H. E. Bird

*Rara avis in terris*

# H. E. Bird

## A Chess Biography with 1,198 Games

### Hans Renette

*Foreword by* Richard Forster

McFarland & Company, Inc., Publishers

*Jefferson, North Carolina*

FIRST EDITION, *first printing*

**Frontispiece: Henry Edward Bird, 1895**

LIBRARY OF CONGRESS CATALOGUING-IN-PUBLICATION DATA

Names: Renette, Hans, 1977–
Title: H.E. Bird : a chess biography with 1,198 games /
Hans Renette ; foreword by Richard Forster.
Description: Jefferson, North Carolina : McFarland & Company, Inc.,
Publishers, 2016 | Includes bibliographical references,
webography and index.
Identifiers: LCCN 2016018981 | ISBN 9780786475780
(library binding : alk. paper) ∞
Subjects: LCSH: Bird, H. E., 1829–1908. | Chess players—England—
Biography. Chess—Collections of games.
Classification: LCC GV1439.B48 R46 2016 | DDC 794.1092 [B] —dc23
LC record available at https://lccn.loc.gov/2016018981

BRITISH LIBRARY CATALOGUING DATA ARE AVAILABLE

**ISBN (print) 978-0-7864-7578-0**
**ISBN (ebook) 978-1-4766-2462-4**

Printed in the United States of America

Edited by Robert Franklin
Designed by Robert Franklin and Susan Ham
Typeset by Susan Ham
(assisted by Wanda Dishmon)

*McFarland & Company, Inc., Publishers
Box 611, Jefferson, North Carolina 28640
www.mcfarlandpub.com*

# TABLE OF CONTENTS

## PART X
## Settling at the Divan, 1888–1890

## PART XI
## The Grand Old Man, 1891–1895

## PART XII
## The Final Years, 1896–1908

# Acknowledgments

This book would not have been possible without the help of various people and institutions. My home university of Leuven requested several documents on my behalf. I made several visits to The Hague, where the National Library preserves the second largest public chess collection in the world. The staff of the Cleveland Public Library were also very helpful: chess columns were digitized and research questions solved. Various of Bird's games and relevant correspondence was discovered.

Tim Harding facilitated the contact with McFarland. Richard Forster read the manuscript, gave many valuable suggestions and was kind enough to write the foreword. Joost Van Winsen responded to various questions and gave me access to some important chess columns. I enjoyed my extensive conversations with Dr. Adrian Harvey. Brian J. Street searched the British Library for me: chess columns were checked and information on Bird's life was found after his suggestions. I brainstormed incessantly about Bird's family with Graeme Rodgers and Mac McCombe, two Australian descendants of Bird's niece. Some unique photographs in this book come from Nigel Webb, a descendant from the Medleys.

Alan Smith made my day more than once when he sent me Bird games that were unknown to me. Many important genealogical matters were solved with the help of people at the Family Tree Forum (www.familytreeforum.com). Without a publishing firm such as McFarland, the chess world would be deprived of the most wonderful books.

My correspondence with many other people and institutions improved the book as well. I never really kept track and had to plough my mailbox searching for them. I hope I did not omit anyone, but here are their names: Bodleian Library, British Library, Hackney Archives, Harvard Library, Kórnik Library, the Museum of Wimbledon, the National Archives, the Savoy Archives, Universtätsbibliothek Leipzig, the Norris Museum, Eduardo Bauzá Mercére, Andrew R. Deane, Roddy Fisher, Tony Gillam, John Grasham, Harrie Grondijs, Barry Henderson, John S. Hilbert, Bob Jones, Thomas A. Lee, Stephen Mann, Dr. Michael Negele, Sarah Sipple (née Bird), Martin Smith, Jan Van Mechelen, David Welch, Edward Winter, Stephen Wright and Fabrizio Zavatarelli.

Being a chess player's wife is perhaps not so easy. It means living with someone who regularly spends time in a parallel universe. What it is to be married to a chess historian is an open question for me. But Els supported me throughout these years and even read the manuscript countless times. Kudos for that. My daughter Lena also likes books.

# FOREWORD
## by Richard Forster

Henry Edward Bird, a great name from a bygone era, was a participant in many glorious international tournaments and some of the most fiercely contested matches of his time. He was the inventor of chess openings and the author of several books. Yet in his heart he was most at home in the world of lightning chess, or "skittles" as it was then known. He rose from the coffee house and always returned to it. A regular at Simpson's Divan in London for over half a century, Bird was perhaps the strongest coffee house player of all time.

His style and attitude to chess were swashbuckling, in the best sense of the word. He could conjure up brilliant ideas in a matter of seconds—and, just as fast, destroy his games through carelessness and impatience.

Those of us who grew up with libraries and books rather than the Internet and databases will always associate his name with many of the highlights of the romantic epoch of chess. Even so, something tragic characterizes virtually all the popular perceptions about him—

—Bird as a participant in the heroic first international chess tournament, in London in 1851—but he is knocked out in the first round.

—Bird as a sparring partner of the dashing young American Paul Morphy—but he is defeated in all their recorded games, while Morphy's fantastic ... R×f2!! and ... Qa3!! combination gains immortal fame.

—Bird and Blackburne, the brilliant and almost inseparable British travel partners, participating in most of the great tournaments between 1870 and 1900, but it is Blackburne who enjoys more success, plays the more famous games, receives more invitations and becomes the public's darling.

—Bird's Opening 1. f4—the ill-bred child of opening theory, never taken seriously and disdained by all the masters, its reputation worse than that of the Dutch Defense even though White is a tempo ahead in Bird's Opening.

—Bird's Variation in the Ruy Lopez with 3. ... Nd4—not just moving the only developed piece for a second time but also immediately exchanging it, the epitome of a dubious opening line.

—Bird as a participant in the last great British tournament of the nineteenth century, London 1899—finishing next to the bottom (not counting Teichmann, who retired after four rounds).

Some other associations are Bird's "Little Bishop's Gambit" (1. e4 e5 2. f4 e×f4 3. Be2), ridiculed at the time and, more recently, at the ChessBase website in an infamous April Fool's prank, or Bird's hopeless literary feud with Wilhelm Steinitz, whose might he could not match, either on or off the chessboard. A few readers may remember Bird as the winner of the first official brilliancy prize, against James Mason in New York 1876. But Bird's queen sacrifice was hardly conclusive, and the notes in the present book show that just before the sacrifice it was Bird's opponent who missed a deep and beautiful tactical idea (29. ... B×d4!!).

Hans Renette's work both confirms and refutes the above conceptions about Bird. His exceptionally deep research results in a multifaceted portrait of a man who was much more than just a player of chess. Henry Edward Bird was an adventurer and a true lover of the game. His impressively light hand at the board is contrasted with his desperate struggle for recognition in the world of chess and some remarkable successes and failures in his personal life.

This volume is full of hitherto unknown facts about Bird's life and about many smaller tournaments held in the second half of the nineteenth century, a period when organized chess was just starting to emerge and the life of a professional or semiprofessional was exceptionally hard and uncertain. Not least, we are offered a wealth of little-known games featuring many unusual twists and turns.

Henry Edward Bird deserves to be honored and remembered on many counts. But above all, he was the first true champion of one of the most dynamic and popular opening variations of all time: the Sicilian Dragon. Long before it was accepted as a viable opening, Bird played it in at least a dozen formal games, between 1883 and 1890. He was not the first to try it, and he was not spectacularly successful with it. But he was the first chess master ever to make it part of his repertoire, regularly playing and exploring the line, and thereby paving the way for future generations of players with the Black pieces.

Nowadays Bird's game against Mackenzie at the London international tournament of 1883 is forgotten because he lost. Considered eccentric and unsound at the time, his play shows a brilliant idea of which most grandmasters today would be exceptionally proud:

### Mackenzie vs. Bird, London 1883

**1. e4 c5 2. Nc3 Nc6 3. Nf3 g6 4. d4 c×d4 5. N×d4 Bg7 6. Be3 Nf6 7. Be2 0–0 8. 0–0 d6 9. Qd2 Bd7 10. Rad1 Qa5 11. Nb3 Qd8 12. h3 Be6 13. Nc1 Rc8 14. f4 Ne8 15. f5 Bd7 16. Bd3 e6 17. f×g6? h×g6 18. N1e2 (see diagram)**

*After 18. N1e2*

Mackenzie's capture on g6 was a positional mistake. Bird exploits it with a truly hypermodern maneuver by his queen to h8—a route made possible by the disappearance of the f5 and h7 pawns:

**18. ... Qa5! 19. Rf2 Qh5! 20. Rdf1 a6 21. Nf4 Qh8! 22. Be2 Ne5 23. Kh1 (see diagram)**

*After 23. Kh1*

Black has outplayed his opponent. 23. ... Bc6, 23. ... b5 or 23. ... Nf6 with the idea of 24. Q×d6 R×c3! 25. b×c3 N×e4 would soon give Black an overwhelming position.

Instead, Bird overlooks some tactics and allows his opponent to launch a dangerous counterattack which culminates in a neat little combination.

**23. ... Nc4? 24. B×c4 R×c4 25. e5 Bc6 26. Qd3 R×c3 27. b×c3 d×e5 28. N×g6 f×g6 29. R×f8† B×f8 30. Q×g6† Qg7 31. R×f8† K×f8 32. Bh6 Kg8 33. B×g7 N×g7 34. Kg1 and Bird resigns.**

A game that perfectly characterizes Bird the chessplayer: a profound, ingenious maneuver, marred by an oversight, and play that was completely misjudged by his contemporaries. May the present volume redress the balance.

*Richard Forster is an International Master and author of* Amos Burn: A Chess Biography *and* The Zurich Chess Club, 1809–2009 *(both McFarland).*

# PREFACE

The final major chess tournament of the 1800s was held in London. The last round, planned on 10 July 1899, started later than foreseen: a photograph taken of most players caused the delay (see the chapter on London 1899 for this photo). On the left side of the picture sat the world's oldest active master. With a somewhat grumpy face, leaning on his stick, Henry Edward Bird looked at the camera. He was clearly bearing the toll of an exhausting tournament of thirty rounds. Bird would turn 70 four days later and he had to cope with several infirmities. Seeing him play must have given the many spectators nostalgic feelings, for they probably felt that this was the last chance to witness Bird in action behind the chessboard.

Even today Bird's name is familiar to almost every serious chess player, but only for the two semidubious lines to which he rendered his name. Almost everything else has long been forgotten: his personality, his chess feats and his eccentric playing style. How different was the perception by Bird's contemporaries: they considered him to be one of the world's strongest masters (even though he fell just short of the absolute top). Bird's love for the game and his creativity gained him their admiration. His personality, his attractive playing style and his extraordinary speed created enthusiasm among the large crowd who witnessed his games.

It would have been hard to predict Bird's popularity when he was a young man. Until 1870 Bird vacillated between two passions: chess and accountancy, with the latter setting the tone. Bird was a distinguished chess player but nothing made him stand out.

At the age of 40 life's circumstances made him abandon a steady middleclass existence and from 1873 onwards Bird started to arrange his life in the playing of chess. At that time he witnessed the ascendency of the so-called modern school as it was propagated by Wilhelm Steinitz. By pointing out and defining the positional foundations of chess Steinitz provided further generations with a compass, due to which the game experienced a rapid development. Like Bird, Steinitz lived in London. While England's capital was easily the world's hotspot for chess it was also a very conservative place during Queen Victoria's era. Acceptance of Steinitz's theories progressed slowly, not only because it cost time to understand them but also because Steinitz's foreign descent, his personality and his chess successes created a lot of envy and jealousy.

Bird was one of many who opposed Steinitz. With the passing of the time most chess masters began to comprehend the value of Steinitz' theories and they, sometimes reluctantly, followed into his footsteps. Bird, however, obstinately stuck to his own opinions and playing style. He lost touch with the evolution and slowly but surely drifted apart from the guild of positional-play chess masters that was rapidly increasing in numbers.

Bird chose to find his joy in the jungle outside the expanding realm of sound chess. He led his opponents to untrodden paths by adopting weird and disparaged openings. Once they were lured onto his minefield, Bird faced them with the idiosyncratic playing style he had developed. Now Bird could employ his great talent for tactics, his legendary combativeness and a stubborn unwillingness to draw. Bird, one could say, was doomed to experiment, triumph, falter and fail.

From time to time he brought about an upset in a tournament, but his real strength lay in offhand chess: chess that was played in crowded coffee houses, amidst incessant waves of chatter and other disturbing sounds. Bird did not consider anyone to be superior to himself in this field and incessantly boasted about his results. At the same time he was the most accessible and good-humored chess master of his day. He enjoyed chess played with amateurs, for a small stake or for honor only. He was willing to play every opponent, no matter how weak or strong.

Among amateurs it was a widespread belief that Bird's popularity and his aggressive playing style would outlast the inheritance of Steinitz. This was not the case. At the end of the century it was clear to everyone that the path chosen by Bird was bound to come to an end.

It is not the sole aim of this book to document and reconstruct the interesting life of a strong chess player. With the collapse of Bird's reputation an important episode in the history of chess ended, halting a tendency to oppose the way chess was going under the influence of Steinitz and his followers. It is the wish of the author to re-immerse the reader in the world in which Bird lived and in which he was widely admired. It is the fate of those who go down a deadend streets: they are often forgotten by history. Let us give back to Henry Edward Bird his rightful place.

The present author's own acquaintance with Bird started at a junior chess tournament, winning at the end of the day a small booklet with the seductive title *Moed en Originaliteit op het Schaakbord* (Courage and originality on the chessboard). The book contained a small biography of Henry Edward Bird after which 16 games were presented to the reader. The fourteenth game, in which Bird opposed James Mason at the New York Clipper tournament of 1876, made a deep impression.

**1.** e4 e6 **2.** d4 d5 **3.** Nc3 Nf6 **4.** e×d5 e×d5 **5.** Nf3 Bd6 **6.** Bd3 0–0 **7.** 0–0 h6 **8.** Re1 Nc6 **9.** Nb5 Bb4 **10.** c3 Ba5 **11.** Na3 Bg4 **12.** Nc2 Qd7 **13.** b4 Bb6 **14.** h3 Bh5 **15.** Ne3 Rfe8 **16.** b5 Ne7 **17.** g4 Bg6 **18.** Ne5 Qc8 **19.** a4 c6 **20.** b×c6 b×c6 **21.** Ba3 Ne4 **22.** Qc2 Ng5 **23.** B×e7 R×e7 **24.** B×g6 f×g6 **25.** Q×g6 N×h3† **26.** Kh2 Nf4 **27.** Qf5 Ne6 **28.** Ng2 Qc7 **29.** a5 B×a5 **30.** R×a5 Rf8 **31.** Ra6 R×f5 **32.** g×f5 Nd8 **33.** Nf4 Qc8 **34.** Nfg6 Re8 **35.** N×c6 Qc7† **36.** Nce5 Q×c3 **37.** Re3 Qd2 **38.** Kg2 Q×d4 **39.** f6 g×f6 **40.** R×f6 Ne6 **41.** Rg3 Ng5 **42.** Ng4 Kg7 **43.** Nf4 Qe4† **44.** Kh2 Nh7 **45.** Nh5† Kh8 **46.** R×h6 Qc2 **47.** Nhf6 Re7 **48.** Kg2 d4 **49.** Ne5 Qc8 **50.** Ng6† resigns.

This game abundantly shows the power, the originality, the courage and the beauty that was often displayed in Bird's games. Bird was rewarded for this exploit with the first brilliancy prize ever awarded in chess history. It is one of the most deeply analyzed games in this book (**game 426**).

Playing over the other games in this booklet convinced this author of Bird's unique talent. Following extensive research on Bird, one can say only that these games were the tip of the iceberg. It will not be easy for the reader to find a positionally fluent and spotless game in this book (there are a few), but thrilling fights there are plenty.

Menno Ploeger, the author of *Moed en Originaliteit*, ended his biographical sketch with the following lines: "But enough about the old master, about whom, hopefully, a thick book will be written." I always kept these words in mind.

During the following years this author focused mainly on improvement across the board, even while keeping a strong interest in chess history and constantly playing over old games. Matters radically changed in 2007 with the purchase of what is perhaps the most wonderful book on chess history: Richard Forster's biography of Amos Burn. While leafing through this immense work I was reminded of Menno Ploeger's words and I decided to write a biography of Bird.

It was not until 2012 that the first historically well-founded essay was written about him. Tim Harding's conclusion presents a fitting state of the art for this biography:

> With all that said, Henry Bird remains an enigma. His books provide sparse information about his life outside chess, and none about his family. Either

through carelessness about dates, or failing memory, much of what he says about his career is subject to correction. Moreover, Bird played so much chess that it would be a mammoth task to collect all his published games. His lengthy chess career and the unavailability of several crucial life facts present severe obstacles to anybody who might attempt a full-scale biography, but he would certainly be a worthy subject [*Eminent Victorian Chess Players*, p. 133].

Harding's essay is a more than worthwhile first attempt to reconstruct the life of Bird, but the format of his book—a chapter on each eminent player—had its restrictions. A monograph devoted entirely to Bird offers the possibility to delve deeply into various aspects of Bird's life. Important gaps can be filled and new discoveries allow us to draw up a more nuanced view.

This book gathers all of the known (to this author) games played by Henry Edward Bird. The majority of the games are presented without notes, but a generous selection (nearly 40 percent of the complete games) have been annotated, often rather deeply. Most historians prefer to publish games with contemporary notes only or, at most, with some short computer-based corrections, but this author found inspiration in analyzing in Richard Forster's approach. These old games are worthy of a closer look and this may be beneficial for the modern player. Thus the reader will find a mix of contemporary and modern notes. The contemporary notes sometimes come from different sources. They are carefully copied and modernized. Some notes that were completely incorrect or less relevant were not necessarily included. This author's own analyses have been augmented by modern computer software, but always in mind has been the aim of improving the reader's understanding of the position.

Contemporary sources are frequently quoted but with minor adaptations for the modern reader intended to speed comprehension, prefer modern terminology in some cases, and impose a mild degree of consistency (capitalization, punctuation). The most nearly correct orthography of proper names has been employed in the game annotations but not in other quoted matter. Quotations in languages other than English have been translated by this author. When the distribution of the colors is unknown "v" has been used to separate the players.

Dozens of sources have been checked as extensively as possible. All major sources have been fully inspected. Games with annotations show the source in which these notes appeared. For other games, the oldest source found has been quoted. Extensive research on Bird's personal and familial life has been possible thanks to the digitization catalogues of archives and newspapers.

# INTRODUCTION

For the sake of clarity this biography begins with an extensive portrait of Henry Edward Bird. The reader will be presented first with an overview of Bird's personal life and chess career, and then a thematic sketch of Bird's personality as it was observed by two of the most influential writers of his day. Their writings contributed to Bird's popularity and created a kind of myth of the man. At the same time they recorded how Bird was strongly opinionated, highly visible in the chess world and not at all weary of quarrels.

A third chapter offers a look at chess themes that were close to Bird's heart. Bird had his convictions, to which he stuck with perseverance.

Then Bird's role in the evolution of chess is set out. The combination of the ascension of the positional school and his reluctance to follow contemporary opening theory made him create his own path in chess. As a result some writers claim that Bird presaged the hypermodern chess school and its most proclaimed advocate, Aron Nimzowitsch.

This part concludes with an attempt to place Bird among his contemporaries and an examination of how he has been perceived by later generations.

## CHESS AND LIFE FACTS

Henry Edward Bird was born in Portsea in 1829. Driven by some misfortune his family led a wandering life during the boy's early years. The Birds ultimately settled in London around 1836. From then on the prospects of the enterprising Henry Bird, the chess master's father, were on the rise.

The young Henry Edward learned the rules of chess at the age of 15. He felt greatly attracted to the game and rapidly climbed the steps of chess mastery. Bird's experiences during these early years decisively formed his chess personality. In 1846 he entered Simpson's Divan, the chess Mecca of London. He immersed himself in the atmosphere, encircled by new chess friends with a similar fascination for the game. The extremely talented Samuel Standidge Boden, a few years older, became his initial mentor. Their friendship lasted until Boden's early death in 1882.

Bird took part in the first two tournaments of significance in chess history. These were held in London in 1849 and 1851. The tournament of 1851 was the first to draw an international field. Bird was eliminated in the first round by the experienced Bernhard Horwitz. A few months later Bird also lost a match against Horwitz. Serious tournament or match play would never be Bird's forte. It was at the margin of the event, at the Divan where all the foreign masters attended almost daily, that Bird definitively made his name by scoring well against them.[1] He developed the reputation of being one of England's most promising players. In his book *Chess History and Reminiscences* Bird gave the impression that the world, or at least the Divanites, thought him ready to storm the Olympus and conquer a spot at the top of the chess world. But other priorities forced their way through. His accountancy career, dramatic events with persistent consequences in his close family circle and his marriage made Bird abstain from any serious chess for five years.

Bird resumed a more intense practice in 1856 when he gave an honorable account of himself in two matches with the Austrian professional Ernst Falkbeer. Bird kept on attending chess events but his main focus turned to accountancy again. During the summer of 1858 the American whirlwind Paul Morphy reached the shores of England. Bird happily returned from his apparent seclusion, only to join his contemporaries in receiving a decisive beating.

Bird continued to play chess leisurely after Morphy's return to the United States. From 1860 onwards his accountancy career was slowly but surely growing. Bird became a worldwide specialist in the field of railway accounting. Intense professional obligations made him abandon chess almost completely.

Bird resurfaced in chess circles in 1866. He committed himself to intense bouts of offhand play and took part in the Challenge Cup tournament of the British Chess Association (the first unofficial British championship). After the summer he agreed to

---

1. "The foreign players, after the tournament, Szén, Löwenthal, Kieseritzky, Mayet, von Jaenisch, Harrwitz and Horwitz frequented Simpson's and Anderssen (like Morphy seven years later) greatly favored the place, and readily engaged in skirmishes of the more lively enterprising, and brilliant description in which he ever met a willing opponent in Bird, who, though a comparatively young player, to the surprise and gratification of all spectators, made even games. This young player who it seems had acquired his utmost form at this time, also won the two only even games he ever played with Staunton, and also two from Szén, which occasioned yet more astonishment, the last-named having been regarded by many deemed good judges, the best player in the world before the tournament was held, and even in higher estimation than his fellow-countryman Löwenthal, and considered not inferior to Staunton himself." H.E. Bird, *Chess History and Reminiscences*. London: Dean and Son, 1893, p. 73.

play a match with Steinitz. This was indeed a serious challenge. Just one month before, the young Austrian had beaten Adolf Anderssen, recognized as the world's strongest active chess player. Steinitz risked his reputation in a new duel. Bird, on the other hand, bore the heavy burden of playing the match at a time when he had several professional obligations running.

Against all odds, the contest was very close. At the point when Steinitz maintained only a small lead, Bird had to resign the match. Bird conceded the stakes to Steinitz, but understood that he would be given the chance of a rematch. Steinitz completely disagreed and their relationship seriously deteriorated. At the same time Steinitz was heavily beset by the British press, personified by Howard Staunton. The Austrian soon found out that the combination of being a foreigner and a chess professional was not enviable. Over the years he began to feel that public sentiment was against him. He believed that Bird had played a malicious role in forming that sentiment.

Bird's reputation greatly benefited from the close call with Steinitz. During the following decades he made ample use of this performance by trumpeting that he was the one who made the narrowest score against the world champion (Johannes Hermann Zukertort and Joseph Henry Blackburne, Steinitz' most important challengers of the 1870s, suffered terribly against him).

Bird's professional high point occurred in 1867 when he played an important role in disclosing the dubious management of the Atlantic and Great Western Railway to the shareholders. A short while later he left the accounting firm to which he had belonged for twenty years. He entered into a partnership and worked as an independent accountant. But then the tide turned. In the span of a few months both his wife and father died and in 1870 he was declared bankrupt. Bird had been playing chess during these years, albeit not very intensively. With his bankruptcy he disappeared completely from the chess scene for almost two years.

Bird's steady family and professional life had been wiped out but he came back and reinvented himself. At the end of 1872 Bird returned to the Divan and his devotion to chess became a crucial element in his new life. A new image of Bird started to emerge in the chess world: "Bird was a born Bohemian; a veritable knight-errant; the Murat of chess; a picturesque figure, unique, historic, impetuous, indomitable" (*Chess Amateur*, June 1913, p. 272).

In 1873, at the age of 44, Bird performed at the chessboard with a previously unseen intensity. Above all his four matches with John Wisker dominated this year. They played 58 games and in the end Bird came out slightly on top. Wisker had become the definitive holder of the Challenge Cup after winning the two last tournaments in 1870 and 1872. While Blackburne or Cecil Valentine De Vere may have been stronger players, these victories gave Wisker ammunition to claim British supremacy. By beating Wisker, Bird had found an effective shortcut to reestablishing his reputation. In the same year Bird also took part in the great tournament in Vienna. He played well and ended in the grouping of strong players just below the absolute top.

After two quieter years Bird mysteriously moved to the United States at the end of 1875. Here his chess activity got intense again. He played a few matches and tournaments but above all excelled in offhand chess. It seems beyond doubt that Bird tasted for the first time the life of professional chess, but his experience was not encouraging. The local players were at first overawed by Bird's international reputation, but Bird's disappointing results changed this feeling soon. Bird believed that he was treated disingenuously on a few occasions and didn't restrict himself in uttering his discontent. The American press created the image of a grumbler and quarreler. A likely collaboration to deprive Bird of a well-earned tournament victory at the New York Clipper tournament led to an outburst of emotions. Bird radically broke with the chess scene and spent most of the year 1877 away from the chessboard.

Early in 1878 Bird returned to Europe. During the following years he succeeded in getting his life back on track. He occasionally played chess, often with decent to very good results. His disinclination towards draws came to the front and gained him a great deal of admiration. At the same time Bird founded a new accountancy firm, even though he was not yet discharged from his bankruptcy of 1871.

Another serious rupture took place at the end of 1880. During that summer great turmoil arose when Bird was not allowed to play in a German chess tournament. Bird was completely fed up with the attitude of his fellow chess masters and, in a long pamphlet, he announced his definitive goodbye from chess. On top of that he disbanded his accountancy firm a few weeks later and left London for some time.

While many must have thought that Bird's goodbye was now definitive he soon became a regular guest at Purssell's, the second chess resort of London to which he remained tied for several years. Bird thus avoided most of his former colleagues who frequented Simpson's Divan.

Bird took part in the major tournaments of Vienna 1882 and London 1883. Especially in Vienna his results were affected by the gout, an illness he was suffering for at least a decade. In London, he delivered several masterpieces. Bird was already over 50 years old, but his level of play seemed intact.

Bird remained active as an accountant for an indefinite number of years. He is reported to have worked hard on statistical tables during the season 1883-84, and it is indeed remarkable that he hardly made any chess appearance. Such a season would follow once more, in 1886-87, but generally speaking it seems that his favorite game preoccupied Bird more and more from 1885 onwards.

The year 1885 saw the rebirth of the British Chess Association (or B.C.A.). Together concurrence with the already well-established Counties Chess Association (C.C.A.), the two invigorated chess in England. The rivalries among a handful of players created a battle for the British chess crown. Bird was so full of self-confidence that he even challenged Steinitz for a rematch, but it was clear that his strength had begun to wane.

The heyday of British chess went hand-in-hand with various private disagreements among several protagonists, players as well as organizers. When Leopold Hoffer, the driving force behind the B.C.A., boycotted Bird in his efforts to commemorate Queen Victoria's Jubilee in 1887 with a tournament, a break between Hoffer and various players occurred. The dissidents, with Bird playing a main role, intensified the chess life at Simpson's Divan. A series of handicap tournaments symbolized this.

By now Bird was represented in the chess press as a veteran. As he easily had the longest experience of all the chess masters one consequently began to call him the "Grand Old Man" of British chess. His love and dedication for the game was greater than ever and made him very popular. Despite his advancing age—he was 60 and over—he still scored excellent results from time to time. His victory at the B.C.A. tournament of 1889 and the third place in 1890 were impressive.

At the end of 1890 Bird underwent another serious attack of gout. It was thought that he was in an awful condition and beyond recovery. To the surprise of many he returned to the Divan in May 1891.

The final decade of Bird's chess career saw him steadily decline in strength. He had slipped from just under the top to the class of the moderate masters. Nevertheless he remained a very dangerous opponent who was able to beat almost everyone on a good day. From time to time he scored a surprising win or good result in a tournament.

The 1890s saw Bird essentially become one with the Divan. He attended on a daily basis and it may have seemed to many, who were perhaps not completely aware of what happened in the five decades before, that he had resided there since the days of his youth. Bird always occupied the same seat and was easily recognizable. This lasted until another severe attack on his health prevented his return to the Divan in 1899.[2]

Bird lived for several more years until death caught him in 1908. He had outlived almost every man of his generation. He was a symbol of the past, overruled by the modern school. His chess beliefs were proved to be obsolete. He was quickly forgotten.

Bird was also a prolific writer. During the last quarter century of his career he published several chess books. These books are important primary sources for they contain much information about Bird's chess career and opinions. It is important to note, however, that Bird was very unreliable with facts. He has more than once given three different versions of the same match or tournament.

His first title, *Chess Masterpieces*, appeared in 1875. Three years later Bird released *Chess Openings*, in which he outlined his favorite opening ideas. *Chess Practice* (1882) was much less relevant. Bird's most worthwhile book is *Modern Chess* (1887), above all a compendium of the best of his games. Bird published two relevant books in the nineties: *Chess History and Reminiscences* (1893) and *Chess Novelties* (1895).

While making a plea to confirm Bird's status as a chess player, the present author does not differ from the predominant opinion that his books were, generally speaking, meager efforts.[3]

Bird also issued a few pamphlets that have become important sources. In 1873 he wrote *A Caution to Investors* about his expe-

riences with the Atlantic and Great Western Railway Company. In 1880 Bird announced his goodbye from chess in *A Slight Chess Retrospect and Explanation*, which counts only four pages. Ten years later the sole issue of *Bird's Chess Reviews* saw the light of day. This small work was dedicated to Steinitz' book *The Modern Chess Instructor* and contained a venomous attack upon the world champion.

Bird was not very active as a chess journalist. His principal column was a syndicated one. It appeared in at least five newspapers from December 1882 until November 1883. In these columns, but also in the London 1883 tournament book, Bird (a bit surprisingly) established himself as an outstanding analyst. Bird also proudly carried the self-imposed title "chess correspondent to *The Times*" and made small contributions to that newspaper.

---

# A Rare Bird

Until 1873 chess was merely a pastime for Bird. He mainly filled his days with his professional duties and only the occasional spare moment was dedicated to the game. Bird was already a well-known and popular figure in England, but not enough to stand out very much in the chess columns and magazines of that day. Bird's character and personality became much more of a hot topic during the second and more intense part of his chess career. The number of magazines and newspapers paying attention to chess increased dramatically from the 1870s onwards and some journalists had a knack in portraying the great masters of that time.

Two of these chess journalists were mainly responsible for what we know about Bird's characteristics. First among equals was without a doubt the Rev. George Alcock MacDonnell. MacDonnell was one of the strongest of the many men of the cloth who spent a lot of their time on chess. For decades he was responsible for the influential chess column in the *Illustrated Sporting and Dramatic News*. This column not only excelled in bringing actuality in the form of news and games, but also more literary as well as gossipy pieces about the condition of chess and its principal practitioners. MacDonnell was a great admirer of Bird's chess style and attitude, as is proven by the countless number of occasions on which he made his support public. MacDonnell wrote two books in the same descriptive style. One of the chapters in *The Knights and Kings of Chess* was dedicated to Bird.

Probably he never made a move on the board that was not instinct with chess. His natural taste for the game is really genius. [...]

Besides genius, Mr. Bird cherishes a love, an unselfish love, for the game, such as no first-class chess player I know anything of ever possessed, excepting,

---

2. On more than one occasion Bird's presence there had been honored by words. Here is one written after Bird's definitive goodbye from the Divan: "Simpson's in the Strand—The Divan, as it is called, is the place where, at some time or other, every chess player of note may be seen. Here is it that the English professional Bird reigns, and unlike some reigning monarchs, he is to be seen almost daily. Entering Simpson's at any hour after noon, he is the first individual you note, and however long you may remain he is certain to be there when you leave. Bird has been playing chess for fifty years, and he is still in the very front rank of the masters; yet he is always ready to play with a young amateur, and will readily explain and assist the novice to a right understanding of the game. Bird is a quick player. During a game, some time ago, with a foreign professional, he made 70 moves in an hour, his opponent occupied nearly four hours in the same number of moves. And Bird won." *The Freemason and Masonic Illustrated: A Weekly Record of Progress in Freemasonry*, 1901, p. 407.

3. As a sample the judgment uttered in *Chess Budget*, 27 October 1924, p. 40, on the occasion of a biographical article on Bird: "Most of them were very poorly edited and are devoid of arrangement, and many chapters are devoted to substantiate his eccentric openings. In addition, they contain many typographical errors, so that as text books they are almost valueless today other than as chess records. [...] By profession he was an accountant, and this fact is evident to an amusing extent in his books, for he presents endless tables showing all sorts of statistics in reference to tournaments, matches and other events."

perhaps, Anderssen. Some men play the game to win money, others to gain a reputation, a few to vindicate their intellectual supremacy, believing chess to be a criterion in this last respect; but Bird plays chess primarily and principally because he loves the game, loves it for itself, as an Irishman loves a free fight, for the fun and pleasure of the thing. But specially does Bird love a good game, the game in which he has to fight hard and put forth all his strength. He prefers losing a good game to winning a bad one, his adversary's part in the game always delighting him as much as his own. His appetite, too, for chess is enormous. No matter how physically fatigued he may be, or gout-afflicted, or game-sated, he is every ready for the fray. No champion's glove is ever thrown down at him without his snatching it up and buckling on his armor at once [*The Knights and Kings of Chess*, pp. 43–44].

At the board Bird is very quick over his moves, and, unlike most quick players, is never impatient with a slow-coach, or ill-humored when unlucky. He never stamps the pieces on the board as if he were crushing an enemy, or flourished his hand about as if he were grinding a hand-organ or striking a cricket ball; never depreciates a rival's skill, or harbors resentment for a defeat; but is always happy in praising other men's games when they deserve it, and in acknowledging the merits to which he himself may have been obliged to succumb. If he cherished any jealousy at all there is not a particle of meanness or pettiness in it. In short, as a chess player, he looks and acts and plays—as genuine John Bull [*The Knights and Kings of Chess*, p. 47].

Similar pieces were written by Robert John Buckley, the chess columnist for the *Birmingham Weekly Mercury*. Also from his hand comes an important article that was published in *Chess Amateur* in 1913.

Bird loved to talk of himself, and invariably gave Bird an excellent character. He had much to say concerning his wrongs: the unfairness with which he was treated; the want of appreciation of the vulgar herd; the tricks that opponents had served him in tournaments [*Chess Amateur*, June 1913, p. 271].

He may have been vain; may have been sudden and quick in quarrel. His temperament betrayed him. His carelessness of consequences accounted for much. Without the craft to conceal his real self, he was ridiculed as conceited, and stigmatized as quarrelsome by men who utilized his courage to fight their battles, and who had the art to conceal a greater vanity and a deeper discontent [*Chess Amateur*, June 1913, p. 272].

This book quotes extensively from articles written by both men. Even though they have a well-deserved reputation for spreading anecdotes not completely free of creativity and embellishment. Thus the reader is advised to take these sources with a grain of salt, but must also realize that MacDonnell and Buckley (and other narrators) offer a unique picture of Bird and many of his contemporaries. For us they bring a long forgotten era to life. For many of Bird's contemporaries the way Bird was depicted often formed the reality if they were unable to witness the veteran playing in real life.

# BIRD'S EYE VIEW

For nearly thirty years Bird practiced the game of chess as a pure amateur for the fun of it. He thoroughly enjoyed a good game, whether won or lost, and was a natural player, gifted with a fast mind that allowed him to throw his spectacular moves on the board unhesitatingly.

During his youth Bird and his companions motivated each other to preserve their best efforts and send them to the press for publication. Once more important matters began to occupy him, Bird did not care much anymore for recording his games. If someone

from the public took the trouble to take down the moves he would object nor bother.[4]

Some of Bird's opponents were more focused on writing down the moves. George Hatfeild Dingley Gossip was notorious for the practice of massively forwarding his wins against the strongest players of his day to the press. This befell Bird in 1873 and caused many collisions between them.

Similar experiences occurred to Bird during his stay in the United States. Almost no win from his sojourn in Philadelphia in 1876 was published, while the New York press also mainly released losses. Bird was mostly bothered by the practice of omitting to publish the score of the series of games, and this awakened him to pay more attention to the recording of games so that he could provide the press with positive examples of his play.

Recording the game score became an obligation during chess tournaments. Bird was not popular among the committee men for as a rule he presented them with illegible manuscripts. The tournament book of Hastings 1895 (p. 357) says that "the scoring of his games is—! [i.e., unreadable] and most had no scores at all at Hastings, the moves having to be obtained from other sources."

When Bird returned to the chessboard in 1873 he found that many practical aspects of the game had changed. While he had been a man of his time during the 1850s he could not connect himself to the ongoing evolutions. Bird was not alone in his resistance to the way chess was evolving, but he was most tenacious in his points of view. He did not miss an opportunity to express his disdain.

One notion that had grown into importance was the regulation of the time limit. Bird never fully agreed with the necessity of this practice and he made his point on every possible occasion. During the chess congress held in Belfast in 1892 Bird and Blackburne agreed to conduct their game without a clock. In *Chess History and Reminiscences* (p. 92), Bird was happy to note that "both players seemed at ease, and glad to be free from the formality and encumbrance of time regulators and it is a happy omen that it proved one of the most interesting [games] in the program."

The use of chess clocks became in vogue from the London 1862 tournament onwards. Until then a player was allowed to take the time he wished on the deliberation of a move. In extreme cases this could lead to the outsitting of one's opponent. Louis Paulsen was notorious for such heavy thinking, while Howard Staunton attributed his own elimination in 1851 to Elijah Williams' time management.

During the last decades of the century, discussions were continuously held about whether fifteen or twenty moves per hour had to be played. Steinitz was an unconditional defender of the slower time limit, while Bird found himself on the other side of the spectrum. After Lasker's victory over Steinitz in 1894 Bird wrote an elucidating letter to the *Daily News*.

Sir,
What is chess; and what constitutes the championship of chess? I see by the *Daily News* this morning that Lasker has beaten Steinitz 10 to 5 at 15

---

4. Bird wrote: "Attaching but little importance to victory or defeat at that time I kept no record of games, and was unaware until recent years that many of these contests had appeared in foreign journals, furnished by whom I know not." H.E. Bird, *Bird's Modern Chess and Chess Masterpieces: Containing a Collection of the Finest Examples of Chess Play*. London: Dean and Son, 1887, pp. 1–2.

moves an hour, and subject to the claims of the invincible Dr. Tarrasch, of Nuremberg, he will be considered for the moment the champion of chess but only of slow chess. There are two other kinds of chess—the useful, the rapid, and the brilliant at the average of half an hour or so a game, and what is known as ordinary chess played at the rates of 50 moves an hour, or an average of near two hours a game. Now, though a player of nearly half a century, I have found sufficient of the old style to more than hold my own against Lasker in more than 100 battles at all round amusement chess (the only chess worth playing) including the range of gambits and the most difficult and enterprising games. It so happens that the few remaining chess experts are rather of the slow school, and will answer that Lasker cannot play his best chess at less than 15 moves an hour. The retort is obvious, neither can the fast English player, like myself, play his best chess at so slow a pace as 15 or 20 moves an hour, our average being 50. If the slow would meet the fast half way at 30 or 35 moves an hour we should, I think, have better chess. Even at that rate a stubborn would take at least four hours, in all conscience quite long enough for any game or player, and prohibitive with most.

Your respectfully,

H.E. Bird, Senior Chess Master, Simpson's, 101, Strand, W.C.

[*Daily News*, 29 May 1894]

On the next day the *Daily News* printed a letter by Samuel Tinsley, who wrote that Bird frequently took half an hour for a single move. Bird's reply came promptly on 31 May. He insisted that he played games at an average of 50 moves per hour. Two recently published games, he claimed, were even played at the rate of 100 moves per hour.[5]

Some of Bird's opponents caught fire when they played him. In his match with Amos Burn (1886) a nominal time limit of 15 moves per hour was adopted, but nevertheless several games per days were played. The same goes for Bird's match with James Mason (1875-76). Even at the advanced age of 60 Bird was considered one of the world's fastest players. Numerous are the anecdotes that highlight his capacities in this field and occasions on which he left his opponent behind in amazement. His physical ailings did not seem to limit him in his movements when performing simultaneously against a large number of opponents.

Bird developed a theory in which he created a distinction between "slow chess and "rapid chess." While he accepted that he was not up to coping with a Lasker or Steinitz in serious games, he at least claimed equality of strength in the field of rapid play. In *Bird's Chess Reviews*, he made a similar difference between "business chess" and "amusement chess," defining the latter as follows: "we mean chess of the day or the evening, limited to an hour or two each game; such chess, in short, as the ordinary mortal seeking recreation cares for or can find time to play" (p. 2). In a footnote Bird boasted about his successes in the late 1880s "as illustrated in his contests with Bardeleben, Prussian champion, in 1888; Weiss, Austrian champion, and Chigorin, Russian champion, in 1889; and also in New York with Lipschütz, Delmar, Martinez and Showalter,

American representatives; also with Burn, the present undoubted English champion, in America, Liverpool and London."[6]

Bird's strength in blitz play easily attracted the attention of the crowd and brought him a lot of popularity. Everyone could wager his chance against him and Bird took care not to deprive his opponent of his dignity. The man was very social. He enjoyed being in good company and celebrating feasts. When he was at ease with the chess world he never missed a banquet or other gatherings built around chess events. Bird never hesitated to offer a toast. In the tournament book of Hastings 1895 (p. 357), it was said that he was a "very ready and fluent speaker, and sometimes assumes an amusingly confident air." His speeches were always well appreciated by the audience. In such an environment, Bird was, as MacDonnell once wrote (*Illustrated Sporting and Dramatic News*, 19 January 1889), "perfectly radiant."

Chess professionals were notorious for their bohemian life style and their poverty, but the game also gave its masters the chance to get in touch with the upper class. Members of the nobility or successful businessmen often took an interest in the game. They joined the elite clubs in London but could also be seen in more public resorts such as the Divan or they made their name as patrons of the game. Bird was very popular and his books provide ample space to the various important men of his time with whom he met. We are not aware of any concrete benefits Bird experienced from his contacts with the upper class, but it seems evident that he must have fared well with these contacts.

It was a recurrent nineteenth century habit to play offhand chess for stakes. A shilling per game was the usual amount. In *Chess History and Reminiscences*, Bird described the evolution he witnessed (pp. 114–116). At Raymond's Coffee House, where he learned the moves of chess in 1844, a cup of coffee was the usual stake. Matters were more serious at the other places where professionals often came. They charged sixpence per game. Even Staunton played games for that rate. Both at the Divan and at St. George's Chess Club a shilling had been the usual tariff.

During his younger days Bird encountered several opponents, such as Boden, MacDonnell and John Cochrane, with whom he never played for money. "Not even for the customary shilling," as he confessed in *Chess History* (p. 77). In the same work (p. 116), Bird also wrote that "Buckle, Lord Lyttleton, and many eminent in chess, were strongly in favor of the customary small stake, and I have seen dignitaries of the Church, and spotless amateurs, pocket their shillings with as much gusto as the poor and much abused professional. It is a kind of voucher to mark the score." The professional's dependence on the stake was often acknowledged by the amateur. In the October 1891 edition of the *British Chess Magazine* (p. 452), John Donaldson recalled how he beat Edward Lowe but "of course would not take the four shillings, and Lowe, who was very poor at the time, was so grateful to me for that little kindness on my part that as long as he lived he would have taken any amount of trouble to oblige me."

In his later years Bird became dependent on earnings from chess. In a letter to Rosario Aspa written in the preamble of his visit to

---

5. MacDonnell extrapolated Bird's view to unrealistic proportions. Steinitz's strength in tournament and match games was radically turned to his disadvantage: "But in important contests Mr. Steinitz is slow in making up his mind. In them he sees too much, and examines unimportant details. Over them he is too apt to waste his time and fatigue his brains. He requires an hour for fifteen moves where many another master would require not half the time. [...] The fact is, he lacks genius of the highest order for chess. The genius that consists in an infinite capacity for taking trouble he undoubtedly possesses, and perhaps to a larger extent than ever was possessed by any other player...; nor does he possess the gift that was Anderssen's, and is Blackburne's and Bird's—the gift of painting beautiful pictures on the chessboard when there is little or nothing there to suggest them." *Illustrated Sporting and Dramatic News*, 15 September 1888.

6. Retrieved at the library of the Harvard University (a gift from Silas W. Howland). This seems to be the sole surviving copy.

Leamington Spa, Bird insisted on playing for a shilling per game. Yet Bird didn't consider himself a professional, and the nuance he made comes to us from an article by Gustavus Charles Reichhelm about the chess masters visiting Philadelphia in the wake of the U.S. Chess Congress in 1889. Unlike players like Blackburne or Gunsberg, Bird did not receive a fee before he would deliver his services. He just played at the rate of a shilling per game, at his usual rapid pace. The local chess community understood that he gained his living this way and they encountered him voluntarily. In the end Bird left with a similar amount of money in the pocket and having made better personal relations than other masters.

Stakes in chess were a recurrent theme in Bird's books about which he could get endlessly agitated. Bird was mostly bothered by the evolution and the rapid ascension of stakes wagered on chess matches. Before 1866, he wrote, common stakes for matches were £10 or £20. When Steinitz and Anderssen met in 1866 for £100, Bird speaks of a "bad example." Later matches involving Steinitz were played for lower stakes, for backers refrained from going higher than £60. The first world championship, however, saw the stakes increased to $2000 a side. This had only bad consequences, according to Bird. In *The Times* of 16 April 1886, he said that the match "has been a disappointment to admirers of chess, on account of the sameness and dullness of the openings, the lack of originality and enterprise in the games, and the absence of well-fought contests." Bird believed that the heaviness of the stakes took a huge toll of Zukertort and contributed to his breakdown.[7]

In his 1886 match with Burn no stakes were involved, although Robert Steel, the organizer of the contest, rewarded Bird for his efforts with a small sum. Shortly afterwards Bird and Gunsberg played a match for £5 a side. On 14 June 1886, Anthony Guest, chess editor of the *Morning Post*, remarked that "the fact, it appears, is becoming recognized that frequent matches for small stakes are preferable to occasional encounters for large sums, and produce examples of chess at least as good in quality."

Bird's focus on playing only for small stakes may not have been a purely principled one. In his column in the *Lincoln, Rutland and Stamford Mercury* of 30 November 1888, Skipworth spoke about the rumor of a match between Bird and Blackburne. Bird, he wrote, couldn't be considered a match for Blackburne and "it is not probable, therefore, that Mr. Bird will find backers for such a match."

The second half of the nineteenth century was characterized by the professionalization of chess. A starting point of this evolution was Staunton's match victory against Pierre Fournier de Saint-Amant in 1843. The popularity of chess gave a few men the opportunity to pursue their livelihood with various kinds of chess activities such as playing, teaching and writing. Staunton himself quickly turned his attention to literary activities and began to condemn "professional" players. He was supported by the rigid morality that characterized the Victorian society. The guilds of chess professionals were mainly formed by foreigners. Many migrants left the continent

due to the political uprisings of 1830 and 1848. England was an attractive destination: the country was politically stable and stood on the verge of an economic boom. Players such as Adolf Zytogorsky, Bernhard Horwitz, Johann Jacob Löwenthal and Ernst Falkbeer tried to find their place in society via chess. Most of these men integrated perfectly.

It was only in the 1870s that the discrepancy between British and foreign chess players came to the fore. The open way in which Steinitz gained his money with chess attracted the attention of several prosecutors. The battle that ensued seriously damaged the chess community in London.

Steinitz' playing style came under fire as, in the eye of some of his contemporaries, his prudent accumulation of small advantages allowed him to win his games, and money, in a much easier not so honorable way, as his opponents adhered to a more romantic playing style. After some time other chess masters began to understand and copy Steinitz's ideas but even then the criticism of Steinitz persisted.

Bird was one of the few players who continued to fight against the modern chess school. He was deeply ingrained in the tradition of chess and, as a counter-reaction, began to idealize the past. Many amateurs shared Bird's opinion that attractive chess, played according to the principles of the romantic school and as a pastime, had given way to a dull and quasiscientific game. An example was the leading art critic John Ruskin. In his obituary, featuring in the *British Chess Magazine* in February 1900, it was remembered how he adored chess from the artistic side, and that "he took great interest in published games of a brilliant description, and was especially fond of Bird's bright games of years ago, and on more than one occasion wrote to that master" (p. 65).[8]

Steinitz was not a peaceful character. Not only did he refuse to take sensibilities into account, on a few occasions he put nearly everyone off with flippant actions. The way he treated Wormald in a book review and the ex-presidents of the City of London Chess Club were exemplary. In *Bird's Chess Reviews* (p. 4), Bird related how he initially took care of Steinitz, and how the latter received the support of the British chess community in his match against Anderssen. At that time, however, Steinitz' "love of self-assertion began to disclose itself," according to Bird.

The combination of antiprofessionalism and xenophobia that rapidly gained ground in chess circles during the second part of the 1870s, seriously damaged Steinitz.[9] As we will see on a few occasions, harsh feelings were quite common at that time. Even Wisker and Potter, relatively mild personalities, can be found uttering extreme

---

7. "There is too much reason to fear that the result of this match, and Zukertort's sensitiveness to supposed coolness towards him afterwards mainly contributed to cause his premature break up and untimely end. I always advised him before the match, in justice to himself, to stipulate for a time limit of 20 or 25 moves an hour, and not to play for more than £100 a side, the previous extreme maximum for the greatest matches, happy for him he had observed this rule, as he himself admitted." Bird, *Chess History and Reminiscences*, p. 115.

8. Ruskin himself was explicit about the way chess developed in a public letter: "Chess, on the contrary, I urge pupils to learn, and enjoy it myself, to the point of its becoming a temptation to waste of time often very difficult to resist; and I have really serious thoughts of publishing a selection of favorite old games by chess players of real genius and imagination, as opposed to the stupidity called chess playing in modern days. Pleasant 'play,' truly! in which the opponents sit calculating and analyzing for 12 hours, tire each other nearly into apoplexy or idiocy and end in a draw or a victory by an odd pawn." *Daily Telegraph*, 6 June 1884.

9. The press, with a man like Patrick Thomas Duffy in front, tackled Steinitz in a merciless fashion: "The West End Chess Club is said to have closed its doors on the 29th ultimo, after a brief life of two years. It was, for a time, the happy hunting-ground of the noisiest German band in London, the gentry who believe that it is highly 'creditable' to 'win' other people's money. Among Englishmen there is a strong preference for earning it." *Land and Water*, 6 October 1877.

statements. At the same time it had become nearly impossible for a foreigner to be fully accepted on British soil.[10]

Bird's myriad of opinions can be summed up with the rather vague term "chivalry." Bird often used it to create a wedge between himself and the ongoing professionalism. Chivalry, so Bird claimed, showed itself in the circumstances of the game. Moderate stakes and a fast time limit were important indicators. A crucial aspect, technically speaking, was also the opening choice.

> The Ruy Lopez, in the opinion of many old players, notably Staunton, Buckle, Cochrane, and Kolisch, has never been considered as a magnanimous opening. I have not played it since my match with Wisker in 1873. In the present instance it was a lapse, or I should not have done so against so chivalrous an opponent as Mr. Mortimer [*Games Played in the London International Chess Tournament*, 1883, p. 287].

Continuing a hopeless game was another point in which a non-chivalrous player could betray himself. In his column Bird wrote:

> The practice which prevails with some players of continuing a hopeless game is one we do not approve of, as not being courteous or respectful to opponents. In this position, if the king could have travelled to the pawns, one would have cost at least a piece. White's skill, however, prevents this, and Black at once resigns [*Sheffield and Rotherham Independent*, 3 March 1883].

Despite his reputation as a dashing and chivalrous player, quite a lot of Bird's games indicate that sometimes circumstances influenced his sportsmanship. It is perhaps characteristic that the two longest nineteenth century games on record were played by Bird. In both cases Bird incessantly tried to grind his opponent down. Against Lipschütz in 1889, in the first game to cross the mark of 150 moves, Bird continued although the position had every appearance of a draw. On other occasions his stubbornness was motivated by the possibility to win a prize (i.e., against Guest in the 1886 tournament at the British Chess Club), or when his opponent was not a personal favorite (i.e., against Gossip in the B.C.A. congresses of 1889 and 1892, twice against Gunsberg in their 1886 match and in his first match game with Mason in 1875).

# A Nimzowitsch Forerunner?

In his book, Tim Harding presents Bird as a precursor of Nimzowitsch and Bent Larsen. He sees a likeness between these players in Bird's "willingness to leave the orthodox paths and set unusual problems for his opponents" (p. 125). Harding situates Bird's heterodoxy in the openings and subsequently offers some of Bird's games to illustrate a few of his favorite lines.

In order to understand Bird it is necessary to have a closer look at the evolution of chess during the nineteenth century. Bird's formative years, from 1844 until 1851, were dominated by the so-called romantic school in chess. Even a superficial look at Bird's early games

reveals that he was a typical adherent of this playing style. Just like most of his contemporaries Bird strived for an open game in which a quick development of his pieces was necessary. Bird reveled in offering gambits and he adored playing wild and aggressive chess. Bird never hid his aim to hunt his opponent's king.

During these years one also witnessed the ascendency of the English chess school. In the wake of Staunton's successes, many players, such as Elijah Williams, propagated a more careful and positional style. From the 1860s onwards a new tendency in chess, the positional school, of which Louis Paulsen and Steinitz were the pioneers, delivered the definitive death blow to the romantic school.

Upon his return to chess in 1873 Bird was above all influenced by the ongoing evolution of opening theory. His favorite lines, such as the Evans Gambit, had lost much of their strength and were replaced by more positionally founded openings. Bird was also not happy with the sudden popularity of the Ruy Lopez, a former favorite of his. An extra burden for Bird was the fast development of the opening theory due to which he often faced theoretically well supported players.[11]

Bird solved the problem by showing a remarkable affinity for the opening phase.[12] In *Chess Openings* he presented the existing theory but also his own favorites and inventions. In the introduction Bird recognized the value of the theoretical work done by Staunton and Wormald and he explicitly denounced any ambition to find improvements in the mainstream openings. Instead Bird strived towards originality by building up his own opening repertoire. His radical choices were fanatically practiced and remained the heart of his successive books.

There undeniably exists a convergence between the opening repertoires of Bird and Nimzowitsch. Both men liked the combination of the moves f4 and b3 (e.g., after 1. f4 d5 2. Nf3 Nf6 3. e3 e6 4. b3) or f5 and b6 (e.g., after 1. d4 f5 2. c4 Nf6 3. Nc3 e6 4. Nf3 b6). Bird's continuous experiments made him discover a few relatively strong setups and he can justly be considered the founder of this system. Yet, regardless of the results he achieved, Bird never lost his motivation to vary his tries and search for innovations.

With the Black pieces Bird firmly believed in the aggressive power of the Dutch Defense. He often followed the strategy of inflicting his opponent with doubled pawns at c3 and c4 by exchanging his bishop at c3. As a result positions that resembled the Nimzo-Indian came on the board from time to time. Bird's play against this pawn structure went reasonably well, though he did not achieve the same precision of play as Nimzowitsch. His game against Mason in Nuremberg 1883 (**game 662**) saw a very fine positional set-up until a perfect example of how Bird completely spoiled a winning position, in typical fashion.

---

10. See for example what Bird wrote at the time of the Belfast 1892 tournament about Lasker and Gunsberg (the latter had been residing for decades in England): "…in which it was at one time proposed that two other eminent players, not British born should participate, but who at the last moment sought certain undue advantages beyond the very liberal bonuses provided, and even a controlling influence never anticipated by the committee, and to which of course it could not, with any full sense of propriety or regard to originally avowed intentions and subscribers views consent." Bird, *Chess History and Reminiscences*, p. 90.

11. Bird's argument is suitable for any era: "Some now come to battle crammed with Gossip or with Cook, their game so to speak, in their hat, the book not unfrequently being there also. They commence full of confidence, but when the opponent is not accommodating enough to play the variation and an unlooked-for move is made they are liable suddenly to collapse." Bird, *Modern Chess*, p. 3.

12. MacDonnell relates a somewhat embellished story: "Formerly he despised book lore, and had no technical knowledge of openings. This nescience often caused him to drift into a bad position in the early part of the game, and so be beaten sometimes by an inferior but book-learned opponent. This weak point in his armor, however, he made good when, some years ago, he resolved to write a book on the openings." G.A. MacDonnell, *The Knights and Kings of Chess*. London: Cox, 1894, p. 46.

One of the openings Bird pioneered was the Wing Gambit against the Sicilian Defense. Now and then he reached positions reminiscent of the Benko Gambit. Though it is generally accepted that the game between Nimzowitsch and Capablanca, played in St. Petersburg 1914, was a forerunner in the demonstration of these ideas, very noteworthy is a consultation game played at Boston in 1880 in which Bird was undoubtedly the driving force behind the sacrifice of the b-pawn. Instead of the later discovered compensation on the queenside, he and his partner focused only on a kingside attack (**game 519**).

Bird's experimental drift left his mind open for innovations and atypical ideas. He picked up the idea to defend against the Ruy Lopez with 3. ... Nd4 from a few contemporaries and then started to personalize this line. Along the way he discovered some motives that still have value today (moves such as h5, Kf8, a5 and Ra6 to develop the rook, the isolated doubled d-pawn). **Game 603** is a fitting example.

Bird was quite fond of the push of the h-pawn, and he made it one of his trademarks in the Dragon Variation. See his game against Isidor Gunsberg in Manchester 1890 (**game 1017**) for a convincing example.

Perhaps at the top of his originality list stands his way to deal with the French Defense. Bird sought and found the sole way to prevent Black from playing 2. ... d5, i.e., with the weird 2. Bb5. He adopted it successfully against a few weaker players in Vienna 1873.

As Bird was certainly not a prominent positional player, the number of games he played flawlessly is small. The two games that overpower most others in this respect are his win against Rosenthal in London 1883 (**game 642**) and, played in consultation with Robert Steel, his game against Blackburne and Hoffer (**game 499**). Also worth mentioning is the brilliant positional idea conceived in his game against Gunsberg in Nottingham 1886 (see **game 815**, moves 22–27). It gave Bird an equal position but he blundered it into a loss.

Bird was not by definition wary of positionally healthy ideas, but they were mostly secondary to his urge to create complications. A good example is his first game with Louis Paulsen in Vienna 1873 (see **game 248**). Bird played some very strong pawn moves, including a promising pawn sacrifice, but he missed the crucial idea of forcing the exchange of queens and thereby intensifying the weaknesses in his opponent's camp. By keeping the pieces on the board, he allowed Paulsen the opportunity for a similar pawn sacrifice that caused his loss.

Bird was appropriately much more famous for his brilliant and dazzling play. On his best moments, and with an opponent who was on the mark, epic fights were created. Besides his immortal game with Mason, five such games stand out in this collection: his win against Horwitz in the London 1851 tournament (**game 69**), the fourth game of Bird's second match with Wisker (**game 219**), his decisive win against Potter in the City of London handicap tournament (**game 505**), a spectacular draw against Blackburne (**game 516**) and the game lost against a consulting team at an exhibition given in Brighton in 1895 (**game 1235**).

Some of Bird's brilliancies were more one-sided affairs. One of his most beautiful combinations, crowned with two underpromotions, was unleashed against MacDonnell (**game 337**). Bird played

some very attractive games in the London 1883 tournament. In their first game Berthold Englisch escaped miraculously with a draw against a most inspired Bird (**game 615**). A few rounds later Mackenzie succumbed to a lasting attack (**game 621**). Equally renowned is Bird's win against Max Weiss in Bradford 1888 (**game 868**).

One contemporary with a very interesting opinion on Bird's playing style was William Norwood Potter. Potter is nowadays largely forgotten. His career record does not look very impressive at first sight, but he is thought to have had a great influence on the development of Steinitz' positional chess ideas. Steinitz and Potter met each other regularly at the City of London Chess Club and analyzed intensively together at the time of the illustrious correspondence match between London and Vienna, played from 1872 until 1874.[13]

Potter deeply analyzed the games from the Paris 1878 tournament for the *Westminster Chess Club Papers*. He came up with a few spot-on descriptions of Bird's chess style. A first one was made in the margin of Bird's game with Mackenzie, played in the penultimate round.

> I have not cared to note or indeed to examine very narrowly the opening dispositions of the players. Mr. Bird's ideas concerning close games and mine would not be likely to come into collision, nor is it at all probable that war will take place between the inhabitants of Greenland, and the subjects of King Mtesa. Viewing the position now arrived at Black seems to have a slight advantage, for he has bishop and knight against two knights, and the opponent is burdened with a doubled pawn [*Westminster Chess Club Papers*, September 1878, pp. 106–107].

Potter even more squarely hit the nail with his summary of Bird's final game of the tournament, which he won against James Mason.

> This game is a good specimen of Bird's vigorous, if somewhat loose, style. Careful elaboration is not a quality that he goes in for, and as long as the opponent's game be broken up, he does not seem to mind his own being in various pieces [*Westminster Chess Club Papers*, August 1878, pp. 88–89].

There are a great number of games in this book that illustrate Potter's point. One fine example showing both Bird's strengths and weaknesses was his second game with Wisker at the B.C.A. Challenge Cup tournament of 1868-69 (**game 187**) *(see diagram)*.

**Black to move**

13. The London team was originally composed of Blackburne, Horwitz, Löwenthal, Wisker, Steinitz and Potter. It did not last long before just Potter and Steinitz conducted the game. They brilliantly won one game and drew the other in a winning position. A very curious anecdote, involving Potter, Steinitz and Bird is worth mentioning. One version came from the hand of Hoffer: "Potter had a peculiar defensive style, so irregular that Steinitz and Zukertort used to say derisively, if you place the Black pieces into a hat and shake them out over the board, you have exactly Potter's style of defense." *The Field*, 31 December 1910. Buckley kept a variation of this story in store: "'Place the contents of the chess box in your hat, shake them up vigorously, and pour them on the board from a height of two feet, and you get the style of Steinitz,' said Bird." *Philadelphia Inquirer*, 26 August 1917. Perhaps, in the eyes of the modern chess player, Bird's playing style best fits this description.

Bird came up with the very strong concrete move: **17. ... g5!** (for another similar move in Bird's practice, see Bird's tenth match game with Steinitz—**game 172**).

Not unsurprisingly, Wisker goes wrong after the apparently innocent sequence **18. d4 Kh8 19. c3?**, when Bird unleashes the crafty **19. ... f5!** Bird continues strongly for a few more moves, but after **20. Bd1 f4! 21. Qf2 f×g3 22. Q×g3 Rf3 23. Nf4 g×f4 24. B×f3** he almost has to start all over again after a typical hasty move, namely **24. ... f×g3?** With a bit more consideration, he would probably have found the conclusive **24. ... Qh6!**

From time to time Bird succeeded in maintaining the high pressure he placed upon his opponent. The task of the defender was not to underestimate in such cases as even the slightest inaccuracy implied the downfall of his position. One such game was played by Bird as White against Maximilian Fleissig in Vienna in 1873 (**game 242**) (*see diagram*).

*White to move*

At first sight the position seems equal, but Bird's **17. f4** is a cunning move. Fleissig reacts a bit too radically with **17. ... f5** and Bird handsomely makes progress: **18. Re5 Bg6 19. g4.** Another intimidating pawn push, and this one is going to be followed by a sudden assault. Black still has enough defensive resources, but he is clearly under pressure. The game continued with **19. ... f×g4 20. f5 Bf7 21. f6!** and now the unforced error comes: **21. ... Bg6? 22. B×g6 h×g6 23. f7†** and Black resigns. Only the most precise defense, starting with **21. ... Nd7!** could have saved him.

Bird did not hesitate to make strange-looking or inferior moves when he thought that they would beneficially complicate the game. Against the weak opposition he faced at the tournament in Gouda in 1880 he purposely played badly, searching in vain for an interesting game. Such a worthwhile effort resulted from another outing in which Bird needlessly took daring risks. The game (Bird was Black) was played against Albert Ensor in the Clipper tournament of 1876 (**game 430**).

**1. d4 e6 2. e4 d5 3. e×d5 e×d5 4. Bd3 Nf6 5. Nf3 Bg4 6. Bg5 h6 7. Bh4 Bd6 8. Nc3 c6 9. Qe2† Kd7** What more needs to be said? Bird's next move was played in the same spirit. **10. B×f6 g×f6 11. 0–0–0 Kc7 12. Qd2 Nd7 13. Be2 Nb6 14. Kb1 Qf8 15. Ka1 a5 16. Nb1** Bird escapes from a true test of his ideas had White found 16. Nh4. Now the battle lingered on for several dozens of moves and in the end Bird succeeded in outplaying his opponent.

Bird's experimental urge and search for complications often made him unhesitatingly submit the most horrendous moves on the board. A notorious example was his seventeenth move in an often published game with Lipschütz (**game 808**).

Bird was a specialist in building up furious, innovative attacks. See for example his twelfth game against Steinitz (1866), in which the strongest player of the world experienced great difficulties. Bird's play was mostly more intuitive than correct (**game 174**) (*see diagram*).

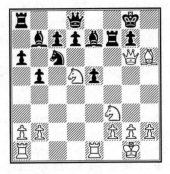

*White to move*

**18. Re4! Qf8 19. Bg5? R×f3! 20. g×f3 B×g5 21. Q×g5 Re8 22. Rae1 Re6 23. N×c7 Rh6? 24. Rg4 Kh7 25. Ne8 Nd4 26. Q×g7† Q×g7 27. R×g7† Kh8 28. Rg3?!** Missing the best transposition into a promising endgame with 28. R×d7. Steinitz managed to safeguard the draw.

With the Black pieces Bird sold his soul to the Dutch Defense. Against solid positional players he often succumbed in passivity, but he equally often enjoyed great pleasure when he massacred an opponent. Even Amos Burn, one of the world's toughest defenders, was sometimes torn to pieces (see **games 781** and **791**). In the following sample Burille (White) was Bird's victim (**game 932**) (*see diagram*).

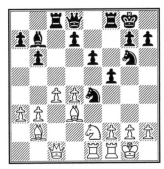

*Black to move*

**16. ... Qh4 17. f3 Ng5 18. Ng3 Nf4! 19. Qc3 Rf6 20. Bc1 Rh6 21. B×f4 Q×h2† 22. Kf2 Nh3†! 23. Ke3 N×f4 24. K×f4 Rg6 25. Ke3 R×g3** and White was ripped apart.

Opponents always had to take Bird's trickiness and inventiveness into account. In many hopeless situations Bird was able to come up with something that could reverse the outcome of the game in a nick of time. A legendary example was his escape against Rudolf Loman in a decisive game of the second Divan tournament of 1891 (**game 1057**). Louis van Vliet went down in a game played at the handicap tournament in the same Divan in 1892 (**game 1095**) (*see diagram*).

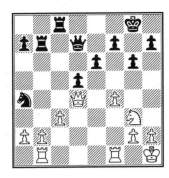

*Black to move*

Van Vliet has just exchanged his bishop at d4 against White's counterpart. The pawn at b2 is now ready to be taken, but only by the knight, as after **27. ... R×b2? 28. Ne4! Qb5 29. Nf6† Kf8 30. N×h7†** Bird has made excellent use of his opponent's undefended queen to activate his knight. Now van Vliet obstinately refuses the draw, giving rise to a crafty follow-up by Bird: **30. ... Ke8? 31. Rbe1! Rc7 32. Qg7 Kd8 33. c4! Qe8 34. c×d5.** Bird seems a bit overconfident, for he misses the immediately winning 34. Nf6! This didn't influence the final result—a White victory.

Bird was arguably at his most vulnerable in the endgame. At its worst, his play in this phase of the game was lamentable. His whole playing style was developed to avoid the endgame by forcing a decision earlier on. This weakness in Bird's play was already known in his early days. In a comment to a match game with Horwitz, Staunton recorded in the London 1851 tournament book (p. 312) that "Nothing more clearly shows the utter incompetence of Mr. Bird, though an amateur of lively imagination and unquestionable ability, to make a stand against such a player as Horwitz, than these endgames." Nevertheless a few worthwhile endgames are to be found in this book. An unique early win was played against George Webb Medley in 1849 (**game 4**). Another fine win in the endgame happened at the B.C.A. consultation tournament in 1885 (**game 733**). Impressive was Bird's victory against Emanuel Lasker on the occasion of the B.C.A. congress of 1892 (**game 1072**).

Bird often experienced difficulties against solid and positionally superior opponents. Some of them seemed to have had a manual on how to beat him. Blackburne suffocated Bird more than once, just as Wisker did. Bird was especially weak in the more positional lines taken against his Dutch Defense. See for example how Lee treated him in their match of 1897 (**game 1276**).

At times Bird was clueless, even in promising positions, as he played often without positional compass. A tragic example was the penultimate game in his match with Mason (**game 377**).

**1. e4 c5 2. Nf3 e6 3. d4 c×d4 4. N×d4 Nf6 5. Bd3 Nc6 6. N×c6 b×c6 7. 0–0 d5 8. e5 Nd7 9. Qe1 Rb8 10. c3 Nc5 11. Be2 Be7 12. b4 Nd7 13. Bd3 c5 14. a3 0–0** The opening has gone very well for Bird, but he refuses to augment the pressure against Mason's queenside with 14. ... a5! (also possible at move 17) **15. Qe2 Qc7 16. f4 g6 17. Qg4 Bb7 18. Be3 Rfd8 19. Ra2 h5** Worse than doing nothing as he needlessly weakens the kingside and offers his opponent a target for free. **20. Qg3 Kh8 21. Re2 Rg8 22. Bd2** Starting a profound maneuvre to exchange his worst piece, but he gets no real value for it. Bird, for his part, has run out of ideas and just sits still and waits. **22. ... Nf8 23. Be1 Rd8 24. Qh3 Nh7 25. Bh4 B×h4 26. Q×h4 a5 27. Qf2 d4 28. b×c5 d×c3 29. Bc4 g5 30. f5 e×f5?** These last few moves fail to impress. This one is a decisive positional concession. **31. N×c3 Rc8 32. Nb5 Q×c5 33. Q×c5 R×c5 34. Nd6 f4 35. Rb1 Bd5 36. B×d5 R×d5 37. N×f7† Kg7 38. Rb7 Kg6 39. Rc2 Ra8 40. Rc6† Kf5 41. Nd6† K×e5 42. Nc4†** and here, a few moves before Bird finally abandoned the game, comes a highly revealing note from Mason: "Mr. Bird remarked, after the game was ended, that the movements of this knight exemplified perfectly what is known as 'chess luck.' If he had not come into the game just as he did, and moved around just as he did, the game would have been different, and would have had a different

conclusion. Mr. Bird also said something about the 'unlucky' [sic] of his own knight. What it was, we cannot recollect at this moment"—Mason.

This game and Mason's final note elucidate how the modern school, here represented by a solidly playing Mason, overcomes Bird.[14]

With his new opening repertoire, and especially in games in which he touched the f-pawn first, Bird often got closed positions that resulted in a true war of trenches. These types of positions could not be more different from those Bird got with his former repertoire, with which he was in line with the so-called romantic school in chess.

With these closed openings, Bird got in the same fairway as, decades later, Aron Nimzowitsch. At times Bird hit upon a beautiful and original idea but only rarely did he follow it consequently. He tested ideas and concepts like a conveyer belt and had no fear of failing. Unlike Nimzowitsch he had no ambition at all to develop a system of thoughts and opinions that would compete with the modern school. He only aspired for a wealth of ideas and originality.

In his introduction to *Chess Novelties*, Professor Louis Hoffmann, the pseudonym of Angelo Lewis, compared Bird with Robert Herrick, an intractable seventeenth century poet. From this point of view Bird was in line with Nimzowitsch, who searched his own way, if necessary, right in opposition to the reigning opinions.

> Mr. Bird's style of play is in some respects peculiar to himself. It was aptly said of Herrick that "it was his pleasure to try the sound of a great variety of rhythms, to find what music the language was capable of." Mr. Bird may be called the Herrick of the chessboard. Throughout his career he has constantly striven after new metres, subtle surprises, unexpected harmonies [*Chess Novelties*, p. xvii].

In his own introduction of the same book, one finds a quotation from Bird that transcended the age he lived in and wherein he even finds connection with the opinions on chess as they stand now.

> Hints to the unwary anent snares to be avoided in the game of chess would be of more practical value than any attempt to define principles without a line as to the exceptions known to arise at every step. The fact is, no hard and fast line can be drawn defining the principles of chess at all [*Chess Novelties*, p. x].

# BIRD'S LEGACY

There exists a huge discrepancy between Bird's reputation during his lifetime and what remained of it a few decades after his death. In 1947 Fred Reinfeld powerfully captured the essence when he reminisced about the veteran in one of his books:

14. A few years later Bird came up with a curious anecdote that reminds us of Mason's remark. Now Bird was on the right side of the board: "A very amiable, but at times somewhat irascible and excitable gentleman in New York had a few chess sittings with Bird when he was last in that city. The latter, giving odds, played what appeared to be a very risky and dangerous sort of game, and his opponent was repeatedly hoping and expecting to give checkmate, but could not succeed in a solitary instance. At last his patience gave way, and he suddenly and almost furiously exclaimed, "There is no combination in your play at all, sir. You have the most confounded luck of any player I ever met with. No matter how your king is placed, you have always the good fortune to get other pieces so situated that nothing can harm his majesty." *Sheffield and Rotherham Independent*, 17 March 1883.

More than one generation of chess players has been familiar with Bird's reputation for originality, waywardness and even eccentricity. To moderns, this reputation is nothing more than an echo of the distant past [*British Chess Masters: Past and Present*, p. 21].

Bird was easily the most popular master among amateurs. His game always stood in the center of attention and he was admired publicly. Some of society's leading men constantly kept an eye at his feats at the chessboard and adored his playing style.[15]

Bird also enjoyed the respect of the greatest masters of his day. His weaknesses were well known but when Bird was at his best nobody doubted his place among the world's leading players. Even Steinitz, despite their bad personal relations, acknowledged more than once that Bird's play could impress him. Steinitz was a fair analyst and his praise has therefore nothing double-edged.

Tarrasch's opinion on Bird can be read between the lines of his analysis of their games in *Three Hundred Chess Games*. In Hamburg 1885, Bird was easily outplayed but he continued to play for tricks as if his opponent was a beginner. The German's attitude was scornful (p. 59): "and I could only smile at the threats ... but he resigned without waiting for my move." Bird deserved much more respect in their high-level duel in Manchester. When Bird contemplated a long time on a move instead of playing instantly Tarrasch was alarmed about the position's subtleties. He delved into it and found Bird's judgment correct. Bird's direct rival Blackburne wrote about him shortly before Bird's death:

We have in England for nearly two-thirds of a century enjoyed the splendid style of Mr. H.E. Bird, especially notable for his originality. He may by his devotion to brilliancy have several times missed the chess crown. He has always apparently set less value on that than on the achievement of some brilliant mate [*The Strand Magazine*, December 1906, p. 723].

Very interesting is the opinion formulated by Samuel Lipschütz in a conversation with some club players. Seeing him quote Löwenthal, who died when Lipschütz was 14, is strange: it must be based on hearsay.

Bird was there, hale and hearty and seeming as brilliant at 70 [*sic*] as he had been at 35. His hair and beard were perfectly white and his step slightly unsteady, but he was the same jolly, good-natured, jovial companion he had been in the days when he manipulated the pieces against Morphy and Staunton. Bird is the most erratic player for an expert I have ever met. He opens his games in a manner peculiar to himself. Before he has played a dozen moves he will have moved his king, doubled pawns on dangerous files, part of his pieces confined, and in fact involved his game in as demoralizing a condition as one would expect from the most ignorant amateur. Then it is that his wonderful fertility of resource develops itself. I have seen him draw and even win games that I should have abandoned in despair. As the genius Löwenthal once pertinently expressed it: "Bird is the best bad player I ever saw" [*Los Angeles Herald*, 13 January 1895].

15. In the obituary of John Ruskin we read: "Here we think of Ruskin as a votary of chess—for he was an enthusiastic lover of the game—that is of chess of a sort, for he would have none of the pawn-gaining, wood-shifting, snail-creeping chess. He loved only the 'grand style,' the sweeping majesty of a game by Morphy or the glittering beauty of a blindfold gem by Blackburne. He regarded chess from its artistic side—as indeed was to be expected of him. He never played chess in public or in any club, reserving it as a relaxation in his own home." *British Chess Magazine*, February 1900, p. 65. The famous science fiction writer H.G. Wells shared the same adoration for Bird: "Compulsory quick moving is the thing for gaiety, and that is why, though we revere Steinitz and Lasker, it is Bird we love. His victories glitter, his errors are magnificent. The true sweetness of chess, if it ever can be sweet, is to see a victory snatched, by some happy impertinence, out of the shadow of apparently irrevocable disaster." H.G. Wells, *Certain Personal Matters*. London: T. Fisher Unwin, 1901, p. 143.

Lively were the reminiscences of William Ewart Napier, who visited Europe at the age of 18. In London he was keen to witness the chess players at the Divan. Napier was an excellent observer and Bird did not escape his eye.

Bird earned the rebuke of playing impulsively in tournaments. It was disrespectful and scandalous, some thought; but if there is genius in chess, Bird, of all players, had it, I believe, in greatest abundance. And his speed and sparkle and eccentricity must have interested Morphy himself, to the degree that he took down some of Bird's games. That's a thought worth more than a stone monument. I like the picture of Morphy, paper and pencil in hand, recording the Bird manoeuvers.

I saw Bird once at Simpson's Divan, but not to speak to. I brought away an impression of fulminating chess, of hearty laughter, and liberty and beefsteak. He romped [*Paul Morphy and the Golden Age of Chess*, p. 97].

It was a common belief that Bird, and many other players with an aggressive playing style, appealed more to the moderate chess fan. Many thought that their memory would easily outlive more "boring" exponents of the game.

The achievements of a Blackburne or a Bird will appeal more heartily to the real lovers of chess than all the scientific wins of the modern school, and it is very possible that the "bits of Blackburne" and "Bird's fancy sketches" will long outlive the results of "playing to win while keeping the draw in hand," even though the latter may win tournament prizes [*Illustrated Sporting and Dramatic News*, 1 November 1890; first published in the *Newcastle Weekly Chronicle*].

Yet Bird's reputation stumbled quickly down after his death. His ideal of pursuing amateurism and his weird opening repertoire and playing style were soon enough outdated. Chess at the top level followed the road towards professionalism. The image of a dubious and overestimated minor master arose.

For over a century no serious study at all was made about Bird. He remained a well-known and recurrent character in British chess magazines and books, but his person and playing style got stereotyped. That there was not much chauvinism about Bird becomes clear from Tim Harding's initial opinion on the man. Harding, arguably well-versed in the subject, wrote (p. 132) that "Research for this chapter began with the impression that Bird was something of a rogue who achieved little of substance."

This point of view was embedded in a certain tradition. An astonishing contribution had been made recently by the late well-respected and influential chess historian Kenneth Whyld. In the May 2001 edition of the *British Chess Magazine* he published the first installment of an article on Gossip. Gossip was a peculiar minor English chess master. He was not very well liked in his time and most often scored disastrously in tournaments. Whyld compared Bird with Gossip (pp. 263–264) and came to a surprising conclusion: "So, was Gossip any good as a player? He was probably better than Bird, who was hugely popular because of his happy nature, and is still respected." To prove his point Whyld published two games that were disastrous for Bird against Gossip in New York in 1889. Whyld's theory was probably built on an earlier article about Gossip. In the *British Chess Magazine* of January 1969 (p. 3), Geoffrey Harber Diggle stated erroneously that "Curiously, however, he [Gossip] never lost a game against Bird." Diggle was referring to four major tournaments (New York 1889, London 1889, Manchester 1890 and London 1892), but he omitted to take several (handicap) tournaments at the Divan in account. In these Bird won repeatedly against Gossip.

On each of these four major tournaments Bird ended well ahead of Gossip, a fact acknowledged by Diggle but not by Whyld. The gap between Bird and Gossip was especially noteworthy at London 1889 (Bird first with 7½/10, Gossip last with 1½/10) and Manchester 1890 (Bird joint third with 12/19, Gossip last with 4/19). In 1889 Bird was even successful against Gossip in a match in which he gave odds.

Harding continued, "The more his life and career were studied, the more that [first] impression altered greatly in his favor." In his conclusion he makes an attempt to qualify Bird (p. 133): "Bird's tournament record looks unimpressive but he would (in today's terms) have earned the IM title in 1873 (if not earlier) by virtue of those match results [against Falkbeer, Steinitz, Wisker and Burn] and his performance in a very strong field in Vienna."

We believe that modern notions, such as an ELO rating or the GM/IM/FM system, are hardly applicable to anything but the present. These concepts are made even more hollow by the enormous inflation to which they have been exposed since their conception. It makes more sense to try to objectify Bird's position amidst his contemporaries.

Until 1872 Bird did not possess the ambition that he exhibited later on. His results were mixed, but mostly not very appealing. A tie against Falkbeer and the close loss against Steinitz demonstrate that he was a player of considerable strength already. The quality of his play was of a decent level, but it was also influenced by his lack of practice. He was considered a moderate master, though nothing exceptional.

The year 1873 was a crucial one. With his victory against Wisker, Bird established himself among the very best players of the United Kingdom. He was eager to test his strength against Steinitz or Blackburne, but both ducked the opportunity as there was not enough financial compensation available.

Bird took part in the major tournaments of the 1870s and solidly placed himself among the world's second-rank grouping. Mostly he convincingly beat the local masters. Bird could sometimes create an upset against a top player, but he never succeeded in putting down a truly excellent result in a strong field. After De Vere's death and Wisker's migration, Bird was considered the nation's number two behind Blackburne. His playing level was arguably on the rise during these years, even though he already approached the age of 50.

Bird's strength slowly declined during the next decade. He participated with little success in the mammoth events of Vienna 1882 and London 1883 but at times his creativity ran high. Bird's activity intensified from 1884 until 1890; his results were mixed. His best performances were his second place (shared) at Hereford 1885 and his match tie with Burn in 1886. At the end of the decade, however, Bird really outdid himself by winning the B.C.A. Congress of 1889 and ending joint third a year later in Manchester.

An ill performance in Hamburg in 1885 ended Bird's presence in tournaments on the European continent. The mammoth event held in New York in 1889 was his sole remaining appearance outside the United Kingdom.

Bird's ranking among the British masters declined further. Blackburne was still considered top of the bill. Players such as Burn and Gunsberg were quickly ascending and became Bird's principal challengers. In match play they mostly overpowered him.

After a severe illness during the winter of 1890-91, Bird returned to chess for a final decade. On his best days Bird could still perform a stunning exploit, but he also had to accept that many minor masters were able to stand alongside him. The year 1892 was Bird's busiest. He received a 5–0 pounding from Lasker, but a few weeks later he nearly played the tournament of his life in Belfast. At Hastings in 1895 Bird was the only strong British representative during the first half of the tournament. Even at his final tournament in 1899, he struggled heroically.

All in all, the feeling remains that Bird did not achieve the maximum of his possibilities. Throughout the years various reasons for his lack of success were put forward.

For decades Bird was troubled by health issues. William Ewart Napier related in *Paul Morphy and the Golden Age of Chess* (p. 97) what Richard Teichmann replied to him when asked his thoughts of Bird's chess: "Same as his health, always alternating between being dangerously ill and dangerously well." Bird's main torment was the gout. Research has found perhaps the first mention of his gout to be in 1873. Even at that time it was spoken of as Bird's "old enemy." Many of his bad performances were blamed on the gout. In the year 1886, for example, we see how excellent results (in a tournament at the British Chess Club, in his match with Burn and in the congress of the Counties Chess Association) were mixed with such dreadful experiences as five straight losses against Gunsberg and the subsequent series of losses at the congress of the British Chess Association.

Bird never allowed the gout to lower his spirits. In 1890 he was hit during a handicap tournament after which he needed more than six months to recover. Heroic was his resistance in Vienna in 1882. Bird had to forfeit five of his games, but in the last round he put himself together for a crucial fight against Steinitz. Afterwards one even feared for his life. Another element that influenced his results was that he despised draws and tried to avoid them at all cost, even when this meant that he had to take unaccountable risks. Bird's match with Burn (1886) counted 18 games but no draws. The same goes for two subsequent international tournaments (Paris 1878 and Wiesbaden 1880): 39 games and no draws.[16] It took some time, but Bird evolved. His stellar results at the B.C.A. congresses of 1889 and 1890 were possible only because of a newfound willingness to submit himself to a draw when necessary. In Hastings 1895 only Carl Schlechter drew more games than Bird.

Another notorious eccentricity of Bird was his choice of openings. He relentlessly chose to go his own way and was averse to theoretically established opinions. His lack of successes rarely influenced his opening repertoire.

> Bird is unquestionably one of the finest living players. For brilliancy and fertility of imagination he has no equal. If he could only put a curb upon his

16. Bird's performance in Wiesbaden was contrasted with the drawing master par excellence, Englisch (who scored 7 wins and 8 draws): "Bird, on the other hand, is well known for his confidence in his own powers, and his scorn of all compromising and draw-producing play. In almost every tournament of this extent he might fairly be credited for one or two games thrown away by play below his strength. When we find him, especially in a tournament where draws are scattered so freely, without a single undecided contest, the result may confidently be set down to his idiosyncrasy, and not to that of his opponents; that is to say, it may be assumed that it is not to be attributed to the failure of his opponents to draw games in which they had the opportunity of drawing, but rather to his playing to win when he might have more successfully attempted to draw." *Glasgow Weekly Herald*, 24 July 1880.

predilection for eccentricities and abandon openings condemned by almost every authority on the subject, there is no doubt that his success would be proportionate to his merit [*Chess Monthly*, March 1889, p. 194].

Bird never put his drift to experiment in doubt, but even beautifully justified it.

For my more humble self Dr. Zukertort has good-naturedly and not unkindly expressed the opinion that if I had been less experimental and less hazardous in my play I might have secured higher positions in tournaments; ... if, however, I have had less success than some other players, I have derived more amusement and real pleasure from the combinations of the game, besides which if I am not original in chess I am nothing [*Modern Chess*, p. 5].

In his notes to a game against Englisch (**game 615**), Bird gave another motivation for his originality: "Change at chess is desirable for real enjoyment like change of air, so I vary my proceedings perhaps more than is consistent with prudence, my desire being to get as much beauty out of the game as I can." Yet Bird could be extremely stubborn in his opening choices and stick to them even when they cost him defeat after defeat. He tried new concepts within his private lines, but did not often look for new horizons.

We believe that one of the most important elements that influenced Bird's results has but rarely been put forward: his age. When one judges Bird's games until 1860 we see a strong player with original concepts. At the same time his play was very error-ridden. The few important games that Bird played between 1860 and 1872 demonstrate that he was absolutely out of practice. The quality of these games is unmistakably lower than those of the older man. Evidently, his accounting career influenced his playing strength.

Bird was nearly 45 years old when his dedication to chess became intense. This had a good impact on the quality of his play. It is very notable that, after a few lesser years, Bird reached what was perhaps his peak in the years 1889–1890, when he was already 60. Even five years later, at Hastings, he was the best British player halfway through.

It is evident that a comparison with the much younger chess players that surrounded him is hardly fair. Seeing what results he put down against these players Bird was indeed a very strong player. What he might have been capable of is difficult to guess, for he hardly played the game during what could have been his heyday.

Most players of Bird's era played without the compass of positional chess. By uncovering the hidden rules of the game Steinitz achieved a status that is nearly impossible to emulate, except by a thinker like Nimzowitsch. Bird remains at a considerable distance from both geniuses of chess, but in one sense his mission was comparable: he was looking for his own compass and bothered not to follow rules or tendencies that influenced and governed the public opinion.

When one takes a close look at Bird's games it is soon remarked that they revel in brilliancy. They repay replaying, one is touched by their beauty. It is especially noteworthy that Bird was able to weave together so many tactical tricks and motives, even though he was notorious for his immensely fast play. The other side of the coin is also abundantly revealed in this book. What might be called his superficial playing style betrayed a lack of depth and a penchant to blunder, his moves aimed for concrete benefits and not long-term consequences. Bird tried to moderate the superficiality by developing his own openings. He came up with his own pointed ideas, and some of them still stand today.

# ◆ Part I ◆

# A Young Bird, 1829–1851

## The Birds of Bridgnorth

The earliest traces of Henry Edward Bird's ancestors lead one back to Bridgnorth. This small historical town is situated near Birmingham in the county of Shropshire, central England. It gained the reputation of being a busy river port in the Middle Ages, ever since a bridge connected both shores of the Severn.

Around 1630 Edward Bird, the first known forefather of Henry Edward, was born there. With a civil war between Parliamentarians and Royalists going on, times were extremely tumultuous. In 1646 Bridgnorth was the center of the battle for a short while, which resulted in huge destructions.

The next few generations of Birds lived in more peaceful times. They married locally and remained firmly tied to their home ground.

## Life in Bristol

The first of Bird's ancestors to look for new and greener pastures was another Edward Bird, the great-grandfather of the chess master. In 1750 he married a girl from Devonshire, a county at about 150 miles from Bridgnorth. The young couple settled in Bristol, a prosperous city halfway between their respective birth counties. They had several children, of whom Edward Bird, born in 1763, was the most important.[1]

Henry Edward's grandfather worked as a watchmaker and silversmith in the center of Bristol. He was an innovative type; his son Henry, the chess master's father, claimed many decades later that his father had invented an unique system for shop owners to open a door automatically. Alas he lacked the financial back-up to materialize his invention with a patent.[2]

Edward's occupation indicates that his family was firmly middle class and led a relatively well-off existence. This was confirmed by his marriage to a young woman of at least equal standing, Mary Pid-

ding, who hailed from Gloucester Lane in Bristol. Their marriage was reported by the *Bath Chronicle and Weekly Gazette* on 14 July 1791.

Mary gave birth to eight children between 1795 and 1806. Henry Bird was her fourth child, born on 30 May 1799. Some of Henry's siblings had their impact on Henry Edward's life, so it is worth mentioning them. Two of Henry's brothers, Daniel Pidding[3] and John, followed in the footsteps of their father and remained active in the jewelry business. The latter son married a member of the Upjohn clan, a very respected family of clockmakers. John and two of his children show up again in the census of 1851.

Henry had two sisters. The youngest, Mary Pidding Bird, died in October 1836. Sarah Pidding Bird was married to Edward Drew, the latter being one of the more unfortunate minor characters in the H.E. Bird story.

## Henry Bird and His Family

On 2 November 1824 Henry Bird, 25 years old, embarked on matrimony with Mary Ellen Baker. His bride was the daughter of William and Honor (sometimes Honour) Baker (who were born respectively in ca. 1781 and 1785). Mary Ellen was born around 1805.

Mary Ellen had two sisters: Jane (born in 1808 in Beaminster, Dorset) and Honor Mary (born ca. 1811). At the time of Mary Ellen's marriage she was living with her parents in Frome, a small town in the vicinity of Bristol.

William Baker earned his living as a linen draper (i.e., a salesman of all kinds of linen), according to *Pigot's and Co's London and Provincial New Commercial Directory for 1822-3*. Henry Bird would follow in his father-in-law's footsteps. Since the abolition of all restrictions on apprenticeships in 1814, it became much easier for young men to become craftsmen. It is therefore possible that he met his future wife while gaining the expertise of the profession in her father's service.

Their marriage was soon blessed with two children. A copy of the original family bible still exists and shows a daughter, Jane, to have

---

1. The pedigree of Henry Edward Bird and his family has been researched by Sarah Sipple (née Bird), a direct descendant of Henry Edward's brother, Edward Daniel Pidding. Much information on the Birds comes from Mrs. Sipple's website, http://www.sarahsipple.co.uk/bird.

2. *The Melbourne Argus*, 15 October 1859. Bird's letter was a reaction to an article that appeared the previous day in the *Argus*. According to this article, a German locksmith claimed the invention of a system that safeguarded a strongbox.

3. It was a recurrent habit in Bird's family to give a child the mother's or grandmother's maiden name as second name. The reader is referred to the family's genealogical chart to keep a clear overview.

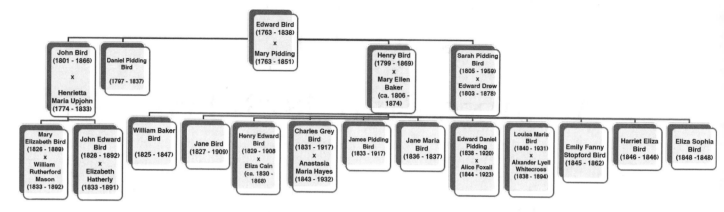

A simplified genealogy of Henry Edward Bird's family.

been born in "1825." Two years later Mary Ellen gave life to William Baker in "1827."[4]

Research in christening records, however, demonstrated that the family bible is in error. William Baker (1825–1847) was actually born first, on 26 November 1825. He was baptized on 2 January 1826 at St. Michael's in Bristol, indicating that the family probably moved to Henry's home town after marrying.[5]

Similar research discloses that Jane Louisa (1827–1909) was baptized on 18 December 1827. In the meantime the family had left Bristol and settled in Portsea, near Portsmouth, where the baptism took place at St. John's.[6] Henry Bird continued his work as a linen draper in Portsea, even though his name wasn't mentioned in *Pigot and Co's National Directory Commercial Directory for 1828-9* (1828).

In 1829 Henry Bird was declared bankrupt. When this failure was pronounced in the *London Gazette* on 6 October 1829, he had already moved further to Brighton.[7] This announcement turns out to be highly relevant for the determination of the birth date of Henry Edward, the third child of Henry and Mary Ellen. While there has never been discussion of his birth place (Portsea), nor of the day on which he was born (14 July), sources diverge on Henry Edward's year of birth.

Throughout the more than 185 years (as of this writing) that separate this author from Bird's birth, the majority of sources have accepted him as being born in 1830. This was supported by such an authoritative voice as *Who Was Who*. On a few rare occasions the year 1829 has been given as Henry Edward's birth year.

Bird's bankruptcy announcement in the *London Gazette* makes it clear that the family had already left Portsea before 1830, implying thus that Henry Edward must have been born in 1829. Proof of this is given by the record of Henry Edward's baptism, which took place at St. Thomas in Portsmouth on 7 August 1829.[8]

Two more boys, Charles Grey (1831–1917) and James Pidding (1833–1917), were born in the early 1830s. They were both baptized on 2 December 1833 at St. Michael's in Southampton.[9] In Southampton Henry Bird re-established a linen draper shop. In December 1831 he unluckily caught the attention of the press when a girl named Mary Newman was remanded on suspicion of stealing from him (*Hampshire Telegraph*, 5 December 1831).

Just like in Portsea, Bird was not able to make a success of his shop. He was facing another bankruptcy which he prevented, according to the *London Gazette* of 15 November 1833 (p. 2117), by making an agreement with two men, James Simes and William Charlesworth. Bird sold the shop while Simes and Charlesworth took care of paying off his debts in return.

During the first decade of his married life Henry thus experienced a few severe setbacks and times were probably hard to support his wife and children. It must be nuanced, however, that it was relatively easy to get rid of business debts.

One had to deal with being declared bankrupt, but discharge followed soon once all the assets had been sold. Legislation was much harsher for insolvent debtors with private debts. These people often ended up in jail. As Henry descended from a family that was relatively well off, financial resources from previous generations of the family, especially from the side of his mother, may have helped him through the difficulties.[10]

## MOVING TO LONDON

Henry Bird's family disappeared from the radar for three years after the baptism of Charles Grey and James Pidding in December 1833. At some point they decided to pack their bags and head for London; which was very common in those years as the British

4. Erroneous family bible data confirmed in private correspondence with Sarah Sipple, who possesses a copy.

5. "England Births and Christenings, 1538–1975," index, *FamilySearch* (https://familysearch.org/pal:/MM9.1.1/NTX7-243: accessed 25 Sep 2014), William Baker Bird, 02 Jan 1826; citing St. Michaels, Bristol, Gloucester, England, reference item 2 p 94; FHL microfilm 1595867.

6. "England Births and Christenings, 1538–1975," index, *FamilySearch* (https://familysearch.org/pal:/MM9.1.1/NTFZ-931: accessed 25 Sep 2014), Jane Louisa Bird, 18 Dec 1827; citing Portsea, Hampshire, England, reference Page 27 #209; FHL microfilm 1596294.

7. On pp. 1835–1836 Henry Bird was called a "linen draper, dealer and chapman."

8. "England Births and Christenings, 1538–1975," index, *FamilySearch* (https://familysearch.org/pal:/MM9.1.1/N1WB-NM4: accessed 25 Sep 2014), Henry Edward Bird, 07 Aug 1829; citing Portsmouth, Hampshire, England, reference p22 no169; FHL microfilm 1,596,260.

9. "England Births and Christenings, 1538–1975," index, *FamilySearch* (https://familysearch.org/pal:/MM9.1.1/NRN3-258: accessed 25 Sep 2014), Charles Grey Bird, 02 Dec 1833; citing Southampton, Hampshire, England, reference p124 rn 986; FHL microfilm 1041739.

10. Two cases that came before the Court of Chancery deal with problems arising from the inheritance of Daniel Pidding, Henry's maternal grandfather. These will be dealt with in detail in Part II.

capital drew large numbers of migrants that quickly transformed it into the world's largest city. Thanks to the positive effects of industrialization and the advent of railways, literally thousands of job opportunities arose.

The very first mention of the Birds after arriving in London concerned the baptism of the newly born Jane Maria (1836–1837). Henry declared that he worked as victualler (i.e., provider of food and drink).[11] In 1838 Mary Ellen gave birth to her last son, Edward Daniel Pidding. He was baptized on 28 December 1838. Henry Edward was baptized a second time on the same occasion. The family had moved their home to the parish of St. Luke's.[12] The same record shows that Henry Bird had switched his profession to become an accountant.

Accounting was a new kind of business, still in its infancy, and there were no requirements nor formal education needed to make it one's profession. In fact, it happened regularly that businessmen, not rarely after being bankrupt in a completely different activity, took up accounting for which they could employ their commercial skills.[13]

The exact address of the Birds, 30 Windsor Terrace, City Road, in the parish of St. Luke's, Finsbury, north London, was discovered in the census of 1841. The youngest child of the family, Louisa Maria (1840–1931), was also registered. Henry's profession was given as clerk.[14] Absent was Charles Grey, 10 years old at the time. He could be found with his grandmother Mary Pidding, in Bristol.[15]

In the meantime William Baker and his family had also moved to London. In the census of 1841 he was recorded at Capel Court in the parish of St. Bartholomew-by-the exchange, in the heart of the City of London. At the same address lived two of his relatives: his wife Honor and his daughter Jane.[16] William lived above the Auction Mart Tavern (which was his property), situated in Throgmorton Street, but Bartholomew Lane was also often given as its address. In the census William was named a tavern keeper, which means he was also a victualler, just like Henry Bird. Perhaps they worked together for a certain period until Henry became an accountant.

William had obtained the license to exploit the Auction Mart Tavern around December 1838 (perhaps it was a prolongation. This was the first date found linking him with this establishment). His business caught much attention of the press when, on 13 December 1842, a servant tried to murder a female colleague, followed by an attempt of suicide (both failed).[17] Several other servants were interrogated, Henry Bird not among them.

On 17 March 1843, the *Era* reported a frightful accident that took place at Lee Bridge Road. William Baker, together with three other gentlemen, were driving in a phaeton when the horse became a runaway, proceeding furiously. Baker jumped out of the carriage but fell very unfortunately. After an agony that lasted a few hours he died in his early sixties. His death received much attention, not only because of the tragic circumstances, but also because he was the chairman of the Licensed Victuallers' Asylum. His funeral, reported in the *Era* of 26 March 1843, was attended by Henry Bird and two of his sons, supposedly William Baker and Henry Edward. William Baker was buried in the grave of his daughter Honor Mary (who died on 28 April 1840).

In his will William Baker specified that he was leaving a dwelling house in Barnstable to his grandson William Baker Bird. He further permitted his wife to carry on his business until his trustees would have sold his license.[18] It is not unlikely that Henry Bird purchased that license. In 1848 he worked as a victualler again (more about this later) and in the *London Post Office Directory* of 1848, one can find "Baker & Bird, Auction Mart Tavern, Throgmorton Street."

At the latest by 1844 Henry Bird and his family moved to a new address, 13 Clapham Road Place in Lambeth. This part of London, on the southern bank of the Thames, was much more central than where Henry had lived previously but it had a bad reputation because of a polluting industry settled there. Within a few decades some 100,000 immigrants changed the former rural suburb into one of London's most overcrowded parts. It is needless to say that many of them lived in terrible conditions. Lambeth became fertile soil for the infamous cholera outbreak of the late 1840s. Yet, the living conditions and financial prospects of the Birds were presumably on the rise as they were able to pay a servant for at least two years.[19]

Lambeth remained the most important parish in the life of Henry Edward and various of his relatives. Both his aunt Jane Baker and his sister Jane died at 44 Clapham Road. Jane Baker married Henry Jacobs, a surgeon, in 1848. Until his death they lived in Kensington. After several wanderings south of the Thames, H.E. Bird definitively returned to Lambeth in 1882 and stayed there until his death.

Some important events occurred at 13 Clapham Road Place during the second part of the decade. In June 1845, Emily Fanny Stopford (1845–1862) was born. She was the last child of Henry and Mary Ellen to grow up into (near) adulthood. Two other children, Harriett Eliza and Eliza Sophia, born in 1846 and 1848, died as infants. An equally sad event was the death of Henry Edward's older brother William Baker, at home on 6 June 1847. He died of tuberculosis.[20] At that time he was working as an accountant for the Shropshire Union Railway and Canal Company. William Baker's death was announced on 12 June in the *Bristol Mercury*, revealing that Henry Bird still had firm links with his native town.

11. London Metropolitan Archives, Bloomsbury St. George, Register of baptisms, P82/GEO1, Item 005.

12. "England Births and Christenings, 1538–1975," index, *FamilySearch* (https://familysearch.org/pal:/MM9.1.1/NP75-4SZ: accessed 25 Sep 2014), Henry Edward Bird, 28 Dec 1838; citing reference; FHL microfilm 585443, 585444, 585445.

13. D. Matthews, M. Anderson, J.R. Edwards, *The Priesthood of Industry: The Rise of the Professional Accountant in British Management*. Oxford: Oxford University Press, 1998, p. 20. The example quoted there involves a former draper.

14. 1841 census: Class: *HO107*; Piece: *666*; Folio: 37; Page: 30.

15. 1841 census: Class: *HO107*; Piece: *377*; Folio: 62; Page: 16.

16. 1841 census: Class: *HO107*; Piece: *720*; Folio: 1; Page: 10.

17. William Cannell, the waiter, shot at Elizabeth Magness and then attempted to cut his throat. Both survived. Cannell was ultimately transported for fifteen years. A few sample articles: *Morning Post* 14 December 1842 and the *Morning Chronicle* 2 March 1843. The process can also be found at the site of the Old Bailey.

18. The National Archives; Kew, England; *Prerogative Court of Canterbury and Related Probate Jurisdictions: Will Registers*; Class: *PROB 11*; Piece: *1982*.

19. This address was mentioned in an extensive article about a theft with Henry Bird as victim. Caroline Taylor, "a respectable looking young female," in the service of Mr. Bird, and George Dean were accused of stealing silver tablespoons, a coffee pot, trousers, etc. from the family safe. *Standard*, 19 November 1844. The trial of the suspects can be found at the online database of the Old Bailey Proceedings.

20. The death registration reference is Lambeth, April-May-June 1847, vol. 4, p. 189.

## Searching Through Life

According to *Who Was Who* (p. 64), Henry Edward received some formal school education during the early part of the 1840s. This period lasted only fifteen months. It is very remarkable that the oldest boys of the family enjoyed but limited schooling. The situation was different for most girls and Edward Daniel Pidding, who were considerably younger. This clearly testifies that Henry Bird's economic prospects were really on the rise towards the end of the decade.

Having spent so little time in school did not limit Henry Edward's chances for the future. The same article in *Who Was Who* pointed out that he was a very keen boy with an extraordinary memory who mostly educated himself. This helped him advance in life, and already by 1846 he had started to work as a clerk for the accounting firm of Alexander and John Young, named Young and Co.

Henry Edward's choice of accountancy is hardly a surprise. He was renowned for his talent for figures and the fact that both his father and his older brother held this profession must have given him a decisive impulse to follow their path. They may also have facilitated Bird's entrance into an office at such a young age, as good connections were often necessary to find a place in this field.[21]

Henry Edward worked as a clerk for more than a decade.[22] Most of Bird's working time was spent on bankruptcies. Since the Bankruptcy Act of 1831, assignees, appointed to liquidate the estate of the bankrupt, increasingly made use of accountants for their investigations.[23]

Bird's name only made it once into the press. A statement before the bankruptcy court was published in the *Standard* on 19 December 1856. For this bankruptcy of a wine merchant, Bird had to draw up a list of bona fide creditors, which led to the debunking of a forger.

## Discovering the Game

Henry Edward Bird was introduced to the game of chess at the age of 15. Unlike many other players, he did not receive his first les-sons from his father or one of his siblings, but became interested when he noticed men playing the noblest of games in a coffee house one day. Bird was already well acquainted with this type of establishment: his grandfather exploited the Auction Mart Tavern until his death when Henry Edward's father probably took over the management.

When Bird wrote his memoirs, almost fifty years later, he still had warm recollections of those early innocent days. With some detail and nostalgia, he described his rapid rise on the chess ladder.

> After about three months looking on at chess play in 1844, at Raymond's Coffee House near the City Road Gate, where Dr. Michaelson of the *Morning Post*, and Mr. Finley, a farrier, were the respective giants, and a cup of coffee the usual stake, I learned the moves at chess, and receiving the odds of a queen for a few games, I happened one day to hear with astonishment that the gentleman conceding me the odds was not as I supposed, the champion of the world, but that better players could be found at Goode's, Ludgate Hill, and Simpson's in the Strand. To the former I soon resorted and found Kling,[24] Kuiper and Muckle,[25] the principal professionals there; a nominal fee of sixpence being the charge per game, and Staunton, the champion, had played many games at that rate. It was some weeks before I mustered resolution to visit Simpson's spacious and handsome hall, but, once arrived there, I made myself at home. Lowe, Williams and Finch were the attendant players there, and extensively they were supported. From each I received the queen soon improving to the odds of the knight, and then playing even with them. Buckle alone, who did not mind hard work, essayed to give me pawn and move, but for a short time only [*Chess History and Reminiscences*, p. 114].

## Clubs and Coffee Houses

The London chess scene around 1850 revolved around two kinds of establishments where all the action took place: clubs and coffee houses.

Two major chess clubs dominated the former category. The London Chess Club was the oldest. Its members were principally middle-class stockbrokers, bank managers, merchants, factory directors, etc. Their rival, the St. George's Chess Club, was more exclusive. Only players from the aristocracy and the upper class were accepted as members. In any case it was quite hard to enter either of these clubs when not belonging to one of the more fortunate classes of society.[26]

From the 1850s onwards the chess clubs softened up their regime. Lineage or other exclusive criteria made room for such a mundane

---

21. Matthews, *Priesthood of Industry*, p. 29.

22. One gets a general insight into Bird's daily tasks from the autobiography of Edwin Waterhouse. Waterhouse was one of the founders of Price Waterhouse which has merged into what is now one of the world's largest auditing firms, PricewaterhouseCoopers. Waterhouse commenced his accountancy career as a clerk in February 1861 (for the firm in which Bird was also working at that time): "My three years at Coleman, Turquand, Youngs and Co. were on the whole very interesting to me, giving me considerable variety of experience. At first I was able to do only the simplest casting or calling over, and found the work very dull, and the meaning of the book entries was often unintelligible to me. Before long, however, I was given little matters of audit or investigation to carry through myself, and the work then soon became of interest." E. Jones, *The Memoirs of Edwin Waterhouse: A Founder of Price Waterhouse*. London: Batsford, 1988, p. 74. ¶ At the time Bird entered the firm of the brothers Young, auditing was still a very minor part of the work.

23. E. Jones, *Accountancy and the British Economy, 1840–1980: The Evolution of Ernst & Whinney*. London: Batsford, 1981, p. 48.

24. Josef Kling, a German chess master and composer. He remains famous for the book *Chess Studies*, written by him and Horwitz. During the 1850s he exploited a famous chess café, Kling's Chess and Coffee Rooms.

25. Perhaps James (?) Mucklow, a participant in the tournament of 1851.

26. "At both clubs membership was exclusive, not so much on account of the annual subscription of three guineas, as, to a much greater extent, the ballot system used for admission of new members. The social style of the members of St. George's Club precluded any intercourse with non-gentlemen, so that the construction or assertion of an identity as a gentleman could fall here for the smallest reason." J. Townsend, *Notes on the Life of Howard Staunton*. Wokingham: John Townsend, 2011, p. 33. Translated from B-P. Lange (1994), "Modernisierung des aristokratischen Habitus: Howard Staunton als viktorianischer Gentleman, Schachmeister und Philologue." *Archiv für Kulturgeschichte, 76* (1), p. 206. In his book Townsend deals in great detail with Staunton's attempts to join the elitist St. George's Chess Club (p. 33ff).

reason as the chess strength of the applicant. Bird became acquainted with the St. George's Chess Club in 1851, as it was the scene of the first international tournament. Around 1857 he started to become a regular visitor.

For the young Bird, there was little hope to join a chess club as he was missing the necessary social background, like the majority of those who wanted to play a game of chess. Yet some confusion is created by the mention of a certain H. Bird on 10 October 1846 in the *Records of the London Chess Club*.[27]

This man paid three guineas for the membership of a year. It seems unlikely that this member was Henry Edward Bird, for he was only 17 years old. His father, Henry Bird, is a more likely candidate to have been allowed to join. It is unknown if he was familiar with chess, but he was, as shall be seen, busy with improving his social position. The membership of a prominent club must have had its appeal to him.

Most people were destined to practice the game in the more accessible coffee houses. Here the public was much more varied. Occasional visitors, regular customers and fanatic amateurs were joined by a select circle of professionals trying to gain their living from chess.

The young Bird was curious. He tested his abilities in a great variety of coffee houses. Charles French Smith, one of his best chess friends, accompanied him on these explorations.

Especially noteworthy is Bird's introduction to the Divan. This establishment saw life as a tobacco bar, which was a great fashion during the 1820s. It gradually evolved into a coffee house when Samuel Reis opened the Grand Cigar Divan in 1828.

Visitors enjoyed reading newspapers and journals while they sipped their coffees or smoked their cigars. When the Westminster Chess Club closed in 1835, Ries (he had respelled his family name in the meantime) managed to draw a part of its chess community into his own establishment. This was the start of the Divan as a gathering place for chess players that would last for decades.[28]

Regular visitors paid one guinea a year for using the facilities. It was also possible to pay a daily entrance fee of 6d. which entitled the visitor to enjoy a cup of coffee and a cigar.

Bird entered the Divan for the first time when he was about 16 or 17 years old. He was soon noticed by Samuel Boden, a slightly older but already strong chess player. In a short span of time, Bird and Boden became good close friends as well as rivals on the chessboard. None of their early games has been preserved.[29]

Henry Thomas Buckle (*Chess Player's Magazine*).

## A TRIAL OF STRENGTH AGAINST BUCKLE 1847–1849

There were a few peculiar forms of chess popular in the nineteenth century that have disappeared completely in more modern times. Apart from consultation chess, about which more later, playing at odds was very often practiced. The concept was that the stronger player offered some advantage to his lesser opponent. There were various forms of odds-giving, but generally material odds were given. The slightest odds gave the weaker player the White pieces and the removal of the opponent's f7 pawn. Players of this strength were considered belonging to the "pawn and move" class or, in later years, class II. The third class received the odds of pawn and 2 moves. Lower ranked players generally took the Black pieces. The fourth class received the knight (most often Nb1). Heavier odds, such as rook and even queen, were equally common to give to absolute beginners. The odds were aimed to more or less equalize the presumed difference in strength. The weaker player was allowed a chance to make a stand against a strong opponent. As games were generally played for stakes, they were induced to part with some money, which became the most important way for the professionals to earn a living.

The young Bird rapidly climbed up from the lowest classes. After just two years of intense practice, only the strongest players were still able to give Bird the smallest odds of pawn and move. Perhaps Henry Thomas Buckle was the last man to concede Bird these odds.

27. See J. Townsend, *Historical Notes on Some Chess Players*. Wokingham: John Townsend, 2014, p. 11.

28. K. Whyld, *Simpson's, Headquarters of the World*. Nottingham: The Chess Player, 2013, pp. 5–6.

29. Many years later, George Alcock MacDonnell, another Divan habitué from 1856 onwards, described Boden's initial impression of the young Bird: "'I remember him well,' said the late S.S. Boden to me, 'when he first came to the Divan in 1846, a pretty-faced boy in a jacket, blue-eyed, fair haired, and rosy-cheeked.'" MacDonnell, *The Knights and Kings of Chess*, p. 44. ¶ Bird eternalized his first visit to Simpson's in another story: "When Bird first visited Simpson's and was playing his first game, he became uneasy at finding so great a mirror at his back, and was greatly troubled at the bare possibility of his coming in contact with it. He was however completely reassured by John, who solemnly informed him that the glass was thicker than his head, and much less likely to crack." Bird, *Chess History and Reminiscences*, p. 77.

Buckle had the good fortune of being born into a very wealthy family. This allowed him the luxury to spend his time with his two great passions: chess and, foremost, history. In the latter field, his studies culminated in his book *The History of Civilization*. Although he died too soon to finish it, this book still enjoys the status of a classic.

When Bird met Buckle for the first time in 1846, many considered the latter to be one of the best players in the world. In 1843, he beat Staunton in a match where he received the odds of pawn and move. Many were eager to see a match with Staunton on equal terms, but Buckle refused to play, for, according to Charles Tomlinson, whose penned portrait of Buckle appeared in July 1891 in the *British Chess Magazine* (p. 328), he wished to retain friendly relations with the man.

Buckle played only a few other formal matches and tournaments. Chess was merely a recreation for him and he could not attach too much importance to the outcome of a game.[30]

Bird wrote that he received the odds of pawn and move from Buckle for just a short while. The turning point appears to have been a small and informal match between both men. The details that exist about this contest were shared by Bird in a biographical article and three of his books. All of them date from many decades after the facts and rather contradict each other, which makes it impossible to ascertain the date and score of this match. In fact, the most likely scenario seems to be that two such matches took place.

In the edition of *Chess Monthly* of March 1889, one of Bird's wins against Buckle was published (p. 219). According to this article, which relied on information given by Bird himself, this game was the fifth of a match played in 1847. Buckle won with 9 against 7.

Bird penned three different versions in his books. The same game was included in *Modern Chess* (p. 10), but now Bird claimed that it was played in 1848 and that he had won all seven match games. In *Chess Practice* (p. 17) he mentions a match with Buckle played in 1849 "for amusement only," without giving a result. Finally, in *Chess History and Reminiscences* (p. 82), he even declared that Buckle gave him odds as late as in 1852, but this is certainly incorrect.[31]

---

30. This attitude was also seen when one observed Buckle in play: "Whether winning or losing Mr. Buckle was a courteous and pleasant adversary, and sat quietly before the board, smoking his cigar, and pursuing his game with inflexible steadiness. He was sometimes harassed when at play by a nervous hiccough, which he would endeavour to suppress by humming some little air." *Westminster Chess Club Papers*, June 1873, p. 24. ¶ Bird, with his genuine love for the game, quickly became one of Buckle's favorite opponents, even though the rapidity of the youngster was a bit to Buckle's dismay: "Buckle called his patiently hard contested games of three, four or five hours each a half-holiday relief; Boden and Bird, two very young rising amateurs, then approaching the highest prevailing force at the time would, to Buckle's dismay, rattle off ten lively skirmishes in half the time he took for one. The younger of the two aspirants became in 1849 a favourite opponent of the distinguished writer and historian whom, however, he somewhat disconcerted at times by the rapidity of his movements and once, and once only, the usually placid Buckle falling into an early snare as he termed it; and emulating Canute of old and Lord Stair in modern times got angry and toppled over the pieces." Bird, *Chess History and Reminiscences*, p. 24.

31. Bird may have based his statement on this note: "With Bird, Buckle won one out of four recorded games, and drew one. But in the two he lost gave the odds of pawn and move." A.H. Huth *The Life and Writings of Henry Thomas Buckle, volume I.* London: S. Low, Marston, Searle & Rivington, 1880, p. 61. Huth referred to the four known games. Bird won both games in which he received odds. Two other games, played in 1852, resulted in a win for Buckle and a draw. Bird, not too focused on exactitude, probably did not think too long about it.

Summing up, it is possible that Bird and Buckle met twice in more or less formal matches in which Bird received the odds of pawn and move. In 1847, Buckle was still too strong for his young opponent and won by a narrow margin, 9–7. One or two years later Bird beat his opponent decisively with 7 wins against 0. It was then that he came on even terms with the strongest players.

## (1) Bird–H.T. Buckle    1–0
Match
London 1849 (?)
*Odds of pawn and move*

**1. d4 e6 2. c4 c5 3. e3 b6 4. Bd3 Nf6 5. e4 Ng8 6. e5 Ne7 7. Bg5 Qc7 8. B×e7 B×e7 9. Be4 Bb7 10. Qh5† Kd8 11. d5 g6 12. Qe2** 12. B×g6 e×d5 13. Nf3 d×c4 14. Nc3 returns the pawn in a more favorable way. Black is caught in a huge bind. **12. ... Q×e5 13. Nf3 Qf4 14. Nc3 Bf6 15. 0–0 B×c3 16. b×c3 e×d5 17. B×d5 B×d5** Correct is 17. ... Nc6, followed by 18. ... Kc7 and 19. ... Rae8. The pawn at d5 hampers the development of his queenside. **18. c×d5 d6** 18. ... Re8 contests the e-file. White has to come up with 19. Qb5! to pose serious problems for Black. **19. Rfe1! Nd7 20. Qe7† Kc7 21. Re4** "He should have played 21. Ng5, winning without much difficulty"—Staunton. **21. ... Qf8 22. Rae1 Q×e7 23. R×e7 Raf8 24. Ng5! Rf5 25. Ne6†** 25. N×h7 is much simpler. **25. ... Kc8 26. c4 a5** 26. ... Re5! unexpectedly gains counterplay at the cost of a pawn. After 27. R×e5 N×e5 28. R×a7 Kb8 29. Ra4 Nd3 White's rook is misplaced. **27. f4! h5** Buckle misses the last chance to complicate the game with 27. ... b5. Bird now smothers all counterplay. **28. g3 Rg8 29. Ng7 Rff8 30. Ne8 g5 31. N×d6†** and after a few more moves Black resigns—*Chess Player's Chronicle* (Staunton), June 1850, pp. 174–175.

## (2) Bird–H.T. Buckle    1–0
Match
London 1849 (?)
*Odds of pawn and move*

"The following, besides being a good game, is the last in which I received odds. It occurred in a match played at the Divan, in which the distinguished author and foremost amateur chess player, Buckle, conceded me the odds of pawn and move in a match of seven games. I was fortunate in winning all and have not accepted odds since"—Bird. In *Chess Monthly* (March 1889, p. 219) Bird writes that this game was the fifth of a match played in 1847 which was won by Buckle with 9 against 7.

**1. d4 e6 2. c4 d5 3. Nc3 Nc6 4. Nf3 Nce7 5. Bg5 c6 6. e4 g6 7. c×d5 c×d5 8. e×d5 e×d5 9. Bb5† Bd7 10. 0–0 Bc6 11. Ne5 Qc7** "If 11. ... B×b5, his opponent would have obtained an overpowering attack by playing 12. Qf3"—Staunton. **12. Qf3 Nh6 13. Rfe1!** "An excellent move, and evidently the result of profound deliberation"—Staunton. **13. ... 0–0–0 14. N×c6 b×c6 15. Ba6† Kb8 16. Bf4 Rd6** (*see diagram*)

**17. N×d5!** "This also is extremely well played, and, as the sequel shows, is as sound as it is brilliant"—Staunton. **17. ... c×d5 18. Rac1 Qb6 19. Q×d5!** "We commend all this to the especial attention of our young aspirants"—Staunton. **19. ... Nhf5** "If

After 16.... Rd6

19. ... N×d5, Black would have been mated in three moves"
—Staunton. **20. Re6 Q×a6 21. R×d6 N×d5 22. Rd8† Kb7
23. Rb8 mates.** This game is perhaps the first testimony to Bird's
brilliance—*Modern Chess* (Bird), p. 10; *Chess Player's Chronicle*
(Staunton), March 1850, p. 76.

# A GHOST TOURNAMENT: LONDON 1848

In the early days of modern chess the practice of the game was
often limited to offhand games, matches between two players
and now and then matches between clubs. It is generally acknowledged that the idea of a tournament, in which several players
took part, was first tested at the Divan during the early winter
months of 1849. Yet, there are some clues that a (handicap) tournament was already held at the same Divan in 1848. Towards the
end of 1847, the Divan closed its doors for some time and underwent
a thorough renovation. At the time of the reopening in December,
Ries was joined in the management by the caterer John Simpson,
after which the establishment was renamed into Simpson's Grand
Divan Tavern. All chess players were eager to move into the refur-
bished Divan and several matches were planned. This may actually
offer a perfect explanation for the introduction of a chess tournament.

Just as it is the case with the matches between Bird and Buckle,
no information about this 1848 affair is available in contemporary
sources, meaning that if any such contest took place it had a very
low-profile. The two references retrieved were recorded much later
and originate from Bird himself.

In *Chess History and Reminiscences* (p. xii), he wrote that the two
first tournaments in England were played at the Divan in 1848 and
1849.[32] In an article in *The Times* of 2 April 1888, most likely written
by Bird, he speaks of a handicap tournament played forty years earlier. Buckle won the tournament while Bird and George Webb Medley were most successful among the juvenile competitors. Both the
success claimed by Bird and the detail that handicaps were given
seem to suggest that this event was not the same as the one that was
definitively played in the following year.

# A TOURNAMENT AT THE DIVAN: LONDON 1849

Under the impressive heading "A Chess Tournament," a new kind
of chess match was proudly announced in the March 1849 edition
of the *Chess Player's Chronicle* (p. 65). The tournament commenced
at the end of January and lasted until about 15 February. The intended number of twelve participants was reached effortlessly. The
first two rounds were played according to the knock-out formula.
The players were paired in lots of six matches and the first to win
two games qualified for the next round. The three remaining players
met each other once in a final pool to determine the final ranking.
They were entitled, respectively, to a half, a third and a sixth of a
prize fund assembled from the participant's entrance fees and subscriptions made by generous supporters.

Bird was evidently extremely eager to test his powers. He was
joined by several other young players as well as some of the Divan's
strongest habitués, notably Buckle and Elijah Williams. Bird hit
upon a strong first round opponent, George Webb Medley. Just like
Bird, G.W. Medley was seen as one of the rising stars. He was three
years older and much more experienced. Thanks to a favorable social
background he had been allowed to become a member of the London Chess Club.

Medley's chess career was largely over by 1851. Being a member
of the club that was much in friction with Staunton about the organization of the tournament of 1851 he had no chance to enter the
field. At the same time his focus shifted away from chess to his work
at the stock exchange. Medley made a fortune but remained
attached to the chess world. He provided financial support to the
game and its players and played a prominent role behind the scenes
of the British Chess Association and the Löwenthal Fund.

Their duel in the tournament was a close contest. Bird initially
suffered in the first game but reached an equal endgame. A blunder
then drastically shortened the game to his disadvantage. The second
game was deservedly won by Bird after a protracted struggle in
which Bird steadily maintained the upper hand. Medley realized
the advantage of the first move by winning the third game, although
not without having flirted with elimination. All in all Bird's performance was very decent.

While Bird in later years confidently asserted that he was ranked
among the better players of his day already, George Walker reported
in his influential chess column in *Bell's Life* on 4 March 1849 that
all losers of the first round, with the exception of John Finch, could
hardly be seen as first-rates.[33]

The final pool was reached by Buckle, the tournament favorite,
and the brothers G.W. and John Racker Medley.[34] Buckle won his
two games to clinch the first prize. A subsequent small match for
the second place was won by G.W. Medley.

33. John Finch must have gained his reputation in the Divan. He did not took
part in any other known tournament or match.
34. John Racker Medley (1828–1902) arrived in Australia in December 1852.
From 1862 until 1881 he was sub-inspector of police at Bourke, Mudgee and the
Gulgong Minefields. For a picture see the site of the National Library of Australia
(http://trove.nla.gov.au/work/192773926?q=%22John+Racker+Medley%22&c
=picture&versionId=211007060).

32. Bird contradicts himself later in the same book (pp. 71–72) by stating that
the first tournament was played in 1849.

**Divan tournament, London, January–February 1849**

*Site:* Simpson's Divan

*Prizes:* 1st, half of the prize fund; 2nd, a third of the prize fund; 3rd, one sixth of the prize fund

*Knock-out phase:*

| | | | | | | |
|---|---|---|---|---|---|---|
| H.T. Buckle | 2 | Buckle | 2 | | | |
| C.F. Smith | 0 | | | | | |
| | | | | Buckle | | |
| E. Williams | 2 | Williams | 0 | | | |
| E.F. Flower | 0 | | | | | |
| G.W. Medley | 2 | G.W. Medley | 2½ | | | |
| H.E. Bird | 1 | | | | | |
| | | | | G.W. Medley | | |
| E. Lowe | 2 | Lowe | 1½ | | | |
| A. Simons | 0 | | | | | |
| J.R. Medley | 2 | J.R. Medley | 2 | | | |
| J.G. Finch | 1 | | | | | |
| | | | | J.R. Medley | | |
| W.J. Tuckett | 2 | Tuckett | 0 | | | |
| J.R. Wise | 0 | | | | | |

*Final pool:*

| | | 1 | 2 | 3 | |
|---|---|---|---|---|---|
| 1 | H.T. Buckle | | 1 | 1 | 2 |
| 2 | G.W. Medley | 0 | | 1 1 | 2 |
| 3 | J.R. Medley | 0 | 0 | | 0 |

## (3) G.W. Medley–Bird    1–0

Divan tournament (round 1, game 1)

London 1849

*A85*

**1. c4 f5 2. d4 Nf6 3. Nc3 d5 4. c×d5 N×d5 5. e3** "5. e4 would perhaps have been better. In that case, the following are likely moves to ensue: 5. … N×c3 (best) 6. b×c3 f×e4 7. Qh5† g6 8. Qe5 Rg8 9. Q×e4 or 9. Bc4 and White has the advantage in position" —Staunton. **5. … e6 6. Nf3 N×c3 7. b×c3 Bd6 8. Bd3 0–0 9. Qc2 b6 10. 0–0 Bb7 11. e4** Correctly played. Bird's inferior reply leaves his position badly compromised. **11. … f×e4 12. B×e4 B×e4 13. Q×e4 Nd7 14. Q×e6†** "We should rather have played 14. Ng5, e.g.,: 14. … Nf6 (or 14. … g6 15. Q×e6† Kg7 16. Qh3 winning easily) 15. Q×e6† Kh8 16. Nf7† winning the exchange and a pawn" —Staunton. **14. … Kh8 15. Ng5 Qe8 16. Qh3 Nf6 17. Bd2** 17. Ne6 Rf7 18. Bg5 gives his opponent no respite. **17. … Qg6** Bird omits making use of Medley's last, somewhat slow, move by heading for complications with 17. … Qe2. Besides the safe 18. Rad1, White has the interesting 18. f4 at his disposal, the surprising point being 18. … Q×d2? when 19. Rf2 wins the queen. Black could better occupy the e-file with a rook, but in both cases White retains a pull thanks to his strong knight: 18. … Rae8 19. Rad1 Qc4 20. f5 and 21. Ne6 or 18. … Rfe8 19. Nf7† and 20. Ne5. **18. f4** White could play 18. Ne6! without any further delay. Bird now takes his opportunities to get rid of his opponent's best piece. **18. … Ne4 19. N×e4 Q×e4 20. Rf2** Anticipating 20. … Qc2. **20. … Rf6** More solid moves are 20. … Rae8 or 20. … Qd5. Absolutely to be avoided is 20. … B×f4 because of 21. Re1. **21. Qf3** Medley continues in his solid style, but more advantage is gained by the space-grabbing 21. f5, which can be followed by 22. Re1 or the sharp 22. g4 and 23. g5. **21. … Q×f3 22. R×f3 Re8 23. Kf2 Re4 24. Re1 R×e1 25. K×e1 g5?** It goes without saying that Bird lacks the necessary

patience for this kind of endgame and he comes up with a badly judged pawn exchange. Despite being a pawn down a draw is still possible, but at least the king had to be brought to the center. **26. f×g5 R×f3 27. g×f3 B×h2 28. f4** "Effectually looking up the enemy's bishop"—Staunton. **28. … Bg3† 29. Ke2 Kg7 30. Kf3 Bh4 31. Kg4 Bf2 32. Kh5 a5 33. f5 b5 34. f6† Kg8 35. g6 h×g6† 36. K×g6** White wins—*Chess Player's Chronicle* (Staunton), March 1849, pp. 71–73.

## (4) Bird–G.W. Medley    1–0

Divan tournament (round 1, game 2)

London 1849

*B45*

**1. e4 c5 2. d4 c×d4 3. Nf3 Nc6 4. N×d4 e6 5. Nc3 Nf6 6. N×c6 b×c6 7. Bd3 d5 8. 0–0 Bc5 9. Kh1 e5 10. f4** Medley's last move was a bit premature, as Bird could have demonstrated by 10. e×d5! Black is then forced to abandon a pawn as 10. … c×d5 11. Qe2 e4? (11. … 0–0 is necessary) loses after 12. Bb5† Bd7 13. N×d5! Not any better is 10. … N×d5 11. Qe2 and Black must castle to save his skin for some time. **10. … Ng4 11. Qe1 d4 12. Ne2 Bd6** Too slow. He should either castle or try the extravagant 12. … e×f4 13. B×f4 g5 14. Bd2 Qc7. **13. h3** 13. Qg3!, forcing the knight back by activating the queen, pursues the same idea as in the game but in an improved form, e.g., 13. … h5 (or 13. … e×f4 14. B×f4 B×f4 15. R×f4 h5 16. e5!) 14. h3 h4 15. Qf3 Nf6 16. N×d4! **13. … Nf6** 13. … Ne3 prevents the subsequent opening of the position. **14. N×d4** The refined 14. Qg3! Nh5 (forced) 15. Qf3 Nf6 16. N×d4 returns to the aforementioned line. **14. … e×d4 15. e5 0–0 16. Qh4** 16. e×f6 ought to be played as White's initiative could have been neutralized at once by the cool 16. … Ne4! **16. … h6? 17. e×f6!** "White plays very well here"—Staunton. **17. … Q×f6 18. Q×f6 g×f6 19. f5 Kh7 20. Bf4 B×f4 21. R×f4 c5 22. Re1 Bb7 23. Re7 Bd5 24. Be4!** "A good move. From this point the game is much in White's favor"—Staunton. **24. … B×e4 25. Rf×e4 Rab8 26. b3 a5 27. Rc7 Rbc8 28. Ree7 Kg8 29. Ra7?!** "Both players appear to have overlooked a decisive advantage now at White's command. Suppose for example he had played thus: 29. R×f7 R×f7 (29. … R×c7 30. R×c7 winning easily two pawns) 30. R×c8†"—Staunton. **29. … Rce8?!** Black gets excellent drawing chances after 29. … c4! Medley's move is not without point either, but Bird can deal adequately with it. **30. R×e8 R×e8 31. R×a5 Re1† 32. Kh2 Rc1 33. R×c5 d3 34. Rd5!** R×c2 "If he had played 34. … d×c2, White would have played 35. Rc5 and have won easily with his pawns" —Staunton. **35. R×d3 R×a2 36. Kg3** Black has but slim chances to save this endgame, despite his active rook. **36. … h5** If 36. … Kf8 37. Rd6! Ke7 38. Rb6! Black faces insuperable difficulties. Either he must bring his king to the queenside, thereby abandoning the pawns on the kingside, or allow White's b-pawn advance. **37. b4 Rb2 38. Rd4 Kg7 39. Kf3 Kh6 40. h4 Kg7 41. g3 Kf8 42. g4** 42. Ke4 is the most straightforward plan to the win as nothing can stop the b-pawn. **42. … Rb3† 43. Kf4 Rh3 44. b5 Ke7** 44. … R×h4 45. Kg3 Rh1, a suggestion made by Staunton, fails after the immediate 46. Rb4!, which supersedes Staunton's 46. g×h5 R×h5, an exchange that simplifies Black's task. **45. b6 Rb3 46. g×h5 R×b6** Black finally conquered the b-pawn, but the apparently very drawish nature of the position is deceitful. **47. h6 Rb8 48. Kg4 Kf8 49. Rd6 Ke7 50. Ra6 Rh8 51. Ra7† Kd6 52. R×f7?!** White's strongest trump is realized after 52. Kh5! Rh7 53. Ra8, when the intended 54. Rg8 and 55. Rg7 will break the final resistance. **52. ... R×h6 53. Rg7 Rh8 54. h5 Ke5** (*see diagram*)

*After 54. ... Ke5*

**55. Rg6?!** After missing some relatively easy chances the win has become problematic but not impossible. It requires a very deep understanding of this endgame to make the most of it and it is therefore not surprising that both players miss the mark on a few occasions from here on. Instead of the text move, 55. Re7†! Kd4 56. Rf7 Ke5 57. Rg7 reaches the same position with Black to move. The advantage of this is very clear after 57. ... Kd4, which now loses offhand: 58. Rg6 Ke5 59. h6. Instead 57. ... Rh6 is much more tenacious. Now 58. Rg6? allows Black to use his remaining pawn to achieve a draw: 58. ... Rh7 59. h6 Rh8! (a useful waiting move as White has to abandon his f-pawn) 60. Kh5 K×f5 61. Rg7 Kf4 62. Kg6 f5 63. h7 Ke4 64. Rg8 R×h7 65. K×h7 f4. Black is a rook behind but the pawn is strong enough to force White to consent with a draw. The correct rejoinder of 57. ... Rh6 is 58. Rg8! After the forced 58. ... Rh7 59. Rg6 Rh8 60. h6 Rh7, the difference with the previous line is minuscule but decisive. Due to the opponent's rook standing at h7 instead of h8, White gains a decisive tempo: 61. Kh5 K×f5 62. Rg7 Rh8 63. h7 Ke4 64. Rf7 f5 65. Kg5! and Black is in zugzwang. **55. ... Rh7?!** 55. ... Rd8! forces White to enter the drawing line given above, e.g., 56. h6 Rh8 57. Kh5 K×f5 58. Rg7 Kf4 etc. **56. h6?!** 56. Rg8! returns to the aforementioned winning plan. **56. ... Rh8 57. Kh5 K×f5 58. Rg7 Ra8?** 58. ... Kf4! is a draw, as we've seen before. **59. Rg1 Ke6 60. h7 Kf7 61. Kh6 Rh8 62. Rg7† Kf8 63. Ra7** and White wins—*Chess Player's Chronicle* (Staunton) March 1849, pp. 73–75.

## (5) G.W. Medley–Bird    1–0

Divan tournament (round 1, game 3)
London 1849
*C01*

**1. e4 e6 2. d4 d5 3. e×d5 e×d5 4. Nf3 Nf6 5. Bd3 Bd6 6. 0–0 0–0 7. h3 h6 8. Nc3 a6 9. Be3 Be6 10. Qd2 Nc6 11. Nh2** "The only objection apparently to 11. B×h6 is that Black, after 11. ... g×h6 12. Q×h6, might play 12. ... Nb4. We believe therefore it was White's best game to prevent that move, by playing 11. a3, threatening 12. B×h6 with great advantage"—Staunton. 12. B×h6 looks rather dangerous, but after 12. ... g×h6 13. Q×h6 Re8 the onus is on White to prove that he has enough for the piece.

**11. ... B×h2†** Staunton's suggestion of exchanging the bishop with 11. ... Nb4 looks best. If White doesn't comply by playing 12. Be2, 12. ... Bf5 gives Black a slight initiative. **12. K×h2 Ne7 13. f4** Impulsive and weakening. 13. Rae1 keeps a very slight edge. **13. ... Bf5 14. Rf2 c5! 15. g4?! B×d3 16. Q×d3 c4 17. Qe2 Qd6** 17. ... Re8 is slightly more subtle. The queen might head for b6 instead. **18. Rg1 Rae8 19. Qf3 Ng6** At this point it is obvious that White cannot advance on the kingside, while Black has good perspectives on the other side of the board. 19. ... b5 is therefore correct. **20. Qg3 Ne4** Each simplification is welcomed by White. Despite the slight inaccuracies made on move 17 and 19, 20. ... b5 is still promising for Black. **21. N×e4 R×e4 22. f5 Q×g3† 23. R×g3 Nh4** (*see diagram*) All of Black's advantage is gone by now. The text move is considerably more exposing the knight to danger than 23. ... Nh8.

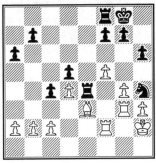

*After 23. ... Nh4*

**24. f6** It was worthwhile to play for the capture of the knight, as Black is forced to weaken his position to save the piece: 24. Bc1 R×d4 25. Rg1 Re8 26. Rgf1 (anticipating the opening of the f-file) 26. ... Re7 27. Kg3 g5 28. f×g6 *e.p.* N×g6 29. B×h6. White enjoys a microscopic edge in this endgame. **24. ... Ng6** 24. ... g5! secures the position of the knight and shuts out the opposite bishop. Black's control over the open file guarantees him the upper hand again. **25. f×g7 K×g7 26. c3 Rfe8 27. Bd2 f6** Too slow, immediately 27. ... Re2 is indicated. **28. Rgf3 R8e6** 28. ... Re2 29. R×f6 R×d2 30. R×g6† K×g6 31. R×d2 Re3 costs a pawn but makes the draw inevitable. **29. Kg3** 29. Rf5 augments the pressure and forces Black to play secure: 29. ... Re2 (not 29. ... Rd6? 30. Rh5) 30. Kg3 R×f2 31. K×f2 Ne7 32. Rh5 f5 33. g5 and White is just a tad better. **29. ... Re2?!** 29. ... Ne7 must be played. Both players missed 30. R×f6!. **30. Rf5?! R×f2 31. K×f2 Rb6 32. Bc1 Ne7 33. Rh5 f5 34. g×f5** Just as in the line starting with 29. Rf5, 34. g5 offers slightly better chances. **34. ... Rf6 35. Bf4 N×f5** "Black cleverly regains a pawn by this manoeuvre, and with proper care and skill ought not from this point to lose the game"—Staunton. **36. Be5 Kg6 37. B×f6 K×h5 38. Kf3 Kg6 39. Bd8 Kf7 40. Kf4 Ke6 41. Bc7 b5 42. Kg4 Kf6 43. Kh5 Kf7 44. Be5 a5 45. a3 a4 46. h4 Ke6?** "He would have given White much more trouble if at this, or rather perhaps on the previous move, he had played 46. ... Ne3 to attack the queenside pawns in the rear"—Staunton. A very expensive oversight of Bird. Both 46. ... Ne3 47. Bf4 Nd1 48. Bc1 Nf2 49. B×h6 Nd3 and 46. ... Kg8 lead to a draw. **47. Bf4 Kf7 48. B×h6 Kg8 49. Bf4 Kg7 50. Kg5 Ne7 51. h5 Ng8 52. Kf5 Kf7 53. Bg5** White wins—*Chess Player's Chronicle* (Staunton), March 1849, pp. 76–77.

# MATCH WITH G.W. MEDLEY 1849

In May or June 1849 Bird and George Webb Medley agreed to play a match. Their duel in the late Divan tournament had been so close that it was certainly justified to find out which player topped the other in a more extended contest. Times were busy for Medley: he had another encounter going on against George Perigal. Information about the match between Bird and Medley is scarce. It is only thanks to a reply of Staunton to a correspondent's request that the final outcome is known: "The match between Messrs. G.W. Medley and Bird, two of the promising players of the day, has just terminated in favor of the former, who won six games to his opponent's three, the two remaining games being drawn" (*Illustrated London News*, 23 June 1849). It is impossible to reconstruct the precise course of the match. Seven games were published in the *Chess Player's Chronicle*, but they come without any further information. Two authors venture upon publishing a partly drawn table, but on which basis is completely unclear.[35]

## (6) G.W. Medley–Bird    1–0
Match
London 1849
*D31*

George W. Medley (courtesy Nigel Webb).

35.  See G. Di Felice, *Chess Results 1747–1900: A Comprehensive Record with 465 Tournament Crosstables and 590 Match Scores*. Jefferson: McFarland, 2004, p. 9, and D. Levy & K. O'Connell, *Oxford Encyclopedia of Chess; volume 1: 1485–1866*. Oxford: Oxford University Press, 1981, p. 132.

**1. d4 d5 2. c4 e6 3. Nc3 Nf6 4. e3 c6 5. a3 Bd6 6. b3 0–0 7. Bb2 b6 8. Nf3 Ba6 9. Bd3 c5 10. d×c5 b×c5 11. c×d5 B×d3 12. Q×d3 e×d5 13. N×d5 N×d5 14. Q×d5 Na6 15. Rd1 Be7 16. Qe5 Q×d1† 17. K×d1 Bf6 18. Qe4 B×b2 19. Qb7 c4 20. Q×a6 c×b3 21. Qa4 Rfc8 22. Ke2 Rc2† 23. Nd2 Bc3 24. Rd1 Rb8 25. Q×a7 Rd8 26. Qc7 Bf6 27. Qb6 b2 28. Qb3 Rdc8 29. a4 R8c3 30. Qb8† Rc8 31. Qb4 Bc3 32. Qb7 Rd8 33. Kf3 Rc1 34. Ne4 Rc×d1 35. N×c3 R1d2 36. Nb1 Rc2 37. Qb3 Rdc8 38. a5 g6 39. a6 R2c7 40. Q×b2 Ra8 41. Qf6 Rca7 42. Nc3 R×a6 43. Qg5 Ra5 44. Qe7 R8a7 45. Qd8† Kg7 46. Nd5 R7a6 47. g4 Rc5 48. g5 Re6 49. h4 Rcc6 50. Nf6 R×f6† 51. g×f6† R×f6† 52. Kg3** and after a few moves Black resigns—*Chess Player's Chronicle*, June 1849, pp. 177–179.

## (7) G.W. Medley–Bird    1–0
Match
London 1849
*D40*

**1. d4 d5 2. c4 e6 3. Nc3 Nf6 4. e3 c5 5. Nf3 b6 6. a3 Bb7 7. b3 Bd6 8. Bb2 c×d4 9. e×d4 0–0 10. c×d5 e×d5 11. Bd3 Nc6 12. 0–0 Bc8 13. h3 Be6 14. Rc1 Ne7 15. Ne2 Ng6 16. Ng3 Qd7** Triggering White to grab the initiative for free. Instead, 16. ... B×g3 17. f×g3 Ne4 is advantageous for Black. **17. Ne5 Qd8 18. f4 Ne7 19. f5 Bd7** "Through his injudicious move of 16. ... Qd7, his subsequent play has been nothing but a succession of retreating moves"—Staunton. **20. Nh5 N×h5 21. Q×h5 f6 22. Rf4** *(see diagram)* "Enterprising, but we doubt its soundness against the best defense"—Staunton. He must take at d7, thereby be content with a minimal edge.

*After 22. Rf4*

**22. ... f×e5** Bird shows himself very eager to accept the offered piece, but hereby he underestimates his opponent's attacking potential. After the calm 22. ... Be8! 23. Qe2 Rc8, everything is kept under control. In case of 24. Rcf1 a5 25. Kh1 Bb8 26. R4f2 Qd6 a war of trenches is going on. It is still dangerous for Black to take the knight, while White would worsen the coordination between his pieces by bringing the knight to safety. **23. f6 e4?!** 23. ... g6 must be played. Attack and defense are in balance after 24. Qh6 Rf7. **24. f×e7 Q×e7 25. Q×d5† Be6 26. R×f8† R×f8 27. Q×e4 g6?** 27. ... Bf5 is preferable, as 28. Re1 would win at once now. **28. d5? Bf5 29. Q×e7 B×e7 30. B×f5?!** Simplifying the position with a pawn up is no more than logical, but the endgame is much trickier than it looks. Preserving the bishop is preferable. **30. ... R×f5 31. Rc8†** White retains some winning chances after 31. Rd1. The text move is certainly not without danger as his king becomes exposed. **31. ... Kf7 32. Rh8 Bc5† 33. Kh2 Bd6†** 33. ... R×d5 is a little more delicate to deal with. After 34. R×h7† Ke6, White may not play 35. R×a7? as 35. ... Bd6† wins a piece. 35. Bc1 is playable, but the ending is obviously more agreeable for Black, thanks to his superior rook. **34. Kg1 R×d5** After 34. ... Bc5† Black has a choice between drawing at once or returning to the previous line. **35. R×h7† Ke6 36. Bh8** 36. Kf1 is safer. **36. ... Bg3** Hoping to catch the king in his box, but this is based on a miscalculation. Instead, 36. ... Rd3! demands precise play from his opponent, for if 37. R×a7? Bg3 38. Kf1 Re3 demonstrates the point of Black's 36th move. Better is 37. Kf1 Be7 38. Rh6 Kf7 39. Rh7† Ke8 40. Rh6 R×b3 41. R×g6 R×a3 when a draw is most likely, although Black's pawns are slightly more dangerous due to the absence of White's king on that side of the board. **37. Kf1 Rd2** 37. ... Rf5† 38. Ke2 Rf2† is very drawish. **38. Rg7 Rf2†?** The final mistake. After 38. ... Rd3! 39. R×g6† Kf5 40. Rf6† Ke4 41. Re6† Kf4 42. Rc6 R×b3 43. Rc4† Kf5 44. Rc3 Rb1† a draw remains the most reasonable result. The text move leaves Bird's bishop posted on a very clumsy square. **39. Kg1 Kf6 40. R×a7† Kg5 41. Ra4 Rf4 42. R×f4 B×f4 43. Bd4 b5 44. a4 b×a4 45. b×a4 Kf5 46. a5 Ke4 47. a6** and Black resigns—*Chess Player's Chronicle* (Staunton), July 1849, p. 211–212.

## (8) G.W. Medley–Bird    1–0
Match
London 1849
*A34*

1. c4 e6 2. e3 c5 3. Nc3 Nc6 4. Nf3 Nf6 5. b3 Be7 6. Bb2 0-0 7. Be2 Ne8 8. 0-0 f5 9. d4 f4 10. d5 Nb8 11. e4 d6 12. d×e6 B×e6 13. Nd5 B×d5 14. e×d5 Nd7 15. Bd3 Bf6 16. Rb1 B×b2 17. R×b2 Nef6 18. Ng5 Qa5 19. Ne6 Rf7 20. N×f4 Ne5 21. Qd2 Qc7 22. Ne6 Qe7 23. f4 N×d3 24. Q×d3 Ng4 25. Ng5 Qe3† 26. Q×e3 N×e3 27. N×f7 N×f1 28. N×d6 Ne3 29. N×b7 Rb8 30. Re2 N×d5 31. c×d5 R×b7 32. d6 Rd7 33. Re8† Kf7 34. Re7† R×e7 35. d×e7 K×e7 36. Kf2 Kd6 37. Ke3 Kd5 38. Kd3 h5 39. g3 a6 40. a3 g6 41. h3 a5 42. a4 and Black resigns—*Chess Player's Chronicle*, July 1849, p. 212–213.

## (9) Bird–G.W. Medley    1–0
Match
London 1849
*C00*

1. e4 e6 2. f4 d5 3. e5 c5 4. Nf3 Nc6 5. Bb5 Qb6 6. B×c6† b×c6 7. 0-0 Nh6 8. Kh1 Be7 9. Nc3 0-0 10. d3 a5 11. b3 f6 12. Ba3 Nf5 13. Qd2 Ba6 14. e×f6 R×f6 15. Ne5 Qc7 16. Rae1 Rd8 17. Qf2 Nd4 18. Na4 Bb5 19. B×c5 B×a4 20. B×d4 Bb5 21. Bb6 and Black resigns—*Chess Player's Chronicle*, July 1849, p. 214.

## (10) Bird–G.W. Medley    0–1
Match
London 1849
*C00*

1. e4 e6 2. f4 d5 3. e5 c5 4. Nf3 Nc6 5. Bb5 Bd7 6. 0-0 N×e5 7. f×e5 B×b5 8. d3 g6 9. Nc3 Bc6 10. Ng5 Nh6 11. Qf3 Qe7 12. Qh3 Bg7 13. Nf3 Nf5 14. g4 Nd4 15. Ng5 f6 16. e×f6 B×f6

**17. Nf3 N×f3† 18. R×f3 0-0 19. Bh6 Bd4† 20. Be3 R×f3 21. Q×f3 B×e3† 22. Q×e3 d4 23. Qe5 d×c3 24. b×c3 Rf8 25. Re1 Qf6 26. Q×e6† Q×e6 27. R×e6 Rf4 28. h3 Rf3 29. Kh2 Rf2†** and Black wins—*Chess Player's Chronicle*, July 1849, p. 215.

## (11) Bird–G.W. Medley    1–0
Match
London 1849
*C00*

**1. e4 e6 2. f4** The French defense was very popular around 1850. White's regular antidote to it was the Exchange Variation, but Bird often preferred this move to deal with it. **2. ... d5 3. e5 c5 4. Nf3 Nc6 5. Bb5 Bd7 6. B×c6 B×c6 7. 0-0 Nh6 8. d3 Be7 9. Nc3 0-0 10. Ne2 f6 11. Ng3 Nf7 12. d4 c×d4 13. N×d4 f×e5?!** Medley misjudges the ensuing tactical opportunities. Both 13. ... Bc5 or 13. ... Qb6 avoid any complications while guaranteeing at least equal play. **14. N×e6 Qb6† 15. Kh1 Bb5 16. Qg4!** *(see diagram)*

*After 16. Qg4*

The most dangerous move. It is also possible to head for 16. N×f8 B×f1 17. Nd7 Qe6 18. N×e5 N×e5 19. f×e5 Ba6 20. Bf4 Rf8 21. Qd4 when White is a pawn up. Black's bishop pair and control over the f-file provide him some compensation nevertheless. **16. ... g6?** Medley immediately stumbles over the various possibilities. Also bad is 16. ... Bf6? 17. Nh5!, but he could hope for a successful defense with 16. ... Ng5! After the relatively forced 17. N×f8 B×f1 18. Nf5 B×f8 19. Q×g5 Rc8 (not good is 19. ... e×f4? 20. B×f4 Qf2 21. Ne3) 20. Be3 d4 21. Bf2 Bb5 22. f×e5 R×c2 23. B×d4 h6 24. Qf4 Qg6 25. Nh4, the situation is quite similar as in the variation given after White's last move. **17. f5! Bd7 18. N×f8 R×f8 19. Qf3 e4 20. Qb3 Bb5 21. Be3 Qc6 22. Rf2 Bc4 23. Qc3 Bf6 24. Bd4 B×d4 25. Q×d4 Nh6 26. f×g6 h×g6 27. R×f8† K×f8 28. b3 Ba6 29. c4 d×c4 30. Rf1† Kg8 31. Qd8† Kg7 32. Qe7† Kh8 33. Rf8†** and White wins—*Chess Player's Chronicle*, July 1849, p. 216–217.

## (12) Bird–G.W. Medley    0–1
Match
London 1849
*C01*

1. e4 e6 2. d4 d5 3. e×d5 e×d5 4. Nf3 Nf6 5. Bd3 Bd6 6. 0-0 0-0 7. Be3 c6 8. Bg5 h6 9. Bh4 Bg4 10. h3 Bh5 11. Nbd2 Nbd7 12. c3 Qc7 13. B×f6 N×f6 14. Qc2 B×f3 15. N×f3 Nh5 16. Rae1 Rae8 17. g3 B×g3 18. R×e8 R×e8 19. f×g3 Q×g3† 20. Kh1 Q×h3† 21. Qh2 Ng3† 22. Kg1 Q×h2† 23. K×h2 N×f1† 24. B×f1 and Black ultimately wins by the strength of his three passed pawns—*Chess Player's Chronicle*, September 1850, p. 264.

# Young Men Explore London

The years prior to the first international chess tournament of London 1851 were very quiet as regards chess among the elite. The allegedly strongest player in the world, Howard Staunton, had played his last serious match in 1846. Since then he engaged in matches only against much weaker players in which he gave odds. Many other top players were in the same situation.

Things were quite different on a lower level. Several young and ambitious players were eager to test their powers in reciprocal combat which created a vibrant and exciting atmosphere. Unlike the professionals, they incessantly encountered each other in countless offhand games and matches. While the talent of several of these youngsters was acknowledged, Bird was the only one to emerge as a strong player in the long run.[36]

One of Bird's most fascinating and obscure early opponents was C.F. Smith. Until very recently his name was completely forgotten, even though he was one of England's most promising youngsters during the years 1848 to 1854. Some revealing research has been done on him by Tim Harding and John Townsend.[37] The latter discovered his full name, Charles French Smith.

Smith was born around 1828. He learned chess at a young age and already in 1847 he was looking for opponents in correspondence chess, as appears from requests that were published in the chess column of the *Illustrated London News*. His first game with Bird was published in 1848 and during the two following years both fanatic players tried to outclass each other by sending in their game scores to the editors of the principal chess columns. As a result many of their games survived.

These games reveal that Bird and Smith explored almost every chess resort and coffee house of the British capital, such as the Divan, Pursell's, Kilpack's Divan (which attracted chess players especially on Sundays, when Simpson's was forbidden ground for them) and also quite often the City Road Chess Club, of which Smith was the president.[38]

Bird and Smith played only casual games with each other, but they tried to spice up their combats by giving it the form of a match. Just on one single occasion the details of such a contest got published.

> The annexed is one of fourteen games recently played, in which Mr. Smith opens with the Evans Gambit and wagers two to one in the event of its being accepted. These parties have produced the following result: Mr. Bird won 10, Mr. Smith won 3, drawn 1 [*Illustrated London News*, 31 August 1850].

36. Bird recalled his rivals from former days in his memoirs: "About forty years ago there were eight young and rising players nearly approaching first class, they were S.S. Boden, the Rev. W. Audrey, Captain Cunningham, G.W. Medley, J. Medley, C.F. Smith, A. Simons and H.E. Bird. Three of these, remarkable for ingenuity and sudden surprises had familiar appellations. One was termed 'The Snake,' another that 'Old Serpent,' I was 'The enemy of the human race.'" Bird, *Chess History and Reminiscences*, p. 117.
37. See www.chesscafe.com, The Kibitzer 177, February 2011, and Townsend, *Historical Notes on Some Chess Players*, pp. 81–90.
38. According to Harding in his Kibitzer article, the City Road Chess Club "seems to have been a club for lower middle-class men, probably artisans or clerical workers in the City of London nearby." It must have been a rather shallow club, as even Staunton was not aware of its exact location (*Illustrated London News*, 2 February 1850). After a few years of nonexistence, a new club with the same name was formed in 1858 (*The Sunday Times*, 19 December 1858).

The games between Bird and Smith have the characteristic romantic character of that age in chess history. The majority of games were opened with 1. e4 e5 and often involved a gambit. From the published games it is clear that both players scored their share. The match score given above suggests that Bird quickly grew into a higher level than his opponent, but this does not readily appear from their preserved games.

**(13) C.F. Smith–Bird   1–0**
Offhand game
London 1848
B21

"Dashing little affair just played between Mr. C.F. Smith and Mr. H. Bird, two young, but highly promising additions to our chess circle"—Staunton.

**1. e4 c5 2. d4 c×d4 3. Nf3 e5 4. c3** "It is needless to point out why he doesn't take the e-pawn"—Staunton. **4. ... d×c3 5. N×c3 Nc6 6. Bc4 d6 7. 0–0 Be6** Unnecessarily weakening his pawn structure. 7. ... Be7 is safe for if 8. Qb3 Na5. **8. B×e6 f×e6 9. Ng5 Qd7 10. Qh5† g6 11. Qh3 Nd4?** *(see diagram)* 11. ... Nd8 is necessary to keep both e6 and f7 defended.

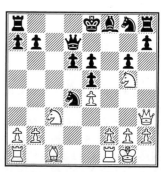

*After 11. ... Nd4*

**12. f4! Be7?!** If the knight were on d8, Black could play 12. ... Bg7, which is impossible now because of 13. f×e5 d×e5 14. Rf7. Relatively best is 12. ... e×f4 13. R×f4 Ne7 14. Rf2 although Black's position remains shaky. Smith's further handling of the game is a wonderful display of his talent. **13. f×e5! B×g5 14. B×g5 d×e5 15. Nd5! h6** "15. ... e×d5 would evidently have cost the queen by 16. Rf8†"—Staunton. **16. Qa3!** "The proper move"—Staunton. **16. ... Ne2† 17. Kh1 Ng3† 18. h×g3 h×g5† 19. Kg1 0–0–0** "Deplorable as this appears, it is about the best thing left for him"—Staunton. **20. Nb6†! a×b6 21. Qa8† Kc7 22. Rac1† Kd6 23. Qa3** mate—*Chess Player's Chronicle* (Staunton), September 1848, p. 272.

**(14) Bird–C.F. Smith   1–0**
Offhand game
Whittington 1849
C37

"Game played at the Whittington Club between Messrs. Bird and Smith. If these two gentlemen frequently favor the Whittingtons with a visit, good players will soon spring up in abundance in their society"—Walker.

**1. e4 e5 2. f4 e×f4 3. Nf3 g5 4. Bc4 g4** The Muzio Gambit, especially suited when playing for the audience. **5. 0–0 g×f3 6. Q×f3 Qf6 7. e5 Q×e5 8. d3 Bh6 9. Nc3 Ne7 10. Bd2 0–0** Modern theory advises 10. ... Nbc6! **11. Rae1 Qc5†** Smith neglects the defense of the f-pawn, which is important as, if it falls one day, White's attack becomes very dangerous. Both 11. ... Qd4† or 11. ... Qf6 are better. **12. Kh1 d5 13. B×d5 c6?** Pointless. He must choose between 13. ... Qd6 (defending the f-pawn) or 13. ... Nd7 (continuing his development). **14. Bb3** 14. Ne4! is already over and out for Black. **14. ... Bf5 15. Qh5 Qd6 16. R×e7** Easy enough. **16. ... Q×e7 17. Q×h6 Nd7 18. R×f4 Rae8 19. Ne4?** Bird is eager to deliver the final punch, but he forgets about the weakness of his back rank. After 19. h3! nothing could stop White from reinforcing the attack, e.g., 19. ... Bg6 20. Ne4 B×e4 (or 20. ... Kh8 21. Nf6 Ne5 22. Bc3 c5 23. Nd7) 21. R×e4 **19. ... B×e4 20. d×e4** Relatively better is 20. R×e4 Qf6 21. Rg4† Kh8 22. Q×f6† N×f6 23. Rb4 (the point of 19. h3! is demonstrated here after 24. Bc3?! Re1†!) 23. ... Nd5 (best). White will gain a second pawn, when he has enough for the exchange but not much more. **20. ... Kh8 21. Rh4 f6 22. Be6 a6?** Smith overlooks the point of Bird's last move. 22. ... Rd8! 23. Qh5 Nc5 keeps the game dynamically balanced. **23. Bf5 Rf7 24. Bg6 Ref8 25. B×f7 Q×f7 26. Bc3 Ne5 27. Rf4 Qg6 28. Q×g6** 28. Q×f8† mates in four moves. **28. ... h×g6 29. R×f6** 29. B×e5 must cause immediate resignation. **29. ... R×f6 30. B×e5 Kg7 31. g3 Kf7 32. B×f6 K×f6 33. Kg2 Ke5 34. Kf3** White wins— *Bell's Life* (Walker), 27 May 1849.

### (15) Bird–C.F. Smith   0–1

Offhand game
London (City Road Chess Club) 1849
*C00*

**1. e4 e6 2. f4 d5 3. e5 c5 4. Nf3 Nc6 5. Bb5 Qb6 6. B×c6† b×c6 7. 0–0 Ba6 8. d3 Nh6** For a few moves Smith had the opportunity to gain the upper hand by executing the thematic push c5–c4. In this case after 8. ... c4†, both 9. d4 c3 and 9. Kh1 Nh6 are favorable for Black. **9. Kh1 Be7 10. Nc3 0–0 11. b3 f6?!** Smith selects an inferior plan that brings him in trouble on the queenside. **12. Na4 Qc7 13. Qe2** 13. Ba3! c4 14. B×e7 Q×e7 15. d×c4 d×c4 16. Qe2 is more than OK for White. Not better is 13. ... Nf5 when 14. Qd2 c4 is met by the exchange of bishops and 16. g4!, pressurizing Black all over the board. **13. ... Rae8** 13. ... Bb5 improves his position by chasing the knight away. The move played by Black leaves White a free hand. **14. Ba3! c4 15. B×e7 c×d3 16. c×d3 Q×e7 17. e×f6** 17. Rac1! attacks the c-pawn. Now 17. ... f×e5 18. N×e5 has to be avoided. Worth trying is 17. ... Qb4, but 18. Nc5! (not 18. R×c6?! Bb5) 18. ... Bc8 19. d4 is rather pathetic for Black. **17. ... Q×f6** 17. ... R×f6 is a must. **18. Ne5 Nf5 19. Qf2** 19. Nc5 and 19. g4 were good alternatives. Bird had to be careful not to get lured into 19. Nd7?! Qh4. **19. ... Re7 20. N×c6?!** He could secure a winning edge after 20. g4! Nd6 21. Qc5. In the game Black obtains dangerous counterplay along the c-file. **20. ... Rc7 21. Ne5 Rfc8 22. b4** Bird pulls himself together just in time. The knight is ready to re-enter the game. **22. ... Rc2** *(see diagram)*

**23. Q×a7?!** Bird shows no fear by taking another pawn, but much more solid was 23. Qe1, keeping h4 under control. **23. ... Qh4 24. Kg1?** 24. Q×a6 forces Black to claim a draw with a perpetual check. Bird is wrong in wanting more. **24. ... Bb5?** 24. ... d4! cuts off the queen from the defense of f2 and initiates the threat 25. ...

*After 22. ... Rc2*

Ne3. If 25. Qf7† Kh8 26. Q×e6 R×g2†!, a similar final as in the game arises. **25. Qf7†?!** Bird misses his chance to divert the rook from g2 with 25. Nc3! Now 25. ... R2xc3 is obligated as 25. ... R8xc3? 26. Qf7† leads to mate and 25. ... d4 26. Qf7† loses quickly as well. After 25. ... R2xc3 26. Qf7† Kh8 27. Q×e6 Nh6 28. a4 White's pawns tend to be stronger than the piece. **25. ... Kh8 26. Q×e6?** Black checkmates in 4 moves. Forced is 26. Nc5, when after 26. ... Ne3 White seems lost, but the stunning 27. Qg6! miraculously gives him a second life. After the logical 27. ... R×g2† 28. Q×g2 N×g2 29. K×g2 Black gets under pressure and has to find 29. ... g5! in order to equalize by opening up the shelter of his opponent's king, e.g., 30. Nf7† Kg8 31. N×g5 h6 32. Ng×e6 Bd7 33. f5 B×e6 34. f×e6 Q×b4. Instead of winning his opponent's queen, 27. ... Be8! is more precise. After 28. Nf3 B×g6 29. N×h4 N×f1 30. K×f1 Bf7 31. Nf3, White has good drawing chances—*Bell's Life*, 8 July 1849.

### (16) Bird–C.F. Smith   1–0

Offhand game
London 1849
*C62*

**1. e4 e5 2. Nf3 Nc6 3. Bb5 d6 4. 0–0 Bg4 5. h3 B×f3 6. Q×f3 a6 7. B×c6† b×c6 8. d4 Qf6?** At this point Black's position was already a bit undermined by the exchange of his bishop. With this offer to exchange queens to reach forthwith an endgame, Smith completely abandons the queenside, which could have been highlighted had Bird retorted with 9. Qb3! **9. Qc3 Ne7 10. Be3 e×d4 11. B×d4 Qg6 12. Nd2 c5 13. Be3 Nc6 14. f4?!** Bird comes up with a plan to break through the center, which certainly looks attractive but doesn't need to be feared that much. The idea mentioned in the previous move, making use of the weakened squares on the queenside by 14. Qb3! is still the most efficient. In case of 14. ... Rb8 15. Qa4 Kd7 16. Rfd1 Rb4 17. Q×a6, the loss of a pawn and the position of his king make Black's struggle a very uphill one. Noteworthy is that 17. ... R×b2?! 18. Nb3! has to be avoided. **14. ... Be7 15. e5 0–0** 15. ... d×e5 might be tried. **16. f5 Qh5 17. f6 g×f6 18. e×f6 Bd8 19. Rf3 Qe5?!** Weak. Not only is it obvious that the king would be safer on h8, while the rook can also be very useful at g8, but this move also abandons the control over one most important square. **20. Qc4?** Staunton rightly judges that 20. Bh6, even though it allows the exchange of queens, only reinforces White's assault. After 20. ... Q×c3 21. b×c3! Re8 22. Rg3† Kh8 23. Bg7† Kg8 24. Nc4, Black is helpless against White's two last pieces joining the attack. Now White's most important pawn gets conquered, making the situation much safer for Black's king, although a safe harbor is not reached yet. **20. ... B×f6 21. Bh6?!** Bird tries to break his opponent's position by force. Instead the calm 21. c3 gives him some compensation for the pawn. **21. ... Qd4†?** Smith's eagerness to exchange queens is understandable, but he overlooks that after 22. Kh1 Q×c4 23. N×c4 two of his pieces are hanging. 21. ... Bg7! completely wards off Bird's attack. **22. Kh1 Rfe8 23. Rg3†?!** White has some choice between a few attractive options, yet not all of them are equally convincing. 23. Raf1 augments the pressure and makes the position dreary for Black. **23. ... Kh8 24. Q×f7 Rg8?** 24. ... Re7! is a very economical way of defending the king. If 25. Qh5 then 25. ... Qh4 kills any attack. **25. R×g8†** Bird misses the prosaic 25. Ne4!, when Black is without resource, e.g., after 25. ... R×g3 26. N×f6 or 25. ... Be7 26. Ng5, and after the exchanges on g5 White's bishop gains decisively in strength. **25. ... R×g8** *(see diagram)*

After 25. ... R×g8

**26. Rf1?** Right now this move is less useful, as the rook doesn't really contribute to the attack. Instead, the knight had to be brought to the front. This could happen in two ways, each time with decisive effects: A—26. Nf3 (the simplest) 26. ... Q×b2 27. Rf1 and whatever Black does (e.g. 27. ... Nd8), the surprising 28. Ng5! wins (e.g. 28. ... B×g5 29. Q×g8†). B—26. Ne4 presents the slow approach. Black's bishop is chased off the long diagonal and its place will be taken by its White counterpart after some preparatory moves: 26. ... Be7 27. Re1 Qe5 28. Re2 Nd8 29. Qf3 Bh4 30. Bd2 Ne6 31. Ng5 N×g5 32. Qd3. **26. ... Bg7?** 26. ... Be7! is preferable. The exchange of his most important defender severely weakens the safety of the king. **27. Nf3 Q×b2?** Smith is apparently completely unconscious of the cunning termination planned by Bird. After 27. ... Qf6 28. Q×c7 B×h6 29. Q×c6 Q×b2 30. Q×d6 Q×c2 31. Rg1 Bg7 32. Q×a6 it is unlikely that White can convert his extra pawn. **28. Ng5! Qe5 29. Qf3 Nd8 30. Qd3** and White wins. A typical game for Bird. Highly dramatic, riddled with mistakes, but also filled with brilliant points and ideas—*Chess Player's Chronicle* (Staunton), August 1849, p. 227.

### (17) C.F. Smith–Bird    0–1
Offhand game
London (City Road Chess Club) 1849
*B21*

1. e4 c5 2. d4 c×d4 3. Nf3 e5 4. Bc4 Qc7 5. b3 b5 6. Bd5 Nc6 7. 0-0 Nf6 8. c3 Bc5 9. c×d4 e×d4 10. Qc2 Nb4 11. Qd1 Nb×d5 12. e×d5 0-0 13. N×d4 Qe5 14. Bb2 Q×d5 15. N×b5 B×f2† 16. K×f2 Ne4† 17. Kg1 Q×b5 18. Kh1 Ba6 19. Rf4 Rae8 20. Na3 Qg5 21. Qd4 Bb7 22. Raf1 Re6 23. Nc4 Rg6 24. Ne3 Re8 25. Q×d7 Nd6 26. Rg4 Q×e3 27. R×g6 h×g6 28. Q×d6 Qf2 and Black wins—*Bell's Life*, 21 October 1849.

### (18) Bird–C.F. Smith    1–0
Offhand game
London 1849
*C56*

1. e4 e5 2. Nf3 Nc6 3. d4 e×d4 4. Bc4 Bc5 5. 0-0 d6 6. c3 Nf6 7. c×d4 Bb6 8. Nc3 Bg4 9. Be3 0-0 10. d5 Ne5 11. Be2 B×f3 12. g×f3 "When the adversary has already castled on the kingside, the opening for the rook obtained in this manner, may often be of great advantage to an attacking player"—Staunton. In this case, the weakness of White's pawn structure is more relevant. Besides the text move, 12. ... B×e3 13. f×e3 Re8 would demonstrate that point just as well, as White has difficulties to defend e4 once the f-pawn is pushed. **12. ... Ng6 13. Kh1** 13. f4 (Staunton) is met by 13. ... Qe7 when e4 becomes vulnerable. **13. ... Nh5 14. Rg1 Nhf4** 14. ... f5 is very interesting at this point. **15. Qd2 Qf6 16. Rg4 N×e2 17. Q×e2 B×e3** Smith selects another plan. Moving away the queen and thus liberating the f-pawn was still good. **18. f×e3 Ne5 19. Rg3 Qh6** The queen is not well placed here. **20. Rag1 Ng6?** 20. ... g6 is obligatory. The knight isn't a good defender. **21. f4! f5 22. Qg2** "Threatening the formidable 23. Rh3"—Staunton. **22. ... Qh4 23. Rg5 f×e4 24. N×e4** "24. f5 looks a troublesome move for Black"—Staunton. **24. ... Rae8 25. Rg3 Qe7 26. Ng5 Rf6 27. Qh3?!** 27. f5! is again stronger. After 27. ... R×f5 28. N×h7! decides the game. **27. ... h6?** The last mistake. 27. ... Nf8 defends the kingside for at least some time. **28. Ne6 R×e6 29. d×e6 Qh4 30. Qf5** and White wins—*Chess Player's Chronicle* (Staunton), November 1849, p. 327.

### (19) Bird–C.F. Smith    1–0
Offhand game
London 1849
*C41*

1. e4 e5 2. Nf3 d6 3. d4 e×d4 4. Bc4 Bg4 5. c3 B×f3 6. Q×f3 Qf6 7. Q×f6 N×f6 8. c×d4 Nc6 "He prudently forbore to seize the bait. If 8. ... N×e4, White would have won a piece by 9. Bd5" —Staunton. **9. d5 Nd4** White has nothing after 9. ... Ne5. At d4 the knight becomes a target. **10. Bd3 0-0-0 11. Be3 c5 12. B×d4** It is easier to win the pawn if he develops first (12. Nd2) and exchanges later. **12. ... c×d4 13. Na3 Re8 14. Rc1† Kb8 15. 0-0 g6** "15. ... N×e4 would have been a great blunder, on account of 16. Rfe1"—Staunton. This becomes clear after 16. ... Nf6 17. R×e8† N×e8 18. Bf5 and a piece is won. **16. f3 Bh6 17. Rc4** White picks up the pawn after 17. Rcd1 a6 18. Bb1 Nd7 19. Nc2, but there is compensation for Black thanks to his excellent bishop and knight. **17. ... a6 18. Nc2 Rc8 19. R×c8†** "It is quite clear he could not take the pawn without loss"—Staunton. **19. ... R×c8 20. Kf2** "The contention which the doubled pawn occasioned, now becomes extremely keen and interesting"—Staunton. **20. ... Re8** "A clever counter move. Intending, if 21. N×d4 N×d5"—Staunton. White should not oblige and instead it was better for Black to leave his rook on the open file and post his bishop at g7, where it commands a promising diagonal. **21. Re1 Bd2** The bishop better remained on the kingside. **22. Re2 Ba5 23. b4 Bb6 24. a4 Rc8 25. Rd2** Here or on the following moves White must play 25. a5. Black on his turn should push his pawn to the same square, as he would gain the

square c5 for his knight by doing so. **25. … Rc3 26. Ke2 Nd7 27. f4 Nf6 28. Kf3 h5 29. h3 Nd7** 29. … h4 determines the kingside structure in a favorable way. **30. g4** Too hasty. The position remains equal after 30. a5 Ba7 31. g3. **30. … h×g4† 31. h×g4 f6** 31. … g5! would have thrown White on the defensive. **32. a5 Ba7 33. Kg2?!** 33. Ne1, so that 33. … g5 can be answered with 34. Rh2, keeps the game in balance. **33. … g5! 34. b5?!** Bird sees his position deteriorating rapidly and burns all his bridges in order to confuse his opponent. 34. Kf3 is the lesser evil. **34. … Nc5! 35. b6 N×d3?!** 35. … B×b6 is a considerable improvement, as 36. a×b6 R×d3 37. R×d3 N×d3 38. f×g5 f×g5 39. N×d4 Ne5 offers excellent winning chances. **36. b×a7† K×a7 37. f×g5** "Purposely giving him the piece" —Staunton. **37. … R×c2?** Smith blindly falls into Bird's trap. After 37. … Nf4† 38. Kf1 d3 39. Nd4 f×g5, Black keeps a slight pull. **38. R×c2 Ne1† 39. Kf2 N×c2 40. g6 Ne3 41. Kf3 Nc4 42. g7** and White wins—*Chess Player's Chronicle* (Staunton), November 1849, pp. 328–329.

## (20) C.F. Smith–Bird    1–0
Offhand game
London (Purssell's) 1849
*B44*

**1. e4 e6 2. c4 c5 3. Nf3 Ne7 4. d4 c×d4 5. N×d4 Nbc6 6. Nb5 Ng6 7. Nd6† B×d6 8. Q×d6 Qe7 9. Q×e7† Ng×e7 10. Nc3 Nb4 11. Kd1 0–0 12. Bf4 a6 13. Bd6 Nbc6 14. Na4 b5 15. c×b5 a×b5 16. B×b5 Re8 17. Rc1 Nd4 18. B×e7 N×b5 19. Nb6 Rb8 20. N×c8 Re×c8 21. Kd2 d6 22. R×c8† R×c8 23. Rc1 R×c1 24. K×c1 f6 25. a4** and White wins—*Chess Player's Chronicle*, November 1849, pp. 329–330.

## (21) Bird–C.F. Smith    1–0
Offhand game
London (Simpson's Divan) 1849
*C62*

**1. e4 e5 2. Nf3 Nc6 3. Bb5 d6 4. 0–0 Bg4 5. d4 e×d4 6. Qd3 B×f3 7. Q×f3 Qf6 8. Qb3 Qd8 9. B×c6† b×c6 10. Qc4 c5 11. Na3 Nf6 12. f4 Be7 13. e5 d5 14. Qb5† Nd7 15. Qc6 0–0 16. Q×d5 Nb6 17. Qf3 c4 18. Bd2 c3 19. Bc1 B×a3 20. b×a3 Qd5 21. Qg4 Rae8 22. f5 Q×e5 23. f6 g6 24. Bh6 Nd5 25. B×f8 R×f8 26. Rae1 Ne3 27. Qh4 Qd5 28. R×e3 Kh8 29. Qh6 Rg8 30. Rh3** White wins—*Bell's Life*, 18 November 1849.

## (22) C.F. Smith–Bird    0–1
Offhand game
London (Kilpack's Divan) 1849
*C54*

**1. e4 e5 2. Nf3 Nc6 3. d4 e×d4 4. Bc4 Bc5 5. c3 Nf6 6. e5 d5 7. Bb5 Qe7?** 7. … Ne4 is the recognized theoretical move. **8. 0–0?!** 8. c×d4 Bb6 9. Nc3 wins a most important pawn. **8. … Ne4 9. N×d4?!** 9. c×d4 still gives White an edge. **9. … 0–0 10. N×c6?** After this final mistake Bird's opening experiment quickly pays off. Both 10. B×c6 and 10. f3 are decent possibilities. **10. … b×c6 11. B×c6** Otherwise the pawn at e5 is lost. Now Bird is in his element. **11. … N×f2! 12. Q×d5 Be6 13. Qf3 Bg4 14. Qd5 Rad8 15. Qb3 Be6 16. c4 Rd3 17. Nc3 Qh4** It doesn't really matter what

Black does. White's king is defenseless against all threats. **18. Bf4 Q×f4 19. R×f2 Q×f2† 20. Kh1 Bd4 21. Ne4 Qe2 22. Nc3 B×c3 23. b×c3 B×c4 24. Qa4 Rd2 25. Rb1 Bb5** Black wins—*Bell's Life*, 2 December 1849.

## (23) C.F. Smith–Bird    0–1
Offhand game
London (Purssell's) 1849
*A65*

**1. e4 e6 2. d4 c5 3. d5 d6 4. c4 Nf6 5. Nc3 Be7 6. f4 e×d5 7. c×d5 Bg4 8. Be2 B×e2 9. Q×e2 0–0 10. Nf3 Nbd7 11. 0–0 Ng4 12. Ng5 B×g5 13. Q×g4 Bf6 14. Rf3 Re8 15. Nb5 Qb6 16. a4 a6 17. Q×d7 a×b5 18. a×b5 Rad8 19. Qf5 Bd4† 20. Kh1 g6 21. Qg5 R×e4 22. Bd2 Rde8 23. Rh3 Q×b5 24. Qh6** and mates in 3 moves—*Bell's Life*, 2 December 1849.

## (24) Bird–C.F. Smith    1–0
Offhand game
London 1849
*C64*

**1. e4 e5 2. Nf3 Nc6 3. Bb5 Bc5 4. c3 Qf6 5. 0–0 Nge7 6. d4 e×d4 7. e5 Qg6 8. c×d4 Bb6 9. Nc3 0–0 10. d5 Nd8 11. Nh4** Black resigns—*Modern Chess*, p. 59.

## (25) C.F. Smith–Bird    1–0
Offhand game
London (Purssell's) 1850
*C38*

**1. e4 e5 2. f4 e×f4 3. Nf3 g5 4. Bc4 Bg7 5. h4 h6 6. h×g5 h×g5 7. R×h8 B×h8 8. Kf2 g4 9. Qh1 g×f3 10. Qh7 Qf6 11. Q×g8† Ke7 12. g×f3 Nc6 13. Nc3 Qh4† 14. Ke2 Qh2† 15. Kd1 Ne5 16. Nd5† Kd6 17. Qf8† Kc6 18. Bb5† K×b5 19. Qb4† Kc6 20. Ne7** mate—*Chess Player's Chronicle*, March 1850, p. 74.

## (26) Bird–C.F. Smith    0–1
Offhand game
London 1850
*C40*

**1. e4 e5 2. Nf3 f5 3. Bc4 Qf6 4. d4 f×e4 5. d×e5 Qe7 6. Ng5 Nh6 7. 0–0 Nc6 8. N×h7 Q×e5 9. N×f8 Ng4 10. g3 Nd4 11. Ng6 Qh5 12. Nh4 Nf3† 13. N×f3 N×h2 14. Nh4 Nf3† 15. Kh1 Qg4** and Black wins—*Chess Player's Chronicle*, April 1850, p. 114.

## (27) Bird–C.F. Smith    1–0
Offhand game
London 1850
*C38*

**1. e4 e5 2. f4 e×f4 3. Nf3 g5 4. Bc4 Bg7 5. 0–0 d6 6. d4 h6 7. g3 g4 8. Nh4 f3 9. c3 Bf6 10. N×f3 g×f3 11. Q×f3 Nc6 12. Bf4 Qe7 13. Nd2 Bd7 14. e5 d×e5 15. d×e5 B×e5 16. B×e5 N×e5 17. Q×b7 Qc5† 18. Rf2 Rd8 19. Re1 Ne7 20. b4 Qc6 21. R×e5 Q×b7 22. B×f7† Kf8 23. Bd5† Kg7 24. R×e7† Kg6 25. B×b7 Bf5 26. g4 B×g4 27. Be4† Kh5 28. Re5† Kh4 29. h3 K×h3 30. Nf1 Bd1** and White forces mate in five [*sic*] moves. Six more

moves do the job: 31. Rg5 Kh4 32. Rg6 Rd3 33. B×d3 Bg4 34. Rh2†
Bh3 35. Rg3 Rg8 36. Rh×h3 mate—*Chess Player's Chronicle*, April
1850, pp. 115–116.

## (28) Bird–C.F. Smith  1–0
Offhand game
London 1850
*C38*

1. e4 e5 2. f4 e×f4 3. Nf3 g5 4. Bc4 Bg7 5. 0–0 h6 6. d4 d6 7. g3
g4 8. Nh4 f3 9. c3 Ne7 10. Bf4 Bf6 11. N×f3 g×f3 12. Q×f3 Ng6
13. e5 d×e5 14. d×e5 Bg7 15. B×f7† Kf8 16. B×g6 Ke7 17. Bg5†
h×g5 18. Qf7 mate—*Chess Player's Chronicle*, May 1850, pp. 143–
144.

## (29) C.F. Smith–Bird  1–0
Offhand game
London 1850
*C38*

1. e4 e5 2. f4 e×f4 3. Nf3 g5 4. Bc4 Bg7 5. d4 h6 6. Nc3 d6
7. h4 g4 8. B×f4 g×f3 9. Q×f3 Be6 10. B×e6 f×e6 11. 0–0–0 Qe7
12. e5 d5 13. Nb5 h5 14. Bg5 Bh6 15. Q×h5† Kd7 16. Kb1 Qg7
17. Rhf1 B×g5 18. Rf7† Kc6 19. Qf3 Qg6 20. R×c7† Kb6
21. Qb3 Qh5 22. Rf1 Nf6 23. e×f6 Qe2 24. Nc3† K×c7 25. N×e2
and White wins—*Chess Player's Chronicle*, June 1850, p. 171.

## (30) Bird–C.F. Smith  1–0
Offhand game
London 1850
*C65*

1. e4 e5 2. Nf3 Nc6 3. Bb5 Nf6 4. d4 N×d4 5. N×d4 e×d4
6. e5 Qe7 7. 0–0 Nd5 8. Bc4 Nb6 9. Bb3 c5 10. Nd2 Qd8 11. Qf3
c4 12. N×c4 N×c4 13. B×c4 Qe7 14. Re1 h6 15. Bf4 g5 16. Bd2
Bg7 17. Bb4 Q×b4 18. Q×f7† Kd8 19. Q×g7 Re8 20. Qf6† Kc7
21. Bf7 Rf8 22. a3 Qc5 23. b4 Qc6 24. Qe7 Rd8 25. b5 Qb6
26. a4 a5 27. c4 d×c3 *e.p.* 28. Rac1 Kb8 29. R×c3 Ka7 30. Rec1
d6 31. Rc7 Rh8 32. R1c6 Qd4 33. b6† Kb8 34. R×b7† B×b7
35. Qc7 mate—*Chess Player's Chronicle*, June 1850, pp. 172–173.

## (31) Bird–C.F. Smith  0–1
Offhand game
London 1850
*C38*

1. e4 e5 2. f4 e×f4 3. Nf3 g5 4. Bc4 Bg7 5. 0–0 d6 6. d4 h6 7. c3
Nd7 8. g3 g4 9. Nh4 f3 10. Nf5 Qf6 11. Bf4 Nb6 12. Bb5† Kf8
13. Ne3 Qe7 14. Re1 h5 15. Nd5 Qd8 16. Nd2 h4 17. Nc4 N×c4
18. B×c4 h×g3 19. B×g3 c6 20. Ne3 Qe7 21. e5 d×e5 22. d×e5
B×e5 23. N×g4 Qc5† 24. Bf2 B×h2† 25. Kh1 Bd6† 26. Kg1
Rh1† and Black wins—*Chess Player's Chronicle*, July 1850, p. 204.

## (32) Bird–C.F. Smith  1–0
Offhand game
London 1850
*C65*

1. e4 e5 2. Nf3 Nc6 3. Bb5 Nf6 4. 0–0 Bd6 "Such a move de-

serves the penalty it usually entails of a cramped position all through,
and defeat at the end"—Staunton. **5. d4 Qe7 6. Nc3 0–0?!** 6. ...
N×d4 relieves the pressure. **7. Bg5!** N×d4? 7. ... e×d4 is necessary.
**8. N×d4** Equally powerful is 8. Nd5 Qe6 9. B×f6 g×f6 10. N×d4
e×d4 11. f4! c6 12. Qh5! c×b5 13. Qh6. **8. ... e×d4 9. Nd5 Q×e4**
9. ... Qe6 leads to the variation mentioned above. **10. N×f6† g×f6**
**11. Bd3!** An excellent piece sacrifice. Black is without resources
against the coming onslaught. **11. ... Qe5 12. f4 Qe3† 13. Kh1**
f×g5 **14. Qh5 f5 15. Q×g5†** 15. Rae1! Qd2 16. Re8 delivers a nice
finishing touch to White's beautiful piece sacrifice. Bird's move is
also sufficient. **15. ... Kh8 16. Rae1 B×f4 17. Qh5 Qd2 18. Re2**
**Qb4 19. R×f4 d5 20. Rh4** and White wins—*Chess Player's Chronicle* (Staunton), August 1850, p. 225.

## (33) C.F. Smith–Bird  1–0
Offhand game
London 1850
*C38*

1. e4 e5 2. f4 e×f4 3. Nf3 g5 4. Bc4 Bg7 5. 0–0 h6 6. g3 g4
7. Nh4 f3 8. c3 Ne7 9. N×f3 g×f3 10. Q×f3 0–0 11. B×f7† Kh8
12. d4 d5 13. Qh5 Ng8 14. e5 c5 15. h4 c×d4 16. Bg5 Qb6 17. Rf6
Bg4 18. Qg6 N×f6 19. e×f6 d×c3† 20. Kg2 R×f7 21. Q×f7 B×f6
22. B×f6† Q×f6 23. Q×f6† and White wins—*Chess Player's
Chronicle*, August 1850, p. 226.

## (34) Bird–C.F. Smith  1–0
Offhand game
London 1850
*C51*

1. e4 e5 2. Nf3 Nc6 3. Bc4 Bc5 4. b4 B×b4 5. c3 Bc5 During
the first decades of Bird's career little attention was given to the retreat of the bishop and both 5. ... Bc5 and 5. ... Ba5 often led to the
same position. In later years it was figured out that 5. ... Ba5! was
the superior move order. **6. 0–0** The previous remark applies here
all the same. It took many decades of practice to find out that 6. d4!,
forcing 6. ... e×d4, is the most precise move order. The point is that
after 6. 0–0 d6 7. d4, Black has the possibility to play 7. ... Bb6!, instead of 7. ... e×d4. This line, invented by Lasker, can always be
reached after 5. ... Ba5 (and not after 5. ... Bc5). **6. ... d6 7. d4 e×d4**
**8. c×d4 Bb6** This was the standard position of the Evans Gambit
in the nineteenth century. **9. Bb2** The major theoretical disputes
occurred after 9. d5 or 9. Nc3. The text move, quite a popular side
line, was adopted by Bird on several occasions. **9. ... Nf6 10. d5**
**Ne7** Black has various options here. 10. ... Na5 returns to one of
the mainlines, the normal move order being 9. d5 Na5 10. Bb2 Nf6
(10. ... Ne7 was more often seen). **11. Nd4?!** 11. B×f6 suggests itself,
but 11. Re1 is also playable. Bird plays for a direct attack, but it isn't
worth a second pawn. **11. ... N×e4 12. Re1 Nf6 13. Bb5† Bd7?**
*(see diagram)* There is no compensation after 13. ... Kf8 14. Nc3 h5
15. h3 Ba5, when White has to be aware not to lose the d-pawn as
well.

**14. Nf5!** "From this point the attack is very lively and amusing"—Staunton. **14. ... B×b5?** 14. ... Kf8 is forced. There could
follow 15. N×e7 B×b5 16. B×f6 g×f6 17. Qc1! h5 18. Qb2 with
lasting pressure. **15. R×e7†?** 15. N×g7† is completely winning.

After 13. ... Bd7

**15. ... Kf8?** 15. ... Q×e7 was overlooked by both players. It reanimates Black's position completely. **16. B×f6 g×f6 17. Qg4 Rg8 18. R×f7†!** "Clever and unexpected"—Staunton. **18. ... K×f7 19. Nh6† Ke8 20. Q×g8† Kd7 21. Qe6** mate—*Illustrated London News* (Staunton), 10 August 1850.

### (35) C.F. Smith–Bird　　0–1

Offhand game
London (City Road Chess Club) 1850
*C51*

　**1. e4 e5 2. Nf3 Nc6 3. Bc4 Bc5 4. b4 d5** Accepting the pawn was by far the most popular reply against the Evans Gambit, but Bird also experimented a few times with the exotic 4. ... d5 against Smith. According to Bird, "this defense may be safely adopted, and leads to a game of an interesting character, although very seldom played." Bird was a pioneer with this line, as the first game in the databases was only played in 1854 (between Urusov and von Jaenisch), six years after Bird put it in practice. Two other fragments of Bird's games with Smith were preserved: 5. e×d5 N×b4 6. c3 (Smith was more successful with 6. N×e5 Qg5 7. d4 Q×g2 8. Qf3 Q×f3 9. N×f3 N×c2† 10. Kd1 N×d4 and White won, C.F. Smith-Bird, 1848) 6. ... N×d5 7. N×e5 Ngf6 8. d4 Bb6 9. 0-0 0-0 and Black won in C.F. Smith-Bird, 1848. **5. e×d5 N×b4 6. N×e5 Nf6 7. Nc3 Bd4 8. Nf3 Qe7† 9. Kf1 Bg4 10. a3 B×f3 11. g×f3 B×c3 12. d×c3 Nb×d5 13. B×d5 0-0-0 14. Bg5 Qe5 15. B×f6 g×f6 16. c4 c6 17. f4 Qf5 18. Qd3 Q×d3† 19. c×d3 c×d5 20. c5 d4 21. Rc1 Rd5 22. Ke2 Kd7 23. Kf3 f5 24. Rc4 Rc8 25. Rhc1 Rc6 26. Ra4 a6 27. Rcc4 Rc×c5 28. R×d4 R×d4 29. R×d4† Kc6 30. Rd8 Rd5 31. R×d5?** This exchange seals his fate. **31. ... K×d5 32. a4 b5 33. a×b5 a×b5 34. Ke3 b4 35. Kd2 Kd4 36. Kc2 b3† 37. Kd2 b2 38. Kc2 h5 39. h4 b1Q† 40. K×b1 K×d3 41. Kc1 Ke4** Black wins—*Family Friend*, vol. II, p. 330; *Chess Practice* (Bird), pp. 55–56.

### (36) C.F. Smith–Bird　　0–1

Match
London 1850
*C51*

　"The annexed is one of fourteen games recently played, in which Mr. Smith opens with the Evans Gambit and wagers two to one in the event of its being accepted. These parties have produced the following result: Mr. Bird 10, Mr. Smith 3, drawn 1"—Staunton.
　**1. e4 e5 2. Nf3 Nc6 3. Bc4 Bc5 4. b4 B×b4 5. c3 Bc5 6. d4 e×d4 7. 0-0 d6 8. c×d4 Bb6 9. Nc3 Nf6** 9. ... Na5 or 9. ... Bg4 are

better. **10. h3** The theoretical recommendation is 10. e5 d×e5 11. Ba3! **10. ... h6 11. e5 d×e5 12. Ba3** Smith spotted the correct continuation. **12. ... Na5?** 12. ... B×d4 or 12. ... N×d4 are much better. Bird's move is much too optimistic. **13. Re1 N×c4 14. Qa4† c6 15. Q×c4 Be6 16. R×e5 Qd7** (*see diagram*)

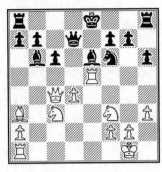

After 16. ...Qd7

**17. Rd1?** "Mr. Smith has opened his game irreproachably, and has obtained a grand position of attack, but he fails, we think, to prosecute his advantages as he might at this moment. Our play now (and the variation well deserves attention) would be 17. R×e6†, for example: 17. ... f×e6 18. Ne5 Qc8 19. Nb5 c×b5 (other moves are 19. ... Bc7 20. N×c7† Q×c7 21. Q×e6† and wins, or 19. ... Kd8, when the loss of the game is alike and immediate) 20. Q×b5† Kd8 21. Nf7† Kc7 22. Rc1† Kb8 23. Bd6† and wins"—Staunton. A tougher defense than 20. ... Kd8 is 20. ... Nd7, when the beautiful 21. Rc1 Qd8 22. Qc4 Qf6 23. Qa4 Qd8 24. d5! e×d5 25. Qg4! wins. **17. ... Bc7 18. d5 c×d5 19. N×d5?** Smith throws everything into the scale for the benefit of his attack, an approach that turns out to be hopeless. After 19. Qb4, Black can consider both 19. ... 0-0-0 and 19. ... a5. **19. ... B×e5 20. N×e5 B×d5 21. Qb4 a5 22. Qc5 b6 23. Q×b6 Qb7 24. Qe3 Be6** 24. ... 0-0-0 provides the king with a safe shelter. The material advantage will decide the game quickly. **25. Ng6 Nd5 26. Qe5 Rg8 27. Nf8 R×f8 28. Q×g7 Nb4 29. Rd6 Ke7 30. Rd2 Rg8** and Black wins—*Illustrated London News* (Staunton), 31 August 1850.

### (37) C.F. Smith–Bird　　0–1

Offhand game
London 1850
*B21*

　**1. e4 c5 2. d4 c×d4 3. Nf3 d6 4. c3 d×c3 5. N×c3 Bg4 6. Bc4 e6 7. Bf4 Nf6 8. 0-0 Nc6 9. Nb5 B×f3 10. Q×f3 a6 11. Nc3 Be7 12. Rad1 e5 13. Be3 Qd7 14. Nd5 Bd8 15. Bc5 N×d5 16. R×d5 Bc7 17. Rfd1 0-0-0 18. Qd3 Qe7 19. B×d6 B×d6 20. R×d6 R×d6 21. Q×d6 Rd8** and Black wins—*Chess Player's Chronicle*, September 1850, p. 263.

### (38) Bird–C.F. Smith　　0–1

Offhand game
In the provinces 1850
*C60*

　**1. e4 e5 2. Nf3 Nc6 3. Bb5 Bd6 4. d4 Qe7 5. 0-0 a6 6. Ba4 b5 7. Bb3 Bb7 8. Bd5 h6 9. d×e5 B×e5 10. N×e5 Q×e5 11. f4 Qe7 12. Nc3 Qc5† 13. Kh1 Nge7 14. f5 0-0 15. e5 N×d5 16. Ne4 Qc4 17. Nf6† N×f6 18. e×f6 Ne5 19. Bf4 Qe4 20. Qd2 Nc4 21. Qf2**

**Q×f5 22. f×g7 Rfe8 23. Qg3 Re2 24. Rg1 Rae8 25. Raf1 Nd2 26. B×d2 R×g2 27. Q×g2 B×g2†** and Black wins—*Chess Player's Chronicle*, November 1850, pp. 338–339.

## (39) C.F. Smith–Bird    0–1
Offhand game
London 1850
C50

**1. e4 e5 2. Nf3 Nc6 3. d4 e×d4 4. Bc4 d6** "Not as good as 4. ... Qf6, 4. ... Bb4† or 4. ... Bc5. White can now take the pawn at d4 without hesitation"—Kieseritzky. **5. N×d4 Ne5** "A vicious way to play the pieces to squares where they will be chased away without loss of time"—Kieseritzky. **6. Bb3** "6. Bd3 was possible as well, to invite Black to exchange their knight against this bishop. White would have taken back with the c-pawn, fortifying the center" —Kieseritzky. **6. ... Nf6 7. 0–0** "A trap. If 7. ... N×e4, Black loses one of his knights after 8. Re1 and 9. f3 or 9. f4 accordingly" —Kieseritzky. **7. ... Be7 8. Nc3 0–0 9. f4 Ng6 10. Bd2** 10. Qd3 places the queen on an active square. White can develop his bishop afterwards. **10. ... c5!** An excellent riposte of Bird, which immediately solves his opening problems. **11. Nf3 b5 12. Bd5** "Instead of this move, we should prefer 12. N×b5 or 12. e5. After 12. N×b5 N×e4 13. Bd5 N×d2 14. Q×d2 Rb8 15. c4, and after 12. e5 d×e5 13. f×e5 Nd7 14. N×b5 Nd×e5 15. N×e5 N×e5 16. Be3. In both cases, White would not be worse"—Kieseritzky. In the first line Black is a bit better thanks to his bishop pair. In the second line 13. ... c4 is an amelioration. The chances are about equal, though Black's bishop pair is agreeable to play with. **12. ... Rb8 13. a3 b4 14. a×b4 c×b4 15. Ne2 N×d5 16. e×d5 Bf6** (*see diagram*) Black holds a comfortable edge.

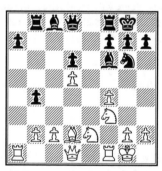

After 16. ... Bf6

**17. Ned4** "17. R×a7 fails to 17. ... Qb6†"—Kieseritzky. The text move is not so good, as it leaves the d-pawn in trouble. Superior are 17. c3 or 17. Kh1. **17. ... Ne7 18. Kh1 Bb7** The exchange of b- for the d-pawn allows White back in the game. Better is 18. ... Qb6, which nets the d-pawn. **19. B×b4 N×d5 20. Bd2 Qb6 21. Nf5?** This loses a pawn. The ugly 21. Bc1 keeps Black's advantage limited. **21. ... Bc8! 22. Ng3 B×b2 23. Rb1 Qc7** White's position is completely joyless. He tries a desperate attack against the king. **24. Ng5 h6** 24. ... Nf6! avoids any weaknesses and controls e4. **25. N5e4 f5 26. Bc1 Be6 27. B×b2** 27. R×b2 is absolutely necessary, although Black's advantage is close to being decisive: 27. ... R×b2 28. B×b2 f×e4 29. Bc1 (e3 needs to be covered) 29. ... Nf6 30. Bb2 Bc4 31. Re1 d5. Only counterplay on the black squares can perhaps save White. **27. ... f×e4** Even stronger is 27. ... Ne3! **28. Qd4 Rb4 29. Qd2 e3**

**30. Qe2 Rb×f4 31. R×f4 N×f4 32. Q×e3 Q×c2** Black wins. "Black has demonstrated a remarkable ability in this game. But we already knew that Mr. Bird, though still quite young, is one of England's distinguished players"—Kieseritzky—*La Régence* (Kieseritzky), November 1850, pp. 346–348.

## (40) Bird–C.F. Smith    1–0
Offhand game
London 1850
C64

**1. e4 e5 2. Nf3 Nc6 3. Bb5 Bc5 4. c3 Qf6 5. 0–0 Nge7 6. d4 e×d4 7. Bg5 Qg6 8. B×e7 N×e7 9. c×d4 Bb6 10. Nc3 0–0 11. Ne5 Qf6 12. f4 d6 13. Nf3 Q×f4 14. Qd3 f5 15. Bc4† Kh8 16. Kh1 f×e4 17. N×e4 d5 18. Nfg5 Q×f1† 19. R×f1 R×f1† 20. Q×f1 Bd7 21. Qf7 d×c4** White mates in three moves—*Horae Divanianae*, pp. 104–105.

## (41) C.F. Smith–Bird    1–0
Offhand game
London 1850 (?)
C51

**1. e4 e5 2. Nf3 Nc6 3. Bc4 Bc5 4. b4 B×b4 5. c3 Ba5 6. d4 e×d4 7. 0–0 Bb6 8. c×d4 d6 9. h3 h6 10. Bb2 Nf6 11. d5 Ne7 12. B×f6 g×f6 13. Nc3 Ng6 14. Nd4 Qe7 15. f4 Bd7 16. Kh1 0–0–0 17. a4 a5 18. Nf5 B×f5 19. e×f5 Nh4 20. Re1 Qd7 21. Qg4 N×f5 22. Bb5 c6 23. d×c6 b×c6 24. Nd5 Bf2 25. Ba6† Kb8 26. Reb1† Ka8 27. Rb7 Q×b7 28. B×b7† K×b7 29. Rb1† Ka7 30. Q×f5 c×d5 31. Q×d5 Bb6 32. Q×f7† Ka6 33. Re1 d5 34. Re7** and White wins—*Chess Player's Chronicle*, March 1851, pp. 78–79.

## (42) C.F. Smith–Bird    1–0
Offhand game
London 1850 (?)
C60

**1. e4 e5 2. Nf3 Nc6 3. Bb5 Bd6** "This move always gives Black a very confined game"—Staunton. **4. c3 Nge7 5. d4 Ng6 6. 0–0 0–0 7. Nbd2 a6 8. Ba4 b5 9. Bb3 Nce7?! 10. a4?!** 10. Ng5! refutes Bird's last move, e.g., 10. ... Bb7 11. Qh5 h6 12. N×f7 R×f7 13. B×f7† K×f7 14. d×e5 B×e5 15. f4. Worse is 10. ... h6 11. N×f7 R×f7 12. B×f7† K×f7 13. f4. The same knight sortie remains at White's disposition for two more moves. **10. ... c6 11. a×b5 c×b5 12. c4 Bb7 13. c5 Bc7** A most unfortunate square. 13. ... Bb8 is about equal. **14. d5 d6 15. c6** The far advanced c-pawn is a major trump for the eventual endgame. **15. ... Bc8 16. Qc2** 16. Nb1 or 16. h3 are stronger moves. Now Bird gets his share of the chances on the kingside. **16. ... f5 17. Re1 f×e4 18. N×e4 Bf5 19. Bg5 h6 20. B×e7** It is better to keep the bishop on the board. **20. ... Q×e7 21. Qc3 Kh7?!** Black has sufficient counterplay after 21. ... B×e4 22. R×e4 Bb6. The text move brings his own king into the frontline. **22. Rad1?!** Black has definite problems after 22. Ng3! Bg4 23. Bc2. The same idea could be executed on the next few moves as well. **22. ... a5 23. Ba2 a4 24. Qc2 Bg4 25. Rd3 Nf4** 25. ... B×f3, inflicting a weakness upon White's kingside, is also interesting. **26. Ra3**

**Kh8 27. Bb1 Bf5** A better way to deal with Smith's reinvigorated threats along the long diagonal is 27. ... g6, threatening to capture at d5 as well as to play 28. ... b4. **28. Qd2 Ba5** "The object of this move apparently was to get a passed pawn on the a-file"—Staunton. **29. b4 Bb6 30. g3** A pawn is lost now, but this is no drama. He could also play the safer 30. Kh1. **30. ... Nh3† 31. Kg2 B×e4 32. B×e4 N×f2** (see diagram)

*After 32. ... N×f2*

**33. Bb1?** Abandoning the blockade of the e-pawn is a very bad idea. Instead after 33. Nh4! a surprising tactical sequence arises: 33. ... N×e4 34. Ng6† Kh7 35. N×f8† R×f8 36. Qd3 Rf2† 37. Kh1 Qf7 38. Q×e4† g6 39. h4 Rf1† 40. R×f1 Q×f1† 41. Kh2 and Black would be wise to take the draw. **33. ... g5?** 33. ... e4! wins easily for if 34. Nh4 Qf6 and now Black has a decisive attack. **34. Rc3?** Once again 34. Nh4! is extremely dangerous and leads to epic variations. Accepting this sacrifice seems like a valid option but is actually playing with fire: 34. ... g×h4 35. Q×h6† Kg8 36. g×h4 Ng4 37. Rg3 Rf2† 38. Kh3 and now 38. ... R×h2† completes the heroic journey of White's king, as after 39. K×g4 Bf2 40. Rf1! B×g3 41. K×g3 Rb2 42. Rf6 Black can resign. 38. ... Qg7 is the only move, but White remains well on top after 39. Qe6† Kh8 40. R×g4 Rf3† 41. Kg2 Rf2† 42. Kg3. Thus Black is almost forced to sacrifice material himself with 34. ... Qf6! After 35. Ng6† Kg7 36. N×f8 R×f8 the position remains extremely tense. **34. ... Ra7 35. Qc2** 35. Nh4 can now be met with 35. ... g×h4 36. Q×h6† Kg8 37. g×h4 Qf6 38. Rg3† Rg7. **35. ... Rf6 36. Qe2 g4?** 36. ... e4! is still the crucial move to find; e.g., 37. B×e4 g4 38. Nd2 Qe5 39. Rcc1 Raf7 and White's king finds itself in the middle of a highway. **37. Nh4 Qf7?** Here, and on the following moves, Bird withdraws into his shell, thereby handing over the victory to his opponent. After 37. ... Bd4 38. Rcc1 Qf7 39. Q×b5 the game is still in full swing. **38. Q×b5** Compared to the previous line, this capture comes with tempo. **38. ... Bd8?!** If now 38. ... Bd4 39. c7 wins. 38. ... Ra8 can be played, for if 39. Q×b6? Q×d5† and Black wins. Better is 39. Bg6 Qc7 40. Ra3 with pressure. **39. Rf1 Nh3** 39. ... a3 is the only way to complicate the game. After 40. Rc2 Ne4 41. R×f6 N×f6 42. Ba2 White's chances to win are still quite good. Now all lines and diagonals are opened, but White remains, fairly simply, master of the situation. **40. R×f6 Q×f6 41. Nf5 e4 42. c7! R×c7 43. Qe8† Kh7 44. R×c7† B×c7 45. Q×e4 Qb2† 46. Bc2 Ng5 47. Qe7†** Black resigns—*Chess Praxis* (Staunton), pp. 211–212.

Another regular opponent during Bird's palmy days was Arthur Simons. Some confusion has been created by the various ways of spelling of his name. Simmons or Simonds were also regularly seen, but there is no doubt they all concerned the same person.

**(43) Bird–Simons    1–0**
Offhand game
London 1848
*C64*

**1. e4 e5 2. Nf3 Nc6 3. Bb5 Bc5 4. c3 Qe7** "Adopted by Boden against Morphy ten years later"—Bird. **5. 0–0 Nf6** "Boden here played 5. ... f6"—Bird. **6. d4 e×d4?** Surrendering the center is a very bad idea. **7. e5 Nd5 8. c×d4 Bb6 9. Bg5?** Already winning is 9. Bc4! Ndb4 10. a3 Na6 and now either 11. Nc3 or 11. d5 wipes away Black's defense. **9. ... Qb4 10. Bd3 N×d4** 10. ... Q×b2 and only then 11. ... N×d4 completely fleeces White. **11. a3?** Such a move is never good when trying to develop an attack. White has compensation for the sacrificed material after 11. Nc3 N×c3 12. b×c3 Q×c3 13. Rc1 Qa5 14. N×d4 B×d4 15. Bc4. **11. ... Q×b2 12. Nbd2 N×f3†?** The queen needed some space but this exchange only benefits his opponent's development. 12. ... Nc3! initiates a strong reorganization, e.g., 13. Qe1 Na4 and 14. ... Nc5. **13. Q×f3 h6 14. Nc4 Qd4 15. Bc1!?** "A very ingenious bait"—Staunton. It certainly is. 15. Bd2! Ne7 16. Rac1 also gives ample compensation for the material. **15. ... Q×a1** 15. ... Ne7, freeing d5 for his queen after 16. Bb2, is much safer. **16. Q×d5?** Bird is blinded by various attacking possibilities. 16. Bb2! is correct, when Black is forced to play 16. ... Q×b2. With rook, bishops and two rooks for the queen, he has enough to claim equality. **16. ... Qd4 17. Qf3 0–0?** "Castling on this side in the face of such a battery was an act of temerity that few players would have had courage for"—Staunton. First 17. ... d5 18. e×d6 *e.p.* and now 18. ... 0–0 is good. **18. B×h6** An incorrect sacrifice. 18. Qf5! g6 19. Qf6 is winning, e.g., 19. ... Kh7 20. B×g6†. **18. ... d5!** "If he had taken the bishop, White would have played 19. Qf5, winning easily"—Staunton. **19. B×g7 d×c4??** In the sight of the finish, Simons becomes a tad too greedy, for which he is severely punished. The cool 19. ... Qg4! returns some material and reaches a winning endgame. **20. Qh5 f5 21. Qh8† Kf7 22. Q×f8† Ke6 23. B×c4†** "Wins the queen if Black retakes and mates in 3 if he doesn't"—Bird. And wins—*Chess Player's Chronicle* (Staunton), February 1851, pp. 43–44; *Modern Chess* (Bird), p. 58.

**(44) Bird–Simons    1–0**
Offhand game
London, 18 December 1849
*C64*

**1. e4 e5 2. Nf3 Nc6 3. Bb5 Bc5 4. 0–0 Nge7 5. c3 0–0 6. d4 e×d4 7. c×d4 Bb6 8. d5 Nb8 9. Bg5 f6 10. d6 c×d6 11. Bf4 a6 12. Bc4† d5 13. B×d5† Kh8 14. Bd6 Bc7 15. B×e7 Q×e7 16. Nh4 Nc6 17. f4 Qc5† 18. Kh1 Ne7 19. Nc3 d6 20. f5 Ba5 21. Rc1 Qe3 22. Rf3 Qg5 23. Rh3 B×c3 24. Rc×c3 Bd7 25. Rcg3 Qf4 26. Rg4 Qe5** mate in 4 moves—*Family Friend*, vol. II.

Late in 1849 or early in 1850 Bird and Simons contested a match. No other details are available but given the fact that all known games were won by Bird it seems fair to assume that he also gained the match.

**(45) Simons–Bird    0–1**

Match
London 1850 (?)
A85

**1. d4 e6 2. c4 f5 3. Nc3 Nf6 4. e3 b6 5. Bd3 Bb7 6. f3 a5 7. a3 Nc6 8. Nge2 Ne7 9. b3 d5 10. Bb2 Ng6 11. Rc1 Bd6 12. c×d5 N×d5 13. N×d5 B×d5 14. Bb5† Kf7 15. 0–0 Rf8 16. e4 Bb7 17. e×f5 e×f5 18. Bc4† Ke7 19. Re1 Kd7 20. d5 Qh4 21. g3 Qg5 22. Bb5† Kc8 23. Qd3 f4 24. g4 B×d5 25. B×g7 Nh4 26. Q×h7 B×f3** and Black wins—*Historic Times*, 25 January 1850.

**(46) Simons–Bird    0–1**

Match
London 1850 (?)
C60

**1. e4 e5 2. Nf3 Nc6 3. Bb5 Bd6 4. c3 Nge7 5. d4 0–0 6. 0–0 f5 7. Bc4† Kh8 8. Ng5 Qe8 9. e×f5 N×f5 10. Re1 Qg6 11. Qg4 Nh6 12. Qh3 Be7 13. Bd3 Qf6 14. Ne4 Qf7 15. B×h6 d5 16. Qe3 d×e4 17. B×g7† Q×g7 18. B×e4 e×d4 19. c×d4 Bg5 20. Qd3 N×d4 21. Nc3 Bf5 22. Rad1 Rad8 23. Kf1 Ne6 24. Qc4 R×d1 25. R×d1 B×e4 26. N×e4 Qe5 27. g3 Rd8 28. R×d8† B×d8 29. f4 Qf5 30. Kg2 c6 31. a4 Qd5 32. Q×d5 c×d5 33. Nd6 Bc7 34. N×b7 Kg7 35. f5 Nd4 36. g4 Nb3 37. Kf3 Kf6 38. Ke3 Ke5 39. Kd3 Bb6 40. Kc3 Nc5 41. N×c5 B×c5 42. h4 Ke4 43. b4 Be7 44. h5 Ke3 45. b5 d4†** and Black wins—*Chess Player's Chronicle*, February 1850, pp. 37–38.

**(47) Simons–Bird    0–1**

Match
London 1850 (?)
C01

**1. e4 e6 2. d4 d5 3. e×d5 e×d5 4. Bd3 Bd6 5. Nc3 Be6 6. Nf3 c6 7. 0–0 Nf6 8. h3 Nbd7 9. Be3 Qc7 10. Qd2 h6 11. Rae1 0–0–0 12. a3 g5 13. b4 g4 14. h×g4 N×g4 15. b5 Rdg8 16. b×c6 b×c6 17. Ba6† Kd8 18. Rb1 Nb6 19. Na4 N×e3 20. f×e3 Bh3 21. Nh4 Rg4 22. Qf2 Rhg8 23. N×b6 a×b6 24. Qf6† Be7 25. Q×f7** and Black gave mate in three moves—*Chess Player's Chronicle*, February 1850, pp. 38–39.

**(48) Bird–Simons    1–0**

Match
London 1850 (?)
C64

**1. e4 e5 2. Nf3 Nc6 3. Bb5 Bc5 4. c3 Nge7 5. 0–0 0–0 6. d4 e×d4 7. c×d4 Bb6 8. Nc3 d6 9. Bg5 Bg4 10. B×c6 b×c6 11. d5 f6 12. Be3 c×d5** 12. ... f5!, breaking up White's center, is interesting. **13. B×b6 B×f3 14. g×f3** Bird overlooks 14. B×c7 which is necessary to maintain the balance. **14. ... a×b6 15. N×d5 Ng6** Either 15. ... f5! or 15. ... N×d5 16. e×d5 f5 is promising for Black. With his knight now undisputed at d5, White has but little to tremble for. **16. Rc1** "Well played. If 16. ... R×a2 17. Qb3"—Bird. **16. ... Rf7?** "This was an oversight, since White can safely take the pawn this rook was thought to guard"—Staunton. **17. N×c7** Good enough, but 17. R×c7! was stronger. **17. ... Ra5** "Suppose 17. ... R×c7

18. R×c7 Q×c7 19. Qd5† and afterwards 20. Q×a8† has gained the exchange and a pawn"—Staunton. **18. Nd5 f5 19. b4?!** Allowing Simons to take the a-pawn after all is a well-considered sacrifice, but against a correct defense, this should lead to little. 19. Qb3 is preferable. **19. ... R×a2 20. Qb3 Nh4?** After 20. ... Raa7! Black has but little problems. **21. Nf6?** "Very well-conceived. The queen cannot take the knight and is prevented to enter at g5"—Bird. This move ought to be winning, but 21. Ne7† or 21. Rc8 would have forced a quicker resignation. **21. ... g×f6 22. Q×a2 N×f3† 23. Kh1 f×e4 24. Qe6 Qe7 25. Rc8†** From this point on Bird slowly but surely starts to drift until an extremely tense position is reached. Most efficient would be 25. Qg4† Rg7 (if 25. ... Ng5 26. h4) 26. Qc8† Qf8 27. Qe6†, winning the queen. **25. ... Kg7 26. Qg4† Kh6** (see diagram)

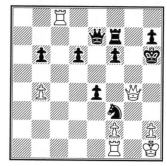

*After 26. ... Kh6*

**27. Rg8?!** Bird chased his opponent's king in a seemingly desperate position, but paradoxically enough his majesty is much safer at h6 than at g8. White is now faced with a whole myriad of possibilities, and it is surprisingly hard to find the correct path. Bird's principal mistake is that he only aims for the Black king while it is more conceivable to reach a very good, or even winning, endgame. After 27. Qh3† Kg7 28. Qg3† Kh6 29. Rd1! Qe5 30. Rd8, the d-pawn falls, soon to be followed by either the f- or the b-pawn. **27. ... f5** Also strong is 27. ... Qe5! 28. Qh3† Qh5 29. Q×h5† K×h5, which reaches a much better version of the same endgame. White will win the d- and b-pawn, but after 30. Rd8 b5 31. R×d6 Kg4 32. Rd5 f5 33. R×b5 Rf6 his king might get in trouble. Either 34. h3† or 34. Rb8 leads then only to a draw, e.g., 34. Rb8 Rh6 35. Rg8† Kf4 36. Rg2 Nh4 37. Rg3 Nf3. **28. Qf4†?!** 28. Qh3† Qh4 29. Q×h4† N×h4 30. Rd8 keeps a minimal edge, but this was the best he could get. **28. ... Kh5 29. Rg3?!** Bird is still aiming at Black's king, but had Simons now played 29. ... Qh4! 30. Q×h4† K×h4, an endgame is reached where Black is better thanks to his strong king. 29. Rd1 is relatively best. **29. ... d5? 30. Rh3† Nh4 31. Rg1 d4 32. Rhg3 h6 33. Qd2** Bird's bluff worked well and after Simons' 29th move, his attack got into full swing again. A direct decision was possible here: 33. Rh3 d3 34. Qg3! **33. ... f4 34. Qd1† f3 35. Q×d4 Qe6 36. Qh8?!** Being faced with the growing menace of Black's advancing pawns makes it tough for Bird to stay cool and find the best way to win the game. It is again crucial to get the queen close to Black's king, which could have been done by 36. Rg4! Re7 37. Rf4, intending 38. Qg7 and 39. Qg3, wins. **36. ... Ng2! 37. Qg8 Qf5?** 38. ... Re7 keeps on raising practical problems for his opponent. After the text move all is over. **38. Rh3† Q×h3 39. Q×f7† Kg5 40. Qe7† Kg6 41. Q×e4† Kf6 42. Qc6† Ke5 43. Rd1 Nf4 44. Qd6† Kf5 45. Rd5† Kg4 46. Qd7† Kh4**

**47. Qe7† Kg4 48. Qg7† Kh4 49. Q×h6† Nh5 50. Qg5** mate
—*Chess Player's Chronicle* (Staunton), February 1850, pp. 39–41;
*Modern Chess* (Bird), p. 61.

## (49) Simons–Bird   0–1

Match (game ?)
London 1850 (?)
*C60*

**1. e4 e5 2. Nf3 Nc6 3. Bb5 Bd6 4. c3 Nge7 5. d4 0–0 6. d5
Nb8 7. Bc4 c6 8. d×c6 d×c6 9. h3 Qc7 10. 0–0 a5 11. a4 Nd7
12. Be3 Nf6 13. Qc2 Ng6 14. Nbd2 Be6 15. B×e6 f×e6 16. Ng5
Rae8 17. Nc4 h6 18. Bb6 Qe7 19. Nf3 Nh5 20. B×a5 R×f3
21. g×f3 Qg5† 22. Kh2 Qf4† 23. Kh1 Q×f3† 24. Kh2 Nhf4
25. Ne3 Q×h3† 26. Kg1 Bc5 27. f3 B×e3† 28. Rf2 Qg2** mate
—*Chess Player's Chronicle*, March 1850, pp. 71–72.

The *Historic Times* of 11 January 1850 announced Simons' retirement from the chess arena but the tournament of 1851 proved an impetus for him to return to the game. He scored his best result of his career by narrowly losing, with 3 against 4, in offhand games against the French master Lionel Kieseritzky. According to the latter in *La Régence* of July 1851 (p. 204), his opponent distinguished himself with his brilliant and lively playing style. Simons took part in two minor tournaments. In the Divan tournament of 1849 he was eliminated in the first round by Edward Lowe. He did not get any further in a small knock-out tournament played at Kling's Chess and Coffee Rooms in 1855.

Another enigmatic and regular opponent of Bird was a certain Hughes. This amateur's activities in chess initially only spanned the years 1849 and 1850. He frequented the City Road Chess Club where he received the odds of pawn and two moves from C.F. Smith.

Hughes played a few matches with the same odds against Bird in January and February 1850. A first game, won by Bird, was published in the *Illustrated London News* on 26 January 1850. According to Staunton it was part of a small match. Two weeks later Hughes informed him that the game was played offhand as Bird had lost all the match games. A return match with the same odds was played in February. Bird easily took his revenge by winning every game. Both these matches had been played to the first five wins. Bird and Hughes agreed to play a third match to bring about a decision, but it is unclear whether it was ever played for no result was published.

Hughes' full name was never published in connection with one of his games. A "Georges Hughes" figures among the list of subscribers of Williams' book *Horae Divanianae*. The present author is, however, inclined to believe that "H. Hughes," active in the late 1850s, is our man.

This player took part in the first two tournaments of the British Chess Association (in 1857 and 1858). Together with Bird and Falkbeer he was recognized as a first-class player in the handicap tournament at Purssell's in 1859. *The Sunday Times* of 12 July 1857 reveals that his full name was Hesketh Hughes. A search on him in the catalogue of the National Archives results in various hits, all of them referring to records of the Patent Office. Around 1850 a "Hesketh Hughes" lived close to the City Road, which presents a clearly possible connection with the player active around that time at the City Road Chess Club.

## (50) Hughes–Bird   0–1

Offhand game
London 1850 (?)
*Odds of pawn and two moves*

**1. e4 & 2. d4 c5 3. Qh5† g6 4. Q×c5 Nc6 5. Qc4 e6 6. c3 d5
7. e×d5 e×d5 8. Qe2† Be7 9. Nf3 Nf6 10. Ne5** 10. Bh6 prevents Bird from castling. **10. … 0–0 11. Qc2** Quite risky, as Bird gets a unique chance to grasp the initiative. 11. Nd2 is good enough for an advantage. **11. … Re8** 11. … N×e5 (Staunton) 12. d×e5 Ng4! looks very good for Black. **12. Bd3** 12. Bb5!, followed by 13. B×c6, avoids all complications, as the knight at e5 cannot be challenged anymore. **12. … Bd6 13. f4** "13. B×g6 looks inviting but is not sound"—Staunton. Even though it appears dangerous, Black can just accept the sacrifice since White will not be able to hold e5. Instead, 13. 0–0! keeps a firm advantage. **13. … Qb6** 13. … B×e5! 14. f×e5 N×e5! is strong. Now 15. d×e5 R×e5† 16. Kf1 Qe7 17. Qd2 Bf5 gives Black a decisive attack, so White is obliged to castle. After 15. … N×d3 16. Q×d3 Bg4 Black has enough compensation for the pawn. **14. Be3?** "Black's last move materially alters the appearances of things, and now we should think 14. B×g6 a perfectly safe and very advantageous move for White. Assuredly much better than the move above"—Staunton. After 14. B×g6 or 14. Nd2 White must win. **14. … Ng4?** 14. … N×e5 15. f×e5 B×e5 wins a pawn with a tremendous position. **15. N×g4??** The final mistake. The quiet 15. Bg1! keeps the center well defended. If necessary, the king can even stay behind these pawns. Black lacks an active plan. **15. … B×g4 16. Kf2 R×e3!** "This is irresistible, let White play as he may, and gives a pretty finish to the game"—Staunton. **17. K×e3 Re8† 18. Kf2 N×d4! 19. c×d4 Q×d4† 20. Kf1 Q×f4† 21. Qf2 Re1† 22. K×e1 Qc1** mate—*Illustrated London News* (Staunton), 26 January 1850.

## (51) Hughes–Bird   1–0

Match 1 (game 1)
London 1850 (?)
*Odds of pawn and two moves*

**1. e4 & 2. d4 e6 3. Bd3 Qe7 4. Nf3 d6 5. e5 Nc6 6. h4 Bd7
7. Be3 h6 8. Bg6† Kd8 9. Nc3 d×e5 10. d×e5 Qb4 11. Rb1 Qg4
12. Be4 Bb4 13. B×c6 b×c6 14. a3 B×c3† 15. b×c3 Ne7 16. Rb4
Q×g2 17. Rg1 Qh3 18. Rd4 Nd5 19. c4 Rf8 20. c×d5 c×d5
21. Rf4 R×f4 22. B×f4 Qf5 23. Be3 g6 24. B×h6 c5 25. Qd3 Qf7
26. Ng5 Qe8 27. Nh7 Qh8 28. Bg5† Kc7 29. Nf6 Rb8 30. c4 Rb2
31. c×d5 Qb8 32. d6† Kc8 33. Qa6† Rb7 34. Kd2 Bb5 35. d7†
B×d7 36. Rb1 Kd8 37. R×b7 Q×e5 38. R×d7** mates—*Historic Times*, 4 January 1850.

## (52) Hughes–Bird   1–0

Match 1 (game ?)
London 1850
*Odds of pawn and two moves*

"The present game was the last of a match in which Mr. Hughes came off decisively victorious"—Staunton.

**1. e4 & 2. d4 d6 3. Bd3 Nc6 4. Be3 e5 5. d5 Nce7 6. Nc3 Nf6
7. f4 e×f4 8. B×f4 Ng6 9. Bg3 Be7 10. Nf3 Bg4 11. Qe2 0–0**

12. 0–0–0 Nd7 13. h3 Bh5 14. Bh2 Nde5 15. B×e5 N×e5 16. g4
R×f3 17. g×h5 Bg5† 18. Kb1 Qd7 19. Bb5 Qf7 20. h4 Bh6
21. Qg2 Rf8 22. Rhf1 a6 23. Be2 Rf2 24. Qh3 Qf4 25. R×f2 Q×f2
26. Rf1 Qe3 27. R×f8† K×f8 28. Qc8† Ke7 29. Q×c7† Nd7
30. a3 b5 31. Ka2 Qf4 32. e5 d×e5 33. Qc6 Qf6 34. d6† Ke8
35. Nd5 Qe6 36. Ka1 Qf5 37. Nc7† Kf7 38. N×a6 e4 39. B×b5
e3 40. Bc4† Kf6 41. Nb4 Bf4 42. Nd5† Ke5 43. Ne7 Qe4 44. Bd5
e2 45. Qc3† Qd4 46. Nc6† K×d5 47. N×d4 and White wins
—*Chess Player's Chronicle* (Staunton), March 1850, pp. 72–74.

## (53) Hughes–Bird  0–1
Match 2 (game ?)
London 1850
*Odds of pawn and two moves*

1. e4 & 2. d4 e6 3. Bd3 Qe7 4. e5 d5 5. Nc3 Nc6 6. Be3
Bd7 7. a3 g6 8. h4 Bh6 9. Nb5 0–0–0 10. f4 Qf7 11. Nh3 Nge7
12. g4 Rdf8 13. Rf1 Qe8 14. b4 Kd8 15. c4 a6 16. Nc3 d×c4
17. B×c4 Nc8 18. d5 N×e5 19. Bb3 e×d5 20. g5 B×h3 21. Q×d5†
Nd7 22. Rf3 Bg7 23. Kd2 B×c3† 24. K×c3 Bg2 and after a few
moves, White resigns—*Chess Player's Chronicle*, May 1850, pp. 136–
137.

## (54) Hughes–Bird  0–1
Match 2 (game ?)
London 1850
*Odds of pawn and two moves*

1. e4 & 2. d4 e6 3. Bd3 Qe7 4. e5 Nc6 5. Nf3 Nd8 6. Bg5 Qb4†
7. Nbd2 Nf7 8. h4 Be7 9. b3 d5 10. a3 Qb6 11. c4 c6 12. c5 Qd8
13. Qc2 g6 14. Be3 Ngh6 15. h5 Nf5 16. B×f5 g×f5 17. 0–0–0 b5
18. Rdg1 Rg8 19. Nh2 Qa5 20. Kb2 b4 21. a4 Ng5 22. g4 f4
23. B×f4 Nh3 24. Q×h7 Rf8 25. Qg6† Kd7 26. Bh6 R×f2 27. Rf1
Ba6 28. R×f2 N×f2 29. Rg1 Bb5 30. a×b5 Qa3† 31. Kb1 Ne4
32. b×c6† Kc7 33. Nhf3 Nc3† 34. Kc2 Qa2† 35. Kd3 Qa6†
36. Ke3 Qe2† 37. Kf4 Qf2 38. Q×e6 Ne2† 39. Kf5 N×d4† and
Black wins—*Chess Player's Chronicle*, May 1850, pp. 138–139.

## (55) Hughes–Bird  0–1
Match 2 (game ?)
London, 28 February 1850
*Odds of pawn and two moves*

1. e4 & 2. d4 e6 3. Bd3 Qe7 4. e5 b6 5. h4 Bb7 6. Qh5† Qf7
7. Q×f7† K×f7 8. f3 Nc6 9. c3 Be7 10. Na3 d6 11. Bf4 Nh6
12. Nb5 d×e5 13. d×e5 a6 14. Nd4 Rad8 15. N×c6 B×c6
16. 0–0–0 Nf5 17. g4 N×h4 18. g5 N×f3 19. g6† h×g6 20. R×h8
R×h8 21. N×f3 B×f3 22. Rg1 g5 23. B×g5 Rh1 24. R×h1 B×g5†
25. Kc2 B×h1 26. B×a6 Be4† 27. Kb3 Be3 28. Kb4 g5 and Mr.
Hughes resigned—*Family Friend*, vol. III, p. 182.

Less fitting in the category of young lions was "Old Lowe" as
Edward Lowe, already over 50, was affectionately called. He was
a very popular and long-lasting visitor of the Divan. Steinitz
wrote a warm-hearted sketch after Lowe's death: "Old Lowe's personality will long be memorable amongst the frequenters of Simpson's Divan, of which classic home of chess he was the oldest

habitué. There was a ringing cheer from all quarters of the room
whenever the old gentleman used to step across the door, his bright
blue eyes beaming with intelligence and good humor" (*The Field*,
6 March 1880).

Bird and Lowe undoubtedly met each other countless times in
offhand games, but there was also some talk about a match in the
contemporary press. Bird, in *Chess Practice* (p. 17), believed that it
was played in 1849 for a stake of £5 a side and that he came out victorious. Contemporary sources, however, indicate that the match
was actually played in September 1850. Bird audaciously challenged
the veteran and both agreed that seven wins were required for
victory. The first game was played on 8 September at the Divan.
Bird started energetically and on 28 September Staunton reported
in his column in the *Illustrated London News* that he had "literally
beaten the Divan 'professor' to a stand-still." A few weeks later Bird's
match victory was announced. Staunton used the opportunity to
criticize both players, especially pointing some poisonous arrows
towards Lowe.

> … the contest between Messrs. Bird and Lowe has terminated in the defeat
> of the latter, Mr. Bird having come off a winner of seven games to four. We
> now hope to hear that Mr. Bird is directing his attention to a match, accepting
> odds from some player of acknowledged skill. In one such struggle he would
> gain more honor and more improvement, than in fifty contests like his last
> [*Illustrated London News*, 19 October 1850].

## (56) Bird–Lowe  1–0
Offhand game
London (Simpson's Divan) 1849
*C64*

"Game just played between Mr. H.E. Bird, one of the most promising among the many rising players of the day, and Mr. Lowe of the
Strand Divan"—Staunton.

1. e4 e5 2. Nf3 Nc6 3. Bb5 Bc5 4. c3 Qe7 5. 0–0 a6 6. Ba4 b5
7. Bb3 d6 Black must hurry up and play 7. … Nf6 to get his king
out of the center. 8. d4 Bb6 9. a4 "This attack is maintained with
all the characteristic energy and correctness of the modern
school"—Staunton. 9. … Rb8 10. Na3 Bg4? 11. a×b5 a×b5
12. N×b5 e×d4 13. c×d4 Nf6 14. Qc2! Na5 15. e5! N×b3
16. e×f6? "A player like Mr. Lowe, whose foresight rarely extends
beyond two moves, and who has no fixed plan of action, stands but
a sorry chance against these vigorous young amateurs. It is quite evident, even at this early stage, that Black's game is hopeless"
—Staunton. Staunton's note comes at the worst possible timing.
16. Q×b3 d×e5 17. N×e5 would indeed have been very good for
White, while Bird's actual move radically turns the tables. 16. …
N×a1 17. f×g7? 17. Qc6† Qd7 18. Re1† is slightly better. 17. …
Rg8 18. Qc6† Qd7 18. … Kd8! is the safest move. If 19. Bg5 f6 and
if 19. Re1? B×f3. Obviously White then has nothing for the rook.
19. Qe4† Be6 20. Q×h7 f6 21. Re1 Kf7?? There is no honor to be
found on this side of the board. 21. … Kd8! stops White's direct attack. He still has some chances to mess around, but that's it.
22. Qh5† K×g7 23. R×e6! "At first view, this looks like lost time,
but it is the best play, for suppose White to make the obvious
23. Bh6†, his opponent might escape from his embarrassments:
23. … Kh8 24. bishop moves and gives check"—Staunton. 23. … Rh8
24. Qg4† Kf8 25. R×f6† Ke8 26. N×d6†! c×d6 27. Qg6† Kd8

**28. R×d6 Rh7 29. Qg8† Kc7 30. R×d7†
R×d7 31. Bf4†** and White wins—*Chess
Player's Chronicle* (Staunton), June 1849, pp.
174–175.

**(57) Bird–Lowe    1–0**
Offhand game (?)
London (Simpson's Divan) 1849 (?)
*B30*

  **1. e4 c5 2. Nf3 Nc6 3. Nc3 e5 4. Bc4 Be7
5. 0-0 Nf6 6. d3 0-0 7. Ne1 Na5 8. Bb3
N×b3 9. a×b3 d5 10. e×d5 N×d5 11. f4
N×f4 12. B×f4 Qd4† 13. Kh1 e×f4 14. Ra4
Qd8 15. Ra×f4 Bd6 16. R4f2 Qh4 17. Nf3
Qh5 18. Ne4 Bc7 19. Qd2 Bg4 20. Qg5
B×f3 21. Nf6† Kh8 22. N×h5 B×h5
23. Q×h5 f6 24. Rf3 Be5 25. Q×e5** and
White wins—*Horae Divianianae*, p. 151.

**(58) Lowe–Bird    0–1**
Match (game 1)
London, 8 September 1850
*B21*

  **1. e4 c5 2. f4 Nc6 3. Nf3 e6 4. c4 g6 5. Nc3 Bg7 6. d3 d6 7. Be2
Nge7 8. 0-0 0-0 9. Be3 b6 10. d4 c×d4 11. N×d4 Bb7 12. Bf3
Rc8 13. Ndb5 B×c3 14. b×c3 Na5 15. N×d6 Rc7 16. N×b7
Q×d1 17. Ra×d1 N×c4 18. Bc1 R×b7 19. Rd4 Rc7 20. Rfd1 e5
21. Rd8 Nc6 22. R×f8† K×f8 23. f5 f6 24. Be2 Ne7 25. g4 g×f5
26. g×f5 b5 27. Bh6† Kf7 28. Bh5† Ng6 29. f×g6† h×g6
30. B×g6†** "This was a mistake. He meant, of course, to withdraw
the attacked piece"—Harrwitz. **30. ... K×g6 31. Bc1 Kf7** The published score omits 31. Bc1 Kf7, and continues at once with 31. Rd3,
which makes no sense at all. **32. Rd3 a5 33. Kf2 Ke6 34. a3 Nd6
35. Kf3 Rc4 36. Re3 N×e4 37. R×e4 R×c3† 38. Be3 f5 39. Rh4
f4 40. Rh8** Here "40. R takes RP" (rook takes a pawn on the h-file)
is given. **40. ... R×e3† 41. Kf2 R×a3** and Black wins—*Family
Friend* (Harrwitz), vol. III, p. 272.

**(59) Bird–Lowe    ½–½**
Match (game 2)
London, 8 September 1850
*B21*

  **1. e4 c5 2. f4 Nc6 3. Nf3 e6 4. Bb5 f5 5. e5 Nh6 6. 0-0 d5
7. Nc3 c4 8. B×c6† b×c6 9. d4 Bb4 10. Ne2 0-0 11. c3 Be7
12. Bd2 c5 13. Ng3 Bd7 14. h3 a5 15. a4 Rb8 16. Qc2 Qb6 17. Bc1
Qb3 18. Rf2 Rb7 19. Be3 Rfb8 20. Q×b3 R×b3 21. Ra2 c×d4
22. B×d4 Nf7 23. Re2 Nd8 24. Nf1 Nc6 25. Ne3 h5 26. g4 h×g4
27. h×g4 f×g4 28. N×g4 N×d4 29. N×d4 Bc5 30. Ne3 B×d4
31. c×d4 Rf8 32. f5 Rd3 33. f6 g×f6 34. Ng4 f×e5 35. N×e5 Rg3†
36. Kh2 Rg7 37. N×d7 Rf5 38. Rg2 R×g2† 39. K×g2 Rf4
40. Nc5 R×d4 41. N×e6 Rd2† 42. Kf3 c3 43. Ra1 c×b2 44. Rb1
Kf7 45. Ke3 Rc2 46. Nd4 Rc4 47. R×b2 R×a4 48. Rb5 Ra1
49. R×d5 a4 50. Ke4 a3** drawn game—*Family Friend*, vol. III, p.
354.

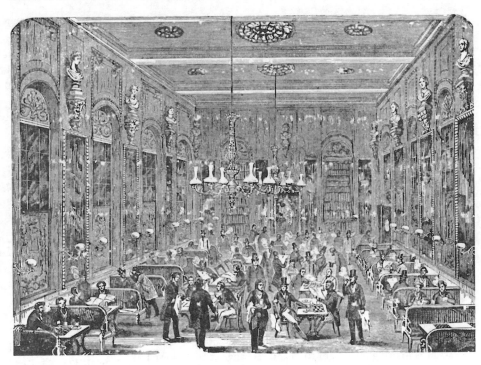

**A Scene at Simpson's Divan (courtesy Savoy Archives).**

# OFFHAND AND VARIOUS 1848–1850

  In the next game Bird faced Elijah Williams. Williams originated
from Bristol but moved to London in 1844 in the hope of earning
his living as a professional chess player. For this noble purpose he
gave up his job as a surgeon. Williams scored his best result in London 1851 where he narrowly missed the final but beat Staunton in
the match for third place. Only three years later Williams succumbed during the cholera epidemic that hit London.

**(60) Bird–E. Williams    1–0**
Offhand game
London 1849
*C01*

  **1. e4 e6 2. d4 d5 3. e×d5 e×d5 4. Nf3 Nf6 5. Bd3 Bd6 6. 0-0
0-0 7. c3 Ne4 8. Nbd2** 8. c4 undermines the stability of the knight.
**8. ... f5 9. c4 c6 10. c×d5** This exchange helps Black as c6 becomes
available for his knight. At once 10. Qb3 is better. **10. ... c×d5
11. Qb3 Kh8 12. Qc2 Nc6 13. a3 h6** A bit slow. There were various
interesting possibilities, e.g., 13. ... Be6, 13. ... Qb6 or 13. ... g5. **14. b4
a6 15. Nb3 Qf6 16. Bb2 g5** Now that the pawn at d4 is well defended this push is a bit too rash. **17. Nfd2** 17. Ne5 tries, at the cost
of a pawn, to profit from the weakening of Black's kingside. There
could follow 17. ... N×e5 18. d×e5 B×e5 19. B×e5 Q×e5 20. f3 Nd6
21. Rfe1 Qf6 22. Qc5 Rd8 23. Rac1. **17. ... g4 18. f4 g×f3 *e.p.*** "The
prudence of exchanging pawns here is rather questionable, since it
affords so much freedom to White's rook"—Staunton. 18. ... g3 is
better for this reason. The pawn at f4 might become weak one day.
**19. R×f3 Qh4** The threat at h2 is a bit too obvious. The disadvantage of this move is that it lures White's rook into a dangerously

offensive position. To avoid this, 19. ... Ng5 could be played. **20. Rh3 Qg5** "20. ... Qf2† seems to answer no good purpose"—Staunton. **21. Re1** 21. Nf3 Qg7 22. Rf1 is more to the point. If 21. ... Qe3† 22. Kf1. **21. ... Rg8 22. Nf3 Qg7 23. Ne5 Bxe5?** The bishop is far too important to exchange. He obtains a solid position with 23. ... Be6. **24. dxe5 Be6** *(see diagram)* "The menacing aspect of the rook at h3 is a serious restraint upon Black's movements"—Staunton.

*After 24. ... Be6*

**25. Bc1?!** 25. Rf1! is the right way to bring fresh powers to the front. If 25. ... f4 26. Rh4 and the pawn is lost. After other moves the rook can join the attack by f4. Another idea, now or at a later stage, is to bring the knight to c5 and exchange at e6, followed by Bxe4, with the purpose of opening the f-file. **25. ... f4 26. Rh4 Raf8?** There is no point in defending this pawn. 26. ... Rac8, 26. ... Ng5 or 26. ... Nxe5 are all playable options, although White's grip on the position remains intact. **27. Bxf4 Ng5 28. Kh1 Ne7 29. Nd4** Black is doomed now. **29. ... Bf7 30. e6!** "The attack is kept up bravely all through"—Staunton. **30. ... Bg6 31. Bxg6** 31. Be5! is the best move. **31. ... Qxg6 32. Qxg6** 32. Qc7 keeps the queens on the board. Since White is attacking, this is in his favor. **32. ... Rxg6 33. Bxg5** Bird is much too keen to gain another pawn. 33. g3 keeps his opponent under pressure. **33. ... Rxg5 34. Rxh6† Kg7 35. Rh3 Re5** 35. ... Rf2 is more tenacious. **36. Rg3† Ng6 37. Rc1 Rc8 38. Rf1 Rf8** "This see-saw is pretty enough. White evidently must not accept the proffered donum"—Staunton. **39. Kg1 Rxf1† 40. Kxf1 Re4 41. e7 Kf7 42. Nf5 Rf4† 43. Rf3 b6 44. Kf2 a5 45. bxa5 bxa5 46. Kg3 Rxf3† 47. Kxf3 Ne5† 48. Ke3 Nc4† 49. Kd4 Nxa3 50. Kxd5 Nb5 51. Nd6† Nxd6 52. Kxd6 Ke8 53. Kc5** and White wins—*Chess Player's Chronicle* (Staunton), September 1849, pp. 262–263.

Bird's opponent in the two following games was the strong amateur James Stanley Kipping (1822–1899). Just as with Simons, his name was often misspelled. In the games below he was respectively named Kepping and Hepping. J.S. Kipping's active period occurred above all during the 1850s. In 1855, he played four matches with John Owen. Each player twice won a match, but Kipping's overall score was one point higher. Kipping played several offhand games with Morphy and Anderssen. He scored a small majority (5 against 4) against the Prussian champion.

**(61) Bird–Kipping   1–0**
Offhand game
London 1849
*C51*

1. e4 e5 2. Nf3 Nc6 3. Bc4 Bc5 4. b4 Bb6 5. 0–0 Nxb4 6. Nxe5

d5 7. exd5 Bd4 8. Nxf7 Kxf7 9. c3 Bf6 10. d6† Kf8 11. Ba3 c5 12. d4 Qxd6 13. cxb4 Qxd4 14. Nd2 Qxa1 15. Qh5 Qxf1† 16. Kxf1 g6 17. Qxc5† Be7 18. Qd5 Nh6 19. Bb2 Rg8 20. Qf3 Bf5 21. Bxg8 Nxg8 22. g4 and White wins—*Chess Player's Chronicle*, September 1849, p. 268.

**(62) Kipping–Bird   ½–½**
Offhand game
London 1850 (?)
*C44*

1. e4 e5 2. Nf3 Nc6 3. c3 Nf6 4. d4 d6 5. Bg5 Be7 6. d5 Nb8 7. Bxf6 Bxf6 8. Be2 0–0 9. 0–0 Be7 10. Nbd2 f5 11. Bd3 f4 12. g3 Bh3 13. Re1 Nd7 14. Bf1 Bg4 15. h3 Bh5 16. g4 Bg6 17. Bg2 h5 18. Nh2 hxg4 19. Qxg4 Rf6 20. Qe2 Bh7 21. Ng4 Rg6 22. Kh2 Nf6 23. Rg1 Qd7 24. Bf3 Rf8 25. Nxf6† Rgxf6 26. Bg4 Qe8 27. Be6† Kh8 28. f3 Rh6 29. Rg2 Bh4 30. Rag1 Bg3† 31. Kh1 Qxe6 32. Rxg3 Rxh3† 33. Rxh3 Qxh3† 34. Qh2 Qxh2† 35. Kxh2 Rf6 36. Nc4 Rh6† 37. Kg2 Rg6† 38. Kf2 Rxg1 39. Kxg1 Kg8 40. Na5 b6 41. Nc6 a5 42. Nd8 g5 43. Ne6 g4 44. Kg2 gxf3† 45. Kxf3 Bg6 46. Nxc7 Bh5† 47. Kf2 Kf7 48. Nb5 Ke7 49. b4 a4 50. c4 Bd1 51. Nc3 Bc2 52. Ke2 a3 53. Kd2 f3 54. Ke3 Kd7 55. Kxf3 Bd3 56. c5 dxc5 57. bxc5 bxc5 58. Ke3 Bc4 59. Kd2 Kc7 60. Kc2 Kd6 61. Nb1 Bxa2 62. Nxa2 Kc7 63. Kb2 Bxd5 64. exd5 Kd6 draw—*La Régence*, November 1850, pp. 348–349.

A short game against a little known habitué of the Divan:

**(63) Nesbitt–Bird   0–1**
Offhand game
London (Simpson's Divan) 1849
*C50*

1. e4 e5 2. Nf3 Nc6 3. Bc4 Be7 4. 0–0 f5 5. exf5 d5 6. Bb5 Bd6 7. Re1 Nge7 8. Nxe5 0–0 9. Nxc6 bxc6 10. Ba4 Nxf5 11. Bxc6 Qh4 12. Bxd5† Kh8 13. g3 Nxg3 14. hxg3 Bxg3 15. fxg3 Qxg3† 16. Bg2 Bb7 17. Re2 Rae8 18. Qe1 Qxe1† 19. Rxe1 Rxe1† 20. Kh2 Rf2 White resigns—*Horae Divanianae*, pp. 105–106.

Finally, a few games in which Bird gave odds to a few weak players have been preserved.

**(64) Bird–Schröder   1–0**
Offhand game
London (Simpson's Divan) 1849
*Odds of Nb1*

1. e4 e5 2. f4 Bc5 3. Nf3 d6 4. c3 Bg4 5. Bc4 Bxf3 6. Qxf3 Nc6 7. b4 Bb6 8. a4 a6 9. Rb1 Nf6 10. b5 Na5 11. Ba2 0–0 12. f5 c5 13. 0–0 c4† 14. Kh1 Ba7 15. g4 Nd7 16. d3 cxd3 17. g5 Nc5 18. f6 g6 19. Qh3 Qd7 20. Qh6 Ne6 21. Rf3 Kh8 22. Rh3 White wins—*Bell's Life*, 28 October 1849.

The history of the following game is curious. It was published in *Bell's Life* and *Horae Divanianae* (p. 29) with Bird giving the odds of removing the Nb1. Bird himself included the game in his column in the *Sheffield and Rotherham Independent* on 17 March

1883. He mentioned that he gave the odds of the knight, but a variation at move 13 suggests the presence of this piece! A year later, the game was published in *Modern Chess* (p. 11), this time without mentioning this variation.

### (65) Bird–Schröder    1–0

Offhand game
London (Simpson's Divan) 1849
*Odds of Nb1*

1. e4 e5 2. Nf3 Nc6 3. Bc4 Bc5 4. b4 B×b4 5. c3 Bc5 6. 0–0 Nf6 7. d4 e×d4 8. e5 Ng4 9. B×f7† Kf8 10. c×d4 Be7 11. Bh5 d6 12. h3 Nh6 13. e6 d5 14. Re1 Nf5 15. Qd3 g6 16. Q×f5† g×f5 17. Bh6† Kg8 18. Bf7† mates—*Bell's Life*, 28 October 1849.

### (66) Bird–Pinkerley    1–0

Offhand game
London (Simpson's Divan) 1850
*Odds of Ng1*

1. e4 e5 2. Bc4 Nf6 3. 0–0 Bc5 4. c3 N×e4 5. d4 Bb6 6. d×e5 0–0 7. Bd5 Ng5 8. Qh5 Ne6 9. Be4 g6 10. Qh6 d5 11. e×d6 *e.p.* Q×d6 12. Na3 Ng7 13. Bf4 Qf6 14. Rae1 Nf5 15. B×f5 Q×f5 16. Be5 f6 and White announced mate in seven moves—*Illustrated London News*, 30 March 1850.

### (67) Bird–Pinkerley    1–0

Offhand game
London (Simpson's Divan) 1850
*Odds of Ra1*

1. e4 e5 2. Nf3 Nc6 3. Bc4 Bc5 4. 0–0 Nf6 5. c3 0–0 6. d4 e×d4 7. c×d4 Bb6 8. e5 d5 9. e×f6 d×c4 10. Bg5 g6 11. d5 Nb8 12. b3 c×b3 13. Q×b3 Bg4 14. Nbd2 B×f3 15. N×f3 Qd7 16. Bc1 c6 17. Ne5 Qc7 18. Bb2 Nd7 19. Ng4 Nc5 20. Qe3 Ne6 21. Qh6 c×d5 22. Qg7† N×g7 23. Nh6† Kh8 24. f×g7 mate—*Sheffield and Rotherham Independent*, 17 March 1883.

# THE CHESS MASTERS GATHER: LONDON 1851

From May until October 1851 the eyes of the world focused on London, at the scene of the Great Exhibition. In a newly constructed building, the Crystal Palace, Great Britain and its colonies demonstrated their modern industrial technology. The Great Exhibition marked the beginning of a series of world's fairs, a very popular feature during the nineteenth century. The interest generated by these fairs was a fertile field for chess organizers, and international tournaments were regularly going to concur with them. The idea to use the opportunity of the Great Exhibition to organize the first international chess tournament was mainly developed and supported by Howard Staunton.[39] An alternative tournament was set up by the London Chess Club, but this could hardly be called a success. The committee had just provided one prize, which made anyone losing their chance to gain it drop out along the way. Ultimately Adolf Anderssen won (also) this tournament.

The main event was organized by and played at the rooms of the St. George's Chess Club. The most prominent foreign players among the 16 participants were Anderssen, the strongest German player, Kieseritzky, who set the tone in Paris, and József Szén from Budapest. Six spots were reserved for the British players. Despite heavy organizational preoccupations, Staunton also entered the field. Bird was the youngest of the participants.

Practically all of the world's strongest players had been invited by Staunton, but several of them were unable to attend. One of the Russians, von Jaenisch, arrived just too late to enter into the fray. Other notable foreign absentees were Saint-Amant, von der Lasa and Petrov. The split between the two largest London chess clubs resulted in the nonappearance of players from the London Chess Club. Some weaker players were called to fill the gaps left by the absent masters.

The adopted knock-out formula was similar to the 1849 event. The players were paired by lot in eight matches that were played for a best-of-three (draws not counting). The losers were excluded from the tournament, while the eight winners were already sure of a part of the considerable prize fund.

In the subsequent rounds matches were played according to a best-of-seven principle. The losers from the second (and also the third) round continued to play, so that an exact ranking among the eight survivors of the first round was determined. It was not long before severe flaws in the pairing system were demonstrated. Already in the first round strong players such as Kieseritzky and Johann Jacob Löwenthal were eliminated. Much more luck had the obscure Mucklow, a very weak substitute. He survived the first round thanks to a favorable pairing and was already entitled to a prize. Despite the criticism it was eleven years, until the congress of London 1862, before the knock-out formula was replaced by roundrobin tournaments.

Another deficiency in the rules was the absence of a time limit. Some players were accused of attempting to out-sit their opponents. A first step to solve this matter was the introduction of chess clocks in 1862. During the subsequent decades the number of moves that had to be made within an hour became a hot topic. Bird was one of the more outspoken voices in that debate.

Bird found himself paired with Bernhard Horwitz in the first round. Their match was widely anticipated: would one of England's finest juniors be able to hold himself against the experienced Prussian? Horwitz already gained his fame during the 1830s when he established himself as a leading player in Berlin. He moved to England in 1845 where he found his means of existence as a chess player and teacher, and as a painter. During his career Horwitz played several matches against the most prominent players of his time but he nearly lost all of them.[40] In fact, his two wins against Bird in 1851,

---

39. The historian Harold Murray summed it up: "It was he who made the first public suggestions that the Great Exhibition offered an appropriate opportunity for the holding of a chess congress. He secured a strong committee, enlisted the active interest of the St. George's Club, and did the preliminary work that was necessary to make the tournament a success. Unfortunately, petty jealousies were aroused, and the London Chess Club resented the prominent part allotted to the St. George's Club, but their action did not affect the success of the official tournament." *British Chess Magazine*, December 1908, p. 515.

40. The reason for the small success of Horwitz was explained in his obituary: "He was seldom successful, but decidedly not on account of lack of ingenuity and skill, but chiefly owing to an excitable temperament, which led him frequently to throw away, by one hasty move, the fruits of hours of hard work and rare talent." *Chess Monthly*, September 1885, p. 8.

in the tournament and in the subsequent match, were considered his best results.

Horwitz opened the first game, which developed an interesting and complicated middle game. Bird managed to extricate some advantage and reached an endgame with two knights against rook and pawn. In this phase his play got flawed and the experienced Horwitz prevailed. By failing to understand some subtleties Bird had to take a painful loss.

The second game was equally tense. Bird sacrificed two pawns to obtain a very menacing position. Horwitz initially defended very well but lost the thread in the continuing complications. Bird now sacrificed his queen against two rooks. Both of his rooks cooperated very well and forced Black to a transition into a lost endgame.

In the third game Horwitz quickly gained a clear advantage but he could not manage to convert it into something real. At move 29, Horwitz committed a major error that resulted in the loss of a piece. All of a sudden Bird was confronted with a winning endgame. Unfortunately he produced some passive moves and Horwitz was able to draw the game.[41]

In the final game of the match Bird's ambition led him to a rapid decision mode of play. The position was not suited for such an aggressive approach and Horwitz needed only a bit of care to convert his material advantage to a full point. By doing so he qualified for the second round and Bird was eliminated from the tournament.

Bird nevertheless gained general praise with his at times brilliant play and his stubbornness. Both players had their share of chances to decide the combat and it is fair to say that Bird's failure was due to his weaker play in the endgame.

The top duel of the second round was played between Anderssen and Szén. Szén enjoyed the reputation of being an extremely strong and solid player and was considered as strong as Staunton. But this reputation did not withstand the aggressive assaults of the Prussian, and Szén was relentlessly eliminated for the main prizes. Three British combatants joined Anderssen in the semifinals: Staunton, Marmaduke Wyvill and Williams.

Once more Anderssen was tested in a clash, now with Staunton himself. The unofficial world champion was easily routed. The tasks of organizing the tournament and playing in it proved to be too

**International chess tournament, London, 27 May–23 July 1851**

*Site:* St. George's Chess Club
*Prizes:* 1st £183 6s. 8d., 2nd £55, 3rd £39 5s. 9d., 4th £27 10s., 5th £20, 6th £13 15s., 7th £9 3s. 4d., 8th £7 10s.

| A. Anderssen | 2½ | | | | | | |
| L. Kieseritzky | ½ | Anderssen | 4 | | | | |
| J. Szén | 2 | | | Anderssen | 4 | | |
| S. Newham | 0 | Szén | 2 | | | | |
| H. Staunton | 2 | | | | | Anderssen | 4½ |
| A. Brodie | 0 | Staunton | 4½ | | | | |
| B. Horwitz | 2½ | | | Staunton | 1 | | |
| H.E. Bird | 1½ | Horwitz | 2½ | | | | |
| M. Wyvill | 2 | | | | | | Anderssen |
| E. Lowe | 0 | Wyvill | 4½ | | | | |
| H.A. Kennedy | 2 | | | Wyvill | 4 | | |
| C. Mayet | 0 | H.A. Kennedy | 3½ | | | | |
| E. Williams | 2 | | | | | Wyvill | 2½ |
| J.J. Löwenthal | 1 | Williams | 4 | | | | |
| J.R. Mucklow | 2 | | | Williams | 3 | | |
| E.S. Kennedy | 0 | Mucklow | 0 | | | | |

*For prize 5–6:*

| Szén | 4 | | |
| Horwitz | 0 | Szén | 4½ |
| H.A. Kennedy | 4 | | |
| Mucklow | 0 | H.A. Kennedy | ½ |

*For prize 7–8:*

| Horwitz | | left unplayed |
| Mucklow | | |

heavy. The other semifinal was the most sensational contest of the whole tournament. Elijah Williams, considered the favorite, started with a hattrick, but by losing four times in a row it was Wyvill, who was also a Member of the British Parliament, who got through.

Though seen as a not so strong amateur, Marmaduke Wyvill fought with resilience against Anderssen. He justified his spot in the final by wringing more points out of the hands of the Prussian than anyone else, but he could not keep from losing with two against four wins. Staunton's fate was a bitter one. He lost the battle for third prize against Williams.

**(68) Horwitz–Bird   1–0**
International tournament (round 1, game1)
London, 27 May 1851
B21

**1. e4 c5 2. f4 d5 3. e×d5 Q×d5 4. Nc3 Qd8 5. Nf3 Nf6 6. Ne5 e6 7. Bb5† Bd7 8. Qf3** "Already the position assumes an aspect unusually interesting at the opening of a close game"—Staunton. **8. ... Qc7 9. B×d7† N×d7 10. 0-0 a6 11. d3 Bd6** More prudent is 11. ... Be7, as the bishop is a bit exposed at d6. **12. Nc4 0-0** If the bishop retreats White can take the initiative with 13. f5! Better however is 12. ... Rb8, as White can snatch the b-pawn without much risk after the coming exchange. **13. N×d6 Q×d6** "I am glad to find

41. According to the tournament book the match started with this draw. This author switched the first and third game, as sources drafted at the time of playing (*Illustrated London News* of 31 May 1851 and *Deutsche Schachzeitung*, June/July 1851, p. 169) state that Horwitz won the first game.

that as a youngster only, I had no prejudice for a bishop over a knight, the only weak drawback in modern play of such masters as Paulsen, Boden, Blackburne, and Steinitz. Further I do not believe that the values assigned by Philidor, Staunton, and other great authorities are correct. They are not in accord with my experience" —Bird. **14. f5 Ne5** The simple 14. ... e×f5 16. Q×f5 Rae8 is slightly better for Black. **15. Qg3 e×f5 16. R×f5 Nfd7 17. Bf4 f6 18. Rf1 Qe6** 18. ... Rae8 completes the development. Now Horwitz had the opportunity to reach a favorable endgame by 19. B×e5! f×e5 (less good is 19. ... N×e5 20. Ne4 Nd7 21. c4! the rook will transfer to d5, when White dominates the game) 20. R×f8† R×f8 21. R×f8† N×f8 22. Qf3 with a slightly better ending. It is no surprise that, against his inexperienced opponent, Horwitz was eager to keep the position complicated. **19. Bd2 Rae8 20. b3 Nc6 21. R5f2 Nd4 22. Bh6 Rf7** Defending the pawn by 22. ... Re7 avoids the coming complications. **23. Ne4! f5?!** Better is 23. ... Ne5, forcing White to agree with mass exchanges after 24. c3 (the alternatives are bad: 24. N×f6†?? Q×f6, 24. N×c5? Qg4! or 24. Kh1? Ng4) 24. ... N×d3 25. Q×d3 Q×e4 26. Q×e4 R×e4 27. c×d4 g×h6 28. d×c5 Kg7. Black should be able to draw the game. **24. Nd6 Q×h6 25. N×e8 Re7?** 25. ... Qe6 is correct, but White's superiority remains undisputed after 26. c3 f4 27. Qh3 Ne2† 28. R×e2 Q×e2 29. Nd6. **26. Qd6!** 26. Qc7 is also very strong. **26. ... Qe3 27. Qd5†** "The play on both sides is highly spirited, but Mr. Horwitz did wrong to give check; he should rather have played 27. Nc7, threatening 28. Nd5"—Staunton. The check is not bad at all, but 27. Nc7! makes his task indeed much easier. **27. ... Kf8 28. Nd6?** *(see diagram)* A surprisingly serious error. After 28. Nc7 White's knight is en route to d5 again. Most tenacious now is 28. ... g6, but after 29. c4! Kg7 30. Qd6, the knight will finally reach d5 with utter dominance.

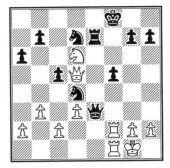

*After 28. Nd6*

**28. ... Nf6!** "White's queen is now in a situation of great peril, and, although Mr. Horwitz acquits himself in this difficulty with characteristic ingenuity, he cannot avoid some loss"—Staunton. **29. N×f5 Q×f2† 30. K×f2 N×d5** "If he had made the very natural 30. ... Re2†, it would have cost him the game, for instance: 31. Kg1 N×d5 32. N×d4† and afterwards 33. N×e2"—Staunton. **31. N×e7 K×e7 32. Re1† Kd6 33. Rc1?** Black's knights are stronger than the rook, but with active play (33. Re8), White could create many practical problems. A passive attitude in such endgames regularly turns out badly. **33. ... Nc3?!** "33. ... Nb4 would have been much stronger"—Staunton. **34. a3 b5 35. Ke3 Kd5?!** Now White gets slightly the better prospects again. Yet, the win is problematic as Black can gain a pawn, but only at the cost of dislocating his knights, e.g., 35. ... Na2 36. Rf1 N×c2† 37. Kd2 Nd4 (not 37. ... N×a3? 38. Rf7 and White comes out on top) 38. Rf7 b4 39. a×b4 N×b3†

40. Kc2 Nd4† 41. Kb2 N×b4 42. R×g7 N×d3† 43. Kc3 Nf4 44. R×h7 N×g2 and it is likely that a drawn endgame with just two knights against bare king will arise. **36. Kd2 b4 37. a×b4 Na2?** After 37. ... c×b4, the game will probably end in a draw. **38. Rb1!** "A masterly coup de repos. If he had played the obvious move which ninety-nine players out of every hundred would have made, of 38. Ra1, his adversary would have played 38. ... N×b4, for if 39. c3 N×b3†, winning the rook"—Staunton. **38. ... c×b4 39. Ra1 Nc3 40. R×a6 Ke5 41. Ra7** "The play of Mr. Horwitz throughout this trying endgame elicited, as it deserved, the highest encomiums from the surrounding spectators"—Staunton. **41. ... Nf5 42. g4 Nd4 43. R×g7 Nf3† 44. Ke3 N×h2 45. d4† Kf6 46. R×h7 N×g4† 47. Kd3 Nd5 48. Ke4 Ke6 49. Ra7 Ngf6† 50. Kd3 Kf5 51. Kc4 Ke4 52. Ra6 Ke3?** Bird fought as a lion, but here he stumbles. After 52. ... Ne3† 53. Kc5 Kf5, a draw remains likely. **53. Rd6 Ke4 54. Kc5** Zugzwang... **54. ... Ne3 55. Re6†** and Mr. Bird surrendered—*Tournament Book* (Staunton), pp. 9–12; *Chess Novelties* (Bird), pp. 214–216.

## (69) Bird–Horwitz    1–0

International tournament (round 1, game 2)
London, May 1851
*C65*

**1. e4 e5 2. Nf3 Nc6 3. Bb5 Nf6 4. d4** Bird's favorite move against the Berlin defense. He also practiced the main line 4. 0–0 and, in later years, 4. Qe2. **4. ... N×d4 5. N×d4 e×d4 6. e5 Nd5 7. 0–0** "Better 7. Q×d4 at once"—Staunton. **7. ... Bc5 8. c3 a6 9. Bc4 Nb6 10. Bb3 d×c3** A bit risky. White has nothing special after 10. ... 0–0. **11. N×c3** A dangerous improvement is 11. Qg4! g6 12. Qf3 Qe7 13. N×c3, when it is hard to see how Black can escape from trouble on his weakened black squares. **11. ... 0–0 12. Ne4 Qe7** 12. ... Be7 is more logical. **13. Qh5** There are two very promising alternatives here: A—13. Re1! Q×e5 14. N×c5 Q×c5 15. Be3 Qa5 16. Rc1 d6 17. R×c7 Bg4 18. Qd2 the bishop pair is very strong. B—13. N×c5! In this line White even sacrifices two pawns, but again counts on his bishop pair for more than sufficient compensation. 13. ... Q×c5 14. Be3 Q×e5 15. Rc1! d5 16. Re1. But also after the text move Horwitz is subject to serious pressure, and he has to play extremely carefully to survive the coming onslaught. **13. ... d6?!** 13. ... Bd4 at the first glance looks stronger, but I believe the following moves will prove that would have been an imprudent move: 13. ... Bd4 14. Ng5 h6 15. N×f7 R×f7 16. B×h6 g×h6 17. Qg4† Kf8 18. B×f7 Q×f7 19. Q×d4 with a capital game" —Staunton. 13. ... d5! appears the only move to avoid an immediate loss. There could follow 14. e×d6 *e.p.* B×d6 15. Re1 Qe5 16. Bg5 Qf5 and the queen joins the defense. White keeps some light pressure. **14. Bg5?** Bird gives away a crucial pawn, although the ensuing complications keep on giving him practical chances. Instead, 14. Re1! remains surprisingly strong, e.g.: 14. ... Nd7 15. e×d6 B×d6 16. Bg5 Qe5 17. N×d6 and 18. Be7 wins material or 14. ... g6 15. Bg5! **14. ... Q×e5 15. Rae1 Nd5?** "Beautifully played. From this moment the game becomes exceedingly animated and instructive"—Staunton. The sober but ice cold 15. ... Qf5! 16. Bc2 Kh8! defends everything. Horwitz' move is intriguing, but renders White new ammunition for his attack. **16. N×c5** 16. Qh4, threatening 17. Nf6†, is also very good. **16. ... Nf6** "All this is very ingenious"—Staunton. **17. Qh4 Q×c5 18. B×f6** 18. Rc1! is very strong. Black cannot deal with the problem pawns c7 and f6. **18. ... g×f6 19. Re3?!** With this move, Bird allows his opponent a chance to build another defensive line. Much better is 19. Q×f6! Bf5 20. Re7, when White completely dominates the board. He may continue his attack by pushing the pawns on the kingside. **19. ... Bf5 20. Q×f6 Bg6 21. Rg3?!** Bird abandons the control over e5, which allows Horwitz to diminish the force of White's attack. Both 21. h4 Qf5 22. Qc3 and 21. Rfe1 keep the pressure intact. **21. ... Qe5! 22. Qh4** Bird refuses to restore material equality with 22. Q×e5 d×e5 23. Re1 Rfe8 24. Rge3 e4 25. Bd5 and ventures everything upon a risky attack. **22. ... Q×b2 23. f4! Qd4†!** "Preventing the advance of the formidable f-pawn"—Staunton. **24. Kh1 Rae8** Good enough, but evacuating the g-file looks safer: 24. ... Kh8 25. Qg5 f5 26. h4 Bf7 27. Rd1 Qb2 28. Rd2 Qa1† 29. Rd1, with a draw. **25. Qg5 Qf2 26. Rf3 Qd2** "Again preventing the advance of the pawn"—Staunton. **27. h4! c6** "With a twofold object; first, to enable him to shut out the opposing bishop; and secondly, to tempt White to march on with his h-pawn. Promising, however, as this move looks, the sequel shows it was not the best, Black in his combination having overlooked one very important coup which White has in store. In this situation Black has two pawns more than his adversary, but the advantage is somewhat counterbalanced by the attack White has obtained. Instead of playing, as Mr. Horwitz did, 27. ... c6, I would suggest that Black should now move 27. ... Kg7 28. Qg3 (White has other moves, but I doubt if he has any one which gives him so good a prospect of success. If he plays 28. h5, Black answers with 28. ... Re5 and wins) 28. ... Kh8 (for the purpose of playing 29. ... Rg8) 29. f5 Bh5. Black now maintains his superiority of force, and must soon have at least an equal position"—Staunton. Staunton's line 27. ... Kg7 is open to a few improvements. Firstly, he underestimates 28. h5. After 28. ... Re5 29. h6† Kg8 30. Qf6 Rh5† 31. Kg1 R×h6 32. f5 d5 33. Rd1 Qe2 34. Qc3, White is slightly better. Secondly, 29. f5? is very bad if Black replies 29. ... Bh5! 30. R3f2 Qe3. Instead, White should play 29. Qg5 Qb2 30. f5 f6 31. Qh6 Bf7 and White can force a draw with 32. R1f2 Qe5 33. Re2 Q×e2 34. Q×f6†. **28. h5 Re5!** *(see diagram)*

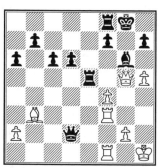

*After 28. ... Re5*

**29. B×f7†!** "A capital counterstroke. This is the move Mr. Horwitz evidently failed to consider when planning his line of attack" —Staunton. **29. ... R×f7 30. Qd8† Rf8 31. Q×f8† K×f8 32. f×e5† Kg7** Safer is 32. ... Ke7 (Staunton), when there could follow 33. h×g6 h×g6 34. Rf7† Ke6 35. e×d6 K×d6 36. R×b7 Q×a2 37. Rd1† Ke6 38. Rbb1 c5 39. Ra1. Although Black has two extra pawns, there are practically no chances that he makes use of them.

After 32. ... Kg7 Black should be able to hold, but any lapse might bring his king in definite problems. **33. h×g6 d×e5 34. g×h7 K×h7 35. Kh2 e4?** Here it is! Both 35. ... Qd6 and 35. ... Qd8 keep f6 and f8 under control, thus forcing White to give perpetual check. **36. Rh3† Kg6 37. Rg3† Kh7 38. Rf7† Kh6 39. Rf6† Kh5** If 29. ... Kh7 30. Rfg6, followed by 31. R6g4. **40. Rf8 Qd4 41. Rh8† Q×h8 42. Rh3† Kg4 43. R×h8 Kf4 44. Rf8† Ke3 45. Kg3** 45. g4 is simple enough. **45. ... c5 46. Rb8 b5 47. Rb6 c4 48. R×a6 c3 49. Rc6 Kd2 50. Kf4 e3 51. Rd6† Ke2 52. g4 Kf2 53. Rh6 e2 54. Rh2† Kf1 55. Kf3 e1N† 56. Ke3 Ng2† 57. R×g2 K×g2 58. g5 b4 59. Kd3** Black resigns—*Tournament Book* (Staunton), pp. 6–9.

## (70) Horwitz–Bird   ½–½
International tournament (round 1, game3)
London, 31 May 1851
*A10*

**1. c4 g6 2. e3 c5 3. f4 Bg7 4. Nf3 Nf6 5. Be2 d6 6. 0–0 Nc6 7. Na3 0–0 8. Nc2 Bf5** It is too early to define the best position of the bishop. 8. ... e5! takes profit of White's strange knight maneuver. **9. d3 Qb6 10. Qe1 e5 11. f×e5** "Surely 11. e4, followed by 12. f5, would have been much stronger"—Staunton. Perhaps 12. f×e5 d×e5 13. Ne3 is better than the pawn sacrifice 12. f5. **11. ... N×e5** Slightly better is 11. ... d×e5, so that the knight can jump to d4 later on. **12. N×e5** "Again, it strikes me that, owing to the situation of Black's knight at f6, White would have done better to play 12. e4"— Staunton. **12. ... d×e5 13. e4 Bg4?** After 13. ... Be6 White is just slightly better. **14. B×g4?** Both players and Staunton miss the directly winning 14. R×f6! **14. ... N×g4 15. Qg3 Nf6 16. Q×e5** Capturing the pawn looks risky. 16. Ne3 Rad8 or 16. Rb1 Rad8 17. Bg5 h6 are quite innocent. **16. ... Nh5 17. Qg5 B×b2** There is no reason for such hurry. First 17. ... Rad8 develops his forces before establishing material equality. **18. Rb1 Bd4†?** Though a pawn is lost, White's advantage is merely symbolic after 18. ... Bf6 19. R×b6 B×g5 20. R×b7 B×c1 21. R×c1 Nf4 22. Rd1 Rfb8. **19. Be3!** "19. N×d4 at first sight gives promise of a winning attack, but I believe Mr. Horwitz's play was the sounder"—Staunton. Horwitz' move is a strong rejoinder, cutting through Bird's plans. Yet, 19. N×d4 is also worth trying, as it demands nerves of steel from his opponent to survive the coming onslaught. But against a correct defense, it turns out that White has nothing, e.g., 19. ... Q×b1 20. Nf5 Kh8 21. Nd6 Q×d3 22. N×f7† R×f7 23. R×f7 Q×c4 24. Bb2† Kg8 25. Rf1 Q×e4 26. g4 Ng7 27. B×g7 K×g7 28. Qf6†. **19. ... B×e3† 20. N×e3 Qd8 21. Q×d8 Ra×d8** *(see diagram)*

*After 21. ... Ra×d8*

**22. Nd5?!** White faced a difficult choice between the text move and the infiltrating 22. R×b7! The latter deserves preference, as after 22. ... R×d3 (this is critical; 22. ... f5 avoids what's coming but at a great cost), he has the unexpectedly strong 23. Ng4! The knight is heading for h6, while 23. ... Rd6 is awful after 24. e5. **22. ... b6 23. a4 f5 24. e×f5 g×f5 25. Rbe1** "He might now have gained the f-pawn, but it would evidently have been at the expense of his own d-pawn. His best move, as I think, was 25. a5"—Staunton. **25. ... Rf7 26. Re5 Ng7 27. g4** 27. a5!, preparing a target for the rook at f1, poses more difficulties for his opponent. **27. ... f4 28. Rf3** More harmonious is 28. Rfe1!, followed by 29. R1e4 and the march of the king to f3. Black is unable to prevent the loss of the f-pawn, while White's pieces take up commanding posts. **28. ... Rd6 29. R×f4??** "A grave error"—Staunton. **29. ... R×d5 30. R×f7 R×e5 31. R×a7 Re6?!** All of a sudden, Bird is a piece ahead with prospects of winning the game. As a reaction, however, he starts to play very passively, thus allowing the endgame specialist Horwitz to escape with a draw. Crucial, here and on the next move, is the activation of his knight, e.g., after 31. ... Ne6! 32. Ra6 Nf4. **32. Kf2 Ne8** 32. ... Rh6, liberating e6 for the knight, is superior. **33. a5** "Mr. Horwitz makes some amends for his carelessness in the preceding moves, by the admirable manner in which he plays the termination of this game"—Staunton. **33. ... b×a5 34. R×a5 Rc6 35. Kf3 Kf7 36. Ra7† Nc7 37. Ke4 Re6† 38. Kf5 Rc6** "38. ... Re7 would have left the rook more freedom. I doubt, however, if any skill on Black's

part could have won the game"—Staunton. **39. h4 Ke7 40. g5 Kf7 41. h5 Kg7 42. Rb7 h6 43. g6 Rf6† 44. Ke5 Re6† 45. Kf4 Re7 46. Kf5 Nd5 47. Rb5** "If White intended only to make a drawn battle, his surest play was to have taken off the rook now"—Staunton. **47. ... Nb4 48. d4 Nd3 49. d×c5 Re5† 50. Kg4 Rg5† 51. Kh4 Nf2 52. Rb7† Kg8 53. Rb8† Kg7 54. Rb7†** and draws by perpetual check—*Tournament Book* (Staunton), pp. 4–6.

**(71) Bird–Horwitz    0–1**
International tournament (round 1, game 4)
London, 2 June 1851
*B30*

1. e4 c5 2. Nf3 Nc6 3. Bb5 Qc7 4. 0-0 e6 5. Nc3 a6 6. B×c6 b×c6 7. e5 Ne7 8. d3 Ng6 9. Re1 Be7 10. b3 f6 11. Ne4 f×e5 12. Bg5 d6 13. B×e7 Q×e7 14. Neg5 h6 15. Ne4 0-0 16. Re3 Nf4 17. g3 Nd5 18. Re1 Bd7 19. c4 Nf6 20. Re3 Be8 21. N×f6† Q×f6 22. Qd2 e4 23. Rae1 e×f3 24. Re4 e5 25. Kh1 Bd7 26. g4 Qg5 27. Qa5 B×g4 28. Rg1 h5 29. Qc7 Qd2 30. Q×d6 Q×f2 31. R×e5 Q×g1† 32. K×g1 f2† and White resigns—*Tournament Book*, pp. 12–13]

# MATCH WITH HORWITZ 1851

The international tournament was accompanied by several side events. In the provincial tournament, for which ten participants signed up, Bird's good friend Samuel Boden emerged as winner.

Immediately after Anderssen gained the first prize, he was challenged to play a match by Staunton. Anderssen principally accepted the offer but as he was unable to stay in London much longer no such contest was ever held. Plans to play a consultation match between the Englishmen and the foreigners also fell through. With the remaining funds, the committee was able to arrange a few matches.[42] In view of their tense match played in the tournament a new encounter between Bird and Horwitz was generally desired. Bird's early sortie was considered to have come hand in hand with a bit of bad luck. A more extended match, the winner the first player to win seven games, could rehabilitate Bird's reputation. The match commenced early in August at the St. George's Chess Club. Just like the other matches between participants of the international tournament (or players of equal standing), £20 was to be divided between Bird and Horwitz. The winner would receive the major share of £16.

Bird had a good start and took the lead twice. After a series of three draws, the seventh game proved to be the turning point. Bird spoiled a winning attack, lost, and also succumbed in the three following games. He drew the eleventh game, won the twelfth but then Horwitz decided the match by scoring two final wins. A return match was suggested, but didn't materialize.

**Bernhard Horwitz (*Chess Monthly*).**

42. "...[T]he committee of management resolved to bring the tourney to an end by a series of picked matches, so arranged as to afford an opportunity for those players who had been unfortunate in the earlier contests to retrieve their laurels and at the same time, to insure an interesting addition of good games for the amusement of the subscribers." H. Staunton, *The Chess Tournament: London 1851*. London: Batsford, 1986, p. lxxii.

| **Match with Horwitz, August–September 1849** | | | | | | | | | | | | | | |
|---|---|---|---|---|---|---|---|---|---|---|---|---|---|---|
| | 1 | 2 | 3 | 4 | 5 | 6 | 7 | 8 | 9 | 10 | 11 | 12 | 13 | 14 |
| B. Horwitz | 0 | 1 | 0 | ½ | ½ | ½ | 1 | 1 | 1 | 1 | ½ | 0 | 1 | 1 | 7 |
| H.E. Bird | 1 | 0 | 1 | ½ | ½ | ½ | 0 | 0 | 0 | 0 | ½ | 1 | 0 | 0 | 3 |

### (72) Bird–Horwitz    1–0

Match (game 1)
London, August 1851
C65

1. e4 e5 2. Nf3 Nc6 3. Bb5 Nf6 4. d4 e×d4 5. e5 Ne4 6. 0–0 f5 7. N×d4 N×d4 8. Q×d4 Bc5 9. Qd3 0–0 10. Nc3 N×c3 11. b×c3 Qe7 12. Bf4 Kh8 13. Qg3 h6 14. h4 a6 15. Bd3 Qe6 16. Rfe1 b6 17. a4 Bb7 18. Re2 Rf7 19. Rd1 Rg8 20. Red2 Bc6 21. B×a6 g5 22. h×g5 h×g5 23. B×g5 Qg6 24. Bc4 Rfg7 25. Qh4† Rh7 26. Bf6† Rgg7 27. B×g7† K×g7 28. R×d7† B×d7 29. R×d7† and Black resigns—*Tournament Book*, pp. 295–296.

### (73) Horwitz–Bird    1–0

Match (game 2)
London, August 1851
C01

1. e4 e6 2. d4 d5 3. e×d5 e×d5 4. Bd3 Nf6 5. Nf3 Bd6 6. 0–0 0–0 7. Bg5 Be6 8. c3 c6 9. Ne5 Nbd7 10. f4 Qb6 11. N×d7 B×d7 12. B×f6 g×f6 13. Qh5 f5 14. Qg5† Kh8 15. Qf6† Kg8 16. Q×d6 Be6 17. b3 Rfe8 18. Nd2 and Black resigns the game—*Tournament Book*, p. 297.

### (74) Bird–Horwitz    1–0

Match (game 3)
London, August 1851
C65

1. e4 e5 2. Nf3 Nc6 3. Bb5 Nf6 4. 0–0 N×e4 5. d4 e×d4 6. Re1 f5 7. N×d4 Bc5 8. R×e4† f×e4 9. Qh5† g6 10. Q×c5 Qe7 11. Qc3 Ne5 12. Bf4 0–0 13. Bc4† N×c4 14. Q×c4† Rf7 15. Be3 c6 16. Qb3 d5 17. Nd2 c5 18. Ne2 d4 19. Bf4 d3 20. c×d3 Be6 21. Qc3 Bg4 22. N×e4 B×e2 23. Bg5 Qd7 24. Nf6† R×f6 25. Q×f6 B×d3 26. Bh6 Re8 27. Rd1 Bf5 28. Rc1 b6 29. h3 Qf7 30. Qc3 Rd8 31. Re1 Rd4 32. Qg3 Rd8 33. Qg5 Rd7 34. Re3 Rd1† 35. Kh2 Rd7 36. Qf4 Rd8 37. Qe5 Qd7 38. f4 Qf7 39. b3 Bb1 40. Re2 Bd3 41. Re3 Bb1 42. g4 c4 43. Qb2 Bd3 44. Qe5 Rc8 45. Qd6 g5 46. f5 c×b3 47. R×d3 Qc7 48. Q×c7 R×c7 49. a×b3 a5 50. B×g5 b5 51. Bf4 Rc2† 52. Kg3 b4 53. Kf3 Ra2 54. Ke4 Ra3 55. Kd4 a4 56. Kc4 a×b3 57. R×b3 Ra7 58. R×b4 Ra3 59. h4 Rh3 60. Bg5 h6 61. Rb8† and White wins—*Tournament Book*, pp. 297–299.

The two following games were published in reversed order in the tournament book:

### (75) Horwitz–Bird    ½–½

Match (game 4)
London, August 1851
B21

1. e4 c5 2. f4 Nc6 3. Nf3 e6 4. Bb5 Qb6 5. Nc3 Be7 6. d3 Nf6

7. B×c6 b×c6 8. 0–0 0–0 9. Na4 Qc7 10. c4 d5 11. Nc3 Ba6 12. b3 Rad8 13. Qe2 Rfe8 14. e5 Nd7 15. Bb2 f6 16. Rae1 f×e5 17. f×e5 Rf8 18. Nd1 Qa5 19. Bc3 Qc7 20. Bd2 Nb6 21. Bg5 Bc8 Both players overlooked 21. ... R×f3 which dissipates White's initiative at once. 22. B×e7 Q×e7 23. Rf2 Bd7 24. g3 Be8 25. Nh4 R×f2 26. N×f2 g5 27. Nf3 Bh5 28. Qe3 h6?! 28. ... B×f3 would have completed Bird's plan and brought him equality. 29. g4 Bg6 30. h4! With this move the game finally bursts open in White's advantage. 30. ... Rf8?! Already a desperate move, but 30. ... d4 31. Qd2 is very annoying. 31. h×g5 d4 32. Qe2 Qf7 "Had he played 32. ... h×g5, White would have retorted with 33. Nh3"—Staunton. 33. Kg2 h5 34. Rh1?! 34. Nd2! decides the game quickly, as the knight will be completely dominant on e4. 34. ... Nd7 35. Nh4? Definitely wrong. 35. b4! is a good try. 35. ... N×e5 36. N×g6?! 36. Rh3 is relatively better as h1 is vacated as a shelter for the king. 36. ... N×g6 37. Kg1 *(see diagram)*

*After 37. Kg1*

37. ... Nf4?! 37. ... Qf4! is very disturbing. There can follow 38. Ne4 h×g4 39. Nf6† R×f6! 40. g×f6 Qc1† 41. Qf1 Qe3† 42. Qf2 Q×d3 and Black must be able to win. After the text move Black has blocked his most important attacking resource, the f-file. 38. Qe4 38. Qe5 is safer as the knight might still go to e4. 38. ... e5 38. ... Ng6 keeps some pressure, e.g., 39. Qe2 (White must lose time now to allow the knight to e4) 39. ... h4 with tricks all over the place. 39. g×h5 N×h5?! Bird shuns absolutely no risk, but opening the h-file is extremely dangerous. 39. ... Qf5, exchanging queens, should lead to a draw. 40. Rh2! Ng3?! The only more or less playable move is 40. ... Qf4. The position remains very tricky, with both kings being in danger. In the end the situation looks more difficult for Black, e.g., 41. Qg6† Ng7 42. Qh7† Kf7 43. Rg2 Qe7 44. Kh1 Ke7 45. Ne4 Rf1† 46. Kh2 Qf4† 47. Rg3. 41. Qh4! Ne2† 42. Kf1 Qf5 43. K×e2 Qf3† 44. Kf1 44. Kd2 Qe3† 45. Kd1 wins immediately. 44. ... Q×d3† 45. Kg1 Qb1† 46. Kg2 Qf5 47. Rh3 e4 48. Q×e4? 48. g6 (Staunton) still wins on the spot. 48. ... Q×f2† and Black draws the game. Now Bird could even continue to press a bit with 49. Kh1 Qf5 50. Q×f5 R×f5, but the outcome should remain a draw—*Tournament Book* (Staunton), pp. 302–303.

### (76) Bird–Horwitz    ½–½

Match (game 5)
London, August 1851
C41

1. e4 e5 2. Nf3 d6 3. d4 e×d4 4. Bc4 Be7 5. N×d4 Nf6 6. Nc3 0–0 7. 0–0 N×e4 8. N×e4 d5 9. B×d5 Q×d5 10. Nc3 Qd8 11. Bf4 Na6 12. Re1 Bf6 13. Ndb5 Bd7 14. Qf3 Bc6 15. Qg3 B×c3

**16. N×c3 Qf6 17. B×c7 N×c7 18. Q×c7 Qg6 19. Qg3 Q×c2
20. Re2 Qf5 21. Rae1 Rad8 22. Re5 Qf6 23. h3 h6 24. b4 a6
25. a4 Rd4 26. b5 a×b5 27. a×b5 Bd7 28. Nd5 Qd6 29. Ne7†
Kh8 30. Qf3 b6 31. g4 Rd3 32. R1e3 R×e3 33. Q×e3 Re8
34. Ng6† f×g6 35. R×e8† B×e8 36. Q×e8† Kh7 37. Qc6 Qd4
38. Kg2 h5 39. g×h5 g×h5 40. Qe6 g6 41. Qf7† Kh6 42. Qf8†
Kh7 43. Qe7† Kg8 44. Qe6† Kg7 45. Qc6** and the game was
drawn—*Tournament Book*, pp. 300–301.

## (77) Horwitz–Bird    ½–½
Match (game 6)
London, August 1851
*C00*

1. e4 c5 2. f4 e6 3. Nf3 d5 4. e5 Be7 5. Bb5† Bd7 6. B×d7†
N×d7 "It is considered better play to take the bishop in similar
cases with the queen"—Staunton. 7. c3 Nh6 8. 0-0 0-0 9. d4 This
pawn will become a target. 9. d3 is safer. 9. ... Qb6 10. b3 f6 11. Ba3
"Mr. Horwitz fails to conduct the opening of this game with his
accustomed skill. 11. Ba3 is comparatively useless"—Staunton. 11. ...
Rad8 12. Kh1 Nf5 13. Re1 f×e5 14. f×e5 Rf7 15. Bc1 Rdf8 16. a4
a5 "Hardly vigorous enough, considering the superior development
of Black's forces. Why not rather have prosecuted the attack with
16. ... Nh4?"—Staunton. 16. ... c×d4 17. c×d4 Nb8! is also good.
17. Na3? c×d4 18. c×d4 Bb4 19. Bd2 B×a3 Not bad, but 19. ...
N×d4! 20. B×b4 N×f3 21. B×f8 N×e1 wins much easier. 20. R×a3
N×d4 21. Be3 Qb4? "He might have obtained a strong but insecure
attack by 21. ... N×f3, sacrificing his queen"—Staunton. 21. ... N×f3
22. B×b6 N×e1 23. Bg1 Rf1 is indeed very good for Black. But
there is a direct win available with 21. ... R×f3! 22. g×f3 Qb4 and
if 23. Ra2 N×f3 24. Ree2, Black has a pleasant choice between 24. ...
d4 and 24. ... N×h2. 22. N×d4 Q×a3 23. N×e6 Re8 24. Ng5
"This portion of the game is extremely animated. White appears
to have extricated himself completely from his embarrassments, and
has now, I think, the advantage of position"—Staunton. 24. ...
R×e5 25. N×f7 K×f7 26. Rf1† Nf6?! 26. ... Kg8 is advisable.
27. Bd4 Re6 28. B×f6 g×f6 29. Q×d5?! "I am strongly of opinion
that White might not only have gained two of the adversary's pawns,
but have acquired a great superiority of position by 29. Qh5†, and
then 30. Q×d5"—Staunton. 29. ... b6 30. Qf5 Q×b3 31. Q×h7†
Kf8 drawn game. White can play on with 32. Qh4 Kg7 33. h3, but
a win will be difficult to realize—*Tournament Book* (Staunton), pp.
304–306.

## (78) Bird–Horwitz    0–1
Match (game 7)
London, August 1851
*C41*

1. e4 e5 2. Nf3 d6 3. Bc4 Be6 4. B×e6 f×e6 5. d4 e×d4 6. N×d4
Qd7 7. 0-0 c5 8. Nf3 Nc6 9. Nc3 0-0-0 10. a4 a6 11. a5 Be7
12. Na4 Kb8 13. Nb6 Qc7 14. Bd2 Nf6 15. Ng5 Nd4 16. c3 h6
17. Nf7 Nc6 18. N×h8 R×h8 19. Qa4 Bd8 20. Rfe1 N×a5
21. Q×a5 Qc6 22. Qa4 Q×b6 23. b4 Ng4 24. h3 Ne5 and Black
eventually won. "Through some inattention on the part of the Secretary, the rest of the game was not recorded. It was won by Mr.
Horwitz"—Staunton. *Tournament Book* (Staunton), pp. 306–307.

## (79) Horwitz–Bird    1–0
Match (game 8)
London, August 1851
*B44*

1. e4 c5 2. d4 c×d4 3. Nf3 e6 4. N×d4 Nc6 5. Be3 g6 6. c3 Bg7
7. Nb5 Be5 8. f4 Bb8 9. e5 Nge7 10. Be2 Nd5 11. Bd2 0-0 12. c4
Nde7 13. Bc3 "The present opening is certainly entitled to the
merit of originality. Who could possibly have anticipated when
Black played his bishop to g7, that he would be found two moves
afterwards in the extraordinary position he now occupies?"—Staunton. 13. ... Bc7 "Owing to the carelessness with which the games
in this match were taken down, I have been repeatedly at a loss to
make out the moves. In the present instance, the manuscript gives
13. ... b6, but this, as the queen is played immediately after to that
square, is evidently not the move made. As the sequel shows, neither
is a6 or a5. In despair of finding the correct move, which appears
to have been a lost one in every sense, I venture to give 13. ... Bc7"
—Staunton. 14. Nd6 If the last move was actually played, 14. Qd3!,
preparing 15. Nd2 and 16. N2e4, would have been very good right
now. 14. ... B×d6 15. e×d6 Nf5 16. Qd3 Qb6 17. Na3 Qe3?! Bird's
ambition to reach an endgame is not well judged, as White gains
an obvious superiority, with his bishop pair, better development
and space advantage. Instead, 17. ... Nb4 18. Qd2 a5 leads to an interesting and balanced middle game. 18. Q×e3 N×e3 19. g4? "The
object Mr. Horwitz had in view by sacrificing the f-pawn is beyond
my comprehension. Was it an oversight?"—Staunton. 19. ... Ng2†
20. Kf2 N×f4 21. h4 f5 22. g5 N×e2 23. K×e2 (*see diagram*)

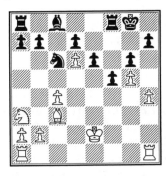

*After 23. K×e2*

23. ... e5?! Everything looks fine for Black, but White does has
some menaces thanks to the possibility to open the h-file. 23. ...
Nd8!, heading for f7, nips them in the bud. The knight would be
excellent at f7, controlling e5, h6 and h8, while attacking the d-
pawn. 24. h5! b6 25. h×g6 h×g6 26. Rh6 Kf7? The cure is worse
than the remedy. Instead, 26. ... Bb7! abandons the g-pawn at once,
but gains important time: 27. R×g6† Kf7 28. Rh6 Rh8 29. Rf6†
Kg7 30. R×f5 Rh2† and White cannot escape the perpetual.
27. Rh7†! Ke6 28. Nb5 Rb8 29. Rd1! "In this situation, instead
of 29. Rd1, White might have played 29. Bb4 with perfect safety.
In this case Black's only mode of escape is to advance his f-pawn. If
29. ... N×b4 30. Re7 mates; and if 29. ... e4 or 29. ... Rb7, his defeat,
though less immediate, is almost equally inevitable. The variations
will be found to be extremely interesting and instructive"—Staunton. Staunton overlooks 29. ... f4! 30. Nc7† Kf5 31. Bc3 Bb7 32. Kf2
Rh8, when White's pressure has led to less than nothing. Black's
central pawns are an important asset for the future. The move

actually made by Horwitz is by far the best. **29. ... f4 30. Nc7†** Strongest here is the thunderbolt 30. N×a7!, e.g., 30. ... Rb7 (not 30. ... N×a7 31. Re7† Kf5 32. R×e5† Kg4 33. Rg1† Kh3 34. Re7) 31. Nb5. **30. ... Kf5 31. Rg1** 31. Nd5 is the only way to keep a small edge. There could follow 31. ... Bb7 32. R×d7 Nd4† 33. B×d4 B×d5 34. c×d5 e×d4 35. R×a7. **31. ... Bb7 32. R×d7** Not so good anymore. Black can dispute the d-file without delay as his bishop is not under attack as in the line above. **32. ... Rbd8 33. Rh7 Ba8?** "Had he taken the d-pawn, White would have answered with 34. Nb5" —Staunton. But 33. ... Bc8! strongly centralizes the bishop. Black now threatens to take at d6, and if 34. Rd1 Rd7 35. R×d7 B×d7 36. Rh1 Be6, he comes out with the better chances. **34. d7 Bb7 35. Nb5 Ba6 36. a4 B×b5 37. a×b5 Nb8 38. Re7?** Horwitz misjudges the position by thinking he can catch Black's king in a mating net. Instead the solid 38. Rd1 nails Black down. **38. ... N×d7 39. Rd1 Nc5 40. R×e5† Kg4 41. Rg1† Kh3 42. Re7 f3† 43. Ke3 Rd7!** He must have overlooked this rejoinder which completely frustrates White's plans to deliver a mate. **44. R×d7 N×d7 45. Kf2 Nc5** An imprecise move that offers White some chances again. 45. ... Rf4! activates the rook. **46. Bf6! Ne4† 47. K×f3 N×g5†** Why not simply 47. ... Nd2† and 48. ... N×c4? **48. Kf4 Kh2?** 48. ... Nf3! is still very drawish. Bird had the same ambition with the text move, but his judgment turns out to be wrong. **49. R×g5 R×f6† 50. Ke5 Rf2 51. R×g6 R×b2 52. Kd5 Rd2† 53. Kc6 Rd4 54. Kb7 Rd7† 55. Ka6 Kh3 56. Rg8 Rc7 57. Ra8 Kg4 58. R×a7 R×c4 59. Rf7!** The winning move. All further resistance is futile! **59. ... Kg5 60. K×b6 Rc2 61. Kb7 Rc5 62. b6 Rc3 63. Kb8** and Black resigns—*Tournament Book* (Staunton), pp. 307–310.

## (80) Bird–Horwitz    0–1
Match (game 9)
London, August 1851
*C62*

1. e4 e5 2. Nf3 Nc6 3. Bb5 d6 4. c3 Bd7 5. d4 e×d4 6. c×d4 Be7 7. Nc3 Nf6 8. 0–0 0–0 9. h3 a6 10. Bd3 b5 11. a3 Ne8 12. b4 f5 13. Qc2 f×e4 14. B×e4 Nf6 15. Ng5 N×e4 16. Nc×e4 Rf5 17. Nf3 R×f3 18. g×f3 N×d4 19. Qd3 c5 20. Kh2 Qf8 21. f4 Qf5 22. Re1 d5 23. b×c5 d×e4 24. Q×d4 Bf6 25. Q×e4 Q×e4 26. R×e4 B×a1 27. Re7 Rd8 28. Be3 Bb2 29. Kg3 Kf8 30. Re4 B×a3 31. Bd4 Bf5 32. Re5 g6 33. Be3 Bb2 34. c6 B×e5 35. f×e5 Rc8 and White resigns—*Tournament Book*, pp. 310–312.

## (81) Horwitz–Bird    1–0
Match (game 10)
London, August 1851
*C01*

1. e4 e6 2. d4 d5 3. e×d5 e×d5 4. Bd3 Nf6 5. Nf3 Bg4 6. 0–0 Be7 7. h3 B×f3 8. Q×f3 0–0 9. c3 c5 10. d×c5 B×c5 11. Bg5 Be7 12. Nd2 Nc6 13. Rfe1 Qd6 14. Qf5 g6 15. Qf3 Ne5 16. Qg3 N×d3 17. Q×d3 Rae8 18. Bh6 Bd8 19. B×f8 R×f8 20. Re2 Bc7 21. Nf3 Nh5 22. Re5 Nf4 23. Qd4 Q×e5 24. Q×e5 B×e5 25. N×e5 Re8 26. Re1 Re6 27. Kf1 Kg7 28. h4 Kf6 29. Ng4† Ke7 30. Ne3 Kd6 31. g3 Nd3 32. Re2 f5 33. Rd2 Nc5 34. R×d5† Kc6 35. Rd4 Ne4 36. Kg2 b6 37. Nd5 b5 38. Nb4† Kb6 39. f3 Nc5 40. Kf2 Nb7 41. Nd5† Kc6 42. Nf4 "Nothing more clearly

shows the utter incompetence of Mr. Bird, though an amateur of lively imagination and unquestionable ability, to make a stand against such a player as Horwitz, than these endgames"—Staunton. **42. ... Rd6 43. R×d6† K×d6 44. Ke3 Nc5 45. b3 a5 46. Kd4 a4 47. b4 Nb3† 48. Kd3 Nc1† 49. Kc2 N×a2 50. Kb2 N×c3 51. K×c3 Ke5 52. Nd3† Kd5 53. Ne1 h6 54. Nc2 Ke5 55. Kd3 Kd5 56. Na3 g5 57. h×g5 h×g5 58. N×b5 Ke5 59. Na3 f4 60. g4 Kd5 61. Kc3 Kd6 62. Kc4** and Black resigns—*Tournament Book* (Staunton), pp. 312–314.

## (82) Bird–Horwitz    ½–½
Match (game 11)
London, August 1851
*C62*

1. e4 e5 2. Nf3 Nc6 3. Bb5 d6 4. c3 Bd7 5. d4 Nf6 6. 0–0 Be7 7. d5 Nb8 8. Bd3 0–0 9. Ne1 b6 10. f4 Bg4 11. Qc2 e×f4 12. B×f4 Nbd7 13. Nd2 Bh5 13. ... Nh5 14. Be3 Bg5 neutralizes White's best piece. **14. Nef3 h6 15. Rae1 Bg6 16. Nd4** The correct move. **16. ... Nc5 17. Bc4 a6 18. b4! Nb7 19. Bd3 Qd7 20. N2f3 Rfe8?!** *(see diagram)* 20. ... Kh8! is necessary, but it was very hard to find out why.

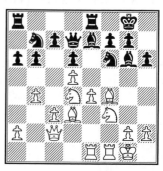

*After 20. ... Rfe8*

**21. c4?!** Bird's pieces are extremely well centralized, and one feels that the position is loaded with possibilities for him. The selected move, planning to open another front on the queenside, doesn't satisfy the demands of the position. Instead a logical consequence would have been 21. Nh4! Bh7 22. Nhf5, which augments the pressure against Black's kingside. But computer analysis reveals an even more forcing and brilliant continuation: 21. B×h6!! A thunderbolt out of the bluest of skies! The critical move is of course 21. ... g×h6 but then White continues with 22. e5! B×d3 23. Q×d3 d×e5 24. N×e5 Q×d5 25. c4 Qd6 and now there follows a beautiful finish: 26. N×f7!! K×f7 27. Qh7† Kf8 28. Q×h6† Kg8 29. Nf5 and wins. **21. ... a5** 21. ... Qg4 22. Bd2 a5 is better. The queen is in danger at d7. **22. Nh4** Better is 22. e5! B×d3 23. Q×d3 d×e5 24. N×e5 and if 24. ... Qc8 an already familiar line is reached where White can play 25. B×h6! **22. ... a×b4** This looks good but the prudent 22. ... Bh7 is better. **23. N×g6 f×g6 24. Nc6?!** Bird continues to divide his attention between both the king- and queenside, which is not bad, but the text move is actually too slow for it allows Black to take control over the all-important e5 square. An important breakthrough is realized by 24. c5! If 24. ... N×c5 25. Bb5 wins some material. After 24. ... Qc8 25. Bb5 Rf8 26. c×b6 c×b6 27. Bc6, White is firmly on top. **24. ... Nc5?!** **25. e5!** N×d3 25. ... d×e5 is relatively risk-free, but gives White a small edge. **26. Q×d3?** Too compliant, for White will now be a pawn down without enough compensation. Instead 26. e6! puts some fuel into the attacking machine. After the forced

26. ... N×e1, White can chose between 27. R×e1, which initiates a dangerous attack after 27. ... Qc8 28. Q×g6 Kh8 29. B×h6 Rg8. His compensation is beyond doubt after 30. Qf7! A crazy line occurs after 27. Q×g6, as 27. ... Q×c6! 28. d×c6 R×a2! is forced. The resulting lines are intriguing and very double-edged, but Black is fighting to survive. A sample line runs as follow: 29. g3! Bf8 30. R×e1 b3 31. Qf7† Kh7 32. Q×c7 b2 33. Q×b6 d5! 34. Qb3 Ra1 35. Qc2† g6 36. Rf1! and now Black's position starts looking grim. **26. ... d×e5** Bird's attack is over, he is material down, and Black's pieces suddenly have good prospects. **27. B×e5 Bc5† 28. Kh1 Kh7 29. B×f6 R×e1 30. R×e1 g×f6 31. d6 Q×d6 32. Qf3 Ra3 33. Qe4 f5** 33. ... R×a2 wins at once. **34. Qe8 Re3?!** 34. ... Qf8 35. Qd7† Qg7 protects the king after which the two pawns more should decide the game. **35. R×e3 B×e3 36. Q×e3 Q×c6 37. Qe7† Kg8 38. Q×b4 Qd6 39. Qb3 Kf7 40. a4 Qc5 41. h3 f4 42. Qd3 Qe3 43. Qd7† Qe7 44. Qd5† Qe6 45. Qd4 g5?** Black is much better after 45. ... Qe1† 46. Kh2 Qe3 47. Qd7† Qe7 48. Qd2 Qd6. The text move exposes the king. **46. c5 Ke7 47. Qg7† Kd8 48. c×b6 Q×b6 49. Qf8† Kd7 50. Qg7† Kc8 51. h4 Qa5 52. Q×h6 Qe1† 53. Kh2 Qg3† 54. Kg1** and the game was agreed to be drawn—*Tournament Book*, pp. 314–315.

## (83) Horwitz–Bird    0–1

Match (game 12)

London 1851

*B32*

**1. e4 c5 2. d4 c×d4 3. Nf3 Nc6 4. N×d4 e5 5. N×c6 b×c6 6. Bc4 Ba6 7. B×a6 Qa5† 8. Bd2 Q×a6 9. Bc3 f6 10. b3 Nh6 11. a4 Rd8 12. Nd2 Bc5 13. Qf3 0–0 14. 0–0–0 d5 15. Bb2 Nf7 16. h4 Bd4 17. Ba3 Rfe8 18. g4 Qb6 19. Rh2 Bc5 20. Bb2 Nd6 21. Re1 Bd4 22. c3 d×e4 23. N×e4 Q×b3 24. Nd2 Q×a4 25. c×d4 e×d4 26. R×e8† R×e8 27. Qb3† Q×b3 28. N×b3 c5 29. f3 d3 30. Ba3 Nc4 31. Kd1 N×a3 32. N×c5 Re3 33. Rd2 Nc4 34. Rf2 d2 35. Ne4 Re1†** and White resigns—*Tournament Book*, pp. 316–317.

## (84) Bird–Horwitz    0–1

Match (game 13)

London 1851

*C41*

**1. e4 e5 2. Nf3 d6 3. d4 e×d4 4. Q×d4 Nc6 5. Bb5 Bd7 6. B×c6 B×c6 7. 0–0 Nf6 8. Nc3 Be7 9. Nd5 B×d5 10. e×d5 0–0 11. Bg5 Qd7 12. Rfe1 h6 13. Bh4 Rfe8 14. Qd2 Qb5 15. Qd4 Qd7 16. c4 a5 17. Re2 g5 18. Bg3 Nh5 19. Rae1 Bf6 20. Qd1 R×e2 21. Q×e2 Ng7 22. Qc2 b6 23. Nd2 Nf5 24. Ne4 Bg7 25. Rd1 Nd4 26. Qd2 f5 27. N×g5 h×g5 28. Q×g5 Ne2† 29. Kf1 N×g3† 30. Q×g3 Re8 31. h4 Re4 32. h5 R×c4 33. f4 Qa4 34. b3 R×f4† 35. Kg1 Rg4 36. Qh3 Qf4 37. Re1 Bd4† 38. Kh1 Rh4** and White resigns—*Tournament Book*, pp. 317–318.

## (85) Horwitz–Bird    1–0

Match (game 14)

London 1851

*C39*

**1. e4 e5 2. f4 e×f4 3. Nf3 g5 4. h4 g4 5. Ne5 h5 6. Bc4 Nh6**

**7. d4 d6 8. Nd3 f3 9. g×f3 Be7 10. Bf4 B×h4† 11. Kd2 g×f3 12. Q×f3 Bg4 13. Qe3 Be7 14. Nc3 Nc6 15. Rag1 Bf8 16. Nd5 Bg7 17. c3 Ne7 18. Bg5 Nhg8 19. Rf1 Be6 20. N3f4 B×d5 21. N×d5 f6 22. N×f6† N×f6 23. B×f6 B×f6 24. R×f6 Qd7 25. Qg5 d5 26. e×d5 0–0–0 27. d6 Rdg8 28. B×g8 R×g8 29. Q×g8† N×g8 30. Rf8† Qd8 31. R×d8† K×d8 32. d×c7† K×c7 33. R×h5 Nf6 34. Rf5 Ne4† 35. Ke3 Nd6 36. Kf4** and Black resigns—*Tournament Book*, pp. 318–319.

---

# OFFHAND AND VARIOUS 1851

Bird grabbed his chance to meet many of the strong foreign players in offhand games. From his account one learns that he pretended having done quite well against the majority of them.

The foreign players, after the tournament, Szén, Löwenthal, Kieseritzky, Mayet, von Jaenisch, Harrwitz and Horwitz frequented Simpson's and Anderssen (like Morphy seven years later) greatly favored the place, and readily engaged in skirmishes of the more lively enterprising, and brilliant description in which he ever met a willing opponent in Bird, who, though a comparatively young player, to the surprise and gratification of all spectators, made even games. This young player who it seems had acquired his utmost form at this time, also won the two only even games he ever played with Staunton,[43] and also two from Szén, which occasioned yet more astonishment, the last-named having been regarded by many deemed good judges, the best player in the world before the tournament was held, and even in higher estimation than his fellow-countryman Löwenthal, and considered not inferior to Staunton himself [*Chess History and Reminiscences*, p. 73].

Bird's result against Anderssen was quite impressive, given that they played eighteen games. Kieseritzky was the only player able to make Bird suffer. In *La Régence* he claimed having beaten the Englishman with eight wins against two losses.[44]

The surviving game between Bird and Anderssen appeared in two of Bird's books and in his column. He dated it alternatively in 1851 or 1854. As Anderssen was not in London in 1854 this game must have been played on the margin of the international tournament.

## (86) Bird–Anderssen    1–0

Offhand game

London (Simpson's Divan) 1851

*C65*

The present game is a typical offhand affair of both Bird and Anderssen. Both players aspired to playing as tactical game as possible. As a result, there are a lot of errors, but their aim was achieved: there is no dull moment.

**1. e4 e5 2. Nf3 Nc6 3. Bb5 Nf6 4. d4 N×d4 5. N×d4 e×d4 6. e5 Ne4 7. 0–0 Qh4** "This premature and unsound attack involves Anderssen in difficulties. The game, however, continues critical and

---

43. On p. 82 of the same book, Bird expresses his admiration for Staunton: "Having witnessed his play during 1845 to 1849, when he was still in full force, deep impressions remain with us of his extraordinary powers of combination, his soundness and accuracy."

44. Kieseritzky dedicated a few nice words to Bird: "Mr. Bird, a very young man with a very remarkable talent, is probably called to occupy the top of British chess one day. His play is powerfully brilliant, but sometimes a bit scatty. Age will modify this impetuosity." *La Régence*, July 1851, p. 204.

interesting to the finish"—Bird. **8. g3** "If 8. Q×d4 Bc5 and White
gets into trouble"—Staunton. **8. ... Qh3 9. Be2 d5 10. e×d6** *e.p.*
**B×d6 11. Q×d4 Bf5?** Black is perfectly fine after the simple 11. ...
Nf6. As usual Anderssen wasn't afraid of experiments and taking
risks in his offhand games. **12. Nc3?** Missing the very convincing,
even decisive, 12. Bf3! **12. ... 0-0-0?** "In order to win the queen, if
White should be tempted to take the knight. The springe, however,
is too obvious, and Black lays himself open to a formidable attack"
—Staunton. **13. Q×a7!** "The right move"—Staunton. **13. ... N×c3
14. b×c3 c6 15. Be3?!** Pointed, but 15. Rb1 causes resignation.
**15. ... Be4 16. Qa8† Kd7** "If 16. ... Kc7 17. Bb6† would be decisive"—Bird. **17. Q×b7† Ke8 18. f3 B×g3** "Attempting to draw the
game"—Bird. **19. Rf2! B×f2†** "He has nothing better and his attack
is now at an end"—Staunton. **20. B×f2 Bd5 21. c4** 21. Re1! also
forces 21. ... Be6, while contributing to the development as well.
**21. ... Be6 22. Q×c6†?!** 22. Bb6! resumes a decisive attack, e.g.,
22. ... Rc8 23. Bc5 Bd7 24. Bf1 Qh4 25. Rd1. **22. ... Ke7?** Much
safer is 22. ... Kf8. His majesty will find shelter further down the
kingside. The rook can be activated with a quick h7–h5. **23. Bc5†
Kf6** (*see diagram*)

*After 23. ... Kf6*

**24. Qc7?** Two successive quiet moves, 24. Bd3 (taking f5 under
control) and only then 25. Qc7, are impossible to meet decently.
The threat would be 26. Qf4†. **24. ... Kg6 25. Kh1 h6 26. Rg1†
Kh7 27. Rg3?** Anderssen's king has reached a safe haven, and it was
time for Bird to start looking for a draw. This could be done with
either 27. Qf4 or the arty 27. Bd4 R×d4 28. Qe5 Bg4 29. R×g4
R×g4 30. Qf5†. The text move only serves to oblige his opponent's
queen to take part in the game again. **27. ... Qh5?** Black is suddenly
much better after 27. ... Qf5!, when his material advantage becomes
the dominant factor again. If 28. Bd3? R×d3! 29. c×d3 Rc8. The
text move reverses the situation once more. **28. Bd3† Bf5 29. Qe5?!**
Now the trick 29. Bd4! works even better than before. After 29. ...
R×d4 30. Qe5 g6 31. Q×d4 B×d3 32. c×d3 Re8, Black has at most
some drawing chances. **29. ... g6 30. Qf6 Rhg8** It is better to defend
the f-pawn. After 30. ... Rd7 31. Bd4 Rg8 everything is covered and
Black may be able to resume the initiative. **31. Q×f7† Rg7 32. Qf6
Rdd7 33. Bd4 Rde7?** 33. ... B×d3 34. c×d3 Rdf7 35. Qe5 Rg8 is
quite drawish. **34. c5?** 34. B×f5 wins offhand. **34. ... B×d3
35. c×d3 g5?** 35. ... Qd5 allows fighting for a draw again. **36. c6?**
The errors follow each other at a rapid pace, but this is no surprise
given the quick play of both players and the difficulty of the
position. 36. Be5! is strong as it closes the e-file and prepares the
march of the d-pawn. **36. ... Re1†** 36. ... Qg6! forces the exchange
of queens and enhances his drawing perspectives. **37. Bg1** A bit dangerous. 37. Rg1 Ree7 38. Qf5† Qg6 is equal again. **37. ... Rf7?!** 37. ...

Rc7 38. Qf5† Qg6 39. Qa5 Ree7 gives Black the same safety as the
previous line, but some perspective since his rook is more active at
c7 than at f7. **38. Qd8?!** 38. Qc3! forces the retreat of the rook, after
which 39. d4 is strong. **38. ... R×f3 39. c7 R×g3 40. Qd7† Kg6
41. Qd6† Kf7 42. Q×g3** Objectively Bird had to take the immediate draw by checking continuously, but it is no surprise to see him
continue. Had Anderssen now played 42. ... Rc1 43. a4 g4!, his
queen joins the game which promises a small edge again. **42. ...
Re8 43. Qf2† Kg8?** After a long, hard, but very interesting struggle,
Anderssen is the one to make the last mistake. After 43. ... Ke6!
44. Qb6† Kd7 45. c8Q†! R×c8 46. Qd4† a draw cannot be avoided
anymore. **44. Qf5** and Black resigns. Staunton's book gives 44. Qc5
as Bird's final move, but this is certainly incorrect as Black can mate
in one in that case. After the text move nothing can be done to keep
the pawn from promotion—*Chess Praxis* (Staunton), pp. 208–209;
*Chess Masterpieces* (Bird), p. 9.

### (87) Bird–Ranken     0–1
Offhand game
London 1851
C65

**1. e4 e5 2. Nf3 Nc6 3. Bb5 Nf6 4. d4 Qe7 5. 0-0 N×d4
6. N×d4 e×d4 7. e5 Nd5 8. Q×d4 c6 9. Bc4 Qc5 10. Qe4 Be7
11. b4 N×b4 12. Be3 d5 13. e×d6** *e.p.* **Q×d6 14. Bf4 Qg6
15. Q×g6 h×g6 16. a3 Nd5 17. B×d5 c×d5 18. Nc3 Be6 19. Rfe1
Rc8 20. Nb5 a6 21. Nd4 Kd7 22. Rab1 b5 23. a4 Rc4 24. Be5
R×a4 25. B×g7 Rh4 26. c3 Bc5 27. Nf3 Rhf4 28. Rbd1 Ra2
29. Bd4 B×d4 30. c×d4 Re4 31. Ne5† Kd6 32. R×e4 d×e4 33. f4
Bd5 34. g4 e3 35. Re1 Rg2† 36. Kf1 Rf2† 37. Kg1 R×f4 38. R×e3
f6 39. N×g6 R×g4† 40. Rg3 R×g3† 41. h×g3 Be4 42. Nf4 b4** and
Black wins—*Chess Player's Chronicle*, November 1854, pp. 351–353.

### (88) Bird–Szén     ½–½
Offhand game
London (Simpson's Divan), 7 June 1851
C67

**1. e4 e5 2. Nf3 Nc6 3. Bb5 Nf6 4. 0-0 N×e4 5. d4 e×d4 6. Re1
f5 7. Ng5 Be7 8. N×e4 f×e4 9. Qh5† g6 10. Qd5 e3 11. f×e3 Nb4
12. Qe5 0-0 13. Bd2 Bf6 14. Qc5 Nc6 15. e4 Qe7 16. Qc4† Kh8
17. B×c6 b×c6 18. Bh6 Re8 19. Nd2 Qe6 20. Qd3 c5 21. Nf3 Bb7
22. e5 Be7 23. Ng5 Qg4 24. Ne4 Bf8 25. h3 B×e4 26. R×e4 Qh5
27. Bf4 Qf5 28. g4 Qe6 29. Rae1 Bg7** draw. "The remainder of the
game, which was played in a subsequent sitting, was not noted down.
It was, as one of the players told us, not very interesting. It ended in
a drawn battle"—*Family Friend* (Harrwitz), vol. III, p. 272.

### (89) Kieseritzky–Bird     1–0
Offhand game
London (Simpson's Divan), 13 June 1851
C01

**1. e4 e6 2. d4 d5 3. e×d5 e×d5 4. c4 d×c4 5. Nc3 Nf6 6. B×c4
Be7 7. Be3 Bf5 8. Nf3 0-0 9. 0-0 c6 10. Ne5 Qc7 11. Rc1 a6
12. Bd3 B×d3 13. Q×d3 Nbd7 14. f4 Bd6 15. Rf3 Rad8 16. Qf5
g6 17. Rg3 Kh8 18. Qh3 Nh5 19. Rg5 f6?** Kieseritzky created some
minimal pressure, but this should not trouble Bird. In fact, after

19. ... N×e5 20. f×e5 Be7, it is White who's drifting into a worse position, e.g., 21. R×h5 g×h5 22. Q×h5 f6! or 21. Rg4 Qd7. The text move is ruinous. **20. N×g6†! h×g6 21. R×g6 Rf7 22. Rh6† Kg8 23. Q×h5** and White wins—*La Régence*, August 1851, pp. 248–249.

**(90) Bird–Baines    1–0**
Offhand game
London 1851
*Odds of Ra1*

**1. e4 e5 2. f4 e×f4 3. Bc4 Qh4† 4. Kf1 g5 5. g3 f×g3 6. Kg2 Q×e4† 7. Nf3 Q×c4 8. d3 Q×a2 9. Nc3 Qa6 10. Re1† Ne7 11. Nd5 Qc6 12. c4 h6 13. Nd4 Qc5 14. Qg4 Na6 15. b4 N×b4 16. Ba3 a5 17. Re5 Kd8 18. Qe4 d6 19. R×e7 Bg7 20. Bb2 N×d5 21. c×d5 B×d4 22. B×d4 f5** and White mates in four moves —*The Chess Player*, 13 December 1851, p. 176.

# ◆ Part II ◆

# THE TURN OF THE TIDE, 1852–1855

## THE DEVELOPMENT OF CHESS

The international chess tournament of 1851 was an obvious success in achieving its aim of gathering a considerable number of the strongest players in the world. The event drew worldwide attention and generated a lot of interest for the game of chess. There was, however, another side to the image that made its impact felt during the next years.

The organization of the event had created great animosity and even enmity between Staunton and other chessplayers and prominents. This exemplified itself in a harsh tension that arose between the St. George's and the London Chess Club. The boost to the game overall that could reasonably be expected, was thus lacking. The chess scene in England remained fragmented and without a serious organization there was no hope of bringing the practice of the game to a higher level.

The following years were characterized by the absence of tournaments. At the same time only a few players were found willing to risk their reputation in a direct confrontation with a foe. Thus chess remained limited to the small scale of chess cafés and clubs.

Being defeated by Anderssen during the tournament, Staunton's hegemony at the chessboard came to an end. He withdrew more and more from practical play and turned his interests to journalistic work and his studies on Shakespeare. Other prominent British players also disappeared from the scene. Williams succumbed during the cholera epidemic of 1854, while Wyvill's spot in the final proved to be a one-hit wonder. Buckle was also a man who belonged to the past.

In their wake the young generation, represented by players such as Bird and Smith, dropped out one by one. None of these players had the ability nor the ambition to carry the leading role of Staunton. Other priorities in life drew them away from what was only a pastime. Bird's name occurred only now and then in the press, when an occasional game was published, but that was about all that was heard about the formerly so enthusiastic youngster.

The vacant places at the top were ultimately filled by a few strong foreigners. Löwenthal and Daniel Harrwitz, later also Falkbeer, took up residence in London. They spiced up the chess life at the capital, became influential as chess journalists and promoted the game in the provinces.

## AN INTRODUCTION TO THE RISE AND FALL OF HENRY BIRD

Henry Edward Bird relinquished any serious chess from the fall of 1851 until the end of 1856. His interest in the game remained but circumstances prevented him from dedicating more attention to pushing pawns. His accountancy career was on the rise, he wed in 1855 and above all severe familial concerns occupied his mind.

Three chapters in this part deal with cases that came for the Court of Chancery. This court had jurisdiction over all matters of equity, including trusts. These cases, Jackson v. Drew, Dyer v. Dyer and Bird v. Drouet, dealt with discords growing out of such trusts. A trust was an asset fund, created by a settlor, and usually managed by one or two trustees for the benefit of the settlor or his offspring.

Trusts had a long history but it was only during the reign of Queen Victoria that they spread among the middle class. The function of trustee was important, difficult and delicate. They had a great liberty of action, mostly did not profit from the trust and had to be wary of putting themselves in a conflicting situation. A trustee was often acquainted with the family. The whole system faded towards the end of the nineteenth century, when it was considered a most thankless job.[1] A pivotal role in these three cases was played by Henry Bird, the chess master's father. Henry Edward Bird was mostly a side figure, but the developments had an heavy impact on his life (and that of his family).

Because of the complicated nature and chronological overlap of these cases they have been separated into three different chapters. These are preceded and followed by other chapters dealing with important personal events.

The files preserved at the National Archives contain a bill of complaint and, in in two cases (a part of) a defense by the defendants. Juridical acts following upon the complaint are also preserved at the National Archives, but they are much harder to retrieve. The traces of all three cases have been pursued up to a point, but no further, for they contain no information that is relevant to the present work.

# Good Years

At the time of the death of his oldest son William Baker in 1847, Henry Bird was appointed the executor of William Baker's will. Since he was the main benefactor of his deceased grandfather, the sum Henry could now lay his hands on was considerable and must have given him a financial boost.

A short while later, on 11 April 1848, Henry leapt an important hurdle on his way up the social ladder. On that day he gained admittance into the Freedom of the City of London.[2] People eligible to become a Freeman had to be over 21 years old, of British descent and good character. Their acceptance into the Freedom confirmed their high status as valuable members of the community. They were consequently expected to live their lives in a honorable fashion.

On his application form Bird wrote that he was "carrying on the business of a victualler." As mentioned before, this probably meant that he exploited the Auction Mart Tavern. At last by 1850 he was no longer the owner of this establishment, and newspaper articles from the 1850s show it being run by a certain Hammond.

Also in 1848, or at last in 1849, the family had moved to new quarters situated at 16 Harleyford Place.[3] Their new home was situated at just a few meters of their previous address.

The census of 1851 was taken on 30 March. One finds Henry

now exploiting the historic Burton Coffee House, situated at Freeman's Court, Cheapside.[4] Henry rented Burton's from June 1850 on. His lease was to last 21 years. The yearly rent was £160 18s. In order to begin his business he submitted to a mortgage of £962 18s. 9p. He borrowed the money from the firm Charrington and Company.[5]

Also present at Burton Coffee House on the evening of 30 March were Mary Ellen and Henry Edward. The recording of the two contains a few remarkable errors. Mary Ellen's name was wrongly transcribed as Ann E., while her age, given as 44, was also definitely incorrect. The young chess master, 21 years old, was correctly listed as an accountant, but his name was distorted into Willie E. Bird. Strangely enough this name resembles the name of his older, and deceased, brother William Baker. About ten other persons were recorded at the same address. Among them were one visitor and one lodger. All others were in service of the Birds, e.g., as cook or housemaid.

It appears obvious that Henry had been faring well during the past few years. Bird confirmed his success in a letter written to his brother-in-law, Edward Drew, on 20 June 1851. Concerning a loan he claimed to be able to repay his debt in two years, as "my position in society (as Liveryman and Citizen of the Ward of Cheap in the City of London) is much improved...."[6] Bird thus evolved from Freeman, for which he fulfilled the criteria in 1848, to Liveryman, a higher membership of the Company. He gained full rights and was now entitled to wear the robes of the Company.

An intriguing remark that also touches upon Henry's financial position was made by his son Charles Grey Bird. Charles Grey moved from England to Australia in 1853. Soon after his arrival he sold a revolver that was a gift from the Hon. C. Fortescue to his father.[7]

It is impossible to identify with certainty which member of this distinguished family had such a close contact with Henry Bird, but an informed guess might point to Chichester Fortescue (1823–1898). Curiously, Fortescue was to become familiar with the Australian territories himself when he became the Under-Secretary of State for the Colonies between 1857 and 1858 and 1859 to 1865. The fact that Henry received a precious gift from him is another clear testimony of the social standing he had achieved by now.

Henry Bird had some other connections that demonstrate his upward social mobility. This was exemplified in a case evolving from the will of Eliza Mason, the deceased wife of John Dyer.[8] Bird was appointed trustee for a few annuities, coming from the estate of Eliza, that were made on behalf of her child. He found himself in

1. See for a detailed study on this subject: C. Stebbings, *The Private Trustee in Victorian England*. Cambridge: Cambridge University Press, 2002.
2. Ancestry.com. *London, England, Freedom of the City Admission Papers, 1681–1925* [database on-line]. Provo, UT, USA: Ancestry.com Operations, Inc., 2010. ¶ Original data: *Freedom admissions papers, 1681–1925*. London, England: London Metropolitan Archives. COL/CHD/FR/02.
3. Henry Bird's name was listed at this address by *Kelly's Post Office London Directory* from 1849 until 1855, with the exception of 1852 and 1853.

4. 1851 census: Class: *HO107*; Piece: *1529*; Folio: 369; Page 3. The history of Burton Coffee House only runs until 1840 in B. Lillywhite, *London Coffee Houses. A Reference Book of Coffee Houses of the Seventeenth, Eighteenth and Nineteenth Centuries*. London: George Allen & Unwin, 1963, p. 142.
5. The National Archives, Public Record Office, 15/179/B76 *Bird v. Drouet*, Bill of Complaint, p. 8.
6. The National Archives, C16/29/I/J17, *Jackson v. Drew*, transcript of Edward Drew's reply, p. 13.
7. C.G. Bird (Alpha), *Reminiscences of the Goldfields in the Fifties and Sixties: Victoria, New Zealand, New South Wales. Part I, Victoria*. Melbourne: Gordon & Gotch, 1915, p. 20. ¶ The pedigree of the Fortescue family goes back to Richard Le Fort. According to the legend, he saved William of Normandy with his shield, hence his adopted name Fort Escu (strong shield). A list of descendants can be found at http://www.fortescue.org/.
8. The National Archives, C15/22/D31, *Dyer v. Dyer*. A close watch of this case follows below, see: Case II—Dyer v. Dyer.

high company. Eliza's husband was born in a branch of the Dyer baronets. His great-grandfather was Sir Thomas Dyer, fifth Baronet.

The second executor was John Clutton. This may have been the John Clutton, born in 1809, who became one of the most eminent surveyors of his time. He founded the London business of Cluttons "prompted by the sudden growth of surveying businesses negotiating land purchases for railway construction."[9] Cluttons is still an important firm in the surveying field.

Eliza Mason also appointed John Lewis as an executor. He was replaced in October 1847 by Thomas Mitchell Hammond, a surgeon.[10]

Back to the census of 1851: James Pidding, nearly 18, was recorded at the family's home at 16 Harleyford Place in Lambeth. Remarkably he was listed as a boarder. Two other persons were registered at this address. E. Yorke, a 48 year old widow was the lodging house keeper. Like Henry Bird she was born in Bristol and thus perhaps an acquaintance. Fanny Yorke, 19 years old and probably her daughter, also lived there.[11]

Charles Grey, 19 years old at the time, had already taken up the adventurous life of a sailor when he was 15 or 16.[12] James Pidding would soon follow into the footsteps of his brother. Both emigrated to Australia in 1853.

The three youngest children were found at two relatively small boarding schools. Edward Daniel Pidding was educated in a school in Brentford, west of London.[13] His two sisters, Louisa Maria and Emily Fanny Stopford, were living at a small boarding school in Wycombe in Buckinghamshire, also well out of London.[14] Jane Bird, the oldest living child of Henry and Mary Ellen, could not be retrieved in the census.

For the next three years Henry Bird remained firmly tied to Burton Coffee House. The last two newspaper mentions found, in the *Morning Post* of 3 March 1852 and a few months later in the *Daily News* of 13 May 1852, relate two thieveries of which he was the victim. In the latter case, Elizabeth Stevens, mentioned as the kitchen maid in the census of 1851, was accused of stealing pieces of silk and coins from her "master and mistress."

# A TOUCH OF AUSTRALIA

From the census of 1851 one learns that Henry Edward's uncle, John Bird, resided in Clerkenwell. Here he was trying to expand his business as a clock and watch trader. After the death of his first wife, Henrietta Upjohn, he married Martha Harford. They lived together with their mutual children.[15]

Mary Elizabeth and John, the children from John's first marriage,

were recorded at 14 Wellington Place in Bristol.[16] They had moved in with their grandmother Mary Pidding, who was 87 or 88 years old at that time. Her death, on 10 November 1851, triggered a series of events that completely upset the life of Henry Edward and his family.

For Mary Elizabeth another person had become important in her life: the seven years younger William Rutherford Mason. William came from a very respectable family. His parents ran a Ladies Seminary in Bath while his brothers purchased a medical career. William gave up the probably traditional prospects that his parents kept in store for him and during the late 1840s he had chosen to live the life of a mariner. A year after Mary Pidding died, the young couple took the radical decision to venture everything and travel to the other side of the world, to the shores of Victoria, Australia. They docked in Melbourne from the ship *Tulloch Castle* on 13 December 1852. Five days later they were married.[17]

The shores of Australia were a great attraction towards fortune seekers since the discovery of gold in Victoria around 1851. The population boomed and already in 1852 Melbourne had become the most popular destination for emigrants leaving Britain. The temptation to settle definitively in the southern hemisphere was especially strong amidst sailors as they were often the first to hear of such discoveries. A symptomatic story appeared on 5 January 1853 in *The Melbourne Argus*. An article related how the whole crew of the *Tulloch Castle*, the ship on which Mary Elizabeth and William Mason Rutherford sailed, abandoned their duties and went for the gold fields in the inhospitable wilderness.

Another ship, the *Agnes Blaikie*, left the harbor of Bristol on 5 February 1853. Five months later, on 7 July, it arrived in Hobson's Bay in the same state of Victoria, Australia. On board were two other young sailors: Charles Grey and James Pidding Bird, the brothers of Henry Edward and the cousins of Mary Elizabeth.[18] The new arrivals witnessed a spectacular scene when they finally had land in sight: "Fully 100 ships of various sizes were lying idle, with scarcely any evidence of life on board, save that of a ship's keeper left in charge, nearly the whole of these vessels having been deserted by their crews" (*Reminiscences of the Goldfields,* p. 16). This observation was written more than sixty years later by Charles Grey Bird. In an autobiographical work he described in great detail his days as a prospector on the gold fields from 1853 until 1865. He published the work anonymously, under the pseudonym "Alpha." It is curious that Charles told only of his own adventures, mentioning his father twice and his brother not even once.

# CASE I. JACKSON V. DREW

At some point, probably in the midst of 1854, Henry Bird followed the trace hewed by his sons and headed for Australia. Such

9. See the website of the Royal Institution of Chartered Surveyors, of which Clutton was the first president. http://www.rics.org/be/news/rics150/surveyors-through-history-john-clutton/.

10. Hammond renounced the probate of her testament and was thus not involved in the further complications, with which we deal below.

11. 1851 census: Class: *HO107*; Piece: *1573*; Folio: 167; Page: 29.

12. C.G. Bird, *Reminiscences of the goldfields*, p. 16.

13. 1851 census: Class: *HO107*; Piece: *1699*; Folio: 155; Page: 3.

14. 1851 census: Class: *HO107*; Piece: *1719*; Folio: 148; Page: 14.

15. 1851 census: Class: *HO107*; Piece: *1518*; Folio: 123; Page: 6.

16. 1851 census: Class: *HO107*; Piece: *1953*; Folio: 171; Page: 13.

17. A great deal of information on the genealogy of the Birds and the Australian part of this story is attributable to Graeme Rodgers and Mac McCombe, two direct descendants of Mary Elizabeth Bird.

18. Public Record Office Victoria. Index to Unassisted Inward Passenger Lists to Victoria 1852–1923. See: http://prov.vic.gov.au/index_search?searchid=23.

a radical choice is in need of explanation, and two of the afore-mentioned court cases are considerably enlightening. The case evolving from a complaint issued by a certain Mary Jackson against Edward Drew, the husband of Henry's sister Sarah Pidding Bird, contains by far the most details. This file, formed in 1861, consists of two major parts. There is first a short but powerful bill of complaint by Mary Jackson against Edward Drew, Henry Bird and the latter's children. Henry Edward and Edward Daniel Pidding declared themselves unaware of both the case and the fate of their father and brothers in Australia. The girls, underage, were equally unaware. Edward Drew's reply is the most fundamental one. At a slow pace he thoroughly explained all the events that culminated in Jackson's complaint. He included snippets of letters from Henry and Mary Ellen, which offer revealing insights about their personal lives. (These will mostly be treated in the following chapters.)

The story starts in 1835 when Mary Pidding Bird, Henry's other sister, wrote down her will. She died on 18 October 1836, at the age of 30. Despite her early death she left a substantial amount of money (including an inheritance from her grandfather, Daniel Pidding) to be divided amongst her close relatives. In her will she determined the precise division and appointed two executors. One, a certain Andrew Thomson, died shortly after Mary, which left her brother-in-law, Edward Drew, as the sole person responsible for managing the inheritance.

Drew took care that each of the parties received their share, but he found out that there was not enough money to reach the figures mentioned in Mary's will. Thus Sarah and Henry, the principal rightful claimants to the estate, did not obtain the destined £1000 per person, but only £497 11s. 2d. Edward Drew invested the money in annuities.

Henry received another inheritance when his mother died in November 1851. She left an annuity of £5000 to be divided among her children. One fifth of this amount, the part initially reserved for the deceased Mary, was divided in proportions. As Edward Drew explained precisely in his defense, the sum of both inheritances, £824 11s., was now invested by him in a "life retreat"— i.e., real estate or personal property. From 1852 onwards Henry Bird thus received twice a year (in April and October) a dividend of £11 10s. 11d. An important element of a life interest stipulated that upon Henry's death the invested money had to be divided among his children.

Henry Bird's prospects were looking bright in the beginning of the decade, and he was very busy making all kinds of investments. In a letter dated 20 June 1851, he informed Edward Drew that he had borrowed £300 with the purpose of "purchasing some leasehold property which will tend very materially to benefit my wife and two daughters." Bird borrowed this sum from a couple of business contacts who were represented by the firm Watson and Sons. Drew was updated on Henry's investments, as he had entered his life interest as a security. In the same letter Bird bragged about being able to pay back the loan in two years thanks to his improved position in society.

As Henry had mortgaged the life interest, Edward Drew was a bit reluctant to forward the dividend to him. He asked Watson and Sons whether they had objections, but there were none, at least so long as Henry Bird kept on repaying his loan on a regular basis.

Edward Drew continued to pay out Henry's life interest until April 1855. In October 1855 he received a letter from Henry's wife containing a letter allegedly written by her husband in London. But Drew was apparently aware that Henry had emigrated to Australia. When confronted, Mary Ellen at first uttered some threats towards her brother-in-law (Drew used the word "threats" but he did not concretize what Mary Ellen wrote to him). In the end she admitted that her husband had been in Australia for more than a year already. As a consequence, proof was needed that Henry Bird was still alive in order to pay out the dividend. Australia was far away, and a stable existence there was not guaranteed. After some time Henry Bird wrote from Australia. He requested that Drew transfer his dividend directly to him, so that he would not be liable to any taxations. Depriving his wife of this money indicates there were problems between them.

The trouble commenced when Drew received a letter from a certain Sarah Willmott in April 1856. She informed him about another loan of £300 which she had granted to Henry Bird in January 1852. Bird had agreed to pay the money back in six months. To obtain this loan, Henry Bird mortgaged the life interest for a second time. Apparently Mrs. Willmott was still waiting for the money and she now claimed the twice-a-year dividend.

Now the case got really complicated and Edward Drew soon found himself caught in a tangle which was difficult to unravel. His main task was to figure out for which of Henry's loans the inheritance he managed was used as a mortgage and whether Henry had actually paid back these loans.

Drew got in contact with Mary Ellen Bird, but she did not make him any wiser. Mary Ellen claimed that Bird had effectively paid off the loans. It turned out that this was partly true. It is evident that Mary Ellen also claimed the dividend. Edward Drew saw no other possibility than postponing the payment. Mary Ellen thereupon broke off all contact with Drew, leaving the unfortunate trustee in the dark about Henry Bird's condition.

Sarah Willmott, evidently fed up with the affair, offered the life interest for sale at a favorable price. A solicitor, Charles Blake, initially pursued it, but then backed away. Ultimately the life interest was purchased by Mary Jackson in October 1857. The change of ownership did not alter the several uncertainties. Edward Drew kept the dividends in a separate bank account, Mary Jackson filed a complaint against him at the Court of Chancery, and the file providing researchers with all this information was formed.

## CASE II. DYER V. DYER

This second case deals much less with the Australian part of this story but more with the friction that existed within the Bird family. Again, the outcome of the case is unknown, but there are at least hints that Henry Bird, the chess master's father, acted dubiously as trustee.

The preserved file is a small one and contains just two documents. Firstly, there is a small note, written by Henry Edward Bird on 16 April 1853, in which he authorized his solicitors, Peter Wickens Fry and John Loxley, to bring the matter before court "in my name as the next friend of the above named plaintiff." The term "next friend" meant that Bird acted on behalf of someone. Bird's "next friend" here was Frederick Swinnerton Dyer. He was born in 1843 and thus only about 10 years old.[19] The second and more important document is the bill of complaint that was filed at the Court of Chancery on 20 April 1853.

The case dealt with the will of Frederick's deceased mother, Eliza Mason. It is uncertain how the chess master was tied to Frederick Swinnerton Dyer, but presumably Eliza Mason was a relative of William Rutherford Mason, the husband of Henry Edward's niece Mary Elizabeth.[20] As an accountant the chess master was probably the best acquainted among them with legal matters.

Eliza had been married for three years to William Frederick Bulmer. Bulmer died in 1839 and left his widow with the management of real and personal estate "of very considerable value," as it was put in the complaint. Eliza then remarried, to John Dyer. Frederick Swinnerton was their only child. On 28 September 1847 Eliza drew up her own will. She appointed Henry Bird, John Lewis and John Clutton as executors. A month later John Lewis was replaced by Thomas Mitchell Hammond. Eliza died on 5 November 1847. With Hammond refusing to be responsible for the execution of Eliza's will, only two executors/trustees were left. They were both the target of the complaint of Frederick and Henry Edward. The third defendant was John Dyer, the infant's father.

The plaintiffs noticed in their complaint that Dyer resided in Jersey at the time and found himself thus out of the jurisdiction of the Court. John Dyer had started a new life after Eliza's death. He married Martha Elizabeth White in 1851 and got two daughters. John Dyer died on 27 August 1855.

The specific complaint made by the plaintiffs against the three defendants becomes clear in the ninth point of the charge.

> That a great part of the said real estate consists of divers messuages[21] let on lease and that the said Henry Bird and John Clutton as such acting trustees ... have ... been in the receipt of the rents and profits thereof but that differences have lately arisen between them as to the management ... and that ... your petitioner's rights and interests are in danger of being prejudiced and that it will be for his benefit that a receiver of the rents and profits of the said real estate should be appointed by this Honorable Court [Dyer v. Dyer, Bill of Complaint, p. 5].

The *London Gazette* of 8 July (p. 1933) summoned "John Dyer and others, the creditors of Eliza Dyer" to come in before 22 July 1853 "and prove their debts at the chambers of the Vice-Chancellor, or in default thereof they will be peremptorily excluded the benefit of the said order." Apparently Frederick and Henry Edward believed that parts of the former's inheritance were unjustly treated by the trustees.

## CASE III. BIRD V. DROUET

The third case, Bird v. Drouet, was filed at the Court of Chancery on 27 April 1855. It enlightens us about the turbulent months before Henry Bird left England. This file mainly consists of a bill of complaint. The plaintiffs were Henry's infant children: Edward Daniel Pidding, Louisa Maria and Emily Fanny Stopford. The defendants were Henry, Mary Ellen, their son James Pidding, William Drouet and Matthew Berry. Charles Grey and Henry Edward had been sold out of this indenture, respectively on 14 February and 22 April 1853. Very curious is that Charles Grey had already embarked to Australia on 5 February 1853.

The complaint was filed by John Streat (written so in his own handwriting. On other occasions one finds John Street), the plaintiff's "next friend." Streat lived in Lawrence Lane at the time. His solicitors were Fry and Loxley, the advocates who represented Henry Edward Bird in Dyer v. Dyer.

The basis of this case was an indenture, arrayed by Henry and Mary Ellen on 1 November 1824, the day before their marriage. With this indenture Henry brought "all his ... share of ... the residuary real and personal estate of Daniel Pidding" in a trust.[22] This sum of £1000, coming from the inheritance of Henry's grandfather from his mother's side, was invested in securities for the benefit of, in that order, Mary Ellen, Henry and their eventual children.[23] Two trustees were appointed: William Baker and Edmund Henry Waller, a candlestick maker from Bristol and probably a friend of Henry. In 1831 Waller resigned the trusteeship upon which a certain Caleb Payne was assigned.

Payne and Baker died, respectively, in 1841 and 1843, after which it became unclear what exactly happened with the money. Assets of the inheritance had been sold, the trustees had received some large sums but there were no receipts and the remainder was "believed to be lost." In December 1852 a "residue" of £721 1s. 4p. was formed, the money coming from the estates of the deceased trustees. This money was invested in bank annuities. Two new trustees, Thomas Tasker and Henry Flower, were appointed.

In the meantime, Bird was "possessed or entitled" to Burton Coffee House, the fittings furniture and appliances. He obtained the right to exploit this establishment for 21 years from 24 June 1850 onwards. Bird paid a yearly rent of £160 18s., "but subject nevertheless to a ... mortgage ... to Messieurs Charrington and Company for the sum of £962 18s 9p."

On 12 April 1854 Henry Flower was replaced as trustee by William Drouet, who was morally more compliant.[24] Eight days

19. It is certain that there was no namesake involved. Bird's address was given as 16 Harleyford Place and his profession as accountant.

20. The Australian companions Graeme Rodgers and Mac McCombe were unable to demonstrate a clear link between Eliza Mason and their branch, coming from William Rutherford Mason. This remains thus a supposition.

21. An archaic legal term that refers to a dwelling house together with its outbuildings and the adjacent land.

22. This practice was very common: "Such settlements ensured that the wife and children would be provided for, and also that the wife had some property for her separate use so as not to be wholly dependent on her husband." Stebbings, *The Private Trustee in Victorian England*, p. 11.

23. There are clearly remarkable similarities with the Jackson v. Drew case, where the decease of Mary Pidding Bird left a lot of money, in all likelihood also coming from Daniel Pidding's inheritance, to be divided among her siblings.

24. William Drouet, but above all his (supposed) brother Bartholomew Peter Drouet, became the talk of the town when 150 children died at the Infant Pauper Asylum at Tooting during the cholera epidemic. Poor conditions and overcrowding resulted in a conviction of manslaughter for Bartholomew Drouet, the superintendent. William Drouet was named as one of the guardians in a child's testimony, published on 21 January 1849 in *The Sunday Times*.

later Henry Bird gave the trustees the order to sell bank annuities worth £503. They were able to sell them only for £440, a considerable loss. Bird now had to secure the retransfer of £503 (and interest) to the trust, for which he demised the leasehold premises—Burton Coffee House—to the trustees. In his complaint John Streat stated that Tasker and Drouet were well aware of the security to Charrington and Company.

On 3 June 1854 Henry requested that the trustees sell off the remaining bank annuities (with a worth of £221 1s. 4p.). These annuities sold for £203 (another loss) and this sum was advanced to the security of Burton's (the annuities worth £503 and those worth £221 1s. 4p. total [loss £3]) the "residue" of £721 1s. 4p. formed in December 1852.

At some point during the following months, probably with the cash in hand, Henry Bird left for Australia. On 4 October 1854, the trustees sold Burton Coffee House by public auction. After paying off Charrington and Company, a sum of £300 or £400 remained, "so that a loss has already resulted to the said trust estate," Streat complained. Streat also denounced the action of 3 June: the investment in the mortgage security was a breach of trust by Tasker and Drouet. Streat also mentioned that Henry Bird had a debt of several hundred pounds to Thomas Tasker.

On 8 February 1855, a few months before John Streat filed his case at the Court, Thomas Tasker died. His inheritance was executed by a certain Matthew Berry. Streat expected from Berry that Tasker's estate would be used to satisfy his plaintiffs.

On a separate page is the defense of Drouet and Berry, and a reaction upon it, presumably from the hand of John Streat. In a first point the trustees stated that Henry Bird was insolvent and that he defrauded his creditors to obtain money. Streat replied that "the contrary was the fact [that] the said Henry Bird having at such respective times been perfectly solvent. He subsequently embarked in speculative transactions which proving unsuccessful he in consequence thereof became for the first time insolvent."

Secondly, the trustee alleged that the mortgage transactions took place with the approbation of Henry Edward and Charles Grey. Again, this was contradicted: "The said Charles Grey Bird was and is in Australia and he has not been informed of the same transactions.... Henry Edward Bird did not approve of the same transactions."

In a last point John Streat criticized Drouet and Berry for having expended money without justifying it.

There is no doubt that Mary Ellen was really on the side of John Streat and her children. In her private correspondence she often damned her husband for disastrous actions he had taken before leaving for Australia. John Streat became a close friend and supporter of Mary Ellen. In 1856 or 1857 he occupied rooms at her home, at 16 Harleyford Place.

his departure for Australia by which he abandoned his business, his marital coexistence with Mary Ellen and contact with his daughters and two of his sons?

Mary Ellen Bird, often quoted by Edward Drew in his lengthy reply to Jackson's bill of complaint, more than once mentions her experiences during those demanding years. Her position was very difficult and sensitive. She initially defended her husband, until the falsification of his letters was revealed. Then her tone about Henry became much harsher, probably an attempt to bring herself forward as his victim and to guarantee the continuing payment of the dividend. When Drew refused to pay out the dividend to her she teamed up with her husband again.

According to Mary Ellen, Henry Bird was still making good investments for his family in 1851. Later transactions, however, were catastrophic.

> As a matter of course I forwarded the receipt for the dividend and cannot but express my regret that Mr. Bird should have remitted the same to me. I can only say I regret to add that it is of a piece with many of his transactions previous to leaving England and had not my eldest son Henry and self-acted with energy in throwing my affairs into Chancery myself and my daughters would have been beggars instead of being possessed of every necessary if not the luxuries of life. I was certainly aware that Mr. Bird borrowed the amount of £300 of a Mrs. Willmott nearly four years since when he nearly ruined himself and his family by his mad speculations in railway shares but had no idea he had the power to assign away his interest under his sisters will [letter from Mary Ellen Bird to Edward Drew, 3 August 1856; source: transcript of Edward Drew's reply, pp. 23–24].

The financial hangover from bad investments may have triggered Henry Bird to start all over again, even if this meant leaving a large part of his family behind. In one of his letters from Australia, Henry Bird explained that he had moved to Australia to help his sons start up their business. While there may be some truth in this statement, the three cases mentioned above suggest that his years of prosperity were over. Bad investments, mismanagement of his proper means, perhaps even the abuse of the trusteeship led to financial and legal problems as well as to serious frictions with his wife and son. That Henry Bird, at the age of 55, still made such an exhausting trip to the other side of the world has something desperate in it. The Bird v. Drouet case indicates that he gathered the money that he could and left, running away from his problems. If one were to believe Mary Ellen's characterization of him, he didn't care much about what would happen with those he left behind.

We were unable to locate a record of Henry Bird on board a ship leaving from a British harbor. This may be explained by the loss of the shipping list, but Edward Drew gave another intriguing alternative. He had heard the rumor that Bird spent some time in France before travelling on. If this was the case, he may have left for Australia from Le Havre, France's most important port.

## A TENTATIVE CONCLUSION

So, what exactly can one learn about the chess master's father Henry Bird and his family in between the census of 1851, when he was still fully confident about his prospects and social advance, and

## THE INTERACTION BETWEEN HENRY BIRD AND HIS FAMILY

Some of Henry Bird's letters are enlightening about his life in Australia. Again, it has to be kept in mind that Henry had a clear agenda—an attempt to salvage the best out of the situation for himself and his wife.

In a letter written on 10 August 1855 from Flinders Street in Melbourne, Bird stated that he had divested himself of Burton Coffee House. Edward Drew claimed that he had heard the rumor that this was not the case, and that Bird had kept Burton's. Henry Bird further explained that his motif to head for Australia was to establish his sons, Charles Grey and James Pidding, in business. Charles definitely had other plans. He did not return to Melbourne and preferred to continue searching for gold at Ovens Diggings. So did James but a few years later he appeared to have set up a branch of his father's newspaper business in the inlands of Victoria.

Bird held on to his plea of sending the dividends to him (as he was not liable to taxes outside of England, the amount would be some £26 instead of £11). He claimed that these dividends were his only income from Great Britain. Bird rounded off his letter by writing that he wouldn't return to England for some years, if ever at all.

In another letter, written about six months later, Bird was even more confident. His business in Melbourne was flourishing and he confirmed his intention to remain in Australia for at least a few more years. But in October 1856, Mary Ellen informed the solicitors of Edward Drew that Henry's return was impending because of health issues. She requested Drew to retain the dividends, hoping he would certainly not pay them out to Mrs. Willmott. Bird's impending return, within twelve months, was again confirmed by Mary Ellen in another letter written on 15 March 1857. Later that year the contact between the Birds and Edward Drew broke off. Drew was from now on left unaware of Bird's condition and eventual return to London.

Edward Drew was undoubtedly the most tormented protagonist in this saga. After a few years of quarreling, his management of the trusteeship was explicitly questioned by Mary Jackson. Forced to defend his own affairs and explain his actions throughout, more than once he threatened to appeal to the Trustee Relief Act, to be relieved of responsibility for administering the trust.

Though it cannot be called a small consolation for him, one should not leave Edward Drew without mentioning that his offspring fared well. The only child of Drew and Sarah Pidding Bird, Ada Drew, was the great-grandmother of Mark Phillips, former husband of Anne Windsor, the daughter of Queen Elizabeth.[25]

## LIFE IN AUSTRALIA

Immediately after their arrival in July 1853 Charles Grey and James Pidding followed the herd to the inlands of Victoria where gold had been discovered earlier on. Their father Henry Bird probably arrived in 1854. Due to his age Henry was less keen to lead a laborious life in the violent surroundings of the boom towns in Victoria and he settled in Melbourne. The versatile man pursued an-

other career switch and started to work as a news agent and newspaper importer in Bourke Street.

During the following years a few mentions of the small contingent of Birds have been found in the press. *The Melbourne Age* of 7 October 1858 contains a small advertisement from James Pidding Bird. He had settled in Rokewood, a gold mining town 80 miles distance from Melbourne. James had opened "Bird's Agency" and now specialized himself as a news agent, bookseller and stationer. He provided the town with newspapers from various continents. The ad explicitly referred to his father's business in Melbourne.

In the edition of *The Melbourne Argus* of 19 September 1860, a cry for help from Henry, his "sick father," was waiting for Charles Grey at the post office in Chiltern, almost 200 miles north of Melbourne. Either Charles did not receive this letter or he neglected his father's bid, as a year later, on 29 June 1861, the same newspaper reported that Charles Grey found gold in the nearby town of Baddaginnie.

Health problems finally made Henry Bird return to England. He left Melbourne on board the *Anglesey* on 3 January 1865.[26] His business in Melbourne went into the hands of Charles Grey, who thereby abandoned the wild life in the outback of Australia.[27] In the same year Charles married a local girl, Anastasia Maria Hayes. He stayed active in the newspaper business, and attempted—unsuccessfully—to become a member of the Parliament of Victoria.[28] On 30 March 1895, the *Melbourne Leader* brought the news of Charles Grey Bird's insolvency, due to "losses in land, falling off in business and heavy expenses in connection with business."

At the end of his long life Charles penned down his memoirs under the pseudonym "Alpha." He nicknamed himself "the Pioneer Prospector." The first part, dedicated to his life as a gold digger in Victoria, was published. A second part, about his experiences in New Zealand and New South Wales, never saw the light of day.

Charles Grey Bird died in Fitzroy North, Melbourne, on 10 August 1917 at the age of 86. His wife survived him until 1932. The couple apparently remained childless.

James Pidding Bird left Australia in 1862 and headed for New Zealand. In his memoirs, Charles Grey wrote that he had been working in New Zealand as well.[29]

James resided on the South Island of New Zealand where he continued to live a tough life. On 14 July 1883 his name featured in a small article in the *Grey River Argus* of 14 July 1883. A lawsuit involving a cow shows that he was at that time working as a miner near Rutherglen.

James probably spent his last years in the hospital in Ross and

---

25. Pointed out by Graeme Rodgers.

26. Public Record Office Victoria. Index to Outward Passengers to Interstate, UK, N and Foreign Ports 1852–1923. See: http://prov.vic.gov.au/index_search?searchid=42.

27. Much to his regret: "owing to the severe illness of my father requiring my presence in town to take charge of his business in Melbourne. This prevented my return to the district, and thus lost me a very profitable business." C.G. Bird, *Reminiscences of the Goldfields*, p. 120.

28. *Supplement to the Victoria Government Gazette*, 22 June 1877.

29. Charles wrote that he was at the Otago goldfields in 1861 and 1862 (p. 90), shortly after he made his discoveries at Baddaginnie. Gold had been found there in May 1861. Only two months later the region was flooded with prospectors.

died there on 5 September 1917, less than a month after his brother. We found no information about a possible wedding or children.[30]

It is unlikely that he ever saw Charles Grey again after 1862 or got in touch with other relatives. According to *De Bernardy's Unclaimed Money Register*, published in London in 1883, James was entitled to an inheritance from Henry Bird that was still unclaimed (p. 6).

# THE STORY OF HENRY EDWARD AND ELIZA

A major life event for H.E. Bird occurred on 10 October 1855: He married Eliza Cain at St. Mary's in Lambeth. With all his direct male adult relatives gone, Bird made an appeal to James Longman Gawler to be his witness. Gawler was for many years the parish clerk at St. Mary's and his signature appears therefore on hundreds of marriage acts.

The marriage certificate contains the names of two close relatives of Eliza. The witness acting on her behalf was Ann Cain. Assuming that Ann was Eliza's sister, which seems likely, one has a starting point from which a trustworthy family tree can be reconstructed. The name of Eliza's deceased father, Robert Cain, is also mentioned on the act. He was a gas meter maker by profession.[31]

On 10 May 1818, a girl named Ann Cain was baptized in the parish of Southwark Christ Church.[32] According to her baptism record she was the daughter of Robert Cain, a lamplighter.[33] This profession is not so different from gas meter maker. The act only registered the first name of the child's mother, Sarah.

More than a decade later, on 27 June 1830, Ann and Rosina Cain were jointly baptized at St. George the Martyr in Southwark.[34] Their parents' names were identical to those given in 1818. It is unclear whether this Ann was the same child as in 1818 or whether she had

died and another child was given the same name. As seen in the case of Henry Edward Bird, it was not completely uncommon to baptize a child twice.

Robert Cain died a short time later. His burial took place on 17 April 1831 in the parish of Southwark Christ Church. At the time of his death he was 36 years old.[35]

Eliza thus had two sisters, Ann and Rosina. Another close family member, in all likelihood her brother, was a certain Robert Kayne.[36] He is mentioned on Eliza's death certificate, in 1868, as the authorities' informant of her demise.

Further research on Robert Kayne only strengthens the presumption of ties with Eliza. Robert wed Naomi Coles on 27 April 1856. The wedding took place at St. John's Church in Lambeth. Naomi died within a year or two, after which Robert remarried Hannah Hyland, a widow. The wedding took place on 18 December 1859 at the Parish Church in St. George's Hannover Square. Both wedding acts identify the groom's father as "Robert Kayne," a lamp maker. Robert Kayne, Eliza's brother, worked as a boot maker. These professions place both men in the class of skilled artisans.

At the time of Eliza's death in 1868, Robert lived at 75 Seymour Place, Bryanston Square in Marylebone, Westminster. The census of 1871 shows him at the same address.[37] According to this document Robert was born in 1824. Most curiously, Edinburgh was given as his birthplace. Robert lived at other addresses when the censuses of 1861 and 1881 were taken, but both his birth year and place were confirmed.[38] Edinburgh hardly seems to fit in with all other familial activities, which occurred in or near Lambeth. Possibly Robert Cain, the father, lived a few years in Scotland during the 1820s. At that time Edinburgh was an important center in the production of gas, the field in which he was professionally active. It remains unclear if Robert, the son, had the same mother as his sisters.

Robert Kayne died in 1882 in Southwark. His death certificate indicates no place of birth. His birth year is given as circa 1828, a marked difference.[39]

---

30. Carl Pfaff, who collected reminiscences of early gold diggers in the beginning of the next century, recorded James' story: "James Pedding [*sic*] Bird came to Dunedin from Melbourne in the *Red Jacket* (Captain Harley R.N., Reserve) in 1862 or the beginning of 1863, and went to the Weatherstone diggings, also Waipouri [Waipori]. Left Waipouri and came to the West Coast in the steamer *Egmont* from Dunedin to Lyttelton, and them tramped overland to the West Coast. Was at Hokitika in 1865, and went to the Auckland Beach Rush, and worked at Cameron's Rush and Brighton and Addison's Flat, Barrytown and Nelson Creek and Moonlight; and was in the Grey District till 1908, till his return to Hokitika; at Takatai for two and a half years, and now an inmate of the Totara Hospital, Ross. Aged 80 years." C. Pfaff, J. Bradshaw, *The Diggers' Story: Accounts of the West Coast Gold Rushes*. Christchurch: Canterbury University Press, p. 162. ¶ Was James Pidding mistaken when he said that he arrived on board the *Red Jacket* in 1862 or the beginning of 1863? We found him on board the *Bruce*, a ship that arrived in October 1862 in Port Chalmers (a suburb of Dunedin). Public Record Office Victoria. Index to Unassisted Inward Passenger Lists to Victoria 1852–1923. http://prov.vic.gov.au/index_search?searchid=23. The newspapers speak of "a ship, supposed to be the *Samuel Appleton* or *Bruce*." It arrived from Melbourne with 12 passengers, general cargo and 159 horses. ¶ The *Otago Daily Times* of 9 February 1863 wrote: "The rush to Otago is commencing in earnest again. The *City of Melbourne* and *Red Jacket* will bring nearly a thousand passengers between them.

31. They "made gas by heating coal to produce gas, which was purified to remove the tar. The coal would be turned into coke. The gas could be used for lighting, heating or powering a gas engine. The tar was used in road surfacing." http://rmhh.co.uk/occup/g.html.

32. "England Births and Christenings, 1538–1975," index, *FamilySearch* (https://familysearch.org/pal:/MM9.1.1/JMR9-C4D: accessed 25 Sep 2014), Ann Cain, 10 May 1818; citing CHRIST CHURCH,SOUTHWARK,LONDON,ENGLAND, reference ; FHL microfilm 908520

33. Lamplighters lit the lights in the evening and put them out at dawn. They were also responsible for more technical interventions. With the introduction of gas light (first used in London in 1807), the job of lamplighter slowly lost its importance. ¶ In the marriage certificates of Robert Cain's children, which originate from the second half of the 1850s and are quoted in this chapter, Robert Cain's profession is given as respectively gas meter maker and lamp maker. With the function of lamplighter having become extinct it seems not illogical that his children, who knew their father only when they were all extremely young, mentioned professions that were more actual but probably had not been that of their father.

34. London Metropolitan Archives, *St. George the Martyr, Register of Baptism, P92/GEO, Item 152*.

35. London Metropolitan Archives, *Christ Church, Southwark, Register of burials, P92/CTC, Item 060*; Call Number: *p92/ctc/060*.

36. Various spellings are possible for Eliza's family name: Cain, Caine, Kayne and Kaine were the most recurrent.

37. 1871 census: Class: RG10; Piece: 166; Folio: 80; Page: 34.

38. Robert's family name was spelled Kaine in 1881.

39. His death was registered in the St. Olave Southwark district, Jan-Feb-Mar 1882, vol. 1d, p. 208.

CERTIFIED COPY OF AN ENTRY OF MARRIAGE     GIVEN AT THE GENERAL REGISTER OFFICE

Application Number 2635376/1

| No. | When Married. | Name and Surname. | Age. | Condition. | Rank or Profession. | Residence at the time of Marriage. | Father's Name and Surname. | Rank or Profession of Father. |
|---|---|---|---|---|---|---|---|---|
| 261 | 19th Oct 1855 | Henry Edward Bird — Eliza Cain | 26th 4 full age | Bachelor Spinster | Accountant | Lambeth | Henry Bird — Robert Cain (decd) | Storekeeper Gas Meter Maker |

1855. Marriage solemnized at *The Parish Church* in the Parish of *St Mary Lambeth* in the County of *Surrey*

Married in the *Parish Church* according to the Rites and Ceremonies of the Established Church, by _____ or after *Banns* by me, C. S. Alexander, Curate.

This Marriage was solemnized between us, { Henry Edward Bird / Eliza Cain } in the Presence of us, { Ann Cain / S. L. Sawter }

CERTIFIED to be a true copy of an entry in the certified copy of a register of Marriages in the Registration District of **Lambeth**
Given at the GENERAL REGISTER OFFICE, under the Seal of the said Office, the    **10th** day of    **September**    **2010**

MXF 033454

Marriage certificate of Henry Edward Bird and Eliza Cain.

## THE TRAGIC FATE OF CHARLES FRENCH SMITH

C.F. Smith, perhaps Bird's most regular opponent during the years 1849 and 1850, disappeared from the chess columns during the year 1851. He was also conspicuously absent from the tournament of 1851. John Townsend discovered what happened and extensively deals with Smith's history in an essay in his book *Historical Notes on Some Chess Players* (pp. 81–90). Townsend found out that from February until October 1851 Smith was interned as a patient at the Royal Hospital of Bethlem. The supposed cause of Smith's insanity was "excessive study and excitement from chess and reading novels." It did not take Smith long to recover: From 1852 onwards he committed himself intensively to chess again. Smith and Bird continued to play each other on a regular basis again between 1852 and 1854.

A few of their games were published in 1852. Two of these featured the same variation of the Evans Gambit, which may mean that they were part of a thematic match, similar to the one played in 1850.

**(91) C.F. Smith–Bird    1–0**
Offhand game
London 1852
*B44*

1. e4 c5 2. d4 c×d4 3. Nf3 Nc6 4. Bc4 e6 5. N×d4 Bc5 6. N×c6 b×c6 7. Qg4 Nf6 8. Qh4 Ba6 9. e5 B×c4 10. Q×c4 Qa5† 11. Bd2 B×f2† 12. K×f2 Q×e5 13. Nc3 Qf5† 14. Qf4 Q×c2 15. Rhc1 Q×b2 16. Rab1 Qa3 17. Rb8† Ke7 18. Nb5 Ng4† 19. Q×g4 Qb2 20. Qb4† Q×b4 21. B×b4† and White wins—*Chess Player's Chronicle*, September 1852, pp. 277–278.

**(92) C.F. Smith–Bird    1–0**
Offhand game
London 1852
*C51*

1. e4 e5 2. Nf3 Nc6 3. Bc4 Bc5 4. b4 B×b4 5. c3 Ba5 6. d4 e×d4 7. 0–0 Bb6 8. e5 Nge7 9. c×d4 0–0 10. d5 Na5 11. Bd3 Ng6 12. Ng5 h6 13. N×f7 R×f7 14. B×g6 Rf8 15. Nc3 Nc4 16. Qh5 Qe7 17. e6 d×e6 18. Bd3 R×f2 19. R×f2 B×f2† 20. Kh1 e×d5 21. B×h6 Be6 22. Bg5 Qd7 23. Rf1 Qf7 24. Qh7† Kf8 25. Bg6 and White wins—*The Chess Player*, 7 November 1852, p. 148.

## (93) C.F. Smith–Bird    0–1
Offhand game
London, 15 December 1852
C51

1. e4 e5 2. Nf3 Nc6 3. Bc4 Bc5 4. b4 B×b4 5. c3 Ba5 6. d4
e×d4 7. 0–0 Bb6 8. e5 Nge7 9. c×d4 0–0 10. d5 Na5 11. Bd3 Ng6
12. Ng5 h6 13. N×f7 R×f7 14. B×g6 Rf8 15. Bc2 Qh4 16. Qd3
R×f2 17. Qh7† Kf7 18. Qg6† Ke7 19. Ba3† Kd8 20. Rd1 Black
mates in two moves—*British Chess Review*, February 1853, p. 56.

The next three games, presented as a series by Staunton, were
published in 1854. Possibly they were played two years earlier; no
other chess-related mention of Bird in 1853 or 1854 has been found.
It is remarkable that Smith won every game convincingly.

## (94) C.F. Smith–Bird    1–0
Offhand game
London 1854 (?)
C51

1. e4 e5 2. Nf3 Nc6 3. Bc4 Bc5 4. b4 B×b4 5. c3 Ba5 6. d4
e×d4 7. 0–0 d6 8. Qb3 Qe7 9. e5 d×e5 10. Re1 Bb6 11. Ba3 Qf6
12. N×e5 N×e5 13. B×f7† Kd8 14. Qd5† Bd7 15. R×e5 c6
16. Re8† Kc7 17. Qd6† Q×d6 18. B×d6† K×d6 19. R×a8 Ke7
20. R×g8 and White wins—*Chess Player's Chronicle*, June 1854,
pp. 172–173.

## (95) Bird–C.F. Smith    0–1
Offhand game
London 1854 (?)
C60

1. e4 e5 2. Nf3 Nc6 3. Bb5 Bd6 4. d4 Qe7 5. 0–0 a6 6. Ba4 b5
7. Bb3 Bb7 8. Bd5 Nf6 9. Bg5 h6 10. B×f6 Q×f6 11. Nc3 Rb8
12. d×e5 N×e5 13. N×e5 B×e5 14. B×b7 R×b7 15. Nd5 Qc6
16. c3 Bd6 17. f4 0–0 18. f5 Qc5† 19. Kh1 c6 20. b4 Qc4 21. Nf6†
g×f6 22. Q×d6 Q×c3 23. Rac1 Qe5 24. Qd2 Kh7 25. Rc3 Rg8
26. Rc5 Q×e4 27. Rf4 R×g2 28. Qc1 Qe2 29. Rh4 Rg5 and Black
wins—*Chess Player's Chronicle*, June 1854, pp. 173–174.

## (96) C.F. Smith–Bird    1–0
Offhand game
London 1854 (?)
C51

1. e4 e5 2. Nf3 Nc6 3. Bc4 Bc5 4. b4 B×b4 5. c3 Ba5 6. d4
e×d4 7. 0–0 Bb6 8. c×d4 d6 9. h3 h6 10. Bb2 Nf6 11. d5 Ne7
12. B×f6 g×f6 13. Nc3 Ng6 14. Nd4 Ne5 Interesting is 14. ... Qe7,
freeing d8 for the king in case of 15. Bb5†. **15. f4 N×c4 16. Qa4†
Bd7 17. Q×c4 Qe7** He could also consider the more active 17. ...
f5. **18. Kh1 0–0–0?!** The queenside is absolutely not safe for the
king. **19. a4?!** 19. Nc6! is very strong. Black has to exchange some
material 19. ... B×c6 20. d×c6 b×c6 21. Q×c6 when White is much
better thanks to his strong knight. **19. ... a6?** Innocent looking at
first sight, but in fact creating an already mortal weakness of the
king's headquarters. After 19. ... Rdg8 Black retains all chances.
**20. Rab1** 20. Rfb1 or 20. Nc6 are winning as well. **20. ... B×d4**

**21. Q×d4 c5** "Desperate indeed, but Black's situation is not one
which admits of half measures"—Staunton. **22. Qc4?** 22. d×c6 *e.p.*
(Staunton) is decisive: 22. ... B×c6 23. Qa7! Qc7 24. Nd5! Qb8
25. Ne7† Kd7 26. N×c6 wins. **22. ... Rdg8 23. Rb2** *(see diagram)*

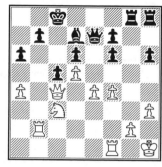

*After 23. Rb2*

**23. ... Rg3?** The situation still looks bad for Black, as White is
ready to double on the b-file and infiltrate at b7. It soon turns out
that Bird's move is too slow to deal with this idea. At once 23. ...
B×h3! is a good way to generate quick counterplay. If White accepts
the sacrifice, Black indeed achieves this aim; e.g., after 24. g×h3
Rg3 25. Kh2 Rhg8 26. Ne2 Rg2† 27. Kh1 Qd7 28. f5 Qe8 29. Rf4
Qe5 with sufficient pressure. The cool 24. Qd3 is more testing. The
retreat 24. ... Bg4 is no option due to 25. Rfb1 (menacing 26. Q×a6!)
25. ... Rd8 26. Rb6 and nothing can be done against 27. Rc6†! So
24. ... B×g2† is forced. After 25. R×g2 Qd7 26. Rfg1 R×g2 27. R×g2
h5 the position is surprisingly murky, as White's knight is pretty
useless. **24. Rfb1 b5 25. N×b5! a×b5 26. R×b5! B×b5 27. Q×b5
Qa7 28. Qc6† Qc7 29. Qa6†** 29. Qa8† picks up the rook. **29. ...
Kd8 30. Rb7 Q×b7 31. Q×b7 Rhg8 32. a5?** Too slow. 32. e5! convincingly breaks through; e.g., in case of 32. ... R×g2 33. Qb8† Kd7
34. Q×d6† Kc8 35. Q×c5†. **32. ... R×g2 33. Qb1 c4 34. a6 Rg1†?**
This must have been a miscalculation. After 34. ... R2g3, Smith has
nothing but to go for a perpetual check. **35. Q×g1 R×g1† 36. K×g1
Kc7 37. Kf2 Kb6 38. e5 K×a6 39. e6** and White wins—*Chess
Player's Chronicle* (Staunton), June 1854, pp. 174–175.

Smith resumed his activities in correspondence chess after he was
dismissed from the hospital. He took part in the first known postal
tournament in chess history which was organized by the periodical
*Home Circle*. Smith succeeded in winning this event.

One of Smith's most frequent opponents in correspondence play
was Valentine Green. In a game published in the *Chess Player's Chronicle* of July 1854 (p. 197), Staunton suggested that Smith had left London by calling him a provincial amateur. A glimpse of Smith's
residence was provided by Falkbeer in *The Sunday Times* of 20 December 1857. He declared that C.F. Smith was living in Birmingham.

A small mystery exists about a "Smith" at the Birmingham tournament in 1858. Supposing that he lived in Birmingham at the time,
possibly it was C.F. Smith who joined the tournament, "in order to
complete the number." Also according to Staunton in the *Illustrated
London News* on 4 September 1858, Smith had "no chance of maintaining a struggle against such powerful opponents."

Staunton's suggestion that Smith was too weak for this field is
strange if indeed it is C.F. Smith, for Staunton was well aware of
his earlier results. It is possible that Staunton did not personally
know the former youngster or did not recognize him anymore.

Smith was paired against Morphy in the first round. The young American visitor ultimately did not play and thus allowed the local player to advance to the next round. Now Smith himself forfeited his game against Brien.

C.F. Smith's name figured a last time in a chess column in 1859. His sad fate was discovered by John Townsend. During the census of 1861 he was recorded as a patient at the Grove Hall Lunatic Asylum, Bow. Smith committed suicide at the same institution on 23 February 1868.

# OTHER OFFHAND GAMES 1852–1855

At the end of 1852 or in January 1853, Bird played a few games against his old antagonist Henry Thomas Buckle. Buckle's days at the chessboard were largely over by now. Around 1851 he had developed the concept of what would become his major historical work, *The History of Civilization*, and he dedicated his remaining years to this work.

The games between Bird and Buckle were played on even terms. Bird was very unlucky to lose to his more experienced opponent, **game 98**, a game he was winning.

## (97) Buckle–Bird   ½–½
Offhand game
London 1852 (?)
*C40*

1. e4 e5 2. Nf3 d5 3. N×e5 d×e4 4. d4 Be6 5. Bc4 B×c4 6. N×c4 Nc6 7. c3 f5 8. Bf4 Nge7 9. Qb3 Rb8 10. Bg5 Qd5 11. B×e7 B×e7 12. Ne3 Q×b3 13. a×b3 0–0 14. Nd2 a6 15. h4 Rbd8 16. f4 e×f3 *e.p.* 17. N×f3 Bd6 18. Kf2 Rde8 19. Rae1 b5 20. b4 a5 21. b×a5 N×a5 22. b4 Nc6 23. Nd5 Re4 24. h5 Rfe8 25. R×e4 f×e4 26. Re1 Nb8 27. Ng5 Rf8† 28. Kg1 Rf5 29. N×e4 R×d5 30. N×d6 c×d6 31. Re8† Kf7 32. R×b8 R×h5 33. Rb7† Kf6 34. Rd7 Rd5 35. Kf2 h5 36. Kf3 g6 37. Ke4 Ke6 38. Rb7 Rg5 39. Kf3 h4 40. Kf2 Rg3 41. R×b5 R×c3 42. Rg5 Kf6 43. Rd5 draw—*The Field*, 22 January 1853.

## (98) Bird–Buckle   0–1
Offhand game
London 1852 (?)
*B30*

1. e4 c5 2. Nf3 Nc6 3. Bb5 e6 4. 0–0 Nce7 5. c4 f5 6. Nc3 g6 7. d3 Bg7 8. Be3 b6 9. Ng5 Kf8 10. e×f5 e×f5 11. Bf4 d6 12. Ba6 h6 13. B×c8 h×g5 14. Bb7 g×f4 15. B×a8 Q×a8 16. Nb5 f3 17. Q×f3 Q×f3 18. g×f3 Nc6 19. f4 Ke7 20. Rae1† Kd7 21. Re2 a6 22. Nc3 B×c3 23. b×c3 Nge7 24. Kg2 d5 25. d4 c×d4 26. c×d4 d×c4 27. Rd1 Nd5 and Black wins—*The Field*, 29 January 1853.

## (99) W.T. Wilson–Bird   1–0
Offhand game
London (Simpson's Divan) 1854
*Bird granted odds of pawn and two moves*

1. e4 & 2. Bc4 e6 3. d4 c6 4. Nc3 d5 5. e×d5 e×d5 6. Qe2† Be7 7. Bb3 Nf6 8. Nf3 0–0 9. 0–0 Bg4 10. h3 Bh5 11. g4 N×g4 12. Qe6† Kh8 13. h×g4 Rf6 14. Qe5 B×g4 15. Ng5 Bd6 16. Qe1 h6 17. f3 Bf5 18. Kf2 h×g5 19. B×g5 Qc7 20. Qe8† Rf8 21. Qh5† Bh7 22. Rh1 g6 23. Qh4 Rf5 24. Rag1 Qf7 25. Rh3 Nd7 26. Rgh1 Nf8 27. Ne4 Bf4 28. Be7 g5 29. B×g5 Qg7 30. Bf6 R×f6 31. N×f6 Bg5 White mates in three moves—*Era*, 12 November 1854.

When Staunton disappeared from the center of British chess after 1851, Daniel Harrwitz took his place as the strongest player in London. While Harrwitz' first passage to England was hardly a success—he had lost by 7 to 0 against Staunton in 1846—he confirmed his new status by beating Williams and Löwenthal in the years following the 1851 tournament. Negotiations for a return match with Staunton were started in 1854 but their bad personal relations stood in the way of a positive outcome.

## (100) Bird–Harrwitz   0–1
Offhand game
London 1854 (?)
*C51*

"Lively game played some time ago between Mr. H.E. Bird and the editor"—Harrwitz.

1. e4 e5 2. Nf3 Nc6 3. Bc4 Bc5 4. b4 B×b4 5. c3 Bc5 6. d4 e×d4 7. 0–0 Bb6 8. e5 Nge7 9. c×d4 d5 10. e×d6 *e.p.* c×d6 11. d5 Nb8 12. Nc3 0–0 13. Ne4 Bf5 14. Re1 Ng6 15. Ba3 Bc7 Needlessly passive. After 15. ... B×e4 16. R×e4 Nd7, White's compensation for the pawn is hard to find. If 17. B×d6? Nf6 18. B×f8 N×e4 Black wins. **16. Rc1 f6?** *(see diagram)* "A weak move, of which White speedily takes advantage"—Harrwitz. 16. ... B×e4 is still fine for Black.

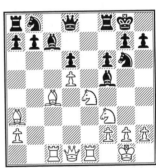

*After 16. ... f6*

17. Nd4! Ne7 18. N×d6! B×d6 19. B×d6 Q×d6 20. R×e7 Bd7 "It is palpable that taking the rook would cost him his queen"—Harrwitz. **21. Re6?** A forceful but innocent continuation. Black is helpless if Bird had started a direct onslaught against the king with 21. Qh5!; e.g., 21. ... Na6 22. Bd3 and wins. **21. ... B×e6 22. Nb5 Qe5 23. d×e6 Kh8 24. Qd5 Nc6 25. Q×e5 f×e5 26. Bd5 Nd4 27. N×d4 e×d4 28. e7 Rfe8 29. Rc7?** A clear-cut mistake. Bird could have drawn easily with 29. B×b7 Rab8 30. Rc7 d3 31. Kf1. **29. ... Rac8 30. R×c8 R×c8 31. Kf1 Re8 32. Ke2** "Had he taken b7 he would not have been able to bring his king out, and must eventually have given his bishop for Black's d-pawn"—Harrwitz. **32. ... R×e7† 33. Kd3 g6 34. K×d4 Kg7 35. f4 Kf6 36. g4 b6**

**37. Be4 Rd7† 38. Bd5 a6 39. Ke4 Re7† 40. Kd4 Re2 41. h4 Rh2 42. h5 g×h5 43. g5† Kf5 44. Ke3 Rh3† 45. Kd4 K×f4** and Black wins—*British Chess Review* (Harrwitz), June 1854, pp. 161–162.

Bird was eager to play more chess in 1855 than in the years before. His name was mentioned on three occasions in connection with a prospective chess event. Firstly, his participation was announced in a tournament at Kling's Chess and Coffee Rooms. This small event, with eight participants, was one of the first tournaments on British soil since 1851. Bird entered the lists, but on arriving too late for the opening round, he found his place taken by Arthur Simons.

Bird's name was also connected with two planned matches. An announcement was made of a duel with Adolf Zytogorsky. This Polish player emigrated to England to escape the Polish-Russian wars of 1830-31. His chess activities mainly occurred between 1854 and 1860 and his most notable result was the tournament victory at the tournament at Kling's, mentioned above. Sadly, no match between Bird and this interesting antagonist appears to have been played.

Finally, there were strange rumors about a match between Bird and Falkbeer. In the December 1855 issue of *Chess Player's Chronicle* (p. 361) it was written that Falkbeer had challenged his British opponent, "but whether a contest will ensue we cannot as yet pronounce with certainty, for, so far as we are aware, Mr. Bird, at the time at which we are writing, knows nothing of the matter."

Perhaps the following offhand game had something to do with this challenge.

**(101) Bird–Falkbeer    1–0**
Offhand game
London 1855
*C60*

**1. e4 e5 2. Nf3 Nc6 3. Bb5 Nge7 4. 0–0 d6 5. d4 e×d4 6. N×d4 Bd7 7. Bc4 Ng6 8. Nc3 Be7 9. N×c6 b×c6 10. f4 0–0 11. Qh5 Bf6 12. Rf3 Qe7 13. f5 Nh4 14. Rh3 d5 15. Bd3 B×f5 16. e5 Q×e5 17. R×h4 Qe1† 18. Bf1 Bg6 19. Qf3 B×h4 20. Rb1 Be4 21. N×e4 d×e4 22. Qe3 Q×e3† 23. B×e3 Rad8 24. B×a7 Rd2 25. c4 Re8 26. Be3 Rc2 27. a4 c5 28. B×c5 e3 29. Bd3 Rd2 30. g3 R×d3 31. g×h4 e2 32. Re1 Rd1 33. Kf2 R×e1 34. K×e1 Re4 35. b3 R×h4 36. a5 R×h2 37. a6 Rh1† 38. K×e2 Ra1 39. a7 h5 40. b4 g5 41. b5 f5 42. Bd4 Kf7 43. B×a1** and Black resigns—*Era*, 26 August 1855.

Bird married Eliza Cain in October 1855 and the priorities in life shifted quite dramatically. For over a year he was totally absent from the chess scene.

---

# ◆ Part III ◆

# THE ACCOUNTANCY YEARS (I), 1856–1865

## BECOMING AN EXPERT ACCOUNTANT 1857–1866

Henry Edward Bird's life stood in quite a contrast with that of his fortune seeking father and brothers. The chess master had opted for the steady career of an accountant in the heart of the city of London. In 1857, when he had been in the service of the Young brothers for over a decade, a major merger occurred. Out of the mêlée the firm Coleman, Turquand, Youngs and Company surfaced. This amalgamation soon enjoyed an excellent reputation as one of the largest accounting firms in London and even in the world. In 1859 they moved their headquarters to 16 Tokenhouse Yard, Lothbury, in the heart of the City of London. Bird fared well during these years. At the time of the merger, he was promoted from clerk to junior partner. There was, however, also a toll to pay in return for his promotion. In *Modern Chess* (p. 1) Bird wrote that he had to travel a lot for his work during the late 1850s.

The accountancy sector was still extremely liable to changes in the legislation. This went hand in hand with a rising number of skills required of accountants, an increase in activities and rapidly growing incomes for the firms.[1]

Auditing received a huge boost during these years. The impor-

---

1. "The Bankruptcy Act of 1861 permitted debtors to absolve themselves of their liabilities by making themselves voluntarily bankrupt; this caused a significant increase in the number of registered failures.... The 'accountant's friend' the Companies Act of 1862, established the position of official liquidators and brought further opportunities, while the Bankruptcy Act 1869, which abolished the position of official assignee and instituted a trustee in his place, also brought a large accession of business to accountants. Under the Act public accountants could be appointed directly as trustees to administer the debtor's estate rather than having to work through an intermediary." Matthews, *Priesthood of Industry*, p. 31.

tance of this task has risen into prominence since the wake of the railway mania of the 1840s. During these years speculators invested loads of money into railways shares of which the price was on the rise for years. The collapse of the British financial markets, the so-called Panic of 1847, put an end to the success. The growing complexity of the accounts of large companies made it impossible for the shareholders to perform an audit themselves. This was a serious problem as neutrality became more and more a requirement. In such complicated and often suspicious cases the appointment of accountants became standard procedure.

During the first part of the 1860s Bird gained more and more expertise by dealing with various such cases and he developed an excellent reputation.[2]

A few of Bird's dossiers were extensively dealt with in the press. In 1863 Bird worked on a balance sheet concerning the bankruptcy of Messrs. Morgan and Adams, proprietors of a bank from Hereford. On 26 September 1863, the *Birmingham Daily Post* reported that he had succeeded in demonstrating a succession of false balances. In 1865 Bird, together with John Edward Coleman, was responsible for auditing the Asiatic Banking Corporation. Bird was also involved in the failure of Overend, Gurney and Company that caused the Panic of 1866.[3]

These few examples mentioned in the press suggest Bird's capability to deal with a variety of cases, but he undoubtedly specialized in railway finances. His most important assignments brought him to the United States on three occasions. Bird's first visit took place in 1860, immediately after he was eliminated from the handicap tournament at the St. James's Chess Club.

Bird's crossing of the Atlantic is well documented. When examining the books and further documents concerning the Great Western Railway of Canada, the committee of shareholders came to the conclusion that an onsite investigation was needed. On 5 May, the *Morning Chronicle* reported the urgent departure of John and Alexander Young to the colony. The passenger lists show the brothers arriving in New York on board the *Africa* on 8 June 1860. On the same page, are entries for three other accountants: Bird, Calder and Sherbrook.[4] As Bird had been working for the Young brothers since the beginning of his professional career it is no surprise to see him selected for such an important undertaking. The

work of the accountants in Ontario, where the railway was situated, ended in July and the company then set off to the United States where they had been engaged on the accounts of the New York Central Railroad.[5] Bird's visit was announced in a local chess column (but with no news about any chess activities).[6]

## PERSONAL CHANGES

Life lingered on for Mary Ellen after Henry had gone to Australia. She continued to live at the family's residence at 16 Harleyford Place. *Kelly's Post Office London Directory* recorded her at that address from 1858 until 1865, the year when her husband returned. From at least 1857, John Streat, professionally a warehouseman, lived at the same address. As seen above, he filed the complaint in the Bird v. Drouet case on behalf of Henry and Mary Ellen's infant children in 1855. At that time he was said to be living at Lawrence Lane. Clearly he became the protégé of the tormented family. John Streat, curiously enough, even lived at the same address until at least 1869, after the reconciliation of Henry Bird and Mary Ellen had taken place.

While her husband stated that he had made provisions for Mary Ellen and her minor aged children before he left England, it remains an open question if this was the case and whether these were sufficient to help her out. She may have had some support from her sister Jane, who lived in comfortable circumstances with her man, a surgeon, at some five miles distance in Kensington.[7]

Mary Ellen lived together with her daughters. In the case of Jackson v. Drew, Louisa Maria and Emily Fanny Stopford Bird were heard. As they were infants they had nothing to add. The aforementioned John Streat was called the children's guardian.

Sad news occurred at 16 Harleyford Place on 10 August 1862, when Emily Fanny Stopford died here. The death of the young girl appeared among the family notices in *The Melbourne Argus* of 14 October 1862. Here it was said that she died "at the family residence."[8]

Henry Edward probably left Harleyford Place shortly after his wedding with Eliza Cain. It remains unknown where the couple

2. MacDonnell learned this from one of Bird's bosses: "Many years ago I happened to be dining with Mr. Turquand, the eminent accountant, and he asked if I knew Bird, then a clerk in his house, and what I thought of his chess. I told him Bird was one of the finest players in England. 'Indeed' he remarked, 'well, he is also one of the cleverest accountants I know; for railway business he is unequalled.'" MacDonnell, *The Knights and Kings of Chess*, pp. 47–48.

3. Bird related a chess anecdote that happened in these juridical circles: "Chief Baron Pigott who also knew it [the rules of chess] presided in the long trial Bartlett v. Lewis, Overend, Gurney, etc., and seemed much surprised at a chess allusion. Said [Isaac] Butt to me 'come, you are not playing chess with me.' Whiteside and Sullivan, two of the six counsel on the other side, almost simultaneously replied, 'A good thing for you brother Butt, for you would surely soon be checkmated.'" Bird, *Chess History and Reminiscences*, p. 125.

4. *New York Passenger Lists, 1820–1957.* Year: *1860*; Arrival: *New York, United States*; Microfilm serial: *M237*; Microfilm roll: *M237_201*; Line: *28*; List number: *432*.

5. A short résumé, containing a few extra details about Bird's activities for Coleman, Turquand, Youngs and Co. in the new world, was published fifteen years later: "Mr. Bird, the eminent English chess player, is by profession a railway accountant. He has been in this country several times before the present visit. In 1860 he was in Canada, as a junior partner of Coleman, Turquand, Youngs and Co., London accountants, and was engaged on the accounts of the Great Western Railroad of Canada, and afterward on the New York Central." *Western Advertiser*, 27 December 1875.

6. "It affords us much pleasure to announce the arrival in America of Mr. Bird, one of the finest chess players in England. We are given to understand that he will soon visit New York, and afford our leading players the long coveted opportunity of comparing their strength with a first rate European chess player. From what we have heard of Mr. Bird's play, and judging also from recorded games played by him, we are inclined to think him a pawn and move, if not pawn and two, stronger than our best players." *Albion*, 7 July 1860.

7. Jane's relative wealth is illustrated by the impressive estate of £9597 she left behind at the time of her death in 1889. Ancestry.com. *England & Wales, National Probate Calendar (Index of Wills and Administrations), 1858–1966* [database on-line]. Provo, UT, USA: Ancestry.com Operations Inc, 2010.

8. London Metropolitan Archives, *All Souls Cemetery, Kensal Green, Kensington, Transcript of Burials, 1862 Jan–1862 Dec, DL/t Item, 041/030*; Call Number: *DL/T/041/030*.

resided until 1861. In 1862, *Kelly's Directory* lists Henry Edward at 16 Williams Terrace, Lorrimore Square. This site had only recently been developed. The first houses at Williams Terrace were built in 1855. The terrace grew in size over the years and the chess master remained here until 1866. By then his lodgings had been re-numbered as 44. It is a pity that the census taken on 7 April 1861 misses large parts of Lambeth. Harleyford Place is been one of the many streets that have been lost. The house at 16 Williams Terrace was given as uninhabited, though *Kelly's Directory* states that a certain William Frederick Tindell lived here in 1861.

**Ernst Falkbeer (*Chess Monthly*).**

## MATCHES WITH FALKBEER 1856–1857

After abstaining for about five years from intense practice of the game, Bird picked up chess again towards the end of 1856. His new favorite resort became Purssell's, a coffee house in the heart of the City of London. Purssell's served as a meeting place between stock exchange men, businessmen, foreigners and lawyers. It was attended by such celebrities as Thackeray and (the future) Napoleon III. Chess had always been a popular activity here but the game received a real boost at the end of 1855 when the London Chess Club moved into the same building. Chess players could now choose between playing in the apartments above Purssell's in which the Club resided or in the rooms of Purssell's on the ground floor. Bird felt very much at ease at the latter location and during some years of his chess career (especially the first part of the 1880s) Purssell's was his home ground.

Bird shared the reputation of strongest player at Purssell's with Ernst Falkbeer. Falkbeer, born in Brno in 1819, led a wandering life consequential to the revolutionary climate in Europe around the year 1848. In 1855 he crossed the Channel and settled in London. His name is still connected with one of the main variations dealing with the King's Gambit. As a player he excelled between 1854 and 1858. His best results were the match win against Bird and the second place at the tournament in Birmingham in 1858. Falkbeer left England definitively in 1864.[9]

At the end of 1856 a small contest for Purssell's chess throne was arranged. Only two wins were sufficient to win the match. The first game, played on Saturday 29 November 1856, was won by Bird.[10] Falkbeer equalized the score on the following Saturday. A week later, Bird decided the match in the third game.

Both players now complied with the general feeling that such a short match was not definitive as to respective playing strengths

and a second match was commenced forthwith. This time the first player to notch five wins would be declared the winner. In *Chess History and Reminiscences* (p. 115), Bird claimed that the stakes were set in between £10 and £20.

This second match between Bird and Falkbeer is more difficult to reconstruct. A part of a table was published in Di Felice's *Chess Results*, but there appears no basis for it.[11]

The match probably began on 27 December 1856 with a draw. With three straight wins following, Falkbeer appeared on his way to a walk-over but, after the pace of the match dropped a bit, Bird surged forward and narrowed the gap until it was just one point after the seventh game. This game was played on 21 February.

From here on the original schedule, one game per week played on Saturdays, was implemented again. After ten games Falkbeer was still in the lead with four wins against three losses, with three draws. The score was flattering for the Austrian. The ninth game was especially dramatic for Bird. He did extremely well out of the opening but failed to convert a winning attack into a full point and even blundered into a loss.

After 12 games the score stood level, with four wins each. The thirteenth game was likely to be the decisive one. It was postponed until Thursday 9 or 16 April. Bird opened well and soon obtained a winning attack. His play combined beauty with vigorousness, but also a vulnerability to commit impulsive blunders. The final one suddenly reversed the roles and Bird's king was busted. The outcome of the match was a disappointment for Bird but he deservedly

9. A good summary of Falkbeer's exorbitant playing style was written down by MacDonnell: "Falkbeer was a very rapid player, original, daring and imaginative. He could be sound when he liked, but he did not covet soundness. He delighted to be fireworky, and courted above all things the admiration of the spectators. As an analyst he occupied a high position. He was at once keen, sound, deep, and, when the humor seized him, even profound. Falkbeer invented many clever and valuable moves in the openings, notably 3. ... e4 in the King's Gambit, evaded 2. ... d5. Referring to which invention, Staunton says: 'It is certainly an embarrassing move for White; for it proves not merely a defense, but a counterattack of considerable power.'" MacDonnell, *The Knights and Kings of Chess*, p. 81.

10. There is some divergence between the sources. The present work follows the most contemporary one (*Era*, 7 December 1856). A few years later, it was written that Falkbeer won the first game (*Chess Player's Chronicle*, April 1859, p. 97).

11. The problem is the absence of a specialized chess magazine during these years. This match was also largely neglected by *The Field* and the *Illustrated London News*, leaving only the *Era* with more or less detailed reports. Falkbeer's important column in *The Sunday Times* took off only after the match was over. The only other source is an article covering the matches of the previous years in the April 1859 edition of the *Chess Player's Chronicle* (particularly p. 97).

received a lot of praise for his strong result against such an experienced opponent.[12]

This match is the first known occasion on which Bird employed his future trademark move, 1. f4. He achieved just one draw out of the four published games with it. With such a dramatic score (two of his games with White are missing), it was easy for his peers to condemn Bird's drift to experiment. Our analysis, however, shows that Bird got very promising positions that were suited for a creative player. His score was unlucky, but certainly open for improvement.

Staunton revealed in the *Illustrated London News* of 25 April that Bird and Falkbeer had plans to arrange a third match in order to "determine who is to be accounted the better player." He spoke of at least 21 games. Falkbeer, however, remained silent about it in *The Sunday Times*. Only towards the end of the year, on 13 December, he mentioned negotiations about a rematch with Bird. Just a week later, Falkbeer reported that the match was postponed due to "some points that remained to be settled." Eventually, no agreement was reached and no match took place.

Patrick Thomas Duffy, a friend and colleague of Bird at Coleman, Turquand, Youngs and Company as well as an influential chess journalist, added some mystery in his review of *Chess Practice*. In the *Illustrated London News* of 4 March 1882 he remarked that Bird had omitted to mention this match in his book, even though "it evoked much interest and some controversy at the time, and was certainly not unimportant." Sadly, the contemporary sources have no particulars to add about any controversy.

---

### First Match with Falkbeer, 29 November–13 December 1856

|              | 1 | 2 | 3 |   |
|--------------|---|---|---|---|
| H.E. Bird    | 1 | 0 | 1 | 2 |
| E. Falkbeer  | 0 | 1 | 0 | 1 |

### Second Match with Falkbeer, 27 December 1856–April 1857

|             | 1 | 2 | 3 | 4 | 5 | 6 | 7 | 8 | 9 | 10 | 11 | 12 | 13 |   |
|-------------|---|---|---|---|---|---|---|---|---|----|----|----|----|---|
| E. Falkbeer | ½ | 1 | 1 | 1 |   |   |   |   | 1 |    |    | 1  |    | 5 |
| H.E. Bird   | ½ | 0 | 0 | 0 |   |   |   |   | 0 |    |    | 0  |    | 4 |

games 5–7: Bird won twice, one game ended in a draw
games 8 and 10: Bird won once, one game ended in a draw
games 11–12: Bird won once, one game ended in a draw

---

## (102) Falkbeer–Bird    0–1

Match 1 (game ?)
London 1856
*C01*

Either game 1 or 3 of the first match.

**1. e4 e6 2. d4 d5 3. e×d5 e×d5 4. Be3** "This move, intended to prevent the advance of Black's c-pawn, has grown much into favor

---

of late"—Staunton. **4. ... Nf6 5. c4 Bb4† 6. Nc3 0–0 7. Qb3 Nc6 8. Nf3 Be6 9. c5 Rb8 10. Bb5** The safe 10. Qc2 avoids all tricks. **10. ... B×c5** "It was with the idea of taking this pawn rather than of defending his own that Black played the rook to b8—a step of which Mr. Falkbeer failed to calculate all the contingencies"—Staunton. **11. Qc2** Too tame. 11. d×c5 d4 12. Qa4 aims for complications. **11. ... Bd6 12. B×c6 b×c6 13. 0–0 Bg4** Losing time and a large part of his advantage. Better is 13. ... Qc8, intending to reply 14. Ne5 with 14. ... Bf5. **14. Ne5! B×e5 15. d×e5 Nd7 16. f4 Nb6 17. Bc5 Re8 18. Rae1** Very risky. After 18. h3! Bc8 19. Ne2, Black's material advantage is largely neutralized by White's strong centralized position. **18. ... Qd7** Bird rates the excellent 18. ... d4!, and if 19. Ne4 d3 20. Qf2 (20. Qc1 Be2 21. Rf2 Qd5 is even worse) 20. ... Be2 gains material. **19. h3 Bf5 20. Qf2 Bd3 21. Ne2 Na4 22. b3 B×e2 23. R×e2 Nc3 24. Rc2 Ne4 25. Qe3 a6** Bird's last moves were all excellent. Here 25. ... a5! would have rendered him some initiative on the queenside. **26. Bd4 Rb5 27. Rfc1 Re6 28. f5** "The game from this point appears to be much in White's favor; for those advanced pawns, properly supported, must surely prove irresistible"—Staunton. **28. ... Rh6?** Giving Falkbeer an unique chance to decide the game at once. 28. ... Re7 is necessary, with a tenable position. After both 29. Qf4 or 29. g4 Black can (and must) give back the pawn with 29. ... c5. The subsequent exchanges will curtail the pressure on his position. **29. Qf4?!** Winning is 29. e6! f×e6 30. R×c6 Rb7 31. Be5, as White is breaking through on two crucial points: c7 and g7, e.g., 31. ... Nd6 32. B×d6 c×d6 33. Rc8† Kf7 34. f×e6† Q×e6 35. Qg5 with a decisive attack. **29. ... Rb4 30. Bc5?!** Blocking his own play on the c-file is an inferior idea. Much better is 30. Be3! **30. ... Rb8 31. Be3** (see diagram)

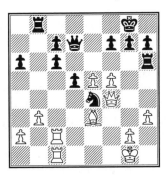

*After 31. Be3*

**31. ... g5!** "This looks desperately hazardous; but it turns the attack, and gives Black time to bring his rook into action, and is thus far commendable; at the same time it weakens the position of his king, and involves the loss of a serviceable pawn"—Staunton. Well defended. The menace was 32. Qg4. **32. Qf3 Re8** 32. ... Qe8 is more tenacious. Falkbeer now finds the correct move to resume his initiative. **33. e6! f×e6 34. R×c6 Qf7 35. R×a6** 35. R×c7? Q×f5 equally leads to nothing, but first 35. Bd4!, covering g7, is very annoying for his opponent. **35. ... Rf6 36. R×e6 Re×e6 37. f×e6 R×f3** It is better to avoid the endgame with 37. ... Q×e6, as White's kingside then needs permanent attention. **38. e×f7† R×f7 39. Rc6 h5 40. Rg6†** Making use of his strongest asset, the a-pawn, by 40. a4 (Staunton) is more straightforward. **40. ... Kh7 41. Rc6 h4 42. Bd4 Kg8** 42. ... Ng3 43. Kh2 Nf1† guarantees an immediate draw. After 43. Rf6 (Staunton), 43. ... Re7 44. Bf2 d4!, White even has to be careful. **43. a4 Ng3 44. Bf6** Risky play, as he takes no account at all

---

12. "The merit of Mr. Bird in these combats was, that after losing the first game in his primary skirmish he gained the victory; and that after losing three games in succession in the second campaign, he all but staved off defeat. In these matches Mr. Bird showed more soundness than opponents to his style of play gave him credit for, and perhaps a little less vigor than is usually the case with our somewhat dashing amateur." *Chess Player's Chronicle*, April 1859, p. 97.

of Bird's d-pawn. **44. Bf2** keeps that little criminal well under supervision. **44. ... Ne4** 44. ... d4! (Staunton) forces White to abandon his bishop, e.g., 45. Kh2 d3 46. B×g5 Rf5 47. Rc3 R×g5 48. R×d3 c5 49. Rf3 Ne2 etc. Black has realistic winning chances. **45. Be5 Rf5 46. B×c7 d4 47. Rc4** White maintains a minor initiative after 47. Re6 Nd2 48. Re1 N×b3 49. Re5. Now Bird's d-pawn becomes an asset after all. **47. ... Rd5 48. Kf1** Falkbeer sacrifices the exchange to reach an endgame that he might be able to draw. Alternatively, he could also consider offering the bishop with 48. Bb6 d3 49. Be3 d2 50. B×d2 N×d2 51. Rb4 Kf7 52. Kf2 Kf6 53. Ke3 Nf1† 54. Ke4 Re5† when the position is still far from being lost. **48. ... Nd2† 49. Ke2 N×c4 50. b×c4 Rc5 51. Bd8 R×c4 52. B×g5 R×a4 53. Kd3 Kf7 54. B×h4?** Surprisingly, after 54. Bd8! there is no easy win for Black in sight. The point is that after 54. ... Ke6 55. Ke4, White's king occupies a dominant square. A sample line illustrates possible tries of the Black king to penetrate White's position: 55. ... Rb4 56. Bg5 Kf7 57. Kd3 Ke6 58. Ke4 Ra4 59. Bd8 Kd6 60. Bb6 Ke7 61. B×d4 (these tries have failed. White can now withdraw his king to h2. Black's king cannot attack g2 without losing h4) 61. ... Ke6 62. Ke3 Kf5 63. Bc5 Rc4 64. Bb6 Rc3† 65. Kf2 Kf4 66. Kg1 Rc2 67. Bf2 Kg5 68. Bb6 Rc4 69. Kh2 Kf5 70. Bf2 Kg5 71. Bb6 Kf4 72. Bf2 Kg5 73. g3. **54. ... Ke6 55. Bg5 Kd5** With the support of the king, the d-pawn will rapidly decide the game. **56. h4 Ra3† 57. Ke2 Ke4 58. h5 Ra5** and White surrendered—*Illustrated London News* (Staunton), 10 January 1857.

### (103) Bird–Falkbeer    0–1
Match 1 (game 2)
London, 6 December 1856
C48

**1. e4 e5 2. Nf3 Nf6 3. Nc3 Nc6 4. Bb5 Bc5 5. 0–0 d6 6. d3 Bg4 7. Bg5 h6 8. Bh4 g5 9. Bg3 Nh5 10. Nd5 N×g3 11. h×g3 a6 12. Ba4 b5 13. Bb3 Nd4 14. c3 N×f3† 15. g×f3 Bh3 16. Re1 c6 17. d4 Ba7 18. Ne3 Qf6 19. d5 c5 20. Kh2 Bd7 21. Kg2 c4 22. Bc2 h5 23. Rh1 Ke7 24. Qe2 h4 25. a4 Bc5 26. a×b5 a×b5 27. Rae1 h×g3 28. f×g3 B×e3 29. Q×e3 R×h1 30. R×h1 Ra2 31. Qc1 g4 32. Bd1 g×f3† 33. B×f3 Qg6 34. Qb1 Ra8 35. Qf1 f5 36. e×f5 B×f5 37. Rh4 Rg8 38. Qf2 Bd7 39. Be4 Qf7 40. Q×f7† K×f7 41. Rh6 Ke7 42. Rh7† Kd8 43. Rh6 Kc7 44. Rh7 Rd8 45. Bf5 Kc8 46. Be4 Rf8 47. Rg7 Bf5 48. Bf3 Bh3† 49. K×h3 R×f3 50. Rg8† Kc7 51. Rg7† Kb6 52. Kh4 Rf2 53. g4 R×b2 54. g5 Rc2 55. Rd7 Kc5** and Black wins—*Bell's Life*, 18 January 1857.

### (104) Bird–Falkbeer    0–1
Match 2 (game 3)
London, 10 January 1857
A03

**1. f4 c5 2. Nf3 e6 3. e3 a6 4. b3 d5 5. Bb2 Nf6 6. Bd3 Nc6 7. 0–0 Bd6 8. Qe2 Nb4 9. Nc3 N×d3 10. Q×d3 Qc7 11. Rae1 Bd7 12. Qe2 Bc6 13. d4 b5 14. Nd1 Bb7 15. Nf2 c4 16. Ne5 c3 17. Bc1 b4 18. Nfd3 g6 19. Ng4 Qe7 20. Nde5 h5 21. Nf2 Kf8 22. Nh3 a5 23. Ng5 Ba6 24. Nd3 Ne4 25. Qf3 f5 26. Rd1 h4 27. Rfe1 N×g5 28. f×g5 B×d3 29. c×d3 Qc7 30. h3 Bg3 31. Re2 Kg7 32. e4 d×e4 33. d×e4 Rad8 34. e5 Qb6 35. Be3 Rd5 36. Bf2 Rhd8 37. Rd3 B×f2† 38. Q×f2 R×d4 39. Kh2 R8d5 40. Re4 f×e4 41. Qf6† Kg8 42. Q×g6† Kf8 43. Qf6† Ke8 44. R×d4 Q×d4**

---

**45. Q×e6† Kd8 46. Qf6† Kc7 47. Qg7† Rd7 48. Qf6 c2 49. Qf4 e3** and White resigns—*Era*, 8 March 1857.

### (105) Falkbeer–Bird    1–0
Match 2 (game ?)
London, January 1857
B06

Either game 2 or 4 of the second match.

**1. d4 g6 2. e4 Bg7 3. e5 d6 4. f4 Nh6 5. Nc3 0–0 6. Nf3 c6 7. Bd3 Bg4 8. h3 Be6 9. g4 d×e5 10. d×e5 f5 11. g5 Nf7 12. Be3 b6 13. Qe2 b5 14. Qg2 Na6 15. h4 Nb4 16. Rd1 Nd5 17. N×d5 B×d5 18. h5 Qa5† 19. Kf2 B×f3 20. Q×f3 Q×a2 21. h×g6 h×g6 22. Qh3 Nh8 23. Qh7† Kf7 24. b3 e6 25. B×f5 Rfd8 26. Bd3 Rd5 27. Be4 Rad8 28. Ra1 Qb2 29. B×d5 Q×c2† 30. Kg3 Rd7 31. Bf3 Kf8 32. Q×h8† B×h8 33. R×h8† Kg7 34. Rah1** and White wins—*Era*, 8 February 1857.

### (106) Bird–Falkbeer    ½–½
Match 2 (game ?)
London 1857
A03

Game 1, 5 or 7 of the second match.

**1. f4 d5 2. Nf3 Nc6** "It may be taken as a general rule to move the c-pawn before developing this knight in close games"—Hoffer. **3. d4 Bf5 4. e3 a6 5. Bd3 Nh6 6. Nc3 e6 7. a3 Be7 8. 0–0 B×d3** "There is no necessity for this exchange; but Black intended to bring his knight to f5, which turns out to be a weak move"—Hoffer. **9. Q×d3 Nf5 10. N×d5! Q×d5 11. e4 Qd7 12. e×f5 e×f5 13. c4** The immediate 13. d5! is stronger. **13. ... f6** Castling the king away towards the kingside is preferable. **14. Be3 0–0–0?** "It was rather hazardous to castle on the queenside in the face of White's much advanced pawns; the more so, as he might have safely castled on the kingside. Still, as there was a chance of getting a good counterattack, White preferred the other mode of play, trusting to the old Latin proverb—audaces fortuna iuvat"—Falkbeer. **15. b4 Rhe8 16. Rfe1 Bf8 17. Rad1 h6 18. d5 g5 19. Qc2** More than good enough, but 19. Qb1 (Hoffer) might be simpler. **19. ... N×b4!** "By this clever sacrifice Black manages to free his game, and places White on the defensive"—Bird. **20. a×b4 B×b4 21. Re2 Re4 22. Bf2 Rde8 23. R×e4** 23. Nd4! destroys Black's initiative. **23. ... f×e4 24. Nd4 e3 25. Bg3 Bc5 26. Qe2** "We prefer 26. Ne2"—Hoffer. **26. ... Re4 26. ... g×f4! 27. B×f4 Re4 offers good counterplay. 27. Nb3 Ba7 28. Kh1?** 28. f×g5 is of course the correct move. **28. ... g×f4 29. Bh4?** A gross mistake, but both players now overlook the winning 29. ... f3! 29. Be1 keeps a small edge. **29. ... Qa4?** *(see diagram)*

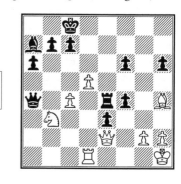

*After 29. ... Qa4*

**30. B×f6?!** Bird snatches away a pawn as it is obvious that his opponent cannot take the knight, which he intended to do so with his last, very impulsive move. Alas, Bird didn't look any further, as there were two interesting and stronger alternatives. Firstly, there is 30. Ra1 Qd7 31. Nd2! Re8 32. Nf3, when he has a solid positional plus. But stronger is 30. d6!, opening a front against Falkbeer's king. After 30. ... c×d6 31. R×d6 Re8 (the knight remains poisoned: 31. ... Q×b3? 32. Qg4† wins) 32. Qh5!, White obtains a fearful attack. **30. ... Bb6** 30. ... Kb8, getting out of reach for White's queen, is much safer. **31. c5** Now it has become time to reactivate the knight with 31. Nd4. After 31. ... Kb8 32. Qd3, Black is forced to offer a pawn with 32. ... e2, as otherwise White plays 33. Ne2 with complete domination. **31. ... Q×b3 32. c×b6 Q×b6 33. d6** "We cannot see any reason for the sacrifice of this pawn"—Falkbeer. Bad timing, as the danger for Black's king is gone. Instead, Bird should switch priorities and head for a draw: 33. Qd3 e2 34. Re1 Qf2 35. Bc3 Re3 36. Qf5† with a perpetual check. **33. ... c×d6 34. Rc1†?** Chasing the king away to a much safer spot. In each case, it would be difficult to cope with Black's pawn mass. **34. ... Kb8 35. Qd3 Re8?** Falkbeer misses a fast win: 35. ... Qb4! defends everything and gets ready for a decisive advance of the pawns. **36. Qg6! Qb5 37. Bd4** It's clear that Black's king is getting in danger again. **37. ... Qd7 38. Q×h6 e2 39. Re1 Qe7!?** A smart trap, for which Bird naively falls. 39. ... Re4 is objectively better, but Black will have a hard time facing White's pressure. He will have to advance his queenside pawns to gain some space for his king, but then both king and pawns are likely to become vulnerable. **40. Q×f4?** First 40. Kg1! kills all back rank threats. If 40. ... Rf8 41. R×e2 and wins. **40. ... Rf8! 41. R×e2** 41. Qd2 Rf1† 42. Bg1 is the shortest way to a draw. White's queen will go for a perpetual after the advance of Black's pawns on the queenside. **41. ... R×f4 42. R×e7 R×d4 43. h3 b5 44. g4 b4 45. g5 b3 46. g6 Rd1† 47. Kg2 b2 48. g7 Rg1† 49. K×g1 b1Q† 50. Kg2** and after a few moves more the game was given up as drawn. "It appears at first sight that White ought to win the game by 50. ... Qg6†, but even by the best play on both sides, we believe, it was but a drawn game, on account of the advance of White's h-pawn"—Falkbeer. A draw is indeed very likely: 50. ... Qg6† 51. Kf2 Kc8 52. Ra7 etc.—*The Sunday Times* (Falkbeer), 7 June 1857; *Modern Chess* (Bird), p. 82; *Chess Monthly* (Hoffer), September 1894, p. 12.

## (107) Bird–Falkbeer    1–0

Match 2 (game ?)

London 1857

C50

Game 5, 7 or 11 of the second match.

**1. e4 e5 2. Bc4 Bc5 3. Nf3 d6 4. 0–0 Bg4 5. c3 Nc6 6. b4** The push of the b-pawn is quite rare in the Italian Game. It became Bird's trademark in later years. **6. ... Bb6 7. b5** First 7. a4 is the right way to continue. **7. ... Na5 8. Be2 f5** Either 8. ... Qd7 or 8. ... Nf6 are much safer. **9. e×f5 B×f5 10. d4 e4** Black has no problems after 10. ... Nf6. If White wins a pawn with 11. d×e5 d×e5 12. N×e5, Black obtains good compensation after 12. ... 0–0 thanks to his superior development and White's weaknesses. **11. Bg5! Nf6 12. Nh4 Bd7 13. c4** Both 13. Nd2! d5 14. f3 and 13. Bh5† g6 14. N×g6 h×g6 15. B×g6† and 16. B×e4 are pressing and very promising continuations. Bird's move is a bit slow. **13. ... 0–0 14. Be3** Bird releases

the pressure without good reason, allowing Falkbeer to force the exchange of knights. Even better, however, would have been 14. ... c6! 15. b×c6 N×c6, weakening White's center and reactivating his knight. **14. ... Nd5 15. c×d5 Q×h4 16. Nc3 Rae8 17. Rc1 c6?!** This comes a bit late as Bird is now fully developed. Various solid moves, such as 17. ... Qf6, 17. ... Bf5 or 17. ... Rf7 were better. **18. d×c6 b×c6 19. Qd2** 19. b×c6 keeps a nice advantage. With the text move Bird wants to catch the queen with 20. Bg5, but both players overlook the trick that equalizes: 19. ... c×b5! 20. Bg5 e3! **19. ... h6 20. b×c6 N×c6 21. Nd5 Ba5?!** *(see diagram)*

*After 21. ... Ba5*

21. ... Ne7 limits his disadvantage. **22. Qc2** 22. Qb2! is the more pointed continuation. It menaces 23. Qb7 as well as 23. Qa3, and there is not much that Black could do against it, e.g., 22. ... Qd8 23. Bh5! Re6 24. Qb7! and Black's position collapses on the queenside. **22. ... Rf5 23. g3** Not bad but 23. Qc4! wins outright; e.g., 23. ... Kh8 24. g3 Qd8 25. Bg4 Rff8 26. B×d7 Q×d7 27. Q×c6. **23. ... Qd8 24. Nf4 Kh7 25. Bg4?!** 25. Bh5! catches the exchange. **25. ... Nb4?!** Falkbeer rates his last chance to trouble Bird. He should sacrifice the exchange with 25. ... R×f4! 26. B×f4 N×d4 when he has an extra pawn for it. After the text move Black seems reasonably well off, but this is an illusion. Bird, for once, harvests the point calmly and with precision. **26. B×f5† B×f5 27. Qe2 g5 28. Ng2 Nd3 29. Rb1 Qd7 30. f4 Bg4 31. Qc2 Bb6 32. f×g5 h×g5 33. Ne1 Bf5 34. a4 Kg6 35. Rb5! d5 36. Qb3 Rd8 37. a5** "White pursues his attack with great spirit, and finishes the game like a master"—Staunton. **37. ... Bc7 38. Rb7 Kh7 39. N×d3 e×d3 40. R×f5! Re8 41. Q×d3 Re4 42. R×d5** Black resigns—*Illustrated London News* (Staunton), 9 May 1857.

## (108) Falkbeer–Bird    ½–½

Match 2 (game ?)

London, February 1857

A40

Either game 6 or 8 of the second match.

**1. d4 e6 2. a3 c5 3. e4 d5 4. e×d5 e×d5 5. Nf3 Nf6 6. Bb5† Nc6 7. 0–0 Bg4 8. Qe1† Be7 9. Ne5 Bd7 10. N×d7 Q×d7 11. d×c5 0–0 12. Be3 Rfe8 13. Qd1 Ne4 14. B×c6 b×c6 15. b4 Rad8 16. Bd4 Qf5 17. Nd2 Bf6 18. B×f6 Q×f6 19. Nf3 Nc3 20. Qd3 Ne2† 21. Kh1 Nf4 22. Qd4 Qf5 23. Rae1 Qg4 24. Nh4 Nh3 25. Q×g4 N×f2† 26. Kg1 N×g4 27. Nf5 Kf8 28. Nd6 R×e1 29. R×e1 Nf6 30. Kf2 Rd7 31. h3 g6 32. a4 a6 33. Re3 Re7 34. R×e7 K×e7 35. Ke3 Ne8 36. N×e8 K×e8 37. Kd4 Kd7 38. Ke5 Ke7 39. b5 f6† 40. Kd4 c×b5 41. a×b5 a×b5 42. K×d5 Kd7 43. c6† Kc7 44. c3 f5** "The game continued for a few more moves, and was ultimately given up as a drawn battle. A bystander, who watched the game, observed that had White played 43. Kc5, he would, probably, have won"—Löwenthal. White picks up the b-pawn and returns in time with his king on the kingside to stop Black's pawns—*Era* (Löwenthal), 8 March 1857.

## (109) Falkbeer–Bird    0–1
Match 2 (game ?)
London 1857
*D46*

Game 6, 8, 10 or 12 of the second match.

**1. d4 d5 2. c4 e6 3. e3 Nf6 4. Nf3 c6** "Novel. The move has never been advised, we believe, at this stage of the game, but 4. ... c5 is usually given by the authorities. The text move, however, is quite safe, but will generally lead to a close game"—Falkbeer. **5. Nc3 Bd6 6. Bd3 Nbd7 7. c×d5 e×d5 8. Bd2 b5 9. Qc2** 9. e4! exploits Bird's last move. **9. ... Bb7 10. Ne2** Falkbeer misses another chance to play 10. e4! **10. ... Rc8 11. Ng3 B×g3** A weak exchange. **12. h×g3 Qe7 13. Rc1 a6** "Obviously necessary, from White's threat to capture at b5"—Falkbeer. **14. Nh4** The immediate 14. a3, leaving the knight centralized, is much stronger. **14. ... g6 15. a3 c5** "To prevent the apparently threatening move 16. Bb4, which must have proved annoying"—Falkbeer. **16. Bb4 0–0** "Ingenious, and seemingly the best reply to the preceding ill-considered move of White, but for which we cannot suppose Black would have ventured to castle in such a ticklish position. If, however, Black had proceeded to capture the bishop instead, then the following would probably have ensued: 16. ... c×b4 17. Q×c8† B×c8 18. R×c8† Qd8 19. R×d8† K×d8 20. a×b4 etc."—Falkbeer. **17. B×c5?!** "There seems to be no other resource for White. If 17. d×c5, Black obtains a good position by 17. ... a5"—Falkbeer. This judgment is not completely correct. After 17. d×c5 a5 (forced) 18. B×a5 R×c5, chances are about even. **17. ... N×c5 18. d×c5** *(see diagram)*

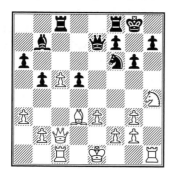

*After 18. d×c5*

**18. ... d4!** "Black drives home his advantage with much tact and force"—Falkbeer. **19. b4 d×e3 20. 0–0 Ng4 21. f4 Rcd8 22. Rce1** The other rook had to occupy this square. **22. ... Nf2! 23. Be2 Ne4 24. Kh2 Nd2 25. Rh1 Qf6 26. Kg1** 26. Rc1 is very stubborn, for after both 26. ... Be4? 27. Qc3 and 26. ... Ne4? 27. c6, the rook demonstrates its function on the c-file. Instead 26. ... Bc6! consolidates his advantage. **26. ... Be4** Good enough, but very strong is 26. ... Ne4! 27. Kh2 g5! and now, for example, 28. Nf3 N×g3! completes the impressive maneuvre of the knight. **27. Qc1 Rfe8** 27. ... g5! remains a clincher. **28. Qa1 Qc6** 28. ... Q×a1! transposes into a winning endgame as Black's pieces cooperate excellently after

29. R×a1 Nb3 30. Re1 Nd4 and there is nothing to be done against 31. ... Nc2. **29. Qc3 f6?!** Too slow. 30. ... Bd5, intending 31. ... Bc4, keeps a firm advantage. **30. Bg4** "Perhaps 30. g4 would have been better play"—Falkbeer. Indeed, after 30. ... Bd5 31. Rh3, Black is on the brink of losing his main trump, the e-pawn. After 31. ... Ne4 32. Qc1 Nd2, the game would end in a draw. **30. ... Rd3! 31. Qc1 Qd5 32. Be2 Rd4** 32. ... Nb3 and 33. ... Rd2 further infiltrate the White ranks. **33. Qc3 g5 34. f×g5 f×g5 35. Q×e3** "A necessary sacrifice of the knight, as his retreat instead would have involved a great inferiority of position. Thus: 35. Nf3 B×f3 36. g×f3 N×f3† 37. B×f3 Q×f3 and White's game is past remedy"—Falkbeer. **35. ... Bg6 36. Qf2 g×h4** 36. ... Ne4! augments his advantage. If 37. Qe3 N×c5! and if 37. Bf3 g×h4 38. R×h4 N×f2 39. R×e8† B×e8 40. B×d5† R×d5. **37. R×h4 R×h4?!** This exchange is much welcomed by White, for Falkbeer finally gets rid of the rook that was so misplaced since move 25. 37. ... Ne4 is again correct. **38. g×h4 Qf7?!** Offering another exchange seems clever, with his piece ahead, but the sudden 39. Bg4! (an improvement over Falkbeer's suggestion 39. Bd1) spoils the fun considerably, as too many pawns will go off the board after, for example, 39. ... R×e1† 40. Q×e1 Ne4 41. h5 Qf4 etc. Fortunately for Bird Falkbeer makes an intuitive choice that rather simplifies his task. **39. Qd4? R×e2!** "The final coup which renders White's game hopeless. We should, however, think that, with the strong position of his pawns, White had before this some chance of a draw, if he had played 39. Bd1"—Falkbeer. **40. Qd8† Kg7 41. Qd4† Kh6 42. R×e2 Qf1† 43. Kh2 Q×e2 44. Qf4† Kg7 45. Qd4† Kf7 46. Qd5† Kf6 47. Qd6† Kf5 48. Qd7† Kf4 49. Qd6† Ke3 50. Qg3† Nf3†** and Black wins—*The Sunday Times* (Falkbeer), 17 May 1857.

## (110) Bird–Falkbeer    0–1
Match 2 (game 9)
London, 7 March 1857
*A03*

**1. f4 d5 2. Nf3 c5 3. b3 Nc6 4. e3 e6 5. Bb5 Bd7 6. Bb2 Nf6 7. 0–0 Be7 8. d3 Qb6 9. B×c6 B×c6 10. Nbd2 Rc8 11. Ne5 0–0 12. Qe2 Ne8 13. Rf3 a5?!** A pointless and bad move that gives Bird the necessary time to launch a promising attack. Better was 13. ... Nd6 or 13. ... f6. **14. Rh3 g6?!** *(see diagram)* 14. ... Nf6 is relatively better.

*After 14. ... g6*

**15. Qg4?!** Strong enough to disturb his opponent, but there were alternative moves that could already doom Black's king. Firstly, White could play 15. Ndf3! Now 15. ... Qd8 is necessary to cover g5 once more, as other moves lose quickly: 15. ... Qc7? 16. Ng5! h5

17. Ng4! B×g5 18. f×g5 or 15. ... f6 16. N×g6! h×g6 17. Nh4 Ng7 18. N×g6 Bd6 19. Qg4 and again Black cannot withstand the attack. After 15. ... Qd8, White calmly pursues the assault with 16. Rf1 Rc7 17. Qf2 b5 18. Ng5 B×g5 19. f×g5 Q×g5 20. N×g6! But 15. Ng4! is actually the strongest continuation. The next moves are forced: 15. ... f6 16. Nh6† Kh8 (16. ... Kg7 is also hopeless. White's pieces slowly occupy their best places, and there is nothing to be done against it: 17. Qg4 Bd7 18. Nf3 Bd8 19. Ng5 Rh8 20. Rg3 Kf8 21. Qh3) 17. Qg4 Bd7 18. Nf5! g×f5 19. Qg6 and wins. **15. ... Ng7 16. Rf1 d4** After 16. ... Be8 White's advantage has diminished into a positional one. This push compromises Falkbeer's position. **17. e4** Alternatively 17. Ndc4 Qc7 18. N×c6 Q×c6 19. a4 is also better for White. **17. ... Qc7 18. Rh6** The alternative is the positional 18. a4, securing c4 for his knights. **18. ... f5?** 18. ... Be8 is necessary to fortify the kingside. Practically speaking the attack plays itself for White, while his opponent has to be extremely secure to hold his position together. But after 19. Qh3 Nh5 20. g4 N×f4 21. R×f4 Q×e5 22. R×h7 Q×f4 23. Rh8†, Black succeeds in forcing White to give a perpetual. If 23. ... Kg7 24. Rh7† Kf6? loses because of 25. Qh4† Qg5 26. e5†. **19. Qh3 Nh5** There is nothing better. **20. g4??** A dreadful mistake that turns a won position into a lost. Instead 20. N×g6! h×g6 21. R×g6† Ng7 22. Qh6 Rf7 23. Rf3 wins. **20. ... N×f4! 21. R×f4 Q×e5 22. Rf3 Bg5 23. R×h7 f×g4** 23. ... B×d2 must cause immediate resignation. **24. Q×g4 K×h7 25. Nc4 Qc7** A slight hiccup in the winning process. 25. ... Qg7 is much better. **26. Rh3† Kg7 27. Q×g5 Qf4 28. Qg2 Rf6 29. Rg3 Rcf8 30. Rg5 b5 31. Rg4 Qf1†** and Black wins—*Deutsche Schachzeitung*, March 1857, pp. 100–102.

## (111) Bird–Falkbeer     0–1
Match 2 (game 13)
London, April 1857
*A03*

"The following brilliant partie was the deciding game in an interesting match just concluded between Mr. Falkbeer the Prussian [*sic*] player, and Mr. Bird, an English amateur, of whose originality and boldness of conception we have often had occasion to speak. The lateness of the hour when the moves were transmitted to us must plead as an apology for the brevity of the annotation"—Staunton.

**1. f4 c5 2. e3 e6 3. b3 Be7 4. Nc3 Bh4†** "In this and similar openings this check may be given with advantage. It deranges and weakens White's position on the kingside, and renders castling of little avail"—Löwenthal. The possibility to fianchetto his bishop is in White's favor, but Bird doesn't make any use of it. **5. g3 Bf6 6. Nf3 d5 7. d4 c×d4 8. e×d4 a6 9. Bd3 Nc6 10. Be3 b5 11. a4 b4 12. Ne2 Bb7** "The present game affords a striking example of the importance, in close openings, of playing the bishop thus, on the diagonal of squares extending to the adverse king's rook's house"—Staunton. **13. Rc1 h5 14. Qd2 Nh6 15. h3 Qd6 16. Ne5 B×e5?** A first clear mistake. This bishop is much too important to exchange. After 16. ... Nf5, the game remains balanced. **17. f×e5 Qe7 18. Bg5 Qd7 19. 0–0** "Who would not now prefer White's position? His forces are well developed, his king securely ensconced, and nothing but ordinary skill and patience seem required to ensure the vic-

tory"—Staunton. **19. ... Rc8 20. Rf4** 20. B×h6! R×h6 21. Qg5 is already totally winning. **20. ... Nf5 21. Rcf1 g6 22. g4 h×g4 23. h×g4 Rg8** "Ingenious—the inspiration of despair—but quite unsound"—Staunton. **24. g×f5 g×f5 25. R4f2 N×e5** "Black must dare boldly or perish miserably"—Staunton. **26. d×e5 d4 27. N×d4** Condemned by both Staunton and Löwenthal as the decisive error, but in fact White is still winning. In any case, 27. Ng3 or 27. Qf4, are more convincing. **27. ... f6!?** *(see diagram)*

*After 27. ... f6*

Falkbeer throws all his possessions into the battle, hoping to confuse Bird, in which he succeeds. At this point nearly each sacrifice that quashes the pawn mass defending Black's king is winning, e.g., 28. N×e6!, 28. N×f5 or 28. B×f5. Bird selects another move of much less strength. **28. e×f6?** Q×d4 29. f7† With nearly all his pieces pinned or unable to move there are but a limited number of candidate moves. This one, followed by the capture at f5, is certainly a valid option. Alternatively he could have opted for the calm 29. Re1! after which a rather forced sequence becomes likely: 29. ... Qg4† 30. Rg2 Q×g2† 31. Q×g2 B×g2 32. R×e6† Kf7 33. Re7† Kg6 34. f7 Rgf8 35. K×g2 with a draw as a probable result. **29. ... K×f7 30. B×f5 Q×d2 31. Bg6†?** Bird appears unable to deal with the changed settings and dropped a brick after which his king suddenly succumbs. After 31. Bh7† Ke8 32. R×d2 R×g5† 33. Kf2, the game must peter out in a draw. **31. ... K×g6 32. B×d2 Kh7† 33. Kh2 Rc5 34. Rf7† Kh8** and White resigns. "White could not, by the best play, save the game. If 35. Rf3 Black mates in three moves. The sacrifice of the rook at f5 would have been equally unavailing"—Löwenthal. *Illustrated London News* (Staunton), 18 April 1857; *Era* (Löwenthal), 19 April 1857.

# OFFHAND CHESS 1857–1858

Judging from his writings one gets the impression that Bird hardly played any chess during the late 1850s. The story was widespread that at the time of Paul Morphy's arrival in England, during the summer of 1858, Bird had retired altogether from chess. Our research demonstrates another picture. After his matches with Falkbeer, Bird continued playing chess until the spring of 1860. At most there were a few intervals of some months. On 21 June 1857, *The Sunday Times* wrote that Bird had played some fine games with the Parisian visitor Alphonse Delannoy. The following game, in which Bird gave odds against an unknown amateur, was probably played around the same time.

## (112) Bird–Mr. E.   1–0

Offhand game
London (Purssell's) 1857
*White gave odds of Ng1*

1. e4 e5 2. Bc4 Bc5 3. b4 B×b4 4. c3 Bc5 5. d4 e×d4 6. 0–0 d3
7. Q×d3 d6 8. Kh1 Be6 9. Bb5† c6 10. Ba4 Nd7 11. f4 Nb6 12. Bb3
Qd7 13. f5 B×b3 14. a×b3 d5 15. e5 f6 16. e6 Qc7 17. Nd2 Ne7
18. Nf3 0–0 19. Nh4 Bd6 20. Qh3 Kh8 21. Rf3 Rg8 and White
gave mate in four moves—*The Sunday Times*, 2 August 1857.

Consultation chess is a nowadays completely neglected form of
chess that was very popular during the nineteenth century. It was
often practiced to give weaker players the chance to combine their
forces and beat a master. Masters could also be joined by amateurs
or patrons, who often paid a fee for the instruction, the amusement
or the honor. During chess tournaments it became a habit to
organize a consultation game between the participants. Nationality
was an often used benchmark of forming teams.

This form of chess was intensely promoted at the St. George's
Chess Club. In February 1856 a series of games was commenced in
which the teams were headed by Staunton and Löwenthal. Notables
such as Thomas Wilson Barnes, Falkbeer and Owen often joined
them. Perhaps Bird also played in one of these games (see the note
at White's sixth move in **game 124**).

Around the turn of the year, however, a rift was created between
Staunton and Löwenthal. Some of the venom trickled out into the
press.[13] It is unclear when the final games of these series were played.
Staunton published the last in the spring of 1857, but they were
probably a few months older.

In May 1857 Löwenthal revitalized the practice of consultation
chess at the St. George's Chess Club. He made use of his column in
the *Era* to promote the weekly "chess soirées." Various masters took
part in consultation games that were mostly contested on Tuesdays
under the attendance of many amateurs.

A successful second soirée was held, probably, on 19 May 1857.
A game opposed Boden, Barnes and Bird against Löwenthal, Horwitz and Joseph Graham Campbell. No result or score was published.

A schedule for the forthcoming weeks was drawn up. According
to the *Era* of 24 May, Bird planned to take part in a game on 2 June.
Some results were given in subsequent weeks but none of them concerned Bird. A high-ranking guest, Adolf Anderssen, attended on
21 July. It was probably on this evening that Bird played the
following crafty game with him. Both players also met each other
for some more duels at the Divan.

## (113) Bird–Anderssen   1–0

Offhand game
London (St. George's C.C.), 21 July 1857
C65

1. e4 e5 2. Nf3 Nc6 3. Bb5 Nf6 4. c3 N×e4 5. d4 e×d4 6. 0–0

13. In the *Illustrated London News* of 10 January 1857 Staunton informed his
readers that Löwenthal declined to continue the series as he "admits what everybody felt, that he was completely overmatched." Löwenthal defended himself in
a reply to an anonymous correspondent in the *Era* of 8 February by writing that
"his [Staunton's] 'chess instinct' is equal to his powers of sarcasm."

Be7 7. Re1 Nf6 8. c×d4 0–0 9. d5 Nb8 10. Nc3 a6 11. Ba4 b5
12. Bc2 d6 13. Bg5! Well played, and posing his opponent some
problems. **13. ... h6** 13. ... Re8, avoiding any concessions, is safer;
e.g., 14. Qd3 Nbd7 15. Nd4 Bb7. **14. Bh4 Nbd7?!** 14. ... Re8 is absolutely necessary by now. **15. Nd4! Bb7 16. Qd3?!** 16. Nf5 Re8
17. Ne4! is an extremely strong assault. Black is forced to give up
material with 17. ... N×e4. **16. ... Re8 17. Nf5 Bf8** Anderssen
gained a crucial tempo for his defense, which makes his position solid, but
the cramped nature of it is not in accordance with his style. **18. Ne4
R×e4** "Necessary, in order to avoid immediate danger"—Löwenthal. **19. R×e4** (*see diagram*)

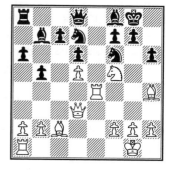

*After 19. R×e4*

Bird bravely brings more pieces to the front. Also tricky to meet
was 19. Q×e4, as 19. ... g5 20. Qe3! and now both 20. ... g×h4
21. N×h6† and 20. ... N×d5 21. Qd3 N7f6 22. Bg3 give White
enough compensation. 19. ... N×e4?! 20. B×d8 has to be avoided
as all of Black's minor pieces are badly placed. **19. ... Nc5?** "Herr
Anderssen correctly remarked that if he had played 19. ... g5, he
would have been free from all danger. We concur in that remark,
and think that the move would not only have arrested the attack,
but have caused it to change hands"—Löwenthal. 19. ... g5? is
just as bad as the text move, though it demands from White to
find the forced sequence 20. B×g5! h×g5 21. Rg4! An improvement is the solid 19. ... g6. In that case White cannot consider a
retreat with his knight as 20. Ng3? Nc5 wins. Instead 20. Rf4!
keeps the pressure high. Not so good now is 20. ... g×f5 21. R×f5
Be7 22. Re1, and White can allow himself the luxury to calmly
bring his pieces to the front. If 22. ... Ne5 23. Qg3† Kf8 24. Qf4
Kg7 25. Re3 Bc8 26. Rf×e5! and White reaches a better endgame
after 26. ... d×e5 27. Q×e5 Qd6 28. Q×e7 Q×e7 29. R×e7. This
leaves 20. ... B×d5 as Black's best attempt. After 21. B×f6 N×f6
22. Ne3 Be6 the game is still fully playable. **20. N×h6†! g×h6
21. Rg4† Bg7 22. Qg3** "Dashingly followed up"—Löwenthal.
**22. ... N×g4 23. B×d8 R×d8 24. Q×g4 B×d5 25. Re1 Be6
26. Qg3 a5 27. Re3 Kf8 28. Qf4 B×a2 29. b3 a4 30. b×a4 b×a4
31. Qh4 f6 32. B×a4 Bf7 33. Bc6 Rb8 34. h3 Rb6 35. Bf3 Nd7
36. Qa4 Ne5 37. Qa8† Be8 38. Bh5** and Black resigns—*Era*
(Löwenthal), 11 October 1857.

The nearing congress of the British Chess Association in Manchester caused the interruption of the soirées. They would not be
resumed after the finish of that event. In all likelihood a struggle
for power was going on behind the scenes of the St. George's Chess
Club. At the end of the year Löwenthal decided to resign his post
as the secretary of the club. Harding believes that he was forced to
do so, as it seemed unlikely that he would have voluntarily departed

from the steady income that this assignment gave him.[14] While this seems perfectly possible, Löwenthal, in his overview of the past year in the *Era* on 3 January 1858, wrote that he resigned himself. Two weeks later he expressly thanked the club for "a very flattering testimonial." The club honored and thanked him by electing Löwenthal an honorary member.

While Staunton probably played a malignant role to bring Löwenthal down, the Hungarian brought up a possible reason for his resignation in the *Era* of 7 March 1858. His function as secretary "prevented him from accepting challenges and … he is now open to play against any one of recognized rank in the chess world."[15] Löwenthal may have stayed away from the St. George's Chess Club for a while, but he certainly did not become a persona non grata. In May 1858, for example, he accompanied de Saint-Amant on his visit to the club.

In the meantime Staunton was trying to revive the tradition of consultation chess at St. George's. In the *Illustrated London News* of 6 February 1858, Staunton confirmed that players like Boden, Falkbeer and Bird were induced to take part as "such an infusion of fresh blood would impart a wonderful degree of spirit and vigor to the contest." Later Staunton wrote that Falkbeer would replace Löwenthal as his standard opponent.

It appears that only two more consultation games were played. The first one, played on Saturday 10 April, saw Staunton and Barnes gain a speedy victory against Bird and Falkbeer. A short while later Bird, now joined by Owen, took his revenge against the same duo. Staunton dismissed the publication of any of these games, as "neither possessed a particle of interest." Fortunately Boden had another opinion, thanks to which now survives a theoretically valuable as well as interesting game.

## (114) Staunton & T.W. Barnes–
## Bird & Owen & T.I. Hampton    0–1
Consultation game
London (St. George's C.C.), April 1858
*C51*

"Mr. Hampton, secretary of the club, acted as Bird's partner, in the absence of Mr. Owen, at the second sitting"—Bird.

**1. e4 e5 2. Nf3 Nc6 3. Bc4 Bc5 4. b4 B×b4 5. c3 Bc5 6. 0–0 d6 7. d4 e×d4 8. c×d4 Bb6 9. d5 Na5** "We think this move better than it is commonly esteemed to be"—Boden. **10. Be2** "10. Bb2 at once is the popular and usual move. 10. Be2 was suggested by Staunton to throw his younger opponents on their own resources. Barnes rather inclined to 10. Bb2"—Bird. "Although there are some points to recommend this square of retreat for the bishop, we doubt if it be not on the whole inferior to the old move of 10. Bd3."—Boden **10. … Ne7** A rather novel concept. This move was generally attributed to Louis Paulsen, who however only played it in 1861 for the first time. In 1874 Bird reacted as stung by a bee

when Zukertort, in an article about the Evans Gambit, omitted to mention that Bird adopted the move already in this consultation game. **11. Bb2 f6 12. Qd2 0–0 13. Nd4 Ng6** "As observed in my notes to other games I incline to think this move may be deferred, and the time utilized in getting the queenside pawns advances"—Bird. **14. Kh1 Bd7 15. f4 c5** As the knight was finally ready to jump to e6, 15. … B×d4 might be considered. **16. Nc2?!** 16. Ne6! is stronger. **16. … Rc8 17. Nba3** The knight must go to the logical c3 square where it defends e4 and keeps the possibility to play a2–a4. **17. … Bc7 18. Rae1 Re8 19. Bf3?!** This move does nothing to obstruct Black's plan of getting the queenside in motion. They could play 19. Bh5, with the hope of refraining their opponents from 19. … b5, although Black has more than enough compensation after 20. f5 Ne5. **19. … b5!** Black is much better now. **20. f5 Ne5 21. Ne3 b4 22. B×e5 R×e5 23. Nac4 N×c4 24. N×c4 Re7 25. Qf4 Bb5 26. Be2 B×c4** A bit hasty. After 26. … Qd7, the bishop is defended and Black can follow up with a7–a5–a4. White's initiative on the kingside is not strong enough to compensate for his disadvantage on the queenside. **27. B×c4 Re5 28. Rf3 Qd7 29. Rg3 Rce8 30. Qg4** After 30. Rge3, keeping the center under control, it is not so easy for Black to make use of his extra material. The text move offers Black the chance to play 30. … h5!, which favorably opens the position after 31. Qe2 R×e4 33. Q×e4 R×e4 34. R×e4 Q×f5. **30. … R8e7** 30. … R×f5? might seem attractive, but loses right away after 31. Bb5. **31. h4 Qe8 32. h5 Kh8 33. Ree3 Bd8** (*see diagram*)

*After 33. … Bd8*

"At this point, the game, having lasted several hours, was adjourned. As the position stands, it is a matter of interesting and difficult analysis to show whether or not Black's pawn is sufficient to insure victory"—Boden. **34. h6?** Maintaining the standstill in the center by moving his rook along the e-file is their only chance. Black has to advance the pawns on the queenside to try to win the game. **34. … g5! 35. f×g6** *e.p.* **R×e4 36. Qf3** 36. g7† is of no avail. **36. … Rh4† 37. Kg1 R×e3 38. Q×e3** 38. g7† doesn't save them: 38. … Kg8 39. Q×e3 Re4! 40. Qd3 Qe5 41. Rf3 f5 and the bishop joins the battle to decide the game. **38. … Q×e3†** 38. … Re4 is simpler, but the text move is also sufficient. **39. R×e3 h×g6 40. Re8† Kh7 41. R×d8 R×c4 42. R×d6 Rd4 43. R×f6 R×d5 44. Rf7† K×h6 45. R×a7 c4 46. Kf2 Rd2† 47. Kf3 c3 48. Rb7 c2 49. Rc7 Rd3† 50. Ke2 Rc3** and Black wins—*The Field* (Boden), 24 April and 1 May 1858; *Modern Chess* (Bird), pp. 153–154.

Morphy's visit was approaching, but one final mention in the *Era* of 23 May 1858 indicates that Bird remained active. In that column Löwenthal showed his interest in receiving games played

14. T. Harding, *Eminent Victorian Chess Players: Ten Biographies.* Jefferson: McFarland, 2012, pp. 84–86.

15. Löwenthal started negotiations with Boden, who was his opponent in the final in Manchester 1857. As Boden had to forfeit this game a duel would be fitting. This led to nothing after which Löwenthal proposed to have a go at Staunton himself—another vain attempt.

between Bird and a certain "S.A." in Newcastle. Bird's opponent was presumably Silas Angas.[16]

# Morphy's First Visit 1858

At the end of 1857, rumors about a young American chess prodigy reached the European shores. At the first American chess congress, held that year in New York, Paul Morphy finalized a flawless track by crushing Louis Paulsen, soon to be recognized as one of the world's strongest players himself. Morphy's fame in America was made but as everybody knew, Europe was considered the real power house of chess. Morphy's supporters encouraged him to cross the Atlantic, especially with the purpose of meeting Howard Staunton in a match. Morphy arrived in Liverpool on 21 June 1858, and immediately headed for Birmingham to participate in the second congress of the British Chess Association. As Morphy learned about its postponement he proceeded his way to the Mecca of chess, London. Here he completely wiped out all opposition. Löwenthal and Owen (the latter accepting the odds of pawn and move) were crushed in set matches while Morphy also proved his superiority over all others in offhand games. Only Staunton avoided a direct confrontation with the American.

The last principal London player to meet Morphy was Bird. Frederick Edge, Morphy's secretary, provided an account from the American point of view.

> The majority of his games in London, Morphy played at the Divan. It was a general subject of regret, after he had vanquished the different amateurs in the capital, that Mr. Bird was absent in the North, and that the American might leave before that gentleman could visit London. Mr. Bird is a terrible fellow for attacking right and left; his game was described as the counterpart of Morphy's, it being added that he was just the antagonist our hero required. At last, Mr. Bird arrived, and the result between the two was more startling than ever, Morphy winning ten to one. It is but just to state that Mr. Bird was somewhat out of play, as he himself observed; adding, however, that he never was a match for his antagonist [*Paul Morphy, the Chess Champion*, pp. 69–70].

Bird himself wrote similarly about his games with Morphy.

> When Morphy appeared in this country I had retired from chess, and was long absent from London; but on my return, upon visiting Simpson's, I cheerfully met him over the board, and though faring badly on that occasion, and at a subsequent meeting, I later on at the St. George's Chess Club won and drew two very fine games which have not been (at least as far as I am aware) ever recorded [*Modern Chess*, p. 1].

The games between Morphy and Bird were played in the second part of August, just before the meeting in Birmingham.

## (115) Bird–Morphy    0–1
Offhand game
London, August 1858
*C41*

**1. e4 e5 2. Nf3 d6 3. d4 f5?!** A favorite line of Morphy, but of dubious value. **4. Nc3** "4. d×e5 is the usual move, and, as has been thought, gives White some advantage. Mr. Morphy, however, seems

to differ from the present authorities, and to agree with the profound Philidor as to the merits of 3. ... f5"—Falkbeer. 4. d×e5 f×e4 5. Ng5 d5 6. Nc3 c6 and now 7. Nc×e4 or 7. e6 are critical. Bird's move isn't bad either. **4. ... f×e4 5. N×e4 d5? 6. Ng3?** "In a dashing game, played between Calthrop vs. Brien, White sacrificed his knight with 6. N×e5. Of course, in mentioning this fact, we say nothing as to the soundness of the sacrifice one way or the other"—Falkbeer. 6. N×e5 is winning: 6. ... d×e4 7. Qh5† g6 8. N×g6 h×g6 9. Q×g6† Kd7 10. Qf5† and the rook will fall. **6. ... e4 7. Ne5 Nf6 8. Bg5 Bd6 9. Nh5?!** This raid comes too late. Undermining the center by 9. c4! is the best continuation. **9. ... 0–0 10. Qd2 Qe8 11. g4?** Bird is faced with a very difficult decision. If 11. Nf4 c6 loses a pawn. 11. N×f6† is playable and demands some precise moves from his opponent, but after 11. ... g×f6 12. B×f6 e3! 13. Q×e3 R×f6, he's better. The best move is the stunning 11. N×g7!, e.g., 11. ... K×g7 12. Bh6† Kh8 13. Bb5! c6 (or 13. ... Q×b5 14. Qg5 Ne8 15. B×f8) 14. Qg5 Qe7 15. B×f8 with unclear play. **11. ... N×g4** 11. ... B×e5! 12. d×e5 N×g4 is clearly superior. **12. N×g4** 12. N×g7 (Boden) is the only move to continue fighting. After 12. ... N×e5 13. N×e8 Nf3† 14. Kd1 N×d2 15. N×d6 c×d6 16. B×d2 R×f2, White has some compensation for the lost pawn. **12. ... Q×h5 13. Ne5 Nc6** 13. ... c5! leads to a more open type of game. After 14. h4 Qe8! 15. c3 c×d4 16. c×d4 Nc6 17. N×c6 Q×c6, there is no more shelter for White's king on the queenside, nor on the kingside. With a pawn ahead as well, Black is simply winning. **14. Be2 Qh3 15. N×c6 b×c6 16. Be3 Rb8** "By the position of Black's queen, castling on the kingside is rendered impossible for White. The text move makes castling on the queenside very hazardous"—Falkbeer. **17. 0–0–0** *(see diagram)*

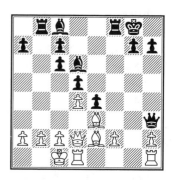

*After 17. 0–0–0*

**17. ... R×f2!!** "A beautiful combination, and sound, inasmuch as in the sequel he can always at least draw"—Boden. There were various quiet moves that gave him excellent perspectives; e.g., 17. ... Be6 18. Rdg1 g6, or 17. ... Bb4 first to seduce White to weaken the position of the king with 18. c3, or 17. ... Bg4, which takes control over the white squares. Morphy's combination immortalizes the game, but it has been unclear for a very long time whether this combination was correct. A discussion of almost 150 years can be concluded nowadays, with the help of computer analysis. It appears that Bird could hope only to reach an endgame offering but slight chances of a draw. **18. B×f2 Qa3!!** Stunning play from Morphy. 18. ... Ba3? 19. Qe3! has to be avoided. **19. c3** "19. Qg5 might have led to a game which Black could, at most, only have drawn"—Boden. That move loses immediately after 19. ... R×b2! **19. ... Q×a2 20. b4 Qa1† 21. Kc2 Qa4†** "All this is beautifully played by Mr. Morphy"—Boden. **22. Kb2?** 22. Kc1 (Boden) is the only move, as it weakens the power of 22. ... B×b4, which now only draws after 23. c×b4 R×b4 24. Qg5 Rb1†! Morphy could also give a perpetual check at once, but there is no reason to renounce a continuance of the game with either 22. ... a5 or 22. ... Bf5. After 22. ... a5, the correct line has been pointed out by Karsten Müller: 23. Qc2 Qa3† 24. Qb2 a×b4! 25. Q×a3 b×a3 26. Bg3 (not 26. Bf1 Bf4†, and Black mates in seven.) 26. ... Be7! (the crucial move. 26. ... a2 gives more drawing chances to his opponent.) 27. h4 e3, and White is lost. (see: http://www.chesscafe.com/text/skittles185.pdf). About at every point White suggestions can be brilliantly refuted by Black. Equally winning, and not worked out in the above article, is 22. ... Bf5! Now 23. Be1 is generally recommended, but this should lose quickly after 23. ... e3!, which is a clear improvement over the formerly analyzed 23. ... Qa1†, when White has more than excellent drawing chances: 24. Kc2 e3† 25. Kb3 e×d2 26. R×a1 Re8 27. Bf3 d×e1Q 28. Rh×e1 R×e1 29. R×e1 B×h2 30. b5! After 23. ... e3!, there follows 24. Qb2 a5! This is the killing move, but is effects are truly hard to estimate. White gets in some kind of zugzwang, e.g., 25. Rg1 (Everything else loses as well, e.g., 25. Bd3 e2 26. Rd2 B×d3 27. R×d3 Rf8) 25. ... a×b4 26. c4 b3 27. c5 B×h2 28. Rg2 Bf4 29. Bc3 g5 30. Rf1 Bg6 White can do absolutely nothing. His opponent can evacuate the king from the g-file, play the bishop to e4 and ultimately the rook will infiltrate via a2. More resilient than the traditional suggestion 23. Be1 is 23. Qe3! Still, the endgame reached after 23. ... a5 24. Kd2 a×b4 25. Ra1 Qb3 26. Rhc1 b×c3† 27. Ke1 c2 28. Q×b3 R×b3 29. R×c2 e3 30. R×c6 e×f2† 31. K×f2 Rb4 is promising for Black. **22. ... B×b4! 23. c×b4 R×b4† 24. Q×b4 Q×b4† 25. Kc2** 25. Ka2 loses after 25. ... c5!, when White cannot hold the center, e.g., 26. d×c5 e3! **25. ... e3!** "First-rate play all this"—Boden. The terrific point of Morphy's combination. **26. B×e3 Bf5† 27. Rd3 Qc4† 28. Kd2 Qa2† 29. Kd1 Qb1†** White resigns—*The Field* (Boden), 4 September 1858; *The Sunday Times* (Falkbeer), 12 September 1858.

### (116) Morphy–Bird　　1–0
Offhand game
London, August 1858
*C30*

1. e4 e5 2. f4 Bc5 3. Nf3 d6 4. c3 Bg4 5. Bc4 Nc6 6. b4 Bb6 7. a4 a6 8. h3 B×f3 9. Q×f3 Nf6 10. d3 Qe7 11. f5 Rd8 12. Bg5 Nb8 13. Nd2 c6 14. Nf1 d5 15. Bb3 Qd6 16. Ng3 0–0 17. Nh5 d×e4 18. d×e4 N×h5 19. Rd1 Qc7 20. B×d8 R×d8 21. R×d8† Q×d8 22. Q×h5 Be3 23. Qd1 Qh4† 24. Ke2 Bb6 25. Kd3 Nd7 26. Qg4 Qf2 27. f6 Black resigns—*The Sunday Times*, 7 November 1858.

### (117) Morphy–Bird　　1–0
Offhand game
London, August 1858
*C39*

1. e4 e5 2. f4 e×f4 3. Nf3 g5 4. h4 g4 5. Ne5 Nf6 6. Bc4 d5 7. e×d5

**Paul Morphy (left) playing a game against Jules Arnous de Rivière (*L'Illustration*).**

Bd6 8. d4 Nh5 9. Nc3 Bf5 10. Ne2 B×e5 11. d×e5 f3 12. g×f3 g×f3 13. Bg5 f6 14. e×f6 Qd6 15. Qd4 f×e2 16. B×e2 Qg3† 17. Kd2 0–0 18. Rag1 and White wins—*Morphy's Games*, p. 314.

### (118) Morphy–Bird　　1–0
Offhand game
London, August 1858
*C51*

1. e4 e5 2. Nf3 Nc6 3. Bc4 Bc5 4. b4 B×b4 5. c3 Bc5 6. d4 e×d4 7. c×d4 Bb6 8. 0–0 "Mr. Boden, in his *Popular Introduction*, has advocated 8. Bb2 here, a move well worthy of the student's attention. A close examination of it has satisfied us of its merits"—Löwenthal. **8. ... d6 9. d5 Na5 10. e5!?** An extremely rare but interesting line. It occurred in only a few games, but the White players were not the weakest: Morphy, Kolisch and Steinitz. 10. Bb2 quickly became established as the mainline in the coming years. **10. ... N×c4 11. Qa4† Bd7 12. Q×c4 d×e5?!** "This move opens too many lines for White. Recommendable is 12. ... Nge7, e.g. 13. e6 f×e6 14. d×e6 Bc6 15. Ng5 0–0 16. Qc2 Ng6 17. h4 Qf6 18. Bb2 Qf4 with a very strong position"—Maróczy. **13. N×e5 Qf6** There is nothing better. **14. N×d7 K×d7** "If 14. ... Q×a1, White would have obtained such an attack as must have won easily, either by forcing the king into a checkmate, or by winning the queen"—Löwenthal. A sample is 15. N×b6 a×b6 16. Q×c7 Ne7 17. Ba3. **15. Qg4†?!** "The attack is maintained with Mr. Morphy's characteristic energy"—Löwenthal. 15. Nc3 is stronger. The aim to hold the king in the center has already been achieved, and pieces should be brought towards the king. **15. ... Ke8 16. Bg5** 16. Qe2† Qe7 17. Qb5† Qd7 18. Re1† Kd8 is

superior, but Black has little to fear as White is far from completing his development. **16. ... Qg6** 16. ... Qd4! allows Black to claim a small advantage after 17. Qf3 h6 18. Re1† Kf8, as White is forced into an endgame a pawn down: 19. Qa3† Qc5 20. Be3 Q×a3. **17. Nc3 Nf6 18. Rae1† Kf8 19. Qb4† Kg8 20. B×f6 Q×f6 21. Ne4 Qg6** 21. ... Qd4 is interesting. **22. Kh1 h5 23. f4 h4** Bird had to stop the f-pawn with 23. ... Qf5! **24. f5 Qh5 25. Rf4** "A masterly move, threatening to win the queen by 26. Nf6†"—Löwenthal. **25. ... f6?** "If 25. ... Kh7 26. Nf6†, winning the queen. But it was observed, at the time, by Mr. Boden, that if, instead of the move played (an oversight which at once costs Mr. Bird the game) Black had moved 25. ... Rh6, Black would have a strong defensible position, with a pawn plus"—Löwenthal. After 25. ... Rh6! 26. h3 Rd8 27. Qe7 R×d5 28. f6 Bd4!, the position is balanced. **26. N×f6† g×f6 27. Rg4† Q×g4 28. Q×g4† Kf8 29. Re6 Rh6 30. Qf4 Kg7 31. Re7†** and White wins—*Morphy's Games* (Löwenthal), p. 315; *Paul Morphy* (Maróczy), pp. 146–147.

## (119) Morphy–Bird    ?
Offhand game
London, August 1858
C40

1. e4 e5 2. Nf3 d5 3. e×d5 e4 4. Qe2 f5 5. d3 Nf6 6. Bg5 Q×d5 7. B×f6 g×f6 8. Nbd2 Be7 9. d×e4 f×e4 10. N×e4 0–0 and the continuation is unknown—*Chess Practice*, p. 54.

# B.C.A. CONGRESS, BIRMINGHAM 1858

Bird's combating with Morphy had aroused his appetite for the game and towards the end of August he travelled to Birmingham. The organizing body, the British Chess Association, was the most important one dedicated to chess on British soil. It had started humbly, in 1841, as the Yorkshire Chess Association. In 1852 the committee announced that the next meeting would be held under the auspices of the Northern and Midland Counties Chess Association. Three years later it was decided to extend its ambitions all over England, and in 1857 the first congress of what was now called the Chess Association took place in Manchester. A field of eight players gathered for a knock-out tournament. Adolf Anderssen was the major asset but he was surprisingly eliminated by the ultimate winner, Löwenthal.

It is noteworthy that the name British Chess Association was effectively adopted only in 1862, on the occasion of the grand chess tournament in London. Since then, this name has been used in hindsight, so that the tournaments from 1857 until 1861 are now reckoned to have been played under the flag of the B.C.A.

The Birmingham congress was originally planned in June but ultimately postponed until the end of August. The ambitions of the B.C.A. were set higher than the year before and the committee hoped for 32 participants. After some difficulties the number of 16 entries was achieved. Two prizes were foreseen, the first one being an attractive £60. The tournament would be a knock-out event,

with two wins needed to qualify for the next round. In the final three wins were necessary.

About every single British player of note signed on, even Howard Staunton, but it was the performance of Paul Morphy that was most anticipated. His easy victory against Löwenthal had left an especially deep impression. Ultimately Morphy decided to withdraw just before the start of the congress, much to the disappointment of the chess fans. Morphy nevertheless made a short trip to Birmingham. He arrived on 26 August and engaged in some skittles play. On the next day, the last of the congress, the tournament was interrupted so that everyone could witness Morphy's blindfold exhibition against eight opponents.

Bird entered his first tournament in seven years. He was paired with a tough opponent, Robert Brien. Each player had scored a win when Bird was obliged to forfeit the third game because of a "pressing engagement" in London.

All favorites survived the first round, hence the second round saw some real clashes. Falkbeer beat de Saint-Amant while Löwenthal disposed of Staunton. This first game of the latter match was fiercely contested and, together with Morphy's blindfold exhibition, was responsible for a serious delay in the tournament schedule. Staunton's elimination marked the practical end of his chess career.

As a result of the delay, a part of the semifinals and the final of the tournament were played out in London. Falkbeer and Löwenthal confirmed their previous result and beat respectively Brien and Owen. Löwenthal repeated his success of the previous year by beating Falkbeer in the final 3–1.

## (120) Brien–Bird    1–0
B.C.A. Congress (round 1, game 1)
Birmingham, 24 August 1858
A20

1. c4 e5 2. e3 Nf6 3. a3 c5 4. Nc3 Nc6 5. b3 d6 6. Bd3 g6 7. Bb2 Bg7 8. Nge2 Be6 9. 0–0 Nh5 10. Re1 f5 11. Ng3 N×g3 12. f×g3 h5 13. Be2 Qg5 14. Rf1 h4 15. g4 Rh7 16. Rb1 Rd8 17. Nd5 Rd7 18. h3 Rf7 19. b4 c×b4 20. a×b4 e4 21. B×g7 Rf×g7 22. Nf4 Bd7 23. d4 Ne7 24. d5 f×g4 25. B×g4 Nf5 26. B×f5 g×f5 27. Qd4 b6 28. c5 Qd8 29. c×d6 Kf7 30. Ra1 a5 31. b×a5 b×a5 32. Qa7 Rg3 33. R×a5 Rhg7 34. Rb1 R×e3 35. Rb8 Re1† 36. Kf2 Q×b8 37. Q×b8 Rc1 38. Qa7 Ke8 39. Nh5 Rc2† 40. Ke3 f4† 41. N×f4 Bf5 42. Qb6 and Black resigns after two or three more moves—*Chess Praxis*, pp. 443–444.

## (121) Bird–Brien    1–0
B.C.A. Congress (round 1, game 2)
Birmingham, 24 August 1858
C01

1. e4 e6 2. d4 d5 3. e×d5 e×d5 4. Bd3 Nf6 5. Nf3 Bd6 6. 0–0 0–0 7. Be3 h6 8. Ne5 Re8 9. f4 a6 10. Nd2 Nc6 11. c3 Ne7 12. Ndf3 Nf5 13. Bf2 Ne4 14. Qc2 f6 15. g4 f×e5 16. f×e5 Bf8 The bishop is out of play at f8 and it prevents his rook from occupying the open file. Either 16. ... Be7 or 16. ... N×d4 maintains the equilibrium. **17. g×f5 B×f5 18. Bg3 Bh3 19. Rfe1 N×g3 20. h×g3 g5?** Under pressure Brien succumbs and makes a crude and unnecessary weakening. After 20. ... Be7 21. Kh2 Bg4 22. Rf1 the control

## 2nd Congress of the B.C.A., Birmingham, 24–27 August 1858

*Site:* Queen's College
*Prizes:* 1st £60, 2nd £20

| | | | | | | | | |
|---|---|---|---|---|---|---|---|---|
| J.J. Löwenthal | 2 | Löwenthal | 2 | | | | | |
| J.S. Kipping | 0 | | | Löwenthal | 2½ | | | |
| H. Staunton | 2 | Staunton | 0 | | | | | |
| H. Hughes | 0 | | | | | Löwenthal | 5 | |
| J. Owen | 2 | Owen | 2 | | | | | |
| T.I. Hampton | 0 | | | Owen | ½ | | | |
| G. Salmon | 2 | Salmon | 0 | | | | | |
| E. de Szabo | 0 | | | | | | | Löwenthal |
| E. Falkbeer | 3½ | Falkbeer | 2 | | | | | |
| C. Ingleby | 1½ | | | Falkbeer | 3½ | | | |
| P. de Saint-Amant | 2 | de Saint-Amant | 1 | | | | | |
| Beetlestone | 0 | | | | | Falkbeer | 3 | |
| R.B. Brien | 2 | Brien | + | | | | | |
| H.E. Bird | 1 | | | Brien | 2½ | | | |
| C.F. Smith | + | Smith | − | | | | | |
| P. Morphy | − | | | | | | | |

over the white squares promise Bird but a small edge. **21. Re2** 21. Bh7† Kh8 22. Bf5 is a more economical way to take control over the white squares and the f-file. **21. ... Bg4?!** The idea to exchange off this bishop and head for an ending with bishops of opposite colors is bad, since Bird has tremendous attacking chances. 21. ... Bg7 is playable. **22. Rf2 B×f3** It is too late now for 22. ... Bg7 as White has complete control over the position: 23. Nh2 Be6 24. Raf1 Re7 25. Qe2. **23. R×f3 Re7 24. Raf1 Qd7 25. Qf2 Bg7 26. Bb1 Qe6 27. Qc2 Bf8 28. Rf6 Qh3 29. Qf2 Bg7 30. Bf5 Qh5 31. Bg6 Qh3 32. Rf7 R×f7 33. B×f7† Kh8 34. e6 Bf8 35. Qe3 Be7 36. Qe5† Kh7 37. Bh5 Rf8 38. R×f8 B×f8 39. e7 Bg7 40. Bg6†** and White wins—*Era* (Löwenthal), 14 May 1865.

**(122) Brien–Bird    1–0**
B.C.A. Congress (round 1, game 3)
Birmingham, 24 August 1858
*Game scored by default*

# A NEW CLUB IN TOWN

Just like Falkbeer, Johann Jacob Löwenthal sought refuge from the continent after the revolutionary year 1848. He initially emigrated to America where he was the first European master to meet Paul Morphy. Though not yet 13 years old, Morphy beat him.

Löwenthal came to London to participate in the international tournament of 1851. His performance there was not a success, as he got eliminated at once by Williams. Nevertheless Löwenthal's reputation started to increase and he was soon established as one of the best British players.

In 1853 he lost a very important and tense match against Harrwitz. At one point Löwenthal was leading 9 to 2, but quite astonishingly it was Harrwitz who first scored the needed 11 wins.

Löwenthal's finest hours came in 1857 and 1858 when he won both the first and second congress of the B.C.A. In the weeks preceding the second congress, he was decisively beaten by Morphy. Löwenthal also took part in the grand tournament of 1862 but played only three games. By now his active career was largely over and more than ever he gained his income from journalistic activities. He remained deeply engaged with the British Chess Association until its end in the early 1870s.

Löwenthal had been on good terms with the influential Staunton since his arrival in 1851 and probably owed the lucrative post of secretary of the St. George's Chess Club to him. Löwenthal's unexpected loss against Harrwitz was a bitter pill to swallow for Staunton and may have put their relationship under some strain.

Without his post at St. George's Chess Club, Löwenthal had his hands free for other initiatives. He did not rest on his laurels and by November 1858 had established a new circle, the St. James's Chess Club. Even though the name of this club contains nowadays less splendor than the St. George's, the Westminster or the City of London Chess Club, it was one of London's major chess centers for more than a decade.

A small advertisement in the *Era* on 5 December 1858 announced the existence of the St. James's Chess Club and contained some basic information. The club assembled at St. James's Hall, a new concert hall in Regent Street. The club attempted to draw chess players from London as well as from the provinces. The latter category were to pay a subscription of half a guinea per year, half of what town members were due. The club opened each day, with special meetings held on Tuesdays and Saturdays, when the experienced players would offer assistance to youngsters. Unlike other clubs, the opportunity was offered to play in the evening, as the club opened from 1 p.m. until midnight.

In the *Era* of 16 January 1859, Löwenthal informed his readers that the Tuesday and Saturday evenings were best attended, while Robert Bownas Wormald and Brien had been among the visitors. One of the club's attractions were the frequently played consultation games. At the end of January, the club was visited with several "influential members of the St. George's," who expressed their satisfaction with the "accommodation afforded to the members." In April 1859, after five months of existence, it already hosted the illustrious blindfold simultaneous exhibition in which Morphy opposed five of the best British players.

A unique record of the chess activity during these first weeks of the club is a small notebook, simply titled *St. James's Chess Club*, which is kept at the library in The Hague. It belonged to Löwenthal and contains mainly games played by him. Quite surprisingly the notebook also includes three games played by Bird. These provide the most important known proof that Bird did not abandon chess completely in between Morphy's visits of 1858 and 1859.

The first two games in the booklet were contested between

**Johann J. Löwenthal (courtesy Nigel Webb).**

Löwenthal and Bird on Saturday 18 December 1858. The second game is especially interesting, as it is the first known game in which Bird adopted the defense against the Ruy Lopez that was ultimately named after him. Bird was also involved in a consultation game that occurred in January 1859. The name of Bird's companion, though hardly readable, was probably George Athelstane Thrupp, the head of the world leading coachbuilding firm Thrupp & Maberly. In the *Era* of 20 February 1859, he was called a "highly-talented amateur." This reputation was affirmed when he was one of the three players to achieve a draw against Paul Morphy in a rather flat game at Morphy's blindfold exhibition on eight boards at the St. George's Club on 20 April. Bird and Thrupp managed to draw against Löwenthal and Frederick Rosenauer, an ardent amateur of whom various games were included in this notebook.

**(123) Bird–Löwenthal    0–1**
Offhand game
London (St. James's C.C.), 18 December 1858
*C90*

**1. e4 e5 2. Nf3 Nc6 3. Bb5 a6 4. Ba4 Nf6 5. 0–0 Be7 6. Re1 b5 7. Bb3 d6 8. Bd5 Bb7 9. d4 N×d5 10. e×d5 N×d4 11. N×d4 e×d4 12. Q×d4 0–0 13. Nc3 Bf6 14. Qd3 B×c3 15. b×c3 Qf6 16. Rb1 Rfe8 17. Bd2 Re5 18. c4 b×c4 19. Q×c4 B×d5 20. Q×c7 h6 21. R×e5 Q×e5 22. Re1 Qd4 23. Qa5 Rc8 24. Be3 Qc4 25. Rd1 B×g2 26. Qf5 Be4 27. Qg4 f5 28. Qh5 Qe6 29. f3 B×c2 30. Re1 Qf7 31. Q×f7† K×f7 32. Kf2 g5 33. f4 g4 34. h3 h5 35. Kg3 Be4 36. Kh4 Rc2 37. h×g4 h×g4** White resigns—*St. James's Chess Club*.

**(124) Löwenthal–Bird    ?**
Offhand game
London (St. James's C.C.), 18 December 1858
*C61*

**1. e4 e5 2. Nf3 Nc6 3. Bb5 Nd4** This game is the first known occasion on which Bird adopted this defense against the Ruy Lopez. He used it a couple of times at the Challenge Cup tournaments of 1866 and 1868/9, but it became his standard defense against this opening from only 1873 onwards. Ultimately the variation received Bird's name. Bird explained his motives to play such a strange move in *Chess Practice* (p. 33): "This [the Ruy Lopez] is the most dreaded of all attacks because Black has to submit to a defensive kind of game without the advantage of a captured pawn as in the other gambits. The exception is in the case of my defense, 3. … Nd4, which, however, is not approved by the recognized authorities, and consequently has not been generally adopted." **4. N×d4 e×d4 5. 0–0 Bc5 6. Bc4** Two earlier games in which 3. … Nd4 had been played have survived. During the first half of 1858 Staunton had beaten Owen and Barnes with it. More interesting is a game played in August or September 1856 during a series of consultation games involving Löwenthal and Staunton played in the St. George's Chess Club. In this game, Löwenthal and Captain Kennedy managed the White pieces. They were opposed by Staunton and an anonymous but skillful amateur. It is possible that Bird was Staunton's companion, even though this game was played in an otherwise blank period of his chess career. Bird had been married for a year and his matches with Falkbeer started only late in November, in Purssell's. Two of Staunton's notes to the game do however fit in with Bird's playing style. This game continued: 6. d3 Ne7 7. Bg5 0–0 8. Qh5 d6 9. f4 f6 10. Bh4 Be6 11. f5 Bf7 12. Qg4 Kh8 13. Rf3 c6 14. Ba4 Qc7 15. Bb3 Ng8 16. Nd2 Nh6 17. Qf4 Qe7 18. Rh3 B×b3 19. a×b3 Qe5 20. Qf3 d5 "The suggestion of this move is due to the skillful amateur who was on Mr. Staunton's side. Mr. Staunton was rather opposed to it, and we believe upon examination it will be found to be, though ingenious, not altogether sound"—Staunton. 21. Rf1 Bb4 22. Bg3 Qe7 23. Bf4 B×d2 24. B×d2 d×e4 25. d×e4 Nf7 26. Bf4 Rae8 27. Re1 Qc5 28. Qf2 Qa5 29. Bd2 Qb6 30. b4 h6 31. Kh1 Ng5 32. B×g5 f×g5 33. Qd2 Qb5 34. Rd3 Qe5 35. g4 g6 36. Rf3 b6 37. h4 Kg7 38. h5 g×h5 39. g×h5 Rd8 40. Qg2 c5 41. b×c5 b×c5 42. Qe2 Rd7 43. Kg2 Rf6 44. Kh3 Rdf7 45. b3 g4† "After suggesting this daring sacrifice, Mr. Staunton was half inclined to forego it from apprehension that White would have time to bring their pieces to the rescue, but his colleague was, fortunately, so much in favor of the move that it was adopted, and, as we shall see, produced a very pleasing bit of endgame manoeuvring"—Staunton. 46. K×g4 Kh7 47. Kh3 Rg7 48. Qh2 Qe8 49. Rg3 Re7 50. Qg1 Q×h5† 51. Kg2 Qe8 52. Kf2 R×e4 53. R×e4 R×f5† 54. Ke2 Q×e4† and in a few more moves White hauled down their colors. *Illustrated London News*, 6 September 1856. Another forerunner of this line appears to have been Francis Burden, a close friend of Bird's at the Divan. He employed Bird's Defense in two games that were published in *The Field* on 28 May and 19 August 1859. **6. ... d6 7. d3 Ne7 8. c3 0–0 9. Nd2 Kh8 10. Nb3 f5?** Enterprising, but plain bad. **11.** c×d4 Bb6 **12.** Bg5 Qe8 **13. f4?** He returns the compliment. 13. Re1 is very good. **13. ... Nc6 14. Bb5?** Now Black gets the upper hand. 14. Kh1 or 14. Re1 are innocent. **14. ... f×e4 15.** d×e4 Q×e4 **16.** Re1 Qd5 **17.** B×c6 b×c6 **18.** Re7 Bf5 **19.** Qd2 a5 The manuscript concludes the game here without giving a result. It is very possible that Löwenthal resigned at this point—*St. James's Chess Club*.

### (125) Löwenthal & Rosenauer–Bird & Thrupp    ½–½
Consultation game
London (St. James's C.C.), 18 December 1858
*C01*

1. e4 e6 2. d4 d5 3. e×d5 e×d5 4. Nf3 Bd6 5. Bd3 Nc6 6. Be3 Bg4 7. Nbd2 Nge7 8. c3 Qd7 9. Qc2 h6 10. h3 Be6 11. Nb3 f5 12. Nc5 B×c5 13. d×c5 0–0 14. 0–0–0 f4 15. Bd4 Bf5 16. Rhe1 B×d3 17. Q×d3 Qf5 18. Q×f5 R×f5 19. Re6 Kf7 20. Rde1 Ng6 21. R×g6 K×g6 22. Nh4† Kg5 23. N×f5 K×f5 24. b4 b5 25. Kb2 g6 26. g4† f×g3 *e.p.* 27. f×g3 a5 28. a3 a×b4 29. a×b4 N×d4 30. c×d4 c6 31. Re7 Rc8 32. Kc3 g5 33. Re5† Kf6 34. g4 Ra8 35. Kb3 Kf7 36. Re1 Ra7 37. Kb2 Ra8 38. Kb3 h5 39. Re5 Kf6 40. h4 Rg8 41. h×g5† R×g5 42. g×h5 draw—*St. James's Chess Club*.

# HANDICAP TOURNAMENT AT PURSSELL'S 1859

In March 1859 Bird entered a knock-out handicap tournament organized at Purssell's. Together with Falkbeer and Hughes, prob-

ably the same player who received odds from Bird in 1850, he gave the odds of pawn and two moves against all the other players. During the first three rounds the first player to win two games qualified for the next round. In the fourth and final round three wins were needed for victory. Three prizes were provided.

Bird's opponent in the first round, Williams, forfeited. In the second round Bird met Falkbeer. Just as in their 1856-57 matches the games were hard-fought and tense, but also full of oversights. Ultimately Falkbeer had the better luck and emerged victorious after four games.

The final was played between Falkbeer and Henry Albert Reeves. The latter, described as a young and promising player, was quite active in 1859. He won a match against Hughes, receiving odds of pawn and two moves. Harrwitz beat Reeves, giving him the same odds. At that time Reeves was 19 years old and studying to become a surgeon. He resurfaced in chess circles in the 1880s and 1890s.

After six games, with each player having scored two wins, Falkbeer beat his opponent in the seventh and clinched to the first prize.

### (126) Falkbeer–Bird    ½–½
Handicap tournament (round 2, game 1)
London, 30 March 1859
*C01*

1. e4 e6 2. Nf3 d5 3. e×d5 e×d5 4. d4 Bd6 5. Bd3 Be6 6. Qe2 Nc6 7. c3 Nf6 8. Bg5 h6 9. Bh4 Ne7 10. Nbd2 c6 11. c4 Nh5 12. Bg3 Bg4 13. c×d5 0–0 14. d×c6 N×c6 15. 0–0 Re8 16. Be4 B×g3 17. f×g3 Nf6 18. Qd3 N×e4 19. N×e4 B×f3 20. g×f3 Q×d4† 21. Q×d4 N×d4 22. Rad1 Rad8 23. Kf2 f5 24. Nc3 Kf7 25. Rd2 Nc6 26. Rfd1 R×d2† 27. R×d2 Re7 28. Rd5 g6 29. f4 a6 30. h3 Re6 31. a3 Ke7 32. b4 Rd6 33. R×d6 K×d6 34. Ke3 b5 35. Kd3 Ke6 and the game was given up as a draw—*The Sunday Times*, 3 April 1859.

### (127) Bird–Falkbeer    0–1
Handicap tournament (round 2, game 2)
London, April 1859
*A03*

1. f4 c5 2. Nf3 d5 3. e3 a6 4. c4 d4 5. d3 Nc6 6. e4 e6 7. g3 Be7 8. Bg2 Nh6 9. 0–0 Bd7 10. a3 0–0 11. Ng5 f6 12. Nh3 f5 13. e5 Nf7 14. Nd2 Kh8 15. Nf3 h6 16. Bd2 g5 17. Ne1 g4 18. Nf2 h5 19. Nh1 Rb8 20. h3 Rg8 21. h×g4 h×g4 22. Rf2 Rg6 23. Qe2 b5 24. b3 b×c4 25. b×c4 Kg7 26. Qd1 Rh6 27. Rb1 Qc7 28. R×b8 N×b8 29. Qb3 Bc6 30. B×c6 Q×c6 31. Rh2 R×h2 32. K×h2 Nd7 33. Nf2 Bd8 34. Kg1 Bc7 35. Qd1 Nf8 36. Ng2 Ng6 37. Kf1 Nd8 38. Kg1 Nb7 39. Kh2 Ba5 40. B×a5 N×a5 41. Ne1 Qb7 42. Qa4 Nb3 43. Qe8 Nf8 44. Qd8 Kf7 45. Qd6 Nd2 46. Q×c5 Nf1† 47. Kg1 N×g3 48. Qd6 Ng6 49. Qd8 Ne2† 50. Kf1 Ne×f4 51. c5 Qb2 52. Ng2 g3 and White resigns—*The Sunday Times*, 10 April 1859.

### (128) Falkbeer–Bird    0–1
Handicap tournament (round 2, game 3)
London, April 1859
*C27*

1. e4 e5 2. Nc3 Bb4 3. Bc4 Nf6 4. f4 0–0 A concession as White

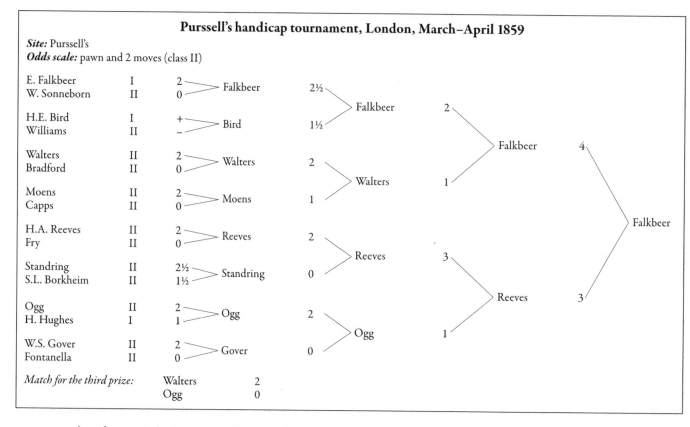

now gains a lot of space. **5. f×e5 N×e4 6. Nf3 B×c3** 6. ... N×c3 is safer. **7. d×c3 Qe7?** 7. ... d6 had to be played. After the text move, Black is rapidly facing a lost position. **8. Qd4! Nd6 9. Bg5 Qe8 10. Bd3 Nc6 11. Qh4** Falkbeer decides to start an immediate attack against Bird's king, but also attractive is 11. Qd5!, when he could completely outplay his opponent after 11. ... Ne7 12. Qc5 Ndf5 13. g4. **11. ... f5 12. 0–0 N×e5** 12. ... Ne4 is the only move to stay more or less in the game. **13. N×e5 Q×e5 14. Rae1** First 14. Be7 is also winning. **14. ... Qc5† 15. Kh1?!** After 15. Be3! Qd5 16. Bd4 White's pieces dominate the board. It won't last long until his rook infiltrates to e7. **15. ... b5** "His best plan to give up the exchange at once"—Boden. **16. Be7** 16. Rf3!, intending 17. Rh3, is another decisive reinforcement of the attack. **16. ... Bb7 17. B×f8 R×f8 18. Re7 Rf6** "From this point to the end the game is extraordinarily interesting and instructive"—Boden. **19. Rfe1** It seems that Bird got away with the loss of the exchange in return for fair attacking chances. These could be nipped in the bud with 19. Qd4! Qc6 20. Rf2 and everything is covered. White threatens 21. Q×a7 on the next move. **19. ... Rg6 20. R7e2** 20. R1e2 is much simpler. **20. ... h6 21. Qd8† Kh7 22. Q×d7 Rg5?** 22. ... Qd5 23. Rg1 c5 is the correct move order, as White is forced to displace his rook with 24. Rf2 to liberate his bishop. White's task is then not an easy one after 24. ... Rg5, as 25. ... Ne4 follows in case the bishop gives way. After 25. B×b5! Ne4 26. Rf3 Nd6, the position remains tense. **23. Qe7 Qd5 24. Rg1 c5 25. h4?** But Falkbeer omits to make use of his more active rook (compared with the line above) by forcing a quick win after 25. Re5! Qc6 26. Re6 Rg6 27. R×g6 K×g6 28. Qe6† and 29. B×f5†. **25. ... Rg4 26. Re5 Qf7?** 26. ... R×h4† 27. Q×h4 Q×e5 limits the disadvantage to a slightly material one. **27. Kh2! Qh5**

**28. g3 Be4 29. Be2??** A dreadful mistake. Though Bird's pieces look threatening, there is nothing to fear and he could just collect material with 29. R×c5. Of course 29. Q×d6?? R×h4† had to be avoided. **29. ... R×h4† 30. g×h4 Q×e2† 31. Kh3 Qf3† 32. Kh2 Qf2† 33. Kh3 Q×g1** White resigns—*The Field* (Boden), 16 April 1859.

### (129) Bird–Falkbeer    0–1

Handicap tournament (round 2, game 4)
London, April 1859
*C43*

**1. e4 e5 2. Nf3 Nf6 3. d4 e×d4 4. e5 Ne4 5. Q×d4 d5 6. e×d6 e.p. N×d6 7. Bg5 f6 8. Be3 Nc6 9. Qd2 Bf5 10. Bd3 Qd7 11. Nc3 Be7 12. 0–0 0–0–0 13. a3 g5 14. b4 h5 15. Nd5 Ne4 16. N×e7† Q×e7 17. Qe1 h4 18. b5 Ne5 19. N×e5 Q×e5 20. f4 Qd5 21. Rd1** A first imprecise move. The chances are even after 21. f×g5 h3 22. B×e4 B×e4 23. R×f6 B×g2, when the presence of the bishops of opposite colors is a dominant factor. **21. ... h3 22. c4?** Certainly better is 22. g3, though the weakened squares around his king are a heavy burden after 22. ... g4. **22. ... Qe6 23. Qa5 h×g2** Winning, just as 23. ... R×d3 24. R×d3 Ng3. **24. Rfe1 R×d3??** The position is greatly in Black's favor but the pressure on Falkbeer to find something decisive is not to be underestimated, as Bird threatens 25. Q×a7 with a decisive attack from his own. Falkbeer's choice should have been a fatal one, and instead 24. ... R×h2! has to be played. It appears that Black's attack is decisive after 25. K×h2 Rh8† 26. Kg1 Rh1† 27. K×g2 Rh4! as nothing can prevent the infiltration of the queen: 28. Rh1 (28. Q×a7 leads to a similar finish 28. ... Bh3† 29. Kf3 Bg2†) 28. ... Bh3† 29. Kf3 Bg2†. **25. R×d3 Nd6 26. Bf2** 26. R×d6!

Q×d6 27. b6, when the bishop is hanging, is the quickest road to victory. **26. ... Qf7 27. R×d6!** "Capital play"—Falkbeer. **27. ... c×d6 28. b6?** "Evidently a mistake. We have no doubt that, had White played 28. Q×a7, he could have won the game"—Falkbeer. **28. ... Qh7!** Covering the bishop and blowing new life into his attack by threatening h2. **29. Bg3 a×b6 30. Qa7** 30. Q×b6 is simpler, but agrees to a certain draw after 30. ... g×f4 31. B×f4 Qc7. **30. ... Bh3** (see diagram)

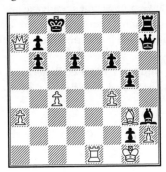

*After 30. ... Bh3*

**31. f×g5??** A third dramatic momentum that turns the outcome of the final game completely upside down. Nerves were clearly taking its toll from both players! There is still a possibility to secure a draw with 31. f5!, a move that's not so easy to find. Black now has to play 31. ... Qc7 (31. ... Q×f5? 32. Qa8† wins offhand, at least as long as White doesn't take the rook after 32. ... Kc7, but plays 33. Re7†!) 32. Qa8† Qb8 33. Qa4 Qc7 34. Qa8†. **31. ... Qd3** "Threatening mate in two moves"— Falkbeer. **32. Qa8† Kc7 33. Re7† Bd7 34. R×d7†** Despair. **34. ... K×d7 35. Q×b7† Ke6 36. K×g2 Q×c4 37. g6 Qd5† 38. Q×d5† K×d5 39. h4 Rh6 40. Kh3 R×g6 41. h5 Rg8 42. Kh4 Ra8 43. h6 R×a3 44. h7 Ra8 45. Kh5 b5 46. Kg6 Ke6 47. Bh4 Rh8 48. Kg7 R×h7† 49. K×h7 b4 50. Kg6 f5 51. Be1 b3 52. Bc3 f4** and White resigns—*The Sunday Times* (Falkbeer), 24 April 1859.

# MORPHY'S SECOND VISIT 1859

After the Birmingham tournament Morphy prolonged his string of victories in France where he beat Harrwitz and Anderssen in regular matches. By now Morphy was generally recognized as the strongest chess player in the world.

On 7 April 1859 Morphy arrived in London for a stay of a few more weeks. He was once again warmly received by the English chess community and was dragged around to visit various chess resorts and clubs in the British capital. Apart from attending several dinners in his honor, Morphy played some chess as well. Besides the usual offhand games he gave two blindfold exhibitions, each time against eight opponents.

Bird and Morphy met again. On 22 April Morphy was humbly taking notes of the games played between Bird and Jules Arnous de Rivière. According to Bird, he and Morphy agreed to commence a match on short notice. Morphy requested a postponement, and sadly nothing came of it.

Morphy's most impressive performance during this visit was a simultaneous display against five of the strongest players present in London. Initially Morphy was going to meet four players, but Bird joined in at the last minute. A great mass of people witnessed the spectacular exhibition on Tuesday 26 April at the St. James's Chess Club. Morphy won twice, against Bird and Arnous de Rivière. Boden and Löwenthal drew, while Barnes succeeded in beating him.[17]

Morphy left England four days later from Liverpool. His impact on chess is well known and hard to overestimate. It is now recognized that he was one of the first chess players to understand the principles of chess as they were formulated several years later by Steinitz. In Bird's time the idea that Steinitz was in fact a successor of Morphy was not orthodox yet and both players were constantly compared with each other.[18]

17. Löwenthal's résumé of the evening is interesting: "On Tuesday evening last the young champion carried out an arrangement..., and contested five games simultaneously.... The large smoking saloon upstairs was thrown open for the benefit of the members of the St. James's and their friends, and so ably were arrangements made that every visitor was enabled with comfort to view the proceedings. Play commenced at six p.m. and was continued until past midnight.... Taking the character of the players into consideration, we consider this to be, perhaps, the most difficult task that Mr. Morphy has yet undertaken, not even paralleled by that, which he so successfully carried out at the London Chess Club. Indeed, on one or two occasions during the evening, we noticed that Mr. Morphy was more or less slow in determining the course that he subsequently followed, while, in playing blindfold, especially at the St. George's, his rapidity of play was the subject of general remark as well as of admiration." *Era*, 1 May 1859.

18. Very interesting in this perspective is an example of Bird's so-called table talk as taken down many years later in 1889: "Morphy had more science than Steinitz— more imagination. His career was very short, though very brilliant, and whether or not he could have held first honors as long as Steinitz has is a matter of some doubt; but Morphy never met his match. He was never compelled to play his best game. His resources were never fully tested. We were taken a little by surprise by Morphy. He was a young man of twenty-one or twenty-two years, with bright eyes and flowing hair and broad forehead. When in England he was cool and calculating, never showing enthusiasm. All that we could provoke from him at the most wonderful sights London affords was, 'Yes I see; that's very pretty.' When he was in London he was all right, but he went to Paris, and foolishly entered upon the gaieties of the gay French capital. His physique was not strong, and he broke down. They say he was never quite right mentally afterwards. At one time they hoped he had recovered sufficiently to play chess once more; in fact, the doctors advised him to play chess as the best means of restoring his mental vigor. We hoped to have him play in the continental tournament of 1878, but were doomed to disappointment." *Philadelphia Times*, 7 July 1889. ¶ A few anecdotes involving Bird and Morphy are worth mentioning here. Bird got along quite well with Morphy and served as his guide by showing him the beauties of London: "Simpson's Divan was naturally the first resort of the incomparable Paul Morphy, and he greatly preferred it to any other chess room he ever saw, he even went so far as to say it was 'very nice,' which was a great deal from him, the most undemonstrative young man we ever met with. Certainly nothing else in London, from St. Paul's, Westminster Abbey and the Tower to our Picture Galleries and Crystal Palace, not even the Duke of Wellington's Equestrian Statue, elicited such praise from him as 'very nice,' at least as applied to any inanimate object." Bird, *Chess History and Reminiscences*, p. 74. ¶ Oscar Conrad Müller, a fellow master of Bird at Simpson's since the late 1880s, recalled an amusing story involving Bird and Morphy in his memoirs: "At the entrance you could hardly fail to notice a fairly large picture, showing the Devil playing chess with a rather despondent-looking young man. H.E. Bird told me that in 1858 Paul Morphy, when visiting Simpson's, looked at the chess position in the picture quite a long time, finally remarking to Bird: 'I don't know whose move it is, but if it is the young man's turn to play, his game is still full of chances.'" *British Chess Magazine*, November 1932, p. 481. ¶ Müller also pointed at a slightly more negative point made by Bird: "Bird, who was a very rapid player himself, had a grievance against Morphy, which he once expressed to me, thus: 'One afternoon Morphy turned up at about one o'clock and offered to play me a skittle game. I accepted the challenge, and the game actually lasted, owing to his slow play, till nine p.m., when I lost it.'" *British Chess Magazine*, December 1932, p. 484. It is quite remarkable that Bird described Morphy as a slow player. Morphy generally used one or two hours to make all his moves. His opponents played markedly slower, sometimes needing eight hours.

**(130) Morphy–Bird    1–0**
Simultaneous game
London (St. James's C.C.), 26 April 1859
*C35*

**1. e4 e5 2. f4 e×f4 3. Nf3 Be7** "Extremely bold play on the part of Mr. Bird to give such an attack as the Cunningham Gambit to a general like Mr. Morphy"—Löwenthal. The Cunningham Defense was another lifelong favorite of Bird. It is a valid defense against the King's Gambit. **4. Bc4 Bh4†** 4. ... Nf6 is nowadays regarded as the main line, but Bird always preferred to give the check. **5. g3** "Simpler was 5. Kf1, as White wins back the gambit pawn with advantageous play. The sacrifice of two pawns surely leads to a sharp attack, but is not completely sound according to the latest insights"—Maróczy. **5. ... f×g3 6. 0–0 g×h2† 7. Kh1 d5 8. B×d5 Nf6 9. B×f7†** 9. N×h4 is preferable, although the text move has often been recognized as White's best. **9. ... K×f7 10. N×h4 Re8** Both 10. ... Nc6 and 10. ... Rf8 (Löwenthal) are better. **11. d3 Bh3** "The game now becomes lively and interesting"—Löwenthal. **12. Qh5† Kg8 13. R×f6** "This highly elegant continuation was not possible had Black played 10. ... Rf8"—Maróczy. **13. ... g×f6 14. Nc3 Re5** Bird gets a bit too ambitious. 14. ... Be6, withdrawing the bishop from the line of fire of the queen, is very safe; e.g., 15. Bf4 Re7 16. Nf5 B×f5 17. Q×f5 Rf7 18. B×h2 Qd7 leaves White struggling for compensation. **15. Qf3 Qd7** Again it is better to retreat the bishop. **16. Bf4** "After 16. Nd5 Black sacrifices the exchange"—Maróczy. **16. ... Nc6** 16. ... Bg4 17. Qg2 Rc5 18. Nd5 R×d5 is a more favorable continuation. **17. K×h2** 17. B×e5! N×e5 18. Q×f6 is very crafty. Morphy probably avoided this line as Black seems able to hang on with 18. ... Ng4, which defends the h-pawn, but then the White knights enter the game with force: 19. Qf3 Rf8 20. Nf5 Kh8 21. Nd5 Qc6 22. c4 a6 23. Qg3, and Black is unable to withstand the pressure very long. **17. ... Bg4 18. Rg1 h5?** The situation looks pretty critical for Bird, but there is salvation in the brilliant 18. ... Rg5! 19. Qe3 Kh8 20. Nd5 (20. B×g5 f×g5 21. Q×g5 Qd6† 22. Kh1 Rg8 defends everything) 20. ... Rgg8 21. N×f6 Qe7 22. e5 Raf8 followed by a sacrifice at f6. The diminished material makes a draw likely. **19. B×e5** "White has regained the sacrificed exchange and obtained positional advantage, as the weak pawn at h5 will soon fall"—Maróczy. **19. ... f×e5 20. Nd5! Nd4 21. Nf6† Kh8 22. Qe3** 22. Ng6† Kg7 23. N×h5† is a much quicker win. **22. ... Qg7 23. N×h5 Qh7 24. R×g4 Q×h5 25. Qh3 Kh7 26. c3 Ne6 27. Rg6 Re8** "It is clear that if he had played 27. ... Nf4, his adversary would have mated him in two moves"—Löwenthal. **28. R×e6 R×e6 29. Q×e6 Q×h4† 30. Qh3 Q×h3† 31. K×h3** "With a pawn ahead White did right in exchanging pieces, and reducing the endgame to one of a simple character"—Löwenthal. **31. ... c5 32. Kg4 Kg6 33. Kf3 Kf6 34. Ke3 Ke6 35. d4 e×d4† 36. c×d4 c×d4† 37. K×d4 Kd6 38. e5† Ke6 39. Ke4 Ke7 40. Kd5 Kd7 41. e6† Ke7 42. Ke5 a6 43. a3 Ke8 44. Kd6** and White wins—*Era* (Löwenthal), 22 May 1859; *Paul Morphy* (Maróczy), pp. 307–308.

# Offhand Chess 1859–1860

Two continental masters followed in Morphy's slipstream and visited London in the spring of 1859. Jules Arnous de Rivière, the strongest French player, accompanied Morphy on his trip to London. Arnous de Rivière played an official match against Thomas Barnes. Barnes had had been the most successful Englishman in the duels with Morphy but was now distinctly beaten 5–2.

Bird and Arnous de Rivière played a dozen informal games with each other. There is some vagueness about the date and location when and where the games were played. According to Boden they were contested at the Divan. In *Modern Chess* (p. 63), Bird wrote that the games were played at George Maude's residence on Good Friday 1858. The year 1858 is definitely wrong, but if one assumes that these games were played on Good Friday, then they were played on 22 April 1859.

The four games between Bird and Arnous de Rivière that went into print show the superiority of Bird. No trace of a score could be retrieved in the sources.

**(131) Arnous de Rivière–Bird    1–0**
Offhand game
London, 22 April 1859
*C51*

**1. e4 e5 2. Nf3 Nc6 3. Bc4 Bc5 4. b4 B×b4 5. c3 Bc5 6. 0–0 d6 7. d4 e×d4 8. c×d4 Bb6 9. d5 Na5 10. e5 N×c4 11. Qa4† Qd7 12. Q×c4 Qg4 13. Bf4 Ne7 14. e×d6 Ng6 15. Re1† Kf8 16. Qb4 c5 17. d×c6 *e.p.* Be6 18. d7† Kg8 19. c×b7 Rb8 20. Q×b6 Q×f4 21. d8Q† Nf8 22. Qbd6** and White wins—*The Field*, 4 June 1859.

**(132) Bird–Arnous de Rivière    1–0**
Offhand game
London, 22 April 1859
*C51*

**1. e4 e5 2. Nf3 Nc6 3. Bc4 Bc5 4. b4 B×b4 5. c3 Bc5 6. 0–0 d6 7. d4 e×d4 8. c×d4 Bb6 9. h3** "Not the strongest move, but a useful one nevertheless, and one often played by McDonnell and the older school of amateurs"—Boden. **9. ... Nf6 10. Bg5 0–0 11. Nc3 Ne7?** Very bad. After 11. ... h6, Black is perfectly fine. **12. e5! d×e5 13. d×e5 Nd7** "This seems to be Black's only move. Had he changed queens he would have lost a piece, as will appear on a very little examination"—Boden. **14. e6** Most precise is 14. Re1!, reinforcing the threat 15. e6. After 14. ... Kh8 (what else?) 15. e6, Black will suffer material losses. **14. ... f×e6 15. B×e6† Kh8 16. Nd5?** 16. B×d7 B×d7 17. Re1 Bc5 18. Qe2! secures a winning advantage. With his next move Arnous de Rivière escapes from Bird's pressure. **16. ... Nf6! 17. B×f6 g×f6 18. B×c8 R×c8 19. Nf4** 19. N×b6 is worth considering. With the bishop a strong piece is eliminated. At the same time the doubling of the pawns diminishes the force of the pawn mass. **19. ... Q×d1 20. Ra×d1 Rcd8** 20. ... Ng6 gives Black a slight advantage in the endgame. White cannot infiltrate on the seventh rank (21. N×g6 h×g6 22. Rd7 Rcd8 22. Re7 Rfe8 24. Rf7 Rd6 wins for Black). In the long run Black's extra pawns on the queenside will start to tell. **21. Ne6 R×d1 22. R×d1 Re8 23. Rd7 Nd5 24. Nd8 Nf4 25. Nf7† Kg8 26. Nh6† Kh8 27. Nh4** *(see diagram)*

**27. ... Re1†** With his last move Bird is putting his opponent to the test. Instead of leaving the back rank with the rook, which is quite dangerous, the solid 27. ... Ne6 ought to draw; e.g., 28. Ng4

*After 27. Nh4*

Rd8 29. Re7 Nf8 30. N×f6 Rd2. **28. Kh2 B×f2?** White announced mate in five moves. In any case, Black is condemned to passivity after 28. ... Re8 29. Ng4 Rf8 30. Nf5—*The Field* (Boden), 25 June 1859.

## (133) Arnous de Rivière–Bird    0–1
Offhand game
London, 22 April 1859
*C51*

**1. e4 e5 2. Nf3 Nc6 3. Bc4 Bc5 4. b4 B×b4 5. c3 Bc5 6. d4 e×d4 7. c×d4 Bb6** "Preferable to checking; in which case White plays 8. Kf1, with a very strong game"—Boden. **8. 0–0 d6 9. d5 Na5 10. Bd3 Bg4 11. Bb2 Ne7** It is hardly a good idea to return the pawn when the g-file blocked by his own bishop. 11. ... f6 is correct. **12. B×g7 Rg8 13. Bf6 Qd7 14. Nc3 Bh5** An immediate raid with 14. ... Bh3 15. Ng5 Bg4 16. Qd2 h6 17. Nh7 Bf3 18. Bg5! is too rash. **15. Bb5 c6 16. d×c6 b×c6 17. B×e7?** Based on a nice trick, which succeeds, but Bird could punish Arnous de Rivière's opportunism decisively with the not so hard to see 17. ... R×g2†! 18. K×g2 Qg4† 19. Kh1 Q×f3† 20. Q×f3 B×f3† 21. Kg1 K×e7! 17. Be2 instead is solid. **17. ... K×e7? 18. Nd5†! Kf8 19. Nf6 Qe6 20. N×h5?!** 20. N×g8! is considerably stronger. Arnous de Rivière undoubtedly overlooked the cunning 20. ... c×b5 21. Nf6! Q×f6 32. Qd5, which saves the knight from being captured for free. **20. ... c×b5 21. Ng3** With this move Arnous de Rivière starts aiming his knights to f5, but this plan is relatively easy to cope with. The subtle 21. Rb1 is an improvement, as after for example 21. ... Rb8, the knight might take better route: 22. Nf4 Qh6 23. Nd5 etc. **21. ... Nc4 22. Nh4 Rg4?!** 22. ... Rd8!, preparing to resolve the weak d-pawn, comes close to equalizing. **23. Nhf5 h5?!** Bird has no interest at all in quiet, positional chess and tries to impress the Frenchman with some idiosyncratic moves. **24. Kh1 Re8?!** A clumsy and inactive square for the rook, as 25. N×h5! becomes possible, given that e4 cannot be taken. 24. ... Rd8 is still preferable. **25. h3 Rg5 26. f4?** *(see diagram)*

*After 26. f4*

Arnous de Rivière loses his patience. With 26. Rb1 a6 27. a4 he'd master the whole board. Bird is now quick to unleash some of his tactical genius. **26. ... Ne3! 27. N×e3 R×g3 28. Nf5 R×h3†! 29. g×h3 Q×e4† 30. Kh2?!** After this move Black obtains good compensation. 30. Rf3! (interposing the queen is less good, as he cannot capture the d-pawn anymore) 30. ... Q×f5 31. Q×d6† Kg7 32. Rg3† Kh7 33. Qd3 forces Black to enter an endgame where only White has chances to win, though a draw remains very likely. **30. ... Q×f5 31. Q×d6† Kg7 32. Rae1?** "We have here a remarkably instructive endgame, and it will be an excellent exercise for the young player to find out how Black now wins by force"—Boden. Arnous de Rivière is clearly struggling on how to deal with the threatened rook invasion. The text move looks like the most natural reply but Bird convincingly refutes it. Alternatively White could have played 32. Rf3, but after 32. ... Re2† 33. Kh1 h4 34. Qd3 Qe6 35. Q×b5 f6, he is completely bottled up and the game should end in a draw. 32. Qd2! is the best try. Step by step White can release himself from the bind of Black's active pieces and reach a slightly better endgame: 32. ... Kh7 (it was crucial to foresee 32. ... Re3 33. Rf3!) 33. Rad1 Re3 34. Qg2 b4 35. Rf3 Rc3 36. Re1 Bc7 37. Kh1 Rc2 38. Qg5 Qg6 39. Rg3 Q×g5 40. R×g5. **32. ... Qc2† 33. Kh1 Qc3!** "A beautiful move, after which White cannot save the game, as he is threatened with mate on the move and the loss of his rook"—Boden. **34. Rg1† Kh7 35. f5 Qf3† 36. Kh2 B×g1† 37. R×g1 Re2†** and Black wins—*The Field* (Boden), 9 July 1859.

## (134) Bird–Arnous de Rivière    1–0
Offhand game
London, 22 April 1859
*C51*

"The following two games were played in the presence of Paul Morphy, who furnished the games to Boden. A match was to have been commenced by Morphy and Bird at this meeting, but was postponed in deference to the wish of the young American"—Bird.

**1. e4 e5 2. Nf3 Nc6 3. Bc4 Bc5 4. b4 B×b4 5. c3 Bc5 6. d4 e×d4 7. c×d4 Bb6 8. 0–0 d6 9. d5 Na5 10. Bb5†** "This is an unusual move; the approved play being either 10. Bd3 or 10. e5"—Boden. **10. ... Bd7** "We do not see any objection to covering with 10. ... c6, so as to gain a move instead of losing one"—Boden. **11. B×d7† Q×d7 12. e5 Ne7 13. Bg5?** Better 13. e6 or 13. Re1, but it's doubtful whether White has enough for the sacrificed material. The text move is worse. **13. ... 0–0–0?!** 13. ... d×e5 is the easiest way to demonstrate the deficit of White's attack: 14. N×e5 Q×d5 15. Qa4† Nac6 16. B×e7 Q×e5 17. Nc3 Qd4. **14. Nc3 f6?!** "Evidently very ill-considered"—Boden. White's compensation is hard to find after 14. ... Rhe8. **15. e6 Qe8 16. Be3 B×e3 17. f×e3 Nc4?** This move is much too time-consuming. With 17. ... Kb8, followed by 18. ... b6 and 19. ... Nb7, he could construct a solid defensive set-up. **18. Qd3** 18. Qb3! initiates an immediately decisive attack; e.g., 18. ... Nb6 19. a4 a5 20. Rab1 Kb8 21. e4 Qg6 22. Nd2 etc. **18. ... Ne5 19. Qd4?** Black is without resource after 19. N×e5 f×e5 20. Rab1; e.g., 20. ... a6 21. Rf7 g6 22. Ne4. **19. ... c5!** "Boldly played. White's reply is, perhaps, his best move, as it prevents the Black queen from leaving her ambush"—Boden. **20. Qd1 Kb8** More in the spirit of the previous move is 20. ... N7g6 and 21. ...

Qe7, when the queen can finally join the defense. **21. Rb1 Nc4 22. Qd3 Nb6 23. a4** There is no need to sacrifice a pawn. The solid 23. e4 leaves Black without any counterplay at all. **23. ... c4?** Tantamount to resignation. 23. ... N×a4 is the only try. **24. Qd1 Qh5 25. e4 f5 26. a5 f×e4 27. a×b6 e×f3 28. b×a7† Ka8 29. R×f3 Rhf8 30. Nb5 R×f3** White mated by force in four moves—*The Field* (Boden), 30 July 1859.

At the end of June, Daniel Harrwitz arrived from Paris. It was Harrwitz's intention to stay for a short while but his visit was ultimately extended until September. He met Bird on several occasions and a few of their games found their way to the press.

### (135) Bird–Harrwitz     0–1

Offhand game
London (Simpson's Divan) 1859
*C41*

**1. e4 e5 2. Nf3 d6 3. d4 e×d4 4. Q×d4 Nc6 5. Bb5 Bd7 6. B×c6 B×c6 7. Nc3 Nf6 8. Be3 Be7 9. h3 0-0 10. 0-0-0 Nd7 11. Qd2 Bf6 12. Nd4 Ne5 13. f4 Nc4 14. Qd3 N×e3 15. Q×e3 Qe7 16. g4 g6 17. g5 Bg7 18. h4 f5 19. h5 B×e4 20. h×g6 h×g6 21. Rh4 Rfe8 22. Re1 c5 23. Ndb5 a6 24. N×e4 a×b5 25. Qb3† c4 26. Q×b5 f×e4 27. Reh1 R×a2 28. Q×c4† Qe6** and Black wins—*Era*, 17 July 1859.

**Daniel Harrwitz (*Chess Monthly*).**

### (136) Bird–Harrwitz     ½–½

Offhand game
London (Simpson's Divan) 1859
*C41*

**1. e4 e5 2. Nf3 d6 3. d4 e×d4 4. Q×d4 Nc6 5. Bb5 Bd7 6. B×c6 B×c6 7. 0-0 Nf6 8. Bg5 Be7 9. Nc3 h6 10. Bh4 0-0 11. Rad1 N×e4 12. B×e7 Q×e7 13. Rfe1 f5 14. Nd2 Qf6 15. Qc4† Kh8 16. Nd×e4 f×e4 17. Qd4 Rae8 18. Re2 Re5 19. Q×a7 d5 20. Qd4 Rfe8 21. Rde1 Qh4 22. Re3 Rf8 23. Rh3 Qe7 24. Rg3 Qf7 25. Re2 Rf5 26. Nd1 b6 27. h3 Bb5 28. Rd2 c5 29. Qe3 Qe6 30. Qb3 Bc4 31. Qa3 d4 32. b4 Qe5 33. Kh2 h5 34. Kg1 h4 35. Rg4 g5 36. b×c5 b×c5 37. Qb2 e3 38. N×e3 R×f2 39. R×f2 Q×e3 40. c3 Qe1† 41. Kh2 Q×f2 42. Q×f2 R×f2 43. c×d4 c×d4 44. R×d4 B×a2 45. Rg4 Rf5 46. g3** and the game was a draw—*Chess Player's Chronicle*, August 1859, pp. 240–242.

### (137) Harrwitz–Bird     1–0

Offhand game
London (Simpson's Divan) 1859
*C42*

**1. e4 e5 2. Nf3 Nf6 3. Bc4 N×e4 4. Nc3 Nf6 5. N×e5 d5 6. Bb3 Bb4 7. 0-0 0-0 8. d4 B×c3 9. b×c3 c6 10. c4 h6 11. f4 d×c4 12. N×c4 Be6 13. f5 B×c4 14. B×c4 Nbd7 15. Bb3 Nb6 16. c4 Re8 17. Qd3 Re4 18. Be3 Qc7 19. Rf3 Ng4 20. Q×e4 Q×h2† 21. Kf1 Qh1† 22. Bg1 Nh2† 23. Kf2 N×f3 24. Q×f3 Qh4† 25. Kf1 Re8 26. Rd1 Re4 27. Be3 Nd7 28. Kg1 Nf6 29. Bc2 Rg4 30. Bf2 Qg5 31. Re1 Qd2 32. Bb3 R×d4 33. Rd1** and White wins—*Chess Player's Chronicle*, August 1859, pp. 244–245.

A final encounter between Bird and Harrwitz took place in September. Both players were worthy of each other on this occasion as they scored two wins each with one game ending in a draw.

### (138) Bird–Harrwitz     1–0

Offhand game
London (Simpson's Divan), September 1859
*C41*

"The following is an interesting game played a few evenings ago"—Boden.
**1. e4 e5 2. Nf3 d6 3. d4 e×d4 4. Q×d4 Be6 5. Nc3 a6 6. Bf4 Nc6 7. Qd2 Nf6 8. Bd3 Be7 9. Ne2 h6 10. Ng3 g5 11. Be3 Ng4 12. Nd4 N×d4 13. B×d4 Bf6 14. Bc3 c5** Further weakening his position for no good reason. Bird reacts competently. **15. Nh5! B×c3 16. Q×c3 Ne5 17. Ng7† Kf8 18. Nh5 Qe7 19. Be2 Rd8 20. Rd1 Rg8 21. 0-0 b5 22. f4!** "This is good bold play"—Boden. **22. ... g×f4 23. N×f4 Rg5?!** After Bird's excellent play, the position has become very difficult to hold for Harrwitz. More tenacious here is 23. ... Kg7. **24. h4** Played with a devilish trick in mind for which Harrwitz immediately falls. Objectively stronger however was 24. Qa5! It is very hard to withstand the infiltration of the queen. **24. ... Rg7?** "Curiously enough this move is, as the sequel shows, fatal to Black. 24. ... Rg8 should have been played so as not to block the king's outlet"—Boden. **25. Q×e5!** "A beautiful move, and one which it is not surprising that even such a quick-sighted player as

Harrwitz should at the moment have overlooked. It is clear that if 25. ... d×e5 26. Q×d8† Q×d8 27. N×e6 wins a piece"—Boden. **25. ... Kg8 26. Qh5 Kh7 27. e5 d5 28. Bd3† Kg8 29. N×e6 Q×e6 30. Rf6 Qg4 31. Q×g4 R×g4 32. R×h6 Re8 33. Bf5 Rg3 34. Kf2 Rg7 35. e6** and White wins—*The Field* (Boden), 17 September 1859.

At the end of the 1850s Bird intensified his visits to Simpson's Divan. His favorite opponent here remained Samuel Boden. Their first recorded game was played in 1859, though they already met in 1846. Samuel Standidge Boden was born in 1826 and thus Bird's senior by three years. Both players were noticed in the late 1840s as two of the most talented British players. During the 1850s Boden's results were markedly superior to Bird's. He achieved the first place in the provincial tournament at London 1851 and reached but forfeited the final at Manchester 1857. In 1858 Boden took the lead of the chess column of *The Field*, thanks to which various of Bird's games survived.

Bird and Boden were both fully occupied with other matters. Boden was a railway employee and a painter. They regularly met at the Divan during Saturday afternoon sessions, which were exceedingly popular, according to Bird.[19]

### (139) Bird–Boden  0–1
Offhand game
London (Simpson's Divan) 1859 (?)
*C77*

1. e4 e5 2. Nf3 Nc6 3. Bb5 a6 4. Ba4 Nf6 5. d4 e×d4 6. e5 Ne4 7. c3 d×c3 8. N×c3 N×c3 9. b×c3 Be7 10. Bf4 d5 11. Nd4 Bd7 12. B×c6 b×c6 13. e6 f×e6 14. Qh5† g6 15. Qe2 Kf7 16. 0–0 Bf6 17. Rae1 Re8 18. Qf3 Kg7 19. Re5 c5 20. Nb3 c4 21. Nc5 Qe7 22. Qe3 B×e5 23. B×e5† Kg8 24. f4 h5 25. Rf3 Rf8 26. Rh3 Rf5 27. N×d7 Q×d7 28. g4 R×e5 29. Q×e5 Qd6 30. Qf6 e5 31. Qg5 Qb6† 32. Kg2 Qb2† 33. Kg3 e×f4† 34. Q×f4 Q×c3† 35. Kh4 Qe1† 36. Rg3 Qe7† 37. Kh3 Rf8 38. Qh6 Qe6 39. Qg5 Kg7 White resigns—*The Field*, 28 January 1860.

### (140) Boden–Bird  0–1
Offhand game
London (Simpson's Divan) 1859 (?)
*C60*

1. e4 e5 2. Nf3 Nc6 3. Bb5 Nge7 4. c3 f5 5. e×f5 d6 6. d4 Bd7 7. B×c6 B×c6 8. Nh4 g6 9. Bg5 Qd7 10. f6 Nf5 11. d×e5 N×h4 12. B×h4 B×g2 13. Rg1 Bc6 14. Qe2 d×e5 15. Q×e5† Kf7 16. Qd4 Re8† 17. Kd1 Bf3† 18. Kc1 Bh6† 19. Nd2 Q×d4 20. c×d4 Re2 21. Bg5 B×g5 22. R×g5 Re1† 23. Kc2 R×a1 24. N×f3 K×f6 25. Rc5 c6 26. Ng5 Re8 27. N×h7† Kg7 and Black wins—*The Field*, 28 January 1860.

**Samuel S. Boden (*Brentano Chess Monthly*).**

### (141) Boden–Bird  1–0
Offhand game
London (Simpson's Divan) 1859
*C43*

1. e4 e5 2. Nf3 Nf6 3. d4 N×e4 4. N×e5 d5 5. Bd3 Nf6 6. 0–0 Bd6 7. Nc3 0–0 8. Bg5 Be6 9. f4 c5 10. f5 c×d4 11. f×e6 B×e5 12. e7 Q×e7 13. N×d5 Qc5 14. N×f6† B×f6 15. B×f6 g×f6 16. Rf5 Qe7 17. Qh5 Kg7 18. Re5 f×e5 19. Q×h7† Kf6 20. Qh6 and mate—*The Field*, 10 March 1860.

Another familiar opponent of Bird was Francis Burden. Burden is so forgotten that calling him underrated is an understatement. Burden was an engineer, travelled a lot through Europe and South America, and played chess when in London. For a few years he accepted odds from the strongest players but in the end he came on even terms with them. As seen above Burden may have been Bird's inspiration for developing his defense against the Ruy Lopez, but they also shared a penchant for a specific playing style.[20] Both Boden and Burden died on 13 January 1882.

---

19. A curious and very typical anecdote about Bird was related by Buckley, years after both men's death: "Said Bird, when parting with a friend very late one night, 'Boden's a great player. He's better than Buckle. He's better than Morphy. He's better than Steinitz. He's good enough to be the world champion.' He paused a little, lost in deep thought. Resuming, he concluded with deep conviction: 'And yet, if he played a match with me, he wouldn't win a game.'" *Chess Amateur*, June 1913, p. 271.

20. Macdonnell wrote about Burden at the time of his death: "He was neither learned nor profound, but for rapidity in moving, combined with brilliancy of style; that is to say, his games produced emotions similar to those excited by witnessing an exhibition of fireworks." *Illustrated Sporting and Dramatic News*, 28 January 1882.

## (142) Burden–Bird   1–0
Offhand game
London (Simpson's Divan) 1859
*C58*

**1. e4 e5 2. Nf3 Nc6 3. Bc4 Nf6 4. Ng5 d5 5. e×d5 Na5 6. d3 Bd6 7. Nc3 h6 8. Nge4 N×e4 9. N×e4 0–0 10. 0–0 f5 11. N×d6 c×d6 12. f4 b5 13. Bb3 Qb6† 14. Kh1 e4 15. d×e4 f×e4 16. Bd2 N×b3 17. a×b3 Bb7 18. c4 Rf6 19. Bc3 Rg6 20. Qh5 Kh7 21. f5 Rg5 22. Qf7 Rc8 23. f6 Rc7 24. Q×c7 Q×c7 25. f7** Black resigns—*The Field*, 1 October 1859.

The overwhelming majority of games played with odds have long since lost their interest for modern players, but the following game is a happy exception. Even though the game is full of mistakes, it is abundant in interesting moments of both strategic and tactical nature.

## (143) Burden–Bird   1–0
Offhand game
London (Simpson's Divan) 1860
*Odds of pawn and move*

**1. e4 Nc6 2. d4 d5 3. e5 Bf5 4. g4 Bg6 5. h4 e6 6. Be3 h5 7. g5 Nge7 8. c4** Burden's opening cannot be called a success. Even with a pawn less, Bird has no problems at all. The text move weakens the white squares around his king, giving Bird plenty of play. **8. ... Nb4 9. Qa4†** The sober 9. Na3 is preferable. Black could reply with 9. ... Qd7, intending 10. ... 0–0–0. White's problem is that he has no good way to resolve the center. If he exchanges on d5, the opening of lines and diagonals is very good for Black. If he pushes the pawn to c5, Bird can break down White's center with b7–b6. **9. ... Nec6 10. Na3 Bd3** This is too expeditious. As White has no active possibilities at all, Black should just finish his development before thinking about active moves; e.g., 10. ... Be7 11. Be2 0–0 12. Qd1 Be4 13. Rh3 Qd7 14. c5 b6. **11. Ne2?** 11. c5! more than remedies his position. After 11. ... Be7 12. B×d3 N×d3† 13. Kf1 0–0 14. Qb3, the exchanges relieved White's position and his space advantage becomes more important. **11. ... Be4! 12. Ng3** The only move. **12. ... B×h1 13. N×h1 g6** Bird would be close to winning had he opened up the position at once with 13. ... d×c4 14. B×c4 Qd7 and 15. ... 0–0–0. **14. Ng3 Be7 15. Nc2 Kf7?** 15. ... d×c4 16. B×c4 Nd5 is correct. **16. c5** Much stronger is 16. a3!. After 16. ... N×c2† 17. Q×c2 Kg7 18. 0–0–0, the white squares in Black's position seem incurable. The winning maneuvre will be Ng3–e2–f4. **16. ... N×c2† 17. Q×c2 Kg7 18. a3 Qe8 19. Bd3** Burden aims for a quick breakthrough. Alternatively the bishop could have been employed on another diagonal with 19. Ne2 Qf7 20. 0–0–0 Rhe8 21. Nf4 Bf8 22. Bh3 Rac8. Black is slightly on top. **19. ... b6?** Opening up the position without delay fulfills his opponent's expectations. After the preparatory moves 19. ... Rf8 20. Ne2 Bd8! 21. 0–0–0 Ne7, and only then 22. ... b6, White's game becomes rather problematic. **20. Ne2!** Bird is not in the position to get e6 and g6 decently covered now. **20. ... b×c5 21. Nf4! c×d4?!** *(see diagram)*

21. ... Qf7 22. B×g6 N×d4 23. Qc1 Qg8 is still more or less playable. **22. N×e6†?** The game could have been concluded with 22. B×g6 Qd7 23. Bf7! **22. ... Kg8?** The position remains extremely

*After 21. ... c×d4*

complicated, hence errors are readily made. It is clear that 22. ... Kh7, keeping g6 defended, looks more logical, but the variation supporting it is less evident: 23. N×c7 Qf7 24. Bf4! Nd8!. 25. N×a8 Q×f4, with mutual chances. **23. N×c7!** The "safe" 23. N×d4? N×e5 is dangerous only for White. **23. ... Qd7 24. N×d5?** Burden misses 24. Bb5! Kh7 25. Q×c6 Q×c6 26. B×c6 Rac8 27. N×d5 R×c6 28. N×e7 Re6 29. N×g6, with excellent winning chances. **24. ... d×e3??** Bird falls for a simple combination. With 24. ... N×e5 he would have augmented the tension in his favor; e.g., 25. 0–0–0 Q×d5 26. Be4 Qe6, and he'll come out of the complications with a piece ahead. **25. Q×c6 e×f2† 26. K×f2 Rf8† 27. Ke1 Rd8** "27. ... Q×c6 evidently loses a piece"—Boden. **28. N×e7† Q×e7 29. Q×g6† Kf8 30. Kd2 Qf7** "Preventing 31. Rf1†, for if White plays now so, Black could take the rook with the queen"—Boden. **31. Qc6??** Incredible, just as Bird's next move! After 31. Qf6, there is no defense. **31. ... Kg7??** The final twist in a comedy of errors is a bitter one for Bird. 31. ... Qf2† 32. Kc3 Qd4† turns the game upside down. **32. Qf6† Q×f6 33. e×f6† Kf7 34. Rf1 Rd4 35. g6† Ke6 36. f7 Rhd8 37. Re1† Kf6 38. Re8 R×d3† 39. Kc2 Rd2† 40. Kb1 Rd1† 41. Ka2** and Black resigns—*The Field*, 26 May 1860.

## (144) "Mr. M."–Bird   0–1
Offhand game
London 1859
*Odds of pawn and two moves*

**1. e4 & 2. d4 c5 3. Qh5† g6 4. Q×c5 Nc6 5. Nf3 Nf6 6. Bd3 e5 7. Qc4 b5 8. Qb3 e×d4 9. e5 Na5 10. Q×b5 Nh5 11. 0–0 Nc6 12. e6 Be7 13. Bh6 Rb8 14. e×d7† B×d7 15. Qd5 Nf6 16. Qg5 Qc7 17. Qg3 Q×g3 18. f×g3 R×b2 19. Nbd2 Ng4 20. Bg7 Rg8 21. B×d4 N×d4 22. N×d4 Bc5 23. Rfe1† Kd8 24. N2f3 Rf8 25. h3 R×f3 26. g×f3 B×d4† 27. Kg2 Ne3† 27. Kh2 N×c2** and White resigns after a few moves—*Chess Player's Chronicle*, May 1859, pp. 148–149.

## (145) Bird–Sanders   1–0
Offhand game
London 1860
*Odds of Nb1*

**1. e4 e5 2. Nf3 d6 3. c3 Bg4 4. Bc4 B×f3 5. Q×f3 Qf6 6. Qd1 Nd7 7. 0–0 Nb6 8. Bb3 0–0–0 9. a4 Ne7 10. f4 e×f4 11. d4 Ng6 12. B×f4 N×f4 13. Qg4† Nd7 14. R×f4 Qg6 15. Qh3 f6 16. Be6 Qe8 17. a5 g5 18. Rf2 Qe7 19. b4 Bg7 20. a6 b6 21. Qf5 c6 22. Qh3 h5 23. Bf5 Kc7 24. Qd3 Nb8 25. c4 Rhf8 26. Rc2 Nd7 27. Rac1 Rc8 28. c5 b5 29. Qa3 h4 30. Qa5† Kb8 31. d5 d×c5**

**32. d×c6 R×c6 33. Q×b5† Rb6 34. Q×d7 Q×d7 35. B×d7 Rd8 36. b×c5 R×a6 37. Rb1† Kc7 38. c6 Rb6 39. R×b6 a×b6 40. Ra2 Kb8 41. Ra6 Kc7 42. Ra7† Kd6 43. c7** and White wins—*Chess Player's Chronicle*, September 1860, p. 262.

## (146) Bird–Unknown     1–0

Offhand game
London (Purssell's) 1860 (?)
*Odds of Nb1*

**1. e4 e5 2. Nf3 Nf6 3. d4 N×e4 4. d×e5 Bc5 5. Qd5 B×f2† 6. Kd1 Nc5 7. Bg5 c6 8. Qd2 Qb6 9. Q×f2 Q×b2 10. Q×c5 Q×a1† 11. Kd2 f6 12. e×f6 g×f6 13. Bc4 Q×h1 14. B×f6 Q×g2† 15. Ke3** and Black resigns—*Chess Player's Magazine*, January 1864, p. 13.

# HANDICAP TOURNAMENT AT THE ST. JAMES'S CHESS CLUB 1860

In the spring of 1860 Bird took part in another handicap tournament, now organized at the St. James's Chess Club. The knockout formula was adopted again. One victory was needed to qualify for the next round. The two finalists were guaranteed of a prize. A bit clumsy was the number of 18 participants, but after the forfeit of Wormald, the situation normalized in the second round.

The pairings took place on 18 March. Bird won his first game against Burden (class II). The place of Wormald, Bird's following opponent, was taken by Arthur Giles Puller (class IV). Despite the serious material disadvantage, Bird won again. In the third round the two strongest players, Bird and Löwenthal (class I), met. Bird succumbed after one serious mistake.

In the final game, played on 14 May, Löwenthal opposed Peter Alexandrovich Sabouroff (class IV). Sabouroff, working at the Russian embassy in London, was much too strong to receive the huge odds of a knight and won the game.

The tournament was considered a great success and a few weeks later a new handicap tournament was started. More participants were attracted, among them the continental chess star Ignaz Kolisch, just arrived in London. Bird, called away on a professional mission in the United States, did not take part.

## (147) Burden–Bird     0–1

Handicap tournament (round 1)
London, March 1860
*Odds of pawn and move*

**1. e4 Nc6 2. d4 d5 3. e5 Bf5 4. g4 Bg6 5. h4 e6 6. Be3 h5 7. g5 Bb4† 8. c3 Ba5 9. a4 a6 10. b4 Bb6 11. Bd3 B×d3 12. Q×d3 Nge7 13. Nh3 Nf5 14. Nf4 Qd7 15. Nd2 Nce7 16. a5 Ba7 17. Nb3 g6** "Considering the odds given, Mr. Bird has got a good game"— Löwenthal. **18. Kd2 Kf7 19. Ne2 Kg7 20. Ng3 N×g3** "We doubt whether the course adopted by Black was a wise one, as the pawn placed at g3 strengthens his game, and enables him eventually to

advance the g-pawn"—Löwenthal. **21. f×g3 Nf5 22. Bf4 Raf8 23. Nc5** The exchange of knight for bishop is welcomed by Bird, as the b-pawn can easily be defended. **23. ... B×c5 24. b×c5 Rf7 25. Rhb1 c6 26. Rb6 Rhf8** 26. ... N×h4! takes immediate profit of Burden's last move. Perhaps Bird noticed that this would only have led to a draw after 27. Rab1 Ng2 28. R×b7 Q×b7 29. R×b7 R×b7 30. Q×a6 Rb2† 31. Kd1 Rf8! **27. Rab1** "Effectually preventing Black's contemplated manoeuvre of 27. ... N×g3"—Löwenthal. **27. ... Qc8 28. Qe2 Re7** "Threatening 29. ... N×h4"—Löwenthal. **29. Qh2 Rff7 30. Kc2 Kh7 31. Kb2 Rd7 32. Ka1 Qd8** Probably an typing error, as with it White's next move would obviously be 33. ... Q×a5†. **33. R6b3 Rfe7 34. Ka2 Qf8 35. Rg1 Qf7 36. Ka3 Ng7** Bird is not content with a draw and moves his knight towards the queenside to support an attack against the king. By thus lifting the blockade of the f-file, he takes great risks. **37. Qc2 Ne8 38. Rf1 Nc7 39. Rbb1 Nb5† 40. Kb4 Qf8?** The transfer of the knight is no real success. At this point, 40. ... Qf5 is necessary, but it is clear that White's situation has ameliorated: 41. Qe2 Rf7 42. Kb3! (White has to be careful. If the bishop moves, Black can pin this piece) 42. ... Nc7 43. Bd2 Qh3 44. Rf6 Ne8 45. Bf4 R×f6 46. e×f6 is very promising for him. Bird's move tests his opponent, but also gives him too many assets to hand. **41. Be3 Rf7 42. Rf6! R×f6 43. g×f6 b6** "The position here is one of uncommon interest and complication. The move made by Mr. Bird is very ingenious, and requires the greatest nicety of play on the part of his opponent"— Löwenthal. **44. a×b6 Rb7** *(see diagram)*

*After 44. ... Rb7*

**45. g4?!** "This was hastily played; and Mr. Burden afterwards pointed out to us the following curious train of play, which would have ensured White of the victory: 45. Ka5 Na3 (this seems best. If 45. ... R×b6 46. c×b6 [or 46. K×b6 Qd8† 47. K×a6 Qa8† 48. Kb6 Qa7† 49. K×c6 Qa6† etc.] 46. ... Qa3† 47. Qa4 Q×a4† 48. K×a4 N×c3† 49. Ka5 N×b1 50. b7 and wins) 46. Qc1 N×b1 47. Q×b1 Qf7 48. Bc1 Qe8 49. Qb2 Qf7 50. Qd2 Qf8 51. Qh6† Q×h6 52. B×h6 K×h6 53. K×a6 and must win"—Löwenthal. An intriguing and correct line. Even though there are a few improvements, Bird's position remains lost. However, to avoid any of these complications, 45. Ka4! (a3 remains covered) is better. The advance of the g-pawn follows at a more appropriate moment. **45. ... R×b6** Bird takes immediate profit of Burden's last move, but even now White's winning chances remained intact. **46. Ka4?** White's situation has suddenly become very problematic and Burden feels forced to abandon some material. Yet, it was still possible to stay out of trouble with 46. Qd3! The king defends the pawn at c3 and the loss of the pawn at d4 is but a Pyrrhic victory for Black, so it becomes clear after 46. ... N×d4† 47. Ka4 R×b1 48. Q×b1 Nb5 49. Qd3

### St. James's Chess Club handicap tournament, London, 18 March–14 May 1860

*Site:* St. James's Chess Club
*Odds scale:* pawn and move (class II), pawn and 2 moves (class III) and knight (class IV)

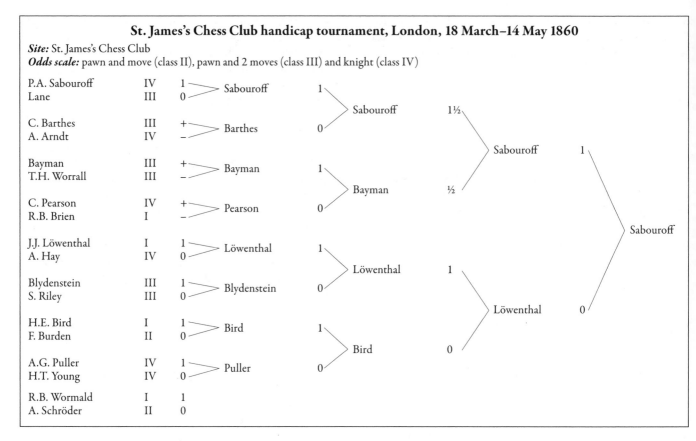

h×g4 50. c4! and depending on Black's reply 51. Qd7† or 51. h5 follows. **46. ... N×c3† 47. Q×c3 R×b1 48. g×h5 Qb8** and Black wins. It is a shame that the score breaks off at this tense moment. Black had the choice between the more defensive 48. ... Qf7 and the wild 48. ... Qb8. In case of 48. ... Qf7, the elaborate 49. Qc2 Ra1 50. Kb4 a5† 51. Kc3 Rh1 52. Qf2 g×h5 53. Qf4 Rh3! keeps the game balanced. Utterly unclear is 48. ... Qb8, when the situation looks extremely dangerous for both parties. Analysis demonstrates that a draw would be the correct result, but a sample line shows how easy it is to lose one's head in such positions, e.g.: 49. h×g5† Kh8 50. Ka3! (the most testing continuation) 50. ... Qb5 51. f7 Qf1 52. Ka2 Kg7 53. h5 Rb5 54. Bg5 Qb1† 55. Ka3 Ra5†! 56. Q×a5 Qa1† 57. Kb3 Q×a5 58. Bh6† K×h6 59. f8Q† K×h5 60. Qf3† K×g6 61. Qg4† when the game will end in a perpetual—*Era* (Löwenthal), 30 September 1860.

**(148) Bird–Löwenthal    0–1**
Handicap tournament (round 3)
London, 23 April 1860
*C84*

1. e4 e5 2. Nf3 Nc6 3. Bb5 a6 4. Ba4 Nf6 5. 0–0 Be7 6. d4 e×d4 7. e5 Ne4 8. N×d4 Nc5 9. B×c6 d×c6 10. Nc3 Ne6 11. N×e6 B×e6 12. Qe2 0–0 13. Be3 f6 14. e×f6 B×f6 15. Bc5 Re8 16. Rad1 Bd5 17. Qd3 B×c3 18. Q×c3 Qg5 19. Qg3 Q×g3 20. h×g3 Re2 21. Rc1 Rae8 22. Be3 R8xe3 23. c4 Re5 24. c×d5 R×d5 25. Rfd1 Rdd2 26. R×d2 R×d2 27. Rb1 c5 28. b4 c4 29. a4 Ra2 30. a5 c3 31. Kf1 c2 32. Rc1 Rb2 33. Ke2 c6 34. Kd3 R×b4 35. R×c2 Rb5 36. Ra2 Kf7 37. Kc4 Ke6 38. f4 h5 39. Re2† Kf6 40. Re5 g6 41. Rg5 R×g5 42. f×g5† Ke6 43. Kc5 Kd7 44. Kb6 Kc8 45. Kc5 Kc7 46. Kd4 Kd6 47. Ke4 c5 and Black wins—*The Field*, 28 April 1860.

## YEARS OF INACTIVITY 1860–1865

Bird did not resume his chess practice after his return from the United States. He chose, until 1866, not to enter any important match or tournament but his name did appear in the press. During these years he was a sporadic visitor to the Divan.

In September 1861 the fourth congress of the British Chess Association took place in Bristol (there had been no congress in 1859, while Cambridge hosted it in 1860). Bird was named as a participant but ultimately was unable to play. According to James Mortimer, Bird visited the Divan at the time of the subsequent match between Louis Paulsen and Kolisch (*British Chess Magazine*, August 1905, p. 294).

In June 1862 the fifth congress of the B.C.A. was held in London. This event was the most important since the first tournament of 1851. The chess throne was considered vacant as Morphy had abandoned the game. Anderssen, the winner of 1851, laid a novel claim to the status of the world's strongest active chess player with his 1862 victory. Louis Paulsen came in second and he was regarded as Anderssen's main rival in the years after. This tournament was a memorable one for several reasons. For the first time in history the flawed format of the knock-out event was replaced by an all-play-all formula. London 1862 was also the first occasion on which a time limit was adopted. Two important players made their entrance in the international tournament arena. Wilhelm Steinitz came over from Austria to play and decided to stay in the British capital and gain a living from chess. London 1862 also marked the beginning of Joseph Henry Blackburne's long career.

In the introduction to *Chess Novelties* (p. xxxv) Bird wrote that he had left the game for the present and was busy travelling around the country. He did kibitz at the tournament and also engaged in various games with Anderssen and the young Steinitz.[21]

The Bird and Steinitz relationship fell under a serious strain. In *Bird's Chess Reviews*, a small booklet published in 1890, Bird scrutinized Steinitz' personality, blaming him for a lack of gratitude to the British chess community that helped him so much. Bird believed he stood out in front when it came to giving support to Steinitz.

> I have known Mr. Steinitz since his first arrival in 1862, when I had been four years out of the active chess circle [*sic*]; and was the first strong player, either amateur or professional, who encountered him. Without dwelling more upon the incidents of those days it may at least be said that I did more to help Steinitz forward, and to popularize his chess, than any other person did, or at that time well could do. This fact he has long recognized, and so recently as the New York meeting [of 1889] admitted with apparent alacrity [*Bird's Chess Reviews*, p. 4].

### (149) Steinitz–Bird    0–1
Match (?)
London, June 1862
C55

1. e4 e5 2. Nc3 Bb4 3. Nf3 Nc6 4. Bc4 Nf6 5. 0–0 B×c3 6. d×c3 d6 7. Bg5 h6 8. Bh4 Be6 9. Bd3 g5 10. N×g5 h×g5 11. B×g5 Rg8 12. Bh4 Bh3 13. Bg3 Bg4 14. Qd2 Nh5 15. f3 N×g3 16. h×g3 Bd7 17. g4 Qh4 18. Qf2 Qh6 19. Rfe1 Ne7 20. Kf1 Ng6 21. g3 Ke7 22. Ke2 Rh8 23. Rh1 Q×h1 24. R×h1 R×h1 25. Qe3 Rah8 26. Qg5† f6 27. Q×g6 R8h2† 28. Ke3 Re1† 29. Be2 Rh×e2† 30. Kd3 Be6 and Black wins—*Bell's Life*, 9 November 1862.

### (150) Steinitz–Bird    1–0
Match (?)
London, June 1862
C42

1. e4 e5 2. Nf3 Nf6 3. Bc4 N×e4 4. Nc3 Nf6 5. N×e5 Bb4 It is hard to believe this has been played because the possibility to take at f7 now. A more realistic move order would have been 5. ... d5 6. Bb3 Bb4 7. 0–0 B×c3 8. b×c3. 6. 0–0 B×c3 7. b×c3 d5 8. Bb3 0–0 9. d4 h6 10. c4 c6 11. f4 Ne4 12. c×d5 c×d5 13. c4 Nc6 14. c×d5 Nc3 15. Qd3 N×d4 16. Bc4 Nde2† 17. Kh1 b5 18. Bb3 Qh4 19. Bd2 Bf5 20. Qe3 Rac8 21. Bd1 N×d1 22. Ra×d1 Bg4 23. d6 Rc4 24. Be1 Qh5 25. N×c4 b×c4 26. d7 Ng3† 27. B×g3 B×d1 28. Qd2 and White wins—*Bell's Life*, 9 November 1862.

### (151) Bird–Anderssen    0–1
Offhand game
London 1862
C65

1. e4 e5 2. Nf3 Nc6 3. Bb5 Nf6 4. d4 e×d4 5. 0–0 Be7 6. e5

Ne4 7. Re1 Nc5 8. c3 d×c3 9. N×c3 0–0 10. Nd5 f6 11. Bf4 f×e5 12. B×e5 N×e5 13. N×e5 Ne6 14. Bc4 Bc5 15. Nd3 Qh4 16. Qc2 Bd6 17. g3 Qh6 18. Re4 b5 19. Bb3 Ng5 20. Qe2 N×e4 21. Q×e4 Kh8 22. Ne3 Rb8 23. Re1 Bb7 24. Nd5 c5 25. Ne5 B×e5 26. Q×e5 c4 27. Bc2 Qd2 28. Qe4 Q×f2† 29. Kh1 B×d5 Black wins—*Bell's Life*, 14 June 1863.

It was perhaps during the course of the same tournament that Bird played with Dr. Hans Anton Westesson Lindehn. The many travels made by this Swedish professor and chess enthusiast gave him the chance to test his abilities against the important players of his time. It is equally possible that this game was played in 1864 when Lindehn was again in London.[22]

### (152) Lindehn–Bird    0–1
Offhand game
London (Simpson's Divan) 1862 or 1864 (?)
C30

1. e4 e5 2. f4 Bc5 3. Nf3 d6 4. d4? "The usual move at this point is 4. Bc4, but the play in the text seems entitled to some consideration. It certainly has the merit of imparting a little life to the stereotyped and spiritless debut"—Staunton. 4. ... e×d4 5. Bd3 It was very dangerous to avoid making a pawn sacrifice from it: 5. N×d4 Nf6 6. Nc3 0–0 7. Be2 Re8 and White's position is shaky. 5. ... Nc6 6. 0–0 Bg4 7. Kh1 Nge7 8. c3 f5 8. ... d×c3 9. N×c3 Qd7 consolidates the extra pawn. Bird prefers an aggressive and speculative line, without a doubt aiming to further complicate the game. 9. e×f5 0–0 10. Qb3† Kh8 "We should have preferred 10. ... d5"—Staunton. 11. Ng5 d5!? Bird abandons the exchange for the sake of eliminating White's knight. Another possibility is 11. ... Qe8. If White then goes out for material gain, he will be punished by a swift attack: 12. Ne6 (better is 12. Re1) 12. ... B×f5 13. N×c7? Qh5 and dark clouds gather around Black's king. 12. Ne6 Qd6 13. N×f8 R×f8 "Black has a full equivalent for the loss of the exchange in the superior disposition of his pieces, which are all in excellent play, while his opponent's game is completely locked"—Staunton. 14. Nd2 B×f5 15. B×f5? A careless exchange that releases several of Bird's pieces. 15. c×d4 N×d4 16. Qc3, followed by 17. Nb3 is better. White completes his development and commences to exchange some pieces along the way. 15. ... N×f5 16. Nf3 16. Rf3 Re8 is also very good for Black. 16. ... Qh6 17. Q×d5 Ng3†? Bird pursued his plan, and it has become obvious that Lindehn's king has ended up in a perilous situation. But here Bird is too eager to deliver the final blow. The preparatory move 17. Qh5! decisively reinforces the attack. After 18. Ng5 Ng3† 19. Kg1 Rf5, Black wins. 18. Kg1 Rf5? *(see diagram)*

Bird foresaw this reply, thinking that his opponent had nothing left now but resignation. For if the queen moves, 19. ... d×c3† 20. Rf2 Ne4 wins a full rook. Alas, White's next move is a complete party spoiler. Correct is 18. ... Bb6 when an equal endgame is reached after the forced sequence 19. Re1 d3† 20. Be3 Ne2† 21. R×e2 d×e2 22. B×b6 c×b6. 19. Re1! "All this is highly ingenious, and renders the game very animated and interesting"—

---

21. In his book on the 1894 world championship, Bird described his acquaintance with the freshly arrived Austrian: "My first meeting with Mr. Steinitz soon after his arrival in London was in this wise. When I was quite out of the chess world ... a small deputation waited on me at 16, Tokenhouse Yard, City (prominent members of which were Messrs. Staunton, Boden and Duffy), asking me to meet a wonderful chess player, who had arrived a week or two before from abroad. This was Mr. Steinitz. I went to Purssell's and we had sixteen offhand games with even results." H.E. Bird, *Steinitz & Lasker Match*, London, 1894, p. 1. ¶ Boden, in *The Field*, 7 June 1862, wrote that Bird and Steinitz played a match at Purssell's where Bird was "in the ascendant."

22. A famous win of Lindehn against Steinitz played in 1864 has been preserved.

*After 18. ... Rf5*

Staunton. **19. ... Qh5 20. Qe6 d3† 21. Be3 Rf6 22. Qc4 B×e3† 23. R×e3 Ne2† 24. Kf2 N×f4 25. Rae1?** Lindehn emerged from the complications with a small material advantage, but more important is the strength of his rooks. He could force a win here with 25. g4!, as Bird is obliged to move the queen to g6, where it blocks the g-pawn. After 26. Rae1, his weak back rank is mortal for Black. **25. ... g5?** "At the first glance this looks doubly hazardous, but on examination we believe it will be found to be perfectly sound"—Staunton. Bad. The king is provided with a lufthole, but there is no safety at all if White continues the attack correctly. After 25. ... g6! the game becomes unclear again. **26. Re8† Kg7 27. Rg8†?!** 27. Qg8† Kh6 28. R1e7 is a quick decider; e.g., 28. ... Qg6 29. R×h7†! **27. ... Kh6 28. R×g5??** Allowing an extreme reverse of situation. 28. h4! g×h4 29. Re4 leaves Black with a very bleak position. **28. ... Nh3†! 29. Kf1 R×f3†! 30. g×f3 Q×f3** mate—*Chess World* (Staunton), August 1865, pp. 175–176.

Bird's name did not occur in print in 1863 and 1864 but he appears to have considered a return to the game during the first months of 1865. According to the *Era* of 26 February, Bird was one of the many prominent witnesses of the telegraphic match held four days earlier between London and Dublin. On 9 April the *Era* brought the report of a chess soirée at the Blackheath Chess Club. The evening was filled with a blindfold exhibition by Blackburne and a lecture by Löwenthal. Bird joined the fray when he and Cecil De Vere played a well contested consultation game against Steinitz and Alexander Petrovich Belaieff. Löwenthal omitted to mention the result.

Bird visited the United States for a second time in 1865, again mainly for professional reasons. Outside of his working hours he found some time to pay an unexpected visit to the New York Chess Club.[23]

### (153) Mackenzie–Bird　　0–1
Offhand game
New York, 22 December 1865
*C51*

　**1. e4 e5 2. Nf3 Nc6 3. Bc4 Bc5 4. b4 B×b4 5. c3 Bc5 6. 0–0 d6 7. d4 e×d4 8. c×d4 Bb6 9. Nc3 Na5 10. Bd3 Ne7 11. h3 0–0 12. d5 Ng6 13. Qc2 c5!** "Adopting and demonstrating the force of this move is one of those masterly emanations of genius in defense by which Mr. Paulsen, above all other players, has rendered his name immortal"—Hazeltine. **14. Kh2** A pointless move that allows Bird to enhance his advantage. 14. Re1, anticipating to reply 14. ... c4 with 15. Bf1, is fully playable. **14. ... c4 15. Be2 Ne5** The quiet 15. ... Bd7, continuing the development of the queenside is Bird's best plan. **16. N×e5 d×e5 17. f4** The exchange of knights give White an unorthodox opportunity in the form of 17. Ba3! Re8 18. Nb5, when Black has concrete problems with his rook. 18. ... Qh4 is now necessary to free d8. After 19. Bb4 Bd7, the chances are about even, as White will soon win back the pawn. **17. ... Bd4 18. f×e5** The plan behind these last two moves, opening up the position, is hardly wise, but after other moves, such as 18. f5 or 18. Rb1, Black can consolidate his extra pawn. **18. ... B×e5† 19. Bf4 B×f4† 20. R×f4 Qc7** "Black has opened the game with his usual ability, and has now acquired a sage position with a pawn ahead"—Löwenthal. Correct, but 20. ... Qd6! is even better. **21. g3 Bd7 22. Raf1 b5** "The pawns on the queenside give Black a very superior game"—Löwenthal. **23. Bd1?!** 23. Bg4 (Löwenthal) fails after 23. ... B×g4 24. R×g4 b4. His best defense is first 23. Qb2 a6 and only then 24. Bg4. **23. ... Rae8** 23. ... b4! is much more straightforward. **24. Qf2 Qb6 25. Qf3?!** Exchanging queens is absolutely joyless but objectively best. **25. ... f5!** "Ingeniously conceived"—Löwenthal. **26. Bc2** "It is evident that 26. e×f5 would have lost White a piece after 26. ... Re3"—Löwenthal. **26. ... b4** This push allows Mackenzie to complicate the game somewhat with 27. Ba4 B×a4 28. N×a4, but after 28. ... Qd6! 29. e×f5 Re5!, the outcome would not be different. Of course, Bird had to avoid 28. ... Qb5?? 29. R×f5 and White's attack is at once extremely dangerous. Instead of the text move 26. ... g5 wins on the spot. **27. Ne2 b3 28. a×b3 c×b3 29. Bd3 g5! 30. Qh5 g×f4 31. g×f4 Kh8 32. e5 Bb5 33. B×f5 R×f5 34. Q×f5 Qg6!** "A capital move, forcing the exchange of queens, thus securing a speedy victory"—Löwenthal. **35. Q×g6 h×g6 36. Re1 B×e2 37. R×e2 Nc4 38. d6 Rb8 39. Re1 Kg7** and Captain Mackenzie resigned—*New York Clipper* (Hazeltine), 24 March 1866; *Era* (Löwenthal), 8 April 1866.

23. "The club was very pleasantly surprised, last week, by a visit from Mr. Bird, who is well known to be in the very foremost rank of English players. His stay in this city was brief, but the club hopes to see him again, on his return from journeys elsewhere. We subjoin a game played, on Friday, the 22nd inst." *Albion*, 30 December 1865.

# ◆ Part IV ◆

# THE ACCOUNTANCY YEARS (II), 1866–1870

## A REUNION AND SOME FAREWELLS

In 1865 Henry Bird (father) returned from Australia. His health had likely deteriorated. Henry reunited with his wife Mary Ellen at their old premises. Around this time 16 Harleyford Place was renumbered and renamed as 274 Kennington Park Road.

With his parents together again, Henry Edward Bird may have decided to leave the noise and pollution of central London and head for Wimbledon, at that time in full development. In 1838 a station connected this rural town with London, while a few years later Wimbledon Park was sold as development property. Several houses, often large and detached, were constructed. A wealthy public was drawn towards the outskirts of the metropolis to live a happy life, often with several servants and in a green environment.

Both the *Metallurgicon Local Directory of Wandsworth, Putney, Wimbledon, etc.,* of 1867 (p. 115) and the *Post Office London Suburban Directory* of 1868 list Bird at St. George's Road. Bird was one of the first inhabitants of this recently built road. In the directory of 1867, Bird is recorded at 5 St. George's Road. The next year he lived at 10 St. George's Road, probably as some renumbering took place. The 1871 census gives an impression: several well-deserving men, such as solicitors, had found their way to this London suburb.[1]

Bird was also mentioned in the electoral register of Wimbledon in 1867, which suggests that he was doing quite well, as one had to own or rent property of a certain value to get the right to vote (about one third of the male population made it into these lists).

Towards the end of 1868, the family was hit by a few tragedies that had a major impact on Bird's life. On 15 October 1868 Eliza Cain died at home in 10 St. George's Road in Wimbledon. The cause of her death was a disease of the liver. Robert Kayne, probably Eliza's brother, reported her death. Eliza died at the age of 39, which implies that she was born in 1828 or, more likely, 1829.[2] The *Era* of 25 October announced her death but supplied no further information. She was buried at the prestigious Kensal Green Cemetery.

Three months later Henry Edward suffered another loss. On 19 January 1869 Henry Bird died at St. Thomas's Hospital. According to his death certificate, he suffered from an enlarged prostate and purulent urine.[3] Obviously these most disturbing symptoms encouraged his return from Australia a few years before. At the time of his death, Bird's estate was much smaller than one might assume. He left effects with a value of less than £200 to divide. His widow was appointed as the sole executrix of his will.[4]

These tragic events had their impact on Henry Edward. He left Wimbledon, settled in the heart of the metropolis again, and would live the bachelor's life until the end of his days. Despite these heavy circumstances Bird found the time and courage to engage himself in playing for the Challenge Cup of the British Chess Association. This is even more surprising as Bird was experiencing turmoil not only in his personal life, but various changes had also taken place in his professional career.

## THE ATLANTIC AND GREAT WESTERN RAILWAY 1865–1867

Between 1865 and 1867 Henry Edwards Bird's business contacts with the United States intensified through his involvement with the Atlantic and Great Western Railway Company. This company was the result of a merger in 1865. At that time a project of long duration came to an end when a railroad connection was established between New York and Saint Louis. It attracted the attention of many European investors, especially after the oil boom started in the late 1850s. But already before the unified company was officially established, its fortunes were turning.

The rapidity with which the railway was constructed intensified the troubles. The necessary time was not given to the deliberation of questions pertinent to the future of the road after the main line was completed. Stock watering was carried to an extreme. Extravagant branch expansion into areas already well supplied with railway facilities was not considered in respect to net profits. The exchange of bonds and the expenditure of cash remittances for branches to the natural resources, together with the financing of the main line, produced financial complications which no auditor could disentangle. The disagreement in accounts caused Reynolds and Kent to resign from the

---

1. 1871 census: Class: *RG10*; Piece: *857*; Folio: 28; Page; 50.
2. The death registration reference is Kingston, Oct-Nov-Dec 1868, vol. 2a, p. 139.
3. The death registration reference is Newington, Jan-Feb-Mar 1869, vol. 1d, p. 186.
4. Ancestry.com. *England & Wales, National Probate Calendar (Index of Wills and Administrations), 1858–1966.* Provo, UT, USA: Ancestry.com Operations, 2010.

CERTIFIED COPY OF AN ENTRY OF DEATH

GIVEN AT THE GENERAL REGISTER OFFICE

Application Number 5351427-1

| | REGISTRATION DISTRICT | | | | | KINGSTON | | | |
|---|---|---|---|---|---|---|---|---|---|
| 1868 DEATH in the Sub-district of Wimbledon | | | | | | in the County of Surrey | | | |

Columns:— 1 2 3 4 5 6 7 8 9

| No. | When and where died | Name and surname | Sex | Age | Occupation | Cause of death | Signature, description and residence of informant | When registered | Signature of registrar |
|---|---|---|---|---|---|---|---|---|---|
| 277 | Fifteenth October 1868 at St Georges Road Wimbledon | Eliza Bird | Female | 39 years | Wife of Henry Edward Bird Accountant | Disease of the Liver Certified | Robert Kayne in Attendance 75 Seymour Place Bryanstone Square London | Fifteenth October 1868 | William Wingfield Registrar |

CERTIFIED to be a true copy of an entry in the certified copy of a Register of Deaths in the District above mentioned.

Given at the GENERAL REGISTER OFFICE, under the Seal of the said Office, the 24th day of December 2013

DYD 621037

See note overleaf

7184667 50656 04/12 5MSSD 031067

AL

---

CERTIFIED COPY OF AN ENTRY OF DEATH

GIVEN AT THE GENERAL REGISTER OFFICE

Application Number 5394427-1

| | REGISTRATION DISTRICT | | | | | NEWINGTON | | | |
|---|---|---|---|---|---|---|---|---|---|
| 1869 DEATH in the Sub-district of St Mary | | | | | | in the County of Surrey | | | |

Columns:— 1 2 3 4 5 6 7 8 9

| No. | When and where died | Name and surname | Sex | Age | Occupation | Cause of death | Signature, description and residence of informant | When registered | Signature of registrar |
|---|---|---|---|---|---|---|---|---|---|
| 70 | Nineteenth January 1869 St Thomas Hospital | Henry Bird | Male | 70 years | Bookseller | Enlarged Prostate Purulent Urine Not certified | J Hooper Present at the death St Thomas Hospital Newington | Twentieth January 1869 | Gasping Young Registrar |

CERTIFIED to be a true copy of an entry in the certified copy of a Register of Deaths in the District above mentioned.

Given at the GENERAL REGISTER OFFICE, under the Seal of the said Office, the 16th day of January 2014

DYD 631186

See note overleaf

7231132 68840 04/13 3MSSD 033108

PDT

*Top:* Death certificate of Eliza Cain. *Bottom:* Death certificate of Henry Bird.

presidency of their respective companies on September 30, 1864 [*The Atlantic and Great Western Railroad*, pp. 126–127].[5]

Bad tidings arrived slowly among European investors and were often met with disbelief. As the matter was extremely complex it was very difficult to create an objective view about the potentiality of railway shares and stocks. Promoters of railway companies thus had ample room to stress the advantages of their undertakings without meeting much well-founded opposition.

Bird got deeply involved in the financial side of the case of the Atlantic and Great Western Railway. At the end of 1865 Coleman, Turquand, Youngs and Company deputed him on behalf of the shareholders to examine their accounts on the spot in America. Bird spent a few months in Pennsylvania amalgamating the books of the three firms. During this stay he paid a short visit to the New York Chess Club.

Bird was back in London just in time to attend a most tumultuous meeting of the shareholders on 29 March 1866. His reports and accounts were ardently awaited by the public which had become worried about the health of their investments. A lengthy report of the meeting appeared on the next day in the *Daily News*. In the company of James A. McHenry, since 1858 the chief European agent for the railway company, Bird confirmed that the earnings exceeded the entire bonded debt charge. The opening of additional lines and miles were also looked forward to. Bird showed himself impressed by the prospects of the railway. He argued that the contrast between the enormous amount of traffic and the great deficiency in the means of carrying it offered the Atlantic and Great Western Railway every chance for success. The good news attracted new shareholders, but a shadow of doubt remained over the whole company. At the end of the year there arose dissatisfaction due to the delay of the annual report. Disappointing traffic receipts also caused unrest. A committee was set up to impose another investigation. Bird was again involved and had to break off his match with Steinitz to perform another independent audit in America. Once more his accounts were eagerly anticipated.

A voluminous report comprising statements by McHenry, L'Hommedieu (the president of the company) and Bird as the London auditor was issued in February 1867. Bird's contribution attracted a lot of attention as there were several discrepancies with the rosy picture painted by McHenry. With a few examples Bird debunked McHenry's presentation. He demonstrated that the working expenses amounted up to 72 percent of income. This was confirmed by Stephen Satterlee L'Hommedieu but contradicted by McHenry, who believed that these costs were the same as in 1863, namely 48.5 percent. McHenry claimed that the earnings would be sufficient to meet all liabilities to the bond and debenture-holders, but it was generally known that traffic was down from before. Bird remarked that the revenue was insufficient to meet the interest of the investors.

All in all there was more than enough reason to hold an assembly of stockholders. A large crowd gathered at the London Tavern on the next Tuesday, 5 March. The *Daily News* reported on the next day that, not unsurprisingly, the meeting took place in a stormy at-

**James A. McHenry.**

mosphere. A near uproar broke out when Bird confirmed allegations that a lucrative line was leased favorably to McHenry, which the latter denied. It became more and more clear to the shareholders that they had been deceived by the management. With not enough money available to pay the dividends, the company could not meet its financial obligations and a receiver was appointed. Thus a few years of high hopes ended in bitter disappointment for various of Bird's daring contemporaries, but also for himself. The immediate future for the company was a sad one.

The resignations and changes in American executive personnel should have warned the English investors that all was not well, but such changes were not published and consequently the first sign of strain was kept secret. Branch extension continued, accounts grew more misleading; no true statement of the railroad's finances could be obtained, even though some investors repeatedly requested an accurate report. Finally legal action was taken. The railroad and property were placed in the hands of Robert Potter as receiver. Potter began the operation of the [rail]road on April 1, 1867, and continued until December 12, 1868. The dilapidated condition of the road, the loss of credit, the inability to purchase supplies except at excessive prices, and the general depression of 1866-1867 brought a temporary reorganization. The new plan did not decrease the over-expanded capital; instead, more stocks and bonds were printed and sold in order to secure money with which to pay interest and debts [*The Atlantic and Great Western Railroad*, p. 127].

5. See P.E. Felton (1943). The Atlantic and Great Western Railroad. *The Western Pennsylvania Historical Magazine*, 26 (3–4), pp. 117–128.

Bird did not let matters rest. He was not only an expert in the matter but also a victim as he had made serious investments in the railway. For the next six years, Bird invested a lot of energy in attempting to form a group of people deceived by the Atlantic and Great Western Railway. In a small announcement, signed by Bird, the case was brought to the attention of the public: "I am desired to request that holders of these bonds, willing to cooperate in the formation of an independent committee for the purpose of establishing their proper legal position, will communicate with me immediately" (*The Times*, 2 November 1869).

In 1873 Bird terminated this important episode by providing a "sketch" of the Atlantic and Great Western Railway Company with the explicit purpose of warning future investors. In his introduction he made it very clear what consequences the whole affair had in England.

> Of the various schemes which have entailed ruin and misery on thousands of the public during the past few years, that, which has perhaps more than any other, led to the disasters which have arisen, is the undertaking known by the name of the Atlantic and Great Western Railway. Even at this late period a slight sketch of the financial history of this company may be useful, as a caution to future investors; for although it is not in liquidation like the principal associations with which it has been connected, it has been the main cause of the collapse of such associations, and it may safely be assumed that the direct losses sustained by the public through their misplaced confidence in this company, and its representatives will be found to exceed the losses by all the financial companies put together [*A Caution to Investors*, pp. 3–4].

Bird finished his text with a desperate plea for attention. He did not neglect to emphasize the personal misery he had experienced during these years.

> I have during the past five years tried to get public attention directed to the proceedings of the agents of the Atlantic and Great Western Railway Company, but in vain; if the press would have stated the real position of its affairs ever so mildly I would not have troubled, for the first time to write a pamphlet. I have however done so ... for it is only reasonable that those interested should have full information as to the property in which their funds are embarked, and how the money they subscribe is applied.
>
> In conclusion I shall only add that if these few lines should have the effect of procuring them the information to which they are entitled, or of putting even one investor on his guard in respect to this undertaking, and saving him and his family from the same ruinous loss which has overtaken many including myself, I shall not regret the trouble I have taken in publishing them [*A Caution to Investors*, p. 14].

# LEAVING THE BUILDING 1867–1870

Soon after he had notified the world about the problems with the Atlantic and Great Western Railway Bird retired as its auditor. Later that year he also separated himself from Coleman, Turquand, Youngs and Company. The circumstances in which this happened are not known. Some conflict may have been the basis for Bird's leaving, but it appears that Bird was ready to make a step forward and start up his own firm (together with a partner). It was not uncommon at all for an accountant to learn the ropes of the trade at an established firm and move on to a more lucrative business from his own.

Bird spent the last months of 1867 finishing a small booklet that was released in January or February 1868 under the rather elaborate title *Railway Accounts: A Comprehensive Analysis of the Capital and Revenue of the Railways of the United Kingdom; With a Few Observations Thereon*.

The contents of this work was quite similar to the research he had done on the Atlantic and Great Western Railway, but now Bird scrutinized the state of affairs in his home country. His knowledge on the matter was recognized by the highest political powers in England as he "gave evidence before Committee of Parliament on Amalgamations of Home Railways; thanked for framing the tables and statistics upon which the Great Eastern Railway was afterwards conducted."[6]

The title page of *Railway Accounts* names Bird's new business premises: Gresham Buildings, Basinghall Street. The Gresham Buildings contained about a hundred separate offices. It was situated at a stone's throw from Tokenhouse Yard. Basinghall Street was the true center of London's accounting firms. The heavy involvement of these firms in insolvency cases is reflected in the mocking remark that "if an accountant were required, he would be found at the bar of the nearest tavern to the Bankruptcy Court in Basinghall Street."[7]

While founding an accounting firm may seem lucrative at first sight one cannot underestimate how much risk such a step contains. In a quite similar situation was Edwin Waterhouse who had left Coleman, Turquand, Youngs and Company in January 1864. He received a large sum of money from his father as starting capital but already after a few weeks, with no work coming in, he believed he made a mistake. Fortunately for Waterhouse his father's network of contacts started to play, and slowly but surely everything turned out all right.[8]

The circumstances in which Bird started off are somewhat ambiguous. At the end of the summer a curious advertisement appeared a couple of times in a local newspaper. "Important Notice! Books kept, Accounts adjusted, Writing executed, on reasonable terms, by an experienced accountant. Address, B., 274 Kennington-Park-Road" (*South London Chronicle*, 15 August 1868). This ad combined the address of Bird's parents with his name hidden behind the single initial "B." One may but guess at Bird's motives for such mysterious behavior. It seems reasonable to assume that he was not drowning in work and could use each additional assignment.

Bird and his partner Edgar Lewis were mentioned together for a first time in 1869, but in all likelihood they combined forces after Bird left his previous firm. Bird and Lewis advertised their services as "public accountants."

Edgar Lewis was born in Tewkesbury, Wales, in 1838. He was the ninth and last child of James Blount Lewis and Carline Brend Winterbotham. His father gained a fortune in the hosiery business in Tewkesbury. A branch was set up in Nottingham once the power machines were introduced and two of Edgar's brothers stepped into the firm.

When Edgar began his accountancy firm he received financial support from his family. At least Lauriston Winterbotham Lewis,

---

6. *Who Was Who*. London: Adam & Charles Black, 1920, p. 64.
7. Matthews, *Priesthood of Industry*, p. 30.
8. Jones, *The Memoirs of Edwin Waterhouse: A Founder of Price Waterhouse*, pp. 76–77.

another brother of Edgar and a solicitor in Walsall by profession, lent him a considerable amount of money.[9]

In 1871, the experienced public accountant David Chadwick pointed out six principal branches in which he and his colleagues were active. They provide a nice overview of what Bird may have been doing during his daily work.

> These [duties] were: the keeping and audit of executor and trust accounts; bankruptcy trusteeships; appointments emanating from proceedings in the Court of Chancery such as corporate liquidations and accounting for wards of court; the audit of companies and other entities; references from courts or private individuals to investigate, arbitrate and report on accounting related matters; and the evaluation of investment opportunities [*Towards the "Great Desideratum,"* p. 12].

Judging from the occurrence of Bird's name in the *London Gazette* in 1868 he was not receiving much work. It was not until 9 October that he was mentioned as the assignee in a bankruptcy case.

A new Bankruptcy Act entered into force in 1869. A most important, though technical, point was the replacement of the function of assignee (created in 1831), by a trustee. This allowed the courts to appoint a public accountant without needing a middleman. The result was that accountants were in higher demand than ever for bankruptcies.[10] In their capacity as trustee they dealt with the bankrupt's assets, monitored their payment of debts and kept an eye on their actions during their period of bankruptcy.

The most media-attentive case for Bird as public accountant concerned the European Insurance Company. Its adventures dominated the discussions of London's financial world for a few months. In September 1869, a certain Joseph Bentley published and sold a pamphlet in which he said the European Insurance Company was insolvent. This pamphlet had a huge impact, especially since a few weeks before, another noted insurance company, Albert Life Assurance Company, had gone under. In the turmoil that arose, the very existence of the European firm got into real danger when several newspapers produced pieces with titles such as "Another Great Assurance Failure." A serious rescue operation was needed to confirm the safety of the company and to reassure the shareholders. Bird was hired to screen the books. In the end he produced comforting figures and the calm was restored. *The Times* report of 16 October 1869 must have caused a sign of relief in financial circles when the condemnation of Joseph Bentley for spreading these unfounded rumors was announced.

# GETTING BACK INTO FORM 1866

The summer of 1866 saw a significant revival of chess in London. The B.C.A. was resuscitated with the organization of a new tournament. Immediately afterwards the British capital was the scene of a change of power. Adolf Anderssen, unofficially back on the chess throne since 1862, lost a match against Steinitz.

After having spent the first months of the year in America, Bird returned to London in the last week of March—just in time to be present at the aforementioned meeting of shareholders of the Atlantic and Great Western Railway on 29 March. Bird subsequently found more time to turn himself back to his great passion and was once more reinvigorated by regularly visiting the Divan. He was especially eager to sharpen his rustiness in play by entering into combat with one of his old antagonists, the Rev. George Alcock MacDonnell.

MacDonnell, above all famous for his witty and sarcastic pen, remained one of Bird's recurrent opponents over the next two decades. As with Bird's countless encounters with Boden and Cochrane these games were played for pleasure and not for any stakes. It is a shame that these chess friends did not pay much attention to preserving the games. None of the games between Bird and Cochrane have survived. The battles between Bird and MacDonnell were mostly fascinating. Both players were loyal adherents of the popular gambits of the time and both were blessed with a lively and bloodthirsty style.

**George A. MacDonnell (*Westminster Chess Club Papers*).**

9. We owe much of the background information of the family to Andrew R. Deane. See http://www.genealogy.japanesegardensonline.com.
10. Jones, *Accountancy and the British Economy*, p. 48.

## (154) MacDonnell–Bird    1–0

Offhand game
London (Simpson's Divan) 1866
C42

**1. e4 e5 2. Nf3 Nf6 3. N×e5 d6 4. Nf3 N×e4 5. d3 Nc5 6. d4 Ne4 7. Bd3 d5 8. 0–0 Be7 9. c4 c6 10. Nc3 N×c3 11. b×c3 Bg4 12. Rb1 b6 13. Re1 0–0 14. h3 Bh5 15. B×h7† K×h7 16. Ng5† B×g5 17. Q×h5† Bh6 18. g4 f6 19. h4 g5 20. h×g5 f×g5 21. Re6 Rf6 22. B×g5 and White wins**—*Illustrated London News*, 26 May 1866.

## (155) MacDonnell–Bird    0–1

Offhand game
London (Simpson's Divan) 1866
C51

**1. e4 e5 2. Nf3 Nc6 3. Bc4 Bc5 4. b4 B×b4 5. c3 Bc5 6. 0–0 d6 7. d4 e×d4 8. c×d4 Bb6 9. Nc3 Na5 10. Ba3 Ne7 11. e5 N×c4 12. Qa4†** This rare line chosen by MacDonnell isn't very promising for him. **12. … c6 13. Q×c4 d5 14. Qb4?** With this move MacDonnell leaves his kingside to its fate. Bird takes immediately profit. **14. … Bg4! 15. Rab1 B×f3 16. g×f3 Nf5 17. Ne2 Qe7** Even better is 17. … Qd7 followed by 18. … 0–0–0 or 17. … Qg5†, as White now gets the chance to exchange queens. **18. Qa4 Qg5†** "Mr. Bird has played his defense extremely well"—Staunton. **19. Ng3 Kd7** "This was obviously necessary, since Black threatened to take off the bishop with his rook"—Staunton. Bird's play during the rest of the game is very convincing. His opponent doesn't stand a chance. **20. Bc1 Qg6 21. Be3 h5 22. Kh1 h4 23. N×f5 Q×f5 24. Qd1 g5 25. Rg1 Rhg8 26. Rg4 f6 27. e×f6 Q×f6 28. f4 g×f4 29. Qf3 Qf5 30. Rbg1 R×g4 31. R×g4 Rf8 32. R×f4 Qb1† 33. Kg2 R×f4 34. Q×f4 Qe4†! 35. Q×e4 d×e4 36. Kh3 Bd8 37. Kg4 Ke6** and Black ultimately wins—*Illustrated London News* (Staunton), 26 May 1866.

The following game was published much later than the previous ones. Hence it may have been played before the summer at the Divan or at a later time in the new Westminster Chess Club.

## (156) MacDonnell–Bird    1–0

Offhand game
London 1866
C51

**1. e4 e5 2. Nf3 Nc6 3. Bc4 Bc5 4. b4 Bb6 5. a4 a6 6. 0–0 Nf6 7. a5 Ba7 8. d3 d6 9. c3 Be6 10. Na3 B×c4 11. N×c4 0–0 12. Be3 Qe7 13. B×a7 N×a7 14. Ne3 g6 15. Ng5 h6 16. Nh3 Nh5 17. Qg4 Kh7 18. Nd5 Qe6 19. Qh4 Nb5 20. g4 c6 21. Nb6 Qf6 22. Q×f6 N×f6 23. N×a8 R×a8 24. g5 Nh5** and White ultimately wins—*The Field*, 5 January 1867.

# THE FIRST CHALLENGE CUP TOURNAMENT, LONDON 1866

After the successful tournament held in 1862 the B.C.A. led a more and more dormant existence in the following years. At the end of 1865 several skeptical voices declared the Association defunct. These voices found a readily available forum in Staunton's column in the *Illustrated London News*, as well as in his magazine *Chess World*.

The criticism provoked Löwenthal and G.W. Medley, respectively the manager and honorary secretary of the B.C.A., to a firm reaction. The B.C.A. was given a formal basis and within a few months a new congress was announced. Besides a handicap and problem tournament the principal appeal was the tournament for the Challenge Cup. This tourney was open to British players only, which made it de facto the first British Championship. The Cup, which had a worth of £50, could become the property of the first player to win the tournament twice. It was the ambition to hold a yearly congress, alternatingly in London and in the provinces.

The clumsy financial arrangements led to a very disappointing field of players. A relatively large entrance fee of £3 3s. was required to enter the tournament, while just one prize was foreseen. Only five players could be lured to take their place behind the chessboard.[11]

Bird's rivals were MacDonnell, James Innes Minchin, John Trelawny and the very young and promising Cecil Valentine De Vere. Each contestant would play a small match for the first three wins against each other. The winner of most matches gained the prize. The tournament opened on 19 June and the first games were played on the next day. For the first three days of the tournament the St. James's Hall was hired. The remainder of the games were played at three locations: the London Chess Club, the St. George's Chess Club and the Divan.

The young De Vere was too far ahead of his adversaries and easily won the Cup and money. With this prize gone, a series of forfeits spoiled the tournament completely.

---

**1st Challenge Cup tournament of the B.C.A., London, 19 June–12 July 1866**

*Site:* St. James's Hall, London Chess Club, St. George's Chess Club, Simpson's Divan
*Prize:* One prize: a cup (worth £50, becomes property if won twice), £10 3s and the entrance fee.
*Time limit:* 20 moves per hour

|   |   | 1 | 2 | 3 | 4 | 5 |   |
|---|---|---|---|---|---|---|---|
| 1 | C. De Vere |   | 1 1 1 | 1 1 1 | 1 1 1 |   | 9/9 |
| 2 | G.A. MacDonnell | 0 0 0 |   | 1 1 ½ 1 |   |   | 3½/7 |
| 3 | J.I. Minchin | 0 0 0 | 0 0 ½ 0 |   | 1 1 0 1 | 1 1 1 | 6½/14 |
| 4 | H.E. Bird | 0 0 0 |   | 0 0 1 0 |   |   | 1/7 |
| 5 | J. Trelawney |   |   | 0 0 0 |   |   | 0/3 |

---

11. The many critics of the B.C.A. had but little trouble to burn down the tournament. Such were the words by "A Looker-On" in Staunton's column: "The country players—the bone and sinew of a real British chess institution—hold themselves aloof from a sham one. The London players have as little affection for it; and so the 'grand Challenge Cup, the guerdon of British championship,' is absolutely going a-begging, not half a dozen competitors being found to enter for it, and of these, I hear, scarcely one of any eminence whatever!" *Illustrated London News*, 16 June 1866.

Bird lost both matches he played. Against Minchin, not a very strong player, he appeared to be completely out of form. Two of his losses were caused by silly blunders. Against De Vere, Bird lost three games in a row.

The handicap tournament was won by Steinitz who was unable to take part in the Challenge Cup tournament due to his nationality. He convincingly eliminated De Vere in the first round.

### (157) Minchin–Bird 1–0

B.C.A. Challenge Cup
London, June 1866
*C42*

1. e4 e5 2. Bc4 Nf6 3. Nf3 N×e4 4. Nc3 Nf6 5. N×e5 d5 6. Qe2 Be6 7. Bb3 c6 8. d4 h6 9. 0–0 Be7 10. f4 g6 11. Bd2 Qd6 12. Rae1 Rg8 13. Kh1 Nbd7 14. g4 Nf8 15. f5 Bc8 16. Bf4 g×f5 17. Nb5 c×b5 18. Ng6 Qe6 19. Q×b5† Bd7 20. Q×b7 f×g6 21. Q×a8† Kf7 22. R×e6 N×e6 23. Q×a7 Bb5 24. Re1 Re8 25. Be5 f×g4 26. B×f6 K×f6 27. R×e6† and White wins—*Tournament Book*, pp. 20–21.

### (158) Bird–Minchin 0–1

B.C.A. Challenge Cup
London, June 1866
*C84*

1. e4 e5 2. Nf3 Nc6 3. Bb5 a6 4. Ba4 Nf6 5. d4 e×d4 6. e5 Ne4 7. 0–0 Be7 8. c3 d×c3 9. Re1 c×b2 10. B×b2 Nc5 11. Bc2 0–0 12. Nc3 d6 13. Nd5 Bg4 14. N×e7† Q×e7 15. Qd5 Nb4 16. Qd4 N×c2 17. Q×g4 Qe6 18. Qh4 N×e1 19. R×e1 Nd3 20. Re4 N×b2 21. Rg4 Qf5 22. h3 d×e5 23. Qg3 g6 24. Ng5 Rad8 25. Qh4 h5 26. Ne4 Rd1† 27. Kh2 h×g4 28. Ng5 Qf4† and Black wins—*Tournament Book*, pp. 21–22.

### (159) Minchin–Bird 0–1

B.C.A. Challenge Cup
London, June 1866
*C50*

1. e4 e5 2. Bc4 Nc6 3. Nf3 Bc5 4. 0–0 Nf6 5. d3 0–0 6. Nc3 d6 7. h3 Be6 8. Bb3 Qd7 9. Ne2 Nh5 10. Kh2 Rae8 11. Ng3 N×g3 12. f×g3 B×b3 13. a×b3 f5 14. e×f5 R×f5 15. Ra4 Ref8 16. Rg4 d5 17. c3 Be7 18. Bg5 h5 19. B×e7 Q×e7 20. Rh4 e4 21. Nd2 e×d3 22. R×h5 R×f1 23. N×f1 Qe2 and White resigns—*Tournament Book*, pp. 22–23.

### (160) Bird–Minchin 0–1

B.C.A. Challenge Cup
London, June 1866
*C84*

1. e4 e5 2. Nf3 Nc6 3. Bb5 a6 4. Ba4 Nf6 5. 0–0 Be7 6. d4 e×d4 7. e5 Ne4 8. Bb3 0–0 9. N×d4 N×d4 10. Q×d4 Nc5 11. Nc3 N×b3 12. a×b3 d6 13. Ne4 d×e5 14. Q×e5 Re8 15. Re1 Bd7 16. Bd2 Bc6 17. Bc3 Bf8 18. Qf4 Qd5 19. f3 Re6 20. Rad1 Qh5 21. Ng5 Bd6 22. N×e6 B×f4 23. N×f4 Qg5 24. Nd5 f6 25. h4 Qh5 26. Ne7† Kf7 27. N×c6 b×c6 28. Rd7† Kf8 29. Ree7 Qc5† 30. Bd4 Q×e7 31. R×e7 K×e7 32. Kf2 Kd6 33. b4 Re8 34. c4

Cecil V. De Vere (*Chess Monthly*).

Ke6 35. g4 g6 36. f4 h5 37. g5 f×g5 38. f×g5 Kf5 and White resigns—*Tournament Book*, pp. 23–24.

### (161) De Vere–Bird 1–0

B.C.A. Challenge Cup
London 1866
*C61*

"I won many games of young De Vere at this defense, but the only one I have yet found recorded is the following; it is a good specimen of the opening, and an excellent example of De Vere's effective style of play"—Bird.

1. e4 e5 2. Nf3 Nc6 3. Bb5 Nd4 4. N×d4 e×d4 5. 0–0 Bc5 6. d3 Ne7 7. Qh5 Bb6 8. Bg5 0–0 9. Bc4 Qe8 10. f4 Kh8 11. e5 d6 11. ... Nf5! would have been an excellent reply to De Vere's omission to exchange at e7. 12. B×e7 "12. Nd2 seems stronger, as White's game would have been thereby developed most rapidly, and his bishop have remained in his powerful position. As a rule, the player who has this kind of attack only relieves his opponent by the exchange of pieces"—Löwenthal. 12. e×d6 is another evident and good move. 12. ... Q×e7 13. Nd2 Be6 14. e×d6 c×d6 15. Rae1 d5 "Black evidently sacrifices his pawn with the view of playing 16. ... Qc5, thinking that by pinning the hostile bishop for a time he must obtain an

equivalent for his lost pawn, but he appears to have forgotten the consequences flowing from 17. Re5"—Löwenthal. **16. B×d5** De Vere falls for Bird's ingenious attempt to liberate his pieces. Black is kept under continuous pressure with 16. Bb3, followed by 17. f5. **16. ... Qc5 17. Re5?** 17. Bf3! keeps a small, but dangerous edge. After 17. ... Q×c2 18. Rf2 it is not easy to find the best move. 18. ... Q×b2?, for example, loses quickly after 19. f5! Correct is 18. ... Qc7, to meet 19. f5 with 19. ... g6 20. f×g6 f×g6 and thanks to the control over e5 Black doesn't lose a piece. **17. ... B×d5 18. R×d5 Q×c2** Bird's position is preferable now as White's attacking plans are undermined by the exchange of his bishop. **19. Nf3 Q×d3 20. f5** This move plans a direct attack against Bird's king, but this would make no chance against a correct defense. Yet, it is hard to find a move by which White doesn't resign himself to passive play. **20. ... Qe2** The evident 20. ... f6! is more than sufficient to stop White's plans, but even better is the cool 20. ... Rac8! for if 21. f6 g×f6 and 22. ... Qg6 follows. **21. Re1 d3† 22. Kh1** *(see diagram)*

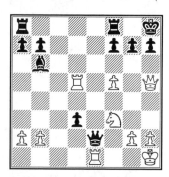

*After 22. Kh1*

**22. ... Qf2?!** The greedy 22. ... Q×b2 could certainly be considered. After 23. Ng5 h6 24. N×f7† Kg8 Black's king is safe, and he is ready to claim an advantage after either 25. Nd6 Bc7 26. R×d3 Rad8, when Black reaches a better ending after White's only move 27. Qd1 B×d6 28. R×d6 R×d6 29. Q×d6 Q×a2, or after 25. N×h6† g×h6 26. R×d3 Bd4! **23. f6!** g×f6?! Not ideal, as the weakening of his kingside, due to the absence of his queen, is telling. White doesn't get any further after the cool 23. ... Rfe8!, when the rook takes over the role of principal defender, e.g., after 24. Rg1 Re6 25. f×g7† Kg8 26. R×d3 Rae8 27. Rd2 Re5 28. Q×e5 Q×g1† 29. N×g1 R×e5. **24. Qh6 Rg8 25. Q×f6†** Rg7 26. g3! "This quiet-looking mode of play was essential, and is also, if rightly looked at, eminently attacking. If he had made the plausible 26. Rg5, Black would have at once gained the day by 26. ... Bd4. Hence we see the importance of Black's 22nd move"—Löwenthal. **26. ... Rag8 27. R×d3 Ba5 28. Red1 Re8 29. b4?!** A forceful move, intending a quick win in case of 29. ... B×b4 30. Rd8, but both players overlooked the saving clause 30. ... Rf8!, instead of 30. ... Reg8? when White delivers mate in four moves. Alternatively, the endgame reached after 29. Rd7! Be1 30. R×f7 Qf1† 31. Ng1 Q×f6 32. R×f6 is quite attractive for White. **29. ... Qb6?! 30. Q×b6 B×b6 31. Rd7 f6 32. a4 Ree7 33. R7d6 Rgf7 34. Nh4 f5?** The endgame was still perfectly manageable after 34. ... Re5!, a move that takes f5 under control. The text move seals the fate of the f-pawn, and with it of the game. **35. R6d5 Rf8** 35. ... f4? 36. Nf5! wins immediately. **36. N×f5 Re4 37. a5 Bc7 38. Rd7 Rc4 39. Ne3 Rc6 40. Nd5 Bd6 41. b5 Rc2 42. R×d6 Rff2 43. Nf4** and Black resigns—*Chess Player's Magazine* (Löwenthal), August 1866, pp. 252–253; *Modern Chess* (Bird), p. 76.

## A Game with the Champion 1866

The most important event of the busy year 1866 was the eagerly awaited match between Steinitz and Anderssen. Just before the commencement of that match Anderssen made a short visit to Simpson's Divan. Despite some fatigue from the long journey he did not hesitate to enter into a game with Bird.

### (162) Bird–Anderssen    0–1
Offhand game
London (Simpson's Divan), 14 July 1866
C65

"The famous German master Anderssen arrived here on Saturday last, for the purpose of playing the match which has been arranged between him and Steinitz. Although somewhat fatigued by a long journey, Anderssen, with characteristic gallantry, on visiting the Grand Cigar Divan that afternoon, accepted the invitation of Bird to a friendly 'passage d'armes,' and the result was the very instructive game which follows"—Staunton.

**1. e4 e5 2. Nf3 Nc6 3. Bb5 Nf6 4. d4 e×d4 5. 0–0 Be7 6. Re1** "We should have preferred 6. e5"—Staunton. **6. ... 0–0 7. e5 Ne8 8. N×d4** "This was hardly prudent. It served to free Black in a great degree from his restrained position, and subjected the White queen to a very disastrous attack"—Staunton. **8. ... N×d4 9. Q×d4 d5 10. Nc3 c6 11. Bd3 Be6 12. Qf4 f5 13. e×f6** *e.p.* **R×f6 14. Qg3 Bd6 15. Qh4 h6 16. Be3 Qc7 17. Ne2?** A major mistake, and Anderssen doesn't hesitate to take immediate profit. After 17. Qh5 Bf7 18. Qh4, neither side can make much progress. **17. ... g5!** "This move, Anderssen had evidently had in view some time, appears to have been quite unforeseen by his usually acute opponent"—Staunton. **18. Qa4** The point of Black's move is 18. Qh5? Ng7. Perhaps the best course would have been to sacrifice the bishop for the two pawns, and trust in the open position of Black's king for compensation. **18. ... b5 19. Qd4 c5 20. Qc3 c4 21. Bd4 b4 22. Qd2 c×d3 23. B×f6 N×f6?** Anderssen could have decided the game with 23. ... B×h2† 24. Kh1 N×f6. Both men, however, neglect the importance of the capture at h2, until Anderssen finally decides to take it after all. **24. Nd4 Bd7 25. Q×d3 Kh8 26. Qg6 B×h2†** *(see diagram)*

*After 26. ... B×h2†*

**27. Kf1?** The wrong direction, even though defending the f-pawn seems logical, but after 27. ... Ng4! White's attack is completely over, for if in that case 28. g3 Rf8 29. Re2 Q×g3 is obvious. Better thus is 27. Kh1, entering the fairly forced but interesting line 27. ... Ng4! 28. g3 B×g3 29. Re7 N×f2† (with the knife against his throat Black has no choice) 30. Kg1 Bh2† 31. K×f2 Rf8† 32. Kg2 Bh3† 33. Kh1 Q×e7 34. Q×h6† Kg8 35. Qg6† Qg7 36. Q×g7† K×g7 37. K×h2 and White has drawing chances. **27. ... Qc4†** Anderssen makes no use of his knight by playing 27. ... Ng4, which again perfectly combines attack and defense. Bird is thus lucky to escape into an endgame. Of course the material balance still favors his opponent. **28. Qd3 Rf8 29. Q×c4 d×c4 30. Re7 Bd6 31. Re2 Ng4 32. Rd1 Bc5 33. c3 Rf4 34. f3 B×d4** Despite some less convincing play, Anderssen could still count on a meaningful edge after 34. ... b×c3 35. b×c3 Rf7. **35. c×d4** Bird suffered during the whole middle game, and after the text move his fate for the endgame isn't any different. With 35. R×d4, he realizes the exchange of rook when he suddenly has excellent drawing chances. **35. ... Bb5 36. Ke1 Nf6 37. Re5 Ba4?!** 37. ... a6, keeping the c-pawn on the board, gives excellent winning chances. **38. b3 c×b3 39. a×b3 B×b3 40. Rb1 Bd5 41. R×b4 Kg7 42. Re7†?!** 42. Ra4 achieves the elimination of the a-pawn without worsening the situation of the central rook. Now both White rooks end up rather offside. **42. ... Kg6 43. R×a7 h5?!** A bit too slow. The situation for White is critical after 43. ... g4! 44. f×g4 B×g2 as the h-pawn will quickly march on. **44. Ra6?!** The only chance to draw the game lies in 44. Rb6! The point of moving this rook to the sixth rank is the fact that the other one has other options than going to a6. But it is very uncertain if this enables him to draw the game. After 44. Rb6!, there may follow 44. ... h4 (another line is 44. ... R×d4 45. Raa6 Rf4 46. Ra5 Rf5 47. g4. Black is still clearly better, but his pieces don't coordinate that well) 45. Rd6 B×f3! 46. g×f3 R×f3 47. Ke2 g4 48. Ra1 h3 49. Rf1 Rf5. White keeps on suffering. **44. ... h4** "The terminating moves are, for the most part, admirably played by Anderssen"—Staunton. **45. Rbb6 g4!** Black crashes through on the kingside. **46. Kf2 h3** Simplest is 46. ... g×f3 47. g×f3 R×f3†. **47. Kg3** 47. g×h3 might be tried, as Black has to be aware of a trick 47. ... R×f3† 48. Kg1! g3! (48. ... g×h3? 49. Kh2 is an immediate draw. The h-pawn has advanced a step too far!) 49. h4 Rf4 50. Rd6 Be4 51. Re6 R×h4! **47. ... Kg5 48. R×f6 R×f6 49. Ra5 Rf5 50. f4†** "Taking either pawn would have been quite unavailing: 50. f×g4 h×g2 51. Kh2 K×g4 or 50. g×h3 R×f3† 51. Kh2 R×h3† 52. Kg1 Rg3† 53. Kf1 (best) 53. ... Rf3† followed by 54. ... Rf5"—Staunton. **50. ... Kg6?** 50. ... Kf6! wins without trouble. **51. g×h3 g×h3 52. Rb5?** The endgame after 52. Ra6† Kh5 53. K×h3 is not so easy to win. Had he played 50. ... Kf6!, 52. ... Be6 would have been possible. **52. ... Be6 53. Re5 Bd7 54. Re3 Rd5 55. Rd3 Kf5 56. Kf3 Bc6 57. Kg3 Ke4 58. Rd1 Bd7 59. Re1† K×d4 60. Re7 Kc3 61. Re2 Rd2 62. Re5 Rg2† 63. Kf3 Bc6† 64. Ke3 h2** and Black wins—*Illustrated London News* (Staunton), 21 July 1866.

# A NEW CLUB AND
# A NEW CHAMPION

During the course of 1866 bad news arrived for the extensive chess community at Simpson's when they were relegated to an inferior part of the building. Several players took the bull by the horns and decided

to leave the Divan and form a new club. This was baptized the Westminster Chess Club, named after its illustrious predecessor.[12] Staunton was appointed president. Rooms were found at the Gordon Hotel in Covent Garden and in just a short time more than a hundred members were affiliated. It was not long before the Westminster Chess Club was acknowledged as the principal club in London. Without any false modesty, and on a proposition from Bird, the club expressed the ambition to represent and promote British chess.

Staunton emphasized the English nature of the club, free from the influence of so-called foreign intrusionists.[13] With this ambition and these lines the new club clearly distinguished itself from the St. James's Chess Club, managed by Löwenthal, the envisaged foreigner, as well as from the British Chess Association. It is therefore quite surprising to find Bird so prominent on both fronts, while Löwenthal and Staunton, the representatives of respectively the B.C.A. and the Westminster Chess Club, were on a hostile footing with each other.

The organization of several activities contributed to the success of the Westminster Club. A handicap tournament was started and the club played a prominent role in the organization of the match between Steinitz and Anderssen. This match was played in several London chess rooms with the Westminster Chess Club taking care of the main part of the finances.[14] The duel was extremely tense and exciting. After 14 games, Steinitz was declared the winner with 8 wins against 6 wins for the Prussian. There were no draws. By winning this match Steinitz gained the reputation of being the world's number one (although nobody disregarded Paul Morphy yet). In retrospect Steinitz claimed this victory as the beginning of his reign as world champion but his results during the next few years were not unambiguous enough to justify such a claim.

# MATCH WITH STEINITZ 1866

Immediately upon the termination of the match between Steinitz and Anderssen, Bird issued a challenge to the new champion. The *Illustrated London News* of 15 September reported that both players quickly agreed on the terms, which indicates there was a good understanding between them. The match was set up with the explicit purpose to "give Mr. Bird an opportunity, by practice with a strong opponent, to recover something of his old proficiency in chess." It was agreed that 11 wins were needed for victory. The stakes were quite moderately set at £15 or £25 per side.[15]

---

12. The first Westminster Chess Club existed in the 1830s. It hosted the famous matches between de la Bourdonnais and McDonnell.

13. *Chess World*, July 1866, p. 132. Staunton established *Chess World* for similar reasons, to counterweigh the, in his eyes, dominant presence of foreigners in chess columns and magazines. At the time Löwenthal was managing his own *Chess Player's Magazine*.

14. *Illustrated London News*, 21 July 1866. Staunton claimed that all the subscribers of the match were connected with the Westminster Chess Club. A few weeks later, after a protest from an important subscriber of another club (*Illustrated London News*, 18 August), he had to adjust his bold statement.

15. As usual, Bird gave different amounts in respectively H.E. Bird, *Chess Practice: Being a Condensed and Simplified Record of the Actual Openings in the Finest Games Played Up to the Present Time*; London: Sampson Low, Marston, Searle and Rivington, 1882, p. 17; and Bird, *Chess History and Reminiscences*, p. 115.

The organization of the match was in the hands of the Westminster Chess Club. After a few games the club found a new home at Haxell's Hotel, on the Strand and thus near the Divan.[16]

No one had the impression that Steinitz put his just-achieved status as the world's strongest player at risk. Anderssen was considered far superior to Bird, who was also out of practice. In *Chess Novelties* (p. xvi), Bird wrote that he worked during the day, which fatigued him considerably and was a heavy burden when playing chess. Yet, against all odds the match turned out to be much more closely contested than widely expected.

The match probably began during the first week of September. The first game ended in a disaster for Bird. He opened with the Black pieces and after merely six moves were played, Staunton's remark in his notes in *Chess World* (October 1866, p. 244) was that "Mr. Bird has evidently forgotten the proper defense of the present opening." After a quick draw, Bird was easily positionally overwhelmed in the third game. Bird tried to with Black with a dubious line of the French. In later years Bird would mostly avoid mainstream theory; in this case his lack of form and long absence from the game explains his choice.

**Wilhelm Steinitz (*A Century of British Chess*).**

16. Apparently the hotel was not a bad location for a chess club: "In its new habitation, the Westminster is by very far the most comfortable, social, and best-appointed chess club in London. The members have the exclusive use of a noble chess saloon and smaller rooms for whist, &. They have the use of a handsome dining-room, smoking-room, lavatory, and the choice of eighty bed-rooms. They can obtain every sort of refreshment at a very moderate tariff, and they can communicate with half the world (there being a telegraph-office in the house) without going beyond the door." *Illustrated London News*, 27 October 1866.

Steinitz' superiority seemed established. After nine games he had a comfortable edge of three points. On 6 October, the *Illustrated London News* informed its readers that "this contest is at a stand for a few days, we are told, owing to Mr. Bird's absence from London." These interruptions were agreed upon in mutual consent. In *A Slight Chess Retrospect and Explanation* (p. 2), Bird wrote that Steinitz received "the stakes, and also presents equivalent thereto for adjournments" (which is taken to mean a sum to compensate for the delays).

Upon the resumption of the match in October a sudden transformation took place. Bird scored two straightforward wins, and failed by a hair's breadth to equalize the score completely in the twelfth game. The steadiness with which he hung on ignited the battle and started to generate increasing public interest.

Steinitz lengthened his lead to two points after the thirteenth game. After two more draws Bird created a sensation when he won the sixteenth game after an abominable blunder of Steinitz. During this game Bird received a telegram requiring him to travel to America as soon as possible on behalf of his firm. The seventeenth game was started and adjourned as early as move 16. The position was already lost for Bird.

The match ended thus with a score of 6 or 7 wins (depending how one interprets the early finish of the last match game. Given the final position on the board, one is inclined to say seven) for Steinitz against 5 wins for Bird.

This close outcome of the match was in fact the first truly excellent result in Bird's chess career and he was justly proud of it. It gave him (even) more confidence to present himself as a leading British player once his return in 1873 proved to be a success. In the years to come he did not restrain this sentiment. He played it out it out in various rather absurd match challenges to Steinitz, at a time when the latter had become much stronger. Bird kept on accentuating that his match loss (of one game in his mind) was the narrowest of Steinitz' victories.

Yet, Bird's good result has to be put in perspective. The much more important match with Anderssen had clearly taken its toll from Steinitz. His level of play was quite dramatic. Most of Steinitz' losses can be attributed to monumental blunders. In three of the five games he lost, Steinitz was completely winning when he lost the thread. But it also has to be said that the reverse was equally true and that Bird's intense occupation with accountancy left its mark. The level of his games played between 1866 and 1870 is considerably lower than in the years before and decades after this period. This match was symptomatic, with Bird blundering in various good or won positions.

### (163) Steinitz–Bird    1–0
Match (game 1)
London 1866
C29

**1. e4 e5 2. Nc3 Nc6 3. f4 Nf6 4. f×e5 N×e5 5. d4 Ng6 6. e5 Ng8 7. Nf3 d5 8. Bd3 Bb4 9. 0–0 Be6 10. Ng5 N8e7 11. N×e6 f×e6 12. Qg4 Qd7 13. Bg5 0–0–0 14. Rf7 Rde8 15. Ne2 Qc6 16. c3 Ba5 17. a4 Qb6 18. b4 B×b4 19. c×b4 N×e5 20. a5 Q×b4 21. Q×e6† Nd7 22. Rb1 Qa3 23. Bf5** and Bird resigns—*The Field*, 27 October 1866.

| Match with Steinitz, September–November 1866 | | | | | | | | | | | | | | | | | | |
|---|---|---|---|---|---|---|---|---|---|---|---|---|---|---|---|---|---|---|
| | 1 | 2 | 3 | 4 | 5 | 6 | 7 | 8 | 9 | 10 | 11 | 12 | 13 | 14 | 15 | 16 | 17 | |
| W. Steinitz | 1 | ½ | 1 | 0 | ½ | 1 | 0 | 1 | 1 | 0 | 0 | ½ | 1 | ½ | ½ | 0 | 1 | 7 |
| H.E. Bird | 0 | ½ | 0 | 1 | ½ | 0 | 1 | 0 | 0 | 1 | 1 | ½ | 0 | ½ | ½ | 1 | 0 | 5 |

## (164) Bird–Steinitz   ½–½

Match (game 2)

London 1866

C65

**1. e4 e5 2. Nf3 Nc6 3. Bb5 Nf6 4. d4 e×d4 5. e5 Ne4 6. 0-0 Be7 7. c3 d×c3 8. N×c3 N×c3 9. b×c3 0-0 10. Qc2 d6 11. Bf4 N×e5 12. N×e5 d×e5 13. Rad1 Bd6 14. B×e5 Bg4 15. Rd4 Bh5 16. Bd3 Bg6 17. B×g6 h×g6 18. Qd2 Qe7 19. B×d6 c×d6 20. Re1 Qc7 21. R×d6 Rad8 22. R×d8 R×d8 23. Qg5 Rc8 24. Rd1** and the game was declared a draw—*Illustrated London News*, 15 September 1866.

## (165) Steinitz–Bird   1–0

Match (game 3)

London, September 1866

C10

**1. e4 e6** The French Defense was a rare appearance in Bird's practice. Against Steinitz, he reinstated this opening in his repertoire after a hopeless loss by forgetting the theory in the first game. For a few games Bird tries the doubtful push f7–f5, but he gets cured of it when Steinitz finally finds the right recipe. **2. d4 d5 3. Nc3 d×e4 4. N×e4 f5 5. Nc3 Nf6 6. Nf3 Bd6 7. Bc4 0-0 8. 0-0 c6 9. Re1 Nd5 10. Ng5 Rf6 11. Qh5 h6 12. Nf3 Bd7 13. Ne5 Be8 14. Qf3 Nd7 15. Bb3 Kh7 16. Bd2 Nf8 17. Ne2 g5 18. c4 Ne7 19. Ng3 Bc7 20. Bc3 h5 21. Ne4 B×e5 22. N×g5† Kg7 23. R×e5 Neg6 24. Ree1 Kh6 25. Nh3 f4 26. d5 Nh4 27. Qe4 Rf5 28. d×e6 Nh7 29. e7 Qd7 30. Rad1 Qc7 31. Qe6† Bg6 32. Rd7** and Black resigns—*Illustrated London News*, 6 October 1866.

## (166) Bird–Steinitz   1–0

Match (game 4)

London, September 1866

C67

**1. e4 e5 2. Nf3 Nc6 3. Bb5 Nf6 4. 0-0 N×e4 5. Re1 Nd6** "This sadly hampers all his men. The move given in *Chess Praxis* and other works on the openings is 5. ... Nf6, with the following as a probable continuation: 6. N×e5 N×e5 7. R×e5† Be7 8. Qe1 c6 9. Ba4 d6 10. Re3 Be6 and the defense is effectual"—Staunton. **6. B×c6 d×c6 7. d4 e4** "Black keeps a pawn plus, but his game is a little exposed"—Boden. **8. Nc3 f5 9. Ne5 Be6 10. d5** "The present game is a great improvement on the previous games in this little match. In those Bird's play is merely tentative, and without much forecast. Here, however, he exhibits considerable ingenuity, and in the course of several complex situations fairly outwits his adversary"—Staunton. Bird heads for unclear complications. Objectively better is 10. f3, when Black is forced to return the pawn to get castled. **10. ... c×d5 11. N×d5 Nf7** "Very interesting situations now arise"—Boden. **12. Nf4** "Well played on White's part"—Boden. **12. ... Qf6** "He would have gained no advantage by exchanging pieces at this point:

12. ... Q×d1 13. R×d1 N×e5 14. N×e6 with the better game"—Staunton. Instead, 13. ... Rd8! 17. R×d8 N×d8 converts the game from a complicated middle game into a very promising endgame for Black. **13. Nf3 Be7** 13. ... Rd8 and 14. ... Bc8 safeguards his extra pawn completely. **14. Nh5 Qg6 15. Nd4** Bird keeps on harassing Steinitz' pieces with enterprising knight moves, but it is very doubtful if this will be enough. He was certainly not interested in the draw he could force with 15. Nf4. **15. ... Bd7 16. c4 0-0-0 17. Nf4 Qd6 18. Nd5 Ne5** 18. ... Bf6! puts an end to Bird's knight sorties. If 19. Bf4 Be5 20. Qd2 c6. **19. Qb3 Rhe8** 19. ... Bf6 is best. Though his compensation for the pawn is still insufficient, Bird now gets a stifling grip on his opponent's position. **20. Bf4 g5?** *(see diagram)*

*After 20. ... g5*

"This oversight loses a piece and the game at once"—Boden. After 20. ... c6! 21. N×e7 Q×e7, there is nothing that can keep Black from playing g5 soon. **21. c5!** Bird doesn't spoil the chance to score his first win in the match. **21. ... Qa6 22. B×e5 Ba4 23. N×c7!** "But for this unforeseen stroke Black's last two ingenious moves would have won him his piece back again"—Boden. **23. ... B×b3 24. N×a6 Bc4 25. Nc7 Rg8 26. N×f5 Bf8 27. Nd6†** and Black resigns—*The Field* (Boden), 15 September 1866; *Illustrated London News* (Staunton), 6 October 1866.

## (167) Steinitz–Bird   ½–½

Match (game 5)

London, September 1866

C10

**1. e4 e6 2. d4 d5 3. Nc3 d×e4 4. N×e4 Nc6 5. Nf3 f5 6. Nc3 Nf6 7. Bc4 Bb4 8. 0-0 B×c3 9. b×c3 0-0 10. Ne5** A unusually antipositional move from Steinitz. Both 10. Re1 and 10. Ba3 are promising. **10. ... Na5 11. Bb3 b6 12. Re1 N×b3 13. a×b3 Bb7 14. Nd3 Ne4 15. Bb2 Qh4 16. f3 Ng5 17. Qe2 Rf6 18. Qf2?** "That a player of Mr. Steinitz's acumen should have committed this error is remarkable, but that his opponent should have omitted to take advantage of it is wonderful"—Staunton. 18. Bc1! crosses all evil plans, e.g., 18. ... Rg6 19. Kh1 a5 20. Bf4 with absolute safety for his king. **18. ... Rg6?!** "A pretty move, but Mr. Bird had here a won game as follows: 18. ... Nh3† 19. g×h3 Rg6† 20. Kf1 (20. Kh1 Q×f2 21. N×f2 B×f3 mate) 20. ... Q×h3† 21. Ke2 Rg2 and wins. The above beautiful demonstration is due originally, we believe, to the keen observation of Mr. Barnes, who was an on-looker at the time of play"—Boden. **19. Q×h4 N×f3† 20. Kf2 N×h4 21. Nf4 N×g2 22. N×g6 N×e1 23. R×e1 h×g6 24. R×e6 Kf7** "Though Black has a pawn more, his game is not a likely one to win against so patient and correct an analyst as Steinitz"—Boden. **25. Re2 Be4 26. Bc1 Rh8 27. Kg3 Ke6?!** 27. ... b5 28. Bf4 c6 29. c4 a5 offers winning chances. **28. c4 c6 29. h4 a5 30. Bf4 Kd7 31. c3 Ra8 32. Be5 a4 33. b×a4 Bd3 34. Re3 B×c4 35. B×g7 R×a4 36. Kf4 Ra1 37. Bh6 Rg1 38. Bg5 Rg4† 39. Ke5 Bd5 40. Re1 Re4† 41. R×e4 B×e4 42. Kf6 f4 43. B×f4** draw—*The Field* (Boden), 22 September 1866; *Chess World* (Staunton), September 1866, pp. 245–246.

## (168) Bird–Steinitz    0–1
Match (game 6)
London, September 1866
*A02*

**1. f4 e5 2. f×e5 d6 3. e×d6 B×d6 4. d4 Nf6 5. Bg5 Nc6 6. Nf3 Bg4 7. e3 Qd7 8. Bb5 0-0-0 9. B×f6 g×f6 10. d5 Qe7 11. B×c6 Q×e3† 12. Qe2 Qc1† 13. Qd1 Rde8† 14. B×e8 R×e8† 15. Kf2 Qe3† 16. Kf1 B×f3 17. g×f3 Bc5 18. Kg2 Rg8†** and White resigns—*The Field*, 22 September 1866.

## (169) Steinitz–Bird    0–1
Match (game 7)
London, September 1866
*C10*

**1. e4 e6 2. d4 d5 3. Nc3 d×e4 4. N×e4 f5 5. Ng5! Be7 6. N1h3 Nc6 7. Bb5 Nf6 8. 0-0 0-0-0 9. B×c6 b×c6 10. Nf4 Qd6 11. c4 c5 12. d×c5 Qc6 13. b4 Ng4 14. Nf3** Steinitz finally found the correct reply that refutes Bird's experimental 4. ... f5. Here he misses a transposition into an excellent endgame with 14. Qf3! Q×f3 15. N×f3, but it isn't long before Bird spoils his own game with an extravagant move. **14. ... Bf6 15. Rb1 g5? 16. Nd3** "We see no objection to 16. Nh5"—Boden. **16. ... e5 17. N×g5 f4 18. b5** "Mr. Steinitz has now very much the better game"—Staunton. **18. ... Qe8 19. Ne4 Bf5 20. f3 N×h2** Bird has been outplayed and decides to try his luck with a desperate sacrifice. **21. K×h2 Qh5† 22. Kg1 Rad8** "A move directly suicidal, if White sees how to profit by it"—Staunton. 22. ... Bh4 (Boden) fails after 23. Nb4, or even 23. B×f4. **23. Qe2** "Steinitz, in this game, is fully a match for his opponent in recklessness. A very little examination of the position would have shown him that Black's last move placed the fortunes of the day at his command. For suppose, instead of 23. Qe2, he had continued the battle thus: 23. N×f6† R×f6 24. N×f4, White has gained a piece and a pawn, and with them, of course, will win the game"—Staunton. **23. ... Bh4** *(see diagram)*

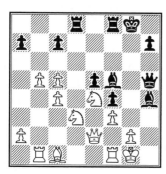

*After 23. ... Bh4*

**24. g4** "This move is worse even than the last. That only threw away an opportunity of winning the game. This throws away all chance of saving it"—Staunton. Even after such a poor move, Steinitz is still winning. Much more conclusive however would have been 24. Ndf2, heading for h3, to block the h-file. **24. ... f×g3 *e.p.* 25. Bb2??** 25. N×e5! Rfe8 26. Bf4 defends against all menaces, while almost completing his development. The text move abandons the control over the most important diagonal on the board. **25. ... B×e4 26. Q×e4 Bg5! 27. Qe2 Be3† 28. Nf2 Qh2** mates—*The Field* (Boden), 29 September 1866; *Illustrated London News* (Staunton), 20 October 1866.

## (170) Bird–Steinitz    0–1
Match (game 8)
London, September 1866
*C65*

**1. e4 e5 2. Nf3 Nc6 3. Bb5 Nf6 4. d4 e×d4 5. 0-0 Be7 6. e5 Ne4 7. Re1 Nc5 8. N×d4 N×d4 9. Q×d4 0-0 10. Nc3 Kh8 11. Be3 Ne6 12. Qe4 f5 13. e×f6 *e.p.* B×f6 14. Bd3 g6 15. Rad1 c6 16. Qb4 d5 17. Be2 Be7 18. Qb3 Nc5 19. Bd4† Kg8 20. B×c5 B×c5 21. Bf3 Qb6 22. Q×b6 a×b6 23. a3 Bf5 24. Rd2 b5 25. g4 Bd7 26. Kg2 Rf7 27. Rd3 Raf8 28. Re2 Kg7 29. b4 Bd6 30. h3 Kh6 31. Red2 Bf4 32. Rd1 Kg7 33. Ne2 Bc7 34. Ng3 h5 35. R1d2 h×g4 36. B×g4 B×g4 37. h×g4 Kh6 38. Re2 Kg5 39. f3 Rh8 40. Nf1 Rfh7 41. Rde3 Rh1 42. Re8 R8h7 43. Rf8 Bd6 44. Rf7 Rh7 45. R×h7 R×h7 46. Re8 Re7 47. R×e7 B×e7 48. Ne3 Bf6 49. Nd1 Kf4 50. Kf2 Bd4† 51. Ke2 b6 52. c3 Bf6 53. Kf2 c5 54. Ne3 d4 55. Nd5† Ke5 56. N×f6 d×c3 57. Ke3 K×f6 58. f4 c4 59. Ke2 Ke6 60. Kd1 Kd5 61. Kc2 Ke4 62. f5 g×f5 63. g×f5 K×f5 64. K×c3 Ke4 65. a4 b×a4 66. K×c4 b5†** and White resigns—*Illustrated London News*, 20 October 1866.

## (171) Steinitz–Bird    1–0
Match (game 9)
London, October 1866
*C10*

**1. e4 e6 2. d4 d5 3. Nc3 d×e4 4. N×e4 Nc6 5. Nf3 Nf6 6. N×f6† Q×f6 7. Bg5 Qf5 8. Bd3 Qg4 9. h3 Q×g2 10. Rh2 Q×h2 11. N×h2 N×d4 12. Bb5†** Black resigns—*The Field*, 6 October 1866.

## (172) Bird–Steinitz    1–0
Match (game 10)
London, October 1866
*C62*

**1. e4 e5 2. Nf3 d6 3. d4 e×d4 4. Q×d4 Nc6 5. Bb5 Bd7 6. B×c6 B×c6 7. Nc3 Nf6 8. Bg5 Be7 9. 0-0-0 0-0 10. h3 Re8 11. Rhe1 h6 12. Bh4 Nd7 13. B×e7 Q×e7 14. Nh2 Nc5 15. f3 f5 16. Nd5 Qf7 17. e5 Ne6 18. Qc4 Nf8 19. f4 Rad8 20. Nf3 Ng6 21. e6 R×e6 22. R×e6 B×d5** "The position here is extremely interesting, and the play on both sides appears very good"—Bird. **23. Q×d5 N×f4 24. Q×b7 N×e6 25. Q×a7 Nc5 26. b4!** A bold, but well-founded advance. Instead of playing it safe to draw the game Bird pursues the straightforward plan of advancing his a-pawn. Steinitz' situation is extremely difficult, as defending this position is far from easy. **26. ... Ne4 27. Kb2 Re8 28. Rd3 Re7 29. Qa8† Kh7 30. Qd5 Qf6† 31. c3 Nf2 32. Rd2 Ne4 33. Rc2** *(see diagram)*

*After 33. Rc2*

**33. ... g6?** This tempo will cost Steinitz dearly. Instead there were two worthy recipes to deal with Bird's a-pawn. With 33. ... Ng3 Black initiates a time-consuming tour with his knight, but after 34. b5 f4! (a crucial move) 35. a4 Nf5 36. Qd3 Kh8 37. a5 Ne3 38. Re2 d5 it becomes clear that the position is full of tension, with White's king not being certain of his life. If White plays 34. a4 instead, Black obtains counterplay with 34. ... c5! 35. b5 Re4. The simpler alternative is 33. ... c5! at once, the point being that after 34. b5 Ra7 35. Qb3 Qd8 White's a-pawn is absolutely not the force it becomes in the game. 36. a4?? even loses outright after the cute 36. ... Qa8! 37. Ka3 c4!! Instead 36. c4 is about equal. **34. a4 c5 35. b5 c4 36. Nd4 Nc5 37. a5 Qf8** "This move is part of an exceedingly clever device, by which Black hoped to turn the tables on his foe"—Staunton. **38. Q×d6 Nd3† 39. Ka2!** "Luckily for Bird, he saw and avoided the trap prepared for him. Had he played 39. Ka3, Black would have played 39. ... Ra7 and scored the game"—Staunton. **39. ... Nc1† 40. Kb1** "It is scarcely necessary to say that he could not take the knight without losing his queen"—Staunton. **40. ... Nd3 41. Re2** and Black resigns. A very neat performance by Bird!—*Illustrated London News* (Staunton), 3 November 1866; *Modern Chess* (Bird), pp. 118–119.

## (173) Steinitz–Bird    0–1

Match (game 11)
London, October 1866
C14

**1. e4 e6 2. d4 d5 3. Nc3 Nf6 4. Bg5 Be7 5. e5 Nfd7 6. B×e7 Q×e7 7. f4 a6 8. Nf3 c5 9. d×c5 N×c5 10. Qd2 b5 11. a3 Bb7 12. Nd4 Nc6 13. Be2 Qh4†** "This check is not, by any means, the unprofitable move it appears to be. White dare not castle on the queenside from fear of his adversary's b-pawn, and when he does so on the other wing his king will be more exposed to attack with the g-pawn advanced than he would be with the same unmoved"—Staunton. **14. g3 Qe7 15. Bf3 Rc8 16. 0–0 0–0 17. Rae1 Rfd8 18. f5?** "The outlook of this step is so unpromising that we suspect the move was the result of an erroneous calculation. In what way did Mr. Steinitz suppose he could recoup himself for the sacrifice of so valuable a pawn?"—Staunton. **18. ... N×d4 19. Q×d4 e×f5 20. Qb4 g6 21. Re2 d4 22. Nd1 B×f3 23. R×f3 Qb7 24. Rf1 Ne4**

**25. Qb3 Re8 26. Qf3 R×e5 27. Nf2 Rce8 28. Rfe1 Qe7 29. Qg2 Re6 30. Nd3 Qb7** "Both parties play well all through the latter portion of the game, but Black's task is incomparably less difficult than his opponent's, and Mr. Steinitz is entitled to high commendation for the coolness and bravery with which he fought out this disheartening battle"—Staunton. **31. Nf4 R6e7 32. Nd3 h5 33. Rd1 Qb6 34. Rde1 Kg7 35. h3 Qd6 36. g4 Kh7 37. b4 h4 38. Nc1 Ng3 39. R×e7 R×e7 40. Qf2 R×e1† 41. Q×e1 Qc6 42. g×f5 g×f5** "We may be wrong; for, in spite of the proverb, lookers-on do not always see so much of the game as the players; but it occurs to us that Mr. Bird would have expedited his victory by playing 42. ... Qh1†, instead of capturing the pawn. Let us see: 43. Kf2 Ne4† (43. ... Qh2† 44. Kf3 N×f5 would have been tolerably conclusive) 44. Ke2 Nc3† 45. Kd2 (45. Kf2 Qh2† followed by 46. ... Q×h3† and 47. ... Q×f5) 45. ... Nb1† 46. Ke2 (46. Kd1 Qf3† 47. Ne2 Nc3†) 46. ... Qe4† and after the king moves to the f-file, the queen takes another pawn, winning offhand"—Staunton. **43. Nb3 Qd5 44. Nc5 Qh1† 45. Kf2 Ne4† 46. Ke2 Qg2† 47. Kd1 Qf3† 48. Kc1 Q×a3† 49. Kd1 Q×h3 50. N×e4 Qg4† 51. Kc1 f×e4 52. Qf2 Qg5† 53. Kb1 h3 54. Q×d4 f5 55. Qa7† Kh6 56. Q×a6† Qg6 57. Qc8 Kh5 58. Qc3 Qg1† 59. Kb2 h2 60. Qh8† Kg4 61. Qg7† Kf3 62. Qc3† Qe3 63. Qh8 Kg2** and White resigns—*Illustrated London News* (Staunton), 10 November 1866.

## (174) Bird–Steinitz    ½–½

Match (game 12)
London, October 1866
C77

**1. e4 e5 2. Nf3 Nc6 3. Bb5 Nf6 4. d4 e×d4 5. e5 Ne4 6. 0–0 a6 7. Ba4 Nc5 8. c3 N×a4** Bird's offering of the c-pawn is not correct, but Steinitz's reply justifies it. 8. ... d×c3 9. N×c3 b5 10. Bb3 N×b3 11. Q×b3 Na5! is the best way to accept the pawn. The difference lies in the control over d5 that Bird obtains in the game. **9. Q×a4 b5 10. Qc2 d×c3 11. N×c3 Be7 12. Nd5! Bb7 13. Bd2 h6 14. Rfe1 0–0 15. Qf5** "White has a pawn less than his opponent, but the superiority of his position fully compensates for the deficiency in force"—Staunton. The direct 15. B×h6 leads to a quick draw: 15. ... g×h6 16. Qf5 Kg7 17. Qg4†. **15. ... f6?!** *(see diagram)* More than dangerous. 15. ... Na7 is necessary, to force a declaration from the knight at d5.

*After 15. ... f6*

**16. B×h6!** "This is well conceived"—Staunton. **16. ... f×e5?!** "If he had taken the bishop, it would have cost him the game: 16. ... g×h6 17. Qg6† Kh8 18. Q×h6† Kg8 19. Qg6† Kh8 20. Re4"—

Staunton. 16. ... N×e5 has more potential as he succeeds in exchanging some pieces. Yet Black is stripped bare after 17. B×g7! B×d5 18. B×f8 Q×f8 19. N×e5 f×e5 20. Q×e5 Be6 21. Q×c7. The bishops offer survival chances, but nothing more. **17. Qg6 Rf7 18. Re4!** Bird continues his attack in brilliant fashion. **18. ... Qf8 19. Bg5!** "What was the objection to 19. Rg4? If 19. ... R×f3 20. B×g7 Qf7/f5 21. Bf6† Q×g6 (best) 22. R×g6† Kf8 (best) 23. g×f3 and Bird has an easy winning game"—Staunton. 22. ... Kf7! keeps the balance in the line above. Instead of 20. B×g7?, White must simply play 20. g×f3! **19. ... R×f3!** "The best move"—Staunton. **20. g×f3 B×g5 21. Q×g5 Re8 22. Rae1 Re6 23. N×c7 Rh6?** "23. ... Nd4 has a look of promise, but the result is not satisfactory: 24. N×e6 N×f3† 25. Kf1 N×g5 26. N×f8 N×e4 27. N×d7 wins"—Staunton. Steinitz' conducted his defense in excellent fashion and neutralized Bird's attack, but here he allows his opponent to blow new life into it. It was not so easy to find the right way. Staunton's line can be ameliorated considerably with 25. ... d×e6!, when the endgame is even slightly favorable for him after 26. Qg6 Nd2†, followed by mass exchanges at e4. But White's play can be improved as well. After 24. R×d4, instead of 24. N×e6, a draw is forced: 24. ... Q×f3 25. Kf1 Qh3† 26. Kg1 etc. **24. Rg4 Kh7 25. Ne8** 25. Kf1! takes the sting out of 25. ... Nd4: 26. R×e5! N×f3 27. Rf5. He can play 25. ... R×h2 instead, but the ending is sad after 26. Rh4†. **25. ... Nd4 26. Q×g7† Q×g7 27. R×g7† Kh8 28. Rg3?!** 28. R×d7 still gives White a better ending after 28. ... Rg6† 29. Kf1 B×f3 30. Re3 Bg2† 31. Ke1 Nc2† 32. Kd2 N×e3 33. K×e3. Compared to the game, White's pieces are much more active. **28. ... N×f3† 29. R×f3 B×f3 30. R×e5 Rg6† 31. Kf1 Rc6 32. Ke1 Rc2 33. Re3 Bg4 34. f3** Giving up his last chance to achieve something by 34. Nf6 Bf5 35. Re2. **34. ... Be6 35. Re2 R×e2†** Keeping his more active rook on the board simplifies his task to draw. **36. K×e2 B×a2 37. b4 Bd5 38. f4 Bc6 39. Ke3 Kg8 40. Kd4 Kf7 41. Nc7 Bb7 42. Kc5 Kf6 43. Kb6 Bf3 44. K×a6 Kf5 45. K×b5** Bird is now even two pawns ahead, but there is no chance of winning the game as Steinitz' bishop can always give its life against the one pawn, the b-pawn, that counts. **45. ... Bc6† 46. Kc5 K×f4 47. b5 Kg4 48. b6 Kh3 49. Nd5 K×h2 50. Nb4 Ba8 51. Kd6 Kg3 52. K×d7 Kf4 53. Kc7 Ke5 54. Kd7 Kd4 55. Kc7 Kc5** drawn game—*Illustrated London News* (Staunton), 17 November 1866.

### (175) Steinitz–Bird    1–0
Match (game 13)
London, October 1866
*C01*

1. e4 e6 2. d4 d5 3. Nc3 Nf6 4. Bg5 Be7 5. e×d5 e×d5 6. Bd3 Bg4 7. f3 Be6 8. Nge2 c5 9. d×c5 B×c5 10. Qd2 Nbd7 11. Bb5 Be7 12. 0-0-0 0-0 13. B×d7 N×d7 14. B×e7 Q×e7 15. Nf4 Nb6 16. Rhe1 Rfd8 17. Qe3 Nc4 18. Nf×d5 Qf8 19. Qf4 B×d5 20. N×d5 R×d5 21. R×d5 Qb4 22. Re4 Q×b2† 23. Kd1 Qb1† 24. Ke2 Q×c2† 25. Ke1 b5 26. Rd7 Rf8 27. R×f7 Qb1† 28. Kf2 Q×a2† 29. Kg3 Qa3 30. R×f8† Q×f8 31. Qg5 Qd6† 32. Kh3 Qd7† 33. g4 h6 34. Qg6 Nd6 35. Rd4 Qb7 36. Q×d6 Q×f3† 37. Qg3 Qf6 38. Qd3 a5 39. Rd8† Kf7 40. Qd5† and Black abandons the game—*Illustrated London News*, 10 November 1866.

### (176) Bird–Steinitz    ½–½
Match (game 14)
London, October 1866
*C65*

1. e4 e5 2. Nf3 Nc6 3. Bb5 Nf6 4. d4 N×d4 5. N×d4 e×d4 6. e5 c6 7. 0-0 c×b5 8. Bg5 Be7 9. e×f6 B×f6 10. Re1† Kf8 11. B×f6 Q×f6 12. Qe2 g6 13. Nd2 d6 14. Q×b5 a6 15. Qd5 Bf5 16. Ne4 B×e4 17. R×e4 Kg7 18. g3 Rac8 19. Rf4 Qe6 20. Q×b7 R×c2 21. Rd1 Q×a2 22. b3 Rf8 23. Qd5 and the game was drawn by mutual consent—*The Field*, 3 November 1866.

### (177) Steinitz–Bird    ½–½
Match (game 15)
London 1866
*C01*

1. e4 e6 2. d4 d5 3. Nc3 Nf6 4. Bg5 Be7 5. e×d5 e×d5 6. Bd3 0-0 7. Nf3 Bg4 8. 0-0 Nc6 9. Ne2 9. Re1 is perfectly safe. Black's best play is 9. ... B×f3! 10. g×f3 Nh5!, with excellent play on the black squares. **9. ... Ne4 10. Be3 f5 11. c3** Both players ignore the strength of 10. ... B×f3. Here 11. Ne5! would have turned the omission of this exchange to his advantage. **11. ... Kh8 12. Nf4 Qd6 13. h3 g5 14. N×d5 B×f3** "Correct play. 14. ... Q×d5 would not have been judicious: 14. h×g4 f×g4 15. c4 etc."—Bird. **15. g×f3 Q×d5 16. f×e4 f×e4 17. Be2** *(see diagram)*

*After 17. Be2*

**17. ... Bd6** 17. ... Rf3 (Staunton) looks threatening, but White can ward off any Black threats: 18. Kg2! Raf8 (the mainline given by Staunton. 18. ... g4? isn't convincing after 19. h×g4! Rg8 20. Rh1 when White's king reaches safety with a material edge in a few moves) 19. Rh1 R3f7 20. Qb3. The material is equal, but the bishop pair favors White (two other lines were refuted by Staunton: 18. Qb3? Qf5 19. Q×b7 Q×h3 20. Q×a8† Kg7 wins, just as 18. B×f3? e×f3 19. c4 Qf5). **18. Bg4 Qf7 19. Qe2** White now enjoys a small but stable edge thanks to his bishop pair. **19. ... Qg6 20. Rae1 Qg8 21. c4 Qg7 22. Rd1 Rab8 23. c5 Bf4 24. d5 B×e3 25. d×c6?!** A badly judged exchange. After 25. f×e3 Ne5 26. d6, White's chances remain preferable. **25. ... B×c5 26. c×b7** 26. Qc4! at once is stronger. **26. ... Qe5!** Bird correctly centralizes his queen. From e5 it threatens White's king. **27. Qc4 h5?!** "Finely played. The only move on the board, we believe, by which the game could have been saved"—Staunton. 27. ... Bd6! is a refinement. White is forced to opt for 28. R×d6! (the endgame after 28. Qc3? Q×c3 29. b×c3 R×b7 is much better for Black. He has real winning chances due to the many weaknesses on the queenside) 28. ... c×d6 29. Bc8 Re8! 30. Qc7 with unclear play. **28. Bc8!**

"The coup juste. If he had taken the pawn, he would have lost the fight: 28. B×h5 Qg3† 29. Kh1 Q×h3†"—Staunton. **28. ... Qg3† 29. Kh1 Qf3† 30. Kh2 Qf4†** 30. ... Bd6†? is not good at all: 31. Kg1! g4 32. Qc3†. **31. Kh1 Qf3† 32. Kh2 Qf4†** and the game was abandoned as a draw—*Illustrated London News* (Staunton), 24 November 1866; *Modern Chess* (Bird), pp. 121–122.

## (178) Bird–Steinitz    1–0

Match (game 16)
London 1866
C84

**1. e4 e5 2. Nf3 Nc6 3. Bb5 Nf6 4. d4 e×d4 5. e5 Ne4 6. 0–0 a6 7. Ba4 Be7 8. c3 d×c3 9. b×c3 0–0 10. Qd5 Nc5 11. Bc2 b6 12. Be3 Bb7 13. B×c5 B×c5 14. e6 d×e6 15. B×h7† K×h7 16. Qh5† Kg8 17. Ng5 Re8??** "It is remarkable that two players of eminence in an important match should commit such palpable errors as these before us. White has sacrificed a piece and his best pawn for an attack which is utterly untenable, since his adversary, by now playing 17. ... Qd3, is at once free from danger, while Black, instead of making the obvious move, which saves his game, adopts one which a child in chess would see must lose it"—Staunton. **18. Q×f7† Kh8 19. Qh5† Kg8 20. Qh7† Kf8 21. Qh8† Ke7 22. Q×g7†** and Black resigns—*Illustrated London News* (Staunton), 29 December 1866.

## (179) Steinitz–Bird    1–0

Match (game 17)
London 1866
C01

**1. e4 e6 2. d4 g6 3. Nf3 Nc6 4. d5 Nce7 5. d×e6 d×e6 6. Q×d8† K×d8 7. Nc3 Nc6 8. Bf4 f6 9. 0–0–0† Bd7 10. Bb5 h5 11. e5 f5 12. Rd2 Ke8 13. Rhd1 Rh7 14. Ng5 Bh6 15. B×c6 b×c6 16. Na4** "And the game was adjourned and remains unfinished, though not undecided, as White has a winning position"—Boden. "Here, Mr. Bird being compelled by business to leave England for a few weeks, the game and the match both came to an abrupt termination. The result is not satisfactory, but the play shows that the English amateur, in practice, and undisturbed by business cares, is quite capable of holding his own against Steinitz"—Staunton. *The Field* (Boden), 10 November 1866; *Illustrated London News* (Staunton), 5 January 1867.

## THE AFTERMATH

Bird thus had to leave the battle scene quite suddenly. He anticipated returning before the end of the year and continuing to play, but his opponent had other plans.

The course of chess matches, like that of true love, seems rarely to run smooth. Since our last notice of the above contest—when the score stood Bird 5; Steinitz 6; and 5 games drawn—the play has been brought to an abrupt close, and will not, it is said, be again resumed. Mr. Bird, it appears, has been obliged by urgent business to leave England for America; but, as his return is not likely to be delayed beyond the end of next month, he endeavored to make arrangements with his opponents for concluding the match at that time. The

latter, however, considering that the struggle had been sufficiently protracted, and finding, perhaps, that it was becoming unpleasantly close, has declined an armistice and claimed the stakes. We are not aware that any fixed time was agreed upon for the duration of the match, but we are told that Mr. Steinitz's demand will not be disputed, and that the contest may, therefore, be considered at an end [*Illustrated London News*, 24 November 1866].

Steinitz thought Staunton's description of his claiming of the stakes highly tendentious as appears from a letter published in the *Illustrated London News* on 8 December.

Sir, Will you allow me to correct some erroneous statements ... respecting the score and the stipulations of my match with Mr. Bird. The final score, when Mr. Bird left for America, was: myself, 7; Mr. Bird, 5; and 5 draws. There had been a stipulation, made in the first instance, practically limiting the duration of the match, as it had been arranged that four games a week should be played at least. ... But, as the match had been protracted already for two months and a half, I had not alone an undoubted right to claim the victory on Mr. Bird's departure for America, but I was bound in honor and duty not to ignore my backer's interest, especially as the latter had left it entirely to my own discretion to decide the question of a further adjournment; and I therefore claimed the stakes, with the full approbation of all the parties concerned in the match. Mr. Bird very chivalrously accepted my proposal of giving him his revenge in another contest on his return from America, which I hope will prove a fairer test of our relative strength than the last one. Mr. Bird had evidently been very much out of play at the commencement of the last match, and would, in consequence, have had to fight against the disadvantage of being two games behind in the score if the match had been resumed; whereas, in a fresh contest, he will start even. Yours obediently, William Steinitz [*Illustrated London News*, 8 December 1866].

In *A Slight Chess Retrospect and Explanation* (p. 2), Bird did not agree with Steinitz' statement on his backer. Backers were usually rewarded with a part of the profit. In this case it is much more likely that is was particularly Steinitz who needed the money. Bird wrote that "the gentleman who backed Mr. Steinitz said that he would have much preferred the match being played out." According to Bird, he did not give Steinitz the authority to demand the stakes.

Staunton's remarks on Steinitz' letter followed promptly. He declared himself unaware of a seventh win by Steinitz and of any arrangements on the number of games that had to be played weekly but he did quote from a column in which some more details on the finish of the match were provided.

Mr. Bird has been obliged to leave England for America, on urgent business, and before his departure proposed to his antagonist that the match should stand over until his return in December. As it is alleged that there had been no stipulation respecting time either for playing or concluding the match, this does not appear a very unreasonable proposal. Herr Steinitz, however, claimed the stakes in default of the match being played out without delay, and as it was impossible to comply with this condition Mr. Bird resigned [*Shields Daily News*, 28 November 1866].

These lines were written by Patrick Thomas Duffy. Bird and Duffy were affiliated with each other, as Bird allegedly made use of his high position in Coleman, Turquand, Youngs and Company to deliver Duffy a post in the same firm during the early 1860s.[17] Duffy also played a role during the termination of the match.

When the 17th game [*sic*] was in progress I received a telegram requesting my early presence in America on business of our firm, and at their request I

---

17. *Letters to John G. White relating to chess*, vol. I, letter 79. This item from the collection of the Cleveland Public Library contains letters written from 1875 until 1900 by the Scottish master George Brunton Fraser to the Cleveland chess bibliophile John Griswold White. These letters mainly deal with purchases of chess works and manuscripts Fraser did for White, but also contain some valuable information concerning Bird.

started two days afterwards. To oblige Mr. Steinitz I commenced the 18th game [*sic*], but was unable to proceed further with it, and my stakes were paid over for me by Mr. P.T. Duffy, my colleague and a representative of our firm, who had full authority to act on my behalf at his own discretion [*Modern Chess*, p. 35].

The outcome of this match had a great influence on British chess in the following decades. Just a few weeks after Steinitz' claim of the stakes Staunton started the process to burn down Steinitz' reputation by severely condemning what he called "professionalism."

> On more than one occasion we have deprecated the spirit of professionalism which of late years has crept into and debased our favorite game. Nowadays, the cause of chess is nothing, courtesy is nothing, justice and honor are nothing, victory is everything [*Illustrated London News*, 29 December 1866].

Many years later, in his own magazine *International Chess Magazine* ( July 1888, p. 211), Steinitz affirmed that the effect of Staun-

**Patrick T. Duffy (courtesy Cleveland Public Library).**

ton's words were soon tangible. Early in 1867 the campaign of the "almighty ruler of public opinion's," as Steinitz called Staunton, obliged him to leave the Westminster Chess Club.

Steinitz continued to reside in London until 1882. These years were marked by a growing tension between amateur and professional chess. The latter category was often despised, especially when a xenophobic element entered the play. It was above all Steinitz who was targeted by the press. Duffy, perhaps one of England's most influential journalists during the 1870s, had a decisive impact when it came to attacking Steinitz.[18]

It is tempting to see the match between Bird and Steinitz and the discussions about the stakes as the watershed in this evolution. Bird clearly stood on Duffy's side, but he nevertheless emphasized in *Modern Chess* (p. 36) that he kept harmonious relations with Steinitz, certainly at the time of the match.[19]

Bird also returned to this point in his chess career in *A Slight Chess Retrospect and Explanation*. Bird cared but little for any possible rise of professionalism in chess at the time. It was Steinitz' unfulfilled promise of a return match that bothered him the most.

> There is also another point which I cannot help thinking at times has something to do with it. When I quitted the chess circle after my closely-contested match with Steinitz in 1867 [*sic*], I was on very pleasant and friendly terms with all classes of the chess community. That match was played shortly after the one between Anderssen and Steinitz, in which the latter was successful. My score was the best ever yet made against Steinitz; but, unfortunately, I had to resign the match at a highly interesting stage after the twenty-first game [*sic*], in consequence of business which called me suddenly to America.
>
> Steinitz, of course, received the stakes, and also presents equivalent thereto for adjournments, but there was an understanding that he should play me a return match on the first convenient occasion, but this engagement he has never fulfilled. The severe comments that were made by the leading chess organ when the stakes were demanded and the subsequent troubles at the Westminster Chess Club took place during my absence in Pennsylvania. I did not sympathize with the complaints against Steinitz; on the contrary, on my return I was his warm supporter. Being my own backer, and having requested that the stakes should be paid over, I could not see what right at the time Staunton, the Committee of the Westminster Chess Club, or anyone else had to complain. I remained, therefore, on very good terms with Steinitz, but these circumstances, nevertheless, I believe have always left an unpleasant feeling on his mind [*A Slight Chess Retrospect and Explanation*, p. 2].

The turmoil around this match left serious scars on Steinitz' soul. At least from his point of view Bird was partly guilty as he continued to emphasize his right for a return match. Many of their future conflicts can be traced back to the 1866 match that started under such favorable auspices.

18. Given the fanaticism with which Duffy attacked Steinitz, Fraser suspected that personal motives played a role. See *Letters to John G. White relating to chess*, vol. I, letter 90.

19. An interesting perspective on the relationship between Bird and Steinitz was given by Buckley, an intimate of both men. He focused on the tension between them in his recollections: "When Bird and Steinitz came together then was the tug of war. Bird detested Steinitz; Steinitz despised Bird. They were fairly matched for bitterness, but Bird was often jocular, while Steinitz was always bitter. In the thrust and riposte of repartee Bird had the advantage, his thought more nimble, his reply more unexpected, the laugh that followed usually disconcerting his opponent and leaving Bird in possession of the field. ¶ "One day, styles of play being discussed by Bird, Steinitz, Captain Mackenzie, and the gallery of Simpson's, Mackenzie said: 'After all, Steinitz, you can't compare yourself with Morphy.' 'Morphy did not create a gambit; I did,' urged Steinitz. 'Therefore I can claim to have the advantage of Morphy.' Bird cut in at once: 'Blackmar has invented two gambits. Therefore he can claim the advantage of Steinitz.' A ripple of subdued laughter ran round the gallery. 'Again,' resumed Steinitz; 'I introduced a bolder play of the king. I bring him out: make him work right in the middle of the board. Now, what did Morphy do? He simply castled!' 'Not a very bad idea,' murmured Mackenzie. Another little ripple. Warming rapidly, Steinitz continued: 'In the opening I play my king—not in the endgame only. With all the pieces on the board! Every one of them! I play him out!! I play him alone!!! I play...' 'You play the fool, mostly,' Bird edged in." *Chess Amateur*, June 1913, pp. 271–2. ¶ Both gambits invented by Blackmar were mentioned in J.W. Miller's book *The American Supplements to the Synopsis Containing American Inventions in the Chess Openings*. W.W. Morgan: London, 1885, p. 84. Besides the well-known Blackmar (later Blackmar-Diemer) Gambit, 1. d4 d5 2. e4 d×e4 3. f3, he used a similar approach against the Dutch Defense: 1. d4 f5 2. e4 f×e4 3. f3.

# QUIET YEARS 1866–1868

Bird claimed that the telegram which arrived during his 17th game with Steinitz obliged him to break off the match urgently. Yet he was in no hurry to leave London. *The Field* was the first to announce the end of the match on 3 November, while Bird arrived in New York on 27 November. As Bird crossed the Atlantic on board the *Scotia* in probably not more than nine or ten days,[20] there is quite a gap, at least two weeks, between the abrupt end of the game and his actual departure from England, time he probably spent making arrangements for his family.

Bird stayed in New York for a month. The *Albion* of 23 February 1867 reported one of Bird's feats at the local chess club, where he narrowly beat Mackenzie with four against three. Bird returned to London on 26 December. In January 1867 the Westminster Chess Club made plans for another grand handicap tournament, even though the first one was not yet finished. Bird was listed as a participant, but he ultimately refrained from playing. Undoubtedly his professional affairs prevented his attendance.

Now a blank period began. Bird's name popped up again only at the end of the spring of 1868, when he and Boden delighted the spectators with their chess sessions.

**(180) Boden–Bird**    ½–½
Offhand game
London (Westminster C.C.) 1868
*C50*

1. e4 e5 2. Bc4 Nc6 3. d3 f5 4. Nf3 Be7 5. Nc3 Nf6 6. Ng5 d5 7. e×d5 Na5 8. d6 Q×d6 9. Nf7 N×c4 10. N×d6† N×d6 11. 0–0 0–0 12. f4 e4 13. d4 Be6 14. Ne2 Rad8 15. c3 c5 16. h3 Bc4 17. b3 Ba6 18. c4 b5 19. Ba3 b×c4 20. B×c5 Nd5 21. Rf2 e3 22. Rf3 Bf6 23. Rc1 c3 24. N×c3 N×c3 25. R×c3 e2 26. Qe1 Ne4 27. Rc1 B×d4† 28. B×d4 R×d4 29. Re3 Rfd8 30. R×e2 B×e2 31. Q×e2 h6 32. Qa6 Kh7 33. Q×a7 R8d6 34. Qa5 R4d5 35. Qe1 Rd2 36. Ra1 Rg6 37. g4 Rd3 38. Qf1 Rg3† 39. Kh2 f×g4 40. Re1 R×h3† 41. Q×h3 g×h3 42. R×e4 Rg2† 43. K×h3 R×a2 given up as a draw—*Westminster Chess Club Papers*, May 1868, p. 17.

In June 1868 Bird got elected to both the managing and general committee of the B.C.A. while he also kept on playing in the Westminster Club and at the Divan.

The following game created some buzz in the press. It was first printed in the *Westminster Chess Club Papers* of August 1868 (p. 55) with Steinitz as Bird's opponent. Five years later the game was reprinted in *The Field*. The game diverged at move 11 and De Vere, then *The Field*'s editor, named himself as being Black. Skipworth commented on this when he republished the game.

**(181) Bird–De Vere**    1–0
Offhand game
London (Westminster C.C.), September 1868
*C65*

"We published a game from the *Westminster Papers*..., which,

we have little doubt, was an imperfect copy of the present game. It purported to be won by Mr. Bird of Mr. Steinitz; but as Mr. De Vere himself edits the chess column in *The Field*, he is not likely to be mistaken as to a game lost by himself. The amended version, moreover, is intrinsically the better of the two, and we feel sure that our readers will like to see it reprinted"—Skipworth.

1. e4 e5 2. Nf3 Nc6 3. Bb5 Nf6 4. d4 e×d4 5. e5 Ne4 6. N×d4 Be7 7. 0–0 N×d4 8. Q×d4 Nc5 9. f4 b6? "The intention of this move was, as will be seen, to win the exchange. Mr. Bird, however, very properly ignored it"—De Vere. **10. f5 Nb3 11. Qg4?!** Actually the move 11. Qe4!, which was the main move when the game was published in 1868, is the superior choice. The termination in that game was very convincing: 11. ... N×a1 12. f6 Bc5† 13. Kh1 Rb8 14. e6 and Black resigns. A possible finish would be very similar as in this game: 14. ... Rg8 15. Q×h7 Rf8 16. e×f7† R×f7 17. Re1† Be7 18. Qg8† Rf8 19. f7 mate. MacDonnell reprinted this version in the *Illustrated Sporting and Dramatic News* of 13 June 1891. **11. ... N×a1 12. Q×g7 Rf8 13. f6 Bc5† 14. Kh1 N×c2?** This move loses quickly after Bird's unexpected reply. First 14. ... c6! creates a different situation: 15. Bc4 (not good is 15. e6?! d×e6 16. B×c6† Bd7 17. B×a8 Q×a8, when White has not enough to compensate for the material disadvantage. Pretty unclear is 15. Bd3 d5) 15. ... N×c2! and now 16. e6? loses offhand. Better is 16. Bh6 d5 17. e×d6 *e.p.* Q×d6 18. Nd2 Bh3 and Black's king escapes from the center. The resulting position is very unclear. **15. e6!** "Capital. White played throughout with great brilliancy and judgment"—De Vere. **15. ... Nd4 16. e×f7† R×f7 17. Re1† Be7 18. Qg8† Rf8 19. f7** mate—*The Field* (De Vere), 5 April 1873; *Chess Player's Chronicle* (Skipworth), June 1873, p. 268; *Westminster Chess Club Papers*, August 1868, p. 55.

In January 1869 the *Westminster Chess Club Papers* was the first magazine to describe Bird in some detail. His accounting career was then in its zenith and this was taken notice of.

We cannot part from Mr. Bird without observing that he is not a mere chess player, the game being to him but an occasional pastime. A nobler ambition than that of attaining excellence in chess has fired his soul and influenced his actions since he passed from boyhood into manhood; and now, by the sheer force of industry, ability and character, he has come to occupy a foremost place in his profession [*Westminster Chess Club Papers*, January 1869, pp. 110–111].

The same article also took a careful look at Bird's playing style. His strengths and weaknesses were meticulously listed.

In dash and vigor of attack, in ingenuity and beauty of combination, as also in rapidity of movement and general brilliancy of style, Mr. Bird is probably unsurpassed by any living player except Anderssen. ...

The truth is, Mr. Bird is wanting in certain moral qualities necessary for the production of a great chess master. He lacks patience, and also that from which patience springs—coolness of temperament. This is his chief defect. Another element of weakness in his game is his imperfect knowledge of openings, and his perfect ignorance of the best published games—in a word, book-ignorance. ...

Shot after shot in rapid succession, with well-directed aim and unflagging vigor, he pours into the enemy's weakest and therefore most vital part, utterly regardless all the time of the cannonading he himself may be receiving [*Westminster Chess Club Papers*, January 1869, p. 110].

---

20. The *Scotia* was the world's fastest vessel from 1863 until 1872.

# THE SECOND CHALLENGE CUP TOURNAMENT, LONDON 1868–1869

In October 1868 the British Chess Association announced the program for their next congress. Although the release came a bit late in the day as events were meant to start but a few weeks later the response was very positive. This was mainly thanks to the extensive program. With four major tournaments and several side events the congress had more the allure of a festival than a tournament.

During the first week of December all activities went through in the spacious St. James's Hall that was rented for four days. Several (blindfold) simultaneous exhibitions, consultation games and a telegraphic match were organized. Bird was present at the preliminary meeting and he took also part in one of the consultation games. Together with his colleague Duffy he defeated Blackburne and Ormond.

The focus of the spectators lay on the second edition of the Challenge Cup tournament. This was the only tournament in which Bird participated. Visitors could follow three other events: a handicap tournament, a knock-out tournament sponsored by the newspaper the *Glowworm* and the Mongredien tournament, with a mild sort of Fischerrandom Chess.[21]

The tournament for the Challenge Cup was open for British players only. The organizing committee had learned from the previous edition and lowered the entrance fee to £1 1s (one guinea). The number of participants doubled when compared with the first tournament. Among them were all the prominent players, such as De Vere and Blackburne. The first prize consisted of the Cup augmented by the sum of the entrance fees collected. A second prize of £10 10s. was foreseen. If De Vere could win the tournament he would be entitled to keep the Cup permanently.

It was determined that participants should play one game with each other but draws had to be replayed. As the tournament had to proceed quickly a strict regime of five games per week was imposed on the participants but it was left to them to arrange a particular date of play. The games were played at four different locations: the London, the Westminster and the St. George's Chess Clubs and at Simpson's Divan.

The course of the tournament is very hard to follow. A scheme with the partition of the colors was drawn up in advance, but not followed at all. A reconstruction has been made by Tony Gillam, and very recently Tim Harding had another look in his book on Blackburne. The present author's research, however, reveals that there remain some slight mistakes. There is no need to dilate on the matter but only to present some refinements in the form of a tournament table.

At a very early stage it had became clear that the tournament would drag on considerably. Only John Owen held himself rigorously to the scheme imposed by the organization. He started with six straight wins but lost his remaining four games against the favorites.[22]

Bird was one of the slow starters. He played two games during the first weeks of the tournament in which he beat Owen and William J. Hampton.[23] Two other players, Cuthbertson and Arthur Bolland Skipworth, rapidly forfeited their remaining games.

Attempts to find a rational path through the very diffuse newspaper reports that were published in December 1868, led ultimately to the conclusion that there is just one trustworthy report: the score of all the players given in *The Field* on 26 December 1868.[24] By adding published results of individual games from three sources (*The Field*, *Glowworm* and *The Weekly Dispatch*) it has been possible to draw up a working, preliminary table. The results put in ***bold italics*** are assumptions.[25] Draws and forfeits are not taken into account for this preliminary table.

| | | 1 | 2 | 3 | 4 | 5 | 6 | 7 | 8 | 9 | 10 | 11 | + | − |
|---|---|---|---|---|---|---|---|---|---|---|---|---|---|---|
| 1 | J.H. Blackburne | | 0 | 1 | 1 | | | 1 | 1 | 1 | 1 | | 6 | 1 |
| 2 | C.V. De Vere | | | 1 | | | *1* | | *1* | 1 | 1 | | 5 | 0 |
| 3 | G.A. MacDonnell | 1 | | | 0 | | | 0 | *1* | | 1 | 1 | 4 | 2 |
| 4 | J. Owen | 0 | 0 | 1 | | 0 | 0 | 1 | 1 | 1 | 1 | 1 | 6 | 4 |
| 5 | R.B. Wormald | 0 | | 1 | | | | 1 | | | 1 | 1 | 4 | 1 |
| 6 | H.E. Bird | | | 1 | | | | 1 | | | 1 | 1 | 4 | 0 |
| 7 | J. Wisker | *0* | 1 | 0 | | | | | | 1 | 1 | 1 | 4 | 2 |
| 8 | W.J. Hampton | 0 | 0 | 0 | 0 | 0 | | | | *1* | 1 | 1 | 3 | 5 |
| 9 | J. Lord | 0 | *0* | 0 | | | 0 | *0* | | | 1 | 1 | 2 | 5 |
| 10 | A.B. Skipworth | 0 | 0 | 0 | 0 | 0 | 0 | 0 | 0 | 0 | | 1 | 1 | 9 |
| 11 | A. Cuthbertson | 0 | 0 | 0 | 0 | 0 | 0 | 0 | 0 | 0 | 0 | | 0 | 10 |

On 9 January *The Field* reported a win for Bird against Wisker and a loss against Lord. It seems probable that the initial draw against Wisker, a young player from Hull who had settled in London to work as a journalist, was played at the end of 1868. This draw was already eventful, but the second game was truly spectacular. Both games were Bird's highlights of the tournament. Probably later in January Bird lost against MacDonnell, a loss that remained unreported.

Bird's chances for a high ranking, or in extraordinary circumstances even the tournament victory, were still existent, but since his form was rather bad nobody expected such an exploit. The game with De Vere was crucial. Bird luckily got out of the opening, obtained some vague chances in the middle game, but ultimately lost. In another important game Blackburne completely outplayed him positionally. Bird drew with his final opponent Wormald. A second, completely irrelevant, game was played only in May. Bird threw it away.

In the end Blackburne and De Vere ended tied for first. Black-

---

21. The starting positions were slightly altered in the Mongredien tournament: the bishops at f1 and f8 were switched with the knights at b1 and b8.

22. Bird was Owen's penultimate opponent. *Glowworm*, 8 December 1868.

23. Hampton's first name is rather unclear. The tournament book uses W., J.W. and W.J. as initials. In his obituary he is named William Hampton (*Land and Water*, 15 February 1873). His brother was Thomas Inglis Hampton.

24. Our main criterion has been that the accumulate positive and negative score of all the players should be 0.

25. Some remarks are necessary here. The chess columns in the *Glowworm* and *The Weekly Dispatch* were managed by Löwenthal, but they are so contradictory that they cannot be trusted. Just one reference found casts a shadow of doubt upon the present reconstruction. A main assumption has been the note in *The Field* of 9 January 1869 that "Mr. De Vere has also scored another Cup game against Mr. Wisker" refers to a game played before 26 December.

burne spoiled De Vere's hope of obtaining the Cup permanently in a deciding game late in March. The narrow difference in strength between Blackburne and De Vere suggested that a longer contest between them would be interesting. A few details were provided by Boden in his column in *The Field*. On 1 May, his readers were informed that the negotiations between Blackburne and De Vere had been broken off as the backer of the latter withdrew.

Bird ended in a modest sixth place far behind the two winners. He nevertheless audaciously challenged Blackburne to play a match with him for a small stake. As no further reference has been found one may assume that either the stakes proposed by Bird were too low or his result in the tournament was too meager, at least according to Blackburne.

## (182) Bird–Owen    1–0
B.C.A. Challenge Cup (round 1)
London, December 1868
*B00*

**1. e4 b6** John Owen's pet move. It was ultimately named after him. **2. d4 Bb7 3. Bd3 e6 4. Ne2 c5 5. 0–0 c4 6. B×c4 B×e4 7. Nbc3 Bb7 8. d5 Qc7 9. Qd3 a6 10. Bf4 e5 11. Bg3 b5?** Bird handled the position with care and the same is now required from his opponent. The text move loses some crucial tempi and creates unnecessary weaknesses. Instead, 11. ... d6 stabilizes the position sufficiently to get out of the opening, e.g., after 12. f4 f6 13. a4 Nd7. **12. Bb3** Bird overlooks a nice tactical sequence that leads to a winning position: 12. B×b5! a×b5 13. N×b5 Qb6 14. B×e5 Ba6 15. a4 and Black's king is hopelessly caught in the center. Nevertheless, Owen's position is already too compromised to survive. **12. ... Bc5 13. Kh1** Alternatively, Bird could initiate decisive play on the queenside: 13. a4 b4 14. Ne4 d6 15. a5 Nd7 16. Ba4 0–0–0 17. c3. **13. ... d6 14. f4! e×f4 15. N×f4 Ne7** (see diagram)

*After 15. ... Ne7*

**16. Qf3** This is a cunning move from Bird, with the intention to prevent his opponent from castling (if 16. ... 0–0 17. Ne6!) A nice win has been suggested by Löwenthal and Medley in the tournament book: 16. Nh5 0–0 17. Ne4 (threatening mate in three moves) 17. ... f5 (equally losing are 17. ... f6 18. Ne×f6† g×f6 19. N×f6† R×f6 20. R×f6 Nd7 21. Re6 Nf8 22. Qe2 N×e6 23. Q×e6† Kh8 24. Bh4 Ng8 25. Rf1 Bc8 26. Bf6† and 17. ... Ng6

18. Qc3 f6 19. N×d6) 18. Qc3 Rf7 (if 18. ... Ng6 19. N×c5 wins a piece, but if 18. ... N×d5, White would reply with 19. B×d5† following the attack up with N×c5, also in this case winning a piece) 19. Ng5. **16. ... Nf5 17. Rae1† Kd8 18. Qg4 Qd7 19. Bh4† Kc7 20. Nd3 N×h4 21. Q×h4 f6 22. Re6 Kb6 23. N×c5 K×c5 24. Qf2† Kb4 25. Qb6** and mates next move. A straightforward and most instructive game—*Tournament Book* (Löwenthal/Medley), pp. 38–39.

## (183) W.J. Hampton–Bird    0–1
B.C.A. Challenge Cup (round 2)
London, December 1868
*C44*

**1. e4 e5 2. Nf3 Nc6 3. c3 d5 4. Bb5 d×e4 5. N×e5 Bd7 6. N×d7 Q×d7 7. Qe2 0–0–0 8. 0–0 f5 9. Rd1 Bd6 10. d4 e×d3 *e.p.* 11. R×d3 Nf6 12. Qf3 Rhe8 13. Qd1 Qe6 14. Nd2 Qe5 15. R×d6 R×d6 16. Bf1 Ng4 17. g3 Red8 18. h3 Ne3 19. f×e3 Q×e3† 20. Kh1 R×d2 21. B×d2 R×d2 22. Qe1 Q×e1 23. R×e1 R×b2 24. Re2 R×e2 25. B×e2 Kd7 26. Kg2 Kd6 27. Kf3 g5 28. Ke3 Ke5 29. Bf3 Nd8 30. Kd3 c6 31. a4 Ne6 32. Kc4 a5 33. Be2 f4 34. g4 Kd6 35. Bf3 Nc5 36. Bd1 h6 37. Kd4 b5 38. a×b5 c×b5 39. c4 b4 40. Bc2 a4 41. Bb1 a3** and White resigns—*Tournament Book*, pp. 36–37.

## (184) Bird vs. Cuthbertson    1–0
B.C.A. Challenge Cup (round 3/4)
London, December 1868
*Game scored by default; colors unknown*

## (185) Bird vs. Skipworth    1–0
B.C.A. Challenge Cup (round 3/4)
London, December 1868
*Game scored by default; colors unknown*

### 2nd Challenge Cup tournament of the B.C.A., London, 24 November 1868–10 March 1869

**Site:** St. James's Hall, London Chess Club, St. George's Chess Club, Westminster Chess Club
**Prizes:** 1st a cup (worth £50, becomes property if won twice) and the entrance fees, 2nd £10 10s.
**Time limit:** 20 moves per hour

|  | 1 | 2 | 3 | 4 | 5 | 6 | 7 | 8 | 9 | 10 | 11 |  |
|---|---|---|---|---|---|---|---|---|---|---|---|---|
| 1 J.H. Blackburne |  | 1 | 0 | 1 | 1 | 1 | ½ 1 | 1 | 1 | + | 1 | 9 |
| 2 C.V. De Vere | 0 |  | ½ 1 | 1 | ½ 1 | 1 | ½ 1 | 1 | 1 | + | 1 | 9 |
| 3 G.A. MacDonnell | 1 | ½ 0 |  | 0 |  | 1 | 0 | ½ 1 | 1 | 1 | + | 6 |
| 4 J. Owen | 0 | 0 | 1 |  | ½ 0 | 0 | 1 | 1 | 1 | 1 | 1 | 6 |
| 5 R.B. Wormald | 0 | ½ 0 |  | ½ 1 |  | ½ 1 | 1 | 1 | 1 | + | + | 6 |
| 6 H.E. Bird | 0 | 0 | 0 | 1 | ½ 0 |  | ½ 1 | 1 | 0 | + | + | 5 |
| 7 J. Wisker | ½ 0 | ½ 0 | 1 | 0 | 0 | ½ 0 |  | 0 | 1 | + | 1 | 4 |
| 8 W.J. Hampton | 0 | 0 | ½ 0 | 0 | 0 | 0 | 1 |  | 1 | + | 1 | 4 |
| 9 J. Lord | 0 | 0 | 0 | 0 | 1 | 0 | 0 |  | 1 | 1 | 3 |
| 10 A.B. Skipworth | – | – | 0 | 0 | – | – | – | – | 0 |  | 1 | 1 |
| 11 A. Cuthbertson | 0 | 0 | – | 0 | – | – | 0 | 0 | 0 | 0 |  | 0 |

*Tie game:*

| J.H. Blackburne | 1 |
| C.V. De Vere | 0 |

## (186) Bird–Wisker   ½–½
B.C.A. Challenge Cup (round 5, game 1)
London, December 1868
C84

**1. e4 e5 2. Nf3 Nc6 3. Bb5 a6 4. Ba4 Nf6 5. d4 e×d4 6. 0–0 Be7 7. Re1 0–0 8. e5 Ne8 9. N×d4 N×d4 10. Q×d4 d5 11. Nc3** A clumsy move. The knight is not particularly well placed, and, more important, the bishop remains out of play on the queenside. First 11. c4! avoids this problem. **11. … c6 12. Qd1 Be6** Routinely played. Stronger is 12. … f6!, opening up the position for his pieces. **13. Bb3 Qd7 14. Na4 Qc7 15. Nc3 h6 16. Bf4 Rd8 17. Ne2 c5 18. c3 Qc6 19. Rc1 f5** Radical, but played with a specific idea in mind. 19. … Bf5 is safe and clean. **20. e×f6 e.p. N×f6?!** (see diagram)

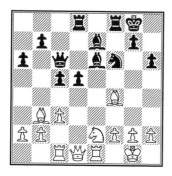

*After 20. … N×f6*

Wisker pursues his plan, and finally gets away with it, as Bird misses 21. Nd4! after which he obtains a most dominant position; e.g., 21. … c×d4 22. c×d4 Bg4 (22. … Qd7 23. Rc7 loses quickly) 23. f3 B×f3 24. Q×f3 Qe8 25. Be5. **21. Ng3?! Ne4!** The point of Wisker's previous moves; he intends to make good use of the open f-file. **22. Be3 c4 23. Bc2?!** Logical, and foreseen by Wisker, but the subtle zwischenzug 23. Ba4! b5 24. Bc2 renders 24. … N×f2 less dangerous. After 25. Qd4!, Black cannot play 25. … Bf6, due to 26. Qb6 (the point of the zwischenzug: the queen is not covered anymore) and he loses a piece. Instead 25. … Ng4 26. Nh5 Bf6 27. Qb6 Rd6 28. Q×c6 R×c6 29. N×f6† N×f6 is nothing special for him. White's bishop pair fully compensates the lost pawn. **23. … N×f2!** "The position is now interesting. If the bishop were to capture the knight, Black would obtain the best game by 24. … R×f2"—Löwenthal/Medley. **24. Qh5** The position is extremely difficult to defend. If 24. B×f2? R×f2†. Still preferable is 24. Qd4! when Black can chose between two moves. 24. … Ng4 seems strong after 25. Nh5 Nf6, as 26. Qb6 is not possible anymore. But White can play the surprising 26. N×g7! K×g7 27. B×h6†! K×h6 28. Qe3† Kg7 29. Qg5† Kh8 30. Qh6† which leads to a draw. 24. … Bf6! might be played with ambition. After 25. Qb6 Nd3 26. Q×c6 b×c6 27. B×d3 c×d3 28. Red1 d4! the endgame is slightly more promising for Black. **24. … Bc5** This move is much too timid. In contrast, harassing the queen with 24. … Bg4! is burdensome for Bird. With g6 covered, he must play 25. Qe5 and now both 25. … Bf6 or 25. … Bd6 are strong suggestions. A sample line: 25. … Bd6 26. Qd4 B×g3 27. h×g3 Ne4 28. B×e4 d×e4 29. Qc5 Qe6 30. Bd4 Rf5 31. Qb6 Q×b6 32. B×b6 Rd2 33. R×e4 R×b2 34. R×g4 R×b6 35. R×c4 Rb2, with much the better ending. **25. Qg6 Rf6?** A blunder that ought to lose the game quickly. 25. … Nd3, to exchange White's

dangerous bishop and return the pawn, was necessary. **26. Qh7† Kf8 27. Nh5 Rf7 28. Bd4?** Very bad. There is no remedy against 28. Bg6 (Löwenthal/Medley). **28. … B×d4 29. c×d4 Qb6 30. Bb1?** Bird goes astray, but all future nuances were very hard to foresee. The cool 30. h3! keeps Black's advantage within bounds. 30. … Q×d4?? is impossible because of 31. R×e6, when there is no mate. The best reply is 30. … Ne4! After 31. B×e4 d×e4 32. R×e4 R×d4, Black has a material as well as positional advantage. **30. … Ne4** Good enough but 30. … Q×d4 (Löwenthal/Medley) is much easier. **31. B×e4 Q×d4† 32. Kh1 d×e4 33. R×e4 Qd1† 34. Re1 Q×h5?** Wisker misses the winning combination, which involves a subtle piece sacrifice. The combination of a weak back rank and strong passed pawn could be exploited thus: 34. … Qd3! 35. Q×d3 c×d3 36. R×e6 d2 37. Rd1 and now 37. … Rc8! wins the house. **35. R×e6 Rd1† 36. Re1 R×e1† 37. R×e1 Re7 38. Rf1† Rf7** game draw by mutual consent—*Tournament Book* (Löwenthal/Medley), pp. 39–40.

## (187) Wisker–Bird   0–1
B.C.A. Challenge Cup (round 5, game 2)
London, December 1868
C35

**1. e4 e5 2. f4 e×f4 3. Nf3 Be7 4. Bc4 Bh4† 5. Kf1 d5 6. B×d5 Nf6 7. Nc3 c6 8. Bb3 Ng4 9. Qe2 0–0? 10. d3 Bg5 11. g3 Ne3† 12. B×e3?** Bird's opening has not been very convincing due to his neglect of the f-pawn, which has now come under fire. This would have been highlighted by the cold-blooded 12. Ke1!, when Black's knight becomes very unstable. After the forced 12. … Bh3 (the h-pawn must be neutralized. If 12. … Qf6? 13. h4!) 13. Rg1!, the knight must retreat by 13. … Ng4. 14. e5! is then a last precise move, after which Black cannot cope decently with the idea 15. Ne4 and 16. g×f4. **12. … f×e3?!** The zwischenzug 12. … Bh3†! renders him equality, e.g., 13. Kg1 f×e3 14. N×g5 Q×g5 15. Re1. **13. N×g5 Q×g5 14. Re1?!** "14. Kg2 would have been the correct play"—Löwenthal/Medley. The point being that Bird's next move is prevented. **14. … Bh3†! 15. Kg1 Nd7 16. Q×e3 Qh5** Despite some complications Bird survived the opening quite well after all. He is a pawn down, but in return White's king is badly placed and the rook is out of play. **17. Ne2 g5! 18. d4 Kh8 19. c3?** (see diagram)

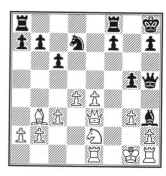

*After 19. c3*

Innocent looking, but in fact a dreadful mistake! Wisker ought to have moved his queen, to d2 or c3, to minimize the impact of the subsequent pawn push. **19. … f5! 20. Bd1** There is nothing better: 20. g4 Q×g4† 21. Qg3 keeps the f-pawn back for a while, but the position is hopeless. If 20. Qd3 f×e4 21. Q×e4 Rae8 23. Qd3 R×e2! **20. ... f4!** Bird is now in his element. **21. Qf2 f×g3 22. Q×g3 Rf3** 22. ... Qf7! decides the game even faster. **23. Nf4 g×f4** "If 23. ... R×g3†?, White could only have obtained in exchange for his queen a rook and minor piece, with no enduring attack"—Löwenthal/Medley. **24. B×f3** "Obviously, he could not have captured the rook with queen, on account of 24. ... Rg8† 25. Kf2 Qh4†"—Löwenthal/Medley. **24. ... f×g3?** Without a doubt played instantly, as Bird saw he would capture the rook at h1 and remain a piece up. But by doing so he allows Wisker to reach an endgame with two pawns for the piece, which is much more than he could have hoped for. The cool 24. ... Qh6! rings down the curtain on the game. **25. B×h5 g2 26. Re3 g×h1Q† 27. K×h1 Be6 28. b3 Rg8 29. c4 Rg5 30. Be2 Kg7 31. Rg3?** A miscalculation. After either 31. h3 or 31. h4 it is no easy task to force a win. **31. ... Kg6?!** Bird could pave a royal way along the black squares for the king with 31. ... R×g3 32. h×g3 c5! 33. d5 Bf7. **32. Kg2** Now the king is in time to prevent an immediate loss. Still, 32. ... c5! is still the best move. **32. ... Nf6 33. Bd3** In the long run, 33. Bf3 should also not be enough to draw: 33. ... h5 34. h4 R×g3† 35. K×g3 Bg4 36. e5 B×f3 37. K×f3 Ng8 38. Ke4 Ne7 39. d5 c×d5† 40. c×d5 Kf7 41. d6 Ng6 42. Kd5 N×h4 43. e6† Ke8. This line is symptomatic for various of the following variations. Black can trigger his opponent's central pawns to move on, after which his pieces will chase White's king from the center. In the end, Black's king will take over the defense, and his own pawns decide the game. **33. ... Nh5 34. R×g5† K×g5 35. c4** (see diagram)

*After 35. c4*

**35. ... h6** He misses 35. ... c5 again. 36. d5 Bg4† wins easy, just as 36. d×c5 Kf6. A nice line is 36. Ke3 c×d4† 37. K×d4 Nf4 38. Bc2 Ng6 39. Kc5 Kf6 40. Kd6 b6 41. Kc7 Ke7 42. Bd3 Ne5 43. Be2 Bh3 44. Bd1 h6 45. Bc2 h5 46. Kb7 Kd8 47. b4 Bc8† 48. K×a7 Kc7 49. Ba4 N×c4. **36. a4 a5** 36. ... Bg4† followed by 37. ... Bd1 wins quickly. **37. d5 Bg4† 38. Ke3 c5 39. e5 Bd1** "This enables White to push his d-pawn forward immediately, but the loss of time is of little consequence, if Black plays correctly afterwards"—Löwenthal/Medley. **40. d6 Bg4 41. Be4 Be6?!** 41. ... Ng7! is the best move here. If 42. B×b7 Kf5 43. Bc8† Ne6 wins. **42. B×b7 Ng7 43. Bc6 Bh3 44. d7?!** Losing quickly. The alternative 44. Kf3 may also lose, but it demands the utmost precise play from his opponent; e.g., 44. ... h5 45. Bd5! (the best move. The bishop now controls e6, the ideal square for Black's knight. But Black can play around it. 45. ... Nf5! (45. ... Ne6 is probably not winning: 46. B×e6 B×e6 47. Ke4 h4 48. d7 B×d7 49. Kd5 Bg4 50. K×c5 Kf5 51. Kb6 Bd1 52. K×a5 B×b3 53. Kb4 Bd1 54. a5 K×e5 55. a6 Bf3 56. c5 Bg2 57. Kc3 Bc6 58. a7 and White's king makes it just in time for the kingside: 58. ...

Kd5 59. Kd3 K×c5 60. Ke3 Kb6 61. Kf4 h3 62. Kg3 Bg2 63. a8B with a draw) 46. Ke4 Nd4 47. Bg8 Bg2† 48. Ke3 (48. Kd3 is inferior 48. ... Kf5 49. Bd5 Bf1† 50. Ke3 Ne6 with zugzwang) 48. ... Bc6 49. Bd5 Bd7 50. Ke4 Bf5† 51. Ke3 h4 52. Be4 Be6 and White is in zugzwang. **44. ... Ne6 45. b4 c×b4 46. c5 Nd8 47. Bb5 Bg2 48. Kd4 Kf5** and Black wins—*Tournament Book* (Löwenthal/Medley), pp. 40–42.

## (188) Bird–J. Lord    0–1
B.C.A. Challenge Cup (round 6)
London, January 1869
*C41*

**1. e4 e5 2. Nf3 d6 3. d4 Nd7 4. Nc3 Ngf6 5. Be3 Be7 6. Bc4 0–0 7. 0–0 c6 8. a4 e×d4 9. B×d4 N×e4 10. N×e4 d5 11. B×d5 c×d5 12. Nc3 Nb8 13. Be5 Be6 14. B×b8 R×b8 15. Nd4 Rc8 16. N×e6 f×e6 17. Qg4 Rf6 18. Rad1 Rg6 19. Qe2 Bd6 20. Rd3 Qh4 21. g3 Qh3 22. f4 Rf8 23. Kh1 Bc5 24. Qg2 Qf5 25. Re1 Rgf6 26. h4 Bb4 27. Kh2 Qg4 28. Re5 h6 29. Nd1 Bd6 30. Nf2 Qg6 31. Re2 Bc5 32. Nh3 Bd6 33. Rd1 Rc8 34. c3 Rc4 35. a5 Bc7 36. Rde1 B×a5 37. f5 Q×f5 38. Rf2 Qg4 39. R×f6 g×f6 40. Nf4 Bc7 41. R×e6 B×f4 42. R×f6 Q×h4†** White resigns—*Westminster Chess Club Papers*, December 1868, p. 103.

## (189) MacDonnell–Bird    1–0
B.C.A. Challenge Cup (round 7)
London, January 1869
*C61*

**1. e4 e5 2. Nf3 Nc6 3. Bb5 Nd4 4. N×d4 e×d4 5. d3 Qh4 6. 0–0 Nf6 7. Nd2 Bc5 8. f4 0–0 9. Nf3 Qh5 10. e5 Nd5 11. Bc4 Ne7 12. Qe1 a6 13. Ng5 b5 14. Bb3 Bb7 15. f5 h6 16. Ne4 B×e4 17. Q×e4 Rad8 18. f6 Ng6 19. g4** Black resigns—*Westminster Chess Club Papers*, January 1869, p. 115.

## (190) De Vere–Bird    1–0
B.C.A. Challenge Cup (round 8)
London, February 1869
*C63*

**1. e4 e5 2. Nf3 Nc6 3. Bb5 f5 4. d3 d6 5. Nc3 Nf6 6. a3 Bd7 7. Bc4 h6 8. Nh4 f4 9. Ng6 Rh7 10. f3 Ne7 11. N×f8 K×f8 12. Bd2 g5 13. Qe2 a5 14. Nd1 b5 15. Ba2 c5 16. c3 h5 17. Nf2 h4 18. d4 Qb6 19. d×e5 d×e5 20. Bd5 Re8 21. c4 b×c4 22. B×c4 Q×b2 23. 0–0 Nc6 24. Rfb1 Qd4 25. Rd1 Qd6 26. B×f4 Nd4 27. R×d4 c×d4 28. B×g5 Rc8 29. Bd3 Kg7 30. Qd2 Kh8 31. Q×a5 Rg7 32. B×h4 Nh5 33. g4 Rc5 34. Qd8† Rg8 35. Qe7 Qc6 36. Bg3 N×g3 37. h×g3 Rg7 38. Qd8† Kh7 39. Kg2 Rc1 40. R×c1 Q×c1 41. f4 Q×a3 42. Qh4† Kg6 43. Qh5†** and White wins—*The Field*, 13 February 1869.

## (191) Blackburne–Bird    1–0
B.C.A. Challenge Cup (round 9)
London, February 1869
*C10*

**1. e4 e6 2. d4 d5 3. Nc3 Nf6 4. Bd3 d×e4 5. N×e4 N×e4**

**6. B×e4 f5 7. Bf3 Be7 8. Ne2 c6 9. 0–0 0–0 10. Re1 Na6 11. g3 Bd7 12. Nf4 Nc7 13. c3 g5 14. Nd3 Bd6 15. Ne5 Be8 16. Bd2 Qf6 17. Qb3 Rb8 18. Re2 h5 19. Rae1 Kh7 20. Qc2 B×e5 21. R×e5 Bg6 22. Qc1 g4 23. Bd1 Bf7 24. Bc2 Rbe8 25. c4 Rg8 26. Bf4 Rg6 27. Qd2 b6 28. Ba4 b5 29. c×b5 c×b5 30. B×b5 N×b5 31. R×b5 Qd8 32. Rb7 Kg8 33. Qc3 Qd5 34. R×a7 h4 35. Re5 Qd8 36. Qc7 Qf6 37. Rb5 Rf8 38. Rb8 Qg7 39. Be5 Qh6 40. Q×f7 mate**—*Tournament Book*, pp. 15–16.

## (192) Bird–Wormald    ½–½
B.C.A. Challenge Cup (round 10, game 1)
London, February 1869
*Game score missing*

Tim Harding informed this author that *The Weekly Dispatch* of 27 February 1869 published the result of a drawn game between Bird and Wormald, which makes the following game a replay.

## (193) Wormald–Bird    1–0
B.C.A. Challenge Cup (round 10, game 2)
London, May 1869
*C61*

**1. e4 e5 2. Nf3 Nc6 3. Bb5 Nd4 4. N×d4 e×d4 5. d3 Bc5 6. 0–0 Ne7 7. Bg5 f6 8. B×f6 0–0 9. Bc4† Kh8 10. Bh4 Qe8 11. Nd2 Ng6 12. Qh5 Bb4 13. Nf3 N×h4 14. Q×h4 Be7 15. Qg3 c5 16. Rae1 d6 17. e5 Qd8 18. e×d6 B×d6 19. Ne5 Qc7** "A palpable oversight, losing the game off-hand. In justice to Bird, however, it ought to be stated that the whole game was little better than a 'skittle,' neither of the competitors, at the time it was played, having any chance of winning the first prize"—Potter. White mates in two moves—*Westminster Chess Club Papers* (Potter), March 1870, p. 170.

## (194) Blackburne & Ormond–Bird & Duffy    0–1
Consultation game
London, December 1868
*C01*

**1. e4 e6 2. d4 d5 3. e×d5 e×d5 4. Nf3 Nf6 5. Be2 Bd6 6. 0–0 Bf5 7. Be3 Ne4 8. c4 c6 9. h3 Nd7 10. Nc3 Qe7 11. N×e4 d×e4 12. Nd2 Bg6 13. f4 e×f3 *e.p.* 14. R×f3 0–0 15. Qb3 b6 16. Re1 Rae8 17. Bd1 c5 18. Rff1?** As they got nothing out of the opening, it was best to head for a draw with 18. Bf2, followed by the exchange of rooks. **18. ... c×d4 19. B×d4 Qh4?** Sacrificing the queen for White's rooks is very profitable at this point. After 19. ... Q×e1 20. R×e1 R×e1† 21. Kf2 (21. Nf1 leads to a speedier loss: 21. ... Nc5 22. Qf3 Bd3) 21. ... Rfe8 22. Nf3 Nc5 23. B×c5 B×c5† 24. Kg3 Rf1 White is completely lost. Either he will experience serious trouble saving his bishop, or his king will stay under fire. **20. Nf3 Qf4 21. Qb5** "For the purpose of playing 22. Qg5, forcing an exchange"—Boden. The queen ends up offside at b5. 21. Qc3 is the best move, after which Black has but a small advantage. **21. ... R×e1 22. R×e1 Nc5 23. B×c5?** A badly judged exchange. The bishops are very powerful in this type of position.

After the more stubborn 23. Be3, the Black allies keep a small advantage with 23. ... Qf5. **23. ... B×c5† 24. Kh1 Be4 25. b4 a6!** "Exceedingly well played, winning a clear pawn"—Boden. **26. Q×a6 B×b4 27. Rf1 Bd6** "This looks good, but 27. ... Bd3, followed by 28. ... Bc5, would have led to Black's acquiring a decisive superiority at once"—Boden. **28. Q×b6** "Very cleverly conceived—the position is now highly instructive and amusing"—Boden. **28. ... B×f3 29. Qg1 Q×c4** The most precise move is 29. ... B×g2†, as White now gets the chance to safeguard his kingside with 30. R×f3. Blackburne and Ormond unwisely prefer to keep their a-pawn on the board, thereby sentencing their king to constant danger. The fact that the bishops are of opposite colors exacerbates White's problems. **30. Bb3 B×g2† 31. Q×g2 Qh4 32. Qf3 Qe7 33. a4 g6 34. Bd5 Kg7 35. Qe4 Qd7 36. Kg2 Re8 37. Qc4 Re7 38. Qg4 Qa7 39. Rd1 f6 40. Bf3 Qc5 41. Qd4 Qg5† 42. Kf1 Bc5 43. Qg4 Qe3 44. Qg3 h5 45. Kg2 Re5 46. h4 Kh6 47. Rd8 Be7 48. Rg8 Qd3 49. Bc6 Re2† 50. Kh3 Qf5†** and Black wins—*The Field* (Boden), 26 December 1868.

---

# A NEW BREAK 1869–1870

Bird's name largely disappeared from the chess columns between the B.C.A. Challenge Cup Tournament and his appearance at the handicap tournament of the City of London Chess Club at the end of 1870. He did occasionally engage in offhand chess, of which a few skittles survive.

## (195) F.H. Lewis–Bird    1–0
Offhand game
London (Westminster C.C.) 1869 (?)
*C65*

**1. e4 e5 2. Nf3 Nc6 3. Bb5 Nf6 4. 0–0 Be7 5. d4 e×d4 6. e5 Ne4 7. Re1 Nc5 8. N×d4 0–0 9. Nc3 Ne6 10. Nf5 g6 11. Qg4 d5 12. N×d5 Bb4 13. Nf6† Q×f6 14. e×f6 B×e1 15. B×c6 b×c6 16. Ne7† Kh8 17. Bh6 Re8 18. Q×e6** and White wins—*Bell's Life*, 9 April 1870.

## (196) Bird–Boden    1–0
Offhand game
London (Westminster C.C.), 1 December 1869
*C84*

**1. e4 e5 2. Nf3 Nc6 3. Bb5 a6 4. Ba4 Nf6 5. 0–0 Be7 6. d4 e×d4 7. e5 Ne4 8. c3 d×c3 9. Re1 Nc5 10. Bc2 c×b2 11. B×b2 Ne6 12. Nc3 0–0 13. Nd5 b5 14. Nf6† B×f6 15. e×f6 g6 16. Qd2 Kh8 17. Qh6 Rg8 18. R×e6 d×e6 19. Ng5** and White wins—*Westminster Chess Club Papers*, June 1870, p. 22.

The following game was published in 1872, in a period when Bird was not actively playing chess. It was probably played in 1869 or 1870.

**(197) Steinitz–Bird    1–0**
Offhand game
London (City of London C.C.) 1870 (?)
*C51*

1. e4 e5 2. Nf3 Nc6 3. Bc4 Bc5 4. b4 B×b4 5. c3 Bc5 6. 0–0 d6 7. d4 e×d4 8. c×d4 Bb6 9. Nc3 Na5 10. Bd3 c5 11. d5 Bg4 12. Ne2 Qf6 13. Bg5 Qg6 14. Nf4 Q×g5 15. Bb5† Ke7 16. N×g5 B×d1 17. Ra×d1 Rf8 18. Rde1 h6 19. Nge6 f×e6 20. Ng6† Kf7 21. N×h8† Kf6 22. f4 Ne7 23. e5† Kf5 24. Bd3† Kg4 25. Re3 R×h8 26. Rg3† Kh5 27. Be2† White wins—*Westminster Chess Club Papers*, February 1872, p. 177.

# HANDICAP TOURNAMENT AT THE CITY OF LONDON CHESS CLUB 1870–1871

At the end of the 1860s a London chess club newly rose to prominence. The City of London Chess Club was founded by a few enthusiastic amateurs on 29 December 1852. During its first fifteen years the club led a rather subdued existence with a small number of members and no strong players. After a decade, from

The Chess Champions of England. Bird is in the first row, seventh from left (*American Chess Magazine*).

## Handicap tournament, London, 22 November 1870–9 June 1871

**Site:** City of London Chess Club
**Prizes:** Four prizes
**Odds scale:** pawn and move (class II), pawn and 2 moves (class III), knight (class IV) and rook (class V)

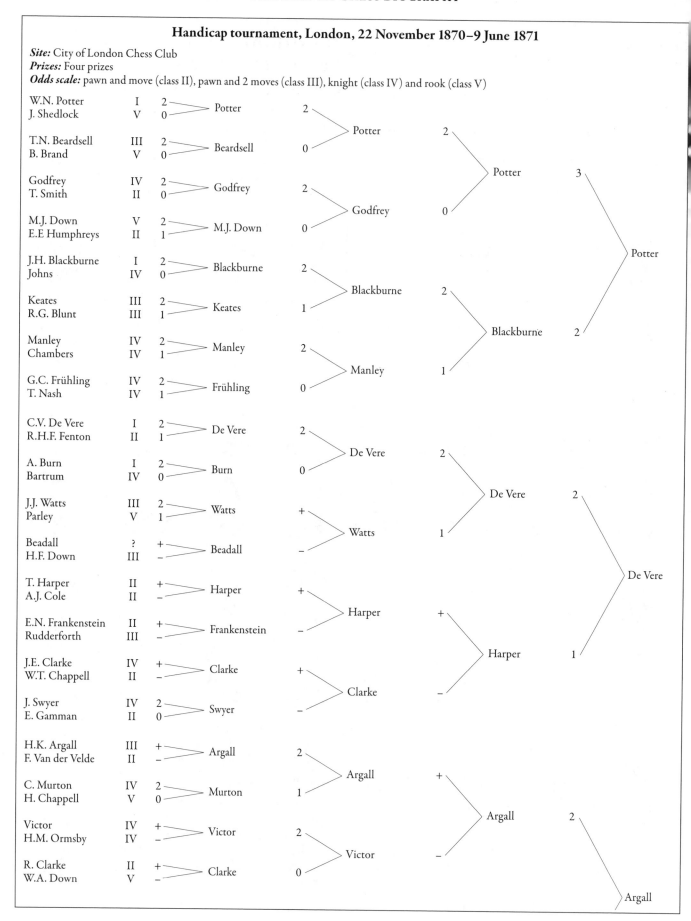

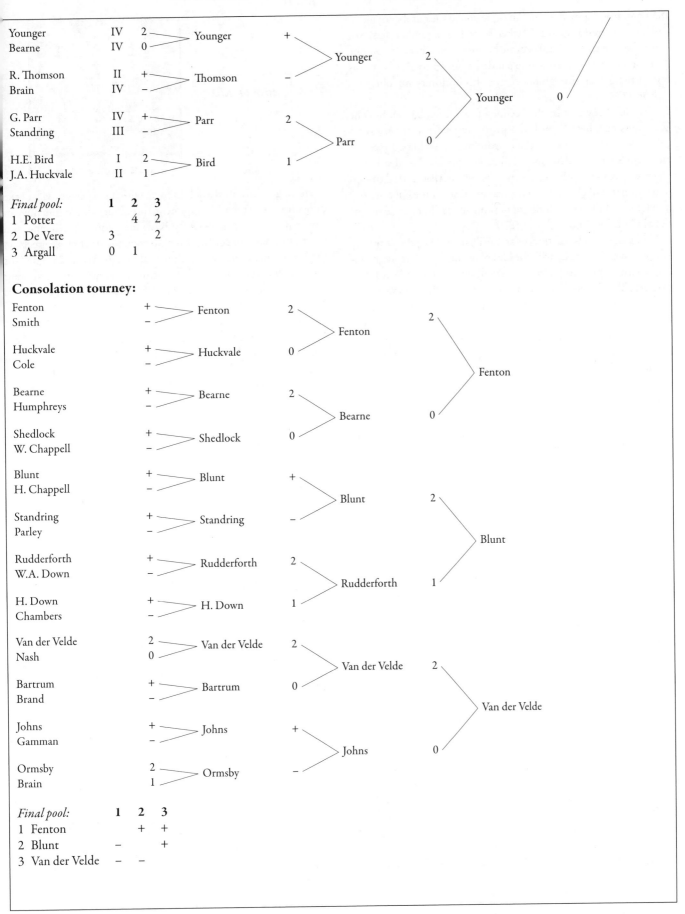

| Younger | IV | 2 |
| Bearne | IV | 0 |

Younger +

Younger 2

| R. Thomson | II | + |
| Brain | IV | – |

Thomson –

Younger 0

| G. Parr | IV | + |
| Standring | III | – |

Parr 2

Parr 0

| H.E. Bird | I | 2 |
| J.A. Huckvale | II | 1 |

Bird 1

| Final pool: | 1 | 2 | 3 |
|---|---|---|---|
| 1 Potter | | 4 | 2 |
| 2 De Vere | 3 | | 2 |
| 3 Argall | 0 | 1 | |

## Consolation tourney:

| Fenton | + |
| Smith | – |

Fenton 2

Fenton 2

| Huckvale | + |
| Cole | – |

Huckvale 0

Fenton

| Bearne | + |
| Humphreys | – |

Bearne 2

Bearne 0

| Shedlock | + |
| W. Chappell | – |

Shedlock 0

| Blunt | + |
| H. Chappell | – |

Blunt +

Blunt 2

| Standring | + |
| Parley | – |

Standring –

Blunt

| Rudderforth | + |
| W.A. Down | – |

Rudderforth 2

Rudderforth 1

| H. Down | + |
| Chambers | – |

H. Down 1

| Van der Velde | 2 |
| Nash | 0 |

Van der Velde 2

Van der Velde 2

| Bartrum | + |
| Brand | – |

Bartrum 0

Van der Velde

| Johns | + |
| Gamman | – |

Johns +

Johns 0

| Ormsby | 2 |
| Brain | 1 |

Ormsby –

| Final pool: | 1 | 2 | 3 |
|---|---|---|---|
| 1 Fenton | | + | + |
| 2 Blunt | – | | + |
| 3 Van der Velde | – | – | |

1864 onwards, a growth set in. An explosion in the number of memberships occurred around 1870 when several strong and professional players joined the club and became honorary members. In just one year the number of members expanded from 35 to 130. Bird was one of them even though he received his honorary membership only in 1873.

The club benefited by the decline of two legendary clubs. The Westminster Chess Club had a promising start, but very soon various squabbles between some prominent members broke out and both Steinitz and Staunton left rather quickly. The deathblow was the upswing of other games, notably whist, that started to suppress the game of chess. Another great impulse for the City of London Chess Club was the influx of new members after the demise of the old London Chess Club in 1870.

Under the impulse of its secretary, William T. Chappell, the City of London club came up with the idea of organizing a massive handicap tournament. No fewer than 48 players took part. With five masters (Blackburne, De Vere, Burn, Potter and Bird) entering the field, even the weakest player had a chance to play for immortality.

The handicap tournament was played according to the knock-out rules. The first player to win two games qualified for the next round. In the end a final pool of three players played for the first two prizes. The losers of the first round played a similar tournament to battle for third and fourth prize. All competitors were divided into classes according to their assumed strength. This class determined the odds that had to be given or taken.

Bird was paired in the first round with James Augustus Huckvale (class II). Bird needed three games to beat his opponent. Against Parr (class IV) Bird had to concede the odds of a knight. This time he lost with similar figures and he was thus eliminated at a very early stage.

Two first-class players, De Vere and Potter, reached the final pool. They were joined by Henry Kempthorne Argall (class III), who did not encounter any real strong opposition in the preliminary rounds. Just as in the previous rounds, small matches according to the best of three were played. In the crucial match Potter beat De Vere 2–1 (and four draws).

### (198) Huckvale–Bird    0–1

Handicap tournament (round 1, game ?)
London 1870
*Odds of pawn and move*

1. e4 Nc6 2. d4 d5 3. e5 Bf5 4. Nf3 e6 5. Bb5 Qd7 6. c3 a6 7. Qa4 h6 8. B×c6 Q×c6 9. Q×c6† "As a rule, it is bad policy, in games at the pawn and move, and pawn and 2 moves, for the player receiving the odds to exchange pieces early in the conflict. There is nothing in the present position, we think, which justified a departure from this rule"—Duffy. 9. ... b×c6 10. Be3 Ne7 11. Nbd2 Nc8 12. 0–0 Be7 13. h3 0–0 14. Nh2 Rb8 15. b4 Nb6 16. f4 Bd3 17. Rf3 Kh7 18. Nb3?! "This move appears to have been an inconsiderate one, and it caused Mr. Huckvale loss of time, and a good deal of embarrassment"—Duffy. 18. ... Be4 19. Rff1 Nc4 20. Bc1 Rf7 21. Ng4 Bd3 22. Rf3 Be4 23. Rf1 Rbf8 24. Kh2 (*see diagram*)

*After 24. Kh2*

24. ... g5? "Mr. Bird avails himself, with his expected skill, of the difficulties by which his opponent is trammeled. He hits now an almost decisive attack"—Duffy. Bird's move looks convincing, and it certainly helps to confuse his weaker opponent, but its effects on the black squares in his position could be dramatic. 25. g3? Not surprisingly Huckvale misses the strongest continuation. There is no satisfying response against 25. Nc5! After 25. ... B×c5 (worse is 25. ... Bf5?! 26. Nf6†!) 26. b×c5, White's knight will reach f6, forcing Bird to try his luck in a rather hopeless sacrifice. 25. ... h5 26. Ne3? The right way to return the pawn is by playing 26. Nf6†, e.g., 26. ... B×f6 27. e×f6 R×f6 28. Nc5 g×f4 29. B×f4 e5!, and White keeps a merely symbolic advantage. 26. ... g×f4 27. g×f4 R×f4 28. R×f4 R×f4 29. N×c4 Rf2† The situation is wholly different now. The cooperation between rook and bishops won't leave the opponent's king a chance to survive. 30. Kg1 Rg2† 31. Kf1 d×c4 32. Nd2 Bd5 33. N×c4 "Well meant, but the adversary has too much hold by this time for any play to shake him off"—Duffy. 33. ... Rh2 34. Ne3 Bf3 35. Kg1 Re2 36. Nc4 Bh4 37. Ba3 Bg3 38. Rc1 Rh2 and checkmate is inevitable on the next move—*Era* (Duffy), 12 March 1871.

## ANOTHER BREAK FROM CHESS 1870–1872

Bird's return to the tournament arena was short-lived. After his elimination he went into seclusion until 1873. In these two and a half years, Bird's name was mentioned just once in relation with a chess contest, namely as participant in the match between the City of London Chess Club and the Westminster Chess Club that was played on 23 June 1871. Ultimately he didn't play.

In the December 1870 edition of the *Chess Player's Chronicle* (p. 183), readers' attention was drawn to the initiative of Heinrich Friedrich Ludwig Meyer, editor of the *Gentleman's Journal*, to construct a "photographic chessboard." Meyer copied the idea from Samuel Loyd, who had released such a photograph with American players in 1868.

Sixty-four portraits, of the most prominents adepts of chess, were required to fill up the board, for which the help of the ordinary chess player was wanted. Meyer published the chessboard in 1871. Among the men pictured is Bird. This is the first known portrait of Bird.

# ◆ Part V ◆

# THE AMATEUR CHESS CHAMPION, 1871–1875

## FAILING ACCOUNTANCY 1870–1871

Fortune did not keep on smiling upon Bird's business interests. As a herald of the approaching catastrophe, the *London Gazette* announced the dissolving of his partnership with Lewis on p. 4484 of its edition of 14 October 1870. Four days later the same newspaper announced that Lewis had left the offices at Gresham Buildings: "In the matter of proceedings for liquidation..., instituted by Edgar Lewis, ..., but now of No. 49, Albion Road, Stoke Newington, in the county of Middlesex."

The following, in general terms, describes the bankruptcy procedure in the nineteenth century:

Under the bankruptcy system, if a debtor failed to pay his creditors, they could file a formal bankruptcy petition in court that triggered the seizure of the debtor's assets; the court distributed the assets on a pro rata basis among creditors after payment of expenses; and, in appropriate cases, the court with creditor approval discharged the debtor from further liability. As part of this process, between the filing of the petition and the closing of the case, the bankrupt "estate" had to be administered according to the provisions of bankruptcy law. Assets had to be collected, managed, and distributed. With larger bankruptcies, assignees or trustees of the estate might have acquired considerable responsibilities, for it was often necessary to continue the operation of the bankrupt's business until it could be profitably sold or otherwise liquidated. In some instances, the administration of a bankrupt estate continued for as long as twenty years [*Victorian Insolvency*, p. 4].

Newspapers, notably the *London Gazette*, the *London City Press* and the *Clerkenwell News*, followed Bird's situation. One article showed that the bankruptcy of Bird and Lewis happened upon the petition of Lauriston Winterbotham Lewis, Edgar's brother.

[The two] were adjudicated bankrupts on the 6th of December last, upon the petition of Mr. L.W. Lewis, of Walsall, Staffordshire, solicitor, for a debt of £108 1s. 1d. money lent.

Mr. Duignan, solicitor, Walsall, appeared by his agent for the petitioning creditor; and Mr. Treherne, of the firm of Treherne and Wolferstan, solicitors, Ironmonger Lane, represented a large number of creditors.

No statement of the bankrupt's affairs had been filed, and several proofs to a large amount were disputed by the bankrupts.

After considerable discussion, the creditors chose Mr. Benjamin Bullock, of 62 Queen's Gardens, gentleman, and Mr. Sillifant, of 24 Old Jewry, accountant, to act as trustees of the bankrupts' estate, and as the creditors could not agree upon the appointment of a committee of inspection, none was chosen.

Upon a former day, upon the application of Mr. Avery, from Messrs. Treherne and Wolferstan's, the Hon. Spring Rice made an order that certain papers should be delivered up to Mr. Bullock, one of the trustees now chosen. The public examination of the bankrupts was fixed to be held before the Chief Judge at Lincoln's Inn Fields on the 22nd of March next, at 12 o'clock.

The proofs tendered by Mr. Treherne amounted to several thousand pounds, and it was understood he would have the future conduct of the case [*Clerkenwell News*, 15 February 1871].

The *London Gazette* wrote on 14 April (p. 1919) that Bird's new unenviable status caused his removal from the bankruptcy cases where he acted as assignee. A public examination, on which the creditors could demonstrate their proof of the bankrupts' debts to the trustees, was to be held on 22 March but postponed until April. A detailed account of the situation appeared in the press.

The joint accounts of the bankrupts, prepared and filed by Mr. Sydney Smith, of Basinghall Street, disclose total debts [of] £736 13s. 9d. and total assets [of] £515.

The separate accounts of the bankrupt Bird are thus summed up, viz.: Debits to unsecured creditors £1324 9s.; creditors fully secured £2600; estimated value of securities £2700; surplus to contra £100; creditors partly secured £922 10s.; estimated value of securities £575; other liabilities £14 6s. 10d.; total debts £1813 5s. 11d. Credits: book debts, about £1298 10s.; estimated to produce £131 10s.; property £140; surplus from securities held by creditors £100; total assets £371 10s. N.B.: Doubtful and bad debts £1167; disputed claims not estimated. ...

Mr. Treherne, after calling the attention of the Court to the large figures in the accounts that had been filed, said he should ask that the bankrupts be ordered to file a cash and goods account, and also an account accounting for their deficiency.

The bankrupt Bird was then briefly examined as to his transactions with Messrs. Cunningham and Co., and ultimately the sitting was adjourned until the 31st of May, and the bankrupts were ordered to furnish the additional accounts asked for by Mr. Treherne [*Clerkenwell News*, 27 April 1871].

In two subsequent meetings Bird and Lewis were somewhat uncooperative with the Court. A long-lasting procedure was now set.

The bankrupts, Henry E. Bird and Edgar Lewis were public accountants at No. 1, Grantham buildings. This was an adjourned public examination sitting, the bankrupts having been required to file additional accounts. The debts and liabilities are to a heavy amount. Mr. Treherne, solicitor, again opposed the bankrupts on behalf of the trustee and creditors, and urged that the bankrupts had failed to file all the accounts which the Court had ordered. He therefore asked for an adjournment. The 5th of July was fixed for the next meeting [*London City Press*, 10 June 1871].

The bankrupts, ..., came up by adjournment for public examination. At the instance of the trustee they had been required to file a statement explanatory of the deficiency which appeared upon their accounts, and the bankrupt Lewis had complied with that order, but the bankrupt Bird had only recently filed the necessary statement; and the accounts as presented were contradictory one of the other.

Mr. Treherne for the trustee asked that the case of both bankrupts should be adjourned until the necessary investigation had been made.

Mr. Reed, who appeared for the bankrupt Lewis, urged that his client should pass, although Bird was not in a position to do so. No rule of law existed for the postponement of the case of one partner merely because his co-partner had not complied with the order of the Court.

His Honor, however, for reasons which he stated, declined to pass one bankrupt without the other, and the meeting stood adjourned as to both [*The Times*, 6 July 1871].

Barely a few bankruptcy files from that era have been preserved and it is hardly a surprise that Bird and Lewis' case is not one of them. An important trigger of their failure seems to have been that Edgar Lewis was asked by his brother to pay his loan back but more motives could have played their role. It can be noted that at that time there was an increased competition among accountants while they were also less frequently appointed by the court. This may have decreased the number of assignments for Bird and Lewis. The curious advertisement published by Bird in 1868 seems to confirm the suggestion that he was wanting for work.

Some accountants lost their reputation because of fraud. Since the Bankruptcy Act of 1869 they could gain full control over the debtor's assets when they were appointed as trustee. This increased the abuse. As Bird's name hardly figured as trustee in the *London Gazette* it is unlikely fraud played any role.

Early in 1871, according to the *Clerkenwell News* of 15 February, Bird resided at 36 Camberwell New Road in Surrey. The census taken on 2 April 1871 shows that he had moved to 104 Stanley Street in Belgrave, where he rented one or more rooms. He lived there with Thomas Austin, the head of the household, and another lodger, the 29 year old Harriet A. Brown.[1]

Edgar Lewis also had left his lodgings at Stoke Newington when the census was taken. He lived now in a lodging house situated at 2 Grenville Street, St. Pancras.[2] Edgar's financial troubles were over when his father died at Tewkesbury on 5 June 1873. In 1881 he was at a hotel in Ross-on-Wye in Herefordshire and by then he derived his income from dividends.[3] A decade later he lived with his family at Dartmouth, in Devonshire. He was still "living on his own means."[4] Lewis died in August 1926, aged 87, in Totnes.

# LOOSE HABITS 1871–1883

Bird was not keen on informing his chess colleagues about his failure in business. About twenty years later he came up with an alternate version of the facts. Bird gave the impression that he had abandoned a prolific accounting career in favor of his greater love, chess.

Mr. Bird may be fairly described as one of these enthusiasts who have given up their lives and their chances in life to the most fascinating of all scientific indoor games. Many years ago he had great opportunities of placing himself in a lucrative position. But he preferred to devote himself to the study of chess, and has sacrificed everything to it [*Western Mail*, 24 May 1893].[5]

1. 1871 census: Class: *RG10*; Piece: 111; Folio: 51; Page: 21.
2. 1871 census: Class: *RG10*; Piece: 215; Folio: 47; Page: 14.
3. 1881 census: Class: *RG11*; Piece: 2585; Folio: 30; Page: 1.
4. 1891 census: Class: *RG12*; Piece: 1710; Folio: 102; Page: 34.
5. This statement has to be taken with a grain of salt. It was made decades after the facts, in a Welsh based newspaper. Yet, with the few details given in the article, it can be assumed that Bird influenced the image that was painted of him.

Bird's chess friends were probably not completely informed about the misfortune which overcame him. In return some gossip circulated about him. In a letter written on 27 November 1877 to John Griswold White, the Scotch master George Brunton Fraser wrote the following intriguing lines.

Bird is I understand back to London and I am sorry to hear that "his habits are somewhat loose" as Mr. Watkinson of Huddersfield writes me. I never heard this hinted before, although I suspected it. He was in a famous firm of accountants in London for many years as partner, and I never learned why he retired [*Letters to John G. White Relating to Chess*, vol. I, letter 76].

It is unclear what John Watkinson meant by ascribing to Bird "loose habits." It may have been related to his stay in America, that lasted from 1875 until 1877, or with his departure from Coleman, Turquand, Youngs and Company to which Fraser unreservedly refers. Fraser may have been aware of Bird's bankruptcy but considered it more prudent not to mention it loud and clear. In any case, Bird's professional as well as his private conduct remains a bit vague for the decade to come. He was not discharged from his bankruptcy yet and, according to English law, was thus not allowed to manage a new firm, whether alone or with a partner. It is likely that he kept on working as an accountant, perhaps in someone's service or for himself but on a much smaller scale. If the latter case is true Bird probably could make good use of the network he had built up during the previous years. It is noteworthy that when the possibility of playing a match with Mackenzie in the United States in 1873 arose, Bird affirmed that he could liberate himself from obligations in short notice.[6]

In 1873 Bird was very busy on the chess front. Perhaps this is an indication of a diminished activity as accountant. Then, chess had to take a step back in 1874 and 1875. The death of his mother, which occurred at 4 Wansey Street on 3 July 1874, is likely to have hurt him a great deal, for he stood closely by her side during the difficult years when her husband had been in Australia. Mary Ellen died of apoplexy and paralysis.[7]

From a letter that was published in the chess column of the *Figaro* on 5 September 1874 one learns that Bird had moved his dwellings to Lupus Street, Pimlico. Bird's new home was actually just around the corner from his previous one in Stanley Street. A 1877 newspaper cutting described Pimlico as "genteel, sacred to professional men ... not rich enough to luxuriate in Belgravia proper, but rich enough to live in private houses." Its inhabitants were "more lively than in Kensington ... and yet a cut above Chelsea, which is only commercial."[8]

The years until 1882 remain blank concerning Bird's bankruptcy. His professional activities are, as far as they are known, fascinating to follow. They will be dealt with in the following parts.

The final phase of Bird and Lewis' bankruptcy commenced when the *London Gazette* of 7 November 1882 (p. 4968) announced that a general meeting of their creditors was called together at the offices of James Pettengill, a solicitor. The bankrupts applied for an order of discharge "upon the ground that his failure to pay a dividend of 10s. in the pound has arisen from circumstances for which the said bankrupt cannot justly be held responsible."

6. *The Spirit of the Times*, 31 May 1873.
7. The death registration reference is St. Saviour Southwark, Jul-Aug-Sep 1874, vol. 1d, p. 97.
8. See http://www3.westminster.gov.uk/spgs/publications/Pimlico%20design%20guide.pdf.

After a pause of a few months, the *London Gazette* contained three articles that dealt with the unwinding of the affair. On 16 February 1883 (p. 906), another call for a meeting was made. The next step followed in the spring. On 30 March (p. 1773), their application for an order of discharge was officially announced for 21 April 1883. And indeed, on that day both Bird and Lewis were officially granted with the requested order, as appeared on 27 April (p. 2290). As a consequence Bird was finally released from all debts and legal constraints. A long ordeal came to an end for Bird and this must at least have given him less worries for the tournament of London that was about to start.

---

# RETURN TO THE CHESS COMMUNITY

When Bird decided to play chess again, late in 1872, it was clear that he had been cut off from that world for the last few years. If one can believe his claim in *Modern Chess* (p. 109), he saw only the games of the match between Steinitz and the freshly-arrived continental star Zukertort (played in September 1872) in 1884. This may be true for Bird completely neglected this important contest in his first book *Chess Masterpieces*.

From 1873 onward Bird's dedication to chess became more intense than ever. This seems not so strange, with the perturbations of his accountancy career in mind. Bird made his reappearance at Simpson's Divan. A revival taking place here was noted by *The Field* on 21 December 1872. Various first-class players, such as Boden, MacDonnell, Zukertort, Wisker and De Vere visited the Divan on daily basis. To the delight of the public they did not hesitate to take up the gauntlet against each other. Just as in former days Bird enjoyed most of his battles with Boden and MacDonnell. Several of their games were published in *Chess Masterpieces*. As they come to the researcher without being properly dated, a bundle of these games are gathered at the end of this part.

The real turning point of Bird's comeback was the first match with Wisker, which commenced in March 1873. A few of his earlier games have been preserved. The first one, published in October 1872, saw William Norwood Potter as Bird's opponent. Potter, one of the best London masters, played a forthright positional style. He gained a lot fame as editor of magazines such as the *Westminster Chess Club Papers* and the *City of London Chess Magazine* while, in later years, he also took care of the chess column in *Land and Water*. The game between Bird and Potter was a real slugfest, full of errors, but mesmerizing until the end.

## (199) Bird–Potter    1–0
Offhand game
London, October 1872
*B27*

**1. e4 c5 2. Nf3 g6 3. c3 Bg7 4. Bd3 Nc6 5. Bc2 d5 6. 0–0 Bg4 7. h3 B×f3 8. Q×f3 e6 9. Qe2 Nge7 10. f4 d4 11. d3 0–0 12. Bd2** It is better to close the center, and especially the long a1–h8 diagonal, at once with 12. c4. **12. ... b5** 12. ... Qb6! is already very

embarrassing. **13. Na3** A real mistake, but having to play such a move as 13. Qf2 is no fun either. Had Potter now opened the long diagonal at once with 13. ... d×c3 14. b×c3 b4, he would have gained a pawn and the control over the important square d4. **13. ... a6 14. Rac1?** Bird insists on pursuing the wrong idea. 14. c4! more or less equalizes. **14. ... d×c3 15. b×c3 Qa5** Back on track! Potter is rewarded with the gain of a pawn. **16. Nb1 Q×a2 17. Be3 Qb2** Too slow. Nothing could stop the advance of the b-pawn: 17. ... b4 18. B×c5 b3 19. Bd1 b2. **18. e5** 18. B×c5 B×c3 19. N×c3 Q×c3 20. Qf2 creates some imbalances. The bishop pair is a force to be reckoned with. **18. ... Nf5! 19. Bf2 b4** Not so bad, but 19. ... Bh6! prevents White's next, and only, move. If then 20. g3 there follows 20. ... Rfc8 21. Kg2 b4! 22. B×c5 b×c3 and White's position is torn apart. **20. g4 b3?** The exchanges following this push clearly favor White. After 20. ... Nfe7 21. B×c5 Rfc8 it looks like Black's strategy has failed, but White still has to be very careful as his position is full of weaknesses, for example after 22. c×b4?! Nd5! Best is 22. Nd2, but after 22. ... b×c3 he is still suffering. **21. g×f5 b×c2 22. R×c2 Qb6 23. f6** Bird doesn't hesitate to push Potter almost off the board on the kingside, but Black is much more vulnerable on the other side of the board. Had Bird played 23. Rb2! Qa7 24. Qe4 Rac8 25. f×e6 f×e6 26. Nd2, his opponent ends up completely bound to his weaknesses. **23. ... Bh6 24. Qg4?!** Senseless, as there is no breakthrough. 24. Nd2! is strong, for if 24. ... B×f4 25. Ne4! wins material. **24. ... Rfd8 25. Qh4 Bf8 26. Qg3 a5!** Potter rightly starts up his counterplay on the queenside. A tad more precise than 26. ... a5 would have been either 26. ... Qb3 or 26. ... Qb5, preventing Bird from developing his knight. **27. Nd2 a4 28. Nc4?!** This move allows 28. ... Qb3! 29. Rfc1 a3 which is impossible to meet in decent fashion. But his position has become quite joyless anyway; e.g., 28. Ra1 Qb5 29. c4 Qb7 with a clear positional edge for Black. Fortunately for Bird, Potter's reply is extraordinarily tame. **28. ... Qa6? 29. Rb1?** "29. Ra1 would have been much better"—Boden. **29. ... Rab8?!** The disadvantage of Bird's move becomes apparent after 29. ... Na5!, which would not be possible had Bird played 29. Ra1, because of 30. R×a4. After 29. ... Na5!, White is bound to lose a pawn, and his position crumbles away at once. **30. Ra1 Rb3 31. Be1?** *(see diagram)* Potter has a brilliant riposte against this move. After 31. Qe3, he might be able to hang on.

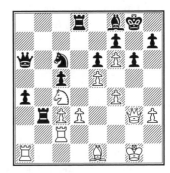

*After 31. Be1*

**31. ... Nb4!! 32. c×b4 Rd×d3?** The false rook. From here on Black's back rank weakness starts to tell! His future looks much rosier after 32. ... Rb×d3! 33. Qg2 c×b4. As both 34. ... b3 and 34. ... a3 are possible now, 34. Nb2 is the only try. Step by step Black can make progress; e.g., 34. ... Ra3! 35. Rb1 Rb3 36. Rc6 Qa7† 37. Bf2 Qa8 38. Rc2 a3 39. Q×a8 R×a8 40. Kg2 h5 (the queens are finally off. Before gaining back the piece it is now important to activate his last piece as well) 41. h4 Bh6 42. Ra1 R×b2 43. R×b2 a×b2 44. Rb1 B×f4 45. R×b2 B×e5 46. R×b4 B×f6. **33. Qg2 R×h3?!** Certainly not without risk, as this capture actually loses valuable time in return for White's least important pawn. At once 33. ... c×b4 34. Nd6 a3 creates a great fight with mutual chances. Compared to the previous line, White's knight really counts. **34. Nd6! c×b4?!** Potter finally realizes his strong pawn pair, but at the cost of opening the c-file, which becomes a decisive factor. Instead, he could fight on after 34. ... Rhf3 35. Qe2 (Black threatened 35. ... Qd3 and 36. ... Qd4†. 35. b5 Qa7 36. Rc4 is another strategy) 35. ... Qa7 36. b×c5. With a strong knight and passed c-pawn, White has thrown his opponent on the defensive. **35. Rc8!** Bird now threatens 36. Ra8, followed by 37. R×f8† and the queen will deliver mate. **35. ... Rbf3 36. B×b4** A particularly brilliant finish ensues after 36. Rac1!, with devilish complications: 36. ... Rf1† 37. Q×f1 Rh1† 38. K×h1 Q×f1† 39. Kh2 Qe2† 40. Kg1 Qg4† 41. Kf2 Q×f4† 42. Kg2 Qg5† 43. Kf3 Qh6 44. R×f8† Q×f8 45. B×b4 Qa8† 46. Kf4 g5† 47. Kg3 and wins. **36. ... Q×c8 37. N×c8 B×b4 38. Rc1 h5** Also losing is 38. ... h6 but White's path to victory is certainly not as evident as in the game: 39. Rc4! Bc3 40. Nd6 Rfg3 41. Q×g3 R×g3† 42. Kf2 Rd3 43. Ke2 Rd2† 44. Ke3 wins. **39. Nd6 Ba5 40. Q×h3 R×h3 41. Rc8† Kh7 42. N×f7** and Black resigns. "Threatening 43. Ng5†, etc."—Boden. *The Field* (Boden), 26 October 1872.

John de Soyres, born in 1849, was a promising young player and became a member of the clergy. Only a few months after this game de Soyres occupied the first board for Cambridge in the very first university chess match between Oxford and Cambridge. He remained active in London chess circles until he emigrated to Canada in 1888.

### (200) de Soyres–Bird    0–1
Offhand game
London (Simpson's Divan), 16 January 1873
C39

**1. e4 e5 2. f4 e×f4 3. Nf3 g5 4. h4 g4 5. Ne5 Nf6** "I have repeatedly expressed the opinion that this move does not bear the test of recent analysis and actual play. 5. ... Bg7 is the best defense"—Wisker. **6. Bc4 d5 7. e×d5 Bd6** "7. ... Bg7, proposed and examined by Dr. M. Lange fifteen years ago, is far better"—Zukertort. **8. d4 Nh5 9. Nc3 Qe7 10. Bb5† Kf8?** Either 10. ... c6, a promising pawn sacrifice, or 10. ... Kd8 are worth considering. The f-file isn't the safest place for the king in this opening. **11. 0–0 B×e5 12. d×e5 Q×h4 13. B×f4** Also interesting is the direct sacrifice of the exchange: 13. R×f4 N×f4 14. B×f4 g3 15. Qf3 Bg4 16. B×g3 B×f3 17. B×h4. **13. ... g3** "Black gets an attack, but it is very short-lived. All his pieces on the queenside are at home—as is usual when this defense is adopted—and the situation is conclusively against him"—Wisker. **14. B×g3!** "Mr. de Soyres thought that at this point he should have played 14. Bh6†. The move he actually adopted is, however, better, although it results in the loss of a rook"—Wisker. **14. ... N×g3 15. Qf3?!** Imprecise. 15. e6! gives his opponent no chance to close the f-file; e.g., 15. ... N×f1 16. Qf3! f6 17. R×f1, with a winning attack. **15. ... Qh1†?** Bird goes hunting for material, but ab-

solute priority had to be given the defense of his king. The wrong way to do this is by playing 15. ... f5 16. e×f6 *e.p.* N×f1 17. R×f1 with lasting pressure. Instead, 15. ... Bf5! is correct. After 16. Bd3 Black can and must force the draw with 16. ... Qd4† 17. Rf2 Qh4 18. Rff1 etc. **16. Kf2 N×f1 17. R×f1 Qh4† 18. Kg1 Qe7 19. d6!** **c×d6 20. e×d6** "Why not 20. Nd5 at once? If then 20. ... Qe6 21. Nc7 and 22. e×d6, winning easily, as the queen cannot abandon the defense of the f-pawn"—Wisker. **20. ... Qe6 21. Nd5 Nd7 22. Qc3?** De Soyres keeps on aiming for a direct attack, but as he is still a rook behind this had to be either decisive or something else had to be found. In this case the simple 22. Nc7 suggests itself to restore the material equilibrium while Black's king and all his pieces remain terribly placed. **22. ... Rg8 23. Qc7?** "Mr. Bird here recommended 23. Re1, as after 23. ... R×g2† 24. K×g2 Q×d5† 25. Kg1, Black could hardly do more than draw"—Wisker. Bird's suggestion loses also after 23. ... Q×d5. Instead 23. Nc7 Q×d6 24. N×a8 Qc5† 25. Q×c5† N×c5 is very drawish. **23. ... f5?** It is difficult to see why he omitted 23. ... Q×d5. **24. R×f5†?** It is rather obvious this move loses outright. Had de Soyres found 24. Ne7!, a draw would be inevitable. 24. ... Nf6 25. N×g8 Qe3† 26. Kh1 K×g8 27. d7 Qh6† **24. ... Q×f5 25. Qd8† Kg7** and Black wins—*Westminster Chess Club Papers* (Wisker/Zukertort), March 1874, p. 230.

The next game was a harbinger of what would come.

### (201) Wisker–Bird    0–1
Offhand game
London, February 1873
C35

**1. e4 e5 2. f4 e×f4 3. Nf3 Be7 4. h4** A radical way to prevent the envisaged bishop check. **4. ... d5 5. e×d5 Bg4 6. Bc4 Nf6** He could already exchange at f3 and take off the h-pawn without many worries. **7. Nc3 c6 8. d4 c×d5 9. Bb5† Nc6 10. B×f4 0–0 11. Qd2?!** 10. B×c6 b×c6 11. Qd3 is a better set-up. With his next move Bird definitively grasps the initiative. **11. ... Bb4! 12. B×c6 b×c6 13. Ne5 Ne4 14. Qd3 Bf5 15. 0–0 B×c3 16. b×c3 Q×h4** All these moves were excellently played by Bird, and he has obtained much the superior position. Steinitz' next comment is therefore incorrect. **17. N×c6?!** "Until now White had rather the better position. The move in the text allows Black's rook to take up a very formidable position"—Steinitz. Not touching the c-pawn is indeed better, but he has no compensation in sight for the lost pawn. **17. ... Rac8 18. g3?** This move ought to lose quickly. He could put up a fight with 18. Bg5 Q×g5 19. R×f5 Qh4, although it is clear that White experiences problems along the c-file. **18. ... Qf6 19. Nb4 N×c3 20. Qe3 Qg6 21. Rae1 Be4 22. Rf2 f6 23. Na6 Rfe8 24. Nc7 R×c7! 25. B×c7** *(see diagram)*

**25. ... Nb5?** Here Bird misses a beautiful combination that would have rewarded him with a quick win: 25. ... Nd1! 26. R×d1 Qh5! 27. Rff1 B×c2. **26. Bf4 Rc8 27. c4?** Suicidal. A win for Black is far away again after 27. a4 or 27. Rc1. **27. ... R×c4 28. Qb3 a6** The immediate 28. ... Rc3! is already possible. **29. a4 Rc3 30. Qb2 R×g3† 31. Kh2** Black announces mate in 4 moves. "31. ... Qg4 (the finish is very neat) 32. B×g3 Qh5† 33. Bh4 Q×h4† 34. Kg1 Qh1 mates"—Steinitz. *The Field* (Steinitz), 1 March 1873.

*After 25. B×c7*

# FIRST MATCH WITH WISKER 1873

On 5 March 1873 Henry Edward Bird sat down for his first serious game of chess in almost three years. He faced John Wisker, one of England's strongest amateurs. Wisker's rise amongst the guild of British chess masters was quite meteoric. He scored a mediocre result at the B.C.A. Challenge Cup in 1868-69, but fared much better at the two following editions. Wisker ended on a joint first place in both of them. In the subsequent tie-breaks he beat Burn (1870) and De Vere (1872). Wisker was less successful in match play. Rosenthal beat him in 1870-71 in a short match, despite losing two games in the beginning. Just like his compatriots Wisker was unable to make a stand against the strongest foreign professionals Steinitz and Zukertort.

Bird's history in chess was much longer, but his ill success at the Challenge Cup tournament and the years of inactivity made it difficult to estimate his actual playing strength.

The agreement to play a match was allegedly the result of an accidental meeting between Bird and Wisker in February.[9] Löwenthal provided a few details on the arrangements.

> Our readers will be gratified to learn that this match was commenced on Wednesday, and, according to arrangements, will be played at the St. George's Chess Club and the Divan alternately. The winner of the first seven games to be declared the victor. This contest will, we feel sure, prove a source of great interest to the members of the St. George's, as well as to the frequenters of the Divan, as the play of both combatants is certain to be characterized by an abundance of skill and ingenuity [*Land and Water*, 8 March 1873].

The course of the match was very tense. Both players won their share of the games and neither of them was able to build up a large advantage in the score. After 12 games Bird was close to winning the match, as he led with 6 against 4. Two subsequent victories brought Wisker up even. It was thought inappropriate to let a single game determine the outcome of the match so a draw was agreed.

9. Bird wrote in *Chess History and Reminiscences*, pp. 114–115: "In 1873, Wisker was holder of the British Chess Association Challenge Cup, but had never seen or played with Bird [*sic*], who had been for six years out of chess [*sic*]. An accidental meeting by them, and the presence and intervention of Löwenthal and Boden, led to the Wisker and Bird four matches, the first for 5 pounds, and the others for credit of victory only." As seen in Part IV, Bird's recollection is incorrect; he met and played Wisker in the Challenge Cup tournament of 1868-69. The matter of the stakes is, as usual, unclear. In other books, namely *Chess Masterpieces* and *Chess Practice*, Bird wrote that the matches were played for chess skills/honor only. MacDonnell pretends that each of the four matches were played for £5 (*Illustrated Sporting and Dramatic News*, 29 March 1884).

**John Wisker (*Chess Monthly*).**

## (202) Bird–Wisker    1–0
Match 1 (game 1)
London, 5 March 1873
*C77*

**1. e4 e5 2. Nf3 Nc6 3. Bb5 a6 4. Ba4 Nf6 5. Qe2** "This move, though it used to be preferred in the days of yore, and is given as the standard line of play in Staunton's *Handbook*, is not to be commended. The queen is stronger for the attack when standing on d1. Her removal, too, renders it more difficult to play d4"—Wisker. **5. ... b5 6. Bb3 Be7 7. c3** "In a subsequent game, White played 7. a4."—Wisker **7. ... d6 8. 0–0 Bg4 9. d3 0–0 10. h3 Bh5 11. Bg5 Rb8 12. Nbd2 Nd7** "By this time Black has attained a perfectly satisfactory defense, but he scarcely makes the most of it. The proper course now was 12. ... Kh8. The knight might afterwards have retired with the view of playing the f-pawn"—Wisker. **13. Be3 Nf6 14. g4** "This course looks hazardous, but it is necessary for White to prevent the advance of the d-pawn, which would ruin White's

| First Match with Wisker, 5 March–5 April 1873 | | | | | | | | | | | | | | |
|---|---|---|---|---|---|---|---|---|---|---|---|---|---|---|
| | 1 | 2 | 3 | 4 | 5 | 6 | 7 | 8 | 9 | 10 | 11 | 12 | 13 | 14 |
| H.E. Bird | 1 | 0 | ½ | 1 | 1 | 0 | ½ | 1 | 0 | 0 | 1 | 1 | 0 | 0 | 6 |
| J. Wisker | 0 | 1 | ½ | 0 | 0 | 1 | ½ | 0 | 1 | 1 | 0 | 0 | 1 | 1 | 6 |

game"—Wisker. **14. ... Bg6 15. g5** "Premature, and giving Black a good chance. I should prefer playing the king, rook and knight to the kingside, keeping Black in a cramped position"—Zukertort. A very good start is 15. Nh4!, when Black has very little to do against the initiative on the kingside. **15. ... Nh5 16. Kh2 Qd7** Too slow. Black could initiate favorable complications with 16. ... Nf4 e.g., 17. B×f4 e×f4 18. h4 Bh5 with good perspectives, thanks to his bishop pair and various possibilities to open up the position. **17. Rg1 Nd8 18. Nh4 Ne6 19. Qg4 Rbd8 20. Nf5** By handing over the important square f4 to his opponent, Bird slowly drifts into an inferior position, but he is full of confidence in his own attacking chances and forsakes to play a move like 20. Ng2 **20. ... Nhf4** "Ill played. Had the other knight been moved here, Black would have had the best of the game. White could then have made nothing of his attack"—Wisker. A strong follow up after 20. ... Nef4 could have been 21. ... Kh8 and 22. ... f6, as suggested by Zukertort. Wisker's move is not bad but it is played with the feeble idea of winning the g-pawn. **21. d4 B×g5?!** "A fatal blunder, losing a clear piece"—Wisker. 21. ... Nd3! is a clear improvement. White has nothing better than 22. d5 Nef4 23. Bc2 Bh5 24. Qh4 Bg6 25. Qg4 with a draw. **22. d5 Kh8?** Though the situation looks desperate for Black, there is salvation to be found in 22. ... Nc5!, when after 23. Q×g5 the following combinational effort renders to Black some pawns for the piece: 23. ... N×h3! 24. K×h3 N×e4 25. N×e4 f6 26. N×f6† R×f6 27. Bc2 B×f5† 28. Kh2 Rdf8 29. B×f5 R×f5 30. Qg4. With a king without shelter, life is not so easy for White either. **23. d×e6 f×e6 24. Ng3?** 24. N×g7! simply snatches a pawn, when Black can resign at once. **24. ... Bh6 25. Nf3 Rf6 26. Rad1 Qc6?** "Another glaring mistake. The game now calls for no comment, except that White finishes it off admirably"—Wisker. **27. N×e5 Qe8 28. Nf3 Qf8 29. Nh4 Be8 30. e5 Rf7 31. Bd2 d5 32. Bc2 c5 33. Ng2 Bd7 34. N×f4 B×f4 35. B×f4 R×f4 36. Qh5 Qg8 37. Rg2 Rdf8 38. Qe2 Bc6 39. Nh5 R4f7 40. Nf6 g×f6 41. R×g8† R×g8 42. e×f6 d4 43. Be4** Black resigns—*Westminster Chess Club Papers* (Wisker/Zukertort), April 1873, p. 192.

### (203) Wisker–Bird    1–0
Match 1 (game 2)
London, 8 March 1873
C35

1. e4 e5 2. f4 e×f4 3. Nf3 Be7 4. Bc4 Bh4† 5. Kf1 d5 6. B×d5 Nf6 7. Nc3 0–0 8. d4 c6 9. Bb3 Bg4 10. B×f4 Nh5 11. Qd2 B×f3 12. g×f3 Kh8 13. Rg1 b5 14. Bg5 Qd7 15. B×h4 Qh3† 16. Rg2 Q×h4 17. Qg5 Qh3 18. Qg4 Q×g4 19. f×g4 Nf4 20. Rf2 g5 21. Ne2 N×e2 22. K×e2 f6 23. Be6 Na6 24. Raf1 Kg7 25. e5 f×e5 26. Rf7† R×f7 27. R×f7† Kg6 28. d×e5 Re8 29. R×a7 R×e6 30. R×a6 R×e5† 31. Kd3 Re6 32. b3 h5 33. a4 b×a4 34. R×a4 h4 35. Re4 Rf6 36. h3 Rf1 37. b4 Kf6 38. c4 Rb1 39. Kc3 Rh1 40. Re3 Rg1 41. b5 c×b5 42. c×b5 Rb1 43. Kc4 Rc1† 44. Kd5 Rd1† 45. Kc4 Rc1† 46. Rc3 Rb1 47. Rb3 Rc1† 48. Kd3 Rd1† 49. Kc2 Rd7 50. b6 Rb7 51. Kc3 Ke5 52. Kc4 Kd6 53. Kb5 Rf7 54. Rd3† Ke5 55. Ka6 Rf1 56. Ra3 Rb1 57. b7 Kd6 58. Ka7 and White wins—*Westminster Chess Club Papers*, April 1873, p. 192.

### (204) Bird–Wisker    ½–½
Match 1 (game 3)
London, 10 March 1873
C90

1. e4 e5 2. Nf3 Nc6 3. Bb5 a6 4. Ba4 Nf6 5. 0–0 Be7 6. Re1 b5 7. Bb3 d6 8. c3 Bg4 9. d3 0–0 10. Be3 d5 11. e×d5 N×d5 12. Nbd2 N×e3 13. R×e3 Bc5 14. Re4 Bf5 15. Re1 B×d3 16. N×e5 N×e5 17. R×e5 Bd6 18. Rd5 Bg6 19. Nf3 Qf6 20. Qd4 Q×d4 21. R×d4 Rae8 22. Kf1 Re4 23. Rad1 Rfe8 24. R×e4 B×e4 25. Ng5 and the game was a draw—*Westminster Chess Club Papers*, April 1873, pp. 192–193.

### (205) Wisker–Bird    0–1
Match 1 (game 4)
London, 12 March 1873
C51

1. e4 e5 2. Nf3 Nc6 3. Bc4 Bc5 4. b4 B×b4 5. c3 Bc5 6. 0–0 d6 7. d4 e×d4 8. c×d4 Bb6 9. d5 Na5 10. Bb2 Ne7 11. Bd3 0–0 12. Nc3 Ng6 13. Ne2 c5 14. Qd2 The major alternative at this point is 14. Rc1. Wisker thought it better and adopted it to score a win in game six of the match. **14. ... Bg4** "This move, which Bird always adopts for the defense, cannot be commended. The bishop occupies a better position at c8, for, as the rook should be played to b8, and the b-pawn thrown up, the bishop then commands both sides, and may often be effectively moved to a6. The bishop at g4 cannot capture the knight, and is therefore of little use in such a situation. Indeed, he may often be attacked with advantage. As an illustration of these remarks, the sixth game may be consulted"—Wisker. Bird was rather fond of the text move (in similar positions), and rightly so, but he often failed to realize the correct idea behind the move—to exchange the piece at f3, inflicting a weakness on White's kingside. White's command of the g-file is not so fearful as thought by Wisker and his contemporaries. **15. Kh1 c4 16. Bc2** 16. Qc3 is advisable to prevent any sacrifice of the c-pawn. **16. ... Bc5** "Black's eccentric movements for the defense ought to have allowed White a great superiority"—Wisker. Black is decidedly better after 16. ... B×f3! 17. g×f3 and now, besides the traditional 17. ... Bc5 and 18. ... b5, he can also play 17. ... c3! 18. Q×c3 Ne5 with powerful piece play. **17. Qc3** "Not the best. The threatened mate only drives Black to a defensive move, which he must make under any circumstances, sooner or later"—Wisker. **17. ... f6 18. Ned4** "18. Nfd4 ought to have been played. White's play at this critical juncture is remarkable for its inefficiency"—Wisker. After 18. Nfd4 B×e2! 19. N×e2 b5, White's attack is absolutely nowhere, while Bird's pawn has started rolling. White's only chance to bring the knight to e6 can smartly be undermined: 20. Ba3 B×a3 21. Q×a3 Qb6 22. Qb4 Rfb8 23. Rad1 Nb7 24. Nd4 Nc5. **18. ... b6 19. Nd2** "Moves 17 and 18 are not good. The knight is played to many different squares on the Evans Gambit, but I never saw it played to d2"—Zukertort. **19. ... Rc8 20. f4 B×d4 21. Q×d4 Qe7** An awkward place for the queen, as it allows Wisker to activate his rook. Had Bird played 21. ... Qc7, he would have triggered the more passive 22. Rac1 (21. Bc3 Nb7 and 22. ... Qc5 with the exchange of queens follows). In any case, there remains a lot of tension in the position, although the onus is on White to prove his compensation. **22. Rae1 Qc7 23. Re3!**

**Rfe8?!** (*see diagram*) The rook is not better here than where it was. Retreating the bishop with 23. ... Bd7 seems logical. There can follow 24. ... b5 and 25. ... Nb7.

*After 23. ... Rfe8*

**24. Rg3?!** "White should not have allowed the bishop to come in"—Wisker. Wisker misses the momentum-gaining move. Quite against expectations, the strength of 24. e5! has been improved considerably after Black's last move, as his bishop is vulnerable at g4 without the rooks opposing along the f-file. Black has a tough choice to make. After the most logical move, 24. ... fxe5, a forcing line arises: 25. fxe5 Nxe5 26. Rxe5! Rxe5 27. Qxg4 c3. Now White can brilliantly force the game with 28. Ba1!; e.g., 28. ... g6 30. Bxg6!! hxg6 31. Ne4! or 28. ... cxd2 29. Bxe5 dxe5 30. Qf5 g6 31. Qe6†! Kg7 32. d6. Less conclusive is 24. ... dxe5, but White's advantage is undeniable after 25. fxe5 Nxe5 26. d6. **24. ... Be2 25. Re1?** "Losing a pawn. By 25. Rf2 White would still have maintained a tenable game. After this, White's rash efforts to retrieve himself are perfectly useless"—Wisker. Bird can in that case return the pawn while realizing an important exchange and keep a slight initiative: 25. ... Bd3! 26. Bxd3 cxd3 27. Rxd3 Qc2 etc. **25. ... Bd3 26. Ba4 Re7 27. Qc3?!** 27. Rc1 is more resilient, but it is hard to overcome the loss of the f-pawn in any case, e.g., 27. ... Nxf4 28. Bd1 Be2 29. Qe3 Nd3 30. Bxe2 Nxc1 31. Bxc1 c3 32. Nb1 c2. **27. ... Nxf4 28. Ree3 Ne2 29. Rxe2 Bxe2 30. Qxf6 Rf8 31. Qg5 Nb7 32. Bf6 Ref7 33. e5 dxe5 34. Ne4 Bd3 35. d6 Nxd6 36. Nxd6 Rxf6** White resigns —*Westminster Chess Club Papers* (Wisker/Zukertort), April 1873, p. 193.

## (206) Bird–Wisker   1–0
Match 1 (game 5)
London, 15 March 1873
C51

**1. e4 e5 2. Nf3 Nc6 3. Bc4 Bc5 4. b4 Bxb4 5. c3 Ba5 6. 0-0 Nf6 7. Ba3 d6 8. d4 Bb6 9. dxe5 dxe5 10. Qb3 Nxe4 11. Bxf7†** and mates next move—*Westminster Chess Club Papers*, April 1873, p. 193.

## (207) Wisker–Bird   1–0
Match 1 (game 6)
London, 15 March 1873
C51

**1. e4 e5 2. Nf3 Nc6 3. Bc4 Bc5 4. b4 Bxb4 5. c3 Bc5 6. 0-0 d6 7. d4 exd4 8. cxd4 Bb6 9. d5 Na5 10. Bb2 Ne7 11. Bd3 0-0 12. Nc3 Ng6 13. Ne2 c5 14. Rc1 Bg4** "A deviation from the usual course, which is 14. ... f6. The position of the bishop at g4 affords

no advantage to Black"—Wisker. **15. Qd2 Bc7** Just as in the fourth match game, both players neglect the exchange at f3. White had to avoid it with 15. Ng3, while Bird could now substantially improve his position with 15. ... Bxf3 16. gxf3 and either 16. ... Qd7!, threatening 17. ... Qh3 and thus forcing White to play the awkward 17. Qg5 f6 18. Qg3 Ne5 19. f4 Nxd3, or 16. ... c4! 17. Bxc4 (or 17. Bc2 Bc5 18. Bc3 b6) 17. ... Nxc4 18. Rxc4 f5! are clearly in Black's favor. **16. Kh1 Qd7** "As the queen retires almost immediately to d8, this also is not advisable"—Wisker. **17. Ng3 Rae8** 17. ... Rab8 (Wisker) is not much better, for White simply continues in the same manner as in the game. He could still play 17. ... Bxf3, but White is now better placed to meet this exchange then he was a few moves ago. For example: 18. gxf3 f6 19. Bc3 b6 20. Rg1 Kh8 21. Nf5 Nb7 22. f4 and Black is under pressure. **18. Ng1** "The proper play, strengthening White's attack on the kingside"—Wisker. **18. ... Qd8** If instead 18. ... Qa4?!, Wisker could demonstrate the reason why Black generally plays f7–f6 in this line: 19. Bxg7! Kxg7 20. Qb2† Kg8? (20. ... Qd4 21. Qxd4† cxd4 22. Rxc7 leads to a difficult, but still tenable, endgame) 21. Bb5. **19. f4 Qh4?** "Black's gyrations with the queen are anything but judicious. Her majesty is locked up by White's next move, and is speedily lost altogether"—Wisker. The position is very hard to defend. 19. ... c4 is one of the better ideas for Black. **20. Qc3?** "This compels Black to shut his queen out of the game"—Wisker. Wisker misses a chance to exchange Bird's strongest defender, chase his knight to a corner and bring another strong piece to the front with 20. Nf5! Bxf5 21. exf5 Nh8 22. Rf3! The threat 23. f6! is now very disturbing for if Black prevents this move with 22. ... f6 the queen is lost after 23. Rh3 Qg4 24. Nf3 and 25. Rh4. **20. ... f6 21. f5?!** Eyeing Bird's queen, but she won't be easy to catch now. More flexible is 21. Qd2, which prepares 22. Bc3, and keeps one of White's most dangerous options, 22. Nf5, in position. **21. ... Ne5 22. Bb5** A loss of time, but White's plan was faulty from the start. **22. ... Re7 23. Rf4** (*see diagram*)

*After 23. Rf4*

**23. ... a6** "Mr. Bird said afterwards the he could win in this position by 23. ... c4. The following would be a probable continuation: 24. Rcf1 Qg5 (or 24. ... Qh6 25. Qc2 g5 26. fxg6 *e.p.* Qxg6 27. h3 Bd7 28. Bxd7 and now after both 28. ... Qxg3 and 28. ... Rxd7, 29. Bxe5 wins) 25. h3 Qh6 26. Kh2 wins a piece"—Zukertort. The situation remains complicated. At the end of Zukertort's main line, it is unclear how White will ever win the piece, as 26. hxg4 is out of the question. It is indeed Black who is better as he can finally get on with his queenside play: 26. ... a6 27. Ba4 b5 28. Bc2 Bb6 29. Qb4 c3! etc. In the sideline 24. ... Qh6, Black's play can be improved with 25. ... Qg5! and if 26. Bc1 a6! But there is an altogether better possibility for Bird. Instead of 23. ... c4, he could play 23. ... Qg5!

Now White can try again to win the queen with 24. Rcf1, but 24. ... a6 changes off the white-squared bishop, securing h5 as a transit square to leave the kingside if necessary: 25. Be2 B×e2 26. N3×e2 Nac4 27. Bc1 Qh5. If 26. N1×e2 Nac4 27. Bc1 Ba5 and Black will always be able to interpose a piece at d2 if the queen is attacked. **24. Be2 Qg5 25. R×g4 N×g4 26. Rf1 h5?** "To give up the piece and exchange queens at e3 would have been better"—Zukertort. An interesting ending arises after 26. ... Qe3! 27. B×g4 Q×c3 28. B×c3 b5. Black's pawn mass on the queenside is a very strong element in his favor. After the text move the game is abruptly decided. **27. Bc1 N×h2 28. B×g5 N×f1 29. B×f1 f×g5 30. N×h5 b5 31. Nf3 b4 32. Qb2 c4 33. N×g5 c3 34. Q×b4** "The best course. The end of the game presents some features of interest"—Wisker. **34. ... g6 35. Q×c3 g×h5 36. f6 Re5 37. f7† Kh8 38. Q×c7 R×g5 39. Qe7** and White wins—*Westminster Chess Club Papers* (Wisker/Zukertort), April 1873, p. 193; *Brisbane Week* (Wisker), 17 March 1877.

**(208) Bird–Wisker    ½–½**
Match 1 (game 7)
London, 17 March 1873
*C77*

1. e4 e5 2. Nf3 Nc6 3. Bb5 a6 4. Ba4 Nf6 5. Qe2 b5 6. Bb3 Be7 7. c3 d6 8. a4 Rb8 9. a×b5 a×b5 10. d4 e×d4 11. c×d4 Bg4 12. Be3 0–0 13. Nbd2 13. Nc3 prevents the following equalizer. **13. ... d5 14. e5 Ne4 15. 0–0 f5** Wisker aims for more with this aggressive but slightly antipositional move. After 15. ... N×d2 16. Q×d2 B×f3, he is perfectly fine. **16. e×f6** *e.p.* **N×f6 17. h3 Bh5 18. Qd3 Kh8 19. Rfc1 Rb6?!** The rook is misplaced here. He could play 19. ... Nb4 20. Qc3 Bd6, when all is defended. **20. Ne5! Nb4 21. Qc3 Bd6 22. Bg5 Be2 23. Re1 Bh5 24. Rac1** Wisker is under pressure, but the text move relieves him a bit. 24. Nf1 slowly improves the position of the knight, while keeping the a-file under control. **24. ... Qc8 25. Bh4 h6 26. g4 Be8 27. Bg3 Na6 28. Ba2** "Mr. Bird has been out of regular chess practice for some years, and his play has deteriorated in consequence. In his best days he would have followed up such an advantage as he obtained early in the present game with far more vigor than he has done here"—Staunton. Directly 28. Bc2 is preferable. The bishop might head for f5. **28. ... c5** "Not sound"—Wisker. It has become hard to sit still and wait. **29. Bb1** Bird's reply is too prudent. He was fully ready to open up the position and make good use of his opponent's many weaknesses with 29. d×c5! Q×c5 30. Qa5 Qd4 31. Nb3 Bb4 32. N×d4 B×a5 33. Re2. **29. ... B×e5** He must aim to keep the position closed with 29. ... c4. The text move gives White an impressive majority on the kingside. **30. d×e5 Nh7 31. Qd3** Bird is eager to smash his opponent, preferably by mating him on the very next move, but he completely underestimates Wisker's resources. After 31. f4!, Black gets in a terrible bind. **31. ... Ng5** This leads to a more or less balanced position. Instead, 31. ... Bg6!, followed by the exchange of the bishops, terminates White's attacking chances. Black will immediately push his own pawns, and get a small advantage in the rat race to the other side of the board. **32. h4** 32. f4 looks sounder. Black must play 32. ... Nb4. **32. ... Bg6 33. Q×d5 Nh3† 34. Kh2?** *(see diagram)* Although it means remaining with his king in the danger zone, the

f-pawn had to be defended at all cost. The position is extremely tricky after 34. Kf1 B×b1 35. R×b1 Qg4 36. Re3.

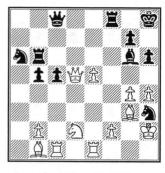

*After 34. Kh2*

**34. ... Q×g4?** An evident capture, but 34. ... N×f2! is very forceful here. Yet it was necessary to foresee, after 35. B×f2 R×f2† 36. Kg3 Qf8 37. Nf3, the extremely forceful and decisive 37. ... Nb4! After 38. Qb3 Nd3, White has no choice but to abandon the queen by playing 39. Q×d3 and 40. K×f2. His perspectives are depressing. **35. f3!** "The only move to save the game"—Wisker. **35. ... Nf4?!** This only implies much welcomed exchanges. **36. f×g4 N×d5 37. Ne4 Nf4?!** Wisker deals too loosely with the situation. 37. ... c4 must be played to keep the c-pawn alive. **38. N×c5?!** Bird in his turn is a bit too greedy. First 38. B×f4 R×f4 39. Kg3 Rf8 and only then 40. N×c5 is a clear improvement. **38. ... N×c5 39. R×c5 B×b1 40. R×b1 Ne6 41. Rd5 Kg8** Much better chances for a draw arise from 41. ... Rc6! If White captures the b-pawn, both his rooks are misplaced. Black gains enough compensation with a swift counterattack. **42. Rbd1** 42. Rd6! puts Black under severe pressure. **42. ... Rc8 43. R1d2 b4 44. Rd6 Rbc6 45. R×c6** This exchange comes too soon. First he should have improved the position of his king, but whether he could force the win by doing it is doubtful. **45. ... R×c6 46. Kg2 b3 47. Kf2 Kf7 48. Ke2 Rc4 49. Rd7† Kg6 50. Rb7 R×g4 51. Kf3 Rc4 52. Bf2 Kf5 53. R×b3** Bird goes a bit far in his bid to win the game, and with 53. ... R×h4! Wisker could change roles and put him on the test. By taking the e-pawn a draw becomes certain. **53. ... K×e5 54. Rb5† Kd6** draw. "This game is considered by both players the best of the series"—Wisker—*Westminster Chess Club Papers* (Wisker), April 1873 p. 193; *Illustrated London News* (Staunton), 24 May 1873.

**(209) Wisker–Bird    0–1**
Match 1 (game 8)
London, 22 March 1873
*C51*

1. e4 e5 2. Nf3 Nc6 3. Bc4 Bc5 4. b4 B×b4 5. c3 Bc5 6. 0–0 d6 7. d4 e×d4 8. c×d4 Bb6 9. d5 Na5 10. Bb2 Ne7 11. Bd3 0–0 12. Nc3 c5 13. Rc1 c4 14. Bb1 Bg4 15. Ne2 Bc5 16. Qd2 Ng6 17. Kh1 "By now moving 17. Bc3 White would have retarded the advance of the pawns on the queenside"—Wisker. **17. ... b5 18. Nfg1?** Bird and Wisker have rattled off a series of similar moves as in their previous encounters with this opening. By doing so, Bird neglected to claim a big advantage with B×f3, a move possible at several opportunities. But with the text move Wisker commits a real mistake. In game six, Wisker also played 18. Ng1. Compared with that position, Bird's pawns on the queenside have now advanced

much further, making it necessary to stop them at once with 18. Bc3. **18. ... b4 19. Bd4 c3 20. Qd3 Rc8 21. f3 Bd7 22. f4 B×d4 23. N×d4 Nc4 24. Nc6 B×c6?** It doesn't take too much imagination to see that 24. ... Nb2 (Wisker) wins easily. **25. Q×c4 Bd7 26. Q×b4 Qb6 27. Q×b6 a×b6 28. Bd3?!** Material equality has been restored, but the pawn at c3 is not to be underestimated. Yet, this is exactly what Wisker does. After 28. Rf3 a draw becomes nearly inevitable. **28. ... f5! 29. g3?!** "Very weak. White should have exchanged pawns and afterwards played 31. Ne2. He would thus have secured at least a draw, for the advanced Black pawn is weak" —Wisker. Wisker overlooks, after 29. e×f5 B×f5 30. B×f5 R×f5 31. Ne2, the riposte 31. ... c2, which wins a pawn and keeps the c-pawn alive. Better is 31. Rf3! R×d5 32. Rf×c3 R×c3 33. R×c3 N×f4. This also nets Black a pawn, but with the c-pawn off the board White's drawing chances increase considerably. **29. ... f×e4 30. B×e4 Rfe8 31. Bd3?!** This is bad. 31. Rfe1 defends the bishop, while the d-pawn remains under control as well. **31. ... Rc5 32. Ne2?** Another bad move after which White is forced to exchange his bishop. **32. ... Re3! 33. B×g6** If 33. Rfd1 Ba4. **33. ... h×g6 34. Rf2 Bg4 35. Nd4 R×d5** White resigns—*Westminster Chess Club Papers* (Wisker), May 1873, p. 8.

## (210) Bird–Wisker     0–1

Match 1 (game 9)
London, 22 March 1873
C77

**1. e4 e5 2. Nf3 Nc6 3. Bb5 a6 4. Ba4 Nf6 5. Qe2 b5 6. Bb3 Be7 7. c3 d6 8. d4 Bg4 9. Be3 0–0 10. Nbd2 d5 11. e×d5 N×d5 12. 0–0 e×d4 13. c×d4 Bf6 14. Qd3 Re8 15. a3 Qd7 16. Rfe1 Bf5 17. Qf1 Nb6 18. Red1 Rad8 19. Rac1 B×d4 20. N×d4 N×d4 21. B×d4 Q×d4 22. R×c7 Bg6 23. Rc3 Bd3 24. Nf3 Q×c3 25. b×c3 B×f1 26. R×d8 R×d8 27. K×f1 Rd3** White resigns—*Westminster Chess Club Papers*, May 1873, p. 8.

## (211) Wisker–Bird     1–0

Match 1 (game 10)
London, 24 March 1873
C51

**1. e4 e5 2. Nf3 Nc6 3. Bc4 Bc5 4. b4 B×b4 5. c3 Bc5 6. 0–0 d6 7. d4 e×d4 8. c×d4 Bb6 9. Nc3 Bg4 10. Qa4 Kf8 11. d5 Nce7 12. Ne2 Ng6 13. Nfd4 h5 14. Kh1 h4 15. h3 B×e2 16. N×e2 Nf6 17. Bg5 Qe8 18. Qc2 N×e4 19. f4 Rh5 20. f5 R×g5 21. f×g6 f6 22. Bd3 Nf2† 23. R×f2 B×f2 24. Nf4 Re5 25. Q×f2 Ke7 26. Re1 Qa4 27. R×e5† d×e5 28. Qc5†** and White wins—*Westminster Chess Club Papers*, May 1873, p. 8.

## (212) Bird–Wisker     1–0

Match 1 (game 11)
London, 27 March 1873
C77

**1. e4 e5 2. Nf3 Nc6 3. Bb5 a6 4. Ba4 Nf6 5. Qe2 b5 6. Bb3 Be7 7. a4 Rb8 8. a×b5 a×b5 9. d3 d6 10. Bg5 0–0 11. B×f6 B×f6 12. Bd5 Ne7 13. Bb3 Ng6 14. g3 Bh3 15. Nc3 c6 16. Nd2 Qd7 17. f3 Ra8 18. Rb1 Kh8 19. Nd1 Bg5 20. Nf2 Be6 21. B×e6 Q×e6**

**22. 0–0 f5 23. Ra1 d5 24. Nb3 Be7 25. Kg2 Rad8 26. e×f5 Q×f5 27. d4 Bd6 28. Nd3 Rde8 29. d×e5 B×e5 30. Qd2 Re7 31. Rae1 Rfe8 32. Re2 h5 33. Rfe1 h4 34. N×e5 N×e5 35. Nd4 h3† 36. Kf2 Qf6 37. Qf4 Q×f4 38. g×f4 Ng6 39. R×e7 R×e7 40. R×e7 N×e7 41. b4 Kg8 42. Kg3 Kf7 43. K×h3 Kf6 44. Kg4 g6 45. h4 Kf7 46. Kg5 Kg7 47. f5 Kf7 48. f4 g×f5 49. N×f5 Ng8 50. Nd4 Ne7 51. f5** Black resigns—*Westminster Chess Club Papers*, May 1873, p. 8.

## (213) Wisker–Bird     0–1

Match 1 (game 12)
London, 31 March 1873
C35

**1. e4 e5 2. f4 e×f4 3. Nf3 Be7** "This move constitutes the Cunningham Defense. It has generally been considered to give Black the inferior game, but Bird has played it with great success against some of our strongest players"—Burn. **4. Bc4 Bh4† 5. Kf1** "This is the best move. If 5. g3 f×g3 6. 0–0 g×h2† and White is three pawns behind, but has a strong attack. With the best play the game should probably be drawn"—Burn. **5. ... d6 6. d4 Bg4 7. B×f4 Qf6 8. Be3 Nc6 9. Nc3 Nge7 10. Be2 B×f3 11. g×f3** "11. B×f3 would probably have been better"—Burn. **11. ... 0–0–0 12. Rg1?!** "Mr. Bird thinks that 12. d5 would have been a better move for Mr. Wisker at this stage"—Burn. **12. ... d5! 13. e5?** White's position was already weakened after allowing the previous move, but this attempt to keep the center closed makes matters only worse. **13. ... Qe6 14. Kg2 Nf5 15. Qd2** *(see diagram)*

*After 15. Qd2*

**15. ... f6!** Excellent play from Bird. He initiates a direct attack against Wisker's king. **16. f4 h5** Even stronger is at once 16. ... g5! **17. Bf3?** A sheer loss of time. With 17. Bb5 he could try to confuse his opponent, but after 17. ... Nce7 and 18. ... g5, Bird's aim remains clear. **17. ... g5! 18. f×g5 f×g5** Here and on the next few moves Bird is riveted on storming forward with his g- and h-pawn, but he overlooks some more forceful continuations. At this point 18. ... f×e5! would have been considerably stronger. **19. Kh1 g4 20. Bg2 Be7 21. Ne2 h4?** Too hasty. The preparatory 21. ... Qd7 is correct. If then 22. Nf4?! Bg5 is good for Black. Against many other moves, Black continues with 22. ... h4. **22. b4?** "A strange mistake. Had White now played 22. Nf4, he would have had the better game"—Wisker. 22. Nf4 is certainly not better for White, but Wisker is correct that this move offers him decent chances to complicate the game. There could follow 22. ... Qf7 23. Rgf1 Qh7 24. B×d5 Ng3† 25. Kg1 Nb4! **22. ... Ng3†** White resigns. "A pretty termination. If 23. h×g3 h×g3† 24. Bh3 R×h3† 25. Kg2 Qf5 and wins or if

23. N×g3 h×g3 24. h3 g×h3 25. Bf1 g2† and wins"—Burn. *West-minster Chess Club Papers* (Wisker), May 1873, p. 9; *Turf, Field and Farm* (Burn, first published in the *Liverpool Weekly Albion*), 16 May 1873.

**(214) Bird–Wisker    0–1**
Match 1 (game 13)
London, 2 April 1873
*C84*

1. e4 e5 2. Nf3 Nc6 3. Bb5 a6 4. Ba4 Nf6 5. d4 e×d4 6. e5 Ne4 7. 0–0 Be7 8. N×d4 Nc5 9. B×c6 d×c6 10. f4 Bg4 11. Q×g4 Q×d4† 12. Kh1 Ne4 13. Qf3 Bc5 14. h3 0–0–0 15. Nc3 N×c3 16. b×c3 Qd5 17. Qe2 Rhe8 18. c4 Qe6 19. Bb2 Bd4 20. c3 Bc5 21. Bc1 f6 22. Rb1 f×e5 23. f5 Qf6 24. a4 e4 25. Bf4 e3 26. a5 Rd2 27. Qh5 Qe7 28. Q×h7 Rf2 29. Bg3 R×f1† 30. R×f1 e2 31. Re1 Bd6 32. Qg6 B×g3 33. Q×g3 Rd8 34. Qf3 Rd1 35. R×d1 e1Q† 36. R×e1 Q×e1† 37. Kh2 Qe5† 38. Qg3 Q×a5 39. Q×g7 Q×f5 40. Qd4 a5 41. h4 a4 42. Qa7 Qf4† 43. Kh3 Q×c4 44. Qe3 b6 45. h5 a3 46. h6 Qf7 47. Qe5 a2 48. c4 Qf1 49. h7 Qh1† 50. Kg3 a1Q and Black wins—*Land and Water*, 19 April 1873.

**(215) Wisker–Bird    1–0**
Match 1 (game 14)
London, 5 April 1873
*C61*

1. e4 e5 2. Nf3 Nc6 3. Bb5 Nd4 4. N×d4 e×d4 5. 0–0 Bc5 6. d3 Qh4 7. f4 Nf6 8. Nd2 c6 9. Nf3 Qh5 10. Bc4 0–0 11. e5 d5 12. Bb3 Ne8 13. Bd2 Nc7 14. h3 f5 15. Nh2 Qg6 16. Kh1 Be6 17. g4 Be7 18. c3 d×c3 19. b×c3 c5 20. Bc2 d4 21. c4 Bd7 22. Ba4 B×a4 23. Q×a4 f×g4 24. Qd7 g3 25. Rg1 Bd8 26. R×g3 Qc6† 27. Q×c6 b×c6 28. Rag1 Ne6 29. Rf3 Rf5 30. Rb1 Bb6 31. a4 Raf8 32. a5 Bc7 33. Rb7 Bb8 34. Kg2 h5 35. Rf1 Kh7 36. Nf3 a6 37. Nh4 R5f7 38. R×f7 R×f7 39. f5 Nf8 40. e6 Rb7 41. Rb1 R×b1 42. e7 Nd7 43. e8Q Black resigns—*Westminster Chess Club Papers*, May 1873, p. 9.

---

# Second Match with Wisker 1873

Because the first match had a peaceful outcome a rematch was commenced forthwith. The conditions remained the same as those of the previous match. Bird opened with a win, but after five games Wisker had taken the lead with three wins and a draw. At this point Bird started to exhibit his tenacity by putting down a winning streak after several closely contested games. After 13 games he managed to obtain a comfortable 6–4 advantage. To the surprise and disappointment of many, Wisker did not attempt to fight back but instead threw in the towel in the fourteenth game due to indispo-

| Second Match with Wisker, April–May 1873 | | | | | | | | | | | | | | | |
|---|---|---|---|---|---|---|---|---|---|---|---|---|---|---|---|
| | 1 | 2 | 3 | 4 | 5 | 6 | 7 | 8 | 9 | 10 | 11 | 12 | 13 | 14 | |
| H.E. Bird | 1 | 0 | ½ | 0 | 0 | 1 | 1 | ½ | 1 | 1 | ½ | 0 | 1 | + | 7 |
| J. Wisker | 0 | 1 | ½ | 1 | 1 | 0 | 0 | ½ | 0 | 0 | ½ | 1 | 0 | – | 4 |

sition. Wisker's loss was generally thought to be caused by the burdens of his professional engagements.[10]

**(216) Bird–Wisker    1–0**
Match 2 (game 1)
London, April 1873
*C77*

1. e4 e5 2. Nf3 Nc6 3. Bb5 a6 4. Ba4 Nf6 5. Qe2 Be7 6. 0–0 b5 7. Bb3 d6 8. a4 Rb8 9. a×b5 a×b5 10. d3 Bg4 11. c3 0–0 12. h3 Bh5 13. g4! "Somewhat hazardous, no doubt, but White, perhaps, saw no other way to develop his forces speedily"—Bird. 13. ... Bg6 14. Nh4 Qd7 15. f4! A crafty follow-up. 15. ... e×f4 16. B×f4 Ne5 17. Nd2 c5 18. B×e5 d×e5 19. Ndf3 Qc7 20. Rf2? "An error, which costs the exchange, and gives Black a won game. It was Black's object to move 20. ... c4 for the double purpose of excluding his adversary's bishop and of bringing his own into play. He can now, of course, throw forward the pawn with proportionately greater advantage"—Wisker. 20. ... c4 21. N×g6 h×g6 22. d×c4 b×c4 More precise is 22. ... Bc5!, as after 23. c×b5 B×f2† 24. K×f2 Qc5†, there is no way for White to maintain his queenside phalanx intact. 23. B×c4 Bc5 24. Raf1 Qb7! 25. b4 "These pawns are too weak to form a balance to the gain of the exchange by Black. Black however, having gained an advantage, took scant pains to preserve it"—Wisker. 25. ... B×f2† 26. Q×f2 N×e4 "The following variation will show how defective would have been 26. ... Q×e4: 27. B×f7† R×f7 28. Ng5 Q moves 29. N×f7 K or Q×f7 30. g5 regains the piece"—Wisker. An improvement over the game, and certainly better than 26. ... Q×e4?, is 26. ... Qc7! 27. Nd2 Rad8, first paying attention to the destruction of White's queenside. 27. Qh4 Qb6† 28. Kg2 Qf6 29. Qe1 Qf4? A very weird move, bad and of no apparent use. Simply 29. ... Nd6! 30. Bb3 Rbe8 consolidates. 30. Bd5! "White plays all this uphill game with great ability"—Bird. 30. ... Nf6 31. N×e5 31. B×f7†! R×f7 32. N×e5 is the more precise move order. 31. ... Qh6 For now 31. ... N×d5! is a promising sacrifice. After 32. R×f4 N×f4† 33. Kf3 g5, Black has to find a way to activate his rook. This is possible on the c- or d-file, but also along the sixth rank; e.g., after 34. ... Rb6! and 35. ... Rh6. 32. Bb3 Rbd8 33. Rf2 Nd5?! This seems good, but f7 turns out surprisingly weak. 33. ... Rde8 or 33. ... Qg5 were fine. 34. Qe4! N×c3?! 34. ... Nf6 35. Qb7 is far from agreeable, but a sad necessity. 35. Q×g6? Bird misses 35. Qf3!, when Black is helpless: 35. ... Rc8 36. B×f7† Kh7 37. Qd3. 35. ... Q×g6 36. N×g6 Ne4 37. Rf5 Rd2† 38. Kf3 Rd3†? A draw becomes unavoidable after 38. ... Nf6 39. N×f8 Rd3† 40. Kg2 R×b3 41. g5. 39. K×e4 R×b3 40. Ne7† and mates next move—*Westminster Chess Club Papers* (Wisker), May 1873, p. 9; *Modern Chess* (Bird) pp. 87–88.

---

10. Bird nevertheless deserved a spot in the sunlight with his performance: "However, be that as it may, Mr. Bird is to be congratulated upon the well-merited success he has achieved. He has fully demonstrated the genius, brilliancy, and high powers which characterize the conduct of his play. In conclusion, we may remark that during the whole match the most friendly spirit prevailed between the combatants, and that the encounter was productive of some exceedingly fine games." *Land and Water*, 31 May 1873.

## (217) Wisker–Bird    1–0
Match 2 (game 2)
London, 9 April 1873
*A80*

**1. e3 f5** "The long series of irregular openings, of which this was the first, was conducted by both parties in the same way throughout—Mr. Bird playing for the attack, whilst his opponent advanced the pawns on the queenside"—Wisker. This was the first game in his career in which Bird adopted the Dutch Defense (if two early games against G.W. Medley and Simons are left out). The Dutch Defense was still quite unexplored in the nineteenth century, and it gave Bird ample room for his creativity and experimentalism. It would be an exaggeration to state that Bird made any lasting theoretical contributions to the opening, but it often led to an entertaining game. The other side of the mirror were some terrible passive defeats suffered by Bird. 1. ... f5 remained Bird's favorite reply against any other opening move than 1. e4 until the end of his career. **2. d4 Nf6 3. Nf3 b6 4. c4 Bb7 5. Nc3 Na6 6. a3 g6 7. b4 c6 8. Bb2 Bg7 9. Qb3 Nc7 10. Be2 e6 11. a4 0–0 12. 0–0 Rb8 13. b5** 13. a5 is a more favorable way to open the queenside. **13. ... c5 14. d×c5 b×c5 15. a5 Qe7 16. Na4 d6 17. Rfd1 e5 18. b6** Wisker recklessly advances his pawns. The opening of lines and diagonals favor his opponent more than him. **18. ... a×b6 19. N×b6 Ne6** 19. ... Na8! demonstrates White's vulnerability along the b-file. After 20. Nd2?! (not 20. N×a8? B×f3) 20. ... Bc6 21. Nb1, Black can chose between 21. ... Nd7! (questioning the knight) or 21. ... f4, heading for an attack. Correct is 20. Qb5, when there is nothing better than 20. ... Nc7. **20. Qa4** Other moves aren't that convincing either, although a more active course should be preferred; e.g., 20. a6 Ba8 21. Ra5. **20. ... f4!** Bird doesn't hesitate a second to take the command of the game. **21. Ne1?** This retreat abandons the control over some crucial squares. Given the various tactical themes that Black has at his disposal, it was necessary to involve his rook in the defense of the center, with 21. Ra3! or 21. Ra2. But in any case, Bird enjoys a very promising position. **21. ... f×e3 22. f×e3 Bh6** "The game hitherto has been singularly devoid of interest. It brightens a little at this point, owing to the attack Mr. Bird has contrived to develop; but we should have hesitated to publish it, where it not for the remarkable variations which spring from Black's 24th move"—Staunton. Staunton and other commentators overlooked a particularly brilliant and unexpected win deeply hidden in the position: 22. ... Nd4!! 23. e×d4 (declining the sacrifice provokes another knight entry: 23. Bf1 Ng4!) 23. ... e×d4 24. Ra3 (saving the bishop loses instantly: 24. Bf1 Qe3† 25. Kh1 Ng4 and mate cannot be averted) 24. ... Q×e2 25. Qc2 Q×c2 26. N×c2 Ng4 wins. **23. Ra3 Ne4** Not bad at all, but the same idea, 23. ... Nd4, is still the most effective one. **24. Nf3** (*see diagram*)

**24. ... N4g5?** "The position from this point was the subject of a lengthy discussion. With the best play on both sides, the attack would probably have succeeded, but it is much easier to discover the best moves for White than for Black. Black somewhat precipitates his onslaught"—Wisker.

Staunton: "By this move Mr. Bird appears to have thrown away an almost certain victory. Had he played the other knight to g5, we believe he could have won the game without difficulty. Let us sup-

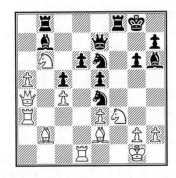

*After 24. Nf3*

pose: 24. ... N6g5 25. a6 R×f3! 26. B×f3 (if 26. Kh1 Nh3! 27. g×h3 Qg5 and then mate follows in three moves or 26. Rf1 Nh3† and mates in three more moves or 26. g×f3 Nh3† 27. Kg2 Qg5† and mates next move) 26. ... N×f3† 27. g×f3 (if 27. Kf1 Qh4 winning immediately) 27. ... Qg5† 28. Kf1 Rf8 29. Ke2 Nc3†! 30. B×c3 (best) 30. ... Qg2† 31. Kd3 (if 31. Ke1 R×f3 and mates directly) 31. ... e4† 32. f×e4 B×e4 mates. There are two major alternatives, **a** and **b**, after 24. ... N6g5:

**a**—25. Qd7 N×f3†; **a1**—26. B×f3 Qh4 27. Rf1 (or 27. g3 N×g3 28. B×b7 R×b7 29. Qe6† [29. Q×b7 Ne4 wins] 29. ... Rbf7 and White cannot save the game) 27. ... Nd2. White [now] has a great choice of moves, but none, we think, by which he can long avert the loss of the game: **a11**—28. Rf2 B×f3 29. g×f3 (best) 29. ... B×e3 30. R×e3 (best) 30. ... Qg5† 31. Kh1 Q×e3 and wins. **a12**—28. Qe6† Kh8 and, whether he takes the e-pawn or plays 29. Nd7 or 29. a6, he must lose in a few moves. **a13**—28. g3 N×f3† 29. R×f3 Qe4 and wins. **a14**—28. e4 Q×e4 29. Qe6† Kh8. **a15**—28. B×e5 N×f1 29. Qe6† Rf7 30. K×f1 (if 30. Nd7 Qe1 and, after enduring a few checks, must win) 30. ... B×f3 31. g×f3 d×e5 and wins. **a2**—26. g×f3 Qg5† (he may also play 26. ... Qh4 and win) 27. Qg4 Q×g4† 28. f×g4 Nf2 (threatening mate next move) 29. e4 (if 29. h4 he must lose the game speedily) 29. ... N×d1 30. B×d1 B×e4 31. h4 Bd2 and White cannot save the game.

**b**—25. Nd7 R×f3 26. B×f3 (best for if 26. g×f3 Nh3† and 26. N×b8 Nh3†) 26. ... N×f3† 27. g×f3 (27. Kf1 Qh4) 27. ... Qg5† 28. Kf1 Qf5 29. Ke2 (best) 29. ... Nc3† 30. R×c3 (best) 30. ... B×f3† 31. Ke1 (best) 31. ... R×b2"—Staunton.

**25. Qd7!** "This turns the scale. The entry of the queen in this fashion ought not to have been permitted"—Wisker. No result is certain after this move. **25. ... N×f3†?!** There were a few alternatives at this point:

25. ... Q×d7 (Wisker) is inferior 26. N×d7 B×f3 (certainly not 26. ... N×f3†?, a suggestion from Wisker, as after 27. B×f3 B×f3 28. g×f3 R×b2 29. N×f8 N×f8 the run of the a-pawn is decisive) 27. B×f3 R×b2 28. N×f8 with excellent winning chances.

Much more interesting is 25. ... Qf6!, which has at least the merit of leading to extremely wild complications. White's best move is 26. Q×d6, as the more defensive 26. Rf1 is slightly better for Black after 26. ... B×f3 27. B×f3 Rbd8 28. Qa4 N×f3† 29. g×f3 (29. R×f3? Qh4! wins) 29. ... Ng5. White must play 30. f4 and is clearly under pressure. Fortunately for him, his queen can still come to the rescue via c6. After 26. Q×d6!, Black has various options. It would be logical to exchange at f3, but in both cases, this doesn't solve his problems completely. The best way to capture is with 26. ... N×f3†, although White keeps a slight pull in the endgame: 27. g×f3 B×f3

28. Q×e5! Q×e5 29. B×e5 B×e2 30. Re1 Bf3 31. B×b8 R×b8 32. Rf1 Bc6 33. Nd5. Black has to watch out for the a-pawn and his pieces don't cooperate optimally. But with a tough defense, a draw is certainly possible. Not so good is 26. ... B×f3? 27. g×f3 N×f3† 28. Kh1 Qf7 29. Qd5, when White has safeguarded his kingside and his pieces dominate the board.

The critical 26. ... Qf7! leads to hair-raising, unclear, but in the end also drawish complications. After 27. a6 or 27. Ba1, Black produces a brilliant sacrifice, after which White's king is boxed in and can't escape from perpetual check, e.g., 27. a6 N×f3† 28. B×f3 B×f3 29. g×f3 Q×f3 30. Q×e6† Rf7 31. Qd5 e4 32. a7 Qf2†. If White, however, plays 27. Q×e5, there follows 27. ... Bg7 28. Rd7! and a forced line arises: 28. ... B×e5 29. R×f7 B×b2 30. R×f8† N×f8 31. Rb3 N×f3† 32. B×f3 Be5 33. Nd7! N×d7 34. B×b7 Bc7 35. a6 Bb6 36. Rd3. Black still has to be careful, but a draw is likely.

**26. B×f3 Qf6?!** White can still go wrong after 26. ... Q×d7 27. N×d7 B×f3 28. g×f3 R×b2 29. N×f8 K×f8, and now he must play the correct 30. a6! Ke7 31. a7 Nc7 32. Rdd3, with excellent winning chances. Very drawish is 30. R×d6?! Ke7 31. Rb6 R×b6 32. a×b6 Kd7. **27. R×d6 Rbd8 28. Q×e6† Q×e6 29. R×e6 B×f3 30. g×f3 Rd1† 31. Kg2 Rd2† 32. Kg3 R×b2 33. R×e5 Bg7 34. R×c5 Re8 35. Rc8 R×c8 36. N×c8 Be5† 37. f4 Bc7 38. a6 Rb8 39. a7 Ra8 40. c5** Black resigns—*Westminster Chess Club Papers* (Wisker), May 1873, p. 9; *Illustrated London News* (Staunton), 14 June 1873.

### (218) Bird–Wisker   ½–½

Match 2 (game 3)
London, 12 April 1873
*A03*

**1. f4 d5 2. Nf3 c5 3. b3 Nc6 4. e3 a6 5. Bb2 e6 6. g3 Nf6 7. Bg2 b5 8. 0-0 g6 9. Nc3 Bg7 10. Ne2 0-0 11. c3 Qb6 12. h3 a5 13. Rb1 Ba6 14. g4 b4 15. c4 Rad8 16. Qc2 d×c4 17. b×c4 a4 18. g5 Nh5 19. B×g7 N×g7 20. Ng3 Ne8 21. Ne4 f5 22. g×f6 e.p. N×f6 23. Neg5 Ne7 24. Ne5 Nf5 25. Rf2 a3 26. Kh2 Rc8 27. Rg1 Rc7 28. Bf3 Bb7 29. B×b7 R×b7 30. Qd1 Rg7 31. e4 Nd4 32. d3 Ra8 33. Nef3 N×f3† 34. Q×f3 Qc6 35. e5 Q×f3 36. R×f3 Nd7 37. N×e6 Re7 38. Ng5 Nf8 39. Ne4 Ne6 40. f5 Nd4 41. Rf2 R×e5 42. f×g6 h×g6 43. R×g6† Kh7 44. Rgg2 Rf5 45. R×f5 N×f5 46. N×c5 Nd4 47. Rg4 Rd8 48. Rf4 b3 49. a×b3 Ra8 50. R×d4 a2 51. Rh4† Kg6 52. Rg4† Kf5 53. Rg1 a1Q 54. R×a1 R×a1 55. d4 Kf4 56. d5 Kf3** drawn game—*Westminster Chess Club Papers*, July 1873, p. 55.

### (219) Wisker–Bird   1–0

Match 2 (game 4)
London, 14 April 1873
*A00*

**1. e3 f5 2. g3 Nf6 3. Bg2 e5 4. Ne2 d5 5. d4 e4 6. 0-0** "The present game is one of the most singular of the series. In thus castling after his g-pawn was moved one square, and before Black had castled, White lays himself open to an attack which ought to have proved irresistible"—Wisker. **6. ... b6** "A lost move, but White's situation is such that the consequence is small"—Wisker. **7. b3** Wisker had to start degrading his opponent's center as soon as possible. The

correct idea therefore is 7. c4 (also good on move 9). If 7. ... d×c4 8. f3! demonstrates the negative side of Bird's last move. By waiting a bit too long before pushing the c-pawn, Bird gets the chance to launch a very dangerous attack against Wisker's king. **7. ... Be6 8. Bb2 h5 9. h4 Ng4 10. Nf4 Bf7 11. c4?!** More drastic measures were already necessary at this point. Black's attack could be warded off with 11. Bh3 g5 12. h×g5 Q×g5 13. B×g4 h×g4 14. Kg2, though the endgame favors Black. **11. ... g5! 12. h×g5 Q×g5 13. Nc3?** Wisker continues playing as if his king were perfectly safe, but the nearby opening of the h-file threatens to be disastrous for him. 13. Bh3 has lost its strength now, as after 13. ... Nf6 and 14. ... h4, the kingside cannot be defended anymore. Paradoxically enough, opening the kingside himself after 13. Qe1 h4 14. f3!, is a good try for it involves the queen in the defense. **13. ... h4! 14. Qe1** This move ought to lose rapidly. Slightly better is 14. Nh3 and there is no direct win in sight after 14. ... Qg6 15. Qe1 h×g3 16. f×g3 but Black's position is so strong that he can just calmly develop his pieces, and only subsequently start a decisive attack against White's king. **14. ... d×c4?** "Black has a winning position, but proceeds to trifle it away. It is quite needless for Black to take precautions on the queenside; he should proceed with his attack. The text move allows White to free himself in a measure"—Wisker. The simple 14. ... h×g3 15. f×g3 Qh6 crowns Bird's idea. **15. Nb5 Na6 16. d5** An understandable move, but 16. f3! remains the right path to take. The ensuing lines are all very complicated, but with spirited play unclear. Black can chose between 16. ... Nf6 and 16. ... Bb4, e.g., 16. ... Nf6 17. d5 Bb4 18. N×c7† Ke7 19. d6†! or 16. ... Bb4 17. Qe2 Nh2 18. K×h2 Q×g3† 19. Kh1 h3 20. B×h3 c6 21. Qg2! etc. **16. ... Rh6** (see diagram)

The loss of tempo of Wisker's last move is punished by the evident 16. ... h×g3! If then 17. f×g3?! Rh2 and 18. ... Bc5 wins. 17. B×h8 is of course crucial: 17. ... Qh4 18. Bh3 g×f2† 19. R×f2 N×f2 20. Q×f2 Q×h8 21. Rf1 0-0-0!, when a very complicated position arises. White can win back his lost pawns, but the strong Black bishop pair will keep on giving him headaches for the rest of the game.

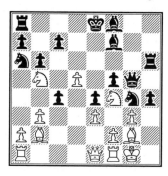

*After 16. ... Rh6*

**17. b×c4** Just as does Bird, Wisker incorrectly attaches more importance to material than to the initiative. Completely unclear complications arise after 17. f3! A few motives for both sides are explained in the following intricate line: 17. ... Nh2 (17. ... e×f3 is an alternative) 18. K×h2 h×g3† 19. Kg1 B×d5 (many other moves lose here; e.g., 19. ... Bc5 20. f×e4, 19. ... 0-0-0 20. N×a7† and 21. Nc6) 20. Rd1! A great move. If now 20. ... c6? 21. f×e4 f×e4 22. N×d5 c×d5 23. b×c4 opens the position in White's favor. If the bishop retreats either 24. Nd4 or 24. f×e4 follows. After 20. ... Qh4 21. Bh3 c6 22. Nd4 the appearance of the game has altered completely. Black's attack is blocked convincingly, while White's knights have occupied the caused holes in the center. Black is thrown upon the defensive. **17. ... Bc5 18. Bd4 0-0-0** "This also was scarcely necessary, but still Black retains a fine game"—Wisker. It is definitely time for Bird to finally open some lines with 18. ... h×g3! After 19. f×g3, he probably missed the winning 19. ... c6! Other moves give White the time to consolidate again. After 19. ... c6! White is forced to retreat his knight, just at the moment when d4 is not available. With this retreat each trace of counterplay disappears; e.g., 20. B×c5 b×c5 21. Nc3 Nb4. **19. N×a7†** Greedy and time-consuming. 19. f3! remains the crucial idea to find. **19. ... Kb7** 19. ... Kb8! prepares a couple of rook sacrifices: 20. Nc6† (other moves are equally bad: 20. Nh3 Qg8 and the attack persists) 20. ... R×c6! 21. d×c6 h×g3 22. f×g3 R×d4! breaks the resistance. **20. Nc6 Re8 21. a4?** This comes way too soon. The kingside had to be stabilized first with 21. Nh3 Qg6 22. f3 e×f3 23. R×f3 h×g3, before 24. a4! becomes interesting. **21. ... h×g3! 22. f×g3 Reh8 23. Ra2** *(see diagram)* Or 23. Rf2 B×d4 24. N×d4 Rh2 and 25. ... Qh6.

*After 23. Ra2*

**23. ... B×d4?** The quiet 23. ... R8h7! is the final step towards a winning attack. White is totally bound and cannot do anything against the threat 24. ... Nh2. Another menace (after 24. Ne5) is 24. ... Rh1†. **24. N×d4?** Necessary is 24. e×d4 when Black's attack has lost much of its strength; e.g., 24. ... Nh2 (the only move to keep some advantage. Stupid would have been 24. ... Rh1†?? 25. B×h1 Qh6 26. B×e4!) 25. Ne5 B×d5 26. N×d5 N×f1 27. Nf7 Q×g3 28. Q×g3 N×g3 29. N×h8 R×h8. Black's winning chances aren't great. **24. ... Rh2** "Up to this Black appears to have conducted his attack irreproachably, but at this moment he unaccountably overlooked the obvious way to win the game in three or four moves by 24. ... Rh1†"—Bird. **25. Rff2 N×f2?!** This knight is far too important to give up for a rook that hindered White more than anything else. 25. ... Nc5! bringing some reserve to the front, leaves little to do for White—for instance 26. Ra3 Qh6!, and the attack decides the game. **26. Q×f2 R2h7?** A sad retreat, that allows White to undertake a counter initiative. 26. ... Nc5! is still very dangerous: 27. a5 Nd3 28. N×d3 Qh6! 29. Kf1 R×g2! 30. Q×g2 Q×e3 etc. **27. a5! Bh5?** Bird, suddenly thrown upon the defensive, is unable to adapt to the difficult situation. White's knights dominate the center and his queen might join the rook in a strong attack against Black's king. Bird's queen is bound to defend f5 and his bishop and rooks look rather offside as well. Black's best idea seems to be 27. ... Rh6, involving the rook in the defense of the king. White should then continue with 28. Qe1!, intending to play the queen to a1. The position is very demanding for Black, as White will soon open the a-file. **28. a×b6 c×b6 29. Nb5?** 29. Nfe6! wins: 29. ... Qg4

30. Ra1! and 31. Qa2! follows with decisive effects. If 30. ... Ra8 31. c5! **29. ... Bf3!** An excellent reaction. Now both kings are in danger. **30. B×f3 e×f3 31. Q×f3 Qg4 32. Q×g4 Rh1† 33. Kf2 f×g4 34. Nd6† Ka7** Bird wants to avoid a draw at all costs, which means taking irresponsible risks. Simply 34. ... Kc7 forces White to take the perpetual 35. Nb5† Kb7 etc. **35. e4!** The knight at d6 now dominates the board. **35. ... R1h2† 36. Ng2 Rf8† 37. Nf5?** 37. Kg1! Rh6 38. e5 is winning, even after 38. ... R×d6. **37. ... Kb7 38. Ke3 Nc5 39. Rf2 Ra8?** A bad remedy to the threat of 40. Nd6†. Instead, 39. ... Kc7! forces the draw: 40. d6† Kb7 41. Kd4 Kc6 41. Ra2 Re8 42. e5 Nb3† etc. **40. Nd6† Kc7 41. Nb5† Kd7 42. Rf7† Kc8 43. Rf8† Kb7 44. R×a8 K×a8 45. Nf4 Rc2 46. Ne6** 46. Nd3 Nd7 47. Nd6 is much cleaner. **46. ... Kb8** 46. ... Nd7 is the only move to prolong the battle. **47. N×c5 b×c5 48. Nd6 Kc7 49. e5 Kd7 50. Kf4 Re2 51. Ne4 Rc2 52. e6† Ke7 53. Ke5 R×c4 54. d6† Kf8 55. e7†** and White wins. This epic game is one of the fiercest struggles in this book—*Westminster Chess Club Papers* (Wisker), May 1873, p. 10; *Modern Chess* (Bird), pp. 44–45.

### (220) Bird–Wisker    0-1
Match 2 (game 5)
London, 16 April 1873
*A03*

1. f4 d5 2. e3 g6 3. Nf3 Bg7 4. c3 a6 5. Bd3 c5 6. 0-0 Nc6 7. Bc2 b5 8. d4 c4 9. b3 Nf6 10. b×c4 b×c4 11. Nbd2 Qa5 12. Nb1 0-0 13. h3 Re8 14. Kh2 e6 15. g4 Rb8 16. Qe1 Re7 17. Rg1 Reb7 18. Nfd2 Nd7 19. Rg2 e5 20. d×e5 Nd×e5 21. f×e5 B×e5† 22. Kh1 B×c3 23. N×c3 Q×c3 24. Ba4 Ne5 25. Qh4 Q×a1 26. Qd8† Kg7 27. Rg1 Bd7 28. Qh4 B×a4 29. Nb3 c×b3 30. e4 Q×c1 31. R×c1 b2 White resigns—*Westminster Chess Club Papers,* May 1873, p. 10.

### (221) Wisker–Bird    0-1
Match 2 (game 6)
London, 19 April 1873
*A10*

1. c4 f5 2. e3 e6 3. g3 Nf6 4. Bg2 c6 5. d4 Bd6 6. Nc3 Bc7 7. b4 a5 8. b5 d5 9. Qa4 0-0 10. Ba3 Re8 11. Nge2 Nbd7 12. c5 Wisker correctly avoids 12. b×c6?! Nb6! **12. ... c×b5 13. N×b5 Nf8 14. 0-0 Bd7 15. Nec3 Bc6 16. Rab1 Ng6 17. Qc2 h5 18. N×c7** 18. h4 is worth considering. **18. ... Q×c7 19. Nb5** "White now attains a superior position. Mr. Bird has again given insufficient attention to the play on the queenside"—Wisker. **19. ... Qd7 20. Nd6** The knight looks extremely strong but Black can neutralize it rather easily. **20. ... Reb8 21. Qe2 Ne7 22. f3** "This was hardly necessary, and somewhat weakens White's situation on the kingside, the more so as it is his intention shortly to remove his bishop to f1"—Wisker. It remains very difficult to find an effective plan. Doubling the rooks on the b-file looks logical, but is unlikely to lead to anything real. White's bishop at a3 remains a problematic piece. **22. ... Nc8 23. N×c8 R×c8 24. Rb6 Qe7 25. Rfb1 Rc7 26. Qd3 g6** 26. ... h4 is an interesting idea to generate counterplay on the kingside. **27. Bf1 Nd7** "Black saw the possibility of capturing the b-pawn, but decided that it would be unsound"—Wisker. **28. R×b7?** Probably Wisker considered this move as the crowning of his positional play, but

there is a serious tactical flaw. Necessary is 28. R6b2, when Bird could equalize with 28. ... e5 or 28. ... g5. **28. ... Rcc8??** Trusting his opponent on his word. 28. ... B×b7 29. c6 Ba6! refutes Wisker's "petite combinaison." **29. Qc3 Qg5 30. f4 Qd8 31. R7b2 Nf6 32. Bd3 Ng4 33. h3 Nf6 34. Rg2 Rab8 35. R×b8 R×b8 36. Rb2 Rc8 37. Rb6 h4 38. Q×a5** A daring looking move, but White can allow himself such luxury. **38. ... h×g3 39. Ra6 Qe8 40. Ra7 g5 41. f×g5 Nh7 42. Qe1 Qh5 43. Q×g3?!** Turning a simply winning position into a much more difficult one. 43. Kg2! prevents any counterplay. **43. ... Qd1† 44. Bf1 Bb5 45. Qf2?** 45. Qf4, hanging on a tad longer onto the g-pawn, is still good enough for a clear advantage; e.g., 45. ... B×f1 46. Q×f1 Qh5 and now 47. g6 or even 47. Kf2 N×g5 48. Ke1 Nf3† 49. Kd1 are promising. **45. ... N×g5 46. Qg2 Kh8 47. h4?** Now he even loses. 47. Q×g5 Rg8 48. Ra8 Q×f1† 49. Kh2 Qe2† is a draw. **47. ... Nf3† 48. Kf2 Rg8 49. Q×g8† K×g8 50. B×b5 N×h4?!** Bird, completely convinced that a win is a mere matter of time, seriously miscalculates himself at this point. After 50. ... Nd2!, Wisker could resign. **51. Be2 Qc2** (see diagram)

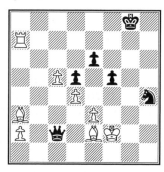

*After 51. ... Qc2*

**52. Rb7?!** The brilliant 52. c6!! saves the day: 52. ... f4 (52. ... Q×c6 leads to a surprising draw 53. Be7! f4 [if 53. ... Ng6 54. Bf6] 54. B×h4 f×e3† 55. K×e3 Qc1† 56. Kd3. Black has nothing) 53. e×f4 (not 53. c7?? f3) 53. ... Q×c6 54. Bc5 Qe8 55. Bd3 Nf5 56. B×f5 e×f5 57. Bd6! with a draw. **52. ... f4! 53. e×f4 Nf5 54. Bb2 Qd2** White's king is helpless now. **55. c6 Q×f4† 56. Ke1 Qg3† 57. Kd1 Qg1† 58. Kd2 Qe3† 59. Kd1 N×d4 60. B×d4 Q×d4† 61. Kc2 Qc5† 62. Kb3 Q×c6** and Black wins—*Westminster Chess Club Papers* (Wisker), May 1873, p. 10.

## (222) Bird–Wisker    1–0
Match 2 (game 7)
London, 21 April 1873
*A02*

**1. f4 c5 2. Nf3 Nc6 3. e3 a6 4. Be2 g6 5. 0-0 d5 6. d4 e6 7. c3 Nf6 8. Nbd2 b6 9. Ne5 N×e5** "This exchange of knights enables White to project a very powerful attack upon the adverse king" —Staunton. **10. f×e5 Nd7 11. e4! Bg7 12. e×d5 e×d5 13. Nf3** A relatively slow continuation. 13. Bf3 is strong but the best move is 13. Qb3 Bb7 and now either 14. Ne4! with a huge positional advantage or 14. Bg4, which wins a pawn after the exchange at d7. **13. ... 0-0 14. Be3 Bb7 15. Qd2 Qe7 16. Rae1 c×d4 17. c×d4 Rac2?!** A routine move that allows White to enhance his advantage again. 17. ... f6! takes the sting out of his opponent's pressure. **18. Bd3 b5 19. a3 Nb6 20. Bg5!** During the last few moves Wisker

had to play 17. ... f6, while Bird could always have made this same move. **20. ... Qe6 21. b3 Rc7 22. Qf4** "White has now an attack, which is exceedingly difficult to resist, but Black might have made a better defense"—Wisker. **22. ... Rc3?!** 22. ... Bc8, hoping to lighten the pressure a bit with 23. ... Qg4, might postpone the inevitable attack a bit. **23. Re3!** "Well played"—Bird. **23. ... Rfc8 24. Bf6 h6** "To prevent 25. Ng5"—Bird. **25. Ne1 Nd7 26. Qg3 Nf8 27. B×g6! B×f6** "If 27. ... f×g6 or 27. ... N×g6 28. R×c3 wins" —Staunton. **28. R×f6** "A decisive move, and threatening 29. B×f7†" —Bird. **28. ... N×g6 29. R×e6** Black resigns. Bird, only he, gave a few more moves: 29. ... R×e3 30. R×g6† f×g6 31. Q×g6† Kf8 32. Q×h6† Black resigns—*Westminster Chess Club Papers* (Wisker), May 1873, p. 10; *Illustrated London News* (Staunton), 28 March 1874; *Chess Masterpieces* (Bird), p. 129.

## (223) Wisker–Bird    ½–½
Match 2 (game 8)
London 1873
*A10*

This game could also have been the seventeenth of the third match. It remains uncertain, however, whether that game of the third match ended in a draw.

**1. c4 f5 2. e3 e6 3. Nf3 b6 4. d4 Bb7 5. Be2 Nf6 6. a3 Be7 7. Nc3 c6 8. b4 a5 9. Rb1 a×b4 10. a×b4 0-0 11. 0-0 d6 12. Qb3 h6 13. c5 d5 14. Ba3 Nbd7 15. Nd2 e5 16. d×e5 N×e5 17. Bb2 Ned7 18. c×b6 N×b6 19. Nf3 Qd6 20. Bd3 Bc8 21. Ne2 Ne4 22. Be5 Qe6 23. Ned4 Qg6 24. Bc7 Nd7 25. b5 Bb7 26. N×c6 B×c6 27. b×c6 Q×c6 28. Bb5 Q×c7 29. Q×d5† Kh7 30. Q×d7 Q×d7 31. B×d7 Ra7 32. Bc6 Nc3 33. Rb3 Bf6 34. g3 Rd8 35. Kg2 Rc7 36. Bb5 g5 37. Re1 g4 38. Nd4 B×d4 39. e×d4 R×d4** drawn game—*The Sportsman*, 29 August 1874.

## (224) Bird–Wisker    1–0
Match 2 (game 9)
London, 21 April 1873
*Game score missing*

## (225) Wisker–Bird    0–1
Match 2 (game 10)
London, 10 May 1873
*A00*

**1. e3 f5 2. c4 e6 3. Nc3 Bb4 4. Qb3 B×c3 5. Q×c3 Nf6 6. g3 Nc6 7. Bg2 Ne7 8. Ne2 0-0 9. d4 c6 10. b3** "This move is played instead of 10. b4, in order to let in the bishop"—Wisker. **10. ... Ng6 11. Ba3 Re8 12. Bd6 b6 13. b4 Bb7 14. a4 Qc8** "A good move, and the only way of rescuing Black from his cramped position"—Wisker. **15. 0-0 c5** "White should have prevented this fine move, at any hazard, by 15. c5"—Wisker. **16. b×c5 B×g2 17. K×g2 b×c5 18. f3** White keeps some pressure after the critical 18. d×c5 Ne4 19. Qd4. The text move allows Bird to favorably open up the game. **18. ... c×d4 19. N×d4 Qa6** The disadvantage of White's 18th move becomes clear after 19. ... Nd5! 20. Qd2 Q×c4 21. Rfc1 Qa6 22. N×f5 Nf6 when his knight is in some trouble, forcing him to play 23. Nh4 N×h4† 24. g×h4. **20. Nb5 Qc6 21. Rfd1 Rec8 22. Rac1?!** It is necessary to play 22. c5. Black's position remains cramped. His control over d5, however, provides certain compensation. **22. ... a6 23. Na3 Q×a4** A bit too materialistic from Bird. Stronger is 23. ... Nd5 24. Qb3 Q×d6 25. c×d5 R×c1 26. R×c1 Rb8 when the exchange of pieces considerably lightens Black's defensive tasks. Here, White can look only to a worse ending after 27. Nc4 Q×g3†. **24. c5** "In giving up a pawn, White calculated that he would gain a greater advantage by the advance of the c-pawn and the move of the knight. He however overlooked one square to which the Black queen could play"—Wisker. **24. ... Nd5 25. Qd3 Re8?!** Black's advantage has slowly slipped away, and after the passive text move, White has ample compensation for the pawn. **26. Nc4 Qb5** "This was the square White did not reckon upon"—Wisker. **27. Kf2 a5 28. Qd4 Nge7 29. Rb1 Nb4 30. B×e7 R×e7 31. Nb6 Rd8 32. Qd6 Ree8 33. N×d7 e5 34. Kg1?!** This move allows a dangerous infiltration. Instead, 34. Rd2! maintains the status quo. **34. ... Qe2! 35. Qd2 Q×f3 36. Rb3?** (see diagram) Allowing Bird to deliver a severe blow. 36. Ra1 h6 37. Qf2 Q×f2† 38. K×f2 e4 isn't very attractive either, but at least tactically much safer.

*After 36. Rb3*

**36. ... f4!** "From this point to the end Black finishes the game in good style"—Wisker. **37. Rf1 Qb7 38. Rd1 f×g3 39. h×g3 Qf3 40. Kh2 e4 41. c6 Qh5† 42. Kg2 N×c6 43. Qd5†** White is allowed to reach an endgame, but there is no consolation to be found in it. **43. ... Q×d5 44. R×d5 Re6** A bit careless. 44. ... Re7 forces an excellent rook endgame. **45. Rb6 Ra8 46. Nc5 Rg6 47. N×e4** 47. Rd2 Ne7 48. R×g6 N×g6 49. Rd4 greatly improves his survival chances. **47. ... a4** 47. ... Ne7 48. R×g6 N×d5 wins easily. **48. Nc3** 48. Nd6 is the last attempt to prolong the game; e.g., 48. ... Nd8 49. Nc4 Ne6 50. Rdb5. Now the finish is near. **48. ... a3 49. Na2 Ne7! 50. Rdb5 R×b6 51. R×b6 Rc8 52. Nb4 Rc3 53. Kf3 Rb3 54. Ra6 R×b4 55. R×a3 Kf7** White resigns—*Westminster Chess Club Papers* (Wisker), July 1873, p. 56.

### (226) Bird–Wisker    ½–½
Match 2 (game 11)
London, May 1873
*Game score missing*

### (227) Wisker–Bird    1–0
Match 2 (game 12)
London, May 1873
*A80*

1. e3 f5 2. d4 Nf6 3. g3 e6 4. Bg2 d5 5. Ne2 c5 6. c4 Nc6 7. b3 b6 8. Bb2 Ba6 9. Nbc3 Rc8 10. c×d5 Nb4 11. 0–0

e×d5 12. a3 Nd3 13. Qd2 Ne4 14. N×e4 f×e4 15. d×c5 b×c5 16. Rfd1 Qb6 17. Rab1 Rc7 18. Nf4 N×f4 19. e×f4 Bd3 20. Be5 Bd6 21. Bf1 B×e5 22. B×d3 Bd4 23. Be2 Re7 24. b4 B×f2† 25. Kf1 c4 26. Q×d5 Bg1 27. Qa8† Kf7 28. Qd5† Re6 29. Qf5† Ke8 30. Bh5† g6 31. Rb2 c3 32. Rg2 Be3 33. Qd5 Bd2 34. Rg×d2 c×d2 35. R×d2 e3 36. Rd4 Qc6 37. Qd8† Kf7 38. Rd7† Q×d7 39. Q×d7† Re7 40. Qd5† Kf8 41. Be2 h5 42. Qd8† Black resigns—*Westminster Chess Club Papers*, July 1873, pp. 55–56.

### (228) Bird–Wisker    1–0
Match 2 (game 13)
London, May 1873
*A03*

1. f4 d5 2. Nf3 c5 3. e3 Nc6 4. c3 g6 5. Be2 Bg7 6. 0–0 e6 "Mr. Steinitz is of the opinion, and we agree with him, that it is not good play in this species of opening to advance the e-pawn. The advance is not needed for any purpose of development, whereas the e-pawn defends f6, a weak point in Black's game"—Wisker. **7. d4 b6 8. Kh1 Nge7 9. Na3 0–0 10. Qe1 Rb8 11. Bd2 Nf5!** An excellent post for the knight. Wisker is challenging Bird to execute a weakening pawn push to chase the knight away and start an attack against Black's king. **12. g4?! Nd6 13. Rd1 Bb7** "Very weak and ineffective, blocking up the rook, whilst the bishop itself does not obtain a good position"—Wisker. This cannot be a bad move, but it is played without a concrete plan. For this purpose, 13. ... c4, intending to play 14. ... b5 and 15. ... b4, looks definitely better. **14. Bd3 c4 15. Bb1 b5 16. Qg3 a5 17. Qh3 b4** Bird's attack has come to a standstill, while his opponent dominates both queenside and center. **18. Nc2 Ba6 19. Nce1 b×c3 20. b×c3?!** 20. B×c3 prevents the following infiltration. **20. ... Rb2! 21. Ng2 Ne4?** A bad mistake that allows Bird to solve his countless problems at once. Had Wisker played 21. ... Ne7!, a strong defensive precaution, he could have slowly built up the pressure with moves as Qd7, Rfb8 and Ba6–b5–Ba4. White would not be able to withstand the pressure against his queenside very long. **22. B×e4 d×e4 23. Ng5 h6 24. N×e4 R×a2** The exchange of e- versus a-pawn is hugely favorable for White. **25. f5** A central push with 25. Nc5 Bc8 26. e4 deserves the preference. **25. ... Qd5?** The correct way to deal with Bird's last move is 25. ... e×f5! 26. g×f5 Bc8! Black would even be a bit better after 27. Ng3 h5 28. e4 Ne5 etc. **26. Nc5 Bc8 27. e4** "And the game is gone"—Wisker. **27. ... Qd8 28. B×h6 e×f5 29. g×f5 Qf6 30. e5 N×e5** "Vainly hoping to draw, but he only obtains one pawn for the piece, and the position is against him"—Wisker. **31. d×e5 Q×e5 32. B×g7 K×g7 33. Nd7 B×d7 34. R×d7 g5** "If 34. ... Rh8 35. f6†, as in the text. Mr. Bird's play throughout is very good"—Wisker. **35. f6† Kg6 36. Re7 Qd5 37. Rd7 Qe4 38. Rd4 Rh8 39. Qg3 Qc6 40. Kg1 Qc5 41. Nf4†** and Black resigns—*Westminster Chess Club Papers* (Wisker), July. 1873, p. 55.

### (229) Wisker–Bird    0–1
Match 2 (game 14)
London, May 1873
*Game scored by default*

# Repertoire Changes

In his first match with Wisker, Bird faced an opponent who was well versed in the rapidly expanding opening theory. Bird's solution to deal with the problems posed to him was radical. He left the well-trodden paths and started to look for openings on the verge of theory. Several of his pet lines are explored in the analyses of his games, but a few of his opening choices already deserve a closer look.

Bird's changing of his White repertoire was the most drastic. He abandoned the Ruy Lopez, to which he had adhered since his youth, in favor of the rarely seen 1. f4. In *Modern Chess* (p. 66) Bird agreed with "Buckle, Staunton, Cochrane, and Kolisch that there are many much finer, more interesting, and certainly more chivalrous debuts which a player of imagination should not be afraid to venture [than the Ruy Lopez]."

Bird may have picked up 1. f4 in his early days at the Divan when Edward Lowe was its first regular practitioner. He adopted this move for the first time as his main weapon in the second match with Falkbeer but had not returned to it since. During and after his matches with Wisker, Bird switched regularly between 1. e4 and 1. f4, but the latter move gained his complete devotion a few years later. Already in 1885, the *Hereford Times* of 8 August baptized 1. f4 the Bird's Opening. Bird's preference for the push of the f-pawn remained intact until his last days over the board.[11]

Wisker himself opened his games of the second match with 1. e3, which allowed Bird to experiment with 1. ... f5. The Dutch Defense thereupon became his favorite system against all kinds of closed games for the rest of his career. The reputation of the Dutch was for a very long time not overly encouraging, even though it had been adopted by some strong players, notably Morphy. Bird found his motivation in the chances he got to launch a rapid kingside attack.

Bird also had to find a reply against the Ruy Lopez, which had become very popular and was on the verge of replacing more romantic lines like the Evans Gambit. The Ruy Lopez had the reputation of submitting Black to a defensive kind of game without having the possibility to complicate the game. Bird ultimately came up with another rare move, 3. ... Nd4, for which he developed a loyal fondness. The purpose of this eccentric move was to create an attack himself on the very first possible occasion. It was no great surprise to see 3. ... Nd4 criticized by nearly all other masters. This variation also received Bird's name.

Also worth mentioning is Bird's choice for the Sicilian Defense at a time when this opening was completely unpopular. He started to experiment with 1. ... c5 in 1876, but his personal grail was only found in 1883, when Bird began to play the Dragon Variation. Just as with several other favorite lines of Bird, this variation enjoyed a very bad reputation.

# Vienna 1873

In the summer of 1873 the focus of the chess world shifted to Vienna where the first international chess tournament since Baden-Baden 1870 was held.[12] Just as in London in 1851 and 1862 and in Paris in 1867, this tournament coincided with the world exposition, or "Weltausstellung."

A pivotal role within the organization of the tournament was played by Ignaz Kolisch. The former world class player had shifted his attention to the world of the haute finance, and in the meantime he was gaining an enormous fortune. Kolisch's fondness for the game remained and he patronized its practice and players. Above all he supported the Vienna tournaments of 1873 and 1882.

When the news of the imminent congress reached the shores of England rumors spread about potential participants. The editor of the *Westminster Chess Club Papers* (July 1873, p. 48), had "not heard that any of our English players purpose taking part, but many amateurs have desired that Mr. Bird should represent us against the German paladins of chess." We do not know any of Bird's motives for his decision to enter the tournament. After a long period of hesitation, he finally made up his mind two weeks before its start. He probably received a good deal of moral support and some financial as well, for an entrance fee of 50 florins was required. Travelling and residence costs may also have been taken care of.

Bird arrived on 17 July in the Austrian capital with Blackburne as his companion.[13] The third London-based player, Steinitz, had reached Vienna before Bird and Blackburne. As the other interna-

---

11. Later Bird declared his love for this cunning move: "That so varied and enjoyable a game, so little analyzed and yet so eminently qualified to exercise and test the skill of the player not well posted in the books has been so long neglected, seems to us somewhat remarkable from a practitioner's point of view; but that it should have been almost ignored in the elaborate and expensive works of writers desiring to be considered the greatest authorities on the subject of the chess openings, is yet more astonishing." H.E. Bird, *Chess Novelties and Their Latest Developments: With Comparisons of the Progress of Chess Openings of the Past Century and the Present Not Dealt With in Existing Works*. London: Warne, 1895, p. 114.

12. During Bird's absence two important tournaments had been played on European soil. In Paris 1867, Kolisch won ahead of Winawer, Steinitz and Neumann. Kolisch retired from chess after this tournament. Neumann beat Winawer in a short match and was eager to revenge his fellow Prussian Anderssen against the Austrian Steinitz, but was not given the chance. In Baden-Baden 1870, Anderssen came out first ahead of Steinitz, Neumann and Blackburne. Gustav Neumann, one of Caissa's brightest stars of that era, fell into oblivion soon afterwards due to heavy mental problems.

13. Perhaps the following undated anecdote occurred on Bird's way to Vienna. Buckley related it many years later, reminiscing about Bird's language capacities and his reluctance to adapt himself to any local habits: "Bird was intensely and peculiarly English. Living in an international atmosphere he knew no word of any foreign tongue. 'Let them speak my language,' quoted Bird; 'it's not the place of a Briton to run after foreigners!' ... He knew nothing of the native names of cities outside the four seas of Britain, and once, when journeying to a German tourney with other masters, stayed for a night at Munich, of which, it appears, Bird had heard. Travelling in the care of his colleagues, Bird resigned himself to their guidance, without much enquiry. One place was no better than another so long as the places were foreign. After the night at Munich, however, Bird emerged from his indifference, and as the morning train in which the party left cleared the city and came upon the fields, addressing the leader, he said: 'Don't forget to recollect to remind me when we get to Munich.' 'What are you growling at now?' asked one of the party. 'I say,—tell me when we get to Munich! I have a sort of commission to execute at Munich, you know.' 'You have, have you? Ha! Ha!' The party cachinnated hilariously. Bird maintained his gravity. 'I promised Boden I would see certain great pictures in the Munich Galleries,' he explained. Samuel Boden, once of Hull, was an artist who spent half his time in excellent chess and half in producing exquisite water-colors. 'Well,' rejoined one of the party, the sternest and hardest of the lot, 'you're a wee bit late! You've missed your chance! You slept in Munich last night! You left Munich this morning! You're a fine—' 'All right, all right' laughed Bird—'Try to deceive the orphan. Get on to the young man from the country. But he's not so green as he looks. I know where we were last night. I copied the name from the hotel notepaper. Here it is—not Munich at all but Muenchen! Put that in your pipe, my boy! Munchin' I call it. How's that, umpire?" *Chess Amateur*, June 1913, p. 271.

tional representatives, namely Anderssen and Louis Paulsen for Germany and Samuel Rosenthal for France, had also arrived before the opening of the congress, a consultation game between them was arranged on 19 July. Baron Rothschild and Kolisch offered a small prize for the game. The French/German combination won after a short struggle, taking revenge for the defeat they suffered at Baden-Baden.

Several other strong players had been invited to enter the tournament but could not attend. England's major absentee was Zukertort. Wisker apparently had other plans as well. Two Americans were hoped for: George Henry Mackenzie and, above all, Paul Morphy. Alas, rumors of the latter's return to the chessboard proved to be unfounded. The six other participants all belonged to the Austro-Hungarian empire and were probably not of the same class as the foreigners.

The most important and innovative rule concerning the tournament was the decision to play according to a system of match points. The competitors met each other in three games. The winner of the match scored one point, in case of a drawn battle each party received half a point. In case of two victories by one player a third game became superfluous and was not played. This experiment wasn't considered a success and never got any imitation. The dense tournament schedule was quite grueling with games planned on each day except Sundays. The time rate per game was 20 moves per player per hour. Good for Bird, but generally condemned as too fast by the British press. All pairings were made before the tournament started. Four prizes were awaiting the best participants.

Bird's results during the first part of the tournament were rather mixed but contained hardly a surprise. He beat three of the weaker masters, disappointingly drew with Josef Heral and lost against Blackburne and Anderssen, two of the favorites. Especially against the latter a few chances to create an upset were missed.

After six rounds Anderssen and Blackburne were in the lead, having won all their matches. Just one player seemed still able to challenge them: Steinitz trailed the leaders by one point. Bird and Rosenthal shared a decent fourth place. They counted 3½ match points.

Bird improved his position during the next two rounds by convincingly beating Meitner and Rosenthal. Blackburne remained untouchable with 8 straight wins, while Steinitz followed at 7. Anderssen, 6 points, had lost both of his matches and gotten within Bird's reach (5½).

Two crucial duels, against Paulsen and Steinitz, were likely to determine whether Bird could clinch to a prize. His match with Paulsen was one between two players with an already weakened condition that was further undermined by the terribly hot weather in Vienna. Paulsen won both games, which made the English press write that Bird's resistance was easily broken. A more detailed study of the games reveals the titanic nature of these battles. Bird was very unlucky to lose them both.

Bird's games with Steinitz were also very worthwhile, and once again he was a bit unlucky to lose in two games. Especially in their first game he came close to inflicting a loss upon Steinitz.

The battle was still not decided. Blackburne had won all his matches but Steinitz remained close behind. The disadvantages of the match point system were clearly demonstrated by now. Steinitz

had won nearly every match with two straight wins while Blackburne often needed three games to secure victory.

Bird finished the tournament excellently by beating a more feasible opponent, Adolf Schwarz, twice. The major upset of the final round was Blackburne's winning streak's coming to an abrupt end against Rosenthal. So Steinitz was able to catch up to him after all. A tie-break was set up in which Steinitz confirmed his superiority with two wins. Bird had a word or two to say about the enticing finish of this tournament. In *Chess Masterpieces* (p. 58) he blamed Blackburne's sudden collapse to his being unwell. Bird then closely watched the tie-break, according himself in *Modern Chess* (p. 86) the role of umpire.

Anderssen recovered well from his temporary setback and with 8½/11 he received third prize. Fourth prize was gained by Rosenthal (7½/11), thanks to his impressive finish. Bird and Paulsen fell out of the prizes by sharing the fifth place with 6½ points. None of the local players left a great impression. They followed at a distance of three points or more behind Bird and Paulsen.

Bird's result was something of a disappointment after his encouraging match win against Wisker. Although he lost his matches against superior opponents another element played a role: towards the end of the tournament Bird had to endure attacks from gout.[14] Bird's gout mostly had its negative effect in the tense duels with Paulsen and Steinitz. In fact this is the first mention of Bird's illness in the chess press, although Duffy described the gout as Bird's "old enemy," thereby more than suggesting that this ailment hit Bird much earlier. In a letter to White, Fraser elucidated that Bird's gout was accompanied by another, similar, chronic disease, sciatica.[15] The gout often troubled Bird during the remainder of his chess career, and it was more than once brought up as the reason for an ill-performance. For a player whose chess was often undermined by his health, the famous expression, credited to Bird by E.B. Osborn in *Chess Pie* (1936, p. 2), that he had hardly ever beaten a healthy player, is quite funny.[16]

When returning to England Bird and Blackburne made a short stop in Paris to visit the legendary Café de la Régence. Bird contested one game with Henri Baucher which ended in a draw.

The Vienna episode concluded on 15 October with a dinner given by the City of London Chess Club. The atmosphere at the dinner was euphoric but at the same time some traces of the future wrangles were already appearing in the specialized press. A positive sound was heard in a speech from de Soyres as he recognized the positive impact of Austrian players (Falkbeer, Hoffer and Steinitz) on British chess.[17] On the other hand there was some, or perhaps even much, disappointment about Blackburne's ultimate defeat against Steinitz, as one "cannot ignore his nationality; and when his compatriots declare that he is but a borrowed sprig in our wreath, candor compels us to admit the truth of the assertion."[18]

14. According to *The Field*, Bird suffered from gout during two weeks of the tournament (30 August 1873). The tournament book (p. 205) remarked that Bird's form was seriously affected during the last days of the tournament due to an increasing "fussübel," (i.e., foot malady).

15. *Letters to John G. White relating to chess*, vol. I, letter 43.

16. The same aphorism has also been attributed to Amos Burn.

17. *Land and Water*, 18 October 1873.

18. *Westminster Chess Club Papers*, October 1873, p. 103.

### International chess tournament, Vienna, 21 July–29 August 1873

*Site:* Wiener Schachgesellschaft
*Playing hours:* 10 a.m.–2 p.m. and 4 p.m. until the end of the game
*Prizes:* 1st 1000 guldens and 200 golden ducats, 2nd 600 guldens, 3rd 300 guldens, 4th 200 guldens
*Time limit:* 20 moves per hour

| | | 1 | 2 | 3 | 4 | 5 | 6 | 7 | 8 | 9 | 10 | 11 | 12 | |
|---|---|---|---|---|---|---|---|---|---|---|---|---|---|---|
| 1 | W. Steinitz | | 0 ½ 0 | 1 1 | 1 1 | 1 1 | 1 1 | ½ 1 ½ | ½ 1 ½ | 1 1 | 1 1 | 1 1 | 1 1 | 10 |
| 2 | J.H. Blackburne | 1 ½ 1 | | 0 1 1 | 0 ½ 0 | 1 1 | 1 0 1 | 1 0 1 | 1 1 | 1 1 | ½ 1 1 | 1 0 1 | 1 0 1 | 10 |
| 3 | A. Anderssen | 0 0 | 1 0 0 | | 0 1 1 | 0 1 1 | 1 1 | 0 1 ½ | ½ ½ 1 | 0 1 1 | 1 1 | 0 1 1 | ½ 1 1 | 8½ |
| 4 | S. Rosenthal | 0 0 | 1 ½ 1 | 1 0 0 | | 0 0 | 1 0 ½ | 1 1 | 1 1 | 1 0 1 | 1 0 1 | 1 1 | 1 1 | 7½ |
| 5 | H.E. Bird | 0 0 | 0 0 | 1 0 0 | 1 1 | | 0 0 | 1 1 | 1 1 | 0 ½ 1 | 1 1 | 1 1 | 1 1 | 6½ |
| 6 | L. Paulsen | 0 0 | 0 1 0 | 0 0 | 0 1 ½ | 1 1 | | 1 1 | ½ 1 1 | 0 1 ½ | 1 1 | 1 0 ½ | 1 1 | 6½ |
| 7 | M. Fleissig | ½ 0 ½ | 0 1 0 | 1 0 ½ | 0 0 | 0 0 | 0 0 | | 0 1 1 | 0 ½ 1 | 1 0 0 | 0 ½ 1 | 1 1 | 3½ |
| 8 | P. Meitner | ½ 0 ½ | 0 0 | ½ ½ 0 | 0 0 | 0 0 | ½ 0 0 | 1 0 0 | | 1 ½ 0 | ½ 1 ½ | ½ 1 1 | 1 1 | 3½ |
| 9 | J. Heral | 0 0 | 0 0 | 1 0 0 | 0 1 0 | 1 ½ 0 | 1 0 ½ | 1 ½ 0 | 0 ½ 1 | | ½ 0 1 | ½ 1 0 | 0 1 0 | 3 |
| 10 | O. Gelbfuhs | 0 0 | ½ 0 0 | 0 0 | 0 1 0 | 0 0 | 0 0 | 0 1 1 | ½ 0 ½ | ½ 1 0 | | ½ ½ ½ | ½ 1 1 | 3 |
| 11 | A. Schwarz | 0 0 | 0 1 0 | 1 0 0 | 0 0 | 0 0 | 0 1 ½ | 1 ½ 0 | ½ 0 0 | ½ 0 1 | ½ ½ ½ | | ½ 1 ½ | 3 |
| 12 | C. Pitschel | 0 0 | 0 1 0 | ½ 0 0 | 0 0 | 0 0 | 0 0 | 0 0 | 0 0 | 1 0 1 | ½ 0 0 | ½ 0 ½ | | 1 |

| *Tie match:* | 1 | 2 | |
|---|---|---|---|
| W. Steinitz | 1 | 1 | 2 |
| J.H. Blackburne | 0 | 0 | 0 |

## (230) Gelbfuhs–Bird    0–1

International tournament (round 1, game 1)
Vienna, 21 July 1873
C61

1. e4 e5 2. Nf3 Nc6 3. Bb5 Nd4 4. N×d4 e×d4 5. d3 Bc5 6. 0–0 Qh4 7. f4 Nf6 8. h3 c6 9. Bc4 d6 10. Qe1 Q×e1 11. R×e1 0–0 12. Bb3 b5 13. a4 b4 14. Nd2 a5 15. Nf3 Nd7 16. g4 Ba6 17. Bd2 Bb8 18. Kg2 Rac8 19. e5 d5 20. f5 Nc5 21. Rad1 N×b3 22. c×b3 c5 23. Bf4 Rfe8 24. Kg3 Bc7 25. h4 Bb8 26. g5 Rc6 27. h5 Bc8 28. f6 h6 29. f×g7 h×g5 30. B×g5 K×g7 31. Kh4 Bc7 32. Rg1 Kf8 33. h6 Rg6 34. Bf4 Bf5 35. R×g6 B×g6 36. Kg3 Kg8 37. Kf2 Bd8 38. Rc1 Be7 39. Ke2 Kh7 40. Kd2 Bh5 41. Rf1 Rg8 42. Rf2 Rg4 43. Ne1 R×f4 44. R×f4 Bg5 45. Ng2 Bg4 46. Ke1 B×f4 47. N×f4 Be6 48. Nh5 K×h6 49. Nf6 Kg6 50. Ne8 c4 51. b×c4 d×c4 52. d×c4 B×c4 53. Nd6 Bb3 54. Nb7 B×a4 55. N×a5 Kf5 56. Nc4 Bb3 57. Nd2 Bd5 58. Ke2 K×e5 59. Kd3 f5 60. Nf1 f4 61. Nd2 b3 62. Nf1 Bb7 63. Nh2 Ba6† 64. Kd2 Ke4 65. Ng4 f3 White resigns—*Tournament Book*, pp. 65–66.

## (231) Bird–Gelbfuhs    1–0

International tournament (round 1, game 2)
Vienna, 22 July 1873
A02

1. f4 f5 2. e4 f×e4 3. d3 e×d3 4. B×d3 Nf6 5. Nf3 e6 6. Ng5 g6 7. h4 Bh6 8. h5 B×g5 9. f×g5 Nd5 10. h×g6 Qe7 11. R×h7 R×h7 12. g×h7 Qb4† 13. Kf1 Qh4 14. Bg6† Ke7 15. Qh5 Black resigns—*Tournament Book*, p. 73.

## (232) Anderssen–Bird    0–1

International tournament (round 2, game 1)
Vienna, 24 July 1873
C51

1. e4 e5 2. Nf3 Nc6 3. Bc4 Bc5 4. b4 B×b4 5. c3 Bc5 6. 0–0 d6 7. d4 e×d4 8. c×d4 Bb6 9. d5 Na5 10. Bb2 Ne7 11. Bd3 0–0 12. Nc3 c5 13. Ne2 f6 14. Qd2 Bg4 15. Rac1 Ng6 16. Ng3 Rc8 17. Kh1 c4 18. Bb1 18. Be2 is necessary to avoid 18. ... B×f3, which is now good for Black. **18. ... c3 19. B×c3 Nc4** "By the sacrifice of the pawn Mr. Bird has converted his defense into an attack, which he maintains with characteristic spirit to the end"—Duffy. **20. Qe1 Re8 21. Nd2 Na3 22. f4 N×b1 23. N×b1 Bd7** "We presently see that the retreat of this bishop was for a very good purpose, and tended considerably to affect the result of the battle"—Duffy. **24. Qd2 Bb5 25. Rfe1 Bc5 26. Ba5 b6 27. Bc3 a5 28. a3 Rc7 29. Bb2 Rce7 30. Nf5?** "A move which promises more than it performs"—Duffy. **30. ... R×e4 31. R×e4 R×e4 32. Nc3 R×f4 33. N×g7** "An evident mistake. But the whole combination depending on 30. Nf5 was miscalculated"—Duffy. **33. ... Rf2 34. Qh6 R×b2 35. Ne6 Qe7 36. h4 f5 37. Ng5 Be3 38. Rd1 Bd7 39. Qh5 B×g5 40. h×g5 R×g2** White resigns—*Era* (Duffy), 17 August 1873.

## (233) Bird–Anderssen    0–1

International tournament (round 2, game 2)
Vienna, 25 July 1873
A02

1. f4 e6 2. Nf3 c5 3. e3 f5 4. c3 Nf6 5. Na3 Be7 6. Nc2 0–0 7. b3 b6 8. Bb2 Bb7 9. Be2 Na6 10. 0–0 Nc7 11. Qe1 Nce8 12. Rd1 Qc7 13. c4 Ng4 14. h3 Nh6 15. d4 Be4 16. Rd2 Bf6 17. Qf2 Rd8 18. Nce1 Nf7 19. Nd3 h6 20. Qg3 Kh7 21. Nf2 B×f3 22. Q×f3 g5 23. Rfd1 g×f4 24. e×f4 Rg8 25. d×c5 b×c5 26. Nd3 B×b2 27. R×b2 Nf6 28. Nf2 Rg6 29. Qe3 Rdg8 30. Bf3 Rg3 31. Rbd2 e5 32. Qc3 R8g6 33. Rd3 e4 34. N×e4 f×e4 35. f5 Rg7 36. Q×f6 e×f3 37. Rd6 R×g2† White resigns—*Tournament Book*, pp. 92–93.

## (234) Anderssen–Bird   1–0

International tournament (round 2, game 3)
Vienna, 26 July 1873
*C61*

**1. e4 e5 2. Nf3 Nc6 3. Bb5 Nd4 4. N×d4 e×d4 5. d3 c6 6. Ba4 Nf6 7. 0–0 d5 8. e×d5 N×d5 9. c3 Bd6 10. c×d4 Qh4 11. g3 Qh3** Bird consequently aims for an attack and neglects the promising 11. ... Q×d4 12. Re1† Be6. **12. Qe2†** "12. Nc3 is the better move. 12. Qe2† brings Black's rook into play"—Wisker/Zukertort. **12. ... Kd8!** Bird prefers this cunning move over the safe 12. ... Be6. **13. f3** The sophisticated 13. Bd1! is a much better way to cure the weakened white squares around his king. If 13. ... Re8 14. Qd2 and 15. Bf3 follows soon. **13. ... Re8 14. Qf2 Bf5 15. Nc3 N×c3 16. b×c3 B×d3 17. Re1 R×e1† 18. Q×e1 Kd7** "With the object of playing 19. ... Re8"—Bird. **19. d5?** "White did not play the opening well, but his last move is ruinous"—Wisker/Zukertort. **19. ... Bc5†!** "Black could now win by: 19. ... Re8 20. d×c6† Kc7 21. Be3 (best) 21. ... Bc5 22. B×c5 (best) 22. ... R×e1† 23. R×e1 b5 24. Bb3 K×c6"—Wisker/Zukertort. Black has nothing in this line, as 25. B×a7 equalizes instantly. 24. ... Qf5 is more promising, though White runs but little risk, especially as 25. Bf2 Q×f3 leads to an interesting forced draw: 26. Re3 Qf5 27. g4! A beautiful move. The c-pawn, supported by rook and bishops forces Black to a perpetual

check: 27. ... Qg6 28. Bd5 Bc4 29. Bg3† Kb6 30. c7 Q×g4 31. B×c4 b×c4 32. Re8. The move played by Bird in the game is the strongest one available. **20. Kh1 b5** *(see diagram)*

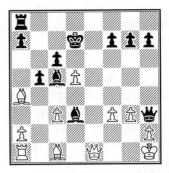

*After 20. ... b5*

**21. Bf4!?** In a critical situation Anderssen comes up with a highly ingenious move. If Bird now naively captures the bishop with 21. ... b×a4?, the roles would be turned at once by 22. Qe5! Rc8 23. d6!, with a winning attack. Alternatively 21. Bb3 leaves the initiative in Bird's hands. After his best move 21. ... Bf1!, the forced 22. d×c6† K×c6 23. Bd5†! Kb6 (certainly not 23. ... K×d5?? 24. Qe4† Kd6 25. Bf4† turns the game upside down again) 24. f4 Rd8 25. Bf3 Rd3 leads to an endgame with bishops of opposing colors by 26. Be3! R×e3 27. Q×f1 Q×f1† 28. R×f1 f6 29. Bd5 R×c3. **21. ... Qh5?** 21. ... b×a4?? 22. Qe5! is still out of the question. But another surprising pawn push, 21. ... g5!, diverts Anderssen's bishop from its excellent diagonal and makes the capture of the bishop at a4 possible after 22. B×g5. If instead 22. d×c6† K×c6 23. B×b5† K×b5!, White has nothing for the piece. After the text move Anderssen averts the loss of a piece. **22. d×c6† K×c6 23. Bd1 Rd8 24. a4 Qd5 25. a×b5† B×b5** 25. ... Kb7, keeping the b-file closed, is safer. **26. Kg2 g5?** Now this move turns out to be a sheer loss of time. Had Bird been aware of Anderssen's intentions, he would have come up with 26. ... Bd3 (preventing his opponent's next move), when position on the board is a mess. **27. Bc2! Kb6?** More resistance is offered by 27. ... Bd3 28. Rd1 Qa2 29. Rd2, although White's position is much improved compared to the previous line. **28. c4!** "Very finely played. Black has now no resources"—Bird. **28. ... Qd7 29. Qa5† Kb7 30. Be4† Bc6 31. Qa6†** and mates in two moves—*Westminster Chess Club Papers* (Wisker/Zukertort), October 1873, p. 110; *Chess Masterpieces* (Bird), p. 10.

## (235) Bird–Heral   0–1

International tournament (round 3, game 1)
Vienna, 28 July 1873
*A03*

**1. f4 d5 2. Nf3 Nc6 3. e3 Nf6 4. b3 Bg4 5. Be2 B×f3 6. B×f3 e6 7. c3 Bd6 8. d4 Ne7 9. Na3 a6 10. 0–0 c6 11. Nc2 Qc7 12. c4 Qb8 13. Bb2 h6 14. Qd3 g5 15. g3 g4 16. Bg2 h5 17. e4 Bc7 18. e5 Nd7 19. Ne3 Qa7 20. c×d5 c×d5 21. Kh1 0–0–0 22. f5 Bb6 23. a3 N×e5 24. d×e5 B×e3 25. f×e6 h4 26. g×h4 f×e6 27. Rae1 Bb6 28. Rf6 R×h4 29. Bc1 Rdh8 30. Bf4 Bf2 31. Rf1 g3 32. B×g3 B×g3 33. Rf8† Kd7 34. R×h8 R×h8 35. Q×g3 Qd4 36. Qg5 Qh4 37. Q×h4 R×h4 38. Bf3 Nc6 39. Re1 Nd4 40. Bd1 Kc6 41. Kg2 Kc5 42. Re3 Nf5 43. Re1 Kd4 44. Bf3 Kc3 45. h3 b5 46. Bg4 d4 47. B×f5 e×f5 48. e6 Rh8 49. h4 d3 50. Re5 d2**

**Adolf Anderssen (*Chess Monthly*).**

**51. Rd5 R×h4 52. Kf3 Re4 53. Rc5† K×b3** White resigns—*Tournament Book*, pp. 103–105.

## (236) Heral–Bird   ½–½
International tournament (round 3, game 2)
Vienna, 29 July 1873
*C47*

1. e4 e5 2. Nf3 Nc6 3. Nc3 Nf6 4. d4 e×d4 5. N×d4 Bb4
6. N×c6 b×c6 7. Qd4 Qe7 8. Bd3 d5 9. Kd1 B×c3 10. Q×c3 0–0
11. f3 d×e4 12. f×e4 Bg4† 13. Ke1 N×e4 14. B×e4 Q×e4† 15. Kf2
Qe2† 16. Kg3 Bf5 17. Re1 Qg4† 18. Kf2 Rae8 19. Bd2 Re6
20. R×e6 f×e6 21. Kg1 Be4 22. Qg3 Qe2 23. Bc3 Bg6 24. Re1
Q×c2 25. R×e6 Qf5 26. Re1 h5 27. h4 Kh7 28. Re7 Qc5†
29. Qe3 Q×e3† 30. R×e3 c5 31. Re7 Rf7 32. Re5 c4 33. Ra5 c6
34. Rc5 Rf4 35. g3 Rf3 36. R×c4 R×g3† 37. Kf2 Rg4 38. R×g4
h×g4 the game, now without interest, lingered on a long time, and
finally ended in a draw—*Tournament Book*, p. 110.

## (237) Bird–Heral   1–0
International tournament (round 3, game 3)
Vienna, 30 July 1873
*C00*

1. e4 e6 2. Bb5 a6 3. Ba4 b5 4. Bb3 Bb7 5. d3 d5 6. e5 Nd7
7. Nf3 h6 8. c3 Ne7 9. a4 Ng6 10. d4 c5 11. Bc2 Nh4 12. 0–0
N×f3† 13. Q×f3 Qb6 14. a×b5 c×d4 15. b×a6 R×a6 16. R×a6
B×a6 17. Re1 Bc5 18. Qg3 d3 19. Ba4 g5 20. b4 Be7 21. Be3 Qb7
22. Bd4 Kd8 23. Qf3 Rf8 24. Nd2 Nb6 25. Bb3 Kc7 26. Ra1
Bb5 27. Ra5 Bc4 28. B×c4 N×c4 29. N×c4 d×c4 30. Ra7 Q×a7
31. B×a7 g4 32. Qe3 Kb7 33. Qb6† Ka8 34. Qa6 Black resigns—
*Tournament Book*, pp. 115–116.

## (238) Bird–Pitschel   1–0
International tournament (round 4, game 1)
Vienna, 31 July 1873
*C00*

1. e4 e6 2. Bb5 a6 3. Ba4 c5 4. c3 b5 5. Bc2 Bb7 6. Ne2 Ne7
7. Ng3 Nbc6 8. a4 d5 9. Qe2 b4 10. d3 g6 11. h4 h5 12. Be3 Ng8
13. Nd2 d4 14. c×d4 c×d4 15. Bg5 f6 16. Nf3 f×g5 17. N×g5 Qd7
18. Bb3 Nd8 19. f4 Qd6 20. e5 Qd7 21. N3e4 Be7 22. 0–0 Bd5
23. Nd6† B×d6 24. B×d5 e×d5 25. e×d6† Kf8 26. Qe5 Qg7
27. Q×d5 Ra7 28. f5 Ke8 29. Rfe1† Kd7 30. Re7† N×e7
31. d×e7† Kc8 32. Rc1† Rc7 33. Qa8† Kd7 34. R×c7† K×c7
35. e×d8Q† Black resigns—*Tournament Book*, p. 122.

## (239) Pitschel–Bird   0–1
International tournament (round 4, game 2)
Vienna, 1 August 1873
*C35*

1. e4 e5 2. f4 e×f4 3. Nf3 Be7 4. Bc4 Bh4† 5. Kf1 d6 6. d4 Bg4
7. Nc3 Nc6 8. Bb5 a6 9. B×c6† b×c6 10. B×f4 Qf6 11. Ne2 B×f3
12. g×f3 g5 13. Rg1 g×f4 14. Rg4 h5 15. R×f4 Qe7 16. Rf5 Bg5
17. Qd3 Nh6 18. Ra5 Qf6 19. Kg2 Rg8 20. Kh1 Kd7 21. f4 Ng4
22. Rf1 Bh4 23. Qf3 Qg6 24. e5 d×e5 25. R×e5 Rae8 26. f5 Qg5

**27. Nf4 Nf2† 28. Q×f2 B×f2** White resigns—*Tournament Book*,
p. 129.

## (240) Bird–Blackburne   0–1
International tournament (round 5, game 1)
Vienna, 4 August 1873
*A02*

1. f4 e6 2. Nf3 b6 3. b3 Nf6 4. Bb2 Be7 5. c3 Bb7 6. e3 0–0
7. Na3 c5 8. Be2 d5 9. 0–0 Nc6 10. Nc2 Ne8 11. Qe1 Nd6 12. Rd1
a5 13. Qg3 a4 14. Bd3 Ne4 15. B×e4 d×e4 16. c4 f6 17. Nfe1 a×b3
18. a×b3 Ra2 19. Bc3 Rf7 20. d4 f5 21. d5 e×d5 22. R×d5 Qc8
23. Rd1 Bf6 24. B×f6 R×f6 25. Rf2 Rg6 26. Qh4 Rh6 27. Qg5
Rg6 28. Qh5 Rh6 29. Qe2 Rb2 30. Qd2 R×b3 31. g4 f×g4 32. f5
Ne5 33. Na1 Rb4 34. Qc3 g3 35. h×g3 Nd3 36. Rf1 Qc7 37. Rd2
Q×g3† 38. Rg2 Q×e3† 39. Rgf2 Rh1† White resigns—*Tournament Book*, pp. 140–141.

## (241) Blackburne–Bird   1–0
International tournament (round 5, game 2)
Vienna, 5 August 1873
*C25*

1. e4 e5 2. Nc3 Bc5 3. Nf3 d6 4. Bc4 Bg4 5. d3 c6 6. Ne2 B×f3
7. g×f3 Ne7 8. Ng3 Nd7 9. Bg5 f6 10. Bd2 d5 11. Bb3 a5 12. a4
Qb6 13. Qe2 g6 14. f4 Bd4 15. 0–0 h5 16. Qd1 Nc5 17. e×d5
c×d5 18. Ba2 h4 19. Ne2 B×b2 20. Rb1 Qe6 21. f3 Ba3 22. d4
Nd7 23. Nc3 Nb6 24. Nb5 Bd6 25. Re1 Rh5 26. d×e5 f×e5
27. Be3 Ra6 28. Bd4 Nd7 29. f×e5 Bb8 30. Qe2 Rg5† 31. Kh1
Rc6 32. f4 Rg4 33. Nd6† Kf8 34. R×b7 Nf5 35. N×f5 g×f5
36. Qb5 Rg7 37. B×d5 Black resigns—*Westminster Chess Club Papers*, October 1873, p. 110.

## (242) Bird–M. Fleissig   1–0
International tournament (round 6, game 1)
Vienna, 7 August 1873
*C00*

1. e4 e6 2. Bb5 "The object of this move was doubtless to vary
the monotonous routine of the safe and dreary French opening.
Any change in the mode of conducting that miserable business is
welcome, but Mr. Bird's variation seems to be destroyed by 2. … a6
3. Ba4 b5 4. Bb3 c5 5. d3 d5"—Wisker/Zukertort. **2. … Qg5** "The
position of his queen, after this sally, is always a trouble to Black"—
Wisker/Zukertort. **3. Bf1 d5** After 3. … Qd8, Bird had to consider
another solution to meet the French. **4. Nf3 Qg6 5. e×d5 e×d5
6. d4 Nf6 7. Ne5 Qe4† 8. Be3 Ng4 9. N×g4 B×g4 10. Qd2 Qe6
11. Bd3 Bd6 12. 0–0 0–0–0 13. Nc3 c6 14. Rae1** "In this case the
result of the opening is very favorable to White. He gains a much
more fully developed game"—Wisker/Zukertort. **14. … Qd7
15. Bf4 Bh5 16. B×d6 Q×d6 17. f4** This ought not to pose too
many problems for Black. 17. Qg5 Bg6 18. B×g6 and 19. Qe7 offers
a slightly better ending. **17. … f5** 17. … Nd7 is very safe. If then 18. h3
f6. **18. Re5 Bg6 19. g4!** A very optimistic, yet also dangerous, assault.
**19. … f×g4** He could also play 19. … Nd7 20. g×f5 Bh5 21. Ne2
Rae8 with an equal position. The text move is very risky. **20. f5** (*see
diagram*)

*After 20. f5*

**20. ... Bf7** The alternative 20. ... Be8 omits to take control of e6. The way this can punished is impressive: 21. Re6 Qb4 and now the powerful 22. f6! is awkward to meet; e.g., 22. ... Nd7 23. a3! (the crucial move. The queen can take a pawn with check, but Black is bound to lose a decisive tempo immediately afterwards) 23. ... Q×d4† (if 23. ... Qb6 24. N×d5 Q×d4† 25. Ne3 or 23. ... Qa5 24. f×g7) 24. Kg2 g6 25. R1f4! Qb6 26. N×d5 with a decisive attack; e.g., 26. ... Qd8 27. Ne7† Kf7 28. Rd6. **21. f6! Bg6?** This move loses at once, but the pressure was huge. Only a few precise moves could neutralize Bird's attack: 21. ... Nd7! 22. f×g7 Rfe8! This last move is necessary to prepare the capture of the g-pawn with the rook; 22. ... K×g7 loses quickly after 23. Qg5†. After 22. ... Rfe8 there may follow 23. Rg5 Re7! 24. R×g4 (he might retain some pressure if he keeps the g-pawn on the board, but after 24. Ne2 Bg6 25. B×g6 h×g6 26. Nf4 R×g7 27. Re1 Nf8 Black is quite solid) 24. ... Bh5 25. Rg3 R×g7 26. R×g7† K×g7. The endgame is equal. **22. B×g6 h×g6 23. f7†** Black resigns—*Westminster Chess Club Papers* (Wisker/Zukertort), October 1873, p. 110.

## (243) M. Fleissig–Bird    0–1
International tournament (round 6, game 2)
Vienna, 8 August 1873
C51

**1. e4 e5 2. Nf3 Nc6 3. Bc4 Bc5 4. b4 B×b4 5. c3 Bc5 6. 0-0 d6 7. d4 e×d4 8. c×d4 Bb6 9. Re1** "A pleasing variation of the Evans Gambit, but hardly strong enough for a match game"—Wisker/Zukertort. "This mode of conducting the attack, if not carefully met, is very dangerous for Black"—Staunton. **9. ... Na5** "9. ... Bg4 at once is the proper play"—Wisker/Zukertort. **10. Nc3 Bg4 11. e5 d5?!** "Mr. Bird's favorite mode of defending the Evans Gambit is to give back the pawn for the sake of neutralizing the attack. In this case however he does not obtain an equivalent for the sacrifice"—Wisker/Zukertort. The text move brings Bird to the verge of losing. Equality is gained after 11. ... N×c4. **12. B×d5 c6 13. Bb3** A logical retreat, but had Fleissig considered 13. e6!, he would have found a winning position after 13. ... f5 14. e7 Qd6 15. B×g8 R×g8 16. d5! **13. ... N×b3 14. Q×b3 B×f3 15. g×f3 Ne7 16. Be3?!** "A poor move, giving Black the very opportunity he needed. 16. Ne4 was the proper play. The capture of the d-pawn by Black would then be evidently fatal to him. If 16. ... 0-0 17. Ba3, with a fine game. The d-pawn need not be regarded"—Wisker/Zukertort. An improvement is 16. Ba3! first, as 16. ... 0-0 is met with 17. e6! If he plays 16. ... Q×d4 17. Ne4! comes in very strong. Black has serious problems in every line. **16. ... 0-0 17. Rad1 Nf5 18. Ne2 Qh4 19. Ng3 Qh3 20. N×f5 Q×f5 21. Bc1 Rfe8** "Black has now a little the better

game"—Wisker/Zukertort. **22. Re4 Re6 23. Rg4 Rg6 24. R×g6 h×g6 25. f4?** An unnecessary and decisive concession. This move both weakens the white squares and further cages in his own bishop, as this piece is now bound to the defense of f4. The flexible 25. Kg2 is much better. **25. ... Rd8 26. Be3 c5!** "Cleverly played. White dare not take the pawn on account of 26. ... Qg4†"—Staunton. **27. d5** This move loses quickly, but other moves would only prolong the game, not change the result of it. **27. ... c4 28. Qa4 Qg4† 29. Kf1 B×e3 30. f×e3 Qf3† 31. Kg1 Q×e3† 32. Kh1 Qf3† 33. Kg1 b5 34. Qc2 R×d5 35. R×d5 Q×d5** "All this is very well managed. The latter portion of the game is excellently played by Mr. Bird"—Wisker/Zukertort. **36. Qc3 Qe4 37. Qd2 Kh7 38. Qf2 g5 39. Q×a7 Q×f4 40. Qd7 b4 41. Qh3† Kg6 42. e6** and White resigns, not waiting for Bird's reply—*Westminster Chess Club Papers* (Wisker/Zukertort), October 1873, p. 111; *Illustrated London News* (Staunton), 14 February 1874.

## (244) Bird–Meitner    1–0
International tournament (round 7, game 1)
Vienna, 11 August 1873
C01

**1. e4 e6 2. Nf3 d5 3. Nc3 Nf6 4. e×d5 e×d5 5. d4 Bd6 6. Bd3 0-0 7. 0-0 c6 8. Bg5 Bg4 9. h3 Bh5 10. Be2 h6 11. Bh4 B×f3 12. B×f3 Nbd7 13. Ne2 Qc7 14. Qd3 Rae8 15. Bg3 Ne4 16. B×e4 d×e4 17. Qb3 B×g3 18. f×g3 Nf6 19. Nf4 Rd8 20. Rad1 Kh7 21. c4 Rfe8 22. Qe3 Re7 23. g4 Qd6 24. Ne2 a6 25. Rf5 g6 26. Rf4 Kg7 27. Rdf1 Nh7 28. h4 Rde8 29. Ng3 Qb4 30. b3 Qa3 31. R1f2 b5 32. c5 Qa5 33. N×e4 Qd8 34. Qf3 Rf8 35. Nd6 Re1† 36. Rf1 Qe7 37. g3 Nf6 38. R×e1 Q×e1† 39. Kh2 Qe7 40. Q×c6 Qe2† 41. Kh3 h5 42. Qg2 Qe6 43. Qd2 N×g4 44. Kg2 Qd5† 45. Kg1 f5 46. Qe2 Nf6 47. Qe5 Qc6 48. Rf1 Kg8 49. Re1 Qf3 50. Qe3 Qc6 51. Qh6 Qf3 52. Q×g6† Kh8 53. N×f5** Black resigns—*Tournament Book*, pp. 170–171.

## (245) Meitner–Bird    0–1
International tournament (round 7, game 2)
Vienna, 12 August 1873
C45

**1. e4 e5 2. Nf3 Nc6 3. d4 e×d4 4. N×d4 Bc5 5. Be3 Qf6 6. c3 Qg6 7. Nb5 B×e3 8. f×e3 Kd8 9. Nd2 Nf6 10. g3 d6 11. Bg2 Qg5 12. Qe2 Bg4 13. Nf3 B×f3 14. B×f3 Re8 15. 0-0 h5 16. Nd4 Ne5 17. Nf5 N×f3† 18. R×f3 N×e4 19. Qb5 Rb8 20. Rd1 Re6 21. Qa5 Kc8 22. Q×a7 Qg4 23. Rff1 Re5 24. Qa4 b5 25. Qa6† Kd8 26. N×d6 c×d6 27. R×d6† Ke7 28. Qa7† K×d6 29. Q×b8† Kd5 30. Q×b5† Kd6 31. Qb6† Ke7 32. Qc7† Ke6 33. Qc6† Nd6 34. b4 Qe2 35. a4 Q×e3† 36. Kh1 Qd3 37. Kg1 Qe3† 38. Kh1 Rd5 39. c4 Rd2 40. Qf3 Q×f3† 41. R×f3 N×c4 42. Rb3 Kd5** White resigns—*Tournament Book*, pp. 176–177.

## (246) Bird–Rosenthal    1–0
International tournament (round 8, game 1)
Vienna, 14 August 1873
A02

**1. f4 e6 2. e3 f5 3. Nf3 c5 4. b3 Nf6 5. Bb2 b6 6. Na3 Bb7 7. c4 Be7 8. Be2 Nc6 9. 0-0 0-0 10. Nc2 Qe8 11. d3 Nd8 12. Qd2 Nf7**

**13. Rae1 Nh6 14. Bd1 Nh5 15. Kh1 Ng4 16. Kg1 Rd8 17. h3 Nh6 18. Qf2 Qg6 19. Ne5 Qe8 20. Bf3 d6 21. B×b7 d×e5 22. Rd1 e×f4 23. e×f4 Qd7 24. Ba6 Bf6 25. B×f6 R×f6** "Much better is 25. ... N×f6"—Wisker/Zukertort. **26. d4** "White now secures a passed pawn, with a fine position. His opponent's knights are badly placed"—Wisker/Zukertort. **26. ... Qc6** The queen is better on c7, out of reach of Bird's d-pawn and pieces. **27. d5! e×d5 28. c×d5 Qd6?** The queen must return to e8 to defend the knight. **29. Be2!** "Well played. This course, followed by 31. Nc4, is far preferable to the more obvious play of 29. Bc4"—Wisker/Zukertort. **29. ... g6 30. Ne3?!** Black is powerless against 30. Qh4 Re8 31. Rde1 Rff8 32. B×h5, when White gains a pawn, while destroying Black's kingside along the way. **30. ... Ng7 31. Nc4 Qf8 32. Qh4 Ne8 33. Ne5 Kg7 34. Bf3 Nd6 35. Rfe1 Ng8** (see diagram)

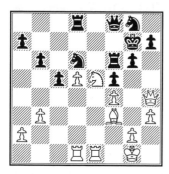

*After 35. ... Ng8*

**36. Re2** Bird's approach is too slow, as Rosenthal now gets a chance to activate his pieces by playing 36. ... Nb5!, which he omits to do. More forceful is 36. Nc6! Rd7 37. Qf2, followed by 38. Re5 or 38. Qb2. White's knight now controls d4. His plan is to make preparations for a breakthrough on the queenside. **36. ... Ne7 37. g4?** Opening the wrong front. Again, 37. Nc6 and 38. Re5 are indicated. **37. ... f×g4 38. N×g4 Rf7 39. Re6 Nef5 40. Qe1 Kh8** A lost move. 40. ... Rb7, making f7 available for his knight, is better. **41. Ne5 Rg7 42. Nc6 Rdd7 43. Qc3** 43. Qe5 is more powerful. Anyway, with his damaged kingside, White's control over the position will never be complete. **43. ... Kg8 44. Rde1 h6** Both 44. ... Nb5 (and 45. ... Nc7) and 44. ... g5 gain sufficient counterplay. Not for the first time during this game, Rosenthal selects an overly passive move. **45. Ne5** Bird immediately points his arrows towards the g-pawn. This pawn is indeed condemned, but the opening of the g-file provides Black enough counterplay. Better is therefore 45. Bg4 or 45. Qf6, keeping the control over e7, and augmenting the pressure. **45. ... Rde7 46. N×g6 Kh7** 46. ... R×e6! is correct. White is bound to sacrifice the exchange, so that anything more than a draw becomes unachievable; e.g., 47. R×e6 Nd4 48. Kh2 Qd8 49. Bg4 N×e6 50. B×e6† Kh7 51. f5 Qg5 52. Nf8†. **47. Bh5! Nb5?** He absolutely needs to simplify the game with 47. ... R×e6, followed by 48. ... Nd4. **48. Qd3** Good enough, but Bird misses a beautiful win after 48. Kh2! N×c3 49. N×f8† Kh8 50. R×e7 R×e7 51. d6! **48. ... R×e6 49. R×e6** This move complicates matters again. After 49. d×e6, Black has great problems to cope with the strong passed pawn. **49. ... Nbd4 50. Kh2 Qf7?** 50. ... Qd8 is correct. **51. Re7?** 51. Qe4! N×e6 52. d×e6 leads to another strong passed pawn that should decide the game. The text move abandons the d-pawn without good reason and as a result a very drawish position appears on the board. **51. ... Q×d5 52. Re5 Qf7 53. Re7 Qd5**

**54. R×g7† K×g7 55. Ne5 Kf6 56. Bg4 Ke6?** Leading to a disaster. After 56. ... Nh4, White is confronted with a direct mate threat. He should defend with 57. Qg3, when 57. ... Ndf5 58. B×f5 Qd2† leads to a perpetual. **57. Qa6!** To the point! Black's attack is suddenly gone. White wins some pawns along the road. **57. ... Qa8** "The only chance, and that a poor one, was to attempt an incursion into the enemy's territory, with an eye to perpetual check. 57. ... Qa8 doesn't save the pawns, as Black is kept continually under pressure"—Wisker/Zukertort. **58. Qa4!** "The queen appears to have been played to the best advantage"—Bird. **58. ... Kf6 59. Qd7 Qf8 60. Q×a7 Qd8 61. Qh7** Missing a mate in one. **61. ... Qe8 62. a4 Ke6 63. Q×h6† Kd5 64. Q×b6 Nd6 65. b4 c×b4 66. Q×b4 Qf8 67. Qa5† Ke4 68. Qe1† Kd5 69. Qf2 Qh6 70. Bf3† Ne4 71. Qa2† Kc5 72. Qc4†** Black resigns—*Chess Masterpieces* (Bird), pp. 52–53; *Westminster Chess Club Papers* (Wisker/Zukertort), October 1873, p. 112.

## (247) Rosenthal–Bird　0–1

International tournament (round 8, game 2)
Vienna, 15 August 1873
*C33*

**1. e4 e5 2. f4 e×f4 3. Bc4 Nf6 4. Nc3 Bb4 5. e5 d5 6. Bb5† c6 7. e×f6 c×b5 8. Qe2† Be6 9. Q×b5†** A doubtful expedition. 9. f×g7 is correct. **9. ... Nc6 10. f×g7 Rg8 11. Nf3 Qd7 12. d4** "White should perhaps castle at this point"—Bird. **12. ... a6 13. Qa4?!** "A singular move for so fine a player, thus shutting the queen completely out of the game"—Bird. 13. Qd3 is much safer. **13. ... R×g7 14. 0–0** (see diagram) "Again unwise"—Bird. 14. B×f4 or 14. Bd2, preparing an exit for the king towards the queenside, is necessary by now.

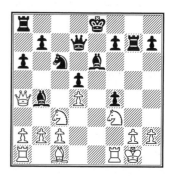

*After 14. 0–0*

**14. ... Bd6** A direct win is available, but it was not easy at all to find: 14. ... B×c3! 15. b×c3 Bh3 16. Rf2 Qg4 17. Ne1 B×g2! 18. R×g2 Qd1 19. Kf2 R×g2† 20. N×g2 0–0–0. Until here the moves were rather forced. Black's compensation for the piece is obvious, but it needs some more moves to demonstrate the real strength of his attack: 21. Bb2 Qd2† 22. Kf3 Rg8 23. Rg1 R×g2 24. R×g2 Qe3† 25. Kg4 f3. **15. Ne2** "Overbold, this, in the face of the Black rook"—Bird. Rosenthal could avoid the following, decisive, attack with 15. Nb5! or with 15. Ne1. Especially the latter move makes it difficult for Bird to obtain anything real. **15. ... Bh3** Bird gave another, probably incorrect, move order in *Chess Masterpieces*: 13. ... Bd6 14. Ne2 R×g2 15. 0–0 Bh3. "This move wins, there is no resource for White. 16. Rf2 would be rather better"—Bird. **16. Ne1 B×g2!** "An excellent stroke of play. Winning the game offhand"—

Staunton. **17. N×g2 Qh3 18. Rf2 f3 19. Ng3 B×g3 20. h×g3 R×g3** and Black wins—*Chess Masterpieces* (Bird), p. 52; *Illustrated London News* (Staunton), 6 December 1873.

## (248) L. Paulsen–Bird    1–0
International tournament (round 9, game 1)
Vienna, 18 August 1873
C25

**1. e4 e5 2. Nc3 Bc5 3. Nf3 d6 4. Na4 Bg4 5. N×c5 d×c5 6. Be2 Qd6 7. h3 B×f3 8. B×f3 Nc6 9. g3 Nge7 10. d3 0-0-0** "10. ... 0-0, followed by 11. ... f5, would have given Black a fine position; in my opinion a better one than that enjoyed by White, despite his bishops. Black might also have played 10. ... Rd8 with advantage. If White on his part had castled on the queenside, the Black pawn could have been thrown up with great facility"—Wisker/Zukertort. **11. Be3 Nd4** Paulsen's opening has been too tame, and Bird comes out of it on top. Here he misses a chance to accentuate his advantage with 11. ... c4! **12. Bg2 h5 13. Qd2 Qa6 14. 0-0 h4** "Black's play for the last two or three moves has not improved his game. This last move deprives him of all chance of making an impression on the kingside"—Wisker/Zukertort. In fact, Bird played very well and kept his advantage. **15. g4 Ng6 16. f4 e×f4 17. B×f4 N×f4 18. R×f4 f6 19. Rf2** *(see diagram)*

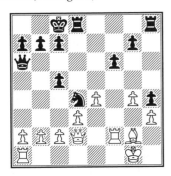

*After 19. Rf2*

**19. ... Ne6** This move releases all the pressure that Bird built so quietly. Again, 19. ... c4! increases White's difficulties. During the following moves both players have trouble finding the strongest plan. Here 20. e5! f×e5 21. Re1 is an excellent way to liberate his pieces. **20. Qc3 Rhe8** 20. ... Qd6! and 21. ... Nd4 takes control over the center again. The loss of time is hardly problematic. **21. b4 c4** "A miscalculation, apparently. Black does regain the pawn, but he irreparably compromises his position"—Zukertort/Wisker. Even at this point 21. ... c4 isn't bad at all, although 21. ... c×b4 or 21. ... Qd6 are certainly superior. **22. d×c4 Rd4 23. c5 Red8** The exchange of queens, realized after 23. ... Qc4!, exploits the several weaknesses in White's camp. **24. a4** 24. a3 consolidates the queenside. Now, Black can play 24. ... Qc4 with a slight advantage again. **24. ... Ng5? 25. e5!** "Another very good move. The course is now clear"—Zukertort/Wisker. Paulsen finds the winning motive which was already an option a few moves ago. By giving up his extra pawn his pieces find the perfect coordination. **25. ... f×e5 26. Qe3 Qh6 27. Q×e5 R×b4 28. c3** "The object of thus driving the rook to b3 becomes apparent presently"—Zukertort/Wisker. **28. ... Rb3 29. Raf1 Qg6 30. Rf5 Ne6 31. Rf6! g×f6 32. Q×e6† Kb8 33. Q×b3 Qd3** "The game, of course, is gone, but the overlooking

**A young Louis Paulsen (left), meeting George W. Medley over the board in 1861 or 1862 (courtesy Nigel Webb).**

of mate on the move is one amongst many proofs that Mr. Bird was unwell when this game was played"—Zukertort/Wisker. **34. Q×b7 mate**—*Westminster Chess Club Papers* (Wisker/Zukertort), October 1873, p. 114.

## (249) Bird–L. Paulsen    0–1
International tournament (round 9, game 2)
Vienna, 19 August 1873
A03

**1. f4 d5 2. Nf3 e6 3. e3 Nf6 4. b3 Be7 5. Bb2 0-0 6. Be2 c5 7. 0-0 Nc6 8. c3 a6 9. Na3 b6 10. Nc2 Bb7 11. Qe1 Qc7 12. c4 Rad8 13. d3 b5 14. c×b5 a×b5 15. Qg3 Qa5 16. a3 c4 17. b4 Qa4 18. Ncd4 N×d4 19. N×d4 Qa6 20. Nf3 Rc8 21. Bd4 Ne8 22. Ne5 Rd823. Qh3 f6 24. Nf3 Bc8 25. Qg3 Nd6 26. Nh4 Qb7 27. Rac1 c×d3 28. B×d3 Ne4 29. Qe1 Bd7 30. Nf3 Bd6 31. Qe2 Rb8 32. B×e4 d×e4 33. Nd2 Bc6 34. Nb3 Bd5 35. Na5 Qd7 36. Bc5 Rfc8 37. B×d6 Q×d6 38. R×c8† R×c8 39. Q×b5 Rc3 40. Qe8† Qf8 41. Qd7 Qf7 42. Qd8† Qf8 43. Qb6 R×a3 44. Rc1 h6 45. h4 Qe8 46. f5 e×f5 47. b5 Kh7 48. Nc6 Ra2 49. Nb4 Rd2 50. N×d5 R×d5 51. Qc6 Qe5 52. b6 Rd2 53. Qc7 Qb2 54. b7 f4 55. Kh1**

R×g2 56. Q×f4 Q×c1† 57. K×g2 Qb2† 58. Kg3 Q×b7 59. Qf5†
Kg8 60. Kf4 Qc7† 61. K×e4 Qc2† 62. Kf4 g5† 63. h×g5 f×g5†
64. Ke5 Q×f5† 65. K×f5 Kf7 66. e4 Ke7 White resigns—*Tournament Book*, pp. 211–213.

## (250) Steinitz–Bird    1–0
International tournament (round 10, game 1)
Vienna, 21 August 1873
C35

**1. e4 e5 2. f4 e×f4 3. Nf3 Be7 4. Bc4 Bh4† 5. Kf1 d6 6. d4 Bg4
7. B×f4 Qf6 8. Be3 Ne7 9. Nbd2 h6 10. h3 B×f3 11. N×f3 Nd7
12. Kg1 Bg3 13. Nd2 Nb6 14. Bd3 Bf4 15. Bf2 h5 16. h4 0-0-0
17. Nf3 d5 18. e5 Qe6 19. Qe2 f6 20. Re1 Nc6 21. g3 f×e5** Both
players treated the opening with care, and as a result the position
has been about equal all the game through. With the text move,
Bird initiates complications. He could also have chosen the quiet
21. ... Bh6. **22. g×f4 Qg4† 23. Kh2 e4 24. Ng5 Q×f4†?!** A very
dangerous capture. Instead 24. ... e×d3! 25. Q×g4† h×g4 26. Nf7
d×c2 27. Rc1 Nd7! (heading for e4) and the closed nature of the
game means that the loss of the exchange is hardly a problem for
Black **25. Bg3 Qf6 26. Bb5?** With 26. Rhf1! e×d3 27. Q×d3 Q×d4
28. Q×d4 N×d4 29. Nf7, Steinitz obtains a similar, but much better
endgame than in the previous note, as his rooks are ready to invade
into Bird's position. The text move, on the other hand, is rather
awful. Bird gains control over the center and a magnificent knight.
**26. ... N×d4 27. Qf1 Rdf8 28. c3 Qe7?!** *(see diagram)* This move
is met by a most unexpected antidote. Bird could consolidate with
28. ... Nf5!, when he has three pawns for the piece and a very harmonious position. White is close to being lost.

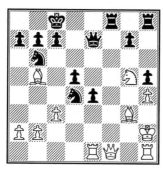

*After 28. ... Qe7*

**29. c×d4!** "Being a piece ahead, White sacrifices (for the sake of
an attack) the queen for two other pieces. The following seems safer:
29. Qh3† Nf5 30. Rhf1 g6 31. Bd3"—Wisker/Zukertort. "A good
move, and as clever and bold as it was unexpected"—Bird. It is unclear what Zukertort and Wisker were hoping to achieve for White
with their line. Bird's appraisal is quite correct. In a very difficult
situation, Steinitz sells his life dearly. **29. ... R×f1 30. Rh×f1 Rf8?**
"Black could recover the attack by 30. ... Qb4. We do not examine
the position resulting from this move, because we hope to see the
two competitors fight over this game on a future occasion"—
Wisker/Zukertort. A possible continuation is 31. Rf7! Na8 32. Bd7†
Kb8 33. Re2 Q×d4 34. Ne6. The position is extremely intriguing
and complicated. It is obvious that both players have their trumps,
which makes a drawish outcome likely, as it would take too many
risks to purchase the win without taking care of his own position.

**31. R×f8†?** Bird's last move was only bad as it contained a tactical
flaw that was so well disguised that both players missed it. 31. N×e4!
would have concluded the game in brilliant fashion: 31. ... d×e4
(31. ... R×f1 32. Nd6†) 32. R×e4! **31. ... Q×f8 32. a3 c6?** Bird
clearly underestimates the danger that threatens his king. With
32. ... a6, his majesty could make use of an escape route and prevent
the worst. **33. Rf1** Or 33. Bf1! Kd7 34. Bh3† Ke8 35. Rf1 wins.
**33. ... Qe8 34. Rf7!** "The coup de grace. If 34. ... c×b5 35. Rc7
and mate or the winning of Black's queen next move"—Bird. **34. ...
Nd7** 34. ... Q×f7 is the only possibility left but the endgame is rather
hopeless. **35. Bf1 Nf6 36. Rc7†** Black resigns. "This game is
probably one of the best won by Steinitz from me"—Bird—*Westminster Chess Club Papers* (Wisker/Zukertort), November 1873, p.
141; *Modern Chess* (Bird), pp. 98–99.

## (251) Bird–Steinitz    0–1
International tournament (round 10, game 2)
Vienna, 22 August 1873
C80

**1. e4 e5 2. Nf3 Nc6 3. Bb5 a6 4. Ba4 Nf6 5. 0-0 N×e4** The
Open Variation of the Ruy Lopez, still a rare bird in 1873. **6. d4 b5
7. Bb3 d5 8. N×e5** "The defense adopted by Black was first recommended by the Leipzig school. If 8. d×e5 Ne7 9. Be3 Bb7 10. Nbd2
N×d2 11. Q×d2 etc."—Wisker/Zukertort. "8. d×e5 is perhaps
slightly better"—Bird. **8. ... N×e5 9. d×e5 c6 10. c3 Bc5 11. Nd2
N×d2 12. B×d2 Qh4 13. Kh1** 13. Be3 is an interesting way to establish equality. After 13. ... B×e3 14. f×e3 Be6 15. Qd4 White has
gained control over the black squares. **13. ... 0-0 14. f4 Bg4** Black
has slightly the more active prospects in the coming endgame. The
difference lies in the mobility of the pawn chains. While Bird cannot
set his majority in motion, the champion can count on his d-pawn
to force matters. **15. Qe1 Q×e1 16. Ra×e1 Bf5 17. Be3 B×e3
18. R×e3 Rad8 19. Rd1 Rd7 20. h3 h5! 21. Rd2 Rfd8 22. Bd1
g6 23. Bf3** "Tame play. 23. g4 would have been better"—Bird. Bird's
suggestion has a serious drawback, as 23. ... d4! opens the position
in Black's favor. An improvement over the text move is 23. Bc2 Be6
24. Rg3 Kf8 25. b4, playing for a blockade. **23. ... c5! 24. g4 h×g4
25. h×g4 Be6 26. Kg2?!** Bird neglects the coming push, and he is
soon faced with a depressing situation. A better way to meet the
coming move would have been 26. Rg2! Kf8 27. a3 d4, as after
28. c×d4 R×d4 29. Be4 Black's advantage is undeniable, but at least
no piece infiltrates into White's lines. **26. ... d4! 27. c×d4 R×d4
28. R×d4 R×d4 29. Kg3 Rd2** There is nothing to be done against
the loss of a pawn. Bird hence tries to find counterplay in an original
way. **30. Kh4 Kf8** Steinitz shows himself impressed by Bird's re-
sourcefulness and wanders off the correct path. The immediate
30. ... R×b2! is stronger. **31. Kg5 Ke7?!** Although the best chance
for it has passed, 31. ... R×b2! is still very good for Black (e.g.,
32. Kf6 Bc4!). **32. f5 B×a2 33. Rc3?!** "The result of the much better
move, 33. Ra3, would be probably a draw"—Wisker/Zukertort.
**33. ... Bc4 34. Bb7** 34. Ra3 is more tenacious. **34. ... g×f5 35. g×f5
a5?!** 35. ... R×b2 is much simpler. **36. b3! Rd3** This move appears
to refute Bird's last move, but there is a hidden salvation. Anyway,
the majority of his advantage has already evaporated; e.g., 36. ...
Bd5 37. Ba6 a4 38. b×a4 b×a4 39. f6† with good counterplay. **37. f6†**

Kd7 38. R×d3† B×d3 39. Bd5? 39. Ba6! stops all Black's winning attempts. The king has to prevent White from playing e6 (e.g. 39. ... Kc6? or 39. ... Kd8? 40. e6 wins), and neither Black pawn can be pushed: 39. ... Ke8 40. Kf4 Kf8 41. Ke3 Bc2 42. B×b5 B×b3 43. Kd3 a4 44. Kc3. 39. ... Ke8 40. Bc6† Kf8 Black's pawns are free to roll now. 41. Kf4 Bc2 42. Bd5 a4 43. b×a4 b×a4 44. e6 f×e6 45. B×e6 Bb3 46. Bf5 a3 47. Bb1 a2 48. B×a2 B×a2 49. Ke3 Kf7 50. Kd3 K×f6 White resigns—*Westminster Chess Club Papers* (Wisker/Zukertort), October 1873, p. 115; *Chess Masterpieces* (Bird), p. 120.

## (252) A. Schwarz–Bird    0–1
International tournament (round 11, game 1)
Vienna, 25 August 1873
C55

1. e4 e5 2. Nf3 Nf6 3. Nc3 Nc6 4. Bc4 Bb4 5. 0–0 d6 6. d3 B×c3 7. b×c3 Be6 8. Bb3 h6 9. Bd2 Bg4 10. Qe2 0–0 11. h3 Bh5 12. g4 Bg6 13. Nh4 Kh7 14. Kh2 d5 15. Rad1 Qd6 16. f3 Ne7 17. Nf5 More in the spirit of the position was 17. f4!, opening lines and diagonals for his pieces. 17. ... B×f5 18. g×f5 Nh5 19. Rg1 g6 20. f4? Very bad timing! The text move attempts to force matters, but he leaves a pawn hanging. By 20. Qf2 g×f5 21. Qh4 Nf4 22. B×f4 e×f4 23. B×d5 a slightly worse endgame could be reached. 20. ... N×f4 20. ... e×f4! keeps the knight on the board. This piece is considerably stronger than the bishop. 21. B×f4 e×f4 22. e5 Qc6 23. f6 Nf5 24. Qf3 Q×c3 25. Q×f4 Rae8?! Bird emerged out of the mêlée with an extra pawn. With 25. ... Qd4! he could force the exchange of queens and, after 26. Q×d4 N×d4 27. B×d5 Ne2, due to the threat of 28. ... Nc3, White has to abandon the exchange. The next move allows his opponent to restore his central pawn structure. 26. d4 c5 27. Rd3 Qb2 28. B×d5 (see diagram)

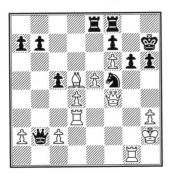

*After 28. B×d5*

28. ... N×d4?! The text move aims to keep the position as complicated as possible, but with the opening of lines and diagonals, a new factor becomes important, namely the safety of the kings. To avoid problems, Bird should have played 28. ... Rd8 29. Be4 R×d4 when a rook gets exchanged. 29. Rg2 Ne6? A gross error, but the tide of the game has turned. After 29. ... Nf5 30. c3 Qb6 31. Be4, Black's position has become increasingly difficult. 30. B×e6 R×e6 31. c3? The thunderbolt 31. R×g6!! terminates the game at once. After the next move, Bird gains control over the crucial d7 square while keeping his extra pawn. 31. ... Qb5 32. c4 Qc6 33. Rg4 Qc7 34. Rd5 34. Rd6! R×d6 35. Rh4! forces a draw. 34. ... Rg8 35. h4 Schwarz throws this pawn forward to finish off Bird's king in a direct attack, but by taking h4 away for the rook, he only kills his own attacking chances. 35. ... Rge8 36. h5? Surrendering the e-pawn is

simply fatal. He was on the defensive anyway, but after 36. Rg3 b6 37. Rgd3, it is not so easy for his opponent to win the game. 36. ... R×e5 37. h×g6† f×g6 38. f7 Re2† 39. Kg1 Q×f4 40. R×f4 Rf8 41. Rd6 R×a2 The game is totally over. 42. Rff6 Ra6 43. R×a6 b×a6 44. Rc6 R×f7 45. R×c5 Kg7 46. Rc8 Kf6 47. c5 Ke6 White resigns—*Tournament Book*, pp. 235–236.

## (253) Bird–A. Schwarz    1–0
International tournament (round 11, game 2)
Vienna, 26 August 1873
C01

1. e4 e6 2. d4 d5 3. e×d5 e×d5 4. Bd3 Bd6 5. Nc3 Nf6 6. Bg5 Be7 7. Nge2 c6 8. Qd2 h6 9. Bh4 Nbd7 10. f4 Bg4 11. 0–0 0–0 12. Ng3 Qc7 13. h3 Bh5 14. Nf5 Bg6 15. N×d6 B×d3 16. Q×d3 Q×d6 17. f5 Rfe8 18. Bg3 Qf8 19. a3 Ne4 20. N×e4 R×e4 21. c4 Rae8 22. Rf3 Qe7 23. c×d5 c×d5 24. Raf1 Re2 25. Qb5 Nf6 26. Be5 Re4 27. Rc3 a6 28. Qb3 b5 29. Rc7 Qd8 30. Rfc1 Re2 31. Qg3 Kf8 32. b4 Ra2 33. Qb3 Re2 34. Qf3 Rd2 35. R1c6 Ne4 36. Qh5 Black resigns—*Tournament Book*, pp. 240–241.

## (254) Steinitz & Blackburne & Bird–Anderssen & Rosenthal & L. Paulsen    0–1
Consultation game
Vienna, 19 July 1873
A10

1. c4 e6 2. e3 f5 3. Nf3 Nf6 4. a3 c5 5. Nc3 Nc6 6. d4 c×d4 7. e×d4 Bd6 8. Bd3 b6 9. 0–0 0–0 10. Re1 Ne7 11. d5 Ng6 12. b4 a6 13. Qb3 Ng4 14. h3 N4e5 15. N×e5 N×e5 16. Bf1 Qh4 17. Be3 Rf6 18. f4 Ng6 19. Ne2 N×f4 20. B×f4 B×f4 21. g3 Rg6 22. Kh2 Be5 23. Bg2 Bb7 24. Qe3 B×g3† 25. N×g3 f4 26. Qe4 Q×g3† 27. Kh1 b5 28. Rad1 b×c4 29. Rf1 Rf8 and the White allies resigns the untenable game—*Tournament Book*, pp. 21–23.

## (255) Jacobi–Bird    1–0
Offhand game
Vienna 1873
C33

1. e4 e5 2. f4 e×f4 3. Bc4 Nf6 4. Nc3 Bb4 5. Nge2 0–0 6. 0–0 B×c3 7. N×c3 N×e4 8. N×e4 d5 9. R×f4 d×c4 10. Qf1 Be6 11. Kh1 Nc6 12. b3 f5 13. Nc5 Qf6 14. Rb1 c×b3 15. Bb2 Qg6 16. a×b3 Rae8 17. N×b7 Bd5 18. Nc5 Ne5 19. c4 Bc6 20. d4 Ng4 21. d5 Qh6 22. h3 Ba8 23. Nd7 Rf7 24. Re1 Re3 25. R×e3 N×e3 26. Qf3 N×d5 27. R×f5 Nb6 28. R×f7 N×d7 29. R×g7† Q×g7 30. Q×a8† Qf8 31. Qd5† Qf7 32. Qg5† Qg6 33. Qd8† Nf8 34. Ba3 Qf5 35. Q×f8† Q×f8 36. B×f8 K×f8 37. Kg1 and White wins.—*Österreichische Schachzeitung*, December 1875, pp. 331–332.

## (256) L. Paulsen–Bird    1–0
Offhand game
Vienna 1873
C61

1. e4 e5 2. Nf3 Nc6 3. Bb5 Nd4 4. Ba4 Qf6 5. Nc3 c6 6. d3 Bc5 7. N×d4 e×d4 8. Ne2 Ne7 9. 0–0 d5 10. Ng3 h5 11. e×d5 N×d5 12. Ne4 Qe7 13. Bg5 Qf8 14. Re1 Be6 15. Qf3 Kd7 16. c3

**Bb6 17. c4 Bg4 18. Qg3 Bc7 19. Qh4 Nb6 20. Bd1 f6 21. N×f6†
g×f6 22. B×f6 Rg8 23. B×g4† h×g4 24. Qh7† Kc8 25. Re7 Bd6
26. Rf7 Qe8 27. c5 Rf8 28. R×f8 B×f8 29. c×b6 a×b6 30. Qf5†
Kb8 31. Be5† Ka7 32. B×d4 Qe2 33. Qa5† Kb8 34. Be5†** and
Black resigns—*New York Clipper*, 5 February 1876.

### (257) Bird–H.F. Down    ½–½
Offhand game
Vienna 1873

*Final position*

"This final position was reached in a game between Bird and the
honorary president of the London City Club, Mr. Down, recently
played in Vienna. Although White, with or without moving first,
should win, the game was adjourned as a draw"—Lehner. Yet,
White cannot win the game—*Österreichische Schachzeitung*, September 1873, p. 284.

## ABOUT AMATEURS
## AND PROFESSIONALS

The first two matches between Bird and Wisker evoked a lot of
interest and both players thought it interesting to broaden the perspective. Their idea was that the winner would challenge the American champion George Mackenzie for a duel.[19] Though the idea was
highly original it is unlikely that it fell upon fertile soil and the execution of it proved to be too difficult. The only realistic possibility
was that the match would be held before or after the Vienna
congress, but as Mackenzie ultimately refrained from his participation in Vienna, nothing came of it.

When Bird's victory over Wisker was a fact he also challenged
Steinitz for a match of five or seven wins. Steinitz accepted the offer
in principal but because of the approaching tournament in Vienna
the match was suspended. The result of the Vienna tournament
changed matters quite radically. Blackburne's performance left a

deep impression on everyone and it was clear that Bird's position
in the chess ranking was not as high as perhaps assumed.

Several match offers between Blackburne, Steinitz and Bird were
launched in the aftermath of Vienna. One rumor spoke of a match
between Bird and Blackburne and it was whispered that the winner
of this duel could challenge Steinitz. The negotiations became very
concrete. On 11 October 1873 *Land and Water* announced an
agreement specifying that the match would be played for the first
seven wins and commence on 13 October. But then Blackburne
suddenly left London for a provincial tour. Upon his return Bird
was already involved in another match with Wisker. Despite persistent mentions in the press, nothing came of it eventually.

In September 1874 Bird challenged Steinitz again. While other
contests, for example between Owen and Burn or Wisker and MacDonnell, were played without much negotiation or with a low stake,
Steinitz's demands had altered radically in the intermediate year:
he demanded stakes of at least £100 a side.[20]

It is not known whether Bird had practical problems to fulfill
the amount of the stakes sought by Steinitz but it is certain he had
objections to such a professional attitude towards chess.[21]

## THIRD AND FOURTH MATCH
## WITH WISKER 1873

Quite suddenly, at least not preceded by lengthy negotiations or
unfounded rumors eked out in the press, a third match between Bird
and Wisker began on 30 October. The rules that were valid for the
first matches remained unaltered. The only difference was that the
games were exclusively played in the rooms of Simpson's Divan.

Just as in the previous matches both players proved to be of equal
strength. After 14 games each had won 6 times. It was agreed to extend the match to the point when one player would have won 10
games. The score meandered a bit further, until it stood 8–8. Then
Wisker decided the match by winning the next two games.

The score between Bird and Wisker was now completely equal,
hence a fourth match commenced immediately afterwards. This
match was played for the first to achieve five wins. After six games,
Wisker had an edge of one point, but by winning three games in a
row Bird grasped away the final victory before Wisker's nose.

---

19. Bird wrote a letter to Mackenzie in which he elucidated their plans. He
proposed Mackenzie to brainstorm about the idea. "Now, to come to the point.
Mr. Wisker proposed that you, as the representative of chess in New York, should
be sounded as to your inclination to play the winner. Should Mr. Wisker win, he
would, I know, propose to get up a large stake and ask you to come over here and
play. Should I win I would suit your convenience, and play either in New York or
here. Just think the matter over, and let me know what sort of a stake would be
raised on your side, and what terms would suit yourself. Much pleasure would be
felt over here at a visit from you, and funds, we think, would be forthcoming on
a liberal scale. For myself, I should like another run across the Atlantic, and would
pay half the expense out of my own pocket, if necessary." *The Spirit of the Times*,
31 May 1873.

20. "Mr. Bird has challenged Mr. Steinitz to play a match of seven or eleven
games, but at the time we write the negotiations have not progressed beyond the
preliminary stage. Mr. Steinitz, we understand, refuses to play for a less stake than
£100 a side." *Illustrated London News*, 10 October 1874.

21. Bird elucidated his point of view: "...there has been no first-class chess play
during the past few years, and consequently, there are no games to record. Time
was when the leading players sought with avidity the opportunity of encountering
each other, the pleasure and exercise of the contest, and the credit of victory being
considered ample inducement. ... Now the aspect of chess policy is changed, match
play is entirely stopped through the largeness of the stakes demanded, and emulatory games, formerly so popular and so frequent, are now of rare occurrence."
H.E. Bird, *Chess Masterpieces: Comprising a Collection of 150 Choice Games of the
Past Quarter of a Century*. London: Dean and Son, [1875], p. 3. Many British amateurs shared Bird's opinion. Wormald's reaction on the matter: "Those who are
behind the scenes know how literally true this is. A modern professional player,
when challenged to a match, invariably declines to play, except for a stake of £100
or £200 a side: and then expects other people to find the money." *Illustrated London News*, 4 September 1875.

The coverage of these last two matches was incomplete. As a result it has been impossible to draw up a complete table for them. With some well-founded guesses it is possible to present nearly full and probably correct tables but it remains possible that the actual course was different.

Opinions about the quality of these two matches rather differed. According to the players, in the *Westminster Chess Club Papers* (December 1873, p. 153), the games in the third and fourth match were decidedly superior, but an opposing point of view came forth from the correspondent of the *Glasgow Weekly Herald*. On 7 March 1874, he, rather impolitely, described the games as rubbish.

The matches with Wisker offered Bird, who did not take part in the 1870 and 1872 Challenge Cup tournaments, an excellent chance to re-establish his reputation as one of Britain's foremost players.

The great majority of contemporary sources attached no special importance to these matches but there were two noteworthy exceptions. The *Morning Post*, a newspaper that had no regular chess column, stated in an incidental article, on 28 May 1873, that the match was played for the Cup of the British Chess Association. This was implicitly confirmed by George Gossip in a private letter to Miron Hazeltine, the chess editor of the *New York Clipper*. Gossip sent Hazeltine a recent game won against Bird, whom he called "the present champion."[22]

All in all it is very likely that these matches were merely played for amusement and training, as Bird regularly emphasized. On a few occasions, however, it seems that Bird tried to refashion his victory to a higher purpose when he presented himself as "the amateur chess champion." He adopted this title for a first time in a letter published on 1 August 1876 in the *New York Herald* and also in *Chess Practice*. Bird's claim resurfaced in the press a decade later, after Wisker's death in 1884. At that time, it was firmly refuted by MacDonnell in his column in the *Illustrated Sporting and Dramatic News* of 29 March 1884.

## (258) Wisker–Bird    ½–½

Match 3 (game 1)
London, 30 October 1873
C33

**1. e4 e5 2. f4 e×f4 3. Bc4 b5?! 4. Bb3 Qh4† 5. Kf1 g5 6. d4 Ne7 7. Nc3 b4 8. Nf3 Qh5 9. Ne5 Q×d1† 10. N×d1 f6 11. Nf7 Rg8 12. h4 Rg7 13. Nh6 Ba6† 14. Kf2 Nbc6 15. Ng4 0-0-0 16. N×f6 N×d4 17. h×g5?** With 17. Nh5 Rg6 18. h×g5 R×g5 19. B×f4 the material balance is restored. With the f-pawn gone, White's game is freed. **17. ... Ng6! 18. c3 Ne6** A first line illustrating the agility of Black's piece play: 18. ... b×c3 19. b×c3 Bc5! 20. Ke1 f3! 21. Ne3 Ne5. **19. B×e6 d×e6 20. Ke1 Bc5** Fortunately for Wisker, his opponent is quite unaware of the various possibilities available to him. 20. ... Ne5! is another quick winner, e.g., 21. Nf2

f3 22. g3 b×c3 23. b×c3 Nd3† 24. N×d3 R×d3. **21. Nf2 b×c3 22. b×c3 e5 23. a4 Nf8 24. Rh5 h6** 24. ... B×f2† 25. K×f2 Rd1 26. g4 Rf1† 27. Kg2 Re1 is quite convincing. **25. N2g4 h×g5 26. N×e5 Ng6?!** While Bird did miss a few quick wins, he did nothing really wrong. Here 26. ... Be7 27. Nfg4 Bb7 is still extremely good for Black. Bird now hoped that Wisker would fall for the picturesque 27. R×g5? N×e5! 28. R×g7 f3! **27. Nf3?!** Instead 27. Nc6 equalizes completely: 27. ... Rf8 28. R×g5 R×f6 29. R×c5 Ne7 30. N×e7† R×e7. **27. ... g4?** Bird insists on returning the pawn. 27. ... Be7 is a last attempt to play for a win: 28. Nd5 Bc4 29. N×e7† R×e7 with excellent chances. **28. N×g4 Rgd7** 28. ... Re7 draws fairly simply. The text move, and certainly Bird's next move, suddenly lead to chances for Wisker. **29. Bd2 Be3?!** 29. ... Be7 must be played. **30. N×e3 f×e3 31. B×e3 Rd3 32. Bd4** The situation would become critical for Bird after 32. B×a7! **32. ... Nf4 33. Rg5 N×g2† 34. Kf2** and the game was given up as a draw. White can still play for more: 34. ... Nf4 35. Rh1 Ne6 36. Rf5 Re8 37. Rh4 Bc4 38. a5 a6 39. Rh8 etc.—*The Field*, 2 November 1873.

## (259) Bird–Wisker    1–0

Match 3 (game 2)
London, 1 November 1873
C52

**1. e4 e5 2. Nf3 Nc6 3. Bc4 Bc5 4. b4 B×b4 5. c3 Ba5** The traditional main line 5. ... Bc5 6. 0-0 d6 7. d4 e×d4 8. c×d4 Bb6 9. d5 was considered very promising for White after the analytical work of some German masters. Other lines of play for Black were researched, restored and made known to the British chess players by Löwenthal in his column in *Land and Water* (24 May 1873). Wisker adopted 5. ... Ba5 here for the first time in an important game. **6. d4 e×d4 7. 0-0 d×c3** The modern move is 7. ... Nge7! **8. e5** "A novelty, and an unsound one. The advanced pawn is weakened; Black is enabled to castle forthwith and the indispensable development of the White pieces on the queenside is retarded"—Wisker. **8. ... Nge7 9. Qb3** "As good as any other move. For if 8. Ng5 N×e5, and remains with a perfectly safe position. If 8. B×f7† K×f7 9. Ng5 Ke8 10. Qb3 (10. Qf3 N×e5) 10. ... d5 11. e×d6 *e.p.* Q×d6 and Black escapes with the advantage of a piece and a pawn, though his position is somewhat cramped"—Wisker. **9. ... 0-0 10. N×c3 Ng6** "This move, intending to sacrifice the exchange, is the best at Black's command"—Wisker. **11. Ba3 Ng×e5 12. N×e5 N×e5 13. B×f8 Q×f8** "Black has now a won position. The pieces are mostly exchanged, and he remains with three united pawns against the exchange"—

22. *Hazeltine's Chess, Autographs, End Games, Games and Problems*, vol. 6, f. 234.

**Third Match with Wisker, 30 October–9 December 1873**

| | 1 | 2 | 3 | 4 | 5 | 6 | 7 | 8 | 9 | 10 | 11 | 12 | 13 | 14 | 15 | 16 | 17 | 18 | 19 | 20 | 21 | |
|---|---|---|---|---|---|---|---|---|---|---|---|---|---|---|---|---|---|---|---|---|---|---|
| J. Wisker | ½ | 0 | 0 | 1 | 1 | ½ | 1 | 0 | • | 0 | • | • | 1 | • | 1 | 0 | 1 | ½ | 0 | 1 | 1 | 10 |
| H.E. Bird | ½ | 1 | 1 | 0 | 0 | ½ | 0 | 1 | • | 1 | • | • | 0 | • | 0 | 1 | 0 | ½ | 1 | 0 | 0 | 8 |

games 9 and 11: each player scored a win  •  games 12 and 14: each player scored a win

**Fourth Match with Wisker, 13 December–late December 1873**

| | 1 | 2 | 3 | 4 | 5 | 6 | 7 | 8 | 9 | 10 | |
|---|---|---|---|---|---|---|---|---|---|---|---|
| H.E. Bird | ½ | 1 | 0 | 0 | 1 | 0 | 1 | 1 | 1 | | 5 |
| J. Wisker | ½ | 0 | 1 | 1 | 0 | 1 | 0 | 0 | 0 | | 3 |

Wisker. "I would prefer 13. ... N×c4 14. Q×c4 Q×f8, remaining with two bishops and three pawns against rook and knight"—Zukertort. **14. Ne4 c6** "Better than exchanging the knight for the bishop, as it gains time, and the Black knight is reserved for an important duty"—Wisker. **15. Be2 d5 16. Ng3 f5 17. f4 Nf7 18. Nh5** "Unwise. The knight is useless at this square, whilst the hostile cavalier takes up a formidable position. Established at d6, he may either advance to e4 or c4, or, remaining where he is, he defends the b-pawn, and enables the bishop to be moved"—Wisker. **18. ... Nd6 19. Rad1 b5 20. Bf3** "Threatening 20. R×d5 or 20. B×d5†"—Wisker. **20. ... Be6 21. Kh1 Nc4 22. Rf2 Re8** "It would have been better first to have seized the opportunity of carrying the queen into the opponent's game by 22. ... Qb4"—Wisker. "I prefer the move in the text to the move proposed by Mr. Wisker in his note. If 22. ... Qb4 23. Qd3 and Black cannot play 23. ... Nb2 on account of 24. Qe2"—Zukertort. **23. a4 a6 24. Be2 Bf7 25. Qh3 B×h5** "Why not 25. ... Bb6, winning the exchange on the move? There is no possible piece sacrifice: 26. Rf3 R×e2 27. Rg3 B×h5 28. Q×h5 Qe8 forces the exchange of queens"—Zukertort **26. B×h5 g6 27. Bf3 Re1†** 27. ... Ne3 (Wisker) or 27. ... b×a4 rapidly decide the game. **28. R×e1 B×e1 29. Re2 Bd2 30. Qh4 Be3 31. a×b5 a×b5 32. Ra2 b4 33. Ra6 Bb6** "Had Black replied to White's last excellent move by 33. ... Qc8, the answer would have been 34. R×c6, and White draws, at once, by perpetual check"—Wisker. **34. Qe1 Kf7** "This and the following move are well played, and Black again gets a winning position"—Wisker. **35. Qa1 Qc5 36. g4 Qf2 37. Qd1 b3 38. g×f5 Qd4?** "The pawn could even now advance: 38. ... b2 39. B×d5† (39. f×g6† K×g6) 39. ... Kf6 40. R×b6 (40. B×c4 b1Q or 40. B×c6 Nd2) 40. ... Q×b6 41. Be4 g×f5 42. Bc2 c5"—Zukertort. **39. f×g6† h×g6 40. Q×d4 B×d4 41. R×c6 Ne3 42. Be2 b2 43. Bd3 Nc4 44. Kg2 Be3** 44. ... Nd2 forces White to abandon his bishop for the b-pawn, securing the draw. **45. Rc7† Kf6 46. Kf3 Bc1?!** 46. ... g5 avoids the loss of the g-pawn. **47. Rc6† Kf7 48. R×g6?!** 48. B×g6†! brings Black on the verge of defeat; e.g., 48. ... Kg7 49. Bd3 Nd2† 50. Ke2 Nc4 51. f5 **48. ... Nd2† 49. Kg4** and Black shortly resigns. The position is still defendable: 49. ... b1Q 50. B×b1 N×b1 51. Rc6 Ba3 52. h4 d4 53. h5 d3 54. Kf3 Kg8 55. f5 Bf8 56. Ke3 d2 57. Ke2 Kh7 etc. Another drawing line is 49. Kf2 b1Q 50. B×b1 N×b1 51. Rg1 B×f4 52. R×b1 B×h2—*Westminster Chess Club Papers* (Wisker/Zukertort), December 1873, p. 164.

## (260) Wisker–Bird   0–1
Match 3 (game 3)
London, 3 November 1873
C33

**1. e4 e5 2. f4 e×f4 3. Bc4 f5** "This defense, which is of very old date, has risen again into favor since the failure of the 'Classical Defense' (3. ... Qh4†) . It is supposed to lead to an even game, but we do not greatly admire it. There are easier and better modes of obtaining an even game for Black"—Wisker. **4. Qe2 Qh4† 5. Kd1 f×e4 6. Q×e4† Ne7 7. Nc3 c6 8. Nf3 Qf6** "We fail to see the equality of the position, though the play has been strictly according to rule. White appears to have decidedly the better game"—Wisker. **9. Re1** 9. d3 is better, but Black has an easy life after either 9. ... g5 or 9. ... d5. **9. ... d5?!** After 9. ... Kd8! he threatens to win a piece

with 10. ... d5. **10. B×d5!** "Quite a sound sacrifice"—Wisker. **10. ... c×d5 11. N×d5 Qd6 12. d3 Kd8** "Any other move would lose the game speedily"—Wisker. **13. N×e7 B×e7 14. B×f4 Qd7 15. Ne5 Qe6 16. Qd4† Bd7** (see diagram)

*After 16. ... Bd7*

**17. Kd2?** "Had White now played 17. N×d7 and 18. Q×g7, he would have had a winning situation"—Wisker. Wisker is a little bit too optimistic. After 17. N×d7 Q×d7 18. Q×g7 Re8 19. g3 Qf5 White has not much attack left. He has sufficient pawns for the piece and a lasting initiative, but nothing more. The text move makes the initiative switch sides, but Bird needs first to make a preparatory move to prevent the check at f7. **17. ... Rf8! 18. Re4** The best move. 18. Re2 (Wisker) is worse as after the same 18. ... Qb6 the queens will be exchanged and White's bishop will be undefended, forcing him to lose further time. **18. ... Qb6! 19. Q×b6† a×b6** With the queens off the board, Black's king is well-placed instead of finding itself in the danger zone. The extra piece becomes more telling. **20. Nc4?!** A very doubtful maneuvre, as it at least loses time after 20. ... b5 21. Nb6 Ra6 22. N×d7. 20. Rae1 is playable. **20. ... b5 21. Ne3?! Bc6 22. Rd4† Nd7 23. c3 g5** More than sufficient, but 23. ... Bc5 wins material at once. **24. Bg3 h5 25. b4 h4 26. Be1 Kc7 27. Nd5† B×d5 28. R×d5 Kc6 29. Rd4 Nf6 30. Kc2 Bd6 31. a4 b×a4 32. Bd2 b5 33. B×g5 Nd5 34. B×h4 B×h2 35. Re4 Bd6 36. g4 Rf3 37. g5 Bg3 38. B×g3 R×g3** and Black ultimately wins. Playing a defensive game was not one of Bird's strengths but here he did a nice job—*Land and Water* (Wisker), 20 June 1874.

## (261) Bird–Wisker   0–1
Match 3 (game 4)
London, November 1873
C52

**1. e4 e5 2. Nf3 Nc6 3. Bc4 Bc5 4. 0-0 Nf6 5. b4 B×b4 6. c3 Ba5 7. d4 0-0 8. d×e5 N×e4 9. Qd5 N×c3 10. Qd3 d5 11. Bb3 Ne4 12. B×d5 Nc5 13. Qc4 Be6 14. B×e6 N×e6 15. Bb2 Qe7 16. Qg4 Qb4 17. Q×b4 N×b4 18. Bc3 b6 19. Na3 Nc2 20. B×a5 N×a3 21. Bc3 Rfd8 22. Rac1 c5 23. Nh4 Nb5 24. Ba1 Nbd4 25. Kh1 g5 26. Nf3 N×f3 27. g×f3 Rd3 28. Rc3 Rad8 29. Rfc1 Rd1† 30. Kg2 Nf4† 31. Kg3 Ne2† 32. Kg4 N×c1** and Black wins—*Land and Water*, 15 November 1873.

## (262) Wisker–Bird   1–0
Match 3 (game 5)
London, 6 November 1873
A40

**1. c4 e6 2. d4 b6 3. a3 f5 4. Nc3 Nf6 5. Nf3 Bb7 6. g3 c6 7. Bg2 Na6 8. b4 Rc8 9. Qb3 Bd6 10. 0-0 0-0 11. c5 Bb8 12. a4 Nc7**

**13. Ne5 Ncd5 14. N×d5 c×d5 15. Nd3 d6 16. f4 Ne4 17. Be3 Kh8 18. Rfc1 d×c5 19. b×c5 Ba6 20. c×b6 Bc4 21. b7 Rc6 22. Qd1 Nd6 23. Nc5 Qe7 24. a5 a6 25. Bd2 Ba7 26. Bb4 Rb8 27. e3 Rc7 28. R×c4 N×c4 29. N×a6 Qd8 30. N×b8 Q×b8 31. a6 N×e3 32. Qa4 Rc2 33. Bc5 R×g2† 34. Kh1 g5 35. B×a7 Q×a7 36. Qe8† Kg7 37. b8Q Q×d4 38. Qf8†** Black resigns—*Westminster Chess Club Papers*, January 1874, p. 185.

## (263) Bird–Wisker   ½–½

Match 3 (game 6)
London, 7 November 1873
*C77*

**1. e4 e5 2. Nf3 Nc6 3. Bb5 a6 4. Ba4 Nf6 5. Qe2 b5 6. Bb3 Be7 7. a4 Rb8 8. a×b5 a×b5 9. d3 d6 10. c3 0-0 11. Bg5 h6 12. B×f6 B×f6 13. h3 Ne7 14. Nbd2 Ng6 15. g3 c5 16. Nf1 Qb6 17. Ne3 Be6 18. B×e6 f×e6 19. Nh2 Bg5 20. Nhg4 Rbd8 21. h4 B×e3 22. N×e3 d5 23. Qh5 d4 24. Ng4 Kh7 25. Rd1 d×c3 26. b×c3 Qa5 27. 0-0 Q×c3 28. Ra1 R×d3 29. Kh2 Rd7 30. Ra6 Qc4 31. Q×g6† K×g6 32. N×e5† Kf6 33. N×c4 b×c4 34. Rc6 Rd4 35. f3 Rb8 36. R×c5 Rb2† 37. Kh3 Rb3 38. Kg4 c3 39. Rc1 Rd3 40. e5† Kg6 41. h5† Kh7 42. Rc2 Rd5 43. R2×c3 R×c3 44. R×c3 R×e5 45. Rc7 Rg5† 46. Kh4 Rf5 47. f4 Rf6 48. Re7 Kg8 49. Kg4 Kf8 50. Rb7 Kg8 51. Rb6 Kf7 52. Kf3 Rf5 53. Rb7† Kf6 54. g4 Ra5 55. Kg3 Ra3† 56. Kh4 Ra4** draw—*Westminster Chess Club Papers*, December 1873, p. 163.

## (264) Wisker–Bird   1–0

Match 3 (game 7)
London, 8 November 1873
*A10*

**1. c4 f5 2. g3 e6 3. Bg2 Nf6 4. a3 d5 5. d4 Nc6 6. Nc3 g6 7. Nf3 Be7 8. 0-0 0-0 9. Bh6 Re8 10. c5 Ne4 11. e3 Bf6 12. h4 Qe7 13. Rc1 Nd8 14. Bf4 Nf7 15. Nb5 e5 16. d×e5 Qd7 17. c6 b×c6 18. e6 R×e6 19. N×c7 Bb7 20. N×e6 Q×e6 21. Nd4 Qd7 22. f3 Ned6 23. B×d6 Q×d6 24. f4 c5 25. Nb5 Qb6 26. Nc3 c4 27. Qe2 Re8 28. N×d5 B×d5 29. B×d5 R×e3 30. B×f7† K×f7 31. Q×c4† Kg7 32. Qc7† Kh6 33. Q×b6 a×b6 34. Rf2 R×g3† 35. Kh2 Rb3 36. Re2 Kh5 37. Rc6 B×h4 38. Rc3 Rb5 39. b4 Rd5 40. a4 Rd4 41. a5 R×b4 42. a6 Ra4 43. Rc7 h6 44. a7** and White wins—*Westminster Chess Club Papers*, December 1873 p. 164.

## (265) Bird–Wisker   1–0

Match 3 (game ?)
London, November 1873
*C90*

Either game 8 or 10 of the third match.

**1. e4 e5 2. Nf3 Nc6 3. Bb5 a6 4. Ba4 Nf6 5. 0-0 Be7 6. Re1 b5 7. Bb3 d6 8. c3 Bg4 9. d3 0-0 10. Bg5 Rb8 11. h3 Bd7 12. d4 h6 13. Bh4 e×d4 14. c×d4 Nh5 15. B×e7 N×e7 16. Nc3 Ng6 17. Nd5 Nf6 18. Qd2 N×d5 19. B×d5 c6 20. Bb3 c5 21. d×c5 d×c5 22. Rad1 Be6 23. B×e6 f×e6 24. Qd6 Qf6** Only now does Black get in trouble. The temporary pawn sacrifice 24. ... Nf4 25. Q×c5 Qf6 equalizes completely. **25. e5 Qf5 26. Q×c5** "Mr. Bird promptly takes advantage of his adversary's weak move"—Löwenthal. **26. ... Nf4** Wisker develops a dangerous looking ini-

tiative in return for the pawn, but Bird defends coolly. **27. Re3 Rbc8 28. Qa7 Rc2 29. Rb3** *(see diagram)*

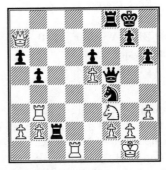

*After 29. Rb3*

**29. ... Qg6?** There were two valid moves at Black's disposal. Still slightly better for White is 29. ... Qh5: e.g., 30. Qb7 Qf5 (not better is 30. ... Qg6 31. Ne1 R×f2 32. K×f2 N×h3† 33. Ke3 and the king escapes or 30. ... a5? 31. Rd7 Qg6 32. Nd4 Rc1† 33. Kh2 and 34. Rg3 decides at once) 31. Q×a6 Qg6 32. Ne1 with a slight plus. The best move is 29. ... a5! By sacrificing a second pawn White's queen is deflected from the kingside for a moment. As a result, Black obtains enough counterplay after 30. Q×a5 (if 30. R×b5? N×h3† wins) 30. ... Qg6 31. Ne1 Qg5 32. Qa7 (the safest. Black now wins back the two pawns, and an equal endgame arises) 32. ... Re2 33. Rg3 Q×e5 34. Nf3 Q×b2. **30. Ne1 Re2 31. Rg3 Qf7 32. Q×f7†?** 32. Rd7 wins on the spot: 32. ... R×e1† 33. Kh2 N×h3 34. Rf3! (better than 34. R×f7). There is little left of White's advantage after the text move. **32. ... R×f7 33. Rb3 R×e5 34. Nf3 Rc5 35. Rd6 a5 36. Nd4** Bird desperately attempts to win the endgame, and thereby risks overstretching his position. 36. Rd2 is safe. **36. ... e5 37. Ne6 Rc1† 38. Kh2 N×e6 39. R×e6 R×f2 40. R×b5 Kf7 41. Ra6 Rcc2 42. Rb7† Kg8 43. Rg6 R×b2 44. Rb×g7† Kf8 45. a4 Rb4 45. ... e4 forces White to take a perpetual check. 46. Ra7 R×a4 47. R×h6 Rf7 48. Ra8† Ke7 49. Raa6 e4 50. Rhe6† Kf8 51. Re5 Re7 52. Re×a5 R×a5? Both rooks had to be kept on the board. 53. R×a5 Kg7 54. Kg3 Kf6 55. Kf4 Re6 56. Ra2 Re7 57. Re2** and White wins—*Land and Water* (Löwenthal), 29 November 1873.

## (266) Wisker–Bird   1–0

Match 3 (game ?)
London, November 1873
*A40*

Probably game 9 or 11 of the third match.

**1. d4 f5 2. c4 e6 3. Nc3 Nf6 4. a3 b6 5. g3 Bb7 6. d5 e5 7. Nf3 d6 8. Bh3 g6 9. e4 f×e4 10. Ng5 c6 11. Ne6 Qe7 12. Bg5 h6 13. B×f6 Q×f6 14. Nc7† Kd8 15. N×e4 Qe7 16. N×a8 B×a8 17. Qg4 Bb7 18. 0-0 g5 19. Rfd1 c5 20. b4 Na6 21. b×c5 b×c5 22. Rab1 Rh7 23. Rb3 Qc7 24. Rf3 Rf7 25. Rdd3 Bg7 26. R×f7 Q×f7 27. Rf3 Qe7 28. Qe6 Q×e6 29. B×e6 Nc7 30. N×d6 Ba6 31. Rf7** and Black resigns—*Land and Water*, 29 November 1873.

## (267) Wisker–Bird   0–1

Match 3 (game ?)
London, November 1873
*C35*

Probably game 9 or 11 of the third match.

**1. e4 e5 2. f4 e×f4 3. Nf3 Be7 4. Bc4 Bh4† 5. Kf1 d5 6. B×d5 Nf6 7. Nc3 N×d5 8. N×d5 f5 9. d3 f×e4 10. d×e4 0-0** and Black wins—*Chess Practice*, p. 59.

## (268) Bird–Wisker　1-0

Match 3 (game ?)
London, November 1873
*A02*

Probably game 10, 12 or 14 of the third match.

**1. f4 e6 2. Nf3 g6 3. e4 d5 4. e5 c5 5. c3 Nc6 6. Bb5 Qb6 7. a4 Bd7 8. 0-0 Nh6 9. Kh1 Be7 10. Na3 0-0 11. Nc2 f5 12. d4 a6 13. B×c6 b×c6 14. d×c5 B×c5 15. b4 Be7 16. Be3 Qc7 17. Rb1 c5 18. a5 Rab8 19. Qd2 Nf7 20. Qf2 Rfc8 21. Rfc1 Bb5 22. Nfe1 Kh8 23. Na3 g5 24. N×b5 R×b5 25. Nd3 g×f4 26. B×c5 N×e5 27. Bd4 Bf6 28. Q×f4 Ng4 29. B×f6† N×f6 30. Qd4 Qg7 31. Nf4 Rc4 32. Qe5 Ne4 33. Q×g7† K×g7 34. N×e6† Kf6 35. Nd4 N×c3 36. N×b5 N×b1 37. R×b1 a×b5 38. a6 Rc7 39. Ra1 Ra7 40. Kg1 Ke5 41. Ra5 Kd4 42. R×b5 R×a6 43. Rb7 h6 44. b5 Ra1† 45. Kf2 Rb1 46. Rb8 Kd3 47. b6 d4 48. b7 Kd2 49. Rd8 R×b7 50. R×d4† Kc3 51. Rd6 Rh7 52. Kf3 Kc4 53. Kf4 Kc5 54. Rg6 Kd4 55. K×f5** and after two or three more moves Mr. Wisker resigns—*Illustrated London News*, 11 July 1874.

## (269) Bird–Wisker　0-1

Match 3 (game ?)
London, November 1873
*A03*

Probably game 12 or 14 of the third match.

**1. f4 c5 2. b3 e6 3. Nf3 Qf6 4. Nc3 Q×f4 5. d4 Qc7 6. d5 d6 7. e4 e5 8. Bb5† Nd7 9. 0-0 Ngf6 10. Nh4 a6 11. Bd3 g6 12. Bg5 Bg7 13. Qd2 0-0 14. Rf3 Nh5 15. Raf1 Nb6 16. h3 c4 17. Be2 c×b3 18. a×b3 Nf4 19. Nd1 h6 20. B×f4 e×f4 21. c4 g5 22. Nf5 B×f5 23. e×f5 Nd7 24. g3 Ne5 25. Rc3 f×g3 26. f6 Bh8 27. R×g3 Qd8 28. R×g5† h×g5 29. Q×g5† Ng6 30. Bd3 Qe8 31. Ne3 Qe5 32. Rf5 Qd4 33. Rf2 Q×d3 34. Nf5 Rae8 35. Nh6† Kh7** and White resigns—*Land and Water*, 17 October 1874.

## (270) Wisker–Bird　1-0

Match 3 (game ?)
London, November 1873
*A10*

Probably game 13, 15 or 17 of the third match.

**1. c4 f5 2. e3 Nf6 3. Nc3 c6 4. d4 e6 5. Nf3 Bd6 6. Bd3 0-0 7. 0-0 Bc7 8. b4 d6 9. Qb3 Qe8 10. a4 Nbd7 11. a5 d5 12. Ne1 g5 13. f4 g4 14. Ra2 Kh8 15. g3 Rg8 16. c×d5 c×d5 17. Nb5 Bb8 18. Rc2 h5 19. Ng2 Nf8 20. Ba3 Ng6 21. Nc7 B×c7 22. R×c7 Ne4 23. B×e4 f×e4 24. b5 Qd8 25. Rfc1 h4 26. N×h4 N×h4 27. Be7 Nf3† 28. Kf2 Bd7 29. B×d8 Ra×d8 30. Qb4 Rg7 31. R1c2 Rh7 32. Kf1 a6 33. R×d7 Rh×d7 34. b6 Kg7 35. Rc7 N×h2† 36. Ke2 Kg6 37. R×d7 R×d7 38. Qf8 Rg7** and after a few more moves Black resigns—*Land and Water*, 13 December 1873.

## (271) Wisker–Bird　1-0

Match 3 (game ?)
London, November 1873
*A10*

Probably game 13, 15 or 17 of the third match.

**1. c4 f5 2. g3 Nf6 3. Bg2 e6 4. a3 Be7 5. d4 c6 6. Nc3 0-0 7. Nf3 Qe8 8. 0-0 Na6 9. b4 Nc7 10. Qb3 d5 11. c5 Qh5 12. Bf4 Nce8 13. a4 Ne4 14. N×e4 f×e4 15. Ne5 Q×e2 16. f3 g5 17. Rf2 Qa6 18. Bd2 b5 19. Rff1 e×f3 20. R×f3 b×a4 21. R×f8† B×f8 22. Qf3 Qb7 23. Rf1 Qg7 24. B×g5 Ba6 25. Rf2 Bb5 26. Bh3 Nc7 27. Bf6 Qh6 28. Qg4† Bg7 29. Bg5 Q×g5 30. Q×g5** Black resigns—*Land and Water*, 13 December 1873.

## (272) Wisker–Bird　1-0

Match 3 (game ?)
London, November 1873
*A85*

Probably game 13, 15 or 17 of the third match.

**1. c4 f5 2. e3 e6 3. Nf3 Nf6 4. a3 Be7 5. Nc3 0-0 6. d4 b6 7. d5 Qe8 8. g3 d6 9. d×e6 B×e6 10. Nd4 Bd7 11. Bg2 Nc6 12. 0-0 Rd8 13. B×c6 B×c6 14. Ne6 Ng4 15. f3 N×e3 16. B×e3 Bf6 17. N×d8 Q×e3† 18. Kg2 R×d8 19. Nd5 Qe5 20. Rf2 B×d5 21. Q×d5† Kf8 22. Rd1 a5 23. Q×e5 B×e5 24. f4 Bf6 25. Rd5 g6 26. Re2 a4 27. Kf3 Kf7 28. h3 c6 29. Rd1 d5 30. c×d5 c×d5 31. g4 d4 32. Rc1 d3 33. Rc7† Kg8 34. Rd2 f×g4† 35. h×g4 Rd6 36. Rc1 g5 37. f5 Be5 38. Rcd1 Rd4 39. R×d3 Rf4† 40. Ke3 B×b2 41. Rd8† Kf7 42. R1d7† Kf6 43. Rf8†** Black resigns—*Illustrated London News*, 13 June 1874.

## (273) Bird–Wisker　1-0

Match 3 (game 16)
London, 21 November 1873
*A02*

**1. f4 c5 2. Nf3 e6 3. Na3 Nc6 4. c3 d5 5. e3 a6 6. Nc2 Nf6 7. Be2 Be7 8. 0-0 0-0 9. Nce1 b5 10. Ne5 N×e5** "10. ... N×e5 in this situation is not advisable. Black should have played 10. ... Qb6 or 10. ... Bb7. Nevertheless, Black gets a very good game as it is"—Wisker. **11. f×e5 Nd7 12. d4 f5 13. Nd3 Qb6 14. Bd2 Bb7 15. Qe1 Rf7 16. Rf3 Kh8 17. Rh3 Rg8 18. Qf2 c4 19. Ne1** "If 19. Nf4 g5 with great effect"—Wisker. **19. ... g5 20. g4** The pawn structure on the kingside is full of tension, but both sides balance each other out for the moment. **20. ... Nf8 21. Qg3 Ng6 22. Ng2 b4 23. Rf1 b×c3 24. B×c3 Nh4 25. Kh1** "If 25. N×h4 g×h4 26. Qf4 Rfg7"—Zukertort. **25. ... Rfg7 26. Qe1 Bc6 27. Bd1?!** Now, after the queen has been evacuated from the g-file the right moment to release the pressure with 27. g×f5 has come. Black can then choose between 27. ... N×f5 or 27. ... N×g2 28. K×g2 e×f5 29. Rh6!, which is equal. **27. ... Be8 28. N×h4?** 28. g×f5 has become mandatory by now, even though the position has slightly altered to Black's advantage as a result of the useless 27. Bd1?! **28. ... g×h4 29. g×f5 e×f5 30. Bc2** *(see diagram)*

**30. ... Qg6?** "Black however obtains an attack, which ought, with the best play, to have drawn at least, but in a few move he fritters it away"—Wisker. Wisker's move loses the crucial tempo

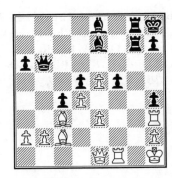

*After 30. Bc2*

hat is needed to win the game. After 30. ... Bd7! 31. Qf2 the queen immediately occupies the strongest position available with 31. ... Qh6! Black's bishops will soon infiltrate with deadly consequences; e.g., 32. Bd1 f4! 33. Rf3 h3 34. e×f4 Bh4 and 35. ... Bf5 decides the contest. In the actual game, White manages to exchange a bishop, thus neutralizing Black's attack. **31. Qf2 Bd7 32. Rf3 Qh6 33. B×f5 B×f5 34. R×f5 h3 35. Be1 Rg4?** For the second time Wisker loses valuable time, now permitting Bird to safeguard his own king. After 35. ... Rg2 36. Qf3 R×b2 37. Bg3 Qe6 38. Rf7 Rg7 no side seems able to fortify his attack. **36. Qf3! Qg6** 36. ... Bh4 (Wisker) is equally hopeless 37. B×h4 R×h4 38. Rg1! **37. Bg3 h5 38. e6 Bd6 39. Q×d5 Bf8 40. R×h5† Bh6 41. Qe5†** Black resigns—*Westminster Chess Club Papers* (Wisker/Zukertort), January 1874, p. 186.

## (274) Wisker–Bird    0–1
Match 3 (game 19)
London, 6 December 1873
C25

1. e4 e5 2. Nc3 Bc5 3. g3 d6 4. Bg2 a6 5. Nge2 Nc6 6. 0–0 h5 7. h4 Nf6 8. d3 Ng4 9. Nd5 Be6 10. c3 Ba7 11. d4 Ne7 12. Ne3 c6 13. f4 N×e3 14. B×e3 Bg4 15. Qd2 Qb6 16. f×e5 d×e5 17. Bf2 Qb5 18. Nc1 0–0–0 19. a4 Qc4 20. b3 Qe6 21. d5 B×f2† 22. Q×f2 c×d5 23. e×d5 N×d5 24. Nd3 f5 25. c4 Nc7 26. Nc5 Qh6 27. N×b7 Rd2 28. Qa7 R×g2† 29. K×g2 Qc6† 30. Kh2 Q×b7 31. Qc5 Rd8 32. Rf2 Qe4 33. Raf1 Rd3 34. Qf8† Kb7 35. Qb4† Kc6 36. a5 f4 37. Qb6† Kd7 38. Rg1 Be6 White resigns—*Westminster Chess Club Papers*, February 1874, p. 211.

## (275) Bird–Wisker    0–1
Match 3 (game 20)
London, 8 December 1873
A03

1. f4 d5 2. e3 g6 3. Nf3 Bg7 4. c3 a6 5. Na3 c5 6. Nc2 Nc6 7. Be2 Nh6 8. 0–0 0–0 9. d4 c4 10. Nce1 b5 11. b3 Rb8 12. Bd2 Nf5 13. Ne5 N×e5 14. f×e5 f6 15. e×f6 R×f6 16. Bf3 Bb7 17. a4 Bh6 18. Qe2 c×b3 19. a×b5 a×b5 20. Nd3 Bc6 21. Rab1 b4 22. c×b4 Bb5 23. g4 Nh4 24. R×b3 Qd7 25. Bg2 N×g2 26. R×f6 e×f6 27. Q×g2 Ra8 28. Nc5 Ra1† 29. Kf2 Qd6 30. Qg3 Qb6 31. Rb2 Bf8 32. e4 d×e4 33. Qb3† Kh8 34. Qf7 Qd6 35. Ke3 Rf1 36. Ne6 Bh6† 37. g5 B×g5† and Black wins—*Chess Player's Chronicle*, February 1874, pp. 6–8.

## (276) Wisker–Bird    1–0
Match 3 (game 21)
London, 9 December 1873
A85

1. d4 f5 2. c4 e6 3. a3 Nf6 4. Nc3 b6 5. d5 Bd6 6. g3 e5 7. Bh3 f4 8. g×f4 e×f4 9. Nf3 0–0 10. Rg1 Qe7 11. Qd4 c5 12. Qd3 Ba6 13. b3 Be5 14. Bb2 d6 15. Nh4 g6 16. Be6† Kh8 17. R×g6 Bc8 18. B×c8 R×c8 19. Nf5 Qf8 20. Rg5 Nbd7 21. 0–0–0 Ng8 22. Rdg1 Nh6 23. Qh3 N×f5 24. R×f5 Qe7 25. Ne4 Rf8 26. B×e5† N×e5 27. R×f8† R×f8 28. Qe6 Q×e6 29. d×e6 Re8 30. Nf6 and Black resigns—*Chess Player's Chronicle*, February 1874, pp. 4–6.

## (277) Bird–Wisker    ½–½
Match 4 (game 1)
London, 13 December 1873
C77

1. e4 e5 2. Nf3 Nc6 3. Bb5 a6 4. Ba4 Nf6 5. Nc3 Be7 6. B×c6 d×c6 7. N×e5 N×e4 8. N×e4 Qd4 9. 0–0 Q×e5 10. d3 Be6 11. f4 Qd4† 12. Kh1 0–0–0 13. a4 c5 14. Bd2 Qd5 15. b3 h6 16. Bc3 Rhg8 17. Qd2 f5 18. Ng3 g5 19. Rae1 g×f4 20. Q×f4 Rg6 21. Qf3 Qd7 22. N×f5 Bg5 23. h4 B×f5 24. Q×f5 Q×f5 25. R×f5 B×h4 26. Re4 Bg3 27. Be5 Rdg8 28. B×g3 R×g3 29. Re2 b6 30. Kh2 R8g7 31. Rf6 R3g6 32. R×g6 R×g6 33. Kh3 Kd7 34. Kh4 Rg5 35. g4 a5 36. Rf2 Ke7 37. Rf4 c6 38. Re4† Kd7 39. c4 Rg6 40. d4 Kd6 41. d×c5† K×c5 42. Kh5 Rd6 43. Re3 Kb4 draw—*Land and Water*, 31 January 1874.

## (278) Wisker–Bird    0–1
Match 4 (game 2)
London, 16 December 1873
A85

1. d4 f5 2. c4 e6 3. a3 Nf6 4. Nc3 d5 "To prevent 5. d5, a move which White played with destructive effect in several of the games in the previous match"—Wisker. **5. Nf3 Be7 6. Bf4 0–0 7. e3 Nc6 8. c5** "8. Nb5 would not have gained anything"—Wisker. **8. ... a6 9. Be2 Ne4 10. h4** "White had better advanced the pawn one square only, retreating the bishop to h2 if Black plays 10. ... g5"—Wisker. **10. ... Bf6 11. Rc1 Qe7 12. Qa4** "The object of this play of the queen is to restrain the development of Black's pieces on the queenside, for if Black now moves 12. ... Bd7, White retires 13. Qb3 and gains a pawn. The queen however renders better service on her own square, where she prevents the advance of e5; 12. b4 and the 13. Qb3 would have given White a good position"—Wisker. **12. ... h6** At once 12. ... N×c3 13. R×c3 e5! equalizes, but he could also play 12. ... Bd7, as after 13. Qb3 Rfc8 14. Q×b7?! Rab8 15. Q×a6 R×b2, Black is better. **13. b4 N×c3 14. R×c3 e5!** "By this timely move Black secures a little the better game"—Wisker. **15. d×e5 N×e5 16. B×e5 B×e5 17. Rd3 c6 18. 0–0** *(see diagram)*

**18. ... f4** Both players neglect the bishop at e5. White should have exchanged it while he could, Black should avoid exchanging. **19. Re1 Bf5! 20. e×f4 B×f4** "He would obviously have lost two pieces after 20. ... B×d3"—Wisker. **21. Rd4 Bc7 22. Qb3 Qf6 23. Bd3 Rae8 24. Qb1** "White might have played 24. R×e8 R×e8

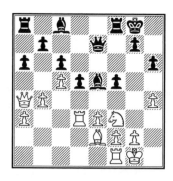

*After 18. 0–0*

25. B×f5 Q×f5 26. Qd3, the game being then perfectly even. As it is, however, the proper result ought to have been a draw"—Wisker. Wisker's line fails due to 25. ... Q×d4! Bird's best choice after the text move is 24. ... Bd7, preserving his bishop pair. **24. ... B×d3 25. R×d3 Re4 26. Rde3** 26. R×e4! d×e4 27. Rd7 e×f3 28. R×c7 f×g2 29. Qb3† and 30. Qg3 is equal. **26. ... Rg4** "He cannot take the h-pawn: 26. ... R×h4 27. N×h4 Q×f2† 28. Kh1 Q×h4† 29. Rh3 and White has the exchange against two pawns, his rooks being in full play"—Wisker. After 29. ... Qg5!, the prospects of the rook at h3 are very meager, which gives Black a lasting initiative. Instead of accepting the sacrifice, 27. Re6 Qf4 28. Re7 Rg4 29. R1e3 is very solid. **27. Qc2 d4?!** "A hazardous move"—Wisker. This push comes too soon, as Bird renders his opponent some important lines and diagonals and a target at d4. A much better execution of the same idea would have been 27. ... a5!, weakening the queenside first, and if then 28. b5 c×b5 29. Qd3 Qf7 30. Q×b5 d4! **28. Qb3† Kh8 29. Re4** At once 29. Re8! is far stronger. **29. ... h5 30. Qd3** "A perfectly satisfactory move if properly followed up. If 30. ... Q×f3 31. Q×f3 R×f3 32. R×g4"—Wisker. **30. ... Qg6 31. Ng5!** "An unsound manoeuvre. White should have played 31. R×d4 and if 31. ... R×g2† 32. Kf1, and Black is compelled to exchange queens, the game remaining a shade in White's favor"—Wisker. Wisker's suggestion is refuted by 31. ... R×f3!, when if anyone it is Bird who'd be better. **31. ... R×h4** Played in despair. 31. ... Qf5 32. Q×d4 is very bad as well. **32. Re8??** Both players missed the neat 32. Rf4!!, winning the queen. **32. ... Bh2†** "White overlooked that, in reply to this check, he could not move 33. Kf1. He had played 32. Re8, thinking to win at once. He loses at once instead"—Wisker. **33. Kh1 Bg3† 34. Nh3 Q×d3 35. R×f8† Kh7 36. f×g3 Q×g3 37. Ref1 R×h3† 38. g×h3 Q×h3†** and Black wins—*Westminster Chess Club Papers* (Wisker), January 1874, pp. 185–186.

## (279) Bird–Wisker    0–1
Match 4? (game 3)
London 1873
C77

Probably game 3 of the fourth match.

1. e4 e5 2. Nf3 Nc6 3. Bb5 a6 4. Ba4 Nf6 5. Qe2 Be7 6. d3 b5 7. Bb3 d6 8. a4 b4 9. a5 0–0 10. Be3 Rb8 11. Nbd2 d5 12. Bg5 Be6 13. 0–0 Qd6 14. Rfe1 d4 15. Bc4 B×c4 16. N×c4 Qe6 17. b3 Rb5 18. Bh4 Ne8 19. Bg3 Nd6 20. Nfd2 Nb7 21. f4 f6 22. f×e5 f×e5 23. Rf1 Bf6 24. Rf5 Nb×a5 25. Raf1 N×c4 26. N×c4 Ne7 27. R5f3 Ng6 28. h4 Nh8 29. Qf2 Nf7 30. Rf5 Qe7 31. h5 Rbb8 32. Bh2 h6 33. Qg3 Nd6 34. R5f3 N×c4 35. b×c4 a5 36. Qg6

a4 37. Rf5 b3 38. c×b3 a×b3 39. R5f2 b2 40. Rb1 Qa3 41. Rd2 Rb6 42. Qg4 Ra8 43. Qd7 Qa5 44. Rdd1 Rb3 45. c5 Kh8 46. Qf7 Rbb8 47. Rf1 Rf8 48. Qd5 Qc3 49. Bg3 Ra1 50. Qc4 R×b1 51. R×b1 Ra8 52. Kh2 Q×c4 53. d×c4 Rb8 54. Kh3 c6 55. Kg4 d3 and Black wins—*City of London Chess Magazine*, February 1874, pp. 16–18.

## (280) Wisker–Bird    1–0
Match 4 (game 4)
London, 18 December 1873
C61

1. e4 e5 2. Nf3 Nc6 3. Bb5 Nd4 4. N×d4 e×d4 5. 0–0 Bc5 6. d3 Nf6 7. e5 Nd5 8. Bc4 Nb6 9. Bb3 d5 10. f4 g6 11. Qe1 Be7 12. Nd2 a5 13. a3 c5 14. Nf3 c4 15. Ba2 Bc5 16. h3 0–0 17. Kh1 f6 18. Bd2 Na4 19. d×c4 f×e5 20. f×e5 Bf5 21. c×d5 B×c2 22. d6† Kg7 23. Bg5 Qe8 24. Qh4 h5 25. Bf6† Kh7 26. Ng5† Kh6 27. Qf4 Black resigns—*Westminster Chess Club Papers*, January 1874, p. 185.

## (281) Wisker–Bird    ?
Match 4 (game ?)
London, December 1873
C61

It seems apparent that this is game 6 of the fourth match. If that is correct, Wisker won it.

1. e4 e5 2. Nf3 Nc6 3. Bb5 Nd4 4. N×d4 e×d4 5. d3 Bc5 6. Qh5 Qe7 7. Bg5 Qf8—*Chess Openings*, p. 5.

## (282) Bird–Wisker    1–0
Match 4 (game 7)
London, 24 December 1873
C77

1. e4 e5 2. Nf3 Nc6 3. Bb5 a6 4. Ba4 Nf6 5. Qe2 b5 6. Bb3 Bb7 "The defense recommended by Herrn Steinitz and Zukertort to this variation of the Ruy Lopez. The move certainly strengthens the queenside after the advance of the b-pawn, but it is very doubtful whether the queen's bishop can be safely withdrawn from the king's flank in such a position"—Wisker. 7. Nc3 Bc5 8. d3 d6 9. 0–0 Ne7 10. Nh4 h6 11. Be3 Qd7 12. B×c5 d×c5 13. f4 e×f4 14. R×f4 Qd4†?! This move only costs him valuable time. After the immediate 14. ... 0–0 15. Qf2 and now 15. ... Qd4 16. a4 Q×f2 17. R×f2 b4, the exchange of queens permits Black to avoid complications. **15. Rf2 0–0** "It is dangerous to castle on either side, and still more dangerous not to castle at all. Black, in fact, has a very bad position"—Wisker. **16. Raf1** The actual point of 13. f4 could have been demonstrated at once with 16. Nf3!—e.g., 16. ... Qd8 17. Ne5. White menaces 18. B×f7†! **16. ... Rad8?** Completely off the mark. Both 16. ... Rae8 (countering on the e-file) or 16. ... c4 (breaking up White's strong center) are decent options. **17. Nf3!** "After this Black's game is virtually indefensible"—Wisker. **17. ... Qb4** "There is no better square for the queen. For if: 17. ... Qd7 18. Ne5 Q any move 19. N×f7 R×f7 20. e5 and wins easily"—Wisker. **18. a3** Bird misses a direct win with 18. Ne5!, threatening 19. B×f7†

gain. **18. ... Qa5 19. Ne5 c4 20. d×c4 b×c4** "He might also have moved 20. ... b4, but the answer would have been 21. Nd5. The attack then becomes as fierce as ever"—Wisker. Still, this line deserves the preference. **21. N×c4 Qg5 22. h3 Rd4 23. Nd2 Qg6 24. Nf3 Nc6 25. e5** "Had he taken the rook Black would have obtained a very fine position in return for the exchange, as follows: 25. N×d4 N×d4 26. Qc4 N×b3 27. Q×b3 B×e4 etc."—Wisker. Calling Black's position "very fine" is a gross exaggeration. 27. e5! is a major improvement, with a winning game for White. **25. ... Ne4 26. Nh4** "The final stroke. The game has been excellently played by White."—Wisker **26. ... Qg5 27. R×f7 R×f7 28. B×f7† Kh7 29. Bg6† Kg8 30. N×e4 Q×h4 31. Rf8† K×f8 32. Qf3† Qf6 33. e×f6** and White wins—*Land and Water* (Wisker), 3 January 1874.

**(283) Wisker–Bird    0–1**
Match 4 (game 8)
London, December 1873
C40

**1. e4 e5 2. Nf3 d5** "This is not a sound defense"—Wisker. **3. e×d5 Q×d5** "If 3. ... e4 4. Qe2, and White permanently retains his pawn"—Wisker. **4. Nc3 Qe6 5. b3** "This, though in the main an unobjectionable move, weakens the position of Nc3, and is inferior to 5. Bb5†. If, then, knight or bishop interposes, White castles. If 5. ... c6, the answer is 6. Ba4 with a very fine game"—Wisker. **5. ... Nc6 6. Bc4 Qg6 7. Qe2 Bd6 8. d4** Wisker has nothing out of the opening. He unwisely tries to force matters with the text move. **8. ... Bg4! 9. Bb5 B×f3** This exchange comes a move too soon, and as a result it liberates White from any worries. After 9. ... Bb4 10. Bd2 and only now 10. ... B×f3! 11. Q×f3 e×d4; the scene has been altered and White has to be very careful to avoid collapsing. **10. Q×f3 0-0-0** "A good move. The Black king appears to be in danger, but is not really so"—Wisker. If now 10. ... Bb4? 11. d5! is possible, e.g., 11. ... B×c3† 12. Q×c3 Qe4† 13. Be3 Q×d5 14. B×c6† Q×c6 15. Q×e5† etc. **11. B×c6 b×c6 12. 0-0** The simplest solution is 12. Q×c6 e×d4 13. Qa6†, with a perpetual check. **12. ... e×d4 13. Ne2 Ne7** He could afford himself to play more actively with 13. ... Nf6 as 14. Q×c6? loses. **14. Bb2 Be5 15. Rfd1 Nf5 16. Rd3** Wisker misses his unique chance to play 16. c3!, which relieves himself from the pressure of the opposing d-pawn. **16. ... Rhe8!** "Well played again. The move not only brings the rook into action, but defends the d-pawn also. For if 17. Rad1, with the intention of taking the pawn, he would evidently expose himself after the exchanges to a deadly check at e1. Black has now a decided advantage"—Wisker. **17. b4 Qe6 18. g3** "This advance certainly prevents the Black knight from posting himself on h4, but it proves disastrous in the end. White would have done better had he pushed forward his a-pawn"—Wisker. Taking control of h4 is the most important thing to do for the moment. After 18. a4? Nh4! 19. Qh5 g5 20. Ng3 Qd5 21. f3 Qc4, White's position is breaking apart. **18. ... g6 19. Nc1** "Much too slow for such a situation"—Wisker. There are no better alternatives. If 19. Rad1 Q×a2. **19. ... Qd5** The infiltrating 19. ... Qc4! puts more pressure. Yet, White can still offer stiff resistance by offering the c-pawn in return for the opening of lines; e.g., 20. Nb3 Q×c2 21. Rd2 Qc4 22. Rc1 Qd5.

**20. Qd1** "Surely it would have been better to have exchanged queens. Black has only a doubled pawn ahead, and the result would very probably have been a drawn game"—Wisker. **20. ... h5** (*see diagram*)

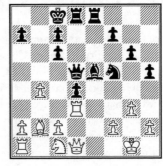

*After 20. ... h5*

**21. Ra3?** "Perfectly useless, but the game is not to be retrieved now"—Wisker. Wisker is too pessimistic about his position. After 21. Nb3 h4, he could choose between 22. g4 Ng7 23. B×d4 Ne6 24. Be3 Qb5 25. Rb1 R×d3 26. Q×d3 Q×b4 27. Qa6†, when Bird isn't much better off despite his extra pawn, or 22. Qf1 h×g3 23. h×g3, and if necessary the queen will go to g2, terminating all attacks. White's position is also solid after 21. ... Bg7, followed by the doubling of the rooks on the e-file. **21. ... h4 22. g4** Wisker's omission to win the d-pawn is fatal. The text move even aggravates the situation, but also after 22. Qf3 Q×f3 (23. ... Bg7 is also possible) 24. R×f3 Nd6, Black's situation has improved considerably. White is saddled with vulnerable holes on the queenside, which his opponent can readily occupy and he is without any prospects of playing the liberating c2–c3. **22. ... Nd6 23. Ra5 Qe4 24. Nd3 Nc4** "The game throughout is well played by Black"—Wisker. **25. Bc1 N×a5 26. b×a5 Bd6 27. Bg5 h3 28. f3 Qe2 29. Q×e2 R×e2 30. B×d8 K×d8 31. Rc1 Rg2† 32. Kf1 R×h2 33. a4 c5 34. c3 c4 35. Nf2 Bg3** White resigns—*City of London Chess Magazine* (Wisker, February 1874), pp. 13–14.

**(284) Bird–Wisker    1–0**
Match 4 (game 5? 9?)
London, December 1873
C77

Either game 5 or 9 of the fourth match.
**1. e4 e5 2. Nf3 Nc6 3. Bb5 a6 4. Ba4 Nf6 5. Qe2 b5 6. Bb3 Be7 7. a4 Rb8 8. a×b5 a×b5 9. Nc3 b4 10. Nd5 0-0 11. Qc4 Bb7 12. d3 d6 13. Be3 Kh8 14. 0-0 Ng4 15. h3 N×e3 16. f×e3 g6 17. Kh1 Bf6 18. N×f6 Q×f6 19. Nd4 d5 20. e×d5 Na5 21. Q×c7 Qg7 22. Ne6 f×e6 23. R×f8† R×f8 24. Q×g7† K×g7 25. R×a5 e×d5 26. B×d5 B×d5 27. R×d5 Rc8 28. Rb5 R×c2 29. R×b4 Re2 30. e4 Rd2 31. Rb3 Kf6 32. Kh2 Kg5 33. Kg3 h5 34. h4† Kf6 35. Kf3 Ke6 36. g3 Kf6 37. g4 h×g4† 38. K×g4 Rg2† 39. Kf3 Rh2 40. Kg3 Rd2** and White wins. "The game was prolonged for some forty more moves, and terminated at length in favor of White, through giving up the b-pawn. The remaining portion of the game was not taken down"—Wisker—*City of London Chess Magazine* (Wisker), February 1874, pp. 19–20.

# Handicap Tournament at the City of London Chess Club 1873-1874

Since Bird's elimination from its handicap tournament in December 1870 the City of London Chess Club had known a continuous growth. By the time of Bird's first match with Wisker the club occupied the dominant position in the London chess scene. Almost all the strong metropolitan players had been invited to join the club as honorary members. These honorary members were allowed to be part of the management committee from 1871 onwards. The power they got with this function would prove to be of no mean relevance within a few years.

The growth of the City Club went hand in hand with the decline of other chess clubs. The principal club of the late 1860s, the Westminster Chess Club, was now close to its end. The ancient St. George's Chess Club was still going strong but clearly lacked the City's star quality.

In January 1873, at the celebration of their twentieth anniversary, the City Club counted some 200 members. Because of this success the club decided to move towards the more spacious rooms of the City Restaurant. On 17 October 1873 a special general meeting took place on which several important decisions for the promotion of the game were taken. Without any doubt the most relevant one concerned the publication of the club's own chess magazine. A few weeks later Potter was appointed editor of the *City of London Chess Magazine*. Several masters, including Bird, joined the editorial board of the new magazine. On the same meeting, the handicap tournament for the winter season was announced. Just as in the previous editions, 48 participants were allowed to enter the knock-out event of the year. While in the edition of 1872-73 just one win was needed to proceed, now the earlier formula of two wins was adopted again. At the end of the knock-out phase a pool of three players was formed, with prizes for the first two players. The losers of the first round continued to play for the third and fourth prize. At least a game per week had to be played, and the time limit was set at 20 moves per hour. This happened not without discussion and proposals were made to play 15 or 25 moves in one hour. Both suggestions, the second one made by Bird, were not upheld. The participants were divided in six classes. The first class was well represented as, besides Bird, De Vere, Lord, Potter, Wisker and Zukertort took part.

The pairings of the first round yielded a clash between two of the strongest players, Bird and De Vere. Bird won the first game, but two subsequent losses (one of them was most unfortunate) eliminated him for the first two prizes. Bird was equally unsuccessful in section B, where the losers of the first round were given a chance for the third and fourth prize. Having each scored a win, he forfeited the decisive game against Joseph Pfahl.

In the winner's section Zukertort and De Vere reached the pool phase together with Sothers, a fourth-class player who received the odds of a knight. Sothers came out on top, to the frustration of both professionals, who claimed that Sothers was classified too favorably

by the handicapping committee. The loser's section was won by Maas (class IV), before Dr. Ballard (class II).

## (285) Bird–De Vere    0–1
Handicap tournament (round 1, game 2)
London, November 1873
C58

**1. e4 e5 2. Nf3 Nc6 3. Bc4 Nf6 4. Ng5 d5 5. e×d5 Na5 6. d3** "We much prefer here Anderssen's variation which generally goes on as follows: 6. Bb5† c6 7. d×c6 b×c6 8. Be2 h6 9. Nf3 e4 10. Ne5 Bc5 11. f4 Qd4 12. Rf1 with a pawn ahead and a safe game"—Steinitz. Recommended by Morphy, 6. d3, was a lifelong favorite of Bird. In theory it was soon superseded by 6. Bb5†. **6. ... N×c4** 6. ... h6 is the major move. **7. d×c4 h6 8. Nf3 Bd6 9. h3 0–0 10. Be3 e4 11. Nd4 Nh7 12. Nc3 f5 13. Ndb5 f4 14. Bd4 f3 15. g×f3** "15. g3 would have been the safest way of playing, as Black has no attack whatever to compensate him for the loss of the pawn, but probably White speculated upon obtaining a strong attack after 0–0–0"—Steinitz. **15. ... e×f3** 15. ... Ng5! initiates strong counterplay against Bird's king. **16. N×d6 Q×d6 17. Be3** "17. Qd2 at once seems stronger, for there was plenty of time to interpose his bishop if Black checked with the rook, and, in that case, the Black rook would not have been subsequently so well posted on the e-file as in his present position, where he defends the f-pawn, which was sure to be attacked sooner or later"—Steinitz. **17. ... Qb4 18. Qc1 A** simple 18. a3! returns the pawn after 18. ... Q×c4 (18. ... Q×b2?? 19. Kd2 catches the queen), but then 19. Qd2 followed by 20. 0–0–0, gives attacking chances in return. **18. ... Q×c4?!** De Vere captures the pawn a bit too hastily. 18. ... Re8 or 18. ... Ng5, to provoke 19. a3, is interesting. White is bound to lose more time to castle after his unlucky eighteenth move. **19. Qd2 Bf5 20. 0–0–0 Nf6 21. Rhg1** Bird restored his initiative. **21. ... Kh7** Although risky, there is no choice but to play 21. ... B×h3 and block the g-file with 22. ... Bg2. Now Bird aims for the win of the f-pawn. **22. Rg3 Ne4 23. N×e4 Q×e4 24. Rdg1** Of no avail, as Black can adequately defend g7; 24. Re1! is problematic to meet; e.g., 24. ... Qh4 25. Bd4 Rf7 26. Qe3 wins the important f-pawn. **24. ... Rf7 25. Qc3 Rg8 26. Rd1 Bg6 27. Rd4 Qe5?** (*see diagram*) 27. ... Qf5 keeps everything under control.

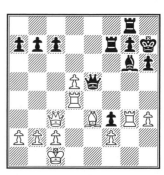

*After 27. ... Qe5*

**28. Qd2?** Bird misses his ticket into the next round with 28. R×g6! **28. ... Be4** 28. ... Rd8, followed by 29. ... Rfd7, takes over the initiative. With everything defended, the d-pawn is becoming a target. **29. b4** "White sacrifices the d-pawn in order to gain the f-pawn for it after a few moves, but we think that Black profits more by this exchange, as he obtains greater liberty of action for his queen and rooks, and White's king is most exposed after the c-pawn is moved"—Steinitz. After 29. Rg4 Bg6 30. Kb1, the position is about equal. **29. ... B×d5** Correct is 29. ... Rd8 30. c4 b5! when he has the clear upper hand. **30. Qd3† Rf5 31. c4?!** Bird ruthlessly pursues his plan, for which he pays the cost of dangerously exposing his king. More considerate is 31. Bf4. **31. ... Bf7 32. R×f3 Bg6 33. Rg3 Rf6 34. Qc3?!** Too compliant: with 34. f4 first and then 34. ... Qe7 35. Qc3, the active post that De Vere's queen reaches in the game would be unachievable. After the text move 34. ... a5! would also have been very strong. **34. ... Qf5 35. Qb2 Re8** 35. ... Rd6! exchanges an important defender of the king. **36. Rd5 Qe4 37. Rg4?** Leaving a pawn hanging. After 37. Rd4, White's position isn't enviable, but defendable. **37. ... Qh1† 38. Rd1 Q×h3 39. Rg3 Q×g3!** This is first-rate play and perfectly sound. Black wins two pieces for the queen with a safe position, in which White can do nothing. The g-pawn is very weak, and must fall very soon, after which the a-pawn wins easily"—Steinitz. **40. f×g3 R×e3 41. g4** "A most singular position. If 41. Rd7 Rf1† 42. Rd1 Rff3 with a winning game. If 41. Qd4 Re2 and if 41. Qd2 R×g3. If 41. Qg2 or 41. Qh2 Rc3† wins at once"—Steinitz. A last try would be 41. Qd2, but both 41. ... Rfe6 and 41. ... R×g3 should win. **41. ... Rf4 42. Kd2** "This may have been a mistake, but there was nothing to be done"—Steinitz. **42. ... Rf2†** and Black wins—*City of London Chess Magazine* (Steinitz), April 1874, pp. 60–61.

**(286) De Vere–Bird    1–0**

Handicap tournament (round 1, game 3)
London, 24 November 1873
C61

1. e4 e5 2. Nf3 Nc6 3. Bb5 Nd4 4. N×d4 e×d4 5. d3 c6 6. Bc4 Qh4 7. 0-0 Nf6 8. e5 Ng4 9. Bf4 h5 10. Nd2 Qd8 11. Qf3 d5 12. e×d6 *e.p.* Be6 13. Rae1 Qd7 14. Ne4 0-0-0 15. Nc5 B×c4 16. N×d7 Bd5 17. N×f8 B×f3 18. d7† Black resigns. "No notes seem to be required to the above game. It is played by De Vere in his usual straightforward style. He always chose the nearest road to the end, and was not one to delight in elaboration where none was required. Of all the strong English players he was perhaps the most clear-headed, and almost up to the last, with a wrecked constitution and the hand of Death visibly upon him, he retained the same faculty of a calm, open-eyed perceptivity by which his play had always been distinguished"—Potter—*City of London Chess Magazine* (Potter), March 1875, p. 50.

**(287) Pfahl–Bird    1–0**

Handicap tournament (round 2, game 1)
London, December 1873
*Odds of pawn and 2 moves*

1. e4 & 2. d4 d6 3. Bd3 Nd7 4. Nf3 e5 5. c3 Ngf6 6. Be3 Be7 7. Qb3 Rf8 8. h3 b6 9. Ng5 Nb8 10. Bc4 d5 11. e×d5 e×d4 12. c×d4 a6 13. Nc3 h6 14. Ne6 B×e6 15. d×e6 b5 16. N×b5 a×b5 17. Q×b5† c6 18. Qb7 Qa5† 19. Bd2 Qa7 20. Qc8† Bd8 21. Bb4 Qb6 22. Bc5 Qc7 23. e7 Rh8 24. e×d8Q† Q×d8 25. Qe6† and mates next move—*Turf, Field and Farm*, 16 January 1874. First published in the *Liverpool Weekly Albion*.

# THE GOSSIP SAGA 1873–1874

The name of George Hatfeild Dingley Gossip, born in 1841, started to pop up in chess circles in the mid–1860s. Gossip was a very active player but he never achieved any significant result in a chess tournament. Yet he had an inclination of presenting himself as a strong player by incessantly sending games won against the recognized masters to magazines. Gossip also made his claim to mastership in his books. As with his games these often received harsh critics.

A conflict between Gossip and Bird arose after the publication of a few of their games in the *Chess Player's Chronicle*. These games, nearly all won by Gossip, were published without any accompanying comment. Potter, in the April 1874 edition of the concurrent magazine *City of London Chess Magazine* (p. 52), denounced the practice of publicizing them this way. According to him second-class players were too apt to rush their games into print. An insulted Gossip reacted by supporting his claims to be regarded as a first-class player: he stated that his score was not any worse than Wisker's in his recent match with Bird.[23]

In the end both Gossip and the *City of London Chess Magazine* seemed to come to an agreement about the necessity of mentioning the scores when games were published. Yet the *Magazine* continued to question Gossip's strength. A battle of words took off in which one point in Gossip's reply provided for a follow-up: "In conclusion, I may add that I shall be most happy to play any English player a match for not less than £15 a side, at the odds of pawn and move, in the course of the ensuing autumn; half the games to be played in London and half at Colchester; Mr. Bird and yourself included. I name this to avoid the reproach of forfanterie [boastfulness]" (*City of London Chess Magazine*, September 1874, p. 188).

With a pawn and move ahead Gossip apparently felt sure enough to take on every English player. Bird at once accepted the challenge. Contemporaries believed that such a duel would be very interesting.

Before further arrangements could be made Gossip had commenced a match with Owen. After five games, with a 3–2 advantage for Owen, Gossip resigned due to illness. After a pause he renewed his challenge to Bird at the end of 1874, but a few additional conditions were met with great skepticism. Gossip demanded "that the game shall be played in a room, from which certain well-known critics can be excluded" (*Westminster Chess Club Papers*, January 1875, p. 171).

It seemed that the duel of words between both men died a silent death, leaving the games that originated the dispute as eternal

23. "...that the exact score of the last thirteen games played between Mr. Bird and myself is as follows: Bird won 7, Gossip won 4, 2 drawn. Out of ten consecutive games played between Mr. Bird and myself in May 1873 the score was: Bird won 5, Gossip won 3, 2 drawn, e.g. exactly the same score as the score in the last match between Messrs. Bird and Wisker, won by the former gentleman. At two sittings Mr. Bird and myself made even games." *City of London Chess Magazine*, June 1874, p. 103. Not surprisingly, Bird had a different opinion of his record against Gossip: "En passant, we may remark, that Mr. Bird is under the impression that he won a much larger majority of games than Mr. Gossip has given him credit for, though, he adds, that he took no particular account, which, we may remark, is usually a characteristic distinguishing a great player." *City of London Chess Magazine*, May 1874, p. 106.

**Handicap tournament, London, November 1873–March 1874**

*Site:* City of London Chess Club
*Prizes:* 1st £5, 2nd £3, 3rd £2 10s., 4th £1 10s.
*Time limit:* 20 moves per hour
*Odds scale:* pawn and move (class II), pawn and 2 moves (class III), knight (class IV), rook (class V) and knight and bishop (class VI)
*Notes:* Not all draws were published. The result between Cutler and Lowson (section B) is unclear. Cutler is given as the winner but Lowson was
   paired into the next round.

**Section A**

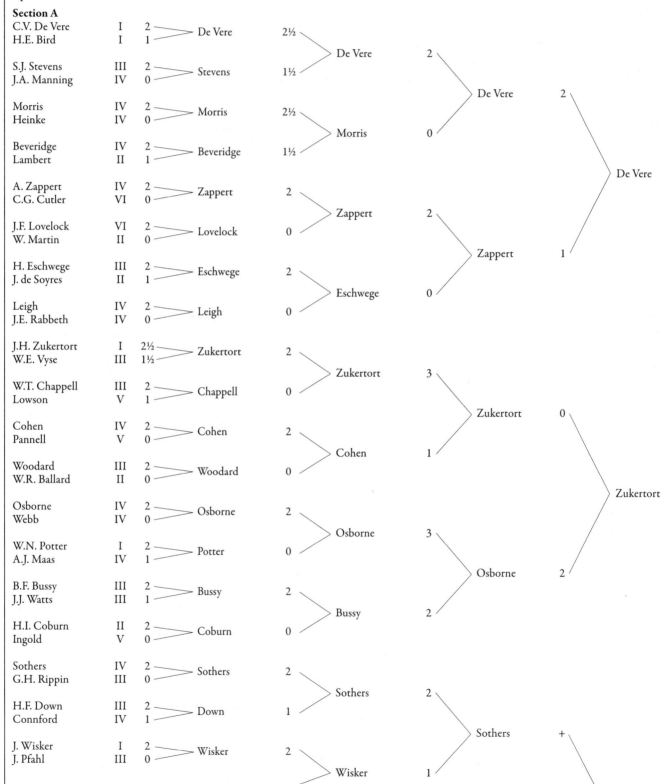

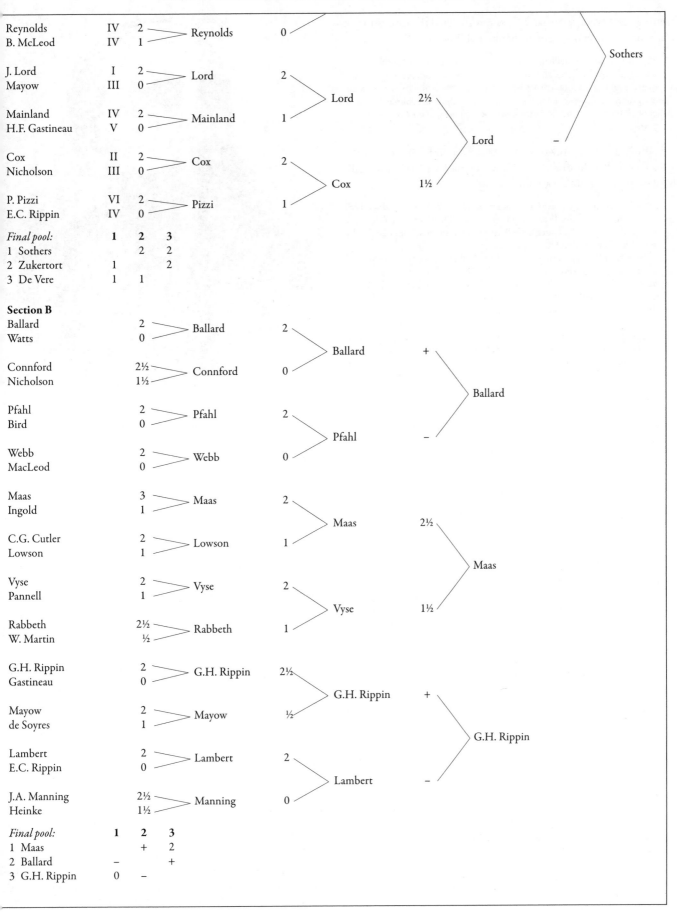

| Reynolds | IV | 2 | | | | |
| B. McLeod | IV | 1 | Reynolds | 0 | | |

Sothers

| J. Lord | I | 2 | | | | |
| Mayow | III | 0 | Lord | 2 | | |

Lord    2½

| Mainland | IV | 2 | | | | |
| H.F. Gastineau | V | 0 | Mainland | 1 | | |

Lord    –

| Cox | II | 2 | | | | |
| Nicholson | III | 0 | Cox | 2 | | |

Cox    1½

| P. Pizzi | VI | 2 | | | | |
| E.C. Rippin | IV | 0 | Pizzi | 1 | | |

*Final pool:*   **1**   **2**   **3**
1  Sothers       2   2
2  Zukertort    1       2
3  De Vere      1   1

**Section B**

| Ballard | 2 | | | |
| Watts | 0 | Ballard | 2 | |

Ballard    +

| Connford | 2½ | | | |
| Nicholson | 1½ | Connford | 0 | |

Ballard

| Pfahl | 2 | | | |
| Bird | 0 | Pfahl | 2 | |

Pfahl    –

| Webb | 2 | | | |
| MacLeod | 0 | Webb | 0 | |

| Maas | 3 | | | |
| Ingold | 1 | Maas | 2 | |

Maas    2½

| C.G. Cutler | 2 | | | |
| Lowson | 1 | Lowson | 1 | |

Maas

| Vyse | 2 | | | |
| Pannell | 1 | Vyse | 2 | |

Vyse    1½

| Rabbeth | 2½ | | | |
| W. Martin | ½ | Rabbeth | 1 | |

| G.H. Rippin | 2 | | | |
| Gastineau | 0 | G.H. Rippin | 2½ | |

G.H. Rippin    +

| Mayow | 2 | | | |
| de Soyres | 1 | Mayow | ½ | |

G.H. Rippin

| Lambert | 2 | | | |
| E.C. Rippin | 0 | Lambert | 2 | |

Lambert    –

| J.A. Manning | 2½ | | | |
| Heinke | 1½ | Manning | 0 | |

*Final pool:*   **1**   **2**   **3**
1  Maas            +   2
2  Ballard        –       +
3  G.H. Rippin   0   –

witnesses. Several years later Gossip revitalized the discussion in the introduction of one of his books, published in 1879.

> The author publicly challenged any English player to a match at the odds of pawn and move for a considerable pecuniary stake. No one accepted his "défi" with the solitary exception of Mr. Bird, who, when the author came to London at considerable expense and inconvenience to play the match, pleaded pressure of other business as his excuse for not playing [*Theory of the Chess Openings*, p. vii].

Bird's detailed reply provides some more information on the background of the discussion. He wrote this letter from the head-quarters of his publisher, Dean and Son.

> Some remarks had just previously appeared in a leading chess magazine which Mr. Gossip considered disparaging to his chess skill. A little paper warfare arose, and Mr. Gossip issued a challenge to play any first-rate player who would yield him the odds of pawn and move.
>
> No other player appearing, I was ultimately asked to accept the challenge, which I did, and to those who know me best in the chess circle it is scarcely necessary for me to state that it was no fault of mine that the match did not take place. When the preliminaries were forwarded to me I at once conceded the questions of "time limit" and "number of games." In regard to the stakes, a substantial amount was at first proposed, but at Mr. Gossip's request I agreed (although in opposition to the advice of many of my friends) to play him for a nominal sum, or, if he preferred it, for the honor of victory only.
>
> The place of meeting only remained to be fixed, and Simpson's chess head-quarters were suggested. When all appeared satisfactorily arranged, I was sur-prised by the receipt of two long letters from Mr. Gossip, containing the fol-lowing proposition, viz., that I should play near his residence at Colchester, paying my own expenses to that place, and whilst remaining there. I was to take my chance of recouping myself out of money which Mr. Gossip supposed might be received in respect of a small charge for admission to witness the games. I recollect that the Town Hall was first suggested, and afterwards a tavern was proposed. I did not think it desirable to adopt the principle of charging for admission, and as I was not prepared to incur the expense of an indefinite stay at Colchester, I was compelled to decline Mr. Gossip's pro-posal.
>
> The match, however, did not fall through on this account. Anxious to play it, I arranged to make things as pleasant as possible for Mr. Gossip to play in London, and he assented.
>
> The St. George's Chess Club and the City of London Chess Club both very kindly granted permission to play at their rooms, and with some glee, I communicated the result to Mr. Gossip. Alas, authorities say, the course of true love never did run smooth. Judge of my disappointment and mortifi-cation to receive a reply from Mr. Gossip agreeing to play, but stipulating that there should be no smoking, and that four of the most eminent chessists in London should be excluded from the room for no other reason than this: that they had, in the exercise of their respective duties, criticized his chess work. This condition, as well as the anti-blast, rendered further negotiation useless. In a private room I might even have consented to forego the weed, but such a proposal for a public match was ridiculous.
>
> In conclusion, I may add, that I am still willing to give Mr. Gossip the odds of pawn and move in a match at chess, either for a substantial or nominal stake.
>
> I am, Sir, yours obediently,
>
> H.E. Bird
>
> 160 Fleet Street, E.C., October 7, 1879 [*Figaro*, 15 October 1879].

According to the *Chess Player's Chronicle* of 1 November 1879, Gossip was not in a condition to accept Bird's novel challenge as he was suffering an ailment to his eye.

A final word can be said about Bird's preserved offhand games with Gossip. Bird's play in these was reckless in the extreme and of an utterly bellicose character. It is obvious that he hardly spent more than a second of his thoughts about the consequences of his moves.

George H.D. Gossip (*Columbia Chess Chronicle*).

### (288) Bird–Gossip    0–1
Offhand game
London (Simpson's Divan) 1873
C39

1. e4 e5 2. f4 e×f4 3. Nf3 g5 4. h4 g4 5. Ne5 Bg7 6. N×g4 d5 7. e×d5 Qe7† 8. Kf2 Bd4† 9. Kf3 B×g4† 10. K×g4 Nf6† 11. Kf3 Qe4 mate—*Chess Player's Chronicle*, October 1873, pp. 341–342.

### (289) Gossip–Bird    1–0
Offhand game
London (Simpson's Divan) 1873
C39

1. e4 e5 2. f4 e×f4 3. Nf3 g5 4. h4 g4 5. Ne5 d6 6. N×g4 h5 7. Nf2 Be7 8. d4 B×h4 9. B×f4 B×f2† 10. K×f2 Qf6 11. Qd2 Ne7 12. Nc3 Nbc6 13. Bb5 Bd7 14. B×c6 B×c6 15. Rae1 Ng6 16. g3 0-0-0 17. d5 Bd7 18. Qe3 h4 19. Ke2 b6 20. Bg5 Bg4† 21. Kd2 Qf3 22. B×d8 K×d8 23. Qg5† Kc8 24. Ref1 Qg2† 25. Kc1 Ne5 26. g×h4 Rh5 27. Qe7 Nc4 28. Qe8† and Black resigns—*Chess Player's Chronicle*, December 1873, p. 371.

### (290) Gossip–Bird    1–0
Offhand game
London (Simpson's Divan) 1873
C35

1. e4 e5 2. f4 e×f4 3. Nf3 Be7 4. Bc4 Bh4† 5. Kf1 d5 6. B×d5 Nf6 7. Nc3 N×d5 8. N×d5 0-0 9. N×f4 f5 10. e5 Nc6 11. d4 g5 12. Nh5 g4 13. N×h4 Q×h4 14. Nf6† Kh8 15. Bf4 Be6 16. Qd2

3 17. c3 R×f6 18. Bg5 Bc4† 19. Kg1 g×h2† 20. R×h2 Q×h2†
21. K×h2 Rg6 22. Bf6† Kg8 23. b3 Bd5 24. Rg1 Kf7 25. g4 Rag8
26. g5 h6 27. Qf4 Be4 28. b4 Ne7 29. e6† Ke8 30. Q×c7 and
Black resigns—*Illustrated London News*, 17 January 1874.

## 291) Bird–Gossip     ½–½

Offhand game
London (Simpson's Divan) 1873
C58

1. e4 e5 2. Nf3 Nc6 3. Bc4 Nf6 4. Ng5 d5 5. e×d5 Na5 6. d3
h6 7. Nf3 e4 8. Qe2 N×c4 9. d×c4 Bc5 10. h3 0-0 11. Nh2 Nh7
12. Nc3 f5 13. Be3 Bb4 14. 0-0-0 B×c3 15. b×c3 b6 16. c5 f4
17. Bd4 Re8 18. Ng4 Q×d5 19. c4 Qg5 20. f3 b×c5 21. Bc3 B×g4
22. h×g4 Nf6 23. Rh5 N×h5 24. g×h5 Rad8 25. R×d8 R×d8
26. Q×e4 Q×g2 27. Qe6† Kh8 28. Q×h6† Kg8 29. Qe6† Kh7
30. Qf5† Kh8 31. Q×f4 Qh1† 32. Kb2 Rb8† 33. Ka3 Q×h5
34. B×g7† K×g7 35. Q×c7† Qf7 36. Q×b8 Q×f3† 37. Qb3 Qc6
38. Kb2 Qf6† 39. Qc3 Q×c3† 40. K×c3 Kg6 41. a4 draw—*Illustrated London News*, 27 December 1873.

## (292) Gossip–Bird     1–0

Offhand game
London (Simpson's Divan) 1873 (?)
C35

1. e4 e5 2. f4 e×f4 3. Nf3 Be7 4. Bc4 d5 5. B×d5 Nf6 6. d4
N×d5 7. e×d5 Bh4† 8. Kf1 Bg4 9. c4 0-0 10. B×f4 c6 11. Nc3
Nd7 12. Qd2 f5 13. b3 Bf6 14. Re1 Nb6 15. Ng5 B×g5 16. B×g5
Qc8 17. Be7 Rf7 18. h3 Bh5 19. Qg5 Bg6 20. d6 f4 21. Kf2 Qd7
22. Ne4 B×e4 23. R×e4 Re8 24. Rhe1 Nc8 25. c5 h6 26. Qh4
N×e7 27. R×e7 Rf×e7 28. R×e7 R×e7 29. Q×e7 Q×e7 30. d×e7
Kf7 31. e8Q† K×e8 32. Kf3 g5 33. Kg4 Kf7 34. Kf5 Kg7 35. Ke5
Kf7 36. b4 a6 37. a3 Ke7 38. a4 Kf7 39. d5 c×d5 40. b5 d4
41. K×d4 Ke7 42. Ke5 Kd7 43. Kd5 h5 44. Ke4 Ke6 45. c6 b×c6
46. b×a6 f3 47. g×f3 and Black resigns—*Chess Player's Chronicle*,
February 1874, pp. 1–3.

## (293) Gossip–Bird     1–0

Offhand game
London (Simpson's Divan) 1873 (?)
C51

1. e4 e5 2. Nf3 Nc6 3. Bc4 Bc5 4. b4 B×b4 5. c3 Bc5 6. 0-0
d6 7. d4 e×d4 8. c×d4 Bb6 9. d5 Na5 10. Bb2 Ne7 11. Nc3 N×c4
12. Qa4† c6 13. Q×c4 0-0 14. e5 d×e5 15. d6 Ng6 16. Ba3 Be6
17. Qe2 f6 18. g3 Qd7 19. h4 Bd5 20. Nh2 Bd4 21. Rac1 b5
22. Rfe1 Qh3 23. N×d5 c×d5 24. Bc5 Q×g3† 25. Kh1 Q×h4
26. Red1 Rfe8 27. B×d4 e×d4 28. Q×b5 Q×f2 29. d7 Rf8
30. Q×d5† Kh8 31. Q×a8 and Black resigns—*Chess Player's
Chronicle*, February 1874, pp. 3–4.

# MATCH WITH J. LORD 1874

In March 1874 Bird commenced a match with John Lord, one
of London's most active amateurs. Accepted as the better player by

far, Bird accepted betting odds of two to one. (The only details available are unclear; the *Illustrated London News*, 2 May 1874: "The ... match between Messrs. Bird and Lord, the former betting two to one—is still unfinished.") It was agreed that the first player to win seven games would win the match. Bird easily imposed himself upon his opponent during the first games of the match and obtained a 4–0 advantage. Then, the match was suspended for a while. In the same *Illustrated London News* article, Staunton annotated the break with a sarcastic comment: "The present pause is not an uncommon feature in a match under such circumstances." Apparently against expectations the match was resumed a short while later. Lord managed to give Bird a bit more opposition by winning two games, but Bird won the final game on Wednesday 27 May. He gained the match with 7 against 2 with one draw.

## (294) J. Lord–Bird     0–1

Match
London 1874
C53

1. e4 e5 2. Nf3 Nc6 3. Bc4 Bc5 4. 0-0 d6 5. c3 Bb6 6. d4 Bg4
7. Bb5 "The correct move. Black has now a more disadvantageous position than he should have at this early stage"—Potter. 7. ... B×f3 "We should have preferred 7. ... Bd7"—Potter. 8. g×f3 Kf8 "We see no other line of play for Black, but that such a move should be necessary shows the weakness of his position. It is evident that 8. ... Kf8 bears no analogy to cases in some variations of the Giuoco Piano, where White can move Kf1 with great advantage"—Potter. 9. B×c6 b×c6 10. d×e5 d×e5 11. Q×d8† "Mr. Lord has played all this with the soundest judgment, and has, according to our opinion, an unmistakable superiority in position. It may be taken as a general rule that isolated doubled pawns, apart from compensating circumstances, constitute a serious disadvantage, and this more especially holds good when the opponent has a knight on the board"—Potter. 11. ... R×d8 12. Na3 Ne7 13. Nc4 Ng6 14. Be3 f6 15. a4 Nh4 16. f4 Kf7 17. a5 B×e3 18. f×e3 "All this has been remarkably well played by Mr. Lord. By a series of well-timed moves he has got rid of what appeared to be the chief obstacle to his ultimate success: his adversary's bishop"—Potter. 18. ... e×f4 19. e×f4 Rd3 20. e5 Re8 "20. ... Rhd8 would have been better"—Potter. 21. Rad1 Red8? "This would seem to be a mistake, and yet, with the open d-file in the possession of White, what chance would Black have had of saving the game?"—Potter. Potter systematically overemphasized the apparent weakness of Black's pawn structure, which has been compensated throughout the game by the dynamic elements in Bird's favor. The text move, however, is a crude tactical mistake. Instead 21. ... Rd5! either maintains the d-file or, in case of an exchange, solves the aforementioned pawn weakness. 22. Nd6† R3×d6 23. e×d6 c×d6 24. Rd3?! Lord misses the chance to continue in the most straightforward fashion. Both 24. f5! and 24. Rd4! are very active continuations. The latter move plans to occupy the b-file. 24. ... Nf5 25. Re1 h5 Superior is 25. ... Rb8! and if 26. b4 d5, followed by 27. ... Nd6. It is clear that White's rooks are much more passive compared to the previous line. 26. Kf2 26. Re4, with the similar idea of bringing a rook to the b-file, is still very good. 26. ... Rb8 27. b4 Rb5?! The immediate 27. ... d5 and 28. ... Nd6 is

necessary. **28. Rb1 d5 29. c4!** "An ingenious reply"—Potter. **29. …d×c4 30. Rd7† Kg6 31. R×a7 c5 32. a6** Certainly not bad, but 32. Rg1† and 33. b×c5 (or 33. a6) avoids any complications. **32. …c×b4 33. Rb7?** "The excellence of Mr. Lord's play during the previous part of the game would not have led us to expect such a miscalculation as this. 33. Ra1, followed by 34. R×g7 or 34. Rb7, would have forced the game"—Potter. **33. … Ra5 34. a7** "It often happens that when a player, by some heedless move, has thrown away a winning advantage, he feels too annoyed to think of salvage, and, rejecting prudent instincts, he, in desperation, still plays to win. This must have been the case, we fancy, in the present instance, for such a move as 34. a7 couldn't have been preceded by a calm analysis of the position. Mr. Lord should have been chiefly anxious at this point to have at least made sure of a draw, which result could have been easily attained by either 34. R×b4 or 34. Rc7"—Potter. **34. … b3?!** After 34. … Ra2† 35. Kg1 (35. Kf3 leads to a perpetual) 35. … b3 none of the players can gain further ground. The text move is far less good, as with 35. Rd7! Lord could now have cut Bird's knight from the scene of action. Subsequently his king could join the fray and march towards the queenside. **35. Rc1? Nd6 36. Rb6?** After Bird's last move the situation has become suddenly very difficult for his opponent, and it is no miracle that Lord loses the thread. He has fighting chances after 36. Rc7 b2 37. Rg1† Kh6. Bad now is 38. Rc×g7? b1Q. The only move to avoid 38. … Ra1 is 38. f5!. The resulting endgame has some surprising points: 38. … R×f5† 39. Ke2 Ra5 40. Kd2 and now 40. … g6 or 40. … g5 is quite unclear, with the practical chances being on Bird's side. Instead the apparently proper 40. … Ra1 leads only to a draw after the surprising 41. Kc3! If White wants more and crosses the third rank with his king, Nb5† is lethal. **36. … R×a7!** "Splendidly played"—Potter. **37. R×d6 b2** "A most curious position. White has two rooks against one, but cannot save the game"—Potter. **38. Rg1† Kh7 39. Rb1 c3 40. R×b2 c×b2** and Black wins—*City of London Chess Magazine* (Potter), June 1874, pp. 126–128.

### (295) Bird–J. Lord    1–0
Match
London 1874
C65

**1. e4 e5 2. Nf3 Nc6 3. Bb5 Nf6 4. Qe2 Be7 5. 0-0 0-0 6. Nc3 d6 7. B×c6 b×c6 8. h3 c5 9. d3 Rb8 10. b3 Ne8 11. Bb2 f5 12. e×f5 B×f5 13. Nd2 Bg5 14. Nde4 Bh6 15. Rae1 Qh4 16. Bc1** "White sees that he cannot allow the hostile bishops to maintain their menacing attitude"—Potter. **16. … Nf6** "We don't consider this a prudent move. The knight occupied an important defensive position where it stood, and while it remained there, Black, being free from any apprehension of immediate danger, could have set about making a quiet, but by no means frivolous, attack on the kingside. For instance he could have played 16. … c6, with a three-fold object: first to enable 17. … Rb7, whence it could have been moved to f7 or g7, secondly to prevent Nd5 or Nb5, thirdly to permit the d-pawn to advance in certain positions"—Potter. Potter's suggestion is not very good: 16. … c6 weakens the central pawn structure and gives White the opportunity to enter a better endgame at once after 17. B×h6 Q×h6 18. Qe3. **17. B×h6 Q×h6 18. N×f6† R×f6** The

less artificial 18. … Q×f6 is certainly better. **19. Nd5** More to the point is 19. f4! Re8 (White is much better after 19. … e×f4?! 20. Nd5! Re6 21. Ne7† Kh8 22. N×f5 R×e2 23. N×h6 R×e1 24. R×e1 g×h6 25. Re7) 20. Nb5!, which wins a pawn, though Black has some compensation for it. **19. … Rf7 20. Qe3 Qe6 21. Nc3 g5** "There is no doubt that Mr. Lord gets a very attacking game by this sacrifice, so we cannot wonder at his making what is really 'a leap into the dark.' Such positions are often fruitful in happy chances" —Potter. Lord gained a comfortable equality, and he should settle himself with it. The text move is too ambitious and poorly thought through. **22. g4! Bg6 23. Q×g5 Rg7 24. Qh6 Qf6 25. Ne4 Qf8 26. Ng3** "26. f4 would appear a forcible move here. 26. … B×e4 27. Qe6†!"—Potter. **26. … Rb5** Either 26. … Qf3 or 26. … Rf7 are better ways to prevent 27. f4, but his prospects remain poor. **27. Re3** "Now that the king is shielded by the knight, we cannot but think that White, by playing 27. f4, must have obtained a most formidable position"—Potter. **27. … Qf4 28. Qh4 Rb8 29. Ne2** Decidedly better is 29. c3, which denies all squares along the fourth rank for the queen. Subsequently she will be thrown back after 30. Ne2. **29. … Qb4 30. f4 Qd2 31. Qf2 Rf8 32. f5 Q×c2 33. Rf3?** The precise 33. Qe1! Bf7 (if 33. … B×f5? 34. Ref3) 34. Nc3 Qb2 35. f6 Rg6 36. Re4! encircles the queen, and forces Black to desperate measures such as 33. … B×b3. **33. … Be8** *(see diagram)*

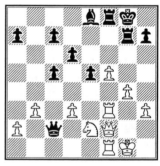

After 33. … Be8

**34. Qe3** The position still looks favorable for Bird, but his attack has come to a standstill, and Lord is ready to nibble away at his queenside. The more prudent 34. Ng3, heading for a slightly better endgame, is therefore indicated. **34. … Bc6?** He must capture the a-pawn at once. White's forces will gather on the kingside, and a battle arises of which the outcome will be unclear. There could follow 34. … Q×a2 35. Ng3 Bd7 36. Nh5 Rgf7 37. f6 Kh8 38. Qg5 Rg8 etc. **35. R3f2 Q×a2** Not good anymore, but there is nothing better. **36. f6! Rgf7 37. Nd4 R×f6** "By this ingenious move Black proffers the capture of the bishop, with the intention, after exchanging both rooks, of taking the b-pawn, remaining then with three pawns against the knight"—Potter. **38. Qg5† Kh8 39. Ne6! R8f7 40. Q×f6† R×f6 41. R×a2 R×e6** "Black is now the exchange behind, with practically only one pawn for it, but with his strong center pawns, as against his adversary's two isolated ditto, on White squares, his game is by no means hopeless"—Potter. In fact, the active White rooks should be able to decide the game in a few moves. **42. Rf7** Or 42. R×a7 followed by 43. Rf8† and 44. Rc8. **42. … Bb5 43. R×a7 Re8 44. Rf3?!** Bird handled the middle game very well, but his endgame play is on a lower level. Instead of this overly passive move, 44. Ra×c7 B×d3 45. Rfd7 wins outright. **44. … Re7 45. Kf2?!** 45. Rf8† Kg7 46. Rc8 is still winning. **45. … d5?**

45. ... Kg7 is much more tenacious. **46. Ke3** After 46. Rf8† Kg7 47. Rc8 Rf7† 48. Ke2 c6 49. R×f7†, Black's position is hopeless. **46. ... B×d3 47. Rf8† Kg7 48. Raa8?** 48. Rc8 wins once more. **48. ... Bc2 49. Rfb8?** 49. ... d4† 50. Kd2 Bg6 51. Ra5 Or 51. Rg8† Kf6 52. Ra5 e4 53. R×c5 e3† 54. Ke1 d3 55. Rd8 Re6 56. R×c7 Ra6 wins. **51. ... e4 52. R×c5 e3† 53. Ke1 d3 54. Rd8 d2†?** First 54. ... Be4!, menacing 55. ... d2 56. Ke2 Bf3†, is the winning procedure. **55. Ke2 Bf7?** 55. ... Be8 (Potter) doesn't allow 56. Rc3 due to 56. ... Bb5†. Hence a draw is quickly forced by 56. Rg5† Bg6 57. Rc5. **56. Rc3 h5 57. R×e3 R×e3† 58. K×e3 h×g4 59. h×g4 B×b3 60. R×d2 c5 61. Rd7† Kg6 62. Kf4** and White wins—*City of London Chess Magazine* (Potter), July 1874, pp. 141–143.

**(296) J. Lord–Bird    1–0**
Match
London 1874
C65

**1. e4 e5 2. Nf3 Nc6 3. Bb5 Nf6 4. d3 Bc5 5. 0–0 d6 6. c3 0–0 7. h3 Ne7 8. d4 e×d4 9. c×d4 Bb6 10. Nc3 Ng6 11. Be3 c6 12. Bd3 Re8 13. Qc2 Be6 14. Rad1 Rc8 15. Rfe1 Ba5** 15. ... Qe7 is correct. **16. a3** Lord misses the very convincing 16. Ng5! Bd7 (16. ... Qe7 17. f4 is also very good for White) 17. Qb3 Qe7 18. Q×b7 Rb8 19. Qa6 B×c3 20. b×c3 and White has won a pawn. **16. ... B×c3 17. b×c3 Bd7 18. Bc1** Here, but also on the next move, 18. Bg5! is strong. **18. ... Qc7 19. Nh2 c5! 20. d5 c4 21. Bf1 Qa5 22. Rd4 Ba4 23. Qe2?** "We cannot approve of this eccentric move. We can see nothing against the obvious reply of 23. Qd2..."—Potter. **23. ... Q×c3 24. Bb2 Qb3 25. R×c4 Nf4?!** 25. ... Bb5! might have elicited a resignation. **26. Qd2 R×c4 27. B×c4 Q×c4 28. B×f6?!** 28. Q×d4 R×e4 keeps slim hopes of a draw. The text move must lose quickly. **28. ... R×e4 29. R×e4 Q×e4 30. f3 Qc4 31. Be7 Qc5† 32. Kh1 N×d5 33. Bh4 Bc6 34. Ng4 h5 35. Bf2 Q×a3 36. Qg5 Qa1† 37. Kh2 Nf6?** Black's easiest road to a win is 37. ... g6, followed by 38. ... Qf6. **38. Nh6† Kf8 39. Nf5 Qe5†??** A draw is likely after 39. ... Ne8! 40. Q×h5 f6 41. Qh8† Kf7 42. Qh5†, since bringing the king out into the open is a bit risky. **40. Bg3 Qb2 41. Q×g7† Ke8 42. N×d6† Ke7 43. Q×f7† Kd8 44. Nc4** White wins—*City of London Chess Magazine* (Potter) 1874-75, p. 144.

**(297) J. Lord–Bird    ½–½**
Match
London 1874
C61

**1. e4 e5 2. Nf3 Nc6 3. Bb5 Nd4 4. N×d4 e×d4 5. 0–0 Bc5 6. d3 Ne7 7. f4 c6 8. Ba4 d5 9. Qh5 Qd6 10. f5 g6 11. f×g6 Q×g6 12. Q×g6 h×g6 13. Nd2 Be6 14. e5 Rh5 15. Nf3 0–0–0 16. Bg5 Re8 17. a3 Bg4 18. Bf6 Ng8 19. Rae1 B×f3 20. R×f3 Bd6 21. Kf2 Bc7 22. Bg7 Re7 23. e6 f5 24. B×d4 R×h2 25. c4 d×c4 26. d×c4 Nh6 27. B×a7 Ng4† 28. Kg1 Reh7 29. Rh3 R2×h3 30. g×h3 Ne5 31. Kg2 Re7 32. Bd4 R×e6 33. b4 Nd3 34. R×e6 Nf4† 35. Kf3 N×e6 36. Bf6 Bd8 37. B×d8 K×d8 38. h4 Ke7 39. Bd1 Kf6 40. a4 Nd4† 41. Ke3 Ke5 42. b5 c×b5 43. c×b5 f4† 44. Kd3 b6 45. h5 g×h5 46. B×h5** draw—*City of London Chess Magazine*, July 1874, pp. 146–147.

# PROPOSING NEW RULES OF CHESS

The June 1874 edition of the *City of London Chess Magazine* (pp. 111–114) contained an article by Bird with a proposal to bring some modifications to the chessboard. Bird suggested the board be enhanced with two files. Between the queen and bishop he would place the *guard*, which combined the moves of rook and knight. Between the king and bishop Bird placed the *equerry*, with the moves of bishop and knight.

Bird adapted his proposition a short while later, for he realized that the force of the new pieces was so great that it would affect the game too much. In the article appearing in *Land and Water* on 4 July, his board had a breadth of nine instead of ten files. The extra piece, "the extended knight," was placed in between the rook and the ordinary knight on the queenside. In Bird's concept this piece could move like a knight, but jump one square farther (i.e., a knight at b1 can go to a4, c4 and e2). Bird bundled both articles into the small pamphlet *Proposed Modification in the Game of Chess*.

Bird's proposal to reform the game was based on his idea that the game had known a decline for a few years. He did not want to replace the old game and its literature completely but merely offer an interesting alternative. This way the immense amount of theory that confers an advantage to the studied player could be circumvented. According to Bird the popularity of the game would fare well with these adaptations. He suggested that a few strong players could test his idea in a match.

Enthusiasm for Bird's innovation was not great. In his introduction to the *Land and Water* article Potter questioned the need for a reform of chess (and the decades since have made it clear that he was right). One stuck to the old game and was more than satisfied with it.

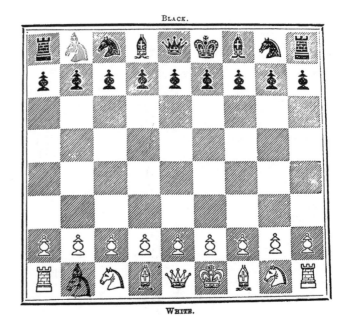

Bird's new form of chess, as proposed in his booklet *Proposed Modification of the Game of Chess as Originally Suggested in the June Number of the City of London Chess Magazine.*

Bird's proposal fell into oblivion but a few decades later José Raúl Capablanca came up with a similar idea. The world champion's motivation to change the game was the allegedly drawish nature of chess. Capablanca presented a board with ten rows. Compared to Bird's original proposal Capablanca left the bishops next to the king and queen and posted the new pieces on the other side of them, next to the knights: On the queenside went an *archbishop*, combining the powers of bishop and knight; on the kingside, the *chancellor*, combining rook and knight. Just as fifty years before it was not seriously considered and everything remained as it ever was.

# Handicap Tournament at the City of London Chess Club 1874–1875

The City of London Chess Club kept on blossoming during 1874. At the annual dinner held in February 1874 the club's president John Edward Rabbeth proudly announced that his club already counted more than three hundred members. But the club wasn't spared of bad news either when in September the rooms in the City Restaurant burnt down after a great fire. A movement was forced and new rooms were found in Horns Tavern. The success of the City Club reflected in the annual handicap tournament where the number of available places was extended from forty-eight to sixty-four. This number was much more convenient, for the pool with three players was now replaced by a straight knock-out formula. One further change subdivided classes II until VI in two sections. This way the player who was considered weaker would enjoy the small advantage of the White pieces (instead of alternating colors) against the stronger esteemed players from the same class.

Bird, Potter, Zukertort and Wisker were the four first-class players present. Some extra alert was paid to the formation of the handicap committee, a clear sign that the outcome of the last edition, won by the underrated Sothers, was not digested very well by many. Potter proposed to select twelve actual participants into that committee, so that those involved could protest against an incorrect classification of a player. Bird was among the committee members.

Bird survived the first three rounds by beating players from class III and IV. Especially his two last matches were won with but little raft after four games. Finally, in the fourth round Bird got thrown out of the tournament by Stow, another player from class IV.

The measures taken by the handicapping committee appeared to be insufficient to protect the strong players. The tournament was won by the 18 year old Arthur Maas (class III) ahead of Potter. Two other low rated players, Peyer (class IV) and Chappell (class III), gained the remaining prizes in the early loser's section.

**(298) Bird–Stow    0–1**
Handicap tournament (round 4, game ?)
London, January 1875
*Odds of Nb1*

**1.** f4 d5 **2.** e3 g6 **3.** c3 c5 **4.** b3 Nf6 **5.** Bb2 Bg7 **6.** Be2 Nc6 **7.** g4 Ne4 **8.** Rc1 e5 **9.** h4 Ng3 **10.** Rh2 N×e2 **11.** Q×e2 e×f4 **12.** h5 f×e3 **13.** d×e3 Qd6 **14.** h6 Bf6 **15.** Rg2 Bh4† **16.** Kd2 Bg5 **17.** Nf3 B×h6 **18.** Rf1 Be6 **19.** Kc1 0-0-0 **20.** Ba3 d4 **21.** g5 d3 **22.** Qd2 Bg7 **23.** Rgf2 Qd5 **24.** c4 Qd6 **25.** e4 Ne5 **26.** Qa5 N×f3 **27.** R×f3 d2† **28.** Kd1 Bg4 **29.** Q×a7 Qd3 **30.** Qa8† Kc7 White resigns—
*City of London Chess Magazine*, February 1875, pp. 28–29.

---

## Handicap tournament, London, October 1874–March 1875

**Site:** City of London Chess Club
**Prizes:** Four prizes
**Odds scale:** pawn and move (class II), pawn and 2 moves (class III), knight (class IV), rook (class V) and knight and bishop (class VI)

**Section A**

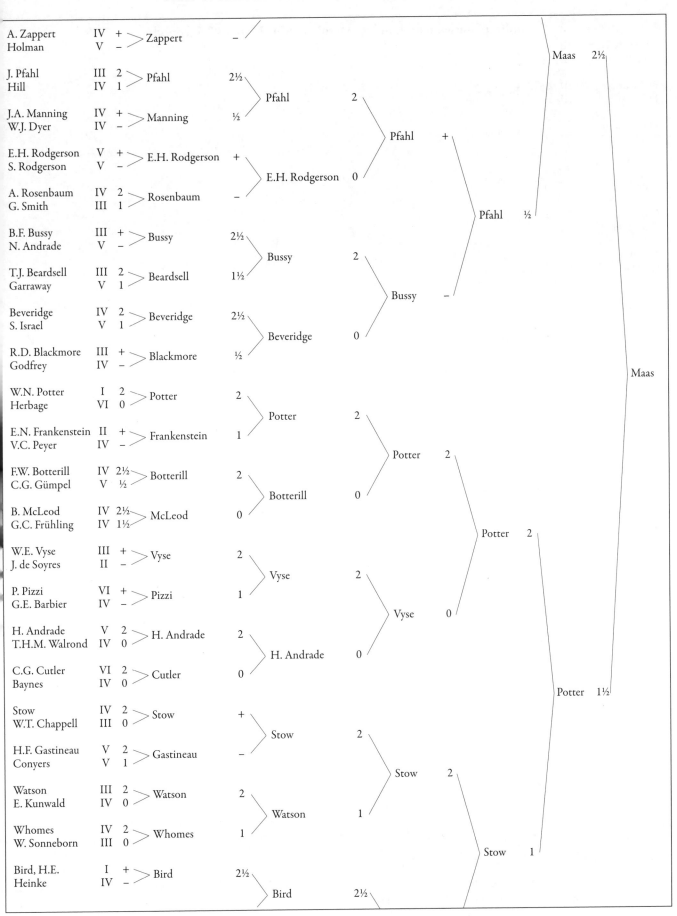

| | | | |
|---|---|---|---|
| A. Zappert | IV | + | > Zappert — |
| Holman | V | – | |

Maas  2½

| | | | |
|---|---|---|---|
| J. Pfahl | III | 2 | > Pfahl  2½ |
| Hill | IV | 1 | |

Pfahl  2

| | | | |
|---|---|---|---|
| J.A. Manning | IV | + | > Manning  ½ |
| W.J. Dyer | IV | – | |

Pfahl  +

| | | | |
|---|---|---|---|
| E.H. Rodgerson | V | + | > E.H. Rodgerson  + |
| S. Rodgerson | V | – | |

E.H. Rodgerson  0

| | | | |
|---|---|---|---|
| A. Rosenbaum | IV | 2 | > Rosenbaum — |
| G. Smith | III | 1 | |

Pfahl  ½

| | | | |
|---|---|---|---|
| B.F. Bussy | III | + | > Bussy  2½ |
| N. Andrade | V | – | |

Bussy  2

| | | | |
|---|---|---|---|
| T.J. Beardsell | III | 2 | > Beardsell  1½ |
| Garraway | V | 1 | |

Bussy  –

| | | | |
|---|---|---|---|
| Beveridge | IV | 2 | > Beveridge  2½ |
| S. Israel | V | 1 | |

Beveridge  0

| | | | |
|---|---|---|---|
| R.D. Blackmore | III | + | > Blackmore  ½ |
| Godfrey | IV | – | |

Maas

| | | | |
|---|---|---|---|
| W.N. Potter | I | 2 | > Potter  2 |
| Herbage | VI | 0 | |

Potter  2

| | | | |
|---|---|---|---|
| E.N. Frankenstein | II | + | > Frankenstein  1 |
| V.C. Peyer | IV | – | |

Potter  2

| | | | |
|---|---|---|---|
| F.W. Botterill | IV | 2½ | > Botterill  2 |
| C.G. Gümpel | V | ½ | |

Botterill  0

| | | | |
|---|---|---|---|
| B. McLeod | IV | 2½ | > McLeod  0 |
| G.C. Frühling | IV | 1½ | |

Potter  2

| | | | |
|---|---|---|---|
| W.E. Vyse | III | + | > Vyse  2 |
| J. de Soyres | II | – | |

Vyse  2

| | | | |
|---|---|---|---|
| P. Pizzi | VI | + | > Pizzi  1 |
| G.E. Barbier | IV | – | |

Vyse  0

| | | | |
|---|---|---|---|
| H. Andrade | V | 2 | > H. Andrade  2 |
| T.H.M. Walrond | IV | 0 | |

H. Andrade  0

| | | | |
|---|---|---|---|
| C.G. Cutler | VI | 2 | > Cutler  0 |
| Baynes | IV | 0 | |

Potter  1½

| | | | |
|---|---|---|---|
| Stow | IV | 2 | > Stow  + |
| W.T. Chappell | III | 0 | |

Stow  2

| | | | |
|---|---|---|---|
| H.F. Gastineau | V | 2 | > Gastineau — |
| Conyers | V | 1 | |

Stow  2

| | | | |
|---|---|---|---|
| Watson | III | 2 | > Watson  2 |
| E. Kunwald | IV | 0 | |

Watson  1

| | | | |
|---|---|---|---|
| Whomes | IV | 2 | > Whomes  1 |
| W. Sonneborn | III | 0 | |

Stow  1

| | | | |
|---|---|---|---|
| Bird, H.E. | I | + | > Bird  2½ |
| Heinke | IV | – | |

Bird  2½

### Handicap tournament, London, October 1874–March 1875 (continued)

```
J.A. Huckvale   III  +
                        > Huckvale   1½
D.H. Wilson     III  −                        \
                                               > Bird   0
H. Eschwege     III  2½                        /
                        > Eschwege   +
J.J. Watts      III  1½              \
                                      > Eschwege   1½
H.I. Coburn     II   2                /
                        > Coburn    −
Norman          III  1

Section B
Peyer                2
                        > Peyer   2
S. Rodgerson         0            \
                                   > Peyer   +
Cox                  2            /            \
                        > Cox    0              \
Sonneborn            1                           \
                                                  > Peyer   +
Stevens              2                            /         \
                        > Stevens  +             /           \
Conyers              0             \            /             \
                                    > Stevens −               \
Hill                 +             /                           \
                        > Hill    −                             \
Rabbeth              −                                           \
                                                                  > Peyer   +
Garraway             2                                           /         \
                        > Garraway  +                           /           \
Walrond              0              \                          /             \
                                     > Garraway  +            /               \
Watts                +              /            \           /                 \
                        > Watts    −              \         /                   \
Sharpe               −                             > Garraway  −                 \
                                                   /                              \
Gümpel               1                            /                                \
                        > Gümpel   2             /                                  \
Heinke               2             \            /                                    \
                                    > Gümpel  −                                       \
Israel               2             /                                                  \
                        > Israel  0                                                    \
Dyer                 0                                                                  > Peyer
                                                                                       /
Chappell             2                                                                /
                        > Chappell  2                                                /
Baynes               1              \                                               /
                                     > Chappell  +                                 /
Godfrey              2              /            \                                 /
                        > Godfrey  0              \                               /
E. Smith             1                            \                             /
                                                   > Chappell  +               /
Norman               2                            /            \             /
                        > Norman   +             /              \           /
G. Smith             1             \            /                \         /
                                    > Norman  −                   > Chappell  −
Frühling             2½            /                             /
                        > Frühling −                            /
Jennings             1½                                        /
                                                              /
Kunwald              2                                       /
                        > Kunwald   2                       /
Wilson               0              \                      /
                                     > Kunwald  2         /
Holman               2              /           \        /
                        > Holman   0             \      /
W.F. Smith           0                            \    /
                                                   > Kunwald  −
de Soyres            2                             /
                        > de Soyres  3            /
N. Andrade           0               \           /
                                      > de Soyres  1
Grady                2               /
                        > Grady     1
Herbage              1
```

---

# THE OXFORD V. CAMBRIDGE
# UNIVERSITY MATCHES 1873–1875

On 28 March 1873 representatives of Oxford and Cambridge universities met each other at the City of London Chess Club for a chess match. It was the first time that such a match between the two principal universities was organized. Inspiration was taken from the annual Boat Race, which was going to take place on the very next day.

The success of the chess match was impressive. Almost 500 spectators witnessed the players. It was the largest crowd ever gathered for a chess contest. Among the notable guests were Bird and Wisker.

The first chess match between the universities of Oxford and Cambridge (*Illustrated London News*).

The second annual match went through on 27 March 1874, also in the City Club, and now in the presence of almost 800 visitors.

One of them was the Frenchman Alphonse Delannoy. He made use of the opportunity to describe all the present British chess stars for *La Stratégie*. Delannoy was full of admiration for the enthusiastic Henry Edward Bird:

> Mr. Bird is a striking example of a gentleman. He is still young with a frank, open, smiling and impressionable personality. He perks up, heats up easily, jumps into difficulties and flourishes in his triumphs. There are drops of blood and tropical regions in this son of Albion.
>
> His game is lively, ingenious and dazzled with brilliancy. His mysterious combinations often hide his true intentions for his opponent. He sometimes seems to lose his head in the investigation of his primitive plans. Waiting, forbearing, almost falling asleep, feeding the hopes of his enemy and facilitate their victory, but then, suddenly, exposing his formidable powers, he releases all pressure at once, chases all runaways with impetuosity, only to succumb himself in the middle of the battlefield from his own fire. His style combines sometimes the depth of Deschapelles, the tricks of Desloges and Mouret, the bedazzlement of Morphy and the thunderbolts of Anderssen and de la Bourdonnais. It is charming.
>
> The spectators gathered around his games are amply recompensed for the wearisome posture to which their number condemns them. He has given me the knight in our first games but trained by my rapidity, surprised by my resistance and my rashness, he lost. Towards the end of the session he had retaken the advantage and I am still fully glorious to have withdrawn from the battlefield as the winner of one game [*La Stratégie*, May 1874, p. 134].

The third match was played on 19 March 1875 in the new rooms of the City of London Chess Club. A few weeks later it became known that Bird had left the committee of the club. The club's magazine of May 1875 (p. 101) noted that Bird gave the difference in opinion "in regard to the proceedings connected with the getting up of the university chess contest" as an explanation for his resignation. More details were provided by Duffy[24] but because of a lack of information on the circumstances these hardly bring light to Bird's decision.

---

24. Bird's departure, "it is said, [was] because he is opposed to the infliction of an annual fine upon some prominent members whose contributions are necessary to the complete success of the universities' chess match. Mr. Bird's consideration for these gentlemen does not appear to be shared by his colleagues, but as we know nothing of the opinions held by the persons most nearly interested, we have not formed any of our own on the subject of controversy." *Westminster Chess Club Papers*, May 1875, p. 1.

# CHESS IN THE CITY OF LONDON CHESS CLUB 1873–1875

From 1873 until 1875 the City of London Chess Club flourished as never before. Besides the annual handicap tournaments, chess life was supported with the organization of many other events: simultaneous exhibitions, consultation games, garden parties, team matches and the like. In May or June 1873 the City of London Chess Club started a regular series of consultation games in which Bird was very active. Most preserved games were played at the City Club, though it is not always certain if they belonged to the series or were played in another context.

## (299) Campbell & Healey–Bird & Boden   0–1
Consultation game
London, 9 May 1873
*C61*

**1. e4 e5 2. Nf3 Nc6 3. Bb5 Nd4 4. Bc4 Qf6 5. N×d4 e×d4 6. 0-0 Bc5 7. d3 d6 8. f4 Be6 9. Nd2 0-0-0 10. Qf3 Ne7 11. b4** "A spirited attempt to open an attack on the hostile king"—Löwenthal. **11. ... B×b4 12. Rb1 Nc6 13. Bb5 B×d2** An ill-judged exchange, as the White allies get the chance to mutilate their opponent's king's position. **14. B×d2** "The White allies failed to take advantage of their superiority of position. Had they first taken off the knight they would have preserved a better game"—Löwenthal. **14. ... Bd7 15. Rb3** Another way to proceed was 15. Rfc1, preparing 16. c3. **15. ... Rde8 16. Rfb1 g5 17. f×g5 Q×f3 18. g×f3 Ne5 19. B×d7† K×d7 20. Kf2 b6 21. f4** Black returned the pawn to obtain an equal endgame. The text move is extremely vigorous. The advanced pawns on the kingside, however, have a tendency to become weak, and therefore 21. Rg1 first would have been more prudent. **21. ... Ng6 22. Kg3 h6 23. Rf1 h×g5 24. f×g5 Rh7 25. h3 d5! 26. Re1?!** Bird and Boden played some very good moves and they exert now a very annoying pressure. With the text move their opponents want to keep the position closed, but the opening of lines after 26. e×d5 seems to give more chances. If then 26. ... Re2 27. Bc1 R×c2 28. Rb2 Rc5 White loses a pawn, but his pieces, especially his rooks, are liberated, and his kingside majority is also not easy to deal with. **26. ... Reh8 27. Rh1 d×e4 28. d×e4 Rh4!** Compared to the previous line the differences are clearly in Black's favor: the adverse kingside majority is kept under control, e4 is a glaring weakness and their opponents lack the active prospects from the line above. **29. Rf3 Ke7 30. Bf4 c5 31. Bd2 c4 32. c3?** This move loses quickly. The position is very difficult, and the possibilities are countless, but the crucial point is that White can keep their drawing chances intact as long as their rooks are active (even if this costs material). Just one sample line to illustrate this: 32. Ra3 a5 33. Rf3 R×e4 34. Rhf1 Ke8 35. R×f7 Reh4 36. R7f6 R×h3† 37. Kg4 R3h4† 38. Kf3 Ne5† 39. Ke2 d3† 40. Kd1 Rh1 etc. **32. ... d3 33. Kg2 R×e4 34. Re3 R×e3 35. B×e3 Ke6** and White resigns—*Land and Water* (Löwenthal), 17 May 1873.

## (300) Bird & Walton–Potter & Ballard   1–0
Consultation game
London (City of London C.C.), 4 June 1873
*A03*

"The friendly challenge issued by Dr. Ballard and Mr. Potter to play any two amateurs, and which led to this game, was originally accepted by Messrs. Boden and Bird. An unexpected engagement precluded Mr. Boden attending, and Mr. Walton, of the Birmingham and the City of London Chess Clubs, kindly took his place" —Bird.

**1. f4 d5 2. Nf3 g6 3. e3 Bg7 4. c3 c5 5. Na3 a6 6. d4 b6 7. Be2 Nh6 8. Bd2 Nc6 9. 0-0 0-0-0 10. Qe1 Kh8 11. Kh1 f6 12. Qg3 e5 13. f×e5 f×e5 14. d×e5** Of course the Black allies come out of the opening with no problems at all. The last move of White was a relatively common mistake at the time. Instead of relieving the tension and activating his own pieces with 14. N×e5, Bird and his companion select an inferior move that keeps their own pieces obstructed. **14. ... Nf5 15. Qf4 Nfd4** "This looks very formidable; but White, by giving up the queen for rook and knight, obtains at least an equivalent"—Steinitz. 15. ... Nd6 16. Qg5 Q×g5 17. N×g5 R×f1† 18. R×f1 N×e5 transposes into an endgame with a riskless edge. **16. Q×f8†** "The soundness of this sacrifice was questioned after the game. I have, however, little doubt that, owing to the force of White's subsequent move of 18. Nh4, the exchange of the queen for the two pieces was judicious play"—Bird. There is no choice for White but to sacrifice the queen, either this way or by playing 16. e×d4. With a rook, knight and pawn for the queen, material is balanced, but the sudden recovery of White's central structure put their pieces into action. **16. ... B×f8 17. e×d4 h6?** *(see diagram)* 17. ... Be7 (Steinitz) or 17. ... Bf5 are considerably stronger. Another suggestion of Steinitz (17. ... Be6?!) only invites White to leash out 18. Ng5!

*After 17. ... h6*

**18. Nh4! Q×h4** Also insufficient is 18. ... Ne7 19. Rf6 g5 20. Raf1 Bg7 21. Ng6† N×g6 22. R×g6 Ra7. All these moves were rather forced, the last one was due to White's threat to play 23. Rf7. White's next target, the d-pawn, is beyond defense; e.g., 23. Be3 c4 24. Nc2 b5 25. Nb4 wins. **19. R×f8† Kg7 20. Raf1 Nd8 21. R8f6!** Aiming at g6 while also cutting off the retreat of the queen. **21. ... Bf5 22. Rf4! Qg5 23. Be3** White's last moves were very strong. Here they miss the correct procedure to encircle her Majesty definitively with 23. Nb1! (threatening 24. R4×f5) 23. ... B×b1 24. h4 Qg3 25. Rg4. **23. ... c×d4 24. c×d4 Rc8** Also possible is 24. ... Ne6, but White's winning chances remain excellent after 25. Re4! (not 25. Rf3? Qh4 26. Bf2 Qg5) 25. ... N×d4 26. B×g5 B×e4 27. R×b6

N×e2 28. Rb7†. **25. g4??** Throwing too much oil on the fire. Calmly 25. Kg1!, preparing 26. Re4 (the immediate 25. Re4?? fails at once due to 25. ... Q×e3) forces Black into a bad endgame after 25. ... Rc6 26. Re4 B×e4 27. B×g5 h×g5 28. B×a6 R×f6 29. e×f6† K×f6 30. Be2. **25. ... Qh4??** The opening of the h1–e4 diagonal is punished severely by 25. ... Ne6!, when all of White's advantage has evaporated, and the material plus of the Black allies will quickly decide the game. For example 26. Rf3 Rc1† is a killer. **26. g×f5 Qe1† 27. Bg1 Q×e2 28. R×g6† Kh7 29. Rg2 Qd1 30. e6** Bird and Walton returned to the right track after their peculiar misstep. There is nothing to be done against the power of White's rooks and pawns. **30. ... Rc7 31. Nc2** "The winning move. Black's best line of play now is 31. ... R×c2, and on 32. R×c2 N×e6. Though much stronger than the course adopted, it would hardly have saved the game"—Steinitz. Black is on the verge of losing after 33. Rff2 Ng5 34. f6 Qd3 35. Rg2 Qf5 36. Rcf2, but it is hard to find any fatal thrust. In hindsight it might have been wiser to commence with the preparatory 31. Rff2, only then to be followed by 32. Nc2. **31. ... Re7 32. Ne3 Qe1 33. N×d5 Rg7 34. R×g7† K×g7 35. Rg4†** and White wins—*The Field* (Steinitz), 7 June 1873; *Modern Chess* (Bird), p. 83.

## (301) Potter & Ballard–Bird & Martin    ½–½

Consultation game

London (City of London C.C.), 4 July 1873

*A81*

"On the evening of Friday, the 4th inst., another game was commenced, in which Mr. Potter and Dr. Ballard consulted together against Mr. Bird and Major Martin. Owing to the lateness of the hour play was adjourned to the following Monday, when the contest ended in a drawn battle"—Löwenthal.

**1. d4 f5 2. g3 Nf6 3. Bg2 c6 4. Nh3 Na6 5. f3 d5 6. c3 Be6 7. Na3 Bf7 8. Bf4 e6 9. Qb3 Qd7 10. Nf2 c5 11. Nb1 Rc8 12. 0-0 Be7 13. Be5 0-0 14. Nd2 c×d4 15. B×d4 Nc5 16. Qc2 Bg6 17. Qd1 Bd6 18. B×f6 R×f6 19. e4 f×e4 20. f×e4 Na4 21. e×d5 Bc5 22. Nb3 R×f2 23. R×f2 B×f2† 24. K×f2 N×b2 25. Qd4 e5 26. Qd2 Nd3† 27. Kg1 Qd6 28. Rf1 Qb6† 29. Kh1 Rf8 30. R×f8† K×f8 31. h3 a5 32. Kh2 a4 33. Nc1 Qb2 34. Qg5 Be4 35. Qd8† Kf7 36. Qd7† Kf8 37. Qd8†** and the game was abandoned as a draw—*Land and Water* (Löwenthal), 16 August 1873.

On the following day various chess players were invited to attend a party at the residence of Henry Francis Gastineau, the club's president. From that occasion comes a well-known photograph (see next page).[25]

The following game was played at an unknown location.

## (302) de Soyres–Bird    1–0

Offhand game

London 1874

*Odds of pawn and move*

**1. e4 Nc6 2. Nc3 e5 3. Bc4 Bc5 4. d3 Nf6 5. Nf3 d6 6. Be3 B×e3 7. f×e3 Qe7 8. 0-0 Be6 9. Nd5 B×d5 10. e×d5 Na5 11. Bb5† c6 12. d×c6 N×c6 13. e4 0-0 14. Bc4† Kh8 15. Ng5 Na5 16. Bb3 Rac8 17. Qd2 N×b3 18. a×b3 h6 19. Nh3 d5 20. e×d5 Qc5† 21. Kh1 Q×c2 22. Q×c2 R×c2 23. d6 Rfc8 24. R×a7 R×b2 25. R×b7 Rcc2 26. R×f6 R×g2 27. Rf8† Kh7 28. Rf2** and White wins—*Liverpool Weekly Albion*, 25 April 1874.

On 13 May 1874 Bird gave a simultaneous display in the City of London Chess Club. He scored an excellent result with 18 wins, 2 losses (against Rabbeth and Walker) and 4 draws (Hutchins, Beveridge, F.W. Lord and Block).[26]

## (303) Bird–Maas    1–0

Simultaneous game

London (City of London C.C.), 13 May 1874

*C37*

**1. e4 e5 2. f4 e×f4 3. Nf3 g5 4. Bc4 g4 5. 0-0 g×f3 6. Q×f3 Qf6 7. b3 Bg7 8. Nc3 Ne7 9. Bb2 Qb6† 10. Kh1 0-0 11. Q×f4 Qg6 12. Rf3 Bh6 13. Q×c7 Qc6 14. Nd5** and Black resigns—*Illustrated London News*, 23 May 1874.

Immediately after the termination of his match with Lord rumors about a match between Bird and Richard Henry Falkland Fenton went around.[27]

No news about Bird's activities during the summer of 1874 is available. These months were dominated by his mother's death on 3 July.

## (304) Bussy–Bird    1–0

Offhand game

London (City of London C.C.), 23 September 1874

*Odds of pawn and 2 moves*

**1. e4 & 2. d4 e6 3. Nf3 Qe7 4. Be2 b6 5. 0-0 Bb7 6. Nc3 g6 7. Bg5 Qd6 8. Ne5 c6 9. Bg4 Bg7 10. f4 Ba6 11. Rf2 c5 12. Nf3 B×d4 13. N×d4 Q×d4 14. Qe1 Qg7 15. Nd5 e×d5 16. e×d5† Kf8 17. f5 Qd4 18. Rd1 Q×g4 19. f×g6† Kg7 20. Qe5† K×g6 21. Rf6† Kh5** and White mates in three moves—*Glasgow Weekly Herald*, 19 January 1878.

---

25. Some lines were dedicated to the party in the chess column of *Land and Water* on 12 July 1873: "On Saturday, 5 July 1873, Mr. Gastineau, the president of the City of London Chess Club, invited a select number of players to meet Messrs. Blackburne and Steinitz, who are about to depart for Vienna, as representatives of the City of London Chess Club at the forthcoming international congress. Among those present we noticed Dr. Ballard, Messrs. Down, De Vere, Horwitz, Potter, Löwenthal, etc. After luncheon, photographs representing most of the distinguished players present were successfully taken by Mr. Barnes of Lewisham High Road, New Cross."

26. The score and details are taken from the *City of London Chess Magazine* (June 1874, p. 109). Several other sources provide us with other scores, but these can be considered less reliable.

27. "A match is being arranged between Messrs. Bird and Fenton at the odds of the pawn and 2 moves. The winner of the first five games will score the match. The friends of the latter gentleman expect that his well-known steadiness of play, and experience of the board, will be too much for his opponent. This may prove to be the case; but we consider it by no means certain that Mr. Bird will not be found equal to the achievement of what might seem an improbable victory." *City of London Chess Magazine*, June 1874, pp. 109–110. No more was heard about this contest.

This famous photograph was taken on 5 July 1873 at one of Henry Francis Gastineau's garden parties. Standing from left to right: James F. Lovelock, Bernhard Horwitz, William N. Potter, Johann J. Löwenthal, Henry F. Down, Joseph H. Blackburne and Dr. William R. Ballard. Seated: Wilhelm Steinitz, Gastineau and Cecil V. De Vere. It was long thought that the man identified as H.F. Down was Henry Edward Bird, despite that the latter was already known to be bald at the time (courtesy Cleveland Public Library).

**21. Qc2† Rc7 22. Q×g6 Qg8 23. a4 Be8 24. Qb1 g5 25. B×g5 B×g5 26. h×g5 Bg6 27. Qb3 Qh7 28. Qf3 Be4 29. R×e4 d×e4 30. Qg2 e3 31. Rf1 e×f2† 32. R×f2 Rc1† 33. Rf1 R×f1† 34. K×f1 Qb1†** White resigns—*City of London Chess Magazine*, December 1874, pp. 283–284.

Gastineau resumed his garden parties in 1874. After having fulfilled a year's service as president he had taken up the post of vice-president, a habit in the City Club. He invited several masters and other notables to his home on 21 April, 4 July and 12 December. Bird was present on all three occasions. The most interesting meeting was the one of 12 December, when two consultation games stood in the center of everybody's attention. Bird was in the winning team in a high-level encounter.

In October Bird was contemplating a match with Valentine Green. Green, slightly younger than Bird, was one of England's most active amateurs. Just like John Cochrane he spent much of his time in India, where he played intensely against the strongest local players. In this match Bird would offer his opponent the odds of pawn and move. It is unclear whether Bird and Green actually played, for any result remained beneath the notice of the chess magazines and columns.

On 23 October 1874 a curious match was played between the City of London Chess Club and the Bermondsey Chess Club. The masters of the former club gave their guests the odds of a knight. Led by Steinitz and Zukertort, the City Club won rather easily, 9–3. Bird lost on board 3 against John J. Watts, one of the first members of the City Club (he joined the club in 1854, a bit more than a year after the establishment of the club). On this occasion Watts defended the colors of the Bermondsey Club.

### (305) Bird–Watts    0–1
City of London C.C. vs. Bermondsey C.C.
London, 23 October 1874
*Odds of Ng1*

1. e4 e6 2. d4 d5 3. e5 c5 4. c3 a6 5. Be2 c×d4 6. c×d4 Bb4† 7. Nc3 Ne7 8. 0–0 Nbc6 9. Bg4 Bd7 10. Ne2 Ng6 11. g3 Qb6 12. a3 Be7 13. h4 h5 14. Bf3 0–0–0 15. b4 Na7 16. Nc3 Nb5 17. N×b5 B×b5 18. Re1 Rd7 19. B×h5 Qd8 20. B×g6 f×g6

### (306) Bird & Zukertort–Wisker & Potter    1–0
Consultation game
London, 19 December 1874
C54

"Played by arrangement on the 19th December, at the residence of Mr. Gastineau, Peckham. Four of the best players in London contended, and chance paired Bird and Zukertort to contend against Potter and Wisker"—Wisker.

**1. e4 e5 2. Nf3 Nc6 3. Bc4 Bc5 4. c3 Nf6 5. b4** "This deviation from the ordinary course in the Giuoco Piano is assuredly not advisable. The White pawns on the queenside become weak, and in order to get up an attack White must expose himself on both flanks"—Wisker. This push in the Italian Opening was another one of Bird's pet lines. In his book *Chess Openings* (p. 27), he wrote: "The following variation, frequently adopted by Mr. Bird in the years 1873 and 1874, against Mr. Boden and Mr. MacDonnell, leads to a very interesting form of game. As to its merits, opinions differ: Mr. Boden, Mr. MacDonnell, and other fine players, rather consider Black's position preferable. Mr. Bird, however, often adopts the variation, believing it to afford a good game, and an enduring, though not very powerful, attack for White." **5. ... Bb6 6. d3 d6 7. a4 a5 8. b5 Ne7 9. Na3 Ng6** "The White allies have gained nothing by the advance of these pawns, whilst on the other hand Black's knight has been driven to a better position"—Wisker. **10. Bg5 h6 11. Be3**

B×e3 12. f×e3 "This exchange is in favor of the Black allies, as it tends still further to disunite the White pawns"—Wisker. **12. ... 0-0 13. 0-0 d5** They could also opt for 13. ... c6, aiming for a strong center. **14. e×d5 N×d5 15. Qd2 Kh7** "Threatening 16. ... f5"— Wisker. This plan is not particularly dangerous. The position is about equal anyway. **16. B×d5 Q×d5 17. e4 Qe6 18. Nc4 b6 19. h4** "A hazardous advance. Properly answered their play gains nothing, whilst it exposes yet another pawn to the assaults of Black"—Wisker. A more positional approach is 19. Ne3 Bb7 20. c4 followed by 21. Nd5. **19. ... f6 20. Ne3 Bb7 21. Nf5 Rad8** "The Black allies have now thoroughly developed their forces, and the superior position of their pawns gives them the better game"—Wisker. **22. Qe3 Rf7 23. g3 Nf8** All of White's last moves have been directed against their opponent's king. This is an inferior strategy compared to Black's piling up their forces against White's central weakness at d3. The text move, however, diverges a bit. The endgame after 23. ... Rfd7! 24. Rfd1 Ne7 25. N×e7 Q×e7 is highly favorable for them. With Nf5 off the board, Black's king is safe, while the weaknesses at d3 and the queenside are glaring. **24. Nh2** "White foresees that the oncoming of the Black knight will end in the loss of a pawn, and they therefore wisely determine to prosecute operations on the kingside. From this point they make the most of their chances"— Wisker. Consequent to their strategy, but 24. Rfe1, so as to be able to push the d-pawn one day, has its advantages. **24. ... Nd7 25. Ng4 Nc5 26. Rad1?** Objectively speaking the passive 26. Nf2 is the only move. **26. ... Rfd7** Immediately 26. ... N×a4 is much simpler. **27. Nf2 N×a4 28. d4 Nb2 29. Rde1 Nc4 30. Qe2 Nd6** "Black have gained a passed pawn and brought back their knight in safety. Their bishop is indeed temporarily shut out, but he can be easily brought into action again at c8"—Wisker. **31. d5 Qe8?!** Evident, but making it much more difficult to actually win the game. Instead 31. ... B×d5 32. N×d6 Bb3 33. Nf5 Bc4 alters the material balance in order to reach a won endgame. The rook and two pawns are far stronger than the knights here. **32. Ng4** *(see diagram)*

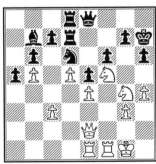

*After 32. Ng4*

**32. ... h5?** "A grave error which throws away the game. By simply 32. ... N×f5 and 33. ... Rd6 Black would have preserved their advantage"—Wisker. **33. N×g7! K×g7 34. N×f6 Qg6 35. N×h5† Kh8 36. Rf6 Qg8 37. g4 Rh7 38. g5 N×e4?** "This attempt to retrieve the fortunes of the day is frustrated by the unfortunate position of the Black bishop"—Wisker. **39. Q×e4 R×h5 40. Q×e5 Qg7 41. Ref1?** The prosaic 41. Qd4! B×d5 42. Re7! crashes through. The text move is the first mistake in a comedy of errors. **41. ... Rg8?** 41. ... B×d5! forces White to head for an instant draw with 42. Rf8† R×f8 43. R×f8† Bg8 44. R×g8† K×g8 45. Qe8†. **42. R1f4! Bc8 43. Kf2** 43. Rc4! is simpler. **43. ... Bd7 44. Q×c7**

Qh7 **45. Rf8?!** And here they miss 45. g6! **45. ... Rh×g5?** Now the game is definitely over. There remain drawing chances after 56. ... Qc2† 57. Kg3 Qd3† 58. Rf3 Qe4 59. Qf4 Q×f4† etc. **46. h×g5 Qh2† 47. Ke3 Qg1† 48. Kd2 Q×g5 49. R×g8† K×g8 50. Qc4 B×b5 51. Qc8† Kh7 52. Qf5† Q×f5 53. R×f5** and White wins— *The Sportsman* (Wisker), 23 December 1874.

On 7 July 1875 Bird gave another simultaneous display in the City of London Chess Club. This kind of event had become a monthly tradition with each time another master taking up the challenge against a large batch of players. Bird was quite successful again. He won 17 games and lost 3, against Bussy, Philp and E.C. Rippin.

Three days later, on a sunny day, another of Gastineau's garden parties took place at Peckham. After dinner the usual consultation game was contested. Löwenthal and Wisker conducted the White pieces against Bird and MacDonnell.

## (307) Löwenthal & Wisker–Bird & MacDonnell    1–0
Consultation game
London, 10 July 1875
C45

**1. e4 e5 2. Nf3 Nc6 3. d4 e×d4 4. N×d4 Bc5 5. Be3 Qf6 6. c3 Qg6 7. Nd2 Nf6 8. Qe2 N×d4 9. c×d4 Bb4 10. f3 0-0 11. Rc1 c6 12. a3 Ba5 13. Rc5 B×d2† 14. Q×d2 d5 15. Bd3 Nd7 16. Rc1 d×e4 17. f×e4 Nb6 18. 0-0 f6 19. Rf3 Be6 20. Rg3 Qe8 21. Qc2 Rd8 22. Rf1 Qd7 23. Rf4 Rf7 24. d5 c×d5 25. e×d5 N×d5 26. B×h7† Kh8 27. Rd4 N×e3 28. R×d7 N×c2 29. R×d8† K×h7 30. Rc3 Na1 31. Rd1 Nb3 32. Rd6 Re7 33. Re3 Nc5 34. b4 Rc7 35. b×c5 Bf7 36. Rc3 Be8 37. Kf2 Kg6 38. Ke3 Bc6 39. Kf2 Kf7 40. g4 g6 41. h4 Bh1 42. Rd1 Be4 43. Ke3 Bg2 44. Kf4 Kg7 45. Rd2 Bh1 46. Rc1 Bc6 47. Re1 Bb5 48. Rd8 Bc6 49. Rd6 Bb5 50. Ree6 Rf7 51. Rd8 Bc4 52. Ree8 Rc7 53. h5 g5† 54. Kf3 Bf7 55. Rc8 Rd7 56. Red8 Re7 57. c6 b×c6 58. R×c6 Be6 59. Rdd6 Kf7 60. R×e6 R×e6 61. R×e6 K×e6 62. Ke4** Black resigns—*Land and Water*, 17 July 1875.

On 24 July the chess community gathered at the residence of Edward Kunwald. Most of the attention went to a long game between Blackburne and Potter against Steinitz and Zukertort. It lasted until four o'clock in the morning and "was worth the candle." Bird engaged in another consultation game. Together with Hoffer he was on the winning side against Dr. Ballard and MacDonnell. Given the outcome, the following game was probably a return game.

## (308) Ballard & MacDonnell–Hoffer & Bird    1–0
Consultation game
London, July 1875
C38

"The following interesting 'alternation' game was contested the other day, Dr. Ballard and the Rev. G.A. MacDonnell playing against Messrs. Bird and Hoffer, each player moving in turn, without any consultation with his partner. The moves were made in the following order: Dr. Ballard, Mr. Hoffer, Mr. MacDonnell, and Mr. Bird"— Wormald.

1. e4 e5 2. f4 e×f4 3. Nf3 g5 4. Bc4 Bg7 5. h4 h6 6. h×g5 h×g5 7. R×h8 B×h8 8. d4 g4 9. B×f4 g×f3 10. Q×f3 Qh4† "The purport of this check is not very obvious, as it simply compels White to advance his g-pawn, which does not appear to be any disadvantage. Mr. Bird, however, who was responsible for the coup, considered it would slightly weaken White's position, and intended on the following move to retire the queen to f6"—Wormald. 11. g3 Qh7 12. Nc3 B×d4?? Much too greedy to be good. 12. ... Nc6 13. 0-0-0 N×d4 leaves the onus on White to prove his compensation for the piece. 13. Nb5! Bb6 14. B×c7 Bc5 15. 0-0-0 a6 16. Nd6† B×d6 17. B×d6 Nc6 18. Rh1 Qg6 19. Rh8 Nce7 20. e5 Qg7 21. Qf6 Qf8 22. B×e7 N×f6 23. B×f8 d5 24. e×d6 *e.p.* and White wins —*Illustrated London News* (Wormald), 7 August 1875.

# C.C.A. Congress, Glasgow 1875

The fourth Challenge Cup tournament held in 1872 turned out to be the swansong of the British Chess Association. John Wisker succeeded in gaining the cup definitively with a second consecutive tournament victory. Together with Löwenthal falling ill, there was hardly an incentive anymore for setting up a new such tournament. The demise of the B.C.A. was characteristic of the decline of master chess in London. The game was still practiced fanatically by Caissa's worshipers at the Divan and in the rooms of various chess clubs, but the lack of organization made itself feel when in the summer of 1875 a few players unsuccessfully tried to set up a tournament at the Divan. The lull lasted until the spring of the following year, when another master tournament was held in London.

There was one other organization with a wide scope active in England at the time. The Counties Chess Association, or C.C.A. as it was commonly abbreviated, was the pet child of the Rev. Arthur Bolland Skipworth. The creation of the C.C.A., out of two predecessors, took place in 1869. Unlike the B.C.A., the C.C.A. did not have an ambition to encompass the whole British chess scene. Instead, they focused on provincial and amateur chess.[28]

The C.C.A. was not a permanent organization. Each year a committee was charged with organizing the next congress. For their 1875 congress, held in Glasgow, the rules of the C.C.A. had been made a bit less stringent. They purposely invited metropolitan and professional players to take part in the handicap tournament as well as in other activities such as blindfold or consultation games. Also,

28. The C.C.A.'s "principal aim is not the fostering of foreign, or indeed native professionals.... It simply excludes London, the hotbed of professionalism, from its competitions, and hence its provincial character and name...." *Glasgow Herald*, 2 August 1875.

## Handicap tournament, Glasgow, 2–7 August 1875

*Site:* Corporation Gallery of Fine Arts
*Prizes:* Four prizes
*Odds scale:* pawn for move (class II), pawn and move (class III) and pawn and two moves (class IV)
*Notes:* second-round pairings for Archdall, Martin, Minchin and Ranken are unknown; Blackburne and Burn shared the first and second prize, Archdall and Ranken the third and fourth prize

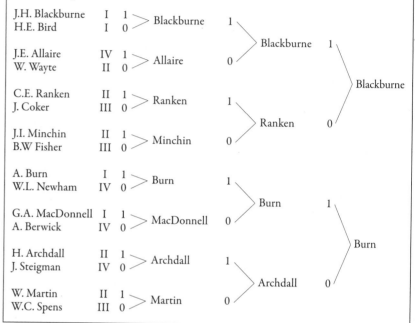

for the first time, "a foreign element" was allowed on these formerly exclusive British meetings.

The invitations were received with enthusiasm. Bird, Blackburne and MacDonnell entered the handicap tournament while Steinitz and Zukertort focused on playing simultaneous or blindfold games.

Sixteen players, divided in four classes, took part in the handicap tournament. The slightest odds were adapted so that the higher rated player gave a pawn in return for the move. As the congress of the C.C.A. only lasted a week a single win was deemed enough to advance into the next round. The pairings of the first round resulted in a regrettable heavyweight contest between Bird and Blackburne. In a short game Bird stood no chance to withstand his powerful opponent.

As foreseen, the outcome of the tournament was spoiled by time pressure, for no duel to decide the 1st–2nd and 3rd–4th prize was played. Respectively Blackburne and Burn, and Ranken and Thomas Hewan Archdall decided to split the money.

Bird played two exciting consultation games in Glasgow. On 4 August, he joint force with MacDonnell against Blackburne and Fraser. This game, with epic allure, was mainly played by Bird. His partner was called away at a crucial moment to play in the handicap. Bird's creative play was not rewarded and he had to resign in the end. Even more notorious is the game played on 6 August when Steinitz, Zukertort and Burn consulted against Blackburne, Bird and MacDonnell and won after a magnificent positional game. The winning team reaped a prize of £8 that was provided by the Glasgow Chess Club.

## (309) Blackburne–Bird   1–0

Handicap tournament (round 1)
Glasgow, 3 August 1875
C48

**1. e4 e5 2. Nf3 Nf6 3. Nc3 Nc6 4. Bb5 Bc5 5. N×e5 B×f2†
6. K×f2 N×e5 7. d4 Neg4† 8. Kg1 c6 9. Be2 d6 10. h3 Nh6
11. Kh2 Be6 12. Rf1 Nhg8 13. Qe1 h5 14. d5 Bd7 15. Bf4 Qe7
16. Rd1 g5 17. B×g5 Ng4† 18. B×g4 Q×g5 19. B×d7† K×d7
20. d×c6† K×c6 21. Rf5 Qg7 22. Qd2** Black resigns. "Bird, like
many other first-class players, more especially those of the English
school, has never gone in for acquiring much scientific knowledge.
The present game is an instance of a natural skill very soon coming
to grief for want of theoretical acquirements. Such incidents sometimes, but not very often, occur, and, in a general way, we are
inclined to think that overloading the memory with variations
doesn't lead to an enhancement of chess power"—Potter. *City of
London Chess Magazine* (Potter), September 1875, p. 252.

## (310) Bird & MacDonnell–Blackburne & Fraser   0–1

Consultation game
Glasgow, 4 August 1875
C38

**1. e4 e5 2. f4 e×f4 3. Nf3 g5 4. Bc4 Bg7 5. 0–0 d6 6. c3** "This
deviation from the usual course, 6. d4, is not very recommendable,
I think"—Zukertort. **6. ... h6 7. Qb3** "We prefer the old-fashioned
7. d4"—Wormald. **7. ... Qe7 8. d4 Nd7 9. Na3 Nb6 10. Bd3 Bd7
11. Qc2 0–0–0 12. b3 Bg4 13. Nc4 d5** 13. ... N×c4 leaves it open
to White to demonstrate their compensation. The opening of the
diagonal is welcomed by White. **14. Ba3** "On the conclusion of the
game, Messrs. Bird and MacDonnell expressed an opinion that they
ought to have played here 14. N×b6†, followed by 15. e×d5"—
Wormald. **14. ... Qf6** "14. ... d×c4 15. B×e7 c×d3 16. Q×d3 N×e7
would not be advisable for Black"—Zukertort. **15. e5** First 15. N×b6†
a×b6 and now 16. e×d5 or 16. Ne5 is best. Generally speaking it is
better for White to prevent the closure of the position. **15. ... Qc6
16. Na5 Qe8 17. Rae1 Kb8 18. b4** Here or on the previous move
18. c4 generates direct compensation for the pawn. The text move
marks the kick-off of a slow plan to bring the knight to c5. Black is
in some kind of bind and has few active counterplans. His first task
is to anticipate the opponents' intentions. **18. ... Be6 19. Qe2 Ne7
20. Nd2 Nf5 21. B×f5** "The result of too many cooks is proverbial.
Untrammeled by the responsibility of partnership, either of the
players would doubtless, in a single encounter have played 21. Ndb3,
and then 22. Nc5, giving up the exchange if 21. ... Ne3"—Wormald.
21. Ndb3 Ne3 22. Nc5 Bg4 23. Rf3! Nbc4 24. Nc×b7 indeed offers
interesting counterplay. The text move isn't bad either. **21. ... B×f5
22. Ndb3 Bc8** 22. ... Na4! hampers White's attacking plans; e.g.,
23. Nc5 N×c5 24. b×c5 Qa4 25. Bb4 Rhe8. **23. Nc5 Na4** "This
move, which results in the opening of the b-file, looks hazardous,
but is in fact very well-conceived. Black's position is at present
cramped, but as soon as White shall be induced to concentrate their
forces on the queenside, Black's counterattack on the kingside will
have every chance of success"—Zukertort. **24. Qc2 N×c5 25. b×c5
Ka8** 25. ... Qb5 forces Black to obstruct the open file with a light
piece. The queen will find a nice spot at a6, but the question remains

whether Black will ever be able to make use of their extra pawn.
**26. Rb1 Qe6** "At this point Mr. MacDonnell was compelled to
withdraw from further participation in the contest, in order to play
in the handicap. Mr. Bird, whose genius for attack is innate,
forthwith attempts by a characteristic coup-de-main to win a game
which legitimately should have been drawn, and pays the inevitable
penalty"—Wormald. **27. Qd3 Rhe8** Black has now managed to put
all their pieces on active squares and now seems ready to liberate
themselves by pushing the f-pawn one square. White has put all his
hopes on the command of the b-file. For the moment b7 is well defended, but it is a hard task to bring more support to it. It is important to notice that the immediate 27. ... f6? gives rise to a rash finish
after 28. R×b7! B×b7 29. c6! Bc8 (29. ... Rb8 is more stubborn, but
in the end White's initiative is obvious: 30. c×b7† R×b7 31. N×b7
K×b7 32. Rb1† Kc8 33. c4! d×c4 34. Qe4 Kd7 35. d5! Q×e5
36. Q×c4 with a decisive attack, for if 36. ... Rc8 37. d6! It is also
worthwhile to have a look at 29. ... Bf8?, which loses due to 30. c×b7
Kb8 31. Bd6!!) 30. Qb5 a6 31. Qb2 Qf5 and now 32. Bd6! brilliantly
decides the contest. **28. Rb2** Now the flashy 28. R×b7 fails by a
hair's breadth after 28. ... B×b7 29. c6 Bc8 30. Qb5 B×e5! 31. Rb1
Ba6!—e.g., 32. Q×a6 Rb8 33. Rb7 B×d4†! and Black mates first.
**28. ... c6** Quite safe and best. 28. ... f6 is also possible, and not without danger for both parties. This is especially the case for White, if
they are triggered into violence without delay and play 29. R×b7?
B×b7 30. c6. This line looks very much to the one given above, after
Black's 27th move, but there is nevertheless a crucial difference:
30. ... Bf8!! is possible and saves the day. After 31. c×b7† Kb8
32. Bd6 c×d6 33. Nc6†, Black's rook at d8 is covered by the other
rook, which was not the case in the line given above. White's attack
is close to being over and out. So, White is forced to build up the
pressure with 29. Rfb1. After the forced 29. ... f×e5, White can
launch their offensive by playing 30. R×b7! B×b7 31. c6! Black now
has a hard choice to make. Best is 31. ... B×c6 32. Qa6 e×d4
33. N×c6 Qe3† 34. Kf1 Qe2† 35. Q×e2 R×e2 36. K×e2 Re8†,
when White's extra piece gives him some winning chances, but there
is still a lot of counterplay left. The other possibility implies a queen
sacrifice, and in the end doesn't turn out well: 31. ... e×d4 32. c×b7†
Kb8 33. Qb5 d×c3 34. Nc6† Q×c6 35. Q×c6 Bd4† 36. Kf1. Black
is now forced to play 36. ... f3, but after 37. Rd1! it is doubtful if he
can survive. **29. Rfb1 Re7** *(see diagram)*

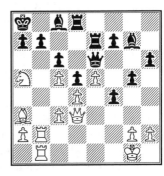

*After 29. ... Re7*

**30. Qd1?** "But why not 30. Qa6? In that case the following is a
probable continuation: 30. ... b6 31. Qf1 (Instead of retiring the
queen, Mr. Bird suggests that White might have possibly given up
the queen and still obtained a drawn game. He submits the following
curious variation: 31. c×b6 B×a6 32. B×e7 Q×e7 [best] 33. b7†

B×b7 34. R×b7 Qe6 [34. ... Qa3 35. N×c6 wins] 35. Rc7 Rb8 36. R×b8† K×b8 37. Re7 Qc8 38. R×f7 Qa6 39. e6 and Mr. Bird thinks the game should probably be drawn. It appears to us, however, that Black might still win by 39. ... B×d4 40. c×d4 Q×a5) 31. b5 best 32. Bb4 and 33. a4"—Wormald. Bird has delivered an extremely brave uphill struggle against two strong opponents. His fierce play has put him on the verge of success, but now he fails finding the best move. Bird's and Wormald's variations are all fascinating and correct. A possible continuation in his main line, after 32. Bb4, would have been 32. ... Ba6 33. a4 Qc8 34. N×c6! Q×c6 35. Ba5 b4! 36. B×d8 B×f1 37. R×b4 a5 38. Rb8† Ka7 39. B×e7 Bd3 40. R1b6 Q×a4 41. R8b7† with a draw. **30. ... Rde8** A successful defense is guaranteed after 30. ... f6! 31. Rb6 Rc7; e.g., 32. Qb3 f×e5 33. N×b7 (33. N×c6 is powerfully met by 33. ... e×d4! 34. c×d4 Q×c6! 35. R×c6 B×d4† 36. Kh1 R×c6) 33. ... B×b7 34. R×b7 Qc8. **31. Qa4 Rc7** "White threatened 32. N×c6"—Zukertort. Strong is 31. ... B×e5! 32. d×e5 Q×e5 33. Qd4 Qf5 34. Qf2 Qf6 35. Bb4 Bf5 with ample compensation for the piece. **32. c4 Kb8** The time was ripe for 32. ... f6 33. c×d5 Q×d5. **33. Rb6** "Very ingenious. The rook clearly cannot be taken"—Wormald. **33. ... B×e5?** "The right moment to dash against the adverse king's quarters, which are deserted by his army"—Zukertort. 33. ... Ka8 avoids all intricacies. After 34. Rd1 Qg4 or 34. R6b3 f6, Black must win. **34. d×e5** "Premature. They ought first to have played 34. c×d5"—Wormald. The text move is still just as good as Wormald's suggestion. **34. ... Q×e5** *(see diagram)*

*After 34. ... Q×e5*

**35. R6b3?** "A drawn battle with Mr. Bird is tantamount to defeat, but it would have been more prudent to play here for a remise, which he might have obtained very prettily by the following mode of play: 35. R×b7† B×b7 36. R×b7† Ka8 37. R×a7†! R×a7 38. Q×c6† Kb8 39. Qb6† Kc8 40. Qc6† Kd8 41. Qb6† and the game is drawn"—Wormald. There could follow 41. ... Qc7 42. Nc6† Kd7 43. Q×a7 Q×a7 44. N×a7 d×c4 45. c6† Kc7 46. Bb2 Re4 47. Kf2 Kb8 48. Nb5 Re6 49. Nd4 Re3 50. Nb5 Re6 with a draw. After the text move the Black allies get an excellent chance to launch a devastating attack themselves. **35. ... Qd4† 36. Kh1 Qf2 37. Qb4 Re2 38. Rg1 g4 39. Rb2 Qh4!** and Black wins. "A beautiful coup, which, in fact, admits of no reply. If 40. R×e2 g3 41. h3 B×h3 42. Rb1 Bg4† and mates in two more moves. If 40. h3 g3 41. Rgb1 B×h3 42. Q×b7† (42. Kg1 Bg4) R×b7 43. R×b7† Kc8 44. Rb8† Kd7 45. R1b7† Ke6 46. Re8† Kf6 wins"—Zukertort. "At this point the game was adjourned, but Black have obviously a winning position. The terminating moves are very cleverly played by Messrs. Blackburne and Fraser"—Wormald. *Illustrated London News* (Wormald), 11 September 1875;

*City of London Chess Magazine* (Zukertort), September 1875, pp. 246–247.

## (311) Burn & Steinitz & Zukertort– Bird & Blackburne & MacDonnell    1-0
Consultation game
Glasgow, 6 August 1875
*C51*

**1. e4 e5 2. Nf3 Nc6 3. Bc4 Bc5 4. b4 B×b4 5. c3 Bc5 6. 0-0 d6 7. d4 e×d4 8. c×d4 Bb6 9. Nc3** "The time limit in this game was fifteen moves per hour. How three players, with an average of only four minutes per move, can consult together, exchange their ideas, and come to a decision without the immorality of chance being introduced, we fail to comprehend. In the particular game before us the difficulty is evaded by both sides adopting the normal eight moves of the Evans with two other easily decided moves to follow"—Potter. **9. ... Bg4 10. Bb5 Kf8** "Anderssen, Neumann and Suhle advocate 10. ... B×f3, and consider that it gives Black an advantage, whereas Morphy objected to that move. As to ourselves, we, as 'old Lowe' would observe, 'say nothing.' Whether this reticence on our part arises from excess of knowledge or otherwise, we must leave for future ages to discover"—Potter. **11. Be3 Nge7 12. Kh1 d5 13. e5 Qd7 14. a4 a5** "We are not able to pledge our positive opinion that 14. ... a6 would have been better, but instinct generally pleads for the latter move in positions of this kind"—Potter. "A contemporary doubts the expediency of this move. We consider it the best, provided that it be followed by Nb4 at the proper moment. The Black allies lost the game through neglecting to strengthen their queenside"—Wisker. **15. Ne2 Ng6** Missing their last chance to exchange at f3. As Potter described above, there was a lot of discussion of the value of such an exchange. Those in favor underlined the weakness of the doubled pawns; those contra principally put faith in their attacking chances along the g-file. History found other ways to deal with Captain Evans' Gambit, but in general it is better to exchange at f3. **16. Nfg1 h5** "Here we feel ourselves on firmer ground, and consider it would be easy to prove that 16. ... h6 must be much better"—Potter. **17. Rc1 Nge7 18. f3 Bf5 19. Qd2 Qc8 20. Nf4 Nd8** Intending to exchange the White knight, which is certainly not bad, but to little avail as White is ready to send a replacement to the front. 20. ... Nb4 (Wisker) is superior, as it leaves White with a superfluous knight for which no suitable task is provided. Black's own knight at b4 hampers White's queenside play. **21. Ngh3** They could consider 21. Qb2 Ne6 22. Qa3 and the queen exerts an annoying pressure on the long diagonal. **21. ... Ne6** Interesting is 21. ... B×h3 22. N×h3 Ne6 to get rid of his bishop that is of no great purpose. **22. N×e6† B×e6 23. Ng5 h4** "An arrow gets weak towards the end of its flight"—Potter. Not necessarily an error, but there was no need for this advance and the pawn might become a target at h4. **24. Bf2** "To open the diagonal for the queen and avoid the exchange of the bishop against the adverse knight, when at f5"—Zukertort. **24. ... c6 25. Bd3 Nf5** Once more it is better to get rid of the mediocre bishop by playing 25. ... Bf5. **26. Qf4 Bd8 27. Rfe1 Rh5 28. N×e6† Q×e6 29. Rb1** "The first thick drop that portends the coming storm"—Potter. **29. ... b6** A second long term weakness (besides the pawn at h4) appears at c6. Perhaps this move was inevitable in the long run, but it could have been postponed with 29. ... Ra7. **30. Qd2 Rb8 31. Rec1 Kg8** "If 32. ... Be7 (intending 33. ... Bb4) 33. Q×a5 with a winning advantage"—Potter. **32. Qc2** "The game was at this point adjourned, having lasted four hours. It is already clearly in White's favor. Black's pieces are in a cramped position, and their pawns very weak on both flanks"—Zukertort. **32. ... Ne7 33. f4 g6 34. h3** "White's play is marked by a delicate skill that is really admirable"—Potter. Slowly but surely, White has neutralized the gambit pawn. It is yet doubtful whether he can crack the solid Black front. The game enters a long maneuvering phase. **34. ... Kg7 35. Be2 Rh8 36. Bg4 f5 37. Be2 Kf7 38. Qc3** "Preparing the attack against the adverse h-pawn, while keeping the storm against the queen's flank. White's play from the 30th move to the end is distinguished by great precision"—Zukertort. **39. ... Rh7 39. Rc2** (see diagram)

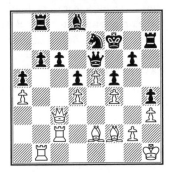

*After 39. Rc2*

**39. ... Qd7?** A move of no special remarkability, but it allows White's plans to burst like an asparagus after the first beams of sun, and the two aforementioned weaknesses seal Black's faith. Instead, after 39. ... Rb7 40. Rbc1 Rc7, there is still no crack to perceive in Black's stronghold. **40. Rbc1 Rc8** Other moves won't help them either: 40. ... Qe8 41. Qa3 (menacing invasion at d6) 41. ... Bc7 (41. ... Qd7 doesn't prevent 42. Qd6) 42. Qb3 (now the menace is 43. R×c6!) 42. ... Ke6 (after 42. ... Kf8 43. Qc3! it seems as nothing has happened, but there is no way to defend h4 anymore. If 43. ... Kf7 44. Bb5!) 43. B×h4! (they could also win with 43. R×c6†! but this move crowns the superb play of Steinitz and his allies on both wings of the board) 43. ... R×h4 44. Qg3 Rh6 45. Qg5 Qf8 46. R×c6† N×c6 47. R×c6† Kd7 48. Rf6 Qg7 49. e6† Kc6 50. Bb5† Kb7 51. Rf7 Qh8 52. R×c7†. **41. Qe1 Ng8 42. Bb5! Ne7 43. Ba6** "All played with consummate art"—Potter. **43. ... Rc7 44. B×h4 Ke6 45. Qg3 Kf7 46. B×e7 B×e7 47. Bb5 Bc5** "They can do nothing better. The game, of course, is lost"—Potter. **48. d×c5 c×b5 49. c6 Qe7 50. a×b5 Qb4 51. Qg5** "The play of White during the greater part of this game, leading up to the end, is simply above praise. Of the merits of the defending parties it is difficult to judge, for their moves seem to have been mostly of a responsive character. We should be inclined to imagine, however, that their styles would not well cohere"—Potter. **51. ... Qe7 52. Q×e7† K×e7 53. Rd2 Ke6 54. Rcd1 g5 55. f×g5 K×e5 56. R×d5† Kf4 57. g6 Rhe7 58. Rd7 Kg3 59. R×e7** Black resigns—*Westminster Chess Club Papers* (Zukertort), September 1875, p. 87; *The Sportsman* (Wisker), 8 September 1875; *City of London Chess Magazine* (Potter), September 1875, pp. 244–245.

# A MAJOR DISPUTE

The management of the City of London Chess Club was reelected at the annual general meeting held on 8 January 1875. Henry Frederic Down became the new president. At the same meeting 16 members of the committee were chosen. Among them were several honorary members, such as Bird, Steinitz, Zukertort, Potter and Wisker.

The past year had been another very successful one for the club. All the events were well attended and the number of participants in the annual handicap had grown to 64. It was reported that the cap of 400 members was broken. The extent of the club was now so vast that ways of expansion were sought. A subcommittee containing several members and the honorary members mentioned above was formed to deal with the problem. It was already deduced that the formation of a chess club in the West End could bring a solution.

A meeting of the subcommittee took place on 2 February at the residence of one of its members, Charles Godfrey Gümpel. It became soon tangible that there were two strong tendencies. After voting the majority supported the establishment of a West End Chess Club as a branch of the club. A minority voted in favor of an independent West End Chess Club.

The decision of the subcommittee was presented at a special general meeting on 5 March. Each faction defended its view in a stormy atmosphere. Another voting was held and again the branch view outweighed those favoring a new and independent club.

A short while later, when Bird resigned his post on the committee of the club (allegedly over the Oxford–Cambridge match), he supported the branch vision so the discussion about the West End Club probably had nothing to do with his abdication.

The future of the West End Club now seemed set as both the general meeting and the subcommittee had voted in favor of a dependent branch of the City of London Chess Club. Yet discord remained among a large group of players and in July they committed a kind of hold-up which resulted in a new independent club in the West End. Potter acted as the spokesman of the new society. For this purpose he made ample use of his editorship of the City of London Club's magazine. Potter articulated the news very prudently when he announced the creation of the West End Chess Club, hoping for a peaceful coexistence between the old and new club. It soon became clear that this was merely wishful.

The principal initiators behind the West End conspiracy were several honorary members (i.e., professional players) of the City Club. Those remaining behind in the City Club immediately announced some measures to restrict their power. One of the club's loyal strong players, John Wisker, supported the proposal to bar honorary members from the committee. In his column in *The Sportsman* of 14 September 1875, he expressed the opinion of many when he wrote that the club had fallen under their control.

It appears that behind the scenes negotiations were going on to pacify the situation. The West End Chess Club effectively made its start with a general meeting on 7 October. It was foreseen that two ex-presidents of the City of London Chess Club, Gastineau and Rabbeth, were going to be elected to the management committee of the new club. This would certainly have kept the ties between both chess clubs intense. But some hidden mechanisms started to play and in the end both men were not elected.[29]

Bird ventilated his disagreement with the running of things in an open letter, in which he said that the denunciation of Gastineau and Rabbeth was the revenge of, above all, Steinitz. Bird believed that the Austrian wanted to take revenge for the tendency in the City of London Chess Club to confine the power of the honorary members.[30]

There was now an open war going on between the two factions which irrupted at a special general meeting of the City of London Chess Club held on 12 November. With a huge attendance it was no surprise to see tensions rising high. A revised code of rules was under discussion. Especially rule 11, which dealt with the status of honorary members in the management of the club, created directly opposing opinions. This rule was already scrutinized by the committee, where the majority was against the decision to exclude honorary members from the general management (hardly a surprise as the relative weight of the honorary members in the committee was very high).

The discussion at the general meeting was held in turmoil. As it was clear that there was no chance for the honorary members to preserve their prerogatives, Steinitz and some other prominent players launched a proposal that allowed honorary members to become ordinary members and thus retain their place in the committee. This was equally opposed by the enemy camp. Bird, one of their spokesmen, pointed out "the injustice of allowing players to vote money for their own benefit."[31] The final voting resulted in an overwhelming majority for the supporters of an unified City Club. The reaction of the group defending the rights of the honorary members followed promptly. Under the leadership of Steinitz and in the company of the likes of Blackburne, Zukertort and Potter, they definitively tore away from the City Club and to the West End Chess Club.

The secession between the both clubs was, at least at first sight, very beneficial for the West End Chess Club. In the following months it saw a great influx of new members. Bird's complaints about the lack of matches between strong chess players were resolved at once. To prove their goodwill, Zukertort started a match against Potter, and the next year Steinitz opposed Blackburne. In *A Slight Chess Retrospect and Explanation* Bird wrote that he was "happy to

remember that I never entered that [West End] club, though frequently invited" (p. 2).

The outcome was less rosy for the City Club. A few weeks after the debacle of 12 November it was decided to bar professional players from its management board. The vast majority of strong chess players had left the City Club for the West End Club, with several important officers and supporters following. One of the direct consequences was the termination of the annual handicap tournament.

## The Expulsion of Steinitz

Steinitz had never been the most popular chess player in London. Small eruptions of the vague hostile feelings that were slumbering under the surface were seen at the time of his match with Bird and his ultimate victory, ahead of the popular favorite Blackburne, in Vienna. The conflict surrounding the West End Club further undermined his standing, but the worst was yet to come.

Steinitz added oil to the fire by publishing a bulky book review in two parts in the November and December 1875 issues of the *City of London Chess Magazine*. The subject of the review was *The Chess Openings* by Wormald. This book appeared in early 1875 and had already been well received by various reviewers; John Wisker claimed in the March issue of the same magazine (p. 44) that "the high praise which has been bestowed upon this work in different quarters seems, on careful examination, to be well deserved."

Steinitz tended to take quite a different angle. He submitted Wormald's analysis to a very detailed and critical examination and came to the conclusion that his contribution to chess theory was close to worthless. Additionally, Steinitz undertook an extremely harsh personal attack on Wormald, stating, among other things, that he had never seen a single good game played by him.

Steinitz' way of dealing with Wormald went over badly in the chess world. Not only was the tone of his article completely misplaced, he also chose the wrong person to point his arrows to, for Wormald was one of the most popular figures in chess. That he had

---

29. Potter showed extensive remorse in the *City of London Chess Magazine*, November 1875, p. 296: "Mr. Potter was one of those who opposed the election of Messrs. Gastineau and Rabbeth.... He now regrets having done so. He considers that the difference of opinion between him and them was not adequate to justify their exclusion from the governing body of a club which they had loyally served. Furthermore, Mr. Potter cannot justify to himself the course he took of not giving Messrs. Gastineau and Rabbeth notice of his intention to vote, and likewise to use his influence, against them, whereby they remained in ignorance thereof until only two days before the election."

30. The letter is worth quoting in full: "It was not until 21 September, a few days before the opening, that the outside world received any official intimation of the club being an accomplished fact. The secretary on that day wrote me a very courteous letter, with an invitation to become a member of the club, and of a council for managing its technical business. I have reason to believe that at this time it was well understood that none of the leading professional players were to be nominated for election on any managing committee, and no one appeared more earnest in this view than Mr. Potter; yet we find him, at the last moment, proposing Mr. Steinitz as a member of the managing committee of the new club, and his election was secured, although with difficulty, and at the bottom of the list; this result only being attained through the resignation of a member in Mr. Steinitz's favour. Amongst the names put forward for nomination were those of the two past presidents of the City of London Chess Club. These gentlemen had acted respectively as chairman and treasurer throughout the earlier stages of the proceedings, and their election, like that of the gentleman who has accepted the office of president, would have been hailed with intense satisfaction by all classes of the chess community; and the fact of their non-election has been, and will continue to be, the subject of universal amazement. That it should be in the power of any section of players, whether professional or non-professional, to bring about such a result, is lamentable enough under any circumstances; but if, as I believe, it has been accomplished through unauthenticated proxies and other irregular means, the matter becomes still more serious, and an election conducted upon fair and open principles appears to be the only proper remedy. At all events, sufficient must be already known to the committee to convince the gentlemen composing it that a close investigation is necessary, not only in their own interests, but in those of the entire chess community." *Illustrated London News*, 30 October 1875.

31. *The Sportsman*, 17 November 1875.

been quite ill for some time also did not help any wish to sympathize with Steinitz' assault.[32]

An additional reason to denounce Steinitz occurred in the early months of 1876 when he convincingly trounced the hope of British chess by beating Blackburne in a match with 7 wins with not a single loss. According to many Steinitz ruthlessly took advantage of Blackburne's health problems to safeguard his position in the chess world. As a result various columnists started an open war against the little liked Austrian. Noteworthy were the contributions of MacDonnell, and above all Duffy. The latter used all his columns to denounce Steinitz on a weekly or monthly basis. Two elements constantly fed the public condemnation of Steinitz. He was still considered a foreigner who refused to integrate himself in his new home town. He was blamed for putting his own interest above his loyalty to England. This sentiment was only strengthened when Blackburne received his pounding from the Austrian.

Bird was far away in the United States at the peak of the enmity, but even more than a decade later he relentlessly attacked Steinitz in his small booklet *Bird's Chess Reviews* (released in 1890). At first Bird scrutinized the first installment of Steinitz's book *The Modern Chess Instructor*, targeting Steinitz' gratitude towards Robert Steel, a patron of the world champion (Steinitz dedicated his book to Steel).

> What right has Steinitz to use the words "generous patron of chess and chess masters" in addressing Mr. R. Steel? He has no title to speak for other chess masters, and chess requires no patron; besides, Mr. Steel has been most distinguished for his patronage of Mr. Steinitz, or, perhaps, of whoever approached him first, or with the most importunity? [*Bird's Chess Reviews*, p. 6].

Bird counted 63 games in Steinitz's book. That only 10 of them involved a British player incensed him.

> When I notice the anti–English tendency of this work I am ashamed to see the names of Anthony and Steel upon it, and I am tempted to strike out the word, Mr. all through when applied to Steinitz, and to restore him to his native Herr. A punishment has been more than once suggested for Mr. Steinitz, almost too horrible to mention. Compared with which the atrocities and cruelties of the most barbarous times sink into utter insignificance, a sentence so dreadful that the mind shudders at the mention of it, a refinement of torture not pronounced till now—to remit him to his native country [*Bird's Chess Reviews*, pp. 6–7].

Many people also had problems with Steinitz's overt aim to live as a professional chess player. The feeling that chess was just a pastime and should be practiced for amusement and honor only was still very much alive in Victorian society and those who diverged too much from the norm were open to disapproval. Playing for money was, during these years, more often than not denigratingly seen as "shilling hunting." The general attitude was quite ambiguous however.

Blackburne was an obvious example of a chess professional, but

he somehow escaped this criticism.[33] Equally, the coming of the American professional Mackenzie in 1878 was generally hailed by the British press.[34]

# THE TERMINATION

The episode of the City of London and the West End Chess Club highlighted the contrast between amateur and professional chess. Since the latter group was symbolized by foreign players as Steinitz and Zukertort, a xenophobic element was added to the discussion.[35]

For Steinitz the situation became more and more difficult as the public indictment he underwent had an undeniable impact on his livelihood. The exclusion from Simpson's Divan, a necessary place to earn his bread for a chess professional, must have hurt him.[36] The attacks by Duffy became more and more virulent while Steinitz himself was not faint-hearted when it came to defending himself.

Yet there remained a handful of loyal supporters and patrons who probably helped Steinitz to get through this difficult period of his life. Steinitz also remained a frequent guest of chess clubs all over the country but, according to Tim Harding, invitations did become rarer after 1876.

Bird's life took a serious turn at the same time when the discussions reached their climax. In November he resigned the co-editorship of the *City of London Chess Magazine* and a few weeks later, on 8 December, he arrived in New York, ready to explore new chess horizons.

The history of the West End Chess Club was bound to be a short one. The club lost its rooms after a change of proprietorship and, when no other suitable alternative was found, disbanded in September 1877.[37]

---

32. Just like many of his friends, Bird was astonished by Steinitz' treatment of Wormald: "A slight skim over the first two pages of the review sufficed to convince me and others at the time that Steinitz was going for the man, who he thought had snubbed him, rather than for the book, which, moreover, is still held in great estimation by the wise in chess. The extreme venom and malignancy of his remarks, many of which were based upon imperfect knowledge, error or misapprehension, created a very painful impression at the time, upon the good English fellows in chess, which has not, to this day, been entirely obliterated." H.E. Bird, *Bird's Chess Reviews*, London, [1890], p. 3.

33. MacDonnell easily forgave Blackburne that for which he blamed Steinitz. After Blackburne's triumph at Berlin 1881 he wrote: "It was ... his staying power—a quality in which ... he has hitherto been singularly deficient. This staying power—or rather capacity for doing nothing and sitting quiet—Blackburne has only developed since his defeat by Zukertort." *Illustrated Sporting and Dramatic News*, 1 October 1881. Blackburne's playing style in tournaments during these years was remarkably boring.

34. In a letter dated 17 September 1878, Fraser wrote: "Mackenzie seems to be well liked by the English players, judging from his reception. A second banquet in his honor took place I believe last week. It is curious to note how 'professionalism' is belauded in Mackenzie and deprecated in Steinitz." *Letters to John G. White relating to chess*, vol. I, letter 90.

35. Such sentiments quickly found their way into the press: "The establishment of the West End Chess Club has had at any rate one good effect—it has cleared away the disturbing foreign element that whilom infected the Divan and the habitués of that classic home of chess and coffee once more breathe freely." *Glasgow Weekly Herald*, 19 February 1876.

36. It is unclear whether the formation of the West End Chess Club had an impact on Steinitz's visits to the Divan. In any case a more formal exclusion happened around August 1877 (according to Harding, *Eminent Victorian Chess Players*, p. 183), when Steinitz was removed from the free access list of which professional players generally enjoyed. After some time the matter was settled and Steinitz returned to the Divan (*International Chess Magazine*, August 1888, p. 236).

37. The announcement of the club's closure was a perfect occasion for Duffy to fire another bullet to Steinitz' direction: "The West End Chess Club is said to have closed its doors on the 29th ultimo, after a brief life of two years. It was, for a time, the happy hunting-ground of the noisiest German band in London, the gentry who believe that it is highly 'creditable' to 'win' other people's money. Among Englishmen there is a strong preference for earning it." *Land and Water*, 6 October 1877.

## Chess Masterpieces

In the summer of 1875 Bird published his first book, *Chess Masterpieces*. He wanted to offer a small and cheap collection of master games played between 1849 and 1875. These games were accompanied by light notes that Bird assembled from various sources. The emphasis of the selected games was put on the 1850s. Modern games were far less present as, in Bird's opinion:

> There has been no first-class chess play during the past few years, and, consequently, there are no games to record. Time was when the leading players sought with avidity the opportunity of encountering each other, the pleasure and excitement of the contest and the credit of victory being considered ample inducement.... Now the aspect of chess policy is changed. Match play is entirely stopped through the largeness of the stakes demanded, and emulatory games, formerly so popular and so frequent, are now of rare occurrence [*Illustrated London News*, 4 September 1875].

The book was received quite favorably. According to Wisker in *The Sportsman* on 27 October 1875, Bird planned an improved edition with additional games played by eminent players from the United States, Canada and the British provinces. In an advertisement promoting the original edition, he was looking for supporters willing to share the risk and the profit of such an undertaking. His plans did not materialize.

There was also well-founded criticism of Bird's approach. Bird failed to select any games from such major tournaments as Paris 1867 and Baden-Baden 1870. The German contingent of players was also largely ignored. The one selected game of Zukertort's was a bit meager. On the other hand Bird was generous with inserting his own games. The majority of these were offhand games played with Boden. These are interesting but objectively speaking there were more than enough arguments to have them replaced with more classic games.

## Two Regular Opponents 1872–1875

The first part of the 1870s formed the heyday of the City of London Chess Club. Any other club, resort or association was overshadowed by its success. That, however, did not mean that chess was not played elsewhere. A principal concurrent for the club remained Simpson's Divan. As the City Club was open only three days a week, Bird could be found on many other afternoons and evenings in the Divan. Here he met his two favorite opponents Boden and MacDonnell. Various of their games that were played between 1872 and 1875 have survived. These games have an obvious offhand character and, as all contenders were known for their sharp and aggressive style, are full of glorious moments as well as stupendous blunders.

### (312) Boden–Bird    1–0
Offhand game
London (Simpson's Divan), 23 November 1872
*C51*

**1. e4 e5 2. Nf3 Nc6 3. Bc4 Bc5 4. b4 B×b4 5. c3 Bc5 6. d4**

e×d4 7. c×d4 Bb6 8. 0–0 d6 9. Bb2 Na5 10. Nc3 Ne7 11. Bd3 Bg4 12. Ne2 0–0 13. h3 B×f3 14. g×f3 d5 15. Kh2 c6 16. Rg1 Ng6 17. e5 f5 18. f4 Qh4 19. Qd2 Rae8 20. Rg3 Re6 21. Rag1 Qe7 22. Bc3 Qc7 23. R1g2 Rf7 24. Ng1 c5 25. d×c5 Q×c5 26. Nf3 Nc4 27. B×c4 Q×c4 28. Ng5 N×f4 29. N×f7 N×g2 30. Nh6† Kf8 31. Qg5 g6 32. N×f5 Qf4 33. Bb4† Q×b4 34. Qh6† Ke8 35. Ng7† Kd7 36. N×e6 Nh4 37. Nf4 Nf5 38. Q×h7† Kc8 39. Qg8† Bd8 40. N×d5 White wins—*Chess Masterpieces*, pp. 48–49.

### (313) Bird–Boden    0–1
Offhand game
London (Simpson's Divan), 18 December 1872
*C30*

**1. e4 e5 2. f4 Bc5 3. Nf3 d6 4. Bc4 Bg4 5. d3 Nd7 6. Nc3 c6 7. f5 Ngf6 8. a3 h6 9. h3 B×f3 10. Q×f3 b5 11. Ba2 a5 12. g4 Qb6 13. Ne2 Rf8 14. Bd2 Qb7 15. Kf1 Bb6 16. Ng3 0–0–0 17. Rc1 d5 18. Rh2 Bc7 19. b4 d×e4 20. d×e4 Nb6 21. b×a5 Nc4 22. B×c4 b×c4 23. Re2 Qa7 24. Bc3 Rfe8 25. Qe3 Rd4 26. Be1 Qa6 27. Rb1 B×a5 28. B×a5 Q×a5 29. Kg2 Nd7 30. Rb4 c5 31. Rb1 f6 32. Qc1 Kd8 33. h4 c3 34. Re3 c4 35. Kh3 Nc5 36. Rb4 Ke7 37. R×c3 N×e4 38. N×e4 R×e4 39. Rb7† Kf8 40. Qb2 Qd5 41. Qb6 Rd4 42. Qb1 h5 43. g×h5 Qe4 44. Rg3 Q×h4† 45. Kg2 Rd2† and Black wins—*The Field*, 21 December 1872.

### (314) Bird–Boden    1–0
Offhand game
London (Simpson's Divan), 15 November 1873
*C56*

**1. e4 e5 2. Nf3 Nc6 3. Bc4 Bc5 4. 0–0 d6 5. c3 Nf6 6. d4 e×d4 7. c×d4 Bb6 8. Bg5 Bg4 9. Bb5 0–0 10. B×c6 b×c6 11. Nc3 h6 12. Bh4 g5 13. Bg3 Nh5 14. a4 a5 15. Qd3 Qf6 16. Rad1 Qg6 17. Qc4 Bd7 18. d5 c5 19. e5 Rae8 20. e×d6 c×d6 21. Qa6 N×g3 22. h×g3 Bd8 23. Rfe1 g4 24. Nd2 R×e1† 25. R×e1 Bf5 26. Qc6 Bg5 27. Nc4 Rd8 28. N×a5 h5 29. Re8† R×e8 30. Q×e8† Kg7 31. Nc6 h4 32. g×h4 B×h4 33. Ne7 B×e7 34. Q×e7 Bd3 35. a5 Ba6 36. Na4 Bb5 37. Nb6 Qf5 38. Qe3 White wins—*Chess Masterpieces*, pp. 45–46.

### (315) Boden–Bird    0–1
Offhand game
London (Simpson's Divan) 1873
*C61*

**1. e4 e5 2. Nf3 Nc6 3. Bb5 Nd4 4. N×d4 e×d4 5. 0–0 Bc5 6. c3 Ne7 7. d3 c6 8. Bc4 0–0 9. Bg5 Kh8** 9. ... d5! is correct. **10. Qh5! f6?!** 10. ... d×c3 11. b×c3 d5 also loses a pawn, but at least Black breaks free and gets a playable game. **11. B×f6! d5 12. B×e7?!** 12. Bh4! consolidates the extra pawn and keeps the important bishop on the board. **12. ... Q×e7 13. e×d5** (*see diagram*)

**13. ... R×f2!** Stunning, but playing 13. ... b5! first even improves the next move. **14. Nd2?** Critical is the following forced line: 14. R×f2! Bg4! (necessary to cover the back rank, see move 18) 15. Q×g4 Qe1† 16. Rf1 d×c3† 17. d4 Q×f1† 18. B×f1 c×b2 19. d×c5 b×a1Q 20. d×c6 Q×b1 21. c7 Rf8 22. Qf3 Re8 23. Qh3 Rf8 and a

*After 13. e×d5*

*After 16. ... h5*

draw is inevitable. **14. ... d×c3 15. Nb3 c×b2 16. Rae1 R×f1†
17. K×f1 Qf6† 18. Qf3 Q×f3† 19. g×f3 Bh3†** and Black wins—
*Chess Masterpieces*, pp. 41–42.

### (316) Bird–Boden    1–0
Offhand game
London (Simpson's Divan) 1874 (?)
*C51*

1. e4 e5 2. Nf3 Nc6 3. Bc4 Bc5 4. b4 B×b4 5. c3 Ba5 6. 0–0
d6 7. d4 e×d4 8. c×d4 Bb6 9. d5 Nce7 10. Bb2 Nf6 11. Bd3 0–0
12. Nd4 Ng6 13. Kh1 Ng4 14. h3 Qh4 15. Kg1 N4e5 16. Nf3
N×f3† 17. Q×f3 Ne5 18. B×e5 d×e5 19. Nd2 Bd7 20. Rac1 Rac8
21. Kh2 c6 22. Nc4 Bc5 23. g4 f6 24. Rce1 c×d5 25. e×d5 g6
26. Re4 b5 27. Ne3 Qg5 28. Rg1 Bd6 29. Qg3 Qh6 30. h4 Qg7
31. h5 Rc3 32. Nd1 Ra3 33. h×g6 h×g6 34. Kg2 R×a2 35. Rh1
f5 36. g×f5 B×f5 37. Re3 Rc8 38. B×b5 Rcc2 39. Bd3 B×d3
40. R×d3 Rc1 41. Qh3 e4 42. Rb3 e3 43. Rb7 Be7 44. d6 e×f2
45. Rb8† Bf8 46. Qb3† Qf7 47. R×f8† K×f8 48. Qb8† Black resigns—*Westminster Chess Club Papers*, April 1875, p. 245.

### (317) Bird–Boden    0–1
Offhand game
London (Simpson's Divan), 17 December 1874
*C59*

1. e4 e5 2. Nf3 Nc6 3. Bc4 Nf6 4. Ng5 d5 5. e×d5 Na5 6. Bb5†
c6 7. d×c6 b×c6 8. Be2 h6 9. Nf3 e4 10. Ne5 Qc7 11. Ng4 Nh7
12. b3 Bd6 13. Bb2 0–0 14. Na3 f5 15. Ne3 B×h2 16. Bc4† N×c4
17. Na×c4 f4 18. Ng4 f3 19. g×f3 B×g4 20. f×g4 R×f2 21. Be5
B×e5 22. N×e5 Raf8 White resigns—*Westminster Chess Club Papers*, April 1875, p. 245.

### (318) Boden–Bird    0–1
Offhand game
London (Simpson's Divan) 1875
*C61*

1. e4 e5 2. Nf3 Nc6 3. Bb5 Nd4 4. N×d4 e×d4 5. Bc4 Nf6 6. d3
Bc5 7. 0–0 d5 8. e×d5 N×d5 9. Qf3 Be6 10. Qg3 Qd7 "Willing
to sacrifice a pawn for the attack he would obtain by castling on the
queenside"—Burn. 10. ... 0–0 is much safer, but rather boring.
**11. B×d5** The pawn at g7 could safely be taken. **11. ... B×d5 12. Bf4
0–0–0 13. Nd2 f6!** "An important move"—Burn. **14. Ne4 B×e4
15. d×e4 g5 16. Bd2 h5** *(see diagram)*

**17. e5?!** Leading to an unfavorable exchange as the g-file will be
opened. There would have been but little fuzz after 17. Qd3. **17. ...**

h4 **18. Qd3 f×e5 19. B×g5?** Speeding up the end. Better is 19. Rae1
h3 20. g3 Qd5 21. Qe4 Be7 22. Q×d5 R×d5, although Black retains
a clear edge. **19. ... Rdg8 20. f4 h3 21. g3 Qd5 22. Rf2 e4 23. Qb3
Q×b3 24. a×b3 d3 25. c×d3 R×g5?** Bird wants to finish style, but
he miscalculates. Simply 25. ... e×d3 would do the job. **26. f×g5
Rf8 27. Raf1?** 27. d4! is an important nuance. After 27. ... B×d4
28. Raf1 a5 29. g6 Bb6 30. g7 Rg8 31. Re1 White ultimately achieves
a draw. **27. ... e×d3 28. g6 R×f2 29. R×f2 d2** giving mate in two
moves—*Liverpool Weekly Albion* (Burn), 15 May 1875.

### (319) Bird–Boden    0–1
Offhand game
London (Simpson's Divan) 1875 (?)
*C58*

1. e4 e5 2. Nf3 Nc6 3. Bc4 Nf6 4. Ng5 d5 5. e×d5 Na5 6. d3
h6 7. Nf3 e4 8. Qe2 N×c4 9. d×c4 Bc5 10. Bf4 0–0 11. Nfd2 Bg4
12. Qf1 c6 13. h3 Bh5 14. Nb3 c×d5 15. N1d2 Bd6 16. B×d6
Q×d6 17. g4 Bg6 18. c×d5 N×d5 19. 0–0–0 Rac8 20. Kb1 e3
21. Nc4 B×c2† 22. K×c2 Qg6† 23. Kc1 Nb4 White resigns—
*Westminster Chess Club Papers*, March 1876, p. 224.

### (320) Bird–Boden    1–0
Offhand game
London 1875
*C58*

1. e4 e5 2. Nf3 Nc6 3. Bc4 Nf6 4. Ng5 d5 5. e×d5 Na5 6. d3
Bd6 7. 0–0 h6 8. Nf3 Bg4 9. Nbd2 Qd7 10. h3 h5 11. Re1 0–0–0
12. h×g4 h×g4 13. Nh2 g3 14. Nhf3 g×f2† 15. K×f2 Bc5† 16. d4
e×d4 17. Bd3 Ng4† 18. Kg1 Ne3 19. Qe2 Q×d5 20. Nf1 Rde8
21. B×e3 d×e3 22. Rad1 Nc6 23. Bb5 Qh5 24. N3h2 f5 25. Rd5
Bb6 26. c3 g6 27. Kh1 Qh4 28. g3 Qf6 29. a4 Re7 30. Red1 Reh7
31. Kg2 Ne5 32. a5 B×a5 33. Q×e3 Bb6 34. Qd2 c6 35. Rd6 Qf8
36. Be2 Bc7 37. Rd4 Qf6 38. Nf3 N×f3 39. B×f3 g5 40. b4 g4
41. Be2 Qe5 42. Rf4 Bb6 43. Qd3 Rh1 44. Q×f5† Q×f5
45. B×g4 Q×g4 46. R×g4 Rg1† 47. Kf3 Re8 48. Rf4 Re7
49. Rf8† Kc7 50. c4 c5 51. b5 a6 52. Kf2 Rh1 53. Rf6 Rh5
54. Rdd6 Ba5 55. b6† B×b6 56. R×b6 a5 57. Rb5 Black resigns—
*Liverpool Weekly Albion*, 3 July 1875.

### (321) Boden–Bird    1–0
Offhand game
London (Simpson's Divan) (?)
*C51*

1. e4 e5 2. Nf3 Nc6 3. Bc4 Bc5 4. b4 B×b4 5. c3 Bc5 6. 0–0

**d6 7. d4 e×d4 8. c×d4 Bb6 9. Re1 Bg4 10. Bb5 Kf8 11. B×c6 b×c6 12. Bb2 h5 13. h3 Qf6 14. a4?!** 14. Re3 avoids the subsequent weakening of the kingside. **14. ... B×f3 15. g×f3 Rh6** 15. ... Ba5 16. Re3 Rb8 avoids all complications. White's subsequent sacrifice contains some hidden poison. **16. a5 Qg5† 17. Kf1 B×a5 18. f4 Qb5† 19. Re2 Bb6** The bishop will be out of play here. A better square was b4. **20. Nc3 Qc4 21. Ra4 Qe6 22. f5 Qf6 23. Bc1 Rh7 24. Qd3 Re8?!** Here Bird falls short in judging the position, and more specifically the situation of his queen. Her majesty finds herself in a somewhat troubled situation. It is possible to withdraw the queen, but then Black will be doomed to passivity. Yet, there is a possibility to remain active while also avoiding any danger of losing her, namely by opening lines and diagonals on the kingside. This seems very risky with the king at f8, but White's pawn center actually hinders his own pieces when it comes to forming an attack. Concretely, 24. ... Ne7! is strong; e.g., 25. f3 Qh4 and 26. ... g6! follows. **25. f3?!** A concrete deficit of Bird's last move is demonstrated after 25. e5!, when 25. ... Qd8 is forced (25. ... d×e5? 26. Ba3† is dramatic for the king). Now after 26. f6! g6 White has excellent compensation for the sacrificed pawns. **25. ... Ne7?!** 25. ... Qh4! returns to the aforementioned idea: 26. Rh2 Ne7 or 26. Rg2 g6! 27. f×g6 Rg7!, when the opening of lines favors Black. It is likely that the rooks will get exchanged, after which his queen is completely free for action again. White has to avoid 28. g×f7? Q×h3 29. f×e8Q† K×e8. **26. Rg2 Qh4** Black is completely boxed in after 26. ... g6 27. Bg5 Qh8 28. f6 Ng8 29. e5 Nh6 30. Ne4 Nf5 31. Bf4. **27. Bg5** 27. Ne2! is a strong refinement. After 27. ... Q×h3 White can move the bishop to a more potent square: 28. Ng1! Qh1 29. Bf4 N×f5 30. Rh2 Q×h2 31. B×h2 Ne7. Black has a rook and four pawns for the queen with a solid position. It remains unclear whether White can crack through. **27. ... Q×h3 28. Ne2** *(see diagram)*

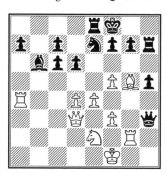

*After 28. Ne2*

**28. ... c5?** Hardly recommendable as this move still neglects the danger his queen is facing. Three other options could be considered: **(a)** 28. ... f6?! is very risky, to say the least. White can chose between 29. Nf4 or, similar to the above, 29. Ng1 Qh1 (29. ... Q×g2† might offer better chances) 30. Bf4. Black is now forced to play 30. ... Nd5 31. Qd2, and the queen is lost or huge sacrifices have to be made. **(b)** 28. ... Qh1† is strong, but only if he would be able to find some celestial moves: 29. Ng1 (29. Rg1 Qh3† draws) and now 29. ... N×f5! forces both sides full speed ahead: 30. e×f5 Re1†! 31. Kf2 h4! (this pawn will advance as much as possible. His counterpart must now do the same) 32. f6! h3 33. Q×h7 Q×g2† 34. K×e1 Q×g1† and at the end it is all peace. **(c)** 28. ... d5! 29. Ng1 Qh1 30. Qc2 f6 31. Rh2 Q×h2 32. Q×h2 f×g5 33. Nh3 g4! is a good way of giving up the queen. White's initiative will peter out quickly,

as his pieces lack active prospects. He will also experience problems with maintaining his center. **29. Ng1 Qh1 30. Raa2 N×f5** The crucial position has arrived. White's intention to close in his opponent's queen is obvious. Bird could still obtain enough material with 30. ... Nc6 31. Rh2 Q×h2 32. R×h2 c×d4 33. Nh3 Ne5. He then counts a rook and four pawns for the queen, but the limited scope of his pieces don't promise him a rosy future. Rather similar is 30. ... c×d4 31. Rh2 Q×h2 32. B×e7† R×e7 33. R×h2 c5 34. Ne2. **31. e×f5 c×d4 32. f6 g6 33. Rae2** "If 33. Rh2 Re1†"—Bird. **33. ... R×e2 34. R×e2 d5 35. Qa3† c5 36. Qa6** Black resigns—*Chess Masterpieces* (Bird), pp. 40–41.

## (322) Boden–Bird    1–0
Offhand game
London (Simpson's Divan) (?)
C51

**1. e4 e5 2. Nf3 Nc6 3. Bc4 Bc5 4. b4 B×b4 5. c3 Bc5 6. d4 e×d4 7. c×d4 Bb6 8. Bb2 Na5 9. Bd3 d6 10. d5 Ne7 11. h3 0–0 12. Nc3 f5 13. Qd2?** Boden intends to sharpen up the game a bit by sending his king to the queenside, but he makes a calculation error. **13. ... f×e4 14. N×e4 Ng6?!** 14. ... N×d5! refutes White's idea outright. Bird probably overlooked that after 15. Bc4 N×c4 16. Q×d5† Kh8 17. Q×c4 he wins back the piece, with two pawns to the good, with 17. ... d5 18. Qc3 Qe7. **15. Qc3 Rf7?!** 15. ... Qe7 keeps a small edge. A later Ne5 is thus supported. **16. 0–0–0** 16. 0–0 is more prudent. **16. ... c6 17. Neg5** Boden avoids the safer 17. d×c6. Bird comes up with an excellent retort. **17. ... Rc7! 18. Ne6 B×e6 19. d×e6 Nf8** A bit overly passive. 19. ... Qe7 or 19. ... d5 promises him a small plus. **20. Rhe1 d5** It might be wise to avoid weakening e5, although White has some play anyway. **21. Qe5 Re7 22. Ng5 Qc7?** Clouds are gathering around Black's king after this careless move. The forceful 22. ... d4! 23. B×d4 Qd5 realizes the exchange of queens. **23. Qf5! Nc4** 23. ... Qd6 24. N×h7 N×e6 25. Qg6! is equally bad. **24. B×c4 d×c4 25. Be5 Qc8 26. Bd6 g6 27. Qf6** Black resigns—*Chess Masterpieces*, p. 42.

## (323) Boden–Bird    1–0
Offhand game
London (?)
C84

**1. e4 e5 2. Bc4 Nf6 3. d4 e×d4 4. Q×d4 Nc6 5. Qe3 b6 6. Nc3 Bc5 7. Qg3 0–0 8. Bg5 Re8 9. 0–0–0 Na5 10. Be2 Be7 11. f4 Bb7 12. Bf3 Kh8 13. h4 c5 14. Nge2 Rc8 15. e5 Ng8 16. B×b7 N×b7 17. f5 f6 18. e6 d6 19. Nf4 f×g5 20. Ng6† h×g6 21. h×g5† Nh6 22. g×h6 Bg5† 23. Kb1 B×h6 24. Q×g6 Re7 25. f6 Qe8 26. f7 Qf8 27. R×h6† g×h6 28. Rh1 R×e6 29. Q×e6 Kh7 30. Ne4 Rc7 31. Ng5†** and mates in two moves—*Chess Masterpieces*, p. 43.

## (324) Boden–Bird    1–0
Offhand game
London (?)
C42

**1. e4 e5 2. Bc4 Nf6 3. Nf3 N×e4 4. Nc3 Nf6 5. N×e5 d6 6. Bb3 Be7 7. d4 Bf5 8. 0–0 c6 9. Bg5 0–0 10. B×f6 g×f6 11. Ng4 Bg6**

12. Ne3 f5 13. f4 Bf6 14. Ne2 Na6 15. Ng3 Qd7 16. c3 Bh4 17. Qf3 Rae8 18. Bc2 B×g3 19. Q×g3 Kh8 20. Qh3 c5 21. B×f5 B×f5 22. Q×f5 Q×f5 23. N×f5 Re2 24. Rf2 Rfe8 25. Kf1 R×f2† 26. K×f2 c×d4 27. c×d4 Nb4 28. Kf3 h5 29. Rc1 Nc6 30. Rc5 Rd8 31. h3 Kh7 32. g4 h×g4† 33. h×g4 f6 34. b4 a6 35. a4 Rd7 36. b5 a×b5 37. a×b5 Nb4 38. g5 Kg6 39. Kg4 f×g5 40. f×g5 Rh7 41. Rc8 Rd7 42. b6 Na6 43. Ra8 Rf7 44. Rd8 and White wins—*Chess Masterpieces*, pp. 44–45.

## (325) Boden–Bird    1–0
Offhand game
London (?)
C42

1. e4 e5 2. Nf3 Nf6 3. Bc4 N×e4 4. Nc3 "This attack was first invented and played by Boden in 1849"—Bird. 4. ... N×c3 5. d×c3 f6 6. 0–0 d6 7. Re1 In a fragment given by Bird in *Chess Practice* (p. 70), Boden continued with 7. Nh4 g6 8. f4 Qe7 9. f5 g5 10. Qh5† Kd8 11. Nf3 Qe8. The game ended in a draw. 7. ... Nc6 8. Nh4 Ne7 9. f4 c6? It is important in this opening to provide a safe haven for Black's king. This could have been done at this point by 9. ... Qd7!, so that both Qf7 as Kd8 are possible if necessary. 10. f×e5 f×e5 11. R×e5! Kd7 12. Bf4 Bird would have been in serious trouble after the simple 12. Re1! The text move gives him the chance to complicate matters with 12. ... Nd5. 12. ... Kc7 13. Qd2 Bird gets and misses another chance to play 13. ... Nd5. Here 13. Rh5! tucks the rook away on a very strong square. 13. ... b5 14. Be6? *(see diagram)* Actually bad, but it is hard to foresee why. 14. Bf7! keeps all trumps in position.

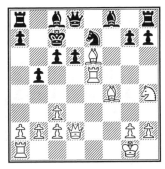

*After 14. Be6*

14. ... B×e6? 14. ... g5! turns the tables, as both ways to capture the g-pawn are obviously bad. White must fight for survival after 15. c4 (menacing 16. Qa5†) 15. ... Bh6! (defending the queen while reinforcing the g-pawn. White is forced to make some dubious sacrifices) 16. Rd1 g×f4 17. c×b5 Bg7! 18. Re2 c×b5 19. c4 White has compensation for the piece, but it remains doubtful if it is enough in the long run. 15. R×e6 Nd5 16. Bg3 Kb7 17. a4 a6 18. Nf5 Decisive. 18. ... g6 19. R×d6 B×d6 20. N×d6† Ka7 21. a×b5 a5 22. Qd4† Qb6 23. R×a5† Kb8 24. Nc4† Black resigns—*Chess Masterpieces* (Bird), pp. 46–47.

## (326) Boden–Bird    0–1
Offhand game
London (Simpson's Divan) (?)
C54

1. e4 e5 2. Bc4 Nf6 3. d3 Nc6 4. c3 Bc5 5. Nf3 d6 6. Bg5 h6

7. Bh4 g5 8. Bg3 Bg4 9. a4 a6 10. b4 Ba7 11. Nbd2 Qd7 12. h4 Rg8 13. h×g5 h×g5 14. Qb3 Be6 15. b5 Nd8 16. d4 B×c4 17. Q×c4 e×d4 18. c×d4 Ne6 19. d5 Nf4 20. Kf1 Bb6? Defending the a-pawn but losing a more important one instead. 20. ... N4h5 creates some weaknesses on the kingside. 21. b×a6 R×a6 22. N×g5 N6h5 23. Ndf3 Qg4 24. B×f4 N×f4 25. g3 Nh5 26. Qe2? 26. Rh4 catches a piece. If 26. ... N×g3† 27. Kg2! 26. ... B×f2! Bird grasps the unexpected chance with both hands. 27. R×h5 27. K×f2 Q×g3† 28. Kf1 seems at least as convincing. Black has to find 28. ... Q×g5! 29. N×g5 Ng3† 30. Kf2 N×e2 to enter a defendable endgame. His knight seems in trouble after 31. Nh7 Ng3 32. Nf6† Kf8 33. Rh6 Rg7 34. Ra3, but the unexpected 34. ... Rb6! 35. Nd7† Ke7 36. N×b6 N×e4† 37. Ke2 c×b6 offers drawing chances. 27. ... Q×h5 28. K×f2 R×g5 29. Qb5†? "White ought to have simply taken the rook. Content to play for a draw, by playing to win he loses"—Bird. 29. ... Kf8 30. a5 Rg6 31. Rg1 Rc6! "This move, like his 26th, is very well planned"—Bird. 32. Qb2 Rc5 33. Rg2 Qg4 34. Nh4 Rh6 35. Qd2 Rf6† 36. Kg1 Q×e4 37. Qg5 Qd4† 38. Kh2 R×d5 39. Qc1 Rh5 White resigns—*Chess Masterpieces* (Bird), pp. 47–48.

## (327) Boden–Bird    0–1
Offhand game
London (Simpson's Divan) (?)
C51

1. e4 e5 2. Nf3 Nc6 3. Bc4 Bc5 4. b4 B×b4 5. c3 Bc5 6. d4 e×d4 7. c×d4 Bb6 8. Bb2 Nge7 9. d5 Na5 10. Bd3 0–0 11. Nc3 d6 12. Qc2 Ng6 13. Ne2 f6 14. h4 Bg4 15. h5 Ne5 16. N×e5 f×e5 17. f3 Bd7 18. 0–0–0 Be3† 19. Kb1 c5 20. d×c6 *e.p.* b×c6 21. Bc4† N×c4 22. Q×c4† Kh8 23. h6 Qf6 24. h×g7† K×g7 25. Ng3 Qg6 26. Nh5† Kh8 27. Qd3 Bc5 28. g4 Rab8 29. Rh2 d5 30. Ka1 d4 31. Rdh1 Be6 32. Ng3 Bg8 33. Rh6 Qf7 34. Nf5 Q×a2 mate—*Chess Masterpieces*, p. 49.

## (328) Bird–Boden    0–1
Offhand game
London (Simpson's Divan) (?)
C58

1. e4 e5 2. Nf3 Nc6 3. Bc4 Nf6 4. Ng5 d5 5. e×d5 Na5 6. d3 h6 7. Nf3 e4 8. Qe2 N×c4 9. d×c4 Bc5 10. h3 0–0 11. Nfd2 Re8 12. Nb3 e3 13. B×e3 B×e3 14. f×e3 Ne4 15. 0–0 Ng3 16. Qf3 N×f1 17. e4 Qg5 18. K×f1 f5 19. Nc3 f×e4 20. N×e4 Qe5 21. Nf2 Rf8 22. Qe2 Qh2 23. Qe4 B×h3 and Black wins—*Chess Masterpieces*, p. 50.

## (329) Boden–Bird    0–1
Offhand game
London (Simpson's Divan) (?)
C44

1. e4 e5 2. Nf3 Nc6 3. c3 d5 4. Bb5 d×e4 5. N×e5 Qd5 6. Qa4 Nge7 7. d4 e×d3 *e.p.* 8. Bf4 Q×g2 9. Rf1 Bh3 10. Nd2 0–0–0 11. N×f7 Qg4 12. Qe4 B×f1 13. N×d8 Be2 14. Qe6† K×d8 15. Q×g4 B×g4 16. B×d3 Nd5 17. Bg5† Be7 18. B×e7† K×e7 White resigns—*Chess Masterpieces*, pp. 50–51.

## (330) Boden–Bird   0–1

Offhand game
London (Simpson's Divan) (?)
C31

1. e4 e5 2. f4 d5 3. e×d5 e4 4. c4 Nf6 5. d4 e×d3 *e.p.* 6. Be3 Bb4† 7. Nc3 0–0 8. Q×d3 g6 9. 0–0–0 Bf5 10. Qd4 c5 11. d×c6 *e.p.* N×c6 12. Q×d8 Ra×d8 13. Nd5 Ng4 14. h3 R×d5 15. h×g4 R×d1† 16. K×d1 B×g4† 17. Be2 Bf5 18. a3 Rd8† 19. Kc1 Na5 20. Bd1 N×c4 21. a×b4 N×e3 22. Bf3 Rc8† 23. Kd2 N×g2 and White resigns—*Illustrated London News*, 31 March 1877.

## (331) Bird–Boden   0–1

Offhand game
London (Simpson's Divan) (?)
C50

1. e4 e5 2. Nf3 Nc6 3. Bc4 f5 4. d4 f×e4 5. N×e5 N×e5 6. d×e5 d6 7. 0–0 Bf5 8. B×g8 R×g8 9. Qd5 Rh8 10. e×d6 Qf6 11. Q×b7 Rc8 12. Qc6† Kf7 13. Qc4† Kg6 14. d7 Rd8 15. Q×c7 Bd6 16. Qc3 Be5 17. Qe3 R×d7 18. Nc3 Qh4 19. g3 Qh3 20. N×e4 h6 21. Re1 Re8 22. Nc3 Kh7 23. Bd2 Rd4 24. Re2 Rh4 25. f4 B×f4 26. Q×e8 B×g3 27. h×g3 Qh1† 28. Kf2 Qh2† 29. Kf3 Bg4† 30. Ke4 Q×g3 and White resigns—*Illustrated London News*, 31 March 1877.

## (332) Bird–Boden   1–0

Offhand game
London (Simpson's Divan) (?)
C51

1. e4 Two fragments in which Bird played 1. f4 against Boden are preserved. One game continued with 1. ... e5 2. f×e5 d6 3. e×d6 B×d6 4. Nf3 Bg4 5. d4 Nc6 6. Bg5 Qd7 7. Be3 0–0–0 8. Bf2 Nb4 9. Nbd2 Nd5 10. a3 Nf4 and Bird ultimately won (*Chess Practice*, p. 78). In a second game, played in 1873, Boden varied with 6. ... f6 7. Be3 Qe7 8. Bf2 0–0–0 9. Nbd2 Nb4 10. a3 Nd5 11. c4 Nf4 12. e3 (*Chess Openings*, pp. 165–166). 1. ... e5 2. Nf3 Nc6 3. Bc4 Bc5 4. b4 Bb6 5. 0–0 d6 6. c3 Nf6 7. d4 e×d4 8. c×d4 Bg4 9. Bb2 0–0 10. b5 Ne7 11. Nbd2 d5 12. e×d5 Ne×d5 13. Qb3 c6 14. Ne5 Bd7 15. Kh1 h6 16. a4 Ba5 17. Ndf3 Re8 18. N×d7 Q×d7 19. Ne5 Qe6 20. f4 Rad8 21. f5 Qc8 22. Rac1 c5 23. B×d5 R×d5 24. R×c5 Qd8 25. R×d5 Q×d5 26. Q×d5 N×d5 27. Rc1 f6 28. Ng6 Kf7 29. g4 Bb6 30. Bc3 Rc8 31. Bd2 R×c1† 32. B×c1 B×d4 the remainder of the game was not recorded, but it was eventually won by White—*Illustrated London News*, 21 July 1877.

## (333) Boden–Bird   1–0

Offhand game
London (Simpson's Divan) (?)
C20

1. a3 e5 2. e4 Nc6 3. Bc4 f5 4. Nc3 Nf6 5. d3 Bc5 6. Nf3 d6 7. b4 Bd4 8. N×d4 e×d4 9. Ne2 f×e4 10. d×e4 N×e4 11. Bd5 Nc3 12. N×c3 d×c3 13. 0–0 Ne7 14. Re1 c6 15. Bb3 Kd7 16. Bg5 Re8 17. Q×d6† K×d6 18. Bf4† Kd7 19. Be6 mate—*Illustrated London News*, 21 July 1877.

## (334) MacDonnell–Bird   1–0

Offhand game
London (Simpson's Divan) 1872
C37

1. e4 e5 2. f4 e×f4 3. Nf3 g5 4. Bc4 g4 5. 0–0 g×f3 6. Q×f3 Qf6 7. e5 Q×e5 8. d3 Bh6 9. Nc3 Ne7 10. Bd2 Nbc6 11. Rae1 Qc5† 12. Kh1 Ne5 13. Qh5 Bg7 14. B×f4 d6 15. B×e5 B×e5 16. R×f7 Kd8 17. R×e7 K×e7 18. Qf7† Kd8 19. Nd5 Re8 20. Bb5 Black resigns—*Westminster Chess Club Papers*, January 1873, p. 139.

## (335) MacDonnell–Bird   1–0

Offhand game
London (Simpson's Divan) 1872 (?)
C37

1. e4 e5 2. f4 e×f4 3. Nf3 g5 4. Bc4 g4 5. 0–0 g×f3 6. Q×f3 Qe7 "This defense to the Muzio, which we believe is invariably adopted by Bird, was brought into notice by Kling and Horwitz, who published an analysis of it in their admirable book on endgames. This analysis was entitled *The defeat of the Muzio Gambit*, but it proved that this formidable opening was not to be so easily disposed of. The inventors had, as not unfrequently happens, overlooked the proper move. 6. ... Qe7 is bad, and ought to lose the game. The best defense is 6. ... Qf6 7. e5 Q×e5 8. d3 Bh6"—Wisker. 7. d4 Nc6 8. B×f4 N×d4 9. Qd3 Bg7 10. B×c7 Nh6 A successful defense is possible after 10. ... d5!—e.g., 11. Qg3 Qc5 12. Rf2 Bf6. 11. e5 Qc5?? 11. ... N4f5! still gives him the much better game. 12. Bd6 Qb6 "The queen is now shut out, as well as the rest of Black's pieces"—Wisker. 13. Kh1 Nhf5 14. Nc3 14. R×f5 wins at once. MacDonnell is aiming to execute a nice combination. 14. ... Q×b2 (*see diagram*) More care is needed after 14. ... N×d6, when White wins as follows: 15. Nd5 Qc5 16. e×d6 Q×d6 17. Qe4† Ne6 and 18. Rad1.

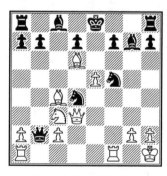

*After 14. ... Q×b2*

15. B×f7†! Kd8 16. Q×d4! N×d4 17. Nd5 Black resigns—*Westminster Chess Club Papers* (Wisker), February 1873, p. 154.

The two games above were reprinted in *The Sportsman* in June 1875. Hence the following game was probably played around the same time.

## (336) MacDonnell–Bird   0–1

Offhand game
London (Simpson's Divan) 1872(?)
C39

1. e4 e5 2. f4 e×f4 3. Nf3 g5 4. h4 g4 5. Ne5 d6 6. N×g4 f5 7. e×f5 B×f5 8. d4 Qe7† 9. Kf2 B×g4 10. Q×g4 Nf6 11. Q×f4

Bh6 **12. Qf5 B×c1 13. Bb5† c6 14. Re1 Ng4† 15. Kf3 Q×e1 16. Qc8† Ke7 17. Q×h8 Nh2** mate—*The Sportsman*, 19 June 1875.

## (337) MacDonnell–Bird   0–1
Offhand game
London (Simpson's Divan) 1874
C39

**1. e4 e5 2. f4 e×f4 3. Nf3 g5 4. h4 g4 5. Ne5 h5** "Mr. Bird retains his preference for this defense, which indeed by no means merits the whole-sale condemnation which has been passed upon it by recent writers"—Wisker. The intriguing Long Whip Variation. It gained a certain popularity during the 1850s. Bird was one of the few who kept on using this line throughout his career. **6. Bc4 Nh6** A better alternative is 6. ... Rh7, but Bird was an adherent of the text move. **7. d4 d6 8. Nd3 f3 9. g3?** The usual move at this point is 9. g×f3, for the opening of lines and diagonals is beneficial for White. **9. ... f5** "Properly this advance must be very prejudicial to Black's game. It exposes the king, whilst it enables White to develop his pieces more rapidly. Black's best move at this point is a moot question. 9. ... Nc6 cannot be bad. 9. ... d5 has been dismissed on account of 10. e×d5, but it has never been properly examined"—Wisker. An interesting but speculative move. Solid and very strong is simply 9. ... c6! **10. Nc3** With the pawn chain tethered to Black's advantage, it deserved preference to continue the strategy of keeping the position closed, by playing 10. e5. **10. ... f×e4 11. N×e4 Nf5!** "If 11. ... d5 12. B×d5"—Wisker. **12. Kf2 Be7?!** As MacDonnell's king is relatively exposed at f2, 12. ... d5! becomes very strong. The point is that after 13. B×d5 Bg7! (covering f6 and thus threatening 13. ... Q×d5) 14. Qe1 B×d4† 15. Kf1 Kf8!, White's king won't find any safe haven. **13. Nf4** The direct danger has been averted, and an unclear position resolved. **13. ... Rh7?** Slow and useless. At least after 13. ... Rf8 the rook fulfills a defensive purpose in covering f6. Also worth considering is 13. ... b5!, gaining some precious time and space for the king in case of 14. B×b5† c6 15. Bd3 Qc7. **14. Ng6??** "White has now the better position, but this move doesn't improve it. He should have occupied the e-file with his rook. Black's game would then have become exceedingly difficult"—Wisker. 14. Re1! Kf8 15. Ng6† Kg7 16. N×e7 Q×e7 17. Bg5 illustrates the point. **14. ... d5 15. N×e7 d×e4!** "White apparently didn't expect this move"—Wisker. **16. Nd5 Be6** "The tide now turns. Nevertheless, but for the brilliant combination Black now commences, he would have fallen into trouble again"—Wisker. **17. Bg5** (see diagram)

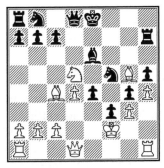

*After 17. Bg5*

**17. ... B×d5!! 18. B×d8** 18. Bb5†! is a good try to disturb the opponent, but in nearly all lines Black's pawn mass proves too strong to withstand. In case of 18. ... c6 19. B×d8 K×d8 20. Bd3, 20. ... e3†! advances without mercy. White is lost. Quite similar is 18. ... Nd7 19. B×d8 K×d8!, a sample line going as follows: 20. Re1 Re7 21. Re3 (White is also lost after 21. Kg1 c6 22. Bf1 e3 23. Kh2 f2 24. Re2 Kc7) 21. ... N×e3 22. K×e3 Nb6 23. b3 Bg8 24. c4 c6 25. Ba4 B×c4! 26. b×c4 N×c4† 27. Kf2 e3† 28. Kg1 f2†. Here 19. ... e3†?! Would have been badly timed for after 20. Kg1 K×d8 21. Qd3! makes good use of the premature push of the e-pawn. **18. ... e3† 19. Kg1** "There is no more favorable square. 19. Ke1 would prove still more disastrous, on account of 19. ... f2† and 20. ... B×c4†"—Wisker. **19. ... B×c4 20. Bg5 f2† 21. Kh2 e2 22. Qd2** (see diagram)

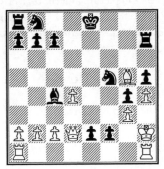

*After 22. Qd2*

**22. ... f1N†?!** Bird's next two moves are impressive, and bestow upon the game a touch of immortality, but waiting one move and playing 22. ... Nc6! first avoids any complications. White is completely helpless, and after, for example, 23. c3 f1N† 24. Rh×f1 e×f1N† 25. R×f1 B×f1 26. Qe1† Nce7 27. Q×f1 0–0–0 Black wins. **23. Rh×f1 e×f1N†** "A manoeuvre of this kind probably never before occurred in actual play"—Wisker. **24. R×f1 B×f1 25. Qe1† Ne7 26. Q×f1?** Here MacDonnell misses a hidden resource that would have drawn the game in an elegant fashion: 26. Qe4! Rf7 27. B×e7 R×e7 28. Q×b7 Ba6 29. Q×a8 Re2† with a perpetual check. **26. ... Nbc6 27. d5 Rf7 28. Qc4** "If 28. Qb5, hoping to win the knight, the attack of the two rooks becomes irresistible"—Wisker. **28. ... Ne5 29. Q×c7 Nf3† 30. Kg2 Rc8 31. Qa5 R×c2† 32. Kf1 N×g5† 33. Ke1 Nf3† 34. Kd1 Rd2† 35. Kc1 N×d5 36. a3 Rc7† 37. Kb1 Nc3†!** "The shortest way. After Black's 38th move mate can be warded off only by the sacrifice of the queen"—Wisker. **38. b×c3 Re7** and Black wins—*Land and Water* (Wisker), 21 March 1874.

## (338) Bird–MacDonnell   0–1
Offhand game
London (Simpson's Divan), March 1874
C77

**1. e4 e5 2. Nf3 Nc6 3. Bb5 a6 4. Ba4 Nf6 5. Qe2 Be7 6. 0–0 b5 7. Bb3 0–0 8. a4 b4 9. Bd5** "From this injudicious attempt to win a pawn we may date the commencement of all White's subsequent difficulties. He ought rather to have played 9. d3"—Wormald. **9. ... N×d5 10. e×d5 Nd4 11. N×d4 e×d4 12. Qc4?!** Continuing his plan to pick up a pawn is very doubtful, but Black is also better after 12. d3 Bb7 13. Qf3 a5, planning 14. ... Ra6. **12. ... c5! 13. d×c6 e.p. d×c6 14. Q×c6 Rb8 15. d3?!** 15. Qf3 can be met by 15. ... d3! After the text move Bird succumbs to a direct attack. **15. ... Bb7 16. Qc4 Rc8 17. Qa2 Bd5 18. b3** (see diagram)

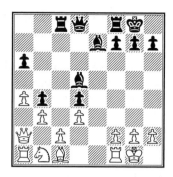

After 18. b3

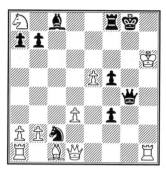

After 22. Kh6

A very sad picture indeed. **18. ... Bd6 19. Qb2 Qh4 20. f4 Qg4 21. Rf2 Rfe8 22. Nd2 Re1† 23. Nf1 R×f1†** and Black mates next move—*Illustrated Sporting and Dramatic News* (Wormald), 4 April 1874.

### (339) Bird–MacDonnell    0–1
Offhand game
London (Simpson's Divan) 1875
C51

According to *Chess Masterpieces* (p. 51), MacDonnell played with the White and Bird with the Black pieces.

**1. e4 e5 2. Nf3 Nc6 3. Bc4 Bc5 4. b4 B×b4 5. c3 Bc5 6. 0–0 d6 7. d4 e×d4 8. c×d4 Bb6 9. Bb5 Kf8 10. B×c6 b×c6 11. Nc3 Bg4 12. Be3 Ne7 13. Ne2 Qd7 14. Qb3 Qe6 15. Qc2 B×f3 16. g×f3 Re8 17. Ng3 h5 18. Kh1 h4 19. Ne2 Qh3 20. Ng1 Qd7 21. f4 c5 22. d×c5 Qc6 23. f3 Nf5 24. Qb3 N×e3 25. Q×e3 B×c5 26. Qc3 Rh6 27. Ne2 Rg6 28. f5 Rf6 29. Nf4 Re5 30. Rad1 Qa4 31. Nd5 Rh6 32. N×c7 Kg8 33. Nd5 h3 34. Rg1 Kh7 35. Rde1 f6 36. Rg4 Q×a2 37. Nc7 Qf2 38. Ne6 R×e6 39. f×e6 Rg6 40. f4** Black mates in two moves—*Liverpool Weekly Albion*, 22 May 1875.

### (340) MacDonnell–Bird    0–1
Offhand game
London (Simpson's Divan) 1875
C35

**1. e4 e5 2. f4 e×f4 3. Nf3 Be7** "The 'books' condemn this defense with edifying unanimity, but it is an especial favorite with Mr. Bird, who has adopted it successfully against some of the best players of the day"—Wormald. **4. Bc4 Bh4† 5. Kf1 d5 6. B×d5 Nf6 7. Nc3 0–0 8. N×h4 N×d5 9. N×d5 Q×h4 10. N×c7?** MacDonnell accepts the challenge, but thereby forsakes his development. **10. ... Nc6 11. N×a8 Nd4!** 12. d3 There is nothing to be done against Bird's idea of playing 12. ... Bg4 and 13. ... Be2†; 12. Qe1 is perhaps more tenacious, but Black's task is not so difficult, as the principal moves remain the same in all variations: 12. ... Qh5 13. d3 (or 13. h3 f3! 14. Qf2 f×g2† 15. K×g2 and now 15. ... f5 launches a fearsome attack; e.g., 16. e5 b5) 13. ... f3! 14. Qe3 f5! Easier to deal with are 12. c3 Bg4 13. Qe1 Be2† or 12. h3 f3! **12. ... f3** The direct 12. ... Bg4! is perhaps stronger. **13. g3** 13. Rg1 loses to the same idea: 13. ... f2 14. Rh1 Bg4. A less prosaic finish occurs after 14. Be3 f×g1Q† 15. K×g1 Bg4, followed by 16. ... Ne2† and 17. ... R×a8. **13. ... Qh3† 14. Kf2** Out for a walk. **14. ... Qg2† 15. Ke3 N×c2† 16. Kf4 f5 17. e5 h6 18. h4 g5† 19. h×g5 h×g5† 20. K×g5 Q×g3† 21. Kh5 Qg4† 22. Kh6** (see diagram)

**22. ... Kf7** and Black wins—*Illustrated London News* (Wormald), 14 August 1875.

### (341) MacDonnell–Bird    1–0
Offhand game
London (Simpson's Divan) 1875
C39

**1. e4 e5 2. f4 e×f4 3. Nf3 g5 4. h4 g4 5. Ne5 h5 6. Bc4 Nh6 7. d4 d6 8. Nd3 f3 9. g×f3 Be7 10. Be3 B×h4† 11. Kd2 g×f3 12. Q×f3 Bg4 13. Qf4 Nc6 14. Nc3 N×d4 15. B×d4 Bg5 16. B×h8 B×f4† 17. N×f4 Qg5 18. Ncd5 Ng8 19. Rag1 Qh6 20. R×g4** Black resigns—*Illustrated London News*, 14 August 1875.

The following game was published a decade after Bird's death in a series "Gems from the masters." The present author could not retrieve it in any contemporary source, nor could any information be found about when the game had been played. It is assumed the game was played in London.

### (342) MacDonnell–Bird    1–0
Offhand game
London (Simpson's Divan) 1875 (?)
C39

**1. e4 e5 2. Nf3 Nc6 3. d4 e×d4 4. Bc4 Bc5 5. Ng5 Nh6 6. Qh5 Ne5 7. Ne6 Qe7 8. Bg5 Qd6 9. N×g7† Kf8 10. B×h6 Kg8 11. Ne8 Qg6** and White mates in two—*Manchester City News*, 14 September 1918.

### (343) Hoffer–Bird    1–0
Offhand game
London (Simpson's Divan) 1874
C51

**1. e4 e5 2. Nf3 Nc6 3. Bc4 Bc5 4. b4 B×b4 5. c3 Bc5 6. 0–0 d6 7. d4 e×d4 8. c×d4 Bb6 9. d5 Na5 10. Bb2 Ne7 11. Bd3 0–0 12. Nc3 Bg4 13. Ne2 Ng6 14. Qd2 B×f3 15. g×f3 Nh4 16. Qf4 h6 17. Kh1 Qg5 18. Rg1 Q×f4 19. R×g7† Kh8 20. Rg4† Qe5 21. B×e5† d×e5 22. R×h4 Kh7 23. Kg2 Rg8† 24. Kf1 c5 25. Rc1 Rac8 26. Rh3 c4 27. Bb1 c3 28. R×c3 Nc4 29. Rd3 Ba5 30. f4 f6 31. f×e5 f×e5 32. Rh5 Kg6 33. Rf5 Rge8 34. Rg3† Kh7 35. Rf7† Kh8 36. Bd3 Nd2† 37. Kg2 a6 38. Nd4 e×d4 39. e5 Rc7 40. Rf6 Rg7 41. R×h6† Kg8 42. Bh7† Kf8 43. Rf6† Rf7 44. Rg8† Ke7 45. d6† Kd8 46. R×e8† K×e8 47. Bg6** Black resigns—*Westminster Chess Club Papers*, June 1874, pp. 29–30.

# ◆ Part VI ◆

# THE NEW WORLD, 1875–1877

## INTRODUCTION

Bird embarked on the *Java* in Liverpool on 27 November 1875. The why and how of his sudden departure was hardly addressed by the British press (the *City of London Chess Magazine* [January 1876, p. 354] suggested that the Divan tournament could be postponed "as he [Bird] may be back again in the early part of the year") but his arrival in New York received attention from the Americans. They informed their readers that Bird intended to stay for about a month, and look into the prospects of the coming chess congress.

Since 1873, plans were afoot to celebrate the 100th anniversary of the independence of the United States with a major chess tournament. Given the city's historical role, this event would take place in Philadelphia. The organizers had great ambition for they wanted European masters to cross the Atlantic and play on American soil for the first time in history. These plans raised the interest of the European chess community but the lack of concrete measures despite years of waiting muffled the initial enthusiasm.

Bird planned a flying visit to the two foremost chess centers on the East Coast, to enjoy a week or two in New York and then travel to Philadelphia, thence to Europe. He would come back to Philadelphia the next summer with all the European greats in his wake. It remains unclear if Bird made this early trip completely on his own or whether his fellows in London rendered him support.

Bird's planned short stay of a month ultimately extended to two years. Clearly other motives induced him to prolong his sojourn again and again. He lingered in New York for nearly two months before he reached Philadelphia. Then his departure for Europe was announced about a dozen times but each time postponed.

Bird was not tied to any obligations whatever in London. Perhaps financial problems concerning his bankruptcy kept him in New York, or he may have found it difficult to get enough accounting work in London to live his life of chess. Upon his arrival in the States he received a few lucrative offers from chess clubs; later he settled at the Café International and played incessantly. His dedication to chess during nearly the whole of 1876 is a clear sign that he was a professional chessplayer, for the first time in his life.

Bird was received with a genuine enthusiasm but this fell off quickly once he became involved in various disputes with other chess players and tournament organizers. Bird dedicated a lot of ink to his grumbles about the tournament held during the spring at the Café International and to the misrepresentation of his score in the newspapers. Tensions increased until the Clipper tournament, held September and October, proved to be the point of no return.

Bird was on his way to winning a first important event when, in all likelihood, a combination was formed against him. Dubious behavior by some fellow competitors cost him the first, and even second prize. Bird felt severely let down and demoralized. He even refrained from bringing the case to the public (many others did this for him), and instead reacted by breaking radically with the professional chess community.

At the end of 1876 Bird found a job in Brooklyn. During his second year in New York he kept on playing chess but only in the company of amateurs of the game. He thoroughly enjoyed a successful stay in Canada and visited some chess clubs in New York. Bird remained distant from the Café International, the gathering place of the professionals. As Fraser put it in a 20 February 1878 letter to White: "I don't think after his American experience of professionalism that he will continue to try longer to earn his livelihood by it."

Bird returned to England at the end of 1877. His motives remain somewhat obscured but some hints have been found that he had opportunities to resume his accountancy work in London.

With Bird leaving the United States, the first visit of a strong European chess player came to an end. Though Bird left with many good chess friends made, the aftertaste was somewhat bitter after the many quarrels that characterized his stay. Bird's results did not fulfill high expectations. The hugely underestimated top Americans, notably Mackenzie and Mason, actually leaned towards the absolute top of the world and they easily confirmed their strength against the over-optimistic Englishman.

## THE NEW CHESS LION ARRIVES

Bird arrived in the port of New York on 8 December 1875. He was received warm-heartedly and his presence was noticed in all the chess columns. (The text of the most interesting article is reproduced in full in Appendix 2: Documents about and by Bird.)

Bird intended to move quickly to Philadelphia but his plans were crossed by the opportunity of heavy chess playing, an irresistible temptation for a fanatic like Bird. His first opponent on American soil was Isaac Rice.[1] Bird started slowly but he ended the series of games with a comfortable win. Each game was for a small stake.

On 11 December Bird accepted the invitation of the Brooklyn

---

1. Rice, in later years a successful businessman, became president of the Manhattan Chess Club. He discovered a variation in the King's Gambit, which became known as the Rice Gambit. Around the turn of the century he sponsored numerous chess tournaments in which this opening was mandatory.

Chess Club to visit their rooms. He impressed the crowd by offering the following amusing finish. His opponent was one of the veteran members of the club.

### (344) Perrin–Bird    0–1
Offhand game
New York (Brooklyn C.C.), 11 December 1875
C33

**1. e4 e5 2. f4 e×f4 3. Bc4 Qh4† 4. Kf1 g5 5. d4 Bg7 6. Nc3 Ne7 7. Nf3** "7. g3 may also be played here, and is preferred by Lange to the text move"—Mackenzie. **7. ... Qh5 8. h4 h6 9. Kg1 g4 10. Ne1 f3 11. g×f3 g×f3 12. N×f3 d6 13. Kf2 Nbc6 14. Be3?** An evident move, but the subsequent pin is extremely annoying. Better options are the quiet 14. Ne2; e.g., 14. ... Rg8 15. Nf4 Qa5 16. Rg1 or 14. Nb5, which leads to complications in case of 14. ... Bg4 15. N×c7† Kd8 16. N×a8 B×d4†. **14. ... Bg4 15. Be2** (see diagram)

After 15. Be2

**15. ... f5!** "Black has well developed his game, and now proceeds with the attack in good style"—Zukertort. **16. e5** "Not satisfactory, but there is hardly anything better; if 16. Qd3 then 16. ... f×e4 17. N×e4 0–0 18. Ned2 Nf5 etc."—Zukertort. **16. ... d×e5 17. d×e5 Rd8 18. Qg1 B×e5 19. N×e5 B×e2** Bird has prosecuted the game with care and is now winning. The text move gives his opponent a single chance to mix up things a bit with 20. Qg7!?, although Black remains firmly on top after 20. ... Rg8 21. N×e2 R×g7 22. Nf4 N×e5! 23. N×h5 Ng4†. All this was easy to avoid with 19. ... N×e5! **20. N×e2** "White dare not play to keep the piece; e.g., 20. N×c6 Rg8 21. Qh2 Qf3† 22. Ke1 Ba6 23. Bc5 (of 23. Bf2) 23. ... Rg2 wins"—Zukertort. **20. ... N×e5 21. Qg3 Ng4† 22. Ke1 Nd5 23. Bd4 0–0 24. c4 f4 25. Qf3 Nde3 26. Rc1 c5 27. Bc3 Rd7**

**28. Bd2** "To resign was certainly the wisest course, but as White chose to proceed with the game, he may as well break the attack by sacrificing the exchange: 25. Q×g4† and 26. Rg1"—Zukertort. **28. ... Ne5!** and Black wins. "A beautiful move, winning the queen or checkmating as White may elect"—Mackenzie. *Turf, Field and Farm* (Mackenzie), 24 December 1875; *Westminster Chess Club Papers* (Zukertort), March 1876, p. 224.

On the following day Bird was received at the Café International. This café was the chess heart of New York. Bird remained for a week to demonstrate his chess powers.[2] Bird encountered George Henry Mackenzie on his first day. A confrontation was eagerly anticipated. Mackenzie's superiority in the States had been beyond doubt since his double victory in the American congresses of 1871 and 1874.[3]

Bird and Mackenzie played a set of three games. Bird has painted a very rosy picture of his powers; see for example the large article in the *New York Sun* in Appendix 2, where he claimed that only Steinitz had a positive score against him, thus it surprised everybody when Mackenzie succeeded in beating his illustrious opponent 2 wins to 1. The press came a bit to the rescue of Bird's nearly invincible reputation by mentioning that the score was a bit flattering for Mackenzie as he made excellent use of Bird's optimistic refusal to draw the final game.

### (345) Bird–Mackenzie    0–1
Offhand game
New York (Café International), 12 December 1875
C77

**1. e4 e5 2. Nf3 Nc6 3. Bb5 a6 4. Ba4 Nf6 5. Qe2 b5 6. Bb3 Bc5 7. d3 d6 8. a4 b4 9. 0–0 0–0 10. Bg5 Bg4 11. Be3 Qe7 12. Nbd2 Nd4 13. B×d4 B×d4 14. Rab1 Nh5 15. Qe1 Ba7 16. Kh1 Nf4 17. Ng1 Kh8 18. f3 Be6 19. Ne2 N×e2 20. Q×e2 B×b3 21. N×b3 f5** Probably an oversight, but a happy side effect of the subsequent pawn loss is that Bird's king goes under fire. **22. e×f5 R×f5 23. Qe4 Raf8 24. Q×b4 Rh5 25. Rbe1 Qg5 26. Qg4 Qh6 27. h3 Rg5?** 27. ... Rh4 demands care from his opponent. After 28. Qd7 Be3! 29. Re2 Bf4 30. Rff2 a standstill is reached. A perpetual arises after 30. ... Bg3 31. Rf1 Bf4 32. Q×c7 R×h3†, while 30. ... Qg5? is bad after 31. Nd2! **28. Qe4?!** At this point, Black is completely unable to deal adequately with 28. Qd7,

2. A vivid portrait of the café was written in 1877 by John G. Belden. These lines make it very clear how the initially favorable opinion of the American players on Bird had been troubled by experience: "This celebrated resort—the Mecca of American chessers—now occupies the basement and first floor of the large building, No. 294 Bowery, New York. The basement is used mainly as a billiard-room, and the front of the ground floor as a restaurant, but it is with the space in the rear of the latter that we have to do. Here are located the chess tables, some thirty in number, under the supervision of Captain Mackenzie, assisted by Messrs. Mason and Becker. The charge for the use of the boards and men is ten cents per day, but the habitués, of course, prefer to 'commute' at the rate of $1 per month. No charge is made for those who do not play, but come merely as spectators. Everything is here subordinated to chess. Conversation is carried on in subdued tones, over-excited individuals are promptly squelched, even dishes seem to clink more softly, and Caissa reigns supreme, worshipped by as faithful devotees as are any goddess of old could boast. Here may generally be found a greater number of the magnates of the game than anywhere else in this country, Mackenzie and Mason, who have yet to settle which is the better player, and at the same time decide the championship of America. The former, a stout genial gentleman, of commanding presence, with full blonde beard and moustache; the latter slight and young looking (he is young, but older than he appears), smooth face: as great a contrast, these two, as could well be found. Bird, portly, almost fat, with a fringe of soft, fluffy, light whiskers about his face, but quite destitute of capillary adornment 'on the top of his head, in the place,' &c Few, very few, are the men who have played as much and as well as he, but he has not been very successful of late, and this has perhaps soured his temper somewhat, for he is perpetually at loggerheads with somebody or something, and perpetually writing letters to the papers complaining of unfair treatment, after the manner of Englishman in general. Ensor, Delmar, and Becker, strong players all three, and well known by reputation throughout chessdom. Perrin, the veteran, and Gilberg, the problemist, who occasionally come over from Brooklyn for a friendly tilt. Stanley, once champion of America, now a mere wreck of his former self, still occasionally striking out some combination that shows traces of his old power. In short, all the strongest players of the vicinity may be found here; and chessers from other places, when visiting this city, invariably make their objective point, and Mr. Lieders, the proprietor, spares no effort to make such visits pleasant and enjoyable." *Hartford Weekly Times*, 7 October 1876.

3. Both in Cleveland and in Chicago Henry Hosmer was the sole player who seemed able to challenge Mackenzie's superiority. Mason did not take part in these tournaments.

or if 28. ... Rh5 29. d4! wins. **28. ... c6
29. f4! Rh5 30. Qf3** The endgame would
be untenable for his opponent after
30. Rf3! e×f4 31. Q×c6 Re5 32. R×e5 d×e5
33. Q×h6 g×h6 34. Nd2. **30. ... d5 31. d4?**
An awful move, especially as Mackenzie's
reply wasn't hard to foresee. Yet, the
winning move is a surprising one: 31. f×e5!
creates an unstoppable e-pawn. Black can
resign at once. **31. ... e4 32. Qg3? Rhf5
33. Qg4?!** This strange dance of the queen
seals Bird's fate. **33. ... g5! 34. g3 g×f4
35. R×f4 R×f4 36. g×f4 R×f4 37. Qc8†
Rf8 38. Qg4 Rg8 39. Qf5 Qg7 40. Qf2
Rf8 41. Qg1 Qf6 42. c3 Bb8 43. Nc5 Qh4
44. Re3 Rg8 45. Qe1 Bg3 46. Qf1 Bf2**
and Black wins—*Canadian Illustrated
News*, 28 July 1879.

Another prominent opponent of Bird
was James Mason, only 26 years old but already a well-known figure in New York
chess circles. With his solid style he was a
very difficult opponent to handle. Since the
late 1860s he had been playing in local tournaments and secured a prize in each of them.

Bird and Mason played a large number social games during Bird's
first week at the Café International. Each was contested for a small
stake. The *New York Herald* closely followed their encounters. On
19 December they reported that Bird crushed his opponent by winning 7 out of 8 games. During the following days the score leveled
out a bit but Bird won the majority of games with a proportion of
more than two to one.[4] His results must have boosted Bird's confidence and undoubtedly he estimated his own powers superior to
those of Mason. Hence it came as a huge surprise to most when
Mason decisively beat him in a straight match around the turn of
the year. Many reasons have been put forward to explain Bird's failure, such as his suffering from the gout and the slower time limit.
It seems nevertheless that in these skittles games, out of which Bird
derived a majority of wins, Mason did not insist on getting a decent
result and that he saved his real power for the match and the purse
that accompanied it.

**(346) Mason–Bird    0–1**
Offhand game
New York (Café International), 13 December 1875
C61

1. e4 e5 2. Nf3 Nc6 3. Bb5 Nd4 4. N×d4 e×d4 5. d3 Bc5
6. Qh5 Qe7 7. Bg5 Nf6 8. Qh4 c6 9. Ba4 d5 10. 0–0 d×e4

4. The *New York Herald* wrote on 6 January 1876, the day after the termination
of the match between Bird and Mason: "Of a large number of offhand games
played with Mr. Mason prior to the match Mr. Bird had won a majority of twelve;
but those who knew the New York player best were satisfied that he had not done
justice to his powers in the games mentioned, and that in a set match his determination and fertility in resource would render his chances very good, even against
such an acknowledged expert as Mr. Bird." *New York Herald*, 6 January 1876.

Bird (right), shortly after his arrival in New York. Opposing him is George H. Mackenzie (*New York Daily Graphic*); the board is set up wrong.

**11. d×e4 Bd7 12. Nd2 0–0–0 13. Rfe1 h6 14. B×f6 g×f6 15. a3
Rhg8 16. b4 Bb6 17. e5** "A showy advance. It must lead to an exchange of pawns, which will clearly improve Black's position"—
Zukertort. **17. ... Rg6 18. Nc4 Bc7 19. Bb3 Be6 20. Rad1 b5** Reckless play from Bird. **21. Na5 B×a5 22. b×a5** (*see diagram*)

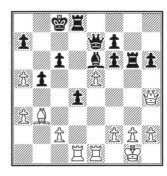

*After 22. b×a5*

**22. ... Bg4?!** This move only activates his opponent's rook. After
22. ... c5 23. e×f6 Q×f6 24. Qe4 Kc7 25. B×e6, Black's position is
a bit loose, but that's it. **23. Rd3 Rd7?! 24. f3?** Bird's last move was
rather clumsy. Mason missed the pointed 24. Rg3! h5 (or 24. ... Bf5
25. Qf4 R×g3 26. h×g3 Bh7 27. Q×h6) 25. e6 f×e6 26. h3 to
demonstrate this. **24. ... Bf5 25. e×f6?!** "25. R×d4 was better. The
move in the text leaves the opponent with four united pawns on
the queenside, which must carry the contest"—Zukertort. 25. R×d4?
loses on the spot after 25. ... Qc5. Better is 25. Rd2, with an equal
endgame arising after 25. ... f×e5 26. Q×e7 R×e7 27. R×d4. **25. ...
Q×f6 26. Re8† Kb7 27. Q×f6 R×f6 28. Rd2 c5 29. Re5 Kc6
30. a4 a6 31. g4 Bg6 32. Rf2?** Allowing Bird the ensuing pawn phalanx is equal to resignation. Though ugly, 32. a×b5 a×b5 33. c4 had
to be tried. **32. ... c4** According to the original score, writes Zukertort, the move order was 32. ... Re6 33. R×e6 f×e6 34. f4 c4 35. Ba2

Kc5. This is in all likelihood incorrect. **33. Ba2 Re6 34. R×e6 f×e6 35. f4 Kc5 36. h4 Kb4 37. a×b5 a×b5 38. h5 Be8 39. Kf1 Ra7 40. c3† K×c3 41. Bb1 d3** White resigns. "Mr. Bird conducts this game all through in good and steady style. He shows skill and judgment vastly superior to that displayed in the match games with the same opponent"—Zukertort. *Westminster Chess Club Papers* (Zukertort), March 1876, pp. 223–224.

### (347) Mason–Bird    1–0
Offhand game
New York (Café International), December 1875
C30

**1. e4 e5 2. Nc3 Bc5 3. f4 d6 4. Nf3 Bg4 5. Bc4 Nc6 6. Bb5 Nge7 7. d3 0–0 8. B×c6 N×c6 9. Na4 e×f4 10. N×c5 d×c5 11. 0–0 f5 12. c3 f×e4 13. Qb3† Kh8 14. d×e4 B×f3 15. R×f3 Qh4 16. B×f4 R×f4 17. g3 Rg4 18. Qb7 Rd8 19. Q×c6 Qe7 20. Re1 h5 21. e5 h4 22. Rf4 R×f4 23. g×f4 Rd2 24. Qg6 c4 25. Qh5† Kg8 26. e6 a6 27. a3 c6 28. Kh1 R×b2 29. Rd1 Rb5 30. f5 Rd5 31. Re1 Rd8 32. f6** and White wins. "The coup de grace, for it will be seen on examination that Black is left absolutely without resource. It is but fair to Mr. Bird to state that he has won a majority of the games played with Mr. Mason"—Mackenzie. *Turf, Field and Farm* (Mackenzie), 24 December 1875.

### (348) Mason–Bird    ½–½
Offhand game
New York (Café International), December 1875
C61

"One of the most interesting games recently contested between Messrs. Bird and Mason"—Mason.

**1. e4 e5 2. Nf3 Nc6 3. Bb5 Nd4** "Mr. Bird is the only great player who has faith in the true goodness of this move in the Lopez. He plays it whenever he has a chance and his success with it is remarkable. 3. ... a6 is supposed to be the correct play"—Mason. **4. N×d4 e×d4 5. d3 c6 6. Bc4 h5** "To prevent 7. Qh5. In another partie Mr. Bird played 6. ... Bc5, and after 7. Qh5 Qe7 8. Bg5 Nf6 White had much the better game"—Mason. **7. Nd2 Bc5 8. Nf3 d5 9. e×d5 c×d5 10. Bb5† Kf8** "Not so bad as it looks. White's bishop is in a very uncomfortable situation, as presently appears"—Mason. **11. 0–0 Qa5 12. c4** "The only move to save the piece"—Mason. **12. ... Bg4** "He might have won a pawn; but White would have more than an equivalent in position"—Mason. There is no reason to refrain from playing 12. ... d×c3 *e.p.* **13. Bd2 Qb6 14. Ne5** After 14. h3 Be6 15. Rc1, Black is thrown on the defensive. The text move is relatively innocent. **14. ... Nf6 15. f3 Be6 16. b4 Be7 17. Qe1 h4 18. a4 a6 19. a5 Qc7 20. Bf4 Qd8 21. Ba4 Nh5** 21. ... d×c4 22. d×c4 d3! activates his pieces. **22. Bd2 Bf5 23. Qe2 Bd6 24. Rfe1 Kg8?** By first omitting to exchange at c4, to give his pieces some scope, and now by losing time (instead 24. ... f6 brings some relief), Mason gets the opportunity to draw the tension out of the position and win a pawn with 25. c5! and 26. Qf2. **25. Bb3 g6 26. c×d5 Kg7 27. Qf2 Bb8** *(see diagram)*
**28. Rac1** "Here Mr. Mason fails to make the most of his position. Had he played 28. N×f7, he must have won with ease; e.g., 28. ... K×f7 29. d6† Kf8 30. Re7 Q×d6 31. Rf7† Ke8 32. Re1† Kd8

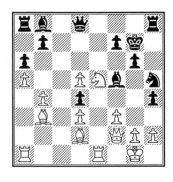

*After 27. ... Bb8*

and wins"—Mason. **28. ... f6 29. Nc4 Nf4 30. B×f4 B×f4 31. Q×d4?** 31. Rcd1 Qc7 32. Q×d4 B×h2† 33. Kh1 consolidates a solid plus. **31. ... B×c1 32. R×c1 Rc8 33. Re1 Re8 34. R×e8 Q×e8 35. Kf2 Rd8 36. Ne3 Qe5 37. N×f5†?!** White has to be careful here. Instead 37. Q×e5 f×e5 38. Ke2 keeps the position closed enough to secure a draw. **37. ... g×f5 38. Q×e5 f×e5 39. Bc4 Kf6 40. Ke3 Rg8 41. Kf2 Rd8 42. Ke3 Rd6** 42. ... f4† 43. Kf2 Ke7 gives excellent winning chances. The king goes to d6 and the rook will support the opening of the b-file. **43. d4** and the game was drawn by mutual consent—*The Spirit of the Times* (Mason), 25 December 1875.

Bird was equally successful against Eugene Delmar, the number three player in New York. The *Buffalo Daily Courier* of 27 December gave a result that is very difficult to decipher. Bird won 9 games, Delmar either 5 or 6. Bird also won a great majority of games played against many other opponents. Just a single one of them has been retrieved:

### (349) Bird–J.E. Clarke    1–0
Offhand game
New York (Café International), December 1875
C33

"This game was contested at the Café International shortly after Mr. Bird's arrival in New York"—Mason.

**1. e4 e5 2. f4 e×f4 3. Bc4 Qh4† 4. Kf1 g5 5. Nc3 Bg7 6. d4 d6 7. g3** "This, we believe, is known as McDonnell's Attack, and gives rise to situations of great complexity. 7. Nf3 or 7. e5, leading to the Petrov Attack, appears to us as preferable"—Mason. **7. ... f×g3 8. Kg2 Qg4** "Well played, and the only way to get the queen out of danger without loss of time"—Mason. **9. Be2** Artificial and time-consuming. The endgame after 9. Q×g4 B×g4 10. Nd5 Kd7 11. h×g3 B×d4 12. B×g5 is not so bad. **9. ... Qd7 10. h×g3 g4 11. Be3 Nc6 12. Bb5 a6 13. Ba4 b5 14. Bb3 Bb7** Thanks to Bird's many bishop moves his opponent has coordinated his pieces excellently and can now count on a serious advantage. **15. d5 Ne5 16. Nge2 h5 17. Nd4 Ne7 18. a4 b4 19. Nce2 a5?!** This move opens new perspectives for the White pieces. There would have been little left for him after 19. ... c5! **20. Nf4 h4** "The best way to give up the pawn. White has now a little better game"—Mason. **21. R×h4 R×h4 22. g×h4 N5g6?!** This move allows Bird to take over the initiative. Either 22. ... 0–0–0 or 22. ... Ba6 keep White tied up. **23. h5 N×f4† 24. B×f4 Ng8?!** *(see diagram)* For the second time in three moves, Clark makes a backward move with a knight, giving

Bird the chance to gain more activity with his own pieces. 24. ...
Ba6 is correct, so as to keep White's bishop out of the game.

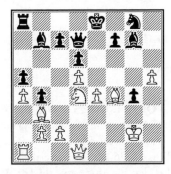

*After 24. ... Ng8*

**25. Nf5! B×b2 26. Rb1** Too slow to upset his opponent. Instead,
26. Bc4! puts Black under serious pressure; e.g., 26. ... Ba6 27. B×a6
R×a6 28. Q×g4 Nf6 29. Qg7 with a dangerous attack. **26. ... Bc3
27. Q×g4 0–0–0** 27. ... Nf6 brings him at least equality. **28. h6
Nf6?!** "This is Mr. Clark's most fatal mistake. 28. ... Kb8, rendering
this check impossible, was the proper move, and had he made it,
his adversary would have found great difficulty in winning"—
Mason. **29. Ne7† Kb8 30. Q×d7 R×d7 31. Nc6† B×c6 32. d×c6
Re7 33. e5! B×e5 34. B×e5 d×e5?** After this capture the game will
soon be over. Much more difficult to beat would have been 34. ...
R×e5, when both 35. Rh1 and 35. B×f7 deserve attention. **35. Rf1
Ng4 36. h7 Re8 37. R×f7 Rh8 38. Rg7 Ka7 39. R×g4 R×h7
40. Rg6 Re7 41. Re6 Rg7† 42. Kf3 Rg5 43. Ke4 Kb6 44. R×e5
R×e5† 45. K×e5** and Black soon resigned—*The Spirit of the Times*
(Mason), 1 January 1876.

# MATCH WITH ALBERONI 1875

Having met nearly every player of note in New York Bird finally
intended to gather his packs and move further to Philadelphia. But
his plans were interrupted by the arrival of another, equally zealous,
worshipper of Caissa: Edward Alberoni.

The elusive Alberoni, of Italian or French descent, emerged seem-
ingly out of nowhere when he made his entrance upon the United
States chess scene in 1874. His meteoric appearance lasted until
May 1876. Alberoni returned to Europe, turned up a final time in
London, and disappeared. During these few years Alberoni scored
well in tournaments and matches, although he was beaten in direct
confrontations by such established masters as Max Judd and Mason.
Alberoni must have heard of Bird's arrival while he was combatting
Albert Ensor in Buffalo. He delayed his plans to visit Saint Louis,
where Judd awaited him, and turned to New York to meet the legendary Englishman over the board.

Bird and Alberoni encountered each other for the first time on
Friday 17 December. Alberoni surprised the spectators by beating
Bird 2 wins to 1. Bird gained his revenge the next day. In the rooms
of the Brooklyn Chess Club he rectified the situation by polishing
off Alberoni 4½–1½.

Around this time Bird accepted the offer from the New York
Down Town Chess Club to perform in their rooms at the Café Cosmopolitan. In all likelihood Bird and Alberoni continued their

series here, with the New York Down Town club offering some financial support.

All in all Bird and Alberoni played 40 games, although it seems
that one cannot speak of a formal match. No arrangements are
known, except that no time control was applied. Bird and Alberoni
played at a blizzard pace in an excellent mutual understanding. They
just cared for chess, and thus values as sportsmanship and chivalry
were riding high. The series of games ended around 25 December.
The score was closely followed by three newspapers: the *New York
Herald*, *Forest and Stream* and *Turf, Field and Farm*.

Bird continued to nurture his initial edge and was at one point
was leading 10 wins to 6. Three successive wins from Alberoni nearly
closed the gap and then he moved to the lead after several more
games (+13 −11 =1 and +17 −15 =2). The contest remained extraordinarily tense. After 40 games the match was settled with a
minor advantage for Bird. He had won 19 games, Alberoni 18 and
just 3 ended in a draw.

**(350) Alberoni–Bird    1–0**
Match
New York, December 1875
*C33*

"Mr. Alberoni played three games with Mr. Bird before leaving
for the West, Mr. Alberoni winning two out of the three. One of
these, a dashing gambit, is a very favorable specimen of Mr. Alberoni's style of play"—*New York Herald*.

**1. e4 e5 2. f4 e×f4 3. Bc4 Qh4† 4. Kf1 g5 5. Nc3 Bg7 6. d4 d6
7. Nf3 Qh5 8. e5** Both players are eager for an open combat. Within
a few moves the board is on fire. **8. ... g4 9. Ne1 f3 10. g×f3 g×f3**
A more precise move order is 10. ... Qh3† 11. Kg1 g×f3, as White's
king is better placed in the game. **11. Q×f3 Qh3† 12. Kf2 Qh4†
13. Ke3** Alberoni pushes it a bit too far. 13. Kg2! keeps all attacking
lines open. Black can at most reach an inferior endgame after, e.g.,
13. ... Nh6 14. e×d6 c×d6 (or 14. ... Rg8 15. Qe4†) 15. Qe4†. **13. ...
Nh6 14. Ng2 Qd8?!** Stronger is 14. ... Qg4, forcing the exchange
of queens. **15. Rf1?** 15. Kf2! is extremely annoying for Black. If 15. ...
0–0? 16. B×h6 B×h6 17. Qh5 Qg5 (17. ... Bg7 18. Rag1 leaves him
defenseless) 18. Q×g5 B×g5 19. Nb5! with a lasting edge in the
endgame. Slightly better is 15. ... Ng4†, though 16. Kg3! 0–0 and
now 17. h3 or 17. e6 should be enough to deliver his opponent an
unpleasant game. **15. ... Nf5† 15. ... 0–0 16. Kf2 d×e5 is more precise. Just as in the game, White's king has come under attack. 16. Kf2
d×e5 17. d×e5** This move at first sight seems to lose the bishop at
c4, but Alberoni has seen a smooth tactical trick. Yet, the move is
open for improvement, as it allows Black to activate his queen. Instead 17. Rd1! keeps the tension in a favorable way. Black has to
avoid 17. ... e×d4 because of 18. Re1†, when White's pieces take up
the attacking positions. An unclear game arises after 17. ... c6. **17. ...
Qd4† 18. Ne3 Qh4†?!** If 18. ... N×e3? 19. Q×f7†.First 18. ... 0–0!
forces White to lose an important tempo to chase away the Black
queen from its post: 19. Nb5 Qh4† 20. Kg1 B×e5. White's best
plan now is to exchange queens with 21. Qg4† Kh8 22. Q×h4
N×h4 23. R×f7 R×f7 24. B×f7 Bd7, but Black keeps a slight plus
in the endgame. **19. Kg1 B×e5?** *(see diagram)* Typical Bird, preferring to utilize his attacking opportunities instead of playing it safe.

19. ... 0–0 had become obligatory. White can spend the move 19. Nb5 saved from the last note above to the present; after 20. N×f5 B×f5 21. Q×f5 Q×c4 22. Ne4 Qe6 23. Nf6†, followed by exchanges at f6 and f5, it is White who has the initiative.

*After 19. ... B×e5*

**20. B×f7†!** This should have been the decisive blow. **20. ... Kd8 21. Qg2** 21. Qd5† Bd6 22. R×f5! is immediately over and out. There is no reason to be afraid of some checks. **21. ... Nd6 22. Nf5?!** Threatening 22. Bg5†, but the same threat would have been much stronger after 22. Nc4; e.g., 22. ... N×f7 23. N×e5! **22. ... Q×h2†! 23. Q×h2 B×h2† 24. K×h2 B×f5 25. Bg5† Kd7 26. Rad1?!** The knight at d6 is too solid to besiege. More chances were offered by 26. Rae1, menacing 27. R×f5! **26. ... Bg6** 26. ... Bg4 gains some extra time; e.g., 27. Rd4 h5 and 27. ... Nc6 comes with tempo. **27. Nb5! Na6?** 27. ... Kc6 is necessary. **28. Rf6?** 28. N×d6 c×d6 29. Rf6 is perhaps simpler. Alberoni's play is quite as good and much more impressive. **28. ... B×f7 29. N×d6! Bh5 30. Rd2 c×d6 31. Rf×d6† Kc7 32. Rd7† Kb6 33. Be3†?!** At least, until now. 33. R2d6† Kb5 34. R×b7† wins back the piece. **33. ... Ka5?** Bird might have held the endgame arising after 33. ... Nc5 34. R2d6† Kb5 35. a4† Ka5 36. Rd5 b6 37. R×h5 Rhc8. **34. R2d5† b5 35. R×h5 Rhe8 36. Bd2† Ka4 37. Rd4† b4 38. Rdd5 Re2† 39. Kh1 Nc5 40. R×c5 a5 41. Bh6** Black resigns—*New York Herald*, 19 December 1875.

### (351) Bird–Alberoni    1–0
Match
New York, 22 December 1875
C39

**1. e4 e5 2. f4 e×f4 3. Nf3 g5 4. h4 g4 5. Ne5 Bg7 6. d4 Nf6 7. B×f4 N×e4 8. Q×g4 B×e5 9. B×e5 d5 10. Qg7 Rf8 11. Nc3 N×c3 12. b×c3 Be6 13. Bd3 c6 14. 0–0 Q×h4 15. Rf4 Qe7 16. Re1 Nd7 17. Bc7 Rc8 18. Ba5 b6 19. Bb4 c5 20. Ba3 Kd8 21. d×c5 b×c5 22. Ba6 Rb8 23. c4 Qd6 24. c×d5 Q×f4 25. d×e6 f×e6 26. Rd1 Qf2† 27. Kh1 Rf7 28. Qc3 Kc7 29. B×c5 Q×c5 30. R×d7† Kb6 31. Q×c5† K×c5 32. R×f7 Rb2 33. a4 e5 34. R×h7 e4 35. c3 Rb1† 36. Kh2 e3 37. Re7** Black resigns—*New York Herald*, 23 December 1875.

### (352) Alberoni–Bird    1–0
Match
New York, 22 December 1875
C33

**1. e4 e5 2. f4 e×f4 3. Bc4 Qh4† 4. Kf1 g5 5. Nc3 Ne7 6. Nf3 Qh5 7. h4 h6 8. B×f7† Q×f7 9. Ne5 Qg7 10. Qh5† Ng6 11. N×g6**

---

**Qf7 12. h×g5 Rh7 13. Nd5 Kd8 14. g×h6 Nc6 15. Qg5† Ne7 16. Ng×e7 B×e7 17. N×e7** Black resigns—*New York Herald*, 23 December 1875.

### (353) Alberoni–Bird    0–1
Match
New York, 23 December 1875
C33

**1. e4 e5 2. f4 e×f4 3. Bc4 Qh4† 4. Kf1 g5 5. Nc3 Bg7 6. g3 f×g3 7. Qf3 Qf4 8. Nd5!** Q×f3†? The plan of exchanging queens is completely faulty. Improvements were possible with 7. ... g2† 8. K×g2 Nh6 or with the ugly 8. ... Qd6. Bird has nevertheless foreseen some deep points with his plan, but after a true slugfest White emerges with a considerable material superiority. **9. N×f3 c6 10. Nc7† Kd8 11. N×a8 d5 12. e×d5 Bh3† 13. Ke2 g2 14. Rg1 g4 15. Ng5 Bd4 16. R×g2 B×g2 17. N×f7† Kd7 18. N×h8 B×h8 19. d×c6† N×c6 20. B×g8 Bf3† 21. Kf1 Be5 22. c4 B×h2 23. Bd5 Nd4 24. B×f3 N×f3 25. d3 h5 26. Be3 Bb8 27. d4 h4 28. d5 h3 29. c5 Be5 30. c6†?** With a full rook up, White's win seemed a matter of time but facing Bird's approaching pawns Alberoni panics. The win is certain after 30. Rc1 h2 31. Kg2 Nh4† 32. Kh1 g3 33. Rc2 where Black's pawns are finally under control. **30. ... b×c6 31. d×c6†** A miracle happened: White can mostly draw this position. A fascinating line, leading to an unique drawing position, is 31. B×a7 g2 32. Bg1 c×d5 33. Nb6† Ke6 34. Rd1 d4 35. a4 d3! 36. Nd7 Bd4 37. B×d4 Nh2†. **31. ... K×c6 32. Rc1†** 32. B×a7 also draws after 32. ... h2 33. Kg2 Nh4† 34. Kh1 g3 35. Rc1† Kb7 36. Rc2 K×a7 37. Nc7 g2† 38. R×g2 N×g2 39. K×g2 B×c7. **32. ... Kb7 33. B×a7** The situation has become extremely delicate for Alberoni and his move has a clear air of desperation. Also not sufficient was 33. Kf2 Nh4 34. Nc7 h2 and Black wins. Yet, a draw was still achievable with 33. Nc7 and now 33. ... B×c7 (if 33. ... Nh4?! 34. Ne6!) 34. Kf2 Nh4 35. Kg1 Bd6 36. Rc4 Nf3† 37. Kf2 h2 38. Kg2 Ne1† 39. Kh1 g3 40. Rg4. **33. ... K×a7 34. Nc7 g3 35. Rc2 h2** White resigns—*Westminster Chess Club Papers*, March 1876, p. 222.

### (354) Alberoni–Bird    0–1
Match
New York, December 1875
C59

**1. e4 e5 2. Nf3 Nc6 3. Bc4 Nf6 4. Ng5 d5 5. e×d5 Na5 6. Bb5† c6 7. d×c6 b×c6 8. Be2 h6 9. Nf3 e4 10. Ne5 Bd6 11. f4 e×f3 *e.p.* 12. N×f3 Qc7 13. 0–0 0–0 14. h3 Rd8 15. d4 c5 16. Be3 Rb8 17. b3 Qe7 18. Bf2 c×d4 19. B×d4 Ne4 20. c3 Nc6 21. Nbd2 N×d4 22. N×e4 N×f3†** White resigns—*New York Herald*, 25 December 1875.

### (355) Alberoni–Bird    1–0
Match
New York, December 1875
C42

**1. e4 e5 2. Bc4 Nf6 3. Nf3 N×e4 4. Nc3** "This was a favorite continuation some years ago, but the sacrifice of the pawn is now admitted to be unsound. Still, in actual play the attack is very embarrassing, and the slightest error on the part of the defense will speedily prove fatal"—Wormald. **4. ... N×c3 5. d×c3 f6 6. Nh4** He may also castle or play 6. Be3 at this point, to either of which moves 6. ... Qe7 is the best reply"—Wormald. **6. ... g6 7. 0–0 d6** Or 7. ... c6, intending 8. ... d5. **8. f4 Nc6?** 8. ... Qe7 is forced so that 9. f5 can be answered with 9. ... Qg7. Alberoni refutes Bird's set-up very convincingly. **9. f5! Ne7 10. f×g6 h×g6** (*see diagram*)

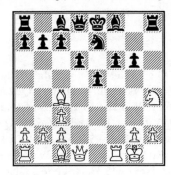

*After 10. ... h×g6*

**11. R×f6!** "Very ingenious. If 11. ... R×h4 White wins in a few moves: 12. Bf7† Kd7 13. Bg5 Re4 (his only move to prevent the fatal check at g4) 14. Qf3 d5 (if 14. ... Ra4 White mates in two) 15. Q×e4 wins"—Wormald. The brilliant text move forms the onset of a decisive assault. White can venture a lot of material due to the situation of Black's king, which is caught in the center. **11. ... d5 12. Bg5! c6** "Had he ventured to take the bishop, White would obviously have won by 13. Q×d8† K×d8 14. N×g6"—Wormald. The alternative, 12. ... Bh6, isn't better: 13. Qc1! Nc6 14. B×d5 Q×f6 15. B×f6 B×c1 16. B×h8, and White is in excellent shape. **13. Bb3** A slight hesitation, but this doesn't make Alberoni's effort less impressive. A quick win results from 13. N×g6!—e.g., 13. ... Qb6† 14. Kh1 N×g6 15. B×d5! Qc7 16. Be4 Ne7 17. Qd3 with a decisive attack. **13. ... Qb6† 14. Kh1 Nf5?!** Equally unimpressive is 14. ... Bh6 due to 15. B×h6 R×h6 16. Qe1! (threatening 17. B×d5) 16. ... Qc7? (16. ... Bd7 is better, but of course White plays 17. B×d5) 17. Qg3 and wins. The only move to prolong the battle somewhat is 14. ... Bf5. White then does best to continue with 15. c4! **15. Qe1** Also good is 15. B×d5. **15. ... R×h4** Despair. Nothing can save him. **16. Q×e5† Be7 17. R×f5 Re4 18. Qh8† Kd7 19. Rf7 Qd8 20. Qg7** Possibly as good as anything, but he might have won a piece by 20. Q×d8 and 21. R×e7"—Wormald. **20. ... Qe8 21. Raf1 Kd6 22. Q×g6† Be6 23. B×e7†** Black resigns—*Illustrated London News* (Wormald), 11 March 1876.

### 356) Bird–Alberoni ½–½

Match
New York, December 1875
C52

"An instructive game in the series between Messrs. Alberoni and Bird"—Mackenzie.

**1. e4 e5 2. Nf3 Nc6 3. Bc4 Bc5 4. b4 B×b4 5. c3 Ba5 6. Qb3 Qf6 7. d4 e×d4 7. ... N×d4! profits from Bird's inferior move order. 8. 0–0 Nge7** 8. ... d×c3 is the critical move. **9. Bg5 Qg6 10. B×e7 K×e7** 10. ... N×e7 was thought to lose after 11. Ne5? according to Mackenzie, but in fact this is an error: 11. ... Q×e4! 12. B×f7† Kd8 13. Nc4 Nc6 with an excellent game. **11. c×d4 d6 12. e5 d×e5 13. d5?!** "Black must now lose a piece, but the attack he obtains is

quite sufficient to counterbalance the loss"—Mackenzie. 13. N×e5 N×e5 14. d×e5 gives enough for the pawn. **13. ... Nd4 14. N×d4 e×d4 15. Qa3† Kd8 16. Q×a5** "The play of Mr. Bird in this opening is not only injudicious, but totally foreign to his style of play. The fact that he here leaves Black with two pawns and a fine attack for a piece proves that his form in America has been considerably below his full strength"—Wisker. **16. ... Bh3 17. g3 Qe4 18. f3 Qe3†?!** 18. ... Qc2 wins back the piece while maintaining a strong attack. **19. Rf2 Qc1† 20. Bf1 Re8 21. d6** 21. Qb4! is marginally better for White, for his opponent's rook will be driven back by force after 21. ... Re1 22. Qf8† Kd7 23. Q×f7† Re7 24. Qh5. **21. ... Re1 22. Nd2?** Bad judgment. 22. d×c7† Kc8 23. Nd2 is a necessary refinement. If now 23. ... Q×a1 24. Qd5! K×c7 25. Q×f7† draws. **22. ... Q×a1 23. Q×c7†** Black also has everything under control after 23. d×c7† Ke7 24. Qc5† Ke8 25. Qh5 B×f1 26. R×f1 R×f1† 27. N×f1 Qc3. **23. ... Ke8 24. d7†** The situation is hopeless, also after 24. Q×b7 Rd8 25. Qc6† Kf8 26. Qc7 Rd7 27. Qb8† Re8. **24. ... B×d7 25. Ne4 Be6 26. Nd6† Kf8 27. Q×b7 Rd8 28. Qc7 Rd7 29. Qb8† Ke7** "The defense is very skilful. With some slight blemishes, indeed, the whole game reflects the greatest credit upon American chess"—Wisker. **30. Nc8† Kf6 31. Qf4† Kg6** Bird struggled heroically, but to little avail. Black's king should be perfectly safe here. **32. Kg2** (*see diagram*)

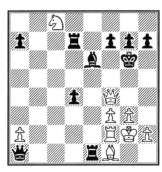

*After 32. Kg2*

**32. ... d3** "Mr. Alberoni probably sacrificed the pawn for the purpose of getting his queen into play, or else overlooked the fact that it could be captured with impunity, for on the 33d move, should Black take bishop with rook, White mates in two moves"—Mackenzie. This sacrifice is not bad at all, but there are various simpler ways to win, one of them being 32. ... Qc1! 33. Bd3† f5. **33. B×d3† f5 34. Nd6 Qe5 35. Qg4† Kf6 36. Qh4† g5 37. Qh6† Ke7 38. Nc8† Ke8** "38. ... Kd8 would never do on account of 39. Qf8†, followed by 40. Rc2† etc."—Mackenzie. **39. Q×g5 f4 40. Qh4 f×g3 41. h×g3 Qd4?** After another tense phase, Alberoni finally makes a crucial mistake by insisting on exchanging queens, which flattens the game too much. A deserved win was within reach with 41. ... Qc5! (e.g., 42. Qa4 Kf8 43. Qf4† Kg7 44. Qd2 Bh3†). **42. Bb5! Q×h4** A spectacular draw rises after 42. ... Qc5 43. B×d7† B×d7 44. Qc4! Bh3†! 45. K×h3 Q×f2. In the game Bird counts two extra pawns but with his knight in trouble the game is certain to devolve into a draw. **43. g×h4 Red1 44. N×a7 Kd8 45. B×d7 B×d7 46. Rb2 Rd5 47. Rb6** 47. Rc2 isn't likely to succeed in liberating the knight either: 47. ... Rd6 48. Rc5 Rg6† 49. Kf2 Rh6 50. Kg3 Rb6 etc. **47. ... Kc7** The draw becomes unavoidable. **48. Rh6 Ra5 49. R×h7 R×a2† 50. Kg3 R×a7 51. h5 Kd6 52. h6 Ra5 53. Kh4 Rf5 54. R×d7† K×d7 55. h7 Rf8 56. Kg5 Ke7**

**57. Kg6 Rh8 58. Kg7 Ke6** "Very pretty; as it is impossible for either player to win in this position, Mr. Alberoni chooses by far the most elegant method of forcing a draw"—Mackenzie. **59. K×h8 Kf7** and the game is drawn—*Turf, Field and Farm* (Mackenzie), 31 December 1875; *The Sportsman* (Wisker), 26 January 1876.

## (357) Bird–Alberoni    0–1
Match
New York, December 1875
C54

"One of the most interesting contests in the series between Messrs. Bird and Alberoni, and played at the rooms of the Down Town Chess Club"—Mason.

**1. e4 e5 2. Nf3 Nc6 3. Bc4 Bc5 4. c3 Nf6 5. b4** "This may be White's strongest move, but we are of opinion that the advance of this pawn is unsound, and that two pawns and the exchange are not a full equivalent for 2 pieces"—Mason. **4. ... Bb6 6. b5 Na5 7. N×e5 0–0 8. d4 d6 9. N×f7 R×f7 10. B×f7† K×f7 11. 0–0** This move doesn't acknowledge the threat 11. ... Qe8, when he loses a pawn. Instead 11. f3! solidly bolsters the e-pawn after which White succeeds in shutting out Black's knight and bishop from the action. **11. ... Kg8 12. Nd2** "12. Bg5 looks stronger here and we mistake if it would not have enabled him to hold his e-pawn, which Black presently wrests from him, and which is, or should be, a considerable element in the attack"—Mason. **12. ... Qe8 13. Qe2 c5 14. Bb2 Bd7 15. a4 Qg6 16. f4** Quite risky play with such a shaky center. 16. Kh1! leaves Black struggling. **16. ... Re8! 17. Rae1 N×e4** Not as good as it looks. Black reaches a better endgame after 17. ... Bf5! For instance, 18. e×f5 R×e2 19. f×g6 R×d2 20. Rf2 c×d4 21. c×d4 R×b2, and the wall of pawns hampering Black's pieces finally falls apart. **18. N×e4 d5 19. f5 Qf7 20. Qf2** 20. d×c5! is rather tricky, but everything turns out well for White after 20. ... R×e4 (20. ... B×c5†? 21. N×c5 R×e2 22. R×e2 Nc4 23. Rfe1 N×b2 24. Re7 is hopeless for Black) 21. Qf2 Bc7 22. R×e4 d×e4 23. Bc1 Nb3 24. Be3. Black's pieces still experience problems becoming active. **20. ... c×d4 21. Ng5 d3?** Unjustly playing for a win. 21. ... d×c3 22. N×f7 B×f2† 23. K×f2 R×e1 24. B×c3 R×f1† 25. K×f1 K×f7 delivers a draw. **22. N×f7 R×e1** *(see diagram)*

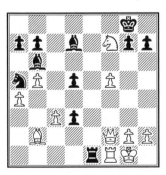

*After 22. ... R×e1*

**23. Nh6†?** Bird probably overlooked that after 23. R×e1 B×f2† 24. K×f2 K×f7 he had an extremely strong silent move that wins the house: 25. Re5! **23. ... g×h6 24. R×e1 d2 25. Rd1 B×f2† 26. K×f2 Nc4** Black has enough compensation for the material disadvantage, but nothing more. **27. g4 h5 28. h3 h×g4 29. h×g4 h5 30. Kg3?** Undoubtedly played without enough consideration.

30. g×h5 B×f5 31. Bc1! is a dead draw. **30. ... h×g4** Here and on the next move 30. ... Ne3 is even stronger. **31. f6 Bf5 32. Bc1 d×c1Q 33. R×c1 Kf7 34. Rd1 Be4 35. Rd4 Ne5 36. Kf4 K×f6 37. c: N×c4 38. K×g4 Ke5** White resigns—*The Spirit of the Time* (Mason), 1 January 1876.

## (358) Bird–Alberoni    0–1
Match
New York, December 1875
C39

**1. e4 e5 2. f4 e×f4 3. Nf3 g5 4. h4 g4 5. Ne5 Bg7 6. d4 d 7. e×d5 Q×d5 8. Nc3 Qd8 9. B×f4 Nf6 10. Bc4 0–0 11. Qd2 Nh 12. Bg5 Qe8 13. 0–0–0 Nc6 14. Rhe1 Be6 15. B×e6 f×e6 16. Bh N×e5 17. d×e5 Rd8 18. Qg5 R×d1† 19. R×d1 Qg6 20. Q×g h×g6 21. B×g7 K×g7 22. Ne4 Rf5 23. Ng5 R×e5 24. Rd7† Kg 25. Kd2 Nf4 26. g3 Nh5 27. Rd3 Rd5 28. Ne4 Kf7 29. c4 R×d3 30. K×d3 e5 31. Ke3 Ke6 32. Nc5† Kf5 33. Ne4 Nf6 34. Nc3 35. b4 e4 36. a4 Ke5 37. a5 b5 38. a×b6 e.p. a×b6 39. b5 c×b 40. N×b5 Nh5 41. Kf2 Ng7 42. Nc3 Kd4 43. Na4 K×c 44. N×b6† Kd3 45. Nd7 Kd2 46. Nf6 e3† 47. Kg2 e2** White re signs—*New York Herald*, 27 December 1875.

## (359) Bird–Alberoni    0–1
Match
New York, December 1875
C52

**1. e4 e5 2. Nf3 Nc6 3. Bc4 Bc5 4. b4 B×b4 5. c3 Ba5 6. d4 e×d 7. 0–0 d×c3 8. Qb3 Qf6 9. e5 Qg6 10. N×c3 Nge7 11. Ne2 b 12. B×b5 Rb8 13. Qa4 a6 14. B×c6 N×c6 15. Ba3 Bb4 16. Nf Qe4 17. Nh5 0–0 18. Ng3 Qc4 19. Bb2 Qb5 20. Qc2 Qc5 21. Qe Qe7 22. Nf5 Qe6 23. Rac1 d5 24. Qh4 Q×f5 25. R×c6 Ba5 26. Ba Re8 27. e6 f×e6 28. Nd4 Qf6 29. Qh5 Bb7 30. Rd1 Bb6 31. R×b c×b6 32. Bd6 Rbd8 33. Be5 Qg6 34. Qh3 Rc8 35. f4 b5 36. Re b4 37. Qb3 a5 38. h4 Qg4 39. Qa4 Qg3 40. Nf3 Bc6 41. Q×a5 Ra 42. Q×b4 R×a2 43. Bb2 d4 44. Rf1 d3 45. f5 Rb8 46. Qe7 Ra×b** White resigns—*Turf, Field and Farm*, 10 March 1876.

---

# THE AMERICAN EAGLE SCREAMS OVER THE ENGLISH BIRD

Bird was not left waiting long for his next opponent. More tha 70 members of the New York Down Town Chess Club contribute to a prize fund that ultimately reached $100. With this money match between Bird and Mason, a honorary member of the club was arranged at the Café Cosmopolitan.[5] The games were playe

5. Further details appeared in the *New York Herald* on 25 December 1875 "The coming match between Messrs. Bird and Mason is exciting great interest in the chess world. Play is to be commenced on Tuesday, December 28. The time of sitting will be from three o'clock until seven o'clock p.m. and from eight o'cloc p.m. until midnight on each day until the match is finished. If a player absent him self from a sitting his opponent may score a game. The winner of the first eleve games shall be declared the winner of the match. The players shall play at the rat of twenty moves per hour, under penalty of the loss of the game. The rooms c the New York Down Town Chess Club, where the match will be played, are ope to the public."

n a small apartment that offered only about a dozen spectators the chance to witness the play. The match proceeded at a pace hardly inferior to that of Bird and Alberoni. Four games a day were played and after a good week the match was already over.

After an initial bloodless fight of more than 100 moves, Bird took the lead in the second game. Mason immediately hit back and took the lead from game five onwards. Until game 13 Bird was able to hang on, with Mason continuously nurturing an advantage of two or three points. While Bird's performance so far was not impressive, he completely broke down in the last part of the match and lost five of the six final games, enabling Mason to secure an easy overall victory.[6]

Various elements that contributed to Bird's loss were analyzed. Above all, the Englishman was severely hindered by his suffering from the gout. On one occasion Bird was unable to return to his hotel and he had to pass the night at the Café Cosmopolitan. Several American columnists acknowledged Bird's health issues but were very reluctant to attach an importance to it when it came to making a substantial difference about the outcome of the match.

There was also some discussion about the quality of the games. Zukertort, who annotated all the games for the *Westminster Chess Club Papers*, was especially severe in his judgment. He concluded that Bird was completely out of form and was hardly convinced of Mason's superiority. Mason attributed the lack of quality to the rapidity of play and thought Zukertort contemptuous in his analysis.

The reputation of James Mason as one of the (two) best American chess players was definitively established by this convincing win. A few weeks later, on 19 January, H. Albert Dimock proposed to back Mason in another match with similar conditions.[7] From this letter it appeared that several players were eligible for Dimock's offer: "…some of the chess-players now in the city will accept the challenge." Bird, not surprisingly, reacted instantly. Though beaten rather decisively, he absolutely did not consider himself of mere perfunctory strength. According to the Englishman, his great majority of wins in the offhand games were enough arguments for a rematch. Alas, his offer to play was plainly refused.[8]

Mason's refusal must have been a telling frustration for Bird and a first experience with the so-called "American professionalism." Bird was always open to play offhand as well as formal games or matches and, thinking along his scheme of chivalry on the board, he expected the same of his opponents. Some of them, however, had other priorities than playing for honor only.

| Match with Mason, 28 December 1875–5 January 1876 | | | | | | | | | | | | | | | | | | | |
|---|---|---|---|---|---|---|---|---|---|---|---|---|---|---|---|---|---|---|---|
| | 1 | 2 | 3 | 4 | 5 | 6 | 7 | 8 | 9 | 10 | 11 | 12 | 13 | 14 | 15 | 16 | 17 | 18 | 19 |
| J. Mason | ½ | 0 | 1 | ½ | 1 | 1 | ½ | 0 | 1 | 1 | 0 | 1 | 0 | 1 | 0 | 1 | 1 | 1 | ½ | 1 | 1 | 11 |
| H.E. Bird | ½ | 1 | 0 | ½ | 0 | 0 | ½ | 1 | 0 | 0 | 1 | 0 | 1 | 0 | 0 | 0 | ½ | 0 | 0 | 4 |

Mason was much too clever to risk his newly earned status so soon.

Mason's challenge to Mackenzie led to discussions and propositions between both men. In the end no arrangements could be made as both players preferred to play the match in their own environment, respectively the Down Town Chess Club and the Café International.

### (360) Bird–Mason   ½–½
Match (game 1)
New York, 28 December 1875
*C54*

**1. e4 e5 2. Nf3 Nc6 3. Bc4 Bc5 4. c3 Nf6 5. b4 Bb6 6. d3 d6 7. Bg5 Be6 8. Nbd2 h6 9. Bh4 g5 10. B×e6 f×e6 11. Bg3 Qe7 12. a4 a5 13. b5 Nd8 14. Nc4 Bc5 15. Nfd2 Nf7 16. Nb3 Bb6 17. N×b6 c×b6 18. h4 Qc7 19. Rc1 0-0-0 20. c4 Nd7 21. Qh5 Nc5 22. N×c5 d×c5 23. Rd1 Qe7 24. Qe2 Qf6 25. h×g5 h×g5 26. Kd2 Nd6 27. Kc2 Nf7 28. Rh5 R×h5 29. Q×h5 Rh8 30. Qg4 Nh6 31. Qe2 Nf7 32. Qd2 Qd8 33. f3 Qe7 34. Rf1 Rh7 35. Qc3 Qd6 36. Qa1 Rh8 37. Rh1 Rd8 38. Qc3 Kd7 39. Bf2 Rh8 40. R×h8 N×h8 41. Qe1 Nf7 42. Qh1 Ke7 43. Qh7 Kf6 44. Be3 Qf8 45. Kd2 Qg7 46. Qh2 Qh8 47. Q×h8† N×h8 48. Ke2 Nf7 49. Kf2 Kg6 50. Kg3 Nh6 51. Bd2 Kh5 52. Bc3 Nf7 53. Bb2 Kg6 54. Ba1 Kh5 55. Bb2 Kg6 56. Kh3 Kh5 57. g3 Kg6 58. Bc3 Kh5 59. Bd2 Kg6 60. f4 e×f4 61. g×f4 g×f4 62. B×f4 e5 63. Bg3 Kg5 64. Kg2 Kh5 65. Kf3 Ng5† 66. Ke3 Nf7 67. Be1 Kg4 68. Bc3 Kg3 69. Be1† Kg4 70. Bc3 Kg3 71. Bb2 Kg4 72. Kf2 Kf4 73. Bc1† Kg4 74. Kg2 Ng5 75. Kf2 Nf7 76. Ke3 Kh4 77. Bb2 Kg4 78. Bc3 Kg3 79. Be1† Kg4 80. Bf2 Ng5 81. Be1 Nf7 82. Ke2 Ng5 83. Kf2 Nf3 84. Bc3 Kf4 85. Bb2 Ng5 86. Bc1† Kg4 87. Bd2 Nf7 88. Kg2 Ng5 89. Be1 Nf7 90. Bg3 Kh5 91. Kf3 Ng5† 92. Ke3 Nf7 93. Kf3 Ng5† 94. Kg2 Nf7 95. Bh2 Kg4 96. Bg3 Kh5 97. Kf3 Ng5† 98. Ke3 Nf7 99. Bf2 Kg4 100. Be1 Ng5 101. Bc3 Nf7 102. Kf2 Kf4 103. Ke2 Ng5 104. Bb2 Nf7 105. Bc1† Kg4 106. Ke3 Ng5 107. Bd2 Nf7 108. Bc3 Kg3 109. Be1† Kg4 110. Kd2 Ng5 111. Ke3 Nf7 112. Bc3 Kg3 113. Bb2 Kg4 114. Kd2 Kf4 115. Kc3 Kg5 116. Bc1† Kg4 117. Kb3 Ng5 118. Bd2 Nf7 and the game was a draw—***Dubuque Chess Journal***, April 1876, pp. 144–148.**

---

6. Mason received some well-deserved praise from Belden: "Mr. Mason has reason to be proud of his triumph, as Mr. Bird is a hard man to beat. He invariably makes a stubborn fight, and never surrenders until he is whipped. He possesses the true Johnny Bull grit, but this time Yankee pluck and skill were too much for him. It is proper that the Centennial year should open by an American victory over an Englishman. The American eagle should be permitted to scream over the defeat of the English Bird. Bird may be a Mason, but it is evident he is not a 'Master (of) Mason.'" *Hartford Weekly Times*, 15 January 1876. ¶ Bird's narrow win against Alberoni as well as his unexpected loss against Mason created quite some stir on the other side of the Atlantic. Wisker's reaction to the news nicely summarized the astonishment in London: "It appears that Mr. Bird has lost [*sic*] a match to Mr. Alberoni, and was, according to latest advices, greatly in the minority against Mr. Mason. The result is unaccountable, for good as are the American players, it could hardly be expected they would compete on even terms with Mr. Bird." *Land and Water*, 22 January 1876. ¶ A short while later Wisker estimated the new balance of power: "At this we rejoice; for it is now probable that the chess intercourse between the two countries will become closer. Such intercourse has hitherto been restrained by the belief—common to both sides of the Atlantic—that the Englishmen and Germans were decisively superior. The time has arrived for a slight revision of this idea." *City of London Chess Magazine*, February 1876, p. 5.

7. Dimock sent a letter that was published in *The New York Sportsman* (unseen). A copy appeared in the *Boston Weekly Globe* on 4 February 1876.

8. "Mr. Bird also signified his willingness to play Mason a return match on the terms proposed, but Mason, in reply, declined to meet the Englishman again on any terms, and stated that the challenge was specially intended for the acceptance of Mackenzie." *Illustrated London News*, 4 March 1876.

## (361) Mason–Bird   0–1

Match (game 2)
New York, 28 December 1875
C33

**1. e4 e5 2. f4 e×f4 3. Bc4 Nf6 4. e5** "4. Nc3 is the right continuation. The text move is justly decried in the books as very inferior"—Zukertort. **4. ... d5 5. Bb3 Ne4 6. Nf3 Bg4 7. d4** "7. 0–0 is the simplest continuation. 7. Nc3 is also good"—Zukertort. **7. ... B×f3 8. Q×f3 Qh4† 9. g3** In his analysis Zukertort suggested 9. Ke2 Ng3† 10. h×g3 as favorable for White, but after 10. ... Q×h1 11. B×f4 Nc6 12. Q×d5 Qh5† and 13. ... Rd8 Black is actually winning. The condemned text move is not that bad. **9. ... f×g3 10. h×g3 Q×g3† 11. Q×g3 N×g3 12. B×d5 c6 13. Rg1 Nf5 14. Rf1 g6 15. Bb3 Be7 16. c3 h5 17. Bf4 Nd7 18. Nd2** (see diagram)

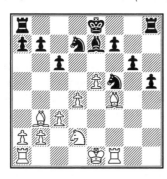

*After 18. Nd2*

**James Mason (courtesy Cleveland Public Library).**

**18. ... Bh4†?!** "Loss of time. This move forces the adverse queen's rook, and certainly doesn't improve the position of the own bishop"—Zukertort. 18. ... Nb6 19. Bc2 Ng7 is a suggestion. **19. Ke2 Nf8 20. Ne4 Ne6 21. B×e6 f×e6 22. Rg1 Kf7 23. Bg5 B×g5 24. N×g5† Ke7 25. Nh3 Rag8 26. Rg5 h4 27. Nf4 Kf7 28. Kf3?** Mason misses a crucial subtlety. With 28. Kf2 he could have maintained the blockade of Black's pawns, albeit at the very last opportunity after 28. ... h3 29. Kg1. **28. ... h3 29. Rh1 h2 30. Kg2 Rh4 31. Nh3 Rgh8 32. R×h2?** "A blunder which loses a piece. 32. Nf2 would have enabled White to prolong the contest, but hardly changed its result"—Zukertort. Indeed, after a few preparatory moves, Black opens the queenside with c6–c5. **32. ... Ne3†** White resigns—*Westminster Chess Club Papers* (Zukertort), February 1876, p. 194.

## (362) Bird–Mason   0–1

Match (game 3)
New York, 28 December 1875
C77

**1. e4 e5 2. Nf3 Nc6 3. Bb5 a6 4. Ba4 Nf6 5. Qe2 b5 6. Bb3 Bc5** "6. ... Bb7, as played first by myself in 1869 against L. Paulsen, and then adopted by Steinitz against Blackburne in the tie of the Vienna tourney, is preferable. It frustrates the advance of the a-pawn"—Zukertort. **7. a4 Rb8** "Black dare not play 7. ... b4 on account of 8. B×f7† and 9. Qc4†"—Zukertort. **8. a×b5 a×b5 9. Nc3 b4 10. Nd5 0–0 11. d3 N×d5 12. B×d5 Nd4 13. N×d4 B×d4 14. Ra2** "Certainly premature"—Zukertort. **14. ... c6 15. Bb3 d5 16. Be3 d×e4 17. d×e4 c5 18. 0–0 Bb7 19. f3 Kh8 20. B×d4 c×d4 21. Rfa1** "To carry the attack against the adversary's queenside at the proper moment, is one of the finest features of the modern school. In the present instance however the doubled rooks resemble Don Quixote fighting the windmills"—Zukertort. Bird may not have been an adherent of the modern school, and he might resemble Don Quixote in more than one case, but here doubling the rooks on the a-file is the best thing to do, even if there is no concrete advantage evolving from it right now. **21. ... f5?!** Mason's last moves were preparatory for this push. Given that White's pieces are better placed than Black's it is unwise to open the position, and the solid 21. ... f6 was called for. Bird then has a small advantage on the queenside, but nothing that should worry Mason. **22. e×f5 R×f5** (see diagram)

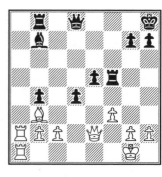

*After 22. ... R×f5*

**23. Bc4?!** 23. Ra5! is the correct rejoinder as 23. ... Qg5? 24. Rb5! wins material. Thus the queen is limited in its movements and has to cover the pawn in another way. If he does so with 23. ... Qd6,

24. Bc4! gives White a clear advantage. **23. … Qg5! 24. Rf1** 24. Kh1 is absolutely safer. **24. … Rbf8** 24. … e4! would have been rather strong: 25. f×e4 R×f1† 26. Q×f1 Qe3† 27. Kh1 B×e4 and White's king is getting under fire. **25. Raa1 R×f3 26. R×f3 R×f3 27. Ba6 Ba8 28. Bc8?** Bird's last moves were rather risky, as they did nothing to get his king out of the danger zone. This would have been no problem had he found 28. h4!, which forces a draw after 28. … Qg3 29. Bc8 Bc6 30. Bd7 Bb7 31. Bc8. At first it seems that the text move is crafty enough for the defense, but after Black's next move its clumsiness becomes clear. A second pawn is lost. **28. … Rf8! 29. h4 Q×g2† 30. Q×g2 B×g2 31. Be6 Bf3 32. Rf1 Rf6 33. Bc4 h5 34. Ra1 Kh7 35. Ra5 e4 36. Rd5 e3 37. Bd3†** "If 37. R×d4 e2 winning a piece"—Zukertort. **37. … g6 38. R×d4 e2** 38. … Rf7! avoids any complications. **39. Rd7† Kh6 40. Re7 Be4** Here or on the next move 40. … Rf4! is the most precise. **41. B×e2 B×c2 42. Rc7 b3 43. Rc4?** Mason's technical skill during the last moves could have been improved, and Bird has obtained drawing chances. Instead of the losing text move, 43. Rc3! was necessary to avoid Mason's following move. A possible continuation would have been 43. … Rf4 44. Rc4 Be4! (exchanging the rooks is very drawish) 45. Rb4 Kg7 46. Bf1 Kf6 47. Bg2 Kf5 48. B×e4 R×e4 49. R×b3 R×h4 etc. **43. … Ra6! 44. Rc7 Ra2 45. Bc4 R×b2 46. Bg8 g5 47. h×g5† K×g5 48. Rc5† Kg4 49. Be6† Kh4 50. Bf7 Bd1 51. Rb5 Kg3** White resigns—*Westminster Chess Club Papers* (Zukertort), February 1876, pp. 194–195.

## (363) Mason–Bird    ½–½
Match (game 4)
New York, 29 December 1875
C61

**1. e4 e5 2. Nf3 Nc6 3. Bb5 Nd4 4. Bc4 Qf6 5. N×d4 e×d4 6. d3 Bc5 7. 0-0 Ne7 8. f4 d5 9. e×d5 h5 10. Nd2 Bg4 11. Qe1 0-0-0 12. Ne4 Qb6 13. a3 N×d5 14. B×d5 R×d5 15. b4 Be7 16. Nd2 Bf6 17. h3 Bf5 18. Nc4 Qc6 19. a4 Rdd8 20. b5 Qd7 21. Qg3 Rhe8 22. Bd2 Re6 23. Rae1 Rde8 24. Qf3 R×e1 25. R×e1 R×e1† 26. B×e1 Be6 27. Q×h5 g6 28. Qc5 b6 29. Qb4 Be7 30. Qd2 B×c4 31. d×c4 Qe6 32. Bf2 Q×c4 33. Q×d4 Q×c2 34. Kh2 Bd6 35. Bg3 Qf5 36. h4 f6 37. Qc4 Bc5 38. Qg8† Kb7 39. Qe8 Bd6** draw—*Westminster Chess Club Papers*, February 1876, p. 195.

## (364) Bird–Mason    0–1
Match (game 5)
New York, 29 December 1875
C43

**1. e4 e5 2. Nf3 Nf6 3. d4 N×e4 4. d×e5 d5 5. Bb5† c6 6. Bd3 Qc7 7. 0-0 Be7 8. Re1 Nc5 9. Bf4 Bg4 10. Be2 B×f3 11. B×f3 Nbd7 12. Nd2 Ne6 13. Bg3 g6 14. c4 d4 15. Bg4 Ndc5 16. Nb3 N×b3 17. a×b3 c5 18. b4 0-0 19. b5 Bg5 20. B×e6 f×e6 21. b4 Be7 22. b×c5 B×c5 23. Qb3 Rf5 24. Rad1 Rc8 25. Rd3 Qe7 26. Rf3 R×f3 27. g×f3 Bb4 28. Ra1 Qc5 29. Ra4 Bc3 30. h4 Rd8 31. Ra2 Qb4 32. Q×b4 B×b4 33. Bf4 d3 34. Bd2 Bc5 35. Bc3 Kg7 36. Kg2 Kh6 37. Ra1 Kh5 38. Re1 Be7 39. Bd2 Rd4 40. Re4 R×e4 41. f×e4 Kg4 42. f3† K×h4 43. Bf4 Bc5 44. Bg3† Kg5 45. Kf1 Be3 46. Ke1 b6 47. Kd1 h5** White resigns—*Deutsche Schachzeitung* (Minckwitz), April 1876, pp. 107–108.

## (365) Mason–Bird    1–0
Match (game 6)
New York, 29 December 1875
C50

**1. e4 e5 2. Nc3 Bc5 3. Nf3 d6 4. Bc4 Nf6 5. d3 Nc6 6. Ne2 Be6 7. Ng3 B×c4 8. d×c4 Ne7 9. 0-0 h6 10. Qe2 Qd7 11. Bd2 a6 12. Rad1 h5 13. Be3 B×e3 14. Q×e3 h4 15. Ne2 Qg4 16. Nc3 Ng6 17. Qg5 Qe6 18. Nd5 0-0-0 19. Qe3 Kb8 20. Ng5 Qe8 21. Nh3 Qc6 22. Qd3 Nh5 23. b3 Qe8 24. Qd2 c6 25. Ne3 Qe6 26. f3 Ngf4 27. N×f4 N×f4 28. Kh1 g6 29. a4 f5 30. Rfe1 Qf6 31. b4 Qg5 32. b5 f×e4 33. f×e4 h3 34. g3 Ng2 35. N×g2 h×g2† 36. Q×g2 Rh7 37. Qf3 Rdh8 38. Re2 Rh3 39. Kg1 Qh6 40. Rdd2 Rf8 41. Qd3 Rd8 42. b×c6 b×c6 43. c5 Ka7 44. c×d6 Qg7 45. Qe3† Ka8 46. Qb6 Qa7 47. Q×a7† K×a7 48. a5 g5 49. c4 Rh7 50. c5 Rb7 51. Rb2 Rb5 52. R×b5 a×b5 53. Ra2 Ka6 54. Kf2 b4 55. Ke2 Kb5 56. a6 b3 57. Rb2 Kc4 58. Kd2 K×c5 59. R×b3 R×d6† 60. Kc3 Rd8 61. a7 Ra8 62. Ra3 Kb6 63. h4** Black resigns—*Turf, Field and Farm*, 7 January 1876.

## (366) Bird–Mason    ½–½
Match (game 7)
New York, 30 December 1875
C41

**1. e4 e5 2. Nf3 Nf6 3. Nc3 d6 4. d4 e×d4 5. Q×d4 Bd7 6. Be3 Nc6 7. Qd2 Be7 8. h3 Ne5 9. Be2 Bc6 10. Bd3 N×d3† 11. c×d3 0-0 12. Nd4 Bd7 13. g4 g6 14. Rg1 Kh8 15. 0-0-0 Re8 16. f4 c5 17. Nde2 b5 18. g5** Bird has put Mason under pressure but this hasty move spoils his game. 18. Ng3 first is necessary to prevent the settling of Bird's knight at h5. **18. … Nh5 19. d4** "Hazardous, as it weakens the e-pawn"—Zukertort. **19. … b4 20. Nd5 Be6 21. d×c5 d×c5 22. Qc2 Qa5 23. Kb1 Rad8 24. b3?!** It was necessary to support the important knight at d5 with 24. Qc4. **24. … R×d5! 25. R×d5 B×d5 26. e×d5 Bf8** 26. … Qb5!, followed by 27. … Bd6 is strong. White now fails to take control over the white squares himself with 27. Qd3. **27. Bc1 Qb5 28. Rg2?!** "As the knight is changed on the next move, the text move proves but loss of time"—Zukertort. **28. … Kg8 29. Ng3 N×g3 30. R×g3 Bd6?!** White cannot hold onto the d-pawn after 30. … Qd7! 31. Qd3 a5 32. Rf3 Rd8. **31. Qd3 Q×d3† 32. R×d3 Re4?** 32. … Re1 keeps White under pressure. Mason overlooks Bird's excellent reply and is suddenly faced with a hardly tenable endgame. **33. Re3! R×e3 34. B×e3 Kf8 35. Kc2 Ke7 36. Kd3 Kd7 37. Ke4!** Another line, suggested by Zukertort, is 37. Kc4 a6 (to prevent the further advance of the king) 38. B×c5 B×f4 39. K×b4 Bd2† 40. Ka4 B×g5 41. Ka5. Here, instead of 41. … f5, 41. … Be7! saves the game. Bird's idea is much more dangerous. **37. … a5 38. f5! Kc7 39. f×g6 f×g6 40. Kd3 Kb6 41. Kc4 Be7 42. Bf4 Bf8 43. Be5 h5 44. h4 Kb7** "Forced. If 44. … Be7, White wins by 45. d6 and 46. Kd5"—Zukertort. **45. Kb5 Kc8 46. K×a5** "46. d6 wins as the following continuation shows: 46. … Kd7 47. K×c5 Ke6 48. Bg3 Kd7 49. Kb5 All the latter led to nought. White cannot do more than draw"—Zukertort. Even better is 46. Kc6! Bird is still winning after the text move, but due to miscalculations he dared not take the c-pawn. **46. … Kd7 47. Kb5 Be7 48. Bf4 Bf8 49. Bd2 Bd6 50. Kc4 Kc7 51. Kb5 Kb7 52. Be1 Kc7 53. Bf2 Kb7 54. Kc4 Kc7 55. Kd3 Bh2 56. Ke4?** Bird overlooks his last opportunity to win the game: **56. B×c5 Bg3 57. B×b4 B×h4 58. Bd2 Bf2 59. a4 Kd6 60. Ke4 h4 61. Bf4† Kc5 62. d6. 56. ... Kd6 57. Be1 Be5 58. Bf2 Bh2 59. Be1 Be5 60. Bd2 Bh2 61. Be3 Bg3 62. Bg1 B×h4 63. Bh2† Kd7 64. Bf4 Bf2 65. Kf3 Be1 66. Ke2 Bc3 67. Kd3 Bg7 68. Kc4 Bf8 69. Bg3 Be7 70. Bh4 Bd6 71. Kb5** draw—*Westminster Chess Club Papers* (Zukertort), February 1876, pp. 196–197.

### (367) Mason–Bird    0–1
Match (game 8)
New York, 31 December 1875
*C32*

**1. e4 e5 2. f4 d5 3. e×d5 e4 4. Bc4 Nf6 5. Nc3 Bc5 6. d4 e×d3 *e.p.* 7. c×d3 0–0 8. d4 Bb4 9. Nf3 Re8† 10. Ne5 N×d5 11. 0–0 B×c3 12. b×c3 f6 13. Qh5 c6 14. Bd3 f5 15. Qf7† Kh8 16. Rf3 Re6 17. B×f5 Rf6 18. B×c8 Q×c8 19. Qh5 g6 20. Qh4 b5 21. Bd2 Nd7 22. Rh3 Nf8 23. g4 Qe6 24. N×g6† R×g6 25. f5 Q×f5 26. Rg3 Qd7 27. Rf1 Ne6 28. Bh6 Rag8 29. h3 Ng5 30. B×g5 R×g5 31. Kh1 Qe6 32. Rgf3 R5g7 33. Re1 Qg6 34. Ref1 Qe4 35. Kh2 Qe7 36. Qg3 Qc7 37. Q×c7 R×c7 38. a4 a6 39. Rc1 Nb6 40. a×b5 a×b5 41. Kg3 Kg7 42. Rcf1 Re8 43. h4 Rce7 44. g5 Re3 45. h5 Nd5 46. R×e3 R×e3† 47. Kg4 R×c3 48. Ra1 Re3 49. Ra6 Nb4 50. Ra7† Kg8 51. h6 Nd5 52. Rg7† Kh8 53. Ra7 Re8 54. Rb7 Ne7 55. Kf4 Kg8 56. Kg4 Kf7 57. d5 c×d5 58. R×b5 Rd8 59. Kf3 Rd6 60. Kg4 Ke6 61. Rb7 Rd7 62. Rb6† Ke5** White resigns—*Westminster Chess Club Papers*, February 1876, p. 197.

### (368) Bird–Mason    0–1
Match (game 9)
New York, 31 December 1875
*A02*

**1. f4 e5 2. f×e5 d6 3. e×d6 B×d6 4. Nf3 Bg4 5. e4 Nf6 6. d3 0–0 7. Bg5 Nc6 8. Be2 B×f3 9. B×f3 Bc5 10. Nc3 Qd4 11. Qd2 Nd7 12. Nd1 Nde5 13. Be3 Qd6 14. B×c5 Q×c5 15. Qf2 Qb4† 16. Qd2 Qc5 17. Nc3 Rfd8 18. Qf2 Nd4 19. Bd1 Rd6 20. Nd5 R×d5 21. e×d5 Qb4† 22. Qd2 N×d3†** and White resigns—*City of London Chess Magazine*, February 1876, p. 18.

### (369) Mason–Bird    1–0
Match (game 10)
New York, 31 December 1875
*C33*

**1. e4 e5 2. f4 e×f4 3. Bc4 f5 4. Qe2 Nf6 5. e5 Ne4 6. Nf3 Be7 7. 0–0 d5 8. e×d6 *e.p.* N×d6 9. Bb3 Nc6 10. d4 Ne4 11. Qc4 Nd6 12. Qd5 Nb4 13. Qe5 Kf8 14. Q×f4 c5 15. d×c5 Ne4 16. Nc3 B×c5† 17. Be3 Qb6 18. B×c5† N×c5 19. Kh1 N×b3 20. a×b3 h5 21. Na4 Qb5 22. Qd6† Kf7 23. Ng5†** and White wins—*Illustrated London News*, 19 February 1876.

### (370) Bird–Mason    1–0
Match (game 11)
New York, 31 December 1875
*C48*

**1. e4 e5 2. Nf3 Nf6 3. Nc3 Nc6 4. Bb5 Bc5 5. N×e5 N×e5 6. d4 Bb4 7. d×e5 N×e4 8. Qd4 B×c3† 9. b×c3 Ng5 10. f4 Ne6**

**11. Qf2 f5 12. Ba3 c5 13. Bc4 Qa5 14. Bb2 Qc7 15. 0–0 b6 16. Rad1 Bb7 17. Rd6 0–0–0 18. Rfd1 Rhe8 19. h4 g6 20. Qd2 Re7 21. Bc1 Rg8 22. Qd3 Reg7 23. Be3 h6 24. a4 Be4 25. Qd2 Bc6 26. Bb5 B×b5 27. a×b5 Qb7 28. Ra1 Re8 29. c4 Kb8 30. Rd3 Kc7 31. Rda3 Ra8 32. Qd6† Kd8 33. Qd5 Kc7 34. Kf2 h5 35. Qd6† Kd8 36. Rd3 Re7 37. Qd5 Kc7 38. Rda3 Ree8 39. Qd6† Kd8 40. Rd3 Qc7 41. Rda3 Qb7 42. Ra4 Rf8 43. Ra6 Re8 44. R6a3 Re7 45. Rd3 Ke8 46. Rda3 Kf7 47. Qd1 Ree8 48. g3 Rec8 49. Rd3 Ke7 50. Rd6 Rd8 51. Ra2 Rac8 52. c3 Kf7 53. Qd5 Qc7 54. Rd2 Ke7 55. Rd3 Rb8 56. Bc1 Qb7 57. Rd2 Qc7 58. Qf3 Qb7 59. Qd1 Rbc8 60. Ra2 Rc7 61. Be3 Rcc8 62. Rad2 Rb8 63. Ra2 Rbc8 64. Qd5 Rb8 65. Rd2 Qc7 66. Rd1 Qb7 67. Qd2 Rbc8 68. Qc2 Rc7 69. R1d5 Re8 70. Qd1 Qc8 71. Rd2 Qb7 72. Ra2 Rcc8 73. Ra1 Rf8 74. Rd2 Qc7 75. Rda2 Ra8 76. Qd5 Rg8 77. Qh1 Rh8 78. Ra3 Rhb8 79. R1a2 Qb7 80. Qd1 Qc7 81. Kg1 Rh8 82. Qa1 Qb7 83. Bf2 Qe4 84. R×a7 R×a7 85. R×a7 Q×c4 86. Qd1 Rd8 87. Qd6† Ke8 88. Q×b6 Q×c3 89. R×d7 R×d7 90. Q×e6† Kd8 91. Qb6† Kc8 92. Qc6† Kd8 93. b6 Qb4 94. e6 Rg7 95. Qd6† Ke8 96. Qb8† Ke7 97. Qc7† Kf8 98. Qd8** mate—*The Spirit of the Times*, 8 January 1876.

### (371) Mason–Bird    1–0
Match (game 12)
New York, 2 January 1876
*C42*

**1. e4 e5 2. Nf3 Nf6 3. N×e5 d6 4. Nf3 N×e4 5. d4 d5 6. Bd3 Bg4 7. 0–0 Be7 8. c4 0–0 9. c×d5 Nf6 10. Nc3 N×d5 11. Be4 Be6 12. Qe2 N×c3 13. b×c3 c6 14. Bc2 Nd7 15. Qd3 g6 16. Bf4 Nb6 17. Rfe1 Bf6 18. Be5 B×e5 19. R×e5 Bc4 20. Qd2 Bd5 21. Qh6 Qf6 22. Ng5 Qg7 23. Qh3 h6 24. Nf3 Rae8 25. Rae1 R×e5 26. N×e5 Re8 27. Re3 B×a2 28. f4 Nd5 29. Rf3 f6 30. N×g6 Bc4 31. Ne5 f×e5 32. Rg3 e×f4 33. R×g7† K×g7 34. Qg4† Kh8 35. h4 Re1† 36. Kh2 Ne3 37. Qc8† Bg8 38. Bb3 Ng4† 39. Q×g4 B×b3 40. Q×f4 Re6 41. Qb8†** and Black resigns—*Land and Water*, 29 January 1876.

### (372) Bird–Mason    1–0
Match (game 13)
New York, 3 January 1876
*C48*

**1. e4 e5 2. Nf3 Nf6 3. Nc3 Nc6 4. Bb5 a6 5. B×c6 d×c6 6. h3 Bd6 7. 0–0 0–0 8. d3 h6 9. Be3 c5 10. Nh2 Be6 11. Qf3 c6** 11. c4 solves all his problems. **12. b3 Kh7 13. Na4 Nd7 14. Qe2 Qa5 15. Bd2 Qc7 16. Nc3 Rae8 17. g4** A valiant attempt at a kingside attack that cannot but be called premature. **17. ... g5** Mason shows himself very impressed by Bird's last move. Instead of this poor and weakening move, 17. ... Ra8 is interesting to make room for his minor pieces to defend the kingside and initiate some play of his own on the queenside. **18. Nd1 f6 19. Ne3 Rf7 20. h4** Bird correctly opens the front. **20. ... Rg7?** Too slow. After 20. ... Nf8 21. Nf5 Ng6 everything turns out fine as the knight gets involved in the defense. **21. Nf5 B×f5** It was not better to let the knight go untouched: 21. ... Rgg8 22. Kg2 Nf8 23. h×g5 h×g5 24. Rh1 Rh8 25. Nf1† Kg8 26. R×h8† K×h8 27. N1g3 and White's initiative is decisive.

22. g×f5 Nf8 23. Kh1 Qf7 24. Rg1?! Bird amasses his powers against g5 but this is useless and time-consuming. By playing 24. Ng4, inviting 24. ... Nd7 and then 25. h×g5 h×g5 26. Kg2, the battleground is cunningly moved towards the edge of the board. 24. ... Nd7 25. Rg3 Rh8 26. Rag1 Kg8 27. Be3 b6 28. Rh3 a5 29. c4 Bf8 30. Rgg3 Rhh7 31. Ng4 h5? His only chance was to sit still and wait with 31. ... Qe8. 32. N×f6†! "Very good. This move ought to have won the game"—Wisker. 32. ... Q×f6 33. h×g5 Qd6 34. g6 Rh8 35. R×h5 Nf6 36. R×h8† K×h8 (see diagram)

After 36. ... K×h8

37. Rh3†?! A logical candidate here would have been 37. Bg5!, but the real point becomes apparent after the forced 37. ... Kg8 and now the surprising 38. d4! Rd7 (if 38. ... c×d4 39. c5! b×c5 40. Qc4† etc.) 39. d5 results in a clear improvement of his pawn structure compared to the game. 37. ... Kg8 38. Bg5 Rd7 39. Qe3 Bg7 40. f4 e×f4 41. B×f4 Qd4 42. Qe2 42. Q×d4 R×d4 43. Be5 Rd7 44. Bc3 might be a better winning attempt. 42. ... Ne8 43. Bh2 Re7 "The attack is now over, and though White has still three good pawns for his piece, his own king is dangerously exposed"—Wisker. More disturbing is 43. ... a4! 44. Bg1 Qe5 45. Qh5 Nf6 46. Qh4 Nd7 47. Rf3 Qf6 48. Qh2?! Bird doesn't resign himself to the draw that would be certain after the exchange of queens. The downside of the text move becomes soon obvious: White's pawn chain is not only paralyzed but will also come under serious pressure. 48. ... Ne5 49. Rg3 Rd7 50. Qh3 Qd6 51. Bh2 Qe7 52. Re3 "White's efforts to maintain an exhaustive attack have brought him into serious jeopardy"—Wisker. 52. ... N×d3 53. Bg3 Ne5 54. Re1 Bf6 55. g7? "An unwise sacrifice. Attack in such a situation is impossible"—Wisker. 55. ... B×g7 56. Bh4 Bf6 57. Rg1† Kf8 58. B×f6 Q×f6 59. Qh5 Rf7 60. Rg3 Ke7 61. Qg5 Rh7† 62. Kg2 Rh2† 63. Kf1 Q×g5 64. R×g5 R×a2 "White has paid the penalty of rashness. With equal pawns and a piece ahead Black ought to have won easily"—Wisker. 65. Rg7† Kf6 66. Rh7 Nf7 67. Rh3 Ra3 68. Rg3 Ne5 69. Rg8 R×b3 70. Rf8† Kg5 71. Re8 Kf4 72. f6 Kf3 73. Ke1 Rb2? "A blunder of the order commonly known as stupendous. 73. ... N×c4 wins easily"—Wisker. 74. R×e5 Ke3 75. Kd1 Kd3 76. Kc1 Rh2? 76. ... Rc2† 77. Kb1 Kd2 still draws. 77. Rf5 Rh8 78. f7 Rf8 79. e5 Ke4 80. e6 Black resigns—*City of London Chess Magazine* (Wisker), February 1876, pp. 20–22.

## (373) Mason–Bird    1–0
Match (game 14)
New York, 3 January 1876
C33

1. e4 e5 2. f4 e×f4 3. Bc4 Qh4† 4. Kf1 Bb4 5. d4 g5 6. Nf3 Qh5 7. h4 Nc6 8. c3 Be7 9. Kg1 g4 10. Ng5 B×g5 11. h×g5 Q×g5

---

12. Qf1 Qg7 13. B×f4 d6 14. Nd2 h5 15. Bg3 Nge7 16. Bh4 f5 17. e×f5 B×f5 18. d5 Qh6 19. d×c6 Q×d2 20. Re1 Rh7 21. Re2 Qh6 22. c×b7 Rb8 23. Q×f5 Kd8 24. Kh2 g3† 25. Kh3 R×b7 26. Rhe1 c5 27. Re6 Black resigns—*Westminster Chess Club Papers,* February 1876, p. 200.

## (374) Bird–Mason    0–1
Match (game 15)
New York, 3 January 1876
C77

1. e4 e5 2. Nf3 Nc6 3. Bb5 a6 4. Ba4 Nf6 5. Qe2 b5 6. Bb3 Bc5 7. c3 Qe7 8. d3 h6 9. Be3 Bb6 "The bishop should be left at c5, or retreated to a7"—Zukertort. 10. B×b6 c×b6 11. Nbd2 0-0 12. Nf1 Nh5 13. Ne3 Nf4 14. Qd2 d6 15. h4 Qd8 16. g3 Nh5 17. Bd5 Qe8 (see diagram)

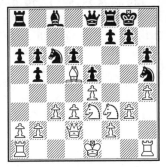

After 17. ... Qe8

18. g4! Nf4 19. h5 Be6 20. g5! Rc8 21. Rg1 Bird managed the opening very well, and Mason is clearly suffering. Instead of the relatively innocent text move, however, more pressing seems 21. g×h6 g×h6 22. d4. 21. ... Kh7 22. a3 Na5 23. b4 B×d5 24. b×a5 Be6 25. g×h6 g×h6 26. a×b6 Qc6 All of Bird's pawn moves served nothing. His attack is now over and he has made too many concessions on the queenside to be well off. 27. b7 Q×b7 28. Ng2 N×g2† 29. R×g2 Qc7 30. Rc1 d5 The opening of the center is not without danger for his own king. With 30. ... Rg8 he gains command over the g-file. 31. e×d5 B×d5 32. Qe3 32. Rg3 was necessary in order to free the knight. The disadvantage of the text move is demonstrated after 32. ... Qb7! 33. Rg3 f5! 32. ... Rce8? This is completely innocuous and allows Bird to get some kind of defense together. 33. Kd2 Qd6 34. Rcg1 Re6? "Ruinous. Black should take the knight"—Zukertort. 35. Rg7† Kh8 36. Ng5! "A fine rejoinder which ought to decide the contest"—Zukertort. 36. ... h×g5 37. Q×g5 Rg6 38. h×g6?? "A frightful slip. 38. R×g6 wins the queen and the game"—Zukertort. 38. ... K×g7 39. g×f7† K×f7 40. Qg7† Ke8 41. Rg6 Be6 42. Qa7 Qd5 43. Qb8† Kf7 44. Rf6† K×f6 45. Q×f8† Bf7 46. Qh6† Bg6 47. Qh4† Kf7 48. d4 Qa2† White resigns—*Westminster Chess Club Papers* (Zukertort), February 1876, p. 200.

## (375) Mason–Bird    1–0
Match (game 16)
New York, 3 January 1876
C33

1. e4 e5 2. f4 e×f4 3. Bc4 f5 4. Qe2 Qh4† 5. Kd1 f×e4 6. Nc3 Kd8 7. N×e4 d6 8. Nf3 Qh5 9. Neg5 Nh6 10. Re1 Bd7 11. d4

Nc6 12. B×f4 Ne7 13. Be6 Bc6 14. g4 Qe8 15. Bg3 B×f3
16. Q×f3 Qb5 17. Qe3 Q×b2 18. Rc1 Qb6 19. Bh4 c5 20. Nf7†
N×f7 21. B×f7 Qc7 22. d×c5 d×c5 23. Re2 b6 24. Qe4 Rb8
25. Rd2† Black resigns—*Westminster Chess Club Papers*, February
1876, p. 200.

## (376) Bird–Mason      ½–½
Match (game 17)
New York, 4 January 1876
*C01*

    1. e4 e6 2. d4 d5 3. e×d5 e×d5 4. Nf3 Nf6 5. Bd3 Bd6 6. 0–0
Be6 7. Bg5 Nbd7 8. Nc3 c6 9. Qd2 Qc7 10. Ne2 Ne4 11. Qe3 f5
12. Bf4 0–0 13. B×d6 Q×d6 14. Qf4 Qe7 15. Rfe1 g5 16. Qc7
Rab8 17. Ng3 Rfc8 18. Qa5 a6 19. Re2 g4 20. B×e4 f×e4 21. Ne1
Kh8 22. Qd2 Rf8 23. c3 Qf6 24. Nc2 Qg6 25. Rae1 Rbe8 26. c4
h5 27. c×d5 c×d5 28. Nf1 h4 29. Re3 Nf6 30. Qb4 Rf7 31. Qd6
Nh5 32. g3 h×g3 33. f×g3 Nf6 34. R3e2 Nh7 35. Nd2 Ng5
36. Kh1 Nf3 37. Rd1 Qh5 38. Nf1 Qh6 39. Nce3 Kh7 40. Rc2
Rd7 41. Rc7 R×c7 42. Q×c7† Qg7 43. Qb6 Ng5 44. Rc1 Qf6
45. Qc7† Re7 46. Qf4 Rf7 47. Q×f6 R×f6 48. Rc7† Rf7
49. R×f7† N×f7 50. Ng2 Nd6 51. Nf4 Bf7 52. Ne3 Nb5 53. N×g4
N×d4 54. N×d5 Kg7 55. Nc3 Be6 56. Ne3 Bd7 57. Kg2 b5 58. a3
a5 59. b4 a×b4 60. a×b4 Bc6 61. Kf2 Kf6 62. h4 Ke5 63. g4 Kf4
64. h5 Kg5 65. Kg3 Nb3 66. Ne2 Bd7 67. Nf4 Nd4 68. Nh3†
Kh6 69. Kf4 Nc6 70. Nd5 e3 71. N×e3 N×b4 72. Nf5† B×f5
73. K×f5 Nc6 74. Nf4 Nd4† 75. Ke4 Nc6 76. Kd5 Nd8 77. Nd3
b4 78. N×b4 Kg5 79. h6 K×h6 80. Ke4 Kg5 81. Kf3 Nf7 draw—
*Westminster Chess Club Papers*, February 1876, pp. 200–201.

## (377) Mason–Bird      1–0
Match (game 18)
New York, 4 January 1876
*B40*

    1. e4 c5 2. Nf3 e6 3. d4 c×d4 4. N×d4 Nf6 5. Bd3 Nc6 6. N×c6
"This may not be so good as 6. Be3. It gives Black a very formidable
center, though White has some little attack as an equivalent"—
Mason. 6. ... b×c6 7. 0–0 d5 8. e5 Nd7 9. Qe1 Rb8 10. c3 Nc5
11. Be2 Be7 12. b4 Nd7 13. Bd3 c5 14. a3 0–0 "It will be seen that
the situation on the queenside is altogether in favor of Black, but
that on the kingside the advantage lies with White"—Mason. The
tension on the queenside has already become critical and with 14. ...
a5!, Bird wins at least a pawn after 15. Bd2 Qc7 16. f4 c×b4 17. a×b4
a×b4 18. c×b4 Qb6† 19. Be3 Q×b4. Worse is 15. b×a5 or 15. b×c5.
The move a7–a5 remains recommended for the following moves.
15. Qe2 Qc7 16. f4 g6 "A little more defensive, we think, than the
exigencies of the position demanded, and certainly quite at variance
with Mr. Bird's usual style of play"—Mason. 17. Qg4 Bb7 17. ... a5!
was now particularly strong, as White's queen left that side of the
board. 18. Be3 Rfd8 19. Ra2 h5 Needlessly weakening his kingside,
and thereby giving his opponent a real target. 20. Qg3 Kh8 21. Re2
Rg8 22. Bd2 Starting a profound maneuvre to exchange his worst
piece, but Mason does not really get any value for it. Bird, for his
part, has run out of ideas and just sits still and waits. 22. ... Nf8
23. Be1 Rd8 24. Qh3 Nh7 25. Bh4 B×h4 26. Q×h4 a5 27. Qf2
d4 After doing nothing for a very long time, Bird decides that the

time is ripe to open up the position, but after 28. Rc2! it turns out
that only White can profit from it. 28. b×c5 d×c3 29. Bc4 g5 "This
might be done later with more advantage"—Mason. Although the
text move is not as bad as it looks, it is certainly wiser to play 29. ...
Rc8 first, getting ready to pick up the c-pawn and exchange queens.
30. f5 (*see diagram*)

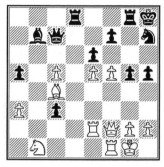

*After 30. f5*

    30. ... e×f5? 30. ... Bd5 31. B×d5 R×d5 32. f×e6 f×e6 doesn't
look nice, but his drawing chances remain very realistic. The text
move is a decisive positional concession. 31. N×c3! "The entrance
of this knight into the game speedily turns the scale in favor of
White"—Mason. 31. ... Rc8 32. Nb5! "White forces the exchange
of queens, as Black's scattered forces will be then easily overpowered"—Zukertort. 32. ... Q×c5 33. Q×c5 R×c5 34. Nd6 f4
35. Rb1 Bd5 36. B×d5 R×d5 37. N×f7† Kg7 38. Rb7 Kg6
39. Rc2 Ra8 40. Rc6† Kf5 41. Nd6† K×e5 42. Nc4† "Mr. Bird
remarked, after the game was ended, that the movements of this
knight exemplified perfectly what is known as 'chess luck.' If he had
not come into the game just as he did, and moved around just as he
did, the game would have been different, and would have had a different conclusion. Mr. Bird also said something about the 'unlucky'
[*sic*] of his own knight. What it was, we cannot recollect at this moment"—Mason. 42. ... Kd4 43. R×h7 Re8 44. R×h5 Rb5 45. Kf2
Kd3 46. Rhh6 g4 47. Rhd6† Ke4 48. Rd2 Black resigns. "This
game is replete with fine points, and was one of the best, if not the
very best, of the match. Mr. Bird good-naturedly admitted that he
was beaten on his own merits"—Hazeltine. *New York Clipper*
(Hazeltine), 22 January 1876; *The Spirit of the Times* (Mason), 29
January 1876.

## (378) Bird–Mason      0–1
Match (game 19)
New York, 5 January 1876
*A02*

    1. f4 f5 2. e3 Nf6 3. b3 b6 4. Bb2 e6 5. Be2 Bb7 6. Bf3 "If there
is any advantage on either side, it is on that of White. By this move
Mr. Bird compels his opponent to exchange or shut in his queen's
bishop, while he preserves the open diagonal for his own"—Mason.
6. ... Nc6 7. Nh3 Be7 8. c4 Rb8 "There is nothing strikingly good
about this, but what was he to do?"—Mason. 9. 0–0 0–0 10. d3 d5
"Leaving the e-pawn weak, but the intention of the move was to
cut off the range of the opposing queen's bishop at any reasonable
hazard"—Mason. 11. d4 Qe8 12. Nc3 These last two moves were
weak, as Black could play 12. ... d×c4 13. b×c4 Na5! with strong
pressure. 12. ... Nd8 "Intending to open an attack on the kingside,

should opportunity occur—that is, if White does not do so himself"—Mason. **13. Rc1 c6 14. Rc2 Ba6** "14. ... a6 15. Be2 Nf7 16. Nf2 Ba8 was given as the game continuation in various publications. This line, however, would have led to the loss of a pawn, as White could often play c×d5 and B×a6. Mason himself emphasized the course with 14. ... Ba6 as the correct one" (*American Chess Journal*, June 1877, p. 28). **15. Be2 Nf7 16. Nf2** "White appears to have no definite object in view just here; not, indeed, for some time afterward. Instead of going on with the attack, he seems willing to act on the defensive, if Black will make a positive forward movement"—Mason. **16. ... Bb7 17. Bd3 Nh6 18. Be2 Rc8 19. Nb1 Kh8 20. Nd2 Rg8 21. Nf3 Nf7 22. Nh3 Ng4** "This begins the attack in earnest—there is now no retreat. It is seldom that the first 22 moves are made in a game without a single exchange taking place"—Mason. **23. Bc1 g5? 24. Ne5?** 24. Nf×g5 opens several lines and diagonals against Black's king. White's bishops especially come to life; e.g., 24. ... N×g5 25. f×g5 Qh5 26. e4! d×e4 27. Bf4 Rgf8 28. Be5† Kg8 29. Rc3 c5 30. Rg3. **24. ... Ng×e5 25. f×e5 g4** This move liberates White's knight. Better is 25. ... c5! **26. Nf4 Ng5 27. Kh1 Qf8 28. B×g4?!** "Bad play. The capture of this bishop would result in leaving Black with three pieces for his queen, and with the superior position"—Mason. Bird has the luxury that he can improve the position of his pieces step by step, but he lacks the patience. **28. ... Qh6?** "Instead of this he could have taken the bishop. Had White deferred correctly, Black could hope for no more than a draw after this move"—Mason. White has not enough for the sacrificed material after 28. ... f×g4 29. N×e6 Qh6 30. N×g5 Q×g5 31. e4 Qg6. **29. Bh3** 29. Bh5! seals Black's fate, as his queen is definitively cut off. **29. ... d×c4 30. b×c4 c5 31. d5!** Mason desperately seeks counterplay, but Bird's center forestalls any attempt, at least for a moment. **31. ... Rcd8 32. e4! Qh4 33. e×f5 e×d5 34. c×d5?** Mason could resign after 34. f6! **34. ... N×h3 35. g×h3?** 35. f6 N×f4 36. B×f4 R×d5 37. Qe1 is far from ideal, but with a miracle a draw is still possible. **35. ... R×d5** "This practically decides the contest"—Mason. **36. N×d5 Qe4† 37. Rf3 B×d5 38. Rcf2 Bh4 39. Rf1 Q×e5 40. Qd2 Bf6 41. Qf4 Qe7** and White resigns—*The Spirit of the Times* (Mason), 22 January 1876.

---

# ANOTHER MONTH IN NEW YORK, JANUARY 1876

Bird remained the guest of the Down Town Chess Club for a few more weeks. He was readily available for every comer with an interest in the game. Bird later claimed that he played some 1,500 offhand games during the first three months of 1876. He generated a lot of interest with a simultaneous exhibition, a rare event in New York, on Wednesday 12 January.[9]

The complete score was given in the *New York Clipper* on 22 January. Bird scored 15 wins and conceded 5 draws (against Becker, Felt, Mickleham, Limbeck and Whittaker). On Saturday 15 January Bird played against a team of four consulting players at the same club. The game began at 8:15 p.m. and lasted several hours. According to Bird he obtained a winning position after just 20 moves but ultimately he had to submit himself to a draw.

A short while later Bird's engagement with the Down Town Chess Club ended. On 24 January, the *New York Evening Telegram* reported that "several ladies have signified their desire to become members of the Down Town Chess Club, and the organization proposes fitting up a room especially for their use." Apparently his visit was quite a success for the club!

For the last days of January Bird relocated to the Café International. Here, consultation chess was the order of the day. The teams were composed in several constellations. Bird opposed Preston Ware and S.R. Dill in a few games. He also joined Ware against Mackenzie and James P. Barnett. The most noteworthy game saw Bird, Ware and Delmar lose against another trio: Mackenzie, Barnett and Philip Richardson.

### (379) von Frankenberg & Becker & Doyle & Teed–Bird   ½–½
Consultation game
New York (Café Cosmopolitan), 15 January 1876
*B40*

"Bird played a consultation game last evening at the rooms of the Down Town Chess Club against Messrs. Frankenberg, Becker, Doyle and Teed. The game commenced at a quarter-past eight and was stubbornly contested by both sides until a late hour"—*New York Herald*.

**1. e4 c5 2. d4 c×d4 3. Nf3 e6 4. N×d4 Nf6 5. Bd3 Nc6 6. Be3 d5** "To this point the moves made on both sides are the best according to the latest authors. It is, however, but fair to state that the allies made the last three moves on general principles, without knowing that they were book, and that their original intention was to leave the book as soon as possible, consistent with safety, since it was known to them that Mr. Bird is thorough master in this respect"—Doyle. **7. N×c6** "7. e×d5 is the move given by the book at this point, but the allies thought it preferable to permit the defense to mass his center pawns rather than to have both of his bishops bearing down upon their king's quarters"—Doyle. **7. ... b×c6 8. Nd2 Be7 9. c3 0-0 10. Qc2** "Threatening the h-pawn and getting the queen into position"—Doyle. **10. ... e5** "The proper reply"—Doyle. **11. 0-0 h6 12. Nb3** "Intending, if the occasion arose, to attempt to permanently establish the knight at c5 after forcing the exchange of bishops"—Doyle. **12. ... a5** "This move at once changes White's program"—Doyle. **13. Rad1** "For the purpose

9. A first partial report of the evening was published in the *New York World*: "Mr. Henry E. Bird ... essayed the task last evening of adding twenty odd games to his victorious record all at once. The playing was at the down-town rooms of the New York Chess Club.... In a long, narrow room twenty-four chess-boards were arranged side by side, and behind these sat four-and-twenty chess-players, like the legendary black-birds, all in a row. Some had at their elbows cups of coffee or chocolate supplied from the cafe below, and took matters leisurely, smoking comfortable pipes as the games progressed. Others were nervous, refreshing themselves with fingernails only. These were all amateurs whom Mr. Bird encountered last evening. The Englishman, ruddy and confident, with a cigar set contemplatively in the corner of his mouth, moved from board to board seemingly heedless of a foot whose ample coverings of flannel proclaimed it a little gouty, advancing his men with scarcely any time lost in deliberation, and apparently at ease concerning each and every one of his two dozen antagonists. ... At 12 o'clock the number of games concluded was six, all of which were won by Mr. Bird." *St. Louis Globe-Democrat*, 16 January 1876; first published in the *New York World*.

of creating a place for the knight at the same time utilizing the rook"—Doyle. **13. ... a4 14. Nc1 Qa5** "We have here a very pretty gambit attack on the part of Mr. Bird, which, without the exercise of great care by the White forces, would have resulted disastrously"—Doyle. **15. Kh1 Be6 16. f4 d×e4** "This attack was unlooked for by the allies, as it was examined by them and pronounced not good. In its result, however, it probably disappointed both parties, as it brought about an even game"—Doyle. **17. B×e4 N×e4 18. Q×e4 Bd5 19. Q×e5?** (*see diagram*) "If 19. Qc2, Mr. Bird might play 19. ... f5 20. f×e5 Be4 20. Qf2 Q×e5 with a good game"—Doyle. Also slightly better for Black were 19. ... Bc4 or 19. ... e×f4, relying on his bishop pair for some lasting pressure. The text move captures a poisoned pawn.

*After 19. Q×e5*

**19. ... Rfe8!** "Mr. Bird has played this series of moves with great judgment, and has now much the best of the game"—Hervey. **20. Qd4** "The only move, for if 20. Bd4, threatening mate, Black plays 20. ... Bf8 and wins"—Doyle. **20. ... Rad8** After 20. ... Red8! there is no escape for White's queen, except to enter a lost endgame with 21. Qb6 Q×b6 22. B×b6 Rdb8. **21. Qa7 Qb5 22. b3 a×b3?!** White's problems with the queen were far from over after the very strong 22. ... c5!, menacing 23. ... Qc6 and 24. ... Ra8. If 23. Q×a4 Qb7!, White is again forced into a hopeless sacrifice to save his queen: 24. R×d5 Q×d5 25. Qb5 Bf6, with a winning advantage. **23. a×b3 B×b3 24. N×b3 R×d1 25. R×d1 Q×b3 26. Qa1 Bh4?!** "This move greatly puzzled the White allies, for they were loath to move the bishop and thus let the rook come to d7. It will be found, however, that the text move is the only one to save the game. The move advocated by some of the party, for instance 27. Rd3, would allow 27. ... c5 and 28. ... c4"—Doyle. The actual reply of the allies consolidates the position. A better attempt would therefore have been 26. ... Bf6, winning a pawn after 27. Bd4 B×d4 28. c×d4 Re4. **27. Bd4 Re2 28. Qa8†** 28. Qb1! neutralizes Black's initiative completely. The excursion of the queen is dangerous. **28. ... Kh7 29. Rg1 Qd5 30. Qc8 Re6 31. Ra1?!** Bird's last move was slightly imprecise (30. ... Re4 is best). With 31. Qf8! Rg6 32. Qc5 his opponents could secure a draw. **31. ... f5?!** "Well played, with the double purpose of stopping the advance of the f-pawn and also of preventing 32. Qh3 in the event of 31. ... Rg6. It has, however, the disadvantage of allowing White's bishop more freedom"—Doyle. The latter element is the most important of the position. After 31. ... Bf6, White remains under severe pressure. **32. Qb7 Rg6 33. Qb2 c5 34. Be5 Qe4 35. Qd2 c4 36. Rd1 Rb6 37. Qd4 Rb1 38. R×b1 Q×b1† 39. Qg1 Qe4 40. Qa7 Qb1† 41. Qg1 Be1 42. h3 h5 43. g3?!** Weakening the kingside is very inadvisable. 43. B×g7! forces a quick draw. **43. ... Qe4† 44. Kh2 B×c3?!** "One of those

hasty moves which even the best players will sometimes make and find too late that they have not such a sure game as they expect"—Doyle. **44. ... Qc2† 45. Qg2 Qd3!** wins the pawn in much more favorable circumstances. The consulting players now find the way to a well-earned draw. **45. Qd1! Bb4 46. Q×h5† Kg8 47. Qe8† Bf8 48. Qe6† Kh7 49. Qf7 Qe2† 50. Kh1 Qf1† 51. Kh2 Qf2† 52. Kh1** draw—*Western Advertiser* (Doyle), 31 January 1876; *Sunday Call* (Hervey), 30 January 1876; *New York Herald*, 16 January 1876.

## (380) Ryan–Bird　1–0
Offhand game
New York (Café Cosmopolitan), January 1876
C35

**1. e4 e5 2. Bc4 Bc5 3. Nf3 Nc6 4. c3 d6 5. d4 e×d4 6. b4 Bb6 7. c×d4 Bg4 8. Bb2 Nf6 9. b5 Ne7 10. Nbd2 0–0 11. Qc2 c6 12. 0–0 d5 13. Ng5 Ng6 14. Bb3 Be2 15. Rfe1 B×b5 16. h4 Kh8 17. Ndf3 h6 18. e5 h×g5 19. e×f6 g×f6 20. h×g5 f×g5 21. Qf5 Kg7 22. N×g5 Bc7 23. Ba3 Bd6 24. Bc2 Kg8 25. N×f7 R×f7 26. Q×g6† Rg7 27. Qe6† Kh8 28. B×d6** Black resigns—*New York Clipper*, 11 March 1876.

## (381) Bird & Delmar & Ware– Mackenzie & Richardson & Barnett　0–1
Consultation game
New York (Café International), 25 January 1876
C52

**1. e4 e5 2. Nf3 Nc6 3. Bc4 Bc5 4. b4 B×b4 5. c3 Ba5 6. d4 e×d4 7. 0–0 d×c3 8. Qb3 Qf6 9. e5 Qg6 10. N×c3 Nge7 11. Ne2** A standard move in a topical line at that time. It has since been overshadowed by 11. Ba3, which promises White compensation for the pawn. **11. ... b5!** First played by Neumann against Minckwitz in Baden-Baden 1870. It was generally thought wise for White to decline the pawn at b5. **12. Bd3 Qe6 13. Qb2 Ng6 14. Nf4 N×f4 15. B×f4 h6 16. Rac1 0–0** "Somewhat premature; 16. ... a6, followed by 17. ... Bb7 seems to be the best line of play, as Black could then castle on either side, according to circumstances"—Mackenzie. **17. Bb1 Rb8 18. Rfd1 Re8 19. Qc2 Qg6** 19. ... g6 is certainly better, as White could now exchange queens and win back one pawn, with enough compensation for the other pawn he has sacrificed. After 19. ... g6, 20. B×h6? is bad because of 20. ... N×e5. **20. Qe2 Qg4 21. Bg3** Rather timid. Better attacking chances gave 21. Qe4 g6 22. h3 Qe6 23. B×h6. **21. ... Bb7** 21. ... Bb6! prevents White's next move and is good enough for some advantage. Bird and his allies now follow up with some strong attacking moves. **22. Q×b5 Bb6 23. Qd3 g6 24. Rc4** "A formidable looking move, though possibly the more simple course 24. Q×d7 might have turned out better in the end"—Mackenzie. After 24. Q×d7?!, 24. ... Re6! is a strong rejoinder; e.g., 25. Qd3?! N×e5! wins the important e-pawn. **24. ... Qe6 25. Rh4 Kg7** It was better not to worry too much about material and gain some activity for his pieces by playing 25. ... Ne7 (hoping for 26. R×h6? Nf5). Then 26. Bc2 seems to be White's best move. After 26. ... Bd5, the position is more or less balanced, with both sides having difficulties to break the opponent's defense. **26. Bf4** Dangerous for Black was 26. Bc2! as the bishop threatens to join the attack—after 26. ... Rbd8 27. Qd2 Rh8 28. Bb3

Qe7 29. Bf4 etc., or after 26. ... a6? 27. Rf4 Qe7 28. Bh4 etc. The best antidote is 26. ... Na5!, ruling out the activation of White's bishop. **26. ... Rh8** The h-pawn remains rather irrelevant. 26. ... Ne7! is a good move here. **27. Qd2 h5?!** A clear concession. 27. ... Kg8 brings the king on a safer spot. **28. Ng5?!** "To this point the attack has been played in fine attacking style, and it is questionable if any of the moves could be improved upon. But here a very weak move, apparently without aim, allows the defense to free their game, and the attack completely collapses"—Hicks. White's main objective should still be the activation of his bishop, which he could achieve with the simple 28. Bc2!—e.g., 28. ... Ba5 29. Qc1 Ba8 30. Bb3, and Black is getting in dire straits. **28. ... Qe7 29. Nf3?!** 29. Qc3 (Mackenzie) 29. ... Kg8 30. Be4 Nd4 or 29. Be4 Bc5 30. Bd5 N×e5 doesn't promise anything for White, but at least it's not worse. **29. ... Nd4!** "From this point the game is in favor of the Black allies"—Mackenzie. **30. Ng5 Ne6 31. N×e6† Q×e6 32. Bg5?** Giving up the e-pawn is equal to suicide, as they don't have enough compensation for two pawns in this position. Although it is clear that White's position is difficult to play, there is hope after 32. Bd3. Black can then chose between 32. ... Qd5 33. Bf1 Q×d2 34. B×d2 Rhe8 35. Bc3 or 32..Rbe8 33. Bc4 Qc6 34. Bf1 Re7 35. Bg3. In each case, White has definite compensation for the deficit of the pawn. **32. ... Q×e5 33. Bf4** If 33. Rf4 Q×g5 34. R×f7† Kh6 (Hicks). **33. ... Qf6 34. Bg5 B×f2†!** "Seemingly very hazardous, but in reality the winning move"—Hicks. **35. Kh1 Qf3!** "Beautifully played"—Hicks. **36. Rg1 Qd5?!** "Curiously enough not one of the three consulting players hit upon the much more potent 36. ... B×h4"—Mackenzie. **37. Bf6†! K×f6** (see diagram)

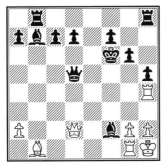

*After 37. ... K×f6*

**38. Q×f2†?** "38. Qb2† might still have left White some chance of drawing the game"—Mackenzie. Not after the astonishing 38. ... Qd4! Although this move is not easy to see, it might have been found by the Black allies by a process of elimination. Worst is 38. ... Ke7? as White wins even after 39. Re4†! Two other moves lead to a draw: 38. ... Ke6?! 39. Q×f2 f5 40. Rd4 Qc6 and Black's damaged kingside gives White enough play; and 38. ... Kg5?! 39. Qc1†. After 38. ... Qd4!, the sequel is forced: 39. R×d4 B×g2† 40. K×g2 R×b2 41. Rf4† Ke5 42. R×f2 R×f2† 43. K×f2 d5. White will find it very difficult to fight against Black's pawn mass, but a miracle remains possible. After the text move Black's king finds shelter and the game is decided. **38. ... Kg7 39. Be4 Qe5 40. B×b7 R×b7 41. Re1 Re8 42. Rf1 f5 43. Rd4 d5 44. Rdd1 Rd8 45. Rfe1 Qf6 46. Qc5 c6 47. Re2 Rdd7 48. Rde1 f4 49. Kg1 Rb5 50. Qf2 c5 51. a4 Ra5 52. Re5 d4 53. Re6 Qf7 54. Qe2 c4! 55. Q×c4 Rg5 56. Qb4 f3 57. Kf1 f2 58. R1e4 R×g2!** White resigns—*Turf, Field and Farm* (Mackenzie), 4 February 1876; *Canadian Illustrated News* (Hicks), 4 March 1876.

**(382) Bird–Alberoni   0–1**
Offhand game
New York (Café International), January 1876
*C51*

1. e4 e5 2. Nf3 Nc6 3. Bc4 Bc5 4. b4 B×b4 5. 0–0 Be7 6. d4 d6 7. c3 Bg4 8. Qb3 Na5 9. B×f7† Kf8 10. Qa4 K×f7 11. Q×a5 B×f3 12. g×f3 c6 13. Qb4 Qd7 14. Be3 h5 15. Rd1 e×d4 16. c×d4 h4 17. Nd2 Nf6 18. Rab1 b5 19. Qb3† d5 20. Kh1 a5 21. Rg1 Qe6 22. Qd3 Bb4 23. e5 Nh5 24. f4 g6 25. Nf3 Qf5 26. Q×f5† g×f5 27. Rg5 Be7 28. Rc1 Rac8 29. Rgg1 b4 30. Ng5† B×g5 31. R×g5 Ng7 32. h3 Rh5 33. f3 R×g5 34. f×g5 Ne6 35. f4 c5 36. d×c5 d4 37. Bf2 R×c5 38. R×c5 N×c5 39. B×d4 Nd3 40. Kg2 a4 41. Kf3 b3 42. a×b3 a×b3 43. Ke3 b2 and White resigns—*Philadelphia Intelligencer*, 31 January 1876.

**(383) Bird–Ware & Dill   0–1**
Consultation game
New York 1876
*C51*

1. e4 e5 2. Nf3 Nc6 3. Bc4 Bc5 4. b4 d5 5. e×d5 N×b4 6. 0–0 N×d5 7. d4 e×d4 8. c3 Ngf6 9. c×d4 Be7 10. Bb2 0–0 11. Qb3 c6 12. Nbd2 Qc7 13. Rac1 Be6 14. Ng5 Ng4 15. Ngf3 Rad8 16. Ne4 Qb6 17. Q×b6 a×b6 18. h3 Ngf6 19. Neg5 Bf5 20. g4 Bc8 21. Rfe1 Bb4 22. Re5 Rfe8 23. R×e8† R×e8 24. Ne5 Be6 25. N×e6 f×e6 26. g5 Ne4 27. h4 Nd2 28. a3 Bd6 29. B×d5 e×d5 30. Kg2 b5 31. f4 Nc4 32. N×c4 b×c4 33. Kg3 B×a3 34. B×a3 Re3† 35. Kg4 R×a3 36. Re1 Kf7 37. Kf5 g6† 38. Ke5 b5 39. Kd6 Ra6 40. Re7† Kf8 41. R×h7 c3 42. h5 c2 43. h6 c1Q 44. Rh8† Kf7 45. Rh7† Kg8 White resigns—*Boston Weekly Globe*, 18 February 1876.

**(384) Ware & Dill–Bird   0–1**
Consultation game
New York 1876
*A80*

1. d4 f5 2. f4 e6 3. Nf3 Nf6 4. e3 c6 5. Bd3 b5 6. 0–0 Na6 7. a3 Bb7 8. Bd2 Be7 9. Nc3 b4 10. Ne2 b×a3 11. b×a3 0–0 12. Ng3 c5 13. c3 Nc7 14. a4 Rc8 15. Rb1 Ba8 16. Ne5 d6 17. Nf3 Ne4 18. Be1 Nd5 19. Qb3 N×g3 20. h×g3 Kh8 21. Bd2 Qe8 22. Kf2 Nf6 23. Rh1 Ne4† 24. B×e4 c4 25. Qd1 B×e4 26. Ra1 Qg6 27. Nh4 B×h4 28. R×h4 Rb8 29. Rh3 Rb2 30. Kg1 Qg4 31. Qe1 h6 32. Rh4 Qg6 33. Rh2 Rfb8 34. Rh4 Rb1 35. R×b1 R×b1 36. Bc1 Qe8 37. Qd2 Ra1 38. Qb2 R×a4 39. g4 a6 40. g5 Qb5 41. Q×b5 a×b5 42. Kh2 d5 43. g×h6 g6 44. Kg3 Ra2 45. Rh2 Kh7 46. Kh3 K×h6 47. Kg3† Kg7 and Black wins—*Boston Weekly Globe*, 3 March 1876.

# BIRD'S VISIT TO PHILADELPHIA

The idea to organize, for the first time in history, an international chess tournament on American soil had been live for several years. In 1873 the decision was made to let the tournament coincide with the 100th anniversary of the independence of the United States. The first information about the congress reached England in 1875. Its prospects were presented very optimistically: a gigantic prize fund and the announced return of Morphy were used as a juicy carrot for the world's strongest players.

Unfortunately the reality was completely different. Two organizations, the American Chess Association and the Philadelphia Chess Club, both had a burning ambition to arrange the tournament and they collided from the start. The Europeans were distant witnesses of their quarrels.

One of Bird's motives to cross the Atlantic was to solve the problems that stood in the way of a successful congress. It was the expectation of many Americans that Bird, with his continental experience, would add considerable value to the project. If he could be convinced of the success of the tournament, so everybody hoped, then all the continental masters would find the trip to Philadelphia worthwhile.

Bird, in the company of Mackenzie and Preston Ware, arrived in Philadelphia on 28 January. Bird and Mackenzie were represented by the *Philadelphia Times* of 29 January 1876 as "honorable secretaries of the committee formed in New York to forward the desire evinced by the Philadelphia Chess Club to work in harmony with all friends to the cause of chess, for a chess congress during the Centennial."

If it really was Bird's ambition to play a role in the setting up of the congress, his mission failed utterly. He was cordially welcomed in Philadelphia but during his whole stay the press paid attention only to his feats on the board and not to any role he played in the preparation of the tournament. People more experienced in politics clearly overruled a mere chess player such as Bird.

Philadelphia was, besides New York, the strongest chess center in the United States. Bird plunged himself into the local chess scene and made himself available for each and every opponent for a variety of offhand games.[10] Yet, Bird's results were even less enticing than they had been in New York. Several newspaper columns punctually followed his score.[11] All sources agree on almost all of the following:

|  | + | − | = |
|---|---|---|---|
| against Neill | 0 | 2 | 0 |
| against Davidson | 2 | 5 | 2 |
| against D.M. Martinez | 24 | 21 | 2 |
| (2 sources mention 0 draws, a bit unlikely) | | | |
| against Barbour | 6 | 4 | 1 |
| against Elson | 5 | 0 | 2 |

10. It is thus not surprising that Bird was initially received with similar enthusiasm as in New York: "Mr. Bird is the very opposite of Mr. Morphy in personal appearance, being a hale, hearty, amiable Englishman, the very counterpart of a good-natured sea captain, and it is evident that he does not allow the play to interfere with his digestion or sleep at nights. He has already become very popular among the Philadelphians although only two days here, and expresses his delight with the city and its people. He will remain here for a week or more as the guest of the club. ... Mr. Bird's play is remarkable for its brilliancy and the ease and quickness with which he makes his moves. He conceived with celerity. He does not play blindfold, but is able to perform the wonderful feat of playing twenty different games at the same time." *Philadelphia Times*, 31 January 1876.

11. For the present work, the following sources were used: *Dubuque Chess Journal*, *Sunday Republic*, *Philadelphia Intelligencer* and Reichhelm's book *Chess in Philadelphia*.

Bird's results against the following players are less certain. They were mentioned in one or more but not all sources:

|  | + | − | = |
|---|---|---|---|
| against Frankenthal | 6 | 6 | 0 |
| against Roberts | 0 | 1 | 0 |
| against Russell (with odds) | 1 | 2 | 0 |
| against Geddes　(a lot of games played, no score given) | | | |

Bird, however, did not agree with the presentation of his results:

As I told Mr. Elson, I went to Philadelphia and did what no first-class player ever did before, or is likely ever to do again—encountered every gentleman there that asked me to play, and contested at least 300 games for amusement only. The Philadelphia chess columns, in return, misrepresent my score and my play. I have been so frequently warned to take no heed of it that I am almost ashamed to allude to it now [*New York Clipper*, 24 June 1876].

The *Philadelphia Intelligencer* confirmed on 30 June 1876 that their printed score was correct. In a private letter written on 19 April 1876 to Miron Hazeltine, the chess editor of the *New York Clipper*, Bird came up with some other reasons to explain his weak results.

... the only instances where I have lost a majority of games was at Philadelphia with Mr. Neill and Mr. Davidson, two games each. With both gentlemen however I played late in the evening when pretty well used up playing with the number of Philadelphia gentlemen who had challenged me during the day [*Hazeltine's Chess, Autographs, End Games, Games and Problems*, vol. 6, 189–190ff].

Bird's opponents were reluctant to engage in battle in suboptimal conditions. When Jacob Elson thought himself unfit to play due to a headache, their planned game was readily postponed. Bird, gout or no gout, recklessly continued battling on the chessboard. Only Dion Martinez appears to have been cut from the same wood as Bird. When Bird left the city both men had fought out nearly 50 games. That Bird only scored marginally better than his much less illustrious opponent shows his mediocre form.

The victory of the very young and talented Harry Davidson, aptly nicknamed the giant-slayer, over Bird was hailed by his club mates.[12] Nearly all of Bird's published games were lost by him. Bird cared but little to record his games or forward them to the disposal of a chess columnist while his opponents often rushed their wins into print. Bird was absolutely not pleased with this habit, and he didn't wait long to denounce it publicly.

### (385) Bird–D.M. Martinez　　1–0
Offhand game
Philadelphia, 29 January 1876
*C51*

**1. e4 e5 2. Nf3 Nc6 3. Bc4 Bc5 4. b4 B×b4 5. c3 Bc5 6. 0–0 d6 7. d4 e×d4 8. c×d4 Bb6 9. Bb2 Nge7 10. Ng5 0–0 11. Qh5 h6 12. N×f7 R×f7 13. Q×f7† Kh8 14. d5 Ne5 15. B×e5 d×e5 16. Nd2**

12. Bird's results revitalized the discussion about the change of power between British and American chess. Albert Roberts, one of the strongest Philadelphian players, gave his view on the matter: "While on this subject we may state that the English papers appear surprised at Mr. Bird's score in America, and express the belief that the American players would have no chance with Mr. Bird were he in good form. This is quite natural when we consider that the American players have tremendously increased in strength during the past ten years, and it was not until Mr. Bird's visit that they had the opportunity of measuring their strength across the board with a celebrated European, the result astonishing them as much as it did Messrs. Wisker and Zukertort...." *Sunday Republic*, 27 February 1876.

Bd7 17. Nf3 Be8 18. N×e5 Qd6 19. Q×e8† and Black resigns—
*Philadelphia Intelligencer*, 15 February 1876.

## (386) D.M. Martinez–Bird   1–0
Offhand game
Philadelphia 1876
*C40*

**1. e4 e5 2. Nf3 d5 3. e×d5 Q×d5 4. Nc3 Qe6 5. Be2 Nc6 6. 0–0
Be7 7. d4 e×d4 8. Nb5 Qd7 9. Bf4 Bd6 10. B×d6 c×d6 11. Nf×d4
a6 12. N×c6 a×b5 13. Re1 Ne7 14. N×e7** Black resigns—*Sunday
Republic*, 9 April 1876.

## (387) H.F. Davidson–Bird   1–0
Offhand game
Philadelphia, 5 February 1876
*C61*

**1. e4 e5 2. Nf3 Nc6 3. Bb5 Nd4 4. N×d4 e×d4 5. d3 Bc5 6. 0–0
c6 7. Ba4 Ne7 8. Qh5 d6 9. Bg5 b5 10. Bb3 0–0 11. Qh4 Re8
12. f4 Be6 13. Rf3 B×b3 14. Rh3 h6 15. a×b3 Qc7 16. f5 d5
17. B×h6 g×h6 18. Q×h6 Qe5 19. f6** and White wins—*Philadelphia Intelligencer*, 7 March 1876.

## (388) Bird–H.F. Davidson   0–1
Offhand game
Philadelphia 1876
*C32*

**1. e4 e5 2. f4 d5 3. e×d5 e4 4. c4** Bird remained loyal to this shallow move for the major part of his career. Shipley, annotating a game
for his column in the *Philadelphia Inquirer* of 27 May 1906, wrote
that "Bird once informed the annotator while playing with him at
Simpson's Divan, London, that this was the only opening in which,
having won a pawn, he attempted to retain it." **4. ... Nf6 5. d4 c6
6. d×c6 N×c6 7. d5 Nb4 8. a3 Na6 9. b4 Nc7 10. Be2** This move
somewhat spoils his set-up. Far more congruent with his previous
moves are 10. Nc3, 11. Nge2 (this square is now taken by the bishop)
and 12. Nd4. Davidson, however, omits to profit from it with the
undermining move 10. ... b5! **10. ... Be7 11. Nc3 0–0 12. Be3 b5
13. Ra2** Davidson's 12. ... b5 came a bit late as 13. d6! would now
have returned the pawn in favorable conditions. Bird hangs on to
his slight material advantage, which gives his opponent the opportunity to destroy his center after all. **13. ... b×c4 14. B×c4 Bd6
15. Rd2 Bd7 16. Nh3 Ng4 17. Qe2 Qh4† 18. Bf2 Qf6?** 18. ... Qh6
or 18. ... N×f2 are better. The text move allows Bird a unique chance
to decide the game at once. **19. Bd4?** "19. N×e4 appears stronger
and sound. If 19. ... Qa1† 20. Qd1"—Brownson. Better is 20. Rd1,
winning a piece. **19. ... Qh4† 20. Kf1 f5** 20. ... e3! opens lines and
diagonals for his pieces. **21. Kg1 Kh8 22. Nd1 Rac8 23. Ne3?** *(see
diagram)* 23. Nc3 avoids Davidson's next move.

**23. ... Nb5!** "A pretty combination"—Brownson. **24. B×b5
B×b5 25. Qd1 Rc7 26. Nf2 N×e3 27. B×e3 B×f4 28. B×f4 Q×f4
29. g3 Qh6 30. d6 Rd7 31. Rd5 Rc8?** Giving his opponent an enormous chance to save the game. The safe 31. ... Bc6 wins effortlessly.
**32. a4?** Bird fails to spot the saving combination 32. R×b5! R×d6
33. Qc2!! Rdd8 34. Rc5 and Black is even thrown upon the defen-

*After 23. Ne3*

sive. **32. ... Rc1 33. a×b5 R×d1† 34. R×d1 R×d6** and Black wins—
*Dubuque Chess Journal* (Brownson), June 1877, pp. 207–209.

## (389) Bird–H.F. Davidson   0–1
Offhand game
Philadelphia 1876
*C43*

**1. e4 e5 2. Nf3 Nf6 3. d4 N×e4 4. Bd3 d5 5. N×e5 Bd6 6. 0–0
0–0 7. B×e4 d×e4 8. Nc4 Nc6 9. N×d6 Q×d6 10. c3 Qg6 11. Kh1
Ne7 12. Bf4 Nd5 13. Bg3 c6 14. Nd2 Bg4 15. Qb3 b5** To stabilize
his strong knight in anticipation of the push of the f-pawn, but
White's queenside play is not to be underestimated. As Bird's last
move abandoned the center a bit (15. Qe1 was safer), he could well
play 15. ... e3! **16. c4 b×c4 17. N×c4 f5 18. Be5** 18. Ne5 Qe6
19. N×g4 clearly demonstrates the flaws in Black's set-up. **18. ...
Be2 19. Rfe1** 19. Rfc1! is much more ambitious. The c-pawn will
come under fire very soon. **19. ... Bd3?** Immediately 19. ... B×c4
safeguards him from pressure along the c-file. This may cost a pawn
but he gets enough counterplay after, e.g., 20. Q×c4 Rf7 21. Rac1
Rb7 22. b3 Re8 23. Q×c6 Q×c6 24. R×c6 Nb4. **20. Rac1 f4
21. Nd6?** 21. Na5! breaks through. Black's attack comes too late:
after 21. ... f3 22. Rg1. **21. ... f3** First 21. ... Rab8 is tricky for White.
If 22. Qa3? f3! wins, both after 23. Rg1 Be2 or 23. g×f3 Qh5 (the
point being that 24. Qd1 is no option anymore). Black's advantage
is undeniable after 22. Nb7 e3 23. f3 Ba6 24. B×b8 R×b8 25. Qa3
B×b7 26. Q×a7 Qd6, but a win seems a hard slog. **22. g×f3 Qh5
23. Re3?** The point of Black needing to play 21. ... Rab8! becomes
apparent now, as White could retort with 23. Qd1! After 23. ...
R×f3? 24. Rg1!, Bird would be the only one with real attacking
chances. It is thus best to enter a drawish endgame with 23. ... Q×f3†
24. Q×f3 R×f3 25. N×e4 B×e4 26. R×e4 R×f2. **23. ... Rab8
24. Nb7 Rf7 25. R×c6 N×e3** and White resigns—*Danbury News*,
8 March 1876.

## (390) Neill–Bird   1–0
Offhand game
Philadelphia 1876
*C61*

**1. e4 e5 2. Nf3 Nc6 3. Bb5 Nd4 4. N×d4 e×d4 5. 0–0 h5 6. d3
Bc5 7. f4 c6 8. Bc4 d5 9. e×d5 c×d5 10. Bb3 a5 11. a3 a4 12. Ba2
Ne7 13. Nd2 Bg4 14. Nf3 Ra6 15. Qe1 B×f3 16. R×f3 Re6 17. Qf2
Nf5 18. Bd2 0–0 19. Re1 Rfe8 20. Re5 Ne3 21. R×h5 g6 22. Re5
Ng4 23. R×d5 Qe7 24. Qg3 Ne3 25. Re5 Kg7 26. B×e6 f×e6
27. f5** Black resigns—*Dubuque Chess Journal*, March 1876, p. 139.

**(391) Bird–Roberts   0–1**
Offhand game
Philadelphia 1876
*A03*

1. f4 d5 2. e3 c5 3. Nf3 e6 4. Bb5† Bd7 5. B×d7† N×d7 6. b3 Bd6 7. Bb2 Ngf6 8. 0–0 0–0 9. Nc3 Rc8 10. Qe1 Ng4 11. Qg3 Ndf6 12. h3 Nh6 13. Qh2 Bb8 14. Rae1 Ne4 15. g4 N×c3 16. B×c3 a6 17. Kh1 b5 18. Qg2 Qe7 19. Rg1 Rfd8 20. f5 e5 21. f6 g×f6 22. g5 f×g5 23. N×g5 Kh8 24. Qf3 Rc6 25. Ref1 f6 26. Ne4 d×e4 27. Q×e4 Qe6 28. Qh4 Nf7 29. Rg6 Qe7 30. Ba5 Rg8 31. R×g8† K×g8 32. Qg3† Kh8 33. Qf3 Re6 34. Qa8 Qf8 35. Rg1 Re8 36. Q×a6 Qh6 37. Rg3 e4 38. Q×b5 Rf8 39. Rg2 Q×h3† 40. Kg1 Ng5 41. Q×c5 Nf3† 42. Kf2 Qh4† and Black wins—*Sunday Republic*, 13 February 1876.

**(392) Bird–Barbour   0–1**
Offhand game
Philadelphia 1876
*C30*

1. e4 e5 2. f4 Nf6 3. f×e5 N×e4 4. Nf3 Ng5 5. h4 Ne6 6. d4 d5 7. Bd3 c5 8. c3 c4 9. Bc2 Be7 10. Be3 Bd7 11. Qe2 b5 12. Nbd2 Nc6 13. Nf1 b4 14. Ng3 b×c3 15. b×c3 Qb6 16. Nf5 Qb2 17. Kd2 Nb4 18. Rhc1 N×a2 19. Rcb1 Q×c3† 20. Kd1 Q×a1 21. R×a1 Nc3† 22. Kd2 N×e2 23. K×e2 g6 24. N×e7 K×e7 25. Bd2 Rhb8 26. Bc1 a5 27. Ba3† Ke8 28. h5 Nf4† 29. Ke3 N×h5 30. Ng5 h6 31. Nf3 a4 and White resigns—*Sunday Republic*, 6 February 1876.

**(393) Bird & Elson–Mackenzie & D.M. Martinez   1–0**
Consultation game
Philadelphia, February 1876
*C52*

1. e4 e5 2. Nf3 Nc6 3. Bc4 Bc5 4. b4 B×b4 5. c3 Ba5 6. d4 e×d4 7. Qb3 Qf6 8. 0–0 d×c3 9. e5 Qg6 10. N×c3 Nge7 11. Ne2 b5 12. Bd3 Qe6 13. Qb2 Ng6 14. Nf4 N×f4 15. B×f4 a6 16. Rac1 h6 17. Rfd1 Bb7 18. a4 b4 19. Bc4 Qf5 20. Bg3 Bb6 21. Nh4 Qg4 22. Kh1 0–0–0 23. B×f7 Rhf8 24. f3 Qg5 25. f4 Qg4 26. Bd5 Be3 27. Bf3 B×c1 28. R×c1 Qe6 29. f5 R×f5 30. N×f5 Q×f5 31. B×c6 B×c6 32. Q×b4 Qe4 33. Q×e4 B×e4 34. e6 Bc6 35. Kg1 Re8 36. e×d7† K×d7 37. Rd1† Kc8 38. Rc1 Re6 39. Rc5 Kb7 40. Be5 R×e5 41. R×e5 B×a4 42. Kf2 g6 43. g4 Bd1 44. h3 h5 45. g5 Bc2 46. Ke3 c6 47. Kd2 Bb1 48. Kc3 Kb6 49. Re1 Bf5 50. Rf1 Be4 51. Kd4 Bc2 52. Rf2 c5† 53. Kc3 Be4 54. Kc4 Kc6 55. Rf6† Kd7 56. h4 a5 57. Ra6 Bc2 58. R×a5 Ke6 59. R×c5 Bb1 60. Kd4 Ba2 61. Re5† Kf7 62. Ra5 Bb3 63. Ke5 Kg7 64. Ra7† Kh8 65. Kf6 Bc2 66. Rg7 and Black resigns—*Turf, Field and Farm*, 24 March 1876.

**(394) D.M. Martinez & Neill & Reichhelm–Bird & Mackenzie & Ware   0–1**
Consultation game
Philadelphia, February 1876
*C80*

1. e4 e5 2. Nf3 Nc6 3. Bb5 a6 4. Ba4 Nf6 5. 0–0 N×e4 6. Re1 Nc5 7. B×c6 d×c6 8. N×e5 Be7 9. Qe2 A feeble idea. 9. d4

---

(Mackenzie) is the normal continuation. **9. ... Be6 10. c3 Nd7 11. N×d7 Q×d7 12. f4** Weakening the kingside isn't very advisable, in view of their opponents' bishop pair. **12. ... g6 13. d4 0–0–0 14. Nd2 Rde8 15. Qf2 Kb8 16. b4 g5** A bit abrupt. They get the g-file open, but in return some long-term weaknesses are created from which White may profit. **17. Nf3** The cleanest solution for all problems would have been 17. f×g5 B×g5 18. Ne4 Be7 19. Nc5, and the bishop pair is neutralized. **17. ... g×f4 18. Ne5 Qc8 19. B×f4 Rhg8 20. Qd2 h5 21. a4** An attack is unlikely to succeed. Thus priority should be given to the formation of a good defense line, with 22. Re2; e.g., 22. ... f6 23. Nd3 Bd5 24. Rae1. **21. ... f6 22. Nf3?!** Now matters become really dangerous for White. **22. ... Bd5 23. Re3 Qg4 24. Bg3 f5** An alternative plan consists of transposing into an excellent endgame after 24. ... Bd6; e.g., 25. R×e8† R×e8 26. Qf2 B×f3 27. Q×f3 Q×f3 28. g×f3 Re3. **25. Ne5?** The immediate occupation of this apparently superior square is but a Pyrrhic victory. Centralization with 25. Rae1 was mandatory. **25. ... Qg7 26. Nf3** *(see diagram)*

*After 26. Nf3*

**26. ... Be4?** Slow, and allowing White to reinforce their defense. The Black allies could have crowned this very well-played game with two well-timed pawn sacrifices: 26. ... h4! 27. N×h4 f4! 28. R×e7 R×e7 29. Q×f4 Rf8 30. Qd2 Bc4. **27. Rf1 h4 28. Bf4** 28. Be5 wins time for the defense. **28. ... Qg4 29. Ne1 Bd6!** White is calmly stripped from his best defenders. **30. Re2 Re7** 30. ... Bd5! gains control over the e-file. **31. Rff2?** White succumbs under the pressure. After 31. B×d6 c×d6 32. Rf4, he may still draw the game. **31. ... B×g2!** "A brilliant coup, suggested by Mr. Bird"—Mackenzie. **32. N×g2 B×f4 33. h3 Qg3 34. R×f4 R×e2 35. Q×e2 Q×f4** and White resigns—*Turf, Field and Farm* (Mackenzie), 11 February 1876.

## A MAN OF LETTERS

Bird resurfaced in New York shortly after 10 February. Many chess fans thought that he was spending his last weeks on American soil, as his return to England was a recurrent topic in the press. During the earlier days of his stay in Philadelphia, Bird suggested that certain obligations could make him leave the United States (*Philadelphia Times*, 31 January 1876). Another Philadelphia newspaper, the *Intelligencer*, suggested on 15 February that Bird would go back to England very soon in order to gather subscriptions for the Centennial tournament and come back to take part in the tournament itself in the summer. Mason even announced Bird's return to England three times in his column in *The Spirit of the Times*.

Yet, against the odds, Bird decided to prolong his stay in New York until the conclusion of the Centennial Congress, according to the *New York Daily Graphic* of 1 March. His final decision was probably influenced by the announcement of a large scale tournament at the Café International.

It was only two months earlier that Bird had exulted in his reception by New York chess circles, but by now the sentiments were slowly turning. His presumed superiority had turned out to be of a mainly imaginary nature while a few characteristics of Bird's personality started to disturb his environment.[13]

The turmoil between Bird and various other players moved apace from March onwards. Bird commenced expressing his dissatisfaction by writing letters that were published in various columns. Very soon his cherished image of being a chivalrous chess player changed into that of a man whose letters aimed to prove his worth. Bird was moved to ventilate his dissatisfaction when a game he lost against Ryan was published. This game was played at the Café Cosmopolitan probably during Bird's engagement in January, but it was published by the *New York Clipper* only on 11 March. Two weeks later, the same newspaper brought Bird's reaction to the attention of the public:

Sir

I beg to call your attention to the very unfair manner in which use is made of my name in the chess column of your paper. The result of my play has been suppressed in your columns, and statements have been made in notes to the game which are not warranted by the facts. In the present number a game appears lost by me to Mr. Ryan, but you omit to mention that I won six games to one of the gentleman. I have won 27 games to 20 games against Mr. Mason of this city, and am one game ahead of Capt. Mackenzie, the American chess champion. I am, on all convenient occasions, ready to meet any player of America for the credit of victory only or for a small or large stake.

Yours respectfully

H.E. Bird [*New York Clipper*, 25 March 1876].

Hazeltine caught the drift of Bird's grievances and promised to pay more attention to the results of game series between players. He also expressed a sincere hope to publish some of Bird's victories accompanied with his own notes. Bird recognized his own responsibility for the publications of many of his losses, as "I have not preserved a single game I have played and it is my own fault that only

**Miron Hazeltine (*British Chess Magazine*).**

my defeats get recorded."[14] Bird referred to other contributors who could deliver to Hazeltine some of his won games. In any case he took Hazeltine's advice to heart and started to contribute his games now and then.

## (395) Bird–Alberoni    1–0
Offhand game
New York, 23 February 1876
*C51*

This game was part of a small match. Bird won all three games.
**1. e4 e5 2. Nf3 Nc6 3. Bc4 Bc5 4. b4 B×b4 5. c3 Bc5 6. d4 e×d4 7. c×d4 Bb6 8. 0–0 d6 9. Bb2 Na5 10. Bd3 Ne7 11. d5 0–0 12. Nc3 Ng6 13. Ne2 f6 14. Ng3 c5 15. Rc1 Rb8 16. Qd2 Bc7 17. h4 b5 18. h5 Ne5** Pushing the h-pawn as far as Bird does is a rarity in the Evans Gambit, and with reason. Black's position is very solid. **19. h6 c4** This impulsive move abrogates his advantage in one move. After 19. … g6! White's attack is over, and Black is ready to get his counterplay going on the other side of the board. **20. h×g7 Rf7 21. Bb1** Bird still aims for an attack against Alberoni's king, but therefore help from his opponent is needed. The bishop would be much better placed on e2. **21. … N×f3†** 21. … R×g7! keeps the diagonals of both of White's bishops closed. **22. g×f3 b4 23. Bd4 c3?** The g-pawn had to be eliminated without any further delay. **24. Qh6!** Suddenly the king is menaced by White's queen and bishop. **24. … Bb6 25. e5 R×g7** (*see diagram*)

---

13. In a private letter written on 19 April to Hazeltine, Bird complained about the isolation he felt at the Café International: "The fact is that under very adverse circumstances I have held my own so well against all comers that there appears to be no player in New York who would care to encounter me. I am always ready and shall be for the short time I shall continue to play chess for to tell you the truth I am wearied with the pressing and blowing common with some of the chess players." *Hazeltine's Chess, Autographs, End Games, Games and Problems*, vol. 6, 188–189ff. ¶ The excitement that was seen when a visitor was able to beat Bird made it into the press. Bird's opponent in this session was William James Appleton Fuller, a veteran of the First American Congress of 1857: "A sensation was produced in the Café International yesterday by the report that a stranger was beating the English champion. Three games had been played of which Mr. Bird had lost two. The other tables were deserted and a throng quickly gathered around the chairs of the contestants. A half dozen games were then played, a majority of which were won by Mr. Bird. At length a final game was announced, at which each player nerved himself to win if possible, and Mr. Bird lost. The stranger, a leading lawyer in this city, whose name was prominently connected with the Singer will case, was formerly well known in chess circles. He is remembered as having played creditably several games with Paul Morphy just after Mr. Morphy's return from his famous tour of conquest in Europe. He played a quick, vigorous, forcing style of game with Mr. Bird, and generally compelled him to remain on the defensive. His initials are W.J.F." *New York Daily Graphic*, 1 March 1876. Thanks to Eduardo Bauzá Mercére for the reference to this article as well as the identification of Bird's opponent.

14. *Hazeltine's Chess, Autographs...*, vol. 6, 186f.

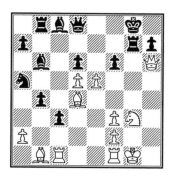

*After 25. ... R×g7*

**26. e×f6?** This serious inaccuracy offers Alberoni an unexpected saving opportunity. The simple 26. B×b6 (if 26. ... Q×b6 27. Kh1! f×e5 28. Nh5) wins quickly. **26. ... R×g3†! 27. f×g3 B×d4† 28. Kh2?** A most complicated position has arisen. By bringing his king to h2, Bird makes an incorrect evaluation, as the h-file is absolutely not safe enough for his majesty. Correct is 28. Kg2!, when there could follow 28. ... Q×f6 29. Q×h7† Kf8 30. Qc7 Nc4! 31. Q×c4 Bh3†! 32. K×h3 Qh6† etc. **28. ... Rb7?** Now 28. ... Q×f6 is winning. White gets mated after 29. Q×h7† Kf8 30. Qc7 Qh6† (hence 28. Kh2? is bad). Not any better is 29. B×h7† Kf7 30. Qh5† Kg7 and the queens will eventually be exchanged. **29. Rce1?!** The subtle 29. Qg5†! Kh8 30. Qh5 B×f6 31. Rce1 keeps a slight initiative. The point being that 31. ... Re7 32. R×e7 R×e7 33. Re1! is promising for White, while 31. ... Be5 32. f4 Nc4 33. f×e5 N×e5 34. Rf4! also favors White. **29. ... Nc4?!** After 29. ... B×f6! (Mason), White can head for a similar line as above with 30. Qh5, but then 30. ... Re7 31. R×e7 Q×e7 32. Re1 simply loses as 32. ... Q×e1 is possible now that Black's king has not been driven to h8. White has better attempts than 30. Qh5, but in all cases Black enjoys a material edge, and with safe defense can play for a win. **30. Qg5† Kh8?** He who makes the last error loses. 30. ... Kf8 is equal after 31. Qh6† Kg8 32. Qg5†. White can try for more, but Black's survival chances are quite good. **31. Re7!** Black resigns—*The Spirit of the Times* (Mason), 4 March 1876.

## (396) Bird–Delmar    0–1
Offhand game
New York 1876
C38

1. e4 e5 2. f4 e×f4 3. Nf3 g5 4. Bc4 Bg7 5. d4 d6 6. c3 h6 7. 0–0 Nc6 8. Na3 Nf6 9. Bd3 0–0 10. Qc2 Bg4 11. h4 B×f3 12. R×f3 Nh5 13. h×g5 h×g5 14. Bd2 Qd7 15. Re1 Rae8 16. Rh3 Ng3 17. e5 f5 18. e6 Qe7 19. R×g3 f×g3 20. B×f5 Qf6 21. Rf1 N×d4 22. c×d4 Q×d4† and White resigns—*Turf, Field and Farm*, 21 June 1878.

## (397) Perrin–Bird    1–0
Offhand game
New York (Café International) 1876
C58

1. e4 e5 2. Nf3 Nc6 3. Bc4 Nf6 4. Ng5 d5 5. e×d5 Na5 6. d3 Bc5 7. Nc3 0–0 8. 0–0 Bf5 9. Qe2 Re8 10. Nce4 Be7 11. N×f6† B×f6 12. Ne4 Be7 13. Bd2 N×c4 14. d×c4 Bg6 15. Bc3 f5 16. Ng3 e4 17. f3 Bc5† 18. Kh1 e3 19. f4 b5 20. b4 Be7 21. Q×e3 B×b4

22. Qd4 Bf8 23. c5 h5 24. Rae1 h4 25. Ne2 Re4 26. Qd3 b4 27. Be5 B×c5 28. c4 Re3 29. Qd2 Qd7 30. Nd4 B×d4 31. Q×d4 Ra3 32. Re2 Bh5 33. Rd2 Rb8 34. c5 b3 35. a×b3 Ra×b3 36. c6 Qf7 37. Q×a7 Rb1 38. Kg1 h3 39. Q×c7 R×f1† 40. K×f1 Rb1† 41. Kf2 Qg6 42. Qd8† Kh7 43. Qg5 Qf7 44. c7 Rc1 45. d6 h×g2 46. K×g2 Rc5 47. Q×g7† Q×g7† 48. B×g7 Be8 49. d7 Black resigns—*The Globe*, May 1876, p. 32.

## (398) Bird–Mason    ½–½
Offhand game
New York (Café International), April 1876
C59

1. e4 e5 2. Nf3 Nc6 3. Bc4 Nf6 4. Ng5 d5 5. e×d5 Na5 6. Bb5† c6 7. d×c6 b×c6 8. Be2 h6 9. Nf3 e4 10. Ne5 Qd4 "Many good players prefer 10. ... Bd6 at this point, considering the attack following from the move in the text more showy than effectual"—Mason. **11. Ng4** 11. f4 is a better way to hope for an advantage. **11. ... B×g4 12. B×g4 e3** A very sharp reply, which demands some cold-bloodedness from Bird. **13. Bf3 e×f2† 14. Kf1 0–0–0 15. d3?** Way too slow. Bird had to remove the thorn in his side at once with 15. Qe2. **15. ... Bc5 16. Nc3 Rhe8 17. Bd2** A nice line, showing that Black's attack can take several forms, is 17. Ne2 Qd7! 18. b3 (to prevent 18. ... Nc4) 18. ... g5 19. h3 and now 19. ... R×e2! 20. B×e2 Ne4! 21. Bf4 (defending the queen) 21. ... Nc3 22. Qd2 Bd4 with complete domination. **17. ... Nc4 18. Ne2 R×e2** Mason has spotted a nice combination, but here, as well as on the next few moves, taking the b-pawn wins much easier. **19. B×e2 N×d2† 20. Q×d2 Nd5 21. c3 Ne3† 22. K×f2** *(see diagram)*

*After 22. K×f2*

**22. ... Qh4†?** 22. ... Ng4† is tricky (for if 23. Kg3 Bd6† and White gets mated), but Black's attack is far from being decisive after 23. Ke1. Much stronger is 22. ... Qf4† 23. Ke1 Bd6, with the poetical menace of 24. ... Qg3†. After 24. Bg4† both 24. ... Kb7 and 24. ... N×g4 look promising. **23. g3 Qh3 24. d4 Qg2† 25. K×e3 Re8† 26. Kd3 Qe4†** and the game was drawn—*The Spirit of the Times* (Mason), 3 June 1876.

## (399) Bird–Alberoni    0–1
Offhand game
New York 1876
C39

This was easily one of the craziest games between Bird and Alberoni. It shows both players aiming for the most brilliant ideas, while at the same time completely neglecting any attempt to refute the play of the opponent. Correct play was about the last of their concerns.

**1. e4 e5 2. f4 e×f4 3. Nf3 g5 4. h4 g4 5. Ne5 Bg7 6. d4 Nf6 7. Bc4 d5 8. e×d5 Ne4?** "An unsound novelty; the usual continuation 8. … 0–0 is the right move"—Zukertort. **9. B×f4 f5 10. Nc3 Nd6 11. Bb3** Also good is 11. Qe2 0–0 12. 0–0–0 (Judd). **11. … 0–0 12. Qd2 b5 13. 0–0–0 a5 14. a4 Bd7** "This style of playing match games may win games occasionally, but we doubt whether it will win against a careful opponent"—Judd. **15. Rdg1** "Instead of this entirely useless move, we would have simply played 15. N×d7 Q×d7 16. a×b5, and we cannot see where Black has an equivalent for the loss of two pawns"—Judd. Judd's suggestion should be enough to secure White a win, but even stronger was 15. Nc6! Qe8 16. N×b5, winning material without allowing any compensation at all. **15. … b×a4 16. Ba2?!** Much easier was 16. N×a4, but once again Bird had eyes only for his own attacking plans. **16. … Na6 17. Nc6?!** Bird is rapidly losing his advantage. With 17. Bg5 Qc8 18. Bh6 he keeps strong pressure. **17. … B×c6 18. d×c6† Kh8 19. Bg5** "Driving the queen just where she wanted to go"—Judd. **19. … Qb8 20. h5 Qb4 21. h6?** Terrible. Bird's sense of reality completely left him during the last few moves. After 21. Nd5, the endgame is about equal. **21. … B×d4 22. Rd1** "All this is beyond our comprehension"—Judd. **22. … Be5 22. … Nb5! ends it all at once. 23. Qd5 Bf4†?** Bad judgment. With this exchange Alberoni abandons the pressure against White's king, especially against b2. At the same time his own king becomes vulnerable. After 23. … Rae8 24. Rhe1 Ne4 White has absolutely nothing at all to compensate for the strong Black pressure. **24. B×f4 Q×f4† 25. Kb1 Nb4 26. Qc5 N×a2?** This exchange allows White to win at once with 27. g3! Qg5 28. Nd5! Nb4 29. Qd4† Kh8 30. Rh5! This line was far from easy to foresee, however. With 26. … Rfe8 Alberoni could have avoided it. **27. N×a2? Qg5** A superfluous move. 27. … Rfe8 is about equal. **28. Rh5** "Bird, throughout the entire game, is unfortunate in moving his rooks, for he invariably places them where they will do least good"—Judd. Bird found the correct idea, but a bit too late. 28. Nc3 is more useful here. **28. … Qf6 29. Nc3 a3 30. Rd4?** "Why not 30. Q×a3? It is this very pawn which ultimately loses the game"—Judd. **30. … a×b2 31. Rd1** That the b-pawn is untouchable becomes apparent after 31. K×b2 Rfb8† 32. Ka2 Rb4! **31. … a4 32. Rhh1 a3 33. Ka2 Ne4 33. … Rfb8! is more direct. 34. N×e4 Qe6† 35. Rd5 f×e4 36. Qd4† Qf6 37. Q×e4 Rab8 38. Qd4 38. Rb1 is the only move to prolong the battle. 38. … Q×d4 39. R×d4 Rf6 40. Rhd1 R×h6 41. Rd8† R×d8 42. R×d8† Kg7 43. Rd7† Kf8 44. R×c7 Rh1** White resigns—*American Chess Journal* (Judd), June 1876, p. 5; *Westminster Chess Club Papers* (Zukertort), July 1876, p. 58.

# THE CAFÉ INTERNATIONAL TOURNAMENT 1876

The year 1876 was the most fertile in American chess life since the days of Morphy. Much of the enthusiasm was generated at one central place: the Café International. It was here that all the strongest players of the city gathered. The proprietor, Siegfried Lieders, was very supportive of the game. He regularly arranged tournaments provided with attractive prize funds. In 1874 and 1875 two massive handicap tournaments (there were even 46 entries in

1875) were held at the Café. A new event was announced to begin in March 1876. Contrary to the previous editions the games were to be played on even terms. With 17 participants the tournament seemed to have been less appealing than in the previous years but the field was stronger than ever with Bird, Mackenzie, Mason, Delmar and Alberoni taking part. The time limit was set on 20 moves per hour. All players would meet each other twice. There was no fixed playing schedule. Present players had to agree when to play their games. It was expected that the tournament would last six weeks. Three prizes were foreseen, the first one mounting up to $100. Captain Mackenzie, responsible for the chess department of the Café International, combined the management of the tournament with taking part in it.

The first games were played around 21 March.[15] Bird commenced hesitatingly with six wins but also two losses against weaker opponents: Dill and Christian Becker. During the following rounds he faced his two principal opponents. Against Mason he lost the first game but then won the second. Bird was less successful against Mackenzie, grasping but one draw from the two encounters. At the end of April Mackenzie was firmly in the lead, having only conceded 1½ out of 12 games. His rivals already followed at some distance. Alberoni, Ensor and Mason had lost 4 points, Bird 4½ and Delmar 5.

A first hiccup spoiling a smooth running tournament occurred on 30 April when Richardson, who claimed to lack the time to complete his games, gave his forfeit. A short while later two other players, J.P. Hind and John H. Parnell, also decided to leave the tournament. The results of all three players were cancelled by the management. The threefold forfeit hardly affected the chances of the strongest players. Richardson, the strongest, succeeded in drawing one game with Alberoni and one with Delmar. This could potentially have favored Bird, Mackenzie and Mason, but it was far from certain that they would all have won their games against him. Yet Bird showed himself absolutely not satisfied with the forfeits.

New York, May 11, 1876
To the chess editor of the *Sunday Call*:

Observing a record in your paper of the score of the games played in the Café International tournament. I beg to remind you that some of the parties in the tournament have taken upon themselves, without any committee meeting, and, as I pretest, without proper authority, to cancel games which have been actually played and won. As I should be one of the competitors most prejudicially affected if this cancellation should be sustained, I propose taking the opinion of the members upon it, and for the present I shall be obliged by your mentioning the fact as it stands as regards my individual score. I have won 18 games, lost 6, and drawn 1.

H.E. Bird [*Sunday Call*, 14 May 1876]

Alberoni was the first player to round off the tournament on 18 May. He had gathered 19 points out of 26 games.[16]

15. According to Bird in a letter which shall be presented later. This date is confirmed by the *New York Evening Telegram* of 22 March. The *New York Herald* gives Monday 19 March as the starting date. *The Sunday Times* gives 20 March.

16. Alberoni left New York for London at the end of May. He received the support of Lieders to visit London with the purpose of setting up a cable match. European reactions, however, were rather tame: "During the last week Mr. Alberoni … paid a flying visit to London, and looked in once or twice at the Divan in the course of his short stay. It was stated that his object was to negotiate a match by telegraph between Philadelphia and London, during the forthcoming Centennial Chess Congress, for $1000 (£200) a side; but the proposal, we hear, did not seem to meet with much favor. The expense of telegraphing alone would, we fear, be an insuperable obstacle." *Illustrated London News*, 10 June 1876.

### Café International Chess Tournament, New York, 21 March–10 June 1876

*Site:* Café International
*Prizes:* 1st $100, 2nd $50, 3rd $25
*Time limit:* 20 moves per hour

| | | 1 | 2 | 3 | 4 | 5 | 6 | 7 | 8 | 9 | 10 | 11 | 12 | 13 | 14 | |
|---|---|---|---|---|---|---|---|---|---|---|---|---|---|---|---|---|
| 1 | G.H. Mackenzie | | 1 0 | ½ 1 | 1 0 | 1 0 | 1 1 | 0 1 | 1 ½ | 1 1 | 1 1 | 0 1 | 1 1 | 1 1 | 1 1 | 20 |
| 2 | E. Alberoni | 0 1 | | 0 0 | ½ ½ | 0 0 | ½ 1 | 1 ½ | 1 1 | 1 1 | 1 1 | 1 1 | 1 1 | 1 1 | 1 1 | 19 |
| 3 | H.E. Bird | ½ 0 | 1 1 | | 0 1 | 1 1 | 1 0 | 0 1 | 0 1 | 1 1 | 1 1 | 1 1 | 1 0 | 1 1 | 0 1 | 18½ |
| 4 | J. Mason | 0 1 | ½ ½ | 1 0 | | 0 0 | ½ 1 | 1 1 | 1 0 | 1 1 | 1 1 | ½ 1 | 1 ½ | 1 1 | 1 1 | 18½ |
| 5 | E. Delmar | 0 1 | 1 1 | 0 0 | 1 1 | | 0 ½ | 0 0 | 0 1 | 1 1 | 1 1 | ½ 1 | 1 1 | 1 1 | 1 1 | 18 |
| 6 | C. Becker | 0 0 | ½ 0 | 0 1 | ½ 0 | 1 ½ | | 1 1 | 1 ½ | 0 1 | ½ ½ | 1 1 | 0 | 1 1 | 1 1 | 15 |
| 7 | A.W. Ensor | 1 0 | 0 ½ | 1 0 | 0 0 | 1 1 | 0 0 | | 0 0 | 1 1 | | | 1 0 | 1 1 | 1 1 | 11½ |
| 8 | F.E. Brenzinger | 0 ½ | 0 0 | 1 0 | 0 1 | 1 0 | ½ 0 | 1 1 | | 0 1 | | | 1 1 | 1 0 | | 10 |
| 9 | F. Perrin | 0 0 | 0 0 | 0 0 | 0 0 | 0 0 | 1 0 | 0 0 | 1 0 | | 0 0 | | 1 1 | 1 0 | | 5 |
| 10 | F.M. Roser | 0 0 | 0 0 | 0 0 | 0 0 | 0 0 | ½ ½ | | | 1 1 | | 0 0 | | 1 0 | 1 | 5 |
| 11 | J.P. Barnett | 1 0 | 0 0 | 0 0 | ½ 0 | ½ 0 | 0 0 | | | | 1 1 | | | | | 4 |
| 12 | S.R. Dill | 0 0 | 0 0 | 0 1 | 0 ½ | 0 0 | 1 | 0 1 | | 0 0 | | | | | | 3½ |
| 13 | J.W. Baird | 0 0 | 0 0 | 0 0 | 0 0 | 0 0 | 0 0 | 0 0 | 0 0 | 0 1 | 0 1 | | | | | 2 |
| 14 | "Smith" | 0 0 | 0 0 | 1 0 | 0 0 | 0 0 | 0 0 | 0 0 | 0 1 | | 0 | | | | | 2 |
| 15 | P. Richardson | | ½ | | 0 | ½ 0 | | 0 0 | 1 0 | | | | 1 1 | | | |
| 16 | J.H. Parnell | 0 0 | 0 0 | 0 0 | | | | 0 0 | | | 1 0 | | | | | |
| 17 | J.P. Hind | 0 0 | | | | | | 0 0 | | 0 | | | 0 0 | 0 0 | | |

Mackenzie remained in pole position to clinch first prize. Alberoni stood best for the second place. Bird's tournament was also coming to an end. He had still one game to play, against Ensor. With 17½ point he could only hope for third prize. Other leading scores were made by Delmar with 16½/23 and Mason with 15½/23.

The tournament ended with a considerable delay on 10 June. As expected, Mackenzie took the first prize with 20/26, one point ahead of Alberoni. Bird and Mason each had 18½ points and divided the third prize sum of $25.

Just before the tournament came to an end Bird poked up the fire again by denouncing the course of events in another public letter.

Sir,

As you have published the official score of this tournament, I shall feel much obliged if you will give also the number of games actually played, a correct statement of which I beg herewith to enclose to you.

There were seventeen entries, the conditions being that each contest should be two games, making 544 games [*sic*] to be played in all. The tournament commenced on the 21st of March, 1876, and might easily have been finished by the end of April, in which case all the games would doubtless have been played. The delay rested not with the amateurs but with the professionals who had the management of the affair. There still remain 186 games [*sic*] to complete the number originally intended. In regard to the retirement and cancellation of games, the names of two gentlemen with whom I played and won have been struck out of the list, although they attended and were ready to play. On the other hand, a gentleman who scored a game with me is retained on the list, although he has not played for upwards of a month, and had ceased to attend for nearly that time. As the only foreigner taking part in the tournament, I very reluctantly appeal to you to notice these facts, as all efforts to get a meeting for their consideration have been unavailing.

I am, sir, yours obediently,

H.E. Bird [*New York World*, 7 June 1876].

Bird obviously had some resentment of the decision to cancel the results of the three aforementioned players (Richardson, Hind and Parnell) while the score of others was retained but did not explicitly contribute any suggestion on how to rectify this injustice. There are a few scenarios he may have had in mind.

In the first scenario the games forfeited by Richardson, Parnell and Hind would be counted as losses for them. In this case Alberoni's draw with Richardson costs him dearly, as Bird and Mason catch up to him.

Secondly, it would have been possible to include the points from the games that were played. The result is that Alberoni gets completely out of reach with 2½/3 against the forfeited trio. Bird adds just 2 points out of two games.

A third reasoning seems most compliant with Bird's wishes. In his letter Bird complained that his loss against a player who ceased playing a month earlier remained included. So Bird suggested that this player, either Dill or "Smith" (a pseudonym), should also be forfeited. A closer look at the final table shows that no fewer than five of the remaining 14 participants omitted to play at least six, but often more than 10 games. As a consequence of Bird's reasoning, only the results made by the first nine players must be counted and the other players forfeited. The result is then indeed favorable for Bird. Mackenzie is still the winner of the tournament, now with 11/16, but he is closely followed by Bird (10/16), who leaves his rivals behind him. Though Bird hints to this solution in his letter, it was completely unthinkable to forfeit half the field, and Bird was well aware of it. It was common practice that players who were eliminated to gain a prize withdrew silently from the tournament. In this case, there is no falsification in consequence of their defaults, as all 14 remaining players had played their games with the top players.

In his letter Bird also dared to criticize Mackenzie who, he believed, was responsible for the long duration of the tournament as well as the (slight) number of official forfeits. Mackenzie's reaction followed swiftly in his column in the *Turf, Field and Farm* of 9 June. Here he defended his decision by referring to one of the rules of the tournament, undersigned by Bird: "If any player shall resign before completing his full quota of games, all games won or lost by such player shall be cancelled."

There was not too much to discuss about Mackenzie's decision. In a final letter on the subject, Bird held his foot down to his principle that all participants were obliged to fulfill the engagements of the tournament. In the end there was some consolation for him.

However, considering the bad start I made, I have no reason to complain; and although the second prize will be allotted to Mr. Alberoni, I have the satisfaction of having scored both my games with him [*New York Clipper*, 24 June 1876].

Bird had lost much of his popularity by now, and his letters were more and more perceived as an irritating way of getting it his own way. Bird's complaint on the course of the Café International tournament was perceived as a personal attack on Mackenzie. Mackenzie was considered an almost untouchable figure, on as well as off the board, and some sharp reactions condemned Bird severely.[17]

The course of the tournament was not the only item that aroused Bird's irritation. In a letter to Hazeltine on 23 June, Bird wrote how difficult it was for him to get hold of the game scores of his own tournament games:

I hope to send you one or more of my games, some demur was at first made to my having even my own games by Mason and Becker here. Capt. Mackenzie of course pulls the strings. I protested against their right to keep my own games from me and with bad grace they consented to let me have them. [*Hazeltine's Chess, Autographs...*, vol. 3, pp. 358–359]

## (400) Bird–Delmar   1–0
Café International tournament
New York, 2 April 1876
*B00*

**1. f4 b6 2. e4 Bb7 3. Nc3 e6 4. a3 d5 5. e×d5 e×d5 6. d4 Nf6 7. Nf3 Bd6 8. Be2 0–0 9. 0–0 Nc6 10. b4 Ne4** Delmar is out for a quick confrontation, but this move only simplifies the position. Better is 10. ... Ne7 and 11. ... a5 to profit from the holes with which White burdened himself. **11. N×d5** "If 11. N×e4 d×e4 12. Ng5 N×d4"—Zukertort. **11. ... N×d4 12. Q×d4 B×d5 13. Bb2 Nf6 14. c4 c5 15. Qc3?!** Careless play. 15. Qd2 defends f4 and thus gives Bird time to play 15. ... Bb7 16. b5, thereby enclosing Black's bishop at d6. After the text move, Bird loses a tempo in defending the f-pawn, allowing Delmar to activate a bishop by exchanging at b4. **15. ... Bb7 16. Nh4 c×b4 17. a×b4 Qe7 18. Bf3?!** Bird resigns himself to the loss of a pawn but he could gain important compensation for it by hampering Black's pieces with 18. c5! After the greedy 18. ... b×c5 the pointed reply 19. Qg3 gives him dangerous counterplay. Thus 18. ... B×c5† is forced. After 19. b×c5 Q×e2 20. Rae1 Qg4 the brilliant resource 21. Re5! makes the position look drawish after 21. ... Q×h4 22. Rg5 Qh6 23. c6 Bc8 24. Q×f6 Q×f6 25. B×f6 g6. But little better is 21. ... h6 22. Qe1! **18. ... B×b4 19. Qb3 B×f3 20. N×f3 Ng4 21. Kh1 Ne3?!** 21. ... Bc5 keeps a decisive advantage. **22. Rfe1 B×e1 23. R×e1 Rfe8 24. Bd4 Qc7 25. B×e3 Re4** "This and the following move are weak"—Zukertort. **26. Ne5 f6? 27. c5† Kf8 28. Qd5!** "Bird seizes the proffered opportunity and finishes

the game in his best style"—Zukertort. **28. ... Re8 29. Nd7† Ke7 30. Q×e4† K×d7 31. Rd1†** Black resigns—*Westminster Chess Club Papers* (Zukertort), September 1876, p. 92.

## (401) Bird–Becker   1–0
Café International tournament
New York, 2 April 1876
*A03*

**1. f4 d5 2. e3 e6 3. b3 Be7 4. Nf3 Bf6 5. c3 Ne7 6. Bd3 Nbc6 7. Na3 0–0 8. 0–0 b6 9. Nc2 Bb7 10. Ncd4 N×d4 11. c×d4 c5 12. Bb2 Rc8 13. Ne5 B×e5 14. f×e5 Ng6 15. Qh5 c4 16. Bb1 f5 17. e×f6 *e.p.* R×f6 18. B×g6 R×g6 19. Qf3 Qe7 20. Ba3 Qf6 21. Qe2 Qg5 22. Rf3 Qh6 23. Be7 Rf6 24. B×f6 g×f6 25. Raf1 f5 26. g4 c×b3 27. a×b3 Qg6 28. Rg3 f4 29. e×f4 Rc2 30. f5** Black resigns—*Chicago Daily Tribune*, 2 July 1876.

## (402) Becker–Bird   1–0
Café International tournament
New York, 4 April 1876
*B44*

**1. e4 c5 2. d4 c×d4 3. Nf3 e6 4. N×d4 Nf6 5. Bd3 Nc6 6. Be3 d5 7. Nd2 e5 8. N×c6 b×c6 9. e×d5 N×d5** "Willfully destroying a good position. 9. ... c×d5 gave Black at least an even game"—Zukertort. **10. 0–0 N×e3?** "Black increases the superiority of the opponents game"—Zukertort. **11. f×e3 Be6 12. Qf3 Rc8 13. Bc4! Qe7 14. Rad1!** Excellently played. Black is all tied up. **14. ... f6 15. Ba6?!** Becker misses a nice tactical shot to finish the game with: 15. Ne4! (Hazeltine) 15. ... B×c4 16. Nd6†. **15. ... Rc7 16. Ne4 Bd5?** *(see diagram)* "16. ... Qf7 was far better here"—Hazeltine. After the text move Bird is picked to pieces by his opponent.

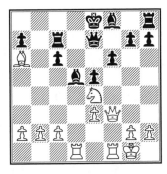

*After 16. ... Bd5*

**17. R×d5! c×d5 18. Bb5†! Kd8 19. Rd1 Qe6 20. c4 Bb4** "If 20. ... Be7 White wins by: 21. c×d5 Qb6 22. d6 Q×b5 23. d×c7† K×c7 24. Nc3"—Zukertort. **21. R×d5† Ke7** 21. ... Kc8 loses to the brute 22. Ng5! f×g5 23. R×e5! Qb6 24. Re6! **22. a3 a6 23. Ba4 Be1 24. Qd1 Rhc8 25. c5 Qf5** "Should Black play here 25. ... h5, intending to answer 26. Rd6 with 26. ... Qg4, White would win by 26. Nd6"—Zukertort. After 26. Rd6 Qg4 27. Qd5! Black is defenseless against the little move 28. h3. If 27. ... Rb8 28. h3 Qc8 29. b4 nails him down. **26. g4 Qe6 27. Rd6 Qc4** and White gave mate in six moves. A brilliant game from Becker, with only a minor slip on move 15—*New York Clipper* (Hazeltine), 19 August 1876; *Westminster Chess Club Papers* (Zukertort), September 1876, p. 93.

17. One of these reactions was written by the Philadelphian Benjamin Milnes Neill: "Mr. Bird is very much aggrieved at American chessers. Has written letters of protest against the management of the Café International tournament. So far very well but he overstepped the line that marks wisdom and courtesy when he went out of his way to slur our champion, Captain Mackenzie. This gentleman's character for fairness is too well known to be injured by Mr. Bird's insinuations, and they can only rebound on Mr. Bird. Let Mr. Bird remember, too, that American chess players, while they esteem him as a man and as a fine player, are not willing to admit his superiority simply because he has a European reputation. Mr. Bird's losses to Mr. Mason and others have probably led him to show the worst side of his chess character, and no doubt, when he goes home it will be with a better impression of American players than he now has, and leave a better impression of himself than is now prevailing here." *Danbury News*, 5 July 1876. ¶ Bird's meager results and his war in the press were known in England as well. Though his countrymen were aware of Bird's sensitivity on this subject, he did not receive full support: "Mr. Bird's exploits in America have disappointed all his friends on this side of the water, and more especially in the fatal facility he has developed for writing to the papers on the subject of his score with American amateurs. Let us hope that in the Centennial tourney he will display the abilities he is known to possess, and leave explanations of isolated defeats to the mediocrities that need them." *Land and Water*, 28 August 1876.

## (403) Mackenzie–Bird    ½–½
Café International tournament
New York, 6 April 1876
*C61*

1. e4 e5 2. Nf3 Nc6 3. Bb5 Nd4 4. N×d4 e×d4 5. 0–0 Bc5
6. Bc4 h5 7. c3 c6 8. c×d4 B×d4 9. Nc3 d6 10. Qb3 Qc7 11. Ne2
Bf6 12. d4 Nh6 13. Be3 Ng4 14. d5 N×e3 15. f×e3 Qb6 15. ... c5!
promises excellent play on the queenside and the black squares.
**16. Q×b6** Giving Bird a nice, flexible pawn structure. More disturbing would have been 16. d×c6! Q×b3 17. a×b3 b×c6 18. Nd4
when both sides suffer from various weaknesses. **16. ... a×b6
17. Nd4 b5 18. Bb3 Bd7 19. d×c6 b×c6 20. Rac1 Ra6 21. e5** "The
object of this sacrifice was, we presume, to stop the diagonal of the
adverse bishop, and thus indirectly to preserve his own b-pawn"—
Wormald. **21. ... d×e5 22. Nf5 B×f5 23. R×f5 Ke7 24. Rf2**
Mackenzie's play has been a bit sloppy, trusting on equality because
of the bishops of different color. Here 24. e4 was needed to block
the opposing bishop out of play. **24. ... Rd8 25. Rfc2 Rd6 26. Kf2
e4 27. Ke2 Be5 28. Rh1 f6** "During the last few moves the game
has looked uncommonly like a draw, and this seemingly ensures
it"—Wormald. Bird is certainly entitled to play for more, as he still
has an extra pawn as well as some very strong pieces. Instead of the
text move, he should have pointed his arrows towards the kingside,
either with 28. ... h4 or 28. ... Rg6 29. g3 h4. In either case White's
prospects appear rather depressing. **29. h3 h4 30. Rhc1 Kd7
31. Rd1 R×d1 32. K×d1 Ra8 33. Rd2† Kc7** The king had to stay
on the kingside to prevent the following transfer of the bishop.
**34. Be6 g5 35. Kc2 Kb6 36. a3 Re8 37. Bf5 Bc7 38. b4 Be5** After
38. ... Bg3 39. Rd4 Re5 some further progress is possible. Mackenzie
now unwisely omits to play 39. B×e4 (or 39. Rd7) with an immediate draw. **39. Rf2 c5 40. Bd7 Rd8 41. Bf5?** Finally a major
mistake, but he has drifted into a very disagreeable endgame. 41. ...
Rd3! creates a free, unstoppable, b-pawn. **41. ... c×b4 42. a×b4**
and the game was abandoned as drawn. Bird still enjoys excellent
winning chances in case of 42. ... Rd3 43. B×e4 Rc3† 44. Kd1
R×e3—*Illustrated London News* (Wormald), 6 May 1876.

## (404) Mason–Bird    0–1
Café International tournament
New York, 6 April 1876
*C30*

1. e4 e5 2. Nc3 Bc5 3. f4 d6 4. Nf3 Nc6 5. Be2 Bg4 5. ... Nf6 is
a cunning attempt to profit without delay from White's mediocre
set-up. If 6. d3? there is a complete refutation with 6. ... Ng4 7. Rf1
N×h2. **6. d3 a6** "Securing a retreat for the bishop in case White
should attack him by 7. Na4"—Mason. **7. f5** "In all likelihood a premature advance. At any rate, most of his subsequent troubles may
be traced directly to this point"—Mason. **7. ... g6 8. f×g6** Mason's
previous move was interesting, but it loses its venom because of this
exchange. After 8. Bg5, Black has to be careful: 8. ... f6 9. Bh4 and
now Bird shouldn't go for material win but leave the pawn structure
intact and play 9. ... B×f3 10. B×f3 Nd4. If, instead, he plays 9. ...
g×f5, there might follow: 10. h3 B×f3 11. B×f3 f×e4? (11. ... Nce7
is equal) 12. Bh5† Kf8 13. N×e4 with a winning attack. **8. ... h×g6
9. Nd5 B×f3 10. B×f3 Nd4 11. c3 N×f3† 12. Q×f3 c6 13. Ne3**

Qh4† 14. g3 Qf6 15. Qg2 0–0–0 16. h4 Qe6 17. Rf1 Nh6 18. Qf3
The only constructive idea at Mason's disposal was to try to head
for the queenside with the king, which is realizable after 18. Bd2
and 19. b3. In reaction to the text move Bird correctly opens up the
center. **18. ... d5! 19. e×d5 c×d5 20. c4?** Mason believed this move
was forced but the result is disastrous. Also inferior is 20. Bd2? when
the expected 20. ... e4! is very strong and indeed leaves few hopes
for survival for White, e.g., 21. Qf6 Q×f6 22. R×f6 Bd6! At once
20. Qf6 is his best possibility. **20. ... d×c4 21. N×c4 Nf5 22. Bg5
f6 23. Rc1 Kb8** More accurate was 23. ... f×g5! Mason, in his notes,
condemned this suggestion, but he missed a few tactical niceties.
After 24. Na5 Rd5! 25. b4, Black has a few ways leading to Rome:
25. ... e4 26. Q×e4 Qe8!, 25. ... b6 or 25. ... Qb6 26. Q×d5 Q×b4†
27. Ke2 Qb2† 28. Kf3 g4† wins as well. **24. Bd2 Qd5?** Bird completely misunderstands the essence of the position. As White's king
is hopelessly caught in the center, Black should certainly not exchange queens. 24. ... Rhe8! prepares 25. ... e4, an essential lever to
crack open White's position. **25. b4?!** This improves the position
of Black's bishop. He must immediately exchange the queens. **25. ...
Be7 26. Q×d5 R×d5 27. Rf3 Rhd8 28. Nb2 Rd4 29. h5?!** *(see diagram)* Mason doesn't shy away from the confrontation, but he
stumbles into an excellent reaction by Bird. Better is 29. Rc4, aiming
for exchanges.

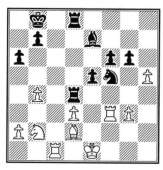

*After 29. h5*

**29. ... Rg4! 30. h×g6 Nd4 31. Re3 R×g6 32. Kf2 Rh8! 33. Rg1
Rh2†** Not bad at all, but 33. ... Rc8 34. Rc1 R×c1 35. B×c1 B×b4
wins a more important pawn. **34. Rg2 R×g2† 35. K×g2 Nf5
36. Re1 R×g3† 37. Kf2 Rg4 38. Re4 Rg8 39. a3 Bd8 40. Be3
N×e3 41. K×e3 Rg2** 41. ... f5! immediately ends the game, for if
42. R×e5 Bf6. **42. Nc4 b5 43. Nd6 Bc7 44. Ne8 Bb6† 45. Kf3
Rd2?!** 45. ... Rg8 46. Nd6 Rd8 wins a second pawn. **46. Kg4 R×d3
47. N×f6 Bd4?!** This allows White to struggle for a draw again.
Winning is 47. ... Bd8 48. Ne8 R×a3 49. Kf5 Ra4 50. Nd6 Kc7
51. K×e5 Be7 52. Nf5 B×b4. **48. Nd7†?!** It is essential to bring the
king towards the e-pawn, so that the b-pawn can be held. After
48. Kf5 R×a3 49. Nd7† Kb7 50. N×e5 he has excellent drawing
chances. **48. ... Kc7 49. N×e5 B×e5 50. R×e5 R×a3 51. Kf5?!**
The path to a win is very narrow and requiring perfect play from
Bird after 51. Re6 Kb7 52. Kf5 Ra4 53. Re4 Kc6 54. Ke5 a5 55. b×a5.
Now 55. ... R×a5! is the winning move; e.g., 56. Re2 Kc5 57. Rc2†
Kb4. After 55. ... b4?! Mason can draw, but again just a single line
guarantees that result: 56. Kf4 Kb5 57. Ke3 R×a5 58. Kd2 Ka4
59. Kc2 Ka3 60. Kb1 Rh5 61. Re3† b3 62. Re1. **51. ... Kd6 52. Kf4
Ra4** It's over now. **53. Re4 Kd5** 53. ... a5 54. b×a5 Kd5! is a humor-
ous way to win. **54. Kf5 Ra1 55. Rh4 Rf1† 56. Kg6 Rc1 57. Kf5
Rc8 58. Kg5 Rc4 59. Rh6 R×b4 60. R×a6 Re4 61. Kf5 Re8**

52. Kf4 Kc4 63. Rc6† Kb3 64. Rc7 b4 65. Kf3 Kb2 66. Kf2 b3
67. Rc6 Kb1 68. Rb6 b2 69. Rb7 Rc8 White resigns—*The Spirit
of the Times* (Mason), 27 May 1876.

## (405) Bird–Mackenzie    0–1
Café International tournament
New York, 21 April 1876
*A02*

1. f4 f5 2. e3 Nf6 3. Be2 e6 4. Nh3 Be7 5. b3 b6 6. 0-0 Bb7
7. Bb2 c5 8. c4 Nc6 9. Nc3 0-0 10. Bf3 Rb8 11. Qe2 Qe8 12. Rad1
Nd8 13. Kh1 B×f3 14. g×f3 Qh5 15. Nf2 Kf7 16. Rg1 h6 17. Rg3
g5 18. f×g5 h×g5 19. Rh3 Qg6 20. Rg1 Nc6 21. Nd3 Rh8
22. Rhg3 Nh5 23. R3g2 Bf6 24. f4 g4 25. Nd1 B×b2 26. N1×b2
Qf6 27. Nd1 Rh6 28. Nc3 Rbh8 29. Qf2 g3 30. Qf3 Qh4 31. Ne2
N×f4 32. Q×g3 Q×g3 33. N×g3 N×d3 and White resigns—*The
Spirit of the Times*, 22 July 1876.

## (406) Brenzinger–Bird    1–0
Café International tournament
New York, 4 May 1876
*C61*

1. e4 e5 2. Nf3 Nc6 3. Bb5 Nd4 4. N×d4 e×d4 5. 0-0 Bc5 6. d3
c6 7. Ba4 Ne7 8. Bb3 d5 9. c3 0-0 10. c×d4 B×d4 11. Nc3 Be6
12. Be3 B×e3 13. f×e3 Qb6 14. d4 d×e4 15. N×e4 B×b3 16. a×b3
Nd5 17. Rf3 Rae8 18. Nc5 Re7 19. Qd3 Rfe8 20. Re1 Qa5 21. Re2
b6 22. Na4 Qb4 23. e4 Nf6 24. e5 Nd5 25. Re4 Re6 26. h4 h6
27. Kh2 h5 28. g4 Nf6 29. R×f6 g×f6 30. d5 Q×e4 31. Q×e4
R×e5 32. Qd4 R×d5 33. Qf2 Red8 34. Q×f6 Rd2† 35. Kg1
Rd1† 36. Kf2 R1d2† 37. Ke3 R2d3† 38. Ke4 c5 39. Qg5† Kf8
40. Nc3 R8d4† 41. Ke5 h×g4 42. Qh6† Ke7 43. Qf6† Ke8
44. Qc6† Ke7 45. h5 Rd6 46. Qb7† Rd7 47. Qg2 R7d4 48. h6
f6† 49. Kf5 Kf7 50. Qb7† Rd7 51. Qa8 Rh3 52. Qh8 Rh5†
53. K×g4 Rg5† 54. Kf4 Rd4† 55. Ne4 Black resigns—*American
Chess Journal*, May 1878, p. 58.

## (407) Ensor–Bird    1–0
Café International tournament
New York 1876
*C54*

1. e4 e5 2. Nf3 Nc6 3. Bc4 Bc5 4. c3 Nf6 5. d3 0-0 6. Bg5 h6
7. Bh4 Be7 8. B×f6 All of these bishop moves give Bird an easy
game. 8. ... B×f6 9. 0-0 d6 10. h3 Ne7 11. d4 Qe8 12. Nbd2 Ng6
13. d×e5 d×e5 14. Kh2 b5 "14. ... Nf4 strikes us as being stronger
play"—Mackenzie. 15. Bd5 c6 16. Bb3 Be6 Bird forsakes his last
opportunity to play 16. ... Nf4. 17. g3 Rd8 18. Qe2 Bc8 19. Rad1
Rd6 20. Ng1 Be6 21. Ndf3 R×d1 22. R×d1 B×b3 23. a×b3 Bd8
24. c4 b4 25. Qe3 Qe7 26. c5 "This looks hazardous, as the isolated
pawn at once becomes a point of attack for Black"—Mackenzie.
26. ... Qb7 27. h4 Re8 28. h5?! This move chases Black's knight
in the right direction. It was not too late to make use of his advanced
c-pawn by playing 28. Nd2, heading for c4. Ensor pursues an attack
against Bird's king. 28. ... Nf8 29. Nh3 Nd7 *(see diagram)*

30. g4 Be7 White's last few moves would have returned as a
boomerang after 30. ... Nf6! In either case, albeit after 31. Rg1 Qd7

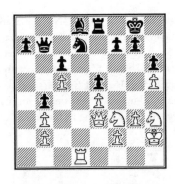

*After 29. ... Nd7*

or 31. Kg3 Qc8 32. Nh2 Be7, his position is full of holes. 31. g5
h×g5 "If 31. ... B×c5, White of course replies with 32. R×d7"—
Mackenzie. 32. Nh×g5 B×g5?! Winning a pawn but the
subsequent exchanges simplify the game. 33. Q×g5 N×c5 34. Rd8
R×d8 35. Q×d8† Kh7 36. Ng5† Kh6 37. Qd6†?! Ensor forsakes
the draw within reach after 37. Qh8† K×g5 38. Q×g7† K×h5
39. Q×e5† Kg6 40. Qf5† 37. ... f6 38. f4 "A very ingenious coup,
the object of which appears to have been overlooked by Black"—
Mackenzie. Very daring, but 38. Nh3 N×e4 is not that appetizing,
although Black's queen's being offside makes this playable for him.
38. ... e×f4? Bird's calculations are infected by the apparent danger
of Ensor's attack. After 38. ... K×h5 39. Q×c5 f×g5 40. Q×e5 he
probably overlooked 40. ... Qb5! when White can resign at once.
39. Q×c5 f×g5? The capture of the knight leads to a speedy mate.
Much less clear is the outcome of 39. ... Qd7! 40. Nh3, when Black
has two choices. Not so good is 40. ... Qg4 41. Qf2 f3 42. Qg3 and
here both 42. ... Q×h5 43. Qf4† Kg6 44. Kg3 and 42. ... Q×e4
43. Qf4† Q×f4† 44. N×f4 Kg5 45. Kg3 f2 46. Ne6† K×h5 47. K×f2
offer but little hope. 40. ... Qd2† 41. Qf2 Q×f2† 42. N×f2 K×h5
is also unclear, but a draw would not come as a great surprise:
43. Nd3 g5 44. N×b4 Kg4 45. N×c6 Kf3 46. e5 f×e5 47. N×e5†
Ke2 48. Ng4 a5 49. Kg2 Kd3. 40. Qf5! K×h5 41. Qh7† and mates
next move—*Turf, Field and Farm* (Mackenzie), 26 May 1876.

## (408) Bird–Ensor    1–0
Café International tournament
New York 1876
*C53*

1. e4 e5 2. Nf3 Nc6 3. Bc4 Bc5 4. c3 d6 5. b4 Bb6 6. Qb3 "This
line of play has been sometimes adopted in games between Bird
with Boden and MacDonnell. It prevents the advance of Black's
d-pawn, but takes White's queen away from the kingside. It makes
an interesting form of the Giuoco Piano, and is not analyzed in the
books to any extent"—Bird. 6. ... Nh6 7. d3 0-0 Ensor is apparently
full of confidence about his knight on the rim, but after 8. Bg5!
Ne7 9. h3 a5 10. a4 Qe8 11. b5 Ng6 12. B×h6, one cannot deny the
weakness of f5. Therefore safer is 7. ... Qf6. 8. a4 a5 9. b5 Ne7
10. Bg5 10. h3 keeps the knight confined to the edge. 10. ... Qe8
Ensor doesn't make use of an opportunity to reactivate the knight:
10. ... Ng4 11. 0-0 (11. Bh4 c6) 11. ... h6 12. Bh4 g5 13. Bg3 Nf6 and
both his knights have the tasty f4-square in sight. 11. 0-0 Kh8
12. Nbd2 Ng4 13. h3 Nh6 Worth considering is 13. ... N×f2
14. R×f2 B×f2† 15. K×f2 f6 16. Be3 f5, as White's pieces don't have
much scope. 14. B×h6 First 14. d4 and if 14. ... e×d4? 15. B×h6 is

a refinement. Instead 14. ... Ng6 is playable. **14. ... g×h6 15. d4 Ng6** Compared to the previous line Black has maintained his stronghold on e5; his position should not be underestimated. His knight is on its way to f4, while f7–f5 can open many lines and diagonals against White's king. **16. Kh1** *(see diagram)* Bird, aware of the open g-file, starts thinking about the defense of his kingside. Besides the text move, 16. Rfe1, freeing f1 for knight or bishop, could be considered.

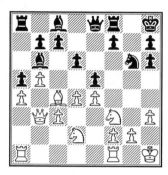

*After 16. Kh1*

**16. ... e×d4?** "Very injudicious, as it gives White's queen access to the kingside, and otherwise develops his game"—Bird. A completely different position is reached after 16. ... Nf4! The untimely exchange at h6 leaves White's kingside vulnerable to Black's pieces, and against nearly all his options, such as 17. Bd5 or 17. Rg1, 17. ... f5! gives Black good attacking chances. A sample line is 17. Rae1 f5!, and if White now goes for the pawn he will quickly go astray: 18. e×f5 B×f5 19. d×e5? (other moves are better but not very attractive) 19. ... Qh5 20. Nh2 N×g2! 21. K×g2 Qg5†. **17. c×d4 Qe7 18. Rae1 Be6 19. Qe3 Kg7** "19. ... Ne5 would lead to many interesting variations, and, we believe, be less prejudicial to Black's game"—Bird. An interesting suggestion from Bird and indeed the best try, though Black is condemned to passivity after 20. Qc3 N×f3 21. N×f3 B×c4 22. Q×c4 with a lame bishop and broken up pawn structure. In case of 19. ... h5 20. e5! is strong. **20. Qc3 B×c4?!** Giving away the very important c4-square to his opponent's knight that is now en route to f5. White is also firmly on top after 20. ... Qf6 21. B×e6 f×e6 22. Nc4 Nf4 23. Rg1 Kh8 24. e5. **21. N×c4 Kg8 22. N×b6** Not bad at all, but 22. Ne3! heads for the king and leaves Black chanceless. **22. ... c×b6 23. d5 Qd8 24. Nd4** "Very forcible. 25. ... Ne7 appears to be the best reply but Black's game is past redemption"—Bird. **24. ... Qg5** In case of 24. ... Ne7 Bird has a nice positional way to conclude the game: 25. Qg3† Kh8 26. Rc1! Rg8 27. Qc3 Rg7 28. Qc7. **25. f4 Qh5** "Black has nothing better than to return to d8. If 26. ... Qf6 27. e5 would be nearly decisive"—Bird. Taking the pawn loses after 25. ... N×f4 26. g3 N×h3 (26. ... Nh5 27. Nf5 wins) 27. Nf5 Rac8 28. Qb2 and Black's knight is lost. **26. g4** and Black resigns—*New York Clipper* (Bird), 24 June 1876.

## FURTHER DISPUTES

Bird's arrival on American soil aroused a lot of authentic enthusiasm. Finally a European master deemed it worthy to cross the Atlantic and bring a visit to the New World. But very soon Bird's image and reputation were scattered by rather meager results against the best players in New York and Philadelphia, so that the assumed superiority of British chess could very well be questioned.

There were several signs of increased unpleasantness between Bird and various American players. Mason's refusal to play a return match, the one-sided publication of games lost by Bird and the little respect shown for his results turned the proud and touchy Bird into a malcontent guest. His airing his opinions in the American press thereby put more oil on the fire. In the letter written to Hazeltine on 19 April, Bird complained about the wrong scores appearing in the press and the lack of recognition of his chess strength.[18]

On a following occasion Bird focused specifically on Mason, stating that he won a clear majority against him.[19] Mason tried to nuance Bird's view, claiming that the press had been misinformed by Bird but ultimately he acknowledged in *The Spirit of the Times* of 22 July that Bird had scored a majority in their mutual games. Although there were certainly grounds in Bird's complaints about the misrepresentation of his results, his letters reinforced his reputation of eternal grousing.

## SUMMER CHESS

Some information about Bird's activity during the dull summer season comes in the form of another letter. Bird wrote it to Hazeltine on 23 June, sitting at his table at the Café International. Bird had been invited by Hazeltine for a farewell visit, as the English master was planning to return home soon. Circumstances prevented Bird to comply with the wish of one of his best friends in New York.

Bird informed Hazeltine that he had bought two recent copies of the *New York Clipper* in which one of his protest letters was printed. Some practical problems prevented him from buying more: "...if funds had been more flourishing with me (as they will be I expect in a few days) I should have bought a few more copies." Bird intended to send his copies to Max Judd and Colonel Bennett.[20]

Bird also informed Hazeltine about his continuous health problems. While the gout troubled his foot and his walking earlier this year, he now had problems "in my right hand and arm. Although better[,] I write with difficulty."[21]

During the first half of July, Neill of Philadelphia, and Ware of Boston were in New York for a few days. The latter contested two games with Bird, in both of which he was victorious.

18. "At New York I have won a majority from Mr. Mason, Mr. Delmar, and all other players—excepting Captain McKenzie, with whom I am even. Of the last 5 games with Mr. Alberoni I won every one, and with Mr. Ensor of Buffalo (who, by the way, stands at the head of the score in the NY Tourney) I have won 11 games to 2." *Hazeltine's Chess, Autographs...,* vol. 6, pp. 185–186.

19. "I have been very successful lately with Mr. Mason. At the last three sittings I won 5 to 2, 9 to 3, and 10 to 4, respectively. Some of these games are considered fine, and I must send you one or two of the best. During the twenty-five years, off or on, I have indulged in the occasional pursuit of chess, I have never felt disposed to mention any successes I may have met with until now; but, looking at the practical record of my results which have hitherto appeared, it is only natural I should wish my efforts fairly recorded." *New York Clipper,* 24 June 1876.

20. Presumably Colonel Clarence E. Bennett, a veteran of the American civil war. At that time he was doing frontier duty (against the Indians) at Fort Abercrombie, North Dakota.

21. *Hazeltine's Chess, Autographs...,* vol. 3, p. 359.

## (409) Bird–Ware    0–1

Offhand game
New York (Café International), 10 July 1876
C30

1. e4 e5 2. f4 Nc6 3. Nf3 d6 4. Bc4 Bg4 5. c3 Nf6 6. 0–0 Be7 7. h3 B×f3 8. Q×f3 h5 9. b4 a6 10. f5 b5 11. Bb3 0–0 12. d3 a5 13. Bd2 a×b4 14. c×b4 Nd4 15. Qd1 c5 16. Bd5 Ra7 17. Nc3 Qd7 18. Bg5 c×b4 19. B×f6 b×c3 20. B×e7 Q×e7 21. Q×h5 Qf6 22. g4 Qh6 23. Q×h6 g×h6 24. Rfc1 c2 25. Kf2 Ra3 26. Ke3 Rc8 27. Kd2 Rcc3 28. Bb3 b4 29. B×c2 N×c2 30. R×c2 R×d3† 31. Kc1 b3 32. Rd2 R×h3 33. Kb2 R×a2† 34. R×a2 b×a2 35. K×a2 Re3 White resigns—*Boston Weekly Globe*, 26 July 1876.

## (410) Perrin & Horner & Barnett–Bird & Field & Wild    0–1

Consultation game
New York (Brooklyn C.C.) 1876 (?)
C54

It is unclear when this game was played. No trace of Bird's presence at the Brooklyn Chess Club has been found since the end of 1875. The publication of this game in September 1876 suggests that he visited the club during the summer months.

1. e4 e5 2. Nf3 Nc6 3. d4 e×d4 4. Bc4 Bc5 5. c3 Nf6 6. c×d4 Bb4† 7. Bd2 B×d2† 8. Nb×d2 d5 9. e×d5 N×d5 10. 0–0 0–0 11. Ne4 Bg4 12. Qd3 Ndb4 13. Qb3 B×f3 14. g×f3 a5 15. d5 a4 16. Qd1 Ne5 17. b3 Qh4 18. Kh1 Nc2 19. Rc1 Nd4 20. Be2 N×e2 21. Q×e2 Rfe8 22. Rg1 a×b3 23. a×b3 f5 24. R×c7 f×e4 25. Rc×g7† Kh8 26. f×e4 Rg8 27. R×g8† R×g8 28. R×g8† K×g8 29. Qe3 Ng4 30. Qg3 Q×g3 31. f×g3 Nf2† 32. Kg2 N×e4 33. h4 Kf7 34. Kf3 Nf6 35. d6 Ke6 36. b4 K×d6 37. g4 Ke6 38. g5 Nd5 39. Kg4 N×b4 40. Kh5 Kf7 41. Kh6 Kg8 42. g6 h×g6 43. K×g6 Nc6 44. Kf5 b5 and after a few moves White resigns—*Illustrated Sporting New Yorker*, 9 September 1876.

In Philadelphia Bird encountered Dr. Lindehn, whom he had already met a decade earlier in London, and competed with in a few offhand games. Lindehn acted as the Swedish commissioner at the International Exhibition. A truncated game appeared in one of Bird's books.

## (411) Lindehn–Bird    ?

Offhand game
Philadelphia, August 1876
C21

1. e4 e5 2. d4 e×d4 3. c3 d×c3 4. Bc4 c×b2 5. B×b2 Bb4† "I have in this position played 6. Kf1 and 7. h4, which, I think, yields a more enduring attack"—Bird. 6. Nc3 Nc6 7. Nf3 d6 8. 0–0 B×c3 9. B×c3 Nf6 10. Ng5 0–0 11. f4 h6 "remaining five [*sic*] pawns ahead with a safe game"—*Chess Practice* (Bird), p. 86.

## CHALLENGING THE CAPTAIN

Bird, still with a speedy return to England in mind, publicly challenged Mackenzie to play a match to fulfill one of his principal reasons to visit the United States.

NY, July 31—

To the Editor of the *New York Herald*: I beg to propose a match at chess with Capt. Mackenzie, the champion of the United States, for $50 a side, leaving all other conditions to be named by him. It is known that the hope of a trial of skill with the Captain (as suggested in our correspondence of 1873) was one of my reasons for visiting America, and I am reluctant to leave without it taking place. I trust, having regard to the desire existing for us to play, he will, in the interest of chess, accept my challenge. The amount of stakes will, perhaps, be considered small, and may possibly be increased. It may be mentioned, however, that some of the most important chess matches on record have been played for a stake within the sum named. Hoping for an early reply, I am, yours obediently.

H.E. Bird

P.S.—Staunton and Horwitz, Morphy and Anderssen, Morphy and Harrwitz, Steinitz and Bird, and Wisker and Bird (London amateur championship), were all played for stakes not exceeding $50 a side [*New York Herald*, 1 August 1876].

Mackenzie's reply followed five days later in the same newspaper. He was not honored by this offer as Bird may have expected and declined it quite categorically, pointing out that Bird first had to re-establish himself in a return match against Mason. Mackenzie's refusal to play fell onto bad soil. Bird replied with another fierce reaction in

George H. Mackenzie (courtesy Cleveland Public Library).

which he combined his frustrations on the score he had made against Mason with the course of the Café International tournament.

To the editor of the *Herald*:

My disappointment at Mr. Mackenzie's rejection of my challenge is only equaled by my regret at the disingenuous reasons which he gives for not accepting it. Mr. Mackenzie would make it appear that I am not worthy of his consideration as a chess opponent, and he alludes to my having been defeated in a match by Mr. Mason, of this city, but he suppresses the fact that I have recently gained many decisive victories from Mr. Mason, and that I have won the large majority of eighteen games from him since my arrival in this country.

Mr. Mackenzie would have acted wisely in not referring to the tournament recently held here. I should be glad to know whether he is prepared to defend the nature of the combination made against me therein. Mr. Mackenzie declined Mr. Mason's challenge on some paltry dispute as to conditions. This he could not do in my case, as I left the terms to be fixed by himself. Anxious to evade a match now, as he has been to avoid encounters with me all through my stay here, Mr. Mackenzie now resorts to the unworthy expedient of attacking my reputation as a chess player. This I submit is scarcely a proper or chivalrous and certainly not a usual way of meeting a challenge, couched in courteous terms, and not worthy of the champion of America.

I am, sir, yours, obediently,

H.E. Bird [*New York Herald*, 9 August 1876].

A third party, Siegfried Lieders, now intervened. In the *New York Herald* of 10 August 1876 he wrote that "Of course there was a combination of victorious chess play against him, but in any other sense this is a most unwarrantable assertion and a slur upon the gentleman who took part in the tournament, which was conducted and decided on rules acceded to and signed by Mr. Bird himself." This reply silenced the complaints for a month or two.

# THE CENTENNIAL CONGRESS 1876

The long-awaited Centennial congress was now rapidly approaching. Despite the mounting criticisms of the organization of the event, the uncertainty had dragged on during the previous months. It lasted until May before the committee of the Philadelphia Chess Club finally published the program. This did not create clarity, and rumors about a lack of funds persisted.

In the meantime, interested chess players were asked to neglect the haziness of the eventual ambitions for the congress and to pay an entrance fee of $20 before 15 July. The amount of prize money would be kept a secret until that same date. In a swift reaction, the most prominent New York players, such as Mackenzie, Mason and Bird, found a unison voice and protested firmly. They wrote an open letter in which they requested exact information about the prize fund and a postponement of the final entrance date until 14 August, a day before the start of the tournament.

European players were hardly enthusiastic to venture upon a quest of such indefinite character. In a razor sharp letter published in the *Westminster Chess Club Papers* (June 1876, p. 30), Zukertort denounced the use (or abuse) of the names of European masters to gather funds for a tournament that was unlikely to be an international event. The discussion kept on for some weeks. It became gradually obvious that the prizes would be way too small to lure the Europeans. The original ambition to gather the world's strongest players thus failed miserably. In the end it was even suggested that

the tournament would be a merely local one, but the participation of a few non–Philadelphia players kept the tournament from a total collapse.

Ultimately nine players entered the tournament. Lorenzo D. Barbour, Davidson, Elson, Martinez and Roberts lived in Philadelphia at the time. The three favorites, Mason, Bird and Judd came from outside the city. The Bostonian Ware completed the field.

The actual American champion, Captain Mackenzie, did not apply. Various reasons may have prevented him from participating. Joost Van Winsen, in his book on James Mason, suggests the bad relations between Bird and Mackenzie, exacerbated by the countless match challenges made by the Englishman, as a possible reason (p. 85). It seems more likely that Mackenzie's decision was influenced by some dissensions he had with the committee about the slow time limit of 12 moves per hour.[22]

Each contestant played two games in succession against every other player. The tournament was planned to last two weeks. The time rate of 12 moves per hour, so criticized by Mackenzie, remained intact. As a result, nearly the whole day was dedicated to chess playing, namely from 9:00 a.m.–1:00, 2:00 p.m.–6:00 and 7:30 p.m.–12:00. With no tight scheme drawn up, the tournament proceeded somewhat irregularly, with some players following a faster pace than others. One participant, Dion Martinez, resigned from the tournament after having met two opponents. His results were cancelled. The first six players were rewarded with a prize. First prize was $300 and a silver cup.

The event opened on 16 August with a smash hit between Bird and Mason. In their first game Bird stubbornly continued to play for a win at all cost. His recklessness cost him dearly again and he lost. The second game ended in a sober draw. During the next rounds Bird recovered reasonably well and he won most of his match-ups. Only Judd withstood him, albeit with some luck. Towards the end of the tournament Bird was struggling with Judd for second prize. By losing his final game against Elson, Bird received a major setback and finished only third. He collected £150 for his efforts.

First prize was decided in the last round duel between Mason and Judd. There was already some tension between them before the tournament, as their attempts to arrange a match had fallen through. Ultimately the favorite, Mason, kept his cool and gained first by beating Judd.

**(412) Bird–Mason    0–1**
Centennial Congress (round 1)
Philadelphia, 16 August 1876
*A02*

**1. f4 f5 2. Nf3 Nf6 3. e3 e6 4. b3 Be7 5. Bb2 0–0 6. d3 b6 7. Be2 Bb7 8. 0–0 c5 9. Na3 Na6 10. c4 Nc7 11. Qe1 Nfe8** "Black plays to shut out the dangerous adverse queen's bishop at once"—Mason. **12. Rd1 Bf6 13. d4 Nd6 14. Ne5 B×e5** "This blocks out the White

<hr>

22. "In New York the grumble is directed against the regulations generally, but more particularly against the extraordinary slow play contemplated in the time limit clause—an hour for every twelve moves. Captain Mackenzie has given forcible expression to the discontent, bluntly intimating, indeed, that unless a revision of the program is agreed to by the Philadelphia committee, New York will hold aloof from the affair altogether." *Land and Water*, 17 June 1876.

## Centennial Chess Congress, Philadelphia, 16–31 August 1876

*Site:* Philadelphia Chess Club
*Playing hours:* 9 a.m.–1 p.m., 2 p.m.–6 p.m. and 7:30 p.m.–12 p.m.
*Prizes:* 1st $300 and a silver cup, 2nd $200, 3rd $150, 4th $100, 5th $50, 6th $8
*Time limit:* 12 moves per hour

|   |              | 1   | 2   | 3   | 4   | 5   | 6   | 7   | 8   | 9   |      |
|---|--------------|-----|-----|-----|-----|-----|-----|-----|-----|-----|------|
| 1 | J. Mason     |     | 1 ½ | 1 ½ | 0 1 | 1 ½ | 1 ½ | 1 1 | ½ 1 |     | 10½  |
| 2 | M. Judd      | 0 ½ |     | 0 1 | 0 ½ | 1 ½ | 1 1 | 1 1 | 1 1 |     | 9½   |
| 3 | H.E. Bird    | 0 ½ | 1 0 |     | 1 ½ | 0 ½ | 1 1 | 1 ½ | 1 ½ |     | 8½   |
| 4 | H.F. Davidson| 1 0 | 1 ½ | 0 ½ |     | 0 ½ | 1 ½ | 0 1 | 1 1 |     | 8    |
| 5 | J. Elson     | 0 ½ | 0 ½ | 1 ½ | 1 ½ |     | ½ ½ | 1 0 | 1 1 |     | 8    |
| 6 | A. Roberts   | 0 ½ | 0 0 | 0 0 | 0 ½ | ½ ½ |     | ½ 1 | 1 1 |     | 5½   |
| 7 | P. Ware      | 0 0 | 0 0 | 0 ½ | 1 0 | 0 1 | ½ 0 |     | ½ ½ |     | 4    |
| 8 | L.D. Barbour | ½ 0 | 0 0 | 0 ½ | 0 0 | 0 0 | 0 0 | ½ ½ |     |     | 2    |
| 9 | D.M. Martinez| 0 0 |     |     | ½ ½ |     |     |     |     |     |      |

bishop effectually, but leaves Black's d-pawn in a very helpless po-sition. In fact, during the entire game Black is hampered by being forced to protect it against continuous attacks"—Mason. **15. d×e5 Ne4 16. Nb1 Qe7 17. Nc3 Rad8** 17. ... d5 solves the problem of the backward d-pawn but opens the long diagonal for the opponent's bishop. White retains the initiative. **18. N×e4 B×e4 19. Qc3 g5** Mason takes risks by aiming to open the position. **20. Bf3 B×f3 21. R×f3 g×f4 22. e×f4 Kh8 23. Qd3** Mason's imprecise moves brought Bird an easy and clearly superior position. Now he has to find a plan to augment the pressure, and this turns out to be no mean feat for him. At this point he could play 23. Rf2! to realize two principal ideas: the occupation of both the d-file, by his rooks, and the long diagonal, by moving his queen to f3. **23. ... Ne8 24. Rh3 Rg8 25. Qf3 Rb8** A similar position as in the last line, but one of White's rooks is rather offside. **26. Rd3 Rg7 27. Qd1 Nc7 28. Rhg3 Rbg8 29. R×g7 R×g7 30. Bc3 Na6 31. a3** With the knight so badly placed at a6, Bird misses a golden opportunity to play 31. Qf3! **31. ... Nb8 32. Be1** 32. b4! is quite strong. **32. ... Nc6 33. Rh3** Bird is losing the thread of the game and Mason takes his chance to equalize the position. **33. ... Rg4 34. Rf3 Nd4 35. Rf2 Qh4 36. Rf1 Qd8 37. h3 Rg6 38. Bc3 Nc6 39. Rf2 Qe7 40. Rf3 a5** Bird gets a free hand again after this move. 40. ... Qg7 keeps him bound to the defense of g2. **41. Rd3 Rg7 42. Be1 Kg8 43. Bf2 h6 44. Qh5 Kh7 45. Kh2 Qf7 46. Qd1 Qe7** (*see diagram*) 46. ... Qg6 covers the important h5 square.

*After 46. ... Qe7*

**47. Qf3** 47. Rd6! is superior. After 47. ... Kg8 48. Qh5 and 49. Bh4, White perfects the coordination between his pieces. **47. ... Kg8 48. Rd6 Kh7 49. Qd3** Stronger is 49. Qd1!, keeping an eye on h5 and thus threatening to infiltrate into Black's position. Mason must then choose between 49. ... Kg8 50. Qh5 Kh7? (50. ... Qf7,

giving up the h-pawn, is more tenacious, but not very attractive) 51. Bh4 Qf7 52. Qd1—and Black's position cracks, since he cannot avert the threat of 53. Bf6—and 49. ... Qe8 50. Bh4 Nd4 51. Bf6 Rg6 52. g4 with very strong pressure. **49. ... Kg8 50. Qd1 Kh7** "Evidently Mr. Mason was willing to declare the game drawn about here, and Mr. Bird, as usual in such cases, paid the penalty for continuing; that is, he lost the game"—Mason. **51. Qe1 Qe8 52. Rd3 Qa8 53. Rg3 R×g3 54. K×g3 Nd4 55. B×d4 c×d4 56. Qd2 Qe4 57. Kf2?!** With this and his next moves Bird denies his king a safe spot for the rest of the game. Right now 57. ... a4! is a strong rejoinder. **57. ... Kg6 58. g3 h5 59. Qe2 h4! 60. Qd2** "White cannot win by exchanging the queens, although his pawns on the queenside could break through, if he had time, by b4, b5 and then c5. But, meanwhile, Black's united center pawns aided by the king, go to queen. For instance: 60. Q×e4 h×g3† 61. K×g3 f×e4 62. h4 (best) 62. ... Kf5 63. h5 d3 64. Kf2 K×f4 etc."—Mason. If one continues Mason's line with a few forced moves it becomes clear that a draw by perpetual check is forced. Black has a forced win only after 62. ... Kh5! instead of 62. ... Kf5, e.g., 63. b4 d3 64. Kf2 d2 65. Ke2 e3 66. b5 K×h4 67. c5 b×c5 68. b6 Kg3 69. b7 d1Q† 70. K×d1 Kf2 71. b8Q e2† 72. Kc2 e1Q 73. Qd6 Qe4† 74. Kc3 Qe3† 75. Kc4 Q×a3. **60. ... h×g3† 61. K×g3 Qb1?** Too hasty. First 61. ... Kf7, bringing his king out of the front line, is far stronger. **62. Q×d4 Q×b3† 63. Kh4 Qb1 64. Qf2 Qd3 65. Q×b6** 65. Qg3† draws, but Bird wants more. **65. ... Q×a3 66. Qd8 Kf7 67. Qf6† Ke8 68. Qh8†?** 68. Qg6† still leads to a draw. Now Black gets the initiative. **68. ... Qf8 69. Qh5† Kd8 70. Qf3 Qb4?!** 70. ... Qc5 is stronger, as the queen is able to reach the kingside when necessary. **71. Qa8†?** 71. Kg5! takes some escape squares of the Black king under control. Black then has only small chances to win. **71. ... Ke7 72. Kg5 Qc3** With 72. ... Kf7!, White's king gets into a mating net, especially as he also has to cope with the a-pawn; e.g., 73. Qa7 Qe7† 74. Kh5 Qd8 and Black has the decisive menace 75. ... Kg7! **73. Qg2 a4?** Mason is very eager to promote his passed pawn, but this move allows Bird to get a perpetual again. 73. ... Q×c4 74. Kh5 Qb4 wins a pawn and allows the queen to return for the protection of the king. **74. Kg6?!** 74. Kh6! Qb4 (74. ... Q×c4? turns out very badly for Black: 75. Qg5† Ke8 76. Qg8† Ke7 77. Kg7 and it is White who has real winning chances!) 75. Kg7! and 76. Qa8 leads to a draw. **74. ... Q×c4 75. Qg5† Ke8 76. Qh4?** 76. Kf6 or 76. h4 must be tried. The battle remains very tense, with Black having the best chances. **76. ... Qb4?!** Much more precise is 76. ... Qc5!, which also controls f2. **77. Qf2 a3 78. h4 Qb2 79. Qc5 a2 80. Qc8† Ke7 81. Qc5†** "The position is peculiar. At first sight it would appear that White might secure a drawn game at this point by 81. Qh8, which would enable him to give perpetual check if his opponent unguardedly pushed his pawn to a1. Bird, however, doubtless saw that Black had an unanswerable reply to the move in question in 81. ... Qa3. The whole of this difficult endgame is very ably played by Mason"—Duffy. **81. ... Kd8 82. Qf8† Kc7 83. Qd6† Kb7 84. Q×d7† Kb6 85. Qd6† Ka5 86. Qc5† Ka4 87. Qc4† Ka3 88. Qc5† Kb3 89. Qb5† Kc3 90. Qc5† Kd3 91. Qd6† Ke3 92. Qc5† Kf3 93. h5 a1Q 94. h6 Qd4 95. Q×d4 Q×d4 96. h7 Qd8** The two following moves were given in the tournament book but not in various other sources. **97. Kg7 K×f4 98. h8Q Q×h8†** and White resigns—*The Spirit of the Times* (Mason), 26 August 1876; *Land and Water* (Duffy), 9 September 1876.

## (413) Mason–Bird   ½–½
Centennial Congress (round 2)
Philadelphia, 17 August 1876
*C33*

**1. e4 e5 2. f4 e×f4 3. Bc4 Nf6 4. Nc3 Bb4 5. e5 d5 6. Bb3 Ne4 7. Nf3 Be6 8. Qe2 B×c3 9. b×c3 Nc6 10. 0–0 0–0–0 11. c4 Ng5 12. N×g5 Q×g5 13. c×d5 Nd4 14. Qf2 N×b3 15. a×b3 B×d5 16. d4 Qg6 17. B×f4 b5 18. Rae1 c6 19. Re3 Rfe8 20. Rfe1 f6 21. Rg3 Qf7 22. e×f6 Q×f6 23. Be5 Q×f2† 24. K×f2 Re7 25. Ke3 c5 26. Kd2 Rae8 27. Rge3 g6 28. Bd6 R×e3 29. R×e3 R×e3 30. K×e3 c×d4† 31. K×d4 B×g2 32. Kc5 Kf7 33. Bb8 g5 34. B×a7 Kg6 35. Kd4 Kf5 36. Ke3 Kg4 37. Kf2 Bc6 38. Bb8** and the game was abandoned as drawn—*Tournament Book*, pp. 53–55.

## (414) Ware–Bird   0–1
Centennial Congress (round 3)
Philadelphia, 18 August 1876
*A80*

**1. d4 f5 2. f4 Nf6 3. Nf3 e6 4. e3 b6 5. Be2 Bb7 6. a3 Be7 7. c3 0–0 8. 0–0 Qe8 9. Ne5 d6 10. Bf3 c6 11. Nd3 Ne4 12. Nd2 d5 13. Be2 Nd7 14. Nf3 Bd6 15. Nde5 Ndf6 16. Bd2 Kh8 17. Be1 B×e5 18. N×e5 Nd7 19. Nf3 a5 20. Rc1 a4 21. Nd2 N×d2 22. Q×d2 b5 23. Bf3 Nb6 24. Qe2 Ba6 25. Qf2 Nc4 26. Rc2 Qe7 27. Be2 Nd6 28. Bd3 Rf6 29. Qf3 Rh6 30. g4 f×g4 31. Q×g4 b4 32. Qd1 B×d3 33. Q×d3 b×a3 34. b×a3 Rg6† 35. Kh1 Nc4 36. e4 Q×a3 37. e5 Qe7 38. Ra2 a3 39. f5 e×f5 40. Q×f5 Ne3 41. Qf7 Q×f7 42. R×f7 Nc4 43. Bg3 h5 44. Rf5 Rb8 45. R×h5† Kg8 46. Rf5 Rb2 47. Rf2 Rg4 48. Kg2 Re4 49. Kh3 Re3 50. Rg2 R×a2 51. R×a2 R×c3 52. Kg4 Kf7 53. Kf5 Rf3† 54. Kg4 Rd3 55. Kf5 g6† 56. Kg5 Rd2 57. Ra1 a2 58. Rf1† Ke8 59. e6 Rb2 60. Ra1 Nd2 61. K×g6 Nb3 62. Rf1 a1Q** and Black wins—*Tournament Book*, pp. 56–58.

## (415) Bird–Ware   ½–½
Centennial Congress (round 4)
Philadelphia, 18 August 1876
*B01*

**1. e4 d5 2. e×d5 Q×d5 3. Nc3 Qd8 4. d4 c6 5. Be3 Bf5 6. Bd3 B×d3 7. Q×d3 e6 8. Nge2 Nf6 9. 0–0 Bd6 10. h3 Nbd7 11. Bg5 Be7 12. Ng3 Qc7 13. Nce2 h6 14. Bf4 Bd6 15. B×d6 Q×d6 16. Qb3 0–0 17. Rad1 Qc7 18. c4 Rad8 19. c5 b6 20. c×b6 a×b6 21. Rc1 Nd5 22. Rfe1 N7f6 23. Rc2 Qd6 24. Rec1 Rc8 25. a3 Rc7 26. Nc3 Rfc8 27. N×d5 N×d5 28. Ne4 Qf4 29. Qd3 Qf5 30. Qe2 Nf4 31. Qe3 Nd5 32. Qe1 Nf4 33. Ng3 Qd5 34. Qe4 Qd6 35. Ne2 Nd5 36. g3 b5 37. Nc3 b4 38. a×b4 N×b4 39. Rd2 Rd8 40. Re1 Qd7 41. Qg4 Kh8 42. Red1 Qe7 43. Qe2 Ra8 44. Ne4 Nd5 45. Nc5 Ra5 46. Rc1 Rb5 47. Ra1 Ra7 48. Rdd1 Qc7 49. R×a7 Q×a7 50. Ne4 Qb8 51. Rd2 Rb3 52. Kg2 Kg8** ...

(continued top of right column)

**53. Nc5 Rb5 54. Rc2 Nb4 55. Rd2 Qd6 56. Kh2 Qd5 57. Ne4 Qd8 58. Nc3 Rb6 59. Qc4 Qd7 60. h4 Nd5 61. Qe2 Rb3 62. Ne4 Rb4 63. Nc5 Qe7 64. Qa6 Qc7 65. Qa3 Qd8 66. f4 Rb5 67. Qf3 Ne7 68. Qe2 Qd5 69. g4 Qd6 70. Qe5 Qd5 71. Qe3 Ra5 72. Rc2 h5 73. f5 Qd6† 74. Qe5 Q×e5† 75. d×e5 e×f5 76. g×h5 Kh7 77. b4 Rb5 78. Rc4 Kh6 79. e6 f×e6 80. N×e6 Re5 81. Nd4 Rd5 82. N×c6 N×c6 83. R×c6† K×h5 84. Rc4 g6 85. Kg3 Rd3† 86. Kg2 g5 87. h×g5 K×g5** and the game was drawn—*Tournament Book*, pp. 59–62.

## (416) Bird–Roberts   1–0
Centennial Congress (round 5)
Philadelphia, 21 August 1876
*C45*

**1. e4 e5 2. Nf3 Nc6 3. d4 e×d4 4. N×d4 Qh4 5. Nb5 Q×e4† 6. Be3 Bb4†?** 6. ... Bb4† is the standard move after 6. Be2. Right here it is already the losing mistake. Correct is 6. ... Qe5! **7. Nd2 B×d2† 8. Q×d2 Kd8 9. 0–0–0 a6** Nothing can save Black. If 9. ... Nf6 (Sayen), 10. Bf4 Nd5 11. Bg3 wins. If 9. ... Qb4 10. c3 Qe7 11. Re1! **10. N×c7!** "Played in Mr. Bird's happiest style. This sacrifice, after careful analysis, appears to be perfectly sound"—Sayen. **10. ... K×c7 11. Qd6† Kd8 12. Qf8†** *The Spirit of the Times* omitted the following repetition of moves 11 and 13. **12. ... Kc7** "If 12. ... Qe8 13. Bb6 mates"—Sayen. **13. Qd6† Kd8 14. Bb6†** "14. Re1 wins at once. Black cannot answer 14. ... Qb4 on account of 15. Q×b4"—Mason. **14. ... Ke8 15. Bd3 Qh4** "The best and only move. If 15. ... Qg4 16. Rhe1† Nge7 17. R×e7† N×e7 18. Re1 Qg5† 19. f4 Qf6 20. Qc7 wins"—Sayen. **16. Rhe1† Nge7 17. Be4! Qh6† 18. Q×h6 g×h6 19. B×c6 b×c6** "Another singular position. If 19. ... d×c6 20. Rd8 mates"—Sayen. **20. Bc5?!** A superficial move that enhances Black's chances to save the game after all. More forceful is 20. Bd4 and 21. Bf6. **20. ... d6 21. R×d6 Be6?!** Black has drawing chances after 21. ... Rb8 22. R×c6 Be6. **22. R×e6! f×e6 23. R×e6 Kf7 24. R×e7† Kf6 25. Rd7 Rhe8 26. Be3** Other moves such as 26. Bd4† or 26. h3 were preferable as the text move loses control over e7. **26. ... Ke6** "26. ... Re7 would have saved one of the h-pawns"—Mason. **27. R×h7 Rh8 28. R×h6† R×h6 29. B×h6 Kf5?** "29. ... Rg8 wins a pawn. If 30. g3 Rh8"—Mason. **30. Be3 Ke4 31. h4 Rd8 32. h5 Rg8 33. g3 Rd8** All these rook moves were perfectly useless. White is winning. **34. h6 Kf3 35. c3 Rd5 36. b4 Rd7 37. Bd4 Kg4 38. Bg7** Black resigns—*Tournament Book* (Sayen), pp. 90–92; *The Spirit of the Times* (Mason), 2 September 1876.

## (417) Roberts–Bird   0–1
Centennial Congress (round 6)
Philadelphia, 21 August 1876
*C80*

**1. e4 e5 2. Nf3 Nc6 3. Bb5 a6 4. Ba4 Nf6 5. 0–0 N×e4 6. Re1 Nc5 7. B×c6 d×c6 8. N×e5 Be7 9. Qe2 Be6 10. c3 Nd7 11. f4 N×e5 12. Q×e5 Bf6 13. Qc5 Be7 14. Qh5 g6 15. Qe2 c5 16. Kh1 Qd7 17. d3 0–0–0 18. Rd1 Bg4 19. Qe1 B×d1 20. Q×d1 Q×d3** and White resigns in a few moves—*Tournament Book*, pp. 93–94.

**418) Bird–Barbour   1–0**
Centennial Congress (round 7)
Philadelphia, 22 August 1876
C40

1. e4 e5 2. Nf3 d5 3. e×d5 e4 4. Qe2 f5 5. d3 Nf6 6. d×e4 f×e4 7. Ng5 Q×d5 8. f3 Bf5 9. Nd2 e3 10. Q×e3† Be7 11. Bc4 Qc5 12. Q×c5 B×c5 13. Nde4 N×e4 14. f×e4 Bg4 15. h3 Bh5 16. Ne6 Bf7 17. N×g7† Kf8 18. Rf1 K×g7 19. R×f7† Kg6 20. Rf5 Bd4 21. c3 Bf6 22. Rf3 Nc6 23. Rg3† Kh5 24. Bf7† Kh4 25. Rg4 mate—*Tournament Book*, pp. 111–112.

**419) Barbour–Bird   ½–½**
Centennial Congress (round 8)
Philadelphia, 22 August 1876
C80

1. e4 e5 2. Nf3 Nc6 3. Bb5 a6 4. Ba4 Nf6 5. 0–0 N×e4 6. Re1 Nc5 7. B×c6 d×c6 8. d4 Ne6 9. N×e5 Be7 10. Be3 0–0 11. c3 f5 12. f4 Rf6 13. Nd2 Nf8 14. Bf2 Ng6 15. N×g6 R×g6 16. Qb3† Kf8 17. Nf3 Qd5 18. c4 Qd8 19. Re2 Re6 20. Ne5 Bf6 21. Rd1 Bd6 22. Rde1 B×e5 23. R×e5 R×e5 24. R×e5 Qf6 25. Qe3 Bd7 26. Be1 a5 27. Bc3 Re8 and the game was abandoned as drawn—*Tournament Book*, pp. 113–115.

**420) Judd–Bird   0–1**
Centennial Congress (round 9)
Philadelphia, 23 August 1876
C45

1. e4 e5 2. Nf3 Nc6 3. d4 e×d4 4. N×d4 Bc5 5. Be3 Qf6 6. c3 Qg6? One of Bird's pet lines. It is refuted by 7. Nb5! 7. Nd2? N×d4 8. c×d4 Bb4 9. f3 Ne7 10. Qc2 c6 11. g3 "In order to free the action of the bishop, which important piece is completely paralyzed by the position of the Black queen"—Sayen. 11. ... d5 12. Bd3 d×e4 13. f×e4 Bg4 14. 0–0 B×d2 15. B×d2 Qd6 16. Bc3 h5 Until now the position has been more or less equal, except for Bird's usual mistake at move 6. With the text move Bird commences maneuvers against White's king, but with the bishop pair and command over the center, there is no need at all for Judd to be afraid of anything. A better alternative was 16. ... Qd7, followed by 17. ... 0–0. Not good at all is the immediate 16. ... 0–0? because of 17. e5! 17. Qf2 17. Bc4! forces serious concessions. Either he must play 17. ... Be6 18. B×e6 f×e6 19. Qf2 or submit to 17. ... 0–0 18. Qb3 Be6 19. B×e6 Q×e6 and now 20. Q×b7. If then 20. ... Q×e4? 21. Rae1. 17. ... f5 "Black obtains a good place for his knight, d5, by sacrificing this pawn, but this is no full equivalent"—Mason. "This is Mr. Bird all over. It is yet doubtful, after a most careful analysis, whether this move was sound, though Mr. Bird contends that it is. The analysis is too extended for publication here, and the reader can best judge from the remainder of the game whether White could have held his advantage"—Sayen. 18. e×f5 Bh3 19. Rfe1 0–0–0 He needs to castle on the kingside, but Bird is still keen on creating maximal complications. 20. Re6 20. d5! opens all diagonals and lines in his favor. A sudden benefit, after 20. ... N×d5 21. B×g7, is the appearance of a passed f-pawn. 20. ... Qc7 21. Rae1 Nd5 22. Bd2 Qf7 23. Bg5

Rde8 24. Qe2 "White ought to exchange both rooks and then play 26. Qe2. This would have left him with a pawn more and two bishops against bishop and knight"—Mason. Mason's suggestion isn't bad, but White loses a large part of his activity with so many exchanges. Best is 24. R6e5!, as Black isn't in a position to exchange at e5. Once the rook is on a stable square, White can look for ways to increase his advantage. 24. ... Nc7 25. Re5 Black now wins back his sacrificed pawn. 25. Re7 Qd5 is but a shade better. 25. ... R×e5 26. d×e5 B×f5 27. Qf2 Bg6 28. B×g6 Q×g6 29. Bf4 Rf8 "Selected with great judgment. The threatening position of this rook paralyzes White's game for many moves, and also prevents the capture of the a-pawn, besides threatening 30. ... Nd5"—Sayen. 30. Kh1 b6 31. Qf3 Kb7 32. Rd1 Nd5 33. h4 Qe6 34. Kg2 Rf5 "Patiently getting his pieces into position, anticipating the removal of Rd1, when he can safely commence the onslaught on the kingside"—Sayen. 35. a3 a5 36. Rc1 g5! "This fine move is worthy of Mr. Bird, and is perfectly sound with the best analysis"—Sayen. 37. h×g5 h4 (*see diagram*)

*After 37. ... h4*

38. Rf1?! 38. Rh1! (Sayen) leaves the rook better placed; e.g., 38. ... h×g3 39. Rh7† Kb8 40. Rh4, and a few exchanges will diminish the danger for both sides. 38. ... Qf7 Stronger is the immediate 38. ... h×g3, forcing the favorable position that arises in the game. 39. Qe4? After 39. Qe2, White sneaks out of danger, as the rook remains defended. Had Bird played 38. ... h×g3 at once, 39. Qe2 would lose a piece. 39. ... h×g3 40. e6 "A blunder, which loses the game. 40. K×g3 was his move"—Mason. Bird should then continue with 40. ... Qe6, exchanging knight for bishop and gaining both the e- and g-pawn. White has but small chances to gain a draw. 40. ... Qh7! 41. e7 "41. K×g3 is useless now: 41. ... R×g5† 42. Kf3 Qh5† 43. Kf2 N×f4 44. e7 Qh4† 45. Ke3 Nd5† 46. Q×d5 R×d5 47. e8Q Qd4† 48. Kf3 Rf5† wins"—Mason. 41. ... Qh2† 42. Kf3 g2 and White resigns, as the game is forced—*Tournament Book* (Sayen), pp. 124–127; *The Spirit of the Times* (Mason), 9 September 1876.

**(421) Bird–Judd   0–1**
Centennial Congress (round 10)
Philadelphia, 24 August 1876
C77

1. e4 e5 2. Nf3 Nc6 3. Bb5 a6 4. Ba4 Nf6 5. Qe2 Bc5 6. c3 b5 7. Bb3 d6 8. a4 Rb8 9. a×b5 a×b5 10. d3 Ne7 11. Be3 Ng6 12. g3 Bb6 13. Nbd2 c6 14. Nf1 0–0 15. B×b6 Q×b6 16. Ne3 Be6 17. B×e6 f×e6 18. h4 Nh8 19. 0–0 h6 20. b4 Ra8 21. Kg2 Ng6 22. Nh2 Ra7 23. h5 Nh8 24. R×a7 Q×a7 25. Nhg4 Qa3 26. N×f6†

**R×f6 27. Qd2 Rf8 28. c4 Rb8 29. Rc1 Nf7 30. c×b5 c×b5 31. Rc3 Qa7 32. Qc1 Rb7?** Abandoning the control of the last rank ought to be fatal, as an important pawn is lost by force. **33. Rc8† Kh7 34. Qc6 Re7 35. Q×b5 Qa2 36. Rc2 Qb1 37. Qc4 Ng5 38. Rc1 Qb2 39. Qc3??** This move is so bad that after Judd's excellent reply his game is instantly lost. 39. Rc2 wards off all threats before then pursuing the win; e.g., 39. ... Qb1 40. Qc8 and 41. Qd8 (Sayen). **39. ... Qe2!** Bird's king becomes the victim of a sudden assault. **40. Rh1 Rf7 41. Nd1 Rf3 42. Qc1 R×g3† 43. K×g3 Qf3†** and White resigns—*Tournament Book* (Sayen), pp. 139–141.

## (422) H.F. Davidson–Bird    0–1
Centennial Congress (round 11)
Philadelphia, 28 August 1876
*C61*

**1. e4 e5 2. Nf3 Nc6 3. Bb5 Nd4** "This move, although generally considered an inferior one, is very formidable in the hands of Mr. Bird, he being well versed in the variations arising therefrom"—Neill. **4. N×d4 e×d4 5. d3 Bc5 6. 0–0** "6. Qh5 seems a strong method of continuing the attack"—Neill. **6. ... c6 7. Bc4 d5 8. e×d5 c×d5 9. Bb5†** "There seems to be little gained by this check, as Black does not intend to castle. 9. Bb3 was better"—Neill. **9. ... Kf8 10. Bf4 h5 11. Re1 Ne7 12. Nd2 Bg4 13. f3 Be6 14. Nb3 Bb6 15. Bg5 Qd6 16. B×e7† Q×e7 17. a4?** With his bishop in apparent trouble Davidson plays a panicking move that allows Bird a very dangerous attack.

**Max Judd (*Book of the Second American Chess Congress*).**

There is nothing lost yet after the tricky 17. f4, a move that not onl[y] blocks the important h2–b8 diagonal, but also threatens 18. f5! (i[n] case of 17. ... Qb4). More prudent is 17. ... Qd6 18. Qf3 Bg4 19. Qg[3] a6 20. Ba4. White can now retreat his knight to d2 if his bishop i[s] threatened. A direct assault on the bishop with 20. ... Qb4 is refute[d] by 21. h3 Be6? (21. ... Q×a4 is correct) 22. f5! B×f5 23. a3. **17. ... a[6] 18. a5 Bc7 19. Ba4 Qd6** 19. ... Qh4! leaves no doubt of the result. **20. g3** 20. f4 Q×f4 21. g3 wins some time for the defense, bu[t] shouldn't rescue him. **20. ... h4 21. f4 h×g3 22. h×g3** (*see diagram*)

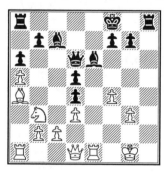

*After 22. h×g3*

**22. ... g5! 23. N×d4** "White's game is hopeless. Mr. Bird finishe[s] it in the same excellent style he has exhibited all through"—Neill. **23. ... g×f4 24. N×e6† f×e6 25. Re2** The endgame reached afte[r] 25. Qg4 Kf7 26. Q×f4† offers no hope to draw the game. **25. ... f3** White resigns—*Tournament Book* (Neill), pp. 168–169.

## (423) Bird–H.F. Davidson    ½–½
Centennial Congress (round 12)
Philadelphia, 29 August 1876
*A03*

**1. f4 d5 2. e3 Nc6 3. Nf3 Bg4 4. Bb5 e6 5. 0–0 Nf6 6. h3 B×f3 7. Q×f3 a6 8. B×c6† b×c6 9. b3 c5 10. Bb2 Be7 11. d3 0–0 12. Nd2 Rb8 13. Rab1 c6 14. e4 Nd7 15. Qg3 Bf6 16. e5 Bh4 17. Qg4 g6 18. Nf3 Be7 19. h4 h5 20. Qh3 Rb4 21. g3 Kg7 22. a4 Rb7 23. Ng5 B×g5 24. h×g5 Qa5 25. Rf2 Qb4 26. Rbf1 d4 27. Rh2 Rbb8 28. Qg2 Rbc8 29. g4 h×g4 30. Q×g4 Rh8 31. R×h8 R×h8 32. Qg2 Nb6 33. Bc1 Nd5 34. Bd2 Qb8 35. Rf3 Rh4 36. Rh3 N×f4 37. B×f4 R×f4 38. Rh7† K×h7 39. Qh2† Kg8 40. Q×f4 Qb4 41. Qf2 Qa3** and the game was abandoned as drawn—*Tournament Book*, pp. 179–181.

## (424) Bird–Elson    0–1
Centennial Congress (round 13)
Philadelphia, 30 August 1876
*A03*

**1. f4 d5 2. e3 f5 3. Be2 Nf6 4. Nf3 e6 5. b3 Be7 6. Bb2 0–0 7. Na3 Ne4 8. 0–0 Bf6 9. c3 Qe7 10. Nc2 c5 11. Qe1 Nc6 12. d3 Nd6 13. d4 Ne4 14. Ba3 b6 15. Bd3 Qd8 16. Rd1 Bb7 17. Ne5 Be7 18. B×e4 f×e4 19. N×c6 B×c6 20. c4 Qc7 21. Qe2 Rf6 22. d×c5 b×c5 23. Bb2 Rh6 24. g4 Rg6 25. c×d5 e×d5 26. f5 Rh6 27. Rf2 Rf8 28. Rg2 Bg5 29. Bc3 Rh3 30. Be1 Re8 31. Bg3 Qb6 32. b4 c×b4 33. Nd4 a5 34. Rf2 Rc8 35. Kg2 Rh6 36. Rff1 Ba4 37. Rc1 Rc3 38. R×c3 b×c3 39. h4 B×h4 40. Bf4 Bf6 41. B×h6 B×d4 42. e×d4 Bb5 43. f6 g×h6 44. Rb1 B×e2 45. R×b6 c2** and White resigns—*Tournament Book*, pp. 182–184.

425) Elson–Bird   ½–½
Centennial Congress (round 14)
Philadelphia, 30 August 1876
C61

1. e4 e5 2. Nf3 Nc6 3. Bb5 Nd4 4. Bc4 Qf6 5. c3 N×f3†
6. Q×f3 Bc5 7. d3 d6 8. Be3 Q×f3 9. g×f3 B×e3 10. f×e3 Be6
11. Nd2 Nf6 12. d4 B×c4 13. N×c4 Nd7 14. Ke2 0-0-0 15. a4
Rhe8 16. Kd3 g6 17. b4 Nf6 18. Rhf1 Re7 19. Rae1 Rde8 20. a5
Nd7 21. Nd2 e×d4 22. e×d4 f5 23. Rf2 Nf6 24. Rfe2 Nh5 25. Kc2
Nf4 26. Rf2 b5 27. h4 a6 28. Rh2 Kb7 29. Rg1 c6 30. Rg5 h6
31. Rg1 Kc7 32. e×f5 g×f5 33. h5 Re2 34. R×e2 R×e2 35. Rg7†
Kb8 36. Rh7 Re6 37. Rf7 N×h5 38. R×f5 Nf6 draw—*Tournament Book*, pp. 185–186.

---

# THE CLIPPER FREE CENTENNIAL TOURNAMENT 1876

The idea to commemorate the centenary of America's independence with a chess tournament was also very much alive in New York. The Café International was the most appropriate place for such an event and with the support of Lieders and the sponsorship of a newspaper the Clipper Free Centennial Tournament was announced. The concrete plans and rules of the Clipper tournament crystallized in the first days of September. The proprietor of the *New York Clipper* provided three prizes of respectively $100, $50 and $25. Twenty moves had to be made per hour. A new kind of additional prize was introduced on this occasion: the winner of the most brilliant game received a silver cup, a donation by Lieders. The problematic outcome of the previous tournament at the Café International caused an intervention by the committee, composed of Mackenzie, Hazeltine and Ira D.J. Sweet.[23] To prevent the tournament from dragging on endlessly it was decided that all the games had to be played within four weeks. The greatest number of victories would be awarded first prize.

The *New York Clipper* of 23 September further stipulated that participants failing to play a game that might change the order of the prize winners would receive the verbal punishment of being called a deserter of the ranks. Although this new rule served a noble goal, it only enhanced the problems and discussions afterwards.

The undeniable favorite for the laurels, thanks to his triumph in Philadelphia, was Mason. Bird, Delmar and Ensor were considered the most dangerous outsiders. For the second time in a row Mackenzie preferred to stay out of the fray. He limited himself to the management of the tournament.

The tournament took off on Wednesday, 20 September. The committee asked each participant to do the utmost to finish all the games before the end of the tournament, which was foreseen to be 18 October. Several of the favorites started the tournament at a very rapid thread. Especially Bird set the tone by scoring win after win. Up to 26 September he played eight games and won them all.

23. Hazeltine and Sweet took care, respectively, of the chess and checkers column in the *New York Clipper*.

Jacob Elson (courtesy Cleveland Public Library).

Highly crucial was his early and beautiful win against Mason. The latter had a terrible start, with two losses in his first four games.

At the end of the following week Bird had finished 12 games. He suffered a single but very surprising loss as it came from the hands of Williams, a very weak player, who ended nearly last in the final ranking.

Early in October the situation still looked fine for Bird. He had lost just 1 point, with his direct rivals Delmar and Mason having already lost, respectively, 2½ and 3 points. Other players were practically eliminated for one of the three prizes. On 12 October, with the end of the tournament in sight, Bird wrote to Hazeltine that he had finished 13 of his 20 games. The games with George A.T. Limbeck (12 October) and John E. Clarke (17 October) were planned in the near future. Four of the other games gave Bird a lot of anxiety. He couldn't get an appointment with Dill and E. McCutcheon. Francis M. Roser had retired, but this was less relevant as he had not met Delmar or Mason either. The worst problem for Bird was the game with Becker. Becker lost against Mason and was out of the city by now. So Mason was granted an extra point that Bird could never earn.[24]

Bird beat Limbeck, Clarke and Delmar, but he unexpectedly lost against Dill. Becker, but also McCutcheon, did not play against

24. *Hazeltine's Chess, Autographs...*, vol. 3, pp. 287–288.

Bird. As they had lost against Mason, the latter was able to outflank Bird in the final ranking.[25]

The committee intervened just before the end of the contest to work out an acceptable arrangement. Two ideas were put forward. One proposal was to extend the tournament. Secondly they suggested to count the forfeited games as wins for Bird and Ensor. Mason could agree with a short extension but he ruled out yielding free points to Bird and Ensor. In a letter written to Hazeltine on 17 October, Mason declared that Bird and Ensor were not free of guilt either as they had the chance to play Becker earlier on.[26]

Delmar was another player who raised his voice in the ensuing discussion. In a letter to the *New York World*, he reacted against the so-called unfair treatment of Bird and Ensor. Delmar claimed that the rules were followed and that "both the defeated candidates have been almost constantly present at the Café International every day from twelve to sixteen hours (and, in fact, may be said to live there)..." (*Hartford Weekly Times*, 28 October 1876; first published in the *New York World*).

Accusing Bird of cowardice seems a bit desperate. There is more than enough proof of Bird's willingness to play and, even though Becker was a strong player, he was obviously not of the same level as Bird. Additionally, Bird was not known for ducking any challenge.

Bird found some consolation in the fact that both Mason and Mackenzie acknowledged that he was the moral winner of the tourney. In a postscript attached to a letter written on 24 October, Bird nevertheless admitted that he was extremely disappointed by getting only the third prize.[27] Bird appears to have made no public announcement about the sad finish of the tournament, but he undoubtedly supported the point of view taken by Ensor. Ensor ended fourth and was also disserved by the absence of few players, though in his case he had only small theoretical chances to gain a prize.

To the Editor of *The World*,
Sir,

I notice in *The World* of yesterday a letter from Mr. Delmar, in which he seeks to palliate the defections in this tournament which deprived Mr. Bird of the first prize. Mr. Delmar knows perfectly well that Mr. Becker and Mr. McCutcheon, like the rest, signed undertakings to play out the whole of their games. He is equally well aware that I have made repeated efforts to induce both of them to come up to the mark. Mr. Bird also informs me that he applied for appointments, and has furnished me with a copy of a card which he wrote

and delivered to Mr. McCutcheon on the day when he first heard that that gentleman had determined to play with Mason and Delmar, and not with him or me. The card ran as follows:

October 11, 1876

"Mr. Bird will feel much obliged by Mr. McCutcheon fixing a time for their tournament game."

No reply came to his card. Mr. Bird and myself applied to the proprietor of the café, Mr. Lieders, and we have reason to believe that Mr. Lieders gave instructions to Captain Mackenzie to see justice done in the matter. Mr. Bird's score in the tournament is the same as Mr. Mason's and Mr. Delmar's [*sic*] and he won from both of those gentlemen. If he could have had the opportunity of playing with Mr. Becker and Mr. McCutcheon, by drawing a game with either of them, he could have secured the first prize. In justice to my own play, I may observe that Mr. Delmar has never yet won or even drawn a game with me [*Hartford Weekly Times*, 28 October 1876].

A week later an anonymous letter about this sordid affair was published in the *Hartford Weekly Times*. The author, who claimed to be a regular visitor of the Clipper tournament, accused Mackenzie of unfairness towards Bird and Ensor. The writer was especially harsh for Becker and McCutcheon.

Mr. Becker, after playing a few unimportant games, and one with Mason which was important, retired from the tourney to go to Chicago; and as he lost the game with Mr. Mason it gave that player a start of one game over the others, impossible to be made up.... But now I come to a case altogether different: Mr. McCutcheon ... played a game with Mason and lost, declined, or being asked, to play with Ensor, and sat down a short time after, on the same evening, to play with Delmar, losing also to him, and offered no opportunity to either Mr. Bird or Mr. Ensor to improve their score. It is said "he is out of town." ... It cannot be said that he was not requested by Bird to play, as Bird wrote to him a letter to that effect which he saw him open [*Hartford Weekly Times*, 4 November 1876].

Slowly but surely all relevant newspapers gave formal notice that Bird was the victim of some foul play. According to the *Brooklyn Daily Eagle* on 18 October, nationality played an important role as the American players (Mason, Delmar, Becker and McCutcheon) conspired against the British representatives (Bird and Ensor). Bird alluded to his nationality as the cause of a combination against him at the previous tournament at the Café International, but in this case the indignation was greater and more supportive to him. Frank Teed resumed the attitude of many Americans towards Bird in an article. In light of the euphoria upon Bird's arrival in December 1875, it becomes clear that much has changed since then.

The trouble arose upon the complaint of Mr. Bird, who stated that no opportunity was given him to win the first prize by reason of two or more gentlemen withdrawing who had lost their games to Messrs. Mason and Delmar. Mr. Bird has been such a chronic grumbler in the past that his complaint, although probably in this instance justly founded, scarcely receives the deserved sympathy [*Brownson's Chess Journal*, February 1877, p. 30].

All developments on the American front were closely followed in other chess centers. In London Wormald compared the situation to the British actuality.

We are sorry to find that professionalism is finding its way into American chess [*Illustrated London News*, 11 November 1876].

A very interesting résumé was written by John Wisker. Bird's former rival had moved to Australia at the end of 1876. When he brought the news to his readers, some months had elapsed:

Mr. Bird, the well-known English amateur, has left the United States and crossed into Canada. Somehow, he found the great Republic a very uncongenial abode. The Englishman was decidedly unpopular—a result we

---

25. "The tournament at the Café International in New York ended last night and the result is the success of Messrs. Mason, Delmar and Bird in winning the three prizes, the former playing [19] games, Delmar [18], Bird [17] and Ensor [15]. The absence of Messrs. Becker, Roser and McCutcheon rather interfered with a satisfactory close of the tournament, as an analysis of the record will show. McCutcheon was defeated by Mason, Delmar and Orchard, four of his five victories being with the weaker players of the tourney. It is very probable that Bird would have won his game with McCutcheon had the latter been on hand to play as he should have been. The fact that Mr. Bird defeated Mason, Delmar and Ensor in the tourney and yet won only third prize, would show that the arrangement of the tourney was not calculated to give the prize to the strongest player." *Brooklyn Daily Eagle*, 19 October 1876.

26. "You know that at the beginning of the tourney Mr. Becker was avoided by the gentlemen to whom you would now give his games. Mr. Becker is a very strong player and so the gentlemen now anxious to score against him because he is unable to play were afraid to meet him during the two weeks he continued in the tourney. I was drawn against him and played him and won after a long and hard fight—and yet you propose to let Bird, Delmar, Ensor and others who would not play him when they had every opportunity, you seriously intend to give them a game each!" *Hazeltine's Chess, Autographs...*, vol. 3, pp. 297–298.

27. *Hazeltine's Chess, Autographs...*, vol. 3, pp. 251–253.

### Clipper Free Centennial Tournament, New York, 20 September–18 October 1876

***Site:*** Café International
***Prizes:*** 1st $100, 2nd $50, 3rd $25
***Time limit:*** 20 moves per hour

| | 1 | 2 | 3 | 4 | 5 | 6 | 7 | 8 | 9 | 10 | 11 | 12 | 13 | 14 | 15 | 16 | 17 | 18 | 19 | 20 | 21 | |
|---|---|---|---|---|---|---|---|---|---|---|---|---|---|---|---|---|---|---|---|---|---|---|
| 1 J. Mason | | 0 | 0 | 1 | 1 | 1 | 1 | 1 | 0 | 1 | 1 | | 1 | 1 | 1 | 1 | 1 | 1 | 1 | 1 | 1 | 16 |
| 2 E. Delmar | 1 | | 0 | 0 | 1 | 1 | 1 | ½ | 1 | 1 | | | 1 | 1 | 1 | 1 | 1 | 1 | 1 | 1 | 1 | 15½ |
| 3 H.E. Bird | 1 | 1 | | 1 | 0 | 1 | 1 | 1 | 1 | 1 | | | 1 | | 1 | 1 | 1 | 1 | 1 | 0 | 1 | 15 |
| 4 A.W. Ensor | 0 | 1 | 0 | | 0 | 1 | | | 1 | 1 | | | 0 | | 1 | 1 | 1 | 1 | 1 | 1 | 1 | 11 |
| 5 S.R. Dill | 0 | 0 | 1 | 1 | | 1 | ½ | 1 | ½ | ½ | | 0 | | | 0 | 1 | 1 | 1 | | | 1 | 9½ |
| 6 H. Wernich | 0 | 0 | 0 | 0 | 0 | | 1 | 1 | 1 | 1 | | 0 | 0 | 0 | ½ | 1 | 1 | | 1 | 1 | 1 | 9½ |
| 7 J.E. Clarke | 0 | 0 | 0 | | ½ | 0 | | | 1 | 1 | | | 0 | | 1 | 1 | 1 | 1 | | 1 | 1 | 8½ |
| 8 A.T. Limbeck | 0 | ½ | 0 | | 0 | 0 | | | 1 | 1 | | 1 | | | 1 | 1 | | 1 | 1 | | 1 | 8½ |
| 9 I.E. Orchard | 1 | 0 | 0 | 0 | ½ | 0 | 0 | 0 | | 1 | 0 | 0 | | 1 | 0 | ½ | 1 | | ½ | 1 | 1 | 7½ |
| 10 J.W. Baird | 0 | 0 | 0 | 0 | ½ | 0 | 0 | 0 | 0 | | | | | | 1 | ½ | 1 | 0 | 1 | 1 | 1 | 6 |
| 11 C. Becker | 0 | | | | | | | | 1 | | | | 0 | | 1 | | | 1 | 1 | 1 | 1 | 6 |
| 12 F.M. Roser | | | | | 1 | 1 | | 0 | 1 | | | | 1 | | | | | 1 | | | 1 | 6 |
| 13 Lissner | 0 | 0 | 0 | 1 | | 1 | 1 | | | | 1 | 0 | | | | 0 | | 1 | | | | 5 |
| 14 E. McCutcheon | 0 | 0 | | | | 1 | | | 0 | | | | | | 1 | | 1 | | | 1 | 1 | 5 |
| 15 W. Dwyer | 0 | 0 | 0 | 0 | 1 | ½ | 0 | 0 | 1 | 0 | 0 | | | 0 | | | 0 | | | 1 | 1 | 4½ |
| 16 J.S. Ryan | 0 | 0 | 0 | 0 | 0 | 0 | 0 | 0 | ½ | ½ | | | 1 | | | | | | | 1 | 1 | 4 |
| 17 A. Cohnfeld | 0 | 0 | 0 | 0 | 0 | 0 | 0 | | 0 | 0 | | | | 0 | 1 | | | 0 | 1 | 1 | 0 | 3 |
| 18 A.L. Grütter | 0 | 0 | 0 | 0 | 0 | | 0 | 0 | | 1 | 0 | 0 | 0 | | | | 1 | | 0 | | 1 | 3 |
| 19 C.H. Fowler | 0 | 0 | 0 | 0 | | 0 | | 0 | ½ | 0 | 0 | | | | | | 0 | 1 | | 0 | 1 | 2½ |
| 20 Williams | 0 | 0 | 1 | 0 | | 0 | 0 | | 0 | 0 | 0 | | | 0 | 0 | 0 | 0 | | 1 | | | 2 |
| 21 Marr | 0 | 0 | 0 | 0 | 0 | 0 | 0 | 0 | 0 | 0 | 0 | 0 | | 0 | 0 | 0 | 1 | 0 | 0 | | | 1 |

cannot well understand, for though of hasty temper, he is by no means singular amongst chess players in that respect. There seems to be no doubt, the American journals admit it, that a combination was formed to prevent Mr. Bird from obtaining first prize in the New York Clipper chess tournament. Certain players systematically absented themselves from play in order to bring Mr. Bird's score, which would have been the highest, below that of other competitors. The scheme succeeded but too well. We are sorry to see the American players lending themselves to such an intrigue against a stranger. The unpopularity of a man has never been accounted a sufficient reason for cheating him [*Brisbane Week*, 5 May 1877].

All the protests were of no avail as no alterations to the final ranking were made. Bird had to be content with the third prize of $25, half the money received by Delmar and a quarter of the first prize gained by Mason.

## 426) Bird–Mason 1–0

Clipper Free Centennial Tournament
New York, September 1876
*C01*

**1. e4 e6 2. d4 d5 3. Nc3 Nf6 4. e×d5 e×d5 5. Nf3 Bd6 6. Bd3 0–0 7. 0–0 h6** "A needless precaution. We certainly prefer 7. ... c6, or even 7. ... c5 as recommended by the German *Handbuch*"—Wormald. **8. Re1 Nc6 9. Nb5** "The opening is much as usual, this move and Mason's play to preserve his bishop from being changed off taking it a little out of the beaten track"—Bird. **9. ... Bb4** "Mr. Mason appears to allow his opponent too much time. Like Steinitz, Paulsen, Boden and some other great players, he may, as a rule, prefer the bishop to the knight, and therefore, wish to avoid changing it off. Except on this supposition, the policy of move 9 is questionable"—Bird. **10. c3 Ba5 11. Na3! Bg4 12. Nc2 Qd7 13. b4 Bb6 14. h3** "Best, as Mr. Mason must now determine whether to take the knight or retreat the bishop to h5 or e6"—Bird. **14. ... Bh5 15. Ne3** 15. b5 Ne7 16. Ba3 Rfe8 17. Ne5 B×d1 18. N×d7 N×d7 19. Ra×d1 is slightly better for White. The actual text move, especially in combination with the astute follow-up, looks threatening as more pieces are kept on the board, but there are still plenty of resources for Black. **15. ... Rfe8 16. b5** These first 15 moves have hardly been tantalizing, especially when compared to the ultimate culmination of this fabulous game. With the space-grabbing text move one gets a first impression that something is going on. **16. ... Ne7 17. g4 Bg6 18. Ne5 Qc8 19. a4 c6** Not bad, but the stronger 19. ... Ba5! not only effectively stops the a-pawn, it also annoyingly targets a weakness in White's own camp. **20. b×c6 b×c6 21. Ba3 Ne4 22. Qc2 Ng5** "Like most of the recent contests between these players, the game early becomes both interesting and critical"—Bird. **23. B×e7 R×e7?** White's knights look very impressive after 23. ... B×d3 (Brenzinger) 24. Q×d3 R×e7 25. Nf5 Re6, but Black's position remains very solid, while White's also counts some weaknesses. **24. B×g6** "Some good judges, witnessing the game, expressed the opinion, after its finish, that 24. N×g6 was better. We incline to the opinion, however, that the knight was more valuable than the bishop in this position"—Bird. **24. ... f×g6 25. Q×g6?!** "Much better than the tempting 25. N×g6"—Bird. After the simple 25. N×g6 Re6 26. Kg2 White has won a pawn with a tremendous position on top of it. Bird prefers to return the pawn and get a ferocious initiative for it. **25. ... N×h3† 26. Kh2 Nf4 27. Qf5! Ne6** "He clearly could not exchange queens without loss: 27. ... Q×f5 28. N×f5 Re6 29. N×c6 etc."—Wormald. **28. Ng2 Qc7** *(see diagram)*

**29. a5!!??** "This move initiates a combination of remarkable interest, besides affording scope for some of the best play of both these well-known players"—Bird. From here on the game is a chain of wonderful combinations, which makes it the most memorable

*After 28. ... Qc7*

of those left behind by Bird. This game was incorporated in various game collections and submitted to analysis. It took generations of players to demonstrate the resources for Black. All these analysis have been overshadowed by the power of modern engines. They have demonstrated that the text move is actually a blunder to which a conclusive riposte is possible. After 29. ... B×d4!! 30. c×d4 N×d4 31. Qf4 R×e5!, White can resign. It is remarkable that in this line Black's knight has similar powers as White's in the game. **29. ... B×a5 30. R×a5! Rf8** 30. ... Q×a5 (Brenzinger) loses by force: 31. Ng6 Qc7† 32. N2f4 etc. **31. Ra6!!?** "This is quite a la Bird. For once in a way our countryman wakes up and comes out in his old brilliant style"—Wormald. "We not only quite concur with the committee in awarding 'the cup' to this game, but pronounce it a grand battle, one of the best that ever came within our observation in America. In this particular coup there is a subtlety of conception and a far-reaching daring not exceeded by the celebrated McDonnell sacrifice, and assuredly not equaled by the Morphy–Paulsen"—Hazeltine. The intended assault of the knights is another brilliant concept from the Englishman. His opponent is completely beset with sharp, concrete, problems. Objectively, Bird's last rook moves have only brought him in deeper trouble. Engine recommendations are 30. Qd3 and 31. Qh5. They obviously pose much fewer practical difficulties to his opponent. **31. ... R×f5 32. g×f5 Nd8 33. Nf4 Qc8 34. Nfg6 Re8 35. N×c6! Qc7†** "If in reply 35. ... R×e1 he loses his queen. If 35. ... Q×a6 he is mated. 35. ... N×c6 was more available, but looked extremely dangerous for White replies 36. R×e8† Q×e8 37. R×c6, threatening to win the queen by 38. Rc8, and with the mating position still in view. Mr. Mason adopts a less risky course, and makes what was supposed at the time to be the most prudent and best reply. Analysis has been devoted to prove that 35. ... N×c6 was best, for, notwithstanding White's then menacing position, Black by playing 37. ... Kh7 and guarding his eighth file would aim at advancing his a-pawn. This would form a highly instructive study"—Bird. Mason's move is the best available, but the line indicated by Bird is absolutely fascinating. Black is winning, but he has to play with extreme care to support the a-pawn and defend his king at the same time: 35. ... N×c6 36. R×e8† Q×e8 37. R×c6 Kh7 38. Rc5 Qd8! 39. Nf4 a5 40. R×d5 (there is no other choice) 40. ... Qc7 41. Kg3 Q×c3† 42. Kg4 a4 43. Rd8 Qc7 44. Ra8 Qc1 45. d5 a3 46. Ne6 Qg1† 47. Kf4 Q×f2† 48. Ke4 Qe1† 49. Kd3 Qb4 (the winning square. White will never be able to deliver mate at f8 as it is covered by the queen) 50. Nd4 Qb1† 51. Kc3 Qb2† 52. Kc4 a2 53. Nb3 h5. **36. Nce5 Q×c3 37. Re3 Qd2** "The pawn could not be taken on this move, on account of 38. Nf3, which

would win the rook"—Bird. With this move Mason leaves the winning path; 37. ... Qc8!, returns to lines similar to those mentioned in the previous note, with an extra pawn to the good. **38. Kg2 Q×d4 39. f6!** "This pawn comes forward now with much force"—Bird. **39. ... g×f6** The game enters a new brilliant phase in which Mason's king suddenly gets under attack. Objectively the position can be held, but in a practical situation the job is no sinecure. Instead of the text move, he could also play 39. ... h5, making space for the king. A crazy line goes 40. Ne7† Kh7 41. Rd6 Qf4 42. R×d5 g×f6 43. N5g6 Qg4† 44. Rg3 Qe4† 45. Kg1 Qb1† 46. Kh2 Nf7 47. R×h5† Nh6 48. Rgh3 Qb8† 49. Kg2 Qb7† with a draw. **40. R×f6 Ne6 41. Rg3** 41. Rf7! also forces a draw: 41. ... Qb 42. R×a7 Nf4† 43. N×f4 Q×f4 44. Ng6 Qg4† 45. Rg3 Qe4 46. Kh2. The text move allows Mason a final chance to turn the result in his favor. **41. ... Ng5 42. Ng4 Kg7** (see diagram) With this move Mason settles for a long defense. A swift and stunning counterattack could be successful: 42. ... Qa1! The queen leaves his majesty to its fate. White is bound to lose one or two tempi, of which Black could make use to condemn White's king: 43. N×h6 Kg7 44. Rc6 Re1! 45. Nf5† Kf7 46. Re3. The only move, as mate was threatened. White can reach a lost knight endgame at most: 46. ... R×e3 47. N×e3 Qb2 48. Ng4 a5 49. N6e5† Ke7 50. Rc7 Ke6 51. Rc6† Kf5 52. Rf6† Ke4 53. Rf4† K×f4 54. Nd3† K×g 55. N×b2 d4.

*After 42. ... Kg7*

**43. Nf4** "Every move is an attack and demands excessive vigilance on the part of Black"—Wormald. **43. ... Qe4† 44. Kh2 Nh7** "Check at f3 would be of no avail. White would take the knight with the rook, winning the queen if the piece were recaptured"—Bird. The final mistake and leading to a grand finale. With 44. ... d4 he could still draw the game: 45. Nh5† Kg8 46. N×h6† Kh8 and as the knight is untouchable (47. R×g5 Qh4†), he must consent with 47. Nf4 Kg7 48. Nh5†. **45. Nh5† Kh8 46. R×h6** "The beginning of the end"—Bird. **46. ... Qc2 47. Nhf6 Re7 48. Kg2 d4 49. Ne5!** "And now it bursts! Bim! Can there be anything prettier than this? What a crash of thunder! The queen starts for home at double-quick, but, alas! Too late. Immediately on her arrival another thunderbolt struck, and in trying to shield her monarch she herself must fall. The gallant and so much feared knight, after razing her castle, hastens to her destruction—and this glorious battle is over"—Brenzinger. **49. ... Qc8 50. Ng6† Kg7 51. N×e7†** and Black resigns. "A most tragic termination, the whole of the remaining army killed with one shot"—Bird—*New York Clipper* (Bird), 14 October 1876; *Illustrated London News* (Wormald), 28 October 1876; *New York Clipper* (Brenzinger/Hazeltine), 30 December 1876; *Modern Chess* (Bird), pp. 6–7.

## (427) B.H. Williams–Bird    1–0

Clipper Free Centennial Tournament
New York, September 1876
C40

**1. e4 e5 2. Nf3 d5 3. N×e5 d×e4 4. Qe2 Nf6 5. h3 Bd6 6. d4 Qe7 7. Bg5 B×e5 8. d×e5 Q×e5 9. Qb5† Nc6 10. Q×e5† N×e5 11. Nc3 Bf5 12. B×f6 g×f6 13. Nd5 Rc8 14. N×f6† Ke7 15. Nd5† Kf8 16. Ne3 Be6 17. Be2 f5 18. a3 Rg8 19. g4 f4 20. Ng2 Ng6 21. f3 Bd5 22. 0-0-0 e×f3 23. R×d5 f×g2 24. Rg1 Nh4 25. Ra5 a6 26. B×f3 N×f3 27. Rf5† Kg7 28. R×f3 Rgf8 29. R×f8 R×f8 30. R×g2 Rf3 31. Rh2 Kf6 32. Kd2 Kg5 33. Ke2 Rf7 34. Rf2 Rd7 35. Rf5† Kh4 36. Kf3** Black resigns—*Land and Water*, 4 November 1876.

## (428) Bird–Orchard    1–0

Clipper Free Centennial Tournament
New York, 27 September 1876
C00

It is not certain whether this game was actually played in the tournament or offhand.

**1. e4 e6 2. Bb5** "This is one of Mr. Bird's eccentricities, but unlike most of his inventions, it is utterly absurd. He has a penchant for this move and plays it against the best players, and not infrequently with success. In a very important match game with Steinitz, Bird adopted this attack [*sic*], and handsomely vanquished his powerful opponent"—Goldstein. **2. ... c6 3. Ba4 d5 4. Nc3 d4 5. Nce2 e5 6. d3 Bd6 7. Bb3 Ne7 8. f4 Ng6 9. f5 Nf8 10. Nf3 f6** The actual outcome of the opening is different from what it could have been. Bird enjoys a small but stable edge thanks to his space advantage. **11. 0-0 Na6 12. a3 Qe7 13. Ng3 Bd7** "Black contemplates castling on the queenside, seeing that White has concentrated his forces on the kingside"—Goldstein. **14. Ba2** "White sees his intention, and opens a way for the advance of his pawns"—Goldstein. **14. ... 0-0-0 15. b4 c5 16. b×c5 B×c5 17. Bc4 b5 18. Bb3 Nc7 19. Qe1 Bc6 20. Kh1 Nd7 21. Bb2 Bb6 22. c3** It has taken him a long time, but Bird finally begins to open up the game. Alas for him, he does it a bit clumsily, and Orchard gets out of it in pretty good shape. Better is 22. a4 b4 23. a5 Bc5, but it is hard to find out what to do next. **22. ... Nc5 23. Bc2 Ba5** (see diagram)

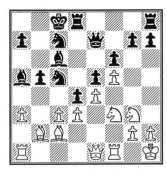

*After 23. ... Ba5*

**24. Ne2** 24. Ng1 is safe enough. Orchard gets play after his next strong move. **24. ... B×e4!** "A most ingenious sacrifice, which gives Black somewhat the advantage"—Goldstein. **25. d×e4 d3 26. Bd1**

d×e2 **27. Q×e2 Nd3 28. a4!** "Mr. Bird, by a magnificent play has wrested the advantage from his opponent, and now the game is about even, though the position is full of difficulties for both players"—Goldstein. **28. ... N×b2** This exchange comes too soon, as it unnecessarily allows White's pieces activity. He had the time to improve his own pieces first: 28. ... Qc5! 29. a×b5 Bb6 30. g3 Qc4. White's extra pawn will shortly fall. Black's edge isn't very significant, but White can do nothing at all. **29. Q×b2 Qc5 30. a×b5 B×c3 31. Qc2 Q×b5 32. Be2 Qb2 33. Q×b2 B×b2 34. R×a7 Bd4?** "A very inconsiderate play. 34. ... Rd6 would have ensued a draw, but this move throws away the game"—Goldstein. With 34. ... Rd6! he could maintain his bishop at b2 (e.g., 35. Rb1 Rb6), and thus gain time to develop his other rook. After the text move Bird wins a piece but it takes him a very long time to conclude the game. **35. N×d4 R×d4 36. Rc1 R×e4 37. Ra×c7† Kb8 38. R1c2** This and the following moves are probably incorrectly recorded, as 38. ... R×e2! is now possible. An alternative course could have been 38. R7c2 Rb4 39. Kg1 Re8 40. Rc7 etc. **38. ... Rb4 39. Kg1 Re8 40. Rc1 Rb7 41. R×b7† K×b7 42. Kf2 Re7 43. Ke3 Rd7 44. Bf3† Kb6 45. g4 h6 46. Rc6† Ka5 47. Rc8 Kb4 48. Rb8† Kc5 49. Rb7 Kd6 50. R×d7† K×d7 51. Bd5 Ke7 52. Ke4 Kd6 53. Ba2 Kc5 54. Kd3 Kb4 55. Bf7 Kc5 56. Kc3 Kd6 57. Kc4 Ke7 58. Bd5 Kd6 59. Be4** The score, as published, gives the impossible moves 59. Be8 Ke7 60. Ba4 Kd6 61. Bb5. **59. ... Ke7 60. Bc6 Kd6 61. Bb5 Ke7 62. Kd5 Kf7** "I have not thought it necessary to make comments on this part of the game, for both players are making the very best moves. Mr. Orchard had played with consummate skill, and though Mr. Bird has won a piece, it is all he can do to force the game. There are very few players who would know how to win in this position"—Goldstein. **63. Bd3 Ke7 64. Kc6 Kf7 65. Kd6 Kg8 66. Bc4† Kh7 67. Ke7 Kh8 68. Kf8 Kh7 69. Bf7 Kh8 70. Bg8 e4 71. Bc4 Kh7 72. Kf7 Kh8 73. h4 Kh7 74. h5 Kh8 75. Ke6 Kh7 76. Kd5 e3 77. Kd4 Kh8 78. K×e3 Kh7 79. Kd4 Kh8 80. Kd5 Kh7 81. Ke6 Kh8 82. Kf7 Kh7 83. Kf8 Kh8** and White forces the game beautifully in three moves. "This terminates a most interesting game. Mr. Orchard deserves great praise for making so gallant a fight against his almost invincible opponent. At the conclusion of the contest, which lasted more than four hours, the British chess athlete said to his youthful antagonist from the land of Morphy: 'Why, Mr. Orchard, you astonish me, you are one of the strongest players I have met in America, and with proper training will make a second Mason'"—Goldstein. *Atlanta Sunny South* (Goldstein), 23 November 1878.

## (429) Bird–Wernich    1–0

Clipper Free Centennial Tournament
New York 1876
C45

**1. e4 e5 2. Nf3 Nc6 3. d4 e×d4 4. N×d4 Qh4 5. Nb5 Q×e4† 6. Be2 Kd8 7. 0-0 d6 8. c4 Nf6 9. N1c3 Qe8 10. c5 Qd7 11. c×d6 B×d6 12. Bg5 h6 13. B×f6† g×f6 14. Qa4 Qf5 15. Rad1 Bd7 16. N×d6 c×d6 17. R×d6 Kc8 18. Rfd1 Ne5 19. R×d7 N×d7 20. Bg4 Qe5 21. Q×d7† Kb8 22. Nb5 a6 23. Qd8†** Black resigns—*Illustrated Sporting New Yorker*, 11 November 1876.

## (430) Ensor–Bird   0–1
Clipper Free Centennial Tournament
New York 1876
C01

**1. d4 e6 2. e4 d5 3. e×d5 e×d5 4. Bd3 Nf6 5. Nf3 Bg4 6. Bg5 h6 7. Bh4 Bd6 8. Nc3 c6 9. Qe2† Kd7** "As a rule, it is considered prudent to get safely castled as early as possible, and this move occasioned some surprise among the numerous on-lookers. In this instance, however, we believe the move not only free from objection, but well-conceived, and its consequences accurately weighed"—Hazeltine. **10. B×f6 g×f6** "Mr. Ensor considered that he gained a slight advantage here; but Mr. Bird was satisfied to double his pawns for the possession of the open file for his rook"—Hazeltine. **11. 0-0-0 Kc7 12. Qd2 Nd7 13. Be2 Nb6 14. Kb1 Qf8 15. Ka1 a5 16. Nb1** "This and the two preceding moves, with the view of forcing his c-pawn forward, are very ingeniously devised; as, however, he is thwarted in this design, it is doubtful whether this line of play was not too slow for the position"—Hazeltine. This plan is not dangerous for Black. Crucial in White's plans should have been the weakened square f5. With 16. Nh4! he could prepare to occupy it. **16. ... a4 17. a3 Rg8 18. Rc1 Be6** 18. ... B×f3! 19. B×f3 Nc4 and 20. ... b5 gives Black the upper hand on the queenside. As White's best knight is eliminated, Ensor is unable to get enough counterplay on the other side of the board. **19. g3 Bg4 20. Qd3 Re8 21. Rhe1 Re6 22. Nfd2?** The doubled f-pawn still promises White a small but nagging edge. This however doesn't mean that he can afford himself everything. After the text move Bird sets up a nasty pin which is very difficult to get rid of. Better was 22. Ng1. **22. ... Qe7! 23. Nf3** *(see diagram)*

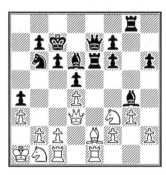

*After 23. Nf3*

**23. ... Re8?** "The veteran Mr. McConnell pointed out, both at the time and after the game, that Mr. Bird, who, having got a grip upon the position, never lost it, might now have achieved a more speedy superiority from 23. ... B×f3"—Hazeltine. A logical continuation would have been 24. Q×f3 Re8 25. Nc3 B×a3! **24. Bf1!** "Well managed"—Hazeltine. **24. ... Re4 25. Red1 f5 26. Nbd2** 26. h3 prevents the undoubling of the f-pawn. **26. ... f4 27. Qc3 f×g3 28. h×g3 Re6** The essential element of the position, here and on the next few moves, are White's weaknesses on f2 and f3. Instead of this untimely retreat, 28. ... Qf6! augments the pressure on White's position, as 29. Re1 is prevented due to the loss of the f-pawn. In the game White succeeds in relieving the pressure with the exchange of rooks. **29. Re1 Qf6 30. R×e6 R×e6 31. Qd3?** Extreme vigilance was still demanded from Ensor, as the danger is far from over. With 31. Nh2 h5 32. Ndf3, he would have built up a very solid position. **31. ... Bf5?** Bird overlooks a chance to conquer the f-pawn with 31. ... Nc4! If now 32. Ka2 (or 32. Kb1 B×f3 33. N×f. Q×f3!) 32. ... N×d2, crashing through on f2 again. **32. Qc3 Be 33. Re1 Qf5 34. Kb1 Be7 35. Bd3?** "Mr. Ensor was pressed fo time at this juncture, or he would doubtless have seen that the ex changes resulting from this move lose him two pawns. Indeed, it i but justice to state that, right in the midst of this difficult position he had only some five minutes to reach and include his 40tl move"—Hazeltine. 35. Re2 or 35. N×e4 are both fully acceptable A draw should be the result. **35. ... B×d3 36. Q×d3?!** 36. R×e( must be played, even though his position is without much joy afte 36. ... B×c2†. **36. ... R×e1† 37. N×e1 Q×f2 38. Ndf3 Q×g. 39. Qf5 Qg6 40. Qe5† Bd6 41. Qe8 Qe6 42. Qg8 Qg6 43. Qe8 Qf5 44. Ka2 Bg3 45. Qe3 B×e1** It was far simpler to preserve th bishop to support the advance of the h-pawn. **46. N×e1 Qg 47. Qf2 f5 48. Nd3 Nc4 49. Qh2† Nd6 50. Nc5** White can ge back in the game with 50. Qe5! **50. ... Qf6 51. Qd2 b6 52. N×a f4** Back en route! **53. Qb4 Nc8 54. Qd2 f3 55. Qf2 Nd6 56. Qf Q×d4 57. b3 f2 58. Nb2 Ne4 59. a4 Nd2 60. Qa6 f1Q 61. Qa7 Kd8 62. Qb8† Ke7 63. Qc7† Kf8 64. Qd6† Kg7 65. Qc7† Qf 66. Qg3† Kh7** and White resigns. "It was anticipated that the meet ing of these athletes would produce a very stubbornly conteste struggle, and the attendance of spectators was, it is believed, equal if not superior, to that at any other game in the tourney"— Hazeltine. *New York Clipper* (Hazeltine), 24 February 1877.

## (431) Delmar–Bird   0–1
Clipper Free Centennial Tournament
New York 1876
A85

**1. c4 f5 2. Nc3 e6 3. d4 Nf6 4. d5** "Premature and weakening— we believe"—Hazeltine. **4. ... e5 5. Bg5 Bb4 6. Qb3 B×c3† 7. b×c3 d6 8. Nf3 0-0** "Black's position already appears preferable to us White must castle on the kingside and delay from the imprisoned bishop costs important time"—Sweet. **9. e3 Nbd7 10. Qc2 Nc5 11. Be2 h6 12. B×f6 Q×f6 13. 0-0 a5 14. Nd2 Bd7 15. Nb3 Ba4 16. Qb2 B×b3 17. a×b3 e4 18. Ra2 b6 19. b4 a×b4 20. c×b4 Q×b2** "This, following the loss of his cavalry, takes much of the usual vivacity out of White's play. Mr. Bird gives us a conspicuou example of the cool, instructive play of the veteran master that he is"—Hazeltine. **21. R×b2 Nd7 22. h3 Ra3 23. Rc1 Rfa8 24. Kh2 Kf7 25. g4 g6 26. g×f5 g×f5 27. Bh5† Kf6 28. Rbc2 Ne5** "Thi knight is now formidable, and increases White's difficulties rap idly"—Sweet. **29. Be2 Rb3 30. b5 Rba3 31. Kg3 Kg5 32. Rc3 R×c3 33. R×c3 Kf6 34. f4 e×f3 e.p. 35. B×f3 Ra2 36. e4 f×e4** "The student will observe that if 36. ... N×f3 37. R×f3 and after wards Black's f-pawn is wholly unprotected"—Sweet. **37. B×e4 Ra4** "The coup juste; virtually winning, with proper consequent play"— Sweet. **38. Rc2 R×c4 39. Rf2† Kg7 40. Bg2 Rc5 41. Rb2 Rc3† 42. Kh4 Ng6† 43. Kg4 Rc4† 44. Kg3 h5 45. Bf1 Rc3† 46. Kf2 Nf4** "Quietly holding the c-file vs. the adverse rook, until the passage of his irresistible pawns is secured"—Sweet. **47. Rd2 N×h3† 48. Kg2 Nf4† 49. Kh2 Kf6 50. Bg2 Ke5 51. Rf2 N×g2 52. R×g2 K×d5 53. Rg5† Kc4 54. R×h5 Kb4 55. Kg2 Rc5 56. Rh6 K×b5 57. Kf2 Kc6 58. Ke3 b5** and Black wins; "though the game wa fought on 14 moves longer"—*New York Clipper* (Hazeltine/Sweet) 18 November 1876.

Eugene Delmar.

## (432) Bird–Clarke    1–0

Clipper Free Centennial Tournament
New York, 17 October 1876
C01

1. e4 e6 2. d4 d5 3. e×d5 e×d5 4. Nf3 Nf6 5. Bd3 Bd6 6. 0–0
0–0 7. Nc3 Nc6 8. Bg5 Be7 9. h3 h6 10. Bh4 Nh7 11. B×e7 N×e7
12. Nh4 f5 13. Re1 c6 14. Qe2 Rf7 15. Na4 b6 16. c4 Bd7 17. Nc3
Kh8 18. Nf3 Ng6 19. c×d5 Nf4 20. Qe3 N×d5 21. N×d5 c×d5
22. Ne5 Rf6 23. f4 Nf8 24. Bc2 Be6 25. g4 f×g4 26. h×g4 Rc8
27. Re2 Bg8 28. g5 Rd6 29. Rf1 Rc7 30. Rff2 Bh7 31. Rg2 Qc8
32. g6 Bg8 33. f5 Qd8 34. Rh2 Re7 35. Reg2 Qe8 36. R×h6†
Nh7 37. R×h7† B×h7 38. Rh2 Rf6 and White's attack gives a mate
in five moves—*New York Clipper*, 23 December 1876.

## THE DISTRIBUTION OF THE LIEDERS CUP

Bird issued no official complaint against the final ranking but he
did put a great deal of effort in an attempt to get hold of the prize
that was not handed out yet: the silver cup for the most brilliant

game. This decision was left to a jury appointed by two members
of the committee. Mackenzie had picked Alfred P. Barnes, a choice
that pleased Bird. Hazeltine selected Frederic Perrin as his referee,
also much to Bird's content.[28] Bird's chances to win the cup were
thus realistic. He had a few of his games sent in while he also
counted on the support of Mackenzie, who liked his win against
Clarke.[29]

About a week later the decision was not taken yet. Barnes complained that he had only received a part of the games that entered
the competition. Perrin decided to decline the invitation to become
part of the jury and no other referee was yet appointed by Hazeltine.

Bird did not hesitate to bring up a new candidate to the chess
editor of the *Clipper*, namely Francis Eugene Brenzinger. Bird also
took the opportunity to defend his candidate games for the cup.
According to him, Mackenzie remained loyal in his support of Bird's
game with Clarke, while Barnes thought the game between Bird
and Mason suitable for the cup.[30]

Brenzinger duly accepted the responsibility to elect the brilliancy
game of the contest. On 11 November, the *New York Clipper* announced that nine games were sent in by a few participants.[31] A
week later they announced that McCutcheon's entry was withheld
due to his unchivalrous behavior during the tournament. The decision of the committee was made public in the same newspaper
on 16 December. Bird deservedly received the cup for his brilliant
win against Mason.

## THE BREAK FROM PROFESSIONAL CHESS

The alleged conspiracy at the Clipper tournament had a great
impact on the small chess scene of New York. While the year 1876
was a very interesting one for American chess, much of the energy
faded away in the next few years. It would not be until 1880 that
another major tournament was organized.

28. The Englishman perhaps influenced Hazeltine's decision by writing him a
letter on 24 October: "In regard to the Cup I may say that the Captain considers
my game with Clarke should get it. I wish the decision rested with the present
Committee viz. yourself, Mr. Sweet and Captain Mackenzie, as it would have saved
time, however the Captain has nominated a gentleman as referee that you will be
as well satisfied with as I am, viz. Mr. A.P. Barnes. I must not of course take the
liberty of suggesting a name to you, at the same time I may say that the name of
Mr. Sweet or Mr. Perrin would conjure confidence. I will copy our my game with
Clarke and send to you unless I find from the Captain that you already have it.
Ensor has a fine ending in one game but makes no claim admitting my games to
be (in his judgment) superior. I shall be waiting anxiously to find the name of
your referee." *Hazeltine's Chess, Autographs...*, vol. 3, pp. 251–253.
29. In another letter to Hazeltine, Bird revealed his true thoughts about the
Captain: "...I shall never have any confidence in him or any of his clique. What a
blessing that there are high minded gentleman like yourself and also Mr. Perrin,
Mr. Sweet, Mr. Barnes to save chess from utter degradation, the interest of our
charming and intellectual favorite will be safe in such hands and truth will in the
end prevail and virtue prove triumphant." *Hazeltine's Chess, Autographs...*, vol. 3,
pp. 291–292.
30. *Hazeltine's Chess, Autographs...*, vol. 3, p. 238.
31. *New York Clipper*, 11 November 1876. Bird, in his undated letter of November, wrote that there were 16 candidates of which only nine games were yet received
by Hazeltine. The number of nine eligible games was confirmed when the decision
was made public in the *Clipper* on 16 December 1876.

Everything that had happened at the tournaments at the Café International left Bird completely fed up with his professional colleagues.[32] The outcome of the Clipper tournament made him leave the Café International. The last known game he played at the Café was against Barnes in November. At the same time he gave up his aspirations to earn money with chess, which was at any rate a delicate point for the man.

Chess players in England were a bit amazed by Bird's sudden absence from the chess columns. In a letter to John G. White, dated on 10 January 1877, Fraser asked what had become of Bird.[33] His sole activity in chess during the last month of the year was a simultaneous exhibition given against 20 opponents at an unknown location. On 22 December, the *New York Herald* reported that he beat 19 of them and lost against Thompson.

On 4 November 1876, Mason, in *The Spirit of the Times*, once more announced Bird's return to England. With his bad experience at the Clipper tournament in mind, thoughts of returning may have occurred but at the same time he was attempting to find his footing in New York away from chess. On 5 January 1877 the *Brooklyn Daily Eagle* published a list of people who were appointed, on 18 December, as commissioner of deeds in Brooklyn. Bird figured among them. The duty of these commissioners was comparable with that of a public notary. They had the authority to take depositions, acknowledgments of deeds, etc., and were also allowed to authenticate legal signatures. Bird's appointment was valid for two years.

The relationship between Bird and his American foes Mason and Mackenzie did not come unharmed out of the year 1876, but time brought solace in at least one case. In later years Bird did get along very well with Mackenzie. During the 1880s Bird regularly praised the chivalry of the long-time American champion—indeed a completely different sound from that heard in 1876. Bird's relation with Mason remained much more ambiguous. When Mason arrived in Europe for the Paris tournament in 1878, he was received and taken care for by Bird, but from time to time both characters kept up a certain discord.

### (433) Bird–A.P. Barnes    0–1
Offhand game
New York (Café International) 1876
C52

1. e4 e5 2. Nf3 Nc6 3. Bc4 Bc5 4. b4 B×b4 5. c3 Ba5 6. Qb3 Qf6 7. d4 e×d4 8. 0–0 d×c3 9. e5 Qg6 10. N×c3 Nge7 11. Ne2 b5 12. Bd3 Qe6 13. Qb2 Ng6 14. Nf4 N×f4 15. B×f4 h6 16. Rac1 a6 17. Rfd1 Bb6 18. Bb1 Bb7 19. Bg3 0–0–0 20. a4 b4 21. Ba2 Qe7 22. Bd5 a5 23. Re1 g5 24. Qb3 Rhf8 25. Qc4 Nb8 26. Qb5 Bc6 27. B×c6 d×c6 28. R×c6 N×c6 29. Q×c6 Qe6 30. Qa8† Kd7 31. Qb7 Rb8 32. Qe4 f5 33. Qd3† Ke7 34. h4 Rbd8 35. Qc2 f4

32. In an anonymous letter from an American source, perhaps written by Bird or an ardent supporter of him, the author wrote of his disgust. It pretty much summed up how Bird must have thought about it. Remarkably enough, this letter was published even before the Clipper tournament began. "I do believe that chess players of note are the most irritable, jealous-pated creatures in existence. To secure success in a great tourney no chess player of any pretensions to a reputation should be allowed to have anything to do with the management; and the chief control should be given to those who know almost nothing of chess." *Illustrated London News*, 26 August 1876.

33. *Letters to John G. White Relating to Chess*, vol. I, letter 48.

36. Bh2 g4 and White resigns—*American Chess Journal*, December 1876, pp. 110–111.

### (434) Bird–McConnell    1–0
Offhand game
New York (Café International) 1876
C33

1. e4 e5 2. f4 e×f4 3. Bc4 Qh4† 4. Kf1 d5 5. B×d5 Bg4 6. Nf? B×f3 7. Q×f3 c6 8. Bc4 Nd7 9. d4 g5 10. g3 Qh3† 11. Kg1 0–0–0 12. Bf1 Qh6 13. h4 Bg7 14. e5 Qg6 15. h×g5 f×g3 16. Bf4 h5 17. Bc4 h4 18. e6 f×e6 19. Q×c6† b×c6 20. Ba6 mate—*Land and Water*, 11 November 1876.

### (435) Bird–McConnell    0–1
Offhand game
New York (Café International) 1876
C33

1. e4 e5 2. f4 e×f4 3. Bc4 d5 4. B×d5 Qh4† 5. Kf1 Bg4 6. Nf? B×f3 7. Q×f3 c6 8. Bc4 Nd7 9. d4 g5 10. Nc3 Nb6 11. Bd3 0–0–0 12. Ne2 Bg7 13. c3 Ne7 14. Bd2 f5 15. e×f5 Rhf8 16. Be1 Qh6 17. h? Nbd5 18. Bf2 Ne3† 19. B×e3 f×e3 20. g3 Nd5 21. h×g5 Q×g? 22. g4 Qf6 23. R×h7 Rh8 24. R×h8 R×h8 25. Kg2 Qg5 26. Bc4 Rh4 27. Kg3 Nf6 28. Be6† Kd8 29. Kg2 R×g4† 30. Kf1 Ne4 31. Rd1 Nd2† 32. R×d2 e×d2 33. Bb3 Qh4 34. Qf2 Qh3† and mates next move—*Brooklyn Chess Chronicle*, 15 October 1884, p. 10?

### (436) Ettlinger–Bird    0–1
Offhand game
New York (Café International) 1876
C61

1. e4 e5 2. Nf3 Nc6 3. Bb5 Nd4 4. N×d4 e×d4 5. 0–0 Bc5 6. c? Ne7 7. b4 Bb6 8. a4 c6 9. Bd3 d5 10. c4 d×c4 11. B×c4 0–0 12. Bb2 Kh8 13. f4 f5 14. e×f5 R×f5 15. Qf3 Ng6 16. Qg3 Qd? 17. d3 N×f4 18. Kh1 Ne2 19. Qe1 and mate in three moves—*Illustrated Sporting New Yorker*, 25 November 1876.

### (437) A.P. Barnes–Bird    1–0
Offhand game
New York (Café International) 1876
C33

1. e4 e5 2. f4 e×f4 3. Bc4 Qh4† 4. Kf1 g5 5. Nf3 Qh5 6. d? Nf6 7. Nc3 g4 8. Ne1 f3 9. g×f3 Qh3† 10. Kg1 g3 11. Bf4 d5 12. Bf1 Qd7 13. h×g3 d×e4 14. N×e4 N×e4 15. f×e4 Nc6 16. Be3 Bg7 17. c3 Qe7 18. Bg2 Bd7 19. Qf3 0–0–0 20. Nd3 Rdf8 21. Rf1 f5 22. e5 Nd8 23. b3 c6 24. c4 Ne6 25. b4 Ng5 26. B×g5 Q×g5 27. Nf4 Re8 28. Re1 Be6 29. N×e6 R×e6 30. Rh5 Qd2 31. Re2 Qd1† 32. Kh2 Rf8 33. Rf2 Q×d4 34. R×f5 Rh6† 35. Bh3 Black resigns—*Cleveland Leader*, 12 October 1876.

### (438) A.P. Barnes–Bird    1–0
Offhand game
New York (Café International) 1876
A85

1. d4 f5 2. c4 e6 3. a3 Be7 4. Nc3 Nf6 5. e3 0–0 6. Be2 b6 7. Nf? Bb7 8. 0–0 Qe8 9. b4 Qg6 10. Bb2 Nc6 11. d5 Nd8 12. Ne5 Qh6

13. f4 e×d5 14. N×d5 B×d5 15. c×d5 d6 16. Nf3 Ng4 17. Bd4 Bf6 18. h3 B×d4 19. Q×d4 Nf6 20. Ng5 Qg6 21. Rac1 h6 22. Ne6 N×e6 23. d×e6 c5 24. b×c5 d×c5 25. Qc4 Kh8 26. Bf3 Rae8 27. Bc6 Re7 28. Rcd1 Ne4 29. Bd7 Qf6 30. Rd5 g5 31. f×g5 Qg6 32. g4 N×g5 33. Rd×f5 R×f5 34. R×f5 b5 35. Qc2 N×h3† 36. Kh2 Q×g4 37. Rf8† Kg7 38. Qc3† K×f8 39. Qh8† Qg8 40. Qf6† Rf7 41. e7 mate—*Baltimore American*, 15 January 1882.

**(439) Bird–A.P. Barnes    1–0**
Offhand game
New York (Café International) 1876
C33

1. e4 e5 2. f4 e×f4 3. Bc4 Qh4† 4. Kf1 g5 5. Nc3 Bg7 6. d4 d6 7. Nf3 Qh5 8. h4 h6 9. Nd5 "The e-pawn should be first advanced. In several games between the same player in this position, Mr. Bird has constantly played 9. Nd5 before pushing 10. e5, not always with the success he meets with in this game"—Barnes. 9. ... Kd8 10. e5 c6 11. Nc3 d5 12. Be2 Bg4 13. Kg1 Qg6 14. Na4 Nd7 15. c4 Ne7 16. Bd2 Qe4 A silly loss of time. Bird commenced playing for an unfounded attack with 14. Na4, which attempt Barnes could now have frustrated with 16. ... B×f3 17. B×f3 d×c4. 17. Nc3 Qg6 18. h×g5 h×g5 19. R×h8† B×h8 20. c×d5 c×d5 21. Nb5 Nc6 Right now 20. ... B×f3 is interesting. One doesn't want to play 21. g×f3, and after 21. B×f3 N×e5! is nice. 22. Rc1! f6? Quite a logical but slow move with which Barnes intends to break down his opponent's center. Nor is 22. ... B×f3 23. B×f3 Nc×e5? possible because 24. Ba5† b6 25. d×e5 b×a5 26. Q×d5 wins. The best move is 22. ... Rb8, preventing the threatened 23. Nd6?! due to 23. ... B×f3! 24. B×f3 Nc×e5 25. d×e5 B×e5 and Black is even better. Instead, White should first play 23. Qa4! and only after 23. ... a6 play 24. Nd6, with an unclear position. 23. Nd6! f×e5 24. N×b7† Ke7 25. d×e5? Bird misses his chance to crown an excellent attack with a quick decision for there is no valid reply to 25. Qa4! If 25. ... Nd8 26. Rc7 and if 25. ... Ncb8 then 26. Qa3† leaves Barnes without any chance. 25. ... B×f3! 26. B×f3 B×e5 27. Bc3 B×c3 28. R×c3 Nce5! 29. B×d5?! Bird grasped the initiative again, thereby putting Barnes under pressure. Instead of the text move Black retains some pressure after 29. Q×d5, but nothing serious: 29. ... g4 30. Bd1 Qb6† 31. Nc5 Rd8 etc. 29. ... Qb6† 30. Kf1 *(see diagram)*

*After 30. Kf1*

30. ... Q×b2 30. ... Rh8! (Barnes) is a considerable reinforcement. The endgame is difficult for White after 31. Qb3 Rh1† 32. Ke2 Q×b3! 33. B×b3 g4. Care is however also needed for Black, for if the endgame is avoided with 32. ... Qg1??, his opponent assumes a decisive attack after 33. Qb4† Kf6 34. Rc6†! **31. Bb3!**

"Beautifully played, and entirely unexpected, it upsets Black's calculation entirely"—Barnes. **31. ... Qa3** "Black is compelled to guard the spot at d6; 31. ... Q×c3 would have lost in the following style: 32. Qd6† Ke8 33. Qe6† Kf8 34. Qg8† Ke7 35. Qg7 Ke8 36. Nd6† Kd8 37. Q×g5† Nf6 38. Q×f6† Kd7 39. Qe6 Kd8 40. Qf6† Kd7 41. Ba4† Kc7 42. Nb5† etc."—Barnes. **32. Rc6?** "It is a pity that the game should be marred by such stupendous blunders as both players commit on their 32nd moves; by a singular coincidence of error, both played here under the remarkable hallucination that Black's knight was pinned"—Barnes. **32. ... Rh8??** A dramatic overview from both players. This move gives White a chance to present an impressive finish. **33. Qd5! Rh1† 34. Ke2 Qb2† 35. Rc2 f3† 36. Kd2 f×g2 37. Qe6† Kf8 38. Qg8† Ke7 39. Qd8** mate—*Illustrated Sporting New Yorker* (Barnes), 2 December 1876.

**(440) Orchard–Bird    1–0**
Offhand game
New York (Café International) 1876
C61

1. e4 e5 2. Nf3 Nc6 3. Bb5 Nd4 4. N×d4 e×d4 5. 0–0 c6 6. Bc4 b5 7. Bb3 Bb7 8. d3 h5 9. e5 At once 9. a4! is very good. 9. ... c5 10. f4 Qb6 11. f5 Qc6 12. Qe2 Nh6? Bird's position is rather skewed already, but the text move is catastrophic. 13. Bg5 a5 14. a4! b4 15. Nd2 d6 and White mates in four moves. "This is an unpardonable blunder for so fine a player as Mr. Bird. From his sixth move he has played in a worse than skittle humor. Mr. Orchard has played well, and finishes this short game by announcing a four move mate, wherein the queen is brilliantly sacrificed, as follows: 16. e×d6† Kd7 17. Be6† K×d6 18. Qe5† K×e5 19. Nc4 mates"—Judd. *St. Louis Globe Democrat* (Judd), 8 April 1877.

**(441) Bird–Orchard    0–1**
Offhand game
New York (Café International) 1876
C52

1. e4 e5 2. Nf3 Nc6 3. Bc4 Bc5 4. b4 B×b4 5. c3 Ba5 6. Qb3 Qf6 7. d4 e×d4 8. e5 Qg6 9. 0–0 d×c3 10. N×c3 Nge7 11. Ne2 b5 12. Bd3 Qe6 13. Qb2 Ng6 14. Nf4 N×f4 15. B×f4 a6 16. Rac1 h6 17. Be4 Bb7 18. Qa3 Bb6 19. Be3 Qe7 20. Bc5 B×c5 21. R×c5 Nd8 22. Qe3 B×e4 23. Q×e4 Q×c5 24. Q×a8 Qc6 25. Q×c6 N×c6 26. Re1 Nb4 and White resigns in a few moves—*Atlanta Sunny South*, 13 July 1878.

**(442) Sweet–Bird    1–0**
Offhand game
New York (Café International) 1876
C37

1. e4 e5 2. f4 e×f4 3. Nf3 g5 4. Bc4 g4 5. 0–0 g×f3 6. R×f3 Bh6 7. d4 Qf6 8. e5 Qg6 9. B×f4 d5 10. e×d6 *e.p.* Nc6 11. c3 Bg4 12. B×f7† Q×f7 13. Re3† Be6 14. B×h6 N×h6 15. d5 0–0 16. Rf3 Bf5 17. d×c6 Qc4 18. c×b7 Rad8 19. Na3 Qc5† 20. Kh1 R×d6 21. Qb3† Be6 22. R×f8† K×f8 23. b8Q† and White wins—*New York Clipper*, 25 November 1876.

# ACROSS THE BORDER 1877

Bird's arrival in New York in December 1875 had the chess community in Canada agog as well. The Canadian press closely followed his results against the New York and Philadelphia chess elite and it was not long before the first suggestions to invite the master to Canada were launched. Already in February 1876 an appeal to arrange a visit of Bird was made to the Canadian Chess Association. A few months later Thomas Workman, a Member of Parliament, used his influence to get Bird to Canada. Bird was willing to pass by before returning to Europe, but he did not find the time in 1876, with his heavy tournament playing. Bird's visit became a topic again at the end of the year. His arrival was announced to happen around Christmas, but in the end Bird left New York for the north in January 1877.

Bird visited a few other cities on his way to Montreal. His first stop was Buffalo. On Thursday 11 January he was the guest of George C. Farnsworth. Several players attended the chess party at which Bird played a large number of simultaneous games. Only Richmond and Thornton managed to beat the master.[34]

Bird continued his way north past the cities of Hamilton and Toronto, not for chess purposes, but to travel and see the Great Western Railway and Grand Trunk Railway, a sweet memory of his accounting work some fifteen years earlier.[35]

Bird finally arrived in Montreal on Saturday 20 January. He immediately visited the Montreal Chess Club to play some offhand games and he proposed that he give a simultaneous display on 20 boards.[36]

On 22 January 15 players assembled in the rooms of the Montreal Chess Club. An extensive report appeared in the *Canadian Illustrated News* on 3 February. Before getting down to business it was necessary to confirm some rules. One of them was "that the pieces were not to be handled in Mr. Bird's absence from the board." Play started at 9 p.m. and lasted well over midnight. Bird managed to win 9 games, lost against 4 players (Dr. Howe, J. Barry, Atkinson and Saunders) and drew the remaining 2 (against Shaw and Hall).

Bird ended the evening by complimenting the Montreal player that they had made a better aggregate score than his opponents at a similar performance in New York. According to the report, Bird "manners as a chess player are most agreeable and in very way calculated to give confidence to his opponents."

One day later Bird met the club members again. Now he opposed four teams of three players each. This contest ended after two days in a small victory (2 wins, 1 loss, 1 draw). The players of the winning team were Ascher, Workman and Shaw.

Bird's willingness to accept every challenge was greatly appreciated in Montreal. Apart from the numerous offhand games, a second simultaneous exhibition between Bird and the Montreal Chess Club was organized on 27 January. This time Bird won 17 games, lost 3 (against Hicks, Ascher and Atkinson) and drew 2 (against Workman and G. Barry). Bird then interrupted his stay in Montreal to visit the nearby town of Sherbrooke. On 30 January, both in the afternoon and in the evening, Bird engaged in simultaneous play. Only one opponent, Robert Short, succeeded in beating and drawing him once.[37]

Back in Montreal Bird performed a third simultaneous exhibition on 10 February. This was his best result: 21 wins, 2 losses (against Saunders and Ascher) and 2 draws (against Hicks and Henderson). Bird's farewell was now rapidly approaching and the guest was treated with a last supper given by Alexander Saunders. The abundant supply of tropical fruits and flowers were hailed with enthusiasm. Finally, on 14 February, Bird returned to the United States.

On 10 March the *Canadian Illustrated News* published a letter in which Jacob Gottschalk Ascher thanked Bird, who had "awakened such a genuine enthusiasm for the noble game." Bird returned the compliment by expressing his thanks for the warm reception.[38]

Several of Bird's Canadian friends used the opportunity to meet him again when visiting in London. At the time of Bird's chess column, in 1882 and 1883, several of his correspondents were people he met during his trip to Canada six years earlier.[39]

---

34. Bird was very enthusiastic about his reception in Buffalo. A few days later, when in Hamilton, he wrote an extensive report for Miron Hazeltine: "I left New York about a week since intending to come on here direct, after spending a few hours at Buffalo, but the unexpectedly warm reception I experienced there induced me to remain until Tuesday midday (yesterday). Please notify that Mr. Bird speaks in rapturous terms of his reception in Buffalo and although winning a large majority in every instance lost three or four very fine games to the president, Henry Richmond, also one to each of the following gentlemen: Messrs. Parker, Thornton and Farnsworth. The interest in chess was somewhat waning when I reached Buffalo, but now it is proposed to carry it on with increased energy, I hope to arrange a match by correspondence between Buffalo and Toronto, Toronto and Montreal, and Buffalo and Montreal. What would you say to a match, by correspondence or telegraph, between New York and Montreal or Canada and America? Such an event would exceed in interest all that has one before, New York and London would be sure to follow." *Hazeltine's Chess, Autographs...*, vol. 6, pp. 113–116.

35. Bird explicitly mentioned travelling over both railways in a letter written on 14 March 1879 to James McHenry, the European agent of the Atlantic and Great Western Railway with whom Bird had collided in 1867. His archives, the *James A. McHenry Papers*, are momentarily in private hands. They are being researched by Barry Henderson, a doctoral candidate at Queens University, Belfast.

36. Bird made a whirling first impression on the club members: "Mr. Bird exhibits all that geniality which seems to characterize the great champions of the chequered board across the Atlantic, and is willing to play any antagonist who may present himself." *Canadian Illustrated News*, 27 January 1877.

37. The whole undertaking was livened up by Major M., one of the present tyros: "In the preliminaries it was understood that no player should move the pieces during Mr. Bird's absence at the other boards—but one gentleman broke through this rule, leading to a laughable episode. Mr. Bird had passed him twice and coming round the third time rather quicker than Major M. had expected found the board in a state of utter confusion, nearly every piece having been moved. Mr. Bird had left his king on e2.... What was the astonishment to find his king at e7 away over in the enemy's territory, and in imminent danger of mate! Major M. in Mr. Bird's absence, had been following out some complicated analysis involving some 16 moves, as it appeared, making of course very bad moves for Mr. Bird, and hunting the latter's poor king all over the board! Major M., caught in the act, very red and guilty, stammered out an apology. 'Mr. Bird,' says he, 'I beg your pardon. I am really very sorry!, but will you be kind enough to pass me again. I really don't recollect quite where your king was! The next time you come round, I will try to get him back into his place!' This, said with perfect politeness and with earnest gravity of countenance, was too much for the equanimity of every spectator— shout of laughter was heard on every side! Mr. Bird said it was the most comical chess incident he had ever known in his life." *Huddersfield College Magazine*, May 1877, p. 220.

38. Even more than a year later, after the Paris tournament, positive appraisal of Bird appeared in the press: "We are the more certain that these will be read with satisfaction here, from the fact that Mr. Bird, during his sojourn in Montreal, gained the goodwill of all by his genial manners, and willingness at all times, even at much personal inconvenience, to gratify any player who was desirous of crossing pawns with him." *Canadian Illustrated News*, 5 October 1878.

39. A small sample of Bird's humor, replying to Ascher: "When is Steinitz expected? Take care you don't lose him in the snow." *Sheffield and Rotherham Independent*, 27 January 1883.

For Bird, being surrounded by amateurs with a genuine love for the game, and being recognized as the strongest chess player among them, must have been a relief after the confrontation with all kinds of special rules and maneuvers in New York.

### (443) Richmond–Bird    ½–½
Simultaneous game
Buffalo, 13 January 1877
C50

1. e4 e5 2. Nf3 Nc6 3. Bc4 Bc5 4. d3 Nf6 5. Be3 d6 6. h3 a6 7. Nc3 h6 8. 0-0 0-0 9. B×c5 d×c5 10. a3 Qd6 11. Ne2 Ne7 12. Ng3 Ng6 13. Kh2 Kh7 14. Nf5 B×f5 15. e×f5 Ne7 16. Nh4 g5 17. Bb3 Qd4 18. g4 Q×b2 19. Nf3 Rad8 20. g5 h×g5 21. N×g5† Kg8 22. Qf3 Qd4 23. Ne4 N×e4 24. d×e4 c4 25. Rg1 Qd2 26. R×g7† Kh8 27. f6 Qf4† 28. Q×f4 e×f4 29. f×e7 K×g7 30. e×f8Q† K×f8 31. Ba2 Rd2 32. Rc1 R×f2† 33. Kg1 Re2 34. Bb1 R×e4 35. c3 Re3 36. Bf5 c5 37. Bc8 a5 38. Ba6 b4 39. a×b4 a×b4 40. c×b4 c×b4 41. B×c4 Rc3 42. R×c3 b×c3 draw—*New York Clipper*, 10 February 1877.

### (444) Bird–Shaw    1–0
Offhand game
Montreal, 20 January 1877
C45

1. e4 e5 2. d4 e×d4 3. Nf3 Nc6 4. N×d4 Bc5 5. Be3 Qe7 6. f3 Qe5 7. c3 Nge7 8. b4 Bb6 9. Na3 d5 10. Be2 f5 11. 0-0 d×e4 12. b5 N×d4 13. c×d4 Qe6 14. Bc4 Nd5 15. Qb3 c6 16. f×e4 f×e4 17. b×c6 b×c6 18. Nb5 Bb7 19. B×d5 c×d5 20. Rf5 a6 21. Re5 Black resigns—*Huddersfield College Magazine*, May 1877, p. 194.

### (445) Bird–J. Barry    0–1
Simultaneous game
Montreal, 22 January 1877
C52

1. e4 e5 2. Nf3 Nc6 3. Bc4 Bc5 4. b4 B×b4 5. c3 Ba5 6. Qb3 Qe7 7. 0-0 h6 8. Ba3 d6 9. d4 Bb6 10. d×e5 N×e5 11. N×e5 Q×e5 12. B×f7† Kf8 13. B×g8 R×g8 14. Nd2 Qe6 15. c4 Kf7 16. Kh1 Rf8 17. f4 Kg8 18. f5 Qf7 19. Rf3 Bd4 20. Raf1 c5 21. Rh3 b6 22. Bb2 Bf6 23. Rg3 Kh7 24. B×f6 Q×f6 25. Rg6 Qe7 26. Qg3 Rf6 27. Rf4 Bd7 28. h4 Rg8 29. Rfg4 Be8 30. R×f6 Q×f6 31. Nf3 Bf7 32. Ng5† Kh8 33. N×f7† Q×f7 34. Q×d6 Q×c4 35. f6 Qf1† 36. Kh2 Q×f6 37. Qc7 Qe6 38. Kg3 Q×a2 39. e5 Qb3† 40. Kh2 Qe6 41. Rg3 Qf5 42. Qe7 Qf4 43. Kh3 a5 44. Rg4 Qf8 and White resigns—*Canadian Illustrated News*, 19 May 1877.

### (446) Shaw–Bird    ½–½
Simultaneous game
Montreal, 22 January 1877
C35

1. e4 e5 2. f4 e×f4 3. Nf3 Be7 4. Bc4 Bh4† 5. g3 f×g3 6. 0-0 g×h2† 7. Kh1 d5 8. B×d5 Nf6 9. B×f7† K×f7 10. N×h4 Re8 Bird commits the same imprecise move as he made nearly 20 years earlier

against Morphy. 10. ... Rf8 and 11. ... Kg8, takes optimal profit of the inferior 9. B×f7†, as Black is ready to occupy the open f-file. **11. Qf3 Kg8 12. d3 Bg4 13. Qf2?!** It is important to keep control over h3. Here Bird could have gone 13. ... Bh3! 14. Ng2 Qd7 15. Qg3 Ng4!, which completely binds White. In the game Shaw forgoes an opportunity to eliminate the h-pawn, and Bird ultimately comes up with the right idea. **13. ... Rf8 14. Bg5 Nc6 15. Nc3 Bh3 16. Rfe1?** Shaw limits himself to passive play. At best he could hope for a weak endgame after 16. Nd5 B×f1 17. B×f6 B×d3 18. c×d3 R×f6 19. N×f6† Q×f6 20. Q×f6 g×f6. **16. ... Ng4! 17. Qd2 Rf2** 17. ... Qd7! first is stronger. The rook will enter White's position on the next move. **18. B×d8** 18. Re2 is relatively better. **18. ... R×d2 19. Bg5 R×c2 20. Re2 R×e2 21. N×e2 Nce5** A nice tactical finish occurs after the forceful 21. ... h6! 22. Bd2 g5 23. Nf5 Nce5 24. d4 Nf2†! 25. K×h2 Nf3† 26. Kg3 N×d2 27. N×h6† Kh7 28. K×f2 Rf8† 29. Ke3 Nc4† 30. Kd3 N×b2† 31. Kc3 K×h6 and Black is a piece up. **22. Nf4 h6 23. N×h3 h×g5 24. N×g5 N×d3** With two pawns ahead, Bird should be able to win without too many problems. **25. Nh3 Rf8 26. Kg2 N×b2 27. Kg3 Ne3 28. K×h2 c5 29. Re1 Ng4† 30. Kg3 Ne5 31. Ng5 c4 32. Nhf3 Ned3 33. Re2 b5 34. e5 b4** (*see diagram*) Bird underestimates the importance of his inactive knight at b2. 34. ... c3! 35. e6 Nc4 reactivates the piece.

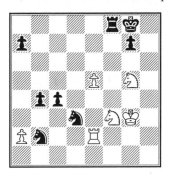

*After 34. ... b4*

**35. e6?** Shaw misses a unique opportunity to save his skin. After 35. Nh4! the position becomes extremely tricky. Bird now does best to avoid 35. ... c3 because after 36. Ng6, he must be very careful. In case of 36. ... Re8? 37. Rh2! he gets mated. There is only one way to save the game, namely 36. ... Rf2! Now it is White who has to be precise. He draws with the magnificent 37. R×f2 N×f2 38. e6! Nc4 39. K×f2 c2 40. e7 Nd6 41. e8Q†! N×e8 42. Ne7† Kf8 43. Ng6†. The best move after 35. Nh4! is at once 35. ... Re8. After 36. e6 Nd1 (not 36. ... c3? 37. Ng6! wins) 37. Re4! (37. Ng6? doesn't work anymore: 37. ... N1f2), White reaches a drawish position. Critical is 37. ... c3, when White equalizes similarly as before: 38. Ng6 Ne3 39. R×e3 c2 40. R×d3 c1Q 41. Ne7†. Black gets minor practical winning chances with 37. ... Nc5 38. R×c4 N×e6 39. N×e6 R×e6 40. R×b4. **35. ... c3 36. Nf7 R×f7** Certainly not necessary, and therefore 36. ... Nc4 must be preferred. **37. e×f7† K×f7 38. Ne5†?!** Losing outright. **38. ... N×e5 39. R×e5 Na4** 39. ... Nd3! is much cleaner. **40. Re2 a5 41. Rc2 Ke6 42. Kf4 Kd5 43. Ke3 Kc4** Played on automatic pilot. 43. ... Nc5, followed by 44. ... a4 wins valuable time. **44. Rg2 Nc5 45. Rg4† Kb5 46. R×g7 a4 47. Rg8 b3 48. Rb8† Kc4 49. a×b3† a×b3 50. Ke2 b2?** Now Bird goes completely astray. 50. ... Ne4! is the only winning move. **51. Kd1 Na6 52. R×b2 c×b2 53. Kc2** draw—*Huddersfield College Magazine*, May 1877, p. 195.

## (447) Henderson & Watkins & Hicks–Bird    1–0

Consultation game
Montreal, 23 January 1877
*B44*

1. e4 c5 2. Nf3 e6 3. d4 c×d4 4. N×d4 Nf6 5. Bd3 Nc6 6. Be3
d5 7. N×c6 b×c6 8. e5 Nd7 9. f4 Nc5 10. 0–0 N×d3 11. c×d3 a5
12. d4 Rb8 13. Qc2 Qb6 14. b3 Ba6 15. Rf3 g6 16. Nc3 Be7
17. Rc1 Bb7 18. Na4 Qa7 19. Nc5 B×c5 20. Q×c5 Q×c5 21. R×c5
Ra8 22. Bd2 a4 23. b4 Kd7 24. Rfc3 Rhc8 25. g4 Ba6 26. Kg2
a3 27. Ra5 Bc4 28. Rc×a3 R×a5 29. R×a5 Rc7 30. a4 h6 31. Ra8
Rc8 32. R×c8 K×c8 33. Kg3 Kd7 34. f5 h5 35. f×g6 f×g6
36. g×h5 g×h5 37. Kf4 Be2 38. Kg5 Bg4 39. a5 Kc7 40. Kf6 Bf5
41. Ke7 h4 42. a6 Kb6 43. Kd6 K×a6 44. K×c6 Bd3 45. b5†
B×b5† 46. Kd6 Kb7 47. K×e6 and ultimately White wins—*Canadian Illustrated News*, 31 March 1877.

## (448) Atkinson–Bird    1–0

Simultaneous game
Montreal, January 1877
*C56*

1. e4 e5 2. Nf3 Nc6 3. d4 e×d4 4. Bc4 Nf6 5. Ng5 Ne5 6. Q×d4
N×c4 7. Q×c4 Qe7 8. 0–0 h6 9. Nf3 d6 10. Nc3 Be6 11. Qb5†
c6 12. Qd3 Nd7 13. Be3 Nb6 14. b3 g6 15. Bd4 Rh7 16. Nd2 c5
17. Be3 f6 18. f4 0–0–0 19. a4 f5 20. a5 Na8 21. a6 b6 22. Nd5
B×d5 23. Q×d5 Kb8 24. Rf3 Qf7 25. Qc6 Rc8 26. Qb5 f×e4
27. N×e4 Qe6 28. Ng3 Qd7 29. Qd3 Rg7 30. Rd1 Nc7 31. Ne4
d5 32. Nf6 Qc6 33. N×d5 Rd7 34. Nb4 c×b4 35. Q×d7 Q×c2
36. Rc1 Qe2 37. B×b6 a×b6 38. a7† Kb7 39. a8Q† R×a8
40. R×c7† Black resigns—*Glasgow Weekly Herald*, 24 March 1877.

## (449) Bird–Shaw    1–0

Offhand game
Montreal, 27 January 1877
*Odds of Nb1*

1. e4 e5 2. f4 d5 3. Nf3 d×e4 4. N×e5 Bd6 5. d4 e×d3 *e.p.*
6. B×d3 B×e5 7. f×e5 Ne7 8. 0–0 0–0 9. Bg5 Qd4† 10. Kh1
Q×e5 11. B×h7† K×h7 12. Qh5† Kg8 13. Rae1 Qc5 14. R×e7
f6 15. R×g7† K×g7 16. Bh6† and White wins—*L'Opinion publique*, 15 February 1877.

## (450) Hicks–Bird    1–0

Simultaneous game
Montreal, 27 January 1877
*D00*

1. d4 d5 2. f4 Nf6 3. e3 Bf5 4. Nf3 h6 5. Bd3 Bg4 6. 0–0 e6
7. c3 B×f3 8. Q×f3 c5 9. Bc2 Qb6 10. b3 Nbd7 11. f5 e5 12. d×c5
B×c5 13. b4 Bd6 14. Nd2 e4 15. Qe2 Qc7 16. h3 Q×c3 17. Nb3
Be5 18. Rb1 Rc8 19. Nc5 N×c5 20. b×c5 Q×c5 21. Ba4† Ke7
22. R×b7† Rc7 23. Rb5 Qc4 24. Ba3† Bd6 25. B×d6† K×d6
26. Qd1 Rhc8 27. Rb3 Q×f1† 28. Q×f1 Rc1 29. Rb6† a×b6
30. Bd1 R8c2 31. Kh2 Rd2 32. Qf4† Kc6 33. Ba4† b5 34. Bb3
Rb2 35. Qb8 Rbb1 36. Qa8† Kc5 37. Qf8† Kb6 38. Q×f7 Rh1†
39. Kg3 Rbe1 40. Kf4 Rhf1† 41. Ke5 R×e3 42. Q×g7 R×b3

43. Q×f6† Ka5 44. a×b3 e3 45. Q×h6 Re1 46. K×d5 Rd1
47. Kc5 Rc1† 48. Kd4 Re1 49. Q×e3 Black resigns—*Canadian Illustrated News*, 30 June 1877.

## (451) Bird–Shaw    1–0

Offhand game
Montreal, 29 January 1877
*Odds of Ng1*

1. e4 e5 2. Bc4 Bc5 3. b4 Bb6 4. a4 a5 5. Ra3 Nf6 6. Rg3 B×f2†
7. K×f2 N×e4† 8. Kg1 N×g3 9. h×g3 d5 10. Bd3 e4 11. Be2 a×b4
12. Bb2 0–0 13. d3 Bf5 14. Nd2 c6 15. d×e4 B×e4 16. Rh4 Qb6†
17. Kh2 f5 18. Ba1 R×a4 19. c4 Ra5 20. N×e4 f×e4 21. Bd4 c5
22. Be5 d4 23. R×e4 Qh6† 24. Rh4 Qe3 25. Bd3 h6 26. Bf4 Qf2
27. Qh5 Ra1 28. Qd5† Kh8 29. R×h6† g×h6 30. Qe5† Kg8
31. Qe6† Rf7 32. Bh7† Kh8 33. Qe8† Kg7 34. Qg8† Kf6
35. Qg6† Ke7 36. Qd6† Ke8 37. Q×b8† Ke7 38. Qd6† Ke8
39. Qe6† Kd8 40. Q×f7 Qg1† 41. Kh3 Qh1† 42. Kg4 Qd1†
43. Kf5 Qc2† 44. Kf6 Ra6† 45. Kg7 Qe2 46. Bc7† Kc8 47. Bf5†
Re6 48. Bd6 Kd8 49. Qc7† Ke8 50. Qc8 mate—*Canadian Illustrated News*, 17 March 1877.

## (452) Ascher–Bird    1–0

Simultaneous game
Montreal, 10 February 1877
*C21*

1. e4 e5 2. d4 e×d4 3. Nf3 Bb4† 4. c3 d×c3 5. b×c3 Bc5 6. Bc4
Qe7 7. 0–0 Nc6 8. e5 b6 9. Bg5 Qf8 10. Re1 h6 11. Bh4 g5 12. Bg3
Nge7 13. Nbd2 Nf5 14. Ne4 Be7 15. Nd6† c×d6 16. e×d6 N×g3
17. h×g3 Kd8 18. d×e7† N×e7 19. Ne5 Rh7 20. Qd3 f5 21. Rad1
Ng8 22. Qd5 Kc7 23. Q×a8 Re7 24. Q×a7† Bb7 25. Ba6 Black
resigns—*New Dominion*, 1 June 1877.

## (453) Bird–Shaw    1–0

Simultaneous game
Montreal, 10 February 1877
*C62*

1. e4 e5 2. Nf3 Nc6 3. Bb5 d6 4. c3 Bg4 5. d4 a6 6. Ba4 b5
7. Bb3 Be7 8. a4 Nf6 9. d5 Na5 10. Bc2 0–0 11. h3 B×f3 12. Q×f3
c6 13. 0–0 c×d5 14. e×d5 Qb6 15. b4 Nc4 16. Na3 Qb7 17. N×c4
b×c4 18. Rd1 h6 19. g4 Nh7 20. Qf5 g6 21. Qe4 Bg5 22. Q×c4
B×c1 23. Ra×c1 Ng5 24. Kg2 Qd7 25. Qe2 f5 26. h4 Nh7 27. f3
f×g4 28. f×g4 Rf4 29. Rd3 Raf8 and White ultimately wins—*Glasgow Weekly Herald*, 17 March 1877.

## (454) Atkinson–Bird    1–0

Offhand game
Montreal 1877
*D00*

1. d4 d5 2. Nc3 g6 3. Bf4 Bg7 4. Nf3 Nc6 5. e3 Nf6 6. Be2 0–0
7. 0–0 Nh5 8. Bg3 N×g3 9. f×g3 Kh8 10. h3 f5 11. Kh2 e5
12. N×e5 N×e5 13. d×e5 B×e5 14. N×d5 B×b2 15. Bc4 B×a1
16. Q×a1† Kg8 17. Ne7 mate—*Chess Player's Chronicle*, May 1877, p. 113.

Jacob G. Ascher (courtesy Cleveland Public Library).

**(455) Bird–Unknown    1–0**
Offhand game
Canada 1877 (?)
C37

This game was published, without a date, years after Bird's visits. It may have been played in 1877 or 1889!

**1. e4 e5 2. f4 e×f4 3. Nf3 g5 4. Bc4 g4 5. 0–0 g×f3 6. Q×f3 Qe7 7. d4 Nc6 8. Nc3 N×d4 9. Qd3 Ne6 10. Nd5 Qc5† 11. Kh1 b5 12. Bb3 Bh6 13. Bd2 Qf8?** Thanks to his opponent's last two rather curious moves, Bird is able to build up a brilliant and decisive attack. **14. Qc3 Bg7 15. N×c7† Kd8** (see diagram)

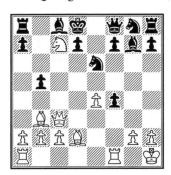

After 15. ... Kd8

**16. Qa5! N×c7 17. Bb4 d6 18. Rad1 Be5 19. R×d6†! B×d6 20. Rd1 Ke8 21. B×d6 Ne7 22. Q×c7 Bd7 23. Qd2 is**

more conclusive. **22. ... Bg4 23. Rd5** Black can resign at once after 23. Qb7 Rd8 24. Q×b5† Bd7 25. Qe5. **23. ... Rc8 24. Qb7 Be6 24.** ... f6 prevents the rook from coming to e5, but there is still plenty of room for Bird to test his opponent's defensive skill with 25. Bb4! Black is almost out of moves after 25. ... a6 26. Rd6! **25. Q×b5† Bd7 26. Qb7 Bc6 27. Ba4 B×a4 28. B×e7 Q×e7 29. Q×c8† Qd8 30. Re5†** and the amateur, who, all things considered, has done very well, here thought the pieces might be reset for another game— *Birmingham Weekly Mercury*, 17 June 1893.

# CHESS IN NEW YORK 1877

Bird returned to New York in February intending to pursue a civil career as commissioner of deeds. Chess, in this scenario, was at most a semiprofessional activity. During the following months Bird was spotted only rarely behind the board, but he nevertheless remained eager to play a match with Mackenzie. Two challenges were issued. Some details became public. Eleven games would be played with a stake of $250 per side. Reactions were rather faint. In his column in the *St. Louis Globe Democrat* of 17 June 1877, Judd gave an abrupt answer to Bird's tries: "Mr. Bird, save your money. The chess championship question is already settled."

**(456) Bird–Channing    1–0**
Offhand game
New York, 6 March 1877
*Odds of Ra1*

**1. e4 e5 2. Nf3 d5 3. N×e5 d×e4 4. Bc4 Be6 5. B×e6 f×e6 6. Qh5† Ke7 7. Qf7† Kd6 8. d4 Nh6 9. B×h6 g×h6 10. Nc3 Qe7 11. Nb5† Kd5 12. c4 mate**—*Canadian Illustrated News*, 24 March 1877.

A new chess resort, Clarke's Chess Room, opened its doors in May. The cream of the New York chess scene, including Mackenzie and Mason, were present. The manager, John E. Clarke, was an avid chess player himself. On 22 May a game between Clarke and Bird was announced by the *Brooklyn Daily Eagle*. No result was published.

Bird's assumed role in the café created some stir on the other side of the ocean. The *Glasgow Weekly Herald* even announced on 28 July that Bird intended to stay in New York, where he planned to open a café similar to Simpson's in London.

Also in May Bird played a match with John S. Ryan at the Crystal Palace, 252 Bowery. On 9 June the *New York Clipper* announced that it had been broken off by mutual consent after 11 of the planned 21 games. At this point the result was slightly in Bird's favor. One game of this contest was published a month later.

**(457) Bird–Ryan    ½–½**
Match
New York 1877
C40

**1. e4 e5 2. Nf3 d5 3. e×d5 e4 4. Qe2 Nf6 5. Nc3 Be7 6. N×e4**

**0–0 7. N×f6† B×f6 8. Qc4 b5 9. Q×b5 Re8† 10. Kd1 Qe7 11. Bd3 Ba6 12. Qb3 Qe2† 13. B×e2 B×e2† 14. Ke1 Bd3†** and the game was here agreed drawn—*New York Clipper*, 7 July 1877.

Bird gave a few simultaneous displays throughout the year. On 31 July he was the guest of the Philidor Chess Club where he encountered 10 opponents. Bird won 9 and lost against C. Marache.

The *Österreichische Lesehalle* of July 1890 (p. 212) recalled Bird's visit to the New York Turn-Verein which took place at an unidentified moment in 1877. This society was established to promote the social, cultural and physical needs of the German immigrants in New York. A chess club was started in the 1850s. Bird gave a simultaneous performance on 17 boards, losing one game against Schomburg. On the next evening, Bird played a small match of four games against a team of four consulting players: Bennecke, Kornfeld, Metzner and Rosenbaum. The match ended with equality. Bird won the second and fourth games. During the summer Bird lived at the Congress Hall Hotel, Chatham Square. From here he made an appeal to his friends and supporters to subscribe to his forthcoming book *Chess Openings*.

Bird increased his presence on the chess scene during his last months in New York. The *Dubuque Chess Journal* (October 1877, p. 294) described him as the leading spirit at the Café Logeling, 49 Bowery. It was here that the Manhattan Chess Club was founded on 24 November 1877. Bird managed the first tournament at this location, which ended mid–December with a victory for David Graham Baird. It is remarkable that Bird's name has disappeared from the annals of this illustrious club.

Bird changed his headquarters to the Brooklyn Chess Club in October or November, just a few weeks before the Manhattan Chess Club was launched. On 12 November the *Brooklyn Daily Eagle* called Bird a resident of Brooklyn. Bird was not present yet at the annual meeting of the club, held in October, where it was decided to organize tournaments on a regular basis and keep a weekly reception. A few weeks later at the third reception of 17 November, Bird was announced as one of the guests.[40]

Bird took part in two consultation games at the reception of 24 November. In a first game he beat Perrin and Wild. It was the second game that was the main dish for the evening, but this game did not end well for the Englishman.[41]

---

40. His appearance did not pass unnoticed: "By 9 p.m. every table in the room was occupied by players, while some were surrounded by spectators eagerly watching the movements on the boards of such noted experts as Mr. Bird, the great English player and chess writer, … Mr. Bird and party came in too late to make up the proposed consultation game, but on the occasion of his next visit it will be played. Mr. Bird sat down with Mr. Thompson for a game or two, and though he won both games Mr. Thompson gave the visitor trouble to beat him." *Brooklyn Daily Eagle*, 19 November 1877.

41. "In the consultation game of the evening Mr. Bird and Dr. Wild played against Messrs. Perrin and De Con. Ordinarily, consultation games are somewhat tedious and lengthy except to chess enthusiasts, but on this occasion a gambit was selected which led to a series of active and decidedly interesting moves. Mr. Bird's side sacrificing a knight in the sixth move for what they intended should be a winning position, but Messrs. Perrin and De Con followed up the advantageous sacrifice so skillfully that the attack lost their hold on the game, and after a finely played game marked on both sides by admirable displays of chess strategy, Mr. Bird's side resigned and the veteran of the club rose from his table smiling. Of course the visiting party will not rest content with this repulse, and next Saturday the return match will be played before the club members." *Brooklyn Daily Eagle*, 27 November 1877.

**Henry Edward Bird ca. 1877 (*Scientific American Supplement*).**

A week later, with a huge crowd attending, Bird and Field consulted against Wild and J. Albert De Con.

### (458) A.P. Barnes–Bird    0–1
Offhand game
New York, October 1877
*C33*

**1. e4 e5 2. f4 e×f4 3. Bc4 Qh4† 4. Kf1 d6 5. Qf3?!** A weak move. **5. … Nc6 6. g3 Qf6 7. Q×f4 Nd4 8. Bd3 h5 9. c3 Ne6 10. Q×f6 N×f6 11. Kg2 h4 12. Bc2 h3† 13. N×h3?** (*see diagram*) Allowing Bird to terminate the game with a nice combination. 13. Kf1 is playable.

*After 13. N×h3*

**13. … R×h3! 14. K×h3 Nf4† 15. Kh4 Ng2† 16. Kg5 Nh7† 17. Kh5 g6 mate**—*Chess Openings*, p. 131.

## (459) A.P. Barnes–Bird    1–0

Offhand game
New York, October 1877
*C33*

1. e4 e5 2. f4 e×f4 3. Bc4 Qh4† 4. Kf1 g5 5. Nf3 Qh5 6. h4 h6
7. B×f7† Q×f7 8. Ne5 Qg7 9. Qh5† Ke7 10. Ng6† Kd8 11. N×h8
Q×h8 12. h×g5 Be7 13. Qf7 Nc6 14. d4 N×d4 15. B×f4 N×c2
16. Be5 Q×e5 17. Q×g8† Bf8 18. Q×f8† Qe8 19. Q×e8† K×e8
20. g×h6 b6 21. h7 Ba6† 22. Kf2 Kf7 23. h8Q R×h8 24. R×h8
N×a1 25. Ra8 Bd3 26. Nc3 a5 27. Ke3 Bf1 28. Kd2 B×g2 29. Ra7
and White wins—*Chess Openings*, pp. 131–132.

## (460) Perrin–Bird    ?

Offhand game
New York, October 1877
*C33*

1. e4 e5 2. f4 e×f4 3. Bc4 Qh4† 4. Kf1 d6 "It appears to us that
by deferring 4. ... g5 until it becomes absolutely necessary to defend
the gambit pawn. Black, having played 4. ... d6, gets his bishop free
in time to frustrate the Fraser Attack, the first move of which 5. g3,
cannot be played in this case without disadvantage; e.g., 5. ... f×g3
6. Qf3 g2† 7. K×g2 Qg4† changing queens, remaining with a pawn
plus, and a fair position"—Bird. 5. Nf3 "If 5. d4 Be6 and White
cannot well change off the bishop, and 6. d5 would be obviously
weak for him"—Bird. 5. ... Qh5 6. d4 g5 7. Nc3 Ne7 8. h4 f6 "By
playing the usual move of 8. ... h6, Black occupies the square on
which he requires to place his bishop. By the text move he leaves
this square open, and also has a retiring place for his queen in the
event of playing Kd8, which in some variations he may require to
do. And Black has retained his pawn, without any disadvantage in
position"—Bird. 9. e5! Perrin finds the critical move. Bird advocated
two weaker lines, 9. Kg1 and 9. Be2 in *Chess Openings*. 9. ... Bg7?
A bad first attempt in this line. Bird adopted it a few times, notably
in his last upsetting win in an important tournament, against
Janowski in 1899. Nevertheless, 9. ... g4 is much better. 10. Ne4??
10. Nb5! refutes Bird's last move. Bird was confronted with it once,
and suffered a terrible loss from the hands of Dr. Ballard. 10. ...
d×e5 11. d×e5 Rf8?! A better try is 11. ... f×e5. 12. e×f6 B×f6
13. N×f6† R×f6 14. Kg1 g4 15. Ng5 Nbc6 16. Bd2 Bd7?! White
is too badly situated to deal with 16. ... f3! The text move retains
only a small advantage. 17. Bc3 Rf8 "and Black will be able to castle,
with a superior game"—Bird. *Chess Openings* (Bird), pp. 127–128.

## (461) Perrin–Bird    ?

Offhand game
New York, October 1877
*C33*

1. e4 e5 2. f4 e×f4 3. Bc4 Qh4† 4. Kf1 d6 5. Nf3 Qh5 6. d4 g5
7. Nc3 Ne7 8. h4 f6 9. e5 g4 10. Ne4 Bg7 11. e×f6 g×f3 12. f×g7

f×g2† 13. Kf2 g×h1N† 14. Q×h1 Rf8 15. g×f8Q† K×f8 16. B×f4
d5 17. Nf6 Qf5 18. Ke3 d×c4 19. Rf1 Bird gave no result of the
game, but after 19. ... Q×c2! 20. Bh6† Kf7, the outcome is predictable: White's attack is clearly over as Black can readily close the
f-file—*Chess Practice*, p. 24.

## (462) Bird & Wild–De Con & Perrin    0–1

Consultation game
New York (Brooklyn C.C.), 24 November 1877
*C39*

1. e4 e5 2. f4 e×f4 3. Nf3 g5 4. h4 g4 5. Ne5 Bg7 6. N×f7?
That's what they call playing for the audience. The master and his
poor companion will never be able to prove their point... 6. ... K×f7
7. d4 d5 8. B×f4 Nc6 9. e5 Be6 10. Be2 Qd7 11. 0–0 Rf8 12. Na3
Ke8 13. Qd2 Nge7 14. h5 h6 15. c3 Nf5 16. b4 Kd8 17. b5 Na5
18. Rfd1 b6 19. c4 Qe7 20. Nc2 Qh4 21. Ne3 g3 22. Nf1 N×d4
23. B×g3 R×f1† 24. K×f1 Q×g3 25. Q×d4 B×e5 26. Qf2 Q×f2†
27. K×f2 B×a1 28. c×d5 Rf8† 29. Bf3 Bd7 30. R×a1 B×b5
31. Re1 Rf6 32. Re4 Bc4 33. Ke3 B×a2 34. Rg4 Ke7 35. Kd4
Bb1 36. Rg7† Rf7 37. Rg8 Nb3† 38. Kc3 Nc5 39. Rh8 Bh7
40. Rc8 Kf6 41. Kc4 Be4 White resigns—*Brooklyn Daily Eagle*,
27 November 1877.

## (463) Bird & Field–De Con & Wild    1–0

Consultation game
New York (Brooklyn C.C.), 1 December 1877
*A03*

1. f4 d5 2. Nf3 c5 3. e3 Nc6 4. Bb5 Bg4 5. 0–0 Qb6 6. c4 0–0–0
7. Qa4 Na5 8. c×d5 R×d5 9. Nc3 B×f3 10. R×f3 Rd8 11. b4 c×b4
12. Q×b4 e6 13. Qa4 Nf6 14. Rb1 Qc7 15. Be2 a6 16. Rf2 Bc5
17. Bf3 Rd3 18. Ne4 N×e4 19. B×e4 Rd6 20. d4 b5 21. d×c5 b×a4
22. c×d6 Q×d6 23. Rc2† Kd7 24. Rd2 Rc8 25. R×d6† K×d6
26. Ba3† Kd7 27. Bb4 Nc4 28. Kf2 a5 29. Be1 f5 30. Bc2 a3
31. Ba4† Ke7 32. Rc1 Nd6 33. R×c8 N×c8 34. B×a5 Kf7 35. Bc7
Ke7 36. Be5 Nb6 37. Bb3 g6 38. h4 h5 39. Ke2 Kd7 40. Kd3
Black resigns—*Brooklyn Daily Eagle*, 3 December 1877.

During the past several months rumors about Bird's return to
Europe had routinely been muttered, so it must have come as a surprise to many when Bird announced his imminent return. In October Bird informed John Griswold White that he would leave for
England early in November. Bird was expecting the visit of Duffy,
his London chess friend and former colleague at Coleman,
Turquand, Youngs and Company. In all likelihood Duffy had taken
steps to facilitate Bird's return to his home country. Ultimately Bird's
stay was prolonged for a few weeks as Duffy arrived in the States
only in December. He visited 19 states in a very short time span and
returned to New York to meet Bird and various American chess
players. Both men visited the Brooklyn Chess Club for the last time
on 22 December. Exactly a week later, they sailed back to England.

# ◆ Part VII ◆

# Success and Controversy
# 1878–1880

## Back Home

Bird returned to English soil on 11 January 1878. He was immediately taken care off by both his business relations and chess friends. Very soon he was back up and running with accounting work, probably by obtaining an assignment thanks to the intervention of his former colleague, P.T. Duffy.[1]

It remains unclear what kind of work Bird performed during the remainder of the year, but at one point, at latest by March 1879, he started up an accountancy firm. His partner, George Brand, was slightly younger than Bird. Their firm, named "Brand & Bird, Auditors & Accountants" found abode at 27 King Street, Cheapside, in the heart of the City of London.

As Bird was not discharged of his bankruptcy of 1871 yet it was in fact illegal to set up a new firm. Research has not turned up an explanation of how this was possible.

Given the precarious situation in which Bird found himself, it seems evident that he did not publicize his return as an accountant. His name did not figure in the *London Gazette* nor was Bird mentioned in any significant case in the daily press. The sole trace of Brand & Bird's existence comes from a letter that was hurriedly penned by Bird on his firm's stationery. This letter (see illustration p. 229), dated 14 March 1879, was addressed to James McHenry. It contains an interesting fragment.

> In case of need Captain Gatton would I am sure speak his opinion of my industry and zeal. Sir H. Tyler who is on your committee was I believe a colleague at the Board of Trade with Captain Gatton.
>
> Some friends of mine interested in Grand Trunk and Great Western of Canada have asked me to enquire about the policy of amalgamation but I am not troubled about it [*James A. McHenry Papers*].

Bird was referring to the merging of two Canadian railroads and was probably aware that McHenry was an advocate. Bird seems to have been on the look-out for interesting information that might influence the business of some of his friends. The two acquaintances he mentioned were highly influential and well respected men. Cap-

tain Douglas Gatton was a Companion of the Most Honourable Order of the Bath (a title awarded by the Queen of England for services to the crown) and Fellow of the Royal Society. Gatton had a considerable knowledge of both financial and technical matters. He had been an accountant for railway companies in the 1850s and had also been busy with railway braking experiments.

Henry Whatley Tyler was appointed Inspecting Officer for Railways in 1853. He had an impressive career and in 1877 became president of the Grand Trunk Railway of Canada. At the 1880 general election he was chosen as a Member of Parliament.

Above all one gets the impression that Bird tried to get a face-to-face meeting with James McHenry. Both men had had a serious difference in point of view on the meeting of the English shareholders of the Atlantic and Great Western Railroad Company on 5 March 1867, where McHenry defended the colors of the Company while Bird, in his function of auditor, severely criticized the current policy. After the collapse of the Company Bird continued to denounce the whole undertaking and its promoter James McHenry in his pamphlet *A Caution to Investors* (1873). Judging from Bird's letter to McHenry both men were on friendly terms again.

Another interesting letter, written by a certain J.M. Connell and published in the *Australasian* of 13 September 1879, sheds a peculiar light on Bird's attempt to reintegrate in British society. On 6 June 1879 this Australian chess amateur, on a visit in Europe, wrote to his home front that "he thinks if encouragement were offered him that that brilliant master, Mr. H.E. Bird, who is an accountant, would be likely to repair to Australia." Apparently Bird was not completely sure yet if his future would be in England. Knowing that his brother Charles Grey was at that time living in Melbourne makes a transfer to the antipodes not as unlikely as it seems at first sight. Nothing came of it.

The address of Bird's private residence during the years 1878 and 1879 cannot be determined with certainty. At the end of 1880 Bird wrote several letters and a pamphlet from which it appears that he was living at 44 Sturgeon Road, Walworth.

## Return to the Divan

With his accountancy career back on track again, chess became mainly confined to an evening and weekend activity for Bird.

---

1.  Early in the year Bird informed his Canadian chess friend Thomas Workman about his activities: "I am fully occupied with accounting work, but leave off early today, Saturday, for two or three hours' play with Boden, at 4 o'clock. In fact, I am writing this at Simpson's whilst waiting. ... A dinner to celebrate my return is announced for next week. It is likely to be an interesting affair, as all grades of the chess community will be represented." *Canadian Illustrated News*, 16 February 1878.

A professional chess career, so thought Fraser, was out of the question after Bird's experiences in New York. It was only during the summer months of 1878 and 1880 that he gave himself completely to the game by taking part in tournaments on the continent.

Bird made his comeback at Simpson's Divan as soon as he was back in London. His reappearance was evidently hailed with hot enthusiasm. He took up with his friends Boden and MacDonnell and they contested several friendly games to the delight of a large number of spectators. On 28 January Bird was celebrated at a dinner given by the City of London Chess Club. He subsequently revealed himself as a loyal member of the club and continued to attend their monthly dinners.

Bird became a familiar face again at all kinds of social meetings related to chess. On Saturday 30 March the automaton chess player Mephisto was presented to the public after a dinner at the house of its constructor, C.G. Gümpel. In the company of various other masters Bird witnessed the first games played between the automaton and some amateurs.[2]

Two months later Bird was eagerly present at the College Chess Club. This club got in the news as it gave women the opportunity to play. On 17 May Blackburne opposed six of the female members in a blindfold exhibition.

A few days later Bird welcomed Mason, who was on his way to the international tournament in Paris. Bird made him familiar with London's ins and outs as well as with the local chess community. Upon his return from Paris, Mason decided to gain a living as a chess professional in London and he became a prominent addition to the British chess scene.

## (464) Bird–Earnshaw    1–0
Offhand game
London (Simpson's Divan) 1878
C30

**1. e4 e5 2. f4 Bc5** "This mode of refusing the gambit is inferior to 2. ... d5"—MacDonnell. **3. Nf3 d6 4. c3 Bg4 5. d4** "This move generally produces an exciting and difficult game, but is not so strong or sound as 5. Be2"—MacDonnell. **5. ... B×f3 6. g×f3 Qh4† 7. Ke2 e×d4 8. c×d4 Bb6 9. Be3 Nc6 10. Nc3 0-0-0 11. Nd5 Nge7** After this move Black becomes subject to a dangerous attack due to the weakening of the queenside. He could choose between the safe 11. ... Kb8 and the interesting 11. ... f5. **12. N×b6† a×b6 13. d5 Nb8 14. Rc1 Ng6 15. Qd2 Rhe8 16. B×b6** More precise is 16. Kd1, preventing 16. ... Na6, and threatening 17. B×b6. **16. ... Na6** "Best. Had he played 16. ... N×f4†, White would have played 17. Q×f4, winning a piece"—MacDonnell. **17. Be3** 17. Qa5 reinforces the attack decisively. The text move allows a counter thrust. **17. ... f5! 18. Kd1 f×e4 19. B×a6 b×a6** (see diagram)

*After 19. ... b×a6*

2. Mephisto remained an attraction for years. That summer it participated in the handicap tournament of the C.C.A. meeting, held in London. During the following year it went "on tour," drawing attention by succumbing gracefully to women chess players.

---

BRAND & BIRD,
AUDITORS & ACCOUNTANTS.

*27, King Street,*
*Guildhall, E.C.*
*14 March 1879*

Dear Sir

I hope you will excuse me for taking the liberty of calling. I should not like to throw a chance away in the event of your caring to serve me, and having time to see me

Very [respectfully?] & truly

H E Bird

In case of need Cap Galton would I am sure speak his opinion of my industry and zeal — Sir H Tyler who is on your Committee was I believe a colleague at Board of Trade with Cap Galton

Some friends of mine interested

in Grand Trunk and Great Western of Canada have asked me to enquire about policy of Amalgamation but I have not troubled about it. I travelled over both lines in 1876 & 1877.

**Letter from Henry Edward Bird to James A. McHenry (courtesy Barry Henderson, curator of the James McHenry Collection).**

**20. Qa5** First 20. f5! is an important improvement. All the crucial lines and diagonals for Bird's lethal attack, including the g-file, are now ready to be taken by White; e.g., 20. ... Ne5 21. Qa5 Rd7 22. Rg1. **20. ... Rd7 21. Q×a6† Kd8 22. Qa8†** An easy check, but it effectively terminates his own attack. Both 22. Re1 and 22. Rc4 keep on posing serious problems for his opponent. **22. ... Ke7 23. Qa4 Qh5 24. Rf1?!** Since a pawn is lost anyway, the more active 24. Re1 must be preferred. **24. ... Q×d5† 25. Ke1?** Bird probably wanted to avoid a depressing endgame after 25. Qd4, when only vague drawing chances await him. The text move keeps the position complicated, but the king is submitted to a fearsome attack. **25. ... e×f3 26. Kf2 Qh5 27. Rh1** "If this is White's best resource, and we have failed to discover a better, then his position is utterly defenseless and all the troubles he has had to endure must be attributed in a large measure to the vagrant disposition of his king, manifested in the very first move made by his majesty"—MacDonnell. **27. ... Qh4† 28. K×f3 Ne5†** "Seeing a good move, Mr. Earnshaw was content therewith; but had he carefully examined the position, he must have seen that 28. ... Qh3† wins the game"—MacDonnell. **29. Ke2 Qg4† 30. Kd2 Qg2†?!** 30. ... Nf3† 31. Kc2 Qf5† 32. Kb3 Kf8 is very convincing. The text move allows Bird another chance. **31. Kc3 Ra8 32. Qb5 Qe4?!** More troublesome for Bird was 32. ... Qh3 33. Rhe1 Nf3. **33. Rhe1 Rb8?** After 33. ... Qc6 the game would have finally calmed down into a likely draw. The text move allows a nice tactical shot, 34. Q×e5†, but Bird misses it. **34. f×e5? Q×e3† 35. R×e3 R×b5 36. e×d6† K×d6 37. Rd1† Rd5?** 37. ... Kc6 is necessary to draw. **38. Rde1?** The exchange of rooks wins: 38. R×d5† K×d5 39. Rd3† Ke6 40. R×d7 K×d7 41. Kd4! Kd6 42. b4! g5 43. a4 g4 44. Ke4 and White wins. **38. ... Kc6 39. b4 Kb6** "The game ought to have been drawn, but was eventually won by White, owing to Black making a slip, of which his adversary unkindly availed himself"—*Illustrated Sporting and Dramatic News* (MacDonnell), 6 April 1878.

### (465) Potter–Bird   ½–½

Offhand game
London (Simpson's Divan) 1878
C35

"The following interesting game occurred recently between Messrs. H.E. Bird and W.N. Potter, two of the best English players"—Duffy.

**1. e4 e5 2. f4 e×f4 3. Nf3 Be7 4. Bc4 d5 5. B×d5 Bh4† 6. Kf1 Nf6 7. Nc3 0–0 8. d3 N×d5 9. N×d5 f5 10. N×h4 Q×h4 11. e5 Nc6 12. B×f4** The disappearance of this pawn strengthens Black's attacking chances. 12. N×c7 Rb8 13. Qf3 N×e5 14. Q×f4 is more solid and slightly better for White. **12. ... Be6 13. Bg3 Qd4 14. N×c7 f4 15. Bf2 Q×e5** *(see diagram)*

**16. N×e6** He doesn't dare to bite the bullet and play 16. N×a8, when the position is very unclear after 16. ... f3! 17. g4! B×g4 18. h3. Alternatively, 16. Qe1 Q×c7 17. Q×e6† Kh8 18. Re1 is completely equal. Now Black obtains a slightly more active position. **16. ... Q×e6 17. Qf3 Qf6 18. c3 Ne5 19. Qd5† Kh8 20. Bd4 f3 21. Rg1?!** After 21. g×f3 a peaceful end is likely; e.g., 21. ... Rae8 22. Rg1 Q×f3† 23. Q×f3 R×f3† 24. Kg2 R×d3 25. B×e5 R×e5 26. Rae1. **21. ... Rad8 22. B×e5 f×g2† 23. K×g2 Qf2†?** Evident, but bad. He could

*After 15. ... Q×e5*

reach a much better endgame with 23. ... Qg6† 24. Kh1 R×d5 25. R×g6 h×g6 26. d4 Rf2. **24. Kh1 R×d5** "Compulsory, for White threatens mate on the move"—Duffy. **25. B×g7† Kg8 26. Bd4†?!** Potter misses his chance to torture his opponent a bit more. After 26. B×f8† K×f8 27. Rgf1 Rf5 28. R×f2 R×f2 29. b3 he'd be two pawns up. His passive pieces, however, offer Bird decent drawing chances. **26. ... Q×g1† 27. R×g1† Kf7 28. Rg7† Ke6 29. R×h7 Rg5 30. h4** "and, after a few more moves, the game was abandoned as drawn"—*Illustrated London News* (Duffy), 27 April 1878.

### (466) Potter–Bird   0–1

Offhand game
London 1878 (?)
C35

**1. e4 e5 2. f4 e×f4 3. Nf3 Be7 4. Bc4 d5 5. B×d5 Bh4† 6. Kf1 Nf6 7. Nc3 0–0 8. d3 N×d5 9. N×d5 f5 10. N×h4 Q×h4 11. e5 Nc6 12. B×f4 Be6 13. Bg3 Qd4 14. N×c7 f4 15. Bf2 Q×e5 16. N×e6 Q×e6 17. Qf3 Qf6 18. c3 Ne5 19. Qd5† Kh8 20. Bd4 f3 21. Rg1 f2** Only here does the game diverges from the previous one. Potter's next move is the decisive mistake. After 22. Q×e5 f×g1Q† 23. K×g1 Qg6 24. Qe4 he has enough compensation for the sacrificed exchange. **22. Rh1? Rae8 23. h3 N×d3 and Black wins**—*Chess Novelties*, p. 247.

### (467) Bird–MacDonnell   1–0

Offhand game
London (Simpson's Divan), 16 March 1878
C58

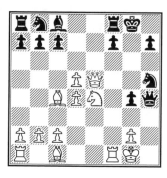

*Black to move*

This was a Kieseritzky Gambit.

**1. ... f6 2. d6† Kh8 3. Bf4 Nc6 4. g3 f×e5 5. B×e5† N×e5 6. R×f8† Kg7 7. Rg8† Kh6 8. g×h4 Nf3† 9. Kf2 N×h4 10. Ng5 or 10. Rh1** White wins—*Chess Openings*, p. 183.

## (468) Bird–MacDonnell   1–0

Offhand game

London (Simpson's Divan), 26 March 1878

C58

**1. e4 e5 2. Nf3 Nc6 3. Bc4 Nf6 4. Ng5 d5 5. e×d5 Na5 6. d3 N×c4 7. d×c4 h6 8. Nf3 e4 9. Qe2 Bd6 10. h3** This move forms the first step of a very ingenious plan. Bird intends to get an attack going along the h-file. **10. ... 0–0 11. Nh2** 11. Nd4 is more solid but Bird pursues his idea. **11. ... b5 12. Ng4 N×g4 13. h×g4 b×c4 14. g5 h×g5 15. Qh5 f6 16. Qh7† Kf7 17. Nc3** After 17. Qh5† Kg8, a draw might be agreed upon, but that was obviously not what Bird was aiming for. **17. ... Bb4** 17. ... Bg4! demonstrates the downside of Bird's plan. His attack is over while his own king becomes vulnerable in the center. **18. Bd2 B×c3 19. B×c3 Q×d5?** On this, and the previous, moves, 19. ... Bg4 was still necessary and OK for Black. **20. Qh5†** Bird failed to spot 20. Rh6!, with the decisive threat 21. R×f6†. **20. ... Ke7** (*see diagram*) As the white squares are obviously safer for him 20. ... Ke6 is correct.

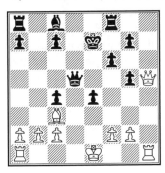

*After 20. ... Ke7*

**21. Rd1 Qf5 22. g4! Qb5 23. Qg6?** 23. a4 first and after 23. ... Qb6 24. Qg6 is winning. In the game d7 remains covered by Black's queen. **23. ... B×g4 24. Q×g7†?** This ought to lead to nothing. Best was 24. Q×e4† Be6 25. a4! Qe8! (25. ... Q×a4 is bad due to 26. Rh7! Kf7 27. Qf3 threatening both 28. Qh5† and 28. Q×f6†, and it becomes obvious that the priority of Black's queen was the defense of the king), with unclear play. 24. Rh7 illustrates that after 24. ... B×d1 25. Q×g7† Ke6, the important square d7 is covered by Black's queen. **24. ... Ke6?** After 24. ... Rf7 25. Qg6 Bf5, there is 26. a4 Qc5 27. Rd7†! B×d7 28. Q×e4† Be6 29. Q×a8 Bd5 30. Qb8 Qb6. **25. Rd4 Qc6?** 25. ... Bf3 is more tenacious. Bird's next move is a killer. **26. Rh7! Rac8 27. R×c4 Qd5 28. Qe7† Kf5 29. Rc5 Rcd8 30. Rf7 R×f7 31. "Q×d8 wins."** Of course, the final move is a misprint. Instead 31. R×d5† must have been played—*Chess Openings*, p. 174.

## CHESS OPENINGS

Bird devoted the first part of 1877 (in the United States) to writing his second book, *Chess Openings*. He finished the manuscript in July but to his disappointment found no American publisher willing to release the book in accordance with his wishes. As Bird thought it too risky to organize the publication himself he made an appeal to subscribers for support. Several of Bird's fans responded positively but this could not prevent several postponements of the publication. When Bird finally left the States the book was not printed yet.

Once in England Bird continued giving priority to the publication of the book. He sent a circular around that Dean and Son, already responsible for his previous work *Chess Masterpieces*, were now occupied with the book. Yet it was not until May that the book finally saw the light of day, in London. Bird now set everything in motion to provide his subscribers from across the Atlantic with their copy, but his troubles were far from over. A large number of books were sent to America in June, but according to the *Turf, Field and Farm* of 13 September 1878, they "were detained at and sent back by the Post Office, for some supposed infringement of our revenue laws."

With *Chess Openings* Bird pursued the aim to present the reader a more condensed opening book than the more exhaustive works by Staunton and Wormald. Besides this overview of generally recognized knowledge Bird felt it was his duty to add a few original variations, namely those that he consistently adopted.

Several reviewers received the book with moderately positive feelings, while some others were critical. In fact, Bird's approach was rather superficial as he restricted himself to presenting variations without too much deep analysis or a critical attitude. The slowly advancing modern (or scientific) school followed another direction.[3]

## PARIS 1878

There had been few important chess events on the European continent during the years that Bird had been in the United States. With the last international gathering of chess players having been the tournament in Vienna in 1873, there existed quite some eagerness for a new such contest. The world exhibition held at Paris from May until November 1878 proved to be an excellent opportunity to gather the world's elite in the French capital. With a liberal prize fund as an extra enticement the aim of the organizing committee was satisfactorily fulfilled. Six prizes, a mixture of cash money and valuable art objects, were foreseen.

---

3. Their criticism was best expressed, in a relatively mild fashion, by their main representative Wilhelm Steinitz: "The author's chief defect as an analyst arises probably from one of his distinguishing qualities as a practitioner over the board. Few chess masters could excel Mr. Bird in rapid survey of position and in the formation and execution of surprising manoeuvers, which, though not always sound—and sometimes, as he admits, even eccentric—tend to raise confusing complications, difficult for the adversary to disentangle at a quick rate. These qualities make Mr. Bird one of the most dangerous opponents in 'skittle play,' or in matches regulated by a fast time limit; but they prove almost antagonistic to the acquirement of excellency as an author on the game. For the first-class analyst is not merely expected to record results, but to judge the causes of success or failure from the strictly scientific point of view, and he has often to supplement with patient research the shortcomings of great masters in actual play. In such cases every move of a main variation becomes a problem which has to be studied for a great length of time, and the best authors have watched the progress of different openings in matches and tournaments for years and pronounced their judgment only after the most careful comparisons. Mr. Bird is, however, too much of an advocate to be a good judge, and he evinces great partiality for ingenious traps and seductive combinations which form an attractive feature of his own style in actual play, but which mostly occur only in light skirmishes. Moreover he often treats his duties as an analyst in a cavalier fashion." *The Field*, 30 December 1879.

Bird was eager to participate, but he was not considered a favorite for the laurels. Anderssen, Blackburne and Zukertort were of much higher esteem. They were joined by experienced representatives of the greatest European chess centers, players like Szymon Winawer and Rosenthal. The modern American school was represented for the first time on European soil by their two flagships, Mackenzie and Mason. Vienna sent a relatively new face to the battle, Berthold Englisch. The addition of a few weaker players completed a field of 12 participants.

Only two of the strongest players in the world failed to take part: Louis Paulsen (the winner of a strong tournament held at Leipzig in 1877) and Wilhelm Steinitz. Steinitz invoked health problems to refuse the invitation but he attended the tournament as a journalist for *The Field*. In this capacity he wrote extremely detailed game reports.

The pairings were made before the start of the tournament. Although much contested it was decided that the tournament would be double round-robin. The players were to meet each other in two consecutive games. The time limit was set at 15 moves per hour. The masters thus faced long working days. Play began at 12:00 noon and the games could last until 12:00 midnight. Only two breaks of an hour each were foreseen.

Bird arrived well on time in Paris but he did not appear completely acclimatized when the tournament started. He only scored one point from his first six games. This dramatically poor start was due to a combination of strong opposition (Bird met Winawer and Zukertort, the two ultimate tournament winners, in the first and third round) and a failing health (his gout bothered him once more). His games from these opening rounds were nevertheless hard-fought and he certainly might have earned a larger reward.

The surprising leader after six games, all of which he won, was Winawer. Blackburne, the hope of the British, had lost a half point. Anderssen followed another half point down.

According to the *Glasgow Weekly Herald* of 27 July, Bird's bad start and health issues demotivated him. He informed their correspondent that he was close to withdrawing altogether from the tournament. Fortunately he decided to continue and in the very next round he frustrated the winning chances of Anderssen by grinding down the German veteran twice.[4]

Slowly but surely Bird fought his way back into the tournament.

He split points with Albert Clerc and Blackburne after which he beat two weaker players, Carl Pitschel and Henry William Birkmyre Gifford, twice each. Bird was somewhat overconfident against his next opponent, Englisch, and he blew a simple second win.

After nine rounds Winawer (13½/18) had maintained his lead and only Zukertort (13) was able to keep up. The battle for the smaller prizes turned out to be a compelling fight among Blackburne and Anderssen (both 11½), Mackenzie (10½) and Bird and Rosenthal (both 10).

The coincidence of the pairings made Bird meet his two American rivals in the final rounds. Each of them was evidently eager to prove his superiority over their rival(s).[5]

Bird and Mackenzie split points after two hard-fought games. Winawer (15½/18) increased his advantage to a full point over Zukertort (14½), but his final opponent was Blackburne. With 13½ points, the latter was not yet completely eliminated from tournament victory. Anderssen, at 12 points, was still within the reach of Mackenzie (11½) and Bird (11).

The last round duel between Bird and Mason was fraught with an even more intense rivalry. The stake of these games was especially high for Bird as he could still gain an important prize. His opponent was the shade of his former self. Both were thus in urgent need of revenge. It turned out that Mason was no party for Bird. Bird must have been extremely pleased that he restored his shattered reputation by beating Mason twice.

Two final wins allowed Zukertort to overtake Winawer. With 16½/22 they ended two points ahead of Blackburne (14½). Anderssen was surpassed by both Mackenzie and Bird (13).

Zukertort and Winawer had to play two more games to distribute the first and second prize. After two draws a prolongation was necessary. By winning both next games Zukertort clinched first prize. MacDonnell, in the *Illustrated Sporting and Dramatic News* of 10 August, hereby pronounced him the "chess champion of the world." Zukertort earned 1000 francs and two expensive Sèvres cups for his performance. These art objects did not interest him much and were sold for much less than their value.

A play-off was also needed for Bird and Mackenzie, although they were not enthusiastic at all to take up the fight again.[6] Both

4. One well-known and popular anecdote about Bird, here related by Buckley, is likely to have occurred after one of these games: "Whether he wanted to give Winawer a knight on this occasion is not known, but a good story is told about Bird, who was gouty even in 1878, and like a true Englishman, declined to speak French for the delectation of the 'Frenche or Paryss' or of anyone else. So it rained and it poured, and the masters who were not gouty went away on the conclusion of play, leaving Mr. Bird to look after himself, being doubtless well aware that he was quite equal to the task, with or without gout, with or without French. So he called on a bystander to get him a cab, and the friendly Parisian understanding either the words or the gesture, obeyed with alacrity, and having chartered a fiacre, very kindly sheltered Mr. Bird with his umbrella during the great master's somewhat slow and painful progress thereto, parting with a very finished bow, which was intended to express the pleasure he had experienced in being of use to our friend, who for once, waiving all prejudice and preference for his countrymen, declared the stranger to be a 'very decent sort.' And when Mr. Bird discovered that his kind attendant was the president of the French Republic, he saw in this no reason to alter his opinion." *Birmingham Weekly Mercury*, 12 August 1899. The president of France at that time was Patrice de Mac-Mahon. ¶ Bird incorporated some differences in his version. He also couldn't resist adding some bewildering reminiscences about his stay in the French capital: "The allegation in *The Field* and elsewhere that he instructed the French president to fetch a cab for him on a busy fête day at the Champs-Élysées, in 1878, is not just, that genial and courteous gentleman having volunteered to do so under exceptional circumstances, and as an act of sympathy, and perhaps on account of Bird's play, who though suffering acutely from gout on that particular day won one of his two best games of Anderssen. If Bird had a carriage and pair to the barbers to get a shave (quite recently asserted) it was because he could not find a conveyance with one horse in time to reach his destination. When he made a late dinner solely off paté de foie grass at the Marquis d'Andigny's banquet at Saint-Germain-des-Prés, Paris, in 1878, when there were any number of courses, he did so because he liked the flavor (certainly did not find it savorless) not comprehending the waiter's surprise or aware of its bilious tendency till afterwards. Even a king once dined off goose livers or something of the sort, and we have heard somewhere of a 'feast of snails.'" Bird, *Chess History and Reminiscences*, p. 124.

5. "As predicted in your last, both the Americans were particularly anxious to win against Bird. The two games between Capt. Mackenzie and him lasted six or seven hours each, a long time, considering that they are both fast players. The games are undoubtedly two of the best in the tournament." *Glasgow Weekly Herald*, 27 July 1878.

6. "The contest between Bird and Mackenzie did not come up to the expectations raised by the well-known rivalry between the two champions which had manifested itself during the former's stay in America. Owing to Capt. Mackenzie being desirous to pay a visit to his relations in Scotland, an application was made to the committee by both players for permission to divide the prizes without playing the tie match. The committee very properly refused to give their sanction to this proposal, and insisted on the games being played, at the same time leaving the disposition over the division of the two prizes to the private arrangement between the two players. Under the circumstances, it was all the more unfortunate and disappointing that the two games were both finished in one afternoon, in the short space of two hours and a half." *The Field*, 3 August 1878.

players rattled of their games. The American won both of them, but this was of no importance as, according to the *Brooklyn Daily Eagle* of 8 March 1880, it was by then known that Bird and Mackenzie had agreed to split the prize money (1400 francs in total) between them.

The rivalry between Bird and Mackenzie, so sharp during Bird's stay in New York, was now officially patched and buried. In the *Glasgow Weekly Herald* of 10 August, Bird exclaimed that Captain Mackenzie had played the finest chess of all the participants. Bird increasingly declared himself an adherent of the playing style and chivalry of the American champion. He supported him a few years later in an attempt to arrange a match with Steinitz. Despite Bird's two final silly losses his result was a very good one and it was received with joy by the chess world.[7] Bird's extremely aggressive playing style, directed to avoid draws at literally all cost, was much appreciated by his fans, but many remarked correctly that it seriously affected and impaired Bird's results, in Paris and in later tournaments.

Some enthusiasts planned to follow up the main event with a smaller tournament at the Café de la Régence. It was rumored that Bird, Blackburne and Mackenzie would play but the plans ultimately failed to eventuate as players were unavailable or had already left Paris.

The tournament was graced by a grand déjeuner, given on 6 July to honor the sixtieth birthday of Adolf Anderssen. At the end of August Zukertort treated some fellow competitors and friends to a dinner at St. James's Restaurant. A more extensive dinner was held at the Criterion Restaurant in November. Fifty chess players attended this meeting to pay tribute to Zukertort's performance. Always on

**Paris 1878. Standing: Berthold Englisch, Henry W.B. Gifford, Samuel Rosenthal, Szymon Winawer and James Mason. Sitting: Adolf Anderssen, Johannes H. Zukertort, Henry E. Bird, Wilhelm Steinitz and Albert Clerc (***A Picture History of Chess***).**

### International chess tournament, Paris, 17 June–31 July 1878

*Site:* Palais de l'Industrie
*Playing hours:* 12 p.m.–12 p.m. with two breaks of an hour each
*Prizes:* 1st 1000 francs and two Sèvres cups (value 4000 and 1800 francs), 2nd 500 francs and a Sèvres cup (value 1900 francs), 3rd 1500 francs, 4th 1000 francs, 5th 400 francs, 6th 200 francs
*Time limit:* 15 moves per hour

|  | 1 | 2 | 3 | 4 | 5 | 6 | 7 | 8 | 9 | 10 | 11 | 12 |  |
|---|---|---|---|---|---|---|---|---|---|---|---|---|---|
| 1 J.H. Zukertort |  | 0 1 | 1 0 | 0 ½ | 1 1 | 1 ½ | ½ ½ | 1 1 | 1 1 | 1 ½ | 1 1 | 1 1 | 16½ |
| 2 S. Winawer | 1 0 |  | ½ ½ | ½ 0 | 1 1 | 1 ½ | 1 0 | 1 1 | 1 ½ | 1 1 | 1 1 | 1 1 | 16½ |
| 3 J.H. Blackburne | 0 1 | ½ ½ |  | 0 1 | 0 1 | 0 0 | 1 ½ | ½ 1 | 1 1 | 1 ½ | 1 1 | 1 1 | 14½ |
| 4 G.H. Mackenzie | 1 ½ | ½ 1 | 1 0 |  | 1 0 | 0 0 | 1 0 | 0 ½ | 0 1 | 1 1 | 1 1 | 1 ½ | 13 |
| 5 H.E. Bird | 0 0 | 0 0 | 1 0 | 0 1 |  | 1 1 | 1 0 | 0 1 | 1 0 | 1 1 | 1 1 | 1 1 | 13 |
| 6 A. Anderssen | 0 ½ | 0 ½ | 1 1 | 1 1 | 0 0 |  | 1 0 | ½ 0 | 1 1 | 1 0 | 1 0 | 1 1 | 12½ |
| 7 B. Englisch | ½ ½ | 0 1 | 0 ½ | 0 1 | 0 1 | 0 1 |  | ½ ½ | 0 1 | ½ ½ | 1 1 | 0 1 | 11½ |
| 8 S. Rosenthal | 0 0 | 0 0 | ½ 0 | 1 ½ | 1 0 | ½ 1 | ½ ½ |  | 1 0 | 0 1 | 1 1 | 1 1 | 11½ |
| 9 A. Clerc | 0 0 | 0 ½ | 0 0 | 1 0 | 0 1 | 0 0 | 1 0 | 0 1 |  | 0 1 | 1 0 | 1 1 | 8½ |
| 10 J. Mason | 0 ½ | 0 0 | 0 ½ | 0 0 | 0 0 | 0 1 | ½ ½ | 1 0 | 1 0 |  | 1 1 | 1 ½ | 8½ |
| 11 H.W. Gifford | 0 0 | 0 0 | 0 0 | 0 0 | 0 0 | 0 1 | 0 0 | 0 0 | 0 1 | 0 0 |  | 1 ½ | 3½ |
| 12 C. Pitschel | 0 0 | 0 0 | 0 0 | 0 ½ | 0 0 | 0 0 | 1 0 | 0 0 | 0 0 | 0 ½ | 0 ½ |  | 2½ |

*Tie matches:*

|  | 1 | 2 | 3 | 4 |  |
|---|---|---|---|---|---|
| J.H. Zukertort | ½ | ½ | 1 | 1 | 3 |
| S. Winawer | ½ | ½ | 0 | 0 | 1 |

|  | 1 | 2 |  |
|---|---|---|---|
| G.H. Mackenzie | 1 | 1 | 2 |
| H.E. Bird | 0 | 0 | 0 |

7. Two positive reviews of Bird's play were written by Potter and Steinitz: "As to Bird, a difficulty arises. He can see far, combine well, and is full of resource; but his ideas are so crotchety, and style so eccentric, that he might be underrated or overrated without any demonstration to the contrary being possible. In such a case as this results are the only reliable test. Competing with the strongest players of the present day, he tied for fourth and fifth prizes, a highly creditable show, most undoubtedly, and if we may say so, rather more than was expected, even by those who wished him well." *Land and Water*, 3 August 1878. "The fifth winner is Bird, an old representative of the London school, with a score specially marked by the absence of any single drawn game, which denotes the vivacity of his dashing style and shows his well-known aptitude for going in to win or lose. His prospects were also unfortunately marred by an indisposition in the early part of the contest, which makes his performance towards the end of the fight still more creditable." *The Field*, 3 August 1878.

the first rank at dinners where speeches were made, Bird spoke of the superiority of Zukertort and Winawer at the Paris tournament.

## (469) Winawer–Bird   1–0
International tournament (round 1, game 1)
Paris, 18 June 1878
*C61*

**1. e4 e5 2. Nf3 Nc6 3. Bb5 Nd4 4. N×d4 e×d4 5. 0-0** "Probably the best continuation"—Potter. **5. ... h5** "Mr. Bird's invention, and there is no doubt, that eccentric as it seems, it affords some scope for a defense if not properly met"—Potter. **6. d3 Bc5 7. h3 c6 8. Bc4 d5 9. e×d5 c×d5 10. Bb5†  Kf8** "Also an essential part of Mr. Bird's defense"—Potter. **11. Ba4** "Necessary, the threat was 11. ... Qa5"—Schallopp. **11. ... g5 12. Re1 Be6 13. f4** A straightforward attempt to crack Black's position, but it comes too hasty as Bird could keep the position closed now with 13. ... Qa5 14. Bb3 g4. Simply 13. Nd2 was preferable. **13. ... b5?** "This ingenious manoeuvre would be by no means unpromising against a less skillful opponent"—Potter. **14. B×b5 Qa5 15. Bc6** Winawer has a promising idea in mind that leads to a position where Bird is almost without counterplay. Even stronger was directly 15. f5 B×f5 16. Bc6 and the opening of lines and diagonals greatly benefits White. **15. ... Rc8 16. R×e6! f×e6 17. Bd7 Rd8 18. B×e6 Re8 19. f5** Winawer has just one pawn for the exchange but Bird's position has been shot to pieces. **19. ... g4 20. Nd2 Qc7 21. Nf1?!** This move gives Bird some respite. All counterplay is prevented by 21. Nb3 Be7 22. Qe1 g×h3 23. g×h3 Rh7 24. Qf2. In this line all relevant squares are kept under control, while preparations to pick up d4 are made. **21. ... g×h3 22. g×h3 Qg7† 23. Kf2?!** A safer spot for the king is h1. **23. ... Nf6** Slightly more precise is 23. ... Bd6 first, to prevent 24. Bf4. **24. Qf3 Bd6 25. Bf4 Qc7** An alternative try is 25. ... B×f4 26. Q×f4 h4. **26. B×d6† Q×d6 27. Re1** First 27. Qg3 is more refined. Black cannot afford to allow the exchange of queens and after 27. ... Qc5 28. Re1! Q×c2 29. Re2, White's king is safe. He gains the all-important d-pawn after 30. Qh4. **27. ... Rb8 28. b3 h4 29. Kg1** Bird's last move was to the point. It makes the kingside less secure for Winawer's king. **29. ... Rh7 30. Qf2 Qb4 31. Re2 Rb6 32. Qf4 Rbb7 33. Qe5** Winawer's moves were all excellent. He centralized his queen and rook and can now aim to gain the d-pawn. **33. ... Rhg7† 34. Kh1 Qe7 35. a3** 35. Nh2! activates his last passive piece. Black apparently has counterplay after 35. ... Rg3, but the straightforward 36. Ng4! R×h3† 37. Kg1 Rg3† 38. Rg2 is convincing. In case of 35. ... Nh5 there follows 36. f6! **35. ... Rg5 36. Q×d4 Qg7 37. Qf2 Re7 38. c4?** Bird defended his last few chances to make something of this game, and this harmless pawn move really allows him to launch a dangerous initiative. The cool 38. Qf4 Rg1† 39. Kh2 keeps complete control as Black is forced to head for the exchange of queens after 39. ... Qg5. With the queens off the board, the activation of his knight offers Winawer excellent winning chances. **38. ... Nh5!** A spirited defense. **39. c×d5** *(see diagram)*

**39. ... Qf6?!** Bird undercuts the principal effect of his previous move. After 39. ... Qa1! 40. Kh2 Q×a3 41. f6, the position looks overwhelming for White, but Black's queen joins the scene in the action just in time. A sample line is 41. ... Rc7 42. Q×h4 Qd6† 43. Kh1 Qf4 and now the exchange of queens is forced. In the resulting endgame White's position is quite mutilated, and he has no

*After 39. c×d5*

realistic hopes for more than a draw. **40. Rc2** 40. d6! wins outright. **40. ... Qa1 41. Rc8† Kg7?** 41. ... Re8 is the only move. There can follow 42. Qc5† Kg7 43. Qc3† Q×c3 44. R×c3 Nf4 This endgame is worse for Black than a few moves ago, but a draw is certainly still possible. **42. Rg8† Kh6 43. R×g5 K×g5 44. Qg1†** 44. d6 is best, but the text move is certainly sufficient. **44. ... Kf6 45. Ne3 Ng3† 46. Kg2 Q×g1† 47. K×g1 Rb7 48. d6 Ne2† 49. Kh2 Nd4 50. Ng4† Kg5 51. d7 Rb8 52. Ne5 Kf6 53. Nf7 Rg8 54. d8Q†** Black resigns—*Westminster Chess Club Papers* (Potter), July 1878, p. 50; *Tournament Book* (Schallopp), pp. 12–13.

## (470) Bird–Winawer   0–1
International tournament (round 1, game 2)
Paris, 19 June 1878
*A02*

**1. f4 c5 2. e3 e6 3. b3 d5 4. Bb5† Bd7 5. a4** "Just one of Mr. Bird's eccentric moves. However, there is always a meaning folded up in what he does. I do not imagine that the bishop thus curiously supported, can be taken off with any particular advantage"—Potter. **5. ... Nc6 6. Nf3 f6** "To provide against the looming fianchetto, but 6. ... Nf6, followed by 7. ... Be7, seems to afford ample security against that danger, while being much preferable in other respects"—Potter. **7. 0-0 Bd6 8. d4 a6 9. B×c6 B×c6 10. Ba3 c×d4** It is preferable to keep the tension with either 10. ... b6 or 10. ... Qe7. **11. N×d4 B×a3 12. N×a3 Bd7 13. Qg4** 13. c4! opens the position in Bird's favor. **13. ... Kf7** "Black's method of conducting defense has not turned out at all well. Mr. Bird has obviously a very fine game"—Potter. **14. Qf3** "Missing here a capital chance: 14. f5 e×f5 15. N×f5 g6 16. Nd6† Kg7 (If, however, 16. ... Ke7 17. Qb4 a5 18. Qc5 b6 19. Q×d5 Be6 20. Qb7† Kf8 21. Nab5 with a superb game) 17. Qf4 and the knight can sooner be supported than attacked"—Potter. Wrong is 15. ... g6? Both 15. ... B×f5 and 15. ... Qf8 limit Bird's advantage to a minimum. **14. ... Ne7 15. c4 Re8** *(see diagram)*

*After 15. ... Re8*

**16. Rad1** Winawer's last move was slightly imprecise (15. ... Qb6 is an improvement), as the h-pawn is undefended for a short while. With 16. f5! e5 17. Ne6 B×e6 18. f×e6†, Bird would succeed in putting a thorn into Black's side, as the e-pawn cannot be taken because of 19. Qh3†. Bird's move allows Winawer to grasp the initiative. **16. ... Kg8 17. Kh1 Qb6 18. e4 Qc5 19. Ndc2 d×e4 20. Q×e4 Qc6 21. Q×c6 B×c6 22. Nd4 Bd7 23. Nac2 Rad8 24. Rfe1 Ng6 25. g3?** This is only apparently harmless. 25. Ne2 is completely equal. **25. ... e5 26. f×e5 f×e5?** "Mr. Winawer having, by good play, worked out of his difficulties seems inclined to play for a win, or otherwise he would, I suppose, take with the knight"—Potter. 26. ... Bg4! leads to a quasi-winning endgame; e.g., 27. Rc1 f×e5 28. Ne2 Rd2. **27. Ne2 Bg4 28. Ne3 R×d1 29. N×d1 Rd8 30. Ne3?!** Bird is still under pressure but there is no reason to panic yet. 30. Nf2 covers d3 and gives better drawing chances. **30. ... Bf3† 31. Kg1 Rd2 32. Kf2?!** 32. Nc1 e4 33. Rf1 Ne5 34. Rf2 is Bird's best chance, but it demands some passive play. **32. ... e4 33. Nd5 Ne5 34. Ke3 Rb2?!** 34. ... Rd3† nets the pawn without allowing any counterplay. **35. Nd4 R×h2 36. N×f3?** 36. Nc3! wins the crucial e-pawn, thereby undermining further winning attempts from Black. **36. ... e×f3 37. Rf1 Re2† 38. Kd4 g5 39. b4 g4** The centralization of the king deserves priority. **40. b5 a×b5 41. a×b5 Nd7 42. Rc1 b6 43. Ra1 Nc5 44. Ra8† Kg7 45. Ra7† Kh6 46. Ne3 Ne6† 47. Kd3 Nc5†**

**48. Kd4 f2 49. N×g4† Kg6 50. N×f2 R×f2 51. Ra8 Rf6 52. Rc8 Rd6† 53. Ke5 Rd1 54. g4 Kf7 55. Rc6 Nd7† 56. Kf5 Rf1† 57. Kg5 Rf6 58. Rc7 Rd6 59. Kf5 Ke7 60. g5 Kd8 61. Ra7 h6 62. Ra8† Kc7 63. Ra7† Kb8 64. R×d7 R×d7 65. g×h6 Kc7 66. Kg6 Kd6 67. h7 Rd8 68. Kg7 Kc5 69. h8Q R×h8 70. K×h8 K×c4** and Black wins. "This game though long, is interesting throughout, and the victor's skill, both when at a disadvantage and after he had obtained the superiority, well deserves the praise implied by his opponent, when he wrote to London after the conclusion of the first round, saying, 'I have lost both my games, but they were very good ones'"—Potter. *Westminster Chess Club Papers* (Potter), August 1878, pp. 74–75.

According to the tournament book, the games between Bird and Rosenthal were played on 22 and 24 June. As nearly all other games of the second round were played on 21 and 22 June, one may assume this is wrong.

### (471) Bird–Rosenthal  1–0

International tournament (round 2, game 1)
Paris, 21 June 1878
C54

**1. e4 e5 2. Nf3 Nc6 3. Bc4 Bc5 4. c3** "This, as I mentioned last month, is Mr. Bird's variation of the Giuoco, and it is given in his new book upon the chess openings. It runs along the same lines as the Evans, when declined by 4. ... Bb6, White following up with 5. a4, and consequently cannot be bad"—Potter. **4. ... Nf6 5. b4 Bb6 6. Qb3 0–0 7. d3 d6 8. a4 a6 9. a5 Ba7 10. Bg5** Played to provoke 10. ... h6, which Bird considered a weakness. **10. ... Qe7 11. 0–0 Nd8 12. Nbd2 Ne6 13. Bh4 Nf4 14. Rfe1 Be6 15. d4 B×c4 16. N×c4 Ng6 17. Rad1** "The bishop ought not to remain at h4 any longer. Of course it is not desirable to take the knight unless absolutely necessary. 17. Bg3 seems good, for Black evidently takes nothing by 17. ... Nh5 18. d×e5"—Potter. **17. ... e×d4 18. c×d4** 18. B×f6 is necessary to avoid any problems. **18. ... Qe6** "This, if it be his best, cuts the legs off my last note, but I fail to see what there is against 18. ... N×h4, followed by 19. ... N×e4. There may be unearthly voices saying 'beware,' but who cares what unearthly voices say?"—Potter. **19. d5 Qg4** An unhappy excursion. **20. B×f6 g×f6 21. h3 Qh5?!** The queen has placed itself out of play. Better was 21. ... Qf4. **22. Qc3 f5 23. e5 Nf4 24. Nd4?!** "This may be a slip, but a slip, if properly utilized, often leads to victory"—Potter. Bird played some very strong positional moves, bringing his opponent on the edge of losing. The text move is pointed, but 24. e×d6, winning a crucial pawn, is far simpler. **24. ... B×d4?** Rosenthal goes for the material win, but he is confronted with his opponent's positional supremacy in a few moves. Centralization with 24. ... Rae8 keeps the game playable. **25. R×d4 Ne2† 26. R×e2 Q×e2 27. Qg3†** After 27. e×d6! c×d6 28. N×d6, the pawn at f5 will also fall. Combined with the exposed position of the king, Black's position must be considered lost. **27. ... Kh8 28. e×d6 Rg8** "Played without looking forward in the slightest degree. It is generally advisable to look at least one move ahead"—Potter. 28. ... c×d6 29. Q×d6 is also much better for White. **29. Qc3 f6 30. d×c7 Rg7 31. d6 Rag8 32. Ne3 Qf3 33. Rg4** "This strong rook, copying Samson of old, drags down the pillars of the enemy's house, and dies a glorious death amongst the

**Samuel Rosenthal (*Chess Monthly*).**

ruins"—Potter. **33. ... R×g4 34. h×g4** and White wins—*Westmin-ster Chess Club Papers* (Potter), August 1878, p. 87.

## (472) Rosenthal–Bird   1–0
International tournament (round 2, game 2)
Paris, 22 June 1878
C01

**1. e4 e6 2. d4 d5 3. Nc3 Nf6 4. e×d5 e×d5 5. Nf3 Bg4 6. Bd3 Nc6 7. Be3 Bb4 8. h3 Bh5 9. a3 Ba5 10. b4 Bb6 11. Ne2 Ne4 12. c4 Qf6 13. c5 B×f3 14. g×f3 Q×f3 15. B×e4 Q×e4 16. Ng3 Qe6 17. Qg4 0–0 18. Q×e6 f×e6 19. f4 Na5 20. b×a5 B×a5† 21. Ke2 c6 22. Rab1 b6 23. Rhf1 b×c5 24. d×c5 Rab8 25. Kd3 Bc7 26. Ne2 g5 27. R×b8 R×b8 28. Kc2 g×f4 29. B×f4** and White wins—*Tournament Book*, pp. 25–26.

## (473) Zukertort–Bird   1–0
International tournament (round 3, game 1)
Paris, 24 June 1878
C01

**1. e4 e6 2. d4 b6 3. Bd3 Bb7 4. Nh3 Nf6 5. f3 c5 6. c3 Nc6 7. Be3 c×d4 8. c×d4 Bb4† 9. Nc3 d5 10. e5 Nd7 11. f4 Ne7 12. 0–0 B×c3 13. b×c3 Rc8 14. Bd2 g6 15. Rc1 Rc7 16. Qe2 Qc8 17. Rf2 Nb8 18. Qg4 Ba6 19. Bc2 Nbc6 20. Qg5 N×d4 21. c×d4 0–0 22. Bb4 Nf5 23. B×f8 Q×f8 24. Rd2 h6 25. Qf6 Qa3 26. Qd8† Kh7 27. Q×c7 Q×c1† 28. Rd1 Qe3† 29. Nf2 N×d4 30. Q×f7†** Black resigns—*Tournament Book*, pp. 44–45.

## (474) Bird–Zukertort   0–1
International tournament (round 3, game 2)
Paris, 25 June 1878
C54

**1. e4 e5 2. Nf3 Nc6 3. Bc4 Bc5 4. c3 Nf6 5. b4 Bb6 6. Qb3 0–0 7. d3 d6 8. Bg5 Ne7 9. Nbd2 Ng6 10. 0–0 h6 11. Be3 c6 12. d4 d5 13. Bd3 d×e4 14. B×e4 N×e4 15. N×e4 Be6 16. Qb2 f5 17. Nc5 B×c5 18. b×c5 f4 19. Bc1 Bd5 20. Qc2 B×f3 21. Q×g6 Rf6 22. Qd3 e4 23. Qc4† Kh8 24. Re1 Rg6 25. g3 Qh4 26. B×f4 Q×f4 27. Rab1 Qc7 28. d5 Qf7 29. Qb4 Qd7** and Black wins—*Tournament Book*, pp. 45–46.

## (475) Anderssen–Bird   0–1
International tournament (round 4, game 1)
Paris, 27 June 1878
C54

**1. e4 e5 2. Nf3 Nc6 3. Bc4 Bc5 4. c3 Nf6 5. d4 e×d4 6. c×d4 Bb4† 7. Bd2 B×d2† 8. Nb×d2 d5** "8. ... N×e4 is slightly prefer-able"—Potter. **9. e×d5 N×d5 10. Qb3 Nce7 11. 0–0 0–0 12. Rfe1 c6 13. Ne5** 13. Ne4 (Schallopp) is slightly better for White. **13. ... Qb6 14. B×d5 N×d5 15. Qd3** "This sacrifice is unduly venture-some"—Potter. **15. ... Q×b2 16. Ne4?!** Anderssen opts for the log-ical idea to attack Bird's king but his opponent is well placed to deal with it. An interesting way to generate pressure is to haunt Black's queen. After 16. Ndc4 Qb5 17. Rab1 Qa6 18. Nd6, his initiative is obvious. **16. ... Nb4?** *(see diagram)* Retreating the queen with 16. ... Qb6 (Schallopp) leaves Anderssen with the difficult task of proving the correctness of his sacrifice.

*After 16. ... Nb4*

**17. Nf6†! g×f6 18. Qg3† Bg4** Necessary, for if 18. ... Kh8 19. N×f7†! **19. Q×g4†?** "19. N×g4 leads to a victory for White. A first line is 19. ... Kh8 20. Nh6 Qd2 21. Re3 Nd5 22. Qh4 followed by 23. Rh3. Alternatives aren't any better: **(a)** 19. ... Q×d4 20. Red1 Qb2 21. Rab1 Qc2 22. Ne3† Qg6 23. R×b4; **(b)** 19. ... Qc2 20. Re4 Nd5 (20. ... Kh8 21. N×f6 Nd5 22. Qe5) 21. Nh6† Kh8 22. Rg4; **(c)** 19. ... Nd5 20. N×f6† Kh8 21. N×d5 c×d5 22. Qe5† f6 23. Q×d5 Rad8 24. Qb3"—Schallopp. This analysis can only be improved in line **c** by both 20. Rab1 Qc2 21. N×f6† and 22. Qe5 and 21. Qd3 N×f6 22. Reb1. **19. ... Kh8 20. Qf5** "20. Rab1 is more promising"—Potter. **20. ... Nd5** Bird plays for more than the draw after 20. ... f×e5 21. Qf6†. **21. Rab1 Qc3?** 22. ... Q×a2 23. Ng4 Rfe8 defends the position. **22. Nd7?** 22. Re4! is close to winning again. If 22. ... Qc2 (best) 23. N×f7†! R×f7 24. Re8†. **22. ... Rfe8 23. Rec1 Q×d4 24. R×b7** Both players keep on playing for a win at all cost. Safer was 24. g3. **24. ... Re6 25. h3?** 25. g3 is necessary. After Bird's reply White experiences problems along the g-file. **25. ... Rg8 26. Nc5** Or 26. Rb8 R×b8 27. N×b8 Nc3 28. Rf1 Qd5 or 26. Kh1 Nf4 27. g3 Nd3 wins. **26. ... Re5?!** 26. ... Nf4! wins at once. **27. Qd3?** "A sad blunder, but with care Black ought to have won whatever is done. 27. Qf3 would be replied to by the rooks being doubled on the g-file"—Potter. 27. Qf3 is indeed his best try. White remains under pressure; e.g., 27. ... Nf4! 28. Rd7 Rd5 29. R×f7 Rh5. **27. ... R×g2†** White resigns—*Tournament Book* (Schallopp), pp. 52–53; *Westminster Chess Club Papers* (Potter), July 1878, p. 53.

## (476) Bird–Anderssen   1–0
International tournament (round 4, game 2)
Paris, 28 June 1878
B30

**1. e4 c5 2. Nf3 e6 3. Nc3 Nc6 4. Bb5 Nd4** "I was, at the first glance, inclined to consider 4. ... Nge7 ought to be a pretty fair de-fense, but after examining cannot but come to a contrary conclu-sion"—Potter. **5. N×d4 c×d4 6. Ne2 Nf6 7. Ng3** Various moves, including 7. 0–0 or 7. e5, are better. On his next few moves Anderssen could harass Bird's knight with 7. ... h5! (Schallopp). **7. ... Bd6 8. Qe2 Bb8 9. b3** "I start with a prejudice against a move so eccentric as this, but am obliged to confess that 'the principles' do not seem to obtain in a position like the present. 9. 0–0 attracts, but a close inspection leads to the discovery of various objections to that movement"—Potter. **9. ... a6 10. Bd3 d6 11. Bb2 e5 12. 0–0 0–0 13. f4 Re8** This move allows Bird to build up an initiative on the kingside. 13. ... Bg4 crosses such plans. **14. Nh5 Ng4 15. Rf3?!**

15. h3 is the evident choice. Bird's reply is extremely clumsy. **15. ...
g6 16. Ng3 Ba7** Bird's position is quite hopeless in case of 16. ...
Qh4 17. Nf1 e×f4 18. B×d4 Ne5! This is clear-cut in case of 19. B×e5
d×e5; another line could be 19. Rf2 Nc6! 20. Bb6 d5. Black's pieces
outstand their White counterparts. **17. f5 d5?!** Retreating the knight
is much safer than opening the position. **18. f×g6** 18. Raf1! (Potter)
introduces the idea 19. e×d5. Black is in a difficult situation then.
If 18. ... b5? 19. e×d5 or 18. ... d×e4? 19. N×e4. His best line is 18. ...
Qh4 19. h3 Nh6 20. Qe1! with strong pressure. **18. ... h×g6
19. Raf1 d×e4?** The situation on the board is critical. The move selected by Anderssen is insufficient as it opens too many lines against
his king. Also not enough are 19. ... Be6? (Schallopp and Potter)
which fails after 20. h3 Nh6 21. Nh5! g×h5 22. Rf6! with a winning
position, and 19. ... f5? 20. e×f5. Two moves are playable: 19. ... Nh6
and the interesting 19. ... N×h2 20. K×h2 Qh4† 21. Kg1 Bg4.
**20. Q×e4!** The previous play from both players had been relatively
weak (though it was hard to get to the bottom of the position), but
now Bird shows his class. **20. ... Be6** (*see diagram*) 20. ... f5 fails
after 21. N×f5!

*After 20. ... Be6*

**21. R×f7!** "A dagger in the heart, but the head should have
guarded the heart better"—Potter. **21. ... B×f7 22. R×f7 Qg5** "The
effect of 22. ... K×f7 is not hidden under a mountain. Of course
23. Q×g6† and after that Bb2 comes on the scene"—Potter.
**23. Q×b7 Qh4** "23. ... Qh6 is more plausible, but 24. h3 seems to
be an effective reply. After points remain, but Hope elevates her
nose with disdain, and walks away"—Potter. **24. h3 Nf6 25. Rg7†
Kh8 26. R×g6 Rg8 27. R×f6 e4 28. Q×e4** and Black resigns—
*Westminster Chess Club Papers* (Potter), August 1878, p. 86; *Tournament Book* (Schallopp), p. 53.

## (477) Clerc–Bird　0–1
International tournament (round 5, game 1)
Paris, 1 July 1878
B23

**1. e4 c5 2. f4 e6 3. Nc3 Nc6 4. Bc4 a6 5. a4 Nge7 6. e5
Nf5 7. Nf3 d5 8. e×d6 *e.p.* B×d6 9. d3 b6 10. Ne4 Be7 11. c3
Bb7 12. Qe2 Na5 13. Ba2 0-0 14. 0-0 b5 15. a×b5 a×b5
16. Bd2 c4 17. d4 Qd5 18. Nf2 Nh4 19. Ng4 N×f3† 20. g×f3
Nc6 21. Be3 Ra6 22. Qc2 f5 23. Ne5 N×e5 24. f×e5 f4
25. Bd2 Rf5 26. Qe4 Qd7 27. Qe2 Bd5 28. Qd1 Qa7 29. Qb1
Bh4 30. Rf2 B×f2† 31. K×f2 Rf8 32. Qc2 R×a2 33. Rg1
Qf7 34. Qb1 Ra7 35. Rg4 Qf5** and Black wins—*Tournament Book*,
pp. 64–66.

## (478) Bird–Clerc　0–1
International tournament (round 5, game 2)
Paris, 2 July 1878
A01

**1. e3 e5 2. b3 d5 3. Bb2 Nc6 4. Bb5 f6 5. Qh5† g6 6. Qe2 Bd7
7. Nc3 a6 8. B×c6 B×c6 9. Nf3 Bd6 10. d4 e4 11. Nd2 Qd7 12. a4
a5 13. f3 f5 14. N×d5 B×d5 15. c4 e×f3 16. g×f3 Nf6 17. c×d5
N×d5 18. Nc4 0-0 19. 0-0 Rae8 20. Ne5 Qe6 21. f4 c6 22. Rf3
Re7 23. Rc1 Rg7 24. Rg3 Kh8 25. Kh1 Be7 26. Rcg1 Rfg8
27. Qf3 Nf6 28. d5 Q×d5 29. Q×d5 c×d5 30. Rc1 Rf8 31. Rc7
Bd8 32. Rc8 Kg8 33. Rg2 Rc7 34. Rc2 R×c2 35. R×c2 Bb6
36. Bc1 Rd8 37. Kg2 Ne4 38. h4 Nc5 39. Ba3 Ne6 40. Be7 Ra8
41. Kf3 d4 42. Nc4 Rc8 43. Rg2 Bc7 44. h5 Kf7 45. Bd6 Kg7
46. h×g6 h×g6 47. Be5† B×e5 48. f×e5 Rc5 49. e4 f4 50. Rd2
g5 51. Kg4 Kg6 52. Rh2 b5 53. Nd6 b×a4 54. Nf5 R×e5 55. Rh6†
Kf7 56. b×a4 d3 57. Rh7† Ke8 58. Rh3 d2 59. Rd3 Kf8 60. R×d2
R×e4 61. Nd6 R×a4 62. Rd5 Ke7 63. Nc8† Kf6 64. Rf5† Kg7
65. Re5 f3† 66. K×f3 Kf6 67. Rd5 Nd4† 68. Kg3 Nf5† 69. Kf2
g4 70. Nb6 Ra2† 71. Kg1 g3 72. Rd1 Kg5 73. Nc4 Kh4 74. Rf1
Nd4 75. Ne3 Kh3 76. Kh1** and Black mates in two moves—*Tournament Book*, pp. 66–67.

## (479) Blackburne–Bird　0–1
International tournament (round 6, game 1)
Paris, 4 July 1878
B24

**1. e4 c5 2. Nc3 e6 3. g3 Nc6 4. Bg2 Be7 5. Nge2 d6 6. d3 Bd7
7. a3 Rc8 8. Be3 Nf6 9. Qd2 Ng4 10. Bf4 Nd4 11. h3 Ne5 12. Be3?**
"This would be comical if it were not melancholy. Mr. Blackburne
was then in the worst stage of his unfortunate illness. I have before
me a letter written to myself on the day previous to this game, in
which Mr. Blackburne says, 'Have no time to write, being laid up
in bed to be ready for Bird tomorrow.' I think that will be as good
a comment as any other, respecting this extraordinary blunder"—
Potter. **12. ... Ndf3† 13. Kd1 N×d2 14. K×d2 Nc6 15. f4 a6 16. g4
Bf6 17. e5 d×e5 18. B×c5 Be7 19. Be3 e×f4 20. N×f4 Ne5
21. Rae1 Nc4† 22. d×c4 Bc6† 23. Kc1 B×g2 24. N×g2 R×c4
25. Bd2 0-0 26. Ne3 Rc6 27. Ref1 Qc8 28. h4 b5 29. Rh2 b4
30. a×b4 B×b4** and after some further moves Black wins—*Westminster Chess Club Papers* (Potter), August 1878, p. 83.

## (480) Bird–Blackburne　0–1
International tournament (round 6, game 2)
Paris, 5 July 1878
A03

**1. f4** "Messrs. Bird and MacDonnell are both very partial to this
opening. I do not believe in its merits myself. What attack it yields,
is only good against a bad defense. Moreover, all the kingside pawns
are weak afterwards, and especially the e-pawn becomes, or should
become as much a source of anxiety as a feeble ailing child to its
parents"—Potter. **1. ... e6 2. e3 Nf6 3. Nf3 b6** "This attacking move
is strong in most openings where e3 has been played, but its offensive
power is greatly enhanced after 1. f4"—Potter. **4. b3** "For the reasons
given in the last note, this is a good continuation"—Potter. **4. ...**

Be7 5. Bb2 0–0 6. a4 Bb7 7. Bd3 Ne4 8. 0–0 f5 "This line of play, which otherwise I should not approve of, is invited by White's seventh move"—Potter. 9. a5 "A kind of continuation, congenial to Mr. Bird's style and taste"—Potter. 9. ... Bf6 "And this agrees with Mr. Blackburne's way of doing things. My own disposition would no doubt have led me to take off the pawn"—Potter. 9. ... Na6 effectively stops the march of the a-pawn. Bird's next move is daring as his advanced pawn may end up as a weakness. 10. a6 Bc8 11. Bd4 c5 12. B×f6 Q×f6 13. Ra4 d5 14. Na3 c4 Interesting, but not so dangerous, as the exchange of the a- for the c-pawn favors White. His central structure is a strong asset. 15. b×c4 Nc5 16. Rb4 Nb×a6 17. Rb1 Rd8 18. c×d5 N×d3 19. c×d3 R×d5 20. d4 Bb7 21. Nc4 Nc7 22. d3 Rdd8 23. Nce5 Nd5 24. Qd2 Qe7 25. Rfe1 Rdc8 26. Rb3 Rc7 27. e4 f×e4 28. d×e4 Nf6 29. Rbe3 Rac8 30. Qa2 Rc2?! "A very bold conception. Not many players would have the nerve to sacrifice those two passed pawns for an attack which does not at once strike the eye as being likely to succeed"—Potter. 31. Q×a7 Ra8 32. Q×b6 Raa2 (see diagram)

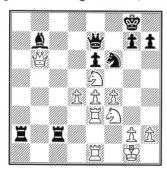

*After 32. ... Raa2*

33. d5? Blackburne achieved his aim of doubling his rooks along the second rank at the cost of two pawns. There is however no reason to panic for Bird, as h2, the crucial point for his defense, is very well defended. The text move is certainly not the best on the board, as it clearly doesn't achieve anything expect returning one of the pawns. The prophylactic 33. Kh1! is very strong and forces Black to make a crucial decision, while the move also hides a tricky trap. The evident 33. ... R×g2? namely loses quickly after 34. Rb1! Bc8 (the point is that 34. ... B×e4? 35. R×e4! N×e4 36. Q×e6† mates, as the rook cannot interpose anymore along the c-file) 35. Qc6 Rgc2 36. Rc3. Perhaps best now is 33. ... h6, but after 34. Ng6, White has everything under control, while compensation for the pawns remains to be seen. 33. ... e×d5 34. Rb3?! The other rook had to go to the b-file, but it was difficult to foresee why. 34. ... Bc8?! 34. ... R×g2† is clearly crucial. Black comes out with a clear edge after 35. Kh1 d×e4 36. Q×b7 e×f3 37. Qc8† Ne8 38. N×f3 (if the rooks were switched on move 34, 38. Ng4 equalizes) 38. ... R×h2†. The position of his king still causes worries for White, but he can hope for a draw. 35. e×d5 N×d5 36. Qd4 R×g2† 37. Kh1 Bb7 38. Re4? After the complications of the past moves, a draw has become likely in case of 38. Rd1, when nothing can keep White from eliminating his opponent's light pieces; e.g., 38. ... h6 39. R×b7 Q×b7 40. Q×d5† Q×d5 41. R×d5. 38. ... Qc7 38. ... Rgc2 is also strong. The weaknesses of the first rank and the long diagonal are too much to deal with for White. 39. Nc4 The position is very difficult for White; e.g., if 39. Nd3 h6 40. Re8† Kh7 41. Qe4† Rg6 with a winning position. 39. ... Qc8?? 39. ... Rge2 frees the long diagonal

for the bishop, when the game seems hopeless for White. 40. Nb2?? Bird misses that 40. R×b7! wins on the spot. 40. ... Rc2 40. ... Rg×b2 gains much quicker. 41. Ne5 Ba8 42. Kg1 Rc×b2 43. R×b2 Qc1† 44. Kf2 R×b2† 45. Kg3 Qc2 46. Ng4 h5 47. Re8† Kh7 48. Nf2 Qg6† 49. Kh3 R×f2 White resigns—*Westminster Chess Club Papers* (Potter), August 1878, p. 83.

## (481) Bird–Pitschel　1–0
International tournament (round 7, game 1)
Paris, 8 July 1878
*A02*

1. f4 f5 2. e3 e6 3. Be2 Nf6 4. b3 Be7 5. Bb2 0–0 6. Nf3 d6 7. a4 "Mr. Bird is rather partial to this advance of the a-pawn. Going by first impressions I should characterize it as bad, but after pausing to survey I see that it is not without its favorable points. Nevertheless, it must be remembered that the c-pawn is never destined in close games to remain at home, and when it moves elements of weakness are introduced"—Potter. 7. ... Ne4 8. d3 Bf6 9. c3 Nc5 10. b4 Ncd7 "All this is of course a wasteful expenditure of time on the part of Black"—Potter. 11. Qb3 Qe8 12. Nd4 B×d4 13. c×d4 d5 12. ... Nf6 deserved the preference, for now the open c-file presents Black with several problems. 14. Nd2 Nf6 15. Nf3 Ng4 16. Kd2 "I had some doubts whether 12. Nd4 was necessary or advisable, and this confirms them somewhat. But I should have preferred 15. 0–0 on the last move, and either taking off the knight when it came to g4, or playing 16. Rf3, the latter for choice. However even as matters stand White's game is superior most decidedly"—Potter. Bird's strategy is certainly not worse. Instead of moving his king, 16. h3! is even stronger, as the e-pawn obviously cannot be captured. 16. ... Nd7 17. h3 Nh6 18. Rhc1 c6 19. b5 Nf6? 19. ... c×b5 is necessary, although it leaves Black with a very cramped game. 20. Ba3 Rf7 21. Ne5 Bd7 "If 21. ... Rc7 22. Bd6. Altogether Black is in a dreadful fix, and no wonder for he gets his pieces into such queer places"—Potter. 22. g4 c×b5 23. g5 b×a4 24. Qb4 Bc6 25. g×f6 Rc7 26. Rg1 Rac8 27. Rac1 g6 28. h4 Kh8 29. Qd6 a5 30. h5 b5 31. Bc5 Ba8 32. h×g6 b4 and White mates in four moves. "This partie is a good specimen of Mr. Bird's vigorous and valorous style. He sometimes slaps safety in the face, but at any rate he abhors all the ways of dullness, and consequently his games nearly always give pleasure"—Potter—*Westminster Chess Club Papers* (Potter), September 1878, p. 110.

## (482) Pitschel–Bird　0–1
International tournament (round 7, game 2)
Paris, 9 July 1878
*B46*

1. e4 c5 2. Nf3 e6 3. Nc3 Nc6 4. d4 c×d4 5. N×d4 a6 6. Be3 Bb4 7. N×c6 B×c3† 8. b×c3 b×c6 9. Qd6 Qe7 10. Bc5 Q×d6 11. B×d6 f6 12. Rb1 Nh6 13. c4 Nf7 14. c5 N×d6 "I look upon Mr. Bird as licensed to do all manner of curious things, and therefore have refrained from making any notes, but how he can expect to sell his pigs at a profit in this market I cannot for the life of me see"—Potter. In fact, White's advantage is quite minimal. 15. c×d6 Kf7 16. Bc4 a5 17. Rb6 a4 18. 0–0 "Castling in an endgame of this description is like eating cream ice in winter. What is the king to

do in that gallery? Better 18. Kd2"—Potter. **18. ... Ra5 19. Rfb1 g5 20. Rb8 Rf8 21. R1b6 a3 22. Bd3 Re8 23. Rb3 g4 24. R8b6** "The office of these two rooks is to keep that bishop in prison, because, if it should once get out goodness knows what might happen. In the meantime they of course require an occasional change of air. Hence the reason of their going up and down that latter"—Potter. A purposeless move, of which Bird makes good use to create his own counterplay. Bird's last move, however, has been a bit risky, and with 24. Be2! h5 25. h3 White could open the kingside in his favor. **24. ... f5 25. f3** Now the opening of the kingside allows Bird to equalize comfortably as White's pieces are cut off on the other side of the board. **25. ... g×f3 26. g×f3 Kf6 27. Rc3 Ke5 28. Rbb3 Rg8† 29. Kf2 f×e4 30. B×e4 K×d6 31. R×a3?** The position is already in Bird's favor, but neglecting the h-pawn costs White dearly. With 31. h3, he could take the sting out of 31. ... Rh5 as 32. f4 is possible. **31. ... Rh5! 32. Ra4 R×h2† 33. Ke3 Kc7 34. Rb3 d5 35. Ra7† Kd6 36. R×h7 Rgg2 37. R×h2 R×h2 38. Bd3 e5 39. Be2** "White has all of a sudden got himself between a cleft stick. His only resource besides this, is 39. c3, whereby he will of course lose a pawn"—Potter. **39. ... d4† 40. Kd2 Ba6 41. Rd3 c5 42. Kd1 B×d3 43. B×d3 Kd5 44. Kc1 c4 45. Be4† Kc5 46. a3 c3 47. Kb1 Rh6 48. Bd3 Rf6 49. Be4 Rb6†** and after some further moves Black wins—*Westminster Chess Club Papers* (Potter), August 1878, p. 88.

## (483) Bird–Gifford   1–0
International tournament (round 8, game 1)
Paris, 8 July 1878
*A02*

1. f4 e6 2. e3 f5 3. Be2 Nf6 4. b3 c5 5. Bb2 b6 6. Bf3 d5 7. a4 Nc6 8. Nh3 Be7 9. Na3 Bb7 10. 0–0 Bd6 11. Nb5 Bb8 12. d4 a6 13. Nc3 Bd6 14. Kh1 Qe7 15. Ne2 0–0 16. Nf2 h5 17. Nd3 Ng4 18. Qd2 Qh4 19. h3 c4 20. Ne5 B×e5 21. f×e5 Nf2† 22. Kg1 Ne4 23. B×e4 f×e4 24. Ba3 R×f1† 25. R×f1 c×b3 26. c×b3 a5 27. Nf4 Re8 28. Kh2 Qg5 29. g3 Kh7 30. Qe2 Kh6 31. h4 Qg4 32. Qb5 g5 33. Ng2 g×h4 34. N×h4 Rg8 35. Rg1 Rc8 36. Qf1 Rg8 37. Bf8† Kh7 38. Qf7† Kh8 39. Q×b7 N×d4 40. Be7 Kh7 41. Bf6† Kh6 42. e×d4 e3 43. Qf7 e2 44. Be7 e1Q 45. Bf8† Black resigns—*Tournament Book*, pp. 109–110.

## (484) Gifford–Bird   0–1
International tournament (round 8, game 2)
Paris, 12 July 1878
*B00*

1. e4 e6 2. d4 b6 3. Nf3 Bb7 4. Bd3 Nf6 5. Qe2 c5 6. 0–0 Nc6 7. e5 Nd5 8. c4 Ndb4 9. d5 N×d3 10. Bg5 Nd4 11. N×d4 Q×g5 12. Nb5 Nf4 13. Qf3 e×d5 14. N1c3 0–0–0 15. N×d5 N×d5 16. c×d5 Kb8 17. Rfe1 f6 18. h4 Q×h4 19. e6 d×e6 20. R×e6 a6 21. R×b6 a×b5 22. d6 Rd7 23. Qc6 Qg4 24. a4 Qe6 25. a×b5 B×d6 26. Kh1 Re8 27. g3 Qe4† White resigns—*Tournament Book*, p. 110.

## (485) Bird–Englisch   1–0
International tournament (round 9, game 1)
Paris, 15 July 1878
*A03*

1. f4 d5 2. e3 e6 3. Nf3 c5 4. b3 Nf6 5. Bb2 Bd6 6. Ne5 Nbd7

7. Bb5 a6 8. B×d7† B×d7 9. 0–0 Qc7 10. a4 b6 11. d3 Bc8 12. Qf3 Bb7 13. Qg3 Rg8 Englisch waited a bit too long to castle and now he experiences some problems, as 13. ... 0–0 14. Nd7 Nh5 15. Nf6† (Schallopp) has to be avoided. A better alternative is 13. ... Qe7. **14. c4** 14. Nd2 is more precise. **14. ... Nd7** 14. ... g5!? is worth a try. After 15. f×g5 Ng4 16. Q×g4 B×e5 17. B×e5 Q×e5 18. Qf4 Q×f4 19. e×f4 0–0–0 the outcome is still open. Had White played 14. Nd2 instead of 14. c4, the line starting with 14. ... g5!? is refuted by 18. Qf3! **15. Nd2 Nf8 16. Qh3** The critical continuation is 16. c×d5. **16. ... f6 17. Nef3 Qf7** Interesting is 17. ... d4 to create counterplay by bruising White's pawn structure. **18. d4 h6?!** *(see diagram)* A lost tempo. Black's position still holds together after 18. ... Rd8.

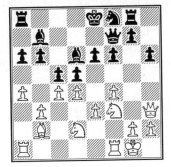

*After 18. ... h6*

**19. f5!** Also interesting is another pawn break: 19. c×d5! e×d5 20. a5 b×a5 21. Ne5! Qe7 22. Nd3, with huge pressure. **19. ... e×f5 20. Q×f5 Qe6 21. Qd3! a5?!** Englisch loses a lot of tempi in a situation where every slight mistake can be lethal, but good moves are hard to find. **22. c×d5 Q×d5 23. e4 Qe6 24. d5 Qd7 25. Nc4 Ba6 26. e5!** Bird's play is very powerful. **26. ... B×c4 27. b×c4 f×e5 28. N×e5 B×e5 29. B×e5 0–0–0 30. Rab1 Qb7 31. Bg3** For sure one of the safest roads to victory, but there were a few more vigorous opportunities to finish Black off: 31. R×f8! Rg×f8 32. Qg6 as well as 31. Rf7! Nd7 (if 31. ... Q×f7 32. R×b6 and Black's king perishes) 32. B×g7 will do. **31. ... Nd7 32. Rf7 g6 33. Qe3 Rde8 34. Q×h6 Re4 35. Qh7 Rge8 36. Q×g6 R×c4 37. Rf4** Black resigns—*Tournament Book* (Schallopp), pp. 119–120.

## (486) Englisch–Bird   1–0
International tournament (round 9, game 2)
Paris, 16 July 1878
*B00*

1. e4 e6 2. d4 b6 3. Bd3 Bb7 4. Nf3 c5 5. c3 c×d4 6. c×d4 Nf6 7. Qe2 Bb4† 8. Nc3 d5 9. e5 Ne4 10. Qc2 0–0 11. 0–0 B×c3 12. b×c3 Na6? 13. B×e4? 13. Ba3 (Potter) 13. ... Re8 14. Bb5 decisively gains material. **13. ... d×e4 14. Ng5 Rc8 15. N×e4 B×e4 16. Q×e4 R×c3 17. Bb2 Rc4 18. Rac1 Ra4** Bird had no problems at all, having the better minor piece and control over the c-file, but placing the rook on the rim is hardly advisable. 18. ... Qd5 is preferable. **19. a3 Qe8 20. Qd3** 20. Rc2 makes work of a total domination of the open file. Englisch pursues another, less convincing, plan. **20. ... Qd7 21. f4 Nc7 22. f5 e×f5 23. R×f5 Ne6 24. Rcf1 Qd5** *(see diagram)*

**25. Qh3** With this move Englisch overstretches the limits of safety. 25. Kh1 is more prudent. **25. ... Rc4!** At once 25. ... N×d4

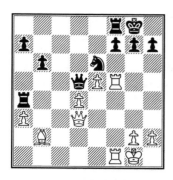

*After 24. ... Qd5*

is tempting but adequately met by 26. R×f7! The preparatory 25. ... g6! is an improvement, though careful play from White reaches to a drawish endgame: 26. Qg4 (26. R5f2 N×d4 is worse) 26. ... Rc4 27. Rf6 (he must find compensation for the nearby loss of his d-pawn by the activation of the rook) 27. ... N×d4 28. Rd6 Ne6 29. R×d5 R×g4 30. Rd7. **26. Rh5?** It was not too late yet to defend the center with 26. Qd3. **26. ... h6 27. Rh4 Rc2?** The time was ripe to take the d-pawn off the board. Bird aims for more. **28. Bc1 Rfc8 29. Be3?** A direct assault forces a quick draw: 29. B×h6! Nf8 30. Rg4 Ng6 31. Qh5 g×h6 32. R×g6†. **29. ... R8c3** "All this has been played by Mr. Bird with first-rate judgment, and he has now a won game"—Potter. **30. Rg4** "A very forlorn hope this must have seemed to Herr Englisch at the time"—Potter. **30. ... Ng5 31. Qg3 Re2 32. Rf3 N×f3†** "Four causes of wonder knock at the mental door in relation to this move. First, that Mr. Bird, with his quick sight, should not see at a glance the effects of this capture; secondly, that he should not look and examine, so as to satisfy himself that everything is all right at this, which is the crisis of the flight; thirdly, that he should not credit the opponent in having an object in giving away a whole rook; fourthly, that the neat but not very difficult method of eliminating every bother, and winning right off, which is at his disposal, should escape his undeniable penetration—e.g., 32. ... R×g2 and 33. K×g2 R×e3 or 33. Q×g2 N×f3†"—Potter. **33. g×f3 Rc×e3??** "I consider that Mr. Bird, by playing 33. ... g6, can still win. Of course White may reply 34. R×g6† but there appears to be no perpetual check if the rook be taken"—Potter. **34. R×g7† Kh8 35. Rg8†** and White wins—*Westminster Chess Club Papers* (Potter), September 1878, p. 109.

## (487) Mackenzie–Bird   1–0
International tournament (round 10, game 1)
Paris, 18 July 1878
*Game score missing*

"Bird, who was in the same position as Rosenthal, with a score of 10, defended against Mackenzie, who headed him by half a game, in his usual way by e6 and b6, followed by exchanging c-pawn and Bb4†, and capturing the knight with the bishop. The middle part appeared much in Mackenzie's favor, who had stuck in a bishop at d6 before the adversary had castled. But the former, by avoiding the exchange of queens, subjected himself to an attack, and in his defensive measures he overlooked a clever conception, whereby a pawn was lost. As it turned out, his game could bear the loss, and he opened an attack soon afterwards by offering a bishop. Bird retorted with the sacrifice of a rook, and created difficulties which enabled

him to recover the exchange and to obtain a perpetual check. But in trying to do more, Bird overrated the strength of his game; and Mackenzie, after having escaped the draw, consolidated his two bishops and the queen, and contrived to obtain a winning endgame position. Duration, six hours and three quarters"—Steinitz. *The Field* (Steinitz), 27 July 1878.

## (488) Bird–Mackenzie   1–0
International tournament (round 10, game 2)
Paris, 19 July 1878
*A03*

**1. f4 d5 2. Nf3 g6 3. e3 Bg7 4. d4 Bf5 5. Nc3 Nf6 6. Bd3 B×d3 7. c×d3 e6 8. Qb3 b6 9. Bd2 0-0 10. Ne2 Nbd7 11. 0-0 c5 12. Rac1 Qe7 13. Qa3 Rfc8 14. Ne5 Bf8 15. Qa6 Rc7 16. b4 Rac8 17. b×c5 b×c5 18. Ba5 Nb8 19. Qb5 Rb7 20. Qa4 Qe8 21. Q×e8 N×e8 22. Rb1 R×b1 23. R×b1 f6 24. Nf3 Nc6 25. Bc3 Kf7 26. Kf2** "White should play 26. d×c5, getting rid of his d-pawn"—Schallopp. **26. ... Nb4 27. B×b4?!** A feeble exchange. **27. ... c×b4 28. Rc1 R×c1 29. N×c1** "I have not cared to note or indeed to examine very narrowly the opening dispositions of the players. Mr. Bird's ideas concerning close games and mine would not be likely to come into collision, nor is it at all probable that war will take place between the inhabitants of Greenland, and the subjects of King Mtesa. Viewing the position now arrived at Black seems to have a slight advantage, for he has bishop and knight against two knights, and the opponent is burdened with a doubled pawn"—Potter. **29. ... a5 30. Ke2 a4 31. Kd2 Nc7 32. Kc2 Nb5 33. Ne2 Be7 34. Kb2 Ke8 35. Ne1 Kd7 36. Nc2 Kc6 37. e4 f5 38. e5 g5?!** "A serious and inexplicable blunder. Presumably the game, but for this false step, would have been soon abandoned as a draw, for Mr. Bird, by good play, had fortified himself against all danger of any mishap, and consequently Black, with whom the initiative rested, could do nothing"—Potter. Even with a pawn less Mackenzie has realistic chances to hold the position. **39. f×g5 Kd7 40. h4 Ke8 41. g3 Kf7 42. Ne1 Bd8 43. Nf3 Bb6 44. h5 Bd8 45. Nf4 Nc7 46. h6 Be7?** "This gives Mr. Bird an opportunity which no one would be less likely to miss. The position is rather curious. Black's only chance of a draw is to move his king and nothing else. By touching any other piece or man a lost game ensues for him"—Potter. Indeed, White cannot force a breakthrough against careful play. **47. g6† Kg8 48. g7 Kf7 49. Nh5** "Mr. Bird has one of the best pair of chess eyes in existence, but where he doesn't see he is not well able to calculate. This knight is of no use at h5 at present, and the same remark applies to the two subsequent occasions when it alights on that square. There is one way of winning, and only one: both knights must be so placed that they can bear on f6. This being so, the correct line of play here is 49. Ng2, followed by 50. Ne3 and 51. g4. White by a process of exhaustion rather than of reflection, ultimately, as will be seen, gets hold of the right bell rope"—Potter. **49. ... Ne8 50. Nf4 Nc7 51. Kc2 Bd8 52. Kb1 Be7 53. Kb2 Kg8 54. Nh5 Ne8 55. Nf4 Nc7 56. Nh3 Nb5 57. Nf4 Nc7 58. Nh5 Ne8 59. Kc2 Kf7 60. Nf4 Nc7 61. Ng2 Kg8 62. Ne3 Kf7 63. g4 f×g4 64. N×g4 Ne8 65. Kb2 Kg8 66. Ng1 Bd8 67. Ne2 Be7 68. Nf4 Nc7 69. Nh5 Ne8 70. a3 b3 71. Nf4** "Two moves later the knight checks, but why not now, seeing that it is the same posiion?"—Potter. **71. ... Nc7 72. Nh5 Ne8 73. Nhf6† N×f6 74. e×f6 Bd8 75. Kb1** Black resigns. "Because the king cannot move on account of 72. Ne5, and if the bishop goes away, then 72. f7†, followed by 73. Nf6, brings on the death rattle, but the bishop must go away after the b-pawn is disposed of"—Potter. *Westminster Chess Club Papers* (Potter), September 1878, pp. 106–107; *Tournament Book* (Schallopp), pp. 130–131.

## 489) Bird–Mason    1–0
International tournament (round 11, game 1)
Paris, 22 July 1878
*Game score missing*

"Bird opened irregular, with 1. e3 and the queenside fianchetto. Mason conducted the early middle part very well, and, by a fine conception, he managed to stick in his knight at d3, supported by a well-fortified e4, after having exchanged all other minor pieces, while the opponent was left with a bishop for the defense. Instead, however, of aiming at dissolving first the pawns on the queenside, he manoeuvred prematurely his knight to f3 for an attack on the other direction, and thereby relieved the adverse queen and left himself open to a counterattack. He finally overlooked the loss of the exchange, which cost the game after some hard struggle in the ending. This victory secured one prize for Bird, whose minimum now overreached the possible maximum of Englisch. The latter lost thereby all hope of coming in for a tie for the last place. Duration, four hours and a quarter"—Steinitz. *The Field* (Steinitz), 27 July 1878.

## (490) Mason–Bird    0–1
International tournament (round 11, game 2)
Paris, 23 July 1878
*C61*

**1. e4 e5 2. Nf3 Nc6 3. Bb5 Nd4 4. N×d4 e×d4 5. 0–0 h5 6. f4** An unfortunate solution to Bird's exotic move. 6. d3 is the main move. **6. ... c6 7. Be2** "Possibly necessary after the last move, and no doubt intended as its follower, but it only shows how completely the nature of the opening has been misconceived. Mr. Mason possesses many of the qualities of a really strong player, and particularly he is by no means apt to break down under difficulties, but he certainly lacks what is called judgment"—Potter. **7. ... d5 8. d3 d×e4 9. d×e4 Bc5 10. Bd3 Nf6 11. f5** 11. h3 is safer. Bird's reply is to the point. **11. ... Ng4! 12. Bf4 Bd7 13. Na3** Each action had to be directed against Bird's predictable plan of bringing the knight to e3. After 13. Qc1 Ne3 14. Rf2 Qe7 15. Nd2 h4 16. h3 Bd6 17. B×d6 Q×d6 18. Nf1 all danger is gone for him. **13. ... Qe7 14. Nc4 b5 15. Na5 Ne3 16. B×e3 d×e3 17. Qe2 Qe5 18. c3 h4** An imprecise move, of which Mason makes immediate use to pull up a defense. Exact is 18. ... Bd6, first provoking a weakness with 19. g3 and only then 19. ... h4. **19. Rf3** The rook is ready to defend h2 if necessary. **19. ... g6 20. Nb3 Bb6 21. Nd4 0–0–0 22. R×e3 g×f5** The opening of the position is welcomed by White. Safe is 22. ... Be8 or 22. ... h3. **23. e×f5 B×d4 24. c×d4 Q×d4 25. Kh1 Rde8 26.** 26. ... Rhe8 is more precise. **26. Be4 h3 27. g3 Re5 28. Rd1 Qb6 29. Qd2 Rd8 30. g4 c5 31. Kg1?** "He cannot stand against 31. ... R×e4, while the king remains at h1, but 31. Bf3 would appear to be more hopeful

than the text move"—Potter. Both sides have handled the game with care and a draw was likely. With this move, Mason throws it all away. **31. ... c4 32. Qf2 Rde8** "Which of course wins"—Potter. **33. Rde1 Bc6 34. B×c6 R×e3 35. R×e3 R×e3 36. Kf1 Qd4 37. Bf3 Qd3†** White resigns. "This game is a good specimen of M. Bird's vigorous, if somewhat loose, style. Careful elaboration is not a quality that he goes in for, and as long as the opponent's game be broken up, he does not seem to mind his own being in various pieces"—Potter. *Westminster Chess Club Papers* (Potter), August 1878, pp. 88–89.

## (491) Bird–Mackenzie    0–1
International tournament (tie match, game 1)
Paris, 27 July 1878
*C77*

**1. e4 e5 2. Nf3 Nc6 3. Bb5 a6 4. Ba4 Nf6 5. Qe2 b5 6. Bb3 Bc5 7. a4 Rb8 8. a×b5 a×b5 9. Nc3 b4 10. Nd5 0–0 11. Qc4 d6 12. d3 N×d5 13. e×d5 Ne7 14. Be3 Bb7 15. Qe4 f5 16. Qh4 B×e3 17. f×e3 h6 18. e4 f×e4 19. d×e4 Rf4 20. Qh5 R×e4† 21. Kd2 B×d5 22. B×d5† N×d5 23. Qg6 Re2† 24. Kd1 Nf4 25. Qg4 R×g2 26. Qf5 g6 27. Qe4 Re2 28. Qc4† d5 29. Qc6 Qd6 30. Q×d6 c×d6 31. Nh4 b3 32. c×b3 R×b3 33. Rg1 Rb×b2** White resigns—*Tournament Book*, pp. 146–147.

## (492) Mackenzie–Bird    1–0
International tournament (tie match, game 2)
Paris, 27 July 1878
*B00*

**1. e4 e6 2. d4 b6 3. Bd3 Bb7 4. Nh3 c5 5. c3 c×d4 6. c×d4 Nc6 7. Be3 Bb4† 8. Nc3 Nf6 9. 0–0 B×c3 10. b×c3 Na5 11. e5 Nd5 12. Qg4 Qc7 13. Rac1 0–0–0 14. c4 f5 15. Qe2 N×e3 16. f×e3 d6 17. Nf4 Rhe8 18. N×e6 R×e6 19. B×f5 d×e5 20. B×e6† Kb8 21. Rf7 Qd6 22. d5 Ba6 23. c5 b×c5 24. Qb2† Ka8 25. Qa3 Nb7 26. Rb1 Rb8 27. Rd7** Black resigns—*Tournament Book*, p. 147.

# AT THE DIVAN 1878-1879

After his return from Paris, Bird fell back on his usual mix of accountancy and chess. During the winter season 1878-79 he participated in just one major tournament: the handicap at the City of London Chess Club. A small number of Bird's offhand games played during this season were published. They were all played at the Divan.

## (493) MacDonnell–Bird    ½–½
Offhand game
London (Simpson's Divan), August 1878
*C51*

"An interesting game played at Simpson's Divan, last August."—MacDonnell

**1. e4 e5 2. Nf3 Nc6 3. Bc4 Bc5 4. b4 B×b4 5. c3 Bc5 6. d4 e×d4 7. c×d4 Bb6 8. 0–0 d6 9. d5** In another, undated, fragment between both players, MacDonnell continued with 9. Nc3 Bg4 10. Bb5 Kf8 11. B×c6 b×c6 12. Be3 B×f3 13. g×f3 h5 14. f5 Qd7 15. Kh1 (*Sheffield and Rotherham Independent*, 13 January 1883). **9. ... Na5 10. e5** "A lively, and by no means unsound form of the Evans attack"—MacDonnell. **10. ... N×c4 11. Qa4† c6 12. Q×c4 Ne7 13. e×d6 Q×d6 14. Re1 Q×d5 15. Q×d5** White's opening has been no great success. He has some initiative for the two sacrificed pawns, but nothing more. **15. ... c×d5 16. Ba3 Be6 17. Nc3 Rd8** 17. ... Ba5! is a serious spoiler for all intended fun. After 18. Rac1 Nc6 19. Red1 B×c3, White has nothing. **18. Nb5 Nc8** This passive move effectively renders White the eagerly sought compensation. With the more active 18. ... Nc6, a successful defense was possible; e.g., 19. Nd6† Kd7 20. N×b7 Rb8 21. Nc5 B×c5 22. B×c5 Rhc8. **19. Rac1 a6 20. Nc7† B×c7 21. R×c7 Nd6 22. Ng5 0–0 23. R×e6?** 23. N×e6 f×e6 24. R×e6 Rfe8 (MacDonnell) is about equal. The text move looks fine but the combination contains a hole. **23. ... f×e6 24. N×e6 Rfe8 25. R×g7† Kh8 26. Bb2 d4 27. B×d4 Nf5?** Bird defended perfectly, but here he commits a serious misstep, as 27. ... Nf7! wins a piece. **28. Rd7† N×d4 29. R×d8 R×d8 30. N×d8** and after a few moves the game was drawn—*Illustrated Sporting and Dramatic News* (MacDonnell), 30 November 1878.

## (494) MacDonnell–Bird   1–0
Offhand game
London (Simpson's Divan), 15 August 1878
C51

"A spirited and interesting game, played on the 15th August last year, between Mr. MacDonnell and a well-known expert"—MacDonnell.

It is very likely that this expert, "Mr. B.," was Bird. The opening of this game at least is very similar to the previous one.

**1. e4 e5 2. Nf3 Nc6 3. Bc4 Bc5 4. b4 B×b4 5. c3 Bc5 6. d4 e×d4 7. c×d4 Bb6 8. 0–0 d6 9. d5 Na5 10. e5 Ne7 11. e×d6 c×d6 12. Nc3 N×c4 13. Qa4† Qd7 14. Q×c4 0–0 15. Re1 Ng6 16. Ba3 Ba5 17. Nb5 B×e1 18. R×e1 Qg4 19. Re4 Qh5 20. N×d6 Bd7 21. Qd4 f5 22. Bb2 Qh6 23. Re3 Rf6 24. Qb4 Rff8 25. Q×b7 Rab8 26. Q×d7 R×b2 27. Qe6† Kh8 28. Nf7†** Black resigns—*Illustrated Sporting and Dramatic News* (MacDonnell), 18 January 1879.

## (495) Smith–Bird   1–0
Offhand game
London (Simpson's Divan), August 1878
A80

**1. d4 f5 2. Bf4 e6 3. e3 Nf6 4. Bc4 b6 5. Nf3 Bb7 6. Nbd2 d5 7. Bb3 a5 8. a3 a4 9. Ba2 Ba6 10. Ne5 Bd6 11. c4 0–0 12. 0–0 B×e5 13. d×e5 Ne4 14. N×e4 d×e4 15. Q×d8 R×d8 16. Rfd1 Nc6 17. c5 Kf7 18. c×b6 c×b6 19. Rd6 R×d6 20. e×d6 Kf6 21. h4 h6 22. Rc1 Na5 23. Rc7 g5 24. h×g5† h×g5 25. Bg3 Rc8 26. f4 g×f4 27. d7 Rh8 28. Bh4† Ke5 29. d8Q R×d8 30. e×f4† K×f4 31. B×d8** and White wins—*Croydon Guardian*, 31 August 1878.

The name of the player behind the Black pieces of the following game was not revealed in the *Illustrated Sporting and Dramatic News*, in which the game was first published. Given the specific

opening variation, an invention by Bird little used by anyone else it is very likely he who is the unnamed one. "Mr. B." was called in the article "one of our most brilliant London amateurs" by MacDonnell, who gave another hint to identify the unknown master when he writes "The *Rupert* of chess almost reveals his identity by this move [29. ... R×e4?]." A search through the digitized newspaper archives shows that MacDonnell probably referred to the HMS *Rupert*, a battleship of the Victorian Royal Navy.

The game was also published in the *Chicago Daily Tribune* on 9 February 1879. Here the identity of Black was given as Samuel Boden. Another publication, the *Brisbane Week*, brought the game on 29 March 1879. Wisker's note at move 4 suggests that Bird managed the Black pieces. One is inclined to believe that it was indeed Bird; the comparison with a warship seems also more fitting for Bird (and his warring manner) than for Boden.

## (496) Mason–Bird   1–0
Offhand game
London (Simpson's Divan) 1878
C33

**1. e4 e5 2. f4 e×f4 3. Bc4 Qh4† 4. Kf1 d6** "Mr. Bird prefers this defense to the 'classical' routine by 4. ... g5 etc. The check preceded or followed by 4. ... d5 and then 5. ... g5 is now a favorite mode of defense. But it is doubtful whether the check can be given at all with any advantage"—Wisker. **5. Nc3 Ne7 6. d4 g5 7. Nf3 Qh5 8. h4 f6** "A pleasing deviation from the hackneyed path, leaving h6 to be occupied by the bishop"—MacDonnell. **9. Kg1** 9. e5 is the critical line. Bird encountered it rarely. **9. ... g4 10. Ne1 Bh6 11. Nd3 f3 12. g3?** "Dangerous. The passed pawn proves very troublesome later in the game"—Wisker. He must absolutely open up the game with 12. g×f3. Bird's position is already structurally won from this point on. **12. ... Bd7 13. Kf2 Nbc6 14. Nf4 B×f4 15. B×f4 0–0 16. a3 Rhf8 17. b4 f5 18. Bg5 Rde8 19. b5 Na5 20. Bd3 f×e4 21. N×e4 Ng8 22. c4 h6 23. Bd2 b6** 23. ... N×c4! robs White of every chance. **24. Re1** Mason probably underestimated 24. B×a5 which affords him best chance to complicate the game. **24. ... d5** 24. ... Nb7 first avoids any risks. **25. c×d5 Q×d5** *(see diagram)*

*After 25. ... Q×d5*

**26. B×a5 Q×d4†?** This capture is very risky as the queen will find itself in danger very soon, while the position of his king is also on the point of being destroyed. At once 26. ... b×a5 keeps the winning chances intact. **27. Re3?** Very clumsy as the rook is being pinned in two ways now. 27. Kf1 b×a5 28. b6! leads to interesting complications; e.g., 28. ... Kd8 29. b×c7† K×c7 30. Qc2† Kd8

1. Rac1 is double-edged. **27. ... b×a5 28. b6** "All this part of the game is very brilliant on both sides"—Wisker. **28. ... Qb2† 29. Bc2 R×e4?** "The *Rupert* of chess almost reveals his identity by this move"—MacDonnell. "Correctly followed up, this move ought to have won"—Wisker. A huge mistake. The simple 29. ... a×b6 stops all future attacks, and three extra pawns should decide the contest with ease. This quest for brilliancy is typical for Bird, and once more he pays dearly for it. **30. R×e4?** The intermediate 30. b×a7! forces a winning transition; e.g., 30. ... Qb7 31. R×e4 Q×a7† 32. Qd4. **30. ... Q×b6†** After 30. ... Nf6 31. Re3 a×b6 the harmony of Black's position has been restored, making it possible for him to play quietly for a win. **31. Rd4?** Still aiming for complications, but the pin he gets in should be fatal. 31. Qd4 leads, for about the first time this game, to a rather equal position. **31. ... Bb5 32. Rb1 Re8??** Here, or on the previous move, 32. ... Ne7! wins rapidly, for if 33. Be4 Nf5 34. B×f5 R×f5 35. Rb2 Re5 36. Rbd2 a4 keeps White bound hand and foot. After some further preparatory moves Black can look for a win, perhaps by pushing the c-pawn. The text move, on the other hand, jeopardizes a piece for free. **33. Bf5† Kb7 34. a4 Re2† 35. Q×e2?** The cool 35. Kf1! keeps a major material advantage. Soon enough Black's position will fall apart. **35. ... Q×d4† 36. Qe3 Q×a4** The resulting endgame is highly interesting. Since Bird's minor pieces are limited in their action, Mason's advantage is indisputable. **37. Qc3?!** More pressure results from 37. Qd3, threatening 38. Qd5†; 37. ... Qa2† 38. Ke3! a6 39. B×g4 forcing 39. ... Qe2† 40. Q×e2 f×e2 41. B×e2, with a good endgame. **37. ... a6?** The wrong pawn, as Mason can force Bird to move the other pawn as well, after which his majesty becomes very vulnerable. **38. Rc1! c6 39. Qg7† Kb6 40. Qe5** "The game would obviously have been lost by the capture of the knight"—Wisker. **40. ... Kb7 41. Qd6?** He errs, but the decisive assault was not easy to construct: 41. Qg7† Kb6 and now a series of three strong moves follow: 42. Rc2! Qb4 43. Bc8! Ne7 44. Qe5! **41. ... Qa2† 42. Rc2 Qf7 43. B×g4 Nf6** The knight joins the party, giving Bird his share of the chances again. **44. Bf5 a4 45. K×f3 a3 46. Qe6 Qf8 47. g4** (*see diagram*) Carelessly playing for a win. 47. Kg2 is safe, but not very ambitious.

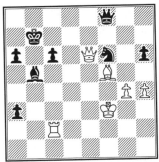

*After 47. g4*

**47. ... h5** "Very weak; a great falling off from Black's previous play"—Wisker. Still good enough for a draw, but in the meantime there was a more testing line: 47. ... Nd5! 48. g5 h×g5 49. h×g5 Ne7 50. Qf6 (the only move: 50. Kg4 N×f5 51. Q×f5 Q×f5† 52. K×f5 Bd3† has to be avoided) 50. ... Q×f6 51. g×f6 N×f5 52. f7 Nd4† 53. Kf2 N×c2 54. f8Q Bc4. A highly spectacular position. The road for the pawn is paved, the only question is whether the king will escape the checks. 55. Qe7† Kb6 56. Qd8† Kb5 57. Qb8† Ka4 58. Qf4 Kb3 59. Qg3† Kb4 60. Qb8† Bb5 61. Qf4† Kb3 62. Qg3† Kb2

63. Qg7† with a draw. **48. g5 Nd5 49. g6 Qb4 50. Qd7† Ka8 51. Q×d5?** "Brilliant and quite sound"—Wisker. Not quite. He had to keep on giving checks, agreeing with a draw. **51. ... c×d5 52. g7 Qb3† 53. Kf2 d4 54. Rc8† Kb7 55. g8Q Qe3† 56. Kg2 Qe2† 57. Kg1 Qf1† 58. Kh2 Q×f5?!** The intermediate 58. ... Qf2† forces a win. This is easy to see after 59. Qg2† Q×g2† 60. K×g2 Bc6†. Far more spectacular is the more accurate 59. Kh1. The strength of Black's initiative is illustrated in the following sample line: 59. ... Q×f5 60. Rb8† Ka7 61. Ra8† Kb6 62. Qd8† Kc5 63. Rc8† Bc6† 64. Kg1 Qg4† 65. Kf2 Kb5 66. Rb8† Ka4 67. Rb6 Qg2† 68. Ke1 Qg3† 69. Ke2 Qe3† 70. Kf1 Bb5† wins. **59. Rb8† Kc7??** "Fatal; but it was probable that the game must be lost in any case at this point"—Wisker. 59. ... Kc6 sets the king on an apparent suicide journey, right into the open field, but the result is quite surprising: 60. Rc8† Kd6 61. Qd8† Bd7 62. Qb6† Ke7 63. Qb4† Ke6 64. Qc4† Qd5 65. Q×a6† Kf7 66. Rc2 Qe5† 67. Kg1 Qe1† 68. Qf1† Q×f1† 69. K×f1 Be6 70. Rc5 a2 71. Ra5 Bc4† 72. Ke1 Ke6 and a draw is most likely, but Black can push his opponent to the limit. **60. Qd8† Kc6 61. Rc8† Q×c8 62. Q×c8†** and White wins. A sad end for Bird but what a tremendous game! *Illustrated Sporting and Dramatic News* (MacDonnell), 28 December 1878; *Brisbane Week* (Wisker), 29 March 1879.

## (497) Mason & MacDonnell–Bird & Blackburne & Earnshaw    ½–½

Consultation game
London (Simpson's Divan) 1879
C38

**1. e4 e5 2. f4 e×f4 3. Nf3 g5 4. Bc4 Bg7 5. 0–0 h6 6. d4 d6 7. c3 Nd7 8. a4 Qe7 9. Na3 Nb6 10. Bd3 Bg4 11. a5 Nd7 12. Qb3 Ngf6 13. Q×b7 0–0 14. Nb5 Rfb8 15. Q×c7 Ne8 16. Qc4 Rc8 17. Qa4 Nf8 18. Qd1 Rab8 19. Na3 Ng6 20. Qe1 B×f3 21. g×f3 h5 22. Nc2 Nc7 23. Rb1 Bh6 24. Qe2 Re8 25. Ne1 Qd7 26. Ng2 Kh8 27. b4 Rg8 28. Kh1 Ne8 29. Bd2 h4 30. e5 h3 31. Ne1 Nh4 32. Rg1 d×e5 33. Q×e5† f6 34. Q×b8 Nd6 35. Q×g8† K×g8 36. c4 Ndf5 37. d5 Nd4 38. Rf1 Kf7 39. b5 g4 40. f×g4 Q×g4 41. Rf2 Nhf5 42. Bc3 Ng3† 43. h×g3 f×g3 44. B×d4 g×f2 45. B×f2 Bd2 46. Rb2 B×e1 47. B×e1 Qf3† 48. Kh2 Q×d3 49. Bg3 Qc3 50. Rf2 Q×c4 51. b6 Q×d5 52. b×a7** draw—*Illustrated Sporting and Dramatic News*, 12 April 1879.

## (498) Bird & Mason–Blackburne & Hoffer    ½–½

Consultation game
London (Simpson's Divan), 15 April 1879
C65

**1. e4 e5 2. Nf3 Nc6 3. Bb5 Nf6 4. Qe2 Bc5 5. B×c6 d×c6 6. N×e5 Qd4 7. Nd3 Bb6 8. f3 Be6 9. c3 Qa4 10. Na3 0–0–0 11. Nf4 Rhe8 12. N×e6 R×e6 13. b3 Qa5 14. Nc4 Qh5 15. N×b6† c×b6 16. d4 g5 17. g4 Qh4† 18. Kd1 h5 19. Qe1 h×g4 20. Q×h4 g×h4 21. Bg5 Rg8 22. B×h4 g×f3 23. e5 Nd5 24. Kd2 Rg2† 25. Kd3 Re2 26. Bg5 f6 27. e×f6 N×f6 28. B×f6 R×f6 29. Raf1 R×a2 30. h4 Ra5 31. Ke4 f2 32. Rh2 Rh5 33. Rf×f2 R×f2 34. R×f2 R×h4† 35. Ke5 Rh7 36. c4 Re7†** and the game was given up as a draw after a few more moves—*Chess Monthly*, September 1879, pp. 13–14.

## (499) Bird & Steel–Blackburne & Hoffer   1–0

Consultation game
London (Simpson's Divan), 7 May 1879
*C77*

**1. e4 e5 2. Nf3 Nc6 3. Bb5 a6 4. Ba4 Nf6 5. Qe2** "This attack
first occurs, we believe, in a game between Paulsen and Zukertort
in the Hamburg tournament of 1869, but it had been lost sight of
until Blackburne adopted it in the tie match against Steinitz at the
Vienna tournament of 1873 and it was afterwards frequently employed in the match between Messrs. Bird and Wisker"—Steinitz.
**5. ... Be7** "Inferior to 5. ... b5, followed by 6. ... Bb7. The advance
of the b-pawn should be made as early as possible—at any rate,
before White has time for 6. c3, which gives the bishop the option
of retreating to the sometimes stronger post at c2. Professor Anderssen favored the following line of defense, which was also based
on the immediate advance of the b-pawn, but different to the continuation by developing Bf8 instead of bishop to b7: 5. ... b5 6. Bb3
Bc5 7. a4 Rb8 8. a×b5 a×b5 9. Nc3 0–0 10. N×b5 d5 followed either
by 11. ... Bg4, or else, if White plays 11. h3, by 11. ... Nh5"—Steinitz.
**6. d3 d6 7. c3 Bg4 8. Nbd2 Qd7 9. Nf1 b5 10. Bc2 d5** "White
have followed the line of attack chosen in a similar position in the
first game of the Steinitz–Blackburne match of 1876, but the defense
is here conducted on different principles, consisting mainly in the
pinning of Nf3 and to an early endeavor to open the d-file, which
apparently gave Black a satisfactory opening"—Steinitz. **11. h3
B×f3** "Best. 11. ... d×e4 would have been answered by 12. h×g4,
and White would have then proceeded with 13. g×f3 in answer of
12. ... e×f3, with an excellent position on the kingside. It was also
of no use to speculate on a counterattack by retreating the bishop
to e6 and giving up the e-pawn: 11. ... Be6 12. e×d5 N×d5 (if 12. ...
Q×d5 13. Ne3 with an attack) 13. N×e5 N×e5 14. Q×e5 Bf6
15. Qe4 (stopping 15. ... N×c3) 0–0 16. d4 g6 17. Qf3, followed
soon by Ne3, with a pawn ahead and an excellent game"—Steinitz.
**12. Q×f3 d4** "But this we consider weak, for the d-pawn remains
fixed, and no opportunity arises of exchanging it advantageously;
while the opponents have the option of capturing it at a point most
convenient for themselves. We should have preferred 12. ... d×e4, as
the entrance of Ne3, which the move in the text apparently provided
against, would do little harm"—Steinitz. **13. Ng3 g6 14. 0–0 h5**
"The attempt at a counterattack is a failure, and subjects them only
to an unfavorable disposition of their forces. They could still obtain
a fair game by 14. ... 0–0, followed by 15. ... Rfd8 in case of
15. Bh6"—Steinitz. **15. Bb3 Rh7** "They were now reduced to that
inconvenient defensive move, for White threatened 16. Bg5 in any
case, which gave White a manifest advantage, if Black had here
adopted 15. ... Na5 or 15. ... h4. In the first place: 15. ... Na5 16. Bg5
Qd6 (if 16. ... N×b3 17. B×f6) 17. c×d4 and in case of 17. ... e×d4
18. e5. Secondly: 15. ... h4 16. Bg5 Qd6 17. Ne2, followed
accordingly by 18. c×d4 or 18. Rac1, with an excellent game"—
Steinitz. 15. ... Rd8 supersedes both the text move and Steinitz' suggestions. If 16. Rd1 (16. Bg5? d×c3 and if 17. B×f6 Nd4) 16. ... a5
17. Bg5 Qd6 Black is but slightly worse. At this point 18. c4 is interesting to improve the prospects of his bishop. **16. Ne2 Ng8?**
"There was time enough for this retreat, if the opponents attacked
by 17. Bg5, and it was preferable to attempt dislodging the adverse

bishop by 16. ... a5. 16. ... Rb8 at once, or else 16. ... Kf8, with th[e]
object of retreating the knight to e8, also deserved more consideration"—Steinitz. Black is bound to lose the fight for the center an[d]
the white squares, but this move leaves their opponents a free hand
**17. a4 Rb8** "Not as good as 17. ... b4, albeit White might have continued then by 18. a5 and 19. Ba4, for in that case Black could firs[t]
remove the queen to d6, and then in answer to 19. Ba4 might castl[e]
safely on the queenside"—Steinitz. 17. ... b4 is also ruinou[s]
(18. c×d4! N×d4 19. N×d4 Q×d4 20. Bd5). 17. ... Rd8 is slightl[y]
stronger, though White's bishop is once again a very strong piec[e]
e.g., after 18. c×d4 e×d4 19. a×b5 a×b5 20. Bd5 or 18. ... N×d[4]
19. N×d4 Q×d4 20. a×b5 a×b5 21. Bd5. **18. a×b5 a×b5 19. Ra[6]
Bc5** *(see diagram)* "[Black] have an uncomfortable game now, i[n]
consequence of having allowed the opponents the open a-file; an[d]
perhaps their best plan was now to oppose the rook at once at b[6]
though it would have subjected them to a doubled pawn. They coul[d]
not well pursue the plan of relieving the c-pawn for the defense o[f]
the d-pawn by 19. ... Nd8, on account of the following continuation
20. Qg3 Bf6 21. c×d4 e×d4 22. e5 Bg7 23. R×g6 h4 24. R×g7 h×g[7]
25. R×g8† and mates in two more moves. An alternative at mov[e]
22: 22. ... Bh8 23. R×g6 f×g6 24. Q×g6† Rf7 25. Q×g8† Rf[8]
26. Qg6†, followed by 27. e6, winning"—Steinitz.

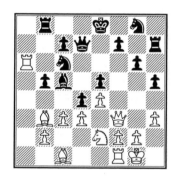

*After 19. ... Bc5*

**20. Bg5!** "An excellent move, which exercises a strong influence
on the subsequent progress of the attack"—Steinitz. **20. ... Bb[6]**
"As the sequence above, this was done with the object of removing
the first obstacle to the advance of the c-pawn, which they tried t[o]
get ready by withdrawing the knight. But the conclusion on which
the plan is based appears to be a misconception, for the bishop wa[s]
more wanted on the kingside, and stood best on its present post
ready for action or protection of both wings. 20. ... Nge7 was better
and the Black allies ought to have kept in view the eventual advance
of the f-pawn, which freed their Rh7 and opened more defensive
prospects than the release of the c-pawn"—Steinitz. Also after 20. ...
Nge7, 21. Rfa1 White's many assets guarantee them a winning positional advantage. **21. Rfa1 Nge7 22. Ra8 Qd8** "As they intended
to retake the adverse rook with the knight, it seems to have been
better to throw the queen back in a manner which also kept Ne7
inactive. Perhaps their best plan was 22. ... Nc8, with the object of
bringing afterwards, according to requirements, either the bishop
or one of the knights to a7. They could not well take the rook with
the view of covering the check by Nd8, for the White allies could
afterwards proceed advantageously with the queen to c6, which
could have led to an exchange of queens, after which White's queenside bishop would have blocked out the rook at Bf6 with an easy-

von game"—Steinitz. 22. ... Nc8 23. Qf6! wins on the spot—
e.g., 23. ... Qd6 24. Bd5. **23. R×b8 N×b8 24. c×d4 e×d4 25. Ra8** "Had they advanced 25. ... c5, the answer 26. e5 was sufficient to paralyze their game, for it threatened a powerful attack either by 27. Qb7, or 27. Ng3, with the object of entering with 28. Ne4"—Steinitz. **26. Qf6 Bc7 27. N×d4 Qd6 28. Q×e7†** Strong enough, but allowing Black to reach an endgame is an unnecessary luxury. 28. Nf3 ends all Black attacking tries, while they keep their mighty bishop pair alive. **28. ... Q×e7 29. B×e7 K×e7 30. R×b8** "The termination is most skillfully played by the White allies"—Steinitz. **30. ... B×b8 31. N×c6† Kd6 32. N×b8 f5 33. Bd5 Rc7 34. Kf1** White wins. "The game was continued for many more moves, which have no further interest, for White was bound to win with the exchange and two pawns ahead"—Steinitz. *The Field* (Steinitz), 7 May 1879.

In the midst of April 1879 the arrival of a young and promising lad from the provinces created quite some stir at the Divan. Julius Jacobsen, 16 years old, had already scored some impressive results in his native Hull and was now taken on a visit to the capital. Here he sensationally succeeded in beating the always available Bird with 4 wins, 2 losses and 1 draw. In his column in *Land and Water* of 19 April 1879, Potter even wrote how many thought that "the long-looked for 'coming man' of English chess is supposed to have been discovered at last in the person of a young gentleman."

Soon after this impressive feat Jacobsen gave up the practice of the game. He left for South Africa around 1880 and some six years later arrived in Australia. Here he took up the game again with great success and in 1897 became the national champion of Australia.

---

# A VISIT TO CROYDON, FEBRUARY 1879

On 18 February Bird visited the chess club of Croydon. This club had become very active recently, having received MacDonnell, Duffy and Blackburne in the months before.

Bird was in the company of Ascher, one of his Montreal friends who was in London at the time.[8]

According to the *Croydon Guardian* of 23 August 1879, only five games were played at the same time during this exhibition. Only L. Browne succeeded in beating Bird.[9]

8. Ascher, a merchant, had beaten Mackenzie in a simultaneous game, played on 14 January 1879 in Montreal. During the summer months the bankruptcy of his firm was announced. See, for example, *Sheffield and Rotherham Independent*, 31 July 1879.

9. "On Tuesday last, Mr. Bird ... paid a visit to the Croydon Chess Club, and, with his usual good nature, played the members simultaneously, winning nearly all the games; Mr. Browne, being a cautious player, won the only game against his powerful antagonist. Leading men in all callings are too apt to allow their better feelings to be warped in estimating the abilities of others, and chess masters are no exception to this rule, but Mr. Bird is happy in being able to avoid giving offence to anyone." *Croydon Guardian*, 22 February 1879.

**(500) Rattenbury–Bird    0–1**
Simultaneous game
Croydon, 18 February 1879
*C33*

"The following is one of several simultaneous games played by Mr. Bird on his recent visit to the Croydon Chess Club"—Hoddinott.

**1. e4 e5 2. f4 e×f4 3. Bc4 Qh4† 4. Kf1 d6** "Black's 4th move is not mentioned by the authorities, but it is a great favorite with Mr. Bird. In his opinion it constitutes a satisfactory defense in this variation of the Bishop's Gambit"—Hoddinott. **5. Nc3 Ne7 6. Nf3 Qh5 7. d4 g5** "Usually played at Black's 4th move; but Mr. Bird considers it a waste of time for Black to protect the gambit pawn, until White threatens to regain it"—Hoddinott. **8. h4 f6** "Another of Mr. Bird's happy inventions. 8. ... h6 is generally played at this point"—Hoddinott. **9. Nb5** Much inferior to 9. e5! **9. ... Kd8 10. Kg1 g4 11. Ne1 Bh6** "The advantage of 8. ... f6 is now apparent. In being able to post his bishop at h6, he strengthens his game considerably"—Hoddinott. **12. d5** "12. Nd3 would have been stronger. The move played enables Black to place his rook on g8, by which he further develops his game on the kingside"—Hoddinott. **12. ... Rg8 13. Qd4 Nd7 14. Nd3** "White marshalls his pieces against his powerful opponent in a manner highly commendable"—Hoddinott. **14. ... f3** "His best move at this point"—Hoddinott. **15. B×h6** If 15. g3 (Hoddinott) 15. ... a6 16. B×h6 Q×h6 17. Nc3 Ne5 and Black's position is much better, besides being a pawn ahead. **15. ... Q×h6 16. g3 f5 17. Nf4 Ne5** "The only way to meet the threatened check on e6"—Hoddinott. **18. Bd3** (*see diagram*)

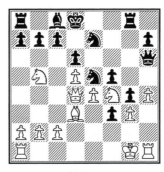

*After 18. Bd3*

**18. ... f×e4** 18. ... a6, a crucial move, is obligatory here. Bird could have played it much sooner as well. **19. B×e4** 19. Qc3 is a better attempt to mix things up as some lines and diagonals are opened after 19. ... c6 20. d×c6 b×c6 21. B×e4. **19. ... Bf5** 19. ... a6 is again much better. **20. B×f5 N×f5 21. Ne6†** "We think White here misses a fine opportunity. 21. Qc3 would have given him a very powerful attack, and would have led to positions of great interest. From the move played, the exchange of queens is inevitable"—Hoddinott. The move 21. Qc3 comes too late. White is lost after 21. ... Rc8 22. N×a7 N×g3. **21. ... Q×e6 22. d×e6 N×d4 23. N×d4 c5** Too hasty. 23. ... Ke7 allows no counterplay at all. **24. Nf5 Kc7** Bird mistakenly continues to ignore the adverse e-pawn. At this point 24. ... Rg6 is therefore a refinement. **25. Rd1 Rad8** Both 25. ... Rae8 and 25. ... Rg6 maintain an important edge. **26. Kf2** 26. e7 Rde8 27. R×d6 leaves nothing of Black's former superiority. **26. ... d5?** "Mr. Bird must certainly have overlooked the very obvious move

26. ... Rg6 which would have been much stronger. The move played probably should have cost him the game"—Hoddinott. **27. Rhe1 Nc4** "There appears no better move"—Hoddinott. **28. b3** "White should have played 28. e7 at once, and his attack would have been almost irresistible"—Hoddinott. **28. ... Nb6 29. e7 Rde8 30. Re6** 30. Re5 is better, as it prevents 30. ... d4, a move Black should have tried now. **30. ... Rg6 31. Rde1** Pointless. 30. Re5 is still good, for it prepares 31. c4. **31. ... Kd7** 31. ... R×e6 is more precise as White could now have played the same 32. R6e5, with a lasting initiative. **32. R×g6 h×g6 33. Nh6 R×e7 34. R×e7† K×e7 35. N×g4 d4** Bird ventures everything to win the game. 35. ... Ke6 or 35. ... Nd7 brings him close to a draw. **36. K×f3 Nd5 37. Ne5 Nb4 38. N×g6† Kf6 39. Nf4 N×c2 40. g4 b5** Not good, but Bird speculates on an error from his opponent. **41. h5** 41. g5† ought to win effortlessly, as the c-pawn falls. 41. ... Kf5 42. g6 Kf6 43. h5. **41. ... c4 42. h6 d3 43. Nd5†?** Throwing away another easy win: 43. g5† Kf7 44. g6† Kf8 45. g7† Kf7 46. Ng6. **43. ... Kg6 44. g5 Nd4† 45. Kg4?** A gross miscalculation. 45. Ke3 draws easily. **45. ... d2 46. Nc3 b4 47. Nd1 c3** White resigns—*Croydon Guardian* (Hoddinott), 15 March 1879.

**(501) Browne–Bird    1–0**
Simultaneous game
Croydon 1879
C40

1. e4 e5 2. Nf3 d5 3. e×d5 e4 4. Ne5 Q×d5 5. d4 e×d3 *e.p.* 6. N×d3 Nc6 7. Nc3 Qd8 8. Be2 Be6 9. Be3 Bd6 10. Ne4 Nf6 11. Bg5 Be7 12. B×f6 g×f6 "We should have taken with the bishop, to prevent the doubling of the pawns, but Mr. Bird ignores such conventional moves"—Hoddinott. **13. c3 f5** The bishop pair is ample compensation for the wrecked pawn structure, and 13. ... Qd5 followed by 14. ... 0–0–0 offers excellent play. The text move is rather weak but ultimately justified after Browne's next move. Much more testing is 14. Nec5! **14. Nd2 Bd6 15. Nf3 Qf6 16. Qd2** "The queen would have had more liberty of action by going to a4"—Hoddinott. **16. ... 0–0–0 17. Nf4** A questionable square for the knight. Black's initiative remains manageable after 17. 0–0. **17. ... Rhg8! 18. g3** *(see diagram)*

*After 18. g3*

**18. ... Rge8** A pity! 18. ... B×f4 19. Q×f4 Rg4 20. Qc1 Re4 would have been a brilliant follow-up of Bird's last move. There is nothing to be done against his attack; e.g., 21. Nd2 R×e2†! 22. K×e2 Qe5† 23. Kf1 Qd5. **19. 0–0 B×f4 20. Q×f4 Bd5 21. Rfe1 Re4 22. Qg5 Qe6 23. Bd3 f6** 23. ... h6 is decidedly better as 24. Qh6 wins a pawn now. **24. Qh5 Ne5?** In his search for tactics Bird makes a decisive

mistake. 24. ... R×e1† 25. N×e1 Be4 is equal, for if 26. B×e4 f×e4 27. Q×h7 e3!. **25. Nd4 R×d4 26. B×f5 Nf3† 27. Q×f3 B×f3 28. B×e6† R4d7 29. B×d7† K×d7 30. Re3 Bd5 31. Rd1** Black resigns—*Croydon Guardian* (Hoddinott), 23 August 1879.

# HANDICAP TOURNAMENT AT THE CITY OF LONDON CHESS CLUB 1878–1879

At the end of 1875 the City of London Chess Club received a heavy blow from the formation of the West End Chess Club. Many members, including almost all the strong players, preferred to transfer to the new club. The prosperity of the West End Chess Club, however, did not last long and it was already disbanded before Bird came back to England. The City Club on the other hand slowly gained back its glory. Upon his return Bird was immediately re-elected as an honorary member and he became a regular attendee at the club evenings and dinners.

Just as in former years the winter season was dominated by the annual handicap tournament. The renewed popularity of the club was illustrated by the large number of 64 entries. The rules and the odds valid for this handicap were still the same as in the previous editions. The committee, with Bird in it, divided the players in the usual classes. Only three players, Bird, MacDonnell and Potter were ranked in Class I. Three lower classes (III to V) were divided in sections A and B. Players of section A gave the move to those of section B.

Bird survived the first four rounds relatively easily by each time beating much lower ranked opponents. One duel in the quarter-finals, between MacDonnell and Frederick William Lord, was becoming a farce when at one point both players threatened to resign their match. In the end Lord forced his way through.

Bird's opponent in the semifinal, Potter, was of a much more substantial level. After an initial draw Bird scored the first victory in the second game. Bird was very close to a quick decision in the third game but drew it.[10] After another draw Potter won the fifth game and thus equalized the score. The sixth game proved to be the decisive one. It was an extremely long fight that lasted over four evenings. After 143 moves Potter ultimately resigned and Bird had reached the final round.

Bird more than once claimed that this game was the longest on record (i.e., *Chess Novelties*, p. 146, which erred by stating it lasted 149 moves). He clearly forgot that his game against Lipschütz in New York 1889 broke that record with 159 moves. That game was the first to pass the 150 mark.

The other semifinal saw the 20 year old James Thomas Heppell (class V) beat F.W. Lord. Heppell was at once the favorite against Bird for the latter had to give him the huge odds of a rook. Not a gift against such an underrated player.

---

10. "The third was resumed, after an adjournment, on Monday night. When I left I thought Mr. Potter had the advantage, but the position was exceedingly difficult. I have since learned that the game was drawn. Just before the end Mr. Bird had a win, but he fell through it." *Glasgow Weekly Herald*, 26 April 1879.

## Handicap tournament, London, October 1878–May 1879

**Site:** City of London Chess Club
**Time limit:** 20 moves per hour
**Odds scale:** pawn and move (class II), pawn and 2 moves (class III), knight (class IV), rook (class V) and knight and bishop (class VI)

**DIVISION A:**

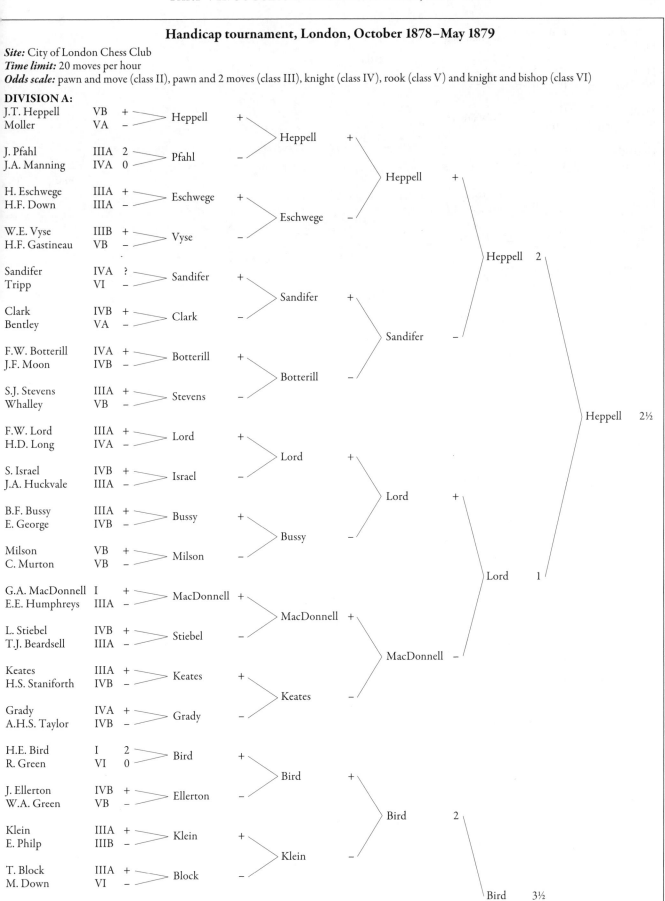

| | | |
|---|---|---|
| J.T. Heppell | VB | + |
| Moller | VA | – |

Heppell +

Heppell +

| J. Pfahl | IIIA | 2 |
| J.A. Manning | IVA | 0 |

Pfahl –

Heppell +

| H. Eschwege | IIIA | + |
| H.F. Down | IIIA | – |

Eschwege +

Eschwege –

| W.E. Vyse | IIIB | + |
| H.F. Gastineau | VB | – |

Vyse –

Heppell 2

| Sandifer | IVA | ? |
| Tripp | VI | – |

Sandifer +

Sandifer +

| Clark | IVB | + |
| Bentley | VA | – |

Clark –

Sandifer –

| F.W. Botterill | IVA | + |
| J.F. Moon | IVB | – |

Botterill +

Botterill –

| S.J. Stevens | IIIA | + |
| Whalley | VB | – |

Stevens –

Heppell 2½

| F.W. Lord | IIIA | + |
| H.D. Long | IVA | – |

Lord +

Lord +

| S. Israel | IVB | + |
| J.A. Huckvale | IIIA | – |

Israel –

Lord +

| B.F. Bussy | IIIA | + |
| E. George | IVB | – |

Bussy +

Bussy –

| Milson | VB | + |
| C. Murton | VB | – |

Milson –

Lord 1

| G.A. MacDonnell | I | + |
| E.E. Humphreys | IIIA | – |

MacDonnell +

MacDonnell +

| L. Stiebel | IVB | + |
| T.J. Beardsell | IIIA | – |

Stiebel –

MacDonnell –

| Keates | IIIA | + |
| H.S. Staniforth | IVB | – |

Keates +

Keates –

| Grady | IVA | + |
| A.H.S. Taylor | IVB | – |

Grady –

| H.E. Bird | I | 2 |
| R. Green | VI | 0 |

Bird +

Bird +

| J. Ellerton | IVB | + |
| W.A. Green | VB | – |

Ellerton –

Bird 2

| Klein | IIIA | + |
| E. Philp | IIIB | – |

Klein +

Klein –

| T. Block | IIIA | + |
| M. Down | VI | – |

Block –

Bird 3½

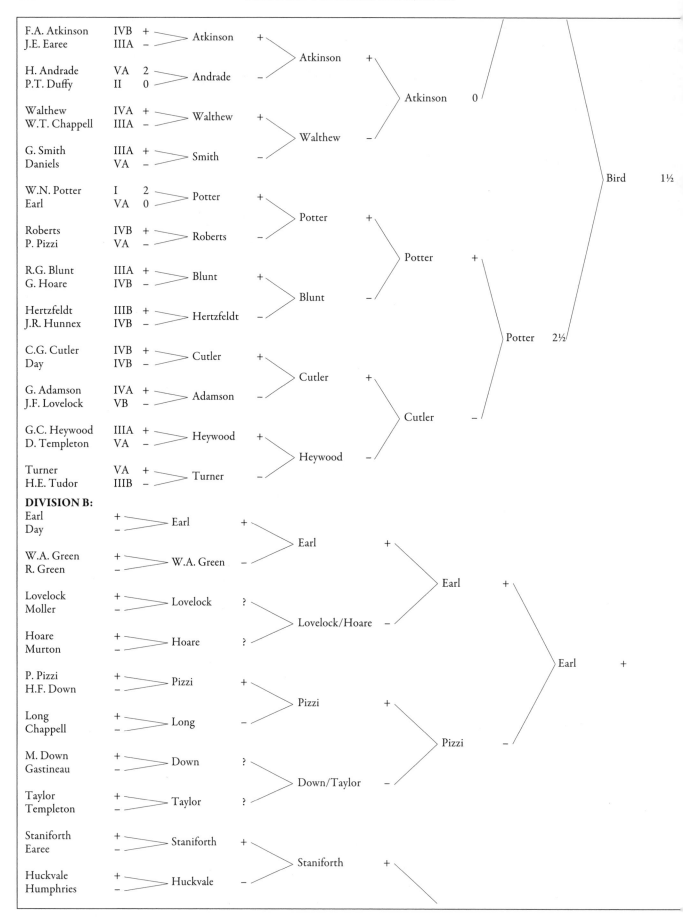

F.A. Atkinson    IVB   +
J.E. Earee       IIIA  −        Atkinson    +
                                               Atkinson    +
H. Andrade       VA    2
P.T. Duffy       II    0        Andrade     −                Atkinson    0
                                                               Potter   2½
Walthew          IVA   +
W.T. Chappell    IIIA  −        Walthew     +
                                               Walthew     −
G. Smith         IIIA  +
Daniels          VA    −        Smith       −

W.N. Potter      I     2
Earl             VA    0        Potter      +
                                               Potter      +
Roberts          IVB   +
P. Pizzi         VA    −        Roberts     −                Potter      +

R.G. Blunt       IIIA  +
G. Hoare         IVB   −        Blunt       +
                                               Blunt       −
Hertzfeldt       IIIB  +
J.R. Hunnex      IVB   −        Hertzfeldt  −

C.G. Cutler      IVB   +
Day              IVB   −        Cutler      +
                                               Cutler      +
G. Adamson       IVA   +
J.F. Lovelock    VB    −        Adamson     −                Cutler      −

G.C. Heywood     IIIA  +
D. Templeton     VA    −        Heywood     +
                                               Heywood     −
Turner           VA    +
H.E. Tudor       IIIB  −        Turner      −

**DIVISION B:**
Earl             +
Day              −              Earl        +
                                               Earl        +
W.A. Green       +
R. Green         −              W.A. Green  −                Earl        +

Lovelock         +
Moller           −              Lovelock    ?
                                               Lovelock/Hoare  −
Hoare            +
Murton           −              Hoare       ?                           Earl    +

P. Pizzi         +
H.F. Down        −              Pizzi       +
                                               Pizzi       +
Long             +
Chappell         −              Long        −                Pizzi

M. Down          +
Gastineau        −              Down        ?
                                               Down/Taylor  −
Taylor           +
Templeton        −              Taylor      ?                Pizzi       −

Staniforth       +
Earee            −              Staniforth  +
                                               Staniforth  +
Huckvale         +
Humphries        −              Huckvale    −

Bird    1½

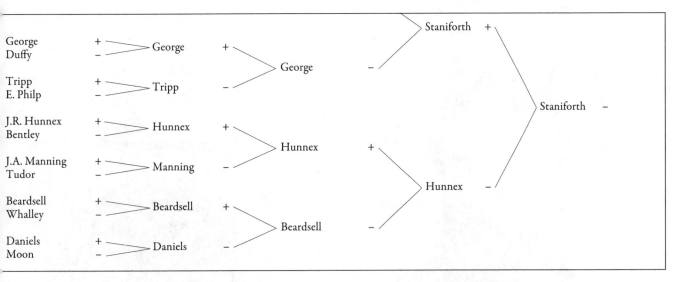

Yet, Bird surprisingly won the opening game. Heppell equalized at once and, after a draw, he realized the widely expected victory by beating Bird a second time. It was the first time in the history of this handicap tournament that a player from fifth class won the laurels.

**(502) Bird–Potter   ½–½**

Handicap tournament (round 5, game 1)

London, April 1879

*C01*

**1. e4 e6 2. d4 d5 3. e×d5 e×d5 4. Bd3 Nf6 5. Nf3 Bd6 6. Nc3 0-0 7. 0-0 Nc6 8. Nb5 Be7 9. Bf4 a6 10. Nc3 Nh5 11. Be3 g6 12. Qd2 Bg4 13. Ne1 Be6 14. Be2 Ng7 15. Nd3 Nf5 16. Nf4 Bf6 17. Bf3 B×d4 18. Nc×d5 N×e3 19. N×e3 B×b2 20. Q×d8 N×d8 21. Rab1 Bd4 22. B×b7 N×b7 23. N×e6 f×e6 24. R×b7 Rf7 25. Rd1 Bb6 26. Ng4 Rf4 27. h3 Raf8 28. Rd2 h5 29. Ne5 R×f2 30. R×f2 B×f2† 31. Kh2 h4 32. Nd3 Bg3† 33. Kg1 c5 34. c4 Rd8 35. Rb3 Rd4 36. Rc3 Bd6 37. Kf2 g5 38. Kf3 Kg7 39. Nf2 Rf4† 40. Ke2 Be5 41. Ra3 R×c4 42. R×a6 Bg3 43. Ng4 Rc2† 44. Kf3 Ra3† 50. Ke4 c3 51. Kd3 c2† 52. K×c2 Ra2† 53. Kd3 R×g2 54. Ke4** draw—*Land and Water*, 5 April 1879.

**(503) Potter–Bird   0–1**

Handicap tournament (round 5, game 2)

London, April 1879

*D05*

**1. e3** "A favorite opening with Mr. Bird, and adopted by him at the Paris congress. We wonder how he felt at having his own weapon turned against himself"—Mackenzie. **1. … e6** "Mr. Bird has the authority of Mr. Potter for considering this superior to 1. … e5"—Mackenzie. **2. b3 d5 3. Bb2 Nf6 4. Nf3 Be7 5. d4 0-0 6. Bd3 Nbd7 7. 0-0 c5 8. c4 b6 9. Nc3 Bb7 10. Rc1 Rc8 11. Qe2 Re8 12. Rfd1 c×d4 13. e×d4 Bb4 14. Ne5 d×c4 15. b×c4 Qe7 16. Nb1 a6 17. f4 N×e5 18. f×e5 Nh5 19. Qe3 Qh4 20. Rf1 Rc7 21. Rf2?** A natural-looking move, but had Bird replied with 21. … Be7, White would have been without resource against a swift attack with 22. … Bg5 and 23. … Bf4 as crucial ideas. It was therefore necessary to

force the exchange of the bishops with 21. Ba3. **21. … f5? 22. Be2?!** Both 22. Ba3 or 22. g3 solve his problems on the kingside. **22. … Be7 23. g3?!** *(see diagram)* 23. Qb3 is relatively better.

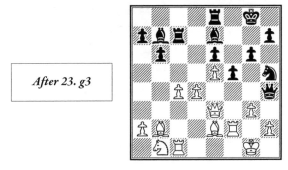

*After 23. g3*

**23. … f4!** "Played in Mr. Bird's happiest style"—Mackenzie. **24. g×f4 Rf8 25. B×h5** 25. Rcf1 R×c4 isn't a pleasure either. **25. … Q×h5 26. Nd2 Bh4 27. d5** "Evidently he cannot save the rook"—Mackenzie. **27. … B×f2† 28. Q×f2 e×d5 29. Qg3 Qe2 30. Bc3 d×c4 31. Re1 Qd3 32. e6 Q×g3† 33. h×g3 a5 34. g4 Re7 35. f5** "Ingenious, but of no avail"—Mackenzie. **35. … g×f5 36. Re5 Rg7 37. Rb5 R×g4† 38. Kf2 Rg2† 39. Kf1 Rg3 40. e7 Re8 41. Bf6 c3 42. Nb3 Ba6 43. Kf2 B×b5 44. K×g3 c2** and White resigns—*Turf, Field and Farm* (Mackenzie), 6 June 1879.

**(504) Bird–Potter   0–1**

Handicap tournament (round 5, game 5)

London 1879

*A03*

**1. f4 d5 2. Nf3 e6 3. b3 Nf6 4. Bb2 Be7 5. e3 0-0 6. Be2 b6 7. a4 c5 8. 0-0 Bb7 9. Qe1 Nc6 10. Bb5 Nb4 11. Na3 c4 12. d4 a6 13. Bc3 N×c2 14. N×c2 a×b5 15. a×b5 c×b3 16. Nb4 R×a1 17. Q×a1 Qd7 18. Rb1 Ra8 19. Qb2 Q×b5 20. Q×b3 Ne4 21. Nd2 N×c3 22. Q×c3 Rc8 23. Qd3 Qa5 24. Qb3 b5 25. Kf2 Kf8 26. Rb2 f6 27. f5 B×b4 28. Q×b4† Q×b4 29. R×b4 Rc2 30. Ke1 Bc6 31. f×e6 Ke7 32. Rb3 K×e6 33. Ra3 Rc1† 34. Ke2 Kf5 35. Ra7 b4 36. Kf3 Rd1 37. g4† Kg6 38. Nb3 Rb1 39. Nd2 Rb2 40. Nf1 h5 41. g×h5† Kh6 42. Ng3 b3 43. Nf5† Kg5 44. h6 g×h6 45. Ng3 Kg6 46. h4 h5 47. Ra6 Bd7 48. e4 Bg4† 49. Ke3**

*Left:* **William N. Potter** (courtesy Cleveland Public Library). *Right:* **James Thomas Heppell** (courtesy London Borough of Hackney Archives)

Rg2 **50. Nf1 Re2† 51. Kd3 d×e4† 52. Kc3 b2 53. Rb6 Re1 54. Nd2 e3** White resigns—*Land and Water*, 3 May 1879.

## (505) Potter–Bird    0–1
Handicap tournament (round 5, game 6)
London, May 1879
*A02*

**1. f4 f5** "We believe that Black ought at least to equalize the game in a few moves by 1. ... d5"—Steinitz. **2. b3 Nf6 3. Bb2 e6 4. Nf3 Be7 5. e3 0–0 6. Be2 c5 7. 0–0 Nc6 8. Ne5 Qc7** "Black loses a great deal of time by this defensive measure, and it was manifestly preferable to exchange the knight; and if then 9. f×e5, the knight could well retreat to e8, with a prospect of activity at c7, or else the knight could enter at e4, and then be brought to f7 by g5"—Steinitz. **9. N×c6 Q×c6 10. Bf3 Qc7** This move is the real, but not so harmful, loss of time. Black obtains a very decent position after the logical 10. ... d5. **11. c4 a6 12. Nc3 Ra7** "In consequence of his tenth move he has now some difficulty to develop the queenside"—Steinitz. **13. g3 b6 14. d4** The resulting central structure is favorable for Black. 14. e4!, on the other hand, leads to a small advantage for White. **14. ... c×d4 15. e×d4 Bb7 16. a3** "We see no use for this; and besides, as the adversary's Ra7 and Bb7 were badly placed, it was not good policy to allow the latter to be exchanged for his own bishop, which had the greatest freedom in all directions. 16. d5

would have kept the advantage of position"—Steinitz. The idea o[f] playing 16. d5 is interesting, and objectively speaking best as wel[l] although Black is a little better after 16. ... b5. **16. ... B×f3 17. Q×f.** **Ng4** This maneuvre doesn't contribute anything to his position. I[t] was time to find adequate spots for the rooks. **18. h3 Nh6 19. Rad[1]** **Bf6 20. Rf2** "The slow manoeuvring is here carried to excess. It i[s] unintelligible to us what the move had to do with the plan carrie[d] into execution on the next move of trying to break through wit[h] the d-pawn"—Steinitz. **20. ... Nf7 21. d5 Raa8 22. Kh1** "Also a[n] aimless waiting move. There was more sense in 22. Kg2, if the kin[g] moved at all; but the best was apparently 22. Rfd2"—Steinitz. **22. ...** **Nd6 23. Re2 Rae8 24. Rde1 Qb7 25. Kg2 B×c3 26. Q×c3 Rf.** **27. Kh2 Ne4 28. Qd4 e×d5 29. c×d5** "29. Q×d5 was stronger. I[f] 29. ... Q×d5 then White could obtain first possession of the ope[n] c-file for one of his rooks; for if 30. ... Rc8, White could oppos[e] 31. Rc1, and after the exchange of one rook would gain undispute[d] possession with the other rook"—Steinitz. **29. ... Qc7 30. b4 Qd6** **31. Qd3 h5 32. h4 Rfe7 33. Be5 Qg6 34. d6 Re6 35. Qf3 b5** **36. Kg2?!** "White has waited so long by choice until he has to wai[t] by compulsion. But again we would not have selected the king fo[r] making an indifferent move. It will be seen that the king is badl[y] posted here later on"—Steinitz. **36. ... Kh7 37. Rd1 Rc8** Finally Both sides could and should have taken possession of the open fil[e] as soon as was possible. **38. Rd3 Rc4 39. Rb2** *(see diagram)* Aban doning the e-file allows Bird to make a very promising sacrifice after, for example, 39. Kh2, 39. ... R×e5 is better for White, as he can quickly return the compliment by taking on e4.

*After 39. Rb2*

**39. ... R×e5!** "Very cleverly played"—Steinitz. **40. f×e5 N×g3 41. Q×g3** "It was his best plan, and it showed a great deal of foresight to give up the queen. The only other alternatives were 41. Kh3 or 41. Kf2, and in both cases Black must have obtained an overwhelming attack; e.g., 41. Kh3 Rg4 42. Rg2 (this seems best. If 42. Qb7 or 42. Qa8, 42. ... R×h4† would win) 42. ... Ne4 43. Re3 Qe6, with a fine game. If 41. Kf2 Ne4† 42. Ke2 Qe6 43. Q×h5† Kg8, with a fine attack"—Steinitz. A desperate move is 41. e6, when after 41. ... Ne2† 42. Kf2 Nf4, Black controls the dangerous e-pawn. **41. ... Rg4 42. Rf2 Qe6 43. Re3 g6** More decisive is 43. ... Qd5†, bringing the queen to the front. Given the relatively closed position, White's rooks are utterly helpless. **44. Kh2 R×g3 45. K×g3 Kg7 46. Rg2** "As it was evidently his plan to try to advance the e-pawn whenever the adverse queen moved away from her present post, 46. Rd2 would have been more consistent in support of that idea; for it gave at once additional strength to the d-pawn, in case it becomes a passed pawn, and it also threatened to obtain perhaps even the superior game by 47. Rd4 and 48. Kf4"—Steinitz. Steinitz misses the tactical hole in his suggestion: 46. ... f4†! snatches a rook. **46. ... Qc4 47. Kf3 Qd5†** "Useless. A strong point could have been here gained by 47. ... Kf7, and, in fact, it would have been difficult for White to find a satisfactory defense. If he tried to utilize the d-pawn, the game might have proceeded thus: 48. e6† d×e6 49. Rd2 Qf1† and wins the pawn next move by 50. ... Qd1†, for the rook must interpose at f2, or else 50. ... f4† follows"—Steinitz. **48. Kf2 f4** "The pawn has not sufficient support to be worth much for the attack, and it must be lost subsequently; going on with the king was better play"—Steinitz. **49. Re1 Kf7 50. Rg5 Qd3 51. Rgg1 Ke6 52. Rg5 Kf7 53. Rgg1** (see diagram)

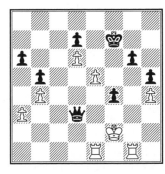

*After 53. Rgg1*

**53. ... Ke8?** Bird commits his first inaccuracy, but it is a serious one. 53. ... Qh3! wins simply enough, as White's last desperate try is doomed to fail: 54. e6† d×e6 55. d7 Q×h4† 56. Ke2 Ke7 etc.

**54. e6 Qd4† 55. Kf3 Qd5† 56. K×f4 d×e6 57. Rd1** "White is defending himself excellently. He has obtained a well-supported passed pawn for himself, and he has separated the adverse dangerous pawns by clever tactics"—Steinitz. Potter misses a most interesting drawing possibility. Compared to a few moves ago, the position is more open, which is very beneficial for White's rooks. As only his own king limits their prospects, the brilliant 57. d7†!, abandoning another pawn for some more open lines, followed, after 57. ... Q×d7, by 58. Kg5! Kf7 59. Kh6! leaves Black without any winning plan at all. **57. ... Qf5† 58. Ke3 Qe5† 59. Kf3 Kd7 60. Rgf1 g5 61. h×g5 Q×g5 62. Rg1 Qf6† 63. Kg3 e5 64. Rgf1 Qe6 65. Kf3 Qc4** The immediate 65. ... h4, possible after Potter's last move, puts much more pressure on White's position. It takes Bird a bit longer to realize the same advance. **66. Rg1 Qf4† 67. Ke2 Qe4† 68. Kf2 Qh7 69. Ke3 h4 70. Rgf1 h3 71. Kf3 Qh4 72. Ke3 h2 73. Rf7† Ke8 74. Rff1** "It would have been bad play to advance the pawn 74. d7†, for the king could take the rook, and if 75. d8Q Q×d8 promote the h-pawn"—Steinitz. **74. ... Kd7 75. Rf7† Ke6 76. Rff1 Qh6† 77. Ke2?** Potter rates his chance to bring his king to the kingside, with 77. Kf2!, forcing Bird to submit to 77. ... Kd7 78. Kg2, and 79. Rf7 renders him counterplay in the form of the d-pawn. **77. ... Qh5†** Not optimal, as the king may still run to g2 after all. At once 77. ... Kd7 was most precise. **78. Ke3 Qg5† 79. Ke2 Qh5† 80. Ke3 Kd7 81. Kf2?!** No longer the right plan, as Bird's following move strongly demonstrates. 81. Ke4 and if 81. ... Qe2† 82. Kd5 may create some trouble for Black. **81. ... Qh3! 82. Ke2 Qb3!** "An excellent move, which leaves White only the choice between blocking out his rook with the king, as actually done, or else of getting into equal inconvenience by 83. Rh1. The two pawns on the queenside are now gained without loss of time, and Black remains well guarded against any counterattack of the adverse rooks"—Steinitz. **83. Kf2** "He had nothing better. 83. Rd2 would have lost, on account of 83. ... Qc4†, followed either by 84. ... Q×f1† and 85. ... h1Q or else by 84. ... e4 if 84. Rd3. For a similar reason the White rook from f1 could not move upwards, as Black would capture 83. ... Q×d1†, and if 83. Rh1 e4 84. R×h2 Qf3† 85. Ke1 (if 85. Kd2 Qf4† wins) 85. ... Qg3† 86. Rf2 e3 and wins"—Steinitz. **83. ... Q×a3 84. Kg2 Q×b4 85. K×h2** "That pawn need not have caused White any anxiety, and it was preferable even to leave it on the board as a protection for the king in some possible contingency. He had an easier fight for a draw by 85. Rf7†, and then to withdraw the same rook to f1. If Black afterwards checked with 86. ... Qb2†, the king would retreat to h1 behind the pawn, and then the advance of White's pawn one step further, or else a draw by checking with 88. Rf7 (in case of 87. ... Kd7) could be secured. With proper play Black would, however, keep the adverse king exposed by advancing the a-pawn, queening before commencing to give the checks"—Steinitz. **85. ... Qc4 86. Kg3 b4 87. Rh1 Qf4† 88. Kg2 Qf7 89. Rhf1 Qg6† 90. Kf3 b3 91. Ke3 a5 92. Rg1 Qh6† 93. Kd3 Kc6?** Bird suddenly abandons the winning plan: advancing the queenside pawns while giving checks to post his queen ideally. Here 93. ... Qh3†! wins in a few moves: 94. Ke4 Qh7† 95. K×e5 b2 96. Rh1 Qc2. **94. d7** "White has defended the latter part of this ticklish endgame remarkably well, but here he suffers again from over anxiety. He could have well kept his d-pawn by 94. Kc3, and if then Black carried out his apparent object of bringing up the king, he ran great danger of losing, e.g. 94. ... Qe3† 95. Kb2 Kb5 (95. ... a4 96. d7 Qe2† 97. Ka3 Kc5 98. Rd5† and wins) 96. d7 Kb4 97. Rg2 and wins"—Steinitz. Steinitz' move is a substantial improvement. With the loss of time on Black's last move, White's king is just in time to neutralize the two dangerous pawns on the queenside. However, there are some reinforcements that allow Bird to keep at least a draw: both 94. ... Kd7 and 95. ... Qf2† will do that job. **94. ... K×d7 95. Kc3† Kc6 96. K×b3 Qf4 97. Rc1† Kb5 98. Rb1 a4† 99. Ka3† Ka5 100. Rgc1 Qf8† 101. Ka2 Qf7† 102. Ka3 Qe7† 103. Ka2 e4 104. Kb2 Qb4† 105. Ka2 Qd2† 106. Ka1 Qd4† 107. Ka2 Qd5† 108. Ka3 Qd6† 109. Kb2 e3 110. Kc3** "He selects obstructing his rook to run after a pawn, which could never reach the eighth square as long as the two rooks guarded the row, while in pursuance of this plan he actually gives greater freedom to the more dangerous adverse a-pawn and king. He had a sure and easy draw if he moved his king alternately to a2 and a3, keeping his rook at b1, while the other rook moved simply at h1 and g1, only excepting to check when the adverse king tried to come nigh, and then to go back again"—Steinitz. **110. ... Qd2† 111. Kc4 e2 112. Rb5† Ka6 113. Rbb1 Qf4†** If 113. ... Qe3 (Steinitz), to keep the king off, 114. Rg1 a3 115. Rg7† draws. **114. Kd3 Qe5 115. Kc4 Qe4† 116. Kc3 Qe3† 117. Kc4** "Again he misses his opportunity of obtaining security by 117. Kb2. If he next withdrew his king to a2 or a3 he would prevent the adverse king from crossing, in accordance with the line of play indicated before."—Steinitz Black has a mate in two after 117. Kb2. **117. ... a3 118. Kb4 a2 119. Ra1 Qd2† 120. Kb3** "120. Ka4 was better. He ought to have stopped the hostile king as long as possible"—Steinitz. **120. ... Kb5 121. Rh1 Qb4† 122. Kc2** "Too timid. He could have taken the pawn safely: 122. K×a2 Ka4 123. Rae1 Qb3† 124. Ka1 Ka3 125. R×e2 Qc3† 126. Kb1 Qd3† (if 126. ... Qb4† 127. Ka1 Qd4† 128. Kb1 Qb6† 129. Ka1 Qf6† 130. Kb1 Qg6† 131. Rc2 is quite safe) 127. Rc2 Kb3 128. Rhc1"—Steinitz. **122. ... Qc4† 123. Kd2 Ka4 124. Rac1 Qb5 125. Rh4† Ka5 126. Rhh1 Qb2† 127. Kd3 Kb4 128. Rh4† Kb3 129. Rhh1 Qe5 130. Rhe1 Qb5† 131. Kd2 Ka4 132. Rh1 Qb2† 133. Kd3 Kb3 134. Rhg1 Qe5 135. Rh1 Qb5† 136. Kd2 Ka4 137. Rh4† Ka5 138. Rhh1 Qe5 139. Rhe1 Qe4 140. Kc3 Ka4** (see diagram)

**After 140. ... Ka4**

**141. Rh1?** "A fatal error. He ought always to have kept on attacking one of the pawns with the king, and therefore he should have moved 141. Kd2. The entrance of the adversary's king at b2 could have done him no harm, so long as he only took care to have both rooks on the first row, but neither of them at a1. One rook at e1 and the other at h1, while the king watched the pawn either at d2 or e3, would have still secured the draw"—Steinitz. **141. ... Qe3†**

**142. Kc2** "Even 142. Kc4 would not have saved the game, for the Black king could be worked up to b2, and then the queen could capture one rook at the first opportunity, which enabled him to queen one pawn and gain the other rook, and win with the remaining pawn"—Steinitz. **142. ... Qd4!** "A beautiful move which cuts off the adverse king and enables his next move safely to threaten mate at c3. Mr. Bird has played this wearisome ending with great patience, and the final combination is very ingenious"— Steinitz. **143. Rhe1 Kb4** White resigns—*The Field* (Steinitz), 3 May 1879.

# LÖWENTHAL TOURNAMENT 1879

In 1876 Johann Löwenthal, one of England's finest chess players died. The deceased had determined in his will that an annual income from the sum realized from his estate should be spent to the promotion of chess. In the *Westminster Chess Club Papers* of February 1878 (p. 174), the surviving trustee of the bequest, G.W. Medley informed the chess world that this sum was not enough to cover Löwenthal's liabilities. However, with other funds provided by Löwenthal's friends to support him, there was enough money to pay all costs and leave an amount of £274 to be spent. Medley declined any responsibility to manage the annual income ensuing from this nucleus and decided to invest parts of the money in concrete projects.

Medley's decision was rapidly taken under fire by Steinitz in his column in the *Figaro* of 20 February 1878. Steinitz thought it disrespectful that Löwenthal's will was so readily overruled by Medley.[11]

Medley nevertheless prevailed and during the following couple of years various initiatives were taken to keep the memory of Löwenthal alive. A problem tourney was held and Medley donated parts of the money to some London clubs, notably the St. George's and the City of London Chess Club. The various plans of the latter club were laid out in the column of *Land and Water* on 15 February 1879. One idea discussed was a consultation tournament with first-class players. In the end, subsequent to a proposal from Blackburne, a first-class tournament with five participants was decided upon. These five players, destined to meet each other once, were Blackburne, Bird, Mason, Potter and MacDonnell. Three small prizes were furnished for the occasion by the Löwenthal fund.

The tournament started towards the end of May. While the preparatory phase did not run smoothly the real problems began

11. Steinitz received support, of which he was probably never aware, from John Wisker in Australia. Wisker was a close friend of Löwenthal and thus well aware of the wishes of the deceased: "As to what Mr. Lowenthal's wishes were, there cannot be the slightest doubt. His will is a most explicit document. The plan was discussed between himself and the present writer before the will was drawn up, and frequently afterwards up to the time of Mr. Löwenthal's decease. The great chess player never hoped that the small sum he could leave would form a chess endowment; he intended the bequest as an example, the money as a nucleus round which an endowment would grow. His intentions have been flagrantly violated—to the great prejudice of chess. Remote as is this corner of the globe from the headquarters of chess-play, we cannot allow such a wrong to pass without a protest." *Brisbane Week*, 25 May 1878.

**Löwenthal tournament, London, 16 May–10 July 1879**

*Site:* City of London Chess Club
*Prizes:* 1st £3 3s, 2nd £2 2s., 3rd £1 1s.

|   |                | 1 | 2 | 3 | 4 |   |
|---|----------------|---|---|---|---|---|
| 1 | H.E. Bird      |   | 0 | 1 | 1 | 2 |
| 2 | J. Mason       | 1 |   | ½ | 0 | 1½ |
| 3 | J.H. Blackburne| 0 | ½ |   | 1 | 1½ |
| 4 | G.A. MacDonnell| 0 | 1 | 0 |   | 1 |
| 5 | W.N. Potter    |   | 0 | ½ |   |   |

...uring the game played between Mason and Potter. The latter overstepped the time limit but was allowed by Mason to continue. Blackburne objected and as a result Potter resigned from the tournament. Blackburne did the same and Potter even announced his retirement from chess altogether.

After some negotiations the tournament took a fresh start. Only four participants remained, as Potter stuck to his decision to forfeit the tournament. He kept on playing chess for a short while, finished his ongoing match with Mason, but then abandoned the game.

When the commotion was over and some more games played Bird was leading with two wins. In his final game Mason succeeded in beating him. Bird was still on top, but the final ranking depended on the result of the last game between Blackburne and Mason. Both players could catch up Bird with a win. It was quite symptomatic for this tournament that even this last game was disputed until the end. After hours of play an endgame was reached in which Mason had a rook and two pawns against a rook and one pawn for Blackburne. The latter claimed a draw but Mason refused and the game dragged on for several moves. Finally a draw could not be avoided.[12]

Bird celebrated his best result in thirty years of chess with his first place in a small but strong field. He earned £3 3s. with his performance.

**506) Bird–MacDonnell   1–0**

Löwenthal tournament
London, June 1879
*Game score missing*

**507) Bird–Blackburne   1–0**

Löwenthal tournament
London, 7 July 1879
*A02*

**1. f4 e5 2. f×e5 d6 3. e×d6 B×d6 4. Nf3 Nf6** "Just as good as the usual move 4. ... Nh6"—Zukertort. **5. d4 Ne4?!** A rare line. Much more critical is 5. ... Ng4. **6. Nc3 f5 7. Qd3 Qe7** Many years later, at Belfast in 1892, Blackburne tried the inferior 7. ... 0–0? against Bird. Though Bird was almost winning after

12. A fitting description for the tournament could be read in the leading Scottish newspaper: "I described the condition of the tourney some time ago as the maximum amount of confusion, capable of resulting from a single arrangement between five players. I am compelled to retract the statement, as an additional element of confusion has since intervened; but, as I have said, the tourney is now dead, and can do no more injury to reporters." *Glasgow Weekly Herald*, 19 July 1879.

8. N×e4 f×e4 9. Q×e4 Bf5? 10. Q×b7, he managed to lose the game. **8. Nb5** Pocketing the bishop pair, but he can do without and play 8. g3. In any case, Black hasn't enough for the pawn. **8. ... Nc6 9. N×d6† Q×d6?!** 9. ... c×d6 looks ugly but at least controls some important squares. **10. c3 0–0 11. g3 Re8** "If 11. ... Bd7 12. Bf4"—Zukertort. **12. Bg2 Qe7 13. 0–0 Nd6?!** Releasing White from any pressure he might have experienced. **14. Re1 Bd7 15. Bg5! Qf8 16. Bf4 Rad8 17. Ng5!** "White has developed his game well: he is a pawn ahead, has the better position, and now begins a promising attack"—Zukertort. **17. ... g6 18. B×d6 c×d6** "If 18. ... Q×d6, White wins the exchange with 19. Qc4†"—Zukertort. **19. Bd5† Kg7** (see diagram)

*After 19. ... Kg7*

**20. Qd2** "Instead of this preparatory move, White may also immediately advance the knight, when the game might proceed with 20. Nf7 Rc8 21. Qd2 Ne7 22. Qh6† Kf6 23. Qg5† Kg7 24. Bb3 d5 25. Ne5 Be6 26. Rf1 etc."—Zukertort. Playing 20. e4! at once favorably breaks open the position. **20. ... Ne7?** "20. ... Re7 was decidedly better. Mr. Blackburne does not conduct this game with his usual skill"—Zukertort. **21. Be6 Ng8 22. d5 Nf6 23. B×d7 R×d7 24. Ne6† R×e6 25. d×e6 Re7** "If 25. ... Rd8 White pursues the attack with 26. Qd4 Qe7 27. e4"—Zukertort. **26. Q×d6 Qe8 27. Rad1 R×e6 28. Qc7† Re7 29. Qd8 Qf7 30. Rd6** "The result is now obvious: neither side has any attack, and the bigger battalions must win"—Zukertort. **30. ... Re8 31. Qa5 b6 32. Qb5 Qe7 33. Qd3 Qf7 34. c4 Re7 35. Rd1 h5 36. Qc3 Rc7 37. b3 Qe7 38. Qd4 Kf7 39. b4 g5 40. c5 b×c5 41. b×c5 Ne4 42. Qd5† Kg7 43. Rd7 R×d7 44. Q×d7 Kf6 45. Q×e7† K×e7 46. c6** Black resigns. A very decent performance by Bird—*Chess Monthly* (Zukertort), October 1879, pp. 43–44.

**(508) Mason–Bird   1–0**

Löwenthal tournament (round 3)
London, 8 July 1879
*C14*

**1. e4 e6 2. d4 d5 3. Nc3 Nf6 4. Bg5 Be7 5. e5 Nfd7 6. B×e7 Q×e7 7. Qd2 a6 8. Nd1 c5 9. c3 Nc6 10. Nf3 f6 11. e×f6 N×f6 12. Bd3 e5 13. d×e5 N×e5 14. N×e5 Q×e5† 15. Qe3 Ng4 16. Q×e5† N×e5 17. Kd2 0–0 18. f3 Bf5 19. B×f5 Nc4† 20. Kc2 R×f5 21. Re1 Rd8 22. Ne3 N×e3† 23. R×e3 Kf7 24. Rae1 Rd7 25. Re5 R×e5 26. R×e5 b6 27. b4 c4 28. Kd2 d4 29. c×d4 R×d4† 30. Kc3 Rd3† 31. K×c4 Rd2 32. a4 R×g2 33. Rh5 h6 34. a5 Rc2† 35. Kb3 Rc6 36. b5 a×b5 37. a6 Kg6 38. R×b5 Rf6 39. a7 R×f3† 40. Ka2 Rf8 41. R×b6†** and White wins—*Illustrated Sporting and Dramatic News*, 19 July 1879.

# Match with Blackburne 1879

Bird's fine result in the Löwenthal tourney soon resulted in match negotiations with Blackburne, although both players refused to speak of a match, and described it as a "small private affair."[13]

The leisurely affair between Bird and Blackburne was quickly arranged and prize money was offered by some amateurs. Two-thirds of the amount was preserved for the first player to win five games, the loser getting the remaining third. The first game was played on Saturday 19 July. Bird confirmed his good form with an initial victory. In the following week Blackburne took the lead with two wins. The struggle remained very tense and after six games Blackburne maintained a narrow lead (+3 −2 =1). He brought the match to an end on 29 July after winning two more games in a row.

In a reaction to the publication of the result in *Chess Monthly*, Bird furnished the October edition of that magazine (p. 36) with a letter in which he claimed that more games had been contested and that the score stood about equal in the end. Bird therefore challenged Blackburne to play another match but perhaps due to Blackburne's obligations in the provinces no quick arrangements could be made.

| Match with Blackburne, 19–29 July 1879 | | | | | | | | | |
|---|---|---|---|---|---|---|---|---|---|
| | 1 | 2 | 3 | 4 | 5 | 6 | 7 | 8 | |
| J.H. Blackburne | 0 | 1 | 1 | | | | 1 | 1 | 5 |
| H.E. Bird | 1 | 0 | 0 | | | | 0 | 0 | 2 |
| games 4–6: Each player won once, one game ended in a draw | | | | | | | | | |

# Offhand Chess 1879–1880

Bird's commitment to chess during the 1879-80 season was comparable with the previous year. He maintained Simpson's Divan as his playing basis but was also present at several important events that occurred in London. Bird took part in just one official tournament, the handicap tournament of the Counties Chess Association in Boston in January 1880.

## (509) Boden–Bird   1–0
Offhand game
London (Simpson's Divan) 1879 (?)
C65

This game was published without any mention of date. It may have been played in 1879, but more likely it took place sooner, as

13.  MacDonnell reacted in his usual arch way: "I referred last week to a friendly fight which had been fought at the Divan, and finished in about ten days, between Messrs. Bird and Blackburne, in which the latter was victorious. I called the second contest a little match, but I am told that I was wrong in so designating it, inasmuch as it was only 'a small private affair.' Well, what's in a name? so let it be called as desired; albeit, it was played in a public room, and was got up as a special test of strength by the admirers of the respective masters. In justice to Mr. Bird, I must state that there was no time limit, and the non-use of it was undoubtedly favorable to Mr. Blackburne, who generally consumes about twice as much time in a match game as Mr. Bird does—not because he is less quick of perception, but because he is deeper in combination." *Illustrated Sporting and Dramatic News*, 9 August 1879.

various sources reported that Boden abstained from chess durin[g] the last years of his life.

**1. e4 e5 2. Nf3 Nc6 3. Bb5 Nf6 4. d4 N×d4 5. N×d4 e×d**[4] **6. e5 Nd5 7. 0-0 Bc5 8. c3 0-0 9. c×d4 Be7 10. Bd3 g6 11. Bh**[6] **Re8 12. Bc4 Nb6 13. B×f7† K×f7 14. Qb3† d5 15. e×d6†** *e.p.* **Be6 16. d×e7 Q×e7 17. Qf3† Kg8 18. Nc3 Qh4 19. Be3 c**[6] **20. Qg3 Q×g3 21. h×g3 Nd5 22. Rae1 N×e3 23. f×e3 Bc**[5] **24. Rf4 Bd5** "and eventually White's skillful manipulation of hi[s] central pawns enabled him to win"—*Illustrated Sporting and Dra-matic News*, 13 September 1879.

Bird suffered a painful loss in an offhand game against D[r] William Robert Ballard. He defended himself against the Bishop['s] Gambit with his own, somewhat dubious, system. His opponent[,] quite a strong amateur, succeeded in completely tearing apart Bird['s] set-up in a beautiful game.

## (510) Ballard–Bird   1–0
Offhand game
London (Simpson's Divan), July 1879
C33

**1. e4 e5 2. f4 e×f4 3. Bc4 Qh4† 4. Kf1 d6** "A very old continu[u]ation, which was advocated in modern times by L. Paulsen"—Zuk[-]ertort. **5. Nf3 Qh5 6. d4 g5 7. Nc3 Ne7 8. h4 f6** "This constitute[s] Mr. Bird's defense. 8. ... h6 is usually played at this juncture"—Zuk[-]ertort. **9. e5!** "Mr. Bird gives here two other variations, beginnin[g] with 9. Kg1 and 9. Be2 respectively. The text move is much stronge[r] than either of the two others"—Zukertort. **9. ... Bg7?** "Given b[y] the author of the defense as best"—Zukertort. Bird kept on playin[g] the text move, although 9. ... g4! is by far preferable. **10. Nb5!** I[n] *Chess Openings* (p. 128) Bird mainly analyzed 10. Ne4 (as playe[d] against him by Perrin in New York), but White's initiative come[s] soon to an end in that case—for example, 10. ... f×e5! 11. d×e5 d×e[5] 12. Ne×g5 Rf8 etc. **10. ... Na6** Black's position is already lost, th[e] text move just hastens matters. 10. ... d5 is perhaps his best optio[n] even though his chances are slim after the simple 11. e×f6 B×f[6] 12. N×c7† and 13. N×d5. **11. e×d6 g4** *(see diagram)*

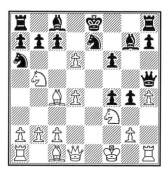

*After 11. ... g4*

**12. Qe1!** "A splendid coup: White carries now, in a most vigorou[s] style, the position of his formidable opponent. The move threaten[s] the hostile king, and cuts off the eventual retreat of the Black quee[n] to a5"—Zukertort. **12. ... c×d6 13. N×d6† Kf8 14. Bf7! Qh**[6] **15. g3! g×f3** "Preferring a desperate but short struggle to a lingerin[g] death. After 15. ... f5 16. B×f4 Qf6 17. Ne5, or 17. Be5 Qh6 18. Ng5 Black's game is hopelessly cramped"—Zukertort. **16. B×f4 Bg4**

7. B×h6 B×h6 18. Qe4! Rd8 19. Re1 Nc6 20. Q×g4 R×d6
21. Re8† K×f7 22. R×h8 R×d4 23. R×h7† Ke8 "If 23. ... Kf8
24. Qg6"—Zukertort. 24. Qg6† Black resigns—*Chess Monthly*
(Zukertort), January 1880, pp. 147–148.

In August the Divan saw a young and promising player from
Southampton try his hand against Bird.

### (511) Blake–Bird   0–1
Offhand game
London (Simpson's Divan), 18 August 1879
C61

"This smart skirmish was played 18th August 1879, at Simpson's
Divan, between the leading Southampton amateur and Mr. Bird"—
Marks.

1. e4 e5 2. Nf3 Nc6 3. Bb5 Nd4 "Mr. Bird's partiality for this
defense is well known; notwithstanding 'the books' look askance
at"—Marks 4. N×d4 e×d4 5. d3 h5 "This bizarre-looking move is
an essential part of Mr. Bird's scheme of defense"—Marks. 6. Bc4
Bc5 7. Qf3 Qe7 8. 0-0 c6 9. Qg3 Kf8 10. f4 "Premature; better
first to develop his game on the queenside"—Marks. 10. ... Nf6
11. e5 Ng4 12. Kh1 This move poses no problems at all to Bird.
12. Re1 makes more sense. 12. ... d5! 13. e×d6 *e.p.* B×d6 14. h3
Nf6 Bird could force a slightly better endgame after 14. ... Qe2
15. Kg1 Ne3 16. B×e3 Q×e3† 17. Q×e3 d×e3 18. Nc3 Bf5. The text
move enhances White's liberty, but the margin of errors also widens.
15. Re1 It is better to keep the f-pawn well defended. 15. ... Qc7
16. Qg5? "Overlooking Black's rejoinder—Marks. After 16. Qf2,
there is nothing big going on. The vulnerability of White's f-pawn
becomes apparent after Bird's excellent reply. 16. ... h4! 17. f5 Rh5
18. Qd2 B×f5 19. c3 "Too late to be of any use." 19. ... Bg3 20. Rf1
Qd7 21. c×d4 B×h3 22. g×h3 Q×h3† 23. Kg1 Rg5 and Black
wins. "The termination is played with Mr. Bird's usual dash"—
Marks. *North Middlesex Magazine* (Marks), September 1879, p. 65.

The following game probably occurred more than once in Bird's
career. Bird included it in his column in the *Sheffield and Rotherham Independent* of 2 December 1882, stating that the game
was played on 12 October 1881 against C. Sfander. In *Modern
Chess* (p. 12), Black's name is given as C. Kauder, with 1882 as
year in which the game was played. Finally, in a biographical article on Bird that appeared in the March 1889 edition of *Chess
Monthly* (p. 206), the player behind the Black pieces was named C.
Pfander.

### (512) Bird–E.J. Taylor   1–0
Offhand game
London (Simpson's Divan), 24 September 1879
*Odds of Ra1*

1. e4 e5 2. f4 e×f4 3. Nf3 g5 4. h4 g4 5. Ng5 h5 6. Bc4 Nh6
7. d4 f6 8. B×f4 f×g5 9. h×g5 Nf7 10. g6 Ng5 11. Qd2 N×e4
12. Bf7† Ke7 13. Nc3 Another version can occasionally be seen:
13. Bg5† N×g5 14. Q×g5† Kd6 15. Qc5 mates. 13. ... N×d2
14. Nd5 mate—*Chess Monthly*, November 1879, p. 83.

### (513) Steel–Bird   1–0
Offhand game
London (Simpson's Divan) 1879
C33

1. e4 e5 2. f4 e×f4 3. Bc4 Qh4† 4. Kf1 d6 5. Nc3 g5 6. Nf3
Qh5 7. d4 Ne7 8. h4 f6 9. e5 Bg7 10. e×d6 c×d6 11. Nb5 g4
12. N×d6† Kd7 13. Bf7 Qa5 14. B×f4 g×f3 15. Q×f3 f5 16. Qe2
Nbc6 17. Qe6† Kd8 18. N×b7† B×b7 19. Qd6† Kc8 20. Be6
mate—*Liverpool Chess Club, Book of Games*, vol. 2.

On 25 October 1879 the *Glasgow Weekly Herald* reported that
a series of offhand games had recently been played between Bird
and Zukertort. The latter had won the majority.

A month earlier, the first edition of a new magazine, *Chess
Monthly*, had appeared. The driving forces behind this valuable addition to British chess were Zukertort, who mainly took care of the
game analysis, and Leopold Hoffer. Hoffer was well known in chess
circles since his arrival in London in 1870 but his role increased
rapidly in the decade to come, and he soon became a pivotal figure.
In the following charming game Hoffer was Bird's antagonist. The
game was probably played toward the end of 1879 or during the
first months of 1880.

### (514) Bird–Hoffer   0–1
Offhand game
London (Simpson's Divan) 1880 (?)
C51

1. e4 e5 2. Nf3 Nc6 3. Bc4 Bc5 4. b4 B×b4 5. c3 Bc5 6. d4
e×d4 7. 0-0 d6 8. c×d4 Bb6 9. d5 Na5 10. Bb2 Ne7 11. Bd3 0-0
12. Nc3 Ng6 13. Qd2 f6 14. Ne2 c5 15. Rac1 Rb8 16. Nf4 Ne5
17. N×e5 f×e5 18. Nh5 Qh4 19. Ng3 Rf6 20. Nf5 B×f5 21. e×f5
c4 22. Bb1 Rbf8 23. Bc3 Rh6 24. h3 Qg3 25. B×a5 R×h3
26. Rfe1 Rh2 27. Be4 Qh4 28. Kf1 Rh1† 29. Ke2 Q×e4† 30. Kd1
R×e1† 31. Q×e1 Q×d5† 32. Bd2 Ba5 White resigns—*Chess
Monthly*, March 1880, pp. 209–210.

On 1 May 1879 the members of the late West End Chess Club
met at Mephisto's Chess Rooms to sort out the balance sheets. It
turned out that a small surplus of £12 was left. It was agreed to invest
this money in a handicap tournament. The games were first played
at the Mephisto's Rooms, which was run by Gümpel, but soon afterwards at Monico's Restaurant. It was here, on 6 March 1880, that
the very last act in the history of the West End Chess Club was written.

On this day, garnered with a dinner, the prizes of the handicap
tournament were distributed (F.W. Lord had won it, ahead of
Minchin and Hoffer). Among the 25 guests were six of the strongest
London chess masters, including Bird. At the end of the evening
an alternation game between these six was held. Steinitz, Hirschfeld
and Mason alternated the moves from the White side. Zukertort,
Bird and Hoffer opposed them in the given order. Mason was responsible for an odd opening choice which had already sown the
germ of defeat. After a spectacular game the Black party succeeded
in winning.

## (515) Steinitz & P. Hirschfeld & Mason– Zukertort & Bird & Hoffer    0–1

Consultation game
London, 6 March 1880
*C33*

"Played on the 6th of March 1880, after the dinner of the West-End Club, at Monico's. The six players moving alternately in the order given and not consulting"—Zukertort.

**1. e4 e5 2. f4 e×f4 3. d4?!** "The following skirmish is certainly not a sample of first-class skill, but rather a lively specimen of after-dinner play with all its unexpected incidents and accidents. The variation chosen by Mr. Mason is a very old form of the King's Gambit. It flourished in Italy at the period which preceded the invention of castling. Zukertort introduced it in modern times, and one of his revivals of this opening (against J.O. Howard Taylor) was published in the chess column of the *Illustrated London News* in 1873"—Zukertort. **3. ... d5** 3. ... Qh4† 4. Ke2 and now 4. ... Qe7 or 4. ... Nf6 are very good. The text move is not critical. **4. e×d5 Qh4† 5. Ke2 Bd6 6. c4 c5 7. Nf3 Bg4 8. Nc3 Na6** "8. ... Nd7 was preferable"—Zukertort. **9. Ne4!** "Apparently a blunder: the move, however, should lead after a series of exchanges to about an even game"—Zukertort. **9. ... Qe7 10. Kf2 Q×e4 11. Bd3 B×f3** "After 11. ... Q×d4† 12. N×d4 B×d1 13. Nb5! Be5 14. R×d1 Ne7, White has some advantage of position while Black is a pawn ahead"—Zukertort. **12. Qa4† Kf8?** "A grave error which should prove fatal: the king should be played to d8"—Zukertort. **13. B×e4 B×e4 14. Re1?** "White's only road to victory was to pursue an immediate attack, without giving the opponents time to develop their forces. The right continuation was: 14. Qd7 Bc7 15. d×c5 (but not 15. d6 Bc6) 15. ... Rd8 (or 15. ... Nf6) 16. Qb5 etc."—Zukertort. After 15. d×c5 Nf6! Black escapes from the worst as there is a fascinating drawing line: 16. Qb5 Ng4† 17. Kf1 Bd3† 18. Ke1 Re8† 19. Kd2 Re3! 20. d6 Bd8 21. c6 Nf2 22. c7 Ne4†. Better is 15. d6 and if 15. ... Bc6 16. Qf5! B×d6 17. B×f4 and the opening of lines turns out to be in White's favor. Black can also play 15. ... Bb6, but White retains an edge with 16. d5 Nb4 17. B×f4 N×d3. **14. ... Nf6 15. Bd2 g5** First 15. ... c×d4 seems better, as White could now improve the position of their bishop with 16. Bc3. **16. b4 c×d4 17. c5 Be5 18. Qa3?** "Certainly a weak move: White would, however, not obtain a winning advantage by 18. c6, as contended by the two other partners; e.g., 18. ... Nc7 19. c×b7 Rb8 20. Q×a7 Nc×d5 21. Rac1 Ne3! 22. h3 (it is evident that after 22. Qc5† Kg7, White dare not take the bishop. The position is of extreme interest: Black threatened to carry the game by immediate assault. Should White play for instance 22. Rc8†, Black would win offhand after 22. ... Kg7 23. R×h8, with 23. ... Nfg4† 24. Kg1 f3!) 22. ... Kg7 23. Rc5 R×b7 24. Qa5 Bd5"—Zukertort. 18. d6 is an alternative, but in each scenario Black is setting the pace. **18. ... Ng4†** "The opponent does not fail to follow suit and makes to a weak move a still weaker reply; he should proceed with 18. ... Nc7, which gave Black the superiority"—Zukertort. **19. Kg1 Ne3 20. B×e3?!** "Why not at once 20. c6? Black dare not reply 20. ... Nc2 21. Qa4 N×e1 22. R×e1 f5 23. c×b7, winning a piece or 20. ... Nc4 21. Qa4 N×d2 22. c×b7 Rb8 23. Q×a6 d3 24. Rad1 and Black cannot avoid serious loss. The text move renders Black's bishops all-powerful"—Zukertort. Both 20. ... Nc2 and

20. ... Nc4 lose on the spot after 21. c×b7. Instead 20. ... Nc7! i[s] strong, as it realizes a perfect coordination between all his pieces e.g., after 21. c×b7 Rb8 22. Q×a7 Kg7. **20. ... d×e3** 20. ... f×e3 i[s] perhaps even better. **21. b5 Nc7 22. c6† Kg7** *(see diagram)*

*After 22. ... Kg7*

**23. Qe7?** "This and the next move lead to rapid ruin. Black woul[d] obtain the superior game in any case; e.g., 23. c×b7 Rab8 24. Q×a7 N×b5 25. Qb6 Nd6 26. Rad1 R×b7 etc."—Zukertort. A final at[-] tempt to mix up matters is 23. d6. The ensuing complications are hair-raising, but generally speaking Black, despite having to fight the queen with but few active pieces, can make life extremely difficult for the White allies. Besides 23. ... B×a1 24. R×a1 Nd5! which is perhaps the best continuation, there is this fascinating line 23. ... N×b5 24. Qc5 Bf6! 25. c×b7 (in case of 25. Q×b5 B×c6, the bishops and pawns are much superior to the opposing queen) and now 25. ... Rad8. In case of White's being greedy with 26. Q×b5 there follows 26. ... R×d6! 27. Rad1 (27. b8Q loses after 27. ... R×b8 28. Q×b8 Rd2! 29. Q×a7 R×g2† 30. Kf1 R×h2 31. R×e3 f×e3 32. Q×e3 Rh1† 33. Kf2 R×a1 34. Q×e4 R×a2†) and now after 27. ... Rb6 28. Qc4 B×b7 29. Rd7 Rf8 and White will have a tough time ahead in defending this position. **23. ... Rhe8 24. Q×g5† Kh8 25. d6 f6! 26. Qh4 N×b5 27. d7 Rg8 28. a4** "Preferring the fire to the frying-pan. 28. g3 Nd4 would prolong the contest a little"—Zukertort. **28. ... B×g2** "Shorter, but more likely to lead to accidents, was 28. ... R×g2† 29. Kf1 Rag8, and White cannot escape a forced mate in a few moves"—Zukertort. **29. a×b5 B×c6† 30. Kf1 B×b5† 31. Re2 f3 32. Raa2 f×e2†** "Extremely mean: 32. ... f2 would save all further trouble"—Zukertort. **33. R×e2 Rad8 34. Qb4 B×e2†** Black can deliver a quick mate after 34. ... B×h2. **35. K×e2 R×d7 36. h4** "Playing for the last resource worthy of the occasion: a stalemate"—Zukertort. **36. ... Bd4 37. h5 f5 38. h6 f4 39. Kf3 Re8 40. Ke2 f3† 41. Ke1 e2** and Black mates after a few more moves—*Chess Monthly* (Zukertort), April 1880, pp. 239–240.

Around the same time Bird and Philip Hirschfeld rattled out a series of offhand games from which Bird emerged victorious.[14]

The major event of the spring was a match held in London between Zukertort and Rosenthal, the French champion. Rosenthal arrived in the British capital in the last week of April and was immediately entertained with a dinner at the City of London Chess Club. Bird was one of the many prominent guests at this dinner but subsequent complications made him follow this match from a distance. The contemporary press omitted to make any mention of this, but Bird enlightened the chess world in his pamphlet written at the end of the year.

14. *Canadian Illustrated News*, 22 May 1880.

# ANOTHER MATCH WITH BLACKBURNE 1879–1880

At the end of 1879 Bird and Blackburne agreed to play a small thematic match of three games at the Divan. Bird backed himself for a small stake, betting that he would score at least two to one while conducting the Black pieces against the Evans Gambit. In *Modern Chess* (p. 128) Bird claimed to have made friendly challenges for such a thematic match to Steinitz and Zukertort as well but only Blackburne accepted the offer. Blackburne withdrew from the match after two games, "to the regret of his backer as well as myself" (*Modern Chess*, p. 145). What Bird did not mention was that the sudden and tragic demise of Blackburne's wife caused this withdrawal.

The first game of the match, a draw, has become a classic. Steinitz analyzed it in depth and did not spare his praise of Bird's play. Bird managed to win the second game but Blackburne's play was not very convincing.

| Match with Blackburne, 27 December 1879–6 January 1880 | | | |
|---|---|---|---|
| | **1** | **2** | |
| H.E. Bird | ½ | 1 | 1½ |
| J.H. Blackburne | ½ | 0 | ½ |

**(516) Blackburne–Bird** ½–½
Match (game 1)
London, 27 December 1879
C51

**1. e4 e5 2. Nf3 Nc6 3. Bc4 Bc5 4. b4 B×b4 5. c3 Bc5 6. 0-0 d6 7. d4 e×d4 8. c×d4 Bb6 9. d5 Na5 10. Bb2 Ne7 11. Bd3 f6** "The best critics recommend the delay of this move as long as possible, and the progress of this game bears out their misgivings respecting its early adoption"—Steinitz. **12. Nh4** "The game takes already an unusual turn, and there is no precedent or book analysis to guide the action of the players. The position is original, and all the more interesting in consequence"—Steinitz. **12. ... 0-0 13. Nd2** "Better than the routine 13. Kh1, with the intention of advancing 14. f4, whereupon the game might have proceeded thus: 13. ... Ng6 14. N×g6 (best, for if 14. Nf5 Black might also reply 14. ... Nf4) 14. ... h×g6 15. f4 f5 with a good game"—Steinitz. **13. ... Ng6** "We think that advancing the c-pawn one or two squares deserved more consideration, for, if White attempted any attack by 14. Qh5, Black's queen could oppose at e8"—Steinitz. **14. N×g6 h×g6 15. Nf3 g5 16. Rc1 Bg4 17. Be2** "White loses all advantage by this untimely retreat. 17. h3 was the right move, for Black could not afford to exchange and let the hostile queen come in at f3, and, if 17. ... Bh5 18. g4 drives him back to g6. White might afterwards move 19. Kg2, and then proceed with the attack by h4, or else by f4, after retreating the knight to d2 in case his e-pawn required defense"—Steinitz. After 19. Kg2, Black is not worse; if 19. ... Re8 20. Nd2 c6. **17. ... Re8 18. Qc2 c6** "Black had a good game, and, we believe, might have made more of it at this point by 18. ... Qe7, attacking the

e-pawn. If 19. Bd3 B×f3 20. g×f3 Kf7 and 21. ... Rh8, with a good attack against the adverse kingside"—Steinitz. **19. d×c6** "Sooner than liberate the adverse knight, we should have been inclined to give up another pawn for the attack, in the following manner: 19. Nd4 B×d4 (best. If 19. ... B×e2 20. N×e2 and 21. Ng3) 20. B×g4 B×b2 21. Q×b2 R×e4 22. Be6† Kf8 (if 22. ... Kh8 23. Qc2, forcing 23. ... Rh4 [for otherwise 24. Qg6 would follow] and then 24. Rfe1, followed by doubling the rooks on the e-file with a dangerous attack) 23. Rfe1 Re5 (he cannot afford 23. ... R×e1† for the hostile queen would afterwards enter on the h-file) 24. R×e5 f×e5 (best; if 24. ... d×e5 25. Qa3† Ke8 26. d6) 25. Rc3 etc."—Steinitz. Steinitz' variation can be improved on several points. First of all, 19. ... B×e2! is his best chance for a small edge: 20. N×e2 c×d5 21. e×d5 Rc8 and there is no trace of an attack for White. In case of 19. ... B×d4, Steinitz' analysis becomes flawed when he suggests 23. ... Re5?. Much better is 23. ... c×d5 24. B×d5 R×e1† 25. R×e1 Qd7, when White has compensation for his offered pawns, but that's it. **19. ... N×c6 20. Rfd1** "For the purpose of strengthening the coming sacrifice, which at present could be easily refuted, for if now 20. N×g5 B×e2 21. Qb3† d5"—Steinitz. **20. ... Qe7** *(see diagram)* This move looks solid enough, but it gives White the chance to execute a dangerous sacrifice. 20. ... Rc8! is safer.

**21. N×g5!** "Very bold, but he was almost bound to play a hazardous game. The sacrifice was not much better now than before"—Steinitz. **21. ... f×g5?!** "He ought to have played 21. ... B×e2 and

**Joseph H. Blackburne (*Chess Monthly*).**

*After 20. ... Qe7*

the game might have proceeded thus: 22. Qb3† d5 23. Q×d5† (if 23. R×d5 then 23. ... f×g5, for White can afterwards do no better than 24. R×g5† [otherwise the queen would interpose accordingly at e6 or f7], and then 24. ... Kh8, and comes out ultimately with four pieces for the queen) 23. ... Kh8 24. Qf5 f×g5 25. Rd7 Qe6 26. B×g7† Kg8 27. Q×g5 Q×d7 28. Bf6† Kf7 and escapes at e6 with a winning game"—Steinitz. Steinitz is correct in suggesting 21. ... B×e2 as the better move, but it only gives a draw after 24. Nf7† (instead of 24. Qf5?) 24. ... Kh7 25. Qf5† Kg8 26. Nh6† Kh8 (26. ... g×h6? 27. Rd7 loses) 27. Rd7 Qe6 28. Nf7† with a perpetual. Steinitz' sideline, 23. R×d5, is instantly refuted by 23. ... Qb4! **22. B×g4 Q×e4 23. Qb3† Kh8 24. Qh3† Kg8 25. Bf5?!** After a few forced moves, Blackburne faced the very difficult choice of finding the best continuation for the attack. Instead of 25. Bf5?!, which allows Bird to interpose the queen, he can play 25. Bf3, but strongest is the silent move 25. Kh1! White has no worries about f2 anymore and can carelessly play for an attack; e.g., 25. ... Re7 26. Bf5 Qh4 27. Qb3† Kh8 28. R×d6 or 25. ... d5 26. Bf5 Qh4 27. Qb3 Kh8 28. R×d5. **25. ... Qh4 26. Qb3† Kh8 27. Qf7?!** "We believe he would have had a better prospect of succeeding with his attack if he had now provided a loophole for his king by 27. g3, forcing 27. ... Qh6. It was of no use for Black in that case to answer 27. ... B×f2† for if then 28. Kg2"—Steinitz. 27. g3 allows 27. ... B×f2†!, and then 28. Kg2 Qh6 29. Qf3 Bc5. The position remains very dangerous for Black, but with correct play he should be able to survive: 30. R×c5! d×c5 31. Rd6 Re2† etc. 27. Kh1 is still the best move, but now Black has gained some valuable time to play 27. ... g4!, and if 28. R×d6 Nd4. Yet White is still clearly better. **27. ... Ne5 28. B×e5 R×e5 29. Bc8 Qf4 30. Q×b7** *(see diagram)*

*After 30. Q×b7*

**30. ... g4!** "A most ingenious trap, and a splendid resource. He actually puts his opponent on the defensive in such a position; for he threatens now, in case of 31. Q×a8 B×f2† 31. Kh1 Q×h2†"—Steinitz. **31. Rc2** 31. Rf1 (Steinitz) loses after 31. ... B×f2†, and if 32. Kh1 Q×h2†. **31. ... Qb4 32. g3** "He could hope

for no more than a draw by 32. Rf1 Re1 33. Rc1 (best; 33. Q×a8 R×f1† wins) 33. ... B×f2† 34. K×f2 (if 34. Kh1 Q×b7 35. B×b7 R×f1† 36. R×f1) 34. ... Qf4† 35. K×e1 (best; if 35. Kg1 Qe3† and 36. ... Q×c1) 35. ... Qe3†, followed by 36. ... Qd3† with a draw. But we think he would have retained at least the best of the game if he had now advanced 32. h3; e.g., 32. ... Re1† 33. Kh2 g3† 34. K×g3 and if now 34. ... R×d1 White may safely play 35. Q×a8"—Steinitz. 32. h3? is a very misplaced try to play for a win for he is lost after 32. ... g3! 33. Rf1 B×f2† 34. Kh1 Re1 35. Rc×f2 g×f2 36. Q×b4 R×f1† etc. **32. ... Rb8** "Such fine play has not been recorded since the Paris tournament, and we almost doubt whether even that great congress produced any specimen of chess skill so full and beautiful and spirited combinations as this. Of course he gives up the rook, not with the intention of winning the queen, as will be seen, but with the object of securing a draw"—Steinitz. **33. Q×b8 Re1** "He could not take the f-pawn, or else he would have lost thus: 33. ... B×f2† 34. R×f2 Q×b8 35. Rf8† Kh7 36. Bf5†"—Steinitz. **34. R×e1 Q×e1† 35. Kg2 Qe4† 36. Kf1 Qh1† 37. Ke2 Qf3† 38. Kd2 Q×f2† 39. Kc3 Qc5† 40. Kd2** "He would have lost if he had played the king on the b-file because of 40. ... Qb5†, followed by a discovered check"—Steinitz. **40. ... Qb4† 41. Kd3 Qd4† 42. Ke2 Qf2† 43. Kd3 Qd4† 44. Ke2** draw. "The game is a beautiful masterpiece, and especially Mr. Bird's play deserves the highest recommendation"—Steinitz. *The Field* (Steinitz), 3 January 1880.

### (517) Blackburne–Bird    0–1
Match (game 2)
London, 6 January 1880
*C51*

"The following game was played on Jan. 6, 1880, in a short match of the best out of three Evans Gambits. Mr. Bird won one game and one was drawn. The third was not played"—Hoffer.

**1. e4 e5 2. Nf3 Nc6 3. Bc4 Bc5 4. b4 B×b4 5. c3 Bc5 6. d4 e×d4 7. c×d4 Bb6 8. 0–0 d6 9. a4** "An inferior move at this stage. It is occasionally played when the odds of the knight is given. Mr. Blackburne tried it as an experiment, but never resorted to it again"—Hoffer. **9. ... Bg4** "Undoubtedly the best reply. It shows conclusively the weakness of White's previous move"—Hoffer. **10. Bb2** "10. Bb5 would seem to give White some prospects of an attack. Anyhow, complication may arise, whereas the text move makes it all plain sailing for Black"—Hoffer. **10. ... B×f3 11. g×f3?!** Though 11. Q×f3 Qf6 seems hardly promising, White has compensation after 12. Bb5 B×d4 13. B×d4 Q×d4 14. Nc3. **11. ... Qf6 12. e5 d×e5 13. d×e5 Qf4 14. Qe2?** Hoffer suggested 14. e6, to open some lines against Black's king, but White gets nothing at all after 14. ... f×e6 15. B×e6 Rd8. The only playable move is 14. Bb5!, keeping Black's knight out of the game. **14. ... Nd4! 15. B×d4 B×d4 16. Rd1 B×a1 17. e6 f5 18. Rd7 Be5 19. Qd3 Nf6 20. Nd2 Bd6 21. Rf7 0–0–0 22. Bb5 Q×h2† 23. Kf1 Bc5 24. Bd7† Kb8 25. Ke2 Q×f2† 26. Kd1 N×d7 27. e×d7 Qd4 28. Q×f5 Bb4** White resigns. "Obviously the queen must defend the knight, then Black would simply reply 29. ... R×d7 etc. The game is by no means a fair specimen of Mr. Blackburne's style, but Mr. Bird played very well"—Hoffer. *The Field* (Hoffer), 21 November 1885.

# A VISIT TO HORNCASTLE 1880

In January 1880 Bird was invited to the annual congress of the Counties Chess Association in Boston. First he visited the Rev. Skipworth in Horncastle. A series of games was played of which Bird won the majority. The most interesting game ended in a victory for Skipworth.

**(518) Bird–Skipworth    0–1**
Offhand game
Horncastle, January 1880
*A03*

**1. f4 e6 2. e3 c5 3. Nf3 a6 4. b3 Nc6 5. Bb2 Nf6 6. Be2 d5 7. 0–0 Bd6 8. Na3 0–0 9. c3 b6** "We prefer Black's game already; as usual in this opening, White's bishops remain shut in for some time, and he is ultimately compelled to weaken his e-pawn by the advance of the d-pawn. Advancing this pawn two steps appears to us, however, much stronger, for Black's game generally resolves itself in an attack on the queenside, and the move we recommend is more adapted for that purpose"—Steinitz. **10. Nc2 Qc7 11. d4 Bb7 12. Ne5 Ne4 13. Bd3 f5 14. B×e4 f×e4 15. Qg4 Rf5 16. c4 Raf8 17. c×d5 e×d5 18. Rac1 Qe7 19. Rfd1 B×e5 20. d×e5 d4** *(see diagram)* "After this well-devised attack, which enables Black to fix a well-supported pawn at d3, Black's game becomes far superior"—Steinitz.

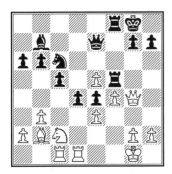

*After 20. ... d4*

**21. g3?** Bird ended up in a position that is more difficult to handle, but still far from hopeless. The surprising 21. B×d4! radically changes the nature of the game. After the forced 21. ... c×d4 22. N×d4 N×d4 23. R×d4, Black's pawn chain is a shambles. Against careless play White's pawns may easily outweigh their opponent's extra piece. **21. ... d3 22. Na3 b5** "It was necessary to shut out the adverse knight. 22. ... Bc8 was inferior, for White might have offered the exchange of queens at h4, and would afterwards rely on getting compensation on the queenside for his broken pawns on the kingside, by Nc4"—Steinitz. And yet, Black is winning after 22. ... Bc8 23. Qh4 Q×h4 24. g×h4 Nb4! for if 25. Nc4 N×a2 26. Ra1 Nb4 27. N×b6 Nc2. **23. Rd2 Nb4 24. Qh3 Ba8?!** "A deep laid scheme, but we believe faulty, as we propose to show. The proper play was 24. ... Nd5, which would have more effectually stopped the advance of the g-pawn; e.g., 25. g4 R×f4 26. e×f4 e3 27. R×d3 N×f4 28. Q×e3 (if 28. Qf1 e2) 28. ... Qh4, threatening 29. ... Nh3†, followed by 30. ... Qf2 mate, and also 29. ... Q×g4"—Steinitz. Steinitz' line is open for improvement, as 25. Re1 defends everything for the moment. Far simpler than the text move was the materialistic 24. ... N×a2. **25. g4 R×f4** "Only the natural and consistent outcome

of the previously conceived brilliant manoeuvre, which, however, turns out unsound in analysis"—Steinitz. **26. e×f4 e3?** It is the quiet 26. ... Nd5! that wins after 27. f5 Qg5 and the e-pawn will be pushed on the next move. **27. Q×e3 Qb7?** Now Black even ought to lose. After 27. ... Nd5! a forced line arises: 28. Qg3 N×f4 29. Rf1 Ne2† 30. R×e2 d×e2 31. R×f8† Q×f8 32. Qf2 e1Q†! 33. Q×e1 Qf3 34. Qd2 Qh1† and Black gives perpetual check. **28. Qg3??** "Very strange that both parties should have overlooked that 28. Rf1 would have completely broken Black's attack. If 28. ... Qh1†, the White king had a safe retreat at e1; and, after losing one or two unimportant pawns, White must have come out with a rook ahead, and if 28. ... Nd5, the answer was 29. Qe4"—Steinitz. **28. ... Qh1† 29. Kf2 R×f4†!** "Notwithstanding that the whole combination was faulty in the main, Mr. Skipworth may be proud at this elegant sacrifice, which demonstrates his opponent's error"—Steinitz. **30. Q×f4 Qg2† 31. Ke1 Qg1† 32. Qf1 Qe3† 33. Re2** "He retained no more chance by 33. Kd1, with the intention of giving up the queen for two rooks; e.g., 33. ... Bf3† 34. Q×f3 Q×f3† 35. Ke1 Qh1† 36. Kf2 Q×h2† 37. Ke3 (best) 37. ... Qg3† 38. Ke4 Q×g4† 39. Ke3 Qg5† and wins the rook"—Steinitz. **33. ... d×e2 34. Q×e2 Nd3† 35. Kf1 Qh3† 36. Kg1 Nf4** Black wins. "White was bound to guard the second row, and whether he went with the queen to f2, c2 or d2, his game was lost; e.g., 37. Qf2 Q×g4† 38. Kf1 (if 38. Qg3 Ne2†) 38. ... Bg2† 39. Ke1 Nd3† and wins. If 37. Qd2 (or 37. Qc2) 37. ... Q×g4† 38. Kf1 (if 37. Kf2 Qf3†, followed by 38. ... Ne2† or 38. ... Nh3 mate) 38. ... Qf3† 39. Qf2 (if the king moves, Black either mates or wins sooner) 39. ... Qd3†, and wins again by the check of the knight"—Steinitz. *The Field* (Steinitz), 24 January 1880.

# C.C.A. CONGRESS, BOSTON 1880

The last time Bird attended a congress of the C.C.A. was in Glasgow in 1875. That edition had seen the one-off experiment to allow London-based masters to enter the handicap tournament and even to invite foreign professionals. The original recipe of organizing a chess meeting with provincial amateurs only was already restored from 1876 onwards.

A crisis occurred in 1879 when the organizing committee, from which Skipworth was absent, had been unable to organize a gathering. The Rev. Skipworth took matters in hand soon enough again and perhaps even avoided the dissolution of the C.C.A. The next meeting was organized in January 1880 and took place in Boston.

Two London-based players, Bird and MacDonnell, were invited to attend the festivities. They gladly accepted the invitation. MacDonnell had also been present in 1878, but only to play in the handicap. For this edition there was some discussion among the inner circle of the C.C.A. whether Bird and MacDonnell were allowed to enter the main tournament (which would have been a complete rupture with the tradition) or the handicap event only.[15] In the end

15. Steinitz commented on the C.C.A.'s actual willingness to consider the participation of Bird and MacDonnell in the main event: "The meeting of this society, which commences at the Guildhall, Boston, on the 19th inst., will be attended by Mr. Bird, who very likely will enter the first-class tournament unless he should be honorably debarred on account of his reputed superior strength over all probable competitors. Mr. MacDonnell is also expected to join the chief tourney." *Figaro*, 28 January 1880.

they were granted access only to the handicap tournament, which, according to MacDonnell in the *Illustrated Sporting and Dramatic News* of 31 January, was perfectly compliant with the rules that excluded "all prize winners in international or any other first class tourneys ... from competing in any of its classes."

Fourteen other candidates joined both masters. Because of their presumed superior strength, Bird and MacDonnell were classified in a special section and they had to concede the odds of the draw (meaning the lesser player in a draw scores a win) against other players from the first class. In the second round de Soyres also received the odds of the draw against Wayte. The tournament offered four prizes. The total amount of prize money, £5, was provided by the Löwenthal fund.

Fate paired Bird against Wayte in the first round. William Wayte was probably the strongest of all the clergymen associated with the C.C.A. As a player from class I he received the aforementioned draw odds, forcing Bird to play as sharp as possible. This was certainly no recipe for success against the solid Wayte. In an equal position, with a draw being very near, Bird was forced to complicate the game at all cost. This was duly punished by his opponent. Wayte and MacDonnell reached the final of the handicap, but the tournament was not played out because of a lack of time.

Bird was given a chance to grasp the third prize in the loser's section, which he managed to do by beating three lesser known players.

The organizing committee strongly supported the occurrence of all kinds of offhand games. Bird was very active in these side events. He beat six opponents in a simultaneous exhibition and played two small matches against Harry Jackson, a 16 year old prodigy. Bird gave the boy the odds of pawn and two moves in the first match, which he won with 3 against 2. A knight was abandoned in the second match and now the veteran was victorious with 3 against 1. A very noteworthy consultation game, with Bird and Skipworth teamed against Wayte and MacDonnell, was commenced. A lack of time caused the game to be broken off a highly crucial moment. It was declared a draw upon Skipworth's proposal.

### (519) Bird & Skipworth–MacDonnell & Wayte    ½–½
Consultation game
Boston, 19 January 1880
*A00*

**1. a3 d5 2. c4 e6 3. e3 Nf6 4. f4 c5 5. Nf3 Nc6 6. c×d5 e×d5 7. Bb5 Qb6** White's set-up isn't very impressive, but this move, and Black's next, justify it. Instead of harassing a bishop that is already willing to exchange itself, 7. ... Bd7 deserves the preference. **8. B×c6† Q×c6** 8. ... b×c6, opening a very nice diagonal for the bishop, might be better. **9. 0–0 Bd6** In view of White's next move, 9. ... Bf5 or 9. ... Bg4 are more exact. **10. b4!** A very strong move. It was probably suggested by Bird, who was toying with the Sicilian Wing's Gambit at the time. Bird and his ally undoubtedly sacrificed this pawn to generate some kind of kingside attack. The truly brilliant idea behind this type of sacrifice, to find compensation along the open lines and diagonals on the queenside, was demonstrated in the famous game between Nimzowitsch and Capablanca (St. Petersburg 1914). **10. ... c×b4 11. a×b4 B×b4** The allies would have done better

to leave the pawn untouched. **12. Ne5 Qb6 13. Na3** A few forced exchanges would have laid bare the weaknesses of their opponents' queenside after 13. Qa4†! Bd7 14. N×d7 N×d7 15. Ba3 B×a3 16. Q×a3 Qc5 17. Nc3 Q×a3 18. R×a3. **13. ... 0–0 14. Rb1 Bf5** The bishop was doing an important job on c8—i.e., defending the b-pawn. Therefore 14. ... Qa5 must be played. **15. d3 Qc5?!** A better square for her majesty is d6. **16. Nc2 a5 17. Nd4 Bd7** 17. ... Bc8 is more exact as it defends b7 again. **18. Bb2?!** Thematic is 18. Bd2! Predictably, Bird and Skipworth aim for Black's king. **18. ... Rfc8?** *(see diagram)* Very imprudent. 18. ... Qe7 or 18. ... Qd6 assists to the defense of f6 and the kingside. White's subsequent attack looks very dangerous.

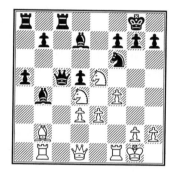

*After 18. ... Rfc8*

**19. N×d7! N×d7 20. Nf5 g6?!** Extending the diagonal of the enemy bishop can hardly be the correct defense. 20. ... f6 suggests itself, but the sharper 20. ... Ra6 also comes into consideration. **21. Qg4?** 21. Nh6†! is very strong. White launches an attack after 21. ... Kf8 22. Bd4 Qe7 23. f5! **21. ... Kf8 22. Rbc1 Qb6** abandoned as a draw. In the *Illustrated Sporting and Dramatic News* of 31 January, MacDonnell wrote that "the consultation game ... was not finished owing to want of time, and a proposal to draw made by Mr. Skipworth was accepted by both sides. At the time the game was broken off Messrs. Bird and Skipworth had a pretty good attack, but their opponents, Messrs. Wayte and MacDonnell, were a pawn ahead, and were in a fair way to extricate themselves from all difficulties." The position is extremely interesting. After 23. Bg7† Ke8 24. Bd4, Black has to give up his queen with 24. ... R×c1 (24. ... Qb5 25. Ng7† and if 25. ... Kf8 26. R×c8† and 27. f5. If 25. ... Ke7 26. Qh4† wins) 25. B×b6 R×f1† 26. K×f1 N×b6. If now 27. Nd4, 27. ... a4 is not without danger for White. Instead 27. Ng7† Kf8 28. Ne6†! strips the defense of the king bare, while also isolating it from the remaining pieces, allowing White soon to end the game with a perpetual check—*Manuscript Games of W. Wayte*, vol. 5, game 858.

### (520) Wayte–Bird    1–0
Handicap tournament (round 1)
Boston, 20 January 1880
*B46*

**1. e4 c5 2. Nc3 e6 3. Nf3 Nc6 4. d4 c×d4 5. N×d4 a6 6. Be2 Qf6 7. Be3 Bb4 8. Qd2 Nge7 9. 0–0 Qg6 10. Bd3 Ne5 11. h3 N×d3 12. c×d3 e5 13. Nc2 B×c3 14. Q×c3 d6 15. Kh2 f5 16. f4 f×e4 17. d×e4 Q×e4 18. f×e5 d×e5 19. Bg5 Nc6 20. Rae1 Qg6 21. Nd4 Be6 22. N×c6 Rc8 23. Q×e5 R×c6 24. Qb8† Kd7 25. Rd1†** Black resigns—*Manuscript Games of W. Wayte*, vol. 5, game 860.

**Handicap tournament, Boston, 19–24 January 1880**

*Odds scale:* pawn and move (class II), pawn and 2 moves (class III) and knight (class IV)
*Notes:* Bird and MacDonnell gave the odds of the draw to other players of the first class.

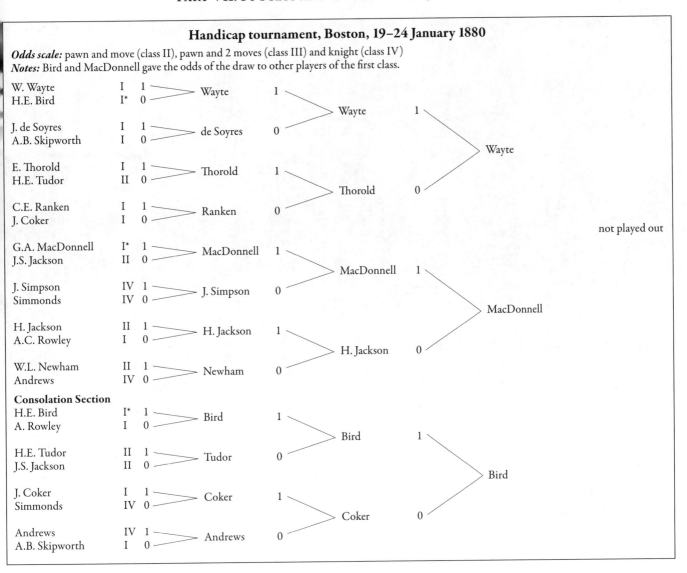

# WIESBADEN 1880

At the end of June, Bird embarked on a chess tour through Germany and the Netherlands. His first important stop was Wiesbaden where an international tournament was held at the Kurhaus. Two other representatives from the London chess scene, Mason and Blackburne, were present. It was the first time in chess history that an English delegation took part in a tournament on German soil. The field was quite strong and could even have been reinforced with the presence of Steinitz and Zukertort had they not preferred to stay on the sidelines. Among the continental favorites were Englisch, Louis Paulsen and Adolph Schwarz, the top three of the tournament held in Leipzig in 1879. Winawer and Blackburne were the highest ranked players present from the Paris 1878 tournament.

The regulations and habits in German tournaments were much more stringent than in England. There were no rest days, not even on Sundays, and two games per day were on the menu. Adjourned games had to be finished in between the regular rounds. A working day was thus quite loaded for the chess players, as they had to demonstrate their powers between 8:30 a.m. and 12:30 p.m., 3:00 and 7:00, and 8:00 and midnight. This allowed the committee to settle the tournament in a mere eight days. At the end of the week only the three best players were rewarded with a prize.

Because of the strict schedule the time limit was changed just before the start of the tournament from 15 to 20 moves per hour. Already in the opening round this led to a dramatic loss when Winawer overstepped his time limit in a crucial game with Blackburne. Bird suffered a loss at the hands of a strong-playing Louis Paulsen. Bird easily won his second game against Carl Wemmers. In the third round Bird overlooked an excellent chance to beat Emil Schallopp. A rather strange queen maneuvre allowed Bird to build up a strong attack but after omitting to play a strong preparatory move at move 33 the worst was over for Schallopp and a draw seemed a logical outcome—though Bird's poor endgame technique even delivered his opponent the full point. Bird was also somewhat unlucky in a lengthy duel with Blackburne where he missed some chances to draw the game.

After this round the tournament was suspended for an afternoon. Alexander Fritz gave a blindfold simultaneous exhibition and a few consultation games were organized. One of them opposed Bird, Blackburne and Winawer against Zukertort and the Paulsen brothers.

262         H.E. BIRD : A CHESS BIOGRAPHY

**A group of players and an official of the Wiesbaden tournament (1880). Sitting: Emil Schallopp, Adolph Schwarz, Joseph H. Blackburne and Louis Paulsen. Standing: Hermann Zwanzig, Berthold Englisch, Wilfried Paulsen, James Mason, Wilhelm Steinitz, Johannes Minckwitz and Johann H. Zukertort. Bird is conspicuously absent** *(Illustrirte Zeitung).*

Bird and his companions played rather badly in the opening and had to suffer through the rest of the game that ended in a well-deserved victory for Black.

Bird's luck returned in the following rounds and he was able to win five games in a row. The game with Carl Friedrich Schmid, played in the fifth round, had a very romantic character. The battle was extremely complicated and only modern analysis seems to be able to demonstrate White's best chances. Schmid missed them and lost. In the sixth round Bird managed to beat Winawer: After a good positional game, one tactical mistake from the Polish champion was punished severely. The

### International chess tournament, Wiesbaden, 3–12 July 1880

*Site:* Kurhaus
*Playing hours:* 8:30 a.m.–12:30 p.m., 3 p.m.–7 and 8 p.m.–12 a.m.
*Prizes:* 1st 1000 marks, 2nd 500 marks, 3rd 250 marks
*Time limit:* 20 moves per hour

| | | 1 | 2 | 3 | 4 | 5 | 6 | 7 | 8 | 9 | 10 | 11 | 12 | 13 | 14 | 15 | 16 | |
|---|---|---|---|---|---|---|---|---|---|---|---|---|---|---|---|---|---|---|
| 1 | J.H. Blackburne | | ½ | ½ | 0 | ½ | 1 | 1 | 1 | 1 | 1 | ½ | ½ | 1 | ½ | 1 | 1 | 11 |
| 2 | B. Englisch | ½ | | ½ | ½ | ½ | ½ | 1 | 1 | ½ | 1 | ½ | ½ | 1 | 1 | 1 | 1 | 11 |
| 3 | A. Schwarz | ½ | ½ | | ½ | 0 | ½ | 1 | ½ | ½ | 1 | 1 | 1 | 1 | 1 | 1 | 1 | 11 |
| 4 | E. Schallopp | 1 | ½ | ½ | | 0 | 1 | 1 | 0 | 1 | 0 | 1 | 1 | 1 | ½ | 1 | 1 | 10½ |
| 5 | J. Mason | ½ | ½ | 1 | 1 | | 0 | 1 | 0 | 0 | 0 | 1 | 1 | 1 | ½ | 1 | 1 | 9½ |
| 6 | S. Winawer | 0 | ½ | ½ | 0 | 1 | | 0 | 1 | 1 | 1 | 0 | 0 | 1 | 1 | 1 | 1 | 9 |
| 7 | H.E. Bird | 0 | 0 | 0 | 0 | 0 | 1 | | 1 | 0 | 1 | 1 | 1 | 1 | 1 | 1 | 1 | 9 |
| 8 | J. Minckwitz | 0 | 0 | ½ | 1 | 1 | 0 | 0 | | ½ | 1 | 1 | ½ | 1 | ½ | 0 | 1 | 8 |
| 9 | L. Paulsen | 0 | ½ | ½ | 0 | 1 | 0 | 1 | ½ | | 0 | ½ | ½ | 0 | 1 | 1 | 1 | 7½ |
| 10 | A. Schottländer | 0 | 0 | 0 | 1 | 1 | 0 | 0 | 0 | 1 | | ½ | 1 | ½ | ½ | 1 | 1 | 7½ |
| 11 | W. Paulsen | ½ | ½ | 0 | 0 | 0 | 1 | 0 | 0 | ½ | ½ | | 1 | 0 | 1 | ½ | 1 | 6½ |
| 12 | C. Wemmers | ½ | ½ | 0 | 0 | 0 | 1 | 0 | ½ | ½ | 0 | 0 | | 1 | ½ | 1 | ½ | 6 |
| 13 | A. Fritz | 0 | 0 | 0 | 0 | 0 | 0 | 0 | 0 | 1 | ½ | 1 | 0 | | 1 | 1 | 1 | 5½ |
| 14 | C. Schwede | ½ | 0 | 0 | ½ | ½ | 0 | 0 | ½ | 0 | ½ | 0 | ½ | 0 | | ½ | ½ | 4 |
| 15 | V. Knorre | 0 | 0 | 0 | 0 | 0 | 0 | 0 | 1 | 0 | 0 | ½ | 0 | 0 | ½ | | 0 | 2 |
| 16 | C. Schmid | 0 | 0 | 0 | 0 | 0 | 0 | 0 | 0 | 0 | 0 | 0 | ½ | 0 | ½ | 1 | | 2 |

game against Victor Knorre is lost and Bird was lucky to win poor positions from Wilfried Paulsen and Johannes Minckwitz.

Bird now counted 6 points out of 9 and had connected with the top players. His chances for a prize, however, were definitively over after two subsequent losses against Schwarz and Mason. Bird recovered well by beating Constantin Schwede, Fritz and Arnold Schottländer. Bird's game with Fritz, the only of these that has been preserved, was easily Bird's highlight of the tournament. The spectators witnessed an extremely complicated battle full of tactical niceties and errors. Fritz missed a few ways to create an upset and in the end the Englishman triumphed. The way Bird lost against Englisch in the final round was a complete anticlimax.

The tournament was won by the trio Blackburne, Schwarz and Englisch.[16] They scored 11 points out of 15 games. Schallopp trailed by a half point. The influence of this quick pace was especially felt by slower players, such Louis Paulsen and Winawer. Their results were worse than ever.

Bird came in sixth, together with Winawer. Undoubtedly a disappointment for the Englishman. Just as in Paris, Bird's unwillingness to draw prevented him from fighting for a prize.[17]

### (521) Bird–L. Paulsen    0–1
International tournament (round 1)
Wiesbaden, 4 July 1880
A03

1. f4 c5 2. Nf3 d5 3. e3 a6 4. b3 Nc6 5. Bb2 Nf6 6. Bd3 e6 7. 0-0 Bd6 8. Na3 0-0 9. Ne5 Nb4 10. Be2 Nd7 11. c3 Nc6 12. N×c6 b×c6 13. c4 e5 14. Qe1 f5 15. Nc2 e4 16. d3 Nf6 17. Rd1 Be6 18. d×e4 N×e4 19. Bd3 Qe7 20. B×e4 f×e4 21. Qc3 Rad8 22. Kh1 Rd7 23. Rd2 Qh4 24. g3 Qh5 25. Rdf2 Bh3 26. Rg1 Re7 27. c×d5 c×d5 28. Qa5 Bg4 29. Ne1 d4 30. Q×a6 Qd5 31. Bc1 Ra8 32. Qf1 d3 33. Rd2 Bc7 34. h3 Qh5 35. h4 Be2 36. Qh3 Ba5 37. g4 Qd5 38. g5 B×d2 39. B×d2 g6 40. Ng2 Qe6 41. Q×e6† R×e6 42. f5 g×f5 43. Nf4 Bf3† 44. Kh2 Rb6 45. Nd5 R×a2 46. N×b6 R×d2† 47. Kg3 Rc2 48. Ra1 d2 49. Nd5 d1Q 50. Ra8† Kf7 51. Ra7† Ke8 White resigns—*Deutsche Schachzeitung*, December 1880, pp. 373–374.

### (522) Wemmers–Bird    0–1
International tournament (round 2)
Wiesbaden, 4 July 1880
C45

1. e4 e5 2. Nf3 Nc6 3. d4 e×d4 4. N×d4 Bc5 5. Be3 Qf6 6. c3 Qg6 7. Nd2 Nf6 8. Qf3 N×d4 9. B×d4 B×d4 10. c×d4 d6 11. Bd3 Qh6 12. Qe3 Q×e3† 13. f×e3 Ng4 14. h3 Nf6 15. Rc1 Kd8 16. 0-0 Re8 17. Rc3 Re7 18. Nf3 h6 19. e5 Nd5 20. Rb3 N×e3 21. Re1 Nd5 22. Be4 Nb6 23. Kf2 d5 24. Bd3 Be6 25. Rc1 c6 26. Rbc3 a5 27. Ra3 Nc4 28. B×c4 d×c4 29. Nd2 b5 30. Ne4 Bd5 31. Nc5 Kc7 32. Rg3 g5 33. a3 Kb6 34. Rh1 f6 35. e×f6 Rf7 36. Ke2 Re8† 37. Kd2 Rd8 38. Rf1 B×g2 39. R×g2 R×d4† 40. Ke3 K×c5 and Black wins—*Deutsche Schachzeitung*, April 1881, pp. 115–116.

### (523) Bird–Schallopp    0–1
International tournament (round 3)
Wiesbaden, 5 July 1880
A02

1. f4 e6 2. Nf3 Nf6 3. e3 Be7 4. b3 0-0 5. Bb2 b6 6. a4 Bb7 7. Bd3 Nc6 8. 0-0 d6 9. Na3 Nb4 10. Be2 Be4 11. d3 Bg6 12. Qd2 c5 13. Nh4 Nd7 13. ... Bh5 crosses Bird's plans to eliminate his bishop pair. 14. N×g6 h×g6 15. c3 "The knight was not dangerous where he stood, and might safely be left alone. We should have played 15. a5, followed by 16. Nc4, if 15. ... b×a5. At any rate, the text move could only serve to weaken White's queenside, and hinder the free action of his pieces"—Ranken. 15. ... Nc6 16. Nc2 16. Bf3 avoids the following annoying complications. 16. ... Na5 "Spotting at once the weak point in the opponent's armor"—Ranken. 17. Ra3 d5 18. b4 c×b4 "Retreating the knight either to c6 or b7 was stronger than exchanging pawns"—Ranken. 19. c×b4 Nb7 "If 19. ... Nc6 White cannot win a pawn after 20. B×g7 K×g7 21. Qc3† because of 21. ... Kg8 22. Q×c6 Rc8"—Ranken. 20. Nd4 Rc8 21. Ra2 a5 22. b5 Bb4 23. Qd1 Bc5 23. ... Nb8 is necessary. 24. Kh1 Preferable is 24. Nc6, a move noticed by contemporary sources, but not evaluated correctly. Black's best move now is 24. ... Qe8 (not 24. ... B×e3† due to 25. Kh1 and now 25. ... Qh4 26. g3 or 25. ... Qe8 26. d4 g5 27. Ba3 with a clear edge), but after 25. d4 Bb4 26. Qb3

16. The end of the tournament was marred by an incident. Through a misunderstanding Blackburne was late to finish an adjourned game with Minckwitz. The latter claimed the game but the committee allowed Blackburne to continue playing. Winawer thereupon demanded the resumption of his first round game, lost on time against Blackburne. This was evidently denied. Steinitz showed himself satisfied with the reception of the English players by their German counterparts: "...and we record with the highest satisfaction; that not alone was every game most fairly and honestly fought by the German players on its merits, irrespective of the score of foreign rivals, but the utmost consideration was shown to a British competitor in a case of dispute, which arose chiefly owing to the English player being unacquainted with the German language." *The Field*, 17 July 1880.

17. MacDonnell was rather critical in this perspective: "Mr. Bird, whose confidence in his own powers, is almost justified by his genius, if not by his success, paid the penalty which generalship usually exacts from the man who scorns to draw and always plays to win. Although he scored nine victories, a number not exceeded by any other competitor, and equalled only by one, yet he failed to gain a prize owing to his having been defeated in all his other contests. Thus did the despised drawn games avenge themselves upon him. Mr. Bird has yet to learn that where draws augment the score they ought to be accepted, unless the probabilities in favor of a victory preponderate." *Illustrated Sporting and Dramatic News*, 31 July 1880. ¶ Besides several of his games an amusing anecdote from Bird's visit to Wiesbaden survived: "At the Wiesbaden tournament the veteran Bird was a competitor. As usual, he carried a big 'grip,' with little in it, but marked on the outside in plain black letters 'correspondent of *The London Times*.' He put up at the leading hotel, and lived on the fat of the land. But when after two weeks no money was forthcoming he was gently reminded by the clerk to attend to the 'needful.' Thereupon Bird grew exceeding wroth, and threatened the hotel folk with the dire vengeance of the 'Thunderer.' Soon afterwards he met his fellow contestants in the tournament, including Blackburne, to whom he unfolded his tale of woe, ending 'Lend me £5, old man.' Blackburne handed over the money, and said 'Just give me your IOU.' A few minutes afterwards Bird was challenging anybody in the room to play him a game of chess for £5. For a few seconds nobody took him up. Then Blackburne quietly said, 'I'll take you.' 'All right,' said Bird, 'put up the money,' and placed on the table the £5 which Blackburne had lent him a few minutes before. Blackburne, with his well-known composure, put his hand in his pocket, took out Bird's IOU and laid it beside Bird's money. 'What,' said Bird, 'you don't expect me to play for that worthless piece of paper, do you?'" *Otago Witness*, 30 July 1891. First published in the *Albany Journal*. With only an American and an Australian source available there seems little basis for this anecdote, but the *Albany* column was managed by William Krause Pollock, a British master well acquainted with Bird and Blackburne.

White's advantage is crystal clear. **24. ... B×d4** "It seems rather bold to let the adversary have two bishops against two knights, but it was almost necessary to prevent the knight occupying c6 presently"—Ranken. **25. B×d4 Nd6 26. Bg4 Qh4 27. g3 Qh6** 27. ... Qe7 equalizes. **28. h4 Nf5 29. B×f5 g×f5** *(see diagram)*

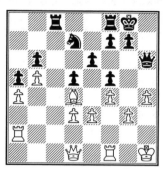

*After 29. ... g×f5*

**30. g4!?** "The commencement of a spirited and well planned attack, which only fails owing to a subsequent mistake"—Ranken. The positional 30. Rc2 is at least as good but much less Bird's style. **30. ... Q×h4†** Very dangerous. 30. ... f6 is his safest option. **31. Rh2 Q×g4 32. Qe1 f6 33. Rh4?** "This is White's error. He should have played 33. Qf2 and then 34. Rg1"—Ranken. After 33. Qf2, the menace of enclosing the queen forces Black to find and play 33. ... e5 34. B×b6 e4! 35. B×a5 e×d3 36. Rg1 Rc2, when he has just enough counterplay. **33. ... Rc1! 34. R×g4 R×e1 35. R×g7† K×g7 36. R×e1 Rh8† 37. Kg2 Rc8 38. e4** The simplification and consequent capturing of the c-file gives Schallopp the better chances. Bird's move considerably worsens his own chances, as he helps his opponent to get rid of the latter's single pawn weakness. **38. ... f×e4 39. d×e4 d×e4 40. R×e4 Kf7 41. Bf2 Rc2 42. Kf3 e5** "Black would have saved himself much trouble by advancing the other pawn: 42. ... f5 43. Rd4 Nc5 44. Bh4 Rc3† 45. Ke2 (if 45. Kf2 or 45. Kg2, then 45. ... Rd3) 45. ... Ra3 46. Bd8 R×a4 winning easily"—Ranken. **43. f5 Nc5?!** This hurried move gives Bird real drawing chances. The position of the king could have been improved considerably by bringing this piece to d5 before making further attempts to enhance his edge. **44. B×c5 R×c5 45. Rh4 Kg7 46. Rg4† Kf7 47. Rh4 Rc3† 48. Ke2 Kg7 49. Rg4† Kf8 50. Rg6** "It would have been more prudent for himself, and more puzzling for Black, had he persevered with his original plan by again playing 50. Rh4"—Ranken. **50. ... Kf7 51. Rh6 Rg3 52. Rh7† Rg7 53. Rh3 Rg4 54. Rh7† Kg8 55. Rb7 R×a4 56. R×b6 Kg7 57. Rb8 Rb4 58. b6 a4 59. Ke3 a3 60. Ra8?** Much better for subtle reasons is 60. b7: 60. ... a2 61. Ra8 R×b7 62. R×a2 and Black has to be careful to win the game: 62. ... Rb4 (not good is 62. ... Kh6 63. Rg2) 63. Rg2† Kf7 64. Rf2 Rg4 and a long battle is ahead. Black has to try to activate his king. White must avoid this. **60. ... R×b6 61. R×a3** White's rook is passive now. Within a few moves the difference with the previous line becomes apparent. **61. ... Rb4 62. Ra2 Rf4 63. Rg2† Kf7 64. Rf2 R×f2 65. K×f2 Ke7 66. Kf3 Kd6 67. Ke4 Kc5 68. Kf3 Kd4 69. Kg3 Ke3** White resigns—*Chess Player's Chronicle* (Ranken), September 1880, pp. 205–206.

### (524) Bird–Blackburne    0–1
International tournament (round 4)
Wiesbaden, 5 July 1880
*B06*

**1. f4 g6 2. e4 Bg7 3. d4 d6 4. c3 Nh6 5. Nf3 b6 6. Bb5† Bd7 7. Bd3 c5 8. d5 Qc7 9. 0–0 b5 10. h3 a5 11. Be3 Na6 12. Qe2 Qb7 13. Qd2 Ng8 14. Re1 Nc7 15. Qf2 b4 16. c4 Na6 17. e5 0–0–0 18. Nbd2 Bf5 19. Bf1 h5 20. a3 b3 21. Nb1 B×b1 22. Ra×b1 Nh6 23. a4 Nf5 24. Bd2 Nb4 25. Bc3 h4 26. Nd2 Nc2 27. Rec1 Nfd4 28. Nf3 d×e5 29. f×e5 Bh6 30. Bd2 N×f3† 31. g×f3 B×d2 32. Q×d2 Qb4 33. Qf4 R×d5 34. Qe4 Rdd8 35. Rd1 Nd4 36. Bg2 Qb7 37. Qe3 e6 38. f4 Qb6 39. Qe4 Kc7 40. Rd3 Rd7 41. Rbd1 Rhd8 42. Kf2 Nf5 43. R×d7† R×d7 44. R×d7† K×d7 45. Kf3 Qc6 46. Q×c6† K×c6 47. Ke2† Kd7 48. Be4 Ng3† 49. Kf3 Ke7 50. Bd3 Nf5 51. Ke4 Nd4 52. Ke3 Kf8 53. Be2 Kg7 54. Bd1 Kh6 55. Ke4 g5 56. Ke3 Kg6 57. Ke4 Nc2 58. Bg4 g×f4 59. K×f4 Nd4 60. Bd1 Nc2 61. Bf3 Nb4 62. Be4† f5 63. e×f6 e.p. K×f6 64. Kg4 Ke5 65. Bg6 Nc2 66. K×h4 Kf4 67. Bd3 e5 68. Kh5 e4 69. Bf1 Nd4 70. h4 Nf5 71. Kg6 N×h4† 72. Kf6 Nf5 73. Ke6 Ng3** White resigns—*The Field*, 10 July 1880.

### (525) Schmid–Bird    0–1
International tournament (round 5)
Wiesbaden, 6 July 1880
*C33*

**1. e4 e5 2. f4 e×f4 3. Bc4 Qh4† 4. Kf1 d6 5. d4 g5 6. Nc3 Ne7 7. g3 Bh3† 8. Kf2 Qh6 9. Qf3 Nbc6 10. g×f4 g4 11. Qg3** It was certainly safer to keep the d-pawn defended with 12. Qe3. Much less precise is 11. Qd3 (Minckwitz) for after 11. ... Nb4 White has to give up c2 and play 12. Qg3, since 12. Qd2? loses immediately: 12. ... Qh4† 13. Ke3 d5! when White's king is in serious trouble, and so is the rook at h1! **11. ... Bg7** The d-pawn could have been taken. Bird probably feared 12. f5. **12. d5 Bf6** This looks very strong, as White's queen is in danger, but 12. ... Nd4 is better. **13. f5!** Schmid spots a fascinating and correct queen sacrifice. **13. ... Qh5 14. N×h3 Bh4** *(see diagram)*

*After 14. ... Bh4*

**15. Nf4** The implication of this move is that the queen sacrifice is unavoidable. Very interesting is 15. d×c6!, for after 15. ... b×c6 16. Kg1 B×g3 17. h×g3, it turns out that Black also cannot avoid the loss of his queen. Better is therefore the radical 15. ... N×f5, when the position remains complicated, e.g., after 16. c×b7 Rb8 17. Bb5† Kf8 18. e×f5 g×h3 19. Bd3 with excellent play in return for the queen. **15. ... B×g3† 16. K×g3 Qh6 17. d×c6 b×c6** Capturing back with the knight is preferable. **18. Nd1?** The point of this move is hard to grasp. Both 18. K×g4 and 18. Bf1 come into consideration. After the latter move, a possible line would be 18. ... Qf6 19. Nh5 Qe5† 20. K×g4 0–0–0 21. Kh3. The king is safe at his exotic position. His three pieces compensate for the loss of the queen. **18. ... d5 19. Be2** "More logical is 19. Bd3"—Minckwitz. **19. ... Rg8 20. B×g4 Qd6** Immediately 20. ... d×e4 soon leads to the conquest of the important f-pawn. **21. Kh3 d×e4 22. Nf2 Qd4 23. Rf1 e3 24. N2d3 h5 25. Bf3 Qf6 26. Be4 Qg5 27. Ne5 N×f5 28. B×c6† Kf8 29. Nfg6† R×g6 30. N×g6† f×g6 31. R×f5† Q×f5† 32. Kg2 Qf2† 33. Kh3 g5** and Black wins—*Deutsche Schachzeitung* (Minckwitz), March 1881, pp. 80–81.

## (526) Winawer–Bird   0–1
International tournament (round 6)
Wiesbaden, 7 July 1880
*C44*

**1. e4 e5 2. Nf3 Nc6 3. c3 d5 4. Qa4 d×e4** The major options at this point are 4. ... Bd7 and 4. ... f6!, a suggestion from Steinitz. **5. N×e5 Qd5 6. N×c6 b×c6 7. d4** Immediately playing 7. Bc4 limits the options of Black's queen as the c-pawn needs to stay defended. **7. ... Bd7 8. Be3 Bd6 9. Nd2 Nf6 10. Qc2 0–0 11. h3 Qf5** Bird completely neglects Winawer's last move, but at least the queen gets out of the center to a less vulnerable spot. Alternatives were 11. ... h5 or 11. ... Rfe8. **12. g4 Qg6 13. Bg2 Rae8 14. 0–0–0 h6 15. c4 Bb4 16. Nf1** A bit too artificial. 16. Kb1, 17. a3 and 18. Nb3 gives White a nice edge. **16. ... Bd6** One point of his previous move could have been 16. ... N×g4 17. h×g4 B×g4 18. f3 e×f3 19. Bh3 Q×c2† 20. K×c2 f5 which is very unclear. **17. c5 Be7 18. Ng3 Bd8 19. Rde1 Re6 20. Bd2 Rfe8 21. Re2 h5** Bird defended himself very well, especially with this well timed counter-move. **22. h4** Winawer doesn't shun a sharp battle. Safer is 22. Ree1. **22. ... h×g4 23. Qa4?!** With a balanced position in the center of the board, this excursion is misplaced. 23. h5 gives enough counterplay for the pawn. **23. ... R6e7?** Bird overlooks the strong 23. ... Nd5, freeing the path of the f-pawn. **24. Rhe1?!** Winawer rates an excellent opportunity to kick his h-pawn forwards. After 24. h5 Qh7 25. h6, the kingside is opened in his favor. **24. ... Nh5 25. R×e4?** A major mistake from the Polish champion. The position remains unclear after 25. Q×a7 f5 26. Qb7. **25. ... N×g3 26. R×e7 R×e7 27. R×e7 B×e7 28. f×g3 Qd3!** An extremely powerful infiltration. Bird's finish is excellent. **29. Qb3 Q×d4 30. Be3 Qe5 31. Bf2 B×c5 32. Qc2 B×f2 33. Q×f2 c5 34. Bf1 Bf5 35. Be2 g6 36. Bb5 c4 37. Ba4 Qe4 38. b4 c3 39. Bc2 Q×c2† 40. Q×c2 B×c2 41. K×c2 f5 42. K×c3 f4 43. g×f4 g3** White resigns—*Deutsche Schachzeitung*, May 1881, pp. 145–146.

## (527) Knorre–Bird   0–1
International tournament (round 7)
Wiesbaden, 7 July 1880
*Game score missing*

## (528) W. Paulsen–Bird   0–1
International tournament (round 8)
Wiesbaden, 8 July 1880
*C46*

**1. e4 e5 2. Nf3 Nc6 3. Nc3 Bb4 4. Bb5 Nge7 5. d4 N×d4 6. N×d4 e×d4 7. Q×d4 c5 8. Qe5 f6 9. Qg3 0–0 10. Bh6 Ng6 11. Bc4† Kh8 12. Bd2 d6 13. 0–0–0 Ne5 14. Bd5 Bg4 15. f3 Bh5 16. Qh3 Bf7 17. f4 B×d5 18. N×d5 B×d2† 19. R×d2 Nc4 20. Rd3**

Qa5 **21. a3 Rae8 22. Nc3 b5 23. Qf5 b4 24. Rh3 g6 25. Qd7 h5 26. Nb1 b×a3 27. b×a3 R×e4 28. Rd1 Re1 29. f5 Rfe8 30. Rc3 R1e7 31. Qc6 Ne3 32. R×d6 N×f5 33. Rd1 Nd4 34. Q×c5 Ne2† 35. Kb2 Rb7† 36. Ka1 R×b1† 37. R×b1 Q×c3†** and Black wins—*Deutsche Schachzeitung*, August–September 1881, pp. 260–261.

## (529) Bird–Minckwitz   1–0
International tournament (round 9)
Wiesbaden, 8 July 1880
*A03*

**1. f4 d5 2. Nf3 Nf6 3. e3 e6 4. b3 Be7 5. Nc3 b6 6. Ne2 Bb7 7. Bb2 c5 8. h3 Ne4 9. g3 Bf6 10. c3 Nd7 11. Bg2 0–0 12. 0–0 c4 13. b×c4 d×c4 14. Ba3 Be7 15. B×e7 Q×e7 16. Qa4 Rfc8 17. Ng5 Ndc5 18. Qb4 N×g5 19. f×g5 Q×g5 20. B×b7 N×b7 21. Rf4 Qc5 22. Qa4 e5 23. Rh4 Qd5 24. Qc2 Qd3 25. Q×d3 c×d3 26. Nc1 Nc5 27. Nb3 Ne6 28. Rb4 Rc6 29. a4 Nc5 30. N×c5 R×c5 31. e4 Rd8 32. Kf2 f6 33. a5 b5 34. a6 Kf7 35. Rab1 Rc6 36. Ra1 Rb6 37. Ra5 Rdd6 38. Ke3 R×a6 39. R×a6 R×a6 40. R×b5 Rb6 41. Ra5 Rb7 42. K×d3 Rd7† 43. Ke3 Rc7 44. Ra3 Ke7 45. d4 e×d4† 46. c×d4 Rb7 47. Kf4 Rd7 48. d5 Kd6 49. h4 Rb7 50. Kf5 Re7 51. Ra6† Kc5 52. d6 Rb7 53. Ke6 Rb4 54. Kd7 R×e4 55. R×a7 Rd4 56. Rc7† Kd5 57. Ra7 Kc5 58. Ra5† Kb6 59. Ra3 Kc5 60. Rc3† Kb4 61. Rc1 Rd3 62. Ke6 Re3† 63. Kf7 Rd3 64. Ke7 Re3† 65. Kd8 R×g3 66. d7 Rd3 67. Kc7 h5 68. d8Q** Black resigns—*Deutsche Schachzeitung*, December 1880, pp. 374–375.

## (530) Bird–A. Schwarz   0–1
International tournament (round 10)
Wiesbaden, 9 July 1880
*Game score missing*

## (531) Bird–Mason   0–1
International tournament (round 11)
Wiesbaden, 9 July 1880
*Game score missing*

## (532) Bird–Schwede   1–0
International tournament (round 12)
Wiesbaden, 10 July 1880
*Game score missing*

## (533) Bird–Fritz   1–0
International tournament (round 13)
Wiesbaden, 10 July 1880
*A03*

**1. f4 d5 2. Nf3 e6 3. e3 b6 4. Be2 Bb7 5. 0–0 Nf6 6. b3 Be7 7. Qe1 Nbd7 8. Nc3 c5 9. Nd1 Ne4 10. d3 Nd6 11. Bb2 Bf6 12. Ne5 B×e5 13. f×e5 Nf5 14. Bg4 Nh6 15. Bh3 Qg5 16. d4 Rc8 17. c3 Ba6 18. Rf3 Bd3** An enterprising move, but it was time to castle, as now 19. Nf2 followed by 20. e4! is strong. **19. Rg3 Qh4 20. Nf2 Bf5** The safer 20. ... Bg6 covers the g-pawn. It seems dangerous now to capture this pawn (21. R×g7 Bg6?), but the refutation comes swiftly with 22. c4! Kf8 23. B×e6! **21. B×f5 N×f5 22. Rh3 Qe7 23. Qe2** Immediately 23. e4 gains a tempo, but it doesn't matter after Fritz' next move. **23. ... Nf8? 24. e4! Nh6 25. Bc1 Ng6 26. B×h6 g×h6 27. Ng4 c×d4 28. c×d4 Qb4 29. Nf6†** This check spoils nothing, but there is no need to forbid castling definitively since it is as bad as it looks. Very strong would have been the centralizing 29. Re3!, anticipating 29. ... Q×d4. The loss of the pawn is more than compensated by the gain of tempo and opening of the king's shelter after 30. Rd1 Qc5 31. e×d5 e×d5 32. Nf6†. **29. ... Ke7 30. Qe3 Nf4!?** *(see diagram)* Fritz doesn't let the chance go by to introduce complications.

*After 30. ... Nf4*

**31. Rf3** Too tame. He'd have excellent winning chances after the evident 31. R×h6 Q×d4 32. Q×d4 Ne2† 33. Kf2 N×d4 34. e×d5. **31. ... Ne2†** The roles are reversed after 31. ... Q×d4 32. Q×d4 Ne2† 33. Kh1 N×d4 34. Rh3 d×e4 35. N×e4. Thanks to the exchange of the queens all danger for his king has disappeared, while the control over the c-file, and soon enough the second rank, gives serious pressure. **32. Kh1 N×d4?** 32. ... Q×d4 33. Raf1 Q×e3 34. R×e3 Nc3 is drawish. Fritz wants more, but this brings him close to losing everything. **33. e×d5?** It remains difficult for Bird to form the right recipe to haunt Fritz' king. After the cool 33. Rff1! Nc2 34. Qf4 N×a1 35. N×d5!, everything comes together and the king perishes. **33. ... Nc2?** Another definite error. After 33. ... N×f3 34. Q×f3 Qc3 35. d6† Kd8 36. Rg1!, White's pieces are dominant enough to neutralize Black's material advantage and secure a draw. **34. d6† Kd8 35. Qg1??** Terribly passive. A win was within reach after 35. Q×h6! N×a1 36. Rf1! and there is nothing to be done against the destructive infiltration of White's queen. **35. ... N×a1 36. Q×a1 Qd2** Black assumes the initiative. Things suddenly look depressing for Bird. **37. Rf1 Rc2 38. Rg1 h5?** 38. ... Kc8 must be played, getting out of reach of Bird's queen. **39. Qf1!** The activation of his queen makes the game tenable once more. **39. ... Qe2 40. Qf4 Kc8 41. Ne4** The other candidate move, 41. d7†! forces Fritz to demonstrate his utmost defensive skills to keep the half point: 41. ... Kd8 (very daring but if 41. ... Kb7? 42. Ne8) 42. Qg5 Ke7! (this tremendous move had to be foreseen. White threatened 43. Qg7) 43. Ng8† K×d7 44. Qf6 Qe3! 45. h3! (both sides are walking on a thin rope. If 45. Q×h8? Rc1 wins) 45. ... Rc1 46. R×c1 Q×c1† 47. Kh2 Qe3 and finally White has to capture at either f7 or h8, in each case leading to a draw. **41. ... Rg8 42. Ng3 Qg4 43. Q×f7** *(see diagram)*

**43. ... Kb8** and White wins. "Until now, Fritz played beautiful and energetic, having obtained a winning advantage, but now his clear overview leaves him. Fritz made various weak moves, returned the quality and resigned at move 84. We don't see how Bird can save the game after 43. ... h4; e.g., 44. Ne2 (44. Q×a7 h×g3 and

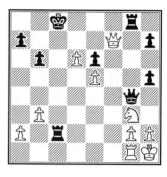

*After 43. Q×f7*

there is no draw for White) 44. ... h3 45. Ng3 h×g2† 46. R×g2 Rc1† 47. Rg1 Qe4† and mate follows"—Minckwitz. 43. ... h4? ought to lose by force, but the line is particularly brilliant, making it therefore very difficult for players and analysts to pierce through. After the forced 44. Q×h7! Rc3 45. Q×a7 h×g3 46. Qa8† Kd7 47. Qb7† Kd8 48. Q×b6† (simpler is 48. Qe7† at once) 48. ... Kc8, a first way to win is 49. Qa6† Kb8 50. Qb5† Kc8 51. d7† Kc7 52. Qa5†. But particularly brilliant is 49. Qa7!, with a stunning zugzwang. If 49. ... g×h2, 50. Qa8† Kd7 51. Qb7† Kd8 52. Qe7† is similar as above. Also simply winning is 49. ... Qg7 50. d7†! Most fascinating is 49. ... Rg7 50. Qa8† Kd7 51. Qb7† Kd8 52. Qb6† Kc8, and now, with the opponent's king at c8, the final blow is delivered by the rook: 53. Rf1 Qf5 54. Qa6† Kb8 55. R×f5. So, the text move is best after all as it leads to a draw after the correct 44. d7 h4 45. Qe8† Kb7 46. d8Q R×e8—*Deutsche Schachzeitung* (Minckwitz), August–September 1881, p. 270.

### (534) Schottländer–Bird    0–1
International tournament (round 14)
Wiesbaden, 11 July 1880
*Game score missing*

### (535) Englisch–Bird    1–0
International tournament (round 15)
Wiesbaden, 11 July 1880
*C40*

1. e4 e5 2. Nf3 d5 3. N×e5 d×e4 4. d4 Be6 5. Be2 f6 6. Nc4 Nc6 7. c3 B×c4 8. B×c4 f5 9. Qb3 Nh6 10. B×h6 Qf6 11. Bf4 0-0-0 12. Bd5 g5 13. B×c6 Q×c6 14. Be5 e3 15. f3 Bd6 16. B×h8 R×h8 17. Na3 Qe8 18. 0-0-0 e2 19. Rde1 Qe3† 20. Kb1 Rd8 21. Nc4 Qd3† 22. Ka1 Bf4 23. Qb5 Kb8 24. Nd6 Q×b5 25. N×b5 Re8 26. Kb1 g4 27. Kc2 Black resigns—*Neue Illustrirte Zeitung*, 12 September 1880.

### (536) Bird & Winawer & Blackburne–Zukertort & L. Paulsen & W. Paulsen    0–1
Consultation game
Wiesbaden, 6 July 1880
*C37*

1. e4 e5 2. f4 e×f4 3. Nf3 g5 4. Bc4 g4 5. Ne5 Qh4† 6. Kf1 Nh6 7. d4 f3 7. ... d6 8. Nd3 f3 9. Nc3 c6 is more precise. The important square d5 remains under control against an invasion from White's knight. **8. Bf4** "8. Nc3, as played by Steinitz in his match against Zukertort in 1872, is here much to be preferred"—Steinitz.

**8. ... d6 9. Nd3 f×g2† 10. K×g2 Nc6 11. Bg3** "It is scarcely possible to play a good consultation game at the quick rate of twenty moves an hour, and it is, therefore, no wonder that the game is early conducted in a shallow manner. The object of this attack was apparently to induce the opponents to 11. ... Qh3†, which would have been a completely lost move, as 13. Nf4, winning the queen, was afterwards threatened by White. It was much more solid play to leave the adverse queen at her outpost, whence she must have retreated ultimately with loss of time, and to withdraw the knight at once to f2. The bishop could then once more protect the d-pawn at e3 if necessary, and he great object was gained of being enabled to bring out the knight to the most favorable attacking square at c3"—Steinitz. Steinitz' suggestion is interesting, but White hasn't got the time to neglect his development by moving two of his developed pieces at his ease. After 12. Nf2 Bg7 13. Be3 f5, the opening of the position is nearly impossible to meet by them. **11. ... Qe7 12. Nf2** 12. Nc3 is necessary. **12. ... Bg7** "The Black allies gain here an important defensive point with fine judgment. They force the opponents to shut out their knight from c3 by their own pawn"—Steinitz. **13. c3 Bd7 14. Nd2 0-0-0 15. b4** "This attack is premature, and even hazardous, in face of the adverse counterattack on the kingside. The better plan of development was 15. Qc2, and then 16. Rae1 and 17. Rhf1"—Steinitz. There is not much left besides this hazardous move. After 15. Qc2 Ng8!, followed by 16. ... h5 and 17. ... h4, White undergoes a cruel attack without any counter-chances. **15. ... f5 16. b5 Na5 17. Re1** "An error of judgment, which we do not think either [*sic*] of the players who acted in concert would have committed when playing separated. They allow thereby one of their most important pieces to be exchanged for the inactive adverse knight. 17. Bd3 was the natural and the best move, and the game might have proceeded thus: 17. ... Rhf8 (if 17. ... Qf7 White may answer 18. Rf1 and if then 18. ... f4 19. Nh1 when 19. ... f3† could do no further harm, and we believe White would ultimately obtain the best of the game, on the queenside mostly, by Nb3 if done in proper time, and after guarding against Nc4) 18. e×f5 N×f5 19. Re1 and 19. ... Ne3† is of no use for 20. Kg1 with a safe game"—Steinitz. Black's attack is reinforced by 19. ... Qf7! (instead of 19. ... Ne3†) 20. Re2 Bh6. **17. ... N×c4 18. N×c4 B×b5 19. e×f5 Qf7 20. Ne3 N×f5 21. N×f5 Q×f5 22. Q×g4 Q×g4 23. N×g4 h5** "All this could have been easily foreseen, and was only the natural consequence of the error pointed out in our last note. Black is now a clear pawn ahead, and has a formidable attack besides against White's exposed king with the combined two rooks and two bishops"—Steinitz. **24. Ne3 h4 25. Bf2** (*see diagram*)

*After 25. Bf2*

**25. ... Rdg8** "This is very fine play. They apparently afterwards lose time with this rook, but in reality gain an important move. It was of great importance to keep the h-pawn defended. Had they played 25. ... Rhg8 the game might have proceeded thus: 26. Kh1 Rdf8 27. B×h4 Bh6 28. d5 B×e3 29. R×e3 Bc4 30. Bg3 and White could make a good fight for a draw with bishops of opposite colors"—Steinitz. The outcome of this line is still much better/winning for Black, but an improvement is possible as 26. ... Bh6 27. Rad1 B×e3 28. B×e3 Bc4 29. f5 Rde8 30. Rd4 B×a2 is very convincing. That said, Steinitz is right in his praise for the text move. **26. Kh1 Rf8** The same idea as pointed out in the note above, 26. ... Bh6 to exchange the knight, is even stronger. **27. Bg1 Rhg8 28. Rad1 Bh6 29. d5** "Their position was now compromised, and there was no means of extrication. Had they played 29. Nd5 the game might have gone on thus: 29. ... Bc4 30. Ne7† Kd7 31. Be3 (best, if 31. d5 Rg7 and 32. Rd4 doesn't save the piece after 32. ... Bf1) 31. ... B×e3 32. R×e3 Rg7 followed by 33. ... Re8 if 33. Rde1. If the knight moves, 33. ... Bd5† follows"—Steinitz. **29. ... Rf3 30. Rd4 R×g1†** This exchange doesn't simplify their job. Winning was 30. ... B×e3 31. B×e3 Re8 32. c4 Ba6. **31. R×g1 B×e3 32. Rg8† Kd7 33. Rdg4** 33. R×h4 Rf1† wins. **33. ... Rf1† 34. Kg2 Rf2† 35. Kh1** "Best. If 35. Kh3 Bf1† 36. Rg2"—Steinitz. **35. ... Ke7 36. c4** "The White allies are defending themselves remarkably well, and give their opponents great trouble"—Steinitz. **36. ... Ba4 37. Re4†** "Better than 37. Rh8 h3 38. R×h3 Rf1† 39. Kg2 Rg1† 40. Kf3 Bd1† 41. K×e3 R×g4 42. Rh7† Kf6 43. R×c7 Rg7 and wins"—Steinitz. **37. ... Kf7 38. Rh8 Bg5 39. Kg1 R×a2 40. Rh7† Kg6 41. R×c7 h3** "After this excellent move White's resistance can only be prolonged without hope of altering the result"—Steinitz. **42. R×b7 Rg2† 43. Kh1 Bc2 44. Re6† Kh5 45. R×a7 Bf4 46. Ra1 R×h2† 47. Kg1 Rg2† 48. Kh1 Rd2 49. Ree1 Bg3 50. Re3 Kg4 51. c5 d×c5 52. d6 Bd1 53. Re4† Kf5 54. Re3 Kf4 55. Raa3 Bb3** White resigns—*The Field* (Steinitz), 21 August 1880.

# BRUNSWICK 1880

Just five days after the closure of the chess activities in Wiesbaden the thirteenth western German chess tournament was held in Brunswick. Bird was eager to join this tournament as well. It is unclear how he spent the few days in between. Leopold Hoffer suggested that he visited the chess club in Frankfurt am Main, while Bird claimed that he prolonged his stay in Wiesbaden for a few days to recover from an attack of gout.

Bird's attempt to play in Brunswick was a failure. He even found himself barred from playing. The whole story lasted several months and eventually became a major dispute that ended with Bird's announcement to retire definitively from chess. The details about all of this will follow at the end of this Part. This chapter focuses on the proceedings in Brunswick and the discussions immediately afterwards.

First of all it must be noted that Bird was the only English player to continue his travel in Germany. Mason and Blackburne returned home after the tournament in Wiesbaden, even though they also had left London with the ambition to participate in Brunswick.[18] Unlike his two colleagues Bird didn't change his plans. He revealed his intentions to play by sending a telegram to the committee of the Brunswick tournament. Bird was convinced that everything was arranged now but he was due for a disappointment when he arrived in Brunswick: his telegram had remained unopened and two competitors now objected to Bird's participation, as the pairings of the tournament had already been made. Wilfried Paulsen and Wemmers were allegedly the players who refused to let Bird in. Bird reacted with a plea to be allowed to take part, but he remained excluded.[19]

Bird was consoled with a match for the best of five games against Gäbler, the strongest local player. A small prize was provided. After two games, with both players having scored a win, Gäbler resigned and declared that he was satisfied that Bird would beat him.

An article in which Hoffer revealed some other motives behind Bird's exclusion inaugurated a revival of the Brunswick saga after the summer.

> An unpleasant incident happened with Mr. Bird and the Brunswick committee, which we only mention to eliminate erroneous impressions, which are sure to creep into the press. The simple facts are: that Mr. Bird was staying at Frankfurt am Main after the Wiesbaden tournament, and enjoying the hospitality of the club. He missed his train; anxious to secure his admission into the Brunswick tournament he telegraphed to the committee; but in consequence of his imperfect knowledge of the German language he directed his telegram: the committee to Mr. Bird, instead of: Mr. Bird to the committee. Naturally the telegram remained unopened until Mr. Bird presented himself and demanded admission to the tournament. The drawing having taken place the previous evening at 6 o'clock p.m. the committee could only admit him by a unanimous vote of the contestants. Two of them, Messrs. Wemmers and W. Paulsen, objected, and Mr. Bird was debarred from participating in the contest. It is very much to be regretted that this happened to the only competitor from England, but law is law, and therewith the matter ends. Had Mr. Bird succeeded in winning the sympathies of the players at Wiesbaden, as Messrs. Blackburne and Mason did, it is more than probable that the players would not have taken the rules to the letter; but the contrary has been the case, and Mr. Bird knew that he had no favor to expect [*Chess Monthly*, August 1880, p. 358].

By suggesting that Bird had created anything but friends at Wiesbaden, this article was surely not the end of the matter for Bird. He wrote a protest letter to *Chess Monthly* but they refused to publish it. Bird went looking for another editor to release his grieves and he found MacDonnell willing.

---

18.   The reasons why they changed their plans remain vague as the sources tend to contradict each other. The *Glasgow Weekly Herald* of 24 July 1880 stated that Mason was unwell but it was also suggested that Blackburne and Mason found a visit to Brunswick not suitable: "Messrs. Blackburne and Mason, having learned at Wiesbaden that this tourney was not intended by the promoters to be of an international character, did not claim to enter the lists. Both players would very probably have received a cordial welcome, but they showed good taste in not intruding upon a number of amateurs who had elected to spend their brief holiday in the exercise of their favorite pastime." *Illustrated London News*, 7 August 1880.

19.   Bird sent his side of the story to the *Glasgow Weekly Herald*, which published it on 31 July 1880: "The president of your committee has had two notices in writing from me for months past of my intention to take part in this tournament. Both of the notices were after conference with and upon the advice of Mr. Steinitz. I attended here just in the same way as I did at Wiesbaden, namely— before the play commenced. The committee had drawn my name at Wiesbaden. I supposed that they would do the same here also. I do not know whether Mr. Steinitz and Mr. Zukertort are on your committee, but both of those gentlemen were well aware of my intention to come to Brunswick. Furthermore, they knew that, health and strength permitting, I had no option in the matter. I came from England for the express purpose of playing in the Wiesbaden and Brunswick tournaments, suffering greatly from pain and illness. I played out all my games at Wiesbaden. In better health, I now claim to do the same at Brunswick."

MacDonnell, in his introduction, pointed out the two grounds for exclusion as mentioned above, and failed to see justice in them.[20]

Bird's own letter was written from a hotel room in Rotterdam. He had already been informed about the article in *Chess Monthly* that had created some stir but having it just seen in Rotterdam he could not reply earlier. Having read the article Bird felt he had no other choice than to publish his version of the facts.

> I was precluded by illness from leaving Wiesbaden for Brunswick until the day before the tournament. I had twice given written notice of my intentions to enter. I had reason to believe that Messrs. Blackburne, Mason, Steinitz, and Zukertort would correctly inform the committee; and all that I understood was necessary was that I should attend punctually in time for play. This I took care to do. I was in no way uneasy during the long journey from Wiesbaden to Brunswick, and congratulated myself very much upon arriving at Brunswick at five in the morning, four hours before the time appointed for play. It is not true, as stated in your article, that I delayed my journey at Frankfurt. It is not true that I enjoyed the hospitality of the club, for I never went to it, and don't know where it is. It is not true that through my imperfect knowledge of the German language I addressed a telegram in error, "The committee to Mr. Bird." It is not true that I did anything to forfeit the sympathies of the Wiesbaden players. I parted on excellent terms with all of them. ... I was surprised and sorry to find that Messrs. Blackburne and Mason were not at Brunswick, and equally disappointed to find that Messrs. Steinitz and Zukertort were. Of course I was astounded to find my name excluded from the list of competitors, and claimed my right to enter; but the committee in concert with Steinitz and Zukertort, had cut and dried the affair beforehand. I protest against the attempt to make Messrs. Paulsen and Wemmers responsible for the affair, the genuine history of which may be gathered from the correspondence published in an independent paper, and with which you are familiar.—Very obediently yours, H.E. Bird [*Illustrated Sporting and Dramatic News*, 2 October 1880].

Clearly, MacDonnell's hinting to a foreign collaboration between Steinitz and Zukertort against him had come from Bird's view on the matter. Bird believed that both men had to announce his arrival and intention to take part in the tournament. This accusation made James Mason take the pen in his hand. In a severe reaction Mason catalogued Bird's opinion as nonsense.

> The suggestion that there was a conspiracy to "exclude a national champion and a chivalrous chess-player," "who had traveled hundreds of miles to uphold the honor of the English flag"—as one of your contemporaries who ought to know better has it—any such motion as that I say is simply absurd. Mr. Bird was denied the fellowship and goodwill of his peers, the contestants in the master tournament at Brunswick, and he was so denied for cause. He had no business to be in Brunswick at all. He should have returned to his own country with the money that was subscribed for that purpose by the players in the tournament at Wiesbaden. The reason why I did not attend the Brunswick tournament was that I knew Mr. Bird would be there, and the same consideration influenced other of the Wiesbaden players [*Glasgow Weekly Herald*, 9 October 1880].

Mason's remark that Bird received money by subscription in Wiesbaden is intriguing but impossible to elucidate for no other reference could be found anywhere else.

The dispute continued in the column of the *Glasgow Weekly Herald*, whose editor was clearly on Bird's side. Another letter from

---

20.   MacDonnell also brought some rumors to the attention of the public. He indirectly hinted that Steinitz and Zukertort, who had followed some players from Wiesbaden to Brunswick and were aware of Bird's intention to play, played a foul part in his excommunication: "How far the committee were influenced in their judgment by the presence of two visitors from England who attended the tournament, not to enhance its glories, but merely to exhibit themselves and busy themselves with arrangements which they ought not to have interfered with, will be best seen by a perusal of Mr. Bird's letter, which I now subjoin, premising that it is addressed to the editors of the *Chess Monthly*, by whom it has been refused admission into their journal." *Illustrated Sporting and Dramatic News*, 2 October 1880.

Mason, published a week later, was cut short into a short fragment which, in the editor's mind, proved that a few players fumbled to damage Bird.

The two gentlemen who took upon themselves the invidious task simply gave expression to a feeling common to all the players who had taken part with Mr. Bird in the Wiesbaden tournament a few days previously. This is the gist of the whole affair. Mr. Bird had made himself impossible at Brunswick if it was within the powers of the players to keep him out [*Glasgow Weekly Herald*, 23 October 1880].

Conspiracy or not, it is clear that there was a serious breach between Bird and his fellow masters. The Brunswick saga brought this to the attention of a worldwide public.

**(537) Gäbler–Bird    1–0**

Match (game 2)
Brunswick, 19 July 1880
C61

1. e4 e5 2. Nf3 Nc6 3. Bb5 Nd4 4. Bc4 b5 5. N×d4 b×c4 6. Nf3 Qf6 7. Nc3 Bb7 8. Qe2 Qe6 9. Nd5 Bd6 10. Q×c4 0–0–0 11. Ng5 Qg6 12. N×f7 Nh6 13. N×h8 Q×g2 14. Rf1 R×h8 15. d3 Q×h2 16. Be3 Ng4 17. B×a7 Qh6 18. a4 Nh2 19. Be3 Qh5 20. Kd2 Kd8 21. Rh1 Nf3† 22. Kc3 Qg6 23. Rh3 Nd4 24. Re1 c6 25. Nf4 Qe8 26. b4 Qf8 27. Rb1 g5 28. Nh5 g4 29. Rhh1 Ne2† 30. Kd2 Qf3 31. b5 Nf4 32. N×f4 e×f4 33. Bb6† Bc7 34. Qd4 B×b6 35. Q×b6† Ke7 36. b×c6 B×c6 37. Qc5† Kd8 38. Rb8† Kc7 39. Qb6† Kd6 40. Rh6† Ke7 41. Qc5† Black resigns—*Deutsche Schachzeitung*, June 1881, pp. 179–180.

# PERFORMING IN HAMBURG 1880

Bird left Brunswick and subsequently headed for Hamburg where he arrived on 29 July. Bird took up his seat in the Neuen Alster-Halle and spread the news that he was available for everyone to play a game of chess.[21] Bird gave a first simultaneous exhibition on 1 August. Against 23 players he scored a solid result: 17 wins, 4 losses and 2 draws. For some time he was also the guest of Alexander Alexander, a prominent local player. On the next Sunday, Bird left another simultaneous exhibition in Altona with 14 wins, 3 losses and 3 draws. According to *Chess Monthly* and *The Field*, Bird pursued his trip to Berlin but no sign of any chess activity in the German capital has yet been traced.

**(538) Bird–Bier    ½–½**

Offhand game
Hamburg, 31 July 1880
C33

1. e4 e5 2. f4 e×f4 3. Bc4 d5 4. B×d5 Qh4† 5. Kf1 g5 6. Nf3 Qh5 7. h4 Bg7 8. d4 Ne7 9. Bc4 "This retreat is weak. We greatly

21. "...Mr. Bird had been playing at Hamburg and Altona for twelve consecutive days, from ten o'clock in the morning until twelve o'clock and later at night.... The enthusiasm of the players was so great that they were waiting patiently in gangs for hours to get a game with the old master. Mr. Bird beat them all with equal impartiality. Simultaneous performances, consultation games (with Herr Bier as opponent), invitations to private houses, and excursions were the order of the day. Tuesday, the 10th of August, Mr. Bird left Hamburg ... for Berlin, where he is now staying, we believe." *Chess Monthly*, September 1880, p. 2.

prefer the established continuation, 9. Nc3"—Zukertort. **9. ... Nbc6 10. Nc3 h6?** 10. ... Bg4 is preferable. **11. Nd5?!** "The initiatory move of an attacking combination which loses a valuable pawn, and should, therefore, prove unsound. 11. Ne2 seems best"—Zukertort. 11. Nb5! is troublesome for Black. **11. ... N×d5 12. e×d5 N×d4 13. Qe1†?!** Bird pursues his very interesting idea, and thereby puts Bier really to the test. Objectively speaking, however, 13. B×f4 is superior; e.g., 13. ... N×f3 14. B×c7 and the piece will be regained. **13. ... Kd8 14. d6 c×d6 15. Qa5† b6** 15. ... Ke8 is also good. **16. Qd5 N×f3?!** White is lost, but only when his opponent is prepared to face the storm after 16. ... Kc7 17. B×f4 Nf5! 18. B×d6† N×d6 19. Rd1 N×c4 20. Q×c4† Kb8 21. Qb4 Qg6. **17. g×f3** "The capture of the exchange would lose the game; e.g., 17. Q×a8? Nh2†! 18. Ke1 (if 18. R×h2 or 18. Kg1, Black mates in three moves) 18. ... Re8† 19. Kd2 Q×h4 20. Be2 Qf2 21. Re1 f3 22. g×f3 R×e2† 23. R×e2 N×f3† mating or winning the queen"—Zukertort. **17. ... Kc7 18. B×f4 Rd8** 18. ... Qg6 a suggestion from Zukertort, must lead to a draw in case of 19. Re1! Qf6 (19. ... g×f4?! 20. Re7† Kd8 21. h5 and Black might lose as well) 20. h×g5 Q×f4 21. Re7† Bd7 22. R×d7†! with a perpetual. **19. Re1 Be6?!** *(see diagram)* Allowing the resourceful Bird to escape with a draw. Anyway, after 19. ... Bf8 20. Bg3 Bb7 21. Q×f7†, the majority of Black's advantage has already vanished.

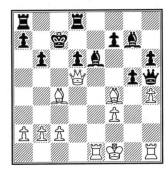

*After 19. ... Be6*

**20. R×e6!** "The ending is played in Mr. Bird's happiest style"—Zukertort. **20. ... f×e6 21. B×d6†! R×d6 22. Q×a8 Rd1† 23. Ke2 R×h1 24. Q×a7† Kc6 25. Qa8† Kc7** With this move Bier shows himself content with a draw. In case of 25. ... Kd7, White draws with 26. Qb7† (and not 26. Bb5†? Ke7 27. Qa3† Kf6 28. Qc3† Kf7 29. Qc7† Kg8 30. Qc8† Bf8 31. Q×e6† Qf7 winning) 26. ... Ke8 27. Qc8† etc. More testing is the eventful 25. ... Kc5!? The continuation is forced, as each misstep might cost him the game: 26. Qc8† Kd4! 27. c3† (there is no time for any preparatory move, like 27. Q×e6, as Black then forces the game with 27. ... Rh2†) 27. ... Ke5 28. Q×e6† Kf4 29. Qe3† (29. Qe4†? and Black wins with 29. ... Kg3) 29. ... Kg3 30. Qf2† Kh3! 31. Be6† g4 32. B×g4† Q×g4 33. f×g4 Rh2 34. Q×h2† K×h2. The perpetual is gone, but there is no way to win the game anymore; e.g., 35. Kf3 Kh3 36. h5 Kh4 37. Kf4 Bh8 38. a4 Bg7 39. Kf5 Bh8. **26. Qa7†** and White drew by perpetual check—*Chess Monthly* (Zukertort), September 1880, pp. 19–20.

**(539) Bird & friends–Bier & friends    0–1**

Consultation game
Altona, 2 August 1880
C77

1. e4 e5 2. Nf3 Nc6 3. Bb5 Nf6 4. Qe2 a6 5. Ba4 b5 6. Bb3 Bb7 7. c3 Be7 8. a4 0–0 9. d3 h6 10. Nbd2 d5 11. Nf1 d×e4

**12. d×e4 N×e4 13. Q×e4 Nd4 14. Q×b7 N×b3 15. Rb1 Qd3 16. N3d2 N×d2 17. N×d2 Bg5** and Black wins—*Deutsche Schachzeitung*, March 1881, p. 89.

## (540) Bird–Bier & Rocamora & Zimmermann    1–0

Consultation game
Hamburg, 3 August 1880
C45

**1. e4 e5 2. Nf3 Nc6 3. d4 e×d4 4. N×d4 Bc5 5. Nb3 Bb6 6. Be2 Qh4 7. 0–0 Q×e4 8. Nc3 Qh4 9. g3 Qd8 10. a4 a6 11. Nd5 Ba7 12. Bc4 d6 13. Re1† Nge7 14. Bg5 Be6 15. N×e7 N×e7 16. B×e6 f×e6 17. R×e6 0–0 18. R×e7 R×f2 19. Qd5† Kh8 20. Be3 Q×e7 21. B×f2 B×f2† 22. K×f2 Rf8† 23. Kg1 Qe3† 24. Kh1 Qe2 25. Qd3** Black resigns—*Deutsche Schachzeitung*, March 1881, pp. 89–90.

## (541) Frensdorf–Bird    1–0

Simultaneous game
Hamburg, 1 August 1880
C71

**1. e4 e5 2. Nf3 Nc6 3. Bb5 a6 4. Ba4 d6 5. B×c6† b×c6 6. d4 e×d4 7. N×d4 Bb7 8. Nc3 g6 9. 0–0 Bg7 10. Nde2 h5** "We do not quite like this, it has too much the appearance of being premature"—Hoddinott. **11. Be3 Nf6 12. Bg5 Qd7 13. f3** "A very cautious move, which secures a safe position, and, we think, much superior to any other more attacking move. It prevents 13. ... Ng4, as evidently intended by him"—Hoddinott. **13. ... Nh7 14. Be3 0–0–0** Fearless play from Bird. 14. ... a5 is a worthy alternative. **15. Bd4 f6 16. b4!** "Very well played. This not only prevents 16. ... c5, but prepares the way for a very strong attack in the right direction"—Hoddinott. **16. ... Ng5 17. a4 Ne6 18. Rb1** "White plays the attack cautiously and well. There is much more mischief in these moves than appears at first sight"—Hoddinott. **18. ... h4** "Not good. Black either underrates White's strength, or, what is more likely, his attention is too much absorbed by the other 22 boards. 18. ... c5 appears to us better play, as it tends to weaken White's attack"—Hoddinott. 18. ... c5?! only weakens the safety of his king. Fine was 18. ... N×d4 19. Q×d4 f5. **19. b5 c5?!** *(see diagram)* "19. ... a×b5 first, followed by 20. ... c5, appears more advantageous"—Hoddinott.

*After 19. ... c5*

**20. b×a6?!** Frensdorf doesn't make the most of it. The quiet 20. Be3! prepares to augment the pressure against Bird's queenside, in order to force him to a most unfavorable exchange. Concrete samples are 20. ... f5 21. b×a6! B×a6 22. Qd5 c6 23. Qb3 or 20. ...

Rde8 21. Qd3. **20. ... B×a6 21. Be3 c6?** This is the wrong way to keep White's queen out. With White's early exchange at a6, it was possible to play 21. ... Bc4. Black has counterplay after 22. Nb5 Rdf8 23. Qd2 f5. **22. Rb6 Nc7 23. Qb1 Qe8** "Forced, in order to prevent the threatened mate by White's rook"—Hoddinott. **24. Rd1** "A very fine move. 24. B×c5 is, however, we think, still more effective, as Black cannot retake the bishop without sacrificing his queen or losing the game"—Hoddinott. **24. ... B×e2 25. N×e2 Rh5 26. Nf4 Bh6** "Very pretty and ingenious"—Hoddinott. **27. Qb3 Re5 28. R×d6!** "Again pretty and ingenious"—Hoddinott. **28. ... R×d6 29. Rb8† Kd7 30. R×e8 R×e8 31. Qf7† Kd8 32. Q×g6 f5** "An oversight. White, however, has anyhow a winning game"—Hoddinott. **33. Q×d6†** Black resigns—*Croydon Guardian* (Hoddinott), 16 October 1880.

## (542) S. Hamel–Bird & Rocamora    1–0

Consultation game
Hamburg 1880
C54

"The subjoined game was played some little time ago at the Alster Pavilion, Hamburg, between Mr. Bird, of London, and Mr. S. Hamel, of Nottingham. The latter is brother to the well-known Melbourne player, to whom we are indebted for the copy"—Wisker.

**1. e4 e5 2. Bc4 Bc5 3. c3 Nf6 4. d3 0–0 5. Nf3** "Though begun as a Two King's Bishop's Game, the opening is soon reduced to that form of the Giuoco which Professor Anderssen used to call 'Pianissimo'"—Wisker. **5. ... Nc6 6. b4 Bb6 7. b5** "A premature and unsound attack"—Wisker. **7. ... Na5 8. N×e5 d6** "Had Black at this point played 8. ... d5, White would speedily have found reason to repent of his ill-starred enterprise for the gain of a pawn"—Wisker. **9. N×f7 R×f7?!** This exchange rewards White's play, as many of Bird's pieces remain out of play for a long time. The unorthodox 9. ... Qe7! leads to a tremendous attack in case of 10. N×d6† N×c4 11. N×c4 B×f2†. Instead 11. Nh6† Kh8 12. Nf7† R×f7 is about equal. **10. B×f7† K×f7 11. 0–0 Bd7** 11. ... Qe8 also forces 12. a4 and prepares, after 12. ... Kg8, the activation of the queen on the kingside. **12. a4 Ng4** "Quite useless and worse, since it enables White to advance his d-pawn, thus at once shutting out the black bishop and improving his own position. The principle of this game differs from that of most others in which one side is supposed to have a superiority of force. The player with the two pieces should avoid exchanges in general, and seek by the cooperation of his queen and minor pieces to gain an advantage before the other can bring his surplus rook into action. It is seldom that this can be prevented"—Wisker. **13. d4 Kg8 14. h3 Nf6 15. Bg5 Qe8** 15. ... h6 prevents the subsequent mutilation of the pawn structure. **16. B×f6 g×f6** "Black has set at nought the principle laid down in the last note. His game has materially altered for the worse"—Wisker. **17. Qf3 Qg6 18. Nd2 Rf8 19. Rae1 Qh6 20. Qe3** "It appears in this position alike contrary to the principles of chess for White to offer the exchange or for Black to accept it. 20. Qd3 is best at this stage"—Wisker. **20. ... Q×e3 21. f×e3** 21. R×e3 keeps the pawns structure more elastic and powerful. **21. ... c6 22. c4 Kg7 23. Rf3 Re8 24. Ref1 Bd8 25. Rf4 Be6 26. d5 Bf7 27. Kh2 Bg6** White's last moves were a bit purposeless and as a result his advantage has evaporated. **28. g4 h6** Bird could take over the initiative with 28. ... c×d5 29. c×d5 Bb6 30. R4f3 Rc8. **29. h4 h5 30. Rg1 Kh6 31. g×h5** B×h5 **32. Rf2 Bg6 33. Rg4 Bh7 34. Rgf4 Re5 35. Rg2 Be7 36. Kh3 a6?** A dreadful move. Black is at least equal after 36. ... c×d5 37. c×d5 b6, when the knight returns to the game. **37. d×c6 b6** "At this point Mr. Bird was called away, and his game was played out by a Mr. Rocamora. The substitute signalized his advent to power by throwing away the game at once. Of course the proper play here is 37. ... a×b5, and if 38. c7 Rc5. In that case Black would still have kept the better game"—Wisker. After 38. c×b7 N×b7 39. c×b5, White is equally winning with the powerful pawns on the queenside. Rocamora's move is even worse. **38. Rg1 a×b5 39. c×b5 Rc5 40. Rfg4 f5 41. Rg7 Bf6 42. Rf7 Bc3 43. Nb1 Bh8 44. Rf8 Be5 45. Re8 Rc2** "It matters not what he does. The game is gone"—Wisker. **46. Re6† Bg6 47. Rg×g6† Kh7 48. Rg2 Rc4 49. e×f5** and White wins—*Australasian* (Wisker), 15 January 1881.

# A SHORT STOP IN AMSTERDAM 1880

While on his way back to England Bird decided to pay a visit to Amsterdam. The local chess community would soon learn to know the flamboyant celebrity and Bird left such an impression that his stay was still spoken of for many years. Some details of the following story were published more than fifty years later, in *De Telegraaf* on 22 September 1932. These romanticized reminiscences were written by the Dutch master Willem Schelfhout. They were based on oral testimonies, above all from one of the last survivors of those early days, Rudolf Loman. Schelfhout is not known as a reliable source but some details in his article are confirmed by contemporary sources.

Bird was welcomed by Joost Pinédo, one of Caissa's most loyal worshippers in Amsterdam. Pinédo was of great service to Bird as he provided him with clients for offhand games that were played for a small stake. Bird allowed himself his usual liberties in these games, such as recklessly advancing his a- and h-pawns, moving his king just one square aside and playing 3. ... Nd4 against the Ruy Lopez, but nevertheless crushed all opposition. His bad examples provoked his opponents for many more years to try his weird moves at inappropriate moments, obviously not with the success that Bird experienced.

Bird's atypical chess style as well as hedonistic life-style did not succeed in pleasing the more Calvinistic part of the club and attempts were made to make the Englishman leave in peace. A farewell simultaneous exhibition for a purse was organized on 22 August. Bird worked off his 20 opponents in merely three hours and succeeded in beating them all. With his earned money Bird dived into the Amsterdam nightlife. When the club's treasurer encountered Bird the next morning, he had but one thing to say: "Fully cleared out, nothing is left!" The treasurer pursued then another cunning plan developed by his club members: they had subscribed Bird as a member of the Dutch chess federation. It happened that the federation's congress was about to start that day in the nearby town of Gouda. Bird was led to the train station and off he went.

## (543) Bird–Pinédo & Mohr    0–1
Consultation game
Amsterdam 1880
*C59*

  **1. e4 e5 2. Nf3 Nc6 3. Bc4 Nf6 4. Ng5 d5 5. e×d5 Na5 6. Bb5† c6 7. d×c6 b×c6 8. Be2 h6 9. Nf3 e4 10. Ne5 Qd4 11. f4 Bc5 12. Rf1 Qd6 13. Nc3 Nb7 14. N×c6 0-0 15. Ne5 Nd8 16. d3 e3 17. Ne4 N×e4 18. d×e4 Qe7 19. g3 Bb7 20. Qd3 Ne6 21. c3 Rad8 22. Qc2 Nd4 23. Qd1 B×e4 24. Bd3 e2 25. Qa4 e×f1Q† 26. B×f1 Nc2†** White resigns—*De Groene Amsterdammer*, 29 September 1889.

## (544) Bird–Pinédo & Mohr    0–1
Consultation game
Amsterdam 1880
*C51*

  **1. e4 e5 2. Nf3 Nc6 3. Bc4 Bc5 4. b4 B×b4 5. c3 Bc5 6. 0-0 d6 7. d4 e×d4 8. c×d4 Bb6 9. Nc3 Bg4 10. e5 d×e5 11. Qb3 N×d4 12. B×f7† Kf8 13. N×d4 e×d4 14. Re1 Nf6 15. Bg5 Qd7 16. Be6 B×e6 17. R×e6 d×c3 18. B×f6 g×f6 19. R×f6† Kg7 20. Rf3 Rhf8 21. Rg3† Kh8 22. Rh3 R×f2 23. Kh1 Raf8** White resigns—*De Groene Amsterdammer*, 29 September 1889.

Bird adopted his novel approach against the Sicilian Defense, the Wing's Gambit, five times against the strong Dutchman Maarten van 't Kruijs. Bird beat him on each occasion. One short sample was published in *Chess Practice*.

## (545) Bird–van 't Kruijs    1–0
Offhand game
Amsterdam 1880
*B20*

  **1. e4 c5 2. b4 c×b4 3. d4 e6 4. Bd3 Nc6 5. Ne2 Nf6 6. a3 b×a3 7. N×a3 Be7 8. c3 0-0 9. 0-0 d6 10. f4 b6** and White ultimately won—*Chess Practice*, pp. 95–6.

# GOUDA 1880

Bird's entry into the tournament of the Dutch chess federation, the Nederlandse Schaakbond, was a start and stop affair. On 23 August, around noon, four players started their games. A fifth participant, Levi Benima, was waiting for his opponent, J.J. Veraart, to arrive. But then, suddenly, Bird hit the scene in the company of G. Mohr and Pinédo. A short while later Loman dropped in. After some discussions Veraart decided to withdraw his participation, and so did Mohr, his alternate. In their place came the sleepy and muzzy Bird. This replacement, supported by the players arriving from Amsterdam, caused an eruption of emotionally intense feelings among the governing members of the chess federation. The participation of a foreigner, it was feared, could even lead to the demise of the federation itself! After a fierce discussion and a vote, Bird was nevertheless allowed to play.

The chatter created about Bird's participation was hardly tolerated by many. One member of the committee resigned from his function and ultimately the rules were adapted so that such an incident could not occur again. Fortunately Bird himself was greatly appreciated and was described in the tournament book (p. 23) as "a joyful person and he plays the most beautiful and genial when he can do so with his generous laugh and not with a dignified a serious face; his playing outside the tournament was entertaining as it was instructive."

Bird's first round game was a tough affair, as he was still experiencing the effects of the night before. Benima, though impressed by the Englishman's reputation, profited maximally and achieved a draw.[22] This initial draw proved to be Bird's only misstep and he duly won the other nine games. Bird did not hide his experimental drifts and even played purposefully bad moves. His quest for brilliancy, however, only resulted in games of a very low quality.

Bird spent some more days in Holland and on 7 September he wrote a letter from the Hotel Leijgraaff in Rotterdam, but nothing can be found that relates Bird to any chess activity in that city.

### (546) Benima–Bird    ½–½
Dutch Chess Congress (round 1)
Gouda, 23 August 1880
C46

**1.** e4 e5 **2.** Nf3 Nc6 **3.** Nc3 Bb4 **4.** Bb5 Nge7 **5.** Nd5 N×d5 **6.** e×d5 Nd4 **7.** N×d4 e×d4 **8.** 0–0 0–0 **9.** c3 Be7 **10.** f4 Bf6

---

**8th Dutch Chess Congress, Gouda,
23 August–late August 1880**

*Site:* Tivoli
*Playing hours:* 1 p.m.–5, 7 p.m.–11
*Prizes:* Four prizes: 1st 150 gulden, 4th 25 gulden. Two other prizes unknown

| | 1 | 2 | 3 | 4 | 5 | 6 | |
|---|---|---|---|---|---|---|---|
| 1 H.E. Bird | | 1 1 | ½ 1 | 1 1 | 1 1 | 1 1 | 9½ |
| 2 C. Messemaker | 0 0 | | 1 1 | 0 ½ | 1 1 | 1 1 | 6½ |
| 3 L. Benima | ½ 0 | 0 0 | | 1 ½ | 0 1 | 1 0 | 4 |
| 4 J.F. Malta | 0 0 | 1 ½ | 0 ½ | | 1 0 | 0 1 | 4 |
| 5 J. Blank | 0 0 | 0 0 | 1 0 | 0 1 | | 1 0 | 3 |
| 6 E.H.E. Van Woelderen | 0 0 | 0 0 | 0 1 | 1 0 | 0 1 | | 3 |

---

22. Not without trouble, however: "We continue with a brief story that we wrote on the occasion of a conversation we had with Bird in Amsterdam. None of the Amsterdam players of that time could cope at all with the Englishman. So, he could safely indulge his lust for eccentric move as nobody knew how to profit from his incorrectness. Honestly, we ourselves fared sadly against this second-rate master. The players outside the capital had no more success. On the national tournament at Gouda, he won 9½ out of 10, only Benima had the luck to achieve a draw. Fate paired Benima already in the first round against the Brit. I was present at this game and will never forget the scene. The provincial player from Groningen sat in his sleeves, trembling as reed, a bottle of medicine next to him to silence his nerves, endlessly meditating each move (in those days the frightening clocks weren't so popular as now). Bird, back from a wild night at the 'Nes' where he had spent the 70 guilders we had collected for him, slept during the largest part of the game and only opened his eyes when it was his turn to play. When Benima, after a long time of shivering and hesitating finally moved a piece, Bird's reply followed as good as instantly and that the game ended in a draw is in fact a greater honor for Bird than for his opponent." *Tijdschrift van de koninklijke Nederlandse schaakbond*, June 1905, p. 113. This story was told by Rudolf Loman. He attended the tournament and played against Bird in some offhand games. The Nes, with its pubs and brothels, was a street famous for its night life.

**11.** Bd3 d6 **12.** g4 g6 **13.** Qf3 Bg7 **14.** Kh1 f5 **15.** g5 Bd7 **16.** Qf2 c5 **17.** c4 Re8 **18.** b3 Qa5 **19.** Re1 R×e1† **20.** Q×e1 Re8 **21.** Qf2 b5 **22.** Qf1 b×c4 **23.** b×c4 h6 **24.** h4 h×g5 **25.** h×g5 Kf7 **26.** Kg2 Re7 **27.** a3 Bc8 **28.** Rb1 Ba6 **29.** Kf2 Qd8 **30.** Bb2 Qh8 **31.** Qh1 Rb7 **32.** Q×h8 B×h8 **33.** Ke2 Rb3 **34.** Rh1 Bg7 **35.** Bc1 Kg8 **36.** Rf1 Bf8 **37.** Rh1 Be7 **38.** Rf1 Bd8 **39.** Rh1 Kg7 **40.** Re1 Ba5 **41.** Rh1 Rb8 **42.** Kd1 Bb6 **43.** Ke2 Bd8 **44.** Kd1 Bc8 **45.** Bc2 Bd7 **46.** Rh3 Ba5 **47.** Rh2 Rh8 **48.** R×h8 K×h8 **49.** Ke2 Kg7 **50.** Kd3 Kf7 **51.** Bb3 Ke7 **52.** Kc2 Kd8 **53.** d3 Be1 **54.** Bd2 Bg3 **55.** Kd1 Kc7 **56.** Ke2 Kb6 **57.** Bc2 Ka6 **58.** Bb3 draw—*Jaarboekje van den Nederlandschen Schaakbond 1880*, pp. 36–38.

### (547) Blank–Bird    0–1
Dutch Chess Congress
Gouda, August 1880
C50

**1.** e4 e5 **2.** Nf3 Nc6 **3.** Bc4 Bc5 **4.** 0–0 Nf6 **5.** d3 d6 **6.** h3 Be6 **7.** Bb3 Qd7 **8.** Kh2 0–0–0 **9.** Ng1 d5 **10.** e×d5 N×d5 **11.** B×d5 B×d5 **12.** Nc3 f5 **13.** f4 Be6 **14.** Nf3 e×f4 **15.** B×f4 h6 **16.** Ne5 N×e5 **17.** B×e5 Rhe8 **18.** Re1 Bg8 **19.** Qf3 g5 **20.** Rad1 g4 **21.** Qf4 R×e5 **22.** R×e5 Bd6 **23.** d4 g×h3 **24.** K×h3 Bh7 **25.** g3 h5 **26.** Kh2 Qg7 **27.** Qh4 B×e5 **28.** d×e5 R×d1 **29.** N×d1 Qg4 **30.** Q×g4 f×g4 **31.** Ne3 Be4 **32.** c4 c6 **33.** b4 Kd7 **34.** Ng2 B×g2 **35.** K×g2 Ke6 **36.** Kf2 K×e5 **37.** Ke3 b6 **38.** a3 a5 **39.** Kd3 a×b4 **40.** a×b4 Kf5 **41.** Ke3 Kg5 **42.** Kf2 h4 **43.** g×h4† K×h4 **44.** Kg2 Kg5 **45.** Kg3 Kf5 **46.** Kf2 Ke4 White resigns—*Jaarboekje van den Nederlandschen Schaakbond 1880*, pp. 31–32.

### (548) Bird–Malta    1–0
Dutch Chess Congress
Gouda, August 1880
A03

**1.** f4 e6 **2.** Nf3 d5 **3.** e3 c5 **4.** b3 Nf6 **5.** Bb2 Be7 **6.** Be2 0–0 **7.** 0–0 Ng4 **8.** h3 Bf6 **9.** c3 Nh6 **10.** Na3 Nf5 **11.** g4 Ng3 **12.** Rf2 Ne4 **13.** Rg2 h6 **14.** Qe1 Nc6 **15.** d3 Nd6 **16.** Qg3 g5 **17.** Rf1 b5 **18.** h4 Kg7 **19.** h×g5 h×g5 **20.** f×g5 B×g5 **21.** N×g5 Q×g5 **22.** Q×d6 Q×e3† **23.** Rff2 Ne5 **24.** Nc2 Qg5 **25.** Rf5 Qd2 **26.** Bf1 Qh6 **27.** R×e5 Rh8 **28.** Rh5 Black resigns—*Jaarboekje van den Nederlandschen Schaakbond 1880*, pp. 32–33.

### (549) Malta–Bird    0–1
Dutch Chess Congress
Gouda, August 1880
A80

**1.** d4 f5 **2.** e3 Nf6 **3.** Nc3 e6 **4.** Nf3 Bb4 **5.** a3 Be7 **6.** Bd3 0–0 **7.** e4 d5 **8.** e5 Ne4 **9.** 0–0 c5 **10.** g3 Nc6 **11.** Be3 b6 **12.** Ne2 g5 **13.** Qc1 g4 **14.** B×e4 d×e4 **15.** Nh4 c×d4 **16.** Rd1 B×h4 **17.** N×d4 N×d4 **18.** R×d4 Qc7 **19.** g×h4 Q×e5 **20.** Qd1 f4 **21.** Q×g4† Kh8 **22.** Bd2 Q×d4 **23.** Bc3 Q×c3 **24.** b×c3 Rg8 **25.** Q×g8† K×g8 **26.** Re1 Bb7 **27.** f3 e3 **28.** Rd1 e2 White resigns—*Jaarboekje van den Nederlandschen Schaakbond 1880*, pp. 33–34.

## (550) Bird–Benima   1–0
Dutch Chess Congress
Gouda, August 1880
A03

1. f4 d5 2. e3 f5 3. Nf3 Nf6 4. b3 c5 5. Bb2 Nc6 6. Bb5 a6
7. B×c6† b×c6 8. 0–0 e6 9. Qe1 Be7 10. Nc3 0–0 11. Na4 Nd7
12. Rd1 Bf6 13. d4 Qe7 14. Ba3 Re8 15. N×c5 N×c5 16. B×c5
Qf7 17. Rf2 Bd7 18. h3 Qh5 19. Rfd2 h6 20. Bd6 Be7 21. Be5 g5
22. Nh2 Bb4 23. Qe2 Qg6 24. Rd3 Kf7 25. c3 Be7 26. Kh1 Rg8
27. g4 Bf6 28. B×f6 K×f6 29. Nf3 Be8 30. Ne5 Qh7 31. c4 h5
32. g×f5 e×f5 33. Qf2 h4 34. Rg1 g4 35. c×d5 c×d5 36. Rc3 Bb5
37. Qc2 g3 38. Rc1 Qh5 39. Rc7 Bc4 40. b×c4 g2† 41. Kg1 Rac8
42. c×d5 Black resigns—*Jaarboekje van den Nederlandschen Schaakbond 1880*, pp. 35–36.

## (551) Bird–Messemaker   1–0
Dutch Chess Congress
Gouda, August 1880
C45

1. e4 e5 2. Nf3 Nc6 3. d4 e×d4 4. N×d4 Qh4 5. Nf3 Q×e4†
6. Be2 Be7 7. Nc3 Qb4 8. 0–0 Nf6 9. Nb5 Kd8 10. c3 Qc5 11. Ng5
Rf8 12. Qb3 d5 13. Be3 d4 14. c×d4 Qf5 15. N×f7† Kd7 16. Bf3
Ne4 17. Ne5† N×e5 18. Qd5† Nd6 19. d×e5 c6 20. e6† Kd8
21. Q×f5 R×f5 22. Nd4 Rf6 23. Rad1 B×e6 24. Bg5 Rg6
25. N×c6† b×c6 26. R×d6† Ke8 27. B×c6† Black resigns—*Jaarboekje van den Nederlandschen Schaakbond 1880*, pp. 38–39.

## (552) Messemaker–Bird   0–1
Dutch Chess Congress
Gouda, August 1880
B40

1. e4 c5 2. Nf3 e6 3. d4 c×d4 4. N×d4 Nf6 5. Bd3 Nc6 6. c3
d5 7. e×d5 N×d5 8. 0–0 Bd6 9. Nf3 h6 10. Be4 Nf6 11. B×c6†
b×c6 12. Be3 Qc7 13. Nbd2 Ba6 14. Re1 0–0 15. c4 c5 16. Qc2
Ng4 17. h3 N×e3 18. R×e3 Bf4 19. Re2 Rfd8 20. Rae1 Bb7
21. Ne4 Qc6 22. Nc3 Rd4 23. Nb5 Rd7 24. Nc3 Rad8 25. Qe4
Qc7 26. Qc2 B×f3 27. g×f3 Bd2 28. Rd1 B×c3 29. R×d7 R×d7
30. Q×c3 Rd1† 31. Kg2 Qf4 32. Qe5 Qc1 33. f4 Q×c4 34. f5
e×f5 35. b3 Qd3 36. Qe3 Qd5† 37. f3 Rd3 38. Qf2 f4 39. Re4
Rd2 40. Re2 Qg5† 41. Kf1 Rd1† 42. Re1 R×e1† 43. K×e1 Qf5
44. Qe2 g5 45. a4 Qe6 46. Kd2 Kg7 47. Qd3 Qe5 48. Kc2 h5
49. Kd2 Qb2† 50. Ke1 Qd4 White resigns—*Jaarboekje van den
Nederlandschen Schaakbond 1880*, pp. 39–41.

## (553) Bird–Van Woelderen   1–0
Dutch Chess Congress
Gouda, August 1880
C59

1. e4 e5 2. Nf3 Nc6 3. Bc4 Nf6 4. Ng5 d5 5. e×d5 Na5 6. Bb5†
c6 7. d×c6 b×c6 8. Be2 h6 9. Nf3 e4 10. Ne5 Qd4 11. f4 Bc5
12. Rf1 Qd6 13. c3 Nb7 14. d4 Bb6 15. a4 Bc7 16. Na3 Nd5
17. Nac4 Qf6 18. g3 Bh3 19. Rf2 g6 20. Ne3 h5 21. N×c6 N×e3
22. B×e3 Bg4 23. Ne5 Rd8 24. N×g4 h×g4 25. Bb5† Kf8
26. Q×g4 Nd6 27. Qg5 Q×g5 28. f×g5 Nf5 29. Bf4 e3 30. Re2

Bird in Holland (1880). Consulting against him were Rudolf Loman and Joost Pinédo. Standing is G. Mohr (*VAS-ASC, Vereenigd Amsterdamsch Schaakgenootschap. Amsterdamsche Schaakclub, 1822–1972*).

B×f4 31. g×f4 Rh4 32. Bd3 Re8 33. B×f5 g×f5 34. 0–0–0 R×f4
35. Kc2 Rg4 36. Kd3 f4 37. Rf1 Kg7 38. h3 Rh4 39. Rf3 Kg6
40. Rg2 Kf5 41. b4 Reh8 42. Rgg3 Re8 43. Rg1 Reh8 44. Rgf1
K×g5 45. c4 Re8 46. c5 Kf5 47. c6 a6 48. b5 a×b5 49. a×b5 Ra8
50. c7 Ra3† 51. Kc4 Ra8 52. R×e3 Rc8 53. Re5† Kg6 Black resigns—*Jaarboekje van den Nederlandschen Schaakbond 1880*, pp.
41–43.

## (554) Van Woelderen–Bird   0–1
Dutch Chess Congress
Gouda, August 1880
C46

1. e4 e5 2. Nf3 Nc6 3. Nc3 Bb4 4. Bb5 Nge7 5. Nd5 N×d5
6. e×d5 Nd4 7. N×d4 e×d4 8. 0–0 Be7 9. Qg4 Bf6 10. Re1† Kf8
11. c4 h5 12. Qe2 b6 13. d3 Bb7 14. Ba4 a6 15. Bb3 d6 16. Bf4
g5 17. Bd2 Be5 18. Qf3 g4 19. Qf5 Bc8 20. Qe4 Qf6 21. Qe2 Bf5

**22. f4 g×f3** *e.p.* **23. Q×f3 Qg6 24. Bc2 Bg4 25. Qe4 f5 26. Rf1 Re8 27. g3 B×g3 28. Qg2 Re2 29. Q×g3 h4 30. Qf4 Bf3† 31. Qg5 Rg2†** White resigns—*Jaarboekje van den Nederlandschen Schaakbond 1880*, pp. 43–44.

**(555) Bird–Blank    1–0**
Dutch Chess Congress
Gouda, August 1880
*Game score missing*

## BIRD'S OWN CHESS PIECES

In November Bird manifested his talents in a new area. He had prepared the design of a new kind of chessmen. The manufacturing of the pieces was handed over to Bird's familiar publishing company Dean and Son. On the advertisement leaf of *Modern Chess* some words of praise recommended Bird's design as a considerable improvement over Staunton's chess pieces.[23] The cover of another of Bird's books, *Chess Novelties*, features a set of pieces that are likely to be Bird's conception.[24] Despite his efforts the versatile veteran's design was not able to compete with the pieces to which Staunton gave his name.

## BIRD'S FAREWELL FROM CHESS

Towards the end of the year Bird's continuing grief towards his colleagues became more and more tangible. He started to isolate himself and was absent from the type of events he would never have missed in former days. Nor did he attend any meeting or event organized by the City of London Chess Club, nor was he present at one of the various expositions of Rosenbaum's paintings depicting the most important players of the day.

Bird's reluctance to make an appearance among his peers was soon enough explained in an extensive circular he spread amongst the press. According to the *Chess Player's Chronicle* of 4 January 1881 (p. 8), Bird first released an anonymous tract. In their next edition of 11 January (p. 19) it was stated that Bird had "revised the original circular, added some new matter, and given it his name." On 18 January the same magazine published a letter by Bird in which he denied ever having written anything on chess anonymously (p. 36).

The pamphlet, *A Slight Chess Retrospect and Explanation*, counts four pages. The copy consulted by the present author was signed "H.E. Bird."[25] Bird unhesitatingly ventilated his opinions on British chess life. Relations with his fellow masters, already

H.E. Bird, photograph forwarded by his nephew, also Henry Edward Bird, and published in *1.P–KB4: A Guide to Bird's Opening.*

unpleasant after the events of the summer, completely broke off when Bird announced his definitive goodbye from the public chess arena.

In his long and controversial monologue Bird laid out his concerns about the decline of chivalry and increasing professionalization of his favorite game. According to Bird's analysis this evolution went hand in hand with the negative role of the foreign chess players. Especially Mason and Steinitz were targeted. Bird's pamphlet in full is presented in Appendix 2: Outtakes.

The *Glasgow Weekly Herald* released a part of Bird's rantings on 27 November 1880. Just as with his earlier grievances concerning the Brunswick tournament, Bird received full support from John Jenkin, its chess editor. Other columnists noticed Bird's literal activities but they were less eager to delve further into the matter while they also offered critical remarks about Bird's own role in recent controversies. One of the most important voices, Potter, recognized Bird's so-called chess spirit, but he also wrote in *Land and Water* (11 December 1880) that "Fairness, however, demands the admission of counterpoising failings, and particularly that by his many quarrels and disputes he has at times done a serious injury to the cause of chess."

A letter by Bird, published on 25 December 1880 in the *Glasgow Weekly Herald*, drew the attention of Potter (it is quoted in Appendix 2: Outtakes). He reacted thoroughly to Bird's statement

---

23. The design of the standard chess pieces was registered by Nathaniel Cook in 1849. Staunton, in return for a fee, advocated for them in his *Illustrated London News* chess column.

24. For a label from a box of Bird chessmen see: http://www.chesshistory.com/winter/winter42.html, item 5383.

25. Retrieved at the Harvard University library (a gift from Silas W. Howland). This appears to be the sole surviving copy.

hat meetings between first-class players had grown much fewer in umber.[26]

Some columnists targeted Bird himself. Max Judd, who had declared himself to be far from a friend of Bird during the latter's stay n New York, described him mildly as "garrulous" in the *St. Louis Globe Democrat* of 2 January 1881. The sharpest reaction came from ohn Wisker. In earlier days he never showed himself as especially ritical of Bird but his opinion of him had completely changed, onsidering the following fragment. This is partly explained by his ersonal acquaintance with Bird, but probably private sources had nformed him of developments in England. If so, these sources are ot in the least favorable to Bird.

> He says nothing about the importance of keeping one's temper—a much more useful subject. It is no secret that Mr. Bird's retirement is mainly caused by the absolute refusal of his contemporaries to play with him. The Brunswick congress, for example, would never have taken place had he been allowed to enter. A temper naturally hot is not likely to be improved by years

and frequent attacks of gout. Latterly Mr. Bird has become an impossibility as a chess player, though when he can govern himself he is a genial and humorous companion, and his genius for the game is undeniable [*Australasian*, 9 April 1881].

Bird's intention to retire was tested when he was challenged for a match by the young Isidor Gunsberg. Judd's reply to the news was poisonous.

> Before resting in some obscure spot where he will be forgotten, Mr. H.E. Bird now has a chance to try the strength of his wins in a flight with Mr. Gunsberg (...) [*St. Louis Globe Democrat*, 2 January 1881].

In merely a few years Gunsberg grew into one of England's strongest players, but in 1880 he was just making his first steps among the chess elite. For a small stake of £10 or £20 he challenged every major British player, with a preference for Bird. Bird nevertheless stuck to his decision to bid chess farewell and he refused the match offer—a unique act in his chess career.[27]

26.  Potter came out with a more nuanced perspective although he also could not hide how deeply he felt about the antiprofessionalism and aversion towards foreign layers: "There is no doubt that, as alleged by Mr. Bird, first-class practice has to a large extent died out, and this is certainly a fact to be regretted. Whether he is right as o the causes of this decadence is very far from being equally clear. Our own views lead us to regard professional play with repugnance, and it would suit our sympathies ery well to attribute the mischief of which Mr. Bird complains to the foreign players now resident amongst us, but we cannot shut our eyes to the fact that in the days which Mr. Bird so fondly recalls professionalism raged rampant at the Divan, and the stories, some of them highly humorous, which have descended to us as to the strange evices of the shilling hunters of that time, show that professionalism was not less repulsive, but very much more so then than now. For ourselves, we wish all the foreigners vould comply with Wisker's tearful request and 'return to the land they (presumably) love so well,' but as they cannot be induced to adopt that course, we are inclined to et the sleeping lion of controversy enjoy his nap, and perhaps he may never awake which would also be a good thing." *Land and Water*, 8 January 1881.

27.  In the letter published by the *Chess Player's Chronicle* on 18 January 1881 (p. 36), Bird wrote "that I should enter into no match except with Steinitz, who has a long tanding engagement with me, as explained in a circular which I have recently issued." This wish to play a rematch with Steinitz was obviously of a vain nature by now. In act Bird was confirming his withdrawal from chess by refusing Gunsberg.

# ◆ Part VIII ◆

# RETURN TO THE CHESSBOARD, 1881–1884

## CHESS IN EXETER

After his renouncement from chess Bird avoided his peers at Simpson's Divan for a few years. He also gave no sign of life when the chess world focused on the tournament held in Berlin in 1881. Then, it came as a surprise to many that Bird was present again in Vienna in May 1882. Yet, strictly speaking he persevered in his voluntary retreat for just a few weeks. The *Glasgow Weekly Herald*, for instance, announced on 12 February 1881 that Bird had been busy for some time with the organization of a new chess club. Rooms were already taken at Anderton's hotel in Fleet Street. The same London correspondent of the *Herald* informed his readers on 5 March that a banquet to inaugurate the club took place on 28 Feb-

ruary. This was the last ever heard about the Anderssen Chess Club, as Bird had baptized it.

On that very same 28 February, according to the *London Gazette* of 11 March 1881 (on p. 1161), the partnership between Bird and George Brand was dissolved in mutual consent. That Bird had been able to manage an accounting firm is curious, George Brand remained officially active as an accountant and is listed among his colleagues in the *Kelly's Directory* for 1882. Bird is absent from that list.

The end of his partnership with Brand coincided perfectly with a new engagement that made Bird travel for the first time to Exeter in Devonshire in March 1881. Perhaps this contract may have persuaded Bird to liquidate his firm with Brand, or it may of course have been the result of a search for a new job.

On 19 March the *Exeter and Plymouth Gazette Daily Telegram* "local intelligence" column noticed the presence of Bird. This aroused the interest of a Mr. W.F. Lambert. Nothing is known about this chess player, but he may have been related to Charles James Lambert of the same city. The latter was a decent player, able to hold his own at a few congresses of the C.C.A.

Bird and W.F. Lambert contested a few friendly matches on the evenings of 24 and 25 March, the outcomes of which were published in the same newspaper on 28 March. Two matches—both with the arrangement that the first game played on even terms, after which Bird gave for the second game the odds of pawn and move and then, for a third, the odds of a knight—ended in a victory for Bird (respectively 3–0 and 2–1). A third match began after an adjustment of the odds and Bird now offered a rook to his opponent. Lambert won the first game. No further results were published.

On the third day of April, when the census of 1881 was taken, Bird was back in London. He had left Sturgeon Road, where he had written his pamphlet a few months earlier, for 167 Mayall Road in Brixton.[1] Brixton, situated in the south of Lambeth, was known to be a middle-class suburb during the second part of the nineteenth century. Compared to his previous and following addresses, Bird probably never lived farther away from the center of London (with the exception of his married years in Wimbledon).

Bird returned to Devonshire in June. His presence was noticed twice by the local *Exeter and Plymouth Gazette*. On 10 June a novel public challenge was made to local gentlemen for a friendly encounter on the chessboard. No follow-up of any of Bird's chess feats was published.

Exactly a week later, on 17 June, the same newspaper recorded the contribution of 2s. 6d. by H.E. Bird to the Beaconsfield Memorial Fund. This fund was established to commemorate the conservative politician Benjamin Disraeli, Earl of Beaconsfield, who had died on 19 April. If this sum hints to Bird's political preference, it comes only as a small surprise, given Bird's patriotism.

Bird's ties with the London chess scene intensified from the fall of 1881 onwards. At that time he started to visit the chess rooms at Purssell's on a regular basis. Early in 1882 he released a new booklet, *Chess Practice*, which contained some personal information besides the chess content.

At the end of this work, Bird included a remarkable advertisement in which he made an appeal for new clients.[2]

In the meantime Bird had changed his dwellings again, for he gave 14 Addington Square as his new home. This address, situated near Walworth Road, was a dwelling house. It was put on sale in an ad that appeared in *The Times* on 23 April 1883, from which one learns that a tenant occupied it at a yearly rent of £42.

Bird himself had left the building earlier on. At the end of 1882 he started to contribute chess articles to various newspapers. Bird signed them with his new address, 5 Heygate Street. Just as were his two previous abodes this address was in the near vicinity of Walworth Road, at some two miles from the heart of the city of London.

Bird finally found stability here and he remained in Heygate Street until he was forced to leave in 1900 when his health broke down.

That Bird's living pattern changed so drastically, from a constant mover to a long time lodger, may have had something to do with the discharge from his aforementioned bankruptcy that he finally received in April 1883.

---

# Match with Maczuski 1881

Bird reappeared on the London chess radar in September when he played a match with Maczuski at Purssell's, for which a nominal purse was assembled by what Bird in *Chess Practice* (p. 20) called the "warm admirers of the brilliant and clever play of Maczuski." It is remarkable that Bird made his, albeit modest, comeback at Purssell's and not at the Divan. Purssell's was situated in the heart of the City of London, and it seems evident that this was the place to be for Bird to arrange his businesses. By avoiding the Divan there was no chance that he would encounter the fellow masters with whom he collided a year earlier.[3]

Ladislas Maczuski was born in Poland around 1838. He only learned the rules of the game in his early twenties but made rapid progress. Maczuski never got involved in serious tournament chess. He made his name as an expert by giving blindfold simultaneous displays, mostly in France and Italy. Around 1881 Maczuski ended up in London where he became an habitué of the City of London Chess Club and Purssell's. Bird and Maczuski had a similar, disorderly style of playing chess with a keen eye for pleasing the onlookers. George MacDonnell visited the match and wrote a short and lively report.

> I visited Purssell's a few days ago and found chess playing there very luxuriant. The room was crowded, and I recognized many old faces, looking as young as ever. The principal attraction was the first game in a short match between

---

1. 1881 census: Class: RG 11; Piece: 622; Folio: 74; Page: 24.

2. Literally: "H.E. Bird begs respectfully to remind his chess friends and the public generally that he will be always happy to devote his personal attention to the arrangement and adjustment of books and accounts at a very moderate charge."

3. In recent times the services offered at the Divan had much declined, according to MacDonnell: "I occasionally look in at Simpson's Divan, not to play chess, but for old acquaintance sake. I cannot, however, help observing how painfully conspicuous by their absence are many of the faces with which I have been long familiar. What has caused this dismal blank? The old Divan, which was thrice as large as the present saloon, was, as a rule, daily crowded with chess players from all parts of the town and country, amongst whom were regularly to be found all the notabilities, English and foreign. ... Thus when you walked into that room in former days you knew exactly where to find the persons whose company you desired. You could find the amateurs or the professionals just as inclination prompted you, or you could retire to some snug corner to read your book or newspaper, or to enjoy a conversation with your friends. But they have changed all that. The present room is so small that readers, smokers, professionals, and amateurs, are all huddled together. There is no privacy possible either for chess, for conversation, or for study. If you sit down to play a game, the chances are that some unwelcome critic will seat himself by your side and keep up a running commentary upon your moves, and if you have an objection to being stifled by smoking, the chances are that two smokers of extra strong tobacco will take up their positions on either side of you." *Illustrated Sporting and Dramatic News*, 30 April 1881. ¶ A similar complaint was made in the *Liverpool Weekly Albion*: "Foreign, and some British, professionals are not ready to compete except for very high stakes; and chess in public is assuming wholly a business form. One chess center is the Strand, a delightful resort ten years ago, is not so now," quoted in the *Chess Player's Chronicle*, 26 April 1882, p. 203.

the veteran Bird and Mr. Maczuski. The game was full of life and prettiness, and many good moves were made on both sides before the on-looking's critics had time to discover them, much less to mention them aloud. The game was finished off in less than one hour, and resulted in a drawn battle, owing to a hasty move made by Mr. Bird when victory was within his grasp [*Illustrated Sporting and Dramatic News*, 17 September 1881].

Bird subsequently scored five straight wins, after which the contest was over.

| Match with Maczuski, September 1881 | | | | | | | |
|---|---|---|---|---|---|---|---|
| | 1 | 2 | 3 | 4 | 5 | 6 | |
| H.E. Bird | ½ | 1 | 1 | 1 | 1 | 1 | 5 |
| L. Maczuski | ½ | 0 | 0 | 0 | 0 | 0 | 0 |

Bird released a fragment of one of his games with Maczuski. If he dated it correctly, the game must have been an offhand one.

**556) Maczuski–Bird    0–1**
Offhand game
London, 22 October 1881
C45

**1. e4 e5 2. Nf3 Nc6 3. d4 e×d4 4. N×d4 Bc5 5. Be3 Qf6 6. c3 Qg6 7. Nd2 Nf6 8. Qf3 N×d4 9. c×d4 Bb4 10. e5 Ne4 11. 0-0-0 B×d2† 12. B×d2 d5 13. h3 Qc6† 14. Kb1 Qa4 15. Bc1 0-0 16. Be2 f6 17. Qe3 f×e5 18. d×e5 N×f2 19. Rd4** Black wins quickly after 19. ... Bf5†! 20. Ka1 Qc2 21. Bd2 N×h1—*Chess Practice*, p. 50.

The following game is considered a highlight of Bird's legacy. His immortal draw. It was in all likelihood an offhand affair, played at Purssell's at the end of 1881 or early in 1882.

**557) Bird–MacDonnell    ½–½**
Offhand game
London 1882 (?)
B20

"The subjoined game was recently played between Messrs. Bird and MacDonnell, and was expressly arranged to test the soundness of the Wing Gambit in the Sicilian Defense. The game is a fine one, abounding in points of interest, though we cannot say it establishes anything in favor of the Wing Gambit"—Wisker.

**1. e4 c5 2. b4 c×b4 3. a3 b×a3 4. d4 e6 5. e5 d5 6. f4 f5 7. N×a3 Bb4† 8. Kf2 Nh6 9. Qh5† Kf8** Both kings are in for a party. **10. Nb5 Ng4† 11. Kf3 g6 12. Qg5 Be7 13. Ba3 Nc6 14. h3 h5** (*see diagram*)

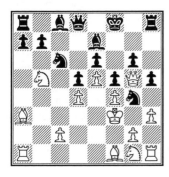

*After 14. ... h5*

**15. h×g4** Played with some brilliant ideas in mind, but settling for a small edge with 15. Ke2 was certainly wiser. **15. ... h×g4† 16. Kg3 R×h1 17. Qf6† Kg8 18. Q×g6† Kh8 19. Kf2 Bh4†** 19. ... Bd7 leaves Bird with the tough task to prove his compensation. **20. Ke3 N×e5** His previous move was not bad at all, as long as he was willing to acknowledge the uselessness of it by playing the silly 20. ... Be7. MacDonnell of course would never risk his reputation with such a whimsical move. **21. d×e5 Qb6† 22. Kd2 Bf2** Both players keep on pursuing their own aims without the slightest consideration for the safety of their kings. After 22. ... Bd7 there is nothing better for White than to take the perpetual. **23. Bd3** A necessary precaution to play for a win is 23. c3. With a safe spot for his king, Bird can accomplish the punishment of MacDonnell's last weak moves, for if 23. ... Bd7 24. Be7 and if 23. ... Bh4 24. Qh6† Kg8 25. Bf8! **23. ... Bd7** A tempo too late, as 24. Be7! (Bird) wins at once. Instead 23. ... Be3† 24. Kc3 (if 24. Ke2 Rh2 25. Be7 R×g2† draws) 24. ... B×f4 25. Be7 B×e5† 26. Kb3 Rh7! maintains the balance. **24. Nf3 R×a1 25. Be7** A nice sample of youthful hubris. **25. ... Be1†! 26. N×e1 Qf2† 27. Kc3 Q×e1† 28. Kd4 Ra4†** These last few moves were perfectly played by MacDonnell. Here 28. ... Qg1† rapidly mates. **29. c4 R×c4†** Wrong. After 29. ... Qa1† 30. Ke3 Qg1†, White's king becomes the victim of Black's queen and rook. **30. B×c4 Qe4† 31. Kc3 Q×c4† 32. Kd2 Q×f4† 33. Kd1** drawn by perpetual check—*Australasian* (Wisker), 17 June 1882; *Sheffield and Rotherham Independent* (Bird), 21 April 1883.

---

## CHESS PRACTICE

Bird's real comeback among his peers occurred in Vienna in May 1882 but a few months earlier his name had already popped up in chess columns when he published his third chess book, *Chess Practice*. *Chess Practice* is a small booklet, with fewer than 100 pages, with a curious construction. The introduction takes up one fifth of the book. It hardly contains anything new, as Bird took the opportunity to explain all over again his views on the merits of amateur, chivalrous, chess in the face of professional chess. Not unexpectedly he remained loyal to his point of view by rejecting the latter. A prominent place was given to tournaments and match results, with an emphasize on Bird's narrow loss against Steinitz in 1866.

On the title page as well as on page 15 Bird comes up with a novel claim when he calls himself the "amateur chess champion" ever since his win against Wisker which, he pretends, was known as the "amateur championship."[4]

When coming to the purpose of *Chess Practice* Bird informed his readers that he wanted to provide an addition to *Chess Masterpieces* in the form of "an additional index which should specify each form of opening under a distinct heading, with variations consecutively arranged in such an order as would admit of a convenient mode of

4. At the time the critics glossed over it, but in 1884, at the time of Wisker's death, MacDonnell ridiculed Bird's presumption: "Several incorrect statements are being circulated in the newspapers respecting the late Mr. John Wisker. The funniest of them all is that his contest with Mr. Bird was for the 'amateur championship.' Why, such a thing was not in existence at the time, nor any time since. It never existed but on paper. Each match was played for £5, and nothing more." *Illustrated Sporting and Dramatic News*, 29 March 1884.

comparing the line of play adopted in each game, and the degree of success which attended it" (p. 5).

Though some of his contemporaries wrote a positive review of *Chess Practice* the general sentiment was one of disappointment. And not undeservedly so since this booklet consists in fact of an index and copied parts from *Chess Masterpieces*. There was not much material for the student either. Bird limited himself to giving just the first moves of all kinds of opening variations, without offering any explanation at all. As usual Bird overemphasized his favorite openings.

# Vienna 1882

By far the principal chess event of 1882 was the tournament organized by the Vienna Chess Club to commemorate its twenty-fifth anniversary. Under the protection and management of Kolisch a serious prize fund, containing six prizes, was set up. The announcement of a special prize, for the player who had scored best against the top three, unleashed an animated discussion in the press. Some believed that the attribution of this prize could be influenced in case a chief prize winner decided to lose on purpose a crucial game. Such suspicions remind one of Bird's problems at the Clipper tournament in New York in 1876, but there had been a more obvious case of fraud at the United States championship of 1880. One of the players involved, Preston Ware, was now present to enter the tournament in Vienna. Thus any suspicions gained extra ground.

There appears to have been no such fallacious incidents in Vienna, but the eventual effect of the extra prize nevertheless led to some grumblings. Zukertort, finishing fifth, made the best score against the top three. His combined prize money (£24 and £32) outnumbered the £48 received by the third prize winner, James Mason.

The prize fund was large enough to attract all the prominent players of the day. The most notable participant was Wilhelm Steinitz. Despite Steinitz's having proven his superiority with match victories against Zukertort (in 1872) and Blackburne (in 1876), his position was somewhat undermined by an absence of nine years from the tournament arena. Steinitz was joined by all of his likely challengers: Blackburne, the winner of the Berlin 1881 tournament, Zukertort and Winawer, joint winners in Paris in 1878, Mackenzie, Mason, Louis Paulsen, et al. Perhaps a bit surprising for his contemporaries, Bird also travelled to Vienna to play in his first major event since the farewell pamphlet written at the end of 1880. All in all 18 players took part. As the event was a double round-robin it would last not less than seven weeks.

The first games were played on 10 May. Bird's opponent, the Russian Mikhail Chigorin, had not arrived yet and their game was postponed until after the fourth round. Bird commenced badly with two losses against the Austrian players Bernhard Fleissig and Englisch. Then he got involved in a major dispute that arose in his game with Mason. This game started quite eventfully. After surviving a badly played opening Bird pursued a magnificent attack which threw his opponent on the ropes. When Mason overstepped the time limit at move 30 he faced a completely lost position. Bird, confident as ever, decided not to claim the game and play it out. A few moves later Bird started making some errors and in the end he was even forced to resign. An account of what happened was given by Steinitz, who combined playing in the tournament with journalistic work for *The Field*.

> On Thursday no play took place, on account of the Catholic holiday, but most of the players assembled in the morning in order to witness the trial of the case "Bird v. Mason." Excepting the parties directly interested, none of the players appeared as witnesses. Mr. Mason averred that he had made his 30th move before the excess of time was alleged, and, in fact, that he had kept within the rule-of-time limit. He admitted, however, that, in order to save time, he had not taken down several moves and it was therefrom concluded that he could not be absolutely certain at which part of the game he passed the hour. On the other hand, besides Mr. Bird, three members of the Vienna club and one American visitor positively testified to Mr. Mason having exceeded his time before making his 30th move, and there was only some discrepancy as regards the extent of the transgression. The rule of the tournament was perfectly clear for such a case, and the committee decided accordingly that the game should be scored for Mr. Bird [*The Field*, 27 May 1882].

Just one crucial element was left out of Steinitz' account, namely that one participant had issued a complaint about Mason's overstepping of the time limit. In a letter to *Chess Monthly* (June 1882 p. 295), the British amateur Wordsworth Donisthorpe debunked the identity of that player, namely Steinitz himself. Donisthorpe sharply condemned Steinitz, whose "sense of rectitude is exquisitely delicate—when self-interest is on the same side." In the next number of *Chess Monthly* several players shed their light on the question. One of them was Mason. He insisted on his previous statement in the conflict that "Mr. Bird claimed that I had lost by time. I declined to admit that claim, and required him to prove it or go on with the play. He did the latter, not from any "disdain" to win from me in any way he could, but because that or resignation on his part was the only alternative" (July 1882, p. 328).

Bird summarized his point of view in his analysis of the game:

> This is the contest in which Mason slightly exceeded his time limit, and lookers-on and Bird called attention to the fact, but the game was not claimed. Mason's score was formidable at this time. Steinitz, Mackenzie, Winawer, and other players initiated a protest, without any concurrence from Bird, who strange to say, actually continued and lost the game. He was suffering severely at the time, and probably the interruption of the game and pain caused him to make the unaccountable slips and loss of a piece subsequently. Donisthorpe one of our best esteemed and finest amateur players, a warm supporter of Mason, considered an injustice had been done on this occasion. I regret that Donisthorpe had not all the facts as well as the game itself before him when he commenced a correspondence with the *Chess Monthly* on the subject. It is to be regretted that Bird's name was imported into the correspondence. In the unfortunate absence of any member of the play committee, he simply did his duty to all in the tournament by calling attention to Mason's exceeding the time limit. The committee managing a tournament should take these delicate questions out of the hands of the players [*Modern Chess*, p. 30].

Bird ultimately received the point. Health issues tormented him and his condition may explain why he did not fare well in the following games of the first cycle. A clear majority of them were lost. One of these losses was interesting: Against Winawer, Bird obtained a powerful attack which he seemed on the verge of crowning by sacrificing a rook in return for two extremely strong passed pawns. Just before he was able to collect the point, however, a huge blunder reversed the situation. Bird ended up in a difficult ending which he ultimately lost.

The strongest player succumbing to Bird was the young but highly promising Austrian Max Weiss. In an innocent-looking

## International chess tournament, Vienna, 10 May–24 June 1882

**Site:** Wiener Schachgesellschaft
**Playing hours:** 10 a.m.–2 p.m., 4 p.m.–12
**Prizes:** 1st 5000 Franken, 2nd 2000 Franken, 3rd 1000 Franken, 4th 500 Franken, 5th 300 Franken, 6th 200 Franken
**Time limit:** 15 moves per hour

| | 1 | 2 | 3 | 4 | 5 | 6 | 7 | 8 | 9 | 10 | 11 | 12 | 13 | 14 | 15 | 16 | 17 | 18 | |
|---|---|---|---|---|---|---|---|---|---|---|---|---|---|---|---|---|---|---|---|
| 1 W. Steinitz | | 1½ | ½½ | 0½ | ½1 | 10 | ½½ | 11 | 01 | 1½ | 01 | 10 | 11 | 11 | 11 | 01 | 1+ | 1+ | 24 |
| 2 S. Winawer | 0½ | | 00 | 1½ | 0½ | 10 | 11 | 10 | 01 | 1½ | 11 | 11 | 11 | 11 | 11 | 11 | 1+ | 0+ | 24 |
| 3 J. Mason | ½½ | 11 | | 0½ | ½1 | ½½ | ½½ | 11 | 11 | 10 | 01 | 11 | ½1 | 1½ | 0½ | 11 | 0+ | ½+ | 23 |
| 4 J.H. Zukertort | 1½ | 0½ | 1½ | | ½½ | 0½ | 0½ | 11 | 11 | 00 | 11 | 01 | 01 | 11 | 1+ | 11 | 1+ | 0+ | 22½ |
| 5 G.H. Mackenzie | ½0 | 1½ | ½0 | ½½ | | 10 | ½1 | 1½ | ½0 | 11 | 11 | 01 | 01 | 11 | 10 | 1½ | 1+ | 1+ | 22½ |
| 6 J.H. Blackburne | 01 | 01 | ½½ | 1½ | 01 | | ½½ | 0½ | 10 | 01 | 10 | 11 | 1½ | 11 | 10 | 11 | 0+ | 1+ | 21½ |
| 7 B. Englisch | ½½ | 00 | ½½ | 1½ | ½0 | ½½ | | 11 | ½0 | ½½ | ½½ | 0½ | ½½ | 01 | 11 | 11 | 1+ | ½1 | 19½ |
| 8 L. Paulsen | 00 | 01 | 00 | 00 | 0½ | 1½ | 00 | | ½½ | ½1 | ½1 | 11 | ½1 | ½1 | ½1 | 11 | ½+ | ½+ | 18½ |
| 9 A. Wittek | 10 | 10 | 00 | 00 | ½1 | 01 | ½1 | ½½ | | ½0 | 01 | 1- | ½½ | ½½ | ½+ | 1½ | ½+ | 1+ | 18 |
| 10 M. Weiss | 0½ | 0½ | 01 | 11 | 00 | 10 | ½½ | ½0 | ½1 | | 0½ | 11 | 0½ | 0½ | 0+ | 00 | 1+ | 1+ | 16½ |
| 11 V. Hruby | 10 | 00 | 10 | 00 | 00 | 01 | ½½ | ½0 | 10 | 1½ | | 10 | ½½ | 11 | 01 | 10 | 0+ | 1+ | 16 |
| 12 M.I. Chigorin | 01 | 00 | 00 | 10 | 10 | 00 | 1½ | 00 | 0+ | 00 | 01 | | 1+ | 00 | 11 | 1½ | 0+ | 01 | 14 |
| 13 A. Schwarz | 00 | 00 | ½0 | 10 | 10 | 0½ | ½½ | ½0 | ½½ | 1½ | ½½ | 0- | | ½0 | 1+ | ½- | 0+ | 1+ | 14 |
| 14 P. Meitner | 00 | 00 | 0½ | 00 | 00 | 00 | 10 | ½0 | ½½ | 1½ | 00 | 11 | ½1 | | 0+ | 01 | 0+ | 1+ | 13 |
| 15 H.E. Bird | 00 | 00 | 1½ | 0- | 01 | 10 | 00 | ½0 | ½- | 1- | 10 | 00 | 0- | 0- | | 11 | ½+ | 01 | 12 |
| 16 P. Ware | 10 | 00 | 00 | 00 | 0½ | 00 | 00 | 00 | 0½ | 11 | 01 | 0½ | ½+ | 10 | 00 | | 0+ | 1+ | 11 |
| 17 J. Noa | 0- | 0- | 1- | 0- | 0- | 1- | 0- | ½- | ½- | 0- | 1- | 1- | 1- | 1- | ½- | 1- | | ½- | 9 |
| 18 B. Fleissig | 0- | 1- | ½- | 1- | 0- | 0- | ½0 | ½- | 0- | 00 | 00 | 10 | 0- | 0- | 10 | 0- | ½+ | | 7 |

*Tie match:*

| | 1 | 2 | |
|---|---|---|---|
| W. Steinitz | 0 | 1 | 1 |
| S. Winawer | 1 | 0 | 1 |

position Bird caught his opponent with a daring sacrifice of the exchange. One single inaccuracy from Weiss was enough to decide the game in a handsome fashion.

Bird's playing level increased in the second cycle and he scored ½ points out of 11 games (one of which was due to the forfeit of osef Noa). Bird beat two strong opponents, Mackenzie and Black-urne, while he drew with Mason, another contender for a high rize. Bird's game with Winawer was again a highlight. A full-ledged battle left Bird with excellent winning chances but in the nd the tenacious Winawer succeeded in reversing the result again. n the meantime Bird's physical condition had gradually worsened. He was not able attend the twenty-ninth round and lost on time. Bird's health did not improve and he forfeited his next four games s well. Then, against all odds, he reappeared to play his last round ame.

In this 34th round, Bird opposed his long-time foe Wilhelm Steinitz. The world's strongest player was leading the tournament with 23 points. Three rivals, Winawer, Mason and Zukertort, ay only a half point behind. The most dangerous of them was Winawer: he still had to play out an adjourned game as well. In this ame, against Weiss, an endgame was reached in which Winawer was a pawn up. Despite having only small winning chances it was vident that the Polish master would try everything he could to defeat Weiss. The resumption of this game was planned after the final ound.

The relevant pairings for the last round were Steinitz–Bird, Englisch–Winawer, Zukertort–Weiss and Meitner–Mason. Steinitz ounted on gaining his game with Bird by forfeit, but to his dismay, he Englishman found it his duty to assemble all his forces. Steinitz, n return, protested and claimed the game. Fortunately the committee allowed Bird to play. In his introduction to this important game Bird wrote about the circumstances:

> The following is an excellent specimen of the opening; it is the notable last game in the Vienna tournament of 1882, and I played it in deference to the wishes of the committee and principal prize winners, being in a lamentable state of health at the time (Steinitz protesting, because several of my previous games, vs. against Zukertort and five others [sic], through my illness and inability to leave the hospital—had been declared forfeited). The game was of the utmost importance as affecting the relative positions of the principal winners, and the ultimate destination of the first, second and third prizes [Modern Chess, pp. 27–28].[5]

The duel turned out to be a compelling affair. Both players had their share of the chances and around move 40 the tension had been driven to extreme heights, especially as Winawer had reached a winning position against Englisch. At the point when Steinitz seemed to have to cede at least a draw, Bird made a decisive error. After missing this unique chance Bird's attack faded away like snow under the sun. It cost Steinitz but little trouble to force his path to a win.

Winawer remained Steinitz's sole rival by beating Englisch. The outcome of the resumed game between Winawer and Weiss would decide about the first prize. After some 40 more moves, a draw was agreed and thus Winawer caught up Steinitz. The match ended in a 1–1 tie and the first two prizes were shared.

5. Some details were provided in an evocative eye-witness report by Adolf Albin: "Master Bird suffered a lot from his gout and it was impossible for him to attend several rounds. One already presumed he would default his game of the last round when suddenly the doors opened and two of the participants (if I remember correctly, these were Mason and the chivalrous Mackenzie) carried Bird on the hands to the board. Bird couldn't resist playing his game against the chess giant. 'I must win the game,' he told anyone surrounding him." *Deutsches Wochenschach*, 11 September 1892, p. 317.

## (558) Bird–B. Fleissig    0–1

International tournament (round 2)

Vienna, 11 May 1882

*C54*

1. e4 e5 2. Nf3 Nc6 3. Bc4 Bc5 4. c3 d6 5. b4 Bb6 6. Qb3 Qe7
7. a4 a5 8. b5 Nd8 9. d3 Nf6 10. Nbd2 Ne6 11. Nf1 Nc5 12. Qc2
Be6 13. Ne3 0–0 14. B×e6 f×e6 15. Nc4 Ncd7 16. N×b6 N×b6
17. Qb3 Nbd7 18. Be3 b6 19. 0–0 Kh8 20. Rae1 Nh5 21. d4 Rae8
22. Bc1 e×d4 23. c×d4 e5 24. Bb2 Nf4 25. g3 Ng6 26. Re3 e×d4
27. N×d4 Nc5 28. Qc2 Rf7 29. Nf5 Qd8 30. Rfe1 Ne5 31. f4
Nf3† 32. R×f3 R×f5 33. Rfe3 Rf7 34. Qc4 Rfe7 35. e5 d5
36. Qd4 Ne6 37. Qd1 d4 38. Rd3 Qd5 39. f5 Ng5 40. h4 Nh3†
41. Kh2 Nf2 42. Qf3 Q×f3 43. R×f3 Ng4† 44. Kg2 N×e5 45. Rf4
Nd3 46. R×e7 N×f4† 47. g×f4 R×e7 48. B×d4 Re4 49. Be5
R×a4 50. B×c7 Rb4 51. Kf3 Kg8 52. B×b6 R×b5 53. Bc7 a4
54. Be5 R×e5 55. f×e5 a3 White resigns—*Allgemeine Sportzeitung*,
18 May 1882.

## (559) Englisch–Bird    1–0

International tournament (round 3)

Vienna, 12 May 1882

*C61*

1. e4 e5 2. Nf3 Nc6 3. Bb5 Nd4 4. Bc4 b5 5. Bb3 Bc5 6. N×d4
B×d4 7. c3 Bb6 8. 0–0 Bb7 9. d4 Qh4 10. Nd2 e×d4 11. c×d4
Nf6 12. Nf3 Qh5 13. e5 Ng4 14. h3 Nh6 15. Ng5 Q×d1 16. R×d1
Nf5 17. d5 Nd4 18. Be3 N×b3 19. a×b3 B×e3 20. f×e3 0–0
21. Nf3 Rfe8 22. Kf2 h6 23. b4 a6 24. Rac1 Rac8 25. Rd4 c6
26. d6 Re6 27. e4 Rce8 28. Ke3 g5 29. Rc5 Kg7 30. g4 Kg6 31. h4
g×h4 32. N×h4† Kh7 33. Kf4 Rg8 34. Rd2 Rg5 35. Rh2 a5
36. Nf5 a×b4 37. Rc1 Rgg6 38. Rch1 c5 39. g5 B×e4 40. K×e4
R×g5 41. R×h6† R×h6 42. N×h6 Kg6 43. Ng8 c4 44. Nf6 c3
45. N×d7 Rg4† 46. Kd5 Rg2 47. b×c3 b×c3 48. Nc5 Rd2†
49. Kc6 c2 50. Rc1 b4 51. d7 Kf5 52. R×c2 Rd1 53. Kc7 Black
resigns—*Allgemeine Sportzeitung*, 18 May 1882.

## (560) Mason–Bird    0–1

International tournament (round 4)

Vienna, 13 May 1882

*A85*

1. d4 f5 2. c4 Nf6 3. Nc3 e6 4. a3 b6 5. Bf4 "Harrwitz invariably
played the bishop thus, and Blackburne and Mason appear to approve of it. I have already expressed an adverse opinion, and I notice
that Messrs. Zukertort and Hoffer consider it not adapted to this
form of opening"—Bird. 5. ... Bb7 6. e3 Be7 7. Nf3 0–0 8. Be2
Ne4 9. N×e4 f×e4 10. Nd2 d6 First 10. ... Bf6, threatening 11. ...
B×d4, is necessary. Mason now overlooks 11. Qc2, winning a pawn,
but this omission is immediately corrected. 11. Bg3 Bf6 12. Qc2
c5 13. N×e4 13. d×c5 (Zukertort) doesn't allow any complications.
13. ... c×d4 14. N×d6 14. 0–0 d×e3 15. f×e3 is the better way to
exchange pawns. Black's position is close to being a ruin. 14. ...
B×g2 15. Rg1 Bc6 16. Bg4 e5 "The sacrifice of the exchange is conceived in Mr. Bird's happiest style: he gets thereby an overwhelming
superiority of position"—Zukertort. 17. Be6† Kh8 18. Nf7† R×f7
19. B×f7 d3 20. Qd2 Na6 21. b4 *(see diagram)*

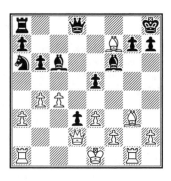

*After 21. b4*

21. ... Nc7 "Very well played: threatening to cut off the retrea[t]
of the White bishop by 22. ... Bf3"—Zukertort. This retreat is rathe[r]
innocent, as Mason's bishop escapes from any trouble easily enough
The straightforward 21. ... Bf3!, on the other hand, effectively threatens to cut off the bishop from the other troops. After the forced sequence 22. Be6 e4 23. Rc1 Qe7 24. Bd5 (24. Bh3 is an option, bu[t]
24. ... Qe8! is a strong rejoinder, after which the pressure is simila[r]
to the following variations) 24. ... Rd8. White's position looks ver[y]
solid, but at the same time it is curiously paralyzed. There are n[o]
constructive ideas at his disposal, while Black has some refined plans
This is illustrated by the following sample lines: (**a**) 25. Bc6 Nc5
26. b×c5 Q×c5 27. Bd5 Q×a3 28. Bc6 Bb2; (**b**) 25. h4 h5 26. Rc[1]
N×b4 27. a×b4 Q×b4 28. Rc1 Qa3 29. Kf1 Bb2 30. Rb1 Bc3; (**c**)
25. Rb1 b5 26. Rc1 Qd7 27. Kf1 b×c4 28. B×c4 Bb2. 22. Bh5 e[4]
23. Rc1 a5 24. b5 Bd7 25. B×c7? Mason played some good defensive moves, but here he completely misjudges the situation. There
is enough play left for him after 25. f3 Bf5 26. f×e4 B×e4 27. Bg[4]
25. ... Q×c7 26. Rg2 Be6 "Not too much purpose. Black shoul[d]
play at once 26. ... Rf8"—Zukertort. 27. Bd1 Rf8 28. Rg3 Bh[3]
29. f4 e×f3 *e.p.* 30. Kf2 "The loss of the exchange was unavoidable
White's game already seems lost. With his last move, Mason exceeded the prescribed time limit of two hours for thirty moves. M[r]
Bird didn't make use of his rights and continued the game in th[e]
conviction that he would win it anyway"—Lehner. 30. ... Bf[5]
31. Bb3 B×g3† "Correct play"—Bird. 32. h×g3 Qd6 33. e4 B×e[4]
"The simple and obvious 33. ... Qd4† would win the game off
hand"—Bird. 34. Re1 Qd4† 35. Re3 Bg6 35. ... Rf5 is the simples[t]
win. It plans to activate the rook along the g- or h-file. 36. Bd1 Be[6]
37. a4 h5 38. Qa2 Bb7 Black's first inferior move, although stil[l]
sufficient to win with a minimum of precision. The immediate 38. ...
h4! crashes open White's kingside before Mason gets the time t[o]
take h4 under control. 39. Qa3 Rd8 40. Qe7 Qb2† 41. Ke1 d2†?
A dreadful move. Not only is Bird's queen at once cut off from th[e]
battlefield, Bird also jeopardizes a piece along the way. 41. ... Rb[8]
consolidates, for if 42. Qc7 Rf8! 42. Kf2 Qd4 43. Q×b7 h[4]
44. Q×f3 h3 45. Qe4 Rf8† 46. Kg1 Qc5 47. Qe5 Q×c4 48. Qh5[†]
Kg8 49. Bb3? Now Mason succumbs to a gross miscalculation.
49. Q×h3! (Zukertort) keeps everything defended. 49. ... Rf1[†]
50. Kh2 Q×b3 51. R×b3 d1Q 52. Q×d1 R×d1 53. Rf3 Rd[4]
54. Rf4 Rb4?! Bird cannot bring himself to accept the draw tha[t]
would occur after 54. ... R×f4. 55. R×b4 a×b4 56. a5 b3 57. a×b[6]
b2 58. b7 b1Q 59. b8Q† Kh7 60. K×h3?! 60. Qe5 was much mor[e]
testing. 60. ... Qh1† 61. Kg4 Qe4† 62. Kg5 Qd5† 63. Kf4 Qd4[†]
64. Kf5 Qd5†? The wrong check. 64. ... Qd3† is a draw. 65. Qe[5]
Qd3† 66. Ke6 Qd8 67. Qe4† Kg8 68. Qd5 Qb8 69. Kd7† Kh[7]

0. Qh5† and then White resigns—*Österreichische Lesehalle* (Lehner),
August 1882, pp. 245–247; *Chess Monthly* (Zukertort), November
882, pp. 76–78; *Modern Chess* (Bird), pp. 29–30.

## 561) Bird–Chigorin   0–1
International tournament (round 1)
Vienna, 14 May 1882
*C59*

1. e4 e5 2. Nf3 Nc6 3. Bc4 Nf6 4. Ng5 d5 5. e×d5 Na5 6. Bb5†
6 7. d×c6 b×c6 8. Be2 h6 9. Nf3 e4 10. Ne5 Qc7 11. Ng4 B×g4
2. B×g4 Bd6 13. h3 0–0 14. Nc3 Nc4 15. b3 Ne5 16. Bb2 Rfe8
7. 0–0 Ne×g4 18. h×g4 Qd7 19. Qe2 N×g4 20. g3 Qf5 21. Kg2
Re6 22. Rae1 Rae8 23. Rh1 h5 24. Ref1 Qg6 25. Nd1 e3 26. Bd4
N×f2 27. R×f2 Q×g3† 28. Kf1 e×f2 29. Ne3 c5 30. Bc3 R×e3
31. d×e3 R×e3 32. Qd1 h4 33. Bd2 h3 White resigns—*Tournament Book*, pp. 60–61.

## 562) Noa–Bird   ½–½
International tournament (round 5)
Vienna, 15 May 1882
*C61*

1. e4 e5 2. Nf3 Nc6 3. Bb5 Nd4 4. N×d4 e×d4 5. c3 Bc5 6. Bc4
d5 7. d3 c6 8. Qc2 b5 9. Bb3 Bb6 10. Qe2 d6 11. h3 Qf6 12. Bd2
Ne7 13. Na3 Ng6 14. 0–0–0 a5 15. Rhf1 a4 16. Bc2 Bc5 17. Nb1
Be6 18. a3 Bb3 19. B×b3 a×b3 20. f4 Qe7 21. Rde1 Qa7 22. Qd1
Qa4 23. c×d4 B×d4 24. Bc3 c5 25. Kd2 Rc8 26. Ke2 Nh4
27. B×d4 c×d4 28. Rf2 Rc2† 29. Kf1 Ng6 30. Ree2 R×e2
31. Q×e2 0–0 32. Qd1 Rc8 33. Nd2 Rc2 34. N×b3 R×f2†
35. K×f2 N×f4 36. Qc2 Kh7 37. Kf3 Ng6 38. Na1 Qa6 39. Nb3
Qa4 40. g3 h4 41. Kg2 h×g3 42. K×g3 Ne5 43. Kh2 g6 44. Na1
Qa5 45. Qe2 b4 46. Nc2 b×a3 47. N×a3 d5 48. e×d5 Q×d5
49. Nc4 N×c4 50. d×c4 d3 51. Qd2 Q×c4 52. Kg3 Qc2 53. Qf4
Qb3 54. Qh4† Kg7 55. Qd4† f6 56. Qa7† Kh6 57. Qe3† g5
58. Qd2 Qc2 59. Qb4 Qc7† 60. Kf3 Qd7 61. Ke3 Q×h3†
62. Kd2 Qf3 63. Qf8† Kh5 64. Qe8† Kh4 65. b4 g4 66. b5 g3
67. Qh8† Kg4 68. Qg7† Kh3 69. Qh7† Kg4 70. Q×d3 Qf2†
71. Kc3 f5 72. Qd2 Kf3 73. Qd1† Kf4 74. Qd6† Kf3 75. Qd1†
Kg2 76. Qd2 f4 77. b6 Q×d2† 78. K×d2 f3 79. b7 f2 80. b8Q
f1Q 81. Qa8† Qf3 82. Qh8 Qf2† 83. Kd3 Kg1 84. Qe5 Qf3†
85. Kd2 g2 86. Qe1† Qf1 87. Qe5 Qf2† 88. Kd1 Qh4 89. Qc5†
Kh2 90. Qe5† Kh1 91. Qd5 Qg4† 92. Kd2 Qf4† 93. Ke2 Kh2
94. Qh5† Kg3 95. Qg6† Kh2 96. Qh5† Kg1 97. Qc5† Kh1
98. Qh5† Qh2 99. Qf3 Qe5† 100. Kf2 Qb2† 101. Kg3 Qe5†
102. Kf2 Qh2 103. Qe4 Qg1† 104. Kg3 Qh2† 105. Kf2 Qg1†
106. Kg3 Qh2† 107. Kf2 draw—*Tournament Book*, pp. 69–70.

## 563) Mackenzie–Bird   1–0
International tournament (round 6)
Vienna, 16 May 1882
*B46*

1. e4 c5 2. Nc3 Nc6 3. Nf3 e6 4. d4 c×d4 5. N×d4 a6 6. Be2
Bb4 7. 0–0 Nf6 8. N×c6 b×c6 9. e5 B×c3 10. b×c3 Nd5 11. Qd4
c5 12. Ba3 f5 13. f4 Ba6 14. B×a6 R×a6 15. Bc5 Ra8 16. Rab1
Rb8 17. Bd6 R×b1 18. R×b1 Ne7 19. B×e7 K×e7 20. Qd6† Kf7
21. Rb7 Kg6 22. h3 Kh5 23. Kh2 g5 24. R×d7 Qg8 25. g3 g×f4

26. g×f4 Qg6 27. Qe7 h6 28. Qg7 Q×g7 29. R×g7 Rd8 30. Re7
Kh4 31. R×e6 Rd2† 32. Kg1 Kg3 33. Rd6 R×c2 34. Kf1 Kf3
35. Rd3† K×f4 36. e6 Ke4 37. e7 K×d3 38. e8Q R×c3 39. Qe2†
Kd4 40. Qd2† Kc4 41. Q×h6 c5 42. h4 Rc2 43. h5 Kc3 44. Qe3†
Kb2 45. Qb3† Kc1 46. Q×c2† K×c2 47. h6 c4 48. h7 a4 49. h8Q
a3 50. Ke2 f4 51. Qd4 f3† 52. K×f3 c3 53. Ke2 Kb1 54. Q×c3
K×a2 55. Kd1 Black resigns—*Österreichische Lesehalle*, November
1882, pp. 340–342.

## (564) Bird–Hruby   1–0
International tournament (round 7)
Vienna, 17 May 1882
*C54*

1. e4 e5 2. Nf3 Nc6 3. Bc4 Bc5 4. c3 Nf6 5. b4 Bb6 6. d3 d6
7. a4 a5 8. b5 Ne7 9. 0–0 0–0 10. Na3 Ng6 11. Be3 c6 12. Nc2 d5
13. e×d5 c×d5 14. Bb3 h6 15. d4 e4 16. Ne5 Bc7 17. N×g6 f×g6
18. Qd2 Ng4 Bird's opening can hardly be called a success. His fifteenth move created some glaring holes along the c-file, while
Hruby's last moves also illustrate the weakness of the position of
Bird's king. But instead of immediately jumping to this attack,
Hruby had better continued his development with 18. ... Be6 first.
**19. g3 Kh7 20. Ne1 Nf6 21. Ng2 Bh3 22. Rfc1 Rc8 23. Rab1 Ng4
24. Bd1 b6 25. Bf4?** Right now 25. c4! can be favorably executed.
In case of 25. ... d×c4 26. B×g4 B×g4 27. R×c4 Be6 28. Rc3 Bd6
29. d5! R×c3 30. Q×c3 B×d5 31. Rd1, Black has problems along
the d-file and will soon lose back his extra pawn, and possibly even
more. The move actually played by Bird is a huge tactical mistake,
at least when met by the decisive 25. ... N×f2; e.g., 26. Q×f2 g5
27. B×c7 R×f2 28. B×d8 R×g2† 29. Kh1 Rf2 30. Bb3 R×d8 31. Kg1
e3. **25. ... g5? 26. Be3** Passive. There was nothing wrong with exchanges at c7 and g4 as his knight, once installed at e3, at least
matches the opponent's bishop. White has a simple and strong plan
in the form of a well-timed push c3–c4. **26. ... Bd6 27. Be2 Rc7
28. c4 d×c4 29. R×c4 N×e3** 29. ... R×c4 30. B×c4 Qf6 31. Bf1
Bb4 keeps strong pressure. The exchange at e3 gives Bird the sudden
chance to besiege the e-pawn. **30. Q×e3 Be6** 30. ... Rcf7 31. Rf1
Re7 keeps the e-pawn well defended. **31. R×c7 B×c7 32. Rc1 Bd5
33. Bc4 Rf3 34. Qe2 Bb8 35. Ne3 Bb7 36. d5 Bd6 37. Rd1** 37. Ba2
Bc5 38. Bb1 finally seals the fate of the sieged pawn. Bird's advantage
is minimal again after the text move, though the d-pawn remains a
strong asset. **37. ... Bc5 38. Ba2 Qe7 39. Bb1 Kh8 40. Ng4 Ra3
41. Ne3 Bc8 42. Qc4 Bd7?** This move loses a fatal tempo. There is
nothing to worry about after 42. ... Qe8, so as to be able to deal adequately with the push of the d-pawn, 43. d6 B×e3 44. f×e3 R×e3
45. Qc6 Bd7 46. Q×b6 Re2 would produce a balanced position.
**43. d6 Qe8 44. Q×e4 Qg8 45. Nf5 Qf8 46. Qe7 Q×e7 47. d×e7
Ra1 48. R×d7 R×b1† 49. Kg2 B×e7 50. N×e7 Rb4 51. h4 g×h4
52. g×h4 Kh7 53. Kg3 Re4 54. Nd5 Rg4† 55. K×g4** Black resigns—*Deutsche Schachzeitung*, May-June 1883, pp. 167–168.

## (565) Blackburne–Bird   1–0
International tournament (round 8)
Vienna, 19 May 1882
*B46*

1. e4 c5 2. Nf3 e6 3. Nc3 Nc6 4. d4 c×d4 5. N×d4 a6 6. Be2

Nf6 7. 0–0 d5 8. e×d5 N×d5 9. N×d5 e×d5 10. Bf3 Be7 11. Re1
0–0 12. B×d5 Q×d5 13. N×c6 Q×c6 14. R×e7 Be6 15. Bf4 Rfd8
16. Qe2 Bd5 17. Rc7 Qf6 18. Qe5 Qb6 19. c4 Bc6 20. Qf5 Q×b2
21. Rb1 Qd4 22. h4 Rf8 23. Re1 Q×c4 24. Re3 Rae8 25. Rg3
Re6 26. h5 g6 27. Be5 Qd5 28. f4 Qd1† 29. Kh2 Qd5 30. h×g6
h×g6 31. Qh3 Q×e5 32. f×e5 Kg7 33. Q×e6 Black resigns—*Tournament Book*, p. 97.

## (566) Winawer–Bird  1–0
International tournament (round 9)
Vienna, 20 May 1882
*B40*

"The following game was regarded as one of the most enterprising in the Vienna tournament. It illustrates the power of advanced pawns, two sacrifices having been made to secure the
winning position shown at move 36, which may be studied with
interest and advantage"—Bird.

**1. e4 c5 2. Nc3 Nc6 3. Nf3 e6 4. b3 d5 5. Bb5 Nf6 6. e×d5
e×d5 7. B×c6† b×c6 8. 0–0 Be7 9. d3** Winawer doesn't find the
modern plan of sieging the doubled c-pawn with 9. Na4, 10. Ba3
and 11. c4. **9. ... 0–0 10. Ne2 d4 11. Ng3 Nd5 12. Bd2 f5 13. Rc1
Bd6 14. Re1 f4** Quite a characteristic push for Bird. It is positionally
not well founded due to the glaring weakness of e4. **15. Ne4 Bg4
16. Qe2** More to the point was 16. c3 to create counterplay along
the c-file. **16. ... Re8 17. Qf1** A compromising move, after Bird's
evident reply. 17. h3 Bh5 and then 18. c3 is still his best chance, but
all hope for an opening edge is gone. **17. ... B×f3 18. g×f3 Re6
19. Qh3?** A severe loss of time that yields to Black a dangerous
attack. With 19. Kh1 White can organize his defense just in time.
**19. ... Rh6 20. Qf1** "The only square for the queen"—Bird. **20. ...
Qh4 21. h3** (see diagram)

*After 21. h3*

**21. ... Ne3!** "Considered over venturesome and rash in a great
tournament game, but yet we believe sound and good"—Bird. Bird's
move is indeed quite strong, with an undeniable surprise value. The
calm 21. ... Bc7 is just as good. **22. f×e3 f×e3 23. Ba5** 23. B×e3
doesn't bring salvation either: 23. ... d×e3 24. N×d6 Rg6† 25. Kh2
Qf4† 26. Kh1 R×d6. **23. ... Bf4** Preserving the bishop at this point
costs valuable time. At once targeting White's f-pawn, his crucial
weakness, with 23. ... Rf8! intending 24. ... Qh5, should have earned
him the full point sooner rather than later. **24. Re2 Re8 25. Be1
Rg6† 26. Kh1 Qh6??** 26. ... Qh5 and 27. ... Rf8 keeps the advantage. After this move Winawer gets, but misses, the chance to consolidate with the surprising 27. h4; e.g., 27. ... Bd6 28. Qh3 Rf8
29. Rg2. **27. c4 Re5** The correct plan remains 27. ... Qh5 and 28. ...

**Szymon Winawer.**

Rf8 and the f-pawn will fall. **28. Rcc2?** The idea 28. h4 and 29. Qh
would be close to winning again. After the text move the chance
are about equal. **28. ... Qh5 29. h4 Qf5** "It was indispensable to
prevent 30. Qh3"—Bird. **30. b4** A good bid for counterplay. **30. ..
c×b4 31. B×b4 Bg3** Bird's attack is in full swing again. Winawer i
almost out of moves, forcing him to bring the bishop to the defense
**32. Be1?** The wrong way! Correct is 32. Bd6!, though the true poin
of the move is deeply hidden. After the forced 32. ... R×e4 33. d×e
Qf6 34. h5 Rg5 35. B×g3 R×g3 36. Qb1 R×f3 37. Qb8† Whit
rescues himself with a draw. **32. ... R×e4!** This was Bird's brillian
conception. **33. d×e4 Qf4 34. Rg2** The difference with the lin
given at move 32 comes to the surface after 34. h5 Rg5 35. B×g
R×g3 36. Qb1 d3, and suddenly Black has covered the crucial squar
b8! **34. ... B×e1 35. Q×e1 d3 36. h5 d2?** "A sudden and unfortu
nate afterthought which White at once takes advantage of by givin
up one of his rooks for the pawns. It will be remembered tha
Winawer tied for first prize with Steinitz, and but for a similar sli
by Bird against the latter in the last game of the tournament woul
have secured its position. The variation by which Black wins i
simple enough but pretty. Why will the finest players overfinesse a
chess, refusing as it were to win a game when they see the way? 36. ..
R×g2 37. R×g2 d2 38. Qg1 Qh4† 39. Rh2 Qe1"—Bird. **37. Rc×d
e×d2 38. Q×d2 Q×d2** As 38. ... Qh4† 39. Rh2 loses a rook. The ex
change of queens is forced. **39. R×d2 Rg3 40. Rd3** It is not obviou
if this rook endgame can be won. The passive text move minimize
Winawer's chances compared to 40. Rd8†. **40. ... Kf7?** An obviou
mistake. 40. ... a5! is the correct defense. **41. Kh2 Rg5 42. Rd7**

Kf6 43. R×a7 43. h6! Rh5† 44. Kg3 R×h6 45. Rc7 is a tactical nicety. **43. ... R×h5† 44. Kg3 Rc5 45. Ra4** 45. a4 is unlikely to win, as Black's rook ends up behind the pawn. **45. ... g5 46. Kf2 g5 47. Ke3 Ke5 48. Kd3 Kf4** 48. ... g4 or 48. ... h4 draws. Abandoning control over d4 is extremely risky. **49. Ra8 Re5 50. Rf8† Kg3 51. Kd4** 51. Rf5, introducing a forced line, may have offered better winning chances, though after 51. ... R×f5 52. e×f5 h4 53. f6 g3 54. f7 h2 55. f8Q h1Q 56. Qd6† Kg2 57. Q×c6 Qf1† a draw is still possible. **51. ... Ra5 52. e5 R×a2 53. Rf5 h4?** 53. ... g4 (Zukertort) gives an easy draw. **54. R×g5† K×f3 55. e6 Rd2† 56. Kc5 Re2 57. Kd6 h3 58. Rh5?** 58. e7 wins offhand. The text move allows Black to gain an important tempo. **58. ... Kg4 59. Rh8 h2?** Bird doesn't use the tempo optimally. 59. ... Rd2† 60. K×c6 Re2 61. Rh6 Kg3 draws. **60. e7 Kg3 61. Kd7?** 61. c5! Kg2 62. R×h2† wins. **61. ... Rd2† 62. K×c6 Re2 63. Kd7 Rd2† 64. Ke8 Rd4?** Correct was 64. ... Rc2 65. Kd7 Rd2† 66. Kc6 Re2 (Zukertort). **65. c5 Rh4 66. R×h4 K×h4 67. Kf8 h1Q 68. e8Q** There is nothing to be done anymore. **68. ... Qf3† 69. Qf7 Qa8† 70. Kg7 Qg2† 71. Qg6 Qb7† 72. Kh6 Qc8 73. Qf6† Kg4 74. c6 Qb8 75. Kg7 Qc7† 76. Kg6 Qb8 77. Qe6† Kf4 78. Kf7 Qc7† 79. Qd7 Qe5 80. c7 Qh5† 81. Kg8 Qg6† 82. Qg7 Qc6 83. Qf8† Ke5** "Even now, when Winawer requesting to hand him a second queen from another table, Bird found it difficult to accept his fate and he pondered several minutes about his last move"—Lehner. **84. c8Q Qd5† 85. Qf7** Black resigns—*Sheffield and Rotherham Independent* (Bird), 7 April 1883; *Österreichische Lesehalle* (Lehner), April 1883, pp. 118–120; *Chess Monthly* (Zukertort), May 1883, pp. 269–271.

## (567) Ware–Bird   0–1
International tournament (round 10)
Vienna, 22 May 1882
A80

**1. d4 f5 2. f4 Nf6 3. Nf3 e6 4. e3 Be7 5. Bd3 0-0 6. 0-0 b6 7. Bd2 Bb7 8. h3 Ne4 9. Be1 d6 10. Nbd2 Nd7 11. c3 Bf6 12. a4 a5 13. Qc2 d5 14. B×e4 f×e4 15. Ne5 N×e5 16. d×e5 Be7 17. Bf2 Ba6 18. Rfe1 Qd7 19. Qd1 Qe8 20. Nb3 h5 21. h4 c5 22. Nc1 Qg6 23. Kh2 Rf5 24. g3 Kh7 25. Rg1 Raf8 26. Rg2 Qg4 27. Q×g4 h×g4 28. Nb3 g5 29. Nd2 Kg7 30. b3 Be2 31. Kg1 g×h4 32. g×h4 Kh6 33. Bg3 Bd3 34. Rh2 Rh5 35. Kg2 Kg6 36. Rah1 d4 37. c4 d×e3 38. Nf1 B×f1† 39. K×f1 Rd8 40. Ke2 Rd3 41. Rb1 Kf5 42. Rhh1 Rd2† 43. K×e3 Rd3† 44. Kf2 e3† 45. Ke2 Ke4 46. Be1 g3 47. Rh3 R×h4 48. R×g3 Rh2† 49. Kf1 Bh4 50. Rg2 Rh1† 51. Rg1 R×g1† 52. K×g1 B×e1 53. R×e1 K×f4 54. Rb1 K×e5 55. Kf1 Ke4 56. Ke2 Rd2† 57. Ke1 Kf3 58. Kf1 e5 59. Ke1 Rd3 60. Rb2 e4 61. Rb1 e2 62. b4 Rd1† 63. R×d1 e×d1Q† 64. K×d1 a×b4** White resigns—*Österreichische Lesehalle*, May 1883, pp. 150–152.

## (568) Bird–L. Paulsen   ½–½
International tournament (round 11)
Vienna, 23 May 1882
B20

**1. e4 c5 2. b4 c×b4 3. d4 d5 4. e5 e6 5. Bd3 Nc6 6. Ne2 Qb6 7. 0-0 Bd7 8. Be3 Nge7 9. a3 Nf5 10. B×f5 e×f5 11. a×b4 B×b4 12. c4 Ne7 13. c5 Qb5 14. Nbc3 B×c3 15. N×c3 Qc6 16. Bg5**

Ng6 17. Qb3 f4 18. g3 h6 19. B×f4 N×f4 20. g×f4 Bh3 21. Q×d5 B×f1 22. Q×c6† b×c6 23. K×f1 a5 24. d5 c×d5 25. c6 Ra6 26. N×d5 R×c6 27. R×a5 Rc1† 28. Kg2 0-0 29. f5 Kh7 30. h4 Rfc8 31. e6 f×e6 32. f×e6 Re8 33. Ra6 Rc5 34. Nf4 g5 35. Nd3 Rd5 36. Ra7† Kg6 37. Rd7 Rd8 38. Ne5† Kf6 39. Ng4† K×e6 40. Rh7 Kf5 41. f3 Rd2† 42. Kg3 g×h4† 43. K×h4 R8d6 44. Kh5 Kf4 45. Rf7† Kg3 46. f4 Rd1 47. Nf6 Rh1† 48. Kg6 K×f4 49. Kg7 Ke5 50. Ng4† Kd4 51. Rf4† Kc5 52. Nf2 Rd7† 53. Kg6 Rg1† 54. K×h6 Rdg7 55. Nh3 R7g6† 56. Kh5 R1g2 57. Rf5† Kd6 58. Ng5 Rg8 59. Ra5 Kc6 60. Rf5 Rd8 61. Kg6 Rd5 62. Rf6† Kc5 63. Rf5 R×f5 64. K×f5 draw—*Österreichische Lesehalle*, August 1883, pp. 245–247.

## (569) A. Schwarz–Bird   1–0
International tournament (round 12)
Vienna, 24 May 1882
C48

**1. e4 e5 2. Nf3 Nc6 3. Nc3 Nf6 4. Bb5 Bc5 5. 0-0 0-0 6. N×e5 N×e5 7. d4 Bb4 8. d×e5 B×c3 9. e×f6 B×f6 10. Bd3 c6 11. f4 B×b2 12. B×b2 Qb6† 13. Kh1 Q×b2 14. e5 f5 15. Bc4† Kh8 16. Qd6 Rd8 17. Rab1 Qc3 18. Qe7 Qa5 19. Rf3 d5 20. Ra3 Rg8 21. R×a5 d×c4 22. e6 b5 23. Ra3 a5 24. Qf7 Rb8 25. Rh3 h6 26. Rd1 Rb7 27. e7 Rd7 28. Q×g8†** Black resigns—*Österreichische Lesehalle*, September 1883, p. 281.

## (570) Bird–Meitner   1–0
International tournament (round 13)
Vienna, 25 May 1882
C54

**1. e4 e5 2. Nf3 Nc6 3. Bc4 Bc5 4. c3 Qe7 5. b4 Bb6 6. a4 a5 7. b5 Nd8 8. 0-0 d6 9. d4 Bg4 10. Be2 Nf6 11. Ba3 e×d4 12. e5 Ne4 13. c×d4 Qd7 14. e×d6 N×d6 15. Ne5 B×e2 16. N×d7 B×d1 17. N×b6 c×b6 18. R×d1 Kd7 19. Nc3 Nc4 20. Nd5 Rc8 21. Rac1 Ke6 22. Ne7** Black resigns—*Österreichische Lesehalle*, November 1883, pp. 342–343.

## (571) Bird–Steinitz   0–1
International tournament (round 14)
Vienna, 26 May 1882
C51

**1. e4 e5 2. Nf3 Nc6 3. Bc4 Bc5 4. b4 B×b4 5. c3 Be7 6. d4 e×d4 7. 0-0 Nh6 8. c×d4 0-0 9. d5 Bf6 10. d×c6 B×a1 11. B×h6 g×h6 12. c×b7 B×b7 13. e5 B×f3 14. g×f3 B×e5 15. f4 B×f4 16. Kh1 Qf6 17. Qf3 Kh8 18. Bd3 Rae8 19. Qh3 Rg8 20. Na3 Qc6† 21. f3 Re5 22. Qh4 Bg5 23. Qg3 Re3 24. Be4 Qa6 25. Rg1 R×a3 26. h4 Qe6 27. Rg2 Q×e4 28. h×g5 R×f3** White resigns—*Österreichische Lesehalle*, January 1884, p. 22.

## (572) Bird–Weiss   1–0
International tournament (round 15)
Vienna, 27 May 1882
C54

**1. e4 e5 2. Nf3 Nc6 3. Bc4 Bc5 4. c3 Nf6 5. b4 Bb6 6. d3 d6 7. a4 a5 8. b5 Ne7 9. Na3 Ng6 10. Be3 B×e3 11. f×e3 0-0 12. 0-0**

d5 13. e×d5 N×d5 14. Qd2 Qd6 15. Ng5 Be6 16. g3 h6 17. N×e6 Q×e6 In view of what's coming 17. ... f×e6 might be interesting. 18. Rf2 If 18. e4 Qb6†. 18. ... Qd6 19. Raf1 Nf6 20. Nc2 Rad8 *(see diagram)*

*After 20. ... Rad8*

21. R×f6! A sparkling sacrifice that generates a dangerous attack. 21. ... g×f6 22. e4 Kg7 23. Ne3 Ne7 24. Ng4! Rh8? Weiss succumbs in a difficult position. Besides the text move, 24. ... Ng8 is worth considering. Now 25. R×f6 seems convincing but 25. ... Qc5† saves the day. The rook has to retreat, as 26. Kg2? Q×c4 loses at once. After 26. Rf2 Rd6 27. Ne3 Ne7 28. Kg2 White has a pawn and a strong center that fully compensates for the sacrifice of the exchange. 25. R×f6 Qc5† 26. Ne3 Nd5 The beautiful point of Bird's combination can be admired after 26. ... K×f6 27. Qf2† Kg5 28. h4† Kh5 29. Q×f7† Ng6 30. Qf3 mate. 27. B×d5 R×d5 28. Qf2! Black resigns—*Österreichische Lesehalle*, February 1884, pp. 57–58.

### (573) Bird–Zukertort　0–1
International tournament (round 16)
Vienna, 30 May 1882
*C54*

1. e4 e5 2. Nf3 Nc6 3. Bc4 Bc5 4. c3 Nf6 5. b4 Bb6 6. d3 d6 7. a4 a6 8. Be3 Ne7 9. 0–0 c6 10. Bb3 Bc7 11. Bg5 h6 12. B×f6 g×f6 13. Nh4 d5 14. Qh5 Be6 15. Nd2 Qd7 16. Qf3 f5 17. b5 f4 18. d4 f6 19. e×d5 c×d5 20. b×a6 R×a6 21. a5 e4 22. Qe2 f3 23. Nd×f3 e×f3 24. N×f3 0–0 25. Nh4 Nf5 26. Ng6 Rf7 27. Rfe1 Rg7 28. Qh5 Qf7 29. R×e6 Q×e6 30. Qf3 R×a5 31. Rf1 R×g6 32. Bc2 Nh4 and White resigns—*Österreichische Lesehalle*, March 1884, pp. 85–86.

### (574) Wittek–Bird　½–½
International tournament (round 17)
Vienna, 31 May 1882
*B46*

1. e4 c5 2. Nc3 Nc6 3. Nf3 e6 4. d4 c×d4 5. N×d4 a6 6. Be2 Bb4 7. 0–0 B×c3 8. b×c3 Nge7 9. N×c6 b×c6 10. Qd6 0–0 11. Ba3 Re8 12. Rab1 a5 13. Rfd1 Ng6 14. c4 e5 15. Rb3 Nf4 16. Bf1 Re6 17. Qc5 h5 18. g3 a4 19. Rbb1 Qg5 20. Rd6 h4 21. Bc1 h×g3 22. h×g3 Qf6 23. Ba3 Ng6 24. Bh3 R×d6 25. Q×d6 Q×d6 26. B×d6 f6 27. c5 Kf7 28. Rb6 Ke8 29. Bf1 Nh8 30. Bc4 Nf7 31. a3 Ng5 32. Bd3 Ne6 33. c3 Ra5 34. Rb8 Kd8 35. Kf1 Nc7 36. Ke2 Ra7 37. Rb1 Ba6 38. Rb8† Bc8 39. f4 e×f4 40. g×f4 Rb7 41. B×c7† K×c7 42. R×c8† K×c8 43. Ba6 Kc7 44. B×b7 K×b7 45. Kf3 Kc7 46. f5 d6 47. Kg4 d5 48. e×d5 c×d5 49. Kh5

Kc6 50. Kg6 K×c5 51. K×g7 Kc4 52. K×f6 K×c3 53. Ke5 d4 54. f6 d3 55. f7 d2 56. f8Q d1Q 57. Qb4† Kd3 58. Qd4† Ke2 59. Q×d1† K×d1 60. Kd4 Kd2 61. Kc4 Kc2 62. Kb4 Kd3 63. K×a4 Kc4 64. Ka5 Kc5 65. Ka6 Kc6 66. a4 Kc7 draw—*Österreichische Lesehalle*, May 1884, pp. 152–153.

### (575) Chigorin–Bird　1–0
International tournament (round 18)
Vienna, 1 June 1882
*B24*

1. e4 c5 2. Nc3 Nc6 3. g3 e6 4. Bg2 g6 5. d3 a6 6. Nh3 d6 7. 0–0 Bg7 8. Ne2 Nge7 9. c3 e5 10. Be3 Bg4 11. f3 Bd7 12. f4 Bg4 13. Nf2 B×e2 14. Q×e2 0–0 15. Rad1 Qa5 16. f×e5 d×e5 17. Ng5 f5 18. Nh6† Kh8 19. e×f5 g×f5 20. Qh5 Q×a2 21. B×c6 b×c6 22. B×c5 Rf6 23. Ng4 f×g4 24. R×f6 B×f6 25. B×e7 Bg7 26. Qg5 Q×b2 27. Bf6 Qb6† 28. d4 Qa7 29. Q×e5 a5 30. Re1 Qf7 31. B×g7† Q×g7 32. Qd6 Qg6 33. Q×g6 h×g6 34. Ra1 Kg7 35. Kf2 Kf6 36. Ke3 g5 37. Kd3 Ke6 38. c4 a4 39. Kc3 Kf5 40. Kd3 a3 41. Ra2 Ra7 42. c5 Ra8 43. Kc4 Ke4 44. Re2† Kf3 45. Ra2 Ra4† 46. Kd3 Ra5 47. Kc4 Ke3 48. d5 c×d5† 49. K×d5 Kd3 50. Kd6 Kc3 51. c6 Kb3 52. c7 Ra8 53. Ra1 Kb2 54. Re1 Rh8 55. Kd7 Rh7† 56. Re7 R×e7† 57. K×e7 a2 58. c8Q a1Q 59. Qh8† Black resigns—*Österreichische Lesehalle*, June 1884, pp. 184–185.

### (576) B. Fleissig–Bird　0–1
International tournament (round 19)
Vienna, 2 June 1882
*C22*

1. e4 e5 2. d4 e×d4 3. Q×d4 Nc6 4. Qe3 Bb4† 5. Bd2 Nf6 6. Nc3 0–0 7. 0–0–0 Re8 8. f3 d5 9. Be1 d4 10. Qf2 Qe7 11. Nb5 Bc5 12. Qg3 Bb6 13. Ne2 Nh5 14. Qh4 Qe5 15. Na3 Be6 16. Kb1 Nf6 17. Nc1 Qc5 18. g4 Qe7 19. Qg3 Bc5 20. Nc4 b5 21. Na5 N×a5 22. B×a5 c6 23. h4 Nd7 24. g5 Nb6 25. b3 Rab8 26. B×b6 a×b6 27. h5 Ra8 28. Bd3 Ba3 29. h6 B×c1 30. K×c1 B×b3 31. h×g7 Qa3† 32. Kd2 B×c2 33. Ke2 B×d1† 34. R×d1 Q×a2† 35. Kf1 Qb3 36. Ke1 Qc3† 37. Kf1 Ra2 38. f4 Rd2 39. R×d2 Q×d2 40. e5 Ra8 White resigns—*Österreichische Lesehalle*, August 1884, pp. 247–248.

### (577) Bird–Englisch　0–1
International tournament (round 20)
Vienna, 3 June 1882
*A03*

1. f4 d5 2. Nf3 Nf6 3. e3 e6 4. b3 Be7 5. Bb2 0–0 6. Be2 c5 7. 0–0 Nc6 8. Ne5 N×e5 9. f×e5 Nd7 10. d4 f6 11. Bg4 Qb6 12. Nc3 c×d4 13. Na4 Qc6 14. e×d4 f×e5 15. d×e5 b5 16. Nc3 R×f1† 17. Q×f1 N×e5 18. Bh3 b4 19. Na4 Ng6 20. Qf2 e5 21. B×c8 R×c8 22. Q×a7 Ra8 23. Qe3 R×a4 24. B×e5 Ra8 25. Bd4 Rf8 26. Re1 Bf6 27. Bc5 Bg5 28. Qe6† Q×e6 29. R×e6 Ra8 30. g3 R×a2 31. h4 R×c2 32. B×b4 Kf7 33. Re1 Bf6 34. Ne5 White resigns—*Österreichische Lesehalle*, September 1884, p. 282.

**(578) Bird–Mason** ½–½

International tournament (round 21)

Vienna, 5 June 1882

*A03*

1. f4 d5 2. Nf3 c5 3. e3 Nf6 4. b3 e6 5. Bb2 Bd7 6. a4 Nc6 7. Bb5 Be7 8. 0-0 0-0 9. Na3 a6 10. B×c6 B×c6 11. Ne5 Rc8 12. Qe2 Ne8 13. Qg4 f5 14. Qh3 Bf6 15. Rad1 Nd6 16. d3 Nf7 17. d4 B×e5 18. d×e5 Qe7 19. c4 Rcd8 20. Qg3 Rd7 21. c×d5 B×d5 22. Rd3 Rfd8 23. Rc1 Be4 24. R×d7 R×d7 25. Bc3 b6 26. Nc4 b5 27. Nd2 Bb7 28. Qe1 Qd8 29. Nf3 b4 30. Ba1 B×f3 31. g×f3 Rd2 32. Bd4 Ng5 33. f×g5 Q×g5† 34. Qg3 Q×g3† 35. h×g3 c×d4 36. e×d4 R×d4 37. Rc6 Rd3 38. Kf2 Kf7 39. R×a6 R×b3 40. Ra7† Kg6 41. Re7 f4 42. g×f4 Ra3 43. R×e6† Kf5 44. Re7 K×f4 45. e6 Ra2† 46. Ke1 b3 47. Rb7 R×a4 48. Kd2 Ra6 49. Rf7† Ke5 50. e7 Re6 51. R×g7 h5 52. Rg5† Kd4 53. R×h5 R×e7 54. Rh4† Kc5 55. Re4 Rf7 56. f4 Kd5 57. Ra4 Rb7 58. Kc1 Kc5 59. Kb2 Rb6 60. f5 Kd5 61. Rf4 Ke5 62. Rf3 Ke4 63. R×b3 R×b3† 64. K×b3 K×f5 draw—*Österreichische Lesehalle*, October 1884, pp. 312–313.

**(579) Bird–Noa   1–0**

International tournament (round 22)

Vienna, 6 June 1882

*Game scored by default*

**(580) Bird–Mackenzie   1–0**

International tournament (round 23)

Vienna, 7 June 1882

*C54*

1. e4 e5 2. Nf3 Nc6 3. Bc4 Bc5 4. c3 Nf6 5. b4 "Bird's favorite attack in this opening. It weakens the pawns on the queenside, but it drives back the pieces of the defense, and the manner in which Bird handles this form of opening certainly deserves attention"— Steinitz. 5. ... Bb6 6. d3 d6 7. a4 a5 8. b5 Ne7 9. Na3 Ng6 10. Be3 c6 "A gross error; surprising in a match game of such importance"— Steinitz. 11. b×c6 Not the most precise. After 11. Qb3! d5 12. e×d5 B×e3 13. d×c6 B×f2† 14. K×f2 0-0 15. Rhe1, the material balance is maintained, but White's development gives him the better prospects. 11. ... b×c6? 11. ... B×e3 rectifies the situation as Black has nothing to fear after 12. c×b7 B×f2† 13. K×f2 Qb6†. The situation becomes at once hopeless after the text move. 12. Qb3 "Promptly taking advantage. It wins a most important pawn, besides subjecting the hostile king to a tremendous attack"—Steinitz. 12. ... B×e3 13. B×f7† Ke7 "The best square under these circumstances, for if White subsequently took the knight, Black would gain an open file for the rook, otherwise the knight could retreat to f8"— Steinitz. 14. f×e3 Nf8 15. Bc4 N8d7 16. 0-0 Rb8 Bird last move was open for improvement, as 16. ... Qb6 would have effectuated the exchange of queens. 16. Qc2 was therefore superior. 17. Qd1 "Loss of time. The queen should have gone to c2 at once"—Steinitz. 17. ... Nc5 18. Qc2 Be6 19. B×e6 N×e6 20. Nc4 Nc5 21. d4 "Mr. Bird conducts the attack in his usual lively and spirited manner"— Steinitz. 21. ... Nc×e4 "It was certainly better to exchange pawns; e.g., 21. ... e×d4 22. e×d4 Nc×e4 23. Rae1 d5 (if 23. ... Kd7 24. R×e4

d5 25. Nce5†) 24. Nfe5 Rc8"—Steinitz. 22. d×e5 d×e5 23. Nc×e5 Qc7 *(see diagram)*

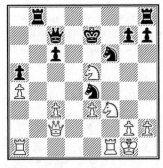

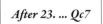
*After 23. ... Qc7*

24. Nd4 "Beautiful play"—Steinitz. 24. ... Rb6 25. Nc4 Rbb8 "25. ... Ra6 was certainly the only move, if anything was of avail"— Steinitz. 26. N×a5 "The two knights playfully make havoc among the hostile pawns"—Steinitz. 26. ... Rb6 27. Nc4 Rbb8 28. a5 "Vigorous and fine, as will be seen. It was important to stop the rook from defending the c-pawn again"—Steinitz. 28. ... Rhe8 29. Ne5 "The manoeuvre with the knight is very elegant, and most ingeniously devised"—Steinitz. 29. ... Kf8 30. Q×e4 R×e5 31. Q×c6 Qe7 32. a6 Qe8 "This loses the exchange but Black had no defense"—Steinitz. 33. Qd6† Kg8 34. Nc6 Reb5 35. N×b8 R×b8 36. a7 Ra8 37. Qd4 h5 38. e4 Qc8 39. e5 Ng4 40. h3 Nh6 41. Qd5† Kh7 42. e6 Black resigns—*The Field* (Steinitz), 24 June 1882.

**(581) Hruby–Bird   1–0**

International tournament (round 24)

Vienna, 9 June 1882

*A85*

1. c4 f5 2. e3 Nf6 3. d4 e6 4. Nc3 Bb4 5. Bd3 B×c3† 6. b×c3 0-0 7. Nh3 b6 8. 0-0 Bb7 9. f3 Na6 10. Qe2 c5 11. d5 Qe7 12. e4 f×e4 13. f×e4 Rae8 14. d6 Q×d6 15. e5 Qc6 16. e×f6 g×f6 17. Bh6 Rf7 18. Rf2 Kh8 19. Ng5 Ree7 20. N×f7† R×f7 21. Raf1 e5 22. Qh5 Re7 23. Qg4 Black resigns—*Österreichische Lesehalle*, April 1885, p. 84.

**(582) Bird–Blackburne   1–0**

International tournament (round 25)

Vienna, 10 June 1882

*A03*

1. f4 d5 2. Nf3 Nf6 3. e3 Bf5 4. b3 e6 5. Bb2 Be7 6. Nc3 0-0 7. Bd3 "I determined here, in opposition to recognized opinions as to the disadvantage of the doubled pawn, especially on the d- and e-file, to challenge exchange of bishops by 7. Bd3. It was evident from Blackburne's long consideration that the move rather perplexed him. He should probably have taken the bishop. He, however, played 7. ... Ne4, [and] to this and some rather undecided subsequent play may be attributed his extraordinary discomfiture in 23 moves, my time for the game being 15 minutes, the whole game not lasting more than an hour and a half"—Bird. 7. ... Ne4 "Instead of this weak move we should have played 7. ... B×d3 8. c×d3 c5, followed, if there is time, by 9. ... Nc6 and 10. ... Bd6; and in case White plays 9. e4, the reply 9. ... d4 would entirely paralyze the White

bishop on b2"—Rosenthal. **8. B×e4 d×e4 9. Ne5 Nd7 10. Ng4 Bg6 11. Nf2 f5 12. Qe2 Bf6 13. 0-0-0 e5** "A dangerous move. Black, not being able to prevent the attack of 14. g4, ought to preserve his pawn at e6, retaking with this pawn on f5 in case of 15. g×f5. The bishop on g6 defends the king against an attack from White's rooks. We should prefer to form an attack on the queenside by 13. ... c6, 14. ... b5, 15. ... a5 and 16. ... a4"—Rosenthal. **14. g4** "Well played. This move gives great superiority of position to White."—Rosenthal **14. ... e×f4 15. g×f5** (*see diagram*)

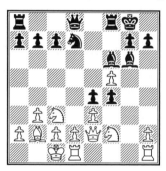

*After 15. g×f5*

**15. ... B×f5** "If 15. ... f3 16. Qc4† Bf7 17. Q×e4 and wins"—Rosenthal. 15. ... B×c3 avoids what is coming. After 16. Qc4† Rf7 17. Q×c3 B×f5 18. e×f4 Nf6, Black has no attack to fear as well as having his own ideas to pursue, such as pressurizing the pawn at f4. **16. e×f4 Re8** This was the last chance for a favorable exchange at c3. **17. Rhg1** The less prosaic 17. Qb5 wins a pawn. **17. ... Nf8 18. Ng4 Kh8** "Weak. 18. ... B×g4 19. Q×g4 e3 20. d3 Ne6 with a defensible game. The knight protecting the g-pawn, and at the same time threatening to go to d4"—Rosenthal. 20. d×e3 is a simple improvement. There is nothing that can save Black, but the text move is equal to immediate surrender. **19. N×f6 g×f6 20. Nd5 Re6** "Black is without resource. If 20. ... Nd7 21. Qh5 Be6 22. Qh6 and wins"—Rosenthal. **21. Ne3 Ng6** "He cannot save the bishop, for if 21. ... Bh3 22. Qh5 and if 21. ... Bg6 22. f5"—Rosenthal. **22. N×f5 N×f4 23. Qe3** Black resigns. "If Black would play 23. ... Ng6, then 24. R×g6, and if 23. ... Nd5 24. Qh6 wins"—Rosenthal. *La Vie Moderne* (Rosenthal), 28 October 1882; *Modern Chess* (Bird), pp. 46–47.

## (583) Bird–Winawer    0–1
International tournament (round 26)
Vienna, 12 June 1882
*A03*

**1. f4 d5 2. Nf3 c5 3. e3 Nc6 4. Bb5 Bd7 5. 0-0 g6 6. B×c6 B×c6 7. d4 e6 8. c3 b6 9. Ne5 Qc7 10. Nd2 a6 11. Ndf3 Bb5 12. Re1 f6 13. Ng4 Bc6 14. Nf2 Qb7 15. a3 Nh6 16. Bd2** "It was better for White to play 16. b3 and develop his bishop to b2"—Lehner. **16. ... Nf5 17. Qc2 Nd6 18. b3 Rc8 19. Bc1 Kf7 20. Bb2 Bg7 21. Nd2 h6 22. Qd1 Rhe8 23. a4 Rcd8 24. a5 c×d4** "Black's play all through was rather eccentric, and its upshot is certainly not very advantageous, as he is now forced to relieve the opponent of his weakest point, the e-pawn, and to open the e-file for his rooks. The next 25 moves represent a series of vain endeavours from both sides to break through into the hostile camp"—Zukertort. **25. e×d4 b5 26. Nd3** Bird's maneuvers on the queenside have been very

strong, and he clearly got the upper hand. **26. ... Qc8 27. Qg4 h5 28. Qh3 Nf5 29. Nf3 Bd7 30. Nh4 N×h4** The exchange of knights is very useful for White. **31. Q×h4 Qc7 32. Nc5 Bc8 33. Rf1 Bh6 34. b4 Rh8 35. Rae1 Bf8 36. Nd3 Bd6 37. Rf3 Rde8 38. Ref1 Kg7 39. Qf2 Rhf8** "A break was held for the lunch"—Lehner. **40. h4 Qd8 41. Rg3 Kh7 42. Bc1 Rf7 43. Qd2 Rg7 44. Re3 Kg8 45. Qe2 Ree7 46. Bd2 Qc7 47. g3 Re8 48. Re1 Rge7 49. Kf2 Qd8 50. Qf3 Bb7?** (*see diagram*) "At last an oasis in the desert: a combination after innumerable shifting manoeuvres. Black threatens 51. ... e5, for if then 52. d×e5 d4, winning a rook, and if 52. f×e5 f×e5, threatening to win the queen"—Zukertort. 50. ... Qc7 to hold back Bird's next move was not less than necessary.

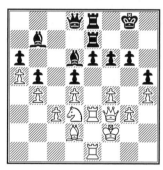

*After 50. ... Bb7*

**51. g4!** "An excellent reply, conceived in Mr. Bird's best style"—Zukertort. **51. ... e5** "Not sufficient to prevent the consequences of White's last coup, but we do not think that Black had any reply which would prevent loss in position or material. After 51. ... h×g4 52. Q×g4 Kf7, White would get a winning advantage with 53. h5, for if 53. ... g×h5 54. Q×h5† Kf8 55. Qh6†, and whether the king moves or the rook interposes, 56. Rg3 decides the game"—Zukertort. **52. g×h5 e4 53. Qg4?** Both 53. Qg3 (Zukertort) and 53. Qg2 enforce a gruesome attack; e.g., 53. Qg3 Qc8 54. Rg1 (54. Q×g6†?? Rg7 wins for Black). Now Black is doomed: 54. ... Rg7 55. h6. The text move on the other hand gives Winawer the needed tempo to bring the bishop to the defense. **53. ... Bc8** 53. ... Qc8! completely puts an end to White's show. After 54. Qg3 Qf5 55. Nc5 Rg7 the roles are reversed. **54. Qg3 Bf5 55. Nc1** Needlessly passive. 55. Nc5! keeps the game in balance. **55. ... Rg7 56. h×g6 Qc7 57. Ne2** It was more important to defend the g-pawn with 57. h5 (Zukertort) when after 57. ... B×f4 58. Qg2 B×e3† 59. K×e3 Black won't be able to crack through White's defensive lines. **57. ... R×g6 58. Qh2 Bg4 59. Rg3 f5!** "Now Winawer's victory is unavoidable. It was a tough battle, lasting 9 hours"—Lehner. **60. h5 Rg7 61. h6 Rg6 62. Rh1 Kh7 63. Qg1 Reg8 64. Qc1 B×e2 65. R×g6 R×g6 66. K×e2 Qc4† 67. Kf2 Qd3 68. Rf1 Rg3** "68. ... Be7 was not bad either"—Lehner. **69. Qb1 Rf3† 70. Kg1 R×f1† 71. Q×f1 Q×d2 72. Qh3 Q×f4 73. Qh5 Qg4†** White resigns—*Chess Monthly* (Zukertort), May 1883, pp. 271–273; *Österreichische Lesehalle* (Lehner), May 1885, pp. 148–149.

## (584) Bird–Ware    1–0
International tournament (round 27)
Vienna, 13 June 1882
*A03*

**1. f4 d5 2. Nf3 f5 3. b3 Nf6 4. Bb2 e6 5. e3 Be7 6. Nc3 0-0 7. Bd3 Bd7 8. 0-0 Be8 9. Qe1 c6 10. Ne2 Ne4 11. B×e4 f×e4**

12. Ne5 Bf6 13. Qg3 Nd7 14. Nd4 Qe7 15. Qh3 Bf7 16. Ng4 c5
17. Ba3 a6 18. N×f6† Q×f6 19. Ne2 b5 20. Rab1 Qe7 21. b4 c4
22. Bb2 Bg6 23. Nd4 Rae8 24. g4 Bf7 25. Bc3 Qd6 26. Qg3 Qb6
27. Rf2 e5 28. Nf5 Bg6 29. f×e5 Qe6 30. Rbf1 h6 31. h4 h5
32. N×g7 K×g7 33. g×h5 R×f2 34. R×f2 Kh7 35. Rf6 N×f6
36. Q×g6† Kh8 37. e×f6 Black resigns—*Österreichische Lesehalle*,
July 1885, pp. 214–215.

## (585) L. Paulsen–Bird    1–0
International tournament (round 28)
Vienna, 14 June 1882
*B01*

    1. e4 d5 2. e×d5 Q×d5 3. Nc3 Qd8 4. Nf3 Bf5 5. d4 e6 6. a3
c6 7. Be2 Bd6 8. Be3 Nd7 9. Qd2 h6 10. h3 Qc7 11. Bd3 Ne7
12. Ne2 g5 13. g4 B×d3 14. Q×d3 0–0–0 15. 0–0–0 f5 16. g×f5
N×f5 17. Kb1 Rhf8 18. Nd2 e5 19. Nc4 Be7 20. Qe4 e×d4
21. N×d4 N×d4 22. B×d4 Bc5 23. Qe6 B×d4 24. R×d4 b5
25. Nd6† Kb8 26. Rhd1 Nb6 27. Q×h6 Nd5 28. N×b5 Qb6
29. c4 Nf6 30. Q×f6 R×f6 31. R×d8† Kb7 32. R1d7† Ka6
33. R×a7† Q×a7 34. N×a7 K×a7 35. Rg8 Rf5 36. Rg6 Kb6
37. b4 Rf3 38. R×g5 R×a3 39. Rg3 Ra4 40. Kb2 c5 41. Ra3 Black
resigns—*Tournament Book*, pp. 337–339.

## (586) Bird–A. Schwarz    0–1
International tournament (round 29)
Vienna, 15 June 1882
*Game scored by default*

## (587) Bird–Wittek    0–1
International tournament (round 30)
Vienna, 16 June 1882
*Game scored by default*

## (588) Zukertort–Bird    1–0
International tournament (round 31)
Vienna, 17 June 1882
*Game scored by default*

## (589) Meitner–Bird    1–0
International tournament (round 32)
Vienna, 19 June 1882
*Game scored by default*

## (590) Weiss–Bird    1–0
International tournament (round 33)
Vienna, 20 June 1882
*Game scored by default*

## (591) Steinitz–Bird    1–0
International tournament (round 34)
Vienna, 21 June 1882
*A80*

"The following is an excellent specimen of the opening. It is the
notable last game in the Vienna tournament of 1882, and I played
it in deference to the wishes of the committee and principal prize-

winners, being in a lamentable state of health at the time (Steinitz
protesting, because several of my previous games, viz. against Zukertort and five others [*sic*], through my illness and inability to leave
the hospital—had been declared forfeited). The game was of the
utmost importance as affecting the relative positions of the principal
winners, and the ultimate destination of the first, second and third
prizes. In the result, Steinitz and Winawer tied for chief honors,
Mason being third. It would have been a serious thing for Steinitz,
chessically speaking, if I had won or drawn the game; the latter I
ought to have done at least at the 41st move. Winawer would then
have had first prize and Steinitz second, and a win would have placed
Mason and Steinitz on an equality for second and third prizes"—
Bird.

    1. d4 f5 2. Nc3 Nf6 3. Bg5 e6 4. e4 f×e4 5. B×f6 Q×f6 6. N×e4
Qe7 7. c3 d5 8. Ng3 Nc6 9. f4 Bd7 10. Bd3 g6 11. h4 0–0–0
12. Nf3 Qf6 13. Ne2 Bd6 14. g3 Ne7 15. Qd2 h6 16. 0–0–0 Kb8
17. Rdf1 h5 18. b4 It was much safer to leave the pawn where it
was. Bird rightly responds by bringing his queen over to the weakened queenside. 18. ... Nf5 19. Ne5 Be8 20. Rf3 Qe7 21. Ng1 B×e5
22. f×e5 Qd7 23. Nh3 Rc8 24. Qg5 Not without risk as the king
is left by itself. 24. ... a5 25. a3 This further weakening of the
position of his king has to be avoided. 25. B×f5 g×f5 26. Qd2 maintains the balance. Of course, due to the tournament situation
Steinitz was obliged to play for a win and take all risks necessary to
achieve this result. 25. ... Rf8 25. ... Qa4! at once is stronger, as the
pawn fortress protecting White's king is blown away in case of
26. Kb2 a×b4 27. a×b4 N×d4! 28. c×d4 Q×b4† 29. Kc1 Qc3†
30. Kd1 Q×d4 with a lasting initiative. 26. Rhf1 Qc6 Both players
missed their chance to get an edge with respectively 26. Kb2 and
26. ... Qa4 again. 27. Kb2 Qb6 28. Rc1 Bb5 29. B×f5 e×f5 30. Nf4
Bc4? Bird achieved nothing and the text move, which blunders an
important pawn, ought to have sealed his fate. The passive 30. ...
Rg8 hardly looks attractive, but is possible because 31. N×d5 Qc6
rids Black of his worries. 31. Rf2? Steinitz's uncertainty makes him
chary of playing 31. Q×g6 (Zukertort). After 31. ... Qb5 32. Q×h5
Qa4 33. Ra1, everything is defended, and thanks to his extra pawns
White should win. There is absolutely no danger in 33. ... Qb3†,
which only loses time for Black, as White threatens, after 34. Kc1,
35. Re3 and 36. Qd1. 31. ... c5? Bird's play is much less restrained
than his opponent's, and he bravely insists that Steinitz capture the
g-pawn. Much better, however is 31. ... Qb5 32. Qe7 b6! 33. Rfc2
Rfe8 34. Qf7 Qa4 with a tense position, where the chances are about
equal. A possible continuation then could be 35. Ra1 Rh8 36. b×a5
(the knight has to remain at f4 to cover d3) 36. ... g5 37. Ng6 (now
that Black has weakened his kingside pawns the knight may go to
g6. White has to avoid 37. h×g5? h4!) 37. ... Bd3 38. Rac1 Qb5†
39. Ka1 B×c2 40. R×c2 Rhe8 41. h×g5. 32. Q×g6 Rc6 33. d×c5
Qb5 34. Qg7 34. Q×h5, to be able to retreat to d1, offers Bird no
counterplay at all. 34. ... Rfc8 35. e6 R×c5 36. Qd7 Qb6 37. Rd2
a×b4 38. a×b4? 38. c×b4! ends Black's attack, as his rook on the
c-file joins the defense. 38. ... Ra5? 38. ... Rb5 draws by force, thanks
to the coming rook sacrifice at b4. 39. Kb1? Steinitz is too impressed
by his opponent's inventiveness to play the cool 39. e7!, which concludes the game in his favor: 39. ... Ra2† 40. Kb1 R×d2 41. Q×c8†
K×c8 42. e8Q† Kc7 43. Ne6†. 39. ... Qe3 39. ... Ra3! (Zukertort)
brings the rook to the dance floor, thus forcing Steinitz to exert the

utmost care. A straight line demonstrating some resources is 40. e7 Qe3 41. b5 (menacing the rook on a3) 41. ... Qe4† 42. Nd3 Ra5 43. Rcc2 B×d3 44. R×d3 Q×d3 45. Q×c8† K×c8 46. e8Q† Kc7 47. Qe5† Kb6 48. Qd4† Q×d4 49. c×d4 Ra3. Bird may still poke his opponent a bit, but a draw is likely. **40. b×a5 Q×d2 41. Rc2** (see diagram)

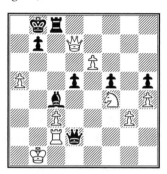

*After 41. Rc2*

**41. ... Qe1†?** "41. ... Qd1† 42. Kb2 Ba2 43. Qd6† Ka8 44. Rc1 Qb3† 45. Ka1 Qa4! (if 45. ... R×c3, White cannot retake on account of 46. ... Qb1 mate, but 46. Qd8† wins. The text move is the correct one) 46. Kb2 Qb3† 47. Ka1 Qa4 and the game would have been drawn [and] Winawer would have won first prize. The fortunate gain of this game by Steinitz placed him on an equality with Winawer; playing off the tie each scored a game, and the first and second prizes were divided between them"—Bird. **42. Kb2 Q×g3 43. Qd6† Ka8 44. e7 Q×h4 45. Qd7 Rb8 46. e8Q Q×f4 47. Qee7 Ba6 48. Qed6 Qf1 49. Q7c7 Qb5† 50. Qb4 d4 51. Q×b5 d×c3† 52. R×c3 B×b5 53. Rc5 Bd3 54. Rd5 Be4 55. Rd8 R×d8 56. Q×d8†** Black resigns—*Modern Chess* (Bird), pp. 28–29; *Chess Monthly* (Zukertort), October 1882, pp. 44–46.

## WRITING A COLUMN

An important addition to the income of various professional Victorian chess players was obtained by writing columns for newspapers and magazines. Many of the strongest players, such as Staunton, Löwenthal, Steinitz and others, wrote some highly interesting columns, through which it is now possible to reconstruct the chess life of the nineteenth century.

Bird often presented himself proudly as the chess columnist of *The Times*. In a letter published in *Chess Monthly* (October 1887, p. 35), he claimed to have started his contributions in 1878, but this has to be taken lightly. Until the 1890s articles dedicated to chess in *The Times* remained very sparse, with no regularity whatever. These articles were not signed, but both the style of writing and the relatively large presence of games played by Bird suggest that they were indeed written by him. It is unclear until what date Bird kept on contributing to *The Times*. When the census of 1891 was taken, he pronounced "journalist" (besides "accountant") as his professional occupation.

Bird's only regular, full-blooded, column appeared from 2 December 1882 until 24 November 1883. This was a syndicated effort that was first published in the *Sheffield and Rotherham Independent* and the *Boston Weekly Journal*. Several other newspapers purchased

Bird's column, which consequently could be seen in the *Nottinghamshire Guardian*, the *Northampton Mercury* and even in the *Illustrated Sydney News* in Australia. The column was quite voluminous and interesting, especially for his numerous fans and chess historians with a predilection for him.

While Bird never cared much about publishing his wins he now had the opportunity to share his best games and he made ample use of that. Bird's surviving offhand games that were played between the great tournaments of Vienna and London offer a much better view of his true strength and creativity, and they demonstrate more than anywhere else in this book that Bird was not such a relatively weak master as he is often thought of. His annotations were also remarkably thorough when compared to the light and superficial analyses in his books.

On 17 November 1883 Bird suddenly announced that his next column would be his last. In a short note, he explained his motives.

> My work on *Railways and National Finances*, referred to in the leading journal will compel me to limit my attentions to chess. This alone would be sufficient to justify my discontinuing the chess article. The jealous and apparent envy of certain local chess representatives, however, is my main reason; and this being my 51st, or last article but one, I take the opportunity of expressing the hope that future chess editors may have to chronicle more enthusiasm than at present appears to prevail out of London.
>
> H.E. Bird
> 5 Heygate street, Walworth Road, London
> [*Sheffield and Rotherham Independent*, 17 November 1883].

At the end of Bird's next and final column, an answer from the secretary of the Sheffield and District chess association appeared. From his reply it becomes clear that a financial dispute was one of the causes of the bad feelings between Bird and the local chess club.

> ... Mr. Bird expressed a desire to come, as shown from the following extract from a letter dated April 10th, 1883:
>
> "Your suggested invitation is also very much appreciated, and I should feel only too delighted to accept it, either with or without a slight fee. I am most desirous to visit Sheffield, etc."
>
> As to remuneration, Mr. Bird also wrote as follows:
>
> "As you, however, thoughtfully make the inquiry, I should say a fee of £3 3s. would be ample remuneration to cover my railway fare and expenses of two days' stay."
>
> The agreement, as stated by Mr. Bird himself, was £3 3s. for two days—he only played on one day, but the association were perfectly satisfied. Mr. Bird went away in a great hurry on the following day (Sunday) following the match, and requested me to pay his hotel bill and forward him the balance. As he also asked for a few of the games played, the remittance was delayed for a few days only, and on their receipt duly forwarded.
>
> With regard to the letter of thanks, I have no recollection of same having been promised; but I am sure that the association would very gladly have forwarded one, as Mr. Bird's visit afforded great pleasure to many, and we knew of no ill-feeling whatever until his letter appeared.
>
> Signed on behalf of the committee,
> H.C. Twist, Hon. Sec.
> [*Sheffield and Rotherham Independent*, 24 November 1883].

## A LOSS FOR BRITISH CHESS

Immediately following the tournament of Vienna various match challenges were made between Steinitz, Zukertort and Mason. Due to a variety of reasons none of them brought any concrete result. In the meantime Steinitz had returned to England where several changes took place. First of all Steinitz resigned his work for the column in *The Field*. The *Figaro*, in which Steinitz maintained another column, even ceased publication when its owner, the chess player James Mortimer, went to prison in a libel case in which he declined to reveal the identity of a contributor. Steinitz lived for twenty years in England and during these two decades he always felt that he had been treated and attacked as a foreigner. Now the time had come for him to make a drastic decision and on 25 October he left for America.

# ON THE ROAD TO LONDON 1882–1883

Bird finished the tournament in Vienna in such poor health that many feared for his further chess career and even for his life. Fortunately, after a recovery that took a few months, Bird was able to play his favorite game again and therefore returned to the fizzling chess community that Purssell's still contained.

The following game, according to Bird in *Modern Chess* (p. 12), "has occurred to me twice before, viz., in early days, 1850, and in New York in 1876." In *Modern Chess*, Bird's opponent was named "J. Jacobsen."

## (592) Bird–James   1–0
Offhand game
London (Purssell's), 26 October 1882
*Odds of Ng1*

1. e4 e5 2. Bc4 Nf6 3. d4 N×e4 4. d×e5 N×f2 5. 0–0 N×d1 6. B×f7† Ke7 7. Bg5 mate—*Sheffield and Rotherham Independent*, 2 December 1882.

In November 1882 Bird and Maczuski agreed to play a return match. Unlike the previous year this one was much more strongly contested. In the end Bird won with 7 wins 4 losses and 2 draws. MacDonnell announced that Bird would publish a booklet with the annotated games for sixpence. But there remain only two games that appeared in Bird's column.

## (593) Bird–Maczuski   1–0
Match (game 7)
London 1882
B00

1. e4 b6 2. d4 Bb7 3. Bd3 e6 4. Ne2 Qe7 5. 0–0 g5 6. c4 Nc6 7. Nbc3 h5 8. f4 g×f4 9. B×f4 d6? 10. d5! Ne5 11. B×e5 Maczuski's weird opening set-up has been refuted by Bird, but here an improvement is possible: 11. c5! N×d3 (11. ... a6 12. Nd4! b×c5 13. B×e5 d×e5 14. Qb3 isn't any better) 12. c×d6 c×d6 13. Q×d3 leaves Black's position ruined. **11. ... d×e5 12. Qa4† Kd8 13. d×e6?!** 13. Rad1 keeps the pressure intact. **13. ... Q×e6 14. Rad1 Bc5†** With the intention of bringing the king to e7, where it is extremely vulnerable. 14. ... Kc8 instead is playable. **15. Kh1 Ke7? 16. b4 Be3 17. c5 Nf6 18. Ng3 Kf8** (*see diagram*)

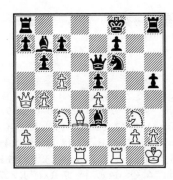

*After 18. ... Kf8*

**19. b5** 19. c6! sacrifices a pawn for a good cause, the gain of a crucial tempo: 19. ... B×c6 20. b5 Bb7 21. Bc4 wins. **19. ... B×c5** 19. ... h4 puts up some fight. **20. Bc4 Qe7 21. R×f6?** 21. Nf5 Qe8 22. Nd6 is the correct procedure to open up the f-file. **21. ... Q×f6 22. Rf1 Qg5 23. B×f7 Kg7** After 23. ... h4! the initiative switches sides—24. Bh5† Ke7 25. Qd1 R×h5 26. N×h5 Rf8. **24. Qc4 Rad8 25. Nf5† Kh7 26. h4 Qf6 27. B×h5 Rhg8 28. Nd5 R×d5?** A fatal error. The game remains utterly unclear after 28. ... B×d5 29. e×d5 e4! 30. Q×e4 Kh8. **29. e×d5 Rd8** 29. ... Kh8 is the only move, but White is close to winning after 30. Bd1!, when he intends to support the center while preparing the march of the pawns on the kingside. Bird now goes for the direct kill. **30. Ng3 Qh6 31. Qe4† Kg8 32. Bf7† Kh8 33. Q×e5† Kh7 34. Nf5 Qf8 35. Qf6 Rd6 36. Bg6†** Black resigns—*Sheffield and Rotherham Independent*, 2 December 1882.

## (594) Maczuski–Bird   0–1
Match (game 12)
London, 11 November 1882
C01

1. e4 e6 2. d4 d5 3. Bd3 d×e4 4. B×e4 Nf6 5. Bd3 c6 6. Nf3 Bd6 7. Nc3 b6 8. 0–0 Bb7 9. Re1 Nbd7 10. Ne4 N×e4 11. B×e4 h6 12. c3 Qe7 13. Be3 g5 14. Qa4 b5 15. Qc2 g4 16. Nd2 Nf6 17. a4 Qc7 18. a×b5 B×h2† 19. Kf1 c×b5 20. B×b7 Q×b7 21. g3 h5 22. Bg5 Nd5 23. Ne4 Kf8 24. Kg2 h4 25. K×h2 h×g3† 26. Kg1 f5 27. Nc5 Qh7 28. N×e6† Kg8 29. Kf1 Re8 30. Ra6 Qh1† 31. Ke2 Qf3† 32. Kd2 g×f2 33. Rf1 Rh1 34. R×h1 Q×h1 35. Q×f5 Qe1† and Black wins—*Sheffield and Rotherham Independent*, 9 December 1882.

## (595) Leonard–Bird   0–1
Offhand game
London (Purssell's), 1 December 1882
*Odds of pawn and two moves*

"The following contest took place on the 1st of December. The position at move 22 ... is one of remarkable interest, resulting from an irregularly lively game, which we publish at the suggestion of many who witnessed it."—Bird

1. e4 & 2. d4 Nc6 3. d5 Ne5 4. f4 Nf7 5. Nf3 c6 6. Bc4 c×d5 7. B×d5 e6 8. Bb3 a5 9. a4 Bc5 10. f5 Nf6 11. e5 Ng4 12. Rf1 N×h2 13. f×e6 N×e5 14. e×d7† B×d7 15. Qd5 Nh×f3† 16. g×f3 Qh4† 17. Kd1 0–0–0 18. Q×e5 Bc6† 19. Bd2 Bd6 20. Be6† Kb8 21. Q×a5 Rhe8 22. Bc4 Bb4 23. Q×b4 B×f3† 24. Kc1 Qe1† 25. R×e1 R×e1† 26. B×e1 Rd1 mate—*Sheffield and Rotherham Independent* (Bird), 16 December 1882.

**(596) Maczuski–Bird    ½–½**
Offhand game
London (Purssell's), 1 January 1883
*C01*

1. e4 e6 2. d4 d5 3. Bd3 d×e4 4. B×e4 Nf6 5. Bd3 Bd6
6. Nf3 Nbd7 7. Nc3 c6 8. 0–0 h6 9. Re1 Qc7 10. Ne4 N×e4
11. B×e4 b6 12. c4 Bb7 13. Bd2 0–0–0 14. b4 Nf6 15. Bc2 g5
16. c5 Bf4 17. g3 B×d2 18. Q×d2 Nd5 19. c×b6 a×b6 20. Rac1
Kb8 21. b5 c5 22. Be4 g4 23. B×d5 R×d5 24. Ne5 f5 25. Qf4
R×d4 26. Q×d4 c×d4 27. R×c7 K×c7 28. Rc1† Kb8 29. Nd7†
Ka7 30. Rc4 Bd5 31. Rc7† Bb7 32. Rc4 Bf3 33. Rc7† Ka8
34. N×b6† Kb8 35. Re7 Rd8 36. Nd7† Kc8 37. Nb6† Kb8
38. Nd7† Kc8 draw—*Sheffield and Rotherham Independent*, 20
January 1883.

The name of Bird's next opponent is uncertain. In his column,
Bird gave the initials "A.W.," while in *Modern Chess* (pp. 13–14),
Black's name is given as "J. Booth."

**(597) Bird–A.W. or J. Booth    1–0**
Offhand game
London (Purssell's) 1883
*Odds of Ra1*

1. e4 e5 2. f4 d5 3. e×d5 Q×d5 4. Nc3 Qe6 5. Nf3 e×f4† 6. Kf2
c6 7. d4 Bd6 8. Bd3 Qe7 9. Re1 Be6 10. d5 c×d5 11. N×d5 Bc5†
12. Kf1 Qd6 13. B×f4 Q×d5 14. Bb5† Kd8 15. Q×d5† B×d5
16. Re8 mate—*Sheffield and Rotherham Independent*, 13 January
1883.

**(598) Unknown–Bird    0–1**
Offhand game
London (Purssell's), 10 January 1883
*Odds of Ra8*

1. e4 f5 2. e×f5 Nf6 3. Be2 Kf7 4. Bh5† Kg8 5. Qf3 d5 6. d3
Nc6 7. c3 e5 8. Bg5 e4 9. d×e4 Ne5 10. Qd1 c6 11. Qd4 Qc7
12. B×f6 g×f6 13. Qe3 Bc5 14. Qg3† Kf8 15. Kd1 d×e4 16. Qf4
Rg8 17. Qh6† Qg7 18. Q×g7† R×g7 19. g4 Nd3 20. Nh3 N×b2†
21. Ke2 b6 22. Nd2 Ba6† 23. c4 N×c4 24. N×c4 B×c4† 25. Kd2
Rd7† 26. Kc3 Rd3† 27. K×c4 Ba3 28. Rab1 b5† 29. R×b5 c×b5†
30. K×b5 R×h3 31. Re1 R×h2 32. R×e4 R×f2 33. Re8† Kg7
34. Ra8 Rb2† 35. Kc6 Rc2† 36. Kb5 Bc5 37. Rc8 Rb2† 38. Kc6
Bb6 39. a4 Rb4 after a few more moves White resigns—*Sheffield
and Rotherham Independent*, 27 January 1883.

**(599) Leonard–Bird    0–1**
Offhand game
London (Purssell's), 26 January 1883
*Odds of pawn and two moves*

"The following position, though given as a problem, really oc-
curred in actual play, on the 26th of January last, in a game between
H.S. Leonard and H.E. Bird, at Purssell's, Cornhill, the latter playing
Black, conceding the odds of pawn and 2 moves"—Bird.

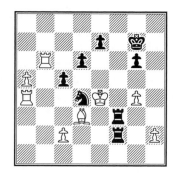

*Black to move*

According to Bird, a mate in two can be found. This is at least
quite optimistic. Black is well on top after **1. … Rf4† 2. Kd5
R×g4**—*Sheffield and Rotherham Independent*, 10 February 1883.

**(600) Bird–Phillips    1–0**
Offhand game
London (Purssell's), 5 March 1883
*Odds of Nb1*

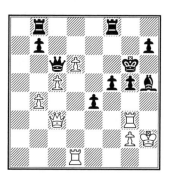

*Black to move*

**1. … B×d1 2. R×g5† K×g5 3. Qg7† Kh5 4. Q×h7† Kg5
5. Qg7† Kh4** and White gave mate in three moves—*Sheffield and
Rotherham Independent*, 17 March 1883.

**(601) Bird–de Galindez    1–0**
Offhand game
London (Purssell's), 5 March 1883
*Odds of Ra1*

"The following very interesting game is presented for the edifi-
cation and improvement of that most numerous class known in
chess circles as rook players, which comprises many rapidly advancing amateurs, from whose list our first-rates may be recruited. We
may add that our opponent in this game is fast overtaking us at this
odds, and at our last sittings made even games, scoring two to our
two"—Bird.

1. e4 e5 2. f4 e×f4 3. Nf3 g5 4. h4 g4 5. Ne5 h5 6. Bc4 Rh7
7. d4 d6 8. Nd3 f3 9. g×f3 g×f3 10. Q×f3 d5 11. e×d5 Bg4
12. Qe4† Qe7 13. Ne5 Nf6 14. Bb5† Kd8 15. Qg2 a6 16. Bd3
Rg7 17. Bg5 Kc8 18. Kd2 Nbd7 19. Rf1 Qd6 20. Nc3 Kb8
21. Nc4 Qe7 22. d6 c×d6 23. Nd5 Qd8 24. N×f6 Be7 25. N×d7†
Q×d7 26. Nb6 B×g5† 27. h×g5 Qe7 28. Qd5 Be6 29. Qa5 Qc7
30. b4 Ra7 31. a4 d5 32. Qc5 Q×c5 33. d×c5 R×g5 34. Rf6 Rg2†
35. Ke3 h4 36. Rh6 h3 37. c4 d×c4 38. B×c4 Kc7 39. B×e6 f×e6
40. Rh8 Black resigns—*Sheffield and Rotherham Independent*
(Bird), 24 March 1883.

Consultation chess was still very popular at Purssell's and Bird must have been one of the most wanted partners. As a rule, a game was arranged at the instigation of a backer who offered a small prize for the experience. From the publication of various of Bird's games one can derive that Cooper was the most liberal sponsor.

## (602) Bird–Maczuski & Cooper & Harper 1–0
Consultation game
London (Purssell's), 2 December 1882
C54

"I visited Purssell's one day last week, and played a few friendly games with Mr. Bird. I found him as potent and brilliant as ever. He presented me with the game which is recorded in our columns today. It was played for a prize given by two or three frequenters of Purssell's"—MacDonnell.

**1. e4 e5 2. Nf3 Nc6 3. Bc4 Bc5 4. c3 Qe7 5. b4 Bb6 6. 0–0 d6 7. a4 a5 8. b5 Nd8 9. d4 f6 10. Na3 Bg4 11. Nc2 Qd7 12. Be2 Be6 13. d5 Bf7 14. Ne3 g5** The allies had to take the opportunity to get rid of their bishop and play 14. … B×e3. Bird now comes up with a very potent idea. **15. Nc4 Bc5 16. b6! c×b6 17. Rb1 Ra6 18. Be3** 18. Nc×e5 is even stronger due to the threat 19. Bb5. Perhaps Bird preferred to offer the allies more value for their money. **18. … Qc7 19. Qb3 Ne7 20. Na3 Ra8 21. Nd2 Nc8 22. Bg4 Bg6 23. Ndc4 B×e3 24. B×c8** This move is very badly judged by Bird. An easy win was still available: 24. Nb5 Qe7 25. f×e3 and d6 falls soon. If 25. … Nf7 26. R×f6! **24. … Bc5 25. Bf5 B×f5 26. e×f5 Ra6 27. Kh1 h5 28. Nb5 Qe7 29. Rbe1 Kd7 30. f4 g×f4 31. R×f4 Qh7 32. Rf3 Rg8** A bit too slow. Black doesn't recognize the importance of the e4 square. Had they done so, they would have played 32. … Nf7 and 33. … Ng5. **33. Nd2 Rg4 34. Ne4 R×e4?** This sacrifice is absolutely not necessary. 34. … Qg7 and 35. … Nf7 is quite all right. **35. R×e4 Nf7 36. h4?!** The cool 36. Rf1 is preferable. **36. … Ra8 37. Na3** 37. Nd4! keeps a clear edge, as the knight will reach e6 (if 37. … e×d4? 38. Qb5†). The text move allows Black to neutralize their disadvantage. **37. … Rg8 38. Nc4 Rg4 39. Nd2 Nh6 40. Qc2 Kc7 41. Qd3 Qd7 42. R×g4 N×g4 43. Qc4 b5 43.** … e4 is interesting. If 44. Q×e4 Nf2†. **44. Q×b5?!** Safer is 44. a×b5, as the endgame becomes suddenly promising for Black. **44. … Q×b5 45. a×b5 a4 46. Ne4 Kb6 47. c4 Bb4 48. Rf1 a3 49. Rb1 Ka5?** Leaving the center with the support of the king gets punished swiftly by Bird. They could equalize with 49. … Bc5 50. N×c5 K×c5 51. Rb3 a2 52. Ra3 K×c4 53. R×a2 e4 54. Kg1 b6 55. Ra3 Nh6. **50. c5! d×c5 51. d6 Nh6** 51. … c4 is also futile: 52. d7 Be7 53. Nd6 Ka4 54. b6. **52. d7 Nf7 53. g4! h×g4 54. h5 c4 55. h6 Be7 56. h7 Kb6 57. Nd6 Nh8** and after a few more moves Black resigns—*Illustrated Sporting and Dramatic News* (MacDonnell), 23 December 1882.

## (603) Maczuski & Cooper & others–Bird 0–1
Consultation game
London (Purssell's), 5 December 1882
C61

**1. e4 e5 2. Nf3 Nc6 3. Bb5 Nd4 4. N×d4 e×d4 5. d3 c6 6. Bc4 h5 7. c3 Bc5 8. h4** "This move appears to be opposed to the theory of White's opening, and is certainly not prudent if White has any attention of castling on the kingside"—Bird. **8. … d5 9. e×d5 c×d5**

**10. Qe2†** "This also seems to me unwise, for Black will play Re8 presently, and White will at least lose a move"—Bird. **10. … Kf8 11. Bb3 a5** 11. … Bg4! and if 12. f3 Qd6 with a steady initiative. **12. Qe5 Ne7 13. 0–0?** "Very objectionable to castle in such a position. We know that uneasy lies the head that wears a crown, but what repose can his Majesty expect in such a position, and why expose him to such discomfort?"—Bird. 13. c×d4 prevents Bird's plans. **13. … a4 14. Bd1 Ng6 15. Qg5?** "White had better have retired his queen at once, so as to play g3. He appears to have wished to secure Black's d-pawn when he retired his bishop"—Bird. **15. … Be7 16. Qd2 N×h4 17. c×d4** *(see diagram)*

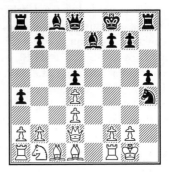

*After 17. c×d4*

**17. … Ra6!** "I consider this rook not utilized sufficiently in the earlier stages of the game, and like to get it into play as soon as possible"—Bird. **18. Kh1 Rg6 19. Rg1 Qd7** "Threatening 20. … N×g2"—Bird. **20. Qe3 Bg5 21. f4 Nf5 22. Qf3 Bf6 23. Nc3 Rg4** "White will, of course, at once guard against the check, but the move made is, nevertheless, sound and good"—Bird. **24. g3 B×d4 25. Rg2 b5 26. Ne2 Bb6 27. d4 h4** "White cannot take the rook without losing the queen after 28. … N×g3†"—Bird. **28. Kg1 R×g3! 29. N×g3 N×d4 30. Qa3†** "The time gained by this check relieves White, and the remainder of the game becomes critical, and requires great nicety of play on both sides"—Bird. **30. … Kg8 31. Be3 h×g3 32. R×g3 Qe6 33. Rc1 Bd7 34. Qd3 Qh6 35. Rg2 Nf5 36. B×b6 Q×b6† 37. Rf2 Rh1†** "This move, or the effect of it, which is decisive, does not appear to have been foreseen by the allies. Instead of 37. Rf2, they would have done better to move their king, and submit the loss of the exchange. Black's two extra pawns would, however, probably ultimately give him the victory"—Bird. **38. K×h1 Q×f2 39. Rc3 d4 40. Rc2 Ng3†** White resigns—*Sheffield and Rotherham Independent* (Bird), 30 December 1882; *Modern Chess* (Bird), p. 77.

## (604) Maczuski & Cooper & others–Bird ½–½
Consultation game
London (Purssell's), January 1883
C61

"The following well contested game took place at one of the Saturday afternoon sittings which have recently become a kind of institution in chess circles, it being a Ruy Lopez attack defended by 3. … Nd4 and 8. … h5. Additional interest may attach to it at the present time, especially with those who wish on occasions to depart from the beaten track. Mr. Cooper provided a special prize"—Bird.

**1. e4 e5 2. Nf3 Nc6 3. Bb5 Nd4 4. N×d4** "If 4. Bc4, he abandons the Ruy Lopez attack, and Black can simplify the opening by 4. …

N×f3†, followed by 5. ... Qf6 or 5. ... Nf6. The sacrifice of the bishop for two pawns by 4. B×d7† and 5. N×e5 is tempting, and has to be met with great care, but it is not sound against correct play, and I do not advise it except by way of experiment, as tending to a lively and spirited game"—Bird. **4. ... e×d4 5. 0–0 Bc5 6. d3 c6 7. Ba4 Kf8** "This move, which has been condemned by the authorities, is still considered eccentric and venturesome, and few players care to adopt it. Black, however, makes it advisedly, and it forms part of his scheme of defense, the object being the advance d5, and having the option, if White captures it, of retaking with the pawn, which he could not do when the king was on e8"—Bird. **8. Qe1 h5** "This is the position which Boden and Steinitz have frequently concurred in thinking uncomfortable and unsatisfactory for Black, and no book on the chess openings, except *Chess Practice* the last published, has approved it"—Bird. **9. f4 d5 10. b4 Bb6 11. Bb3** 11. e×d5 is the best try for some advantage. **11. ... d×e4 12. d×e4 Nf6** "Advancing the d-pawn at this juncture would have been weak play"—Bird. **13. Na3?** Much more prudent is 13. Kh1. **13. ... d3†!** "Now as White threatens 14. Nc4, to disturb the bishop, Black determines to advance the pawn at once. However, 13. ... a5 14. Nc4 Bc7 were open to him, and would have been both sound and steady play. Black, however, preferred to commence an attack at once in anticipation of White's knight's sortie into his position"—Bird. **14. Kh1 Qd4 15. Rb1 N×e4?!** The correct continuation is 15. ... h4! White's king is likely to perish in the assault arising after 16. c×d3 h3 17. g3 Bg4, with the threat 18. ... Qg1†, while 18. ... Q×d3 is also possible. **16. c3?** Wrong. 16. Bb2 is a good fighting move. **16. ... N×c3 17. Bb2 d2 18. Qg3 Ne4 19. B×d4 N×g3† 20. h×g3 B×d4 21. Nc2 Bb6 22. Na3 Bd7** Why not try to open the h-file with 22. ... h4? **23. Bc2 Rh6 24. f5 Rf6 25. Rbd1 Re8 26. R×d2 B×f5** Bird cannot resist the ensuing complications. Safer was 26. ... Bc8. **27. B×f5** 27. R×f5 must be played, although White's situation remains critical—e.g., 27. ... Re1 28. Kh2 Bg1† 29. Kh3 R×f5 30. B×f5 Be3 31. Rd8† Ke7 32. Rd7† Kf6 33. g4 h4. **27. ... R×f5 28. R×f5 Re1† 29. Kh2 Bg1† 30. Kh3 Be3 31. R×h5 B×d2 32. Rh8† Ke7 33. Rb8 f5 34. R×b7† Kf6 35. Kh2 Be3 36. g4 f4 37. Nc4 Bg1† 38. Kh3 Bf2?** 38. ... Bd4! 39. Kh2 Re8 closes White's king definitively into its coffin. **39. g3?** 39. g5†! gives a very drawish endgame, since g7 isn't defended and after 39. ... Kg6?! 40. Kg4 Black would be in trouble. **39. ... f×g3 40. Rc7 Rh1†** 40. ... Re2 is perhaps simpler. **41. Kg2 Rg1†?** A win is still likely after 41. ... Rh2† 42. Kf3 Be1 43. g5† (this pawn has to be abandoned to keep Black from promoting his g-pawn) 43. ... K×g5 44. R×g7† Kf6 45. Rg4 R×a2. **42. Kf3** "and after a little more skirmishing the game was abandoned as drawn." Bird could still try with 42. ... Rb1, but in view of 43. R×c6†, which leaves him but small winning chances, he calls it a day, and a draw was agreed—*Sheffield and Rotherham Independent* (Bird), 17 February 1883; *Modern Chess* (Bird), pp. 78–79.

## (605) Bird & Cooper–Gunsberg & Fenton    ½–½
Consultation game
London (Purssell's) 1883
*C54*

"This was a game for a small prize presented by Mr. Cooper. A consultation game played in a nice friendly spirit is a very enjoyable affair, especially if the competitors engaged will play it at a reasonable pace, say one hour for a contest if it happens to turn out smart and lively, or two hours, or three at the most, if it probe a very well contested game. In view of the instructive tendency of consultation parties, and the advantages afforded to the younger player from conference with the more experienced, I am sure these contests might be popularized, and would become more frequent. They are productive of good feeling also, and the disappointment of losing is found not to be so great when there is a partner to share the responsibility"—Bird.

**1. e4 e5 2. Nf3 Nc6 3. Bc4 Bc5 4. c3 Nf6 5. b4 Bb6 6. Qb3 0–0 7. d3 d6 8. a4 a6 9. a5 Ba7 10. 0–0 Qe7 11. Na3 Be6 12. Be3 Rad8 13. Rae1 B×e3 14. R×e3 Nh5 15. g3 Kh8 16. d4 Bg4 17. d5 Nb8 18. Be2 f5 19. e×f5 B×f5 20. N×e5 d×e5 21. B×h5 Nd7 22. c4 Nf6 23. Bf3 e4 24. Nc2 Qf7 25. Bg2 Ng4 26. Re2 N×h2 27. Rfe1 Qh5 28. Nd4 Ng4 29. f4 Qh2† 30. Kf1 e3 31. N×f5 R×f5 32. R×e3 N×e3† 33. Q×e3 Rdf8 34. Qf3 h5 35. Ke2 Re5† 36. f×e5 R×f3 37. K×f3 h4 38. g×h4 Kg8 39. e6 Kf8 40. Re4 Qg1 41. c5 Qd1† 42. Kg3 Ke7 43. Rf4 Qe1† 44. Kh3 Qe3† 45. Kg4 Qe2† 46. Bf3 Qe1 47. Kg5 Qe5† 48. Kg4 g6 49. Be4 Qh5† 50. Kg3 g5 51. h×g5 Q×g5† 52. Kf3 Qh5† 53. Rg4 c6** "drawn by mutual consent, the time of the sitting having expired. White thought that they might win, but Black felt confident of drawing"—*Sheffield and Rotherham Independent* (Bird), 10 March 1883.

The following skirmish was played around the turn of the year.

## (606) MacDonnell–Bird    ½–½
Offhand game
London (Purssell's), December 1882 (?)
*C38*

**1. e4 e5 2. f4 e×f4 3. Nf3 g5 4. h4 g4 5. Ng5** The Thorold-Allgaier Gambit was, although very popular in the nineteenth century, a rarity in Bird's games; this is the first known game with Bird defending against it. **5. ... h6 6. N×f7 K×f7 7. d4 f3 8. Bc4† d5 9. B×d5† Kg7 10. g×f3 Bd6 11. Be3 Nf6 12. Nc3 Bb4 13. Kd2 N×d5 14. e×d5 B×c3† 15. b×c3 Q×d5 16. Qg1 Re8 17. Re1 Bd7 18. B×h6† K×h6 19. R×e8 B×e8 20. Qe3† Kh7 21. Q×e8 Nc6 22. Q×a8 N×d4 23. c×d4 Q×d4†** drawn by perpetual check—*Illustrated Sporting and Dramatic News*, 13 January 1883.

## (607) Bird–MacDonnell    ½–½
Offhand game
London (Purssell's), 8 February 1883
*C38*

**1. e4 e5 2. f4 e×f4 3. Nf3 g5 4. Bc4 Bg7 5. 0–0 d6 6. g3 g4 7. Nh4 f3 8. Nc3 Nc6 9. d3 Be6 10. Nd5 Ne5 11. Bb3 Ng6 12. Nf5 Be5 13. d4 Bf6 14. N×f6† Q×f6 15. Qd3 h5 16. Qb5† Kf8 17. Q×b7 B×f5 18. Q×a8† Kg7 19. e×f5 h4 20. Be3 h×g3 21. Qd5 R×h2 22. R×f3 g×f3 23. Q×f3 Qh4 24. f×g6 Nf6 25. g×f7 g2 26. Bf4 Rh1† 27. K×g2 R×a1 28. Bh6† Q×h6 29. Qg3† Kf8** and eventually the game was drawn. "It may interest our readers to learn that the above game was played with great rapidity on both sides, especially Mr. Bird's, and was the last in a long series of encounters"—MacDonnell. *Illustrated Sporting and Dramatic News* (MacDonnell), 24 February 1883.

Bird's strongest opponent at Purssell's was Isidor Gunsberg. Born in Hungary in 1854 Gunsberg arrived in London at the age of 22. He initially earned a living as professional chess player in coffee houses and as the hidden operator of the Mephisto automaton. Mephisto's identity had been a mystery for some years until Bird clumsily revealed it in his column of 13 January 1883.[6]

Gunsberg's ambitions started to surpass an existence in coffee houses when he challenged some established masters at the end of 1880. Bird was his preferred opponent but after Bird's announced goodbye from chess Gunsberg had to find another one. Blackburne was willing not only to play but also to give him a lead of 2–0, in a match where the first player to win seven games would be the winner. Gunsberg showed his class by narrowly losing with the margin of just one game.

Early in 1883 Bird suggested that a match between him and Gunsberg would be interesting. Negotiations were started but surprisingly dragged on for a couple of months. It is a good indication of Gunsberg's already considerable strength that, at the point when it became clear that there would be a master and minor section in the approaching London tournament, Bird's major concern about an eventual match was whether he would preserve the right to take part in the master tournament, even in case of a loss.[7] The last mention of a match between both men was given in Bird's column on 3 March. As no further information could be found, it is unlikely a real match ever happened. All their published games were offhand affairs. In the following game Gunsberg played under the disguise of Mephisto.

## (608) Gunsberg (as "Mephisto")–Bird   1–0
Offhand game
London (Purssell's), January 1883
C30

**1. e4 e5 2. Nc3 Bc5 3. f4 d6 4. Nf3 Nc6 5. Bb5 Bd7 6. d3 Nf6 7. B×c6 B×c6 8. f×e5 d×e5 9. N×e5** "A dangerous capture, therefore not advisable"—Gunsberg. **9. ... Qd4 10. Ng4 N×g4 11. Q×g4 0-0** "A very good move, and better than 11. ... Qf2†, for after 12. Kd1 0-0 13. Qf3, Black's chances of attack is diminished"—Gunsberg. 11. ... Qf2† is a decent try. Black is bound to win back his pawn after 12. Kd1 0-0 13. Qf3 f5 14. Q×f2 B×f2 15. Rf1 f×e4 16. N×e4 B×e4 17. d×e4 Rae8, but the diminished material makes a win difficult. **12. Rf1?!** "In consequence of Black's good play the position is full of difficulties. Black threatens the dangerous 12. ... f5, and thereby to open up the f-file for his rook, or even the e-file for the other rook, which would be fatal. The only other possible move seems to be 12. Ne2, which, however, would also result badly; e.g., 12. ... Qf2† 13. Kd1 f5 14. e×f5 (if 14. Qg3 f×e4 with advantage), 14. ... Q×g2 and Black must win the exchange by 15. Q×g2 B×g2 16. Re1 Bf2"—Gunsberg. Gunsberg overlooks the more pru-

dent 12. Qg3 f5 13. Ne2 Qd7 14. e5 Qd5 15. c3, which keeps the center closed. Black can win back his pawn again with 15. ... Q×g2 16. Rf1, but he cannot demonstrate an advantage anymore. **12. ... f5!** "Brave, and destroys White's hopes for peace and quietness. Watch the following ingenious combination: 13. R×f5 Bd7! 14. R×f8† R×f8 15. Qg5 Qf2† 16. Kd1 Qf1† 17. Kd2 Rf2† and mate in two moves"—Gunsberg. **13. Qg3** "White of course expected an attack when he ventured on 9. N×e5, but when there is an attack there is also a defense. This move must be taken in connection with the following one as being the soundest reply"—Gunsberg. **13. ... f×e4 14. Bf4** *(see diagram)*

After 14. Bf4

**14. ... R×f4?!** "If now 14. ... e×d3 15. 0-0-0, White will recover his pawn, and turn a dangerous position into one of comparative safety"—Gunsberg. Not completely true. Besides the simple 15. ... B×g2, 15. ... Rf5! is awkward to meet. The idea is to pile up the pressure along the f-file; e.g., after 16. R×d3 Qf6!. Other moves are but little better: 16. B×c7 d2† 17. Kb1 R×f1 18. R×f1 Re8, and Black will take up the attack with a quick Bb4. **15. R×f4 Bd6** 15. ... Bb4 16. 0-0-0 B×c3 17. b×c3 Q×c3 forces a perpetual check. Bird wants more, but there is nothing in it. **16. Qf2 Qb4 17. 0-0-0 e3** "A fine

**Isidor Gunsberg (*Illustrirte Zeitung*).**

6. It seems reasonable to assume that the secret was already known in the inner circle of London's chess community.

7. Minchin explained in the tournament book that there was some objection to allow Gunsberg (and MacDonnell) in the minor tournament (p. xxii). This makes it very unlikely that Bird had to fear being relegated to that event.

specimen of Black's noted brilliancy. If 17. ... B×f4† 18. Q×f4, and White stands somewhat better"—Gunsberg. **18. R×b4** "The only move to avoid loss"—Gunsberg. **18. ... e×f2** "We can now better point out Black's plans, and why he did not take the rook. He now threatens the rook as well as 19. ... B×g2. If to prevent this White plays 19. Rg4, then follows 19. ... Rf8 20. Rf1 h5 21. Rg6 Kh7 22. R×d6 B×g2 23. R×f2 R×f2 24. Rd7 Bc6 25. R×c7 R×h2, and Black has two passed pawns"—Gunsberg. A few improvements are possible, simplest of all 21. Re4 with probably a quick draw. **19. Re4** "The right move. It avoids all danger and if 19. ... B×e4, White remains with a fair ending of knight against bishop"—Gunsberg. **19. ... Rf8 20. Rf1 B×h2** "Although 20. ... B×e4 was sound play, we cannot condemn this bold move, because with the pawn on f2, Black could fairly reckon upon drawing the game, but it also left him a (very) remote chance of winning. Had he played 20. ... B×e4 he would have had nothing left but to play for a draw"—Gunsberg. **21. Re2 Bg3 22. Ne4 B×e4 23. R×e4 h5 24. Kd2 Kh7 25. Ke2 h4 26. Rh1** "The ensuing ending is most interesting. White must now endeavor to utilize his advantage—by no means an easy task. 26. Rh1 is the beginning of a series of moves to arrive at a favorable position to sacrifice a rook for the bishop with advantage"—Gunsberg. The plan is completely innocent, as such a rook endgame would be plainly drawish. Instead, 26. Rd1, followed by the activation of his pawn majority, offers good winning chances. **26. ... g5 27. Re6** "A most important move, as it cuts off the king from the bishop and wins time ultimately. If White takes the bishop (the only way of winning) he would lose unless he could also get some pawns. There would be no hope of doing this if the king were near the bishop"—Gunsberg. **27. ... Rf5 28. Kf1 Kg7 29. Rh3 Kf7 30. Re3 Rb5 31. b3 Ra5 32. a4 b5 33. Rh×g3 h×g3 34. R×g3 b×a4 35. b×a4 Kg6?** The game is decided by a subtlety. 35. ... Kf6 brings the king that necessary step closer to the center. After 36. Rg4 Rc5 37. Rc4 R×c4 38. d×c4 Ke5 39. K×f2 Kd4 40. Kg3 K×c4, followed by picking up the a-pawn, this draws. **36. Rg4 Kh5** Bird's situation has become very difficult, as the logical move 36. ... Rc5 is losing now: 37. Rc4 R×c4 38. d×c4 Kf5 39. K×f2 Kf4 40. c5 c6 41. a5 a6 42. c3 g4 43. g3† Ke4 44. Ke2 Kd5 45. Kd3 K×c5 46. c4 Kb4 47. Kd4 K×a5 48. Kc5 Ka4 49. K×c6 a5 50. c5 Kb3 51. Kd5 a4 52. c6 a3 53. c7 a2 54. c8Q. **37. Rc4 g4** This pawn will become a mere target, but good advice is hard to find. **38. K×f2 Kh4 39. g3† Kh3** Right into the coffin, but all chances were gone. **40. Rf4 Rc5 41. c4 Rh5 42. Rf7 Rh8 43. d4 Kh2 44. d5 Rh3 45. c5 Rh6 46. d6 c×d6 47. c×d6 Kh1 48. d7 Rh2† 49. Kf1 Rh8 50. d8Q** Black resigns—*Knowledge* (Gunsberg), 26 January 1883.

**(609) Bird–Gunsberg   1–0**
Offhand game
London (Purssell's), 10 February 1883
*C51*

1. e4 e5 2. Nf3 Nc6 3. Bc4 Bc5 4. b4 B×b4 5. c3 Bc5 6. d4 e×d4 7. c×d4 Bb6 8. Bb2 Na5 9. d5 f6 10. Bd3 d6 11. 0-0 Ne7 12. Nc3 Ng6 13. Ne2 Ne5 14. N×e5 f×e5 15. Kh1 g5 "An ill-judged move for so skillful a player as Mr. Gunsberg to make. Its object appears to be to check the advance of 16. f4, but this it did not satisfactorily prevent"—Bird. 15. ... 0-0 is certainly safer. After 16. f4 Bg4 17. f×e5

R×f1† 18. Q×f1 d×e5 Black returns his extra pawn but succeeds in completing his development. **16. f4! g×f4** (*see diagram*)

*After 16. ... g×f4*

**17. N×f4** 17. Bb5† is a refinement. Black has to be very careful now: 17. ... c6 (17. ... Bd7 18. N×f4 is worse. Black's best is now 18. ... 0-0, but his position is lost after 19. B×d7) 18. N×f4 0-0 (18. ... c×b5 19. Qh5† wins at once) 19. d×c6 b×c6 20. B×c6 N×c6 21. Qd5† Kg7 22. Q×c6 with a clear edge. **17. ... 0-0?** "The most promising move order under the circumstances. By keeping White's bishops out of his game, Black hoped to get into a safe position"—Bird. Bird doesn't take the coming infiltration of his queen into account. A defendable position could be reached after 17. ... Qg5 as White is forced to offer the exchange of queens. After 18. Qh5† Q×h5 19. N×h5 White certainly has enough compensation for the pawn, but a forced win is not possible yet. **18. Qh5!** "This appears to be the most effective move. Black could not, without speedy loss, take the knight. For example: 18. ... e×f4 19. e5 Qe7 20. e×d6 c×d6 21. Rae1 wins"—Bird. **18. ... Bd7 19. Ne6** 19. Rf3! is much more direct; e.g., 19. ... R×f4 20. R×f4 e×f4 21. e5! **19. ... B×e6 20. d×e6 Qe7 21. Rf5 R×f5** "If 21. ... Q×e6 22. Qg4†, winning the queen"—Bird. **22. e×f5 Qf6 23. Rf1 Nc6** "If 23. ... Be3 with the view of getting to h6 and g7, White's reply of 24. Rf3 would frustrate his object. The bishop would be lost"—Bird. **24. Bc1 e4 25. Bg5 Qg7 26. f6 Qg6 27. Q×g6†** "Unpretentious but sure"—Bird. **27. ... h×g6 28. B×e4 Ne5 29. B×b7 Rf8 30. Bd5 c6 31. f7† N×f7 32. e×f7† Kg7 33. Bf6†** Black resigns—*Sheffield and Rotherham Independent* (Bird), 24 February 1883.

**(610) Gunsberg–Bird   1–0**
Offhand game
London (Purssell's), 5 March 1883
*C30*

1. e4 e5 2. Nc3 Bc5 3. f4 d6 4. Nf3 Nf6 5. Bc4 Nc6 6. d3 a6 7. f×e5 d×e5 8. Qe2 Bg4 9. Be3 Nd4 10. B×d4 B×d4 11. Nd1 Qd6 12. c3 Ba7 13. Ne3 Bd7 14. 0-0-0 0-0 15. d4 N×e4 16. Bd5 Bc6 17. Nf5 N×c3 18. b×c3 Qa3† 19. Qb2 Q×b2† 20. K×b2 B×d5 21. Ne7† Kh8 22. N×d5 c6 23. Ne3 e4 24. Nd2 f5 25. g3 g5 26. h4 f4 27. Ng2 f3 28. Ne3 g×h4 29. R×h4 c5 30. Rdh1 Rf7 31. N×e4 c×d4 32. Nd6 d×e3 33. N×f7† Kg7 34. R×h7† Kf6 35. R1h6† Kf5 36. Nd6† Black resigns—*Sheffield and Rotherham Independent*, 3 March 1883.

**(611) Bird–Gunsberg   1–0**
Offhand game
London (Purssell's), February 1883
*C51*

1. e4 e5 2. Nf3 Nc6 3. Bc4 Bc5 4. b4 B×b4 5. c3 Bc5 6. d4

e×d4 7. c×d4 Bb6 8. Bb2 Na5 9. d5 f6 10. Bd3 d6 11. Qd2 c5 12. Nc3 c4 13. Bc2 Bc7 14. Ne2 Ne7 15. Bc3 Ng6 16. 0–0 0–0 17. Kh1 b5 18. Nfg1 Bb6 19. f4 Nb7 20. Nf3 a5 21. a3 Nc5 22. Ng3 Bd7 23. e5 f×e5 24. f×e5 Bf5 25. e6 Bd3 26. B×d3 c×d3 27. Rab1 Nf4 28. R×b5 N×d5 29. Bd4 Qe8 30. Rbb1 Q×e6 31. Rfe1 Qf7 32. Ba1 Nd7 33. Re4 Nf4 34. Ng5 Qg6 35. Re7 Ne5 36. B×e5 d×e5 37. Qa2† Kh8 38. Nf7† R×f7 39. Q×f7 d2 40. Q×g6 h×g6 41. Rd7 Bd4 42. Ne4 Nd3 43. h3 g5 44. N×d2 g4 45. Ne4 Rf8 46. h×g4 Rf4 47. Ng5 Nf2† 48. Kh2 N×g4† 49. Kg3 Bf2† 50. Kh3 Nf6 51. Rd8† Ng8 52. g3 Rf5 53. Ne4 Black resigns—*Sheffield and Rotherham Independent*, 3 March 1883.

# LONDON 1883

The success of the chess tournament held in Vienna aroused some envy in London chess circles. England's capital was the cradle of international chess competitions, having hosted the first two great tournaments in chess history in 1851 and 1862—but this has now been more than twenty years ago. During the quiet summer season of 1882, the first few steps were made towards the organization of a new tournament. A subscription list was started in September. G.W. Medley offered the remainder of the Löwenthal fund for the cause, while several well-known patrons also gave their financial support. In October a managing committee was formed. The appointed chairman was Frederic Hyman Lewis with Minchin acting as the honorary secretary. They widened the appeal for support to chess clubs all over the country. The seeds of the ambitious plans fell onto fertile soil and before the end of the year the envisaged £1000 prize fund was achieved.

One contributor deserving a special mention was the Maharajah of Vizayanagaram. This Indian nobleman offered £200, enough to set up a large side event. The Vizayanagaram tournament drew 26 participants and was won by the young German Curt von Bardeleben.

The committee presented the official program early in January 1883. It was a recurrent factor in the nineteenth century that each tournament provided an incentive for long discussions about the rules. The London committee based their rules on those used to manage the Vienna tournament, but they also came up with a controversial addition. This new rule concerned the eternal problem of solving the high number of draws. The solutions adopted in earlier tournaments (draws didn't count in Paris 1867, while in Vienna 1873 small matches were played) were no longer deemed suitable. Now it was agreed that games that ended in a draw had to be replayed, even twice if necessary. Only in the case of three draws a half point would be added to the score of both players. Bird was elated about this idea and defended it passionately.[8] With the majority of the players also in favor, this rule was adopted. The tournament was a double round-robin and would consequently last much longer than originally expected. Another decision that prolonged the endeavors of the players was the setting of the time limit at a rather slow 15 moves per hour.

The prize fund of the tournament was the largest yet in chess history, exceeding an amount of £1000. Ultimately eight prizes were offered. The major bait for the chess masters was a first prize of £300. Consolation prizes were distributed among the non–prize winners.

Bird, although coping with health problems, could not hide his eagerness to play in his home town. His recovery and decision to participate was loudly applauded by his many chess fans.[9]

Bird was not the only player in doubt about his presence. Both Steinitz and Zukertort reported health issues but they recovered in time to play. They were joined by all the other prize winners of Vienna: Winawer, Mason, Mackenzie and Blackburne. Additionally Rosenthal and Englisch took part. Only four of the 14 players could be considered a bit weak for such a field full of stars: Alexander G. Sellman, Noa, Mortimer and Skipworth. Everybody was quite ready for the spectacle to start.[10]

Bird opened the tournament quite well. After eight rounds he had scored five points with his drawn game with Rosenthal still needed to be replayed. Bird's play throughout these first rounds was particularly brilliant as his games against Englisch an Mackenzie testify.

But from then on, with a few of the strongest opponents to meet, Bird started to lose focus. He lost against the very strong Steinitz and Zukertort but also against the much weaker Noa. More satisfying was his win against Blackburne. With 7 out of 13 points at the end of the first cycle Bird occupied a decent place in the middle of the pack.

Bird was not able to maintain the same high playing standard during the second cycle. He repeated his two losses against Zukertort and Steinitz. His struggle against Zukertort was heroic and Bird was somewhat unlucky not to drag a draw and then replay out of it. Bird subsequently beat the weak Sellman but his tournament finish was mediocre. He suffered a second very painful loss at the hands of Noa, but on the positive side scored a surprising point against Chigorin after an epic blunder of the latter (Bird never beat the Russian master again). In the penultimate round Bird crowned his tournament by delivering a positional masterpiece against

8. In the *Sheffield and Rotherham Independent* of 31 March 1883 he declared: "Notwithstanding the objections urged to playing over again to decide the win on account of time and convenience, we hope that the committee will be able to carry out their original intention not to allow draws to count half each, as formerly. This rule, we repeat, has given rise to abuses in tournament, such as draws by consent and so on, and has been found to militate against the spirit in which every game should be played in a tournament."

9. Bird greatly appreciated the encouragements: "The participation of Bird (retired from the more active and prominent chess circle through ill-health) was scarcely expected, and his adhesion has caused great satisfaction, the rapidity and liveliness of his play imparting additional spirit to the contests." *Sheffield and Rotherham Independent*, 12 May 1883.

10. Hoffer described the scene for his readers: "At twelve o'clock all the players took their seats, their places having been marked by large printed slips, and as soon as the signal was given by the sounding of the gong, play commenced. The Victoria Hall at the Criterion is divided by two rows of settees, standing back to back, one-third being allotted to the masters and two-thirds to the twenty-six competitors of the minor tournament. Ropes have been fixed all round to ensure the comfort of the players, and at the same time to give free circulation to the numerous spectators, who have every facility for seeing the games from both sides, as each pair of players is sitting back to back to the next pair. The boards and men are of the largest size, Staunton pattern; and the clocks, by an ingenious contrivance—the invention of Mr. T.B. Wilson, of Manchester—fixed together on a balance so that the two clocks can never be going at the same time. On setting one in motion the other must necessarily stop. Therefore, the greatest bone of contention in former tournaments is removed." *The Field*, 28 April 1883.

**Sketches at the London 1883 tournament (*Illustrated London News*).**

### International chess tournament, London, 26 April–23 June 1883

*Site:* Victoria Hall, Criterion
*Playing hours:* 12 p.m.–7 and 7 p.m.–11
*Prizes:* 1st £250, 2nd £150, 3rd £120, 4th £90, 5th £70, 6th £50, 7th £25
*Time limit:* 15 moves per hour
*Notes:* The duel between Blackburne and Rosenthal (second cycle) was not played out.

| | 1 | 2 | 3 | 4 | 5 | 6 | 7 | 8 | 9 | 10 | 11 | 12 | 13 | 14 | |
|---|---|---|---|---|---|---|---|---|---|---|---|---|---|---|---|
| 1 J.H. Zukertort | | 0 1 | r1 1 | 1 r1 | rr1 1 | 1 r0 | 1 1 | 1 1 | r1 r1 | 1 1 | 1 1 | 1 0 | 1 0 | 1 + | 22 |
| 2 W. Steinitz | 1 0 | | 1 0 | 0 0 | 0 rr1 | 1 1 | 1 r1 | r0 r0 | 1 1 | 1 1 | 1 r1 | 1 1 | 1 r1 | 1 + | 19 |
| 3 J.H. Blackburne | r0 0 | 0 1 | | 0 1 | 1 rr0 | r0 0 | 1 r1 | r1 r* | rr½ rr1 | 0 r1 | 1 r1 | r1 1 | 1 1 | 1 + | 16½ |
| 4 M.I. Chigorin | 0 r0 | 1 1 | 1 0 | | 0 r1 | 1 1 | r0 1 | 0 rr1 | 1 0 | 1 0 | r1 0 | 1 r1 | 1 0 | 1 + | 16 |
| 5 B. Englisch | rr0 0 | 1 rr0 | 0 rr1 | 1 r0 | | rr½ rr½ | rr0 0 | rr½ rr1 | 0 1 | r0 1 | 1 1 | r1 1 | 1 1 | 1 + | 15½ |
| 6 G.H. Mackenzie | 0 r1 | 0 0 | r1 1 | 0 0 | rr½ rr½ | | 0 r1 | r0 r1 | 0 1 | 0 r1 | 1 r1 | rr½ r1 | r1 1 | 1 + | 15½ |
| 7 J. Mason | 0 0 | 0 r0 | 0 r0 | r1 0 | rr1 1 | 1 r0 | | r1 0 | r1 0 | 1 1 | rr½ 1 | 1 rr1 | r1 1 | 1 + | 15½ |
| 8 S. Rosenthal | 0 0 | r1 r1 | r0 r* | 1 rr0 | rr½ rr0 | r1 r0 | r0 1 | | rr½ rr1 | r1 0 | 0 1 | r0 1 | 1 1 | r1 + | 14 |
| 9 S. Winawer | r0 r0 | 0 0 | rr½ rr0 | 0 1 | 1 0 | 1 0 | r0 1 | rr½ rr0 | | r0 1 | rr1 0 | 1 r1 | 1 1 | r1 + | 13 |
| 10 H.E. Bird | 0 0 | 0 0 | 1 r0 | 0 1 | r1 0 | 1 r0 | 0 0 | r0 1 | r0 1 | | 0 0 | 1 1 | r1 1 | r1 + | 12 |
| 11 J. Noa | 0 0 | 0 0 | 0 r0 | r0 1 | 0 0 | 0 r0 | rr½ 0 | 0 r0 | rr0 1 | 1 1 | | 0 1 | 1 1 | 0 + | 9½ |
| 12 A. Sellman | 0 1 | 0 0 | r0 0 | 0 r0 | r0 0 | rr½ r0 | 0 rr0 | r1 0 | 0 r0 | 0 0 | 1 0 | | 1 1 | 0 + | 6½ |
| 13 J. Mortimer | 0 1 | 0 r0 | 0 0 | 0 1 | 0 0 | r0 0 | r0 0 | 0 0 | 0 0 | r0 0 | 0 0 | 0 0 | | 0 1 | 3 |
| 14 A.B. Skipworth | 0 – | 0 – | 0 – | 0 – | 0 – | 0 – | 0 – | r0– | 0 – | r0 – | 1 – | 1 – | 1 0 | | 3 |

*Notes:* "r" means a draw was replayed; "*" means this mini-match was not played and thus ended after the first draw.

Rosenthal. This game was one of the most sober-looking highlights of his chess career. Bird came in tenth with 12 points out of 26. He could leave only the four minor masters behind him. This was disappointing, certainly when considering that his playing level during this tournament was much more elevated than in Vienna.[11]

The balance of the Löwenthal fund, £50, was divided among the non–prize winners. Bird earned £11 15s. for his effort.

While the tournament in Vienna excelled in a lasting tension that ascended into a climax, the outcome of this tournament was clear halfway, as Zukertort had gathered 12 out of 13 points. Mason already trailed at 2½ points. Steinitz, the sole player able to beat Zukertort with a good portion of luck, and Chigorin both had 9 points. Zukertort continued his winning streak until he achieved a nearly unbelievable 22 out of 23. That he lost his three final games (for 22 out of 26 overall) had no impact on first place. Steinitz, whose dominance over the chess world was now in real danger as an explicit contender had stood up, ended with a respectable 19. He clearly topped Blackburne, who came third at 16½.

As a consequence of the London 1883 tournament, negotiations for a world championship match were started between Steinitz and Zukertort. To the frustration of the chess world, and certainly of someone like Bird, these negotiations lasted three years.

At the end of the year a voluminous tournament book was released. Bird contributed analyses of his (and others') games and was

thus closely involved in the production. In the preface, the editor of the book, Minchin, thanked him and other contributors (Zukertort, Steinitz and Mason were the other participants of the major tournament who sent in game annotations).[12]

### (612) Rosenthal–Bird    ½–½
International tournament (round 1, game 1)
London, 26 April 1883
C44

**1. e4 e5 2. Nf3 Nc6 3. d4 e×d4 4. Bc4 Bc5 5. 0–0 d6 6. c3 Bg4 7. Qb3 B×f3 8. B×f7† Kf8 9. g×f3 Nf6 10. Bd5 Qc8 11. Be6 Qe8 12. Bf5 Bb6 13. Bf4 Qh5 14. Nd2 Re8 15. Qd1 Qf7 16. Kh1 Ne7 17. Bh3 d×c3 18. b×c3 N×e4 19. f×e4 Q×f4 20. Bd7 Rd8 21. Qg4 Q×g4 22. B×g4 h5 23. Bh3 Ng6 24. f4 Rh6 25. Nf3 Ke7 26. Nd4 Nh4 27. Rab1 Rf6 28. a4 Rdf8 29. f5 B×d4 30. c×d4 b6 31. Rbc1 c5 32. d×c5 d×c5 33. Rg1 R8f7 34. e5 R×f5 35. B×f5 N×f5 36. Rg6 Nd4 37. e6 Rf2 38. Kg1 Re2 39. R×g7† Kf6 40. R×a7 K×e6 41. Ra6 Kd5 42. R×b6 Ra2 43. Rf1 c4 44. Rh6 c3 45. R×h5† Kc4 46. Rh8 c2 47. Rc8† Kd3** draw—*Tournament Book*, pp. 251–252.

### (613) Bird–Winawer    ½–½
International tournament (round 2, game 1)
London, 27 April 1883
C54

**1. e4 e5 2. Nf3 Nc6 3. Bc4 Bc5 4. c3 Nf6 5. b4** "I am the only

---

11.  Bird judged his own performance in *The Times* on 25 June 1883: "The low score of Bird, 12 only out of a possible 26, has occasioned more disappointment and regret than surprise. The slow time limit of 15 moves an hour and the formalities and the clock it was known would militate against his chance of success. It may be remarked, however, that by availing himself of the several drawn games offered—notably with Zukertort, Winawer, Englisch and Noa, he would have materially improved his score and have gained an important prize. His lack of judgment in this respect is to be lamented. During the latter part of the tournament he was suffering from gout and was daily fearful of having to withdraw altogether." A similar sound could be read in *Chess Monthly* (July 1883, p. 323): "Bird made good progress in the first round, and was expected to be among the prize-winners; but failing health coupled with an old hankering after favorite variations of his own and a certain unwillingness to be satisfied with a legitimate draw made him lose ground."

12.  Minchin couldn't resist to give his readers a warning considering Bird's opinions: "The opinions of Mr. Bird on some points of theory are well known to be heterodox, and the reader may be amused at finding such opposite views propounded within one volume as will meet him in this collection. I can only suggest to the young student that on all questions of theory he will find Zukertort and Steinitz thoroughly safe guides, while if he attempt to put in practice some of Mr. Bird's opinions he must be prepared for difficulties only to be surmounted by that master's chess genius and originality." J.I. Minchin, *Games Played in the London International Chess Tournament,* 1883. London: Wade, [1884], p. i. Now, that must have been a challenge to Bird's fans.

player who has yet ventured upon this line of play in the Giuoco Piano. Until quite recently Zukertort, Steinitz, Blackburne, and all the book authorities were unanimous in condemning the advance of the pawns on the queenside as premature and unsound. Deep and profound, in some cases all but exhaustive, analysis has somewhat narrowed the choice of openings at chess, and the question, therefore, of the validity or otherwise of this form of the Giuoco Piano must be of considerable interest and importance to all who do not wish to be confined continually in their choice of openings. I cannot venture my opinion in favor of this opening abstractedly as equal in value to that of any one of the great authorities objecting to it, but I recommend the student to examine the positions I obtained in the following games, at any move he may select: v Zukertort 29th move of White, v Englisch 26th move of White, v Rosenthal 26th move of White; v Winawer 25th move"—Bird. **5. ... Bb6 6. d3 d6 7. a4** "By the advance of the a-pawn I make space to bring my rook early into the game. It also gives the option Nb1–a3–c2, a mode of bringing this knight into the game which I am very partial to, especially in the 1. f4-opening"—Bird. **7. ... a5** "Zukertort prefers 7. ... a6"—Bird. **8. b5 Ne7 9. 0–0** "I sometimes play 9. Qb3, 10. Ra2 etc."—Bird. **9. ... Ng6 10. Be3** "Against Englisch I played 10. Bg5"—Bird. **10. ... d5 11. e×d5 B×e3 12. f×e3 N×d5 13. Qb3 Be6 14. B×d5 B×d5 15. c4 Be6 16. Nbd2 Qe7 17. d4 f6 18. Ne4 b6 19. d5 Bf7 20. Ng3 Qd7** Bird played well and obtained a small but annoying advantage. The text move allows him to further expand this edge, as Black gives up control over the Black squares, especially c5. 20. ... 0–0 is correct. **21. Rad1 Ne7 22. Nh4 0–0 23. e4 Nc8** Bird omitted to play at once 21. e4 and 22. c5!, and this gave Winawer the chance to rectify the situation with 23. ... Qd6. **24. c5** The correct idea, but the execution could be better: 24. Rc1! g6 25. c5, followed by 26. Nh4–f3–e1–d3. **24. ... b×c5 25. Rc1** *(see diagram)*

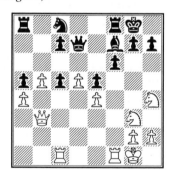

*After 25. Rc1*

**25. ... g6?** "A very ingenious, not to say artful, move; whether perfectly sound is another question. White considered the consequences of 26. R×f6, and, notwithstanding Winawer's plans, determined to do it. 26. R×c5 would, however, have been sounder play. White could soon after have won c7, and the game then would be indefensible for Black."—Bird The move order selected by Bird allows Winawer to play 25. ... c6, which lightens up the pressure a bit, although White keeps an initiative; e.g., 26. b×c6 Q×c6 27. Ngf5 Qc7 etc. **26. R×f6!** 26. R×c5 (Bird) is also very strong, but the text move is certainly more decisive. **26. ... Qe7 27. Rcf1 Nd6 28. Qe3 Ne8 29. Qg5** "White, strange to say, here misses a very pretty and conclusive way of finishing the game: 29. Qh6 N×f6 30. Ngf5 g×f5 31. N×f5 wins"—Bird. **29. ... N×f6 30. Ngf5?**

30. R×f6!, followed by 31. Nhf5, leaves Black with no choice but a quick resignation. **30. ... Qd8 31. Nh6† Kh8** 31. ... Kg7 secures the draw: 32. R×f6 Be6 33. R×g6† h×g6 34. Q×g6† Kh8 35. Qh5 etc. **32. R×f6 Bg8?!** 32. ... B×d5 is the only decent move. The endgame is but slightly better for White: 33. R×f8† Q×f8 34. e×d5 e4 35. Qe5†. **33. N×g8?** With this move Bird shows himself content with a draw. He could certainly test his opponent further with 33. R×g6! Q×g5 34. R×g5, which is very tricky to meet. One faulty line for Black is 34. ... Rae8? 35. N4f5 Rf6 36. Rg3, with various threats, like 37. Rc3, and in case of 36. ... Rff8? 37. R×g8! poetically mates on the next move. A better chance is offered by 34. ... Bf7, but after 35. R×e5, White can count on a firm advantage. **33. ... K×g8 34. R×g6† h×g6 35. Q×g6† Kh8 36. Qh5† Kg8 37. Qg4†** draw—*Tournament Book* (Bird), p. 285; *Modern Chess* (Bird), pp. 20–22.

## (614) Winawer–Bird    0–1
International tournament (round 2, game 2)
London, 28 April 1883
*B30*

**1. e4 c5** "The Sicilian reply has probably undergone more vicissitudes in regard to its estimation and appreciation than any other form of defense. In 1851, it was entirely out of favor, but its successful adoption on so many occasions by Anderssen entirely restored it to confidence. Its rejection by Morphy in 1857-8, and by Steinitz in 1862, caused it again to lapse in consideration as not being a perfectly valid and reliable defense. Its fortunes have ever since continued in an unsettled state. Staunton (three weeks before his death), dining with Kolisch and myself, pronounced it to be quite trustworthy, and on the same day Löwenthal expressed a similar opinion. Baron Kolisch, who has a vivid recollection of the meetings, concurs in these views"—Bird. **2. Nf3 e6** "I now rather prefer 2. ... Nc6, followed by 3. ... g6 and 4. ... Bg7"—Bird. **3. Nc3 Nc6 4. Bb5 Nd4 5. 0–0 Ne7 6. N×d4 c×d4 7. Nb1** "Curious play, but Winawer never moves unadvisedly. Doubtless he required e2 for his bishop"—Bird. **7. ... a6 8. Be2 d5 9. d3 Bd7 10. e×d5 N×d5 11. Bf3 Bc6 12. Nd2 Be7 13. Re1 Rc8 14. Nc4** "Commencement of a long combination, with the hope of winning the exchange by Nb6, with the option also of playing to e5"—Bird. **14. ... 0–0 15. Bd2 b5 16. Ba5 Qd7 17. Ne5** "If 17. B×d5, Black of course replies 17. ... Q×d5, threatening mate"—Bird. **17. ... Qb7 18. c4 d×c3 e.p. 19. b×c3 Bf6 20. c4 Ne7 21. N×c6 N×c6 22. Rb1** "This part of the game is interesting and well played on both sides"—Bird. **22. ... Qd7 23. B×c6 Q×c6 24. c×b5 a×b5 25. Qb3 Qc2 26. Kf1 g6 27. Q×c2 R×c2 28. Re2 Rfc8 29. R×b5 R×e2 30. K×e2 Rc2† 31. Ke3 R×a2 32. Rb8† Kg7 33. Bb4 Be5 34. Bf8† Kf6 35. Rb1 Bb2** "A very good move on the part of Black which materially influences the subsequent course of the game"—Bird. White's slight pawn weakness shouldn't cause him to lose the game, but it is enough reason for Bird to continue trying to force something. **36. h4 h5 37. d4 Kf5 38. f3 f6 39. Rg1 e5 40. g4† Ke6 41. d×e5 f×e5 42. Kd3 Bd4 43. Rh1?** Natural but wrong; 43. Rg3 instead abandons a pawn after 43. ... Rh2 (if 43. ... h×g4 44. R×g4) 44. g×h5 g×h5 45. Bh6 R×h4, but the tactical trick 46. Rg6† Kf5 47. Rg5† Kf6 48. f4 saves his skin. **43. ... h×g4 44. f×g4 Kd5** "Black as now attained a winning position, I believe, against the best play"—Bird. **45. Re1 Rg2** 45. ... Rb2! forces matters at once as 46. ... e4† is threatened. **46. Re2 e4† 47. Kd2 R×g4 48. Be7 Rg1 49. Bg5 Rg3 50. Kc2 Ra3 51. Kd1 e3 52. Rc2 Ke4 53. Ke2 Ra1 54. Rc6 Ra2† 55. Ke1 Kf3! 56. B×e3 B×e3 57. Rf6† Bf4 58. Kd1 Rd2† 59. Ke1 Rg2 60. Kf1 Rg4 61. Ra6 Kg3 62. h5 g×h5 63. Kg1 Kf3† 64. Kf1 h4 65. Ra2 h3 66. Rf2† Ke4 67. Re2† Be3 68. Rh2 Rg1† 69. Ke2 Rg2†** White resigns—*Tournament Book* (Bird), pp. 286–287.

## (615) Bird–Englisch ½–½

International tournament (round 3, game 1)
London, 30 April 1883
C54

**1. e4 e5 2. Nf3 Nc6 3. Bc4 Bc5 4. c3 Nf6 5. b4 Bb6 6. d3** "6. Qb3 was the move originally played by Bird, and he frequently still adopts it"—Bird. **6. ... d6 7. 0-0 0-0 8. Bg5** "Whether bishop played thus to pin the knight or planted on e3 be preferable must ever remain a debatable point. I have latterly inclined to prefer the latter as probably the sounder course. Change at chess is desirable for real enjoyment like change of air, so I vary my proceedings perhaps more than is consistent with prudence, my desire being to get as much beauty out of the game as I can"—Bird. **8. ... Be6** 8. ... h6 9. Bh4 g5 might be more interesting. **9. Nbd2 Qe7** "Zukertort plays 9. ... Ne7. Rosenthal also did so, but rather later. The move in the text is certainly inferior"—Bird. **10. a4 a6 11. a5 Ba7 12. Kh1 h6 13. Bh4 Rad8 14. b5** "The play now becomes quite animated, and the way the pawns get on is very curious. I recommend the chess aspirant to carefully study the progress of the game from this point; it is far above average interest"—Bird. **14. ... B×c4 15. N×c4 a×b5 16. Ne3** "The knight assumes a threatening attitude"—Bird. **16. ... B×e3** "And Black accordingly walks him off"—Bird. **17. f×e3 Qe6** Other valid moves are 17. ... Nb8, 17. ... Ra8 or 17. ... d5. **18. Qb1!** "Very useful"—Bird. **18. ... g5?!** A crude weakening; 18. ... Na7 is safe. **19. Bg3?** 19. N×g5 h×g5 20. B×g5 Nd7 21. B×d8 gives White two pawns and rook against knights, as well as some attacking chances on both queen- and kingside. With the text move Bird has some brilliant ideas in his sleeve, but objectively these should fail. **19. ... Na7?!** A strong central reaction with 19. ... d5! is much better, as it is obvious that White has nothing concrete after 20. e×d5 N×d5. **20. c4 c6** (*see diagram*)

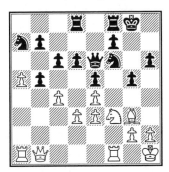

*After 20. ... c6*

**21. c5** Bird continues playing in intimidating style. Perhaps 21. a6 is the better option. **21. ... Nh5?!** 21. ... d×c5 obtains a pawn mass on the queenside. White can try to mix things up but with careful

**Berthold Englisch (courtesy Cleveland Public Library).**

play Black holds the extra pawn with a strong position as well—e.g., 22. B×e5 Nd7 23. Bc7 (retreating is no option: 23. Bg3?! b4! and 24. ... Nb5 activates the knight) 23. ... Rc8 24. Bb6 Ra8 25. Rc1 Qd6! (more precise than 25. ... Qe7 26. B×c5) 26. e5 Qe7 and now 27. B×c5 is not so good as in the previous line, while after 27. d4 c4 28. Bc7 Nc8 29. Rf1 White has counterplay for the pawn, but it's doubtful that it is enough. **22. a6! b×a6 23. R×a6 Qd7?** Abandoning a pawn, which Bird mysteriously doesn't capture with 24. c×d6. The retreat of the knight, 23. ... Nc8, seems to imply the loss of another pawn after 24. R×c6, but Black wins it back with precise play: 24. ... g4 25. Nh4 Qd7 26. Ra6 N×g3† 27. h×g3 d×c5. White keeps a slight initiative after 28. d4! **24. d4?! N×g3† 25. h×g3 Nc8** "Black apparently has nothing better; besides, he cannot make the essential move of 25. ... f6 now, for White could check at a2, which would practically decide the game"—Bird. **26. c×d6 f6?** A consolidating move too much. 26. ... Qb7! is correct as White's active rook is chased away. After 27. Ra3 N×d6 28. N×e5 Rde8 29. Rc3 b4 30. R×c6 R×e5 31. R×d6 Re6, the contours of a drawn endgame become apparent. **27. Rc1!** Better than 27. d×e5 (Bird) 27. ... f×e5 28. Qa2† Qf7. **27. ... N×d6 28. Rc×c6 Ne8 29. Q×b5** "Instead of thus hurriedly capturing the b-pawn, White should have played 29. d5, which would have given him a splendid game"—Bird. 29. d5?! Qg4! offers Englisch decent chances to defend himself. The text move isn't bad at all, but his best continuation would have been 29. d×e5!, crashing through Black's sixth rank. **29. ... g4 30. Nh4 e×d4 31. e×d4** 31. Qb3†! Rf7 32. Nf5 d×e3

33. Q×e3 is immediately winning. **31. … Q×d4 32. Nf5?!** 32. Qh5! is a killer. **32. … Q×e4 33. Re6!** "It was not judicious on White's part to surrender these strong center pawns unless he could see his way to win right off. White was playing at a very rapid pace; by taking a little more time he might, perhaps, have seen that 33. N×h6† would win thus: 33. … Kg7 (best) 34. Qb7† K×h6 35. R×f6† N×f6 36. Q×e4 Kg7 (if 36. … Rd1† 37. Kh2 and owing to the position of Black's knight, White must win with proper play) 37. Qe7† Kg6 38. R×f6† and wins"—Bird. 35. … R×f6! overthrows Bird's evaluation: Black is winning. **33. … Rd1†** 33. … Nc7 is the alternative. White keeps excellent winning chances after 34. R×e4 and 35. R×g4†. **34. Kh2 Qb1 35. Q×b1 R×b1 36. Ra7?!** 36. Ra8 Ng7 37. R×f8† is better, though it's not easy to win the endgame. **36. … Rb5 37. N×h6† Kh8 38. N×g4 Rg5 39. R×e8** This leads to a draw, but that result was likely anyway, after 39. Ne3. **39. … Rh5† 40. Kg1 R×e8 41. N×f6** (see diagram)

*After 41. N×f6*

**41. … Rh1†!** "A capital resource for Black, which White should have foreseen"—Bird. **42. K×h1 Re1† 43. Kh2 Rh1† 44. K×h1** stalemate. "This game throughout occasioned much interest, and the stalemate at the finish caused much amusement to all excepting White"—Minchin. *Tournament Book* (Bird/Minchin), pp. 171–173

### (616) Bird–Chigorin　0–1
International tournament (round 4)
London, 1 May 1883
*C58*

　1. e4 e5 2. Nf3 Nc6 3. Bc4 Nf6 4. Ng5 d5 5. e×d5 Na5 6. d3 h6 7. Nf3 e4 8. Qe2 N×c4 9. d×c4 Bc5 10. h3 0–0 11. Nh2 b5 12. Nc3 b×c4 13. Q×c4 Qd6 14. 0–0 Ba6 15. Nb5 Qb6 16. a4 N×d5 17. Q×e4 c6 18. Ng4 f5 19. Qe6† Kh7 20. N×h6 Rf6 21. Qe5 g×h6 22. c4 c×b5 23. a×b5 Bb7 24. c×d5 Bd4 25. Qe7† Kh8 26. Bf4 Rg8 27. g3 Rg7 28. Qe8† Kh7 29. Ra4 Rfg6 30. Qb8 B×d5 31. Ra6 R×g3† 32. B×g3 Q×b8 White resigns—*Tournament Book*, pp. 143–144.

### (617) Englisch–Bird　0–1
International tournament (round 3, game 2)
London, 2 May 1883
*A85*

　1. d4 f5 "If the view of the very highest authorities that 1. f4 is not advisable, the reasons for Black not adopting it should be still more forcible. My opinion is that 1. … f5 is the best move on the board for the party commencing. It at once effects something by stopping e4. I speak with the utmost diffidence and respect, know-

ing that Zukertort, Steinitz, Blackburne, and Mason all oppose it, and never adopt it. On the other hand, it is only right to mention that both Anderssen and Morphy approved it for White. At the same time I cannot quote any great authority (except practice) to justify its adoption for Black"—Bird. **2. c4 Nf6 3. Nc3 e6 4. a3 Be7 5. Bf4** "A very favorite move of Mason's, and also of Blackburne's. Harrwitz used to adopt it so successfully that Morphy expressed a high opinion of it. I boldly oppose the Bf4 by Bd6, and have been fortunate with it against both Mason and Blackburne"—Bird. **5. … 0–0 6. e3 b6 7. Nf3 Bb7 8. Bd3 Ne4 9. h4** A weird move, allowing Bird to inflict upon his opponent a weakness along the c-file. 9. B×e4 is perfectly playable, as Black is forced to push his d-pawn to d5 within a few moves. **9. … N×c3 10. b×c3 Bd6 11. B×d6 c×d6 12. Qc2 h6** Englisch's last move invited Bird to create another doubled pawn, but Bird neglects the opportunity. **13. h5 Nc6 14. Nh4 Na5** Black is now in excellent shape on the queenside, while White has nothing to boast about. **15. f3 Rc8 16. g4?** A desperate attack, asking for a swift punishment. **16. … N×c4** 16. … f×g4 can be played without hesitation. **17. B×c4 R×c4 18. g×f5 Qg5 19. Kf2 Rfc8** "I considered that the possession of the c-file was more than an equivalent for White's attack, which, moreover, I did not regard with great apprehension"—Bird. **20. Rag1** The passive 20. Rac1 deserves the preference. **20. … R×c3 21. Q×c3 R×c3 22. R×g5 h×g5 23. Ng6 Kf7** Correct is at once 23. … g4! Englisch's reply however gives Bird a second chance. **24. Nh8†** 24. f×e6† d×e6 25. Rg1 had to be tried. The endgame remains miserable for White. **24. … Kg8 25. Ng6 g4** "Quite necessary to play thus without loss of time, as White could otherwise play 26. h6, threatening to draw, make a queen, or checkmate"—Bird. **26. d5 g×f3 27. Rh4 Rc2† 28. Kg3 f2** The win becomes a piece of cake after 28. … e×d5! **29. Rf4 e5** 29. … e×f5 is certainly better (30. R×f5 Kh7 31. e4 Re2). **30. Rf3?** The endgame is far more difficult to win for Bird had Englisch taken the pawn at once. **30. … Ba6** "After the exchange of rooks the endgame became very interesting. Black's extra pawn on the queenside required so much attention from the White king that Black was enabled to get his majesty to f4 just in time to secure victory"—Bird. **31. R×f2 R×f2 32. K×f2 Kf7 33. e4 Bb5** The immediate 33. … Bd3 34. Ke3 Bc2 35. Nh4 b5 gives White much less liberty. **34. Ke3 a5 35. Nh4 Ba4 36. Kd2 Kf6 37. Nf3 b5 38. Kc1 b4 39. a×b4 a×b4 40. Nd2 Bb5 41. Kb2 Kg5 42. Kb3 K×h5 43. K×b4 Bd3 44. Ka5 Kg4 45. Kb6 Kf4 46. Kc7 B×e4 47. K×d7 B×d5 48. K×d6 Ba2 49. Nf1 e4 50. Ke7 K×f5 51. Ng3† Ke5 52. Kf8 g5 53. Kg7 Kf4 54. Nh5† Kf3 55. Kf6 e3** White resigns—*Tournament Book* (Bird), pp. 173–174.

### (618) Bird–Mortimer　½–½
International tournament (round 5, game 1)
London, 3 May 1883
*C65*

　1. e4 e5 2. Nf3 Nc6 3. Bb5 Nf6 4. Qe2 Bc5 5. c3 0–0 6. 0–0 a6 7. Ba4 b5 8. Bc2 d6 9. d3 Bg4 10. h3 B×f3 11. Q×f3 Ne7 12. Be3 Ng6 13. B×c5 d×c5 14. g3 Qd7 15. Kh2 Ne8 16. a4 c6 17. Nd2 Nd6 18. Nb3 Nb7 19. Qg2 Qd8 20. f4 f6 21. f5 Nh8 22. Nd2 Nf7 23. Nf3 Qc7 24. Qe2 Rfd8 25. Bb3 Kh8 26. Nh4 Nh6 27. a×b5 a×b5 28. Be6 Nd6 29. Qe3 Nb7 30. g4 Qe7 31. Nf3

Nf7 32. R×a8 R×a8 33. Rf2 Nbd8 34. Bb3 Qd6 35. Rg2 h6 36. h4 Qe7 37. Kg3 Nd6 38. g5 c4 39. d×c4 b×c4 40. Bc2 N8f7 41. Kh2 Qa7 42. Qd2 Rd8 43. g6 Rd7 44. g×f7 N×f7 45. Qe2 Nd6 46. b3 Qa3 47. b×c4 Q×c3 48. Qd3 Q×d3 49. B×d3 N×f5 50. Rd2 Ne3 51. h5 Kh7 52. Be2 R×d2 53. N×d2 Nc2 54. Bg4 g6 55. Kg3 Nd4 56. c5 g×h5 57. Bd7 Kg7 58. Kh4 Kf7 59. K×h5 Kg7 60. Bg4 Kh7 61. Bd1 Ne6 62. Nb3 Nf4† 63. Kg4 Kg6 64. Bc2 h5† 65. Kh4 Kh6 66. Na5 Ne6 67. Nb7 Nd4 68. Bd1 f5 69. Nd6 f×e4 70. N×e4 Nf5† 71. Kh3 Nd4 72. Kg2 Kg6 73. Nd6 h4 74. Bg4 Kg5 75. Bd7 Kf4 76. Be8 e4 77. N×e4 K×e4 78. Kh3 Kd5 79. B×c6† draw—*Tournament Book*, pp. 287–288.

## (619) Mason–Bird    1–0

International tournament (round 6)
London, 4 May 1883
*B40*

1. e4 c5 2. Nf3 e6 3. Nc3 Ne7 4. d4 c×d4 5. N×d4 Ng6 6. Be2 Nc6 7. 0–0 Be7 8. Be3 0–0 9. Kh1 Bb4 10. Nb1 d5 11. c3 Bd6 12. e×d5 e×d5 13. Nd2 N×d4 14. B×d4 Qc7 15. g3 Bd7 16. Bf3 Bc6 17. Bg2 a6 18. f4 f6 19. Qh5 Qf7 20. Rfe1 Rfe8 21. Nf1 Ne7 22. Q×f7† K×f7 23. Ne3 Rad8 24. Rad1 Bc7 25. Kg1 h5 26. Kf2 b6 27. h4 g5 28. h×g5 f×g5 29. f×g5 b5 30. Bf3 Kg6 31. Rh1 K×g5 32. R×h5† Kg6 33. Rdh1 Ng8 34. Rh7 Re7 35. R1h6† N×h6 36. R×e7 B×g3† 37. K×g3 Rg8 38. Kh4 Nf5† 39. N×f5 K×f5 40. Rf7† Ke6 41. Rf6† Kd7 42. Bg4† Kc7 43. Rf7† Kb8 44. Rh7 Rg6 45. Rh8† Kb7 46. b4 Kc7 47. Be5† Kb7 48. Kh5 Black resigns—*Tournament Book*, pp. 224–225.

## (620) Mortimer–Bird    0–1

International tournament (round 5, game 2)
London, 5 May 1883
*C33*

1. e4 e5 2. f4 e×f4 3. Bc4 Qh4† 4. Kf1 d6 "This move I adopted with much success in America in 1877. Although it is not recommended in the works of any of the leading authorities on the openings, it has stood the test of practice well, and I believe is better than 4. ... g5, the move usually played in the magnificent games of Anderssen, Harrwitz, Löwenthal, Kieseritzky, and other great masters who were most partial to the unrivalled Bishop's Gambit opening"—Bird. 5. Qf3 "5. Nc3 is justly considered the best move at this point, as it at once threatens to go to d5, a formidable square. 5. Nf3 or 5. d4 are also frequently played, the order of them being varied. The move in the text, 5. Qf3, has the sanction of Staunton, and has been regarded as free from objection by other leading authorities. With due respect, however! I do not regard it as perfectly satisfactory. The Bishop's Gambit is rarely ventured in tournaments or great games, being an opening of a dangerous and decisive character"—Bird. 5. ... Nc6 6. g3 Qf6 7. Q×f4 Nd4 8. Bb3 For the next few moves, Bird's play is a bit slack. 8. ... Q×f4† 9. g×f4 f5! 10. d3 N×b3 11. a×b3 f×e4 12. d×e4 d5! gives him excellent prospects in the endgame. 8. ... Be6 9. Nc3 h5 This move doesn't fit in well in the position, but it succeeds in mesmerizing his opponent. 10. d3 h4 11. Q×f6 N×f6 12. Kg2? 12. g×h4 neutralizes the dangerous pawn once and for all. 12. ... B×b3 13. c×b3 Nc2 "Our talented and at times brilliant opponent failed to see the full effects of this

move, fearing the loss of a pawn only. It will be seen upon examination that there is no valid reply to Black's combination"—Bird. 14. Rb1 Ne1† 15. Kf1 h×g3 "Threatening 16. ... g2† to win rook and make a queen"—Bird. 16. h×g3 "Deplorable as this is there appears nothing better"—Bird. 16. ... R×h1 17. Bg5 R×g1† 18. K×g1 Nf3† 19. Kf2 N×g5 20. Ke3 Kd7 21. d4 Re8 White resigns—*Tournament Book* (Bird), pp. 288–289.

## (621) Mackenzie–Bird    0–1

International tournament (round 7)
London, 7 May 1883
*C61*

1. e4 e5 2. Nf3 Nc6 3. Bb5 Nd4 4. Ba4 Bc5 5. c3 N×f3† 6. Q×f3 Ne7 "If Black had desired to make the move most likely to lead to a draw he would probably have selected 6. ... Qf6"—Bird. 7. Qg3 The more active 7. Qh5 Ng6 8. d4 is interesting. 7. ... 0–0 "Abandoning an important pawn, but gaining time to organize an attack"—Ranken. 8. Q×e5 "Whether judiciously or not, White captures the proffered e-pawn"—Bird. 8. ... d5 9. d3 a5 "This move is a favorite of mine. I like to utilize my rook as speedily as possible, and in the present game I employed that valuable officer quite early, and, as will be seen, with much advantage"—Bird. 10. 0–0 Ra6! "This rook is destined to become a very useful officer in the attack"—Bird. 11. e×d5 11. d4 or 11. Qh5 (11. ... Rg6 12. Bd1) are valuable alternatives. Taking this pawn is risky. 11. ... Rg6 "With a view to 12. ... Bh3, which it is to White's interest to prevent"—Bird. 12. Kh1 "A little examination will show that 12. Bf4 for White would lose a piece"—Bird. 12. ... Bd6 13. Qe2 13. Qd4 is a better try—13. ... N×d5 14. Q×d5 (14. Bd1 is an alternative) 14. ... Qh4 15. g3 Q×a4, though Black's compensation is obvious. 13. ... N×d5 Bird has now an excellent position, with great attacking chances. 14. f4? *(see diagram)* 14. g3 or 14. Bb3 are playable.

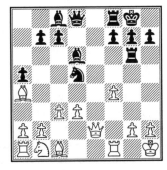

*After 14. f4*

14. ... Bg4 Certainly not a bad move, but it doesn't enhance Black's advantage, as does 14. ... b5!—e.g., 15. B×b5 Bb7, when g2 and f4 cannot be defended both. 15. Qf2 c6 "To enable him to bring Rf8 in action. Had White now played 16. f5, Black would have taken it and then played 17. ... Qh4"—Ranken. 16. Bd1 Bf5 17. Be2 Re8 Both sides had their alternatives, but the result would have remained the same: Black has a terrific attack going on. 18. Rd1 Rge6! "A sledge-hammer stroke, recovering his lost pawn, with a winning position"—Ranken. 19. Bf3 "Had White played 19. Bf1, then 19. ... Bg4 would have been almost decisive"—Bird. 19. ... N×f4 20. B×f4 B×f4 21. Na3 Qg5 "Threatening 22. ... Rh6, which would be fatal"—Bird. 22. g3 Be3 23. Qg2 Qh6 "24. ... Bh3 again must be

provided for"—Bird. **24. g4 Bg6 25. Nc2 Ba7 26. Qg3** "In order to push the g-pawn, but Black doesn't object to the exchange of queens"—Ranken. **26. ... Bb8!** **27. g5** "Black plays in very fine attacking style, and carries all before him. White, being hard pressed, thought an exchange of queens would relieve the strain"—Gunsberg. **27. ... B×g3 28. g×h6 Bh4 29. h×g7 Rd8** The exchange of queens diminished Bird's attack, but not enough to doubt his eventual win. This move, on the other hand, offers Mackenzie some unexpected chances of resistance. Winning is 29. ... Rf6! 30. Bg2 Rf2 31. Re1 R×e1† 32. N×e1 R×b2. **30. Nd4** "If 30. Be4 then Black plays 30. ... R×e4 31. d×e4 R×d1 32. R×d1 B×e4† and 33. ... B×c2"—Bird. **30. ... Rf6 31. Kg2** 31. Be4 is better, although Black remains firmly in the driving seat after 31. ... Rf2 32. Rab1 c5 33. Nb5 Bg5. **31. ... K×g7 32. Nb3 Rf5** *(see diagram)*

After 32. ... Rf5

"From this point to the end Mr. Bird plays beautifully, leaving his skillful opponent really nothing to do. Captain Mackenzie's conduct of the early part of the game was weak, and having got thereby into difficulties, he was never able to recover himself"—Ranken. More precise is 32. ... Kh6! (intending 33. ... Rg8) 33. Be4 Rf2† 34. Kh1 f5 35. Bg2 f4. **33. d4 Kh6 34. Rd2?** 34. Rf1 is the last chance to offer resistance. After 34. ... Rg8 35. Kh1 Rb5 White remains under severe pressure, but there is nothing decisive for the moment. **34. ... Rg8 35. Be4** "It is not often that the Captain makes so ill-judged a move as this. 35. Rf1 would have been much more to the purpose"—Bird. Of course, this fails after 35. ... Bh5†. **35. ... Rg5†!** "Much stronger than the discovered check, which would allow the king to retreat to h1, whereas this fetches him out"—Ranken. **36. Kf3 f5 37. Bc2 Re8!** "It was considered by the large concourse of visitors that Black had managed this somewhat adroitly; his 31st and subsequent moves were well planned. There is now no satisfactory move for White"—Bird. **38. Nc5 Bh5† 39. Kf4 Rg4† 40. K×f5 Rgg8** "Threatening mate in four moves"—Bird. **41. Ne6 Bg4† 42. Ke4 R×e6† 43. Kd3 b5** "To prevent an escape by 44. Kc4"—Gunsberg. **44. c4 Bg5 45. Rg2 Re3†** White resigns. "For if 45. Kd2 Rg3† and wins. Black's play in the latter part of the game has been very telling and ingenious"—Gunsberg. *Tournament Book* (Bird), pp. 197–198; *Knowledge* (Gunsberg), 18 May 1883; *British Chess Magazine* (Ranken), June 1883, pp. 211–212; *Modern Chess* (Bird), pp. 72–73.

## (622) Skipworth–Bird  ½–½
International tournament (round 8, game 1)
London, 8 May 1883
A04

**1. Nf3 f5 2. e3 e6 3. Be2 Nf6 4. c4 b6 5. 0–0 Bb7 6. b3 Bd6**

**7. Bb2 0–0 8. d3 Nc6 9. Nbd2 Qe8 10. d4 Qg6 11. g3 Be7 12. Nh4 Qh6 13. Ng2 Nd8 14. f3 d5 15. Rc1 c6 16. c5 Nf7 17. f4 Nd7 18. b4 g5 19. Qb3 Rfb8 20. Qc3 Nf6 21. a4 Nd7 22. b5 b×c5 23. d×c5 Bf6 24. Qc2 g×f4 25. g×f4 Kh8 26. Nf3 Rg8 27. b×c6 B×c6 28. Bb5 R×g2 29. K×g2 B×b5 30. B×f6† N×f6 31. a×b5 Ne4 32. Qb2† d4 33. Q×d4† Kg8 34. Rg1 Rd8 35. Qb2 e5 36. Kh1† Kf8 37. c6 Qh5 38. Qg2 Ke7 39. c7 Rc8 40. f×e5 h6 41. Rgf1 Qg4 42. Qb2 Qh3 43. Qb4† Ke8 44. Qe1 h5 45. Ng1 Qg4 46. Rf4 Qg6 47. Nf3 Qe6 48. Nd4 Qd5 49. Kg1 N×e5 50. R×f5 Kd7 51. Kf1 Nd6 52. Rg5 Rf8† 53. Kg1 Ne4 54. c8Q† R×c8 55. R×c8 N×g5 56. Qg3 Ngf3† 57. N×f3 N×f3† 58. Kf2 K×c8 59. Q×f3 Q×b5** draw—*Tournament Book*, pp. 289–290.

## (623) Bird–Skipworth  1–0
International tournament (round 8, game 2)
London, 10 May 1883
D63

**1. c4 e6 2. Nc3 Nf6 3. d4 d5 4. Bg5 Be7 5. e3 0–0 6. Nf3 Nbd7 7. Rc1 d×c4 8. B×c4 Nb6 9. Bd3 Nfd5 10. B×e7 Q×e7 11. 0–0 N×c3 12. b×c3 Nd7 13. Rb1 b6 14. e4 Bb7 15. Re1 e5 16. Qa4 c6 17. h3 Rfd8 18. Re3 c5 19. d5 Nf8 20. c4 Rd6 21. Nh2 Bc8 22. Nf1 Rh6 23. Rg3 Qh4 24. Ne3 Rf6 25. Rf1 Bd7 26. Qd1 Re8 27. Nf5 B×f5 28. e×f5 h5 29. Re3 e4 30. f4 R×f5 31. B×e4 g6 32. Qf3 Rf6 33. Kh2 Rd6 34. f5 Qf6 35. g3 Nd7 36. Qe2 Qd4 37. Rd1 Qe5 38. Rdd3 Qg7 39. f×g6 f×g6 40. Bg2 R×e3 41. R×e3 Rf6 42. Re7 Rf7 43. d6 Nf6 44. Qe6 Kf8** and White mates in two—*Tournament Book*, pp. 290–291.

## (624) Zukertort–Bird  1–0
International tournament (round 9)
London, 10 May 1883
C30

**1. e4 e5 2. Nc3 Bc5 3. f4 d6 4. Nf3 Nf6 5. Bc4 Be6** "In theory doubling a pawn thus is considered bad. We, however, played it as a novelty, and considered we gained time by it getting also two files open for our rooks"—Bird. **6. B×e6 f×e6 7. f×e5 d×e5 8. Qe2** 8. N×e5 is the critical test of Bird's idea. **8. ... Nc6 9. Qc4 Qe7 10. Ng5?!** Zukertort is convinced of his advantage and rushes in to demonstrate it as soon as possible, but in fact this move permits Bird to obtain excellent play in the center. 10. Na4 is better, though Black has good play after 10. ... Bd6 11. 0–0 Nd4! **10. ... Nd4 11. Nb5 N×e4** "A trap. Black's best course would be 11. ... 0–0–0 12. d3 (if 12. N×d4 R×d4) 12. ... N×b5 13. Q×b5 Ng4 etc."—Zukertort. "Although this move was ingenious and tempting, Black rather regretted that he did not follow his first impression and play 11. ... 0–0–0"—Bird. Contrary to the player's opinion, the text move is at least as good as 11. ... 0–0–0. **12. N×c7†?** "Of course, not 12. N×e4 on account of 12. ... Qh4† and if 13. Ng3 then 13. ... Nf3†"—Zukertort. The best and only playable move is 12. N×d4, when Black retains his superiority after 12. ... N×g5 13. Nb3 Bb6 14. Qa4† c6. **12. ... Kd7?!** "Too enterprising. 12. ... Q×c7 would have given Bird a decided advantage. White would ultimately lose his c-pawn and have to move his king. Black's game is obviously much better developed"—Bird. The continuation could have been 13. N×e4 0–0! 14. Q×c5 Q×c5 15. N×c5 N×c2†, and Black is clearly winning. **13. Nc×e6 N×e6??** With this serious error Bird digs his own grave. Things could have been completely different after 13. ... Bd6!, when White is fighting for survival; e.g., 14. N×d4 ·×d4 15. N×e4 Q×e4† 16. Kd1 Q×g2. **14. N×e4 Bb6** Or 14. ... Rac8 (Bird) 15. Qd5† Kc7 16. Q×e5† Bd6 17. Q×d6†. **15. Qd5† Kc8 16. d3 Rd8** 16. ... Nd4 is a better attempt but 17. Kd1 and 18. c3 defends against all threats. **17. Q×e5 Bc7 18. Qf5 Rf8 19. Qh3 Kb8 20. Bd2 a5 21. 0–0–0 Ra6 22. Rhf1 Rc8 23. Rde1 Be5 24. Nc3 Bf6 25. Re4 Rac6 26. Qf5 Qd6 27. Rfe1 Nc7 28. Bf4 Qf8 29. Q×a5 b6 30. Qb4 Qd8 31. Re6 B×c3 32. b×c3 Qd5 33. R×c6 Q×c6 34. Re7** Black resigns—*Sheffield and Rotherham Independent* (Bird), 26 May 1883; *Tournament Book* (Zukertort), p. 16.

## (625) Noa–Bird    1–0

International tournament (round 10)
London, 11 May 1883
*B40*

**1. e4 c5 2. Nf3 e6 3. d4 c×d4 4. N×d4 Nf6 5. Nc3 Bb4 6. Bd3 Nc6 7. N×c6 b×c6 8. Bd2 d5 9. e5 Nd7 10. Qg4 Bf8 11. f4 Rb8 12. b3 g6 13. 0–0 Be7 14. Rae1 Nc5 15. Be2 h5 16. Qh3 Bb7 17. b4 Nd7 18. a3 c5 19. b×c5 B×c5† 20. Kh1 Bc6 21. Bd3 B×a3 22. B×g6 Nc5 23. B×h5 Kd7 24. f5 Qg8 25. Ne2 Bb4 26. B×b4 R×b4 27. Nf4 Qg5 28. f×e6† f×e6 29. N×e6 N×e6 30. Rf7† Kd8 31. Q×e6 Rh6 32. Rf6 Bd7 33. Qd6 R×f6 34. Q×f6† Q×f6 35. e×f6 Rf4 36. f7 Be6 37. g3** Black resigns—*Tournament Book,* pp. 291–292.

## (626) Steinitz–Bird    1–0

International tournament (round 11)
London, 14 May 1883
*C46*

**1. e4 e5 2. Nc3 Nc6 3. Nf3 Bc5 4. N×e5 N×e5 5. d4 Bd6 6. d×e5 B×e5 7. Bd3 Ne7 8. 0–0 c6 9. Qh5 d6 10. f4 Bd4† 11. Kh1 g6 12. Qe2 Kd7 13. Bc4 f5 14. Rd1 B×c3 15. b×c3 f×e4 16. Ba3 d5 17. Q×e4 b5 18. B×b5 c×b5 19. B×e7 Kc6 20. Qe5 Qd7 21. Q×h8 Q×e7 22. Re1 Qd6 23. Re8 Qd7 24. Rae1 Qc7 25. Qf6† Kc5 26. R1e6 B×e6 27. R×e6** Black resigns—*Tournament Book,* pp. 72–73.

## (627) Bird–Blackburne    1–0

International tournament (round 12)
London, 15 May 1883
*A02*

**1. f4 e6 2. Nf3 Be7 3. e3 b6 4. Be2 Bb7 5. 0–0 c5 6. d3 Nc6 7. Nbd2 Qc7 8. Ne4 f5 9. Ng3 0–0–0 10. Bd2 Nf6 11. a3** "This quiet and modest looking move is mostly of the greatest importance, and particularly so in close games. It forms a starting point and basis for White's designs in the present game"—Bird. **11. ... h5 12. b4 h4** "It becomes apparent thus early that each player is bent upon instituting an attack with as little delay as possible"—Bird. **13. Nh1 h3 14. g3 Rdg8** It was possible to accept the offered pawn without great risk. **15. b5 Na5 16. Ne5** "16. Ng5 would have been good here,

not so forcible at first sight, but in reality safer and sounder than the one made in the text, which would have effectually foiled Black's contemplated attack, commencing with 16. ... g5"—Bird. **16. ... g5 17. Bf3 g×f4 18. e×f4 Bd6 19. B×a5** At once 19. Nf7 Rh7 20. N×d6† Q×d6 and now 21. Nf2 or 21. Bc3 neutralizes Black's attacking chances. The exchange is beneficial for White whose weakest piece disappears from the board at the cost of a crucial White defender. The weakening of his queenside is of no importance. **19. ... b×a5** *(see diagram)*

*After 19. ... b×a5*

**20. Nf7?** "Bird played throughout this tournament at times with a singular lack of judgment, and more than usual impetuosity, utterly forgetting or ignoring the paramount importance of safety. In the present position White's pawns are obviously so much stronger than Black's that his policy should be to avoid complications and play so as to bring about an endgame. 20. B×b7† and 21. Qf3 would help to bring about this result"—Bird. **20. ... B×f4! 21. Rf2** Other moves end up bad as well: 21. N×h8 Be3† 22. Rf2 B×f2† 23. K×f2 R×h8. **21. ... Rh7 22. Qe2 R×f7 23. B×b7† Q×b7** "Both Zukertort and Steinitz, on looking through the game at its conclusion, inclined to think that Blackburne should have taken with the king (I thought so, too), interposing the knight when 24. Qf3†. 25. c4 would not have been so formidable as at first sight it appeared. For example: 23. ... K×b7 24. Qf3† Nd5 25. c4 Qe5 26. Raf1 Be3 and White loses the exchange without any equivalent in position"—Bird. **24. R×f4 Qc7** Better is 24. ... Q×b5 or 24. ... Nd5 (Zukertort) 25. Rf2 f4. **25. Raf1 Nd5 26. Rh4 f4 27. R×h3 Rfg7?!** This move allows Bird some time to set up a line of defense. 27. ... Ne3! 28. Re1 Qe5 is close to winning. Black's queen is heading for c3. **28. Qf3** 28. Qe4! is more precise, as Blackburne now has, but fails to take, the opportunity to open an important diagonal against White's king by playing 28. ... c4! **28. ... Qe5 29. c4 Qd4† 30. Nf2 f×g3 31. R×g3 Ne3?!** Stronger is 31. ... Qe3!, obliging Bird to exchange queens after which White's last kingside pawn will be lost. **32. Re1!** "After due consideration White could not see that anything better than a draw by perpetual check would result by venturing with the queen to a8, unless he determined to sacrifice his queen and rook for Black's two rooks, knight and two pawns. This would have been extremely hazardous, though very tempting. White, it is true, would have had two passed pawns, but Black would have got his a-pawn passed also. Liking his position and prospects, White, prudent for once, did not venture on a ending of this very complicated and doubtful character. It would, however, have been so interesting that I cannot refrain from giving as a variation this probable continuation. Suppose: 32. Qa8† Kc7 33. Q×a7† Kd8 34. Qb8† Ke7 35. Q×g8 R×g8 36. R×g8 N×f1 37. K×f1 Qa1†

38. Kg2 Q×a3 39. h4 Qc1 40. b6 (if 40. h5, 40. ... Kf7 appears a good reply). White with the best play could not win"—Bird. Two decisive reinforcements, 36. ... Kf7! as well as 40. ... Qb2 41. h5 Kf7 42. Rb8 a4, make the move actually played by Bird the best one. The attack is beaten off, material equality restored, and Black's initiative is clearly much less threatening than it was before. **32. ... Nf5 33. R×g7 Q×g7† 34. Kh1 Kc7 35. Ne4 Qh6 36. Qf2 d6** "White had long been anxious to compel Black to advance this pawn in order to direct his attack on c6. He now promptly takes advantage of the occasion"—Bird. **37. Qf3 Rh8 38. Qg2 Nd4** "A very fine, not to say insidious move, as he threatens 39. ... Q×h2†, and also 39. ... Nf3"—Bird. **39. Ng5** "A very potent reply, which effectually demolished Black's chance of a coup. He could not afford to take the knight; e.g., 39. ... Q×g5 40. Q×g5 R×h2† 41. K×h2 Nf3† 42. Kg3 N×g5 43. Kg4 and should win easily"—Bird. **39. ... Rg8 40. Rg1 Kb6 41. Qg3 e5 42. Qg4 Qf6?** A very clumsy square for the queen, allowing Bird to realize a surprising turnaround of the game. After 42. ... a6 or 42. ... Qf8 (and if 43. Qe4 Qf6), the game is quite balanced. **43. Ne4!** "Well played, bringing matters at once to an issue"—Bird. **43. ... R×g4 44. N×f6 R×g1† 45. K×g1** The h-pawn will decide the game. **45. ... Ne2† 46. Kf2 Nf4 47. Ke3 Kc7 48. Ke4 Nh3 49. Kf5 a4 50. Nd5† Kd7 51. b6** "The finishing stroke"—Bird. **51. ... a×b6 52. N×b6† Kc6 53. N×a4 Nf2 54. Nb2 d5 55. h4 e4 56. c×d5† K×d5 57. d×e4† N×e4 58. a4 Nd6† 59. Kg6 c4 60. h5 c3 61. Nd1 c2 62. Ne3† Ke6 63. N×c2 Nf5 64. Nd4† N×d4 65. h6 Nc6 66. h7 Ne5† 67. Kg7** Black resigns. "This game for the last 40 moves engaged nearly the undivided and continuous interest of the large company present. Blackburne played with remarkable ingenuity, and made several very clever attempts to force the game, but Bird was in good form, and played—as he occasionally does—with commendable patience and accuracy"—Bird. *Tournament Book* (Bird), pp. 118–120; *Chess Monthly* (Zukertort), July 1883, pp. 326–327.

## (628) Bird–Rosenthal 0–1

International tournament (round 1, game 2)
London, 16 May 1883
*A03*

**1. f4 d5 2. e3 e6 3. Nf3 Nf6 4. Bd3 Nc6 5. 0–0 e5 6. f×e5 Ng4 7. Bb5 Bd7 8. B×c6 b×c6 9. d4 Be7 10. Nc3 f5 11. Ne2 Be6 12. a4 g5 13. Qd3 0–0 14. h3 Nh6 15. Bd2 Qe8 16. Nh2 c5 17. Ng3 c4 18. Qe2 Rb8 19. Ra2 c5 20. Bc3 c×d4 21. B×d4 a6 22. Qh5 Qg6 23. Q×g6† h×g6 24. Ne2 Nf7 25. h4 Nd8 26. h×g5 B×g5 27. Nf3 Be7 28. a5 Nc6 29. Bb6 Nb4 30. Ned4 N×a2 31. N×e6 Rfc8 32. Nfd4 Nb4 33. Nf4 Bg5 34. Nde6 B×f4 35. N×f4 Kh7 36. c3 Nc6 37. Rf3 N×e5 38. Rh3† Kg7 39. Kf1 Nc6 40. Ne6† Kf7 41. Nc7 Rh8 42. N×d5 R×h3 43. g×h3 Rh8 44. Nc7 R×h3 45. Kg2 Rh8 46. N×a6 Ke6 47. Nc7† Kd7 48. a6 Rc8 49. Nd5 Kd6 50. Nb4 Ra8 51. Bd4 N×b4 52. c×b4 R×a6 53. Kf3 Ra4 54. b5 Rb4 55. Kf4 R×b5 56. Kg5 Kd5 57. Kf4 Rb7 58. Bf6 Rb6 59. Bc3 Re6 60. Bg7 Re4† 61. Kf3 g5 62. Bh6 g4† 63. Ke2 Re6 64. Bg7 f4 65. Bd4 Ke4 66. Bc5 g3 67. e×f4 K×f4† 68. Kd2 g2 69. Bg1 Kf3 70. Kc3 Re1 71. Bd4 Re3†** White resigns—*Tournament Book*, pp. 252–253.

## (629) Sellman–Bird 0–1

International tournament (round 13)
London, 17 May 1883
*B33*

**1. e4 c5 2. Nc3 Nc6 3. Nf3 e6 4. d4 c×d4 5. N×d4 Nf6 6. Ndb5 d6 7. Bf4 e5 8. Bg5 a6 9. Na3 Be6 10. Nd5 B×d5 11. B×f6 Qa5† 12. c3 B×e4 13. Nc4 Qc7 14. Bh4 d5 15. f3 d×c4 16. f×e4 Be7 17. Bf2 Nd8 18. Qd5 Rc8 19. Be2 Ne6 20. g3 0–0 21. Qd1 Rfd8 22. Qc2 Bg5 23. Rb1 Qc6 24. Rd1 R×d1† 25. B×d1 Rd8 26. 0–0 Rd2 27. Qb1 Nc5 28. B×c5 Q×c5† 29. Kh1 Qe3 30. Bf3 g6 31. Qc1 Qb6 32. Bg2 f6 33. Qe1 Q×b2 34. Rg1 Q×c3 35. Qb1 Qb2 36. Qf1 Qd4 37. Qf3 Qf2 38. Qg4 Kf7 39. Qh3 Kg7 40. Rf1 Q×g2† 41. Q×g2 R×g2 42. K×g2 c3 43. Rf2 Bd2** White resigns—*Tournament Book*, pp. 292–293.

## (630) Bird–Zukertort 0–1

International tournament (round 14)
London, 28 May 1883
*C54*

**1. e4 e5 2. Nf3 Nc6 3. Bc4 Bc5 4. c3 Nf6 5. b4 Bb6 6. d3 d6 7. a4 a5** "The usual continuation is 7. ... a6. The text move, however, is equally satisfactory"—Zukertort. "I rather regret that Zukertort is entirely silent in regard to White's opening, his first note to the game being at move 7"—Bird. **8. b5 Ne7 9. Be3 B×e3 10. f×e3 c6 11. 0–0 0–0 12. Na3 Ng6 13. Bb3 d5 14. e×d5 c×d5 15. Qd2** This and his next move lead to a passive and weak center. Instead 15. c4 forces some simplifications that tend to equalize the position. **15. ... Bg4 16. d4 B×f3 17. R×f3 Rc8 18. Bc2 e4 19. Rh3** "Any direct has no chance of success, and the awkward position of the rook must finally prove very troublesome"—Zukertort. **19. ... Qc7 20. Nb1 Ne7** "Ill-judged. This knight was required at g6 for defensive purposes and has finally to return there after a promenade of six moves. Black had two promising continuations: 20. ... Nd7 followed by 21. ... f5 or 21. ... Nb6 and 20. ... Rd8, 21. ... Rd6 and 22. ... Nd7"—Zukertort. **21. Bd1 Nf5** 21. ... h6, followed by 22. ... Nh7 and 23. ... f5, is another interesting way to defend the kingside. **22. Qf2 Nd6 23. Ra2 Rfd8 24. Qh4 Nf5 25. Qg5 Ne7 26. Rf2 Rd6 27. Rg3 Ng6 28. Bb3** "Very tempting, but disastrous would be: 28. c4 Q×c4! (if 28. ... d×c4? 29. Nc3 and White will soon recover the sacrificed pawn with a fine position) 29. Rc2 Q×c2 30. B×c2 R×c2 31. Na3 Rc1† 32. Kf2 Ra1 33. Qf5 (if 33. h4 then 33. ... h6) 33. ... Nd7 34. Ke2 R×a3 with a decisive superiority"—Zukertort. **28. ... Qd7 29. Qf5** "Of course, White dare not prepare the advance of the c-pawn with 29. Rc2, for Black would then win the queen with 29. ... h6. Mr. Bird proposed here the continuation 29. R×f6 R×f6 (?) 30. Q×d5 Qf5 31. Q×f5 R×f5 32. Bc2. The sacrifice of the exchange would have been absolutely unsound, however, for I would have retaken with the pawn, and if 30. Qh6 then 30. ... f5 31. Rh3 Nf8 etc."—Zukertort. "In this position I saw just too late the potency of capturing the knight or sacrificing the exchange by 29. R×f6. In his notes Zukertort states that 29. R×f6 would be unsound, for he says that he would have retaken with the pawn, and he gives the following variation: 29. ... g×f6 30. Qh6 f5 31. Rh3. But why does the champion gives 31. Rh3? Can he possibly have overlooked the far more potent move 31. h4? I am anxious to know what reply Zukertort would suggest to this"—Bird. Black has a strong diversion at his proposal after 31. h4: 31. ... f4! 32. e×f4 e3! 33. R×e3 Re8. The exchange of the rooks is forced and followed by the decisive entry of Black's queen into the game. **29. ... Q×f5 30. R×f5 Ne7 31. Rf2 Nd7** 31. ... g6! initiates a far better concept. The knight will soon head for f5, and his h-pawn will advance and harass the rook. **32. Kf1** "Threatening to continue with 33. Nd2 R×c3 34. N×e4 d×e4 35. R×f7! White could not at once enter on this line of play, for Black would first check at c1 and exchange rooks, and then capture the knight"—Zukertort. **32. ... g6 33. h4 h5 34. Ke1 Kf8 35. Rh3 Nf5 36. Kd2 Nf6 37. Bd1** "White still dare not play the knight; e.g., 37. Na3 Ng4 38. Rf1 (or 38. Rf4) 38. ... Nf×e3 39. R×e3 N×e3 40. K×e3 R×c3†"—Zukertort. **37. ... Ng4 38. Rf4** "After 38. B×g4 h×g4 39. Rh1 Black would get a winning advantage with 39. ... Rc4"—Zukertort. **38. ... Kg7 39. Be2** The raid of Black's knights made a great impression, but ultimately it appeared to be rather innocent. A move ago, the knight at g4 had to be supported by 38. ... Nfh6. Now Bird forgoes taking the offered pawn—strange, for if 39. B×g4 h×g4 40. R×g4 Rc4 41. Kc2 R×a4 42. Kb3 Rc4 43. Na3 a4†! 44. Kb2 Rc8 45. c4 d×c4 with reasonable drawing chances. **39. ... Rf6 40. c4!** "It is difficult to suggest any other continuation for White. It is obvious that neither the king nor Rh3 dare move. If 40. Na3 Nf×e3 41. R×f6 K×f6 42. R×e3 N×e3 43. K×e3 R×c3† or if 40. Bd1 Nf×e3 41. R×f6 Nc4† and if at last 40. B×g4 h×g4 41. R×g4 Rc4 42. h5 R×a4 43. h×g6 Ra2† 44. Kd1 R×g6"—Zukertort. **40. ... d×c4** (see diagram)

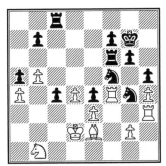

After 40. ... d×c4

**41. Nc3?** Logical, but Bird is apparently unaware of the coming blow. If he had noticed it, he would probably have chosen to play 41. B×g4 h×g4 42. R×g4 Ne7 43. Nc3 Rf2† 44. Kd1 f5 45. Rgg3 Kh6 46. Rg5 with an extremely solid position. **41. ... N×d4! 42. B×g4** "Best, for if 42. R×f6 then 42. ... Nb3† 43. Ke1 N×f6. If 42. N×e4 R×f4 43. e×f4 N×e2 44. K×e2 Re8 45. Kf3 c3! 46. Rh1 R×e4"—Zukertort. **42. ... Nb3† 43. Ke1 h×g4 44. R×g4 Nc5 45. Ke2** "After 45. N×e4 N×e4 46. R×e4, Black wins with 46. ... c3"—Zukertort. **45. ... Re6** In his notes Zukertort advocated 45. ... Rd8, arguing that the e-pawn was in no need of protection, but he overlooked that after 46. N×e4 N×e4 47. R×e4 c3, 48. Rd4! (instead of 48. Rc4) equalizes. There is no harm at all in the text move, but 45. ... Rd6 is a slight improvement. The obvious idea is that the rook at c8 was ideally placed. **46. h5 Rd8 47. h×g6 R×g6 48. R×g6† K×g6 49. Rg3† Kf6** "Throwing away an easy win which I could force with: 49. ... Kf5 50. Rg7 f6 51. g4† (or 51. Rc7 b6 52. Rc6 Rd3) 51. ... Ke6 52. Rc7 b6 53. Rc6† Rd6 54. R×d6† (or if 54. Rc7 Rd3 or 54. R×c5 b×c5

55. N×e4 Rd8 56. N×c5† Ke5 57. b6 c3 58. b7 [58. Nd3† Kd5 and 59. ... Kc4] 58. ... c2 and must win) 54. ... K×d6 55. Kd2 Ke5 56. Kc2 f5 57. g×f5 K×f5 58. Kd2 Kg4 59. Ke2 Kg3 60. Ke1 Kf3 etc."—Zukertort. **50. Rg4 Ke5 51. Rg5† f5 52. g4 Rf8 53. g×f5 R×f5 54. Rg8 Rh5 55. Re8† Kf5 56. Rf8† Ke6 57. Rf2** 57. Rd8! (a move that could be played one or two moves before with equal effect) makes a Black win problematic. **57. ... Rh1 58. Rf4 Rh2†** 58. ... Rc1! is far more decisive as the c-pawn will be a strong asset in the endgame. For instance, 59. N×e4 N×a4 60. Kd2 Rh1 61. Kc2 Rh2† 62. Nd2 Nb6 63. Rd4 Nd5 64. e4 Nb6 65. Kb1 c3 66. Nc4 N×c4 67. R×c4 Rb2† 68. Ka1 R×b5 69. R×c3 Ke5. **59. Kd1 Ke5 60. Rg4 Rh1† 61. Kd2 Rh2† 62. Kd1 b6 63. Rg5† Kf6 64. Rd5 Rh1† 65. Kc2 Rh2† 66. Kd1 Rh3 67. Ke2 Rh2† 68. Kd1 Rh1† 69. Kc2 Ra1 70. R×c5!** "An ingenious sacrifice which secures the draw, but nothing more. It was over and over stated in the daily press that Mr. Bird got a winning position against me. I do not know on whose authority the statement was made, but it has no foundation whatever, cf. the next note"—Zukertort. "This move was intended to be, and should have been, decisive. It was made at a few minutes to 11, many anxious spectators waiting to see the game finished. White played very hurriedly, though he had abundant time (an hour and a half to spare) and forgot to take e4 with check"—Bird. **70. ... b×c5 71. b6 Rh1 72. b7?** "A hasty advance which proves fatal. White should have continued with: 72. N×e4† Ke7 (Black would lose after 72. ... Ke5 by 73. b7 Rh8 74. N×c5 and 75. Nd7 or 75. Na6 wins) 73. b7 (if 73. N×c5 then 73. ... Rh6 74. b7 Rb6 75. Kc3 Kd6 and now 76. K×c4 loses) 73. ... Rh8 74. N×c5 Rb8 75. Kc3 Kd6 76. K×c4 Kc6 77. e4 Rh8 and draws"—Zukertort. **72. ... Rh2†!** "The winning reply: the White king loses one move, which proves decisive"—Zukertort. **73. Kc1 Rh8 74. N×e4† Ke7 75. Kc2 Rb8 76. N×c5 Kd6 77. Ne4† Kd5 78. Nf6† Kc6 79. Kc3 R×b7 80. K×c4 Rb4† 81. Kd3 R×a4 82. Ne4 Ra3† 83. Kd4 Kb5 84. Nd6† Kb4** "The game was here adjourned after nine hours' play"—Zukertort. **85. Nc4 Ra1 86. Nb2 a4 87. Nd3† Kb3 88. Nc5† Kc2 89. e4 a3 90. Kc4 a2** White resigns. "If 91. Nd3 then 91. ... Rb1, if 91. Nb3 then 91. ... Re1"—Zukertort. *Tournament Book* (Zukertort), pp. 26–28; *Modern Chess* (Bird), pp. 17–19.

## (631) Bird–Steinitz    0–1
International tournament (round 15)
London, 29 May 1883
*C51*

**1. e4 e5 2. Nf3 Nc6 3. Bc4 Bc5 4. b4 B×b4 5. c3 Ba5 6. 0-0 Bb6 7. d4 e×d4 8. c×d4 d6 9. Bb2 Nf6 10. d5 Ne7 11. B×f6 g×f6 12. a4 0-0 13. Kh1 f5 14. Ng5 h6 15. Nh3 f×e4 16. Ra3 Ng6 17. Rg3 Kh7 18. Qh5 Qh4 19. Ng5† Kg8 20. Q×h4 N×h4 21. Ne6† Ng6 22. N×f8 K×f8 23. Na3 Nf4 24. Nc2 c6 25. d×c6 b×c6 26. a5 Rd8 27. Nd4 Bd7 28. Rb3 d5 29. Ba6 c5 30. g3 c×d4 31. g×f4 B×a5 32. Bb7 Rd8 33. Ra1 Bb6 34. B×d5 Bf5 35. Bc4 d3 36. Rb5 Bg4 37. Rd5 Rc8 38. Bb3 B×f2 39. Kg2 Bb6 40. Bd1 Be6 41. Rh5 e3 42. f5 Bd5† 43. Bf3 Rc2† 44. Kg3 B×f3 45. K×f3 Rf2† 46. Ke4 e2 47. K×d3 Rf1** White resigns—*Tournament Book*, pp. 79–80.

## (632) Bird–Sellman   1–0

International tournament (round 16)
London, 31 May 1883
*C10*

**1. e4 e6 2. d4 d5 3. Nc3 Nf6 4. Bg5 Be7 5. B×f6 B×f6 6. Nf3 Nc6 7. e5 Be7 8. a3 0–0 9. Bd3 f5 10. h4 Qe8 11. Ne2 Nd8 12. c4 c6 13. Nf4 b6 14. Rc1 Qd7 15. Qa4 d×c4 16. Q×c4 Bb7 17. Qb3 c5 18. Bc4 Kf7 19. d5 e×d5 20. e6† N×e6 21. Ne5†** Black resigns—*Tournament Book*, p. 293.

## (633) Bird–Skipworth   1–0

International tournament (round 17)
London, 1 June 1883
*Game scored by default*

## (634) Englisch–Bird   1–0

International tournament (round 18)
London, 4 June 1883
*B73*

**1. e4 c5 2. Nf3 Nc6 3. Nc3 g6 4. d4 c×d4 5. N×d4 Bg7 6. Be3 Nf6 7. Be2 d6** "This move I adopted now for the first time, having usually played 7. ... e6 at this point. I like this better, however"—Bird. **8. 0–0 0–0 9. h3 Bd7 10. Qd2 Rc8 11. N×c6 B×c6 12. f3 a6 13. Rad1 Nh5 14. Bd4 Qa5 15. Rf2 B×d4 16. Q×d4 Nf4 17. Kh2 Qg5** "This move is good. If White plays 18. Qe3 N×h3 would win an important pawn. If 18. Qd2 Qh4 attacking the rook"—Bird. **18. g3 Ne6 19. Qd2 Qc5 20. Bd3 Qb6** "With the object of compelling advance of the b-pawn, which weakens White"—Bird. **21. b3 Qc5 22. Bc4 b5 23. Bf1** "Zukertort thought 23. B×e6 would have been the proper move. I should not have objected. With the two open files for my rooks and the pawns in the center, my game, I think, would have been preferable"—Bird. **23. ... Bb7** Bird's play has been quite impressive. Here he could have continued in good style with 23. ... f5! **24. Nd5** "The best move"—Bird. **24. ... B×d5 25. e×d5 Ng7 26. h4 e5 27. d×e6 *e.p.* f×e6 28. c4 b×c4 29. B×c4 a5 30. Bd3 d5 31. Qe1 Qc3 32. Qe3 Qf6 33. f4 Rc3 34. Re2 Rfc8 35. Qb6 Qd8 36. Qd4** 36. R×e6 N×e6 37. Q×e6† Kg7 38. Bc4 gets rid at once of the annoying pressure. **36. ... Qd6 37. Qf6 Rc1 38. Rdd2** Risky. But little could happen to him after the exchange of all rooks after 38. R×c1 R×c1 39. Rc2. **38. ... Qb6 39. Rf2 Re1** 39. ... Qe3! is quite strong as it paralyzes both White rooks while also threatening 40. ... Nf5. White can force the exchange of queens by 40. Qe5, but then a fresh weakness in the form of a pawn at e5 arises. **40. Kg2** 40. Rc2 was absolutely necessary. **40. ... Nh5** 40. ... Rcc1! 41. Bf1 Nf5! is killing. 41. Rf1 is better, but defending remains a tough task. **41. Qg5** In case of 41. Qe7 Bird could force a better endgame with 41. ... Qb4! **41. ... Re3!** 41. ... Rcc1! 42. Rf1 Kf7 leaves White nothing but drastic measures, that must ultimately fail; e.g., 43. f5 e×f5 44. g4 Ng3! 45. R×e1 R×e1 46. K×g3 Qd4 47. g×f5 Rg1†. **42. Rf3 R×f3 43. K×f3 Qg1** *(see diagram)* The situation looks now extremely grave for White, but due to the exchange of rooks he can still fight.

**44. Rc2** "An excellent conception for forcing a draw"—Bird. **44. ... Qd1† 45. Ke3 d4†** "Black should not have sacrificed a valuable pawn unless he could calculate on certain victory. 45. ... Qe1†

*After 43. ... Qg1*

46. Kf3 Rf8 was the proper play. Black then threatens 47. ... e5. White's king must apparently retire to 47. Kg2. 47. ... Qe3 would then be decisive"—Bird. This was indeed Bird's best play, but the game would be far from over. **46. K×d4 Qg1† 47. Ke4 N×g3† 48. Kf3 Qd1† 49. Ke3?** Offering Bird new ammunition. 49. Kg2 draws by force: 49. ... R×c2† 50. B×c2 Q×c2† 51. K×g3. **49. ... Nf1† 50. Kd4 Qa1† 51. Ke4 Qe1† 52. Kf3 Nd2†?** 52. ... Qd1† 53. Ke4 Rf8! keeps Englisch's king in critical condition. **53. Kg2 Rf8?** Bird pushes it too far, loses a crucial tempo, and as a result Englisch carries the attack. It was necessary to exchange rooks and be content with a draw. **54. Qg3! Qd1 55. h5! e5 56. h×g6 Nf1 57. Qh3 h5 58. Qe6† Kg7 59. Rc7†** Black resigns. "Thus terminated a very critical and eventful game, Englisch remarking, with much candor: 'I have picked it up in the street'"—Bird. *The Times* (Bird), 5 June 1883; *Tournament Book* (Bird), pp. 186–187.

## (635) Bird–Mackenzie   ½–½

International tournament (round 19, game 1)
London, 5 June 1883
*B20*

**1. e4 c5 2. b4** "An experiment tried with singular success against van 't Kruijs in Amsterdam in 1880, but somewhat hazardous in a tournament, and against a player of Mackenzie's great powers. It, however, usually leads to most enterprising and critical games. The present is no exception to the rule"—Bird. **2. ... c×b4 3. d4 e6 4. Bd3 Nc6 5. Ne2 d5 6. e5 g6 7. a3 Bd7** "Had Black played 7. ... b×a3 White would have replied with 8. c3, followed probably by 9. N×a3 or 9. 0–0"—Bird. **8. 0–0 Nh6 9. Bd2 Nf5 10. B×f5 g×f5 11. a×b4 B×b4 12. c3 Bf8 13. Ng3 Bg7 14. Na3 a6 15. Qh5 0–0 16. Qh3 f6 17. Nh5 Rf7 18. f4 Ne7 19. Nc2 Bb5 20. Rf3** "Perhaps it would have been better to prevent this bishop reaching e7. I regretted that I did not play 20. e×f6. Black must have replied with 20. ... B×f6. White by then playing 21. Rfe1, attacking e6, obtains a very commanding position and in a few moves an attack of a very formidable character"—Bird. **20. ... Be2** First 19. ... f×e5, and only then 20. ... Be2 is the correct procedure as Bird is now able to transpose to the aforementioned line. **21. e×f6 B×f6 22. Re3 Bg4 23. Qg3 Ng6 24. N×f6† Q×f6 25. Rae1** "The last few moves since 22 have been exceedingly critical and interesting on both sides. White has several courses open to him, but the line of play selected appears good, and with due skill in continuation he has now a winning advantage in position"—Bird. Bird is far too optimistic, as Black's position is still a tough nut to crack. **25. ... Re8 26. Nb4 Ree7** 26. ... Rfe7 is the simplest way to defend everything. **27. Nd3 Rg7 28. Qf2**

Nf8 29. Bc1 Nd7 After this move Black gets into a serious bind. 9. ... Rc7 seems impossible due to 30. Ba3 R×c3 31. B×f8 Q×f8 2. R×e6 R×d3 33. Re8, but Black still has fair drawing chances after 3. ... Q×e8 34. R×e8† Kf7 35. Re5 Rd1† 36. Re1 R×e1† 37. Q×e1 Bf3 38. g3 Be4. **30. Ba3 Re8 31. Bd6 Bh5 32. Qb2 b6 33. Ne5** 33. Nb4 at once would be sound play, winning a center pawn. White commits the fault common to him throughout the tournament of playing for too much instead of availing himself of the small but certain advantages offered"—Bird. 33. Nb4! a5 34. Na6! is especially strong. The e-pawn is sieged and will soon fall. **33. ... Qd8 34. N×d7 R×d7 35. Be5 b5 36. Rg3† Bg6 37. Qf2 Kf7 38. Rg5 Rg8 39. Qh4 Re8 40. Qg3 Kf7** "Black has managed his defense capitally. Powerful as White's position has appeared, it does not appear that he could have done better since missing his opportunity at 33"—Bird. **41. Qh4 Re8 42. Re3 Rf7 43. Qe1** "In ordinary play I should probably see at a glance that 48. g4 would render this attack irresistible: 43. ... Rgf8 44. Qh6 Qe7 45. g×f5 R×f5 46. h4"—Bird. Such attempt to decide the game in his favor is doomed to fail. Black can just throw his a-pawn forward, as 47. h5 is no threat due to 47. ... R×g5 48. f×g5 Qf7. **43. ... h6 44. Rgg3 Kd7 45. Bd6 Rf6 46. Bc5 Qb8 47. Re5 Qb7 48. Rge3 Bf7 49. Qh4 Rfg6 50. Rg3 Kc8 51. R×g6 R×g6 52. Re3 Be8 53. Qe1 Qf7 54. Re2 Bc6 55. Ra2 Bb7 56. Qe5 Qc7 57. Qh8† Qd8 58. Qe5** "If White now plays 58. Qh7, Black's reply of 58. ... Qg8 would force a draw"—Bird. **58. ... Qc7 59. Qe3 a5 60. g3** draw—*Tournament Book* (Bird), pp. 212–213.

## (636) Mortimer–Bird    0–1

International tournament (round 20)
London, 7 June 1883
C33

**1. e4 e5 2. f4 e×f4 3. Bc4 Qh4† 4. Kf1 d6 5. Nf3 Qh5 6. h4** "I do not recollect to have observed this move at this point before in an important contest. It appears, moreover, worthy of attention, and, I think, strong. It compels Black to play 6. ... g5 at once if he intends to attempt to keep the gambit pawn, and this deprives him of a numerous choice of moves which he might otherwise select"— Bird. **6. ... Nf6** "Black preferred not to attempt to maintain the gambit pawn"—Bird. **7. Nc3 Bg4 8. d4 Nc6 9. Bb5 0-0-0** Not as good as 9. ... Be7, intending to castle on the kingside. **10. B×c6 b×c6 11. B×f4 d5** "In a position fairly developed, as Black's is, I doubt the prudence of this, which appears to lose important time, unless a definite object was sought to be obtained by it"—Bird. **12. Qd3** "Correctly played"—Bird. **12. ... B×f3** "It was essential to take the knight now, as otherwise it would go to e5 and be very embarrassing to Black"—Bird. **13. g×f3 d×e4 14. f×e4** *(see diagram)*

After 14. f×e4

**14. ... R×d4!** "Good and sound play, I believe"—Bird. **15. Q×d4 Qf3† 16. Qf2?** "Black calculated on White playing 16. Kg1, losing the bishop and not the rook. Black would then have obtained an equivalent in position for the sacrifice of a rook for bishop and pawn"—Bird. After 16. Kg1 Qg4† 17. Kf2 Q×f4† 18. Ke1, a forceful way to a draw is 18. ... Bc5 19. Q×c5 N×e4 20. N×e4 Re8 21. Qf2 Q×e4† 22. Kd2 Rd8† 23. Kc3 Qe5†. 18. ... Bd6 also offers enough compensation. **16. ... Q×h1† 17. Ke2 Q×a1** "Black left himself open to considerable attack by taking the rook"—Bird. **18. Q×a7 Ne8 19. Na4 Qh1?** 19. ... Bb4! 20. c3 Qh1 forces the win; e.g., 21. Nb6† c×b6 22. Qb8† Kd7 23. Qb7† Ke6 24. Qc8† Ke7 and the king finds a safe spot. **20. Nb6† c×b6 21. Qb8† Kd7 22. Qb7† Ke6 23. Q×c6†?** "A mistake. 23. Qc8† would still draw (23. ... Kf6 24. Q×c6† Ke7) and if he interposes a piece he loses his queen, and White draws by perpetual check"—Bird. **23. ... Nd6 24. B×d6 Qg2† 25. Ke3 Qg1† 26. Kd2 Qd4† 27. Kc1 B×d6** White resigns—*Tournament Book* (Bird), p. 294.

## (637) Bird–Mason    0–1

International tournament (round 21)
London, 8 June 1883
C14

**1. e4 e6 2. d4 d5 3. Nc3 Nf6 4. Bg5 Be7 5. B×f6 B×f6 6. e5 Be7 7. Bd3 c5 8. d×c5 B×c5 9. Qh5 g6 10. Qh6 Bf8 11. Qh3 Nc6 12. f4 Bb4 13. 0-0-0 B×c3 14. b×c3 Qa5 15. Nf3 Q×c3 16. Ng5 Qa3† 17. Kd2 Qb4† 18. Ke3 h6 19. Rhf1 Qf8 20. Nf3 Bd7 21. Rb1 Qc5† 22. Ke2 Nd8 23. Qg3 a6 24. h4 Bb5 25. Rfc1 Rc8 26. h5 g×h5 27. Qg7 Qf8 28. B×b5† a×b5 29. Q×f8† K×f8 30. R×b5 Rg8 31. Kf2 Rc4 32. g3 Ra4 33. Rb2 Kg7 34. Rh1 Nc6 35. R×h5 Rga8 36. R×b7 R×a2 37. g4 R×c2† 38. Kg3 Ra3 39. g5 Nd4 40. g×h6† Kg6 41. Rg5† K×h6 42. R×f7 R×f3† 43. Kh4 Rh2† 44. Kg4 Rg2† 45. Kh4 R×g5 46. f×g5† Kg6** White resigns—*Tournament Book*, pp. 245–246.

## (638) Mackenzie–Bird    1–0

International tournament (round 19, game 2)
London, 9 June 1883
B73

**1. e4 c5 2. Nc3 Nc6 3. Nf3 g6 4. d4 c×d4 5. N×d4 Bg7 6. Be3 Nf6 7. Be2 0-0 8. 0-0 d6 9. Qd2 Bd7 10. Rad1 Qa5 11. Nb3 Qd8 12. h3 Be6 13. Nc1 Rc8 14. f4 Ne8 15. f5 Bd7 16. Bd3 e6 17. f×g6 h×g6 18. N1e2 Qa5 19. Rf2 Qh5 20. Rdf1 a6 21. Nf4 Qh8 22. Be2 Ne5 23. Kh1 Nc4 24. B×c4 R×c4 25. e5 Bc6 26. Qd3 R×c3 27. b×c3 d×e5 28. N×g6 f×g6 29. R×f8† B×f8 30. Q×g6† Qg7 31. R×f8† K×f8 32. Bh6 Kg8 33. B×g7 N×g7 34. Kg1** Black resigns—*Tournament Book*, p. 213.

## (639) Chigorin–Bird    0–1

International tournament (round 22)
London, 11 June 1883
A80

**1. d4 f5 2. Bg5** "This move was first adopted against me by Captain Mackenzie, in New York. Black can reply 2. ... d5, but this is supposed to be disadvantageous, as leaving the e-pawn weak when it is played to e6. This is a stock objection of both Zukertort and Steinitz, but with the greatest possible respect I submit that practical experience proves that their objections are very remote, and that there is very little in them. If 2. ... Nf6, White would probably capture the knight, and Black upon retaking would have a doubled pawn. I should not consider this of any particular disadvantage"—Bird. **2. ... h6 3. Bh4 g5 4. Bg3** "White would gain nothing by 4. e4; 4. ... e6 would answer the same purpose and be a good sound move. I rather expected it"—Bird. If 4. ... e6? 5. Qh5† and 6. B×g5† wins. 4. ... Bg7 is the theoretical move. **4. ... d5** "4. ... f4, with the view of winning the bishop would probably have resulted thus: 5. e3 h5 6. e×f4 h4 7. Be2 d5. White, it appears, could then prevent Black's castling and get three pawns for his bishop; yet Black's game would really, I think, be better, though an awkward one to play"—Bird. **5. e3 Be6 6. h4 g4 7. Na3** "Players of the Chigorin and Bird stamp care little for such trifling disadvantages as doubled pawns"—Bird. **7. ... Nf6 8. Ne2 c6 9. Nf4 Bf7 10. c4** 10. Nd3, taking e5 under control and liberating f4 for the bishop, is more prudent. **10. ... Qa5†** Aiming for complications instead of an endgame is preferable: 10. ... e5! (10. ... Ne4 is also interesting) 11. d×e5 Qa5† 12. Ke2 B×a3 13. b×a3 Ne4 14. Qd4 Na6 15. e6 0-0-0 with an extremely dangerous initiative. White is forced to close the position with 16. c5. **11. Qd2 Q×d2† 12. K×d2 e6 13. Bd3 B×a3 14. b×a3 d×c4 15. B×c4 Ne4†** "Black played judiciously here. The check was given at once to secure the e4 square for the knight and option to capture g3. Had the move been delayed White could have played 16. Bd3, which would have prevented it unless made at a disadvantage"—Bird. **16. Ke2 Ke7 17. Bh2** 17. Rhc1 is the alternative. **17. ... e5** "A happy device which may not have been foreseen by White"—Bird. Bird's idea looks effective, but it might contain the effect of a boomerang. 17. ... g3 is a good move to disorganize White's position. **18. B×f7 e×f4 19. Bg6 Kf6** 19. ... g3 is the safest option. **20. h5** "The position stands thus: strangely enough, it appears quite in Black's favor, but it is not so in reality. In a few moves which appear naturally to result from the position White gets at least an even game, if not an advantage"—Bird. **20. ... g3 21. f×g3** "21. Bg1 would be very bad. Black, of course, would not play 21. ... g×f2, but proceed to develop, and White's bishop would be entirely out of play"—Bird. **21. ... f×g3 22. Raf1!** "This move is (unexpectedly to both players) so potent, that it actually compensates for the loss of the piece. Favorable positions at chess, which frequently crop up far in advance of the calculations of either player, constitute an element of luck in the game, which element, of course, is only incidental to the lack of power of any exponent to calculate beyond a certain point with accuracy"—Bird. **22. ... g×h2 23. R×f5† Kg7** "Otherwise Black loses the knight"—Bird. **24. Rf7† Kg8 25. R×h2 b6** "25. ... Na6 would have been better. Even then Black's position is very embarrassing, and the best he could hope for is a draw"—Bird. **26. Rh4 Ng5 27. Rc7 Na6 28. Be8??** "A remarkable blunder, the only instance of a piece left actually en prise in the tournament"—Bird. **28. ... N×c7** White resigns—*Tournament Book* (Bird), pp. 160–161; *Modern Chess* (Bird), pp. 30–31.

## (640) Bird–Noa   0–1
International tournament (round 23)
London, 12 June 1883
*C14*

1. e4 e6 2. d4 d5 3. Nc3 Nf6 4. Bg5 Be7 5. B×f6 B×f6 6. Nf⸮ 0-0 7. Bd3 Nc6 8. e5 Be7 9. 0-0 Nb4 10. Be2 c5 11. Kh1 Nc⸮ 12. d×c5 B×c5 13. Bd3 b6 14. a3 Bb7 15. b4 Be7 16. b5 Nb⸮ 17. Ng1 Qc7 18. Qe1 Nd7 19. f4 Rac8 20. Nce2 Nc5 21. Nf⸮ N×d3 22. c×d3 Qc2 23. d4 Qa4 24. Ng3 Q×b5 25. f5 e×f⸮ 26. N×f5 Qd7 27. N3h4 g6 28. Qg3 B×h4 29. Q×h4 g×f⸮ 30. Qg5† Kh8 31. Qf6† Kg8 32. R×f5 Rfe8 33. Rg5† Kf8 34. Rf⸮ Qe6 35. Qg7† Ke7 36. Q×h7 Rh8 37. Qd3 R×h2† 38. K×h⸮ Qh6† 39. Qh3 Q×g5 40. Qh7 Qg8 41. Qh4† Ke8 42. Rf5 Qg⸮ 43. Rf6 Qg7 44. Rh6 Rc2 45. Rh8† Kd7 46. Qd8† Ke6 47. Qe8⸮ Kf5 48. Qd7† Ke4 49. Rh4† Ke3 50. Qh3† Kd2 51. Rg4 Qf⸮ 52. Rg3 Bc8 53. Qh4 Rc3 54. Rg5 Be6 55. Qf2† Kc1 56. Rh⸮ Q×a3 57. Rh4 Rc2 58. Qe1† Kb2 59. Rf4 Qh3† White resigns— *Tournament Book*, p. 295.

## (641) Blackburne–Bird   ½–½
International tournament (round 24, game 1)
London, 14 June 1883
*B72*

1. e4 c5 2. Nc3 Nc6 3. Nf3 g6 4. d4 c×d4 5. N×d4 Bg7 6. Be3 Nf6 7. Be2 0-0 8. Qd2 d6 9. Rd1 Bd7 10. 0-0 N×d4 11. B×d4 Bc6 12. f3 a6 13. Qe3 Qa5 14. a3 Qh5 15. B×f6 B×f6 16. Nd5 Qe5 17. c3 B×d5 18. R×d5 Qe6 19. Rfd1 Qc8 20. f4 e6 21. R5d3 Be7 22. Kh1 Qc7 23. f5 e×f5 24. e×f5 Rfe8 25. f×g6 h×g6 26. Bf3 Bf6 27. Qf2 Be5 28. Bd5 Kg7 29. Rf3 f6 30. Rf1 Rae8 31. h3 Rae8 32. c4 b6 33. Rb3 Rb8 34. Qd2 Qc5 35. Rd3 Rh8 36. b4 Qc7 37. Rdf3 Qe7 38. Qe2 Rbf8 39. Rb1 g5 40. Rfb3 Rh4 41. a4 Rfh8 42. a5 Qd7 43. Qf1 Rf4 44. Rf3 R×f3 45. Q×f3 g4 46. Qe4 f5 47. Qe3 f4 48. Q×b6 Qf5 49. Qb7† Kh6 50. Be4 Qf6 51. Qd7 g×h3 52. g×h3 f3 53. Qf5 Q×f5 54. B×f5 Rf8 55. Be4 Bc3 56. b5 a×b5 57. a6 f2 58. Kg2 Bd4 59. c×b5 Re8 60. a7 Rg8† 61. Kf3 B×a7 62. Bd3 Bb6 63. Bf1 Rf8† 64. Kg2 Kg5 65. Rb3 Rf4 66. Rg3† Kf6 67. Rf3 Ke5 68. R×f4 K×f4 69. h4 Kg4 70. h5 K×h5 71. Kf3 Kg5 72. Ke4 Kf6 73. Kd5 Ke7 74. Bh3 Bc5 75. Kc6 Kf6 76. Kd5 draw— *Tournament Book*, pp. 133–134.

## (642) Bird–Rosenthal   1–0
International tournament (round 25)
London, 15 June 1883
*C54*

1. e4 e5 2. Nf3 Nc6 3. Bc4 Bc5 4. c3 Nf6 5. b4 Bb6 6. d3 d6 7. a4 a6 8. 0-0 Ne7 9. Be3 c6 10. Nbd2 Ng6 11. Qb3 0-0 "Black could not now play 11. ... d5 without disadvantage. White would reply with 12. B×b6 and play as Black may he would lose a pawn"— Bird. **12. Ng5 Nh8 13. B×b6 Q×b6 14. a5 Qd8 15. Qc2** "It was necessary now to make room for the bishop to retire, as Black could now play 15. ... d5"—Bird. **15. ... h6 16. Ngf3 Ng6 17. Rfe1 Nh5 18. d4 Nhf4 19. d×e5 d×e5 20. Bf1** "Preparing for defense, and at the same time freeing c4 for the knight, with the option of advancing queen's pawns"—Bird. **20. ... Qf6 21. Re3 Be6** *(see diagram)* **22. g3** "Judiciously played. Black must now check with the knight or retire it to h5, where it would be quite out of play"—Bird. **22. ... Nh3† 23. B×h3 B×h3 24. Nb3 Rad8 25. Nc5** "This move, as will be seen, exercised a material influence on the game. The knight at c5 became very formidable, especially for the endgame. It could

*After 21. ... Be6*

not, moreover, be displaced"—Bird. **25. ... Qe7 26. Rd1 Bc8 27. Red3** "White considered it desirable in this position to exchange rooks, with a view to the endgame, having in view also the importance of keeping possession of the d-file"—Bird. **27. ... R×d3 28. Q×d3 Bg4 29. Rd2 f5** This move creates new weaknesses, which Bird exploits in a masterful fashion. Complete passivity was the alternative. **30. Ne1 f×e4 31. Q×e4 Bf5 32. Qc4† Kh7 33. Ng2 e4** "This move requires care in answering. 34. Ne3 would not be good, as White must guard against the impending sally of the knight"—Bird. **34. Qe2! Ne5 35. Nh4** "Apparently the best"—Bird. **35. ... Kg8** "35. ... g6 appeared a little more hopeful for Black"—Bird. After 36. Rd4 White wins a pawn anyway. **36. N×f5 R×f5 37. Kg2 Nf3 38. Rd7 Qg5 39. Q×e4 Qh5 40. Rd8† Kh7 41. h3 Qg6 42. Nd7 Nh4† 43. Kg1** "If White had at this move taken knight with queen then Black would have played 43. ... R×f2† with some chance of a draw by perpetual check. If the knight had checked again, 44. Kh1 would have saved risk in this respect"—Bird. There is no perpetual after 43. Q×h4, but neither is there any objection to Bird's playing it safe. **43. ... Rf3 44. Nc5** "It is practically over now. White has played the long game with continued attention throughout, and it is one of his best played games"—Bird. **44. ... Q×e4 45. N×e4 Ng6 46. Rd7 Ne5 47. R×b7 Rd3 48. Rc7 Rd1† 49. Kg2 Re1 50. Nf6† Kg6 51. Ng4 Nd3 52. R×c6† Kh7 53. f4 Rc1 54. Ne5 Rc2† 55. Kf3 Nc1 56. Rc8 h5 57. f5 Na2 58. h4 R×c3† 59. R×c3 N×c3 60. Nc6 Kg8 61. Nb8 Kf7 62. N×a6 Nb5 63. Nc5 Ke7 64. Kf4 Kd6 65. Kg5** Black resigns. A magnificent positional masterpiece by Bird. From move 13 onwards he played perfect chess—*Tournament Book* (Bird), pp. 265–266; *Modern Chess* (Bird), pp. 23–24.

## (643) Bird–Blackburne   0–1

International tournament (round 24, game 2)
London, 16 June 1883
*A02*

**1. f4** "It appears worthy of remark that neither Steinitz, Zukertort, nor Blackburne ever open with 1. f4. The first-named has, in fact, openly expressed his disapproval of it. On the other hand, Anderssen approved it, and Morphy played it many times, especially against Harrwitz. At Vienna, in 1873, Anderssen, Paulsen, and Rosenthal, playing in consultation against Steinitz, Blackburne, and Bird, also commenced with 1. f4, and were successful. I adopt it against Blackburne because he never ventures on an open game with me, 1. ... e6 (commonly called the French), which leads to the most monotonous and dullest of all games, being his invariable reply. In

the present tournament I am the only player except Chigorin (once) who has started with 1. f4, and I have found no reason to modify the opinion which I have always held in its favor. Another most important consideration is that it invariably leads to highly-interesting games. Steinitz, at Vienna last year, when the first prize depended on the result, opened with 1. d4 against Bird, who replied with 1. ... f5, and not only maintained his ground through the opening, but obtained a winning position in the middle game"—Bird. **1. ... e6 2. Nf3 b6 3. e3 Bb7 4. Nc3 d5 5. d4 Nf6 6. a3 Be7 7. Bd3 Nbd7 8. 0-0 Ne4 9. Ne5 0-0 10. N×e4 d×e4 11. Be2 N×e5 12. f×e5 Rc8 13. c3 Qd7 14. Bd2 c5 15. Rf4 Bg5 16. Rg4 Bh6 17. Rg3 f5 18. e×f6** *e.p.* **R×f6 19. Qb3 Rcf8 20. Re1 Rf2 21. Qd1 c×d4 22. c×d4 Bd5 23. Bb4 R8f7 24. Ba6 b5 25. Qh5 Bc4 26. h3 Qc7 27. Kh2 R2f5 28. Q×h6 Q×g3† 29. K×g3 g×h6 30. Bd6 Rg5† 31. Kh4 R×g2 32. b3 Be2 33. Rc1 Rf5 34. Rc5 Rgg5 35. R×f5 R×f5 36. a4 Bd3 37. a5 Rf3 38. Bc5 Bf1 39. B×a7 B×h3 40. Bb8 R×e3 41. Bb7 Bf5 42. Bg3 R×b3 43. d5 Ra3 44. d6 Kf7 45. a6 e5 46. Bd5† Ke8 47. Bc6† Bd7 48. Bb7 Kf8 49. Bd5 R×a6 50. B×e5 Ra3 51. Bg3 Rc3** White resigns—*Tournament Book* (Bird), pp. 134–136.

## (644) Winawer–Bird   1–0

International tournament (round 26)
London, 18 June 1883
*C61*

**1. e4 e5 2. Nf3 Nc6 3. Bb5 Nd4 4. N×d4 e×d4 5. 0-0 h5 6. Bc4 Bc5 7. Qf3 Qf6 8. Q×f6 N×f6 9. d3 d6 10. a3 Be6 11. b4 Bb6 12. Nd2 c6 13. B×e6 f×e6 14. Nc4 Bc7 15. Bg5 b5 16. B×f6 g×f6 17. Nd2 Kd7 18. Nb3 Bb6 19. f4 a5 20. f5 e5 21. a4 a×b4 22. a×b5 c×b5 23. R×a8 R×a8 24. Ra1 Ra3 25. Kf2 d5 26. Kf3 Kc6 27. g3 Bc5 28. h3 d×e4† 29. K×e4 Bf8 30. g4 h×g4 31. h×g4 R×a1 32. N×a1 Bh6 33. Nb3 Bg5 34. Na5† Kb6 35. Nb3 Kc6 36. Na5† Kd6 37. Nb7† Kc7 38. Nc5 Kd6 39. Nb7† Kc7 40. Nc5 Kc6 41. Ne6 Bh6 42. g5 f×g5 43. K×e5 g4 44. N×d4† Kd7 45. Ne2 Ke7 46. Ng3 Be3 47. Ne4 Kf7 48. f6 Kg6 49. d4 Bg1 50. d5 g3 51. N×g3 Bh2 52. Ke6 B×g3 53. f7** Black resigns—*Tournament Book*, p. 296.

---

# A VISIT TO SHEFFIELD 1883

Bird's column in the *Sheffield and Rotherham Independent* increased his popularity in that region. The local club soon thought it fitting to invite the master for a simultaneous exhibition. Bird found one free date in his agenda: Saturday 25 May, right in between the two cycles of the London tournament. His visit turned out to meet all expectations.

The proceedings were thoroughly enjoyable, and Mr. Bird's genial manner and quick and skillful play gained him many friends. He played 25 games simultaneously in the afternoon, but some of them were prolonged into the night, and throughout the competition Mr. Bird was never engaged with fewer than 25 players. He also made a somewhat unusual concession to his opponents under the circumstances, as, instead of commencing the attack, he drew with each player for the right to move first, thus giving them a chance of leading off. From three o'clock until eleven o'clock, with one short interval, Mr. Bird was kept engaged, and at the close it was found that he had lost 6, won 20, and drawn 7 games, 6 others being unfinished [*Sheffield and Rother-ham Independent*, 28 May 1883].

#### (645) Carr-Smith–Bird    ½–½
Simultaneous game
Sheffield, 26 May 1883
C56

1. e4 e5 2. Nf3 Nc6 3. Bc4 Nf6 4. d4 e×d4 5. e5 d5 6. Bb5 Ne4 7. N×d4 Bd7 8. N×c6 b×c6 9. Bd3 Nc5 10. 0–0 N×d3 11. c×d3 Be7 12. f4 g6 13. Nc3 Rb8 14. Ne2 c5 15. d4 Bb5 16. Rf2 c6 17. Ng3 h5 18. f5 c×d4 19. Qf3 Kd7 20. e6† f×e6 21. f×e6† Kc7 22. Qf4† Kb6 23. a4 Ba6 24. a5† Kb7 25. Q×d4 Ka8 26. Rf7 Rb4 27. Qf2 h4 28. Ne2 B×e2 29. Q×e2 Re4 30. Qa6 R×e6 31. Be3 d4 32. Bg5 Qe8 33. R×e7 R×e7 34. B×e7 Q×e7 35. Q×c6† Qb7 36. Q×g6 h3 37. Qg3 Q×b2 38. Qf3† Qb7 39. Q×b7† K×b7 draw—*Sheffield and Rotherham Independent*, 28 May 1883.

#### (646) H. Davy–Bird    1–0
Simultaneous game
Sheffield, 26 May 1883
C53

1. e4 e5 2. Nf3 Nc6 3. d4 e×d4 4. Bc4 Bc5 5. c3 d6 6. c×d4 Bb6 7. 0–0 Bg4 8. Qb3 B×f3 9. B×f7† Kf8 10. B×g8 R×g8 11. Q×f3† Qf6 12. Q×f6† g×f6 13. d5 Nd4 14. Bh6† Kf7 15. Nc3 Rg6 16. Be3 Nc2 17. B×b6 N×a1 18. B×c7 Nc2 19. B×d6 Rd8 20. Bg3 Nb4 21. Rd1 Rgg8 22. a3 Na6 23. f4 h5 24. e5 Rg4 25. e6† Ke7 26. f5 h4 27. d6† Black resigns—*Sheffield and Rotherham Independent*, 28 May 1883.

#### (647) Bird–Pullen    ½–½
Simultaneous game
Sheffield, 26 May 1883
C57

1. e4 e5 2. Nf3 Nc6 3. Bc4 Nf6 4. Ng5 d5 5. e×d5 N×d5 6. N×f7 K×f7 7. Qf3† Ke6 8. Nc3 Ncb4 9. 0–0 c6 10. d4 N×c2 11. Qe4 N×d4 12. f4 Qd6 13. Re1 Kd7 14. f×e5 Qc5 15. e6† N×e6† 16. Kh1 Kd8 17. B×d5 c×d5 18. N×d5 Bd7 19. Be3 Qb5 20. Qh4† Ke8 21. Rad1 Kf7 22. a4 Q×a4 23. Bd4 Kg8 24. Rd3 N×d4 25. R×d4 Qc6 26. Qg3 h6 27. Rf1 Kh7 28. Nf6† g×f6 29. Qd3† Kg8 30. R×d7 Bg7 31. Rd1 Rf8 32. Qg6 Rh7 33. Rd8 Qc5 34. R×f8† Q×f8 35. Re1 Rh8 36. Re8 b6 37. h4 a5 38. g4 Q×e8 39. Q×e8† Kh7 40. Qe4† Kg8 41. Qe6† Kh7 42. Q×b6 Re8 43. Q×a5 Re5 44. Qa4 Re1† 45. Kg2 Re2† 46. Kf3 R×b2 draw—*Sheffield and Rotherham Independent*, 9 June 1883.

#### (648) Makings & Helliwell–Bird    0–1
Simultaneous game
Sheffield, 26 May 1883
C41

1. e4 e5 2. Nf3 d6 3. Bc4 f5 4. d3 Nc6 5. B×g8 R×g8 6. 0–0 f4 7. d4 Qf6 8. d×e5 d×e5 9. Nc3 Bg4 10. Nd5 Qf7 11. Ng5 B×d1 12. N×f7 B×c2 13. N×c7† K×f7 14. N×a8 Bd6 15. Re1 R×a8 16. Re2 Ba4 17. Rd2 Ke6 18. b3 Bb5 19. Bb2 Nd4 20. B×d4 e×d4

21. Rad1 Be5 22. a4 Bc6 23. f3 a5 24. Kf2 b5 25. a×b5 B×b5 26. Ra2 g5 27. b4 a4 28. Ra3 h5 29. h3 Rc8 30. Ra2 Rc4 31. Rb1 d3 32. Kg1 Rc3 33. Kf2 Bd4† 34. Ke1 Be3 35. Kd1 a3 36. Rba1 Ba4† 37. Ke1 d2† 38. Ke2 Ke5 39. R×d2 B×d2 40. K×d2 Kd4 41. Rc1 R×c1 42. K×c1 Kc3 43. Kb1 K×b4 44. Ka2 Bb3† 45. Ka1 Kc3 46. Kb1 Bc4 47. e5 Kd4 48. e6 B×e6 White resigns—*Sheffield and Rotherham Independent*, 16 June 1883.

#### (649) A.C.J. Wilson–Bird    1–0
Simultaneous game
Sheffield, 26 May 1883
C45

1. e4 e5 2. Nf3 Nc6 3. d4 e×d4 4. N×d4 Qf6 5. Be3 Qg6 6. Nd2 Nf6 7. Qf3 Ne5 8. Qf5 Q×f5 9. N×f5 d5 10. Ng3 h5 11. Bd4 Bd6 12. f4 Nc6 13. B×f6 g×f6 14. e×d5 Nb4 15. Bb5† Kf8 16. 0–0 h4 17. Nge4 N×c2 18. Rac1 Ne3 19. Rf3 N×d5 20. N×d6 c×d6 21. Ne4 Bg4 22. Rf2 a6 23. Bc4 Rc8 24. N×d6 Rc6 25. N×f7 Rh5 26. Nd8 Rc8 27. N×b7 Ne3 28. Nd6 Rc6 29. Rd2 Ke7 30. Re1 R×d6 31. R×e3† Kd7 32. R×d6† K×d6 33. Be2 B×e2 34. R×e2 Kd5 35. Re3 Kd4 36. Re6 Rc5 37. Kf2 Rc2† 38. Re2 Kd3 39. R×c2 K×c2 40. g4 Black resigns—*Sheffield and Rotherham Independent*, 23 June 1883.

---

# NUREMBERG 1883

Three weeks after the termination of the London chess tournament, a few of its participants as well as several German masters came together at Nuremberg to play at the third tournament of the German Chess Association. The Deutsche Schachbund was founded in 1877 at the Leipzig tournament, six years after the proclamation of the German empire. Until then, the majority of tournaments in Germany were organized by regional associations, such as the West German Chess Association. The first tournament played under a unified flag took place in Leipzig in 1879. Two years later the first British participants showed up at the second tournament in Berlin. The third opened on 15 July with a preliminary meeting. All players minus one were present: Bird had missed his train twice, in Cologne and again a few miles out of Nuremberg.[13] Hoffer secured Bird's entry in the tournament so that a Brunswick scenario was avoided.

---

13. Bird expounded on his adventures in the countryside: "Starting only on Friday night, and having had the misfortune to miss one train and be left behind by another, we only arrived late on Sunday night. Mr. Hoffer, of *The Field* and *Chess Monthly*, with his usual courtesy, did all that was necessary for us in regard to voting entrance to the tournament. To console those who may sympathize with us in the misfortunes attending our journey, we may mention that our mishaps were not without incident. At the last place where the train rushed on rudely without stopping for us, we had to wait a small matter of six hours, but, thanks to the kindness of the station master (there being no refreshment room), we were conducted to the village, and had the gratification of an interview with the entire population, consisting of say 26 people, minus one lady too ill to leave the house, though the day was beautifully fine." *Sheffield and Rotherham Independent*, 28 July 1883. Thanks to Hoffer more details are known: "We learned afterwards, that the place of the accidental delay was a hamlet of about 25 inhabitants with due honors, and in acknowledgment of such an unexpected reception he ordered bumpers, which were filled and emptied over and over again. The story goes that on this memorable occasion the local supply of beer for the next fortnight was entirely exhausted." *Chess Monthly*, August 1883, p. 354.

Blackburne, Mason and Winawer[14] were the tournament favorites. Gunsberg, made his debut on the international scene. The majority of the participants lived in Germany or Austria, but besides Louis Paulsen none of them could count on much experience at an international level.

As was usual in German tournaments, the playing schedule was very demanding. The games were played from 8:30 a.m. to 12:30 p.m. and from 3:00 to 7:00 p.m. Three games had to be played every two days while unfinished games were played out during the intervals. As Hoffer wrote, everything here was done "as by steam." The time limit was 20 moves per hour. The games were played at the Gesellschaftshaus of the Museum. Initially five prizes were foreseen but during the tournament this was expanded until nine prizes. A few of the other activities included by the hospitable German organization, such as sight-seeing and feasting at banquets, were approved by the foreign masters.

Nuremberg was the first tournament on German soil in which Bird took part since he failed to enter the field in Brunswick in 1880. It is therefore likely that there was still some tension between Bird and a few of the local players or organizers. On the other hand, disputes between players of different countries, not so rare, were due to linguistic and cultural differences. A few incidents occurred during the tournament. There were hints that at least one game was arranged by the players (this will be discussed further) and there was also a copyright issue that troubled Bird even before the start.[15]

Bird's play throughout the first part of the tournament was rather atypical: he drew five of his games, won once and lost twice. By far the most attractive game was played with Fritz. Bird was very unlucky not to score the full point.

Bird turned loose from the ninth round onwards. He switched from 1. e4 to 1. f4 and beat Louis Paulsen and Lange. Bird continued his winning streak with the Black pieces at the expense of Weiss, von Bardeleben and, after a bye, Wilfried Paulsen. With 8 points in 12 games Bird had established a connection with the leading players. But then a setback followed in two crucial and hard-fought games with his countrymen. Out of a very modern-looking opening, Bird got a promising position against Mason. Bird was two pawns up but much too eager to exchange queens. Mason ultimately won the game. Bird was certainly not mismatched against Blackburne either. A draw seemed at first inevitable, but Bird's misplaced determination for more sealed his fate yet again.

As the organization had extended the number of prizes in the meantime Bird was still in the running for one of the smaller. His results during the following rounds were rather mixed. He was very

successful with 1. f4 against both Hruby and Riemann[16] but also had to accept a loss in a crucial game against Schallopp.

Bird enjoyed a relatively easy final round pairing as he met Carl Leffmann, the tail-ender. Whether Bird still had a chance for a profitable prize was very dependent from the results of Schallopp and Riemann. To Bird's profit, both players lost their games. Bird's game was rather boring, with a position that was obviously leading to a draw. Yet, Bird made desperate tries to grind a win out of nothing. The tournament book (p. 258) noticed that, after the draw was ultimately agreed, Leffmann remarked: "I would have moved the rook for eight days if it was Mr. Bird's wish." The principal winner of the last round was Curt von Bardeleben.[17]

Bird and Riemann had to be content with a shared sixth and seventh prize. This brought each of them 110 marks, or about £5 10s. In fact, a tie match was foreseen, but Riemann wished to split the prizes on account of a funeral he had to attend. The battle for the first place was a tense struggle between Winawer and Blackburne. In the end Winawer, apparently well recovered from his toothache, took the laurels with 14 points (of 18 games). Blackburne followed at a half point. Mason completed the stage.

## (650) Bird–J. Schwarz   ½–½
International tournament (round 1)
Nuremberg, 16 July 1883
*C14*

Bird's (questionable) "infringement" of the copyright rules from the Nuremberg committee preserved the major part of his game against Schwarz. The tournament book only gives the first few moves.

**1. e4 e6 2. d4 d5 3. Nc3 Nf6 4. Bg5 Be7 5. B×f6 B×f6 6. Nf3 a6** Here the course of the game diverges from the tournament book, where 6. ... 0–0 7. Bd3 c5 8. d×c5 B×c3† 9. b×c3 Qa5 10. 0–0 Q×c5 is given. These moves were provided by Schwarz with the following notes: "I recall the game until this point. White built up a very beautiful attack with queen, rook, bishop and knight against Black's castled king. Black succeeded in beating off the attack with a piece up.

14. Winawer's entry was unusual: in need of a dentist he stopped in Nuremberg while he was travelling from Hamburg to Vienna. He met Mason along his way and was persuaded to play in the tournament.

15. In the *Sheffield and Rotherham Independent* of 28 July 1883 Bird objected "to an unprecedented proceeding on the part of the committee, resident treasurer, and secretary (all amalgamated in one person), in claiming to charge for [the publication of] every game played in the tournament at the rate of 5s. or 10s. per game. At the recent London tournament, and in all previous gatherings, it has been the rule to allow each player to publish his own games, or a number equivalent thereto, and this has been regarded as satisfactory. We append two of the games played, which we shall pay for, under protest, if required. A late intimation, however, has been made to us to the effect that our protest is under consideration." This was the only reference found dealing with copyright issues. As there was no follow-up in Bird's column one may assume that the dispute was settled peacefully.

16. Riemann was quite bitter about his defeat that cost him dearly in the final ranking: "Black [*Riemann*] underestimated his opponent, who was inferior to Gäbler [*sic*], a player who shortly after received a knight from Riemann, in a small match played in Brunswick in 1880. ... This game lasted some 45 minutes. Black, to his own harm, allowed such a fast game, even though Bird was excellent in such blitz games, and despite the importance of the game for him in the rankings." F. Riemann, *Schach-Erinnerungen des Jüngsten Anderssen-Schülers*. Berlin: De Gruyter, 1925, p. 485.

17. Von Bardeleben's win caused a small scandal. Hoffer set matters afire in *The Field* of 4 August 1883: "and von Bardeleben had a dead lost game with Fritz. A disagreeable incident happened with the latter game; Fritz had only one minute to spare, and von Bardeleben two minutes, when the game was broken off. At three o'clock, when play had to be resumed, Fritz did not put in an appearance; his clock was set in motion, and he arrived just three minutes too late. The game was consequently scored to the credit of von Bardeleben, who stands fifth instead of, as it would otherwise have been, a tie for the seventh prize with Schallopp." Many players, Bird included, thought a dishonorable agreement had been made: "By an accident or fault at Nuremberg on the part of one of the foreign players von Bardeleben scored a game, which he should have lost in a few moves, making him 11 (instead of 10) to Bird's 10½ games won over the board [implying that von Bardeleben gained a point for free]. He thus obtained the fifth prize to the detriment of both Bird and Riemann. Favoritism on the part of the players when their chances of prizes are gone is a drawback to tournaments, and the rules of the committees cannot be too stringent to guard against abuse in this respect." *Sheffield and Rotherham Independent*, 11 August 1883.

## 3rd Congress of the German Chess Association, Nuremberg, 15–30 July 1883

**Site:** Gesellschaftshaus des Museum
**Playing hours:** 9 a.m.–1 p.m., 2 p.m.–6 and 7:30 p.m.–12
**Prizes:** 1st 1200 marks, 2nd 800 marks, 3rd 500 marks, 4th 300 marks, 5th 200 marks, 6th 120 marks, 7th 100 marks, 8th 80 marks, 9th 70 marks
**Time limit:** 20 moves per hour

| | 1 | 2 | 3 | 4 | 5 | 6 | 7 | 8 | 9 | 10 | 11 | 12 | 13 | 14 | 15 | 16 | 17 | 18 | 19 | |
|---|---|---|---|---|---|---|---|---|---|---|---|---|---|---|---|---|---|---|---|---|
| 1 S. Winawer | | 0 | 1 | 1 | 1 | 1 | ½ | 1 | 1 | 1 | 0 | 1 | 1 | 1 | 1 | 1 | 0 | + | ½ | 14 |
| 2 J.H. Blackburne | 1 | | 0 | ½ | ½ | 1 | 1 | 0 | 1 | 1 | 1 | ½ | 1 | ½ | 1 | 1 | 1 | 1 | ½ | 13½ |
| 3 J. Mason | 0 | 1 | | ½ | ½ | 1 | ½ | ½ | ½ | ½ | ½ | 1 | + | 1 | ½ | 0 | 1 | 1 | 1 | 12 |
| 4 J.N. Berger | 0 | ½ | ½ | | 0 | ½ | ½ | 1 | 1 | ½ | 1 | ½ | 1 | ½ | ½ | ½ | 1 | + | 1 | 11½ |
| 5 C. von Bardeleben | 0 | ½ | ½ | 1 | | 0 | ½ | 0 | 1 | 0 | ½ | ½ | 1 | ½ | 1 | 1 | 1 | 1 | 1 | 11 |
| 6 H.E. Bird | 0 | 0 | 0 | ½ | 1 | | 1 | 0 | ½ | 1 | 1 | 0 | 1 | 1 | 1 | ½ | ½ | 1 | ½ | 10½ |
| 7 F. Riemann | ½ | 0 | ½ | ½ | ½ | 0 | | 1 | 0 | 0 | ½ | ½ | 1 | 1 | 1 | 1 | 1 | ½ | 1 | 10½ |
| 8 E. Schallopp | 0 | 1 | ½ | 0 | 1 | 1 | 0 | | 0 | 1 | 1 | 0 | ½ | 1 | 0 | 0 | 1 | 1 | 1 | 10 |
| 9 J. Schwarz | 0 | 0 | ½ | 0 | 0 | ½ | 1 | 1 | | ½ | ½ | ½ | 0 | 1 | ½ | 1 | ½ | 1 | 1 | 9½ |
| 10 V. Hruby | 0 | 0 | ½ | ½ | 1 | 0 | 1 | 0 | ½ | | ½ | ½ | ½ | ½ | ½ | 1 | 1 | 0 | 1 | 9 |
| 11 M. Weiss | 1 | 0 | ½ | 0 | ½ | 0 | ½ | 0 | ½ | ½ | | 1 | ½ | 0 | ½ | 1 | 1 | + | ½ | 9 |
| 12 A. Schottländer | 0 | ½ | 0 | ½ | ½ | 1 | ½ | 1 | ½ | ½ | 0 | | 0 | ½ | 0 | 1 | 1 | ½ | ½ | 8½ |
| 13 M. Bier | 0 | 0 | – | 0 | 0 | 0 | 0 | ½ | 1 | ½ | ½ | 1 | | 0 | 1 | ½ | 1 | + | 1 | 8 |
| 14 L. Paulsen | 0 | ½ | 0 | ½ | ½ | 0 | 0 | 0 | 0 | ½ | 1 | ½ | 1 | | + | ½ | 1 | 1 | 0 | 8 |
| 15 W. Paulsen | 0 | 0 | ½ | ½ | 0 | 0 | 0 | 1 | ½ | ½ | ½ | 1 | 0 | – | | 0 | 0 | + | 1 | 6½ |
| 16 A. Fritz | 0 | 0 | 1 | ½ | 0 | ½ | 0 | 1 | 0 | 0 | 0 | 0 | ½ | ½ | 1 | | 0 | 0 | ½ | 5½ |
| 17 I. Gunsberg | 1 | 0 | 0 | 0 | 0 | ½ | 0 | 0 | ½ | 0 | 0 | 0 | 0 | 0 | 1 | 1 | | 0 | 1 | 5 |
| 18 M. Lange | – | 0 | 0 | – | 0 | 0 | ½ | 0 | 0 | 1 | – | ½ | – | 0 | – | 1 | 1 | | 1 | 5 |
| 19 C. Leffmann | ½ | ½ | 0 | 0 | 0 | ½ | 0 | 0 | 0 | 0 | ½ | ½ | 0 | 1 | 0 | ½ | 0 | 0 | | 4 |

White continued the game masterfully and gained back the piece. The result was a rook endgame where Black had active chances, compensating [for] White's extra pawn." **7. Bd3 c5 8. d×c5 B×c3† 9. b×c3 Qa5 10. 0–0 Q×c5 11. e×d5 Q×d5 12. Re1 Nc6** From here on Schwarz obstinately refuses to provide his king with a safe shelter at the kingside. As a consequence, Bird slowly but surely develops a dangerous initiative. **13. Qe2 Qc5 14. Qd2 Bd7 15. Rab1 Rb8 16. Re4 b5 17. Rbe1 Rc8 18. Rg4 g6** *(see diagram)*

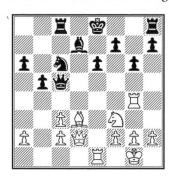

*After 18. ... g6*

**19. c4!** Correctly augmenting pressure on both sides of the board. **19. ... b4 20. Rh4 Rd8 21. Qh6 Qf8 22. Qf4 Qg7 23. c5 a5 24. Ng5** Bird completely outplayed his opponent. With the text move he keeps adding oil on the fire, but he could already start to harvest his bounty with 24. Bb5! 0–0 25. Qc7 Nb8 26. Q×a5. **24. ... e5?!** It is not surprising to see Schwarz missing the best, but difficult to find, defensive moves. Here, he should go for 24. ... h6 25. Ne4 g5 26. Qg3 0–0 27. Rh5 f5 with an unclear position. **25. Qf3 f6 26. N×h7?** A serious mistake, just when it seemed that nothing could go wrong! Instead 26. Ne6! wins a pawn while retaining an excellent position: 26. ... B×e6 27. Q×c6† Qd7 28. Qb6 0–0 29. Q×a5. **26. ... f5?** 26. ... Ke7 completely turns the tables! White is forced to play 27. Rh6!? R×h7 28. R×g6, hoping on a misstep of

his opponent to obtain full compensation. **27. Bb5 Rc8 28. Qd5?** Bird gets a bit too confident. Simply 27. Qh3! retains the knight while the position of Black's king is untenable in the long run. **28. ... R×h7 29. R×h7 Q×h7 30. B×c6 R×c6 31. Q×e5† Kf8 32. h4** Bird feels that his attack is slipping away and decides to jeopardize another pawn. A more restrained approach with 32. c3 to effectuate some exchanges gives good drawing chances. **32. ... Qg7?** A terrible way to spoil a simple win with 32. ... Q×h4!—e.g., 33. Qd5 Qh7, intending 34. ... Be8 and 35. ... Qd7. **33. Q×g7† K×g7 34. Re7† Kf6 35. R×d7 R×c5 36. Rd2** Such a passive move should never be considered in rook endings. 36. Ra7 secures an easy draw. **36. ... Rc3 37. Rd6† Kf7 38. Rd5?** Bird is playing for a win, but this could get punished severely. **38. ... Ra3 39. h5 g×h5?!** 39. ... R×a2! is game over. **40. R×f5† Kg6 41. Rb5 R×a2?!** His best chance was 41. ... h4. Neither side played the endgame at a master's level. **42. g3 Kf6** adjourned and finally a draw—*Sheffield and Rotherham Independent*, 28 July 1883; *Tournament Book* (Schwarz), p. 91.

### (651) Schottländer–Bird    1–0
International tournament (round 2)
Nuremberg, 16 July 1883
*B73*

**1. e4 c5 2. Nc3 Nc6 3. Nf3 g6 4. d4 c×d4 5. N×d4 Bg7 6. Be3 Nf6 7. Be2 0–0 8. 0–0 d6 9. Qd2 Bd7 10. h3 Rc8 11. Rad1 a6 12. f4 Qc7 13. Bf3 b5 14. a3 Rfd8 15. Qf2 Na5 16. Nd×b5** The tournament book gives 16. Nc×b5, but this is probably a misprint as 16. ... a×b5 wins obviously. **16. ... B×b5 17. N×b5 Q×c2 18. Bb6 Rf8 19. Q×c2 R×c2 20. Nd4 Nc4 21. N×c2 N×b6 22. b3 Nfd7 23. b4 Rc8 24. Ne1 Bb2 25. Be2 Nf6 26. B×a6 Ra8 27. Bb5 R×a3 28. Rf3 N×e4 29. R×a3 B×a3 30. Nd3 Nc3 31. Re1 N×b5 32. R×e7 Nd5 33. Rb7 Ndc3 34. Kf2 Kg7 35. g4 Kf6 36. Ke3**

Coryphees of the Nuremberg 1883 chess tournament. Blackburne (left) is seen playing Mason. Arnold Schottländer is standing behind them. Three other faces are well-known (foreground): Louis Paulsen, Bird and Winawer. On the left, J. Adolf Roegner, the local president, is depicted. At far right is Hermann Zwanzig, president of the German chess federation (*Daheim*).

6 37. h4 Ke6 38. Kd2 d5 39. Kc2 Nd6 40. Rb8 Nce4 41. Rh8 Kf6 42. Ra8 Nc4 43. Ra6† Ke7 44. Ra7† Kf6 45. Kb3 Ned2† 6. Kc2 Nf3 47. Kb3 Nd4† 48. Ka2 Nb5 49. Ra6† Ke7 50. Ra8 4 51. Kb3 Nbd6 52. Ne5 B×b4 53. N×c4 N×c4 54. K×c4 Bd6 5. K×d4 B×f4 56. Ra3 Kf6 57. Rf3 g5 58. h5 Kg7 59. Ke4 Bc1 0. Kd5 Bb2 61. Kd6 Kf8 62. Kd7 Be5 63. Rf5 Bb2 64. Rb5 Bf6 5. Rb6 Kg7 66. Ke8 Bd4 67. Rb7 Kf6 68. R×f7† Ke5 69. Rf5† e4 70. Kf7 Be3 71. Kg6 Bf4 72. K×h6 Kf3 73. R×g5 Kg3

74. Kg6 Kh4 75. Rf5 Black resigns—*Tournament Book*, pp. 96–98.

## (652) Winawer–Bird   1–0
International tournament (round 3)
Nuremberg, 17 July 1883
*C61*

1. e4 e5 2. Nf3 Nc6 3. Bb5 Nd4 4. N×d4 e×d4 5. 0–0 h5 6. Bc4

Bc5 7. d3 d6 8. c3 Qe7 9. c×d4 Bb6 10. Nc3 c6 11. Be3 Qf6 12. e5 Qg6 13. e×d6 Bh3 14. Qf3 Bg4 15. Qe4† Kf8 16. Q×g6 f×g6 17. d5 Nf6 18. d×c6 b×c6 19. b4 Rd8 20. Bc5 h4 21. Rae1 Rh5 22. Re7 Rd7 23. h3 Bf5 24. Rfe1 g5 25. f3 Bg6 26. d4 Rh6 27. b5 c×b5 28. B×b5 Rd8 29. d7 B×c5 30. d×c5 Bf7 31. c6 Black resigns—*Tournament Book*, pp. 106–107.

## (653) Bird–Bier   1–0
International tournament (round 4)
Nuremberg, 18 July 1883
*C14*

1. e4 e6 2. d4 d5 3. Nc3 Nf6 4. Bg5 Be7 5. B×f6 B×f6 6. Nf3 a6 7. Bd3 c5 8. d×c5 B×c3† 9. b×c3 Bd7 10. 0–0 0–0 11. e5 Bc6 12. Nd4 Qe7 13. f4 Nd7 14. B×h7† K×h7 15. Qh5† Kg8 16. Rf3 f5 17. Rh3 N×c5 18. Rf1 Qe8 19. Qh7† Kf7 20. Rh6 Rg8 21. N×e6 Q×e6 22. R×e6 N×e6 23. Q×f5† Ke7 24. Qh3 g6 25. c4 Rad8 26. Qa3† Ke8 27. c5 d4 28. h4 Rd5 29. Qh3 Ke7 30. h5 g×h5 31. Qh4† Kd7 32. Rf2 R×c5 33. Q×h5 Rg7 34. Qh4 Rb5 35. f5 Ng5 36. e6† Kc7 37. Qg3† Kc8 38. f6 Nf3† 39. Q×f3 B×f3 40. f×g7 Rg5 41. R×f3 R×g7 42. Rf8† Kc7 43. Rf7† Black resigns—*Tournament Book*, pp. 121–122.

## (654) Bird–Fritz   ½–½
International tournament (round 5)
Nuremberg, 18 July 1883
*C54*

"The following game is remarkable on account of its many vicissitudes and the interesting positions which frequently arose. Fritz is a dashing and ingenious player, as his victories over Mason and von Bardeleben will attest. He had a little good fortune, however, in the game submitted"—Bird.

1. e4 e5 2. Nf3 Nc6 3. Bc4 Bc5 4. b4 Bb6 5. c3 "This is a less forcible continuation for White; but Mr. Bird is fond of this form of the Giuoco Piano, which the game now assumes"—Hoffer. **5. ... d6 6. Qb3 Qe7 7. a4 a5 8. b5 Nd8 9. d3 Ne6 10. 0–0 Nf6 11. Na3 Nh5 12. Be3 g5** "Perhaps a little too impetuous. The instituted counterattack is not strong enough to allow Black to disregard the consequences of having his queenside weakened if White exchanges bishops. 12. ... B×e3 is preferable"—Hoffer. **13. Nc2** "This is a good square for the knight. If Black intends to take the bishop he should do so before it is defended with the knight or White would now on retaking have it at e3, which would be potent in this position"—Bird. Stronger is 13. B×b6!, when b6 will become a target in the long run. Fritz' counterattack is not to be underestimated. **13. ... g4** "Here it would not be any more advisable to take the bishop, because White would bring his knight into play. Black must, therefore, continue with his original plan"—Hoffer. **14. Nd2 Nef4 15. d4 Rg8 16. Rfe1 Be6 17. d5 Bd7 18. B×b6** *(see diagram)*

**18. ... c×b6** Some thorough computer analysis demonstrates here that 18. ... g3! initiates a brilliant attack. After the forced 19. h×g3 N×g3 20. f×g3 R×g3 White is obliged to defend g2. He has three possibilities: (**a**) 21. Re2 Qg5 22. Ne1 N×e2† 23. B×e2 Q×d2 24. Bf2 R×c3 with a clear edge; (**b**) 21. Ne3 Qh4 22. Qb2 Rh3!

Alexander Fritz (*Illustrirte Zeitung*).

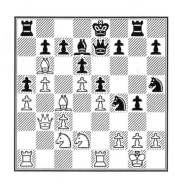

*After 18. B×b6*

23. g×h3 Qg3† 24. Kh1 Q×h3† 25. Kg1 Ke7 26. Kf2 Qh4† 27. Kf Rg8 28. Rg1 Qh5† 29. Kf2 Nh3† 30. Ke1 R×g1† 31. Ndf1 Qh4 32. Kd1 c×b6 with an advantage; (**c**) 21. Bf1 Qh4 22. Ne3 c×b 23. Qa3 Rg6 24. Nf3 Qg3 25. Nh2 Nh3† 26. Kh1 Qf2 wins b force. **19. Ne3 Qg5 20. Ndf1** The safest move. **20. ... Ng7** Makin way for the h-pawn, but this plan is too slow. Valid alternatives ar 20. ... Nf6 (Bird) or 20. ... Rg6. **21. Qa3! Ke7 22. Ng3** 22. Ba planning 23. Nc4, is interesting. **22. ... h5** "We should hav preferred 22. ... Rac8, when White could not have executed his ma noeuvre, as the bishop would have remained en prise. Black coul then have continued 23. ... Rc5, followed by 24. ... Rgc8, thereb keeping up a double attack on both queen- and kingside"—Hoffe Schallopp proposed 22. ... f6 23. Bf1 Rac8 24. Nc4 Rc5 25. N×b h5, stating that Black has good attacking chances. In fact, White i able to defend successfully and keep a clear edge: 26. Ne2 g 27. h×g3 N×e2† 28. B×e2 h4 29. Qc1 Qg6 30. N×d7. **23. Nef5** A bit too hasty. 23. Bf1 Rac8 24. Nef5 N×f5 25. e×f5! Rc5 26. Ne wins the exchange. Black's position remains hard to crack. **23. ...**

N×f5? The knight was indispensable to defend d6. After 23. ... B×f5 24. e×f5 Ne8!, Black's position would be perfectly safe, even at the cost of a pawn as 25. R×e5† is possible. **24. e×f5 f6** 24. ... Qh6 25. R×e5† is equally joyless. **25. Ne4 Q×f5 26. Q×d6† Kf7 27. Ng3** *(see diagram)* "The text move is the best on the board, and wins the game right off, if Mr. Bird had seen the full force of it. As the sequel shows, however, he was taken by surprise, through Herr Fritz's ingenious but unsound rejoinder. If, therefore, Bird made the text move unconscious of Black's possible reply, he might have chosen a more favorable line of play with 27. N×f6, or a simpler course still would have been 27. Q×b6, threatening 28. Nd6†. Black could then not play 27. ... Nh3†, because of 28. Kf1"—Hoffer.

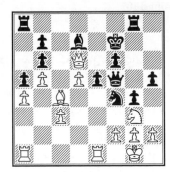

*After 27. Ng3*

**27. ... Nh3† 28. g×h3** "As hinted above, Bird could here win the game as follows: 28. Kh1 N×f2† 29. Kg1 Nh3† 30. g×h3 g×h3 31. Rf1 Qg4 (31. ... R×g3† 32. h×g3 h2† 33. Kh1 Qe4† 34. K×h2 Qc2† 35. Kg1 and wins) 32. R×f6† Ke8 33. Q×e5† Kd8 34. d6 and wins"—Hoffer. Bird's move should be good enough for a simple win. **28. ... g×h3 29. Q×b6** "The simple move of 29. Bd3, which Bird was on the eve of making, would win speedily"—Bird. **29. ... Rac8 30. Bf1 h4 31. Re3** "Well played, because after 31. ... h×g3 32. f×g3, Black would reply 32. ... Qf3, followed by 33. ... R×g3†"—Hoffer. **31. ... h×g3 32. f×g3 Qc2 33. Rf3 Rg6 34. Q×b7 Ke8 35. Re1** "35. c4, cutting off the communication between queen and rook, would have been very serviceable"—Bird. Also excellent is 35. d6!. It threatens 36. B×h3. **35. ... R×c3 36. Re2 Qc1 37. Qb8† Rc8 38. R×e5† f×e5 39. Q×e5† Be6 40. b6?** "White's play continues of the most fanciful character. He is playing for a mate. 40. d×e6 would have been quite good enough"—Bird. **40. ... Qc5† 41. Re3 Q×b6 42. d×e6** This move is not without danger. A forced draw arises after 42. B×h3 Qb1† 43. Re1 Rc1 44. Qh8† Ke7 45. d6† Kd7 46. B×e6† R×e6 47. Qg7†. **42. ... Ke7! 43. Qe4 Rc1** Allowing his opponent a perpetual. 43. ... Rh6! (Bird's suggestion according to Schallopp) controls the h-file and leaves White without any active chances. He will probably be obliged to exchange queens in a few moves, after which a tough defensive task awaits him. **44. Qh4† Kd6?** 44. ... Rf6 45. Qh7† Kd6 46. Qd7† Kc5 47. Qe7† Kd5 48. Qd7† is the way to draw. **45. Qf4† Kc6 46. Qe4† Kc7 47. Qe5†?** "47. e7, threatening to make queen or knight, should win"—Bird. **47. ... Kb7 48. e7 Rf6** "White can now only draw"—Bird. **49. Qd5† Ka7 50. Qd7† Qb7 51. Qd4† Qb6** draw. Later that day Fritz gave a blindfold exhibition, for which he was renowned, against ten opponents. He won 5 games and drew 5—*The Field* (Hoffer), 29 September 1883; *Sheffield and Rotherham Independent* (Bird), 13 October 1883; *Modern Chess* (Bird), pp. 22–3; *Tournament Book* (Schallopp), pp. 130–131.

## (655) Gunsberg–Bird   ½–½
International tournament (round 6)
Nuremberg, 19 July 1883
B34

1. e4 c5 2. Nc3 Nc6 3. Nf3 g6 4. d4 c×d4 5. N×d4 Bg7 6. Be3 Nf6 7. f4 Qa5 8. Nb3 Qc7 9. e5 Ng8 10. Nd5 Qd8 11. Qd2 e6 12. Nc3 d5 13. e×d6 *e.p.* Nf6 14. Bb5 0–0 15. 0–0–0 Bd7 16. h3 Nb4 17. Bd4 N×a2† 18. N×a2 B×b5 19. Nc3 Bc4 20. Nc5 Q×d6 21. b3 Ba6 22. B×f6 Q×c5 23. Ne4 Qc7 24. B×g7 K×g7 25. Qd4† f6 26. Ng5 Rae8 27. Rhe1 e5 28. Qd7† Q×d7 29. R×d7† Kg8 30. N×h7 Rf7 31. R×f7 K×f7 32. f×e5 R×e5 33. R×e5 f×e5 34. Kd2 Kg7 35. Ng5 Kf6 36. Ne4† Ke7 37. c4 b6 38. g3 Bc8 39. g4 Bd7 40. Ke3 Bc6 41. Nc3 Ke6 42. h4 Kf6 43. Nd5† Ke6 44. h5 g×h5 45. g×h5 Kf7 46. Ke4 b5 47. K×e5 b×c4 48. b×c4 a5 49. Kd6 Be8 50. Kc5 Kg7 draw—*Tournament Book*, pp. 133–134.

## (656) Bird–Berger   ½–½
International tournament (round 7)
Nuremberg, 20 July 1883
C54

1. e4 e5 2. Nf3 Nc6 3. Bc4 Bc5 4. c3 Nf6 5. b4 Bb6 6. d3 d6 7. a4 a6 8. a5 Ba7 9. 0–0 Ne7 10. Be3 0–0 11. Na3 Ng6 12. Re1 c6 13. Bb3 Re8 14. Nc4 Be6 15. B×a7 R×a7 16. Ne3 d5 17. e×d5 N×d5 18. B×d5 B×d5 19. d4 B×f3 20. Q×f3 e×d4 21. Rad1 d3 22. Rd2 Ra8 23. Red1 Qe7 24. Qg3 Rad8 25. R×d3 R×d3 26. R×d3 Qe4 27. Rd1 Nf4 28. Kf1 Nd5 29. Qf3 N×e3† 30. Q×e3 Q×e3 31. f×e3 Kf8 32. Kf2 Ke7 33. Kf3 Rc8 34. Rd4 c5 35. Rc4 Kd6 36. h4 Rc7 37. Rf4 Ke6 38. g4 f6 39. b×c5 R×c5 40. Rb4 Rc7 41. Ke4 Rd7 42. Rb6† Ke7 43. h5 g6 44. c4 Kf7 45. h6 Ke7 46. c5 Rc7 47. Kd5 Rd7† 48. Rd6 Rc7 49. e4 Kf7 50. c6 b×c6† 51. R×c6 Ra7 52. Kd6 Re7 53. Rc7 R×c7 54. K×c7 Ke6 55. Kb6 Kd6 56. K×a6 Kc6 57. Ka7 Kc7 58. a6 g5 draw—*Tournament Book*, pp. 145–147.

## (657) Bird–L. Paulsen   1–0
International tournament (round 8)
Nuremberg, 20 July 1883
A03

1. f4 c5 2. Nf3 d5 3. e3 a6 4. d4 e6 5. Bd3 Nf6 6. 0–0 Nc6 7. c3 Bd6 8. Ng5 c×d4 9. e×d4 Qc7 10. Qf3 h6 11. Nh3 Bd7 Preparing to bring the king to the queenside, but his majesty is certainly not safer there than on the other side of the board. **12. Nd2 Ne7 13. Qe2 0–0–0 14. a4 Nf5** "Black wants to transfer the knight to e4 but this plan is much too time-consuming"—Schallopp. **15. Nf3 g6 16. Ne5 Be8 17. Bd2 Kb8 18. b4** Bird has grasped the initiative, making the position extremely difficult to deal with for Paulsen. **18. ... Be7 19. b5 a5 20. Rab1** At once 20. Rfc1 loses no time. **20. ... Nd6?** Instead of this feeble text move, 20. ... Rc8 and if 21. b6 Qd8 at least leaves Black's pieces coherently placed. An amelioration is 21. Nf2, followed by 22. Rfc1. **21. b6! Qc8 22. Nf2** The time was ripe for a more direct approach: 22. Rfc1!, followed by 23. c4 (if 22. ... Nf5 23. g4). **22. ... Nd7 23. Nfg4** Rather innocent. 23. N×g6! destroys Black's position. **23. ... Nf8?** "Black loses too much time"—

Schallopp. **24. c4 h5 25. c5 Ne4 26. Nf2** Certainly not bad, but 26. c6! is more forceful. **26. ... f6 27. Nf3 f5 28. Bb5 Bf6 29. B×a5 Nh7 30. Bb4** There was another opportunity to play 30. c6! **30. ... g5 31. B×e8 Rd×e8 32. Ne5 g×f4 33. Qb5** 33. Nfd3 is still very convincing; e.g., 33. ... Nhg5 34. c6 b×c6 35. b7. **33. ... B×e5 34. d×e5 Qc6** "Black incorrectly thought that mate could not be avoided after 35. Qa5. He should have played 34. ... Nhg5"—Schallopp. There could follow 35. N×e4 N×e4 36. R×f4 Qc6 37. Ra1, planning 38. Q×c6 and 39. a5, when White keeps a close to winning initiative. **35. N×e4 f×e4 36. R×f4 Rhf8 37. Rbf1 Kc8 38. Rf7 R×f7 39. R×f7 Q×b5 40. a×b5 Nf8 41. c6** Black resigns—*Tournament Book* (Schallopp), pp. 155–157.

## (658) Bird–Lange    1–0
International tournament (round 9)
Nuremberg, 21 July 1883
*A02*

**1. f4 e6 2. Nf3 f5 3. b3 Nf6 4. Bb2 Be7 5. e3 c5 6. Nc3 Nc6** "These first six moves premise a well contested game"—Bird. **7. Bb5** "A move favored by Potter, but it will have been noticed that I have more than once expressed the opinion that Black should not allow this knight to be pinned. Until recently I was alone in that view, but Steinitz inclines to the same opinion, and Winawer is decided to the same effect"—Bird. **7. ... Qc7 8. 0–0 d5** "Now, due to White postponing to exchange at c6, 8. ... Nd8, followed by 9. ... Nf7 and 10. ... a6, might be recommended"—Schallopp. **9. Qe2 Bd7 10. B×c6 B×c6 11. Nd1 0–0 12. Nf2 Nd7** "Subject to the question of allowing the knight to be pinned at move 7, and which perhaps, may be still regarded as a debatable point, the opening, I think, may be regarded as unexceptional, each of those old players entertaining due respect for the skill of his adversary"—Bird. **13. Nh3 Bf6 14. d4 Rfe8 15. Ne5 c×d4 16. e×d4 N×e5 17. f×e5 Bd8 18. a4 Qd7 19. Rf2 a6 20. Raf1 Kh8?!** *(see diagram)* Losing time. After 20. ... b5 21. a×b5 a×b5, Black has sufficient counterplay. Also possible is the interesting 20. ... g5, preparing to answer 21. g4 with 21. ... f4.

*After 20. ... Kh8*

**21. g4!** "Somewhat unexpected at the time, but now regarded as an excellent move"—Bird. **21. ... Bh4?** He must think about fortifying the f-file with 21. ... g6. **22. Rg2 Qf7?!** 22. ... g6 is the lesser evil (23. g5 h6). **23. g5** "Black ought not to have permitted his bishop to be locked in thus. It is difficult however to find a satisfactory move for him. To retire his bishop would be disastrous, for he at once loses his f-pawn, besides having his queen and Ra8 shut out of play. If he plays 22. ... f×g4, then 23. Q×g4 Qe7 24. Ba3 wins, or if 23. ... Bd8, doubling the rooks and Rf7 would be decisive"—Bird.

**23. ... h6 24. g6** Simpler is 24. Bc1!, e.g., 24. ... b5 25. g×h6 g 26. Ng5. **24. ... Qf8 25. Qh5 Be7 26. Bc1! Kg8 27. B×h6 g×h 28. g7 Q×g7** "Compulsory. If 28. ... Qf7 29. Q×h6 and mat follows in two moves"—Bird. **29. R×g7† K×g7 30. Kh1 Rg 31. Nf4 Be8** "With the idea 32. N×e6† Kh7 33. Q×f5†?? Kh 34. Qh3 Be4† 35. Rf3 Rg6 36. Nf4 Rf8"—Schallopp. **32. N×e6 Kh7 33. Qh3 Bg6 34. Nf4 Bg5 35. N×g6 R×g6 36. Q×f5 Rag 37. Rg1 Be3 38. R×g6 R×g6 39. e6 Bg5 40. Q×d5** and Whit wins—*Tournament Book* (Schallopp), pp. 163–164; *Modern Che* (Bird), pp. 50–51.

## (659) Weiss–Bird    0–1
International tournament (round 10)
Nuremberg, 23 July 1883
*B73*

**1. e4 c5 2. Nf3 Nc6 3. Nc3 g6 4. d4 c×d4 5. N×d4 Bg7 6. Be Nf6 7. Be2 0–0 8. 0–0 d6 9. h3 Bd7 10. Qd2 Rc8 11. Rad1 Ne 12. Bh6 Qb6 13. B×g7 K×g7 14. Nb3 Nc4 15. B×c4 R×c 16. Rfe1 Rfc8 17. Qe3 Q×e3 18. R×e3 b5 19. a3 a6 20. e5 d×e 21. R×e5 Kf8 22. Nd4 Be8 23. Rd2 Nd7 24. Ree2 Nb6 25. Nb R4c7 26. Na5 Na4** "Well calculated. White's knight is exclude from play after 27. N×a4 b×a4"—Schallopp. **27. Nd5** 27. Nd1 passive but it avoids all tricks. **27. ... Rd7 28. b3 Nc3** 28. ... Rc5 another possibility. **29. N×c3 R×c3 30. Kf1** "White starts a lon trip with his king to liberate his knight. In the end, this will no help"—Schallopp. **30. ... Rdc7! 31. Ke1 Bd7** A small improvemen is 31. ... b4, though after 32. a×b4 Bb5 33. Nc4 B×c4 34. b×c R3xc4 Black's advantage is meant to remain symbolic. **32. Kd1 Be 33. Re3 R3c5** Slim chances for a win were obtained by exchangin rooks and thus inflicting a weakness upon his opponent. **34. Kc h5 35. h4 Bf5 36. Ree2 Kg7 37. Kb2 Kf6 38. b4 Rc3 39. Nb R3c4 40. g3 g5 41. h×g5† K×g5 42. Nd4 Bg6 43. Nf3† Kf 44. Ne5?** "A miscalculation, on which Black speculated with hi last moves"—Schallopp. After 44. Nd4, a draw is inevitable. **44. ... R×c2†! 45. R×c2 B×c2 46. N×f7 Bd3 47. Re3** "White saw to late that 47. Rd2 is very dangerous for his knight: 47. ... Bc4 48. Nd e6!, followed by 49. ... Bd5 and 50. ... Ke7. He prefers to fight wit a pawn less, but a big mistake makes Black's task easy"—Schallopp **47. ... Rc2† 48. Kb3 R×f2 49. Ne5 Bf5 50. Kc3 e6 51. Kd4 Rd2 52. Kc3 Rd5 53. Nf3 e5 54. Nd2 Rd4 55. R×e5?** His position i very difficult to hold anyway; e.g., 55. Nf1 Rd7! 56. Nd2 Rc7 57. Kb3 Bh7 and if the knight moves 57. ... e4 follows, if the roo moves 57. ... Rd7 is the winning move. **55. ... Rd3†** White resigns— *Tournament Book* (Schallopp), pp. 172–173.

## (660) von Bardeleben–Bird    0–1
International tournament (round 11)
Nuremberg, 23 July 1883
*A81*

**1. d4 f5 2. g3 e6 3. Bg2 d5 4. e3 Nf6 5. b3 c6 6. Bb2 Bd6 7. Nf Ng4 8. c4 0–0 9. Nc3 Nd7 10. Qe2 Ndf6 11. 0–0 Bd7 12. Nd Qe8 13. h3 Nh6 14. f4 Qg6 15. Kf2 Rad8 16. c5 Bc7 17. Rg1 Kh 18. Raf1 Be8 19. Bf3 Qf7 20. Ke1 b6 21. b4 b×c5 22. b×c5 Ne 23. g4 Rb8 24. Nb3 Bd8 25. g5 Ng8 26. h4 Qb7 27. Qc2 Qb 28. Rg2 a5 29. Nc1 a4 30. Q×a4 Ba5 31. Q×b4 R×b4 32. Ba**

b1 33. Kd1 R×a1 34. N×e4 d×e4 35. Be2 Bd7 36. Bc4 Rb8 7. Bb3 Bb4 38. Kc2 Ba3 39. Rgg1 Bc8 40. Ne2 R×f1 41. R×f1 Ne7 42. Nc3 Ba6 43. Re1 Nd5 44. N×d5 Bd3† 45. Kd1 e×d5 6. Rh1 Kg8 47. h5 Kf7 48. Rg1 Bb4 49. g6† h×g6 50. R×g6 h8 51. Rg5 g6 52. h×g6† Kg7 53. Rg1 Rh2 54. Kc1 Bd2† White esigns—*Tournament Book*, pp. 184–185.

Bird had a bye in the 12th round.

**661) W. Paulsen–Bird    0–1**
nternational tournament (round 13)
Nuremberg, 25 July 1883
*24*

**1. e4 c5 2. Nc3 Nc6 3. g3 d6 4. Bg2 Nf6 5. d3 h5 6. h4 Qb6 . Nh3 Bg4 8. f3 B×h3 9. B×h3 g6 10. Bd2 Bg7 11. Rb1 e6 2. Ne2 Nd7 13. Bc3 Nd4 14. N×d4 c×d4 15. Bd2 Rc8 16. 0-0 Qc5 17. Rc1 Qb6 18. b3 Rc6 19. Rf2 Qc7 20. f4 f5 21. e×f5 g×f5 2. Qe1 Kf7 23. Ba5 b6 24. Bb4 Nf6 25. Bg2 d5 26. Re2 a5 7. Ba3 b5 28. Bf3 b4 29. Bb2 Ng4 30. B×g4 h×g4 31. Qf2 Qb6 2. a3 b×a3 33. B×a3 Bf6 34. Qe1 Qc7 35. Qd2 Rc8 36. Bb2 Kg6 37. Qe1 Qb6 38. Ba3 Kf7 39. Qf2 Qb5 40. Qh2 Kg6 41. Ra1 Kh5 42. Qf2 a4 43. b×a4 Q×a4 44. Bb2 Qb4 45. Bc1 Qb7 6. Qe1 Qd7 47. Ra2 Kg6 48. Kg2 Kf7 49. Qb4 Qc7 50. Qb1 Qe7 51. Re1 R8c7 52. Bd2 Kg6 53. Bb4 Qd7 54. Bd2 Qc8 5. Rc1 Be7 56. Kf2 Bd6 57. Kg2 Kh5 58. Kf2 e5 59. f×e5 B×e5 0. Kg2 Rb7 61. Qa1 Rf7 62. Ra8 Qc7 63. Ra6 Bg7 64. Qa4 R×a6 65. Q×a6 Rf6 66. Qa5 Q×a5 67. B×a5 Rc6 68. Bd2 Bf8 9. c4 Ba3 70. Rc2 Kg6 71. Ra2 Bd6 72. c×d5 Rb6** “and after an- ther four moves were made, the game was declared a loss for White n account of overstepping the time-limit”—*Tournament Book*, pp. 99–200.

**662) Mason–Bird    1–0**
nternational tournament (round 14)
Nuremberg, 25 July 1883
*185*

**1. d4 f5 2. c4 e6 3. e3 Nf6 4. Nc3 Bb4 5. Qb3** “An interesting noment in this opening. Black is resolving the problem of his ingside bishop by exchanging it on c3. This is why we suggest o play 4. a3 before developing the knight to c3. The move of the queen seems superfluous to us. Developing the kingside is more mportant at the moment”—Schallopp. **5. … B×c3† 6. b×c3 b6 . f3** A slow way of developing. Black gets time to besiege the veak pawn at c4. **7. … 0-0 8. Bd3 Nc6 9. Nh3 Na5 10. Qc2 3a6 11. Qe2** “White should have resolved his doubled pawns: fter 11. c5 B×d3 12. Q×d3 b×c5 13. Qb5 c6 14. Q×c5 d6 15. Qa3 Nd5 16. Bd2 Nc4 17. Qc1 he could work himself out of a pressed osition without losing material. Now, after 11. … c5, Black tarts attacking the doubled pawns”—Schallopp. After 14. … Qb6!, a major improvement, White is left with several weaknesses. **1. … c5! 12. Ba3 Qc7** “Much stronger was 11. … d6, intending to ransfer the queen to d7 and a4”—Schallopp. There were several ttractive options; e.g., 12. … d5 13. c×d5 B×d3 14. Q×d3 Q×d5, vhen White is faced once more with the weakness at c4. **13. 0-0 6 14. Rac1?** 14. e4, starting active play himself, was necessary.

**14. … Rae8?!** At once 14. … Qd7!, planning 15. … Qa4, is very strong. Bird eventually wins the c-pawn anyway, but only after mak- ing some sub-optimal moves. **15. Rfd1 g6 16. e4 Qc6 17. Rb1 Qa4 18. Bc1 B×c4 19. Bh6** Mason lacks any real compensation for the lost pawn. He must create something on the kingside. **19. … Rf7 20. Ng5 Rfe7 21. e5?!** Mason considers it already necessary to make desperate attempts to gain some counterplay. **21. … d×e5 22. Q×e5 Nd7** The patient 22. … Nd5! improves the position of the knight. **23. Qg3 B×d3 24. R×d3 Q×a2 25. Rbd1 Qd5 26. d×c5 Q×c5† 27. Kh1 Nf6** 27. … Ne5! (Schallopp) 28. Rd8 Nac6 is very strong. **28. Nh3 Nh5 29. Qh4 Nc6 30. Bg5 Rf7 31. Be3** Mason defends with tenacity. The coordination of Bird's pieces isn't what it was a few moves ago. **31. … Qe7?!** Bird wants to realize his advantage by playing for exchanges. In this case such a strategy is inferior, as Mason gets the chance to occupy some important squares. Much better is 31. … Qb5!, limiting the prospects of the adverse queen. **32. Qa4! Ne5?** “32. … Qb7, again intending to advance the queen- side pawns, [should have been in] its place”—Schallopp. Now, de- spite being two pawns behind, White puts a real bind on his oppo- nent. **33. Bg5 Rf6?** This way of returning material is rather desperate. Yet, after 33. … Nf6 (Schallopp) Black is also suffering: 34. Rd6! Rff8 35. Qh4 a5 36. Nf4 Qf7 37. Bh6. **34. Re3 Nf7 35. Rd7 Qc5 36. Rc7 Qf8 37. B×f6 N×f6 38. R×a7 Nd5 39. Re1 N×c3 40. Qb3** 40. Qc6! snatches an important pawn without much further ado. **40. … Nd5 41. Qb5 Rc8 42. Qd7 Nf6 43. Q×e6 Re8 44. Re7 R×e7 45. Q×e7 Q×e7 46. R×e7 Kf8 47. Rb7 Nd5 48. Nf2 Kg7 49. Nd3 Kf6 50. Kg1 h5 51. Ra7** 51. Nb4 wins the pawn at once. **51. … Nd6 52. Ra4 g5 53. Kf2 f4** Determining the pawn structure on the kingside makes White's task considerably lighter. **54. h4! Nf5 55. h×g5† K×g5 56. Re4 Nc3** “Black cannot do anything. Further opposition is useless”—Schallopp. **57. R×f4 Nd1† 58. Kg1 b5 59. Rb4 Nc3 60. Kf2 h4 61. Nb2 Ne7 62. Rg4† Kh5 63. Nd3 Ng6 64. Nf4† N×f4 65. R×f4 Kg5 66. Rb4 Nd1† 67. Ke2 Nc3† 68. Kd2 h3 69. K×c3 h2 70. Rb1 Kf4 71. g4 K×f3 72. g5 Kg2 73. g6** Black resigns—*Tournament Book* (Schallopp), pp. 210–212.

**(663) Bird–Blackburne    0–1**
International tournament (round 15)
Nuremberg, 26 July 1883
*B06*

**1. f4 g6 2. Nf3 Bg7 3. e4 d5 4. e5 Nc6 5. Bb5 Bd7 6. Qe2 a6 7. B×c6 B×c6 8. d4 e6 9. a4 Nh6 10. Be3 Qd7 11. Nc3 Nf5 12. Bf2 h5 13. 0-0 Bf8 14. b3 Be7 15. Rfd1 b6 16. Na2 Bb7 17. c4 0-0 18. Nc3 Rfc8 19. Ng5 B×g5 20. f×g5 Qe7 21. c×d5 B×d5 22. N×d5 e×d5 23. h4 Qe6 24. Rac1 c6 25. Rc2 a5 26. Rdc1 Rc7 27. Rc3 Rac8 28. g4 h×g4 29. Q×g4 Ng7 30. Qe2 Nh5 31. Qf3 Ng7 32. Qf6 Qg4† 33. Kh2 Nh5 34. Qf3 Q×f3 35. R×f3 Ng7 36. Rf6 Ne8 37. Rf3 Ng7 38. Kh3 Ne6 39. Kg4 Kg7 40. h5 g×h5† 41. K×h5 c5 42. d×c5 b×c5 43. Rg1 Rb7 44. Kg4 Rb4† 45. Kf5 Rh8 46. Rg4 Rh5 47. Rfg3 R×g4 48. R×g4 Rh3 49. Rg2 R×b3 50. Be1 Rf3† 51. Kg4 Rf4† 52. Kh5 R×a4 53. Bd2 Nf4† 54. B×f4 R×f4 55. Rc2 c4 56. e6 f×e6 57. Rb2 c3 58. Rb7† Rf7 59. Rb5 Rc7** White resigns—*Tour- nament Book*, pp. 228–229.

## (664) Bird–Hruby    1–0

International tournament (round 16)
Nuremberg, 27 July 1883
*A03*

**1. f4 d5 2. Nf3 c5 3. e3 a6** "As observed in examples v. Blackburne, Mason, Winawer and Riemann, this move is now considered desirable, it being thought better not to allow the option of pinning the knight"—Bird. **4. Bd3 Nf6 5. 0-0 Nc6 6. Nc3** "The manner in which this knight is to be played is one of the most difficult points in this opening. In some of my former games I first played c4, Na3–c2. The move in the text I now rather prefer, and so far I have found it answers well"—Bird. **6. ... e6** A set-up with 6. ... g6 is very promising here. **7. b3 Be7 8. Bb2 b6 9. Ne5** "This move tends to free the game, but should only be made after due consideration"—Bird. **9. ... Bb7 10. Qf3 Qc7 11. Qg3 Rg8** Black is driven by fear. There is no need to avoid the simple 11. ... 0-0, with a perfectly safe position; e.g., 12. Ng4?! N×g4 13. Q×g4 d4! **12. Nd1 Nb4 13. a3 N×d3 14. c×d3** *(see diagram)* "I do not object to the doubled pawn in this position, and having no prejudice in favor of a bishop over a knight, make no attempt to avoid the exchange, if I think that by doing so time is lost"—Bird.

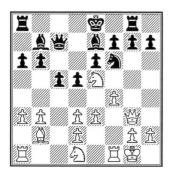

*After 14. c×d3*

**14. ... Nd7 15. Nf2 N×e5 16. f×e5 0-0-0** 16. ... f5 is an interesting alternative. Castling is a bit risky as White is ready to occupy the c-file. **17. Rac1 Kb8 18. b4 Qd7 19. b×c5 b×c5 20. Rb1 d4?!** Simply 20. ... Ka7 is much safer. Black should avoid any opening of the position. **21. e×d4 c×d4 22. Ne4! Qd5** "Black considering it impossible to maintain the f-pawn makes a highly ingenious and dashing attack, which, however, is exceedingly well met by White" —Bird. 22. ... Ka8 23. R×f7 B×e4 24. d×e4 d3 isn't amusing either, but the text move is hopeless. **23. R×f7 Qa2 24. Rbf1 B×e4 25. d×e4 Bc5 26. Qd3** "Threatening to win Black's queen if he takes b2"—Bird. **26. ... Rgf8 27. R×f8 R×f8 28. R×f8† B×f8 29. Q×d4 Bc5 30. Q×c5 Q×b2 31. Qb4† Q×b4 32. a×b4 Kb7 33. d4 Kc6 34. Kf2 g5 35. g4 h6 36. Ke3** Black resigns—*Modern Chess* (Bird), pp. 47–48.

## (665) Schallopp–Bird    1–0

International tournament (round 17)
Nuremberg, 27 July 1883
*C61*

**1. e4 e5 2. Nf3 Nc6 3. Bb5 Nd4 4. Ba4** "We believe this defense was first suggested by Rosenthal. We consider it better than 4. N×d4, but 4. Bc4 has many good points which recommend it to popularity"—*Chess Player's Chronicle*. **4. ... Bc5 5. 0-0 N×f3†**

**6. Q×f3 Ne7 7. Bb3 0-0 8. d3 a5 9. Be3 d6 10. Nc3 c6 11. Rad[1] Ng6 12. d4 e×d4 13. B×d4 B×d4 14. R×d4 b5 15. a4 c5** A ver[y] weakening move. More prudent is 15. ... b4, e.g., 16. Ne2 Ba6 17. Rd[1] Ne5. **16. Rd2 b×a4 17. N×a4** 17. B×a4! (Schallopp) is superio[r]. The bishop is quite active here, while the knight keeps its eye o[n] d5. **17. ... c4** "A pretty little move. If 18. B×c4 Ne5 19. Qb3 N×c[4] 20. Q×c4 Ba6. White, by refusing the proffered pawn gets, numer[]ically, the superior game"—*Chess Player's Chronicle*. **18. Ba2 Be[6]** 18. ... Rb8 is more active, for if 19. B×c4 Ne5 20. Qe2 N×c[4] 21. Q×c4 Rb4 22. Qa2 Qg5. **19. Qg3! Qb8** An interesting mov[e] that leads to some intriguing lines. 19. ... Ra6 is however safe[r]. **20. Q×d6** 20. R×d6 is better, but trickier 20. ... c3! 21. B×e6 f×e[6] 22. Rb6! (if 22. b×c3? Nf4!, and the advantage changes sides). **20. ...[] Qb4?** 20. ... c3! complicates matters considerably. After 21. N×c[3] B×a2 22. N×a2 Q×b2, White's advantage is limited. After the tex[t] move 21. Nc5! would have been decisive. **21. b3? Rfb8 22. Rb[1] Q×d6** 22. ... Ra6 or 22. ... c×b3 pre-empts the activation of White[']s rook. **23. R×d6 c×b3 24. B×b3 Rb4 25. f3 Kf8 26. Rb6** "Effe[c]tually stopping Black's intended move 26. ... Rab8"—*Chess Player[']s Chronicle*. **26. ... Nf4?!** 26. ... B×b3 27. c×b3 Rb8 is more tenaciou[s.] **27. R×b4 a×b4 28. Nc5?!** 28. B×e6! R×a4 29. Bb3 is a superio[r] version of the ending. White's rook will occupy the d-file, while hi[s] bishop is clearly better than the knight. **28. ... B×b3 29. N×b[3]** Preferable over 29. c×b3, as the adverse b-pawn is kept under fire[.] **29. ... Rc8 30. Rb2 h5 31. Nc1 Rd8 32. Nd3 N×d3 33. c×d3 Rb[8]** "33. ... R×d3 would doubtless have afforded a better chance"– *Chess Player's Chronicle*. Instead of an almost certain draw, Bird ge[ts] an almost certain loss. **34. Kf2 Ke7 35. Ke3 Kd6 36. Kd4 Rc[]** **37. h4 Rc1 38. R×b4 Rg1 39. Rb5 g6 40. Rg5 Rh1 41. g3 Ke[]** **42. f4 Rf1** "Here White wins 'right away.' Bird has not played thi[s] game with his accustomed spirit. Move 17 is smart in its way, bu[t] was not followed up in the same freshness of style with which thi[s] player usually follows up an advantage, however small"—*Ches[s] Player's Chronicle*. **43. f5† g×f5 44. e×f5† R×f5 45. R×f5 K×f[] 46. Kd5 Kg4 47. Ke5 K×g3 48. d4 Kg4 49. d5 f5 50. d6 f4 51. d[] f3 52. d8Q f2 53. Qd3 K×h4 54. Kf5** Black resigns—*Tournamen[t] Book* (Schallopp), pp. 239–241; *Chess Player's Chronicle*, 22 Augus[t] 1883 pp. 93–94.

## (666) Bird–Riemann    1–0

International tournament (round 18)
Nuremberg, 28 July 1883
*A03*

**1. f4 d5 2. e3** "I now rather prefer playing 2. e3, reserving 3. Nf[3] for my third, or even later, according to the play of my opponent[.] Bf1 is free a move earlier, and if Black plays 2. ... Nc6 at once, it ca[n] be pinned with advantage. This knight commands e5 and d4, and[,] in my opinion, Black should endeavour to preserve it, and not allo[w] the opinion of changing it off"—Bird. **2. ... c5 3. Nf3 Nc6** "As jus[t] observed, it is desirable to prevent the knight being pinned in thi[s] form of opening"—Bird. **4. Bb5 Qb6** "Wisker in 1873 also adopte[d] this move against me in our match. It does not, however, appear t[o] afford the most favorable development for Black"—Bird. **5. c4** "De[]cidedly the best move. This opinion was endorsed by Andersse[n] when I played it against him in one of our best games, which ha[]

ever been recorded"—Bird. **5. ... d×c4** "5. ... d4 would be bad play"—Bird. 5. ... e6 (Schallopp) is the most solid option. **6. B×c4** 6 **7. Nc3 Nf6 8. 0–0 a6** "With the view of retiring the queen to 7 and advancing b5. Riemann was Anderssen's most successful pupil, and is Berlin champion. As is common with the greatest players, he wished the option of castling on either side"—Bird. "8. ... 6 and 9. ... Bg7 should be played. Black underestimated his opponent, who lost a small match against Gäbler in Brunswick in 1880 [sic]. A short while earlier I gave the odds of a knight to Gäbler"—Riemann. **9. b3 Qc7 10. Bb2 b5 11. Be2 Bb7 12. Qe1 Rd8 13. Rc1** Bd6 **14. Qg3** *(see diagram)*

*After 14. Qg3*

"The full design of my 12th and 14th moves seems not to have been sufficiently considered or appreciated by Black. He cannot now castle without immediately disastrous results. For example suppose 14. ... 0–0 15. Ne4 (15. N×b5 or 15. Nd5 would either give White an advantage, but this was intended) 15. ... Nh5 (best, in fact the only move not immediately fatal) 16. Nf6† N×f6 17. B×f6 6 18. Qh4 Be7 19. Ng5 h5 20. Ne4. White threatens 21. B×h5, which will be conclusive"—Bird. **14. ... Rg8?** Bird's play looks very simple, yet Black is confronted with serious difficulties. He probably had to submit himself to the ugly 14. ... Bf8, intending a complete regrouping of his pieces. White then can slowly build up further pressure, with 15. d3 and now 15. ... Ne7 is probably best (if 15. ... Qb6 16. f5! e×f5 17. Nh4); e.g., 16. Ne5 Nf5 17. Qh3 Bd6 18. g4 with the initiative. Another playable alternative is 14. ... Kf8 (Schallopp). **15. N×b5! a×b5 16. B×f6 Ra8 17. B×b5 Kf8 18. Be5!** "Well played, for if Black takes the bishop an irresistible battery is at once opened upon him"—Bird. **18. ... R×a2 19. R×c5** "This is a serious loss for Black."—Bird. **19. ... f6 20. B×c6** "Threatening 20. ... B×c6 1. Nd4"—Bird. **20. ... f×e5 21. f×e5 B×c5 22. Nd4†** Black resigns. This game was an important one, being at the close of the tournament. Riemann's score being formidable at the time, its result materially affected the ultimate destination of the prizes"—Bird. "The game lasted some 45 minutes. Black, to his damage, was tempted to follow Bird in playing his moves in blitztempo even though the game was important for the final ranking"—Riemann. *Tournament Book* (Schallopp), pp. 248–249; *Modern Chess* (Bird), pp. 48–49; *Schacherinnerungen* (Riemann), p. 485.

**(667) Leffmann–Bird   ½–½**
International tournament (round 19)
Nuremberg, 30 July 1883
873

**1. e4 c5 2. Nf3 Nc6 3. Nc3 g6 4. d4 c×d4 5. N×d4 Bg7 6. Be3** Nf6 **7. Be2 0–0 8. 0–0 d6 9. Qd2 Bd7 10. Rad1 Rc8 11. f4 N×d4**

**12. B×d4 Ne8 13. B×g7 N×g7 14. Qd4 a6 15. Rd2 Bc6 16. Bf3** Qa5 **17. a3 f5 18. Nd5 Rf7 19. e5 B×d5 20. B×d5 e6 21. Bb3 d5** **22. Rff2 b5 23. h4 Qd8 24. g3 Rd7 25. c3 Qc7 26. Rd1 Qc6** **27. Rdd2 Ne8 28. Rde2 Nc7 29. Rc2 Na8 30. Rcd2 Nb6 31. Rd3** Kg7 **32. Rd1 a5 33. Rfd2 a4 34. Ba2 Qc5 35. Kf2 Nc4 36. B×c4** b×c4 **37. Q×c5 R×c5 38. Re2 Rb5 39. Rdd2 Kh6 40. Kf3 Rb3** **41. Ke3 Kh5 42. Kd4 Rb5 43. Rh2 h6 44. Rc2 Kg4 45. Rcf2 Rh7** **46. Rfg2 Rh8 47. Rf2 Rhb8 48. Rhg2 Rh8 49. Rh2 Rh7 50. Rfg2** Rg7 **51. Rf2 g5 52. h5 Rg8 53. Rfg2 Rgb8 54. Rf2 Rb3 55. Rfg2** R8b7 **56. Rf2 Rd7 57. Rc2 Rb8 58. Rcf2 Rg7 59. Rc2 Rgg8** **60. Rcf2 Rb7 61. Rc2 Rgb8 62. Rcf2 Rb3 63. Rc2** draw—*Tournament Book*, pp. 257–258.

---

# HANDICAP TOURNAMENT AT PURSSELL'S 1883

During the following months Bird continued to attend Purssell's. A few of his offhand games were published.

**(668) Bird–C.F.M.   1–0**
Offhand game
London (Purssell's), 16 August 1883
*Odds of Nb1*

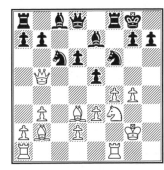

*White to move*

The game proceeded thus: **1. g5 a6 2. B×h7† N×h7 3. Qd5†** Kh8 **4. g6 Bh4 5. Rh1 Ne7 6. R×h4 N×d5 7. R×h7† Kg8 8. Rah1** Black resigns—*Sheffield and Rotherham Independent*, 1 September 1883.

**(669) Bird–Israel   1–0**
Offhand game
London (Purssell's), 18 August 1883
*Odds of Nb1*

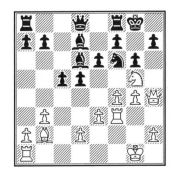

*Black to move*

Bird revealed the name of his opponent in *Modern Chess* (p. 32). In his column in the *Sheffield and Rotherham Independent* he gave the initials "J.J."

**1. ... Re8 2. N×h7 N×h7 3. Q×h7† K×h7 4. Rh3† Qh4 5. R×h4† Kg8 6. Rh8** mate—*Sheffield and Rotherham Independent*, 1 September 1883.

### (670) Gunsberg–Bird    1–0
Offhand game
London (Purssell's) 1883
*A80*

**1. Nf3 f5 2. d4 e6 3. e3 b6 4. c4 Bb7 5. Be2 Nf6 6. 0–0 Bd6 7. b3 0–0 8. Bb2 Nc6 9. Nc3 Qe8 10. Rc1 Qg6 11. Nb5 a6 12. N×d6 c×d6 13. Ba3 Ne4 14. Nd2 Ng5 15. B×d6 Rf6 16. Bh5 Qh6 17. Bf4 g6 18. Be2 Nd8 19. Kh1 Ndf7 20. Bf3 Be4 21. B×e4 f×e4 22. Qg4 e5 23. d×e5 Rf5 24. N×e4 N×e5 25. B×e5 R×e5 26. N×g5 R×g5 27. Q×d7** Black resigns—*Our Corner*, November 1883.

### (671) Bird–Unknown    1–0
Offhand game
London (Purssell's), 16 November 1883
*Odds of Ng1*

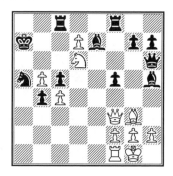

White to move

**White mated in two moves**—*Sheffield and Rotherham Independent*, 24 November 1883.

Chess life at Purssell's was spiced up with the organization of a handicap tournament that ran in October and November. A powerful triumvirate, consisting of Bird, Gunsberg and Hoffer, designed the contours of the event. Twenty players were allowed to take part and all places were swiftly taken. Several participants were professionally active in the City of London, so the games were played on evenings during the week. The best players were rewarded with five money and three chess book prizes. All players were divided into six classes. The stronger players received a privilege: Instead of the usual pawn and move, they gave to the players of the class below them the milder odds of two moves to start with. Two balanced sections of ten players each were formed. Bird found himself in the relatively stronger group, with Maczuski and Anthony Guest (class II). Gunsberg was the only class I player in the other section.

On the opening day of the tournament, 8 October, Bird disposed of Guest. His results from the next three games showed that securing first place in his section would not be a walk in the park. Bird beat Clark but lost against Ledger and Leonard. These two players ap-

peared to be Bird's most dangerous opponents for the first spo[...]. Bird recovered well by winning his next games against Skelto[...], Thomas and Hardy. In the last round Bird took the measure [...] Maczuski, the other class I player in his group. This was Bird's la[...] game since De Vecchi had left the tournament at an early stage, fo[...] feiting all subsequent games. With 6 points out of 8 Bird share[...] the top spot with Ledger. By beating Ledger in a tie game Bir[...] reached the final.

In the other group the weakly-esteemed E.T. Smith (class V[...] surprised his opponents and came out first before Heppell (cla[...] III), the winner of the handicap tournament of the City of Londo[...] Chess Club in 1879. Gunsberg played no role of importance.

In the final game Bird had to concede the huge odds of a roo[...] to Smith. After a protracted struggle, of which two fragments wer[...] preserved, Bird won the game and with it the first prize.[18]

Bird enthusiastically announced another handicap at Pursell'[...] but his plans did not materialize. It is worth mentioning that a ha[...] year later a similar tournament took place at the Divan. It appea[...] that slowly but surely Bird considered returning to this resort a[...] well. In an article in *The Times* of 30 May 1884 he expressed h[...] regret at being prevented from taking part.

### (672) Guest–Bird    0–1
Handicap preliminary (round 1)
London, 8 October 1883
*Odds of a move*

**1. e4 & 2. d4 g6 3. Bd3 e6 4. Be3 Bg7 5. Nf3 b6 6. Nc3 Ne[...] 7. Qe2** "7. Qd2 would, we think, have been preferable"—Bird. **7. [...] a5 8. a4** "Black at his previous move played 7. ... a5 to open his a-fil[...] with the view of 8. ... Na6 and possibly 9. ... c5. White's reply, how[...] ever, appears without object, and was unobjectionable as it let Black's knight in at b4, and gets rid of Bd3"—Bird. **8. ... Na6 9. 0–[...] Nb4 10. Rfe1 0–0 11. Qd2 N×d3 12. c×d3 Ba6 13. Bh6 f6** "T[...] guard against the contingency of 15. Ng5 after 14. B×g7, also to de[...] velop the rook, and in case of need to get Qf8"—Bird. **14. Rad[...] Rf7 15. e5 f5 16. d5** "Well conceived and requires very careful pla[...] in reply, and against a lesser experienced player might perhaps hav[...] answered. The sacrifice of the pawn, however, against best play wa[...] not sound"—Bird. Creative but absolutely not necessary. Quietl[...] 16. Bf4 keeps everything under control. **16. ... N×d5 17. N×d[...] e×d5 18. e6 d×e6 19. R×e6 Bc8** "This move was necessary to pro[...] vide for White's intended doubling of rooks on the e-file. Black ha[...] to exercise caution in this and his subsequent moves"—Bird. 19. ..[...] Qd7 looks more natural. **20. Bg5?** 20. Re2, intending to exchang[...] Black's most dangerous bishop still guarantees equal play. This mov[...] costs a tempo after which Bird is able to consolidate his extra pawn[...] **20. ... Qf8 21. Re2 Bd7** "The bishop arrives just in time to defen[...] e8, which is one of the points of White's intended attack"—Bird[...]

---

18. Bird was very positive in his evaluation: "The tournament has been a mos[...] enjoyable affair, and a genuine success from every point of view. It has also estab[...] lished the fact that gentlemen greatly immersed in business have been able to tak[...] part without the slightest interference with ordinary pursuits. The games hav[...] not averaged more than two hours each, the three finest played having occupie[...] rather less than one hour and a half each. The arrangements of this tournamen[...] would serve as a model, and the competitions having proved so keen and spirited[...] and the times of playing so convenient for business men, these contests will becom[...] regular." *Sheffield and Rotherham Independent*, 10 November 1883.

**22. b3 h6?!** 22. ... f4! is difficult to meet. **23. Bf4 c5** The endgame after 23. ... g5 24. B×c7 B×a4 25. B×b6 B×b3 26. Rde1 a4 27. Bd4! is certainly tenable thanks to the excellent centralization of his pieces. With the text move Bird aims higher, but the closed nature of the position makes the defense for White easier. **24. Rde1 Re8 25. Ne5 B×e5 26. B×e5 d4** "26. ... f4 appeared tempting, but the text move was sounder"—Bird. **27. f4?** "After this, which shuts in the queen, Black has more freedom, and makes the best of his position"—Bird. **27. ... Bc6 28. Rb1 Rd7 29. Qe1 Qf7 30. Qg3 Kh7 31. Kf1 Bd5 32. Reb2 Rde7 33. Qf2 g5 34. g3 g4** 34. ... g×f4 35. g×f4 Qh5 is at once decisive. **35. Qe1 Qh5 36. Kg1 Qh3 37. Rf2 Qh5** "On second thoughts Black determined to avoid change of queens, which White could enforce if Black played 37. ... h5"—Bird. This exchange would be hopeless as well: 37. ... h5! 38. Qf1 h4! 39. Q×h3 g×h3 40. g×h4 Rg8† and both rooks will be transferred to the g-file. **38. Rfb2 Qf7 39. Qf2 h5 40. Kf1 Qe6 41. Ke1 Qc6 42. Kd1 Bf3†** "Travelling away from the threatened danger on the kingside, White gets into more speedy trouble on the queenside"—Bird. **43. Kc2 b5 44. a×b5 Q×b5 45. Re1 a4 46. b×a4 Q×a4† 47. Kb1 Ra8 48. Ra2 Qb3† 49. Qb2 Q×d3† 50. Ka1 R×a2†** White resigns. "51. Q×a2 Qc3†, winning the rook at once and the queen two moves afterwards"—Bird. *Sheffield and Rotherham Independent* (Bird), 20 October 1883.

### (673) Bird–E.T. Hardy   1–0
Handicap preliminary (round 7)
London 1883
*Odds of Ng1*

**1. e4 e5 2. Bc4 Nf6 3. d4 e×d4 4. 0–0 N×e4 5. Re1 d5 6. B×d5 Q×d5 7. Nc3 Qc6 8. N×e4 Be7 9. Bg5** "This is a good move. Black cannot well take the bishop, on account of 10. Nd6† Kd7 11. N×f7"—Bird. **9. ... Be6 10. B×e7 K×e7 11. Q×d4** "White is now threatening 12. Q×g7, which would make a serious breach in the Royal ramparts"—Bird. **11. ... Rg8?!** Very cramped play. 11. ... Nd7 just continues to complete his development while White has no real threats. **12. Qb4†** "White's object is to prevent Nb8 and Ra8 getting into play before he can gain an advantage in position sufficient to compensate to some extent for the piece given. This check appears desirable, for it compels Black to retire to his first rank, and will enable White for a time to prevent communication between the two Black rooks"—Bird. **12. ... Kd8** "12. ... Ke8 would have been better. It would have left the knight free after Nd7"—Bird. **13. Nc5** "This move is well judged. Keeping Rd1† in reserve is good for many reasons. If 13. ... Nd7 14. R×e6 would be the soundest and most effective reply"—Bird. **13. ... Bc8??** "The position is somewhat embarrassing for Black. We believe 13. ... Re8 was best here. Bird's chance of a leading prize would have been defeated had he lost this game, so he would, we think, have had to be content with winning two pawns and fighting as best as he could against the extra piece. The retirement of the bishop was extremely injudicious"—Bird. 13. ... Kc8! refutes White's attack. After the text, Hardy is indeed an easy prey for Bird. **14. Qh4†** "White saw

---

that 14. Rad1† would win easily if 14. ... Bd7, but he omitted to see that he equally did so in reply to 14. ... Nd7 15. N×b7† B×b7 and mates in three moves. 14. Qh4†, though good, was by no means best, and certainly not artistic"—Bird. **14. ... g5 15. Q×h7 Qg6 16. Rad1† Nd7 17. Qh3 g4 18. Qe3 Qg5 19. Qd4 Qf5 20. Re5 Qg6** White mates in two moves—*Sheffield and Rotherham Independent* (Bird), 10 November 1883.

### (674) Bird–E.T. Smith   1–0
Handicap final
London, 13 November 1883
*Odds of Ra1*

*White to move*

**1. Qe6† Qf7** "If 1. ... Kh8 2. Q×h6; if 1. ... Rf7 1. Rd8† would be immediately fatal"—Bird. **2. Rd7 Q×e6?** Bird could resign after 2. ... Re8. **3. R×g7† Kh8 4. Rf7†** "White has a draw in hand, and playing to win was considered venturesome"—Bird. **4. ... Kg8**

**5. Rg7† Kh8 6. Rg6†? Rf6 7. B×f6† Q×f6 8. R×f6 Kg7 9. Rc6**
Objectively speaking, Black should win this endgame rather easily.
The game ultimately arrived at the following position.

White to move

**1. Rd3 Be1 2. Ra3† Ba5 3. Ra4** Black resigns. "The success of
an old and popular player as Bird was hailed with much satisfaction,
not to say enthusiasm. The young and rapidly advancing amateur,
Mr. Smith, was also warmly congratulated, and this was the first defeat sustained by him in the tournament"—Bird. *Sheffield and
Rotherham Independent* (Bird), 24 November 1883; *Modern Chess*
(Bird), p. 32.

## A Testimonial for Bird

During the winter season 1883-84 Blackburne fell seriously ill.
This was not the first, nor the last, mention of health problems involving Blackburne, who suffered from chronic nasal inflammation.
As these problems affected his income as a chess professional a committee was set up to arrange a testimonial for him.

On 30 May 1884 Bird informed his readers in *The Times* that
some of his own friends were planning to present him, Bird, with a
similar gift. Three men, Herbert Baldwin, C.C. Davison and Minchin
(the latter apparently back on good terms after Bird's exclusion from
the match between Zukertort and Rosenthal (see Appendix 2, Bird's
Farewell to Chess); he and Bird cooperated fruitfully for the London 1883 tournament book), volunteered to receive the subscriptions. At the end of September, the nice sum of £45 14s. could be
presented to Bird. Minchin informed the public that Bird showed
his gratitude by writing on a new work, *Modern Chess*.[19]

With their purses opened up to help Bird and Blackburne, their
friends tried to arrange a friendly match between them along the
way. In *The Times* of 21 July 1884, Bird optimistically believed in

James I. Minchin (courtesy Cleveland Public Library).

the success of such a scheme, but Blackburne's condition would not
allow it. He left England for Australia in October, only to return
just in time for the summer tournaments of 1885.[20]

## C.C.A. Congress, Bath 1884

The only important chess event of 1884 was the meeting of the
C.C.A. in Bath. In the preamble to the congress Skipworth had
made attempts to widen its perspective by nationalizing it. In an
appeal that appeared on 8 March 1884 in the *Illustrated Sporting
and Dramatic News* he launched an idea to establish a tournament
for all comers for which a first prize of £50 was foreseen. Extra funds
would be required and Skipworth was contemplating working with
a London secretary and treasury in addition to the existing officers.
A follow-up letter appeared in the same column on 7 June. Skipworth had to admit that "it seems to be a general feeling not to have

---

19. "It was at first suggested that the fund should be devoted to the cost of
printing some railway statistics prepared with much labor by Mr. Bird, well known
as a professional accountant. This has been done in part, but it was not considered
advisable to spend more of the funds on the printing of expensive tables, which
would prove of interest chiefly to experts." *Chess Monthly*, October 1884, p. 35.
Bird's book about railway accountancy saw the light of day only in 1886 under the
title *Railway Accounts: a concise view for the last four years, 1881 to 1884, and an
estimate for 1885. With remarks on the relation of capital to revenue, etc.* It was
(partly) preceded by *Modern Chess* of which the first installment appeared towards
the end of 1884. Here Bird expressed his appreciation for the support: "I cannot
allow the first part of Bird's *Modern Chess* to appear without expressing my heartfelt acknowledgements to the many kind friends who have joined in the testimonial
to me as an old English chess player. I trust I shall never forfeit their approbation,
and am unable to express the pride I feel at such a proof of their goodwill—H.E.B."
Bird, *Modern Chess*, p. 32.

20. MacDonnell found the initiative to arrange a match between Bird and
Blackburne highly inappropriate: "Mr. Bird's friends offer to back him for £25 a
side against Mr. Blackburne. It is not usual to ask a sick man to play a match? And
yet Mr. Bird himself is undoubtedly sincere as to this challenge and usually chivalrous in his proposals." *Illustrated Sporting and Dramatic News*, 9 August 1884.

## 14th Congress of the C.C.A., Bath, 28 July–1 August 1884

*Site:* Guildhall  /  *Prizes:* 1st £12, 2nd £5, 3rd £2  /  *Time limit:* 20 moves per hour

|   | 1 | 2 | 3 | 4 | 5 | 6 | 7 |    |
|---|---|---|---|---|---|---|---|----|
| 1 W. Wayte |   | 1 | ½ | 1 | ½ | 1 | 1 | 5 |
| 2 A.B. Skipworth | 0 |   | 1 | 1 | 0 | 1 | 1 | 4 |
| 3 H.E. Bird | ½ | 0 |   | 1 | 0 | 1 | 1 | 3½ |
| 4 J.I. Minchin | 0 | 0 | 0 |   | 1 | 1 | ½ | 2½ |
| 5 E. Thorold | ½ | 1 | 1 | 0 |   | 0 | 0 | 2½ |
| 6 G.A. MacDonnell | 0 | 0 | 0 | 0 | 1 |   | 1 | 2 |
| 7 C.E. Ranken | 0 | 0 | 0 | ½ | 1 | 0 |   | 1½ |

### Handicap tournament

*Prizes:* 1st £5 5s., 2nd £3 3s., 3rd £1 1s.  /  *Odds scale:* pawn and move (class IB), pawn and 2 moves (class II) and knight (class III)

*Notes:* no draws after the first round were mentioned in the press

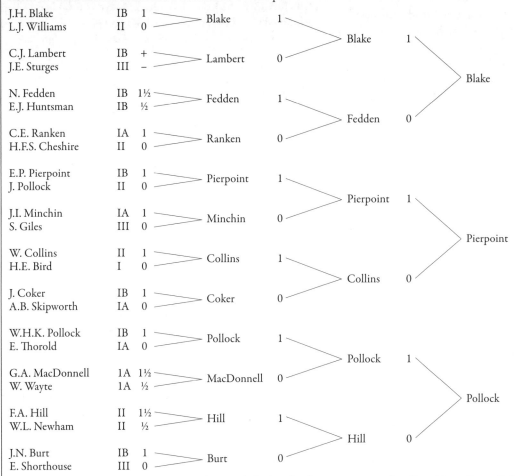

The final pool was won by Joseph Henry Blake, ahead of Edward Pelham Pierpoint and William Henry Krause Pollock.

### Consolation handicap tournament

*Prizes:* 1st £2, 2nd 2/6 of the entrance fees  /  *Odds scale:* pawn and move (class IB), pawn and two moves (class II) and knight (class III)

*Notes:* no draws were mentioned in the press G.A. Hooke played either in class IB or class II

| H.E. Bird | IA | 1 | Bird | 1 |  |  |  |
| G.A. Hooke | IB/II | 0 |  |  | Bird | 1 |  |
| E. Thorold | IA | 1 | Thorold | 0 |  |  |  |
| A.B. Skipworth | IA | 0 |  |  |  |  | Bird |
| F.G. Jones | II | 1 | Jones | 1 |  |  |  |
| W.L. Newham | II | 0 |  |  | Jones | 0 |  |
| F.A. Hill | II | 1 | Hill | 0 |  |  |  |
| G.A. MacDonnell | IA | 0 |  |  |  |  |  |

an entirely open class in connection with this society, but rather that British amateurs only should be allowed to compete for its prizes and honors." As a consequence the principal tournament (Class I, Division I) was open for former first prize winners but also for players who had distinguished themselves in the eyes of the committee. MacDonnell and Bird were thought eligible in the latter category and were consequently invited. Both men accepted the offer to play. The fact that Bird and MacDonnell were born in the provinces may have ratified their participation.[21]

The Association opened its festivities on Monday 28 July. Seven players entered the major tournament. The cliché that the C.C.A. was a very religious-dominated organization hit the nail once more. Besides Bird, only Minchin and Edmund Thorold had not taken up the vows. When, a few years later, a game of Bird identified with the title "Rev.," the free-willed veteran replied "that he has not 'taken orders,' and never will do so from any man."[22]

The C.C.A. contest was held at the Guildhall and drew a great attendance from players from all over the country. The main tournament offered three prizes of respectively £12, £5 and £2. The time limit was set on 20 moves per hour.

A handicap tournament was held along the way. A single loss would lead to elimination. Three prizes were distributed among the players able to reach the final pool.

Bird received a bye in the first round. On the next day he beat Charles Edward Ranken. In the evening he got eliminated in the first round of the handicap tournament by Collins.

On Wednesday Bird lost against Skipworth and drew with Wayte. This seriously damaged his chances to win the tournament, for which Skipworth and Wayte were now the favorites. The next day again brought some mixed results with a win against MacDonnell and a loss against Thorold. Wayte claimed the tournament victory by beating Skipworth. In the last round Bird beat Minchin to gain the third prize, a meager consolation.

Skipworth was especially delighted with such a result. In his column in the *Lincoln, Rutland and Stamford Mercury* of 2 March 1888 he based his claim that the wall between London masters and amateurs was diminished by the results achieved by him and Wayte at Bath. It is ironic that this imaginary wall was erected by Skipworth himself by excluding London-based and professional players from tournaments organized by the C.C.A. MacDonnell, in the *Illustrated Sporting and Dramatic News* of 9 August 1884, pointed to "his gouty state of health and total lack of training for the contest" as an explanation for Bird's mediocre result.

Towards the end of the week a "Consolation Handicap" tournament started. A small prize fund was provided by the Reverend J. Greene. Eight players participated and Bird was more successful this time. He managed to win the tournament and clinch the first prize of £2 2s.

---

21. Or so one can assume, since their place of birth was specifically mentioned in an article in *The Times* on 21 July 1884.

22. *Illustrated Sporting and Dramatic News*, 4 June 1887. Buckley recalled a similar amusing story in his reminiscences of Bird: "Another friend of mine wanted me to become a clergyman of the Church of England. Curious that a son of his spoke to me about it the other day; he asked me what was my objection to taking orders. I told him that I had no objection to taking orders—for my forthcoming book, *Chess Masterpieces*, and he ordered six copies instantaneously." *Chess Amateur*, June 1913, p. 271.

## (675) Collins–Bird    1–0
Handicap tournament (round 1)
Bath, 29 July 1884
*Odds of pawn and two moves*

**1. e4 &  2. d4 e6 3. Bc4 Qe7 4. Nc3 g6 5. Nf3 Qg7 6. Be3 Nh6 7. h3 Nf7 8. Qd2 Bb4 9. a3 Ba5 10. b4 Bb6 11. Ne2 a5 12. c3 a×b4 13. c×b4 Nc6 14. 0–0 Ne7 15. a4 0–0 16. a5 Ba7 17. Ng5 Nd6 18. Ba2 h6 19. e5 h×g5 20. e×d6 c×d6 21. B×g5 Nf5 22. g4 N×d4 23. N×d4 B×d4 24. Rad1 Qe5 25. Q×d4 Q×g5 26. Q×d6 Rf8 27. Kg2 Ra3 28. Bb1 Qh4 29. f3 b6 30. Q×b6 Rb3 31. Rf2 Qf6 32. Be4 Ra6 33. Qc5 Rc3 34. Qd4 Kg7 35. Q×f6† K×f6 36. Rb2 d5 37. Bb1 Bd7 38. Rd3 Rc1 39. Rdd2 g5 40. Bd3 Ra8 41. Ra2 Ke5 42. b5 Rc5 43. Rdb2 Kd4 44. Bf1 Ke3 45. a6 d4 46. b6 Bc6 47. Kg3 d3 48. B×d3 K×d3 49. b7 Rf8 50. b8Q R×f3† 51. Kh2** and after a few more moves Black resigns—*Western Daily Press*, 31 July 1884.

Bird was bye in the first round.

## (676) Ranken–Bird    0–1
C.C.A. Congress (round 2)
Bath, 29 July 1884
*Game score missing*

## (677) Skipworth–Bird    1–0
C.C.A. Congress
Bath, 30 July 1884
*B34*

**1. e4 c5 2. Nc3 Nc6 3. Nf3 g6** "This move was adopted by Mr. Bird in the London tourney against Blackburne. It is, we believe, the invention of Paulsen"—Ranken. **4. d4 c×d4 5. N×d4 Bg7 6. Be3 Nf6** If he wished to avoid the coming sequence, 6. ... d6 is the correct move order. **7. N×c6** "Forcing back Black's knight, but leaving his e-pawn rather weak. Mr. Blackburne played here 7. Be2"—Ranken. **7. ... b×c6 8. e5 Ng8** "Black does not seem to lose much time by being driven back, for he immediately occupies an attacking position at h6, and the bishop has an unobstructed game"—Skipworth. **9. f4 Nh6** "We prefer 9. ... f6 at once, and if White replies with 10. Bd4 then 10. ... Qc7"—Ranken. **10. Bd3 d5 11. e×d6 *e.p.*** Opening the position, especially the long diagonal of the bishop, is rather dangerous. With Black's knight offside, he could very well set up a blockade on the black squares, starting with 11. Bc5. **11. ... e×d6 12. 0–0** 12. Qf3 (Skipworth) isn't any better: 12. ... 0–0 13. Q×c6 Rb8 with excellent compensation. **12. ... 0–0** 12. ... Ng4!, picking up White's best bishop, is certainly considerable. **13. Qf3 d5 14. Bc5 Re8 15. Rae1 R×e1 16. R×e1 Be6 17. h3 Qa5 18. b4 Qa3 19. Nd1** "Anticipating the move which Black actually made"—Skipworth. Not a very favorable square, with 19. Ne2 available. **19. ... Nf5?** *(see diagram)* Very bad timing from Bird. After 19. ... a5, he submits Skipworth's queenside to a lot of pressure. White is forced to act quickly on the other side of the board, but after 20. g4 a×b4 21. f5 Qa5, Black's attack has progressed more.

**20. R×e6?!** "In this combination, prepared by the last move, Mr. Bird was fairly outplayed, and the advantage which his opponent here obtained was quite sufficient for victory. We are sorry, however, that honesty compels us to spoil the variation. It is not quite sound, but it came off. Take the following way of playing it: 20. ... f×e6

*After 19. ... Nf5*

21. B×f5 Q×f3 22. B×e6† Kh8 23. g×f3 Re8, and Black must win back a piece for the loss of a pawn. He would then have had the exchange to the good against two pawns, and the game would probably have been a draw! Neither of the players nor an able annotator who examined the game at the time saw the whole: but all's well that ends well"—Skipworth. Bird's reply is certainly not inferior to the line suggested by Skipworth. However, with the text move Skipworth overlooks another possibility that would have posed Bird severe problems: 20. g4! Bd4† (forced) 21. B×d4 N×d4 22. Qf2 c5 (after 22. ... Nb5 23. f5! White has a decisive attack. Relatively best is 22. ... N×c2 and 23. ... Q×b4) 23. c3 Rf8 24. f5 and the game is very difficult to hold for Black. **20. ... Nd4 21. B×d4 B×d4† 22. Re3 Re8 23. Kh2 B×e3 24. N×e3 Q×b4 25. Ng4 Re1?!** The game is quite balanced, which is clearly not to Bird's liking. His attempt to harass White's king is misplaced and allows Skipworth a dangerous initiative. Had he taken control over the black squares in his king's neighborhood with, 25. ... Qd6 or 25. ... Kg7, little could go wrong. **26. Qf2** "Having an ingenious plan, which he presently carries out, for getting his queen to d4 or c5. It has, however, this objection, that Black can immediately force the knight to move, and the check at f6 will soon be seen to be premature. It would therefore we think be stronger to push 26. f5 here, threatening 27. f6, and preventing Black from driving the knight"—Ranken. 26. f5 is weakening the position of his own king too much; for instance, 26. ... h5 27. Nf2 Qd6† 28. g3 h4 gives attacking chances. **26. ... h5?** A serious concession. The immediate 26. ... Ra1 still gives perspectives for a draw. **27. Nf6†?** 27. Ne5 nets a pawn, for if 27. ... c5? 28. B×g6! f×g6 29. Nd3 is no fun. **27. ... Kg7 28. Nd7 Ra1** This escapade, condemned by Ranken, looks dangerous (contrary to 28. ... Re7), but Black is still fine. **29. c4 Qc3?** Only this move marks the end of Bird's long struggle for survival. The obvious check at d4 is now prevented, but White's queen possesses another, even much stronger, entry square that quickly decides the game. The drastic 29. ... Qe1 leaves nothing more than a draw in it for his opponent; e.g., 30. Qd4† Kg8 31. Nf6† Kf8 32. Q×a7 h4 and a perpetual is inevitable. **30. Qc5! Kh7 31. Qe7 Qg7 32. Nf6† Kh6 33. Ne8!** and White wins—*British Chess Magazine* (Ranken), October 1884, pp. 359–360; *Lincoln, Rutland and Stamford Mercury* (Skipworth), 6 July 1888.

## (678) Bird–Wayte    ½–½

C.C.A. Congress
Bath, 30 July 1884
*A13*

**1. c4 e6 2. g3** "An interesting departure from the usual shape of the English, but somewhat against its principles. There accordingly

arise disadvantages, but these are not very serious, and taking everything into account this combinations of the English and kingside fianchetto may well be occasionally adopted"—Potter. **2. ... d5 3. c×d5 e×d5 4. Bg2 Nf6 5. Nf3 Bd6 6. 0–0 0–0 7. b3 b6** "7. ... c6 8. Bb2 Re8 has claims"—Potter. **8. Bb2 Bb7 9. Nc3 c6 10. Nd4 Qd7 11. e4?!** Bird's last two moves don't fit well into the position. **11. ... c5?!** 11. ... d×e4! is the sternest test of Bird's antipositional set-up. As 12. N×e4? Be5 has to be avoided, White has to go through some trouble to get his pawn back. After 12. Nc2 Be5 13. Re1 c5 14. Rb1 Nc6 15. N×e4 B×b2 16. R×b2 N×e4 17. B×e4 Rfe8, material equality is restored, but Black's position is much more harmonious. **12. Nf5! Be5** "If 12. ... d×e4, then 13. N×e4 B×e4 14. B×e4 N×e4 15. Qg4. Black cannot play 15. ... g6 on account of 16. Nh6 mate, and White, therefore, wins back the piece with a good game. The effects of 12. ... N×e4 are also obviously unsatisfactory. There is likewise 12. ... d4 13. N×d6 d×c3 14. B×c3 Q×d6 15. e5, winning back the piece with a fine game. The text move is Black's best resource, but White retains an advantage, though whether it will lead to victory depends as much upon his adversary as himself"—Potter. **13. Bh3** 13. f4 forces 13. ... B×c3, when he gets rid of the weak d-pawn. **13. ... Kh8 14. e×d5 N×d5** *(see diagram)*

*After 14. ... N×d5*

**15. Qg4** 15. Re1! Nc6 16. Qg4 is an important refinement. Due to threat 17. R×e5!, Black has to lose an important tempo with 16. ... Bf6, which allows Bird to equalize with 17. Ne3! Another defensive option is 16. ... g6, but then 17. Qh4! g×f5 18. N×d5 B×b2 19. Nf6 forces a draw. **15. ... N×c3** 15. ... Nb4! is the move he could now play favorably. White's attack is being controlled while his weaknesses are becoming glaring. **16. B×c3 Qc6** "Black attacks in his turn and it serves for a good defense"—Potter. **17. f3 Qf6** "Here comes in the ruling passion. He wants to keep the adverse d-pawn weak for the endgame, but in doing so he runs risks. The bishop should be captured, after which a draw would be the legitimate result. We do not, however, mean to say that White can even now force a winning advantage"—Potter. **18. B×e5 Q×e5 19. Rae1** 19. d4 finally gets rid of the weak pawn. **19. ... Qf6 20. Re7?** An adventurous move. Bird's initiative seems threatening, but Black is well placed to deal with it and ultimately his chances in an endgame are promising due to White's weak d-pawn. A more defensive approach was by far preferable—e.g., 20. f4 g6 21. Ne3. **20. ... Ba6 21. Rfe1 Nc6 22. Rc7** "All this is in Mr. Bird's own courageous style. He examines the immediate present with a quick, keen glance, and trusts the future. It is this kind of valorous 'go' that enables him in the winter of his life to stand well against the best players of the day"—Potter. Even if the rook stays on the e-file, 22. ... Rad8 is clearly better for Black. **22. ... Ne5?** Wayte misses his chance to deliver the decisive blow with 22. ... Rae8! right now as White is in no position to keep everything closed: 23. Re4 (or 23. Re3 Qa1† 24. Kf2 Rd8!) 23. ... Ne5 24. Qf4 Bd3. **23. Qe4 Rae8 24. Re3** Right in time to defend everything. **24. ... g6** "The position is complicated and perplexing. Many things attract, but they shrink up when closely investigated. 24. ... Qd8 smiles very alluringly, but against best play it would come to nothing"—Potter. 24. ... Qd8 also leads to a draw: 25. R×a7 Bd3 26. Qh4 N×f3† 27. R×f3 Re1† 28. Bf1 B×f1 29. R×f1 R×f1† 30. K×f1 Qd3†. **25. f4 g×f5 26. f×e5 Qd8 27. Q×f5** "This assures a draw and gives a chance of something more. It does not appear that any better line is open to him. If 27. Qc6 Q×d2 28. Qf6† Kg8 29. Qg5† Kh8, and now as White dare not to play 30. B×f5, nor can get any good by 30. R×a7 he has no position to work with as far as victory is concerned"—Potter. **27. ... Q×c7 28. Qf6† Kg8 29. Re4 Bd3** "Claiming the draw, and it must be allowed to him. That a game of this kind should thus end is more satisfactory than that either party should be defeated"—Potter. **30. Qg5†** draw by perpetual check—*Land and Water* (Potter), 16 August 1884.

**William Wayte's carte de visite at Eton (courtesy of Provost and Fellows of Eton College).**

### (679) MacDonnell–Bird ½–½
C.C.A. Congress
Bath, 31 July 1884
*Game score missing*

### (680) Bird–Thorold 0–1
C.C.A. Congress
Bath, 31 July 1884
*A02*

**1.** f4 f5 **2.** Nf3 e6 **3.** e3 b6 **4.** Be2 Bb7 **5.** 0–0 Nf6 **6.** c4 c5 **7.** Nc3 Nc6 **8.** a3 a6 **9.** d3 Qc7 **10.** Ng5 g6 **11.** Bf3 h6 **12.** Nh3 0–0–0 **13.** Bd2 g5 **14.** Be2 g4 **15.** Nf2 d5 **16.** c×d5 e×d5 **17.** Qb3 c4 **18.** d×c4 d×c4 **19.** Qc2 Ne7 **20.** Rfd1 h5 **21.** Bf1 h4 **22.** Be1 R×d1 **23.** Nc×d1 b5 **24.** Bb4 g3 **25.** Nh3 g×h2† **26.** K×h2 Be4 **27.** Qd2 Nfd5 **28.** Ba5 Qc6 **29.** Ndf2 Bg7 **30.** N×e4 f×e4 **31.** Rd1 Qg6 **32.** Ng5 Bf6 **33.** Bc3 B×c3 **34.** b×c3 Qb6 **35.** Re1 Nf6 **36.** Be2 Nf5 **37.** N×e4 Rd8 **38.** Qc2 Q×e3 **39.** Bf3 Q×e1 **40.** N×f6 Ng3 **41.** Kh3 Rd3 **42.** Kg4 Nf1 **43.** Qe2 Nh2† **44.** Kh5 N×f3 White resigns—*Illustrated Sporting and Dramatic News*, September 1884.

### (681) Bird–Minchin 1–0
C.C.A. Congress (round 7)
Bath, 1 August 1884
*Game score missing*

---

# A VISIT TO MANCHESTER 1884

On 8 November the Athenaeum Chess Club of Manchester hosted the second match between the counties of Lancashire and Yorkshire. (The first match was played on 20 January 1883 and won by the team from Lancashire.) Bird, but also Gunsberg and Hoffer, were among the prominent visitors from London. Bird was hired to act as umpire. His services were called upon to adjudicate the large number of unfinished games. Just as on the previous occasion, Lancashire proved their superior strength and won easily with 74 wins against 34 losses and 27 draws.

The different chess clubs in Manchester engaged Bird for three simultaneous performances immediately afterwards. On 10 November Bird was welcomed by the Manchester Chess Club where he played 20 games. After four hours and a half he had won 15 games, lost 2 (against J. Parker and G. Hicks) and drawn 2 (W. Horrocks and F.J. Hamel). One game was left unfinished.

On the following day Bird was the guest of the Athenaeum Chess Club. In an exhibition that lasted four hours Bird remained unbeaten. He scored 13 wins and 5 draws (against J.M. Pollitt, T. Higginbotham, C.A. Dust, R.H. Whatham and J.B. Rayner) with two unfinished games. One of these games, with J. Parker, and a second game with Miniati were to be played out on 12 November when Bird gave a last séance at the St. Ann's Chess Club. The games of the previous evening both ended in a draw. Besides them only a limited number of opponents took up the gauntlet against Bird. He won against 4, lost 2 (against Berry and Whatham) and drew 3 games (with H. Jones, J. Parker and J. Leake). One game remained unfinished.

According to the *Morning Post* of 10 November Bird would pro-long his visit to Liverpool and the north of England, but no source confirms that he actually did this.

### (682) Bird–T.B. Wilson　1–0
Simultaneous game
Manchester (Manchester C.C.), 10 November 1884
A03

1. f4 Nf6 2. b3 e6 3. Nf3 Be7 4. Bb2 0–0 5. e3 d5 6. Be2 Nc6 7. 0–0 Ne8 8. Qe1 f6 9. c4 Nb4 10. Na3 Nd6 11. d4 Ne4 12. Nd2 N5 13. N×e4 f×e4 14. c5 a5 15. Bc3 Nc6 16. Nc2 b6 17. c×b6 c×b6 18. Qg3 Bh4 19. Qh3 e5 20. Bg4 e×f4 21. e×f4 Bf6 22. Rad1 b5 23. Ne3 Ne7 24. Be6† Kh8 25. f5 b4 26. Bb2 Ra6 27. Rc1 Qd6 28. B×c8 N×c8 29. Ng4 Ne7 30. Ne5 h6 31. Qh5 Bg5 32. Rc5 g6 33. Qe2 N×f5 34. g4 Nh4 35. R×f8† and White wins—*Manchester Weekly Post*, 24 January 1885.

### (683) Bird–F.J. Hamel　½–½
Simultaneous game
Manchester (Manchester C.C.), 10 November 1884
C51

1. e4 e5 2. Nf3 Nc6 3. Bc4 Bc5 4. b4 B×b4 5. c3 Bc5 6. d4 e×d4 7. c×d4 Bb6 8. Bb2 Nge7 9. Ng5 d5 10. e×d5 Na5 11. Bd3 Q×d5 12. Nf3 Bg4 13. Nbd2 Qe6† 14. Kf1 0–0 15. Qc2 Bf5 16. Re1 B×d3† 17. Q×d3 Qg6 18. Q×g6 N×g6 19. h4 Rad8 20. g3 Rfe8 21. Kg2 Nc6 22. h5 Nge7 23. Re4 f6 24. Rhe1 Kf7 25. g4 Nd5 26. Nc4 R×e4 27. R×e4 Re8 28. R×e8 K×e8 29. N×b6 N×b6 30. g5 Nd5 draw—*Nottinghamshire Guardian*, 28 August 1885.

### (684) Bird–Higginbotham　½–½
Simultaneous game
Manchester (Athenaeum C.C.), 11 November 1884
C51

1. e4 e5 2. Nf3 Nc6 3. Bc4 Bc5 4. b4 B×b4 5. c3 Bc5 6. d4 e×d4 7. c×d4 Bb6 8. 0–0 d6 9. d5 Na5 10. Bb2 Nf6 11. Bd3 0–0 12. Nc3 c6 13. Ne2 Kh8 14. Ng3 c×d5 15. e×d5 N×d5 16. B×h7 Nf6 17. Bd3 Bg4 18. Qd2 B×f3 19. g×f3 Nc6 20. Qg5 Ne5 21. B×e5 d×e5 22. Nf5 Rg8 23. Nd6 Q×d6 24. Qh4† Nh5 25. Q×h5† Qh6 26. Q×e5 Rac8 27. Qg3 Rc5 28. h4 Rh5 29. Rac1 R×h4 30. Kg2 g5 31. Rh1 f6 32. Bf5 Bd4 33. Be6 Rf8 34. f4 b6 35. Rcd1 Bc5 36. f×g5 f×g5 37. Qe5† Qf6 38. R×h4† g×h4 39. Qh5† Kg7 40. Rd7† Be7 draw—*Manchester Weekly Post*, 22 November 1884.

### (685) Bird–H. Jones　0–1
Simultaneous game
Manchester (St. Ann's C.C.), 12 November 1884
C54

1. e4 e5 2. Nf3 Nc6 3. Bc4 Bc5 4. c3 Nf6 5. b4 Bb6 6. a4 a6 7. Qb3 0–0 8. d3 h6 9. Na3 d6 10. 0–0 Kh7 11. B×f7 Qe7 12. Bc4 Bg4 13. Be3 B×f3 14. g×f3 B×e3 15. f×e3 Nh5 16. Qd1 Qg5† 17. Kh1 Q×e3 18. Nc2 Qf4 19. Ne1 Qf6 20. Rg1 Ne7 21. Ra2 c6 22. d4 Ng6 23. e×d5 c×d5 24. Bd3† Kh8 25. d×e5 Q×e5 26. Rag2

Rf7 27. Bc2 Rd8 28. Qd3 Nf5 29. Qd2 Nf4 30. Rg4 Ne3 31. Nd3 N×d3 32. Q×d3 N×c2 33. Q×c2 Rc8 34. Qg6 Rcc7 35. Rh4 Qe3 36. Rg3 Rf6 37. Qg4 Q×c3 38. Kg2 Qc2† 39. Kh3 Qf5 40. Rh5 Q×g4† 41. f×g4 g5 42. Rd3 Rd6 43. Kg3 d4 44. h4 Rc3 45. R×c3 g×h4† 46. K×h4 d×c3 White resigns—*Nottinghamshire Guardian*, 16 January 1885.

---

# VARIOUS AND OFFHAND 1883–1884

Bird's name hardly figured in any chess column from November 1883 until July 1884. With his own column in the *Sheffield and Rotherham Independent* abruptly closed down, the main source for news about him dried up. He probably continued practicing the game, but only at Purssell's. In May 1884 all chess players of note assembled at the Divan for a handicap tournament, but Bird's absence persisted. At the same time he was still intensely occupied with accounting work, preparing a work on railway statistics.

On 8 December MacDonnell reported in the *Illustrated Sporting and Dramatic News* that Bird was active in the City of London Chess Club. Curiously enough Bird's name was hardly ever connected with this club during the 1880s and 1890s.

Bird's single known public appearance was on 3 April, when he acted as the umpire of the 12th match between Cambridge and Oxford, held in the rooms of the St. George's Chess Club. At the end of the day he had to adjudicate two games, which must have cost him but little effort.

Bird's only known game from this period was played two days earlier, at an unknown location, where Gunsberg was handsomely crushed.

### (686) Bird–Gunsberg　1–0
Offhand game
London, 1 April 1884
A03

1. f4 d5 2. e3 e6 3. Nf3 c5 4. b3 Be7 5. Bb2 Bf6 6. d4 c×d4 7. e×d4 Ne7 8. Bd3 0–0 9. 0–0 Nbc6 10. c3 g6 11. Nbd2 Bg7 12. Ng5 "Adopted successfully by the same player against von Bardeleben and Paulsen. The object being to give room for the other knight, and to allow full play and combination for both"—Bird. 12. … h6 "Von Bardeleben did not attack this knight at once. Black appears here to rather force White's development on the g-file after the king has ensconced himself in snug quarters under efficient protection at h8"—Bird. 12. … f6 safeguards the king against all kinds of threats. It also takes control of the important e5-square. 13. Nh3 Kh7 14. Nf3 Qc7 15. Rc1 Bd7 16. Ba3 Rae8 17. Qe1 "An excellent move in this kind of position, and in the present instance the key move to White's combination"—Bird. 17. … Rg8? "An unfortunate move, which White promptly takes advantage of"—Bird. Many moves were still fully playable: e.g., 17. … f6, 17. … Qa5 or 17. … Kg8, although White's advantage remains undisputed. 18. Nhg5† Kh8 19. N×f7† Kh7 20. N3g5† h×g5 21. N×g5† and mate follows in two more moves—*The Times* (Bird), 5 January 1884.

Samuel Israel, a regular opponent of Bird in these years, was an old member of the City of London Chess Club and an avid correspondence player. This seriously physically infirm man who, as Potter noted in his obituary in *Land and Water* on 2 May 1885, lived in "a world that could not have afforded him much happiness," died in April 1885.

## (687) Israel–Bird    ½–½
Offhand game
London 1884
*Odds of pawn and two moves*

**1. e4 & 2. d4 c5 3. Qh5† g6 4. Q×c5 Nc6 5. c3 Nf6 6. e5 d6 7. e×d6 e×d6 8. Qg5 Kf7 9. Bd3 Kg7 10. Nf3 Qe8† 11. Be3 h6 12. Qb5 a6 13. Qb3 Ng4 14. 0–0** "Judiciously conceived, and its ultimate effects are such as to neutralize Black's skillful combination"—Potter. **14. ... N×e3 15. Re1 Na5 16. Qb4 Qd8 17. R×e3 d5 18. Qa4 Bd6 19. Ne5 g5 20. Nd2 Rf8 21. Rae1 Qc7 22. Qc2 b5 23. h3** "There is here an asterisk, and a previous acquaintance with Mr. Israel's score sheets tells us that he asks for analytical information. We examine 23. Bh7 and find that its complicated issues do not promise any adequate advantage; nor will any good purpose be served by 23. B×b5. White's best move is 23. b3"—Potter. The move played, as well as the three suggestions, are easily winning for White who is two pawns ahead with a great position. His best move is 23. B×b5!, for if 23. ... a×b5 24. Qg6† Kh8 25. Q×h6† Kg8 26. Qg6† Kh8 27. g4! forms a clear punishment. **23. ... Nc4 24. Nd×c4 b×c4 25. Be2** "25. Bh7 is now advisable. The following two variations will illustrate points and disperse apprehensions, but they are not to be considered as implying forced play in all respects: 25. ... B×e5 26. R×e5 Kh8 27. Re7 Qf4 28. Qe2, or 28. Bg6, with a sound game, and there are also other safe moves. There is also 28. g4, which bold line is fraught with much advantage assuming good nerves and a calm mind. The other variation is 25. ... Rf6 26. Ng4 B×g4 27. h×g4, with a sound position; or, after 25. ... Rf6, White could play 26. Rf3 Qe7 27. Ree3, with a perfectly safe game"—Potter. Israel missed two opportunities (both 24. B×c4 and 25. B×c4) to transpose into the variation given above. **25. ... Bf5 26. Qd2 Rab8 27. Bh5 Be4** "This queer-looking though shrewd and well-judged move is quite in Mr. Bird's own style"—Potter. **28. f3 Bf5 29. a3 Rb7 30. R3e2 Qb8 31. Nc6** "Which is what the enemy invites, and yet it is probably the best course at White's disposal, seeing that all other lines open out grave difficulties"—Potter. **31. ... Bh2† 32. Kh1 Qd6 33. Re7† R×e7 34. N×e7 Bd3 35. Qe3?** "Skillfully played, and it is just in time to save the game"—Potter. Until now, Israel was playing strongly, even if he was drifting a bit after the 25th move, but here he finally goes astray. 35. N×d5! frees the square e7 for his rook which intensifies the power of his attack. Yet, precise calculation is required to force the game—e.g., 35. ... Bg3 36. Re7† Kh8 37. Bf7 R×f7 38. R×f7 Q×d5 39. Re7, and the queen will infiltrate the position along the e-file. If Bird prevents this with 39. ... Bd6 40. Ra7 Qe6, White wins another pawn and Black has no way to threaten White's king. **35. ... Bg3 36. Qe6 Q×e6 37. R×e6 Rb8 38. N×d5 R×b2 39. Re7†** White draws by perpetual check. "Having regard to previous positions, both parties may be complimented on this result"—Potter—*Land and Water* (Potter), 4 October 1884.

## (688) Israel–Bird    0–1
Offhand game
London 1884
*C61*

**1. e4 e5 2. Nf3 Nc6 3. Bb5 Nd4 4. Bc4** "Favored by some authorities, and their preference is not wholly baseless"—Potter. **4. ... b5?** "An ingenious but unsound novelty"—Potter. **5. Bb3?** "In itself good, though an expert of Mr. Bird's own rank would look for more profit. There is 5. N×d4 b×c4 6. Nf3 d6 7. Qe2 Be6 8. Na3 d5 9. e×d5 Q×d5 10. Q×e5 Q×e5† 11. N×e5 B×a3 12. b×a3 with a pawn ahead and not much per contra, seeing that both parties have doubled pawns. Other lines are still more favorable for White"—Potter. 5. B×f7† instantly refutes Bird's invention, for if 5. ... K×f7 6. N×d4 e×d4 7. Qh5† wins the rook. **5. ... Bc5 6. 0–0 Qf6 7. N×d4 e×d4 8. d3 Ne7 9. f4 Bb7 10. f5 0–0–0 11. Bf4 g5 12. Bg3 h5** Thanks to Israel's cooperative play Bird got rid of his problems and now is able to start a promising attack. Instead of 12. Bg3, 12. f×g6 *e.p.* was still good for White. Earlier on he could have played his queen to h5. **13. h3 Rdg8 14. Nd2 h4 15. Bh2 g4 16. h×g4 h3 17. g3?!** White organizes the funeral of his own bishop. 17. Rf2 is indicated. **17. ... d5?!** The quiet 17. ... Rh7, going after g4 with 18. ... Rhg7, is hard to deal with by his opponent. **18. Qe2 Qg5 19. f6** (see diagram)

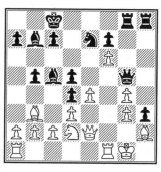

*After 19. f6*

**19. ... Ng6?!** Rather compliant, as the important square f5 is handed over to his opponent. Either 19. ... Bb4 or 19. ... Qe3† keeps the game chaotic but well balanced. **20. Rf5** "White has stood well against his opponent's fierce onslaught, and now obtains an advantage, but dangers come with it"—Potter. These dangers were avoidable had he played 20. B×d5! B×d5 21. Rf5. **20. ... Qe3† 21. Q×e3 d×e3 22. Nf3 d×e4 23. d×e4 Bb6** "23. ... B×e4 yields some attractive variations, but White meeting it well comes out with a profit"—Potter. Indeed, if 23. ... B×e4?! 24. R×c5 B×f3 25. B×f7 with a big advantage. **24. B×f7** "The game is full of complications however White may play. Perhaps 24. Kf1 B×e4 25. B×f7, though decidedly intricate enough, would have kept the game more under White's control. However, the text move cannot be theoretically condemned seeing that it should win"—Potter. **24. ... e2† 25. Kh1 B×e4?!** A mistake but very pardonable in such a complicated position. An unclear but balanced position arises after 25. ... Rd8!—e.g., 26. Bd5 c6 27. Be6† Kc7 etc. **26. B×g8 R×g8 27. Bg1! Rd8! 28. Re1 Rd1 29. Kh2??** "Mr. Israel points out that he should have played 29. R×e2, and he claims that, with care, he might expect to win afterwards. To the first proposition an unhesitating affirmative must be returned, and that there would be a theoretical win must also be admitted. It must be remembered, however, that Mr. Israel, though one of our best correspondence players, usually receives pawn and 2 moves from Mr. Bird over the board, and therefore it cannot be held as improbable that the eminent veteran would have managed to secure a draw. The move in question might run as follows: 29. R×e2 R×g1† 30. Kh2 Rg2† 31. R×g2 h×g2 32. K×g2 B×f5 33. g×f5 Nf8, and though White, best play assumed, should win, yet, practically, Mr. Bird would expect to have something to say about it"—Potter. Black keeps reasonable drawing chances after 32. ... Kd7 33. R×b5 as when White's pawns on the kingside won't decide the game so easily as they would after 32. ... B×f5. **29. ... B×f3** White resigns—*Land and Water* (Potter), 22 November 1884.

## (689) Wayte–Bird    1–0

Offhand game

London (St. George's C.C.), 4 November 1884

C30

**1. e4 e5 2. Nc3 Bc5 3. f4 d6 4. Nf3 a6 5. d4 e×d4 6. N×d4 Nf6 7. Be2 0–0 8. 0–0 Re8 9. Bf3 c6 10. Be3 b5 11. Qd3 a5 12. Rfd1 b4 13. Na4 Ba6 14. c4 b×c3 *e.p.* 15. Q×c3 B×d4 16. B×d4 N×e4 17. B×e4 R×e4 18. B×g7 R×f4 19. Be5 Rg4 20. R×d6 Nd7 21. Rad1 Bc8 22. Nc5 Ra7 23. Qh3 Rg6 24. R×g6† f×g6 25. Qb3†** Black resigns—*Manuscript games of W. Wayte*, vol. 11, game 1177.

## (690) Bird–Seymour    1–0

Offhand game

London (Gatti's), 6 November 1884

C52

**1. e4 e5 2. Bc4 Bc5 3. Nf3 Nc6 4. b4 B×b4 5. c3 Ba5** "This move is favored by Zukertort, and is generally adopted by the Berlin and Vienna masters. Bird, the English player, prefers 5. ... Bc5, and Steinitz in the last great tournaments also selected it"—Bird. **6. d4 e×d4 7. Qb3 Qf6 8. 0–0 d×c3 9. e5 Qg6 10. N×c3 Nge7** "These are approved opening moves in this form of defense; the choice of continuations considered best rests between 11. Ba3, 11. Bb2, 11. Re1, 11. Nd5 and 11. Ne2. White's knight at c3 is rarely captured by Black, as White, though two pawns minus, secures an attack which is seldom successfully resisted. Blackburne concurs in this view"—Bird. **11. Ne2 b5** "The advance of this pawn is made with the object of instituting a counterattack, which Black obtains by 12. ... Rb8, if White captures the pawn"—Bird. **12. Bd3 Qe6 13. Qb2** "Considered best, though 13. Qb1 or 13. Qd1 have many supporters"—Bird. **13. ... Ng6** "The knight here, besides attacking the e-pawn, again occupies a powerful position, both for defense and attack. Now it is deemed desirable to dislodge it by playing 14. Nf4"—Bird. **14. Nf4 N×f4 15. B×f4 h6** "A necessary precaution before castling, on account of 16. B×h7†, and as a guard against other contingencies"—Bird. **16. Rac1 0–0** "Previous to this move the game had followed the line of play most approved by modern analysts of the Compromised Defense. The book continuation here is 16. ... a6"—Dust. **17. Rfd1 Bb6** "Still willing to lose the b-pawn to divert the attack"—Bird. **18. Bb1 Ne7 19. Qc2** Bird doesn't hide his intentions to attack Black's king, but his opponent is relatively well placed to defend himself. Therefore he could consider 19. Q×b5 instead.

**19. ... Ng6 20. Nh4 Bb7 21. Nf5** "If Black now threatened mate, or exchange of queens by 21. ... Qc6, White, by retorting with 22. Ne7†, would win Black's queen or give checkmate"—Bird. **21. ... Rfe8 22. Qd3 Rad8 23. Bg3 a6 24. h4 Bc6 25. Kh2 Nf8?!** White's task would have been very difficult after 25. ... N×e5! **26. Qd2** Suddenly, after 26. h5! White has good pressure against Black's king. Subsequently, he can maneuvre his knight towards g4. **26. ... h5?** A lethal weakness. The onus to prove his compensation remains on White after 26. ... Ng6. **27. Qg5 g6** (*see diagram*) "From this point to the end the game is very instructive"—Dust. Against 27. ... Ng6, White plays 28. Q×h5 and afterwards prepares the march of the h-pawn.

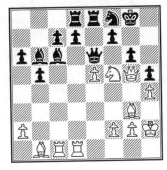

*After 27. ... g6*

**28. R×c6!** "The plausible moves of 28. Qh6 or 28. Nh6† would be useless, and to retire the knight would leave Black with an impregnable position and two pawns advantage. The curious and instructive finish planned by White was quite overlooked by his opponent, as well as the spectators"—Bird. **28. ... Q×c6** "If 28. ... d×c6, he loses a piece for two pawns and gets a bad game"—Dust. **29. Nh6†** "Very well-conceived by White, Black naturally moves to g7 to avoid losing his valuable f-pawn, and White, instead of simply gaining a material advantage, secures the gain of the queen, or checkmate"—Bird. **29. ... Kg7 30. Rd6!** "A very fine move, by which White obtains a decisive advantage"—Dust. **30. ... c×d6 31. Qf6† K×h6 32. Qh8† Nh7 33. Bf4† g5 34. Q×h7** mate—*The Times* (Bird), 28 November 1884; *Manchester Weekly Post* (Dust), 29 November 1884.

---

## MODERN CHESS

Thanks to the financial support received from his recent testimonial Bird was able to spend time working on his new chess book. A first installment was ready during the summer months of 1884.[23] According to the *Illustrated London News* of 1 November 1884, it was Bird's design to publish 12 installments on a monthly basis. Other sources and Bird himself in the introduction (p. 2) speak of ten parts. At any rate, with the price set at 1s., each booklet was affordable for anyone.

23. MacDonnell was one of the first to have a look: "Mr. H.E. Bird has in the press a primer entitled *Modern Chess*. Having glanced at the proof a few days ago, I am happy to be able to say that the preface is highly racy and amusing, while the lessons on the game are conveyed in a form and manner that every reading and writing child will be able easily to comprehend and thoroughly to enjoy. The price of the book is one shilling, and the publisher is James Wade, 18, Tavistock Street, Covent Garden." *Illustrated Sporting and Dramatic News*, 9 August 1884.

With *Modern Chess* Bird wanted to present his readers with a kind of follow-up to his well acclaimed *Chess Masterpieces*, which offered a selection of the best games between the greatest players. But this time the emphasis was placed on his own worthwhile efforts. Bird would of course not betray himself, and included "select games played by myself and others illustrative of novel lines of play in the openings, which in opposition to the generally-received opinions of chess theorists, I have long advocated and practiced, alike in important contests and in ordinary play, and I shall bring to special notice such débuts as have been least analyzed in the books, but which have led to many of the best recent games" (p. 2). The first installment (32 pages) of what would become *Modern Chess*, contained some of Bird's most highly reputed games. Bird also gave a survey of two of his favorite lines: the advance of the b-pawn in the Giuoco Piano and the Dutch Defense.

The second installment, which appeared in February 1885, was divided into two sections. In section A, Bird paid some more attention to the same openings as in the first installment, while he also introduced another favorite of his, 1. f4. Section B was dedicated to a selection of games played by Bird during his younger days.

The third installment was released in March 1885: The Ruy Lopez, of which Bird was no longer an adherent, was the main subject. Bird gave special attention to his own antidote, 3. ... Nd4.

In the fourth installment, which appeared in May 1885, Bird responded to some critics who accused him of publishing too much of his own games. In it, he published several games played by Steinitz, Anderssen and Zukertort, but nevertheless included some of his own best achievements as well as the complete run of his match with Steinitz from 1866.

Now there came a serious hiatus in the production process and for nearly two years nothing more was heard about a fifth installment. It was probably friction with his publisher that caused the delay, for from the fifth installment onward, it was Dean and Son who released Bird's writings.

The fifth installment did not appear until March 1887. Its 36 pages were dedicated to the Evans Gambit. By now the games played by Bird were mainly replaced by a selection of games played by a variety of his colleagues. With this fifth installment, the first volume of *Modern Chess* came to an end, according to the *Nottinghamshire Guardian* of 18 March 1887. Five more installments had been planned but the considerable delay in publishing the fifth installment showed that interest was waning.

Bird released a sixth installment in April 1887, and this proved to be the final one. The Evans Gambit as well as various forms of the King's Gambit nearly completely filled the last pages of *Modern Chess*.[24] Three months later the entire book was released as a whole for the price of 7s.

24. An interesting, yet critical review about Bird's suggested improvements in the Evans Gambit appeared in the June 1887 edition of the *British Chess Magazine* (pp. 237–238). Edward Freeborough was the man holding the pen: "His details are fragmentary and distributed about generally. He gives the day-book instead of the ledger and leaves his readers to make a debtor and creditor account for themselves. It will, however, be seen from the above that the general character of his suggestions is that the player should take the risk of an uncomfortable game in consideration of a possibly compensating advantage in the end. ... Says Mr. Bird frankly, "it is urged, I know, by the great authorities that I like hair-breadth games, and that they suit me, and even my best friends in the circle are not disposed to accept any dictum of mine at variance with defenses adopted and sanctioned by Anderssen, Morphy, Steinitz, and other great players, and which are still recommended by the book authorities."

# ◆ Part IX ◆

# THE HEYDAY OF THE ASSOCIATIONS, 1885–1887

## A NEW TURN

The year 1885 was the threshold to a new era in Bird's life. At the beginning of the year he was 55 years old and one of England's most experienced and respected players. Up till then his relationship with chess had mostly been intense, although there were times when he had abandoned the game. Bird's last "farewell" occurred at the end of 1880 with a long pamphlet that clearly shows his annoyance with the evolution of chess—but even within a couple of months Bird

suffered withdrawal symptoms and started to revisit the chess rooms of Purssell's. In 1882 Bird rejoined the guild of chess masters in Vienna and he would never give up the game again (not counting absences due to health issues).

Bird's ties with accountancy, on the other hand, became more loose. After the break-up of his partnership with George Brand, Bird fell back on his existing network of friends and acquaintances to find the necessary jobs to survive. In the summer of 1884 he planned to release a work on railway statistics. The money gathered by his chess friends in the form of a testimonial (see end of Part

VIII) created the conditions in which he could pursue this work. Early in 1885 he received another welcome assignment when he was appointed to audit the books of the rejuvenated British Chess Association.

Bird's cherished status of chess amateur came under pressure. His fascination for the game was still intact, and perhaps greater than ever, but contrary to the previous decades it started to become a necessity for him to find ways to make chess supplement his income. Bird remained a visitor to the many London chess resorts, but from 1888 onwards his presence at Simpson's Divan easily stands out. Here he built a network of friends, admirers and clients. His accessibility, conversational skills and attractive playing style made him the most popular player there who was trying to earn his living from the game. From a venerated veteran player he evolved into a living legend. A man of myth.

Bird also started to undertake chess tours throughout the provinces. He gave simultaneous displays and made himself available for consultation and offhand chess against anyone interested in meeting him over the board. The usual standards of a shilling per game were applied to these skittles.

## SKIPWORTH'S ANGUISH

At first sight the year 1884 seemed to be a quiet one in the history of chess but this was not so. There had been no major tournaments nor matches, but a lot was going on behind the scenes. The tournament of 1883 had left a great enthusiasm for the game. British chess was living in its heyday and the call for a strong national organization that included all chess players (provincial and metropolitan, amateurs as well as professionals) became louder and louder. The British Chess Association, the last organization with such ambitions, was seen as defunct since its last major tournament was held in 1872. While the B.C.A. was just a memory, the other major association, the Counties Chess Association, was still active. The attitude of the C.C.A. towards metropolitan and professional chess players had since its founding been skeptical. They had relaxed some of their rules for their congress in Glasgow in 1875, but this experience hardly appeared satisfying and a more stringent approach was adhered to during subsequent congresses.

Skipworth had always been the man behind the ideological legacy of the C.C.A., but his experiences in the international tournament of London as well as his contacts with metropolitan chess circles eventually convinced him that his group had to widen its perspective and allow all British amateurs to join their ranks. If Skipworth would abstain from the nationalization of the C.C.A. its finances, that were already under the gun, were likely to become problematic. In a public letter published in *Land and Water* on 8 March 1884, he announced his plans to broaden the scope of the C.C.A. by organizing a tournament open to "all comers," whether professionals or not. For this purpose he was on the look-out for new funds. Potter, the column's chess editor, and Bird supported his initiative, but some representatives from within the C.C.A. placed a burden on Skipworth's, in their view, willful plans.

Putting Mr. Minchin and his logic aside, we turn to Mr. Bird, who argued that the Counties Chess Association ought to be the national association of this country. In this opinion there would be much force were it not out of date. Mr. Skipworth, in his original letter to our column, expressed his wish to "nationalize" the C.C.A., and with that object he proposed to start an all comer's tournament. He had to abandon the project owing to strong opposition from his own camp [*Land and Water*, 16 August 1884].

## THE FORMATION OF A NATIONAL ASSOCIATION

The most widely anticipated chess event of the year 1885 took place on 19 January. For the second time in history a match was fought between the two major chess clubs residing in London: the City of London and the St. George's. Their first duel had been played in March 1881 and was won by St. George's Chess Club. A large number of witnesses, with Bird among them, saw the City of London Chess Club gain their revenge convincingly: 12 to 8. The presence of many prominent figures caused Leopold Hoffer to arrange the first general meeting of the just established British Chess Association on 20 January.

A few months earlier, Hoffer had made ample use of his column in *The Field* and his magazine *Chess Monthly* to promote the revitalization of the British Chess Association. He worked out a scheme according to which the various chess clubs, societies and associations within the United Kingdom could federate with the B.C.A. at the cost of a nominal subscription. His proposal was presented for the first time at a meeting at the Divan on 24 July 1884.

**Leopold Hoffer (courtesy Cleveland Public Library).**

A large number of chess players and club representatives from all over the country attended this meeting. At the end of the evening a council was elected and the already familiar name of the British Chess Association got officially adopted. Just a week later Hoffer visited the congress of the Counties Chess Association in Bath. The changes in London had evidently been observed with suspicion. The question everybody wanted to ask was whether the B.C.A. intended to organize their tournaments out of London, on terrain supposedly appertaining to the C.C.A. Hoffer obviously did not exclude this option, not wanting to limit his association from the start. Thus he acknowledged that the relationship between both associations was likely to be a complex one. Quite an ambiguous element in the whole story was the presence of several of the C.C.A.'s representatives (Skipworth above all, but also Wayte and Thorold, who were however less hostile towards what happened in London) within the council of the B.C.A. This encompassed a possible collaboration, but might just as well weaken the B.C.A. from the inside.

On 15 December 1884 a meeting of the council of the B.C.A. took place at the Divan. On this occasion a constitution was drawn up and the first general meeting was planned on the day after the important club match. The constitution was officially adopted at the general meeting of 20 January 1885. At the same time the first chess congress was announced to be held within a few months notice at the rooms of Simpson's Divan. Bird was involved in the B.C.A. from the beginning. Thomas Hewitt proposed to appoint him as the auditor of the organization. This was seconded with much approval for "a bird in hand is worth two in the bush."

While the B.C.A. was now really under way, its start was not as rosy as Hoffer and his companions would have wished. Already at the general meeting Skipworth expressed his fear of an interference with his C.C.A. He therefore proposed to limit all the activities of the B.C.A. to London, but this was to no avail.[1]

The federation idea, so it became clear during the next few months, was not hailed in every corner of the country. Among the various clubs that did not wish to join the B.C.A. the City of London Chess Club was the most important.[2]

---

1. Hoffer in *Chess Monthly*, February 1885, p. 162 retorted: "Mr. Hoffer contended that the very name of the association implied that it is their duty to hold their meetings in the provinces as well as in town, otherwise they could not possibly apply to the provinces for support, and the association would then not be British but metropolitan. Both societies must leave it to the country which association they would support."

2. Their (and other's) arguments to refuse the invitation were reiterated by the London correspondent of the *International Chess Magazine*: "I believe that it is no secret that the federation idea never met with the sympathies of the officials of the club, and undoubtedly the great bulk of the members shared their views. ... Many disliked the childish idea (as they termed it) of conferring degrees for proficiency, in what after all is not a science, but merely a game, though it may be the most scientific of games. Others thought the ostensible committee of the Association but a lot of 'ornamental figure heads' (these are not my words, bien entendu, but others) and that the real power would be in the hands of one or two persons, perhaps not the best fitted for such a position. Again others thought in the organization of the Association too little consideration had been shown to such strong clubs as the City, which club indeed, in the opinion of many, had been practically ignored in laying the lines upon which the Association could be run. There were yet again some who thought the real management of the Association too despotic, and one under which it would not be well for the City to place itself, and these argued that a club of nearly 300 members, and one standing at the head of all English clubs in playing strength, was not likely to gain anything by being at 'beck and call' of the officials of another association." *International Chess Magazine*, June 1885, p. 164.

## THE BRITISH CHESS HEGEMONY

While the enthusiasm for chess remained intact after the London 1883 tournament, there certainly was a drain from talent in the British capital. Steinitz had already left London in 1882. Subsequent to his triumph in London, his main rival Zukertort was absent for longer times undertaking chess tours throughout the United States. Blackburne already had the habit of spending a lot of time touring the provinces. In an attempt to remedy a faltering health, he left England towards the end of 1884 for a recovery journey that brought him to Australia.

The arrival of the B.C.A. was a blessing for the remaining British chess masters. The rivalry with the C.C.A was often filled with intrigues and trouble, but it also had the beneficial side effect that they both tried to outbid each other in organizing the best and strongest tournament.

As a consequence the matter of the so-called British chess hegemony gained in importance. With Steinitz gone and Zukertort preparing an attempt to wrest the title from Steinitz, Blackburne, back from Australia to play a few tournaments during the summer of 1885, was considered the strongest player. Yet, several others found themselves eligible to challenge his position. Two of these rivals are worth mentioning as they would rapidly gain in status and occupy a top spot in the British chess hierarchy.

First there was Amos Burn. Burn had pursued a merchant career and adapted his chess ambitions to this. For twenty years he had mostly limited himself to playing in and around his home town Liverpool. Burn was the most successful participant at the congresses of the C.C.A. From 1886 onwards he enhanced his playing spectre. Despite his already relatively advanced age he was increasingly successful at tournaments and matches.

Another player making great leaps forward was Isidor Gunsberg. His previous results had not been very remarkable. He ended, respectably, fourth at the Vizayanagaram tournament of 1883 while his international debut in Nuremberg a few weeks later was a failure. The year 1885, however, saw him as the world's most successful and ambitious player.

Bird clearly wished to measure his strength with all aspiring rivals but it was clear to almost everybody (he himself the notable exception) that his status as a top player was in decline. While, until a few years ago, he could present himself as a worthy challenger of Blackburne, there were now a great deal more rivals in the field. With the increase of tournaments a real battle among them had developed. Bird's results were mixed at best, and it became more and more obvious that he had slipped back from the front rank.

A turnaround in the revival of British chess began in 1887. The B.C.A. and the C.C.A. begrudged each other and a poisonous atmosphere was created. For their congress of 1887 the C.C.A. returned to their old recipe of banning professional players. In the meantime, the discontent had matured and a serious row broke out about Skipworth's autocratic ways. He resigned his position as secretary in 1888 and the C.C.A. came to an end. (There was a final, but less meaningful revival in the 1890s.)

Also in 1887 Hoffer experienced trouble setting up the congress of his B.C.A. Bird nearly stole his wind by taking steps to arrange a Jubilee tournament in honor of Queen Victoria's fiftieth year on the throne. Bird's efforts were cut short by Hoffer, which generated quite some grumpiness in certain corners. One of the effects was the start-up of a series of handicap tournaments that invigorated chess life at Simpson's Divan for the next decade. Bird was one of the backers of this project.

The three following editions of the B.C.A. congresses (1888–1890) were more successful, but the congress of 1891 was postponed until February 1892. This was clearly a sign: Most of life had faded from the B.C.A. and later that year Hoffer announced its demise.

The battle for British chess hegemony became closely interwoven with the world championship once Zukertort was beaten by Steinitz in 1886. It became the source of an endless number of quarrels and disputes within the small arena of the London chess world. Matches were played to test each other's strength, but players often avoided each other to keep their reputations intact. With the demise of the B.C.A., the ambition-driven British chess hegemony was also nearing its end. Gunsberg skillfully guaranteed himself an attempt at the crown, but he was also beaten by Steinitz in 1891. By then foreign players such as Tarrasch and Lasker were lining up one tournament victory after another. Their British counterparts were older gentlemen, who had to be content with lower places in the international tournaments and who were clearly superseded by the younger generation.

# MEETING THE CLERGY IN LONDON, JANUARY 1885

Skipworth was enjoying a longer stay in London in January 1885. He defended the colors of the St. George's club in the grand match of 19 January and did the same for the C.C.A. at the general meeting of the B.C.A. Bird made good use of the Reverend Skipworth's presence in the capital to play a number of offhand games. A few of the more remarkable ones Skipworth released to the press.

**(691) Bird–Skipworth    0–1**
Offhand game
London (St. George's C.C.), 14 January 1885
C30

**1. e4 e5 2. f4 Bc5 3. Nf3 d6 4. c3 Nc6 5. Bc4 Nf6 6. d3 a6 7. b4 Ba7 8. Qe2 Bg4 9. f5 B×f3 10. Q×f3 N×b4 11. Na3 Nc6 12. Rb1 Na5 13. Bg5 0–0 14. Nc2 b5 15. Bb3 N×b3 16. R×b3 c5 17. Ra3 b4 18. R×a6 Bb6 19. R×a8 Q×a8 20. 0–0 Q×a2 21. B×f6 g×f6 22. Ne3 c4 23. d4 b×c3 24. Ng4 B×d4† 25. Kh1 Qd2 26. N×f6† Kh8 27. Qh3 h6 28. Ng4 c2 29. N×h6 c1Q 30. N×f7† Kg8 31. Qg3† K×f7 32. Qg6† Ke7 33. Qe6† Kd8 34. Q×d6† Kc8 35. Q×f8† Kb7 36. Qe7† Ka6 37. Qd6† Bb6** White resigns—*Glasgow Weekly Herald*, 21 February 1885.

**(692) Skipworth–Bird    1–0**
Offhand game
London (St. George's C.C.), January 1885
C24

**1. e4 e5 2. Bc4 Nf6 3. Qe2 Nc6 4. c3 Be7 5. d3 d6 6. Nf3 Bg4 7. Nbd2 a6 8. Nf1 Na5 9. Ng3 0–0 10. Bg5 Re8** "10. ... N×e4 could

be played. Neither injury nor benefit would accrue from it: 11. N×e4 B×f3 12. B×e7 B×e2 13. B×d8 Ra×d8 14. K×e2 d5, winning back the piece with an even game. 10. ... N×e4 yields many other variations, but they are all colored with a neutral tint. In one of them White may give up the pawn for an attack, but he gets no more than the pawn's worth. As to the text move it is not very good. 10. ... N×c4 11. d×c4 Ne8 is Black's best line"—Potter. **11. h3 Bd7 12. Bb3 N×b3 13. a×b3 Qc8 14. Nh4 g6** Some important weaknesses on the black squares are hereby created. 14. ... Nd5! 15. B×e7 Nf4 relieves the tension without submitting to any concessions. **15. Qf3 Nd5** 15. ... Kg7 (Hoffer) is not bad. **16. B×e7 N×e7 17. Qf6 Qd8 18. Qg5 Nc6 19. Qh6 Qf6** 19. ... Qe7 is safer. Now the queen ends up in a strange spot and White retains some pressure. **20. Nh5 Qh8 21. g4?** A cocky sacrifice, the acceptance of which would have left Skipworth empty-handed. Instead 21. Qg5 Re6 22. f4 maintains the pressure. **21. ... Re6?** *(see diagram)*

*After 21. ... Re6*

**22. Rg1! f6 23. f4! e×f4** "Taking the knight might have the following result: 23. ... g×h5 24. g×h5† Kf7 25. Nf5 Rg8 26. R×g8 Q×g8 27. Kf2, which threatens 28. Rg1 with a very strong attack. Other ways of playing are conceivable, but this would be our way, and probably Mr. Skipworth had it in view also, seeing that but for his move 23. f4 this line would not be at White's disposal"—Potter. **24. N×f4 Re7 25. Nd5 Rf7 26. 0–0–0?** "The stage of violence is over, but let it not be rashly imagined that White's attack is gone. On the contrary, he has obtained what we regard as a won game"—Potter. Both Skipworth and Potter didn't appreciate the simple 26. N×c7, when Black has absolutely nothing for the pawn. **26. ... Be6 27. d4** After this move, all advantage vanishes after 27. ... B×d5! (Potter). 27. Nf5 maintains some pressure. **27. ... Qg7 28. Nf5! Qf8?** 28. ... B×f5 is perhaps passive but yet absolutely necessary. **29. Qh4 g5 30. Qh5** 30. Nh6† Kg7 31. Qh5 and 32. h4! keeps the attack going on at full speed, but there is nothing wrong with Skipworth's way of dealing either. **30. ... B×f5 31. g×f5 Re8 32. h4 h6 33. h×g5 f×g5 34. Qg6†** "White now reaps the fruits of skill, and the long innate victory assumes shape and form"—Potter. **34. ... Qg7 35. Nf6† R×f6 36. Q×e8† Kh7 37. Qh5 Na5 38. Kc2 d5 39. e5 R×f5 40. Rdf1 Qf8 41. Qe2 Kg6 42. e6 Nc6 43. Kd2 Ne7 44. R×f5 N×f5 45. Rf1 h5 46. Qd3** Black resigns. "Mr. Skipworth's play during the greater part of the game is characterized by much tactical skill, and also by a continuous exercise of insight to an extent that we do not often find in offhand games"—Potter. *Land and Water* (Potter), 28 February 1885.

Bird also encountered William Wayte, the strongest player of the St. George's Chess Club. One game, found in the notebooks of Wayte, resulted in a merciless slugfest.

## (693) Bird–Wayte    0–1

Offhand game
London (St. George's C.C.), 27 January 1885
C33

**1. e4 e5 2. f4 e×f4 3. Bc4 d5 4. B×d5 Qh4† 5. Kf1 g5 6. Nf3 Qh5 7. B×f7†** An inspired, but incorrect, sacrifice. **7. ... Q×f7 8. Ne5 Qf6** 8. ... Qg7, keeping f6 open for the knight, saves him a lot of trouble. **9. Qh5† Ke7 10. d4 Nd7 11. Nc3 c6 12. h4 N×e5 13. d×e5 Q×e5 14. h×g5 Bg7 15. Qh4 Be6 16. B×f4 Qc5 17. Rd1 Bc4†** 17. ... Rd8!, with the idea of liberating his knight after 18. R×d8 K×d8, is much better. Thanks to the text move, Bird gains some chances. **18. Ke1 Be5** 18. ... Rd8 is still the best possible move. **19. g6†** Wayte's fault in offering the exchange of bishops is highlighted in the severe weaknesses of the black squares around his king after 19. Qg3! B×f4 20. Q×f4 Ke8 21. e5, when the imminent arrival of the knight spells trouble. **19. ... Nf6** The knight joins the defense and this ought to terminate Bird's attack quickly. **20. g7 Rhg8 21. Qg3 B×f4 22. Q×f4 R×g7 23. e5 Ng4 24. Rd4 N×e5** Extremely risky, as the king now enters the front. 24. ... Be6 is simple enough. **25. Re4 Ke6** *(see diagram)* Wayte goes completely wrong, but he probably noted and wished to avoid the drawing tendencies after 25. ... Rf8 26. R×e5† Kd7 27. Qd2† Qd6.

*After 25. ... Ke6*

**26. Rh6†** But 26. b4! wins at once; e.g., 26. ... Qd6 27. Rh6†! (more precise than 27. Rh5 when 27. ... Kd7 escapes from the worst) 27. ... Rg6 28. Rh5, and if now 28. ... Kd7 29. R×h7† is another story. **26. ... Rg6 27. Qg4†** 27. b4 Qg1† is not good anymore. 27. Na4! is the way to go: 27. ... Qa5† 28. Nc3 and now 28. ... Qc5, planning 29. ... Rf8, is correct, but allows a repetition of move. **27. ... Kf6** 27. ... Kf7! 28. Qf4† Kg8 escapes definitively. **28. Qh4†?** 28. Qf4† Ke6 29. Na4 returns to the previous drawing line. **28. ... Ke6 29. Qh3† Kd6** The king finally reaches a safe haven. **30. Re3 Bd5 31. R×h7 Re8 32. Ne2 Q×e3 33. Q×e3 Nf3†** White resigns—*Manuscript games of W. Wayte*, vol. 11, game 1189.

# IN THE PROVINCES, MARCH–JUNE 1885

Bird embarked on his first fully-fledged chess tour through the provinces in the spring of 1885. A few days before he left the capital Bird delighted his fans with a brilliancy played at Gatti's Café, one of London's minor chess resorts.

## (694) Bird–Maltby    1–0

Offhand game
London (Gatti's), 23 March 1885
A02

**1. f4 f5 2. e4** "This opening, greatly in vogue about 1861, was the precursor of From's Gambit, which appeared in 1862. The latter is a reversal of the above opening, Black assuming the attack as follows: 1. f4 e5 2. f×e5 d6 3. e×d6 B×d6 4. Nf3 Nh6 etc. Both openings enjoyed a short-lived popularity on account of their questionable soundness"—Hoffer. **2. ... f×e4 3. d3 e×d3 4. B×d3 Nf6 5. Nf3 d6 6. f5 Nbd7 7. Be3 Ne5 8. N×e5 d×e5 9. 0–0 Qd6** After this move, the queen is likely to end in the line of fire. Black's position is fine after 9. ... e6. **10. Nc3 Bd7 11. Qe2 a6 12. a3** Bird takes his time to begin the assault, but this is of little use. Better is 12. Rad1 at once. **12. ... e6** 12. ... 0–0–0 is still playable. **13. f×e6** 13. Ne4! is very strong now; 13. ... Qe7 (13. ... N×e4 14. Qh5† loses instantly) 14. f×e6 Q×e6 15. N×f6† g×f6 16. Bf5 Qf7 17. B×d7† Q×d7 18. R×f6. **13. ... Q×e6 14. Bf5 Qf7 15. B×d7† Q×d7 16. Rad1 Bd6 17. Qc4 Qf7** Bird's attacking play hasn't been very convincing and here 17. ... 0–0–0 (Hoffer) would have ended it. **18. Nd5 0–0 19. Bg5 Kh8** *(see diagram)* The best move.

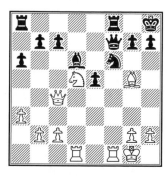

*After 19. ... Kh8*

**20. R×f6** 20. B×f6 g×f6 21. R×f6 Qg7 22. Rdf1 R×f6 23. R×f6 Rf8 24. Qh4 etc., a line suggested by Hoffer, gives White a small initiative. The text move is much trickier. **20. ... g×f6?** Maltby is taken by surprise by Bird's unexpected move. Some expertise was needed to spot that 20. ... Qh5! was the correct defense. After 21. Rff1 Q×g5 22. N×c7 b5 23. Qc6 B×c7 24. Q×c7 h6 the position is equal. **21. B×f6† Kg8 22. Rd3 e4 23. Rg3†** "A very pretty finish. There is another mate in reversing the moves with 23. Ne7† B×e7 24. Rg3 mate"—Hoffer. **23. ... B×g3 24. Ne7** mate—*The Field* (Hoffer), 17 October 1885.

Bird spent the last days of March in the Manchester region as the guest of Joseph Buckley Reyner. Reyner's family has been connected to the cotton spinning industry for decades, and he was one of the pivotal figures of his hometown, Ashton-under-Lyne. On 27 March Bird gave a simultaneous performance against 17 opponents.

## (695) J.D. Waterhouse–Bird    0–1

Simultaneous game
Ashton-under-Lyne, 27 March 1885
C56

**1. e4 e5 2. Nf3 Nc6 3. Bc4 Bc5 4. c3 Nf6 5. d4 e×d4 6. 0–0 0–0 7. c×d4 Bb6 8. Bg5?** 8. e5! is strong. The text move simply throws a pawn away. **8. ... h6 9. Bh4 g5 10. Bg3 N×e4 11. Qd3** 11. d5 is necessary to complicate the position. **11. ... d5 12. Bb3 Be6 13. Nc3 f5 14. Be5 g4 15. Nd2 Kh7 16. Ne2 N×e5 17. d×e5 Qh4 18. g3 Qe7** 18. ... N×f2 19. R×f2 B×f2† 20. K×f2 Q×h2† 21. Ke3 c6 leaves White's king in danger. **19. Nf4 Rad8 20. Qe2 Kg7 21. Bc2 c5 22. Bd3 Ng5 23. b3 Bc7 24. Rae1 Ba5 25. Rd1 B×d2 26. R×d2 Bd7 27. Bb5** "Had White played 27. N×d5, then something of this kind would have followed: 27. ... Nh3† 28. Kh1 Bc6 etc. The text move is in accordance with the score sheet, but it seems probable that this and White's next move have been transposed in copying, otherwise Black might now reply with 27. ... B×b5 and 28. ... Nf3†, winning a piece"—Dust. **27. ... d4 28. Kg2 Nf3 29. B×d7 Q×d7 30. Rdd1 Qc6 31. e6 Rfe8 32. Rh1 d3 33. Qb2† Rd4 34. h3 R×e6** Various roads lead to Rome. Bird, not unexpectedly, selects the prettiest. **35. N×e6† Kg8 36. Nf4 R×f4 37. g×f4 Nd4† 38. Kg1 Ne2† 39. Kh2 Qf3** and Black wins—*Manchester Weekly Post* (Dust), 4 April 1885.

Bird spent the two following days near Heathfield. He contested two games with Reyner and three with James Dean Waterhouse's wife, Elizabeth Walmsley. Bird thanked his opponents for their hospitality with the publication of two games.

### (696) E.W. Waterhouse–Bird   ½–½
Simultaneous game
Heathfield, 28 March 1885
C54

**1. e4 e5 2. Nf3 Nc6 3. Bc4 Bc5 4. 0-0 Nf6 5. d3 0-0 6. c3 d6 7. Bg5 Be6 8. B×e6 f×e6 9. h3 Qe8 10. b4 Bb6 11. Nbd2 Nh5 12. Nc4 Nf4 13. Nh4 h6 14. B×f4 e×f4 15. N×b6 a×b6 16. d4 g5 17. b5 Ne7 18. Qg4 Kh7 19. Nf3 Qg6 20. h4 g×h4 21. Q×g6† N×g6 22. Kh2 Rg8 23. Kh3** draw. "In this, as well as in two other contests my fair opponent showed wonderful skill and judgment for so young a player"—Bird. *Modern Chess* (Bird), p. 112.

### (697) Bird–Reyner   ½–½
Offhand game
Heathfield, 29 March 1885
C51

"This was the second of two interesting games played with Mr. Reyner"—Bird.

**1. e4 e5 2. Nf3 Nc6 3. Bc4 Bc5 4. b4 B×b4 5. c3 Bc5 6. d4 e×d4 7. c×d4 Bb6 8. Nc3 d6 9. 0-0 Bg4 10. Be3 Nf6 11. a4 a6 12. Nd5 N×d5 13. B×d5 B×f3 14. g×f3 Rb8 15. f4 Ne7 16. Ba2 c6 17. Qh5 d5 18. e5 g6 19. Qf3 Nf5 20. Rad1 N×e3 21. f×e3 0-0 22. Kh1 f6 23. Rg1 f5 24. Rg5 Qd7 25. Rdg1 Rf7 26. Bb1 Rbf8 27. Qh5 Rg7 28. Qh6 Bd8 29. R5g2 Qe7** draw—*Modern Chess* (Bird), pp. 112–113.

Bird, who enjoyed a great popularity among Mancunians (especially among the young ones, according to the chess press), was the guest of the Athenaeum Chess Club on 14 April. Even though the exhibition was organized on short notice, 21 players opposed the master. Bird worked hard and after four and a half hours, he had scored 16 wins, 1 loss, against F.J. Hamel, and 4 draws (with J. Symes, J.P. Kenrick, G. Worrall and A.B. Rink).

### (698) Bird–Whatham   1–0
Simultaneous game
Manchester (Athenaeum C.C.), 14 April 1885
C51

**1. e4 e5 2. Nf3 Nc6 3. Bc4 Bc5 4. b4 B×b4 5. c3 Bc5 6. d4 e×d4 7. c×d4 Bb6 8. Bb2 Nf6 9. d5 Na5 10. Bd3 d6 11. Nc3 0-0 12. Ne2 c6 13. Bc3 c×d5 14. e×d5 h6 15. Bc2 a6 16. Rb1 Ba7 17. Qd3 g6 18. Qd2 Nc4 19. Q×h6 B×f2† 20. Kd1 Ne3† 21. Kc1 Neg4 22. Qh3 Be3† 23. Kb2 Nf2 24. Qh4 Kg7 25. Ng5 Rh8 26. Qg3 B×g5 27. Q×g5 N×h1 28. Rf1 Kg8 29. B×g6 Qb6† 30. Kc2 Kf8 31. Q×f6** Black resigns—*Morning Post*, 27 April 1885.

### (699) F.J. Hamel–Bird   1–0
Simultaneous game
Manchester (Athenaeum C.C.), 14 April 1885
C45

**1. e4 e5 2. Nf3 Nc6 3. d4 e×d4 4. N×d4 Qh4 5. Nb5 Kd8 6. Be2 a6 7. N5c3 Nf6 8. g3 Qh3 9. Nd2 Bc5 10. Nb3 Qg2 11. Rf1 Ba7 12. Bf3 Q×h2 13. Qe2 Qh3 14. Bg5 Nd4 15. N×d4 B×d4 16. Nd5 Qe6 17. 0-0-0 Be5 18. Bg4 B×b2† 19. Kb1 Qc6 20. K×b2 h6 21. B×f6† g×f6 22. Rd3 Qb5† 23. Ka1 c6 24. Rb1 Qc5 25. Qf3 Qd6 26. Q×f6† Q×f6† 27. N×f6 Ke7 28. e5 b5 29. B×d7 Bb7 30. Bf5 Rad8 31. Rbd1 R×d3 32. R×d3 Bc8 33. B×c8 R×c8 34. Rd7† Ke6 35. f4** Black resigns—*Manchester Weekly Post*, 25 April 1885.

### (700) Bird–Riddell   1–0
Simultaneous game
Manchester (Athenaeum C.C.), 14 April 1885
C21

**1. e4 e5 2. d4 e×d4 3. c3 d×c3 4. Bc4 c×b2 5. B×b2 Nf6 6. e5 Bb4† 7. Kf1 d5 8. e×f6 d×c4 9. Qe2† Be6 10. f×g7 Rg8 11. Nc3 Qd3 12. Ne4 Nd7 13. Rd1 Q×e2† 14. N×e2 0-0-0 15. Nf4 Nc5 16. R×d8† R×d8 17. N×c5 B×c5 18. Bf6 Re8 19. N×e6 f×e6 20. Ke2 Kd7 21. Rd1† Bd6 22. Rd4 e5 23. Rh4 Ke6 24. R×h7 K×f6 25. Rh8 K×g7 26. R×e8 a5 27. Kd2 b5 28. Rb8 b4 29. Rb5 b3 30. a×b3 c×b3 31. Kc3 Bb4† 32. K×b3 c5 33. Kc4 Kg6 34. h4 Kh5 35. g3 Kg4 36. Kd3** and White wins—*Manchester Weekly Post*, 9 May 1885.

On 25 April Bird made a friendly call at the thirtieth annual meeting of the West Yorkshire Chess Association in Wakefield. Also present on the occasion was Isidor Gunsberg.

Bird gave his fifth and final simultaneous exhibition of the season in Manchester on Monday 26 April. Thirteen opponents awaited him at the Manchester Chess Club. Fourteen games were played that evening. Quite uncharacteristically the amateurs scored extremely well with 6 wins (by Boyer, A.R. Marriott, Whatham, Rink, Hart and Morton) and 1 draw (by Charles). Bird barely topped them with 7 wins. It was perhaps on this occasion that Bird was elected as an honorary member of the club.

At the end of the week, on 30 April, Bird arrived at the Huddersfield Junior Chess Club. This club had been established only six weeks earlier as a branch of the Huddersfield Chess Club. The circular that announced Bird's visit was sent out only the day before but nevertheless the attendance was very good.

Bird had few problems with his 20 opponents. He suffered 1 loss, from the hands of A.P. Wilson. Afterwards Bird explained some of his favorite openings to the audience. He concluded the evening with an encouraging word for the young players. With sufficient practice, he told them, they would be able to give him a good beating within a few years.

### (701) A.P. Wilson–Bird    1–0
Simultaneous game
Huddersfield, 30 April 1885
C35

**1. e4 e5 2. f4 e×f4 3. Nf3 Be7 4. Bc4 Bh4† 5. N×h4 Q×h4†
6. Kf1 Nc6 7. d4 f5 8. e5 f3 9. c3 f×g2† 10. K×g2 b6 11. Bd5 Nge7
12. Bf3 f4 13. Bd2 d6 14. e×d6 Bh3† 15. Kg1 c×d6 16. B×c6†
N×c6 17. Qe1† Q×e1† 18. B×e1 0–0 19. Kf2 f3 20. Bd2 Rae8
21. Re1 R×e1 22. B×e1 Bg2 23. Bd2 Re8 24. Be3 Ne7 25. Nd2
Nd5 26. Re1 Nf6 27. N×f3 B×f3 28. K×f3 Nd5 29. Bd2 R×e1
30. B×e1 b5 31. Bg3 Nb6 32. B×d6 Nc4 33. Ba3 a6 34. d5 Kf7
35. Kf4 N×a3 36. b×a3 Ke7 37. Ke4 Kd6 38. a4 g5 39. a×b5
a×b5 40. Kd4 h5 41. c4 b×c4 42. K×c4 g4 43. a4 h4 44. a5 g3
45. h×g3 h3 46. a6 Kc7 47. d6† Kc8 48. d7† and Black resigns—**
*Bradford Observer Budget*, 2 May 1885.

A few weeks later Bird gladly accepted the offer to spend a week at the Liverpool Chess Club as the guest of Sir William Watson Rutherford. The club had just moved into new rooms and a visit by Bird was seen as an excellent way to inaugurate them. During the week Bird played various exhibition and consultation games. On 16 May he gave a successful simultaneous performance: 15 players were beaten, three held the master to a draw. Two days later a seat was reserved for Bird at the club dinner.

### (702) Bird–Hvistendahl & Rutherford    0–1
Consultation game
Liverpool, May 1885
C33

**1. e4 e5 2. f4 e×f4 3. Be2** The first known occurrence of Bird playing this Lesser (Limited or Little were more used in Bird's days) Bishop's Gambit, which remained a favorite of his for the rest of his years, as "there is no opening from which the writer has derived more interesting or enjoyable games than this" (*Chess Novelties*, p. 41). According to MacDonnell, Bird also had a knack for an extremely obscure line in the King's Gambit: "The so-called American or Palmetto Gambit (1. e4 e5 2. f4 e×f4 3. g3) was frequently played many years ago by Mr. H.E. Bird" (*Illustrated Sporting and Dramatic News*, 2 July 1881). No games with this line have been found. **3. ...
Qh4† 4. Kf1 g5 5. d4 Nc6 6. g3 f×g3 7. Kg2 Q×e4† 8. Bf3 Q×d4
9. Qe2† Be7 10. Nc3 d5** Bird sacrificed half his pawns for nothing but an interesting game. He wouldn't even have that had the allies played 10. ... Qf2†. As Dust remarked in his notes to the game, such a move would have been advisable in a serious match game. **11. h×g3
g4** 11. ... Be6 leaves White with no trace of attack at all. **12. B×d5
Nf6 13. B×c6† b×c6 14. Bf4 Be6 15. Rd1 Qc5 16. B×c7** Bad

again, as Black gains some important tempi. **16. ... Nd5 17. Bf4
N×c3 18. b×c3 Bd5† 19. Kh2 Bc4 20. Qe3 Qh5† 21. Kg2 Bd5†
22. R×d5 Q×d5† 23. Kh2 h5 24. c4 Qf5 25. Ne2 h4 26. Nd4
Qg6** 26. ... Qc5 defends both c6 and e7. White can resign. The final phase of the game is marred by mistakes but is nevertheless fascinating. **27. Re1** If now the passive 27. ... Qf6 28. Nf5 h×g3† 29. Kg1 Bird would finally have conquered the initiative. The allies are correct to try their chance with a sharp counterattack. **27. ... h×g3†
28. Kg1 Rh1†! 29. K×h1 Qh5† 30. Kg1 Qh2† 31. Kf1** (*see diagram*)

*After 31. Kf1*

**31. ... 0–0–0?** The evident 31. ... g2† 32. Ke2 g1Q† 33. B×h2 Q×h2† 34. Kd3 Qd6 might have seemed a disappointment, as there is no direct win, but it leaves White struggling. **32. B×g3 Qh3†
33. Kf2** There are no more tricks after 33. Kg1! Rh8 34. Qf4. **33. ...
Bh4 34. Nf5?** Correct is 34. B×h4 Q×h4† 35. Kg1 Rh8 36. Qe4 or even simpler 34. Ne2. **34. ... Qh2†?** The brilliant 34. ... Rd2†! forces a draw; e.g., 35. Re2 Qh2† 36. Kf1 Rd1† 37. Re1 Qh1† 38. Kf2 Qh2†. **35. Kf1 Qh1† 36. Ke2** 36. Qg1 starts a winning regroupment: 36. ... Qf3† 37. Qf2 Qh1† 38. Ke2 Qe4† 39. Ne3. **36. ...
Qg2† 37. Bf2?** A blunder which is the result of Bird's effort to win at all cost. After 37. Qf2 (Dust) 37. ... Re8† 38. Kd2 Rd8† 39. Ke2 the outcome would be a draw. **37. ... B×f2 38. Ne7†** If 38. Q×f2 Rd2†. **38. ... Kb7 39. Rb1† Ka8** White resigns—*Manchester Weekly Post* (Dust), 30 May 1885.

### (703) Bird–Rutherford & Unknown    0–1
Consultation game
Liverpool, May 1885
C33

**1. e4 e5 2. f4 e×f4 3. Bc4 d5 4. B×d5 Nf6 5. Nc3 Bb4 6. d4
N×d5 7. e×d5 0–0 8. Nf3 Re8† 9. Kf2 c5 10. d×c5 B×c5† 11. Kf1
b6 12. a4 Ba6† 13. Nb5 g5 14. h4 g4 15. Ne1 Qd7 16. c4 B×b5
17. a×b5 Re4 18. b3 Qf5 19. Bb2 Nd7 20. Nd3 f3 21. g×f3 Re3
22. N×c5 R×f3† 23. Kg2 N×c5 24. Qd4 Qc2† 25. Kg1 Rg3†**
White resigns—*Liverpool Weekly Courier*, 21 November 1885.

### (704) Rutherford & Marke Wood–Bird    0–1
Consultation game
Liverpool, 13 May 1885
C44

**1. e4 e5 2. Nf3 Nc6 3. c3 d5 4. Bb5 d×e4 5. N×e5 Qd5 6. Qa4
Nge7 7. f4 e×f3 *e.p.* 8. N×f3 Bd7 9. 0–0 0–0–0 10. c4** "10. d4 was clearly a better move here"—Dust. **10. ... Qh5 11. Nc3 Nf5 12. d4
Bd6** A crucial loss of time. White can already resign after the

igorous 12. ... N×d4! 13. N×d4 N×d4 14. B×d7† R×d7 and if 5. Q×a7 Ne2† 16. N×e2 Bc5†. **13. c5 Be7 14. B×c6** Equality is ept by 14. Nd5 Rhe8 15. Nf4, keeping the kingside under solid rotection. **14. ... B×c6 15. Q×a7 b6** "Very risky even for an expert; ut Mr. Bird seems to have bent upon bringing about a critical potion at all hazards"—Dust. 15. ... N×d4 wins easily enough. The ext move is instantly losing after 16. Bf4. Instead the board gets on re. **16. Ne5 R×d4 17. N×c6 B×c5** "Threatening 18. ... Q×h2†; nd if 19. K×h2 Rh4 mate"—Dust. **18. Be3** 18. N×d4 (Dust) is far mpler. **18. ... N×e3** (see diagram)

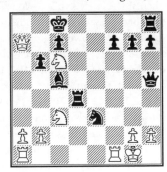

After 18. ... N×e3

**19. R×f7** 19. Nb5! wins. **19. ... Rd1†** Bird could narrowly save imself with 19. ... Q×f7 20. Qa6† Kd7 21. Ne5† Ke7 22. N×f7 Ng4! 23. Kh1 Nf2† 24. Kg1 Ng4 with a repetition of moves. **0. R×d1** 20. N×d1! wins, but only after an impressive series of rilliant tactical shots. 20. ... Ng4† 21. Nf2 Q×f7 22. Qa8† Kd7 3. Rd1† Bd6 24. Q×h8 Q×f2† 25. Kh1 K×c6 26. Qa8† Kd7 7. Qa4†. **20. ... Ng4† 21. Nd4 Q×h2†?** 21. ... B×d4† 22. R×d4 Q×h2† 23. Kf1 Qh1† 24. Ke2 Q×g2† 25. Kd1 Ne3† 26. Ke1 Nc2† s another narrow drawing line. **22. Kf1 Qh1† 23. Ke2 Q×g2† 4. Kd3??** The king traps itself in a mortal situation. The cool 4. Ke1 leaves Black with nothing; e.g., 24. ... Re8† 25. Nde2 R×e2† 6. N×e2 Bf2† 27. Kd2 Be3† 28. Kd3. **24. ... Ne5† 25. Ke3 Nc4† 6. Kd3 N×b2† 27. Ke3 Re8† 28. Kf4 Bd6† 29. Kf5 Qg6** mate— *Manchester Weekly Post* (Dust), 30 May 1885.

Bird interrupted his tour for a short while to fight out his match with Skipworth. Immediately after his victory he travelled north gain for an engagement in Newcastle. On 5 June he played 32 games in a simultaneous exhibition. These games were played on s few as six or as many as nine boards at once (the number varying f players joined or left without being replaced). Beaten players were hus offered a chance for a rematch. Bird remained in excellent form s he won 26 games, drew 4 (against Kersey, Downey, Campbell nd W. Mitcheson) and lost only 2, to Nicholson and W. Mitcheson. On his second and last day in Newcastle Bird played a lot of offhand kirmishes against the local amateurs.

**705) Bird–Unknown      1–0**
Offhand game
Newcastle, 6 June 1885
Odds of Ng1

**1. e4 e5 2. Bc4 Bc5 3. b4 B×b4 4. c3 Bc5 5. d4 e×d4 6. c×d4 Bb4† 7. Nd2 Nf6 8. e5 d5 9. e×f6 d×c4 10. f×g7 Rg8 11. Qh5 Qf6 12. 0-0 Q×d4 13. Re1† Kd8 14. Nf3 Q×g7 15. Bg5† f6**

**16. Rad1† Bd7 17. Nd4 Kc8 18. Ne6 B×e6 19. R×e6 Qg6 20. Qg4 Nd7 21. Re7 f5 22. Re×d7 Bd6 23. R7×d6 c×d6 24. Q×c4† Kb8 25. h4 a5 26. R×d6 Qg7 27. Qd5** and White wins—*Leeds Mercury*, 13 June 1885.

Before returning to London, Bird made a flying visit to the chess club in Leeds. He opposed 17 players on 8 June, scoring 13 wins, 2 draws (with J. Parker and J. White) and 2 losses (against T.Y. Stokoe and A.G. Dowling).

**(706) Bird–J. Parker      ½–½**
Simultaneous game
Leeds, 8 June 1885
C59

In a letter published in the *British Chess Magazine* (December 1928, p. 478), Diggle stated that Joys Parker, one of the founding fathers of the chess club in Grimsby (1875) never lost a game against a master in a simultaneous display. He has drawn with Bird and Pollock and has beaten Skipworth, Zukertort, Blackburne (twice), Yates and Capablanca.

**1. e4 e5 2. Nf3 Nc6 3. Bc4 Nf6 4. Ng5 d5 5. e×d5 Na5 6. Bb5† c6 7. d×c6 b×c6 8. Be2 h6 9. Nf3 e4 10. Ne5 Bd6 11. d4 Qc7 12. Bf4 0-0 13. Nd2 Nd5 14. Bg3 e3 15. Ndf3 e×f2† 16. B×f2 Nf4 17. 0-0 Re8 18. Bd3 c5 19. c3 Bb7 20. Bb5 Re7 21. Bg3 Nd5 22. Qa4 a6 23. Bd3 Nc6 24. Rae1 c×d4 25. c×d4 N×d4 26. N×d4 B×e5 27. Nf5 Re6 28. B×e5 R×e5 29. R×e5 Q×e5 30. Qd7 Qc7 31. Ne7† Kf8 32. Ng6† Kg8 33. Q×c7 N×c7 34. Bc4 Kh7 35. B×f7 Bd5 36. Ne5 B×f7 37. R×f7 Nd5 38. Rb7 Rc8 39. h4 Rc2 40. g4 Nf4 41. Rb3 Re2 42. Rf3 Re4 43. Kf1 Nd5 44. Nd7 R×g4 45. Ra3 R×h4 46. R×a6** and after a few more moves the game was drawn—*British Chess Magazine*, August-September 1885, pp. 295–297.

**(707) Bird–White      ½–½**
Simultaneous game
Leeds, 8 June 1885
A03

**1. f4 e6 2. Nf3 d5 3. e3 Nf6 4. b3 Bd7 5. Bb2 Be7 6. c4 c6 7. Bd3 Na6 8. Nc3 Nc5 9. Bb1 Qb6 10. d4 Na6 11. c5 Qc7 12. 0-0 b6 13. c×b6 a×b6 14. Ne5 c5 15. N×d7 Q×d7 16. Bd3 Nc7 17. a4 0-0 18. d×c5 b×c5 19. Nb5 Qc6 20. Qf3 Rac8 21. N×c7 Q×c7 22. Be5 Qb6 23. Qh3 g6 24. Bb5 Ne8 25. Rab1 f6 26. Ba1 Rf7 27. g4 Nd6 28. Bd3 f5 29. g5 d4 30. e×d4 c×d4 31. Qf3 Rd8 32. Rfe1 Ne4 33. B×e4 d3† 34. Kh1 d2 35. Red1 f×e4 36. Q×e4** "and at this point Black was considering his reply, which required some little thought to make its result sure, and being past midnight, Mr. Bird suggested a draw. This was agreed to"—*Leeds Mercury*, 13 June 1885.

**(708) Stokoe–Bird      1–0**
Simultaneous game
Leeds, 8 June 1885
C22

**1. e4 e5 2. d4 e×d4 3. Q×d4 Nc6 4. Qe3 Bb4† 5. Bd2 Nf6 6. Nc3 0-0 7. 0-0-0 Re8 8. f3 d6 9. Bb5 Bd7 10. Qf4 Ne5**

11. B×d7 Q×d7 12. Nd5 N×d5 13. e×d5 B×d2† 14. R×d2 Qb5
15. Rd1 Nc4 16. Qd4 Ne3 17. Rd3 N×g2 18. Nh3 Re1† 19. R×e1
N×e1 20. Re3 Qf1 21. Qd1 Q×h3 22. Q×e1 g6 23. Qg3 Q×g3
24. h×g3 Kf8 25. Kd2 Re8 26. Ra3 a6 27. Rb3 b6 28. Rc3 Re7
29. b4 h5 30. Ra3 f5 31. R×a6 g5 32. Ra7 Kf7 33. c4 Kf6 34. c5
b×c5 35. b×c5 h4 36. g×h4 g×h4 37. c×d6 c×d6 38. R×e7 K×e7
39. Ke3 Kf6 40. f4 Ke7 41. a4 Kd7 42. a5 Kc7 43. Kf2 Kb7
44. Kg2 Ka6 45. Kh3 K×a5 46. K×h4 Kb5 47. Kg5 Kc5
48. K×f5 K×d5 49. Kg6 and Black resigns—*Leeds Mercury*, 31
October 1885.

# MATCH WITH SKIPWORTH 1885

Bird's unsatisfying result at the congress of the C.C.A. in Bath
increased the versatility of a man like Skipworth. His, and Wayte's,
results formed the basis of his opinion to place provincial chess on
equal footing with the metropolitan and professional representatives
of the game. The results booked by both clergyman against Bird in
January were equally encouraging. Hence, a set match between Bird
and Skipworth was a good opportunity for both players to, respectively, restore or improve their reputation. MacDonnell was the first
to announce a short match to be played in May.[3]

As both Skipworth and Bird lacked the time for a long duel the
match was limited to seven games. The St. George's Chess Club
hosted the match. A time limit of 20 moves per hour was agreed
to.

The match commenced with a win for Skipworth. Despite his
confidence this result was still seen as a surprise. After four games
the score stood equal and everything still seemed possible. But then
Skipworth's momentum was in the past and he lost three games in
a row.

Suggestions for a match between Bird and Wayte, arguably the
strongest representative of the C.C.A. (except the inactive Burn),
were made but ultimately did not materialize, perhaps mainly because of Bird's busy summer schedule.

**(709) Bird–Skipworth    0–1**
Match (game 1)
London, 21 May 1885
*Game score missing*

**(710) Skipworth–Bird    0–1**
Match (game 2)
London, 22 May 1885
*A04*

**1. Nf3 f5 2. e3 Nf6 3. b3 b6 4. Bb2 e6 5. d4 Bb7 6. Bd3 Nc6**
"As a rule it is better, in close openings such as the present, to play
6. ... c5 before playing 7. ... Nc6"—MacDonnell. **7. 0–0 Nb4 8. a3**
"8. Be2 would have been a fit rebuke to Black's knight-errantry"—

---

3. MacDonnell eagerly anticipated what he thought would be a close contest:
"Mr. Skipworth's play has been for some time past so steady, so spirited, and also
so successful that it will need all the skill and genius even of a Bird to compete
with it victoriously." *Illustrated Sporting and Dramatic News*, 11 April 1885.

| Match with Skipworth, 21–29 May 1885 | | | | | | | | |
|---|---|---|---|---|---|---|---|---|
| | 1 | 2 | 3 | 4 | 5 | 6 | 7 | |
| H.E. Bird | 0 | 1 | 1 | 0 | 1 | 1 | 1 | 5 |
| A.B. Skipworth | 1 | 0 | 0 | 1 | 0 | 0 | 0 | 2 |

MacDonnell. **8. ... N×d3 9. c×d3** Condemned by MacDonnell
but not a bad try as e4 is kept under control. **9. ... Bd6** A typical
square to which Bird would develop his bishop. **10. Nbd2 0–0**
"Here 10. ... g5 is perfectly right, and is certainly more accordan[t]
with Mr. Bird's dashing style: then, if 11. N×g5 B×h2†"—MacDonnell. **11. Qe2 a5 12. Rfc1** "'In the brave days of old,' the other roo[k]
would have marched to the c-file, but Mr. Skipworth, preferring th[e]
Steinitzian style, proceeds to mass his forces on the queenside"—
MacDonnell. **12. ... Rc8 13. e4 Nh5 14. g3 Qe8 15. Nh4 Be7** 15. ...
g5 (MacDonnell) is possible, but not as sound as the text move
**16. Ng2 Qg6 17. f4 Bd6 18. e5 Be7 19. Rc2 Bd5 20. Rac1 c5** Ver[y]
optimistic play from Bird. White has the best chances on the queen[-]
side and it is therefore in Bird's interest to keep this side of the boar[d]
as closed as possible and avoid any weaknesses, which he could d[o]
with 20. ... c6. **21. d×c5** 21. Qf2! combines two assets. Not onl[y]
does it point the queen towards the queenside, it also defends f[4]
and prepares 22. Ne3. **21. ... R×c5 22. d4 Rc6** The simplest solutio[n]
to deal with the pressure is 22. ... R×c2 23. R×c2 d6. **23. R×c6 d×c[6]**
**24. Nc4 Bd8 25. Nce3 Be4 26. Nd1** "White skillfully manoeuvers
his knights, with the object of exchanging one of them for the ob[-]
noxious queenside bishop"—MacDonnell. **26. ... c5** "With the tru[e]
instinct of a master, Black resolves to retain his well-posted bishop
even at the cost of weakening his pawns"—MacDonnell. Better wa[s]
26. ... Qh6, and if 27. Nc3 B×g2 and 28. ... g5, gaining counterpla[y]
on the kingside. The text move results in the weakening of th[e]
a-pawn. **27. d×c5 b×c5 28. Nde3 Be7** Passive. 28. ... Qh6 remains
the correct idea. **29. Bc3 Ra8 30. Qb5** *(see diagram)* "In this gam[e]
the superiority of the old classical school to that of the modern is
finely illustrated, White nibbling away at pawns whilst Black pound[s]
away at the king"—MacDonnell. MacDonnell's criticism of Steinit[z]
is quite unfounded. Bird has been overplayed on the queenside afte[r]
some slow moves on his part. The text move is a bit too rash[,]
however, and allows Bird to venture a swift counterattack. First
30. a4 and then 31. Nc4 safeguards a small edge.

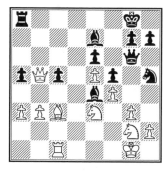

*After 30. Qb5*

**30. ... Qf7 31. B×a5** Skipworth is too eager to snatch this pawn.
In the meantime, Bird freed his g-pawn, and some attention had to
be paid to its potential with the prudent 31. Be1; for instance, 31. ...
g5 32. f×g5 B×g5 33. R×c5 f4 34. Qc4, and White keeps contro[l]
over the position. **31. ... g5** "The first of a series of powerful strokes

which White's defenses are rapidly demolished"—MacDonnell. **2. Rf1?** Skipworth's situation has become troublesome in just a few moves. More resilient than the text move was 32. f×g5 B×g5 33. Q×c5, although Black keeps the attack going on with 33. ... f4! 34. Rf1 Qg7 etc. **32. ... g×f4 33. g×f4 Kh8** An inattentive move that gives Skipworth the chance to prevent the worst with 34. Rf2! Rg8 35. Kf1, when his king is out of the line of fire; e.g., after 35. ... Qc8 36. Be1 R×a3 31. Rd2 etc. Instead of 33. ... Kh8, the precise 33. ... Qg6! prevents 34. Rf2 as this fails to 34. ... Bh4. White has to find another move, but then 34. ... Kh8 and 35. ... Rg8 gains in strength. **34. b4? Qg6** "The terminating moves by Mr. Bird presents a fine specimen of his mode of consummating a victory. It is but fair towards Mr. Skipworth to observe that his play throughout this game is so good that it would have triumphed over any other play but that of the very highest order"—MacDonnell. **35. Rf2 Bh4 36. Rf1 Rg8 37. Qe2 c4 38. Kh1 Qh6** 38. ... Ng3†! would also be cutting. **39. Q×c4 N×f4 40. R×f4 Q×f4 41. Qe2 R×g2** White resigns—*Illustrated Sporting and Dramatic News* (MacDonnell), 6 June 1885.

## 711) Bird–Skipworth    1–0
Match (game 3)
London, May 1885
*Game score missing*

## 712) Skipworth–Bird    1–0
Match (game 4)
London, 26 May 1885
*B34*

1. e4 c5 2. Nf3 Nc6 3. Nc3 g6 4. d4 c×d4 5. N×d4 Bg7 6. N×c6 b×c6 7. Be3 d6 8. Be2 Rb8 9. Bd4 Nf6 10. e5 d×e5 11. B×e5 R×b2 12. Q×d8† K×d8 13. Na4 Rb4 14. Rd1† Ke8 15. Bf3 Rc4 16. 0–0 Rg8 17. c3 Nd7 18. B×g7 R×g7 19. Rd4 Ba6 20. Rfd1 R×d4 21. c×d4 Bb5 22. Nc3 e6 23. a4 Bc4 24. B×c6 Ke7 25. Rb1 Ba6 26. B×d7 K×d7 27. Ne4 Kc6 28. Nf6 g5 29. Rc1† Kb6 30. Rc5 Rg6 31. a5† Kb7 32. Ne8 e5 33. d5 Bd3 34. d6 Bf5 35. Rc7† Ka6 36. R×f7 Bd3 37. d7 Rc6 38. Rf6 Black resigns—*Illustrated Sporting and Dramatic News*, 13 June 1885.

## 713) Bird–Skipworth    1–0
Match (game 5)
London, 27 May 1885
*Game score missing*

## 714) Skipworth–Bird    0–1
Match (game 6)
London, 28 May 1885
*A10*

1. c4 f5 2. e3 e6 3. Nf3 b6 4. d4 Bb4† 5. Nc3 Nf6 6. a3 "Now the text move might be dispensed with, in favor of a developing move. The pawn at a2 is better placed than at a3, which might be a good square for the bishop"—Hoffer. **6. ... B×c3† 7. b×c3 0–0 8. Bd3 Nc6 9. 0–0 Na5 10. a4 d6 11. Ba3 c5 12. Qc2 Qe8 13. d5** White cannot play here 13. e4, because of 13. ... f×e4 14. B×e4 N×e4 15. Q×e4 Bb7 etc."—Hoffer. **13. ... e×d5 14. c×d5 Ne4 15. ...**

**Arthur B. Skipworth (*Dubuque Chess Journal*).**

N×d5! would have crowned Bird's superb play. After the text move Skipworth is able to restore equality at once. **15. c4 Qg6 16. Bb2 Bd7 17. Ra3 Rae8 18. Ne1 Re7 19. Kh1 Qh5 20. Be2 Qh6 21. Kg1 Qg6 22. Nd3 Qe8** The game has come to a standstill and a draw would be a logical conclusion. Bird, trying to avoid this, switches his attention to the queenside. **23. Nf4 Nb7 24. Bh5 Qc8 25. Bd1 Nd8?** From this point onwards, both players neglect the important a5-square. With a well-timed a5 White can now weaken Black's pawn structure. **26. Nh5 Be8 27. Ng3?** Skipworth unjustly refrains from the winning 27. N×g7! R×g7 28. B×g7 K×g7 29. a5, followed by 30. a×b6 and 31. Qb2. Black's pieces can't cope with the activity of their counterparts. **27. ... Bg6 28. Ne2 h6 29. Nf4 Bh7** Bird's last moves have been weak. 29. ... Be8 is necessary to keep some counterplay. **30. Ba1** "We certainly should have tried here to get rid of one of the weaknesses with 30. a5"—Hoffer. **30. ... Nf6 31. Qb2 Rff7 32. Nh5 N×h5 33. B×h5 Rf8 34. e4 f4** "Of course, if 34. ... f×e4, than 35. Rg3 would be very strong; but White could hardly expect Mr. Bird to be so accommodating. Again 35. a5 might have been played"—Hoffer. Releasing the tension against e4 is not good. 34. ... Qd7 could be played. **35. Re1** More straightforward is 35. f3, followed by 36. Qa2 and 37. Bc3, preparing a4–a5. **35. ... Nb7 36. Qc3 Na5 37. Ra2 Re5 38. f3 Qa6 39. Bg4 N×c4?** "The capture of the pawn seems premature, if properly met by White"—Hoffer. **40. Qd3! Rg5 41. Bd7?** Winning is 41. Ree2 followed by 42. Rec2. **41. ... Qa5!** "Of course Black gains now an important move in attacking the adverse rook"—Hoffer. **42. Bc3?** Turning the tables completely. After 42. Rf1 Ne5 43. B×e5, a draw becomes a reasonable result. **42. ... Ne5** "The saving clause, which gives Black

the advantage"—Hoffer. **43. B×a5 N×d3 44. Rd1 Ne5 45. Be6†
Kh8 46. Bc3 N×f3† 47. Kf2 Nh4 48. Kf1 B×e4 49. Rdd2 Nf5
50. B×f5 Rg×f5** The game score doesn't state which rooks recaptured the bishop. **51. Kg1 f3 52. g3 B×d5 53. Kf2** "This is probably an oversight, but even if the rook moves Black would win with 53. ... f2†, exchanging both rooks, when the pawns on the queenside could not be stopped, in spite of the bishops of opposite color"—Hoffer. **53. ... B×a2** White resigns—*The Field* (Hoffer), 13 June 1885.

## (715) Bird–Skipworth    1–0
Match (game 7)
London, 29 May 1885
*C15*

**1. e4 e6 2. d4 d5 3. Nc3 Bb4 4. Bd3 c5 5. d×c5 d4 6. a3 Ba5
7. b4 d×c3 8. b×a5 Q×a5 9. Be3 Nc6 10. f4 Nf6 11. Nf3 Bd7
12. Ne5 h5 13. Nc4 Qc7 14. Nd6† Ke7 15. e5 Ng4 16. Bg1 Rad8
17. Be2 f5 18. h3 Ng×e5 19. f×e5 N×e5 20. Qd4 Nf7 21. Q×g7
Rhf8 22. Bf2 Bc6 23. Bh4† Kd7 24. Rd1** Black resigns—*Manchester Weekly Post*, 6 June 1885.

# B.C.A. Congress, London 1885

The constitution of the B.C.A. determined its ambition to organize a yearly master tournament of an alternatingly national and international character. The first tournament was held at Simpson's Divan and was open for British players only. The tournament was initially planned for the summer, but the organizers thought it wise to avoid interference with the congresses of the C.C.A. and the German Chess Association. Therefore, the start was brought forward to 15 June. The master tournament was the eye-catcher of the congress. Several side events proceeded at the same time: two minor tournaments, a consultation tourney, a solution tournament and a four-handed chess event.

Sixteen participants entered the major contest. The relatively meager prize fund (five prizes, the first being £25) was only able to convince three representatives of the master class, Bird, Gunsberg and MacDonnell, to try their luck. Twenty moves per hour had to be made.

Bird had an excellent start with six straight wins. In the seventh round he lost his first half point against Loman. In the ensuing

round Bird met Gunsberg, the sole player with the maximum point[s]. Despite the importance of the game, Bird's play was very apatheti[c] and he lost without standing a chance. Gunsberg did not look bac[k] drawing twice and finished with an overwhelming 14 out of 1[5] With this result his career as a British top player was definite[ly] launched.

Bird won the majority of his remaining games but he also had t[o] concede three more draws. This allowed the young Anthony Gues[t] to catch him. In *The Times* of 6 July Bird claimed the right to pla[y] a tie-break match with Guest. This did not come off, perhap[s] because of Bird's going to Hamburg or perhaps Guest found ou[t] that the veteran's claim was based on nothing. So, Bird had to spl[it] the second and third prize, of respectively £15 and £10.[4]

Bird took part in three side events, the most interesting bein[g] the consultation tournament. Four pairs, each composed of a maste[r] and an amateur, entered this single-round event. Mason and Don[-] isthorpe gained the laurels and with it a prize of £5 5s., ahead o[f] Bird and Thomas Hewitt, who netted £3 3s. for their effort. As wa[s] often the case with this type of chess, a lot of interesting battles wer[e] produced.

Gunsberg was the first to solve the four-move problem in the so[-] lution tournament, ahead of Bird, who gained £1 1s. The prize fo[r] the three-mover was gained by Herbert Jacobs.

Finally, a small "four-handed chess tournament" was held. Thi[s] game was an invention of Major Verney.[5]

All agreed that the first congress of the B.C.A. was quite a succes[s] There was a large attendance every day. No conflicts burst out an[d] the tournament continued steadily as planned with a minimum o[f] delay.

This certainly didn't mean that the tournament was completel[y] spared by the critics. In Steinitz' new magazine, the London corre[-] spondent pointed out, and quite justly so, that the ambition to rep[-] resent British chess turned out to be a failure.[6]

## (716) Pollock–Bird    0–1
B.C.A. Congress (round 1)
London, 15 June 1885
*B72*

**1. e4 c5 2. Nc3 Nc6 3. Nf3 g6 4. d4 c×d4 5. N×d4 Bg7 6. Be3
d6 7. Bc4 Nf6 8. 0–0 0–0 9. Qd2 Ng4 10. N×c6 b×c6 11. Rad1
Be6 12. B×e6 f×e6 13. Bg5 Rf7 14. h3 Nf6 15. Qe2 Qa5 16. Bd2
Qb4 17. Rb1 Raf8 18. Nd1 Qa4 19. b3 Q×a2 20. Rc1 Qa3 21. f4
Nd7 22. Qg4 Nc5 23. Nf2 Bd4 24. f5 e×f5 25. e×f5 B×f2†**

4. The specialized press was rather critical of Bird's performance in this tournament: "Mr. H.E. Bird can hardly be said to have increased his reputation by hi[s] performance in the present tourney, though now and again his play showed all his old fire. His games with Pollock, Mills, Mortimer and Donisthorpe were really fine specimens of his chess powers, but in some of the other wins, however, luck as well as skill was on his side. This was especially the case in his game with Mr. de Soyres." *International Chess Magazine*, August 1885, p. 233.

5. The Major encountered no problems worth mention in managing the tournament firmly: "Major Verney appropriated with military authority one-third of th[e] saloon for the four-handed chess match. The major brought three tables with his own chessmen. The construction of these tables is ingeniously contrived. They can be taken to pieces and put up again, all the parts being numbered, and brought into action as rapidly as a field-battery. Two games in the four-handed match were playe[d] between Major Bull and Mr. Hales against Major Verney and Mr. Hughes-Hughes; and Major Bull and Mr. Hales against H.E. Bird and A. Rosenbaum. Major Bull an[d] Mr. Hales were the victors in both games." *Standard*, 24 June 1885. Later that year, on 13 October 1885, the London Four-handed Chess Club met for the first time a[t] the Holborn Restaurant. Among the famous players trying their chance were Blackburne, Gunsberg, Hoffer and MacDonnell. *Illustrated London News*, 24 Octobe[r] 1885.

6. "Were one inclined to be critical these names might be suggestive, for at first sight, with two or three exceptions, they hardly represent an encounter betwee[n] English (not to say British) first-rates. It will be noticed that names of eminent provincial experts are 'conspicuous by their absence'; it will be further noticed tha[t] amongst the list are several players whose claims to anything like first-class strength, are more than open to question, and lastly it will be noticed that with few (and ver[y] few) exceptions the whole sixteen are the ordinary Divan players! Call this a meeting of a British Chess Association!" *International Chess Magazine*, July 1885, p. 197.

## 1st Congress of the B.C.A., London, 15 June–3 July 1885

*Site:* Simpson's Divan
*Playing hours:* 12 p.m.–5 and 7 p.m.–11
*Prizes:* 1st £25, 2nd £15, 3rd £10, 4th £5, 5th £4
*Time limit:* 20 moves per hour

| | 1 | 2 | 3 | 4 | 5 | 6 | 7 | 8 | 9 | 10 | 11 | 12 | 13 | 14 | 15 | 16 | |
|---|---|---|---|---|---|---|---|---|---|---|---|---|---|---|---|---|---|
| 1 I. Gunsberg | | 1 | 1 | 1 | 1 | 1 | ½ | 1 | 1 | 1 | 1 | ½ | 1 | 1 | 1 | 1 | 14 |
| 2 H.E. Bird | 0 | | ½ | 1 | ½ | ½ | 1 | 1 | ½ | 1 | 1 | 1 | 1 | 1 | 1 | 1 | 12 |
| 3 A. Guest | 0 | ½ | | ½ | 1 | 1 | 1 | 1 | 1 | 1 | 0 | 1 | 1 | 1 | 1 | 1 | 12 |
| 4 W.H.K. Pollock | 0 | 0 | ½ | | 1 | 0 | 1 | 0 | 1 | 1 | 1 | 1 | 1 | 1 | 1 | 1 | 10½ |
| 5 R. Loman | 0 | ½ | 0 | 0 | | 0 | 1 | 1 | 1 | ½ | 1 | 1 | 1 | 1 | 1 | 1 | 10 |
| 6 G.A. MacDonnell | 0 | ½ | 0 | 1 | 1 | | 1 | 0 | 1 | 0 | 1 | 1 | 1 | ½ | 1 | 1 | 10 |
| 7 G.E. Wainwright | ½ | 0 | 0 | 0 | 0 | 0 | | 1 | 1 | 1 | 1 | ½ | 1 | 1 | 1 | 1 | 9 |
| 8 W. Donisthorpe | 0 | 0 | 0 | 1 | 0 | 1 | 0 | | 0 | 1 | 1 | 1 | 0 | 1 | 1 | 1 | 8 |
| 9 T. Hewitt | 0 | ½ | 0 | 0 | 0 | 0 | 0 | 1 | | 1 | 1 | 0 | 1 | 1 | ½ | 1 | 7 |
| 10 J. Mortimer | 0 | 0 | 0 | 0 | ½ | 1 | 0 | 0 | 0 | | ½ | 1 | 1 | 0 | 1 | 1 | 6 |
| 11 H.A. Reeves | 0 | 0 | 1 | 0 | 0 | 0 | 0 | 0 | 0 | ½ | | ½ | 1 | 1 | 1 | 1 | 6 |
| 12 D.Y. Mills | ½ | 0 | 0 | 0 | 0 | 0 | ½ | 0 | 1 | 0 | ½ | | 0 | 1 | 1 | 1 | 5½ |
| 13 A. Rumboll | 0 | 0 | 0 | 0 | 0 | 0 | 0 | 1 | 0 | 0 | 0 | 1 | | 0 | 1 | 1 | 4 |
| 14 J. de Soyres | 0 | 0 | 0 | 0 | 0 | ½ | 0 | 0 | 0 | 1 | 0 | 0 | 1 | | 1 | ½ | 4 |
| 15 R. Rabson | 0 | 0 | 0 | 0 | 0 | 0 | 0 | 0 | ½ | 0 | 0 | 0 | 0 | 0 | | 1 | 1½ |
| 16 W.W. Mackeson | 0 | 0 | 0 | 0 | 0 | 0 | 0 | 0 | 0 | 0 | 0 | 0 | 0 | ½ | 0 | | ½ |

## Consultation tournament, 26 June–3 July 1885

*Site:* Simpson's Divan
*Prizes:* 1st £5 5s., 2nd £3 3s., 3rd £2 2s.
*Time limit:* 20 moves per hour

| | 1 | 2 | 3 | 4 | |
|---|---|---|---|---|---|
| 1 J. Mason & W. Donisthorpe | | 1 | ½ | 1 | 2½ |
| 2 H.E. Bird & T. Hewitt | 0 | | 1 | 1 | 2 |
| 3 I. Gunsberg & A. Hunter | ½ | 0 | | 1 | 1½ |
| 4 G.A. MacDonnell & W.H.K. Pollock | 0 | 0 | 0 | | 0 |

26. R×f2 R×f5 27. R×f5 R×f5 28. Qd4 Ne6 29. Qh4 Qc5†
30. Kh1 Rf6 31. Qe4 d5 32. Qa4 Qf2 33. Qb4 c5 34. Qb8† Rf8
35. Qe5 Qf5 36. Qe2 Rf7 37. Qa6 Ng5 38. Q×a7 d4 39. Qc7 Kg7
40. Ra1 e6 41. Qb8 Ne4 42. Ba5 e5 43. Bc7 Nf2† 44. Kg1 e4
45. Be5† Kh6 46. Kh2 e3 47. b4 N×h3 48. g×h3 Q×c2† 49. Kh1
Qe4† 50. Kg1 Rf2 51. Bg7† K×g7 52. Ra7† Kh6 53. R×h7†
K×h7 and Black wins—*Pollock Memories*, pp. 26–28.

### (717) Bird–Rabson   1–0
B.C.A. Congress (round 2)
London, 15 June 1885
*C54*

1. e4 e5 2. Nf3 Nc6 3. Bc4 Bc5 4. c3 Nf6 5. b4 Bb6 6. Qb3
0–0 7. d3 d6 8. a4 a6 9. a5 Ba7 10. Bg5 h6 11. Be3 B×e3 12. f×e3
Ng4 13. Ke2 Ne7 14. Qc2 c6 15. h3 Nf6 16. Bb3 Ng6 17. g4 Nh7
18. Nbd2 Be6 19. Raf1 d5 20. Rhg1 d4 21. c×d4 e×d4 22. N×d4
B×b3 23. Q×b3 Qd6 24. Rf2 Ne5 25. Nf5 Qd7 26. d4 Rad8
27. Qc3 Ng6 28. d5 f6 29. d6 Rf7 30. h4 Ne5 31. Nf3 N×f3
32. R×f3 Nf8 33. g5 f×g5 34. h×g5 h5 35. Nh6† g×h6 36. g×h6†
Kh7 37. R×f7† Black resigns—*Standard*, 16 June 1885.

### (718) Rumboll–Bird   0–1
B.C.A. Congress (round 3)
London, 16 June 1885
*Game score missing*

### (719) Bird–Mills   1–0
B.C.A. Congress (round 4)
London, 16 June 1885
*A03*

1. f4 d5 2. Nf3 e6 3. e3 Nf6 4. b3
Be7 5. Bb2 c5 6. Bd3 Nc6 7. 0–0 b6
8. Ne5 Bb7 9. Bb5 Qc7 10. d3 0–0
11. B×c6 B×c6 12. Qf3 Rac8 13. Nd2
Bb7 14. Qg3 Ne8 15. Ndf3 f6 16. Ng4
Kh8 17. Qh3 Bd6 This move looks innocent enough, but it had to be replaced by 17. ... Nd6 or 17. ... d4, as it
creates the momentum for Bird to deliver his opponent a severe blow with
18. Nge5! After 18. ... f×e5, the most
logical reply, the situation of Black's
king becomes at once critical: 19. f×e5
Be7 20. Ng5 R×f1† 21. R×f1 h6
22. N×e6 etc. Relatively better but not
attractive is 18. ... B×e5 19. f×e5 Qe7
20. e×f6 etc. 18. Nh4 Qf7 19. f5! e×f5
20. N×f5 Rc7? 20. ... Bb8 or 20. ...
Qg6 are correct. 21. N×d6 N×d6
22. Be5! Qe7?! Slightly better is 22. ...
Qe6, preventing the annoying pin after
Bird's next move, but White can reach
a very nice endgame with 23. N×f6!
Q×h3 24. g×h3 g×f6 25. B×d6.
23. Qh4! Kg8 (*see diagram*)

*After 23. ... Kg8*

24. N×f6†! Bird doesn't miss his chance to conclude the game
with a devastating attack. 24. ... R×f6 25. B×f6 g×f6 26. R×f6
Black's pieces cannot withstand White's queen and rooks. 26. ...
Ne8 27. Qg4† Ng7 28. Raf1 Bc8 29. Qf3 h5 30. Q×d5† Kh7
31. Qg5 Be6 32. e4 Rd7 33. Rh6† Kg8 34. Qg6 Black resigns—
*The Field*, 20 June 1885.

### (720) Bird–Mortimer   1–0
B.C.A. Congress (round 5)
London, 17 June 1885
*Game score missing*

### (721) Donisthorpe–Bird   0–1
B.C.A. Congress (round 6)
London, 17 June 1885
*Game score missing*

**(722) Loman–Bird**    ½–½

B.C.A. Congress (round 7)

London, 18 June 1885

*B25*

1. e4 c5 2. Nc3 Nc6 3. Nf3 g6 4. g3 Bg7 5. Bg2 d6 6. d3 h5 7. Be3 Bg4 8. h3 Bd7 9. Qd2 Nd4 10. Nd1 Qc8 11. Ng1 Ba4 12. B×d4 c×d4 13. b3 Bc6 14. f4 e5 15. Ne2 Bd7 16. Rc1 h4 17. g4 Qd8 18. Qb4 Bc6 19. 0–0 a5 20. Qd2 Qb6 21. Nb2 Ne7 22. Nc4 Qc7 23. Qe1 b5 24. Nd2 b4 25. Nf3 f5 26. e×f5 g×f5 27. Ng5 B×g2 28. K×g2 Qb7† 29. Kg1 Bf6 30. g×f5 Rg8 31. Kh2 N×f5 32. Ne4 0–0–0 33. Rg1 Be7 34. Qf2 Ne3 35. f×e5 d×e5 36. Qf7 Rgf8 37. Qe6† Kb8 38. Rg7 Nf5 39. Rh7 Qd7 40. Nc5 Qd6 41. Q×d6† R×d6 42. Rf1 Ng3 43. R×f8† B×f8 44. N×g3 h×g3† 45. Kg2 Bh6 46. Nd7† Kc8 47. N×e5 Bf4 48. Nc4 Re6 49. Kf3 Bc7 50. Rf7 Re1 51. Rg7 Rf1† 52. Ke4 Rf2 53. Kd5 Rf5† 54. Kc6 Rf6† 55. Kd5 Rh6 56. K×d4 R×h3 57. Kc5 Rh5† 58. Kc6 Rh6† 59. Kc5 Rh5† 60. Kc6 Rh6† draw—*Chess Monthly*, November 1885, pp. 73–74.

**(723) Gunsberg–Bird**    1–0

B.C.A. Congress (round 8)

London, 20 June 1885

*B34*

1. e4 c5 2. Nc3 Nc6 3. Nf3 g6 4. d4 c×d4 5. N×d4 Bg7 6. Be3 d6 7. Nd5 Nf6 8. Nb5 N×d5 9. e×d5 Ne5 10. Bd4 0–0 11. f4 a6 12. Nc3 Bg4 13. Qd2 Nd7 14. B×g7 K×g7 15. h3 Bf5 16. g4 e5 17. g×f5 e×f4 18. 0–0–0 Qh4 19. Ne4 Rfe8 20. N×d6 Re3 21. Rg1 Ne5 22. f×g6 Qf6 23. g×f7† Kh6 24. Qf2 Ng6 25. Nc4 Re7 26. h4 b5 27. h5 Nf8 28. Rd4 b×c4 29. R×f4 Qe5 30. Rf6† Black resigns—*Standard*, 22 June 1885.

**(724) Mackeson–Bird**    0–1

B.C.A. Congress (round 9)

London, 22 June 1885

*Game score missing*

**(725) Bird–de Soyres**    1–0

B.C.A. Congress (round 10)

London, 22 June 1885

*C50*

1. e4 e5 2. Nf3 Nc6 3. Bc4 Nf6 4. d3 "This turns the Two Knight's Defense into a Giuoco Piano, which is rather surprising, as Mr. Bird used to play numerous very fine games of this opening with the late Mr. Boden"—*Standard*. 4. ... Bc5 5. 0–0 d6 6. h3 "Not advisable after castling, as weakening the defensive power of the pawns"—*Standard*. 6. ... h6 7. Be3 Bb6 8. a3 g5 9. Nh2 Ne7 10. Nc3 Ng6 11. Na4 Nf4 12. N×b6 a×b6 13. B×f4 g×f4 14. d4 Qe7 15. d×e5 d×e5 16. Qd3 Bd7 17. Rfe1 Rg8 18. Qb3 0–0–0 19. Rad1 Rg7 Black attacking chances on the kingside are due to Bird's indifferent play. 20. Kh1 Rdg8 21. Bf1 Bc6 22. f3? The tricky 22. Nf3 keeps the kingside well defended, for if 22. ... N×e4? 23. R×e4! B×e4 24. Qa4. 22. ... Bd7 22. ... Nh5! is even stronger. 23. Ng4 N×g4 24. f×g4 h5 25. g×h5 Rg3 26. Qb4 Qh4 "A very powerful move, which compels White to sacrifice his rook for the

bishop, in order to avoid immediate loss"—*Standard*. 27. R×d7 (*see diagram*)

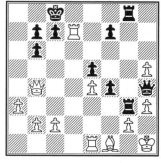

*After 27. R×d7*

27. ... K×d7 "Mr. F.H. Lewis pointed out a beautiful variation, which gives Black an absolute win, with 27. ... R×h3† 28. g×h3 Qf2 and wins. Upon examination, it will be found that White must continue with 29. R×c7† Kb8 30. R×b7† K×b7 and if 31. Ba6† Ka8 32. Bb7† K×b7 33. Qe7† Ka8 and wins. Of course these brilliant combinations are easier detected in analysis than in actual play"—*Standard*. 28. Qa4† Ke7 "And here again the reply should have been 28. ... c6, when, after a few checks, the king may escape into a safe position"—*Standard*. 29. Rd1 f3 30. Qd7† Kf6?! "30. ... Kf8 would have yielded a good game still to Black. Mr. de Soyres observed that he made the text move under a misapprehension"—*Standard*. 31. Qf5† Kg7 32. Rd7 f×g2† 33. B×g2 Kh6?? 33. ... Rf8 34. Q×e5† Kh6 is still good for Black. The text move is an enormous blunder. 34. R×f7 R×h3† 35. Q×h3 Black resigns—*Standard*, 25 June 1885.

**(726) Wainwright–Bird**    0–1

B.C.A. Congress (round 11)

London, 24 June 1885

*Game score missing*

**(727) Bird–MacDonnell**    ½–½

B.C.A. Congress (round 12)

London, 25 June 1885

*Game score missing*

**(728) Bird–Hewitt**    ½–½

B.C.A. Congress (round 13)

London, 29 June 1885

*Game score missing*

**(729) Reeves–Bird**    0–1

B.C.A. Congress (round 14)

London, 29 June 1885

*Game score missing*

**(730) Guest–Bird**    ½–½

B.C.A. Congress (round 15)

London, 30 June 1885

*B34*

1. e4 c5 2. Nf3 Nc6 3. d4 c×d4 4. N×d4 g6 5. Be3 Bg7 6. c3 Nf6 7. Nd2 0–0 8. Be2 d6 9. h4 h5 10. Qc2 N×d4 11. B×d4 e5

2. Be3 d5 13. Bg5 d4 14. c×d4 Q×d4 15. 0–0 Bg4 16. Be3 Qd7
7. Nf3 B×f3 18. B×f3 Rfc8 19. Qb3 b6 20. Rad1 Qb7 21. Rfe1
Rd8 22. Bg5 R×d1 23. R×d1 Nd7 24. Qd5 Q×d5 25. R×d5 Nc5
26. Be7 Ne6 27. Rd7 Nd4 28. Bd1 Rc8 29. Rd8† R×d8 30. B×d8
Ne6 "several more moves were played, and the game was eventually
adjudicated as drawn"—*Morning Post*, 9 November 1885.

## (731) Bird & Hewitt–Mason & Donisthorpe   0–1
Consultation tournament (round 1)
London, 26 June 1885
C14

1. e4 e6 2. d4 d5 3. Nc3 Nf6 4. Bg5 Be7 5. B×f6 B×f6 6. Nf3
f6 7. Bd3 Bb7 8. 0–0 0–0 9. e5 Be7 10. Ne2 Ba6 11. c3 B×d3
12. Q×d3 c5 13. Nf4 c4 14. Qc2 Nd7 15. Rfe1 Re8 16. a4 Nf8
17. b3 c×b3 18. Q×b3 Qc7 19. Rac1 Rec8 20. Rc2 Qc4 21. Rb1
Rc7 22. g3 Rac8 23. h4 Q×b3 24. R×b3 Rc4 25. a5 b×a5 26. Ne2
Bb4 27. Nd2 R4c7 28. Ra2 B×c3 29. N×c3 R×c3 30. R×a5 R8c7
31. Rb8 Rd3 32. Nb3 g6 33. Rc5 R×c5 34. d×c5 Rc3 35. Kf1
Kg7 36. Rb7 a5 37. N×a5 R×c5 38. Nb3 Rc4 39. Re7 Re4 40. f4
Re3 41. Nd4 R×g3 42. Kf2 Rg4 43. Kf3 R×h4 44. Nb5 g5 45. f5
Rf4† 46. Kg3 R×f5 47. Nd6 Rf4 48. Ne8† Kg6 49. Nf6 R×f6
50. e×f6 K×f6 and Black wins—*The Field*, 11 July 1885.

## (732) Bird & Hewitt–Gunsberg & Hunter   1–0
Consultation tournament (round 2)
London, 27 June 1885
C14

1. e4 e6 2. d4 d5 3. Nc3 Nf6 4. Bg5 Be7 5. B×f6 B×f6 6. Nf3
Nc6 "The knight should not be brought out before the c-pawn is
moved to c5. 6. ... b6 is preferable at this stage"—Zukertort. 7. e5
Be7 8. a3 "Loss of time, which enables Black to lose a move, too,
in retreating the knight, and to rectify the omission pointed out
above"—Zukertort. 8. ... Nb8 9. Ne2 c5 10. c3 Nc6 11. Nf4 Bd7
12. Bd3 c×d4 13. c×d4 Qb6 "Black played to win a pawn with the
text move without taking sufficiently into consideration White's
clever continuation. They might have castled or moved 13. ... Rc8
instead"—Zukertort. 14. 0–0 N×d4 14. ... g5 15. Ne2 g4 and 16. ...
N×d4 would have crossed White's trick and left Black with an excellent position. 15. N×d4 Q×d4 16. N×e6! "This pretty combination the Black allies did not foresee. Obviously the knight cannot
be taken without the loss of the queen"—Zukertort. 16. ... Q×e5
17. Re1 Qd6 18. N×g7† Kf8 19. Nh5 19. Nf5 is much simpler.
19. ... Rg8 20. Ng3 Rg7 21. Qb3 b6 22. Rad1 Bg4 23. Be2 Be6
24. Bf3 Rd8 25. Qa4 a5 26. Nh5 Rg5 27. Qd4 Kg8 28. h4 Rg6
29. Re5 Qc5 30. g3 30. Q×c5 and 31. Nf4 continues to impose a
serious bind on Black, which is not the case in the actual game.
30. ... Q×d4 31. R×d4 Bc5 32. Rd2 d4 "Perhaps the advance of
the pawn was premature. 32. ... Bd6 seems somewhat better; but
there is not much in the game now. Black labors under the disadvantage of the isolated pawn, and ought to remain masterly inactive"—Zukertort. 33. Be4 Rh6 34. Bf3 Bc4 "At this stage the game
was adjourned and the text move enclosed in an envelope according
to the conditions"—Zukertort. 35. Kg2 Re6 36. Rf5 Rdd6?! This
eventually leads to some exchanges that enhance White's advantage
again; 36. ... d3 generates sufficient counterplay to draw comfort-

ably. 37. Nf4 Re1 38. Bd5 B×d5†?! This exchange helps White
considerably. 39. R×d5 R×d5 40. N×d5 Re5 41. Nf4 a4 42. Kf3
f6 43. Re2 Kf7 44. Re4 h5 45. R×e5 f×e5 46. Nd3 Ke6 47. Ke4
Bd6 48. f3 b5 49. f4 e×f4 50. N×f4† B×f4 51. g×f4 d3 52. K×d3
Kf5 53. Ke3 Kg4 54. Ke4 K×h4 55. f5 Kg5 56. Ke5 Black resigns.
"Obviously White queens first and wins the adverse queen with
two checks"—Zukertort. *Chess Monthly* (Zukertort), July 1885, p.
334–336.

## (733) Bird & Hewitt–MacDonnell & Pollock   1–0
Consultation tournament (round 3)
London, 2 July 1885
A02

1. f4 f5 2. e3 Nf6 3. b3 e6 4. Bb2 Be7 5. Nf3 0–0 6. Bd3 "One
of Mr. Bird's eccentricities which frequently succeed, but we should
not recommend less experienced players to follow the example"—
Zukertort. 6. ... b6 7. 0–0 Bb7 8. Nc3 Na6 9. Bc4 c5 10. Ng5 h6
10. ... Nc7 avoids White's plans, but the text move appears intimidating enough. 11. Nf3 "It seems as if it had been White's intention
to exchange two pieces for rook and two pawns; but the allies must
have changed their minds at the last moment and retreated the
knight. White might have continued here with 11. B×e6† d×e6
12. N×e6, which would have been an equivalent for the two pieces.
To retreat the knight is loss of time"—Zukertort. 11. ... Kh7
12. Ne5 Qe8 "Black should have played here 12. ... d6 13. Nf3 Nc7,
with a good pawn position in the center"—Zukertort. 13. Be2 Nc7
14. Bf3 d5 15. a4 a6 16. Qe2 Bd6 17. Nd1 Rb8 "Perhaps 17. ... Rd8
would have been a better place"—Zukertort. 18. Nf2 Rg8 "Black
might have advanced 18. ... g5, if such was their intention, followed
by the text move, when White could not have prevented it as they
actually did"—Zukertort. 19. h4 Ne4 After the subsequent exchange the pawn structure in the center is very advantageous for
White. 20. B×e4! d×e4 21. Nh3 White relentlessly pursues an
attack against the king. A central strategy is certainly not inferior;
e.g., 21. Nc4! Qe7 22. h5 Bd5 23. N×d6 Q×d6 24. Rfd1 and 25. d3
will follow. 21. ... Nd5 22. g4 "A clever way of preventing 22. ...
Nf6"—Zukertort. 22. ... f×g4 23. Ng5†?! "Very tempting and brilliant but too hazardous; in this instance the defense seems to maintain the advantage resulting from the sacrifice"—Zukertort. 23. ...
h×g5 24. h×g5 B×e5 25. B×e5 Rd8 26. Kg2 Rh8 27. Q×g4 Kg8
"The following might be suggested here for Black: 27. ... Qg6 28. f5
(if 28. Rh1† Kg8 and we do not see any danger for Black) 28. ...
e×f5 29. R×f5 Bc8 and we do not see any danger for Black. The
chief object of the suggested move is to guard the e-pawn, and enable
Black to play Ne7. This knight once established at f5 White's attack
would be at an end"—Zukertort. 28. c4 Nb4 "Illustrating our remark in the preceding note"—Zukertort. 29. Bc3 Bc8 30. Rh1
R×h1 31. R×h1 Qg6 32. Rh5 Na2?! This contributes nothing at
all to the defense. Alternatives were 32. ... Nd3, 32. ... e5 or 32. ...
Kf7. 33. Qh4 Kf7? *(see diagram)* Another bad move after which the
balance seems definitely tilted in favor of White. Correct is 33. ...
Re8! 34. Rh8† Kf7 35. B×g7 R×h8 36. Q×h8 Qf5 when a draw is
becoming likely.

34. B×g7! "A very ingenious resource and the only chance of
continuing the attack. Obviously Black dare not capture the bishop,

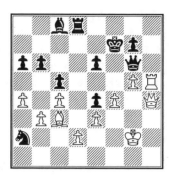

*After 33. ... Kf7*

for if 34. ... K×g7 35. Rh6 Qf5 36. g6 should win"—Zukertort. **34. ... R×d2† 35. Kg3??** "White did not make the most of their opportunities. 35. Kf1 would have left Black scanty defensive resources"—Zukertort. **35. ... Nc1! 36. Rh7** "The White allies observed afterwards that their original intention was 36. Rh6. We quite agree with them. They certainly would have secured a draw with that move"—Zukertort. 36. Rh6 is equally destined to lose quickly after 36. ... Ne2† 37. Kg2 Nd4† 38. Kf1 Rd1† 39. Kf2 Nf5. **36. ... Ne2†** "The text move might have been kept in reserve, especially as 36. ... Kg8 would have put the king in a safe position; e.g., 37. Rh8† (if 37. Rh6 Q×g7 38. g6 Ne2† 39. Kf2 N×f4† followed by 40. ... N×g6) 37. ... K×g7 38. R×c8 (if 38. Rh6 Qf5 39. Rf6 Ne2† and wins in a few moves) 38. ... Ne2† 39. Kf2 N×f4† 40. Kf1 Qh5 wins"—Zukertort. **37. Kf2 N×f4†?** 37. ... Kg8! returns to the line above. The text move loses all advantage. **38. Kg1 Nh3†** Another crazy line goes like this 38. ... Kg8 39. Rh8† K×g7 40. e×f4 e3 41. f5 e×f5 42. R×c8 with equality. **39. Q×h3 Q×g5†** **40. Kf1 Qf5†** 40. ... Kg6! is the safest move. **41. Q×f5† e×f5 42. Bc3† Kg6 43. Rg7† Kh6 44. Rc7 Rd3 45. Be5 Bd7 46. Bf4† Kh5 47. Rb7 Kg4 48. Ke2 Be8 49. R×b6 Bh5 50. R×a6** "At this stage the game was adjourned, White having made this move in the enclosed envelope. On the following day Messrs. Bird and MacDonnell concluded the game without their partners"—Zukertort. **50. ... Kh3†** **51. Kf2 R×b3 52. Rh6 Kg4 53. a5 Bf7 54. a6 Ra3 55. Rh7 Ra2† 56. Ke1 Ra1†** After 56. ... Bg6! 57. Ra7 Kf3, Black runs no risk of losing the game. **57. Kd2 B×c4 58. a7 Bd5 59. Rd7 Ba8** "59. ... Be6, remaining on the diagonal, would have prevented the White king from advancing at least for a time"—Zukertort. **60. Kc3 Kf3?** Bird's squeeze worked quite well, as he comes close to winning. Black's last attempt to prevent the defeat was by playing 60. ... Ra4 here, keeping the king out. **61. Kc4 Ra5 62. Rf7 Bc6 63. R×f5 Ke2 64. R×c5 Ra6 65. R×c6 Ra4† 66. Kd5 R×a7 67. K×e4 Ra4† 68. Kf5 Kf3 69. e4 Ra3 70. Be5** Black resigns. "Mr. Bird cleverly won a game which he willingly would have given up as drawn"—Zukertort. *Chess Monthly* (Zukertort), July 1885, pp. 332–334.

The following offhand game took both players five minutes to finish. It was played either just before or after the Hamburg tournament.

**(734) MacDonnell–Bird　　1–0**
Offhand game
London, July 1885
*C37*

　　**1. e4 e5 2. f4 e×f4 3. Nf3 g5 4. Bc4 g4 5. Nc3 g×f3 6. Q×f3**

Bh6 7. d4 Nc6 8. B×f4 N×d4 9. B×f7† Kf8 10. B×h6† N×h6 11. Qf2 N×f7 12. 0–0 Qe8 13. Q×d4 Rg8 14. R×f7† Q×f7 15. Rf1 Q×f1† 16. K×f1 Rg7 17. Kg1 d6 18. Qf6† Rf7 19. Qd8† Kg7 20. Nd5 h6 21. N×c7 Rd7 22. Q×d7† B×d7 23. N×a8 Bc6 24. Nc7 Kf6 25. Nd5† Ke5 26. Nc3 b5 "and after a few more moves Black gracefully surrendered"—*Illustrated Sporting and Dramatic News*, 6 September 1885.

# German Chess Congress, Hamburg 1885

A few days later Bird set sail for Hamburg where the fourth congress of the German Chess Association was going to be held. The festivities opened on Sunday 12 July with a general meeting of the players. Three of the 21 competitors dropped out for different reasons. The case of Alexander Fritz was very similar to Bird's attempt to enter the tournament in Brunswick in 1880: A telegram announcing his arrival remained unread and as a result Fritz appeared on the scene when the games had already started and his bid to be included was refused by his fellow masters.

The scheme of the tournament did not deviate a lot from the usual in German tournaments: three games and adjournments had to be worked off every two days. The field was filled with star players. Blackburne, back just a week from Australia, Mason and Gunsberg had crossed the North Sea. They were joined by other foreign masters such as Mackenzie and Weiss. From the German front Schallopp was the most experienced player in Louis Paulsen's absence. One eagerly watched the performance of Siegbert Tarrasch who had gained the master title at Nuremberg two years earlier.

Play commenced on Monday 13 July. Very soon it became clear that Bird would not repeat his Nuremberg performance as he was only able to pull one single draw out of his first five games. In a few of these games, especially those with Mason and Hermann von Gottschall, Bird deserved a better reward than two losses.

Bird hit back with three straight consecutive wins with the White pieces against weaker opposition. His next three games were also played as White, making six in a row, but these all ended in losses. Bird's finish was more tolerable, with 4½ points out of six games. Bird thus ended the tournament with 8 points in 17 games, sharing eleventh place in the company of Berger. As eight prizes were foreseen, Bird came out empty-handed.

The battle for first place was extremely tense. With a loss in the final round, the 23 year old Siegbert Tarrasch was overtaken by an impressive Gunsberg, who thereby more than confirmed his excellent result made at the B.C.A. meeting. No fewer than five rivals counted but a half point less in the final ranking.

**(735) Blackburne–Bird　　1–0**
International tournament (round 1)
Hamburg, 13 July 1885
*A81*

　　**1. d4 f5 2. g3 e6 3. Bg2 Nf6 4. Nh3 c6 5. 0–0 Be7 6. c4 d5 7. b3 Na6 8. Nc3 0–0 9. Bb2 Bd7 10. Rc1 Nc7 11. e3 Ng4 12. Qe2 Ne8**

3. f3 Nh6 14. e4 d×c4 15. b×c4
Qa5 16. Rfd1 f×e4 17. N×e4
Rd8 18. Bc3 Qf5 19. Nhf2 Nc7
0. Nd3 Rfe8 21. Ne5 Bc8
2. Rb1 Qf8 23. f4 Nf5 24. Qf2
Na6 25. c5 Bf6 26. Ba5 B×e5
7. f×e5 Rd7 28. Nd6 N×d6
9. Q×f8† K×f8 30. e×d6 Rf7
1. Bh3 Nb8 32. Re1 Rf6
3. Bc3 Rh6 34. Bg4 Kf7
5. Bd2 Rf6 36. Bg5 Nd7
7. B×f6 N×f6 38. Bf3 g5
9. Rf1 Kg6 40. Rbe1 Bd7
1. Be4† Kg7 42. Bg2 b5 43. Re3
5 44. h3 h6 45. Rf2 g4 46. Rf4
g×h3 47. B×h3 Nh7 48. Bg4
Ng5 49. Kf1 Rb8 50. Ke1 b4
51. Bd1 Nh3 52. Rf1 Ng5
53. Ba4 Be8 54. Kd2 Rd8
55. Kc1 Bd7 56. Kb2 Kg6
57. Bc2† Kg7 58. a3 Rb8
59. Rb3 e5 60. a×b4 Be6
61. b×a5 B×b3 62. B×b3 e×d4
63. a6 Ne4 64. Rf7† Kg6
65. Rb7 Rf8 66. Bc2 Rf2 67. Kb3 Rf3† 68. Kc4 Rc3† 69. K×d4
R×c2 70. K×e4 Rc4† 71. Kf3 Rc3† 72. Kg2 Rc2† 73. Kh3 R×c5
74. a7 Black resigns—*Tournament Book*, pp. 47–48.

## (736) Mason–Bird   1–0
International tournament (round 2)
Hamburg, 13 July 1885
*A85*

1. d4 f5 2. e3 Nf6 3. c4 e6 4. Nc3 Bb4 5. Bd2 0-0 6. Bd3 b6
7. a3 B×c3 8. B×c3 Bb7 9. Nf3 Qe8 10. Qe2 d6 11. 0-0-0 Ne4
12. B×e4 f×e4 13. Ng5 d5 14. c×d5 e×d5 15. f4 a5 16. g4 Ba6
17. Qg2 Nc6 18. f5 b5 19. Be1 b4 20. a4 b3 21. Ne6 Nb4 22. B×b4
a×b4 23. Nc5 Bc4 24. Kd2 R×a4 25. N×a4 Q×a4 26. Ra1 Qc6
27. Rhc1 Ra8 28. R×a8† Q×a8 29. Ke1 Qa2 30. Qd2 Qa4 31. Kf2
Qc6 32. Ra1 Qf6 33. Kg3 h5 34. h3 c5 35. Qf2 c×d4 36. e×d4
h4† 37. Kg2 Qg5 38. Re1 Bd3 39. Qe3 Qf6 40. Ra1 Kh7 41. Kh1
Bc2 42. Qf4 e3 43. Q×e3 Be4† 44. Kg1 Qd6 45. Rf1 Qb6 46. g5
Kg8 47. f6 g6 48. Qf2 Kf7 49. Q×h4 Q×d4† 50. Qf2 Q×f2†
51. R×f2 Bf5 52. Rd2 Black resigns—*Tournament Book*, pp. 58–
59.

## (737) von Gottschall–Bird   1–0
International tournament (round 3)
Hamburg, 14 July 1885
*A85*

1. e3 f5 2. d4 e6 3. c4 Nf6 4. Nc3 Bb4 5. Bd2 0-0 6. Nf3 b6
7. Bd3 "Injudicious for two reasons: the bishop is not well posted
in all openings in which the opponent starts with 1. … f5. Secondly,
he should be played to e2 on account of the adverse fianchetto development"—Zukertort. 7. … Bb7 8. Qb3 a5 9. 0-0-0 White's
opening can hardly be called a success. The text move is not good,

but Bird's reaction could have been better. 9. … Na6 9. … Ne4!
10. Rhf1 Qf6 11. Kb1 B×c3 12. B×c3 Qg6 gives excellent play. Black
can further strengthen his position with some pawn pushes, such
as a5–a4–a3, d7–d6 or c7–c5. 10. a3 B×c3 11. B×c3 Ne4 12. Be1
d6 13. h4 h6 14. Rh2 An awkward way to defend the g-pawn and
liberate his knight. He could obtain good decent play with 14. Ng1!,
intending 15. Ne2 and 16. f3. 14. … c5 15. Nd2 The logical continuation, but safer is 15. Kb1. 15. … Qc7 16. f3 N×d2 16. … d5! would
have been very good. White's rook is hanging, and after 17. Rh3
c×d4! 18. f×e4 Nc5 19. Qc2 f×e4 he is forced to return the piece
with a destroyed position. 17. R×d2 c×d4 18. e×d4 d5 Bird's way
of coming to d5 isn't bad either. White is on the brink of defeat.
19. g3 a4 *(see diagram)*

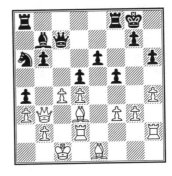

*After 19. … a4*

20. Qa2 20. Q×a4 is better, although after 20. … Rfc8! (superior
to Zukertort's 20. … Nc5, which unnecessarily exchanges a pair of
pieces at d3) 21. Qb5 Bc6 22. Qb3 d×c4 23. Q×c4 Qd7 Black gets
an extremely dangerous initiative. 20. … b5 20. … d×c4! is simple
and sufficient to win: 21. Q×c4 Qd7 (he can also take the f-pawn,
but keeping the attack going on is more dangerous for his opponent)
22. Bc2 b5 23. Qd3 b4. The text move allows von Gottschall to close
the position. 21. c5 b4 Bird continues his push on the queenside.

### 4th Congress of the German Chess Association, Hamburg, 12–26 July 1885

*Site:* Sagebiel's Etablissement
*Playing hours:* 9 a.m.–1 p.m. and 4 p.m.–8
*Prizes:* 1st 1000 marks, 2nd 750 marks, 3rd 500 marks, 4th 300 marks, 5th 200 marks, 6th 150 marks, 7th 120 marks, 8th 100 marks
*Time limit:* 20 moves per hour

|  | 1 | 2 | 3 | 4 | 5 | 6 | 7 | 8 | 9 | 10 | 11 | 12 | 13 | 14 | 15 | 16 | 17 | 18 |  |
|---|---|---|---|---|---|---|---|---|---|---|---|---|---|---|---|---|---|---|---|
| 1 I. Gunsberg |  | 1 | 0 | ½ | ½ | 1 | 1 | 0 | 1 | 1 | 0 | 1 | 1 | 1 | 0 | 1 | 1 | 1 | 12 |
| 2 J.H. Blackburne | 0 |  | 0 | ½ | 1 | 1 | 1 | 1 | 0 | 1 | ½ | 1 | 1 | 1 | 1 | 1 | ½ | 0 | 11½ |
| 3 J. Mason | 1 | 1 |  | ½ | ½ | 0 | 1 | 0 | 0 | ½ | ½ | 1 | 1 | 1 | ½ | 1 | 1 | 1 | 11½ |
| 4 M. Weiss | ½ | ½ | ½ |  | 0 | 0 | 1 | ½ | 1 | 1 | ½ | 1 | ½ | 1 | 1 | ½ | 1 | 1 | 11½ |
| 5 B. Englisch | ½ | 0 | ½ | 1 |  | 1 | 0 | 0 | 0 | 1 | ½ | 1 | 1 | 1 | 1 | 1 | 1 | 1 | 11½ |
| 6 S. Tarrasch | 0 | 0 | 1 | 1 | 0 |  | 0 | 1 | 1 | 0 | ½ | 1 | 1 | 1 | 1 | 1 | 1 | 1 | 11½ |
| 7 G.H. Mackenzie | 0 | 0 | 0 | 0 | 1 | 1 |  | ½ | 1 | 1 | 1 | ½ | ½ | 1 | ½ | ½ | 1 | 1 | 10 |
| 8 F. Riemann | 1 | 0 | 1 | ½ | 1 | 0 | ½ |  | 1 | 0 | ½ | 0 | 1 | ½ | 0 | ½ | 1 | 1 | 9½ |
| 9 E. Schallopp | 0 | 1 | 1 | 0 | 1 | ½ | 0 | 0 |  | 0 | 1 | ½ | 0 | 1 | 1 | 1 | 1 | 1 | 9½ |
| 10 J. Minckwitz | 0 | 0 | ½ | 0 | 0 | 1 | 0 | 1 | 1 |  | ½ | 0 | 1 | 1 | 1 | ½ | ½ | 1 | 9 |
| 11 J. Berger | 1 | ½ | ½ | ½ | ½ | ½ | ½ | ½ | 0 | ½ |  | ½ | ½ | 0 | ½ | ½ | ½ | ½ | 8 |
| 12 H.E. Bird | 0 | 0 | 0 | 0 | 0 | 0 | 0 | 1 | ½ | 1 | ½ |  | 0 | 1 | 1 | 1 | 1 | 1 | 8 |
| 13 H. von Gottschall | 0 | 0 | 0 | ½ | 0 | 0 | ½ | 0 | 1 | 0 | ½ | 1 |  | 0 | 1 | 1 | 0 | 1 | 6½ |
| 14 J. Taubenhaus | 0 | 0 | 0 | 0 | 0 | 0 | ½ | ½ | 0 | 0 | ½ | 0 | 1 |  | 1 | ½ | 1 | 0 | 5 |
| 15 J. Noa | 1 | 0 | ½ | 0 | 0 | 0 | 0 | 1 | 0 | 0 | ½ | 0 | 0 | ½ |  | ½ | ½ | 4 | 4 |
| 16 A. Schottländer | 0 | 0 | 0 | ½ | 0 | 0 | ½ | ½ | 0 | ½ | ½ | 0 | 0 | 0 | 0 | ½ |  | ½ | 4 |
| 17 W. Paulsen | 0 | ½ | 0 | 0 | 0 | 0 | 0 | 0 | 0 | ½ | ½ | 0 | 0 | 0 | 1 | ½ | ½ |  | 3½ |
| 18 M. Bier | 0 | 1 | 0 | 0 | 0 | 0 | 0 | 0 | 0 | 0 | ½ | 0 | 0 | 1 | ½ | ½ |  |  | 3½ |

The central break 21. ... e5 is an alternative: 22. Rc2 e×d4 23. c6 (best) 23. ... B×c6 24. B×b5 Rfe8 25. Bd2 Q×g3 with mutual chances, although Black is still on top. **22. Rde2 b3** With this move his showy run on the queenside draws to a close. The result is an equal position. Much more chanceful was 22. ... N×c5! White is now in difficulties and has to be extremely careful. His best way is 23. d×c5 Q×c5† 24. Kd1 Rfc8 25. Qb1 b×a3 26. b×a3 d4 27. Bb4 Qc7 28. R×e6 Q×g3 29. Bd6 Q×f3†. It is clear that Black still has a dangerous attack. **23. Qb1 e5** "An oversight. Black expected the immediate 24. d×e5, which would be met, of course, with 24. ... N×c5."—Zukertort **24. B×a6 B×a6 25. R×e5** Bird's series of ecstatic moves has come to an end. He lost a pawn along the way, but with the bishops of opposed colors on the board, this is merely trivial. **25. ... Rae8 26. f4 R×e5 26.** ... h5 is more likely to draw. **27. f×e5 f4** "We suspect that Black is underrating the skill of his youthful opponent. Otherwise he would avoid all reckless schemes, and try to secure the draw by hard play"—Zukertort. **28. Rf2! Qd7 29. Qg6 Qb5 30. g×f4** White is now in the possession of a nice pawn phalanx, but Bird succeeds in setting up a blockade. **30. ... Bc8 31. Bc3 Bf5 32. Qg3 Qd7 33. Kd2 Bh7 34. Rg2 Rf7 35. Qg4 Bf5 36. Qh5 Be4 37. Rf2** It is far from certain if White would get any further with 37. Rg3 R×f4. The text move guarantees Bird practical chances with the infiltration of his queen. **37. ... Qh3 38. Qe2 Q×h4 39. Qe3 Qg4** (see diagram) 39. ... g5! annuls the tension completely; e.g., 40. Rf1 R×f4 41. R×f4 g×f4 42. Qg1†.

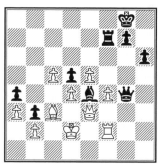

*After 39. ... Qg4*

**40. Ba5!** von Gottschall finds a strong maneuvre that virtually puts a knife on Black's throat. **40. ... h5 41. Bd8 h4 42. e6 Rf8?** Bird accepts a passive position with the vague hope of obtaining chances later on. It was necessary to exchange the passed pawns to fight for a draw: 42. ... Q×e6 43. B×h4 Rf8 44. Bg5 Qd7. **43. e7 Re8 44. Qe2 Qf5 45. Kc3 h3 46. Qe3** 46. Rh2! Kf7 47. Kb4 Bg2 48. R×g2 wins in a most prosaic way. A sample line: 48. ... h×g2 49. Q×g2 Rh8 50. K×a4 Rh3 51. Ka5 Rh6 52. Qe2 Re6 53. Qf3 Re4 54. Q×b3. **46. ... Bg2 47. Qg3 Qe4 48. Rd2 Kf7 48.** ... Qb1 isn't sufficient either after 49. R×g2 h×g2 50. Q×g2 Qc1† 51. Kb4 Qc4† 52. Ka5 Q×d4 53. Kb5 and the mightier king wins. Or 48. ... Bf1 49. f5! Q×f5 50. Qd6 and the king will advance decisively. **49. f5** "The final struggle in a very interesting game"—Zukertort. **49. ... Kg8 50. f6 g6 51. Re2!** Qb1 "If 51. ... Qf5 52. Rf2, winning at once"—Zukertort. **52. Qf4 Kf7 53. Kb4** 53. Qh6 wins at once, but the text move is more than enough as well. **53. ... Qd3 54. Qh6 Q×d4† 55. Kb5 Qc4† 56. Kb6 Q×e2 57. Qg7† Ke6 58. f7 R×e7 59. B×e7 Kd7 60. f8Q** Black resigns—*Chess Monthly* (Zukertort), August 1885, pp. 373–375.

## (738) Bird–Schallopp  ½–½
International tournament (round 4)
Hamburg, 15 July 1885
*C58*

**1. e4 e5 2. Nf3 Nc6 3. Bc4 Nf6 4. Ng5 d5 5. e×d5 Na5 6. d.** **h6 7. Nf3 e4 8. Qe2 N×c4 9. d×c4 Bc5 10. h3 0-0 11. Nh2 b** **12. Nc3 b×c4 13. Q×c4 Bd6** This retreat hampers his own play After 13. ... Qd6 Black has excellent play for the pawn. **14. Be3 a** **15. 0-0-0 Ba6 16. Qd4 Re8 17. Ng4 N×g4 18. h×g4 Be5 19. Qd** **B×c3?** Schallopp is too eager to win back his pawn. **20. Q×c3 Be** **21. Rd4** Not bad at all, but immediately decisive is 21. Rd2 B×g **22. B×h6! f6 23. Bf4**, with great preponderance on each part of th board. **21. ... B×g4 22. f3 Bf5 23. g4 Bg6 24. f4 f5 25. g×f5 B×f** **26. Rg1** 26. Rc4 Re7 27. Rc5 gains the important a-pawn. Blac has nothing to show for in return. **26. ... g6** More prudent is 26. .. Re7. Bird now finds the correct idea. **27. Rc4! Re7 28. Rc6 Kh** (see diagram)

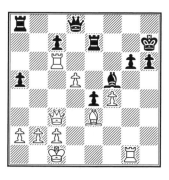

*After 28. ... Kh7*

**29. Qc5** 29. Rg×g6! decisively tears the kingside apart; e.g. 29. ... B×g6 30. f5! Rg7 31. f×g6† R×g6 32. R×g6 K×g6 33. Qc6† and Black can resign. **29. ... Rd7 30. c4 Rc8** Abandoning the a-pawn is bad, but Bird wrongly didn't take the time to capture it. **31. Rh1 Rd6!** A very strong reply, that forces White to make such concessions that a win becomes unlikely. **32. Bd2** Relatively innocent. The same idea, capturing the opponent's a-pawn remains critical; e.g., 32. a4 R×c6 33. d×c6 Qe8 34. Q×a5 Q×c6 35. Qb5 Qe6 36. a5. **32. ... Bd7?** A bad mistake, just when a draw seems inevitable after 32. ... R×c6 33. d×c6 Qd6. **33. R×d6 c×d6 34. Q×d6 R×c4† 35. Bc3 h5 36. Qe5 R×c3† 37. b×c3 Qc8 38. Rh2 Qc5 39. Qd4 Qa3† 40. Rb2 Bf5 41. d6 e3 42. Q×e3 Q×d6 43. c4 h4 44. c5 Qf6 45. Qe5 Q×e5 46. f×e5 g5 47. c6** 47. Kd2 secures a relatively easy win. Now the Black pawns get unexpectedly strong. **47. ... g4 48. c7?** Only precise play is enough to bring the full point home. Concretely, after 48. e6! B×e6 49. Rb7† Kg6 50. c7, Black is bound to lose crucial time with his bishop being vulnerable at e6. After 50. ... Kg5 51. Rb6 Bd7 52. Rd6 Bc8 53. Rd8 Ba6 54. Ra8 Bb7 55. Rb8 Ba6 56. Kd2 the king arrives in time. **48. ... h3 49. Rf2 Be6 50. Kd2** Another line is 50. Kb2 Kg7 (50. ... g3 51. Rf7† wins) 51. Rd2 g3 52. Rd6 Bc8 53. Rd8 h2 54. R×c8 h1Q 55. Rg8† K×g8 56. c8Q† and the draw is inevitable. **50. ... Kg7 51. Rf6 Bc8 52. Rf1 g3 53. Ke2 g2 54. Rg1 Kf7 55. Kf2 h2 56. K×g2 h×g1Q† 57. K×g1 Ke6 58. Kf2 Kd5 59. Ke2 Kc4 60. Kd2 Kb4 61. Kc1 a4 62. Kb1 Ka3** draw—*Tournament Book*, pp. 80–81.

**(739) Mackenzie–Bird   1–0**

International tournament (round 5)

Hamburg, 15 July 1885

C61

1. e4 e5 2. Nf3 Nc6 3. Bb5 Nd4 4. N×d4 e×d4 5. 0-0 h5 6. d3 Bc5 7. Nd2 c6 8. Ba4 d6 9. Bb3 Bg4 10. f3 Be6 11. Qe1 h4 12. B×e6 f×e6 13. h3 Bb6 14. f4 Qe7 15. Nf3 0-0-0 16. a4 c5 17. a5 Bc7 18. b4 d5 19. e5 Rd7 20. Bd2 Kb8 21. Qf2 b6 22. Rfb1 Nh6 23. b×c5 Q×c5 24. Bb4 Qc6 25. N×d4 Qb7 26. N×e6 Nf5 27. N×c7 K×c7 28. a×b6† a×b6 29. Bc5 Rh6 30. B×b6† Black resigns—*Tournament Book*, pp. 88–90.

**(740) Bird–Taubenhaus   1–0**

International tournament (round 6)

Hamburg, 17 July 1885

A02

1. f4 e6 2. Nf3 Nc6 3. e3 b6 4. b3 Bb7 5. Bb2 Nf6 6. Bb5 Ne7 7. 0-0 Ng6 8. Nc3 Be7 9. Qe2 0-0 10. Bd3 Ne8 11. Ne4 f5 12. Neg5 h6 13. Nh3 Bf6 14. c3 Nd6 15. Rae1 Ne4 16. B×e4 f×e4 17. Nd4 e5 18. Nf5 Ne7 18. ... d6 is perfectly fine. Bird now exchanges knights, instead of playing the more testing 19. Ng3, followed by 20. Qg4 and 21. f5, when Black's e-pawn is coming under fire. **19. N×e7† Q×e7 20. f×e5** Activating his opponent's pieces at the expense of its own isn't a good idea. 20. c4 or 20. f5 equalizes. **20. ... B×e5 21. Nf4 Rf6 22. Rf2 Raf8 23. Ref1 d5?** Taubenhaus carelessly falls in a trap. Instead, 23. ... Qd6 leaves White struggling against the bishop pair, e.g., 24. g3 g5 25. Qg4 (or 25. Nh5 Rf3) 25. ... Ba6 26. Rd1 Kh8 27. Nh3 Bd3. **24. Ng6** White wins the exchange. Despite stubborn defensive play, Taubenhaus doesn't come close to drawing. **24. ... R×g6 25. R×f8† Kh7 26. Qh5 Bc6 27. Rh8† K×h8 28. Q×g6 Be8 29. Qf5 Kg8 30. Ba3 c5 31. d4 c×d3 *e.p.* 32. Q×d3 Bc6 33. g3 Qd6 34. Rf2 Be8 35. Rd2 Bf7 36. Bb2 B×g3 37. h×g3 Q×g3† 38. Rg2 Qe1† 39. Qf1 Q×e3† 40. Qf2 Qd3 41. Rg3 Qb1† 42. Kh2 d4 43. Qg2 g5 44. c×d4 Qf5 45. d×c5 b×c5 46. Qe2 Kh7 47. Qe3** Black resigns—*Tournament Book*, pp. 101–102.

**(741) Bird–Bier   1–0**

International tournament (round 7)

Hamburg, 17 July 1885

*Game score missing*

**(742) Bird–Riemann   1–0**

International tournament (round 8)

Hamburg, 18 July 1885

A03

1. f4 d5 2. Nf3 c5 3. e3 Nc6 4. Bb5 Bd7 5. 0-0 e6 6. b3 Nf6 7. Bb2 Be7 8. B×c6 B×c6 9. Ne5 Qc7 10. d3 Rg8 11. Nd2 Nd7 12. Qh5 g6 13. Q×h7 0-0-0 14. Q×f7 Rde8 15. Q×e6 Bd6 16. Qg4 Kb8 17. N×c6† b×c6 18. Rae1 g5 19. Qf3 g×f4 20. e×f4 R×e1 21. R×e1 B×f4 22. Nf1 d4 23. Bc1 Bd6 24. Qf7 Rf8 25. Re8† R×e8 26. Q×e8† Kb7 27. Bg5 Ne5 28. Qd8 Q×d8 29. B×d8 Kc8 30. Bh4 Nd7 31. Nd2 Bf8 32. Ne4 Nb6 33. Be1 Kd7 34. Bd2 Ke6 35. g4 Nd7 36. h3 Be7 37. Kg2 Bh4 38. Kf3

Ne5† 39. Ke2 Be7 40. Bf4 Nd7 41. Kf3 Nb6 42. Kg3 Nd5 43. Bd2 Nc7 44. a4 Nd5 45. h4 Nb6 46. a5 Nd7 47. h5 Ne5 48. Kf4 Nd7 49. g5 Ne5 50. g6 Bf8 51. Ng5† Kd5 52. Kf5 Bh6 53. Bf4 Nd7 54. a6 Nf8 55. Ne6 Black resigns—*Tournament Book*, pp. 119–120.

**(743) Bird–Tarrasch   0–1**

International tournament (round 9)

Hamburg, 20 July 1885

C77

1. e4 e5 2. Nf3 Nc6 3. Bb5 a6 4. Ba4 Nf6 5. Qe2 Bc5 6. c3 b5 7. Bc2 0-0 8. d3 d5 9. Bg5 d4 10. h3 Qd6 11. Nbd2 Nd7 12. g4 f6 13. Bh4 d×c3 14. b×c3 Ba3 15. Nf1 Qc5 16. Bb3† Kh8 17. Qd2 b4 18. c4 Nd4 19. N×d4 Q×d4 20. Rb1 Nc5 21. Ke2 N×e4 22. d×e4 Q×e4† 23. Ne3 Bb7 24. Rbg1 Rad8 25. Qc2 Qf3† 26. Ke1 Be4 27. Qe2 Qf4 28. Bg3 Qh6 29. Rh2 Bd3 30. Qf3 Bb2 31. Nd5 R×d5 32. Bf4 Bc3† 33. Kd1 Be4† 34. Kc1 Bd2† 35. Kb2 B×f4 36. Q×e4 Rd2† 37. Kb1 B×h2 38. g5 Qg6 39. Q×g6 h×g6 40. Rg4 White resigns—*Tournament Book*, pp. 133–134.

**(744) Bird–Englisch   0–1**

International tournament (round 10)

Hamburg, 20 July 1885

C77

1. e4 e5 2. Nf3 Nc6 3. Bb5 a6 4. Ba4 Nf6 5. Qe2 b5 6. Bb3 Bc5 7. a4 Rb8 8. a×b5 a×b5 9. 0-0 0-0 10. d3 d6 11. Bg5 h6 12. Be3 B×e3 13. f×e3 Be6 14. Nbd2 Ra8 15. B×e6 f×e6 16. Nb3 Qd7 17. Nh4 Ne7 18. Qd2 Qc6 19. h3 Qb6 20. Kh2 R×a1 "All through the game Herr Englisch—the 'ex drawing master,' for Herr Berger has now greater claims to that position—seizes every opportunity to simplify matters, whilst Mr. Bird tries to avoid the dreaded result of a draw"—Zukertort. Zukertort is doing Englisch some injustice. Bird's last moves were positionally unfounded. Black could have obtained an edge here with 20. ... Ra4! **21. R×a1 Nd7 22. Nf3 Nf6 23. Qe1 Qc6 24. c3 Ra8 25. Na5 Qb6 26. b4 Kh7 27. Nd2 Ng6 28. d4 Rf8 29. Qe2 e×d4 30. c×d4** Bird hopes to exploit the open c-file, but had Englisch replied 30. ... c5!, it would have become clear that he only got trouble: 31. b×c5 d×c5 and he must choose between allowing a strong passed pawn or the destruction of his center. Thus, the natural 30. e×d4 was preferable. **30. ... c6 31. Rc1 Ne7 32. Qd3 Kh8 33. Qb3 d5 34. e5 Nd7 35. Nf3** Thanks to his opponent's doubtful 30th move, Bird succeeded in obtaining a slight initiative. **35. ... Nb8 36. Qd3 Qd8 37. Nb3** 37. Nb7 and the knight reaches greener pastures. **37. ... Nd7 38. e4 Nb6 39. Nc5 Qc8 40. Ra1 d×e4 41. Q×e4** Bird played well, forcing Englisch to demonstrate his defensive powers. **41. ... Nbd5 42. Ra7 Rf4 43. Qb1 Qg8** *(see diagram)*

**44. Nd3** Losing time. He could have crowned his positional play by outmaneuvring his opponent with 44. Rd7! Rf7 45. Rd6. **44. ... Rf8 45. Qc1 Qf7 46. Qc5 Qf5 47. Ra3** 47. R×e7 forces the draw after 47. ... Q×d3 48. R×e6 R×f3! 49. Q×c6 R×h3† 50. g×h3 Qe2† etc. **47. ... Qe4 48. Nf2** 48. Qc1 has the benefit of avoiding the following activation of Englisch's queen. **48. ... Qe2 49. Kg1 Qb2 50. Ra7 Ne3** A highly promising endgame for Black is reached after 50. ... Qb1†! 51. Kh2 R×f3! 52. g×f3 Qf1 53. Ra2 Nf4 54. Ne4

*After 43. ... Qg8*

Q×h3† 55. Kg1 Q×f3 56. Nf6 Ng8! **51. Q×e7 Qb1† 52. Nd1** "It does not matter, whether White plays at once 52. Kh2 or interposes first: in either case Black should finally draw by perpetual check with the knight at f1 and g3"—Zukertort. **52. ... Q×d1† 53. Kf2?** "Playing hurriedly, White overlooked probably the check at d2: a tragi-comic conclusion"—Zukertort. **53. ... Qd2† 54. Kg3 Q×g2† 55. Kh4 Nf5†** and mates in two more moves—*Chess Monthly* (Zukertort), September 1885, pp. 17–18.

### (745) Bird–Weiss    0–1
International tournament (round 11)
Hamburg, 21 July 1885
A03

1. f4 d5 2. Nf3 Nf6 3. e3 e6 4. b3 Be7 5. Bb2 a6 6. Be2 c5 7. 0–0 Nc6 8. Qe1 0–0 9. Qg3 d4 10. Bd3 Nb4 11. e×d4 N×d3 12. c×d3 b5 13. Ne5 Bb7 14. Qf2 Rc8 15. d×c5 B×c5 16. d4 Bb6 17. Na3 Qd5 18. Rac1 Ne4 19. Qf3 B×d4† 20. B×d4 Q×d4† 21. Qe3 Qb2 22. R×c8 R×c8 23. Nac4 b×c4 24. N×c4 Qf6 25. d3 Nc3 26. Nd6 Rb8 27. Rc1 Bd5 28. Rc2 Nb5 29. Nc8 h6 30. a4 Qd4 31. Kf2 Q×e3† 32. K×e3 B×b3 33. Rc6 B×a4 34. Nb6 Nd4 White resigns—*Tournament Book*, pp. 156–157.

### (746) Schottländer–Bird    0–1
International tournament (round 12)
Hamburg, 22 July 1885
C61

1. e4 e5 2. Nf3 Nc6 3. Bb5 Nd4 4. Ba4 Bc5 5. d3 Qf6 6. N×d4 B×d4 7. 0–0 h5 8. c3 Bb6 9. Nd2 g5 10. Nc4 Ne7 11. Ne3 c6 12. Nc4 Bc7 13. d4 Qg7 14. Be3 Ng6 15. Bb3 Nf4 and Black wins. At this point von Bardeleben and Minckwitz lost track in Bird's untraceable manuscript. It can be called a small miracle that Bird has been able to win this game after 37 moves. He'd be completely lost after 16. d×e5 h4 17. Nd6 B×d6 18. e×d6—*Tournament Book*, pp. 168–169.

### (747) W. Paulsen–Bird    0–1
International tournament (round 13)
Hamburg, 22 July 1885
C22

1. e4 e5 2. d4 e×d4 3. Q×d4 Nc6 4. Qe3 Bb4† 5. c3 Ba5 6. Qg3 Nf6 7. Be2 Qe7 8. Be3 d6 9. Nd2 Be6 10. Nh3 Bb6 11. Nf4 0–0 12. 0–0 B×e3 13. Q×e3 Bd7 14. Rae1 Rfe8 15. Bd1 Ne5 16. Qg3

Ng6 17. N×g6 h×g6 18. Bc2 Bb5 19. c4 Bc6 20. f4 Qd7 21. f[...] g×f5 22. R×f5 N×e4 23. Qf4 N×d2 24. Q×d2 R×e1† 25. Q×e[...] Qe6 26. Q×e6 f×e6 27. Rg5 Rf8 28. h4 Rf4 29. h5 Kf7 30. b[...] Rd4 31. a4 b6 32. Rg3 e5 33. Kf1 Rd2 34. Bf5 Kf6 35. Bh3 Be[...] 36. Re3 d5 37. Ke1 Rb2 38. Kf1 c6 39. Kg1 Bc2 40. Rc3 d[...] 41. Rf3† Kg5 42. Rf7 K×h5 43. R×a7 Kh6 44. Bg4 d3 45. a[...] b×a5 46. R×a5 Kg5 47. Bf3 Kf4 48. Ra1 Ke3 49. Bh5 d2 50. c[...] Rb1† 51. R×b1 B×b1 52. Bd1 Bd3 White resigns—*Tournamen[...] Book*, p. 172.

### (748) Berger–Bird    ½–½
International tournament (round 14)
Hamburg, 23 July 1885
B72

1. e4 c5 2. Nc3 Nc6 3. Nf3 g6 4. d4 c×d4 5. N×d4 Bg[...] 6. Be3 d6 7. Bc4 Bd7 8. 0–0 Nf6 9. h3 0–0 10. Qd2 Rc[...] 11. Bd3 Ne5 12. Qe2 a6 13. f4 N×d3 14. c×d3 Qa5 15. Rac[...] Rfe8 16. Qf2 e6 17. Nde2 Rc6 18. d4 Rec8 19. a3 Be8 20. e[...] Nd5 21. Bd2 N×c3 22. R×c3 Qb6 23. R×c6 B×c6 24. Bc3 Bb[...] 25. Re1 Bf8 26. Ng3 d5 27. Qd2 Qd8 28. Nh1 Qh4 29. Qf[...] Q×f2† 30. N×f2 B×a3 31. g4 Be7 32. g5 Bc4 33. Ng4 b[...] 34. Nf6† Kg7 35. Rc1 Bd3 36. Bd2 R×c1† 37. B×c1 Bb4 38. Kf[...] a5 39. Nd7 a4 40. Nc5 Bc4 41. Na6 Ba5 42. Nc5 Kf8 43. Ke[...] Bf1 44. Bd2 B×d2† 45. K×d2 B×h3 46. Kc3 Bf1 47. Kb4 Kg[...] 48. Nb7 h5 49. g×h6† *e.p.* K×h6 50. Nd6 Kh5 51. N×f7 Kg[...] 52. Ng5 Kf5 53. Kc3 Be2 54. Kb4 Bd3 55. Kc5 Be2 56. Kb4 Bg[...] 57. K×b5 K×f4 58. Nh7 Bd1 59. Nf6 g5 60. Kc5 g4 61. Nh5 [...] Kg5 62. Ng3 Kh4 63. Nf1 g3 64. Ne3 Bg4 65. Kb4 Bf3 66. K×a[...] g2 67. N×g2† B×g2 68. b4 Bf1 69. b5 Kg4 70. Ka5 B×b[...] 71. K×b5 Kf4 72. Kc5 Ke4 73. Kd6 draw—*Tournament Book*, [...] 183–184.

### (749) Bird–Gunsberg    0–1
International tournament (round 15)
Hamburg, 24 July 1885
C77

1. e4 e5 2. Nf3 Nc6 3. Bb5 a6 4. Ba4 Nf6 5. Qe2 Bc5 6. c3 Qe[...] 7. 0–0 b5 8. Bb3 d6 9. a4 b4 10. d3 Rb8 11. Bd1 a5 12. Be3 B×e[...] 13. f×e3 Ba6 14. c4 0–0 15. Nh4 g6 16. Qf2 Ne8 17. b3 Bc[...] 18. Nd2 Ng7 19. Qg3 f5 20. e×f5 N×f5 21. N×f5 B×f5 22. Bf[...] Nd8 23. Be4 B×e4 24. R×f8† K×f8 25. N×e4 Ne6 26. Rf1† Kg[...] 27. Qg4 Rf8 28. R×f8 K×f8 29. h4 Kg7 30. Ng3 Qf7 31. d4 e×d[...] 32. e×d4 c5 33. d×c5 N×c5 34. Ne4 Qf5 35. Q×f5 g×f[...] 36. N×c5 d×c5 37. Kf2 Kf6 38. Ke3 Ke5 39. g3 h5 40. Kd3 f[...] 41. g×f4† K×f4 42. Ke2 Kg4 43. Ke3 K×h4 44. Kf4 Kh3 45. K[...] h4 46. Kf2 Kg4 47. Kg2 Kf4 48. Kh3 Ke4 49. K×h4 Kd4 Whit[...] resigns—*Tournament Book*, pp. 198–199.

### (750) Noa–Bird    0–1
International tournament (round 16)
Hamburg, 24 July 1885
B34

1. e4 c5 2. Nf3 Nc6 3. d4 c×d4 4. N×d4 g6 5. c3 Bg7 6. Nc[...] d6 7. Be3 Nf6 8. f3 0–0 9. Qd2 d5 10. e×d5 N×d5 11. Bh6 B×h[...]

2. Q×h6 Qd6 13. Nd2 Qe5† 14. Kd1 White's opening has ~~b~~een a complete failure. Taking his seat in the center the king is ~~b~~ound to perish. 14. ... Bf5 15. g4 B×c2† 16. K×c2 Ne3† ~~1~~7. Kc1 Rfd8 18. Bb5 Nd4! 19. Re1 "19. c×d4 fails after ~~1~~9. ... Q×d4 20. Rd1 Qc5† 21. Bc4 Q×c4† 22. N×c4 R×d1 mate" —Von Bardeleben. 19. ... Ndc2 20. Nc4 N×e1 21. Q×e3 Q×b5 White resigns—*Tournament Book* (von Bardeleben), pp. 202– ~~2~~03.

**(751) Bird–Minckwitz   1–0**
International tournament (round 17)
Hamburg, 25 July 1885
*A03*

1. f4 d5 2. e3 e6 3. Nf3 Nf6 4. b3 Be7 5. Bb2 c5 6. Nc3 Nc6
7. Bb5 0–0 8. B×c6 b×c6 9. 0–0 Qc7 10. Qe1 Ba6 11. d3 Rab8
12. Qg3 Ne8 13. Ne5 f6 14. Ng4 c4 15. d×c4 B×c4 16. Rf3 Ba6
17. Qh3 f5 18. Ne5 Nf6 19. Rg3 Bd6 20. Qh6 Rb7 21. Na4 Bb5
22. Nd7 Q×d7 23. B×f6 Rf7 24. Bc3 B×a4 25. b×a4 c5 26. Rf1
Rf8 27. Be5 g6 28. R×g6† Bg7 29. B×g7 R×g7 30. R×g7† Q×g7
31. Q×e6† Qf7 32. Qc8† Kg7 33. Q×c5 Qe6 34. Rd1 Rd7
35. Qd4† Kg6 36. c4 Qd6 37. c×d5 Qa3 38. d6 Q×a2 39. e4 f×e4
40. Q×e4† Kg7 41. Qe5† Kf7 42. Qf5† Ke8 43. Re1† Kd8
44. Qf8 mate—*Tournament Book*, pp. 217–218.

**Josef Noa (courtesy Cleveland Public Library).**

# C.C.A. CONGRESS, HEREFORD 1885

Immediately after the tournament in Hamburg the British masters returned to England. They were expected in Hereford to attend the congress of the Counties Chess Association (of which the start date was postponed a week).

The association existed twenty years (this count is only correct when one includes the forerunners; the first congress held under the auspices of the C.C.A. was in 1870), and this was the proclaimed reason to organize, for the first time, a master tournament. The arrival of the B.C.A. was an undoubted and crucial stimulant that finally broadened the perspective of the rather conservative C.C.A. Thanks to the generous support of Charles Anthony, the proprietor of the *Hereford Times*, the C.C.A. was able to warrant a well-filled prize fund. The first four players were entitled to a prize, while the entrance fees were distributed among the non–prize winners. Especially the first prize of £60 attracted the attention of the participants.

Skipworth's attempts to outflank the B.C.A seemed to be a success. Eleven players entered the master tournament. Among them were all the leading British players except Zukertort, who was in negotiations with Steinitz to play a match for the world championship. Several German players were expected, but nearly all of them ultimately refrained from undertaking the trip as the number of prizes was considered too small to cover their expenses.

Just before the tournament took off, the players had a word to say about whether it would be a single or double round-robin and which time limit would be used. The majority settled for the slower rate of 15 moves per hour and a single round event. Bird and Pollock were the sole dissonant voices. The games were played at the Green Dragon Hotel.

People were moderate in their expectations of Bird after his two consecutive ill-successes, but the veteran surprised the field by taking an excellent start with three straight wins at the expense of Owen, Pollock and Schallopp. After a draw with Mason a clash with Blackburne, the sole leader, was programmed for round five. A tense game was adjourned and only finished after the eighth round. Bird missed an easy win at one point and ultimately had to agree to a draw. Bird scored another win in the sixth round, against Thorold, but then he suffered his usual defeat from Gunsberg, who otherwise had a dreadful tournament. Bird's follow-up during the next rounds was on par with his previous results. He beat Skipworth, drew Mackenzie and won against Ranken in the final round.

The end of the tournament brimmed with surprises. Schallopp took the lead after the tenth and penultimate round by beating the leader, Blackburne. In the final round Thorold, one of the tail-enders, created a major upset when he made use of a blunder by the nervous German. Blackburne recovered well, beat Mason and came out first after all with 8 points. Thanks to his final win, Bird caught up the unlucky Schallopp. Both players counted 7½ points. The committee decided to determine the second and third prize with a tie-break match. Schallopp won the first game and could have decided the match rather easily in the second game. Careless play,

**Hereford 1885. Standing from left to right:** Isidor Gunsberg, Edmund Thorold, Henry E. Bird, William H.K. Pollock, T. Smith, E. Schallopp, the Rev. John Owen, the Rev. Arthur B. Skipworth. **Seated:** James Mason, Joseph H. Blackburne, Charles Anthony (the president), Capt George H. Mackenzie, the Rev. Charles E. Ranken (*Illustrated London News*).

however, turned the tables and Bird made excellent use of the opportunity to launch a strong counterattack. It was subsequently decided to share both prizes between them.

The tournament in Hereford was received with enthusiasm (even

Hoffer called it a "complete success"). The future looked prosperous for the C.C.A., and many believed there was ample room in England for two organizations.

Bird supplied a nice postlude on p. 24 of his *Chess Novelties*. Immediately after the end of the tournament Bird went for a tour in the company of two "less successful competitors," as he, not subtly characterized his American rivals Mackenzie and Mason. Bird's idea was to show the visitors (Mason definitely settled in England seven years earlier but as usual it took a long time before foreigners were completely accepted) the idyllic scenery of such towns as Ross, Monmouth and Tintern.

## (752) Owen–Bird    0–1

C.C.A. Congress (round 1)
Hereford, 4 August 1885
*A80*

1. Nf3 f5 2. d4 Nf6 3. e3 b6 4. Be2 e6 5. 0–0 Bb7 6. Nbd2 "A very awkward method of proceeding with the development"—Zukertort. 6. … Be7 7. Ne1 "7. c4, followed up by 8. b3, would be more to our taste"—Zukertort. 7. … 0–0 8. Nd3 Qe8 9. Bf3 Ne4 10. Bh5 g6 11. Be2 Nc6 12. f3 Nf6 13. c3 d5 14. b3 Bd6 15. f4 Ne4 16. Bb2 Nd8 17. Ne5 Qe7 18. Rf3 c5 19. Rh3 B×e5 20. d×e5 Nc6 21. Nf3 Rad8 22. Qf1 Rf7 23. Rd1 Rg7 24. Bd3 g5 Bird decides to take his chance on the kingside. Otherwise, there is not much play in the

### 15th Congress of the C.C.A., Hereford, 3–12 August 1885

*Site:* Green Dragon Hotel
*Prizes:* 1st £60, 2nd £25, 3rd £15, 4th £5 entrance fees distributed among non–prize winners
*Time limit:* 15 moves per hour

|  | 1 | 2 | 3 | 4 | 5 | 6 | 7 | 8 | 9 | 10 | 11 | |
|---|---|---|---|---|---|---|---|---|---|---|---|---|
| 1 J.H. Blackburne |  | 0 | ½ | ½ | 1 | 1 | 1 | 1 | 1 | 1 | 1 | 8 |
| 2 E. Schallopp | 1 |  | 0 | 1 | ½ | 1 | 1 | 0 | 1 | 1 | 1 | 7½ |
| 3 H.E. Bird | ½ | 1 |  | ½ | ½ | 0 | 1 | 1 | 1 | 1 | 1 | 7½ |
| 4 G.H. Mackenzie | ½ | 0 | ½ |  | 0 | 1 | 1 | 1 | 1 | 1 | 1 | 7 |
| 5 J. Mason | 0 | ½ | ½ | 1 |  | ½ | 1 | 1 | 0 | 0 | 1 | 5½ |
| 6 I. Gunsberg | 0 | 0 | 1 | 0 | ½ |  | ½ | 1 | 1 | 1 | ½ | 5½ |
| 7 A.B. Skipworth | 0 | 0 | 0 | 0 | 0 | ½ |  | 1 | 1 | 0 | 1 | 3½ |
| 8 E. Thorold | 0 | 1 | 0 | 0 | 0 | 0 | 0 |  | 0 | 1 | 1 | 3 |
| 9 W.H.K. Pollock | 0 | 0 | 0 | 0 | 1 | 0 | 0 | 1 |  | 1 | 0 | 3 |
| 10 C.E. Ranken | 0 | 0 | 0 | 0 | 1 | 0 | 1 | 0 | 0 |  | 1 | 3 |
| 11 J. Owen | 0 | 0 | 0 | 0 | 0 | ½ | 0 | 0 | 1 | 0 |  | 1½ |

*Tie match:*    1    2
H.E. Bird    0    1    1
E. Schallopp    1    0    1

position. **25. B×e4 g4 26. Rh6 f×e4?** Too venturesome. Safe, but leading to a rather boring position, is 26. ... d×e4 27. Ng5 Bc8. **27. Ng5 Bc8 28. Qf2?** Simply overlooking 28. ... N×e5!, but he's not alone. Instead 28. c4! breaks down Black's center. With 28. ... Nb4 29. c×d5, each way of recapturing the pawn has grave consequences. **28. ... Rf8?! 29. Qh4 Rf5?!** Though it has lost some of its value, 29. ... N×e5 was still the right move. **30. Q×g4?!** *(see diagram)* The same idea as above, 30. c4!, remains hard to meet. After 30. ... d×c4 31. Rf6! c×b3 32. a×b3 Na5 33. N×e4 Bird's position looks desperate.

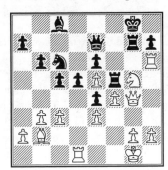

*After 30. Q×g4*

**30. ... N×e5!** Bird finally hits upon the correct rejoinder. By losing a crucial pawn, White is faced with serious difficulties. **31. Qe2 c4** Much better was 31. ... Nd3 at once, as the knight is far less impressive after 32. b×c4! (instead of the text move) 32. ... N×c4 33. Bc1!, due to the threat of 34. N×e4. **32. Kh1? Nd3 33. g4 Rf×g5!** The game has finally stabilized, and with this correct sacrifice Bird definitively launches a winning attack. **34. f×g5 Q×g5 35. Rh3 N×b2 36. Rg1** "If 36. Q×b2 Q×g4, attacking both rooks, and one must fall. Bird has well calculated the points of the position"—White. **36. ... Nd3 37. Rh5 Qg6 38. h4 e5 39. Rg5 Qh6 40. Rh5 Qe6 41. Kh2 Bd7 42. Rg3 Be8 43. Rf5 Bg6 44. Qg2 B×f5 45. g×f5 Qf6 46. b×c4 R×g3 47. Q×g3† Qg7 48. Qh3 d×c4 49. f6 Q×f6 50. Qg2† Qg6** White resigns—*Leeds Mercury* (White), 12 September 1885; *Chess Monthly* (Zukertort), May 1886, pp. 280–281.

**(753) Bird–Pollock    1–0**
C.C.A. Congress (round 2)
Hereford, 4 August 1885
*Game score missing*

**(754) Schallopp–Bird    0–1**
C.C.A. Congress (round 3)
Hereford, 5 August 1885
*Game score missing*

**(755) Bird–Mason    ½–½**
C.C.A. Congress (round 4)
Hereford, 6 August 1885
*Game score missing*

**(756) Blackburne–Bird    ½–½**
C.C.A. Congress (round 5)
Hereford, 6 August 1885
*B25*

**1. e4 c5 2. Nc3 Nc6 3. g3 d6 4. Bg2 g6 5. Nd5 Bg7 6. d3 Nf6 7. N×f6† B×f6 8. Ne2 h5 9. h4 Bg4 10. f3 Bd7 11. c3 Qb6 12. Qc2**

**Bg7 13. Be3 Qa6 14. f4 Bg4 15. Bh3 0–0–0 16. B×g4† h×g4 17. Nc1 e5 18. a4 c4 19. Qe2 e×f4 20. B×f4 f5 21. 0–0 Rhe8 22. Qd1 c×d3** Bird played very well and obtained pressure against White's position. With his last move Blackburne gave up the defense of the b-pawn which Bird could have picked up with 22. ... Qb6†. **23. e×f5 g×f5 24. Q×d3 Qb6† 25. Kh1 Re4** 25. ... Q×b2 26. Rb1 Q×c3 is certainly playable. The text move loses the tempo that allows Blackburne to get his position in order. **26. Qb5 Ne5 27. Q×b6 a×b6 28. Nb3** Both players play somewhat hesitatingly. At once 28. a5! opens the queenside and nurtures a small edge. **28. ... Nf3 29. Rf2 Be5 30. Nd2 N×d2 31. B×d2 B×g3 32. R×f5 B×h4 33. Bg5 B×g5 34. R×g5 Kc7** The game transposed into an endgame that is slightly better for Bird. But despite the extra material, a win is hard to realize. **35. Rf1 R×a4 36. Kg2 Re8 37. Rf2 Re7 38. Rd2 Rae4 39. Kf2 Kc6 40. Rg6 R7e6 41. R×e6 R×e6 42. Rd4 Rg6 43. Kg3 Kc5 44. Rb4 d5 45. Rd4 b5 46. Rf4 Kd6** 46. ... Re6! is a well-timed opportunity to go for the full point: 47. R×g4 Re4 48. Rg8 b4 etc. **47. Rb4 Kc6 48. Rd4 Kc5 49. Rf4 Rg8 50. Rf7 Rd8** Bird's suggestion 50. ... d4! wins after 51. c×d4† K×d4 52. Rf4† Kd3 53. Rf7 Kc4 54. R×b7 b4 55. Rf7 Kb3 56. Rf2 Rc8 etc. **51. K×g4 d4 52. c×d4† R×d4† 53. Kf3 Rb4 54. Ke2 R×b2† 55. Kd1 b6 56. Kc1 Rb4 57. Kc2** draw—*The Times* (Bird), 13 August 1885.

**(757) Bird–Thorold    1–0**
C.C.A. Congress (round 6)
Hereford, 7 August 1885
*Game score missing*

**(758) Gunsberg–Bird    1–0**
C.C.A. Congress (round 7)
Hereford, 8 August 1885
*B34*

**1. e4 c5 2. Nc3 Nc6 3. Nf3 g6 4. d4 c×d4 5. N×d4 Bg7 6. Be3 Nf6 7. Be2 h5 8. h3 d6 9. 0–0 Bd7 10. f4 N×d4 11. B×d4 Bc6 12. Qd3 Qa5 13. a3 Qc7 14. Rad1 0–0–0 15. B×a7 e6 16. Qe3 Nd7 17. Bd4 e5 18. f×e5 d×e5 19. Bc5 N×c5 20. Q×c5 Rd4 21. R×d4 e×d4 22. Nb5 B×b5 23. Q×c7† K×c7 24. R×f7† Kb6 25. B×b5 Bh6 26. Bd3 Bc1 27. b3 g5 28. a4 Kc6 29. b4 b6 30. Rf6† Kc7 31. a5 b×a5 32. b×a5 Rb8 33. a6 Rb1 34. Kf2 Ra1 35. e5 Bf4 36. Rf7† Kb6 37. Rb7† Kc5 38. e6 h4 39. e7 g4 40. h×g4 Bg3† 41. Kf3 Re1 42. Be2** Black resigns—*Morning Post*, 17 August 1885.

**(759) Bird–Skipworth    1–0**
C.C.A. Congress (round 8)
Hereford, 10 August 1885
*Game score missing*

Bird had a bye in the ninth round.

**(760) Mackenzie–Bird    ½–½**
C.C.A. Congress (round 10)
Hereford, 11 August 1885
*B73*

**1. e4 c5 2. Nc3 Nc6 3. Nf3 g6 4. d4 c×d4 5. N×d4 Bg7 6. Be3**

d6 7. Be2 Nf6 8. 0-0 0-0 9. f4 Bd7 10. h3 N×d4 11. B×d4 Bc6 12. Bf3 Ne8 13. Kh2 Qc7 14. B×g7 N×g7 15. Qd2 e6 16. Rae1 Rad8 17. Qf2 b5 18. g4 With his next moves, Bird grasps the initiative. **18. ... b4 19. Nd1** "19. Ne2 would be better"—Zukertort. **19. ... d5 20. e5 d4** 20. ... f5 stops all his opponent's attacking aspirations. **21. B×c6 Q×c6 22. Re2 f6 23. Qg2 Qa6! 24. b3 Q×a2 25. Nf2 f×e5 26. f×e5 Qa5** Bird relieves the pressure a tad too soon, thus allowing White to get back in the game again. 26. ... Rc8 forces 27. Rc1, when Black is better. **27. Nd3** White concentrates his forces in good style to a strong attack, which, however, has not much chance of success considering the previous exchange of the minor pieces. **27. ... Qb5 28. Rf6 a5 29. Ref2 Qb8 30. Kg1 Kh8** The difference in activity of Bird's pieces since a few moves is more than obvious. Here 30. ... Qc8 was necessary to prevent 31. Nc5, which would have been very strong right now. **31. Qf3 Rg8 32. Rf7 Rc8 33. Qf4 Rc7 34. Qh6** Throwing away all his advantage at once. 34. Rf8 retained some initiative. **34. ... R×f7 35. R×f7 Qe8 36. Ra7** 36. Rc7 looks strong and dangerous, but the cold-blooded 36. ... Qa8! 37. Nf4 Qe4 defends everything. **36. ... g5** "A superfluous sacrifice. He might have played 36. ... Qc6"—Zukertort. **37. Q×g5 Qc6 38. Qd2** "If 38. Nf4, Black would capture the c-pawn, defending g6. It is obvious that White might draw at once with 38. R×g7 and 39. Qd8†"—Zukertort. **38. ... Qf3** 38. ... Nf5 39. Qg2 Qc8 is relatively better, but after 40. Rf7 h5, Black is struggling. **39. Qg2** 39. Kh2! calmly defends. If 39. ... Nf5 40. Qf2! forces Black into a difficult endgame. **39. ... Qe3† 40. Kh2 h5 41. R×a5 h×g4 42. h×g4 Nh5 43. Ra8 Nf4 44. R×g8† K×g8 45. N×f4 Q×f4† 46. Qg3 Qd2† 47. Qg2 Qf4†** draw—*Chess Monthly* (Zukertort), May 1886, pp. 278–279.

## (761) Bird–Ranken 1–0
C.C.A. Congress (round 11)
Hereford, 12 August 1885
*C65*

**1. e4 e5 2. Nf3 Nc6 3. Bb5 Nf6 4. Qe2** "Mr. Staunton used to maintain that this is White's best move here"—Ranken. **4. ... Bc5 5. 0-0 Nd4 6. N×d4 B×d4 7. c3 Bb6 8. d3 h6 9. Nd2 c6 10. Ba4 d6 11. Bc2 Bg4 12. Qe1 0-0 13. Nc4 Bc7 14. f4 e×f4 15. B×f4 Be6** Ranken makes a temporary sacrifice of a pawn to relieve his position, but both he and Bird overlooked a hidden nuance at move 18. Instead 15. ... Re8 gives Black a flexible position. **16. N×d6 Qb8** 16. ... B×d6 (Ranken) loses at once after 17. B×d6. **17. e5 Nh5 18. Qh4** Alternatively he could play 18. Bc1! After 18. ... B×d6 19. e×d6 Q×d6 20. Qh4 Qd5 21. d4 Black's knight is in trouble and White has a powerful bishop pair. **18. ... N×f4 19. Q×f4 B×d6 20. e×d6 Rd8 21. d4 Q×d6 22. Qe4 f5** Best. If 22. ... g6 23. Qh4! **23. Qf3 g6 24. Rae1 Bc4** "A scheme for gaining possession of the open e-file, for if now 25. Bd3, Black can safely take the a-pawn, and if instead 25. Rf2 Re8 26. Re3 f4, whereupon if 27. Q×f4 he loses a piece by 27. ... Q×f4 28. R×e8† R×e8 29. R×f4 Re1† etc."—Ranken. **25. Bb3 B×b3 26. a×b3 Re8** (*see diagram*) "The somewhat exposed position of Black's king renders it desirable that he should get rid of the adverse queen. Had he, however, challenged the exchange by 26. ... Qd5, the answer would have been 27. Qe3."—Ranken

*After 26. ... Re8*

**27. Re3 R×e3** "There was no need to give up the open file, for the proper course was likewise 27. ... Re6, doubling rooks if White did the same, and then bringing the king to f7"—Ranken. **28. Q×e. Kg7 29. Re1 Rf8 30. g3 g5** Not bad yet, but 30. ... Rf7 (Ranken) is very safe. **31. Kf2 Kf6** A risky move. **32. h4 Rf7 33. h×g5† h×g. 34. Rh1 Qe7?** "If 34. ... Kg6 now White can answer with 35. Rh. and Black dare not then push 35. ... f4 on account of 36. Qe4†, bu. he might without danger play 35. ... Rf8. After once allowing the rook to check at h6, Black has no further chance of recovering him self"—Ranken. **35. Rh6† Kg7 36. Re6 Qd8 37. Qe5† Kh. 38. Re8** 38. Qe2! is more conclusive. **38. ... Qd7 39. c4 a6 40. Kg. Rg7 41. Rf8 Rf7 42. Re8 Rg7 43. d5** "The advance of this pawn i. decisive. When the game was over, Mr. Bird remarked that he shoul. have proposed a draw about the 40th move, but did not like to do so because he thought his opponent had rather the best of it. Any advantage of position, however, which he may have had was entirely thrown away by his subsequent weak moves"—Ranken. **43. ... c×d. 44. c×d5 f4 45. Qe4† Kh6 46. Rh8†** Black resigns—*British Che. Magazine* (Ranken), October 1885, pp. 348–349.

## (762) Schallopp–Bird 1–0
C.C.A. Congress (tie match, game 1)
Hereford, 13 August 1885
*B34*

**1. e4 c5 2. Nc3 Nc6 3. Nf3 g6 4. d4 c×d4 5. N×d4 Bg7 6. Be3 d6 7. Nd5** "Sacrificing tempi to weaken the d-pawn"—Schallopp. **7. ... e6 8. Nc3 Nge7 9. Qd2** "Worth considering was 9. Ndb5 B×c3† 10. N×c3 or 9. ... Be5 10. f4 B×c3† 11. N×c3"—Schallopp. **9. ... 0-0 10. Ndb5 d5 11. e×d5 N×d5 12. N×d5 e×d5 13. 0-0-0 Be6** From here on Bird slowly but surely drifts into a bind. 13. ... a6 14. Nd4 Re8 offers enough active play to compensate for the isolated pawn. **14. h4 h5 15. Be2 a6 16. Nd4 N×d4 17. B×d4 Rc8 18. B×g7** "Not good was 18. Bf3 because of 18. ... Bf5 19. c3 Qa5 20. a3 Rfd8, when Black retains a good attacking game (Qa5–a4–b3–a2)"—Schallopp. **18. ... K×g7 19. Qd4† Qf6** Each further exchange is profitable for White. 19. ... Kg8 must be played. **20. Bf3 Rfd8 21. Rhe1 Rc4 22. Q×f6† K×f6 23. g3 Rdc8 24. Re2 R8c5 25. Rdd2** "Intending 26. Kd1 and 27. c3, to free the movement of the rooks"—Schallopp. **25. ... Bg4** Once more offering an exchange, and thereby blowing new life into Schallopp's small initiative. **26. B×g4 R×g4 27. Re8 g5** Bad timing. 27. ... Re4 is still good enough. **28. Rd3** Bird's last, auto-mutilating move, would have given Schallopp a nice course with 28. h×g5 R×g5 29. Rb8 Re5 30. b3 Re7 31. Rd8 Re5 32. Rd7. The German instead selects a tricky continuation. **28. ... g×h4 29. Rf3† Kg6 30. g×h4 Rc7?!** Passive, and thus inferior. A quick draw is achieved after 30. ... Rgc4! 31. Rg8† Kh7 32. Rg5 R×c2†. **31. Rg8† Kh7?!** 31. ... Kh6 is, as will soon be clear, substantially better. **32. R×g4 h×g4 33. Rf4 Rc4 34. R×f7† Kg6?!** At first sight it doesn't matter whether the king would have gone to this square or h6, but the difference is nevertheless crucial. In case of 34. ... Kh6, namely, White has to be most careful and play 35. Kd2!, which maintains his edge. If White plays 35. R×b7 instead, another tricky choice awaits him after 35. ... Rf4! Now 36. Rb6†! Kh5 37. Rb8 R×f2 38. Rh8† draws, while 36. Rd7? even loses because of 36. ... R×f2 37. R×c5 g3, thereby unmasking the importance of 34. ... Kh6, as 38. Rg5 is now without check. **35. Rf8?!** In this situation 35. R×b7! is close to winning, for if 35. ... Rf4 36. Rd7 Rf5 37. Kd1 Kh5 38. Ke1 K×h4 39. a3 Kh5 40. Rd6 a5 41. b4 etc. If 36. ... R×f2 37. R×d5 and thanks to the check available at g5 Black can resign. **35. ... Kg7?!** 35. ... Kh5 had to be tried. Due to his continued passive play Bird rapidly succumbs. **36. Rf5 Kg6 37. R×d5 Rf4 38. Rg5† Kf6 39. Kd1 b5 40. Ke1 Rc4 41. c3 b4 42. c×b4 R×b4 43. b3 Re4† 44. Kf1** Black resigns—*Deutsche Schachzeitung* (Schallopp), November 1885, pp. 348–349.

## (763) Bird–Schallopp     1–0

C.C.A. Congress (tie match, game 2)
Hereford, 13 August 1885
*C33*

**1. e4 e5 2. f4 e×f4 3. Be2 d5 4. e×d5 Q×d5 5. Bf3 Qg5 6. d4 Qh4† 7. Kf1 Bd6 8. c4 c6 9. Nc3 Ne7 10. g3 Qh6** Bird's opening selection doesn't hide his intention to complicate the game at all costs. Critical is 10. ... f×g3. **11. h4 Nf5 12. Nge2 Ne3† 13. B×e3 f×e3 14. g4 B×g4 15. Ng1** If 15. B×g4 Qf6†. **15. ... Qf4 16. Ke2 0–0 17. B×g4 Q×g4† 18. Nf3 Qg2† 19. Kd3 Re8 20. Rg1 Q×b2 21. Rb1 Qa3 22. Rb3 Qa6 23. Ng5 b5** Bird invested some more pawns in order to alienate Schallopp's queen from the kingside. This would not have been a problem after the intermediate 23. ... e2! 24. N×e2 b5 which obliges White's knight to move to a most inferior square where it hampers his most important piece in her journey to the kingside. **24. c×b5 c×b5 25. Qh5 b4† 26. Kc2** *(see diagram)*

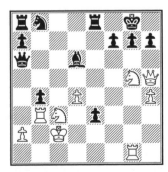

*After 26. Kc2*

**26. ... Qc4?** Bird's practical compensation is now beyond dispute, and nerves of steel are required from Schallopp. It all comes down to leaving his king to its mercy (there is no choice anyway) and, that's the difference with the text move, launch a sweeping counterattack. 26. ... Rc8 might be suitable, but best is the very direct 26. ... Nc6! After 27. Q×h7† Kf8 28. N×f7! N×d4† 29. Kb1, it is

**Emil Schallopp (*Chess Monthly*).**

29. ... Bg3!! that clinches to the victory. The rook is drastically cut off from the action (30. R×g3 Qf1†). **27. d5!** A stunning move that completely turns the tables. Bird's attack is suddenly nearly decisive. **27. ... Qc7?** Black is struggling after 27. ... Nc6 28. Q×f7† Kh8 29. d×c6 Q×h4 30. Ne2 or 27. ... Qf4 28. Q×h7† Kf8 29. Ne6† R×e6 30. Q×g7† Ke7 31. d×e6. After the text move he is doomed. **28. Q×h7† Kf8 29. Qh8† Ke7 30. Q×g7 Kd8 31. N×f7† Kc8 32. Qg4†** Good enough but 32. Qg6! would have been very awkward to meet. **32. ... Nd7 33. N×d6† Q×d6 34. R×b4 Kd8 35. Qg5† Nf6 36. Rf4 Rf8 37. Rgf1 Ke7 38. R×f6 R×f6 39. Qg7† Ke8 40. R×f6 Qh2† 41. Kd3 Qd2† 42. Kc4 Rc8† 43. Rc6 R×c6† 44. d×c6 Qd6 45. Qd7† Q×d7 46. c×d7† K×d7 47. Kd3** Black resigns—*Megabase 2010*.

# IN THE PROVINCES, SEPTEMBER–OCTOBER 1885

The rest of the summer season went by in the usual dullness. On 1 September, Mackenzie was treated to a farewell dinner by the City of London Chess Club. The next day he left the capital in the company of Bird. On their way to a port in the west of England a few stops in chess centers were planned. For this purpose Bird had written to the local chess clubs in the hope to have some exhibitions arranged.

Both men were received the evening of 2 September at the Birmingham Chess Club. While Mackenzie gave a simultaneous exhibition, Bird was engaged in a game against the consulting William Cook and Alderman Avery, respectively the strongest player and the president of the club. A perpetual check ended the game in a draw.

Bird had informed the editors of local newspapers that he and Mackenzie would pass by in Cardiff (on 3 September) and Swansea. In all likelihood last-minute arrangements were set up, but no reports of their visit have been found.

On 24 September Bird visited the Junior Liberal Association Chess Club in Maidstone. The opposition was not so strong here and Bird scored a convincing twenty wins, conceding but one draw.

In October Bird made a second and more extended visit to the Birmingham Chess Club. He was invited to inaugurate the new rooms of the club at the Midland Institute. Bird opened the festivities on Tuesday 6 October with an exhibition against 15 locals. No result was published, but if one subtracts the results of the other performances from the general result given, it appears that actually 16 games were played that evening of which Bird won 10, lost 2 and drew 4.

The following three days were arranged according to a fixed scheme. The evening started with a match game between Bird and Cook. Afterwards the indefatigable veteran opposed the interested amateurs in a simultaneous exhibition.

Synopsis Cook, as Bird's match opponent was nicknamed after the publication of his famous work, *Synopsis of the Chess Openings*, was not to be underestimated. At the C.C.A. meeting held in Birmingham in 1883 he beat Burn in the duel for third prize. Bird apparently kept matters firmly under control. He drew both of his games with the Black pieces and scored the decisive victory in the second game.

Bird's results in the exhibitions were rather mixed. On Wednesday he won 9 games, lost 3 and drew 3, while two games remained unfinished. His best score was made on Thursday, with 15 wins, 2 draws and no losses. Tiredness may explain his relatively meager result on the final evening, when he won 14 games, lost 5 and drew 4. The club committee was extremely pleased with Bird's performance, as his exhibitions attracted a lot of attention from both club members and many interested players living in the neighborhood.

## CHANGES IN LONDON

On 30 October the B.C.A. resumed its activities with a meeting of the governing council at Simpson's Divan. On this occasion several of the world's strongest chess players, among them Bird, were elected to the rank of "Master of the B.C.A." A more controversial point on the agenda was the nature of the relationship between the B.C.A. and the C.C.A. Immediately after the C.C.A. congress at Hereford, Skipworth and Owen made an appeal which was interpreted as a proposal to enhance the cooperation between both organizations. The council of the B.C.A. declared that they "do not see their way to limit their operations or alter their constitution as is proposed by Mr. Owen, but at the same time the council are of opinion that if the C.C.A. federates with the B.C.A., they are

willing, with hearty goodwill, to consider any proposal made by the official executive of the C.C.A. for an arrangement for meetings in the provinces, to be held under the joint auspices of the two associations" (*Chess Monthly*, November 1885, p. 65). Skipworth's reply, not unsurprisingly, insisted on the independence of the C.C.A. He believed his organization was much better suited for organizing provincial meetings, while each Association's having its own meeting in the provinces would be overkill. He ended his exposé with a swipe towards the B.C.A.

> I am bound also to think it a little unreasonable to expect an old, prosperous, and prospering society, national in the support it obtains, national in its work, and having every claim to nationality, to "federate" with a new society, whose very existence as a national one has not yet been assured [*Chess Monthly*, December 1885, p. 97].

Hoffer reacted promptly by pointing out that it was Skipworth who had approached the B.C.A. and not the other way around. It is needless to say that no form of collaboration was agreed to.

Hoffer had more irons in the fire than the management of the B.C.A. and his journalistic work for *Chess Monthly* and *The Field*. At the end of the year he played a crucial role in the foundation of a new chess club in London, the British Chess Club. In its nomenclature the new club was clearly linked with the British Chess Association. With this initiative Hoffer wanted to drain away the popularity of the Divan, to which end he succeeded to a certain degree, especially among those who found the Divan's closing hour, 11 p.m., too early to finish the night.

The start of the club was announced rather bombastically in *Chess Monthly*. According to Hoffer the club was the only place in London where everyone could play a game of chess on every moment of the day from 11 a.m. until 12 midnight. Immediately after the notification of the existence of the British Chess Club a flood of new members joined. Five masters, Bird, Blackburne, Gunsberg, Mackenzie and Zukertort were elected as honorary members. An inaugural dinner took place on 9 January at the Victoria Hall of the Criterion Restaurant. The start of the club was launched with a great deal of various activities such as (handicap) tournaments, consultation games and simultaneous exhibitions. Bird "advocated frequent play between masters for small stakes, and stated that the four matches he had played with Wisker for no stakes had excited much interest."

## HANDICAP TOURNAMENT AT PURSSELL'S 1886

Bird opened the new year by taking part in a handicap tournament at Purssell's. Seventeen other participants joined the event. Two sections with nine players each were formed. The winners of each section were to play for the 1st and 2nd prize, the second for 3rd and 4th, and the thirds for the 5th prize. The players were divided in five classes. The lightest odds were that of an extra move, instead of pawn and move.

Gunsberg triumphed easily in section A. A tie for the second and third place was won by Anger ahead of Sheppard, while Hooke fell off. Bird played in section B. Due to persisting health problems he

## Purssell's handicap tournament, London, January–February 1886

**Site:** Purssell's
**Prizes:** 1st £6, 2nd £4, 3rd £3, 4th £2, 5th £1
**Odds scale:** two moves (class II), pawn and move (class III), pawn and two moves (class IV) and knight (class V)

| Section A | | 1 | 2 | 3 | 4 | 5 | 6 | 7 | 8 | 9 | |
|---|---|---|---|---|---|---|---|---|---|---|---|
| 1 I. Gunsberg | I | | 0 | 1 | 1 | 1 | 1 | 1 | 1 | 1 | 7 |
| 2 F. Anger | III | 1 | | 0 | 1 | 0 | 1 | 1 | ½ | 1 | 5½ |
| 3 W. Sheppard | V | 0 | 1 | | ½ | 1 | ½ | 1 | ½ | 1 | 5½ |
| 4 G.A. Hooke | III | 0 | 0 | ½ | | 1 | 1 | 1 | 1 | 1 | 5½ |
| 5 A. Guest | II | 0 | 1 | 0 | 0 | | 1 | 1 | 1 | 1 | 5 |
| 6 Lee | IV | 0 | 0 | ½ | 0 | 0 | | ½ | 1 | 1 | 3 |
| 7 A.W. Hamilton-Gell | V | 0 | 0 | 0 | 0 | 0 | ½ | | 1 | 1 | 2½ |
| 8 Thomson | IV | 0 | 0 | ½ | 0 | 0 | 0 | 0 | | 1 | 1½ |
| 9 W. Knight | V | 0 | ½ | 0 | 0 | 0 | 0 | 0 | 0 | | ½ |

| Section B | | 1 | 2 | 3 | 4 | 5 | 6 | 7 | 8 | 9 | |
|---|---|---|---|---|---|---|---|---|---|---|---|
| 1 Fenton | IV | | ½ | 1 | 1 | 1 | 1 | 1 | 1 | 0 | 6½ |
| 2 J.T. Heppell | III | ½ | | 0 | 1 | 1 | 1 | + | 1 | + | 6½ |
| 3 W.H.K. Pollock | II | 0 | 1 | | 1 | 1 | ½ | + | 1 | + | 6½ |
| 4 Jacobs | III | 0 | 0 | 0 | | 1 | 1 | + | 0 | + | 4 |
| 5 Chapman | IV | 0 | 0 | 0 | 0 | | 1 | ½ | 1 | 1 | 3½ |
| 6 Marshall | IV | 0 | 0 | ½ | 0 | 0 | | + | 1 | + | 3½ |
| 7 H.E. Bird | I | 0 | – | – | – | ½ | – | | 1 | 1 | 2½ |
| 8 Gladstone | IV | 0 | 0 | 0 | 1 | 0 | 0 | 0 | | + | 2 |
| 9 Carter | V | 1 | – | – | – | 0 | – | 0 | – | | 1 |

Play-off section A: Anger ahead of Sheppard and Hooke
Play-off section B: Fenton ahead of Heppell and Pollock
Play-off 1st and 2nd: Gunsberg wins against Fenton

fared miserably. He had spent the last weeks of the previous year in bed and now, at the point when he had scored 1½ out of 3, he got ill again. In all likelihood Bird forfeited his other games. Three players shared first place. The tie match was won by Fenton (a player from class IV, not the master Richard Fenton), ahead of Heppell. Pollock gathered the same number of points but he seems not to have taken part in the tie games.

Finishing the tournament in style was no mean job. The tie games produced some delay while at the same time the chess room at Purssell's disappeared as the establishment was being rebuilt. It took a few weeks to find a new venue for the players. On top of that the chess columns lost their interest in the affair: All the attention was drawn towards the world championship match between Steinitz and Zukertort and the master tournament held at the British Chess Club. It lasted until early April when it became known that Gunsberg had won the event ahead of Fenton. No further information about the other prize winners could be retrieved.

# MASTER TOURNAMENT AT THE BRITISH CHESS CLUB 1886

The first important event hosted by the British Chess Club was a master tournament in February and March 1886. Thanks to the financial support of some wealthy patrons, of whom F.H. Lewis was the most prominent, a prize fund was amassed. Four prizes, the first being £18, attracted the attention of the British chess elite and in

the nick of time eight players, a good mix of professionals and promising amateurs were ready to play.

Bird was pitted against Blackburne in the first round. After a rather dry game the players agreed to a draw. In the next rounds Bird met two of his "bêtes noires." For the first time since long, Bird was able to beat Mason, but he was less successful against Gunsberg. For the fourth time in a row Bird played with the Black pieces and once again his Sicilian Defense failed utterly against the chess star of the past year. Bird's next opponents were of another caliber and he beat MacDonnell, Pollock and Reeves one after another. His game with Reeves had been postponed as Bird had obligations out of town. With one round to go Bird still had a good chance for a high prize. Blackburne was leading the field with 5½ of 6. Gunsberg followed at a half point while Bird stood third with 4½. The other players followed at a respectable distance.

Blackburne finished the tournament elegantly with another win. All attention now focused on the games of Bird and Gunsberg. Gunsberg dug his own grave when he took a poisoned pawn against Reeves. The underdog surprisingly grasped the point. A sole second place was now within Bird's reach. With Anthony Guest as his opponent he also enjoyed a favorable pairing and the veteran expectedly tried everything he could to drag a full point out of a drawn position (queen against rook and pawn). After two adjournments Bird nevertheless had to concede the draw. Thus Bird and Gunsberg ended tied for 2nd–3rd and shared £10. The press raved about the veteran's exploit.[7]

## Master tournament, London, 17 February–9 March 1886

**Site:** British Chess club
**Prizes:** 1st £18, 2nd £12, 3rd £8, 4th £4
**Time limit:** 20 moves per hour

| | | 1 | 2 | 3 | 4 | 5 | 6 | 7 | 8 | |
|---|---|---|---|---|---|---|---|---|---|---|---|
| 1 J.H. Blackburne | | | ½ | 1 | 1 | 1 | 1 | 1 | 1 | 6½ |
| 2 H.E. Bird | | ½ | | 0 | 1 | 1 | 1 | ½ | 1 | 5 |
| 3 I. Gunsberg | | 0 | 1 | | 1 | 1 | 1 | 1 | 0 | 5 |
| 4 J. Mason | | 0 | 0 | 0 | | 1 | ½ | 1 | 1 | 3½ |
| 5 W.H.K. Pollock | | 0 | 0 | 0 | 0 | | 1 | + | 1 | 3 |
| 6 G.A. MacDonnell | | 0 | 0 | 0 | ½ | 0 | | ½ | 1 | 2 |
| 7 A. Guest | | 0 | ½ | 0 | 0 | – | ½ | | 1 | 2 |
| 8 H.A. Reeves | | 0 | 0 | 1 | 0 | 0 | 0 | 0 | | 1 |

**(764) Bird–Blackburne**    ½–½

B.C.C. tournament (round 1)
London, 17 February 1886
C13

**1. e4 e6 2. d4 d5 3. Nc3 Nf6 4. Bg5 Be7 5. B×f6 B×f6 6. Nf3 d×e4 7. N×e4 b6 8. c3 Bb7 9. Bd3 Nd7 10. Qe2 Qe7 11. 0–0 0–0–0**

7. Once again MacDonnell came first in declaring Bird his admiration: "Bird's play from first to last was, with one exception, truly grand. The one exception was in his game with Gunsberg, where, with a draw certain and a win probable, over-anxious to terminate the fight he blundered into defeat. Bird's drawn game with Blackburne is regarded by the latter as a masterpiece. Again and again did Blackburne essay to lure him on to do something, to risk his draw and fight for victory; but the wily veteran eschewed the snares, refusing to look at, much less to pick up, the chaff thrown to him." *Illustrated Sporting and Dramatic News,* 27 March 1886.

12. Rfe1 Rfd8 13. Ng3 Nf8 14. Be4 B×e4 15. Q×e4 Ng6 16. Nh5 Rac8 17. Rad1 Qd6 18. N×f6† g×f6 19. g3 Qd5 20. Q×d5 R×d5 21. Re4 Rcd8 22. Rde1 Kg7 23. Kg2 R5d7 24. h4 h5 25. Kh3 Rd5 26. Rg1 Rf5 27. Kg2 Kh6 28. Ne1 Rg8 29. Kf1 Rd5 30. Nc2 f5 31. Re2 Rdd8 32. f4 Ne7 33. Ne1 Nd5 34. Nf3 Nf6 35. Ng5 Kg7 36. Kg2 Rd6 37. Rge1 Re8 38. Re5 Kg6 39. Nf3 Ne4 40. Ng5 Nf6 41. R5e2 Red8 42. a3 Nd7 43. Nf3 Kg7 44. b4 b5 45. Ne5 N×e5 46. R×e5 Rd5 47. R×d5 R×d5 48. Kf3 Rd6 49. Ke3 Kf6 50. Kd3 Ke7 51. Kc2 Kd7 52. Kb3 Kc6 53. a4 a6 54. a5 Rd8 55. Kc2 Rg8 56. Re3 Kd5 57. Kd3 c6 draw—*Chess Monthly*, May 1886, p. 272.

### (765) Mason–Bird   0–1
B.C.C. tournament (round 2)
London, 20 February 1886
*B56*

1. e4 c5 2. Nf3 Nc6 3. Nc3 g6 4. d4 c×d4 5. N×d4 Bg7 6. Be3 d6 7. Bb5 "7. Be2 is preferable. The move played loses time as the knight cannot well be taken, and the bishop has to retire to e2"—Guest. 7. ... Bd7 8. 0-0 Nf6 9. Qd2 Ne5 10. Be2 0-0 11. h3 "With a view to playing 12. f4, and to prevent the reply 11. ... Neg4"—Guest. 11. ... Rc8 12. Bh6 Qb6 13. B×g7 K×g7 14. b3 This move costs him a pawn. 14. Nd5 N×d5 15. e×d5 promises a small space advantage. 14. ... Qc5 15. Nd1 N×e4 16. Qe3 Nc3 17. N×c3 Q×c3 18. Bd3 Rfe8 The first of a few moves that only harden Bird's task to convert the extra pawn. Here, or on the next move, exchanging the bishop is much simpler. 19. Rad1 f5 20. Rfe1 Qc5 20. ... a6 is still very good for him. 21. Bb5! "Of course if 21. ... B×b5 22. Ne6† wins the queen. The move considerably improves White's prospects of drawing"—Guest. 21. ... Kh8 22. B×d7 N×d7 23. Qe6 The immediate 23. c4 offers enough compensation for the pawn thanks to the central pressure. The intrusion of his queen leads to nothing. 23. ... Nf6 24. Qf7 26. c4 was still fully playable. 24. ... Ne4! Threatening 25. ... Ng5, and if 25. Ne6 Q×f2†. White's queen is suddenly in serious troubles. 25. b4 Mason panics. The calm 25. Qe6 is much better, though after 25. ... a6 26. c4 b5 Bird has excellent play. 25. ... Qe5 25. ... Q×b4 captures a second pawn for free. If 26. Ne6 Qc3! 26. f3 Qf6 27. Qb3 Ng5 28. Rd2 a6 29. Qd5?! 29. Ne6 radically prevents the following. 29. ... e5 30. Nb3 (see diagram)

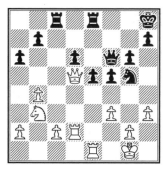

*After 30. Nb3*

30. ... Red8 Bird is bound to return his extra pawn, but this could be done in a far more favorable way. After 30. ... e4! White is forced to go for 31. f4, as after 31. Rde2 Rc7 he will not regain the pawn. In case of 31. f4, the forced 31. ... Ne6 32. Q×d6 Rcd8 33. Qe5

Q×e5 34. f×e5 R×d2 35. N×d2 Rc8 36. c4 Nf4 makes Black holds all the trumps in the resulting endgame. 31. Q×b7 e4 32. f4 32. h4 Nf7 33. f×e4 breaks up Black's pawn phalanx. 32. ... Ne6 33. Q×a6 N×f4 34. Qf1? Much too passive. Instead, 34. Qb6 Rb8 35. Qf2 Qg5 36. Qe3 leads to a very tense position, where it is unclear who has the better chances. 34. ... Qg5 35. Kh2 Rc3! Bird's pieces now infiltrate decisively due to Mason's lack of control over the black squares. 36. Qf2 Rdc8 The immediate 36. ... Kg8!, avoiding any check at d4, wins quickly; e.g., 37. b5 N×h3 38. g×h3 e3. 37. Re3 Kg8! "A well-judged move, which prevents White subsequently checking at d4, and enables Black to make an artistic finish"—Guest. 38. R×c3 R×c3 39. Qd4 Qg3† White resigns. "Black would play 40. ... Re3 and win"—Guest. *Morning Post* (Guest), 22 March 1886.

### (766) Gunsberg–Bird   1–0
B.C.C. tournament (round 3)
London, 23 February 1886
*Game score missing*

### (767) Bird–Reeves   1–0
B.C.C. tournament (round 4)
London, 3 March 1886
*Game score missing*

### (768) MacDonnell–Bird   0–1
B.C.C. tournament (round 5)
London, 2 March 1886
*B73*

1. e4 c5 2. Nf3 Nc6 3. Nc3 g6 4. d4 c×d4 5. N×d4 Bg7 6. Be3 d6 "Mr. Bird's new and favorite continuation"—MacDonnell. 7. Be2 Bd7 8. 0-0 Nf6 9. Qd2 0-0 10. Rad1 N×d4 11. B×d4 Bc6 12. Bd3 Ng4 13. B×g7 K×g7 14. h3 Nf6 15. Qe3 "To prevent 15. ... Qb6"—MacDonnell. 15. ... Qa5 16. Rfe1 Nd7 17. Nd5 B×d5 18. e×d5 Nf6 19. Bc4 "Taking the e-pawn would involve the loss of a rook"—MacDonnell. 19. ... Rac8 20. Bb3 Rfe8 21. Rd4 "The series of manoeuvers by which White forces Black to advance his queenside pawns, and thereby weaken the flank, is very instructive and interesting"—MacDonnell. 21. ... Qc5 22. Qd2 b5 Bird responds positively to MacDonnell's plans, while 22. ... Rc7 grants his opponent nothing. 23. Rd3 He could make good use of Bird's last move with 23. c4!, which forces the win of a pawn—23. ... a6 (23. ... b×c4? is clearly worse: 24. R×c4 Qb6 25. R×c8 R×c8 26. R×e7) 24. c×b5 a×b5 25. a4! Ra8 26. Rc1 Qb6 27. Rb4 Qa5 28. a×b5 Reb8 29. Bc4. Of course, White will have some difficulties in reorganizing his pieces and exploiting his pawn, but he is clearly better. 23. ... Qb6 24. a4 b4 25. Rd4 a5 26. Bc4 "Here he ought to have carried out his original intention, which would have given him an easy victory. Thus 26. Rh4 h5 27. g4. White now threatening to sacrifice the rook for a knight, and then after checking with the queen to play Re3 with a won game. Play as he may, Black cannot avoid serious loss"—MacDonnell. There is no reason to panic. After 26. Rh4 Rc7 27. Qh6† Kh8 28. Re3 Rg8 everything is well defended. 26. ... Rc5 27. Rh4 h5 Better than in MacDonnell's

previous line, as the bishop would be hanging after 28. g4?? (Mac-Donnell). **28. Qd4 Qc7 29. b3** *(see diagram)* Creating a significant weakness. 29. Bb3 keeps everything well defended.

*After 29. b3*

**29. ... e5! 30. d×e6** *e.p.* **f×e6 31. B×e6?** "Very stupid. Clearly he ought to have taken with rook, emerging from the fray with superior position, thus: 31. R×e6 R×e6 32. B×e6 R×c2 33. Rf4 Qe7 34. Re4 followed by 35. Bd5 etc."—MacDonnell. 31. R×e6 is equally bad because of 31. ... R×e6 32. B×e6 Re5!, and if 33. Bc4 g5. Best was 31. f4, when after 31. ... e5!, MacDonnell's surviving chances are held together by only a thread. Every deviation from the following path leads to an immediate defeat: 32. f×e5 R×e5 33. Rf1 g5 34. Qf2 Rf5 35. Qg3 Qa7 36. Kh1 Kh6 37. Rd4 R×f1† 38. B×f1. **31. ... Re5!** "Gaining a decisive advantage"—MacDonnell. **32. R×e5 d×e5 33. Qc4 Q×c4** 33. ... Qd6 34. Bf7 Re7 wins the bishop without allowing any counterplay. **34. R×c4** If 34. B×c4 g5. **34. ... R×e6 35. Rc5** White wins back a pawn, making it not so easy for his opponent to use his extra piece. **35. ... Rd6 36. R×a5 Rd1† 37. Kh2 Nd5 38. Rb5** Loss of time. The immediate 38. Rc5 is more resolute. **38. ... Kf6 39. Rc5 Ke6 40. Rc6† Kf5 41. a5 Ra1 42. a6 h4 43. g3 g5 44. g×h4 g×h4 45. Rh6 Nf4 46. Rb6 Ra2 47. R×b4 R×a6 48. Rc4 Rg6 49. b4 Rg2† 50. Kh1 R×f2** "and at the 58th move White surrendered"—*Illustrated Sporting and Dramatic News* (MacDonnell), 20 March 1886.

## (769) Pollock–Bird    0–1

B.C.C. tournament (round 6)
London, 6 March 1886
*B27*

**1. e4 c5 2. d4 c×d4 3. Nf3 g6 4. Q×d4 Nf6 5. e5 Nc6 6. Qf4 Nd5 7. Qe4 e6 8. Nc3 N×c3 9. b×c3 d5 10. e×d6** *e.p.* **Bg7 11. Qd3 0–0 12. Be2 e5 13. 0–0 Bf5 14. Qd1 e4 15. Ne1 B×c3 16. Rb1 Be5 17. R×b7 B×d6 18. Kh1 Rb8 19. Rb3 Qe7 20. Qd2 Rbd8 21. Qh6 Be5 22. Ba3 Bd6 23. g4 Be6 24. Rh3 f6 25. Bb2 Rf7 26. Ng2 Ne5 27. Ne3 Qb7 28. Ba1 Rg7 29. c4 Nf7 30. Qh4 g5 31. Qh5 Be5 32. B×e5 N×e5 33. Nd5 B×d5 34. c×d5 Q×d5 35. Ra3 e3† 36. f3 Qd2 37. Rd1 Q×d1† 38. B×d1 R×d1† 39. Kg2 Ng6 40. Ra4 e2 41. Re4 Nf4† 42. R×f4 e1Q 43. Re4 Rd2† 44. Kh3 Qf1† 45. Kg3 Qg2** mate—*Morning Post*, 15 March 1886.

## (770) Bird–Guest    ½–½

B.C.C. tournament (round 7)
London, 9 March 1886
*Game score missing*

# SIMULS AND VISITS, JANUARY–APRIL 1886

Bird's tournament and match activity during the first part of the year did not leave him much time to embark on a grand provincial tour. Instead he made two short excursions out of London. In both cases old acquaintances facilitated the negotiations. Bird also engaged himself for a few separate exhibitions in London clubs.

On 28 January, barely recovered from a long period of illness, Bird made his second visit in a few months to the Maidstone Chess Club. He was as successful as on his previous visit. Only one player out of 24 succeeded in drawing his game.

The British Chess Club hosted a simultaneous exhibition by Bird on 13 February. With spirited and rapid play he overwhelmed 11 of his opponents. W.W. Mackeson drew his game while Ree and Jones were successful.

Bird postponed his fourth round game with Reeves in the master tournament at the British Chess Club in order to keep an appointment outside the capital. On 27 February he was for the second time in a year the guest of J.B. Reyner in Ashton-under-Lyne. The host, consulting with a friend, managed to beat Bird in a well contested game.

## (771) Verdon & Reyner–Bird    1–0

Consultation game
Brookfield, Ashton-under-Lyne, 27 February 1886
*C51*

**1. e4 e5 2. Nf3 Nc6 3. Bc4 Bc5 4. b4 B×b4 5. c3 Bc5 6. d4 e×d4 7. c×d4 Bb6 8. 0–0 d6 9. Bb2 Nge7 10. d5 Na5 11. Bd3 f6 12. Nc3 0–0 13. h3** "The usual move here is 13. Ne2. The allies probably try to prevent 13. ... Bg4, which, however, would be favorable to White, because an open file on the kingside would add to the dangers of the defense, which are already numerous enough in this form of the Evans"—Hoffer. **13. ... c5 14. Ne2 c4 15. Bc2 Bc5 16. Ned4** There is no counterweight for the advance of Black's pawn mass on the queenside after this move. Instead 16. Nfd4 b5! 17. Nf4 (not 17. N×b5 Rb8) forces Black to cede with his bishop pair. After 17. ... B×d4 18. B×d4 Nb7 19. Qb1 White can blockade the pawns with 20. Qb2 and 21. Bc3. Also 16. Bc3 Bd7 17. Rb1 b5 18. a4 a6 19. Nfd4 is a valid option. White has reached a standstill on the queenside. **16. ... Bd7** 16. ... b5 and if 17. Qd2 b4, the pawn structure has reached a nearly decisive strength. The text move is too slow and gives White time to reorganize his pieces. **17. Qd2 b5** More solid is 17. ... b6. Thus a field is provided for the offside knight, while he avoids a break-up of his pawns with 20. a2–a4, after White has blockaded the pawn chain (see variation 16. Bc3 at move 16). **18. Bc3 Nb7 19. Rfb1 a6 20. a4** White have realized their plans on the queenside and obtained sufficient compensation. **20. ... Qb6** *(see diagram)*

**21. a5?** "This move, which secures the position of Black's pawns, ought only to be made under compulsion. 21. a×b5, followed by 22. Ba4, would lead to interesting complications, out of which White would emerge with at least the gain of a pawn"—Hoffer. All the pressure built up against Black's pawns evaporates with the text

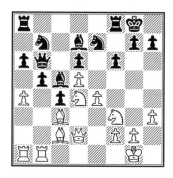

*After 20. ... Qb6*

move. It is worth looking a bit deeper into the correct line, as suggested by Hoffer. Black maintains his extra pawn with 21. a×b5 a×b5 22. Ba4 B×d4 23. N×d4 Nc5, but with correct play a draw is still feasible 24. B×b5 N×e4 25. Qc2 N×c3 26. Q×c3 R×a1 27. Q×a1 Rb8 28. Re1 B×b5 29. R×e7 Rb7 30. Qa8† Rbb8 31. Qa1. **21. ...  Qc7 22. Nh4 Rae8** Putting the rook on the semi-open file is thematic but 22. ... Nd8! is also strong. The knight heads to f7, where it would be excellently placed. After 23. ... Rab8, Black plans to set his b-pawn in motion. White is forced to focus himself on the defense of the queenside, and doesn't get a chance to move his pieces towards the kingside. **23. Re1** Though they have the liberty to play for a kingside attack, this shouldn't make much headway against a correct defense. **23. ... B×d4 24. Q×d4 Ng6** Certainly not bad, but 24. ... Nd8, heading for e5, remains the best idea. **25. N×g6 h×g6 26. Qb6** "The exchange of queens renders Black's pawns stronger than ever, and ought to have been avoided rather than sought for"—Hoffer. **26. ... Q×b6 27. a×b6 Ra8 28. e5** "Simply keeping up the semblance of an attack, so as to delay the threatened advance of the queenside pawns"—Hoffer. **28. ... f×e5 29. B×g6 a5 30. Re4 Rf6 31. Bh5 a4 32. Bg4 B×g4 33. R×g4 Ra6 34. Bd2 R×b6 35. f4 Nc5 36. f×e5 d×e5 37. Be3 Nd7** "37. ... Nb3 seems the obvious reply here"—Hoffer. **38. B×b6 N×b6?** Bird's manner of advancing his queenside pawns was already questionable (31. ... a4), but this move is plain bad. He loses the most important of his pawns. **39. Rb1 N×d5 40. R×b5 Ne3 41. Re4 Rf1† 42. Kh2 Re1?** "42. ... c3 would have secured a draw, at least. Afterwards White has the advantage"—Hoffer. Following this, 43. R×e3 c2 44. Rc5 c1Q 45. R×c1 R×c1 46. R×e5 is a sample line. **43. Rb×e5 Nf1† 44. Kg1 Ra1 45. Re1 R×e1 46. R×e1 Nd2 47. Ra1 c3 48. R×a4 Kf7 49. Ra7† Ke6 50. Kf2 Ne4† 51. Ke3 Nc5 52. Ra3** Black resigns—*The Field* (Hoffer), 1 May 1886.

On 4 April Bird refereed the fourteenth annual match between Oxford and Cambridge, held at the St. George's Chess Club. After four hours of play Bird had to adjudicate the unfinished games.

On 17 April Bird gave a second exhibition at the British Chess Club. He fared well against 13 opponents as he had to concede but 2 draws.

**(772) Bird–Locock    0–1**
Offhand game
London, April 1886
C59

**1. e4 e5 2. Nf3 Nc6 3. Bc4 Nf6 4. Ng5 d5 5. e×d5 Na5 6. Bb5† c6 7. d×c6 b×c6 8. Be2 h6 9. Nf3 e4 10. Ne5 Qd4 11. Ng4 B×g4**

**12. B×g4 e3 13. Be2 e×f2† 14. Kf1 0-0-0 15. c3 Qh4 16. Ba6† Kc7 17. Qf3 Re8 18. Q×f2 Q×f2† 19. K×f2 Ng4† 20. Kf1 Re6 21. h3 Bd6 22. h×g4 Bg3 23. Be2 Rhe8 24. Rh3 R×e2 25. R×g3 Re1† 26. Kf2 R8e2† 27. Kf3 Re6 28. g5 Rf1† 29. Kg4 Rg6 30. Na3 R×g5† 31. Kh4 Rf4† 32. Kh3 Rh5** mate—*Chess Monthly*, October 1891, pp. 43–44.

**(773) Bird–H.    1–0**
Offhand game
London (British C.C.), July 1886
B20

**1. e4 c5 2. b4 e5 3. f4 d6 4. Nf3 Bg4 5. Bc4 Nc6 6. 0-0 Nd4 7. N×d4 B×d1 8. Bb5† Ke7 9. Nf5† Ke6 10. Nc3 c×b4 11. Nd5 Nf6 12. N×g7† B×g7 13. f5** mate—*Illustrated Sporting and Dramatic News*, 18 May 1889.

---

# CONTROVERSIES WITH BURN, GUNSBERG AND STEINITZ

The British chess boom continued in full force in the new year. Both the B.C.A. and the C.C.A. would organize international tournaments and once spring arrived in the country it started raining match challenges. Bird confidently played a role in them.

Challenges seem to be the rage. Mr. Gunsberg has challenged Mr. Blackburne to play a match. The latter has accepted on condition that the stakes be not less than £500, to which Mr. Gunsberg rejoined: "Stake the money with the editor of ___ and I will consider the matter." Whereupon Blackburne laughed and Gunsberg disappeared. Mr. Bird is prepared to play Mr. Gunsberg a match for £5. Quite enough, too. Mr. Burn longs to tackle Mr. Bird. Mr. Bird is ready to play Steinitz for the championship. Stakes (I suppose) to be provided by the president of the USA and Her Majesty Queen Victoria. ... Joking apart, I believe the veteran Bird and the aspiring Burn will meet in deadly strife about a fortnight hence at the British Chess Club [*Illustrated Sporting and Dramatic News*, 15 May 1886].

MacDonnell's prophecy blossomed. At the end of May Bird and Burn combatted each other, while immediately afterwards Bird met Gunsberg in a match. But before the hostilities on the chessboard started Bird had drawn worldwide attention by challenging Steinitz for a match. Steinitz had just brought the first world championship match to a good end by decisively beating Zukertort. This was reason enough for the, so-called, irrepressible Bird to spur their 20 year old rivalry on by sending a letter to the *New York Herald* in which he defended his rights for a return match.

London, May 2, 1886

To the Editor of the *Herald*:

In a letter to Captain G.H. Mackenzie, the American chess champion, who is very highly esteemed in this country, I have just ventured to express the opinion that the play in the recent match affords no indication of superiority over British born, recognized leaders, adding my belief that in a series of games or a match the gallant Captain himself would make matters very lively for Steinitz, the now acknowledged world's chess champion.

As a veteran chess player and old opponent of Paul Morphy, as well as of Steinitz, I make bold to ask you to favor me with a short portion of your very valuable space to state reasons why I feel it not unduly presumptuous to wish to play with Steinitz, deferring, however, entirely to Captain Mackenzie, if so desirable an event as a match between him and Steinitz can be brought

**Leading chess players of the world in 1886. Standing from left to right: George H. Mackenzie, Ignaz Kolisch, Szymon Winawer, Henry E. Bird, Jules Arnous de Rivière, Samuel Rosenthal, James Mason, William N. Potter, Emil Schallopp, Louis Paulsen, George A. MacDonnell and Isidor Gunsberg. Seated: Joseph H. Blackburne, Wilhelm Steinitz, Johannes H. Zukertort, Berthold Englisch (*Graphic*).**

about. Briefly, my own pretentions or claims are that I have the best match record extant against Steinitz in an unfinished match with him, which he frequently agreed to resume and complete.

In 1866 Steinitz, fresh with victory over Anderssen by 8 to 6, engaged in a match with myself. I was deeply engaged in business at the time, and at a very interesting stage, when I was only one game behind, out of a total played of twenty-one or twenty-two [*sic*], I had unexpectedly to sail for New York on business and to forfeit stakes and match.

I am aware that Steinitz's victories over Zukertort and Blackburne have been of a very decisive character and would make him greatly the favorite in a contest with myself. So much the better for Steinitz. My style, however, is very different, as the champion knows; and even conceding, as I must do, the slow time limit, so favorable to Steinitz, I shall yet hope to make as good a score as I did when out of practice in 1866. I trust that Steinitz will take a chivalrous view of my wishes for a match, and fix a moderate sum for resumption and completion of our 1866 match, or engage in a new one. If the match be fixed at a stake of say double what we originally played for, I will meet Steinitz's time, terms and convenience in every respect, and visit New York upon receiving due intimation of acceptance.

H.E. Bird [*International Chess Magazine*, June 1886, p. 169].

Steinitz unhesitatingly inserted Bird's letter in his magazine. With an irritated reaction he wiped away Bird's proposition. The champion's pamphlet nicely illustrates his view on the British master.

Of course I shall wait patiently, in the first place, for a message from Captain Mackenzie who is delegated in preference to return thanks for the "match" of 1866, but a few remarks on Mr. Bird's epistle may be appropriate. The "match" to which he alludes might form an item of biographical chess history, but it will be sufficient to state now that after my match with Anderssen,

which was played for £100 a side for the first eight games a "friendly contest," was arranged between me and Mr. Bird for a small sum, the winner of the first ten games to be the victor, and Mr. Bird receiving the odds of four to three in betting, namely £20 to £15. He chivalrously now appeals to my chivalry to play him a champion match for double the amount, which would mean that, on his part, he offers $150 as stakes. This ought to be enough to characterize the genuineness of Mr. Bird's challenge, especially as he cunningly conceals the amount he wishes me to play for.

Mr. Bird's claims to come forward before the public as a champion representative are naturally of like character. I am supposed to know his "different style," as he fondly calls it, though he would give to understand that he had never played with me again for twenty years. The six games which I won of him since in three international tournaments, in none of which, by the way, Bird won a single prize, are passed over in silence, not to speak of a very large number of offhand games in which I beat him at the rate of about seven to one at least. (Bird is welcome to deny this and in order to facilitate his doing so, I shall state that I have kept no record, and I promise to call no witnesses.)

It must also appear somewhat remarkable that Bird does not endeavor first to make some impression with his "different style" on either Blackburne or Mason who have each decisively defeated him in set matches within the last ten years, as well as at least in the general score of tournaments. For my part, I must confess that I have not much noticed the "different style" of the "British born leader," which only seems to me as imaginative as his statement of facts, and apparently he is quite alone in thinking that he can succeed with either.

Mr. Bird has already given several different accounts on various occasions of his score against me in 1866, and a big dose of salt will have to be swallowed with his statement in the *Herald* that we played twenty-one or twenty-two games in the match, and that I was only one game ahead. For the true score, which can be easily verified by the chess columns and periodicals of the time, was seven to five and five draws in my favor, and I may add that he never made even games during the "friendly contest," as I was led to believe it would be, and that I always kept the lead by two or three games, which, as far as I can remember, he only once reduced to one game majority, about at the beginning of the match. Nor is there an atom of truth in his allegation that I had "frequently promised to resume the unfinished match," and as far as I am aware, this is the first time that even the "British born leader" has had the impudence to make such an assertion which is perfectly absurd on the face of it. For it would imply that I consented to accept the odds of two games in a match of which the stakes had already been forfeited, as Bird admits. But I may mention what the "British born leader" has conveniently forgotten (and is also quite welcome to deny), namely, that I offered at the time either to play him a match for the first three won games (which was the number he would have had to score if the match for ten games up had proceeded) for a small amount, or to contest a new match for a larger stake. But he declined either alternative, being apparently quite satisfied with the newspaper clamor made on his behalf by a certain London press clique which was only then in its growth. In all probability Mr. Bird will now rest contented with having fooled the *New York Herald* into giving a cheap advertisement to his name [*International Chess Magazine*, June 1886, pp. 169–170].

Bird's unworldly challenge to Steinitz was subject to some mild mockery. In the next edition of the *International Chess Magazine*, James Gavin Cunningham, Steinitz' London correspondent, cast his eye on the quarrel. His affirmation of Bird's seriousness when challenging the champion is worthwhile.

Mr. Bird's challenge, or supposed challenge, to Mr. Steinitz has caused some little amusement among those who do not know Mr. Bird, as they look upon it as a joke on his part. I do not share their opinion, for I am inclined to think he means it in "sad and sober earnestness." At any rate, I have often heard him declare that he had the best match record against Steinitz, and that that gave him a title to challenge him. In making this assertion, he was quite serious, for he forgets the lapse of time, the results of the tournament play between them, and the fact that one of the players occupies now a much lower level than he did then, whilst the other stands at the very top of the masters. I like Mr. Bird personally and admire his pluck and energy after so many years of battle, but yet it does not always do to take a man at his own estimate [*International Chess Magazine*, July 1886, p. 196].

# Match with Burn 1886

One of the strongest, yet not so well-known, British masters was Amos Burn. Burn lived and worked in Liverpool, far away from the London chess mecca. In 1886, at the age of 38, he could look back on a very successful professional career. Burn had played at regular times, but mostly in Liverpool and its environments. After a break from serious chess that had lasted a few years, he thought the time fit to put his business affairs aside and dedicate more time to his favorite game. With the support of the wealthy chess patron Robert Steel, also a Liverpudlian, he challenged all British players, excluding Blackburne, to a match. Not surprisingly, Bird did not hesitate to accept the offer. Without much ado, arrangements were set up and agreed to. Only ten days later the match started at Simpson's Divan. An excellent overview of the circumstances was given by the London correspondent of the *International Chess Magazine*.

| | **Match with Burn, 25 May–4 June 1886** | | | | | | | | | | | | | | | | | |
|---|---|---|---|---|---|---|---|---|---|---|---|---|---|---|---|---|---|---|---|
| | **1** | **2** | **3** | **4** | **5** | **6** | **7** | **8** | **9** | **10** | **11** | **12** | **13** | **14** | **15** | **16** | **17** | **18** | |
| H.E. Bird | 1 | 1 | 0 | 0 | 1 | 1 | 0 | 1 | 0 | 0 | 0 | 1 | 0 | 0 | 0 | 1 | 1 | 0 | 1 | 9 |
| A. Burn | 0 | 0 | 1 | 1 | 0 | 0 | 1 | 0 | 1 | 0 | 1 | 1 | 0 | 1 | 1 | 1 | 0 | 0 | 1 | 0 | 9 |

The principal event of late in the chess world here has been the match between Messrs. Bird and Burn. Both gentlemen have long been connected with chess and both have made their mark as players. Mr. Bird has undoubtedly the wider reputation, as he has played in so many master tournaments, whilst Mr. Burn's fame has been more of a provincial nature, yet his record, taken all round, is a very good one, and his friends were very sanguine that he would prove the winner. The player who first scored seven games was to be the victor. The time limit was nominally fifteen moves per hour, but many of the games were played at more like thirty moves per hour than fifteen. This is manifest when I mention that three games a day were got through. It is an open secret that Mr. Bird prefers rapid play when it is carried out on both sides, and undoubtedly the present match has been played much more quickly than any match of late years. Whether the quality of the games suffer from the rapid play remains to be seen. The match commenced at Simpson's Divan, on Tuesday, 25th May, at noon. The two opponents were punctual to time, and play at once commenced. In appearance they presented a marked contrast. Mr. Bird has a fine, open face and wears his whiskers trimmed in a somewhat old-fashioned style. His head is large and finely developed, and as time has sadly thinned his locks, you have a good opportunity of noting its "bumps" if inclined to phrenology. Tall, erect and almost military in his bearing, he looks all over English. Mr. Burn is a much shorter man, and with bearded face and spectacled eyes he has a very thoughtful countenance. [*International Chess Magazine*, July 1886, p. 194]

The battle had a fierce start. Almost four games were worked off on the opening day and the players maintained the furious tempo during the first part of the match. After 12 games, each player had scored 6 wins and there was still no draw. As it was thought undesirable that the outcome of the match would depend on the next win, both players agreed to extend the match until one of them had won ten games. The match continued now at a slower pace of one game a day. Yet both players remained very bloodthirsty and after the eighteenth game, won by Bird, the score was equal again with 9 wins each and still no draws. Hereupon the players decided to leave the match as a draw.

The matter of the stakes is a bit unclear. At the beginning of the match the *Morning Post* of 26 May spoke of a stake of £20 a side. On the next day this was corrected in the same newspaper with the words, "neither player has any monetary interest in the match, and whatever sum is staked upon it in no way concerns them." The rumors about the stakes made Cunningham, in the *International Chess Magazine* (July 1886, p. 196), stress that Burn had no pecuniary interest at all in the match. Bird received £10 from the hands of Robert Steel, who declared himself very pleased with the aesthetic qualities of the games.

**(774) Bird–Burn    1–0**
Match (game 1)
London, 25 May 1886
*C33*

**1. e4 e5 2. f4 e×f4 3. Be2** "Although recommended by von Jaenisch, this opening is seldom played. Mr. Bird, who is the champion of neglected debuts has tried it before. He calls it the Little Bishop's Gambit. The *Chess Monthly* has disparagingly styled it the Bishop's Gambit Limited, no doubt coming to the conclusion that it does not pay"—Green. **3. ... d5** "A defense recommended by Zukertort. Max Lange advocates 3. ... g5"—Green. **4. e×d5 Q×d5 5. Nf3 Nc6 6. Nc3 Qa5** "The queen does not seem well placed here, and Black's future difficulties may be traced to this move. Perhaps 6. ... Qd8 would have been better. Evidently Black is scheming to castle on the queenside and to throw up the kingside pawns"—Green. **7. 0–0 Be6** "The bishop's position is subsequently a source of embarrassment to Black, on which account 7. ... Bd7 is to be preferred"—Green. **8. Bb5 0–0–0 9. B×c6 b×c6** "A misconception. If 9. ... Qb6† White recovers the gambit pawn with a superior game by 10. d4"—Green. **10. d3 g5 11. Ne4 h6 12. Bd2 Qb6† 13. Kh1 f5** "The Bishop's Gambit does not usually afford such a free opening to Black as we see here"—Duffy. **14. Nc3 Nf6** This move puts the knight on a tricky square. 14. ... Rh7 is interesting. **15. Na4 Qa6** "The queen is unfortunately placed here, and throughout the remainder of the game exercises very little influence"—Duffy. **16. b3** Too slow, and it allows Black to correct his error on the fourteenth move. After 16. Bc3, Black loses material with the clumsy position of his queen (e.g., 16. ... Bg7 17. Nc5 or 16. ... Be7 17. Qe2) **16. ... Ng4** Burn embarks on a doubtful maneuvre that leaves his hinterland completely undeveloped. Both 16. ... c5 and 16. ... Rh7 are in Black's favor. **17. h3 Ne3** "If 17. ... Nf6 18. Bc3 wins a piece"—Green. **18. Qe1 g4 19. Nh4 g×h3** This move results in the break-up of his own position. After 19. ... Bd6! 20. h×g4 f×g4 21. B×e3 f×e3 22. Q×e3 Rhe8 White is facing a dangerous bishop pair. **20. R×f4 h×g2†** 20. ... N×c2 21. Q×e6† Kb8 22. Rd1 Q×d3 23. Q×f5 brings no relief. White dominates the board. **21. Kg1** Throwing away the advantage that he could obtain with 21. N×g2 N×c2 22. Q×e6† Kb8 23. Raf1. **21. ... Bd6?** 21. ... N×c2 is much better now as Black's queen gets into the game. After 22. Q×e6† Kb8 23. Rc1 Q×d3 24. Q×c6 Q×d2 25. Qb5† White must take the draw. **22. Q×e3 Bd7 23. N×f5 Rdf8** Nothing helps anymore: 23. ... B×f4 24. Ne7† Kb8 25. Q×f4 Rhf8 26. Qh4. **24. N×d6† c×d6 25. R×f8† R×f8 26. Q×h6 Rg8 27. Q×d6 Bh3 28. Bf4 Qb7 29. Re1** Black resigns—*Liverpool Weekly Courier* (Green), 29 May 1886; *Illustrated London News* (Duffy), 5 June 1886.

## (775) Burn–Bird    0–1
Match (game 2)
London, 25 May 1886
*B30*

1. e4 c5 2. Nc3 Nc6 3. Nf3 g6 4. Bc4 Bg7 5. d3 a6 6. a4 d6 7. 0–0 Nf6 8. h3 0–0 9. Nh2 e6 10. Bg5 h6 11. B×f6 B×f6 12. Ng4 Bg7 13. Qd2 Kh7 14. Rae1 h5 15. Ne3 Bd7 16. f4 Qh4 17. Re2 Nd4 18. Ref2 b5 19. Ba2 b4 20. Ncd1 B×a4 21. f5 b3 22. Nc3 b×a2 23. N×a4 Be5 24. Ra1 Bg3 25. Rff1 Bf4 26. R×a2 g×f5 27. N×f5 e×f5 28. R×f4 Q×f4 and Black wins—*Games of the Liverpool C.C.*, vol. 2.

## (776) Bird–Burn    0–1
Match (game 3)
London, 25 May 1886
*A03*

1. f4 d5 2. Nf3 c5 3. e3 Nc6 4. Bb5 e6 5. b3 Nf6 6. Bb2 Be7 7. 0–0 0–0 8. B×c6 b×c6 9. Nc3 Ba6 10. Re1 c4 11. Na4 c×b3 12. a×b3 Nd7 13. d4 Bb7 14. Ne5 Nf6 15. Qf3 Ne4 16. Rad1 Bb4 17. Re2 Qa5 18. Nd3 Ba6 19. Ra1 B×d3 20. c×d3 Nd2 21. R×d2 B×d2 22. Nc5 Qb5 23. e4 Bb4 24. Nd7 Rfd8 25. Ne5 Bd6 26. Rf1 Q×b3 27. Ba1 B×e5 28. f×e5 Rd7 29. h4 Rb8 30. h5 h6

Amos Burn.

31. e×d5 c×d5 32. Kh2 Rc7 33. Qg3 Qa3 34. Rf4 Rb1 35. Rg4 Qf8 36. Qf4 R×a1 37. Q×h6 Rf1 and Black wins—*Liverpool Weekly Courier*, 10 July 1886.

## (777) Burn–Bird    1–0
Match (game 4)
London, 25 May 1886
*A84*

1. c4 f5 2. e3 Nf6 3. Nf3 e6 4. Be2 b6 5. 0–0 Bb7 6. d4 Be7 7. Nc3 0–0 8. Qb3 d5 9. Rd1 c6 10. Bd2 Ne4 11. Rac1 Nd7 12. Be1 Qe8 13. Bd3 Qg6 14. Ne2 Bd6 15. Nf4 The knight becomes a target here. 15. c×d5 c×d5 16. Bb4 takes the sting out of Bird's attacking plans. **15. ... Qh6 16. g3 g5 17. Ng2 Ndf6 18. h4 g×h4 19. Ng×h4** The wrong knight recaptures the pawn, as it becomes now very risky to exchange at e4 and lose time by moving the knight away from f3. Better was 19. Nf×h4 Rf7 20. c×d5 c×d5 21. Rc2, when Black's attack is not strong and Burn can slowly improve his position on the queenside with such moves as Rfc1, Qa4, Nf4 or Bb4. **19. ... Rf7 20. c×d5?** 20. B×e4 f×e4 21. Nh2 Rg7 22. Ng2 Rf8 might be a better way to deal with Black's attack, although White is under serious pressure. **20. ... c×d5 21. Bf1** 21. B×e4 comes too late. Black's attack is decisive after 21. ... f×e4 22. Nh2 Rg7 23. Ng2 Qh3 24. Rc2 Rg6. Another typical line is 21. Bb5 Ng4 22. Bc6 Raf8. All of Black's pieces are eyeing the

opponent's king, while White has nothing to show in return. Black is likely to sacrifice soon to force a breakthrough; e.g., 23. B×b7 R×b7 24. Rc6 Rg7 25. Rdc1 Ng×f2 26. B×f2 B×g3 and wins. **21. … Rg7 22. Bg2 Ng4 23. Rc2** *(see diagram)*

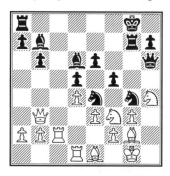

*After 23. Rc2*

**23. … Ng×f2** 23. … B×g3! delivers a decisive blow. After 24. f×g3 Q×e3† 25. Q×e3 N×e3 26. Rdd2 N×c2 27. R×c2 Rc8 White's minor pieces are awfully placed. **24. R×f2 N×f2 25. B×f2 R×g3** Once again 25. … B×g3! is stronger. Black can trust his positional advantage after 26. B×g3 R×g3 27. Kf2 Rg7 28. Rg1 Rf8 29. Bf1 R×g1 30. K×g1 f4. **26. Qd3** 26. B×g3 is crucial, though Black remains firmly in the driver's seat in case of 26. … B×g3 27. Qa4 Q×e3† 28. Kh1 Qh6 29. Qd7 Ba6 30. Qe7 Be2 31. Rg1 B×f3 32. B×f3 f4. White can't escape material losses, and his counterplay after 33. Bg4 is probably not strong enough to rescue himself. **26. … Rg4 27. Rc1 Kh8 28. Qe2 Rag8 29. Rc2 Qh5 30. Kf1 Be7?** Bird finds the correct idea, but his execution is not perfect. First 30. … R8g7! denies White any counter; Black's next move 31. … Be7 would decide the game at once. **31. Rc7 B×h4?** Bird misjudges the resulting position. Equality is achieved after 31. … R×g2 32. R×e7 R2g7 33. R×e6 Bc8 34. Rc6. **32. B×h4 Qh6** 32. … R×g2 and 32. … R×h4 are much inferior. **33. Bg5** A trick that succeeds very well. He could also play 33. R×b7 R×g2 34. Q×g2 R×g2 35. K×g2 Q×e3 36. Bg5 with later Bg5–h6. Black's king gets in trouble. **33. … R4xg5?** The wrong rook! After 33. … R8xg5 34. N×g5 Q×g5 35. R×b7 Rg3 36. Qf2 R×e3 37. Re7 f4 38. R×a7 White's extra piece is not so telling that Black is without drawing chances. **34. N×g5 Q×g5 35. R×b7 f4 36. Qc2!** Bird is forced on the defense. **36. … Qh6** 36. … Rg6 isn't any better: 37. Rb8† Kg7 38. Rc8 f×e3 39. Qc7† Kh6 40. Qh2† and the endgame is Burn's. **37. Qc7 Rf8 38. Qe5† Kg8 39. Ke2 Qg6 40. Bf3 f×e3** There is no perpetual after 40. … Qc2† 41. Ke1 Qc1† 42. Bd1 Q×e3† 43. Q×e3 f×e3 44. Bg4. **41. R×a7 Rc8 42. Rg7† Q×g7 43. Q×e6†** and White wins—*Games of the Liverpool C.C.,* vol. 2.

**(778) Bird–Burn    1–0**
Match (game 5)
London, 26 May 1886
*A03*

1. f4 d5 2. Nf3 e6 3. e3 Nf6 4. b3 Be7 5. Bb2 0–0 6. Bd3 c5 7. 0–0 Nc6 8. Kh1 a6 9. a4 Bd7 10. Nc3 Nb4 11. Ne5 Be8 12. Ne2 b5 13. Ng3 N×d3 14. N×d3 b×a4 15. b×a4 Rb8 16. Be5 Rb7 17. f5 Ne4 18. N×e4 d×e4 19. Qg4 f6 20. Q×e4 Qb6 21. Bc3 e5 22. Qg4 Bc6 23. Nf2 Rd8 24. Ne4 c4 25. Ng3 Bd5 26. e4 Bf7 27. a5 Qc6 28. h3 Rdb8 29. Rfe1 Bd8 30. Qf3 Rb5 31. Qf2 R8b7

32. Qg1 Bc7 33. Reb1 h6 34. R×b5 R×b5 35. Qe3 Qb7 36. Kh2 Bb8 37. Nf1 Ba7 38. Qf3 Rb1 39. Ne3 R×a1 40. B×a1 Qb1 41. Qd1 Qa2 42. Bc3 B×e3 43. d×e3 Qa4 44. Qd8† Kh7 45. Qe7 Be6 46. B×e5 Qd7 47. B×f6 Q×e7 48. B×e7 Bc6 49. e5 Be4 50. g4 B×c2 51. Bb4 h5 52. Kg3 h×g4 53. h×g4 Ba4 54. Kf4 Kg8 55. e6 c3 56. B×c3 Bb3 57. g5 Black resigns—*Morning Post,* 14 June 1886.

**(779) Burn–Bird    0–1**
Match (game 6)
London, 26 May 1886
*Game score missing*

**(780) Bird–Burn    0–1**
Match (game 7)
London, 26 May 1886
*Game score missing*

**(781) Burn–Bird    0–1**
Match (game 8)
London, 27 May 1886
*A84*

1. c4 f5 2. e3 e6 3. d4 Nf6 4. Nf3 Bb4† 5. Nbd2 Nc6 6. Be2 "He might as well free his game at once by 6. a3, when Black would have to take the knight. It is often a troublesome piece in this opening. Black, it will be observed, has already provided a future for his b8-knight"—Freeborough. **6. … 0–0 7. 0–0 b6 8. Qc2 Bb7 9. Rd1 Qe8 10. a3** Why not 10. Nf1, securing his kingside and making the bishop at b4 look foolish. It is quite strange that Bird now avoids exchanging the knight, the point of his opening. **10. … Bd6 11. b4 Nd8 12. c5** "Premature: White should proceed with his development, and then advance the pawns according to the requirements of the position"—Zukertort. **12. … Be7 13. Bb2 Qg6 14. Rac1 Nf7 15. g3?** "An altogether injudicious move. We would hardly expect such a ruinous advance from a careful player like Mr. Burn in a match game"—Zukertort. A concession which creates a crucial weakness. There was a way out: 15. Nh4 Qh6 16. Nhf3 g5?! (16. … Qg6 takes the draw, 16. … Bd5 is also possible, but doesn't give any advantage, and 16. … g5 is workable, but White can now counterstrike in the center) 17. Ne5 Bd5 18. Bf3 with a positional plus. **15. … Qh6 16. Bf1** *(see diagram)* The drastic 16. h4 demands precise play from Black, but White's defensive task is not so easy: 16. … g5 17. b5 Bd5 18. Bc4 g×h4 19. N×h4 Ng4 20. B×d5 B×h4 21. g×h4 e×d5 22. Nf3 Rae8 23. Re1 Re4 and soon the f-pawn will advance. If 16. Nf1 Qh3 17. Ne1 Ng5 18. f3 avoids any mate, but Black's position is far better.

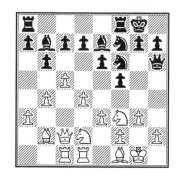

*After 16. Bf1*

**16. ... Ng4!** "Mr. Bird carries now the attack in his happiest style: every move tells"—Zukertort. **17. h3** 17. Bg2 (Freeborough) is interesting. A sample: 17. ... Ng5 18. h4 Ne4 19. Rf1 N×g3 20. f×g3 N×e3 (20. ... Q×e3† is nearly as good) 21. Qd3 N×f1 22. N×f1 Be4 23. Qd2 Qh5 24. Ne5 d6 with an ongoing attack. **17. ... Ng5!** "This disregarded coup wrecks White's fortune"—Freeborough. **18. N×g5 B×g5 19. Qc3 N×e3! 20. f×e3 B×e3† 21. Kh2 f4 22. h4** If 22. g4 Qh4 wins. **22. ... f×g3† 23. K×g3 Rf4** White resigns—*Chess Monthly* (Zukertort), May 1886, pp. 281–282; *British Chess Magazine* (Freeborough), August–September 1886, pp. 315–316.

## (782) Bird–Burn  0–1

Match (game 9)
London, 27 May 1886
A03

1. f4 d5 2. Nf3 e6 3. e3 Nf6 4. b3 Be7 5. Nc3 0–0 6. Bb2 c5 7. Ne2 Nc6 8. Ng3 Qc7 9. Bb5 Bd7 10. 0–0 Rfd8 11. B×c6 B×c6 12. d3 d4 13. e×d4 B×f3 14. R×f3 c×d4 15. f5 e5 16. Rf2 Nd5 17. Qh5 f6 18. Ne4 Rac8 19. Bc1 Qd7 20. a3 Rc7 21. Qg4 Rdc8 22. Ra2 Rc6 23. Qh5 Qe8 24. Qh4 R8c7 25. Ng3 Bf8 26. Qg4 Qc8 27. Bh6 Kh8 28. Bd2 R×c2 29. R×c2 R×c2 30. h4 B×a3 31. h5 Bc1 32. h6 g5 33. B×c1 R×c1† 34. Kh2 Qf8 35. Qh5 Nf4 36. R×f4 e×f4 37. Ne4 Rc6 38. b4 b6 39. b5 Rc7 40. Kh3 Rf7 41. Kg4 Qg8 42. Kf3 Rf8 43. Qh1 Qd5 44. Kg4 Q×b5 45. N×f6 Q×d3 and Black wins—*Games of the Liverpool C.C.*, vol. 2.

## (783) Burn–Bird  1–0

Match (game 10?)
London, 27 May 1886
A84

1. d4 f5 2. e3 Nf6 3. Nf3 e6 4. Be2 b6 5. 0–0 Be7 6. c4 Bb7 7. Nc3 0–0 8. Qc2 Qe8 9. d5 Na6 10. Rd1 Bb4 11. Bd2 c6 12. a3 B×c3 13. B×c3 Ne4 14. d×e6 d×e6 15. Be5 Nac5 16. b4 Nd7 17. Bd6 N×d6 18. R×d6 c5 19. Rad1 Nf6 20. Ne5 Qe7 21. b×c5 b×c5 22. Qb2 Bd5 23. Ra6 Rab8 24. Qc3 Ba8 25. Qa5 Ne4 26. f3 Qg5 27. f4 Qh4 28. Qe1 Q×e1† 29. R×e1 Rb3 30. Bf3 Nd2 31. R×a7 B×f3 32. g×f3 Rd8 33. Kf2 h5 34. Rg1 Ne4† 35. f×e4 Rb2† 36. Kf3 Rdd2 37. Rg×g7† Black resigns—*Chess Monthly*, May 1886, pp. 282–283.

## (784) Bird–Burn  1–0

Match (game 11?)
London, 28 May 1886
A35

1. c4 c5 2. Nc3 Nc6 3. e3 e6 4. f4 Nf6 5. Nf3 Be7 6. Be2 0–0 7. 0–0 d5 8. Ne5 Qc7 9. Nb5 A stroke into thin air, but Black's position was already excellent. **9. ... Qb6 10. b3 Rd8 11. Qe1 Bd7 12. Bf3** It was time to retreat the knight to a3, and be content with meager equality. **12. ... Be8** 12. ... N×e5 13. f×e5 B×b5 14. c×b5 Nd7 wins a pawn. **13. Nc3 d4 14. Ne4 N×e5 15. f×e5 Nd7?!** A passive move. With the knights on the board, and all of White's pieces pointing towards the kingside, Black's king is vulnerable. Instead, heading for an endgame with 15. ... N×e4 16. B×e4 Bc6 is at least equal. **16. Qg3 Qc7 17. e×d4 c×d4 18. d3 N×e5?!** (*see diagram*)

*gram*) This was Burn's purpose, but the opening of the diagonal is extremely dangerous for him. Other moves are also clearly better for White; e.g., 18. ... Kh8 19. Bf4 Rac8 20. Nd6 or 20. Nf6.

*After 18. ... N×e5*

**19. Bf4** 19. Bg4! is even stronger, if 19. ... Bd6 20. Bf4. **19. ... N×f3†?** A blunder that loses at once. 19. ... f6 20. Bg4 remains excellent for White (20. ... Bf7 21. Rae1 Re8 22. B×e5 f×e5 23. Qh3 Qa5 24. Re2). **20. R×f3 Qc6 21. Be5 Bf8 22. Nf6† Kh8 23. Qh4 h6 24. Rg3** Black resigns. For 25. Q×h6† g×h6 26. Rg8 mate was on the schedule—*Games of the Liverpool C.C.*, vol. 2.

## (785) Burn–Bird  1–0

Match (game 12?)
London, 29 May 1886
A80

1. d4 f5 2. e3 Nf6 3. Nf3 e6 4. Be2 b6 5. 0–0 Bb7 6. c4 Bd6 7. Nc3 0–0 8. Qc2 Nc6 9. Rd1 Nb4 10. Qb3 Be4 11. N×e4 f×e4 12. Ne5 c5 13. Bd2 Qc7 14. f4 e×f3 *e.p.* 15. N×f3 Ng4 16. h3 Bh2† 17. Kf1 Nf6 18. B×b4 c×b4 19. Bd3 a5 20. Rd2 Nh5 21. Ke2 Rf6 22. Rc1 Bd6 23. Qa4 Raf8 24. Qb5 Ng3† 25. Kd1 Nf5 26. Re2 Ng3 27. Re1 h6 28. Rc2 Rc8 29. Kc1 Qc6 30. Q×c6 R×c6 31. Kb1 Rc7 32. b3 Rf8 33. Rec1 Rfc8 34. Bg6 Be7 35. e4 Rf8 36. e5 Rf4 37. Re1 Kf8 38. Rd2 Ra7 39. d5 e×d5 40. c×d5 Bc5 41. d6 Ra8 42. e6 d×e6 43. d7 Ke7 44. Ne5 Rf1 45. R×f1 N×f1 46. Rd3 Bd6 47. d8Q† K×d8 48. R×d6† and White wins—*Games of the Liverpool C.C.*, vol. 2.

## (786) Bird–Burn  0–1

Match (game 13)
London, 29 May 1886
A03

**1. f4** "A favorite opening of Mr. Bird. It belongs to the close games and of necessity involves the adoption of the fianchetto later on, unless he wants to resort to the Stonewall Opening of Ware, which weakens the e-pawn. It presents the difference and perhaps slight advantage over the queen's fianchetto proper that it does not allow the advance of e5"—Steinitz. **1. ... d5 2. e3 e6 3. b3 Nf6 4. Nf3 Be7 5. Bb2 0–0** "No more than in the open game do we approve of castling too early, especially when Black, and before it is certain on which side the opponent will lodge his king"—Steinitz. **6. Bd3** "And it might have proved somewhat dangerous if White had hit on the expedient which the editor has often adopted in similar positions when giving the odds of a knight, viz., 6. Qe2 which is likely to lead to the following continuation: 6. ... c5 7. g4. Obviously White has now a strong attack with his pawns against the adverse king who has indiscreetly castled too early, but especially at odds we have often found Black falling into the following trap: 7. ... N×g4 8. B×g7 K×g7 9. Qg2 f5 10. h3 h5 (it makes no difference whether or not Black checks at h4 and drives the king to d1) 11. Ne5 Bf6 12. h×g4 h×g4 13. N×g4 f×g4 (best) 14. Q×g4† Bg5 (best) 15. Rh5 with a pawn ahead and an excellent attack"—Steinitz. Not surprisingly, there are a few errors in this long and speculative line. 8. ... Bh4† 9. Kd1 Nf2† wins simply. The losing mistake is the tame 11. ... Bf6. Much better is 11. ... Rh8! **6. ... c5 7. Nc3 Nc6 8. Bb5** "The bishop has lost a move, and besides he can gain little by its exchange for the knight. 8. a3 seems to be indicated here"— Steinitz. **8. ... Qc7** 8. ... d4! exploits Bird's loss of tempo. **9. B×c6 Q×c6 10. Ne5** One now has a rather typical Bird opening, with a slight edge for White. **10. ... Qc7 11. Ne2 Rd8 12. Ng3** The maneuvring with the knight allows 12. ... d4! once more. **12. ... Bd7 13. 0–0 Be8** "How to utilize this bishop without causing too much obstruction, is the important question which has to be decided by the player who has early played 2. ... e6, and correspondingly it is the object of the attack to keep that bishop shut up or have it displaced without being of much use. Formerly the adoption of the fianchetto in order to play Bb7, or else the further advance of the e-pawn, were held to be the only alternatives. In the last championship match the editor first introduced in a similar position the plan of bringing out the queen and then to let the h-rook occupy d8 before developing the bishop to e8 via d7. On principle the treatment of the two analogous positions is alike, and the new idea is applied under slightly modified circumstances which in no way diminish its good effect"—Steinitz. Forster, in his biography on Burn (p. 215), points out that Eduard Pindar was the first to adopt this maneuvre in his first match with Blackburne in 1861. **14. Ng4 d4** "Which scores the first point on the queenside. White's bishop is blocked and will remain so for a long time"—Steinitz. The thematic push of the d-pawn is less strong than it would have been a few moves earlier. **15. e4** 15. N×f6† B×f6 16. Qg4 with some pressure. White can play 17. e4 or 17. Nh5 on the next move. **15. ... N×e4** The exchange of knights helps Bird, whose pieces are kind of congested on the kingside. This is nicely demonstrated by 15. ... Nd7! **16. N×e4 f5 17. Ng5** "Mr. Bird seems to have speculated on the strength of the open f-file, but it was much better to preserve this knight which ought to have retreated to g3 and to keep the e-pawn weak"—Steinitz. **17. ... B×g5 18. f×g5 f×g4 19. Q×g4 e5** *(see diagram)*

*After 19. ... e5*

**20. c3** Contrary to Steinitz' opinion, expressed in his last remark, the actual continuation chosen by Bird appears to be the best, and

it is sufficient to give him a very small edge. But here he designs a very original, but antipositional plan to release his bishop. Instead 20. Rae1 Bf7 21. d3 gives White a slight edge. The bishop will return to c1, his future plan being the push of the h-pawn until h6. **20. ... Bg6 21. Qg3 Rd7 22. Rac1** "Not as good, we think, as 22. Rae1, albeit the move in the text prepares some interesting manoeuvring"—Steinitz. **22. ... Qd6** 22. ... Qa5 exploits Bird's last move: 23. a3 Re8 24. Rce1 e4 with the initiative. **23. h4 Re8 24. b4** "A very ingenious effort to extricate himself with advantage"—Steinitz. 24. b4 doesn't lead to the much wanted complications, but to an endgame that is simply better for Black. In fact, White's position has some trumps of its own, and by pursuing these the balance could be maintained: 24. c×d4 c×d4 25. Qh3 Rf7 26. h5 R×f1† 27. R×f1 Be4 28. h6. **24. ... d×c3! 25. d×c3 c4** The materialistic 25. ... Qe6 is even stronger; e.g., 26. Rce1 Rd3 27. Rf3 R×f3 28. Q×f3 Q×a2. **26. Qg4** 26. Rce1 is tougher, although the passed pawn and open d-file are hard to compete with (e.g., 26. ... Qb6† 27. Kh2 Rd3). **26. ... Qe6** The exchange of queens, which Bird unwisely avoids, would offer him some drawing chances. Much better was 26. ... Qb6† and 27. ... Rd2 with active play. **27. Qg3?** 27. Q×e6† R×e6 28. Rce1 Rd3 (Steinitz) and now 29. b5 might be playable. **27. ... e4** 27. ... Rd2! decides the game at once. If 28. Ba3 Qb6† 29. Kh2 Qa6. **28. Qf4** "From bad to worse. 28. Rce1 e3 29. Bc1, followed by 30. Rf3 was his best resource"—Steinitz. 29. ... e2 30. Rf3 and now 30. ... Rd3 or 30. ... Bh5 guarantee the win anyway. **28. ... e3 29. Rfd1 Rf7 30. Qg3 Rf2 31. Ba3 R×a2 32. Rd6** "It was all hopeless. If 32. Ra1 e2, and exchanging rooks wins easy"—Steinitz. **32. ... Qf7 33. Rf1 Q×f1†** "An elegant termination. Burn's play after the opening has been faultless"—Steinitz. **34. K×f1 e2† 35. Ke1 Ra1†** White resigns—*International Chess Magazine* (Steinitz), July 1886, pp. 206–207.

**(787) Burn–Bird　1–0**
Match (game 14)
London, 31 May 1886
*Game score missing*

**(788) Bird–Burn　1–0**
Match (game 15)
London, 1 June 1886
A03

1. f4 d5 2. Nf3 e6 3. e3 Nf6 4. b3 Be7 5. Bb2 c5 6. Bb5† Nbd7 7. 0–0 0–0 8. Qe1 Ne4 9. B×d7 B×d7 10. d3 Bf6 11. Ne5 Nd6 12. Nd2 Be7 13. e4 d4 14. Qg3 f6 15. Nef3 Nf7 16. Rae1 Rc8 17. h4 Nh6 18. Nh2 f5 19. Ndf3 Bf6 20. Ng5 Qa5 21. a3 Rce8 22. Re2 Qd8 23. e5 Be7 24. Qh3 Bc8 25. Bc1 Qd5 26. g4 b5 27. Rg2 Bb7 28. Rg3 f×g4 29. N×g4 Nf5 30. Rgf3 c4 31. b×c4 b×c4 32. Ne4 h5 33. Ngf2 B×h4 34. Qg2 c×d3 35. c×d3 Rc8 36. Qg6 Rc2 37. Q×h5 Qd8 38. Rh3 Qe7 39. Qg6 B×f2† 40. N×f2 Rfc8 41. Qh7† Kf8 42. Qh8† Kf7 43. Qh5† g6 44. Qh7† Ng7 45. f5 e×f5 46. Bf4 Rg8 47. Rg3 Qe6 48. Nh3 Qc6 49. Ng5† Kf8 50. Nf3 Qd5 51. R×g6 Rc6 52. Rg3 Rc7 53. Bh6 Rf7 54. Rf2 f4 55. Rg6 Qb3 56. e6 Rc7 57. B×f4 Rc6 58. Bd6† R×d6 59. N×d4† Black resigns—*Games of the Liverpool C.C.*, vol. 2.

**(789) Burn–Bird    0–1**

Match (game 16)
London, 2 June 1886
*A80*

1. d4 f5 2. e3 Nf6 3. Nf3 e6 4. Be2 b6 5. 0–0 Bb7 6. c4 Bd6 7. Nc3 Nc6 8. Bd2 0–0 9. Qc2 Qe8 10. Rfd1 Qg6 11. Be1 Ne4 12. a3 Ng5 13. N×g5 Q×g5 14. d5 Ne7 15. f4 Qh6 16. Bg3 e×d5 17. c×d5 Rae8 18. Bf3 Ng6 19. Qf2 Bc5 20. Re1 a5 21. Rab1 Rf7 22. b4 a×b4 23. a×b4 Bf8 24. h4 c6 25. Red1 Ne7 26. d×c6 B×c6 27. Rd3 B×f3 28. Q×f3 Nc6 29. Nd5 Re4 30. Be1 Qe6 31. Bc3 Ne7 32. N×e7† B×e7 33. g3 Rf8 34. Kf2 Re8 35. Qd1 d5 36. R×d5 R×e3 37. Be5 Re4 38. Rd4 R×d4 39. Q×d4 Rd8 40. Qb2 Rd3 41. Qe2 Qd5 42. Rb2 B×b4 43. R×b4 Rd2 44. Rb2 R×e2† 45. R×e2 b5 46. Rc2 b4 47. Rc7 b3 48. R×g7† Kf8 49. R×h7 b2 50. Rh8† Kf7 51. Rh7† Kg6 52. Rg7† Kh6 53. B×b2 Qd2† 54. Kf1 Q×b2 55. Rg5 Qd2 56. Kg1 Qe2 57. Kh1 Qf2 and Black wins—*Games of the Liverpool C.C.*, vol. 2.

**(790) Bird–Burn    0–1**

Match (game 17)
London, 3 June 1886
*A03*

1. f4 d5 2. e3 e6 3. Nf3 Nf6 4. b3 Be7 5. Nc3 c5 6. Bb5† Nbd7 7. 0–0 0–0 8. Qe1 Qc7 9. Bb2 Rd8 10. Be2 Nf8 11. Nb5 Qb6 12. Be5 Ne8 13. a4 f6 14. a5 Qc6 15. Bb2 Bd7 16. c4 Nd6 17. Nc3 d×c4 18. b×c4 Be8 19. d4 c×d4 20. N×d4 Qc7 21. Ncb5 Qd7 21. … N×b5 fixes White's pawn structure, but avoids the following strong move. **22. a6! b6 23. Rd1 Rac8?** (*see diagram*) 23. … N×b5 is necessary, but obviously better for White after 24. c×b5 Qc7 25. Bf3. It is curious that Bird gets such a promising position despite some time-consuming maneuvers in the opening phase.

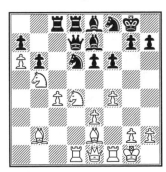

*After 23. ... Rac8*

**24. Qg3?** Bird misses an excellent chance to get very close to the win of the match with the quiet 24. Nf3! Suddenly all of Black's pieces lack space and the a-pawn is a target. The Black queen is also extremely uncomfortable on the d-file. After 24. … Ra8 25. Ba3 Qc6 26. Nfd4 Qc8 27. Bf3 Rb8 28. B×d6 B×d6 29. N×a7 White wins the exchange. **24. … Bg6 25. N×d6 Q×d6 26. Nb5 Qb8 27. Qf3 Be8** Bird still has reason to be confident but the exchange of a piece on each side has relieved Burn greatly. He would have kept a slight initiative after 28. Qb7. **28. R×d8 R×d8 29. Nd4 Bc5 30. Ra1 Qd6** 30. … e5! 31. f×e5 Q×e5 throws White on the defensive, as his position counts several weaknesses while Black's pieces gain some activity. **31. Rd1 Qe7 32. Kf2 Rc8 33. Qe4 Bg6 34. Qb7** A decent reply. **34. … Rc7 35. Qa8 e5 36. f×e5 f×e5 37. Qd5†?** Bird faced

a difficult choice. 37. Nf3 might have rescued the game, though the complications are difficult to foresee. After 37. … B×e3† 38. K×e3 Qc5† 39. Kd2 Rd7† 40. Ke1 Qb4† 41. Kf2 R×d1 42. B×d1 Q×b2† 43. Be2, White will win the pawn at e5 since 43. … e4 44. Qd5† Kh8 45. Qd6 Kg8 draws at once. The endgame is just slightly better for Black. **37. … Qf7 38. Q×f7† R×f7† 39. Kg1 e×d4 40. e×d4 Bb4 41. c5 Rf6 42. c×b6 R×b6 43. d5 Bc2 44. Bd4 B×d1 45. Bc4 Nd7 46. Kf1 Bc5 47. Bc3 Bb3** White resigns—*Games of the Liverpool C.C.*, vol. 2.

**(791) Burn–Bird    0–1**

Match (game 18)
London, 4 June 1886
*A80*

1. d4 f5 "This defense gives the opening the name of a strong Dutch player [Elias Stein] who first suggested it. Morphy, after having lost the defense of a Queen's Gambit against Harrwitz, declared the latter opening to be so strong that he avoided it subsequently in three more games against the same opponent by the defense in the text"—Steinitz. **2. e3 Nf6 3. Nf3 e6 4. Be2 b6 5. c4 Bb7 6. 0–0 Be7 7. Nc3 0–0 8. Qb3** "We do not like this as much as 8. Qc2, which Burn often adopted in this match"—Steinitz. **8. … Ne4 9. Rd1 Qe8 10. Bd2 d6** "The weakening of the e-pawn by 10. … d6 seems to be a necessity for Black in this opening, and on that ground alone the defense appears unsatisfactory"—Steinitz. **11. Rac1 Qg6 12. Be1** "With the exception of one or two games only close openings of the same description as the present one occurred in this match. For Mr. Bird mostly opened with 1. f4, while Mr. Burn adopted 1. d4 or 1. c4, to which Mr. Bird replied 1. … f5. It is noteworthy that Burn, whether White or Black, invariably chose to make almost exactly the same preparations for the attack in the center or on the queenside as those which were introduced by the editor in the defense of the Queen's Gambit in the late championship match—Steinitz. **12. … Nd7 13. a3** "13. d5 would have been better. The move in the text loses time"—Duffy. **13. … f4! 14. d5?!** "It was perhaps a little better to reserve this advance which could never be prevented, and to make a preliminary preparation by 14. Qc2. He could also safely play 14. Bd3 f×e3 15. f×e3 R×f3 16. B×e4 B×e4 17. N×e4"—Steinitz. This is a worthy alternative. After 17. … Raf8, Black retains a small edge, but he loses the possibility of playing for an immediate kingside attack. **14. … Ndc5! 15. Qc2 f×e3 16. f×e3** (*see diagram*)

*After 16. f×e3*

**16. … e×d5 17. N×d5?** "This was an error, and 17. c×d5 was clearly better, for White threatened then 18. b4, and if 17. … Bg5

18. N×g5 N×c3 19. Q×c3 Q×g5 20. b4 Nd7 (best) 21. Qd4 Rac8 22. Bg3 with the superior game"—Steinitz. An improvement here is 17. ... Bc8!, e.g., 18. N×e4 Bf5, with a lasting initiative. Bird's play after Burn's move is close to perfect, and he convincingly equalizes the match score. **17. ... B×d5 18. c×d5** The alternative capture isn't better. Black's attack remains decisive after 18. R×d5 c6! 19. Rd4 Bf6 20. Rdd1 Bg5 21. Bf2 Qf6 22. b4 N×f2 23. K×f2 Rae8. **18. ... Bg5! 19. Bf2** "Most unpleasant, but he had nothing better. If 19. N×g5 Q×g5. Or if 19. Bd2 N×d2 20. Q×d2 (best; if 20. Q×g6 N×f3†, winning a piece) 20. ... Nb3"—Steinitz. **19. ... Qh6** Just as in all variations, White's e-pawn is doomed thanks to Black's overwhelming knights. **20. b4 N×f2** "Good enough, but 20. ... B×e3 at once was still better and might have led to Philidor's Legacy; e.g., 21. B×e3 Q×e3† 22. Kh1 Nf2† 23. Kg1 Nh3† 24. Kh1 Qg1†, followed by 25. ... Nf2 mate"—Steinitz. **21. K×f2 B×e3† 22. Ke1 Rae8!** "Mr. Bird is noted to be unrelenting in his attack once he holds the grip of it"—Steinitz. **23. Rb1** "If 23. b×c5 R×f3! 24. B×f3 (best) 24. ... B×c1† 25. Kf1 B×a3 with a winning game"—Steinitz. **23. ... Ne4 24. Rb3 Bf2† 25. Kf1 Ng3†!** "One of those happy inspirations for which Bird is justly famous"—Steinitz. **26. h×g3 B×g3 27. Kg1 R×f3** White resigns—*Illustrated London News* (Duffy), 12 June 1886; *International Chess Magazine* (Steinitz), July 1886, pp. 207–209.

# MATCH WITH GUNSBERG 1886

Burn's match challenge towards the British chess world excluded Blackburne, recognized by all as the strongest English player. Behind him, several players attempted to work themselves up to a position worthy to challenge the Black Death, as Blackburne was aptly nicknamed. Besides Burn and Bird, Isidor Gunsberg was a player with such ambitions. The unexpected draw between Burn and Bird (many had anticipated a win for the younger and calmer Burn) was a huge motivation for him to meet Bird in a similar contest. If he could beat the veteran, his position on the chess ladder would clearly elevate. Thus Gunsberg issued a challenge to Bird, "for chess supremacy only, the stake being merely nominal," as the *Leeds Mercury* of 19 June put it.

The negotiations between Bird and Gunsberg went as fluently as between Bird and Burn. Just four days after the termination of the latter match the two met at the British Chess Club. The match was played for five wins. The time limit was set on 20 moves per hour with the stakes being £5 per side.

Bird started uncharacteristically with a draw, a win and two consolidating draws. Game five and six saw some very resourceful play by Bird. He had more than his share of the chances but was not rewarded at all and suffered two bitter defeats. Three subsequent losses sealed his fate quickly. According to the press Bird's suffering from the gout once more deprived him of his best abilities to make something out of it.

The battle for chess hegemony continued in full rage during the summer months with strongly occupied congresses of the B.C.A. and the C.C.A. Towards the end of August, Gunsberg issued a match challenge to Burn. Burn declined on the ground that he had finished ahead of Gunsberg in both London and Nottingham. At

that time Burn tried to negotiate a match with Blackburne, which ultimately did not materialize. Gunsberg was not convinced by Burn's argument. In a public letter he referred to his match win against Bird, as opposed to Burn's inability to beat the veteran.

Bird was far from happy at being brought into the discussion and he reacted as if stung by a bee. In a firm letter he had a retrospective look on his match with Gunsberg. It turned out that this one had been far less agreeable for Bird than his match with Burn.

> To Mr. Gunsberg must belong the credit of making an umpire necessary in a chess match; for I appeal to all who were present at the British Chess Club when the interruptions in play occurred during the third and fourth games in our match, and ask would it be wise for any master or amateur to engage in a match with Mr. Gunsberg without an umpire? Can it be tolerated that a man shall slam the pieces, jump from the chair, and parade the room after a move, and finally wind up by quitting the room altogether for the period of three-quarters of an hour without a word of explanation or apology? The very essence and enjoyment of chess consists in the nice feeling and spirit with which the game is all but universally played. When it is otherwise, then away with chess. With the fourth game, when I had won one game and drawn three, I determined to abandon the match, but, to oblige others, weakly hesitated to do so. I threw away three games in succession when I had much advantage, and lost the match in which my interest had departed. Mr. Gunsberg has certainly been very successful against me at chess lately; but why a few victories (some very lucky ones) over a broken-down old chess-player in bad health should be put forward as a plea to justify him in challenging Burn, I do not know [*Bradford Observer Budget*, 11 September 1886].

Gunsberg retaliated by questioning Bird's sportive attitude during the match. He referred, by memory, to the positions of their match games 3 and 4 (see below).

> Now, Mr. Bird continued playing both these positions for nearly 200 moves, objecting to allow me to count 50 moves, and also objecting to an adjournment, which I proposed in the fourth game, after ten p.m. In spite of the tone of injured innocence which Mr. Bird adopts in his letter, I cannot possibly believe that he has played chess for 40 years without possibly knowing that at least the position in game 4 was a hopeless draw. I can, therefore, confidently leave it to the public to decide whether I or Mr. Bird was most at fault [*Bradford Observer Budget*, 25 September 1886].

| Match with Gunsberg, 14–23 June 1886 | | | | | | | | | | |
|---|---|---|---|---|---|---|---|---|---|---|
| | 1 | 2 | 3 | 4 | 5 | 6 | 7 | 8 | 9 | |
| I. Gunsberg | ½ | 0 | ½ | ½ | 1 | 1 | 1 | 1 | 1 | 5 |
| H.E. Bird | ½ | 1 | ½ | ½ | 0 | 0 | 0 | 0 | 0 | 1 |

**(792) Bird–Gunsberg   ½–½**
Match (game 1)
London, 14 June 1886
*Game score missing*

**(793) Gunsberg–Bird   0–1**
Match (game 2)
London, 15 June 1886
C25

**1. e4 e5 2. Nc3 Nc6 3. f4 e×f4 4. Nf3 Bb4 5. d4 d5 6. e5 Nge7 7. B×f4 Be6 8. Bd3 h6 9. 0–0 Qd7 10. Na4** "The intention is to drive back the bishop, and then exchange it at b6 for the knight. White might, however, have foreseen Black's reply, and, instead of losing time with the text move, should have played 10. Ne2, when the adverse bishop would have been temporarily out of play"—Hoffer. **10. ... Ng6** "Now Black has a good square for his bishop, and the adverse knight is inactive"—Hoffer. **11. B×g6 f×g6 12. c3 Be7 13. b4** "Compulsory for the protection of the knight"—Hoffer. **13. ... 0–0 14. Be3 g5 15. Nb2 a5 16. a3 b5 17. Nd3 Nd8 18. Qd2 Nf7 19. Rf2 Nh8 20. Raf1 Ng6** "A cleverly executed knight's tour"—Hoffer. **21. Nc5** Allowing, even obligating, an exchange that is welcomed by Black. 21. Qb2, liberating d2 to bring the knight towards b3, is a better plan. **21. ... B×c5 22. b×c5 c6 23. Ne1** Black's control over the white squares is enhanced after the exchange of rooks. **23. ... R×f2 24. R×f2 Rf8 25. R×f8† N×f8 26. g3 Ng6 27. Bf2 Qf7 28. Ng2 Qf5 29. Ne3?** Hoffer criticized Gunsberg's last few moves (suggesting 27. Qf2), but the actual error is made only here, as the entry of Bird's queen, which has decisive effects, could still be prevented with precise play: 29. Qd1 Qe4 30. Ne3 Bh3 31. Qc2 Q×c2 32. N×c2 Bf5 33. Ne1 with a considerable drawing margin. **29. ... Qb1† 30. Qd1 Qb2 31. Qc2 Qa1† 32. Kg2 Ne7** Excellent play from Bird. He wins a pawn. **33. g4 Q×a3 34. Nf5 Ng6** The best retort. White is helpless. **35. N×h6† Kh7 36. Nf5 Nf4† 37. Kf3 g6** As there is no dangerous discovery check available, 37. ... b4! at once is very strong. Now White misses his last straw to perhaps save the game, by playing either 38. h4 or 38. Be3. **38. Ne7 Qa1 39. Bg3 Qf1† 40. Ke3 B×g4 41. Kd2 a4 42. B×f4** "White has no saving move. Black threatens 42. ... h3, which leads to a mate"—Hoffer. **42. ... Q×f4† 43. Ke1 Qe3†** White resigns—*The Field* (Hoffer), 12 June 1886.

## (794) Bird–Gunsberg    ½–½
Match (game 3)
London, 16 June 1886

*Position as published; game status unknown*

Finally a draw—*Bradford Observer Budget*, 25 September 1886.

## (795) Gunsberg–Bird    ½–½
Match (game 4)
London, 17 June 1886

*Position as published; game status unknown*

Again a draw—*Bradford Observer Budget*, 25 September 1886.

## (796) Bird–Gunsberg    0–1
Match (game 5)
London, June 1886
*A03*

**1. f4 d5 2. Nf3 e6 3. e3 Nf6 4. b3 c5 5. Bb2 Be7 6. Nc3 a6 7. Bd3** "With the threatened advance of Black's pawns on the queenside, this is not a square where the bishop can maintain itself. 7. Be2 is the usual move. The text move may be played if Black adopts a different development, or if there is a possibility of moving the c-pawn, and to post the bishop at c2"—Hoffer. **7. ... 0–0 8. 0–0 b5 9. Qe1 Nc6 10. Ne5 N×e5 11. f×e5 Nd7 12. Nd1 c4 13. Be2 Qc7** "13. ... Bh4, intending to prevent the queen from supporting e5 would not have helped, because of 14. Nf2, 15. g3 and 16. Ng4"—Hoffer. **14. b×c4 b×c4 15. Qg3 f6** 15. ... Rb8 gains a valuable tempo or binds White's knight to the passive square d1. **16. Nf2** *(see diagram)* "An ingenious move of protecting the e-pawn, and leading to interesting variations"—Hoffer.

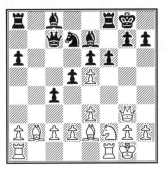

*After 16. Nf2*

**16. ... N×e5** "If 16. ... f×e5, White obviously would reply 17. Ng4 with more effect"—Hoffer. 16. ... Rb8 is again an interesting zwischenzug. Little is changed with the lines as played in the game, but the extra tempo counts in some positions; e.g., 17. Bd4 N×e5 18. Ng4 Bd6 19. N×f6† R×f6 20. R×f6 Ng6 21. R×g6 B×g3 22. R×g3? (22. R×g7† is decidedly better, but here the difference with the position in the game becomes visible after 22. ... Q×g7 23. B×g7 K×g7 [or 23. ... B×h2† 24. K×h2 K×g7 and Black controls the b-file] 24. h×g3 Rb2 25. Bd1 e5 when Black holds all trumps, but it's unclear whether he can force a breakthrough) 22. ... e5. **17. Ng4 Bd6 18. N×f6† R×f6 19. R×f6 Ng6 20. R×g6! B×g3 21. R×g3!** "Very bold. White of course could have equalized the game as far as material is concerned, but Black would have emerged with a more advantageous position; e.g., 21. R×g7† Q×g7 22. B×g7 K×g7 23. h×g3 Rb8 taking the open file. Less advantageous would have been 22. ... B×h2† 23. K×h2 K×g7, because White would then have occupied with 24. Rb1"—Hoffer. After 24. Bd1 Rb2 25. Kf2, a draw can be agreed upon. Bird's move is not bad, just unnecessarily risky. **21. ... g6 22. Rf1** "The variations resulting from 22. Bf6, intending to play it ultimately to h6 are very interesting; but hardly so good as those which occurred in the actual game"—Hoffer. Bird selects by far the most competitive move. 22. Bf6 Bd7 23. Bg5? c3! is certainly not what he wants. **22. ... Bd7 23. Rgf3 e5** Bird gains sufficient counterplay now. **24. Rf7 Qd6 25. R1f6 Be6** A simpler line to force the draw was 25. ... Qb8 26. R×d7 Q×b2 27. Rff7 e4 28. c3 and White must soon take a perpetual. **26. Bg4 Re8** *(see diagram)*

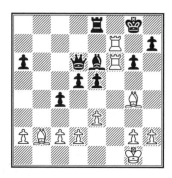

*After 26. ... Re8*

**27. h4** 27. Rb7! is surprisingly testing. After an innocent-like move as 27. ... Qc6 (Hoffer), it turns out that White's rook are extremely strong, e.g., 28. B×e6† R×e6 29. Rff7 Qa4 30. Rg7† Kf8 31. Rbf7† Ke8 32. R×h7 Q×c2 33. h3 Qa4 (33. ... Qb1† 34. Kh2) 34. Ra7 wins. The only possibility to draw appears to be 27. ... d4! Black is just in time to create the much wanted counterplay; e.g., 28. B×e6† R×e6 29. Rff7 d×e3 30. Rg7† Kf8 31. Rbf7† Ke8 32. Ra7 Kf8 33. Raf7† and he must take the perpetual. **27. ... Qb8!** Getting the queen out of the pin and attacking the White bishops at the same time brings serious difficulties to his opponent. **28. B×e6 R×e6 29. Rf8† Q×f8 30. R×e6 e4?!** 30. ... d4! 31. e×d4 Qf4 32. d5 Q×d2 33. d6 c3 is the way to go. After the text move, the bishop continues to take part in the game. **31. Bc3?!** Black has nothing but equality after 31. R×a6 Qe7 32. Bf6 Qb7 33. Ra5 Qb6 34. Bc3. **31. ... Qa3! 32. Re5 Q×a2** 32. ... d4! 33. e×d4 Q×a2 34. R×e4 Q×c2 is more precise. **33. R×d5 Q×c2 34. Rd4?!** White's position goes rapidly downhill after this calm move. Aiming for the opponent's king is the right procedure to draw the game, certainly as it delivers him the h-pawn by force after 34. Rd8† Kf7 35. Rd7† Ke8 36. R×h7 Qd1† 37. Kh2 Qg4 38. Kg1. **34. ... Qb1† 35. Kf2 Qb7 36. Kg3 Qc6 37. Kh3 Qe6† 38. Kh2 Kf7 39. g3?** With cool play Gunsberg managed to safeguard his king and he only needs this voluntary weakness to deliver Bird the final stab. If the veteran had just moved his majesty to and fro, his opponent still had to find a clean cut win. **39. ... h6 40. Rd8 g5 41. h×g5 h×g5 42. Ra8 Kg6 43. Rb8 Kf5 44. Rf8† Kg4 45. Rf6 Qe8 46. Rh6 Qa8** The quickest way to win the game would have been 46. ... Qb8 47. Rh3 Qf8 etc. **47. Rb6 a5 48. Rb5 a4 49. Ra5 Qe8 50. Rc5 Qf7 51. Kg1 Qf3 52. Be5 Kh3** White resigns—*The Field* (Hoffer), 26 June 1886.

### (797) Gunsberg–Bird    1–0
Match (game 6)
London, 19 June 1886
*A82*

**1. d4 f5 2. e4** "This move of voiding a close opening was first tried by Staunton in a game with Horwitz. We believe most experts would prefer to stick to the close opening in which Black, as a natural consequence of the first move, would have the inferior position"—Green. **2. ... f×e4 3. Nc3 Nf6 4. Bg5 e6** "Horwitz against Staunton introduced 4. ... c6, a good move giving Black an advantage in position"—Freeborough. **5. B×f6 Q×f6 6. N×e4 Qe7** "6. ... Qg6 is the book move, but Mr. Bird's play seems justified by results up to a certain point"—Green. **7. Bd3 d5** "Black might win a pawn by 7. ... Qb4†, but it would not be good play"—Green. **8. Nc3** "Needs must. No doubt he would like 8. Ng3, but then 8. ...

Qb4†, which is a point to the credit of Mr. Bird's sixth move"—Green. **8. ... Nc6 9. Nf3 Bd7 10. a3** "Which permits Black to take the lead, and he is not the sort of player to object. White is apparently afraid of losing his bishop and being left with two knights against two bishops. There is also a possible advance of the c-pawn to be considered. It will be seen, however, that he doesn't escape a little disadvantage"—Freeborough. **10. ... Qf6** "Black's tactics are directed towards advancing the e-pawn, and thus getting rid of the weak point in his game. 10. ... Qf6 is played not so much to attack the d-pawn as to allow Bd6, and thus facilitate the ultimate e5"—Green. **11. Qd2 Bd6 12. Ne2** "This permits of the immediate advance of Black's e-pawn, which obviously could not stir while the knight was at c3"—Green. With 12. Bb5, intending to get the knight off the board at some point, White keeps the position equal. **12. ... e5 13. d×e5 N×e5 14. N×e5 B×e5 15. c3 0–0** "Which compels White to follow suit. The net result of the opening is decidedly in Black's favor. He has the majority of pawns on the queenside, two bishops against bishop and knight, and in addition a game so superior that it is surprising he lost"—Green. **16. 0–0 Bd6 17. Rae1 Rae8 18. Ng3 R×e1 19. R×e1 Bc5 20. Rf1 c6 21. c4 Bd4** Immediately exploiting the deficiencies of Gunsberg's last move. **22. b4 Qh4?!** "An unfortunate continuation which causes immediate loss of material. Black could still maintain a slight advantage with 22. ... Be6"—Zukertort. **23. c×d5 c×d5 24. Be4! Qf6?** 24. ... d×e4 25. Q×d4 Bc6 is still more or less playable. The text move is tantamount to resignation. **25. B×d5† Kh8 26. Ne4 Qe5 27. B×b7 Bb5 28. Rd1 Rd8 29. Kh1 Rd7 30. Ng5 Qf6 31. Qc1** "Mr. Gunsberg avails himself ingeniously of the position of Black's king; the constantly threatened mate prevents Black from winning a piece, and gives White time for the final onslaught"—Green. **31. ... g6 32. Bf3 Ba4 33. Re1 Bb2 34. Re8† Kg7 35. Ne6† Kf7 36. Rf8† K×e6 37. R×f6† B×f6 38. Bg4†** Black resigns—*Liverpool Weekly Mercury* (Green), 26 June 1886; *British Chess Magazine* (Freeborough), August–September 1886, pp. 318–319; *Chess Monthly* (Zukertort), September 1886, pp. 9–10.

### (798) Bird–Gunsberg    0–1
Match (game 7)
London, 21 June 1886
*A03*

**1. f4 d5 2. Nf3 g6 3. e3 Bg7 4. d4 Nf6 5. c4 e6 6. Nc3 0–0 7. Be2 b6 8. b3 Bb7 9. 0–0 Nbd7 10. Ne5 c5 11. Ba3 Re8 12. Bf3 N×e5 13. f×e5 Ne4 14. B×e4 d×e4 15. Nb5 Qg5 16. Qe1 Red8 17. Qf2 Rd7 18. Nd6 Rf8 19. h4 Qg4 20. Rae1 f5 21. Qf4 Q×f4 22. e×f4 c×d4 23. N×b7 R×b7 24. B×f8 B×f8 25. Kf2 d3 26. g4 Bc5† 27. Kg3 Rd7 28. Rh1 d2 29. Rb1 Rd3† 30. Kg2 f×g4 31. b4 Be3 32. Kg3 Rc3 33. K×g4 Bf2 34. Rb3 h5† 35. Kg5 R×b3 36. a×b3 e3 37. K×g6 B×h4 38. Ra1 e2** White resigns—*Hackney Mercury*, 3 July 1886.

### (799) Gunsberg–Bird    1–0
Match (game 8)
London, 22 June 1886
*B73*

**1. e4 c5 2. Nc3 g6 3. Nf3 Bg7 4. d4 c×d4 5. N×d4 d6 6. Be3**

Nf6 7. Be2 0–0 8. 0–0 Nc6 9. f4 Bd7 10. Qd2 N×d4 11. B×d4
[B]c6 12. Bf3 Qa5 13. a3 e5 14. Be3 Qc7 15. Rad1 Rad8 16. Qf2
[Q]6 17. Qh4 Nd7 18. f5 f6 19. f×g6 h×g6 20. Be2 b5 21. N×b5
[B]×b5 22. B×b5 Nb6 23. Kh1 Kf7 24. Rf2 Rh8 25. Qg3 Rh5
[2]6. Be2 Rh7 27. Rdf1 Rdh8 28. h3 Nd7 29. b3 Qc3 30. Bc4†
[K]e7 31. Rf3 Q×c2 32. Q×g6 Bf8 33. Rc1 Qb2 34. Rf2 Q×a3
[3]5. Qf5 Bh6 36. Bb5 Kd8 37. B×d7 Black resigns—*Morning
Chronicle*, 19 August 1886. First published in the *Glasgow Weekly
Herald*.

**(800) Bird–Gunsberg   0–1**
Match (game 9)
London, 23 June 1886
*Game score missing*

---

# B.C.A. CONGRESS, LONDON 1886

At the annual meeting of the B.C.A., held on 3 March 1886, some
important decisions were taken. First of all Bird received a new assignment for auditing the accounts of the past year. For this job he
was rewarded with £2 2s. On the same occasion plans for the
coming congress were revealed. The previous edition was not a
unanimous success since it only drew the attention of the habitués
of the Divan. According to the statutes of the organization this congress was intended to gather an international representation. From
the previous congress of the C.C.A. in Hereford, Hoffer had learned
that more prizes had to be provided, so that at least the expenses of
the foreign masters would be covered. Non–prize winners received
a part of the entrance fees.

This intervention proved to be successful as interest for the tournament was raised in all the important chess countries. Schallopp
from Germany, Jean Taubenhaus from France and Mackenzie, James
Moore Hanham and Samuel Lipschütz from America promised to
take part. At the last moment Hoffer's C.C.A. nemesis Arthur Skipworth also requested approval to play in the master tournament.
Since the Reverend Skipworth was only able to commence playing
a few days after the start of the tournament he was not included in
the lists.

Bird's play in this tournament turned out to be dramatic. Apart
from one draw, he lost all his games from the first eight rounds. In
several of them he was unable to offer any resistance worth mentioning. Then Bird won twice, against Pollock and Mortimer, but
this was to no avail when it came to avoiding the bottom place. He
concluded the tournament with another two losses. More than ever
Bird suffered from the gout which even—very unusual for the
plucky veteran—made him miss the banquet at the end of the tournament.

The congress offered the British chess elite another chance
to fight for the so eagerly wanted chess hegemony over the Isles.
All of the usual suspects, Blackburne, Gunsberg, Mason and Burn,
were present, just as the defeated candidate for the world crown,
Zukertort. The star of the first rounds was Amos Burn, but losses
against Blackburne and Gunsberg brought him back among his
peers. The fight for the major honor remained exciting until the
very end, when finally Blackburne and Burn came out on top with
8½ points out of 12. They were closely followed by Gunsberg and
the surprising Taubenhaus (8 each). A tie-break match ended in
Blackburne's favor who hereby reconfirmed his status as England's
number one. Burn proved that he was a worthy and dangerous challenger.

Hoffer was euphoric in his evaluation of the tournament. Against all critical expectations, he stated,
the ambitions of the B.C.A. were realized, and it had
established itself as a crucial factor in British chess.

---

## 2nd Congress of the B.C.A., London, 12–29 July 1886

*Site:* Victoria Hall, Criterion
*Playing hours:* 12 p.m.–4 and 7 p.m.–11
*Prizes:* 1st £80, 2nd £50, 3rd £40, 4th £25, 5th £15 entrance fees divided among
  non–prize winners
*Time limit:* 20 moves per hour

|   |                | 1 | 2 | 3 | 4 | 5 | 6 | 7 | 8 | 9 | 10 | 11 | 12 | 13 |      |
|---|----------------|---|---|---|---|---|---|---|---|---|----|----|----|----|------|
| 1 | J.H. Blackburne |   | 1 | 1 | 0 | ½ | ½ | ½ | 1 | 1 | 0  | 1  | 1  | 1  | 8½   |
| 2 | A. Burn        | 0 |   | 0 | 1 | ½ | 0 | 1 | 1 | 1 | 1  | 1  | 1  | 1  | 8½   |
| 3 | I. Gunsberg    | 0 | 1 |   | 0 | ½ | 1 | 1 | 1 | 0 | ½  | 1  | 1  | 1  | 8    |
| 4 | J. Taubenhaus  | 1 | 0 | 1 |   | ½ | 1 | ½ | 0 | 1 | 1  | 0  | 1  | 1  | 8    |
| 5 | J. Mason       | ½ | ½ | ½ | ½ |   | 1 | 1 | ½ | 0 | 1  | 0  | 1  | ½  | 7    |
| 6 | S. Lipschütz   | ½ | 1 | 0 | 0 | 0 |   | 1 | 1 | 1 | 0  | 1  | 0  | 1  | 6½   |
| 7 | G.H. Mackenzie | ½ | 0 | 0 | ½ | 0 | 0 |   | 1 | 1 | 0  | 1  | 1  | 1  | 6    |
| 8 | J.H. Zukertort | 0 | 0 | 0 | 1 | ½ | 0 | 0 |   | 1 | 1  | 1  | ½  | 1  | 6    |
| 9 | E. Schallopp   | 0 | 0 | 1 | 0 | 1 | 0 | 0 | 0 |   | 1  | 0  | 1  | 1  | 5    |
| 10| W.H.K. Pollock | 1 | 0 | ½ | 0 | 0 | 1 | 1 | 0 | 0 |    | 0  | 1  | 0  | 4½   |
| 11| J. Mortimer    | 0 | 0 | 0 | 1 | 1 | 0 | 0 | 0 | 1 | 1  |    | 0  | 0  | 4    |
| 12| J.M. Hanham    | 0 | 0 | 0 | 0 | 0 | 1 | 0 | ½ | 0 | 0  | 1  |    | 1  | 3½   |
| 13| H.E. Bird      | 0 | 0 | 0 | 0 | ½ | 0 | 0 | 0 | 0 | 1  | 1  | 0  |    | 2½   |

| *Tie matches*     | 1 | 2 |     |
|-------------------|---|---|-----|
| J.H. Blackburne   | 1 | ½ | 1½  |
| A. Burn           | 0 | ½ | ½   |

|                   | 1 | 2 |     |
|-------------------|---|---|-----|
| I. Gunsberg       | ½ | ½ | 1   |
| J. Taubenhaus     | ½ | ½ | 1   |

**(801) Bird–Burn   0–1**
B.C.A. Congress (round 1)
London, 12 July 1886
*A03*

**1. f4 d5 2. b3 e6 3. Bb2 Nf6 4. Nf3 Be7 5. e3 c5
6. Bb5† Nbd7 7. 0–0 0–0 8. Qe1 Qc7 9. Nc3 Rd8
10. Nd1 Nf8 11. Be2 Bd7 12. Ne5 Be8 13. d3 Rac8
14. Nf2 b5 15. Nfg4** Bird immediately launches his
usual kingside attack, but Burn is excellently placed
to deal with it. Instead, 15. c4 stops Burn's plans on
the queenside. **15. ... N×g4 16. B×g4 f6 17. Nf3 Bf7**
A bit slow. Playing 17. ... a5! immediately is promising.
**18. Qg3** Bird incorrectly continues his demonstration
on the kingside; 18. a4, again questioning Black on
the other side of the board, restores equality. **18. ...
Bd6** 18. ... c4 is correct. The text move allows Bird to
transpose to a very promising endgame. **19. Qe1** Bird
overlooked 19. B×f6 g×f6! 20. B×e6† Ng6 21. B×c8
Q×c8 22. c3. White has enough material to compen-

sate for Black's two pieces. Besides, he has all the time of the world to post his rook on central files and advance his pawn mass in either the center or on the kingside. **19. ... Rb8 20. Bc3 b4 21. Bd2** The bishop has few prospects here. **21. ... a5** 21. ... c4! at once is also possible; e.g., 22. d×c4 d×c4 23. c3 Rdc8, with an annoying pressure. **22. a3 Re8 23. a×b4 a×b4 24. Nh4?** Bird still hasn't abandoned his attacking plans yet, but here he finds a strong Burn on his way. 24. Qh4, to connect his rooks, is better, but Black's position is very harmonious and difficult to combat anyway. **24. ... g5!** A very convincing retort that wins material. **25. Nf3 f5** 25. ... h5! is the superior way to continue: 26. Bh3 g4 27. Qg3 f5. **26. N×g5 f×g4 27. Qh4 Bg6 28. Q×g4 Qg7 29. Ra6 Rbd8 30. Rfa1 Rd7** 30. ... c4! quickly decides the game as White cannot hold his center together. **31. h4 h6 32. Nf3 Bf5?!** 32. ... h5! 33. Qg5 c4 and Black's initiative on the queenside is decisive again. The exchange of queens looks logical from Burn's side, but his extra piece is not so valuable, as his knight has but little prospect. **33. Q×g7† K×g7 34. Rc6 Nh7?!** The knight is badly placed here. White now gets the time to reorganize his pieces and this offers him equal chances again. 34. ... Ng6 (intending 35. ... Ne7) would have kept an advantage. **35. Raa6** 35. Bc1 is also possible. **35. ... Red8 36. Ne5 B×e5 37. f×e5 Nf8** 37. ... c4 could be tried. Black probably hasn't enough to win anyway: 38. b×c4 d×c4 39. R×c4 b3 40. c×b3 R×d3 41. Ra7† R8d7 42. R×d7† R×d7 43. Bc3. **38. R×c5 Ng6** The b-pawn had to be defended. **39. B×b4 N×h4?!** *(see diagram)* This pawn is not safely captured. 39. ... Kh7 is safe, but it is Black who has now to fight for the draw.

*After 39. ... N×h4*

**40. Be1?!** 40. Ra4! is very dangerous for Black. This move indirectly attacks the knight, but also, in case of its retreat by 40. ... Ng6?, he is ready to win the bishop by 41. g4! Black is thus forced to play artificially to even survive. For instance, 40. ... Rb8 41. Rc3 (41. Bc3 is met by 41. ... Ng6 42. g4 B×d3 43. c×d3 R×b3) 41. ... d4 (something had to be done against the menace 42. Bd6) 42. Rc4 Kh7 43. Be1 Ng6 44. R×d4 with a slight edge. **40. ... Ng6 41. d4** The defense of the e-pawn was not necessary and even has a downside as it brings Black's bishop into action again. Both 41. Ra4 or 41. b4 are fully playable. **41. ... Kf7 42. Rcc6 Ne7 43. Rcb6?!** 43. Rd6 is correct: 43. ... Nc8 44. Rdc6 with equality. **43. ... Rg8** 43. ... Rc8! is much stronger. After 44. c3 Bd3 and 45. ... Nf5 the situation of Black's minor pieces has improved drastically. **44. c4 Rc7 45. c5 Bd3 46. Ra2** Bird's position has suddenly become very precarious. Here 46. Ra3 is an improvement, for the e-pawn is in need of support. If 46. ... Be4 47. g3 h5 48. b4 with a sharp endgame that offers chances to both sides. **46. ... Nf5 47. Rf2** This proves to be too time-consuming. With 47. b4 the e-pawn is sacrificed, but the time gained may allow him to hold the game; e.g., after 47. ...

N×e3 48. b5 Nf5 49. Rd2 Bc4 50. Rf2 Ra7 51. Rf4. **47. ... Ra7 48. Bc3 h5 49. Kh2?!** Another move that is too passive, which is bad timing as Black's pieces are truly coming to life. 49. b4 might offer more chances. **49. ... h4 50. b4** 50. c6 can't save him either 50. ... Rc8 51. b4 Ra3 52. Bd2 Kg8 and the c-pawn will eventually fall. **50. ... Ke7 51. Bd2 Ng3 52. Be1 Nf1† 53. Kh3 N×e3 54. b5 Bf5† 55. R×f5 N×f5 56. c6 Kf7 57. Bf2 Ra3† 58. Kh2 Ra2 59. Rb7† Kg6 60. c7 Rc8 61. b6 Raa8 62. Be1 Kf7 63. Bb4 Ke8 64. Bd6 N×d6 65. e×d6 Kd7 66. Kh3 K×d6 67. K×h4 Kc6** White resigns— *The Field*, 17 July 1886.

### (802) Schallopp–Bird  1–0
B.C.A. Congress (round 2)
London, 13 July 1886
*C61*

**1. e4 e5 2. Nf3 Nc6 3. Bb5 Nd4 4. N×d4 e×d4 5. d3 h5 6. 0–0 Bc5 7. c3 c6 8. Ba4 Ne7 9. b4 Bb6 10. c4 d6 11. Qc2 Bg4 12. f4 h4 13. h3 Bd7 14. c5 Bc7 15. Bb2 d5 16. e5 Nf5 17. Qf2 Rh6 18. Re1 Rg6 19. B×d4 N×d4 20. Q×d4 B×h3 21. Re2 Bf5 22. Kh2 a6 23. Nc3 Kf8 24. Nd1 Qd7 25. Ne3 Rg3 26. Bc2 Re8 27. Qb2 Bh3 28. d4 Bg4 29. Ree1 g6 30. Nf1 Bf3 31. N×g3 h×g3† 32. Kg1 Bh5 33. f5 g×f5 34. Qc1 Qe6 35. Qf4 Bg4 36. Re3 Ke7 37. Rf1 Rh8 38. Qg5† Ke8 39. R×g3 Bd8 40. Qg7 Rh5 41. Qg8† Ke7 42. R×g4 f×g4 43. Rf6** Black resigns— *Deutsche Illustrirte Zeitung.*

### (803) Bird–Mason  ½–½
B.C.A. Congress (round 3)
London, 14 July 1886
*Game score missing*

### (804) Mackenzie–Bird  1–0
B.C.A. Congress (round 4)
London, 15 July 1886
*B73*

**1. e4 c5 2. Nc3 Nc6 3. Nf3 g6 4. d4 c×d4 5. N×d4 Bg7 6. Be3 d6 7. Be2 Nf6 8. 0–0 0–0 9. f4 Ne8 10. f5 e6 11. f×g6 h×g6 12. Qd2 e5 13. Nf3 Be6 14. Rad1 Qa5 15. Kh1 Rc8 16. Qe1 Bg4 17. Qh4 B×f3 18. R×f3 Nd4 19. B×d4 e×d4 20. Nd5 Rc7 21. Rh3 f6 22. N×c7 Q×c7 23. R×d4 Kf7 24. Bc4† Ke7 25. Bb3 Qa5 26. Rd5 Qa6 27. Rhd3 Rh8 28. Qg3 Rh6 29. h3 Kd7 30. Qg4† Kd8 31. Qe6 Bf8 32. e5 f×e5 33. R×e5 Qc6 34. Ree3 g5 35. Qf7 Rh8 36. Rc3 Qd7 37. R×e8†** Black resigns— *Illustrated Sporting and Dramatic News*, 7 August 1886.

### (805) Bird–Blackburne  0–1
B.C.A. Congress (round 5)
London, 16 July 1886
*A02*

**1. f4 e5 2. f×e5 d6 3. e×d6 B×d6 4. Nf3 Nh6 5. d4 Ng4 6. Bg5 f6 7. Bh4 g5 8. Bf2 N×f2 9. K×f2 g4 10. Nh4 f5 11. g3 f4 12. Qd3 0–0 13. Kg1 Qf6 14. Bg2 f×g3 15. h×g3 Qf2† 16. Kh2 Rf3 17. Qc4† Kh8** White resigns— *British Chess Magazine*, August–September 1886, p. 342.

**806) Gunsberg–Bird   1–0**

B.C.A. Congress (round 6)
London, 17 July 1886
*B73*

**1. e4 c5 2. Nc3 Nc6 3. Nf3 g6 4. d4 c×d4 5. N×d4 Bg7 6. Be3 d6 7. Be2 Nf6 8. 0–0 0–0 9. f4 Ne8 10. f5**
Only the finish of this game was given in *The Field (see diagram)*.

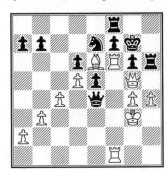

*Black to move*

**37. ... Ng8 38. R×f7† R×f7 39. R×f7† Kh8 40. Rf8 Qe1† 41. Kg2 Qe2† 42. Rf2 Qe4† 43. Kg3 Qd3† 44. Kh2 Qd4 45. Kg1 Qc3 46. B×g8** and after a few more moves Black resigns—*The Field*, 24 July 1886.

**807) Bird–Zukertort   0–1**

B.C.A. Congress (round 7)
London, 19 July 1886
*C33*

**1. f4 e5 2. e4 e×f4 3. Be2 f5 4. e5 d6 5. e×d6 Qh4† 6. Kf1 B×d6 7. d4 Ne7 8. Nf3 Qf6 9. c4 c6 10. c5 Bc7 11. Nc3 Be6 12. h4 Nd7 13. Qa4 h6 14. Bd2 g5 15. d5 N×d5 16. N×d5 B×d5 17. Bc3 Ne5 18. Qd4 0–0–0 19. Qa4 Kb8 20. Rh3 g4 21. N×e5 B×e5 22. B×e5† Q×e5 23. Ra3 B×g2† 24. K×g2 Q×e2† 25. Kg1 a6 26. Q×f4† Ka8 27. Re3 Q×b2 28. Rf1 Rd2 29. Qc7 Rhd8 30. Kh1 Q×a2 31. Qe5 Qd5†** White resigns—*Standard*, 20 July 1886.

**808) Lipschütz–Bird   1–0**

B.C.A. Congress (round 8)
London, 20 July 1886
*B73*

**1. e4 c5 2. Nf3 Nc6 3. Nc3 g6 4. d4 c×d4 5. N×d4 Bg7 6. Be3 d6 7. Be2 Nf6 8. 0–0 0–0 9. Qd2 N×d4 10. B×d4 Ne8 11. Bc4 Be6 12. Nd5 Rc8 13. Bb3 B×d5 14. e×d5 B×d4 15. Q×d4 Rc5 16. Rfe1 Ng7 17. Re4 f5 18. Re2 a5 19. Rae1 Rf7 20. Qh4 b5 21. a4 b×a4 22. B×a4 Rc7 23. f4 Nh5 24. Bc6 Nf6 25. Qf2 Qb8 26. Qd4 Ne4 27. Ra1 Qa7 28. Q×a7 R×a7 29. b4 Rf8 30. R×a5 Rc7 31. b5 Rb8 32. c4 Kf7 33. Rb2 Rb6 34. Rba2 Nc5 35. R2a3 Kf6 36. Ra7 R×a7 37. R×a7 Rb8 38. Kf2 h5 39. h4 e5 40. g3 Ne4† 41. Kg2 Nd2 42. b6 N×c4 43. b7 Nb6 44. Ra6 Nc4 45. Ra8** Black resigns—*Daily News*, 21 July 1886.

**809) Bird–Pollock   1–0**

B.C.A. Congress (round 9)
London, 21 July 1886
*C45*

**1. e4 e5 2. Nf3 Nc6 3. d4 e×d4 4. N×d4 Bc5 5. Be3 Qf6 6. c3**

**Nge7 7. Be2 B×d4 8. c×d4 d5 9. Nc3 Be6 10. e5 Qg6 11. 0–0 h5** "He is obliged to provide against 12. Bh5 followed by 13. g4"—Freeborough. **12. Kh1 Rd8 13. Na4 Nf5 14. Nc5 Bc8 15. Rc1 h4 16. Bd3 h3 17. g3** The more assertive 17. g4 is very attractive. If 17. ... N×e3 18. f×e3 Q×g4 19. Q×g4 B×g4 20. Bb5! and White holds all the trumps for the ensuing endgame. **17. ... b6?!** "He finds the waiting game intolerable"—Freeborough. 17. ... 0–0 had to be played. **18. Nb3 Nb4** "The whole manoeuvre, commencing with 17. ... b6, was unsound, especially as the c-pawn remains unguarded. Black entangled himself still more afterwards in attempting to save that pawn"—*Standard*. **19. Bb1 Ba6** "His game is clearly worthless unless he can save it by counterattack"—Freeborough. **20. Qf3** "But Bird is too versed in wiles to be frightened. This move deprives Black of the resource 20. ... N×e3 upon which he has been relying for some moves, in default of a better"—Freeborough. **20. ... Nd3** "Very well if White would only take the knight, but he is not likely"—Freeborough. **21. Rfd1** It will soon turn out that White cannot make use of the pinned knight after all in the near future. Therefore 21. R×c7 was decidedly superior. **21. ... N×e3 22. f×e3** 22. Q×e3 Qe4† is a first point. **22. ... Rd7 23. Nd2** "If 23. Rc3 Qe4"—Freeborough. **23. ... f5?!** "He might play 23. ... Qh5, for if 24. B×d3 he is not compelled to exchange queens. He could hardly hope for anything better than to get out of the complication without loss, and with his c-pawn protected"—Freeborough. **24. Rc3 N×b2 25. B×f5 0–0 26. B×g6 R×f3 27. Rb1** "This resource wins a piece, more by good luck than good management it would seem"—Freeborough. **27. ... Rf2 28. R×b2 Be2 29. e6 Re7 30. Bf7† Kh7 31. Rc1 Bd3** "Black could win the exchange, but it would be of little avail: 31. ... Bf3† 32. N×f3 R×b2 33. Ne5, followed by 34. Nc6"—*Standard*. **32. Nc4 Rf3 33. Ne5 R×e3 34. N×d3 R×d3 35. Rf2 R×d4 36. Rf4 R×f4 37. g×f4 d4 38. Rg1 c5 39. f5 c4 40. Rg4 Kh6 41. R×d4 Rc7 42. Rd7 Rc5 43. e7 R×f5 44. Rd1** Black resigns—*Standard*, 22 July 1886; *British Chess Magazine* (Freeborough), August–September 1886, pp. 324–325.

**(810) Mortimer–Bird   0–1**

B.C.A. Congress (round 10)
London, 22 July 1886
*C61*

**1. e4 e5 2. Nf3 Nc6 3. Bb5 Nd4 4. N×d4 e×d4 5. 0–0 h5 6. d3 c6 7. Bc4 Bc5 8. f4** It couldn't harm him to wait with this push. 8. e5!? is interesting. **8. ... d5 9. e×d5 c×d5 10. Bb5† Kf8** "Part of Bird's plan. White is obliged to move his bishop again, and so let Black take the attack"—Freeborough. **11. Ba4 Ne7 12. Nd2** "He has to provide against 12. ... Nf5, 12. ... Bg4 and 12. ... h4. The choice of a move good enough to meet all these contingencies is certainly embarrassing, and merits sympathetic attention. The final decision rests between the move actually made, 12. Re1, and 12. Qe1"—Freeborough. **12. ... h4 13. Nf3** "Black has abandoned 12. ... Bg4 for the moment, but White has still a difficult choice between 13. Nf3, 13. Nb3, 13. Qf3 and 13. h3. It is not clear that he hits upon the best move this time; his scarcity of minor pieces on the kingside must be taken into account"—Freeborough. **13. ... h3 14. g3 Qa5** First 14. ... Bg4 is stronger. The queen can head for another square; e.g., c7, if desired. **15. Bb3 Bg4 16. Bd2 Qa6** This leaves her majesty a bit out of play. Centralization is therefore preferable—16. ... Qd8 17. Qe1 f6 18. Nh4 Qd7. **17. Qe1 B×f3 18. R×f3 Qc6 19. g4** "Black's vagaries with his queen have given White time for a free move, and 19. Bb4 suggests itself. The same thought is in Bird's mind, as is shown by his subtle offer of a pawn on the following move. White's play provides an opening for a fresh attack"—Freeborough. 19. Bb4 is not so convincing, as White will be left with the inferior minor piece after an exchange. The text move is much better, just as 19. f5! would have been. **19. ... a5** Trying to confuse his opponent, which works perfectly as Mortimer obstinately refrains to take the a-pawn, which he could have done now without any negative repercussion. Much better tries were 19. ... Qg6 or 19. ... b6. **20. a4 Ng6? 21. Qf1 Rh4 22. Rg3** A bit slow. At once 22. f5! R×g4† 23. Kh1 results in the fall of the h-pawn when Black's king ends up in terrible misery. **22. ... Re8 23. Re1?** Very peaceful play from Mortimer. He misses the same motive as above: 23. f5! Ne5 24. Bg5 R×g4 25. R×g4 N×g4 26. Q×h3. **23. ... Re3** Bird is pushing his luck to win the game. 23. ... R×e1 or 23. ... Bd6 are objectively better, but only good enough for drawing purposes. **24. B×e3** 24. f5! is once more the strongest idea. If 24. ... Ne7 25. B×e3 d×e3 26. Re2 with a clear superiority. 24. Re×e3? would be a blunder due to 24. ... d×e3 25. B×e3 B×e3† 26. R×e3 R×g4† wins. **24. ... d×e3 25. Qf3 d4** The strong passed pawn compensates for the material deficit. **26. Bd5 Q×a4** *(see diagram)* 26. ... Qc7 is safer.

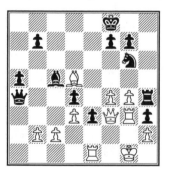

*After 26. ... Q×a4*

**27. Be4** "In possible reply to some solitary student I may say that 27. B×f7 has not been overlooked. Mr. Bird finishes the game with the skill of a grand old master; impelling an apparently free rook to immolate himself with the best intentions. Mr. Mortimer's motives are well worth examining, nevertheless it would be 'holding a farthing candle to the sun' to explain them in detail"—Freeborough. Bird is rewarded for his courageous play after this passive move. Interesting and complicated is 27. B×b7 Qb4 28. Rb1 Bd6. The seductive 27. B×f7? is refuted by the intermediate move 27. ... Qb4! The prophylactic 27. Rf1! is perhaps the strongest possibility. If 27. ... Q×c2? 28. Bc4! e2 29. Re1 and the e-pawn is a goner. Better is 27. ... Bb4 28. B×f7! e2! (White's attack is frightening after 28. ... K×f7 29. f5 Ne7 30. f6) 29. Q×e2 K×f7 30. f5 Nf8 31. g5 with complex play. **27. ... Q×c2 28. B×g6 f×g6** 28. ... Qd2! 29. Re2 Qc1† 30. Qf1 Q×f1† 31. K×f1 f×g6 reaches a better endgame. White will lose the f- or g-pawn soon after 32. ... Bd6. **29. Qe2?** A howler. 29. Rf1 leads to a quick draw after 29. ... Bb4 30. Q×b7 e2 and White's queen is obliged to check perpetually. **29. ... Q×e2 30. R×e2 Bd6 31. Rf3 R×g4† 32. Kf1 R×f4 33. R×f4† B×f4 34. Kg1 Ke7 35. Rc2 Kd6 36. Rc8 Ke6 37. Re8† Kf5 38. Re4 Kg4 39. R×d4 Kf3 40. Re4 e2 41. R×f4† K×f4 42. Kf2 e1Q†**

White resigns—*British Chess Magazine* (Freeborough), August–September 1886, pp. 335–336.

### (811) Bird–Taubenhaus    0–1
B.C.A. Congress (round 11)
London, 23 July 1886
*Game score missing*

### (812) Hanham–Bird    1–0
B.C.A. Congress (round 12)
London, 26 July 1886

*Black to move*

Bird now played **58. ... Be7?** and the game proceeded **59. Ne8 B×g5† 60. K×g5 Re7 61. Nd6** and the ending was reduced to rook and knight against rook, and should have been draw but Bird played wildly and lost—*British Chess Magazine*, August–September 1886, pp. 358–359.

The tragicomic finish of the game is to be found in the tournament book compiled by Tony Gillam.

*White to move*

**112. Kg4 Rf1 113. Nf3 Ra1 114. Kf5 Rf1 115. Rg3 Kh6** Moving the rook along the first rank is the simplest way to draw. **116. Kf6 Kh5** 116. ... Kh7 117. Kf7 Rh1 118. Rg2 Kh8 119. Rg8† Kh7 120. Ng5† is the other way. **117. Kg7!** Black resigns.

Bird had a bye in the final round.

## MATCH WITH LEE 1886

Immediately after the B.C.A. tournament Bird played a short match against Frank James Lee, 29 years old at the time, a new face in the London chess scene. It is no surprise that a confident Bird insisted on giving the young man his usual treatment by offering him the odds of pawn and two moves. According to the *Manchester Evening News* of 11 August 1888, Bird received a serious hammering for he lost 5 games and scarcely managed 2 draws. The *Pictorial World* gave a better result for Bird on 16 October 1890, stating that Lee won 5 games, lost 2 and 3 ended in a draw.[8]

# C.C.A. CONGRESS, NOTTINGHAM 1886

The congress of the C.C.A. started a few days later in Nottingham. With the presence of such a variety of strong players in London the committee refrained from their original intention to return to the old formula of a provincial chess tournament. Instead an international event was announced.[9] Skipworth was able to guarantee four prizes, the first one £40. Several masters continued their way to Nottingham, some even by foot, only to find out that a whole range of amateurs had entered the same tournament. This was not to the liking of players like Mason and Mackenzie and they retracted their participation. Ultimately a field of 12 players remained but then Blackburne forfeited at the last moment while on top of that the start of the tournament had to be postponed because of the late arrival of the chess clocks. Skipworth himself further complicated matters by forfeiting after having finished one game and adjourned another (against Pollock).

Bird had recovered from his gout attack and entered into the fray. After an initial bye, due to Blackburne's late forfeit, he started hesitatingly with two draws and a loss. But then he fought back and beat Taubenhaus, Pollock and Zukertort. Thorold escaped with a draw. In the penultimate round Bird lost the crucial encounter against Schallopp. Even though he beat James Alexander Porterfield Rynd in the final round he could only secure fifth place. Bird was rewarded with his part of the entrance fees and he earned £4 7s.

It was obvious to all that the course and management of the tournament was far from flawless and Hoffer took the opportunity to launch his arrows upon the C.C.A. He claimed that instead of allowing amateurs to the master tournament, it would have been better to organize a separate Class I tournament for them, as the year before. He also raised his hand against Skipworth by questioning his position as the representative of the C.C.A. by hinting at financial mismanagement, or worse.[10]

Bird was bye in the first round.

**(813) Hanham–Bird   ½–½**
C.C.A. Congress (round 2)
Nottingham, 3 August 1886
*Game score missing*

**(814) Bird–Burn   ½–½**
C.C.A. Congress (round 3)
Nottingham, 4 August 1886

The final of this game was reconstructed by Richard Forster in his book on Burn (p. 231).

*White to move*

**47. R×f4** Bird miscalculates that after the forced line 47. e5! h3 48. e×d6 h2 49. d7 h1Q 50. d8Q, Black has no perpetual. **47. ... h3 48. Rf8 Kh4 49. Rh8† Nh5 50. Rb8 h2 51. Rb1 Ng3 52. Ke3?** An expensive miscalculation. The correct move was still 52. e5!— e.g., 52. ... Ne2† 53. Kc4 Ng1 54. e×d6 N×f3 55. Kc5 (of course not 55. d7? Ne5†) 55. ... Ne5 56. Kb6 and wins. **52. ... h1Q 53. R×h1† N×h1 54. e5** 54. f4 isn't enough for the win either: 54. ... Ng3 55. Kf3 Nh5 56. e5 d×e5 57. f×e5 Kg5 58. Ke4 Ng7. **54. ... Ng3 55. Kf4 Ne2† 56. Ke3 Ng3 57. Kf4 Ne2† 58. Kf5**

---

## 16th Congress of the C.C.A., Nottingham, 3–9 August 1886

*Site:* Mechanics' Lecture-hall
*Prizes:* 1st £40, 2nd £20, 3rd £10, 4th £5 entrance fees divided among non-prize winners
*Time limit:* 20 moves per hour

|    |                     | 1 | 2 | 3 | 4 | 5 | 6 | 7 | 8 | 9 | 10 | 11 |      |
|----|---------------------|---|---|---|---|---|---|---|---|---|----|----|------|
| 1  | A. Burn             |   | 1 | 1 | ½ | ½ | 1 | 1 | 1 | 1 | 1  |    | 8    |
| 2  | E. Schallopp        | 0 |   | 1 | 1 | 1 | 1 | 0 | 1 | 1 | 1  | 1  | 7    |
| 3  | I. Gunsberg         | 0 | 0 |   | ½ | 1 | 1 | 1 | 1 | 1 | ½  |    | 6    |
| 4  | J.H. Zukertort      | ½ | 0 | ½ |   | 0 | 1 | 1 | 1 | 1 | 1  |    | 6    |
| 5  | H.E. Bird           | ½ | 0 | 0 | 1 |   | 1 | 1 | ½ | ½ | 1  |    | 5½   |
| 6  | J. Taubenhaus       | 0 | 0 | 0 | 0 | 0 |   | 1 | 1 | 1 | 1  |    | 4    |
| 7  | W.H.K. Pollock      | 0 | 1 | 0 | 0 | 0 | 0 |   | 0 | 1 | 1  |    | 3    |
| 8  | J.M. Hanham         | 0 | 0 | 0 | 0 | ½ | 0 | 1 |   | 0 | ½  |    | 2    |
| 9  | E. Thorold          | 0 | 0 | 0 | 0 | ½ | 0 | 0 | 1 |   | ½  |    | 2    |
| 10 | J.A.P. Rynd         | 0 | 0 | ½ | 0 | 0 | 0 | 0 | ½ | ½ |    |    | 1½   |
| 11 | A.B. Skipworth      | 0 |   |   |   |   |   |   |   |   |    |    |      |

---

8. An anecdote from this match survives: "Two or three years ago Lee, the young London master, decisively upset Bird, who gave him pawn and 2 moves in a match. A few months later on the veteran, in public, referred of this match saying, 'By the way, when is our return match at pawn and 2 moves coming off?' This was too much for Lee, who has since played in a master tournament. 'Who of us,' said he, 'is to concede the odds? As I came out a game ahead of you in the tournament, I suppose I am to give you pawn and 2 moves!'" *Baltimore Sunday News*, 5 January 1890. First published in the *Hereford Times*.

9. *British Chess Magazine*, September 1886, p. 360. Skipworth confirmed that the master tournament was set up in a hurry, which makes it strange that MacDonnell had already announced at the end of the previous year that another master event with a prize fund of at least £100 would be organized by the C.C.A. (*Illustrated Sporting and Dramatic News*, 26 December 1885).

10. It is worth quoting Hoffer's attack in full: "There is not the slightest doubt that, without the masters' tournament, the Counties meeting would have been an utter failure. A great falling off in the attendance as compared with former meetings was noticeable, and the reason is not far to seek. An entire recasting of the constitution of the C.C.A. is necessary. The 'unwritten' laws of the Association must be put in tangible shape, and the one-man system of government, so highly distasteful to English notions, must cease. The Rev. A.B. Skipworth is a very able hon. secretary, he is unceasing in his propaganda for the C.C.A. during the interval between one meeting and the other, but the return he provides or the money subscribed in the provinces is not adequate to the outlay." *Chess Monthly*, June 1886, p. 289.

Nd4† **59. Ke4 d×e5 60. d6?!** Careless. Instead both 60. K×e5 and 60. f4 force a draw without delay. **60. ... Kg3?** 60. ... Nc6 puts White to a true test. After 61. d7 Kg3 62. Kd5 Nd8 63. K×e5 K×f3 64. Kf6 Ke4 65. Ke7 Nb7 66. d8Q N×d8 67. K×d8 he luckily just draws. **61. d7?** Time trouble or nerves are killing the instincts of both players. 61. Kd5! shuts the opposite knight out. **61. ... Nc6 62. Kd5 Nd8 63. K×e5 K×f3** and the game was ultimately drawn—*The Times*, 6 August 1886; *International Chess Magazine*, October 1886, p. 298.

### (815) Gunsberg–Bird    1–0
C.C.A. Congress (round 4)
Nottingham, 5 August 1886
*C13*

**1. e4 e6 2. d4 d5 3. Nc3 Nf6 4. Bg5 d×e4 5. N×e4 c6** "This irregular defense is very characteristic of the player who so often turns irregularities to brilliant account. Mr. Bird leaves a pawn to be doubled that he may have an open g-file for an attack"—Skipworth. **6. Nf3 Nbd7 7. Bd3 Qb6 8. 0–0 N×e4 9. B×e4 Nf6** Bird could safely capture the b-pawn at this point. After Gunsberg's next move, he lacks active counterplay and White gains the upper hand. **10. B×f6** "Having counted the cost and prepared himself for attack, White now obliges his opponent and opens the desired file"—Skipworth. **10. ... g×f6 11. Re1 Bd7 12. c4 Be7 13. c5! Qc7** "It would not all along have paid to have taken the b-pawn. Black therefore quietly retires, hoping that there are better things in store for him"—Skipworth. **14. b4 f5 15. Bd3 Qf4 16. g3 Rg8 17. Bf1 h5?!** A desperate attack in a very difficult position. **18. Bg2** It would have been very frustrating to deal with 18. Ne5! After 18. ... h4 19. Qh5 0–0–0 20. Bg2 Qg5 21. Q×g5 Black's initiative belongs to the past, leaving White with a winning endgame. **18. ... Qg4 19. Qd3** Better was 19. Qb3. **19. ... Bf6 20. Rab1?!** 20. Ne5 is still the best move. Bird now gains counterplay against White's kingside. **20. ... h4 21. Rb3 h×g3 22. h×g3** *(see diagram)*

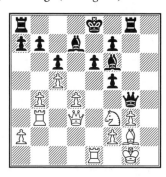

*After 22. h×g3*

**22. ... Rd8** The king would be perfectly safe after 22. ... 0–0–0, and the rook might quickly join in the attack if necessary. Yet, Bird has found another, quite elaborate, idea that works out fine as well. **23. Qc4 Kf8 24. Rd3 Be8 25. a4 Qh5 26. Qc1 Rg4 27. Qd2 Qh8** The point. White is tied down to the weak spot in his position, the pawn at d4. **28. Ne5 Rg8** 28. ... B×e5 (Skipworth) crowns Bird's past moves. His position is comfortable after both 29. R×e5 a6 30. Bf3 Rg7 and 29. d×e5 R×d3 30. Q×d3 R×b4 31. a5 a6 32. Qc3 Ra4. **29. f4 Qg7 30. Kf2 B×e5 31. R×e5 Bd7?!** After a long battle, Bird makes an inaccuracy of which Gunsberg takes immediate

profit. Instead of the text move he should have played 31. ... a6 32. b5 a×b5 33. a×b5 Ra8 with a drawish endgame. **32. b5 Qh6?** Bird hasn't the foggiest idea about what to do next against White's upcoming infiltration on the queenside. Right was 32. ... Be8, making 33. Qa5? a blunder because of 33. ... R×d4 and Black wins. Far better is 33. d5! first, though after 33. ... e×d5 34. Qa5 Qf6 35. Q×a7 c×b5 36. Q×b7 Bc6 37. Qa6 b×a4 38. B×d5, the position is still full of tension. **33. Qa5 Kg7 34. Re1 Qf6 35. Q×a7 c×b5 36. B×b7** 36. Q×b7! is the most accurate move. **36. ... b×a4 37. c6 Bc8 38. Q×a4** 38. c7! wins quickly. **38. ... Rh8 39. Rg1 B×b7 40. c×b7 Qe7 41. Qb5 Rb8?!** 41. ... Qc7 offers much more resistance. **42. Rb1 Kg6 43. Qc6 Rhd8 44. Ke3 Rd6 45. Qf3 Rd5 46. Rh1** and Black resigns—*Tournament Book* (Skipworth), p. 83.

### (816) Taubenhaus–Bird    0–1
C.C.A. Congress (round 5)
Nottingham, 5 August 1886
*Game score missing*

### (817) Bird–Pollock    1–0
C.C.A. Congress (round 6)
Nottingham, 6 August 1886
*C62*

**1. e4 e5 2. Nf3 Nc6 3. Bb5 d6 4. 0–0** "A somewhat risky departure from the beaten track. 4. d4 is no doubt stronger"—Marriott. **4. ... Bg4 5. h3 Bh5 6. d4** "Bird seems to have played for the opportunity of sacrificing this pawn. The combination is probably unsound, but it relieves the monotony of the Lopez Opening"—Marriott. **6. ... B×f3** "If 6. ... e×d4 White has the advantage by 7. g4 Bg6 8. N×d4"—Marriott. **7. Q×f3 e×d4 8. e5** A bit rash. White enjoys a normal opening advantage after 8. Rd1 Nge7 9. R×d4. **8. ... Qd7 9. e×d6 B×d6 10. Nd2?!** White has very little to show for his sacrificed pawn now. A better try was 10. Bc4 forcing Black to abandon his f-pawn, though the position remains very much OK after 10. ... 0–0–0 11. Q×f7 Q×f7 12. B×f7 Nf6. **10. ... 0–0–0** 10. ... Nge7! (Marriott) gives him an excellent position with a pawn more. **11. Nc4 f6?** "Not fully realizing the danger. 11. ... a6 would still save him"—Marriott. **12. Na5 Nge7** *(see diagram)*

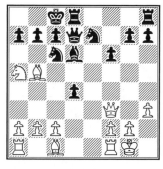

*After 12. ... Nge7*

**13. Qb3!** "After this ingenious coup Black has a lost game"—Marriott. **13. ... g5?** "If 13. ... a6 14. B×c6 and Black must give up his queen to avoid mate. If 13. ... b6 14. Qa4 and the knight can only be taken under penalty of mate in three. Seeing no way of saving the queen Black commences a desperate counterattack with his pawns on the kingside. He overlooks the force of 13. ... Qf5, which would at least prolong the game, and perhaps enable him to pull through his difficulties. If 14. B×c6 b×c6 and 15. Qb7† would lose its sting. After 13. ... Qf5 White must do something to prevent 14. ... N×a5; the best course appears to be 14. N×b7, followed (if the rook moves) by 15. Ba6 Kd7; and though Black is hardly in smooth water he is not threatened with anything disastrous"—Marriott. The position is extremely difficult for Pollock, and it is no surprise that he didn't find the only way to prolong the game. Marriott's ultimate suggestion (13. ... Qf5) is equally disastrous, as he demonstrates clearly. The sole try seems 13. ... Qe8 14. B×c6 b×c6 15. Qc4 Qh5 when an escape route for the Black king has been made. Alas for him, White stays well on top after 16. Qa6† Kd7 17. Nb7 Rb8 18. N×d6 K×d6 19. Bf4†. **14. B×c6 Q×c6 15. N×c6 N×c6 16. Bd2 Qh5 17. Qe6† Kb8 18. Q×f6 g4 19. h4 Be7 20. Qe6 B×h4 21. Rae1 Rdg8 22. b4 a6 23. a4 Rg7 24. b5 Nd8 25. Qe5 Rhh7 26. b6 Ka8 27. Bf4** Black resigns—*Nottinghamshire Guardian* (Marriott), 1 October 1886.

## (818) Bird–Thorold    ½–½
C.C.A. Congress (round 7)
Nottingham, 7 August 1886
*Game score missing*

## (819) Bird–Zukertort    1–0
C.C.A. Congress (round 8)
Nottingham, 7 August 1886
*A02*

**1. f4 e5 2. f×e5 d6 3. e×d6 B×d6 4. Nf3 Nf6 5. d4 Ng4 6. Bg5** 6. Qd3 is the best move. **6. ... f6 7. Bh4 g5 8. Bf2 N×f2 9. K×f2 g4 10. Nh4 f5 11. g3 f4 12. e4?** "The first eleven moves are identical with those played in a game in the B.C.A. tournament between Messrs. Bird and Blackburne"—Zukertort. Much better was 12. Qd3, as played against Blackburne. **12. ... Nc6 13. Bb5** "If 13. e5, Black would obviously reply 13. ... B×e5. White loses now a pawn which he could protect only with 13. c3. It is questionable, however, whether he could afford to adopt this slow development"—Zukertort. 13. c3 is not much better: 13. ... Rf8 14. Nf5 B×f5 15. e×f5 R×f5 with a decisive attack. **13. ... f×g3†?** "It would be better to postpone that capture and to proceed first with 13. ... 0–0"—Zukertort. If then 14. Kg2, Be7 is extremely strong. The text move looks equally dangerous but Black's attack can be met adequately. **14. h×g3 0–0† 15. Kg2 Qf6 16. Rf1 Q×d4 17. R×f8† B×f8 18. Nc3 Bc5 19. Qe2** Zukertort has problems coping with his opponent's advance in development. **19. ... Be6** A logical move, but there is a strong reply. 19. ... Bd6 is better. **20. Rd1** Two subsequent exchanges, 20. B×c6! b×c6 21. Nf5 B×f5 22. e×f5 spell trouble for Black; e.g., after 22. ... Kh8 23. Rd1. **20. ... Qe5 21. Bc4 Kh8 22. B×e6 Q×e6 23. Rd5** More intimidating than dangerous. 23. Nf5 is logical as it reactivates a crucial piece. **23. ... Bb6** 23. ... Bd4 24. Nf5 B×c3 25. b×c3 Rg8 with a solid defense is also interesting. **24. Nf5 Ne5 25. Qd2** "Threatening to continue with 26. Rd8†"—Zukertort. **25. ... c6 26. Rd6 Qf7 27. Qh6** (*see diagram*)

**27. ... Ng6** "The position requires delicate handling: if 27. ... Rf8, White would proceed with 28. Re6 (threatening 29. Re7), and if 28. ... Ng6, then, of course, 29. R×g6"—Zukertort. Both 28. Na4

**Johannes Hermann Zukertort (*Daily Graphic*).**

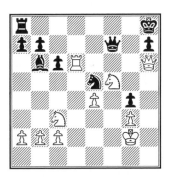

*After 27. Qh6*

and 28. Ne2 are better attempts in case of 27. ... Rf8 for 28. Re6 is poignantly met by 28. ... Be3! **28. Qg5** "Threatening 29. Rd7, and if 29. ... Q×d7, White mates in two moves"—Zukertort. **28. ... Rf8!** A keen pawn sacrifice by Zukertort. Bird is happy to accept, but would have done better had he calmly played 29. Rd1 Bc7 30. b3 Ne5 31. Na4, retaining some pressure. **29. Q×g4 Bc7 30. Rd1 Nf4† 31. Kh2 Nh5 32. Ne2** 32. Rd3 is the superior way to defend the pawn. Black hasn't a dangerous attack, but White is in no position to claim his extra pawn. A draw would be very likely. The text move allows Zukertort to win his pawn back. **32. ... Nf6 33. Qf3** Far more active is 33. Qh4. If then 33. ... Q×a2 34. Nf4 Qf7! 35. Nd6 B×d6 36. R×d6 N×e4 37. Re6 Re8 and White can hope for a successful defense. **33. ... Q×a2 34. Qc3** 34. Nfd4 is solid. For instance, 34. ... c5 (34. ... Q×b2? 35. Ne6) 35. Nc3 Qc4 36. b3 Qf7 37. Nf5 offers nearly equal play. After the text move the e-pawn comes under immediate fire. **34. ... Qe6 35. Nf4 B×f4** "A grave error, which leads to the following blunder and the loss of the game, which was probably won for Black after 35. ... Q×e4 36. Nd6 Qe7 37. Nf5 Qe5 etc."—Zukertort. White still has fair drawing chances if he'd continue with 38. Q×e5 B×e5 39. Ne6 Re8 40. Nd8 Bc7 41. N×b7 Rb8 42. Nbd6. **36. g×f4 Q×e4?** A stupendous blunder! Correct was 36. ... h5 37. Re1 Kh7, bringing the king out of reach of the queen. Neither side can make further progress without allowing his opponent a decisive advantage. **37. Q×f6†** Black resigns—*Chess Monthly* (Zukertort), July 1886, pp. 334–336.

### (820) Bird–Schallopp    0–1
C.C.A. Congress (round 9)
Nottingham, 9 August 1886
*A03*

**1. f4 d5 2. e3 c5 3. Nf3 Nf6 4. b3 e6 5. Bb2 Bd6 6. Nc3 a6 7. Ne2 Nc6 8. Neg1 0–0 9. Ne5 d4 10. Ngf3 Qa5 11. Nc4 Qc7 12. Be2 Rd8 13. N×d6 R×d6 14. e×d4 c×d4 15. 0–0 b5 16. a4 b4 17. Bd3 Rd5 18. Ng5 h6 19. Ne4 Nd7 20. Qe2 Rf5 21. g3 Bb7 22. Nf2 Ras 23. Be4 f5 24. Bg2 e5 25. Qc4† Kh8 26. f×e5 Rc5 27. Qe6 R×e5 28. Qc4 Rc5 29. Qe2 R×c2 30. Nd3 Na5 31. B×d4 Qd6 32. Be3 B×g2 33. Q×g2 Re8 34. Ne1 Rb2 35. R×f5 N×b3 36. Rd5 Qc6 37. Nd3 N×a1 38. N×b2 Nc2 39. Nd1 Ne1 40. Qh1 Rf8 41. Qe4 Nf6 42. Q×b4 Re8 43. d4 Nf3† 44. Kh1 N×d5** White resigns—*Deutsche Schachzeitung*, December 1886, p. 355.

### (821) Bird–Rynd    1–0
C.C.A. Congress (round 10)
Nottingham, 9 August 1886
*C31*

**1. e4 e5 2. f4 d5 3. e×d5 e4 4. c4 c6 5. Qc2 Bf5 6. Ne2 c×d5 7. c×d5** 7. Ng3! is a strong intermediate move. Black is forced to make a concession if he doesn't want to lose a pawn. **7. ... Q×d5 8. Nbc3 Qc5** 8. ... Qd7 is much safer. **9. b4!** Powerful play from Bird. 9. Ng3 was also very good for him. **9. ... Qc8 10. Ng3 B×b4?** The pawn remains poisoned. **11. Qa4† Nc6 12. Nd5?** Rynd gets another chance from the veteran. After 12. N×f5 Q×f5 13. Bb5, he can resign. **12. ... Bd6 13. Bb2 f6 14. Rc1 e3?** Houdini-like capacities are needed to balance out the game with 14. ... Nge7 15. Bb5 N×d5 16. B×c6† b×c6 17. R×c6 Qd7 18. N×f5 Bb4. In fact, after 19. Re6† Kd8 20. Q×d7† and a draw would become likely. A possible improvement, however, is 15. Ba6. **15. d×e3 Qd7** A blunder, but 15. ... Nge7 16. Bc4 also looks very bad. **16. Nb6 Bb4† 17. Bc3** Black resigns—*Tournament Book*, p. 62.

---

# GIVING EXHIBITIONS 1886-1887

Bird did not undertake a major tour through the provinces during the 1886-87 season. He limited himself to some successful exhibitions in London and near environment. Following concrete invitations Bird also visited particular chess clubs throughout the country. A first contract brought Bird to the north once again. On 18 October he was a guest at the Wigan Chess Club. With 16 wins, 1 loss and 1 draw he delivered a neat performance. Three days later Bird paid a flying visit to Leeds to face 18 opponents. One of them, Toothill, managed to win. Three games ended in a draw.

### (822) Bird–Toothill    0–1
Simultaneous game
Leeds, 21 October 1886
*C00*

**1. e4 e6 2. Bb5 c6 3. Ba4 d5 4. e×d5 e×d5 5. Nf3 Qe7† 6. Kf1 Bd7 7. d3 h6 8. Nc3 Nf6 9. Bb3 Be6 10. h3 Qc7 11. Ne2 Bd6 12. g3 Nbd7 13. a4 b6 14. Nf4 0–0–0 15. a5 Kb7 16. c3 g5 17. N×e6 f×e6 18. Nd4 Rde8 19. Ba4 b5 20. a6† Kb8 21. Bc2 Rhf8 22. Kg2 Nb6 23. Re1 Qd7 24. c4 e5 25. Nb3 Qf7 26. f3 b×c4 27. d×c4 e4 28. c×d5 e×f3† 29. Kf2 R×e1 30. Q×e1 Nh5 31. Qe6 B×g3† 32. Kf1 Re8** Black wins—*Leeds Mercury*, 30 October 1886.

### (823) Bird–R. Taylor    ½–½
Simultaneous game
Leeds, 21 October 1886

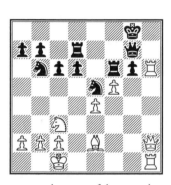

*Black to move*

The position here given represents the state of the game between Mr. Bird and Mr. Richard Taylor in the simultaneous encounter on Thursday the 21st. inst., at the rooms of the Leeds Club. **25. ... Nf7 26. Rh7 Qf8 27. f×g6 R×g6 28. R×f7 K×f7 29. Bh5 Qh6† 30. Kd1 Kg7 31. B×g6 Q×h2 32. R×h2 K×g6 33. b3 Rh7 34. R×h7 K×h7 35. Ke2 Kg6 36. Kf3 d5 37. e×d5 N×d5 38. N×d5 c×d5 39. Ke3 Kf6 40. Kd4 Ke6 41. Kc5 Ke5 42. a4 Ke6 43. a5 Ke5 44. b4 Ke6 45. b5 Ke5 46. a6 b×a6 47. b×a6 d4 48. Kc6 Ke6 49. Kc7 Ke7 50. Kb7 Kd7 51. K×a7 Kc7 52. Ka8 Kc8** draw—*Leeds Mercury*, 30 October 1886.

Tougher opposition awaited Bird at the British Chess Club. On 27 November he took up the gauntlet against 19 players. He won 17 games (two players were beaten twice), but suffered 4 defeats, against Mills, Lowe, Gwinner and Crawford. The session lasted only three hours. It was calculated that Bird had spent an average of nine minutes on each game.

### (824) Bird–Shepheard    1–0
Simultaneous game
London (British C.C.), 27 November 1886
*C51*

**1. e4 e5 2. Nf3 Nc6 3. Bc4 Bc5 4. b4 B×b4 5. c3 Bc5 6. d4 e×d4 7. c×d4 Bb6 8. Bb2 d6 9. d5 Ne5 10. N×e5 d×e5 11. Nd2 Qd6 12. 0–0 Ne7 13. Bb3 Ng6 14. Nc4 Qf6 15. Ba4† Kf8 16. Kh1 h5 17. f4 Bg4 18. f×e5 B×d1 19. e×f6 B×a4 20. f×g7† Kg8 21. g×h8Q† N×h8 22. N×b6 a×b6 23. B×h8 K×h8 24. R×f7** Black resigns—*Morning Post*, 29 November 1886.

**825) Bird–Mills   0–1**

imultaneous game
ondon (British C.C.), 27 November 1887
C55

1. e4 e5 2. Nf3 Nc6 3. Bc4 Nf6 4. Nc3 N×e4 5. B×f7† K×f7
. N×e4 d5 7. Neg5† Kg8 8. d3 h6 9. Nh3 Bg4 10. c3 Bc5 11. Be3
4 12. Bc1 Qd7 13. Nhg1 Kh7 14. h3 Be6 15. Ne2 Rhf8 16. b4
d6 17. b5 Ne7 18. c4 a6 19. b×a6 R×a6 20. Ng3 Ng6 21. Ne4
e7 22. h4 Bf5 23. h5 B×e4 24. d×e4 Nf4 25. N×e5 Bb4†
6. Kf1 Qe8 27. B×f4 R×f4 28. Ng6 R×e4 29. g3 Re1† 30. Q×e1
×e1 31. R×e1 Qc6 32. Rh4 Q×c4† 33. Kg1 Q×a2 34. Re8
×g6 35. h×g6† K×g6 36. Rf4 c5 "Black queened in a few moves
nd White resigns"—*Morning Post*, 31 January 1887.

In *The Times* of 29 November 1886 Bird announced two other
xhibitions where he and Zukertort would play against 12 strong
mateurs, but these plans appear to have fallen through. On 27 Jan-
ary Bird visited the club of Putney to meet the local members.
ird won 13 games and drew 2.[11]

Two months later Bird popped up in Nottingham for two ex-
ibitions. The first one was held on 29 March in the rooms of
he Nottingham Chess Club. Bird won 18 games, lost against
Derbyshire and drew with Dr. Hatherly.[12] On the next evening Bird
vas the guest at the Mechanics Institute. Against 19 players he won
6 games, lost against Gerrard and drew 2, with Sander and Gille-
pie.

**826) Bird–Marshall   1–0**

imultaneous game
Nottingham (C.C.), 29 March 1887

White to move

1. e×f6 Q×e4 2. f×g7† Ke7 3. Bf6 mate—*Nottinghamshire
Guardian*, 8 April 1887.

**(827) Derbyshire–Bird   1–0**

Simultaneous game
Nottingham (C.C.), 29 March 1887
C51

1. e4 e5 2. Nf3 Nc6 3. Bc4 Bc5 4. b4 B×b4 5. c3 Bc5 6. 0–0 d6
7. d4 e×d4 8. c×d4 Bb6 9. Nc3 Na5 10. Bd3 Ne7 11. Bb2 Bg4
12. Ne2 Ng6 13. d5 B×f3 14. g×f3 Nh4 15. Ng3 Qg5 16. e5 Qf4
17. Be4 d×e5 18. Re1 0–0–0 19. B×e5 Q×e5 20. Bf5† Q×f5
21. N×f5 N×f5 22. Rc1 Nd6 23. Re7 Rhe8 24. Qe1 R×e7 25. Q×e7
Re8 26. Q×d6 Re1† 27. Kg2 R×c1 28. Qf8† Kd7 29. Q×f7† Kd8
30. Qg8† Kd7 31. Q×g7† Ke8 32. Qg8† Kd7 33. Qe6† Kd8
34. Qg8† Kd7 35. Qe6† Kd8 36. h4 Rc2 37. Qf6† Kc8 38. Qf5†
Black resigns—*Nottinghamshire Guardian*, 22 April 1887.

**(828) Bird–Hatherly   ½–½**

Simultaneous game
Nottingham (C.C.), 29 March 1887
C58

1. e4 e5 2. Nf3 Nc6 3. Bc4 Nf6 4. Ng5 d5 5. e×d5 Na5 6. d3
N×c4 7. d×c4 Bd6 8. h3 Bf5 9. Nc3 a6 10. Nf3 h6 11. 0–0 Qe7
12. Re1 0–0–0 13. Be3 g5 14. Nh2 Rde8 15. a3 e4 16. Bd4 B×h2†
17. K×h2 Rhg8 18. c5 g4 19. d6 c×d6 20. B×f6 Q×f6 21. Q×d6
Q×d6† 22. c×d6 Kd7 23. Nd5 Rg6 24. Ne3 Be6 25. Rad1 g×h3
26. g×h3 Rg5 27. Rg1 Reg8 28. R×g5 R×g5 29. h4 Rh5 30. Kg3
draw—*Nottinghamshire Guardian*, May 6, 1887.

**(829) Bird–Rowe   1–0**

Simultaneous game
Nottingham (Mechanics Institution), 30 March 1887
C33

1. e4 e5 2. f4 e×f4 3. Bc4 d5 4. B×d5 Nf6 5. Nc3 c6 6. Bc4 Bg4
7. Nf3 Bc5 8. e5 Nd5 9. d4 N×c3 10. b×c3 Bb6 11. B×f4 Nd7
12. 0–0 0–0 13. h3 B×f3 14. Q×f3 Kh8 15. Qh5 f5 16. Bd3 g6
17. Qh6 Qe8 18. Rae1 Qe6 19. Kh2 Ba5 20. c4 B×e1 21. R×e1
Rae8 22. h4 Rf7 23. c5 Nf6 24. e×f6 Q×e1 25. Bc4 R×f6 26. Qg5
Ree6 27. Be5 R×e5 28. Q×f6 mate—*Nottinghamshire Guardian*,
8 April 1887.

**(830) Bird–Gerrard   0–1**

Simultaneous game
Nottingham (Mechanics Institution), 30 March 1887
C30

1. e4 e5 2. f4 Bc5 3. Nf3 d6 4. c3 Bg4 5. d4 B×f3 6. g×f3 Qh4†

11. MacDonnell witnessed the display and painted a lively picture of the evening: "On Thursday, the 27th January, I visited the club, and found a goodly company
ssembled to do battle with the veteran Mr. H.E. Bird. Precisely at 7.45 the champion opened an attack on each of the 15 boards. In half an hour he had winning games
n three or four instances, and in less than an hour and a half he had victory within his grasp at every board. By the end of the second hour, however, Mr. Bird began to
lay a little too wildly, and Mr. E. Rabbeth, Mr. Ingoldsby, and Mr. Challis had each of them wrested the attack from Mr. Bird's hands, and were rushing on to victory.
But the two former missed the right road, and stumbled into defeat. Ultimately Mr. Bird prevailed over 13 of his foemen, and divided honors with two, Mr. Challis and
Mr. Osprey. ... Mr. Bird's usual pace in walking is about half a mile an hour, but on this occasion he rolled or wheeled round the room quite at the rate of five miles an
our. 'By Jove,' said a terrified youngster, 'he has only left me this moment, and here he is again. I don't believe he has since then been round to all the others.' 'Oh yes, I
have,' said the champion, and the crowd cheered him." *Illustrated Sporting and Dramatic News*, 5 February 1887.
12. "The Nottingham Chess Club was the scene of unusual animation on Tuesday evening, in consequence of a flying visit from Mr. H.E. Bird. The genial chess
master arrived at Bingham's restaurant late in the afternoon, and soon after four o'clock commenced to play simultaneously against several members of the club who
vere present to receive him. Mr. Bird said he was prepared to play at 25 or 30 boards at once, but unfortunately the clubroom is only large enough for about 14. As the
evening wore on all the available space was taken up, until the performer was engaged in a peripatetic battle against 14 opponents simultaneously. Though suffering from
n attack of his old enemy, the gout, Mr. Bird moved from board to board with astonishing rapidity, leaving consternation and disaster behind him in nearly every case.
An exceedingly pleasant contest ended in the single player winning 18 games, losing 1 (to Mr. Derbyshire), and drawing 1 (with Dr. Hatherly)." *Nottinghamshire Guardian*,
April 1887.

7. Ke2 Bb6 8. Be3 Nf6 9. f5 Nc6 10. Na3 N×e4 11. f×e4 Q×e4
12. Bh3 e×d4 13. c×d4 N×d4† 14. Kd2 Nf3† 15. Q×f3 Q×f3
16. B×b6 Q×h3 17. Rae1† Kd7 18. Be3 Rae8 19. Nc2 Re5
20. Re2 Q×f5 21. Rf2 Qe6 22. Rhf1 f6 Black wins—*Notting-hamshire Guardian*, 13 May 1887.

# A QUIET SEASON

In a book dealing with a modification of the chessboard, the author Frank Vigor Morley presents a game played between his father Frank Morley and Bird.

### (831) F. Morley–Bird　　1–0
Offhand game
London, 17 September 1886
C45

1. e4 e5 2. Nf3 Nc6 3. d4 e×d4 4. N×d4 Bc5 5. Be3 Qh4 6. Nc3
B×d4 7. B×d4 N×d4 8. Q×d4 Nf6 9. g3 Qg4 10. Be2 Qe6 11. e5
Ng8 12. 0-0-0 a6 13. Bg4 Qc6 14. e6 Nf6 15. e×d7† B×d7
16. B×d7† N×d7 17. Rhe1† Kd8 18. Q×g7 Re8 19. R×e8† K×e8
20. Re1† Kd8 21. Qg8† and White wins—*My One Contribution to Chess*, p. 30.

At the end of the year Bird tested a new defense against the Steinitz Gambit. Guest, Edwyn Anthony and Burn (probably in 1887) took up the gauntlet against him. Three of Bird's games were included in *Modern Chess*.

### (832) Guest–Bird　　0–1
Offhand game
London 1886
C25

1. e4 e5 2. Nc3 Nc6 3. f4 e×f4 4. d4 Qh4† 5. Ke2 g5 6. Nf3
Qh5 7. Nd5 Bg7? "This line of defense is, we believe, quite original"—Bird. Original and bad, for Black doesn't has enough compensation after 8. N×c7† Kd8 9. N×a8 g4 10. Ne5 N×e5 11. B×f4!
Instead 7. ... Kd8! is excellent. 8. c3? Nf6 Bird insists on the sacrifice of his rook. By now it is worth a try. 9. N×c7† Kd8 10. N×a8 N×e4
11. Qa4 11. Qc2! is a better version of the text move. The queen covers the important square f2. 11. ... Re8! *(see diagram)* "The force of this move had not been foreseen by Mr. Guest, who was taken by surprise in the opening"—Bird.

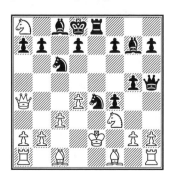

After 11. ... Re8

12. Kd3? 12. Kd1 is the only move. After 12. ... g4 (12. ... Nf2
13. Kc2 N×h1 14. d5 is more promising for White) 13. Ne5 Nf2
14. Kc2 B×e5 15. d×e5 Qf5† 16. Kb3 N×h1 17. B×f4 the position is extremely muddy. 12. ... Qg6! "A strong and well-judged move of what the late Mr. Boden would call a very high order"—Bird.
13. Kc4 b5† 14. K×b5 Nd6† 15. Kc5 Qe6 16. d5 Nb7† 17. Kc[...]
Qe4† and Black wins—*Modern Chess* (Bird), p. 190.

### (833) E. Anthony–Bird　　0–1
Offhand game
London (Simpson's Divan), September 1886
C25

1. e4 e5 2. Nc3 Nc6 3. f4 e×f4 4. d4 Qh4† 5. Ke2 g5 6. Nf[...]
Qh5 7. Nd5 Bg7 8. N×c7† Kd8 9. N×a8 Nf6 10. e5 g4 11. e×f[...]
B×f6 12. Nd2 Re8† 13. Kd3 Re3† 14. Kc4 b5 mate—*Modern Chess*, pp. 190–191.

### (834) Unknown–Bird　　0–1
Offhand game
London (Simpson's Divan) 1886
C25

1. e4 e5 2. Nc3 Nc6 3. f4 e×f4 4. d4 Qh4† 5. Ke2 g5 6. Nf[...]
Qh5 7. Nd5 Bg7 8. N×c7† Kd8 9. N×a8 Nf6 10. e5 g4 11. e×f[...]
B×f6 12. Ne1 Re8† 13. Kd2 f3 14. g×f3 Qg5† 15. Kd3 Nb4[...]
16. Kc3 Qa5 17. Kb3 b5 18. B×b5 Q×b5 19. h4 Qb7 20. Ka[...]
Be7 21. c4 Q×a8 22. c5 a5 23. Rg1 Qd5 24. R×g4 d6 25. Re[...]
Bf5 26. R×e7 R×e7 27. Bd2 Rb7 28. b3 Nc2† White resigns—
*Modern Chess*, p. 191.

On 15 November 1886 a cable match was started between th[e] British Chess Club and the St. Petersburg Chess Club. Each team consisted of five players. Chigorin and Emanuel Stepanovich Schiffer were the leading figures on the Russian team. Bird was the bigges[t] name among the five British players. He was joined by Donisthorpe, Hoffer, Guest and Daniel Yarnton Mills. Two games were played.
The Russians caused no great surprise by selecting the Evans Gambit. The London team opened with 1. Nf3, a move that was criticize[d] in various reports as being boring. Bird followed the match close[ly] by supplying small articles for *The Times*. This lasted until 4 January 1887, when just move 8 had been made. A month later other ches[s] columns announced the news that Bird had withdrawn from th[e] playing committee, allegedly due to a difference of opinion in the 1. Nf3 game. The small match ultimately ended in a victory of 1½–½ in favor of the Russians.
During the first part of the winter season Amos Burn was in London for business reasons. Burn used his spare time to join fellow masters like Pollock and Bird at the Divan. According to Bird in *Bird's Chess Reviews* (p. 2), Bird and Burn were at that time "the only leading living players who play amusement chess together."

### (835) Bird–Burn　　1–0
Offhand game
London (Simpson's Divan), 17 November 1886
C51

1. e4 e5 2. Nf3 Nc6 3. Bc4 Bc5 4. b4 B×b4 5. c3 Ba5 6. 0-0

**6** 7. d4 e×d4 8. c×d4 Bb6 9. Bb2 Nf6 10. e5 d×e5 11. Ba3 Bg4 White has no compensation after 11. ... B×d4! 12. Qb3 Qd7. **12. d5** 12. Qb3 is an amelioration. After the text move 12. ... Nd4! is very strong. **12. ... B×f3 13. Q×f3 Ne7 14. Re1 Bd4 15. Bb5† c6** 15. ... Kf8 is perfectly safe. The d-pawn will soon fall. **16. d×c6 b×c6** 16. ... 0–0 evacuates the king at the cost of some pawns. Now Bird gets in his element and obtains a very dangerous attack. **17. B×c6† N×c6 18. Q×c6† Nd7 19. Nd2! B×a1 20. Ne4 Bb2 21. Nd6† Kf8 22. Qd5 Qf6 23. Q×a8† Ke7 24. Nc8† Ke8 25. Ne7† Nb8 26. Q×b8† Kd7 27. Qb7† Ke6 28. Qd5** mate—*The Field*, 4 December 1886.

**(836) Bird–Burn     1–0**
Offhand game
London (Simpson's Divan), 17 November 1886
C54

**1. e4 e5 2. Nf3 Nc6 3. Bc4 Bc5 4. c3 Nf6 5. b4 Bb6 6. Qb3** "This attack, though not recommended by other authorities, is much favored by Bird, who has often played it with success in important matches"—Guest. **6. ... 0–0 7. d3 d6 8. Bg5 h6 9. Bh4 g5** "This dangerous move leads to Black's subsequent difficulties. He should have developed quietly by 9. ... Bd7"—Guest. **10. Bg3 Ne7 11. Nbd2 c6** "Doubtless with the intention of playing 12. ... d5. 11. ... Ng6 would have been a better move"—Guest. **12. d4** The queen ought to have retreated to provide some space for the bishop. **12. ... e×d4 13. N×d4 N×e4?** *(see diagram)* "Falling into a trap which his opponent has ingeniously laid for him. Bird is now able to make a pretty finish"—Guest. 13. ... d5! breaks up White's game.

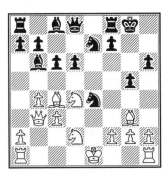

*After 13. ... N×e4*

**14. N×e4 d5 15. Nf6† Kg7 16. Nh5† Kg6 17. Bd3† K×h5 18. Qd1† Bg4 19. Q×g4† K×g4 20. Be2** mate—*Morning Post* (Guest), 29 November 1886.

**(837) Burn–Bird     0–1**
Offhand game
London (Simpson's Divan), 17 November 1886
A85

**1. d4 f5 2. Nf3 Nf6 3. e3 e6 4. c4 Be7 5. Nc3 0–0 6. Be2 d6 7. 0–0 Bb7 8. Qc2 Qe8 9. Bd2 Nc6 10. Rfd1 Nd8 11. d5 Bd6 12. Be1 Qg6 13. Rac1 Nf7 14. Bf1 Qh6 15. g3 g5 16. Nb5 Ng4 17. Bg2 Nfe5 18. N×d6 N×f3† 19. B×f3 Q×h2† 20. Kf1 N×d6 21. e4 Rac8 22. b4 Ba6 23. Qd3 f×e4 24. Q×e4 R×f3 25. Q×g4 Rcf8 26. Q×g5† Kh8 27. Rd2 R×g3 28. Qe7 Qg2† 29. Ke2 Qf3† 30. Kf1 Rfg8** White resigns—*The Field*, 25 December 1886.

This period of Bird's life was not without disputes. In December 1886 an article about the chess masters of the day, drafted by Leopold Hoffer, appeared in the *Fortnightly Review*. It created quite some stir. One of its critics was Cunningham in the *International Chess Magazine* (February 1887, p. 42). He found Hoffer's selection of masters very doubtful: two dead players were included while various first ranked contemporaries were lacking. The sentiment among the British masters was expressed by Bird. A reply from his hand was published a few months later. In the most interesting paragraph of the letter, Bird took up the defense of Steinitz, who was once more on the receiving end of Hoffer's criticism: "As a player he is considered unrivalled, his record has never been surpassed; he is a real chess artist, and a painstaking and conscientious amateur. It is true that his temper at times has been found to be touchy, and even litigious, but chess-players like other mortals are not perfect in this respect, nor indeed in any other. Why he alone should be singled out for so much ridicule does not appear upon the surface, and will be unintelligible to the outer chess world" (*Fortnightly Review*, March 1887, p. 471).

Bird also pointed his arrows at Zukertort in a letter of complaint that was published in the December 1886 edition of *Chess Monthly* (p. 99). Bird proved himself touchy by remarking that *Chess Monthly* never mentioned his name in the openings "with which my name is by this time, in all other chess quarters, literally familiarly identified." Bird then referred to some lines in the Evans Gambit, the Lesser Bishop's Gambit and his 1. f4. On top of that Bird accused Zukertort of demolishing the "English chess notions." Zukertort's reaction followed promptly. He pointedly refuted Bird's complaints by referring to the occasions when games with these lines were played long enough before Bird adopted them. Bird's accusations were justifiably ridiculed by Zukertort when he quoted the work of Stamma, written nearly 150 years earlier, in which there was already some space devoted to the Lesser Bishop's Gambit.

Bird was also dragged into a discussion with his good friend Amos Burn. Burn himself had been in a controversy with Gunsberg for a few months already, as he refused to accept the match challenge made by the ambitious Gunsberg. In a letter written on 14 December 1886 Burn was so unwise as to mention that he beat Bird.[13] Cunningham averred in the March edition (p. 71) that both players acknowledged that their score, including the results during Burn's visit of 1887, was balanced. But Bird, in a letter dated 14 April, could not resist poking up the fire again.

> Dear Sir: I feel certain that your desire is to give a faithful record of the performances and scores of chess players, and as a very great misconception has appeared in your columns regarding Burn and myself, I shall be glad if you will state that it is agreed between us that there is a balance in my favor, as explained to your London correspondent of about 15 games ... [*International Chess Magazine*, May 1887, p. 145].

In the June issue of the *International Chess Magazine* (p. 178), Cunningham denied Bird's statement, having written a memorandum on the subject on 9 February that up to that date Burn and Bird had made an even score.

13. "I have just returned from London, where I have been having a little chess feast. I played chiefly with Bird and Pollock, the result being that I won a majority of 21 games from Bird...." *International Chess Magazine*, January 1887, p. 8.

## (838) MacDonnell–Bird    0–1
Offhand game
London (Simpson's Divan), February 1887
C35

     1. e4 e5 2. f4 e×f4 3. Nf3 Be7 4. Bc4 Bh4† 5. Kf1 d5 6. B×d5
Nf6 7. Nc3 N×d5 8. N×d5 0–0 9. d3 Bg4 10. B×f4 f5 11. Qe2
f×e4 12. d×e4 Nc6 13. Rd1 Qe8 14. g3 Ne5 15. N×c7 R×f4
16. N×e8 R×f3† 17. Kg2 R×e8 18. Qb5 Ref8 19. Q×e5 Rf2†
20. Kg1 Bh3 and Black wins—*Chess Monthly*, March 1889, p. 218.

## (839) Unknown–Bird    0–1
Offhand game
London (Purssell's), 18 February 1887
*Odds of Ra8*

     1. e4 e5 2. Nf3 d6 3. Bc4 f5 4. d3 Nc6 5. Ng5 Nh6 6. 0–0 f4
7. Ne6 Qf6 8. N×f8 R×f8 9. Nc3 Qg6 10. Kh1 f3 11. g3 Qg4
12. Rg1 Qh3 13. Qf1 Ng4 White resigns—*Modern Chess*, pp. 193–
194.

On 22 March Bird was hired as the umpire at the third match
between a team of university students of Oxford and Cambridge
against second-class players from the City of London Chess Club.
Six games remained unfinished and were adjudicated by Bird. Contrary to the previous matches, the university team was now victorious. On Monday 18 April Bird signed present at the 35th annual
dinner of the City of London Chess Club. On Thursday 12 May
Bird witnessed the fourth match between the two major chess clubs
of London: St. George's and the City of London Chess Club. The
former won narrowly, 8 against 7.

After a few calm months a chess event of importance took place
in May 1887. A short match between Blackburne and Zukertort,
played for the first five wins, ended in a convincing victory for Blackburne. A rare occurrence, as Blackburne generally succumbed in a
direct confrontation with a top player. His opponent, however, was
only a shadow of his former self after the defeat he suffered in the
world championship match. Subsequent rumors spoke of a similar
match between Bird and Blackburne. In the June 1887 edition of
the *British Chess Magazine* (p. 263) several details leaked out: a
purse of £25 was the stake (£15 for the winner). Five wins were required to gain the match. The time limit was set at 20 moves per
hour. The match would commence a fortnight after the finish of
the contest between Blackburne and Zukertort. MacDonnell mentioned in the *Illustrated Sporting and Dramatic News* of 4 June that
he was requested to act as umpire and stakeholder. Two weeks later
he specified the starting date as Jubilee day (20 June) or shortly after.
But then, maybe through the sudden hot summer weather, a
lethargy set in and rumors about the match slowly abated.

# C.C.A. CONGRESS,
# STAMFORD 1887

The attention of the chess world shifted to Frankfurt am Main
where the fifth German Chess Congress started on 18 July. Bird was

reported by the British press to be scheduled to play but ultimate[l]
he didn't leave for Germany.[14] The tournament ended in a con[-]
vincing victory for Captain Mackenzie. Blackburne came in secon[d]
while the other British participants (Burn, Gunsberg and Zukertort[)]
disappointed by finishing in the second half of the list.

Bird found a worthy alternative by spending his days at Stamfor[d]
where the annual congress of the C.C.A. was held the first week o[f]
August. After two outings with a strong master tournament, th[e]
C.C.A. returned to its roots. Several tournaments were organize[d]
for traditional players: mostly provincial amateurs.

The major tournament, named Class I Division I, saw seven en[-]
tries. Bird and MacDonnell were the experienced London repre[-]
sentatives, Thorold was the only veteran of the C.C.A., and fou[r]
young and promising players completed the field: Blake, Mills, Pol[-]
lock and Charles Dealtry Locock. With these antagonists Bir[d]
could be considered the only favorite, but things ran far fro[m]
smoothly for him. He beat Locock after an attractive game but the[n]
lost three in a row. After a bye and two final wins Bird only narrow[ly]
shared third prize with Pollock and Thorold. Blake scored an im[-]
pressive tournament victory while Mills took second prize.

The disappointing results of the established masters Bird an[d]
MacDonnell was a topic for some time in the chess world. Mac[-]
Donnell especially created some controversy by bringing in a su[-]
perfluity of excuses.[15]

Bird was more successful in two side events. Together wit[h]
Thorold he won the problem solution contest, while the handica[p]
tournament also ended in a win for Bird (he beat Pollock in th[e]
final game).[16] His performance brought him £2. A consolatio[n]
handicap was won by MacDonnell. On Friday 5 August the com[-]
pany spent the afternoon in Burghley Park. The evening saw a col[d]
collation served at Stamford Hotel. A series of toasts were mad[e]
and, as usual, Bird didn't miss the chance to speak:

> Mr. Bird, who rose in response to repeated calls, said he hardly knew in wha[t]
> capacity it was that he did rise; but he presumed it was to respond to the toas[t]
> of the chess masters—(applause) to which he had responded in America, o[n]
> the continent, and almost all over the world. Proceeding, he said that of al[l]
> the places he had been to he had never enjoyed a meeting better than thi[s]
> one; and he had never seen a town better adapted for the formation of a ches[s]
> club. It was reserved for Stamford, too—this pretty, ancient, hospitable littl[e]
> place—to provide the only celebration by chess players of the Queen's Jubile[e]
> (laughter and applause) [*Lincoln, Rutland and Stamford Mercury*, 12 Augus[t]
> 1887].

While until now everything ran in accordance with the usua[l]
scheme of a meeting of the C.C.A., the organization and it[s]
secretary were nothing less than undermined during the annua[l]
meeting that took place later that evening. After a tumultuous dis[-]
cussion all hidden disagreements, undoubtedly brewing for a fe[w]

14. *The Field* wrote on 16 July 1887: "..., and Bird has written to the committe[e]
to keep his place open, as it is doubtful whether he will be able to play."

15. MacDonnell was however quite fair about Bird's performance: "Mr. Bir[d]
played at times with all his old force, fury, and brilliancy, but at other times h[e]
launched into a recklessness that seemed begotten of anger or surprise at his oppo[-]
nent for daring to defend himself, and cherishing even a vague hope of escapin[g]
from the wily veteran's clutches." *Illustrated Sporting and Dramatic News*, 2[?]
August 1887.

16. Sources as the *Lincoln, Rutland and Stamford Mercury* of 12 August an[d]
the *Illustrated Sporting and Dramatic News* of 13 August claim that the tournamen[t]
was not played out and that Bird and Pollock shared the first two prizes. The deci[-]
sive game, published in the *Horncastle News*, however, proves the opposite.

## 17th Congress of the C.C.A., Stamford, 1–6 August 1887

*Site:* Stamford Hotel
*Playing hours:* 10 a.m.–3 p.m. and 7 p.m.–11
*Prizes:* 1st £10, 2nd £4, 3rd £2

|   |                | 1 | 2 | 3 | 4 | 5 | 6 | 7 |   |
|---|----------------|---|---|---|---|---|---|---|---|
| 1 | J.H. Blake     |   | 1 | 1 | 1 | ½ | ½ | 1 | 5 |
| 2 | D.Y. Mills     | 0 |   | 1 | 1 | ½ | ½ | 1 | 4 |
| 3 | H.E. Bird      | 0 | 0 |   | 1 | 1 | 0 | 1 | 3 |
| 4 | E. Thorold     | 0 | 0 | 0 |   | 1 | 1 | 1 | 3 |
| 5 | W.H.K. Pollock | ½ | ½ | 0 | 0 |   | 1 | 1 | 3 |
| 6 | G.A. MacDonnell| ½ | ½ | 1 | 0 | 0 |   | 0 | 2 |
| 7 | C.D. Locock    | 0 | 0 | 0 | 0 | 0 | 1 |   | 1 |

### *Handicap tournament*

*Prizes:* 1st £2, 2nd £1
*Odds scale:* two moves (class II), pawn and move (class III), pawn and 2 moves (class IV) and knight (class V)
*Notes:* Twenty players signed up to play. Two, M.E. Thorold (class IV) and Walker (class V), were not paired and fell off. Mills received a bye in the second round and replaced Newham in the third. Perhaps they played a tie game.

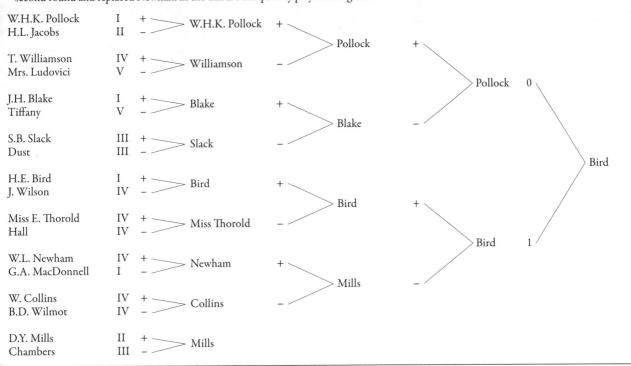

years under the surface, erupted. As a result the congress ended in a tarnished atmosphere. In his column of 12 August in the *Lincoln, Rutland and Stamford Mercury*, Skipworth tipped a veil of the events of that evening. Under discussion was the proposition to appoint a committee for the preparations of the following congress. Skipworth interpreted this proposal as a motion of censure; he considered himself the sole decision-maker, and reacted by offering his resignation as secretary in case this proposition were accepted. This dry and factual message completely ignored the deeply rooted discontent among a large number of the C.C.A.'s members. The Reverend Greene took the lead of the opposition against Skipworth. He described why the proceedings of the evening were very dissatisfactory for him and a large number of allies. An open letter from his hand was published by the *Glasgow Weekly Herald* on 3 September. Greene complained how difficult it was to even just organize the annual meeting as Skipworth just wanted to get rid of it.

Skipworth also had to confess that he had already fixed the place of next year's meeting, without acknowledging any other member of the C.C.A.

The meeting got really stormy when two other points were raised: the formation of a committee, to which Skipworth responded by threatening to resign his function as secretary, and the demand for a written constitution of the C.C.A. At this point Skipworth invited Bird, MacDonnell and Pollock, the London guests, into the meeting—according to his opponents as an attempt to force a decision into his favor. Ultimately no vote was taken and the meeting broke off abruptly. All in all, a great part of the members of the C.C.A. was fed up with the autocracy of Skipworth and demanded a democratization of the organization of which he had been the figurehead for twenty years.

As usual very little was heard about the C.C.A. during the winter season but in the preamble of the new congress, Skipworth resigned his post as honorary secretary because he disapproved of the committee's proposal to hold the meeting in Clifton instead of Newcastle. Herewith the C.C.A. actually ceased to exist.

Three years later, in 1890, Skipworth made a successful attempt to reanimate the C.C.A. and a few more congresses were held.[17]

### (840) Bird–Locock    1–0
C.C.A. Congress (round 1)
Stamford, 1 August 1887
A03

**1. f4 d5 2. Nf3 c5 3. e3 Nc6 4. b3 e6 5. Bb2 Nf6 6. Bb5 Bd7 7. 0–0 Be7 8. Qe1** "A standard move in this opening, threatening to play any convenient time Qg3. Also when the opponent's queen's knight is gone, White's unprotected c-pawn is in no immediate danger"—Skipworth. **8. ... 0–0 9. Nc3** At once 10. B×c6 is more precise as it avoids 9. ... Nb4. **9. ... a6 10. B×c6 B×c6 11. Ne5 Rc8 12. Ne2 Ne4 13. d3 Nd6 14. Ng3 Nf5 15. N×f5 e×f5 16. Qg3 Bf6 17. Qh3 g6 18. Qh6** Bird goes a bit too far in his attempts to create an attack. He leaves his center on its own, counting on a rather simple trap. **18. ... d4** "Mr. Locock is too good a player to fall into the trap. Had he played 18. ... Bg7, attacking the queen, White would have replied 19. Q×g7†, regaining his queen by a discovered check, and winning a piece!"—Skipworth. **19. Rae1 B×e5** After 19. ... Re8 Black has all the chances in the coming endgame. With this exchange Locock perhaps wanted to secure a draw, but he only improves the prospects of White, whose pieces are better placed for the opening up of the position. **20. f×e5 Qd5 21. Qg5 Rfe8** 21. ... h6 appears to be the best defense. After 22. Qg3 d×e3 23. R×e3 Kh7 24. e6 Black's position is nevertheless not very comfortable; e.g., 24. ... f×e6 25. Re5 Qd7 26. R×c5 with very active piece play. **22. e4?** Bird could win a pawn and reach a very promising endgame with 22. R×f5 h6 23. Qg3 Q×g2† 24. Q×g2 B×g2 25. Rf2. The bishops are of different colors, but the impressive White pawn chain will make life hard for Black. Bird's move is horrible and should have lost quickly. **22. ... Q×e5 23. e×f5 Qd5?** (see diagram) 23. ... Q×e1 24. R×e1 R×e1† 25. Kf2 Re5! gives Black everything he could have dreamt of. White can already resign.

**24. c4!** A strong move that truly tries his opponent's hand. Either

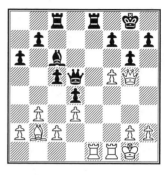

After 23. ... Qd5

he must leave the strong diagonal with his queen, and be content with a more passive position, or play 24. ... d×c3 e.p., when White' bishop comes alive. **24. ... Qd8?** Locock picks out the wrong option. After 24. ... d×c3 e.p. 25. B×c3 R×e1 26. R×e1 Rf8! 27. Re7 f6 28. Qg3 Rf7 both parties keep each other in balance. **25. f6!** Black is now subject to a very dangerous attack. **25. ... R×e1 26. R×e1 Qf8?!** Locock again chooses the passive solution, which is quite forcibly lost. Yet, the alternative was not attractive at all: 26. ... Qd6 27. Ba3! b6 28. Bc1 h6 29. Q×h6 Q×f6 30. Bg5 Qh8 31. Q×h8† K×h8 32. Re7 and Black is bound to lose at least one of the pawns on the queenside (after 32. ... Kg7 33. Bf4). He will have a hard time defending this position, but a draw is still possible. **27. Bc1?!** Too slow. 27. Re7! deprives his opponent from his last chance, namely 27. ... Bd7 and 28. ... Bf5. Locock selects another move after which his fate is sealed. **27. ... Re8?! 28. Re7! b6 29. Qe5 Bd7 30. h4 h5 31. Bf4 Kh7 32. Qg5 R×e7 33. f×e7 Qg7 34. Be5 f6** "A very ingenious effort to get out of difficulty. Had he played 34. ... Qh6 White would have played 35. Qf6, and there was no escaping mate or had he played 34. ... Qg8, White would still have replied 35. Qf6 and Black's queenside pawns could not have been defended"—Skipworth. **35. B×f6 Qh6** "Now he can safely play the queen to h6 and get an exchange of queens, hoping with the bishops on opposite colors to have just a chance for a draw. There was, really however no hope, for another pawn must go, and the White pawn at e7 was as good as a piece, for a piece must be on guard to prevent its queening. There is nothing brilliant about the game, but a steady attack has been maintained in Mr. Bird's best style, from Black's 12th move"—Skipworth. **36. Qe5 Qe3† 37. Q×e3 d×e3 38. Bg5 Kg7 39. Kf1 Kf7 40. Ke2 Ke6 41. K×e3 Ke5 42. g3 Kf5 43. d4 Ke6 44. d5† Ke5 45. Bf4† Kf6 46. Bd6 Kf7 47. b4 c×b4 48. B×b4 Ba4 49. Kf4 b5 50. c5 K×e7 51. c6† Kd8 52. d6** and Black resigns "Nothing can prevent 53. d7, and then 54. Ba5†"—Skipworth. *Lincoln, Rutland and Stamford Mercury* (Skipworth), 29 November 1889.

### (841) Bird–MacDonnell    0–1
C.C.A. Congress (round 2)
Stamford, 2 August 1887
A02

**1. f4 f5 2. b3 Nf6 3. Bb2 e6 4. Nf3 b6 5. e3 Bb7 6. Be2 Be7 7. 0–0 0–0 8. c4 c5 9. Na3 Nc6 10. Nc2 Qc7 11. Ng5 h6 12. Nh3 Rad8 13. Qe1 Rf7 14. Bf3 d5 15. c×d5 e×d5 16. Rc1 Ba6 17. Be2 B×e2 18. Q×e2 Ng4 19. Ne1 Bf6 20. B×f6 R×f6** Bird's opening experiment didn't turn out well. Thanks to some well-planned exchanges, MacDonnell built up a nice positional advantage. His

17. From this period comes the following extremely critical piece in which Gunsberg publicly denounced Skipworth's management style. It enlightens one about the dissatisfaction that brewed before the implosion at Stamford occurred: "The program doesn't say what will become of the money in case the entrance fees in all the four tournaments exceed the total amount of the prizes, viz., £42, and what will be done with the funds which the noble and right reverend lords and the forty other vice-presidents have no doubt (?) subscribed. The utter absence of the sense of fairness is exemplified by the following rules: 'The committee reserve themselves the power to alter any rule or add any rule,' and 'reserve themselves the right of refusing any entry.' Further also a clause which is an old enemy of every journalist trying to do his duty to his employers and the public, namely, 'all the games played are the property of the committee,' which simply means that the reverend gentleman will himself try and traffic in the games, as he has done before. Fines are provided for a variety of offences, among others for leaving the room without permission. Oh, the happy days of our youth! And, lastly, a most decided intimation that Mr. Skipworth is not to be trifled with is found in the following rule: 'any person who refuses to comply with any rule, or any resolution of the committee, or who in any way shall disturb the meeting (means in plain English get drunk), renders himself liable (at the discretion of the committee) to forfeit all entrance fees he has paid, his right to further competition, and his right to any prize, and to be dealt with as the committee shall order.'" *Evening News and Post*, 17 May 1890.

main idea is to play d5–d4 at a good moment. **21. Nf3 Qe7 22. Rfe1 Re6 23. Qd3** 23. Qf1 gets the queen out of the line of fire. MacDonnell now replies with the best preparatory move for 24. ... d4. **23. ... Re4! 24. a3 Kh7** But here MacDonnell misses the momentum to play 24. ... d4!, which is very strong. There is no reason to fear 25. Qc4† Kf8, nor other lines such as 25. e×d4 N×d4 26. R×e4 Q×e4 27. Q×e4 f×e4 28. N×d4 R×d4 or 25. Qb5 d×e3 26. d×e3 Qe6 and the pawn at e3 falls. **25. Qb5 Rd6 26. Nf2** 26. b4 c4 takes the sting out of Black's strong center. Bird's move is not so good, as it allows Black to push d4 after all. **26. ... N×f2 27. K×f2 d4** A tad too hasty. First 27. ... Qf6 neutralizes 28. b4 due to 28. ... c×b4 and the knight is defended. **28. b4 a6** MacDonnell doesn't stray from the correct path, at least not now. **29. Q×a6 g5?** Way too enterprising for this position. Not only is there no decisive attack against White's king in sight, this move also jeopardizes the protection of his own royal. Right was 29. ... c×b4! and White has to be extremely careful: both 30. a×b4? N×b4 and 30. Q×b6 Ne5 lead to a swift conclusion as Black's knight deadly enters at d3. If instead 30. Qb5 Qd7 31. a4 Qe6 Black has good pressure, although the position remains very unclear. **30. b×c5** *(see diagram)*

*After 30. b×c5*

**30. ... d×e3†** Or 30. ... b×c5 31. Qc8! Qf6 32. f×g5 h×g5 33. R×c5 and the tragedy of MacDonnell's 29th move becomes clear. His knight is a completely different piece from the one it could have been in the previous variation, while the weakness of his kingside is obvious by now. **31. d×e3?!** The sharp 31. R×e3! decides the game in a short while. The motives remain the same: 31. ... b×c5 (or 31. ... R×d2† 32. N×d2 R×e3 33. c×b6 Nb8 34. Qb5) 32. Qc8. **31. ... b×c5 32. Qc8 Qf6** 32. ... Ree6 is more solid. Then 33. R×c5 g×f4 is nothing, but 33. Rcd1! is strong. The curious thing about this position is that exchanges are good for White, as they eliminate Black's defenders. **33. R×c5 Ne7 34. Qc7?** 34. f×g5 h×g5 35. Qe8 Kh6 36. h3 leaves Black with absolutely nothing to show for his two lost pawns. **34. ... g×f4?** 34. ... g4 is the correct move. The situation suddenly seems critical for White (moving the knight loses at once due to 35. ... Qh4†), but he has an unexpected drawing line: 35. R×f5! Q×f5 36. Q×d6 g×f3 37. K×f3 Re6 38. Qd1. After 34. ... g×f4? White's king also appears to be hunted, but this is only illusionary due to a whole series of pins. **35. e×f4 Rd2† 36. Kf1** "Of course he cannot take the rook with the knight because of 36. ... Qd4†"—Duffy. **36. ... Qa6† 37. Rc4 Rd7 38. Q×d7 Q×c4† 39. Kf2** The king belongs on h1. **39. ... Qc5† 40. Kg3 Q×a3 41. Rd1 Qc3 42. Qa7?!** Losing his extra pawn and the advantage. 42. Rd4! is still likely to win. **42. ... Qg7† 43. Kf2 R×f4 44. h3 Re4 45. Rd7 f4 46. Qc5 Re3**

**47. Kg1?!** 47. Qc2† forces the exchange of queens. He will probably conquer the f-pawn, though it is unlikely that this is enough to win the game. **47. ... Re2 48. Nh4?** Bird panics and this costs him dearly. He'd have good drawing chances after 48. R×e7 Q×e7 49. Qf5† Kh8 50. Q×f4 Qe3† 51. Q×e3 R×e3 52. Kf2. **48. ... Re1†** and White resigns—*Illustrated London News* (Duffy), 24 September 1887.

**(842) Bird vs. Mills   0–1**
C.C.A. Congress (round 3)
Stamford, 2 August 1887
*Game score missing; colors unknown*

**(843) Bird vs. Blake   0–1**
C.C.A. Congress (round 4)
Stamford, 3 August 1887
*Game score missing; colors unknown*

**(844) Bird vs. Pollock   1–0**
C.C.A. Congress (round 6)
Stamford, 4 August 1887
*Game score missing; colors unknown*

**(845) Thorold–Bird   0–1**
C.C.A. Congress (round 7)
Stamford, 4 August 1887
C35

**1. e4 e5 2. f4 e×f4 3. Nf3 Be7 4. Bc4 Bh4† 5. g3 f×g3 6. 0–0 d5 7. B×d5 Nf6 8. B×f7†** True to his reputation, Thorold opens the game as sharply as possible. Alas for him, this sacrifice is completely incorrect, and it doesn't take Bird long to prove it convincingly. **8. ... K×f7 9. N×h4 Qd4† 10. Kg2 Q×e4† 11. Nf3 g×h2 12. Nc3 Qg6† 13. Kh1 Re8 14. d3 Kg8 15. Bf4 Bg4 16. Qd2 Nc6 17. N×h2 Nd4 18. Rf2 Bd7 19. Ne4 N×e4 20. d×e4 Q×e4† 21. Rg2 Bc6 22. Rag1 Ne2 23. B×c7 N×g1 24. K×g1 Q×g2† 25. Q×g2 B×g2 26. K×g2 Re2† 27. Kg3 R×c2** and White resigns—*Aspa Chess Miscellanies*, vol. 1.

**(846) Bird–Pollock   1–0**
Handicap tournament (round 4)
Stamford, August 1887
C54

**1. e4 e5 2. Nf3 Nc6 3. Bc4 Bc5 4. c3 Nf6 5. b4 Bb6 6. Qb3 0–0 7. d3 h6 8. a4 a6 9. a5 Ba7 10. Be3 B×e3 11. f×e3 d6 12. Nbd2 Qe7 13. 0–0 Be6 14. Nh4 N×e4 15. Ng6 Qg5 16. N×e4 B×c4 17. Q×c4 Q×g6 18. b5 a×b5 19. Q×b5 Nd8 20. Ng3 c6 21. Qb1 f5 22. d4 e4 23. Qb3† d5 24. c4 c5 25. c×d5 c×d4 26. d6† Ne6 27. Qd5 d×e3 28. N×f5 Kh7 29. Ne7 Qg4 30. h3 Qh4 31. Nf5 Nf4 32. Qe5 Ne2† 33. Kh2 Qg5 34. Q×e4 Kh8 35. g4 Rae8 36. Ne7 Qc5 37. Ng6† Kg8 38. R×f8† R×f8 39. Qe6† Rf7 40. Rf1 Q×d6 41. Q×d6 R×f1 42. Qd8† Kh7 43. Nf8† Kg8 44. Ne6†** and Black resigns—*Horncastle News*, September 1886.

## Working for a Jubilee Tournament

Quite in contrast with the two previous years, 1887 was rather stodgy. The C.C.A. had returned to their format of smaller meetings. The state of the B.C.A. seemed even worse as several voices publicly wondered whether it even still existed after the summer had passed without their congress. It appeared that the summer restored its reputation as "the dead season." Yet there was more than enough reason to hold a major tournament. Queen Victoria celebrated the Golden Jubilee of her reign. Bird saw it as his task to bring the matter to the attention of the public. Hereby he invited the B.C.A. to take the initiative.[18]

No immediate reaction followed, above all because Bird wrote his appeal in the midst of the summer. He therefore energetically took matters in own hand by sending letters to supporters and patrons of the game.[19] A short while later a more elaborated version of Bird's plans became publicly known.[20] The fact that the B.C.A. was kept outside Bird's scenario became more and more a thorn in Hoffer's eye. As matters grew more concrete he started undermining Bird's plans with the use of his magazine, *Chess Monthly*. In the edition of October, on p. 36, an anonymous letter was published. The writer, allegedly a member of the British Chess Club, thought it disreputable for players to organize their own tournaments and expressed the hope that patrons of chess would not be seduced into supporting them.

Hoffer did not need much more inducement to express his worries about Bird's proposition. He thoroughly burnt down Bird's initiative.[21] At the same time he announced the start of the long-awaited third congress of the B.C.A. in November. Hoffer's claim that he already announced the B.C.A. congress before Bird published his plans to hold a Jubilee tournament, was ridiculed. Both the *International Chess Magazine* and the *British Chess Magazine* recognized that Bird's initiative had spurred the B.C.A. to organize their master tournament. While the congress of the B.C.A. was now definitively going on, Bird kept on trying and hoping, at a much lower profile, to realize his Jubilee chess congress. But, as generally expected, being without support and with almost no time left before the end of the year, his initiative died a slow death.

## In the Provinces, October 1887

Bird did not remain idle when his plans to commemorate Queen Victoria ascension to the throne fell through and he headed for the provinces during October. On 5 and 6 October Bird's tour took off in Sunderland. Bird held two sessions per day, from 3 until 6 p.m. and from 7 until 10 p.m., at the Assembly Hall. Tickets to attend the meeting were sold at the prize of a shilling per day. The event opened with speeches by R.K.A. Ellis, the club president and Bird, after which a first exhibition against 16 players started. Bird was in quite a peaceful mood, with 7 wins, 2 losses (against Gibson and Downey) and 7 draws. For the evening session 19 opponents turned up. Bird beat 16 of them and drew 1 game, while 2 games remained unfinished.

During the afternoon of 6 October Bird met 15 players. One of them (Pattison) won his game, 2 ended in a draw and Bird won the remaining 12 games. For the last exhibition 20 opponents assembled. Bird won 19 games and succumbed for a second time to Gibson.

On the next day Bird arrived in Newcastle. The opposition was very strong and the rare feat occurred that the master was nearly beaten by the locals. Bird won 6 games, suffered 5 losses and 5 games ended in a draw.

**(847) Bird–Downey    0–1**
Simultaneous game
Newcastle (Art Gallery), 7 October 1887
C33

**1. e4 e5 2. f4 e×f4 3. Be2 d5 4. e×d5 Nf6 5. c4 c6 6. d×c6 N×c6 7. Nf3 Bc5 8. Nc3 Bf5 9. Qb3 Nd4 10. N×d4 Q×d4 11. Q×b7**

---

18. Bird's letter appeared in *The Times* on 2 August 1887. A fragment: "It certainly seems a pity, and some of the more enthusiastic among us feel sad at the fear that the Jubilee year, for all others, should be reserved for a blank page in the glorious chapter of the history of the royal game of chess; but as it is, and, notwithstanding the many willing workers ready, so it is likely to remain, unless some of its many distinguished friends will sound the keynote, or our chess clubs shake off their apathy. Surely the British Chess Association, which is honored with the names of Tennyson, Ruskin, Churchill and Peel, will do something in appreciation of the patronage accorded it. As a member of that body, and its auditor, and also as the oldest of the leading exponents of the game, I humbly appeal to its executive to make one good move in chess."

19. An example was published in *Chess Monthly*, October 1887, p. 35.

20. The full text appeared in the *Illustrated Sporting and Dramatic News* of 17 September 1887: "Mr. H.E. Bird proposes the holding of an international congress in London about the middle of October, and in a series of letters to me has elaborated his scheme with his usual care and ability. The veteran very properly observes that we owe some return to the foreigners for the many open-to-the-world tourneys which they have held during the last ten years, and in which Englishmen have taken part, and gained good prizes. Since 1877 France and Germany have organized no less than eight international contests. This, being the Jubilee year, Mr. Bird naturally considers to be a very fitting time for such a congress. To meet the expenses of such a meeting, Mr. Bird proposes to form a select and influential committee at once, who shall proceed to raise funds by issuing transferable tickets—say, 500 at one guinea each; the holders thereof, besides having the right of admission to the tournament and of introducing a friend on each occasion, also to be entitled to a copy of the book of the congress containing the games played. I understand that this scheme is sanctioned and will be supported by Messrs. Gunsberg, MacDonnell, Guest, Mason, Mackenzie, Burn and Pollock. The names of subscribers—who will not be asked to pay up unless by October 1st the scheme is assured of success—will be received by H.E. Bird, 5 Heygate Street, Walworth, S.E."

21. "It appears that Mr. Bird received, to the great number of applications made, some favorable replies, and, armed with these, he called a meeting at Simpson's, but no meeting took place, for the simple reason that nobody attended. ... The next step of Mr. Bird's was to invite the hon. sec. of the British Chess Association to take the management of the affair in hand. The latter, however, declined to join a movement which was so ostensibly started in opposition to the B.C.A. ... Another meeting was then called, this time at the British Chess Club; but again a few gentlemen, who were asked to form a committee, consented to adjourn into the committee room, under the conditions that Mr. Bird consented to leave the whole matter in the hands of the British Chess Association. He reluctantly agreed, and only then the following members of the B.C.C. and B.C.A. held a meeting. ... It would be much better if Mr. Bird were to use his undoubted energy and goodwill in endeavouring to lend a helping hand to those gentlemen who have always conscientiously worked to promote the interest of the game, and to drag it out of the taverns, by establishing a worthy home for it at the British Chess Club." *Chess Monthly*, October 1887, pp. 36–37.

0–0 12. Rf1 Rfe8 13. b4 Ne4 14. R×f4 Qg1† 15. Rf1 N×c3 16. d×c3 R×e2† and mates in a few moves—*Newcastle Weekly Chronicle*, 21 May 1892.

Before heading to his following arrangement in Manchester, Bird made a first stop in Bradford. Here he engaged in some offhand chess with the local club members and kibitzed the ongoing match between Blackburne and Gunsberg. Such a match had been awaited for a long time. Except for the duel between Blackburne and Zukertort, the past year had brought but little real struggle around the formerly so burning question about the British hegemony. Because of his long list of achievements and excellent result at the German Congress in Frankfurt, Blackburne was considered the favorite but he was outclassed by Gunsberg, who thus considerably improved his reputation at the cost of a somewhat indisposed opponent.

On 12 October Bird finally arrived in Manchester. His simultaneous exhibition here aroused a lot of interest and several members of nearby clubs and villages headed to the place of action. After three hours of play only 10 games were finished. Time was up to play out the remaining 9 games and Bird took up the job of referee. He claimed 4 wins while granting 5 draws. This brought the final result to 12 wins, 2 losses (against A.B. Rink and F.D. Frankland) and 5 draws.

A second performance was announced at the Athenaeum Chess Club, but these plans ultimately fell through.[22]

### (848) F.J. Hamel & Pescall & Hargreaves–Bird   1–0
Consultation game
Manchester, 12 October 1887
C45

1. e4 e5 2. Nf3 Nc6 3. d4 e×d4 4. N×d4 Qh4 5. Nb5 Bc5 6. Qf3 Nf6 7. N1c3 Nd4 8. N×d4 B×d4 9. Ne2 Bb6 10. Ng3 d5 11. Bd3 Ng4 12. Be3 B×e3 13. f×e3 N×h2 14. Qf4 Q×f4 15. e×f4 Ng4 16. e×d5 g6 17. Kd2 Kf8 18. Raf1 Bd7 19. f5 Kg7 20. Rh4 h5 21. f×g6 f×g6 22. Ne4 Raf8 23. Rhh1 b6 24. c4 Ne5 25. Be2 Bg4 26. B×g4 R×f1 27. R×f1 N×c4† 28. Kc3 Ne3 29. Be2 N×d5† 30. Kb3 Re8 31. Bf3 Ne3 32. Rc1 c5 33. Rc3 Nf5 34. Rd3 h4 35. Ng5 Kf6 36. Nh3 b5 37. Kc3 c4 38. Rd7 a5 39. Bc6 Re3† 40. Kd2 Rg3 41. Nf4 b4 42. Bf3 h3 43. N×h3 Nh4 44. Nf2 N×f3† 45. g×f3 R×f3 46. Ke2 Rf5 47. Rc7 Rf4 48. Ke3 g5 49. Ne4† Kf5 50. Rc5† Ke6 51. N×g5† Kd6 52. R×a5 Rf1 53. Ne4† Ke6 54. Nd2 Rc1 55. Kd4 c3 56. b×c3 R×c3 57. Ra4 Ra3 58. R×a3 b×a3 59. Nc4 and White wins—*Manchester Evening News*, 12 November 1887.

On 14 October Bird returned to Bradford. He gave a simultaneous exhibition against 20 opponents. The veteran stumbled into fervid opposition and had to suffer 4 defeats (against J.E. Hall, T. Spencer, W.W. Simpson and J.A. Guy) and concede 4 draws (versus J.A. Woollard, H.O. Pudgett, E. Dobson and C.A. Müller).[23]

After a short break Bird appeared on 22 October at the annual general meeting of the Surrey County Chess Association. Opposing 20 players he scored 13 wins, 2 losses and 5 draws.

22. *Manchester Evening News*, 13 October 1887. The exhibition at the Athenaeum Chess Club is not mentioned in the overview given in *The Field* (15 October 1887) or *The Times* (17 October 1887).

23. *Leeds Mercury*, 22 October 1887. According to Bird himself only 2 draws were played (*The Times*, 17 October 1887).

Bird then returned to London to attend of the coming congress of the B.C.A. One offhand game contested at the Divan shows him dismantling a well-known amateur.

### (849) Braund–Bird   0–1
Offhand game
London (Simpson's Divan), 4 November 1887
C33

1. e4 e5 2. f4 e×f4 3. Bc4 Qh4† 4. Kf1 d6 5. d4 g5 6. Nc3 Ne7 7. Nf3 Qh5 8. h4 f6 "8. ... f6 and h6 form the special trade mark of the defense favored by Mr. Bird in the Bishop's Gambit"—Zukertort. 9. Qd3? "A very weak continuation; we would prefer 9. e5 or 9. Ne2"—Zukertort. 9. ... Nbc6 10. a3 g4 11. Ne1 Bh6 12. Ne2 Ng6 13. g3 "Giving Black a telling superiority of position, while the pieces of White are hopelessly displaced"—Zukertort. 13. ... f3 14. Nf4 N×f4 15. B×f4 B×f4 16. g×f4 Bd7 17. c3 0–0–0 18. b4 Rhe8 19. a4 f5 20. e5 d×e5 21. f×e5 f4 22. Qe4 Qf5 More than enough to win comfortably. Also strong was 22. ... N×e5. 23. Q×f5 B×f5 24. a5 Be4 25. b5 N×e5 "The sacrifice of the knight opens the file for the rook, which easily forces the advance of the Black pawns"—Zukertort. 26. d×e5 R×e5 27. b6 c×b6 28. a×b6 a6 29. Rh2 g3 30. Rha2 Rd6 31. Ra5 R×a5 32. R×a5 g2† 33. Kf2 Rd2† 34. Kg1 Rd1 "Simpler would be 34. ... f2† 35. Kh2 g1Q etc."—Zukertort. 35. Be6† Kb8 White resigns—*Chess Monthly* (Zukertort), March 1888, p. 215.

## B.C.A. CONGRESS, LONDON 1887

Hoffer unfolded the plans for the third master tournament of the B.C.A. in September, after which a committee to prepare the tournament was formed. Perhaps as a consolation for hampering his plans to organize a jubilee tournament to commemorate the ascendancy of Queen Victoria, Hoffer invited Bird to join it together with Frederick Anger, Guest and Reeves. It is unclear whether Bird remained a member of the committee until the beginning of the tournament.

The committee succeeded well in its mission and was rewarded with the participation of all players belonging to the chess elite: Blackburne, Burn, Gunsberg, Zukertort, Mason and Bird. Four other players with a smaller reputation completed the field. With ten players the minimum to keep the tournament a single round-robin was attained. But then the Reverend Skipworth, the usual suspect, attempted to derail the tournament for an obscure reason: games were to be played in the British Chess Club instead of in the Victoria Hall. Skipworth refused to play in a private club. This shallow argument resulted in an outburst from Hoffer which brought sharp tensions between the C.C.A. and the B.C.A. back again.[24]

24. "Now we cannot help commenting upon Mr. Skipworth's unjustifiable action. It is not the first time that he has caused so much unnecessary trouble. It is whispered pretty loud that the object of Mr. Skipworth is to have his name advertised as a master, and that he has not the least intention to jeopardize this cheaply gained notoriety. This is, however, the last time that his entry will be accepted upon trust, without the accompanying entrance fee and deposit, the same as the other competitors.... Mr. Skipworth is an avowed enemy of the B.C.A., in spite of his name figuring amongst the members of the council." *Chess Monthly*, December 1887, pp. 97–98.

The pairings had to be redone and, more importantly, with only nine participants the tournament had to become a double round-robin according to the rules of the B.C.A. Disorderly chaos was prevented only by the late addition of Anthony Guest.

In the first round Bird was paired with Guest. To give the last-minute volunteer some time to come to himself this game started three hours later than the other ones. Bird confidently pushed his luck but was severely punished with a loss when he overstretched in a drawn position. This was rather symptomatic for his tournament. In the second round Bird rapidly crushed Mortimer in a game highly appreciated by the spectators, but from then on he was not up to the task of converting various promising positions into a win. Bird's worst experience was against Gunsberg in the penultimate round. At this point Gunsberg and Burn were in the lead. Bird played a magnificent game and, at one point, could have mated his opponent with a queen sacrifice. He missed it and was duly punished. Bird's last round game, against Zukertort, also could have turned out differently. Bird lost again and ended at a joint sixth to ninth place. It was clear that he deserved much better.[25]

Burn and Gunsberg dominated the tournament and each ended with an astonishing 8 out of 9. A tie match, played for the first two wins was commenced, but broken off after five games, at the point where each player had won one game.

## (850) Guest–Bird   1–0
B.C.A. Congress (round 1)
London, 29 November 1887

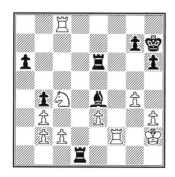

Black to move

**38. ...** **Rh1†** **39. Kg3** **Rg1†** **40. Kh2** **Rh1†** **41. Kg3** **Rc1** As pointed out by the *British Chess Magazine*, Bird overestimates his attack and refuses to settle with the draw after 41. ... Rg1†. **42. Rc7 R×c2 43. Rff7 Rg6 44. Ne5 R×c7 45. R×c7 Re6 46. Nd7 Rd6 47. Kf4 Bc6 48. Ke5 R×d7 49. R×c6 Rd3 50. Ke4 R×b3 51. R×a6 R×b2 52. Rb6 b3** "and after about a score more moves, Guest won the game with the passed e-pawn." With correct play, the game

25. See for example the *British Chess Magazine* (January 1888, p. 44): "The most disappointing score in the whole tournament was that of Bird's. The veteran's play in almost every game was of a very high order, and indeed some of the very best games played were those at his board, but unfortunately his score is no index to his play, for in some cases after obtaining a winning position by excellent play, he threw all away by a fearful blunder at the end, whilst in other cases, players who had hardly done themselves justice against other players, seemed to play their level best against the old man. Gunsberg's was a case in point of the former class, whilst Blackburne, Lee an Pollock come under the second. 'Ah!' said Bird, in the hearing of the writer of this report, 'these young dogs'—alluding to Lee and Pollock—'played pawn and move stronger against me than they did against anyone else in the tournament!' And indeed there is much truth in this."

---

### 3rd Congress of the B.C.A., London, 29 November–8 December 1887

*Site:* British Chess Club
*Playing hours:* 2 p.m.–6 and 8 p.m.–11
*Prizes:* 1st £30, 2nd £20, 3rd £10, 4th £5 entrance fees divided among non–prize winners
*Time limit:* 20 moves per hour

|  |  | 1 | 2 | 3 | 4 | 5 | 6 | 7 | 8 | 9 | 10 |  |
|---|---|---|---|---|---|---|---|---|---|---|---|---|
| 1 | A. Burn |  | 1 | 1 | 0 | 1 | 1 | 1 | 1 | 1 | 1 | 8 |
| 2 | I. Gunsberg | 0 |  | 1 | 1 | 1 | 1 | 1 | 1 | 1 | 1 | 8 |
| 3 | J.H. Blackburne | 0 | 0 |  | 1 | 1 | 1 | ½ | 1 | 1 | 1 | 6½ |
| 4 | J.H. Zukertort | 1 | 0 | 0 |  | ½ | ½ | 1 | 1 | 1 | 1 | 6 |
| 5 | W.H.K Pollock | 0 | 0 | 0 | ½ |  | 1 | ½ | 0 | 1 | 1 | 4 |
| 6 | F.J. Lee | 0 | 0 | 0 | ½ | 0 |  | ½ | 1 | ½ | 1 | 3½ |
| 7 | H.E Bird | 0 | 0 | ½ | 0 | ½ | ½ |  | 0 | ½ | 1 | 3 |
| 8 | A. Guest | 0 | 0 | 0 | 0 | 1 | 0 | 1 |  | 0 | 1 | 3 |
| 9 | J. Mason | 0 | 0 | 0 | 0 | 0 | ½ | ½ | 1 |  | 1 | 3 |
| 10 | J. Mortimer | 0 | 0 | 0 | 0 | 0 | 0 | 0 | 0 | 0 |  | 0 |

| *Tie match:* | 1 | 2 | 3 | 4 | 5 |  |
|---|---|---|---|---|---|---|
| I. Gunsberg | 0 | ½ | 1 | ½ | ½ | 2½ |
| A. Burn | 1 | ½ | 0 | ½ | ½ | 2½ |

---

should have ended in a draw. *British Chess Magazine*, January 1888, p. 45.

## (851) Bird–Mortimer   1–0
B.C.A. Congress (round 2)
London, 30 November 1887
*C33*

**1. e4 e5 2. f4 e×f4 3. Be2 d5 4. e×d5 Nf6 5. c4 Bd6 6. d4 b6 7. Nc3 0–0 8. Nf3 Re8 9. 0–0 Ng4 10. Bd3 c5 11. Ne4 Bf5 12. N×d6 B×d3 13. N×f7 Qf6 14. Q×d3 Q×f7 15. Ng5 Qh5 16. B×f4 N×h2 17. Rfe1 Na6 18. Ne6 Ng4 19. Qg3 Qg6 20. Be5 N×e5 21. Q×e5 c×d4 22. Q×d4 Rac8 23. Re4 Nc5 24. N×c5 R×c5 25. R×e8† Q×e8 26. Rd1 Rc8 27. d6 Rd8 28. b4 Qa4 29. c5 b×c5 30. b×c5 Qe8 31. d7 Qe2 32. c6 Qc2 33. Qd5† Kh8 34. Re1 Qg6 35. Qe6** Black resigns—*The Times*, 1 December 1887.

## (852) Mason–Bird   ½–½
B.C.A. Congress (round 3)
London, 1 December 1887
*C61*

**1. e4 e5 2. Nf3 Nc6 3. Bb5 Nd4 4. N×d4 e×d4 5. 0–0 h5 6. d3 Bc5 7. Nd2 c6 8. Bc4 d5 9. e×d5 c×d5 10. Bb3 Bg4 11. f3 Be6 12. Re1 Ne7 13. Nf1 Nf5 14. Bf4 a5 15. a3 a4 16. Ba2 h4 17. Qe2 Kf8 18. Bc1 Qc7 19. Bd2 Kg8 20. Bb4 B×b4 21. a×b4 Rh6 22. Rac1 Rg6 23. Qe5 Qd8 24. f4 Rc8 25. c4 d×c3 *e.p.* 26. b×c3 Qb6† 27. d4 Rd8 28. Bb1 Rf6 29. Ne3 N×e3 30. R×e3 Qd6 31. f5 Bd7 32. g4 h×g3 *e.p.* 33. h×g3 Bb5 34. g4 a3 35. g5 Q×e5 36. R×e5 Rfd6 37. Ba2 f6 38. g×f6 g×f6 39. Re3 Kf7 40. Kf2 Rh8 41. Kg2 Rdd8 42. Rce1 Rhg8† 43. Kf3 Rd7 44. Bb3 Rg5 45. Kf4 Bc4 46. B×c4 d×c4 47. Ra1 Rd5 48. R×a3 Rd×f5† 49. Ke4 Rf1 50. Rf3 Re1† 51. Kf4 Kg6 52. Ra8 Rf5† 53. Kg3 Rg1† 54. Kf2 Rf1† 55. K×f1 R×f3† 56. Ke2 R×c3 57. Rb8 Rd3 58. R×b7 R×d4 59. Rc7 Kf5 60. b5 Rd5** "and after a few more moves the game was abandoned as drawn"—*Daily News*, 2 December 1887.

## (853) Bird–Burn    0–1
B.C.A. Congress (round 4)
London, 2 December 1887
*A03*

1. f4 d5 2. e3 e6 3. Be2 Nf6 4. Nh3 c5 5. 0–0 Nc6 6. b3 Be7 7. Bb2 0–0 8. Qe1 Bd7 9. Bd1 Qc7 10. d3 Rad8 11. Nd2 Ne8 12. Nf3 f6 13. d4 b6 14. a3 Nd6 15. c3 Be8 16. Nf2 Bg6 17. Nh4 Be4 18. Rc1 c4 19. N×e4 N×e4 20. b×c4 d×c4 21. Bc2 Nd6 22. Qe2 f5 23. Nf3 b5 24. Nd2 Rde8 25. e4 Nd8 26. e5 Nc8 27. a4 a6 28. a×b5 a×b5 29. Ra1 Nc6 30. Rf3 Nb6 31. Rh3 g6 32. Rf1 Nd5 33. g4 Rf7 34. g×f5 g×f5 35. Rg3† Kh8 36. Qh5 Bd8 37. Rf2 Rg8 38. R×g8† K×g8 39. Rg2† Kh8 40. Qf3 Nce7 41. Nf1 Ng6 42. Rg3 Bh4 43. Rh3 Be1 44. Kh1 Qb7 45. Bd1 Ng×f4 46. Rh6 B×c3 47. Bc1 B×d4 48. Rh4 B×e5 49. Ng3 Ng6 White resigns—*British Chess Magazine*, March 1888, pp. 160–161.

## (854) Blackburne–Bird    ½–½
B.C.A. Congress (round 5)
London, 3 December 1887
*C45*

1. e4 e5 2. Nf3 Nc6 3. d4 e×d4 4. N×d4 Qh4 5. Nb5 Bc5 6. Qf3 Nd4 7. N×d4 B×d4 8. c3 Bc5 9. g3 Qe7 10. Bg2 d6 11. Be3 Bb6 12. Nd2 Nf6 13. h3 Bd7 14. 0–0 B×e3 15. Q×e3 0–0 16. Rfe1 Bc6 17. Nb3 Rfe8 18. Nd4 Bd7 19. Rad1 Qe5 20. Qd2 Qh5 21. g4 Qc5 22. Qf4 h6 23. Qg3 a5 24. Kh2 a4 25. f4 g5 26. e5 g×f4 27. Qh4 d×e5 28. Q×f6 Ra6 29. Qh4 e×d4 30. R×d4 R×e1 31. Q×e1 Re6 32. Qd2 Bc6 33. B×c6 Q×c6 34. Q×f4 Rf6 35. Qe3 Rf3 36. Qe2 a3 37. Rd8† Kg7 38. Qe5† Qf6 39. Q×f6† K×f6 40. Rd2 a×b2 41. R×b2 b6 42. Rc2 Kg5 43. Kg2 Rd3 44. c4 Kh4 45. c5 Rg3† 46. Kf1 R×h3 47. c×b6

**William H.K. Pollock (courtesy Cleveland Public Library).**

c×b6 48. Rc6 K×g4 49. R×b6 f5 50. Kg2 Rh5 51. a4 f4 52. Rb5 Rh3 53. Rb6 Rg3† 54. Kf2 Rh3 55. Kg2 f3† 56. Kf2 Rh2† 57. Kg1 Rg2† 58. Kf1 h5 59. Rg6† Kh3 60. Rf6 Kg3 61. Rg6† Kh2 62. Rf6 Ra2 63. R×f3 R×a4 64. Rf2† Kh1 65. Rf3 Rh4 66. Kf2 Kh2 67. Rf5 Rh3 68. Rg5 Rh4 69. Rg2† draw—*The Field*, 10 December 1887.

## (855) Bird–Pollock    ½–½
B.C.A. Congress (round 6)
London, 5 December 1887
*C54*

1. e4 e5 2. Nf3 Nc6 3. Bc4 Bc5 4. c3 Qe7 5. b4 Bb6 6. a4 a5 7. b5 Nd8 8. 0–0 d6 9. d4 f6 Pollock adopts a fairly daunting set-up against Bird's pet line in the Giuoco Piano. **10. Ba3** 10. B×g8 can be considered. Black then has problems disputing White's central control and his king will have a hard time finding a safe shelter. **10. ... Bg4 11. Be2 Ne6 12. Nh4 B×e2 13. Q×e2 e×d4** "Rather shortsighted and losing his advantage. 13. ... Nh6 or 13. ... g6 are better moves"—Pollock. **14. Nf5 Qd7 15. Rd1! g6** Losing valuable time. 15. ... 0–0–0 is perfectly fine for Black after all. **16. N×d4 Nf4 17. Qf3 Ne6** (*see diagram*)

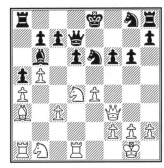

*After 17. ... Ne6*

**18. e5!** Bird continues playing in a spirited fashion. Though facing danger, Black can still ward off the worst. **18. ... f×e5 19. N×e6 Q×e6 20. Q×b7 Rd8** 20. ... Rc8 is the correct defensive move, as the c-pawn remains well defended in case of 21. c4 Bd4 22. R×d4 e×d4 23. Nd2 Ne7. **21. Qc6†** 21. c4! is now particularly strong. Hunting pawns is not to be advised for Black; e.g., 21. ... Q×c4 22. Nd2 Q×a4 (or 22. ... Qe6 23. Ne4 Ne7 24. N×d6† demonstrates White's powerful attack) 23. Qc6† Kf7 24. B×d6. Possible is 21. ... Bd4, but then after 22. R×d4 e×d4 23. Nd2 Ne7 24. Q×c7, White's pawn mass on the queenside forms a considerable power. **21. ... Rd7 22. Nd2 Ne7 23. Qc4 Qd5?** He should play 23. ... Q×c4 and continue playing for a draw. The text move is a blunder. **24. Qe4??** Graver than worse, as not only he misses the simply winning 24. Q×d5 N×d5 25. Ne4, but had Pollock now found 24. ... 0–0!, Bird could have resigned at once. **24. ... Qf7? 25. Rf1 g5?!** Hunting an impossible line of attack. The simple 25. ... 0–0 leads to a balanced game. After the text move, Bird restores his former initiative on the queenside. **26. Nc4 Qd5 27. Qe2 Ng6** It was necessary to support the queenside with 27. ... Nc8. **28. Rfd1 Qb7?!** 28. ... Qe6 is obligatory. **29. N×b6** Not bad but 29. B×d6! wins easily: 29. ... c×d6 30. R×d6, threatening 31. R×g6. **29. ... Q×b6 30. Bc1** Equally good was the thematic 30. c4, as Black's threats are not very real. **30. ... Nf4 31. B×f4 g×f4 32. Rd5** A move with a rather simplistic idea (32. R×e5†). 32. Qg4! forces a structural concession, such as 32. ... Kd8, from his opponent. **32. ... 0–0** 32. ... Rg7 regains control over the kingside. **33. Rad1 Rg7 34. Qf3 Qb8 35. Kh1** Bird allows his opponent to reorganize his forces. At move 33 as well as now, 35. c4! is still very good for him. **35. ... Qe8 36. Qe4 Qh5** The thematic 36. ... f3 puts an eternal thorn into White's kingside, tying at least one of his pieces to the defense of the king. With his next move Bird safeguards his kingside. **37. f3 Rf6 38. Qe1?** 38. R5d2, and if necessary 39. h3, offers more than enough support to the defense. **38. ... Rh6?** Strange; Pollock ordinarily would have found 38. ... R×g2! 39. K×g2 Rg6† 40. Kf1 Q×f3† 41. Qf2 Qh3† 42. Ke1 Rg2 43. Qa7 Q×c3† 44. R5d2 f3 and wins. **39. Qg1 Qh4 40. b6!** "Very well played, although truly he has little else to do"—Pollock. **40. ... c×b6 41. R×d6 R×d6 42. R×d6 Rg6 43. R×g6†?!** Equivalent to agreeing to a draw. If he wanted to realize his positional edge, it was necessary to keep the rooks on the board. **43. ... h×g6 44. Qd1 Qf2 45. h3 Kh7 46. Qb1 Kh6 47. Qe4 Qc5 48. Qe1 Kg5 49. h4† Kf6 50. Qd2 Ke7 51. Qd3 Kf6 52. Kh2 Qc6 53. Qe4?** Bird goes unusually far in trying to win the game. The text move should lose offhand. **53. ... Qc5?** "53. ... Q×e4 54. f×e4 b5 wins at once"—Pollock. **54. Qd3 Qc6 55. Qc2 Ke7 56. Kh3 Qe6† 57. g4 Qc4 58. Kg2 b5 59. a×b5 Q×b5 60. c4 Qc5 61. g5 Qe3 62. Qb2 a4 63. Qb7† Kd8 64. Qb8† Kd7 65. Qb5† Kd6** draw—*Pollock Memories* (Pollock), pp. 45–46.

**(856) Lee–Bird    ½–½**
B.C.A. Congress (round 7)
London, 6 December 1887
*Game score missing*

**(857) Bird–Gunsberg    0–1**
B.C.A. Congress (round 8)
London, 7 December 1887
*C77*

**1. e4 e5 2. Nf3 Nc6 3. Bb5 a6 4. Ba4 Nf6 5. d3 d6 6. Nc3 h6 7. 0–0 Bg4 8. h3 Bh5 9. Ne2** Bird is seeking complications—but allowing Gunsberg to mutilate his pawn structure is not recommendable. **9. ... B×f3 10. g×f3 Qd7 11. Kh2 d5 12. c3 Rd8 13. Ng3 b5** He waited a long time but finally played this important move. **14. Bc2 d4 15. a4 Bd6** Bird's last move was rather weak, but Gunsberg fails to make optimal use of it with 15. ... d×c3 16. b×c3 b4! and the d4-square falls into his hands. **16. Rg1 g6 17. a×b5 a×b5 18. Bd2 Nh7 19. Kg2 f5** 19. ... Ng5 20. Rh1 Ne6 is still good for Black. The text move gives Bird a chance to open up the game for his bishops. **20. Rh1** 20. e×f5! g×f5 21. f4 is suddenly very promising. If 21. ... e×f4 22. Qh5† Qf7 23. Rge1† Ne7 24. Bb3. **20. ... f4 21. Ne2 Bc5 22. Ra6** An expedition that leads to nothing. 22. Bb3, activating the bishop, is the clue to an equal game. If 22. ... d×c3 23. B×c3. **22. ... Bb6 23. b4** A very weakening move. **23. ... Ng5 24. h4 Nf7 25. Qg1 Ke7 26. Qh2 g5 27. Qh3 Qd6** He could reach an excellent endgame after 27. ... Q×h3† 28. R×h3 Rhg8 29. Kf1 Ra8 30. R×a8 R×a8 31. Nc1 d×c3 and the same weakened pawn structure presages heavy going for Bird. **28. Bb3** Once again, the activation of this bishop is the best way to obtain play. **28. ... Rdf8** *(see diagram)*

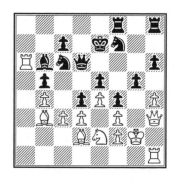

*After 28. ... Rdf8*

**29. c×d4?!** Very strong is the surprising 29. c4! After the forced 29. ... b×c4 30. B×c4, Black's pieces on the queenside are hemmed in. An immediate reorganization, by playing 30. ... Nb8, followed by 31. ... Qd7 is best. If instead 30. ... g4?!, White is much better after 31. f×g4 N×b4 32. Ra4 Nc6 33. Rha1. **29. ... g4! 30. f×g4 N×d4** A serious oversight, but it is understandable that both players miss the consequences of Black's last move: Instead 30. ... Ng5! gains the queen, although after 31. h×g5 f3† 32. Q×f3 R×f3 33. K×f3 N×d4† 34. N×d4 Q×d4 35. R×b6 c×b6 36. Be3 Q×d3 37. Bd5, the position is quite difficult, if even possible, to win for Black. **31. N×d4 Q×d4 32. R×b6** The simple 32. Be1 consolidates the extra pawn. The sacrifice is not necessary, but it warrants interesting complications. **32. ... Q×b6 33. Rc1 Rhg8 34. Rc5 Qd6 35. Bd5 Qd7 36. f3 Rg6 37. h5?!** This only helps his opponent to activate his pieces. 37. Bc3 retains the standstill. **37. ... Ra6 38. Qh1 Kf6** The position is very tense. Each move can see the initiative switch from side to side (which happens incessantly). 38. ... c6! is a concrete improvement. Piling up on the c-file by 39. Qc1 is met by the equally refined 39. ... Rd8!, getting equal play after 40. Be1 c×d5. **39. Qc1 c6 40. B×c6** Bird wants to cash in, but 40. B×f7 R×f7 41. Qc3 is the way to go. White wins a second pawn with a great position. **40. ... Qa7?** 40. ... Qd4! keeps the game tense but equal. The text move should lose. **41. B×b5** Not bad but 41. Bd5! wins quickly, as Black can do nothing against the infiltration of White's heavy pieces; e.g., 41. ... Qb8 42. Rc7 or 41. ... Ra1 42. Qc3 Qa3 43. Rc6† Kg7 44. Rg6† Kh7 45. Qc6. **41. ... Ra1 42. Qc3 Rc8** 42. ... Ra3 is necessary to prolong the game. The rook will continue to harass the queen. She might go to e2 while preserving attacking chances. **43. Bc4 R×c5 44. b×c5 Nd6** "And this hazardous move is the connecting link of the combination alluded to in the previous note. The conception is very pretty, but should have proved disastrous for Black had Bird not been too precipitate with his reply"—Hoffer. Alternatively 44. ... Qa3 loses after 45. c6! and 44. ... Rb1 after 45. Bd5. **45. B×f4?** "Here White could have announced mate in two moves with 45. Q×e5 K×e5 46. Bc3 mate. This beautiful mate was discovered by Bird in showing the game to the spectators after its conclusion. The game would have been a perfect gem with this termination. The text move lost the game right off, and secured Gunsberg his prominent position"—Hoffer. **45. ... N×c4 46. d×c4?** There is still a draw possible after 46. Q×c4 e×f4 47. Qd4† Kf7 48. Qd5† Kg7 49. Qe5†. **46. ... Qa2† 47. Bd2 Rd1 48. Kf2 R×d2† 49. Ke3 Rh2** White resigns—*The Field* (Hoffer), 10 December 1887.

**(858) Zukertort–Bird    1–0**
B.C.A. Congress (round 9)
London, 8 December 1887
*C30*

**1. e4 e5 2. Nc3 Bc5 3. f4 d6 4. Nf3 Nf6 5. Bc4 0–0 6. d3 c6 7. f×e5 d×e5 8. Bg5 Nbd7 9. Qd2 b5 10. Bb3 a5 11. a4 Qb6** Allowing 12. B×f6 N×f6 13. N×e5, which Zukertort strangely omits to do. 11. ... b4 is the correct move. **12. Nh4 Ng4** An optimistic outburst of activity. **13. Nf5 Ndf6 14. h3?** This loss of time allows Bird to insert a wonderful knight into the heart of White's position. Zukertort could secure himself with enough counterplay with 14. N×g7!, hampering Bird's kingside. A possible continuation then would have been 14. ... Bf2† 15. Ke2 K×g7 16. Bh6† Kh8 17. B×f8 Be3 18. Qe1 Bf2 19. Qc1 Be3 20. Qf1 Bg5 21. Qg1 Be3 and a draw is unavoidable. **14. ... B×f5! 15. e×f5 Be3 16. B×e3 N×e3 17. g4 Rad8 18. Qf2** *(see diagram)* As ugly as it looks, 18. Ke2 had to be played.

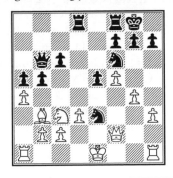

After 18. Qf2

**18. ... Qd4?** Much too slow and therefore losing all of his advantage. The crafty 18. ... e4! doesn't permit White the luxury of keeping the position closed—with 19. d×e4 (or 19. g5 e×d3 20. g×f6 Rfe8) 19. ... Rfe8 20. Qf3 Qd4 White is completely helpless, thanks to the magnificent knight at e3. **19. Rg1** 19. Ke2 forces some key exchanges. **19. ... e4** Far stronger is 19. ... Rde8, for the subtle reason that after 20. Rg3 b4! is possible, as his queen is still defended. After 21. Nd1 N×d1 22. Q×d4 e×d4† 23. K×d1 Re5, White's set-up is spoiled, and the control over the e-file promises Black the better endgame. Worse is 20. Ke2? for the king is bound to perish after 20. ... e4! **20. Rg3 b4?!** The false choice, after which Bird gets an endgame with a pawn down. After 20. ... e×d3! 21. R×e3 b4 22. Nd1 d×c2 23. B×c2 Rfe8 the position of White's king gives him enough compensation. **21. Q×e3 e×d3 22. Q×d4 R×d4 23. R×d3** Good enough, but he could easily save the piece with 23. Nd1. **23. ... R×d3 24. c×d3 b×c3 25. b×c3 Rb8 26. Rb1 Nd5 27. Kd2 g5?!** The endgame is already rather good for White, the text move makes it even better. Bringing the king to f8, thus liberating the knight, might enable him to play for a draw. **28. f×g6 *e.p.* h×g6 29. h4** 29. Kc1! forces the exchange of some pieces and wins easily. **29. ... Kg7 30. Ba2 R×b1 31. B×b1 Nf6** 31. ... g5! was the last chance to make something of it. **32. g5 Nd5 33. d4 f5 34. g×f6 *e.p.* K×f6 35. Be4 Ne7 36. Ke3 Ke6 37. Kf4 Kf6 38. c4 Ke6 39. B×c6 Nf5 40. d5† Kf6 41. c5 N×h4 42. d6 g5† 43. Kg4 Ng6 44. Be4 Ne5† 45. Kh5 Nc4 46. Bd5 Ne3 47. c6 Nf5 48. c7 N×d6 49. Bb7** Black resigns—*Morning Post*, 9 December 1887.

---

# ◆ Part X ◆

# SETTLING AT THE DIVAN, 1888–1890

## TOURING THE NORTH, JANUARY–FEBRUARY 1888

In the beginning of the new year Bird returned to some northern chess clubs where he had already been in October. On Wednesday 31 January he played 30 games simultaneously at the Sunderland Chess Club. He conceded only two draws. On the next two days he gave exhibitions in Newcastle, scoring respectively 13 wins and 3 losses (against Vaughan, Kersey and Greenwell) and then 18 wins, a draw and a loss against Dr. Newton. Bird finished his small tour against 12 opponents on 3 February in Sunderland. He lost twice, against Gibson and Halcro, and won the other games. On 16 February Bird gave an exhibition against 21 opponents in Newport. No result of this meeting is known, but one game gained some notice:

**(859) Hutchins–Bird    0–1**
Simultaneous game
Newport, 16 February 1888
*C45*

**1. e4 e5 2. Nf3 Nc6 3. d4 e×d4 4. N×d4 Qh4 5. N×c6 b×c6 6. Bd3 Nf6 7. 0–0 Bc5 8. Qf3 h5 9. h3 d6 10. e5 Ng4 11. Q×c6†**

Kd8 12. Q×a8 Qg3 13. Bf4 Q×f4 14. g3 B×f2† 15. Kh1 Q×g3 16. Qg2 Bb7 17. R×f2 Qh2 mate—*Chess Monthly*, March 1889, p. 211.

## QUARRELING WITH SKIPWORTH

Skipworth's last minute withdrawal from the B.C.A. tournament at the end of 1887 had raised some instant anger. Just a few months later the man ended up in argument again. Through his column of the *Lincoln, Rutland and Stamford Mercury* of 2 March 1888 he informed the chess world that he had issued a match challenge to Zukertort, the former contender for the world championship title. The challenge was picked up by the national press. Skipworth was generally condemned for showing so little respect for the much stronger player whose play and health were visibly affected by the events of the last years. Not only Leopold Hoffer, who was always on the first rank when it came to denigrating the cleric, but also Bird was agitated by this challenge. In a letter published in *Chess Monthly* (May 1888, p. 261), Bird issued a typical counterproposal: "I now beg to say that, having regard to the decisive beating which I gave you in our match at the St. George's and our relative estimate of force, I feel quite justified and prepared to play you a match at any time, conceding the odds of pawn and move." Skipworth not only promptly accepted but also requested that stakes running as high as £10 per side would be brought in.[1]

Bird showed his astonishment and turned down Skipworth's condition.[2]

## HANDICAP TOURNAMENT AT SIMPSON'S DIVAN, MARCH–APRIL 1888

The way Bird's project to celebrate Queen Victoria's Jubilee had been hijacked by Hoffer and his B.C.A. had an impact in London chess circles. Many chess players and supporters condemned the way Hoffer had treated the popular Bird. In their mind Hoffer and

his organizations, the B.C.A. and the British Chess Club, had become too dominant.[3]

The malcontents united at Simpson's Divan, which had remained the meeting point for many adherents of the game. With the recent developments it was considered the perfect location to come up with alternative tournament activities outside the B.C.A. and C.C.A. A first initiative was the organization of a handicap tournament. Bird played a major role in invigorating chess at the Divan. The first handicap tournament was officially organized by Lee with the support of J.D. Henley, the proprietor of Simpson's. Bird would regularly take his responsibility and act as the tournament's secretary during the following years. His impact is illustrated by the abrupt suspension of the regular series of handicap tournaments when he fell ill at the end of 1890.

The prize fund consisted originally of £15. Two-thirds of this amount was reserved for the winner. With 18 players entering the field the tournament was an unexpected success and the prizes were increased. Game scores were sold at 5s. each to cover the extra cost. Ultimately five prizes were offered. The exact amounts are unknown.

The players were divided in five classes. Eight familiar names were allotted to the first class: Bird, Gunsberg, Lee, Mason, Mortimer, Pollock, Zukertort and Oscar Conrad Müller. The latter, a young German player, had just arrived in London. A scheme of pairings, drawn up before the start of the tournament, gave special attention to a balanced division of games with the White and Black pieces between first-class players.

Bird was one of the strongest starters. After eight games he had lost only against Mortimer. Bird was full of confidence for the outcome. The *Manchester Guardian* of 5 April noted that he had loudly declared that "the young ones are not in it this time." A loss against Gunsberg put Bird's opponent on the road to tournament victory. Mason, by also winning a crucial game against Bird, was underway to the second place. Bird lost a fourth game against Pollock, but this was no threat to his third place. Considering his ailing health, this result was quite good.[4]

On 28 April, with just a few less important games remaining, the success of the tournament was celebrated with a dinner where Bird took the chair. Besides entertaining the public, he handed over the brilliancy prize to Pollock for his win against Lee.

### (860) Zukertort–Bird    0–1
Handicap tournament
London, 10 April 1888
*C30*

---

1. Skipworth's reply was published in his column in the *Lincoln, Rutland and Stamford Mercury* on 15 June 1888: "At first I thought your challenge, of a weeks ago, to play me a match at pawn and move was a joke or something of that nature, and I treated it in my reply accordingly, but I have lately learnt that you have spoken about the challenge in public, and it would therefore seem that you meant what you said. Anyway I will now consider the challenge as a bona fide one, and I beg to say that I have pleasure in accepting it…. That each party within a week from the date of the letter (May 21) should deposit £10 as a stake in the hands of the hon. sec. of the St. George's Chess Club, London, Mr. Minchin, a mutual friend. (A friend of Mr. Skipworth would find the £10, he as a clergyman preferring not to do so.)"

2. Bird was asked for his reply by Hoffer, who explained his amazement to Skipworth's behavior: "Mr. Bird, who is, we are sorry to state, seriously ill, informs us that he will reply to Mr. Skipworth as soon as able to do so. In the meantime he desires us to state that, having on the occasion of their match on even terms obliged Mr. Skipworth by agreeing to play for a nominal stake, or nothing, is a little surprised that a stake of £10 is named upon this occasion and considers it quite unnecessary, especially so as Mr. Skipworth, being a clergyman, should prefer not to find the stakes. The only object Mr. Bird has in view is to test Mr. Skipworth's real strength, and to put a stop to the long series of articles which have appeared in Mr. Skipworth's chess column." *Chess Monthly*, June 1888, p. 292.

3. In the *Illustrated Sporting and Dramatic News* of 19 May 1888, MacDonnell supported the initiative taken at the Divan for "The management of tourneys should never be confined to any one man, no matter how capable or independent he may be, but should always be assigned to a committee, and the best of all committees for such a purpose is the whole of the competitors, or a select number chosen therefrom by the competitors themselves. The signal success that attended the recent tournament at the Grand Divan was, no doubt, owing in a great measure to the adoption of self-government."

4. "What shall I say of our old veteran, H.E. Bird, with his good score of 13 out of 17, and that score made whilst suffering from indisposition? He is in some respects a wonder, for age and infirmity combined do not seem to impair the force and vigor of his play. He lost to Gunsberg, Mason, Mortimer and Pollock, but won all his other games in good style. His play at odds has always been of a 'slashing' style, and it was so during the present encounter, and the 'weaker brethren' went down like shuttlecocks before the old man." *British Chess Magazine*, June 1888, p. 280.

## Handicap tournament, London, 22 March–3 May 1888

*Site:* Simpson's Divan
*Prizes:* Five prizes. 1st £10
*Time limit:* 20 moves per hour
*Odds scale:* two moves (class II), pawn and move (class III), pawn and two moves (class IV) and knight (class V)

| | | | 1 | 2 | 3 | 4 | 5 | 6 | 7 | 8 | 9 | 10 | 11 | 12 | 13 | 14 | 15 | 16 | 17 | 18 | |
|---|---|---|---|---|---|---|---|---|---|---|---|---|---|---|---|---|---|---|---|---|---|
| 1 | I. Gunsberg | I | | ½ | 1 | 1 | 1 | 1 | 1 | 1 | 1 | 1 | 1 | 1 | 1 | 1 | 1 | + | 1 | + | 16½ |
| 2 | J. Mason | I | ½ | | 1 | 1 | 1 | | 1 | 1 | ½ | 1 | 1 | 1 | 1 | 1 | 1 | + | 1 | + | 15 |
| 3 | H.E. Bird | I | 0 | 0 | | 1 | 1 | 0 | 1 | 0 | 1 | 1 | 1 | 1 | 1 | 1 | 1 | + | 1 | 1 | 13 |
| 4 | T.C. Gibbons | V | 0 | 0 | 0 | | 1 | ½ | 0 | 1 | 1 | 1 | 1 | 1 | 0 | 1 | 1 | + | + | + | 11½ |
| 5 | E.L. Sellon | IV | 0 | 0 | 0 | 0 | | 1 | 1 | 1 | 0 | 1 | 0 | 1 | 1 | 1 | 1 | + | + | + | 11 |
| 6 | W.H.K. Pollock | I | 0 | | 1 | ½ | 0 | | 0 | 1 | 1 | 0 | 1 | 1 | 1 | 0 | 1 | + | + | + | 10½ |
| 7 | J.H. Zukertort | I | 0 | 0 | 0 | 1 | 0 | 1 | | 1 | 1 | ½ | ½ | ½ | 1 | 1 | 1 | + | + | + | 10½ |
| 8 | J. Mortimer | I | 0 | 0 | 1 | 0 | 0 | 0 | 0 | | 1 | 1 | ½ | 1 | 1 | 1 | 1 | + | + | + | 10½ |
| 9 | F.J. Lee | I | 0 | ½ | 0 | 0 | 1 | 0 | 0 | 0 | | ½ | 1 | 0 | 1 | 1 | 0 | + | 1 | + | 9 |
| 10 | H. Hicks | V | 0 | 0 | 0 | 0 | 0 | 1 | ½ | 0 | ½ | | 0 | 1 | 1 | 1 | 1 | + | + | + | 9 |
| 11 | O.C. Müller | I | 0 | 0 | 0 | 0 | 1 | 0 | ½ | ½ | 0 | 1 | | 1 | 1 | ½ | 1 | + | + | + | 8½ |
| 12 | F.L. Kinderman | V | 0 | 0 | 0 | 0 | 0 | 0 | ½ | 0 | 1 | 0 | 0 | | 1 | | 1 | + | + | + | 6½ |
| 13 | Rolland | V | 0 | 0 | 0 | 1 | 0 | 0 | 0 | 0 | 0 | 0 | 0 | 0 | | 1 | 1 | + | + | + | 6 |
| 14 | J.B. Purchase | V | 0 | 0 | 0 | 0 | 0 | 1 | 0 | 0 | 0 | 0 | ½ | | 0 | | 1 | + | + | + | 5½ |
| 15 | W. Gaitskill | V | 0 | 0 | 0 | 0 | 0 | 0 | 0 | 0 | 1 | 0 | 0 | 0 | 0 | 0 | | + | + | + | 4 |
| 16 | W.P. Ball | II | – | – | – | – | – | – | – | – | – | – | – | – | – | – | – | | – | 1 | |
| 17 | T.F. Evans | IV | 0 | 0 | 0 | – | – | – | – | – | 0 | – | – | – | – | – | – | + | | | |
| 18 | Jackson | V | – | – | 0 | – | – | – | – | – | – | – | – | – | – | – | – | 0 | | | |

**1. e4 e5 2. Nc3 Bc5 3. f4 d6 4. Nf3 a6 5. Bc4 Nf6 6. d3 Be6** "Mr. Bird played the same move on a previous occasion against Zukertort, but it can hardly be recommended, as Black remains with a weak double pawn"—Hoffer. **7. B×e6 f×e6 8. f×e5 d×e5 9. Ne2** "White could capture the e-pawn, and reply to 9. ... Qd4 with 10. Ng4 N×g4 11. Q×g4 Qf2† 12. Kd1 etc."—Hoffer. **9. ... Nc6 10. Ng3 Ng4 11. Qe2 0–0 12. h3? Nf6?** Zukertort's last move, a bad one, could have been exploited by 12. ... Nf2! (a move out of the question, according to Hoffer) 13. Rf1 Nd4! 14. N×d4 Q×d4. **13. Be3 B×e3 14. Q×e3 Nd4 15. 0–0–0 Qd6 16. c3 Nc6** 16. ... N×f3 is perfectly safe and probably leads to a draw. Bird prefers to keep the pieces on the board and generate an attack on the queenside. Zukertort anticipates perfectly and obtains the better chances. **17. Kb1 b5 18. Ne2 b4 19. d4! b×c3** 19. ... e×d4 is absolutely necessary. 20. c×d4 gives White an ideal center and the advantage. **20. d×e5 Qb4 21. N×c3 Rab8 22. Rd2** 22. b3! forces the knight to h5. **22. ... Nd7 23. Qg5** The queen goes out on the rim. 23. b3 is correct. **23. ... h6** 23. ... Na5 is interesting. Black's knights rapidly approach the king. **24. Qg6 Rfe8** *(see diagram)*

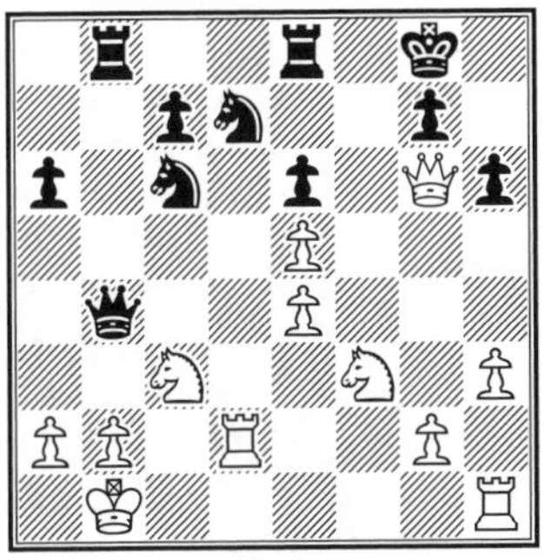

*After 24. ... Rfe8*

**25. Qg3?** Zukertort's position deteriorates rapidly from this point onward. One possibility was 25. Nd5 (Hoffer) 25. ... e×d5 26. Q×c6 and now 26. ... Q×e4† instead of 26. ... d×e4 keeps a pull. Also playable was 25. Ka1 and if now 25. ... Nd×e5 26. N×e5 N×e5 27. Qg3 Nc4 28. Rc2 and everything is defended. The dangerous-looking 25. ... Na5 can be coolly met by 26. Rf2 Nc4 27. Ng5 and Black is forced to admit perpetual check. **25. ... Nc5 26. Qg6 Na5** He was hoping for 26. ... Q×c3?? 27. Q×e8† wins. **27. a3 Qb7 28. Nd1 Nc4 29. Re2 N×a3† 30. Ka2 Qb3† 31. Ka1 Nc2† 32. Kb1 Nb4 33. Nc3 Na4 34. N×a4 Q×a4** and White resigns after two more moves—*The Field* (Hoffer), 14 April 1888.

### (861) Pollock–Bird 1–0
Handicap tournament
London, April 1888
*C48*

**1. e4 e5 2. Nf3 Nc6 3. Nc3 Nf6 4. Bb5 Bc5 5. N×e5 N×e5 6. d4 Bb4 7. d×e5 N×e4 8. 0–0 B×c3 9. b×c3 N×c3 10. Qg4 Qe7 11. Bg5 Qe6 12. Qb4 N×b5 13. Q×b5 b6 14. f4 Bb7 15. Rad1 Qc6 16. Qe2 h6 17. Bh4 Qe4 18. Qg4 g5 19. Rfe1 Qc6 20. f×g5 0–0–0 21. g6 Rdg8 22. g7 Rh7 23. Bf6 h5 24. Qh3 Rh6 25. Re3 Rg6 26. Rd2 Qb5 27. g3 Qc6 28. Red3 Qc5† 29. Kf1 Ba6 30. Q×d7† Kb7 31. Q×f7 R×f6† 32. Q×f6 Qe3 33. Kg2 B×d3 34. R×d3 Qe2† 35. Qf2 Q×e5 36. Qf3† Kb8 37. Qf8† Kb7 38. Qf3† Kb8 39. Rd5 Q×g7 40. R×h5 Qc3 41. Q×c3** Black resigns—*Pollock Memories*, pp. 59–60.

### (862) Bird–Mason 0–1
Handicap tournament
London, 25 April 1888
*A03*

**1. f4 d5 2. e3 Nf6 3. Nf3 e6 4. b3 c5 5. Bb2 a6 6. Bd3 Be7 7. 0–0**

The Divan in the mid–1880s (*Punch*). MacDonnell extensively described the cartoon in the *Illustrated Sporting and Dramatic News* of 11 April 1885: "It is a fancy sketch in some particulars, but at the same time perfectly true to life. The central figure, with hat on head, arms folded, and fun-flashing eyes, is Sir Robert Peel. Next to him is the world renowned J.H. Blackburne ... On the extreme left of the picture is Mr. P.T. Duffy, so long known as the president of the defunct *Westminster Papers*, and now the ruler of the *Illustrated London News* column. Next to him is Mr. Wordsworth Donisthorpe, one of the pillars—a pillar of fire, I may say, for he is a guide as well as support—of the Grand Chess Divan. Over a chess board are two warriors engaged—one of them, with the massive head and beetling brow, is the hero of the last Bath meeting, the Rev. W. Wayte. His opponent ... is ... the world's champion, J.H. Zukertort. Resting on the back of the professor's chair, with flowing beard and amused aspect, is the portly form of G.A. MacDonnell. Between Mr. Wayte and Mr. Duffy, sits, calm and contemplative, the racy writer and acute analyst whose lucubrations weekly grace the pages of *The Field*, L. Hoffer. Between the combatants, peering at the board, shines the genial countenance of the uncrowned king of the City Club, H.F. Gastineau. In front of and to the right of the picture, two brawny personages are portrayed, evidently engaged in friendly duel for Caissa's honors.... In them we recognize J.W. Abbott, the eminent composer, and Thomas Hewitt, a grand tower of strength in the kingdom of chess. ... Behind Mr. Hewitt ... sits ... Mr. Norwood Potter—a striking likeness this, but for the hat, which is not quite high enough. Still further behind the duellists are Mr. E. Thorold and the back of Mr. Horwitz's venerable head.... Two other figures deserve notice; one is that of the quondam champion, W. Steinitz, a player second to no man living.... Sadly looks he, as though musing upon his past triumphs, and mourning over departed friends." It is remarkable that Bird, in 1885, was still conspicuously absent from this sketch and presumably from the Divan as well.

b5 8. Qe1 c4 9. Be2 Nbd7 10. Nc3 0–0 11. Nd1 Bb7 12. Qg3 Rc8 13. Nf2 b4 14. Bd4 Bc5 15. Qh3 B×d4 16. N×d4 Qb6 17. g4 Ne8 18. g5 Nd6 19. Ng4 Nb5 20. N×b5 a×b5 21. Rf3 d4 22. Rg3 Be4 23. d3 Bg6 24. e4 c×b3 25. c×b3 Rc2 26. Bd1 Rc5 27. Nf2 Qd6 28. e5 Qc7 29. Qg4 Bf5 30. Qh4 Rc1 31. R×c1 Q×c1 32. Kg2 Ra8 33. Bg4 R×a2 34. B×f5 e×f5 35. g6 Qc6† 36. Kh3 h×g6 37. Qd8† Nf8 38. Q×d4 Ne6 39. Qe3 g5 40. R×g5 N×g5† 41. f×g5 Qe6 42. Kg3 Q×b3 43. g6 Qe6 44. g×f7† Q×f7 45. Nh3 Qh5 46. Qf4 Qg4† 47. Q×g4 f×g4 48. Ng5 b3 White resigns— *The Field*, 12 May 1888.

# SOME OFFHAND GAMES, SPRING 1888

The following game was printed in the spring of 1888 in a few provincial newspapers. On 26 January 1889 MacDonnell published the game in the *Illustrated Sporting and Dramatic News* with a slightly different finish. Here Bird's opponent was called "Mr. F (Cambridge University)." In later publications (see Bird's visit to Albany just after the chess tournament in New York in 1889 but also *Chess Novelties*, p. 80) the name of Bird's opponent was altered to "Cantab," the Latin-abbreviated nickname of alumni of Cambridge university.

## (863) Unknown–Bird    0–1

Offhand game
London (Simpson's Divan) 1888
C45

**1. e4 e5 2. Nf3 Nc6 3. d4 e×d4 4. N×d4 Qh4 5. Nb5 Bc5 6. Qf3 Nf6 7. N×c7† Kd8 8. N×a8 Re8 9. Bd3 N×e4 10. 0–0 N×f2 11. R×f2 Re1† 12. Bf1 Nd4 13. Bg5†** MacDonnell, publishing the game in the *Illustrated Sporting and Dramatic News* on 26 January 1889, gave another continuation: 13. Q×f7 Ne2† 14. Kh1 R×f1† 15. R×f1 Ng3 mate. **13. ... Q×g5 14. Q×f7** and Black announced mate in five moves—*Bristol Mercury and Daily Post*, 14 April 1888.

## (864) Bird–Three Unknowns    1–0

Consultation game
London (Simpson's Divan) 1888
C30

**1. e4 e5 2. f4 Bc5 3. Nf3 d6 4. c3 Bg4 5. d4** "A somewhat rare continuation, leading to the displacement of the king"—White. **5. ... e×d4 6. c×d4** "If 7. Qa4† Qd7 8. Q×d7 N×d7 and White will lose a pawn"—White. **6. ... B×f3 7. g×f3 Qh4† 8. Ke2 Bb6 9. Rg1** "As the allies need not be afraid of capturing the h-pawn, they have, after this move, a decided advantage in the opening"—White. **9. ... Q×h2† 10. Rg2 Qh6** Retreating the queen to h4 doesn't lose a tempo. **11. f5 Qf6 12. Nc3** "A bold conception, but it is evident that the d-pawn must be abandoned to its fate (12. Be3 Nc6)"—White. **12. ... Q×d4** It was better not to capture this pawn yet and continue with the development; e.g., with 12. ... Nc6 13. Be3 Nge7. Bird has compensation for the pawn, but not enough to claim equality. **13. Q×d4 B×d4 14. Nd5** Much more forcing is 14. Nb5 Bb6 15. Be3! Na6 16. Rc1 Nf6 17. B×b6 a×b6 18. N×c7† with a position that tends to be drawish. **14. ... Na6** 14. ... Kd8 15. Bg5† Kc8 leaves White without compensation for the two sacrificed pawns. **15. Kd1** 15. Be3 B×e3 16. K×e3 Ne7 17. N×e7 K×e7 18. Rc1 is the best continuation. Black loses one of his extra pawns after which White's active rook gives him plenty of play. **15. ... 0–0–0 16. B×a6 b×a6 17. Rc2 c5 18. Bg5 Nf6 19. B×f6 g×f6 20. Kd2 Kd7 21. Rh1** *(see diagram)*

**21. ... Rdg8** 21. ... h5 keeps better chances to win. The text move allows a strong reply. **22. Rh6 Rg2† 23. Kd3 R×c2** This exchanges

*After 21. Rh1*

off his only active piece. **24. K×c2 Rg8 25. R×h7 Rg2†** Hoping that exchanging all the pawns will bring them a draw, but they underestimate the perilous situation their king is facing. Better is 25. ... Ke8 which keeps the activity of the adverse rook limited to the kingside. **26. Kd3 R×b2 27. R×f7† Ke8 28. R×a7 R×a2 29. Nc7† Kd8 30. Kc4! Ra4†?** The fatal error. 30. ... Rd2 doesn't abandon the d-pawn, as happened in the game. White retains strong pressure, but a breakthrough is not in sight; e.g., 31. Ne6† Ke8 32. R×a6 Kd7 33. f4 Be3. **31. Kd5 Be3 32. f4!** "This elegant and effective stroke may have been overlooked by Black. It is quite fatal, of course"—White. **32. ... Rd4† 33. Kc6 R×e4 34. f×e5 R×e5 35. K×d6 Kc8 36. Kc6 Kd8 37. Ne6† Ke8 38. Kd6 R×e6† 39. f×e6** and the Black allies resign—*Leeds Mercury* (White), 7 July 1888.

# HANDICAP TOURNAMENT AT THE BRITISH CHESS CLUB, JUNE–JULY 1888

Hoffer's response to the handicap tournament at the Divan came quickly. A month later a similar event was set up at the British Chess Club. Hoffer went one up on the Divan by offering six instead of five prizes. The first prize consisted of £12 instead of the £10 at Simpson's.

On 5 June, 15 participants opened the fights. The field of top players was largely the same as at Simpson's, with the addition of Blackburne. At the last moment Mason decided to withdraw.

The tournament ran quite fluently. After two weeks of play Bird was leading (+8 −1 =1), ahead of Zukertort (+7 −1), apparently in much better shape than the month before, and George Edward Wainwright (+7 −2). The two favorites, Gunsberg and notably Blackburne (who had paused his tournament games for a while due to a provincial engagement), were seriously lagging in number of games played. As the first-class players still had to meet each other nothing was decided yet.

Then, on the evening of 19 June, the tournament was struck by a tragedy. While playing at Simpson's, Zukertort suffered a stroke. He was first brought to the British Chess Club and only then to the hospital. It was too late to hope for his recovery and he died the next morning. The tournament was suspended for a week and then resumed. It ended around 17 July. Ultimately Blackburne and Gunsberg came out on top. They shared the first and second prize without playing a tie-break match.

## Handicap tournament, London, 5 June–17 July 1888

**Site:** British Chess Club
**Prizes:** 1st £12, 2nd £10. Four other prizes £13 in total, so presumably 3rd £6, 4th £4, 5th £2, 6th £1
**Time limit:** 20 moves per hour
**Odds scale:** two moves (class II), pawn and move (class III), pawn and two moves (class IV), knight (class V) and rook (class VI). Odds for classes
    VIII and IX unknown. = used for Zukertort's unplayed draws

|   |   |   | 1 | 2 | 3 | 4 | 5 | 6 | 7 | 8 | 9 | 10 | 11 | 12 | 13 | 14 | 15 |    |
|---|---|---|---|---|---|---|---|---|---|---|---|----|----|----|----|----|----|----|
| 1 | J.H. Blackburne | I |   | ½ | = | 1 | 1 | 0 | 1 | 1 | 1 | 1 | 0 | 1 | 1 | 1 | 1 | 11 |
| 2 | I. Gunsberg | I | ½ |   | 0 | 1 | 1 | 1 | 0 | ½ | 1 | 1 | 1 | 1 | 1 | 1 | 1 | 11 |
| 3 | J.H. Zukertort | I | = | 1 |   | = | 0 | = | = | 1 | 1 | 1 | = | = | 1 | 1 | 1 | 10 |
| 4 | H.E. Bird | I | 0 | 0 | = |   | 1 | 1 | 0 | 1 | 1 | 1 | ½ | 1 | 1 | 1 | 1 | 10 |
| 5 | G.E. Wainwright | II | 0 | 0 | 1 | 0 |   | 1 | 1 | 0 | 1 | 1 | 1 | 1 | 1 | 1 | 1 | 10 |
| 6 | W.M. Gattie | I | 1 | 0 | = | 0 | 0 |   | 1 | 1 | 0 | 1 | 1 | 0 | 1 | 1 | 1 | 8½ |
| 7 | W.H.K. Pollock | I | 0 | 1 | = | 1 | 0 | 0 |   | 1 | 0 | 0 | 1 | 1 | 1 | 0 | 1 | 7½ |
| 8 | J. Mortimer | I | 0 | ½ | 0 | 0 | 1 | 0 | 0 |   | 1 | 0 | 0 | 1 | 1 | 1 | 1 | 6½ |
| 9 | A. Michael | II | 0 | 0 | 0 | 0 | 0 | 1 | 1 | 0 |   | 1 | 1 |   | ½ | 1 |   | 5½ |
| 10 | V. Jetley | V | 0 | 0 | 0 | 0 | 0 | 0 | 1 | 1 | 0 |   | 1 | 0 | ½ | 1 | 1 | 5½ |
| 11 | W.J. Ingoldsby | V | 1 | 0 | = | ½ | 0 | 0 | 0 | 1 | 0 | 0 |   | ½ |   | 1 |   | 4½ |
| 12 | E.L. Sellon | IV | 0 | 0 | = | 0 | 0 | 1 | 0 | 0 |   | 1 | ½ |   | 0 | 1 | 1 | 4 |
| 13 | H.G.H. Wyman | VIII | 0 | 0 | 0 | 0 | 0 | 0 | 0 | 0 | ½ | ½ |   | 1 |   | 1 | 1 | 4 |
| 14 | Alderson | IX | 0 | 0 | 0 | 0 | 0 | 0 | 1 | 0 | 0 | 0 | 0 | 0 | 0 |   | 1 | 2 |
| 15 | A. Hirschfeld | VIII | 0 | 0 | 0 | 0 | 0 | 0 | 0 | 0 | 0 |   | 0 | 0 | 0 | 0 |   | 0 |

The remainder of Zukertort's games were declared draws. The deceased ended in a shared third place in the company of Bird and Wainwright.

## (865) Bird–Blackburne   0–1

Handicap tournament
London, 7 June 1888
C54

1. e4 e5 2. Nf3 Nc6 3. Bc4 Bc5 4. c3 Nf6 5. b4 Bb6 6. Qb3 0-0 7. d3 d6 8. Bg5 Ne7 9. B×f6 g×f6 10. 0-0 c6 11. d4 d5 12. e×d5 c×d5 13. Be2 Ng6 14. g3 e4 15. Ne1 f5 16. f4 Kh8 17. Ng2 Rg8 18. Na3 Be6 19. Nc2 Rc8 20. Nce3 Rc7 21. a4 a5 22. b5 Qd7 23. Kh1 Rgc8 24. Nd1 f6 25. Nge3 Ne7 26. Ra3 Rg8 27. Ra2 Qe8 28. Rd2 Qf7 29. Ng2 Nc8 30. Nde3 Nd6 31. Qa3 Qf8 32. Bd1 Nc4 33. N×c4 R×c4 34. Qb2 Qh6 35. Ne3 Rc7 36. Rg2 Rgc8 37. Bb3 R×c3 38. B×d5 R×e3 39. B×e6 Rcc3 40. d5 Qh3 41. Rc1 Qg4 42. d6 Qf3 43. Bc4 R×c1† 44. Q×c1 Rc3 45. Qa1 Qe3 46. Bf1 White resigns—*Bradford Budget Observer*, 23 June 1888.

## (866) Pollock–Bird   1–0

Handicap tournament
London 1888
B34

1. e4 c5 2. d4 c×d4 3. Nf3 Nc6 4. N×d4 g6 5. N×c6 b×c6 6. Qd4 f6 7. Nc3 Bg7 8. Bc4 Qb6 9. Qd3 Nh6 10. 0-0 Ng4 11. Qg3 d6 12. h3 Ne5 13. Bb3 Ba6 13. ... h5! 14. Be3 h4 secures Black a comfortable game. **14. Be3 Qb7** *(see diagram)*

**15. f4!** The solid 15. Rfd1 promises White a slight plus but Pollock prefers to complicate the game. Not a bad choice as he runs no risks at all. **15. ... B×f1 16. f×e5 Ba6** It was hard to make a choice. Speaking afterwards, the less materialistic 16. ... Bc4 is perhaps preferable as it keeps the position closed, but in the end it is likely that White's minor pieces outweigh the rook: 17. B×c4 Q×b2

*After 14. ... Qb7*

18. Qe1 Qb4 19. Be6. **17. e×d6 Rd8 18. Bc5** It appears that not too much has happened, but after 18. e5 f×e5 19. d×e7 Q×e7 20. Ne4 Black is already lost. The game continuation is also very strong. **18. ... e×d6 19. B×d6 Bf8 20. e5 B×d6 21. e×d6 Kf8 22. Ne4 Qb6† 23. Kh1 Qd4 24. Re1 Kg7 25. c3 Qe5 26. Q×e5 f×e5 27. Nc5 Bc8 28. Rd1 Bd7 29. Be6 B×e6 30. N×e6† Kf6 31. N×d8 R×d8 32. c4 c5 33. Rd5** and White wins. Bird's resignation comes quite soon after all, as this rook endgame may still be held. Perhaps he wanted to pay tribute to Pollock's magnificent play—*Illustrated London News*, 11 August 1888.

# B.C.A. CONGRESS, BRADFORD 1888

Just a few months after the conclusion of the B.C.A. congress of 1887 everything was set in motion to organize the fourth congress. In February Hoffer found the Bradford Chess Club willing to host a whole set of tournaments. The provincial exploration by the B.C.A. was probably easier to achieve without the rivalry of the nearly defunct C.C.A. It could also be that the generous provincial support for the B.C.A. gave the C.C.A. the death blow.

An attractive prize fund was necessary to fulfill Hoffer's wish to organize an event with international allure. With 18 players affirming their participation success was guaranteed. Apart from the best British players and some amateurs who were more affiliated with the C.C.A., a few strong foreign masters undertook the trip to Bradford: von Bardeleben, Weiss, Taubenhaus and Mackenzie.

**4th Congress of the B.C.A., Bradford, 6–18 August 1888**

***Site:*** Alexandra Hotel
***Playing hours:*** 11 a.m.–3 p.m. and 5 p.m.–9
***Prizes:*** 1st £80, 2nd £50, 3rd £40, 4th £30, 5th £20, 6th £10 entrance fees divided among non-prize winners
***Time limit:*** 20 moves per hour

| | 1 | 2 | 3 | 4 | 5 | 6 | 7 | 8 | 9 | 10 | 11 | 12 | 13 | 14 | 15 | 16 | 17 | |
|---|---|---|---|---|---|---|---|---|---|---|---|---|---|---|---|---|---|---|
| 1 I. Gunsberg | | 1 | ½ | ½ | 1 | 1 | ½ | 1 | 1 | 1 | 1 | 0 | 1 | 1 | 1 | 1 | 1 | 13½ |
| 2 G.H. Mackenzie | 0 | | 0 | ½ | ½ | 1 | ½ | ½ | 1 | 1 | 1 | 1 | 1 | 1 | 1 | 1 | 1 | 12 |
| 3 C. von Bardeleben | ½ | 1 | | ½ | 1 | 0 | 1 | 1 | ½ | 0 | 1 | 1 | 0 | 1 | 1 | ½ | 1 | 11 |
| 4 J. Mason | ½ | ½ | ½ | | 0 | 0 | ½ | ½ | 1 | 1 | 1 | 1 | 1 | ½ | 1 | 1 | 1 | 11 |
| 5 A. Burn | 0 | ½ | 0 | 1 | | 1 | 1 | 0 | 0 | 1 | 1 | 1 | 1 | 0 | 1 | 1 | 1 | 10½ |
| 6 J.H. Blackburne | 0 | 0 | 1 | 1 | 0 | | 0 | ½ | 1 | 1 | ½ | 1 | 1 | 0 | 1 | 1 | 1 | 10 |
| 7 M. Weiss | ½ | ½ | 0 | ½ | 0 | 1 | | ½ | 0 | 1 | 1 | 0 | 1 | 1 | 1 | 1 | 1 | 10 |
| 8 J. Taubenhaus | 0 | ½ | 0 | ½ | 1 | ½ | ½ | | 1 | 0 | 1 | 0 | 1 | 1 | 0 | 1 | 1 | 9 |
| 9 H.E. Bird | 0 | 0 | ½ | 0 | 1 | 0 | 1 | 0 | | 0 | ½ | 1 | ½ | 0 | 1 | 1 | ½ | 7 |
| 10 W.H.K. Pollock | 0 | 0 | 1 | 0 | 0 | 0 | 0 | 1 | 1 | | 0 | 0 | 1 | 1 | 0 | 1 | 1 | 7 |
| 11 C.D. Locock | 0 | 0 | 0 | 0 | 0 | ½ | 0 | 0 | ½ | 1 | | 1 | 1 | ½ | 1 | 0 | 1 | 6½ |
| 12 E. Thorold | 1 | 0 | 0 | 0 | 0 | 0 | 1 | 1 | 0 | 1 | 0 | | 0 | 1 | 1 | 0 | ½ | 6½ |
| 13 J. Mortimer | 0 | 0 | 1 | 0 | 0 | 0 | 0 | 0 | ½ | 0 | 0 | 1 | | 1 | 0 | 1 | 1 | 5½ |
| 14 F.J. Lee | 0 | 0 | 0 | ½ | 1 | 1 | 0 | 0 | 1 | 0 | ½ | 0 | 0 | | 0 | 0 | 1 | 5 |
| 15 J. Owen | 0 | 0 | 0 | 0 | 0 | 0 | 0 | 1 | 0 | 1 | 0 | 0 | 1 | 1 | | 1 | 0 | 5 |
| 16 J.E. Hall | 0 | 0 | ½ | 0 | 0 | 0 | 0 | 0 | 0 | 0 | 1 | 1 | 0 | 1 | 0 | | 0 | 3½ |
| 17 A. Rumboll | 0 | 0 | 0 | 0 | 0 | 0 | 0 | 0 | ½ | 0 | 0 | ½ | 0 | 0 | 1 | 1 | | 3 |
| 18 A.B. Skipworth | | 0 | | 0 | 0 | | | 0 | | | 0 | | | | ½ | | | |

The beginning of the tournament was mainly characterized by another incident involving the Reverend Skipworth. Even after his misbehavior on the previous congress. Hoffer foolishly gave him another chance to create some chaos. Skipworth had lost five out of his first six games when he announced his retirement due to illness. While another forfeit from Skipworth was already enough to bring up an intense war of letters, things were especially set on fire when he tried to get his deposit back. Hoffer informed him that this amount had been divided amongst his six opponents. Skipworth insisted and pointed to the rules of the program that, so he believed, gave him the right to reclaim the money. But he went away empty-handed.[5]

Bird started excellently with two wins against the local player John Edmund Hall and Weiss. This second game became one of Bird's most well-known and memorable games. Bird employed one of his favorite obscure lines, the Lesser Bishop's Gambit. Though the value of this opening is just as limited as the name it has received, Bird was relatively successful with it. Almost forty years later it got a second life when Tartakower employed it in the tournament of New York 1924.

Bird subsequently suffered two losses against the tournament favorites Gunsberg and Blackburne. After a disappointing draw with Alfred Rumboll, he succeeded in beating Owen and, after another beautiful game, Burn. With 4½ out of 7, he was doing well but then Bird broke down in a way that can only be explained by emerging health problems. From the remaining nine games he drew a few and scored just one win, against a weakly playing Thorold. Bird finished with 7 points, far behind all the strongest players but still ahead of the local amateurs. He received a small consolation prize of £3 16s. 8d. from the entrance fees.

Von Bardeleben had started the tournament impressively with a series of six straight wins. After a few lesser results he was caught up to by Gunsberg, Mackenzie and Mason. Gunsberg, who lost surprisingly in the first round against Thorold, set down a remarkable series of wins. In the twelfth round he won a crucial game against Mackenzie and as he continued to score better than his rivals in the ensuing rounds he secured first place. Mackenzie ultimately took second, ahead of von Bardeleben and Mason. Blackburne and Burn did not fulfill the high expectations of the public.

With his tournament victory Gunsberg not only demonstrated that he was the best British player of the moment, but also that his possibilities still had not reached their limits. Slowly but surely he was joining the short list of possible world championship contenders.

At the B.C.A.'s annual banquet, held at the Alexandra Hotel on 16 August, F.H. Lewis announced that he offered a prize of 10 guineas for a consultation game between Bird and Blackburne, representing England, against von Bardeleben and Weiss, representing Germany [*sic*]. The game was especially remarkable as it appears to have been the second game on English soil that was opened with the Caro-Kann (the first one was Noa–Winawer, London 1883). This opening was already fairly well analyzed by the German and Austrian chess community. The game ended in an eventless draw.

## (867) Hall–Bird 0–1

B.C.A. Congress (round 1)
Bradford, 6 August 1888
*Game score missing*

5. Hoffer's retort was more potent than ever: "It was thought that, after the severe comment so freely expressed in the press about Mr. Skipworth's conduct; his fiasco in Bradford, after clamoring for a match with the late Dr. Zukertort and others; and his losing a match with Mr. Locock, four to one and two draws, before the Bradford congress, would be sufficient to induce the irascible gentleman to seek in the quiet seclusion of Horncastle that oblivion from the unenviable notoriety he has made such efforts to obtain. Mr. Skipworth 'being a clergyman,' the same friend perhaps who was willing 'to find the money' for the stakes in the matches he wanted to play, has also 'found' his deposit money, and hence probably his anxiety to get it back. But we may inform him that it has been divided according to Rule XIV, and was spent the same evening in champagne, the Rev. J. Owen proposing 'Mr. Skipworth's better form.' This toast was duly honored!" *Chess Monthly*, September 1888, p. 9.

## (868) Bird–Weiss    1–0
B.C.A. Congress (round 2)
Bradford, 7 August 1888
C33

**1. e4 e5 2. f4 e×f4 3. Be2** "The Limited Bishop's Gambit, a favorite with Mr. Bird. A variation will be found in Staunton's *Praxis* showing the difficulty for Black of retaining the gambit pawn"—Pollock. **3. ... f5** "This defense, when White has played 3. Bc4, is very old, and, we may add, unreliable. Zukertort, we believe, hit upon this reply to White's last move, and the *Chess Monthly* views it very favorably. The other defenses are 3. ... Qh4† and 3. ... d5. The latter is also favored by Zukertort, and gives Black a good game"—Green. Weiss' choice is rare, but certainly not bad. **4. e5** "If 4. e×f5 then Black would get a good game with 4. ... Qh4† and 5. ... d5"—Green. **4. ... d6 5. Nf3 d×e5 6. N×e5 Qh4† 7. Kf1 Bd6 8. Nf3 Qf6 9. d4 Ne7 10. c4 c6** 10. ... b6 is worth considering. It opens a nice diagonal for the bishop. **11. Nc3 Nd7 12. Bd2 Qh6** Loss of time. 12. ... g5! grasps a lot of space on the kingside and makes it difficult for Bird to demonstrate his compensation for the pawn. **13. c5 Bc7 14. Qb3 Nf6** 14. ... b6! is the thematic move to liberate his pieces. **15. Bc4 Ne4 16. Re1** Weiss' knight moves cost some valuable time that Bird spent well with developing his pieces. With Black's king stuck in the middle, Bird obtained full compensation for the sacrificed pawn. **16. ... N×d2†** "If 16. ... Ng3† 17. Kg1 N×h1 18. d5 c×d5 19. N×d5 Bd8 20. B×f4 Qh5 21. R×e7† Kf8 (best) 22. Re1 and wins"—Pollock. **17. N×d2 Kd8?** A prudent move that surprisingly enough allows Bird to form a decisive attack. Necessary was 17. ... b6, breaking down White's central bind. **18. Nf3 b5 19. Be6** 19. c×b6 *e.p.* a×b6 20. h4 intending 21. Ng5 also gives him a very dangerous attack. **19. ... b4** (*see diagram*)

*After 19. ... b4*

**20. d5!** "An excellent reply, which deprives Black of all power of resistance"—Abbott. **20. ... b×c3** 20. ... c×d5 loses after 21. B×c8 b×c3 22. Be6 Qg6 23. Nd4. **21. d6!** "The right line of play, nothing daunted by Black's efforts to create a diversion"—Pollock. **21. ... Rb8 22. d×e7† K×e7 23. Bd7†?** Both 23. B×c8† Kd8 24. Bb7 (Pollock) and 23. Bg8 win immediately. The text move might have changed the result. **23. ... Kd8 24. Qf7 B×d7** "The only move. Bad was 24. ... Ba6† 25. Kg1 Bd6 26. c×d6 Q×d6 27. Q×g7 Qc5† 28. Nd4 c×b2 29. B×f5 and wins"—Pollock. **25. Rd1 Kc8?** Allowing Bird to decide this well-played game in a beautiful way. At this point, Weiss missed a brilliant chance to prolong the game and perhaps save half a point in doing so: 25. ... Bd6! 26. R×d6! (after 26. Ne5 Qe6 27. Q×e6 B×e6 28. R×d6† Ke7 29. N×c6† Kf7 30. Ne5† a draw is forced) 26. ... Q×d6 27. c×d6 c×b2 28. Kf2 b1Q 29. R×b1 R×b1 30. Q×g7 Re8 31. Ne5 Rb7. So far the moves have been fairly forced. It is clear that White still has some advantage, but it is of much more positional than tactical nature. His best plan is to advance the a-pawn, relocate his knight to c5, and try to pick up some pawns with the queen. Black has to sit tight and fight for a draw. **26. Q×d7† Kb7 27. Rd6 Qh5 28. Q×c6† Kc8 29. Qa6†** Black resigns—*Liverpool Weekly Courier* (Green), 18 August 1888; *British Chess Magazine* (Pollock), September 1888, pp. 372–373; *Illustrated London News* (Abbott), 6 October 1888.

## (869) Gunsberg–Bird    1–0
B.C.A. Congress (round 3)
Bradford, 7 August 1888
B73

**1. e4 c5 2. Nc3 Nc6 3. Nf3 g6 4. d4 c×d4 5. N×d4 Bg7 6. Be3 d6 7. Be2 Nf6 8. 0–0 0–0 9. h3 Bd7 10. Qd2 N×d4 11. B×d4 Bc6 12. Bf3 Qa5 13. a3 b5 14. B×f6 e×f6 15. Q×d6 Rac8 16. Qb4 Qb6 17. Bg4 Rcd8 18. Rad1 h5 19. Be2 a5 20. Qb3 R×d1 21. R×d1 Rb8 22. Nd5 Qb7 23. f3 Re8 24. Bf1 Qb8 25. Nc3 Re5 26. Kh1 Bf8 27. B×b5 Rg5 28. Bf1 Qg3 29. Qb6 Rc5 30. Ne2 Qe5 31. c3 Kg7 32. Qd8 Be7 33. Qd4 Qb8 34. b4 Re5 35. Nc1 Re6 36. Bc4 Rd6 37. Bd5 a×b4 38. a×b4 Rd8 39. Nd3 Bd7 40. f4 Bb5 41. c4 Ba4 42. Rd2 Bd6 43. e5 Be7 44. b5 Qc8 45. Qa7 R×d5 46. c×d5 Qc3 47. Q×e7 Q×d2 48. e×f6†** Black resigns—*Yorkshire Post and Leeds Intelligencer*, 9 August 1888.

## (870) Bird–Blackburne    0–1
B.C.A. Congress (round 4)
Bradford, 8 August 1888
C32

**Max Weiss (*Chess Monthly*).**

1. f4 e5 2. e4 d5 3. e×d5 e4 4. c4 Nf6 5. Nc3 c6 6. Qc2 Bf5
7. Nge2 Bc5 8. Ng3 Bf2† 9. Kd1 B×g3 10. h×g3 0–0 11. Be2 Na6
12. Ke1 c×d5 13. c×d5 Nb4 14. Qb3 Nb×d5 15. N×d5 Q×d5
16. Q×d5 N×d5 17. a3 Rac8 18. b4 Rfd8 19. g4 Bd7 20. g3 f6
21. Bd1 Be6 22. Kf2 Rc7 23. f5 Bf7 24. Re1 Re7 25. Bc2 Rde8
26. Ba4 Rc8 27. Bb2 Nb6 28. Bd1 Nc4 29. Bc3 Rd8 30. Re2 Rd3
31. Rc1 Bd5 32. Re1 N×d2 33. B×d2 R×d2† 34. Be2 e3† 35. Kg1
a6 36. Rc8† Kf7 37. Rd8 Bb3 38. Rh8 Rc7 39. g5 f×g5 40. Bh5†
Kf6 41. Rf8† Bf7 42. B×f7 R×f7 43. R×f7† K×f7 44. R×e3 h5
45. a4 Rb2 46. Re4 Kf6 47. g4 h×g4 48. Re6† K×f5 49. Rb6 g3
50. R×b7 Kg4 51. b5 a×b5 52. R×b5 Ra2 53. Rb8 R×a4 54. Kg2
Ra2† 55. Kg1 Re2 56. Ra8 g2 57. Rb8 Kf3 58. Rf8† Kg3 59. Re8
Rf2 60. Rf8 Rf1† White resigns—*The Field*, 25 August 1888.

## (871) Rumboll–Bird    ½–½

B.C.A. Congress (round 5)
Bradford, 9 August 1888
*Game score missing*

## (872) Bird–Owen    1–0

B.C.A. Congress (round 6)
Bradford, 9 August 1888
*C01*

1. e4 e6 2. d4 c6 3. f4 d5 4. e5 Na6 5. c3 Nc7 6. Be3 b6 7. Nf3
Nh6 8. Be2 Be7 9. 0–0 0–0 10. h3 c5 11. g4 Kh8 12. Rf2 Ne8
13. Nbd2 a6 14. Nf1 Ra7 15. Rg2 c4 16. Ng3 Rg8 There are no
weaknesses in Black's position after 16. ... Ng8, while his counterattack on the queenside must not be underestimated. **17. Ng5 g6**
17. ... Rf8 was still perfectly playable. **18. Nf3 Ng7 19. f5** "The
utmost ingenuity cannot now save the game for Black, who, nevertheless, makes a gallant effort. It must be borne in mind, also, that
Owen, at the critical moment, may very probably have been harassed
by the exigencies of the time limit, and unable to 'get into his new
hour' just when the difficulty of working out the best defense demanded a few minutes' breathing time"—Pollock. **19. ... Nh×f5
20. g×f5 e×f5 21. Qd2 Ne6 22. Rf1** 22. Kh1 and 23. Rag1 is a more
threatening set-up. Now Owen had the time to start up his counterplay with 22. ... b5. **22. ... f4 23. B×f4 N×f4 24. Q×f4 g5** 24. ...
B×h3 is a last desperate try. White should be winning after 25. Q×f7
B×g2 26. K×g2. **25. Q×f7 B×h3 26. Qh5** Winning, but it is a bit
strange that Bird didn't play 26. Rh2. **26. ... B×g2 27. K×g2 Bf8
28. e6** "Bird finishes the game with the same elegance and precision
which characterizes his play throughout the game on his master-
days"—Pollock. **28. ... Rg6 29. Ne5 Rf6 30. Nc6** Black resigns—
*British Chess Magazine* (Pollock), October 1888, pp. 414–416.

## (873) Burn–Bird    0–1

B.C.A. Congress (round 7)
Bradford, 10 August 1888
*A84*

1. d4 f5 "This is [Arnous] de Rivière's defense and was adopted
by Morphy in his match against Harrwitz throughout the contest
after the former had lost the first game in which he had replied 1. ...
d5. The opening has, however, fallen into disfavor and we think
justly, for it either compels Black to retain the d-pawn or else to

leave the e-pawn weak"—Steinitz. **2. e3 e6 3. c4 Nf6 4. Nf3 b6
5. Be2 Bb7 6. 0–0 Bd6 7. Nbd2** "Mr. Burn's favorite development
for the knight. We prefer placing it at c3 and more so now when it
threatens Nb5 at an opportune time, which at least would have
compelled Black to waste a move by a6"—Steinitz. **7. ... 0–0 8. Qc2
c5** Atypical in this set-up. 8. ... Ne4 would have been good for Black.
**9. Rd1 Nc6 10. Nf1 Rc8 11. d×c5 B×c5 12. Bd2 Ne4 13. Be1 Qe8
14. Rac1 Be7 15. Qb1** Burn played his favorite game of just developing his pieces very calmly and getting ready for the storm. Active
plans seem absent. Bird has thus a perfectly fine position and he
correctly starts looking for an attack against his opponent's king.
**15. ... Rf6! 16. b4 Rg6 17. a4** "White has been playing on the
system we generally recommend and especially in this opening,
namely: of leaving the kingside almost to take care of itself and
pressing the attack in the center and on the queenside. But it is essential in adopting that style to look ahead of possible brilliancies
on the part of the opponent at the right time. The simple precaution
by 17. Ng3 was due at this juncture"—Steinitz. **17. ... d6** "For Black
might have instituted an excellent attack at once by 17. ... Ne5. Obviously White could not capture the knight on account of the reply
18. ... Nc3, followed by 19. ... R×g2†"—Steinitz. **18. Qb2** Loss of
time. 18. Ng3 is necessary to relieve some of the pressure. **18. ... Bf6
19. Qa3 Ne5** It was better to play 19. ... Nd8; e.g., 20. a5 Qe7, with
a flexible position. The text move allows Burn to fortify his kingside
after an exchange of knights. **20. N×e5 B×e5 21. f3 Ng5 22. Bg3
Rh6 23. a5** 23. c5 is certainly as interesting. Burn's initiative on the
queenside has become dangerous. **23. ... Qh5** Bird prefers to wager
on an attack instead of the more solid but passive 23. ... B×g3
24. N×g3 Nf7 25. a×b6 a×b6 26. Ra1 Qe7. **24. B×e5?!** "This unnecessary exchange deprives his kingside of a most important protection. 24. Rd2 would have provided against the adverse unpleasant
entrance of 24. ... Ne4 and would have still left him with a telling
superiority on the queenside. Of course if Black then exchanged
bishops, the pawn would have to retake, but this was safe enough"—
Steinitz. 24. Kf2! evacuates the king from the danger zone and provides some additional support to f3. Bird would then have no choice
but to play 24. ... B×g3 25. h×g3 Qf7, when 26. b5! launches a very
strong initiative on the other side of the board. **24. ... d×e5 25. Rd7**
*(see diagram)* 25. c5 makes hell break loose: 25. ... B×f3 26. c×b6
Qg4! (there is no alternative but to sacrifice his whole queenside.
If 26. ... R×c1 27. Q×c1) 27. R×c8† Kf7 28. Ng3 R×h2! This is the
point. Perpetual check is unavoidable after 29. Rf8† K×f8 30. b5†
Kf7 31. K×h2 Qh4† 32. Kg1 Q×g3 33. B×f3 Nh3†.

*After 25. Rd7*

**25. ... B×f3!!** "The combination point has arrived and Mr. Bird
plays now in the highest style"—Steinitz. **26. B×f3** "More difficult

to play against was 26. g×f3, but Black would win with 26. ... N×f3†
27. Kf2 (27. B×f3 leads to the position in actual play) 27. ... Qh4†
28. K×f3 Rg6 29. Ng3 Q×h2 30. Rg1 e4† and wins, for if 31. Kf4
Black mates in a few moves commencing with 31. ... Qh4†"—
Steinitz. 29. Bd3! provides the necessary flight square for the king.
Black has no win after 29. ... e4† 30. Ke2 Rg2† 31. Kd1, making it
necessary for him to settle for a draw. Winning, however, is 26. ...
Nh3† 27. Kh1 Qg6! 28. Ng3 Nf4! **26. ... N×f3† 27. g×f3 Q×f3**
The immediate 27. ... Rg6† should make no difference. **28. Qd3**
"White has no good defense. If 28. Ng3 Rg6 29. Rf1 R×g3†
30. h×g3 Q×g3† 31. Kh1 R×c4 and wins"—Steinitz. **28. ... Rg6†
29. Ng3 h5 30. Rc2?!** 30. Rf1 is the cleanest way to bring Black as
far as forcing the game. After 30. ... R×g3† 31. h×g3 Q×g3† 32. Kh1
Qh4† 33. Kg1 R×c4, 34. Rf4! offers his opponent no choice but to
give a perpetual check. **30. ... h4!** Burn lost some time and as a result
Bird's attack increased in danger. **31. Rd8† R×d8 32. Q×d8† Kh7
33. Rg2?** 33. Q×h4† is the only chance. After 33. ... Rh6 34. Qd8
Q×e3† 35. Rf2 (also possible is 35. Kg2 b×a5 36. b×a5 f4 37. Qd2
Qb3 38. c5 f×g3 39. h×g3 Qa4. It is difficult to estimate whether
Black has real winning chances) 35. ... b×a5 36. b×a5 Qc5, Bird has
just two pawns for the piece but the position of White's king will
always be a source of trouble for his opponent. Added to this, Black's
central pawns have a great potential. Black has the better chances
but each result is still possible. **33. ... h3** 33. ... Q×e3† is more accurate, though the text is certainly sufficient. **34. Ra2** 34. Rf2
R×g3† 35. h×g3 Q×g3† 36. Kf1 h2 37. R×h2† Q×h2 is White's
ultimate try. The endgame should be winning for Black. **34. ... f4
35. a×b6 a×b6 36. Qa8 Q×e3† 37. Kf1 f×g3 38. Qa3 Rf6†** White
resigns—*International Chess Magazine* (Steinitz), September 1888,
pp. 278–279.

## (874) Bird–Taubenhaus    0–1
B.C.A. Congress (round 8)
Bradford, 11 August 1888
*Game score missing*

## (875) Locock–Bird    ½–½
B.C.A. Congress (round 9)
Bradford, 11 August 1888
*C22*

1. e4 e5 2. d4 e×d4 3. Q×d4 Nc6 4. Qe3 Bb4† 5. c3 Ba5
6. Qg3 Nf6 7. Bd3 Qe7 8. Ne2 d6 9. Nd2 Ne5 10. Nc4 N×c4
11. B×c4 Bb6 12. Bd3 Bd7 13. Be3 0-0-0 14. B×b6 a×b6
15. f3 d5 16. e×d5 Nh5 17. Qf2 Nf4 18. 0-0-0 N×d3†
19. R×d3 Bf5 20. Rd2 h5 21. Ng3 Bh7 22. Re1 Qd7 23. Qd4
Bg6 24. h4 Qb5 25. b3 f6 26. Qc4 Q×c4 27. b×c4 Kd7 28. Rde2
Rhe8 29. R×e8 R×e8 30. R×e8 K×e8 31. Kd2 Kd7 32. Ke3
Kd6 33. Kd4 c5† 34. d×c6 *e.p.* b×c6 35. f4 f5 36. Ke3 Ke6
37. Kd2 Be8 38. Kc2 g6 39. Kb3 c5 40. Nf1 Bc6 41. g3 Bf3
42. Ne3 Kd6 43. a4 Kc6 44. Ka3 Be4 45. Kb3 Bf3 46. a5
b×a5 47. Ka4 Kb6 48. Nd5† Ka6 49. Ne7 Bd1† 50. Ka3 Be2
51. N×g6 B×c4 52. Ne5 Kb5 53. Nf3 Bd5 54. Nd2 a4 55. Kb2
Bg2 56. Ka3 Bd5 57. Kb2 Bc4 58. Ka3 draw—*Tournament Book*,
pp. 40–41.

## (876) Bird–Mackenzie    0–1
B.C.A. Congress (round 10)
Bradford, 13 August 1888
*A03*

1. f4 d5 2. e3 g6 3. Nf3 Bg7 4. d4 Nf6 5. c3 b6 6. a4 a6 7. Na3
Bf5 8. b4 Ne4 9. Bb2 e6 10. Be2 Nd7 11. 0-0 h5 12. Nc2 g5 13. b5
a5 14. Ne5 g4 15. Nc6 Qh4 16. Ne1 Nf8 17. g3 N×g3 18. h×g3
Q×g3† 19. Ng2 Be4 20. Rf2 h4 21. Bd3 B×d3 22. Q×d3 h3
23. Raf1 Ng6 24. f5 Nh4 25. Rd2 h×g2 White resigns—*Tournament Book*, p. 44.

## (877) Mason–Bird    1–0
B.C.A. Congress (round 11)
Bradford, 14 August 1888
*A84*

1. d4 f5 2. Nf3 e6 3. e3 Nf6 4. c4 b6 5. Nc3 Bb4 6. Bd2 Bb7
7. Be2 0-0 8. 0-0 a5 9. a3 B×c3 10. B×c3 Ne4 11. Nd2 N×c3
12. b×c3 d6 13. Bf3 c6 14. Rb1 Ra7 15. Qb3 Nd7 16. c5 d5
17. c×b6 Ra6 18. Qa4 R×b6 19. R×b6 Q×b6 20. Rb1 Qc7 21. c4
Ba6 22. Rc1 Qb7 23. Q×a5 Rb8 24. h3 B×c4 25. N×c4 d×c4
26. Qc3 Nb6 27. a4 Ra8 28. a5 Nd5 29. Q×c4 Ra6 30. B×d5
e×d5 31. Qc5 Kf7 32. Qd6 Qe7 33. Qb8 Kf6 34. Rb1 R×a5
35. Rb7 Rb5 36. R×b5 c×b5 37. Q×b5 Qd6 38. Qe8 g6 39. Qh8†
Kg5 40. Q×h7 Qb4 41. g3 Qb1† 42. Kh2 Qe4 43. Qh8 Qg2†
44. K×g2 Black resigns—*Tournament Book*, pp. 51–52.

## (878) Bird–Mortimer    ½–½
B.C.A. Congress (round 12)
Bradford, 14 August 1888
*Game score missing*

## (879) Bird–von Bardeleben    ½–½
B.C.A. Congress (round 14)
Bradford, 16 August 1888
*Game score missing*

## (880) Lee–Bird    1–0
B.C.A. Congress (round 15)
Bradford, 17 August 1888
*Game score missing*

## (881) Bird–Thorold    1–0
B.C.A. Congress (round 16)
Bradford, 17 August 1888
*C33*

1. e4 e5 2. f4 e×f4 3. Be2 Qh4† 4. Kf1 f3 5. B×f3 d6 6. g3 Qf6
7. Nc3 c6 8. Kg2 h5 9. h4 He could easily take the offered pawn.
9. ... g6 10. d4 Bh6 11. e5 d×e5 12. Ne4 Qd8 13. B×h6 N×h6
14. d×e5 Q×d1 15. R×d1 0-0 Thorold came out of the opening
with a fairly acceptable position, but here he makes a stereotypical
move that permits Bird to retain annoying central pressure. Instead
15. ... Nf5 poses his opponent more concrete problems. After
16. Nd6† (worse is 16. Kf2 Nd7 17. Re1 Ke7 18. Ng5 Nb6) 16. ...
N×d6 17. e×d6 Na6 followed by 18. ... Bd7 and 19. ... 0-0-0 equality
is maintained. **16. Nh3 Nf5 17. Rhe1 Na6 18. Nf4 Nc7 19. Nd6**

**Ne6?** A serious overlook after which Black is immediately lost. A decent move was 19. ... Rd8. **20. N×h5 g×h5 21. N×f5 Nf4† 22. g×f4 B×f5 23. B×h5 B×c2 24. Rd7 Bf5 25. R×b7 Be6 26. Bf3 Rab8 27. R×b8 R×b8 28. b3 Rc8 29. Be4 f5 30. Bf3 Rd8 31. Rd1 R×d1 32. B×d1 a5 33. Kf2 Kg7 34. Ke3 c5 35. Be2 Bf7 36. Bc4 Bg6 37. Kd2 Kh6 38. Be2 Bf7 39. Kc3 Kg7 40. a4 Kf8 41. Bc4 Bg6 42. Bd5** Black resigns—*Bradford Observer Budget*, 25 August 1888.

## (882) Pollock–Bird   1–0
B.C.A. Congress (round 17)
Bradford, 18 August 1888
*C41*

**1. e4 e5 2. Nf3 d6 3. d4 f5 4. d×e5 f×e4 5. Ng5 d5 6. e6 Nf6 7. Nf7 Qe7 8. N×h8 B×e6 9. Be2 Nc6 10. Bh5† Kd7 11. Nc3 Rd8 12. 0-0 Kc8 13. Bg5 Ne5 14. Qe2 g6 15. f4 Nc6 16. f5 g×f5 17. Rad1 Qg7 18. Nf7 B×f7 19. B×f6 Q×f6 20. R×f5 B×h5 21. Q×h5 Qe6 22. Qh3 Bc5† 23. Kh1 Bd6 24. Rf×d5 Q×h3 25. g×h3 e3 26. Re1 Re8 27. Rd3 Bf4 28. Nd5 Bh6 29. N×e3 Nb4 30. Rb3 c5 31. a3 Nc6 32. Kg2 b5 33. Rd3 Bf4 34. Kf2 B×h2 35. Nf5 Rf8 36. Rf3 Kd7 37. Rd1† Kc7 38. Ng7 R×f3† 39. K×f3 Nd4† 40. Ke4 Ne2 41. Ne6† Kc6 42. Rd2 Ng3† 43. Kf3 Nf1 44. Rf2 Be5 45. c3 Nh2† 46. Kg2 h5 47. Ng5 Kd5 48. Rf5 b4 49. a×b4 c×b4 50. c×b4 Kd4 51. R×e5 K×e5 52. K×h2 Kd4 53. Ne6† Kc4 54. Nd8 a6 55. Nc6** Black resigns—*Tournament Book*, pp. 73–74.

F.H. Lewis offered a prize of £10 for a consultation game between two British and two continental representatives. The balanced and at first sight uneventful game received a lot of criticism in the press. It was seen as a most boring affair, but in fact both sides played it very well and succeeded in solving all the problems in ingenious ways.

## (883) Bird & Blackburne– Weiss & von Bardeleben   ½–½
Consultation game
Bradford, August 1888
*B18*

**1. e4 c6 2. d4 d5 3. Nc3 d×e4 4. N×e4 Bf5 5. Ng3 Bg6 6. c3 e6**

**7. Nh3 Bd6 8. Be2 Ne7 9. 0-0 0-0 10. Nf4 Nd7 11. N×g6 N×g6 12. Bd3 Qh4 13. B×g6 h×g6 14. f4 g5 15. Ne4 B×f4 16. B×f4 g×f4 17. Rf3 g6 18. Rh3 Qe7 19. Qg4 Kg7 20. Rf1 Rh8 21. R×h8 R×h8 22. Q×f4 e5 23. d×e5 N×e5 24. Nf6 Nd3 25. Qd4 Qe5 26. Q×d3 Q×h2† 27. Kf2 K×f6 28. Ke1† Ke7 29. Qe4† Kd8 30. Qd4† Kc8 31. R×f7 Qg3† 32. Qf2 Re8† 33. Kd2 Rd8† 34. Kc1 Qd6 35. Qf1** draw—*Tournament Book*, pp. 78–79.

The following little game occurred probably more than once in Bird's practice. In *Chess Novelties* (p. 257), Bird reproduced a diagram that greatly resembled the final position. According to Bird here, this position occurred in a game played at Huddersfield in 1885.[6]

## (884) Bird–H.   1–0
Offhand game
Bradford 1888
*C37*

**1. e4 e5 2. f4 e×f4 3. Nf3 g5 4. Nc3 g4 5. Ne5 Qh4† 6. g3 f×g3 7. Q×g4 g2† 8. Q×h4 g×h1Q 9. Qh5 Be7 10. N×f7 Nf6 11. Nd6† Kd8 12. Qe8†** and mate on the next move—*Illustrated Sporting and Dramatic News*, 6 April 1889.

---

# THE ZUKERTORT CHESS CLUB

Bird dedicated a lot of his time in the summer of 1888 to the realization of one of his pet ideas, the introduction of chess among the working classes.[7] His intention was not to emancipate those who were less well off. In November 1887 (p. 437) the *British Chess Magazine* wrote about a speech given by Bird at the Sunderland Chess Club on 5 October 1886 in which the chess master ventured that he wanted them to accept their often wretched situation and try to make the best of it. Bird's concrete attempts to realize these plans popped up in the press for the first time in June 1888.[8]

A few weeks later a club was founded in the East End. Bird decided to memorialize the name of his good friend, the just deceased Zukertort, by naming the club after him.[9] The Zukertort Chess

6.  This game, or better said these moves, has been the subject of an article at Edward Winter's website (see: http://www.chesshistory.com/winter/extra/gamelet.html). Richard Forster directed attention to the December 1910 edition of the *British Chess Magazine* (p. 526) where the same game was said to have been played in Munich in 1907. Three months later (p. 101) a story was published, taken from the *Hull Times*, in which the editor claimed that he played that game in 1904 or 1905. Later the editor discovered that Bird played it earlier in Huddersfield in 1886 [*sic*, he found this date in *Chess Novelties*, p. 257]. A slightly different version of the game was said to be published in the *Cape Times*, going 4. d4 g5 5. Ne5 Qh4† 6. g3 f×g3 7. Q×g4 g2† 8. Q×h4 g1Q 9. Nc3 Nc6 10. Qh5 Be7 11. N×f7 Nf6 and White mates in three. All the versions to be found at the chesshistory website start with 4. Nc3.

7.  Bird had explained his thoughts about the matter a few years earlier, in one of his books: "Chess, regarded as an amusement only, is admittedly a very innocent and pleasing one, yet but a comparatively small portion of the community are fully aware of the enjoyment, and even at times, solace and comfort it affords. As a recreation for the working classes, it is reasonable to assume that it would be highly welcome, and it appears desirable, therefore, to place a knowledge of the various most approved methods of commencing and conducting the opening of the game within their reach in as simple, condensed, and cheap a form as possible. ... The press has, within the past month, fully directed attention to its advantages—harmless, quiet, peaceable, temperate, appeasing, and last not least in importance to the humbler or poorer classes, inexpensive; it requires only to be known to be appreciated." Bird, *Chess Practice*, p. 4.

8.  Bird's "chess mission" met with some critical comments. "A CHESS MISSION [is being pursued] in the East End of London, in order to encourage the noble art amongst the working men of Whitechapel. He believes that men who are inoculated with a love of chess cease to drink hard and to gamble, and he intends to play the pedagogue in a room which he has taken not far from Toynbee Hall. Mr. Barnett and some of his fellow-workers are disposed (I understand) to look favorably on Mr. Bird's experiment." *Bristol Mercury and Daily Post*, 30 June 1888. ¶ Samuel Barnett (1844–1913), an Anglican cleric and social reformer, was the warden at Toynbee Hall, the home of a charity with the same name.

9.  Bird's relations with Zukertort were somewhat ambiguous nevertheless. Both men collided in 1886, when Bird accused Zukertort of attacking English chess notions. Tensions also existed in 1880, at the time of Zukertort's match with Rosenthal. In *Chess History and Reminiscences* (pp. 115–116), however, Bird presents himself as a close friend: "Zukertort lived in the Walworth Road just past my single eleven years lodging—5 Heygate Street, and he voluntarily confided many matters to me during the last twelve months of his life, which were for certain reasons fortunate. His two beautiful daughters, the sole care of his life, are now provided for, one nine years of age, and the other thirteen years of age, are being educated at or near Berlin by Zukertort's mother and his married sister." See also Harding, *Eminent Victorian Chess Players*, pp. 256–258.

Club experienced a tremendous start. Several well-known players, such as Gunsberg and von Bardeleben attended the club to give simultaneous performances.[10]

At the end of September it was reported that the club already counted more than 100 members. Branches were planned in several towns. The young German chess professional O.C. Müller was appointed as a chess teacher.

All enthusiastic messages in the press ended abruptly just a few weeks later. After a simultaneous exhibition by Hoffer, held on 10 October, the name of the club suddenly disappeared from the chess columns. It is certain that the club existed with a lower profile for a few years, but its name cannot be retrieved anymore on the list of British clubs, published in the *Chess Player's Annual* of 1892. Various guesses about the situation might be made. A speculative one is that the excitement around the club waned when the panic caused by Jack the Ripper's murders hit the East End during the fall of 1888.

# A FEW EXHIBITIONS, OCTOBER 1888–JANUARY 1889

On Monday 15 October Bird visited the chess club in Dover for an exhibition. After four hours of play three of his opponents were successful. Buckman managed to beat the veteran while Haward and England achieved a draw.

On 16 November, 27 opponents awaited Bird at the Cambridge Conservative Club. Bird scored 23 victories, 2 draws and 2 losses (against Neville Goodman and Robinson).

Bird's final exhibition of the year was given at Hampstead Hall on 15 December, right in the middle of the handicap tournament at the Divan. Despite his illness and incomplete recovery, Bird could not resist a fulfilling this engagement. Against 18 foes he won 13 and lost 5 games.[11]

A fourth exhibition in four months was given at the Twickenham Chess Club on 14 January. Against 16 opponents Bird was only able to win 9 games. He lost to 5 players, G.E.N. Ryan, C.A.L. Bull, H. Barton, E. Henderson and T. Gwyn. Two opponents, W. Britten and Franci, succeeded in drawing their game.

The few offhand games preserved from this period were probably all played at the Divan. They once again show how popular and entertaining consultation chess still was.

## (885) Lee & Pollock–Bird & Unknown   1–0
Consultation game
London (Simpson's Divan) 1888 (?)
*A02*

**1. f4 f5 2. e3 b6 3. Nf3 Bb7 4. Be2 c5 5. 0-0 Nf6 6. Ne5 e6 7. Bh5† g6 8. Bf3 d5 9. b3 Bg7 10. Bb2 Nc6 11. c4 Qe7 12. c×d5**

10. Around this time Bird gave von Bardeleben a serious beating in offhand chess, winning a series of 18 games with 16 against 2—*Illustrated Sporting and Dramatic News*, 13 October 1888.

11. MacDonnell wrote that "this large number of defeats is a very unusual thing with Bird, and may be attributed to his ill health. He had been in bed nearly all the week, suffering from a bad attack of gout." *Illustrated Sporting and Dramatic News*, 22 December 1888.

e×d5 13. Na3 Ne4 14. d3 N×e5 15. f×e5 Ng5 16. d4 a6 17. Rc1 Rd8 18. Qe1 Ne6 19. Qg3 0-0 20. Be2 c×d4 21. e×d4 f4 22. Qd3 Ng5 23. Nb1 Rf7 24. Ba3 Qe6 25. Nd2 Ne4 26. Bf3 g5 27. h3 Ng3 28. Bg4 Qe8 29. Rfe1 h5 30. e6 Rf6 31. e7 Rb8 32. Be6† Kh8 33. Bd6 Ra8 34. Rc7 R×e6 35. R×e6 Bc8 36. Re1 Bf5 37. Qc3 Qg6 38. Rc8† R×c8 39. Q×c8† B×c8 40. e8Q† Kh7 41. Nf3 g4 42. h×g4 h×g4 43. Q×g6† K×g6 44. Ne5† Kf5 45. Nc6 Bd7 46. Ne7† Kg5 47. Be5 Bf8 48. N×d5 Nh5 49. N×b6 Bc6 50. Rc1 Be4 51. d5 Bb4 52. Rc4 Ba5 53. Bc7 Ng3 54. d6 Bd2 55. R×e4 N×e4 56. d7 Kh4 57. d8Q† Black resigns—*Aspa Chess Miscellanies*, vol. 1.

## (886) Bird & Rushworth–Mason & Pollock   0–1
Consultation game
London (Simpson's Divan), November 1888
*C33*

**1. e4 e5 2. f4 e×f4 3. Be2 d5 4. e×d5 Nf6 5. Nf3 Bd6 6. d4 0-0 7. c4 c5** "A natural and correct rejoinder, but the opening early assumes features of originality and instructiveness"—White. **8. d×c6 e.p. N×c6 9. 0-0 Bg4 10. Nc3 Rc8** "Without reference to the policy of allowing their opponents to establish a powerful passed pawn in the center, Black have developed their game in a classical manner, and in bringing this last piece into play they not only provide a secure retreat for Bg4, but threaten 11. ... B×f3 and 12. ... N×d4"—White. **11. d5** Less compromising was 11. Kh1. **11. ... B×f3 12. B×f3 Ne5** 12. ... Na5 13. b3 Be5 14. Bd2 b5 is an interesting line, but after 15. N×b5!, Black has nothing special. The text move secures them a slight positional advantage. **13. Ne4?** 13. b3 was necessary. It would have been interesting if Black, then, had found 13. ... a6 and 14. ... b5. **13. ... N×e4 14. B×e4 g5** 14. ... R×c4 wins a pawn. If 15. R×f4 f5 16. Bf3 Qb6† 17. Kh1 Ng4! 18. B×g4 B×f4 wins. **15. b3 f5** Black's advantage is considerable anyway. **16. Bc2 Qf6 17. Bb2** "To prevent the loss of the exchange by 17. ... Nf3†"—White. **17. ... Qh6** (*see diagram*)

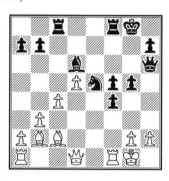

*After 17. ... Qh6*

**18. Qd2 g4?** Too rash. Close to winning was 18. ... Ng4! 19. h3 Ne3 and if White wants to save the rook, 20. ... g4! is decisive. **19. B×e5** After 19. Rae1! Rce8 20. Kh1 White's centralized position renders Black's attack harmless. **19. ... B×e5 20. Rae1 Rce8 21. R×e5** Played with a little trick in mind, but ultimately this combination is not completely sound. The quiet 21. Kh1 would have led to more peaceful positions. **21. ... R×e5 22. R×f4 Qf6** The menace was 23. R×g4†. More precise than the text move was 23. ... Qb6† and 24. ... Qe3, forcing the exchange of queens. **23. c5 Rfe8** Better than 23. ... Rd8?! 24. b4. **24. b4?** Now it was necessary to get e2 covered by 24. Bd3. **24. … Re1† 25. Rf1 Qh4?** 25. … R8e2 wins on the spot. **26. d6?!** 26. g3! wins valuable time, after which the d-pawn becomes a major trump; with 26. … R×f1† 27. K×f1 Qf6 28. d6 Kf8 29. b5, Black has to fight for a draw. **26. … R8e2 27. Qd5† Kg7 28. Qd4† Kg6** Relatively better was 28. … Qf6 29. Qd3 R×f1† 30. K×f1 Re4 31. Qd2 Rd4 with a slight pull. **29. B×f5†! Kh5 30. B×g4† Q×g4 31. Q×g4†?** Being a rook down, the situation looks hopeless for White, but there was an unexpected way to draw the game after all: 31. Qd5† Kh6 32. d7! Q×b4 (32. … R×f1† 33. K×f1 Re4 34. Q×e4 is completely equal as well) 33. Qd6† Kh5 34. Qd5†. **31. … K×g4 32. b5 R×f1† 33. K×f1 Rd2 34. Ke1 Rd5** Black wins—*Leeds Mercury* (White), 8 December 1888.

## (887) Lee & Pollock–Bird & Rushworth　0–1

Consultation game
London (Simpson's Divan), November 1888
C39

**1. e4 e5 2. f4 e×f4 3. Nf3 g5 4. h4 g4 5. Ne5 h5** "Old and sound and pregnant with beauties"—MacDonnell. **6. Bc4 Nh6 7. d4 d6 8. Nd3 f3 9. g3?** "9. g×f3 is generally preferred"—MacDonnell. **9. … f5** "One of Mr. Bird's many ingenious conceptions"—MacDonnell. **10. Nc3** 10. e5 avoids a rapid finish. **10. … f×e4 11. N×e4 Nf5 12. Kf2 Bg7 13. Re1** "A little more than bold, and less than good. They ought to have played 13. c3. But both parties seem in this game to play more for the fun of the thing than for glory or victory"—MacDonnell. **13. … B×d4† 14. Kf1 d5?** Allowing their opponents an unexpected chance, which 14. … Kf8 would have avoided. **15. B×d5?** 15. Bg5! d×e4 16. R×e4† Kf8 17. B×d8 N×g3† 18. Ke1 N×e4 19. B×c7 leads to quite an unclear position. **15. … Q×d5! 16. Nf6† Kd8** White resigns—*Illustrated Sporting and Dramatic News* (MacDonnell), 2 February 1889.

---

# MATCH WITH BLACKBURNE 1888

At the end of November a match between Bird and Blackburne was held at the British Chess Club. The prize money was provided by F.H. Lewis, a barrister and one of the principal patrons of the game in the British capital.[12] Lewis had supported a variety of tournaments and was often especially eager to reward the winner of the brilliancy prize. On this occasion Lewis proposed that all the games should open with the Evans Gambit. Blackburne, however, defended the cause of variety and just two Evans were agreed to be played. Bird won the opening game, but lost then four in a row. Blackburne's striking success was, everyone agreed, more than deserved.[13]

---

12. Lewis died less than a year later: "We deeply regret to announce the death of Mr. Frederic H. Lewis…, which took place on Sept. 23.… Mr. Lewis was a barrister in fine practice, and the brother of Mr. George Lewis, the head of the eminent firm of Lewis and Lewis, solicitors, of Ely Place. He made a munificent use of his simple means, and was quite the largest benefactor to chess of late years in England." *Lincoln, Rutland and Stamford Mercury*, 11 October 1889.
13. Bird complimented his opponent with some exquisite words: "Bird magnanimously said to me a few evenings ago, 'Blackburne's play against me was very grand. I think it was the finest exhibition of combined force and beauty that I have ever seen on Blackburne's part.'" *Illustrated Sporting and Dramatic News*, 22 December 1888.

### Match with Blackburne, 26–30 November 1888

|  | 1 | 2 | 3 | 4 | 5 |  |
|---|---|---|---|---|---|---|
| J.H. Blackburne | 0 | 1 | 1 | 1 | 1 | 4 |
| H.E. Bird | 1 | 0 | 0 | 0 | 0 | 1 |

## (888) Blackburne–Bird　0–1

Match (game 1)
London, 26 November 1888
C51

**1. e4 e5 2. Nf3 Nc6 3. Bc4 Bc5 4. b4 B×b4 5. c3 Bc5 6. 0–0 d6 7. d4 e×d4 8. c×d4 Bb6 9. Nc3 Bg4** "This prevents the favorite continuation 10. Bg5, often adopted in reply to 9. … Na5"—Ranken. **10. Bb5** "Modern analysis prefers this move to 10. Qa4 (Fraser's Attack), which is now considered unsound on account of 10. … Bd7"—Ranken. **10. … Kf8 11. Be3** "He can also play 11. B×c6 b×c6 12. e5 or 12. Be3. In the St. Petersburg–London match game, the text move was followed by 11. … Nge7 12. a4 a5 13. Bc4"—Ranken. **11. … h5** "A favorite move of Mr. Bird. We prefer 11. … Nce7"—Steinitz. **12. a4** 12. B×c6 b×c6 13. h3 is all right for White. Black should certainly have played 12. … B×f3 now. **12. … a6** "12. … Na5 is now Black's best defense. The move in the text compromises his superiority on the queenside"—Steinitz. **13. Be2** "[We] agree with *The Field* that 13. B×c6 b×c6 14. a5 was better, and we would add that White should afterward obtain a strong attack by 15. Qd3"—Steinitz. **13. … Qd7 14. d5** "A good way of pursuing the attack, albeit it involves some exchanges of minor pieces"—Steinitz. "Which leads to a disastrous series of exchanges. It would have been better to play 14. Nd5 and if 14. … Ba7 15. Qd2, bringing Rf1 in action on the queenside"—Ranken. **14. … B×f3 15. B×b6** 15. d×c6! (Steinitz) is definitely better. After 15. … Q×c6 16. B×f3 B×e3 17. Qd3 Bf4, the position is unclear. **15. … B×e2 16. d×c6 b×c6 17. N×e2 c×b6 18. Qb3 Qc7 19. Rac1 Re8** Bird is two pawns up but here he gives one up too easily. At once 19. … Rh6 is very strong. **20. Qc4 Ne7 21. Q×a6 Rh6 22. Nc3 h4 23. f4** "23. h3 was more prudent"—Ranken. **23. … h3 24. g3 Re6 25. Rc2** "A good move, threatening now 26. Nd5, which he could not have done before on account of 25. Nd5 N×d5 26. e×d5 Re2 etc."—Ranken. **25. … c5** "A bad move which weakens the pawns on the queenside. The proper play was 25. … Nc8, threatening 26. … Qa7; or else if 26. Rb1 Qe7 followed mostly by 27. … f5"—Steinitz. **26. Rb1 Nc6** "In making this and his last move, Mr. Bird evidently intended sacrificing another pawn for the sake of the attack, and to get the exchange of queens. A very fine manoeuvre"—Ranken. **27. Q×b6** The alternatives are worse: 27. R×b6 Nb4 or 27. Nd5 Qd8 28. R×b6 Nd4 (Ranken). **27. … Q×b6 28. R×b6 Nd4 29. Ra2** (*see diagram*)

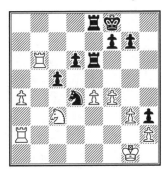

*After 29. Ra2*

**29. ... f5!** "Excellent, for if 30. e×f5 Re1† and then 31. ... Rh1 wins"—Ranken. **30. a5** "Quite sound if properly pursued"—Steinitz. **30. ... f×e4 31. a6 e3 32. Ne2?** A cruel mistake after which Black's pawns become much too strong to cope with. With correct play White should obtain at least a draw: 32. a7 e2 (or 32. ... Ra8 33. Rb8† Re8 34. R×a8 R×a8 and neither side can get any further) 33. N×e2 N×e2† 34. Kf2 N×f4! (an improvement over 34. ... Ra8, suggested by Steinitz, which loses quickly after 35. Rb8† Re8 36. R×a8 R×a8 37. K×e2) and a draw is very likely. **32. ... N×e2† 33. R×e2 d5 34. R×e6 R×e6 35. a7 Ra6 36. R×e3 R×a7 37. Re5 Rd7 38. Kf2 c4 39. Rf5†** "No doubt he had to move the rook from the e-file in order to be enabled to cross with his king, for otherwise Black would reply 39. ... Re7 in reply to 39. Ke3 and would easily win after exchanging rooks, but the move selected only helps the opponent. 39. Rg5 instead would have kept the adverse king aloof for some time, but no doubt by best play Black was bound to win: 39. ... d4 40. Rc5 d3 41. Ke1 d2†"—Steinitz. **39. ... Ke7 40. Ke3 d4† 41. Kd2 Kd6 42. Ra5 Rb7 43. Kc2 Kc6 44. g4 Re7 45. Kd2 Re3 46. Rg5 Rf3 47. R×g7 Rf2† 48. Ke1 R×h2** White resigns—*British Chess Magazine* (Ranken), January 1889, pp. 24–27; *International Chess Magazine* (Steinitz), January 1889, pp. 22–24.

### (889) Bird–Blackburne     0–1

Match (game 2)
London, 27 November 1888
C51

**1. e4 e5 2. Nf3 Nc6 3. Bc4 Bc5 4. b4 B×b4 5. c3 Bc5 6. d4 e×d4 7. c×d4 Bb4†** "A risky defense. 7. ... Bb6 is now with good reason preferred"—Ranken. **8. Kf1 Qe7 9. a3** "The old move 9. e5 leads to a much more complicated and doubtful issue: 9. ... d6 10. a3 (if 10. Qa4 Kf8 [best] 11. d5 N×e5 12. Q×b4 N×f3 13. g×f3 Bh3†† 14. Kg1 Qf6 15. Bd3 Q×f3 and wins) 10. ... Ba5 11. Ra2 and the game becomes difficult for both sides, but we prefer White's position, as he now threatens 12. Bg5, 13. Re2 and 14. Qa4"—Ranken. **9. ... Ba5 10. Ra2 b5** "Offering a pawn to gain time and to free his pieces, for 10. ... d6 would be dangerous, and the alternatives 10. ... b6 or 10. ... a6 would be too slow"—Ranken. It's difficult to see why 10. ... a6 first is too slow according to Ranken. White hasn't any real threats yet. **11. Bd3** "We see no cause for refusing to take the pawn, but if the bishop retreated, it should be to b3"—Ranken. **11. ... Rb8 12. Re2 d6 13. e5 d5 14. Qc2 Nd8 15. Bg5 Qd7** 15. ... Qe6 is correct. After 16. B×d8 K×d8 17. B×h7 b4 the position is murky. **16. B×d8** "Mr. Bird here misses an important chance. He should have played 16. e6, whereupon, if 16. ... N×e6 or 16. ... f×e6 (best) 17. Ne5, followed by 18. Nc6 or 18. B×d8 and then 19. Nc6"—Ranken. **16. ... Q×d8** (*see diagram*)

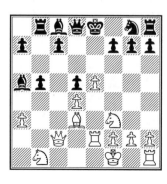

*After 16. ... Q×d8*

**17. e6** "He might have taken the h-pawn, we believe, with safety here, preserving then an equal number of pawns and a good position"—Ranken. **17. ... B×e6 18. B×h7** "Another tempting line of play, perhaps, was 18. Qc6† Kf8 (18. ... Qd7 19. Ne5), but there was no good continuation, as neither 18. B×h7 nor 18. Qa6 would have been sound"—Ranken. **18. ... Ne7 19. Ng5 Rb6 20. Qd3** "The position of White's bishop looks perilous, and he might release it now by 20. N×e6 f×e6 21. Bg6† Kd7 22. Bd3, but the result would be to throw away the attack"—Ranken. **20. ... Qd7 21. h4 Rc6** That White's attack failed becomes clear after 21. ... g6! and any attempt to release the bishop is doomed: 22. h5 Qc6! 23. Qd1 Bg4 24. f3 B×h5. **22. g3 Bg4** The beginning of a false plan that leads to a least an important loss of time or, as in the game, to the complete misplacement of the bishop. **23. f3 Rf6 24. Kg2 Bh5 25. Nd2 B×d2 26. Q×d2 Kd8 27. Bd3 Nf5?** Not good, as Bird gets the opportunity to eliminate his opponent's most important defender. Instead 27. ... a6, preparing 28. ... Nc6, offers equal chances. **28. B×f5 Q×f5 29. Qe3** 29. Qc3! initiates an unanswerable assault against the queenside and center. If 29. ... Qd7 30. Rc1 a6 31. Qc5 Rb6 32. Re5 **29. ... Kc8 30. Rc1 Rd6** 30. ... Qd7 31. Qc3 (if 31. Rec2 Bg6 and 32. R×c7† is not so dangerous) 31. ... Kb7 32. Qc5 Rd6 33. Rce1 is no pleasure either. **31. Qc3?!** The disadvantage of Blackburne's last move is demonstrated after 31. Rec2!, when the c-pawn falls with decisive effect: 31. ... Qd7 32. R×c7† Q×c7 33. R×c7† K×c7 34. g4 Bg6 35. h5. **31. ... Qd7 32. Qc5 Kb7 33. a4?!** The positional 33. Rce1! is much stronger. Black remains tied hand and foot after 33. ... a6 34. Re7 Qd8 35. a4. **33. ... f6 34. Nh3 g5** (*see diagram*) 34. ... b×a4 looks very risky, but is possible. White's attack is far from decisive while this extra pawn may become important one day.

*After 34. ... g5*

**35. Rec2** A few alternatives are worth looking at. 35. Q×b5†! restores his positional superiority and the material balance at once; e.g., 35. ... Q×b5 36. a×b5 g×h4 37. Re7. More double-edged is 35. Rb2: 35. ... g×h4 36. Nf4 h3† 37. Kf2 (bad is 37. N×h3? Q×h3† while 37. Kh2 B×f3 is reasonable) 37. ... h2. **35. ... Rh7** Black's position remains uncomfortable, despite Bird's last sloppy move. Inferior now is 35. ... b×a4? due to 36. Qb4†! (if 36. Q×c7†?! Q×c7 37. R×c7† Kb6 and Black can hold) 36. ... Rb6 37. R×c7† Q×c7 38. R×c7† K×c7 39. Q×a4 must win. 35. ... c6 also looks dangerous: 36. a×b5 c×b5 37. Qa3 a6 38. g4 B×g4 39. f×g4 Q×g4† 40. Kf1 Qd7 41. Rc7† Q×c7 42. R×c7† K×c7 43. h×g5 f×g5 44. Qc5† with complicated play. **36. a×b5** 36. Qa3, threatening 37. R×c7†, retains strong pressure. The counterattack launched by 36. ... Qf5 is not sufficient; e.g., 37. a×b5 g×h4 38. Ra2 a5 39. b×a6† *e.p.* Ka8 40. g4 and White must win. The defensive 36. ... Rb6 won't help either against best play—37. a×b5 g×h4 38. Nf4 Qf5 39. Ra2 and lack is left without defense. **36. … B×f3†!** A nice and unexpected ounter-blow. **37. K×f3 Q×h3 38. Ra1** Bird picks up the wrong ook to move to the a-file. The rook on c2 is now destined for the -file, but due to the weakness of the second rank it cannot infiltrate nto the heart of Black's position. This rook is also a liability at c2. **8. … Qf5†** Or 38. … Kc8 39. Q×d6 Qf5† and it becomes apparent hy the other rook should have moved to the a-file. Too optimistic, n the other hand, would have been 38. … g×h4?, for he gets mated fter 39. Q×a7† Kc8 40. Qa8† Kd7 41. R×c7†! Ke6 42. Qg8† Rf7 3. Q×f7† Kf5 44. Qh5† Ke6 45. Re1. **39. Kg2 Qe4† 40. Kh2 Rb6 41. Rca2 a5 42. b×a6e.p.†?** "Mr. Bird has still a drawn game y 42. R×a5, for then Black would have been obliged to resort to erpetual check, whereas now he wins, owing to his king being shel-ered by White's pawn"—Ranken. **42. … Ka7 43. Qc2 Qe7 43. … ×h4 44. Q×e4 d×e4 45. g×h4 f5!** wins as well. **44. Re1** "These at-empts at exchanges are unavailing now, for Black will not let to go is grip"—Ranken. **44. … Qd7 45. Qe2 g×h4 46. g4 Qd6† 7. Kh1 Rb3 48. Rb2** "48. Qf1 would stave off for a time, but only or a time, the impending disaster"—Ranken. **48. … Rh3†** White esigns—*British Chess Magazine* (Ranken), January 1889, pp. 27– 9.

## 890) Blackburne–Bird   1–0

Match (game 3)
London, 28 November 1888
B22

**1. e4 c5 2. Nf3 g6 3. d4 Bg7 4. c3 c×d4 5. c×d4 d6 6. Nc3 Nc6 . Be3 Nf6 8. d5 Nb8 9. Rc1 0–0 10. h3 Nbd7 11. Bd3 a6 12. 0–0 Ne8 13. Qd2 f6 14. Nd4 Nc7 15. Nce2 Ne5 16. Bb1 e6 17. f4 e×d5 8. f×e5 d×e5 19. Nf3 d4 20. Bh6 Be6 21. B×g7 K×g7 22. Qb4 Nb5 23. Bd3 Rf7 24. a4 Nd6 25. Rc5 a5 26. Qd2 Qb6 27. Rfc1 Rc8 28. R×c8 B×c8 29. Kh2 Bd7 30. Qc2 Bc6 31. Ng3 Rd7 2. Qc5 Qd8 33. b3 Re7 34. Nh4 Re6 35. Rf1 Be8 36. Qc1 Bf7 7. Rf2 Re8 38. Qc5 Be6 39. Bb5 Re7 40. Bd3 Qc7 41. Qa3 Qb6 2. Bc4 Kf7 43. B×e6† K×e6 44. Qa2 Qb4 45. Qc2 Kf7 46. Nf3 Kg7 47. Nd2 Qb6 48. Qd1 Qd8 49. Qg4 Rf7 50. Rf1 Kf8 51. Qe6 5 52. Rc1 Kg7 53. Rc5 Re7 54. Qd5 Rd7 55. Rc1 h4 56. Nh1 Nf5 57. Qc5 Ne3 58. Nf2 b6 59. Qc6 f5 60. Nf3 Rf7 61. Nd3 Qf6 2. Q×f6† R×f6 63. Nd×e5 f×e4 64. N×d4 Rf2 65. Rc7† Kh6 6. Ng4† N×g4† 67. h×g4 Rd2 68. Ne6 Rd3 69. g5† Kh5 0. Nf4†** Black resigns—*The Field*, 15 December 1888.

## 891) Bird–Blackburne   0–1

Match (game 4)
London, 29 November 1888
402

**1. f4 e5 2. f×e5 d6 3. e×d6 B×d6 4. Nf3 Nf6 5. d4 Ng4 6. Bg5 6 7. Bh4 g5 8. Bf2 N×f2 9. K×f2 g4 10. Nh4 f5 11. g3 f4 12. Qd3 0–0 13. Ke1 Nc6 14. Nd2 Qe7 15. c3 Bd7 16. Ne4 Rae8 17. N×d6 ×d6 18. Rd1 Qg5 19. Qd2 Qd5 20. Ng2 f3 21. Nf4 f×e2 22. Bg2 ×d1Q† 23. K×d1 Qf5 24. Kc1 Ne7 25. h3 Qg5 26. h×g4 B×g4 7. B×b7 Ng6 28. Bd5† Kh8 29. Bc6 Re7 30. Rf1 N×f4 31. g×f4 e2 32. Q×e2 B×e2 33. f×g5 B×f1** White resigns—*The Field*, 22 December 1888.

## (892) Blackburne–Bird   1–0

Match (game 5)
London, 30 November 1888
B00

**1. e4 e6 2. d4 b6 3. Bd3 Bb7 4. Nh3 Nf6 5. f3 c5 6. c3 c×d4 7. c×d4 Nc6 8. Be3 Bb4† 9. Nd2 d5 10. e5 Nd7 11. 0–0 Be7 12. Rc1 f5 13. f4 Nb4 14. Bb1 Ba6 15. Rf2 Rc8 16. Nf3 h6 17. g4 R×c1 18. B×c1 f×g4 19. Bg6† Kf8 20. Nfg5 h×g5 21. Q×g4 Bd3 22. f×g5† Nf6 23. g×f6 g×f6 24. e×f6 Bd6 25. Bf7 K×f7 26. Qg7† Ke8 27. f7†** Black resigns—*The Field*, 29 December 1888.

A return match was envisaged to be played at the Divan, but did not materialize. Instead F.H. Lewis enticed Bird and Blackburne into one exhibition game, for which both players got a small finan-cial reward.

## (893) Bird–Blackburne   ½–½

Offhand game
London (Simpson's Divan), 5 January 1889
C32

**1. e4 e5 2. f4 d5 3. e×d5 e4 4. c4 c6 5. Nc3 Nf6 6. Qc2 Bf5 7. Nge2 Bc5 8. Qb3 Qd7 9. Ng3 0–0 10. Be2 Na6 11. Nd1 c×d5 12. c×d5 Nb4 13. Ne3 B×e3 14. d×e3 Nf×d5 15. 0–0 Rfe8 16. Bd2 Nd3 17. Rad1 Rad8 18. Qa3 b6 19. N×f5 Q×f5 20. g4 Qd7 21. h3 h5 22. Kh2 h×g4 23. h×g4 Qd6 24. Q×d6 R×d6 25. B×d3 e×d3 26. Rf3 Nf6 27. g5 Ne4 28. Bb4 Rd5 29. Kg2 Rc8 30. Rff1 a5 31. Be1 f5 32. g×f6 e.p. g×f6 33. Kf3 f5 34. Rh1 Rc7 35. Bc3 N×c3 36. b×c3 Rd6 37. Rdg1† Rg7 38. R×g7† K×g7 39. e4 f×e4† 40. K×e4 d2 41. Rd1 Kf6 42. Ke3 Kf5 43. R×d2 R×d2 44. K×d2 K×f4 45. Kd3 Ke5 46. Kc4 Kd6 47. Kb5 Kc7** draw—*The Field*, 12 January 1889.

# HANDICAP TOURNAMENT AT SIMPSON'S DIVAN, DECEMBER 1888–JANUARY 1889

As the handicap tournament held in the spring at the Divan was considered a great success it was no surprise that the proposal for a second outing was well received. Henley, Simpson's proprietor, acted as the treasurer. Bird agreed to take up responsibility as secretary. The tournament was planned to start on 1 November but because of Bird's travelling in the provinces it was deferred for a month. This was the reason why some of the announced participants, notably Blackburne and von Bardeleben, dropped out. The tournament fi-nally began under huge publication on 1 December. On that day Bird drew with Loman.[14] Bird marred his start as he drew another

14. MacDonnell was an eye-witness: "On Saturday, 1st of December, I visited Simpson's Divan, and was pleased to see a large and goodly company assembled there to witness the opening of a grand handicap tournament which took place on that day. Many battles were fought, perhaps the most interesting of them being one on even terms between Mr. H.E. Bird and Mr. R. Loman, which, greatly to the credit of the junior master, resulted in a draw." *Illustrated Sporting and Dra-matic News*, 8 December 1888.

game with Müller and even lost against H. Hicks, one of the weaker amateurs.[15]

Bird inexorably fought back by winning one game after another and with 9 out of 11, he was in third place, behind Pollock and Lee. A heavy attack of gout tied Bird a week to his bed around the middle of December. Fortunately he recovered enough to give the Hampstead Hall simul (see the chapter "A Few Exhibitions, 1888–1889" above) and pick up his games in the tournament again.

Bird mounted one place in the ranking by beating Pollock in a crucial game. With the game against tournament leader Lee still ahead, a miraculous resurrection seemed in the making. The solid Lee, however, had the fortune to play with the White pieces. He refrained from taking any risks and the game ended in a draw, offered respectfully to Bird at the point when Lee had achieved a winning position.

Lee (11½ out of 14) thus gained the first prize ahead of Bird (10½). Pollock collapsed in the final rounds, lost all his games against the strongest players and was overrun by Loman and Müller (9½). Those two did not benefit from the early forfeit of Frederick Louis Kinderman, the weakest player of the lot. Without playing him, they were deprived of a chance to share second place with Bird. At the banquet held a few days before the closing off of the tournament on 10 January, Bird was found "perfectly radiant. Indeed, the countenance of the latter gentleman from first to last glowed with delight, and presented a very pretty picture."[16]

### (894) Bird–Loman    ½–½

Handicap tournament (round 1)
London, 1 December 1888
*A03*

**1.** f4 d5 **2.** Nf3 b6 **3.** e3 Bb7 **4.** Be2 e6 **5.** 0-0 Nf6 **6.** b3 Be7 **7.** Bb2 0-0 **8.** Qe1 c5 **9.** d3 Nc6 **10.** Nbd2 Ng4 **11.** Qg3 Bf6 **12.** Ne5 Ng×e5 **13.** f×e5 Bh4 **14.** Qh3 d4 **15.** Nc4 Rb8 **16.** Bg4 Bg5 **17.** e×d4 c×d4 **18.** B×e6 f×e6 **19.** Q×e6† Kh8 **20.** Nd6 Be3† **21.** Kh1 h6 **22.** N×b7 R×b7 **23.** Q×c6 Rbf7 **24.** R×f7 R×f7 **25.** Ba3 Rf2 **26.** Qe4 Qg5 **27.** h3 Bf4 **28.** Qa8† Kh7 White draws by perpetual check—*Morning Post*, 31 December 1888.

### Handicap tournament, London, 1 December 1888–January 1889

*Site:* Simpson's Divan
*Prizes:* Five prizes
*Time limit:* 20 moves per hour
*Odds scale:* pawn and move (class II), pawn and 2 moves (class III) and knight (class IV)
*Notes:* The tournament table may be incomplete. The sources are contradictory about the outcome of the game between Pollock and Cole. The present author believes Pollock won.

| | | | 1 | 2 | 3 | 4 | 5 | 6 | 7 | 8 | 9 | 10 | 11 | 12 | 13 | 14 | 15 | |
|---|---|---|---|---|---|---|---|---|---|---|---|---|---|---|---|---|---|---|
| 1 | F.J. Lee | I | | ½ | 1 | 0 | 0 | 1 | 1 | 1 | 1 | 1 | 1 | 1 | 1 | 1 | 1 | 11½ |
| 2 | H.E. Bird | I | ½ | | ½ | ½ | 1 | 1 | 1 | 1 | 1 | 0 | 1 | 1 | 1 | 0 | 1 | 10½ |
| 3 | R. Loman | I | 0 | ½ | | | 1 | 1 | 0 | 1 | 1 | 1 | 1 | ½ | ½ | 1 | | 9½ |
| 4 | O.C. Müller | I | 1 | ½ | 0 | | | 1 | 1 | ½ | 1 | ½ | 1 | 1 | 1 | ½ | 1 | 9½ |
| 5 | Rolland | IV | 1 | 0 | 0 | 0 | | 1 | ½ | 1 | ½ | 0 | 1 | 1 | 1 | 1 | 1 | 9 |
| 6 | S.F. Smith | II | 0 | 0 | 1 | 0 | 0 | | 1 | 0 | 1 | 1 | 1 | 1 | 1 | 1 | 1 | 9 |
| 7 | T.C. Gibbons | III | 0 | 0 | 0 | ½ | ½ | 0 | | 0 | 1 | 1 | 1 | 1 | 1 | 1 | 1 | 8 |
| 8 | W.H.K. Pollock | I | 0 | 0 | 0 | 0 | 0 | 1 | 1 | | 0 | 1 | 1 | 1 | 1 | 1 | 1 | 8 |
| 9 | E.L. Sellon | III | 0 | 0 | 0 | ½ | ½ | 0 | 0 | 1 | | | 1 | | | | | 3 |
| 10 | J.B. Purchase | IV | 0 | 1 | 0 | 0 | 1 | 0 | 0 | 0 | | | | 0 | 1 | 0 | | 3 |
| 11 | Cole | IV | 0 | 0 | 0 | 0 | 0 | 0 | 0 | 0 | 0 | 1 | | 0 | 0 | 1 | 1 | 3 |
| 12 | T.G. Sampson | IV | 0 | 0 | ½ | 0 | 0 | 0 | 0 | 0 | | | 1 | | | | | 1½ |
| 13 | F. Humphreys | III | 0 | 0 | ½ | ½ | 0 | 0 | 0 | 0 | | 0 | 1 | | | | | 2 |
| 14 | H. Hicks | IV | 0 | 1 | 0 | 0 | 0 | 0 | 0 | 0 | | 1 | 0 | | | | | 2 |
| 15 | F.L. Kinderman | IV | 0 | 0 | | | 0 | 0 | 0 | 0 | | | 0 | | | | | 0 |

### (895) Pollock–Bird    0–1

Handicap tournament
London, December 1888
*B34*

**1.** e4 c5 **2.** Nc3 Nc6 **3.** Nf3 g6 "A move of late frequentl⟨y⟩ adopted"—Anthony. **4.** d4 c×d4 **5.** N×d4 Bg7 **6.** Be3 h5 "Char⟨⟩acteristic of Mr. Bird. The play of this veteran master is more origina⟨l⟩ than that of any other English player of note and perhaps the mos⟨t⟩ marked feature of his style is his predilection for an early advance⟨⟩ of the pawns on one or other of the two flanks"—Anthony. **7.** Be⟨2⟩ d6 **8.** 0-0 Nf6 **9.** h3 h4 "The last move on both sides appears to u⟨s⟩ ill-advised"—Anthony. **10.** f4 Nh5 "An exception to the rule tha⟨t⟩ the knight should not be played to a side of the board. For Whit⟨e⟩ cannot permit it to enter at g3, and is therefore compelled to ex⟨⟩change it for his bishop"—Anthony. **11.** N×c6 This and the follow⟨⟩ing exchanges facilitate Black's position. 11. B×h5! R×h5 12. f5 is far sharper and more troubling continuation for his opponent. **11. ...** b×c6 **12.** B×h5 R×h5 **13.** f5 Rh8 **14.** Bd4 B×d4† **15.** Q×d4 Qb⟨6⟩ **16.** Q×b6 a×b6 **17.** f×g6 f×g6 "We now prefer Black's position⟨.⟩ His pawns are united, and his bishop has considerable freedom o⟨f⟩ action, while White has an isolated pawn on a white square"—An⟨⟩thony. **18.** Rae1 Ra5 **19.** a3 Re5 **20.** Na2 c5 **21.** Nc3 Be6 **22.** Na⟨4⟩ b5 **23.** Nc3 "The peregrinations of the knight have not improve⟨d⟩ White's game"—Anthony. **23. ...** b4 **24.** a×b4 c×b4 **25.** Ra1 Kd⟨7⟩ **26.** Ra7† Kc6 **27.** Na4 Bc4 **28.** Re1 Rf8 **29.** b3 Bb5 **30.** c4 B×a⟨4⟩ **31.** R×a4 Kc5 **32.** Rd1 "White apparently gives up a pawn to set ⟨a⟩ trap"—Anthony. **32. ...** R×e4 **33.** Ra6 "He cannot play 33. Rd5⟨†⟩ followed by 34. R×b4, because Black would answer 34. ... Re1† an⟨d⟩ 35. ... Rff1, and White cannot avert the mate at h1. The text mov⟨e⟩ threatens mate on the move"—Anthony. **33. ...** Rf5 **34.** Ra5† Kc⟨6⟩ **35.** Ra6† Kd7 **36.** Rb6 Re2 **37.** Rf1 Rg5 **38.** Rf2 Re3 **39.** R×b⟨4⟩ R×h3 "and the game was prolonged for many moves, Black's extra⟨⟩ pawn finally gaining the day."—*Hereford Times* (Anthony), 2 Feb⟨⟩ruary 1889.

---

15. The *British Chess Magazine* (January 1889, p. 3) gave a peculiar explanation to Bird's failure: "Many of the games have been excellent specimens of chess, and some of Bird's, at odds, have been played in all his old style, indeed, he lost a game to a fourth-class player by playing too well, that is he gave his opponent credit for seeing a very fine move and played to avoid it, whereas none under first-class strength could have seen it, and, as a matter of fact, had the old man gone on and braved the danger, ten to one he would have scored the game."

16. *Illustrated Sporting and Dramatic News*, 19 January 1889.

**(896) Lee–Bird**  ½–½
Handicap tournament (round 15)
London, January 1889

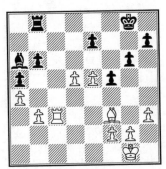

*Final position*

"This game was with Bird, and their respective scores were Lee 11, Bird 10, and if Mr. Bird had won, the first place would have been tied for. The old man defended with a Sicilian, following it up by a fianchetto development, but Lee held his game together well, and ultimately Mr. Bird had to give up a pawn with no commensurate attack. Lee, risking nothing, played steadily for the draw, and on the 31st move the draw was agreed upon. I give a diagram of the game at the point where it was drawn"—*British Chess Magazine*. *British Chess Magazine*, February 1889, p. 53.

# HANDICAP TOURNAMENT AT SIMPSON'S DIVAN, JANUARY–FEBRUARY 1889

Henry Edward Bird (*Chess Monthly*).

Immediately following the closure of the second handicap tournament at the Divan another similar tournament commenced, also with great public attention. Bird started with a string of 11 straight wins and although he had to concede a draw and a loss in the following rounds his final victory was never in danger. The winner of the previous tournament, Lee, captured second prize ahead of Müller. This tournament was but sparsely covered by the press and no games played by Bird were published.

## Handicap tournament, London, 26 January–February 1889

*Site:* Simpson's Divan
*Prizes:* Four prizes
*Odds scale:* pawn and move (class II), pawn and 2 moves (class III), knight (class IV) and rook (class V)

|  |  |  | 1 | 2 | 3 | 4 | 5 | 6 | 7 | 8 | 9 | 10 | 11 | 12 | 13 | 14 | 15 | 16 |  |
|---|---|---|---|---|---|---|---|---|---|---|---|---|---|---|---|---|---|---|---|
| 1 | H.E. Bird | I |  | ½ | 1 | 1 | 0 | 1 | 1 | 1 | 1 | 1 | 1 | 1 | 1 | 1 | 1 |  | 12½ |
| 2 | F.J. Lee | I | ½ |  | ½ | 0 | 1 | 0 | 1 | 1 | 1 | 1 | 1 | 1 | 1 | 1 | 1 | 1 | 12 |
| 3 | O.C. Müller | I | 0 | ½ |  | 1 | 0 | 1 | 1 | 1 | 1 | 1 | 0 | 1 | 0 | 1 | 1 | 1 | 10½ |
| 4 | E.O. Jones | II | 0 | 1 | 0 |  | 1 | 0 | 1 | ½ | 1 | 0 | 1 | 1 | 1 | 0 | 1 | 1 | 9½ |
| 5 | T.E. Greatorex | IV | 1 | 0 | 1 | 0 |  | 0 | 0 | 1 | 1 | 0 | 1 | 0 | 1 | 1 | 1 | 1 | 9 |
| 6 | E.L. Sellon | III | 0 | 1 | 0 | 1 | 1 |  | ½ | 0 | 0 | 1 | 0 | 1 |  |  | 1 | 1 | 6½ |
| 7 | T.C. Gibbons | III | 0 | 0 | 0 | 0 | 1 | ½ |  | 1 |  |  | 0 | ½ | 1 | 0 | 1 | 1 | 6 |
| 8 | Rolland | III | 0 | 0 | 0 | ½ | 0 | 1 | 0 |  | 0 | 1 | 1 | 1 | 1 |  |  |  | 5½ |
| 9 | H. Hicks | IV | 0 | 0 | 0 | 0 | 0 | 1 |  | 1 |  | 1 | 1 |  | 1 |  |  |  | 5 |
| 10 | Cole | IV | 0 | 0 | 0 | 1 | 1 | 0 |  | 0 | 0 |  | 1 | 1 |  | 1 |  |  | 5 |
| 11 | F.L. Kinderman | IV | 0 | 0 | 1 | 0 | 0 | 1 | 1 | 0 | 0 | 0 |  | 1 | 1 |  |  | 1 | 5 |
| 12 | Wellington | IV | 0 | 0 | 0 | 0 | 1 | 0 | ½ | 0 |  | 0 | 0 |  | 0 |  | 1 |  | 2½ |
| 13 | Roberts | V | 0 | 0 | 1 | 0 | 0 |  | 0 | 0 |  | 0 | 1 |  |  |  | 0 |  | 2 |
| 14 | Day | VI | 0 | 0 | 0 | 1 | 0 |  | 1 |  | 0 | 0 |  |  |  |  | 1 | 0 | 2 |
| 15 | Morresey | IV | 0 | 0 | 0 | 0 | 0 | 1 | 0 |  |  |  | 0 |  | 1 | 0 |  | 1 | 2 |
| 16 | J.B. Purchase | IV |  | 0 | 0 | 0 | 0 | 0 | 0 |  |  |  |  | 1 | 1 | 0 |  |  | 1 |

# A TOUR IN WALES, FEBRUARY 1889

In February Bird ventured upon a tour through the south of Wales. The local chess clubs cooperated to receive Bird appropriately. His first stop was Cardiff where he was the guest of J.C. Goodall. On 15 February he began his tour with some offhand chess. Bird engaged in a few well crowded consultation games. One of them got published.

On 18 February a first simultaneous exhibition was planned in the same city. A special room at the Park Hotel was reserved for the event which drew a large gathering of players from all parts of the country. Bird played 23 games of which he won 17, lost 2, to W.F. Pethybridge and G.W. Lennox and drew 1 with Bisgood. Three games were left unfinished.

On 20 February Bird met players of the United Rhondda Chess Club in Porth. Out of 21 games he won 19, drew with George Parry and lost to Dr. Parry.

Two days later Bird was back in Cardiff for a final exhibition. He combined offhand chess with a successful simultaneous display in which he beat 12 opponents, lost against Dr. Arthur and drew with F. and A.H. Hybart. Three games were not played out.

Bird's tour also brought him to Newport and Aberdare (as the guest of Rees Williams), but no reports of these visits appeared in the press. On 23 February Bird returned to London, leaving behind a very favorable impression. During the following years Bird could be spotted on various occasions in Wales.

## (897) Bird & Morris & Gibbings– Lennox & Cook & Goodall    1–0

Consultation game
Cardiff, 15 February 1889
C51

According to the *Illustrated Sporting and Dramatic News*, this game was played on 16 February, with only Bird and Gibbings playing as White. **1. e4 e5 2. Nf3 Nc6 3. Bc4 Bc5 4. b4 B×b4 5. c3 Bc5 6. d4 e×d4 7. c×d4 Bb6 8. Bb2 Nge7 9. d5 Na5 10. Bd3 d6 11. Qd2 f6** "Not usually called for (unless, of course, White plays 12. Qc3) until White's knight reaches g3. 11. ... 0–0 is the correct play"—Blake. **12. Na3** "A favorite move with Mr. Bird. 12. Nc3 is generally preferred"—Blake. **12. ... c5 13. h4 Bd7** "The last opportunity of castling with comfort, and that of a rather dubious kind now"—Blake. A bit too slow. 13. ... a6, 14. ... Bc7 and 15. ... b5 sets the queenside in motion. **14. Qf4** The attack against d6 is relatively simple to deal with. With 14. h5 they could try their chance on the kingside. **14. ... Rc8** "A trap to win the exchange. White's reply should have been a warning against setting traps for the rest of the game"—Blake. "Cleverly tempting White to destruction, thus: 15. Q×d6 Bc7 16. Q×c5 Nb3"—MacDonnell. 14. ... Bc7 is perhaps preferable as the trap is not too difficult to pierce through. **15. Nb5 0–0** "Showing that the warning was lost upon the Black allies. 15. ... Bc7 16. N×d6† B×d6 17. Q×d6 c4 and 18. ... c3 promised some slight compensation for the loss of the gambit pawn"—Blake. **16. N×d6 Bc7 17. e5** *(see diagram)*

**17. ... N×d5?** "Tantamount to giving up further resistance. 17. ...

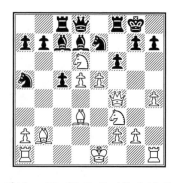

*After 17. e5*

B×d6 18. e×d6 Ng6 (best, if 18. ... N×d5 19. Qe4 Re8 20. Be5) may not afford very bright prospects, but is not entirely hopeless"— Blake. Blake's evaluation of 20. Be5? is completely wrong, for White ends up in a terrible pin after 20. ... f5! 21. Qe2 (21. Q×d5† Be6 is obviously worse) 21. ... c4 22. Bc2 Rc5! Another interesting try at move 18 is 18. ... c4!, when Black reaches a promising endgame after 19. d×e7 Q×e7† 20. Be2 Qb4† 21. Qd2 c3 22. B×c3 Q×c3 23. Q×c3 R×c3. **18. Qe4 B×d6 19. Q×h7† Kf7 20. Bg6† Ke6 21. Bf5† Ke7 22. Q×g7† Rf7 23. e×f6† Ke8 24. Qg8†** "They have now a brilliant mate in four—a termination befitting their conduct of the game"—Blake. The score in the *British Chess Magazine* stopped here. **24. ... Bf8 25. Q×f7† K×f7 26. Ng5** Black resigns— *British Chess Magazine* (Blake), April 1889, pp. 156–157; *Illustrated Sporting and Dramatic News* (MacDonnell), 2 March 1889.

## (898) Bird–Lennox    0–1

Simultaneous game
Cardiff, 18 February 1889
C33

According to the *Hereford Times*, this game was played together with 17 others during a simultaneous exhibition. The number of games fits the exhibition of 22 February, but Lennox did not win his game on that occasion. Hence, one suspects that this game was played a few days earlier, on 18 February.

**1. e4 e5 2. f4 e×f4 3. Be2 d5 4. e×d5 Bd6 5. d4 Nf6 6. c4 Ne4 7. Nf3 c5 8. b4 b6 9. 0–0 0–0 10. Bd3 f5 11. Ne5 c×d4 12. B×f4 Qc7 13. B×e4 f×e4 14. c5 b×c5 15. b×c5 Q×c5 16. Nd2 Q×d5 17. Ndc4 Ba6 18. N×d6 B×f1 19. Q×f1 d3 20. Qc1 R×f4 21. N×d3 Rf8 22. Ne5 Q×d6 23. Qc4† Kh8 24. Rf1 R×f1† 25. Q×f1 Qc5† 26. Kh1 Nc6** White resigns—*Hereford Times*, 30 March 1889.

# MATCH WITH GUNSBERG 1889

Bird did not enjoy a long rest after his return from Wales. On 26 February he began a short match with Gunsberg. The contest was arranged and provided with stakes by F.H. Lewis. The games were played at the British Chess Club.

The match conditions remained largely the same as Bird's previous match with Blackburne: five games would be played with a time limit set on 20 moves per hour. No more mention was made about any opening regulations, but Gunsberg's choice for the King's

Gambit in both preserved games may have been part of the deal, or, at least, must have pleased the sponsor of the match.

    The course of this contest was very tense. Bird was quite unfortunate to lose narrowly with 1 win against 2 losses and 2 draws and he certainly deserved better. Once again his enemy the gout was taking its toll.

| Match with Gunsberg, 26 February–2 March 1889 | | | | | |
|---|---|---|---|---|---|
| | **1** | **2** | **3** | **4** | **5** |
| I. Gunsberg | 1 | | 0 | ½ | 3 |
| H.E. Bird | 0 | | 1 | ½ | 2 |

games 2 and 4: Gunsberg won one game, the other ended in a draw

## (899) Gunsberg–Bird     1–0

Match (game 1)
London, 26 February 1889
*C33*

    **1. e4 e5 2. f4 e×f4 3. Bc4 Qh4† 4. Kf1 d6** "This is Mr. Bird's own variation. We think it inferior to the Classical Defense 3. ... d5, 4. ... Qh4† and 5. ... g5"—Guest. **5. Nf3 Qh5 6. d4 g5 7. h4 f6 8. Nc3 Ne7** 9. ... c6 is the most solid option for Black. White's next move creates chances for him. **9. e5 Bg7?** An exchange of pawns at e5 was mandatory **10. e×d6 c×d6 11. Nb5 d5** Sacrificing some material for counterplay. 11. ... Kd8 12. N×d6 or 11. ... Nf5 12. Nc7† Kd8 13. N×a8 Ng3† 14. Kh1 N×h1 15. Qd3! offers only depressing prospects. **12. Nc7†?!** Playing into his opponent's hand. The simple 12. Be2 is winning. **12. ... Kd8 13. N×a8 d×c4 14. d5?!** Weakening and time-consuming. 14. Kf2 is preferable. **14. ... Nf5 15. Kg1 Ng3 16. Rh2?** *(see diagram)* 16. Qe1 is tricky as it threatens 17. Qa5†. The right remedy consists of playing 16. ... b6.

*After 16. Rh2*

    **16. ... Qg4?** Losing a crucial tempo. The sudden hopelessness of White's position is accentuated after 16. ... Bf8! **17. Bd2 Bf8 18. Bc3 Bc5† 19. Bd4 B×d4† 20. N×d4 f3?** Bird takes irresponsible risks to pursue his attack. 20. ... Q×d1 leads to an equal endgame. **21. g×f3 Ne2† 22. Kh1 Q×d4 23. Q×e2 Re8 24. Qf1 Bf5** With his former attack gone, his king in peril and a material deficit, Bird's fate is sealed. All other moves lose are equally hopeless, e.g., 24. ... Qc5 25. h×g5 or 24. ... Re3 25. h×g5. **25. h×g5 f×g5 26. Re1 R×e1 27. Q×e1 Nd7 28. d6 Q×d6** 28. ... Ne5 (Guest) fails after 29. Re2 Qd5 30. Qc3 etc. **29. Qa5† Kc8 30. Q×f5 Qd1† 31. Kg2 Qe2† 32. Kg3 Qe1† 33. Rf2 Qg1† 34. Rg2 Qe1† 35. Kh2 Qh4† 36. Qh3 Qf4† 37. Qg3 Ne5 38. Q×f4 g×f4 39. Rg8† Kd7 40. Kg2 c3 41. b×c3 Nc4 42. Rg7†** Black resigns—*Morning Post* (Guest), 4 March 1889.

## (900) Bird–Gunsberg     ?

Match (game 2)
London, 27 February 1889
*Game score missing*

    Either Gunsberg won this game or it ended in a draw.

## (901) Gunsberg–Bird     0–1

Match (game 3)
London, 28 February 1889
*C39*

    **1. e4 e5 2. f4 e×f4 3. Nf3 g5 4. h4 g4 5. Ng5 h6 6. N×f7 K×f7 7. d4 f3** "An older defense, which was superseded by 7. ... d5"—Hoffer. **8. g×f3 d5 9. Bf4** Intending to meet 9. ... Be7 with 10. Bg3. **9. ... Nf6** Nevertheless better was 9. ... Be7 10. Bg3 d×e4 11. f×e4 Nf6 12. Nc3 Nc6, and White has to make a central concession in favor of one of Black's knights; e.g., 13. d5 Nh5 14. Bf2 Ne5. **10. e5 Nh5 11. f×g4** "This is compulsory. White remains now with two pawns for a piece, and the utmost he can expect is a draw, the attack having failed so far"—Hoffer. **11. ... N×f4 12. Qf3 Kg7 13. Q×f4 Bb4† 14. c3 Rf8 15. Qg3 Be7 16. Nd2 c5!** "Black commences now an effective counterattack on the side on which White is compelled to castle"—Hoffer. **17. Nf3 Nc6 18. 0-0-0 c×d4 19. c×d4?** *(see diagram)* The decisive error, though Black's attack was not easy to foresee. Necessary was 19. N×d4, attempting to relieve some pressure with exchanges.

*After 19. c×d4*

    **19. ... Be6** Immediately 19. ... Nb4 and 20. ... Qa5 leaves White chanceless. Now he retains some small hope to rescue himself. **20. Bd3 Nb4 21. Bf5** 21. Kb1 is the only move. Black nets White's second bishop after 21. ... Qd7 22. a3 N×d3, with a clear edge. **21. ... Qd7 22. Kb1 Kh8** Black's king is safe. Gunsberg is without resources against the coming attack. **23. B×e6 Q×e6 24. a3 a5 25. Ka1** "Obviously if 25. a×b4, Black would win with 25. ... Qg6† 26. Ka2 a×b4† 27. Kb3 Qc6 and mate next move; and if 26. Kc1 then 26. ... Rac8† 27. Kd2 Rc2† 28. Ke1 Qe4† and wins"—Hoffer. **25. ... Qg6 26. h5 Qc2 27. Nd2 Nd3 28. Rb1 B×a3** White resigns. "If 28. ... Q×d2 White wins the piece back with 29. Rhd1. If, after 28. ... B×a3, 29. b×a3 Qc3† 30. Ka2 Q×d2† 31. Ka1 Qc3† winning the queen on the next move"—Hoffer. *The Field* (Hoffer), 16 March 1889.

## (902) Bird–Gunsberg     ?

Match (game 4)
London, 1 March 1889
*Game score missing*

    Either Gunsberg won this game or it ended in a draw.

**(903) Gunsberg–Bird**　½–½
Match (game 5)
London, 2 March 1889
*Game score missing*

# American Chess Congress, New York 1889

The first match for the world championship between Steinitz and Zukertort, which was played in various American cities, greatly spurred the interest for the game in the new world. Soon after its termination plans for a first international tournament on American soil were drafted. The initial proposal came from the New York Chess Club. At a meeting held on 4 September 1886 it was decided to hold a sixth American Chess Congress that was accessible by foreign masters. At least $2500, a bit later boosted to $5000, were to be devoted to the organization of the event. Concrete plans, however, proved to be more difficult to realize as the promoters of the idea had a hard time collecting the necessary funds. Attempts were made to increase the amount of subscriptions. Steinitz, involved from the start, announced the project of a tournament book. The book was promised to be a valuable one, as after the first printing the plates were to be destroyed. Suggesting that the winner of the tournament would gain the right to play a match for the title with Steinitz was another thought to raise the money. At least one player on the other side of the ocean was very enthusiastic about the plans made in New York. Bird loudly declared that it certainly would be possible to collect $500 in England for every $1000 gathered in America.

After some time it became clear that the project was lacking support. Some New York clubs had withdrawn and several prominent names were absent from the committee list. A short while later it became known in England that only $860 of the required $5000 had been collected; this was allegedly due to a quarrel between Steinitz and some other prominent players. Yet, the plans were abandoned and the committee continued to gather money. Finally, a disencumbering message reached England at the end of the summer of 1888: the necessary $5000 had been found, so that tournament plans could finally become concrete. The event was scheduled for the next year.

Early in 1889 Steinitz prolonged his world title by convincingly beating Chigorin. In the meantime the committee issued the preliminary program. This led to some agitation in England. Especially the long duration of the tournament was questioned. Further definitive tidings only sparsely reached the shores of England. Yet, early in March, six of the strongest British masters finally sailed to New York. Ranking among them was Bird.[17]

Twenty players entered the fray. A great disappointment for the committee, as well as for the whole chess world, was Steinitz' decision to retire from playing in the tournament. Instead he focused on writing the tournament book. Two other notable absentees were Mackenzie and Tarrasch. Ten participants made the voyage from Europe, the ten others lived in the New World. Apart from the three players mentioned above, every player of note was present in New York. A few of the favorites for the first place were Chigorin, Gunsberg and Blackburne. The tournament schedule was very rigid. Six games per week had to be played. Working days counted eight hours. The time limit was set on 15 moves per hour, despite the heavy European protest that this would cause further delay. Curiously enough, the tournament was even prolonged by the decision that draws in the second cycle had to be replayed.

The players met a first time on 23 March at the annual diner of the Manhattan Chess Club and several of them, including Bird, made the speeches. Two days later the tournament finally began.[18]

Bird started poorly with a draw and two losses. His usual problems with the gout made him forfeit his game against Delmar. Bird then recovered excellently with four straight wins and a well-deserved draw against Weiss, after which he fell seriously back in the ranking when he could gather but two points out of the next eight games. Against each player of repute Bird lost his game.[19]

A final win against the young Nicholas Menelaus MacLeod brought Bird to 8½ out of 19 after the first cycle. The surprising leader was the Austrian Max Weiss. He assembled 15½ points, and remarkably didn't lose a single game. Closely behind was Blackburne with 15 points. Other rivals trailed: Gunsberg (14), Chigorin (13½) and Burn (13).

Bird started the second leg as he finished the first one: by losing

---

17. MacDonnell saw Bird just before he went off to New York: "I saw Bird a few evenings ago at the Divan, and although still suffering from gout, he looked remarkably well and was as hopeful and good-humored as ever. It was pleasant to see old stagers, and young ones too, crowded round him to wish him good luck and a speedy return to the Strand." *Illustrated Sporting and Dramatic News*, 16 March 1889.

18. Three months later, when the public must have been well acquainted with all the participants, an extensive article lavishly described every player. The part consecrated to the oldest participant was certainly generous: "Bird is past his 60th [*sic*] year. He is tall, very well built, and in his younger days must have been a handsome, muscular man of presentable appearance. His skin is fair, and his light blue eyes, under a well-shaped brow, beam with intelligent good humor except when they are clouded by twinges of pain from rheumatism. It has already bent his form, and he walks with difficulty. Toward the end of the tournament he frequently appeared with his right hand swollen and bandaged up. When playing, Mr. Bird's face becomes grave and thoughtfully intent upon the game before him. He does not scan the face of his adversary, and seldom takes his eyes off the board. Every now and then he painfully shifts from side to side, as though seeking relief from pain, and smokes a great deal. He prefers a Cuban cigar, but when he cannot get one he fills his pipe and puffs away at that. Although Bird did not make a high score in the last tournament, his past record is a good one. He has played against several of the strongest men in Europe, and gave them severe tussles. He is the chess reporter for *The Times*, and knows every prominent chess player in the world. When not at work he likes to sit down to a glass of beer and a pipe, and to engage in a running conversation. He speaks with a broad London accent, although he studiously avoids the vulgar cockney mutilation of the letter h; nor does he aspirate the a. Neither does he pronounce his r like a w, which so many dudes imagine is English. When in London he is a great frequenter of the Criterion. Mr. Bird soon took a liking to American rye, and when he drank a glass of the genuine old Kentucky stuff he fell in love with it at once. But he missed one London attraction, and that was the pretty barmaids, and he expressed his regret at their absence. 'I'm an old fellow now,' he used to say, 'and the girls won't flirt any more with me, but still I like a pretty barmaid to hand me my glass of beer, you know.'" *New York Times*, 16 June 1889.

19. Typical for Bird's conduct was his game with Blackburne: "The course of events in Blackburne's game with Bird merges on the ridiculous. At the adjournment Bird thought that he had a winning game, and with characteristic modesty he reported to London that he had won the game. Lo and behold! on resuming the game in the evening Blackburne turned the tables and won the game. Moral: A bird in hand is worth two in the bush." *Evening News and Post*, 6 July 1889.

he majority of his games. From round 26 until round 33 he got nto the flow again and scored 6½ of 8, including a win against Mason and a draw (in fact two draws as they had to be replayed ow) with Weiss. But then four consecutive games against a few faorites brought him 0 points, after which he was definitively thrown ack among the second half of the players. A win in the final round gainst MacLeod made him finish with 17 points out of 38. Bird hared the 12th-13th spot with Taubenhaus.

The battle for the chief honor was interesting until the very end. Weiss continued playing solid chess but he could not prevent a few osses. Only Chigorin and Burn were able to follow the Austrian's ace. Towards the end of the tournament it became more difficult o preserve an overview as various games were adjourned. Weiss was eading four rounds before the end with 25½ points and two replays head of him. Burn and Chigorin counted 25 points and had one eplay to the good. At this point Burn lost his chance after losing wice to weaker opponents. After the final round Chigorin counted 9 points with one more game to finish. Weiss and Gunsberg had 6½ points and respectively four and two adjourned games. Bird layed a role at this point as he still had to replay his first draw with Weiss. Chigorin lost his remaining game against Gunsberg, while Weiss also did not score maximally as Bird kept him to a draw. Ultimately Chigorin and Weiss joined up at the first spot with 29 oints. A playoff consisting of four games was played. These all nded in a draw. Both Weiss and Chigorin preferred not to be compelled to continue this strenuous tournament, with his world championship match coming up against Steinitz.

### (904) Bird–J.W. Baird ½–½

American Congress (round 1)
New York, 25 March 1889
*C30*

**1. e4 e5 2. f4 Bc5 3. Nf3 d6 4. c3 Bg4 5. Qb3 B×f3 6. g×f3 Qh4† 7. Kd1 Bb6 8. a4 Qf2 9. Be2 a5 10. f×e5 d×e5 11. Na3 Nf6 12. Nc4 Nc6 13. N×b6 c×b6 14. Rf1 Qc5 15. Qb5 0–0 16. Q×c5 b×c5 17. b3 Rfd8 18. Kc2 Rac8 19. d3 Nd7 20. f4 Re8 21. f5 f6 22. Rg1 Kh8 23. Bh5 Re7 24. Rg3 Nf8 25. Ba3 b6 26. Rag1 Rd7 27. Bc1 Rcc7 28. Bh6 Na7 29. Kd2 Re7 30. Be8 Nc8 31. Bb5 Nd6 32. Bc4 N×c4† 33. b×c4 Rf7 34. h4 Rce7 35. h5 Nd7 36. Ke2 Nf8 37. Be3 h6 38. Rb1 Rb7 39. d4 c×d4 40. c×d4 e×d4 41. B×d4 Rfc7 42. Rc3 Nd7 43. Rb5 Nc5 44. B×c5 R×c5 45. Ke3 Kg8 46. Kd3 Kf7 47. Rcb3 Rc6 48. R×a5 Rbc7 49. Rd5 R×c4 50. Rd7† R×d7† 51. K×c4 Ra7 52. Kb4 Ke7** and after a few more moves the game was a draw—*Tournament Book*, p. 421.

### (905) Delmar–Bird 1–0

American Congress (round 2)
New York, 26 March 1889
*Game scored by default*

### (906) Bird–Burn 0–1

American Congress (round 3)
New York, 27 March 1889
*C65*

### 6th American Chess Congress, New York, 25 March–27 May 1889

***Site:*** Hall at 8 Union Square
***Playing hours:*** 1 p.m.–5, 7 p.m.–11
***Prizes:*** 1st $1000, 2nd $750, 3rd $600, 4th $500, 5th $400, 6th $300, 7th $200
***Time limit:*** 15 moves per hour

| | | 1 | 2 | 3 | 4 | 5 | 6 | 7 | 8 | 9 | 10 | 11 | 12 | 13 | 14 | 15 | 16 | 17 | 18 | 19 | 20 | |
|---|---|---|---|---|---|---|---|---|---|---|---|---|---|---|---|---|---|---|---|---|---|---|
| 1 | M.I. Chigorin | | ½r1 | 0r0 | ½ 1 | 1 1 | 1 0 | 0 0 | 1 1 | 0 1 | ½ 1 | 1r1 | 1 1 | ½ 1 | 1 1 | 1 0 | 1 1 | 1 1 | 1r1 | 1 1 | 1 1 | 29 |
| 2 | M. Weiss | ½r0 | | ½ 1 | 1 0 | ½r½ | ½r1 | 1r½ | 1 1 | 1 1 | 1 1 | 1 0 | ½r½ | ½ 1 | 1r0 | 1 1 | 1 1 | ½ 1 | 1r1 | 1 1 | 1 1 | 29 |
| 3 | I. Gunsberg | 1r1 | ½ 0 | | 0 1 | ½ 0 | ½ 0 | 1r½ | 1 0 | 1 1 | 1 1 | ½ 1 | 1 1 | 0r1 | 1r1 | 0 1 | 1r1 | 1 1 | 1 1 | 1 1 | 1 1 | 28½ |
| 4 | J.H. Blackburne | ½ 0 | 0 1 | 1 0 | | 0r1 | 1 0 | 1r0 | 0 1 | 1 1 | 1 0 | 1 1 | 1 1 | 1 1 | 1r1 | 1 1 | 1r0 | 1 1 | ½ 1 | 1 1 | 1r0 | 27 |
| 5 | A. Burn | 0 0 | ½r½ | ½ 1 | 1r0 | | 1r½ | 0 0 | 1 1 | 1 1 | 1 0 | 1 1 | 1 1 | 0 1 | 0 0 | 1r1 | 0 1 | 1 1 | 1 1 | 1 1 | 1 1 | 26 |
| 6 | S. Lipschütz | 0 1 | ½r0 | ½ 1 | 0 1 | 0r½ | | ½ 1 | 0 0 | 1 1 | ½ 1 | 1 0 | ½ 0 | ½r1 | 1 1 | 1 1 | 1r1 | 1r0 | 1 1 | 1 1 | 1 1 | 25½ |
| 7 | J. Mason | 1 1 | 0r½ | 0r½ | 0r1 | 1 1 | ½ 0 | | ½ 0 | 0r0 | 1 1 | ½ 0 | 1 0 | 0r1 | 0 1 | ½ 1 | 1r½ | ½r1 | ½r½ | 1r1 | 1 1 | 22 |
| 8 | M. Judd | 0 0 | 0 0 | 0 1 | 1 0 | 0 0 | 1 1 | ½ 1 | | 1 0 | +r1 | 0 1 | 0 0 | 1 1 | 0 0 | ½ 1 | ½ 0 | 1 0 | ½ 1 | 1 1 | 1 1 | 20 |
| 9 | E. Delmar | 1 0 | 0 0 | 0 0 | 0 0 | 0 0 | 0 0 | 1r1 | 0 1 | | ½ 0 | 1 0 | + 1 | 0r½ | 1 0 | 0 1 | 1r1 | 1r0 | 1 1 | 1 1 | 0r1 | 18 |
| 10 | J.W. Showalter | ½ 0 | 0 0 | 0 0 | 0 1 | 0 1 | ½ 0 | 0 0 | –r0 | ½ 1 | | ½ 1 | 1 0 | 1 0 | 1 0 | 1 1 | ½ 1 | 0r1 | ½ 1 | 1 1 | 1 1 | 18 |
| 11 | W.H.K. Pollock | 0r0 | 0 1 | ½ 0 | 0 0 | 0 0 | 0 1 | ½ 1 | 1 0 | 0 1 | ½ 0 | | 0 1 | ½ 1 | ½r1 | 0 1 | 1 1 | 0 0 | 0r0 | 1 1 | 1 1 | 17½ |
| 12 | H.E. Bird | 0 0 | ½r½ | 0 0 | 0 0 | 0 0 | ½ 1 | 0 1 | 1 1 | – 0 | 0 1 | 1 0 | | ½ 0 | 1 1 | ½ 1 | 1 1 | 0 0 | 1 0 | ½r0 | 1 1 | 17 |
| 13 | J. Taubenhaus | ½ 0 | ½ 0 | 1r0 | 0 0 | 1 0 | ½r0 | 1r0 | 0 0 | 1r½ | 0 1 | ½ 0 | ½ 1 | | 0 1 | 0 0 | 0r½ | ½ 1 | 1 0 | 1 1 | 1 1 | 17 |
| 14 | D.G. Baird | 0 0 | 0r1 | 0r0 | 0r0 | 1 1 | 0 0 | 1 0 | 1 1 | 0 1 | 0 1 | ½r0 | 0 0 | 1 0 | | 1r0 | 0 0 | 0 1 | 1 1 | 1r0 | ½ 1 | 16 |
| 15 | C.F. Burille | 0 1 | 0 0 | 1 0 | 0 0 | 0r0 | 0 0 | ½ 0 | ½ 0 | 1 0 | 0 0 | 1 0 | ½ 0 | 1 1 | 0r1 | | ½ 1 | 1r½ | 0r0 | ½r1 | 1 1 | 15 |
| 16 | J.M. Hanham | 0 0 | 0 0 | 0r0 | 0r1 | 1 0 | 0r0 | 0r½ | ½ 1 | 0r0 | ½ 1 | 0 0 | 0 0 | 1r½ | 1 1 | ½ 0 | | 0r0 | 0 1 | 0r½ | 1 1 | 14 |
| 17 | G.H.D. Gossip | 0 0 | ½ 0 | 0 0 | 0 0 | 0 0 | 0r1 | ½r0 | 0 1 | 0r1 | 1r0 | 1 1 | 1 1 | ½ 0 | 1 0 | 0r½ | 0r1 | | 0 0 | 1r½ | 0 0 | 13½ |
| 18 | D.M. Martinez | 0r0 | 0r0 | 0 0 | ½ 0 | 0 0 | 0 0 | ½r½ | ½ 0 | 0 0 | ½ 0 | 1r1 | 0 1 | 0 1 | 0 0 | 1r1 | 1 0 | 1 1 | | 0 1 | 0 1 | 13½ |
| 19 | J.W. Baird | 0 0 | 0 0 | 0 0 | 0 0 | 0 0 | 0 0 | 0r0 | 0 0 | 0 0 | 0 0 | 0 0 | ½r1 | 0 0 | 0r1 | ½r0 | 1r½ | 0r½ | 1 0 | | 1 0 | 7 |
| 20 | N. MacLeod | 0 0 | 0 0 | 0 0 | 0r1 | 0 0 | 0 0 | 0 0 | 0 0 | 1r0 | 0 0 | 0 0 | 0 0 | 0 0 | ½ 0 | 0 0 | 0 0 | 1 1 | 1 0 | 0 1 | | 6½ |

*The note "r" means a replay of a draw*

| *Tie match:* | 1 | 2 | 3 | 4 | |
|---|---|---|---|---|---|
| M.I. Chigorin | ½ | ½ | ½ | ½ | 2 |
| M. Weiss | ½ | ½ | ½ | ½ | 2 |

1. e4 e5 2. Nf3 Nc6 3. Bb5 Nf6 4. Qe2 d6 5. c3 Bd7 6. d3 g6 7. Nbd2 Bg7 8. Nf1 0–0 9. Bg5 h6 10. Be3 Qe7 11. h3 d5 12. Ng3 Nd4 13. c×d4 B×b5 14. Qd2 d×e4 15. d×e4 e×d4 16. N×d4 Rad8 17. Qc2 N×e4 18. N×e4 B×d4 19. B×h6 Rfe8 20. f3 Qh4† 21. g3 Q×h6 White resigns—*Tournament Book*, p. 217.

### (907) Hanham–Bird    0–1
American Congress (round 4)
New York, 28 March 1889
*B34*

1. e4 c5 2. Nf3 Nc6 3. Nc3 g6 4. d4 c×d4 5. N×d4 Bg7 6. Be3 d6 7. Bc4 Bd7 8. 0–0 h5 9. f4 Nf6 10. h3 h4 11. f5 Ne5 12. Be2 Rc8 13. f×g6 f×g6 14. Bb5 Kf7 15. B×d7 Q×d7 16. Nf3 Nc4 17. Bd4 e5 18. Bf2 N×b2 19. Qd2 Qc6 20. Be1 Nc4 21. Qd3 Nb2 22. Qe2 Kg8 23. Rb1 Nc4 24. B×h4 Nb6 25. Rb3 Nh5 26. Nd5 N×d5 27. e×d5 Qc5† 28. Bf2 Q×d5 29. Ng5 Nf4 30. Qg4 Rf8 31. Rd1 Qc4 32. Rd2 Rh5 33. h4 Bh6 34. R×b7 B×g5 35. h×g5 d5 36. Rb3 d4 37. Rf3 Q×a2 38. B×d4 Qb1† 39. Kf2 Rh1 40. Kg3 Nh5† 41. Q×h5 R×h5 and Black wins—*Tournament Book*, pp. 426–427.

### (908) Bird–Pollock    1–0
American Congress (round 5)
New York, 29 March 1889
*B01*

1. e4 d5 2. e×d5 Nf6 3. Bb5† c6 4. d×c6 b×c6 5. Be2 e5 6. d3 Bc5 7. Nf3 e4 8. d×e4 Qb6 9. 0–0 N×e4 10. Qe1 0–0 11. Nbd2 Re8 12. N×e4 R×e4 13. Qd1 Nd7 14. Bd3 Re7 15. c3 a5 16. Qc2 h6 17. Bf4 Nf6 18. Rae1 Be6 19. Be5 B×a2 20. B×f6 R×e1 21. R×e1 g×f6 22. c4 Rd8 23. Bf1 Bb3 24. Qe2 B×c4 25. Qc2 B×f1 26. R×f1 Qb5 27. Nh4 Rd5 28. g3 Qd3 29. Qa4 Qb5 30. Qg4† Rg5 31. Qc8† Kh7 32. Qd7 Qc4 33. Rd1 Qe6 34. Qd3† Kg7 35. Qc2 Re5 36. Kg2 Bb6 37. Rd2 Rc5 38. Qd1 Rd5 39. f3 Re5 40. f4 Re1 41. Nf5† Q×f5 42. Q×e1 a4 43. Qe2 h5 44. Qd3 Qc5 45. Qf3 Kh6 46. Re2 Qd4 47. Q×c6 Qg1† 48. Kh3 Qf1† 49. Qg2 Qd1 50. f5 Bd4 51. Qf3 Kg7 52. Q×h5 Qf1† 53. Kh4 Qc1 54. Qg4† Kf8 55. Qf4 Qc5 56. Qh6† and mates in two more moves—*Tournament Book*, p. 405.

### (909) D.M. Martinez–Bird    0–1
American Congress (round 6)
New York, 30 March 1889
*A02*

1. f4 f5 2. Nf3 e6 3. e3 Be7 4. c4 Nh6 5. b3 Bf6 6. Nc3 0–0 7. Rb1 d6 8. Bb2 Bd7 9. d4 Qe8 10. Bd3 Nc6 11. a3 e5 12. d×e5 d×e5 13. Nd5 e4 14. N×c7 Qd8 15. B×f6 Q×c7 16. Bb2 Rad8 17. Bc2 e×f3 18. Qd5† Rf7 19. Q×f3 Re8 20. 0–0 Ng4 21. e4 Qb6† 22. Kh1 Ne3 23. Bd3 N×f1 24. c5 Q×c5 25. R×f1 f×e4 26. B×e4 Rfe7 27. b4 Qd6 28. Bb1 Re1 29. Ba2† Kh8 30. B×g7† K×g7 31. Qg3† Qg6 32. Qc3† Qf6 33. Qg3† Kh6 34. R×e1 R×e1† 35. Q×e1 Q×f4 36. Be6 B×e6 37. Q×e6† Kg7 38. h3 Qe5 39. Qd7† Qe7 40. Qg4† Kh8 41. Qc8† Kg7 42. Qg4† Kf7 43. Qh5† Ke6 44. g4 Kd7 45. Qf5† Kc7 46. Kg2 Ne5 47. h4 Kd6 48. Qf2 b6 49. Qd2† Ke6 50. Qa2† Kd7 51. Qd5† Kc7 52. Qe4

Kd6 53. Kg3 h6 54. Qf4 Qe6 55. g5 h5 56. Qf8† Kd5 57. Qd8† Ke4 58. Qa8† Ke3 59. Kg2 Qg4† 60. Kf1 Qe2† White resigns—*Tournament Book*, p. 430.

### (910) Bird–Judd    1–0
American Congress (round 7)
New York, 1 April 1889
*A03*

1. f4 c5 2. e3 e6 3. Nf3 Nf6 4. b3 d5 5. Bb2 Be7 6. Be2 Nc6 7. 0–0 0–0–0 8. Qe1 Ne4 9. d3 Bf6 10. Ne5 Nd6 11. Nd2 11. N×c6 b×c6 12. B×f6 Q×f6 13. Qc3 offers White a small advantage. **11. ... B×e5 12. f×e5 Nf5 13. Bg4 Nce7** 13. ... Nb4 is annoying for White **14. B×f5 e×f5 15. Nf3 Be6 16. a4 a5 17. Nh4 Rc8 18. Rd1 b6** 19. Qg3 Kh8 20. Rd2 Rc6 21. Rdf2 Rg8 22. Qg5 Qf8 "The king side was better guarded if he had not crowded his heavy pieces on that wing and tried a diversion on the other flank by 22. ... c4"—Steinitz. 22. ... c4 has the disadvantage of losing control over d4, of which White can make immediate use with 23. Nf3. The position is in fact completely equal, no side being able to make progress with correct play. **23. h3 g6** "Unnecessary and weak"—Steinitz. **24. e4 d4** "It was much better to capture the center pawn, which either allowed him the time for the defense that his opponent required to recover the pawn, or left him a pawn ahead as some compensation for the attack which the adversary had anyhow"—Steinitz. 24. ... d×e4 25. d×e4 h6 26. Qe3 Kh7 27. e×f5 N×f5 28. N×f5 g×f5 29. Qf3 is no real improvement for Black. White will occupy the d-file next. Instead 24. ... h6 25. Qd2 d4 is the correct continuation **25. Bc1!** 25. ... h6 is prevented and White's domination of the black squares gives him an advantage. **25. ... Bc8** *(see diagram)* Black has to consider the organization of his defense. With the weakness of h6 and f6 in mind, 25. ... Rg7 comes up as the correct move—if 26. Nf3 then 26. ... f×e4 27. d×e4 Ng8. The important f6 square is covered, so that he can exchange White's bishop once it arrives there in a few moves: 28. Qh4 Qb8 29. Bg5 h6 30. Bf6 N×f6 31. e×f6 Rh7 and Black has good chances to stand the assault.

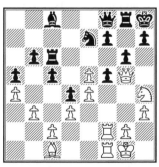

*After 25. ... Bc8*

**26. Qg3** 26. Nf3! initiates a strong regrouping of his pieces. For instance, 26. ... Rg7 27. Qh4 Ng8 28. Bg5 f×e4 29. Q×e4 Rc7 30. Bf6 N×f6 31. e×f6 Rg8 32. Ng5 Bb7 33. Qh4 h5 34. Qf4 Rd7 35. Ne6 f×e6 36. f7 and wins. **26. ... h6** The best move, the holes on the kingside are plugged for a while. **27. Qh2 Be6 28. Kh1** Not so good, as Black is now able to form a pawn majority on the queenside. 28. e×f5 g×f5 29. Qf4 Bc8 30. Qf3 keeps a lasting pressure. **28. ... Kh7 29. g4 f×e4 30. d×e4** There is not much left of White's attack, so Judd could start thinking about some

CAPT. GEORGE HENRY MACKENZIE.  ISIDOR GUNSBERG.  AMOS BURN.  CURT. V. BARDELEBEN.

WILHELM STEINITZ.  MAX JUDD.  MICHAEL TSCHIGOUIN.  C. H. D. GOSSIP.

CONSTANTINE SCHUBERT.  S. LIPSCHUETZ.  J. H. BLACKBURNE.  JAMES MASON.

Some players attending the New York congress. Schubert is Constant Burille; Mackenzie, von Bardeleben and Steinitz ultimately didn't play (courtesy Cleveland Public Library).

active play of his own. 30. ... Qg7 31. Qg3 Rgc8 and 32. ... Ng8 covers all squares around his king once more, while the plans on the queenside are also taking shape. Judd is less patient and plays an inferior move. **30. ... c4 31. Rf3** 31. Nf3 Qd8 32. Bb2 exploits the hasty 30. ... c4. 32. ... d3 or 32. ... c3 is forced, in each case these moves are very easy for White to deal with: 32. ... d3 33. Nd4 d×c2 34. R×f7† and 32. ... c3 33. Ba3. **31. ... c×b3 32. c×b3 Rc3?!** Judd again omits to think about his king's safety first. After 32. ... g5! 33. Nf5 N×f5 34. g×f5 Bc8 all of White's attacking lines are closed. The weaknesses on the queenside grant him a promising game. **33. Qd2 R×f3 34. N×f3 B×b3?** The decisive mistake. Bird wins the important d-pawn and can immediately follow up with a decisive attack. 34. ... Nc6 is likely to lead to a drawish endgame of bishops of opposite colors. **35. N×d4 Bc4 36. Rf6 Qg7 37. e6!** "With his usual energy Mr. Bird grasps the winning opportunity"—Steinitz. **37. ... g5**

**38. R×f7 Q×f7 39. e×f7 B×f7 40. Nf5 Ng6 41. Qd4 Bb3 42. Qd7†** Black resigns—*Tournament Book* (Steinitz), p. 330.

**(911) Mason–Bird   1–0**
American Congress (round 8)
New York, 2 April 1889
*B30*

1. e4 c5 2. Nf3 Nc6 3. Nc3 g6 4. Bc4 Bg7 5. d3 d6 6. 0–0 a6 7. a3 Nf6 8. h3 0–0 9. Be3 e6 10. e5 d×e5 11. B×c5 Re8 12. Ne4 b6 13. Be3 Nd5 14. Qd2 f6 15. Rad1 b5 16. Ba2 f5 17. Bg5 Qc7 18. B×d5 e×d5 19. Nf6† B×f6 20. B×f6 Qd6 21. Bg5 Bb7 22. d4 e4 23. Bf4 Qe6 24. Ne5 Rac8 25. N×c6 Q×c6 26. c3 Re6 27. Rfe1 Rf8 28. Re3 Rf7 29. Rg3 Qe8 30. h4 h5 31. Re1 Kh7 32. Ree3 Qe7 33. Rg5 Bc6 34. Reg3 Be8 35. Qd1 Rf8 36. Re3 a5 37. Qd2 Bf7

**38. Qe2 b4 39. a×b4 a×b4 40. c4 d×c4 41. Q×c4 Ra8 42. d5 Rea6 43. Qd4 Qa7 44. Q×b4 Rb6 45. Qc3 Qa1† 46. Re1 Q×b2 47. Qc7 Rb7 48. Qc6 Ra2 49. Rf1 Qb5 50. Q×b5 R×b5 51. d6 Rd5 52. Rc1 Kg7 53. Rg3 Kf6 54. Rgc3 Be6 55. Rb1 Rda5 56. Rb6 Ra1† 57. Kh2 Rd1 58. Rc7 Raa1 59. d7 Rh1† 60. Kg3 Rad1 61. Bg5† Ke5 62. Rc5†** Black resigns—*Tournament Book*, pp. 297–298.

## (912) Bird–Burille    ½–½
American Congress (round 9)
New York, 3 April 1889
*A03*

**1. f4 d5 2. e3 Nf6 3. Be2 e6 4. Nf3 Bd6 5. Nc3 a6 6. 0–0 c5 7. Qe1 Nc6 8. d4 b6 9. Qg3 0–0 10. Ne5 Bb7 11. N×c6 B×c6 12. Qh3 Ne4 13. N×e4 d×e4 14. c3 f5 15. g4 Qe7 16. Rf2 Be8 17. Rg2 c×d4 18. e×d4 b5 19. Be3 Bc6 20. g×f5 e×f5 21. Kh1 Qe6 22. Rag1 Rf7 23. b3 Bd5 24. Rg5 Be7 25. Rh5 g6 26. c4 b×c4 27. b×c4 B×c4 28. R×g6† Q×g6 29. B×c4 Rb8 30. B×f7† K×f7 31. Q×f5† Q×f5 32. R×f5† Bf6 33. Ra5 Rb6 34. d5 Rd6 35. Kg2 Kg6 36. Ba7 Bd8 37. Rc5 Kf5 38. h3 Rg6† 39. Kf1 K×f4 40. Rc6 R×c6 41. d×c6 Bc7 42. Ke2 h5 43. Bf2 Kf5 44. Bd4 Ke6 45. Ke3 Kd5 46. Ba7 Bd6 47. Bd4 Bc7 48. a4 Bd6 49. Bf6 Bc7 50. Bg5 a5 51. h4 K×c6 52. K×e4 Bg3 53. Be7 Be1 54. Kf5 Kd5 55. Kg5 Kc4** draw—*Tournament Book*, pp. 423–424.

## (913) Weiss–Bird    ½–½
American Congress (round 10)
New York, 4 April 1889
*B25*

**1. e4 c5 2. Nc3 Nc6 3. g3** "One of Louis Paulsen's innovations. It is a good way of leading White's game in this opening"—Steinitz. **3. ... g6 4. Bg2 Bg7 5. d3 d6 6. Nge2 h5 7. h3** "Good and necessary in order to be enabled to advance 8. g4 should Black try to open his h-file by 7. ... h4"—Steinitz. **7. ... Bd7 8. Be3** "We prefer 8. Nd5 and then leaving himself the option as long as possible of retreating Ne3, which latter square is now blocked"—Steinitz. **8. ... Nd4 9. Qd2 Rb8** "The meaning of this at such an early stage is not clear"—Steinitz. **10. Nd1 Qc8** "10. ... Qc7 was a better development, though the text move threatened eventually 11. ... B×h3, and whichever piece would take the bishop, then queen might retake, followed by 12. ... Nf3†"—Steinitz. **11. c3 Nc6** "Black finds a hitch in his contemplated plan. If 11. ... B×h3 12. B×d4 B×g2 13. B×g7 and wins"—Steinitz. **12. d4 b6 13. f4 Na5 14. b3 Nh6 15. Nf2 Qa6 16. 0–0 Bb5 17. c4 Bd7 18. Rad1 Qc8 19. Kh2** Bird's last move was a bit careless, as could have been demonstrated by 19. d×c5 d×c5 20. f5! g×f5 21. Bf4 Rb7 22. e×f5 and he wins material. **19. ... Nc6** 19. ... Nb7, giving some more support to c5, seems preferable. **20. d×c5** "Attack and defense have been well conducted by the two respective players. But here we would have preferred 20. d5, followed soon by 21. Nd3, which would have made the subsequent attack by e5 much stronger"—Steinitz. 20. d5 Nd8 21. Nd3 allows Black to undermine his opponent's position with 21. ... h4 (the slower 21. ... a6 is also good enough) 22. g×h4 b5. **20. ... b×c5** The other pawn had to capture at c5 to minimize the impact of White's next move. **21. e5! d×e5 22. B×c5 Nf5 23. Nd3** *(see diagram)*
**23. ... h4?** "The sacrifice of the pawn to which this leads, though

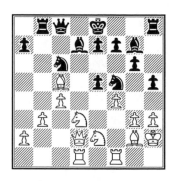

*After 23. Nd3*

it opens the h-file, is not warranted by the position"—Steinitz. Bird's attempt to escape from a precarious situation seems rather desperate. Relatively better was 23. ... Qc7 24. Nc3 (24. B×c6 is not so strong) 24. ... e×f4 25. N×f4, although White's central dominance secures him a safe edge. **24. g4 Ng3 25. N×g3 h×g3† 26. K×g3 Qc7 27. B×c6!** "Best, if 27. f×e5 N×e5 30. Qf4 (or 30. N×e5 B×e5† and wins) 30. ... g5, and wins"—Steinitz. **27. ... B×c6 28. N×e5 B×e5 29. f×e5 f6** "29. ... Q×e5† 30. Qf4 would clearly effect no more than an exchange of queens, for, obviously, if 30. ... Q×c5, White mates by 31. Q×f7†, but, nevertheless, this was his best play under the circumstances, and gave him better prospects of drawing than the plan which he pursues"—Steinitz. **30. Qe3** 30. Bd6! initiates a wonderful attack: 30. ... e×d6 31. R×f6 Qe7 32. Qg5 Rg8 33. Rd×d6. **30. ... Kf7 31. Qf4** "After Black's last bold move the sacrificing tactics were quite appropriate, and we believe that 31. B×e7 K×e7 32. R×f6, followed by 33. Qg5, were good enough to win"—Steinitz. **31. ... Qa5 32. Be3** "Again a little more enterprise on the part of White would, we think, have secured him the victory thus: 32. e6† Kg7 33. B×e7 Qc3† 34. Rf3 Q×f3† 35. Q×f3 B×f3 36. K×f3 R×h3† 37. Ke4, followed by 38. Rd7, and then he may capture the a-pawn or advance the c-pawn, with a winning game"—Steinitz. 34. Kf2 even improves this line. **32. ... Q×a2 33. Rd2 Qa5 34. c5** 34. Rd6! is decisive. **34. ... Rb4 35. Rd4?** 35. Qg5! and once more there is nothing to be done against a rook sacrifice at f6. After Bird's next move White's king goes under sudden fire. **35. ... R×b3 36. Qg5** "White has no other means of parrying the adverse attack. If 36. e×f6 e5 37. Q×e5 Re8 wins. Or if 36. Rd6 R×e3† 37. Q×e3 e×d6 38. R×f6† Kg7 39. R×d6 (or 39. e×d6 Re8 40. Re6 [if 40. Qf2 Qc3† wins] 40. ... R×e6 41. Q×e6 Qc3†, followed by 42. ... Qf6, and the passed a-pawn will win) 39. ... Qc7 etc."—Steinitz. In the mainline, starting with 36. Rd6, Black can have no aspirations to win as at the end of this line White forces a quick perpetual check after 40. Qg5. **36. ... Qe1†!** "An ingenious answer which secures a draw at least, with better prospects of winning for his own side on account of his strong a-pawn"—Steinitz. **37. R×e1 f×g5 38. Rdd1** This allows Bird to take the initiative. 38. e6†! K×e6 39. Rd2 keeps Black's king under fire. **38. ... Ke6!** A perfect shelter for the king. **39. Rb1 Rhb8 40. R×b3 R×b3 41. h4 a5** "By best play on both sides the game was drawn under any circumstances, but it would have given White more trouble to effect that result if Black had exchanged pawns here, so as not to allow the opponent to form a passed pawn."—Steinitz. There are still possibilities for Bird to make some progress; e.g., 41. ... g×h4† 42. K×h4 a5 43. Kg5 a4 44. Bd2 Rd3 45. Ba5 Rd4 46. Re3 Be8 47. Bb6 Rb4 48. Ra3 Rb3 49. Ra1 Re3. **42. h5 g×h5 43. g×h5 a4** 43. ... Kf5 must be played, to pick up the h-pawn once it advances. If 44. Rf1†, then 44. ... K×e5 is very strong. **44. Kg4 a3 45. h6 Be4 46. c6 B×c6 47. h7 Rb8 48. Ra1 Rh8 49. R×a3 R×h7 50. B×g5 Rh1 51. Ra6 Rg1† 52. Kf4 Rf1† 53. Kg4** draw—*Tournament Book* (Steinitz), pp. 68–69.

## (914) Bird–Gossip   0–1
American Congress (round 11)
New York, 5 April 1889
*A03*

**1. f4 d5 2. Nf3 e6 3. e3 Nf6 4. b3 Bd6 5. Bb2 0–0 6. Nc3 c5 7. Ne2 Ne4 8. Ng3 Nc6 9. d3 Nf6 10. Ne5 d4 11. e×d4 c×d4 12. N×c6 b×c6 13. Qf3 Qa5† 14. Kd1 Nd5 15. B×d4 B×f4 16. c4 Qd2** mate—*Tournament Book*, p. 425.

## (915) Showalter–Bird   1–0
American Congress (round 12)
New York, 6 April 1889
*C51*

**1. e4 e5 2. Nf3 Nc6 3. Bc4 Bc5 4. b4 B×b4 5. c3 Bc5 6. 0–0 d6 7. d4 e×d4 8. c×d4 Bb6 9. Nc3 Bg4 10. Qa4 Kf8 11. Bg5** "New in this position, but not of much use, as it drives Black's queen to a better post"—Steinitz. **11. ... Qc8 12. d5 B×f3 13. g×f3 Ne5 14. Be2 Qh3 15. Qd1 Nf6 16. Na4 h5** 16. ... h6! 17. Bc1 h5 is an important improvement. He threatens 18. ... Ng6 and 19. ... Nh4, thus forcing White to seek the exchange of queens with 18. Qb3 Ng6 19. f4 Q×b3 20. a×b3, when White's e-pawn is lost. Instead of 17. ... h5, 17. ... Ng6 18. Kh1 Nh4 19. Rg1 B×f2 is also possible. **17. N×b6?** *(see diagram)*

*After 17. N×b6*

**17. ... a×b6?!** 17. ... Nfg4! (Steinitz) opens up a decisive attack. Two principal lines are 18. f×g4 h×g4 19. Bf4 Nf3† and 18. Bf4 Ng6! (a crucial move. Steinitz mistakenly suggests 18. ... g5?, but then 19. Bg3 N×h2 20. Nd7†! escapes) 19. Bg3 Nh4. **18. Qb3 Nh7 19. Bd2 Nd7 20. Rfc1 Nc5 21. Qe3 Nf6 22. Bf1 Qd7 23. Qc3 Re8** "The rook stood better on the open a-file, and he ought to have proceeded with 23. ... h4 at once"—Steinitz. **24. a4 h4 25. a5 Rh5?!** 25. ... b×a5 26. R×a5 Nf×e4! 27. f×e4 Qg4† maintains a strong attack. **26. Be3 h3 27. Bf4 Rh4** "Loss of time which could have been much better used for the purpose of making his queenside safe by 27. ... b×a5"—Steinitz. **28. Bg3 Rh6 29. a×b6 c×b6 30. Rab1 Qd8 31. Qb4 Nfd7 32. Bb5 Qf6 33. Qc3 Ra8 34. B×d7 Q×c3** "The exchange of queens deteriorates his game. There was no danger to be apprehended from the adverse queen remaining on the board, and if White exchanged, Black evidently gained time by retaking with the rook and attacking the f-pawn"—Steinitz. **35. R×c3 N×d7**

**36. Kf1 Ke7 37. Rc7 Kd8 38. Rbc1 Rb8 39. f4 f6?** This leads to the loss of a pawn in a few moves. 39. ... Ke8 is fine, although White has an annoying pressure after 40. f5. **40. f5** "White's ending play is remarkably fine, and he has now arrived at a winning position"—Steinitz. **40. ... Ke7 41. Rb1 Kd8 42. B×d6 Rc8 43. R×b7 g6 44. f×g6 R×g6 45. Bg3 Rg4 46. f3 R×g3 47. h×g3 Rc2 48. Kg1 Rg2† 49. Kh1 R×g3 50. Rg1 R×g1† 51. K×g1** and White wins—*Tournament Book* (Steinitz), pp. 383–384.

## (916) Bird–D.G. Baird   1–0
American Congress (round 13)
New York, 8 April 1889
*C30*

**1. e4 e5 2. f4 Bc5 3. Nf3 d6 4. c3 Bg4 5. Bc4 Nc6 6. Qb3 B×f3 7. B×f7† Kf8 8. B×g8 R×g8 9. g×f3 Qh4† 10. Kd1 Qf2 11. Kc2 Re8 12. Qc4 e×f4 13. Qf1 Q×f1 14. R×f1 g5 15. d4 Bb6 16. a4 a5 17. Nd2 Nb8 18. Nc4 Nd7 19. b3 Re6 20. Kd3 Rh6 21. Ra2 Rh3 22. Rg2 Rg6 23. Ke2 Kf7 24. Rfg1 Kf6 25. Bd2 Rh5 26. Be1 Kg7 27. Bf2 Kh6 28. Nb2 c6 29. Nd3 Bd8 30. h4 Nf8 31. h×g5† B×g5 32. Be1 Rf6 33. c4 b6 34. Bc3 Rf7 35. e5 d5 36. c5 b×c5 37. N×c5 Ra7 38. Bd2 Ra8 39. R×g5** Black resigns—*Tournament Book*, pp. 419–420.

## (917) Lipschütz–Bird   ½–½
American Congress (round 14)
New York, 9 April 1889
*B34*

**1. e4 c5 2. Nc3 Nc6 3. Nf3 g6 4. d4 c×d4 5. N×d4 Bg7 6. Be3 d6 7. Be2 Bd7 8. 0–0 h5 9. Qd2 h4 10. h3 Nf6 11. a3 N×d4 12. B×d4 Bc6 13. Bd3 Qa5 14. Qe2 Nh5 15. B×g7 N×g7 16. Rae1 Ne6 17. Qe3 g5 18. Be2 Nf4 19. Bg4 Qe5 20. Rd1 Rg8 21. Qd4 Q×d4 22. R×d4 Bd7 23. B×d7† K×d7 24. f3 Rgc8 25. Rf2 Rc5 26. Nd1 Rac8 27. Ne3 Rb5 28. c3 Rc6 29. Rdd2 e6 30. Ng4 f5 31. e×f5 e×f5 32. Ne3 Re5 33. Nc2 Rc8 34. Nd4 Rce8 35. Rf1 Nh5 36. Rfd1 Ng3 37. Kf2 g4 38. f×g4 Ne4† 39. Kf1 N×d2† 40. R×d2 f×g4 41. h×g4 Re4 42. g5 Rf8† 43. Nf3 h3 44. Rf2 h×g2† 45. K×g2 Rff4 46. Nh2 R×f2† 47. K×f2 Ke6 48. Nf3 Kf5 49. Nd4† K×g5 50. Nb5 d5 51. N×a7 Rh4 52. Ke3 Kf5 53. Nb5 Ke5 54. Nd4 Rh3† 55. Kd2 Rh2† 56. Kc1 Ke4 57. Kb1 Kd3 58. Ka2 Kc4 59. Nb3 b6 60. Nd4 Rh6 61. Nf5 Re6 62. Nd4 Re4 63. Nb3 Re2 64. Nd4 Rd2 65. Nc6 Re2 66. Nd4 Re4 67. Nb3 Rf4 68. Nd2† Kd3 69. Nb3 Re4 70. Nc1† Kc2 71. Nb3 Kd3 72. Nc1† Kc4 73. Nb3 Re2 74. Nd4 Rd2 75. Nc6 Re2 76. Nd4 Re5 77. Nc6 Re3 78. Nd4 Re8 79. Nf5 Re6 80. Nd4 Rf6 81. Nc2 Re6 82. Nd4 Re5 83. Nb3 Rf5 84. Nd4 Rf2 85. Nb3 Re2 86. Nd4 Re1 87. Nc6 Re4 88. Nd4 Kd3 89. Nb3 Kc2 90. Na1† Kd1 91. Nb3 Rf4 92. Kb1 Re4 93. Ka2 Kc2 94. Na1† Kd3 95. Nb3 Ke3 96. Kb1 Rf4 97. Ka2 Kd3 98. Nc1† Kc2 99. Nb3 Rf1 100. Na1† Kd3 101. Nb3 Rd1 102. Nd4 Kc4 103. Nb3 Rd3 104. Nc1 Rd2 105. Nb3 Rd1 106. Na1 d4 107. c×d4 R×d4 108. Nb3 Rd1 109. Na1 Rd2 110. Nb3 Re2 111. Na1 Rf2 112. Nb3 Rf4 113. Nd2† Kd3 114. Nb3 Rc4 115. Na1 Rc8 116. Kb3 Rc4 117. Ka2 Rh4 118. Kb3 Rh2 119. Ka2 Kc4 120. Nb3 Re2 121. Na1 Re5 122. Nb3 Rd5 123. Na1 Rd2 124. Nb3 Re2 125. Na1 b5 126. Nb3 b4 127. a×b4 K×b4 128. Nc1 Re3 129. Kb1 Kc4 130. Kc2**

**Kd4 131. Nb3† Kc4 132. Nd2† Kb4 133. Kd1 Kc5 134. Kc2 Rh3 135. Nb3† Kc4 136. Nd2† Kd4 137. Nb1 Rh2† 138. Kb3 Kd3 139. Nc3 Rh8 140. Kb4 Rb8† 141. Nb5 Ke4 142. Kc4 Rc8† 143. Kb4 Kd5 144. Nc3† Kc6 145. Kc4 Kb6† 146. Kb4 Ka6 147. Nd1 Rd8 148. Ne3 Rb8† 149. Kc3 Rc8† 150. Kb4 Kb6 151. Nd5† Ka6 152. Ne3 Rb8† 153. Kc3 Ka5 154. Nc4† Ka4 155. Nd2 Rc8† 156. Nc4 Kb5 157. b3 Kc5 158. Nb2 Rh8 159. Nd3† Kb5** drawn by decision of the umpire after a count of fifty moves had taken place at the request of White—*Tournament Book* (Steinitz), pp. 257–259.

## (918) Bird–Blackburne   0–1
American Congress (round 15)
New York, 10 April 1889
*D70*

1. c4 g6 2. d4 d5 3. c×d5 Nf6 4. Nf3 Bg7 5. e3 0–0 6. Be2 N×d5 7. Nc3 N×c3 8. b×c3 Nd7 9. a4 c5 10. Qb3 c×d4 11. c×d4 Nc5 12. Qc2 b6 13. Ra3 Bf5 14. Qd1 Ne4 15. 0–0 Rc8 16. Bb2 Nd6 17. Nd2 Rc7 18. a5 b5 19. Rc3 a6 20. Qa1 R×c3 21. B×c3 Qb8 22. Nb3 Rc8 23. Bf3 Be4 24. Nc5 B×f3 25. g×f3 Nf5 26. Bb4 Nh4 27. Qd1 Bf8 28. f4 h5 29. f3 Qa7 30. Kh1 Nf5 31. Qd3 Bg7 32. Rd1 Qa8 33. d5 Qa7 34. e4 Nd4 35. e5 Nf5 36. Rc1 h4 37. Kg2 Qa8 38. Kh3 Rd8 39. Rd1 Qc8 40. e6 Bd4 41. Rc1 R×d5 42. Qe4 Ne3 43. f5 R×f5 44. Re1 B×c5 45. B×c5 Q×c5 46. R×e3 f6 47. f4 Kg7 48. Rd3 Qc1 49. Rf3 Qc4 50. Qe3 g5 51. Qb6 R×f4 52. R×f4 Q×f4 53. Qc6 Qf1† White resigns— *Tournament Book*, pp. 172–173.

## (919) Gunsberg–Bird   1–0
American Congress (round 16)
New York, 11 April 1889
*B00*

1. d4 e6 2. e4 b6 3. Bd3 Bb7 4. Nf3 g6 5. 0–0 Bg7 6. c3 h5 7. Be3 d6 8. Qc2 Nd7 9. Nbd2 Qe7 10. Rae1 h4 11. h3 Bh6 12. e5 d×e5 13. d×e5 0–0–0 14. Be4 B×e3 15. B×b7† K×b7 16. R×e3 Nh6 17. Qe4† Ka6 18. c4 Nc5 19. Ra3† Black resigns—*Tournament Book*, p. 125.

## (920) Bird–Chigorin   0–1
American Congress (round 17)
New York, 12 April 1889
*C55*

1. e4 e5 2. Nf3 Nc6 3. Bc4 Nf6 4. Qe2 Bc5 5. Nc3 d6 6. d3 Na5 7. a3 N×c4 8. d×c4 0–0 9. Bg5 c6 10. h3 Qe7 11. Rd1 Qe6 12. b4 Bb6 13. Nh4 Bd4 14. Nb1 d5 15. e×d5 c×d5 16. c3 Bb6 17. c5 Bc7 18. B×f6 Q×f6 19. Nf3 Qg6 20. g3 Bd7 21. b5 a6 22. Nh4 Qf6 23. a4 a×b5 24. a×b5 Ra5 25. c4 Qe7 26. Nc3 d×c4 27. b6 Bb8 28. Ne4 Be6 29. Qh5 f6 30. Nf5 B×f5 31. Q×f5 g6 32. Qf3 Qe6 33. 0–0 Rb5 34. Qe2 h6 35. Qc2 f5 36. Qa4 Rb2 37. Nc3 e4 38. Nd5 c3 39. Nc7 B×c7 40. b×c7 Rd2 41. R×d2 c×d2 42. Qd4 Qc6 43. Qd6 Kf7 44. Q×d2 Q×c7 45. Qd5† Kg7 46. Rb1 Rf7 47. Rb6 Re7 48. Rd6 Kh7 49. Kg2 h5 50. g4 Rg7 51. Kg3 Qe7 52. Qd2 Qe5† 53. Qf4 h4† White resigns—*Tournament Book*, pp. 9–10.

## (921) Taubenhaus–Bird   ½–½
American Congress (round 18)
New York, 13 April 1889
*B56*

1. e4 c5 2. Nf3 Nc6 3. d4 c×d4 4. N×d4 d6 5. Nc3 Nf6 6. Bb5 Bd7 7. 0–0 h5 8. f3 g6 9. Nce2 Bg7 10. c3 h4 11. Be3 Ne5 12. h3 a6 13. B×d7† Q×d7 14. f4 Nc4 15. Qd3 N×b2 16. Qc2 Nc4 17. Bf2 Rc8 18. Rad1 Qc7 19. Rfe1 Nd7 20. Nf3 Bf6 21. Ned4 e5 22. Ne2 b5 23. a4 b×a4 24. f×e5 d×e5 25. Nh2 Be7 26. Ng4 a3 27. Rd3 Qc6 28. Rd5 f6 29. Nc1 Ndb6 30. Rd3 Rd8 31. Rf1 R×d3 32. Q×d3 Nd7 33. Kh1 Nd6 34. Re1 Qc4 35. Qc2 Nb5 36. Na2 Nd6 37. Nb4 a5 38. Nd5 a2 39. Nge3 Qc6 40. N×e7 K×e7 41. Nd5† Kf7 42. Q×a2 Qc4 43. Qa3 Qc6 44. c4 Re8 45. B×h4 a4 46. c5 Nb7 47. Nb4 Q×c5 48. Q×a4 Nb6 49. Qb3† Qc4 50. Q×c4† N×c4 51. Rf1 Re6 52. Nd5 Nd2 53. Rc1 Nd6 54. Rc7† Kf8 55. B×f6 N2×e4 56. Be7† Kg8 57. B×d6 N×d6 58. Rc6 Kf7 59. Kg1 Ne8 and the game was finally a draw—*Tournament Book*, pp. 432–433.

## (922) MacLeod–Bird   0–1
American Congress (round 19)
New York, 15 April 1889
*C20*

1. e4 e5 2. c3 d5 3. Nf3 d×e4 4. N×e5 Nf6 5. Qa4† Bd7 6. Qb3 Be6 7. Q×b7 Bd6 8. Q×a8 B×e5 9. Bb5† c6 10. B×c6† N×c6 11. Q×c6† Bd7 12. Qc4 Qb8 13. d4 e×d3 *e.p.* 14. Q×d3 0–0 15. Be3 Q×b2 16. 0–0 Q×a1 17. Qc2 Be6 18. f4 Bb8 19. c4 Ng4 20. Bc5 Qf6 21. B×f8 Qd4† 22. Kh1 K×f8 23. Qb3 Bd6 24. Qf3 g6 25. h3 Ne3 26. Rf2 N×c4 27. Nc3 Bc5 28. Re2 Qg1 mate— *Tournament Book*, pp. 428–429.

## (923) J.W. Baird–Bird   ½–½
American Congress (round 20, game 1)
New York, 18 April 1889
*B54*

1. e4 c5 2. Nf3 Nc6 3. d4 c×d4 4. N×d4 d6 5. Be3 Bd7 6. Bd3 Nf6 7. 0–0 g6 8. Nc3 Bg7 9. Nce2 Ng4 10. Qd2 h5 11. N×c6 b×c6 12. Bd4 B×d4 13. N×d4 Qb6 14. Qc3 0–0 15. h3 Ne5 16. Be2 c5 17. Nf3 f6 18. Nh4 Kh7 19. f4 Nc6 20. f5 Nd4 21. f×g6† Kg7 22. Bc4 e6 23. Qd2 d5 24. e×d5 e×d5 25. B×d5 Rad8 26. c3 Qd6 27. Bf7 Qg3 28. c×d4 Q×h4 29. Qf4 Q×f4 30. R×f4 c×d4 31. R×d4 Bf5 32. Rad1 Rb8 33. b3 Rbc8 34. Rd5 B×g6 35. B×g6 K×g6 36. Rd7 a5 37. R1d2 Rfe8 38. R7d4 Rc3 39. Rf2 Re6 40. h4 Rc1† 41. Kh2 Ree1 42. Rd6 Rh1† 43. Kg3 Rc3† 44. Rf3 R×f3† 45. K×f3 Ra1 46. a4 Rb1 47. Rb6 Rf1† 48. Kg3 Rd1 49. Rb5 Rd3† 50. Kh2 Re3 51. R×a5 R×b3 52. Ra8 Kf5 53. a5 Rb4 54. Kh3 Rb3† 55. g3 Rb1 56. Rh8 Rh1† 57. Kg2 Ra1 58. R×h5† Kg4 59. Rb5 Ra2† 60. Kf1 draw—*Tournament Book*, pp. 422–423.

## (924) Bird–Delmar   0–1
American Congress (round 21)
New York, 19 April 1889
*A03*

1. f4 e6 2. e3 d5 3. Nf3 Bd6 4. b3 Nf6 5. Bb2 c5 6. Bb5† Bd7
. a4 a6 8. Bd3 Bc6 9. 0–0 Nbd7 10. Qe1 Qc7 11. Qg3 Rg8
2. Ne5 g6 13. Na3 Nh5 14. Qf3 f6 15. N×c6 Q×c6 16. c4 f5
7. g4 Nhf6 18. g5 Ne4 19. Rad1 0–0–0 20. c×d5 e×d5 21. Be2
4 22. b×c4 Q×a4 23. Nb1 Qb3 24. Bd4 Bc5 25. d3 B×d4
6. e×d4 Nc3 27. N×c3 Q×c3 28. Q×d5 Nb8 29. Qc5† Nc6
0. d5 Qd4† 31. Q×d4 N×d4 32. Kf2 Rge8 33. Bf3 b6 34. Rb1
c7 35. Rb2 Rb8 36. Bg2 Kd6 37. h4 b5 38. Ra2 Rb6 39. Rc1
c8 40. Ke3 Nb3 41. Rc3 Re8† 42. Kf2 b×c4 43. R×c4 Nc5
4. Rc3 Rb4 45. Rac2 R×f4† 46. Bf3 Rc8 47. Kg3 Rb4 48. Kh3
5 49. d4 R×d4 50. Rb2 Rd3 51. Rb6† Ke5 52. Re6† N×e6
3. R×d3 Nf4† White resigns—*Tournament Book*, pp. 356–257.

## (925) Burn–Bird  1–0
American Congress (round 22)
New York, 20 April 1889
*325*

1. e4 c5 2. Nc3 Nc6 3. g3 g6 4. Bg2 Bg7 5. d3 d6 6. Nf3 a6
7. h3 Bd7 8. 0–0 Ra7 9. Nd5 h5 10. c3 Nf6 11. N×f6† B×f6
12. Be3 Qc8 13. Kh2 h4 14. g4 Be5† 15. N×e5 N×e5 16. f4 Nc6
17. d4 b6 18. d5 Nd8 19. Qf3 f6 20. e5 d×e5 21. f×e5 Qb8
22. Kh1 f×e5 23. Qe4 Rg8 24. Bg5 Qd6 25. Rae1 Rh8 26. Q×e5
Q×e5 27. R×e5 Bb5 28. Rfe1 Rh7 29. Be4 Kf8 30. B×g6 Rh8
31. B×e7† Kg7 32. Bh5 Nf7 33. Rf5 R×h5 34. R×h5 Rd7 35. b3
Bd3 36. R×h4 R×d5 37. g5 Bf5 38. Bf6† Kg6 39. Re2 Rd3
40. Kh2 a5 41. Rg2 b5 42. c4 b4 43. Be7 a4 44. b×a4 Ra3
45. B×c5 R×a4 46. Be7 Ra3 47. B×b4 Rd3 48. Be7 Re3 49. Bf6
Nd6 50. Rh6† Kf7 51. g6† Black resigns—*Tournament Book*, p.
218.

## (926) Bird–Hanham  1–0
American Congress (round 23)
New York, 21 April 1889
*A03*

1. f4 d5 2. e3 e6 3. Nh3 Nh6 "The unusual development of the
knight which both parties adopt is more favorable for Black who
has good prospects of forming a center, commencing with 4. ...
f6"—Steinitz. 4. b3 f6 5. Be2 Bd6 6. Nc3 a6 "Much better was
6. ... c5 or 6. ... Nf7"—Steinitz. 7. Bh5† g6 8. Bf3 Nf7 9. Bb2 Nd7
10. 0–0 h5 "We see no positive object in this advance which loosens
his kingside"—Steinitz. 11. Qe1 Qe7 12. a4 Rh7 13. Qe2 c6 14. a5
e5 *(see diagram)*

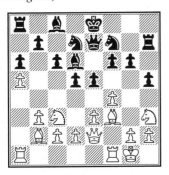

*After 14. ... e5*

15. f×e5 At once 15. B×d5! denies Black any escape. There could
follow 15. ... c×d5 16. N×d5 Qe6 17. c4 Kd8 18. f×e5 Nf×e5 19. Nhf4

Qe8 20. d4 Nc6 21. e4 with huge play. 15. ... f×e5 15. ... Nf×e5! was
necessary. 16. B×d5! "A high-spirited sacrifice, based on fine position
judgment"—Steinitz. 16. ... c×d5 17. N×d5 Qe6 18. Qc4 Nf8
19. Ba3 Rg7 20. B×d6 N×d6 21. Nc7† 21. Qa4† Nb5 22. c4 and
23. Nb6 is much simpler. If 21. ... Bd7 22. Nc7† Ke7 23. Qh4†. 21. ...
R×c7 22. Q×c7 Qe7 23. Q×e7† K×e7 24. Ng5 Bf5 25. d3 e4
"25. ... Rc8 was much better"—Steinitz. 26. d4 Ne6 27. N×e6 K×e6
28. c4 Rc8 29. Ra4 Rc7 30. Rb4 Ke7 31. Kf2 Be6 32. Ke1 Bc8
33. Kd2 Be6 34. h4 Bf5 35. Rf4 Kd7 36. Kc3 Nb5† 37. Kd2 Nd6
38. d5 Rc5 39. Ra4 Ke7 40. Kc3 Rc7 41. Kd4 Kf6 42. Rb4 Rd7
43. Rb6 Ke7 44. c5 Nc8 45. R×f5 "The culmination at this juncture
of White's finely-conceived plan has been led up to with consummate
skill"—Steinitz. 45. ... g×f5 46. Rh6 Kd8 47. R×h5 Ne7 48. d6
Nc6† 49. Kd5 Rf7 50. Ke6 Rf8 51. g3 Nd4† 52. Ke5 N×b3
53. R×f5 Re8† 54. Kd5 N×a5 55. h5 Nc6 56. g4 a5 57. h6 a4
58. Rf7 Re5† 59. Kc4 Re6 60. Rf8† Kd7 61. h7 Rh6 62. h8Q and
White wins—*Tournament Book* (Steinitz), pp. 427–428.

## (927) Pollock–Bird  1–0
American Congress (round 24)
New York, 23 April 1889
*B72*

1. e4 c5 2. d4 c×d4 3. Nf3 Nc6 4. N×d4 d6 5. Be3 g6 6. Nc3
Bg7 7. Be2 Nf6 8. Qd2 h5 9. h3 0–0 10. 0–0–0 Bd7 11. f4 N×d4
12. B×d4 Bc6 13. Bd3 Qa5 14. Kb1 e5 15. Be3 Rfd8 16. f5 d5
17. Bh6 d×e4 18. B×g7 K×g7 19. N×e4 Q×d2 20. N×d2 e4
21. Bc4 g×f5 22. Kc1 b5 23. Be2 Nd5 24. Rdf1 Ne3 25. Rf4 Kg6
26. Re1 Kg5 27. Rf2 Nd5 28. g4 h×g4 29. h×g4 e3 30. R×f5†
Kg6 31. Nf3 f6 32. Nh4† Kg7 33. g5 Rh8 34. g×f6† N×f6
35. Rg1† Kf7 36. Rg6 R×h4 37. Rg×f6† Ke7 38. R×c6 Rh2
39. B×b5 Rh1† 40. Rf1 R×f1† 41. B×f1 Rf8 42. Be2 Rf2 43. Kd1
Rg2 44. Ke1 Black resigns—*Tournament Book*, p. 406.

## (928) Bird–D.M. Martinez  0–1
American Congress (round 25)
New York, 24 April 1889
*A25*

1. c4 e5 2. Nc3 Nc6 3. g3 f5 4. Bg2 Nf6 5. a3 Bc5 6. e3 0–0
7. Nge2 Re8 8. b4 Bf8 9. 0–0 d6 10. Bb2 e4 11. Nf4 Ne5 12. Qe2
g5 13. Nfd5 Nfd7 14. f3 Nd3 15. f×e4 N7e5 16. Nd1 N×b2
17. N×b2 f×e4 18. Nf6† Kh8 19. Qh5 Re7 20. B×e4 h6 21. d4
Nd7 22. Qg6 N×f6 23. Q×f6† Bg7 24. Qg6 Qg8 25. Rf2 c6
26. Raf1 Bh3 27. Bg2 B×g2 28. K×g2 R×e3 29. Rf3 Re2†
30. R1f2 Rae8 31. Q×d6 Qh7 32. Nd3 Qe4 33. R×e2 Q×e2†
34. Nf2 Q×c4 35. Qd7 Re1 36. Qc8† Kh7 37. Qf5† Kh8 38. Kh3
Q×d4 39. Rd3 Qf6 40. Q×f6 B×f6 41. Rd6 Kg7 42. Ng4 Bb2
43. N×h6 B×a3 44. Nf5† Kf7 45. Rd7† Kf6 46. Nh6 B×b4
47. R×b7 a5 48. Rc7 Rc1 49. Ra7 Rc4 50. Kg2 Kg6 51. Nf7 Kf5
52. R×a5† Kf6 53. Ra7 Rc2† 54. Kh3 c5 55. Nd8 c4 56. Kg4
Bd2 57. Ra6† Ke5 58. Nf7† Kd4 59. h3 c3 60. Ra4† Kc5
61. N×g5 Kb5 62. Ra8 Rb2 63. Nf3 Rb4† 64. Kf5 c2 65. Rb8†
Ka6 66. Rc8 c1Q 67. R×c1 B×c1 68. h4 Kb7 69. h5 Kc8 70. Ne5
Rb5 71. Ke6 Rb6† 72. Kf5 Kd8 73. g4 Rb5 74. Ke6 Ke8 75. Ng6
Rg5 76. Ne5 Bb2 77. Nc4 Bg7 78. Nd6† Kf8 White resigns—
*Tournament Book*, pp. 431–432.

**(929) J.W. Baird–Bird  1–0**
American Congress (round 20, game 2)
New York, 25 April 1889
*C61*

1. e4 e5 2. Nf3 Nc6 3. Bb5 Nd4 4. N×d4 e×d4 5. 0–0 h5 6. d3 Bc5 7. Bf4 g5 8. Bd2 c6 9. Bc4 d5 10. e×d5 c×d5 11. Qe2† Kf8 12. Qe5 Qf6 13. Q×d5 Be7 14. B×g5 Qg6 15. B×e7† N×e7 16. Qd8† Kg7 17. Q×e7 Rf8 18. Qe5† Kh7 19. Nd2 Rg8 20. g3 Bh3 21. Ne4 Rg7 22. Nf6† Kh6 23. Qf4† Qg5 24. Q×g5† and White wins—*Tournament Book*, p. 423.

**(930) Judd–Bird  0–1**
American Congress (round 26)
New York, 26 April 1889
*C61*

1. e4 e5 2. Nf3 Nc6 3. Bb5 Nd4 4. N×d4 e×d4 5. d3 "The *Modern Chess Instructor* recommends 5. 0–0, and continues 5. ... c6 6. Ba4 Nf6 7. Re1"—Steinitz. **5. ... h5 6. c3 c6 7. Bc4 Bc5 8. Qf3 Qe7 9. 0–0 d6 10. h3 Be6 11. Nd2 g5 12. B×e6 f×e6 13. Nb3 g4 14. Qg3** 14. h×g4 h×g4 15. Q×g4 is possible, although the open lines against White's king look a bit dangerous. **14. ... g×h3 15. Q×h3 d×c3 16. b×c3 Bb6 17. Be3** "It was preferable to shut out the bishop and to form a strong center by 17. d4. His own bishop had more scope of action in all directions than that of the opponent"—Steinitz. **17. ... B×e3 18. f×e3 Nf6 19. Rf3** *(see diagram)* This weak move overturns the course of the game. Instead of consolidating a small edge with 19. Rf4, Bird gets excellent practical chances with his reply.

*After 19. Rf3*

19. ... Ng4! 20. Nd4 0–0–0 21. Raf1 Rh7 22. Ne2 Re8 23. Nf4 Ne5 24. Rg3? "Overlooking or underestimating the opponent's ingenious reply which gives Black just the sort of a lively attack that suits Mr. Bird's style"—Steinitz. 24. R3f2 is forced. Bird could continue with 24. ... Rh6 (24. ... Ng4 25. Rf3 Rg8 is also interesting) 25. a4 Rg8 with strong pressure. 25. d4 leaves the e-pawn weak after 25. ... Ng4 26. Rf3 Qh7. **24. ... h4! 25. Ng6 Qg7 26. N×h4 Qh8 27. Rf4 N×d3 28. Rfg4 Kc7 29. Qh1 Q×c3 30. Kh2 Reh8 31. Qf1 R×h4† 32. R×h4 R×h4† 33. Kg1 Qe1 34. Q×e1 N×e1 35. Rg7† Kb6** White resigns—*Tournament Book* (Steinitz), p. 331.

**(931) Bird–Mason  1–0**
American Congress (round 27)
New York, 27 April 1889
*A03*

1. f4 d5 2. e3 c5 3. Nf3 a6 4. b3 Nc6 5. Bb2 e6 6. Be2 Nf6 7. 0–0 Be7 8. Qe1 0–0 9. d3 Ne8 10. Ne5 Bd7 11. Qg3 f5 "As usual, we condemn such a move that leaves a hole in the center. 11. ... f6 was by far better"—Steinitz. **12. Nd2 Bf6 13. Ndf3 b5 14. Qh3 N×e5 15. B×e5 B×e5 16. N×e5 Nd6 17. Rf3 Be8 18. g4 Ra7 19. Kh1 a5** Not bad, but 19. ... Qa5 prevents White from bringing his last piece to the kingside. **20. Rg1 b4 21. Rfg3 a4 22. g×f5 N×f5 23. Rg5 a×b3 24. a×b3 Qf6** First 23. ... h6 and then 24. Rg4 Qf6 prevents the elimination of an important defensive piece. **25. Bg6 h6 26. B×f5 e×f5 27. R5g3 d4 28. e4** 28. Qg2 d×e3 29. Qd5† Kh7 30. Q×c5 Rff7 31. Q×e3 wins a pawn, but Black manages to hold the balance thanks to 31. ... Bc6† 32. N×c6 Q×c6† 33. R3g2 Rfe7 34. Qf2 Ra2. The text move is not without risk. **28. ... g5?** "The opponent has formed his attack most skillfully, and it is difficult to suggest anything good for Black. Of course, if 28. ... f×e4 29. Ng4 followed by 30. N×h6† with a winning game"—Steinitz. 28. ... Kh7! is the correct move. The king evades the g-file, after which Black threatens to play 29. ... f×e4. It is not in White's advantage to exchange at f5, as this only creates weaknesses in his own camp. Best is 29. Qg2 but this was very difficult to estimate had Black then replied with 29. ... g5! With his position on the verge of a breakdown, White had to find the brilliant 30. Nd7! R×d7 31. f×g5 to demonstrate the downside of 29. ... g5. Now 31. ... h×g5 32. R×g5 Qh6 33. Rg3 Bh5 34. Rh3 is probably a draw: White will win back his piece and the exchange of queens is also likely. More testing is 31. ... Qe5—e.g., 32. g×h6 f4 33. Rg5 f3 34. R×e5 f×g2† 35. R×g2 c4! 36. b×c4 Ra7 and a draw is still possible. **29. Qg2?** The knight could be abandoned at once, as after 29. f×g5! Q×e5 30. g×h6† Kh8 31. h7 Black can resign. **29. ... Rg7 30. e×f5 Q×f5** Interesting is 30. ... Kh7, and after 31. Qd5 Re7 the position remains full with tension. **31. Qd5† Bf7 32. Q×c5 Rd8?** *(see diagram)* Just as a few moves earlier, the position is extremely difficult to pierce through. Black could win a piece with 32. ... Qc8! 33. Nc6 (taking a pawn—e.g., 33. Q×d4?—is very unwise due to the weakness of the long diagonal demonstrated by 33. ... Qa8† and 34. ... Bd5) 33. ... Kh7 34. f×g5 Rg6, but the resulting endgame is hard to convert into a win.

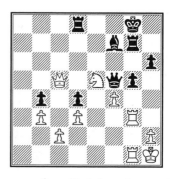

*After 32. ... Rd8*

**33. Rf1!** A brilliant calm move from Bird that wins outright. Had Mason now defended more tenaciously with 33. ... g×f4, White had to find 34. R×g7† K×g7 35. Qe7 Rf8 36. Rf2! (another silent move that neutralizes the bishop check that occurs after the immediate 36. Rg1† Kh7 37. Q×f8?? Bd5†) 36. ... Kg8 37. Rg2†. **33. ... Rd5 34. N×f7** "In Mr. Bird's happy mood. Of course, he recovers the queen immediately by 35. N×h6†, but still this is very pretty"—Steinitz. **34. ... R×f7 35. Q×b4 Kh7 36. Rgf3 g4 37. R3f2 h5**

**38. Qe1 Qd7 39. Re2 Rdf5 40. Re4 Qd5 41. Kg1 Kh6 42. Qf2 Rd7 43. Rfe1 Qf7 44. Re6† Kh7 45. R1e4 Rfd5 46. Qh4 Qf5 47. Rf6** Black resigns. "Virtually his victory was secured for some time, but the queen is here caught very neatly"—Steinitz. *Tournament Book* (Steinitz), p. 299.

## (932) Burille–Bird    0–1
American Congress (round 28)
New York, 29 April 1889
*A85*

**1. d4 f5 2. c4 Nf6 3. Nc3 e6 4. e3 Bb4 5. Qb3 c5 6. Bd3 b6 7. Nge2 Nc6 8. a3 B×c3† 9. Q×c3 0–0 10. b3** "10. d5 was stronger as Black could not capture twice, for then White, after pinning with 12. Bc4, could also bring Nf4 and Qd3 to bear upon it. 10. b4 was also better"—Steinitz. **10. ... Bb7 11. Bb2 c×d4 12. e×d4 Ne7 13. 0–0 Rc8 14. Rae1 Ng6 15. Qd2 Ne4 16. Qc1** *(see diagram)* Sheer loss of time. 16. B×e4 was necessary, but not very ambitious.

*After 16. Qc1*

**16. ... Qh4** A very interesting and complicated position has been reached. Bird's move is logical, but it wouldn't lead to anything against a correct defense. As g2 is the weak spot in White's camp, 16. ... Nh4 appears workable. Now White does best to play 17. B×e4 so that the long diagonal will be closed. Yet, after 17. ... f×e4 18. Ng3 d5 it is clear that the pawn structure is in Bird's favor. White has some other options, but they are all surprisingly bad due to the weakness of the long h1–a8 diagonal. A few lines illustrate Black's attacking ideas: 17. f3 Ng5 (threatening 17. ... Ng×f3†) 18. Qe3 f4! 19. N×f4 Ng×f3† 20. R×f3 B×f3 21. g3 R×f4 wins or 17. Ng3 Ng5 18. f3 B×f3 19. g×f3 Ng×f3† 20. Kh1 N×e1 21. Q×e1 Qg5, when material is about equal but Black's initiative very annoying. **17. f3 Ng5 18. Ng3?** This move allows the second knight to enter the game with decisive effect. Preventive measures such as either 18. Kh1 or 18. d5 e×d5 19. Qd1 are necessary. In the latter line White sacrifices a pawn but he has more than enough piece play to compensate. **18. ... Nf4!** Decisive. There appear to be no major threats yet, but besides the knight sacrifices that were seen in the variations at move 16, something is bound to happen on the h-file. Bird manages the attack perfectly. **19. Qc3 Rf6! 20. Bc1 Rh6** "Beautiful and decisive"—Steinitz. **21. B×f4 Q×h2† 22. Kf2 Nh3† 23. Ke3 N×f4 24. K×f4 Rg6 25. Ke3 R×g3 26. Rf2 R×g2 27. Ref1 f4† 28. Ke2 B×f3†! 29. Ke1** "There was no better answer to White's last master move, for if 29. K×f3 then followed 29. ... Qg3† and 30. ... Qe3† winning the rook"—Steinitz. **29. ... R×f2 30. R×f2 Qg1† 31. Bf1 Be4 32. R×f4 Rf8 33. R×f8†**

**K×f8 34. c5 Bg2** White resigns—*Tournament Book* (Steinitz), pp. 424–425.

## (933) Bird–Weiss    ½–½
American Congress (round 29, game 1)
New York, 3 May 1889
*A03*

**1. f4 d5 2. e3 Nf6 3. Nf3 a6** "Such a wing pawn move should be retained at least"—Steinitz. **4. b3 e6 5. Bb2 Be7 6. Be2 c5 7. 0–0 0–0 8. Qe1 Nc6 9. a3 b5 10. d3** "White's disposition of pawns is quite contrary to modern maxims of play. His center is thoroughly weak"—Steinitz. **10. ... Bb7 11. Nbd2 Rc8** The thematic 11. ... d4! saddles White with some weaknesses. After the text move 12. c4 is fine for White. **12. Qg3 Ne8 13. Qh3 Bf6** "Black fails here to disorganize the adverse center and queenside, which he could have done apparently by 13. ... d4 14. e4 f5 15. e5 (if 15. e×f5 e×f5, and Black will soon obtain the stronger position on the open e-file, owing to the bad placement of White's pieces) 15. ... Nc7, followed by 16. ... Nd5, and White's two holes at e3 and c3 will be sore points in the latter's game"—Steinitz. Either pawn move at move 15 is a concession. 15. Rae1 keeps the strong center intact. **14. Ne5 N×e5 15. B×e5 Nd6 16. Bg4 c4 17. Nf3 Re8 18. Nd4 c×b3** "We can see nothing for Black to fear that was not on the board before, and the opening of the adverse game was quite premature, for it could be well reserved with advantage, as White could not well initiate the exchange of pawns. 18. ... g6 at once was the right play; and if, for instance, 19. b×c4 d×c4 20. e4 B×e5 21. f×e5 N×e4 etc.; for if 22. N×e6 Qb6† and wins"—Steinitz. 18. ... g6?! is certainly not without danger, as White can commence a terrible attack with 19. Rf3, threatening 20. Qh6 and 21. Rh3. If 19. ... Kg7 20. B×e6! is strong. The same sacrifice is a motive if Black plays Bg7 at some point. **19. c×b3 g6 20. Rac1** The same idea, 20. Rf3, remains powerful. The text move promises a slight, rather innocent, pull. **20. ... R×c1** "Allowing the opponent the open file for the rook without good cause. 20. ... Nf5, with the probable continuation 21. R×c8 B×c8 22. B×f5 e×f5 23. Nf3 Kg7 24. Qg3 Qa5 was good enough"—Steinitz. The consequences of 20. ... Nf5 are less favorable than abandoning the c-file, which White cannot use anyway, 21. R×c8! B×c8 22. Nc6! Qb6 23. B×f6 Q×c6 24. B×f5 e×f5 25. Bd4 with a lasting initiative. **21. R×c1 Nf5 22. B×f5 e×f5 23. B×f6 Q×f6 24. b4 Rc8** This exchange is beneficial for White, who can activate his queen much easier now. 24. ... Qe7 defends c7 and posts the queen on a superior square. **25. R×c8† B×c8 26. Qf3 Qe7 27. Kf2 Qh4† 28. Qg3 Qe7** "Black rightly distrusts his position for the ending with bishop against knight, for with one pawn isolated and another doubled he would have been at a disadvantage after exchanging queens"—Steinitz. **29. Ke2 a5 30. Qe1** "An excellent answer if properly pursued"—Steinitz. **30. ... a×b4 31. a×b4** "White ought to have retaken with the queen, forcing the exchange. It was then an easy matter for him to get his king in at d4, after withdrawing the knight, which could then manoeuvre to c5. Being sure of breaking in finally by e4, he could so time his knight and pawn moves as to make it at least extremely difficult for the opponent to save the game, whereas he himself would not run the slightest risk"—Steinitz. **31. ... Bd7 32. g3 Qd6 33. Qc3 Qa6 34. Qb2 Be6**

**35. h4 h6 36. Kd2 Qa4 37. Nc2 d4** "The sacrifice of the pawn is, we believe, in no way justifiable. We see no danger for Black in moving bishop or king, and sometimes even the queen, backward and forward, as White could gain nothing by 38. Qe5, for he could not well get his knight into play without leaving himself open to perpetual check or the loss of a pawn"—Steinitz. **38. N×d4 Bd7** *(see diagram)*

*After 38. ... Bd7*

**39. Kc3** "A very weak move just at the time when he had a winning game in hand by 39. h5 (an ingenious move adopted later on by Mr. Bird at a critical juncture) 39. ... g×h5 (if 39. ... g5 40. f×g5 h×g5 41. Nf3, threatening 42. h6, and wins) 40. Ne2 or 40. e4, with a fine game"—Steinitz. Steinitz' line doesn't promise White much progress. Instead Bird could, step by step, infiltrate Black's position with his queen; e.g., 39. Qc3 Qa2† 40. Qc2 Qa3 41. Qc5 Qa2† 42. Nc2 Qa8 43. Kc3 h5 44. Qc7. **39. ... Qd1 40. Qf2** Completely innocent. But 40. Nc2 Qg1 41. Qa2 Q×g3 42. Qd5 Be6 43. Q×b5 Q×h4 44. Qb8† is also far from winning. **40. ... Qa1† 41. Kd2 Qa2†** "Very fine and deep play, for, as will be seen, he has to keep on the a-file in order to play subsequently 44. ... Qa4, which recovers the pawn and gives him some winning chances. 41. ... Qb2† would not have served that purpose, for after 42. Nc2 Be6 43. Qe1, followed by 44. Qc1, Black will have to struggle for a draw only"—Steinitz. 41. ... Qb2† equally draws without a chance for more: 42. Nc2 Be6 43. Qe1 Bb3 44. Qc1 Qa2. **42. Nc2 Be6 43. Kc1 Bb3 44. Qd2 Qa4 45. Qc3 B×c2 46. Q×c2 Q×b4 47. Kd1 Qa3 48. Kd2 b4 49. h5** "An ingenious move that in actual play succeeds to save a hopeless game"—Steinitz. **49. ... g×h5** "But not in analysis, we think, for the following line of play seems to win: 49. ... b3 50. Qc8† Kg7 51. Qc3† (or 51. h×g6 Qa2† 52. Kd1 b2 53. Qc3† K×g6 54. Qc6† Kh7 and wins) 51. ... Kh7 52. h×g6† K×g6 53. Qc6† Kh7 54. Qf6 Qa2† 55. Kd1 b2 56. Q×f5† Kg8 (the only move to win) 57. Qg4† Kh8 58. Qc8† Kg7 59. Qg4† Kf6 60. Qh4† Ke6 61. Q×h6† (or 61. f5† Kd7) 61. ... Kd7 and wins"—Steinitz. The cunning 52. Kd1! is the saving clause. A draw occurs after 52. ... Qa2 53. Qc4 Qb1† 54. Ke2 Qb2† 55. Kf3 Kg7 56. h×g6 K×g6 57. Qc8 etc. **50. Qc8† Kg7 51. Q×f5 Qb2† 52. Kd1 Qb1† 53. Ke2 Qc2† 54. Kf3 b3 55. Qe5† Kf8 56. Qd6† Kg8 57. Qd8† Kg7 58. Qd4† Kg8 59. Qd8† Kg7** draw—*Tournament Book* (Steinitz), pp. 69–71.

**(934) Gossip–Bird     1–0**
American Congress (round 30)
New York, 4 May 1889
*A85*

**1. d4 f5 2. c4 Nf6 3. Nc3 e6 4. e3 Bb4 5. Qb3 c5 6. a3 B×c3† 7. b×c3 Na6 8. Nf3 b6 9. Be2 0-0 10. 0-0 Bb7 11. Ne5 d6 12. Bf3 Ne4 13. Nd3 Qg5 14. B×e4 f×e4 15. Nf4 Qf5 16. a4 g5 17. Ne2 Bc6 18. Ng3 Qg6 19. a5 Rab8 20. Qd1 d5 21. a×b6 R×b6 22. d×c5 N×c5 23. Ba3 Nb3 24. B×f8 N×a1 25. Q×a1 h5 26. Q×a7 Rb7 27. Qc5 Rc7 28. Bd6 Rc8 29. Be5 h4 30. Ne2 h3 31. Ng3 h×g2 32. Rb1 Qf7 33. Ne2 Rf8 34. Bg3 Be8 35. c×d5 e×d5 36. Nd4 Kh7 37. Rb6 Bd7 38. Qd6 Qh5 39. Q×d7† Rf7 40. Qa4** and White wins—*Tournament Book*, p. 426.

**(935) Bird–Showalter     1–0**
American Congress (round 31)
New York, 6 May 1889
*A03*

**1. f4 d5 2. e3 c5 3. Nc3 Nf6 4. Nf3 e6 5. Ne2 Nc6 6. Ng3** "The manoeuvers of this knight so early in the game are original and worth trying, considering that this piece is generally difficult to place at a later stage of this opening after the common development"—Steinitz. **6. ... Be7 7. Bd3 a6 8. 0-0 b6 9. c3 Bb7 10. Bc2 Rc8** "10. ... c4, and if 11. b3 Na5 would have been good play here"—Steinitz. **11. d4 h5 12. f5 h4 13. Nh1 Ne4 14. f×e6 f×e6 15. Nf2 N×f2 16. R×f2 Kd7** *(see diagram)* A suicide move, but his position was already difficult as he didn't play 13. ... e×f5 so as not to allow his pawn structure weakened.

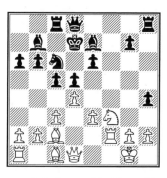

*After 16. ... Kd7*

**17. e4!** Rf8 **18. Be3** More straightforward is 18. e×d5 e×d5 19. Ng5 and Black's king is a bird for the cat. **18. ... Kc7 19. d×c5 b×c5 20. Qe2 d4 21. Bd2 e5** "21. ... Kb8 was much better"—Steinitz. **22. Bd3 Ra8 23. c×d4 e×d4 24. Rc1 Kb8 25. Rc4 a5 26. Rc1 Nb4 27. a3** Bird nurtured a small initiative with care but allowing the exchange of his bishop should end his attacking chances. **27. ... N×d3 28. Q×d3 Ba6** "Useless. 28. ... Ra6 or 28. ... a4 were evidently superior"—Steinitz. **29. Qb3† Bb7?** This careless move allows Bird to execute a powerful series of moves that force the win of the game. With 29. ... Ka7 Black could still hope for survival, even though he will soon lose the a-pawn. **30. Ne5! Ra6 31. R×f8 B×f8 32. Rf1 Ka7 33. Rf7 Qc8 34. Nc4 Bd6 35. B×a5 Ka8 36. Nb6† R×b6 37. B×b6 Qc6 38. R×g7 c4 39. Rg8† Bc8** "If 39. ... Bb8 39. Qb4, threatening 40. Qa5†. White now finishes an excellently-conducted attack with great energy and precision"—Steinitz. **40. R×c8† Q×c8 41. Qa4† Kb7 42. B×d4 Qg4 43. Qb5† Kc8 44. Q×c4† Bc7 45. Qa6† Kd7 46. Qb5† Ke7 47. Bc5† Kd8 48. Qd3† Kc8 49. Qh3** Black resigns—*Tournament Book* (Steinitz), pp. 384–385.

## (936) D.G. Baird–Bird    0–1

American Congress (round 32)
New York, 7 May 1889
*B34*

"Bird beat the time record against D.G. Baird. He was fifty minutes late, but caught up like a steam engine and rattled off a win before Baird knew what o'clock it was. Patriarch Bird has more chess in him to the square minute than any player living"—Reichhelm.

**1. e4 c5 2. Nf3 Nc6 3. d4 c×d4 4. N×d4 g6 5. N×c6 b×c6 6. Bd3 Bg7 7. 0–0 h5 8. Nc3 h4 9. h3 Rb8 10. Qf3 e6 11. Re1 Qa5 12. Bc4 Be5 13. Bb3 Nf6 14. Bd2 Qc7 15. Bg5 Nh5 16. Rad1 f6 17. Bc1 Kf7 18. Ne2 c5 19. c3 Kg7 20. Qd3 Rb6 21. Be3 g5 22. Qc4 d6 23. Nd4 Re8 24. Nf3 Bf4 25. Qe2 B×e3 26. Q×e3 Qe7 27. c4 e5 28. Rd2 Nf4 29. Red1 Rh8 30. Nh2 Be6 31. Rc1 Rhb8 32. Nf3 a5 33. Qc3 Rb4 34. Qc2 Qd7 35. Rcd1 R8b6 36. Qc3 a4 37. N×e5 f×e5 38. R×d6 Ne2† 39. Kh2 Q×d6 40. R×d6 N×c3 41. R×e6 R×e6** White resigns—*Philadelphia Times* (Reichhelm), 12 May 1889; *Tournament Book*, p. 420.

## (937) Bird–Lipschütz    1–0

American Congress (round 33)
New York, 9 May 1889
*A03*

Francis J. Lee shared the following anecdote about this game with the readers of his column in the *Hereford Times* on 31 October 1891: "In the first round [*sic*] of the American International Tournament of 1889 Mr. Bird was 52 minutes late on the occasion of his game with Mr. S. Lipschütz, a celebrated American master. His clock was, in accordance with the rules, set in motion at the appointed time for the commencement of play, and by the time Mr. Bird was seated and ready for the combat, he had only eight minutes (instead of the usual hour) in which to make the first 20 moves of the game. Nothing daunted, however, the veteran English player set to work, made the moves in time, and won the game in fine style in about 40 moves." This anecdote probably relates to Bird's game against D.G. Baird, here above.

**1. f4 d5 2. e3 e6 3. Nf3 Nf6 4. b3 c5 5. Bb2 Be7 6. Nc3 a6 7. Bd3** "The bishop is not well posted here, as he is liable to be driven back by the advance of the adverse pawns on the queenside"—Steinitz. **7. … b5 8. 0–0 Qc7** "8. … c4 would have been also good play"—Steinitz. **9. Qe1 Nc6 10. a4 Nb4** "Well conceived"—Steinitz. **11. Rc1** "If 11. a×b5 c4 12. b×c4 d×c4 13. Be4 N×e4 14. N×e4 N×c2 and wins"—Steinitz. **11. … N×d3 12. c×d3 Qb6 13. a×b5 a×b5 14. Qg3 0–0 15. Nd1** 15. Ne2 leaves the knight better placed. **15. … Rd8 16. Ne5 Ne8 17. Nf2 Ra2** 17. … f6 was the safer option. **18. Rb1** Bird's reply is however not critical. Instead 18. Rc2! is very dangerous for his opponent. The actual continuation in the game is quite similar to this variation but the rook is better placed on c2; e.g., 18. … f6?! (18. … f5 is substantially better here) 19. Nfg4! f×e5? (19. … Nd6 is preferable but after 20. Nc6! Q×c6 21. B×f6 it becomes clear that with the rook at c2 White wins material) 20. f×e5 Kh8 21. Qf4 h6 22. N×h6! g×h6 23. Q×h6† Kg8 24. Qg6† Ng7 25. Qf7† wins. **18. … f6 19. Nfg4** "A fine idea"—Steinitz. **19. … Nd6!** "If 19. … f×e5 20. Nh6† draws at least at

White's option, for 20. … Kh8 is his best answer (if 20. … Kf8 21. f×e5† with a winning attack), and then White may check alternately at f7 and h6, or he may proceed with 21. Nf7† Kg8 22. f×e5 and keep up a strong attack"—Steinitz. **20. Nf3 Nf5 21. Qh3 b4 22. e4?** Bird's attack has stopped; he tries to blow new life into it but this should fail quickly, were Black's response proper. **22. … Nd4?** Bad, as it allows Bird to keep the position completely closed. There was no remedy against 22. … d×e4 23. d×e4 Ba6! 24. e×f5 B×f1 25. K×f1 Qa6† 26. Kg1 Qd3. **23. B×d4** "White has much improved his game. His bishop was rather an encumbrance to him, and he has now exchanged it for an adverse active piece and formed an ugly doubled pawn in the hostile center"—Steinitz. **23. … c×d4 24. e5 f5 25. Nf2 Bd7 26. g4 Rf8 27. Kh1 Be8 28. Rg1 Bg6 29. g×f5 R×f5** "Not well judged. 29. … B×f5, followed by 30. … Rf7, was now his best play"—Steinitz. **30. Qg3 Ra8 31. Nh3 Raf8?** *(see diagram)* "Black proceeds with his attack, being evidently unaware of his own danger and underrating the force of White's last capital move. 31. … Rf7 was still his best play"—Steinitz.

*After 31. … Raf8*

**32. Nfg5!** With this move the tide has definitively turned. **32. … B×g5 33. N×g5 R×g5** "There was no other remedy, for White threatened 34. N×h7, and if 33. … Qb7 34. N×e6, with a winning game"—Steinitz. **34. Q×g5 Qa6 35. Rg3 Qa7 36. Rbg1 Qf7 37. Qg4 Ra8 38. h4 Ra7 39. Qg5 Qe8 40. Kh2 Qd7** "This is fatal. 40. … Bf5 and then moving the queen alternately to c8 and e8 furnished a much better defense"—Steinitz. **40. … Bf5 41. Ra1!** and the rook conquers the a-file. **41. h5 Bf5 42. Qf6** "Mr. Bird makes, as usual, the most of a fine kingside attack once he has it in his grasp"—Steinitz. **42. … Qf7 43. R×g7† Q×g7 44. Qd8† Kf7 45. R×g7† K×g7 46. h6† Kf7 47. Qb6 Re7 48. Q×d4 Rb7 49. Qg1 Ke8 50. Qc5 Kd7 51. Kg3 Rb8 52. Qd6† Kc8 53. Kf2** "With true insight into the position, White enters on a march with his king right up to c6, which cannot be prevented unless Black leaves one of his pawns undefended, and in either case White wins with ease"—Steinitz. **53. … Rb7 54. Ke3** Black resigns—*Tournament Book* (Steinitz), pp. 260–261.

## (938) Blackburne–Bird    1–0

American Congress (round 34)
New York, 10 May 1889
*A91*

**1. d4 f5 2. g3 Nf6 3. Bg2 e6 4. Nh3 d5 5. 0–0 Be7 6. b3 0–0 7. c4 c6 8. Bb2 Na6 9. Nc3 Bd7 10. Nf4 Qe8 11. e3 Bd6 12. Nd3 Rd8 13. Qe2 Bc8 14. c5 Bb8 15. b4 Ne4 16. f3 N×c3 17. B×c3 Nc7 18. f4 Qg6 19. Ne5 Qf6 20. a4 a6 21. Rfb1 Bd7 22. Bf1 Qh6**

**23. Qf2 Be8 24. Nf3 Qf6 25. Nd2 g5 26. Nb3 Bd7 27. Na5 g×f4 28. e×f4 Bc8 29. b5 a×b5 30. a×b5 c×b5 31. B×b5 Qg7 32. Ra3 e5 33. d×e5 Ne6 34. Bd4 Rf7 35. Be2 Ba7 36. Nb3 Bb8 37. Nd2 Bc7 38. Kh1 Qf8 39. Rbb3 Qe7 40. Nb1 Bb8 41. Nc3 N×d4 42. Q×d4 Be6 43. Nb5 Rc8 44. Rc3 Rff8 45. Nd6 B×d6 46. c×d6 Qd7 47. Kg2 Rc4 48. B×c4 d×c4 49. R×c4 Qb5 50. Rc2 Kg7 51. Rac3 Ra8 52. Rc5 Qb1 53. Qb2 Ra1 54. Q×b1 R×b1 55. Rd2** Black resigns—*Tournament Book* (Steinitz), pp. 173–174.

## (939) Bird–Gunsberg    0–1
American Congress (round 35)
New York, 11 May 1889
B00

**1. f4 b6 2. e4 Bb7 3. d3 e6 4. Nf3 d5 5. e5 c5 6. Be2 Nc6 7. c3 Rc8 8. a3 g6 9. b4 d4 10. b5 Nce7 11. c4 Nf5 12. a4 Ngh6 13. Na3 Ng4 14. Nc2 B×f3 15. B×f3 Qh4† 16. g3 N×g3 17. h×g3 Q×g3† 18. Kd2 Q×f4† 19. Ke2 Q×e5† 20. Kf1 Nh2† 21. Kg2 Bd6 22. Qe1 N×f3 23. K×f3 Qf5† 24. Ke2 Qg4† 25. Kf1 Qf3† 26. Kg1 Q×d3 27. Na3 h5 28. Ra2 h4 29. Qf1 Qb3 30. Rf2 Qg3† 31. Rg2 Qc3 32. Nb1 Qb3 33. Bg5 h3 34. Nd2 h2† 35. Kf2 Qc2 36. Qe2 Rh3 37. Ne4 Q×e2† 38. K×e2 Bc7 39. Nf6† Kf8 40. Ng4 f5 41. Nf2 Ra3 42. Bc1 Ra2† 43. Kf3 Kf7 44. Nh3 R×a4 45. Re2 e5 46. Ng5† Kf6 47. Kg2 e4 48. Rf1 e3 49. Nf3 Rh8 50. Kh1 R×c4 51. Bb2 Re8 52. Rd1 Re4 53. Ba1 g5 54. N×h2 Rh4 55. Kg1 R×h2 56. R×h2 B×h2† 57. K×h2 Rc2† 58. Kg3 f4† 59. Kg4 e2 60. Re1 Ra2 61. Kf3 Kf5** White resigns—*Tournament Book*, pp. 126–127.

## (940) Chigorin–Bird    1–0
American Congress (round 36)
New York, 13 May 1889
C44

**1. e4 e5 2. Nf3 Nc6 3. c3 d5 4. Qa4 d×e4 5. N×e5 Qd5 6. N×c6 b×c6 7. Bc4 Qd6 8. d3 e×d3 9. 0–0 Be7 10. B×d3 Bd7 11. Rd1 Nf6 12. Na3 Ng4 13. Bf4 Qc5 14. Bg3 Bd6 15. Qe4† Kf8 16. Qf3 Be6 17. b4 Q×c3 18. Nb5 Q×b4 19. N×d6 c×d6 20. Bf5 Kg8 21. B×e6 f×e6 22. Q×c6 Kf7 23. Rab1 Qc5 24. Qd7† Kg6 25. Rb7 Rag8 26. Qf7† Kh6 27. Q×e6† Nf6 28. Bf4† Kg6 29. Rb3 h6 30. Rg3† Kh7 31. B×d6 Qh5 32. Rc1 Rc8 33. Rb1 Rhe8 34. R×g7† K×g7 35. Rb7† Kg6 36. Qf7† Kf5 37. Rb5† Ke4 38. f3† Ke3 39. Qb3† Ke2 40. Qb2† Kd3 41. Qb1† Ke2 42. Rb2† Ke3 43. Qe1† Kd4 44. Qd2† Kc4 45. Rb4 mate**—*Tournament Book*, pp. 10–12.

## (941) Bird–Taubenhaus    0–1
American Congress (round 37)
New York, 14 May 1889
A03

**1. f4 b6 2. Nf3 Bb7 3. e3 e6 4. Be2 d5 5. 0–0 Bd6 6. b3 Ne7 7. Bb2 0–0 8. Nc3 a6 9. Bd3 Nd7 10. Qe2 Ng6 11. Ng5 e5 12. B×g6 h×g6 13. Qg4 Be7 14. Ne6 f×e6 15. Q×e6† Kh7 16. f×e5 Nc5 17. Qh3† Kg8 18. d4 Bc8 19. Qg3 Ne6 20. Q×g6 c6 21. R×f8† B×f8 22. Rf1 Qe7 23. e4 N×d4 24. e×d5 Bf5 25. R×f5 N×f5 26. Ne4 Qh4 27. Nf6† Kh8 28. g3 Qh3 29. Ng4**

**Bc5† 30. Nf2 B×f2† 31. K×f2 Q×h2† 32. Kf3 Rf8** White resigns—*Tournament Book*, p. 433.

## (942) Bird–MacLeod    1–0
American Congress (round 38)
New York, 15 May 1889
C30

**1. e4 e5 2. f4 d6 3. c3 Nc6 4. Nf3 Nf6 5. Bb5 Bd7** "If 5. ... N×e4 6. Qe2 Nc5 7. f×e5 Be7 8. d4, with the better game"—Steinitz. **6. d3 a6?!** "Losing a pawn. It was necessary now to capture the f-pawn"—Steinitz. **7. B×c6 B×c6 8. f×e5 d×e5 9. N×e5 N×e4** "Not deep enough, though rather ingenious up to the point of its incorrectness"—Steinitz. **10. Qe2?!** With this move Bird condemns his king to an uncomfortable stay in the middle of the board. 10. 0–0 gains an initiative. **10. ... Qh4† 11. Kd1 0–0–0** "It only amounted to a transposition of moves if he checked at once by 11. ... Nf2†, for he had then to guard against 13. N×c6† or 13. Ng6†"—Steinitz. **12. N×c6 Nf2† 13. Kc2 b×c6 14. g3 Qf6 15. Rf1 Bc5 16. d4 Qf5†?** The outcome of the game could have been different had the queen given the check from g6: 16. ... Qg6† 17. Kb3 (if 17. Kd2? B×d4) 17. ... Nd3! 18. d×c5? (18. Rd1 is necessary, but Black has the initiative thanks to the position of the White king) 18. ... Rhe8 19. Qg2 N×c5† 20. Ka3 Nd3 and his attack is fearsome due to the situation of his opponent's king. Three alternatives: (**a**) 21. Bd2 Qd6† 22. Kb3 a5 (or 22. ... Re5) 23. Qf3 a4, and if 24. Kc2 Qg6!; (**b**) 21. Nd2 Rd5 22. Nc4 Rc5 23. b3 Qh5; or (**c**) 21. Bf4 Re4. **17. Kb3 Qd5† 18. Qc4** MacLeod now loses a piece without obtaining sufficient attack. **18. ... Qg2 19. d×c5 Nd3 20. Nd2 N×c1† 21. Ra×c1 Q×d2?** "The loser. He could at least prolong the struggle by 21. ... R×d2 22. Q×a6† Kb8! 23. Ka3 g5, etc."—Steinitz. **22. Q×a6†?** is premature, for Black can play 22. ... Kd7! and he is safe (White can take at f7, but gains nothing from it). First 22. Ka3! is something else. Black must play the weakening 22. ... f6. After 23. Q×a6† Kd7 24. Rfd1 White is well on top. **22. Q×a6† Kb8 23. Rf4 Qd5† 24. Ka3** Black resigns—*Tournament Book* (Steinitz), p. 429.

## (943) Weiss–Bird    ½–½
American Congress (round 29, game 2)
New York, 16 May 1889
B34

**1. e4 c5 2. Nc3 Nc6 3. Nf3 g6 4. d4 c×d4 5. N×d4 Bg7 6. Be3 d6 7. Be2 Bd7 8. 0–0 h5 9. f4 h4 10. Qd2 h3 11. g3 Nf6 12. Rad1 Ng4 13. N×c6 b×c6 14. Bd4 B×d4† 15. Q×d4 Qb6 16. B×g4 B×g4 17. Rd2 Rh5 18. b3 Q×d4† 19. R×d4 Rc5 20. Rd3 f5 21. Rf2 Ra5 22. Re3 Rb8 23. Rd2 Kf7 24. a4 Rb4 25. e×f5 g×f5 26. Kf2 Rc5 27. Na2 Re4 28. c4 d5 29. c×d5 c×d5 30. Rc3 R×c3 31. N×c3 Rb4 32. Rb2 e6 33. Ke1 a6 34. Kd2 Ke7 35. Kd3 Kd6 36. Na2 Re4 37. Nc3 Re1 38. b4 e5 39. f×e5† K×e5 40. Rb1 R×b1 41. N×b1 Bf3 42. Nd2 Be4† 43. Kc3 d4† 44. Kc4 Bd5† 45. Kc5 d3 46. b5 a×b5 47. a×b5 Be6 48. b6 Bc8 49. Kc4 Ba6† 50. Kc3 Kd5 51. b7 B×b7 52. K×d3 Ke5 53. Ke3 Bd5 54. Nb1 Bb7 55. Nc3 Ba6 56. Nd1 Bc4 57. Nf2 Bf1 58. Nd1 Ba6 59. Nc3 Bc4 60. Na4 Ba6 61. Nc5 Bc4 62. Nd7† Ke6 63. Nf8† Kf7 64. Nh7 Kg6 65. Nf8† Kf7 66. Nd7 Ke6** draw—*Tournament Book*, pp. 71–73.

# TOURING THROUGH THE UNITED STATES AND CANADA, MAY–JULY 1889

After the termination of the tournament, several competitors were engaged for simultaneous and blindfold exhibitions by clubs situated in the wider vicinity of New York. Bird extended his stay in America for financial reasons. According to the *Yenowine's News* of 9 June, he "'blew in' all his funds during the congress and will display his talents in Albany and Montreal to replenish his depleted exchequer." On 7 July the same newspaper related that "even the blithesome Bird, it seems, could not escape the contagion, but had to borrow $25 of the president of the chess congress to get to Montreal with. When dunned for the loan, he wrote back: 'Please deduct the amount due you from my share of the Gelbfuhs prize money, and send me a check for the balance!'"[20]

## Albany, 24–26 May 1889

Bird's first stop on his American tour was Albany. The arrival of the British master on 24 May aroused great interest in the game and the local newspapers dedicated several columns to his visit. They offer a unique insight in the course of such an exhibition and are quoted in full in Appendix 2: Outtakes.

Bird played a few offhand and consultation games and offered two simultaneous exhibitions. On Friday 24 May he opposed 16 players. Just one player could win, Deyo. Bird beat all others. On the next day Bird won on all 12 boards.

### (944) Bird–R.B. Leake    1–0
Offhand game
Albany, 24 May 1889
*Odds of Ra1*

1. e4 e5 2. f4 Bc5 3. c3 d6 4. d4 Bb6 5. Be3 Nd7 6. Nd2 Ne7 7. f5 f6 8. Bc4 c6 9. Qh5† g6 10. f×g6 N×g6 11. Ngf3 d5 12. e×d5 c×d5 13. B×d5 Ndf8 14. Ne4 Qe7 15. N×e5 Be6 16. 0-0 0-0-0 17. B×e6† Q×e6 18. R×f6 Q×a2 19. Qh3† Kb8 20. Nf7 Qb1† 21. Rf1 Q×e4 22. Bg5 Rd5 23. Qh6 Rg8 24. Bf6 Nf4 25. Q×f4† Q×f4 26. R×f4 Bc7 27. Re4 a6 28. Re8† Ka7 29. Nh6 Rg6 30. R×f8 R×h6 31. g4 B×h2† 32. Kg2 Bd6 33. Rf7 Rh2† 34. Kf3 h6 35. c4 Ra5 36. c5 Bb8 37. c6 Rb5 38. c7 Rb3† 39. Ke4 Re2† 40. Kf5 Rf3† 41. Kg6 B×c7 42. R×c7 Re6 43. Rf7 a5 44. d5 Rd6 45. Kg7 R×d5 46. K×h6 a4 47. g5 a3 48. Bd4† R×d4 49. R×f3 a2 50. Ra3† Kb8 51. R×a2 White wins—*Albany Evening News*, 24 May 1889.

### (945) Bird–Leake    0–1
Offhand game
Albany, 24 May 1889
*Odds of Ra1*

1. g4 Bird attempted the same opening move in one or two games on even terms with Boden. In *Chess Openings* (p. 167) he writes that this move "gives a slightly inferior game to White, and has, we fear, little beyond novelty to recommend it." The beginning of one game went so: 1. g4 d5 2. e3 c5 3. h4 e5 4. b3 a6 5. Bb2 Nc6 6. Nc3 f5 7. g×f5 B×f5 8. Bg2 Nf6. **1. ... d5 2. e3 e6 3. h4 b6 4. g5 Bb7 5. Rh3 Qe7 6. b3 Nd7 7. a4 0-0-0 8. Bd3 g6 9. Qe2 Bg7 10. a5 Nc5 11. Bb5 a6 12. d4 a×b5 13. Ba3 b4 14. d×c5 Q×c5 15. a6 b×a3 16. a×b7† K×b7 17. c4 d×c4 18. e4 Qb4† 19. Kf1 c×b3 20. e5 a2 21. Qb2 Rd1† 22. Kg2 R×b1** White resigns—*Albany Evening News*, 24 May 1889.

### (946) Bird–Goold    1–0
Offhand game
Albany, 24 May 1889
*Odds of Ra1*

1. e4 d5 2. e5 e6 3. f4 Bc5 4. Qg4 g6 5. Nh3 h5 6. Qg3 Nh6 7. b4 Nf5 8. Qc3 Bd4 9. Qb3 c5 10. c3 c4 11. Qd1 Bb6 12. Ng5 Nd7 13. Na3 a6 14. d3 c×d3 15. B×d3 Ne3 16. Qe2 Ng4 17. c4 Bf2† 18. Kf1 d4 19. Qe4 Qe7 20. c5 Ne3† 21. K×f2 Nf5 22. Nc4 0-0 23. g4 h×g4 24. Nd6 Ra7 25. Qg2 Ne3 26. Qg3 N×e5 27. f×e5 Q×g5 28. Ne4 Qf5† 29. Ke1 Qf3 30. Q×f3 g×f3 31. Nf6† Kg7 32. Kf2 Rh8 33. h4 g5 34. h5 g4 35. B×e3 d×e3† 36. K×e3 Rh6 37. N×g4 Bd7 38. Rg1 R×h5 39. Nf6† Kf8 40. N×h5 Bc6 41. Nf6 Ke7 42. Be4 B×e4 43. K×e4 f2 44. Rg8 Black resigns—*Albany Evening News*, 24 May 1889.

## Montreal, 27 May–20 June 1889

Albany was a short visit for Bird who was on his way to Montreal to fulfill an engagement for the local chess club. It had been 12 years since Bird visited the capital of Quebec. At that time he was the first major master to visit Canada and his arrival was met with genuine enthusiasm. Since then various of his stronger colleagues, such as Mackenzie and Zukertort, had been the guest of the club. This time Bird was preceded by Blackburne, who stunned the local population with his power in blindfold simultaneous exhibitions.

Bird was only engaged for a short span of time, probably for a week, but he ultimately stayed for three weeks. He threw himself into playing countless numbers of offhand games, allegedly 150 during his first week. As usual he was available for every comer during the afternoon and evening. Bird gave at least three simultaneous exhibitions at the chess club, but only sparse details were revealed in the press. Blackburne ran away with most of the attention.

### (947) Bird–Binmore    0–1
Simultaneous game
Montreal, 28 May 1889
*A03*

1. f4 c5 2. e3 d5 3. b3 e6 4. Bb2 Nf6 5. Nf3 Be7 6. Be2 b6 7. 0-0 0-0 8. Nc3 Nc6 9. Qe1 d4 10. e×d4 c×d4 11. Nb5 Bc5 12. d3 Bb7 13. Qh4 a6 14. Na3 Ne7 15. Qh3 Nfd5 16. Ng5 Nf6 17. Nc4 Ng6 18. Ne5 h6 19. Ngf3 Kh7 20. N×g6 f×g6 21. Ne5 Nd5 22. Bc1 Qe8 23. g3 Nf6 24. Bf3 B×f3 25. R×f3 Nd7 26. Ng4 e5 27. f5 e4 28. B×h6 e×f3 29. B×g7† K×g7 30. Qh6† Kg8 31. f×g6

---

20. It was a common practice that the entrance fees were distributed among the non-prize winners. To calculate the share each would receive the Gelbfuhs system was used. It is curious, however, that the New York 1889 tournament book only speaks of seven main prizes and not of any consolation prizes.

f2† 32. N×f2 Qe7 33. Ne4 Qg7 34. Qg5 Ne5 35. Kg2 N×g6 36. Re1 Ra7 37. Qd5† Kh8 38. Ng5 Qb7 39. Q×b7 R×b7 and Black wins—*Montreal Gazette*, 11 September 1889.

## (948) Bird–Fleming　0–1
Offhand game
Montreal, 30 May 1889
C33

**1. e4 e5 2. f4 e×f4 3. Be2 Be7 4. d4 Bh4† 5. Kf1 Nf6 6. Nc3 d6 7. g3 f×g3** "Black prefers to sacrifice the bishop for the pawns on the kingside to letting White establish a strong center"—*Montreal Daily Herald*. **8. h×g3 B×g3 9. Kg2 Nc6 10. K×g3 Qe7 11. Bf3 Bd7 12. Bg5 0-0-0 13. Kg2** "Threatening 14. Nd5. Had he played 13. Nd5, Black would have answered 13. ... N×e4†"—*Montreal Daily Herald*. An intriguing alternative was 13. Nh3, giving priority to the development of his pieces. This line required some precise calculation, but promises a clear edge after 13. ... h6 14. Nd5 N×e4† 15. Kh2 Qe6 16. Ndf4 Qf5 17. B×e4 Q×e4 18. B×d8. **13. ... h6 14. B×f6 Q×f6** Better than 14. ... g×f6. **15. Nge2 g5 16. Nd5 Qg7 17. Bh5 f5 18. Rf1** Dangerous. It was better to sweep this pawn off the board. **18. ... f4 19. c3 Ne7 20. N×e7† Q×e7 21. Qd3 Rdf8 22. d5 Rf6** (*see diagram*)

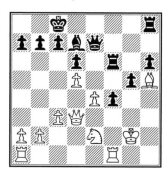

*After 22. ... Rf6*

**23. Qd4** The queen is vulnerable here. The patient 23. Rf2 demands some creativity from his opponent to come up with constructive ideas. **23. ... Rhf8** "Black's intention was to play 23. ... Kb8, but he was afraid of 24. N×f4, on account of the queen attacking Rh8. Had he played 21. ... Rhf8, 23. ... Kb8 would have been possible"—*Montreal Daily Herald*. Fleming misjudges the situation. After 23. ... Kb8 24. N×f4 g×f4 25. R×f4, there is a saving check at g8. **24. Q×a7 Kd8?** 24. ... c5 is the only move. **25. Qb8† Bc8 26. Bg4 Q×e4† 27. Kh2 Rf5 28. Nd4** "It is obvious that the rook could not be captured"—*Montreal Daily Herald*. **28. ... f3 29. Ne6†?** Bird had a difficult and far-stretching choice to make here. The text move appears to be the wrong one: moving the knight to e6 closes his own attacking lines. On the other hand, White's attack breaks through after 29. Rae1! Q×g4 30. Ne6† Ke7 31. Q×c7† Bd7 32. N×f8! Re5 33. Ng6† Kf7 34. N×e5† d×e5 35. R×f3†! **29. ... Ke7 30. Q×c7† Bd7 31. Nd4 Q×g4 32. N×f5†** 32. Rae1† is less materialistic, but the exchanges ensuing after 32. ... Re5 33. R×e5† d×e5 34. Q×e5† Kd8 35. Qb8† Ke7 36. d6† Kf7 37. R×f3† Q×f3 38. Q×f8† K×f8 39. N×f3 improve his drawing prospects. **32. ... R×f5?** Bird's bluff is paying off. Necessary is 32. ... Q×f5, so that the king can evacuate from the center as quickly as possible. After 33. Rae1† Kf7 34. Rf2 Kg8 a most unclear position arises. **33. Rae1†**

Re5 34. R×e5† d×e5 35. Q×e5† Kf7 36. Qg3 Warding off the attack. White has the upperhand. **36. ... Qh5† 37. Kg1 g4 38. Qf4† Bf5 39. Re1 Kg6 40. Qd6† Kg5 41. Qe7† Kf4 42. Qe3† Kg3 43. Qe5† Kh4 44. Qf4 Qg6 45. Re5** 45. d6! wins quickly. **45. ... Qb6† 46. Kh1??** A dreadful mistake that allows Black to force the exchange of queens after which his pawns decide the day. White has no chance against Black's pawns. 46. Re3! effectively safeguards the position of his king, while keeping ammunition for his own attack that will be decisive after, for example, 46. ... Bd7 47. Kh1 Q×b2 48. R×f3. **46. ... Qf2 47. Qh2† Q×h2† 48. K×h2 g3† 49. Kg1 f2† 50. Kg2 Bh3†** White resigns—*Montreal Daily Herald*, 24 December 1892.

## (949) Bird–Henderson　0–1
Simultaneous game
Montreal, 1 June 1889
C58

One of 17 simultaneous games.

**1. e4 e5 2. Nf3 Nc6 3. Bc4 Nf6 4. Ng5 d5 5. e×d5 Na5 6. d3 h6 7. Nf3 e4 8. Qe2 N×c4 9. d×c4 Bc5 10. h3 0-0 11. Nh2 Qe7 12. Ng4 Bf5 13. Be3 B×g4 14. h×g4 B×e3 15. f×e3 Qb4† 16. c3 Qd6 17. Rh3 Qd7 18. g5 h×g5 19. Nd2 Rfe8 20. 0-0-0 g6 21. Rf1 Kg7 22. Nb3 Rh8 23. Qf2 Ng4 24. Qd2 R×h3 25. g×h3 Nf6 26. Qd4 Qe7 27. Nc5 Re8 28. N×e4 Q×e4 29. Q×f6† Kh6 30. Qf3 Q×e3† 31. Q×e3 R×e3 32. R×f7 R×h3 33. R×c7 g4 34. Rc8 Kg5 35. Re8 g3 36. Re1 g2 37. Kd2 Rh1** White resigns—*Quebec Weekly Chronicle*, 20 June 1889.

## (950) Bird–Fleming　0–1
Simultaneous game
Montreal, June 1889
C56

One of 13 simultaneous games.

**1. e4 e5 2. Nf3 Nc6 3. Bc4 Nf6 4. d4 e×d4 5. Ng5 d5 6. e×d5 Na5 7. Qe2† Be7 8. d6 N×c4 9. Q×c4 0-0 10. d×e7 Q×e7 11. Qe2 Qb4† 12. Qd2 Re8† 13. Kd1 Qb6 14. f3 h6 15. Nh3 Ne4 16. Qf4 B×h3 17. f×e4 B×g2 18. Re1 Qg6 19. Bd2 R×e4 20. Qg3 Rae8 21. Rg1 Bf3† 22. Kc1 Rg4 23. b3 R×g3 24. R×g3 Qc6 25. Kb2 Be4 26. Na3 Bg6 27. Rd1 Re2 28. h4 Qf6 29. h5 Qf2 30. h×g6 Q×g3 31. g×f7† K×f7 32. Bb4 c5** White resigns—*Montreal Gazette*, 23 October 1889.

## (951) Fleming–Bird　1–0
Offhand game
Montreal, June 1889
C25

**1. e4 e5 2. Nc3 Bc5 3. Nf3 d6 4. d3 a6 5. Be3 B×e3 6. f×e3 c6 7. Be2 Qb6 8. Qc1 Nf6 9. 0-0 0-0 10. h3 Nh5 11. N×e5 Ng3 12. Nc4 Qd8 13. Rf3 Qg5 14. Qe1 N×e2† 15. N×e2 Qd8 16. Qg3 d5 17. Ne5 d×e4 18. d×e4 Be6 19. Raf1 Nd7 20. Nd3 Qe7 21. Nef4 Bc4 22. Nh5 g6 23. e5 B×d3 24. Nf6† N×f6 25. e×f6 Qc5 26. c×d3 Rfe8 27. Qh4 h5 28. d4 Qd5 29. Rf5 Qe4 30. R1f4 Q×e3† 31. Kh2 Qe1 32. Qg5 Qb4 33. Rc5 Kh7 34. Rh4 Re2 35. R×h5† Kg8 36. Rh8†** Black resigns—*Montreal Gazette*, 9 October 1889.

Group portrait of the Canadian Chess Association, 1889. Standing from left to right: T. Taylor, Robert Short, M. St. John, J.P. Cooke, J.W. Shaw, G.W. Liddell, J.R. Robertson, Jacob G. Ascher, J.E. Narraway. Seated: J. Nolan, John Henderson, J. Barry, H.A. Howe, Prof. Hicks, R.B. Hutchison (courtesy Cleveland Public Library).

## Rochester, end of June 1889

After leaving Montreal, Bird headed for Rochester, where the local club had engaged him for a short while. Every trace of his appearance there, however, is lacking.[21]

## Philadelphia, 27 June–early July 1889

Bird's next stop was Philadelphia. The Franklin Chess Club, one of the strongest in the United States, had made every possible effort to gain the attention of the visiting European masters. During the past few weeks Weiss, Gunsberg and Blackburne had already demonstrated their powers. While their visits were a source of enjoyment for the true chess lover, they did not pass in complete harmony. Blackburne departed in a bitter atmosphere due to a financial dispute. The English professional had requested he be released before the fulfillment of his engagement so that he could make another profitable visit to Baltimore. That he subsequently did not receive his full fee was found outrageous by Blackburne.

Bird's visit enjoyed an entirely different atmosphere. He was invited by Walter Penn Shipley and arrived on 27 June. Bird and Shipley immediately agreed to a short match, played for the first five wins. Shipley managed to leave the battlefield honorably, with 3 wins and 1 draw against 5 losses. This contest was obviously a friendly affair, given the time limit of 40 moves an hour.

Bird also met the other prominent Philadelphians. They were

strong players and already well versed due to heavy playing with the other visitors during the past weeks, making it no great surprise that Bird was unable to prove his superiority against them. Charles Martinez (+4 −4 =4) and Elson (+0 −0 =1) maintained the balance, Charles John Newman gained a slight superiority (+3 −4 =0). Bird narrowly beat Alfred K. Robinson (+4 −3 =3). Only Hermann G. Voigt and August Priester suffered considerably against the veteran.[22]

Bird left Philadelphia with excellent relations and a well-filled purse. Reichhelm interestingly pointed out that Bird had not required a fee in advance for his appearance in Philadelphia, quite unlike his colleagues, but that he gained a similar amount of money because he correctly trusted on his abilities in offhand chess. Such attitude was praised by the local amateurs who stood in line to play the master and support him.

21. While on his way to Philadelphia Bird wrote a letter to the Baltimore Chess Club, in hopes of arranging a visit, in which he mentioned that he had just been in Albany, Montreal and Rochester. *Baltimore Sunday News*, 7 July 1889.

22. On this occasion Bird gained a lot of attention by his so-called "table talk," (to which there was a reference above in the chapter on Paul Morphy's second visit to England). In the *Philadelphia Times* of 7 July 1889, Bird compared Morphy with Steinitz: "Probably with the exception of Steinitz, Blackburne is the finest living player. Steinitz is a slow player and is always pretty well crowded for time, and I doubt if he could have made as good a showing against Zukertort had the latter been less confident and arranged the match at a time limit of 20 moves to the hour instead of 15. I trotted Steinitz the closest heat he ever contested. He beat me 8 to 7 with 6 draws [*sic*]. This was in '67 [*sic*]. In '58 Morphy beat me 10 to 1 with 1 draw. Steinitz claims that he is a better player than ever Morphy was, but I think my record with each is a fair test of the strength of the two. Steinitz claims that when I played with Morphy I was out of practice, but I cannot explain away my crushing defeat by that great player in any such way. I never played better chess in my life than when he beat me." This quoted text offers an interesting insight into Bird's mindset. Unsurprisingly, Bird's outspoken opinions were frequently copied by other chess columns and resonated loudly throughout the world.

## (952) Bird–Shipley 0–1

Match
Philadelphia, June 1889
C55

1. e4 e5 2. Nf3 Nf6 3. Nc3 Nc6 4. Bc4 Be7 5. 0–0 d6 6. d4 Bg4 7. Be3 e×d4 8. B×d4 N×d4 9. Q×d4 0–0 10. Rad1 Nd7 11. Nd5 Ne5 12. N×e5 d×e5 13. Q×e5 Bd6 14. Qc3 B×d1 15. R×d1 Qh4 16. e5 B×e5 17. Q×e5 Q×c4 18. Rd4 Q×c2 19. g3 Rfe8 20. Qg5 Re1† 21. Kg2 Qc6 22. f3 Rae8 23. Rg4 Qc2† 24. Kh3 Q×h2† and mates in two moves—*International Chess Magazine*, August 1889, pp. 247–248.

## (953) Shipley–Bird 0–1

Match
Philadelphia, June 1889
B34

1. e4 c5 2. Nc3 Nc6 3. Nf3 g6 4. d4 c×d4 5. N×d4 Bg7 6. Be3 h5 7. Be2 d6 8. 0–0 h4 9. h3 Nf6 10. f4 Nh5 Shipley's last move was a bit too confident. Instead of the inferior text move Bird could get a decent position with 10. ... Bd7. **11. B×h5 R×h5 12. f5 N×d4 13. B×d4** The intermezzo 13. f×g6 greatly improves his attacking chances. **13. ... B×d4† 14. Q×d4 Qb6 15. Q×b6 a×b6 16. f×g6 f×g6 17. Nd5** The endgame looks worse for Bird than it actually is. **17. ... Ra5 18. b4** *(see diagram)* Shipley overlooked or underestimated Bird's reply. First 18. a4! is decidedly stronger.

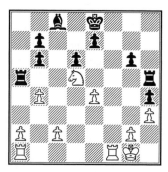

*After 18. b4*

**18. ... Ra3!** A temporarily pawn sacrifice, as Bird is bound to get his investment back soon. **19. N×b6 Be6 20. c4 Rg5 21. Kh2 Re5 22. Rfe1 Rc3 23. Rac1 R×c1 24. R×c1 R×e4 25. a4 Kd8 26. a5 Re2 27. Rf1 Bf5 28. Rf4 Re4 29. R×e4 B×e4 30. g3 g5 31. g×h4 g×h4 32. Na4 Kc7 33. Nc3 Bc6 34. Kg1 e5 35. Nd5†?** Allowing Bird to exchange pieces is extremely risky, to say the very least. 35. Kf2 leads to a certain draw. **35. B×d5 36. c×d5 b6 37. a6** 37. Kf2 is to no avail. See the following long but forced line 37. ... b×a5 38. b×a5 Kb7 39. Kf3 Ka6 40. Kg4 K×a5 41. K×h4 Kb4 42. Kg5 Kc4 43. h4 e4 44. Kf4 Kd3 45. h5 e3 46. h6 e2 47. h7 e1Q 48. h8Q Qe3† 49. Kg4 Qd4†. **37. ... b5 38. Kf2 Kb6 39. Kf3 K×a6 40. Kg4 Kb7 41. K×h4 Kc7 42. Kg5 Kd7 43. h4 Ke7 44. Kf5 Kf7 45. Kg5 Kg7 46. Kh5 Kh7 47. Kg5 Kh8 48. Kh5 Kh7 49. Kg5 Kg7 50. h5 Kh7 51. Kh4 Kh6 52. Kg4 e4 53. Kf4 K×h5** and Black must win, as White will not be able to save his pawn—*Philadelphia Times*, 7 July 1889.

## (954) C.S. Martinez–Bird 1–0

Offhand game
Philadelphia 1889
C45

1. e4 e5 2. Nf3 Nc6 3. d4 e×d4 4. N×d4 Qh4 5. Nf3 Q×e4† 6. Be3 Be7 7. Bd3 Qg4 8. 0–0 d6 9. Nc3 Kd8 10. Ne4 Nh6 11. h3 Qd7 12. Qe2 Nf5 13. Rad1 h6 14. Nc5 Qe8 15. B×f5 B×f5 16. N×b7† Kd7 17. Qb5 B×c2 18. Nd4 Kc8 19. N×c6 a6 20. N×e7† Q×e7 21. Qc6 Be4 22. N×d6† Q×d6 23. Q×e4 and White wins—*Philadelphia Times*, 14 July 1889.

## (955) C.S. Martinez–Bird 1–0

Offhand game
Philadelphia, June 1889
C45

1. e4 e5 2. Nf3 Nc6 3. d4 e×d4 4. N×d4 Qh4 5. Nf3 Q×e4† 6. Be3 Bb4† 7. c3 Bc5 8. Bd3 Qe7 9. 0–0 B×e3 10. Re1 d6 11. R×e3 Be6 12. Bb5 0–0–0 13. B×c6 b×c6 14. Nd4 Qd7 15. Qa4 Kb7 16. c4 Ne7 17. Ra3 Nc8 18. Qa6† Kb8 19. N×c6† and White wins—*Philadelphia Times*, 4 August 1889.

## *Baltimore, 6 July–middle of July 1889*

Bird subsequently headed for Baltimore, another hotspot for the European chess masters. Just before Bird arrived, Blackburne had passed through. Another English player, Pollock, even decided to take up his residence in the city. He quickly found a way of obtaining an income by taking over the chess column in the *Baltimore Sunday News*.

A few days before his arrival Bird had sent a letter to the Baltimore Chess Club, expressing the hope he might complete his tour by visiting that city. As several organizations had been made to receive Blackburne such a short time ago, no arrangements for fixed exhibitions could be set up, although Bird of course remained very welcome. Bird arrived on 6 July. He did not lose any time discovering what kind of opposition awaited him.

Mr. Bird has made himself a general favorite in Baltimore, and the fact of his visit having been a private and sociable one (no formalities) seems rather to have enhanced the enthusiasm of his reception, though we think the phenomenal quickness and freshness of his play over the board did a great deal towards enticing players to brave the sweltering hot evenings and emulate the energy and courage of the brave old islander.

Within an hour after his arrival Mr. Bird was confronted with an array of ten players, seated in the following order: Messrs. Prangley, Kemper, Koch, Schofield, Dallam, Renshaw, Broadbent, Hinrichs, Uhthoff and Maas, every one of whom were compelled to strike their colors except Mr. Prangley, who played a fine game to a draw. We are not able to give very many specimens of the play on this and subsequent occasions, because only one or two were quick enough to record their games, and as for the rest, well—there was no instantaneous photographer present to preserve to memory the positions on the chequered fields.

On the following Monday evening Mr. Bird encountered a team composed of Messrs. Hinrichs, Bentley, Uhthoff, Schofield, Jackson, Broadbent, Pachholder and Adler. Of these Messrs. Uhthoff and Pachholder won capital games, and the remaining six fell to the prowess of the single player.

Tuesday evening was devoted to a consultation match, consisting of three parties conducted simultaneously, Messrs. Bird and Pollock captaining the respective sides. These games were keenly contested up to a late (or early) hour, but finally were left uncompleted, all parties agreeing that they had done their duty by the games, which were of an interesting nature.

On Wednesday evening, 10th instant., Mr. Bird was entertained at supper at the Hotel Bennert by President E.L. Torsch [*Baltimore Sunday News*, 14 July 1889].

## (956) Pollock & Hinrichs–Bird & Uhthoff   ½–½
Consultation game
Baltimore, July 1889
*C51*

"The following beautiful consultation game was played at a small though brilliant gathering promoted by the genial and hospitable Mr. Hinrichs to celebrate the visit of England's veteran hero to Maryland."—Pollock

**1. e4 e5 2. Nf3 Nc6 3. Bc4 Bc5 4. b4 B×b4 5. c3 Bc5 6. d4 e×d4 7. c×d4 Bb6 8. 0–0** "One of Bird's favorite lines of attack, (revived by him lately, but practiced years ago by Boden and Mac-Donnell) is to proceed with 8. Bb2, and postpone castling, in some cases even castling on the queenside later on"—Pollock. **8. ... d6 9. Nc3 Bg4 10. Qa4** "The old Fraser Attack, long discarded in favor of 10. Bb5, but adopted by the White allies for the sake of variety"—Pollock. **10. ... Kf8** "The retreat of the bishop to d7 leads into the mazes of the historical Fraser-Mortimer Attack, analyzed in nearly every modern work on chess"—Pollock. **11. d5 Na5 12. Be2 B×f3 13. g×f3 Ne7 14. Kh1 h5 15. Be3 Ng6** 15. ... B×e3, followed by 16. ... b6, 17. ... Nb7 and 18. ... Nc5 looks certainly not worse than Bird's plan. The knight won't be very stable at e5. **16. Rac1 Ne5 17. Rg1 Qh4** "A somewhat premature rally, resulting in a slight loss of time"—Pollock. Instead, 17. ... c6 is worth considering. **18. Rg3** Very good would have been 18. Nb5! Qd8 19. Qb4. Black is almost forced to commit himself to 19. ... c5 20. d×c6 *e.p.* Na×c6 21. Q×d6 when he is much worse. **18. ... Qe7 19. Nb5 h4** The immediate 19. ... a6 is preferable. **20. Rgg1 a6 21. Nd4** *(see diagram)* Black has lost control over g4 with his 19th move. His knight at e5 is in difficulties.

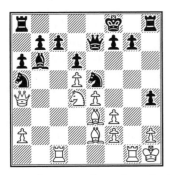

*After 21. Nd4*

**21. ... Qd7?** 21. ... g6 was the only playable move, though 22. f4 Nec4 23. R×c4 doesn't look very appetizing for him. After the text move his central knight is in real trouble. **22. Qa3! Rh7 23. f4 Ng6 24. f5** More than sufficient for a winning position, but some other moves were more conclusive; e.g., 24. R×g6 B×d4 (24. ... f×g6 25. Ne6†) 25. B×d4 f×g6 26. Q×a5 or 24. Ne6†. **24. ... Ne7** "If 24. ... Ne5 25. f4 and the knight is lost"—Pollock. **25. Bg4** The quiet 25. Nf3! is impossible to meet satisfactorily. The bishops will get exchanged after which White has a free hand—25. ... f6 26. B×b6 c×b6 27. Nd4 or 25. ... Nc8 26. B×b6 c×b6 27. Qc3! **25. ... Qe8** 25. ... Qd8 seems better but White has the same strong continuation: 26. f6! g×f6 27. Qc3, and there is nothing to do against

a strong sacrifice coming up; e.g., 27. ... Nc8 28. Ne6†! f×e6 29. B×e6 and wins. **26. f6! g×f6 27. Ne6†?** Right here the knight sacrifice is incorrect. White breaks through on the queenside with the calm 27. Nf5! B×e3 28. N×e3 b6 29. R×c7. **27. ... f×e6 28. B×e6** 28. B×b6 c×b6 29. Q×d6 Rd8 30. Q×b6 e×d5 is utterly unclear. **28. ... Qh5!** Certainly not 28. ... B×e3? 29. Q×e3 Qh5 30. R×c7 Rh6 31. Bg4 Qg5 32. f4 which gives White too much compensation. **29. B×b6 c×b6 30. Rc7 Re8 31. Qc3 Qe5 32. Q×e5?** This exchange is too confident. They should keep the queens on the board with 32. Qe3, obtaining enough compensation for the huge amount of sacrificed material. **32. ... f×e5 33. f4 e×f4 34. e5 d×e5 34. ... Rd8!** would have killed all fun for White at once. **35. d6 Nac6 36. R×b7 Rg7?** 36. ... Ng6! 37. Bd7 R×d7 38. R×d7 Re6 transposes into an easily won endgame. **37. R×g7 K×g7 38. Bd7! Rd8 39. B×c6 R×d6 40. R×e7† Kf6 41. Rh7** "The Black party had not included this neat move in their calculations. The game is now drawn, by correct play"—Pollock. **41. ... Kg5 42. Bf3 Rd2 43. Rh5† Kf6 44. R×h4 R×a2 45. Rh6† Kf5 46. Rh5†** here the game was drawn by mutual consent—*Baltimore Sunday News* (Pollock), 14 July 1889.

## (957) Bird–Pachholder   0–1
Simultaneous game
Baltimore, 8 July 1889
*A02*

**1. f4 d6 2. Nf3 Bf5 3. b3 e6 4. Bb2 Nf6 5. e3 Be7 6. Be2 0–0 7. 0–0 h6 8. d3 d5 9. Nd4 c5 10. N×f5 e×f5 11. Qe1 Nc6 12. c3 d4 13. c×d4 c×d4 14. Bf3 Bc5 15. e4 f×e4 16. d×e4 Re8 17. Nd2 Rc8 18. a3 a5 19. Rc1 Ba7 20. Qg3 d3† 21. Kh1 Nd4 22. e5 Nh7 23. Be4 R×c1 24. R×c1 Ne2 25. Qg4 N×c1 26. e6 Nf6 27. e×f7† K×f7 28. Qg6† Kf8 29. B×f6 Q×f6** and Black wins—*Baltimore Sunday News*, 14 July 1889.

## *Philadelphia, middle of July 1889*

Bird's days left in the United States were dwindling by now. He made a brief visit to Washington, which remains undocumented, and then headed for the second time to Philadelphia. Here he worked off a series of six games at a rattling pace with John Welsh Young. Bird came out well on top with five wins and one loss.

## (958) J.W. Young–Bird   1–0
Match (game 4)
Philadelphia, July 1889
*C51*

**1. e4 e5 2. Nf3 Nc6 3. Bc4 Bc5 4. b4 B×b4 5. c3 Bc5 6. 0–0 d6 7. d4 e×d4 8. c×d4 Bb6 9. Re1 Bg4 10. Qa4 B×f3 11. d5 Qh4 12. Be3 Qg4 13. Bf1 Nge7 14. d×c6 b×c6 15. Nd2 B×g2 16. B×g2 0–0 17. h3 Qg6 18. Kh2 Kh8 19. Nf3 f5 20. e5 B×e3 21. R×e3 Nd5 22. Nh4 Qh6 23. B×d5 c×d5 24. Nf3 f4 25. Re2 Qh5 26. Qb3 d4 27. Rae1 c5 28. e×d6 c4 29. Qb7 d3 30. Re5 Qh6 31. Q×a8** and White wins—*Philadelphia Times*, 21 July 1889.

**(959) Bird–
J.W. Young　1–0**
Match (game 5)
Philadelphia, July 1889
C58

1. e4 e5 2. Nf3 Nc6 3. Bc4
Nf6 4. Ng5 d5 5. e×d5 Na5
6. d3 Bg4 7. f3 Bh5 8. Qe2 Bd6
9. Nc3 0–0 10. Bd2 c6 11. d×c6
N×c6 12. 0–0–0 Nd4 13. Qf1
b5 14. N×b5 N×b5 15. B×b5
Rb8 16. Bc4 a5 17. Ne4 a4
18. N×d6 Q×d6 19. Bc3 Nd5
20. Qe1 Rfe8 21. B×d5 Q×d5
22. Kb1 f6 23. Qe4 Qd7 24. d4
Bg6 25. Qe3 Qf5 26. Rd2 e4
27. d5 Qc8 28. d6 e×f3
29. Q×f3 Be4 30. d7 B×f3
31. d×c8Q Re×c8 32. g×f3
R×c3 33. Rf1 Rc5 34. Rfd1

### Handicap tournament, London, 13 September–26 October 1889

*Site:* Simpson's Divan
*Prizes:* Five prizes
*Odds scale:* pawn and move (class II), pawn and 2 moves (class III), knight (class IV) and two pieces (class V)

|  |  | 1 | 2 | 3 | 4 | 5 | 6 | 7 | 8 | 9 | 10 | 11 | 12 | 13 | 14 | 15 | 16 |  |
|---|---|---|---|---|---|---|---|---|---|---|---|---|---|---|---|---|---|---|
| 1 O.C. Müller | I |  | 1 | 1 | 1 | 1 | 1 | 1 | 0 | 1 | 1 | ½ | 1 | ½ | 1 | 1 | 1 | 13 |
| 2 E.L. Sellon | III | 0 |  | 1 | 0 | 1 | 1 | 1 | 1 | 1 | 1 | 1 | 1 | ½ | 1 | 1 | 1 | 12½ |
| 3 H.E. Bird | I | 0 | 0 |  | 1 | 1 | 1 | ½ | 1 | 1 | ½ | 1 | 1 | 1 | 1 | 1 | 1 | 12 |
| 4 F.J. Lee | I | 0 | 1 | 0 |  | 0 | 1 | ½ | 1 |  | ½ | 1 | 0 | 1 | 1 | 1 | 1 | 9 |
| 5 G.H.D. Gossip | I | 0 | 0 | 0 | 1 |  | ½ | ½ | 0 | 1 | 0 | 1 | 1 | ½ | 1 | 1 | 1 | 8½ |
| 6 E.O. Jones | I | 0 | 0 | 0 | 0 | ½ |  | 1 | 1 | 1 | ½ | 0 | 1 | 1 | 0 | 1 | 1 | 8 |
| 7 S.F. Smith | I | 0 | 0 | ½ | ½ | ½ | 0 |  | 1 | 1 | 0 | 0 | 0 | 1 | 1 | 1 | 1 | 7½ |
| 8 W. Ward-Higgs | IV | 1 | 0 | 0 | 0 | 1 | 0 | 0 |  | 0 | 1 | 0 | 1 |  | 1 | 1 | 1 | 7 |
| 9 T.E. Greatorex | IV | 0 | 0 | 0 | 0 |  | 0 | 0 | 1 |  | 1 | 1 | 0 | 1 | 1 | 1 | 1 | 7 |
| 10 W.J. Ingoldsby | I | 0 | 0 | ½ | ½ | 1 | ½ | 1 | 0 | 0 |  |  |  |  | 1 | 1 | 1 | 6½ |
| 11 J.B. Purchase | IV | ½ | 0 | 0 | 0 | 0 | 1 | 1 |  | 0 |  |  | 1 | 0 |  | 1 | 1 | 5½ |
| 12 Alderson | V | 0 | 0 | 0 | 1 | 0 | 0 | 1 | 0 | 1 |  | 0 |  | 1 | 1 | 0 |  | 5 |
| 13 J.E. Hetley | II | ½ | ½ | 0 | 0 | ½ | 0 | 0 |  | 0 |  | 1 | 0 |  | 1 | 1 |  | 4½ |
| 14 Grossbach | II | 0 | 0 | 0 | 0 | 0 | 1 | 0 | 0 | 0 | 0 |  | 0 | 0 |  | 1 |  | 2 |
| 15 T.C. Gibbons | I | 0 | 0 | 0 | 0 | 0 | 0 | 0 | 0 | 0 | 0 | 0 | 1 | 0 | 0 |  | 1 | 2 |
| 16 Wilkinson | III | 0 | 0 | 0 | 0 | 0 | 0 | 0 | 0 |  | 0 | 0 | 0 |  |  | 0 |  | 0 |

and won finally through White's pawns—*Philadelphia Times*, 21 July 1889.

On Wednesday 17 July, Bird boarded ship and 11 days later, on 28 July, he arrived on English shores.[23]

## HANDICAP TOURNAMENT AT SIMPSON'S DIVAN, SEPTEMBER–OCTOBER 1889

The summer season in London had been rather dull, with all the important prelates of the royal game absent. London chess circles were stirred in September when the opening of the new season coincided with a new handicap tournament. As usual, such an event attracted many participants and onlookers to the Divan.

The secretary of the handicap was Lee, who oversaw the entry of 16 players in the tournament. The participation of masters such as Bird, Lee and Müller was rather predictable. They were joined by Gossip who had spent the past decade in France, Australia and America. In the summer of 1889 he returned to Europe to take part in the German Congress at Breslau and he subsequently resettled in England.

A notable feature of this tournament was the realization that the most successful days of chess with odds were over. Several players

who were used to being divided in lower classes joined the first class for the first time. Thus they received the opportunity to meet the masters on equal terms. Such an arrangement hardly affected their chances to win a high prize, as even with giving odds the masters generally ended ahead of the others.

Müller had the best start, winning 8 games out of 9. Bird also played quite well in the earliest rounds, scoring 3½ out of 4. Two of his games were published worldwide. Against Edward Owen Jones, Bird launched a successful attack out of nothing. The game abounds with beautiful complications. The name of his opponent in the other game, where Bird gave the huge odds of rook and knight but nevertheless won in seven moves, was not mentioned in any source. Given these odds, one imagines that Bird's victim must have been Dr. Alderson.

Towards the end of September, Bird marred his strong start with two losses. Especially the one against Müller was unnecessary and also highly crucial for the final ranking, as Bird ended a full point below the young German. The surprising Ernest Lyttlehales Sellon (class III) pushed Bird from the second to the third spot. The awarding of prizes happened on 26 October. Immediately afterwards Bird to his satisfaction beat Müller with the Black pieces in what he called a match game in *The Times* on 28 October.

**(960) E.O. Jones–Bird　0–1**
Handicap tournament
London, September 1889
C45

1. e4 e5 2. Nf3 Nc6 3. d4 e×d4 4. N×d4 Bc5 5. c3 Qf6 6. Be3 Nge7 7. f4 B×d4 8. c×d4 d5 9. Nc3 d×e4 10. d5 Nd8 This looks bad after White's next move, but Bird had seen further. If he wanted to play it safe, 10. ... Nf5 11. Bc5 Nd8 was an alternative. **11. Nb5 0–0 12. N×c7 Nf5 13. Bc5 e3!** *(see diagram)*

**14. Be2** This move loses on the spot, but it was very difficult, probably even impossible, to cope with Bird's strong attack. 14. N×a8

23. His old friend MacDonnell remarked a new and youthful look when observing the veteran for the first time in five months: "Mr. H.E. Bird returned from America last Sunday, and I have pleasure in announcing that he looks remarkably well; in fact, so young and radiant, that by special request of his friends he has abandoned the title of the 'veteran,' and is henceforth to be known as 'young Bird.' He has lost three stone in weight, but for this he has found full compensation in the supernatural growth of his hair, aided by some American invention." *Illustrated Sporting and Dramatic News*, 3 August 1889.

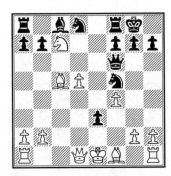

*After 13. ... e3*

fails after 14. ... Qh4† (15. g3 N×g3 or 15. Ke2 b6), thus leaving 14. Qc2 as White's best try. After 14. ... Qh4† 15. Kd1 Nc6!!, White has some major options. 16. Qd3 loses quickly after 16. ... Rd8 17. N×a8 Qf2 18. Be2 Q×g2 or 18. Nc7 b6 19. Ba3 Nfd4 20. Be2 N×e2. An improvement is 16. Qe4, with the point that g2 is defended. After 16. ... Rd8 17. N×a8 Qf2 18. Be2 the position remains extremely murky. Better is the intriguing 16. ... Rb8!, when White can chose between 17. B×f8 Qf2 18. Qc2 Q×f4, with a raging attack (19. d×c6 Nd4 wins immediately) and 17. g3 Qf6 18. Kc1 Bd7! (a very strong move. It is nearly unbelievable, but Black keeps his attack going even with several of his pieces disappearing from the board); e.g., 19. B×f8 R×f8 20. Bb5 Qd6! 21. Kb1 Nfd4 etc. Though 16. Qe4 is certainly still playable in a practical situation, the critical line seems to be 16. d×c6 Rd8† 17. Bd3 b×c6 18. Kc1 (18. N×a8 turns out to be too greedy after 18. ... Ba6) 18. ... Rb8. White still enjoys a material advantage, but Black's compensation is more than obvious. **14. ... Qh4† 15. g3 N×g3 16. B×e3 Ne4† 17. Kf1 Qh3† 18. Ke1 Q×e3 19. Rf1 Bh3 20. Rf3 Qg1† 21. Bf1 B×f1** White resigns—*Evening News and Post*, 28 September 1889.

## (961) Bird–Alderson    1–0
Handicap tournament
London, September 1889
*Odds of Ra1 and Ng1*

**1. b3 b6 2. Bb2 Bb7 3. e3 f6 4. h4 h5 5. Bd3 Rh6 6. Q×h5† R×h5 7. Bg6** mate—*Evening News and Post*, 28 September 1889.

## (962) Bird–Müller    0–1
Handicap tournament
London, 24 September 1889
*A03*

**1. f4 d5 2. Nf3 Nf6 3. e3 e6 4. b3 Be7 5. Bb2 b6 6. Bb5† c6 7. Be2 Nbd7 8. 0–0 Nf8 9. Ne5 Qc7 10. a4 a6 11. d3 Ng6 12. d4 Ne4 13. Bd3 f6 14. Nf3 c5 15. c4 Bb7 16. Nbd2 0–0 17. Rc1 a5 18. Qe2 Bd6 19. c×d5 e×d5 20. d×c5 B×c5 21. Nd4 Qf7 22. N×e4 d×e4 23. Bb5 Rfc8 24. Rcd1 Bd5 25. f5 Nf8 26. Ne6 B×b3 27. Rd2 N×e6 28. Rd7 Qf8 29. f×e6 B×e6 30. Rb7 Qd6 31. Bc4 B×c4 32. Q×c4† Kh8 33. Qf7 B×e3† 34. Kh1 Qf8 35. R×f6 Q×f7 36. Rf×f7 Bh6 37. g4 Rc2 38. Bd4 e3 39. B×g7† B×g7 40. R×g7 Rf2 41. R×h7† Kg8 42. Rbg7† Kf8 43. Kg1 Rd8 44. Rd7 R×d7 45. R×d7 Rf4 46. h3 e2** White resigns—*Chess Player's Chronicle*, 28 September 1889, p. 69.

# A SECOND VISIT TO WALES, OCTOBER 1889

Bird's first passage through Wales in February pleased him and his hosts, as is warranted by his speedy return in October. The visit took place under the auspices of the South Wales Chess Association.

Bird commenced his tour in Cardiff with exhibitions at the Park Hotel. On Thursday 10 October Bird contested 23 games. He succeeded in winning all but 2, which he lost from C. Bisgood and E. Possart. His audience greatly appreciated Bird's approach of introducing new opening lines.

On 11 October Bird played 18 games. Only G.W. Lennox succeeded in beating him, while 2 players (E.N. Bisgood being one of them) drew their game. Bird won against the remaining 15 opponents.

Bird's travelling to more remote towns are less documented. On Tuesday 15 October Bird scored 15 wins out of 16 games at the Black Lion Hotel, the home of the Aberdare Chess Club. The fortunate winner was Flooks. On the next day the veteran was in Pentre. Against 15 members of the United Rhondda Chess Club, Bird played a total of 27 games. Just one player, Rees T. Jones, beat him. In *Bird's Chess Reviews* (p. 1) the chess master also thanked people from Merthyr and Dowlais, implying that he also visited these towns.

## (963) Bird–Eachran    1–0
Simultaneous game
Cardiff, 10 October 1889
*C55*

**1. e4 e5 2. Nf3 Nc6 3. Bc4 Nf6 4. Qe2 d5 5. e×d5 Nb4 6. N×e5 Be7 7. d4 0–0 8. 0–0 Nb×d5 9. Nc3 Be6 10. Bb3 N×c3 11. b×c3 B×b3 12. a×b3 c5 13. Be3 Qc8 14. Rfe1 Qc7 15. Bf4 Bd6 16. Qc4 c×d4 17. c×d4 Q×c4 18. b×c4 b6 19. Bg5 B×e5 20. d×e5 Nd7 21. Be7 Rfe8 22. Bd6** and White wins—*Nottinghamshire Guardian*, 16 November 1889. First published in the *Glasgow Weekly Herald*.

## (964) Bird–Lennox    0–1
Simultaneous game
Cardiff, 11 October 1889
*C33*

**1. e4 e5 2. f4 e×f4 3. Be2 d5 4. e×d5 Nf6 5. c4 Bd6 6. d4 b6 7. Nc3 a6 8. b4 c5 9. b×c5 b×c5 10. d×c5 B×c5 11. B×f4 0–0 12. Rb1 Bf5 13. Rb3 Re8 14. Nf3 Nbd7 15. Nd4 Be4 16. Nc6 Qc8 17. Na4 B×g2 18. N×c5 B×h1 19. Nb7 Ne4 20. Kf1 Ndc5 21. N×c5 N×c5 22. Rg3 Qf5 23. Qd4 f6 24. Bg4 Nd3 25. R×d3 Q×g4 26. Qf2 Re4 27. Bg3 Rae8 28. Qd2 Re2 29. Kg1 Re1†** and White resigns—*Western Mail*, 14 October 1889.

## (965) Bisgood–Bird    ½–½
Simultaneous game
Cardiff, 11 October 1889
*C51*

1. e4 e5 2. Nf3 Nc6 3. Bc4 Bc5 4. b4 B×b4 5. c3 Bc5 6. 0–0 d6 7. d4 e×d4 8. c×d4 Bb6 9. Nc3 Na5 10. Bg5 f6 11. Bf4 N×c4 12. Qa4† c6 13. Q×c4 Ne7 14. e5 d5 15. Qb3 Ng6 16. Bg3 f5 17. Ne2 0–0 18. Nf4 N×f4 19. B×f4 h6 20. Qe3 g5 21. N×g5 h×g5 22. B×g5 Qd7 23. Bf6 R×f6 24. e×f6 Qf7 25. Qg5† Kh8 draw—*Weekly Mail*, 29 November 1890.

The following game, published in 1892, presents something of a mystery. According to the *Oldham Chronicle*, it was part of a recent match that was played in Cardiff between Bird and the strong Welsh player George W. Lennox. Research, however, has not unearthed a visit made by Bird to Wales after the one that took place in October 1889. The game itself is a fascinating battle.

**(966) Lennox–Bird    1–0**

Match
Cardiff 1889 (?)
C47

**1. e4 e5 2. Nc3 Bc5 3. Nf3 d6 4. Be2** "A rather cautious development, but perhaps a good tactic against such an aggressive player as Mr. Bird. White might have played 4. Bc4 without any danger"—*Oldham Chronicle*. **4. ... Nc6 5. d3 Nf6 6. Na4 Bb6 7. N×b6 a×b6 8. c3 Be6 9. b3** White's queenside is somewhat weakened after this move. Bird immediately points to this part of the board. **9. ... h6 10. 0–0 Ra5 11. Be3 Qa8 12. Qc2 Ra3 13. Rfb1 0–0 14. Bc1 Ra5 15. d4 e×d4 16. N×d4 N×d4 17. c×d4 c5** White reacted by occupying the center. Bird's last move contains a certain logic but also freely grants his opponent a space advantage. Also slightly better for White is 17. ... c6 18. Bd2. Perhaps his best try is the unorthodox 17. ... N×e4 as the evident 18. Q×e4?! Bf5 19. Qh4 B×b1 20. R×b1 R×a2 followed by 21. ... Ra1 provides Black with more than enough material and positional compensation for the two bishops his opponent gets. Preferable is 18. Rb2 Bf5 19. Q×c7 Rc8 20. Q×b6 Nc3 21. a4 and now the surprising 21. ... N×a4 22. b×a4 R×a4 23. Rab1 B×b1 24. R×b1 Rc6 25. Qb2 Ra2 is at least equal for Black. **18. d5** Playing 18. a4! at once is good. Black has nothing better than 18. ... c×d4 19. Bb2 d5 20. e5 Rc5 21. Qd3 Nd7 22. B×d4 when White's superiority is obvious. He maintained control over the center and prevented any counterplay on the queenside. **18. ... Bd7 19. Bd2 Ra7** "Black now moves this rook for the fourth time, without obtaining any advantage, while White again gains time to develop his forces"—*Oldham Chronicle*. **20. Bc3** 20. a4 obstructs Black's intended counterplay with a clever trick. If at once 20. ... b5? 21. Bc3 wins a pawn or completely destroys Black's kingside with 22. B×f6. **20. ... Nh7** It was time to give up his play on the a-file and pay some more attention to the center with 20. ... Qd8. Though White enjoys a small initiative, Black's position is still fine. **21. f4 b5 22. Qb2** Lennox misses the opportunity to make the thematic push 22. e5! b4 23. Bb2 d×e5 24. f×e5. **22. ... f6 23. b4** "We greatly prefer 23. a3. The text move allows Black a dangerous passed pawn, and gives him at least an even game"—*Oldham Chronicle*. **23. ... c4 24. e5 Bf5 25. Rd1 Re8** "Black ought to exchange the pawn on e5. By the move made he also allows his opponent to establish a well-supported passed pawn"—*Oldham Chronicle*. 25. ... f×e5 26. f×e5 Qe8 27. e×d6 Qg6 offers adequate counterplay. **26. e6** 26. Bh5 Rf8 (26. ... Re7

27. Bd4 Ra6 28. e×d6) 27. e6 improves White's chances. Black is forced to keep the e-pawn nearing promotion under control. **26. ... Ra3** (*see diagram*) "Mr. Bird seems absolutely determined to win the game with this rook"—*Oldham Chronicle*.

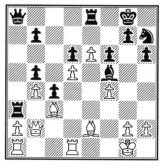

*After 26. ... Ra3*

**27. g4?!** White is losing his patience in dealing with Bird's obstinate resistance. 27. Bh5 Re7 28. Bd4 Kh8 29. Qf2 keeps a slight initiative, though Black's position is quite solid. **27. ... Be4** Many of White's pieces are now misplaced. His next move doesn't improve the situation. **28. Rd4 Qa7 29. Kf1 f5 30. R×e4** He had no choice. Yet, the sacrifice is certainly not without danger for his opponent. **30. ... f×e4 31. Bd4?** With the undisguised aim of gaining back his material. But the resulting position is very disappointing for White. Instead he should try his luck with 31. B×g7!, which sets the board on fire. Now 31. ... Ra8 is necessary, forcing a declaration of White's bishop. (If instead 31. ... b6?, White has the luxury to play 32. B×h6!, when 32. ... c3? 33. Qc2 even wins quickly.) So, after 31. ... Ra8, 32. B×h6 has to be avoided, as 32. ... c3! 33. Qc2 Qd4 is another story, the Black queen not being cut off from d4 yet. Forceful measures are thus necessary in the form of 32. Bh8, finally forcing Black to play 32. ... b6 to cover the mate, but this move effectively cuts off the queen from a transfer to the kingside via e3. Now there are a few possibilities for White. 33. Kg1 is playable, but after 33. ... Qc7!, with the threat of pushing the c-pawn, White has to retreat his bishop to c3. This is an extremely complicated position, with perhaps the better chances for Black. More critical is 33. f5 (*see diagram*), aiming for some targets of his own. Here are three options for Black, each demonstrating the extreme difficulty of the position.

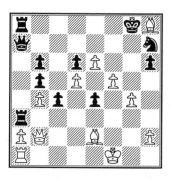

**Analysis position after 33. f5**

(**a**) A first try is 33. ... Qe7, bringing the queen towards the kingside without any delay, but after 34. Kg2!, Black is forced to change plans with 34. ... Qb7 35. h4, and White has gained important time for his attack. The crucial element of this line is that 34. ... Qg5? 35. h4! completely turns the tables. (**b**) An important refinement is 33. ... Qc7!, forcing the retreat of White's bishop (as in the line given above) by 34. Bd4, and only now 34. ... Qe7! If then 35. Kg2 (best) 35. ... Qg5! is possible, and Black is ready to break down White's pawn shelter by 36. ... h5! A spicy line illustrating this is 36. Bh8 h5! 37. h4 Qh6 38. g5 N×g5 39. h×g5 and 39. ... Q×g5† initiates a lethal attack. (**c**) While 33. ... Qc7! thus seems to be the best move, 33. ... Ng5 also deserves consideration, if only for the crazy lines resulting from it. Two samples, both arising after 34. h4, are 34. ... Qh7 35. Bc3 Nh3 36. f6 Qg6 37. f7† Kf8 38. Be5 d×e5 39. Q×e5 Rg3 40. Ke1 Rg1† 41. Bf1 Q×g4 42. Qh8† Ke7 43. d6† K×d6 44. f8Q† or 34. ... Nf3 35. Bd4 Qh7 36. B×b6 h5 37. f6 Ne5 38. Bd8 h×g4 39. f7† Kf8, both leading to extreme complications. Black is likely to end on top as he can sacrifice his knight against the most dangerous White pawns at an opportune moment. **31. ... b6** If the queen retreats, the g-pawn is ready to be taken. **32. B×b6 Q×b6?!** 32. ... Qa8! 33. Bd4 Rc8 makes good use of the time lost by his opponent. He threatens to push the c-pawn, while the pawns at d5 and a2 are worth taking when the opportunity arises. Suddenly the situation appears very difficult for White. **33. Q×a3** White is now a pawn ahead, but his king is feeling a distinct draft while some of his pawns (d5, f4) remain weak. **33. ... Nf6?!** 33. ... Rf8 puts much more pressure on White; e.g., 34. f5 (34. Qc1 Qd4) 34. ... Qd4 35. Rd1 Qe5 36. Qg3 Q×g3 37. h×g3 Ra8 and Black has good chances. **34. Rd1 Qb7 35. Qe3 Qa8 36. Rd2?** In view of the game continuation, the far-seeing 36. Ke1 is very strong. Black now had to find 36. ... N×d5 37. Q×e4 N×f4! to keep the game equal (37. ... N×b4 38. Q×a8 R×a8 39. R×d6 Kf8 40. f5 is better for White), for even though White is a piece up after 38. Q×f4 R×e6 39. R×d6 Re8, Black has chances to hold the game. **36. ... N×d5 37. Q×e4 N×f4!** "A splendid coup. White dare not take the knight on account of 38. Rf8"—*Oldham Chronicle*. **38. Q×a8 R×a8 39. R×d6 N×e2?** An incomprehensible exchange. 39. ... Kf8 wins without much problems. **40. e7 Re8 41. Rd8 Kf7 42. R×e8 K×e8 43. K×e2 K×e7 44. Ke3 Kd6 45. Kd4 Kc6 46. a4 b×a4 47. K×c4 a3?** "An unaccountable blunder, which loses the pawn and thereby an otherwise well contested game. Black's correct course here was 47. ... Kb6"—*Oldham Chronicle*. **48. Kb3 g6 49. K×a3 h5 50. g5 h4 51. Kb3 h3 52. Kc4** and White wins—*Oldham Chronicle*, 30 January 1892.

# B.C.A. CONGRESS, LONDON 1889

The principal chess event of the autumn was the fifth congress of the British Chess Association. Compared to the previous congresses, a few important changes were made. While the previous congresses were very busy with the overlapping tournaments, the master tournament was now held in advance in order to give Captain Beaumont the chance to witness the play before he had to undergo an operation. Beaumont had namely proposed to make a donation of £50, on the condition that the prize money would be divided according to the Sonneborn-Berger tie breaking system. The committee duly accepted the offer and promised to feed the prize fund with the usual entrance fees as well as with an undefined sum provided by the B.C.A.

This year's B.C.A. congress was destined for British players only. The elite was expected to take part, but after a few days of ambiguity, three of the best players dropped out. Mackenzie was allowed to enter the tournament but he was too ill to participate. Burn was prevented for business reasons. Blackburne's late dropping out had more impact as he had initially given his word to attend and play. Gunsberg, Bird and Mason were considered the favorites among the remaining 11.

Bird opened the tournament with Black against Müller. The game took a rather quiet course and a draw appeared in the making when Bird suddenly forced the opening of the queenside with some powerful moves. Müller was helpless against Bird's infiltrating forces and soon had to resign.

In the second round Bird enjoyed a bye due to Blackburne's not turning up. It was only on the third day that Blackburne announced his withdrawal officially.

In the next round Bird faced a dilemma. He was bound to meet Gossip but also wished to attend the Lord Mayor's Show, one of London's most renowned and longest-established annual events. In the end Bird was able to obtain a remarkable exception from the organization: his game would start two hours later.[24] Poor Gossip could not count on any mercy from Bird's side. The veteran was determined to do everything to win the game, but Gossip clung to a draw.[25]

Bird was also unable to force a win in either of his two following games. The position against Blake was sterile from the opening onwards and both players quickly agreed upon a draw. The game between Bird and Louis van Vliet saw much more excitement. This time, Bird was very lucky, for after the game Hoffer pointed out how van Vliet could have won.

It was only in the sixth round that Bird got to handle the White pieces for the first time. Against Wainwright he unleashed his habitual 1. f4. His young opponent was not very familiar with Bird's pet line yet and got in difficulties after the opening. Bird commenced a solid attack that Wainwright was not able to withstand. At this point Gunsberg was leading the field, half a point ahead of Bird.[26]

A hard fight lay ahead in the seventh round when Bird had the Black pieces again against Lee. The veteran won relatively easily.

Another tough opponent awaited Bird in the eighth round. Only a handful of years earlier Mason had been one of the top players in the world and he had been a true nemesis of Bird ever since they met—but alcoholism had broken down the American. In this game

24. "Even then he arrived half an hour later, but, much to the amusement of the onlookers, he made up his lost time in a very few moves." *Pall Mall Gazette*, 11 November 1889.

25. "At the adjournment at six o'clock the game between Gossip and Bird was unfinished. Resumed at 8 p.m., it was still undecided at 11, and again adjourned, after 85 moves and seven hours play. In the course of the game Bird won a piece which he was subsequently compelled to give up for a queened pawn, and the position of affairs now is thus: Bird: king, rook and 2 pawns vs. Gossip king, rook and pawn. Bird's king, however, is prevented from crossing to the aid of his rooks and pawns, and Gossip has commenced counting the moves for a draw." *Daily News*, 11 November 1889.

26. Bird was very ambitious and optimistic at this point of the contest: "I shall come out at the top. I feel I have it in me. I don't intend to go in for rapid and risky play.... If I can help it. I don't intend to lose a game." *Baltimore Sunday News*, 8 December 1889. First published in the *Leeds Mercury*.

Bird was close to winning, but Mason's defensive skills brought about a draw.[27]

In the ninth round Bird disposed of Mortimer. This game was of a lower quality and it was thanks to a blunder by his opponent that Bird won. He still occupied an excellent position in the general ranking, a half point behind the leader, Gunsberg.

Bird was able to catch up with Gunsberg in the penultimate round. Just as with Wainwright a few rounds earlier, the inexperienced Nicholas Theodore Miniati was not prepared to match Bird's 1. f4. Bird slaughtered him in a beautiful game that left a spectator, a certain Mr. Peek from Redcar, so struck that he gave a special prize for it. All was set for a tremendous last round with the game between the two leaders Bird and Gunsberg.[28]

Both players were well aware of the strain and decided to take as little risk as possible. When the game threatened to end in a quick draw Bird started an attack against Gunsberg's queenside. Gunsberg defended patiently and with a well-timed sacrifice he seemed to gain the upperhand. Bird replied correctly and, offering a similar sacrifice, brought about a drawn position. On the 61st move hands were shaken to confirm the splitting of the point. The enthusiasm of Bird's supporters exploded when their favorite achieved sole possession of first place thanks to the Sonneborn-Berger system.

Bird and his colleagues were due for a cold shower when Hoffer announced that the B.C.A. would not come up with extra money, thus limiting the prize fund to slightly more than £74. Bird caught £12 0s. 6d. of this fund, while Gunsberg received only £11 18s. Hoffer gave various arguments to defend the decimation of the prize fund, such as the absence of several strong players and the difficulty in finding enough means to organize a yearly congress. One other reason is worth mentioning in detail, as it certainly will not have done any good to his relationship with some of the masters:

> Now, looking calmly and without bias at the result, it must be admitted that the achievement of the two first prize winners is not so remarkable as to entitle them to exceptional remuneration. ...
>
> It must, therefore, be admitted that such a mediocre result does not warrant a larger share than was received by them according to the system of division. They were rewarded according to the quality of their games, and if their share was not larger, it is not the fault of the system, but their own [*Chess Monthly*, December 1889, p. 100].

Hoffer's remarks clearly refer to the great number of draws made by Bird and Gunsberg. Five draws in a total of ten games was indeed rare for Bird, and it was the result of a deliberate decision by of the

| | | 1 | 2 | 3 | 4 | 5 | 6 | 7 | 8 | 9 | 10 | 11 | |
|---|---|---|---|---|---|---|---|---|---|---|---|---|---|
| 1 | H.E. Bird | | ½ | ½ | 1 | 1 | 1 | ½ | ½ | 1 | 1 | ½ | 7½ |
| 2 | I. Gunsberg | ½ | | ½ | ½ | 1 | 1 | 1 | ½ | 1 | ½ | 1 | 7½ |
| 3 | J. Mason | ½ | ½ | | 0 | 0 | ½ | ½ | 1 | ½ | 1 | 1 | 5½ |
| 4 | O.C. Müller | 0 | ½ | 1 | | 1 | 0 | 0 | 1 | 0 | 1 | 1 | 5½ |
| 5 | N. Miniati | 0 | 0 | 1 | 0 | | ½ | ½ | 1 | 1 | ½ | 1 | 5½ |
| 6 | F.J. Lee | 0 | 0 | ½ | 1 | ½ | | 1 | ½ | ½ | ½ | ½ | 5 |
| 7 | J.H. Blake | ½ | 0 | ½ | 1 | ½ | 0 | | 0 | 1 | ½ | 1 | 5 |
| 8 | L. van Vliet | ½ | ½ | 0 | 0 | 0 | ½ | 1 | | 1 | 1 | ½ | 5 |
| 9 | G.E. Wainwright | 0 | 0 | ½ | 1 | 0 | ½ | 0 | 0 | | 1 | 1 | 4 |
| 10 | J. Mortimer | 0 | ½ | 0 | 0 | ½ | ½ | ½ | 0 | 0 | | 1 | 3 |
| 11 | G.H.D. Gossip | ½ | 0 | 0 | 0 | 0 | ½ | 0 | ½ | 0 | 0 | | 1½ |

**5th Congress of the B.C.A., London, 7–19 November 1889**
*Site:* British Chess Club
*Playing hours:* 1 p.m.–6 and 8 p.m.–11
*Prizes:* £72 divided among the participants according to the Sonneborn-Berger system
*Time limit:* 20 moves per hour

veteran. For the first time in his long chess career he managed to keep his most aberrant ideas under control and off the board. Instead, Bird's play was characterized by a very atypical prudence and temperance attitude. One cannot really say that Bird played positionally well-founded chess, but he adopted a more rational version of his own style. While his ideas were generally rejected by his peers, one cannot deny that they at least posed several problems to players (of lower, same or even superior class). Even more remarkable was that Bird succeeded in maintaining this standard in his last three major tournaments during the 1890s, at Manchester, Hastings and London. At Manchester he scored another brilliant result, at Hastings he was by far the best British exponent, until his health started playing its role during the second half of the tournament. Even at London 1899, despite disastrous results, his play troubled much younger and superior opponents. During this 5th congress of the B.C.A. tournament Bird saved himself from one or two dangerous situations and generally played chess at a level superior to that of his opponents. The voices in the press, even Hoffer's when it did not came down to the money issue, showered Bird's performance with praise.[29]

Bird's victory was celebrated with a dinner at Simpson's on 6 December. In the presence of many of his admirers and opponents an overview of Bird's career was given while numerous reminiscences and anecdotes, alas not repeated in the press, caused widespread amusement.

27. A report appeared in the *Daily News* on 16 November 1889: "Bird played 1. f4 against Mason. After a few preliminary moves, Bird inaugurated a strong attack on his adversary's kingside, and it required all the well-known defensive skill of Mason to resist the onslaught. The battle raged for five hours and was then adjourned. Resumed at eight o'clock, it was found that the forces and position on both sides were equal, and after a few ineffectual efforts to accomplish a decisive termination it was agreed to abandon the game as drawn, at the 77th move."

28. "When the news reached the clubs on Monday night that Bird had come out of the ten rounds with a score equal to that of Gunsberg, and that these two masters would meet next day to compete for the first prize and the championship of Great Britain, excitement ran high, and an extraordinarily large number of spectators attended at the 'British' on Tuesday in order to watch the championship game." *Bradford Observer Budget*, 23 November 1889.

29. "Mr. Bird deserves high credit, not only for his distinguished place in the tournament, but for the style in which he played. Although his games were tempered with caution, they gave evidence in several instances that, in spite of over forty years constant public play, and in spite of advancing age, he has preserved an unimpaired intellect. In fact, his games will compare well with any he ever played; whilst in soundness and depth of combination we might aim to say, surpassed himself. For his game with Miniati, which we publish this week, he was awarded (Mr. Hoffer being umpire) a prize for brilliancy, offered by one of the spectators, who constantly watched Mr. Bird's play." *The Field*, 23 November 1889. ¶ "I am very pleased that Mr. Bird took part in this contest, and I join with all true lovers of our game in congratulating him upon his victory. Had Mr. Bird retired a year or two ago from match contests—that is, retired without having won a first prize in a grand tournament—the magic chatter of redundant juvenility might have buzzed away his reputation into obscurity, or at all events assigned to him a place behind that occupied by the great masters. But now, by his late victories, Bird has proved that whilst in brilliancy of style he is as splendid as ever, in steadiness and strength—in superiority to weak moves—he is not a whit behind the most consummate match-player." *Illustrated Sporting and Dramatic News*, 30 November 1889.

**(967) Müller–Bird   0–1**
B.C.A. Congress (round 1)
London, 7 November 1889
B73

1. e4 c5 2. Nc3 Nc6 3. Nf3 g6 4. d4 c×d4 5. N×d4 Bg7 6. Be3 d6 7. Be2 Bd7 8. 0–0 Nf6 9. Qd2 0–0 10. f4 N×d4 11. B×d4 Bc6 12. Qe3 Nd7 13. Rad1 B×d4 14. Q×d4 Qb6 15. Nd5 B×d5 16. e×d5 Rac8 17. c4 Q×d4† 18. R×d4 f5 19. g4 Nf6 20. g5 Nd7 21. Bf3 Rc7 22. Re1 Kf7 Bird experienced no problems whatsoever and now has slightly better prospects for the endgame. **23. Kg2 a6 24. a4 Nc5 25. Bd1 a5 26. b3 h6 27. h4 Rh8 28. Re3 h5 29. Bf3 Re8 30. Rd1 Ra8 31. Rde1 Ra6 32. Bd1 Rb6 33. Bc2 Rb4** Despite extensive maneuvring Bird didn't get any further along, mainly because of the unnecessary closure of the kingside with 28. ... h5. The activation of his rook should be innocent. **34. Kf2?** *(see diagram)* A most unhappy square for the king. If his majesty had gone to f3 or g3 nothing could happen to him.

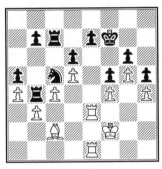

*After 34. Kf2*

**34. ... b5!** Bird immediately clinches his chance. **35. a×b5 a4 36. b×a4 R×c4 37. Bd1 R×f4†** Here is the point: the f-pawn is undefended. **38. Kg3 Rb4 39. Ra3 Ra7 40. Bc2?!** 40. Rf3 is more stubborn, but not sufficient against careful play: 40. ... Rc7! (a win becomes problematic after 40. ... N×a4 41. Ra3 Ra8 42. B×a4 Ra×a4 43. R×a4 R×a4 44. Rb1 Ra7) 41. Ra3 Ne4† 42. Kh3 Rb1. Black's pieces are sovereign. White is already forced to play 43. a5 and abandon his b-pawn. **40. ... R×b5 41. a×b5 R×a3†** White resigns. The b-pawn is doomed—*The Field*, 9 November 1889.

Bird had a bye in the second round.

**(968) Gossip–Bird   ½–½**
B.C.A. Congress (round 3)
London, 9 November 1889

*White to move*

"The game was adjourned here (having already lasted afternoon and evening), but, on resumption, Bird could not get his king into action. Gossip here played 1. Rf2†, and the Black king could never cross the line and the game was drawn"—Cunningham. *International Chess Magazine* (Cunningham), December 1889, p. 366.

**(969) Blake–Bird   ½–½**
B.C.A. Congress (round 4)
London, 11 November 1889
*Game score missing*

**(970) van Vliet–Bird   ½–½**
B.C.A. Congress (round 5)
London, 12 November 1889
B73

1. e4 c5 2. Nc3 Nc6 3. Nf3 g6 4. d4 c×d4 5. N×d4 Bg7 6. Be3 Nf6 7. Be2 d6 8. 0–0 0–0 9. h3 Bd7 10. Qd2 N×d4 11. B×d4 Bc6 12. Bd3 Nd7 13. Be3 Nc5 14. f3 Qc7 15. Rae1 e6 16. Be2 a6 17. Rd1 Rfd8 18. Kh1 b5 19. a3 Rac8 20. Qe1 Qe7 21. Bd2 Bb7 22. Qf2 B×c3 23. B×c3 Na4 24. Bb4 e5 25. b3 Nc3 26. Rd2 Rd7 27. Qe3 N×e2 28. Q×e2 Qe6 29. Rfd1 d5 30. e×d5 R×d5 31. R×d5 B×d5 32. Re1 Re8 33. Bc3 f6 34. Bb2 Qf5 35. Kh2 h5 36. c4 b×c4 37. b×c4 Bc6 38. Qe3 Rd8 39. Qb6 Qc8 40. Bc3 Rd3 41. Re3 R×e3 42. Q×e3 Qe6 43. Qc5 e4 44. Bb4 Qe8 45. f×e4 B×e4 46. Qd6 Qe5† 47. Q×e5 f×e5 48. Bc3 Bd3 49. c5 e4 50. c6 Bb5 51. c7 Bd7 52. Kg3 Bc8 53. Kf4 Bb7 54. Ke5 Kf7 55. Kd6 Ke8 56. Bd4 Bc8 57. Be3 Kf7 and van Vliet proposed a draw, which was accepted. He could hardly miss the win had he continued playing—58. a4 Ke8 59. a5 Kf7 60. Kc6 Ke7 61. Kb6 Kd7 62. h4 Kd6 63. Bf4† Kd7 64. Ka7 e3 65. Kb8—*The Field*, 16 November 1889.

**(971) Bird–Wainwright   1–0**
B.C.A. Congress (round 6)
London, 13 November 1889
A03

1. f4 d5 2. e3 Nf6 3. Nf3 e6 4. b3 Be7 5. Bb2 a6 6. Be2 c5 7. 0–0 Nc6 8. Qe1 b5 9. a4 b4 10. Ne5 Bb7 11. d3 d4?! "Black's development is inferior to that of White; and this attempt to open the diagonal for his bishop makes matters worse"—Anthony. Alternatives such as 11. ... N×e5 or 11. ... 0–0 promise him equal play. **12. Bf3!** "Taking immediate advantage of the weak position, and securing a manifest advantage in position"—Abbott. **12. ... Rc8 13. e×d4 c×d4 14. Nd2 Nd5** This way the d-pawn gets cut off from the rest of the army. White can already capture that pawn as after 15. N×c6 B×c6 16. B×d4 Nf6 17. Qf2 everything is defended. Bird's treatment of the position is not worse. **15. Ndc4 0–0?** Black had to play 15. ... Nc3 to avoid the capture of the d-pawn. **16. Qg3? N×e5** 16. ... Bh4! (Abbott) takes maximal profit from Bird's last move. After 17. N×c6 B×c6 18. Qh3 N×f4 19. Qg4 B×f3 20. Q×f4 Bd5 21. B×d4 Black's bishop pair is an important asset. **17. f×e5 Bc5** As the d-pawn would be lost now after 18. Qf2!, the text move makes little sense. 17. ... Rc7 covers the bishop and gives the knight freedom of liberty again. If 18. B×d4, he can harass his opponent's queen and gain counterplay, 18. ... Bh4 19. Qg4 h5 20. Qe4 Nc3 21. Qe3 Bg5 22. Qf2 B×f3

23. B×c3 B×g2 24. Q×g2 b×c3 with but a slight advantage for White. **18. Kh1 Rc7 19. Bc1** "Being of no more use on b2, the bishop quietly reoccupies his original diagonal, at the same time threatening 20. Bh6"—Moon. **19. ... f6** "19. ... Kh8 appears much better"—Anthony. **20. e×f6 Kh8?** "Especially if this be the best reply to White's last move; but we confess to fail to see the objection to 20. ... N×f6"—Anthony. **21. f×g7† R×g7 22. Qe5 Qh4** "An imprudent sally. 22. ... Qf6 would have broken the attack, though of course White's pawns must win in the long run"—Anthony. **23. Bd2 Rfg8 24. g3 Qh3 25. Rf2** 25. Be4 is more potent. **25. ... Ba7** 25. ... Rf8 offers some resistance. **26. Nd6 Rf8 27. N×b7 Bb8 28. Nd6 Rf5 29. Nf7† R×f7 30. Q×b8† Rg8 31. Qe5†** "For if 31. ... Nf6 32. Be4. If 32. ... Rgg7 33. Bg4 and if 32. ... Rfg7 33. B×d5 e×d5 34. Rf7"—Anthony. *Hereford Times* (Anthony), 23 November 1889; *Illustrated London News* (Abbott), 1 March 1890; *Hampshire Telegraph* (Moon), 31 May 1890.

## (972) Lee–Bird   0–1
B.C.A. Congress (round 7)
London, 14 November 1889
*Game score missing*

## (973) Bird–Mason   ½–½
B.C.A. Congress (round 8)
London, 15 November 1889
*Game score missing*

## (974) Bird–Mortimer   1–0
B.C.A. Congress (round 9)
London, 16 November 1889
*A03*

**1. f4 e6 2. e3 Nf6 3. Be2 Be7 4. b3 b6 5. Bb2 Bb7 6. Nf3 0–0 7. 0–0 d6 8. c4 c5 9. Qe1** "It will be convenient if this development were at once named 'Bird's Opening,' if only out of compliment to its most successful exponent"—Abbott. **9. ... Ne8 10. Nc3 Nd7 11. Rd1 Kh8 12. Qg3 f5 13. d4 Rf6** "In a close game it is hazardous to bring out a rook at so early a stage as the present, as the sequel proves"—Abbott. **14. d5 Rg6 15. Qf2 Nc7?** 15. ... e×d5 doesn't look attractive but is necessary. **16. d×e6 R×e6 17. Nd5** Black is allowed to simplify the game a bit. Very strong was 17. Bd3 Qf8 18. Ng5 Rg6 19. Qc2, putting the f-pawn under fire. If now 19. ... B×g5 20. B×f5 Bf6 21. B×g6 h×g6 22. Q×g6 Qe7 23. Rfe1 with a great position. **17. ... N×d5?!** "17. ... B×d5 is better, as that piece is now shut out of play for the rest of the game"—Abbott. **18. c×d5 Rh6 19. Qg3?** This way the attack is easy enough to repel, while Black even gets the chance to take the initiative. Far less agreeable for him would have been 19. Bd3!, which once more pinpoints the weakest spot in Black's camp, the f-pawn. **19. ... Bf6 20. Ng5 Qe7 21. Bc1 Re8** 21. ... a5 is interesting. **22. h4 a6 23. Qh3 Nf8 24. g3** White enjoys the freer position in the center and kingside. Any trace of an initiative from Black on the queenside is gone. **24. ... B×g5?** "This move only seems to add to Black's difficulties. 24. ... Bc8 appears the correct move"—Abbott. To say the least for the text move is an outright blunder. After 24. ... Bc8 25. Bd3 g6 the position of his rook causes Black worries. **25. f×g5 Q×g5** "The rook

now pays the penalty of his temerity"—Abbott. **26. e4** "Here White does not make the most of his position. If 26. h×g5 R×h3 27. Kg2, the rook is lost and the game virtually finished"—Abbott. **26. ... Qg6 27. B×h6 Q×h6 28. Q×f5 Ng6 29. Qg5** "With White's numerical superiority this is perhaps the shortest way to victory"—Abbott. **29. ... Q×g5 30. h×g5 Ne5 31. Rf4 Kg8 32. Bg4 Bc8 33. Bf5 b5 34. Kg2 c4 35. b×c4 b×c4 36. Rh1 B×f5 37. e×f5 Nd3 38. R×c4 Re2† 39. Kf3 R×a2 40. Rc8† Kf7 41. R×h7 Ne5† 42. Ke3 Ng4† 43. Kd3 Ne5† 44. Kc3 Ra3† 45. Kb4 R×g3 46. Rc7† Kg8 47. Rc×g7†** and White wins—*Illustrated London News* (Abbott), 11 January 1890.

## (975) Bird–Miniati   1–0
B.C.A. Congress (round 10)
London, 18 November 1889
*A03*

**1. f4 d5 2. Nf3 Nf6 3. e3 e6 4. b3 a6 5. Bd3** "A favorite move of Mr. Bird's, who plays this opening with great predilection and to perfection"—Hoffer. **5. ... c5 6. Bb2 Be7 7. 0–0 Nc6 8. c3 Qc7 9. c4 d×c4 10. b×c4 b6 11. Nc3 Bb7 12. Be2** "Perceiving Black's intention to castle on the queenside, the bishop is better placed at e2, for it can be brought to f3, where it occupies an unobstructed diagonal"—Hoffer. **12. ... h6 13. Qe1 0–0–0?!** "We confess that it is a daring venture to castle on this side with an open b-file, and the threat of White's bishop to be brought to f3, after the removal of the knight"—Hoffer. **14. Na4! Rdg8** "All this is well intended, and very bold on the part of the younger master, but the counterattack is hardly expected to succeed against the veteran"—Hoffer. **15. Rb1 Nd7 16. Ne5 Nc×e5 17. B×e5 Qc6** (*see diagram*) "17. ... Bd6 is the right move here. Obviously, if 17. ... N×e5 18. N×b6†"—Hoffer. 17. ... Bd6 18. Bc3 leaves Black bound hand and foot; e.g., 18. ... B×g2 19. N×b6† N×b6 20. K×g2 Na4 21. Bf3 with a decisive attack.

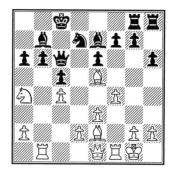

*After 17. ... Qc6*

**18. N×b6†!** "A brilliant, and to all appearances, a sound conception"—Hoffer. **18. ... N×b6** "Compulsory. If 18. ... Kd8 19. Bf3 wins the queen"—Hoffer. **19. Bf3 Nd5** "Equally compulsory"—Hoffer. **20. c×d5 e×d5 21. d3 f6 22. Bg4† Kd8 23. Qa5† Ke8 24. Bc7 Ba8 25. Rf2 Kf7 26. Rfb2** "Obviously, White would win the queen with 26. Rb6; but he would have to give more for it than necessary in such a powerful position"—Hoffer. **26. ... h5 27. Bf5 d4 28. e4 Bd6 29. B×d6 Q×d6 30. Rb6 Bc6 31. Q×a6!** "And now comes the brilliant termination to this pretty game"—Hoffer. **31. ... Ra8 32. Rb7† B×b7 33. R×b7† Qe7 34. Qe6† Kf8 35. Q×e7†** and Black resigns—*The Field* (Hoffer), 23 November 1889.

**976) Bird–Gunsberg** ½–½

B.C.A. Congress (round 11)
London, 19 November 1889
*A02*

**1. f4 b6 2. e3 Bb7 3. Nf3 g6 4. Be2 Bg7 5. 0–0 e6 6. c3 Ne7 7. Na3 0–0 8. Nc2 d5 9. Qe1 c5 10. Qf2 Nbc6 11. d4 c4 12. Nce1 b5 13. Ne5 f6 14. N×c6 B×c6 15. Bg4** "In irregular openings each player asserts his own individuality, and the development is shaped according to his style and predilection. We dispense, therefore, with any remarks on the game so far. Here, however, it seems as if this move was unnecessary and loss of time"—Hoffer. **15. ... Qd6 16. Nf3** And so is this move. As the sequel shows, the bishop is placed hors de combat almost right up to the ending, and nearly jeopardized White's game"—Hoffer. 16. Nc2 is therefore more logical. **16. ... b5 17. Bd2 b4 18. a3** This merely leads to a weakness at a3 or b2. 18. Rfc1 is less harmful. **18. ... b×a3** "Obviously not 18. ... b3, which would be a protection to White's queenside, and give him time for an attack on the kingside"—Hoffer. **19. R×a3 Rfb8 20. Bc1 Nc8 21. Qh4** "This move does not improve White's prospects—on the contrary. After Black's reply, White's bishop is out of play. He will have to retire his queen before pushing the g-pawn and so lose still more time. No doubt, Black has the better game at this stage"—Hoffer. **21. ... h5** 21. ... f5 is a safer way to put his opponent's bishop in seclusion. **22. Bh3 Ne7 23. Qg3 Bd7 24. Qe1 Qc6 25. Nd2 f5 26. Qh4 Nc8 27. Nf3 Be8 28. Ne5?!** The knight had to remain in a position from where it would be able to challenge its Black counterpart which is underway to e4. **28. ... Qc7 29. Rf3?! Nd6 30. Rf1 Ne4** Bird lost a lot of time. Gunsberg is close to forcing the decision on the queenside. **31. Nf3 a4 32. Qe1 Bf8 33. Ra2 Rb3?!** 33. ... a3! breaks down White's defense. He can't handle the vigorous opening up of his queenside; 34. b×a3 Qb6 35. Ng5 Qb1 36. Re2 N×g5 37. f×g5 Qd3 38. Bb2 B×a3 wins. **34. Nd2 N×d2 35. Q×d2 Rab8 36. g3 Qa5 37. Qe2** "A subtle move which Mr. Gunsberg did not appreciate at its full value, although it constitutes the turning point of the game"—Hoffer. **37. ... a3 38. e4?** Complications enter the game, but this should have resulted in a quick instead of slow death for White. **38. ... d×e4 39. Q×c4 Qd5?!** 39. ... Qb5! 40. Q×b5 B×b5 41. Rf2 Bd3 completely binds White. 40. Q×e6† is even worse. **40. Q×d5 e×d5 41. Rf2 Kf7 42. Bf1 Bd6** "Black should have prevented the advance of the c-pawn with 42. ... Rc8"—Hoffer. **43. c4 Rc8?** 43. ... Be7 is still much better for him, as each step of the c-pawn is very bad for White (44. c5 Bf6 and 44. c×d5 Rc8). If instead 44. b×a3 Rb1 45. Rfb2 R8xb2 46. B×b2 d×c4 leaves his opponent struggling as well. **44. c5 B×c5** The logical consequence of the previous move, but Gunsberg made a false evaluation of the resulting position and his advantage evaporates. **45. d×c5 R×c5 46. Ra1 a2 47. Rd2 Rb4?** After 47. ... Ke6 there is a standstill. This was no option for Gunsberg as the tournament situation demanded his taking risks. **48. b3 R×b3 49. Rd×a2 d4 50. Bb2?** Bird misses the chance to win the tournament on his own with a direct assault: 50. Ra7† Ke6 51. R1a6† Bc6 52. Ba3 Rc2 53. Re7† Kf6 54. Rc7. **50. ... d3 51. Bd4 Rcb5 52. Kf2 R5b4 53. Be5 Rb1 54. Ra7† Ke6 55. R1a6† Rb6 56. R×b6† R×b6 57. Ra2 Rb1 58. Rd2 Bb5 59. Bg2 Bc4 60. Bd4 Kd5 61. Be5** draw. "An interesting and difficult ending, which, after the sacrifice of the piece by Black,

might have been won by Mr. Bird. But a draw securing him a division of first honors, he was well advised not to venture upon hazardous ground"—Hoffer. *The Field* (Hoffer), 23 November 1889.

# MATCH WITH GOSSIP 1889

Bird did not rest on his laurels for long. Just a week after his tournament win he brought to a conclusion the discussion with Gossip that had lasted more than 15 years. Gossip had finished in sole possession of last place at the congress of the B.C.A., but he had drawn with Bird and beaten him twice in New York. This was, however, no reason for the obstinate veteran to adjust his long-standing offer of playing a match with Gossip giving odds. Bird even augmented the stakes by offering the heavy odds of pawn and two moves instead of pawn and move. Three games were played and the outcome came quite as a surprise:

> Mr. Bird and Mr. Gossip have just played a short match, the former giving the odds of pawn and 2 moves. The result was a tie, but the two players have since contested other games at the same odds, with the result that Mr. Bird has won the majority [*Manchester Evening News*, 14 December 1889].

Charles A. Dust, the chess editor of the *Manchester Evening News* seems to have been misinformed about the second duel, where the odds were actually lowered to pawn and move. This contest was planned to be a longer one, but no report about the final result of it could be retrieved.

**(977) Gossip–Bird 1–0**
Match 1 (game 1)
London, 25 November 1889
*Odds of pawn and two moves*

**1. e4 & 2. Nf3 c5 3. d4 c×d4 4. N×d4 Nf6 5. Nc3 Qa5 6. Bd2 Qb6 7. Nb3 d6 8. Nd5 N×d5 9. e×d5 Nd7 10. Ba5** Black resigns—*Hereford Times*, 7 December 1889.

The second game ended in a draw while Bird equalized by winning the third game in brilliant style. A second match was started early in December.

**(978) Gossip–Bird 0–1**
Match 2 (game ?)
London, December 1889
*Odds of pawn and move*

**1. e4 Nc6** "A very old and frequently adopted move. How ancient we know not, further than that it is to be found in Salvio (1604)"—Anthony. **2. Nf3** "2. d4 and 2. Nc3 are the book replies. We have failed to find any analysis or actual game in which the text move occurs"—Anthony. **2. ... g6 3. Bb5** "Loss of time as it appears to us"—Anthony. **3. ... Bg7 4. d4 Nh6** "Here 4. ... e6 seems stronger"—Anthony. **5. d5 Nb8 6. Be3 c6** "If 6. ... B×b2 7. B×h6 B×a1 8. c3"—Anthony. **7. Be2 Nf7 8. Nc3** "White might have seized the opportunity of exchanging the powerful Black bishop by playing 8. Bd4"—Anthony. **8. ... 0–0 9. Qd2 d6 10. Nd4** "10. 0–0 is more to our taste"—Anthony. **10. ... c5 11. Ne6 B×e6**

**12. d×e6 Ne5 13. 0–0–0** "Threatening 13. B×c5. Castling on the other side would, however, have been more prudent, besides enabling him to defend with greater ease the pawn at e6, which, if it can be retained, should prove a thorn in Black's side"—Anthony. **13. ... Na6 14. f4 Nc6 15. Bc4** "White should prosecute his attack on the kingside by 15. g4"—Anthony. **15. ... Nc7 16. a3** "Weak play, being worse than loss of time, since it aids rather than retards the coming assault"—Anthony. **16. ... b5** "An admirable rejoinder, if the pawn be taken, the open b-file for Black's rooks would prove irresistible"—Anthony. **17. Bd5** *(see diagram)*

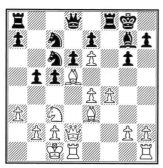

*After 17. Bd5*

**17. ... b4!** "Bird here initiates one of his famous original combinations. Move 19 is part of it, and particularly brilliant"—Pollock. **18. Ne2** 18. B×c6 b×c3 19. b×c3 Rb8 20. Qd3 Rb6 21. Bd5 still keeps everything under control for White, although Black is far from being lost as well. Bird conquers the initiative after the text move. **18. ... N×d5 19. Q×d5** Or 19. e×d5 b×a3 20. b×a3 Rb8. **19. ... b×a3! 20. Q×c6?** He has no choice but to play 20. b×a3 when Black is a little bit better after 20. ... Qb6 21. Kd2 Qa6. **20. ... a×b2† 21. Kd2** "If 21. Kb1 Qa5 wins instantly"—Pollock. **21. ... Qa5† 22. c3 b1Q 23. R×b1 Qa2† 24. Kc1 Q×e2 25. Bd2 Q×g2** "The remaining play lacks interest, as Mr. Bird now has an easily won game"—Anthony. **26. Rd1 Qh3 27. Qd7 Rae8 28. Kc2 c4 29. e5 Qd3† 30. Kc1 Rb8 31. Rb5 R×b5 32. Q×b5 a6 33. Qb7 d×e5 34. f×e5 B×e5 35. Bh6 Q×c3† 36. Kb1 Qa1†** "Too old to be caught in a trap! If 36. ... Rb8 White mates in two moves"—Pollock. **37. Kc2 Rf2† 38. Rd2 Qa4†** White resigns—*Hereford Times* (Anthony), 14 December 1889; *Baltimore Sunday News* (Pollock), 12 January 1890.

# Visiting the North, December 1889–January 1890

Bird dedicated the last month of the year and the beginning of the next one to extensive touring throughout the country. Before leaving home he engaged in an interesting consultation game in which he beat a duo lead by Mason.

**(979) Bird & Lee–Mason & Cook    1–0**
Consultation game
London (British C.C.), 27 November 1889
*A02*

**1. f4 e5 2. f×e5 d6 3. e×d6 B×d6 4. Nf3 g5** "Black here leaves the beaten track, 4. ... Nh6 is usually played"—Lee. This game is of theoretical importance as it is the first known occasion where 4. ... g5 was played in the From's Gambit. This move, however, only gained real popularity when Lasker adopted it in 1892 to beat Bird in their match in Newcastle. **5. d4** Time would point out 5. g3 as the main move. Bird tried several alternatives during his career. **5. ... g4 6. Ng5** Certainly better is 6. Ne5, forcing Black into an endgame after 6. ... B×e5 7. d×e5 Q×d1. This was the continuation in the aforementioned game between Bird and Lasker. **6. ... f5** "Threatening to win the knight by 7. ... h6"—Lee. **7. d5 Qe7** There is no need to refrain from the planned 7. ... h6; 8. Qd4 Nf6 9. Qe3† Qe7 10. Q×e7† K×e7 11. Ne6 N×d5 with the better endgame. **8. Qd4 Be5 9. Qc4 h6 10. Ne6 B×e6 11. d×e6 Qh4†?!** Until now the Black allies had the game firmly under control, but this sudden outburst tilts the balance into White's favor. 11. ... Nc6 is advantageous for them. **12. g3!** "White voluntarily gives up the exchange and pawn here, in anticipation of an attack which proves successful"—Lee. **12. ... B×g3† 13. h×g3 Q×h1 14. Q×c7 Ne7 15. Nc3 Nbc6 16. Bd2** Both here and on move 18 White's play is a bit slow. After 16. Kf2! Qh5 17. Bg2 Rd8 18. Q×b7 they possess a strong attack. **16. ... 0–0 17. 0–0–0 Rad8 18. e3** 18. e4! is very powerful. Black is forced to return some material with 18. ... R×d2, as White threatens 19. Bb5, 20. B×c6 and 21. e7. **18. ... Rc8 19. Qf4 Ng6 20. Qf2 Qf3?** *(see diagram)* Not good at all as the queen remains a target for White's pieces. With 20. ... Qh5 his position would be acceptable.

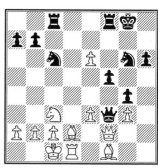

*After 20. ... Qf3*

**21. Qh2 Nce5 22. Bg2 Qf2 23. e7!** "An ingenious conception. If 23. ... N×e7 24. Bd5† wins the queen"—Lee. **23. ... Rf7 24. Nd5 N×e7 25. N×e7† R×e7** "A pretty trap. If 26. Bd5† Kh7 27. Q×f2 Nd3† and captures the White queen with the better game"—Lee. **26. Rf1! Nf3** "The only move. If 26. ... Qe2 27. Bd5† wins"—Lee. **27. R×f2 N×h2 28. Bd5† Kh7 29. R×h2 Rd8 30. Bc4 Kg6 31. Bd3 h5 32. Kd1 Rh8 33. Rf2** "The winning move. Black's reply is as good as any, but there is no satisfactory defense"—Lee. **33. ... Rf7 34. e4 h4** "Desperation. the battle is won for White"—Lee. **35. e×f5† Kh5 36. Rh2 h3** "Black has a choice of mates here and elects to give White a pretty termination"—Lee. **37. R×h3† g×h3 38. Be2** mate—*British Chess Magazine* (Lee), January 1890, p. 28.

The first part of his tour brought Bird to several cities in the north. On 21 December he witnessed Blackburne's blindfold exhibition at Stockton-on-Tees. Two days later Bird gave two exhibitions at the chess club of Sunderland. In the afternoon he opposed 20 players, winning against 18 of them and losing 2, against Halcro and J. Nicholson. About 16 games were played in the evening; Bird was victorious in 13, drew 1 with R. Forster, and lost 2, against Dr. Marshall and, once more, Nicholson.

## (980) Bird–Halcro    0–1

Simultaneous game
Sunderland, 23 December 1889
C14

1. e4 e6 2. d4 d5 3. Nc3 Nf6 4. Bg5 Be7 5. Bxf6 Bxf6 6. Nf3 Be7 7. Bd3 c5 8. dxc5 Bxc5 9. exd5 exd5 10. Nxd5 Bxf2† 11. Kxf2 Qxd5 12. Re1† Be6 13. Re5 Qd8 14. Bb5† Nc6 15. Nd4 0–0 16. Bxc6 bxc6 17. Nxc6 Qb6† 18. Nd4 Rad8 19. Re4 Bf5 20. Rf4 g5 21. Rxf5 Rxd4 and Black wins, as White must give up his queen or he gets mated—*Newcastle Weekly Chronicle*, 1 February 1890.

## (981) Bird–J.R. Marshall    1–0

Simultaneous game
Sunderland, 23 December 1889
C14

1. e4 e6 2. d4 d5 3. Nc3 Nf6 4. Bg5 Be7 5. Bxf6 Bxf6 6. Nf3 0–0 7. h4 c5 8. Bd3 cxd4 9. e5 Be7 10. Bxh7† Kxh7 11. Ng5† Bxg5 12. hxg5† Kg6 13. Qh5† Kf5 14. g4† Kxe5 15. Qh2 mate—*Illustrated London News*, 12 April 1890.

## (982) Bird–Halcro    1–0

Simultaneous game
Sunderland, 23 December 1889
C14

1. e4 e6 2. d4 d5 3. Nc3 Nf6 4. Bg5 Be7 5. Bxf6 Bxf6 6. Nf3 Be7 7. Bd3 c5 8. dxc5 Bxc5 9. Qe2 Nc6 10. e5 0–0 11. h4 Bd7 12. Bxh7† Kxh7 13. Ng5† Kg8 14. Qh5 Re8 15. Qxf7† Kh8 16. Qh5† Kg8 17. Qh7† Kf8 18. Qh8† Ke7 19. Qxg7 mate—*Newcastle Weekly Chronicle*, 4 January 1890.

Bird visited some other towns as well, Sheffield and Redcar certainly being among them, but his stay there remains undocumented.

Bird prolonged his tour in the new year. On 8 January he was the guest of the club in Plymouth. Against 31 members he scored 21 wins, 3 losses (against W. Edwin Turner, J.T. Wright and T.G. Pearse) and 7 draws (against C. Winter-Wood, W. Binns, R.H. Fison, D.W. Earle, E.P. Clark, W.J. May and E.A. New). Bird drifted with a remarkable pace along the boards, and impressed his adversaries by correcting the exact position when one of them had been shifting the pieces on his own initiative.

Bird continued his way to the west of England and on 10 January he arrived in Penzance. The master succeeded in grinding down 13 opponents. He lost 4 games, against Hedgeland, V. Douglas, C. Staples and Russell Pengelly. R. Davy and Gartrell each earned a draw. Before leaving town Bird complimented his opponents by stating that they were about evenly matched with the major club of Plymouth.

## (983) Bird–R. Davy    ½–½

Simultaneous game
Penzance, 10 January 1890
C39

1. e4 e5 2. f4 exf4 3. Nf3 g5 4. h4 g4 5. Ng5 h6 6. Nxf7 Kxf7

7. d4 h5 8. Bxf4 d6 9. Nc3 Bh6 10. Bc4† Be6 Bird succeeds in gaining material after this careless move. 10. ... Kg7 leaves White to demonstrate his compensation for the piece. **11. 0–0! Bxc4 12. Bg5† Nf6 13. Rxf6† Qxf6 14. Bxf6 Kxf6** Black has enough material for the queen, but the position of his king may cause him worries. **15. d5?** Bad, as it concedes the important central e5 square to Black's knight. Instead 15. b3 Bf7 16. e5† keeps Black's king under fire. **15. ... Nd7 16. Qd4† Ne5 17. b3 Ba6** The closed character of the center favors Black's bishop pair and rooks for they have some weaknesses to attack. **18. a4 Ke7** 18. ... Bg7 19. b4 Kg6 20. Qe3 Bc4 was very good. For no good reason Black doesn't play the thematic Bg7 on his next moves either. **19. Nb5 Kd7 20. c4 Rhf8 21. Na3 Ng6 22. b4 b6 23. b5 Bb7 24. Nc2 Nxh4** Even though Davy's play had been planless he couldn't do much wrong, since Bird's pieces lack active play. The capture of the h-pawn allows Bird an unexpected chance, that he omits to take. **25. a5** With this push Bird had some sharp ideas in mind. Also possible was 25. e5, trying to make use of the absence of Black's knight. Black nevertheless retains control after 25. ... Rae8 26. e6† Kc8 27. Qd3. **25. ... Rae8 26. axb6 axb6 27. Ra7 Kc8 28. Qa1 Bd2?** *(see diagram)* Allowing Bird to make his point. 28. ... g3! initiates a decisive attack (29. c5 Rf2).

*After 28. ... Bd2*

**29. c5! dxc5 30. d6!** A second pawn is sacrificed, a new front is opened, and suddenly Bird obtains fantastic counterplay. The immediate threat is 31. Qg7. **30. ... Rf7** With 30. ... Bf4! the bishop takes up the important task of gaining control over the black squares around its king, White has to try 31. Ra8† Kd7 32. Qg7† Kxd6 33. Rxe8 Rxe8 34. Qf6† Kd7 35. Qxh4 (35. Qxf4 Rxe4 36. Qf7† Re7 37. Qxh5 Nxg2 is also slightly better for Black) 35. ... Be5 36. Qxh5 g3. Black's king can escape from the perpetual check, after which he will attack the e-pawn. White isn't without chance to achieve a perpetual in a later stage, when Black needs to redeploy his pieces to attack White's king. **31. Rxb7!** 31. Ra8† equally secures the draw. **31. ... Kxb7 32. Qa6† Kb8 33. dxc7† Rxc7 34. Qxb6† Kc8 35. Qa6† Rb7?** Blundering a rook, but Bird overlooks 36. Qc6†. **36. Qa8† Rb8 37. Qc6† Kd8 38. Qd6† Kc8 39. b6?** The situation would be completely different after 39. Qxc5† Kd7 40. Qd5† Ke7 41. Qxh5 Rh8 42. Qe5† Kf7 43. Qd5† Kg6 44. Qxd2 when Black is lost. **39. ... Bf4!** Excellently played by the amateur! **40. Qxf4** 40. Qc6† Kd8 41. Qxc5 Kd7 42. Qxh5 Be5 43. Qxg4† Re6 44. Qxh4 Rbxb6 is a bit similar to the previous line, but a much better version for Black, as he enjoys now excellent drawing chances. **40. ... Rxb6 41. Qg5 Rb1†?!** 41. ... Ng6 is safer. Black's pieces cooperate well enough to avoid losing. **42. Kh2 Rb2?** The position is extremely complicated, hence it is no surprise to see Bird's opponent stumbling. The point is that Black's knight at h4 is in trouble and that 42. ... Rd8 solves this, for after 43. Q×c5† Kb7 44. Qe7† Kc8, Black in case of 45. Q×h4? Rd3 46. Q×h5 g3† at least draws. He'd still be suffering after 45. Qe6† Kb7 46. Nb4, but the text move is much worse. **43. Q×c5† Kb8 44. Qc3 Rb7 45. Qg3† Rc7 46. Nb4 Kc8 47. Nd5 Nf3† 48. g×f3 Rc2† 49. Kg1 g×f3 50. Qg6?** A terrible mistake. 50. Q×f3 wins easily. **50. ... Rg2† 51. Q×g2 f×g2 52. K×g2** draw—*The Cornishman*, 23 January 1890.

On 15 January Bird arrived unexpectedly at the chess club of Trowbridge. Twenty players were assembled to play him. Bird lost one game, against A. Gregory, who received some hints from the master while playing.

On 28 December 1889 an announcement had appeared in the *Manchester Times* that Bird would visit the Liverpool Chess Club from 20 until 25 January. As no traces of his actual staying there have been found, it is unclear if this visit actually went through. Instead the following game may have been played around this time, if Bird was back in London for some days.

### (984) Unknown–Bird    0–1
Offhand game
London, January 1890
C45

**1. e4 e5 2. Nf3 Nc6 3. d4 e×d4 4. N×d4 Bc5 5. Be3 Qf6 6. c3 Nge7 7. Qd2 B×d4 8. c×d4 d5 9. e5 Qg6 10. Nc3 Bf5 11. 0-0-0 0-0-0 12. f4 f6 13. Bd3 f×e5 14. f×e5 Nb4 15. B×f5† N×f5 16. Bg5 N×d4 17. B×d8 N×a2† 18. N×a2 Nb3 mate**—*Manchester Examiner and Times*, 28 January 1890.

On 25 January Bird attended the annual meeting of the Surrey County Chess Association in Croydon. He was invited by Captain Beaumont to give a simultaneous exhibition on 20 boards against members of the association. After three hours of play, Bird had won 14 games, lost 3 (against A.W. Air, Hillier and Sargent) and drawn 3 (Henderson, Rawson and Barton).

Two days later Bird commenced an engagement for the Manchester Chess Club. It was arranged that the members would meet the British champion for three weeks in offhand games, consultation chess, simultaneous exhibitions. Also some opening instruction was foreseen.

A detailed program was drafted but only a few details of the proceedings leaked into the press. On Thursday 30 January, Bird gave two simultaneous exhibitions. In the afternoon he won all 20 games. In the evening 13 opponents succumbed and 2 earned a draw. On Friday 14 February another exhibition was given. Against 20 opponents Bird won 12, lost 4 and drew 3 games. One game remained unfinished.

At this time his engagement with the Manchester Chess Club belonged to the past and Bird immediately continued his way to Liverpool to meet Lasker during the last two weeks of February.

### (985) Bird–Pierce    ½–½
Simultaneous game
Manchester (Manchester C.C.), 30 January 1890
C25

**1. e4 e5 2. Nc3 Nc6 3. f4 e×f4 4. Nf3 Bc5 5. d4 N×d4 6. N×d4 Qh4† 7. Ke2 d5 8. Qd3 Bg4† 9. Nf3 Nf6 10. Qb5† Nd7 11. B×f4 Qf2† 12. Kd1 B×f3† 13. g×f3 Q×f3† 14. Qe2 Q×f4 15. e×d5 Qe5 16. Q×e5† N×e5 17. Bg2 0-0-0 18. Rf1 f6 19. Rf4 c6 20. Ke2 Rhe8 21. Kf1 Be3 22. Rh4 h6** draw—*Manchester Examiner and Times*, 31 January 1890.

### (986) Bird–Unknown    ½–½
Offhand game
Manchester (Manchester C.C.), 31 January 1890
C58

Bird's opponent was a local first class player.

**1. e4 e5 2. Nf3 Nc6 3. Bc4 Nf6 4. Ng5 d5 5. e×d5 Na5 6. Bb5† c6 7. d×c6 b×c6 8. Bd3 Bc5 9. 0-0 Bg4 10. Qe1 Qc7 11. b3 0-0 12. Ne4 N×e4 13. B×e4 f5 14. Bf3 B×f3 15. g×f3 Rf6 16. Kh1 Re8 17. Rg1 Bd6 18. Rg2 Re7 19. Bb2 Nb7 20. Na3 Nc5 21. Nc4 Nd7 22. N×d6 Q×d6 23. Qe2 Nf8 24. f4 Ng6 25. f×e5 N×e5 26. Re1 Rfe6 27. B×e5 R×e5 28. Qc4† Kh8 29. Reg1 Re4 30. Qc3 Qd5 31. f3 Rd4 32. d3 Qd6 33. Qa5 c5 34. Qb5 Rh4 35. b4 Qf4 36. Q×c5 R×h2† 37. R×h2 Q×f3† 38. Rhg2 Qh3** draw—*Manchester Examiner and Times*, 1 February 1890.

### (987) Mills & Hardman & Wright–Bird & Mitchell & Wahltuch    1–0
Consultation game
Manchester (Manchester C.C.), 1 February 1890
C11

**1. e4 e6 2. d4 d5 3. Nc3 Nf6 4. e5 Nfd7 5. f4 c5 6. d×c5 Nc6 7. a3 N×c5 8. Nf3 Be7 9. b4 Ne4 10. Bb2 f5 11. e×f6 e.p. B×f6 12. Ne5 B×e5 13. f×e5 Qh4† 14. g3 N×g3 15. h×g3 Q×h1 16. Ne2 0-0 17. Nf4 R×f4 18. g×f4 Qh4† 19. Kd2 Q×f4† 20. Kc3 Bd7 21. Kb3 a5 22. b5 Ne7 23. Bd3 Be8 24. Qg1 Bg6 25. Rf1 Qh4 26. Qb6 Qh3 27. Q×b7 Rf8 28. R×f8† K×f8 29. b6 B×d3 30. c×d3 Q×d3† 31. Ka2 Qc4† 32. Ka1 Qb5 33. Qc7 Qf1† 34. Bc1 Qc4 35. Qd8† Kf7 36. Bb2 Qf1† 37. Ka2 Qb5 38. a4 Qc4† 39. Kb1 Qe4† 40. Ka2 d4 41. Ba3 Qc2† 42. Ka1 Qc3† 43. Ka2 Qc4† 44. Ka1 Nc6 45. Qd7† Kg6 46. b7 Qc3†** and White wins as Black avoided the repetition of moves—*Manchester Examiner and Times*, 3 February 1890.

### (988) Mills & Wright–Bird & Mitchell    1–0
Consultation game
Manchester (Manchester C.C.), 8 February 1890
B34

**1. e4 c5 2. Nf3 Nc6 3. d4 c×d4 4. N×d4 g6 5. Nc3 Bg7 6. Be3 d6 7. Qd2 h5 8. Be2 Bd7 9. f4 Nf6 10. h3 N×d4 11. B×d4 Bc6 12. Bf3 Kf8 13. 0-0 Qa5 14. e5 Ne8 15. Rae1 Rd8 16. Qe3 d×e5 17. f×e5 e6 18. B×a7 B×e5 19. B×c6 b×c6 20. Bc5† Bd6 21. R×f7† K×f7 22. Q×e6† Kg7 23. Bd4† Kh6 24. B×h8 Qa7† 25. Kh1 Qf2 26. Qe2 Bg3 27. Rf1 Q×e2 28. N×e2 Bc7 29. Bc3 Nd6 30. Bd2† g5 31. h4 Ne4 32. h×g5† Kg6 33. Nf4† B×f4 34. B×f4 Ra8 35. a3 Ra5 36. g3 Rc5 37. c3 Rb5 38. b4 Rd5 39. Re1 N×g5 40. B×g5 K×g5 41. Kg2 Rd3 42. Re5† Kg4 43. Re4† Kf5 44. Rc4 Rd6 45. a4** Black resigns—*Manchester Examiner and Times*, 10 February 1890.

## (989) Bird & T.B. Wilson–Miniati & Mills   ½–½
Consultation game
Manchester (Manchester C.C.), 8 February 1890
*C30*

1. e4 e5 2. f4 Bc5 3. Nf3 d6 4. c3 Nc6 5. b4 Bb6 6. a4 a6 7. a5 Ba7 8. b5 a×b5 9. B×b5 Bd7 10. a6 b×a6 11. R×a6 Bb6 12. Qa4 R×a6 13. Q×a6 Nge7 14. f×e5 d×e5 15. Ba3 0-0 16. Qa4 Be8 17. d3 f5 18. Nbd2 Rf6 19. B×c6 N×c6 20. e×f5 Nd4 21. Qd1 N×f3† 22. Q×f3 g6 23. g4 g×f5 24. g×f5 Bg6 25. Qg3 R×f5 26. Ne4 Qa8 27. Bb2 Qf8 28. h4 Rf3 29. Q×e5 B×e4 30. Qe6† Qf7 31. Q×f7† K×f7 32. d×e4 Ke6 33. Rh2 Ke5 34. Ke2 K×e4 35. h5 Rg3 36. Kd2 Be3† 37. Kc2 Kf3 38. Rh4 Bg5 39. Rd4 h6 40. Rd7 Bf4 41. c4 Rg5 42. Rf7 R×h5 43. Bc1 Rh4 44. B×f4 R×f4 45. R×c7 draw—*Manchester Examiner and Times*, 10 February 1890.

On 10 March Bird gave an exhibition at the Huddersfield Chess Club against 13 players. At the conclusion of the evening Bird had won 8 games and drawn 4. He lost 1 game in which he gave odds.

It was Bird's intention to make an extended visit to Birmingham but unexpected accounting work made him postpone his visit for several weeks. Bird finally succeeded in fulfilling the wish of the eager chess clubs of Birmingham at the end of April. On 24 April he gave a simultaneous exhibition against 15 opponents at the St. George's Chess Club. Only the talented young player Frank Hollins was able to snatch a point from the master.

On 25 April Bird was a guest at the Midland Institute, the home of the Birmingham Chess Club. Here 17 players awaited of whom two would score a win from the master (Binns and Clere).

Bird finished his visit the next day, when he was probably the guest of Buckley, the editor of the chess column in the *Birmingham Weekly Mercury*. He entertained the assembly with some offhand skittles.

## (990) Bird–Buckley   1–0
Simultaneous game
Birmingham (St. George's C.C.), 24 April 1890
*C50*

1. e4 e5 2. Nf3 Nc6 3. Bc4 Be7 4. b4 d6 5. c3 Nf6 6. Qb3 0-0 7. d3 Qe8 8. a4 Nd8 9. Qc2 Be6 10. Na3 B×c4 11. N×c4 Ne6 12. g3 Nd7 13. Ne3 Ng5 14. N×g5 B×g5 15. Nf5 B×c1 16. Q×c1 Qe6 17. h4 c6 18. Qg5 Qf6 19. 0-0-0 a5 20. b5 c×b5 21. a×b5 Rfd8 22. Ne7† Kh8 23. Nd5 Q×g5†? 23. … Qe6 24. Kc2 a4 25. Ra1 h6 26. Qf5 Ra5 is equal. The text move allows Bird to impose a lasting bind on Black. 24. h×g5 Nf8 25. Rh3 Ne6 26. f4 a4 27. Rdh1 Nf8 28. f5 a3 29. Kb1 a2† 30. Ka1 Ra5 31. c4 Ra3 32. g4 Rda8 (*see diagram*)

33. Ne7 33. Nb6 chases one rook off the a-file after which the conquest of the a-pawn happens without allowing his opponent chances; e.g., 33. … Rd8 34. Kb2 Ra7 35. R3h2. 33. … Rb3 34. g6?! It was possible to return to the previous line with 34. Rd1 when Black has nothing better than 34. … Rba3 35. Nd5. 34. … Rb1†! 35. R×b1 a×b1Q†† 36. K×b1 Re8 37. Nd5 f×g6 The pawn is won back and a lot of White's pressure has vanished together with the exchange of a pair of rooks. 38. Kb2 Kg8 39. g5 g×f5 40. e×f5 e4

*After 32. … Rda8*

It was a better option to sit still and move the rook to and fro. 41. f6 An improvement is 41. Re3 and push the d-pawn later on to d4. By avoiding the exchange of this pawn White improves his chances for a breakthrough on the queenside. 41. … e×d3 42. R×d3 Re2† 43. Kc3 g×f6? The point of the last note is demonstrated after 43. … Kf7 44. f×g7 K×g7 45. Ne3 Kg6 46. R×d6† K×g5 47. Nd5 when Buckley can offer his knight for the remaining pawns in some circumstances. 44. N×f6† Kf7 45. R×d6 Re5 46. Rd5? 46. Rb6! R×g5 (46. … Re7 47. c5) 47. Ne4 wipes away the final resistance on the queenside. 46. … R×d5 47. c×d5 Kg6? Missing a small but decisive tactic. 47. … h6 keeps serious drawing chances. 48. d6 K×g5 49. N×h7† and White wins—*Birmingham Weekly Mercury*, 3 May 1890.

## (991) Buckley–Bird   1–0
Offhand game
Birmingham (St. George's C.C.), 24 April 1890
*C63*

1. e4 e5 2. Nf3 Nc6 3. Bb5 f5 4. B×c6 d×c6 5. N×e5 Qd4 6. Nf3 Q×e4† 7. Qe2 Be7 8. Nc3 Q×c2 9. Nd4 Black resigns—*Birmingham Weekly Mercury*, 3 May 1890.

## (992) Macaulay–Bird   1–0
Offhand game
Birmingham (St. George's C.C.), 24 April 1890
*C61*

1. e4 e5 2. Nf3 Nc6 3. Bb5 Nd4 4. N×d4 e×d4 5. d3 h5 "Another step out of the orthodox path. Referring to this move, Mr. Bird himself says, in *Modern Chess* p. 126: 'I sometimes play this, but not always; it depends on the state of mind I am in, and whether I want a lively and critical game or a steady contest—one, in fact, in which my adversary considers that I treat him with becoming respect. A well-known and esteemed reverend gentleman once objected that I would not make so silly a move against one of the greatest players.' But Mr. Bird has 'tried it' on Winawer"—Buckley. 6. f4 Bc5 7. Qf3 Ne7 8. 0-0 c6 9. Bc4 d5 10. Bb3 Bg4 11. Qg3 d×e4 12. d×e4 d3† 13. Be3 Qb6 14. B×c5 Q×c5† 15. Kh1 d×c2 16. Nc3 f5 "To enable him to play 17. … h4"—Buckley. 17. h4 Both 17. h3 and 17. Qd3 offer White a small advantage. 17. … 0-0-0 18. Rac1?! The irritating pawn at c2 had to be eliminated without delay. 18. B×c2 Kb8 19. e×f5 Rd2 is just slightly better for Black. 18. … f×e4 19. N×e4 Qd4 (*see diagram*)

20. f5? A blunder but other moves, such as 20. B×c2 or 20. Ng5, would be answered with 20. … Nf5! with material gain. 20. … B×f5?

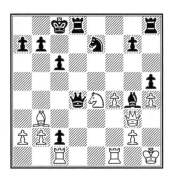

*After 19. ... Qd4*

20. ... Q×e4 21. Rfe1 N×f5 was overlooked by Bird. **21. R×f5!** A balanced tactical struggle now follows. **21. ... Q×e4** If 21. ... N×f5 22. Be6†. **22. Re5 Rd1†** **23. Kh2 Qd4** **24. R×d1 c×d1Q** **25. B×d1 Qd6** Bird is playing for a win at all cost. The exchange of knight against bishop after 25. ... Ng6 26. Rg5 Q×d1 27. R×g6 makes a drawish outcome unavoidable. **26. Bb3** 26. B×h5 is possible. **26. ... Rd8 27. Kh3** 27. Be6† Kb8 28. R×h5 is sufficient to secure a draw, but Macaulay shows himself not afraid of his opponent's reputation and prefers a risky line. **27. ... Ng6** 27. ... g6 secures the safety of his extra pawn. **28. Rg5 Nf4† 29. Kh2 g6** This sly move doesn't help to consolidate. A better try for more is 29. ... Qf6, forcing the exchange of queens after 30. R×g7 Rd2! 31. Rg8† Kc7 32. Qg7† Q×g7 33. R×g7†. It remains doubtful if all this is enough to win in case of precise play from White: 33. ... Kd6 34. R×b7 R×g2† 35. Kh1 R×b2 36. R×a7. **30. Bf7! Qf6 31. B×g6 Rd5** Not unexpectedly Bird keeps on searching for imbalances to test his opponent. 31. ... N×g6 would safeguard the draw. **32. Be4** 32. R×d5 c×d5 33. B×h5 wins an important pawn. The remaining endgame is unappetizing for the master. **32. ... R×g5 33. Q×g5 Qd6 34. Bf5†** 34. Bf3 is a better try, as the pawn at h5 remains a target. **34. ... Kc7 35. Qg3 c5** Reckless. 35. ... Qd4 annuls all further White tries by covering e4 and g7. **36. Be4 Qe5 37. Qf3** Macaulay designs a devilish trick for which Bird falls without hesitation. Objectively better was 37. Bf3, menacing 38. B×h5. If 37. ... Qd6 38. Qg7†. White is also on top after Black's best: 37. ... b5 38. B×h5 c4 39. Bd1 b4. **37. ... Ne2†?** Exposing his own king to a decisive attack. With White's forces momentarily uncoordinated, the advance of his queenside pawns should enable him to play for a draw: 37. ... b5 (37. ... Nd3† is also playable) 38. Kg1 c4 39. g3 Ne6 40. Ba8 Kd8 41. Qd5† Q×d5 42. B×d5 Nc5. **38. g3 Q×b2 39. Qf7† Kd8 40. Qd5† Ke8 41. Q×h5† Kd7 42. Qd5† Ke8 43. Bg2** A direct attack is decisive, but not so easy to calculate: 43. Qe6† Kf8 44. Qd6† Kf7 45. Qd7† Kf6 46. Qd8†. **43. ... Nd4 44. h5** Better was 44. Q×c5. **44. ... Qe2** 44. ... Qc2 would have prolonged the battle. **45. h6 Kf8 46. h7** Black resigns—*Birmingham Weekly Mercury* (Buckley), 17 May 1890.

## (993) Binns–Bird　0–1
Simultaneous game
Birmingham (Birmingham C.C.), 25 April 1890
C39

**1. e4 e5 2. f4 e×f4 3. Nf3 g5 4. h4 g4 5. Ng5 h6 6. N×f7 K×f7 7. Bc4† d5 8. B×d5† Kg7** 8. ... Ke8 keeps the option of developing the bishop to g7. After the text move White has a forced drawing line at his disposal: 9. B×b7 B×b7 10. Q×g4† Kf7 11. Qh5† etc. **9. 0–0 f3** White's attack is already over and done. **10. g3 c6 11. Bb3**

**Qd4† 12. Kh1 Bd6 13. Qe1 Nf6 14. c3 Qb6 15. d4 Nh5 16. Rg1 Re8** All is set for the final. **17. Qe3** (*see diagram*) "Well intended, no doubt"—Buckley.

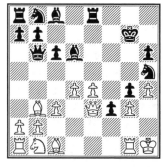

*After 17. Qe3*

**17. ... Bf4!** "One of Bird's characteristic moves, which appears to turn the tables on White"—Buckley. **18. g×f4 Qd8** "Do you catch my meaning?' said Bird"—Buckley. **19. Qf2 R×e4 20. Bc4 Kh8** "So that White may not take the g-pawn with check in the little combination the Grand Old Man thinks he sees"—Buckley. **21. Bd3** "Intended as an attack"—Buckley. **21. ... g3** "Same—one size larger!"—Buckley. **22. R×g3 Q×h4†** "Bird wings his airy way to victory!"—Buckley. **23. Qh2 Re1† 24. Rg1 Ng3** mate—*Birmingham Weekly Mercury* (Buckley), 31 May 1890.

## (994) Buckley–Bird　1–0
Offhand game
Birmingham, 26 April 1890
C39

**1. e4 e5 2. f4 e×f4 3. Nf3 g5 4. h4 g4 5. Ng5 h6 6. N×f7 K×f7 7. d4 d5 8. B×f4 d×e4 9. Bc4† Ke8 10. 0–0 Nf6 11. Nc3 Nc6 12. d5 Bc5† 13. Kh1 Nh5 14. N×e4 Q×h4† 15. Bh2 g3 16. Q×h5† Q×h5 17. Nf6† Kd8 18. N×h5 g×h2 19. d×c6 Bd6 20. Bd5 b×c6 21. B×c6 Rb8 22. b3 Bg4 23. Nf6 Be6 24. Rae1 Bf7 25. Ne4 Rb6 26. N×d6 c×d6 27. R×f7 R×c6 28. R×a7 R×c2 29. Rd1** Black resigns—*Pictorial World*, 7 March 1891.

## (995) Buckley–Bird　1–0
Offhand game
Birmingham, 26 April 1890
C50

**1. e4 e5 2. Nf3 Nc6 3. Bc4 Bc5 4. d3 d5 5. e×d5 Nd4 6. N×d4 e×d4 7. Qe2† Kf8 8. 0–0 h5 9. Nd2 Ne7 10. Ne4 Bb6 11. Bg5 f6 12. N×f6 g×f6 13. B×f6 Rh6 14. Bg5 Qd6 15. Qf3† Kg7 16. Rae1 Ng8 17. B×h6† N×h6 18. Q×h5 Bg4 19. Qg5† Qg6 20. Re7† Nf7 21. Qe5† Kf8 22. R×f7† Q×f7 23. d6 Qg7 24. Qf4† Ke8 25. Re1† Kd8 26. Re7 Qh8 27. Q×g4** Black resigns—*Birmingham Weekly Mercury*, 24 May 1890.

Probably just before or just after his visit to the chess clubs in Birmingham, Bird was the guest of the nearby Dudley Chess Club. Here Bird lost one single game, against the very talented, 15-year-old George Bellingham. In the same year the young boy also beat Blackburne in a simultaneous display. Bellingham was soon to be one of Britain's most promising players until he suddenly gave up the game in 1905.

# BIRD'S CHESS REVIEWS

Besides playing chess Bird was always deeply engaged in all kinds of literary work. His interest in the origins and history of the game made him assemble information that ultimately culminated in his book *Chess History and Reminiscences*.

On 1 February 1890, Bird released the first issue of an eight page booklet, *Bird's Chess Reviews*. The booklet could be obtained from Bird for a price of 3d. This issue dealt with Wilhelm Steinitz.

Bird started to work on this text while giving exhibitions in Cardiff in October. He had just received the first installment of Steinitz's recent work *The Modern Chess Instructor*. Bird praised Steinitz's work, above all because of his pre-eminency in the world of "business chess," which he opposed against "amusement chess." Under amusement chess Bird understood "chess of the day or the evening, limited to an hour or two each game; such chess, in short, as the ordinary mortal seeking recreation cares for or can find time to play" (p. 2). Bird reckoned himself to be a forerunner of this category.[30]

Bird continued with some reminiscences about his personal experiences with Steinitz and his relationship with the British chess world. Furthermore he severely criticized what he thought were Steinitz's pretenses. For nearly a page Bird enumerated a whole list of luminaries of the game whose strength and qualities "were to sink into utter insignificance when compared with the prodigious standard production of the great W.S." (p. 2). Bird declared himself disappointed by Steinitz's book for he "search[ed] in vain for the fresh developments and instructions we had hoped to gather from it." Bird consequently ranted about the absence of the various opening lines that were dear to his heart.[31]

MacDonnell read Bird's work a few weeks before its publication.

> The article thus produced is one of a series which Mr. Bird purposes writing. It is slashing, indeed in some respects scathing, and therefore I need scarcely add very amusing. I have glanced at it, and am inclined to think that it does something very like justice to the merits as well as the demerits of W.S. Whether it is perfectly fair to Mr. Steinitz' book I cannot say, not having seen, much less read, the magnum opus [*Illustrated Sporting and Dramatic News*, 11 January 1890].

Bird spoke of a continuation of *Bird's Chess Reviews*, but no issues appear to have been released.[32]

30. Bird mentioned a few of his results: "(...), as illustrated in his contests with Bardeleben, Prussian champion, in 1888; Weiss, Austrian champion, and Chigorin, Russian champion, in 1889; and also in New York with Lipschütz, Delmar, Martinez and Showalter, American representatives; also with Burn, the present undoubted English champion, in America, Liverpool and London." Bird, *Bird's Chess Reviews*, p. 2.

31. "The Lesser Bishop's Gambit, the terror of the Vienna and Berlin champions, and not successfully met by players such as Chigorin, of St. Petersburg, the Russian champion, or by Delmar, of New York, and others, must surely receive due attention." Bird, *Bird's Chess Reviews*, p. 5.

32. Bird filled the last page with the announcement of a second number: "The second part of this sketch will be devoted: first, to a chapter on each of the openings given by Mr. Steinitz; second, to chess players in history; third, to longevity of chess players; fourth, to his mistaken views, based on Philidor's and Staunton's estimates, of the relative value of the pieces; fifth, to the American chess congress, 1889; and, sixth, to chess champions and Steinitz' play and comparison." Bird, *Bird's Chess Reviews*, p. 8.

# MATCH WITH LASKER 1890

During Bird's stay in Manchester it was announced that he would soon play a match in nearby Liverpool against a freshly arrived chess star: Emanuel Lasker. The 21-year-old Lasker was relatively unknown in England. During the previous summer he had gained the master title with his victory at the Hauptturnier (the major side event) of the German Chess Congress held in Breslau. In a subsequent master tournament in Amsterdam he ended second, ahead of Mason and Gunsberg. In the winter of 1890 Lasker crossed the Channel in the hope of contesting a match with one of the strongest British players: Blackburne, Mason or Gunsberg.[33] What Lasker omitted to take into account was that players of such stature were not eager at all to risk their reputation in a direct confrontation with a hot newcomer. Lasker consequently travelled from London to Liverpool to meet Amos Burn. Burn had shown superior strength by gaining the first prize in Amsterdam. On that occasion he had promised Lasker to meet him in a match. Other obligations, however, prevented Burn from keeping his promise. He suggested Bird as a possible opponent for Lasker.

Bird was in the vicinity, busy touring the provinces, and efforts were made to arrange a match. The veteran's reputation of being available to encounter any opponent anytime proved still true. On 17 February the match commenced in the rooms of the Liverpool Chess Club. It was agreed that the first player to win seven games would clinch the match victory. One game per day was played. In case of a draw both players could agree to start another game. The time limit was set at 20 moves an hour. Everybody was eager to witness the duel between the reputed Bird and the young, brilliantly playing hero of Amsterdam. What could be imagined by only just a few happened and surprised the British chess community.

> One of the most interesting of the provincial displays has been the match between Mr. H.E. Bird and Herr Lasker which commenced at Liverpool on the 17th February and concluded on the 28th in a decisive victory for the young Berlin player. From the first Herr Lasker had the advantage, and he led right through, indeed at one time it looked as if he would win the match without his opponent scoring a single game, for at the end of the first week's play the score stood: Lasker 5; Bird 0; draws 2. With the opening of the second week victory still continued to smile on Lasker, for he again won his game, thus bringing up his score to 6 and leaving him but one more game to win in order to gain the match. The next day, however, Mr. Bird managed to draw, and on the day following he did still better, for he got a decided advantage and at last forced a win, thus breaking the series of "duck's eggs." Mr. Bird followed this up on Thursday by scoring another game, but this was the last of his wins, for on Friday Herr Lasker carried off the victor's palm, the final score being: Lasker 7; Bird 2; draws 3 [*International Chess Magazine*, April 1890, p. 97].

Though this distinguishing result established Lasker's reputation in England, several excuses were found to explain Bird's failure.

> I have not seen any of the games, and therefore have no right to entertain, much less to express, an opinion respecting them; but I am told that Mr. Bird played at times as if his opponent was a knight player. In any case, the result by no means proves Mr. Bird's inferiority. ...
>
> That being quite true, surely it is not to be expected that a man sixty years of age, and suffering from chronic gout, can accomplish such an impossibility.

33. When in Paris for a week Lasker expressed his intention to challenge Gunsberg. *Revue des Jeux*, 28 March 1890, p. 177.

In the eyes of competent and fair judges, Mr. Bird's reputation suffers not a jot by his recent defeat. ...

One of Mr. Bird's special weaknesses is to undervalue the strength of an unknown opponent. Unknown no doubt to him was Herr Lasker's play, and hence his mistake in supposing him unworthy to cope with a master [*Illustrated Sporting and Dramatic News*, 8 March 1890].

Lasker continued looking for new opponents but he stumbled into a complicated world full of egos and feuds. Gunsberg, who had just tied a match with Chigorin, preferred to avoid Lasker and to save his power for a much wanted match for the world title with Steinitz. A possible loss against Lasker would considerably narrow his chances for such a match.

A whole myriad of other match challenges were offered and refused. Lasker was negotiating with Blackburne but, much to the amusement of the English press, the German was not able to get the necessary stakes together. Lee was another player interested in delivering combat with Lasker, while Bird hoped to restore order with a return match. The veteran even gallantly proposed to take the winner of the young ones, Lee or Lasker, but none of these plans materialized. Lasker's days in England were momentarily over and he left the island before the upcoming congress of the B.C.A. in Manchester.

### Match with Lasker, 17–28 February 1890

| | 1 | 2 | 3 | 4 | 5 | 6 | 7 | 8 | 9 | 10 | 11 | 12 | |
|---|---|---|---|---|---|---|---|---|---|---|---|---|---|
| E. Lasker | 1 | ½ | 1 | ½ | 1 | 1 | 1 | 1 | ½ | 0 | 0 | 1 | 7 |
| H.E. Bird | 0 | ½ | 0 | ½ | 0 | 0 | 0 | 0 | ½ | 1 | 1 | 0 | 2 |

**Emanuel Lasker (*Chess Monthly*).**

**(996) Bird–Lasker   0–1**
Match (game 1)
Liverpool, 17 February 1890
*A03*

1. f4 d5 2. e3 g6 3. Nf3 Bg7 4. c3 Nf6 5. Na3 0–0 6. Be2 a6 7. 0–0 Nc6 8. Nc2 Re8 9. Ne5 N×e5 10. f×e5 Nd7 11. d4 f6 12. Nb4 Nb6 13. e×f6 e×f6 14. b3 Be6 15. Nd3 Bf7 16. Qe1 Nd7 17. Qf2 Qe7 18. Bf3 Rac8 19. a4 c6 20. Bd2 f5 21. g4 Be6 22. Qg2 f×g4 23. B×g4 B×g4 24. Q×g4 Nf6 25. Qg2 Ne4 26. Rf3 Bh6 27. Ne5 Bg7 28. Nd3 Bh6 29. Ne5 Bg7 30. Nd3 Rc7 31. c4 d×c4 32. b×c4 c5 33. Nf4 N×d2 34. Q×d2 Qe4 35. Raf1 c×d4 36. Nd5 R×c4 37. Qg2 d×e3 38. N×e3 Rc3 39. Nd5 R×f3 40. Q×f3 Bd4† 41. Kh1 Q×f3† 42. R×f3 Re1† 43. Kg2 Re2† 44. Kf1 R×h2 45. Rb3 Rb2 46. Rd3 Bc5 47. Rc3 b6 48. a5 Rf2† 49. Ke1 Rf5 White resigns—*Liverpool Daily Courier*, 18 February 1890.

**(997) Lasker–Bird   ½–½**
Match (game 2)
Liverpool, 18 February 1890
*B26*

1. e4 c5 2. Nc3 Nc6 3. g3 g6 4. Bg2 Bg7 5. d3 d6 6. Be3 h5 7. h3 Bd7 8. Qd2 Nd4 9. Nd1 e5 10. c3 Nc6 11. Ne2 f5 12. d4 Qe7 13. Bg5 Bf6 14. B×f6 N×f6 15. e×f5 g×f5 16. Ne3 0–0–0 17. d5 "Up to this point the positions were about equal, but the move in the text is weak, as it blocks the important diagonal of Bg2, leaving Black with a slight advantage"—Burn. 17. ... Nb8 18. Qc2 Qh7 19. 0–0–0 Rhg8 19. ... h4 is interesting as it keeps White's kingside pawns under a lasting pressure. 20. Rdg1 Na6 21. Bf1 Nc7 "Black has now clearly the better game, his pieces having more scope for action than those of his opponent"—Burn. 22. c4 Rg7 23. h4 Na6 24. a3 Rdg8 25. Bh3 Ng4 26. Nd1 Qh6† 27. Qd2 Q×d2† 28. K×d2 Nf6 29. Ne3 Ng4 30. Nd1 Kc7 31. b3 b5 32. c×b5 B×b5 33. Nec3 Bd7 34. Bf1 Kb6 35. Rg2 Nf6 36. Ne3 Nb8 37. Rhg1 Kc7 38. Bd3 e4 39. Bb5 Ng4 40. B×d7 N×e3 41. f×e3 *(see diagram)*

*After 41. f×e3*

41. ... K×d7? Inaccurately calculated by Bird. He now loses a pawn and White's pieces get activated along the road. The natural 41. ... N×d7 only implies a temporary material loss. After 42. Nb5† Kd8 43. N×d6 Ne5, with his knight activated, the lost pawn will very soon be compensated by one of his adversary's. 42. Rf1 R×g3 43. R×g3 R×g3 44. R×f5 Rg2† 45. Ne2?! Lasker unnecessarily selects a passive defense. The active 45. Ke1 Rb2 46. Rf7† Ke8 47. Rb7 wins quickly. 45. ... Ke7 46. R×h5 "White has emerged out of the melee with a pawn ahead, and but for the cramped

position of his king might have obtained a winning advantage"—Burn. **46. ... Nd7 47. Rh7† Kd8 48. Rh6 Kc7 49. h5?!** Just as Bird on move 41, Lasker forgets to bring his knight into the game. 49. Ke1 Nb6 50. Kf1 Rh2 51. Nc3 is very good for White. **49. ... Ne5 50. Rh7† Kb6 51. h6 Rh2 52. Rh8 Nf7 53. Rb8† Kc7 54. Re8 Ng5 55. Re7† Kd8 56. R×a7 Nf3† 57. Kd1 R×h6?** Bird fails in sight of the finish. A forced perpetual check is possible with 57. ... Rh1† 58. Kc2 Rh2 59. h7 R×e2† 60. Kc3 R×e3† 61. Kc2 Re2†. **58. Nf4?** Luckily for the veteran, Lasker also stumbles. 58. Ng3! wins the all-important e-pawn, and with it the game. **58. ... Rh1† 59. Kc2 Re1** Black now wins back his pawn, and it was agreed to dismiss the game as a draw—*Liverpool Daily Courier* (Burn), 19 February 1890.

## (998) Bird–Lasker 0–1
Match (game 3)
Liverpool, 19 February 1890
*A03*

1. f4 d5 2. e3 g6 3. Nf3 Bg7 4. c3 Nf6 5. d4 0–0 6. Bd3 b6 7. b4 Bb7 8. a4 Nbd7 9. 0–0 Rc8 10. a5 c5 11. a×b6 a×b6 12. Ra7 Bc6 13. b5 Ba8 14. Ne5 Rc7 15. Ra2 e6 16. Nd2 Qb8 17. Ndf3 Ra7 18. R×a7 Q×a7 19. Bb2 c4 20. Bc2 Qa5 21. Qa1 N×e5 22. Q×a5 N×f3† White resigns—*Liverpool Daily Courier*, 20 February 1890.

## (999) Lasker–Bird ½–½
Match (game 4)
Liverpool, 19 February 1890
*B26*

1. e4 c5 2. Nc3 Nc6 3. g3 g6 4. Bg2 Bg7 5. d3 d6 6. Be3 h5 7. h3 Bd7 8. Qd2 Nd4 9. Nd1 e5 10. c3 Ne6 11. Ne2 Bc6 12. d4 d5 13. c4 c×d4 14. e×d5 d×e3 15. N×e3 Ne7 16. d×e6 Q×d2† 17. K×d2 f×e6 18. Nc3 0–0 19. Ke2 B×g2 20. N×g2 Nf5 Black's weakened pawn structure is sufficiently compensated by his control over d4 and the pressure along the f-file. **21. Rhd1 Nd4† 22. Kf1 Rac8 23. b3 b5** Bird plays this phase very well and obtains an annoying pressure against White's queenside. **24. Ne4 b×c4 25. Nd6 Rc7** 25. ... Rc6! 26. N×c4 Ra6 menaces 27. ... Nc2, while 27. ... e4 is also a strong option after 27. Rdc1. **26. N×c4 Rcf7 27. Rd2 g5 28. Nd6 Rc7 29. Ne4 Bh6 30. Rb2 g4 31. h×g4 h×g4 32. Ne1 Rf5 33. Kg2 Bf8 34. Nd3 Nf3 35. Rh1 Ba3 36. Re2 Be7 37. Nb2 Nd4 38. Rd2 Bb4** Bird missed the sharpness to keep his opponent on the defensive and step by step Lasker consolidated his position. Here Bird goes wrong and loses a pawn. 38. ... Nf3 should be sufficient for a draw; e.g., 39. Rd3 Rc2 40. Nd1 Rh5 41. R×h5 Ne1† 42. Kg1 N×d3. **39. Rdd1 Rc2 40. Nd3 Be7 41. N×e5 R×e5 42. R×d4 Rd5 43. Ra4 a5 44. Re1 Kf7 45. Re3 Rf5 46. Rc3** The more patient 46. Rd3! and then 47. Rd2 takes away the pressure of the f-pawn. Subsequently, White can point toward g4. **46. ... Re2?** Missing his best chance for a draw by exchanging one pair of rooks and diminishing the number of pawns with 46. ... Rf×f2† 47. N×f2 R×c3 48. Rf4† Ke8 49. N×g4 Rc2† 50. Rf2 Rc3. **47. Rc7 Ke8 48. Kf1 Rb2 49. Ra7 Rd5 50. R7×a5?** A careless move. Priority had to be given to the safety of his king: 50. Kg2! Rd1 51. Ra8†

Kd7 52. Rg8 and White should win comfortably. **50. ... Rd1† 51. Kg2 Rbb1 52. Ra8† Kf7 53. f3?!** This is only dangerous for White! After 53. Ng5† B×g5 54. R×g4 a draw is inevitable. **53. ... Rb2† 54. Nf2 e5 55. R×g4 Rdd2 56. Re4 R×f2† 57. Kh3 R×f3 58. Kg4** draw. The game ended in a draw at this point, with the last move being imprecise (58. R×e5 would be correct). Bird could even win after 58. ... Rbf2 59. Ra6 Bf6 60. Ra7† Ke6 61. Ra6† Kd5—*Deutsches Wochenschach*, 30 March 1890, p. 107.

## (1000) Bird–Lasker 0–1
Match (game 5)
Liverpool, 20 February 1890
*A03*

1. f4 d5 2. Nf3 g6 3. e3 Bg7 4. Be2 Nf6 5. 0–0 0–0 6. b3 Ne4 7. c3 Nc6 8. Bb2 Re8 9. d3 Nd6 10. Na3 e5 11. d4 e×f4 12. e×f4 Ne7 13. Nc2 c6 14. Bd3 Bf5 15. B×f5 Ne×f5 16. Qd3 Ne4 17. Ne5 Rc8 18. Rad1 Rc7 19. c4 Bf8 20. Rf3 Bd6 21. Rh3 f6 22. g4 f×e5 23. c×d5 e×f4 24. g×f5 Qg5† 25. Kf1 c×d5 26. Qb5 Nf6 27. Qd3 g×f5 28. Bc1 Qg4 29. Rd2 Rg7 White resigns—*Liverpool Daily Courier*, 21 February 1890.

## (1001) Lasker–Bird 1–0
Match (game 6)
Liverpool, 21 February 1890
*B73*

1. e4 c5 2. Nc3 Nc6 3. Nf3 g6 4. d4 c×d4 5. N×d4 Bg7 6. Be3 d6 7. Be2 Bd7 8. 0–0 Nf6 9. h3 0–0 10. Qd2 N×d4 11. B×d4 Bc6 12. Bf3 Qa5 13. Rfe1 Nd7 14. B×g7 K×g7 15. Qd4† Kg8 16. b4 Qb6 17. Q×b6 N×b6 18. b5 Bd7 19. Nd5 N×d5 20. e×d5 Rfe8 21. c4 Rac8 22. Rac1 Rc5 23. Kf1 Kf8 24. a4 Rec8 25. Be2 e6 26. Rcd1 e5 27. g4 f5 28. f3 Kf7 29. Kg2 Kf6 30. Kg3 Kg5 31. h4† Kf6 32. g5† Kg7 33. f4 e4 34. Kf2 a6 35. Ke3 Be8 36. Kd4 Ra8 37. Ra1 h6 38. Reb1 a×b5 39. a×b5 Rcc8 40. b6 h×g5 41. h×g5 Ba4 42. Rb2 Bd7 43. Rba2 Rab8 44. Ra5 Kf7 45. Rh1 Rh8 46. R×h8 R×h8 47. Ra7 Bc8 48. c5 d×c5† 49. K×c5 Rh2 50. Ba6 Ra2 51. Bc4 Rc2 52. Ra8 Bd7 53. Rd8 Ke7 54. Rb8 Ba4 55. R×b7† Kd8 56. Ra7 Bb3 57. Kd6 Black resigns—*Liverpool Daily Courier*, 22 February 1890.

## (1002) Bird–Lasker 0–1
Match (game 7)
Liverpool, 22 February 1890
*C14*

1. e4 e6 2. d4 d5 3. Nc3 Nf6 4. Bg5 Be7 5. B×f6 B×f6 6. Nf3 0–0 7. e5 Be7 8. Bd3 c5 9. d×c5 B×c5 10. 0–0 Nc6 11. a3 a6 12. Ne2 f6 13. b4 Be7 14. e×f6 B×f6 15. Rb1 e5 16. b5 a×b5 17. B×b5 R×a3 18. Qc1 Ra8 19. Rd1 Kh8 20. Ng3 Be6 21. c4 d4 22. Re1 Qc7 23. Ne4 Bf5 24. c5 Nd8 25. Rb2 B×e4 26. R×e4 Ne6 27. c6 b6 28. Re1 Nc5 29. Qc4 e4 30. N×d4 Qe5 31. Rd2 Nd3 32. Ne6 N×e1 33. Ra2 Nd3 34. g3 R×a2 35. Q×a2 Q×b5 36. N×f8 Q×c6 37. Qf7 Qc1† 38. Kg2 Ne1† 39. Kh3 Qh6† 40. Kg4 Qg5† 41. Kh3 Qf5† White resigns—*Liverpool Daily Courier*, 24 February 1890.

**(1003) Lasker–Bird    1–0**
Match (game 8)
Liverpool, 24 February 1890
*B00*

1. d4 e6 2. Nf3 b6 3. e4 Bb7 4. Bd3 g6 5. Nc3 Bg7 6. Bf4 d6
7. Qe2 a6 8. Rd1 Ne7 9. 0–0 0–0 10. Qe3 Nd7 11. e5 d5 12. Ne2
c5 13. c3 c4 14. Bb1 b5 15. Ng5 h6 16. Nh3 Kh7 17. Bg3 Rh8
18. f4 Kg8 19. Rf3 Qb6 20. Bh4 Nf5 21. B×f5 e×f5 22. Nf2 Re8
23. g4 f×g4 24. N×g4 f5 25. Nf2 Nf8 26. Bg3 Ne6 27. h4 Rh7
28. Nh3 Bf8 29. Rf2 Rg7 30. Rg2 b4 31. Be1 a5 32. h5 g×h5
33. Ng3 b×c3 34. B×c3 Kh7 35. Qf3 h4 36. N×f5 R×g2†
37. K×g2 Nc5 38. Qh5 Qc6 39. Qf7† Kh8 40. N×h4 Bg7
41. Ng6† Kh7 42. Ng5† h×g5 43. Rh1 mate—*Liverpool Daily
Courier*, 25 February 1890.

**(1004) Bird–Lasker    ½–½**
Match (game 9)
Liverpool, 25 February 1890
*A03*

1. f4 d5 2. b3 c5 3. e3 a6 4. Nf3 Nc6 5. Bb2 e6 6. Be2 Nf6 7. 0–0
Be7 8. Qe1 0–0 9. Qg3 Ne8 10. d4 Nd6 11. Nbd2 c×d4 12. e×d4
Qc7 13. Qf2 Rd8 14. c3 Bd7 15. Bd3 Be8 16. Ng5 h6 17. Ngf3
Bf8 18. Rae1 Ne7 19. g4 Rac8 20. Ne5 b5 21. Qg3 f5 22. h3 Ne4
23. B×e4 d×e4 24. c4 Nc6 25. N×c6 B×c6 26. Rf2 Rd7 27. g×f5
e×f5 28. d5 Bc5 29. Kh2 B×f2 30. Q×f2 B×d5 31. c×d5 R×d5
32. Rc1 Qd7 33. R×c8† Q×c8 34. Nf1 Qd7 35. Be5 Rd1 36. Qg2
Kh7 37. h4 h5 38. Bc3 g6 39. Qf2 Rd3 40. Qc5 Qd8 41. Kg2 Rd5
42. Qf2 Qc7 43. Ba1 Rd1 44. Be5 Qd7 45. Qc5 R×f1 46. K×f1
Qd1† 47. Kf2 Qd2† 48. Kg3 Qd3† 49. Kh2 Qd2† 50. Kg1 Qd1†
draw—*Liverpool Daily Courier*, 26 February 1890.

**(1005) Lasker–Bird    0–1**
Match (game 10)
Liverpool, 26 February 1890
*A93*

1. d4 f5 2. g3 Nf6 3. Bg2 e6 4. Nf3 Nc6 5. 0–0 Be7 6. c4 d5
"This move brings about, for Black, a position very similar to the
Stonewall Opening, invented by Mr. Preston Ware. It is usually considered somewhat disadvantageous for the player adopting it, on account of the weak pawn at e6"—Burn. 7. b3 0–0 8. Bb2 Qe8 9. Nc3
Qh5 10. Ne5 Rd8 11. e3 Qh6 12. Qe2 a6 13. Rfd1 Ne4 14. Rac1
N×e5 15. d×e5 N×c3 16. R×c3 16. B×c3, to answer 16. ... c6 with
17. Ba5, is a better line than the small promise of the text move. 16. ...
c6 17. Rcd3 Bd7 18. Bc1 Qg6 19. e4 f×e4 20. B×e4 Qf7 Immediately 20. ... Qe8 gains some important time. 21. Rf3 Qe8 22. Bb1
Kh8 23. Qc2 Lasker produced some excellent chess during the last
few moves, but this one is a bit premature as it allows Bird to defend
the h-pawn optimally. First 23. Be3 or at once 23. g4, controls h5
and thus improves the attack. 23. ... Qh5 24. Rf7 Bc5 25. Rf4 Rf8
Bird is now fully developed and has even obtained some pressure
against f2. 26. Rf1 "If 26. Rh4 R×f2"—Burn. 26. ... Be7 27. Be3
R×f4 28. B×f4 Rf8 29. Qd1 "White evidently doesn't like his position, and offers the exchange of queens with a view to playing for
a draw"—Burn. 29. ... Qh3 29. ... Q×d1 30. R×d1 Be8 31. c×d5
Bh5 32. Rc1 e×d5 is slightly better for Black. 30. Bd3 Be8 31. Be2

g5 Bird wants to force matters, but he is the only one taking risks.
32. Bg4 Qh6 33. Be3 Qg6 34. Qb1 34. c×d5 c×d5 35. Qd4 h5
36. Be2 and White's central dominance is not to be underestimated.
34. ... Qg8 35. Qd1 c5 36. c×d5 e×d5 37. f4 d4 38. Bc1 g×f4
39. B×f4 b6 The exchanges of the central pawns drastically changed
the nature of the position, but not the evaluation. Both sides have
their trumps and the game is in balance. 40. Be2 Bc6 (*see diagram*)

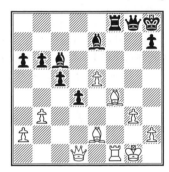

*After 40. ... Bc6*

41. Bd3? The first of a few very bad moves, maybe caused by time
trouble. 41. Bc4 prevents the queen from occupying the long diagonal. After 41. ... Qg6 42. Bd3 Be4 (42. ... Qg8? is wrong 43. e6!)
43. B×a6 Ra8 44. Bc4 R×a2 45. Rf2 the position stands equal. 41. ...
Qf7? The obvious 41. ... Qd5 wins directly: 42. Qd2 Bg5! 43. Qc2
Qh1† 44. Kf2 R×f4†. 42. Bc4? 42. e6! opens up several lines and
diagonals. After 42. ... Qg7 43. Qh5 Be8 44. Qd5, Black is forced
to abandon the a-pawn (and with it all his play on the queenside)
for if 44. ... b5 45. Be5 R×f1† 46. B×f1 Bf6 47. Qa8 B×e5
48. Q×e8† Qg8 49. Qd7 B×g3 50. e7 renders further resistance futile. 42. ... Qf5 43. Qe2 Bird gains important time after this careless
move which allows him to safeguard his queenside. Instead, 43. Bd3
Qh3 44. Qd2 maintains equality. 43. ... b5 44. Bd3 Qe6 45. Be4?!
45. Qh5 keeps Black busy with the defense of the king. The exchange
of bishop on the other hand liberates him from all dangers. 45. ...
B×e4 46. Q×e4 Rd8 "Black's majority of pawns on the queenside
now comes in with telling effect, whereas White's extra pawns on
the kingside are perfectly useless, the one at e5 serving no other purpose than to block his own pieces. Bird has played the game splendidly throughout"—Burn. 47. Rd1 c4 48. Kg2 d3 49. b×c4 b×c4
50. Bd2 Hereby Black's pawns are stopped and it will take Bird a
lot of creativity to crack through White's defense. 50. ... Bf8 Bird's
next few moves are too slow to trouble his opponent. More to the
point was 50. ... Rf8 51. Bc3 Kg8 52. Rb1 h5 and 53. ... Qf7 might
follow. Even here a direct win is out of sight. 51. Bc3 Bg7 52. Rb1
h6 53. Rb2 Kg8 54. Qe3? Lasker, having played his last moves with
the back against the wall, succeeded in minimizing Bird's edge.
Here, however, he makes a fatal mistake. After 54. Kg1 h5 55. Rf2
Lasker's defensive line will be very difficult to crack. 54. ... Rf8?!
54. ... Qd5† 55. Kh3 Rf8 with a strong attack, or White has to abandon the e-pawn at least. 55. Qe4 Qf7 56. e6? 56. g4 or 56. h4 prolongs the game considerably. 56. ... Qf1 mate—*Liverpool Daily
Courier* (Burn), 27 February 1890.

**(1006) Bird–Lasker    1–0**
Match (game 11)
Liverpool, 27 February 1890
*A13*

**1. c4** "This move constitutes the English Opening, which was greatly favored by the late Mr. Howard Staunton"—Burn. **1. ... e6 2. e3 Nf6 3. f4** "The usual continuation here is 3. d4. The move in the text is a variation the merits of which it would be difficult to decide upon without very careful analysis. It has at any rate the merit of bringing about a somewhat open game, which is more suitable to Mr. Bird's attacking style than the usual form of this close opening"—Burn. **3. ... d5 4. Nf3 c5 5. c×d5 e×d5 6. Bb5† Bd7 7. B×d7† Nb×d7 8. b3 g6 9. Bb2 Bg7 10. 0–0 0–0 11. Na3 a6 12. Nc2 Ne4 13. B×g7 K×g7 14. Nce1 b5 15. Qc2 Re8 16. Nd3 Qb6 17. Qb2† f6 18. Nf2 Rab8 19. Rae1 c4** Abandoning d4 has no grave consequences. **20. b4 Rb7 21. N×e4 d×e4 22. Nd4 Kg8 23. g4** Too aggressive. 23. Ra1, intending to initiate play on the queenside, is a better plan. **23. ... Nf8 24. Rf2** "White wisely refrains from the tempting move of 24. f5, which would enable Black very soon to occupy a menacing position with his knight at e5"—Burn. **24. ... Rf7 25. Ref1 h6 26. Kh1 Kh7 27. Ne2 f5 28. g×f5 g×f5 29. Rg2 Qf6 30. Q×f6 R×f6 31. Rfg1 Rf7 32. Rg8 Rd8** 32. ... Re6! **33. Nd4 Ne6** The exchange of a pair of rooks gives White reason to play for more. He wouldn't get any further after 33. ... Rdd7 34. Nc6 Rf6 35. Ne5 Re7 and 35. ... Nd7 the next move. **34. R×d8 N×d8 35. a4!** "Very finely played. Mr. Bird seizes with unerring instinct on the weak point of his adversary's position"—Burn. **35. ... b×a4 36. Ra1 Rf6 37. R×a4 Kg6 38. Kg2 Nc6 39. Ne2** "White is playing to win. 39. R×a6 would lead to the exchange of both pieces, followed by a draw"—Burn. **39. ... Na7 40. Kf2 Nb5 41. Ra5 Rd6 42. Ra2 Rb6 43. Ra5 Rd6 44. Ra2 Rb6 45. Ra1 Nc7 46. Rg1† Kf6 47. h4** 47. Rg8 R×b4 48. Rc8 Nd5 49. Rc6† is a draw. **47. ... Nd5 48. h5** *(see diagram)*

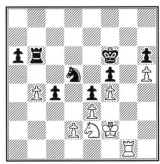

*After 48. h5*

**48. ... Ne7?!** 48. ... Kf7 denies White any starting point to get any further. A possible continuation would be 49. Nd4 N×b4 50. N×f5 Nd3† 51. Kg2 a5. **49. Ra1! Nd5?!** 49. ... Nc6 makes it difficult for White to develop his initiative. He must try 50. Nd4, but the drawing margin remains wide, e.g., after 50. ... N×d4 51. e×d4 R×b4 52. R×a6† Kg7 53. Rg6† Kf7 54. Ke2 Rb2 55. Rc6 Rb3 56. R×h6 Rd3. **50. Nd4** An excellent square for the knight. The f-pawn is getting under fire. **50. ... N×b4 51. Ra5** "After four hours play the game was at this point adjourned, Mr. Bird apparently having the best of the position"—Burn. **51. ... Nd3† 52. Kg3 Ke7 53. N×f5† Kd7 54. Nd4 Rb2** Lasker prefers to venture his fate with a counterattack, as "doing nothing" is not an option: if 54. ... Ke7 55. Kg4 Kf6 56. Ne2 Rd6 57. Kg3! (a brilliant waiting move. If directly 57. Nc3 Nf2† and 58. ... R×d2) 57. ... Re6 58. Ra4 Rc6 59. Nc3 and wins and if 54. ... Nc1 55. Rd5† Ke7 (55. ... Rd6

56. R×d6† K×d6 57. Nf5 wins) 56. Nf5† Kf7 57. Rc5 should also win. **55. R×a6 R×d2 56. R×h6 Ne1 57. Rh7† Kd6 58. h6 c3 59. Rh8 Kd7 60. h7 c2 61. Rd8† K×d8 62. h8Q† Kd7 63. Qg7† Kd6 64. Qe5† Kd7 65. Qb5† Kc8 66. Qc5† Kd7 67. Qd5† Kc8 68. Qa8† Kd7 69. Qb7†** Black resigns. White will play 70. N×c2 on the next move—*Liverpool Daily Courier* (Burn), 28 February 1890.

### (1007) Lasker–Bird    1–0
Match (game 12)
Liverpool, 28 February 1890
*A81*

**1. d4 f5 2. g3 Nf6 3. Bg2 e6 4. Nf3 c6 5. 0–0 Be7 6. Nbd2 0–0 7. c3 d6 8. Qc2 d5 9. Rd1 Qe8 10. Nf1 Na6 11. Bf4 Qh5 12. h4 Ne4 13. a3 Nb8 14. c4 Nd7 15. c5 h6 16. Ne1 g5 17. h×g5 h×g5 18. Bc7 Rf7 19. f3 Ne×c5 20. d×c5 B×c5† 21. e3 f4 22. b4 B×e3† 23. N×e3 f×e3 24. g4 Qh6 25. Qd3 e5 26. Q×e3 e4 27. Bd8 Nf6 28. B×f6 R×f6 29. Rd4 Qh4 30. Ra2 Rh6 31. Rf2 Bd7 32. f×e4 c5 33. R×d5 Qh2† 34. Kf1 Bb5† 35. Nd3 Kh8 36. R×c5 B×d3† 37. Q×d3 Rd6 38. Qc3†** Black resigns—*Liverpool Daily Courier*, 1 March 1890.

# HANDICAP TOURNAMENT AT SIMPSON'S DIVAN, APRIL–JUNE 1890

The fifth handicap tournament played at the Divan started on 7 April with 19 participants. Apart from Blackburne and Gunsberg, all the best London masters competed again. Just as on the previous occasion a few weaker amateurs took the liberty to play in a higher class than their actual strength.

Bird started off very strongly, despite an early loss to Thomas Charles Gibbons. Only Lee appeared on his way to overtaking him. Towards the end of the tournament Bird suffered another loss, which made it unlikely to catch up the tournament leader. In their mutual game—a draw—Lee showed his most solid side and Bird had to be content with second place.[34]

As usual with this type of tournaments, it lasted several weeks before the final games were played. Around 7 June the committee decided to bring the event to a close by declaring a few games forfeited.

### (1008) Sellon–Bird    0–1
Handicap tournament (round 1)
London, 7 April 1890
*Odds of pawn and move*

**1. e4 Nc6 2. d4 d5 3. e5 Bf5 4. c3 e6 5. h3 Qd7 6. Nd2 h6 7. Qh5† g6 8. Qf3 h5 9. Bd3 0–0–0 10. Nb3 Be7 11. B×f5 g×f5**

---

34. Bird's performance was appreciated by the press: "Mr. H.E. Bird has played some excellent chess, and at one time he looked a likely winner of the first prize, but his old enemy, the gout, laid its finger upon him, and for some days he was unable to play at all. All hopes of his winning the first prize were crushed when he was beaten by Mortimer, and Lee on the other hand beat Mason." *British Chess Magazine*, June 1890, p. 218.

### Handicap tournament, London, 7 April–7 June 1890

***Site:*** Simpson's Divan
***Prizes:*** Five prizes
***Odds scale:*** pawn and move (class II), pawn and 2 moves (class III) and knight (class IV)

| | | | 1 | 2 | 3 | 4 | 5 | 6 | 7 | 8 | 9 | 10 | 11 | 12 | 13 | 14 | 15 | 16 | 17 | 18 | 19 | |
|---|---|---|---|---|---|---|---|---|---|---|---|---|---|---|---|---|---|---|---|---|---|---|
| 1 | F.J. Lee | I | | ½ | 1 | 1 | 1 | ½ | ½ | 1 | 1 | 1 | 1 | 1 | 1 | 1 | 1 | 1 | 1 | 1 | 1 | 16½ |
| 2 | H.E. Bird | I | ½ | | ½ | 1 | 1 | 1 | 0 | 1 | 1 | 0 | 0 | 1 | 1 | 1 | 1 | 1 | 1 | 1 | + | 14 |
| 3 | J. Mason | I | 0 | ½ | | 0 | 1 | 1 | 0 | 0 | 1 | 1 | 1 | ½ | + | 1 | 1 | 1 | 1 | 1 | + | 13 |
| 4 | S. Tinsley | I | 0 | 0 | 1 | | ½ | 0 | 0 | 1 | 1 | 1 | 1 | ½ | 1 | 1 | 1 | 1 | 1 | 1 | 1 | 13 |
| 5 | O.C. Müller | I | 0 | 0 | 0 | ½ | | 0 | 1 | 1 | 0 | 1 | ½ | 1 | 1 | 1 | 1 | 1 | 1 | 1 | 1 | 12 |
| 6 | L. van Vliet | I | ½ | 0 | 0 | 1 | 1 | | 1 | 1 | ½ | 0 | 1 | 0 | 0 | 1 | 1 | 1 | 1 | 1 | 1 | 12 |
| 7 | G.H.D. Gossip | I | ½ | 1 | 1 | 1 | 0 | 0 | | ½ | ½ | 1 | 0 | 1 | | 0 | 0 | 1 | | 0 | | 7½ |
| 8 | A.G. Davidson | I | 0 | 0 | 1 | 0 | 0 | 0 | ½ | | 1 | 1 | | | ½ | 1 | 1 | 0 | 0 | | ½ | 6½ |
| 9 | N. Jasnogrodsky | I | 0 | 0 | 0 | 0 | 1 | ½ | ½ | 0 | | 0 | 1 | ½ | 0 | 0 | 1 | 1 | | 1 | | 6½ |
| 10 | T.C. Gibbons | I | 0 | 1 | 0 | 0 | 0 | 1 | 0 | 0 | 1 | | 1 | 0 | 0 | ½ | 0 | 0 | 1 | 0 | 1 | 6½ |
| 11 | J. Mortimer | I | 0 | 1 | 0 | 0 | ½ | 0 | 1 | | 0 | 0 | | | | | 1 | 1 | | | 1 | 5½ |
| 12 | R. Loman | I | 0 | 0 | ½ | ½ | 0 | 1 | 0 | | ½ | 1 | | | 0 | | | 1 | | | | 4½ |
| 13 | E.L. Sellon | II | 0 | 0 | – | 0 | 0 | 1 | | ½ | 1 | 1 | | 1 | | 0 | 0 | | 0 | | | 4½ |
| 14 | A.J. Curnock | II | 0 | 0 | 0 | 0 | 0 | 0 | 1 | 0 | 1 | ½ | | | 1 | | 0 | 0 | | 1 | | 4½ |
| 15 | T.E. Greatorex | III | 0 | 0 | 0 | 0 | 0 | 0 | 1 | 0 | 0 | 1 | 0 | | 1 | 1 | | ½ | 0 | | | 4½ |
| 16 | J.E. Hetley | II | 0 | 0 | 0 | 0 | 0 | 0 | 0 | 1 | 0 | 1 | 0 | 0 | | 1 | ½ | | | | | 3½ |
| 17 | W. Ward-Higgs | III | 0 | 0 | 0 | 0 | 0 | 0 | | 1 | | 0 | | | 1 | | 1 | | | | | 3 |
| 18 | Cole | IV | 0 | 0 | 0 | 0 | 0 | 0 | 1 | | 0 | 1 | | | | 0 | | | | | | 2 |
| 19 | J.B. Purchase | IV | 0 | – | – | 0 | 0 | 0 | | ½ | | 0 | 0 | | | | | | | | | ½ |

**12. Ne2 Nh6 13. Nf4 h4 14. Be3 Rdg8 15. a4 Nf7 16. Qe2 Ng5 17. a5 a6 18. Nd2 Ne4 19. Nf3 Nd8 20. 0–0 Bf8 21. Rfc1 Bh6 22. Ne1 B×f4 23. B×f4 Nc6 24. b4 Rg6 25. Ra2 Rhg8 26. b5 Nb8 27. c4 d×c4 28. Q×c4 a×b5 29. Qd3 Na6 30. Rb2 b4 31. f3 Nc3 32. Ra1 Nd5 33. Bc1 Rg3 34. Kh2 Qg7 35. Qf1 c5 36. Rc2 Kb8 37. d×c5 Q×e5 38. Bb2** mate in two moves—*New York Herald* (London edition), 11 May 1890.

## (1009) Loman–Bird 0–1

Handicap tournament
London, 11 April 1890
*B25*

**1. e4 c5 2. g3 g6 3. Bg2 Bg7 4. Nc3 Nc6 5. Nge2 d6 6. d3 Bd7 7. Be3 Nd4 8. Qd2 Qa5 9. B×d4 c×d4 10. Nd1 Qa6 11. Qb4 e5 12. 0–0 Ne7 13. f4 Rc8 14. Qd2 h5!** Bird obtained an excellent position on each part of the board. **15. h3 Qb6 16. Kh2 Bh6 17. c3 h4 18. g4 e×f4 19. N×f4 Bg7** Prolonging the long diagonal for his bishop by 19. ... d×c3 keeps a small advantage. Now White takes countermeasures. **20. c4 Be5 21. Kh1 Bc6 22. b3** 22. b4, creating his own chances on the other side of the board, is more disturbing for Black. **22. ... f5 23. Nf2 Kd7 24. Nd5** Allowing the subsequent exchange comes as a relief, as Bird's king will now find a quiet spot at b8. 24. b4! was still promising for White. **24. ... B×d5 25. c×d5 f4 26. g5 Kc7 27. Bf3 Kb8 28. Rfc1 Rc3 29. Nd1 R×c1 30. R×c1 Rc8 31. Rc4 R×c4 32. d×c4** *(see diagram)* White has a small edge as he has the possibility of bringing his knight to d3. Bird's next move is not good. Instead, 32. ... Nc8, and if 33. Nb2 Qd8, keep his chances intact.

**32. ... Qa6?! 33. a4?!** Loman misses a series of forced moves that catch a pawn after 33. Nf2 Nc8 34. Nd3 b6 35. Kg2 Qa3 36. Bg4 Ne7 37. Kf3. **33. ... Qb6! 34. b4** Further weakening his pawn structure is risky. 34. Qc2! is equal but not very ambitious. **34. ... a5! 35. b5** 35. Nb2 a×b4 36. Nd3 b3 37. Bd1 Qd8 38. B×b3 Nc8 39. Qg2 Qa5 is an interesting possibility to complicate the game.

*After 32. d×c4*

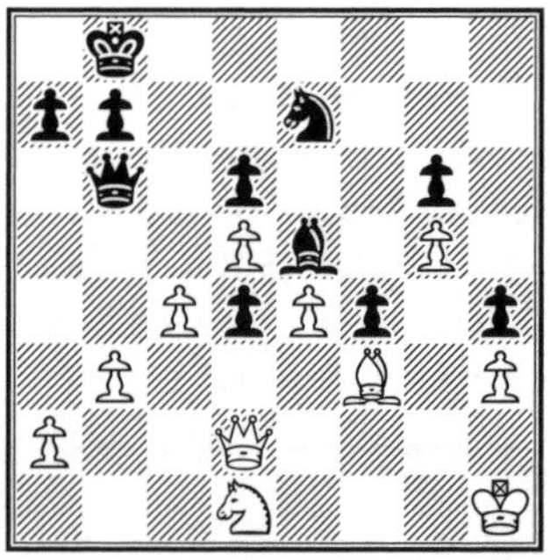

**35. ... Qc5** The exchange of pawns is not well timed, as Black's king might get in jeopardy. First 35. ... Nc8 safeguards his majesty against the intruding of the queen. If 36. Bg4 Qd8 and the g-pawn will soon fall. White has problems. **36. Q×a5 Q×c4 37. Qd8† Nc8** He should start thinking about a draw with 37. ... Ka7. **38. Kg2** Losing a crucial tempo. Both sides come to a standstill after 38. b6! Qc2 39. a5 d3 40. Kg1 Bd4† 41. Kf1 Qc5 42. Bg4. **38. ... Q×a4 39. b6 Qc2† 40. Nf2 d3 41. Bg4?** Another lost move, now with much graver consequences. The immediate 41. Bd1 leads to similar lines as in the game, with the crucial difference that Black's d-pawn falls, after which White's drawing chances are excellent; e.g., 41. ... Qc3 42. Qc7† Q×c7 43. b×c7† K×c7 44. N×d3. **41. ... d2 42. Bd1 Qc3 43. Qc7† Q×c7 44. b×c7† K×c7 45. Nd3 Nb6 46. Bb3 Nc4 47. Kf3 b5 48. Ke2 Kb6 49. Ba2 f3† 50. Kd1 Bc3** White resigns—*New York Herald (London edition)*, 13 April 1890.

## (1010) Bird–Gossip 0–1

Handicap tournament
London, May 1890
*A03*

**1. f4 d5 2. Nf3 e6 3. e3 Nf6 4. b3 Be7 5. Bb2 0–0 6. Bd3 c5 7. 0–0 Nc6 8. Ne5 Nb4 9. Be2 Nc6 10. N×c6 b×c6 11. d3 d4**

12. e4 Rb8 13. Nd2 Ba6 14. Bc1 Qc7 15. h3 Kh8 16. Qe1 Qa5
17. Nf3 Q×e1 18. R×e1 Bd8 19. Bd2 Bc7 20. g3 g6 21. Kg2 Kg8
22. g4 h5 23. g×h5 N×h5 24. Ne5 B×e5 25. f×e5 Kh7 26. Rf1
f5 27. B×h5 g×h5 28. e×f5 e×f5 29. Bg5 Bc8 30. Rf4 Rg8 31. h4
Be6 32. Kf2 Rg6 33. Rg1 Rb7 34. Ke2 a5 35. a4 Rd7 36. Rff1
Rdg7 37. Kf3 Bd5† 38. Kf4 Be6 39. Rc1 Rd7 40. Bf6 Rg4†
41. R×g4 h×g4 42. Kg5 Rd5 43. Kf4 Rd7 44. h5 Kh6 45. Bg5†
Kg7 46. Kg3 Rd5 47. Re1 Rd7 48. Bd2 Ra7 49. Kh4 Kh7
50. Rg1 Rg7 51. Kg3 Ra7 52. Bg5 Rd7 53. Kf4 Kg7 54. Rh1 Kh7
55. Bh4 Kg7 56. Be1 Ra7 57. Kg5 Rf7 58. Rf1 Kh7 59. h6 Rf8
60. Rg1 f4 61. B×a5 f3 62. Kh4 f2 63. Rf1 Rf3 64. R×f2 R×f2
65. Be1 R×c2 66. Kg5 Rb2 67. a5 R×b3 68. Kf6 Bc8 69. e6 B×e6
70. K×e6 R×d3 71. Kd6 Rd1 72. Bg3 Ra1 73. K×c5 d3 74. Bf4
g3 White resigns—*Chess Pocket Manual*, pp. 161–163.

## (1011) A.G. Davidson–Bird    0–1

Handicap tournament
London 1890
*B30*

    1. e4 c5 2. Nf3 Nc6 3. Nc3 g6 4. Bc4 Bg7 5. Ne2 Qc7 6. c3 a6
7. a3 e6 8. d3 b5 9. Ba2 Bb7 10. d4 c×d4 11. c×d4 Nce7 12. Bf4
Qa5† 13. b4 Qb6 14. Bb1 Nf6 15. Ng3 h5 16. Be3 Ng4 17. 0-0
h4 18. Ne2 h3 19. g3 f5 20. Ng5 N×e3 21. f×e3 Bh6 22. N×h3
B×e3† 23. Nf2 f×e4 24. Qb3 Nf5 25. g4 N×d4 26. N×d4 B×d4
27. Ra2 Qd6 28. Qg3 Q×g3† 29. h×g3 e3 30. Ne4 e2† and Black
wins—*Illustrated Sporting and Dramatic News*, 7 June 1890.

## (1012) Bird–Mortimer    0–1

Handicap tournament
London 1890
*A03*

    1. c4 e6 2. f4 d5 3. e3 Nf6 4. Nf3 b6 5. Nc3 Bb7 6. c×d5 e×d5
7. Bb5† c6 8. Be2 Bd6 9. 0-0 Nbd7 10. b3 Nf8 11. Bb2 Ng6
12. Bd3 Rc8 13. Nd4 0-0 14. Nf5 Bb8 15. Ne2 c5 16. Qe1 c4
17. b×c4 d×c4 18. Bc2 Re8 19. Bc3 Bd6 20. a4 Bf8 21. Rb1 Ne4
22. a5 Rc5 23. a×b6 R×f5 24. b×a7 Qc7 25. Bd4 Bc5 26. Rb5
Qc6 27. Ba4 Nd6 28. R×b7 Q×a4 29. Qb1 N×b7 30. Q×f5 B×d4
31. N×d4 Q×a7 32. Rb1 Nd6 33. Qg4 Ne4 34. f5 N×d2 35. Rd1
Ne5 36. Qg3 Ne4 37. Qf4 Nf6 38. h3 h6 39. Kh2 Nd3 40. Qf3
Qc7† 41. g3 Qe5 42. Qc6 Q×e3 43. Q×c4 Qf2† 44. Kh1 Ne4
45. R×d3 N×g3† White resigns—*The Field*, 21 June 1890.

## (1013) Lee–Bird    ½–½

Handicap tournament
London, 16 May 1890
*A81*

    1. d4 f5 2. g3 Nf6 3. Bg2 e6 4. Nf3 Be7 5. Nc3 d5 6. 0-0 0-0
7. Ne5 Na6 8. Kh1 c5 9. e3 Nc7 10. Ne2 Bd6 11. b3 b6 12. Bb2
Qe8 13. d×c5 b×c5 14. c4 Bb7 15. Nf4 g5 16. Nfd3 Rd8 17. Qe1
d×c4 18. b×c4 B×g2† 19. K×g2 Ng4 20. N×g4 f×g4 21. Qc3
Qg6 22. Qh8† Kf7 23. Ne5† B×e5 24. Q×e5 Ne8 25. Rad1
R×d1 26. R×d1 draw. A merciful decision, since White holds all
the trumps—*Daily News*, 17 May 1890.

# CHAPMAN IN LONDON

    A few weeks after the termination of the handicap tournament
Bird was struck once more by a couple of severe attacks of gout.
The first one occurred in early June and lasted about ten days. More
serious was the second attack which confined him to his bed for
two months.

    Just before the suffering began, Bird indulged in a series of con-
sultation games at the Divan. In these games Bird had a permanent
companion: Horace Edward Chapman. Chapman, who would soon
gain notoriety as the innovative president during the heyday of the
Hastings Chess Club, was a well-known patron of the game. Above
all he enjoyed supporting and taking part in consultation games.
In his obituary, which appeared in the *British Chess Magazine* of
April 1907 (p. 162), it is remarked that "he always advocated enterprising tactics and experiments in the openings." It comes thus as
no surprise to find him making an excellent pair with Bird. Three
other couples, Müller and van Vliet (2–0), Blackburne and Lee
(2–1) and Lee and Müller (1½–½) all went down against them.

## (1014) Müller & van Vliet–Bird & Chapman    0–1

Consultation game
London (Simpson's Divan), 15 May 1890
*C51*

    1. e4 e5 2. Nf3 Nc6 3. Bc4 Bc5 4. b4 B×b4 5. c3 Bc5 6. 0-0
d6 7. d4 e×d4 8. c×d4 Bb6 9. Nc3 Bg4 10. Bb5 Kf8 11. Be3 h5 A
curious invention of Bird and his partner. Better was 11. ... B×f3

Horace E. Chapman (*American Chess Magazine*).

12. g×f3 Na5, followed by 13. ... c6 and a later d5, with a very good game. **12. a4** A lost move. White has compensation for the pawn after 12. B×c6 b×c6 13. h3 (von Bardeleben and von Gottschall), as his strong center is secure then. **12. ... B×f3 13. g×f3 Nge7** The idea of playing 13. ... Na5, 14. ... c6 and 15. ... d5, remains interesting. During the next few moves White should have taken the opportunity to exchange his bishop for the knight. **14. f4 a5 15. Qd2 d5 16. e5 Nf5** The center has become locked, which is beneficial for Black. 16. ... Nb4, keeping both knights, looks very attractive. **17. Ne2 Nh4 18. f3 Nf5 19. Kh1 h4 20. B×c6** Finally! **20. ... Ng3†** *(see diagram)*

*After 20. ... Ng3*

**21. h×g3?** 21. Kg2 was no option either because of the simple 21. ... N×f1. The White allies probably saw that they were on the verge of losing their queen after 21. N×g3!, but it was very difficult to estimate the real consequences of it. Ultimately Chigorin came up with the solution by pointing out the following line: 21. ... h×g3 22. B×b7 Rb8 23. Ra2 R×h2† 24. Q×h2 g×h2 25. R×h2 Ke7 26. Bc6 and it is very difficult for Black to crack White's position. **21. ... h×g3† 22. Kg1 Rh1† 23. Kg2 Rh2† 24. Kg1 Qh4** White resigns—*Deutsche Schachzeitung* (von Bardeleben and von Gottschall), July 1890, pp. 204–205; *St. Petersburg Novoe Vremya* (Chigorin), 21 July 1890.

### (1015) Bird & Chapman–Blackburne & Lee    1–0

Consultation game
London (Simpson's Divan), 3 June 1890
C58

The second in a series of three consultation games.
**1. e4 e5 2. Nf3 Nc6 3. Bc4 Nf6 4. Ng5 d5 5. e×d5 Na5 6. d3 Be7 7. d6 Q×d6 8. B×f7† Kf8 9. Bh5 g6 10. Bf3 Bf5 11. Nc3 Kg7 12. 0–0 Rad8 13. Qe2 Nc6 14. Be3 Nd4 15. B×d4 e×d4 16. Nb5 Qc5 17. b4 Q×b4 18. N×c7 Rd7 19. Rab1 Qd6 20. Nce6† B×e6 21. N×e6† Kf7 22. Ng5† Kg7 23. R×b7 h6 24. R×d7 Q×d7 25. Rb1 Re8 26. Rb7 Qd6 27. Qe6 Qa3 28. Qf7† Kh8 29. Q×f6†** and White wins—*Evening News And Post*, 14 June 1890.

### (1016) Blackburne & Lee–Bird & Chapman    1–0

Consultation game
London (Simpson's Divan), 4 June 1890
C25

The third and final game of the series.
**1. e4 e5 2. Nc3 Bc5 3. Bc4 a6 4. Qh5 Qe7 5. Nd5 Nf6 6. N×e7**

N×h5 7. Nd5 Kd8 8. g4 Nf6 9. N×f6 g×f6 10. B×f7 d6 11. f3 Ke7 12. Bh5 Nc6 13. c3 Be6 14. Ne2 d5 15. d3 Rad8 16. Ng3 d4 17. c4 b5 18. c×b5 a×b5 19. Bd2 Ra8 20. Rc1 Kd6 21. a3 b4 22. a×b4 N×b4 23. Ke2 Ra2 24. Rb1 Rb8 25. Nf5† B×f5 26. g×f5 Nc2 27. Bc1 Ke7 28. Rg1 Na3 29. Rg7† Kd6 30. Bf7 N×b1 31. B×a2 Ra8 32. Bd5 Ra1 33. Bh6 Bb6 34. Rf7 Kc5 35. R×f6 Nc3† 36. b×c3 d×c3 37. Rc6† Kb4 38. Bf8† Black resigns—*Evening News and Post*, 7 June 1890.

---

# B.C.A Congress, Manchester 1890

At the end of the August the sixth congress of the B.C.A. began in Manchester. There had been considerable doubt, instigated by some chess columnists, whether the tournament would go forward. Once the summer months were there, and the upcoming tournament had become a certainty, another popular criticism gained ground: namely that the event would merely be of local nature while, according to the statutes of the B.C.A., an international event should be aimed for. Hoffer replied by sending invitations to all the great masters in the world (with the exception of the inactive Rosenthal and Steinitz). The response was great: 20 players from a great variety of countries showed up. Mostly missed was Lasker but as a consolation Tarrasch, the German player with by far the strongest reputation, travelled to Manchester to make his début on English soil. Tarrasch was the logical favorite for the tournament victory. He had won the last German Chess Congress held a year earlier in Breslau.

Bird's participation was absolutely not certain. He spent the weeks preceding the tournament on his sick bed, but unexpectedly rose from it to play in Manchester.[35]

Initially six prizes and the usual consolation money gathered from the entrance fees were provided to reward the participants. A last minute decision from the committee to replace the consolation money by a seventh price bred some ill will among the participants. In fact, the whole tournament was overshadowed by the increasing tension between Hoffer and several of the most prominent British chess masters. On 16 August, just prior to the tournament, Gunsberg openly denounced Hoffer as well as some of his colleagues in his column in the *Evening News and Post*, aptly titled "Chessmen at war." Gunsberg accused Hoffer, but also Mason and Burn, of forming a combination against him in order to obstruct his chances for a world championship match with Steinitz. They refused to acknowledge Gunsberg as being the best British chess player and a logical challenger for Steinitz. A few months before Mason had challenged Gunsberg to a match for hegemony in England, but evidently Gunsberg was not willing to jeopardize his chances against a player whose recent results had been anything but appealing.

35. Robert John Buckley described a select group of players in the *Birmingham Weekly Mercury* on 6 September 1890. Bird was one of them: "Bird never doffs a tall silk hat, which he wears with a jaunty and youthful air. He smokes incessantly, and varies the proceedings by silent greetings and hand-shakings with his innumerable friends, for Bird is immensely popular, and we may add, deservedly so."

Gunsberg waited until the very last moment to enter the B.C.A. Congress.[36]

The strain of the tournament was very heavy. Players were expected to play alternately two games and one game per day. The remaining time was spent on adjourned games. As a consequence the tournament suffered from such a delay that an extension appeared unavoidable. The great number of adjourned games made it difficult to follow the exact course of the tournament.

Though the field was outclassed by Tarrasch, the two actual heroes of the tournament were the veterans Bird and Mackenzie. Especially the latter's performance gained a lot of respect as Mackenzie was clearly suffering from a severe illness.[37] Others lauded Bird even before the start of the tournament.

> Bird is up to the present undoubtedly the hero of the tournament, his grand and totally unexpected victory over Gunsberg having elicited innumerable congratulations from all sorts and conditions of men. As he hobbled goutily and painfully into the large lecture room of the Athenaeum immediately before the commencement of play he was at once surrounded by a number of friends, who bore the heavy tidings that the formidable Hungarian would be his first opponent. But Mr. Bird exhibited no symptoms of alarm. On the contrary he said, "I'm not afraid of Gunsberg; he won't get over me this time. I'm not going to be fascinated by his brilliancy" [*Birmingham Weekly Mercury*, 30 August 1890].

And Bird was getting it his way! He responded to Gunsberg's 1. e4 with his usual 1. ... c5, well aware that he had lost on nearly each previous occasion with his Dragon Variation. Gunsberg did not achieve much out of the opening and when he tried to push for more he got severely punished. Bird took his time to grind his opponent down slowly.

Bird also fared well against his next, relatively weak, opponents. Locock managed to wrest a draw out of the veteran's hands, while Owen and Simon Alapin lost their games. These wins brought Bird to the top of the ranking where he enjoyed the company of Mason.

The duel between the leaders was planned for the fifth round. Not for the first time their meeting created a lot of turmoil, this time because Mason claimed the game on account of Bird overstepping the time limit. Such discussions were quite representative of this event. A few days later a similar situation arose, now with Lee claiming the point against Mason. In both cases the committee decided that the games had to be played out, which was accepted by all.[38] Mason succeeded in beating Bird on the board after all.

The real quarreling began when, in a third game, Tarrasch made the same claim to win his game on time against William Hewison Gunston. Blackburne and Gunsberg were under the impression that a member of the committee (instead of the committee as a whole) had taken an offhand decision in the matter and they refused to commence their mutual game. They were reassured that it was the task of the complete committee to decide about the outcome, and ultimately both players started playing.

This did not mean the settling of the dust, as a group of players, including Gunsberg, Tarrasch and Lee, sent in a letter of protest in which they disagreed with the decision of the committee to interpret the time limit rule loosely. A reply by another faction of the participants, with Bird and Mason among them, got published the other day.[39]

Bird suffered two more losses in the next few rounds from the hands of Schallopp and Mackenzie. With 3½ out of 7 he was now a long distance behind Mason and Blackburne (both with 6) and Tarrasch (5½).

Bird's recovery was more than impressive, for he stayed undefeated during a string of ten games. In the eighth round he could not get more than a draw out of his game with Gunston but then

36.   He elaborately explained his motives in his column: "To show how entirely he is out in interpreting the situation, I will tell him that the reason why both myself and Mr. Blackburne—myself in particular—have not yet entered the list of competitors, much as I should like doing so, is because he (Hoffer) having shown hostility towards me which is as persistent as it was unprovoked, I do not think him a fit and proper person to conduct a tournament in which I am competing, and I naturally want to know before I enter, and commit my reputation to his care, whether the gentlemen of the Manchester committee intend that he shall have the sole and arbitrary power of managing this tournament, which he had on previous occasions. Mr. Blackburne has expressed himself somewhat to the same effect in a letter to the Manchester committee, and other strong players are of a similar opinion." *Evening News and Post*, 16 August 1890. ¶ The concrete effect on the playground becomes clear from the reports written by the chess correspondent of the *New York Sun*: "Gunsberg is in a peculiar position at this congress. Hoffer and he cross to the other side of the room to avoid each other. Gunsberg is, at the moment of writing, playing with Lee, with whom he is on pretty similar terms. They blackguard each other upon every possible occasion, and don't speak." *New York Sun*, 7 September 1890. ¶ "My statement about the secretary's kindness in allowing me to copy games for the *Sun* must be taken back. Hoffer is very difficult to manage, and I am getting just about sick of going round begging for them. ... Bird, it is said, intends to object to the constitution of the committee with a view to securing the removal of Hoffer. In accomplishing this, there is no doubt he would be cheerfully aided by a great many of the other masters. ... A pretty little incident took place today [20 August]. Bird has a habit of talking very loudly, as the readers will remember from his presence in New York. This is particularly exasperating to Gossip, who was playing on the next board today. Gossip turned round excitedly and said: 'I wish you would give over talking; it is impossible for me to play,' to which Bird testily responded 'Shut up.' Gossip thereupon suggested that the old veteran should go to the devil, and as this little conversation was carried on in a high one, one can imagine that there was something like a scene." *New York Sun*, 9 September 1890. ¶ "Blackburne and Gunsberg allege that Hoffer has been backing Mason considerably, and is even coaching him during the tournament. This may be as it is, but what I do know from Hoffer's remarks himself, is that he (Hoffer) is watching Mason like a dog, and that he dare not let him out of his sight for fear he will go out and get—well, everyone knows what he will get, any a stimulant or so." *New York Sun*, 12 September 1890.

37.   Another veteran, John Owen, declared his admiration to an American reporter: "'During my long chess career, I have seen a lot. I have seen poor De Vere worsting the amateurs at Simpson's Divan, I have seen the crippled Schottländer making fine combinations, I have seen the wonderful Zukertort, a man of very weak constitution, playing sixteen games blindfolded and repeating them forward and backward six hours after they were finished. I have seen the immortal Morphy here in Manchester, when he drove the people mad with delight by his classical style of play. But I cannot remember a case where a man like Mackenzie has played chess when his body must be considered almost dead. Here you have genius at its best. His games against Blackburne, Schallopp and Alapin are chess, sir, chess of that beautiful elegance and fineness that is rarely being exhibited in tournament play, and certainly never in match play.' The same reporter was equally interested in Bird's opinion of the Captain: "'Look at me,' said old Bird, the genial veteran of England's champions, 'I can't move, the gout is almost beating me. I have done my little share of brilliancies only a few months ago at Simpson's handicap, but the Captain is supreme.'" *New York Daily Tribune*, 7 September 1890.

38.   Before the decision of the committee was taken, one journalist claimed that "I hear that the committee will keep their decision dark until the end of the tournament, for fear if the decision was against Bird that he would retire." *New York Sun*, 9 September 1890.

39.   From this reply Bird's opinion on the matter of exceeding the time limit can be filtered: "All the claims made under the time limit have been fully examined by the committee, and the infractions have been so unimportant that it has not been deemed necessary to enforce in any instance a penalty so severe as the loss of a game. It is also held that ordinary courtesy between the contestants demands that before making a claim under the time limit rule fair and loyal warning should be given by a player to his opponent." *Manchester Guardian*, 4 September 1890.

Thorold and Blackburne fell victim to Bird's will to win. His victory over Blackburne was brilliant. Bird subsequently drew Gossip and beat Taubenhaus. In the thirteenth round Bird met Tarrasch, who had conquered the leading place a few rounds before. Bird played at his best and pushed the extremely strong German doctor to the utmost to reach a draw.[40]

Bird unleashed an impressive finish. In the fourteenth round he drew with Lee, then beat Mortimer, drew another game with Samuel Tinsley (one of Bird's few preserved games, from which it becomes clear that Bird was not without luck either) and beat van Vliet.

**6th Congress of the B.C.A., Manchester, 25 August–8 September 1890**

***Site:*** Athenaeum
***Playing hours:*** 12 p.m.–4 and 6 p.m.–10
***Prizes:*** 1st £80, 2nd £60, 3rd £50, 4th £40, 5th £30, 6th £20, 7th £10
***Time limit:*** 20 moves per hour

| | | **1** | **2** | **3** | **4** | **5** | **6** | **7** | **8** | **9** | **10** | **11** | **12** | **13** | **14** | **15** | **16** | **17** | **18** | **19** | **20** | |
|---|---|---|---|---|---|---|---|---|---|---|---|---|---|---|---|---|---|---|---|---|---|---|
| 1 | S. Tarrasch | | 1 | ½ | ½ | 1 | 1 | ½ | ½ | ½ | 1 | 1 | ½ | 1 | 1 | 1 | 1 | 1 | 1 | ½ | 1 | 15½ |
| 2 | J.H. Blackburne | 0 | | 0 | 0 | ½ | ½ | 1 | 1 | 1 | 0 | 1 | 1 | 1 | 1 | 1 | 1 | 0 | ½ | 1 | 1 | 12½ |
| 3 | G.H. Mackenzie | ½ | 1 | | 1 | 0 | ½ | 1 | 0 | 1 | ½ | 1 | 0 | 1 | ½ | 1 | 1 | 1 | 0 | 0 | 1 | 12 |
| 4 | H.E. Bird | ½ | 1 | 0 | | 0 | 1 | 0 | ½ | 1 | 1 | 0 | ½ | ½ | 1 | 1 | 1 | 1 | ½ | 1 | ½ | 12 |
| 5 | J. Mason | 0 | ½ | 1 | 1 | | 0 | 0 | ½ | 0 | ½ | ½ | 1 | 1 | 1 | 0 | 1 | 1 | 1 | ½ | 1 | 11½ |
| 6 | I. Gunsberg | 0 | ½ | ½ | 0 | 1 | | 1 | 0 | ½ | ½ | 1 | ½ | 0 | 1 | 0 | 1 | 1 | 1 | 1 | 1 | 11½ |
| 7 | T. von Scheve | ½ | 0 | 0 | 1 | 1 | 0 | | 1 | 0 | ½ | 1 | ½ | 1 | 1 | 1 | 0 | 0 | 1 | 1 | ½ | 11 |
| 8 | S. Tinsley | ½ | 0 | 1 | ½ | ½ | 1 | 0 | | 0 | 0 | 1 | ½ | 1 | 0 | ½ | 1 | 1 | 1 | 1 | ½ | 11 |
| 9 | S. Alapin | ½ | 0 | 0 | 0 | 1 | ½ | 1 | 1 | | 0 | 0 | ½ | ½ | 1 | 1 | 1 | ½ | 1 | 1 | ½ | 11 |
| 10 | J. Taubenhaus | 0 | 1 | ½ | 0 | ½ | ½ | ½ | 1 | 1 | | 0 | 0 | 1 | 1 | 0 | 0 | ½ | 1 | 1 | 1 | 10½ |
| 11 | E. Schallopp | 0 | 0 | 0 | 1 | ½ | 0 | 0 | 0 | 1 | 1 | | ½ | ½ | 0 | ½ | 1 | 1 | 1 | 1 | 1 | 10 |
| 12 | F.J. Lee | ½ | 0 | 1 | ½ | 0 | ½ | ½ | ½ | ½ | 1 | ½ | | ½ | 0 | 0 | ½ | 1 | 0 | ½ | 1 | 9 |
| 13 | W. Gunston | 0 | 0 | 0 | ½ | 0 | 1 | 0 | 0 | ½ | 0 | ½ | ½ | | 1 | ½ | 1 | ½ | 1 | 1 | 1 | 9 |
| 14 | J. Mortimer | 0 | 0 | ½ | 0 | 0 | 0 | 0 | 1 | 0 | 0 | 1 | 1 | 0 | | 1 | ½ | ½ | 1 | 1 | 1 | 8½ |
| 15 | J. Owen | 0 | 0 | 0 | 0 | 1 | 1 | 0 | ½ | 0 | 1 | ½ | 1 | ½ | 0 | | 0 | 0 | 1 | 1 | 0 | 7½ |
| 16 | O.C. Müller | 0 | 0 | 0 | 0 | 0 | 0 | 1 | 0 | 0 | 1 | 0 | ½ | 0 | ½ | 1 | | 1 | ½ | 1 | ½ | 7 |
| 17 | E. Thorold | 0 | 1 | 0 | 0 | 0 | 0 | 1 | 0 | ½ | ½ | 0 | 0 | ½ | ½ | 1 | 0 | | 0 | ½ | ½ | 6 |
| 18 | C.D. Locock | 0 | ½ | 1 | ½ | 0 | 0 | 0 | 0 | 0 | 0 | 0 | 1 | 0 | 0 | 0 | ½ | 1 | | 0 | 1 | 5½ |
| 19 | L. van Vliet | ½ | 0 | 1 | 0 | ½ | 0 | 0 | 0 | 0 | 0 | 0 | ½ | 0 | 0 | 0 | 0 | ½ | 1 | | 1 | 5 |
| 20 | G.H.D. Gossip | 0 | 0 | 0 | ½ | 0 | 0 | ½ | ½ | ½ | 0 | 0 | 0 | 0 | 0 | 1 | ½ | ½ | 0 | 0 | | 4 |

After seventeen rounds the tournament victory was definitively for Tarrasch. With 14/17 he was too far ahead of every other contender. Trailing at three points were Bird, Blackburne, Mackenzie and Mason. Gunsberg and Tinsley followed just behind.

Tarrasch and Blackburne succeeded in winning their games in the penultimate round. Bird, Mackenzie and Mason lost. Theodor von Scheve was too strong for the veteran.

In the final round Bird beat Müller. Tarrasch rounded off his tournament with a draw, realizing a fantastic 15½ points in 19 games. His superiority over the field was beyond dispute. Only in his games with Schallopp and Bird had he experienced some problems.

The older and experienced players ended at a respectable distance. With a draw against Mason, Blackburne secured second place. The third and fourth prize were shared, very surprisingly, by Bird and Mackenzie. Mackenzie took part against the explicit advice of his doctor to rest. Towards the end of the congress, he declined and suffered some unnecessary losses. He died six months later.

Bird's performance was equally magnificent. At the age of 61 he was the second oldest participant, behind Owen.[41]

## (1017) Gunsberg–Bird 0–1

B.C.A. Congress (round 1)
Manchester, 25 August 1890
*B34*

**1. e4 c5 2. Nc3 Nc6 3. Nf3 g6 4. d4 c×d4 5. N×d4 Bg7 6. Be3 d6 7. Be2** "We much prefer 7. Nd5, for the opponent will not be able to get rid of this piece without weakening his center"—Steinitz. **7. ... Bd7 8. 0–0 Nf6 9. f4 h5 10. h3 h4 11. Qd2 Qa5 12. Rad1 Rc8** Stronger is the immediate 12. ... Nh5 13. B×h5 R×h5 with equal chances. Not so good for White then is 14. Nb3 B×c3. **13. a3** 13. Nb3! leaves Black with a cramped position. If 13. ... Qd8 (best) 14. e5 d×e5 15. f×e5 N×e5 16. B×a7 and White is well on top. **13. ... Nh5 14. B×h5 R×h5!** *(see diagram)*

*After 14. ... R×h5*

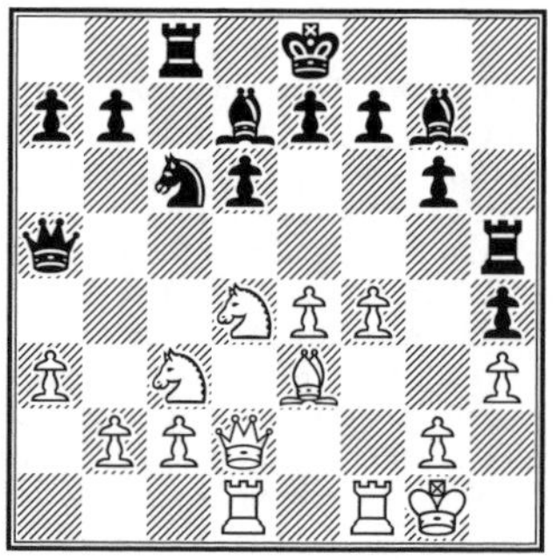

**15. b4?** "The sacrifice of pawns which White here institutes are [*sic*] not sound"—Steinitz. Black has no problems anymore after the previous exchange. Gunsberg wants to get an advantage by all means and simply throws material and the game away. A quiet move,

40. Buckley, more than ever an astute admirer of Bird, got lyrical in his descriptions: "Bird followed up his defeat of Gunsberg by beating his old friend Blackburne, and drawing a game with Tarrasch. 'The G.O.M. plays like a demon against the strongest players,' remarked one who knows. On Monday morning we met the veteran toiling painfully up the 75 steps leading to the battleground. After each step he rested, leaning against the wall. But the light of battle was in his eye—he wore a determined look, and evidently meant mischief." *Birmingham Weekly Mercury*, 6 September 1890.

41. In fact, it had not been the strain of the tournament that bothered Bird most: "Bird too went straight from a sick room to the battlefield, and his score is therefore most creditable. I am sure if your readers could have seen the veteran painfully toiling up the many steps that lead to the play-room in the Athenaeum, they would wonder at the old man's pluck. ''Tisn't the moves on the board so much that bothers me as the moves up those confounded stairs,' was his reply to a person who complimented him on his score. Bird, sitting at the board, looks a strong healthy old fellow, Bird, walking across the room, looks a decrepit old man. But, gout or no gout, Bird is a tough customer, and so he proved himself at Manchester." *International Chess Magazine*, September 1890, p. 259.

such as 15. Kh1 or 15. Rf2 gives equal play. **15. … Q×a3 16. Ra1 Q×b4 17. Ra4** "The opponent makes now his escape, but he could not hold him more tightly either by 17. Rfb1 Qc4 18. Ra4 Nb4"— Steinitz. **17. … Qb6 18. Nd5** "The promising appearance of the position is deceptive. If, for instance, 19. Ne6 B×c3 20. Q×c3 Nd4 and White will effect no more than exchanges that are to his disadvantage in view of Black's strong passed pawns"—Steinitz. **18. … Qd8** 18. … Qb2 is more forceful; e.g., 19. e5 N×d4 20. B×d4 Qb5 21. Ra5 R×c2. **19. N×c6 b×c6 20. Nc3 Ra5 21. Rfa1 R×a4 22. R×a4 c5 23. R×a7 Qb6 24. Ra3 Qb2 25. Rb3 Qa1† 26. Nd1 Bc6 27. Bf2 B×e4 28. Re3 f5 29. Re1 Qa4 30. B×h4 Qd4†** "His finely planned attack forces now a victorious ending, with plenty of material ahead"—Steinitz. **31. Q×d4 c×d4 32. Nf2 d5 33. Re2 R×c2 34. Re1 d3 35. N×d3 B×d3 36. R×e7† Kf8 37. Re6 Bd4† 38. Kh2 Be4 39. R×g6 Kf7** White resigns. "For if 40. Rg3 Bf2 wins or if 40. Rg5 Bf6 41. Rh5 B×h4 42. R×h4 R×g2† 43. Kh1 Rg4†"— Steinitz. *International Chess Magazine* (Steinitz), October 1890, pp. 311–312.

## (1018) Bird–Locock ½–½
B.C.A. Congress (round 2)
Manchester, 25 August 1890
*Game score missing*

## (1019) Owen–Bird 0–1
B.C.A. Congress (round 3)
Manchester, 26 August 1890
*Game score missing*

## (1020) Bird–Alapin 1–0
B.C.A. Congress (round 4)
Manchester, 27 August 1890
*Game score missing*

## (1021) Mason–Bird 1–0
B.C.A. Congress (round 5)
Manchester, 27 August 1890

*Black to move*

**40. … Nd8 41. Nd4 Kg6** 41. … Ne6 42. N×e6† Q×e6 43. b5 Qd6! draws. After the text move White develops a bind. **42. c3 e3?** From which Bird attempts to escape, but a better possibility doing so consisted of playing 42. … Qd6; e.g., 43. b5 Q×f4! 44. Q×d8 Qc1† 45. Kf2 e3† 46. Kf3 Qf1† 47. K×e3 Qe1† 48. Ne2 f4† 49. K×f4 Qf2† 50. Ke5 Q×e2† 51. Kd6 c×b5 52. Q×h4 Q×g2 53. Kc5. The endgame remains difficult for him. **43. Qc7 Ne6 44. Q×c6 N×f4 45. Qe8† Kh6 46. Q×e3 Qg5 47. Qf3 N×g2**

**48. Q×g2 Qc1† 49. Kh2 Qf4† 50. Kh1 Qc1† 51. Qg1 Q×c3 52. Qe3† Q×e3 53. N×f5† Kg5 54. N×e3** and White wins—*Chess Monthly*, November 1890, p. 94.

## (1022) Mackenzie–Bird 1–0
B.C.A. Congress (round 6)
Manchester, 29 August 1890
*Game score missing*

The postmortem of this game was described by the Canadian chess player John Henderson in a letter published in the *Montreal Gazette* on 24 September 1890: "Bird and Mackenzie then proceeded to finish a game they had on. The position was not far removed from an equal game at the time of adjournment, but Mackenzie very soon obtained an advantage, which he continued until he had a won game. Mr. Bird, however, kept the game on for some moves, until Mackenzie threatened a mate almost on the move. Mr. Bird said it was a most mortifying game to lose, as he considered he had the better position at the adjournment. He set up the position and proceeded to argue thereupon. 'But look,' said Captain Mackenzie, 'your rook is out of play.' 'And so is yours,' retorted Mr. Bird. 'No, no, that is just my strong point. Look how it is supporting that pawn.' Then Captain Mackenzie leaving Mr. Bird alone, he was joined by Mr. L. Hoffer, the energetic secretary of the B.C.A. who unsuccessfully endeavored to prove to Mr. Bird that the odds were against him in the position before them. For nearly half an hour, Mr. Bird sat there moving piece after piece, and trying one variation after another. Mr. Bird's success in the tournament is wonderful, considering that he is suffering most acutely from rheumatic gout, and that he can only labor along a few yards at a time, with two stout sticks. If he had only been in good health he might have given even Tarrasch cause for apprehension as to the destination of the first prize."

## (1023) Bird–Schallopp 0–1
B.C.A. Congress (round 7)
Manchester, 28 August 1890
*C58*

**1. e4 e5 2. Nf3 Nc6 3. Bc4 Nf6 4. Ng5 d5 5. e×d5 Na5 6. Bb5† c6 7. d×c6 b×c6 8. Bd3 Nd5 9. Nf3 Bd6 10. 0-0 0-0-0 11. Re1 Qc7 12. Bf1 f5 13. d3 Bd7 14. c4 Nf6 15. c5 B×c5 16. R×e5 B×f2† 17. Kh1 Ng4 18. Re2 Rae8 19. Bd2 R×e2 20. B×e2 Bb6 21. Be1 Rf6 22. d4 Rh6 23. h3 Ne3 24. Qd3 f4 25. Nbd2 Bf5 26. Ne4 Qd7 27. h4 Nac4 28. Rc1 Nd6 29. Nfg5 N×e4 30. N×e4 Q×d4 31. Q×d4 B×d4 32. Ng5 B×b2 33. Rc5 Bd4 34. Ra5 Rd6 35. Bf2 Bc2 36. Nf3 Bb6 37. Re5 h6 38. Re8† Kf7 39. Rb8 Bd1 40. Rb7† Kf6 41. B×d1 R×d1† 42. Ng1 Rd2 43. Nh3 g5 44. Rh7 Kg6 45. Re7 R×a2 46. Re6† Kf5 47. R×c6 g4 48. Ng1 R×f2** White resigns—*Deutsches Wochenschach*, 7 September 1890, pp. 297–298.

## (1024) Bird–Gunston ½–½
B.C.A. Congress (round 8)
Manchester, 29 August 1890
*Game score missing*

## (1025) Thorold–Bird    0–1
B.C.A. Congress (round 9)
Manchester, 30 August 1890
*A85*

**1. Nf3 f5** "The English veteran is very partial to this reply. In fact he is said to claim that 1. ... f5 is the best move on the board when White has not opened with 1. e4"—Séguin and Maurian. **2. d4 Nf6 3. c4 e6 4. Nc3 Bb4 5. Bd2 0–0 6. e3 d6 7. Qc2 Nc6 8. a3 B×c3 9. B×c3 Qe8 10. 0–0–0 d5** 10. ... e5 is much more in the spirit of the position, but Bird adopted the Stonewall whenever he could. **11. Ne5 a5 12. f3 Ne7 13. h3** "Preliminary to this attempt to open the h-file by his next move"—Séguin and Maurian. **13. ... c6 14. g4 Nd7 15. f4 N×e5 16. d×e5 b5** 16. ... c5 or 16. ... b6 are fine. The text move offers Thorold the opportunity to close the position, which he incorrectly does. Having the bishop pair it was interesting to go for 17. c×b5. **17. c5 Bd7 18. b4** Thorold is apparently eager to block the whole position and escape with a draw but the text move limits his own bishop as well as allows Bird to open the a-file. **18. ... a×b4 19. B×b4** He should have played 19. a×b4. **19. ... Ra7 20. Rd4 Qa8 21. Kb2 Be8 22. Bd3 Bg6 23. Qg2** 23. g5 seems consistent. After 23. ... Bh5 24. Be2 B×e2 25. Q×e2 Ng6, it is not clear whether Black has enough trumps in hand to force the position. **23. ... Qe8 24. h4?!** Worse than the approach proposed above. This move only saddles him with weakened white squares without obtaining a trace of an attack in return. **24. ... f×g4 25. Q×g4 Bf5 26. B×f5 N×f5 27. Rd3 Qf7** 27. ... h5 is strong. The knight can head to g4 at once. **28. Rg1 Rfa8 29. h5** *(see diagram)*

**Edmund Thorold (*Chess Monthly*).**

*After 29. h5*

**29. ... Ra4!** "A very fine move. He threatens 30. ... R×b4† followed by 31. ... Qa7! with unanswerable effect"—Séguin and Maurian. **30. Qd1 Qa7 31. Qb3 Qf7 32. Qd1 h6 33. e4?** "Entirely too precipitate, to say the least. The sacrifice is unsound and virtually loses the game"—Séguin and Maurian. **33. ... d×e4 34. Rd7 Qe8 35. Rg2 R4a7 36. Rgd2 R×d7 37. R×d7 Ne3 38. Qd4 Nc4† 39. Kc2 e3 40. f5 Q×h5 41. f6 Qf5† 42. Kc1 g×f6 43. e×f6 e5** "The accuracy of the defense, culminating in this decisive stroke, with which the old master has met the formidable counterattack, initiated at White's 40th move, is admirable"—Séguin and Maurian. **44. Rd8†** "If, instead, 44. f7† Kf8 45. Rd8† R×d8 46. Q×d8† K×f7 soon escaping from check and winning easily."—Séguin and Maurian. **44. ... Kf7 45. Qd7† Q×d7 46. R×d7† K×f6** and after a few more moves, White resigns—*New Orleans Times Democrat* (Séguin and Maurian), 21 September 1890.

## (1026) Blackburne–Bird    0–1
B.C.A. Congress (round 10)
Manchester, 1 September 1890
*A81*

On 2 September, the correspondent of the *Birmingham Gazette* gave another fitting introduction to the duel of the two British masters: "Bird appeared fifteen minutes late and consequently had to make his first twenty moves in 45 minutes. This, however, is no special disadvantage to the grand old man who, despite his advanced age, is far away the quickest player engaged in the tournament. Blackburne, departing from his usual custom, took off his hat, and appeared to prepare himself for a supreme effort. The 'ancient master' on the contrary retained his headgear as well as the jaunty and light-hearted air which he is popularly supposed to have worn for half a century at least."

**1. d4 f5 2. g3** "Creating a weakness which proved fatal in the end. 2. Nf3 is far preferable, followed by 3. e3 and castling on the kingside later"—Tinsley. **2. ... Nf6 3. Bg2 e6 4. Nh3 d5 5. 0–0 Be7 6. Nd2 0–0 7. c3 Qe8 8. Re1 c5 9. e3 Nc6 10. f3** "Apparently to prevent 10. ... Ne4, and to get 11. Nf2, but further weakening his position on this side. His game is bad. He has no attack, and his pieces are mostly on the wrong squares"—Tinsley. **10. ... b6 11. Nf2 Bb7 12. Nb3 Nd8** 12. ... Qf7 makes a future push of the e-pawn very dangerous for his opponent. **13. d×c5 b×c5 14. e4** As the result of this move, both sides end up with a decimated pawn structure. The chances are about equal. **14. ... f×e4 15. f×e4 Rc8** "If now 15. Na5 Ba8 and the knight remains out of the game"—Tinsley. **16. e×d5 B×d5!** The correct way of recapturing the pawn. An important defender of White's king is neutralized. **17. B×d5 N×d5 18. Nd2 Qf7 19. Nde4 Nb7 20. Nd3 c4 21. Nf4** 21. Ne5 is a better spot for the knight; e.g., 21. ... Qf5 22. Nd7 Rfd8 23. g4 Qg6 24. Ne5 with light pressure, albeit nothing that could have worried Bird. **21. ... Nc5! 22. N×c5** Blackburne clearly underestimates the chances of his opponent in this position. 22. Qe2 limits the activity of Bird's pieces. **22. ... B×c5† 23. Kg2** *(see diagram)*

*After 23. Kg2*

**23. ... Qb7** "Fearfully strong. Threatening among other things, mate in two by 23. ... N×f4†. But all this is merely the result of the foregoing"—Tinsley. The refined 23. ... Rce8! is even stronger. White is nearly without moves and with the e-pawn covered, Black threatens 24. ... N×f4 25. B×f4 Qb7†. The endgame after 24. N×d5 e×d5 25. R×e8 R×e8 26. Bf4 d4 is also unattractive. Perhaps best is 24. Qe2 e5 25. Nh3 h6 26. Kh1 Nf6, once again with magnificent play for Black. **24. Kh3 Rf6** 24. ... Rf5! leaves his opponent with the question about what to do. If 25. R×e6 Qd7. Almost no other piece can move; e.g., 25. Qe2 e5 26. Ne6 Nf6 27. Ng5 Bb6, covering c4 and menacing 28. ... Qd7 or 28. ... Rf2. **25. Re5** Trying to escape into an endgame is no solution either: 25. N×d5 e×d5 26. Re5 d4! 27. c×d4 Bd6 28. Re1 Rf2 wins. **25. ... Rd8!** Very strong. White is without resource. **26. N×d5?** 26. N×e6 is not a free bite as becomes clear after 26. ... R×e6! 27. R×e6 Qc8 28. Qg4 h5 29. Qf5 Ne7. 26. Qe2! is the only good try. It calmly completes the development and, after 26. ... Bd6 27. N×d5 e×d5 28. Re8† R×e8 29. Q×e8† Bf8 30. Bg5 Rf7, the exchanges have lightened his task to fight for equality. **26. ... R×d5 27. R×d5 e×d5 28. Bf4 Bd6?** A single moment of hesitation allows Blackburne a second life. Very strong was 28. ... d4! 29. c×d4 Bd6. White's king is in serious trouble. A possible line would be 30. Qh5 Qd7† 31. Qg4 Rf5! 32. Kg2 B×f4 33. g×f4 h5 34. Qf3 Q×d4. **29. Be3 Qf7 30. Kg2** With his king back on a safe square his position has normalized. **30. ... Qe6 31. Qd4 Qf5 32. Rd1?** *(see diagram)* A blunder that inspires Bird to a swift execution. After 32. Kg1 Qf3 33. Bf2 a5 34. Qe3 the game should have a peaceful outcome.

*After 32. Rd1*

**32. ... Qf3† 33. Kg1 Bc5!** "As the 'G.O.M.' of chess lifted his gouty hand to make this move, his face was a study for a painter. The rest is not worthy of publication. Of course if 34. Q×c5, White is mated in two. Our great English champion played this game feebly, and in a way to assist the attacking propensities of his opponent"—Tinsley. **34. Q×d5† Q×d5 35. R×d5 B×e3† 36. Kg2 Rf2† 37. Kh3 R×b2 38. Rd8† Kf7 39. Rd7† Kf6 40. Rc7 Bg1 41. R×c4 R×a2 42. Rf4† Ke6 43. Re4† Kd6 44. Kg4 R×h2 45. a5 46. Re1 Bd4** White resigns—*British Chess Magazine* (Tinsley), October 1890, pp. 423–424.

**(1027) Bird–Gossip** ½–½
B.C.A. Congress (round 11)
Manchester, 1 September 1890
*Game score missing*

**(1028) Taubenhaus–Bird** 0–1
B.C.A. Congress (round 12)
Manchester, 2 September 1890
*Game score missing*

**(1029) Bird–Tarrasch** ½–½
B.C.A. Congress (round 13)
Manchester, 2 September 1890
*A03*

**1. f4 d5 2. Nf3 c5 3. e3 Nf6 4. b3 e6 5. Bb2 a6 6. Be2 Be7 7. 0-0 Nc6 8. Ne5 Qc7 9. d3 0-0 10. Nd2 Nd7 11. Ndf3 f6 12. N×c6 Q×c6 13. Qe1 b5** "Both sides played the opening correct in the character of the game, and Black is better on the queenside, while he is exposed to some attacking threats on the kingside"—Tarrasch. **14. a4 Bb7 15. Qg3 Nb6** "Black intends a queenside break with c5–c4. Another very good plan is to advance the e-pawn after 15. ... Bd6 and 16. ... Rae8"—Tarrasch. **16. a×b5 a×b5 17. Nh4 c4 18. Bg4!** "This is a very well thought up trap. If 18. ... c3?, there follows 19. B×c3 Q×c3 20. B×e6† Rf7! (20. ... Kh8? 21. Ng6† and mate next move) 21. Nf5 g6 22. R×a8† B×a8 23. Nh6† Kg7 24. N×f7 and White is an exchange ahead with a good position. A combination like this causes anxiety, thus I played 18. ... Bc8"—Tarrasch. **18. ... Bc8** "Better would have been 18. ... R×a1 19. B×a1! Bc8 or 19. ... Ra8. White could not play 19. R×a1 as then 19. ... c3 can be played and the above mentioned combination would not work"—Tarrasch. **19. b×c4 b×c4 20. Bd4 Bd7 21. Be2 Bc5 22. R×a8 N×a8** "Not 22. ... R×a8 23. B×f6"—Tarrasch. **23. d×c4 B×d4 24. e×d4** "On 24. c×d5 Q×d5 25. e×d4 Q×d4†, Black gets a good game"—Tarrasch. **24. ... d×c4** "The interesting skirmish of the last few moves seems to have led to a slightly inferior position for Black and the next moves tend to confirm this fact"—Tarrasch. **25. f5 Qe4!** "On 25. ... e×f5 26. N×f5 B×f5 27. R×f5, White's position would be excellent because of his passed pawn and Black's weak c4-pawn. Together with the next move, 25. ... Qe4! is the only correct defense"—Tarrasch. **26. Qg4** "The only way to guard e2, d4 and f5"—Tarrasch. The offensive 26. Qd6! is an improvement. Black has to retreat his queen 26. ... Qd5 (after 26. ... Q×e2 27. Q×d7 Black's king might end up in trouble) when the position remains balanced (27. Qf4 e×f5 28. Bf3 Qb5 29. Qd6). **26. ... Qe3†** "The queen's trade would be unfavorable for Black"—Tarrasch. **27. Kh1 Nb6** "Here a strange thing happened to me. I was under the impression that with the last moves I had consolidated my position again and that I now had fair drawing chances. Then it struck me that Mr. Bird, who is known for playing fast, took an extraordinarily long time for his next move. Then I began to ask myself what I would do as White, and the longer I thought about it, the more I found to my amazement that the situation had completely changed and that White had great trouble finding a plausible continuation, and that it was he and not I, who was trying to draw the game. This underestimating of my own position had never happened to me before"—Tarrasch. **28. Bf3** "White hardly has a choice; e.g., 28. f×e6 B×e6 29. Nf5 B×f5 is good for Black"—Tarrasch. **28. ... e×f5** 28. ... Re8! keeps the tension a moment longer. White cannot make a very constructive move, and Black reaches a similar position with a slightly more active rook and the better chances: 29. h3 e×f5 30. N×f5 B×f5 31. Q×f5 Q×d4 32. Rd1 Qe5 33. Q×e5 R×e5. The drawing margin nevertheless remains large. **29. N×f5 B×f5 30. Q×f5 Re8?** "Should Black capture the d-pawn, White will develop a strong attack with 31. Qe6† Kh8 32. Rd1 Qc5 33. Rd6, followed by 34. Rc6, with penetration of the seventh rank by rook and queen. Worse than 30. ... Re8 would be 30. ... Rd8, because of 31. Be4"—Tarrasch. Tarrasch wrongly considers 30. ... Q×d4 the inferior move, for he overlooks 32. ... Qf2! instead of 32. ... Qc5? At f2, the queen forces White's rook to remain passive on the first rank. 30. ... Re8? gave Bird a unique chance to create a major upset. **31. Qb5! Re6** (see diagram)

After 31. ... Re6

**32. Bd5?** "Better was 32. d5 Rd6, but the best White could do here was to draw as the further advance of the passed pawn was blocked"—Tarrasch. A convincing riposte against 32. d5 is 32. ... Qe1! Surprisingly strong is 32. Bg4!, for if then 32. ... Rd6 33. h3 Kf8 (he cannot capture the d-pawn) 34. Qb4! Qe7 35. Rb1 g6 36. Qc5 Nd7 37. Q×c4. After several precise moves White can finally reap the important c-pawn. Black, facing a strong pair of pawns on the queenside, lacks compensation. **32. ... N×d5 33. Q×d5 Qe2 34. Rg1** "34. Rb1 would have been answered by the same move, but it would have saved White a tempo"—Tarrasch. **34. ... g6 35. h3 Kg7 36. Rb1 Re7** "Black, because of time pressure, chose to make the simplest possible moves and did not really do justice to the position. 36. ... c3 would have given winning chances, as the c- and d-pawn would have been exposed to danger and there was no danger of mate by 37. Rb7† Kh6 38. Qd7, as Black would have 38. ... Qf1†, followed by 39. ... Qf4† and mates"—Tarrasch. Instead of 37. Rb7†?, 37. Kh2! saves the day. **37. c3** "White should play 37. Rb7 at once, since Black might still have winning chances by

playing 37. ... Re3"—Tarrasch. **37. ... Qd3 38. Rb7 Qf1† 39. Kh2 Qf4†** and drawn by perpetual check—*Three Hundred Chess Games* (Tarrasch), pp. 207–208.

### (1030) Lee–Bird    0–1
B.C.A. Congress (round 14)
Manchester, 3 September 1890
*Game score missing*

### (1031) Bird–Mortimer    1–0
B.C.A. Congress (round 15)
Manchester, 4 September 1890
*Game score missing*

### (1032) Tinsley–Bird    ½–½
B.C.A. Congress (round 16)
Manchester, 4 September 1890
*A84*

**1. d4 d5 2. c4 e6 3. Nf3 c6 4. e3 Bd6 5. Nc3 Nd7 6. Bd3 f5 7. c×d5 c×d5 8. Bd2 a6 9. Rc1 Nh6 10. Qb3** "With some idea of sacrificing the knight if Black castles"—Pierce. **10. ... Nf7 11. 0–0 0–0 12. Kh1 Nf6 13. Ng1 Ne4 14. B×e4 f×e4 15. f4 Nh6 16. Nge2 Kh8 17. Na4 b5** A thoughtless advance that offers his opponent the juicy square c5. Fortunately for Bird, there are no direct consequences involved. **18. Nc5 Ra7 19. a4 Qe8 20. a×b5 a×b5 21. Be1 Ng4 22. h3 Nh6 23. Bg3 Nf5 24. Bh2 B×c5 25. d×c5 Ra4 26. Nc3** (see diagram)

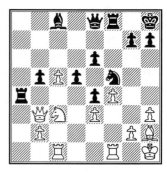

After 26. Nc3

**26. ... Ba6** "Black is almost compelled to lose the exchange for a pawn, but this ingenious move equalizes things very nicely. 26. ... N×e3 would also lead to some interesting play, as he could then proceed with 27. ... N×f1 and 28. ... N×h2 in certain events"—Pierce. 26. ... N×e3 27. Rfe1 N×g2! 28. K×g2 Rd4! is a very strong piece sacrifice. Black's rook is activated in highly original fashion as is shown by a few sample lines. First of all, after 29. Re2? Qh5! Black's attack is already decisive. More critical is 29. N×b5, when Black has but a pawn for the knight, but his threats to the king are nevertheless very real—for instance, 29. ... Rd3! 30. Rc3 Rd2† 31. Kg1! (31. Kh1?! d4 becomes dangerous for White) 31. ... e5! All gates are opened now. It is only with drastic measures that White can withstand the assault: 32. Nd6 Qh5 33. N×c8 d4 34. Nd6 (34. Rg3 e×f4 is certainly not what he wants) 34. ... d×c3 35. Q×c3 Rd3 36. Q×e5 Q×h3 37. N×e4 Qg4† 38. Kh1 Qf3† with a perpetual. **27. N×a4** 27. Rfe1 is preferable. **27. ... b×a4 28. Qc3 B×f1 29. R×f1 e5** "One of Mr. Bird's surprises. As 30. ... d4 is threatened, this compels White to exchange rook for knight; but it is not really good for Black. His knight is strong at f5, and the bishop is badly situated except for defense. The passed pawn, too, is an important element"—Pierce. The slower 29. ... Qc6 30. Ra1 Rc8 gives Black nice chances in the endgame. Bad is now 31. g4? d4! **30. f×e5 Ng3† 31. B×g3 R×f1† 32. Kh2 Rf8 33. c6 Qe6 34. Qc5 Rc8 35. Qd6?** "A miscalculation. The obvious move of 35. c7 was better, as it could be supported by the bishop later"—Pierce. 35. c7 Qd7 36. e6 Q×e6 37. Qb5 Ra8 38. Qb7 Rc8 39. Qb5 is a forced draw. **35. ... R×c6 36. Qd8† Qg8 37. Qd7 Rg6** 37. ... Ra6 is definitely superior. **38. Q×a4 h6 39. Be1 Kh7 40. Bc3 Qf7 41. Qc2 Qf5** Why not 41. ... Qf1? **42. Qe2 Qg5 43. Qf2 Rc6 44. Bd4 h5?** This move allows the dangerous advance of the b-pawn. At the same time Bird weakens his king's resources and minimizes his winning chances. 44. ... Qe7 is a reasonable try to win the game. **45. b4! h4 46. b5 Rc4 47. b6 Rc8 48. e6 Rb8?** It goes from bad to worse for Bird. He could draw with 48. ... Rc1 49. e7 Q×e7 50. Qf5† Kg8 51. Q×d5† Kh7 52. Qh5†. **49. Bc5?** 49. g4! cannot be met decently; e.g., 49. ... Qe7 50. Qf7 Rb7 51. Q×e7 R×e7 52. Bc5 wins. **49. ... Re8?** 49. ... Qe5† 50. Kg1 Qa1† is a simple draw. Bird ventures everything to win. **50. e7** 50. Bd6, preparing the promotion of the b-pawn guarantees the win. The text move makes his task more complicated. **50. ... d4 51. e×d4 e3 52. Qf3 R×e7 53. B×e7 Q×e7** draw. "The ending is of the highest interest, and was watched by one of the largest galleries of the tournament. At first sight it appears an easy draw. Closer examination will show that White wins at once by 54. b7. Players get tired after four hours under exciting conditions. The most preferable continuation would be 54. ... Qc7† 55. Kg1 Qc1† 56. Qf1 Qc7 57. Qf5† Kh6 (or 57. ... g6) 58. Qc8 and there is no reply. If Black plays 54. ... e2 55. Qh5† Kg8 56. b8Q†"—Pierce. *Pictorial World* (Pierce), 16 October 1890.

## (1033) Bird–van Vliet   1–0
B.C.A. Congress (round 17)
Manchester, 5 September 1890
*Game score missing*

## (1034) von Scheve–Bird   1–0
B.C.A. Congress (round 18)
Manchester, 6 September 1890
*Game score missing*

## (1035) Bird–Müller   1–0
B.C.A. Congress (round 19)
Manchester, 6 September 1890
*Game score missing*

# TO HOLLAND 1890

Bird left Manchester in a reasonable physical condition. Two weeks later he surprised the Dutchmen by suddenly arriving in Amsterdam. Even though no worthy reception could be set up, the Amsterdam chess society did their best to meet the master adequately. Bird took his headquarters in one of the rooms of the coffee house

De Roode Leeuw, and here he engaged in offhand and consultation chess. Among his opponents were some of the best Dutch players, such as Jan Diederik Tresling, Dirk van Foreest, Hendrik Meijer and others. Bird tried to puzzle them by reinstating the extravagant playing style that he had employed to destruct the opposition at the Dutch Chess Congress in Gouda ten years ago, but his pet opening lines brought him mediocre success at best. Bird gave at least one simultaneous exhibition, on 20 September. In two and a half hours he disposed of nine opponents, two of whom secured a draw. The large number of visitors was deeply impressed by the action.[42]

## (1036) Bird–van Foreest   ½–½
Offhand game
Amsterdam 1890

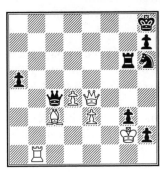

*White to move*

**1. Qe5† Rg7 2. Rb8†?** 2. d5 forces Black to give a perpetual with 2. ... Qe2†. **2. ... Ng8 3. R×g8† Q×g8 4. d5 Qf8 5. Q×g3 h1Q†?** 5. ... Kg8! is the winning move. **6. K×h1 Qf1† 7. Kh2 Qe2†** draw. "Here Bird offered a draw, which was accepted by Black. Unjustly because Black wins easily after 8. Kh3 Qh5† 9. Kg2 Q×d5† 10. Kh2 Qa2† 11. Kh3 Qe6† 12. Kh2 Qh6† 13. Qh3 Qd6† and Black wins after 14. ... Qd1† and 15. ... Qg1 mate"—Loman. 10. Kf2! is a decisive amelioration after which Black must be happy with a draw after all—*De Groene Amsterdammer* (Loman), 29 November 1891.

## (1037) Bird–Tresling   0–1
Offhand game
Amsterdam, 18 September 1890
C00

**1. e4 e6 2. Bb5 a6 3. Ba4 b5 4. Bb3 Bb7 5. Qe2 c5 6. c3 c4 7. Bc2 Bc5 8. Nh3 Ne7 9. 0–0 d5 10. a4 Nbc6 11. d4 Bb6 12. e5 b4 13. Nd2 b3 14. Bb1 g6 15. Nf3 h6 16. Kh1 Qd7 17. Be3 0–0–0 18. Qd2 g5 19. Ne1 Rdg8 20. f3 Nf5 21. Bg1 Bd8 22. Nf2 h5 23. Nd1 h4 24. B×f5 e×f5 25. Ne3 Ne7 26. h3 f4 27. Ng4 Nf5 28. Bf2 Ng3† 29. B×g3 h×g3 30. a5 Kb8 31. Nc2 b×c2 32. Q×c2 Be7 33. b3 Ka8 34. Rfb1 Rb8 35. b×c4 d×c4 36. Rb6 Qd5 37. Qe2 Bc8 38. R×b8† K×b8 39. Rb1† Ka7 40. Qb2 Qb5 41. Qa2 Qd5 42. Qb2 Bb7 43. Qb6† Ka8 44. Nf6 B×f6 45. Q×f6 R×h3† 46. Kg1 Rh2 47. Q×g5 R×g2† 48. Kh1** Black mates in four moves—*De Groene Amsterdammer*, 28 September 1890.

42. Once back in England Bird spoke happily of the reception he was given by the Dutchmen: "Mr. Bird is very pleased with his hosts, who gave him an enthusiastic reception, and treat him in princely style. The G.O.M. now distinctly may 'call him a Dutchman' and he will regard the epithet highly complimentary." *Birmingham Weekly Mercury*, 27 September 1890.

**(1038) Bird–van Foreest & Tresling 0–1**
Consultation game
Amsterdam, 20 September 1890
*C00*

One assumes Bird's opponent in this game was Dirk van Foreest, as he certainly played Bird during his visit in Amsterdam, and not his brother Arnold.

**1. e4 e6 2. Bb5 a6 3. Ba4 b5 4. Bb3 Bb7 5. d3 c5 6. Nd2 Bd6 7. Nh3 Ne7 8. c3 Nbc6 9. 0–0 Bc7 10. Qh5 Ne5 11. d4 c×d4 12. c×d4 Nd3 13. Qe2 N×c1 14. Ra×c1 0–0 15. e5 f5 16. Nf4 Ng6 17. Nd3 Bb6 18. Nc5 B×c5 19. d×c5 Nf4 20. Qe3 Qg5** White resigns—*De Groene Amsterdammer*, 28 September 1890.

**(1039) Bird–Pilger 1–0**
Simultaneous game
Amsterdam, September 1890
*C21*

**1. e4 e5 2. d4 e×d4 3. Nf3 c5 4. Bc4 d6 5. c3 Nc6 6. c×d4 c×d4 7. 0–0 Bg4 8. Qb3 Qd7 9. Ng5 Nh6 10. f4 Na5 11. Qd3 N×c4 12. Q×c4 f6 13. Nf3 B×f3 14. R×f3?!** 14. g×f3 is necessary in order to eliminate the pawn at d4 as soon as possible. **14. ... Rc8 15. Qf1 Be7** The crafty 15. ... d5! 16. e×d5 Bc5 completely frees his game. **16. Nd2 Bd8 17. Kh1 Ng4 18. Nb3 Bb6 19. h3 h5 20. Bd2 a6 21. Rc1** After some slow moves of his opponent Bird misses another opportunity to eliminate the troublesome pawn with 20. Rd3. **21. ... R×c1 22. N×c1 Qc6 23. Qd3 Kd7 24. Rf1 Ne3 25. B×e3 d×e3 26. Ne2?** 26. e5 puts the board on fire. The text move on the other hand could have brought White into a lost ending after 26. ... Qb5! 27. Q×b5 a×b5 28. Nc3 Re8 29. g3 Ba5. **26. ... Re8? 27. e5 f×e5 28. Qf5† Re6 29. f×e5 d×e5 30. Rc1 Qd6 31. Qf3** 31. Qe4 or 31. Q×h5 prevents Black's from taking the initiative with his next move. **31. ... e4 32. Q×h5 Bc7 33. g3 Qf8** It would have been wise to leave the zone of fire with 33. ... Kc8. **34. Nd4** 34. Qd5† finally wins back the pawn. **34. ... Rf6 35. Qg4† Kd8 36. Qe2** Too passive. 36. Kg1 is reasonable. **36. ... B×g3?** First 36. ... Qd6 secures the position of his king. After 37. Q×e3 Q×g3 38. Q×g3 B×g3 Black has excellent winning chances. **37. Qc4 Rc6?** Pilger panics completely in face of Bird's heavy artillery. He was close to a draw if his king would have fled towards the kingside: 37. ... Ke7 38. Qb4† Kf7 39. Qc4† Kg6 40. Rg1 Kh7 41. R×g3 Rf1† 42. Rg1 R×g1† 43. K×g1 Qf2†. **38. N×c6† b×c6 39. Q×e4 Qf2 40. Rd1† Kc7 41. Qe7† Kb6 42. Qb4† Kc7 43. Qa5†** Black resigns—*De Groene Amsterdammer*, 28 September 1890.

## Handicap Tournament at Simpson's Divan, October–December 1890

The task of managing the sixth handicap tournament at Simpson's Divan fell to O.C. Müller. The conditions as well as the participants list were very similar to the previous ones. One entry that drew some attention was that of Skipworth, but not surprisingly that gentleman failed to turn up at the beginning of the tournament. After the first two weeks of play all candidates for the first prize had already dropped some important points. The better placed players were Müller (8 points in 11 games), Bird (6½ in 9) and William John Evans (4 out of 5). But before the real fight for a high prize began, Bird, already tormented by gout

**Handicap tournament, London, 13 October–5 December 1890**

***Site:*** Simpson's Divan
***Prizes:*** Five prizes
***Time limit:*** 20 moves per hour
***Odds scale:*** pawn and move (class II), pawn and 2 moves (class III) and knight
***Notes:*** The game between Mortimer and Evans was not played and adjudicated as a draw

| | | | 1 | 2 | 3 | 4 | 5 | 6 | 7 | 8 | 9 | 10 | 11 | 12 | 13 | 14 | 15 | 16 | 17 | 18 | 19 | |
|---|---|---|---|---|---|---|---|---|---|---|---|---|---|---|---|---|---|---|---|---|---|---|
| 1 | O.C. Müller | I | | 1 | 1 | ½ | ½ | ½ | 1 | 1 | + | 1 | 1 | 1 | 0 | ½ | 1 | 0 | 1 | 1 | 1 | 14 |
| 2 | F.J. Lee | I | 0 | | 1 | 0 | 0 | 1 | 1 | 1 | + | 1 | 1 | 1 | 1 | 1 | 1 | 1 | 1 | 1 | 0 | 14 |
| 3 | G.H.D. Gossip | I | 0 | 0 | | 0 | 1 | 0 | 0 | 0 | + | 1 | 1 | 1 | 1 | 1 | 1 | 1 | 1 | 1 | 1 | 12 |
| 4 | A.J. Curnock | II | ½ | 1 | 1 | | 1 | 0 | 0 | 0 | 0 | 0 | 1 | 0 | 1 | 1 | 1 | 1 | 1 | 1 | 1 | 11½ |
| 5 | J. Mortimer | I | ½ | 1 | 0 | 0 | | 1 | ½ | 1 | + | 1 | 1 | 1 | ½ | 0 | 0 | 1 | – | 1 | 0 | 10½ |
| 6 | L. van Vliet | I | ½ | 0 | 1 | 1 | 0 | | 1 | ½ | + | 0 | 1 | 0 | 0 | ½ | 1 | 1 | 1 | 1 | 0 | 10½ |
| 7 | N. Jasnogrodsky | I | 0 | 0 | 1 | 1 | ½ | 0 | | 0 | 1 | 1 | 1 | ½ | ½ | ½ | 1 | 1 | ½ | ½ | 0 | 10 |
| 8 | J.E. Hetley | III | 0 | 0 | 1 | 1 | 0 | ½ | 1 | | ½ | 1 | 0 | ½ | + | 1 | 0 | ½ | | 0 | 1 | 9 |
| 9 | H.E. Bird | I | – | – | – | 1 | – | – | 0 | ½ | | 1 | 0 | – | + | 1 | – | 1 | – | 1 | 1 | 7½ |
| 10 | T.C. Gibbons | I | 0 | 0 | 0 | 1 | 0 | 1 | 0 | 0 | 0 | | 0 | 1 | 1 | 0 | 1 | 1 | 1 | | ½ | 7½ |
| 11 | E. Atfield | IV | 0 | 0 | 0 | 0 | 0 | 0 | 0 | 1 | 1 | 1 | | 1 | 0 | 0 | 1 | 1 | ½ | | 1 | 7½ |
| 12 | F.B. Osborn | III | 0 | 0 | 0 | 1 | 0 | 1 | ½ | ½ | + | 0 | 0 | | + | 1 | | 0 | | | 1 | 7 |
| 13 | W.J. Evans | I | 1 | 0 | 0 | 0 | ½ | 1 | ½ | – | – | 0 | 1 | – | | 1 | 1 | – | – | – | 1 | 7 |
| 14 | Rolland | I | ½ | 0 | 0 | 0 | 1 | ½ | ½ | 0 | 0 | 1 | 1 | 0 | 0 | | 0 | 0 | ½ | 0 | 1 | 6 |
| 15 | J.E. Maitland | IV | 0 | 0 | 0 | 0 | 1 | 0 | 0 | 1 | + | 0 | 0 | * | 0 | 1 | | 1 | ½ | | | 5½ |
| 16 | G.C. Frühling | IV | 1 | 0 | 0 | 0 | 0 | 0 | 0 | ½ | 0 | 0 | 0 | 1 | + | 1 | 0 | | 1 | 0 | | 5½ |
| 17 | A. Clayton | I | 0 | 0 | 0 | 0 | + | 0 | ½ | | + | 0 | ½ | | + | ½ | ½ | 0 | | | | 5 |
| 18 | E.N.R. Harvey | III | 0 | 0 | 0 | 0 | 0 | 0 | ½ | 1 | 0 | | | | + | 1 | | 1 | | | | 4½ |
| 19 | W. Ward | III | 0 | 1 | 0 | 0 | 1 | 1 | 1 | 0 | 0 | ½ | 0 | 0 | 0 | 0 | | | | | | 4½ |

for some months, suffered a violent attack directly after a tournament game.[43]

Bird's condition improved somewhat during his stay in the hospital but he was facing a long recovery and therefore had to forfeit the tournament. The tournament was further decimated by the forfeit of another candidate with prospects of winning it, Evans.

The tournament ended in the beginning of December with a joint victory of Lee and Müller, ahead of Gossip. One player who deserves a special mention was the young Frenchman Rolland. He progressed in merely two years from the fifth into the first class and now had ambitions of living as a professional chess player. Rolland's full name remains an enigma. Most often he is found mentioned as M. Rolland (in all likelihood the abbreviation of Monsieur), but he's also called L., A.J.B. and J.B. Rolland on various other occasions.

With this tournament the unbroken string of Divan handicap tournaments that started in 1888 came to an end. It is probable that Bird's serious illness undermined the organization of another handicap but there brewed also some dissatisfaction among the players. In any case, Hoffer jumped on the occasion to heavily criticize the management. In his report on the tournament in *Chess Monthly* of January 1891 (p. 132), he suggested that leaving the management in the hands of a professional player, in this case Müller, was a mistake.

## (1040) Jasnogrodsky–Bird    1–0

Handicap tournament
London, October 1890
*A90*

1. d4 f5 2. g3 Nf6 3. Bg2 e6 4. c4 Bb4† 5. Bd2 Qe7 6. Nc3 0–0 7. Nf3 c6 8. 0–0 d6 9. a3 B×c3 10. B×c3 Nbd7 11. e3 Ne4 12. Qc2 Ndf6 13. Nd2 Ng5 14. f3 e5 15. f4 Nf7 16. e4 e×d4 17. B×d4 c5 18. Bc3 f×e4 19. N×e4 Ne8 20. Rae1 Bf5 21. Qe2 Qd7 22. Qd2 Rc8 23. Nf2 b5 24. c×b5 Q×b5 25. Re7 Nc7 26. Rfe1 Qb3 27. g4 d5 28. R×c7 R×c7 29. B×d5 Qb6 30. g×f5 Kh8 31. Ba5 Qd6 32. B×c7 Q×c7 33. B×f7 Q×f7 34. Qc2 c4 35. Qe4 h6 36. Qe6 Qh5 37. Qg6 Q×f5 38. Q×f5 R×f5 and after a few more moves Black resigns—*New York Herald (London edition)*, 26 October 1890.

## FALLING ILL

The attack of gout that hit Bird was exacerbated by bronchitis and made one fear for his life. After a stay of three months at St.

Thomas's Hospital he was dismissed to recover at home. Though there seemed a great chance that Bird would remain an invalid,[44] he did not allow his misfortune to lower his spirits.[45]

On 5 April 1891 the census was taken. As can be expected Bird's presence was recorded at his home in 5 Heygate Street. He lived here in the company of Cecelia Webb, the head of the household. She was a 63-year-old widow who lived on her own means. The second lodger was Susan J. Mellors.

Bird stated accountant and journalist when asked for his occupation.[46]

When a new tournament at the Divan was anticipated in June 1891, Bird's condition did not seem good enough yet to consider participating. Great was the surprise when the veteran suddenly reappeared at the Divan. His arrival was saluted with a great enthusiasm.

Last week I met Mr. Bird at Simpson's Divan, and was pleased to find him looking very well; indeed, wonderfully well, considering that he has now been suffering for more than six months from a painful and exhausting illness. True, he is only able to limp about, but his complexion is clear, and his countenance has assumed quite a spiritualized expression. He told me he had found his principal occupation and enjoyment during his illness in studying the Bible from a certain standpoint. "I took up the study," said he, "as an amusement and soon found in it exquisite enjoyment." Addressing several who gathered about us, he discussed the subject with his usual clearness and enthusiasm; and told us he had embodied his ideas and arguments in a work that would contain about 300 pages small octavo.

The veteran was as lively and good-humored as ever. He then gave an exhibition of his chess skill, reviving in undiminished beauty the glories of his best days. The Divan was very full on the occasion, and I noticed with much pleasure how every visitor when he entered the room marched straight up to Bird and warmly congratulated him upon the recovery. I myself felt ten years younger as I gazed at the heroic veteran. Long life to him! More study and more honors! [*Illustrated Sporting and Dramatic News*, 13 June 1891].

Bird definitively had more strings in his bow than just a book dealing with the Bible. His booklet *Steinitz & Lasker Match with Comments, Review and Original Notes*, issued in 1894 and dealing with the world championship match, pointed at various other works.

Bird was able to use his accountancy capacities in a series called "Condensations to be published in cheap form." A first title was *Bible Essence*. The promotional text reveals the statistic nature of the work: Deduced from an analysis of the 23,648 verses in the Old and 7957 verses in the New Testament, including the 2045 verses of prophecies, 368 Messianic, and 119 of promises to David and Soloman, the 17 Gentile verses, and 220 verses of the most significant and consolatory character [*Steinitz and Lasker Match*

---

43. Rudolf Loman was one of the witnesses of the scene: "Many will hear with regret that Mr. Bird is dangerously ill. Saturday 25 October, after having finished a tournament game with great difficulty, Bird was struck by a serious attack of rheumatism at Simpson's Divan and had to be transferred to St. Thomas's Hospital in a cab. His condition has worsened a lot since then and there is but little hope of recovery." *Groene Amsterdammer*, 9 November 1890.

44. The chess community tried to comfort Bird's needs by raising a subscription: "For two months his recovery was doubtful. Thanks to the special care taken by the medical staff, he has so far recovered that he was able to leave the hospital; but it is feared that he will remain a confirmed invalid. The latest information we have is that a week ago 'he attempted to walk from chair to chair, and this was the first day he could stand upright.' Mr. Bird is endowed with indomitable courage and exceptional recuperative powers, and he may be able in time, and with care, to rely upon his own resources. It is no secret that the veteran chess player has no private means to fall back upon, and whilst he is convalescent his position is a precarious one. We have laid his case before Mr. James Innes Minchin, hon. sec. of the St. George's Chess Club, and he has kindly undertaken to start a subscription at the St. George's, whilst we have taken a similar step at the British Chess Club." *Chess Monthly*, February 1891, p. 166.

45. MacDonnell was deeply impressed with Bird's ability to cope with the situation: "Truly the energy of the man is even more remarkable than his ability, which is saying a good deal. Enfeebled by prolonged sickness, crippled by gout, confined for months to bed, with scarcely a friend to cheer or solace him, he yet works on with all the enthusiasm of youth at his chess works, and even ventures into fresh woods and pastures new, where I trust he will find much enjoyment and reap a rich harvest. The subscription to Mr. Bird's testimonial now amounts to £45, and I trust before the end of April it will be augmented to £100." *Illustrated Sporting and Dramatic News*, 28 March 1891.

46. 1891 census: Class: *RG12*; Piece: *367*; Folio: 68; Page: 1.

*with comments...*]. More interesting was *Vocabularies from Existing Dictionaries*. One does not gain much understanding of the purpose of this booklet from Bird's explanatory text, where he stated that it was "deduced from existing dictionaries from a classification of 60,000 words in the English, French and German. Bird's inability

in both foreign languages was clearly no obstacle. Bird also advertised another work of his, *Great Men of the World*. He finished the advertisement page by pointing the reader's attention to his service of preparing "statistics, balance sheets and accounts expeditiously and most economically."

# ◆ Part XI ◆

# The Grand Old Man, 1891–1895

## Introduction

Bird required the first four months of 1891 to complete his recovery at home. His return to the Divan occurred in May and came somewhat as a surprise. Everybody was pleased to see the old man back in such good form, even though his illness had left a decided mark on him.[1] Bird must have been glad to witness how buzzing chess was at his favorite place. He was just in time to join his colleagues in an even tournament that was bound to take place. The field consisted of a mix of habitués of the Divan, such as Lee and Müller, and some new faces wagering their chance: Tinsley, Fenton and Nikolai Jasnogrodsky. These three were still mainly tied to the chess community of Purssell's. Purssell's, however, definitively closed its doors a few month later. They made the transfer to the Divan, which thus became more than ever the beating heart of London chess.

> Simpson's is about the only place in London where there is any play worthy of the name to be seen just now. Mr. Blackburne is a daily visitor, and, besides playing occasional games with amateurs, he fills in his leisure time by composing a three-move problem. Mr. H.E. Bird, always a host in himself is never absent except when he has an attack of his old enemy the gout. The distinguished veteran is engaged in play during most of the day and evening, but when, perchance he has an hour to spare, he may be seen compiling sheet upon sheet of manuscript. What the nature of the great work is which Mr. Bird has in hand is only known to those who are strictly in his confidence [*Newcastle Courant*, 30 September 1893].

The chess professionals residing at the Divan were bound to deliver a tough struggle for clients. Bird, on account of his weighty historical status, enjoyed more privileges than his colleagues. Thanks

to the steady and central spot he occupied in the room he easily drew the attention from any potential visitor.[2]

Playing for stakes had become a *conditio sine qua non* for Bird. It was part of the ritual and an essential contribution to his means of living. Shipley, a visitor to the Divan in the summer of 1887, elucidated the practical proceedings in his obituary of Bird.

> We first had the pleasure of meeting the great English player at Simpson's Divan in London, in the summer of 1887 and contested a large number of games with him. The total result of several days rapid skittle play being about 2–1 in favor of the veteran.
>
> We vividly recall the summer evenings spent at the Divan and can still see the pleasure it gave the Englishman at the end of the evening's play to deduct from the pile of matches on his side a number equal to the matches on our side of the board and inform us that we owed him so many "bobs." During the play, as each player scored a game, he would take a match out of the box and lay it on his side of the board. Frequently as a result of three hours play there would be as many as 15 or 16 matches on the table, and the majority with the exception of one evening was always in favor of the veteran [*Philadelphia Inquirer*, 17 May 1908].

More fascinating details about the proceedings at the Divan and Bird's role were given by the chess amateur Thomas E. Haydon.

> The recognized stake when playing with one of the professionals was 1s. They would give such odds as would enable you to make a game of it, and you were entitled to deduct wins (if any) from losses. Or, if you went in with a friend you could each have a professional to assist you in a consultation game, the losing amateur paying 2s. 6d. to the winning professional.
>
> These consultation games were certainly the best for improving one's play, since the professional partner would suggest, and give reasons for, the move that he thought the best, and would thus reveal to his amateur partner something of the depth and beauty of the game which, unaided, he would never have seen.
>
> There were a number of tables in the room. On the left as you entered was

---

1. Cunningham reported that "He has lost a great deal of flesh and walks with great difficulty; otherwise he is in fair health and in the best of spirits." *International Chess Magazine*, July 1891, p. 193.

2. "Of all the masters I have known none was more interesting than H.E. Bird, who in his character of veteran was for many years accorded the best commercial position in the historic room known to chess players over the whole world as Simpson's Divan. He usually sat at a table by the end window which faced you as you entered the room. A convenient window looking on the Strand which Bird called his back garden; one of his innumerable witticisms. Bird could be bitter, but he had a sense of the humorous, and loved to repeat a joke." *Chess Amateur*, June 1913, p. 270.

Four prominent chess amateurs. Left to right, from top: Joseph Henry Blake, Anthony Guest, Daniel Yarton Mills, Herbert Jacobs (all four images courtesy London Borough Hackney Archives).

Mr. Bird's table, which was always of great interest to onlookers. In 1892 he was an old man, crippled and bent with rheumatism. As he played he would manoeuvre his lower set of false teeth in a most alarming fashion, what time he carried on a wordy warfare with his opponent. With a constantly replenished glass of whisky and water (for which his opponent paid as a matter of course), he played a remarkably rapid and brilliant game. I have seen him in the short space of an hour take as many as ten games off a City gentleman who rather fancied himself.

On one occasion the old gentleman had a serious downfall. I persuaded my friend Mr. Herbert Jacobs, who at lightning chess had few equals and no superior, to dine with me at Simpson's and play Mr. Bird afterwards. In an evening filled with sparkling chess, the old warrior was heavily defeated, and became vociferously indignant, to the great amusement of everybody. He was a great character, and sadly missed.

I often saw Mr. Bonar Law playing with Mr. Bird. On those occasions Mr. Bird was unusually quiet and deliberate. I imagine that he had to give of his best in order to make sure of a winning balance [*Singapore Free Press and Mercantile Advertiser*, 16 February 1927].

Descriptions of Bird himself often have this nostalgic touch, but some other visitors carry more negative experiences. J.L. Garner, a chess tourist from Milwaukee who played some games at the Divan while touring through Europe, painted a miserable picture of the present masters.

As a rule, the chess professionals in London and Paris are a dilapidated lot of tramps, with cot sleeves out at elbows, toes projecting from their boots, hats badly caved in and a ghoulish eagerness to fasten upon some wandering amateur, and bleed him at the rate of a shilling a game [*Yenowine's News*, 13 October 1889].[3]

In 1893 Bird prophesied the extermination of the British professional chess player. He proclaimed that the lack of patronage, a habit still relatively prominent when Steinitz lived in London, had become a major problem. Bird himself was quite fortunate in this field. Many of his hours were taken by clients and he was backed by several patrons. For the first part of the 1890s, two names stand out as Bird's benefactors. Horace Chapman, already mentioned above, had a knack for arranging to have Bird on his team when it came to playing consultation games. They encountered various teams of professional players and scored excellently against them.

Even more intense was the relationship Bird had with William John Evelyn. Evelyn descended from a wealthy family and made a name of his own as a member of the House of Commons. Evelyn had been a member of the St. George's Chess Club for decades, but none of his chess feats gained much attention. He greatly admired Bird and they often teamed up in consultation games. Bird and Evelyn also immersed themselves in opening analysis. In *Chess Novelties* Bird attributed many innovations in his favorite lines to his friend.

Bird maintained his regime of playing for stakes when he visited the provinces. In a few letters written to Rosario Aspa in the preamble of his visit to Leamington Spa in August 1892, Bird hinted how the local chess club could attract many spectators by suggesting that "a press notice in advance perhaps would attract visitors as my fast and original style seems as popular as ever." He also informed Aspa that he wished to play skittles games at the usual rate of a shilling per game.[4]

From the point of view of many nineteenth century chess players

**William John Evelyn.**

there nevertheless remained an important difference that distinguished Bird from the cliché of the "professional chess player." Players from the latter category wished to get a financial compensation before they would undertake a visit to a chess club or give an exhibition. Blackburne, for example, received about £2 or £3 for a simultaneous exhibition in England. After the American congress of 1889, Blackburne, Gunsberg and Weiss all visited Philadelphia. Each of these masters was lured with a fee of $75. In the *Philadelphia Times* of 28 July 1889, Reichhelm explained that Bird's approach was completely different. Bird arrived without formal invitation, and thus had no right for a financial reward. But the enthusiasm that he generated among his opponents made it that "the financial result of his visit was quite as large as that of any of the other masters. Every one played rapidly with him, so as to make his stay both profitable and pleasant."

Bird's touring through the provinces diminished gradually during the last decade of his active chess career. He needed 1891 to recover fully from his illness (as MacDonnell noted, he still looked frail at the end of the year). The ensuing year saw him travel nearly incessantly—including three visits to Newcastle. But from 1893 on there were no larger tours anymore. Bird's annual visit to the Hastings festival, from 1894 to 1898, formed the main part of his chess playing outside of London.

Bird's number of admirers increased year by year. Many amateurs appreciated his lively chess style that was so different from the positional school of chess as propagated by Steinitz and followed by nearly every chess master. Bird was also considered, not unjustly, to be the last link with the long-gone days of Staunton and Morphy. Bird's advancing age also gained him a lot of respect. His obvious infirmities failed to lower his spirits and the image of a tormented man struggling with stairs to reach the battlefield made him emerge

---

3. Especially Lee was targeted by Garner for knocking shillings out of his pocket.

4. Letter from Bird to Aspa, undated. *Autographs of Noted Chess and Checker Players*, vol. 1 A–G, f. 79b.

even more as a chess hero. The combination of all these elements resulted in a new and rather affectionate epithet which rapidly gained a great following in the press. According to MacDonnell, the title "Grand Old Man" was unanimously accorded to Bird at a meeting held in July 1890.[5] This nickname really caught on, also by the extensive use of it in especially the columns of MacDonnell and Buckley (of the *Birmingham Weekly Mercury*). The same epithet was used a few years earlier to honor William Ewart Gladstone, then prime minister of the United Kingdom.

The struggle for British chess hegemony slowed during the last decade of the nineteenth century. Slowly but surely Gunsberg had reached the top spot among the London-based chess masters. In 1889 he confirmed his high rank with a third place at the tournament in New York. Later that year he was invited to contest a match with Chigorin. As Gunsberg wrote in his column in the *Evening News and Post* of 28 September 1889, "this match may prove the stepping stone to an encounter with Steinitz, and be the means of bringing back to England the chess championship of the world." The duel between Gunsberg and Chigorin took place in January and February 1890 and ended in a tie. Thus Gunsberg kept his chances for a world championship match with Steinitz intact. From now on Gunsberg carefully avoided each obstacle to achieve his aim. When a match challenge by Mason was refused the tensions that were so imminent in England came to the surface (see the Part X chapter on Manchester 1890).

Gunsberg's match with Steinitz effectively came off in December 1890. The world champion kept matters under control and prolonged his title. This was actually the last major feat of Gunsberg's career. Upon his return he was confronted with serious problems. The death of his wife had left him with three young children to care for. Living as a chess professional became thus problematic and Gunsberg had to give his priority to journalistic and organizing work.[6] As a consequence his former chess strength crumbled away at a fearful speed.

Blackburne had scored a decent second place at Manchester but his results in the following years were more unstable. Just like Mason, his zenith was past.

Burn can be called an exception as his greatest triumph was still years ahead of him, but between 1889 and 1895 he refrained from playing chess at an international level and was therefore not a factor of importance. Bird was still eager to play chess, but it became very hard for him to get access to the class of tournaments to which he automatically belonged in former days.

The major problem for British chess was the absolute lack of new, young and talented players. That such talent arose in other parts of the world became clear when Lasker wiped away the whole British chess contingent in 1892. The cramped way in which Lasker's success was dealt with exemplifies the local frustration. With the demise of the B.C.A., a lethargy set in until 1895 when the Hastings chess club blew new life in the practice of the game.

Bird was essentially barred from playing outside England: almost no one on the Continent thought he was strong enough for a top tournament anymore. Yet his results on British soil were still spectacular from time to time. He won the 1889 congress of the B.C.A. and brilliant play in Manchester brought him third place there. In Hastings (1895) he made by far the best start of all the British participants. It lasted until the second half of the tournament before a mixture of strong opposition and exhaustion took its toll. The attention and support of the public motivated him to shine on these occasions, while his playing style also strikes the modern observer as much more pragmatic than ever before. This translated itself into a relatively high number of draws.

Bird's playing strength nevertheless slowly declined. Upon the return from his sickbed he encountered players belonging to a lower class than him at the Divan tournaments of 1891. He clearly experienced problems to distance himself from them. His results at a handful of tournaments played in 1892 and 1893 were rather mixed. He managed to hold up in the B.C.A. congress of 1892, but in an encounter with only top players (Quintangular, 1892) it was hardly a surprise that his uncompromising playing style made him finish alone at the last spot with a meager 1 out of 8. Later that year Bird was trashed by Lasker 5–0, even though he offered decent resistance. His good form was confirmed at Belfast, which could have been one of Bird's major career triumphs, for his playing level was cracking. Six months later he ended desperately last in the event supported by the *Black and White* newspaper.

---

## CHESS: A MANUAL FOR BEGINNERS

Bird's return to the chess front was accompanied by the release of a new chess book, titled *Chess: A Manual for Beginners*. As usual Bird and his publishers, Dean and Son, took care of keeping the price low. Hoffer gave an adequate summary of the work:

As the title indicates, this is an elementary treatise, which comprises all that is required for the student who is desirous to become acquainted with the rudiments of the game. Mr. Bird has added a valuable portion in an appendix, which will prove interesting to chess players of all degrees of strength, as it is in part a criticism of Mr. Steinitz's "*Modern Chess Instructor*." The eighteen pages of the appendix alone are worth the shilling, which is the price of this little book [*Chess Monthly*, June 1891, p. 324].

---

## SIMPSON'S DIVAN TOURNAMENT, JUNE–JULY 1891

The string of handicap tournaments that livened up the Divan since 1888 had come to an end with Bird's illness. When the summer months of 1891 were approaching, plans were made for a small tournament, but now on even terms. The idea was received with enthusiasm and generosity, for £20 was collected from voluntary

---

5. MacDonnell candidly remarked that the club of Bath had conferred upon himself the epithet "G.A.M.," his initials, many years earlier. *Illustrated Sporting and Dramatic News*, 26 July 1890.

6. Harding, *Eminent Victorian Chess Players*, pp. 299–300. Buckley got almost lyrical when describing Gunsberg's success in the latter field: "Gunsberg is a capital man of business. While the London masters are discussing the affairs of the round world and all that therein is, Gunsberg is acting. ... The Divanians argue and vapor, and challenge and counter-challenge, with no result until Gunsberg comes on the scene. Then a match is arranged, the money is provided, a room is found.... Meanwhile Gunsberg is shoveling in the shekels." *Birmingham Weekly Mercury*, 8 August 1891.

subscriptions by the habitués of the Divan. As a result the participants were dismissed from paying the usual entrance fee. The tournament was set to begin on 15 June and a novel and strict scheme of two games per day, one in the afternoon and one in the evening, was adopted to maximize the interest of the public. All the pairings were determined in advance. With 10 participants, the tournament would last a little less than a month.

Among the 10 were all the minor chess professionals from London. They were joined by two amateurs, Mortimer and Loman. The latter was considered a rising star after his recent victories in the Dutch as well as in the City of London Chess Club Championship.

The prize fund was not rich enough to lure Blackburne, Gunsberg or Mason into battle. Bird was not the man to care too much for the financial rewards, but given his frail health it was thought unlikely that he would be recovered enough to defend his chances. Against all odds, however, he got much better in a short time and thus became the sole participant with international fame.[7]

Bird opened the tournament against two tough opponents. He drew with Müller and succeeded in beating Lee. His next two games demonstrated that Bird was still not fully recovered. Both Mortimer and Jasnogrodsky beat him. Bird was after four games well behind the amateurs Loman (4 points) and Mortimer (3).

The fifth round saw a crucial duel between Bird and Loman. An extremely tense fighting game mesmerized the many spectators. Both sides played far from perfect chess but in the end it appeared that Loman was coming out on top.[8] A dramatic 40th move by Loman completely reversed the outcome of the game and Bird scored the point a dozen moves later, thereby renewing the tension for the remainder of the tournament.

Bird continued in excellent style by winning his three following games against Tinsley, Gossip and Fenton. All these games were well-fought but his game with Gossip easily stood out. Bird did not miss his chance to lash out with a queen sacrifice that was not necessarily winning but clearly put the pressure on his opponent. In a difficult situation Gossip made the final mistake. While this game did not garner the brilliancy prize, Bird was rewarded with an extra prize of £1 1s. offered by Anton Hvistendahl.[9]

With one round to go Loman led the field with an excellent 7 points in 8 games, ahead of van Vliet (6 of 7 with one adjourned game left against Mortimer) and Bird (5½ of 8). Mortimer (4½ of 7) still had a small chance to wrestle the third prize out of Bird's hands.

7. Gunsberg wrote: "Last but not least we have to record the welcome intelligence of the participation in this tournament of Mr. Bird. One must admire the abounding vitality of the veteran player, who after experiencing eight months of severe illness, literally crawls up to Simpson's, as enthusiastic a chess player as ever, and showing by a cleverly won game from Lee and a hard-fought drawn game with Müller that his chess faculties are still in full and unimpaired vigour. Mr. Bird in the past has belonged to a higher class of chess players than any of his fellow competitors and while hoping for his success, we may say that the fact of his competing will, at all events, give great additional interest to the contest, and improve the standard of play." *Evening News and Post*, 20 June 1891.

8. According to Cunningham, Loman "played somewhat timidly, as if a little overweighted by the veteran's fame." *International Chess Magazine*, August 1891, p. 226.

9. The famous problem composer Edward Nathan Frankenstein offered a guinea to the winner of the most brilliant game. He selected Tinsley's against Lee. In a letter to Bird, Hvistendahl admitted that he did not think much of that game. He believed that Bird's win against Loman was entitled to win Frankenstein's prize. *Chess Monthly*, September 1891, p. 5.

## Divan tournament, London, 15 June–14 July 1891

*Site:* Simpson's Divan
*Playing hours:* 1 p.m.–5 and 6 p.m.–10
*Prizes:* Prize fund of ca. £20. Four prizes divided into respective fractions of 1st 9/24, 2nd 7/24, 3rd 5/24, 4th 3/24
*Time limit:* 20 moves per hour

| | | 1 | 2 | 3 | 4 | 5 | 6 | 7 | 8 | 9 | 10 | |
|---|---|---|---|---|---|---|---|---|---|---|---|---|
| 1 | R. Loman | | 1 | 0 | 1 | 1 | 1 | 1 | ½ | 1 | 1 | 7½ |
| 2 | L. van Vliet | 0 | | ½ | ½ | 1 | 1 | 1 | 1 | 1 | 1 | 7 |
| 3 | H.E. Bird | 1 | ½ | | 0 | 1 | ½ | 1 | 1 | 1 | 0 | 6 |
| 4 | J. Mortimer | 0 | ½ | 1 | | ½ | 0 | 1 | 1 | ½ | 1 | 5½ |
| 5 | G.H.D. Gossip | 0 | 0 | 0 | ½ | | 1 | ½ | 1 | ½ | 1 | 4½ |
| 6 | O.C. Müller | 0 | 0 | ½ | 1 | 0 | | 1 | ½ | ½ | ½ | 4 |
| 7 | R.H.F. Fenton | 0 | 0 | 0 | 0 | ½ | 0 | | ½ | 1 | 1 | 3 |
| 8 | S. Tinsley | ½ | 0 | 0 | 0 | 0 | ½ | ½ | | 1 | ½ | 3 |
| 9 | F.J. Lee | 0 | 0 | 0 | ½ | ½ | ½ | 0 | 0 | | 1 | 2½ |
| 10 | N. Jasnogrodsky | 0 | 0 | 1 | 0 | 0 | ½ | 0 | ½ | 0 | | 2 |

In his final game Bird tried his best to beat van Vliet with the Black pieces. Another tough fight ultimately ended in a draw. Bird thus finished with 6 out of 9. The tournament was convincingly won by Loman ahead of van Vliet. Given his status Bird could not be very pleased with but third prize, but the circumstances were clearly not in his favor. After the two early losses that eliminated him for a run for the top, he fought back in an excellent fashion.[10]

**(1041) Müller–Bird**	½–½
Divan tournament (round 1)
London, 15 June 1891
*Game score missing*

**(1042) Lee–Bird**	0–1
Divan tournament (round 2)
London, 17 June 1891
*A90*

**1. d4 f5 2. g3 Nf6 3. Bg2 e6 4. Nf3 d5 5. 0–0 Bd6 6. c4 c6 7. b3 0–0 8. e3 Bd7 9. Ba3** "Not good, as White loses time in the development of his knight. 9. Be2 was better"—Lee. **9. ... B×a3 10. N×a3 Be8 11. Nb1 Nbd7 12. Nbd2 Bh5 13. Qc2 Ne4 14. Rfc1 Qf6** Exchange his bad bishop is interesting. **15. a4 Qh6 16. Ne5 N×e5 17. d×e5 Ng5** A time-consuming maneuvre. 17. ... a5 stops White's initiative on the queenside and equalizes. **18. f4 Ne4 19. N×e4** More precise is first 19. c×d5 c×d5 and only then 20. N×e4 f×e4 (20. ... d×e4 21. Qc7 Rf7 22. Qd6 is worse for Black) and White gains access into Black's position with 21. Qc7. **19. ... f×e4** The right way to recapture is 19. ... d×e4, for the d-file belongs to Black. The text move keeps alive the prospects of a White queenside attack. **20. a5 a6 21. h3 g5** "This move appears at first sight somewhat risky, but it is nevertheless a strong attacking move as Black has his pieces well posted for a kingside attack"—Lee. **22. c×d5**

10. Bird's performance was judged very positively in the press. Buckley expressed himself once more as a fan: "Mr. Bird is playing chess as vigorously as ever, and, notwithstanding his advanced age and his chronic gout, he persists in the bold and imaginative style of play which usually characterizes ardent and enthusiastic beginners. In the recently concluded tourney at Simpson's Divan, the veteran has acquitted himself to the admiration of all. Will anyone be kind enough to tell us what will become of British chess when we no longer have Bird and Blackburne?" *Birmingham Weekly Mercury*, 1 August 1891.

George H.D. Gossip (right) and Francis J. Lee meeting each other in New York in 1893 (courtesy Cleveland Public Library).

c×d5 23. Qd2 g×f4 24. e×f4 "The lesser evil probably is that chosen by Mr. Lee, although it gives Black two passed pawns. 24. g×f4 would be too dangerous"—Hoffer. **24. ... Rf7 25. Qd4 Rg7 26. Rc3** "Had he first doubled his rooks and then opened the file, he might have been able to exchange one of the rooks, thus somewhat reducing Black's attacking forces"—Hoffer. **26. ... Rf8 27. Rac1 Be8 28. Kh2 Qg6** (see diagram) "Black fixes his opponent's rook now. Besides, he has his bishop in a better position, and makes room to advance the h-pawn"—Hoffer.

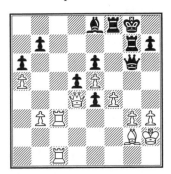

*After 28. ... Qg6*

**29. Rf1** This move makes no sense at all: it forsakes the possibility of forcing the exchange of a pair of rooks along the c-file and gives Bird the chance to activate his bishop with tempo. Instead 29. Qf2 comes into consideration. **29. ... h5 30. h4** "Forced, as the future advance of Black's h-pawn would be fatal to White. The text move

also opens a good square for the bishop at h3"—Lee. **30. ... Bb5 31. Rg1 Be2 32. Bh3 Bg4 33. Bg2 Kh7 34. b4 Kh6 35. Qe3 Bf5 36. Bh3 Kh7 37. B×f5 Q×f5 38. Rgc1 Rff7 39. R3c2 d4** "A very fine move. If 40. Q×d4 R×g3, with a winning attack"—Hoffer. This is based on a miscalculation as White can draw by force after 40. Q×d4 R×g3 41. K×g3 Q×f4† 42. Kh3! (this move was probably overlooked by both players and the commentator. After 42. Kg2? Black mates his opponent) 42. ... Qg4† 43. Kh2 Q×h4† 44. Kg1 Rg7† 45. Rg2. 39. ... Rd7 is correct, even though it is very difficult to crack the blockade that arises after 40. Qd4. **40. Qf2? e3 41. Qf3 d3?** Bird advances his pawns too rashly. They could have used some support with first 41. ... Rd7. **42. Rc3 Q×e5 43. Rc5** "If 43. f×e5 R×f3 winning easily"—Lee. **43. ... d2 44. Rd1 Qd4 45. Q×h5†** "If 45. R×h5†, then 45. ... Kg8 and White cannot play 46. Re5 because of 46. ... Q×e5, and if 46. Qe2, to prevent 46. ... Qd3, Black would win by 46. ... R×f4"—Hoffer. **45. ... Kg8 46. Rc8†?** The surprising 46. Re5! leads to a drawn position. The pawn at e3 is kept under control for a second while he is just in time to create his own counterplay: 46. ... Qd3 47. R×e6 e2 48. Re8† Rf8 49. R×e2 Q×g3† 50. Kh1 Q×f4 51. Re×d2. **46. ... Rf8 47. Rc5 Qd3 48. Re5 e2 49. R×e2 Q×g3† 50. Kh1 Rg4?!** "A hasty move, which might have thrown away a splendidly played game. Mr. Bird could have won the game offhand with 50. ... Rf5"—Hoffer. **51. Q×g4† Q×g4 52. Rg2 R×f4 53. Rd×d2 R×b4?** The real mistake. The endgame after 53. ... Kf8 54. R×g4 R×g4 55. Rf2† Ke7 56. h5 Rh4† 57. Rh2

R×b4 wins for Black. **54. Rd8†?** "Here White overlooks a certain draw; e.g., 54. R×g4† R×g4 55. Rg2 Rg7 (if 55. ... R×g2 White wins) and draws for, although White can win all Black's pawns, by the time he captures the last at a6, Black with the best play is enabled to reach c6 with his king after having first captured White's h-pawn, and the game is drawn"—Lee. **55. ... R×g2** also draws. **54. ... Kf7 55. Rd7† Kf6 56. R×g4 R×g4 57. R×b7 R×h4† 58. Kg2 Ra4** White resigns. "Mr. Bird, with the exception of his 50th move, played this game with his usual dash and vigor"—Hoffer. *Hereford Times* (Lee), 27 June 1891; *The Field* (Hoffer), 4 July 1891.

### (1043) Mortimer–Bird    1–0
Divan tournament (round 3)
London, 23 June 1891
*B34*

1. e4 c5 2. Nc3 Nc6 3. Nf3 g6 4. d4 c×d4 5. N×d4 Bg7 6. Be3 h5 7. Be2 d6 8. h3 Nf6 9. Qd2 Nd7 10. Rd1 Qa5 11. Ncb5 Q×d2† 12. R×d2 0–0 13. c3 Nf6 14. f3 Bd7 15. g4 N×d4 16. N×d4 Rfc8 17. Kf2 Be6 18. N×e6 f×e6 19. Bd3 h×g4 20. h×g4 Rf8 21. Kg2 Nd7 22. f4 Rac8 23. e5 Kf7 24. Bb5 Nc5 25. e×d6 e×d6 26. R×d6 a6 27. Bd7 Rc7 28. B×c5 R×c5 29. Rhd1 e5 30. f5 g×f5 31. B×f5 Rb5 32. b3 Bh8 33. b4 e4 34. Be6† Ke7 35. Bc4 Re5 36. Rd7† Kf6 37. Rf1† Kg5 38. R×f8 Black resigns—*Daily News*, 24 June 1891.

### (1044) Bird–Jasnogrodsky    0–1
Divan tournament (round 4)
London, 24 June 1891
*C54*

1. e4 e5 2. Nf3 Nc6 3. Bc4 Bc5 4. c3 Nf6 5. b4 Bb6 6. d3 d6 7. a4 a5 8. b5 Ne7 9. Be3 Ng6 10. Nbd2 0–0 11. 0–0 Ng4 12. Bg5 Nf6 13. Nh4 Kh8 14. Qb3 Qe7 15. Kh1 h6 16. N×g6† f×g6 17. Be3 Nh5 18. d4 Nf4 19. B×f4 R×f4 20. g3 Rf6 21. d×e5 d×e5 22. Kg2 Qd7 23. Rad1 Qh3† 24. Kh1 Bg4 25. f3 Raf8 26. f×g4 Rf2 White resigns—*Norwich Mercury*, 4 July 1891.

### (1045) Bird–Loman    1–0
Divan tournament (round 5)
London, 27 June 1891
*A03*

1. f4 d5 2. e3 e6 3. Nf3 a6 4. b3 Nf6 5. Bb2 Be7 6. Be2 c5 7. 0–0 Nc6 8. Qe1 0–0 9. Qg3 b5 10. d3 g6 "The game has, up to this point, proceeded on the usual lines of most of Mr. Bird's games at this opening. The only thing that would complete White's happiness would be to have his bishop on d3. Black now seeks to prevent the pressure on his kingside growing into a dangerous attack, but we do not agree with his way of doing it. We think 10. ... Ne8 would have been better"—*Daily News*. **11. Nbd2 Nh5 12. Qf2 Bf6** 12. ... f6 is a better way to close the diagonal once and forever. **13. Ne5** "An excellent move, as it puts the Black knight into a difficulty at once. Black cannot play 13. ... N×e5 on account of 14. f×e5 followed by 15. B×h5"—*Daily News*. **13. ... B×e5 14. f×e5 Ng7 15. Qf4 Bb7 16. Qh6** Loman's last move was a bit too naive, as White's pieces are gathering around his king and 15. ... Bb7 doesn't contribute any-

thing to the defense. Yet, Bird's actual move is overly energetic. First 16. Nf3 Qe7 17. e4 makes his position ready for 18. Qh6 and 19. Ng5. His opponent is forced to make detrimental concessions. **16. ... Nf5 17. R×f5** "The charm of Mr. Bird's play consists in the fact that he never hesitates to sacrifice when he sees a prospect to get up an attack. His vigorous play in this instance leads to some very interesting complications"—*Daily News*. **17. ... e×f5 18. Nf3 f6** "The only way to prevent White mating by playing 19. Ng5"—*Daily News*. **19. e×f6 Qd7 20. Ng5 d4 21. f7†** Bird gains back his sacrificed material with this move, but the resulting position is favorable for Black. Instead, 21. Ne6! Rf7 22. N×c5 Qd6 23. N×b7 R×b7 24. Bf3 Rd8 25. e×d4 Q×f6 26. c4 provides him with a dangerous initiative. **21. ... R×f7 22. N×f7 Q×f7 23. Bf3 Re8 24. e4** 24. e×d4 N×d4 25. B×d4 c×d4 26. Qf4 B×f3 27. Q×f3 leaves the e-file in the hands of his opponent, but this is not so dangerous. **24. ... f×e4** Bird's aim for complications should have been stopped by 24. ... Nb4! when he is forced into a difficult endgame: 25. Rf1 Qe7 26. e×f5 B×f3 27. R×f3 Qe1† 28. Rf1 Qe3† 29. Q×e3 d×e3. **25. B×e4 Rf8 26. Qd2 Ne5 27. B×b7 Q×b7** *(see diagram)*

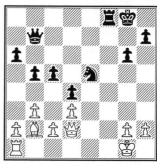

*After 27. ... Q×b7*

**28. b4!** "A very serviceable move"—*Daily News*. **28. ... Ng4 29. Qe2 Qd7** 29. ... Ne3! 30. b×c5 Qd5 31. Re1 Rc8 32. Qf2 Re8 33. B×d4 makes a draw inevitable. **30. h3** "Mr. Bird points out that he ought to have played 30. b×c5, to be followed by 31. c6"—*Daily News*. **30. ... Ne3 31. b×c5 Qd5 32. c3** 32. Re1 again prepares 33. B×d4, with a clear draw. **32. ... d×c3 33. Ba3?** Bird is pushing it very far, but 33. B×c3 Q×c5 34. Rc1 Nd5† 35. d4 Nf4 36. Qe6† N×e6 37. d×c5 N×c5 is a rather joyless ending, where he has to fight for a draw. **33. ... Qd4 34. Kh1 Nf5 35. Qe6† Kg7 36. c6 b4 37. c7 Ng3† 38. Kh2 Nf1†?** 38. ... Qf4! 39. Kg1 Nf1 40. Qe7† Kg8 41. R×f1 (the only move against 41. ... Qh2 mate) 41. ... Q×f1† 42. Kh2 Qf4† 43. Kg1 b×a3 wins. The text move could be met by a cunning maneuver. **39. R×f1** "This is the second time in this game that White has sacrificed the exchange"—*Daily News*. **39. ... R×f1 40. Qe7†?** 40. Bc1! forces Black to take the perpetual check at g1 and f2. **40. ... Kh6??** A dramatic blunder that was probably caused by time trouble. 40. ... Rf7 41. Q×f7† K×f7 42. c8Q b×a3 is a winning endgame for Black. **41. Bc1†!** "Very fine play throughout. Black threatened to draw by 41. ... Qg1† and 42. ... Qf2†, but this ingenious sacrifice makes this impossible"—*Daily News*. **41. ... R×c1 42. Qf8† Qg7** "A very disagreeable necessity. If 42..Kh5 46. g4† Kg5 44. Qd8†, which forces the exchange of queens just the same"—*Daily News*. **43. Q×g7† K×g7 44. c8Q Rd1 45. Qc7† Kh6 46. Qf4† Kg7 47. Qd4† Kh6 48. Qe3† Kg7 49. Qe7† Kh6 50. Qf8† Kg5 51. h4† K×h4 52. Qf4†** Black resigns—*Daily News*, 1 July 1891.

## (1046) Bird–Tinsley   1–0
Divan tournament (round 6)
London 1891
*A03*

**1. f4 g6 2. Nf3 Bg7 3. e3 d5 4. d4 Nf6 5. c4 c6 6. Nc3 0–0 7. Bd3 d×c4 8. B×c4 Nbd7 9. 0–0 Nb6 10. Bd3 Nbd5 11. Qe1 Nb4 12. Bb1 b6 13. Ne2 Ba6 14. Ne5 Rc8 15. Bd2 Nbd5 16. e4 Nc7 17. N×c6 Qd7 18. Ne5 Qd8 19. Be3 e6 20. Rf3 Nce8 21. Nc3 Nd6 22. Bf2 Bb7 23. Bd3 a6 24. Rd1 b5 25. a3 Re8 26. Bh4 Qc7 27. Qe3 h5 28. Rg3 Nh7 29. Nf3 Qb6 30. e5 Nc4 31. B×c4 R×c4 32. Ne4 Rc2 33. Nd6 Rb8 34. Qb3 Qc6 35. R×g6 Rc1 36. Rg3 Kf8 37. Be7† Kg8 38. N×b7 Qc4 39. Q×c4 R×d1† 40. Qf1 R×f1† 41. K×f1 R×b7 42. Bf6** Black resigns—*The Field*, 11 July 1891.

## (1047) Bird–Gossip   1–0
Divan tournament (round 7)
London, 6 July 1891
*A03*

**1. f4 d5 2. e3 e6 3. Nf3 Nf6 4. b3 Be7** "This set-up looks better than the one Tinsley played"—Loman. **5. Bb2 c5 6. Bb5† Nbd7 7. 0–0 0–0 8. Qe1 a6 9. Bd3** "In some cases this move has some great advantages. However, here 9. Be2 was better, since White loses a tempo"—Loman. **9. ... b5 10. Be2 Ne4 11. d3 Bf6 12. Ne5 Nd6 13. Nd2 Bb7?!** 13. ... B×e5 is excellent for Black. The text move could have cost him dearly. **14. Bg4?!** Bird misses a forced tactical sequence that renders him a pawn: 14. N×d7! B×b2 (14. ... Q×d7 15. B×f6 g×f6 16. Rf3 submits Black to a dangerous attack) 15. N×f8 B×a1 16. N×e6 Qc8 17. Q×a1 Q×e6 18. Qe5. **14. ... Bh4 15. Qe2 f5 16. Bh3 Bf6 17. Rad1** 17. a4 b4 18. N×d7 Q×d7 (18. ... B×b2? 19. N×f8 is bad for him) 19. B×f6 releases some of the tension, which was not unwise as Gossip could now launch an initiative on the queenside with 17. ... b4, followed by the push of the a-pawn until a4 and Nb5. **17. ... B×e5 18. f×e5 Nf7 19. Nf3** Innocent looking but not good; 19. e4 dissolves the doubled pawn and gives equal chances. **19. ... Qc7** 19. ... Qe7! is surprisingly strong. Given White's last move, 20. e4 isn't an option anymore and he lacks other plans. Black can continue with his play on the queenside, starting with the advance of the a-pawn to open that file. **20. Qf2** "A subtle defense of the e-pawn, for if Black plays 20. ... Nf×e5, then 21. N×e5 N×e5 22. Qg3 etc."—Hoffer. The reason why 19. ... Qc7 is inferior to 19. ... Qe7 is of a tactical nature. White could solve his problems here with 20. B×f5! **20. ... Rae8 21. d4 a5! 22. g4** "For everyone else this move would be dangerous to play. However, it suits completely with Mr. Bird's style of play"—Loman. **22. ... f×g4 23. B×g4 Ng5** *(see diagram)* "Gossip was of course totally unaware of the brilliant sacrifice Bird wants to play. Otherwise he would for certain have played 23. ... Nh6. Only a few chess players would have guessed the veteran's plan"—Loman. Both 23. ... Nh6 and 23. ... c4 are excellent. Bird's next move has a great surprise value, making it difficult to deal with in a practical situation.

**24. N×g5!** "A magnificent concept that proves Bird's magnificent taxation skills, because the consequences were difficult to calculate. Bird, as usual, only thought very shortly about this move. As soon

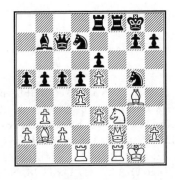

*23. ... Ng5*

as he starts calculating he gets confused. Everything on him is chess instinct, he says"—Loman. **24. ... R×f2 25. R×f2 Nf8** Another interesting option is 25. ... Qb6. Just as in the game, there are plenty of attractive opportunities, e.g., 26. d×c5! Qc6 27. Bd4 Bc8 28. Rdf1 N×c5 29. Bh5 g6 30. Rg2 (30. N×h7 leads also to a draw 30. ... K×h7 31. B×g6† K×g6 32. Rg2† Kh5 33. Rf3 Kh4 34. Rf4†) 30. ... Re7 31. N×h7 R×h7 32. B×g6 Rg7 33. Rf3 Bd7 34. Bf7† Kf8 35. B×e6† Ke8 36. B×d7† R×d7 37. Rg8†. White has but a rook for the queen but given the situation of his opponent's king his compensation is sufficient to draw. Or 25. ... Qc6 26. Nf7 Re7 27. Nd6 c×d4 28. B×d4 and White has enough compensation for the queen. **26. Rdf1 Bc8?** The losing move, but the situation was extremely difficult to cope with. Correct was 26. ... Qe7! (Hoffer) when White can play on with 27. Kh1 (for example) or take a forced draw arising after 27. R×f8† R×f8 28. B×e6† Kh8 29. R×f8† Q×f8 30. Nf7† Kg8 31. Nd6† Kh8. **27. d×c5?** "Mr. Bird points out that he just saw a moment too late the following pretty variation: 27. R×f8† R×f8 28. B×e6† B×e6 29. R×f8† K×f8 30. N×e6† and 31. N×c7 with two piece ahead"—Hoffer. **27. ... Q×c5 28. Bd4 Qe7 29. h4** 29. Nf7 Bd7 30. Nd6 is slightly better. After 30. ... Rb8 31. Rf7 Qg5 32. Kh1 Qg6 33. Bd1 White can keep on trying to confuse his opponent but with careful play Black is always able to reach a drawn endgame by returning his queen at the right moment. **29. ... h6 30. Rf7** 30. Bh5 looks strong, for if 30. ... Rd8 31. Rf7 Qa3 32. Bb6 Re8 33. Rc7 Rd8 34. Nf7 Re8 35. N×h6† wins. After the stronger 30. ... g6! 31. Nf7! g×h5 32. N×h6† Kh7 33. Rf7† K×h6 34. R×e7 R×e7 35. R×f8 White is marginally better. **30. ... Qb4 31. Nh3 Ng6 32. Bh5 Ne7 33. c3 Qa3 34. R7f2 g6 35. Be2** 35. B×g6 is also possible. A standstill arises after 35. ... N×g6 36. Rg2 Re7 37. Nf4 Rf7 38. R×g6† Kh7 39. Rg2. **35. ... Bd7 36. Bd3 Nf5 37. B×f5** This exchange of dubious value as Black is in a better position to make use of the opening of the g-file. After 37. Nf4 White obtains slight pressure; e.g., 37. ... Kf7 38. h5 g×h5 39. B×f5 e×f5 40. N×d5 Rg8† 41. Kh2 Rg4 42. Nf6 Qe7 43. N×g4 Qh4† 44. Kg1 h×g4 45. Rh2 Qg3† 46. Rg2 Qh3 with a draw. **37. ... g×f5 38. Nf4 Kh7** The worst possible square for the king. Both alternatives give him a slight edge: 38. ... Kf7 39. Nh5 Rg8† 40. Kh1 or 38. ... Kh8 39. Kh2 Rg8. **39. Nh5 Rg8† 40. Kh2 Rd8?** This leaves the king to the mercy of White's pieces. 40. ... Rg6 41. Nf6†! was probably misjudged by Gossip, for he comes out on top after 41. ... R×f6! 42. e×f6 Qd6† 43. Kg1 e5. White has a better option in 41. Rg1 R×g1 42. K×g1 Kg6 43. Nf6 Bc6 44. Rg2†, when another drawn endgame is reached. **41. Nf6†** The king is caught now. **41. ... Kh8 42. Rg1 Bc6 43. Rfg2 Qf8 44. Bc5** Black resigns—*The Field* (Hoffer), 11 July 1891; *De Groene Amsterdammer* (Loman), 26 July 1891.

**(1048) Bird–Fenton   1–0**
Divan tournament (round 8)
London, July 1891
*A03*

1. f4 d5 2. e3 c5 3. Nf3 e6 4. Bb5† Bd7 5. B×d7† N×d7 6. b3 Ngf6 7. Bb2 Be7 8. 0–0 0–0 9. d3 Rc8 10. Qe1 b5 11. a4 a6 12. Nbd2 c4 13. b×c4 b×c4 14. Bd4 c×d3 15. c×d3 Bb4 16. Qg3 B×d2 17. N×d2 Rc2 18. Nf3 h6 19. f5 Qc7 20. f×e6 f×e6 21. Qh3 Rc6 22. B×f6 R×f6 23. Nd4 Rb6 24. a5 Rd6 25. R×f6 N×f6 26. N×e6 Qc3 27. Rf1 Q×d3 28. N×g7 Rc6 29. Nf5 Black resigns—*Illustrated London News*, 18 July 1891.

**(1049) van Vliet–Bird   ½–½**
Divan tournament (round 9)
London, July 1891

"Van Vliet–Bird (1. d4 f5) was a very hard fight, being played at a time when a point either way was of vital importance to both players, Bird being 5½ and van Vliet 6 with an adjourned game with Mortimer on hand. After many manoeuvers Bird had what seemed a winning position with a pawn ahead, three pawns being passed, as follows":

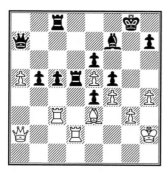

*Black to move*

1. ... R×d2† 2. Q×d2 b4 3. R×c5 R×c5 4. Qd8† and draw—*British Chess Magazine*, August 1891, p. 377.

# LASKER'S RETURN

Bird did not fall idle after the Divan tournament and he was full of plans for the summer. One of his priorities was to reach Oxford where the congress of the reinstated Counties Chess Association was going on. Bird's intentions did not materialize, quite likely because of his still delicate health.

At the end of July it became known that Emanuel Lasker was invited to give a few simultaneous exhibitions at the German Exhibition, held during the next month in London. His visit was very much anticipated but, according to Loman in the *De Groene Amsterdammer* of 26 July, only Bird and Mason had declared themselves willing to meet Lasker in a match.

Two months later the *Liverpool Mercury* of 12 September confirmed that a short match between Lasker and Bird, played for the first five wins, was in the bag but it turned out that Lasker was not

so interested in beating Bird again. Mason and his supporters were also in for a disillusion.[11] Only Lee succeeded in obtaining an agreement for a match of six games. With the score standing 1½–½ in Lasker's favor the Englishman resigned the match due to health issues. While the British press emphasized the eagerness with which some British players attempted to meet Lasker over the board, quite another sound was heard from Lasker himself. He declared that during these months he was ready to play anyone but felt boycotted by the overall chess scene of London (see below).

# SIMPSON'S DIVAN TOURNAMENT, SEPTEMBER–OCTOBER 1891

The first even tournament at the Divan was considered a great success. The atmosphere revived and reminded one of former days.[12] Already at the closing dinner plans were made for a follow-up after the summer months.[13] With more money in the pocket, Bird, acting as the secretary, maintained the distinguished ambition of composing the strongest possible field. Lasker, Blackburne, Gunsberg and Mason were consulted to take part. Unfortunately all these attempts failed and the contingent of players was largely the same as in June. Loman was considered the favorite by most. Bird, by now in better condition, was a dark horse for tournament victory. The conditions of the tournament remained untouched. The idea to spread the games over a few weeks to attract the maximum of interest was maintained.

The veteran opened rather hesitatingly, with two draws and a loss against Müller in the third round. A win against Mortimer put him back in business, even though Tinsley (3½ of 4) and Loman (3) were ahead of him. The third week of the tournament resulted in a gathering of the field. Bird beat Jasnogrodsky and Gossip, thereby catching up to the leaders Fenton and Loman (now 4 of 6). Tinsley lost both his games and was joined by Müller (3½ out of 6). In the next two rounds Bird beat Rolland and Loman. The win against Loman was crucial and spectacular. Bird had a completely lost position during the whole game but a final blunder ruined Loman. Bird was now the clear leader with 6 of 8. His narrowest pursuers were Müller (5) and Loman and Tinsley (4½). In the final round, a draw against van Vliet was enough for a solo first place. The year 1891 had been a very difficult one for Bird and it was a miracle that

11. Buckley wrote that Mason was "perfectly ready, and, to oblige the Berliner, will play for the small sum of £20. It is to be hoped that Lasker will cover the stakes. ... We remember how Blackburne took up the gauntlet [in 1890] and waited several weeks for Lasker to raise the money in Berlin. And we remember how the British master withdrew in disgust." *Birmingham Weekly Mercury*, 8 August 1891.

12. Gunsberg was most enthusiastic: "The Divan was well filled during most part of the week and presented a very animated appearance. Everyone seemed to have caught the spirit of the fray, and watched the various games with an attention which could not have been exceeded.... It also reminded one of old times to see Bird, Blackburne, Gunsberg and Mason also take an active interest in the play of the various competitors and, by their lucid and friendly remarks and comments, on the game assist in imparting the greatest interest to the inevitable post-mortem examination." *Evening News and Post*, 27 June 1891.

13. W.H. Cubison subscribed £5 for another tournament. Other guests gave an aggregate sum of £9. *Chess Monthly*, August 1891, p. 358.

he concluded it with such a sterling tournament victory.[14] Tinsley clinched to a sole second place with 5½ of 9.

This second tournament at the Divan seems to have generated less enthusiasm. The character of the games was not very appealing for the public: the style of many players was described as steady more than brilliant. This resulted in long games where the players were unable to keep the attention of the public.[15] The experiment of playing just two games per day, one in the afternoon and one in the evening, was not repeated. As weaker players were also eager to join the fray again, the next tournament at the Divan returned to the handicap formula.

### Divan tournament, London, 28 September–28 October 1891

*Site:* Simpson's Divan
*Playing hours:* 1 p.m.–5 and 6 p.m.–10
*Prizes:* Prize fund of ca. £30.
*Time limit:* 20 moves per hour

|   |                  | 1 | 2 | 3 | 4 | 5 | 6 | 7 | 8 | 9 | 10 |     |
|---|------------------|---|---|---|---|---|---|---|---|---|----|-----|
| 1 | H.E. Bird        |   | ½ | 0 | 1 | 1 | ½ | 1 | 1 | 1 | ½  | 6½  |
| 2 | S. Tinsley       | ½ |   | 1 | ½ | 0 | 1 | ½ | 0 | 1 | 1  | 5½  |
| 3 | O.C. Müller      | 1 | 0 |   | 0 | ½ | 1 | 1 | 0 | ½ | 1  | 5   |
| 4 | N. Jasnogrodsky  | 0 | ½ | 1 |   | 0 | 1 | 0 | 1 | ½ | ½  | 4½  |
| 5 | R. Loman         | 0 | 1 | ½ | 1 |   | 0 | ½ | 1 | 0 | ½  | 4½  |
| 6 | R.H.F. Fenton    | ½ | 0 | 0 | 0 | 1 |   | 1 | 1 | ½ | 0  | 4   |
| 7 | J. Mortimer      | 0 | ½ | 0 | 1 | ½ | 0 |   | 1 | 1 | 0  | 4   |
| 8 | Rolland          | 0 | 1 | 1 | 0 | 0 | 0 | 0 |   | 1 | 1  | 4   |
| 9 | G.H.D. Gossip    | 0 | 0 | ½ | ½ | 1 | ½ | 0 | 0 |   | 1  | 3½  |
| 10| L. van Vliet     | ½ | 0 | 0 | ½ | ½ | 1 | 1 | 0 | 0 |    | 3½  |

**(1050) Bird–Fenton   ½–½**

Divan tournament (round 1)
London, 29 September 1891
*Game score missing*

**(1051) Bird–Tinsley   ½–½**

Divan tournament (round 2)
London, 2 October 1891
*A03*

**1. f4 g6 2. Nf3 Bg7 3. e3 d5 4. d4 a6 5. Bd3 c5 6. c3 c4 7. Bc2 Nf6 8. a4 Nc6 9. 0-0 Bd7 10. Nbd2 Rc8 11. Qe1 e6 12. Ne5 0-0 13. Qg3 Rc7 14. Ndf3 Bc8 15. Bd2 Ne7 16. Qh3 b6 17. g4** A rather optimistic assault, which however achieves its aim as Black forgoes the thematic reaction 17. ... h5! 18. g×h5 N×h5. **17. ... Ne8 18. Ng5 h6 19. Ngf3** The consequent 19. Ng×f7 R×f7 20. N×f7 K×f7 implies

a small material investment, but in return Black's position lacks all active prospects. White can continue with the activation of his bishop to h4. **19. ... Nd6 20. Be1 Ne4 21. Nh4 g5 22. Ng2** (*see diagram*)

*After 22. Ng2*

**22. ... f6** A loss of time. 22. ... f5 is satisfactory. **23. Nf3 Qe8 24. f×g5 h×g5 25. Bg3 Ra7** It's better to cover d6 with 25. ... Rc6. **26. Bd6** Bird has obtained a promising position. **26. ... Rf7** "If 26. ... N×d6, White mates in two moves: 27. Qh7† Kf7 and the knight mates"—Hoffer. **27. Ba3 Bf8 28. B×e4 d×e4 29. Nd2 Qc6 30. Rf2 Bg7?** Tinsley has been suffering for more than about a dozen of moves already, but only this thoughtless one leads to a rapid decline. 30. ... Ng6, bringing down the pressure with an exchange, is indicated. **31. Qg3** Bird's continuation of the attack is far from perfect, though for a long time he never really lets his opponent escape. Here 31. Qh5! radically augments the pressure. A possible line would be 31. ... Qd5 32. Raf1 Bd7 33. h4 g×h4 34. Q×h4 with a steady attack. **31. ... Rd7 32. h4** 32. a5 b5 33. Raf1 and now 34. h4 can be played under much better conditions. **32. ... g×h4** 32. ... Bh6 is preferable as it keeps the position as closed as possible. **33. N×h4** Tinsley's last move gave Bird free access to both f4 and h4. 33. Q×h4 is optimal as f4 is kept as the knight's destination. **33. ... Bb7 34. Raf1** 34. B×e7 eliminates a crucial defender; e.g., 34. ... Rf×e7 35. Ng6 Re8 36. Rh2 with a decisive attack. **34. ... Nd5 35. g5** The preliminary 35. Ng6 Bh6 reinforces this push: 36. g5 B×g5 37. Rh2 Rh7 38. R×f6! and White's attack cracks through. **35. ... f×g5** 35. ... Qc7 is the only move to prolong the battle. Now 36. Q×g5! is more precise. **36. R×f7 R×f7 37. R×f7 K×f7 38. Q×g5 Nf6 39. Qg6† Kg8 40. Be7 Nh7 41. Qg3 b5 42. a5 Qd5 43. Nf1 Bc8 44. Ng6 Kf7 45. Nh2?!** 45. Nh4 would have kept a large advantage. **45. ... e5! 46. Bh4 e×d4 47. c×d4 b4?** 47. ... Bd7 finally breaks the band of White's pressure. **48. Ne7 Qe6 49. d5 Qh3 50. Qg6† Kf8 51. Q×h7?** Now Tinsley escapes after all. Both 51. N×c8 and 51. Q×e4 win quite easily. **51. ... Q×e3† 52. Kh1 Qc1† 53. Kg2 Q×b2† 54. Bf2 e3 55. Ng6†** "He has nothing better now than to draw the game. If 55. N×c8 Q×f2† 56. Kh3 e2 wins"—Hoffer. **55. ... Kf7 56. Nh8†** draw. "Black played his king to f8 and f7 in answer to White's check and a draw was agreed upon. If Black played his king anywhere else he would lose the e-pawn"—Hoffer. *The Field* (Hoffer), 10 October 1891.

**(1052) Bird–Müller   0–1**

Divan tournament (round 3)
London, 6 October 1891
*A03*

**1. f4 d5 2. e3 g6 3. Nf3 Bg7 4. d4 Nf6 5. Bd3 0-0 6. 0-0 c5**

---

14. MacDonnell, visiting the Divan at the end of the year, penned a mused description of his old and apparently again ailing friend: "I visited the Divan not many days since, and was glad to recognize many old faces and some young ones. I had a long and pleasant chat with the veteran champion, H.E. Bird. Occasionally he brightened up during our converse, and his hearty laugh rang out clear and joyous as in the olden days. But on the whole he seemed weak in body and depressed in spirit. However, we played a few games together, he showing all his best powers of skill and resource, laughing heartily and enjoying thoroughly my desperate efforts to 'kill' him. I think Bird is about the pleasantest opponent I ever encountered." *Illustrated Sporting and Dramatic News*, 26 December 1891.

15. Probably Bird himself wrote down the following lines, advocating a quicker pace: "The time limit allowed ... 20 moves an hour, which represents five or six hours for a contest of 50 or 60 moves. As a sitting is limited to four hours, a game lasting more than that time has to be adjourned, which is disappointing to lookers-on, and not altogether satisfactory to many players." *The Times*, 12 October 1891.

Three minor professionals: Nikolai Jasnogrodsky, Samuel Tinsley and Richard Fenton (*British Chess Magazine*).

7. c3 b6 8. Nbd2 Bb7 9. Qe1 Nc6 10. Ng5 e6 11. Ndf3 h6 12. Nh3 Ne4 13. Nf2 Ne7 14. B×e4 d×e4 15. Nd2 Ba6 16. Nd×e4 c×d4 17. e×d4 Qc7 18. Nh3 B×f1 19. Q×f1 Nf5 20. Qe1 Rfd8 21. Be3 N×e3 22. Q×e3 Rac8 23. Nhf2 Qc4 24. Nd2 Qb5 25. Nd3 Rc7 26. Nf3 Qf5 27. Re1 Bf6 28. h3 Qd5 29. a3 Kh7 30. Kh2 g5 31. Nde5 Rg8 32. Qd3† Kh8 33. Ng4 Bg7 34. f×g5 h×g5 35. Nfe5 f5 36. Ng6† Kh7 37. N4e5 Bf6 38. g4 R×g6 39. N×g6 K×g6 and Black wins—*Evening News and Post*, 24 October 1891.

### (1053) Mortimer–Bird    0–1
Divan tournament (round 4)
London, 9 October 1891
*Game score missing*

### (1054) Gossip–Bird    0–1
Divan tournament (round 5)
London, 13 October 1891
*Game score missing*

### (1055) Bird–Jasnogrodsky    1–0
Divan tournament (round 6)
London, 15 October 1891
*Game score missing*

### (1056) Rolland–Bird    0–1
Divan tournament (round 7)
London, 20 October 1891
*Game score missing*

### (1057) Loman–Bird    0–1
Divan tournament (round 8)
London, 22 October 1891
*B72*

1. e4 c5 2. Nc3 Nc6 3. Nf3 g6 4. d4 c×d4 5. N×d4 Bg7 6. Be3 d6 7. Be2 Bd7 8. Qd2 Nf6 9. h3 h5 "Typical Bird"—Loman. 10. Rd1 N×d4 Bird follows his usual approach, but with his pawn at h5, the exchange is rather doubtful. 10. ... a6 can be advised. 11. B×d4 Qa5 12. f4! Bc6 13. 0–0 h4? Castling is necessary. Loman's reaction is up the mark. 14. e5! d×e5 15. f×e5 Nh5 (*see diagram*)

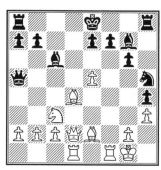

*After 15. ... Nh5*

**16. e6?** This move leaves a convincing first impression, but it turns out to be much more double-edged than that. Very strong was 16. Qg5!, a move which contains the menace 17. R×f7. The white squares around Black's king remain a telling weakness for him; e.g., in the line 16. ... e6 17. Bg4 (threatening 18. B×e6) 17. ... Rh6 18. Be3 Ng3 19. R×f7! K×f7 20. B×e6†! Ke8 21. Qf4 and Black is helpless. **16. ... f6** 16. ... 0-0-0! brings about a very tense situation in the center. White is forced to allow a transposition into an endgame that is favorable for Black: 17. Qe3 R×d4 18. R×d4 B×d4 19. Q×d4 f6 etc. **17. Qd3** 17. Bf3 rips the Black king of an important defender (if he exchanges and castles to the queenside) or forces the weakening of Black's position in case of 17. ... Ng3 18. B×c6† b×c6 19. Rfe1 0-0 20. Qf2 with some advantage. **17. ... Qg5?** More important than the g-pawn is the safety of the king. After 17. ... 0-0-0! 18. Q×g6 Ng3 19. Rf2 N×e2† 20. R×e2 Bh6, Black has more than enough play for the pawn. One idea is to bring the bishop to b8, a rook will occupy the open g-file and with Qc7 coming up, Black's attack becomes very dangerous. **18. Ne4! B×e4 19. Q×e4** Now White possesses the bishop pair and Black's king is in mortal danger. Loman's follow-up is very crafty. **19. ... Ng3 20. Bb5†! Q×b5 21. Q×g6† Kd8 22. Q×g7 Ne2† 23. Kh2 Re8 24. B×f6† Kc7 25. Rd7† Kb6 26. Bd4† Ka6 27. Rf3** "Here one expected Black to resign the game. That it was justified not do appears from the following"—Loman. **27. ... Qh5 28. Ra3†** "When replaying the game it seems that White, till now, played the best move possible, and, starting from the 28th move, the worst move possible. It was, by the way, not an easy task to lose this position! The best was 28. c4 Ka5 29. Ra3† Kb4 30. Rc7"—Loman. Loman is wrong in condemning this move, his best, that could force a mate in six. **28. ... Kb5 29. Bc3** 29. Rc7! (Loman) 29. ... Kb4 30. c4 and only 30. ... Qc5 postpones the mate. **29. ... b6 30. R×e7?** Both 30. Rb3† and 30. Qe5† win easily. **30. ... Qc5! 31. Qe5?** "31. Rb3† draws the game. The end of this true comedy of errors costs the editor no less than the first price, of which he would be certain if he had won this game"—Loman. *De Groene Amsterdammer* (Loman), 1 November 1891.

### (1058) Bird–van Vliet   ½–½
Divan tournament (round 9)
London, 26 October 1891
*Game score missing*

---

# OFFHAND GAMES 1891

Immediately after the Divan tournament Bird was reported to be playing a match with odds. Neither the opponent's name nor the final result of this affair could be uncovered.[16]

### (1059) Bird & Two Unknowns– Lee & Tinsley & Preston   1–0
Consultation game
London 1891
C14

16. Bird's opponent was a well-known amateur of the City of London Chess Club. Ten wins were required to win the match, with the score 8–7 to Bird's disadvantage when the news was reported. *Liverpool Mercury*, 21 November 1891.

1. e4 e6 2. d4 d5 3. Nc3 Nf6 4. Bg5 Be7 5. B×f6 B×f6 6. Nf3 0-0 7. Bd3 b6 8. h4 Ba6 9. e5 Be7 10. B×h7† K×h7 11. Ng5† Kg6 12. Qg4 B×g5 13. f4 Nc6 14. 0-0-0 Rh8 15. f×g5 Qe7 16. Ne4 Kh7 17. Nf6† g×f6 18. e×f6 Qf8 19. h5 Rg8 20. g6† Kh8 21. Qf4 Re8 22. Rh3 N×d4 23. Q×d4 Qh6† 24. Kb1 Rd8 25. Qe5 Rd7 26. Rdh1 d4 27. g7† R×g7 28. f×g7† Q×g7 29. Qe4 Rd5 30. Ra3 Bc8 31. R×a7 f5 32. Qf3 Qe7 33. Qg3 e5 34. h6 Rd8 35. Re1 Re8 36. Qg6 Rg8 37. Q×b6 Qh4 38. Qa5 Re8 39. R×c7 Ba6 40. Ra7 Bc4 41. Ra8 Rg8 42. Q×e5† Kh7 43. R×g8 Black resigns—*The Times*, 30 June 1891.

### (1060) Ward–Higgs–Bird   0–1
Offhand game
London (Simpson's Divan), 27 September 1891
C33

**1. e4 e5 2. Nc3 Bc5** "This defense is usually adopted by Mr. Bird in this opening. 2. ... Nf6 or 2. ... Nc6 can also be safely played"— Lee. **3. Nf3 d6 4. Bc4 a6** "Played to prevent White from proceeding 5. Na4 and 6. N×c5. The bishop, if attacked, can now retire to a7"— Lee. **5. d3 Nc6 6. Be3 Bg4 7. h3 Bh5 8. g4** "This advance of pawns thus early in the game is not to be commended, as they remain weak in the event of matters being decided in the endgame. White, however, contemplates a dashing attack on the kingside"—Lee. **8. ... Bg6 9. Qd2 B×e3** "Correct play. Fully aware of the weakness already created in the hostile ranks, Black at once proceeds to simplify matters by exchange"—Lee. **10. f×e3 Nf6 11. a3 Nd7 12. h4 h5 13. g5** "This blocks on the kingside does not turn out to the advantage of White. 13. g×h5, followed by 14. Ng5 was apparently better"—Lee. **13. ... Nc5 14. b4** "Decidedly vigorous. Under the circumstances, White's best chance is to attack, but against a correct defense these all-round pawn onslaughts usually end in disaster"— Lee. **14. ... Ne6 15. d4** "Well played. White makes the best of his much compromised position"—Lee. **15. ... e×d4 16. e×d4 Ne7 17. 0-0-0** "Too soon. Here 17. d5, followed by 18. Nd4, was unquestionably stronger"—Lee. **17. ... c6** "The 'coup juste.' Anticipating White's plan of action Black prepares for the opening of the c-file, which ultimately gains him the victory, as will be seen"—Lee. **18. d5 c×d5 19. e×d5** White, despite Lee's tendentious comments, nurtured a small edge until now, and he did it well. Instead of the innocent text move, 19. B×d5 N×d5 20. e×d5 realizes a promising exchange, for Black's king is destined to remain in the center. **19. ... Nc7 20. Rhe1 0-0 21. Bd3 Nb5** "The complications now begin, and Mr. Bird, in his well-known style, sacrifices a pawn for the attack. The game from this point to the end is very interesting"— Lee. Correct is 21. ... a5!, with counterplay along the c-file after 22. b5 Rc8. **22. B×g6** 22. N×b5 a×b5 23. Kb2 is preferable, for now, after the text move, 23. ... N×g6! is good for Black. Bird prefers to mix up the game with a dubious pawn sacrifice. **22. ... N×c3?! 23. B×f7† R×f7 24. Q×c3 Rc8** "The key of a very formidable attack Mr. Bird here expressed the opinion that he had more than an equivalent for the pawn minus"—Lee. **25. Qe3** 25. Qd3! is an improvement. As c2 is covered, 25. ... Qc7 can be met with 26. Nd4!, for if 26. ... N×d5? 27. g6! and 27. ... Rf2 28. Qb3 or 27. ... Rff8 28. Ne6 both win. The endgame is excellent for White after 26. ... Qc3 27. Q×c3. **25. ... Qc7 26. Re2** "The best way of defending the threatened checkmate. If 26. Rd2 or 26. Nd4, Black replies 26. ... N×d5"—Lee. **26. ... Nf5 27. Qe6 Kh8** (*see diagram*)

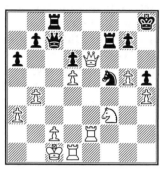

*After 27. ... Kh8*

**28. g6??** All of a sudden the position is full of tension and White appears unable to find his way out. 28. Qe8†! initiates interesting complications. Very bad for Black now is 28. ... R×e8?, as becomes clear after 29. R×e8† Kh7 30. g6†! K×g6 31. Rg1† Kh7 (there is a pretty mate after 31. ... Ng3 32. R×g3† Kf5) 32. Ng5†. Far more balanced is the position arising after 28. ... Rff8 29. Q×h5† Kg8 30. g6 Nh6 31. Rd3 Qc4!, when neither side seems unable to deliver a telling blow. It is obviously a thin rope both players are walking on. **28. ... Rf6!** "Best. If 28. ... Re7 29. Q×f5 R×e2 30. Q×h5† Kg8 31. Qh7† Kf8 32. Qh8† Ke7 33. Q×g7† Kd8 34. Q×c7† followed by 35. Nd4 with a winning position"—Lee. **29. Qe4** "This loses at once. The only alternative, e.g., 29. Qe8† Rff8, followed by the doubling of the rooks on the e-file was better, but the end would probably have been the same"—Lee. **29. ... Ng3** White resigns—*Hereford Times* (Lee), 3 October 1891.

Frank Preston Wildman, a prominent member of the Leeds Chess Club, probably played the following game with the veteran during a visit to London.

### (1061) Bird–Wildman 0–1

Offhand game
London (?) 1891
C33

**1. e4 e5 2. f4 e×f4 3. Be2 d6 4. d4 g5 5. h4 Bg7 6. h×g5 Q×g5 7. Nf3 Qg3† 8. Kf1 Nc6 9. Nc3 Bd7 10. Nd5 0-0-0 11. B×f4 Qg6 12. Qd3 Re8 13. Ng5 h6 14. Bh5 h×g5 15. B×g6 R×h1† 16. Kf2 B×d4† 17. Kf3 g×f4 18. Qb3 Ne5† 19. Ke2 Bg4† 20. Kd2 R×a1 21. Bf5† B×f5 22. e×f5 Rf1 23. Qa4 Rf2† 24. Ke1** and Black mated the Grand Old Man in two moves—*Birmingham Weekly Mercury*, 24 October 1891.

### (1062) G.F. Hardy–Bird 1–0

Offhand game
London 1891
C51

**1. e4 e5 2. Nf3 Nc6 3. Bc4 Bc5 4. b4 B×b4 5. c3 Bc5 6. 0-0 d6 7. d4 e×d4 8. c×d4 Bb6 9. Nc3 Bg4 10. d5 B×f3 11. Q×f3 Ne5 12. Qe2 Qh4 13. Bb5† Kf8 14. Be3 Nf6 15. h3 N×e4 16. N×e4 Q×e4 17. Rae1 Q×d5 18. B×b6 a×b6 19. f4 R×a2 20. Qg4 Q×b5 21. f×e5 d×e5 22. Qe6 Qc5† 23. Kh1 Rf2 24. R×f2 Q×f2 25. Q×e5** and White wins—*Morning Post*, 2 November 1891.

### (1063) Shepheard–Bird 0–1

Offhand game
London 1891
*Odds of pawn and two moves*

**1. e4 & 2. d4 Nc6 3. f4 d5 4. e5 g6 5. Nf3 Bg4 6. Bb5 Nh6 7. h3 B×f3 8. Q×f3 e6 9. Be3 Nf5 10. B×c6† b×c6 11. 0-0 N×e3 12. Q×e3 Bh6 13. g4 0-0 14. Kh2 Qb8 15. b3 Qb6 16. Nd2 Rf7 17. g5 Bf8 18. h4 a5 19. h5 c5 20. h×g6 h×g6 21. c3 c×d4 22. c×d4 c5 23. d×c5 B×c5 24. Qd3 Rf5 25. Rac1 Raf8 26. Qh3 R8f7 27. Kg2 Qb4 28. Qc3 R×g5† 29. f×g5 Qg4† 30. Qg3 Qe2†** and Black wins—*Birmingham Weekly Mercury*, 12 December 1891.

### (1064) Bird & Martineau–Müller & Maas 0–1

Consultation game
London (Simpson's Divan), 8 December 1891
C30

**1. e4 e5 2. f4 Bc5 3. Nf3 d6 4. c3 Nc6 5. b4 Bb6 6. b5 Na5 7. d4 e×d4 8. c×d4 Bg4 9. Be2 Qe7 10. Nc3 0-0-0 11. Qd3 Nf6 12. Ba3 Nh5 13. Nd5 Qd7 14. Rc1 f5 15. Ng5 f×e4 16. Qd1 B×e2 17. Q×e2 Nf6 18. N×b6† a×b6 19. 0-0 d5 20. f5 Kb8 21. Bb4 Nc4 22. a4 h6 23. Ne6 Rde8 24. R×c4 d×c4 25. Q×c4 g6 26. Rc1 Nd5 27. a5 g×f5 28. a×b6 R×e6 29. b×c7† Q×c7 30. Bc5 Qd7 31. Qa2 b6 32. Ra1 Qb7 33. Bb4 Rg6 34. Be1 Rhg8 35. g3 f4 36. Qe2 e3 37. Qh5 Qf7 38. Qe5† Nc7 39. d5 Re8 40. Qd4 f3** White resigns—*Hereford Times*, 26 December 1891.

---

# Match with Loman 1892

In January 1892 Bird was challenged by Loman for a short match. Such a duel was interesting not only as it would oppose the oldest with the youngest London master.[17] It was also well justified by Loman's string of tournament successes of the past year. Both Bird and Loman had each won one of the Divan tournaments. The direct confrontations ended to Bird's advantage but a close look at the games shows that the reverse had easily been possible.

The games created a lot of interest at the Divan but the coverage of the match by the press was somewhat sparse as the world championship match between Steinitz and Chigorin was being played at the same time. The Bird–Loman match was limited to seven games. Bird rectified an opening loss by winning three games in a row. He suffered a second loss in the fifth game but his next victory made the gap between both players insuperable and the final game redundant.

| Match with Loman, 22–30 January 1892 | | | | | | | |
|---|---|---|---|---|---|---|---|
| | 1 | 2 | 3 | 4 | 5 | 6 | |
| H.E. Bird | 0 | 1 | 1 | 1 | 0 | 1 | 4 |
| R. Loman | 1 | 0 | 0 | 0 | 1 | 0 | 2 |

17. According to *The Times* of 2 February 1892 Loman had turned 30 years old a few months earlier. From the participants at the Divan tournaments, only van Vliet was definitively younger. Rolland's birth year is unknown, but it is likely that he was also in his twenties.

**(1065) Bird–Loman    0–1**
Match (game 1)
London, 22 January 1892
*Game score missing*

**(1066) Loman–Bird    0–1**
Match (game 2)
London, January 1892
*Game score missing*

**(1067) Bird–Loman    1–0**
Match (game 3)
London, January 1892
*A03*

**1. f4 d5 2. Nf3 c5 3. b3 e6 4. e3 Nf6 5. Bb2 Be7 6. Bd3 0–0 7. 0–0 Nc6 8. Nc3 a6 9. a3 b5 10. Qe1 Bb7 11. Qg3 Ne8 12. Nd1 c4 13. Be2 c×b3 14. c×b3 Na5** "The game has gone very steadily and carefully so far, but here Black embarks on a useless diversion. The forces of his opponent are being massed on the king's wing, and to this he ought to have directed his attention. 14. ... f5, followed by 15. ... Bf6, would have relieved his position"—Abbott. **15. b4** 15. Rb1 is a more flexible way to deal with Black's last move. **15. ... Nc4 16. Bd4** "The bishop is invaluable to White, and is here most usefully posted"—Abbott. **16. ... a5** 16. ... Bf6 would have neutralized all kingside pressure. **17. b×a5** This move abandons a pawn for less than enough. Instead 17. Nc3! promises good play. **17. ... R×a5 18. Nf2 R×a3** Loman is a little bit too eager to secure his extra pawn. He must first deal with Bird's attempts to launch an attack on the kingside with 18. ... Bf6! **19. R×a3 B×a3** "Black has won a pawn, and in certain positions the b-pawn would be dangerous, but there is no relief from the risks of the other side of the board"—Abbott. **20. Bd3 Be7 21. Qh3** Hardly effective due to Loman's following move. An alternative approach is 21. Ng4 f5 22. Nh6† Kh8 23. B×c4 d×c4 24. Ne5 with interesting play. **21. ... f5! 22. g4 Ned6 23. g5** Played with a specific, yet harmless plan in mind. Each possible alternative would have left him struggling, but the closing of the kingside has a pernicious effect on his attacking chances. **23. ... g6** *(see diagram)*

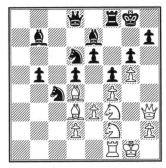

*After 23. ... g6*

**24. Ra1** "An unexpected but ingenious move that practically wins the game. The position is such that White has time to bring his only ineffective piece to a most advantageous post"—Abbott. This evaluation is far too optimistic. The only important element of the position is Black's extra pawn. Instead of the text move, 24. Be2, intending 25. Nd3, to control e5 as well as some squares

Rudolf Loman (*British Chess Magazine*).

on the b-file, is much better. **24. ... Ne4?** The calm 24. ... b4! continues the logical plan to make good use of the extra pawn. **25. Ra7?** Bird overlooks the winning 25. N×e4! d×e4 (forced) 26. B×c4 b×c4 27. Qh6 Rf7 28. Ne5. **25. ... Qc8?** 25. ... N×f2 26. K×f2 Qc8 restores his advantage. **26. B×c4?** 26. N×e4 remains very strong. **26. ... d×c4?** This game is an excellent example of the adage that the last mistake decides the game. After this unlucky move everything is settled, while 26. ... N×f2 keeps the outcome of the game unclear. **27. N×e4 f×e4 28. Ne5 Rf5 29. Ng4 B×g5 30. f×g5 R×g5 31. Qg3!** "White ends with his usual vigor and elegance"—Abbott. **31. ... Kf7 32. Qf4† Rf5 33. Qh6** Black resigns—*Illustrated London News* (Abbott), 9 April 1892.

**(1068) Loman–Bird    0–1**
Match (game 4)
London, January 1892
*Game score missing*

**(1069) Bird–Loman    0–1**
Match (game 5)
London, January 1892
*A03*

**1. f4 d5 2. e3 g6 3. Nf3 Bg7 4. Be2 c5 5. d4 Nc6 6. 0–0 Qb6 7. c3 Nh6 8. a4 a5 9. Na3 e6 10. Nb5 0–0 11. Ng5 Bd7 12. b3 c×d4 13. e×d4 Na7 14. Ba3 N×b5 15. a×b5 Rfc8 16. Bc5 Qd8 17. Qd3 b6 18. Ba3 Rc7 19. Bb2 Nf5 20. Nf3 Nd6 21. Ne5 B×b5 22. Qf3 Qe8 23. Rfe1 B×e2 24. R×e2 a4 25. b4 B×e5 26. f×e5 Ne4 27. Re3**

Rac8 28. Qh3 b5 29. Rf1 Qe7 30. Rf4 Qg5 31. Rg4 Qf5 32. Qh4 N×c3 33. B×c3 R×c3 34. Rf4 Rc1† 35. Kf2 R8c2† 36. Kg3 g5 White resigns—*De Groene Amsterdammer*, 13 March 1892.

## (1070) Loman–Bird    0–1
Match (game 6)
London, 30 January 1892
*A90*

**1. d4 f5** "Scarcely to be recommended, except to a player of Bird-like genius"—MacDonnell. **2. g3** "2. c4 leads to a more manageable opening"—MacDonnell. **2. ... Nf6 3. Bg2 d5** "This weakens the e-pawn, but Black evidently intended to lure his opponent to early castling, then at once to attack him fiercely"—MacDonnell. **4. Nf3 e6 5. 0-0 c6 6. c4 Bd6 7. b3 0-0 8. Ne5 Nbd7 9. Nd3 Qe8 10. c5 Bc7 11. Qc2** "The queen is here comparatively useless. 11. Nc3 would have been more effective"—MacDonnell. **11. ... g5?** "If 12. B×g5, Black plays advantageously 12. ... Ng4"—MacDonnell. Bird's bluff pays off, as after 13. h3 Qh5 14. Bf4! he could resign. Instead of the daunting 11. ... g5? the thematic 11. ... e5 solves all of Black's problems. **12. Nc3? Ne4 13. f3 N×c3 14. Q×c3 Qg6 15. f4** "Of doubtful import, but it stops the advance of Black's f-pawn, which would have been troublesome"—MacDonnell. **15. ... g4 16. Ne5 Qg7 17. Kf2** "A very daring and clever conception"—MacDonnell. **17. ... Nf6 18. Rh1 Bd7 19. h3 g×h3 20. R×h3 Ng4† 21. Ke1 Be8** "Rightly strengthening his weak points"—MacDonnell. **22. Be3 Rf6** "Black henceforward conducts his game with a skill and force that almost overawe resistance"—MacDonnell. **23. Kd2 h5 24. Rah1 Rh6 25. Bf3 Nf6** "Mr. Bird rarely condescends to erect such fortifications, but he gauges aright his opponent's valor and ingenuity"—MacDonnell. **26. g4** "A beautiful move, which is answered still more beautifully"—MacDonnell. Despite MacDonnell's continuous praise of Bird's play, Loman carefully nurtured his small edge, but Bird's solid defense proved difficult to crack. With his actual move Loman switches to a more aggressive approach. **26. ... f×g4 27. N×g4 h×g4** "The grand style; rare and refreshing in these do-nothing, long-match days"—MacDonnell. **28. R×h6 g×f3 29. e×f3** "Of course if 29. Rg1 Ne4†"—MacDonnell. **29. ... Qg2† 30. Kc1 Q×f3 31. Qe1 B×f4 32. B×f4 Q×f4† 33. Kb2?** An evident blunder. 33. Kb1 puts the king on a safe spot. Black now has to meet the threat 34. Q×e6† by 33. ... Kg7 34. Qg1† Ng4 35. R1h4 Qf3. Because of his hanging rook White cannot take at g4 right now. Black threatens 36. ... Bg6†, so after the forced 36. Kb2 Black succeeds in exchanging queens. The endgame after 36. ... Qf2† 37. Q×f2 N×f2 is still slightly better for White as Black still has some development problems. **33. ... Q×d4† 34. Ka3** (see diagram)

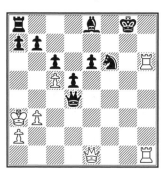

*After 34. Ka3*

**34. ... Kg7??** "Most subtle and effective"—MacDonnell. After 34. ... Ne4! 35. Rg1† Kf8!, White's attack is over and done, despite the bare kingside of his opponent. In his column in *De Groene Amsterdammer* Loman published a fragment of this game. He started with the position before move 26. g4 (which he gave as the 32nd move). The score diverged at this point from MacDonnell's version: 34. ... Qe4 35. Qg3† Qg4 36. Rh8† Kg7 37. R8h7† Kg6 38. R1h6† Kg5 39. Rg7† K×h6 40. R×g4 N×g4 41. Q×g4 Bf7 42. Qf4† Kg7 43. Qc7 Re8 43. Q×b7 e5 44. Q×c6 e4 45. Qd6 e3 and White resigns. **35. Qg3† Qg4 36. Rh7† Kg6** "Into the jaws of death seemingly"—MacDonnell. **37. R1h6† Kg5 38. Rg7†?** Both 38. Qe5† Qf5 39. Qh2 and 38. Qe3† Qf4 39. Q×f4† close the jaws and swallow the prey. **38. ... K×h6 39. R×g4 N×g4 40. Q×g4 Bf7** 40. ... Bd7 41. Qf4† Kg6 42. Qc7 Bc8 is, curiously, rock solid. White's queen is destined to keep Black's queenside locked, and after 43. Kb4 Kf5 44. Kc3 e5 45. Kd2 Kf4, it is his king itself which maintains the balance. With the text move Bird abandons the queenside in return for development and the advance of the central pawns. **41. Qf4† Kg7 42. Qc7 Re8 43. Q×b7 e5 44. Q×c6 e4 45. Qd6** 45. Qa4 e3 46. Qd4† Kg8 47. Qg4† Kf8 48. Qe2 is unclear. The text move is relatively innocent. **45. ... e3 46. b4 e2 47. Qg3† Bg6 48. Qe1 d4 49. Kb2 d3 50. Kc3 Rf8 51. Kd2?** The final mistake, as the queen is now lost. A draw can be achieved with 51. Qg3 Rf1 52. Qe5†. **51. ... Rf1 52. b5 R×e1 53. K×e1 Kf6 54. a4 Ke5 55. a5 Kd4 56. c6 Ke3** and Black wins the game and the match by 4 games to 2—*Illustrated Sporting and Dramatic News* (MacDonnell), 20 February 1892; *De Groene Amsterdammer* (Loman), 21 February 1892.

---

# B.C.A. Congress, London 1892

After several months of silence Hoffer finally announced the seventh congress of the B.C.A. at the end of 1891. At the same time he made it clear in the December 1891 edition of *Chess Monthly* (p. 99) that he would convene a general meeting on which he would tender his resignation, which was due to other obligations and "chiefly through the persistent opposition of some of those who have mostly benefited by the establishment of the Association."

The congress was planned to commence in early January, but it was held up and the definitive starting date was ultimately set on 7 March. This outing was of a national character, yet foreigners residing on the island were not hindered in their attempts to take part. Lasker made good use of this opportunity to improve his reputation. Two other notables, Gunsberg and Blackburne, refused to play. Gunsberg claimed that the prize fund was not enough to compete. In his column in the *Evening News and Post* of 12 March 1892, he assured that the same reason withheld Blackburne from playing. There were however rumors that they protested against the participation of a player of German nationality.[18]

18. So Lasker declared a few years later when being interviewed: "A diplomatic campaign, which was much more difficult to conduct than the ensuing matches, began. I was hushed for a half year, I got no opportunity to encounter the famous players. And when finally, under Bird's urge, a tournament for English players was arranged, then Blackburne and Gunsberg protested against my participation, while I am a German. The public voice however was for fair play so I entered the tournament." *Welt am Montag*, 24 January 1896.

Just two other participants of international stature took part: Mason and Bird. Nine minor masters completed the field. All of them, except Rumboll, were well settled in the London chess scene. The prize fund consisted of £65 and the entrance fees. Four prizes were provided. The tournament was held in the excellent commodities of the British Chess Club.[19]

After a silly first-round loss against van Vliet, Bird was bound to face Lasker. Against expectations the German encountered a tough client and was beaten in the end.[20] Bird won two more games in fine style against Locock and Mortimer. With 3 points out of 4 games he shared the top spot with Lasker—but then the fifth round saw a turnaround. Weak play resulted in losses against Mason and Loman. Bird beat Fenton in the seventh round, but not without flirting once more with a loss. In the following round Lee proved too strong; the latter's beautiful, but rather evident, sacrifice of the exchange was afterwards rewarded with the brilliancy prize. Bird kept on fighting and succeeded in beating Jasnogrodsky and Rumboll. With one round to go Lasker, with 8½ of 10 was close to clinching the first prize. Mason (7½) was his only rival. Bird, Locock and Loman, all counting 6 points, were in contention for third place.

Lasker secured the tournament victory with a quick draw with Locock. Mason surprisingly lost, but this did not make any difference. Loman surpassed Locock by beating van Vliet, thus putting the onus on the veteran to catch him. Bird's game with Gossip, the tail-ender, resolved into an endgame where Bird had a rook and pawn versus a single rook. A seemingly endless number of tries were not enough to realize a miracle and after 132 moves Bird agreed to a draw.

Bird and Locock had to split fourth prize of £5. Bird's amount was augmented with £4 6s., his share of the entrance fees.

This tournament turned out to be the swan song of the British Chess Association. After many months full of rumors, an explicit article revealed what was going on behind the scenes.

> It is apprehended that a similar fate [as the end of the Austro-Hungarian Association] will befall the British Chess Association, unless the constitution is revised. As originally constituted, under the presidency of the late Lord Tennyson, with Mr. Ruskin, Lord Randolph Churchill and Sir Robert Peel as vice-presidents, it was intended to be a federation of chess associations and chess clubs of the United Kingdom, at a nominal annual subscription. It was

### 7th Congress of the B.C.A., London, 7–18 March 1892

*Site:* British Chess Club
*Playing hours:* 1 p.m.–6 and 8 p.m.–11
*Prizes:* 1st £30, 2nd £20, 3rd £10, 4th £5 entrance fees divided among non-prize winners
*Time limit:* 20 moves per hour

|   |                  | 1 | 2 | 3 | 4 | 5 | 6 | 7 | 8 | 9 | 10 | 11 | 12 |     |
|---|------------------|---|---|---|---|---|---|---|---|---|----|----|----|-----|
| 1 | E. Lasker        |   | 1 | 1 | 0 | ½ | 1 | 1 | 1 | 1 | ½  | 1  | 1  | 9   |
| 2 | J. Mason         | 0 |   | 1 | 1 | ½ | ½ | ½ | 1 | 1 | 0  | 1  | 1  | 7½  |
| 3 | R. Loman         | 0 | 0 |   | 1 | ½ | ½ | 0 | 1 | 1 | 1  | 1  | 1  | 7   |
| 4 | H.E. Bird        | 1 | 0 | 0 |   | 1 | 1 | 0 | 1 | 0 | 1  | 1  | ½  | 6½  |
| 5 | C.D. Locock      | ½ | ½ | ½ | 0 |   | 1 | ½ | 0 | ½ | 1  | 1  | 1  | 6½  |
| 6 | R.H.F. Fenton    | 0 | ½ | ½ | 0 | 0 |   | ½ | 1 | ½ | ½  | 1  | 1  | 5½  |
| 7 | F.J. Lee         | 0 | ½ | 1 | 1 | ½ | ½ |   | 0 | 1 | 1  | 0  | 0  | 5½  |
| 8 | N. Jasnogrodsky  | 0 | 0 | 0 | 0 | 1 | 0 | 1 |   | 1 | 0  | 1  | 1  | 5   |
| 9 | L. van Vliet     | 0 | 0 | 0 | 1 | ½ | ½ | 0 | 0 |   | 1  | 1  | ½  | 4½  |
| 10| J. Mortimer      | ½ | 1 | 0 | 0 | 0 | ½ | 0 | 1 | 0 |    | 0  | ½  | 3½  |
| 11| A. Rumboll       | 0 | 0 | 0 | 0 | 0 | 0 | 1 | 0 | 0 | 1  |    | 1  | 3   |
| 12| G.H.D. Gossip    | 0 | 0 | 0 | ½ | 0 | 0 | 1 | 0 | ½ | ½  | 0  |    | 2½  |

then calculated that a sufficient sum could thus be raised from the holding of an international and a national congress alternately each year. Since 1885, when the British Chess Association was established, such congresses have taken place, without the aid of associations or clubs (with few exceptions), but only owing to the liberality of individual members. The honorary secretary, however, does not feel justified in applying again to the generosity of the few for the benefit of the many. A general meeting will be convened, when the matter can be thoroughly discussed, and upon the result of that meeting the fate of the British Chess Association depends [*Standard*, 24 October 1892].

In his introduction of *Chess History and Reminiscences*, Bird claimed that the B.C.A. "had practically lapsed since the year 1889, when last any efforts were made to collect in annual or promised subscriptions" (p. xv). Hoffer offered some proposals to reanimate the B.C.A.:

> Instead of "a federation of associations and clubs" it must be in future a federation of chess players, and the Association will then find plenty of individual supporters. Further, there must be two hon. secretaries; the work is too much for one. It is contemplated holding a general meeting for the ventilation of these questions, when, it is hoped, the B.C.A. will emerge with a new lease on life, and continue its usefulness, not as hitherto, by artificial means, but as a vigorous and healthy institution [*Chess Monthly*, November 1892, p. 70].

His efforts turned out to be in vain. In the meantime another movement was gaining ground. In the fall of 1892 a first series of counties associations joined forces and the Southern Counties' Chess Union was formed. In 1897 and 1899, respectively the counties of the Midlands and the North followed their example. The movement towards centralization was crowned in 1904, these unions and the London Chess League came together to create the British Chess Federation.[21]

The definitive demise of that other association, the C.C.A., followed soon after. Its last congress was organized in 1893 in Woodhall Spa.[22]

---

19. The *Daily News* gave some details on 10 March 1892: "The British Chess Club is one of the most commodious chess resorts in the metropolis. Lighted by incandescent electric light, the onlookers move noiselessly about on the soft carpets on their tours of inspection of the various games in progress, the players being located in a railed enclosure in the center of the room."

20. Hoffer's game description is interesting: "Bird played remarkably well, atoning amply for the defeat he sustained on the first day. His favorite 1. f4 was well defended by Lasker, but the veteran, who evidently suspected that Lasker would anticipate this opening, changed tactics by posting his queen on c1 instead of e1, as is his custom. Lasker wanted to secure at least a draw, brought about exchanges, and remained with bishops of opposite color. But now the real fight commenced, and the veteran has seldom shown to better advantage than in this ending. He played with great tenacity, and quite contrary to his usual impetuous style, won pawn after pawn, and at the adjournment he was three pawns to the good, which won the game in spite of the bishops of different colors. The game extended to over a hundred moves." *The Field*, 12 March 1892.

21. At the time of the B.C.A.'s collapse, Samuel Tinsley was "advocating the formation of a genuine British Chess Union," according to the *New York Daily Tribune* of 13 November 1892.

22. Years after they were written, the words of Ranken turned out to be prophetic: "There is plenty of room for both associations to co-exist, but neither can be long-lived if they continue to bite and devour one another." *Land and Water*, 30 May 1885.

## (1071) van Vliet–Bird   1–0
B.C.A. Congress (round 1)
London, 7 March 1892
*A81*

1. d4 f5 2. g3 e6 3. Bg2 Nf6 4. Nf3 b6 5. Ne5 c6 6. 0–0 Be7 7. c4 Bb7 8. Nc3 d6 9. Nd3 0–0 10. Nf4 Bc8 11. d5 e5 12. d×c6 e4 13. Nfd5 Na6 14. b4 Nc7 15. Bb2 Be6 16. N×c7 Q×c7 17. Nd5 N×d5 18. c×d5 Bf7 19. f3 Bg6 20. Rc1 b5 21. Bc3 Bg5 22. f4 Bd8 23. e3 Bf6 24. B×f6 R×f6 25. Qe2 Rb8 26. Qd2 Rff8 27. Rf2 Bf7 28. g4 f×g4 29. B×e4 Rfe8 30. Bg2 Re7 31. e4 g5 32. e5 g×f4 33. e×d6 Q×d6 34. Q×f4 Q×f4 35. R×f4 h5 36. d6 Re2 37. R×f7 K×f7 38. c7 Black resigns—*Daily News*, 8 March 1892.

## (1072) Bird–Lasker   1–0
B.C.A. Congress (round 2)
London, 8 March 1892
*A03*

1. f4 d5 2. Nf3 Nf6 3. e3 g6 "Rather contrary to modern principles. 3. ... e6 or 3. ... c5 is the usual and better order of development"—Steinitz. 4. d4 "A Stonewall Opening, which was the invention of the late Mr. Ware, of Boston, is now formed. The drawback of White's position is the hole at e4"—Steinitz. 4. ... Bg7 5. Bd3 0–0 6. 0–0 c5 7. c3 Nbd7 "The movements of both sides from this point up to that of our next comment are distinctly marked with the judgment of modern science"—Steinitz. 8. Bd2 Qb6 9. Qc1 Ne4 10. Be1 Nd6 11. Nbd2 Re8 12. a4 "The opponent's clever answer which creates a hole on White's queenside shows the objection to this advance"—Steinitz. 12. ... c4 13. Bc2 Nf6 14. a5 Qc7 15. Bg3 Bf5 16. Nh4 Pursuing the exchange of the bishop but the opening the e-file is very promising for Black. 16. ... e6 17. N×f5 e×f5 18. Re1 Re6 19. Nf3 Nde4 20. Ng5 "Well played. Obviously Black dare not retake or else he would lose a piece"—Steinitz. 20. B×e4 N×e4 21. Qc2 is positionally bad, but it was necessary to be able to defend the a-pawn. 20. ... Re7 20. ... Ra6 wins a pawn. White has nothing in return for it. 21. Bh4 N×g5 22. B×g5 Rc8 23. Bd1 Rd7 24. B×f6 B×f6 25. Bf3 Rd6 26. Qc2 Bd8 27. g3 Rd7 *(see diagram)* "Incautious. 27. ... Be7, in order to double the rooks on the d-file if necessary, was called for"—Steinitz.

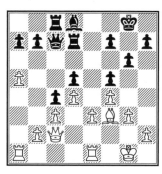

*After 27. ... Rd7*

28. Qg2! "The veteran has been on the lookout and gains a strong point with this fine move and its immediate sequence"—Steinitz. 28. ... Qc6 29. g4! Kh8 "If 29. ... f×g4 30. B×g4, winning the exchange, for 30. ... f5 then would be of no use on account

of 31. B×f5"—Steinitz. 30. g×f5 Bh4 31. Re2 Rg8 32. Qh3 g×f5† 33. Rg2 R×g2† 34. B×g2 Qf6 35. Rf1 Rd8 36. Kh1 Rd6 37. Qf3 Qg6 37. ... Qe6 is correct. If 38. Bh3 Qe4 draws. 38. Bh3 Bd8 39. Rg1 Qe6 40. Qh5 It is understandable that Bird wishes to avoid an endgame with bishops of opposite colors, but the version reached after 40. Qg2! Qe4 41. B×f5 Q×g2† 42. K×g2 B×a5 43. Ra1 Bb6 44. Bc8 is very promising for him. 40. ... Qe4† 41. Bg2 Qe6 42. Bh3 Qe4† 43. Bg2 Qe6 44. Rf1 Qg6 "If 44. ... B×a5 45. Rf3 Qg6 46. Qh3, followed by 47. Rg3 and 48. Rg5, with an excellent game"—Steinitz. The text move is good enough. At the end of Steinitz' line, 46. ... Qg4! is even better for Black. White could improve with 45. Bh3 Qe4† 46. Bg2 with a draw. 45. Qf3 Qg4 46. Qf2 Bh4 47. Qc2 Rh6 48. Bf3 "This and the next are forced as Black threatens 48. ... Bg3"—Steinitz. 48. ... Qh3 49. Qg2 Q×g2† 50. K×g2 Rd6 51. Ra1 51. Rb1 is slightly more active. If 51. ... Bd8 52. b4. 51. ... Bd8 52. Ra4 Rd7 53. Rb4 "Another nice point gained by the veteran, who now threatens 54. Rb5, to avoid which Black has to commit all his pawns to squares of the color of the adverse bishop. White's pawns are no doubt similarly situated, but they are obviously in more compact order and present a better front against attacking attempts"—Steinitz. 53. a6 b×a6 54. R×a6 Bb6 and the d-pawn will remain a target. The text move offers Black better defensive chances. 53. ... a6! Ruling out any a5–a6 ideas. 54. Ra4 Kg7 55. Kf2 Kf6 56. Bg2 Ke6 57. Bh3 Re7 Both 57. ... Bc7 and 57. ... Rc7 avoid the dangerous complications initiated by Bird's next move. 58. e4! "A bright idea, such as very seldom has been carried out in an ending. Combined with White's two last introductory moves, this beautiful stroke forms a charming scheme for a winning decision under conditions which to all appearances would offer very large odds in favor of Black being able to draw, since the two parties have bishops of opposite colors with even pawns"—Steinitz. 58. ... d×e4 59. R×c4 Rc7 "59. ... B×a5 60. Rc5 Bb6 61. R×f5 f6 gave Black more freedom of action and promise of equalization"—Steinitz. Steinitz overlooked that 62. Rb5† wins a piece. 60. Ra4 Rd7 61. Ke3 Rd5 62. b4 Bf6 63. Bf1 Rd8? 63. ... Ke7 keeps control over b5, which is crucial. 64. b5! "In splendid style."—Steinitz 64. ... a×b5 65. B×b5 Rc8 66. c4 Ra8 67. c5 Kd5 "White threatened 68. Bc4†, followed by 69. Rb4 and 70. Bd5"—Steinitz. 67. ... Ke7 could offer some more resistance but the pawns are hard to deal with anyway: 68. a6 b×a6 69. R×a6 R×a6 70. B×a6 Kd7 71. Bc4 Ke7 72. d5. 68. Bc4† Kc6 69. B×f7 Kb5 70. Ra2 Rd8 "If 70. ... R×a5 71. Rb2† and either wins the b-pawn or the bishop"—Steinitz. 71. Rd2 K×a5 72. Be6 Kb5 73. B×f5 b6 74. c×b6 K×b6 75. B×h7 Kb5 76. B×e4 "The rest explains itself. The bishops are of opposite color, but White has three pawns which often are sufficient to win even against a piece ahead. The game is a masterpiece of play on the part of the veteran Bird, but as will be seen, the young German giant dies fighting"—Steinitz. 76. ... Kc4 77. d5 Kc5 78. Rc2† Kd6 79. Rc6† Ke7 80. Kf3 Rh8 81. Kg2 Rg8† 82. Kf3 Rh8 83. Rc2 Kd6 84. Ra2 Bd8 85. Ra6† Ke7 86. Re6† Kf7 87. Bg6† Kg7 88. Kg3 Bf6 89. Be4 Kf7 90. Bf3 Rg8† 91. Bg4 Rd8 92. Ra6 Be7 93. h4 Bd6 94. h5 Kg7 95. Bf3 Kf6 96. Be4 Kg7 97. Ra7† Kf6 98. h6 Rg8† 99. Kf3 Rg1 100. h7 Rh1 101. Ra8 Kg7 102. Rg8† Black resigns—*New York Daily Tribune* (Steinitz), 26 June 1892.

## (1073) Bird–Locock   1–0
B.C.A. Congress (round 3)
London, 9 March 1892
*Game score missing*

## (1074) Mortimer–Bird   0–1
B.C.A. Congress (round 4)
London, 10 March 1892

*White to move*

In this very tense position, every result is still possible. With the following move, Mortimer goes wrong.
**1. Ke1?** It is the brave 1. Ke3! that may gain him the full point, e.g., 1. ... Ng2† 2. Kd4 Rd2† 3. Ke5 R×d7 4. B×d7 Ne3 5. c5. **1. ... Ng2† 2. Kf1 Ne3† 3. Kg1?** Mortimer lands from the frying-pan into the fire. Necessary was 3. Ke1. Bird can then evidently draw, but he could also opt for a highly complicated position, in which each side can still lose: 3. ... f4 4. Rf7 R×h2 5. c5 f3 (5. ... Nc2† is an alternative) 6. c6 Kg3 7. c7 Rc2 8. Bd3 Ng2† 9. Kd1 Rc5 10. B×g6 Nf4. An artistic drawing line now is 11. Bf5 f2 12. Rg7† Kf3 13. Bg4† Ke4 14. Re7† Kd4 15. Rd7† Nd5 16. Ke2. **3. ... f4** 3. ... Rg2† wins in a fascinating way. White must lose a crucial tempo to save himself from mate: 4. Kh1 Ra2 5. Kg1 f4 6. Rf7 g5 7. c5 Rg2† 8. Kh1 Rb2 9. Bd7† Kf3 10. Bc6† Kf2 11. Rb7 Rc2 12. Rb1 g4. **4. R×a7 f3 5. Rf7** and Black mates in three—*British Chess Magazine*, April 1892, p. 144.

## (1075) Mason–Bird   1–0
B.C.A. Congress (round 5)
London, 11 March 1892
*B73*

1. e4 c5 2. Nf3 Nc6 3. Nc3 g6 4. d4 c×d4 5. N×d4 Bg7 6. Be3 d6 7. Be2 Nf6 8. 0–0 0–0 9. Qd2 N×d4 10. B×d4 Ne8 11. f4 e6 12. Rad1 Qa5 13. Kh1 Bd7 14. B×g7 K×g7 15. f5 e×f5 16. Qd4† f6 17. e×f5 B×f5 18. Rd2 Qd8 19. Bf3 Rf7 20. Bd5 Re7 21. g4 Bd7 22. g5 Re5 23. Re2 Qc7 24. Qh4 Bf5 25. Qh6† Black resigns—*New York Sun*, 12 March 1892.

## (1076) Loman–Bird   1–0
B.C.A. Congress (round 6)
London, 12 March 1892
*B25*

1. e4 c5 2. Nc3 Nc6 3. g3 g6 4. Bg2 Bg7 5. Nge2 d6 6. d3 Bd7 7. 0–0 h5 8. h3 Qc8 9. Kh2 Nd4 10. N×d4 c×d4 11. Ne2 Qc7 12. Bd2 Qb6 13. Rb1 Nf6 14. f4 e5 15. f×e5 d×e5 16. c4 h4 17. g4 B×g4 18. h×g4 N×g4† 19. Kh1 h3 20. Bf3 Ne3 21. B×e3 d×e3

22. Nc3 0–0 23. Qe2 Bh6 24. Nd5 Qd4 25. Bg4 b5 26. c×b5 f5 27. Ne7† Kg7 28. B×f5 Bg5 29. Rg1 g×f5 30. R×g5† Kf6 31. Nc6 K×g5 32. N×d4 e×d4 33. Rg1† Kf6 34. Qf3 Ke7 35. e×f5 Rg8 36. Qe4† Black resigns—*Morning Advertiser*, 14 March 1892.

## (1077) Bird–Fenton   1–0
B.C.A. Congress (round 7)
London, 14 March 1892
*Game score missing*

## (1078) Bird–Lee   0–1
B.C.A. Congress (round 8)
London, 15 March 1892
*A03*

1. f4 d5 2. e3 g6 3. Nf3 Bg7 4. d4 Nd7 5. c4 e6 6. Nc3 Ngf6 7. b3 0–0 8. Bd3 b6 9. 0–0 Bb7 10. a4 c5 11. Ne5 Ne4 12. B×e4 d×e4 13. Ba3 N×e5 14. f×e5 Qg5 15. Qe2 Rfd8 16. Nb5 a6 17. Nd6 R×d6 18. e×d6 c×d4 19. Qf2 f5 20. h4 d×e3 21. Qe2 Qg3 22. Bb2 f4 23. B×g7 f3 24. Be5 Qg4 25. Qb2 e2 26. Rf2 e3 27. Bh8 e×f2† 28. K×f2 Q×h4† 29. g3 Qh2† 30. Ke3 Qh6† 31. Kd3 Qf8 32. Be5 Qf5† 33. Ke3 Qe4† 34. Kf2 Rd8 35. Qc3 Qc6 36. b4 a5 37. Bf4 a×b4 38. Q×b4 Kf7 39. Rb1 Rd7 40. Qc3 Qc5† 41. Be3 Qh5 42. Bf4 g5 43. g4 Qg6 44. R×b6 g×f4 45. R×b7 R×b7 46. Q×f3 e1Q† 47. K×e1 Qb1† 48. Qd1 Q×d1† 49. K×d1 Rb4 White resigns—*Hereford Times*, 23 April 1892.

## (1079) Bird–Jasnogrodsky   1–0
B.C.A. Congress (round 9)
London, 16 March 1892
*A03*

1. f4 d5 2. e3 e6 3. Nf3 g6 4. c4 Bg7 5. d4 Nf6 6. Nc3 b6 7. Bd3 Bb7 8. 0–0 0–0 9. Bd2 Nbd7 10. Ne5 Ne4 11. B×e4 d×e4 12. Be1 f5 13. Qb3 N×e5 14. d×e5 Qd3 More flexible is 14. ... Qe7. He experiences some problems with his c-pawn after Bird's reply. **15. Nb5 Rfc8 16. Rd1 Q×b3 17. a×b3 a6 18. Nd4 Kf7 19. b4 Rd8 20. Bh4 Rd7** This looks like being a tricky square for the rook, but Black is still fine; e.g., after 21. Nf3 Bc8! 22. R×d7† B×d7 23. Ng5† Kg8 24. Rd1 Ba4 25. Ra1 Bd7 26. b5 h6 27. Nh3 Bc8 or 21. c5 b×c5 22. b×c5 Rd5. Yet, the unattractive 20. ... Rdc8 might have been preferable. **21. b5 a×b5** This exchange allows Bird to come into action. The quiet 21. ... Bc8 (sit and wait) would be the perfect strategy here. Bird hasn't enough to force a breakthrough anywhere. **22. N×b5 Ke8?** Apparently the only move, but he overlooks the same idea that was so crucial in the lines above. After 22. ... Bc8 he is perfectly fine; e.g., 23. R×d7† (23. Ra1 is the only way to achieve a slight initiative) 23. ... B×d7 24. N×c7 Rc8 25. Nb5 B×b5 26. c×b5 Bf8 27. Ra1 Rc2 with complete equality. **23. R×d7 K×d7 24. Rd1† Kc6 25. Nd4† Kc5 26. N×e6† K×c4 27. N×g7 Kb3 28. e6 Kc2 29. Rd7 Ra1† 30. Kf2 Ba6 31. e7 Rf1† 32. Kg3** Black resigns—*Standard*, 17 March 1892.

## (1080) Rumboll–Bird   0–1
B.C.A. Congress (round 10)
London, 17 March 1892
*Game score missing*

**(1081) Bird–Gossip**   ½–½
B.C.A. Congress (round 11)
London, 18 March 1892
*Game score missing*

---

# Quintangular Tournament 1892

Despite his first place at the B.C.A. congress, Lasker's superiority over the guild of British masters was still questioned by many. Mason, so it was argued, had been troubled by his health, while the mutual games between Lasker, Bird and Mason showed no winner. George Newnes, a well-known publisher, MP and chess patron, decided to provide £25 for a small additional tournament between these three rivals. Gunsberg and Blackburne thought the time was fit to make their entry against the young German and showed their interest in participating. Newnes gladly called them in and doubled the prize money in return. Suddenly it was not only Lasker's strength that was put to a real test, but the hot disputes between Blackburne, Mason and Gunsberg about British supremacy could be settled as well.

A few rules were determined. The tournament would be a double round-robin with a time limit of 20 moves per hour. The prize money would be divided according to the Sonneborn-Berger system. The tournament arena was once more the British Chess Club.

The games started on 28 March, just a week after the B.C.A. Congress, with a huge attendance. Mason tried to postpone the start by a week. According to *The Times*, which brought a report on the first round on 29 March, Mason failed to appear on the first day and it was decided to continue playing with four and make the players meet each other three times. On the following day Mason did sign present and the original idea of a double round-robin tournament was ultimately maintained.

In the first round Lasker gained his revenge for his defeat at the B.C.A. Congress by outplaying Bird. Bird's play in his second game against Mason was a bit too eccentric. While he was already fighting for a draw, Bird made a far too adventuresome move which sealed his fate. After a bye he then opposed Gunsberg. Here Bird played with determination and he was able to exploit his opponent's errors and score the point. In the fifth round Bird fared miserably against Blackburne's From's Gambit. After suffering through a whole game he had to strike the flag. At halfway Lasker and Blackburne were leading with 3 points, far ahead of the others.

Before Bird commenced his second game with Lasker in the sixth round he pleased a dense crowd with a dissertation about chess openings. Bird paid extra attention to his personal favorite opening move, 1. f4. Against expectations he selected the d-pawn to open his game against Lasker. Bird sacrificed a pawn and reached a complicated position. Lasker's solid play swiftly consolidated the game and in the endgame Bird was unable to cope with his material disadvantage.

Bird went completely astray during the final three rounds. Against

both Mason and Gunsberg he refused to split the point, even though any other decision did not make sense. His stubbornness cost him dearly against both. Even more dramatic was Bird's last round game with Blackburne. Though he was still in the running for the tournament victory, Blackburne played weakly and Bird obtained a winning position. But then he blundered it all away: a first mistake allowed a perpetual check, a second mistake offered Blackburne a mate in two.

Bird ended thus desolately last with 1 out of 8, for which he gained a scrimpy £1 1s. 1d. His playing style, it was generally accepted, was not of the kind to pose problems for his stronger opponents. Objectively he could have improved his score with at least two points, but his tendency to play too sharply, too optimistically and blunder once in a while were once more fatal for him. His opponents were of the kind that made merciless use of these vulnerabilities.[23]

The battle for first place was between Lasker and Blackburne. Lasker kept the upperhand throughout the tournament and a final draw with Mason made him emerge with 6½ out of 8, half a point ahead of Blackburne. Quite telling was the fact that Lasker won both games against the Englishman. Mason (twice) and Gunsberg were responsible for wresting half points from Lasker.

Now both Gunsberg and Blackburne were in demand of a match with Lasker. Gunsberg's candidature was easily overshadowed by a potential duel between Lasker and Blackburne. After a few weeks of negotiations and a short delay because of Blackburne's health problems, the match commenced towards the end of May at the British Chess Club. Lasker stilled all critical voices by reaching the required six wins after only ten games. The four other games ended in draws. By now it was clear to everybody that Lasker outranked all British players and was already a candidate for the scepter of the chess world.

---

**Quintangular chess tournament, London, 28 March–8 April 1892**

*Site:* British Chess Club
*Prizes:* £50 divided among the participants according to the Sonneborn-Berger system
*Time limit:* 20 moves per hour

| | 1 | 2 | 3 | 4 | 5 | |
|---|---|---|---|---|---|---|
| 1 E. Lasker | | 1 1 | ½ ½ | ½ 1 | 1 1 | 6½ |
| 2 J.H. Blackburne | 0 0 | | 1 1 | 1 1 | 1 1 | 6 |
| 3 J. Mason | ½ ½ | 0 0 | | 0 1 | 1 1 | 4 |
| 4 I. Gunsberg | ½ 0 | 0 0 | 1 0 | | 0 1 | 2½ |
| 5 H.E. Bird | 0 0 | 0 0 | 0 0 | 1 0 | | 1 |

---

**(1082) Lasker–Bird**   1–0
Quintangular tournament (round 1)
London, 28 March 1892
*B30*

---

23. "Bird was entirely too rash, considering who his opponents were. He sought too much after brilliancy, instead of waiting for it to come to him. To this course, moreover, he was tempted maliciously by his opponents, and often fell a victim to their cunning. On two or three occasion, with victory in his grasp, he was beaten, succumbing not to the superior prowess of the enemy but to the wayward force of his own genius. The chivalry of the man, however, is splendid, and if a painful, certainly no finer sight was witnessed at the tournament, than when this heroic veteran occasionally left his seat at the board and limped across the room to welcome one of his admirers, whilst his industrious opponent was poring over the board, and cudgelling his brains to the uttermost." *Illustrated Sporting and Dramatic News*, 23 April 1892.

1. e4 c5 2. Nf3 Nc6 3. b3 e5 4. Nc3 d6 5. Bc4 h6 6. d3 Be6 7. B×e6 f×e6 8. 0–0 Be7 9. Ne2 g5 10. c3 g4 11. Nd2 Qb6 12. Nc4 Qc7 13. d4 b5 14. Na3 b4 15. Nc2 b×c3 16. d×c5 Nf6 17. c×d6 B×d6 18. N×c3 Nd4 19. Bb2 Rd8 20. Rc1 Qf7 21. Qd3 Qh5 22. N×d4 e×d4 23. Qb5† Kf7 24. Q×h5† N×h5 25. Nb5 Nf4 26. B×d4 Ne2† 27. Kh1 Bf4 28. Rc4 Rhg8 29. B×a7 Rg5 30. Nd4 B×h2 31. N×e2 Rh5 32. g3 B×g3† 33. Kg2 Be5 34. Bd4 Bb8 35. Rh1 R×h1 36. K×h1 e5 37. Be3 h5 38. Nc3 Rd3 39. Nd5 h4 40. Rc8 Bd6 41. Rh8 Rd1† 42. Kh2 Rd4 43. Rh7† Ke6 44. Rh6† Kd7 45. R×h4 Black resigns—*Standard*, 29 March 1892.

## (1083) Bird–Mason    0–1
Quintangular tournament (round 2)
London, 29 March 1892
*A03*

1. f4 d5 2. e3 c5 3. Nf3 Nf6 4. b3 g6 5. Bb2 Bg7 6. Bb5† Bd7 7. Be2 Nc6 8. c3 0–0 9. 0–0 Qc7 10. Na3 Rae8 11. Qe1 a6 12. c4 d×c4 13. N×c4 Nb4 14. Qh4 Bf5 15. a3 Bd3 16. B×d3 N×d3 17. Bc3 Nd5 18. B×g7 K×g7 19. f5 Nf6 20. e4 b5 21. Ne3 Qf4 22. g4 h6 23. f×g6 f×g6 24. e5 N×e5 25. N×e5 Q×e5 26. Rae1 Qg5 27. Qg3 Ne4 28. R×f8 R×f8 29. Qg2 Qf6 30. Rf1 Qd4 31. R×f8 K×f8 32. Qh3 Kg7 33. d3 Nf6 34. Qf3 N×g4 35. Q×g4 Q×e3† 36. Kg2 Qd2† 37. Kh1 Q×d3 38. h4 Q×b3 39. Qe4 Qd1† 40. Kh2 Qd6† 41. Kh1 c4 42. h5 Qd1† 43. Kg2 Qd6 44. a4 g×h5 45. a×b5 a×b5 46. Kg1 c3 47. Qe2 Qd4† White resigns—*Daily News*, 30 March 1892.

Bird had a bye in the third round.

## (1084) Gunsberg–Bird    0–1
Quintangular tournament (round 4)
London, 31 March 1892
*B01*

1. e4 d5 2. e×d5 Q×d5 3. Nc3 Qd8 4. d4 c6 5. Bc4 e6 6. Nf3 Nd7 7. 0–0 Ngf6 8. Re1 Be7 9. Ne2 0–0 10. Bd3 b6 11. Ne5 Bb7 12. c3 c5 13. Nc4 Rc8 14. Ne3 c×d4 15. c×d4 Nd5 16. N×d5 B×d5 17. Nc3 Nf6 18. Bf4 Bb7 19. Be5 Bd6 This move compels Bird to exchange soon at e5 after which Gunsberg gains promising play on the kingside. 19. ... Nd7 avoids this altogether. **20. Re3 g6 21. Rh3 B×e5 22. d×e5 Nd5** Better options were 22. ... Nd7 or the more elaborate 22. ... Nh5 23. Qd2 Rc4! 24. Rd1 Rg4 25. Bf1 Q×d2 26. R×d2 Nf4. **23. Qd2 f5** (*see diagram*)

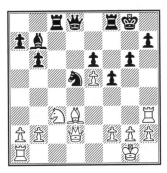

*After 23. ... f5*

**24. Qh6** At once 24. Nb5! is a clear improvement. The knight dominates the board once it reaches d6. **24. ... Rf7 25. Nb5 Rc5**

**26. Nd6 Rfc7** Thanks to the activation of his rooks the situation is now less dramatic for Bird. **27. Bc4 Qf8 28. Qh4 Qe7 29. b3 Q×h4 30. R×h4 g5?!** With the exchange of queens Bird crowned his defense but this doesn't mean that he has the luxury to recklessly open up the kingside. 30. ... Bc6, followed by 30. ... b5, is a better plan. **31. Rh6** Entering with the rook in the enemy lines is not without risk and had to be well calculated. **31. ... Nf4 32. Ne8?!** The critical point of the game. Though this maneuvre looks very attractive, Bird comes out of the complications with slightly the better chances. Gunsberg perhaps abstained from the relatively simple way to win a pawn with 32. g3 Ng6 33. B×e6† Kg7 34. N×f5† Kh8 because the position of his king becomes tricky. After the prudent 35. Kf1 Bf3 36. Bc4 b5 37. Nd4, White is nevertheless well on top. **32. ... Re7 33. Nf6† Kh8 34. g3 Ng6 35. N×h7?** Based on a miscalculation. 35. Re1? N×e5 loses immediately due to the threats 36. ... Nf3† and 36. ... Kg7. 35. f4 is the best move as, at the price of a pawn at f4, the more important stronghold at e5 is held a bit longer. This allows him counterplay after 35. ... g×f4 36. g×f4 N×f4 37. Rd1 Rc8 38. Rd6. **35. ... Kg7! 36. Rh3 g4 37. Rh5 N×e5 38. Ng5 Kg6 39. N×e6 K×h5 40. N×c5 b×c5 41. Be2 Nf3† 42. B×f3 B×f3 43. Kf1 Re2** White resigns—*Standard*, 1 April 1892.

## (1085) Bird–Blackburne    0–1
Quintangular tournament (round 5)
London, 1 April 1892
*A02*

1. f4 e5 2. f×e5 d6 3. e×d6 B×d6 4. Nf3 Nf6 5. d4 Ne4 6. Qd3 f5 7. Nc3 0–0 8. N×e4 f×e4 9. Q×e4 Bf5 10. Q×b7 Nd7 11. Qb3† Kh8 12. Bg5 Qe8 13. Qe3 Qh5 14. c3 Rab8 15. Qd2 Nb6 16. b3 Nd5 17. Rc1 h6 18. Bh4 Bf4 19. Qb2 Ne3 20. Bf2 Rbe8 21. B×e3 B×e3 22. c4 Be4 23. Rc3 B×f3 24. R×e3 R×e3 25. g×f3 Q×f3 26. Kd2 Q×h1 27. K×e3 Q×f1 28. Kd3 Rf3† 29. Kd2 Rf2 30. Kd3 Qh3† White resigns—*Daily News*, 2 April 1892.

## (1086) Bird–Lasker    0–1
Quintangular tournament (round 6)
London, 2 April 1892

*Black to move*

Bird opened with 1. d4 and got what seemed a strong center, but this Lasker broke up at the right time. Above is the position of the game at a critical point. The game went on: **1. ... 0–0 2. Rd1 g6 3. Qf2 Q×f2† 4. K×f2 Ng4† 5. Ke2 f6 6. Bc1 Kg7** and White ultimately lost the game—*British Chess Magazine*, June 1892, p. 203.

## (1087) Mason–Bird    1–0
Quintangular tournament (round 7)
London, 4 April 1892

White to move

In their second game, Bird adopted a Center Counter, and early lost a pawn. Then he played very well for some time, and Mason had to keep his weather eye open to avoid danger. The end was singular, for Bird had a dead draw in the position shown on the diagram above. The game continued: **76. a6† Kc7** 76. ... Ka7 would have drawn easily, but hours of play had evidently told upon the older man. The line runs: 77. Ka5 Kb8 78. Kb6 Ka8 79. Nf6 h2 80. Nd5 h1Q 81. Nc7† Kb8 82. a7† Kc8 83. a8Q†. **77. Nh2 Kc8 78. Kc6 Kb8 79. Kb6 Ka8 80. Ng4 Kb8 81. a7† Ka8 82. Nf6 h2 83. Nd5** and Black resigns—*British Chess Magazine*, June 1892, p. 206.

Bird was bye in the eighth round.

## (1088) Bird–Gunsberg    0–1
Quintangular tournament (round 9)
London, 6 April 1892

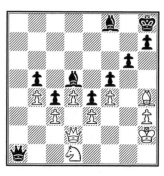

White to move

The game early got somewhat blocked, and then rooks were exchanged and Gunsberg offered a draw, but Bird refused, and the play went on till the diagrammed position resulted. Here again, Bird seemed to lose all sight of the board for a moment, for he played **1. Nf2?** and Gunsberg seized his chance **1. ... B×b4 2. c×b4 c3! 3. Qe2 Bc4 4. Q×c4** Herr Lasker pointed out afterwards that White got a chance of counterattack and drawing by 4. Qc2 Qb2 5. Qd1, for if 5. ... c2 6. Qg1, and White will get perpetual check if 6. ... c1Q. Black, however, can improve this line anywhere, by playing 5. ... Kg7, followed by 6. ... h6 or even 6. ... Kg8 7. Qg5 Q×b4. **4. ... b×c4 5. d5 c2** White resigns—*British Chess Magazine*, June 1892, p. 207.

## (1089) Blackburne–Bird    1–0
Quintangular tournament (round 10)
London, 8 April 1892
*A02*

**1. f4 f5 2. b3 e6 3. Bb2 Nf6 4. g3 c5 5. Bg2 d5 6. Nf3 Bd6 7. 0–0 0–0 8. Ne5 Na6 9. e3 Nc7 10. c4 Bd7 11. Na3 Bc6 12. Nc2 Qe7 13. Ne1 B×e5 14. f×e5 Ng4 15. Qe2 Rad8 16. Rc1 Na6 17. Nc2 Qd7 18. d4 d×c4 19. B×c6 Q×c6 20. b×c4** The unorthodox 20. Q×c4, intending 21. d×c5, looks ugly but in return for a wrecked pawn structure White gets control over the important square d4. After the text move, White is bound to suffer with his weak pawn at d4. **20. ... Rd7 21. Rcd1 Rfd8 22. h3 Nh6 23. Ne1 Nf7 24. Ng2 Nc7 25. Nf4 Qe4 26. Kh2?** 26. Rb1 b6 27. Ba1 keeps Black's advantage limited. **26. ... c×d4 27. R×d4** If 27. B×d4 g5. Of course, 27. e×d4 Q×e2 28. N×e2 N×e5 wins a pawn. Therefore it was better to leave the d-file with the rook on the previous move. **27. ... Qc6** Bird forgoes the simple material win after 27. ... R×d4 28. B×d4 N×e5. He aims for Blackburne's king instead. **28. Rfd1 Ng5 29. R×d7 R×d7 30. R×d7 Q×d7 31. h4 Ne4 32. Bd4 b6 33. Nd3 Qa4** 33. ... Qc6 prevents 34. c5. **34. Nf4 g6 35. Nh3 Na6 36. Nf4 Qc6 37. Qd3** Losing time. 37. g4 was worth a try. **37. ... Nf2 38. Qf1 Ng4† 39. Kg1 Nc5 40. Qd1 Ne4** 40. ... Nd7 wins the pawn at e5. **41. Ne2 Q×c4** 41. ... Nef2 now even conquers the queen. **42. B×b6 a×b6?** 42. ... Kg7! wins easily. **43. Qd8† Kg7 44. Qe7† Kh6??** A suicidal attempt to avoid the perpetual. **45. Qf8† Kh5 46. Nf4** mate—*Standard*, 9 April 1892.

# HANDICAP TOURNAMENT AT SIMPSON'S DIVAN, APRIL–JUNE 1892

In April 1892 the Divan was the scene of a handicap tournament. The rules applied at earlier such tournaments remained unaltered. The field consisted of 17 players. Bird was back and he was joined by masters such as Lee and Loman. Another strong German player made his first appearance on the London chess scene: Richard Teichmann. Teichmann enjoyed the reputation of being one of Berlin's stronger players, though the self-confidence of the British players, with Bird at first place, made them claim that nothing of his professed strength was proven in England yet.

Bird started enthusiastically. He gained 4½ points from his first six games. One of his noteworthy wins was against Teichmann. In this game Bird treated the Sicilian in a very modern way. His play left such an impression on his opponent that Teichmann showed his respect by resigning rather early. Bird then suffered a loss against Loman. Subsequent losses against Müller and the weak Martineau made Bird lose touch with the leaders. With 5½ out of 9 and eliminated from the higher prizes, he took a rest that lasted ten days. Bird was experiencing health issues and it was even suggested that he might have to forfeit his remaining games. Fortunately he recovered well and finished with 10½ out of 16. Maas and Teichmann, whose play was doubtlessly affected by all kinds of practical problems related with his arrival in England, shared fourth place with Bird.

## Handicap tournament, London, 25 April–June 1892

***Site:*** Simpson's Divan
***Prizes:*** Four prizes
***Time limit:*** 20 moves per hour
***Odds scale:*** two moves (class II), pawn and move (class III), pawn and two moves (class IV), knight (class V), knight and move (class VI) and two pieces (class VII)

| | | | 1 | 2 | 3 | 4 | 5 | 6 | 7 | 8 | 9 | 10 | 11 | 12 | 13 | 14 | 15 | 16 | 17 | |
|---|---|---|---|---|---|---|---|---|---|---|---|---|---|---|---|---|---|---|---|---|
| 1 | F.J. Lee | I | | 1 | 0 | ½ | 1 | ½ | 0 | 1 | 1 | ½ | 1 | 1 | 1 | 1 | 1 | 1 | 1 | 12½ |
| 2 | J.P. Mollard | II | 0 | | 1 | 1 | 0 | 1 | 1 | 1 | ½ | 1 | 0 | 1 | 1 | 1 | 1 | 1 | 1 | 11½ |
| 3 | R. Loman | I | 1 | 0 | | ½ | 1 | 1 | ½ | ½ | 1 | 1 | 1 | 1 | 1 | 1 | ½ | 0 | 1 | 11 |
| 4 | R. Teichmann | I | ½ | 0 | ½ | | 0 | 1 | 1 | 1 | ½ | 1 | 1 | 1 | 0 | 1 | 1 | 1 | 0 | 10½ |
| 5 | H.E. Bird | I | 0 | 1 | 0 | 1 | | ½ | ½ | 1 | 1 | 0 | ½ | 0 | 1 | 1 | 1 | 1 | 1 | 10½ |
| 6 | A.J. Maas | V | ½ | 0 | 0 | 0 | ½ | | 1 | 1 | 1 | ½ | 1 | 1 | 1 | 0 | 1 | 1 | 1 | 10½ |
| 7 | N. Jasnogrodsky | I | 1 | 0 | ½ | 0 | ½ | 0 | | 1 | 1 | 1 | ½ | ½ | 1 | 1 | 0 | 1 | 1 | 10 |
| 8 | L. van Vliet | I | 0 | 0 | ½ | 0 | 0 | 0 | 0 | | 1 | 1 | 1 | 1 | 0 | 1 | 1 | 1 | 1 | 8½ |
| 9 | Rolland | I | 0 | ½ | 0 | ½ | 0 | 0 | 0 | 0 | | ½ | 1 | 1 | 1 | 1 | 1 | 1 | 1 | 8½ |
| 10 | O.C. Müller | I | ½ | 0 | 0 | 0 | 1 | ½ | 0 | 0 | ½ | | 1 | 0 | 1 | 1 | 1 | | 1 | 7½ |
| 11 | Law | VI | 0 | 1 | 0 | 0 | ½ | 1 | ½ | 0 | 0 | 0 | | | | | | 1 | | 4 |
| 12 | G. Martineau | IV | 0 | 0 | 0 | 0 | 1 | 0 | ½ | 0 | 0 | 1 | | | | 0 | ½ | 1 | | 4 |
| 13 | J.E. Hetley | IV | 0 | 0 | 0 | 1 | 0 | 0 | 0 | 1 | 0 | 0 | | | | | | | 1 | 3 |
| 14 | E.O. Jones | I | 0 | 0 | 0 | 0 | 0 | 1 | 0 | 0 | 0 | 0 | | 1 | | | 1 | | | 3 |
| 15 | Cruesmann | IV | 0 | 0 | ½ | 0 | 0 | 0 | 1 | 0 | 0 | 0 | | ½ | | 0 | | | | 2 |
| 16 | Alderson | VII | 0 | 0 | 1 | 0 | 0 | 0 | 0 | 0 | 0 | | 0 | 0 | | | | | | 1 |
| 17 | E.L. Sellon | III | 0 | 0 | 0 | 1 | 0 | 0 | 0 | 0 | 0 | 0 | | | 0 | | | | | 1 |

The battle for victory turned out to be a race between Loman and Lee. Loman started with 6½ out of 8 and, having already met most of the first-class opponents, was considered the favorite. Lee scored 7 points out of his first 8 games, but he still had to do battle with many strong players. Van Vliet, with 5½ of 7, also did well at the start, but he dropped some points in the following rounds. The struggle remained tense, with constantly changing front-runners. Towards the end of the tournament, Lee (11 of 14) restored his slight advantage over Loman (11 of 15) once more. Lee still had to face Teichmann and Bird, while Loman seemed to have an easy pairing with Alderson. Alderson enjoyed the odds of two pieces, but given his very low score, a win would be unexpected. Lee managed to draw Teichmann and ensured victory by beating Bird. Loman, to the surprise of everybody, lost his game against the odds-taker and finished with 11 out of 16. This allowed the weaker James Percival Mollard to surpass him and take second place with 11½.

### (1090) Bird–E.O. Jones 1–0

Handicap tournament (round 1)
London, 25 April 1892
*A03*

**1. f4 d5 2. Nf3 e6 3. e3 Nf6 4. b3 Be7 5. Bb2 a6 6. Nc3 0–0 7. Bd3 c5 8. 0–0 Nc6 9. a3 b5 10. Qe1 Qb6 11. Nd1 c4 12. Be2 Bb7 13. Qg3 Ne8 14. Nf2 Bf6 15. Ne5 B×e5 16. f×e5 d4 17. Ng4 d×e3 18. Nh6† Kh8 19. N×f7† R×f7 20. R×f7 e×d2† 21. Qf2 Q×f2† 22. K×f2 Kg8 23. R×b7 Rd8 24. b×c4 Na5 25. Re7 b×c4 26. Bc3** Black resigns—*Standard*, 26 April 1892.

### (1091) Loman–Bird 1–0

Handicap tournament (round 2)
London, 25 April 1892
*C61*

**1. e4 e5 2. Nf3 Nc6 3. Bb5 Nd4 4. Bc4 Bc5 5. N×d4 B×d4** "If 5. ... e×d4 6. B×f7† and 7. Qh5†"—Loman. **6. c3 Bb6 7. d4 Qh4 8. 0–0 d6 9. Qb3 Nf6?** Bird sacrifices a pawn to pursue a hopeless attack. **10. B×f7† Ke7 11. Nd2 Bg4 12. Nc4 Be2 13. Ne3** "13. Re1 was not possible due to 13. ... Ng4. White menaces now 14. Nf5†"—Loman. **13. ... Q×e4 14. Bd5** "14. Qe6† leads to nothing"—Loman. His actual move is not bad, but at once 14. Re1! is a strong improvement. **14. ... N×d5 15. N×d5† Kd7 16. Re1 e×d4 17. N×b6† a×b6 18. c×d4?** After this slow move Bird is completely back into the game again. 18. Qf7†! Kc8 19. Q×g7 and 20. c×d4 puts Black with his back against the wall. **18. ... Rhe8! 19. Be3 Bd3** 19. ... Qd3 is objectively better, but the endgame is much too drawish to Bird's taste. **20. Rac1 Qg6 21. d5 Be4?!** An error as he neglects the defense of his own king which resides in precarious conditions. 21. ... b5, fortifying the white squares on the queenside, is his best plan. **22. g3 Qf7?!** Bird continues his plan to attack Loman's king along the White squares, but the sudden 23. B×b6! would have put an immediate end to this. Therefore it was necessary to consent with the ugly but still playable 22. ... c5 23. d×c6 *e.p.* B×c6. **23. Qb5† c6 24. Q×b6 Reb8** *(see diagram)*

*After 24. ... Reb8*

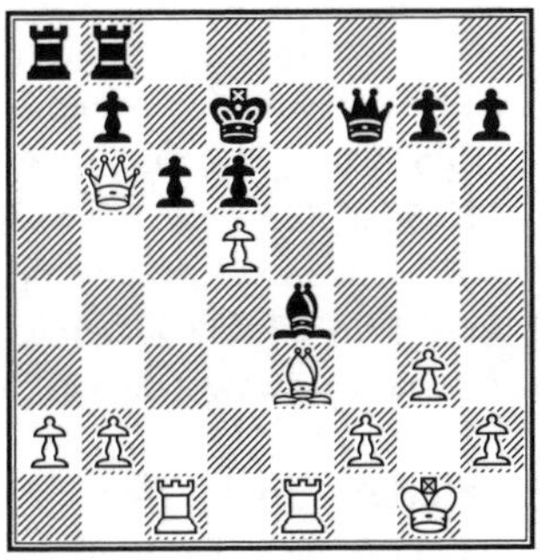

**25. R×c6!** "This sacrifice was impossible with Black's rook at e8"—Loman. **25. ... b×c6** 25. ... Qf3 brings no avail after 26. R×d6†

Ke8 27. Re6† Kf7 (27. ... Kf8 28. R×e4! Q×e4 29. Bc5†) 28. Re7†!! K×e7 29. Qe6† and mates next move. **26. Q×c6† Ke7 27. Bg5†** 27. Bf4! Qg6 28. B×d6† wins at once. After the text move Black's king momentarily escapes from the worst. **27. ... Kf8 28. R×e4 Kg8 29. Q×d6** 29. Bf4 prevents Black from taking at b2. **29. ... R×b2 30. Rf4 Qh5** 30. ... Qe8, to keep e6 under control, is more stubborn. A possible continuation would have been 31. Be7 Qb5 32. Qe6† Kh8 33. Kg2 White stays well on top, but he must remain alert. **31. Qe6† Kh8** (*see diagram*)

*After 31. ... Kh8*

**32. Qe7?** "A mistake that loses an important pawn. Blackburne expected 32. Qf5, but we don't see more than a draw for White after 32. ... Qd1† 33. Kg2 Rbb8. The position is very interesting. The strongest continuation is probably 32. Be7 and, if possible, 33. Bf8"—Loman. The text move is a blunder as it leaves the d-pawn to be captured. However, both players overlook Black's best way to deal with it. Finding a good alternative is far from easy. 32. Qf5 is only sufficient for a draw, but not by 32. ... Qd1† 33. Kg2 Rbb8 as 34. Bf6! is handsomely strong. Correct is 32. ... h6! 33. Rh4 Qd1† 34. Kg2 R×f2†! 35. Q×f2 Q×d5†. Loman's other suggestion, 32. Be7 also turns out to be a draw after 32. ... Re2 33. Qd7 Re1† 34. Kg2 Qe2 35. Bf8 Qf1† etc. Winning is the immediate 32. Bf6!— e.g., 32. ... g×f6 33. Q×f6† Kg8 34. Q×b2 or, a bit better, 32. ... Rb7 33. Bd4 Qg6 34. Re4 Rc7 36. Bb6 Rb7 37. Bc5 etc. **32. ... Qd1† 33. Kg2 Q×d5† 34. Kh3 Qg8?!** The situation changed dramatically: White's king has come under fire from Black's heavy artillery. At this point 34. ... Kg8!, intending 35. ... Rb7, is the correct procedure. White's pieces are placed somewhat clumsily. **35. Rf7 Rb6** 35. ... Re8 36. R×g7 R×e7 is also very drawish. **36. Be3 Re8 37. R×g7 Qe6†?** A dreadful mistake. 37. ... R×e7 secures an easy draw. **38. Q×e6 Rb×e6 39. Bd4** Black is bound up. **39. ... h6 40. a4 Re4 41. Re7†?!** 41. Bc3 leaves Black no option but a quick resignation. **41. ... Kg8 42. R×e8† R×e8 43. a5 Re4 44. Bb6 Ra4 45. Kg2 Kg7 46. Kf3 Kf6 47. h4 Ke6** 47. ... h5! is the crucial idea to stop White from progressing. **48. Ke3 Ke5** As White omitted to push the h-pawn himself, 48. ... h5 is still a valid defense. White, for example, doesn't get any further after 49. Kd3 Kd5 50. Kc3 Ra2 51. Kb4 Ra1 52. Kb5 Rb1† 53. Ka6 Kc6. **49. Kd3 Kd5 50. Kc3 Kc6 51. Kb3 Rg4 52. Be3** Black's condition has worsened, and he is unable to cope with the a-pawn now. **52. ... h5 53. a6 Kb5 54. a7 Ra4 55. g4! h×g4 56. h5** and White wins— *De Groene Amsterdammer* (Loman), 1 May 1892.

## (1092) Hetley–Bird    0–1

Handicap tournament (round 3)
London, 27 April 1892
*Odds of pawn and two moves*

**1. e4 & 2. d4 Nc6 3. c3 e5 4. Nf3 Qe7 5. Be3 d6 6. h3 Nf6 7. Bg5 Bd7 8. d5 Nd8 9. B×f6 g×f6 10. Nbd2 Nf7 11. g4 Bh6 12. Bg2 0–0 13. 0–0 Nh8 14. Nh2 Ng6 15. a4 Nf4 16. Nc4 b5 17. Ne3 b×a4 18. Nf5 B×f5 19. g×f5 Kh8 20. Ng4 Bg7 21. f3 h5 22. Nf2 Bh6 23. Nd3 Rg8 24. N×f4 B×f4 25. Kh1 Rg3 26. Rf2 Rag8 27. Qe2 Qg7 28. Rg1 R×h3†** White resigns—*Morning Post*, 20 June 1892.

## (1093) Teichmann–Bird    0–1

Handicap tournament (round 4)
London, 27 April 1892
*B73*

**1. e4 c5 2. Nf3 Nc6 3. Nc3 g6** "Mr. Bird's favorite defense, and splendidly as a rule does conduct it"—MacDonnell. **4. d4 c×d4 5. N×d4 Bg7 6. Be3 d6** "Another 'Bird' move; unorthodox, but also unhackneyed, and therefore not to be despised"—MacDonnell. **7. Be2 Bd7 8. 0–0 Nf6 9. h3 0–0 10. f4 N×d4 11. B×d4 Bc6 12. Kh2 Qc7** Here 12. ... e5! 13. f×e5 N×e4 leads to an excellent position for Black. Such a radical freeing move was still a rare find in the nineteenth century. **13. B×f6** This exchange is not the solution of his problems. Fine is 13. Qd3. **13. ... B×f6 14. Qd3 a6 15. Rad1** A stereotypic move that seriously compromises his queenside. The prophylactic 15. Nd1, intending 16. c4, would stabilize his position. **15. ... Rac8 16. Bf3** (*see diagram*)

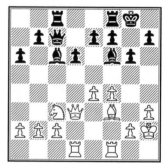

*After 16. Bf3*

**16. ... Qb6!** Bird's reply is excellent here. **17. Rb1 B×c3! 18. b×c3 Qa5 19. c4** He must either lose a pawn or the exchange. In any case White's position is in ruin. **19. ... Q×a2 20. Bg4 Rc7 21. f5 Qa5 22. Rbe1 Qe5† 23. Kh1 Be8** White resigns. "Of course he might have prolonged the game for many moves—or many hours, but he chivalrously preferred by early resignation to testify his consciousness of the inferiority of his position, and his appreciation of Mr. Bird's generalship. Herr Teichmann is well known as one of the leading players in Berlin"—MacDonnell. Teichmann's resignation is perhaps a little bit premature, but well founded. He is a pawn behind and has no chance to withstand his opponent on the queenside— *Illustrated Sporting and Dramatic News* (MacDonnell), 7 May 1892.

## (1094) Bird–Rolland    1–0

Handicap tournament (round 10)
London, 17 May 1892
*A03*

**1. f4 c5 2. Nf3 Nc6 3. e3 d5 4. b3 Nf6 5. Bb2 e6 6. Bb5 a6** "This is a wasted move. 6. ... Bd7 would have been better"—Guest. **7. B×c6† b×c6 8. 0–0 Be7 9. Qe1 0–0 10. d3 Nd7** "Apparently to prevent White from playing 11. Ne5. In view of the threatened attack of 12. Qg3 etc., the knight had better not have been moved from the protection of the kingside"—Guest. **11. Nc3 f6 12. Qg3** Now that Black consolidated his kingside, it is perhaps more interesting to switch his attention towards the center with 12. e4. Yet Bird's approach is certainly not without venom either. **12. ... Bd6 13. Nd1 Qe7 14. Nf2 e5 15. Ng4 e×f4 16. e×f4 Kh8** "White threatened 17. Nh6†, followed by 18. Nf5 winning a piece"—Guest. **17. Nh4** Bird pursues his attack with all possible means, which demands the utmost care of his opponent. As a perfect defense is possible, objectively speaking 17. Rae1 deserves the preference. **17. ... Nb6 18. Qh3 Qf7 19. f5 Kg8?** *(see diagram)* Rolland finally makes the single mistake that Bird needs to win the game. 19. ... Qh5 20. N×f6 R×f6 (if at once 20. ... g×f6 21. g4!) 21. B×f6 g×f6 gives him equality.

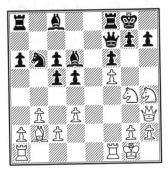

*After 19. ... Kg8*

**20. B×f6!** Qh5 "Obviously if 20. ... g×f6 21. Nh6† wins the queen"—Guest. **21. Be5 Be7 22. Bg3 B×h4 23. Q×h4 Q×h4 24. B×h4 R×f5 25. R×f5 B×f5 26. Ne5 Bd7 27. a4 Re8** Losing quickly, but White's positional advantage is indisputable. **28. a5 R×e5 29. a×b6 Bc8 30. Ra5! c4 31. b×c4 Re2 32. Rc5 d×c4 33. R×c4 Bb7 34. Rd4 R×g2† 35. K×g2 c5† 36. Re4** Black resigns—*Morning Post* (Guest), 19 May 1892.

## (1095) Bird–van Vliet 1–0
Handicap tournament (round 12)
London, 18 May 1892
*A03*

**1. f4 d5 2. e3 g6 3. Nf3 Bg7 4. Nc3 c5 5. Ne2 Nc6 6. d4 Nf6 7. c3 Qb6 8. Ng3 0–0 9. Bd3 e6 10. 0–0 Rd8 11. Kh1 Bd7 12. Ne5 Be8 13. Qe2 Nd7 14. N×c6** "Up to now both games are well developed, but this exchange does not please us, as it affords Black the possibility of dissolving the center and of getting an attack on White's queenside. Further it renders the development of Bc1 difficult. Why not let the knight at e5 and play 14. Rb1, and bring the bishop to f2, followed by e4?"—Lasker. **14. ... b×c6 15. Qc2** 15. d×c5 is the lesser evil. Black's two c-pawns now open the center in an extremely favorable way for him. **15. ... c×d4 16. e×d4 c5 17. d×c5 N×c5 18. Be2 Na4** The immediate 18. ... d4! is very awkward to meet. **19. Bd3 Rdc8 20. Rb1 Rab8 21. Qe2?** 21. f5!? creates some chances of his own, as with 21. ... e×f5 (21. ... e5 is an improvement and keeps a positional edge after 22. Re1 Bb5) 22. N×f5!? g×f5 23. Bf4 Rb7 24. B×f5. **21. ... Bb5** 21. ... Nc5! cleverly exploits the weakness of the f1–a6 diagonal. He gains material after 22. Be3 d4!, followed by exchanges at d4 and d3. **22. Be3 B×d3 23. Q×d3**

Richard Teichmann (courtesy Cleveland Public Library).

Qc7?! 23. ... N×b2! nets a pawn. **24. Qc2 Qd7?!** Not an ideal square. 24. ... Nb6 remains clearly better for Black. **25. Qf2?** After 25. Ne2 Nb6 26. Bd4 the worst would be over. **25. ... Rb7** 25. ... Rc7 is more precise as the queen remains defended in some crucial lines (see move 28). **26. Bd4 B×d4 27. Q×d4** "The object of the last queen moves is now obvious, Mr. Bird has cleverly exchanged the dangerous bishop, in order to equalize the position"—Lasker. If correctly followed up, this ought to lose. The passive 27. c×d4 is obligatory. **27. ... R×b2?** *(see diagram)* Black falls into Bird's little trap. Correct is 27. ... N×b2, snatching the pawn while keeping the queen defended.

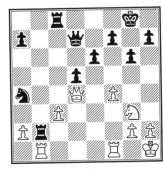

*After 27. ... R×b2*

**28. Ne4! Qb5 29. Nf6† Kf8 30. N×h7† Ke8?** A dreadful way to lose. 30. ... Kg8 forces the draw. **31. Rbe1! Rc7 32. Qg7 Kd8 33. c4!** Now the transformation is complete. This crafty move considerably fortifies the attack. **33. ... Qe8 34. c×d5** Bird misses the immediately winning 34. Nf6! **34. ... Rcc2 35. Rg1 Nc5 36. Qd4 Qd7 37. d6 Kc8 38. Rc1 Qc6 39. R×c2 R×c2 40. Ng5 Qd5 41. Qh8† Kb7 42. Rb1† Nb3 43. Nf3** Black resigns—*London Chess Fortnightly* (Lasker), 14 July 1893, pp. 153–154.

**(1096) Bird–Lee　0–1**
Handicap tournament (round 15)
London, June 1892
*A03*

1. f4 d5 2. e3 g6 3. Nf3 Bg7 4. d4 c5 5. c3 Qb6 6. Nbd2
Nf6 7. a4 0–0 8. Bd3 Nc6 9. 0–0 Bd7 10. Ne5 N×e5 11. f×e5
Ng4 12. a5 Qc7 13. Qf3 Be6 14. h3 Nh6 15. e4 Rad8 16. e×d5
B×d5 17. Be4 Qc6 18. d×c5 Q×c5† 19. Kh1 B×e4 20. N×e4
Q×e5 21. Bf4 Qb5 22. Qf2 a6 23. Bg5 f6 24. Be3 Nf5 25. Bb6
Rd5 26. Rfe1 Re5 27. Nc5 Qc6 28. Nd3 R×e1† 29. R×e1 e5
30. Nb4 Qe6 31. Qd2 Bh6 32. Qf2 Bg5 33. g4 Bh4 34. Qg1
Ne7 35. Rd1 Nc6 36. N×c6 Q×c6† 37. Qg2 Q×g2† 38. K×g2
f5 39. g×f5 g×f5 40. Bc5 Rf7 41. Rd5 e4 42. Re5 Kg7 43. Re6
Bf6 44. Kg3 Rd7 45. Be3 Kf7 46. Rb6 Be5† 47. Kh4 f4 and
after a few more moves White resigns—*Hereford Times*, 25 June
1892.

# Some Offhand Games,
# Spring 1892

**(1097) Fish–Bird　0–1**
Offhand game
London 1892
*C40*

1. e4 e5 2. Bc4 f5 3. Nf3 f×e4 4. N×e5 Nf6 5. Nf7 Qe7 6. N×h8
d5 7. Be2 Nc6 8. Bh5† g6 9. N×g6 h×g6 10. Be2 Qe5 11. 0–0
d4 12. d3 e3 13. f×e3 d×e3 14. Rf3 Ng4 15. Rg3 Bc5 16. c3
Bf5 17. a3 Rd8 18. b4 R×d3 19. Qe1 Bb6 20. R×g4 B×g4
21. B×d3 e2† 22. Kh1 Bf2 23. B×g6† Ke7 24. Bg5† Q×g5
25. Q×f2 Qc1† Black wins—*Illustrated London News*, 6 February
1892.

**(1098) Fish–Bird　0–1**
Offhand game
London 1892
*C40*

1. e4 e5 2. Bc4 f5 3. Nf3 f×e4 4. N×e5 Nf6 5. Nf7 Qe7 6. N×h8
d5 7. Be2 Nc6 8. Bh5† g6 9. N×g6 h×g6 10. B×g6† Kd8 11. h4
Bg4 12. f3 e×f3† 13. Kf2 f×g2 14. Re1 Ne4† 15. R×e4 Q×h4†
16. Ke3 Qg3† 17. Qf3 Q×f3 mate—*Illustrated London News*, 30
April 1892.

**(1099) Buckley–Bird　1–0**
Offhand game
London (British C.C.), 4 April 1892
*C37*

1. e4 e5 2. f4 e×f4 3. Nf3 g5 4. Bc4 g4 5. 0–0 g×f3 6. Q×f3
Qf6 7. e5 Q×e5 8. d3 Bh6 9. Bd2 Ne7 10. Nc3 Nbc6 11. Rae1
Qc5† 12. Kh1 d6 13. Nd5 Ne5 14. R×e5 d×e5 15. Bb4 Qc6

16. Bb5 Q×b5 17. N×c7† Black resigns—*Birmingham Weekly Mercury*, 16 April 1892.

**(1100) Bird & Chapman–Blackburne & Lee　1–0**
Consultation game
London (Simpson's Divan) 1892
*C58*

1. e4 e5 2. Nf3 Nc6 3. Bc4 Nf6 4. Ng5 d5 5. e×d5 Na5 6. Bb5†
c6 7. d×c6 b×c6 8. Bd3 Bg4 9. Be2 Bf5 10. d3 Qc7 11. Bd2 h6
12. Nf3 Bd6 13. Bc3 Rd8 14. Nbd2 Nd5 15. Nb3 Nb7 16. Nfd2
0–0 17. Nc4 Rfe8 18. Qc1 e4 19. N×d6 R×d6 20. 0–0 Rg6
21. Re1 Nf4 22. g3 Nh3† 23. Kg2 Nf4† 24. Kh1 e×d3 25. Bf3
R×e1† 26. Q×e1 Ne6 27. c×d3 B×d3 28. Qe3 Bc4 29. Q×a7 Bd5
30. Bg2 Ng5 31. Re1 Qd7 32. Nd2 B×g2† 33. K×g2 Rd6 34. h4
Re6 35. R×e6 N×e6 36. Nf3 c5 37. a4 Nf4† 38. g×f4 Qg4†
39. Kf1 Q×f3 40. Qb8† Kh7 41. Qe5 Qd1† 42. Be1 Qd3† 43. Kg1
Qg6† 44. Kf1 Nd6 45. Qe3 Nf5 46. Q×c5 N×h4 47. Qd5 Qa6†
48. Qb5 Qg6 49. Qc4 Nf3 50. Ke2 N×e1 51. K×e1 h5 52. a5 h4
53. a6 h3 54. a7 h2 55. a8Q Qg1† 56. Kd2 h1Q 57. Q×h1† Q×h1
58. Q×f7 Qf3 59. Qf5† Kh8 60. Ke1 Qc6 61. Qe5 White wins—
*Daily News*, 25 May 1892.

**(1101) Bird–Jasnogrodsky & Unknown　1–0**
Consultation game
London 1892
*A03*

1. f4 d5 2. Nf3 g6 3. e3 Bg7 4. c4 e6 5. Be2 Nf6 6. Nc3 b6 7. 0–0
0–0 8. d4 Nbd7 9. Ne5 Bb7 10. Bd2 Ne8 11. Bg4 Ndf6 12. Bh3
Nd6 13. c×d5 e×d5 14. Be1 Nfe4 15. Qb3 N×c3 16. b×c3 Re8
17. Bd7 Rf8 18. Bc6 B×e5 19. B×b7 N×b7 20. f×e5 Na5 21. Qd1
Nc4 22. Qf3 Qg5 23. Bf2 Nd2 24. Q×d5 N×f1 25. R×f1 Rad8
26. Qe4 f5 27. Qc6 Qe7 28. Bg3 Qd7 29. Qc4† Qd5 30. Qe2 b5
31. Bh4 Rd7 32. Bf6 Rdf7 33. h3 a6 34. g4 f×g4 35. h×g4 Qe4
36. Rf4 Qb1† 37. Kg2 Qc1 38. Qd3 Qb2† 39. Rf2 Qa3 40. g5
Re8 41. d5 Rd7 42. e4 b4 43. Qh3 Qa4 44. e6 Rde7 45. c4 Qa3
46. Q×a3 b×a3 47. B×e7 R×e7 48. Rf3 Kg7 49. e5 h6 50. Rf7†
R×f7 51. g×h6† K×h6 52. e×f7 Kg7 53. e6 and in a few more
moves Black resigns—*Illustrated London News*, 25 June 1892.

Dr. Reeves, a strong chess amateur, fanatically tested his favorite
move against the Ruy Lopez, 3. … f5, against a varied contingent of
masters.

**(1102) Bird–Reeves　0–1**
Offhand game
London 1892
*C63*

1. e4 e5 2. Nf3 Nc6 3. Bb5 f5 4. Qe2 f×e4 5. B×c6 d×c6
6. Q×e4 Bd6 7. d4 Nf6 8. Qe2 e4 9. Nc3 Qe7 10. Ng5 Bf5 11. h4
0–0–0 12. Be3 Rhe8 13. Qc4 Bb4 14. 0–0–0 h6 15. Nh3 Be6
16. Qf1 B×c3 17. b×c3 Qa3† 18. Kd2 Nd5 19. Ke1 Q×c3†
20. Bd2 Q×c2 21. Rc1 Q×a2 22. Qc4 Q×c4 23. R×c4 e3 White
resigns—*Standard*, 11 July 1892.

# IN THE PROVINCES,
# JULY–AUGUST 1892

The highlight of the summer of 1892 was the 7th congress of the German Chess Association in Dresden. Seventeen players entered the main tournament, which was convincingly won by Tarrasch. The three British entries, Mason, Blackburne and Loman (who competed for the first and last time in such a field) were radically overshadowed by such young continental newcomers as Moritz Porges, Gyula Makovetz and Carl August Walbrodt. Bird was willing to test his luck in Dresden, but he abandoned this opportunity as the chance to meet Lasker arose.[24]

In a letter to MacDonnell, published in the *Illustrated Sporting and Dramatic News* on 16 July, Bird asserted that a match between him and Lasker was already arranged for a long time and could commence without any further ado. Bird travelled to Newcastle in the second part of June, but he was left in the dark when he did not encounter his opponent there. Lasker, who did not go to Dresden, had in the meantime issued a private challenge to the first prize winner of the German congress (few thought this could have been anyone but Tarrasch). He obviously wanted to have his schedule free in case of the latter's acceptance. Tarrasch publicly refused to play Lasker as long as the latter had not proven himself to be of similar stature by winning an international tournament. So nothing came of it and Bird's planned contest with Lasker was only postponed for a few weeks instead of annulled. Bird did not, however, spent his time in Newcastle in vain. The local clubs arranged a busy program for him during his stay of a week.

Mr. H.E. Bird, the veteran English chess master, has been the guest of the Newcastle Chess Club since Saturday last, and during his stay has played a number of simultaneous games with the members, delighting one and all by his brilliant performances. Mr. Bird has been opposed on each occasion by a very strong contingent, including nearly all the first-class players in the club, and his score—considering the rapidity of his play and the number and strength of his opponents—is phenomenal.

On Saturday last Mr. Bird played 30 games, of which he won 25, drew 3 and lost only 2. The fortunate winners were Messrs. Greenwell and Hamond, whilst Messrs. Graham and Heywood secured drawn games. On Monday evening Mr. Bird played no less than 33 games, winning 23, drawing 4 and losing 6. Messrs. Zollner, Greenwell, Graham, Hamond, Bennett, and Downey won one game each, and Messrs. Downey, Bennett and Heywood drew. Sixteen games were played on Tuesday night, of which the veteran single player won 15, lost none, and drew 1 with Mr. Heywood [*Newcastle Weekly Chronicle*, 30 July 1892].

On Wednesday 27 games were played, Mr. Bird winning 18, losing 7, and drawing 2. The winners were Messrs. Greenwell, Zollner, Downey, Bennett, and Mason, whilst Mr. Graham secured a draw. On Thursday 23 games were played, and resulted in the single player placing 15 to his credit, 7 being lost by him, and 1 drawn. Messrs. Greenwell, Keiffenheim, Wright, Graham, and Heywood secured wins, and Mr. Blackett drew a game. This concluded Mr. Bird's visit to the Newcastle Chess Club, but at the request of the officials of the Art Gallery Club he consented to remain another day in Newcastle in order to give the Art Gallery members an opportunity of breaking a lance with him. This meeting took place on Friday, July 29th, at Taylor's Restaurant,

24. "Mr. H.E. Bird states that he did not go to Dresden, since the Newcastle players have offered £10 each to himself and Lasker for a match to be played at Newcastle. If Lasker will be content to play in addition for a stake of £20 or £30, the match may come off." *Belfast News-Letter*, 21 July 1892.

Blackett Street, when 24 games were played, of which Mr. Bird won 21, drew 2, and lost 1. Mr. Heywood was the solitary winner, and Messrs. Wadsworth and Vincent drew their games. Adding up the whole of these totals, we find that Mr. Bird has played no less than 153 games during his visit. Of these he has won 117, lost 23, and drawn 13. We consider this a remarkable performance, when it is remembered that at the Newcastle Club Mr. Bird did not encounter a long list of names, including a lot of weak players, but played repeated games against a select and very strong contingent. The visit to Newcastle of the G.O.M. of chess has been a very interesting and enjoyable one. A distinguishing characteristic of Mr. Bird is his genuine and disinterested love for the game. A brilliant sortie or subtle waiting move affords as much pleasure to the veteran as to the neophyte who sits opposite to him. Mr. Bird left Newcastle on Saturday to fulfill an engagement with the Glasgow Chess Club [*Newcastle Weekly Chronicle*, 6 August 1892].

## (1103) Greenwell–Bird    1–0
Simultaneous game
Newcastle, 23 July 1892
*A82*

1. d4 f5 2. e4 f×e4 3. f3 e×f3 4. N×f3 Nf6 5. Bd3 g6 6. Ng5 Bg7 7. N×h7 R×h7 8. B×g6† Kf8 9. B×h7 N×h7 10. 0-0† Kg8 11. Qh5 Nc6 12. Rf7 Nf8 13. R×g7† K×g7 14. Bh6† Kh8 15. B×f8† Kg8 16. Qg6† and White wins—*Newcastle Courant*, 24 June 1893.

## (1104) Greenwell–Bird    1–0
Simultaneous game
Newcastle, 23 July 1892
*C24*

1. e4 e5 2. Bc4 Nf6 3. f4 N×e4 4. d3 Qh4† 5. g3 N×g3 6. Nf3 Qh5 7. Rg1 e4 8. d×e4 N×e4 9. Qe2 d5 10. Rg5 Qh6 11. Re5† Be6 12. B×d5 Nc5 13. f5 Q×c1† 14. Kf2 Nc6 15. B×c6† b×c6 16. f×e6 N×e6 17. R×e6† f×e6 18. Q×e6† Be7 19. Q×c6† Kd8 20. Q×a8† Kd7 21. Qd5† Bd6 22. Ne5† Kd8 23. Nf7† Kd7 24. N×h8 Qf4† 25. Qf3 Q×h2† 26. Kf1 Black resigns—*Newcastle Courant*, 1 April 1893.

## (1105) Bird–D. Cook    1–0
Simultaneous game
Newcastle, 23 July 1892
*C52*

1. e4 e5 2. Nf3 Nc6 3. Bc4 Bc5 4. b4 B×b4 5. c3 Ba5 6. Qb3 Qe7 7. 0-0 Nf6 8. d4 0-0 9. Ba3 d6 10. Nbd2 e×d4 11. e5 N×e5 12. Rae1 N×f3† 13. N×f3 Qd7 14. N×d4 a6 15. Ne6 Re8 16. Ng5 d5 17. R×e8† Q×e8 18. B×d5 N×d5 19. Q×d5 B×c3 20. Qd3 g6 21. Q×c3 h6 22. Bb2 Qf8 23. Qh8 mate—*Newcastle Weekly Chronicle*, 30 July 1892.

## (1106) Bird–Keiffenheim    1–0
Simultaneous game
Newcastle, 26 July 1892
*C21*

1. e4 e5 2. d4 e×d4 3. c3 d×c3 4. Bc4 c×b2 5. B×b2 Bb4† 6. Kf1 Nf6 7. e5 d5 8. Bb3 Ng4 9. h3 Nh6 10. g4 Be6 11. Nd2 Qg5 12. Ndf3 Qe7 13. Rc1 Nc6 14. Ba4 Ba3 15. R×c6 0-0 16. R×c7

Q×c7 17. B×a3 Qc4† 18. Ne2 Rfc8 19. Nfd4 a6 20. Bb3 Qc7 21. Nf4 Q×e5 22. Nd×e6 f×e6 23. N×e6 Kh8 24. Q×d5 Q×d5 25. B×d5 Rc2 26. Bb3 Rd2 27. Ke1 Rd7 28. Bb2 Re8 29. f4 Ree7 30. Ke2 Ng8 31. Rc1 h6 32. Rc8 Kh7 33. Kf1 Rd2 34. f5 R×e6 35. B×e6 Nf6 36. Bf7 h5 37. g5 and Black resigns—*Newcastle Weekly Chronicle*, 30 July 1892.

## (1107) Downey–Bird   0–1
Simultaneous game
Newcastle, 26 July 1892
*C21*

1. e4 e5 2. d4 e×d4 3. c3 d×c3 4. Bc4 c×b2 5. B×b2 Qe7 6. Nc3 c6 7. Nge2 Nh6 8. 0–0 Qc5 9. Bb3 Na6 10. Ng3 b5 11. Nf5 N×f5 12. e×f5 Q×f5 13. Re1† Kd8 14. Ne4 Nc5 15. Nd6 B×d6 16. Q×d6 Re8 17. R×e8† K×e8 18. Ba3 Qf6 19. B×c5 Q×a1† White resigns—*Newcastle Weekly Chronicle*, 6 August 1892.

The following game was played at the simultaneous exhibition of either 25 or 27 July.

## (1108) Zollner–Bird   1–0
Simultaneous game
Newcastle, July 1892
*C21*

1. e4 e5 2. d4 e×d4 3. c3 d×c3 4. Bc4 c×b2 5. B×b2 Nc6 6. Nf3 Nh6 7. 0–0 d6 8. Nc3 Be7 9. Qe2 Bg4 10. Rad1 0–0 11. Qe3 B×f3 12. g×f3 Ne5 13. Bb3 Qd7 14. Kh1 Qh3 15. Nd5 Bd8 16. Rg1 Kh8 17. Rg3 Qh5 18. Nf4 Qh4 19. Rh3 Qe7 20. Nd5 Qe6 21. f4 Neg4 22. Rg1 f6 23. R×g4 N×g4 24. R×h7† K×h7 25. Qh3† Kg8 26. N×f6† R×f6 27. B×e6† R×e6 28. Q×g4 Re7 29. h4 c6 30. h5 Bb6 31. h6 d5 32. Bf6 Rf7 33. e5 Bd8 34. B×g7 Kh7 35. f5 Black resigns—*Newcastle Weekly Chronicle*, 6 August 1892.

## (1109) Greenwell & Hamond–Bird   1–0
Consultation game
Newcastle, July 1892 (?)
*C35*

1. e4 e5 2. f4 e×f4 3. Nf3 Be7 4. Bc4 Bh4† 5. g3 f×g3 6. 0–0 g×h2† 7. Kh1 d5 8. B×d5 Nf6 9. Bb3 Bg3 10. e5 Nd5 11. Nc3 Be6 12. d4 0–0 13. Ng5 N×c3 14. b×c3 Bd5† 15. B×d5 Q×d5† 16. Qf3 Q×f3† 17. R×f3 Bh4 18. N×h7 Rd8 19. Bg5 Rd7 20. Raf1 K×h7 21. B×h4 Kg8 22. Rg3 Kh7 23. Bf6 Black resigns—*Newcastle Courant*, 27 May 1893.

Bird left Newcastle to embark on a short tour that had him spend the first few days of August in Glasgow. Here he gave a few exhibitions of which no specific results were published.[25]

25. "Mr. Bird, the well-known English player, has been in town for the last few days, and has been giving exhibitions of his skill at the Glasgow Chess Club. The veteran was in good form, and of course won a large majority of games. Some of our local experts, however, were successful in securing wins or draws, Messrs. Long-will, Gilchrist, Court and Jonas giving a good account of themselves against the great player." *Glasgow Weekly Citizen*, 6 August 1892.

## (1110) Bird–Gilchrist   ½–½
Offhand game
Glasgow, August 1892
*C33*

1. e4 e5 2. f4 e×f4 3. Be2 d5 4. e×d5 Q×d5 5. Nc3 Qd8 6. d4 Bd6 7. Nf3 Nf6 8. Nb5 0–0 9. 0–0 a6 10. N×d6 Q×d6 11. Ng5 h6 12. B×f4 Qe7 13. c3 h×g5 14. B×g5 Nbd7 15. Rf3 b5 16. Qc2 Bb7 17. Rh3 Qd6 18. Rf1 Qd5 19. Rg3 Rfe8 20. Bd3 Ne4 21. B×e4 R×e4 22. Qf2 Rae8 23. Bf6 N×f6 24. Q×f6 g6 25. R×g6† f×g6 26. Q×g6† draw—*Glasgow Weekly Herald*, 13 August 1892.

## (1111) Finlayson–Bird   0–1
Offhand game
Glasgow, 1 August 1892
*C33*

1. e4 e5 2. Nf3 Nc6 3. d4 e×d4 4. N×d4 Bc5 5. Be3 Qf6 6. c3 Nge7 7. Be2 B×d4 8. c×d4 d5 9. e5 Qg6 10. 0–0 h5 11. Nd2 h4 12. Nf3 h3 13. g3 Bg4 14. Kh1 Qe4 15. Bf4 N×d4 16. Qd3 B×f3† White resigns—*Glasgow Weekly Citizen*, 13 August 1892.

On 4 August Bird made a quick visit to the Leeds Chess Club. He gave a small exhibition on 13 boards, which he concluded by winning 7, losing 2 (against F.P. Wildman and I.M. Brown) and drawing the remaining 4 games (v. Carter, Elson, Harris and West).

## (1112) I.M. Brown–Bird   1–0
Simultaneous game
Leeds, 4 August 1892
*C61*

1. e4 e5 2. Nf3 Nc6 3. Bb5 Nd4 4. Bc4 N×f3† 5. Q×f3 Nf6 6. d4 d6 7. Bg5 Be7 8. d×e5 d×e5 9. B×f6 B×f6 10. Nd2 0–0 11. 0–0–0 Qe7 12. h4 g6 13. g4 Be6 14. g5 Bg7 15. h5 B×c4 16. N×c4 Q×g5† 17. Kb1 Rad8 18. Rdg1 Qf4 19. Qb3 Q×e4 20. h×g6 h×g6 21. Qh3 f6 22. Qe6† Rf7 23. Re1 Qd5 24. Qg4 f5 25. Qe2 e4 26. Ne3 Qe5 27. Nc4 Qf6 28. c3 b5 29. Ne3 Rb8 30. Rd1 b4 31. Nd5 Qe5 32. Qc4 b×c3 33. N×c3 Bf6 34. Rd7 R×b2† 35. Ka1 R×a2† 36. K×a2 Qa5† 37. Kb1 Qb6† 38. Kc2 Q×f2† 39. Ne2 Black resigns—*Newcastle Weekly Chronicle*, 3 September 1892.

Bird, somewhat fatigued by now, left Leeds and headed for Brighton (according to a few sources; e.g., the *Leeds Mercury* of 5 August 1892), where the annual meeting of the Counties Chess Association was going on. The main guest there was Emanuel Lasker and Bird continued to pursue his aim of meeting Lasker once more in a match. Yet, it seems that he did not reach the coastal town in the south of England as no single mention at all has been made about Bird's presence in Brighton.

Bird's course for the week following his visit to Leeds is lost to the researcher. It is likely that he spent some time giving exhibitions at chess clubs. On Thursday 11 August Bird emerged in Leamington Spa after having made arrangements with Rosario Aspa. Aspa was an avid chess player and talented musician of Italian origin who spent the major part of his life in Leamington Spa. His archives, which include letters as well as newspaper cuttings, have made it to the Cleveland Public Library collection. Two of these letters were written by Bird, at the end of July and on 2 August, in anticipation of his visit to Aspa's home town. They offer a unique insight in Bird's way of fixing his engagements. Bird received his invitation to visit Leamington Spa while he was playing in Newcastle. He was not reluctant and asked if his usual conditions could be applied during his stay: "If I should be passing Leamington and were to halt there are there any of your gentlemen who would like to test skill with me at the old classic rate of one shilling a game?"[26]

Apparently, Aspa immediately agreed to Bird's conditions and focused on finding a date for his visit. No report appeared in the press. Just one, albeit very interesting, game between Bird against Aspa and Sherrard was published.[27]

## (1113) Aspa & Sherrard–Bird     1–0

Consultation game
Leamington Spa, 11 August 1892
B50

**1. e4 c5 2. Be2 Nc6 3. Nf3 g6 4. d3 Bg7 5. Nc3 d6 6. 0–0 h5 7. Be3 Nd4 8. B×d4** This exchange solves all opening problems Bird may have experienced. **8. ... c×d4 9. Nb1 Bd7 10. Nbd2 e6 11. Nb3 Qb6 12. Nfd2 Rc8 13. Nc4 Qc7 14. Rc1 b5 15. Ncd2 Ne7 16. f4 Qb6 17. Nf3 d5** 17. ... Bh6 exploits White's last move. The pin after 18. Qd2 e5 19. g3 Nc6 is quite burdensome. **18. Kh1 a5 19. Nbd2** Better was to close the center with 19. e5 as 19. ... Nf5 is forbidden: 20. Qd2! a4 21. Nb×d4! N×d4 22. Qe3. **19. ... a4 20. Qe1** *(see diagram)*

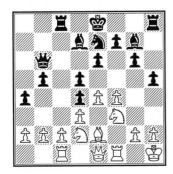

*After 20. Qe1*

**20. ... Bf6** 20. ... Qc7, inciting his opponents to play 21. e5 secures the future of his weak d-pawn after 21. ... Nf5. **21. Qf2 Bg7 22. Ne5 22. c3!** wins the disputed pawn with an excellent position on top

26.  Bird gave Aspa a useful hint to make his exhibition a success: "A first notice in advance perhaps would attract visitors as my fast and original style seems as possible as ever. This however for your better judgment." *Autographs of Notes Chess and Checker Players*, vol. 1 A–G, f. 79a–79b. ¶ It is interesting to make a comparison with Blackburne, whose letters involving his exhibitions at Leamington Spa are in the same Cleveland collection. Blackburne visited Leamington Spa on 22 and 23 December 1890. He played against all comers (simultaneous or otherwise) and gave a blindfold exhibition against six opponents. His fee for these two days was 5 guineas. Blackburne made two other arrangements in February 1894 and October 1895. On the latter occasion he proposed to give a simultaneous exhibition against 20 to 25 opponents for £2. It is unclear whether these visits materialized. *Autographs of Noted Chess and Checker Players*, vol. 1 A–G, f. 80a, 85b, 86a, 86b and 87a.

27.  Charles Hugh Sherrard, 24 years old, was no mean player himself in later years. In 1905 he took a shared 2nd–3rd place at the British Championship. He died a year later.

**Letter from Henry Edward Bird to Rosario Aspa (courtesy Cleveland Public Library).**

of it. **22. ... d×e4?!** The position is extremely difficult for Black to defend. Opening it with exchanges will not help him. 22. ... h4 is interesting. **23. N×d7 K×d7 24. d×e4 Rhd8 25. Bd3 Rc5?!** Black is bound to lose an extra tempo after White's evident reply. **26. e5 Ke8 27. Ne4 Rc6 28. Qe2 Rd5 29. Nf6†** The allies could have crowned their strong play with 29. Nd6†! Kf8 30. B×b5. **29. ... B×f6 30. e×f6 Nf5** With their 29th move the allies intended to gain the exchange. This was unavoidable, but 30. ... Ng8 would at least have brought Bird a pawn in return. **31. Be4 Rcd6 32. B×d5 R×d5 33. Rfe1 Qc5 34. Qd3 h4 35. c3 Qc4 36. Q×c4 b×c4 37. c×d4 R×d4 38. Re5 R×f4 39. Ra5** Going after the a-pawn but Bird gets chances to reorganize his pieces in return. 39. Rd1! maintains a strong grip. **39. ... Nd6 40. Ra6 Rd4 41. R×a4 e5 42. Re1 Kd7 43. Kg1 Ke6 44. b3 K×f6 45. b×c4 e4 46. Ra6 Ke5 47. c5 Nf5 48. c6 Rc4 49. Ra7 R×c6 50. R×f7 Rc2 51. a4 Ra2 52. Ra7 e3 53. g4?** A very impulsive move that creates several weaknesses around his king and gives Bird some real perspectives for a draw. Pushing their passed pawn was sufficient to win as Black is bound to run out of ideas; e.g., 53. a5 Kf4 54. a6 Kg4 55. Kh1 Kg5 56. Ra8 Nd4 57. h3 e2 58. a7 Nc6 59. Kg1. **53. ... h×g3 e.p. 54. h×g3 Ra3?**

Very passive. After 54. ... Ke4 55. g4 Nh4 56. Re7† Kf4 White cannot escape the draw. **55. Kg2 Ke4 56. a5?** The king lacks some space to escape from his opponent's rook. 56. g4 was therefore correct. **56. ... Ra2† 57. Kh3 Kf3 58. g4 Nd6 59. Rd7 Nc4 60. Rf7† Ke4 61. Rg7 Ne5 62. Ra7 Kd3 63. a6** Ignoring the adverse e-pawn is not risk free. 63. Re7 R×a5 64. Rd1† Ke4 65. Re1 draws by force. **63. ... Kd2 64. Rh1 e2 65. Re7 Nd3** 65. ... Ra3† forces a rapid promotion, but a theoretical draw arises after 66. Kg2 Nd3 67. a7 e1Q 68. Rh×e1† N×e1† 69. Kf1 Nd3 70. g5 Nb4 71. Re6. **66. Rh2 Kd1?** 66. ... Nf4† 67. Kg3 g5 forces White to give a perpetual check. In the game Black's knight is unprotected at f4, which White may exploit. **67. Kh4 Nf4 68. Kg5 Ra4** Or 68. ... Ra5† 69. K×f4 g5† 70. Kf3 e1Q 71. R×e1† K×e1 72. Rh1† Kd2 73. Rh6 with excellent winning chances. **69. Rh1† Kd2 70. a7** Threatening 70. a8Q. Black is forced to lose a tempo. **70. ... Ng2** If 70. ... Nd3 71. Rh2 Nc1 72. Rc7 Nd3 73. Rd7 Ra5† 74. Kh6 g5 75. Rg2 and Black is in zugzwang. **71. Rh2?!** 71. Rh8! is much more convincing. If 71. ... R×a7 72. Rd8†. **71. ... Ne3?!** 71. ... R×a7! 72. R×a7 e1Q 73. R×g2† Kc3 with fair drawing chances. **72. Rd7† Ke1 73. Rh8?** 73. Rh1† Kf2 74. Rf7† Kg3 75. Re1 Ra5† 76. K×g6 leaves no doubt about the result. **73. ... Kf2 74. Rh2† Ng2 75. Re7 Kg3?** Bird misses a final chance to draw: 75. ... R×a7 76. R×e2† K×e2 77. R×g2†. **76. R×g2† K×g2 77. R×e2† Kf3 78. Re7 R×g4† 79. Kf6 Ra4 80. K×g6** White wins—*Leamington Spa Courier*, 20 August 1892.

Herewith Bird's tour through the provinces came to an end and he could permit himself a short rest of a few weeks before the match with Lasker finally happened.[28]

# MATCH WITH LASKER 1892

At the end of the summer the agreement between Bird and Lasker finally materialized. Both players appeared ready for their match on Saturday 27 August in Newcastle. It was agreed to play for the first five wins. The time limit was set on 20 moves an hour. Each player, with the support of friends, took care of a stake of £25. The Newcastle club offered Bird and Lasker £10 each to cover their expenses.

Lasker's tournament and match record, albeit a short one, clearly exceeded Bird's, but the veteran nevertheless remained quite confident in his own chances. He informed the journalists that he had won a majority of offhand games against Lasker.[29]

The first game commenced on 29 August at 2 p.m. Lasker won

the toss and opened the match with the White pieces. The favorite obtained a hugely favorable position, but overlooked a few quick ways to decide the game. Bird reached an endgame with drawing chances but ultimately went wrong and lost.

Bird opened the second game with his favorite 1. f4. Lasker replied with the From Gambit and then came 4. ... g5, an extremely rare continuation at that time. Thanks to this game this line gained a great popularity. Bird selected a variation that transposed into an endgame where he could nurture an extra, albeit weak, pawn. Lasker steadily augmented the pressure, and the defense proved to be too difficult for the Englishman. Bird got decently out of a Sicilian Opening in the third game when a badly judged move spoiled his position at once. The fourth game was the most absorbing one of the match. After an equal, but curious, opening phase, Lasker treated the middle game inadequately. Bird, on the other hand, played very strong chess and obtained a winning position. Things were never simple, however, and ultimately Bird blew a drawish position by blundering a rook. With four straight losses Bird was doubtless demoralized. In the fifth game, he thoughtlessly lost a pawn just after the exchange of queens. His further play lacked Bird's usual stubbornness and at move 43 he had to resign game and match.

The clean sweep achieved by Lasker was somewhat misrepresentative of Bird's strength. That the youthful German was superior to Bird could not be denied (except perhaps by Bird). Yet, the veteran made a honorable fight of it, which certainly deserved to be rewarded with some half or even full points.[30]

Despite the decisive defeat, Bird was still extremely combative. Some reports in the English press stated that the veteran lost the match because he could not expunge the conviction that he ought to be able to give Lasker the odds of a knight. Foolhardy, Bird distributed his opinion that out of 130 games played he had won the majority.

On Monday 5 September Bird and Lasker were still present at the ceremony and prize-giving of a local tournament. The major entertainment, however, was a blitz match between both masters. Twelve games were played in two hours. The game score survives of a famous miniature, in which Bird mated the future world champion in 12 moves. Afterwards Lasker jokingly remarked "that his arm, not his head, ached; such was the rapidity of the moves and the large amount of wood-shifting!"[31]

Shortly after his victory Lasker accepted the invitation of the Manhattan Chess Club to travel to New York. Therefore his match with Bird was, for a while, his last chess feat in England. Lasker's name had been linked with the congress in Belfast, which was planned two weeks later, but he ultimately declined to play there. Typically for the English chess scene some sarcastic voices suggested that he wanted to leave England with a string of tournament and match victories without suffering a single defeat. But of course

---

28. Bird's contemporaries were deeply impressed by the youthful energy of the 63-year-old veteran: "Mr. Bird has been running around the country like a young 'un and at Newcastle, Leeds, and other northern towns gave wonderful displays of his powers as a simultaneous player meeting strong teams of twenty and more players and fairly jumping on them—that is, metaphorically, for Mr. Bird, alas, cannot jump at all; gout holding him down as with a vice." *American Chess Monthly*, September 1892, p. 172.

29. Bird's arguments did not impress everyone: "May vs. December would be an appropriate designation of the contest arranged at Newcastle-on-Tyne between Lasker and Bird. ... The match cannot in any way be regarded as a serious test of Lasker's playing strength, but it certainly will be productive of some very interesting play, as Bird, in spite of his years, has a wonderful amount of fighting capacity in him." *Daily News*, 31 August 1892.

30. Bird received respect from the whole chess playing community. It is no great surprise to find MacDonnell among them: "Bird's visit to Newcastle proved a great success, notwithstanding his defeat in the match. So great, indeed, was the interest taken in the contest, that there was a very large number of visitors from a distance covering an area from Whitby in the south to Berwick in the north. Bird played with his usual rapidity and flashed out some brilliant strokes, but was obliged to yield to the youthful vigor and profound judgment of his ambitious antagonist." *Illustrated Sporting and Dramatic News*, 17 September 1892.

31. *Illustrated Sporting and Dramatic News*, 8 October 1892.

Lasker had nothing to prove anymore after having beaten all major English players in such a decisive way. In the States he could find new and highly reputed opponents, and perhaps make a deal with Steinitz to play a match for the world championship.

| Match with Lasker, 29 August–2 September 1892 | | | | | | |
|---|---|---|---|---|---|---|
| | **1** | **2** | **3** | **4** | **5** | |
| E. Lasker | 1 | 1 | 1 | 1 | 1 | 5 |
| H.E. Bird | 0 | 0 | 0 | 0 | 0 | 0 |

## (1114) Lasker–Bird   1–0
Match (game 1)
Newcastle, 29 August 1892
*C61*

**1. e4 e5 2. Nf3 Nc6 3. Bb5 Nd4 4. Bc4** "Scarcely as strong as 4. N×d4. But the latter is apt to give rise to a class of position in which Mr. Bird is much at home, and which therefore it was his adversary's purpose to avoid"—Mason. **4. ... N×f3† 5. Q×f3 Nf6** "5. ... Qf6 appears decidedly preferable"—Mason. **6. d4 d6** "6. ... e×d4 7. e5 Qe7 8. Qe2 Ng8 would leave Black a dangerously undeveloped game. Or 7. ... d5 8. e×f6 d×c4 9. Bg5, and White has a manifest advantage"—Mason. Black equalizes in the latter line with 9. ... Qd7! **7. Qb3 Qe7 8. d×e5 d×e5 9. 0–0 c6 10. Qf3** "The best way of defending the pawn. 7. Qb3 was simply a temporary measure, compelling Black to take precautions not fitted to his general plan. If 9. ... N×e4 then perhaps 10. B×f7† Q×f7 11. Qa4† etc."—Mason. **10. ... h6 11. Nc3 g5** "Bold play, but seemingly without any sufficient object; unless the intention was 12. ... Bg7 and 13. ... 0–0"—Mason. 11. ... b5, initiating play on the queenside, is a more interesting plan. **12. a4** "An advance good in itself, and also as partly making way for the bishop to go to a3, if desirable, in case his opponent decided to castle as just mentioned"—Mason. **12. ... Be6 13. Qe2 Nd7 14. Rd1 Qf6 15. Be3 Bb4 16. Na2 Be7 17. b4** This advance is perhaps too rash. After 17. Nc1 0–0 18. Nb3, White commands the board. **17. ... Nb6 18. Bb3 0–0** "Were he to exchange bishops, the unguarded f5 might eventually be taken by opposing the knight, with serious consequences; and, at the same time, White's already strong position on the queenside would be further strengthened"—Mason. **19. a5 Nc8 20. Rab1 Nd6 21. Nc3 a6?!** A serious weakness at b6 occurs now, after which Black cannot dispute the d-file anymore. Better was 21. ... Rfd8 22. h3 Bf8 and it is White's task to come up with something. **22. Bb6 Ne8?!** This overly passive move allows White to conquer the queenside and the d-file. 22. ... Nb5 or 22. ... Nc8 are more stubborn options. **23. Na4!** Lasker plays this part of the game extremely well and Bird is left without any counterplay. **23. ... Ng7 24. c3 B×b3 25. R×b3 Ne6 26. g3 Bd8 27. Rb2 Qg6 28. Rbd2 h5** 28. ... g4 (Mason) loses after 29. Rd7! **29. B×d8?!** Here Lasker misses the immediately conclusive 29. Rd7! **29. ... Ra×d8 30. R×d8 R×d8 31. R×d8† N×d8 32. Nc5** The endgame remains extremely unpleasant for Bird. **32. ... g4** "For, now, supposing the other play not to have varied, the Black king could go to g7 with every chance of holding his own"—Mason. **33. Qd3 Ne6 34. N×e6 Q×e6 35. Qd8† Kh7 36. Qg5 f6 37. Q×h5† Kg7 38. Kg2 Qd7 39. h3** "The ending is instructive, simple though it seems, and worthy of the closest attention"—Mason. **39. ... g×h3† 40. Q×h3 Qd6 41. Qg4† Kf7** (see diagram)

*After 41. ... Kf7*

**42. Qf3** Both sides prefer to burden their queens with more defensive tasks. A few moves earlier 40. ... Qd2 offered counterplay. Here Lasker could strongly infiltrate with 42. Qc8. **42. ... Qe6 43. Qe3 Ke7 44. f3** Lasker weakens the position of his king, which endangers his winning chances. 44. Qa7! is rather disturbing for his opponent. **44. ... Kd6 45. Kf2 Qa2† 46. Qe2 Qe6 47. Qd2† Kc7 48. g4 Qc4 49. Qe3 Qa2† 50. Kg3 Qa1 51. g5** Lasker has been drifting for the past few moves. The text move is an optimistic attempt to conclude the game rapidly. **51. ... f×g5 52. Kg4 Qb2** 52. ... Qh1! tries to make use of the vulnerable position White's king is in; e.g., 53. K×g5 Qh3 54. Kf6 Qh5 55. Ke7 Qh7†. **53. K×g5 Kd7** Bird is wrong in putting his king in the center, most importantly as this enhances his opponent's opportunity to exchange queens. **54. Kg4** Both 54. Kf6 (Mason) and 54. Kf5 promise a quick victory. **54. ... Qh2 55. Kf5** 55. Qg5! improves the position of the queen and eliminates Black's drawing chances. If 55. ... Qg2† 56. Kh5 Q×f3† 57. Qg4† forces the exchange of queens. More tenacious, but also insufficient is 55. ... Ke6 56. Qf5† Ke7 57. c4 Kd6 58. Qf6† Kd7 59. Kg5 Qd2† 60. Kg6 Q×b4 61. Qf5† Kd8 62. Q×e5, which must win relatively easy. **55. ... Qg3?** "After this the case becomes desperate. 55. ... Qh5† would have enabled him to prolong the contest almost indefinitely, with many chances of a draw at the last"—Mason. For example: 55. ... Qh5†! 56. Kf6 Qh8† 57. Kg6 Qe8† 58. Kg5 Kc8. **56. Kf6! c5 57. Qg5 Qh2 58. Qf5† Kc6 59. Qc8† Kb5 60. Q×c5† Ka4 61. Q×e5 Qh8† 62. Ke6 Qc8† 63. Ke7 Qc4 64. f4** Black resigns—*British Chess Magazine* (Mason), October 1892, pp. 436–437.

## (1115) Bird–Lasker   0–1
Match (game 2)
Newcastle, 30 August 1892
*A02*

**1. f4 e5** "The invention of the Danish player, Herr From, after whom it is named. The pawn given up yields a counterattack productive of entertaining varieties"—Steinitz. **2. f×e5 d6 3. e×d6 B×d6 4. Nf3 g5** "A novelty of considerable importance. Usually Black proceeds with 4. ... Nf6 or 4. ... Nh6, and then the proper answer is 5. d3"—Steinitz. **5. d4** "A safe plan of defense is now, we believe, 5. c3, and if 5. ... g4 6. Qa4† Nc6 (to prevent 7. Qd4) 7. Qe4† Be6 (if 7. ... Nge7 8. Nh4) 8. Nd4 N×d4 (or 8. ... Qh4† 9. g3) 9. Q×d4 with a good game"—Steinitz. The text move was Bird's preferred move here but he also tried 5. c3 and 5. g3. The latter move later became established as the main line against 4. ... g5. **5. ... g4 6. Ne5 B×e5 7. d×e5 Q×d1† 8. K×d1** "White's advantage is already nil, it being almost impossible to retain the pawn. He has lost his privilege of castling, and otherwise has no satisfactory game"—Mason. **8. ... Nc6 9. Bf4 Be6 10. e3 Nge7 11. Bb5 0-0-0† 12. Kc1 Bd5 13. Rg1 a6 14. Be2 Be6 15. Nc3 h6** The direct 15. ... Ng6 is preferable. White is bound to lose his extra pawn and his remaining e-pawn will be a weakness. On the other hand, his bishop pair should not be underestimated. **16. Bd3 Ng6 17. B×g6 f×g6 18. Rd1** He'd have better chances with both rooks on the board. After 18. b3 Black has to work hard to win his pawn back while White can use this time very well: 18. ... g5 19. Bg3 Rhe8 20. Kb2 Bd7 21. Rad1 N×e5 22. Rgf1 with a small initiative. **18. ... Rde8** 18. ... R×d1†! 19. K×d1 g5 20. Bg3 h5 takes the initiative. **19. e4** 19. b3 remains the best move. The situation is becoming tricky for Bird. **19. ... g5 20. Bg3 Rhf8 21. b3 h5 22. Rd2 h4 23. Bf2 N×e5 24. Be3** (see diagram) 24. Bd4 or 24. Kb2 are more to the point. Lasker's reply is excellent and puts White under pressure.

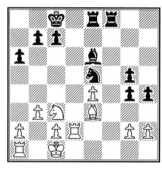

*After 24. Be3*

**24. ... h3! 25. B×g5?** Overlooking what Lasker was keeping in store for him. Speeding up his development maintains equality, with 25. Kb2 h×g2 26. R×g2 Nf3 27. Rf1. **25. ... g3!** "Enchanting play in an original position, and the young German master has created his opportunity by previous generalship with marvelous skill"—Steinitz. **26. h×g3** 26. g×h3 is also insufficient: 26. ... Nf3 27. h×g3 N×g5 28. h4 Nh3 29. Rd3 Nf2 and Black must win. **26. ... Rf1† 27. Kb2 R×a1 28. K×a1 h2 29. Rd1 Ng4 30. Rh1 Bf7** 30. ... Rh8! is the most precise road to victory. A series of exact moves then leads to the win of the e-pawn: 31. Bh4 Rf8 32. Nd1 (keeping the rook out) 32. ... Bd7 (on its way to harass the e-pawn) 33. Bg5 Rh8! (33. ... Re8? or 33. ... Bc6? 34. Ne3 leaves White off the hook) 34. Kb1 (if 34. Be3 Re8) 34. ... Bc6. **31. Kb2** "If 31. Nd5 B×d5 32. e×d5 Re2 and not alone does Black win the g-pawn, but White as no means in the interval to prevent the winning 34. ... Rg1"—Steinitz. **31. ... c6** "To prevent 32. Nd5 after 31. ... Bg6"—Mason. **32. Kc1 Bg6 33. Kd2 R×e4!** "Beautiful play! Taking the rook would mean the loss of a piece for White"—Mason. **34. Nd1** "And singularly enough this leads to the like result. At most, however, he could only prolong the agony, as the paralyzing influence of the Black passed pawn should ultimately prove fatal"—Mason. **34. ... Rd4† 35. Ke2 R×d1! 36. R×d1 Be4 37. Rd8† Kc7 38. Rd1 B×g2 39. Bd8† Kc8 40. Bb6** "Attempting a mate which Black easily stops. With the loss of the rook following, the game virtually comes to an end. However, White struggled on to the 63rd move before giving in"—Mason. **40. ... Bd5 41. c4 h1Q 42. R×h1 B×h1** White resigns the hopeless struggle on the 63rd move—*New York Daily Tribune*

(Steinitz), 25 September 1892; *British Chess Magazine* (Mason), October 1892, p. 438.

## (1116) Lasker–Bird    1–0

Match (game 3)
Newcastle, 31 August 1892
*B34*

**1. e4 c5 2. Nf3 Nc6 3. d4 c×d4 4. N×d4 g6 5. N×c6 b×c6 6. Qd4 f6 7. Nc3 Bg7 8. Bc4 Nh6 9. 0-0 Nf7 10. Be3 0-0 11. Qd2 e6 12. Rfd1 Qa5 13. Rab1 Re8 14. b4 Qc7 15. Bf4 Ne5 16. Bb3 Bf8 17. b5 Rb8 18. a4 Be7 19. Bg3 Kg7 20. f4 Bc5† 21. Kh1 Nf7 22. f5 e5 23. B×f7 K×f7 24. Qh6 g5 25. Q×h7† Kf8 26. Qh6 Ke7 27. Qg7† Kd8 28. Q×f6† Be7 29. Q×e5 d6 30. f6 Bf8 31. Q×g5 Qf7 32. B×d6 B×d6 33. R×d6†** and White wins—*Newcastle Weekly Chronicle*, 17 September 1892.

## (1117) Bird–Lasker    0–1

Match (game 4)
Newcastle, 1 September 1892
*C58*

**1. e4 e5 2. Nf3 Nc6 3. Bc4 Nf6 4. Ng5 d5 5. e×d5 Na5 6. Bb5† c6 7. d×c6 b×c6 8. Bd3** "Seldom played and inferior to the usual 8. Be2. Black's best reply is 8. ... Bc5"—Mason. **8. ... Ng4 9. Nf3 f5 10. h3 e4 11. h×g4 e×d3 12. c×d3** A strange move even to consider. 12. g5 gives White a healthy extra pawn. **12. ... f×g4 13. Qe2† Be7 14. Ng5 0-0 15. Ne6** "If 15. N×h7 Re8 with speedy trouble for White"—Mason. **15. ... B×e6 16. Q×e6† Kh8 17. Nc3 Nb7** "17. ... Q×d3, leading to an exchange of queens, would not be favorable"—Mason. **18. Qe4 h6 19. b4** "Designing to get the bishop into action as much as to keep the knight from c5"—Mason. Bird is in for a real struggle, but his king is in serious danger. Forcing a draw with 19. Q×c6 Nc5 20. R×h6† is the best he could get. **19. ... a5** Far stronger is 19. ... Bf6! Bird's king has then the choice between hiding on the kingside with 20. 0-0, which is refuted by 20. ... g3! (and if 21. Bb2 Bd4), and 20. Kd1 when Black has a huge initiative after 20. ... Qd7 21. Qg6 Nd6. **20. Ne2 Bf6 21. Rb1 a×b4 22. d4** A pipe dream. 22. Q×b4 keeps the position playable as Black is bound to lose time defending the knight. **22. ... Qd6** 22. ... Qd7! is slightly more precise. The idea is that h7 will be covered in case of a sacrificial attack; after 23. d3 R×a2 24. B×h6 g×h6 25. R×h6† Kg8. **23. d3 Rae8** As said, 23. ... R×a2 24. B×h6! subjects him to a very dangerous attack. Instead of the text move, however, 23. ... Rfe8 leaves both rooks better placed. **24. Q×g4 B×d4** "Here it is said that Black overlooked the fact that his opponent could castle. 24. ... Q×d4 was the correct move"—Mason. 24. ... Q×d4 25. Q×d4 B×d4 26. Kd1 B×f2 27. R×b4 Nc5 28. Rh3 is equally drawish. **25. 0-0** "Throwing Black on the defensive. The difference between 24. ... Q×d4 and the text move is easily seen"—Mason. **25. ... Bf6 26. Nf4 Bg5?!** A pawn is hereby abandoned. 26. ... Kh7 is safe. **27. R×b4** "All the play hereabouts is extremely ingenious"—Mason. **27. ... Nc5 28. Rd4 R×f4 29. R×f4 B×f4 30. B×f4 Qd5** "If 30. ... Q×d3 31. Qh5, regaining the pawn at the very least. Neither can he take it on the next move for the same reason"—Mason. **31. d4 Ne6?!** Bird's next move had to be prevented with 31. ... Nd7. Also quite stubborn is 31. ... Q×d4 32. Qh5 Qe4 33. B×h6 Re5. **32. Be5 c5**

**33. Qg6 Ra8 34. f4** "White maintains his attack in the finest style, and Black's defense is a model one. With an eye to the end, it was necessary for the latter to get rid of the a-pawn, as he does on the 36th move, though the risk was great"—Mason. **34. ... c×d4 35. Q×h6†** Too greedy and losing an important tempo. The activation of his rook with 35. Rc1 ties his opponent's rook to the back rank. White threatens—in case of 35. ... d3—to play 36. Rc7. After 35. ... Qd7 36. f5 Nf8 37. Q×h6† Black's position is torn apart. **35. ... Kg8 36. Qg6 R×a2** 36. ... d3 creates dangerous counterplay. The text move favors White again. **37. Rc1 Ra7 38. Rc8† Nf8 39. Qe8?** 39. Qd6! forces a winning endgame: 39. ... Q×d6 40. B×d6 Rf7 41. g4 d3 42. B×f8 R×f8 43. R×f8†. **39. ... Rf7 40. Rd8 Qe4 41. Qe6?** "A terrible blunder. Anxious to stop the threatened perpetual check, Mr. Bird here simply throws away the game. The position was not to be won for White"—Mason. **41. ... Qe1† 42. Kh2 Qh4† 43. Kg1 Q×d8** White resigns—*British Chess Magazine* (Mason), October 1892, p. 440.

## (1118) Lasker–Bird    1–0
Match (game 5)
Newcastle, 2 September 1892
B32

1. e4 c5 2. Nf3 Nc6 3. d4 c×d4 4. N×d4 N×d4 5. Q×d4 f6 6. Nc3 g6 7. Bc4 Nh6 8. 0–0 e6 9. Be3 b6 10. Rad1 Nf7 11. f4 Bc5 12. Qd2 Qc7 13. Bb3 Ba6 14. Rf2 Rd8 15. B×c5 Q×c5 16. Qd4 Q×d4 17. R×d4 Ke7 18. Ra4 Bb7 19. R×a7 Bc6 20. Ba4 Ra8 21. R×a8 R×a8 22. B×c6 d×c6 23. a4 Rd8 24. Re2 Rd4 25. Kf2 Nd8 26. b3 c5 27. Ke3 f5 28. Rd2 R×d2 29. K×d2 Kd7 30. e×f5 g×f5 31. Ke3 Nb7 32. h3 Na5 33. Ne2 Nc6 34. g4 Nb4 35. c3 Nc6 36. g5 Kd6 37. h4 e5 38. f×e5† K×e5 39. Nf4 Na5 40. h5 N×b3 41. h6 Na5 42. g6 Nc4† 43. Ke2 Black resigns—*Newcastle Weekly Chronicle*, 17 September 1892.

## (1119) Bird–Heywood    0–1
Offhand game
Newcastle, 3 September 1892
A02

1. f4 e5 2. f×e5 d6 3. e×d6 B×d6 4. Nf3 Nf6 5. c3 Ng4 6. Qa4† Nc6 7. Qe4† Be6 8. d4 0–0 9. Bg5 Qd7 10. Qc2 Rae8 11. Na3 Bf5 12. Qd2 h6 13. Bf4 B×f4 14. Q×f4 Re4 15. Qg3 Rfe8 16. Nc4 Qe6 17. e3 R×e3† 18. Kd2 Re2† 19. Kd1 Q×c4 20. Ne5 R8xe5 21. d×e5 Nf2† 22. Q×f2 Qd3† and Black mates next move—*Newcastle Weekly Chronicle*, 14 July 1894.

The following game was part of the series of blitz games between Bird and Lasker. It went around the world.

## (1120) Bird–Lasker    1–0
Offhand game
Newcastle, 5 September 1892
C21

1. e4 e5 2. d4 e×d4 3. c3 d×c3 4. Bc4 c×b2 5. B×b2 Qg5 6. Nf3 Q×g2 7. Rg1 Bb4† 8. Ke2 Qh3 9. B×f7† Kd8 10. B×g7 Ne7 11. Ng5 Qh4 12. Ne6 mate—*Newcastle Weekly Chronicle*, 17 September 1892.

# BELFAST 1892

Bird left Newcastle for Belfast to take part in an important chess tournament. The planning for this tournament lasted several months and underwent some important changes. At the end, four native British players took part in the master tournament.[32] In his book *Chess History and Reminiscences*, which appeared a short while after the congress was finished, Bird expressed his content with such composition. At the same time he hinted at what he saw as a few negative characteristics of the contemporary foreign players.

> It seems desirable … to say a few words about the inceptions of the great matches in which it was at one time proposed that two other eminent players, not British born should participate, but who at the last moment sought certain undue advantages beyond the very liberal bonuses provided, and even a controlling influence never anticipated by the committee, and to which of course it could not, with any full sense of propriety or regard to originally avowed intentions and subscribers views consent [*Chess History and Reminiscences*, p. 90].

The tournament offered four prizes, worth of £75 in total. The games were played at the Central Hall in Belfast during the second part of September.

Bird opened the tournament against Blackburne. This game was played without time regulation. Bird missed a win on several occasions and the game ended in a draw, just like Bird's next one with Lee. In the third round he unnecessarily lost against Mason but recovered well in the second cycle by beating Blackburne and Lee in two well played games. A second loss was suffered against Mason. Blackburne and Mason now had 4 points, Bird following with 3.

Bird opened the third and final cycle with two draws against Blackburne and Lee. Especially the draw against the latter cost Bird dearly. Before the start of the last round Mason was leading with 5½ out of 8, just ahead of Blackburne (5). Bird (4) was eliminated from first place. Blackburne did not succeed in beating Lee, but the surprise of the final round was the crushing win of Bird over Mason.

Blackburne and Mason tied for first with Bird a half point behind, thus demonstrating that he was still able to hold himself against capable opponents. Lee ended last at a serious distance. Bird's scoring but 2 out of 3 against Lee while his rivals had 2½ was decisive in the final ranking. That no foreign players were needed for discontent (however mild) appeared from Bird's remark in *Chess History and Reminiscences* (p. 92) "that Lee went out of the running, directed a care and energy against Bird which he did not against Blackburne and Mason." All in all, Bird's play in this tournament was of a very high level and in fact he would at least have deserved a shared tournament victory. This was acknowledged by J.A.P. Rynd, the Irish champion, in his column in the Dublin *Saturday Herald* of 24 September: "The games were as a whole exceptionally well

---

32. The different stages gone through were summarized in the *British Chess Magazine* (October 1892, p. 428): "The congress was really the outcome of a proposed match between Messrs. Blackburne and Gunsberg for the championship of England, and the arrangements were in an advanced stage when Mr. Blackburne succumbed to Herr Lasker; after this, Herr Lasker was, with the consent of all parties, included in the proposed match. Two weeks later he withdrew, and on his place being filled by Messrs. Bird and Mason, Mr. Gunsberg withdrew. The match, therefore, finally resolved into a quadrangular contest, between Messrs. Bird, Blackburne, Lee and Mason, in which each player contested three games with each of the other competitors, under a time-limit of twenty moves an hour."

contested, Mr. Bird's vivacious aggressiveness being a distinguishing feature throughout."

Several side events were held along with the main tournament: the amateur championship of Ulster, a handicap tournament and several simultaneous exhibitions given by the visiting masters. Bird performed against 20 opponents on 21 September. After three hours and a half, he had won 16 games, drew 3 (vs. W. Clugston, J. Allen and Courtenay Johnston) and lost 1, against S. Gault.

**(1121) Bird–Blackburne   ½–½**
North of Ireland Congress (round 1)
Belfast, 12 September 1892
C54

**1. e4 e5 2. Nf3 Nc6 3. Bc4 Bc5 4. b4 Bb6 5. c3 Nf6 6. d3 d6 7. a4 a6 8. Bg5** "This looks very much like a lost move, since the bishop returns presently to e3; but Mr. Bird's object, perhaps, was to prevent his opponent from playing 8. ... d5"—Ranken. **8. ... Qe7 9. 0–0 Bg4 10. Na3** "Intending, probably, to bring the knight via c2 to e3, but 10. Nbd2 was better"—Ranken. **10. ... h6 11. Be3 B×e3 12. f×e3 0–0 13. Qe1 B×f3** "Because the knight threatens to go to h4, and then either to g6 or f5"—Ranken. **14. R×f3 Rad8 15. Qg3 d5 16. e×d5 N×d5 17. B×d5 R×d5 18. e4 Rd7 19. Nc4 Kh7 20. b5** 20. Ne3 is the quiet option. **20. ... a×b5 21. a×b5 Qc5† 22. Kh1 Q×b5 23. Raf1** Winning the pawn alienated Black's queen from the king. It is therefore logical that Bird seeks his chances on the kingside, but there is nothing he can force on the f-file. Instead 23. Qg4, planning to put the g-pawn under fire, generates counterplay; e.g., 23. ... Rfd8 24. Rg3 f6 (less good is 24. ... g6 25. Rf1 h5 26. Qg5 and White's attack has become very dangerous) 25. Ne3 Q×d3 (other moves are possible, but not better) 26. Nd5 Qd2 27. N×f6† with a forced draw. **23. ... f6 24. h4 Rff7 25. h5 Qc5 26. Ne3** *(see diagram)*

*After 26. Ne3*

**26. ... Qf8** Bird's last move was a tricky one. Terribly wrong would have been 26. ... R×d3?? 27. Qg6† Kg8 28. Nf5 (Ranken). If 26. ...

Q×c3? 27. Qg6† Kh8, White has to avoid 28. Nf5? due to 28. ... Nd4! Instead 28. Nd5 maintains the balance. The superior reply to Bird's idea is the subtle 26. ... Kh8!, the point being that after 27. Nf5 Black can immediately challenge this piece with 27. ... Ne7. White is forced to exchange, as otherwise Black simply plays 28. ... Q×c3. **27. Ng4** 27. Nf5 is preferable. If 27. ... Ne7 28. Nh4 and Black stands quite passively. **27. ... Kh8 28. Qf2 Nd8 29. d4** White is forced to act before Black has plugged all the holes on the kingside. **29. ... e×d4 30. c×d4** 30. e5 d×c3 31. e×f6 Rd5 is perhaps a better try to complicate the game. **30. ... Qd6 31. d5 f5** A badly timed bid for activity, for White can crack Black's kingside with a well-timed f5-f6. Possible alternatives are 31. ... Rde7 or 31. ... b5. In the latter case, White can continue with 32. Qb2 b4 33. N×f6 (Ranken suggests that this threat may have urged Blackburne to push his f-pawn), but the cool 33. ... Rde7! wards off all the threats, while making himself ready to take over the initiative. **32. e×f5 Q×d5 33. Qh4 Nc6 34. f6 Nd4?** Very dangerous. It was time to adopt some prudence and play for a draw with 34. ... Qg5. **35. Rf4?!** Already Bird misses a chance to decide the game: 35. f×g7† K×g7 36. Rf6! (the crucial move) 36. ... Qg5 37. Q×g5† h×g5 38. Rg6† Kh8 39. Nf6 forces Black into a hopeless ending after 39. ... R×f6 40. Rf×f6. **35. ... Ne6?!** 35. ... Qg5 is the only playable move. **36. Rf5! Qd4 37. Qg3!** "The exchange of pawns and rooks and queens would have enabled White to win a pawn here, but, on account of the distance of his king from the queening square of the Black b-pawn, it would have been a fatal gain"—Ranken. **37. ... g×f6 38. R×f6 R×f6 39. R×f6** Bird played very well and Blackburne landed in an extremely difficult position. His best try now was 39. Ng5 40. R×h6† Rh7. **39. ... Rg7 40. R×h6†?** 40. R×e6! makes the win a cinch; e.g., 40. ... Q×g4 41. Re8† Rg8 42. Q×g4. **40. ... Kg8 41. R×e6 Q×g4** "If 41. ... R×g4, then of course 42. Rg6†"—Ranken. **42. Re8† Kf7 43. Q×g4 R×g4 44. Rc8 Rc4 45. Kh2** "White's game is not easy: he has temporarily recovered his pawn, but must apparently lose it again, for before he can bring up his king and pawn to its support, Black can advance his passed pawns too far to be stopped"—Ranken. **45. ... b5 46. Kh3 b4** "Mr. Blackburne plays endgames so well that we are surprised he did not retire his rook now to c6, in order to interpose it at b6 if White played 47. Rb8. It seems to us that this manoeuvre must have given him the victory"—Ranken. 46. ... Rc6 47. Rb8 Rb6 48. Rc8 draws. **47. Rb8 Kf6 48. g4 Kg5 49. Rg8† Kh6 50. Kh4 Kh7 51. Rb8 Kh6 52. Rb5 c6 53. Re5 b3?** 53. ... c5 or 53. ... Kg7 should lead to a draw. The text move allows a maneuver that sets White's g-pawn in motion. **54. Re6† Kg7 55. Re7† Kf6 56. Rb7 Rc3 57. g5† Kf5 58. g6 Rc4† 59. Kg3?** A subtle mistake that costs him the win after all. 59. Kh3 Kg5 60. R×b3 Rh4† 61. Kg2 secures the promotion of the g-pawn. **59. ... Kg5 60. g7 Rg4† 61. Kf3 K×h5** and the game was drawn after 64 moves—*British Chess Magazine* (Ranken), October 1892, p. 448–450.

**(1122) Bird–Lee   ½–½**
North of Ireland Congress (round 2)
Belfast, 13 September 1892
B01

**1. e4 d5 2. e×d5 Q×d5 3. Nf3 c6 4. Be2 Bg4 5. 0–0 B×f3 6. B×f3 Qd8 7. b3 e6 8. Bb2 Nf6 9. d3 Nbd7 10. Nd2 Be7 11. g3**

0-0 12. Bg2 Ne8 13. Ne4 Nd6 14. Qe1 N×e4 15. d×e4 Qb6 16. Kh1 Qc5 17. Qe2 Bf6 18. c3 e5 19. a4 Qb6 20. Qc2 Rfd8 21. a5 Qc7 22. Rfd1 Nf8 23. b4 Ne6 24. Qe2 a6 25. Bh3 Qe7 26. B×e6 Q×e6 27. c4 R×d1† 28. R×d1 Rd8 29. R×d8† B×d8 30. Kg2 Qd6 31. Bc3 Qe6 32. Qd3 Bc7 33. h3 Qd6 34. Qe3 Bb8 35. Qe2 Qd7 36. Qe3 Qd6 37. g4 h6 38. Qe2 Qd7 39. Qf3 Qe6 40. Qe2 Qd7 41. f3 Qd8 42. Be1 Ba7 43. c5 Qd4 44. Qc2 Bb8 45. Qc3 Q×c3 46. B×c3 g5 draw—*Bristol Mercury and Daily Post*, 24 September 1892.

## (1123) Mason–Bird    1–0
North of Ireland Congress (round 3)
Belfast, 14 September 1892
*B01*

**1. e4 d5 2. e×d5 Q×d5 3. Nc3 Qd8 4. d4 g6 5. Bf4 Bg7 6. Nb5 Na6 7. c3 c6 8. Na3 Nc7 9. Nf3 Nf6 10. h3 Nfd5 11. Bd2 0-0 12. Bd3 Re8 13. 0-0 Ne6 14. Re1 b5 15. Be4 Bb7 16. B×d5** Bird's position was a bit inferior (mainly because of 14. ... b5), but this exchange offers him the bishop pair as well as the important lever c6–c5. **16. ... Q×d5 17. b4** Mason wishes to avoid 17. ... c5, but Bird's reply exploits the downside of this move. **17. ... a5! 18. Nc2 a×b4 19. N×b4 Qd6** 19. ... Qf5 is a much better spot for the queen. The threat 20. ... c5 is very annoying for White and forces 20. g4 Qf6 with 21. ... c5 still to follow. **20. Qe2 c5!** The idea remains the same. White is struggling to keep his position together. **21. d×c5 Q×c5 22. Rac1 Rad8** This rook belongs to the c-file. The other one had to go to d8. **23. Red1** 23. Be3 is necessary. The text move makes matters much worse. **23. ... Qh5 24. Be3 R×d1† 25. Q×d1 Rd8 26. Nd4** *(see diagram)*

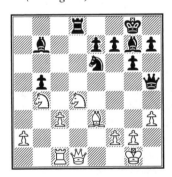

*After 26. Nd4*

**26. ... Qe5** 26. ... Q×d1 is not so convincing, as after 27. R×d1 N×d4 28. c×d4 e5 29. d5 Bf8 Black will gain a pawn but an ending with bishops of opposite color minimizes his winning chances. A better alternative was 26. ... Qh4, retaining strong pressure. If 27. Nbc2 Nf4! and White has to say farewell to his second bishop. Therefore 27. Qg4 is forced. Black now enters a similar endgame as mentioned above but he wins an extra pawn: 27. ... Q×g4 28. h×g4 N×d4 29. c×d4 B×d4. **27. Qe1** 27. Qc2 seems to be a better spot for the queen for if then 27. ... Nf4? 28. Ndc6 wins. **27. ... N×d4** 27. ... Nf4 is more dangerous to meet. Two possibilities are 28. B×f4 Q×f4 29. Ndc6 B×c6 30. N×c6 Rd6 or 28. Nbc6 N×g2 29. N×e5 N×e1 30. R×e1 B×e5 31. N×b5 Rd3. In both cases Bird's edge is clear. **28. c×d4 Qe4 29. f3 Q×e3† 30. Q×e3 B×d4 31. Kf2 e5** Bird incorrectly assumes that he has enough time to take the queen. A small edge could be nurtured after 31. ... B×e3† 32. K×e3 Kf8.

**32. Rc5! B×e3† 33. K×e3 Rd4?** The text move seriously mortgages his drawing chances. **34. R×b5 Bc8 35. R×e5?** Far stronger is 35. a4!, keeping the pieces on the board while advancing the extra pawn as much as possible. A rook endgame is much welcomed by Black. **35. ... R×b4 36. Re8† Kg7 37. R×c8 Rb2 38. a4 R×g2 39. a5 Ra2 40. Rc5 Ra4 41. Kd2 Ra3 42. Kc2** Mason speculates on Bird's not always convincing endgame play. **42. ... R×f3 43. Rc3 Rf6 44. Kb3 Ra6** 44. ... Re6 followed by the advance of his pawns draws fairly simple. **45. Kb4 g5** 45. ... Ra8! is good enough for a narrow save. If 46. Ra3 f5 47. Kb5 f4 etc. If 46. Kb5 Rb8† 47. Ka6 Ra8† 48. Kb6 Rb8† 49. Kc7 seems winning, but Black surprisingly draws—49. ... Rb1 50. a6 Ra1 51. Rc6 f5 52. Kb7 f4 53. a7 f3 54. a8Q R×a8 55. K×a8 f2 56. Rc1 Kh1 etc. **46. Kb5 Ra8 47. Kb6** 47. a6 doesn't win either: 47. ... f5 48. Kb6 f4 49. Kb7 Rf8 50. a7 Kf6 51. Rc8 Rf7† 52. Kb6 R×a7 53. K×a7 Ke5. **47. ... Kg6 48. a6 h5?** Wrong; the unopposed f-pawn had to advance, with a similar ending as in the variations given above. **49. Kb7 R×a6** There was nothing better than 49. ... Re8 50. a7 g4 51. h4 Kf5 (if 51. ... f5 52. Rc6†) 52. Rc8 Re7† 53. Rc7 Re8 54. R×f7† Ke4 55. Ka6! g3 56. Re7† and wins. **50. K×a6 g4 51. h×g4?** After 51. Kb5 the king is back in time to stop the pawns: 51. ... f5 52. Kc4 f4 53. Kd4 Kg5 54. Ke4 f3 55. Ke3. **51. ... h×g4 52. Kb5 Kg5?** The wrong square! 52. ... Kf5 draws as the journey of the White king is interrupted after 53. Kc4 Ke4. **53. Kc4 Kf4 54. Kd3 Kf3 55. Kd2† Kf2** This move took Bird 30 minutes to make. He used his time a few moves too late. **56. Rc5 g3 57. Rf5† Kg1 58. Ke2 g2 59. Kf3 f6 60. R×f6 Kh1 61. Rh6† Kg1 62. Rg6** Black resigns—*Belfast News-Letter*, 15 September 1892.

## (1124) Blackburne–Bird    0–1
North of Ireland Congress (round 4)
Belfast, 15 September 1892
*C61*

**1. e4 e5 2. Nf3 Nc6 3. Bb5 Nd4 4. N×d4 e×d4 5. d3 h5** "A form of counterattack to a certain extent imposed as a consequence of 3. ... Nd4"—Mason. **6. c3** "It would be better to castle. On its merits, Black's attack can be brought to a standstill, with a reaction in favor of White, usually decisive. But the latter must be content to defend for a time, or affairs may easily take a serious turn against him"—Mason. **6. ... Bc5 7. 0-0 c6 8. Ba4 d6** "On other occasions Mr. Bird has played 8. ... Ne7, and afterwards advanced this pawn to d5, with good results"—Mason. **9. Qe1 Qf6 10. Kh1** "This and his next move seem to be enforced chiefly by the masked action of the Black bishop—which but for 6. c3 would of course be quite inoperative"—Mason. **10. ... Nh6 11. f3 h4 12. Bc2** Here, and on the next moves, both sides are unaware of the importance of playing h3. For White this is a preparatory move for 13. f4. Black on the other hand would create some lasting weaknesses on White's kingside after 12. ... h3. **12. ... Bd7 13. c×d4** This exchange gives Bird the control over the position. **13. ... B×d4 14. Nc3 0-0-0 15. Be3 Rde8 16. B×d4** "An interesting variation here would be 16. Qf2 B×e3 (16. ... B×c3 17. b×c3 Q×c3 for the sake of a pawn would be dangerous) 17. Q×e3 Nf5! 18. Q×a7 Ng3†! 19. Kg1 N×f1 20. K×f1 and some players would be inclined to take White for choice, the utility of the exchange being so much deferred. It may be added that if in the above White were to play 19. h×g3, his game would be lost, through 19. ... h×g3† and 20. ... Rh1†"—Mason. White comes very bad out of this line. Instead of 20. K×f1? h3! (which wins at once), at least 20. R×f1 had to be played. **16. ... Q×d4 17. Qf2** The opening has been a success for Bird. Blackburne is forced to rescue himself in the endgame, as 17. Q×h4? loses immediately after 17. ... Ng4. **17. ... Q×f2 18. R×f2 g5** 18. ... f5 may be a bit better. In any case, Bird has no problems. **19. b4** "Time was pressing, no doubt. There is little force in this either for attack or defense. Some such moves as 19. d4, or 19. Re2, or 19. Kg1 or even 19. h3 would be stronger"—Mason. **19. ... f5 20. Re2 g4 21. f4 Rhf8 22. Rf1** "White has a much more difficult game to play than appears at first sight. 22. g3, in an effort to get the king more into the center of things, would afford a better prospect than this"—Mason. **22. ... Kc7 23. Bd1 Be6 24. Rc2 f×e4 25. d×e4 Bc4 26. Be2 B×e2 27. R×e2 d5!** "Fine play. The pawn must be taken, because if 28. e5 Nf5, threatening all sorts of mischief; and the four pawns against two on the queenside would soon become intolerable"—Mason. **28. e×d5 R×e2 29. N×e2 c×d5** Bird obtained a passed pawn, but Blackburne should be able to cope with it. **30. Nd4 Re8 31. f5?!** (see diagram) Advancing his passed pawn looks logical, but Bird can stop it easily and at the same time activate his rook. Both 31. g3 and 31. Rc1† Kd7 32. Rd1 keep the game in balance.

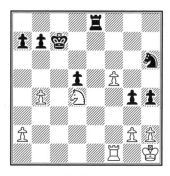

*After 31. f5*

**31. ... Re4!** "Black's game is a winning one from this point, as his opponent's exposed pawns are an easy prey to the active king and rook"—Mason. **32. Ne6† Kd6 33. Ng7?!** It was necessary to bring the king towards the front, thus avoiding any mating threats. After 33. Kg1 Nf7 White remains in trouble anyway as he is likely to lose a pawn soon; e.g., 34. a3 (34. b5 Ra4 35. Rf2 Rb4 36. Re2 R×b5 37. Kf2 Rb4) 34. ... Re3 35. Nf4 R×a3 36. Rd1 Ke5 37. N×d5 h3 38. g×h3 g×h3 39. Ne7 Kf6 40. Nd5† K×f5 and although White can still play for a draw his task is not easy. **33. ... R×b4** The immediate 33. ... d4 is also very good. **34. f6 Nf7 35. Nf5† Ke5 36. N×h4 d4 37. Ng6† Ke4 38. Kg1 Rb2 39. h4** This loses, but there is nothing else. If 39. Ne7 d3 40. Re1† Kf4 41. Nd5† Kf5 42. Ne3† K×f6 43. N×g4† Kg5 44. Nf2 d2 and Black should win. **39. ... g×h3 e.p. 40. g×h3 d3 41. Re1† Kf5 42. Ne7† K×f6 43. Nd5† Kf5 44. Ne3† Kg6 45. Nc4 R×a2 46. Rd1 b5 47. Nd2 Ng5** "Getting rid of White's last pawn, as it threatens 48. ... R×d2. The whole game is an excellent specimen of Mr. Bird at his best, and in several respects one of the most interesting in the tournament. On the other hand, it must be said, Mr. Blackburne was not so well, and consequently failed to display anything like his full resources. He might have resigned here"—Mason. **48. Kf1 N×h3 49. Kg2 Ng5 50. Kf1 Rb2 51. Ke1 a5 52. Ra1 a4 53. Ra3 Ne4 54. N×e4 Re2† 55. Kd1**

R×e4 56. R×d3 Rc4 57. Rd6† Kf7 58. Ra6 Ke7 59. Ra5 Rc5 60. Kd2 Kd6 61. Kd3 Kc6 62. Ra8 Kb7 63. Ra5 Kb6 64. Ra8 Rc7 65. Rb8† Ka5 66. Kd2 Kb4 67. Rb6 a3 68. Rh6 a2 69. Rh1 Ka3 70. Kd3 Rd7† 71. Kc3 b4† 72. Kc4 Kb2 73. Rh2† Ka3 74. Rh1 b3 75. Kb5 Rd2 and White resigns. 75. ... b2 76. Rh3 would have been painful—*Belfast News-Letter*, 16 September 1892; *British Chess Magazine* (Mason), October 1892, pp. 446–447.

### (1125) Lee–Bird　　0–1
North of Ireland Congress (round 5)
Belfast, 16 September 1892
*D46*

**1. d4 d5 2. Nf3 e6 3. c4 Nf6 4. e3 Nbd7 5. Bd3 Be7 6. Nc3 0–0 7. 0–0** "A carefully played opening on both sides, and at this point White has nothing more than the first move advantage"—Lee. **7. ... Re8 8. b3 c6 9. Bb2 Bd6 10. Qc2 d×c4** It wasn't necessary to hand over the center so easily. **11. b×c4 Bb8** "Eccentric as this move seems, it is the best place for the bishop, if it is to remain on the diagonal for an attack on the kingside, contemplated by Black" —Hoffer. Bird's move is above all a loss of time. The thematic 11. ... e5 gives him a reasonable game. **12. Ne2** "12. e4, neglected for several moves previously, might now be played with advantage. He cannot play the tempting 12. Ng5 because of 12. ... B×h2† and 13. ... Ng4†"—Hoffer. Both after the text move and 12. e4, Bird could equalize with 12. ... e5! Decidedly better was 12. Ne4!, completely preventing Black's liberating push. **12. ... Qa5** "A favorite move of Bird. It appears to be very good here, preventing White from playing 13. Ne5, and with a view to posting the queen advantageously at h5"—Lee. **13. c5** "Needlessly afraid that Black will bring his queen over to the kingside. We should still have preferred 13. e4. The text move weakens the center, and gives Black an opportunity to play e5"—Hoffer. A good move, and certainly better than 13. e4 when 13. ... e5 solves all Black's problems. **13. ... e5 14. Bc3** 14. Ng5! is a very strong reaction against Black's untimely opening of the center: 14. ... h6 (14. ... g6 15. Bc4 Rf8 16. B×f7† R×f7 17. Qb3 wins at once) 15. N×f7 K×f7 16. Bg6† Kg8 17. B×e8 N×e8 18. Qc4† Kf8 19. Rfd1 results in a complete bind. **14. ... Qd8 15. Ng3 e×d4 16. B×d4** "Weak. 16. e×d4 was much better. The text move leaves White with bad pawns for the ending, without much compensation in the shape of attack"—Lee. The text move has the strong benefit of gaining active piece play. His weakness at c5 is compensated by the one at b7. White can also assume a space advantage and the better development. 16. e×d4, on the other hand, would have closed in his own bishop and created a strong field at d5 for his opponent's use. **16. ... Ne5 17. B×e5 B×e5 18. N×e5** This exchange comes too soon. After 18. Rad1 Qc7 19. Ne4 N×e4 20. B×e4 g6 21. N×e5 Q×e5 22. Rd4, White has a small, but undeniable plus. **18. ... R×e5 19. Rfd1 Qe7** Now the weakness at c5 starts to tell. **20. Rac1 Bg4 21. f3 Be6 22. Re1** Undeveloping his own rook isn't wise. Lee thought that 22. e4 Nd7 would lose the pawn at c5, but 23. Qb2! saves this precious pawn. **22. ... g6 23. f4 Rd5 24. e4 Rd4 25. f5 Rad8!** "Fine play, much better than retiring the bishop. In the interesting complications that follow, Black obtains the advantage by good play"—Lee. **26. e5** "Further complicating matters. Taking into consideration the White queenside pawns, the venturesome line of play selected is probably as good as any"—Lee. "26. f×e6 R×d3 27. e×f7† Q×f7 28. e5 would be better, because he could advance his e-pawn to e6"—Hoffer. **26. ... Ng4 27. f×e6 R×d3 28. e×f7† Q×f7** (*see diagram*)

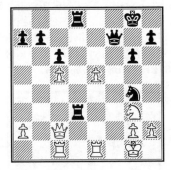

*After 28. ... Q×f7*

**29. Ne4?** "A bad move, after which White's game cannot be saved. 29. e6 was the only move to give White any chance"—Lee. 29. e6 is a better try, but the position remains favorable for Bird: 29. ... Qf6 30. Qc4 (30. e7 is inferior—30. ... Qd4† 31. Kh1 Re8) 30. ... Qf2† (30. ... Ne5 allows White better chances to save the game: 31. Ne4! Qe7 32. Qc2 Q×e6 33. Qb2 and Black will probably lose the b-pawn soon, when White has good survival chances. The position remains very complicated) 31. Kh1 Ne3 32. Qe4 R8d4. Black's pieces have infiltrated his opponent's position in a fascinating way. White is forced into an inferior endgame: 33. Qf3 Q×f3 34. g×f3 Kf8. **29. ... Qf4 30. Qc4†?!** It was necessary to abandon the e-pawn with 30. Nf6†, achieving the exchange of Bird's deadly knight. **30. ... Kg7 31. g3 Qh6 32. Rc2** "There is no satisfactory defense for White at this stage. If 32. Qc2, then 32. ... Rd2 and wins. Black has conducted his counterattack in forcible and elegant style"—Lee. **32. ... Rd1 33. Qe2 R×e1† 34. Q×e1 Qe3† 35. Kf1** "If 35. Q×e3 Rd1† wins a piece"—Lee. **35. ... Qf3† 36. Rf2** "If 36. Nf2 Ne3† wins"—Hoffer. **36. ... Qh1†** White resigns. "An interesting and brilliant termination"—Hoffer—*Hereford Times* (Lee), 24 September 1892; *The Field* (Hoffer), 24 September 1892.

### (1126) Bird–Mason    0–1
North of Ireland Congress (round 6)
Belfast, 19 September 1892
C59

**1. e4 e5 2. Nf3 Nc6 3. Bc4 Nf6 4. Ng5 d5 5. e×d5 Na5 6. d3 h6 7. Nf3 e4 8. Qe2 N×c4 9. d×c4 Bc5 10. h3 0–0 11. Nh2 b5 12. Ng4 b×c4 13. N×f6† Q×f6 14. Nc3 Re8 15. 0–0 Qe5 16. Re1 Bd6 17. g3 B×h3 18. Bf4 Qf5 19. B×d6 Bg4 20. Qf1 c×d6 21. Nb5 Bf3 22. Nd4 Q×d5 23. N×f3 e×f3 24. Qh3 Re2 25. g4 Rae8 26. Red1 Qe4 27. R×d6 R×c2 28. Rad1 R×b2 29. g5 h×g5 30. Rd8 Rb8 31. R8d7 c3 32. Qh5 Qf5 33. R×a7 c2 34. Rf1 Rb1 35. Rc7 R×f1† 36. K×f1 Rd8** White resigns—*Belfast News-Letter*, 20 September 1892.

### (1127) Bird–Blackburne    ½–½
North of Ireland Congress (round 7)
Belfast, 20 September 1892
D00

**1. e3 d5 2. d4 Nf6 3. c3 Nbd7 4. f4 Ne4 5. Nf3 e6 6. Bd3 Ndf6**

**7. 0–0 Be7 8. Na3 0–0 9. Nc2 c5 10. Nce1 c4 11. Bc2 b5 12. Ng5 N×g5 13. f×g5 Ne4 14. B×e4 d×e4 15. h4 Qc7 16. Qg4 Qc6 17. Nc2 a5 18. Bd2 Rb8 19. a3 Qd5 20. Be1 Rb7 21. Bg3 f5 22. Qe2 Bd7 23. Be5 Bd6 24. B×d6 Q×d6 25. Qf2 Bc6 26. Qf4 Q×f4 27. R×f4 g6 28. g3 Rff8 29. Kf2 h5 30. Ke2 Bd5 31. Rf2 Rf8 32. Kd2 Rfb8 33. Rff1 Kf7 34. Rfc1 Kg7 35. Rh1 Bc6 36. Rhb1 Bd5 37. Ke2 a4 38. Nb4 Rb6 39. Rf1 Rf8 40. Rf2 Rd6 41. Rd1 Ra8 42. Rd2 Rf8** draw—*Belfast News-Letter*, 21 September 1892.

### (1128) Bird–Lee    ½–½
North of Ireland Congress (round 8)
Belfast, 22 September 1892
A01

**1. e3 e5 2. b3** "Mr. Bird is on quite unfamiliar lines here, and the result, though interesting in a way, is not very encouraging. In practical play we have tried this sort of thing a good deal, and cannot say we consider it strong. Better is 2. d4 at once"—Tinsley. **2. ... d5 3. Bb2 Bd6 4. Nf3 Qe7 5. c4 c6 6. c×d5 c×d5 7. Nc3 Nf6 8. Nb5** "White is well advised in getting rid of the bishop. Besides he threatens still to win the e-pawn"—Tinsley. **8. ... Nc6 9. N×d6† Q×d6 10. Bb5 e4 11. Ne5 0–0 12. B×c6 b×c6 13. Rc1 Bb7 14. 0–0 Nd7 15. f4 N×e5 16. B×e5 Qe7 17. Bd4** Although a position with bishops of opposite color has come on the board, Black is under great pressure. Bird's bishop is clearly the superior one and gives him chances to attack the kingside. The possession of the semi-open c-file is also a trump for him. **17. ... Rfe8 18. Qg4 f6 19. Rc5 a6 20. Rfc1 Rac8 21. f5! Kh8 22. Rf1 Rc7 23. Rf4 Qf7 24. Qh3 Rf8 25. g4** "In offhand play Mr. Bird would doubtless have tried 25. Rh4 here, forcing Black to play 25. ... h6 or 25. ... Qg8 at once"—Tinsley. Bird wants to crack his opponent's kingside with his pawns. Lee has nothing to show in return. **25. ... Kg8 26. Qg3 h6 27. b4 Rd7 28. Rc1 Ra8 29. h4 Qe7** (*see diagram*)

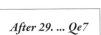

*After 29. ... Qe7*

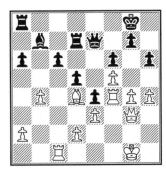

**30. Rc5** "Playing for safety. The bishop is it will be noted carefully kept at d5, and this rook does duty instead of the tempting 30. Bc5"—Tinsley. The thematic 30. g5 secures a quick win—e.g., 30. ... h×g5 31. h×g5 f×g5 32. Rg4 Qd6 33. Q×d6 R×d6 34. R×g5 Rd7 35. Kf2, and the assault can be strengthened with 36. Rcg1 and 37. f6. **30. ... Rf8 31. a3 Rf7 32. Kh2 Qd8 33. Rc1 a5 34. Rg1 a×b4 35. a×b4 Qe7 36. Bc5** 36. g5! still breaks through: 36. ... f×g5 37. h×g5 h×g5 38. Q×g5 Q×g5 39. R×g5 Kf8 40. Rh4 Ke8 41. Rh7. **36. ... Qd8 37. Bd4 Qe7 38. Bc3 Ba6 39. Qh3 Be2 40. g5** After dragging his feet for a while, Bird decides to play the crucial push, which hasn't lost anything of its strength. **40. ... f×g5 41. h×g5**

**d4** "The culminating point of a really interesting game. No doubt White intends if 41. … h×g5, to reply 42. f6 g×f6 43. R×f6! R×f6 44. R×g5† with an attack which seems to win"—Tinsley. **42. B×d4** 42. g×h6 forces the decision in a few moves: 42. … Qf6 43. B×d4 R×d4 44. h×g7 R×g7 45. R×g7† Q×g7 46. e×d4. **42. … R×d4** A desperate try. If 42. … h×g5 43. f6! wins. **43. e×d4?** Rather too impetuous. First 43. g6! and if 43. … Rf6 44. e×d4 makes the situation hopeless for Black. **43. … h×g5 44. Rf2 g4 45. Qg3 Bf3 46. Ra1 R×f5 47. Ra8† Kh7 48. Kg1** During the past few moves a complete transformation took place. Both kings find themselves in a troublesome situation, but they are also very hard to get at. Bird's move is, not surprisingly, very risky. 48. Ra5, which neutralizes Lee's rook, is good enough for a draw. **48. … Q×b4 49. Qh4† Kg6 50. Rh8 g3 51. Qh7† Kf6 52. Qh4† Kg6 53. Qh7† Kf6 54. Qh4† Kg6 55. Qh7† Kf6 56. Qh4† Rg5** Black has a mate threat. **57. Qf4† Kg6 58. R×f3** Securing the draw after all. **58. … e×f3 59. Qe4† Rf5 60. Qe8† Rf7** and the game was drawn after 73 moves—*British Chess Magazine* (Tinsley), November 1892, pp. 507–508.

## (1129) Mason–Bird    0–1

North of Ireland Congress (round 9)
Belfast, 23 September 1892
*B54*

**1. e4 c5 2. Nf3 Nc6 3. d4** "Long ago discarded in favor of Paulsen's move 3. Nc3"—Steinitz. **3. … c×d4 4. N×d4 d6** "A favorite move of Bird in this opening, and with which he is more successful than with 4. … g6"—Lee. **5. Nc3 Bd7 6. N×c6** "Not commendable at such an early stage. He should delay this exchange at least until the opponent plays g6, when he afterwards will gain time by Qd4"—Steinitz. **6. … B×c6** "Much inferior to 6. … b×c6 with the view of following it up by 7. … e6 and 8. … d5"—Steinitz. **7. Bd3 e6 8. 0–0 g6** Adopting the fianchetto after having played 7. … e6 is positionally suspect. **9. f4** This thrust is double-edged. **9. … h5** "In the old style, which is the style of Bird, who cannot resist following the semblance of an attack on the kingside even at great risk to himself"—Steinitz. **10. f5 g×f5** "White's attack seemed promising, but Black, who plays the whole game with excellent judgment, goes only so far in response as to open the g-file for his own attacking purposes"—Abbott. **11. e×f5 Qb6† 12. Kh1 0–0–0?** Black must keep the position absolutely closed and play 12. … e5, as White's rook and bishops become much more active than his now. **13. f×e6 f×e6 14. Qe2 e5** "He suffers much now from his previous boldness, as his kingside is open to all sorts of aggressions, and the weakening of his center has now become almost compulsory. He could not play 14. … Re8 on account of the rejoinder 15. Bg6, but probably his best plan was the more defensive 14. … Bd7, though this involved his abandoning prospects of attack with this bishop against the adverse king"—Steinitz. **15. Be4** "15. Ne4 gave him more surely the advantage, for Black had no better answer than 15. … B×e4, when White would retake with the bishop followed by 17. c4, or accordingly 17. Bf5†. If, however, 15. … d5 16. Ng5 e4 17. Nf7 Rh7 (or 17. … e×d3 18. Qe6† Bd7 19. Q×b6 etc.) 18. N×d8 Q×d8 19. Bb5 and should win"—Steinitz. After 15. … Be7!, Black is well placed to meet 16. Ng5 with 16. … Nh6. More fruitful possibilities are 16. c4, 16. a4 or 16. Be3. But better is directly playing 15. Be3 Qa5 16. Qf2,

which puts Bird with his back against the wall. If then 16. … Kb8, there is a stunning continuation: 17. Q×f8! R×f8 18. R×f8† Kc7 19. Bg5! b6 20. Bd8† Kb7 21. Raf1, with a decisive initiative. **15. … Ne7** 15. … B×e4 eliminates another dangerous piece. **16. Bg5! d5** Steinitz suggests 16. … Q×b2, but this is equally dreadful after 17. B×e7 B×e7 18. Qc4! **17. B×e7?** A dramatic exchange that not only throws away a decisive advantage, but delivers to Black the initiative as well. After 17. Bf6! Rh6 18. Bf5† N×f5 19. B×d8 Bird could resign. **17. … B×e7 18. Bf5† Kb8** *(see diagram)*

*After 18. … Kb8*

**19. b3?!** 19. Q×e5† (Steinitz) 19. … Bd6 gives Black a dangerous attack, but the text move is worse as it simply loses time. **19. … e4 20. Na4** Chasing the queen to a more threatening place. Mason's last moves were very weak. **20. … Qc7 21. c4** "This does not improve matters. White has, however, now a very inferior game, which cannot be saved against the best play on the part of Black"—Lee. **21. … Qe5 22. c×d5 Bd6!** "The veteran is now in his element with his forces well directed against the adverse king"—Steinitz. **23. g3 B×d5 24. Rac1 e3† 25. Kg1 Rdg8!** "Ingeniously threatening the sacrifice of the rook by 26. … R×g3†"—Steinitz. **26. Rf3 B×f3 27. Q×f3 Rf8** Black wins "This is one of the few important tourney games in which the Sicilian Defense has recently proved successful. Mr. Bird's play is as accurate and vigorous as ever, Mr. Mason being scarcely at his best. We may point out that Mr. Mason only lost one game to Mr. Bird in this contest"—Abbott. *Hereford Times* (Lee), 1 October 1892; *Illustrated London News* (Abbott), 15 October 1892; *New York Daily Tribune* (Steinitz), 30 October 1892.

## MATCH WITH HEYWOOD 1892

Bird interrupted his return from Belfast to London to stay another two weeks in Newcastle. The highlight of Bird's third visit of 1892 was a friendly match between him and George Carm Heywood. Heywood was an old acquaintance of Bird. They had met in the 1870s at the City of London Chess Club. Later Heywood became the president and driving force of the young Newcastle Art Gallery Chess Club (established in 1891). A peculiar match set-up was designed to give the amateur a reasonable chance for success. The match was divided in three cycles of three games each. The first game was played on even terms, while Bird gave the odds of respectively pawn and move and pawn and 2 moves in the following games.

Play commenced on Monday 3 October. Bird was successful in the first cycle, winning with 2 against 1. Heywood gained his revenge by terminating the next three games with the same score. Both players consequently won one game in the last cycle. With each player counting 4 points, and having to concede the heavy odds of pawn and two moves in the final game, Bird decided that he could not hope even to draw and preferred to resign the match instead of playing it out. This was accepted by his opponent. Immediately afterwards, Bird and his allies, scored a brilliant victory against a team headed by Heywood.

The match between Bird and Heywood was interrupted twice for simultaneous exhibitions. On Wednesday 5 October Bird met 20 eager opponents. Within two hours of play, and despite his age and chronic lameness, as respectfully remarked in the newspapers, he had beaten them all except one, S.C. Lockerby, who drew his game. Bird scored a similar impressive result on the next Wednesday, 12 October. Once again 20 opponents showed up. Bird conceded just 1 draw, now against C.L. Cummings.

A month after Bird left, he was elected honorary member of the club at a special general meeting held on 16 November.

George C. Heywood (*British Chess Magazine*).

**Match with Heywood, 3–15 October 1892**

| | 1 | 2 | 3 | 4 | 5 | 6 | 7 | 8 | 9 | |
|---|---|---|---|---|---|---|---|---|---|---|
| G.C. Heywood | 0 | ½ | ½ | 1 | 0 | 1 | 0 | 1 | + | 5 |
| H.E. Bird | 1 | ½ | ½ | 0 | 1 | 0 | 1 | 0 | – | 4 |

### (1130) Heywood–Bird    0–1

Match (game 1)
Newcastle, 3 October 1892
*C61*

1. e4 e5 2. Nf3 Nc6 3. Bb5 Nd4 4. N×d4 e×d4 5. 0–0 h5 6. d3 c6 7. Ba4 Bc5 8. Nd2 d6 9. Nf3 Bg4 10. Bd2 h4 11. h3 Bh5 12. Re1 g5 13. e5 g4 14. e×d6† Kf8 15. Ng5 g×h3 16. Qc1 h×g2 17. K×g2 h3† 18. Kh2 Nf6 19. f3 B×d6† 20. Bf4 Qc7 21. B×d6† Q×d6† 22. Kh1 Qg3 23. Rg1 B×f3† 24. N×f3 Q×f3† 25. Kh2 Re8 White resigns—*Newcastle Weekly Chronicle*, 8 October 1892.

### (1131) Heywood–Bird    ½–½

Match (game 2)
Newcastle, 3 October 1892
*Odds of pawn and move*

1. f4 c5 2. Nf3 Nf6 3. e3 Nc6 4. b3 g6 5. Bb2 Bg7 6. a3 0–0 7. Bd3 d6 8. Nc3 e6 9. 0–0 Qe7 10. Qe1 Bd7 11. Nh4 Be8 12. Ne4 Nd8 13. Ng5 b5 14. Qe2 Rb8 15. Rab1 a5 16. Ba1 d5 17. Nhf3 Qa7 18. c4 a4 19. Be5 Rb6 20. b×a4 b×c4 21. Bc2 h6 22. Nh3 Nd7 23. R×b6 Q×b6 24. Rb1 Qa6 25. B×g7 K×g7 26. Nf2 Nc6 27. Nd1 Bf7 28. d3 c×d3 29. B×d3 c4 30. Qb2† Nf6 31. Qb5 Ra8 32. Bc2 Qc8 33. Qb7 Q×b7 34. R×b7 Nd8 35. Rb1 Be8 36. Nc3 Ng4 37. Re1 Rb8 38. h3 Nf6 draw—*Newcastle Weekly Chronicle*, 8 October 1892.

### (1132) Heywood–Bird    ½–½

Match (game 3)
Newcastle, 4 October 1892
*Odds of pawn and two moves*

1. e4 & 2. d4 Nc6 3. Nf3 d6 4. Bd3 e5 5. d×e5 d×e5 6. Bd2

Bg4 7. Bc3 Bd6 8. Nbd2 Qf6 9. h3 Bh5 10. Qe2 Nge7 11. Qe3 h6 12. Nh2 0–0–0 13. Ng4 B×g4 14. h×g4 Ng6 15. g3 Bb4 16. a3 B×c3 17. b×c3 Rhf8 18. 0–0 Nge7 19. Rab1 Qe6 20. Qe2 Na5 21. Nb3 N×b3 22. R×b3 Rd6 23. Rfb1 Rb6 24. a4 Nc6 25. Kg2 Rf6 26. Rh1 g5 27. Bb5 Na5 28. Rbb1 a6 29. Bd3 R×b1 30. R×b1 Qa2 31. Qf1 Qa3 32. Qe1 Rc6 33. c4 Qc5 34. Qb4 Q×b4 35. R×b4 draw—*Newcastle Weekly Chronicle*, 8 October 1892.

### (1133) Bird–Heywood    0–1

Match (game 4)
Newcastle, October 1892
*C50*

1. e4 e5 2. Nf3 Nc6 3. Bc4 Be7 4. d4 d6 5. c3 Nf6 6. Nbd2 0–0 7. Bb5 e×d4 8. c×d4 Bg4 9. B×c6 b×c6 10. h3 Be6 11. Qc2 Qd7 12. Nf1 d5 13. Ne5 Qe8 14. e×d5 B×d5 15. Ne3 Bd6 16. N5g4 Nh5 17. 0–0 Be4 18. Qd1 f5 19. Ne5 Nf4 20. f3 Bd5 21. N×d5 N×d5 22. Re1 Qh5 23. Qa4 Qh4 24. Bd2 c5 25. f4 Kh8 26. d×c5 B×c5† 27. Kh1 Nf6 28. Qc4 Bb6 29. Bb4 c5 30. Bc3 Qh5 31. Rad1 Rae8 32. Rd6 Bc7 33. Rc6 B×e5 34. B×e5 Qh4 35. Qc3 Rf7 36. R×c5 Ne4 37. Rc8 Q×e1† 38. Q×e1 R×c8 39. g4 Rd7 40. Kg1 Rcd8 41. Qa5 Rd1† 42. Kg2 R8d2† 43. Kf3 Rf1† 44. Ke3 Re1† 45. Kf3 Rf2 mate—*The Field*, 15 October 1892.

### (1134) Heywood–Bird    0–1

Match (game 5)
Newcastle, 8 October 1892
*Odds of pawn and move*

1. e4 Nc6 2. d4 d5 3. Nc3 e6 4. Nf3 Bb4 5. Bd3 Nf6 6. Bg5 h6 7. B×f6 Q×f6 8. 0–0 B×c3 9. b×c3 Ne7 10. Ne5 0–0 11. f4 Rd8 12. g4 c5 13. Qd2 c4 14. g5 Qf8 15. Be2 d×e4 16. g×h6 g×h6 17. Kh1 b5 18. Rg1† Kh7 19. Bh5 Bb7 20. Qg2 Qf6 21. Ng4 Qg7 22. Ne3 Q×g2† 23. R×g2 Nd5 24. Rag1 Rd7 25. Re1 N×f4 26. Bg4 N×g2 27. K×g2 Rg7 28. Kf2 Rf8† 29. Ke2 Bd5 30. Rb1 Rf4 31. N×d5 e×d5 32. h3 a6 33. Ke3 Rgf7 34. Rg1 Rf1 35. R×f1 R×f1 36. Be6 Rf3† 37. Kd2 Rf2† 38. Kd1 Kg6 39. B×d5 Kf5 40. Bb7 Kf4 41. B×a6 Ke3 42. Kc1 Rf1† 43. Kb2 Rf5 44. a4 b×a4 45. B×c4 Kd2 White resigns—*Newcastle Weekly Chronicle*, 15 October 1892.

### (1135) Heywood–Bird　　1–0
Match (game 6)
Newcastle, 10 October 1892
*Odds of pawn and two moves*

1. e4 & 2. d4 Nc6 3. d5 Ne5 4. f4 Nf7 5. Nf3 Ngh6 6. c4 c6 7. Be3 g6 8. Bd4 Rg8 9. Nc3 d6 10. Bd3 Qc7 11. Ne2 Bg7 12. B×g7 R×g7 13. h3 Bd7 14. Qc2 0–0–0 15. Qc3 Rgg8 16. Qd2 Kb8 17. g4 Rgf8 18. 0–0–0 Ng8 19. Kb1 Rc8 20. Ned4 Nd8 21. f5 h6 22. Rhf1 g×f5 23. g×f5 Nf7 24. Ne6 B×e6 25. d×e6 Nd8 26. Nh4 c5 27. Ng6 Re8 28. Nf4 Nc6 29. Nd5 Qd8 30. Be2 Ne5 31. b3 Rf8 32. Rg1 Nf6 33. Nc3 Rg8 34. Q×h6 Rh8 35. Qe3 Rh4 36. Bg4 Qh8 37. Qe2 Rg8 38. Nd5 N×d5 39. e×d5 Qf6 40. Rg2 Kc7 41. Rdg1 b5 42. Rg3 b×c4 43. b×c4 Rb8† 44. Rb3 N×g4 45. R×b8 K×b8 46. R×g4 Q×f5† 47. Qc2 Q×c2† 48. K×c2 R×h3 49. Rg7 Black resigns—*Newcastle Weekly Chronicle*, 15 October 1892.

### (1136) Heywood–Bird　　0–1
Match (game 7)
Newcastle, 11 October 1892
C01

1. e4 b6 2. d4 e6 3. Bd3 Bb7 4. Be3 Na6 5. c3 c6 6. Ne2 Nc7 7. 0–0 g6 8. Nd2 h5 9. Nf3 Qe7 10. a4 Nh6 11. h3 Bg7 12. b4 Ng8 13. Qc2 Bh6 14. B×h6 N×h6 15. Qd2 d5 16. e×d5 N×d5 17. a5 Kf8 18. a×b6 a×b6 19. R×a8† B×a8 20. Nf4 Kg7 21. Re1 c5 22. d×c5 b×c5 23. b5 Rd8 24. N×d5 B×d5 25. Qf4 f6 26. Qe3 Nf7 27. Be4 B×e4 28. Q×e4 e5 29. Ra1 f5 30. Qc2 e4 31. Nd2 Qd7 32. Nf1 Q×b5 33. c4 Qe8 34. Ne3 Qe5 35. Ra7 Rb8 36. Qd1 Qd4 37. Rd7 Q×d1† 38. R×d1 Ne5 39. Rd5 Rb1† 40. Kh2 Nd3 41. Rd7† Kf6 42. Nd5† Ke5 43. Rg7 N×f2 44. R×g6 h4 45. g3 h×g3† 46. R×g3 Rc1 47. Nb6 f4 48. Rg5† Kd4 49. Rd5† Ke3 and White resigns—*Newcastle Weekly Chronicle*, 15 October 1892.

### (1137) Heywood–Bird　　1–0
Match (game 8)
Newcastle, 13 October 1892
*Odds of pawn and move*

1. e4 g6 2. d4 Bg7 3. Nf3 Nh6 4. Bd3 Nf7 5. Nbd2 d6 6. Nf1 0–0 7. Ng3 e6 8. Be3 a5 9. Qd2 b6 10. h4 c5 11. h5 Ba6 12. h×g6 h×g6 13. e5 Nh8 14. Bh6 Qd7 15. Ne4 d×e5 16. N×e5 B×h6 17. Q×h6 Qg7 18. 0–0–0 c×d4 19. Ng5 B×d3 20. R×d3 Ra7

21. Q×g7† R×g7 22. Rdh3 Nf7 23. Ne×f7 Rg×f7 24. Rh8† Kg7 25. R1h7† Kf6 26. R×f7† Black resigns—*Newcastle Weekly Chronicle*, 22 October 1892.

### (1138) Heywood–Bird　　1–0
Match (game 9)
Newcastle, October 1892
*Game scored by default*

### (1139) Bird–Cummings　　½–½
Simultaneous game
Newcastle, 12 October 1892
D31

1. d4 d5 2. c4 e6 3. Nc3 Bb4 4. e3 B×c3† 5. b×c3 Nf6 6. Ba3 c6 7. Nf3 h6 8. Bd3 Qa5 9. Bb4 Qc7 10. Ne5 Nbd7 11. f4 c5 12. Ba3 Qa5 13. Qc1 0–0 14. 0–0 Qc7 15. Qe1 b6 16. Qg3 Bb7 17. f5 N×e5 18. d×e5 Ne4 19. B×e4 d×e4 20. f6 g6 21. Qf4 Kh7 22. Rad1 Rg8 23. Rd6 Rad8 24. Rfd1 g5 25. Qg3 h5 26. h4 g4 27. Qf4 R×d6 28. R×d6 g3 29. Qf1 Bc6 30. Bc1 Rg4 31. R×e6 f×e6 32. f7 Rg8 33. f×g8Q† K×g8 34. Qf4 Qg7 35. Bd2 Qg4 36. Be1 Bd7 37. B×g3 Q×f4 38. B×f4 Ba4 39. Kh2 Bd1 40. Bg5 Be2 41. Kg3 B×c4 draw—*Sunderland Daily Echo*, 13 October 1892.

### (1140) Bird–Blackett　　1–0
Simultaneous game
Newcastle, 12 October 1892
C14

1. e4 e6 2. d4 d5 3. Nc3 Nf6 4. Bg5 Be7 5. B×f6 B×f6 6. e5 Be7 7. Qg4 0–0 8. Bd3 c5 9. d×c5 B×c5 10. Nf3 f5 11. Qf4 Nc6 12. 0–0–0 B×f2 13. Nb5 d4 14. Kb1 Be3 15. Qg3 a5 16. Nd6 a4 17. c3 d×c3 18. N×f5 Rf7 19. Nd6 Rd7 20. Qh3 g6 21. Q×e6† Kg7 22. Bc4 Qe7 23. N×c8 R×d1† 24. R×d1 Q×e6 25. B×e6 b5 26. Rd7† Kh6 27. Nd6 Bf4 28. g3 B×e5 29. Nf7† Kh5 30. N7xe5 Black resigns—*Newcastle Weekly Chronicle*, 15 October 1892.

### (1141) Bird & Fox & R.N. Hanks & C. Hanks–Heywood & Hawks & Hawdon　　1–0
Consultation game
Newcastle, 15 October 1892
C52

The names of the participants was given in the *Newcastle Weekly Chronicle* on 22 October 1892. The publication of the game followed six years later.

1. e4 e5 2. Nf3 Nc6 3. Bc4 Bc5 4. b4 B×b4 5. c3 Ba5 6. d4 e×d4 7. 0–0 d×c3 8. Qb3 Qf6 9. e5 Qg6 10. N×c3 Nge7 11. Ne2 b5 12. Bd3 Qe6 13. Qb1 Ng6 14. Bf5 Qe7 15. a4 b4? Bird selected a line that was very popular twenty years before this game was played. Black's ample compensation for the pawn was demonstrated in various games. After the text move, however, White does get their counterplay, which their opponents could have denied with the principal 15. ... Nc×e5 16. N×e5 N×e5 17. a×b5 Bb6 18. Bb2 Bb7 19. Ng3 0–0–0. With his king in safety and two pawns in the pocket,

the future looks bright for Black. **16. Bg5 Qf8** (*see diagram*) This move condemns the Black king to a long stay in the center of the back rank without any chance of escaping the annoying pressure. The other choice, 16. ... Qc5, is however not much better; e.g., 17. Rc1 Qb6 18. Be3 Qb7 19. Be4.

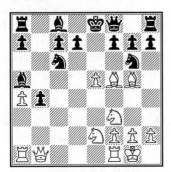

*After 16. ... Qf8*

**17. Qe4! Nge7 18. Rfd1 N×f5 19. Q×c6! Rb8 20. Qd5 c5** Black's position has become critical after his error on the fifteenth move. **21. Ng3 N×g3 22. h×g3 Bd8 23. Bf4** 23. B×d8 K×d8 24. Ng5 Ke8 25. Ne4 wins quickly, but 23. Bf4 doesn't spoil anything. **23. ... Rb6 24. Rac1 Qe7 25. Bg5 Qe6 26. Q×c5 B×g5 27. Q×c8† Bd8 28. Nd4 Qg4 29. f3 Qg6 30. a5 0–0 31. a×b6 B×b6 32. Qc4 a5 33. g4 h5 34. g×h5 Q×h5 35. Qb5 Qh6 36. Qd3** 36. Q×d7 Rd8 37. Rc8 wins quickly. **36. ... g6 37. Rc4 Kg7 38. Qd2 Qh5 39. Qf4 Rh8 40. Qf6† Kh7 41. Q×f7†** Black resigns—*Newcastle Courant*, 26 February 1898.

---

# IN THE PROVINCES, 1892–1893

On 4 November, Bird was the guest of the Whitgift Chess Club in Croydon, where he opposed 16 players. A few defeated players were granted another game, so that Bird contested 20 games in total, of which he won 19 and lost only 1, to Leonard Percy Rees.

From 16 until 21 December Bird was received by the chess clubs in Birmingham. His first exhibition on 16 December at the Midland Institute, the home of the Birmingham Chess Club ended in a complete rout in Bird's favor: he won all 18 games. A few days later, on 19 December, Bird met stronger opposition at the St. George's Chess Club. The play commenced rather late which explains the large number of 8 draws out of 16 games. Bird won 6 and lost the remaining 2. On 20 December he returned to the Birmingham Chess Club. Bird's less successful result here was due to a combination of stronger opposition and an attack of gout. He still won 11 games, lost 4 and drew 5. The farewell exhibition was given on 21 December at the Bohemian Club, a recent addition to the local chess scene. After three hours of play Bird had won 11 games, lost 2 and drawn 1. In a few games consulting players opposed Bird.

### (1142) Bird–Buckley    ½–½
Offhand game
Birmingham, December 1892
C44

**1. e4 e5 2. Nf3 Nc6 3. c3 Nf6 4. d4 N×e4 5. d×e5 d5 6. Bb5**

Bc5 **7. Nd4 Bd7 8. B×c6 b×c6 9. 0–0 0–0 10. Be3 Bb6 11. a4 a6 12. a5 Ba7 13. b4 Qe7 14. f3 Ng5 15. f4 Ne4 16. Kh1 Qh4 17. Qe1 Q×e1 18. R×e1 B×d4 19. B×d4 Bg4 20. Na3 Rfe8 21. Nc2 Bd7 22. Ne3 Rab8 23. Ra2 Rb5 24. g4 Reb8 25. Kg2 Bc8 26. Nf5 g6 27. Nh6† Kf8 28. R×e4 d×e4 29. f5** and the game was drawn for lack of time, Black being the exchange ahead—*Birmingham Weekly Mercury*, 24 December 1892.

### (1143) Bird–Stallmann    0–1
Simultaneous game
Birmingham (St. George's C.C.), 19 December 1892
C51

**1. e4 e5 2. Nf3 Nc6 3. Bc4 Bc5 4. b4 Bb6 5. a4 a6 6. c3 d6 7. Na3 Nf6 8. d3 h6 9. 0–0 0–0 10. Be3 Bg4 11. Nc2 d5 12. e×d5 N×d5 13. B×d5 Q×d5 14. c4 B×f3 15. g×f3 Qe6 16. c5 Ba7 17. f4 Rad8 18. f×e5 Qg6† 19. Kh1 R×d3 20. Qe2 N×e5 21. Bf4 Qc6† 22. f3 N×f3 23. Qg2 Nd4 24. Q×c6 b×c6 25. N×d4 R×d4 26. Rab1 Re8 27. Bg3 Ree4 28. Be1 a5 29. b×a5 B×c5 30. Bf2 Rc4 31. B×c5 R×c5 32. a6 R×a4 33. Rb8† Kh7 34. R×f7 Rc2 35. Rb1 R×a6 36. R×c7 Raa2** White resigns—*Birmingham Weekly Mercury*, 14 January 1893.

### (1144) Bird–Binns    0–1
Simultaneous game
Birmingham (Birmingham C.C.), 20 December 1892
C45

**1. e4 e5 2. d4 e×d4 3. Nf3 Nc6 4. N×d4 Bc5 5. Be3 Qf6 6. c3 Nge7 7. Be2 d5 8. Na3 B×a3 9. b×a3 d×e4 10. Nb5 0–0 11. 0–0 Rd8 12. Qc1 Qg6 13. Bf4 Nd5 14. Bg3 f5 15. c4 Nf6 16. N×c7 Nd4 17. Bd1 Be6 18. N×a8 R×a8 19. Rb1 b6 20. Qe3 Rd8 21. Be5 Nf3† 22. B×f3 e×f3 23. Bg3 B×c4 24. Rfc1 Bd5 25. Rc7 f4 26. Qc1 f×g3 27. h×g3 Qf5 28. Rb4 f×g2 29. Rf4 Qh3 30. f3 Qh1† 31. Kf2 Re8 32. Rh4 g1Q† 33. Q×g1 Q×f3** mate—*Birmingham Weekly Mercury*, 7 January 1893.

### (1145) Bird–Lowes    0–1
Simultaneous game
Birmingham (Birmingham C.C.), 20 December 1892
C52

**1. e4 e5 2. Nf3 Nc6 3. Bc4 Bc5 4. b4 B×b4 5. c3 Ba5 6. Qb3 Qe7 7. Ba3 d6 8. d4 N×d4 9. N×d4 e×d4 10. Qb5† c6 11. Q×a5 Q×e4† 12. Kd1 b6 13. Qb4 c5 14. Qb2 d×c3 15. Bb5† Bd7 16. B×d7† K×d7 17. N×c3 Q×g2 18. Re1 Nf6 19. Qb5† Kd8 20. Qd3 Kd7 21. Nb5 Q×h2 22. Qf3 Qh5 23. Q×h5 N×h5 24. Kc2 a6 25. Nc3 Nf6 26. Bc1 h6 27. Bf4 d5 28. Be5 Kc6 29. B×f6 g×f6 30. Re7 Rhf8 31. Rh1 Rae8 32. R×e8 R×e8 33. R×h6 Re6 34. Rh8 d4 35. Nd1 Re2† 36. Kd3 R×a2 37. Rh6 Kb5 38. R×f6 c4† 39. K×d4 Rd2†** "and the knight being lost, Mr. Bird shortly cried peccavi"—*Birmingham Weekly Mercury*, 25 March 1893.

### (1146) Bird–Three Unknowns    1–0
Consultation game
Birmingham (Bohemian C.C.), 21 December 1892
A03

1. f4 d5 2. Nf3 Nc6 3. e3 Nf6 4. Bb5 Bd7 5. 0–0 e6 6. c4 d×c4 7. B×c4 Bd6 8. Nc3 a6 9. a3 0–0 10. b4 b5 11. Be2 e5 12. f×e5 N×e5 13. d4 Neg4 14. e4 Be7 15. e5 Ne8 16. h3 Nh6 17. B×h6 g×h6 18. Bd3 Kg7 19. Bc2 f5 20. d5 Kh8 21. e6 Bc8 22. Qd2 Bg5 23. N×g5 Q×g5 24. Qd4† Ng7 25. Ne4 Qe7 26. Nc5 Kg8 27. Rf3 Qd6 28. Re1 Qe7 29. Rg3 Rf6 30. Qe5 Kf8 31. Nd3 Bb7 32. Nf4 Rd8 33. R×g7 K×g7 34. Nh5† Kg6 35. Qg3† and the allies resign—*Birmingham Weekly Mercury*; 21 January 1893.

## (1147) Bird–McCarthy　0–1

Simultaneous game
Birmingham (Bohemian C.C.), 21 December 1892
*A00*

1. g4 e5 2. h4 d5 3. e3 Nf6 4. g5 Ne4 5. d3 Nd6 6. Bg2 c6 7. Nc3 Be6 8. Bd2 Na6 9. Nf3 f6 10. a3 Bg4 11. Bh3 Bh5 12. Qe2 Nc5 13. d4 Nd7 14. d×e5 f×e5 15. e4 Nc5 16. e×d5 e4 17. N×e4 Nc×e4 18. d×c6 b×c6 19. Bf4 Be7 20. 0–0–0 0–0 21. B×d6 B×f3 22. Qc4† Kh8 23. Be5 B×g5† 24. Kb1 B×h1 25. R×d8 Ra×d8 26. Qb4 c5 27. Qa5 B×h4 28. Qc7 Bf6 29. B×f6 N×f6 30. Q×c5 Ne4 31. Q×a7 R×f2 32. Be6 Rff8 33. Ka2 Nd2 34. Qc5 Be4 35. b4 Rfe8 36. Qc7 Ra8 37. Bb3 N×b3 38. K×b3 Rec8 39. Qe5 B×c2† and Black wins. "We have named this extraordinary opening the Birdswing Gambit to distinguish it from the Wing Gambit, and because no one but Mr. Bird would play it against a strong opponent. It has been objected that a gambit means the giving up of a pawn or a piece, and that this opening sacrifices nothing. To this we answer that White brings the opening under the gambit denomination by giving himself away. The greatest of all gambits this. The game is full of real chess, and Mr. McCarthy plays very cleverly, completely outmanoeuvring the G.O.M., who evidently lacked time to look deep enough"—Buckley. *Birmingham Weekly Mercury* (Buckley), 7 January 1893.

Bird was also reported to be visiting chess clubs in Yorkshire, just before or after his visit to Birmingham, but the relevant chess columns do not reveal any information. He spent the first days of 1893 in Herne Bay, a popular late Victorian holiday resort in the far southeast of England. Whether he was the guest of a local chess club or just enjoying the quiet life is unknown.

Bird was mentioned as a participant in the massive annual match between the North and South of England which was planned for 28 January, but his name was ultimately scratched from the lists.

On Monday 13 February Bird visited the Brixton Chess Club. Against 16 opponents he won 11 games, lost 3 (against Britton, Neville and Weston) and drew 2 (against Dr. Dunstan and another).

# LONDON 1893

Hoffer mainly remained active as a journalist after the B.C.A.'s demise, but he also kept on organizing chess events. In February 1893 he convinced the weekly magazine *Black and White*, for which he wrote a chess column, to support a small master tournament. In return for the sponsorship the magazine obtained the rights to pub-lish the games. Six prominent players of the London chess scene were invited. Bird played his first game against Tinsley. After a protracted and uphill struggle, at the point when he could finally equalize, a slip made Bird's position untenable. Bird played better against van Vliet but he ruined his own chances by giving one check too many. With two powerful strokes his opponent built up a decisive attack. With two losses against the weakest players of the lot, Bird's prospects were turning grim. In the third round he was overrun by a superior Blackburne. Bird put up a more stubborn fight in his next game against Teichmann. He reached a safe endgame but then inexplicably lost thread and threw away a game that could even have turned out in his favor. Bird's last round game against Mason was decisive for the first prize, as Mason still had a chance to catch up to Blackburne. Seeing that Bird obtained a risk-free position, Blackburne drew his game. For once in this tournament Bird did not spoil his chances and he earned his only half point.

Scoring but ½ out of 5 was a clear failure. It seemed that age and illness had him definitively in their grip.[33] Yet, as one can see, the old crocodile kept on battling until the very end.

---

**Black and White chess tournament, London, 27 February–5 March 1893**

*Site:* Simpson's Divan
*Playing hours:* 2 p.m.–6 and 7:30 p.m.–11
*Prizes:* 1st £30, 2nd £20, 3rd £10
*Time limit:* 40 moves in 2 hours, 20 moves per hour

|   | | 1 | 2 | 3 | 4 | 5 | 6 | |
|---|---|---|---|---|---|---|---|---|
| 1 | J.H. Blackburne | | ½ | ½ | 1 | ½ | 1 | 3½ |
| 2 | J. Mason | ½ | | 1 | ½ | ½ | ½ | 3 |
| 3 | R. Teichmann | ½ | 0 | | ½ | 1 | 1 | 3 |
| 4 | S. Tinsley | 0 | ½ | ½ | | 1 | 1 | 3 |
| 5 | L. van Vliet | ½ | ½ | 0 | 0 | | 1 | 2 |
| 6 | H.E. Bird | 0 | ½ | 0 | 0 | 0 | | ½ |

---

## (1148) Tinsley–Bird　1–0

Black and White tournament (round 1)
London, 27 February 1893
*A85*

1. d4 f5 2. c4 e6 3. Nc3 Nf6 4. e3 Bb4 5. Qb3 c5 6. d×c5 B×c5 7. Nf3 Nc6 8. Be2 0–0 9. 0–0 b6 10. Rd1 Bb7 11. Na4 Be7 12. c5 Na5 13. Qa3 Ne4 14. b4 Nc6 15. Rb1 Qe8 16. Bb2 a5 17. b5 Nb8 18. Bd4 b×c5 19. N×c5 Bd5 20. Rbc1 d6 21. Na6 N×a6 22. b×a6 a4 23. Rc7 Rc8 24. R×c8 Q×c8 25. Q×a4 Bf6 26. B×f6 g×f6 27. Re1 Nc3 28. Qc2 Rf7 29. Kh1 Rc7 30. Kg1 N×a2 31. Qb2 Nc3 32. Bf1 e5 33. Ra1 Ba8 34. a7 Kf7 35. Qb8 Nd5 36. Rb1 Ne7 37. Nd2 Nc6 38. Nc4 Ke6 39. Qb3 d5 40. Nb6 Qd8 41. N×d5 Rb7 42. Nf4† Ke7 43. Qe6† Kf8 44. R×b7 B×b7 45. Nh5 Qe7 46. Q×f5 N×a7 47. N×f6 Bc8 48. Q×h7 Qc5 49. Qg8† Ke7 50. Qg7† Kd8 51. h4 Nc6 52. h5 Black resigns—*Black and White*, 11 March 1893.

---

33. A more favorable than realistic review was given by Bird's olden days companion MacDonnell: "Bird played with all his usual brilliancy, but on several occasions broke down when he was heading his opponents in the race. The fact is 'hard' chess—or rather patience-exhausting-chess—does not quite suit Bird's style. It does not afford full scope to the exercise of his peculiar genius. Often, indeed, has his genius triumphed over all obstacles, but as years increase genius is obliged to succumb to dullness and slowness." *Illustrated Sporting and Dramatic News*, 11 March 1893.

## (1149) Bird–van Vliet    0–1
Black and White tournament (round 2)
London, 28 February 1893
A03

1. f4 d5 2. Nf3 g6 3. e3 Bg7 4. c4 e6 5. Nc3 Nf6 6. d4 b6 7. Bd3
Bb7 8. c×d5 e×d5 9. 0–0 Nbd7 10. Ne5 Ne4 11. N×e4 d×e4
12. Bb5 B×e5 13. f×e5 Qe7 14. Bc4 f5 15. Bd2 0–0–0 16. Qb3
N×e5 17. Bb4 c5 18. d×c5 b×c5 19. Be6† Kb8 20. Bc3 Qc7 21. h3
Nf3† 22. R×f3 e×f3 23. B×h8 Rd2 24. e4 R×g2† 25. Kf1 Rg1†
26. Kf2 Qg3† 27. Ke3 f2† White resigns—*Black and White*, 18
March 1893.

## (1150) Bird–Blackburne    0–1
Black and White tournament (round 3)
London, 1 March 1893
C55

1. e4 e5 2. Nf3 Nc6 3. Bc4 Be7 4. 0–0 Nf6 5. Nc3 d6 6. h3 Be6
7. B×e6 f×e6 8. d3 0–0 9. Bd2 Qe8 10. Ne2 Nh5 11. c3 Qg6
12. Kh1 Nf4 13. B×f4 e×f4 14. Qb3 Nd8 15. Rad1 Kh8 16. e5
d×e5 17. N×e5 Qh5 18. Nf3 g5 Bird kept his advantage all during
the opening phase. Being under pressure Blackburne makes a drastic,
but not a bad, advance on the kingside. Bird's reply is testing, but
perhaps could be ameliorated by Hoffer's suggestion. **19. Qb5** "Allowing Black to bring his rook into play without loss of time, Mr.
Bird pursued a set plan for the last half-dozen moves—viz., to bring
his queen into the enemy's camp; but the whole combination proved
faulty. The queen is quite harmless at d7, as will be seen. White has
already a bad game, and should have defended his king's position
at the eleventh hour with his knights, although under less favorable
circumstances now than when suggested above. Still, he might have
played 19. Nfg1, and if 19. ... g4 20. f3, and if 19. ... f3 20. Ng3, and
the position was not so hopeless at all"—Hoffer. **19. ... Rf5 20. Qd7**
*(see diagram)*

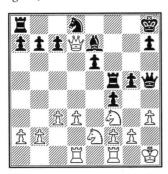

*After 20. Qd7*

**20. ... g4?** Blackburne opens the hostilities, but with a defense
possible this could have been punished severely. Instead the sober
20. ... Bd6 is still fine. **21. Nfg1?** The refutation was far from easy
to design. Namely, after the brave 21. Nfd4! g×h3 22. g4! f×g3 *e.p.*
23. N×g3 Qg4 24. Q×e7, only despair rests upon Black. After 24. ...
Nc6 25. Q×e6 N×d4 26. Qe4! Rf4 27. Qe5† Kg8 28. Qd5† Ne6,
the mating threats are finally under control and White is ready to
take over by placing the rooks on the open files. **21. ... g×h3
22. g×h3?** White's position is under a cloud, but only after this
move does it deteriorate. Better survival chances were possible after
22. N×h3 f3 23. Ng3. **22. ... Bd6!** Very well played. Everything is

defended and after the following nice maneuvre, White's queen is
offsided. **23. Nd4 Rg5! 24. Ndf3 Rg7 25. Qa4** "Now the queen
has to retreat from its useless excursion, and for that he endangered
his king's position"—Hoffer. **25. ... Nf7** Initiating the final attack.
**26. Rde1 Rag8 27. Qe4 Ng5 28. N×g5 R×g5 29. Q×e6 R5g6
30. Qd7 Qg5** "This is decisive. White could abandon now"—Hoffer. **31. Qg4 Qd5† 32. f3 R×g4 33. h×g4 R×g4 34. Re8† Kg7
35. Re2 Rh4† 36. Rh2 R×h2† 37. K×h2 Q×d3 38. Rf2 Bc5
39. Rg2† Kf6** White resigns. "This pretty game was played by Mr.
Blackburne quite in his former style"—Hoffer. *Black and White*
(Hoffer), 8 April 1893.

## (1151) Teichmann–Bird    1–0
Black and White tournament (round 4)
London, 2 March 1893
B54

1. e4 c5 2. Nc3 Nc6 3. Nf3 d6 4. d4 c×d4 5. N×d4 Bd7 6. Be3
g6 7. Be2 Bg7 8. 0–0 h5 "This advance, of course, precludes castling
on the kingside, and castling on the queenside is rare in the Sicilian,
because the king would be exposed on that side too much. It is,
therefore, a sure indication that Mr. Bird means fighting"—Hoffer.
**9. f4 Nf6 10. h3 N×d4 11. B×d4 Bc6 12. Bf3** 12. Qd3 develops
the queen and prepares 13. e5! **12. ... Kf8** He could castle here.
**13. Qd2** 13. e5! is critical again. **13. ... Nd7 14. Rad1 B×d4†
15. Q×d4 Qb6** Correctly heading for exchanges. The closer Black
is to an endgame, the better. **16. Rf2 Q×d4 17. R×d4 Nc5** The
knight was well placed at d7: it could head to e5 in case of White
pushing the f-pawn. Fine was 17. ... Rc8. **18. Be2 Kg7 19. f5 Nd7
20. Bc4 g×f5** Keeping the position closed with 20. ... g5 deserves
the preference. **21. e×f5 Nf6 22. Re2 Kf8 23. Nd5 B×d5 24. B×d5
Rb8** 24. ... N×d5 would have secured the draw. The bishop is a bit
stronger than the knight in the present endgame. **25. Bf3 Rg8** It
was necessary to think about the defense of the queenside. 25. ...
b5 is therefore best. **26. h4** 26. Ra4! means trouble for Black; e.g.,
26. ... Rg5 (26. ... a6 27. Rc4 Rg5 28. Rc7 Ng8 29. R×b7) 27. R×a7
d5 28. Re5 e6 29. h4. **26. ... b5 27. Rb4** 27. Rd3 forces 27. ... b4
28. Rde3 Nd7 (28. ... Re8 29. Rb3 a5 30. c3 is also promising for
White) 29. B×h5 Ne5 30. Bf3 Rb5 White has won a pawn but
Black's knight provides certain compensation. A win for White is
far from evident. **27. ... a5 28. Rb3** *(see diagram)*

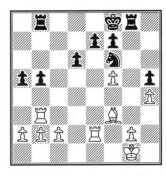

*After 28. Rb3*

**28. ... Nd7** "Now commences really the pretty part of the game.
Mr. Bird abandons a pawn designedly in order to get his pieces into
play. But he could have played 28. ... Ng4 with the probable continuation: 29. B×g4 R×g4 30. g3 a4 31. Rbe3 Rb7 threatening 32. ...

Rc4, followed by 33. ... Rcc7, so as to bring his king to f6, or 33. ... Rc5 so as to remove the pressure from his e-pawn. The line of play chosen by Mr. Bird is highly ingenious, but complicated in proportion"—Hoffer. After 29. ... Ng4, 29. Rc3! is the best continuation (also possible and strong after the text move). Bird's best line seems to be 28. ... b4, though 29. c3 is disturbing. **29. Bc6 Ne5 30. B×b5 Rg4 31. g3 Rc8 32. Rd2 a4 33. Re3 Rb4 34. c4 Kg7 35. b3 Kf6** Bird has plugged the center well and gained considerable terrain on the queenside during the past few moves. Now the opening of the a-file would have put his opponent under pressure. After 35. ... a×b3 36. a×b3 Ra8 37. Kg2?! Ra3 Black is very active. Necessary, to gain some counterplay, is 37. f6†. White is delivering an uphill fight: in case of 37. ... K×f6 38. Ba4 Kg7 (the direct 38. ... N×c4 demonstrates the point of 37. f6: 39. Rf2† Kg6 40. b×c4 Ra×a4 41. R×e7 with equality) 39. Rc3 f6 leaves a very small edge for Black. Not good is 39. ... N×c4 on account of 40. Rd4. **36. Rde2 a×b3** Much more likely than 36. ... Ra8? 37. Kg2? (the simple 37. B×a4 K×f5 38. Bb5 is close to winning) 37. ... a×b3 38. a×b3, the score given by Hoffer. **37. a×b3 Ra8 38. Kg2 Ra3 39. Ba4 K×f5 40. Rf2† Ke6** "40. ... Kg6 would have been better"—Hoffer. **41. Be8** "Threatening 41. B×f7†"—Hoffer. **41. ... f6 42. B×h5** As this pawn wasn't running away, first 42. Rb2 was superior. **42. ... Rb×b3 43. R×b3 R×b3 44. Be2 f5** "He should not have touched the center, which he maintained intact with so much trouble all through the game. He might have played 44. ... Rc3 45. Rf4 Kf7 followed by 46. ... Kg7 so as to attack the h-pawn with the king if it advances"—Hoffer. **45. h5 Kf6** There seems to be no point behind this move. Instead 45. ... Rb2 puts White under severe pressure: 46. Kf1 Kf6 47. Rf4 Kg5 48. Rh4 and now 48. ... Nd7 and 49. ... Nf6 is very strong. **46. g4 e6 47. g×f5 e×f5 48. Bd1 Rb8** "Why not 48. ... Rc3?"— Hoffer. **49. Rc2 Kg5 50. c5 d5** Teichmann's last move was a bit rash (50. Be2 is safer). Strong here was 50. ... Nd3! 51. Kf1 d×c5. **51. c6 Nc4** 51. ... Rc8 52. Rc5 R×c6 53. R×d5 with a draw. **52. Kf2 Kf4** Simpler is 52. ... Rc8 53. Bf3 Ne5 54. B×d5 Nd3† 55. Ke3 Nb4. **53. Be2 Nd6?** Forsaking the draw that was in reach with 53. ... Rc8 after all. **54. c7 Rh8 55. Rc6 Ke5 56. Ba6 d4 57. h6 R×h6** "The game is lost now. If 57. ... Nc8 58. B×c8 R×c8 59. h6 and queens either one or the other pawn. Mr. Bird has thrown away a pretty game"—Hoffer. **58. R×d6 Rh2† 59. Kg1 Rc2 60. Rd7** Black resigns—*Black and White* (Hoffer), 6 May 1893.

**(1152) Mason–Bird**    ½–½
Black and White tournament (round 5)
London, 5 March 1893
*C50*

    1. e4 e5 2. Nc3 Bc5 3. Nf3 Nc6 4. Bc4 a6 5. d3 Nf6 6. Be3 d6 7. B×c5 d×c5 8. h3 Qd6 9. 0–0 h6 10. Nd5 Bd7 11. c3 Rd8 12. Ne1 Ne7 13. N×e7 Q×e7 14. f4 b5 15. Bb3 c4 16. f×e5 Q×e5 17. Bc2 B×h3 18. d4 Qg5 19. Qf3 Bg4 20. Qf4 0–0 21. Q×g5 h×g5 22. Nf3 B×f3 23. R×f3 Rfe8 24. e5 Nd5 25. Be4 Nf4 26. Re1 g6 27. g3 Ne6 28. Bb7 Re7 29. Bc6 g4 30. Rf6 Ng5 31. Bg2 Re6 32. R×e6 f×e6 33. Rf1 Kg7 34. Rf4 c5 35. R×g4 Nf7 36. Re4 c×d4 37. c×d4 b4 38. Bf1 Ng5 39. Rg4 c3 40. b×c3 b×c3 41. Bd3 Nf3† 42. Kf2 N×e5 43. d×e5 R×d3 44. Rc4 a5 45. a4 Kh6 46. Rc6 Rd5 47. R×c3 R×e5 48. Kf3 Kg7 49. Rc7† Kf8 50. Kf4

Rd5 51. Ke4 g5 52. Ra7 Ke8 53. Rg7 Kd8 54. Ra7 Rc5 55. Kd4 Rf5 56. Ke4 Rd5 57. Rg7 Kc8 58. Re7 Rc5 59. Kd4 Rd5† 60. Ke4 draw—*Black and White*, 13 May 1893.

---

# IN WALES, MARCH 1893

Bird commenced a week-long tour through Wales on Friday 10 March at the Newport Chess Club. In the afternoon Bird played simultaneously offhand games against two local players, Williams and Merriman. In the evening 14 members of the club gathered to oppose Bird. Williams scored 1 win, while Bird also had to agree to some draws.

Bird went to Cardiff after the weekend. On 13 March he gave a simultaneous exhibition against an unknown number of opponents. Bird lost 3 games (against Dr. Arthur, H. Francis and E.A. Edwards), while G.W. Lennox achieved a draw.

Subsequently Bird moved to Aberdare where he was the guest of Rees Williams. On Tuesday 14 March he was tremendously successful as he won all his 30 games in an exhibition. On Wednesday Bird succeeded in avoiding a loss during simultaneous and offhand play. A last stop, which remains undocumented, was made in Rhondda Valley.

---

# CHESS HISTORY AND REMINISCENCES

Medio 1893, just before Bird's match with Jasnogrodsky, Dean and Son released *Chess History and Reminiscences*, which would become one of Bird's best known works. Already in 1888 MacDonnell informed his readers that Bird was planning a major work dealing with various historical subjects of chess.[34]

Bird combined two different subjects in his book. Firstly he provided the reader with an overview of the history of the game from the early legends about the arrival of chess in Europe until the changes it underwent in the nineteenth century. Secondly, he devoted ample space to his own melancholic reminiscences of bygone days when, in his opinion, chess chivalry was still existent. Bird was his usual self by maintaining a more negative attitude about the recent times. He also presented the reader with information and games of the recent tournament in Belfast. All in all, the book was a very mixed offering, as was pointed out by some reviewers.

Bird alluded to the much larger work he had in mind to explain the diffuse character of *Chess History and Reminiscences*, but there are more remarks to be made. Bird collected his information on the history of chess by making uncritical and clumsy use of various other sources. Not only is his text full of factual errors, his apparent lack of knowledge of other languages caused him to commit dozens of

---

34. Bird was not able to fulfill his plans completely: "This little work is but a condensation and essence of a much larger one, containing the result of what can be discovered concerning the origin and history of chess, combined with some of my own reminiscences of 46 years past both of chess play and its exponents...." Bird, *Chess History and Reminiscences*, p. xi.

**Henry Edward Bird (*Chess History and Reminiscences*).**

misspellings. The chapters on Bird's memoirs suffer from the same flaws and lack a systematic approach. His habit of speaking about himself in the third person and his over-confidence were also likely to annoy the reader.

Yet, *Chess History and Reminiscences* managed to raise some interest as well. Bird was the last man standing between the late Victorian generation and the long gone days of Staunton, Buckle and Morphy, and several of his thoughts, stories and opinions possess a lasting value.

# MATCH WITH JASNOGRODSKY 1893

During the last two weeks of May the Divan was the scene of a trial of strength between Bird and Jasnogrodsky. Nikolai Jasnogrodsky was 33 years old and already a familiar face as he had arrived in London in the late 1880s.[35] Soon after this match Jasnogrodsky migrated to the United States.

35. Jasnogrodsky's appearance was described in some detail by James White of the *Leeds Mercury* on 26 March 1892: "Jasnogrodsky is eminently a solid man. His face is square cut, and his features somewhat heavy, and he speaks in monosyllables as a rule. He has been trying for the last two years to Anglicize his name, but he has not yet succeeded to his perfect satisfaction. As it is a mouthful, so his friends indifferently call him 'Jas,' or the 'Russian-Pole.' He answers cheerfully to either appellation. He is a steady, all-round player, and a thoroughly decent fellow."

The conditions of the match were rather straightforward. The winner would be the first player to win seven games. The stakes were set on £10 per side. The first game was played on 17 May.

The match between Bird and Jasnogrodsky, which for over a fortnight has been in progress at Simpson's Divan, was concluded yesterday, when a draw was mutually agreed upon, each player having won six games, while three had been drawn. The match, which was a friendly affair, arranged to fill up a portion of the off-season of chess, has excited an unusual amount of interest. In the first few games Bird obtained a strong lead, but Jasnogrodsky, by his successes last week, made matters level, the score on Monday being four each, with two draws. Of the next three games each player won one, and one was drawn. Two more games were played yesterday, and an even result was again obtained.[36] The deciding number originally agreed upon was seven games, but it was generally felt that the issue of a so closely disputed a contest should not depend upon a single game, and that a draw was a suitable termination. The match has produced several good games of a spirited character [*Morning Post*, 2 June 1893].

| Match with Jasnogrodsky, 17 May–1 June 1893 | | | | | | | | | | | | | | | | |
|---|---|---|---|---|---|---|---|---|---|---|---|---|---|---|---|---|
| | **1** | **2** | **3** | **4** | **5** | **6** | **7** | **8** | **9** | **10** | **11** | **12** | **13** | **14** | **15** | |
| H.E. Bird | 0 | 1 | 1 | 1 | 0 | ½ | 0 | ½ | 0 | 1 | 0 | ½ | 1 | 1 | 0 | 6 |
| N. Jasnogrodsky | 1 | 0 | 0 | 0 | 1 | ½ | 1 | ½ | 1 | 0 | 1 | ½ | 0 | 0 | 1 | 6 |

## (1153) Jasnogrodsky–Bird    1–0
Match (game 1)
London, 17 May 1893
*A81*

**1. d4 f5 2. g3 e6 3. Bg2 Nf6 4. Nf3 Be7 5. Nc3 c6 6. 0–0 Na6 7. Ne1 d5 8. Bf4 0–0 9. Nd3 Bd7 10. Be5 Nc7 11. e3 Nce8 12. f3 Nd6 13. Qe2 Nc4 14. b3 Nd6 15. Nd1 Nf7 16. N1f2 Qa5 17. c4 Rac8 18. c5 Qa6 19. Qd2 N×e5 20. N×e5 Be8 21. Nfd3 Nd7 22. b4 N×e5 23. N×e5 Bf6 24. Nd3 b6 25. Rfb1 Qb7 26. a4 Qe7 27. f4 g5 28. Kh1 Kh8 29. Ra2 g×f4 30. g×f4 Bh5 31. c×b6 a×b6 32. a5 b×a5 33. b×a5 Qg7 34. Nc5 Rb8 35. Rab2 R×b2 36. R×b2 Re8 37. a6 Be7 38. Rb7 Rg8 39. Qf2 Qf6 40. Nd7 Qg7 41. a7 Bd6 42. Qg3 Bg6 43. Qh4 Be7 44. Qg3 Bd6 45. Qg5 Be7 46. Nb8 B×g5 47. R×g7 R×g7 48. a8Q** Black resigns—*Belfast News-Letter*, 21 June 1893. First published in the *Hereford Times*.

## (1154) Bird–Jasnogrodsky    1–0
Match (game 2)
London, 18 May 1893
*A03*

**1. f4 d5 2. e3 Nf6 3. Nf3 e6 4. b3 Be7 5. Bb2 c5 6. Bd3 Nc6 7. 0–0 Bd7 8. Nc3 Nb4** "This seems a loss of time, for the knight must presently return. 8. ... 0–0 or 8. ... Rc8 tends to a speedier development"—Abbott. **9. Be2 0–0 10. a3 Nc6 11. Qe1 Ne8 12. Nd1 Bf6 13. Ne5 B×e5** A slight concession. Instead, 13. ... Bh4 gives equal play. **14. f×e5 Qg5 15. d4 b6 16. Rf3 f5** Another weakening move. White could now best play 17. e×f6 *e.p.* **17. Nf2 Qe7 18. Nd3 g5** "Generally a hazardous move after castling, and in this case particularly so"—Abbott. **19. Rg3** With the bishop pair in hand,

36. The *Daily News*, the only newspaper that followed the match day by day, declared on 1 June that Bird and Jasnogrodsky had buried the hatchet on the last day of May when each player had scored *five* wins. Such a finish seems untimely, given that seven wins were needed for match victory.

opening up the game was a valid option—e.g., with 19. d×c5 b×c5 20. Qc3 Rc8 21. Q×c5 Q×c5 22. N×c5 N×e5 23. B×e5 R×c5 24. Rc1. **19. … Ng7 20. c4** Correctly switching his attention towards the center and queenside. **20. … d×c4 21. b×c4 c×d4?!** This exchange is beneficial for White's bishop pair. 21. … g4 is very solid. **22. e×d4** White's center gained much in flexibility. The overwhelming menace is d4–d5 at some point. **22. … f4** This moves weakens the white squares. **23. Rh3 Na5** 23. … Nf5 24. d5 Ncd4 offers central counterplay. The text move leaves White's pieces the free hand. **24. Nf2 Rac8?! 25. Ng4** 25. Bc3, threatening 26. Bb4, is an improvement. Black is defenseless after 25. … Qd8 26. Bb4 Rf7 27. B×a5 b×a5 28. Ng4. **25. … N×c4 26. B×c4?!** Once again 26. Bc3 is a subtle refinement. If 26. … a5 27. Qb1 Nf5 28. B×c4 R×c4 29. Q×b6 wins a pawn. **26. … R×c4 27. Rc1 R×c1 28. Q×c1 Ne8** *(see diagram)* 28. … h5 is the best defensive move. 29. Nf6† can be met by 29. … Kf7.

*After 28. … Ne8*

**29. d5!** Excellently played from Bird. **29. … Qc5† 30. Q×c5 b×c5 31. Rh6** 31. d6! puts Black into a serious bind. On his next move, White can switch his attention to the queenside with 32. Rc3. **31. … e×d5?** 31. … Kf7, keeping e6 defended at all cost, must be played. After 32. R×h7† Ng7, there is not much special for White. **32. e6 Bb5 33. e7 Rf7 34. Re6! d4 35. Nh6†** 35. Re5! is much stronger. **35. … Kg7 36. N×f7 K×f7 37. Re5 d3 38. R×c5 Nd6 39. Bc3 h6 40. Rd5 Ne4 41. Rf5† Ke8 42. Bb4** Black resigns— *Illustrated London News* (Abbott), 10 June 1893.

**(1155) Jasnogrodsky–Bird   0–1**
Match (game 3)
London, 19 May 1893
*A81*

**1. d4 f5** "Morphy adopted this successfully against Harrwitz, after having failed in the defense of a Queen's Gambit. Nevertheless, it is now rarely played, and we believe that it is justly discarded on the ground that the weakening of the e-pawn is seemingly a necessary consequence"—Steinitz. **2. g3** "The editor first experimented with this move against the late Mr. Wisker, in the London tournament of 1872"—Steinitz. **2. … Nf6 3. Bg2 d5 4. Nf3 e6 5. 0–0 Bd6 6. Nc3 0–0 7. Ne1 c5 8. e3** "8. d×c5, with probabilities like 8. … B×c5 9. Nd3 Bd6 10. Nb5 Nc6 11. c4 d×c4 12. N×d6 Q×d6 13. Bf4 Qd8 14. Ne5 might have been fruitful of a more favorable position in which the pawn was sure to be recovered with the better game"—Steinitz. **8. … Nc6 9. Ne2 b6 10. c4** "An imprudent advance, though safe for the time"—Steinitz. **10. … Ba6** "Correct and telling. Sooner or later White will be compelled to

exchange the c-pawn or lose it, and Black at least gets rid of his isolated e-pawn with the superior position"—Steinitz. **11. c×d5 e×d5 12. d×c5 B×c5** 12. … b×c5! is possible and very good as White cannot head for 13. B×d5†? N×d5 14. Q×d5† Kh8 15. Q×c6 B×e2. **13. Nd3 Rc8 14. N×c5** "If 14. b3, 14. … d4 would also have been embarrassing for White"—Steinitz. **14. … b×c5 15. Re1 Re8 16. b3 Ne4** Too slow to upset his opponent. 16. … Ne5! is very strong. **17. Bb2 Nb4 18. Nc1** *(see diagram)* A passive move. After 18. Nf4, White stands slightly better.

*After 18. Nc1*

**18. … c4!** "The energy of the veteran in the conduct of the attack reminds of the dash of his best days"—Steinitz. **19. b×c4** "Some defensive possibilities arose from 19. Ba3 Nd3 20. N×d3 c×d3 21. B×e4 d×e4 22. Bb4 (if 22. Rc1 Qa5) 22. … Rc2 23. Bd2; but by best play Black must have won, though no doubt with some difficulty, on account of the bishops of opposite colors"—Steinitz. **19. … d×c4 20. Qa4?** The losing move. White is but slightly worse after the superior 20. Bd4. If then 20. … c3 (better is 20. … Qd7) 21. Qa4 and White's pieces are activated. **20. … c3!** "The rare opportunity for such well-directed play on the queenside so early in the game is seized by the old master with powerful energy"—Steinitz. **21. B×c3** "A forlorn hope, but he was helpless. If 21. Q×b4, Black would either win by 21. … Rb8 or 21. … Qd2 22. Ne2 c×b2"—Steinitz. **21. … R×c3 22. Q×b4 Qd2 23. Ne2 B×e2** and after a few more moves White resigns—*New York Daily Tribune* (Steinitz), 4 June 1893.

**(1156) Bird–Jasnogrodsky   1–0**
Match (game 4)
London, 20 May 1893
*C54*

**1. e4 e5 2. Nf3 Nc6 3. Bc4 Bc5 4. c3 d6 5. b4 Bb6 6. Qb3 Qe7 7. a4 a5 8. b5 Nd8 9. 0–0 Nf6 10. d4 0–0** This and the following move surrender the center of which Bird happily makes use. 10. … Ne6 is a considerable improvement. **11. Ba3 e×d4 12. e5 Ne4** The knight was better off at g4. **13. c×d4 Ne6?!** There is not much room for Black's pieces left after this move. After 13. … Be6 some exchanges could relieve the pressure. **14. Qd3! N4g5 15. Nbd2 Rd8?! 16. Rae1** Black is under great pressure, especially after forgoing 15. … N×f3. **16. … Qd7 17. N×g5 N×g5 18. d5 h6** 18. … d×e5 19. R×e5 h6 20. Rfe1 is no option at all for Black. **19. h4 Nh7 20. e6 f×e6 21. d×e6 Qe7 22. Nf3 Nf8 23. h5 B×e6** "This loses a piece, and of course the game, but Black's position is too hopeless to save in any case"—Abbott. **24. R×e6 N×e6 25. Re1 Kh8 26. R×e6 Qf8 27. R×h6† g×h6 28. Bb2†** and White wins—*Illustrated London News* (Abbott), 17 June 1893.

**(1157) Jasnogrodsky–Bird   1–0**
Match (game 5)
London, 22 May 1893
*A84*

1. d4 d5 2. c4 e6 3. Nc3 c6 4. e3 Bd6 5. Nf3 Nd7 6. Bd3 f5 7. 0-0 Nh6 8. b3 0-0 9. Bb2 Nf7 10. c×d5 c×d5 11. Rc1 a6 12. Ne2 g5 13. Re1 Qf6 14. Nd2 Qh6 15. Nf1 Nf6 16. f3 Bd7 17. Nc3 Bc6 18. Rc2 Rad8 19. Bc1 Bb8 20. g3 Rfe8 21. f4 Kh8 22. Rg2 Ne4 23. B×e4 d×e4 24. Bb2 e5 25. Ne2 g×f4 26. g×f4 e×f4 27. d5† Be5 28. B×e5† N×e5 29. N×f4 Nf3† 30. Kh1 Qf6 31. Ree2 Bb5 32. Rc2 B×f1 33. Q×f1 Rg8 34. Qc1 Qe5 35. R×g8† R×g8 36. Rc8 b6 37. R×g8† K×g8 38. Qc8† Kf7 39. Qd7† Kf6 40. Qc6† Kg5 41. Qc1 b5 42. Kg2 b4 43. Kg3 Qc3 44. h4† Kf6 45. Qf1 Qe1† 46. Q×e1 N×e1 47. d6 Nd3 48. h5 a5 49. Ne2 Nc5 50. Nd4 Kg5 51. Nc6 K×h5 52. Ne5 Kg5 53. d7 N×d7 54. N×d7 and White wins—*Daily News*, 23 May 1893.

**(1158) Bird–Jasnogrodsky   ½–½**
Match (game 6)
London, 23 May 1893
*Game score missing*

**(1159) Jasnogrodsky–Bird   1–0**
Match (game 7)
London, 24 May 1893
*A90*

1. d4 f5 2. g3 Nf6 3. Bg2 e6 4. Nf3 d5 5. c4 c6 6. Qc2 Bd6 7. 0-0 0-0 8. b3 Qe7 9. Bb2 Na6 10. a3 Bd7 11. e3 Rac8 12. c5 Bb8 13. b4 Be8 14. Qe2 Nc7 15. Nbd2 Bh5 16. Qd3 Ne4 17. Ne5 Ne8 18. f3 N×d2 19. Q×d2 Nf6 20. a4 Be8 21. Bc3 Nd7 22. N×d7 B×d7 23. f4 Qe8 24. Kh1 a6 25. Bf3 Bc7 26. Qe2 Bd8 27. g4 Qe7 28. Rg1 Be8 29. g5 g6 30. h4 h6 31. Rg2 Rc7 32. Rag1 h×g5 33. h×g5 Rf7 34. Rh2 Rh7 35. Rgg2 Qf8 36. Kg1 Rcg7 37. Qf2 R×h2 38. R×h2 Rh7 39. Be2 Qe7 40. Kf1 Bc7 41. Ke1 Qg7 42. Kd2 Qh8 43. R×h7 Q×h7 44. Qg2 Qh4 45. Kc2 Bd7 46. Kd1 Kf7 47. Be1 Qh8 48. Qf1 Qh2 49. Qf2 Qh8 50. Qh4 Qg7 51. Kc2 Be8 52. Kb3 Bd8 53. Bd3 Kg8 54. Qf2 Qc7 55. Qe2 Be7 56. b5 c×b5 57. a×b5 a×b5 58. B×b5 Bf7 59. Qa2 e5 60. Qa8† Kg7 61. Ba5 Black resigns—*Morning Post*, 12 June 1893.

**(1160) Bird–Jasnogrodsky   ½–½**
Match (game 8)
London, 25 May 1893
*Game score missing*

**(1161) Jasnogrodsky–Bird   1–0**
Match (game 9)
London, 26 May 1893
*A90*

1. d4 f5 2. g3 Nf6 3. Bg2 e6 4. Nf3 Be7 5. c4 Bb4† 6. Bd2 Qe7 7. Nc3 0-0 8. 0-0 d6 9. Ne1 Nc6 10. Nd3 B×c3 11. B×c3 Ne4 12. Qc2 Qf6 13. e3 N×c3 14. Q×c3 Bd7 15. b4 Nd8 16. Rfc1 Qh6 17. a4 g5 18. f4 g4 19. b5 a6 20. Nb4 a5 21. Nd3 c6 22. b6 Nf7 23. c5 e5 24. d×e5 d×e5 25. N×e5 N×e5 26. Q×e5 Rae8

27. Qd4 Qe6 28. Re1 Qf7 29. e4 Rd8 30. Qc3 f×e4 31. R×e4 Bf5 32. Re3 Qf6 33. Qc4† Kg7 34. Rae1 Qd4 35. Qc3 Q×c3 36. R×c3 Rd4 37. Rce3 R×a4 38. Re7† Rf7 39. R×b7 R×b7 40. B×c6 Rc4 41. B×b7 R×c5 42. Bg2 Rb5 43. b7 Kf7 44. Ra1 Bd7 45. R×a5 Rb1† 46. Kf2 Rb2† 47. Ke3 Ke6 48. Ra8 Rb3† 49. Kd4 Black resigns—*Morning Post*, 27 May 1893; *British Chess Magazine*, June 1893, p. 257.

**(1162) Bird–Jasnogrodsky   1–0**
Match (game 10)
London, 27 May 1893
*C11*

1. e4 e6 2. d4 d5 3. Nc3 Nf6 4. e5 Nfd7 5. Nf3 c5 6. Bg5 Qb6 7. Bb5 Nc6 8. B×c6 b×c6 9. d×c5 Q×b2 10. Bd2 Qb8 11. Rb1 Qc7 12. 0-0 N×e5 13. Bf4 N×f3† 14. Q×f3 Qd8 15. Qg3 Qf6 16. Bd6 Qg6 17. Qf4 f6 18. B×f8 R×f8 19. Qc7 Bd7 20. N×d5 c×d5 21. Rb7 Rf7 22. Rfb1 Re7 23. c6 Rd8 24. c×d7† R×d7 25. Qc6 Ke7 26. h3 Qe8 27. Qc5† Kf7 28. Q×a7 Qe7 29. a4 Ke8 30. a5 Black resigns—*Morning Post*, 29 May 1893.

**(1163) Jasnogrodsky–Bird   1–0**
Match (game 11)
London, 29 May 1893
*A81*

1. d4 f5 2. g3 Nf6 3. Bg2 d5 4. c4 d×c4 5. Qa4† Bd7 6. Q×c4 Bc6 7. Nf3 Bd5 8. Qa4† Qd7 9. Qd1 Nc6 10. Nc3 e6 11. 0-0 Bd6 12. Nb5 0-0 13. Nc3 Ne4 14. N×d5 e×d5 15. e3 Rae8 16. Ne1 Qe6 17. Nd3 Rf6 18. f3 Ng5 19. e4 N×f3† 20. R×f3 N×d4 21. Rf1 f×e4 22. Nf4 Qe5 23. Be3 Bc5 24. Kh1 c6 25. b4 Bb6 26. a4 Nf5 27. B×b6 a×b6 28. Re1 Ref8 29. Ra2 Rh6 30. Kg1 Qc3 31. Qd2 Qb3 32. Qb2 Qc4 33. Rc1 Qa6 34. Qe5 b5 35. a5 Qa7† 36. Rf2 Rhf6 37. Rc5 Qb8 38. Q×b8 R×b8 39. Nh5 Rf7 40. a6 g6 41. Nf4 Nd4 42. Bh3 e3 43. Rf1 b6 44. Rcc1 e2 45. Rfe1 Nf3† 46. Kh1 Re8 47. R×c6 N×e1 48. Be6 R×e6 49. R×e6 g5 50. N×e2 Rf1† 51. Ng1 Nf3 52. Kg2 R×g1† 53. K×f3 Ra1 54. R×b6 Kf7 55. Ke3 Ra3† 56. Kd4 Ra4 57. K×d5 R×b4 58. Kc6 Ra4 59. Kb7 Black resigns—*St. James's Budget*, 2 June 1893.

**(1164) Bird–Jasnogrodsky   ½–½**
Match (game 12)
London, 30 May 1893
*Game score missing*

**(1165) Jasnogrodsky–Bird   0–1**
Match (game 13)
London, 31 May 1893
*Game score missing*

**(1166) Bird–Jasnogrodsky   1–0**
Match (game 14)
London, 1 June 1893
*A18*

1. c4 e6 2. Nc3 Nf6 3. e4 d5 4. e5 Nfd7 5. d4 d×c4 6. B×c4 c6 7. Nf3 Nb6 8. Bd3 Be7 9. h4 N8d7 10. Qe2 Nd5 11. Ne4 N7b6

**12. Bg5!** Bird comes out of the opening with a serious advantage. **12. ... f6 13. e×f6 g×f6 14. Bh6 Bb4† 15. Kf1 Qe7?** Allowing a very unfavorable exchange. **16. a3 Bd6 17. N×d6† Q×d6 18. Nd2 Qe7 19. Ne4 Bd7 20. Qh5†?!** 20. Nc5! is superior. If 20. ... 0-0-0 21. Ba6! **20. ... Kd8 21. Nc5 Kc7 22. a4** An alternative plan was 22. Re1. **22. ... Be8 23. Qf3?!** 23. Qg4! keeps Black under pressure. **23. ... Nd7 24. Ne4 Bg6** 24. ... e5 is interesting at this point. **25. h5 B×e4 26. B×e4 Rae8 27. B×d5 e×d5 28. Bf4† Kc8 29. Qc3 Qe4 30. Bg3 f5 31. Rh4 Qe2† 32. Kg1 Nb6?** Now the knight becomes a target. 32. ... Rhg8 leads to a balanced game. If necessary, the knight might go to b8. **33. Qa5?** 33. Qc1! Re4 34. R×e4 Q×e4 35. Qh6 is a strong maneuvre to bring Black's king into the vicinity of his queen. **33. ... Re4?** He must absolutely play 33. ... Q×b2 when a draw is imminent: 34. Q×a7 Q×a1† 35. Kh2 Re1 36. Qb8† Kd7 37. Q×b7†. **34. R×e4 f×e4 35. Q×a7 Q×b2** Bird has a rook to the good compared to the last variation. **36. Qb8† Kd7 37. Q×b7† Ke8 38. Q×c6† Nd7 39. Rc1 Qb6 40. Q×d5 Qd8 41. Qe6† Kf8 42. Bd6† Kg7 43. h6** mate—*Morning Post*, 2 June 1893.

### (1167) Jasnogrodsky–Bird   1–0
Match (game 15)
London, 1 June 1893
*Game score missing*

---

# THE REMAINDER
# OF THE YEAR 1893

Bird stuck to his post in the Divan throughout the year. With the decline of chess becoming more and more remarkable, Simpson's remained standing like a rock with the veteran in the middle of it.

Mr. H.E. Bird, always a host in himself, is never absent except when he has an attack of his old enemy the gout. The distinguished veteran is engaged in play during most of the day and the evening, but when, per chance he has an hour to spare, he may be seen compiling sheet upon sheet of manuscript. What the nature of the great work is which Mr. Bird has in hand is only known to those who are strictly in his confidence. Various guesses are made from time to time, one being that he is compiling a classical dictionary, and a second that he is to present the world with a brand new collection of English and German synonyms. For ourselves, we have a strong suspicion, judging by Mr. Bird's recent letter in the *St. James's Budget*, that his forthcoming work will be entirely devoted to prove that the Romans played chess, notwithstanding all that has been written to the contrary [*Newcastle Courant*, 30 September 1893].

Bird's preserved offhand games were played either during the spring or after the summer months of 1893. A visit to Newcastle was planned in July or August, but probably the gout made Bird postpone this trip (no record has been found).

### (1168) Bird & Chapman–van Vliet & Rolland   1–0
Consultation game
London (Simpson's Divan) 1893
C52

**1. e4 e5 2. Nf3 Nc6 3. Bc4 Bc5 4. b4 B×b4 5. c3 Ba5 6. d4 e×d4 7. Qb3 d×c3 8. B×f7† Kf8 9. 0-0 Qf6 10. B×g8 R×g8 11. Ng5 Qg6 12. f4 Bb6† 13. Kh1 Nd4 14. Qd5 Rh8 15. f5 Qe8**

**16. f6 g6 17. e5 Ne6 18. f7 Qe7 19. N×e6† Q×e6 20. Bh6† Ke7 21. f8Q† R×f8 22. B×f8†** and White wins—*Illustrated London News*, 22 April 1893.

### (1169) Blackburne & Jasnogrodsky–Bird & Chapman   1–0
Consultation game
London (Simpson's Divan) 1893
C30

**1. e4 e5 2. Nc3 Bc5 3. f4 d6 4. Nf3 a6 5. Bc4 Be6 6. B×e6 f×e6 7. d4 e×d4 8. N×d4 Qf6 9. Nb3 Ba7 10. Qe2 Nc6 11. Be3 B×e3 12. Q×e3 Nh6 13. 0-0-0 0-0 14. Rhf1 b5 15. h3 b4 16. Na4 e5 17. f5 Nf7 18. Kb1 Kh8 19. g4 Qh4 20. c4 Ng5 21. c5 Rad8 22. c×d6 c×d6 23. Nb6 N×h3 24. Rc1 Nd4 25. Rh1 Q×g4 26. R×h3 d5 27. Rch1 Q×e4† 28. Q×e4 d×e4 29. R×h7† Kg8 30. Nc5 e3 31. Ne6 N×e6 32. f×e6 Rf1† 33. R×f1 K×h7 34. e7 Re8 35. Nd5 Kg6 36. Re1 Kf5 37. R×e3 e4 38. Re1 Ke5 39. N×b4 g5 40. Kc2 g4 41. Kd2 a5 42. Nc6† Kd5 43. Rc1 g3 44. Ke3 a4 45. b4 a×b3 *e.p.* 46. a×b3 Rg8 47. Rd1† Ke6 48. Rd8** Black resigns—*Newcastle Courant*, 20 May 1893.

### (1170) Bird–van Vliet & Schwann   0–1
Consultation game
London (Simpson's Divan) 1893
C62

**1. e4 e5 2. Nf3 Nc6 3. Bb5 d6 4. c3 f5 5. d4 f×e4 6. N×e5 d×e5 7. Qh5† Ke7 8. Bg5† Nf6 9. B×c6 b×c6 10. d×e5 Qd5 11. Bh4 Ba6 12. c4 Qa5† 13. Nc3 Ke6 14. B×f6 g×f6 15. Qh3† f5 16. 0-0 B×c4 17. Rfe1 Bd3 18. N×e4 B×e4 19. R×e4 Qd5 20. Rae1 Bg7 21. R4e3 Rad8 22. Rf3 Qe4 23. Rc1 Qc2 24. Rf1 Rd1 25. g4 R×f1† 26. K×f1 Qc4†** White resigns—*Leeds Mercury*, 24 June 1893.

### (1171) Bird–Evelyn   0–1
Offhand game
London (Simpson's Divan) 1893
C52

**1. e4 e5 2. Nf3 Nc6** Two fragments played by the same players in the line 2. ... d6 3. d4 f5 were published by Bird in *Chess Novelties*. Bird selected 4. Nc3 and his opponent had an edge after 4. Nc3 f×e4 5. N×e5 Nf6 6. Bg5 d×e5 7. d×e5 Q×d1† 8. R×d1 h6 9. B×f6 g×f6 10. Nd5 Kd8 11. Nb6† Nd7 12. N×a8 f×e5 (p. 99). In another game, played with reversed colors, Evelyn opted for 4. d×e5 f×e4 5. Ng5 d5 6. e6 Nh6 7. Nc3 Bb4 8. Qh5† Kf8 (p. 98). **3. Bc4 Bc5 4. b4 B×b4 5. c3 Ba5 6. d4 Nf6 7. Ba3 N×e4 8. Qb3 Nd6 9. B×d6 c×d6 10. B×f7† Kf8 11. 0-0 g6 12. Nbd2 Kg7 13. Bd5 Rf8 14. Ne4 Bc7 15. Rad1 a5 16. c4 Rf4 17. c5 Ra6 18. Qa3 Ne7 19. d×e5 d×e5 20. Ng3 b5 21. Qb2 Raf6 22. N×e5 B×e5 23. Q×e5 Qf8 24. Bf3 Nc6 25. Qc7 Qd8 26. Q×d8 N×d8 27. Ne4 Rc6 28. Rd5 Nf7 29. Rfd1 Re6 30. R5d4 Bb7 31. Ng5 N×g5 32. R×f4 B×f3 33. R×f3 N×f3† 34. g×f3 Re7 35. Kg2 Kf7 36. Kg3 Ke8 37. Rd2 Kd8 38. f4 Kc7 39. h4 Kc6 40. Rc2 Re4 41. Kg4 h6 42. f3 Rd4 43. Rc3 Rd5 44. Rc1 h5†** White resigns—*Daily News*, 10 August 1893.

## (1172) Evelyn–Bird    0–1
Offhand game
London (Simpson's Divan) 1893
C45

**1. e4 e5 2. Nf3 Nc6 3. d4 e×d4 4. N×d4 Qf6 5. c3 Bc5 6. Bc4 N×d4 7. c×d4 B×d4 8. 0–0 h5 9. Kh1 Nh6 10. f3 d5 11. e×d5 Nf5 12. Nc3 h4 13. Ne2 Ng3† 14. N×g3 h×g3 15. Re1† Kf8 16. Be3 R×h2† 17. Kg1 Rh1† 18. K×h1 Qh4† 19. Kg1 Qh2† 20. Kf1 Qh1† 21. Ke2 Q×g2† 22. Kd3 Bf5† 23. K×d4 Q×b2† 24. Kc5 Qb6** mate—*Illustrated London News*, 6 January 1894.

## (1173) Bird–Moules    1–0
Offhand game
London (Simpson's Divan) 1893
A03

**1. f4 d5 2. Nf3 c5 3. e3 e6 4. b3 Nc6 5. Bb2 Nf6 6. Nc3 Bd6 7. Ne2 0–0 8. Ng3 Re8 9. Ne5 Bd7 10. Bd3 d4 11. e×d4 N×d4 12. 0–0 Qb6 13. c4 Bc6 14. Nh5 Ne4 15. Qg4 Nf5 16. N×c6 Q×c6 17. B×e4** Black resigns—*Illustrated London News*, 7 October 1893.

## (1174) Alapin–Bird    1–0
Offhand game
London (Simpson's Divan), 22 November 1893
C50

**1. e4 e5 2. Nf3 Nc6 3. Bc4 Bc5 4. 0–0 Nf6 5. b4 B×b4 6. d4** "If 6. c3, the right answer is 6. ... Be7"—Alapin. **6. ... 0–0** "Better to play 6. ... e×d4 7. c3 Be7!"—Alapin. **7. d×e5 N×e4 8. Bd5 Nc3** 8. ... Nc5 is safe. **9. N×c3 B×c3 10. Ng5!** "That Black can never safely take the rook is distinctly curious"—Alapin. **10. ... N×e5** If 10. ... B×a1? 11. Qh5 h6 12. N×f7 R×f7 13. Q×f7† Kh8 14. B×h6! (Alapin considered 14. Bg5? to be the winning move, but 14. ... N×e5 15. B×d8 N×f7 16. B×f7 Be5 is equal) 14. ... g×h6 15. R×a1 N×e5 16. Qf4 and wins. **11. f4! Ng6 12. Qh5** *(see diagram)*

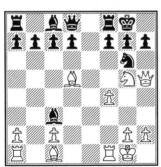

*After 12. Qh5*

**12. ... h6?** This doesn't diminish White's attacking potential; on the contrary. The drastic 12. ... Q×g5! however alters the course of the game. Possible then was 13. Q×g5 B×a1 14. f5 Bf6 15. f×g6! (15. Qg3 Ne7 16. Be4 d5 17. Bd3 Nc6 is even better for Black!) 15. ... B×g5 16. g×f7† Kh8 17. B×g5. During the following moves both sides must focus on the f-pawn: 17. ... d6 18. Be7 Bg4 19. Re1 Bh5 20. B×f8 R×f8 21. Re7 c6 22. Be6 b5 23. g4 Bg6 24. R×a7 B×c2 and after 25. ... g5, Black has excellent drawing chances! **13. Q×g6 h×g5 14. f×g5 Qe7 15. Ba3! d6 16. R×f7?** After some magnificent

play, Alapin misses the forced win after 16. Rae1 Qd7 (16. ... B×e1 17. Bb2 Bc3 18. B×c3 Qe3† 19. Kh1 Q×c3 20. R×f7 also ends badly) 17. Qh5. **16. ... R×f7 17. Rf1 Qe3†?** 17. ... Bf6! is another surprising move that neutralizes White's winning ambitions: 18. B×f7† (18. g×f6? Qe3† 19. Kh1 Be6 and Black wins) 18. ... Q×f7 19. Qd3 Be6 20. Rf4 Bd4†! 21. Q×d4 Qg6. **18. Kh1 Be6 19. B×e6** Black resigns—*Birmingham Weekly Mercury* (Alapin), 6 January 1894.

## (1175) Alapin–Bird    1–0
Offhand game
London (Simpson's Divan), 22 November 1893
C20

**1. e4 e5 2. Ne2 d5 3. e×d5 Q×d5 4. Nbc3 Qd8 5. d4 e×d4 6. Q×d4 Bd7 7. Qe5† Ne7 8. Bf4 Nbc6 9. Q×c7 Q×c7 10. B×c7 Rc8 11. Bd6 Ng6 12. B×f8 R×f8 13. 0–0–0 f5 14. Nd4 N×d4 15. R×d4 Bc6 16. Bb5 Kf7 17. B×c6 R×c6 18. Rd7† Kf6 19. R×b7 a6 20. Re1 Nf4 21. g3 Nh3 22. Nd5† Kg5 23. R×g7† Kh6 24. Ree7 Rh8 25. Ne3 Rf6 26. f4 Nf2 27. Rg5 Rhf8 28. Re5** Black resigns—*La Stratégie*, December 1893, p. 372.

## (1176) Bird & Evelyn–van Vliet & Müller    1–0
Consultation game
London (Simpson's Divan) 1893
A02

**1. f4 e5 2. f×e5 d6 3. e×d6 B×d6 4. Nf3 g5 5. c3** A very interesting and playable idea. **5. ... g4 6. Qa4† Nc6 7. Nd4** 7. Qe4† is a refinement. **7. ... Qh4† 8. Kd1 Nge7?** They must play 8. ... g3 themselves to gain compensation for the pawn. **9. g3 Qh5** "If 9. ... B×g3 then 10. Bg2 Bd6 11. N×c6 N×c6 12. B×c6† and wins"—Abbott. **10. Bg2 Bd7 11. N×c6** 11. Nb5 0–0 12. N×d6 eliminates Black's strongest piece. White is winning. **11. ... N×c6 12. Qe4† Be6 13. d4 0–0–0 14. Qc2 f5 15. e3 Qf7 16. b3 Bd5 17. Rf1 B×g2 18. Q×g2 Qg6 19. Qc2 Rhf8 20. Nd2 Be7 21. a4** "A good move. White has the best of the opening, and steadily gains as the game proceeds"—Abbott. **21. ... Bg5 22. Nc4 h6 23. Qd3 Rf7 24. Kc2 Qe6 25. Ba3 a6 26. a5 Qd5** *(see diagram)*

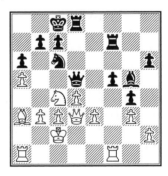

*After 26. ... Qd5*

**27. Rf2** 27. Bc5 is correct. Black could have now taken the pawn at a5 without problems. **27. ... Re8 28. Raf1** 28. Bd6!, followed by 29. Bf4, is a smooth tactical trick to neutralize Black's pressure along the e-file. **28. ... Re4** 28. ... N×a5 is again best for Black; e.g., 29. N×a5 Q×a5 30. Bc1 Rfe7. **29. Bc5 h5 30. Re2 Rd7 31. Rd1 Rd8 32. b4** Black's last move was an error (31. ... Kb8, keeping the f-pawn well defended was correct). White could break the position open with a direct assault: 32. Rf2! Rd7 33. Qf1 Rf7 34. Qh1 Qd7

35. Rdf1 Rf6 36. h4 Bh6 37. Q×e4. **32. ... Rde8 33. Kb2 f4** 33. ... h4 is the right pawn push. **34. g×f4 B×f4 35. Rde1** He could have made excellent use of the opening of the f-file: 35. Rf1! Bg5 36. Ref2 B×e3 37. Rf5 Qd8 38. R×h5 and White is on top. **35. ... Bh6 36. Nd2?** 36. Rf2 Nd8 37. Qf1 B×e3 38. Rf5 is still very favorable for White. **36. ... Ne5! 37. Qc2 Nc4† 38. N×c4 Q×c4** Black has made a very important exchange that makes White's extra pawn valueless. **39. Qd2 c6** Even 39. ... Bg5, slowly preparing the advance of the kingside majority, was becoming promising for him. **40. Qc2 B×e3?** 40. ... Bf4! 41. Rd1 Kb8 42. Rdd2 B×e3 leads to an excellent ending for Black. With the text move Black captures a poisoned pawn. **41. Kb1 Qf7 42. d5! Qf4** 42. ... Bd2 is hardly enticing, but at least prolongs the game; e.g., 43. R×e4 B×e1 44. R×e8† Q×e8 45. Qf5† Qd7 46. Qf8† Qd8 47. Qf7. **43. d×c6** and White wins—*Illustrated London News* (Abbott), 16 December 1893.

## (1177) Rolland & Unknown–Bird   0–1

Consultation game
London (Simpson's Divan) 1893
*C61*

1. e4 e5 2. Nf3 Nc6 3. Bb5 Nd4 4. N×d4 e×d4 5. d3 h5 6. c3 Bc5 7. Nd2 c6 8. Ba4 d6 9. Nb3 b5 10. N×c5 d×c5 11. Bc2 Bg4 12. f3 Be6 13. Qe2 Qf6 14. Bd2 Ne7 15. Qf2 h4 16. f4 h3 17. f5 h×g2 18. Q×g2 N×f5 19. e×f5 Bd5 20. Qe2† Kd7 21. 0–0 Rh4 22. Rae1 Rah8 23. Bf4 R×h2 24. B×h2 and Black mates in three moves—*Illustrated London News*, 13 January 1894.

# HASTINGS CHESS FESTIVAL 1894

The decline of British chess during the 1890s was interrupted by one magnificent spark: the tournament in Hastings in 1895, arguably the strongest chess event of the nineteenth century. That such a famous event took place in a small and relatively remote town can be explained by the exceptionally fruitful local chess life. The Hastings Chess Club started to show its ambition to rise to prominence in the early 1890s when several strong masters, such as Blackburne and Gunsberg, were invited for simultaneous play. The club received a major impulse at the end of 1893 when the club officers succeeded in convincing Blackburne, still the flag-bearer of British chess, to move to the seaside resort to promote the royal game.[37] In December the club's secretary, Herbert Edward Dobell, proudly announced a chess festival to be held in Hastings.

Bird, not yet a familiar face to most club members, was invited to appear, with Blackburne. Gunsberg was equally charmed by the initiative of the Hastings Chess Club and he succeeded in getting invited. The club subsequently changed their program so that the festival would last three days. Each day was well filled, with a simultaneous exhibition by one of the masters and a consultation game with the two other masters and two amateurs involved.[38]

During the afternoon of the opening day, Wednesday 10 January, Gunsberg and Blackburne were engaged in two consultation games. Bird took care of the simultaneous exhibition which started at 7:00 p.m. After four hours of play, he had won 17 games, lost 1 (against Toddenham), with 3 draws—against Colonel Gillies, O. Earl and J. Watney.

On Thursday Bird accompanied Locock in the first consultation game of the day. They played White against Blackburne and Horace Fabian Cheshire. The game was adjourned in a winning position for the Black allies. Bird and Locock resigned the game before the resumption.

The most attractive game of the festival was played on the final day. Gunsberg and George Anderson Ballingall transposed a strong attack into a convincing win against a team consisting of Bird and Chapman.

## (1178) Bird & Locock–Blackburne & Cheshire   0–1

Consultation game
Hastings, 11 January 1894
*C54*

1. e4 e5 2. Nf3 Nc6 3. Bc4 Bc5 4. b4 Bb6 5. c3 Nf6 6. d3 d6 7. a4 a5 8. b5 Nb8 9. Be3 Nbd7 10. Nbd2 0–0 11. Bb3 B×e3 12. f×e3 Nc5 13. Bc2 Qe7 14. 0–0 d5 15. e×d5 N×d5 16. Qe1 Bg4 17. d4 e×d4 18. c×d4 Q×e3† 19. Kh1 Q×e1 20. Ra×e1 Nd7 21. Ne5 N×e5 22. R×e5 Rad8 23. h3 Be6 24. Nf3 h6 25. Rc1 Rd7 26. Be4 b6 27. Kh2 Nb4 28. Rc3 Rfd8 29. g4 Bd5 30. Bf5 Rd6 31. Ng1 g6 32. Bb1 Rf6 33. Be4 B×e4 34. R×e4 Nd5 35. Rc2 Rf1 36. Ne2 Ra1 37. Rc4 Rd7 38. Nf4 Ra2† 39. Kg3 Ra3† 40. Kh2 Nb4 41. Re8† Kg7 42. Rc8 Re2 43. Rc1 Rf3 44. Ng2 Re2 45. Re1 Rc2 and Black wins. Most sources suggest that this game was adjourned and not resumed. However, according to the *Sussex Daily News* of 15 January 1894, two or three moves were played on Saturday morning, after which Bird declined to continue and abandoned the game—*Daily News*, 15 January 1894.

## (1179) Gunsberg & Ballingall–Bird & Chapman   1–0

Consultation game
Hastings, 12 January 1894
*C25*

1. e4 e5 2. Nc3 Nc6 3. f4 e×f4 4. Nf3 Be7 5. Bc4 Bh4† 6. Kf1 d6 7. d4 Bg4 8. B×f4 B×f3 9. g×f3 Bf6 10. Be3 Nge7 11. Ke2 Qd7 12. Qg1 g6 13. Rd1 Bg7 14. Kd2 Rf8 15. Kc1 a6 16. h4 h5 17. f4 Bh6 18. d5 Na5 19. Bd3 b5 20. f5 B×e3† 21. Q×e3 c5 22. f6 Nc8 23. e5 d×e5 24. Q×c5 Qd6 25. Qf2 Kd8 26. Ne4 Qb6 27. Nc5 Ra7 28. d6 Rd7 29. Rhf1 R×d6 30. B×g6 Kc7 31. B×h5 R×d1† 32. R×d1 Rd8 33. R×d8 K×d8 34. B×f7 Qc6 35. Qd2† Kc7 36. Q×a5† Nb6 37. Ne6† Kb8 38. Qe1 e4 39. Qg3† and White wins—*Daily News*, 15 January 1894.

---

37. Blackburne's decision may also have been influenced by health issues, for the air in Hastings was surely much purer than in London. From his letters to Aspa (quoted before), one learns that he lived at 62 Mount Pleasant Road.

38. This formula would be maintained throughout the following years. On the practice of consultation chess Blackburne offered this: "Mr. Blackburne says that much the best practice for the members is for them to play three consultation games against him, as not only the players, but the onlookers, gain experience by the discussions on the moves." *Illustrated Sporting and Dramatic News*, 23 December 1893.

Three matadors of English chess: Henry Edward Bird, Isidor Gunsberg and Joseph H. Blackburne (courtesy National Archives).

# A Small Tour in the Provinces, March 1894

During the first two weeks of March, Bird visited several major cities in the north. This tour is badly documented and may have been more extended than appears from the few reports found and the games given below.

Bird spent three days, from 1 until 3 March, in Liverpool. Here he played an unknown number of offhand games at the classic rate of a shilling per game. On the final day he gave a simultaneous exhibition against 20 opponents. He won 16, lost 2 and 2 players achieved a draw (R.W. Johnson was one of them).

## (1180) Kaizer–Bird   0–1
Offhand game
Liverpool, March 1894
C30

1. e4 e5 2. Nc3 Bc5 3. f4 d6 4. Nf3 a6 5. fxe5 dxe5 6. Nxe5 Qd4 7. Nd3 Ba7 8. Nd5 Nc6 9. Nxc7† Kd8 10. Nxa8 Qxe4† 11. Be2 Nf6 12. Kf1 Nd4 13. Bf3 Nxf3 14. Qxf3 Qxf3† 15. gxf3 Bh3† 16. Ke2 Re8† 17. Ne5 Rxe5† 18. Kd3 Bg2 19. Rd1 Bxf3 20. Rf1 Be2† White resigns—*Newcastle Courant*, 17 March 1894.

## (1181) Bird–Johnson   ½–½
Simultaneous game
Liverpool, 3 March 1894
C30

1. e4 e5 2. f4 Nc6 3. Nf3 d5 4. exd5 Qxd5 5. Nc3 Qe6 6. Be2 Bc5 7. Ne4 Qe7 8. d3 Nd4 9. Nxd4 Bxd4 10. c3 Bb6 11. fxe5 Qxe5 12. Kd2 Bf5 13. Bf3 0–0–0 14. Kc2 Bxe4 15. Bxe4 Nf6 16. Qf3 Nxe4 17. Qxe4 Qxe4 18. dxe4 Rhe8 19. Re1 Re6 20. Bf4 draw—*Bristol Mercury and Daily Post*, 10 March 1894.

On Monday 5 March Bird gave a simultaneous exhibition in the rooms of the Manchester Chess Club. Nothing more has been found about Bird's stay here.

Bird extended his visit to Newcastle later that week. Newcastle appears to have been the final stop of the tour. Bird was extremely successful here, not only with his anecdotes of old and legendary players, but also with his play in offhand as well as simultaneous games.

On Thursday evening Mr. Bird played a number of games at the Newcastle Chess Club, encountering several of its strongest members. The visitor won a large majority of the games played, his most successful opponent being Mr. W.F. Graham, one of Newcastle's most accomplished amateurs. Friday evening was the occasion of a members' social at the Art Gallery, when Mr. Bird played all comers simultaneously in the chess room of Mr. Barkas's popular institution. Playing with all his accustomed verve and brilliancy, Mr. Bird completed 21 games in a little over two hours, of which he won 16, lost none, and drew 5. The players who succeeded in making drawn games were Messrs. P. Forsyth, H.W. Hawks, J.H. Lowes, James Wadsworth, and Capt. Smith. Mr. Bird concluded his visit by playing some offhand games at the Art Gallery on Saturday afternoon, and at the Newcastle Chess Club in the evening [*Newcastle Weekly Chronicle*, 17 March 1894].

## (1182) Bird–Lowes    ½–½
Simultaneous game
Newcastle, 9 March 1894
C30

1. f4 Nc6 2. e4 e5 3. Nf3 d6 4. c3 Bg4 5. Qb3 Rb8 6. Bc4 Qf6 7. f×e5 d×e5 8. 0-0 Na5 9. Qa4† Nc6 10. d4 Bd7 11. d5 Nd4 12. Q×a7 N×f3† 13. R×f3 Qb6† 14. Q×b6 c×b6 15. d6 f6 16. Rd3 Rc8 17. B×g8 R×g8 18. Na3 Bc6 19. Be3 Rd8 20. Nc4 Bb5 21. b3 B×c4 22. b×c4 B×d6 23. Rad1 Bc7 24. R×d8† B×d8 25. Rb1 Rf8 26. B×b6 B×b6† 27. R×b6 Rf7 28. Kf2 Rc7 29. Rb4 Kd7 30. Ke3 Kd6 31. Kd3 g6 32. Rb6† Ke7 33. a4 f5 34. e×f5 g×f5 35. Rh6 Kf8 36. Rf6† Rf7 37. R×f7† K×f7 38. c5 Ke6 39. Kc4 e4 40. g3 Kd7 41. h3 h5 42. h4 Kc6 43. a5 Kc7 44. Kd4 Kc6 45. c4 draw—*Newcastle Weekly Chronicle*, 17 March 1894.

## (1183) Bird–Heywood    1–0
Offhand game
Newcastle, 10 March 1894
A02

1. f4 e5 2. f×e5 d6 3. e×d6 B×d6 4. g3 h5 5. d4 h4 6. Bg2 h×g3 7. h3 Nc6 8. Nf3 Be6 9. e4 Bc4 10. a3 Qd7 11. Nbd2 With this move he blocks his own development. **11. ... Ba6 12. c4 Bf4 13. d5 Be3!** A very brave and correct sacrifice, even though the calm 13. ... Nce7 certainly comes into consideration. **14. d×c6 Bf2† 15. Ke2** "The only move. If 15. Kf1 B×c4† and mates in two more moves, but the veteran is not to be caught napping"—Heywood. **15. ... Q×c6 16. Qb3 Nf6 17. Ne5 Qc5 18. Nd3 Qe3† 19. Kd1 0-0-0 20. Kc2 Rd4 21. N×f2** Risky, for the defense of his king gets stripped. **21. ... Q×f2 22. Qf3 R×c4† 23. Kb3 Qb6†** The cool 23. ... Rd4! nearly stalemates White: 24. Q×f2 g×f2 25. Kc2 Bd3† 26. Kc3 c5 etc. **24. Ka2 Rd4 25. Q×g3 Rhd8 26. e5?** This push is too aggressive. 26. Bf1! eliminates an important piece. **26. ... R×d2! 27. B×d2 R×d2 28. Rab1 Bc4† 29. Ka1 R×g2??** "Black plays as usual for the 'gallery' of which there were a considerable number present. Of course 30. Q×g2 would be met by the fatal 30. ... Qb3, but the master has a surprise in store for his too ingenious opponent"—Heywood. 29. ... Rd3! successfully realizes the same idea of bringing the queen to b3. If 30. Q×d3 B×d3 31. Rbd1 Be4. **30. Qc3! Ne4?!** Though not attractive, the endgame after 30. ... Nd5 31. Q×c4 Ne3 32. Qd3 Nc2† is his only chance. **31. Q×c4 Nd2 32. Q×f7 c5 33. Rhd1 Nb3† 34. Ka2 Nd4 35. R×d4 c×d4 36. Rc1†** Black resigns—*Newcastle Weekly Chronicle* (Heywood), 17 March 1894.

# Two Tournaments at the Divan 1894

After a break of two years another handicap tournament was organized at the Divan in April and May 1894. With only 11 players signing up (of which seven played in the first class), the handicap formula had clearly become frayed. In fact, this tournament appears to have been the last one played with odds at the Divan.

Bird and Teichmann were the most respected among the participants and their game was played on one of the early days of the tournament. An impetuous sacrifice sealed Bird's fate after he had reached an interesting position. Bird lost a second game against James Ernest Manlove. He replied to his opponent's unorthodox 1. e4 e5 2. Bb5 with the bizarre 2. ... Qg5. Bird underestimated Manlove severely and was punished with a defeat. Bird completed his other games in a few weeks which gave him the chance to witness the end of the tournament at ease. Teichmann won relatively simply with 9 points out of 10 games. A short draw given to Rolland permitted the Frenchman to clinch second place with 7½. Bird secured he third spot thanks to a final win against Rolland. It was reported, by the *Standard* on 14 May, that Manlove was still able to catch up to Bird, but the lack of adequate press coverage prevents the drawing of conclusions. The final results of all the other players are also unknown.

The winners of the three prizes were already known early in May. The remaining competitors decided to spend their prize money, which compassed some £10 assembled from the entry fees, for the prize fund of another small tournament. Teichmann, Rolland and Bird were joined by Müller, which may be an indication that he finished fourth in the handicap tournament, to form a quadrangular tournament.

Games in this tournament were played at a rate of one per day. Teichmann took the lead by beating Rolland on 28 May. On the next day Bird had to concede a draw against Müller in an endgame with bishops of opposite colors, despite having an extra pawn. Bird opposed Teichmann on the third day. The queens were exchanged rapidly and the endgame was much in favor of the young man. Bird

| | | | 1 | 2 | 3 | 4 | 5 | 6 | 7 | 8 | 9 | 10 | 11 | |
|---|---|---|---|---|---|---|---|---|---|---|---|---|---|---|
| 1 | R. Teichmann | I | | ½ | 1 | 1 | 1 | ½ | 1 | 1 | 1 | 1 | 1 | 9 |
| 2 | Rolland | I | ½ | | 0 | 1 | 0 | 1 | 1 | 1 | 1 | 1 | 1 | 7½ |
| 3 | H.E. Bird | I | 0 | 1 | | | 0 | ½ | | | | | | 7 |
| 4 | O.C. Müller | I | 0 | 0 | | | 1 | ½ | | | | | | |
| 5 | J.E. Manlove | I | 0 | 1 | 1 | 0 | | | | | | | | |
| 6 | A. Guest | I | ½ | 0 | ½ | ½ | | | | | | | | |
| 7 | T.C. Gibbons | I | 0 | 0 | | | | | | | | | | |
| 8 | L.R. Manlove | III | 0 | 0 | | | | | | | | | | |
| 9 | Smith | II | 0 | 0 | | | | | | | | | | |
| 10 | Cruesmann | III | 0 | 0 | | | | | | | | | | |
| 11 | Fabius | IV | 0 | 0 | | | | | | | | | | |

**Handicap tournament, London, 2 April–May 1894**

*Site:* Simpson's Divan
*Prizes:* Prize fund of ca. £20. Three prizes. Entrance fees divided among non–prize winners.
*Odds scale:* pawn and move (class II), pawn and two moves (class III) and knight (class IV) and two pieces (class VII)

**Quadrangular tournament, London, 28 May–2 June 1894**

*Site:* Simpson's Divan
*Prizes:* Prize fund of ca. £10. Four prizes.

| | 1 | 2 | 3 | 4 | |
|---|---|---|---|---|---|
| 1 R. Teichmann | | ½ | 1 | 1 | 2½ |
| 2 O.C. Müller | ½ | | ½ | 1 | 2 |
| 3 H.E. Bird | 0 | ½ | | 1 | 1½ |
| 4 Rolland | 0 | 0 | 0 | | 0 |

was not able to draw it. In his final game, Bird beat Rolland, and thus came out third behind Teichmann (2½) and Müller (2).

## (1184) Teichmann–Bird    1–0

Handicap tournament
London, 3 April 1894
C30

1. e4 e5 2. Nc3 Bc5 3. f4 d6 4. Nf3 a6 5. f×e5 d×e5 6. N×e5 Qd4 7. Nd3 Ba7 8. Qf3 Nc6 9. Be2 Nf6 10. Nf2 Nb4 11. Bd1 h5 12. h3 Be6 13. d3 0-0-0 14. a3 Nc6 15. Ne2 Qc5 16. b4 Qe5 17. Rb1 Ng4 18. N×g4 h×g4 19. Qf1 g3 20. Qf4 Bf2† 21. Kf1 f6 22. Bb2 Qg5 23. Bc1 Qg6 24. Be3 B×h3 25. R×h3 R×h3 26. g×h3 B×e3 27. Q×e3 g2† 28. Kg1 Ne5 29. Nf4 Qf7 30. d4 Nc4 31. Qc3 f5 32. e5 g5 33. N×g2 Qd5 34. Bf3 Q×d4† 35. Q×d4 R×d4 36. Re1 c6 37. e6 g4 38. h×g4 f×g4 39. Be2 Kd8 40. B×c4 R×c4 41. Nh4 Rc3 42. e7† Ke8 43. Nf5 Black resigns—*Morning Post*, 5 April 1894.

## (1185) Bird–Rolland    1–0

Handicap tournament
London, 18 April 1894
A03

1. f4 d5 2. Nf3 Nf6 3. e3 e6 4. b3 Be7 5. Bb2 0-0 6. Nc3 c5 7. Ne2 Ne4 8. d3 Bf6 9. c3 Nd6 Black's early knight sally forced some concessions from his opponent. 10. Ng3 Qa5 11. d4 c×d4 12. e×d4 Nc6 13. Ne5 g6 14. a4 "Presumably to prevent 14. ... Nb5, which might have proved troublesome"—*Daily News*. 14. ... Bh4 15. b4 A rather weakening move. Black's reply could be improved by 15. ... Qc7. 15. ... Qd8 16. Bd3 Ne7 17. 0-0 f6 18. Nf3 B×g3 19. h×g3 Ndf5 Rolland came out of the opening quite well. The text move wasn't necessary, and it encourages Bird to play g3–g4, an idea that he wanted to execute anyway. 20. Qe1 Bd7 21. b5 Qc7 *(see diagram)* It was time to prevent White's next move with 21. ... h5.

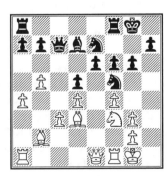

*After 21. ... Qc7*

22. g4! Nh6 23. g5 A calm approach is at least as promising. White completely dominates the board after 23. Ba3! Rae8 24. Nh2 Kh8 25. Qh4 Nhg8 26. Bb4. 23. ... Nhf5? 23. ... f×g5 24. f×g5 Ng4 25. Qh4 Ne3 is playable. The text move looks more logical, but there is a tactical downside. 24. g×f6 R×f6 25. Qe5 "This practically decides the day. Black is compelled to exchange, after which White has a marked superiority in position for the ending"—*Daily News*. White has a great luxury in excellent moves. Besides the text move 25. Ne5 or 25. Ba3 are equally problematic to deal with. 25. ... Q×e5 26. f×e5? But this move, which closes the important e-file, demonstrates that Bird was not aware of the crucial elements of the position. Far stronger is 26. N×e5 Rd8 27. Ba3 with a similar set-up as in previous lines. Black's position still looks reasonable but White's pieces are so dominant that they will undeniable win material very soon; e.g., 27. ... Be8 28. Ng4! Rf7 29. Rfe1 h5 30. R×e6! h×g4 31. Rae1. 26. ... Rff8 27. Ba3 Rae8 28. Ng5 h6 29. Nh3 h5? Rolland wanders off the right path again. 29. ... g5 is positionally correct. The text move only creates new holes in his position. 30. Rf3?! A direct assault grants him a winning attack; 30. Ng5 Bc8 31. c4! (31. a5 and 32. Bc5 is another plan. Black is unable to defend the queenside) 31. ... d×c4 32. B×c4 N×d4 33. R×f8† K×f8 34. Rf1† Nd5 35. N×e6†. Just as in previous lines, everything turns out fine for White if he utilizes the power of his strong bishops. 30. ... Kh7 31. Raf1 b6 32. Nf2 Rf7 33. g4 h×g4 34. N×g4 Kg7 35. c4? Extremely badly timed. The plain 35. Nf6 crowns White's plan: 35. ... Rd8 36. Rh3. 35. ... Rh8? Rolland misses his chance to bring his pieces to life with 35. ... d×c4 36. B×c4 Bc8. 36. Nf6? 36. c5! obtains a pawn steamroller. Now, Rolland doesn't miss his chance. 36. ... d×c4! "He could not play 36. ... N×d4 on account of 37. Nh5† winning the exchange"—*Daily News*. 37. B×c4 Bc8 38. d5 Much too impatient. 38. ... e×d5 39. N×d5 N×d5 40. B×d5 Rc7? Rolland fought back well. Here he missed the crucial tempo gain 40. ... Rd7! 41. Bb3, when a draw is certain after 41. ... Rh4 42. Rc3 Rg4†. 41. e6! Bird's bishops rule the board. 41. ... Rh4 42. Bb2† Kh7 43. Rf4 Rather passive. 43. Bf6! is very strong. Black can hunt Bird's king for a while, but the result is that White threatens to occupy the h-file. In the end Black is forced to sacrifice material to reach an endgame: 43. ... Rg4† 44. Kf2 Rc2† 45. Ke1 B×e6 46. B×e6 Re4† 47. Kd1 R×e6 48. Rh1† Kg8 49. K×c2. 43. ... R×f4 The exchange of rooks safeguards White's king. 43. ... Rh5 offers more resistance. 44. R×f4 Rc2 45. Bf6 Re2 46. e7 Bd7 "Of course it is obvious that the pawn cannot be taken, for White would give checkmate at h4"—*Daily News*. 47. Bc6 B×c6 48. b×c6 N×e7 49. c7? After 49. Rh4† Kg8 50. Rh8† Kf7 51. B×e7 the road is paved for the advanced c-pawn. 49. ... Rc2 "There was nothing better. If 49. ... Nc8 50. Rh4† Kg8 51. Rh8† Kf7 52. R×c8 and wins"—*Daily News*. 50. Rh4† Kg8 51. B×e7 R×c7 52. Bf6 Rd7 "and the game was prolonged for about 20 moves, but was finally won by Mr. Bird." With the wrong bishop to cover the promotion field of the a-pawn, it is extremely doubtful if White can win the game against correct defense—*Daily News*, 19 April 1894.

## (1186) Bird–Teichmann    0–1

Quadrangular (round 2)
London, 30 May 1894
A03

**1.** f4 d5 **2.** Nf3 g6 **3.** e3 Bg7 **4.** d4 c5 **5.** c3 Nc6 **6.** Bd3 Nf6 **7.** 0–0 0–0 **8.** a4 b6 **9.** Nbd2 Bb7 **10.** Qe1 e6 **11.** Qh4 Ne7 **12.** Ng5 Nf5 **13.** B×f5 e×f5 **14.** Ndf3 h6 **15.** Nh3 Ne4 **16.** Q×d8 Rf×d8 **17.** a5 f6 **18.** Nf2 Kf7 **19.** Rd1 Bf8 **20.** Nd3 c4 **21.** a6 Bc8 **22.** Nf2 Rb8 **23.** N×e4 f×e4 **24.** Nd2 b5 **25.** b3 b4 **26.** Bb2 c×b3 **27.** c4 d×c4 **28.** N×c4 Be6 **29.** Na5 Bd5 **30.** Rdc1 Rdc8 **31.** Rcb1 Rc2 **32.** Nb7 B×b7 **33.** a×b7 R×b7 **34.** h3 Be7 **35.** Kh2 g5 **36.** d5 g×f4 **37.** e×f4 Bd6 **38.** Kg3 Kg6 **39.** Ra6 Rc3† **40.** Kg4 h5† **41.** Kh4 B×f4 **42.** B×c3 b×c3 **43.** g4 Bg5† **44.** Kg3 c2 **45.** Rf1 h4† White resigns—*Morning Post*, 11 June 1894.

---

# A Book on the World Championship

For about two and a half months, from March until May 1894, the world championship match between Steinitz and Lasker took the attention of the chess world. On 25 May, Lasker dethroned Steinitz by winning the nineteenth game. He thereby achieved the aim he had set for himself a few years earlier. The games were published around the globe and commented on by the best players. Bird contributed his part four months later, when he covered the match in a small booklet of some 40 pages. It was published in London by George Bell and Co. for the prize of one shilling. It was also available in New York, where its prize was 35 cents.

In his introduction of *Steinitz & Lasker Match with Comments, Review and Original Notes*, Bird related how he had met Steinitz for the first time in 1862. Bird then described all the championship games and discussed the outcome of the match. Given the time that had passed since the conclusion, Bird was able to consult all relevant sources, but he emphasized the originality of his own notes. As one contemporary remarked, these may not have been the most correct ones.[39]

---

# Offhand Games 1894–1895

Just a few of Bird's offhand games played during the second part of 1894 and the first part of 1895 have been preserved.

### (1187) Bird–van Vliet & Unknown    1–0
Consultation game
London (Simpson's Divan) 1894
*A02*

**1.** f4 e5 **2.** f×e5 d6 **3.** e×d6 B×d6 **4.** g3 h5 **5.** Bg2 h4 **6.** d4 h×g3 **7.** h3 Qf6 **8.** Nf3 Bf5 **9.** Nc3 Bb4 **10.** e4 B×e4 **11.** Qe2 B×c3† **12.** b×c3 Qe7 **13.** 0–0 Nf6 **14.** Bg5 Bc6 **15.** Qd3 0–0 **16.** B×f6 g×f6 **17.** Rae1 Qd7 **18.** Nh4 B×g2 **19.** K×g2 Qd5† **20.** Re4 Re8

39. A positive review was published in the *Illustrated London News* on 6 October 1894: "This is a collection of the games in the latest match for the championship, with notes in Mr. Bird's well-known style. They are always interesting, sometimes humorous, and never without point. He has admiration for the winner, and sticks to his belief in the merits of the loser, and the chief fault he finds is the slowness of the play. But that is only saying the critic is Mr. Bird."

**21.** Rff4 R×e4 **22.** R×e4 Nd7 **23.** Qf3 Q×a2 **24.** Qg4† Kf8 **25.** Nf5 Q×c2† **26.** Re2 Black resigns—*Newcastle Courant*, 12 May 1894.

### (1188) Rolland–Bird    1–0
Offhand game
London (Simpson's Divan) 1894
*A43*

This game was attributed to the Divan tournament, but given the result this cannot be correct.

**1.** e4 c5 **2.** Nf3 g6 **3.** d4 Bg7 **4.** d5 d6 **5.** Nc3 a6 **6.** Bd2 b5 **7.** a3 h5 **8.** Be2 Nd7 **9.** Ng5 Ne5 **10.** 0–0 Rb8 **11.** f4 Nc4 **12.** Bc1 Bg4 **13.** B×g4 h×g4 **14.** Q×g4 Bd4† **15.** Kh1 Nf6 **16.** Qf3 Qd7 **17.** Ne2 B×b2 **18.** B×b2 N×b2 **19.** e5 d×e5 **20.** f×e5 Qg4 **21.** e×f6 Q×g5 **22.** f×e7 Rh7 **23.** d6 Kd7 **24.** Nf4 Rh4 **25.** Rae1 Rhh8 **26.** Nd5 f5 **27.** Qc3 Nc4 **28.** Nf6† K×d6 **29.** Qd3† Kc7 **30.** e8Q Rb×e8 **31.** Qd7† Kb6 **32.** N×e8 Qg3 **33.** Qd8† Black resigns—*Illustrated London News*, 12 May 1894.

### (1189) Bird–Rolland    1–0
Offhand game
London (Simpson's Divan) 1894
*C33*

**1.** e4 e5 **2.** f4 e×f4 **3.** Be2 Qh4† **4.** Kf1 g5 **5.** Nc3 d6 **6.** d4 Nf6 **7.** Nf3 Qh6 **8.** h4 Nh5 **9.** Kg1 Ng3 **10.** Rh2 g4 **11.** Nd5 g×f3 **12.** B×f3 Na6 **13.** B×f4 Qg7 **14.** e5 Be7 **15.** c3 Be6 **16.** N×e7 K×e7 **17.** d5 Bd7 **18.** e×d6† Kd8 **19.** Qb3 Rb8 **20.** Qa3 Rc8 **21.** d×c7† N×c7 **22.** Q×a7 Re8 **23.** d6 Na8 **24.** Qa5† b6 **25.** Qg5† Q×g5 **26.** B×g5† Re7 **27.** B×e7† Ke8 **28.** Re1 Be6 **29.** Bb7 Rb8 **30.** Bc6† Bd7 **31.** Bg5† Ne2† **32.** R×e2† Kf8 **33.** Bh6† Kg8 **34.** B×d7 Black resigns—*Illustrated London News*, 27 October 1894.

### (1190) Rolland–Bird    0–1
Offhand game
London (Simpson's Divan) 1894 (?)
*A85*

**1.** d4 f5 **2.** c4 Nf6 **3.** Nc3 e6 **4.** e3 b6 **5.** Nf3 Bb7 **6.** Be2 a6 **7.** 0–0 Bb4 **8.** Qb3 B×c3 **9.** b×c3 Nc6 **10.** a4 Na5 **11.** Qa2 Ne4 **12.** Bb2 "White's queen is badly posted, and is practically useless throughout"—Abbott. **12. ...** Qf6 **13.** d5 0–0 **14.** Rac1 Kh8 **15.** Ba3 d6 There was nothing wrong with snatching the pawn at c3. **16.** Bb4 e5 Better was 16. ... Qf7, augmenting, instead of giving up, the pressure against d5. **17.** B×a5 b×a5 **18.** Rc2? Too slow. 18. Nd2 would have questioned Black's best piece. **18. ...** Bc8 Here, or on the next moves, Bird could have opened the attack with 18. ... f4! 19. e×f4 Q×f4 20. Ne1 Bc8 21. Nd3 Qg5. Black has a great positional advantage as well as excellent prospects on the kingside. **19.** Bd1 Bd7 **20.** Nd2 "White's play is distinctly inferior to his usual form"—Abbott. **20. ...** Nc5 **21.** Rb2 e4! Taking space on the kingside and laying a claim on d3. **22.** Qa3 f4 **23.** e×f4 Q×f4 **24.** Kh1 Rf6 Bird can permit himself everything from now on. As Abbott pointed out, 24. ... Nd3 also wins. **25.** g3 Qh6 **26.** f4 Qh3 **27.** Be2 Rh6

**28. Rf2 e3 29. Bf1 e×d2 30. B×h3 d1Q† 31. Rf1 Qd3 32. Rfb1 R×h3 33. Rb8† Be8 34. R×a8 Q×b1† 35. Kg2 Qe4† 36. K×h3 Nd3 37. Qa2 g5 38. Qd2 N×f4† 39. Kg4 Ne2† 40. K×g5 h6†** "Or 40. ... Qg6† 41. Kh4 Qh5 mate"—Abbott. **41. Kf6 Qg6†** 41. ... Qe5 delivers mate. **42. Ke7 Qf7† 43. Kd8 Qd7 mate**—*Illustrated London News* (Abbott), 19 January 1895.

Toward the end of 1895, Bird published a new chess book, *Chess Novelties*. It contained the following friendly game that was played by correspondence from 6 January until 6 April. Bird mentioned no year, but it is likely that this game was played during the first months of 1895. Bird, apparently on his own, represented the chess community of the Divan, while the opposing allies defended the colors of the St. George's Chess Club. Bird's principal opponent was only mentioned by his initials, "E.M.J." This nicely fits the strong amateur Edward Mackenzie Jackson.

### (1191) Jackson & Allies–Bird   ½–½
Correspondence game
London 1895 (?)
C41

**1. e4 e5 2. Nf3 d6 3. Bc4 f5 4. d3 c6 5. Nc3 Be7 6. 0-0 Qc7 7. Ng5 B×g5 8. B×g5 f4 9. g3 g6 10. B×g8 R×g8 11. g×f4 Qg7 12. f×e5 d×e5 13. Qd2 Na6 14. Bh6 Qe7 15. Qg5 Bh3 16. Rfe1 Nc5 17. Re3 Bd7 18. Q×e7† K×e7 19. Bg5† Kd6 20. f4 Ne6 21. Rf1 Rae8 22. f×e5† K×e5 23. d4† Kd6 24. Bf6 Kc7 25. d5 Ng7 26. Bd4 Nh5 27. Rf7 Kc8 28. R×h7 Rgf8 29. Re2 Rf4 30. Rf2 c×d5 31. N×d5 Rfxe4 32. B×a7 Rg4† 33. Rg2 R×g2† 34. K×g2 Bc6** draw—*Chess Novelties*, pp. 294–296.

Bird's opponent in the following game was a chess friend of his from Cardiff.

### (1192) Goodall–Bird   1–0
Offhand game
London (Simpson's Divan), January 1895
D00

**1. d4 d5 2. e4 d×e4 3. f3 f5 4. f×e4 f×e4 5. Ne2 Nf6 6. Ng3 Nc6 7. Be3?** Much to passive. Equality was still within reach with 7. Bb5. **7. ... e5! 8. c3 e×d4 9. c×d4 Bb4† 10. Nc3 Nd5 11. Qh5† g6** (see diagram)

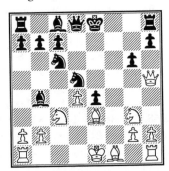

*After 11. ... g6*

**12. Be2!?** A highly innovative but desperate sacrifice. To avoid all complications Bird could reply with 12. ... N×e3, but that would

have been perhaps not so chivalrous. **12. ... g×h5 13. B×h5† Ke7 14. Bg5† Kd7 15. Bg4† Ke8 16. Bh5† Kf8 17. 0-0† Kg7 18. Rf7† Kg8 19. B×d8 N×c3??** Bird changes off a crucial defender. Easily winning is 19. ... B×c3. **20. b×c3?** 20. Bf6! Nd5 21. N×e4 grasps the attack. In that case, Black does best to flee into a bad endgame with 21. ... Bf8 22. R×f8† K×f8 23. B×h8. **20. ... B×c3** Goodall gets another chance. 20. ... N×d8 spoils White's fun. **21. Bf6 Be6?** 21. ... B×a1 deprives White of the necessary ammunition to deliver the final blow. His initiative still looks menacing but will eventually fade away: 22. Rg7† Kf8 23. R×c7 N×d4 24. B×h8 e3 25. Bg7† Kg8 26. Bh6 Be6. **22. Rg7† Kf8 23. Rf1 Bc4 24. Rf4 Bd2 25. R×e4 Bd5 26. Re2 Bb4 27. Rf2 Be1 28. Rf1** Black resigns—*Cambrian*, 1 February 1895.

---

# IN THE PROVINCES 1894

Bird gave several simultaneous exhibitions in chess clubs during the fall of 1894. The present author succeeded in retrieving four of them, but it is very likely that his playing schedule was busier than that. On Saturday 6 October Bird opened the season of the Chess Bohemians at their new rooms in the Ludgate Café. Bird beat 17 players in excellent style. He drew 1 game and lost 2, against W.H. Wood and Percy Howell. Both winners were given an autographed copy of one of Bird's books for their effort.

### (1193) Bird–Daniels   1–0
Simultaneous game
London (Chess Bohemians), 6 October 1894
C57

**1. e4 e5 2. Nf3 Nc6 3. Bc4 Nf6 4. Ng5 d5 5. e×d5 N×d5 6. N×f7 K×f7 7. Qf3† Ke6 8. Nc3 Nce7 9. d4 b5 10. Bb3 c6 11. a4 b4 12. Ne4 Kd7 13. d×e5 Kc7 14. Nd6 Be6 15. Bg5 h6 16. Bh4 g5 17. Bg3 Nc8 18. Ne4 Be7 19. 0-0-0 g4 20. Qe2 Kb7 21. Nd6† N×d6 22. e×d6 Bg5† 23. Kb1 Re8 24. Qd3 Qd7 25. a5 Rab8 26. Rhe1 Bf5 27. a6† Ka8 28. Q×d5 c×d5 29. B×d5† Rb7 30. R×e8† Q×e8 31. a×b7† Kb8 32. d7† Bf4 33. B×f4† Qe5 34. B×e5 mate**—*Morning Post*, 19 November 1894.

On Tuesday 16 October Bird was received at the Victoria Hall, the home of the Ealing Chess Club and played 22 games, conceding 3 draws. On Monday 12 November he visited the Caterham Institute. All in all he played 23 games that evening. Various players had the opportunity to meet the veteran twice. Bird's success rate was high again. He won 20 games and lost 2, against Greenwood and J. de Lacy Abbott, and was held to a single draw (Goodwin-Barnes). Bird rewarded his victors, as well as those he considered had played a strong game, with some of his books.

Bird's last known exhibition of the year passed on Wednesday 21 November in Brighton. He played 16 games of which he won 11; 3 players, A.J. Field, P. Isaac and Miss M. Parkinson won their games, and the games with T. Smith and T. Duff Barnett ended in a draw.

# HASTINGS CHESS FESTIVAL 1895

The second festival of the Hastings Chess Club ran from 17 until 19 January 1895. The "guest list" remained the same as the previous year, and Bird, Blackburne and Gunsberg were glad to be there. They were joined by some other outstanding London players and even a complete chess team from the capital.

Bird, in the company of MacDonnell, arrived three days before the festival commenced. On Monday 14 and Tuesday 15 January, Bird played two casual games with Blackburne. The younger veteran succeeded in winning this small duel with 1½ against ½. On Wednesday the attention of the club was focused on a consultation game in which Blackburne and MacDonnell opposed Bird and Chapman; Bird was once more on the losing side.

The actual festival opened on Thursday 17 January. Its set up was identical to the previous year, with a consultation game in the afternoon and a simultaneous exhibition in the evening. Bird gave his exhibition on the first evening. It was not a great success for the veteran, who was considerably ailing.[40] He won and lost eight games (Bird lost against F.S. Toddenham, G.A. Herington, H.E. Dobell, A.H. Hall, H.S. Leonard, W. Young, J.E. Watson and J. Fitzpatrick). Three games ended in a draw.

On Friday Bird and Frederick William Womersley played with the Black pieces against Gunsberg and Locock. Bird and his partner got the better of it, but—notably—they had to be aware of techniques that were mastered only decades later to make the most of it. That they reached such a position was unique for the time. Overall, Bird and his ally missed their best chances and were beaten in the end. In the third consultation game, played on Saturday 19 January, Bird and Chapman opposed Blackburne and Colonel Gillies. Against all expectations, Bird and his colleague rapidly won their game. Another game was set to fill the afternoon. Bird and Chapman now played a pet variation of the veteran against Gunsberg and Wayte, but were not successful. According to the 21 January *Daily News*, which published the game, Bird and Chapman played with the Black pieces, but given the opening this seems unlikely.

On the same day, a match between the Hastings Chess Club and the Athenaeum Chess Club ended in a tie: 8–8.

## (1194) Blackburne–Bird    1–0
Offhand game
Hastings, 14 January 1895
C50

1. e4 e5 2. Nc3 Bc5 3. Bc4 a6 4. Nf3 Nc6 5. d3 d6 6. Bg5 Nf6 7. Nd5 Be6 8. B×f6 g×f6 9. Nh4 b5 10. Bb3 Nd4 11. c3 N×b3 12. a×b3 c6 13. Ne3 h5 14. Nef5 d5 15. Qc2 Bf8 16. 0–0 Qb6 17. c4 d4 18. c5 Qc7 19. b4 Kd7 20. Ra5 Be7 21. Rfa1 Qb7 22. b3 Ra7 23. Qa2 Rha8 24. Qe2 Rh8 25. R5a3 Qa8

---

26. Qa2 Bd8 27. R×a6 R×a6 28. Q×a6 Q×a6 29. R×a6 B×b3 30. Kf1 Bc7 31. Ke2 Be6 32. Ra7 Kc8 33. Nd6† Kd7 34. Nhf5 Rg8 35. g3 Rb8 36. Ng7 Kd8 37. Nde8 Rc8 38. N×f6 h4 39. g4 Ke7 40. g5 Kf8 41. N×e6† f×e6 42. g6 Ke7 43. R×c7† R×c7 44. g7 Black resigns—*British Chess Magazine*, February 1895, pp. 92–93.

## (1195) Bird–Blackburne    ½–½
Offhand game
Hastings, 15 January 1895
A02

1. f4 e5 2. f×e5 d6 3. e×d6 B×d6 4. g3 h5 5. Bg2 5. d4 is the correct move. 5. ... h4 6. d4 h×g3 7. h3 Nc6 8. c3 Qe7 9. Na3 9. e4 was possible and good. The text move is in Black's favor were it countered with 9. ... B×a3 10. b×a3 Bf5 and 11. ... Be4. 9. ... Nf6 10. Qd3 Rh5 11. Nb5 Bf5 12. N×d6† 12. Qe3 reaches a promising endgame. 12. ... c×d6 Giving away the g-pawn for no good reason at all. 12. ... Q×d6 suggests itself and would be good for Black. 13. Q×g3 Ne4 14. Qf4 Qe6 15. h4 0-0-0 16. Bf3 Rh7 17. Nh3 Bird played very well, and the compensation Blackburne hoped for didn't materialize. His next move clearly underplays some tactical possibilities in the position. Instead, 17. ... Ne7 or 18. ... Re8 keep his prospects alive. 17. ... Rdh8? 18. Nf2? Bird misses a quick win with 18. d5! Q×d5 19. Ng5. 18. ... g5?! *(see diagram)* 18. ... d5 was necessary.

*After 18. ... g5*

19. d5! g×f4 20. d×e6 N×f2 21. K×f2 f×e6 22. B×f4 e5 23. Bg3 The bishop would have been much more influential on g5. 23. ... e4 Rather impetuously played as this move blows new life into the prospects of the bishop at g3. 23. ... Rf7 is considerably stronger. 24. Bg2 Rf7 25. Bf4 Rg8 26. Rag1 d5 27. e3 Kd8 28. h5 Bird consolidated his position and seems on his way to win the game. 28. ... Rh7 29. h6 29. Rd1! wins the important d-pawn. 29. ... Ne7 30. Bf1 Ke8 31. Be2 Kf7 32. c4 R×g1 33. R×g1 Ng6 34. Rg5 34. Bg5 keeps the bishop pair alive. 34. ... Kf6 35. c×d5 N×f4 36. e×f4 R×h6 37. Rh5 R×h5 38. B×h5 Ke7 39. Ke3 Kd6 40. Bf7 b6 41. Be6 Bh7 42. Kd4 a6 43. Bg4 43. f5 (MacDonnell) is much simpler. 43. ... a5 44. f5? 44. Be6 would have rectified his last move. With the text move, Bird blunders away a pawn. 44. ... Bg8 45. b3 B×d5 46. f6 e3 47. Bh5 Bc6 48. Bg4 Be8 49. K×e3 Ke5 50. Kd3 K×f6 51. Kd4 Bc6 52. Bc8 Ke7 53. Ke5 Bf3 "The ending requires great care on Black's part; and he handles it with his usual ingenuity and judgment"—MacDonnell. 54. Be6 Bc6 55. a3 Bf3 56. b4 a×b4 57. a×b4 Bc6 draw—*Illustrated Sporting and Dramatic News* (MacDonnell), 26 January 1895.

## (1196) Blackburne & MacDonnell–Bird & Chapman   1–0

Consultation game
Hastings, 16 January 1895
C01

1. e4 e6 2. d4 d5 3. Be3 Nf6 4. Nd2 Be7 5. e5 Nfd7 6. Bd3 c5 7. c3 Nc6 8. Ne2 Nf8 9. 0–0 Bd7 10. f4 Qb6 11. Nf3 Rc8 12. d×c5 B×c5 13. B×c5 Q×c5† 14. Kh1 Ne7 15. Nfd4 g6 16. Qe1 Nf5 17. Qf2 h5 18. Rac1 a6 19. c4 d×c4 20. R×c4 Qa5 21. R×c8† B×c8 22. Rc1 Ne7 23. Ng3 Nh7 24. Ne4 0–0 25. Nd6 Rd8 26. Nb3 Q×a2 27. Bc4 Qa4 28. Qh4 Nc6 29. Nc5 Qb4 30. Nce4 Q×b2 31. Rf1 b5 32. f5 Rf8 33. f×g6 f×g6 34. R×f8† N×f8 35. Qf4 N×e5 36. Nf6† Kg7 37. Nfe8† Kg8 38. Qf6 Qc1† 39. Bf1 Qh6 40. Q×e5 Black resigns—*British Chess Magazine*, February 1895, p. 93.

## (1197) Gunsberg & Locock–Bird & Womersley   1–0

Consultation game
Hastings, 18 January 1895
C46

1. e4 e5 2. Nf3 Nc6 3. Nc3 g6 4. d4 e×d4 5. N×d4 Bg7 6. Be3 Nge7 7. Bc4 d6 8. f4 Bd7 9. 0–0 0–0 10. Nce2 An inferior move that allows Black to unleash the power hidden in their position. The correct 10. f5 keeps Black in a bind. **10. ... Na5! 11. Qd3 N×c4** As the bishop was a target it could have been left on the board and pursued; e.g., by 11. ... c5 12. Nf3 (12. Nb5 d5!) 12. ... a6. **12. Q×c4 c5 13. Nb5 Qb6 14. Nbc3 Rfe8** The sharp 14. ... Q×b2! is critical. After 15. Rab1 Q×c2 16. Rfc1 Be6! 17. Qb5 a6 18. Q×b7 Qd3, they have fantastic piece play and are a pawn up. **15. Rab1 Qc6 16. Qd3 Rad8** At once 16. ... b5! is strong. **17. Bf2 b5** Not so good anymore, as the advance of the b-pawn doesn't fit very well with 16. ... Rad8. Promising was 17. ... Bg4 to prepare the push of the d-pawn. Whatever White tries, he keeps being thrown on the defensive. **18. Ng3** (18. Bh4 is harmless now; after 18. ... Rd7 19. Rbe1 d5 Black is better) 18. ... d5 19. Qb5 d×e4 20. Ng×e4 b6 with a superb game. **18. Bh4 c4 19. Qd2?!** 19. Qf3 to keep the e-pawn supported is logical. Black retains slight pressure after 19. ... f5! 20. Ng3 Qc5† 21. Kh1 Bc6 22. Rbd1 Bd4. **19. ... b4 20. Nd5 N×d5 21. B×d8** 21. e×d5 Qb6† 22. Bf2 Qa5 23. c3 Rb8 is also very bad for White. **21. ... R×e4 22. Bh4 Ne3** 22. ... Bg4! 23. Rbe1 B×b2 24. Rf2 f5 leaves Black in complete control over the position. **23. Rf3** *(see diagram)*

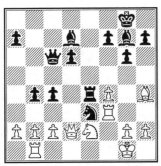

After 23. Rf3

**23. ... Nf5** There was an interesting alternative here: 23. ... N×g2! 24. K×g2 Bg4 25. Rbf1 B×b2 26. Kg1 B×f3 27. R×f3 Bg7. With

three pawns for the piece, material is equal, but Black's pawns are clearly stronger than the White knight that is kept passive by these pawns. **24. Bf2 B×b2??** A terrible blunder. They should have played 24. ... Qa4 25. a3 c3 26. b×c3 b×a3 with a lasting initiative. **25. R×b2 c3 26. N×c3 b×c3 27. R×c3** White has a material advantage and is rid of the pressure; they are winning. **27. ... Qa4 28. Rc7 Nd4 29. h3 B×h3 30. Rb8† Kg7 31. Qc3 Be6 32. B×d4† R×d4 33. Re8** 33. a3! prepares the decisive 34. Rb4. **33. ... Kf6 34. Rc6?** White goes after the wrong pawn. Winning is 34. Rd8 Qb4 35. Q×b4 R×b4 36. R×a7. **34. ... Kf5?** 34. ... Qb4 is now playable; e.g., 35. Q×b4 R×b4 36. Ra8 Ra4 37. R×d6 R×a2 with good drawing chances. **35. R×d6 R×f4 36. Rd5† B×d5 37. Re5†** Black resigns—*Daily News*, 21 January 1895.

## (1198) Bird & Chapman–Blackburne & Gillies   1–0

Consultation game
Hastings, 19 January 1895
C32

1. e4 e5 2. f4 d5 3. e×d5 e4 4. c4 c6 5. Nc3 Nf6 6. d4 c×d5 7. c×d5 N×d5 8. Bb5† Nc6 9. Qh5 Be6 10. f5 Nf6 11. Qh3 Bd7 12. Nge2 Nb4 13. B×d7† Q×d7 14. 0–0 Nc2 15. Rb1 N×d4 16. N×d4 Bc5 17. Rd1 B×d4† 18. Kh1 Black resigns—*Daily News*, 21 January 1895.

## (1199) Bird & Chapman–Gunsberg & Wayte   0–1

Consultation game
Hastings, 19 January 1895
A02

Published with reversed colors. Undoubtedly, this was erroneous, given the selected opening, as also appears from various reports.

1. f4 e5 2. f×e5 d6 3. e×d6 B×d6 4. g3 Nf6 5. Bg2 h5 6. d4 Ng4 7. Qd3 h4 8. Bf4 Qf6 9. Nc3 B×f4 10. g×f4 Q×f4 11. Nh3 Qh6 12. Nd5 Na6 13. Qe4† Qe6 14. Qf4 c6 15. Ng5 Qf5 16. Be4 Q×f4 17. N×f4 f6 18. Nf3 g5 19. Ng6 Rh6 20. h3 Ne3 21. Kf2 Nf5 22. c4 R×g6 23. d5 Nc5 24. Bc2 c×d5 25. c×d5 Rg7 26. b4 Na6 27. a3 Ng3 28. Rhc1 B×h3 29. Bd3 Rd8 30. e4 Re7 31. Rc4 Bg4 32. Rac1 B×f3 33. K×f3 Nb8 34. Rd4 a6 35. Bb1 Nd7 36. a4 Ne5† 37. Ke3 f5 38. d6 f×e4 39. Kf2 Re6 40. Rc5 Nf7 41. b5 Re×d6 42. R×d6 R×d6 43. e5 Re6 44. Rc8† Kd7 White resigns—*St. James's Budget*, 25 January 1895.

## (1200) Bird & MacDonnell–Gunsberg & Locock & Wayte   1–0

Consultation game
Hastings, January 1895
C58

1. e4 e5 2. Nf3 Nc6 3. Bc4 Nf6 4. Ng5 d5 5. e×d5 Na5 6. Bb5† c6 7. d×c6 b×c6 8. Qf3 Qc7 9. Be2 h6 10. Ne4 N×e4 11. Q×e4 Bd6 12. c3 0–0 13. b4 A typical Bird sortie. There was nothing wrong with the simple 13. d3. **13. ... f5 14. Qc2 Nb7 15. a4 Bd7 16. Na3 Qd8 17. Nc4** 17. Ba6 Qc7 18. d3 is quite good. The bishop on a6 is troublesome for Black. **17. ... Bc7 18. b5** An interesting way of returning his extra pawn, but hardly necessary at all. 18. d3 would still secure him a clear advantage. **18. ... c×b5 19. a×b5 B×b5**

**20. Qb3 Qd5** An effective move that denies their opponents all advantage. **21. Rb1** At once 21. Qa2 was necessary, but such a move illustrates how toothless White's position is. **21. ... Bc6** Very strong is the tactical intermezzo 21. ... Nc5! 22. Qa2 (22. Q×b5 Rab8 wins the queen) 22. ... Ne6. Normally in this opening Black is a pawn down and saddled with an offside knight. As both deficiencies are cured in this case, Black can count on an important edge. White is even forced to play 23. Bf1. **22. Ne3?!** The exchange of queens is much welcomed by Black. 22. Ba3 first is preferable. **22. ... Q×b3 23. R×b3 f4 24. Bc4† Kh8 25. Nd5 Bd6 26. Ba3 Rfd8 27. Ne7 B×e7** 27. ... B×g2 28. Rg1 Na5 is extremely critical for White. **28. B×e7 Rd7 29. Ba3 B×g2** 29. ... Na5! 30. Rb4 N×c4 31. R×c4 B×g2 is an improvement for the position of White's king is highly insecure. **30. Rg1 Bf3** 30. ... Na5 is still very good. **31. Be6 Rc7 32. c4 Bc6 33. d3** *(see diagram)*

*After 33. d3*

**33. ... Re8** White succeeded in keeping his bishop pair which provides compensation for Black's active pieces. Now a new intriguing phase takes off, in which the push of his e-pawn is Black's key to consolidate his initiative. In this case, 33. ... Rd8 is the best preparatory move. If then 34. Bf5 e4! 35. d×e4 Na5 36. Rc3 Ba4 **34. Bf5** 34. Rg6! equalizes, for if 34. ... e4?! 35. Bb2! **34. ... Bf3** Again 34. ... e4 is very combative. Exchanging at e4 is evidently out of the question, and other moves are also not agreeable. One recurrent motive in these lines—e.g., after 35. B×e4—is the activation of Black's knight by 35. ... Na5! **35. Kd2 Rd8 36. Kc3? Bc6?** It would have been better had the king stayed away from the front line (by 36. Kc2), for now 36. ... e4! 37. d×e4 (37. B×e4 B×e4 38. d×e4 Na5) 37. ... Be2 offers excellent winning chances, as the cover of the king, his c-pawn, will fall. Had the king gone to c2 then 38. Rc3 would prevent the worst. **37. Rg6** "Here Mr. Wayte took Mr. Gunsberg's place; but Black's game is scarcely saveable"—MacDonnell. **37. ... Na5** From here on Black's position starts to lose it dynamics. Once more 37. ... e4 is good, but in this case only for equality. The line is very interesting and exemplary for this position: 38. d×e4 Ba4 39. Rb1 Be8 40. Ra6 Bf7 41. Be6 B×e6 42. R×e6 Rdc8 43. Kd3 Na5 44. c5 Nb7. **38. Rb1 Rf7** A very passive move, but White is ready to get a solid grip on the position in any case; e.g., 38. ... e4? 39. Bd6 Rf7 40. d×e4 and wins or 38. ... Bd7 (best) 39. Rd6 Nc6 40. Be4. **39. Rd6 Ra8 40. Be6** A sloppy move that offers their opponents a last chance to save their skin. 40. Bg6! brings the bishop to a much more useful post. If then 40. ... Rf6 41. R×f6 g×f6 42. Be7 Kg7 43. Rg1. **40. ... Rb7?** The allies miss their chance to stay in the game with 40. ... Rc7. Everything is then defended and 41. ... e4 is once more a menace. 41. Bf5 is the only logical move. Then 41. ... Bf3 42. Rb5 Nc6 43. Bd7 Nd8 44. Be8 Nf7 45. B×f7

R×f7 46. R×e5 is favorable for White, but no walk in the park yet. **41. R×b7 B×b7 42. Rd7 Bf3 43. Bd6 Nc6 44. Bd5** The fall of the pawn at e5 rapidly decides the game. **44. ... B×d5 45. c×d5 Nd4 46. B×e5 Nf3 47. B×f4** and White wins—*Illustrated Sporting and Dramatic News* (MacDonnell), 2 February 1895.

---

## ANOTHER TRIP TO HASTINGS

In March Bird returned to Hastings for a stay that must have lasted at least two weeks. Several of his consultation games were published. On each occasion Blackburne opposed Bird in the other team. Details about Bird's visit did not receive coverage in the press.

**(1201) Bird & Colborne–**
**Blackburne & Chapman    1–0**
Consultation game
Hastings, March 1895
*A02*

**1. f4 e5 2. f×e5 d6 3. e×d6 B×d6 4. g3 f5 5. d4 Nf6 6. Bg5 Nbd7 7. c3 h6 8. B×f6 N×f6 9. Qd3 0–0 10. Nd2 Re8** 10. ... f4 is interesting. **11. Nc4** Better first 11. Ngf3 Qe7 12. Bh3, and only then 13. Nc4, with occupation of e5 following. **11. ... b5** "A forcible move that yields a rapid development of the bishop at c8"—Abbott. **12. N×d6 c×d6** 12. ... Q×d6 must be preferred. Black now gets into a bind again. **13. Bg2** "The White allies evidently thought it imprudent to take the proffered pawn, we believe with great judgment"—Abbott. **13. ... Rb8 14. Nh3 d5** More dynamic was 14. ... Ng4, heading for e3. **15. 0–0 Rb6** It seems that White has some weak spots in his position, notably e2, e3 and e4, but Black has no concrete plan to make use of them. White's extra pawn and strong minor pieces yield them a secure advantage. **16. Nf2** 16. a3, to prevent any b5–b4, was more precise. **16. ... Rbe6 17. Rae1 b4 18. Kh1** Passive and useless. There is no reason to refrain from entering the forced line 18. c×b4 Ba6 19. b5 Re3 20. Q×f5 B×b5 21. Bf3 B×e2 22. B×e2 R×e2 23. R×e2 R×e2 24. Rc1 with a small advantage. **18. ... b×c3 19. b×c3** *(see diagram)*

*After 19. b×c3*

**19. ... Re3** 19. ... f4! grasps the initiative; e.g., 20. g×f4 (or 20. Bf3 Ba6 21. Qc2 f×g3 22. h×g3 Qe7) 20. ... Ba6 21. Qb1 B×e2. **20. Qc2 Ba6 21. Nd1** 21. Bf3 maintains the extra pawn, but Black stands at least equal. **21. ... R×e2 22. R×e2 R×e2 23. Q×f5 Qe7** 23. ... Qe8 is more precise. **24. Rg1** "Necessary, as 24. ... Re1 was threatened"—Abbott. The pawn capture, 24. B×d5† N×d5 25. Q×d5† is hardly advisable, as the opening of the long diagonal is likely to be lethal for him. **24. … Bb7** Had they played 23. … Qe8, 24. … Bc8! would have been possible. After 25. Qf4 R×a2, d5 is well covered. Instead 25. B×d5†? may be met by 25. … Kh8 26. Qf3 Bg4! 27. Qf4 R×h2†! If Black plays 24. … R×a2 in the current position, 25. B×d5 is slightly better for White. **25. Nf2 Qe3 26. Ng4 N×g4 27. Q×g4 Re1 28. Rf1** Better than 28. Bf1? Q×c3. **28. … Ba6 29. Qf5 R×f1† 30. B×f1 B×f1 31. Qc8† Kf7 32. Qf5† Ke7 33. Q×f1 Q×c3 34. Qe2† Kf7 35. Qh5† Kf6 36. Q×d5 Qe1† 37. Kg2 Qe2† 38. Kh3 Qf1†?!** 38. … g5! forces a draw. **39. Kg4 h5†?** After the precise 39. … Qa6!, Black's position is still defendable; if 40. Qf5† then Ke7 41. Qe4† Kd8 42. d5 g6. **40. Kh4!** and White wins—*Illustrated London News* (Abbott), 10 August 1895.

## (1202) Bird & Hickman–
## Blackburne & Chapman ½–½
Consultation game
Hastings, March 1895
*C31*

1. e4 e5 2. f4 d5 3. e×d5 e4 4. c4 c6 5. Nc3 Nf6 6. d3 Bb4 7. Qc2 c×d5 8. c×d5 0–0 9. d×e4 N×e4 10. Bd3 Nf6 11. Bd2 Re8† 12. Nge2 Na6 13. 0–0 Bc5† 14. Kh1 Nb4 15. Qb1 Ng4 16. B×h7† Kh8 17. Be1 Ne3 18. Rf3 Bg4 19. Rg3 f5 20. R×g4 f×g4 21. Qg6 Qf6 22. Rc1 Bb6 23. Ne4 R×e4 24. Qh5 Qh6 25. Q×h6 g×h6 26. B×e4 Nb×d5 27. Bg3 Re8 28. Bg6 Rf8 29. f5 N×f5 30. Be5† Kg8 31. Ng3 N×g3† 32. h×g3 Ne7 33. Be4 Rf2 34. Bf4 R×b2 35. a4 Nc6 36. Bd5† Kh7 37. Be4† Kg8 draw—*Illustrated London News*, 25 May 1895.

## (1203) Blackburne & Chapman–Bird & Cheshire 1–0
Consultation game
Hastings, March 1895
*C51*

1. e4 e5 2. Nf3 Nc6 3. Bc4 Bc5 4. b4 B×b4 5. c3 Bc5 6. d4 e×d4 7. c×d4 Bb6 8. Nc3 d6 9. Bg5 Nce7 10. Qb3 f6 11. Bd2 Bg4 12. Ne2 Kf8 13. h3 Bd7 14. e5 Ng6 15. Bb4 a5 16. Ba3 a4 17. Qb2 Ba5† 18. Kf1 Bc6 19. d5 Be8 20. Nfd4 Bf7 21. e×d6 c×d6 22. Q×b7 Rb8 23. Qa6 N8e7 24. Q×d6 Kg8 25. Qg3 Qc8 26. Rc1 Bd2 27. Ba6 Qd8 28. Rd1 Bb4 29. B×b4 R×b4 30. d6 Qb6 31. d×e7 Q×a6 32. Nc2 Black resigns—*Illustrated London News*, 27 April 1895.

## (1204) Bird & Cheshire–
## Blackburne & Chapman 0–1
Consultation game
Hastings, 14 March 1895
*A02*

1. f4 e5 2. f×e5 d6 3. e×d6 B×d6 4. g3 f5 5. d4 Nf6 6. Bg5 0–0 7. Bg2 Nc6 8. c3 h6 9. B×f6 Q×f6 10. Nd2 Bd7 11. Qb3† Kh8 12. 0–0–0 Qg5 13. Qd5 Rae8 14. Nh3 Qe3 15. Rhe1 g5 16. Qf3 Qe7 17. Nf2 Qf7 18. Nb3 a5 19. Kb1 f4 20. g×f4 g×f4 21. Nd3 Re3 22. Qf2 Bf5 23. Bf3 Qh7 24. Nbc1 a4 25. Qh4 Na5 26. Rg1 c5 27. Ka1 c×d4 28. c×d4 a3 29. b×a3 Qc7 30. Q×h6† Bh7 31. Rd2 B×a3 32. Rc2 Qd7 33. Rg5 Re6 34. Qh5 Q×d4† 35. Kb1

Nc4 36. Nb3 Rb6 37. Rg6 Rc8 38. R×c4 R×c4 39. Rg8† K×g8 40. Bd5† Kg7 41. Qf7† Kh6 White resigns—*The Field*, 1 June 1895.

## (1205) Bird & Hickman–
## Blackburne & Chapman 0–1
Consultation game
Hastings, 29 March 1895
*C58*

1. e4 e5 2. Nf3 Nc6 3. Bc4 Nf6 4. Ng5 d5 5. e×d5 Na5 6. Bb5† c6 7. d×c6 b×c6 8. Qf3 c×b5 9. Q×a8 Bc5 10. Qf3 0–0 11. d3 e4 12. N×e4 N×e4 13. d×e4 f5 14. e5 f4 15. Nc3 Bb7 16. Qg4 h5 17. Qe6† Kh7 18. 0–0 Qg5 19. Qh3 Nc4 20. Ne2 B×g2 21. Qg3 f×g3 22. B×g5 B×f1 23. R×f1 N×e5 24. Kg2 g×f2 25. Nf4 Rf5 26. h4 g6 27. Rd1 Be3 28. Ne6 Ng4 29. Rf1 Kg8 30. Kg3 Kf7 31. Nd8† Ke8 32. Ne6 Kd7 33. Nf4 B×f4† 34. B×f4 Rd5 35. Kf3 Ke6 36. Ke2 Rd4 37. Bg3 a5 38. c3 Ra4 39. a3 Re4† 40. Kf3 Re3† 41. Kf4 Re2 42. b4 a×b4 43. c×b4 Ra2 44. Kg5 R×a3 45. B×f2 Rf3 46. Re1† Kf7 White resigns—*British Chess Magazine*, August 1895, pp. 357–358.

## (1206) Bird & Dobell–Blackburne & Chapman
Consultation game
Hastings 1895

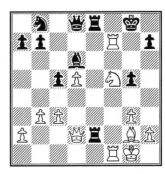

*White to move*

This position was given, without further ado, in one of Bird's books. White's most convincing continuation is **1. Qd3**—*Chess Novelties*, p. 293.

---

# PREPARING FOR HASTINGS

With the international congress of Hastings approaching, chess life at the Divan intensified considerably by the arrival of various masters who were eager to restore their former force by some practice. Bird had a first much-witnessed blitz session with Amos Burn on Saturday 1 June. A second duel had a high-profile public watching.

One day recently there was assembled at Simpson's Divan in the Strand a team of famous players such as we have not seen in that historic chess resort for years. The center of the group was formed by the veteran Bird, who was playing some lightning chess with Mr. A. Burn, who has returned from the United States as full of chess enthusiasm as ever. There was Lasker, looking on with an Olympian smile. Herr von Bardeleben stood on tip-toe, amazed at the reckless pace; Mr. van Vliet facetiously criticized a bold sacrifice of a piece, while Messrs. Müller and Loman having caught the infection, started an opposition of their own, and in the attempt to imitate Mr. Bird's speed and brilliant tactics, Mr. Müller captured one of his own pieces [*Otago Witness*, 12 September 1895; first published in the *Glasgow Weekly Citizen*].

# HASTINGS 1895

With the tournament of Manchester already five years in the past, the wish to organize another international event in England became more insistent. In the beginning of the year 1895 the amateurs of the Hastings and St. Leonards' Chess Club secured support from a few key figures and a nucleus fund of £250 was raised. As substantially more was needed to attract the attention of the principal chess masters an appeal for support was made towards the British chess community. The plea for financial help was met with general enthusiasm. With seven prizes, amounting to £500, and £150 foreseen for the winner, dates were fixed in August. Alongside the major tournament an amateur championship was held.

The committee originally aimed for 16 players but in the end no fewer than 38 candidates tried to secure a spot, of which 22 were allowed to enter the main tournament. Among them were literally all the chess greats of the time, which makes Hastings 1895 the most important tournament of the nineteenth century.

Above all, Emanuel Lasker's performance as the newly bred world champion was closely watched. His predecessor, Steinitz, took part, as did Tarrasch and Chigorin, two of the principal contenders. The strength of several young players, such as Dawid Janowski, Carl Schlechter, Teichmann, Walbrodt and Harry Nelson Pillsbury was more difficult to estimate. Finally there was a contingent of more experienced chess players. This group counted above all the British masters. First among equals was still Blackburne. Burn returned after an absence from the international scene of six years. Gunsberg, practically inactive for three years, and Mason, a shade of his former self, were also granted a place on account of their results during the previous decade. Finally, the nestor of the tournament was Bird. He was thought to be too weak for such a field but his popularity guaranteed him a spot amongst the best.

The pairings were made beforehand, but it was only just before each round that they were made public. The games were played from Monday until Saturday. Thursdays were preserved for unfinished games. A time limit of 30 moves in two hours was applied. All these rules were pretty grueling for the old and crusty Bird, but with his performance he earned more veneration than ever before.

Bird commenced the tournament fiercely with a fascinating game against Albin. A double-edged queen sacrifice eventually turned out well for him. The veteran continued with three solid draws. In the fifth round Bird, not unexpectedly, succumbed to Lasker.

Bird's next game, against Georg Marco, was noteworthy. After excellent middle-game play he obtained a devastating attack, but blundered it terribly. Marco attempted to reach the time control before starting to convert his advantage. He fell into a threefold repetition, and found the veteran attentive enough to unhesitatingly claim the draw. In the seventh round Bird beat Beniamino Vergani, the weakest player of the tournament.[41]

Bird subsequently beat Steinitz. This duel was fascinating and Bird handsomely exploited a few tactical mistakes from the strategically superior Steinitz. Bird consolidated his score with two decent draws against Schlechter and Chigorin. So after ten rounds, nearly halfway, Bird was in sixth place with 6 points. He was by far the best English representative. It was very remarkable that Bird, just as in London 1889 and Manchester 1890, adopted a style of play that did not avoid draws at all costs. He fared much better this way, but it was of course not unexpected to see the health-tormented old man fall back in the second half of the tournament.

In the eleventh round Bird lost to his old nemesis Mason. Bird continued with two draws, including a highly spectacular one against Burn, but then the final breakdown occurred: during the six following rounds he could score but one draw. A final win, in the penultimate round against Gunsberg, would doubtlessly have brought a great deal of satisfaction to Bird. His last game with Jacques Mieses ended in a draw after a tough fight.

Bird ended the tournament with a minus score of 9 points in 21 games. Only slightly ahead of him were a few other veterans of many wars, such as Gunsberg, Burn, Mason and Blackburne. The British chess elite was outclassed by the new generation, a feat that the press enjoyed pointing out. Only Bird gained good credits with his performance. On the monetary front, Bird left the arena with £4 20s.: a pound for each win and 10s. per draw against a prize winner.[42]

Chigorin and von Bardeleben set the pace during the first part of the tournament. Pillsbury and Lasker were their closest pursuers. Von Bardeleben crashed in the second half, a setback to which his famous loss against Steinitz contributed. After 17 rounds Pillsbury, Chigorin and Lasker each had 13½ points. Pillsbury was the first to lose another game, in the eighteenth round, but several missteps by both of the others allowed the American to gain first place with one round to go. With a final win, he consolidated this position and scored thus the greatest triumph of what would be a sadly short career.

---

41. During this game the Australian visitor R. Meller depicted Bird: "With Bird, the oldest of the competitors at Hastings, the physical question is evidently a serious one. Bent nearly double with rheumatism or lumbago, he was in great fear that he should be unable to play all his games. 'I've had to bully it,' I heard him say at breakfast time in the hotel, referring to his complaint, 'or I couldn't have got up this morning.' That he should have persevered to the end, and done so well as he did, speaks volumes for the pluck of this 'Grand Old Man'" *Maitland Weekly Mercury*, 30 May 1896. ¶ Another noteworthy description of Bird comes from the hand of the young strong Dutch chess player Norman Willem van Lennep, who had won the master title in the last German chess congress, held in Leipzig in 1894. His bid to enter the tournament of Hastings was denied, but he asked to serve as the first reserve. He wound up with no chance to play but in return wrote a most interesting booklet on the tournament. "Bird certainly has not a brilliant appearance. He moves around with effort, helped by a cane, and when he has finally taken his place behind the board his face adopts such a comically lamentable expression that one cannot help laughing. It seems that he dies a thousand deaths during each game. Thereby he chews alternately on his pipe and on his teeth, which constantly threaten to fall out of his mouth, and he wears clothes and a high hat that must have been familiar to his grandfather. Maybe this overawes his opponents, for they are likely to be made uneasy by the venerable size of the old gentleman and the huge velocity with which he makes his moves. Even Chigorin, who succeeded in winning eight games in the first nine rounds, relaxed, as if it was already the weekend, into a little trap that Bird had shrewdly set out for him, and, though already several pawns up, had to allow a perpetual. What is bred in the man will show in every act!" N.W. Van Lennep, *Hastings 1895*. Amsterdam: Andriessen, p. 17.

42. Bird was unable to beat a player from the top-3, which would have earned him £2.

Several participants and officials of the Hastings 1895 tournament. The photograph was taken on 8 August during a visit at Battle Abbey. Sitting: Carl A. Walbrodt, Giovanni B. Vergani, Adolf Albin, Jacques Mieses, Siegbert Tarrasch, John Watney, Wilhelm Steinitz, Henry E. Bird, Georg Marco and Mikhail Chigorin. Standing: Arthur H. Hall, Joseph H. Blackburne, Dawid Janowski, Richard Teichmann, Harry N. Pillsbury, Emmanuel Schiffers, Isidor Gunsberg, Carl Schlechter, Norman W. Van Lennep, Herbert E. Dobell and Thomas H. Cole.

During free moments various offhand and consultation games were contested between the participants. Two of these consultation games with Bird survived. Another, more famous game, saw Bird lose against Géza Maróczy, the winner of the amateur championship. This game was often presented as a demonstration of the defensive powers of the new generation. Actually a triumph of Bird's eccentric style was but a hair's breadth away, but then he blundered...

**(1207) Albin–Bird    0–1**
International tournament (round 1)
Hastings, 5 August 1895
*A04*

**1. Nf3 f5 2. b3 Nf6 3. Bb2 e6 4. e3 Be7** "Here 4. ... Bd6 can also be played. See move 11"—Schiffers. "Mr. Bird has been criticized for not at once playing 4. ... Bd6, as he does at move 11. We believe that he was right now and wrong then"—Wayte. **5. Nc3 b6 6. d4 Bb7 7. Bd3 0–0 8. 0–0 Qe8 9. Ne2 Nc6** 9. ... B×f3 10. g×f3 Qh5 11. Ng3 Qh4 favors of Black, but Bird is quite effective with his bishop. **10. c4 Nd8 11. Nf4 Bd6** "This move invites the aggressive advance 12. Ne5, when its capture with the bishop soon becomes compulsory"—Wayte. **12. Ne5 Nf7 13. Be2** 13. f3 halts Bird's attacking plans. **13. ... B×e5** "I think this move is not advantageous for Black, but that 13. ... c5 followed by 14. ... Bc7 would be better"—Schiffers. **14. d×e5 Ne4 15. f3** 15. Bh5 is a good party spoiler. For instance, 15. ... Qe7 (15. ... g6 16. B×g6 h×g6 17. N×g6 must even win. White's rook and easily pawns outmatch the opposing knights) 16. f3 Nc5 17. b4 Na6 18. B×f7† R×f7 19. a3 with a positional plus. **15. ... Nc5 16. b4 Na6 17. Qd2 Qe7 18. a3 c5 19. Rad1 Rfd8 20. b5 Nc7 21. Qc3** *(see diagram)*

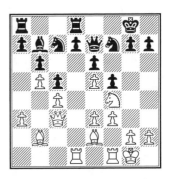

*After 21. Qc3*

**21. ... Nh8** 21. ... d6 22. e×d6 N×d6, suggested by Schiffers, looks a bit too dangerous. The text move isn't good either since White is given a free hand for a queenside attack. Best is 21. ... Ne8 22. a4 a6 23. Rd3 a×b5 24. a×b5 d6 25. e×d6 R×d6 26. R×d6 Q×d6. Black has gotten rid of the weak d-pawn while the dangerous long diagonal is completely under control. **22. Kh1** "In this and the following move White prepares for g4, but afterwards changes his mind. The position of the White king on h1 with Black's bishop at b7 is fraught with danger. It would have been better at once to double the rooks on the d-file."—Schiffers. Doubling the rooks is a bit slow, and lessens the possibility of battling for the a-file. Instead, direct action is likely to bring him some advantage: 22. a4!, for if 22. ... a6? 23. Rd6! **22. ... Ng6** 22. ... Ne8, to reply 23. a4 with 23. ... a6 must still be played. On his part, White could gain a considerable advantage were he to exchange the knight and push the a-pawn. The same idea remains true for the next few moves. Albin choses another path that leads to a less pressing advantage. **23. Rg1 Rf8 24. Rd2 Rf7 25. Rgd1 Rd8 26. Rd6 N×f4 27. e×f4 Ne8 28. R6d2 g6?!** The same idea, 28. ... a6, remains Black's best. Albin, now master of the d-file, correctly assumes the

**International chess tournament, Hastings, 5 August–2 September 1895**

***Site:*** Brassey Institute
***Playing hours:*** 1 p.m.–5 and 7 p.m.–10
***Prizes:*** 1st £150, 2nd £115, 3rd £85, 4th £60, 5th £40, 6th £30, 7th £20 consolation prizes for the non–prize winners
***Time limit:*** 30 moves in 2 hours, 15 moves per hour

| | | **1** | **2** | **3** | **4** | **5** | **6** | **7** | **8** | **9** | **10** | **11** | **12** | **13** | **14** | **15** | **16** | **17** | **18** | **19** | **20** | **21** | **22** | |
|---|---|---|---|---|---|---|---|---|---|---|---|---|---|---|---|---|---|---|---|---|---|---|---|---|
| 1 | H.N. Pillsbury | | 0 | 0 | 1 | 1 | 1 | + | 1 | 0 | ½ | ½ | 1 | 1 | 1 | 1 | 1 | 1 | ½ | 1 | 1 | 1 | 1 | 16½ |
| 2 | M.I. Chigorin | 1 | | 1 | 1 | 0 | 0 | 1 | 1 | 1 | 1 | ½ | 1 | 0 | 1 | ½ | 1 | ½ | 1 | 1 | ½ | 1 | 1 | 16 |
| 3 | E. Lasker | 1 | 0 | | 0 | 1 | 1 | 0 | 1 | 1 | 0 | 1 | 1 | 1 | ½ | 1 | 1 | ½ | 1 | 1 | ½ | 1 | 1 | 15½ |
| 4 | S. Tarrasch | 0 | 0 | 1 | | 1 | 1 | ½ | 0 | ½ | 1 | 1 | 1 | 1 | 0 | 1 | ½ | 1 | 1 | 0 | ½ | 1 | 1 | 14 |
| 5 | W. Steinitz | 0 | 1 | 0 | 0 | | 1 | 1 | ½ | ½ | 1 | 1 | ½ | 0 | 1 | 0 | 1 | 1 | 1 | 0 | ½ | 1 | 1 | 13 |
| 6 | E.S. Schiffers | 0 | 1 | 0 | 0 | 0 | | ½ | ½ | 0 | 1 | 1 | ½ | 1 | ½ | 1 | 1 | 0 | ½ | 1 | ½ | 1 | 1 | 12 |
| 7 | C. von Bardeleben | – | 0 | 1 | ½ | 0 | ½ | | ½ | ½ | 0 | 0 | 1 | ½ | 1 | ½ | 1 | ½ | 1 | 1 | 1 | 0 | 1 | 11½ |
| 8 | R. Teichmann | 0 | 0 | 0 | 1 | ½ | ½ | ½ | | ½ | 0 | 0 | 1 | ½ | 1 | 1 | 0 | ½ | 1 | ½ | 1 | 1 | 1 | 11½ |
| 9 | C. Schlechter | 1 | 0 | 0 | ½ | ½ | 1 | ½ | ½ | | ½ | ½ | 1 | 0 | 1 | ½ | ½ | ½ | ½ | ½ | ½ | 1 | 0 | 11 |
| 10 | J.H. Blackburne | ½ | 0 | 1 | 0 | 0 | 0 | 1 | 1 | ½ | | 0 | 1 | 1 | 0 | ½ | 0 | 1 | 0 | 1 | 0 | 1 | 1 | 10½ |
| 11 | C.A. Walbrodt | ½ | ½ | 0 | 0 | 0 | 0 | 1 | 1 | ½ | 1 | | 0 | 0 | ½ | ½ | ½ | 0 | ½ | ½ | 1 | 1 | 1 | 10 |
| 12 | A. Burn | 0 | 0 | 0 | 0 | ½ | ½ | 0 | 0 | 0 | 0 | 1 | | 1 | 0 | ½ | 0 | 1 | 1 | 1 | 1 | 1 | 1 | 9½ |
| 13 | D. Janowski | 0 | 1 | 0 | 0 | 1 | 0 | ½ | ½ | 1 | 0 | 1 | 0 | | ½ | ½ | 0 | 0 | 1 | ½ | 1 | 0 | 1 | 9½ |
| 14 | J. Mason | 0 | 0 | ½ | 1 | 0 | ½ | 0 | 0 | 0 | 1 | ½ | 1 | ½ | | 1 | 0 | ½ | 0 | 1 | 1 | 0 | 1 | 9½ |
| 15 | H.E. Bird | 0 | ½ | 0 | 0 | 1 | 0 | ½ | 0 | ½ | ½ | ½ | ½ | ½ | 0 | | 1 | 1 | ½ | 0 | ½ | ½ | 1 | 9 |
| 16 | I. Gunsberg | 0 | 0 | 0 | ½ | 0 | 0 | 0 | 1 | ½ | 1 | ½ | 1 | 1 | 1 | 0 | | 1 | ½ | 0 | 1 | 0 | 0 | 9 |
| 17 | A. Albin | 0 | ½ | ½ | 0 | 0 | 1 | ½ | ½ | ½ | 0 | 1 | 0 | 1 | ½ | 0 | 0 | | 0 | 0 | 1 | 1 | ½ | 8½ |
| 18 | G. Marco | ½ | 0 | 0 | 0 | 0 | ½ | 0 | 0 | ½ | 1 | ½ | 0 | 0 | 1 | ½ | ½ | 1 | | 1 | 1 | 0 | ½ | 8½ |
| 19 | W.H.K. Pollock | 0 | 0 | 0 | 1 | 1 | 0 | 0 | ½ | ½ | 0 | ½ | 0 | ½ | 0 | 1 | 1 | 1 | 0 | | 0 | 0 | 1 | 8 |
| 20 | J. Mieses | 0 | ½ | ½ | ½ | ½ | ½ | 0 | 0 | ½ | 1 | 0 | 0 | 0 | 0 | ½ | 0 | 0 | 0 | 1 | | 1 | 1 | 7½ |
| 21 | S. Tinsley | 0 | 0 | 0 | 0 | 0 | 0 | 1 | 0 | 0 | 0 | 0 | 0 | 1 | 1 | ½ | 1 | 0 | 1 | 1 | 0 | | 1 | 7½ |
| 22 | G.B. Vergani | 0 | 0 | 0 | 0 | 0 | 0 | 0 | 0 | 1 | 0 | 0 | 0 | 0 | 0 | 0 | 1 | ½ | ½ | 0 | 0 | 0 | | 3 |

initiative on the queenside. **29. a4 Ng7 30. a5 Qh4?** A desperate attempt, but of course Bird wouldn't consider a move like 30. ... Rb8. **31. g3** Missing a forced win: 31. a×b6 a×b6 32. Rd6 Nh5 33. Bf1 N×f4 34. R×b6 Ba8 35. Ra6 and White can go after the c-pawn. Bird's counterattack is much too slow to be successful. **31. ... Qh6** 31. ... Qe7 32. Rd6 Rb8 takes up a passive position without much perspective. **32. a×b6 a×b6 33. Rd6 g5 34. R×b6** Good enough, but 34. f×g5 Q×g5 35. Bc1, as suggested by Schiffers, avoids any complications. **34. ... g×f4 35. Bc1** "35. R×b7 will not do on account of 35. ... f×g3"—Schiffers. **35. ... Nh5 36. Rg1 Rb8 37. Rd6?** 37. Qa3! completes the assault. If 37. ... Rg7 38. R×b7. **37. ... Rg7! 38. Rg2?** "38. Qe1 was better. Black could now force the win by 38. ... N×g3† 39. R×g3 (if 39. Kg1 N×e2†) 39. ... R×g3 40. B×f4 R×f3 41. B×f3 (if 41. B×h6 Rf1 mate) 41. ... Q×f4 42. Kg2 Kh8 and wins"—Schiffers. In case of 38. Qe1, 38. ... Kh8 39. B×f4 N×f4 40. g×f4 Rbg8 41. R×g7 R×g7 42. Rb6 d5! is rather unclear, but this is all he could hope for by now. Also possible is 38. B×f4, heading for the endgame. **38. ... Kh8? 39. Qe1 Rbg8 40. Kg1 f×g3?** A very challenging and brilliant queen sacrifice from Bird. In hindsight it can be said that 40. ... Qg6, keeping White under severe pressure, is superior. After 41. Rb6 f×g3 42. h4 Ba8 43. Ra6 f4 the direct confrontation on the kingside has passed. Each side has its own strengths and weaknesses, but an overall evaluation favors Black. **41. B×h6 g×h2† 42. K×h2 R×g2† 43. Kh3** "If 43. Kh1 R×e2"—Schiffers. **43. ... R2g6 44. Be3?!** So far so good, but here 44. Qc1! (Wayte) was very strong. Both bishop and queen retain a maximal liberty of movement. After, for example, 44. ... Rg3† 45. Kh4 Rg2 46. Qf1 Rh2† 47. Qh3 R×h3† 48. K×h3, White, despite being a pawn down, must win, with his superior pieces and dangerous b-pawn. Another move consolidating an important edge is 44. Bc1! **44. ... f4** *(see diagram)*

*After 44. ... f4*

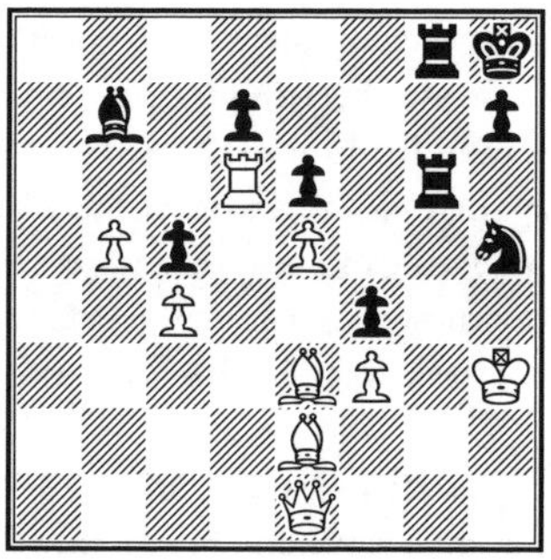

**45. Bf2?** This move cuts off his queen from the defense of the king, which turns out to be the decisive mistake. Correct is 45. Bd2, when only a narrow path allows Black to keep the balance: 45. ... Rg3† 46. Q×g3 R×g3† 47. Kh2 B×f3! (the crucial move. If 47. ... Rg7 48. Rb6 Ba8 49. Rb8† Rg8 50. R×g8† K×g8 51. Kg2 with the much better endgame. The idea is to play 52. Bd3 and 53. Be4 or 53. B×h7) 48. B×f3 R×f3 49. R×d7 Rb3 and White cannot make much progress. **45. ... Rh6! 46. Bh4 Ng3** White cannot properly meet the threat 47. ... Nf5. **47. R×d7 N×e2 48. Rd8** "If 48. R×b7 Ng1† wins"—Schiffers. **48. ... R×d8 49. Kg2 Rg8† 50. Kf2 R×h4 51. K×e2 Rh3 52. Qc3** Wayte believed Albin played 52. Qa5. **52. ... B×f3†** White resigns—*Tournament Book* (Schiffers), pp. 22–24; *British Chess Magazine* (Wayte), September 1895, pp. 388–389.

## (1208) Bird–Walbrodt ½–½

International tournament (round 2)
Hastings, 6 August 1895
*A03*

1. f4 d5 2. Nf3 e6 3. e3 c5 4. b3 Nc6 5. Bb2 Nf6 6. Nc3 Be7 7. Ne2 Nh5 8. Ng3 Nf6 9. a3 Qb6 10. Rb1 Bd7 11. Bd3 h6 12. 0–0 g6 13. Ne5 Rg8 14. Qf3 Qc7 15. Rf2 Nd8 16. c4 Bc6 17. c×d5 N×d5 18. Qe2 Bd6 19. Ne4 f5 20. N×d6† Q×d6 21. Rc1 Ne7 22. Nc4 Qd7 23. e4 Nf7 24. Na5 f×e4 25. B×e4 B×e4 26. Q×e4 Nd6 27. Qc2 b6 28. Nc4 N×c4 29. Q×c4 Qd5 30. Re1 Q×c4 31. b×c4 Kd7 32. Rfe2 Nc6 33. R×e6 Raf8 34. g3 Rf7 35. Bc3 Re7 36. R×e7† N×e7 37. Kg2 draw—*Tournament Book*, pp. 36–38.

## (1209) von Bardeleben–Bird   ½–½
International tournament (round 3)
Hastings, 7 August 1895
*C00*

1. e4 e6 2. d4 d5 3. Be3 Nf6 4. e5 Nfd7 5. Nf3 c5 6. c3 Nc6 7. Nbd2 Qb6 8. Rb1 c×d4 9. c×d4 Be7 10. Be2 0–0 11. 0–0 f5 12. e×f6 *e.p.* N×f6 13. h3 Bd7 14. Nb3 Nd8 15. Nc1 Bd6 16. Ne5 Be8 17. Ncd3 Ne4 18. Bh5 Bb5 19. Re1 Qc7 20. Rc1 Qe7 21. Bf3 Ng5 22. Bg4 B×d3 23. Q×d3 Ne4 24. Bf3 Ng5 25. B×g5 Q×g5 26. Rc2 draw—*Tournament Book*, p. 55.

## (1210) Bird–Blackburne   ½–½
International tournament (round 4)
Hastings, 9 August 1895
*A02*

1. f4 e5 2. f×e5 d6 3. e×d6 B×d6 4. g3 h5 5. Bg2 Nc6 6. Nc3 h4 7. Ne4 h×g3 8. h3 Nf6 9. N×d6† Q×d6 10. d3 Be6 11. c3 0–0–0 12. Qa4 Nd5 13. Bd2 g5 14. B×g5 N×c3 15. Qf4 Q×f4 16. B×f4 Nd5 17. B×g3 Rdg8 18. Kf2 Rh6 19. B×d5 B×d5 20. Nf3 Nb4 21. Be5 Rh5 22. d4 Nd3† 23. Ke3 N×b2 24. Rag1 R×g1 25. R×g1 R×h3 26. Kf4 Nd3† 27. Kf5 B×f3 28. e×d3 Bd5 29. Kf6 Kd7 30. Rc1 Rh6† 31. Kg7 Rg6† 32. Kh7 Rc6 33. Rb1 Rc2 34. Rb5 Kc6 35. Ra5 a6 36. a3 Bb3 37. Bf4 Kd7 38. Kg7 Rg2† 39. Kf6 Be6 40. d5 Rg6† 41. Ke5 Bh3 42. Rc5 Bg2 43. Kd4 c6 44. d6 Bd5 45. Rc2 Rg4 46. Rf2 b5 47. Kc5 a5 48. d4 Rg8 49. Re2 Re8 50. Rh2 b4 51. a4 Rg8 52. Kb6 Rg4 53. Bd2 R×d4 54. K×a5 c5 55. Be3 Rc4 56. Kb6 K×d6 57. a5 Be4 58. a6 Rc3 59. Rd2† Rd3 60. B×c5† Ke5 61. Re2 Rd8 62. a7 b3 63. Kb5 Kf5 64. Kb4 Bc2 65. Ka3 Ra8 66. Re7 Kg6 67. Rb7 Be4 68. R×b3 f5 69. Kb4 Kf7 70. Kc3 Ke6 71. Rb8 Ke5 draw—*Tournament Book*, pp. 64–65.

## (1211) Bird–Lasker   0–1
International tournament (round 5)
Hastings, 10 August 1895
*A02*

1. f4 e5 2. f×e5 d6 3. e×d6 B×d6 4. g3 f5 5. d3 Nf6 6. c3 Nc6 7. Bg2 Ne5 8. Nd2 Qe7 9. Nf1 Bd7 10. Bf4 0–0 11. B×e5 B×e5 12. Qc2 Kh8 13. Bf3 Rab8 14. Qd2 Rfe8 15. h3 Qd6 16. Kf2 c5 17. e3 Bb5 18. Rd1 Rbd8 19. c4 Bc6 20. Qe2 b5 21. b3 b×c4 22. b×c4 Ba4 23. Rb1 Rb8 24. Nd2 B×g3† 25. Kg2 Bh4 26. Rh2 Bc2 27. R×b8 R×b8 28. d4 c×d4 29. e×d4 Re8 30. Qf1 Re1 31. c5 Q×d4 32. Q×e1 B×e1 33. Nb3 B×b3 34. a×b3 Q×c5 White resigns—*Tournament Book*, pp. 77–78.

## (1212) Marco–Bird   ½–½
International tournament (round 6)
Hastings, 12 August 1895
*C61*

1. e4 e5 2. Nf3 Nc6 3. Bb5 Nd4 4. N×d4 e×d4 5. Bc4 h5 "Somewhat eccentric, and regardless of the established principles of development; but Mr. Bird likes to go his own way"—Teichmann. 6. d3 Bc5 7. 0–0 d6 8. f4 c6 9. f5 An interesting idea to restrict the activity of his opponent's bishop. 9. ... d5 The correct reply. Bird obtains a decent position. 10. e×d5 c×d5 11. Bb3 f6 12. Qf3 Ne7 13. h3 a5 "Very well played. The rook is thus brought into play without loss of time"—Teichmann. 13. ... B×f5 14. Re1 is only chanceful for White. 14. a4 Kf8 15. g4 h×g4 16. h×g4 Ra6 17. Bf4?! *(see diagram)* This move, for one moment, neglects the defense of the kingside pawns and Bird doesn't hesitate to take profit from it. 17. Bd2 or 17. Rf2 is completely equal.

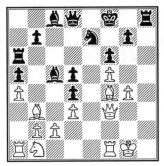

*After 17. Bf4*

17. ... g6! "This fine move initiates a powerful attack on the exposed White's king position, whilst the Black king will be perfectly safe at g7"—Teichmann. 18. f×g6 Kg7?! The immediate 18. ... Rh4! forces White to enter a rather tactical line: 19. g5 (there are other moves, but the result doesn't vary) 19. ... N×g6 20. Bd2 Qc7. White is suffering to deal with a strong attack. 19. Nd2? Bird gets a second chance and now he strikes. Instead 19. g5 N×g6 20. Q×d5 Q×d5 21. B×d5 N×f4 22. R×f4 f5 23. Nd2 restores equality. 19. ... Rh4! 20. g5 Rg4† Black's attack is even stronger now than before. 21. Kh1 "If 21. Kf2 N×g6 22. Bg3 f×g5 winning in a few moves"—Teichmann. 21. ... Qh8†! All of Bird's pieces aim directly at White's king, which resides rather helpless on the h-file. On the next move Bird eliminates a very dangerous pawn of his opponent, giving relative safety to his king. 22. Bh2 R×g5 23. Rf2 Bg4 24. Qf4 Rf5 25. Qg3 Bd6 26. Qg1 R×f2 26. ... Rh5 wins quickly. There is nothing to be done against the approach of the knight (27. ... Nf5 and 28. ... Ng3). 27. Q×f2 f5?? "So far Black has played very well, but with this curious oversight he throws away what should have been an easily won game. The simplest way would have been to exchange queens by 27. ... Q×h2†, leaving him with a strong passed pawn ahead for the endgame"—Teichmann. A dramatic blunder from Bird. He just overlooks that the pawn at d4 is en prise. Teichmann's suggestion is not bad, as it promises an endgame edge, but stronger is 27. ... Qh5! 28. Kg1 N×g6 29. B×d6 R×d6 30. Qg3 Qg5 31. Rf1 Qe3†. White has to exchange queens after which Black's advantage is decisive. 28. Q×d4† Kg8 29. B×d5† N×d5 30. Q×d5† Kg7 31. Qd4† Kg8 32. Qc4† Kg7 33. Qc3† Kg8 34. Qc4† Kg7 35. Qc3† Kg8 36. Qb3† Kg7 37. Qc3† draw. "The position being

very difficult, Herr Marco tried to gain time by these checks; but he overlooked that with this move the same position occurred for the third time, which, according to the rules in forces, permitted his opponent to claim a draw. White had a won game. It seems however, difficult to force the game by the exchange of queens, although White would be a pawn ahead in the endgame"—Teichmann. Teichmann proceeds by giving a long winning line, that can however be reinforced at a few instances. To cut a long story short, after 37. Qf7† Kh6 38. B×d6 R×d6, 39. Qh7†! (instead of Teichmann's 39. Kg2) 39. ... Q×h7 40. g×h7 K×h7 41. Re1, White is close to winning—*Tournament Book* (Teichmann), pp. 102–103.

## (1213) Bird–Vergani　1–0
International tournament (round 7)
Hastings, 13 August 1895
A03

　　1. f4 e6 2. Nf3 Nc6 3. e3 d5 4. Bb5 Bd6 5. b3 Nge7 6. Bb2 f6 7. 0-0 0-0 8. Nc3 a6 9. Be2 Bc5 10. d4 Ba7 11. Qe1 Nf5 12. Nd1 Nce7 13. Bd3 Nd6 14. Nf2 f5 15. c4 Ne4 16. Nh3 c6 17. Ne5 Rf6 18. Rd1 Ng6 19. B×e4 d×e4 20. Kh1 Ne7 21. Qg3 Qe8 22. Ng5 Bb8 23. Rd2 B×e5 24. d×e5 Rf8 25. Rd6 Qg6 26. Rfd1 h6 27. N×e6 B×e6 28. Q×g6 N×g6 29. R×e6 Kf7 30. Red6 Rfe8 31. Rd7† Re7 32. Ba3 Rae8 33. B×e7 R×e7 34. R×e7† K×e7 35. Kg1 Nf8 36. Kf2 Ne6 37. b4 g5 38. g3 g4 39. Rd6 h5 40. b5 a×b5 41. c×b5 c×b5 42. Rb6 Black resigns—*Tournament Book*, p. 110.

## (1214) Steinitz–Bird　0–1
International tournament (round 8)
Hastings, 14 August 1895
D31

　　1. d4 d5 2. c4 e6 3. Nc3 c6 "This defense of the Queen's Gambit is not worse than the usual one, but gives White for a long time the freer game"—Tarrasch. 4. e3 "The c-pawn must now be protected at once. 4. e4 would be stronger"—Tarrasch. 4. ... Nd7 5. Nf3 Bd6 6. e4 "By this move White gets the freer game. To prevent the advance of this move Black might play 4. ... f5 as I played in this tournament against Gunsberg and Burn"—Tarrasch. 6. ... d×e4 7. N×e4 Bb4† "The more natural move is 7. ... Bc7"—Tarrasch. 8. Nc3 "I should have played 8. Bd2, for Black could here (or in the following move) have doubled White's pawns in a very disagreeable manner by exchanging the bishop for knight, and have prevented an advance by c5 (besides playing eventually Qa5). Later on, Black after all does exchange, but under far less favorable circumstances"—Tarrasch. 8. ... Ndf6 9. Bd3 Qa5 "This move is not good now, for Black is forced to exchange his bishop for the knight in a few moves, and to retreat the queen also"—Tarrasch. 10. Bd2 Ne7 11. 0-0 0-0 12. a3 B×c3 13. B×c3 Qc7 "Now White has the better position"—Tarrasch. 14. Ne5 Rd8 15. Qe2 b6 16. b4 Bb7 17. f4 "With this quite simple move White gives up his advantage, for the knight at f6 threatens to establish itself on e4, and Black makes admirable use of his opponent's mistake"—Tarrasch. 17. ... Nf5 18. Qf2 "18. B×f5 is disadvantageous for White on account of 18. ... e×f5 and 19. ... Ne4"—Tarrasch. 18. ... c5! "Exceedingly well played. With this fine pawn sacrifice Black not only frees his game but ob-

tains the better one. White ought not to have accepted the gift, but should have played 19. d5"—Tarrasch. A very ingenious sacrifice of Bird, that is however excellently met by the former world champion. Less creative would have been 18. ... Nd7, hoping to lighten up the pressure with some exchanges. 19. d×c5 b×c5 20. Q×c5 "Also after 20. b×c5 Be4, or if 20. b5 Be4 or even 20. ... Nd4, and Black's position is a very good one"—Tarrasch. 20. ... Q×c5† 21. b×c5 Be4 22. Rfd1 Rdc8 23. c6 "In order to make a trebled pawn after 23. ... B×c6 by 24. N×c6 R×c6 25. B×f6 g×f6 26. B×f5"—Tarrasch. 23. ... B×d3 24. R×d3 (see diagram)

After 24. R×d3

　　24. ... Ne4 "Black's knights are now very menacing, besides which Black threatens to drive away the knight by 25. ... f6, and then to take, first, the pawn at c6, after which the second pawn becomes weakened. Steinitz decides therefore to sacrifice a piece, in order to utilize his pawns. This truly beautiful plan of the old master is only wrecked by the circumstance that Black gets in the endgame (thanks to the favorable position of his knights) an attack which could not be foreseen"—Tarrasch. Bird continues to play actively, but once more Steinitz's reaction is up the mark. Less risky is 24. ... Ne8 when the pawn will be gained back after White's knight has been chased away; e.g., 25. c5 f6 26. Nc4 Ne7 (better than 26. ... R×c6 27. Bb4 and the rook stands rather clumsy). Equality is within reach for Black. 25. Bb4 a5 If now 25. ... f6 26. Re1 f×e5 27. R×e4 R×c6 28. f×e5 with better prospects. The text move is however no improvement. 26. Rad1 26. Re1! is far more pressing. After 26. ... a×b4 27. a×b4, Black is forced to return the piece, for 27. ... Nf6? 28. b5 wins. After 27. ... Nc5 28. b×c5 f6 29. g4! Nh4 30. Nd7 R×c6 31. g5, Black's task is not easy at all. 26. ... a×b4 Bird doesn't duck the challenge, but Steinitz's judgment of the resulting position is excellent. Far less promising for White is 26. ... f6 27. Nd7 R×c6, when Black's pieces are more active and c4 has become a nice target. 27. c7 The best try. 27. ... g5 A radical solution to meet the threatened mate, but the text move does nothing to improve his position and leaves the initiative to White. Better is 27. ... Nfd6 28. a×b4 R×c7 29. R×d6 N×d6 30. R×d6 Rca7 and the chances are about equal. 28. Rd8† Kg7 29. a×b4 Ne3?! "The decisive move. With it Black locks up White's king completely and forces the exchange of a rook"—Tarrasch. 29. ... g×f4 is better, but White can still test him: 30. b5 Nfd6 31. Rd7 Kf6 32. Ng4† Kg5 33. Nf2 N×f2 34. R1×d6 Ne4 35. b6 N×d6 36. R×d6 R×c7 37. b×c7 Rc8 38. Rd7 Kf6. A draw would be the logical outcome. 30. R×c8 R×c8 31. Rd4 "After 31. Rd7, 31. ... Ra8 wins at once"—Tarrasch. 31. ... f5?! 31. ... Nc2 32. R×e4 N×b4 33. c5 Nd5 gives White much the better endgame, but the text move ought to lose. 32. Rd7† Fascinating is 32. b5, a suggestion made by Colin Crouch. His most beautiful

variation, 32. ... Ra8 33. R×e4! f×e4 34. f×g5 is winning for White. After 32. ... g×f4 33. Rd8 R×c7 34. b6 Rb7 35. Rd7† R×d7 36. N×d7 Nd6 37. c5 Nec4, however, a draw is likely. **32. ... Kh6 33. f×g5† K×g5** (*see diagram*)

*After 33. ... K×g5*

**34. h4†??** "If White plays 34. Nc6, in order to block the a-file with 35. Na5 after 34. ... Ra8, we get the following surprisingly beautiful termination: 34. ... Kf6 35. Na7 Rg8 36. g3 f4 37. c8Q R×c8 38. N×c8 f3 and wins"—Tarrasch. This magnificent line can be decisively reinforced with 37. Rd4! Ng5 38. R×f4†, which radically changes the outcome of the game. Black can resign. **34. ... Kf6 35. Nc6 Rg8** White resigns. "A true, genuine, master game, well played on both sides"—Tarrasch. *Tournament Book* (Tarrasch), pp. 130–131; *Hastings 1895 The Centenary Book* (Crouch), pp. 127–130.

## (1215) Schlechter–Bird    ½–½
International tournament (round 9)
Hastings, 16 August 1895
*C14*

**1. e4 e6 2. d4 d5 3. Nc3 Nf6 4. Bg5 Be7 5. e×d5 N×d5 6. B×e7 N×e7 7. Nf3 c6 8. Bd3 Nd7 9. 0–0 Nf6 10. Ne2 0–0 11. c3 Qb6 12. Qb3 Qc7 13. Ng3 Rd8 14. Rad1 Bd7 15. Rfe1 Be8 16. Qc2 Ned5 17. Ng5 g6 18. N5e4 N×e4 19. N×e4 b6 20. Qc1 Qf4 21. Q×f4 N×f4 22. Bf1 Kg7 23. g3 Nd5 24. Bg2 h6 25. Nd2 Rac8 26. Nc4 Rc7 27. Ne5 Rdc8 28. Nd3 Ne7 29. Be4 c5 30. d×c5 b×c5 31. Ne5 Bb5 32. Bg2 Rb8 33. Rd2 Rb6 34. Red1 Ra6 35. c4 Ba4 36. b3 f6 37. Nd3 Be8 38. Nf4 g5 39. Ne2 Bh5 40. Re1 B×e2 41. Rd×e2 Nf5 42. R×e6 R×a2 43. Bd5 Nd4 44. Re8 f5 45. Rg8† Kh7 46. Ree8 g4 47. Rh8† Kg6 48. Reg8† Rg7 49. Rd8 Ra6 50. h3 g×h3 51. Kh2 N×b3 52. K×h3 Nd4 53. Rc8 Nb3 54. f3 Rd6 55. g4 Kg5 56. Kg3 f×g4 57. f×g4 Rf6 58. Rce8 Nd2 59. Re5† Kg6 60. Rh5 Rh7 61. Rg8† Rg7** draw—*Tournament Book*, pp. 153–155.

## (1216) Bird–Chigorin    ½–½
International tournament (round 10)
Hastings, 17 August 1895
*C52*

**1. e4 e5 2. Nf3 Nc6 3. Bc4 Bc5 4. b4 B×b4 5. c3 Ba5 6. Qb3 Qf6 7. 0–0 Bb6 8. d4 e×d4 9. e5 Qg6 10. c×d4 N×d4 11. N×d4 B×d4 12. Nc3 Nh6 13. Be3 B×e5 14. B×h6 Q×h6 15. g3 0–0 16. Rfe1 d6 17. Rac1 c6 18. Qb1 b5 19. Bd3 Bb7 20. Nd1 a6 21. Ne3 c5 22. Nf5 Qf6 23. Be4 B×e4 24. Q×e4 Rae8 25. Kg2 Re6 26. Qg4 Rfe8 27. Rc2 Qg6 28. Qf3 h5 29. Rce2 c4 30. Nh4**

Qd3 31. Qc6 Bf6 32. R×e6 R×e6 33. R×e6 f×e6 34. Qe8† Kh7 35. Q×h5† Kg8 36. Qe8† draw—*Tournament Book*, p. 165.

## (1217) Mason–Bird    1–0
International tournament (round 11)
Hastings, 19 August 1895
*C14*

**1. e4 e6 2. d4 d5 3. Nc3 Nf6 4. Bg5 Be7 5. B×f6 B×f6 6. e5 Be7 7. Qg4 Kf8 8. Bd3 c5 9. d×c5 Nc6 10. Nf3 h5 11. Qg3 h4 12. Qg4 B×c5 13. 0–0 Bd7 14. a3 Kg8 15. Rae1 Be7 16. Ne2 Rh6 17. Ned4 Rc8 18. c3 Kh8 19. Re2 a6 20. Rfe1 Na5 21. Kh1 Nc6 22. N×c6 R×c6 23. Nd4 Rc8 24. f4 g6 25. Qh3 Bc5 26. Nf3 Kg7 27. Ng5 Be7 28. Nf3 Qb6 29. Qg4 Bb5 30. B×b5 Q×b5 31. Nd4 Qd7 32. f5 e×f5 33. e6 f×e6 34. N×f5† Kh7 35. N×h6 Rc4 36. Q×e6 Q×e6 37. R×e6 Bf8 38. Nf7** Black resigns—*Tournament Book*, pp. 180–182.

## (1218) Tinsley–Bird    ½–½
International tournament (round 12)
Hastings, 20 August 1895
*A84*

**1. d4 d5 2. c4 e6 3. Nf3 c6 4. e3 Nd7 5. Nc3 Bd6 6. Bd3 f5 7. c×d5 c×d5 8. Bd2 a6 9. Rc1 Nh6 10. Qb3 Qe7 11. g3 Nf7 12. h4 0–0 13. h5 b5 14. h6 g6 15. Nh4 Nf6 16. f4 Bd7 17. Be2 b4 18. Na4 Ne4 19. Nb6 N×g3 20. Rh3 N×e2 21. K×e2 Bb5† 22. Kf2 Rab8 23. Na4 N×h6 24. Rch1 Qe8 25. Nc5 Ng4† 26. Ke1 Bc4 27. Qc2 B×c5 28. b3 Bb5 29. Q×c5 Rc8 30. Q×b4 Nf6 31. a4 Bd3 32. Nf3 Be4 33. Kf2 Rc2 34. Rc1 R×c1 35. B×c1 B×f3 36. K×f3 Rf7 37. Rh2 Rc7 38. Ba3 Ne4 39. Qb6 Qc8 40. Qb4 Kg7 41. a5 h6 42. Qb6 g5 43. f×g5 N×g5† 44. Kg3 Rc6 45. Qa7† Qc7† 46. Q×c7† R×c7 47. Bc5 Ne4† 48. Kf3 N×c5 49. Rc2 Kf6 50. R×c5 Rb7 51. Rc6 R×b3 52. R×a6 Rb8 53. Kf4 Rb4 54. Kf3 h5 55. Ra8 Ra4 56. a6 h4 57. a7 Kg7 58. Re8 R×a7 59. R×e6 Ra1 60. Re5 Rg1 61. Kf2 Rg5 62. R×d5 h3 63. Rc5 Rg2† 64. Kf3 Rg1 65. Rc2 Rh1 66. Kg3 Kf6 67. Re2 Kg5 68. Rh2 R×h2 69. K×h2 f4 70. e×f4†** draw—*Tournament Book*, pp. 197–198.

## (1219) Burn–Bird    ½–½
International tournament (round 13)
Hastings, 21 August 1895
*A84*

**1. d4 f5 2. c4 e6 3. e3 Nf6 4. Nf3** "4. Bd3 and 5. Ne2, as between Steinitz and Albin, seems a better development"—Pillsbury. **4. ... b6 5. Be2 Bb7 6. 0–0 Nc6 7. Nc3 Bb4** "A favorite idea of Mr. Bird is to exchange the Black bishop for White's knight"—Pillsbury. **8. Bd2 0–0 9. Qc2 B×c3 10. B×c3 Ne4 11. Be1 d6 12. Rd1 Qf6 13. Nd2** "The main objection to this form of opening for Black has always been that at some point White by advancing d4–d5 could block the adverse bishop out, or else in some way take advantage of e6. This point seems to have now arrived, and 13. d5 would seem difficult to answer satisfactorily. If, for instance, 13. ... e×d5 14. c×d5 Ne7 15. Bc4 with the better game (White could not attempt to win two pieces for a rook, however, by 15. Q×c7 B×d5 16. R×d5 etc., on account of 16. ... Rfc8 17. Qb7 Rab8 and Black would win. If Black plays 13. ... Nd8 then 14. Nd4 and if 14. ... e×d5 (14. ... e5? 15. N×f5 Q×f5 16. Bd3 should win) 15. c×d5 B×d5 16. N×f5 Q×f5 17. R×d5 with the better game"—Pillsbury. Pillsbury overlooked the more modern concept of abandoning the e-pawn for a short while. After 13. d5 Ne7 14. d×e6 Nc5! the chances are equal. **13. ... Ne7 14. f3 Ng5** Here, and on the next moves, Bird's pieces end up somewhat clumsily placed on the kingside. With 14. ... N×d2 15. Q×d2 Rad8 chances would be completely equal. **15. Bf2 Qh6 16. Rfe1 Ng6 17. Bd3 c6 18. c5!** After careful opening play, Burn takes profit from Bird's last moves to initiate an initiative on the queenside. Bird cannot prevent some weaknesses being created. **18. ... b×c5 19. d×c5 d5 20. Nb3 Bc8 21. Nd4 Bd7 22. Re2?** A lost move, that could have serious consequences. After 22. Bg3! Nf7 23. b4 Black is condemned to passivity. **22. ... Qh5** There was no reason to delay 22. ... e5! **23. Qa4** (see diagram) The coming advance of the e-pawn had to be foreseen with 23. f4. If then 23. ... e5 24. f×g5 e×d4 25. e×d4 with equal play.

*After 23. Qa4*

**23. ... e5!** The e-pawn marches forward at last and this means trouble for Burn. **24. N×c6 e4** "Of course, if 24. ... Rac8 25. Ne7†. The attack which Black now obtains is very beautiful, and almost wins"—Pillsbury. **25. Bb5?!** Bird obtains a decisive attack after this bad move. Yet, the better 25. Ne7† is very good for him as well after 25. ... N×e7 26. Q×d7 e×f3. **25. ... e×f3 26. Red2 f×g2 27. Be2 Nh3† 28. K×g2 Qg5† 29. Bg3 f4 30. R×d5 Nh4†** 30. ... Qh6 brings the queen to safety after which the attack becomes at once decisive. It had to be foreseen that 31. Rh5 is refuted by 31. ... f×g3! **31. Kh1 B×c6?** 31. ... Nf5! forces White to head for 32. R×f5 R×f5 33. e×f4 R×f4! 34. Qb3† Kh8 35. R×d7 but then 35. ... Q×c5 rounds White off. **32. Q×c6 Qe7** 32. ... Nf2† retains some attack, but nothing decisive; e.g., 33. Kg1 Nf5 34. Qe6† Kh8 35. R×f5 R×f5 36. e×f4 Nh3† 37. Kh1 N×f4 38. B×f4 R×f4. White has good drawing chances. **33. Rd7 f×g3** "All very fine chess indeed, but there appears to be no more than a draw, a just ending to a most interesting game"—Pillsbury. **34. Bc4† Kh8 35. R×e7 Nf2† 36. Kg1 Nh3†** draw—*Tournament Book* (Pillsbury), pp. 201–202.

## (1220) Bird–Pillsbury    0–1
International tournament (round 14)
Hastings, 23 August 1895
C51

1. e4 e5 2. Nf3 Nc6 3. Bc4 Bc5 4. b4 B×b4 5. c3 Bd6 6. d4 Nf6 7. Ng5 0–0 8. N×f7 R×f7 9. B×f7† K×f7 10. f4 e×d4 11. e5 Be7 12. e×f6 B×f6 13. 0–0 d5 14. Nd2 d×c3 15. Nf3 Kg8 16. Rb1 b6

17. Be3 Bg4 18. Qa4 B×f3 19. R×f3 Qd6 20. Rd1 Rd8 21. Rh3 d4 22. Bc1 Qe6 23. Qc2 d3 24. Rh×d3 Nd4 25. f5 Qe4 26. Ba3 c5 27. Qf2 Ne2† 28. Kf1 R×d3 29. R×d3 Q×d3 30. Q×e2 Q×f5† 31. Kg1 Qb1† 32. Kf2 Bd4† 33. Kg3 Qg6† 34. Kh3 h5 35. g3 Qg4† 36. Q×g4 h×g4† 37. K×g4 Be3 38. Kf3 Bh6 39. Ke2 c2 White resigns—*Tournament Book*, pp. 229–230.

## (1221) Pollock–Bird    1–0
International tournament (round 15)
Hastings, 24 August 1895
C29

1. e4 e5 2. Nc3 Nf6 3. f4 d5 4. f×e5 N×e4 5. Nf3 Be7 6. d4 0–0 7. Bd3 f5 8. e×f6 *e.p.* Bb4 9. 0–0 B×c3 10. b×c3 R×f6 11. c4 Bg4 12. c×d5 B×f3 13. g×f3 Nc3 14. Qe1 N×d5 15. Kh1 Nf4 16. Bc4† Kh8 17. Qe4 Qd6 18. Q×b7 Nc6 19. Q×a8† Rf8 20. B×f4 Qf6 21. Be5 Black resigns—*Tournament Book*, p. 239.

## (1222) Bird–Janowski    ½–½
International tournament (round 16)
Hastings, 26 August 1895
A03

1. f4 d5 2. e3 Nf6 3. Nf3 c5 "The development of White's bishop in this opening is the most difficult point, and for that reason Black should not play 3. ... c5. Instead of that 3. ... e6 or any other move would be much better, and if White then plays 4. Bb5†, then 4. ... c6"—Albin. **4. Bb5† Nc6 5. B×c6† b×c6 6. Ne5 Qc7 7. 0–0** "White gets now the better position"—Albin. **7. ... e6 8. b3 Ba6** "Superfluous. 8. ... Bb7 at once is the proper move"—Albin. **9. d3 Rd8 10. Qf3 Bb7 11. Bb2 Be7 12. Qg3 0–0 13. Nd2 Ne8 14. Ndf3** Instead of heading for a kingside attack, Bird could gain a central superiority with 14. e4. **14. ... f6 15. Ng4 Nd6 16. Nh4** "16. f5 is stronger. If then 16. ... e×f5 17. Nh6† Kh8 18. N×f5 Rg8 19. Nfh4 g6 20. N×e7 and wins. Or if 16. ... e5 17. N×e5 f×e5 18. f6 B×f6 (if 18. ... g×f6 19. N×f6† and 20. B×e5!) 19. R×f6 R×f6 20. N×f6† Kh8 21. B×e5 and wins"—Albin. Albin overlooks 16. ... Bc8! (the move actually played in the game) with equal chances. **16. ... Bc8 17. Rae1 Nf5 18. N×f5 e×f5 19. Nf2** Janowski has beaten off Bird's attacking aspirations without any difficulty. With the bishop pair, the open e-file and White's weaknesses on the queenside, he has at least compensation for his doubled pawns. **19. ... Bd6** 19. ... Qa5 20. a3 c4 is an interesting way to open the position for his bishops. The same idea, c5–c4, remains a possibility on the next moves. **20. Qf3 Rde8 21. Nh1 Rf7 22. Ng3 Rfe7 23. Re2 Qd7 24. Rfe1 Qe6 25. Nh5 Qf7 26. Ng3** "White gets no more chances"—Albin. **26. ... Bc7** Janowski wants to activate his bishop by bringing it to b4, but the result of this maneuvre favors only Bird. **27. Ba3 Ba5 28. Rd1** 28. Rc1 and if 28. ... Bb4 29. B×b4 c×b4 30. c3 exploits the downside of his opponent's idea. **28. ... Bb4 29. Bb2 g6 30. c3** "I would prefer at once 30. h4, and if possible 31. h5"—Albin. **30. ... Ba5 31. h4 h5 32. Kf2 Bb6** Bird's last move was an inaccuracy. Janowski, however, overlooks the best reply against it: 32. ... c4!, when White is forced to make some serious positional concessions—e.g., 33. b×c4 d×c4 34. d4 Bb7 35. Kg1 c5. **33. c4 a5 34. a4** Bird manages to keep the position closed and a draw becomes likely. **34. ... Rb7 35. Bc3 Be6 36. Nf1 Kg7 37. Qg3 Qe7 38. Rb2 Bg8**

**39. Re1 Qe6 40. Rbe2 Bd8 41. Nd2 Rbe7 42. Kf1 Bc7 43. Qf2 Qd6 44. Qf3 d×c4** Janowski is the first to make an explicit effort to avoid a draw. **45. d×c4 Qd3 46. e4 Q×f3† 47. g×f3 B×f4 48. e×f5 R×e2 49. R×e2 R×e2?** A gross misjudgment, for after this exchange White will win the pawn at c5 in the long run. Abandoning control over the e-file in White's hands looks dangerous, but this is very relative: 49. ... Rb8 50. Re7† Kf8 51. Ra7 B×d2 52. B×d2 g×f5 with a clear draw. **50. K×e2 g×f5 51. B×a5 Be6 52. Nf1 Bc8 53. Bd2 Bd6 54. f4 Ba6 55. Be3 Bc7 56. Kf3 Bb6 57. Ng3 Kg6 58. Ne2 Kf7 59. Bd2** Bird experiences great trouble with winning the doomed c-pawn. Here 59. Nc1 Ke7 60. Nd3 Kd6 61. Bg1! Bc8 (Black is in zugzwang) 62. b4 is a quick road to victory. **59. ... Bc7 60. Ke3 Bb6 61. Kd3 Bc7 62. Be3 Bd6 63. Kc3 Bc7 64. B×c5 Ba5† 65. b4 Bc7 66. Be3 Bc8 67. a5 Ba6 68. Nc1 Ke6 69. Nd3 Bd6 70. Bc5 Bb8 71. Kd4 Kd7 72. Bb6 Bb7 73. Nc5† Kc8 74. Ke3 Bd6 75. N×b7 K×b7 76. b5 Bb4 77. Kf2 Be7 78. Bd4 c5 79. a6† Kb6 80. Bc3 Ka7 81. Bd2 Bd6 82. Ke2 Bc7 83. Kd3 Bd8 84. Kc2 Bc7 85. Kb3 Bd6 86. Ka4 Bc7 87. Be3 Bd6 88. Kb3** 88. Ka5 Bc7† 89. b6† B×b6† 90. Kb5 wins. **88. ... Kb6 89. Kc2 Ka7 90. Kd3 Be7 91. Ke2 Bd6 92. Kf3 Be7 93. Bd2 Bd8 94. Bc3 Kb8 95. Ke2 Ka7 96. Kd3 Kb8 97. Kc2 Ka7 98. Kb3 Bc7 99. Bd2 Bd6 100. Ka4 Bc7** draw—*Tournament Book* (Albin), pp. 248–250.

## (1223) Tarrasch–Bird 1–0
International tournament (round 17)
Hastings, 27 August 1895
B34

**1. e4 c5 2. Nf3 Nc6 3. Nc3 g6 4. d4 c×d4 5. N×d4 Bg7 6. Be3 h5 7. Be2 d6 8. Qd2 Bd7 9. 0–0 Nf6 10. h3 Qc8 11. f4 Kf8 12. Rad1 h4 13. N×c6 B×c6 14. e5 d×e5 15. f×e5 Nh5 16. Bg4 Qc7 17. Qf2 Be8 18. Nd5 Q×e5 19. N×e7 Bf6 20. Nd5 Bg7 21. Bc5† Kg8 22. Ne7† Kh7 23. Rd5 Ng3 24. R×e5 B×e5 25. Re1 B×b2 26. Bd4 B×d4 27. Q×d4 f5 28. N×g6** Black resigns—*Tournament Book*, pp. 267–268.

## (1224) Bird–Teichmann 0–1
International tournament (round 18)
Hastings, 28 August 1895
A03

**1. f4 d5 2. e3 g6 3. Nf3 Bg7 4. Nc3 Nf6 5. d4 b6 6. Ne5 Bb7 7. Be2 Nbd7 8. Bb5 0–0 9. 0–0 Nb8 10. Bd2 a6 11. Be2 c5 12. Be1 Nc6 13. Bh4 e6 14. Ng4 c×d4 15. e×d4 Nb8 16. Qe1 Nbd7 17. Bd3 Qc7 18. Ne5 Rac8 19. Rd1 b5 20. Ne2 Ne4 21. Ng3 f5 22. c3 N×e5 23. f×e5 Bh6 24. N×e4 d×e4 25. Bc2 Bd5 26. Bb3 g5 27. Bf2 Qf7 28. Qe2 Qg6 29. h3 Rc7 30. g3 f4 31. Qg4 e3 32. Be1 Rc4 33. Kh2 Qe4 34. Rg1 f3 35. Q×e4 B×e4 36. B×c4 b×c4 37. Bf2 e×f2 38. Rgf1 g4 39. R×f2 Be3 40. Re1 B×f2 41. R×e4 B×g3† 42. Kg1 Bh2† 43. Kf1 g3 44. Rg4† Kh8 45. b3 g2† 46. Kf2 Bg1†** White resigns—*Tournament Book*, p. 287.

## (1225) Bird–Schiffers 0–1
International tournament (round 19)
Hastings, 30 August 1895
C58

**1. e4 e5 2. Nf3 Nc6 3. Bc4 Nf6 4. Ng5 d5 5. e×d5 Na5 6. Bb5† c6 7. d×c6 b×c6 8. Qf3 Qc7 9. Be2 Bd6 10. Nc3 0–0 11. d3 Rb8 12. h4 Bg4 13. Qe3 B×e2 14. Q×e2 c5 15. Nge4 N×e4 16. N×e4 f5 17. Ng5 Qd7 18. b3 Nc6 19. c3 Rbe8 20. Be3 a5 21. Qf3 Ne7 22. Qh3 Nd5 23. Bd2 h6 24. Ne4 Nf4 25. B×f4 e×f4 26. 0–0 Be7 27. Nd2 Rd8 28. Nc4 Bf6 29. Rac1 Q×d3 30. Q×d3 R×d3 31. N×a5 B×c3 32. Nc4 Re8 33. Rc2 Bf6 34. h5 f3 35. Ne3 f×g2 36. K×g2 f4 37. Ng4 f3† 38. Kh3 Bd4 39. Rfc1 Re2 40. Kg3 Bb2 41. R×b2 R×b2 42. R×c5 Rbd2 43. Ra5 Rd5 44. Ra8† Kh7 45. Ra7 Rf5 46. b4 Rd4 47. Ne3 Rg5† 48. K×f3 R×b4 49. a3 Rh4 50. Ke2 Rh×h5 51. Rd7 Rh4 52. Rd3 Ra4 53. Rc3 Rg1 54. Nc4 h5 55. Nb2 Re4† 56. Kd2 Rge1 57. Kd3 Rf4 58. Rc2 Rf3† 59. Kd4 R×a3 60. Nc4 Rf3** White resigns—*Tournament Book*, pp. 300–302.

## (1226) Gunsberg–Bird 0–1
International tournament (round 20)
Hastings, 31 August 1895
C14

**1. e4 e6 2. d4 d5 3. Nc3 Nf6 4. Bg5 Be7 5. B×f6 B×f6 6. e5 Be7 7. Qg4 Kf8** "The foregoing line of play is the invention of J.W. Showalter, of New York. At this point Black has several moves; 7. ... g6 is weakening. 7. ... Bf8, while somewhat backward, is perfectly safe. Castling is also safe, but requires correct afterplay. In the match Showalter–Albin, New York City, occurred the following: 7. ... 0–0 8. Bd3 f5 9. Qh3 c5 10. d×c5 Nd7 11. f4 N×c5 12. 0–0–0 b5 etc. The text move also appears perfectly safe"—Pillsbury. **8. f4 c5 9. d×c5 Nc6 10. Nf3 Qa5 11. Nd2** "Losing a pawn. Castling is safe and correct"—Pillsbury. **11. ... Qb4 12. 0–0–0 N×e5 13. Qg3 Nc6 14. Nb3 Na5 15. Nd4 Q×c5 16. f5 Bf6 17. Ncb5?** Poor. There is enough compensation for the pawn after 17. f×e6 B×e6 18. N×e6 f×e6 19. Re1! If now 19. ... B×c3 20. b×c3 and Black's king is not so safe anymore. **17. ... e5 18. Nb3 N×b3† 19. Q×b3 d4 20. g4 a6 21. Na3 h5** "With this powerful move Black forces the entrance of the rook and queen's bishop, and, with a pawn behind, White has little to do but await developments, his game being virtually lost"—Pillsbury. **22. Bc4 h×g4 23. B×f7 Rh3!** "Correctly forcing the exchange of queens"—Pillsbury. **24. Qd5 Q×d5 25. B×d5 B×f5 26. B×b7 Ra7 27. Bg2 Rh6 28. Rdf1 Bg5† 29. Kb1 Bf4 30. Nc4 Rf6** "White threatened 31. N×e5"—Pillsbury. **31. b3 d3!** "The winning move. Black's bishops become all-powerful"—Pillsbury. **32. c3 d2† 33. Kb2 Bd3 34. N×d2 B×f1** "White offers up only the exchange, for if 34. ... B×d2 35. R×f6† g×f6 36. Rd1 regaining the piece"—Pillsbury. **35. N×f1 Rd7 36. c4 Rd1 37. Ka3 e4 38. c5 e3** "The advance of the pawn settles matters, and White's remaining moves are merely desperate attempts to save an untenable game"—Pillsbury. **39. N×e3 R×h1 40. c6 R×h2 41. Bd5 Bd6†** White resigns—*Tournament Book* (Pillsbury), pp. 308–309.

## (1227) Bird–Mieses ½–½
International tournament (round 21)
Hastings, 2 September 1895
C50

**1. e4 e5 2. Nf3 Nc6 3. Bc4 Be7 4. d4 e×d4 5. N×d4 Nf6 6. N×c6 d×c6 7. Bd3 Be6 8. 0–0 Qd7 9. Qe1 0–0–0 10. Qa5 Kb8**

11. Be3 b6 12. Qe1 Ng4 13. Nd2 Bd6 14. Nf3 f5 15. h3 h5 16. Bg5 Rde8 17. Qc3 Bf7 18. Nd4 Bc5 19. N×f5 g6 20. Nh4 Ne5 21. Be2 Bd4 22. Qg3 Bc4 23. B×c4 N×c4 24. c3 Bc5 25. b3 Nd2 26. Rfd1 N×e4 27. R×d7 N×g3 28. b4 Ne2† 29. Kf1 Bd6 30. Be3 N×c3 31. Bd4 B×b4 32. B×h8 R×h8 33. a3 Bc5 34. N×g6 Re8 35. a4 Re2 36. Rf7 Rd2 37. Ne5 Kb7 38. a5 b×a5 39. Nc4 Rc2 40. N×a5† Kb6 41. Nc4† Kb5 42. Ne3 B×e3 43. f×e3 a5 44. Rf2 R×f2† 45. K×f2 a4 46. g4 h×g4 47. h×g4 Kb4 48. Kf3 a3 49. g5 Nd5 50. e4 Ne7 51. Kf4 Kb3 52. Ke5 c5 53. Kf6 Ng8† 54. Kf7 c4 55. K×g8 c3 56. g6 c2 57. Kf7 Kb2 58. Rh1 a2 59. g7 a1Q 60. R×a1 K×a1 61. g8Q c1Q 62. Qa8† Kb2 63. Qb7† Ka3 64. e5 Qf4† 65. Ke6 Qh6† 66. Kf5 Qh5† 67. Kf4 Qh2† 68. Kf5 Qh5† 69. Kf6 Qh6† 70. Kf7 Qh7† 71. Ke6 Qg6† 72. Kd7 Qg7† draw— *Tournament Book*, pp. 323–325.

### (1228) Bird–Maróczy    0–1
Offhand game
Hastings, August 1895
*C00*

1. e4 e6 2. Nf3 d5 3. Bd3 Nf6 4. e5 Nfd7 5. c3 c5 6. Bc2 Nc6 7. d4 Be7 8. h3 a6 9. Be3 b5 10. b3 Bb7 11. Nbd2 c×d4 Bird's treatment of the French cannot be called convincing and Maróczy already gains the better position. Here, he missed the stronger 11. ... b4! 12. c×b4 c×d4 13. N×d4 B×b4. If White can limit the damage to losing a pawn, he can be happy. 12. c×d4 0–0 12. ... Ba3! pinpoints the several weakened black squares on the queenside. 13. h4 A nifty as well as tricky move that demands utmost care from his opponent. The direct threat is 13. B×h7†! 13. ... f6? 13. ... h6! is the correct reply. After 14. Ng5, 14. ... h×g5 has of course to be avoided, but 14. ... Bb4 slightly favors Black. 14. Qb1? Bird misses two possible ways to claim an advantage. A rather brutal approach is 14. B×h7† K×h7 15. Ng5† Kg8 16. N×e6 Qe8 17. Qg4 Qf7 18. N×f8 with the better chances for White. This line can be reinforced by 14. Ng5!, and now there are a few possibilities: 14. ... f×g5 15. B×h7† K×h7 16. h×g5† Kg8 17. Rh8† or 14. ... Qe8 15. B×h7† (many other moves such as 15. e×f6, 15. N×h7 and 15. N×e6 win as well) 15. ... Kh8 16. h5! f×g5 17. Bg6 Rf7 18. h6 Nf8 19. Qh5 wins. 14. ... f×e5 14. ... f5! is much safer. White should then reply with 15. Bg5, with equal chances. 15. B×h7† 15. Ng5 is not so good: 15. ... e×d4 16. N×e6 Qb8 17. N×f8 N×f8. 15. ... Kh8 16. Ng5 Too rash, for he abandons the center without getting enough attacking play in return. 16. Bg6 keeps his opponent under serious pressure. With correct play Black can claim equal chances after 16. ... Bb4 (if 16. ... e×d4 17. N×d4 N×d4 18. B×d4) 17. Qd1 e×d4 18. N×d4 Nf6. 16. ... Rf6 (*see diagram*) The more vigorous 16. ... e×d4 17. N×e6 Qb8 18. N×f8 N×f8 gains a piece and terminates White's attack.

*After 16. ... Rf6*

17. Qd1?! 17. Bg6! prevents 17. ... Qe8. Black is forced to enter an inferior line to deal with White's approaching queen: 17. ... Qg8 18. Qd1 R×g6 19. Qh5† Rh6 20. Nf7† Q×f7 21. Q×f7 Rf8 22. Q×f8† N×f8 23. B×h6 g×h6 24. d×e5 N×e5 when a strange material balance has been reached. Black's pieces cooperate very well and this will compensate for the deficits. 17. ... Qe8 18. h5 Pursuing his attack gives him the best practical chances, but his opponent has enough defensive resources to come out triumphant. Certainly not attractive was 18. d×e5 Nd×e5 when White has to fight hard for a draw. 18. ... e×d4 19. Bg6 Qf8? Maróczy, famous for his defensive skills, allows Bird a chance to get a well-deserved draw after all. Winning was 19. ... Qg8. 20. Nh7? Overlooking a clever queen sacrifice that effectively terminates his attack. 20. h6!, abandoning a piece, is the right way to proceed. After the forced 20. ... R×g6 (White even wins in case of 20. ... g×h6? 21. Nf7† Kg8 22. B×h6) 21. h×g7† K×g7 22. Rh7† Kg8 23. Qh5 Qf5 24. Rh8† White gives a perpetual check with the rook. 20. ... d×e3! 21. N×f8 e×d2† 22. Kf1 Ra×f8 23. f3 Nde5 24. Q×d2 N×f3 25. g×f3 R×f3† 26. Kg2 Bb4 27. Qc1 Rf2† 28. Kg1 Nd4 29. Bd3 Bd2 30. Qc5 Be3 White resigns—*Birmingham Weekly Mercury*, 7 December 1895.

Consultation games were promoted and arranged on free days. Participants were rewarded with 30 shillings for each winner, while 20 shillings went to each loser. A first game with Bird included was played in the evening of 8 August, the day when the participants visited Battle Abbey.

### (1229) Burn & von Bardeleben–Bird & Pillsbury    0–1
Consultation game
Hastings, 8 August 1895
*C37*

1. e4 e5 2. f4 e×f4 3. Nf3 g5 4. Bc4 g4 5. 0–0 g×f3 6. Q×f3 Qf6 7. d3 Not as aggressive as the usual 7. e5. 7. ... Bh6 7. ... d6 8. B×f4 Nd7 9. Qh5 Qg6 is a good antidote to White's attack. 8. Nc3 Ne7 9. B×f4 B×f4 10. Q×f4 Q×f4 11. R×f4 Despite the game's transposing into an endgame so quickly, White's excellent compensation for the sacrificed piece is due to Black's undeveloped queenside. 11. ... Nbc6 12. B×f7† Kd8 13. Raf1 d6 14. Bb3 Ng6 "Black can hardly afford to lose the h-pawn at present. So the exchange of rooks with that consequence is avoided"—Mason. 15. Rf7 Bd7 16. Rg7 Nce7 Preferable was 16. ... Nd4, to get White's bishop off the board. 17. Nd5 N×d5 18. B×d5 Nf8 19. Rf6 "Naturally, 19. B×b7 would be worse than useless, as at once freeing the Black rook"—Mason. 19. ... c6 20. Bg8 Kc7 21. d4 Re8 22. d5 c×d5 23. e×d5 Ng6 24. Be6 Ne5 25. B×d7 N×d7 26. Rff7 Rd8 27. g4?! Both sides played good and correct chess and a draw would be a logical outcome after 27. R×h7 R×h7 28. R×h7 Re8 29. h4 Re1† 30. Kh2 Kd8 31. Rg7 Re7 (31. ... Re2 32. h5 is not risk free) 32. Rg8† Re8. 27. ... h6 It will take a lot more trouble for White to win the h-pawn now. Black makes good use of the extra time given. 28. Kg2 Rhe8 29. Rh7 Re2† 30. Kg3 It is dangerous to allow their opponents to keep this active rook. 30. Rf2 offers probably enough compensation in the form of the advanced kingside pawns. 30. ... R×c2 30. ... Kc8! is the most precise move as it rapidly evacuates the seventh rank and thereby allows the knight to move. If now

31. R×h6 Ne5 32. Rff6 R×c2 33. R×d6 Rg8 or 31. Rf2 R×f2
32. K×f2 Nf6 win. Also 31. h4 R×c2 32. R×h6 Ne5 33. Rff6 R×b2
should win relatively easily for Black. **31. R×h6 Rd2 32. g5 R×d5
33. h4 Kc6 34. Rhh7 Rd1 35. Rhg7?** A much more effective plan
is organizing the defense of the king's quarters and the queenside.
An interesting way to do so is 35. Rf3 Nc5! (the best chance; the
idea is to hinder the advance of the g-pawn, as well as paving the
path of his d-pawn. If 35. … Rd2?! 36. g6 R×b2 37. g7 Rg8 38. Rf7
with full compensation) 36. Kg4 d5 37. b4 Ne4 38. Rh6† Nd6 with
the better chances. **35. … Ne5 36. R×b7 Rf8** White's king is faced
with unsurmountable troubles now. 37. **Rb3 Rg1† 38. Kh3 Rf2
39. h5 Nf3 40. R×f3 R×f3† 41. Kh2 Rb1 42. g6 R×b2† 43. Kg1
Rd3 44. Rf7 Rg3† 45. Kh1 Rh3† 46. Kg1 R×h5** White resigns—
*British Chess Magazine* (Mason), May 1896, pp. 203–204.

**(1230) Bird & Burn–Pillsbury & Schiffers    ½–½**
Consultation game
Hastings 1895
C58

**1. e4 e5 2. Nf3 Nc6 3. Bc4 Nf6 4. Ng5 d5 5. e×d5 Na5 6. Bb5†
c6 7. d×c6 b×c6 8. Qf3 Qc7 9. Be2 Bd6 10. Nc3 0–0 11. d3 Rb8
12. Nge4 N×e4 13. N×e4 Be7 14. Ng3 f5 15. 0–0 Be6 16. Bd1
Bd5 17. Qe2 c5 18. c4 Ba8 19. Re1 Bd6 20. Qh5 g6 21. Qh6 Nc6
22. Bf3 Nd4 23. B×a8 R×a8 24. Rb1 Qa5 25. Bd2 Q×a2 26. Bc3
Qb3 27. f4 Rae8 28. Ra1 Qb7 29. B×d4 e×d4 30. R×e8 R×e8
31. N×f5 Bf8 32. Qg5 Q×b2 33. Rf1 Qd2 34. Ng3 Q×d3
35. Qd5† Kh8 36. f5 g5 37. f6 Qe3† 38. Kh1 Qe5 39. f7 Re7
40. Qd8 Qg7 41. Qe8 d3 42. Nh5 Qh6 43. g4 d2 44. Kg1 a5
45. h3 a4 46. Rd1 Re1† 47. R×e1 d×e1Q† 48. Q×e1 Qd6
49. Kg2 a3 50. Qc3† Qd4 51. Q×a3 Q×c4 52. Qb2† Qd4
53. Q×d4† c×d4 54. Kf3 h6 55. Ke4 Kh7 56. K×d4 Kg6 57. Ke5
K×f7 58. Kf5 Bd6** draw—*British Chess Magazine*, June 1896, pp.
245–247.

# CHESS NOVELTIES

A short while after the finish of the Hastings tournament Bird
released a new book. *Chess Novelties* was written similarly to much
of Bird's previous work. He presented a series of variations that he
considered to be unjustly neglected in chess literature. Noteworthy
is the attention given by Bird to his two principal patrons, Chapman
and Evelyn. Especially the latter is brought into the spotlight: Bird
called him the inventor of several variations and he also dedicated
the book to him. The "cooperation" between both men had started
when Bird and Captain Mackenzie met Evelyn shortly after the
Manchester tournament.[43]

Bird's work received mixed critics. Some editors raved about the

**Harry N. Pillsbury (courtesy Cleveland Public Library).**

veteran's effort, but more critical voices found plenty of ammunition
to take Bird's approach under fire. An excellent sample is the extensive review in the edition of November 1895 of the *British Chess
Magazine* (pp. 460–464). The reviewer paid tribute to Bird's unique
status in chess, but was relentless when it came to discussing various
aspects of the book. In his criticism one can see several points
coming back that were also relevant for Bird's earlier books. Bird
stressed that he dealt with eccentric openings and novelties that are
omitted in all other opening books, but the unjustness of his
opinion was amply demonstrated. Bird also continued his inferior
habit of presenting samples of games without the slightest attempt
to analyze them. Breaking those games off after about a dozen moves
with the note "won in 70 moves" hardly contributed to the reader's
understanding. Finally a large number of historical errors were
pointed out by the reviewer. Precision was not a priority for a hasty
Bird.

**(1231) M.–Bird    0–1**
Offhand game
London (?)
C64

**1. e4 e5 2. Nf3 Nc6 3. Bb5 Bc5 4. c3 Qe7 5. 0–0 Nf6 6. d4 Bb6
7. B×c6 d×c6 8. N×e5 N×e4 9. Re1 Q×e5 10. d×e5 N×f2
11. Qb3 Ng4† 12. Kh1 Nf2† 13. Kg1 Ng4† 14. Kf1 N×h2†
15. Ke2 Bg4† 16. Kd2 0–0–0† 17. Kc2 Bf5†** and mate in two—
*Chess Novelties*, pp. 70–71.

43. Bird gave quite some details how he got re-acquainted with Evelyn: "At Manchester in 1890 the Captain and myself, both very low down on the sick list, did
equally well in the international chess competition and on return I suggested a glimpse of Surrey scenery, Leatherhead to Box Hill and on to Dorking and round about
these delightful parts. Our thoughts incidentally wandered to an esteemed opponent and friend of early days, W.J. Evelyn, Esq., who, I informed the Captain, lived in
that beautiful neighborhood. We radiated at the hotel a day or two and returned to Heygate Street. Mr. Evelyn we think must in some way, probably through the Dorking
paper, have heard of our visit. Kindnesses from him following health inquiries shortly afterwards led also to chess comparisons and retrospects and certain ideas concerning
debatable openings with which he has favored and honored the writer, combined with his own stock of disregarded and unnoticed though available and successful
moves, has been the incentive to this little work." *Chess Novelties*, pp. 24–25.

### (1232) Bird–M.　1–0
Offhand game
London (?)
*A03*

"This has occurred to me more than once in actual play. Early mates are abundant in this opening."—Bird

**1. f4 d5 2. e3 c5 3. Nf3 e6 4. b3 Nc6 5. Bb2 Nf6 6. Bd3 Be7 7. a3 0–0 8. 0–0 b6 9. Qe1 Bb7 10. Qh4 g6 11. Ng5 h5 12. g4 N×g4 13. Q×h5 g×h5 14. Bh7** mate—*Chess Novelties* (Bird), pp. 117–118.

### (1233) J.C.–Bird　0–1
Offhand game
London (?)
*C35*

**1. e4 e5 2. f4 e×f4 3. Nf3 Be7 4. Bc4 Bh4† 5. Kf1 d5 6. B×d5 Nf6 7. Nc3 N×d5 8. N×d5 0–0 9. N×h4 Q×h4 10. N×c7 Nc6 11. N×a8 Nd4 12. Nc7 f3 13. Rg1 Bh3 14. g×h3 Q×h3† 15. Ke1 Q×h2 16. Rf1 N×c2† 17. Q×c2 Qe2** mate—*Chess Novelties*, pp. 247–248.

---

# A TOUR THROUGH THE SOUTH, OCTOBER–NOVEMBER 1895

Bird made a small tour through the south of England around the end of October. His first known stop was the remote town of Petworth. Here he gave an exhibition against 20 opponents on 28 October. The opposition was relatively weak, as Bird won the majority of his 16 wins straight out of the opening. Bird was beaten by W. Bridger, later a Sussex champion, and conceded 3 draws against A.C. Holland, Hunt and J. Bridger.

Bird thereupon travelled to Brighton for two exhibitions. In an ordinary simultaneous display he played eleven opponents, beating 7 of them while losing 2 and drawing 2. On 30 October he opposed four opposed teams of two players each at the same time. No result of this performance is known. Two of these games were published. Bird dominated both of them but came out of the fray with two losses. His game with Emery and Macdonald was especially fascinating.

### (1234) Bird–E. Baird & Butler　0–1
Consultation game
Brighton, 30 October 1895
*C31*

**1. e4 e5 2. f4 d5 3. e×d5 e4 4. Bb5† Bd7 5. Qe2 f5 6. Nc3 Nf6 7. Bc4 Bd6 8. Nh3 Qe7 9. 0–0–0 10. d4 h6 11. a3 Be8 12. Nd1 Bh5 13. Qe1 B×d1! 14. Q×d1 Nbd7 15. Be2 Rac8 16. c4 c5 17. d×c6** *e.p.* **b×c6 18. c5 Bb8 19. Bc4† Kh8 20. Nf2 Rfe8 21. Be3 Nf8 22. b4 Ne6 23. g3 Nc7 24. Re1 Ncd5 25. Qb3 Qd7 26. Rad1 Red8 27. b5 N×e3 28. R×e3 Nd5 29. B×d5 Q×d5 30. Q×d5 R×d5 31. b×c6 R×c6 32. Rb3 Bc7 33. Rb7 e3 34. Nh3 Rc×c5**

---

**35. Kf1 Rc2 36. Ng1 Rf2† 37. Ke1 Ba5†** White resigns—*Brighton Society*, 9 November 1895.

### (1235) Bird–Emery & MacDonald　0–1
Consultation game
Brighton, 30 October 1895
*C54*

**1. e4 e5 2. Nf3 Nc6 3. Bc4 Bc5 4. b4 Bb6 5. c3 Nf6 6. Qb3 Qe7 7. d3 d6 8. a4 a6 9. a5 Ba7 10. 0–0 Nd8 11. Re1 Ne6 12. Ba3 Ng4 13. Ra2 Qf6 14. h3?** Bird's experimental sortie of the bishop to a3 leaves this piece completely useless. It was better to redirect it to the kingside without further delay. **14. ... Nh6?** Bird's opponents readily contribute to his bid to retreat the knight. A very strong and lasting attack is launched after 14. ... Ng5!—e.g., 15. h×g4 N×f3† 16. g×f3 Q×f3 17. d4 Q×g4† 18. Kh1 Qf3† 19. Kh2 Qh5† 20. Kg1 Qg6† 21. Kh1 Bg4 22. Nd2 0–0. **15. b5?** Bird insists on giving his bishop a perspective along the a3–f8 diagonal, but the state of his kingside is lamentable, as his opponents now amply demonstrate. Once more, admitting the failure of his twelfth move and playing 15. Bc1 maintains the equilibrium. **15. ... Nf4 16. d4 N×h3†** Snatching a pawn for free, but the loss of time involved allows Bird an initiative on the queenside after all. The refined 16. ... Qg6! 17. g3 N×h3† 18. Kf1 Qh5 is far harder on their opponent. **17. Kf1 Nf4 18. b6 c×b6?!** The intermediate 18. ... Qg6! drastically changes in the evaluation of the position. After 19. g3 Qh5 20. g×f4 Q×f3 21. f5 Qh1†! 22. Ke2 Q×e4† 23. Kd2 Qf4† and 24. ... Bb8, White lacks compensation for the sacrificed material. **19. a×b6 Bb8 20. d×e5 Qg6 21. g3 Bh3†?** The allies fail to find the best way to propel their attack, and as a result their own pieces block each other in their attempts to hunt down Bird's king. Correct was, as above, to improve the position of their queen first, as after 21. ... Qh5 22. Nh4 Bh3†! 23. Kg1, the push of the g-pawn really sets the board on fire. **22. Kg1 0–0** If instead 22. ... Qh5 23. Nbd2 0–0 24. e×d6 and Black's attack runs out of steam. **23. e×d6 Qh5 24. Nh4?!** Bird succeeded in blasting his opponents' center away, but with this move he hands them some free ammunition against his king. The calm 24. Nh2 or 24. Nbd2 finishes Black's attack. **24. ... g5** *(see diagram)*

*After 24. ... g5*

**25. f3!** Bird selects a strong and interesting, but also very daring, way to create problems for his opponents. Equally intriguing is the endgame arising after 25. Qd1 g×h4 (25. ... Bg4? 26. f3 Nh3† 27. Kg2 Bd7 28. Nf5 wins) 26. Q×h5 N×h5 27. Bd5 Be6 28. B×b7. White has but two pawns for the piece but some of the pawns are dangerous. **25. ... g×h4** Given the possibilities White has after the text move, 25. ... Rd8 may have been preferable. Once more, the game stands very unclear after 26. Qd1 g×h4 27. g×f4 B×d6! 28. B×d6 Qg6† etc. **26. g×f4 Q×f3 27. Qd1** These last few moves were rather forced. The material balance is almost equal now. Black seems attacking, but the position is still full of resources. **27. ... Q×f4** Black has a difficult choice to make between the text move and 27. ... Qg3†. Black gains material after 28. Kh1 Bg4 29. Rg2 B×d1 30. R×g3† h×g3 31. R×d1, but White's compensation is of plenty nature. A sample line runs 31. ... Ng4 32. Re1! Nf6 33. e5. **28. Bf1??** A decent try at first sight, but it turns out that Black's attack now gains serious proportions. The alternative 28. Qd3! is much more convincing, as g3 is covered and the bishop attacked. Retreating this piece is no option (28. ... Bd7 29. Bc1!), so they must wager their chances on a direct attack with 28. ... Kh8 29. Q×h3 Rg8†. Cool defense consolidation now repels Black's attack: 30. Kh1 Rg3 31. Qf1 Rf3 32. Qg2 Rg3 33. Rf2! etc. **28. ... Qg3† 29. Kh1 Ng4 30. B×h3 Q×h3† 31. Kg1 Kh8?!** A slightly imprecise move order with serious consequences. Black's attack is fearsome after 31. ... Ne3 32. Qd2 Kh8! **32. Rg2!** Hereby Bird has survived the assault so far. Now 32. ... Ne3? 33. Qd4† must be avoided. **32. ... Rg8 33. Qd4† f6** A beautiful and subtle alternative here is 33. ... Rg7! White's pieces, shattered as they are, don't have a single target point while Black has a slow but effective idea, namely 34. Nd2 B×d6! 35. B×d6 Rag8 and White is faced with the threat 36. ... Ne5! or 36. ... Ne3, if necessary after 36. ... f6. The sole defense in this complicated position seems the suicidal-looking 36. R×g4 Q×g4† 37. Kf2 Rd8 38. Nf3, with an extremely obscure position. **34. Nd2** *(see diagram)*

*After 34. Nd2*

**34. ... a5?** This move is obviously too slow to be good, but it is a very tough task to find the way forward among a myriad of variations. One move that can thematically be dismissed is 34. ... Ne5?, for after 35. R×g8† K×g8 36. Re2 White gains control over the g-file and Black's army is out of play. White has various possible ideas to improve his position: Rg2, Qd5, Bc5–d4, Nc4.... 34. ... Rg7? echoes to the variation given above. White has a clever solution in 35. Rf1! Ne5 36. R×g7 K×g7 37. Rf2 which makes Black's life extremely difficult. Once more the control of the g-file is crucial (37. ... Qe6 38. Rg2† Kf7 39. Qc5! h3 40. Rg3). Worth considering is 34. ... h6, but perhaps 34. ... h5 is best. The position of their knight is improved and White's move is certainly not easy

to find. We'll have a look at two fascinating lines, in both of which Black sacrifice their bishop to bring their rook into play. Though a piece down in both cases, their compensation in the form of a king-side attack is stunning. **(a)** First, the attempt to break through with 35. e5, a pawn that cannot be captured, must be met by 35. ... Ba7!! The rooks are connected, so 36. b×a7? Ne3! even wins on the spot! Instead 36. e×f6 B×b6! 37. Q×b6 draws the queen away from the scene of the action. Now 37. ... Ne3 seems fatal to White, were it not that he has the marvelous 38. Rg7! Nd5 39. Q×b7 N×f6 40. Ree7 R×g7† 41. R×g7 Qe3† and a draw is forced. **(b)** The safer option is 35. Ree2. As everything is covered well (Ne3 is neutralized), Black must limit themselves to the calm, preparatory 35. ... Rg7 when a standstill is reached. White's position still seems to justify playing for more, but he has to be extremely careful, for if 36. Qc5?! B×d6! Now 37. Q×h5† Rh7 38. Q×g4 is best, but after the exchange of queens Black win back their piece and this relatively simple endgame is clearly in their favor. But much worse, instantly losing even, is 37. Q×d6? Rag8!!, and whatever White does he is lost, for example 38. Qf4 Q×c3 39. Qf3 Qd4† and 40. ... h3. So 36. Qd5 is the way to go (after 35. Ree2 Rg7). It is easy to err, but with correct play a draw can be forced by means of a perpetual check; e.g., 36. ... Rg5 37. Q×b7 Q×c3 38. Q×a8 Qd4† 39. Ref2 N×f2 40. Q×b8† Kh7 41. Qb7† Kh6 42. Qc8 N×e4† 43. Kh1 R×g2 44. Qh8†. **35. Bb2?!** This move initiates a relatively slow and harmless plan. Still very good was 35. Rf1!, forcing Black to take drastic measures as their queen is in danger of being lost. After 35. ... B×d6 36. B×d6 Ne5 (36. ... Qe3† 37. Kh1) 37. Rff2 everything is defended. **35. ... a4 36. c4 h5?!** The idea to consolidate the knight is not what the position requires right now. Instead 36. ... Rg7 prepares against doom coming via the long diagonal. There could follow 37. Rf1 (37. e5 N×e5 38. R×g7 K×g7 39. R×e5 Qg3† 40. Kf1 f×e5 41. Qd5 and Black has a perpetual again) 37. ... B×d6 38. Q×d6 Qe3† with a draw. **37. Rf1** Certainly good enough, but he misses the thematic 37. e5! f×e5 38. R×e5! and Black is fighting an uphill struggle. **37. ... B×d6** They could also try to find salvation in an endgame: 37. ... Qe3† 38. Q×e3 N×e3 39. R×g8† K×g8 40. R×f6 a3. This pawn is Black's only trump, but it is far from being enough. 41. Ba1 Nc2 42. Bc3 a2 43. d7 Bg3 44. e5 wins. **38. Q×d6 Qe3† 39. Rff2 h3 40. B×f6† Kh7 41. Qd7†??** The climax of a wonderful battle has arrived but this move completely spoils it for Bird. With this spite check Bird's queen leaves a crucial diagonal and, being cut off from the defense, White is now bound to lose. Winning was 41. Bd4, though the main line was very hard to calculate precisely: 41. ... h2† 42. Kh1 N×f2† 43. R×f2 Qe1† 44. Rf1 Rg1† 45. B×g1 h×g1Q† 46. R×g1 Qh4† 47. Qh2, and the outcome is finally clear. **41. ... Kh6 42. Bd4** Other moves don't help either, for instance, 42. Qe6 Rg6. **42. ... h2† 43. Kh1 N×f2† 44. K×h2** 44. R×f2 loses now: 44. ... Rg1† 45. K×h2 Qg3 mate. **44. ... Qf4† 45. Kg1 R×g2† 46. K×g2 Rg8† 47. Kf1 N×e4†** White resigns— *Daily News*, 18 November 1895.

# ◆ Part XII ◆
# The Final Years, 1896–1908

## Introduction

With the conclusion of the international tournament in Hastings, the winter of Bird's chess career continued to grow. During the four years of intense chess that remained for him, Bird took part in two tournaments, one match and a cable match. Even though his results were further in decline, Bird remained a strong and tough to beat player until the very end.

Bird made it to the selection for the first cable match between England and the United States. He even occupied third board, behind Blackburne and Burn. On this occasion it was mainly over confidence that did him in, in his game against Constant Ferdinand Burille. Much worse was Bird's play during the Divan tournament that followed a short while later. His playing level was clearly influenced by the gout.

Bird lost a match against Lee during the summer of 1897. Once again, there were some excuses for his mediocre performance. Severe blunders, caused by tiredness after hours of play, cost him at least two games.

The following year passed by without any important event. In 1899 Bird, to the surprise of many, was allowed to enter the field of the strong London tournament. At the age of 70 he was considered a relic from another—long gone—time by a large part of the public. His score, at first sight, indeed does not seem to justify his participation, but a closer look at his games testifies how he succeeded in making life difficult for the majority of his opponents. Bird's belief in his own opinions remained unshaken and many of his strong adversaries were lucky to get half or whole points out of the hands of the veteran by making use of his weariness inspired blunders.

Bird rarely left London during these years, but this was certainly not his own will. He amazed the chess world, and along the way earned great sympathy, when he made a public appeal to support him in his candidature for the international tournament in Berlin in 1897. During these final years Bird remained a loyal guest at the Hastings festival. Despite great pain he performed in simultaneous exhibitions. From time to time he visited chess clubs around London and in the countryside. Towards the end of 1898 he was prepared for some kind of a farewell tour through the north. These exhibitions continued to please Bird and generated great enthusiasm in the midst of a much younger audience.[1]

The major part of Bird's final years in chess passed at the Divan. One extended article described the atmosphere of a working day in Bird's life with a lot of detail.

Among the chess rooms patronized by the better class of London players, Simpson's is probably the best known. This is a large, gloomy apartment, whose high, dust-covered window look down on the Strand. It has an interesting history, for here many of the most famous chess masters have met.

About 10 o'clock every morning the habitués of Simpson's begin to make their appearance. Unlike the practice which prevails in most other resorts of a similar nature, a fee of 6d. is charged for admission. Those who arrive first are usually professional players, each of whom earns a meager livelihood by playing with and instructing amateurs. They are all shabbily dressed and most of their faces show a reprehensible lack of intimacy with a razor. Despite their seedy appearance, however, most of them are masters whose names are honored on two continents.

Upon entering the room they while away the hours of the morning reading the papers or lazily watching the traffic on the Strand. If among the visitors there should be any desirous of entering into conversation with Blackburne, Bird, Gunsberg, or other champions, this is the opportunity, for after 1 o'clock all hope to be engaged in play. The scanty fees vouchsafed these famous players by amateurs are all the most of them have to depend upon for a living, and they watch eagerly for the arrival of their patrons. It is noticeable that they seldom play with one another, nor do they seem to evince any interest in the games that are going around them. Their enthusiasm for their favorite game has kept them out of commercial or professional pursuits, and now it seems to one who observes them closely that even this youthful enthusiasm has spent its force, leaving nothing to compensate them for the comfort-winning faculties it has robbed them of.

By 2 o'clock the room begins to fill, and little groups silently surround the tables. The stillness of the apartment is broken only by the low calls for drinks or sandwiches, or the rattle of the chessmen as they are replaced on the board.

It is amusing to watch the idiosyncrasies of the masters as they silently study their games. Blackburne is an inveterate whisky drinker, and the amount of liquor which he is able to consume in the course of the day is marvelous. From the time that the pieces are arranged for play until the game is finished he sips his whisky and water continually, consuming about five glasses of the mixture in the course of an hour.

He moves promptly and apparently plays with little effort. Gunsberg, who probably ranks next to Steinitz as an analyst, plays slowly and carefully, and is a staunch believer in coffee as a mental stimulant. Unlike Blackburne, he is extremely patient with his pupils, evincing no disposition to rally them on the time they require to work out their moves.

Of all the habitués of Simpson's, however, none affords so much amusement to the visitor as the solid-faced Bird, who enjoys the distinction of ranking next to Blackburne among the native-born chess masters of England. He is

---

1. A nice reminiscence of a small undercover operation by Bird, written down by A.R. Davies, appeared in print nearly forty years later: "On a second visit of Blackburne, as we were indulging in 'skittles' before his arrival, a stout elderly gentleman wandered in, wearing a heavy great coat and a cheerful smile. He sat down and puffed at his pipe, and was taken for an ordinary spectator. He knew chess, for on a game opening with 1. e4, he remarked that he believed he had seen that move somewhere before. However, there was an unexpected delay, and the visitor departed as quietly as he had arrived. We found out later that he was Bird, and were much concerned that he was unrecognized, for he would have had the warmest of welcomes. He appeared exactly as Mrs. Anderson cleverly depicted him in *Chess Pie*, pipe and all." *British Chess Magazine*, June 1932, p. 244.

usually to be seen seated at a table in a corner of the room, with his badly worn top hat tilted over his eye. He is always ready with his move, and after it has been made he immediately forces his false teeth outward from his lips, and proceeds to work his jaws vigorously over the plate, looking for all the world like a cocky old squirrel nibbling a nut. When his opponent has replied to his move, the teeth go in for a few moments as he surveys the situation; then he moves a piece, takes a sip of whisky, places his arms akimbo and resumes his nobbling [*Daily Inter Ocean*, 8 September 1896; first published in the *New York Evening Post*].

Early in 1898, an article in the *Daily Mail* elaborated on the decline of chess. One fragment related to the situation of Bird (and other professionals) at the Divan.

Today the attendance at Simpson's, partly owing to the increasing number of clubs, and still more, perhaps, to the 6d. charged for admission, is not what it used to be. Bird, the father of English chess, whose faculties, after fifty years of chess-playing, are as clear as ever, still attends nightly, to talk over the palmy days and play all comers at the usual fee, but antagonists are not too numerous. Foreigners prefer the Vienna Café, in Oxford Street, where chess, since the great Lasker patronized the place, has greatly flourished [*Daily Mail*, 15 February 1898].

Bird's goodbye from the international chess world took place in July 1899 at the tournament in London. Only a short while later a severe attack of gout obliged him to leave Simpson's Divan forever. On 16 February 1903, the *Morning Post* brought the sad tidings that Simpson's Divan would be closed for rebuilding. At this point ended the history of London's principal chess resort of the nineteenth century.

Bird's illness condemned him to a wheelchair and consequently confined him to his rooms. With this sad event, his active chess career was over while his source of income suddenly dried up as well. Bird was dependent on the chess community for his survival. His numerous friends came to the rescue and guaranteed him eight more quiet years, in which he slowly faded away.

## (1236) Bird–North   0–1
Simultaneous game
Hampstead C.C., 11 February 1896
*C33*

On 11 February Bird opposed twenty players at the Hampstead Chess Club. No result of this exhibition is known.

**1.** e4 e5 **2.** f4 e×f4 **3.** Be2 g5 **4.** h4 Bg7 **5.** d4 d5 **6.** e×d5 Q×d5 **7.** c3 Q×g2 **8.** Bf3 Qg3† **9.** Kf1 g4 **10.** Qe2† Ne7 **11.** Be4 f3 **12.** Qc2 Nd7 **13.** Be3 Nf6 **14.** Bd3 Nfd5 **15.** Bc1 Ng6 **16.** Qf2 Qg2† **17.** Q×g2 f×g2† **18.** K×g2 Ngf4† **19.** B×f4 N×f4† **20.** Kg3 N×d3 **21.** Ne2 h5 **22.** b3 Bf5 **23.** Na3 0-0-0 **24.** Rad1 Rhe8 **25.** R×d3 B×d3 White resigns—*Nottinghamshire Guardian*, 7 March 1896.

## (1237) Bird–Unknown   1–0
Offhand game
London (Simpson's Divan) 1896
*Odds of Ng1*

**1.** e4 e5 **2.** Bc4 Bc5 **3.** b4 Bb6 **4.** a4 Qf6 **5.** 0-0 Ne7 **6.** a5 d5 **7.** a×b6 d×c4 **8.** R×a7 R×a7 **9.** b×a7 Qa6 **10.** a×b8Q 0-0 **11.** Q×c7 Black resigns—*Birmingham Weekly Mercury*, 11 April 1896.

## (1238) Unknown–Bird   0–1
Offhand game
London (Simpson's Divan) 1896
*C39*

**1.** e4 e5 **2.** f4 e×f4 **3.** Nf3 g5 **4.** h4 g4 **5.** Ne5 h5 **6.** d4 d6 **7.** Nd3 f3 **8.** g3 f5 **9.** e5 Nc6 **10.** Nf4 d×e5 **11.** Ng6 N×d4 **12.** N×h8 f4 **13.** Nc3 Qd6 **14.** Kf2 Qc5 **15.** Na4 and mate in a few moves—*Birmingham Weekly Mercury*, 25 April 1896.

## (1239) Buz–Bird   1–0
Offhand game
London (Simpson's Divan), 12 August 1896
*C62*

**1.** e4 e5 **2.** Nf3 Nc6 **3.** Bb5 d6 **4.** d4 Bd7 **5.** B×c6 B×c6 **6.** d×e5 d×e5 **7.** Q×d8† R×d8 **8.** N×e5 B×e4 **9.** 0-0 B×c2 **10.** Nc3 Bb4 **11.** Nb5 c6 **12.** N×a7 Nf6 **13.** Na×c6 b×c6 **14.** N×c6 Be7 **15.** N×d8 K×d8 **16.** Be3 Nd7 **17.** Rac1 Bf5 **18.** Rfd1 Bf6 **19.** Bd4 B×d4 **20.** R×d4 Ke7 **21.** Re1† Be6 **22.** f4 g6 **23.** g4 Kf6 **24.** g5† Kf5 **25.** Kg2 h6 **26.** h4 h×g5 **27.** h×g5 Rc8 **28.** Kg3 Rc5 **29.** Re3 Rd5 **30.** R×d5† B×d5 **31.** a4 Be4 **32.** a5 Nc5 **33.** b4 Nd3 **34.** R×e4 K×e4 **35.** a6 Black resigns—*Deutsche Schachzeitung*, October 1896, pp. 307–308.

## (1240) Pillsbury & Chapman–Bird & Allen   ½–½
Consultation game
London (Simpson's Divan) 1896 (?)
*C33*

**1.** e4 e5 **2.** f4 e×f4 **3.** Bc4 Qh4† **4.** Kf1 d6 **5.** Nf3 Qh5 **6.** d4 g5 **7.** Nc3 Ne7 **8.** h4 f6 **9.** Kg1 As pointed out in several earlier games, this flat move is inferior to the critical 9. e5! **9. ...** g4 **10.** Ne1 Bh6 **11.** Nd3 f3 **12.** g3? The position needs to be opened up by exchanging at f3. **12. ...** Nbc6 **13.** Nf4 B×f4 **14.** B×f4 Bd7 **15.** b4 0-0-0 **16.** Rb1 Ng6 **17.** Be3 f5 **18.** d5 Nce5 **19.** Qd4 N×c4 **20.** Q×c4 f×e4 Bird and his partner caught a second pawn, for this one cannot be recaptured, as otherwise to many lines and diagonals would be opened. Though Black is doubtlessly winning, the second pawn win results in a pawn structure that is a bit too closed to comfortably open up the game. Had they played 20. ... f4!, there is no doubt that White would succumb quickly. **21.** Kf2 Rde8 **22.** b5 b6 **23.** a4 Ne5 **24.** Qd4 Bf5 **25.** a5 Kd7 **26.** Rhe1 Rhg8 "Bird thought afterwards that 26. ... Ng6 might have been better, but 27. Qc4 would then have to be reckoned with"—Bird. **27.** Bf4 Qg6 **28.** Re3 Qg7 **29.** B×e5 d×e5? Not only self-destructive of his pawn structure but also causing his king to land up in a drafty condition. **30.** Qc4 Rb8 "More effective than it looks"—Bird. **31.** d6? Either played for the public or for a vain kind of attack. Indeed, after 31. N×e4, both sides will probably keep each other in balance until the end of times. **31. ...** c×d6 **32.** Qc6† Ke6 **33.** Rd1 Qd7 **34.** Qd5† Ke7 **35.** N×e4 B×e4 **36.** Q×e4 Rg6 **37.** Red3 Q×b5 **38.** h5 Rg7? 38. ... Qc5† is very problematical, as each reply does definite damage; e.g., 39. Kf1 Q×c2. **39.** R×d6 Qe2† The exchange of queens allows Black to reach an endgame with two extra pawns and nearly no winning chances. But 39. ... Qc5† 40. R1d4 Q×d6 was, despite the exciting appearance, hardly any more enticing. **40.** Q×e2 f×e2

**41. K×e2 b×a5 42. Rd7† Kf8 43. R×g7 K×g7 44. Rd7† Kh6 45. R×a7 Rb5** draw. "Here the White allies offered a draw, which, owing to the lateness of the hour, Black accepted, though the extra pawn might perhaps have won"—Bird. *New York Daily Tribune* (Bird), 14 March 1897.

## (1241) Allies–Bird  0–1
Consultation game
London (Simpson's Divan) 1897 (?)

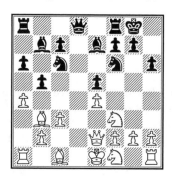

*Black to move*

**1. ... N×e4 2. Q×e4 Nd4 3. Q×b7 N×b3 4. Rb1 Qd3 5. N3d2 N×d2 6. N×d2 Bg5** "and the allies gave in"—*Birmingham Weekly Mercury*, 29 May 1897.

## (1242) Rolland & Unknown–Bird  0–1
Consultation game
London (Simpson's Divan) 1897 (?)
C44

**1. e4 e5 2. Nf3 Nc6 3. c3 f5 4. d4 f×e4 5. N×e5 Nf6 6. Bg5 Be7 7. Be2** 7. Bb5! is extremely strong. Black now cannot move the c-pawn while he also loses after 7. ... 0–0? 8. Qb3† or 7. ... a6 8. Ba4 b5 9. Bb3. 7. ... Nb8 is in fact his best move. **7. ... Nd5? 8. B×e7?** This exchange relieves Black considerably. A curious line that is likely to end badly for Black is 8. Bh6! Bf6 9. Bc4! The queen is ready to enter the scene of action at h5, forcing Black to consent with 9. ... B×e5 10. B×d5 Qf6 (if 10. ... Bf6 11. B×g7!) 11. Qh5† Qg6 12. Q×g6† h×g6 13. Be3 and the pawn at e4 falls. **8. ... Nc×e7 9. Nd2 d6 10. Nec4 Nf4 11. 0–0 d5 12. Ne5 0–0 13. f3?** White is clearly suffering, but the text move is far from being a solution, and could have been punished decisively with 13. ... Nf5! The ugly 13. g3 is still playable. **13. ... e3 14. Nb3 Neg6 15. N×g6 h×g6 16. Kh1 Qg5 17. g3 Bh3 18. Rg1 N×e2 19. Q×e2** *(see diagram)*

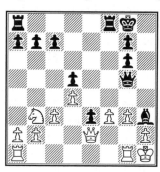

*After 19. Q×e2*

**19. ... R×f3!** Rolland's play has been rather bad, but this is not detrimental to Bird's pretty final combination. **20. Q×f3 Rf8**

**21. Qe2 Rf2 22. Qe1 Bg4 23. Rf1 Bf3†** and Black wins—*Otago Witness*, 11 February 1898.

## (1243) Bird & Lee–Blackburne & Chapman  1–0
Consultation game
London (Simpson's Divan), 30 July 1897
C58

**1. e4 e5 2. Nf3 Nc6 3. Bc4 Nf6 4. Ng5 d5 5. e×d5 Na5 6. Bb5† c6 7. d×c6 b×c6 8. Bd3 Be7 9. 0–0 0–0 10. Re1 Qc7 11. Nc3 h6 12. Nf3 Bd6 13. Bf1 Re8 14. d3 Nd5 15. Ne4 Bf8 16. Bd2 Be6 17. c4** Black hasn't found sufficient compensation for the sacrificed pawn at all. Here White misses the win of a second pawn with 17. B×a5 Q×a5 18. N×e5. **17. ... Ne7 18. b4 Nb7 19. c5 Bd5 20. Bc3 f6 21. Qc1 Ng6 22. Qc2 Qf7 23. g3 Nh8 24. Bg2 g5 25. d4!** Bird and Lee find a strong move hidden in the position. It could have been played a few moves earlier as well. **25. ... f5 26. Ned2 e4 27. Ne5 R×e5** A desperate try for counterplay, but there is nothing that works. As the White allies refuse to take any risks, the game drags on for a while. **28. d×e5 g4 29. Bd4 Qe6 30. Bf1 Nf7 31. Nc4 Ng5 32. Be2 Nf3† 33. B×f3 g×f3 34. Ne3 Bg7 35. N×d5 c×d5 36. Kh1 Nd8 37. b5 Nf7 38. b6 Nd8 39. Rab1 Nc6 40. Qa4 Qe8 41. b7 Rb8 42. Red1 Kh7 43. Qb3 Qe6 44. Be3 Rd8 45. Bf4 B×e5 46. B×e5 Q×e5 47. Qa4 Qc7 48. Qb3 Qd7 49. Qe3 d4 50. Qf4** and White wins—*Illustrated Sporting and Dramatic News*, 21 August 1897.

## (1244) Bird & Chapman–Lee & Jenkins  0–1
Consultation game
London (Simpson's Divan) 1897
C30

**1. e4 e5 2. f4 Bc5 3. Nf3 d6 4. c3 Nf6 5. Bc4 Bg4 6. h3 B×f3 7. Q×f3 Nbd7 8. f5 c6 9. d3 h6 10. b4 Bb6 11. a4 a5 12. b5 Qe7 13. Nd2 Nc5 14. Nf1 d5 15. e×d5 c×d5 16. Ba2 e4 17. d×e4 d×e4 18. Qg3 Nd3† 19. Ke2 0–0–0 20. Ba3 Qd7 21. Bc4 Nh5 22. Qd6 Q×d6 23. B×d6 R×d6** White resigns—*Illustrated Sporting and Dramatic News*, 4 December 1897.

## (1245) Unknown–Bird  0–1
Offhand game
London (Simpson's Divan) 1898
C44

**1. e4 e5 2. Nf3 Nc6 3. c3 d5 4. Bb5 d×e4 5. N×e5 Qg5 6. Qa4 Q×g2 7. B×c6† b×c6 8. Q×c6† Kd8 9. Rf1 Bh3 10. Q×a8† Ke7 11. Nc6† Kf6 12. Qd8† Kg6 13. Ne5† Kh5 14. Ke2 Q×f1† 15. Ke3 Nf6 16. Qd4 Qe1† 17. Kf4 g5† 18. Kg3 Qg1† 19. K×h3 g4† 20. N×g4 Q×g4** mate—*Hereford Times*, 11 June 1898.

---

# CABLE MATCH 1896

The first Anglo-American cable match was played on Friday 13 and Saturday 14 March 1896. Almost exactly one year earlier a similar match between the Manhattan Chess Club and the British

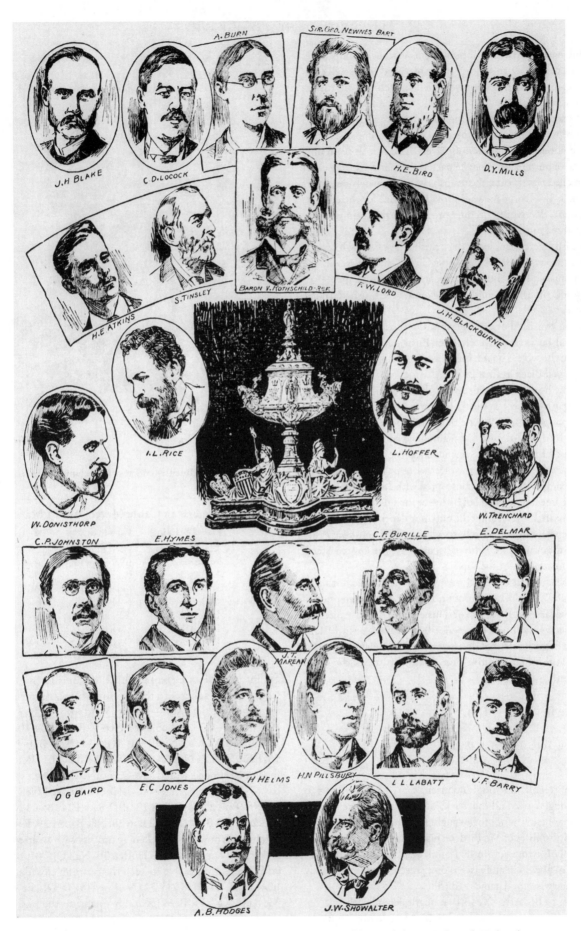

**British and American participants and officials of the 1896 cable match** (*New York Daily Tribune*).

Chess Club had ended in a disappointment. Various circumstances resulted in a great delay, and with just one playing day foreseen eight of the ten games remained unfinished. The match was unsatisfactorily adjourned as a draw.

Now the stakes were set much higher, as both countries gathered their best representatives to combat each other. Some discussion was caused about the eligibility of players. The British team only wanted native born players to take part, the Americans were eager to let domiciled players enter the teams as well. Ultimately foreigners were banned. Sir George Newnes provided a prize for the contest, a silver trophy, that would become property of the team winning the match three times in a row.

The British team assembled at the British Chess Club while their opponents met at the Brooklyn Chess Club. On the first day the games were played from 3 until 7 p.m. and from 8 p.m. until 0:30 a.m. (London time). The adjourned games were finished on the following day.

Each team consisted of eight players. On the first board Blackburne and Pillsbury opposed each other, Burn met Jackson Whipps Showalter on the second board. Bird was assigned to the third board where he played Black against Burille.

After a few hours of play it seemed that the English team was well on its way to success, as Blackburne and Jackson could already boast winning positions. But the tide turned when a catastrophe occurred on Bird's board. Bird had maintained equality throughout the game until his opponent sacrificed a piece to force his way through. The veteran accepted the offer without a second thought and just two moves later he was confronted with an inevitable mate. Some other games also turned out badly for the English team. With an equal score after seven games the outcome depended on the final game between Tinsley and John Barry which at this point was easily winning for the American. With 4½ against 3½ the United States became the first holder of the cup.

Bird's appearance at the Anglo-American match was not to be repeated. In 1897, despite heavy protest, amateurs were given priority above such notables as Bird, Lee or Tinsley. The Anglo-American matches lasted, with a break between 1904 and 1906, until 1911. In that year the English team took possession of the Newnes cup after winning for a third consecutive time. With this streak the series came to an end.

## (1246) Burille–Bird   1–0
Anglo-American Cable Match
London/New York, 13 March 1896
*B00*

"It was an irregular opening, and interesting to me from start to finish. Although I tried all the 'tricks of the trade' in the middle game, my opponent was not to be caught napping, and, considering the age and infirmities of Mr. Bird, he played a wonderful game up to the time of his error at move 48. I think that analysis will demonstrate that I had a win in any case, so on that score it unfortunately spoils an otherwise good game"—Burille.

**1. d4 e6 2. e4 b6** "After 2. e4 Black might defend with 2. ... d5, it being now a French Defense; but Mr. Bird frequently adopts the fianchetto in that opening, turning the game, as happened here later

**Constant F. Burille (courtesy Cleveland Public Library).**

| Anglo-American Cable Match, 13–14 March 1896 | | |
|---|---|---|
| **Great Britain** | **United States** | **3½–4½** |
| J.H. Blackburne | H.N. Pillsbury | 1–0 |
| A. Burn | J.W. Showalter | 0–1 |
| H.E. Bird | C.F. Burille | 0–1 |
| S. Tinsley | J.F. Barry | 0–1 |
| C.D. Locock | E. Hymes | ½–½ |
| D.Y. Mills | A.B. Hodges | ½–½ |
| H.E. Atkins | E. Delmar | ½–½ |
| E.M. Jackson | D.G. Baird | 1–0 |

on, into a Sicilian Defense; whilst Mr. Burille, in establishing a strong center, adheres to the development recommended against the fianchetto defenses"—Hoffer. **3. Bd3 Bb7 4. Be3 Nf6 5. Nd2 Be7 6. f3 0–0 7. Nh3 c5 8. c3 Nc6 9. Rc1 c×d4 10. c×d4 Nb4 11. Bb1 Rc8 12. a3 Nc6 13. 0–0 d6 14. Nb3 Ba6 15. Rf2 Qd7 16. Rfc2 Nb8 17. Nf2 R×c2 18. R×c2 Rd8** "18. ... Rc8, and to play for a draw at once, would have been advisable now, especially as he has to oppose rooks later on"—Hoffer. **19. Rc3 Ne8 20. Nd3 g6 21. Nf4 Bb7 22. Qc2 Rc8 23. Bd2 R×c3 24. B×c3 Ng7 25. Nd2 Bg5 26. Nh3 Be3† 27. Nf2 Ba6 28. Nf1 B×f2† 29. K×f2 f5** "Black commences now a self-weakening process with an attempt at an attack in an even position"—Hoffer. **30. Ng3 Qe7 31. Bb4** Not very effective, as Bird is able to keep the position closed and drawish. Instead 31. e×f5! N×f5 32. N×f5 e×f5 (if 32. ... g×f5 33. d5!) 33. Ba2† Kg7 34. Be6! favorably opens up the position for the bishop pair. **31. ... Qd7 32. Ba2 d5 33. e×d5 e×d5 34. Ne2 Ne6 35. Bc3 Nc6 36. Qd2 Qd6 37. Qe3 Kg7 38. g3 g5** "The object being to prevent 39. Ng1, 40. f4, and eventually 42. Ne5. But simply 38. ... B×e2, followed by 39. ... f4, would have been good enough to draw"—Hoffer. **39. f4 B×e2 40. Q×e2 Kg6** 40. ... g×f4 takes away all pressure. White is able to win back the pawn with correct play, but the endgame is plain sailing for Black, for example after 41. Qh5 f×g3† 42. h×g3 Nc7 43. Bb1 Qg6 44. Q×f5 Q×f5† 45. B×f5 Ne7 and the knights hold thread with the bishops. **41. Bb1 Nc×d4?!** This pawn, on the other hand, is a dangerous one to capture. 41. ... h6 is very solid. **42. B×d4?!** The smart 42. Qd2 Nc6 43. B×f5†! is much stronger. The bishop pair comes alive again. **42. ... N×d4 43. Qe8† Kg7 44. f×g5 f4** The best try. **45. B×h7** "A very pretty move indeed"—Hoffer. **45. ... f×g3† 46. h×g3 K×h7?** "Mr. Bird made this move without a moment's consideration, although he had more than half an hour's time to spare. Of course he could have saved the game with 46. ... Qe6, forcing the exchange of queens"—Hoffer. 46. ... Qe6 47. Qh5 Nf5 48. B×f5 Q×f5† 49. Qf3 Q×g5 is completely drawn. **47. Qf7† Kh8 48. g6** Black resigns—*Boston Daily Advertiser* (Burille), 16 March 1896; *The Field* (Hoffer), 31 March 1896.

---

# HASTINGS CHESS FESTIVAL 1896

The third festival of the Hastings chess club was held during the week that followed the cable match. Three masters were invited. Bird and Blackburne were now joined by Teichmann. The formula remained untouched, except that the program was extended to last four days.

On Monday 16, March Bird opened the festivities with a simultaneous exhibition on 25 boards. He won 17 games, lost 5 others against G. Herington, T.H. Cole, J.A. Watt, J.T. Pughe and A.R. Henry; there were 3 draws, with Miss Watson, J.E. Watson and G. McCormick. On Tuesday Bird lost, together with Dr. Colborne, against Teichmann and Dr. Ballingall. Wednesday afternoon the game between Blackburne and G. Herington against Bird and Chapman drew attention. The former were victorious. Bird also lost his third consultation game on Thursday, with Wayte against Blackburne and Chapman. That evening a new kind of event was tested. Each master played three games simultaneously against consulting teams of two players each. Bird beat A.C. Jenour and F.G. Mann. Two pairs held him to a draw: F.W. Womersley and A. Wisden, and Aloof and Cpt. Gardiner.

## (1247) Bird & Colborne–
**Teichmann & Ballingall    0–1**
Consultation game
Hastings, 17 March 1896
C37

     **1. e4 e5 2. f4 e×f4 3. Nf3 g5 4. Bc4 g4 5. Nc3 g×f3 6. Q×f3 d5 7. N×d5 Be6 8. d3 c6 9. N×f4 B×c4 10. d×c4 Nd7 11. Bd2 Ne5 12. Qh5 Bd6 13. c5 Bc7 14. Ne6 Qd7 15. Ng7† Kd8 16. 0-0-0 Kc8 17. Bc3 Qg4 18. Qf5† Q×f5 19. N×f5 Nf6 20. Nd6† B×d6 21. R×d6 Nfd7 22. Rf1 Re8 23. b4 Re7 24. Rh6 f6 25. Rf5 Kc7 26. Rfh5 Rgg8 27. g3 Rgg7 28. Rf5 Rg6 29. Rh4 b6 30. c×b6†**

**N×b6 31. B×e5† f×e5 32. Rfh5 Rgg7 33. g4 Nc4 34. c3 Kb6 35. h3 Rd7 36. Rf5 Rd2 37. a4 Rgd7 38. Rf3 Na3** White resigns—*Standard*, 24 March 1896.

## (1248) Blackburne & Herington–
**Bird & Chapman    1–0**
Consultation game
Hastings, 18 March 1896
C51

     **1. e4 e5 2. Nf3 Nc6 3. Bc4 Bc5 4. b4 B×b4 5. c3 Bc5 6. d4 e×d4 7. c×d4 Bb6 8. Bb2 Na5 9. d5 Ne7 10. Bd3 d6 11. Nc3 c5 12. Ne2 0-0 13. Rc1 f6 14. Nh4 Ng6 15. N×g6 h×g6 16. h4 Qe8 17. h5 c4 18. Bb1 Bg4 19. f3 Bd7 20. Qd2 c3 21. R×c3 g×h5 22. Ng3 Qg6 23. N×h5 Rac8 24. Bd3 Bc5 25. a3 b5 26. g4 b4 27. R×c5 d×c5 28. Nf4 Qg5 29. Rh5 Nb3 30. Qh2 b×a3 31. R×g5 f×g5 32. e5 Nd4 33. Qh7† Kf7 34. Bg6† Ke7 35. Q×g7†** Black resigns—*Liverpool Mercury*, 11 April 1896.

The next game fell outside of the official program. Blackburne's companion was likely the well-known lady player Kate Belinda Finn. Yet, the source speaks of "Messrs. Finn and Blackburne," suggesting (if correct) the player was male.

## (1249) Bird & Chapman–
**Blackburne & K.B. Finn    0–1**
Consultation game
Hastings, March 1896
C58

     **1. e4 e5 2. Nf3 Nc6 3. Bc4 Nf6 4. Ng5 d5 5. e×d5 Na5 6. Bb5† c6 7. d×c6 b×c6 8. Bd3 Be7 9. Nc3 0-0 10. Qe2 h6 11. Nf3 Bd6 12. 0-0 Re8 13. Be4 Rb8 14. a3 c5 15. d3 Bf8 16. Nd2 N×e4 17. d×e4 Nc6 18. Nb3 Nd4 19. Qd1 Ba6 20. Re1 Qh4 21. Be3 Rbd8 22. Nd2 Rd6 23. Nf3 Qd8 24. B×d4 e×d4 25. e5 Rb6 26. Na4 Rg6 27. Re4 Bb7 28. Rf4 R×g2† 29. Kf1 Rg6 30. c4 Qd7 31. b4 Qh3† 32. Ke1 B×f3** and Black wins—*Illustrated London News*, 4 July 1896.

---

# SIMPSON'S DIVAN TOURNAMENT 1896

During the first months of 1896 the rooms at Simpson's were thoroughly rejuvenated. Immediately afterwards an inauguration chess tournament was held. This tournament also gave the amateurs the opportunity to test their skills with a few of the best London masters. The field was formed by 12 regular frequenters. The outspoken favorite among them was Richard Teichmann. Bird, newly recovered from another bad attack of gout, also entered into the fray even though he was completely out of form and still ailing. The tournament rules did not diverge a lot from previous occasions, which gave rise to the usual criticism. With no playing schedule drawn up before the start, the players were at great liberty to choose the moment when they played which opponent. The games were spread during the afternoon and evening, which dented some of the public's interest. Players were obliged to play at least three games per week, a number that was impossible to achieve by the amateur players. As usual the tournament dragged on for a few more weeks. The final game was not played until around the middle of June.

Bird lost his first game against Mortimer. The old man recovered quite well by beating Loman and by at first playing well with Teichmann in a tense duel. This game was adjourned, but then Bird fell back upon his old habit of playing for a win when a draw was all he could hope for. Teichmann duly punished him, and this victory put the young German well on his way to the expected tournament victory. For Bird, matters went from bad to worse. He nearly lost all his remaining games, scoring just a few points along the way.

Bird ended with a disappointing 4 points in 11 games, in the company of Mortimer, Rolland and Reeves (playing under the pseudonym Dr. Farrow). Only William Joseph Ingoldsby, who forfeited several of his games due to illness, was below them. Bird's failure to fulfill the expectations of many, bore more on him than the defeats themselves.[2]

---

### Divan tournament, London, 18 April–June 1896

**Site:** Simpson's Divan
**Prizes:** Prize fund of ca. £40. 70% divided among the four prize winners, 30% divided among the other contestants
**Time limit:** 20 moves per hour

|  | | 1 | 2 | 3 | 4 | 5 | 6 | 7 | 8 | 9 | 10 | 11 | 12 | |
|---|---|---|---|---|---|---|---|---|---|---|---|---|---|---|
| 1 | R. Teichmann | | 1 | ½ | 1 | 1 | 0 | 1 | 1 | 1 | 1 | 1 | ½ | 9 |
| 2 | F.J. Lee | 0 | | ½ | 1 | 1 | 1 | 1 | 1 | ½ | 1 | 1 | ½ | 8½ |
| 3 | L. van Vliet | ½ | ½ | | ½ | 1 | 1 | 1 | 1 | 1 | 0 | 1 | 1 | 8½ |
| 4 | R. Loman | 0 | 0 | ½ | | 1 | 1 | ½ | 0 | 1 | 1 | 1 | 1 | 7 |
| 5 | O.C. Müller | 0 | 0 | 0 | 0 | | 1 | 1 | 0 | 1 | 1 | 1 | + | 6 |
| 6 | E. Creswell | 1 | 0 | 0 | 0 | 0 | | ½ | 1 | 1 | 1 | 0 | + | 5½ |
| 7 | R.H.F. Fenton | 0 | 0 | 0 | ½ | 0 | ½ | | 1 | ½ | 1 | 0 | + | 4½ |
| 8 | H.E. Bird | 0 | 0 | 0 | 1 | 1 | 0 | 0 | | 0 | 0 | 1 | + | 4 |
| 9 | H.A. Reeves | 0 | ½ | 0 | 0 | 0 | 0 | ½ | 1 | | 0 | 1 | + | 4 |
| 10 | J. Mortimer | 0 | 0 | 1 | 0 | 0 | 0 | 0 | 1 | 1 | | 0 | + | 4 |
| 11 | Rolland | 0 | 0 | 0 | 0 | 0 | 1 | 1 | 0 | 0 | 1 | | + | 4 |
| 12 | W.J. Ingoldsby | ½ | ½ | 0 | 0 | – | – | – | – | – | – | – | – | 1 |

The course of the tournament can be more or less reconstructed thanks to the table published each week in *The Field*. What remains unclear is whether Bird's game with Ingoldsby was actually played or not.

### (1250) Bird–Mortimer    0–1
Divan tournament (round 1)
London, 20 April 1896
C54

1. e4 e5 2. Nf3 Nc6 3. Bc4 Bc5 4. c3 Nf6 5. b4 Bb6 6. Qb3 0–0 7. d3 h6 8. 0–0 d6 9. a4 a5 10. b5 Ne7 11. Be3 Bg4 12. Nbd2 Ng6 13. Rfe1 Nh5 14. d4 Qe7 15. Bf1 Nhf4 16. g3 Nh5 17. Bg2 Kh7 18. h3 Bd7 19. d×e5 d×e5 20. B×b6 c×b6 21. c4 Rac8

22. Qe3 Qc5 23. Bf1 Be6 24. Rac1 Rfd8 25. Q×c5 R×c5 26. Nb3 Rc7 27. Nfd2 Ne7 28. Rc2 Rcd7 29. Rec1 f5 30. Nf3 Ng6 31. e×f5 B×f5 32. Rc3 Nf6 33. Re3 e4 34. Ne1 Ne5 35. Rcc3 Nd3 36. g4 Bg6 37. Ng2 Nb2 38. Rc1 N×a4 "and Black wins in 75 moves"—*St. James's Budget*, 3 July 1896.

### (1251) Loman–Bird    0–1
Divan tournament (round 2)
London, 23 April 1896
A85

1. d4 f5 2. e3 Nf6 3. c4 e6 4. Nc3 b6 5. Bd3 Bb7 6. f3 Be7 7. Nge2 0–0 8. 0–0 Na6 9. d5 Qe8 10. a3 c6 11. d×e6 d×e6 12. b4 Nc7 13. e4 f×e4 14. N×e4 c5 15. N×f6† g×f6 Positionally dubious but resulting in an interesting position. 15. ... B×f6 16. Rb1 is rather dry. 16. Qe1 Bd6 17. Nf4 17. Bf4 or 17. Qh4 are better tries for an advantage. 17. ... Rf7 18. Qh4 Rd8 19. Bc2 Be5 20. Rb1 c×b4 21. a×b4 Rd4 (*see diagram*) Bird succeeded in overcoming the small disadvantage and now even wins a pawn. White has enough play to compensate for it as he is able to neutralize Black's strong bishop.

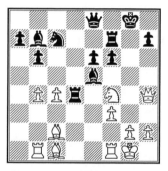

*After 21. ... Rd4*

22. Be3 R×c4 23. Bb3 B×f4 24. B×f4 Rd4 "If 24. ... R×b4 25. B×e6"—Gunsberg. 25. Rfd1 R×d1† 26. R×d1 Nd5 27. Bh4 Kh8 28. Re1 Qg8? Both 28. ... Nc7 and 28. ... Qd7 are perfectly fine. It is hard to see why Loman didn't play 29. R×e6. 29. Qe4? Qg6 29. ... Re7 gives better chances to play for more than a draw. 30. Qh4 "If 30. Q×e6 Re7, but he could have played 30. Q×g6 h×g6 31. R×e6 or 31. B×d5, remaining with bishops of different color and chances for a draw"—Gunsberg. 30. ... Re7 31. Rc1 Re8 32. B×d5 Keeping the bishop pair is the best way to preserve his compensation. 32. ... B×d5 33. Rc7 "The position is more difficult now but he could have played 33. Kf2 to save the f-pawn"—Gunsberg. 33. ... B×f3 34. Bg7† Kg8 35. Qh3? "And here 35. Qg3 Q×g3 36. h×g3 Be4 37. B×f6 etc. If 35. ... Bg4 36. h3 with a probable draw still"—Gunsberg. 35. ... Bg4? This offers White an ultimate defense with 36. Qh6!, when 36. ... Qb1† is neutralized by 37. Rc1. Correct is 35. ... Bh5!, forcing 36. Qb3 to cover b1, and then 36. ... Qe4! is strong. 36. Qc3? Qb1† 37. Kf2 Qf5† 38. Kg1 "38. Kg3 would be equally bad"—Gunsberg. 38. ... Rd8 39. h3 Rd1† 40. Kh2 Qf4† 41. Qg3 Rh1† White resigns—*Standard* (Gunsberg), 27 April 1896.

---

2. MacDonnell kept his faith in Bird: "Bird has not done well. Years and the gout do tell upon a man, however iron in constitution and sprightly in temperament or brilliant in imagination; but everybody hopes, and even believes, that the grand old champion will yet do wonderful deeds before this tournament is over." *Illustrated Sporting and Dramatic News*, 16 May 1896. ¶ Tinsley touched upon another cause of Bird's losses: "Turning to the play, some attention must be devoted to the doings of Mr. Bird. This veteran of both the past and present has been most unfortunate in the present contest. On several occasions he has by hard and good play obtained excellent games, but has come to grief by failing to make the best use of opportunities, or by making some glaring oversight at the critical juncture." *British Chess Magazine*, July 1896, p. 268.

## (1252) Bird–Teichmann　0–1

Divan tournament (round 3)
London, April 1896
*C65*

1. e4 e5 2. Nf3 Nc6 3. Bb5 Nf6 4. Qe2 Bc5 5. 0–0 0–0
6. c3 Re8 7. d3 h6 8. b4 Bf8 9. Ba4 d6 10. h3 Bd7 11. Bc2
Ne7 12. Rd1 Ng6 13. Be3 Qe7 14. Nbd2 Nh5 15. d4
Nhf4 16. B×f4 N×f4 17. Qf1 g5 18. Nc4 Bb5 19. a4 B×c4
20. Q×c4 Bg7 21. Qf1 c5 22. b5 b6 23. Re1 Rad8 24. d5
Qd7 25. Re3 Bf6 26. Nh2 h5 27. Bd1 Kg7 28. Rg3 Rh8
29. Ra2 Rdg8 30. Qc4 Kf8 31. Qf1 g4 32. h×g4 Bh4
33. c4 f6 34. Raa3 B×g3 35. f×g3 h×g4 36. N×g4 Nh5
37. N×f6 N×f6 38. Q×f6† Ke8 39. Rf3 Rh7 40. Rf5 Qe7
41. Bh5† Kd8 42. g4 Q×f6 43. R×f6 Rhh8 This and the
following move are in all likelihood transcription errors.
44. Re6 Kd7 45. Bg6 Kc8 46. g3 Kd8 47. Bh5 Rg7
48. Kg2 Rf8 49. Kh3 Rf1 50. Re8† Kd7 51. Rh8 Rh1†
52. Kg2 Rc1 53. Kh3 R×c4 54. g5 R×g5 55. Rh7† Kd8
56. Rh8† Ke7 57. g4 Rg7 58. Re8† Kd7 59. Re6 R×e4
60. Be8† Kd8 61. Bc6 Rg8 62. g5 Re1 63. Kh2 Rf1
White resigns—*The Field*, 9 May 1896.

## (1253) Bird v. Reeves　0–1

Divan tournament (round 4)
London, 2 May 1896
*Game score missing*

*The Sunday Times* of 25 January 1914, which reported
the death of Reeves, wrote: "In 1896, as 'Dr. Farrow,' Mr.
Reeves entered for a tournament at 'Simpson's' with the
late H.E. Bird … and several strong amateurs, for the express
purpose of testing his variations in actual practice. But sad
to say, he got very little chance, as with the exception of
Bird, who had the courage of a lion, no one ventured to
play the Ruy Lopez against him."

## (1254) Lee–Bird　1–0

Divan tournament (round 5)
London, May 1896
*A85*

1. d4 f5 2. c4 Nf6 3. Nc3 e6 4. a3 b6 5. e3 Bb7 6. Nf3 Be7 7. Be2
0–0 8. 0–0 a6 9. Ne5 Qe8 10. Bf3 Ne4 11. Bd2 Bf6 12. Bh5 g6
13. Be2 d6 14. Nd3 Bg5 15. f4 Bh6 16. Nf2 N×d2 17. Q×d2 Nd7
18. Nh3 Nf6 19. Bf3 B×f3 20. R×f3 Rc8 21. Qe2 c5 22. d×c5
b×c5 23. e4 Rb8 24. e×f5 e×f5 25. Re3 Qc6 26. Ng5 Rb7 27. Rd1
B×g5 28. f×g5 Ng4 29. Re6 Rd7 30. h3 Ne5 31. Q×e5 d×e5
32. R×c6 R×d1† 33. N×d1 Rd8 34. Nc3 Rd2 35. R×c5 e4
36. Na4 e3 37. Re5 Rd1† 38. Kh2 f4 39. c5 Rd2 40. c6 Rd6 41. c7
Black resigns—*Morning Post*, 18 May 1896.

## (1255) Bird v. Rolland　1–0

Divan tournament (round 6)
London, May 1896
*Game score missing*

Simpson's Divan around 1900 (courtesy Savoy Archives).

## (1256) Bird v. Fenton　0–1

Divan tournament (round 7 or 8)
London, May 1896
*Game score missing*

## (1257) Bird v. Ingoldsby　1–0

Divan tournament (round 7 or 8)
London, May 1896
*Game score missing*

## (1258) Bird–van Vliet　0–1

Divan tournament (round 9 or 10)
London, May 1896
*D00*

1. d4 d5 2. e3 Nf6 3. Bd3 c5 4. c3 e6 5. Nd2 Nbd7 6. f4 Bd6

7. Nh3 b6 8. 0–0 Bb7 9. Qf3 Qc7 10. Re1 0–0–0 11. a4 h6 12. Qf1 Nb8 13. Nf3 Ne4 14. Bd2 f6 15. Red1 g5 16. B×e4 d×e4 17. Ne1 Ba6 18. c4 c×d4 19. b3 d3 20. a5 Bb7 21. b4 Rhg8 22. a×b6 a×b6 23. c5 b×c5 24. b×c5 B×c5 25. Rdc1 Rd5 26. f×g5 Rf5 27. Nf2 Rg×g5 28. g3 Nc6 29. Qg2 Ne7 30. Ra4 Bc6 31. Rac4 Re5 32. Nh3 Bd6 33. N×g5 R×g5 34. Kh1 Kd7 35. Qh3 h5 36. Ng2 Qb7 37. Nf4 B×f4 38. g×f4 Rb5 39. Rd4† Bd5 40. Q×h5 Rb2 41. Qd1 Nc6 42. Bc3 N×d4 43. B×d4 Re2 44. Qg1 Rc2 45. Rb1 Qc8 46. B×f6 Qf8 47. Be5 Qh6 48. Ra1 Bb7 49. Rc1 Q×h2† White resigns—*British Chess Magazine*, July 1896, pp. 268–269.

## (1259) Bird v. Creswell    0–1
Divan tournament (round 9 or 10)
London, May 1896
*Game score missing*

## (1260) Bird v. Müller    1–0
Divan tournament (round 11)
London 1896
*Game score missing*

# The Divan Chess Association

On Saturday 25 April 1896 a new chess organization was formed at the Divan. It was fittingly baptized the Divan Chess Association. The driving force and main representative behind it was Emanuel Lasker. In a public letter he presented the Divan Chess Association as a gathering of professional chess players. They were open for match arrangements against strong amateur as well as against foreign teams. All the London chess masters, Bird included, were present at the inaugural meeting and all supported Lasker's initiative.

The new Association contested just one match during its short existence. On 15 May the amateurs of the City of London Chess Club managed to obtain a draw (4–4) against a strong master team that was headed by Lasker himself. Bird did not take part in this match.

The limited scope of the Divan Chess Association soon proved to be a considerable burden, and even before the match with the City of London Chess Club, the constitution had been rewritten in order to make first-class amateurs eligible for membership. Despite this change, the whole idea did not catch on, and a short while later the Association was declared defunct.

# Hastings Chess Festival 1897

The fourth Hastings chess festival took place in February 1897. Bird and Blackburne (the latter living in London again) were joined once more by Gunsberg. Lasker had also received an invitation but he was not able to make it in time, being on his return from Moscow. The program was scrupulously the same as the previous year.

On Monday afternoon, 15 February, Bird and Dobell quickly succumbed to Gunsberg and Locock. The following evening Bird gave his simultaneous exhibition. Bird defeated 13 of his 24 oppo-

nents. Three men beat him, H.E. Chapman, J.A. Watt and H.W. Trenchard. Eight games ended in a draw: against Miss Garland, Miss Thomas, Mrs. Ridpath, Dr. Lewis, Messrs. H.E. Dobell, R. Kay, H.R. Mackeson, and G.W. Bradshaw.

On Wednesday afternoon the consultation game between Blackburne and Aloof as White and Bird and Womersley as Black was adjourned in a hopeless position for the former. That evening Blackburne and Chapman produced a magnificent finish in their game against Bird and Trenchard. On the next day Bird and Trenchard succumbed again, now against Blackburne and Jenour. Finally, the event was closed with an exhibition against consulting teams. Bird won against two teams (team one: Hall, A.C. Jenour, H. Dowsett and C.G. Skyrme, team two: J.E. Watson, H.R. Mackeson and Miss Watson). The third team (H.E. Dobell, J.A. Watt, A.G. Ginner and G.W. Bradshaw) achieved a draw.

Bird's performance was appreciated abundantly. It was considered that his force was highly suited for this kind of events, much more than for a serious contest such as the second cable match between England and America, for which Bird fell out of the selection.[3]

## (1261) Bird & Dobell–Gunsberg & Locock    0–1
Consultation game
Hastings, 15 February 1897
*A02*

1. f4 e5 2. f×e5 d6 3. e×d6 B×d6 4. Nf3 g5 5. c3 g4 6. Qa4† Nc6 7. Nd4 Qh4† 8. Kd1 g3 9. b3 Q×h2 10. N×c6 Q×h1 11. Ke1 Qg1 12. Ne5† c6 13. Nd3 Bf5 14. e4 0–0–0 15. e×f5 Nf6 16. Kd1 Q×f1† 17. Kc2 Q×f5 18. Q×a7 Q×d3† and Black wins—*Pall Mall Gazette*, 22 February 1897.

## (1262) Bird & Trenchard–Blackburne & Chapman    0–1
Consultation game
Hastings, 17 February 1897
*C31*

1. e4 e5 2. f4 d5 3. e×d5 e4 4. Bb5† c6 5. d×c6 b×c6 6. Bc4 Nf6 7. Be2 Bc5 8. Kf1 0–0 9. Nc3 Na6 10. a3 Nc7 11. Qe1 Ne6 12. g3 Nd4 13. Qd1 a5 14. Kg2 Re8 15. h3 Nf5 16. Bg4 N×g3 17. K×g3 Nh5† 18. Kg2 Qh4 19. N×e4 R×e4 20. Qf3 R×f4 21. d4 R×f3 22. N×f3 Qg3† White resigns—*British Chess Magazine*, March 1897, p. 93.

## (1263) Blackburne & Aloof–Bird & Womersley    0–1
Consultation game
Hastings, 17 February 1897
*C33*

1. e4 e5 2. f4 e×f4 3. Nf3 Be7 "There are alternative moves, such as 3. ... d6 or 3. ... Nf6, but this line of play, which we believe is a speciality of Mr. Bird's, has the advantage of producing a very promising counterattack"—Guest. 4. h4 Not such a clever idea. 4. ... d5

3. MacDonnell wrote: "Bird, however, is essentially a rapid player, and brilliantly as he is able to acquit himself in exhibition games or at ordinary chess, it is doubtful whether he is constituted to conduct a slow and patient struggle extending over a couple of days, like some of those by virtue of which England recovered the International Trophy." *Illustrated Sporting and Dramatic News*, 27 February 1897.

**5. e×d5 Bg4 6. Be2 Nf6** He could just as well execute his idea of playing 6. ... B×f3 and capture the h-pawn. **7. Nc3 0–0 8. d4 Nh5 9. 0–0** Matters could have been much worse for White. **9. ... Nd7 10. Ne4** 10. Ng5! leads to a complicated game with chances for White as well. **10. ... h6** The h-pawn could be taken again. **11. Ne5** 11. Nh2 is correct. **11. ... B×e2** 11. ... N×e5! 12. B×g4 N×g4 13. Q×g4 Q×d5 is joyless for White. **12. Q×e2 Ng3** Another serious inaccuracy. After 12. ... N×e5 13. Q×h5 Ng6, the game turns out to be equal. The text move gives White some time that he can use to build up an attack. **13. N×g3 f×g3 14. Qg4** More dangerous is 14. Ng4!, aiming for a possible sacrifice at h6. The text move implies a simplification. **14. ... N×e5 15. d×e5 Q×d5 16. B×h6 Q×e5** *(see diagram)* Black is a pawn up again. His king looks in danger as White can gain a few tempi by harassing the queen. The White allies try to make use of their chances, but ultimately they fall short.

*After 16. ... Q×e5*

**17. Rae1 Bc5† 18. Kh1 Q×b2!** "This looks dangerous at first glance, and it is evident that Black must have looked very deeply into the position to venture upon such a course"—Guest. **19. c3?** As said, Blackburne and Aloof try everything to enforce their attack, but the position just holds for Black. Therefore 19. Rb1 is the only possibility. White regains his pawns and reaches an endgame after 19. ... Qd4 20. Rf4 f5 21. R×d4 f×g4 22. R×g4 Rf7 23. Bf4 b6 24. B×g3 Re8. The better placed rooks and more intact pawn structure remain to favor for Black. **19. ... Q×c3 20. Rc1 f5** 20. ... Qd4 is the best way to consolidate his edge, especially as 21. Rf4 isn't possible due to 21. ... Qb2! 22. Rff1 Bd6. **21. R×f5** 21. Qh5 is the only playable move. Black retains a great advantage. **21. ... Rae8!** This strong move effectively terminates the struggle. **22. R×f8† B×f8 23. Qd1 Qe5 24. Bd2 b6 25. Rc3 Bc5 26. Qb3† Kh8 27. R×g3 Bd6 28. Qd1 Rf8 29. Rh3 Rf2 30. Be3 R×a2 31. Bd4 Qe2 32. Q×e2 R×e2 33. g4 Re4 34. Bf2 R×g4 35. h5 Kh7 36. h6 g×h6 37. B×b6 Ra4** White resigns—*Morning Post* (Guest), 22 February 1897.

## (1264) Locock & Trenchard–Bird & Chapman    0–1

Consultation game
Hastings, February 1897
*C44*

**1. e4 e5 2. Nf3 Nc6 3. c3 d5 4. Qa4 d×e4?! 5. N×e5 Qd5 6. N×c6 b×c6 7. Bc4 Qd7 8. 0–0 Bd6 9. f3?!** The simple 9. Re1 picks up a pawn. **9. ... e×f3 10. R×f3 Nf6 11. d4 0–0 12. Nd2 Qe7 13. Nf1 Bg4 14. Re3 Qd7 15. Bd2 Be6** Avoiding the drawish 15. ... Nd5. **16. B×e6 f×e6 17. Rae1 Ng4 18. R×e6?** This must have been the move Bird and Chapman were counting on to be played. After

**18. Rf3** White remains a solid pawn up, but their chances to convert it into a win are limited. **18. ... R×f1† 19. K×f1 Qf7† 20. Kg1 B×h2† 21. Kh1 Rf8 22. Qc4** "The only move to prevent an immediate checkmate, or the loss of the queen. Black, nevertheless, was able to announce mate in five moves. The game is one of the prettiest we have seen for some time, and is worth several 60 moves drawn games played in the classic style"—van Vliet. **22. ... Nf2† 23. K×h2 Qh5† 24. Kg3 Qg4† 25. Kh2 Qh4† 26. Kg1 Qh1** mate—*Hereford Times* (van Vliet), 27 February 1897.

## (1265) Blackburne & Jenour–Bird & Trenchard    1–0

Consultation game
Hastings, 18 February 1897
*C51*

**1. e4 e5 2. Nf3 Nc6 3. Bc4 Bc5 4. b4 B×b4 5. c3 Bc5 6. d4 e×d4 7. c×d4 Bb6 8. Nc3 d6 9. a4 a5 10. Nd5 Bg4 11. Bb2 Nge7 12. Ne3 Bh5 13. g4 Bg6 14. d5 Nb4 15. Nf5 B×f5 16. g×f5 f6 17. Rg1 Rg8 c1 Kd7 19. Bd4 Nc8 20. B×b6 N×b6 21. Bb5† Kc8 22. Nd4 g6 23. Ne6 g×f5 24. Ke2 R×g1 25. Q×g1 Qh8 26. R×c7† Kb8 27. Qc1 Na6 28. Re7 Ka7 29. B×a6 Rc8 30. Qb2 Qg8 31. R×b7† Ka8 32. Q×b6 Qg4† 33. Kd2 Rc2† 34. K×c2 Q×e4† 35. Kb2** Black resigns—*British Chess Magazine*, March 1897, pp. 95–96.

---

# MATCH WITH LEE 1897

The traditionally dull summer season was invigorated by a match between Bird and Francis J. Lee. This match was not an ordinary one, as both Bird and Lee had the aspiration that it would be the first in a series of matches to serve as qualification contests for the future Anglo-American cable matches.[4] Both players agreed that the match would be played for the first five games won. The games were to be played on Mondays, Tuesdays, Thursdays and Fridays between 4 and 7 p.m. An unusual time limit of 23 moves an hour was agreed upon. The match commenced on 12 July and was immediately set on fire.

This encounter has produced some remarkably good games, and has proved very enticing to those visitors who enjoy a hard-fought and spirited contest. Mr. Bird, despite age and gout, always contrives to impart animation to his games, and, although he has an opponent of a peculiarly solid type, there has been no lack of sprightliness in the play. Mr. Lee won the first two games in good style, but this only had the effect of inducing the old warrior to pull himself together, and he thereupon won three running. In the next three games, however, Mr. Bird was unsuccessful. He had some chances, but his impetuosity perhaps was greater than his discretion, so that at the conclusion of play on Monday night his score was only three to five [wins] [*Illustrated Sporting and Dramatic News*, 31 July 1897].

Lee thus started off with two wins but Bird overhauled him and took the lead after the fifth game. After seven games, with Lee in the lead again, Bird proposed to extend the match until the first player would have won seven games. Lee agreed and subsequently enhanced his advantage by winning the eighth and eleventh game

4. See the *Illustrated Sporting and Dramatic News*, 17 July 1897: "If a series of such matches could be arranged they would be of great value in determining the qualifications of our own representatives in the Anglo-American cable contests."

and drawing the other two. Bird narrowed the gap a last time, to 6–4, by winning the twelfth game. In the thirteenth game Lee forced the decision.

Though being defeated with clear figures, Bird's performance was perceived as a decent one. He blundered away a win in at least two games. Everyone was aware that the advancing age of the veteran played a crucial role in his defeat.[5]

| Match with Lee, 12 July–6 August 1897 | | | | | | | | | | | | | | |
|---|---|---|---|---|---|---|---|---|---|---|---|---|---|---|
| | **1** | **2** | **3** | **4** | **5** | **6** | **7** | **8** | **9** | **10** | **11** | **12** | **13** | |
| F.J. Lee | 1 | 1 | 0 | 0 | 0 | 0 | 1 | 1 | 1 | ½ | ½ | 1 | 0 | 1 | 7 |
| H.E. Bird | 0 | 0 | 1 | 1 | 1 | 0 | 0 | 0 | 0 | ½ | ½ | 0 | 1 | 0 | 4 |

**(1266) Lee–Bird    1–0**
Match (game 1)
London, 12 July 1897
*C26*

1. e4 e5 2. Nc3 Nf6 3. g3 Nc6 4. Bg2 d6 5. Nge2 Bg4 6. h3 Be6 7. d4 Bd7 8. d5 Nb8 9. f4 Be7 10. Be3 g6 11. Qd2 h5 12. 0–0–0 a6 13. Ng1 b5 14. Re1 b4 15. Nd1 a5 16. Nf2 Bb5 17. Nf3 Nbd7 18. g4 Qb8 19. g5 Ng8 20. f5 g×f5 21. e×f5 f6 22. Ne4 Qb7 23. Nh4 f×g5 24. Ng6 Rh7 25. N×g5 B×g5 26. B×g5 Ngf6 27. B×f6 N×f6 28. Qg5 Rf7 29. Nh8 Rf8 30. Qg6† Kd8 31. Nf7† Ke7 32. R×e5† d×e5 33. d6† c×d6 34. B×b7 Ra7 35. Bd5 Be8 36. Qg1 Rd7 37. Be6 B×f7 38. B×d7 N×d7 39. Qa7 Bd5 40. Rg1 Black resigns—*Morning Post*, 2 August 1897.

**(1267) Bird–Lee    0–1**
Match (game 2)
London, 13 July 1897
*Game score missing*

**(1268) Lee–Bird    0–1**
Match (game 3)
London, 15 July 1897
*Game score missing*

**(1269) Bird–Lee    1–0**
Match (game 4)
London, 16 July 1897
*A03*

1. f4 d5 2. b3 c5 3. Bb2 e6 4. Nf3 Nf6 5. e3 Be7 6. Bd3 0–0 7. 0–0 Nc6 8. Nc3 a6 9. a3 b5 10. Qe1 c4 11. Be2 Bb7 12. Nd1 c×b3 13. c×b3 Na5 "A rather tempting but an injudicious move, since White has a good reply to it, and the knight has to remain out of play for a considerable time"—Guest. 14. Rb1 Rc8 15. Nf2 Ne4 16. Nd3 g6 17. Bd1 Nc6 18. b4 Bf6 19. Nfe5 Bg7 19. ... d4 cuts down all White's attempts to grasp the initiative. 20. Bf3 "Threatening to win a pawn by 22. B×e4 and 23. Nc5"—Guest. 20. ...

5. Bird was particularly upset with the way Lee treated his trusted Dutch Defense: "The veteran, indeed, is himself inclined to admit that the opening on which he has relied in so many memorable engagements is hardly trustworthy when opposed by this kind of strategy. Bird is not the man to ride his hobby-horse to death, and he has fully made up his mind to adopt new tactics at Berlin, if he can arrange, as he desires, to compete in the tournament that commences there in mid–September." *Illustrated Sporting and Dramatic News*, 14 August 1897.

Francis J. Lee.

N×e5 21. B×e5 Nd6 21. ... B×e5 leads to an equal endgame. After White's next move, he is positionally better. 22. Nc5 Rc7 23. d4 Much better was 23. d3, keeping c4 under control. Black is then bound up. 23. ... B×e5 24. f×e5 Nc4 25. Rb3 Bc8 26. Be2 Nb6 26. ... f6, to free the bishop in the long run, is a constructive plan. 27. Qg3 Nd7 28. Qf4 N×c5 29. d×c5 The difference with the last line is clear. Black's bishop is a dead piece. 29. ... f5 *(see diagram)*

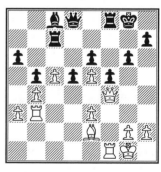

*After 29. ... f5*

30. Rd3 Now the position tends to be too closed. Although after 30. e×f6 *e.p.* Rcf7 31. Qb8 R×f6 32. Rbb1 Black has won back the pawn, the infiltrated White queen causes him a lot of worries. 30. ... Bb7 31. h4 Qe7 32. Rd4 Qg7 33. Rf3 Qe7?! Black hasn't the luxury to do nothing, as his kingside is in need of defense. Therefore 33. ... Bc6, intending to support the g-pawn, is safe. 34. Rg3 Qe8 34. ... Rf7 was absolutely necessary as the g-pawn becomes untenable now. 35. h5 Rg7 36. Qh6 g5 37. R×g5 Rff7 38. R×g7† R×g7 39. Bf3 Kh8 40. Qf4 Qe7 41. h6 Rg6 42. Bh5 Rg5 43. Qh4 Qd8

**44. Kh2 Rg8 45. Bf7** and White wins—*Morning Post* (Guest), 26 July 1897.

**(1270) Lee–Bird   0–1**
Match (game 5)
London, 20 July 1897
*Game score missing*

**(1271) Bird–Lee   0–1**
Match (game 6)
London, 22 July 1897
*C54*

1. e4 e5 2. Nf3 Nc6 3. Bc4 Bc5 4. c3 Nf6 5. b4 Bb6 6. d3 d6 7. Bg5 Ne7 8. 0–0 Ng6 9. Nbd2 h6 10. Be3 c6 11. Bb3 Bc7 12. Re1 0–0 13. d4 Qe7 14. h3 Be6 15. Qc2 Nh5 16. d×e5 d×e5 17. Nc4 Qf6 18. Nh2 Nhf4 19. Kh1 Rfd8 20. B×f4 N×f4 21. Ne3 Rd7 22. B×e6 Q×e6 23. Nf3 Rad8 24. Nf5 Kh7 25. Kh2 Bb6 26. g3 Rd3 27. N3d4 e×d4 28. g×f4 d×c3 29. Re2 g6 30. Ng3 h5 31. f5 Qe5 32. f×g6† f×g6 33. h4 B×f2 Black wins—*Illustrated London News*, 14 August 1897.

**(1272) Lee–Bird   1–0**
Match (game 7)
London, 23 July 1897
*Game score missing*

**(1273) Bird–Lee   0–1**
Match (game 8)
London, 26 July 1897
*Game score missing*

**(1274) Lee–Bird   ½–½**
Match (game 9)
London, 27 July 1897
*Game score missing*

**(1275) Bird–Lee   ½–½**
Match (game 10)
London, 29 July 1897
*Game score missing*

**(1276) Lee–Bird   1–0**
Match (game 11)
London, 3 August 1897
*A81*

1. d4 f5 2. g3 Nf6 3. Bg2 e6 4. Nh3 Bd6 5. 0–0 0–0 6. c4 c6 7. Nc3 Bc7 8. e4 d5 9. e5 Ne4 10. Ne2 h6 11. b3 c5 12. c×d5 e×d5 13. f3 Ng5 14. N×g5 h×g5 15. f4 c×d4 16. N×d4 g4 17. Kh1 Nc6 18. Nb5 d4 19. Ba3 Rf7 20. Rc1 Be6 21. Nd6 B×d6 22. B×d6 Qa5 23. Rf2 Bd5 24. Rc5 B×g2† 25. R×g2 Qb6 26. Qd3 g6 27. h4 Rd8 28. Qc4 Kg7 29. Kh2 Rh8 30. b4 Qd8 31. b5 Na5 32. Q×d4 Kh6 33. Rgc2 b6 34. Rc8 Q×c8 35. R×c8 R×c8 36. e6 Rh7 37. Qf6 Rb7 38. e7 Black resigns—*Hereford Times*, 14 August 1897.

**(1277) Bird–Lee   1–0**
Match (game 12)
London, 5 August 1897
*Game score missing*

**(1278) Lee–Bird   1–0**
Match (game 13)
London, 6 August 1897
*A81*

1. d4 f5 2. g3 Nf6 3. Bg2 d5 4. Nf3 e6 5. Nbd2 c5 6. e3 Nc6 7. 0–0 Be7 8. b3 0–0 9. Bb2 Bd7 10. Ne5 N×e5 11. d×e5 Ng4 12. h3 Nh6 13. c4 Bc6 14. Qe2 Qc7 15. Rfd1 Rad8 16. c×d5 B×d5 17. Kh2 Nf7 18. f4 B×g2 19. K×g2 Rd7 20. Nf3 Rfd8 21. R×d7 Q×d7 22. Kf2 g5 23. Rc1 b5 24. Rc2 Qc6 25. Rd2 Rc8 26. Bc3 b4 27. Bb2 Kf8 28. Qc4 g4 29. h×g4 f×g4 30. Nh2 h5 31. e4 Rd8 32. R×d8† B×d8 33. Bc1 Be7 34. Be3 a5 35. Nf1 Kg7 36. Nd2 h4 37. Qe2 Nh6 38. g×h4 B×h4† 39. Kg1 a4 40. Kf1 a×b3 41. a×b3 Kh7 42. Qd3 Be7 43. f5 e×f5 44. e×f5 Qh1† 45. Ke2 Bf8 46. f6† Kh8 47. Qe4 Qh5 48. e6 Nf5 49. Bf4 Nd4† 50. Kd3 N×e6 51. Q×e6 Qh3† 52. Be3 Qh5 53. Ne4 g3 54. N×g3 Qd1† 55. Ke4 Qc2† 56. Kf3 Qd1† 57. Kg2 Qc2† 58. Bf2 Qg6 59. Qf5 Q×f5 60. N×f5 Kg8 61. Ne7† Kf7 62. B×c5 Black resigns—*St. James's Budget*, 20 August 1897.

---

## ATTEMPTS TO ENTER A GERMAN CONGRESS

The decline of British chess at a top level was revealed by the number of British players making it into German tournaments. Gone were the days when almost the complete British chess elite travelled to the bi-annual congresses. At the international tournament held in Nuremberg in 1896 just one genuine British player, Blackburne, was allowed to enter the field. The British press could further boast only the participation of the temporary residents Lasker and Teichmann. Lee, Tinsley and Bird were a few of the other players sending in their candidature, but they were all refused.

A similar scenario developed in 1897 when the Berliner Schachgesellschaft commemorated seventy years of existence with a major tournament. Bird was among various British players to make another attempt to play in Germany. At first the veteran had been very optimistic about his chances to head for the German capital as his name figured on an initial list of competitors. Bird, however, lacked the financial resources to undertake the trip. For this purpose he wrote a public letter to further his nomination and ask for the support of the British chess community.

Reminiscences of over 45 years and recollections of a visit to Berlin in 1882 [*sic*], and exchange of promises then, have made me wish to take part in the international chess tournament to commence there on September 12, so on receipt of program I sent in my name as a player. I may mention that I have not participated in any of the tournaments (five in number) which have taken place abroad since 1885, and those English representatives who did play were not fortunate. Perhaps it is not unnatural that I should like to have one more bout. If any chess friends would like to cooperate with me in the outlay of the little venture I shall be glad to hear from them, and shall feel much obliged.

The tournament play will take about three weeks [*Morning Post*, 16 August 1897].

Bird gained a lot of sympathy with his plans, but saw his entry refused by the committee. Lee and Mason were in the same situation. Various columnists showed little understanding for this decision.

There is no man living at the present moment who can boast, as Mr. Bird can, of having played with all the strong players of half a century. Granting that Mr. Bird's play in the natural order of things may have lost some of its keenness, it would have been, as we have said, as human nature goes, a peculiarly ungracious act to exclude a player with such a famous past, who has 50 years of work in the cause of chess to his credit, even if it were justified; that is to say, if his exclusion had taken place in order to admit men of greater strength than he is at the present time. But the result of play shows this was not the case, and that his exclusion was not justified even by any such flimsy pretext. Players have been admitted in this tournament who are inferior in strength to Mr. Bird over the board [*Birmingham Weekly Mercury*, 2 October 1897; first published in the *Birmingham Daily Gazette*].

# A FEW EXHIBITIONS, 1897–1898

Bird gave about half a dozen of exhibitions between March 1897 and March 1898. The first one brought him to the Ideal Café, the new quarters of the Ladies' Chess Club.[6] This club, a gathering place for chess enthusiasts of the fair sex, existed since January 1895. The ladies succeeded in scoring very decent results against chess masters in simultaneous exhibitions as well as in matches against other teams. Bird was their guest on Monday 30 March 1897. During the afternoon, the 15-year-old George Thomas was delivered by his mother, the club's vice-president, to perform a first simultaneous exhibition. Already a year earlier he had beaten Emanuel Lasker, and he would grow into one of England's finest masters of the early twentieth century. The boy was followed, at 7 p.m., by Bird. He opposed 15 ladies: 3 of them, Mrs. Fagan, Miss Fox and Miss Field dealt ably with Bird's frivolities.[7]

## (1279) Bird–Miss Fox  0–1
Simultaneous game
London (Ladies C.C.), 30 March 1897
C33

1. e4 e5 2. f4 e×f4 3. Bc4 d5 4. B×d5 Nf6 5. Nc3 Bb4 6. Qf3 Bd6 7. d4 Bg4 8. Qf2 Qe7 9. Bd2 N×d5 10. Kf1 N×c3 11. B×c3 0–0 12. e5 Bb4 13. Q×f4 Bh5 14. Nf3 f6 15. Re1 f×e5 16. Qe4 Nd7 17. Q×b7 B×c3 18. b×c3 Rab8 19. Q×c7 B×f3 20. g×f3

R×f3† 21. Ke2 Rbf8 22. Kd1 e4 23. Q×a7 e3 24. Qa5 Qe4 25. Re2 Rf1† 26. R×f1 R×f1† 27. Re1 Qf3† White resigns— *Lady's Pictorial*, 10 April 1897.

In October Bird remained in Cirencester for a week as the guest of the local chess club. It appears that he gave just one simultaneous exhibition against 21 opponents. Bird was beaten by the club's president, Herbert Ellis Norris, and the Rev. G.A.E. Kempson. H. Zachary drew his game. The two games that survive were probably played offhand.

## (1280) Norris–Bird  0–1
Offhand game
Cirencester, October 1897
C55

1. e4 e5 2. Nf3 Nc6 3. Bc4 Bc5 4. 0–0 Nf6 5. d4 e×d4 6. e5 d5 7. e×f6 d×c4 8. Re1† Be6 9. Ng5 Qd5 10. Nc3 Qf5 11. Nce4 Bb6 12. g4 Qg6 13. f×g7 Rg8 14. f4 0–0–0 15. f5 B×f5 16. g×f5 Q×f5 17. Rf1 d3† 18. Kh1 Qd5 19. R×f7 h6 20. Qg4† Kb8 21. Ne6 Ne5 22. Qf5 N×f7 23. Q×d5 R×d5 24. Nf6 Rd6 25. N×g8 R×e6 26. Nf6 Re1† 27. Kg2 Rg1† 28. Kh3 R×g7 29. c×d3 c×d3 30. Bd2 Bd4 White resigns— *Morning Post*, 1 November 1897.

## (1281) Norris–Bird  1–0
Offhand game
Cirencester, October 1897
C58

1. e4 e5 2. Nf3 Nc6 3. Bc4 Nf6 4. Ng5 d5 5. e×d5 Na5 6. Bb5† c6 7. d×c6 b×c6 8. Qf3 c×b5 9. Q×a8 Bc5 10. Qf3 Bb7 11. Qe2 0–0 12. d3 h6 13. Nf3 e4 14. d×e4 N×e4 15. Be3 B×e3 16. f×e3 Nc4 17. Nc3 N×c3 18. b×c3 N×e3 19. Q×e3 Re8 20. Ne5 B×g2 21. Rg1 Qh4† 22. Kd1 Q×h2 23. Ng4 Qd6† 24. Qd4 Bf3† 25. Kc1 Qa3† 26. Kb1 Be4 27. N×h6† and White wins— *Morning Post*, 8 November 1897.

A short while later Bird was in Dover. Against 23 opponents, Bird won 19 games and drew 4, losing none.

On Wednesday 15 December Bird played 17 games at the North Kensington Chess Club. He beat 10 opponents, lost 3 games and drew 4.

Bird opened the new year on Sunday 13 January with a second visit to the Ladies' Chess Club. This time Gunsberg took care of the afternoon session; against 18 opponents he scored 14 wins, 3 losses and 1 draw. In the evening Bird improved his younger colleague's performance: 19 ladies opposed him, of whom Bird beat 15, losing 2 and drawing 2.[8]

On Tuesday 15 and Wednesday 16 March, Bird gave simultaneous exhibitions at the Mechanics' Institution in Nottingham. On

---

6. On 3 April 1897, the change of quarters was announced in the *Lady's Pictorial*: "They have secured a large and more commodious room, where there is very good catering, at the favorably known resort for intellectual people, the Ideal Café, 185 Tottenham Court Road...."

7. "Fifteen ladies in this contest [against] the single player [were] treated with that chivalrous consideration to the fair sex for which he is famed, his chief object being not so much to make sure of winning every game, as to afford enjoyment to his opponents, by treating them to all sorts of fanciful attacks in which pieces flew in all directions. But the veteran, after a couple of hours' play, soon saw that the ladies were too strong for such generously intended frivolities. He had to button himself up to his task, but he could not avoid defeat on several boards, the winners, Mrs. Fagan, Miss Fox and Miss Field being much gratified by their success." *Lady's Pictorial*, 10 April 1897.

8. Bird seemed to have been slightly uncomfortable amidst the female violence: "Their reception in the new rooms that they occupy, at 185, Tottenham Court-road, was a dazzling success. Mrs. Bowles did the honors, and a brilliant array of members and visitors sympathetically watched the valiant struggle that the old master, Mr. Bird, mad to overcome his embarrassment when surrounded by nineteen young mistresses of the game, whom he had rashly undertaken to encounter simultaneously. How he managed to win fifteen of the games I cannot imagine; but strange things happen in chess." *Illustrated Sporting and Dramatic News*, 21 January 1898.

**Herbert E. Norris (by kind permission of Norris Museum).**

the first day Bird met 13 players. He lost against E. Dale and Gerard. On the second day he suffered his only loss, once again against Dale.

## (1282) Bird–Dale    0–1
Simultaneous game
Nottingham, 15 March 1898
C33

1. e4 e5 2. f4 e×f4 3. Bc4 Nf6 4. e5 d5 5. Bb5† c6 6. e×f6 c×b5 7. Qe2† Be6 8. f×g7 B×g7 9. Nf3 a6 10. d4 Nc6 11. c3 Qf6 12. 0–0 0–0 13. Qd2 Bh6 14. Na3 Kh8 15. Nc2 Rg8 16. Nce1 Rg4 17. Nd3 Rag8 18. Rf2 Ne7 19. Nfe5 R4g7 20. N×f4 Qh4 21. g3 Bh3 22. Qe2 B×f4 23. B×f4 f6 24. Nd3 Nf5 25. Kh1 R×g3 26. B×g3 N×g3† 27. h×g3 Bg2† 28. K×g2 R×g3† 29. Kf1 Qh1 mate—*Nottinghamshire Guardian*, 26 March 1898.

# HASTINGS CHESS FESTIVAL 1898

The fifth Hastings Festival proceeded between 24 and 27 January 1898. As a winning formula was in no need of being changed, each day was filled with consultation games and simultaneous exhibitions. Bird, Blackburne and Gunsberg were the already well-known matadors for the Hastings chess public. They were complemented

by a representative from France, Dawid Janowski. Bird was too exhausted to give a simultaneous exhibition and he limited himself to a variety of consultation games.

On the opening day, Monday afternoon 24 January, Bird, "after consulting his companion, very chivalrously decided to accept a Hamppe-Allgaier" from Gunsberg and H.E. Dobell. Without much success: Bird and A.C. Jenour had to resign after 39 moves. Bird did better the next day, when he beat Janowski and Dr. J.G. Colborne after a long battle. Trenchard played on his side. Finally, on Thursday, Blackburne and Mann had White against Bird and Watt. A wild game ended in White's favor. In the evening Bird won one game and drew another against consulting teams.

## (1283) Gunsberg & Dobell–Bird & Jenour    1–0
Consultation game
Hastings, 24 January 1898
C25

1. e4 e5 2. Nc3 Nc6 3. f4 e×f4 4. Nf3 g5 5. h4 g4 6. Ng5 h6 7. N×f7 K×f7 8. Bc4 d5 9. B×d5† Kg7 10. d4 f3 11. g×f3 Nf6 12. Bf4 Ne7 13. Bb3 Rh7 14. Nb5 Ng6 15. Bg3 Nh5 16. B×c7 Qe8 17. Qd3 Bd7 18. Nd6 B×d6 19. B×d6 Kh8 20. 0–0–0 g3 21. Rdg1 Rg7 22. Qd2 Kh7 23. B×g3 Qe7 24. Bd5 Bc6 25. Bc4 Qf6 26. e5 Q×f3 27. Be2 Qf7 28. B×h5 B×h1 29. Qd3 Bc6 30. Bh2 Qf2 31. B×g6† Kh8 32. Qd2 Q×h4 33. e6 Rf8 34. Be5 Rf2 35. Qe3 Rg2 36. R×g2 B×g2 37. B×g7† K×g7 38. e7 Bc6 39. e8Q Black resigns—*St. James's Budget*, 28 January 1898.

## (1284) Bird & Trenchard–
## Blackburne & Chapman    0–1
Consultation game
Hastings, 24 January 1898
B00

1. e4 Nc6 2. d4 e5 3. d×e5 N×e5 4. f4 Nc6 5. Bc4 Bb4† 6. c3 Ba5 7. Nf3 Qe7 8. Qe2 d6 9. 0–0 Be6 10. Na3 Nf6 11. B×e6 Bb6† 12. Be3 Q×e6 13. B×b6 a×b6 14. Nb5 0–0–0 15. Ng5 Qe7 16. Qc4 h6 "Involving the sacrifice of a piece for a promising attack. We say sacrifice advisedly, for we assume that the White allies foresaw the consequences, when advancing the knight"—Hoffer. 17. N×f7 d5 18. Qa4 Q×f7 19. Qa8† Kd7 20. Q×b7 Ne8? There were better purposes thinkable for this knight. Instead 20. ... Rc8 forces White to close the d-file with 21. e×d5 (for if 21. Rad1? N×e4), and now after 21. ... Na5 22. Qa6 Ra8 23. Na7 N×d5 24. Rad1 Ke7 a very interesting position arises. 21. Rad1 Rb8 22. Qa6 Nf6 23. e×d5 Na5 *(see diagram)*

*After 23. ... Na5*

**24. d6** Compared to the line given instead of Black's twentieth move above, his king is still in a very hazardous zone. While the text move is good enough to nurture what should be a decisive attack, first 24. b4! and if 24. ... Nb7 25. d6 is even stronger. **24. ... c6 25. Rfe1?!** Not so good as 25. b4! c×b5 26. b×a5 Kd8 27. Rfe1 and Black's defense is stripped. **25. ... Rhe8 26. Re7†?!** The point of their previous move. The exchange of rooks and win of the d-pawn are, however, a dream coming true for Black. A dangerous initiative is kept with 26. Nd4 Nd5 27. b4 Ra8 28. Qf1 Nb7 29. c4, though this line is far less critical for Black than the situation would have been had their opponents played 24. b4! **26. ... R×e7 27. d×e7† K×e7 28. Nd6 Qh5 29. Qd3?** This retreat inaugurates the termination of his attack, but it was very hard to foresee that 26. Rd3 still gave enough play to justify the sacrificed material. Black has various possibilities, of which 29. ... Qc5† 30. Kf1 Nd5 31. Qa7† and 29. ... Qe2 30. Nf5† Kf8 31. Rd8† are to be avoided. Best is 29. ... Rd8, when a sacrifice of the knight forces a draw after 30. Qa7† Rd7 31. Re3† K×d6 32. Qb8† Rc7 33. Qd8†. **29. ... Kf8 30. b4** 30. Nf5 is a bit more stubborn. White's pieces have some activity, but after 30. ... Re8 they must lose nevertheless. **30. ... Nb7 31. N×b7 R×b7 32. Qd6† Kg8 33. Re1 Qd5** White resigns. "As a matter of fact the game was adjourned at this stage, but resigned the following day without playing it out"—Hoffer. *The Field* (Hoffer), 29 January 1898.

## (1285) Janowski & Colborne–Bird & Trenchard    0–1

Consultation game
Hastings, 25 January 1898
*D31*

**1. d4 d5 2. c4 e6 3. Nc3 c6** "Mr. Trenchard's latest predilection; but it is to be hoped he will abandon it"—Hoffer. **4. Nf3 Nd7 5. e3 Bd6** "The best move now would be the Stonewall Defense 5. ... f5, to prevent White opening the game with 6. e4; which they should have done on the previous move"—Hoffer. **6. e4 d×e4 7. N×e4 Bb4† 8. Bd2 B×d2†** Even after losing so much time with the bishop, it was decidedly better to keep it on the board. Above all, d6 is extremely weak now. **9. Q×d2 Ndf6 10. N×f6† Q×f6** "10. ... N×f6 is preferable"—Hoffer. **11. Bd3** "We suggested after the conclusion of the game 11. Ng5, threatening 12. Ne4, 13. c5 and to establish the knight at d6; but Janowski found eventually a defense: 11. ... Qe7 12. Ne4 Nf6 etc."—Hoffer. **11. ... Ne7 12. 0–0 Ng6 13. Rfe1 0–0 14. B×g6 Q×g6** "14. ... h×g6 would lose in a few moves in various ways"—Hoffer. 14. ... h×g6 15. Re4! Bd7 16. Ne5 Rad8 17. Qb4 Bc8 18. Qa3 is indeed very good for White. **15. Ne5 Qh5** "A good move. It enables them to bring the queen back to e8 subsequently"—Hoffer. **16. Re3** Black's idea behind 15. ... Qh5 is correct, but it is only thanks to this move that he obtains a defendable position. Immediately 16. c5 and 17. Nc4 will make them suffer the rest of the game. **16. ... f6 17. Rh3** "This tempting move turned out inferior. The simple 17. Nd3 would have left White the preferable game"—Hoffer. **17. ... Qe8 18. Nd3** "Instead of this move a complicated variation has been tried, but we have no time at present to exhaust its ramifications. It commences with 18. Qd3 g6 19. Ng4 e5 20. Nh6† etc. At present we incline to believe that Black can get out of the difficulties eventually"—Hoffer. This line leads

**Dawid Janowski (courtesy Cleveland Public Library).**

to equal play. 18. Qc2 is a better place for the queen, but nothing more. 18. Nf3 is the most logical and best move. **18. ... e5 19. Re3 e4?!** Bird and his companion intend to exchange the e-pawn for their opponent's c-pawn. This way White is saddled with an isolated pawn, but this turns out to be a pawn of no mean strength. Equality is gained after the refined 19. ... Bf5 20. d×e5 Rd8 21. e×f6 Qg6 22. Rd1 R×f6 when White's clumsy pieces on the d-file gives Black enough compensation. **20. Rae1 Qf7 21. R×e4 Q×c4 22. b3** 22. Nf4! launches a dangerous initiative; e.g., 22. ... Bd7 23. b3 Qb5 24. Re7 Rf7 25. d5! c×d5 26. N×d5. White has the much more active pieces. **22. ... Qd5 23. Nf4 Qd6 24. Re7** Innocent. 24. Ne6 and 25. Nc5 generates some pressure. **24. ... Bd7 25. Qc1 Rae8 26. Qc4† Kh8 27. Qc5 Q×c5 28. d×c5 Kg8 29. Kf1 R×e7 30. R×e7 Rf7 31. Re4 Kf8 32. Ra4** "The last dozen moves are the prettiest part of the game. The text move is also good, as White forces the advance of the a-pawn, thus weakening Black's queenside pawns, and leaving an open road to the White king to approach these pawns"—Hoffer. **32. ... a6 33. Ke2 Bf5 34. Kd2** "Here White throws the game away. He should have withdrawn 34. Rd4 followed by the intended march of the king"—Hoffer. Hoffer exaggerates in his judgment. Both his suggestion and the text move give equal chances. **34. ... Rd7†** *(see diagram)*

**35. Kc1?!** A bit risky. 35. Ke1 would certainly lead to a draw. **35. ... g5! 36. Ne2?!** 36. Nh5 forces Black to lose a tempo with the defense of the f-pawn. Now Black's pieces gain ground. **36. ... Rd5 37. b4** There was no way of saving the pawn, the text move making matters only worse. **37. ... Bd3 38. Nc3 Rd4** 38. ... Rf5! 39. Nd1 Bf1 40. g3 Be2 wins a little guy after all. **39. Kb2 Bb5** 39. ... Bf1 40. g3 Rd2† is a much simpler win. **40. N×b5 c×b5 41. Kc3 Rc4†**

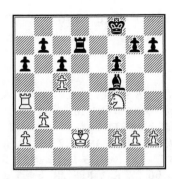

*After 34. ... Rd7*

**42. Kb3 Rf4 43. Ra5 R×f2 44. c6 b×c6 45. R×a6 R×g2 46. R×c6 R×h2 47. R×f6† Ke7** "Black might have won this ending easier, but they have kept just enough in hand to win eventually. The remainder of the moves is all forced. There is only to add that on the 60th move Janowski proposed a draw, to which his opponents replied 60. ... g2, and wins"—Hoffer. **48. Rf5 Rh3† 49. Kb2 g4 50. R×b5 g3 51. Rg5 h5** 51. ... h6! is much more precise as some time is gained after 52. Rg6 Kf7 53. Rg4 h5. **52. b5 h4 53. a4 Rh2† 54. Kb3 g2 55. b6 Rh3†?** 55. ... Kd7 wins. After the text move White has good practical chances to achieve a draw. **56. Kc4 Rg3 57. R×g3 h×g3 58. b7 g1Q 59. b8Q Qf1†** 59. ... Qe3 is a theoretical win. The queen will occupy e4, the pawn advances to g2 after which the king comes to the help. **60. Kc3 g2 61. Qe5† Kf7 62. Qh5† Kf6 63. Qh6† Kf5 64. Qh5† Kf4 65. Qh4† Kf3 66. Qh3† Kf2 67. Qh4† Kg1 68. Qd4† Qf2 69. Qd1† Kh2 70. Qh5† Kg3 71. Qg5†?** 71. Qg6† Kh3 72. Qe6† draws. **71. ... Kh3 72. Qh5† Qh4 73. Qf5† Kh2 74. Qc2 Kh1** White resigns—*The Field* (Hoffer), 29 January 1898.

**(1286) Bird & Mann–Janowski & Chapman      0–1**
Consultation game
Hastings, January 1898
*B40*

1. e4 c5 2. Nf3 e6 3. d4 c×d4 4. N×d4 Nf6 5. Nc3 Bb4 6. f3 Nc6 7. N×c6 b×c6 8. Bd3 d5 9. 0–0 Nd7 10. e×d5 c×d5 11. Ne2 0–0 12. c3 Bd6 13. Qc2 f5 14. Nf4 Ne5 15. Re1 Qh4 16. Re2 Rf6 17. R×e5 B×e5 18. g3 Qh6 19. N×d5 Qh5 20. N×f6† g×f6 21. f4 Bc7 22. Bf1 Bb6† 23. Kh1 Bb7† 24. Bg2 Qh3 25. Qe2 B×g2† 26. Q×g2 Q×g2† 27. K×g2 Rd8 28. Kf3 Rd1 29. a4 e5 30. a5 Bc7 31. f×e5 f×e5 32. b4 e4† 33. Ke2 Rh1 34. Bf4 R×a1 35. B×c7 Kf7 36. b5 Ke6 37. b6 a×b6 38. a×b6 Kd7 39. Be5 Kc6 40. Bd4 Ra2† 41. Ke3 R×h2 42. Kf4 Rd2 43. g4 R×d4 44. c×d4 e3 45. K×e3 f×g4 46. Kf4 h5 47. d5† K×b6 48. Ke5 Kc7 White resigns—*British Chess Magazine*, March 1898, pp. 115–116.

## BIRD AGAINST THE WORLD

During the spring of 1898 a suggestion made by Donald L. Anderson, a deaf and dumb member of the British Chess Club, was realized by the London magazine *Pearson's Weekly*. On 12 March, Bird began two correspondence games simultaneously against their readers. Members of the latter cohort were invited to send in their reply against Bird's moves. Bird played with the White pieces in

both games and opted twice for the King's Gambit to make the game attractive. Although the concept was considered interesting there was but little doubt about the outcome of these games, as the majority of Bird's opponents would be up to the mark.

The games commenced with a pace of one move per week, but quite soon the moves came only biweekly. The experiment did not last long. The last couple of moves were published on 16 July after which the games were suddenly and silently interrupted.

**(1287) Bird–Readers of Pearson's Weekly      Unfinished**
Correspondence game
London 1898
*C33*

1. e4 e5 2. f4 e×f4 3. Bc4 Qh4† 4. Kf1 g5 5. Nc3 Bg7 6. d4 d6 7. Nf3 Qh5 8. h4 h6 9. Kg1 Qg6 10. e5 g4 11. h5—*Pearson's Weekly*, 16 July 1898.

**(1288) Bird–Readers of Pearson's Weekly      Unfinished**
Correspondence game
London 1898
*C33*

1. e4 e5 2. f4 e×f4 3. Bc4 Qh4† 4. Kf1 d5 5. e×d5 Bd6 6. Nc3 Nf6 7. d4 0–0 8. Nce2 Bg4 9. Qd3 Re8 10. Nf3 B×f3 11. Q×f3—*Pearson's Weekly*, 16 July 1898.

The reason for the termination of the correspondence games may be found in Bird's condition. During the month July he was supposedly stricken with paralysis due to which he lost the use of his arms. The bad tidings, made public by the *British Chess Magazine* (August 1898, p. 337), were however soon nuanced when it appeared that Bird, though saddled with very frail health, was not as ill as presumed.[9]

## AMONG OLD FOLKS

Two major tournaments colored the summer of 1898. A mammoth event in Vienna, consisting of 20 players and 38 rounds, captured the chess world's attention during the months of June and July. Tarrasch and Pillsbury came out as joint winners. Immediately afterwards a mix of tired veterans from Vienna and fresh players gathered in Cologne. One of the diehards present on both occasions was Amos Burn; while his result in Vienna was nothing to write home about, he played the tournament of his life in Cologne. With 11½ out of 15 he won ahead of Wilhelm Cohn, Rezső Charousek and Chigorin. Steinitz came in fifth.

Early in September both Burn and Steinitz were in London where they met a brittle Bird. The *Hereford Times* reported on 10 September 1898 that "In the afternoon [of Wednesday 7 September] Mr. Burn played a number of offhand games with Mr. Bird, and Mr.

9. Details about Bird's condition were given in the *Hereford Times* on 13 August 1898: "Mr. Bird, during July, was laid up for a few days with a severe cold, and one of his periodical twinges of his ancient enemy the gout. He has, however, been able to get about again, and is ready to meet all comers—from Lasker, Tarrasch and Pillsbury upwards (!), and is as youthful and agile as ever."

Steinitz acting as umpire. Mr. Bird, considering his precarious condition, played with surprising vigor, none being more surprised than Mr. Burn. But the latter had of course been travelling all night."

Various sources mentioned Bird as a guest at the coming congress of the Southern Counties' Chess Union in Salisbury which would start on 12 September. Blackburne was engaged for a blindfold exhibition while Bird would assist in consultation games. As reports of the activities at the congress do not mention him, most likely Bird did not attend.

# The Final Tour

At the end of the year Bird made two sorties into the provinces. It turned out that these short visits were his farewell from some of the clubs where he had been enthusiastically received during the past fifteen years.

On 29 October Bird was the guest at the Liverpool Chess Club. He encountered 17 players in an exhibition. With 13 wins, 2 losses and 2 draws he made a creditable score.

### (1289) Bird–Greig    0–1
Simultaneous game
Liverpool, 29 October 1898
C21

1. e4 e5 2. d4 e×d4 3. Nf3 c5 4. Bc4 Nc6 5. 0–0 Nf6 6. c3 Na5 7. e5 N×c4 8. e×f6 g×f6 9. Qe2† Ne5 10. c×d4 c×d4 11. N×e5 Qe7 12. Qh5 f×e5 13. Bg5 Qe6 14. Nd2 Qg6 15. Qh4 Rg8 16. Ne4 Be7 17. g3 B×g5 18. N×g5 Q×g5 19. Qe4 d6 20. Rac1 Qf5 21. Qd5 Rg6 22. Rc7 Rf6 23. f3 Qd3 24. Rf2 Bh3 25. Rc1 Qe3 26. Ra1 Rc8 White resigns—*Illustrated London News*, 3 December 1898.

Bird's last tour was more comprehensive. He left London on 5 December and arrived the next day in Newcastle. From the preserved games it seems that Bird was active only in consultation games and that he skipped the traditional simultaneous exhibition. Bird confided to his friends here that he was busy writing another book, but this work is unlikely to have ever seen the day of light.

### (1290) Bird–Sergeant & Greenwell    0–1
Consultation game
Newcastle 1898
C32

1. e4 e5 2. f4 d5 3. e×d5 e4 4. Nc3 Nf6 5. d3 Bb4 6. d×e4 N×e4 7. Qd4 Qe7 8. Kd1 B×c3 9. b×c3 Nc6 10. Bb5 Bg4† 11. Nf3 0–0–0 12. B×c6 b×c6 13. c4 c×d5 14. c5 Rhe8 15. Ba3 Qf6 16. Q×f6 B×f3† 17. g×f3 N×f6 18. Kd2 Nh5 19. Rae1 N×f4 20. c6 Re6 21. R×e6 N×e6 22. c3 d4 23. c4 d3 24. Rg1 Nd4 25. R×g7 N×f3† 26. Kd1 Re8 27. Be7 Ne5 28. R×h7 N×c6 29. Bc5 Ne5 30. Kd2 Kd8 31. B×a7 N×c4† 32. Kd1 d2 White resigns—*Newcastle Courant*, 10 December 1898.

### (1291) Sergeant & Greenwell–Bird    1–0
Consultation game
Newcastle 1898
C30

1. e4 e5 2. Nc3 Bc5 3. f4 d6 4. Nf3 a6 5. Bc4 Nc6 6. d3 Nf6 7. h3 Be6 8. Bb3 Qe7 9. f5 B×b3 10. a×b3 h6 11. g4 Bb4 12. Bd2 0–0–0 13. Nd5 N×d5 14. e×d5 B×d2† 15. K×d2 Nd4 16. c3 N×f3† 17. Q×f3 Qg5† 18. Kc2 h5 19. Rag1 h4 20. Ra1 g6 21. f6 Rhe8 22. Ra4 Kd7 23. Re1 Ra8 24. Rae4 c5 25. Qf2 Rac8 26. b4 b6 27. Ra1 Ra8 28. b×c5 d×c5 29. b4 Rec8 30. Rae1 c×b4 31. R×e5 R×c3† 32. Kb2 Qh6 33. Re7† Kc8 34. Re8† Kb7 35. R1e7† Rc7 36. R×c7 K×c7 37. Qh2† Black resigns—*Newcastle Courant*, 10 December 1898.

### (1292) Greenwell & Graham–Bird    1–0
Consultation game
Newcastle 1898
C44

1. e4 e5 2. Nf3 Nc6 3. c3 d5 4. Bb5 d×e4 5. N×e5 Qg5 6. Qa4 Q×g2 7. Rf1 Bh3 8. N×c6 b×c6 9. B×c6† Kd8 10. Qc4 Rb8 11. B×e4 Q×h2 12. Rh1 Be6 13. Qd4† Qd6 14. Q×a7 Rb6 15. b3 Bd5 16. d3 Qe6 17. Be3 B×e4 18. d×e4 Q×e4 19. Rh5 Nf6 20. Nd2 Qe7 21. Ra5 Nd7 22. 0–0–0 Qe6 23. Nc4 Rc6 24. Qa8† Ke7 25. Re5 R×c4 26. R×e6† f×e6 27. Bg5† Nf6 28. b×c4 Black resigns—*Newcastle Courant*, 17 December 1898.

Bird's farewell to Scotland is only meagerly documented. In Edinburgh he won every one of his 18 games in a simultaneous exhibition. Among his opponents was the strong amateur Mills. Bird consequently headed for Glasgow where he played some 150 games against all comers.

### (1293) Bird–Mills    1–0
Simultaneous game
Edinburgh, December 1898
C58

1. e4 e5 2. Nf3 Nc6 3. Bc4 Nf6 4. Ng5 d5 5. e×d5 Na5 6. Bb5† c6 7. d×c6 b×c6 8. Qf3 Qb6 9. Be2 Bd6 10. d3 0–0 11. Nc3 Re8 12. 0–0 h6 13. Nge4 N×e4 14. N×e4 Bc7 15. Qe3 c5 16. f4 f5 17. Nc3 Bb7 18. Bf3 B×f3 19. Q×f3 e4 20. Qf2 Nc6 21. Be3 Nd8 22. Nd5 Qd6 23. c4 Bb6 24. Rae1 Nc6 25. b4 c×b4 26. B×b6 a×b6 27. Q×b6 Rab8 28. Qf2 e×d3 29. Qg3 Qc5† 30. Kh1 R×e1 31. R×e1 Nd4 32. Qg6 d2 33. Nf6† and mates in two—*Falkirk Herald*, 14 December 1898.

Bird left Scotland in the early morning of 10 December to arrive after a few hours in Newcastle. He encountered groups of players during the afternoon and evening, and left the battlefield with 16 wins, 5 losses (against Zollner, Hemy, Martin, Sergeant and Laserson) and 5 draws (against Hawks, Hemy, Greenwell, Ogilvie and Nixon).

# LONDON 1899

The final major tournament of the 1800s was held during the summer of 1899 in London. The committee collected a prize fund of £800 for a double round-robin tournament for which 16 players were invited. The £800 were divided among nine prizes! The other participants received consolation money for each win (£2 for wins against a player from the top 3, £1 for other wins).

The games were played from Monday through Saturday. Adjourned games were finished on Thursdays. The time limit was set at 15 moves an hour. The tournament was played at St. Stephen's Hall in the Royal Aquarium, Westminster. A spacious, but rather depressing, room, according to the contemporary journalists. Certainly a disappointment when compared to the playing halls of the tournaments of 1883 and 1895.

The committee had more success with the gathering of a strong field. The old guard was represented in generous numbers with former world champion Steinitz, and Chigorin, Blackburne, Mason and Bird. The most forceful young players were Lasker, Pillsbury, Janowski, Maróczy and Schlechter. Only two players were unable to accept their invitation, Tarrasch and Charousek. Some distress was caused by two cancellations just before the commencement of the tournament. Horatio Caro fell ill, but especially Burn's last-minute refusal to play in his own country caused a huge disappointment. Anticipations of him had been very high after his stunning victory in Cologne. Burn's decision to pass up the tournament found its ground in his refusal to endorse some rules as decided by the committee. Just one of the vacant places was filled, by Lee, so that 15 players commenced the combat. After the fourth round the number of participants became 14 after all when Teichmann was obliged to forfeit his further games due to an eye injury.

It was a genuine, but satisfying, surprise for many to find Bird among the participants. For Bird himself it was a formidable recognition. Exactly fifty years previously he commenced his tournament career in an already forgotten tournament at the Divan.

Not everyone, however, was as enthusiastic about the appearance of the veteran. Louis van Vliet, chess editor of *The Sunday Times*, wrote on 4 June 1899 that Bird, "had he been wise, would have preferred to rest on his laurels rather than attempt in his declining years to do battle with the modern giants."

The pairings of each round were made on the playing day, just before the games began. Lasker had the honor of drawing the first envelope—in which Bird was paired with Showalter.[10] Bird opened the tournament very badly with four losses in a row. He collected his first point in the fifth round but it was because Teichmann forfeited his first game. Bird lost the next three rounds.[11] His game with Blackburne particularly drew the attention of the press.

Bird's score of 1 point, thanks to the forfeit, out of eight games gives a distorted view of his actual strength. A closer look at his games demonstrates that he had his chances for half and whole points, and that he was actually even playing quite strongly and much less erratically than usual. His style was still very idiosyncratic but the resulting positions were often satisfying and presented good practical chances. Bird's aforementioned game with Blackburne was symptomatic. Bird concluded the opening phase a pawn up but at the cost of a dreary pawn structure. He stubbornly defended the extra pawn and after a tenacious on both sides combat, a complicated middle game arose. Both players had their chances, made some mistakes, but Bird got the best share of play. Only after move 40, after several hours of exhausting play, Bird committed a mistake after which Blackburne becomes master over the game and wins.

In the ninth and tenth round, Bird was finally able to break the slump, scoring a draw and a win.

On Thursday 15 June no adjourned games were played as a dinner took place at the City of London Chess Club. Bird showed himself confident in his speech, from which the *Westminster Budget* selected the following outtake on 23 June: "I will make some of the boys sit up yet." Bird kept his word and beat one of the tournament's strongest players, Janowski, on the following day. Bird ended the first cycle with 4 points out of 14 games.[12]

The second going went similarly. Bird had not used up his characteristic fighting spirit but the rewards remained very slender. He had to be satisfied with two wins and two draws. His win against

---

10. An amusing scene arising at the game's adjournment was described by the journalist of *La Stratégie* in the June 1899 number (pp. 168–169): "With his shaved moustache and his collar of white beard, the veteran Bird, who plays against Showalter, has all the appearance of an old seaman.... After the bell sounded warning the players that the next move must be sealed, Showalter, who was absorbed in thought and failed to hear it, made his move. The veteran Bird, who had not left his seat, regards with interest the move which Showalter has just made, and, after attentively examining the position, he got up and said to Showalter, 'the bell has sounded. Place that move in the envelope.' 'But,' said Showalter, 'are you not going to place your move in the envelope?' 'No, no,' said Bird, going away doubled up and leaning on his cane. 'You have made the move since the bell sounded; you ought to have written down the move instead of playing it.' And, to the general amusement, Showalter, smiling, writes down the move he had just made. At half past 6 exactly play is resumed. The spectators are more numerous than in the afternoon. ... Bird finds himself constrained to lay down his arms to Showalter. Bird seems much disappointed by his defeat, and tries to show, after he has resigned, that at a given point of the game he might have been able to turn the tables on his opponent."

11. Another excellent description of Bird was published in the *Adelaide Observer* on 29 July 1899: "A very interesting table is that whereon a game is progressing between two veterans of great repute. Blackburne is handling the Black men and Bird the White—a pair of jolly old players, who treat their chess as a game and not as a matter of life and death.... Bird is equally cheery, though it is plain that years are laying a heavy burden on him; gout makes him walk very lame, his hand is not very steady, and his head is very bald, but the grey-whiskered face, which is of the foxhunting squire description, is full of placid good humor, and his eye can still light up with a merry twinkle. But at the same time I longest watched his game there was no room for much twinkling. He leaned his head to the right, and looked at the board sidewise; then took a spell, with his head leaning to the left. The veteran had made a hot attack, parried by Blackburne with judgment and coolness, and now was being himself pressed into a corner. They have been fighting against each other these two for the last 30 years, and ought to know each other's tactics by this time, but Bird spent himself in vain against a rock, and at adjournment time all the experts seemed to think his case hopeless. In the evening he struggled on to no purpose, for after two hours of it he had no choice but to resign."

12. The performances of all the players, now that the tournament was halfway, were discussed in the *British Chess Magazine* of July 1899 (p. 302): "What shall be said of the perennial Bird, the boyish competitor in the 1851 tournament—the first of its kind, be it remembered—the veteran competitor of 1899? Bird not only essayed the task of meeting the youthful giants of today, but he boldly announced his intention of playing gambits whenever he was White and got the chance. He played the gambits, but as a rule did not win them, but then he is handicapped by age and gout. Apart from his bald head he does not look his age when seated, for his features retain much of the vivacity of his earlier days. As the play proceeded he seemed to 'harden to the fight,' and it may be he will do better in the next half of the tournament. His final score in the first half was 4 (thereby equaling Lee), made up of 3 wins and 2 draws."

**A photograph from the final round of the London 1899 tournament. Sitting: Henry E. Bird, Emanuel Lasker, Mikhail Chigorin, Joseph H. Blackburne and Carl Schlechter. Standing: Dawid Janowski, Géza Maróczy, Francis J. Lee, Junius L. Cope, J. Walter Russell, Samuel Tinsley, Herbert W. Trenchard and Wilhelm Cohn (*Black and White*).**

Cohn, especially his 22nd move, demonstrated a spark of Bird's genius. Bird drew with the giants Pillsbury and Maróczy after having obtained a winning position in both cases.[13]

Bird's final score of 7 points in 27 games (a win due to the forfeit of Teichmann included) rendered him thirteenth. Only Tinsley and Teichmann were left behind. Bird received only £5 as a consolation prize, but the applause Bird got on final appearance on the chess stage may well have outdone the ones given to the other players.

The tournament was dominated by Emanuel Lasker. The world champion made his first appearance in a serious contest since he renewed his world championship title against Steinitz, early in 1897. Many thought that his former superiority would have faded, but this was absolutely not the case. Second place was shared by three youngsters: Maróczy, Pillsbury and Janowski. Bird's contemporary, Wilhelm Steinitz, ended at a creditable 10th-11th place, but for the first time in his career he ended outside the prizes. London 1899 turned out to be Steinitz swan song. He died a year later in miserable conditions. First place in the minor event fell to Frank Marshall whose international chess career was hereby at once launched.

13. Now the *British Chess Magazine* (August 1899, p. 330) became very brief on Bird: "Mr. Bird would rather lose a good game than win a bad one, and at his best his score in tournament play never was a true index of his ability as a player." ¶ A decade later, at the time of Bird's death, more straightforward words were written down: "But it must be remembered that he was now but a wreck of his old self—advancing years and that fell master, gout, having made sad inroads into his constitution." *British Chess Magazine*, June 1908, p. 250.

Five participants entered one or more of their games for the brilliancy prize competition. Bird selected two of his games (against Janowski and his win against Tinsley from the 28th round). Janowski even believed six of his games were eligible, but they were all outdone by Lasker who gained £10 10s., offered by H.S. and Mrs. F.S. Lewis, for his brilliant win against Steinitz and a gold medal presented by the Ladies' Chess Club for his first win against Showalter.

### (1294) Bird–Showalter 0–1
International tournament (round 1)
London, 30 May 1899
*C11*

1. e4 e6 2. d4 d5 3. Nc3 Nf6 4. e5 Nfd7 5. Nce2 c5 6. c3 Nc6 7. f4 Qb6 8. Nf3 Be7 9. g3 0-0 10. Bh3 c×d4 11. c×d4 f5 12. 0-0 Rf7 13. Kh1 Nf8 14. Bg2 Bd7 15. Rf2 Rc8 16. Nc3 Na5 17. Bf1 Be8 18. Rg2 Bb4 19. Bd3 Rfc7 20. Bd2 Nc4 21. Rb1 N×d2 22. R×d2 Bh5 23. Rf2 B×f3† 24. Q×f3 Q×d4 25. Ne2 Qb6 26. Rg2 g6 27. g4 f×g4 28. R×g4 Rg7 29. h4 Bd2 30. Rg3 Rcc7 31. h5 g×h5 32. Rbg1 h4 33. R×g7† R×g7 34. R×g7† K×g7 35. f5 Qe3 36. f6† Kh6 37. Qg4 Qg5 38. Qg2 Be3 39. Nc3 Bd4 40. Nb5 Q×g2† 41. K×g2 B×b2 42. Nd6 Kg5 43. N×b7 B×e5 44. f7 Kf6 45. Nd8 Bc7 White resigns—*Tournament Book*, pp. 110–111.

## International chess tournament, London, 30 May–10 July 1899

**Site:** St. Stephen's Hall
**Playing hours:** 12 p.m.–4:30 and 6:30 p.m.–10:30
**Prizes:** 1st £250, 2nd £165, 3rd £100, 4th £80, 5th £65, 6th £50, 7th £40, 8th £30, 9th £20; consolation prizes for the non–prize winners
**Time limit:** 15 moves per hour

| | | 1 | 2 | 3 | 4 | 5 | 6 | 7 | 8 | 9 | 10 | 11 | 12 | 13 | 14 | 15 | |
|---|---|---|---|---|---|---|---|---|---|---|---|---|---|---|---|---|---|
| 1 | E. Lasker | | 1 ½ | ½ 1 | ½ 1 | ½ 1 | 0 1 | 1 1 | 1 1 | 1 ½ | 1 ½ | ½ 1 | 1 1 | 1 1 | 1 1 | + | 22½ |
| 2 | D. Janowski | 0 ½ | | 0 1 | 1 0 | 1 1 | 1 ½ | 1 1 | ½ 1 | 0 0 | 1 1 | 1 0 | 1 1 | 0 1 | 1 ½ | + | 18 |
| 3 | G. Maróczy | ½ 0 | 1 0 | | ½ ½ | ½ ½ | ½ 1 | 0 1 | 1 ½ | 1 0 | 1 1 | ½ 1 | ½ 1 | 1 ½ | 1 1 | + | 18 |
| 4 | H.N. Pillsbury | ½ 0 | 0 1 | ½ ½ | | ½ 1 | 0 0 | 1 0 | ½ ½ | 1 1 | 1 1 | 1 1 | 1 1 | 1 ½ | 1 1 | ½ | 18 |
| 5 | C. Schlechter | ½ 0 | 0 0 | ½ ½ | ½ 0 | | 1 ½ | 1 0 | ½ 1 | ½ 1 | 0 ½ | 1 1 | 1 1 | 1 1 | 1 1 | + | 17 |
| 6 | J.H. Blackburne | 1 0 | 0 ½ | ½ 0 | 1 1 | 0 ½ | | ½ 0 | 0 1 | 1 ½ | 0 1 | 1 0 | 1 ½ | 1 1 | 1 1 | ½ | 15½ |
| 7 | M.I. Chigorin | 0 0 | 0 0 | 1 0 | 0 1 | 0 1 | ½ 1 | | 1 ½ | 1 ½ | 1 0 | ½ 1 | 1 0 | 1 1 | 1 0 | 1 | 15 |
| 8 | J.W. Showalter | 0 0 | ½ 0 | 0 ½ | ½ ½ | ½ 0 | 1 0 | 0 ½ | | 0 ½ | 0 ½ | 1 ½ | 1 1 | 1 1 | 0 1 | + | 12½ |
| 9 | J. Mason | 0 ½ | 1 1 | 0 1 | 0 0 | ½ 0 | 0 ½ | 0 ½ | 1 ½ | | 0 1 | 0 0 | 1 1 | ½ 1 | + | 12 |
| 10 | W. Cohn | 0 ½ | 0 0 | 0 0 | 0 0 | 1 ½ | 1 0 | 1 0 | 1 ½ | 1 1 | | 0 ½ | 1 ½ | 1 0 | 0 0 | + | 11½ |
| 11 | W. Steinitz | ½ 0 | 0 1 | ½ 0 | 0 0 | 0 0 | 0 1 | ½ 0 | 0 ½ | 1 0 | 1 ½ | | ½ 0 | ½ 1 | 1 1 | + | 11½ |
| 12 | F.J. Lee | 0 0 | 0 0 | ½ 0 | 0 0 | 0 0 | 0 ½ | 0 1 | 0 0 | 1 1 | 0 ½ | ½ 1 | | ½ 1 | ½ ½ | + | 9½ |
| 13 | H.E. Bird | 0 0 | 1 0 | 0 ½ | 0 ½ | 0 0 | 0 0 | 0 0 | 0 0 | 0 0 | 0 1 | ½ 0 | ½ 0 | | 1 1 | + | 7 |
| 14 | S. Tinsley | 0 0 | 0 ½ | 0 0 | 0 0 | 0 0 | 0 0 | 0 1 | 1 0 | ½ 0 | 1 1 | 0 0 | ½ ½ | 0 0 | | 0 | 6 |
| 15 | R. Teichmann | – | – | – | ½ | – | ½ | 0 | – | – | – | – | – | 1 | | | 2 |

## (1295) Mason–Bird    1–0

International tournament (round 2)
London, 31 May 1899
C50

**1. e4 e5 2. Nf3 Nc6 3. Bc4 Bc5 4. Nc3 Nf6 5. d3 a6** "In anticipation of 6. Na4"—Hoffer. **6. Be3 d6** "Mason's favorite variation. Obviously if 7. B×c5 the open d-file, and the prospective undoubling of the pawn compensate for the temporary doubled pawn"—Hoffer. **7. Qd2 Bg4** "The queen being removed, 7. ... Bg4 does not pin the knight. 7. ... Be6 is therefore preferable"—Hoffer. **8. B×c5 d×c5 9. Ng5 Bh5 10. f3 h6 11. Nh3 Nd4 12. Qf2 g5 13. Nd1 b5** Mason's last passive move could have been exploited with 13. ... g4! **14. Bb3 Qd6 15. Ne3 Bg6 16. 0–0 0–0** "16. ... Nh5 17. g3 Ng7 with a view of a kingside attack might have been tried"—Hoffer. **17. Kh1 Rad8 18. Qd2 Kh7 19. Rad1 Qb6 20. Nf2** "20. c3 N×b3 21. a×b3 followed by removing the queen from d2 would have been better"—Hoffer. **20. ... c4!** "Bird excels in this sort of desultory fighting. The text move reveals the subtle combination which he had prepared. White, however, helped him by his last queen's move"—Hoffer. **21. c3** "The only move to save the piece"—Hoffer. **21. ... c×b3 22. c×d4 e×d4 23. Neg4 N×g4 24. f×g4 b×a2 25. b3 Rd6** "He should have played 25. ... a5 26. Q×a2 a4 27. b×a4 Ra8 with a passed pawn. If 28. Rb1 R×a4 29. Q×a4 b×a4 30. R×b6 c×b6 with two passed pawns."—Hoffer. **26. Q×a2 Rc6** Bird forgoes his chance to create a strong pawn mass with 26. ... c5. **27. b4** "This excellent move improves White's game considerably"—Hoffer. **27. ... Rc3 28. Ra1 Ra8 29. Qd5 Rf8 30. Kg1 Rc6 31. Nh1 Rd6** "Having to return with the rook to d6, the intermediate moves are loss of time"—Hoffer. **32. Qb3 Rf6 33. R×f6 Q×f6 34. Rf1 Qd6 35. Qa3 Re8 36. Ng3 Re5 37. Rc1** "Obviously to prevent 37. ... c5"—Hoffer. **37. ... Re6 38. Re1 Rf6 39. Nf5 B×f5 40. g×f5 Qe5 41. Qc1 Rb6 42. Qc2 Kg7 43. Rc1 Qf4 44. Q×c7 Qe3†** Or 44. ... Qd2 45. Qc2 Q×b4 when he is a pawn up again. White gains some initiative in return with 46. e5. **45. Kh1 Rf6 46. Qc2 h5 47. Rf1 g4 48. g3 Rd6 49. Kg2 Rh6 50. Rf4 Qe1 51. Qc5** Mason sacrifices a pawn again

in return for an initiative. Both sides have to play precisely. **51. ... Qe2† 52. Rf2 Q×d3 53. f6† Kh7 54. Qe7 Qc4 55. e5 d3 56. h4?** Both players go to the limit to win the game. With this move, however, Mason drives it too far, as the opening of the kingside is extremely dangerous. **56. ... g×h3† e.p. 57. Kh2** (see diagram)

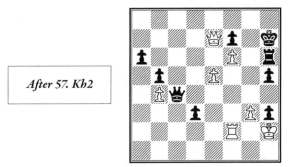

*After 57. Kh2*

**57. ... h4! 58. g×h4 d2?** An error, probably due to a miscalculation or fatigue. First 58. ... Qd5! takes the sting out of White's idea. In case of 59. e6 Black can quickly force mate with 59. ... Qe5†. **59. e6 Q×e6?** Apparently played out of despair, for it is obvious that both sides promote their pawn and that White's attack comes first. After 59. ... R×f6! 60. Q×f6 Qc7† 61. K×h3 d1Q, White has no choice but to take the perpetual check. **60. Q×e6 f×e6 61. f7 d1Q 62. f8Q Qd4 63. Rf7† Kg6 64. Qg8†** Black resigns—*Tournament Book* (Hoffer), pp. 31–33.

## (1296) Bird–Pillsbury    0–1

International tournament (round 3)
London, 2 June 1899
C31

**1. e4 e5 2. f4 d5 3. e×d5 e4 4. Bb5† c6 5. d×c6 b×c6 6. Bc4 Nf6 7. Qe2 Bc5 8. Nc3 0–0 9. Qf1 Qe7 10. Nd1 a5 11. Ne3 Na6 12. a3 Nc7 13. g3 Ncd5 14. h4 N×e3 15. d×e3 Qa7 16. Qe2 Rd8 17. Bd2 Bg4 18. Qf2 R×d2 19. Q×d2 B×e3 20. Qg2 Qd4 21. Be2 Bd2† 22. Kf1 Nd5 23. B×g4 Ne3† 24. Kf2 N×c2† 25. Kf1 Ne3†**

**26. Kf2 N×g4† 27. Ke2 Qd3†** White resigns—*Tournament Book*, pp. 73–74.

## (1297) Maróczy–Bird   1–0
International tournament (round 4)
London, 3 June 1899
C49

**1. e4 e5 2. Nf3 Nc6 3. Nc3 Nf6 4. Bb5 Bb4 5. 0–0 0–0 6. d3 Re8 7. h3 B×c3 8. b×c3 Na5** "In order to dislodge the bishop before moving the d-pawn"—Hoffer. **9. Ba4 c6 10. c4 b6** "If 10. ... a6, to be followed by 11. ... b5, White would stop the advance with 11. c5 d6 12. Bd2 d×c5 13. Qe1 b6 14. B×a5 b×a5 15. B×c6 and wins"—Hoffer. **11. Bb2** 11. Re1, waiting to determine the position of the bishop, is preferable. **11. ... Qc7 12. Nh4 Nb7 13. f4 d6** "If 13. ... e×f4 then 14. B×f6 g×f6 15. Nf5 threatening 16. Qg4†"—Hoffer. **14. Bb3 a5** White's bishops are both adequately neutralized. **15. a3 Nc5 16. Ba2 Qe7** 16. ... Ne6 is also interesting. **17. f×e5 d×e5 18. Nf5?!** Allowing Bird a very favorable exchange. His knights are much more powerful than the bishops in this type of position. **18. ... B×f5 19. R×f5 Qd6** 19. ... Nfd7 20. Rb1 Ne6 is the most direct approach. Now 21. B×e5? g6 is a small trick White has to avoid. **20. Qe1 Re6 21. Qg3 Nfd7 22. Raf1 Rg6?** "Overlooking his opponent's subtle combination. 22. ... f6 was necessary"—Hoffer. Black is indeed extremely solid after 22. ... f6 23. Rh5 Nf8 24. Kh2 Kh8. He may subsequently prepare the transfer of a knight to d4, followed by an increase of activity on the queenside. Also good is Maróczy's suggestion 22. ... Rf8. **23. B×e5!** "Very pretty. Maróczy had the move in view for some time"—Hoffer. **23. ... Qe7** "If 23. ... R×g3, White wins another pawn, and the game would have been lost less violently. Maróczy finishes this pretty game brilliantly"—Hoffer. **24. Qf2 Rf8** 24. ... N×e5 25. R×e5 Re6 is miserable, especially since White can liberate his bishop quickly after exchanging the rook and 27. d4. The text move is much worse. **25. Bc7 Ne6 26. c5! b×c5 27. e5 Ng5 28. Kh1 h6 29. Bd6 R×d6 30. e×d6 Q×d6 31. h4 Ne6 32. R×f7 Re8 33. R×g7† Kh8 34. Rf7 Nd4 35. Rh7†** Black resigns—*Tournament Book* (Hoffer), pp. 69–70; *Maróczy's Hundert Schachpartien* (Maróczy), pp. 42–43.

## (1298) Bird–Teichmann   1–0
International tournament (round 5)
London, 5 June 1899
*Game scored by default*

## (1299) Bird–Blackburne   0–1
International tournament (round 6)
London, 6 June 1899
C41

**1. e4 e5 2. Nf3 d6 3. d4 Bg4** "An inferior move abandoned years ago. 3. ... e×d4 or 3. ... Nf6 is preferable"—Hoffer. **4. d×e5 Nd7** "A variation played by Albin, 1886. It involves giving up a pawn for a quick development. White, however, should be able to retain the pawn"—Hoffer. **5. e×d6 B×d6 6. Nc3** "6. Bb5 Ngf6 7. Bg5 might be suggested"—Hoffer. **6. ... Ngf6 7. h3 Bh5 8. Bg5 h6 9. Be3** "If he had pinned both knights he could have now exchanged both, thus relieving the pressure on the e-pawn. Anyhow he should have taken off the knight, as Be3 hinders the e-pawn being adequately

defended"—Hoffer. **9. ... Qe7 10. Qd4 Bc5 11. Qc4** A highly interesting choice. 11. Qd3 0–0–0 is certainly not without danger for White. With the text move Bird gets his queen out of the way while trusting that his extra pawn can be maintained. **11. ... B×e3 12. f×e3 Nb6 13. Qb3 0–0–0** 13. ... N×e4 14. N×e4 Q×e4 15. Qb5† hangs a piece. **14. Bd3 Qc5 15. Kf2 g5 16. Qa3 Q×a3 17. b×a3 Rhe8 18. Rhf1 Bg6 19. Nd2 c6 20. Rab1 Nfd7 21. Ke2 Nc5 22. Rb4** All these moves show top-notch prophylaxis from Bird's side. **22. ... Re7 23. a4 Red7** Blackburne is champing at the bit to win the pawn back. 23. ... Nbd7 keeps his position more harmonious. **24. a5 N×d3 25. c×d3 R×d3 26. Ncb1** More natural looks 26. Ndb1, especially as a small material reward is gained after 26. ... Na8 27. Nd5 R8xd5 28. e×d5 R×d5 29. a6 b6 30. Rf6, though Black doesn't need to be overly worried about losing. **26. ... Na8 27. Nb3 R3d6** "Because of the threat 27. R×b7 K×b7 28. Nc5†"—Hoffer. **28. N1d2 c5** The pushing of the c- and b-pawn renders Bird some chances to put them under fire. **29. Rc4 b6 30. a4 f6 31. Rc2 Be8 32. Ra1 Kb8 33. a×b6 a×b6** (see diagram)

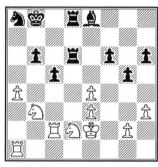

*After 33. ... a×b6*

**34. Rb2** The immediate 34. a5! is not to be underestimated. Black's king is getting in trouble. **34. ... Kc7** Blackburne fears what is coming and panics a bit. 34. ... Rc8 defends c5 and demands some attention of his opponent due to the threatened advance of the c-pawn. After the text move Bird should absolutely play 35. a5!, with much the better game. **35. Nc4 Re6 36. Nbd2** 36. Ncd2 had to be played in the hope to return to the previous line. **36. ... Bc6 37. a5** Badly timed, for the advance of Black's b-pawn reinforces his pawn structure. A calm move such as 37. g3 leaves it to Black to prove he has something. **37. ... b5 38. Na3 b4 39. Nac4 Bb5 40. Rc1 Kb7** But this contains no venom at all. On the other hand, after 40. ... Kc6 41. Rbc2 Nc7 42. Kf3 B×c4 43. R×c4 Na6, his king becomes very active. **41. Nb3 Ka7 42. Kf3 Rc8 43. Rd2 Ba4 44. Rb1?** Very cooperative, for Bird's firm blockade will be abruptly broken down after the following exchange. The refined 44. Rd6 Ree8 45. Nbd2 keeps the situation under control. **44. ... Rcc6 45. Rd5 B×b3 46. R×b3 Nc7 47. Rf5 Ka6 48. e5 Kb5 49. Nd6† Ka4 50. Rb1 R×e5 51. Ra1† Kb3 52. R×f6 Rd5 53. R×h6 Rc×d6 54. Rh7 Na6 55. Ra7 c4 56. e4 Re5 57. Rb7 c3 58. Rb6 Rde6 59. g4 R×e4** White resigns—*Tournament Book* (Hoffer), pp. 7–8.

## (1300) Schlechter–Bird   1–0
International tournament (round 7)
London, 7 June 1899
B34

**1. e4 c5 2. Nf3 g6 3. Nc3 Bg7 4. d4 c×d4 5. N×d4 Nc6 6. Be3**

h5 7. Be2 Nf6 8. h3 d6 9. 0–0 Bd7 10. f4 N×d4 11. B×d4 Bc6
12. Bf3 e6 13. Qd3 a6 14. Rad1 Qc7 15. e5 d×e5 16. B×e5 Qb6†
17. Bd4 Qc7 18. Be5 Qb6† 19. Qd4 Q×d4† 20. R×d4 B×f3
21. R×f3 0–0 22. a4 Rfc8 23. Rb4 Nd5 24. N×d5 e×d5 25. B×g7
K×g7 26. c3 Rc7 27. Rd3 a5 28. Rbd4 Rc4 29. R×c4 d×c4
30. Rd7 Re8 31. R×b7 Re1† 32. Kf2 Ra1 33. g4 R×a4 34. Rb5
Ra1 35. g×h5 g×h5 36. R×h5 a4 37. Ra5 Ra2 38. Ke3 R×b2
39. R×a4 Rh2 40. R×c4 R×h3† 41. Ke4 Kf6 42. Rc6† Ke7 43. c4
Kd7 44. Ra6 Rc3 45. Kd5 Rd3† 46. Ke5 Rc3 47. Ra7† Ke8
48. Rc7 Re3† 49. Kf6 Re6† 50. Kf5 Kf8 51. c5 Kg7 52. Rb7 Re1
53. c6 Re2 54. c7 Rc2 55. Ke5 Kg6 56. Kd6 Rd2† 57. Kc6 Rc2†
58. Kd7 Rd2† 59. Kc8 Kf5 60. Rb4 Black resigns—*Tournament
Book*, pp. 99–100.

## (1301) Bird–Chigorin   0–1
International tournament (round 8)
London, 9 June 1899
*C51*

1. e4 e5 2. Nf3 Nc6 3. Bc4 Bc5 4. b4 B×b4 5. c3 Ba5 6. d4
e×d4 7. 0–0 d6 8. c×d4 Bb6 9. Nc3 Na5 10. Bd3 Ne7 11. Nd5
0–0 12. N×b6 a×b6 13. d5 Ng6 14. Qc2 c5 15. Rb1 Bg4 16. Be2
Re8 17. Bb5 B×f3 18. B×e8 Nh4 19. g×f3 Qf6 20. Bd7 Qg6†
21. Bg4 N×f3† 22. Kh1 Q×g4 23. Qe2 Re8 24. R×b6 R×e4
25. R×d6 h5 26. Rd8† Kh7 27. Qc2 f5 White resigns—*Tournament Book*, p. 36.

## (1302) Lee–Bird   ½–½
International tournament (round 9)
London, 10 June 1899
*A91*

1. d4 f5 2. g3 e6 3. Bg2 Nf6 4. Nh3 Be7 5. 0–0 0–0 6. c4 d6
7. Nc3 Qe8 8. f4 Nc6 9. Nf2 Qh5 10. e3 Qg6 11. a3 a6 12. b4 Nd8
13. e4 f×e4 14. Nc×e4 Bd7 15. N×f6† B×f6 16. Ne4 Bc6 17. Re1
d5 18. N×f6† Q×f6 19. c5 Nf7 20. a4 Nh6 21. Ra2 Be8 22. Bh3
Bf7 23. Re5 Rfe8 24. Qe1 Kh8 25. Rae2 Rf8 26. Qf2 Qg6
27. B×e6 B×e6 28. R×e6 Qb1 29. Qe1 Qa1 30. Bb2 Q×a4
31. Re7 Rac8 32. R7e5 Qd7 33. Kg2 Ng4 34. Re7 Qf5 35. h3
Nf6 36. R2e5 Qc2† 37. Qe2 Qb3 38. Qd2 Ne4 39. R×e4 d×e4
40. d5 Qf3† 41. Kh2 Rg8 42. Qd4 Qe2† draw—*Tournament
Book*, pp. 166–167.

## (1303) Tinsley–Bird   0–1
International tournament (round 10)
London, 12 June 1899
*A81*

1. d4 f5 2. g3 e6 3. e3 d5 4. Bg2 c6 5. Qh5† "There is nothing
gained by the check, as the queen retires to d1. There would be
some justification for the move if he could play 6. Qh3"—Hoffer.
5. ... g6 6. Qd1 Bd6 7. c3 Nd7 8. Ne2 Qe7 9. Nd2 Ngf6 "9. ... e5
would be an excellent move, improving Black's position considerably"—Hoffer. 10. b3 0–0 11. f4 "White now stops the suggested
advance. The game is converted into a Stonewall on both sides, and
nothing can be done in the center"—Hoffer. 11. ... Ng4 12. Nf3
a5 13. h3 Nh6 14. 0–0 Nf7 15. Kh2 Re8 16. Ne5 Nb6 17. N×f7

Q×f7 18. Ng1 Bd7 19. Nf3 Qg7 20. Ne5 "All White has done up
to this point is to exchange one knight and to bring the other one
to e5, also to be exchanged"—Hoffer. 20. ... Rec8 20. ... a4! obtains
the initiative on the queenside. 21. Bb2 "There is not much scope
for the bishop on this crowded diagonal, especially if Black takes
the knight. He might have played 21. a4, followed by 22. Ba3 or
22. Bd2, with the option of 23. Be1, with an outlet eventually at g3,
h4 or via c3"—Hoffer. 21. ... Be8 22. c4 "This advance should have
been supported by 22. Rc1. As it is, he gets a bad game thereby"—
Hoffer. 22. ... B×e5 23. d×e5 "Compelled to retake with the
d-pawn, else a pawn would be lost"—Hoffer. 23. ... d×c4 24. Qd4
Qc7 25. b×c4 Rd8 26. Qc3 Na4 27. Qb3 c5 28. Bc1 Bc6 29. Rb1
B×g2 30. K×g2 Qc6† 31. Kg1 Rd7 32. Qb5? Tinsley's passive
play is painful to see. Bird cannot avoid the exchange of queens, but
this shouldn't matter as the endgame is very favorable for him. 32. ...
Q×b5 33. R×b5 b6 34. Re1 Rad8 35. Rb3 Rd3 36. Kf2 Rc3
37. e4 R×c4 "He could have captured the pawn, and kept it with
37. ... f×e4 38. R×c3 N×c3 and the knight could not be attacked
either with rook or bishop without losing the exchange"—Hoffer.
38. e×f5 g×f5 39. g4 Rc2† 40. Kg3 c4 41. Rbe3 Nc5 42. g×f5
e×f5 43. Kh4 Ne6 "A very good move, and better than the tempting
43. ... Ne4"—Hoffer. 44. Rg3† Kf7 45. Be3 b5 46. Rb1 b4 47. Bb6
Rd3 "He could well defend the a-pawn with 37. ... Rd5, but there
is no need for it. A game very well played on the part of Bird"—
Hoffer. 48. B×a5 N×f4 49. R×b4 Ng6† 50. R×g6 h×g6 51. Rb7†
Ke6 52. Bc7 R×a2 53. Rb6† Kd7 54. Bb8 Re2 55. Kg5 Rb3
56. Rd6† Kc8 57. Ba7 R×e5 58. h4 Rh3 White resigns—*Tournament Book* (Hoffer), pp. 167–168.

## (1304) Bird–Cohn   0–1
International tournament (round 11)
London, 13 June 1899
*C45*

1. e4 e5 2. d4 e×d4 3. Nf3 Nc6 4. N×d4 Bc5 5. Be3 Qf6 6. c3
Nge7 7. Be2 d5 8. Na3 N×d4 9. B×d4 B×d4 10. c×d4 d×e4
11. Qd2 0–0 12. Rc1 c6 13. 0–0 Nd5 14. Nc4 Nf4 15. Rfd1 Be6
16. Bf1 Rad8 17. g3 Nh3† 18. B×h3 B×h3 19. Ne5 Rfe8 20. Qe3
c5 21. Q×e4 c×d4 22. f4 Qb6 23. Qd3 f6 24. Nc4 Qc6 25. Rc2
Qb5 26. Rf2 Qd5 27. b3 b5 28. Na3 a6 29. Nc2 Re4 30. Re1 f5
31. Rfe2 Qc5 32. Kf2 Kf7 33. Rd2 Re3 34. N×e3 d×e3†
35. R×e3 R×d3 36. Rd×d3 Qc2† 37. Ke1 Qc1† White resigns—
*Tournament book*, pp. 3–4.

Bird had a bye in the twelfth round.

## (1305) Janowski–Bird   0–1
International tournament (round 13)
London, 16 June 1899
*C33*

1. e4 e5 2. f4 e×f4 3. Bc4 Qh4† 4. Kf1 d6 "An old defense,
which Bird plays with predilection and considerable skill"—Hoffer.
5. d4 g5 6. Nc3 Ne7 7. Nf3 Qh5 8. h4 f6 "This move is the sequel
to Bird's treatment of this variation; but it would not stand analysis.
It is good enough for an isolated attempt"—Hoffer. 9. e5 Bg7? 9. ...
g4 leads to a complicated, but fairly equal, game; e.g., 10. Ne4 Nd7

11. e×f6 g×f3 12. f×e7 Bg7 13. Ng5 f×g2† 14. K×g2 Q×d1 15. R×d1 Nb6. **10. e×f6?** "The beginning of Janowski's weak play. Obviously the text move brings the inactive bishop into the game, whereas 10. e×d6 c×d6 11. Ne4 would have subjected Black to a strong attack"—Hoffer. After 11. ... d5 12. Nd6† Kd8 13. Be2 g4 White gets nothing special. Instead 11. Nb5! is decisive. **10. ... B×f6 11. Ne4?** Janowski completely misunderstands the position. It was time to think about getting away with a draw by preparing the exchange of queens with 11. Qe2 Rf8 12. N×g5. If at once 11. N×g5 Q×d1 12. N×d1 B×d4. **11. ... Rf8 12. Qe1** "This square is required for the retreat of the knight in answer to Black's g4"—Hoffer. **12. ... h6 13. Kg1 g4 14. N×f6† R×f6 15. Nd2 Nbc6 16. Ne4 Rf8 17. c3** "This, of course, is an unaccountable mistake; but Black has by far the better game, and would have won it even without this blunder"—Hoffer. **17. ... d5 18. Bd3 d×e4 19. B×e4 Bd7 20. d5 Ne5 21. Qf2 g3 22. Qd4 f3 23. Bg5 f2† 24. Kf1 Bb5†** White resigns—*Tournament Book* (Hoffer), pp. 72–73.

### (1306) Steinitz–Bird    ½–½
International tournament (round 14)
London, 17 June 1899
*A85*

1. d4 f5 2. c4 e6 3. Nc3 Bb4 4. e3 Nf6 5. Bd3 Nc6 6. Nge2 0-0 7. 0-0 B×c3 8. b×c3 b6 9. f3 Bb7 10. e4 f×e4 11. f×e4 Nh5 12. g4 R×f1† 13. Q×f1 Nf6 14. g5 Nh5 15. Qh3 g6 16. Ng3 N×g3 17. Q×g3 d6 18. Be3 Qe7 19. c5 Rf8 20. c×d6 c×d6 21. Rf1 R×f1† 22. K×f1 Nd8 23. Ke2 Nf7 24. Kd2 Qd7 25. Kc1 Qa4 26. Kb2 Ba6 draw—*Tournament Book*, pp. 170–171.

### (1307) Lasker–Bird    1–0
International tournament (round 15)
London, 19 June 1899
*A82*

1. d4 f5 2. e4 f×e4 3. Nc3 e6 4. N×e4 Nf6 5. N×f6† g×f6 6. Qh5† Ke7 7. Bd3 Qe8 8. Qh4 Nc6 9. c3 Qf7 10. Ne2 Kd8 11. Nf4 Ne7 12. Nh5 Bg7 13. g4 h6 14. Rg1 d6 15. Bd2 Bd7 16. 0-0-0 a6 17. Rde1 b5 18. Re2 a5 19. Rge1 b4 20. Bc4 d5 21. Bd3 Rb8 22. f4 b×c3 23. B×c3 Nc6 24. f5 e×f5 25. B×f5 Rb6 26. Qf2 Kc8 27. Qf3 Kb7 28. N×g7 Q×g7 29. Q×d5 Rd8 30. Qf3 B×f5 31. g×f5 Ka7 32. d5 Nb4 33. Bd4 Qg5† 34. Kb1 R×d5 35. B×b6† K×b6 36. a3 R×f5 37. Qb3 Qg6 38. a×b4 Black resigns—*Tournament Book*, pp. 172–173.

### (1308) Bird–Maróczy    ½–½
International tournament (round 16)
London, 20 June 1899
*C47*

1. e4 e5 2. d4 e×d4 3. Nf3 Nc6 4. N×d4 Nf6 5. Nc3 Bb4 6. N×c6 b×c6 7. Bd3 d5 8. e×d5 c×d5 9. 0-0 0-0 10. Bg5 c6 11. Qf3 "White deviates with 11. Qf3 from Steinitz's continuation 11. Ne2, as played by him in his match with Zukertort, New York, 1886, which seems preferable, as Black has to retire his bishop nevertheless"—Hoffer. **11. ... Be7 12. h3 h6 13. Bh4 Rb8 14. Rab1 Rb4 15. Bg3 Bd6 16. a3 Rb8 17. Rfe1 Re8 18. b4 Rb7 19. B×d6**

R×e1† 20. R×e1 Q×d6 21. Na4 "Neither 21. Ba6 nor 21. Qe2 leads to a more favorable position. Pieces are being exchanged too freely to enable either side to achieve more than the draw, which so frequently results from this form of the Scotch game"—Hoffer. **21. ... Re7 22. R×e7 Q×e7 23. Qe3 Q×e3 24. f×e3 Nd7 25. Kf2 Kf8 26. Nc3 Nb6 27. a4 Be6 28. a5 Nc8 29. e4 Ne7** Safer is 29. ... d×e4, keeping open the most direct road for the king towards the center. **30. Ke3 f5?** 30. ... d×e4 was still feasible. Now Bird obtains a very dangerous initiative. **31. e×f5 N×f5† 32. B×f5 B×f5 33. b5! c×b5 34. N×b5 B×c2 35. N×a7 Be4 36. g3** At once 36. a6 B×g2 37. Nc8 forces the decision. Black must give up his bishop for the a-pawn. Although White is only left with his h-pawn, this is enough to win the game; e.g., 37. ... d4† 38. K×d4 Ke8 (or 38. ... B×h3 Nb6) 39. Nb6 Kd8 40. a7 Kc7 41. Kc5. **36. ... Bg2 37. h4 Ke7 38. Nb5 g5** There are other possibilities, but all of them look very bad for Black. **39. Nd4 Bf1 40. Nf5†?** The following exchange of pawns results in an inevitable draw. By keeping the position closed, with 40. h5 Kf6 41. Ne2, Bird could have created a major upset. **40. ... Kf6 41. N×h6 g×h4 42. g×h4 Kg6 43. Ng4 Kh5 44. Nf6† K×h4 45. N×d5 Kg5 46. Kd4 Be2 47. Kc5 Kf5 48. Nc3 Bf1 49. Nb5 Ke6 50. a6 Kd7 51. a7 Bg2 52. Kb6 Ba8 53. Nc7 Bg2 54. Na6 Ba8 55. Nb8† Kc8 56. Nc6 Kd7 57. Ne5† Kd6 58. Nc4† Kd7 59. Ka6 Kc7 60. Nb6 Bb7† 61. Kb5 Bc6† 62. Ka5 Bb7 63. Kb5 Bc6† 64. Kc5 Bg2** draw—*Tournament Book* (Hoffer), pp. 4–5.

### (1309) Bird–Steinitz    0–1
International tournament (round 17)
London, 21 June 1899
*A03*

1. f4 d5 2. e3 e6 3. Nf3 Bd6 4. b3 Qe7 5. Bb2 f6 6. Nc3 a6 7. Bd3 b5 8. Qe2 c5 9. Qf2 c4 10. Be2 Nc6 11. 0-0 Nh6 12. Rae1 0-0 13. Bd1 Rb8 14. Nd4 N×d4 15. e×d4 Qa7 16. Ne2 a5 17. Ng3 a4 18. b×c4 a3 19. Bc3 b×c4 20. Be2 Qa4 21. f5 e×f5 22. Bf3 Qc6 23. h3 Nf7 24. Rb1 Be6 25. Rfe1 Ng5 26. Nf1 Ne4 27. B×e4 f×e4 28. R×b8 R×b8 29. Ne3 Bc7 30. g4 Qd6 31. Kh1 g6 32. Rg1 Kf7 33. g5 B×h3 34. Q×f6† Q×f6 35. g×f6 Be6 36. Rf1 Bd8 37. Kg2 Rb5 38. d3 c×d3 39. c×d3 e×d3 40. Rd1 B×f6 41. R×d3 h5 42. Kf3 g5 43. Be1 Rb1 44. Bg3 Be7** White resigns—*Tournament Book*, pp. 211–212.

### (1310) Cohn–Bird    0–1
International tournament (round 18)
London, 23 June 1899
*B73*

1. e4 c5 2. Nf3 Nc6 3. Nc3 g6 4. d4 c×d4 5. N×d4 Bg7 6. Be3 d6 7. Be2 Bd7 8. 0-0 Nf6 9. f4 0-0 10. f5 "A weak and premature attack. In this particular form of the Sicilian the advance of the f-pawn never yields an enduring attack, whilst it weaken the e-pawn and gives Black a strong square at e5"—Hoffer. **10. ... N×d4 11. B×d4 Bc6 12. Bf3** 12. Bc4 keeps his opponent under some pressure. Cohn's next moves allow Bird to liberate himself. **12. ... Qa5 13. Qe1 Qb4 14. Rd1 Nd7 15. Qe3?** "With this move White gives a pawn for the attack; but Black, playing very well from this point, demonstrates that the pawn can safely be taken. 15. B×g7 K×g7 16. b3 might have been played, though White would always suffer

from the weakness of his isolated and fixed e-pawn"—Hoffer. **15. ... B×d4 16. R×d4 Q×b2 17. Rb1 Qa3** "Of course not 17. ... Q×c2 on account of 18. Rd2 winning the queen"—Hoffer. **18. h4 Qc5 19. h5 Qe5 20. Nd5** (see diagram)

*After 20. Nd5*

**20. ... Kh8!** Many other moves, such as 20. ... Rae8, 20. ... Nf6 or even 20. ... g×h5 are simpler. Bird's idea is deep and brilliant. **21. h×g6 f×g6 22. f×g6 Qg7!** "A very good move, which gives Black a winning attack. White cannot answer 23. g×h7, as Black would win a piece by 23. ... R×f3"—Hoffer. **23. Rbd1** 23. Nc7! forces the utmost from Bird, but after 23. ... R×f3! 24. g×f3 Rg8! 25. Kf1 Q×g6 26. Ke2 Ne5 his attack takes decisive proportions, e.g., 27. Qf2 Qh5 28. Nd5 N×f3 29. Q×f3 Qh2† and wins. **23. ... B×d5 24. e×d5 Ne5 25. Be4 Rf6?!** 25. ... h×g6 suggests itself. Black is a solid pawn up, with a promising position as well. **26. g×h7?!** Opening the g-file renders a whole lot of fresh life into Bird's attack. Better is 26. Rb4 N×g6 (if 26. ... b6 27. g×h7 Raf8 28. Rb3) 27. R×b7 Ne5 Black still stands better, but there is a tough struggle ahead. **26. ... Raf8 27. Qe2 Qg3 28. R4d3** "There is no other defense to the threatened 28. ... Rf2. The sacrifice of the exchange of course means the loss of the game. About the following ending nothing need to be said, except that Bird played it very well, as he did, indeed, the whole game"—Hoffer. **28. ... N×d3 29. R×d3 Qe5 30. Bf3 Q×e2 31. B×e2 K×h7 32. Ra3 Ra8 33. Bg4 Rf4 34. Be6 Kg7 35. Rc3 Kf6 36. Kh2 b5 37. g4 Rc4 38. Rf3† Ke5 39. c3 Rf4 40. Re3† Kf6 41. Kg3 Kg5 42. Bf5 Rc4 43. Bd7 Rd8 44. Bf5 Rh8 45. Rf3 Rf8 46. Re3 a5 47. Rf3 b4 48. c×b4 a×b4 49. Rf2 Rc3† 50. Kg2 Ra3 51. Rb2 Rfa8 52. Bb1 R8a5 53. Rd2 K×g4 54. Rd4† Kg5 55. Kf2 b3 56. a×b3 R×b3 57. Bd3 Raa3 58. Be2 Rb2 59. Re4 Kf6 60. Re6† Kf7 61. Ke1 Ra1† 62. Kf2 Raa2 63. Kf3 R×e2 64. R×e2 R×e2** White resigns—*Tournament Book* (Hoffer), pp. 97–98.

### (1311) Blackburne–Bird  1–0
International tournament (round 19)
London, 24 June 1899
A82

**1. d4 f5 2. e4 f×e4 3. Nc3 Nf6 4. f3 e×f3 5. N×f3 d5 6. Bd3 Bg4 7. 0–0 Nc6 8. Ne2?** 8. Bb5 is a clear improvement. **8. ... B×f3 9. g×f3** Blackburne has two not so good moves to choose from; 9. R×f3 is relatively better although White has nothing at all for the pawn after 9. ... e5! **9. ... Qd7 10. c3** "Having to fend the d-pawn retards Nf4, with the view of Ne6, which would be a fine post for the knight"—Hoffer. **10. ... e5 11. Bb5 Bd6 12. d×e5 B×e5 13. f4 Bd6 14. Nd4 0–0 15. Kh1 a6 16. B×c6 b×c6 17. f5 Rae8** Bird is

distracted by the approaching invasion of White's knight at e6. Had he pursued his own attack, Blackburne's case would soon be hopeless; e.g., 17. ... Ne4! 18. Qf3 (18. Ne6 brings him nothing: 18. ... Qe7! 19. Qf3 Qh4 20. Bf4 R×f5) 18. ... Rae8 19. Be3 g6 20. Bh6 Rf6 21. Qg2 Bc5 and White's position crumbles. **18. Bg5 Be5** Not as good as 18. ... Ne4 19. Qh5 c5 20. Ne6 R×f5! 21. R×f5 g6 and Black lives happily ever after. **19. Ne6 Rf7 20. Bh4** Hugely underestimating the power of Black's knight, which had to be swapped off immediately. Then each side has its own strengths, but Bird is still a pawn ahead. **20. ... Ne4! 21. Qh5** (see diagram)

*After 21. Qh5*

**21. ... c5?!** Too slow. Instead 21. ... d4!, followed by the occupation of the long diagonal by moving the queen to d5, decisively strengthens his attack. **22. Rae1 Bf6 23. Rf4 B×h4 24. R×h4?** Wagering it all on a direct attack, that could have been ended at once by 24. ... h6! **24. ... Nf6 25. Qf3 Qd6?** 25. ... Ne4 is the correct rejoinder. The text move doesn't seem to be a mistake, but the tempo thrown away with it allows Blackburne to create some real threats. **26. Rg1! c6 27. Ng5 Rfe7 28. N×h7** Pretty, and 28. ... N×h7? 29. Qh5 loses at once, but that's it. **28. ... Re1 29. N×f6†** A bit slow, as his heavy pieces don't coordinate yet. 29. Qh3 R×g1† 30. K×g1 Re1† 31. Kf2 Qe5 32. N×f6† Kf7 33. Ne4 R×e4 34. R×e4 is an improvement as the draw seems certain. **29. ... Q×f6 30. Rhg4 R×g1† 31. R×g1 Re5** 31. ... Rf8 (Hoffer) 32. Rf1 Qe5 coordinates his pieces perfectly, implying that White has to be precise for the remaining endgame. **32. Rg6 Re1† 33. Kg2 Qe5?** A horrendous blunder at the end of an extremely well-played game by Bird. After 33. ... Qe7 34. f6 Qe2† 35. Q×e2 R×e2† 36. Kg3 R×b2 37. R×g7† the game will end in a draw. **34. Re6 Q×e6 35. f×e6 R×e6 36. Qf5 Re2† 37. Kg3 R×b2 38. Qc8† Kh7 39. Q×c6** Black resigns—*Tournament Book* (Hoffer), pp. 173–175.

Bird had a bye in the 20th round.

### (1312) Bird–Lasker  0–1
International tournament (round 21)
London, 27 June 1899
C47

**1. e4 e5 2. Nf3 Nc6 3. d4 e×d4 4. N×d4 Nf6 5. Nc3 Bb4 6. N×c6 b×c6 7. Bd3 h6** "Better than to allow 8. Bg5, and then to attack the bishop"—Hoffer. **8. 0–0 d6 9. Bf4** "We see no utility in this move, unless he intended 10. e5. Probably he refrained from the latter course, seeing that Black would reply 10. ... B×c3 and 11. ... Nd5"—Hoffer. **9. ... 0–0 10. Na4** "10. Ne2 would have been better if the bishop were not at f4; but he cannot now do it, because it allows 10. ... Nh5"—Hoffer. **10. ... Re8 11. c3 Ba5 12. Qc2 Nh5**

**13. Bg3 N×g3 14. h×g3 Qg5 15. Rae1 c5 16. Re3 Bd7 17. f4 Qh5 18. c4 c6 19. Be2 Qg6 20. Nc3** *(see diagram)* "The knight now has to return from its useless journey because of the threat of 20. ... d5"—Hoffer.

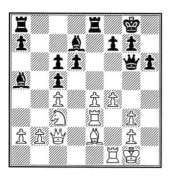

*After 20. Nc3*

**20. ... d5** "With the object of winning the exchange. But as it costs a bishop and two pawns, it would not be favorable if he had not also the advantage in position. These are exactly the positions in which Lasker excels"—Hoffer. **21. c×d5 c4 22. B×c4 Bb6 23. Qf2 Rad8 24. Rfe1 B×e3 25. Q×e3 c×d5 26. N×d5 Bc6 27. f5 Qd6 28. Kf2 B×d5 29. B×d5 Qb4 30. Qc3** "If 30. Q×a7 R×d5"—Hoffer. **30. ... Qb6† 31. Kf3 Rc8 32. Qb3 Qc7 33. Re2 Re7 34. Qd3 Qc1 35. Kf2 Rec7 36. Bb3** "After the loss of the exchange White made the best possible defense. He now prevents Black's design of changing rooks"—Hoffer. **36. ... Qc5† 37. Qe3 Kf8 38. g4 f6 39. Be6 Rd8 40. Q×c5†** "Compulsory, as Black threatens to force the exchange with 40. ... Rd3"—Hoffer. **40. ... R×c5 41. Ke3 Ke7 42. Bb3 Rc1 43. Kf4?** Bird defended himself extremely well against a persistent world champion. After 43. Kf2 Rd3 44. Bc2 Rd4 45. Ke3 he can still claim decent drawing chances. Lasker's next move brings Bird's king in serious problems. **43. ... Rd3! 44. Rf2 Re1 45. Bc4 Rde3 46. Bd5 R3e2** "Having forced his rooks into the enemy's camp Black must win"—Hoffer. **47. Rf3 R×g2 48. b4 Kd6 49. Bc4 Reg1 50. Rd3† Kc7 51. Rd5 R×g4† 52. Kf3 R1g3† 53. Kf2 Rg2† 54. Kf3 R4g3† 55. Kf4 Rc3 56. Rc5† Kd6 57. Rd5† Ke7 58. Rc5 h5** White resigns—*Tournament Book* (Hoffer), pp. 20–22.

Bird had a bye in the 22nd round.

## (1313) Bird–Janowski   0–1
International tournament (round 23)
London, 30 June 1899
*C47*

**1. e4 e5 2. Nf3 Nc6 3. d4 e×d4 4. N×d4 Nf6 5. Nc3 Bb4 6. N×c6 b×c6 7. Bd3 0-0 8. 0-0 d5 9. e×d5 c×d5 10. Bg5 c6 11. Qf3** "Preferable would have been 11. Ne2 Bd6 12. Qd2. Zukertort (vs. Steinitz, New York 1886) played the inferior 12. Ng3"—Hoffer. **11. ... Be7 12. h3 Be6 13. Rad1 h6 14. B×f6** "With this exchange he leaves Black two bishops, and consequently the better game"—Hoffer. **14. ... B×f6 15. Na4 Be7 16. b3 Bd6 17. Rfe1** "He might have ventured upon 17. c4. There are several continuations favorable for White"—Hoffer. **17. ... Bc7 18. Bf5 Qd6 19. g3 g6?!** A provocative move that really heats up the game. Janowski's conviction that the open f-file and central pawns will compensate for the lost pawn and the weaknesses on his kingside is dubious.

**20. B×e6 f×e6 21. Qe3 Rf6** 21. ... e5 22. Q×h6 Rf7 gives some compensation, but not enough. **22. Q×h6 e5** *(see diagram)*

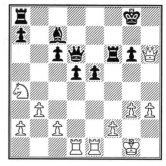

*After 22. ... e5*

**23. Re2** Too timid. 23. c4! d4 (if 23. ... e4 24. Nc3) 24. Re4 Qf8 25. Qd2 determines Black's pawn mass advantageously. The knight will soon reach d3, after which White can calmly proceed with a kingside attack. Black has little to show in return. **23. ... Raf8 24. Rd3?** This blunder allows Janowski to end the game quickly, but White already has to be careful, as is shown by the following sample line: 24. c4 e4 25. Qd2 Rf3 26. c×d5 R8f5 27. Rf1 c×d5 28. Re3 R×e3 29. Q×e3 Rf3 30. Qg5 e3 31. Kg2 d4! 32. K×f3 Qc6† with a perpetual. **24. ... e4 25. R×e4 R×f2 26. Re1 R2f3?** A surprising hiccup in the winning process. 26. ... Qf6! terminates the game. **27. Qg5?** After 27. R×f3 R×f3, the smart 28. Kh1! leaves White with surprisingly good counter-chances after 28. ... R×g3 29. Re8† Kf7 30. Rc8!, when he seems on the verge of winning himself. The simplest way now to secure the draw is by sacrificing the rook on g1, but more testing is 30. ... d4, when a few sacrifices lead to a slightly better endgame for Black: 31. R×c7† Ke6 32. Nc5† Q×c5 33. Kh2 Qe5 34. Qg7 Rc3† 35. Q×e5† K×e5 36. Re7† Kf4 37. Re2. **27. ... R3f5 28. Qe3 Qf6 29. h4 Rf1† 30. Kg2 Qf2†** White resigns. "A remarkably smart ending"—Hoffer. *Tournament Book* (Hoffer), p. 22.

## (1314) Bird–Lee   0–1
International tournament (round 24)
London, 1 July 1899
*C11*

**1. e4 e6 2. d4 d5 3. Nc3 Nf6 4. e5 Nfd7 5. Nce2 c5 6. c3 Nc6 7. f4 Qb6 8. Nf3 Be7 9. g3 0-0 10. Bh3 f5 11. 0-0 Qd8 12. Kh1 b6 13. Rg1 Kh8 14. Be3 Bb7 15. g4 g6 16. Qe1 Ba6 17. Rd1** "This is necessary, to prevent 17. ... Bd3"—Hoffer. **17. ... Rc8 18. Rg2** "We suggest 18. g×f5 g×f5 19. Ng3 followed by 20. Bf1, and doubling rooks on the open g-file. White would then get a telling attack"—Hoffer. **18. ... Na5 19. b3 Rg8 20. g×f5 g×f5 21. R×g8† K×g8 22. Ng3 Kh8 23. Bf2 Nc6 24. Bf1 Bb7 25. Bg2 Qf8 26. Ne2 Ba6 27. Neg1 Nd8 28. Nh3 Nf7 29. Bh4 Qe8 30. Qg3 Nf8?** The game's set up has been quite solid from both sides. Bird enjoyed a small initiative during most of it. Lee's last move could have been a decisive error, but not for the first time in this tournament, Bird failed to exploit it maximally. **31. Bf6†! B×f6 32. e×f6 Ng6 33. Ne5?!** 33. Re1! eyes the glaring weakness at e6, while keeping open several paths for the knights. A sample line is 33. ... Nd6 34. Ne5 c×d4 35. c×d4 Qg8 36. Ng5 N×e5 37. f×e5 Ne4 38. B×e4 f×e4 39. Qf4 and 40. Rg1! follows. **33. ... Qg8 34. Ng5 Ng×e5**

**35. d×e5 N×g5 36. f×g5** Bird is still clearly better, but Lee averted direct defeat. **36. ... Be2 37. Re1 Bg4 38. Qf4 Rd8 39. h3 Bh5 40. Re3?** Allowing Black to make an important move with a gain of tempo. Bird goes quickly astray now. **40. ... d4 41. Rg3?!** 41. Rd3 d×c3 42. Qc4 R×d3 43. Q×d3 Q×g5 44. Q×c3 loses a pawn, but the strong f-pawn offers counterplay. **41. ... d×c3 42. R×c3 Rd4 43. Qg3?! f4** Lee is granted another free move. White is lost. **44. Qh4 Qg6 45. Kh2 h6 46. f7 Q×f7 47. Bf3 Rd2† 48. Kg1 Qg6 49. Qe1 Q×g5† 50. Kf1 Rd4 51. Qe2 Qg3 52. Qg2 Q×g2† 53. K×g2 B×f3† 54. K×f3 Kg7 55. Kg4 Kg6 56. Rf3 h5†** White resigns—*Tournament Book*, pp. 113–114.

**(1315) Chigorin–Bird    1–0**
International tournament (round 25)
London, 3 July 1899
*C44*

**1. e4 e5 2. Nf3 Nc6 3. c3 d5 4. Qa4 d×e4 5. N×e5 Qd5 6. N×c6 b×c6 7. Bc4 Qd7 8. 0-0 Nf6 9. d3 e×d3 10. B×d3 Bb7 11. Re1† Be7 12. Qb3 0-0 13. Q×b7 Q×d3 14. Q×c6 Bd6 15. Qf3 Qc2 16. Bg5 Nd7 17. Qe2 Rae8 18. Be3 Qg6 19. Nd2 Ne5 20. B×a7 Nd3 21. Q×e8 R×e8 22. R×e8† Bf8 23. Nf3 Nf4 24. Ne1 Qc6 25. Rb8 f5 26. Nf3 Qd5 27. Re1 Kf7 28. Ne5† Kg8 29. Nf3 Kf7 30. c4 Qa5 31. Bd4 Nd3 32. Rb5 Q×a2 33. R×f5† Kg6 34. Nh4†** Black resigns—*Tournament Book*, pp. 17–18.

**(1316) Pillsbury–Bird    ½–½**
International tournament (round 26)
London, 4 July 1899
*D53*

**1. d4 d5 2. c4 c6 3. Nc3 Nf6 4. Nf3 e6 5. Bg5 Be7 6. e3 h6 7. Bh4 Nbd7 8. Bd3 Nb6 9. c×d5** "Pillsbury must have had some particular variation in view, otherwise it would be difficult to explain why he opened Black's cramped position with this exchange of pawns instead of 9. c5, which in this position seems to be favorable"—Hoffer. **9. ... e×d5 10. h3 Ne4 11. B×e7 Q×e7 12. 0-0 Bf5 13. a4 a5 14. B×e4 B×e4 15. N×e4 d×e4 16. Nd2 0-0 17. Qc2 Rfe8 18. f3** White came out of the opening with less than nothing. The text move could receive the strong riposte of 18. ... Nd5! **18. ... Qg5 19. Qb3 Nd5 20. Rae1 e×f3 21. N×f3** 21. R×f3 equalizes. Bird's reply is excellent. **21. ... Qe7 22. e4 Qb4! 23. Qc2 Nf4 24. Rd1 Rad8 25. Rf2 Ng6 26. g3** *(see diagram)*

*After 26. g3*

**26. ... c5!** "After Black's challenge of queens on his 22nd move the position was quite even, and here Black gets the best of it by isolating White's e-pawn"—Hoffer. **27. Rfd2 c×d4 28. R×d4 Qb6**

**29. Qf2 R×d4 30. Q×d4 Qc6 31. Re1 Rc8** 31. ... Nf8! 32. Re2 Ne6 33. Qd2 Nc5 tends to become untenable for White. Bird's approach isn't bad, but not forceful enough. **32. Re2 Qe6 33. Kg2 Qb3 34. h4 Nf8 35. Ne5 Rc2 36. R×c2 Q×c2† 37. Kh3 Qe2 38. Qc4 Qf2 39. b3 Ne6 40. Ng4?** 40. Qb5 Qg1 41. Ng4 Qh1† 42. Nh2 g5 is no pleasure either, but White keeps on writhing. **40. ... Qf3?!** The temporary sacrifice 40. ... Nf4†! 41. g×f4 Qf3† 42. Kh2 Q×f4† transposes into a winning endgame. **41. e5** "The only move, 41. ... Nf4† being threatened"—Hoffer. **41. ... Qf5 42. Kg2 h5?!** Bird picks a hasty and imprecise approach to conquer an enemy pawn. He'd be excellent after 42. ... b6 43. Qc8† Kh7 44. Qc4 h5 45. Ne3 Q×e5. **43. Nf2 Kh7 44. Qb5 g5 45. h×g5 N×g5 46. Q×b7** This capture secures the draw but Bird is evidently not convinced yet. **46. ... Q×e5 47. Qb5 Qf6 48. Qd5 Kh6 49. Nd3 Qg6 50. b4 a×b4 51. N×b4 Qb1 52. Qd6† Ne6 53. Qd2† Ng5 54. Qd6† Ne6 55. Qd2† Kg7 56. Nc2 Qb7† 57. Kh2 Qe4 58. a5 h4 59. Qg2 Qe5 60. a6 h×g3† 61. Q×g3† Q×g3† 62. K×g3 Nc7 63. a7 Kf6 64. Kf4 Ke6 65. Nd4† Kd7** draw—*Tournament Book* (Hoffer), pp. 130–131.

**(1317) Showalter–Bird    1–0**
International tournament (round 27)
London, 5 July 1899
*A85*

**1. d4 f5 2. c4 e6 3. Nc3 Nf6 4. Nf3 Bb4 5. Qb3 Nc6 6. e3 0-0 7. Bd3 b6 8. 0-0 B×c3 9. b×c3 Bb7 10. Ba3 d6 11. c5 Re8 12. c×d6 c×d6 13. Ng5 d5 14. Nf3 Ne4 15. Rac1 Rc8 16. Qb2 Na5 17. Ne5 Nd6 18. B×d6 Q×d6 19. f4 Rc7 20. Rf3 Rec8 21. Rh3 g6 22. g4 Nc4 23. Qb3 N×e5 24. f×e5 Qe7 25. g×f5 g×f5 26. Rg3† Kh8 27. Kh1 Rg8 28. R×g8† K×g8 29. Rg1† Kh8 30. Qb2 Qf8 31. Qd2 Bc6 32. h3 Be8 33. Kh2 Qh6 34. Be2 Rg7 35. R×g7 K×g7 36. c4 Qh4 37. Bd3 Bc6 38. Qg2† Kh6 39. Qg3 Qe7 40. h4 Qg7 41. Qf4† Kg6 42. B×f5† e×f5 43. Qg5† Kf7 44. e6† Kf8 45. Q×f5† Kg8 46. c×d5 Qc7† 47. Kh3 Be8 48. Qg5† Kf8 49. Qf6† Kg8 50. Qg5† Kf8 51. Qf6† Kg8 52. Qf3 Qe7 53. Qg3† Kf8 54. Qf4† Kg8 55. Qe5 Qf8 56. Kg2 Bb5 57. Qg3† Kh8 58. Qe5† Kg8 59. Qg3† Kh8 60. Qe5† Kg8 61. Qg3† Kh8 62. Kh2 Qa3 63. Qe5† Kg8 64. d6 Q×a2† 65. Kg3** Black resigns—*Tournament Book*, pp. 171–172.

**(1318) Bird–Tinsley    1–0**
International tournament (round 28)
London, 7 July 1899
*C13*

**1. e4 e6 2. d4 d5 3. Nc3 d×e4 4. N×e4 Nf6 5. Bg5 Nbd7 6. Nf3 Be7 7. N×f6† N×f6 8. c3 Nd5 9. Be3 N×e3 10. f×e3 Bh4† 11. g3 Bg5 12. Kf2 0-0 13. h4 Be7 14. Bd3 f5 15. Kg2 Bd7 16. Rf1 Bc6 17. Qe2 Bd6 18. Rg1 Rf6 19. Kf2 Rg6 20. Rg2 Qf6 21. Rag1 Rg4 22. Bb5 Be4 23. Bd3 Bc6 24. Bb5 Bd5 25. Bc4 c6 26. Bb3 Rf8 27. Ke1 Qg6 28. Qf2 Bb3 29. a×b3 f4 30. g×f4 Qb1† 31. Ke2 Q×b2† 32. Kf1 Qb1† 33. Ne1 R×g2 34. Q×g2 Rf7 35. Qc2 Qa1 36. Ke2 Qa5 37. Rg5 Qc7 38. Nf3 h6 39. Rg6 Qe7 40. Qe4 Rf6 41. h5 R×g6 42. Q×g6 Qf7 43. Qg4 Qf5 44. Q×f5 e×f5 45. b4 b5 46. Kd3 Kf7 47. Nh4 Ke6 48. e4 f×e4† 49. K×e4 g5 50. f5† Kf6 51. Ng6 Bg3 52. Ne5 Be1 53. Ng4† Kg7 54. f6† Kf7 55. Kf5**

B×c3 56. N×h6† Kf8 57. Kg6 B×b4 58. Ng4 a5 59. h6 Kg8 60. h7† Kh8 61. Nh6 Black resigns—*Tournament Book*, pp. 108–109.

## (1319) Bird–Schlechter    0–1
International tournament (round 29)
London, 8 July 1899
C45

1. e4 e5 2. Nf3 Nc6 3. d4 e×d4 4. N×d4 Bc5 5. Be3 Qf6 6. c3 Nge7 7. Qd2 0–0 8. f4 d6 9. Na3 N×d4 10. B×d4 B×d4 11. c×d4 d5 12. e5 Qb6 13. Nb5 c6 14. Nc3 f6 15. 0–0–0 Ng6 16. g3 Rf7 17. Na4 Qc7 18. Bd3 f5 19. Rdf1 Nf8 20. Be2 Ne6 21. Qc3 Bd7 22. Bf3 Re8 23. h4 b6 24. b3 Qd8 25. Rd1 Qe7 26. Qb2 Bc8 27. Kb1 Ba6 28. Rh2 Rd8 29. Rc2 Bb7 30. b4 Ba6 31. Qc3 Bc4 32. Nb2 b5 33. Qa3 a5 34. Q×a5 Rff8 35. N×c4 b×c4 36. Qa4 Rb8 37. Q×c6 Q×b4† 38. Ka1 Rb6 39. Q×e6† R×e6 40. B×d5 Rfe8 41. R×c4 Qb5 42. Rc5 Qe2 43. Rcc1 Kf8 44. Bc4 Qf2 45. Bb3 Rb6 46. Rd3 Ra8 White resigns—*Tournament Book*, pp. 18–19.

## (1320) Bird–Mason    0–1
International tournament (round 30)
London, 10 July 1899
C42

1. e4 e5 2. Nf3 Nf6 3. Nc3 d6 4. Bc4 Be7 5. 0–0 Bg4 6. Re1 Nbd7 7. d3 Nf8 8. h3 Be6 9. B×e6 N×e6 10. d4 e×d4 11. N×d4 N×d4 12. Q×d4 0–0 13. Be3 Ne8 14. Qd3 Qd7 15. Ne2 Bf6 16. c3 g6 17. f4 Bg7 18. Ng3 a6 19. Rf1 Qc6 20. Rad1 Rd8 21. e5 Rc8 22. Bd4 d×e5 23. f×e5 Rd8 24. Qe4 Q×e4 25. N×e4 b6 26. b4 Rd7 27. Rde1 Rd5 28. Rf3 a5 29. a3 h6 30. g4 Kh8 31. e6 B×d4† 32. c×d4 f5 33. b×a5 R×a5 34. Ng3 f4 35. Re4 g5 36. Nh5 Rg8 37. Re5 R×e5 38. d×e5 Rg6 39. e7 Re6 40. Nf6 R×e7 White resigns—*Tournament Book*, p. 13.

---

# THE FINAL YEARS

A few months after the tournament of London Bird suffered another serious, and now definitive, breakdown of his health. He was admitted for treatment at Guy's Hospital in London but only a few weeks later he was discharged as being incurable. At the time Bird's condition became publicly known some of his friends had already arranged a stay for him at a private nursing home in Tooting.[14]

Under the impetus of Dr. Robert Dunstan and H.A. Richardson, the secretary of the St. George's Chess Club, a public subscription was set up. The appeal for supporting Bird's cause went worldwide: even a few clubs from other continents contributed. At the end of the year a little over £425 was gathered to invest in an annuity. Some

£150 more was required to guarantee a full annuity and a second appeal was made forthwith. By March 1901 there was enough money gathered to offer Bird an annuity of £72. Late additions increased this amount still further.

Despite his grave condition, but maybe thanks to the generosity shown to him by the chess community, Bird did not allow his circumstances to lower his spirits. On 20 March 1901, the *Manchester Evening News* brought the news that "Mr. Bird is unable to walk, but otherwise his general health is good, and he declares that he plays chess now better than ever." A few months later Bird's life was nearly drastically cut short by an incident at his lodgings. On 13 June 1901 the *Aberdeen Journal* reported that "Mr. H.E. Bird, the chess-player, has had a narrow escape. He is an invalid confined to his bed, and the upsetting of a light, which set fire to the bed, placed him in serious danger. He was saved by the promptitude of Mrs. Hartland, his landlady, who was severely burnt in putting out the flames."

Just a few days later Bird made his last public appearance. On 22 June he was present, in a bath-chair, at a garden party given by Doctor and Mrs. Dunstan to the members of the Nightingale Lane Chess Club on the occasion of the presentation of a testimonial to W.T. Marshall, the club's secretary.

The last known photograph depicting Bird was taken on this occasion.

Information from the electoral rolls allows one to find a few traces of Bird during his final years. In 1902 and 1903 he lived at 338, Balham High Road, renting "two rooms, 1st floor, furnished." His injured landlady Fanny Hartland lived at the same address. For the years 1905, 1906 and 1908 Bird was listed as a lodger at 16, Chetwode Road, with F.J. Merryweather as his landlord. Bird occupied a furnished room in the front part of the building. Just as at Balham High Road, Bird lived on the "first floor"—the level above the ground floor—access to which must have been very difficult given his condition.

Bird did not lose his interest in the game, nor was he forgotten by his fellows of whom several were among his regular visitors. Bird found in correspondence chess an alternative to his inability to play chess outside his lodging.[15]

With the passing of the years Bird's condition slowly worsened. At the same time he became forgotten by the younger generation while many of his younger contemporaries died well before him. Bird's solitude increased. Early in 1908, H.A. Richardson released an appeal on behalf of the old man in *The Sunday Times* of 16 February: "[Richardson] suggests that it would be a real kindness if some of his old friends were occasionally to pay the old gentleman a visit, just to show that he is not quite forgotten."

Less than two months later, on 11 April 1908, Henry Edward Bird left this world at the age of 78. He died at his home at 16 Chetwode Road. As his cause of death was noted a "chronic enlargement of [the] prostate. Cystitis Exhaustion."[16] These symptoms are re-

---

14. See the *Pall Mall Gazette*, 13 February 1900. It has been remarkable how long Bird withstood his infirmities: "Mr. H.E. Bird has been a sufferer for many years past, but he astonished both his friends and his doctors by the cheerfulness of spirits and the physical strength which gave him the power to bear his infirmity, and continue playing, both in private and in public competitions, in spite of them. Now, however, his illness has taken a more serious shape, confining him absolutely to his couch."

15. Bird remained constantly on the lookout for opponents. A snippet from the *Exeter and Plymouth Gazette* of 31 January 1905 advertised: "The veteran master, Mr. H.E. Bird, will be pleased to play a game by correspondence with any Devonian. Here is a chance for someone. Address: Mr. H.E. Bird, 16, Chetwode-road, Upper Tooting, London, S.W."

16. The death registration reference is Wandsworth, Apr-May-Jun 1908, vol. 1d, p. 307.

**Garden party at the Dunstans on 22 June 1901. Bird is sitting in his wheelchair (*CHESS*).**

markably similar to those of his father, Henry, at the time of his death in 1869.

Henry Edward's death was reported by Louisa Maria Whitecross, his youngest sister. She inherited his estate, worth £35 0s 10d.[17] The chess master was buried at Streatham Cemetery on Thursday 16 April.[18]

---

## OBITUARIES AND MEMORIALS

Bird's death was merely mentioned as a side note by most newspapers and magazines. One of the more fundamental obituaries appeared in the *British Chess Magazine*, where four pages were dedicated to the master. Besides a summing up of Bird's tournament and match results, he was sketched for a final time:

To see Mr. Bird in his glory one had to see him occupying his favourite end seat at Simpson's, just opposite the door. Then, when he had a congenial opponent, he fairly beamed with delight, and that without much reference as to whether he was winning or losing. He was one of the best odds-givers at lightning speed. He gave a rook or a queen to a weaker brother, and thought nothing of it. He played with great rapidity, conjuring up the strangest combinations, making the most extraordinary moves, sacrificing a piece here, giving up a pawn there, winning a queen as if by sleight of hand, and mating his opponent by some sort of hypnotism. Amidst it all he laughed and joked, and was happy. For this veteran of many summers really enjoyed his game like a schoolboy out for a holiday. Chess was his pastime and his life pleasure. He claimed to be the chess champion of the world at lightning speed—say, at 1000 moves per hour! [*British Chess Magazine*, June 1908, p. 251].

Another extensive portrait containing some details about his final years was written by Isaac McIntyre Brown, the chess editor of the *Manchester Guardian*:

H.E. Bird was the possessor of a marvellous amount of vitality and zest for life, in spite of his great age, and in spite of his sufferings—he was confined to his bed for nearly ten years,—he invited visitors almost to the last to come and play chess with him. This fact may be accepted as a proof of an enthusiasm for the game which probably will never be surpassed in the future. His enthusiasm was so great that it proved his undoing, for he started life with the best prospects as a member of a leading firm of London accountants. His genius for figures was only equalled by his genius for chess, but he allowed his love for the game to outrun his discretion. He was a player who trusted more to inspiration than to theory. Whenever Bird met a player of his own school and his own line of thought he produced wonderful games and had a fair amount of success; but opposed to players trained in the modern theory he could not hold his own so well. However, he often wrested a game from

---

17. Ancestry.com. *England & Wales, National Probate Calendar (Index of Wills and Administrations), 1858–1966* [database on-line]. Provo, UT, USA: Ancestry.com Operations Inc., 2010.

18.   The information about Bird's final years is gathered, besides the quoted sources, from various newspapers and magazines. One of the most important articles was republished from the *Western Daily Mercury* by the *British Chess Magazine* in January 1917 (pp. 13–14). In this article, written to refute the statements made by a visitor of the Torquay Chess Club that Bird died in poverty, it was stated that Bird entered Guy's Hospital in May 1900. More contemporary sources (such as the quoted article from the *Pall Mall Gazette*) suggest this occurred earlier.

CERTIFIED COPY OF AN ENTRY OF DEATH    GIVEN AT THE GENERAL REGISTER OFFICE

Application Number    5394427-2

| REGISTRATION DISTRICT | WANDSWORTH | |
|---|---|---|
| 1908 DEATH in the Sub-district of Streatham | in the County of London | |

Columns:— 1 2 3 4 5 6 7 8 9

| No. | When and where died | Name and surname | Sex | Age | Occupation | Cause of death | Signature, description and residence of informant | When registered | Signature of registrar |
|---|---|---|---|---|---|---|---|---|---|
| 464 | Eleventh April 1908 16 Shetwode Road | Henry Edward Bird | Male | 75 years | Annuitant | Chronic Enlargement of Prostate. Cystitis Exhaustion Certified by H. Thompson Barron M.D.Lond. | L. M. Whitecross Sister 129 Brixton Road Brixton | Fifteenth April 1908 | Charles J. Smith Registrar |

CERTIFIED to be a true copy of an entry in the certified copy of a Register of Deaths in the District above mentioned.

Given at the GENERAL REGISTER OFFICE, under the Seal of the said Office, the    16th    day of    January    2014

DYD 631393    See note overleaf

CAUTION: THERE ARE OFFENCES RELATING TO FALSIFYING OR ALTERING A CERTIFICATE AND USING OR POSSESSING A FALSE CERTIFICATE ©CROWN COPYRIGHT
**WARNING: A CERTIFICATE IS NOT EVIDENCE OF IDENTITY.**

7231132 68840 04/13 3MSSD 033108    CM

**Death certificate of Henry Edward Bird.**

first prize winners in tournaments in which he occupied but an inferior position [*Manchester Guardian*, 21 April 1908].

Hoffer's offering seems rather short for his longtime acquaintanceship.

It is with great regret that we record the death of Mr. H.E. Bird, which took place in London on Tuesday. Mr. Bird, who had reached his seventy-eighth year, was the *doyen* of chess masters, but during the present century his old resorts had seen little of him, and, a victim to gout and other infirmities, he had passed a life of retirement at Balham. The deceased master was by profession an accountant, and was employed by the firm of Messrs. Turquand, Young, and Co. but very early in life he fell beneath the spell that chess casts upon its votaries. Almost his first recorded games were played with Buckle, the historian. He competed in the great London tournament of 1851, and practically his last appearance in public was in the London tournament of 1899. In the interval he took part in many tournaments, but his vivacious style was little suited to the onerous conditions of a prolonged contest. His most notable performances were at Vienna, in 1873, when he took fifth prize; at Philadelphia, in 1876, when he finished third; whilst he won the first prize at the London congress of the now defunct British Chess Association in 1889. Bird also competed in many matches [*The Field*, 18 April 1908].

Also interesting are the reminiscences of the editor of a New Zealand newspaper:

Having met and played with the veteran, we can endorse what has been said about his geniality. On the occasion referred to, while playing, he kept up a continual conversation with the bystanders on various subjects, architecture amongst other things. There was nothing offensive to his opponent in this, and it did not interfere with his conduct of the game in any way. It was one of the irregular openings to which he was so partial, and we have a lively recollection of how he overwhelmed us with his pawns; it seemed quite impossible to stop them advancing, and he did it all so easily, without hesitation and apparently without consideration, that it looked the simplest thing in the world on his side, and the most difficult from our side of the board [*Otago Witness*, 1 July 1908].

In an article consecrated to the different schools in chess, a contributor to *The Times* paid some attention to Bird.[19]

He detested a safe, common-place game and would indulge in the wildest eccentricities to avoid it. His love of the bizarre and the humorous often caused him to lose a won game, and he never achieved the highest honors in a great tournament. But he produced games of an uncanny, almost diabolical, brilliance at times, and the strongest of his opponents, even when winning at his leisure to all appearance, could never feel safe against the wizardry of his wayward imagination. At his best he out–Morphyed Morphy, and that should be his epitaph [*The Times*, 27 January 1910].

During the following years and decades Bird from time to time reappeared in various memoirs, from which the present work has

19. From 1903 until 1912 the chess column in *The Times* was in the hands of the three sons of the deceased chess master Samuel Tinsley. One of them, Samuel, shared a few lines on Bird in his book *Across the World*: "Henry Bird was another great player of Blackburne's day. Dear old Bird, who was called the 'amorous bird,' because he was 'always looking for a mate.'"

already quoted extensively. A final interesting story comes from O.C. Müller:

> The senior of the British-born masters (he was born in 1830 [*sic*]) was H.E. Bird, always a humorous and cheerful old soul, in spite of the gout which often tormented him in his later years. He also was invariably very friendly to me, and on many occasions I acted for him as his "substitute," as he would say. He was a very versatile and ingenious chess player; fond of playing very quickly, and in tournaments, and in particular, in "exhibition games" he was often successful. Even against Steinitz, Blackburne, and Zukertort he occasionally won games in my presence. He also wrote numerous books on chess, the most enduring of which will probably be his collection of *Chess Masterpieces* [*British Chess Magazine*, November 1932, pp. 483–484].

It may be a fitting tribute to Bird's passion for chess to place two testimonies describing the young and old Bird next to each other. They come respectively from Samuel Boden and Philip Sergeant.

> "I remember him well," said the late S.S. Boden to me [MacDonnell], "when he first came to the Divan in 1846, a pretty-faced boy in a jacket, blue-eyed, fair haired, and rosy-cheeked"—a strange picture to one who, like the present writer [Sergeant], was near Bird's then age, and in a jacket, when he first saw the master at Simpson's, still blue-eyed, still rosy-cheeked, it is true, but otherwise *quantum mutatus ab illo*; majestic in his stature, in his girth, in the baldness of his great head, less majestic in the constant litter of tobacco-ash upon the creases of the waistcoat of his broadcloth suit and the frequent disarray of manuscripts or proofs upon the table at which he sat. He seemed, for all his pleasant smiling countenance, too venerable for the jacketed boy to approach [*A Century of British Chess*, p. 80].

# APPENDIX 1:
# CHESS PROBLEMS

The composition of chess studies and problems was a very popular activity in the nineteenth century. It formed the basis of about every chess column that was published. In many cases, a column even existed of a sole problem and the solution of the last week's one. In a time when any remoteness from the chess centers implied great difficulties in finding a worthy opponent over the board, creating and solving problems were a valuable alternative.

Bird, unlike many other masters, hardly had any interest in creating brain teasers for the chess addicts, which is testified to by the very slight number of compositions he left behind. Only a handful of them appeared in print. They were nevertheless well appreciated and reprinted several times over the course of many years.

Buckley, in a story that is situated just before the Quintangular tournament of 1892, shows us why Bird preferred a real chess game by describing the reaction of the veteran to Lasker's showing a problem to other masters at the Divan.

Bird looked at it with contempt: he cared little for problems; there was no fight in them [*Birmingham Weekly Mercury*, 5 January 1901].

Bird's first known problem appeared in the *Chess Player's Chronicle*, October 1853, p. 319:

**Problem 1**
**White to mate in three moves**

The key move is **1. Nf4!** The two main lines are 1. ... R×c5 2. Ne6† Kc6 3. Qc8 mates and 1. ... Bb3 2. Bb6† and mate on the next move.

The following position actually occurred in a game witnessed by Bird. The *Albion*, 7 December 1867:

In the ... position (which occurred between two good players, in a London chess room), White had to move and played 1. Qg1, which allows Black to

escape safely; but an onlooker, Mr. Bird, observed that White had at command a move which would speedily have won by force. It will be an instructive exercise to chess to find the path to victory.

**White to move and win**

Bird perhaps had **1. Qb7** in mind, which seems White's trickiest option, for if 1. ... Qc6 2. Rc4† and in case of 1. ... Rhb8 there is a pretty mate: 2. R×d5†! Q×d5 3. Be7† Kc4 4. Qa6+! Qb5 5. Qe6† Qd5 6. Qe2 mate. But 1. ... a5! is a strong rejoinder after which White may resign.

___

Bird's principal activity in composing may be situated in the 1870s. Problems number 2 and 5 are almost identical. The *Westminster Chess Club Papers*, July 1873, p. 52:

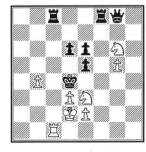

**Problem 2**
**White to mate in four moves**

The solution is **1. Rc6 R×c6 2. Ne7**, followed by **3. N3f5†** and **4. e3**.

___

The *City of London Chess Magazine*, September 1874, p. 194:

**Problem 3**
**White to mate in two moves**

The key move is **1. Rd6**. If 1. ... N×d6 or 1. ... R×d6 then 2. Ne5 mates. If 2. ... Q×d6 3. Nh8 mates.

*The Sportsman*, 13 November 1875:

**Problem 4**
**White to mate in two moves**

**1. Re5** is the initial move.

The *Scientific American*, 2 October 1877:

**Problem 5**
**White to mate in four moves**

The main line is **1. Rb6 R×b6 2. N×d7 Qf6 3. N3e5+ Q×e5 4. d3 mate.**

Regarding Bird, Loyd wrote in the same column:

[W]e cannot close without adding our tribute to his skill as a composer of chess problems of great beauty and merit, ... and are particularly pleased to find a player like Mr. Bird, who has encountered the champions from almost every clime, gives it as his candid opinion that he has never known a good problemist who was not a fine chess player [*Scientific American*, 2 October 1877].

In *Sheffield and Rotherham Independent*, 8 September 1883:

**Problem 6**
**White to mate in two moves**

The key move is **1. Ne5.**

Three weeks later Bird informed his readers that in preparing problem 6 (above) he had followed the advice of E.N. Frankenstein, one of England's top composers, to simplify the design of his original version. On this occasion (*Sheffield and Rotherham Independent*, 29 September 1883) Bird published his first version:

**Problem 7**
**White to mate in two moves**

The key move remains **1. Ne5.**

The following problem was included in Bird's book *Chess Openings*. It was devised and dedicated to Bird by his admirer Samuel Loyd. The problem has the form of the letter B:

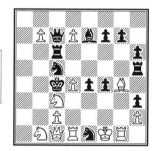

**Problem 8 by Samuel Loyd**
**White to mate in four moves**

After **1. Nd2† Kb4 2. Qa3† K×a3 3. Rb1** and mate follows promptly.

Another problem dedicated to Bird was composed by Dr. Joseph Law. Dr. Law contributed a weekly problem that was published in the chess column of the *Sheffield and Rotherham Independent*. This is from the 14 April 1883 edition:

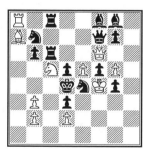

**Problem 9 by Joseph Law**
**White to mate in three moves**

The key move is **1. B×b6**, e.g., **1. ... R×b6 2. Q×b6 B×c5 3. Ra4 mates.**

# Appendix 2: Documents about and by Bird

## The New Chess Lion Arrives

*The most interesting and extensive portrait describing Bird upon his arrival in the United States appeared in the* New York Sun *on 19 December 1875.*

**THE NEW CHESS LION**

A Man Who Holds His Own with the Strongest Players of the World.

The arrival in New York of Mr. H.E. Bird, the distinguished English chess player, is a circumstance of much interest to all devotees of the game. Mr. Bird has already tried his hand with some of the best of the New York players, and has manifested his strength and skill to the satisfaction of all. He is nearly every evening in the Café International chess room at 294 Bowery, the main chess resort of the city, where he sits in the center of a large gathering of chess players, come to see him and witness his games. For the last two or three days he has been playing with Alberoni, a comparatively new man in American chess circles, and not long from Europe, but one who aspires to a high rank among the exponents of the game. About the players sit and stand chess enthusiasts as far as a glimpse of the board can be obtained. They are of every tongue and clime. They look very much like the cuts in Kladderadatsch, in which all the nations are represented by appropriate physiognomies. ... The best chess player is the most interesting man. These all stand and watch the games for hours upon hours.

Mr. Bird is a quiet, good-natured, gentlemanly-looking person of forty-five: bald, short, portly, of round, florid face, fringed with light, soft whiskers. He might be mistaken for a sea captain on a merchant vessel. He moves the pieces gently, but without hesitation, and plays very rapidly. He is remarkable for the rapidity of his play. No English player of note equals him in this respect. He seems to have great endurance. Since his arrival here he has sometimes played ten or fifteen games, or even more, in a day. To be sure, they were not for a stake.

Mr. Bird ranks with the best of the European players. He has played with Anderssen, Steinitz, Wisker, Boden, MacDonnell, Blackburne, Zukertort and Staunton, and with Buckle. ... He played with Anderssen in the tournament of 1851; a match with Steinitz

in 1866—a very-hotly contested match, which was left unfinished in consequence of Mr. Bird's trip, on important business, to America, the score standing: Steinitz 7; Bird 5; drawn 5. Mr. Bird's games with Anderssen and Boden are some of the finest on record. With Mr. Wisker, who was the winner of the Challenge Cup of the British Chess Association in 1873 [*sic*], he recently played a match. Steinitz is the only one with whom he has won less than his half of the games.

He lives in London, where he is honorary member of the City of London Chess Club, and is a favorite frequenter of St. George's Chess Club, the fashionable club, to which the nobility and members of Parliament belong. He was a warm friend of Staunton's during the latter's lifetime. He is a railway accountant by profession, of large experience, and well-known in connection with railway investigations. He has recently produced a book on chess—*Chess Masterpieces*—a collection of choice games, with notes, dedicated to Kolisch, which is rapidly going through the edition. He has been in New York three times heretofore, in 1860, 1865 and 1866.

In 1866 he came in the capacity of auditor of the Atlantic and Great Western Railway. Many persons are acquainted with him who know him only in business connections, and are not aware that he plays chess at all, although in 1866 he met Mackenzie here and played him a number of games. That was the only time before the present that he played in America. Having more leisure this trip, he will, probably, play a good deal. He has given notice that he is ready to enter the arena with anybody. He has already been playing with Mackenzie, Mason, and Alberoni, and with other players, such as Perrin and Ries [Rice]. He will soon meet Delmar, and is likely to try the players of Philadelphia and Buffalo. It is thought that he will receive an invitation from the chess players of Philadelphia, and will be suitably entertained by them. The Brooklyn Chess Club has received him very hospitably. Bird's games with Mackenzie were very fine. Mackenzie won the odd game, but since Bird had the opportunity of making it a draw, and chivalrously declined to do it, it can hardly be called a lost game.

He goes to Philadelphia next week with Mackenzie to see what arrangements can be made for a chess tournament in connection with the Centennial. If the result is satisfactory a whole galaxy of suns and stars of the chess universe will probably shed lustre upon the Centennial celebration. From London will come Bird, Zukertort, Steinitz, MacDonnell and Wisker.

Mr. Bird's present stay is fixed at about a month, of which several days will be spent in other cities.

---

# Bird's Farewell to Chess

*At the end of 1880 Bird released a long pamphlet in which he announced his goodbye from chess. He did not take the trouble to spread copies of his text to the British chess columns for, he claimed, they were nearly all in foreign hands. The* Glasgow Weekly Herald *devoted quite some space to the subject. Only the New York–based* Turf, Field and Farm, *of which the chess content was managed by Mackenzie, published the pamphlet (nearly) in full on 24 December 1880. The few paragraphs that Mackenzie omitted are put in bold below. The sole surviving copy (the present researcher could find) is preserved at the library of Harvard University.*

Sir,

In relinquishing any further active participation in public chess play, I would gladly follow the example of the other three leading English amateurs, and withdraw (like them) from the chess circle unnoticed and unperceived.[1]

I am, however, in a somewhat different position to my contemporaries, and cannot emulate the modesty and dignity of their retirement. Not only have I been longer in the chess world, but I have been far more identified with the vicissitudes and ups and downs of the game than either of them; in addition to which I am the last link of the old chess chain which bound the players of the past quarter of a century together in friendly rivalry, generous emulation, and complete unity during a period when dissensions were unknown.

It is thirty-five years since I first played chess, and thirty years since I first encountered Anderssen, Buckle and Harrwitz on even terms. I have had the good fortune to meet with Kieseritzky, Löwenthal and Szén, and have held my own against all of them. In later years Barnes, Macdonnell, and notably Boden were my regular competitors, and some scores of delightful games took place only six years since between Cochrane and myself. In fact, I do not suppose that any amateur ever existed who has played with greater masters. I have lived at a time when first-class chess encounters were of everyday occurrence, now such a thing is unknown. During the past two or three years I do not recollect any casual games between leading players, excepting those in which I have taken part. Boden, Blackburne, Hoffer, Macdonnell, Mason, Potter and Zukertort have each contested more or less with me, but no two of them ever played together. I have upheld the good old cause in America on four different occasions. In Canada, at Montreal and elsewhere, I assisted in awakening quite a genuine enthusiasm for the game, and my recent gratifying receptions at Hamburg, Berlin, Amsterdam and Rotterdam, and my successes, although not noticed in the London chess press,

are well known to have exercised a beneficial influence on the fortunes of chess in these places. The present generation of professional players dislike first-class amateurs, because they are at times expected to play with them, and will not do so. Notwithstanding this, at first sight, it may appear strange that they should single out an old enthusiast like myself as an object of their jealousy, their envy, their attacks. The reason, however, is not so very difficult to explain, for it has arisen mainly through my remaining too long an active and prominent member of the circle, forming at times opinions upon chess matters of policy not entirely in accordance with their views. There is also another point which I cannot help thinking at times has something to do with it. When I quitted the chess circle after my closely-contested match with Steinitz in 1867 [*sic*], I was on very pleasant and friendly terms with all classes of the chess community. That match was played shortly after the one between Anderssen and Steinitz, in which the latter was successful. My score was the best ever yet made against Steinitz; but, unfortunately, I had to resign the match at a highly interesting stage after the twenty-first game [*sic*], in consequence of business which called me suddenly to America.

Steinitz, of course, received the stakes, and also presents [money] equivalent thereto [in compensation] for adjournments [i.e., delays], but there was an understanding that he should play me a return match on the first convenient occasion, but this engagement he has never fulfilled. The severe comments that were made by the leading chess organ when the stakes were demanded and the subsequent troubles at the Westminster Chess Club took place during my absence in Pennsylvania. I did not sympathize with the complaints against Steinitz; on the contrary, on my return I was his warm supporter. Being my own backer, and having requested that the stakes should be paid over, I could not see what right at the time Staunton, the committee of the Westminster Chess Club, or anyone else had to complain. I remained, therefore, on very good terms with Steinitz, but these circumstances, nevertheless, I believe have always left an unpleasant feeling on his mind.

I did not resume active chess until the year 1872, but in 1873, through the kind instrumentality of Löwenthal, a match was arranged, for chess honor merely, between Wisker, the winner of the British Chess Association Challenge Cup, and myself. The match, or rather matches, which ensued between us were of the most agreeable character, and created much interest, especially in the St. George's Chess Club, where they were played.

It is scarcely necessary to observe that I was still on excellent terms with all the chess circle, and it was not until sometime afterward that the foreign professionals began to exhibit unmistakable signs of jealousy toward the leading English amateurs. The change in the management of the St. George's Chess Club materially increased the influence of the foreign trio [Steinitz, Zukertort, Hoffer], who no longer were members of the City of London Chess Club.

The leading amateurs, who, in the days of Mr. Hampton, Mr. Cochrane and Mr. Löwenthal, were always received and regarded with due consideration, have, since the accession to power of the present honorary secretary [James Innes Minchin], been ever treated with marked disrespect.

Circumstances had arisen about the time which rendered it necessary that the trio should secede from the City of London Chess

---

1. Which three players had Bird in mind? Quite certainly Potter was one of them. Perhaps Bird also alluded to Boden, although he was inactive towards the last years of his life.

Club. I will not further allude to this, nor do I care even to make a point of its dissolution, beyond observing that I am happy to remember that I never entered that club, though frequently invited.

There can, I think, be no doubt that the death of Mr. Hampton, the former highly popular secretary of the St. George's Chess Club, and the irreparable loss of Mr. Cochrane and Mr. Löwenthal, caused quite a revolution in the interests of the game. These three staunch lovers of chess knew not what jealousy meant. They exulted in first-class play, and never missed an opportunity of promoting it. With the present honorary secretary a new era arose. His contempt for the skill of the leading English players has been openly expressed in their presence on two noteworthy occasions. His admiration of the powers of the foreign players appears to know no bounds, and to border on enthusiasm. With such a supporter in such a position it has, no doubt, appeared an easy task to extinguish the small remnant of the old English chess school, and especially a humble member like myself. My desire also to play a match with either Steinitz or Zukertort has long been well known, and my (perhaps, too) persistent efforts to bring such an event about would appear to have occasioned both of them some annoyance. The fair and business-like protest which I made at the request and on the part of Rosenthal against umpires and referees being all selected from the club supporting Zukertort appears to have afforded the honorary secretary a capital opportunity of gratifying his caprice and avenging an old grudge. My wish to see Rosenthal supported, as I was informed his friends in Paris expected him to be, was just and reasonable, yet I understand that under the silly and shallow pretext that I had conveyed imputations or shown disrespect to the club, an attempt was made to pass a resolution requesting me not to visit the club again.[2] This, however, was not carried. The honorary secretary still, however, appears to have determined to proceed on his own authority, for recently, on my return from the continent, I happened to look in at the club, and was told by the hall porter that the honorary secretary had given instructions that I was not to be admitted, but he knew of no order of the committee to that effect.

The question, however, between the honorary secretary and myself is of little interest and minor import; the depressed condition of chess and the lack of chivalry in the present day are what real lovers of the game deplore. Should an English amateur come forward worthy to succeed in the footsteps of Staunton, Buckle, or Cochrane, he could get no practice with the professionals when he attained a certain force. The aspect of chess policy is, in fact, entirely changed. Match play is stopped through the largeness of the stakes demanded. Emulatory games, formerly so popular and so frequent, are now unknown. The old chess spirit seems quite to have died out. The practice of the St. George's Chess Club in making what

2. MacDonnell gave his version in the *Illustrated Sporting and Dramatic News* of 15 May 1880: "M. Rosenthal called upon me a few days ago to complain of the treatment he had received at the St. George's Club, and to ask for my assistance in obtaining justice for him. He complained of two things: first, the partisanship manifested in a very open and offensive manner by one of the spectators; secondly, that the non-presence of any of his friends tended to injuriously affect his game. ... In these circumstances M. Rosenthal requested the secretary to invite some of the leading English players to witness the match, naming at the same time three gentlemen well-known in chess literature, but this request was refused by the secretary on the ground that the presence of any of the gentlemen named would be disagreeable to Mr. Zukertort!"

were formerly, and ought still to be, public exhibitions of skill into private matches is detrimental to public interest in the game. The present plan also of avoiding strong opponents and taking complete possession of the weak must be fatal to any advancement in the cause. This is the policy of the foreign professionals. Not satisfied with the monopoly of influence of a certain sort, and also of a monopoly of weak play, they have aimed at the control of the chess press also. In this effort, however, they have not been altogether successful; yet, strange to say, the prizes that they have failed to secure have fallen into hands equally respectable no doubt, but from a chess point of view not more worthy than their own. The result is that, with one exception, there is not one independent chess column with an important circulation in existence, and so keenly do I feel this that I will not take the trouble to ask any of them to publish these lines. No, I will rather put the friends that are supporting me in this matter to the little expense of printing and publishing rather than coquette with those that I have known for a lifetime, and have regarded as bosom friends.

Writing somewhat impetuously, I may have been guilty of some digression, but returning to the impression always on my mind, I say, without fear of contradiction, that these professionals have (with one exception) been treated with the greatest consideration and courtesy by English chess admirers and amateurs, and instead of showing gratitude they have, by a process which Anderssen, Kolisch and myself long since agreed to christen buttonholing, succeeded in alienating every person they come in contact with from English chess enthusiasts. What have they done? Look at poor Wormald's book on the *Chess Openings*, the best for an every-day, or, rather, I should say, ordinary chess player, extant. What did they do? Why, go systematically through it, pick out what defects they could, and make the most of the few faults which a chess author, no matter how conscientious or how able, must, in the course of things, be guilty of. No wonder that the Berlin and Vienna champions, who, with the Divan player, are what I mean by the foreign professionals, have begrudged me any credit for the original ideas contained in my works, *Chess Masterpieces* and *Chess Openings*, when they have been bold enough to despise the brilliant efforts of my gifted predecessor.

They will, owing to the audacity inspired by the encouragement of some of their supporters, the aforesaid buttonholers, treat any other English author of first-class standing as a chess player no better than they have Wormald and myself. The fact is, that they deny us credit for anything. "Live and let live" is no part of their motto. Have they no friends who will advise them that they are sufficiently great to be able to afford a little toleration to their inferiors? Surely they have it all to themselves now; all masters and no pupils. What more do they want? Can they not see that, powerful as they are, a little chivalry will yet do them and the cause of chess good?

The ease with which Steinitz defeated Zukertort and Blackburne every game, would tend to indicate that he is far in advance of either of them, or possibly of any other player, whether professional or amateur. Possibly he can beat me with equal facility, and prove that our score of 1867 [*sic*] was owing to his not being in best form. Let him, therefore, redeem his promise, and play a return match for the same moderate stake which we then played for. No other English player is at all likely to wish to test conclusions with him. If not quite worthy of him in force, I am admitted even by the foreign professionals here to be as agreeable and pleasant an opponent as ever sat at a chessboard. I do not ask for which I like best, a fast time limit; I leave all terms but stakes to him. Some good and possibly fine games will result. High stakes do not as a rule produce fine games. Those in the match between Zukertort and Rosenthal, for example, were not equal to many played in memorable matches for a tenth part the money. Such a match would tend to arrest the waning popularity of chess, and perhaps revive a little enthusiasm for the game. One thing is certain, that for the time of its progress at least it would tend to allay the chess differences and squabbles which have been so prevalent of late.

**In penning the foregoing lines I have not even alluded to the recent tournaments at Wiesbaden and Brunswick. I will, however, now simply express the hope that arrangements between players similar to those made therein will not be repeated at any future meetings.**

**The foreign professionals are well aware of the unpleasant incidents which attended the tournaments in America. They have been recently exposed by impartial and warm supporters of chess out there.[3] This unsuccessful attempt to deprive me of the first prize in the New York Clipper tournament was well known to the chess editor of *The Field* at least, and probably, also, to his colleagues.[4] That the American player who connived at the ignoble proceedings in American tournaments should have been put forward as apologist for the recent objectionable dealing in Germany is, to my mind, the most significant and disagreeable feature in that unsatisfactory campaign, and that any supporter of chess can be found to encourage such proceedings is also to my mind most remarkable.**

I am, Sir, yours, etc. / H.E. Bird / 44 Sturgeon Road, S.E., November 1880 [*A Slight Chess Retrospect and Explanation*].

*A few weeks later Bird wrote an interesting letter to the* Glasgow Weekly Herald *in which he summarized the reactions he received (without mentioning the names of his correspondents). It offers another unique insight into Bird's personality.*

In all the letters which I have received in reference to my statements, not one of the writers ventures to differ from me in regard to my expressed opinions as to the depression in leading chess, and the reasons for it.

I should like you very much to see some of the communications which I have received. In the main you may understand that the little inner circle of foreign supporters, with a few of the Divan regular frequenters, condemn me for issuing my circular. C. has written fiercely attacking me. In a defense of ten pages I have replied him warmly, but in a polite and dignified manner which he will not easily forget. He is a very fine man, but his intellect and judgment have become impoverished by the constant button-holing of X., Y., Z. and one or two others. ...

Not one of the above-mentioned gentlemen have attempted to answer my allegation that first-class chess practice has died out. They cannot consistently do so. One glance in at the Divan on a Saturday afternoon will at once establish my assertion. Contrast the view with the time when Barnes, Boden, Buckle, Bird, Burden, De Vere, Löwenthal, and MacDonnell (and when he visited England), Anderssen were seen eagerly and constantly playing together. Even Williams and Lowe would forsake their lessons for a time, for the chivalry which then existed was, in fact, contagious.

Resuming reference to the letters which I have received, there are several from the outside circle which accord me unqualified approval; but the most valuable of all is one from a distinguished English amateur, written in his usual impartial, able, and masterly style.

He commences by saying that there are so many good points in my circular that he regrets that I have been carried away by my feelings to write harshly of the foreigners; he discusses the question fully and clearly from their point of view; appears to think that the professionals are entitled to take a business view of their position, and demand the highest stakes that they can get. This view I do not agree with. He concludes a letter which, taken with my circular, may go some way to form a common standing ground on the basis of which the merits of chess policy may be considered, and he adds a most flattering compliment to my style of play, my chivalry, and my long devotion to the cause. ...

Anyway, I suppose that I shall remain, as I always have been, a somewhat reckless and impetuous individual, but at the same time a courteous, chivalrous, and upright player, and a thoroughly independent member of the chess circle, and one whose popularity with the impartial chess world cannot be easily destroyed.

H.E. Bird [*Glasgow Weekly Herald*, 25 December 1880].

---

3. **Note by Bird**: "Peruse Mr. A. Möhle's pamphlet, Mr. Chadwick's strictures and the American press on treatment of another Englishman in the last New York tournament." ¶ Preston Ware, one of the participants of the fifth American chess congress, in New York 1880, claimed that he was paid by the British participant, James Glover Grundy, to draw their final game. Grundy consequently broke their arrangement by beating him, after which he tied with Mackenzie for first and second place. ¶ Bird's reference to the "treatment of another Englishman" seems to put him on the side of Grundy, who in this case was blamed for the cheating. ¶ Bird referred to a pamphlet titled *The American Chess Congress and the Manhattan Chess Club*. The writer, Adolph Möhle, took up the defense of Grundy. This pamphlet was discussed by Henry Clay Allen in the chess column of *Turf, Field and Farm* on 7 and 14 May 1880. He dismissed it as a complete lie and an abject attempt to defend the low behavior of some participants at the U.S. congress of 1880. ¶ Henry Chadwick, the editor of the *Brooklyn Daily Eagle*, had opened fire in an article about morals in chess (published on 9 February 1880). He also dedicated some lines to the selling of games in *De Witt's American Chess Manual* (pp. 56–58). See also: J. Van Winsen, *James Mason in America* (Jefferson, NC: McFarland, 2011, pp. 97–99).

4. Steinitz gave the final table of the Clipper tournament in *The Field* of 11 November 1876, stating that Bird gained only third place. Without naming anyone, he suggested that the final standings were influenced by some foul play. On 30 June 1877, *The Field* published a letter by Arthur Jackson from New York, who wrote that "I cannot but observe, with feelings of regret, that your popular paper displays some prejudice against the eminent chess player, Mr. H.E. Bird, of your city. This was particularly noticeable when you omitted to give him first honors in the Clipper tournament here, and your failure to record his many victories creates much surprise in chess circles here." ¶ Steinitz pointed out that Bird's third place was in accordance with the tournament rules that he accepted by starting in the tournament. Concerning the latter reproach he defended himself as follows: "Respecting the charge that we have unduly neglected to record Mr. Bird's general chess performances, we are authorized by the chief editor to state that the omission is due to Mr. Bird's wish, personally expressed to [the chief editor] nearly four years ago, on the occasion of Mr. Steinitz taking charge of the chess department of *The Field*. Since that time none of Mr. Bird's matches, whether in England or America, have been reported in our columns, except when he has played in a public tournament, such as that above mentioned, when the omission of his name would vitiate the report."

# Bird's Visit to Albany (24–26 May 1889)

*Albany was Bird's first stop on his American tour following the tournament of New York. The local newspapers dedicated several columns to describe the master's visit. Their articles offer a unique insight in the course of Bird's visit.*

## PROF. BIRD SHOWS THE ALBANY CHESS CLUB SOME FINE POINTS

Only members of the Albany chess club were present this morning when, in the club's rooms in the south wing of the Albany academy, Prof. Henry E. Bird, the professional English player, began a series of exhibitions before the club, which are to continue until tomorrow evening at 10 o'clock. Social games between the members and their distinguished visitor were the program this morning, and a very interesting séance was held between 11 a.m. and 1:30 p.m.

## EVIDENTLY AN ENGLISHMAN

Prof. Bird is obviously English or Scotch. His face is round and ruddy. A short but thick growth of gray beard fringes his face and becomes heavier under his chin. He is quite bald, a scant supply of long gray hair being brushed forward above his ears, another bunch from there over the top. He is about 65 years of age, courteous in the extreme and a good conversationalist, though seldom speaks during his game.

## THE FIRST, A GOOD GAME

The first game played this morning was between Prof. Bird (White) and Mr. Leake of the club (Black). Mr. Leake played a very strong game and won several admiring comments from his opponent. Prof. Bird gave him odds, removing his queen's rook. This is the score: **Bird–R.B. Leake 1–0** [see game **944**]

## PROF. BIRD RESIGNS THE SECOND

The second game also was an excellent one on the part of Mr. Leake, who again played Black, with the same odds in his favor. The game was shorter, only 22 moves being made, and Mr. Leake finally drove Mr. Bird to cover, the latter resigning at the end of a game, whose score follows: **Bird–R.B. Leake 0–1** [see game **945**]

## PROF. GOOLD VANQUISHED

The third and last game was longer and more stubborn. Prof. Gould, of the academy, played Black against Prof. Bird, the same odds, queen's rook, being in his favor. After 44 moves, however, Prof. Goold resigned. The score follows: **Bird–Goold 1–0** [see game **946**]

## PROF. BIRD'S "GEMS OF CHESS"

"There are two pretty games that I have played and would like to show you," Prof. Bird said after the third game had been discussed. "The first I played last year in London with Mr. Pfander." Rapidly he placed his men, removing the White queen's rook, and his trained fingers moved them through the 12 steps with great swiftness. "Here we are," he said. "We start with 1. e4, like this":

**1. e4 e5 2. f4 e.×f4 3. Nf3 g5 4. h4 g4 5. Ng5 h6 6. Bc4 Nh6 7. d4 f6 8. B×f4 f.×g5 9. h.×g5 Nf7 10. g6 Ng5 11. Qd2 N×e4 12. Nc3**

"At this point, you see," the player continued, "the case for the Black begins to look hopeless, for the game is lost by analysis, but you can go on and lose it actually if you like, after this fashion":

**12. ... N×d2 13. Bf7† Ke7 14. Nd5 mate.**

"It's a very pretty game" he added, "and almost anybody would fall into the trap."

"By Jove," interposed Marion Randolph, "that's lovely!"

## A GEM IN 15 MOVES

"Then there's another pretty one," said Prof. Bird, "not so well known; the question of the strength of the sacrificing of the queen's rook never has been thoroughly settled. I played the game in London last year with F. Cantab. This is the game; it has 15 moves":

**1. e4 e5 2. Nf3 Nc6 3. d4 e.×d4 4. N×d4 Qh4 5. Nb5 Bc5 6. Qf3 Nf6 7. N×c7† Kd8 8. N×a8 Re8 9. Bd3 N×e4 10. 0–0 N×f2 11. R×f2 Re1† 12. Bf1 Nd4 13. Q×f7 Ne2† 14. Kh1 R×f1 15. R×f1 Ng3 mate.**

## PROF. ROGERS'S DARING

At 1:30 the game broke up, and the meeting was adjourned until this afternoon; and in accordance with the notice then given, Prof. Howard J. Rogers of the academy is playing with Prof. Bird, but accepting no odds, though it was announced at first that rook odds would be given. The contest is continued this evening and tomorrow [*Albany Evening News*, 24 May 1889].

*The continuation of Bird's performance was extensively discussed in the newspaper of the following day.*

## HE CAN PLAY CHESS

Prof. Howard J. Rogers of the Albany academy is secretary of the chess club, and he is a very excellent player. The first game played when the club came together again yesterday afternoon was between Prof. Bird, the English expert, and Prof. Rogers. All the games played in the morning had been with rook odds in favor of the Albanian, but Prof. Rogers refused odds and played a first-class game, which resulted in a draw at the forty-first move. Prof. Rogers plays a very conservative but very strong game, and Prof. Bird was enthusiastic in commending his playing. After this W. Boardman won an offhand game with Prof. Bird.

## SIXTEEN GAMES AT ONCE

In the evening the distinguished visitor displayed his remarkable skill by vanquishing 15 players at once; that is, he played 16 different games simultaneously, the players, with their boards, being arranged around him in a circle, and one by one he drove them out, until only Prof. Deyo remained; and when the contest closed in between the two Prof. Deyo won. ...

## EXPLAINING TO LADIES

This morning at 11 o'clock the two-hours' session devoted exclusively to ladies began, and a most entertaining it was. Several fair devotees of the noble game were present, and Prof. Bird spent the entire morning in explaining the intricacies of chess and illustrating peculiarly strong or beautiful situations. He varied the proceedings with anecdotes regarding chess playing and players, or reading articles of his own writing with reference to the origin and history of the game. The expert's audience beyond a doubt was greatly fascinated.

## WILL HAVE HIS HANDS FULL

This afternoon Prof. Bird has two games in progress at once—

one a consultation game, in which he plays against the members of the club who have made the best scores in single games: Messrs. Boardman, Deyo, Barber [*Albany Evening News*, 24 May 1889].

*An article dealing with Bird's activities during the remainder of the weekend was published in another Albany newspaper. Again, it is worth quoting in full as it provides unique insight and details.*

Saturday evening, Mr. Bird played eleven simultaneous games and one consultation game at the same time. Result: Bird won 11 simultaneous games and won 1 consultation game.

It should be noted that when the English player lost the first consultation game Saturday afternoon, he was at the same time playing offhand games against Messrs. Heyward, Gould and Lansing.

After the conclusion of play Saturday evening, May 25th, Col. W.G. Rice moved, "that the president of the club fittingly express to Prof. Bird the great pleasure the members and guests of the club have experienced in his visit, and that he convey to Prof. Bird the thanks of the club for his kindness and courtesy." This resolution having been unanimously adopted, President Underhill said:

"Mr. Bird, it is my pleasant privilege, as the spokesman of this club, to express to you, although perhaps in halting and ill-chosen words, the great gratification we have all derived from your visit, as well as to thank you for your considerate courtesy to all of us (a courtesy uniform with you, sir); and I cannot do better than to quote the words of one of our famous speakers to another noted English guest on a memorable occasion: 'And when you return to your home across the seas, may He who holds the waves in the hollow of His hand, be gracious to you, sir.' It is hardly possible that, at your advanced age, we should all meet again, but we have intended that this your visit to Albany shall always be to you, as it certainly will be to us, a pleasant memory. We do not play chess at this club on Sunday, and as you leave tomorrow evening, we shall in considerable numbers pay our respects to you at your hotel."

Prof. Bird seemed for a moment amazed, but quickly recovering, responded: "Mr. President and Gentlemen of the Albany Chess Club. I must say I have enjoyed my visit to you in no ordinary degree, and I shall certainly cherish the memory thereof for my lifetime. In all my visits I have never been treated with so much kindness and consideration. My visit has been an extremely pleasant one, and I have been quite surprised to find among gentlemen who lack the opportunity for practice with experts such excellent play—I may say remarkable play. And to you, Mr. Underhill, to whom I am mainly indebted for the honor of the invitation to visit the club, I desire to add my heartfelt thanks. I shall be pleased to meet any and all of you at my rooms at the Globe hotel tomorrow."

With applause for the distinguished guest, the club dispersed. Mr. Bird departed for Canada on a late train Sunday night. His visit has had the effect of inducing ten gentlemen to have their names posted for admission to the club. It is being discussed among the members whether it would not be well to invite Capt. Mackenzie, the champion of America, to visit the club this fall [*Albany Evening Times*, 27 May 1889].

# Buckley's Recollections of Bird

*Towards the end of May 1892, Robert John Buckley travelled to London to witness and cover the beginning of the long-awaited match between Lasker and Blackburne. To his surprise this contest was delayed for three days. He found a worthy alternative in paying a visit to the Divan, where Bird's star was shining amidst his fellow masters.*

But we immediately adjourned to Simpson's Divan, and there received a hearty welcome. The Grand Old Man beamed radiantly, and all creation smiled. Lasker relaxed his disappointed look, and for the moment seemed consoled. Van Vliet stretched forth the fellowshipial hand. F.J. Lee looked as if he might be happy yet. Even Jasnogrodsky seemed pleased, and for a moment the settled melancholy which is supposed to arise from the burden of his name, was chased away. Tinsley smiled the broadest, but then he learned his manners in the country, where people are too unsophisticated to conceal their joy.

It was, indeed, a memorable moment. Loman was deeply engaged in the handicap tourney, but even he found time to bestow a greeting on your humble representative. James Mason emerged from a dark and remote corner, where he hides from the light of day, and engaged us in animated conversation. Müller, who has forsworn chess, and has determined to become a millionaire in some other way, warmly gripped the editorial fin. It was clear that something ought to be done. We challenged Lasker, offering to concede to him the odds of the rook. He declined the gage of battle. Perhaps this was best. We have no desire to ruin the reputation of the young. He may have wanted the queen. Mr. Bird rushed into the breach, and lifting the gauntlet, cast defiance at our head. The metaphor is not so mixed as we would wish, but no matter.

Mr. Bird said, "Come on, Macduff." Mr. Bird has always been a reckless kind of man. We moved to a roomy corner, where Mr. Bird could get his back to the wall. (His back was up.) The crowd followed. There was an awful struggle for position. The masters climbed on each other's shoulders, perched on the chimney-piece, clambered on the tables, fought for the chairs. Infinitesimal advantages were cast to the winds. There was a breathless silence, during which Mr. Bird, with affected calmness, inquired what odds we proposed to concede. We declined to give any odds whatever, on the ground of Mr. Bird's marked improvement during the last sixty or seventy years, to which we added the expression of our conviction that he was still improving. Mr. Bird led off with 1. e4, and we accepted a Bishop's Gambit. The silence was profound. You might have heard a dynamite explosion.

In the mid-game we sprung a little min, which won the veteran's queen, and shortly after he resigned. The next game was a Muzio, in which we sacrificed several pieces, emerging with a splendid position, but no men. This, of course, might happen to anybody. The subsequent progress of the game was devoid of interest. We gave it up, after a tremendous struggle, lasting (inclusive of the setting up of the pieces) a period of more than thirty seconds. A third game was commenced by Mr. Bird playing in the hope of getting an Evans Gambit. We made it a Two Knight's Defense, got up a hot counter attack, sacrificed a piece, and again captured the queen, amid a scene of wild excitement, one master falling off the chimney-piece—Jasnogrodsky for choice. We do not know who it was, but give the preference to Jasnogrodsky, as being a deserving young fellow, and the most picturesque. We emerged with a queen against a rook for the endgame. Mr. Bird proposed a draw. We accepted, and Mr. Bird caught his bus. Score: 1½ each. Time occupied by the three games: ten minutes. No such chess has been seen in Europe since the days of Morphy [*Birmingham Weekly Mercury*, 28 May 1892].

*Buckley's stories about nineteenth century chess masters are a treat, as they excel in painting this epoch so evocatively that those long-gone players get their humanity back. While such stories may, from an historical point of view, be taken with more than one grain of salt, they seem essential to our understanding of Henry Edward Bird. In 1913, some extensive portraits by Buckley were printed in the low-budget magazine* Chess Amateur. *In January (1913) Zuk-ertort was Buckley's main subject. Bird played an important role in one of Buckley's long stories.*

It was our last meeting. Years had elapsed since we had played together. I was not recognized. He [Zukertort] sauntered into Simpson's with a walk like that of the ghost in Hamlet. He wore a long overcoat, with side-pockets, in which his hands were buried. On his head a battered silk hat of ancient fashion. A small, cadaverous, Semitic man, moving slowly and sleepily. The world was wearisome. What was the good of anything? From board to board he moved without a word. Pollock, Mason and Bird were there, the first two-named two playing amateurs for shillings, after the manner of Simpson's from time immemorial.

Now it so happened that Bird and I had been fighting ferociously. Having lost a game or two, the old man declared that unless he gave odds he could not play his best with rural amateurs at Simpson's. There was truth in this. Bird was hasty and careless when skittling for shillings with "young men from the country." So was Mason. Both were Bohemians, detesting trouble, aiming to get the best of life with the least exertion.

Bird, in his explosion of opinion, had said that if he were giving me the knight, he would win every game. This was just like Bird who would have given Lasker a rook without the smallest compunction. Bird was the most audacious of the masters, and the quickest player. He said "I can't play better when I play slower—I haven't the patience to work things out." We played at the odds, Bird taking off Nb1, and dashing on in the grand old avian manner. But the knight was too much, especially as the reply to his gambit was always a counter-gambit. Bird had not the defensive temperament: he must be forever attacking. Therefore to attack him boldly, to put him on his defense, was good policy. Two or three games sufficed, Mason, Pollock, and others looking on.

Then Pollock asked for a game at the odds; he saw where Bird had erred, and would go on different lines. He would, in fact, concede the rook, if required. It was agreed that he should concede the rook when he had beaten me at the knight. We played: Pollock failed to score, and Mason cut in. Mason was not a brilliant odds-giver, and two games satisfied him. He and Pollock took more profitable customers, and Bird talked with me until Zukertort swam in.

The sight of him was the germ of a conspiracy. He came to our corner by the fireside. "Hello! Zukertort!" cried Bird. "Just the man we want. Friend of mine from the country wants to play. I'm tired; everybody else is busy. I gave him a knight. So did Pollock. So did

Mason." Bird kicked me under the table. Zukertort looked at me inquiringly. I said a game would be agreeable and Zukertort took off the knight, remarking: "Ze usual shillink, I subbose?" I agreed, determining to decline his shilling if he lost. I never took a coin from any player, and this occasion, of course, was exceptional. It was meant for a joke on Zukertort. The masters at Simpson's were children in their notions of fun.

As Zukertort made the first move, Bird called out: "I'll have a shilling on the rural, Zukertort, eh?" Before Zukertort could reply, both Mason and Pollock cried, "And I!" "And I!" which aroused the Semitic suspicion of J.H.Z. He looked around gravely. He was grave by nature. Very solemn was Zukertort, always on his dignity. "Vat you risk all your money for, like dis?" he wanted to know. "We want you to shovel in the shekels," laughed Bird. "Dot is shust like you all tree," snarled Zukertort. "Alvays you vos anxious for oders to rake in de doubloons! I see vot dis game look like first. Den p'rps I bet you."

There was a glorious gallery. Early I sacrificed a knight for two pawns and a smart attack. Zukertort turned to Bird. "You give him a knight, you say. How many you vin?" Bird chuckled. The end of this story may be found disappointing. To me the affair was intensely amusing.

Zukertort won! He pocketed the shilling, and declined another game at the odds. "I tink I rather play you lefel," he opined. "De knight give me too much drubble." A pupil he awaited carried him off, and I never saw Zukertort again [*Chess Amateur*, January 1913, pp. 102–3].

*In the June edition of the* Chess Amateur *Buckley sketched his pit-toresque picture of Bird, parts of which have been quoted in the present work. One slight addition is worthwhile for it reveals Bird's view, in a rather surreal description, of his position at the Divan.*

Off all the masters I have known none was more interesting than H.E. Bird, who in his character of veteran was for many years accorded the best commercial position in the historic room known to chess players over the whole world as Simpson's Divan. ... "So many humbugs around me make me mad," he once said. "Some of them, because they think I'm old—which I'm not, and never shall be—try to cast foul scorn on my play. Do you know what the worm said?" I had to confess a deplorable ignorance of what the worm had remarked on the particular occasion present to the mind of my eminent friend.

"Just so, just so," Bird chortled. "We're all alike. Things slip from our memories. At school we learn Latin and lying. We forget—the Latin! So with you and the saying of the celebrated worm; the worm that turns. You've not forgotten the worm that turns, I hope?" I hastened to assure Mr. Bird that the turning worm was one of my cherished recollections.

"Good! Well, the heel of the tyrant came down on him, and he turned after his manner and said—'You don't know what he said?'" I feared not. Addressing the tyrant, probably a peasant with hob-nailed shoes, he asked with dignity: "Do you wish to kick up a row? The worm did his turn: I do mine. If you make yourself a lamb at Simpson's, you'll find that the wolves are not all dead. So I rebel: though I'm the most amiable man in the world, when fairly treated."

I remembered Sir Anthony Absolute's: "Let me have my own way and a child can lead me" [*Chess Amateur*, June 1913, p. 270].

# APPENDIX 3:
# TOURNAMENT RECORD

Bird's results in tournaments, including tie-breaks. Points from unplayed games are separately represented.

| | | Place | Players | + | – | = | Unplayed games + | – | = |
|---|---|---|---|---|---|---|---|---|---|
| 1848 | London | ? | ? | ? | ? | ? | | | |
| 1849 | London | - | 12 | 1 | 2 | 0 | | | |
| 1851 | London | - | 16 | 1 | 2 | 1 | | | |
| 1858 | Birmingham | - | 16 | 1 | 1 | 0 | | 1 | |
| 1859 | London Purssell's Handicap | - | 16 | 1 | 2 | 1 | 2 | | |
| 1860 | London St. James's Handicap | - | 18 | 2 | 1 | 0 | | | |
| 1866 | London B.C.A. Challenge Cup | 4 | 5 | 1 | 6 | 0 | | | |
| 1868/9 | London B.C.A. Challenge Cup | 6 | 11 | 3 | 5 | 2 | 2 | | |
| 1870/1 | London City Handicap | - | 48 | 3 | 3 | 0 | | | |
| 1873 | Vienna | 5–6 | 12 | 14 | 9 | 1 | | | |
| 1873/4 | London City Handicap | - | 48 | 1 | 3 | 0 | | | |
| 1874/5 | London City Handicap | - | 64 | 6 | 4 | 2 | | | |
| 1875 | Glasgow C.C.A. Handicap | - | 16 | 0 | 1 | 0 | | | |
| 1876 | New York Café International | 3–4 | 17 | 20 | 7 | 1 | 2 | | |
| 1876 | Philadelphia | 3 | 9 | 6 | 3 | 5 | | | |
| 1876 | New York Clipper | 3 | 21 | 15 | 3 | 0 | | | |
| 1878 | Paris | 4–5 | 12 | 13 | 9 | 0 | | | |
| 1878/9 | London City Handicap | 2 | 64 | 9 | 3 | 2 | | | |
| 1879 | London Löwenthal Cup | 1 | 4 | 2 | 1 | 0 | | | |
| 1880 | Boston Handicap | - | 16 | 0 | 1 | 0 | | | |
| 1880 | Boston Consolation Handicap | 1 | 8 | 3 | 0 | 0 | | | |
| 1880 | Wiesbaden | 6–7 | 16 | 9 | 6 | 0 | | | |
| 1880 | Gouda | 1 | 6 | 9 | 0 | 1 | | | |
| 1882 | Wien | 15 | 18 | 9 | 15 | 4 | 1 | 5 | |
| 1883 | London | 10 | 14 | 11 | 14 | 7 | 1 | | |
| 1883 | Nuremberg | 6–7 | 19 | 8 | 5 | 5 | | | |
| 1883 | London Purssell's Handicap | 1 | 20 | 9 | 2 | 0 | | | |
| 1884 | Bath C.C.A. | 3 | 7 | 3 | 2 | 1 | | | |
| 1885 | London B.C.A. | 2 | 16 | 10 | 1 | 4 | | | |
| 1885 | London B.C.A. Consultation | 2 | 4 | 2 | 1 | 0 | | | |
| 1885 | Hamburg | 11–12 | 18 | 7 | 8 | 2 | | | |
| 1885 | Hereford | 2–3 | 11 | 7 | 2 | 3 | | | |
| 1886 | London Purssell's Handicap | - | 18 | 2 | 1 | 1 | | 4 | |
| 1886 | London B.C.C. | 2–3 | 7 | 4 | 1 | 2 | | | |

| | | (Place) | (Players) | (+) | (−) | (=) | (Unplayed games) (+) | (−) | (=) |
|---|---|---|---|---|---|---|---|---|---|
| 1886 | London B.C.A. | 13 | 13 | 2 | 9 | 1 | | | |
| 1886 | Nottingham C.C.A. | 5 | 11 | 4 | 2 | 3 | | | |
| 1887 | Stamford C.C.A. | 3–5 | 7 | 3 | 3 | 0 | | | |
| 1887 | Stamford C.C.A. Handicap | 1 | 16 | 4 | 0 | 0 | | | |
| 1887 | London B.C.A. | 7–9 | 10 | 1 | 4 | 4 | | | |
| 1888 | London Simpson's Handicap | 3 | 18 | 12 | 4 | 0 | 1 | | |
| 1888 | London B.C.C. Handicap | 3–5 | 15 | 9 | 3 | 1 | | | 1 |
| 1888 | Bradford B.C.A. | 9–10 | 18 | 5 | 7 | 4 | | | |
| 1888/9 | London Simpson's Handicap | 2 | 15 | 9 | 2 | 3 | | | |
| 1889 | London Simpson's Handicap | 1 | 16 | 12 | 1 | 1 | | | |
| 1889 | New York | 12–13 | 20 | 14 | 17 | 8 | | 1 | |
| 1889 | London Simpson's Handicap | 3 | 16 | 11 | 2 | 2 | | | |
| 1889 | London B.C.A. | 1–2 | 12 | 5 | 0 | 6 | | | |
| 1890 | London Simpson's Handicap | 2 | 19 | 12 | 3 | 2 | 1 | | |
| 1890 | Manchester B.C.A. | 3–4 | 20 | 9 | 4 | 6 | | | |
| 1890 | London Simpson's Handicap | 9–11 | 19 | 6 | 2 | 1 | 1 | 8 | |
| 1891 | London Divan | 3 | 10 | 5 | 2 | 2 | | | |
| 1891 | London Divan | 1 | 10 | 5 | 1 | 3 | | | |
| 1892 | London B.C.A. | 4–5 | 12 | 6 | 4 | 1 | | | |
| 1892 | London Quintangular | 5 | 5 | 1 | 7 | 0 | | | |
| 1892 | London Simpson's Handicap | 4–6 | 17 | 9 | 4 | 3 | | | |
| 1892 | Belfast | 3 | 4 | 3 | 2 | 4 | | | |
| 1893 | London | 6 | 6 | 0 | 4 | 1 | | | |
| 1894 | London Simpson's Handicap | 3 | 11 | 6 | 2 | 2 | | | |
| 1894 | London Simpson's | 3 | 4 | 1 | 1 | 1 | | | |
| 1895 | Hastings | 15–16 | 22 | 4 | 7 | 10 | | | |
| 1896 | London Simpson's | 8–11 | 12 | 3 | 7 | 0 | 1 | | |
| 1899 | London | 13 | 15 | 4 | 18 | 4 | 1 | | |
| | | | | 355 | 245 | 118 | 13 | 19 | 1 |

# Appendix 4: Match Record

Bird's results in (more or less) set matches. Informal encounters are not included.

|      |                     |              | **Result**          | **+** | **−** | **=** |
|------|---------------------|--------------|---------------------|-------|-------|-------|
| 1847 | Buckle (odds)       | London       | Lost (7 against 9)  | ?     | ?     | ?     |
| 1849 | Buckle (odds)       | London       | Won                 | 7     | 0     | 0     |
| 1849 | G.W. Medley         | London       | Lost                | 3     | 6     | 2     |
| 1850 | Hughes (odds)       | London       | Lost                | 0     | 5     | 0     |
| 1850 | Hughes (odds)       | London       | Won                 | 5     | 0     | 0     |
| 1850 | Hughes (odds)       | London       | ?                   | ?     | ?     | ?     |
| 1850 | Lowe                | London       | Won (7–4)           | ?     | ?     | ?     |
| 1851 | Horwitz             | London       | Lost                | 3     | 4     | 7     |
| 1856 | Falkbeer            | London       | Won                 | 2     | 1     | 0     |
| 1856/7 | Falkbeer          | London       | Lost                | 4     | 5     | 4     |
| 1866 | Steinitz            | London       | Lost                | 5     | 7     | 5     |
| 1873 | Wisker              | London       | Draw                | 6     | 2     | 6     |
| 1873 | Wisker              | London       | Won                 | 7     | 4     | 3     |
| 1873 | Wisker              | London       | Last                | 8     | 10    | 3     |
| 1873 | Wisker              | London       | Won                 | 5     | 3     | 1     |
| 1874 | J. Lord             | London       | Won                 | 7     | 2     | 1     |
| 1875 | Alberoni            | New York     | Won                 | 19    | 18    | 3     |
| 1875/6 | Mason             | New York     | Lost                | 4     | 11    | 4     |
| 1879 | Blackburne          | London       | Lost                | 2     | 5     | 1     |
| 1879/80 | Blackburne       | London       | Won                 | 1     | 0     | 1     |
| 1880 | Gäbler              | Wiesbaden    | Draw                | 1     | 1     | 0     |
| 1881 | Maczuski            | London       | Won                 | 5     | 0     | 1     |
| 1882 | Maczuski            | London       | Won                 | 7     | 4     | 2     |
| 1885 | Skipworth           | London       | Won                 | 5     | 2     | 0     |
| 1886 | Burn                | London       | Draw                | 9     | 9     | 0     |
| 1886 | Gunsberg            | London       | Lost                | 1     | 5     | 3     |
| 1886 | Lee (odds)          | London       | Lost                | ?     | 5     | ?     |
| 1888 | Blackburne          | London       | Lost                | 1     | 4     | 0     |
| 1889 | Gunsberg            | London       | Lost                | 1     | 2     | 2     |
| 1889 | Shipley             | Philadelphia | Won                 | 5     | 3     | 1     |
| 1889 | Gossip (odds)       | London       | Draw                | 1     | 1     | 1     |
| 1889 | Gossip (odds)       | London       | Won                 | ?     | ?     | ?     |
| 1890 | Lasker              | Liverpool    | Lost                | 2     | 7     | 3     |
| 1892 | Loman               | London       | Won                 | 4     | 2     | 0     |
| 1892 | Lasker              | Newcastle    | Lost                | 0     | 5     | 0     |
| 1892 | Heywood (odds)      | Newcastle    | Lost                | 3     | 4     | 2     |
| 1893 | Jasnogrodsky        | London       | Draw                | 6     | 6     | 3     |
| 1896 | Burille             | Cable match  | Lost                | 0     | 1     | 0     |
| 1897 | Lee                 | London       | Lost                | 4     | 7     | 2     |
|      |                     |              |                     | 143   | 151   | 61    |

# APPENDIX 5:
# RESULTS AGAINST MASTERS

Here follows an overview of Bird's results against masters in regular tournaments and matches. Not included are forfeits, informal encounters, simultaneous games or games in which odds were given or accepted.

| | Games | Won | Lost | Drawn | Total | % |
|---|---|---|---|---|---|---|
| Alapin | 1 | 1 | 0 | 0 | 1/1 | 100 |
| Alberoni | 42 | 21 | 18 | 3 | 22½/42 | 54 |
| Albin | 1 | 1 | 0 | 0 | 1/1 | 100 |
| Anderssen | 5 | 3 | 2 | 0 | 3/5 | 60 |
| D.G. Baird | 2 | 2 | 0 | 0 | 2/2 | 100 |
| J.W. Baird | 5 | 2 | 1 | 2 | 3/5 | 60 |
| Barbour | 2 | 1 | 0 | 1 | 1½/2 | 75 |
| von Bardeleben | 3 | 1 | 0 | 2 | 2/3 | 67 |
| Becker | 2 | 1 | 1 | 0 | 1/2 | 50 |
| Benima | 2 | 1 | 0 | 1 | 1½/2 | 75 |
| Berger | 2 | 0 | 0 | 2 | 1/2 | 50 |
| Bier | 2 | 2 | 0 | 0 | 2/2 | 100 |
| Blackburne | 50 | 10 | 31 | 9 | 14½/50 | 29 |
| Blake | 2 | 0 | 1 | 1 | ½/2 | 25 |
| Brenzinger | 2 | 1 | 1 | 0 | 1/2 | 50 |
| Brien | 2 | 1 | 1 | 0 | 1/2 | 50 |
| Burille | 3 | 1 | 1 | 1 | 1½/3 | 50 |
| Burn | 25 | 10 | 13 | 2 | 11/25 | 44 |
| Chigorin | 9 | 1 | 7 | 1 | 1½/9 | 17 |
| Clerc | 2 | 1 | 1 | 0 | 1/2 | 50 |
| W. Cohn | 2 | 1 | 1 | 0 | 1/2 | 50 |
| H.F. Davidson | 2 | 1 | 0 | 1 | 1½/2 | 75 |
| De Vere | 6 | 1 | 5 | 0 | 1/5 | 20 |
| Delmar | 4 | 3 | 1 | 0 | 3/4 | 75 |
| Donisthorpe | 1 | 1 | 0 | 0 | 1/1 | 100 |
| Elson | 2 | 0 | 1 | 1 | 1½/2 | 25 |
| Englisch | 9 | 2 | 6 | 1 | 2½/9 | 28 |
| A.W. Ensor | 3 | 2 | 1 | 0 | 2/3 | 67 |
| Falkbeer | 21 | 7 | 8 | 6 | 10/21 | 48 |
| R.H.F. Fenton | 4 | 2 | 1 | 1 | 2½/4 | 63 |
| B. Fleissig | 2 | 1 | 1 | 0 | 1/2 | 50 |
| M. Fleissig | 2 | 2 | 0 | 0 | 2/2 | 100 |

| | (Games) | (Won) | (Lost) | (Drawn) | (Total) | (%) |
|---|---|---|---|---|---|---|
| Fritz | 2 | 1 | 0 | 1 | 1½/2 | 75 |
| Gelbfuhs | 2 | 2 | 0 | 0 | 2/2 | 100 |
| Gifford | 2 | 2 | 0 | 0 | 2/2 | 100 |
| Gossip | 8 | 3 | 3 | 2 | 4/8 | 50 |
| von Gottschall | 1 | 0 | 1 | 0 | 0/1 | 0 |
| Guest | 4 | 0 | 1 | 3 | 1½/4 | 38 |
| Gunsberg | 32 | 5 | 20 | 7 | 8½/32 | 27 |
| Gunston | 1 | 0 | 0 | 1 | ½/1 | 50 |
| Hanham | 4 | 2 | 1 | 1 | 2½/4 | 63 |
| Heral | 3 | 1 | 1 | 1 | 1½/3 | 50 |
| Horwitz | 18 | 4 | 9 | 5 | 6½/18 | 36 |
| Hruby | 3 | 2 | 1 | 0 | 2/3 | 67 |
| Janowski | 3 | 1 | 1 | 1 | 1½/3 | 50 |
| Jasnogrodsky | 21 | 9 | 8 | 4 | 11/21 | 52 |
| Judd | 4 | 3 | 1 | 0 | 3/4 | 75 |
| Lange | 1 | 1 | 0 | 0 | 1/1 | 100 |
| Lasker | 23 | 3 | 17 | 3 | 4½/23 | 20 |
| Lee | 31 | 9 | 12 | 10 | 14/31 | 45 |
| Lipschütz | 3 | 1 | 1 | 1 | 1½/3 | 50 |
| Locock | 4 | 2 | 0 | 2 | 3/4 | 75 |
| Loman | 14 | 8 | 4 | 2 | 9/14 | 64 |
| J. Lord | 11 | 7 | 3 | 1 | 7½/11 | 68 |
| Löwenthal | 1 | 0 | 1 | 0 | 0/1 | 0 |
| MacDonnell | 6 | 3 | 2 | 1 | 3½/6 | 58 |
| Mackenzie | 16 | 3 | 10 | 3 | 4½/16 | 28 |
| Maczuski | 20 | 13 | 4 | 3 | 14½/20 | 73 |
| Marco | 1 | 0 | 0 | 1 | ½/1 | 50 |
| Maróczy | 2 | 0 | 1 | 1 | ½/2 | 25 |
| D.M. Martinez | 2 | 1 | 1 | 0 | 1/2 | 50 |
| Mason | 54 | 12 | 31 | 11 | 17½/54 | 32 |
| G.W. Medley | 14 | 4 | 8 | 2 | 5/14 | 36 |
| Meitner | 3 | 3 | 0 | 0 | 3/3 | 100 |
| Messemaker | 2 | 2 | 0 | 0 | 2/2 | 100 |
| Mieses | 1 | 0 | 0 | 1 | ½/1 | 50 |
| Mills | 2 | 1 | 1 | 0 | 1/2 | 50 |
| J.I. Minchin | 5 | 2 | 3 | 0 | 2/5 | 40 |
| Minckwitz | 2 | 2 | 0 | 0 | 2/2 | 100 |

| | (Games) | (Won) | (Lost) | (Drawn) | (Total) | (%) | | (Games) | (Won) | (Lost) | (Drawn) | (Total) | (%) |
|---|---|---|---|---|---|---|---|---|---|---|---|---|---|
| Miniati | 1 | 1 | 0 | 0 | 1/1 | 100 | Sellman | 2 | 2 | 0 | 0 | 2/2 | 100 |
| Mortimer | 16 | 10 | 4 | 2 | 11/16 | 69 | Shipley | 9 | 5 | 3 | 1 | 5½/9 | 61 |
| O.C. Müller | 12 | 6 | 3 | 3 | 7½/12 | 63 | Showalter | 4 | 1 | 3 | 0 | 1/4 | 25 |
| Noa | 4 | 1 | 2 | 1 | 1½/4 | 38 | Skipworth | 11 | 7 | 3 | 1 | 7½/11 | 68 |
| Owen | 4 | 4 | 0 | 0 | 4/4 | 100 | Steinitz | 26 | 6 | 14 | 6 | 9/26 | 35 |
| L. Paulsen | 6 | 1 | 4 | 1 | 1½/6 | 25 | Tarrasch | 3 | 0 | 2 | 1 | ½/3 | 17 |
| W. Paulsen | 3 | 3 | 0 | 0 | 3/3 | 100 | Taubenhaus | 7 | 3 | 3 | 1 | 3½/7 | 50 |
| Pillsbury | 3 | 0 | 2 | 1 | ½/3 | 17 | Teichmann | 6 | 1 | 5 | 0 | 1/6 | 17 |
| Pitschel | 4 | 4 | 0 | 0 | 4/4 | 100 | Thorold | 6 | 4 | 1 | 1 | 4½/6 | 75 |
| Pollock | 15 | 9 | 5 | 1 | 9½/15 | 63 | Tinsley | 8 | 4 | 1 | 3 | 5½/8 | 69 |
| Potter | 6 | 2 | 1 | 3 | 3½/6 | 58 | van Vliet | 9 | 3 | 3 | 3 | 3½/7 | 50 |
| Ranken | 2 | 2 | 0 | 0 | 2/2 | 100 | Wainwright | 2 | 2 | 0 | 0 | 2/2 | 100 |
| Riemann | 2 | 2 | 0 | 0 | 2/2 | 100 | Walbrodt | 1 | 0 | 0 | 1 | ½/1 | 50 |
| Roberts | 2 | 2 | 0 | 0 | 2/2 | 100 | Ware | 4 | 3 | 0 | 1 | 3½/4 | 88 |
| Rolland | 6 | 6 | 0 | 0 | 6/6 | 100 | Wayte | 1 | 0 | 0 | 1 | ½/1 | 50 |
| Rosenthal | 7 | 4 | 2 | 1 | 4½/7 | 64 | Weiss | 7 | 3 | 1 | 3 | 4½/7 | 64 |
| Schallopp | 9 | 2 | 6 | 1 | 2½/9 | 28 | Wemmers | 1 | 1 | 0 | 0 | 1/1 | 100 |
| von Scheve | 1 | 0 | 1 | 0 | 0/1 | 0 | Winawer | 9 | 2 | 6 | 1 | 2½/9 | 28 |
| Schiffers | 1 | 0 | 1 | 0 | 0/1 | 0 | Wisker | 59 | 26 | 23 | 10 | 31/59 | 53 |
| Schlechter | 3 | 0 | 2 | 1 | ½/3 | 17 | Wittek | 1 | 0 | 0 | 1 | ½/1 | 50 |
| Schottländer | 3 | 2 | 1 | 0 | 2/3 | 67 | Wormald | 2 | 0 | 1 | 1 | ½/2 | 25 |
| A. Schwarz | 4 | 2 | 2 | 0 | 2/4 | 50 | Zukertort | 9 | 2 | 7 | 0 | 2/9 | 22 |
| J. Schwarz | 1 | 0 | 1 | 0 | 0/1 | 0 | **All Opponents** | **850** | **334** | **362** | **154** | **411/850** | **48** |

# BIBLIOGRAPHY

This bibliography contains the most important manuscripts, books, reference works and websites consulted during the research for this book. The numerous chess magazines and newspapers referenced in the text are not listed here.

## Works and Typescripts by Henry Edward Bird (Chronological)

Bird, H.E. *Railway Accounts: A Comprehensive Analysis of the Capital and Revenue of the Railways of the United Kingdom; With a Few Observations Thereon*. London, Dean and Son, [1868].

_____. *A Caution to Investors. A Brief Sketch Concerning the Position and Career of the Atlantic and Great Western Railway Company*. [London], 1873.

_____. *Proposed Modification of the Game of Chess as Originally Suggested in the June Number of the City of London Chess Magazine*. [London], [1875].

_____. *Chess Masterpieces: Comprising a Collection of 150 Choice Games of the Past Quarter of a Century*. London: Dean and Son, [1875].

_____. *The Chess Openings, Considered Critically and Practically*. London: Dean and Son, 1878.

_____. *A Slight Chess Retrospect and Explanation*. London, 1880.

_____. *Chess Practice: Being a Condensed and Simplified Record of the Actual Openings in the Finest Games Played Up to the Present Time*. London: Sampson Low, Marston, Searle and Rivington, 1882.

_____. *Railway Accounts: A Concise View for the Last Four Years, 1881 to 1884, and an Estimate for 1885. With Remarks on the Relation of Capital to Revenue, etc.* London: Effingham Wilson, 1886.

_____. *Bird's Modern Chess and Chess Masterpieces: Containing a Collection of the Finest Examples of Chess Play*. London: Dean and Son, 1887.

_____. *Bird's Chess Reviews*. London, [1890].

_____. *Chess: A Manual for Beginners*. London: Dean and Son, [1891].

_____. *Chess History and Reminiscences*. London: Dean and Son, 1893.

_____. *Steinitz and Lasker Match*. London, 1894.

_____. *Chess Novelties and Their Latest Developments: With Comparisons of the Progress of Chess Openings of the Past Century and the Present Not Dealt With in Existing Works*. London: Warne, 1895.

## Manuscripts/Typescripts

Cleveland Public Library: 789. 6918M F862 Volume 1–2, *Letters to John G. White relating to chess*.

Cleveland Public Library: 789. 691M H338 Volume 1–10, *[Hazeltine's] Chess Autographs, End Games, Games and Problems*.

Cleveland Public Library: 789. 21 MA W369G Volume 1–13, *Wayte, W. Games*.

Cleveland Public Library: Q 789. 31 O1A Volume 1–2, *[Aspa's] Chess Miscellanies*.

Cleveland Public Library: Photographic collection.

Den Haag, Koninklijke Bibliotheek: KB : 66 C 8, *St. James's Chess Club*.

*James McHenry archives* (in private possession).

Liverpool Chess Club. *Games of the Liverpool Chess Club* Volume 2.

London, Metropolitan Archives. *Electoral Rolls*.

London, The National Archives: Public Record Office, C 15/179/B76, *Bird v. Drouet*.

London, The National Archives: Public Record Office, C 15/22/D31, *Dyer v. Dyer*.

London, The National Archives: Public Record Office, C 16/29/I/J17, *Jackson v. Drew*.

[Möhle, Adolphe] *The American Chess Congress and the Manhattan Chess Club*. [New York, 1880].

## Reference Works

Bland, W.R. *Chess Player's Annual and Club Directory 1892*. London, 1892.

Di Felice, G. *Chess Results 1747–1900: A Comprehensive Record with 465 Tournament Crosstables and 590 Match Scores*. Jefferson, North Carolina: McFarland, 2004.

_____. *Chess Periodicals: An Annotated International Bibliography, 1836–2008*. Jefferson, North Carolina: McFarland, 2010.

Eales, R. *Chess: The History of a Game*. London: Batsford, 1985.

Hooper, D., and K. Whyld. *The Oxford Companion to Chess*. Oxford: Oxford University Press, 1992.

Le Lionnais, F. *Les Prix de Beauté aux Echecs*. Paris: Payot, 2002.

Levy, D., and K. O'Connell. *Oxford Encyclopedia of Chess; Volume 1: 1485–1866*. Oxford: Oxford University Press, 1981.

*The Metallurgicon Local Directory. Wandsworth, Putney, Wimbledon, Roehampton, Clapham, Balham, Tooting, Battersea, Barnes, etc.* Wandsworth: J.W. Gray, [1867].

*National Union Catalog. Pre-1956 Imprints: A Cumulative Author List Representing Library of Congress Printed Cards and Titles Reported by Other American Libraries*. London: Mansell, 1968–1981.

*Oxford Dictionary of National Biography: From the Earliest Times to the Year 2000*. Oxford: Oxford University Press, 2004.

*Pigot's and Co's London and Provincial New Commercial Directory for 1822–3*. Manchester: Pigot, [1822].

*Pigot and Co's National Directory Commercial Directory for 1828–9*. London: Pigot, [1828].

*The Post Office London Directory, 1848–1869 and 1882*. London: Kelly & Co, 1848–1869 and 1882.

*The Post Office London Suburban Directory 1868*. London: Kelly & Co, 1868.

*Who Was Who*. London: Adam & Charles Black, 1920.

Whyld, K. *Chess Columns: A List*. Olomouc, Czech Republic: Moravian Chess, 2002.

## Tournament Books with Bird
## as a Participant (Chronological)

### London 1851

Staunton, H. *The Chess Tournament: London 1851*. London: Batsford, 1986.

Ziegler, M. *Das Schachturnier von London 1851*. St. Ingberg: ChessCoach, 2013.

### Birmingham 1858

Whyld, K. *English Tournaments 1857–1866*. Nottingham: The Chess Player, 2003.

### London 1866

Löwenthal, J.J. *The Transactions of the British Chess Association: For the Years 1866 and 1867*. London: Longmans, Green, Reader and Deyer, 1868.

### London 1868–69

Löwenthal, J.J. *The Transactions of the British Chess Association: For the Years 1868 and 1869*. London: Longmans, Green, Reader and Deyer, 1869.

Gillam, A.J. *The Meeting of the British Chess Association, London 1868/9*. Nottingham: The Chess Player, 2003.

### Vienna 1873

Lehner, H.F. *Der Erste Wiener Internationale Schachkongress im Jahre 1873*. Zürich: Olms, 1986.

### Philadelphia 1876

*The Second, Third and Fourth American Chess Congress: Cleveland 1871, Chicago 1874, Philadelphia 1876*. Zürich: Olms, 1985.

### Paris 1878

Schallopp, Emil. *Der Internationale Schachkongress zu Paris im Jahre 1878*. Leipzig: Veit, 1879.

### Gouda 1880

*Jaarboekje van den Nederlandschen Schaakbond 1880*. Gouda: G.B. van Goor Zonen, 1881.

### Vienna 1882

Bijl, C.M. *Das II. Internationale Schachmeisterturnier Wien 1882*. Zürich: Olms, 1984.

### London 1883

Minchin, J.I. *Games Played in the London International Chess Tournament, 1883*. London: Wade, [1884].

### Nuremberg 1883

Schallopp, E. *Der Erste, Zweite und Dritte Kongress des Deutschen Schachbundes, Leipzig 1879—Berlin 1881—Nürnberg 1883*. Zürich: Olms, 1979.

### Hamburg 1885

Bardeleben, C. von. *Der Vierte und Fünfte Kongress des Deutschen Schachbundes, Hamburg 1885 und Frankfurt a.M. 1887*. Zürich: Olms, 1982.

### Hereford 1885

Skipworth, A.B. *The Book of the Counties' Chess Association: Parts I and II*. Lincoln: Williamson; London: Wade, 1885–1886.

### London (February) 1886

Gillam, A.J. *London Feb/Mar 1886 and Nottingham 1886*. Nottingham: The Chess Player, 2007.

### London (July) 1886

Gillam, A.J. *London July 1886*. Nottingham: The Chess Player, 2008.

### Nottingham 1886

Skipworth, A.B. *The Book of the Counties' Chess Association. Parts II and III*. Lincoln: Williamson; London: Wade, 1886–1887.

Gillam, A.J. *London Feb/Mar 1886 and Nottingham 1886*. Nottingham: The Chess Player, 2007.

### Stamford 1887

Skipworth, A.B. *The Book of the Counties' Chess Association: Part III*. Lincoln: Williamson; London: Wade, 1887.

### London 1887

Gillam, A.J. *London 1887*. Nottingham: The Chess Player, 2000.

### Bradford 1888

*The Bradford Tournament: A Selection of Games Played in the International Masters' Tournament of the British Chess Association and Yorkshire County Chess Club, Held in Bradford, Yorkshire, 6th August 1888*. Leeds: British Chess Magazine, 1888.

Gillam, A.J. *Bradford 1888*. Nottingham: The Chess Player, 2012.

### New York 1889

Steinitz, W. *The Book of the Sixth American Chess Congress: Containing the Games of the International Chess Tournament Held at New York in 1889*. Zürich: Olms, 1982.

### Manchester 1890

Gillam, A.J. *Manchester 1890*. Nottingham: The Chess Player, 2011.

### London B.C.A., London Quintangular and Belfast 1892

Gillam, A.J. *London March 1892, London March/April 1892, Belfast 1892*. Nottingham: The Chess Player, 2008.

### Hastings 1895

Cheshire, H.F. *The Hastings Chess Tournament 1895: Containing the Authorised Account of the 230 games Played Aug.–Sept. 1895*. London, Chatto & Windus, 1896.

Van Lennep, N.W. *Hastings 1895*. Amsterdam: Andriessen, 1978.

Crouch, C.S. and K.D. Haines. *Hastings 1895: The Centenary Book*. Sheffield: Waterthorpe Information Services, 1995.

### Cable Match 1896

Gillam, A.J. *Great Britain Versus America: Cable Matches 1895–1901*. Nottingham: The Chess Player, 1997.

### London 1899

*The Book of the London International Chess Congress, 1899*. London: Longmans, Green and Co, 1900.

## Biographies, Other Tournament Books
## and Game Collections

Bachmann, L.E.A. *Schachmeister Steinitz: Ein Lebensbild des Ersten Weltschachmeisters, Dargestellt in einer Vollständigen Sammlung Seiner Partien*. Zürich: Olms, 1980.

Blackburne, J.H., P.A. Graham and D.V. Hooper. *Blackburne's Chess Games*. New York: Dover, 1979.

Brownson, O.A., Jr. *Book of the Second American Chess Congress Held at Cleveland, Ohio: December 1871*. Dubuque, Iowa: Privately printed, [1872].

Edge, F.M. *The Exploits and Triumphs in Europe of Paul Morphy, the Chess Champion*. New York: Appleton, 1859.

Forster, R. *Amos Burn: A Chess Biography*. Jefferson, North Carolina: McFarland, 2004.

_____, S. Hansen, M. Negele and W. Angerstein. *Emanuel Lasker: Denker, Weltenbürger, Schachweltmeister*. Berlin: Exzelsior, 2009.

Gillam, A.J. *Emil Schallopp*. Nottingham: The Chess Player, 2008.

Gottschall, H. von. *Adolf Anderssen: Der Altmeister Deutscher Schachspielkunst*. Zürich: Olms, 1980.

Harding, T. *Eminent Victorian Chess Players: Ten Biographies*. Jefferson, North Carolina: McFarland, 2012.

_____. *Joseph Henry Blackburne: A Chess Biography*. Jefferson, North Carolina: McFarland, 2015.

Hilbert, J.S. *Napier: The Forgotten Chessmaster*. Yorklyn, Delaware: Caissa Editions, 1997.

_____. *Walter Penn Shipley: Philadelphia's Friend of Chess*. Jefferson, North Carolina: McFarland, 2003.

Hindle, O.M., and R.H. Jones. *"The English Morphy?": The Life and Games of Cecil De Vere, First British Chess Champion*. Exmouth, England: Keverel Chess Books, 2001.

Huth, A.H. *The Life and Writings of Henry Thomas Buckle, Volume 1*. London: Sampson Low & Co., 1880.

Landsberger, K. *William Steinitz, Chess Champion: A Biography of the Bohemian Caesar*. Jefferson, North Carolina: McFarland, 1993.

Lawson, D. *Paul Morphy: The Pride and Sorrow of Chess*. Lafayette: University of Louisiana at Lafayette Press, 2010.

Löwenthal, J.J. *Morphy's Games: Selection of the Best Games Played by the Distinguished Champion, in Europe and America*. New York: D. Appleton and Company, 1860.

_____. *The Chess Congress of 1862: A Collection of the Games Played, and a Selection of the Problems Sent in for the Competition*. London: Bohn, 1864.

Maróczy, G. *Paul Morphy: Sammlung der von ihm Gespielten Partien mit Ausführlichen Erläuterungen*. Berlin: De Gruyter, 1909.

_____. *Maróczy's Hundert Schachpartien*. Zürich: Olms, 1984.

Ploeger, M. *Moed en Originaliteit op het Schaakbord*. Venlo, Netherlands: Van Spijk, 1984.

Pope, J.N. *Harry Nelson Pillsbury: American Chess Champion*. Ann Arbor, Michigan: Pawn Island Press, 1996.

Riemann, F. *Schach-Erinnerungen des Jüngsten Anderssen-Schülers*. Berlin: De Gruyter, 1925.

Rowland, F.F. *Pollock Memories: A Collection of Chess Games, Problems, &*. Dublin: Rowland, 1899.

Steinitz, William. *The Steinitz Papers: Letters and Documents of the First World Chess Champion*. Edited by Kurt Landsberger. Jefferson, North Carolina: McFarland, 2002.

Tarrasch, S. *Three Hundred Chess Games*. Park Hills, Oklahoma: Hays Publishing, 1999.

Townsend, J. *Notes on the Life of Howard Staunton*. Wokingham, England: John Townsend, 2011.

_____. *Historical Notes on Some Chess Players*. Wokingham, England: John Townsend, 2014.

Whyld, K. *The Collected Games of Emanuel Lasker*. Nottingham: The Chess Player, 1998.

Winsen, J. van. *James Mason in America: The Early Chess Career, 1867–1878*. Jefferson, North Carolina: McFarland, 2011.

## Anthologies, Chronicles, Textbooks, etc.

Chadwick, H. and C.H. Stanley. *De Witt's American Chess Manual: Containing Full Instructions for Young Players*. New York: De Witt, 1880.

Gossip, G.H.D. *The Chess Pocket Manual: A Pocket-guide for Beginners and Advanced Players*. London: Edward Arnold, [1894].

Grondijs, H. *The International Chess Tournament 1883: in Letters*. Rijswijk: RUEB, 2010.

Harding, T. *Correspondence Chess in Britain and Ireland, 1824–1987*. Jefferson, North Carolina: McFarland, 2011.

Hilbert, J.S. *Writings in Chess History*. Olomouc, Czech Republic: Moravian Chess, 2012.

Krabbé, T. *VAS-ASC, Vereenigd Amsterdamsch Schaakgenootschap. Amsterdamsche Schaakclub, 1822–1972*. Amsterdam: VAS-ASC, [1973].

MacDonnell, G.A. *Chess Life-pictures: Biographical Sketches, Caïssana, and Character-sketches*. London, 1883.

_____. *The Knights and Kings of Chess*. London: Cox, 1894.

Mason, J. *Social Chess: A Collection of Short and Brilliant Games with Historical and Practical Illustrations*. London: Horace Cox, 1900.

McCormick, G.H., and A. Soltis. *Bird's Defense to the Ruy Lopez*. Jefferson, North Carolina: McFarland, 1981.

Miller, J.W. *The American Supplements to the Synopsis Containing American Inventions in the Chess Openings*. London: W.W. Morgan, 1885.

Morley, F.V. *My One Contribution to Chess*. London: Faber and Faber, 1947.

Napier, W.E. *Paul Morphy and the Golden Age of Chess*. New York: McKay, 1957.

Reichhelm, G.C. *Chess in Philadelphia: A Brief History of the Game in Philadelphia, Illustrated by Numerous Charts, Tables, Games and Problems*. Philadelphia: Reichhelm, 1998.

Reinfeld, F. *British Chess Masters: Past and Present*. London: Bell and Sons, 1947.

_____. *A Treasury of British Chess Masterpieces: One Hundred Games*. London: Chatto & Windus, 1950.

Robinson, R.E. *1. P–KB4: A Guide to Bird's Opening*. Liverpool: Daily Post Printers, [1950].

Sergeant, P.W. *A Century of British Chess*. London: Hutchinson, [1934].

Soltis, A. *Chess to Enjoy*. New York: Stein and Day, 1978.

Staunton, H. *Chess Praxis: A Supplement to The Chess Player's Handbook: Containing All the Most Important Modern Improvements in the Openings, Illustrated by Actual Games; a Rev. Code of Chess Laws; and a Collection of Mr. Morphy's Matches, &., in England and France*. London: Bohn, 1860.

Steinitz, W. *The Modern Chess Instructor*. New York, Putnam, 1889–1895.

Taylor, T. *Bird's Opening: Detailed Coverage of an Underrated and Dynamic Choice for White*. London: Everyman Chess, 2005.

Whyld, K. *Simpson's. Headquarters of the World*. Nottingham: The Chess Player, 2013.

Williams, E. *Horae Divanianae: A Selection of One Hundred and Fifty Original Games at Chess by Leading Players, Principally Played at the Grand Divan*. London, 1852.

Wilson, F. *A Picture History of Chess*. London: Dover Publications, 1981.

Winter, E. *Chess Explorations: A Pot-pourri from the Journal "Chess Notes."* London: Cadogan, 1995.

_____. *Chess Facts and Fables*. Jefferson, North Carolina: McFarland, 2006.

_____. *A Chess Omnibus*. Milford, Connecticut: Russell, 2003.

_____. *Kings, Commoners and Knaves: Further Chess Explorations*. Milford, Connecticut: Russell, 1999.

## Websites

www.sarahsipple.co.uk/bird/index.html. Genealogy of the Bird family.

www.familysearch.org. Genealogical website.

www.ancestry.com. Genealogical website.

www.edochess.ca. Historical chess ratings.

www.britishnewspaperarchive.co.uk. British historical newspapers.

newspaper.library.wales/home. Welsh historical newspapers.

trove.nla.gov.au/newspaper. Australian historical newspapers.

Paperspast.natlib.govt.nz. New Zealand historical newspapers.

www.chesscafe.com. Historical chess articles.

www.chessarch.com. Historical chess columns.

www.chesshistory.com. Website specialized in chess history.

www.sjmann.supanet.com/Yorkshire%20Chess%20History%20Home.htm. Yorkshire chess history.

streathambrixtonchess.blogspot.com. A great blog, with much attention to chess history.

www.chessdevon.co.uk. Devonshire chess history.

www.thegazette.co.uk. The *London Gazette* (digitized).

prov.vic.gov.au/index_search?searchid=23. Index to unassisted inward passenger lists 1852–1923.

www.oldbaileyonline.org. The proceedings of the Old Bailey, 1674 to 1913.

## Non-Chess Works

Bird, C.G. (Alpha), *Reminiscences of the Goldfields in the Fifties and Sixties: Victoria, New Zealand, New South Wales. Part I, Victoria*. Melbourne, Australia: Gordon & Gotch, 1915.

De Bernardy Brothers, *De Bernardy's Unclaimed Money Register: Being a List of Names of Persons Entitled to Property at Home and Abroad*. London: De Bernardy Brothers, 1883.

Felton, P.E. "The Atlantic and Great Western Railroad." *The Western Pennsylvania Historical Magazine*, Volume 26, Number 3–4, pp. 117–128.

Jones, E. *Accountancy and the British Economy, 1840–1980: The Evolution of Ernst & Whinney*. London: Batsford, 1981.

_____. *The Memoirs of Edwin Waterhouse: A Founder of Price Waterhouse*. London: Batsford, 1988.

Lee, T.A. "Bankrupt Accountants and Lawyers: Transition in the Rise of Professionalism in Victorian Scotland." *Accounting, Auditing & Accountability Journal*, Volume 24, Number 7, pp. 879–903.

Lester, V.M. *Victorian Insolvency: Bankruptcy, Imprisonment for Debt, and Company Winding-up in Nineteenth-Century England*. Oxford: Clarendon Press, 1995.

Lillywhite, B. *London Coffee Houses: A Reference Book of Coffee Houses of the Seventeenth, Eighteenth and Nineteenth Centuries*. London: George Allen & Unwin, 1963.

Matthews, D., M. Anderson and J.R. Edwards. *The Priesthood of Industry: The Rise of the Professional Accountant in British Management*. Oxford: Oxford University Press, 1998.

Pfaff, C. (J. Bradshaw, ed.) *The Diggers' Story: Accounts of the West Coast Gold Rushes*. Christchurch, New Zealand: Canterbury University Press, 2014.

Simmons, J. and G. Biddle. *The Oxford Companion to British Railway History; From 1603 to the 1990s*. Oxford: Oxford University Press, 1997.

Stebbings, C. *The Private Trustee in Victorian England*. Cambridge: Cambridge University Press, 2002.

*Supplement to the Victoria Government Gazette*, 22 June 1877.

Thomas, A.J. *The Lambeth Cholera Outbreak of 1848–1849*. Jefferson, North Carolina: McFarland, 2009.

Walker, S.P. *Towards the "Great Desideratum": The Unification of the Accountancy Bodies in England, 1870–1880*. Edinburgh: Institute of Chartered Accountants of Scotland, 2004.

Wells, H.G. *Certain Personal Matters*. London: T. Fisher Unwin, 1901.

# INDEX OF OPPONENTS
## (by game number)

All references are to games involving Bird. **Bold** numbers indicate that the player had the Black pieces. Numbers in parentheses refer to games for which the score is completely missing or which were decided by forfeit. *Italics* indicate consultation games. Unnamed opponents are gathered under "Unknown."

# INDEX OF ANNOTATORS
## (by game number)

# INDEX OF NAMED OPENINGS
## (by game number)

Games at various odds are listed at the end of this index

# INDEX OF OPENINGS—ECO CODE
## (by game number)

# GENERAL INDEX
## (to page numbers)